JANUARY – DECEMBER 2017

Los Angeles I London I New Delhi
Singapore I Washington DC I Melbourne

Published by CQ Press, an Imprint of SAGE Publications, Inc.
2600 Virginia Ave., N.W., Suite 600, Washington, DC 20037

Photo credits, clockwise from top left: AFP/Getty Images/Adem Altan; Getty Images/Chip Somodevilla; AFP/Getty Images/Ed Jones; Getty Images/Anadolu Agency/Mustafa Yalcin; Getty Images/Anadolu Agency/Aydin Palabiyikoglu; AFP/Getty Images/Nicholas Kamm

ISBN 978-1-54430-057-3
ISSN 1056-2036

CQ Researcher

CQ Researcher is the choice of researchers seeking accurate, in-depth information on issues in the news. Investigated and written by an experienced journalist, each *CQ Researcher* offers a comprehensive, balanced examination of a controversial topic. Now in its 95th year, *CQ Researcher* has received the prestigious Sigma Delta Chi Award for Journalism Excellence for a 10-part series on health care and the American Bar Association's Silver Gavel Award for a nine-part series on liberty and justice issues.

Each *CQ Researcher* report opens with an overview, followed by a discussion of three key questions that drive the debate surrounding the topic. The answers provided are not conclusive but serve to highlight the range of opinions among experts and political parties. The overview and issue questions are followed by a "Background" section that places the topic in historical context.

"Current Situation" examines the activities of legislators, citizen groups, courts and others influencing the debate. "Outlook" offers insights by experts on what may happen in the future. Each report also features illuminating photographs, graphs and tables, as well as a presentation of views from representatives on opposing sides of the debate. A chronology identifying milestones in the debate and bibliographies of key sources for further research round out the report.

CITING *CQ RESEARCHER*

Sample formats for citing these reports in a bibliography include the ones listed below. Preferred styles and formats vary, so please check with your instructor or professor.

MLA STYLE
Mantel, Barbara. "Coal Industry's Future." CQ Researcher, 17 June 2016: 529-552.

APA STYLE
Mantel, B. (2016, June 17). Coal Industry's Future. *CQ Researcher*, 6, 529-552.

CHICAGO STYLE
Mantel, Barbara. "Coal Industry's Future." *CQ Researcher*, June 17, 2016, 529–52.

ACCESSING *CQ RESEARCHER*

CQ Researcher is available in print and online. For access, visit your library or
http://library.cqpress.com/cqresearcher.

For subscription pricing and a free trial, call 1-800-818-7243, or email librarysales@sagepub.com.

CONTENTS JANUARY – DECEMBER 2017

Trump Presidency — January 6 1

U.S.-Russia Relations — January 13 25

China and the South China Sea — January 20 49

Guns on Campus — January 27 73

Civic Education — February 3 97

Forensic Science Controversies — February 10 121

Reducing Traffic Deaths — February 17 145

Immigrants and the Economy — February 24 169

Women in Prison — March 3 193

Charter Schools — March 10 217

'Alt-Right' Movement — March 17 241

Reviving Rural Economies — March 31 265

Troubled Brazil — April 7 289

Rethinking Foreign Aid — April 14 313

High-Tech Policing — April 21 337

Sports and Sexual Assault — April 28 361

Native American Sovereignty — May 5 385

Anti-Semitism — May 12 409

North Korea Showdown — May 19 433

Pandemic Threat — June 2 457

Trust in Media — June 9 481

Food Labeling — June 16 509

Future of the Christian Right — June 23 533

Hunger in America — July 7 557

Funding the Arts — July 14 581

Medical Marijuana — July 21 605

Muslims in America — July 28 629

New Space Race — August 4 653

Redistricting Showdown — August 25 677

National Debt — September 1 701

Universal Basic Income — September 8 725

Medical Breakthroughs — September 15 749

Climate Change and National Security — September 22 773

Think Tanks in Transition — September 29 797

Cyberwarfare Threat — October 6 821

Future of the Democratic Party — October 13 845

Democracy Under Stress — October 20 869

Workplace Sexual Harassment — October 27 893

Military Readiness — November 3 917

Stolen Antiquities — November 10 945

Affirmative Action and College Admissions — November 17 969

Future of Marriage — December 1 993

Privatizing Government Services — December 8 1017

Species Extinction — December 15 1041

CQ RESEARCHER

In-depth reports on today's issues

Published by CQ Press, an Imprint of SAGE Publications, Inc.

www.cqresearcher.com

Trump Presidency

Can he carry out his policy agenda?

D onald Trump rode a populist wave to the presidency, vowing to roll back government regulations, renegotiate free-trade agreements, repeal the Affordable Care Act, cut taxes and rebuild infrastructure. It's all part of his plan, he says, to accelerate economic growth, revive manufacturing and help the working class. But critics say his policies could ignite a trade war and eventually harm the economy. They also worry about how racial and religious minorities will fare during the next four years. Trump's Cabinet selections are proving controversial as well. Supporters praise them as talented and successful; others see some of them as out-of-touch millionaires and billionaires too closely tied to Wall Street and the industries they are supposed to oversee. Trump's foreign policy team is heavy on military experience but is facing questions about its diplomatic experience, possible ties to Russia and how it will deal with complex challenges, ranging from terrorism to China's and Russia's growing assertiveness.

President-elect Donald Trump, speaking in Des Moines, Iowa, on Dec. 8 during his "thank you tour," has said he will put America first again by sparking economic growth, challenging free-trade agreements, restricting immigration and re-evaluating foreign alliances. He also has pledged to help workers by reviving manufacturing and placing renewed attention on left-behind communities.

THIS REPORT

I N S I D E

THE ISSUES 3

BACKGROUND 10

CHRONOLOGY 11

CURRENT SITUATION 16

AT ISSUE.........................17

OUTLOOK 19

BIBLIOGRAPHY 22

THE NEXT STEP 23

CQ Researcher • Jan. 6, 2017 • www.cqresearcher.com
Volume 27, Number 1 • Pages 1-24

CQ RESEARCHER

Jan. 6, 2017
Volume 27, Number 1

EXECUTIVE EDITOR: Thomas J. Billitteri
tjb@sagepub.com

ASSISTANT MANAGING EDITORS: Kenneth
Fireman, kenneth.fireman@sagepub.com,
Kathy Koch, kathy.koch@sagepub.com,
Scott Rohrer, scott.rohrer@sagepub.com

SENIOR CONTRIBUTING EDITOR:
Thomas J. Colin
tom.colin@sagepub.com

CONTRIBUTING WRITERS: Marcia Clemmitt,
Sarah Glazer, Reed Karaim, Peter Katel,
Barbara Mantel, Chuck McCutcheon,
Tom Price

SENIOR PROJECT EDITOR: Olu B. Davis

EDITORIAL ASSISTANT: Anika Reed

FACT CHECKERS: Eva P. Dasher,
Michelle Harris, Betsy Towner Levine,
Nancie Majkowski, Robin Palmer

◆SAGE Publishing | CQPRESS

Los Angeles I London I New Delhi
Singapore I Washington DC I Melbourne

An Imprint of SAGE Publications, Inc.

SENIOR VICE PRESIDENT,
GLOBAL LEARNING RESOURCES:
Karen Phillips

EXECUTIVE DIRECTOR, ONLINE LIBRARY AND
REFERENCE PUBLISHING:
Todd Baldwin

CQ Press is a registered trademark of Congressional Quarterly Inc.

CQ Researcher (ISSN 1056-2036) is printed on acid-free paper. Published weekly, except: (March wk. 4) (May wk. 4) (July wks. 1, 2) (Aug. wks. 2, 3) (Nov. wk. 4) and (Dec. wks. 3, 4). Published by SAGE Publications, Inc., 2455 Teller Rd., Thousand Oaks, CA 91320. Annual full-service subscriptions start at $1,131. For pricing, call 1-800-818-7243. To purchase a *CQ Researcher* report in print or electronic format (PDF), visit www.cqpress. com or call 866-427-7737. Single reports start at $15. Bulk purchase discounts and electronic-rights licensing are also available. Periodicals postage paid at Thousand Oaks, California, and at additional mailing offices. POSTMASTER: Send address changes to *CQ Researcher*, 2600 Virginia Ave., N.W., Suite 600, Washington, DC 20037.

THE ISSUES

3
- Would exiting trade agreements or imposing stiff tariffs damage the U.S. economy?
- Would American workers benefit from a more restrictive immigration policy?
- Would Trump's demand that U.S. allies pay more of the cost of common defense weaken European and Asian security?

BACKGROUND

10 **The Family Legacy**
The president-elect's roots are in real estate.

12 **Learning the Business**
Trump expanded the family company.

14 **Betting on Atlantic City**
Casinos, Trump Shuttle dragged company down.

16 **Reinvention**
"The Apprentice" put Trump in the limelight.

CURRENT SITUATION

16 **Cabinet Controversies**
Wealth of appointees raises eyebrows.

18 **The ACA**
Trump hopes to repeal and replace the health care law.

18 **The Environment**
Oklahoma Attorney General Scott Pruitt has twice sued the agency he is slated to lead.

OUTLOOK

19 **Hopes and Fears**
Trump's supporters are confident of success; his critics are nervous.

SIDEBARS AND GRAPHICS

4 **Trump Turns to Conservatives, Business Executives**
Trump's closest advisers are loyal supporters and multi-millionaires and billionaires.

5 **Trump's Business Ties Spark Concerns**
A majority of Americans are worried about potential conflicts of interest.

8 **Trump's Businesses Span Globe**
Male cologne, hotels among enterprises.

11 **Chronology**
Key events since 1946.

12 **Foreign Policy to Test Trump From the Get-Go**
Critics fear advisers lack diplomatic touch.

14 **Supreme Court an Early Battleground**
Stakes high as Trump prepares to nominate a new justice.

17 **At Issue:**
Will Trump be able to unify the country?

FOR FURTHER RESEARCH

21 **For More Information**
Organizations to contact.

22 **Bibliography**
Selected sources used.

23 **The Next Step**
Additional articles.

23 **Citing *CQ Researcher***
Sample bibliography formats.

Cover: Getty Images/Bloomberg/Daniel Acker

Trump Presidency

BY BARBARA MANTEL

THE ISSUES

Donald Trump, the populist disrupter who set off a political earthquake by winning the Nov. 8 presidential election, continues to shake up the American landscape as his Jan. 20 inauguration nears.

In a storm of tweets, Cabinet appointments and controversies since becoming the president-elect, Trump has called the Democrats sore losers; horrified environmentalists with the selection of a climate-change skeptic to head the Environmental Protection Agency (EPA); mocked the CIA and its findings about Russia's suspected meddling in the election; angered China with his questioning of longtime U.S. policies on Taiwan; and done little to assuage the fears of civil-rights advocates worried about how Muslims and other minorities will fare over the next four years.

At the same time, Trump has thrilled many of his supporters by nominating conservatives for sensitive Cabinet posts; sparked a stock market surge with his plans to cut taxes and federal regulations; energized rank-and-file workers by pushing Carrier Corp. to reverse its plan to move some factory jobs from Indiana to Mexico; and pleased deficit hawks by threatening to pull the plug on expensive military weapons programs such as the F-35 fighter plane. [1]

"Things will change. I know he's not going to be perfect. But he's got a heart," said Doug Ratliff, of the battered coal-country town of Richlands, Va., who owns strip malls in the area. "And he gives people hope." [2]

Since Trump pulled off an upset against Democratic nominee Hillary

Trump protesters rally in Chicago on Nov. 19. Critics fear his presidency will harm civil liberties and set back race relations. Anti-Trump groups include Muslims worried about being targeted by a national watch list, gays and transgender people afraid their gains of the past eight years will be erased and women's rights groups angered by Trump's misogynistic statements. Critics also worry Trump's policies could eliminate medical insurance for millions.

Clinton — winning the Electoral College and losing the popular vote — many Americans have tried to discern what the mercurial businessman and former reality-television star will do in office. Recent polling finds that only 41 percent of American adults approve of the job Trump is doing so far, and just 40 percent approve of his Cabinet selections and other high-level appointments. Those are historically low numbers for a president-elect during the postelection "honeymoon" phase. [3]

Trump and his strongest defenders appear unperturbed by the tepid support. During a "thank-you" tour visit to Cincinnati on Dec. 1, a confident Trump told a raucous crowd that he will restore America's greatness. "Never again will anyone's interests come before the in-

terests of the American people," Trump declared. "It's not going to happen." [4]

Although Trump has sent conflicting messages about the details of his intentions, he has indicated he plans to press ahead with the ambitious agenda he outlined during his campaign, including restricting immigration, curbing free trade and repealing the Affordable Care Act (ACA), President Obama's signature legislative achievement.

In addition, Trump wants to:

• Rebuild roads, bridges, the electricity grid and other infrastructure by issuing tax credits to encourage private investment.

• Place a moratorium on new government regulations and roll back rules that "destroy jobs."

• Lower personal income tax rates and collapse seven tax brackets into three and eliminate the estate tax.

• Lower the business tax rate from 35 percent to 15 percent, and tax repatriated corporate profits held offshore at a onetime rate of 10 percent.

• Renegotiate the North American Free Trade Agreement (NAFTA) and stiffen punishment for countries engaging in unfair trade practices. [5]

The Trump team says his policies will work synergistically to boost economic growth to as much as 4 percent annually and create 25 million jobs over 10 years — goals many economists doubt are feasible. Gregory Daco, chief U.S. economist at Oxford Economics, a global economic advisory firm headquartered in Oxford, England, says he is skeptical that Trump's plans will spark such robust growth. The positive effects of personal income tax cuts on consumer spending will be less than Trump thinks

Continued on p. 5

Trump Turns to Conservatives, Business Executives

To staff his administration, President-elect Donald Trump is relying on loyalists from the campaign trail, titans from the business world, conservatives from Congress and retired generals from the military. Trump's Cabinet nominees are notable for their wealth — they had combined assets of nearly $10 billion as of late December, according to The Wall Street Journal, *the highest of any Cabinet in U.S. history.*

Key Cabinet Appointments

Elaine Chao
Secretary of Transportation
Served for eight years as President George W. Bush's secretary of Labor. Married to Majority Leader Sen. Mitch McConnell, R-Ky.

Betsy DeVos
Secretary of Education
Prominent GOP advocate for school choice, charter schools and voucher programs.

James Mattis
Secretary of Defense
Retired general who led a Marine division to Baghdad in the 2003 invasion of Iraq.

Steven Mnuchin
Secretary of the Treasury
Former Goldman Sachs executive and hedge fund owner. Will take the lead to enact Trump's proposed economic policy changes.

Rick Perry
Secretary of Energy
Former Texas governor. Proposed eliminating the Energy Department in 2011 while seeking Republican nomination for president.

Andrew Puzder
Secretary of Labor
Top Trump campaign donor and CEO of parent company of food chains Hardee's and Carl's Jr.

Wilbur Ross
Secretary of Commerce
Billionaire investor has advocated for steep tariffs and will be in charge of trade deals.

Rex Tillerson
Secretary of State
President and CEO of Exxon Mobil. Is close to Russian President Vladimir Putin.

Ryan Zinke
Secretary of the Interior
Republican U.S. representative from Montana. Is skeptical of the science behind human-caused climate change.

All photos by Getty Images

Other Key Appointments

Stephen Bannon
Chief Strategist
Former executive chair at so-called "alt-right" media company Breitbart who played an instrumental role in Trump's election.

Gary Cohn
Director of the National Economic Council
Former options trader and president of Goldman Sachs.

Kellyanne Conway
Counselor
Former Trump campaign manager and Republican pollster and strategist. Upon appointment became the highest-ranking woman in the White House.

Michael Flynn
National Security Adviser
Retired Army lieutenant general and former director of the Defense Intelligence Agency. Has encouraged closer relations with Russia.

Carl Icahn
Special Adviser on Regulatory Reform
Billionaire investor and economic adviser during Trump's campaign. Will help select new Securities and Exchange Commission chairman.

Peter Navarro
Director of Trade and Industrial Policy
Professor at the University of California, Irvine. China critic and only credentialed economist in Trump's inner circle.

Reince Priebus
Chief of Staff
Current chairman of the Republican National Committee.

Scott Pruitt
Environmental Protection Agency Administrator
Oklahoma's attorney general. Currently in a legal battle to dismantle two major environmental rules.

Continued from p. 3

and private investment in infrastructure will fall short, says Daco. Oxford is predicting the economy will grow 1.6 percent in 2016 and 2.3 percent this year.

Others say cutting taxes and boosting infrastructure spending will ignite inflation and eventually hurt growth. They also note that Trump is inheriting a strong economy with low unemployment, rising wages, low inflation and steady growth. The Federal Reserve is actually concerned that the economy is growing too fast; it announced on Dec. 14 that it was raising its benchmark interest rate for only the second time since the financial crisis of 2008. Nevertheless, interest rates remain historically low. [6]

In any case, Trump's Democratic critics deny he has a mandate for sweeping change. Trump, they point out, lost the popular vote to Clinton by 2.8 million, and 54 percent voted for someone other than him. [7] A poll by *The Washington Post* and George Mason University found that only 29 percent of respondents said Trump has a mandate to carry out his agenda. That is sharply lower than the 50 percent who said Obama had a mandate when he was first elected in 2008. [8]

But Republican leaders in Congress are hopeful. "Welcome to the dawn of a new unified Republican government," House Speaker Paul Ryan, R-Wis., told reporters days after the election. [9] For the first time since 2006, Republicans will control the executive branch and both houses of Congress. Democrats, however, picked up two Senate seats, which could make it more difficult for Senate Majority Leader Mitch McConnell, R-Ky., to round up the necessary 60 votes to overcome a Democratic filibuster of Republican-backed legislation.

"Even though we didn't get the majority, those two votes will be invaluable in stopping Republicans from doing bad, bad things," said Sen. Chuck Schumer, D-N.Y., whose colleagues chose him to be the next Senate minority leader. Schumer said he was ready to

Trump's Business Ties Spark Concerns

Sixty-five percent of Americans are "very" or "somewhat" concerned that Donald Trump's business and foreign-government ties could affect his ability to serve the country. But the public is split along party lines. More than 90 percent of Democrats say they are "very" or "somewhat" concerned versus 31 percent of Republicans.

Public Concern Over Trump's Business and Foreign Government Ties

Total / Democrat / Republican

	Very	Somewhat	Not too	Not at all
Total	45%	20%	14%	20%
Democrat	70%	22%	3%	5%
Republican	13%	18%	27%	41%

Source: "Views of President-elect Trump and his administration," Pew Research Center, Dec. 8, 2016, http://tinyurl.com/z7rj3tx

work with the new president on proposals for infrastructure spending and trade but would hold the line on tax cuts for the wealthy, repealing the ACA and reversing banking regulations put in place after the 2007-09 recession. [10]

Congressional leaders seem to be united on at least one point: They are planning to look into the CIA's conclusion that the Russian government tried to help Trump, who has praised Russian President Vladimir Putin, by using computer hackers to steal and release emails from the Democratic National Committee and Clinton's campaign chairman, John Podesta. Although House and Senate leaders are debating how to proceed, leaders from both parties agree that Congress needs to learn more about what Russia did and how to prevent such interference from happening again. Any congressional action will likely be over Trump's objections; he has dismissed the CIA's findings as "ridiculous" and politically motivated. [11]

Trump faces opposition on other fronts. He must deal with critics who say his worldwide businesses present serious conflicts of interest and who warn he must take steps to avoid violating government ethics rules. (*See graphic, above.*) Trump has said his

two eldest sons would run the family business, but the U.S. Office of Government Ethics said that wouldn't be enough. In a postelection tweet it said: "Only way to resolve these conflicts of interest is to divest." Trump, who canceled a mid-December press conference on the topic, said he would reveal his plan for resolving conflicts of interest sometime this month. Trump already took some steps in December, canceling licensing deals for hotels in Brazil and Azerbaijan, for example. [12]

Following in the footsteps of "Not My President" protests in the days after the Nov. 8 vote, numerous groups plan to protest his inauguration in Washington. [13] Anti-Trump protesters span a diverse group of American society: Muslims worried about being targeted if the Trump administration establishes a national watch list; minorities from the Black Lives Matter movement and other groups fearful that Trump's presidency will further inflame racial bigotry; gays and transgender people afraid their gains of the past eight years will be erased; and women's rights groups angered by Trump's statements they consider misogynistic.

The Southern Poverty Law Center, a liberal civil-rights group in Montgomery,

Ala., said the United States has experienced "a national outbreak of hate, as white supremacists celebrate Donald Trump's victory"; it said it documented 867 reports of harassment and intimidation in the 10 days after the Nov. 8 election. It added that many of the harassers invoked Trump's name. [14]

Since winning, Trump, at times, has vowed to be a president for all Americans, saying "it is time for us to come together as one united people." [15]

"I am going to instruct my Treasury secretary to label China a currency manipulator," Trump said in June. "Any country that devalues their currency in order to take advantage of the United States will be met with sharply." [16] Such devaluation makes a country's exports cheaper. Yet experts agree China is no longer guilty of weakening its currency, as it did for two decades. [17]

Democrats and Republicans who favor open markets and free trade have

Gadbaw, a senior fellow at Georgetown University's Institute of International Economic Law. But it's also "pretty clear that the president would have to come back to Congress to get agreement to any renegotiated deal."

In September, billionaire investor Wilbur Ross and University of California-Irvine business professor Peter Navarro wrote a paper defending Trump's trade agenda. Ross is Trump's pick for Commerce secretary and Navarro is to be director of trade and industrial policy.

The United States has entered into "a series of poorly negotiated trade deals that have not distributed the gains from trade fairly," they wrote. Since President Bill Clinton signed NAFTA in 1993, "the U.S. has lost over 850,000 jobs and its trade deficit with Mexico has soared from virtually zero to roughly $60 billion." Trump, they said, will renegotiate NAFTA to increase U.S. economic growth, decrease the U.S. trade deficit and strengthen the U.S. manufacturing base. [19] NAFTA's critics point to the loss of hundreds of thousands of jobs in the U.S. auto sector in particular. [20]

But Navarro and Ross are mistaken about NAFTA, says Marcus Noland, director of studies at the Peterson Institute for International Economics, a centrist think tank in Washington. "All the studies show that the bulk of job loss over the last 20 years in manufacturing is due to technological change, with the exception of the garment sector and maybe apparel or textiles more broadly," Noland says.

Although NAFTA produced wrenching changes in the beginning as some manufacturing shifted across borders, "we have accommodated ourselves to being very close trading partners," says Gary Burtless, an economist at the Brookings Institution, a centrist research group in Washington. Canada, Mexico and the United States each specializes in what it manufactures most efficiently and cost-effectively, he says, "and that has advantages on both sides of the border. The

President-elect Trump visits a Carrier Corp. plant in Indianapolis, Ind., on Dec. 1. Trump and Vice President-elect Mike Pence arranged for Carrier to receive state tax breaks in exchange for the company agreeing not to move some factory jobs to Mexico. Trump's supporters say he will renegotiate the North American Free Trade Agreement to boost U.S. economic growth and strengthen manufacturing. But many economists say factory job losses over the last 20 years are due mainly to technological change, not free trade.

AP Photo/Evan Vucci

As Trump readies to take office, here are some of the questions politicians, analysts, voters and others are asking:

Would exiting trade agreements or imposing stiff tariffs damage the U.S. economy?

If Trump's campaign rhetoric is any guide, he wants to radically change U.S. trade policy. He has said he would walk away from NAFTA if Mexico and Canada don't agree to renegotiate it; withdraw from the Trans-Pacific Partnership (TPP), a new trade agreement between Pacific Rim countries, which Congress has yet to ratify; and punish China for its trade practices.

attacked Trump's comments, saying they fear he will start a trade war. Unlike Trump's other promises, such as repealing the Affordable Care Act, many of his trade policies would not require congressional approval.

Abandoning the Trans-Pacific Partnership "would be a no-brainer for Trump," said Billy Melo Araujo, a lecturer in international economic law at Queen's University in Belfast, Ireland. Once Trump is sworn in, "it would simply be a matter of not putting it to a vote before Congress." [18]

As for NAFTA, "Trump has inherent authority to terminate the agreement, so he also has inherent authority to call for a renegotiation," says R. Michael

notion that we have fewer jobs than we would without NAFTA is really a stretch."

"Without NAFTA, [our company] would be out of business," said Rich Turner, a senior manager of a denim-manufacturing plant in Mauldin, S.C. The plant exports 85 percent of its denim duty-free to Mexico, where it is made into jeans that are then shipped to the United States. [21]

Trump has also threatened to impose a 35 percent tariff on some Mexican goods, a move that experts say would violate international law and could prompt Mexico to retaliate. "I don't see how that's a win," said Turner. He said he worries that tariffs on Mexican goods would make the finished jeans too expensive for the U.S. market and depress orders for his denim. Forty percent of the parts in Mexican-manufactured exports originate in the United States, according to the Congressional Research Service. [22]

Navarro denied tariffs would put U.S. jobs at risk. "The tariff is not an end game; it's a strategy — a strategy to renegotiate trade deals," he said. [23]

Trump has threatened to impose an even larger tariff, 45 percent, on China. Most economists agree that when China was allowed to join the World Trade Organization (WTO) in 2001, many U.S. communities suffered as manufacturing shifted to the low-wage nation. In addition, U.S. companies found it difficult to sell in China because the Chinese "don't allow competition with their state-owned enterprises," says Derek Scissors, Asia economist at the American Enterprise Institute, a conservative think tank in Washington.

But an across-the-board tariff is a bad idea, Scissors says. For one thing, "we import consumer goods [from China], so prices for clothing, for computers, prices for cellphones would all rise," he says, "and it's going to disproportionately hit the poor." And many American-made products have Chinese components.

In addition, says Burtless, high tariffs against China or Mexico are no guarantee that jobs would return to the United States. Companies might instead move production to "Vietnam and Malaysia and [South] Korea. . . . Are we going to put tariff barriers on every country on Earth?"

And finally, say Burtless and Scissors, China is sure to retaliate. The answer to gaining access to China's markets has to be negotiation, says Noland. "Donald Trump likes to make deals. Wilbur Ross, same thing," he says.

Would American workers benefit from a more restrictive immigration policy?

From the beginning of his presidential campaign, Trump vocally — critics say unfairly — attacked undocumented immigrants. He called the United States a "dumping ground for everybody else's problems" and said Mexico is "sending people that have lots of problems," including some who are criminals and rapists. He promised to build a wall on the nation's southern border, with Mexico footing the bill, and vowed to deport the roughly 11 million foreigners in the United States illegally. [24]

He later softened his position to say he wanted to focus deportation on the 2 million to 3 million undocumented immigrants with criminal records. (Experts say the actual number is closer to 820,000. [25])

Trump's critique didn't focus solely on crime. In an August speech, he said "most illegal immigrants are lower-skilled workers with less education who compete directly against vulnerable American workers" and blamed these immigrants for lowering wages. [26] Sen. Jeff Sessions, R-Ala., Trump's pick for attorney general, shares his views, blaming what Sessions' website calls the "unprecedented flow of immigration" for "sapping the wages and job prospects of those living and working here today." [27]

Immigrants — both documented and undocumented — constituted 16.9 percent of the U.S. civilian labor force in 2015, up from 12.4 percent in 2000 but little changed since 2010, according to the Washington-based Migration Policy Institute, a nonpartisan think tank that analyzes worldwide migration trends. Those in the country illegally accounted for 5 percent of the civilian labor force in 2014, up from 3.9 percent in 2000 but less than the 5.4 percent peak in 2007, according to the Pew Research Center, a nonpartisan polling and research think tank in Washington. [28]

Business owners in sectors dependent on immigrant labor, such as agriculture and construction, say the problem isn't too many immigrant workers but too few. [29] They point to Mexico, which saw the net flow of migration across its U.S. border fall to zero five years ago as Mexican birth rates declined, the country's employment opportunities improved and the Obama administration increased deportations. [30]

"Right now, if I had 80 guys, I could put every one of them to work," said Steve Johnson, who harvests Florida oranges. Said Nelson Braddy Jr., owner of King of Texas Roofing Co.: "Without Mexican labor, our industry is at a standstill." Braddy raised wages twice last year, with most of his workers now earning more than $20 an hour, and he still cannot attract enough people, he said. [31]

That's partly because immigrants tend to move to regions of the United States that are economically robust with low unemployment, says Randy Capps, the Migration Policy Institute's director of research for U.S. programs. "So it's not as if removing large numbers of unauthorized immigrants would immediately open up jobs to U.S.-born workers because many of those workers don't live in the right places. They're not employed in the right sectors, and they don't have the right job experience," he says.

Trump adviser Navarro disagrees. "These are jobs that many American citizens would gladly take if they weren't being pushed out by illegal immigrants," he said. [32]

Trump and his supporters also partly blame immigration for the decline in the percentage of native-born American adults in the labor force, which shrank

Trump's Businesses Span Globe

President-elect Donald Trump has amassed what experts estimate to be a net worth of $3.5 billion in a global network that consists of licensing deals and business ventures, most of which are housed under the Trump Organization. Businesses range from a vineyard in Charlottesville, Va., to hotels overseas. Several of his earlier ventures, such as Trump University and his Atlantic City, N.J., casinos, are defunct.

Notable Business Holdings

Getty Images/NurPhoto/Cheriss May

The Trump Organization

Trump's parent company, based in Trump Tower in Manhattan, oversees his real estate development, entertainment, hospitality and retail divisions. The Trump Organization owns or has licensing agreements with properties in Florida, New Jersey, Nevada and elsewhere, as well as in such countries as Panama, South Korea, Canada and India. These properties include hotels, golf courses, residential real estate and office buildings.

Along with its real estate holdings, the Trump Organization oversees Success by Trump, a male cologne that is produced in collaboration with Five Star Fragrance Co. The organization also partners with private-jet company Sentient Jet, whose planes transported Trump and his aides throughout the campaign.

Trump Productions LLC

The television production company serves the entertainment business slice of the Trump Organization, and Trump is chairman and CEO. The production company is behind Trump's reality-TV competition show "The Apprentice" and its spinoff "Celebrity Apprentice"; Trump will retain his executive producer title for the latter when he becomes president.

Trump Model Management

Started in 1999, Trump's modeling agency is based in New York City and formerly represented socialite Paris Hilton. The agency also represented Trump's wife, Melania Trump, before her 2005 marriage to the president-elect.

Sources: "The Companies Donald Trump Owns," Investopedia, Nov. 9, 2016, http://tinyurl.com/ju4xmxg; "Trump Productions," the Trump Organization, http://tinyurl.com/jq7jqgm

from 67 percent in 2000 to 62 percent in 2015. [33] But Theresa Cardinal Brown, director of immigration policy at the Washington-based Bipartisan Policy Center, a centrist think tank, says immigration isn't to blame. Instead, many native-born Americans leaving the workforce are retiring or going on disability as the population ages, or are returning to school, she says.

In fact, "most evidence and research suggests immigration is good for the country, including its effects on the wages of most workers," said Daniel Costa, director of immigration law and policy research at the Washington-based Economic Policy Institute, a liberal think tank. [34]

That's also the conclusion of a recent report from the National Academy of Sciences, Engineering, and Medicine, an independent group of leading researchers that reviewed relevant studies. [35] (Those studies did not distinguish between illegal and legal immigration.)

More immigrants mean more people to demand more goods, says Rutgers University economics professor Jennifer Hunt, one of the report's authors. Higher sales mean firms will need to raise production, which means hiring more workers and investing in more equipment. In the end, immigration's impact on native-born Americans' wages is about zero, she says.

But that doesn't mean there aren't losers. The report also looked at immigration's impact on the 10 percent of native-born workers without a high school diploma. "We came to a consensus" that immigration hurts these high school dropouts because many of the immigrants themselves do not have diplomas, and when they land poorly paying jobs it depresses wages for native-born Americans, Hunt says. But by how much is something researchers disagree on, she says.

One set of studies the academy reviewed simulated the impact of a 20-year increase in immigration that swelled the number of high school dropouts by 25 percent. They estimated it would depress the wages of native-born dropouts by 2 percent to 5 percent over that period. But when researchers assumed that firms were able to adjust to the flow of workers by investing in capital equipment and increasing production, the estimated effects were much less, ranging from lowering wages for native-born high school dropouts by 2 percent to increasing them by 1 percent. [36]

Would Trump's demand that U.S. allies pay more of the cost of common defense weaken European and Asian security?

During the campaign, Trump threatened, if elected, to pull U.S. troops from Europe and Asia if allied countries did not pay more toward the cost of maintaining the forces. He called the North Atlantic Treaty Organization (NATO) "obsolete" and then stunned its 28 members when he suggested that he would not automatically come to the defense of NATO members, including the Baltic nations Lithuania, Latvia and Estonia, if they were attacked by Russia, unless they increased their military spending. [37]

NATO was formed after World War II to deter Soviet expansion in Europe and to prevent the re-emergence of militant nationalism on the continent. A central principle, enshrined in the alliance's founding treaty, is the notion of collective defense, "that an attack against one or several members is considered as an attack against all." [38]

For decades, American presidents have demanded that NATO members pay more for defense. NATO's agreed-upon target for each member's military spending is at least 2 percent of the nation's gross domestic product (GDP), which only Estonia, Greece, Poland, the United Kingdom and the United States met last year. [39] But Trump would be the first American president to question the core notion of collective defense by making a U.S. military response contingent on a member's meeting that goal.

Many experts are uncomfortable with Trump's challenge. "I think it makes provocations by Putin and future aggression by Russia much more likely," says Jorge Benitez, a senior fellow at the Washington-based Atlantic Council, a private research organization that was formed to support NATO. The Russians "may doubt that we will defend our allies," says Benitez, noting that Russia invaded two states that aren't NATO members, Georgia in 2008 and Ukraine in 2014.

Doug Bandow, a senior fellow at the Washington-based Cato Institute, a libertarian public policy research organization, says Russia doesn't pose a threat to Europe, but he also doesn't like Trump's ultimatum.

"While Putin is happy to keep the West off balance, what evidence is there that he plans on attacking the Baltics?" says Bandow. "I think he knows that he would lose a war." But Trump was wrong to question the U.S. commitment to collective defense, he says, and "I cannot believe in a crisis that he would not fulfill obligations that had been undertaken by previous presidents."

Bandow says Trump has other means to pressure NATO members to increase their military spending, including "ostentatiously" holding a planning exercise at the Pentagon with a reduced U.S. presence in Europe and canceling President Obama's budget request to return to Europe troops that he had brought home before Russia's invasion of Ukraine.

"The combined GDP of the European Union countries is quite high, and they easily could spend more and provide more for their defense," says William Ruger, vice president for research and policy at the Washington-based Charles Koch Institute, a libertarian research group.

Judy Dempsey, a nonresident senior fellow at Brussels-based Carnegie Europe, an international affairs think tank, agrees that NATO members take U.S. security guarantees for granted but says reducing American troop strength in Europe has drawbacks. "Europe does still very much benefit America precisely because of its geographic proximity to the trouble areas that America has to deal with." For example, U.S. bases in Germany support operations in Afghanistan and the Middle East, she says.

Abrupt American policy changes in Europe could bring about regional and domestic instability, said Stephen Sestanovich, a Columbia University professor of international diplomacy and an ambassador at large for the former Soviet Union during the Clinton administration. "Hotheads" among Latvia's large Russian minority could become emboldened and threaten national unity while the country's security officials, worried that the United States "might not be with them in a crisis," might respond with harsh crackdowns, said Sestanovich. [40]

Dempsey says even more important than increasing NATO members' military budgets is changing what they spend money on. "There's duplication of helicopters, of tanks, of armaments for one thing," she says. In addition, European countries need to overcome their mutual mistrust and do a better job of sharing intelligence with one another," she says. "I hope Trump's rhetoric snaps them out of their comfort zone."

Trump has also questioned America's military commitment to Asia. Last March he told *The New York Times* that he would be open to Japan and South Korea developing their own nuclear weapons rather than relying on the U.S. nuclear deterrent and that he would consider withdrawing troops from the two countries if they didn't pay more to keep them. "We will not be ripped off anymore," he said. [41]

Bandow agrees with Trump's promise to draw down troops. "South Korea has 40 times the GDP and twice the population of North Korea. Why have [U.S.] troops there at this point 63 years after the [Korean] War concluded?" he asks. "South Koreans could do a lot more, and they don't because they rely on the U.S. How does that make sense for America?"

But U.S. military experts say Japan and South Korea pay billions of dollars a year to help maintain U.S. bases there. For example, South Korea covers about half of

U.S. personnel costs and is contributing 92 percent of the cost of constructing a new U.S. base in the country, according to Army Gen. Vincent Brooks, the top U.S. commander in South Korea. [42]

Zack Cooper, a fellow at the Washington-based Center for Strategic and International Studies, a centrist policy research organization, said it would be far more expensive to bring these troops home. "If you were to shift U.S. forces currently in Japan and Korea back to the U.S., you would have to place them somewhere, and those facilities are fairly expensive to build and maintain." [43] ∎

BACKGROUND

The Family Legacy

Donald Trump has been a celebrity nearly all of his adult life. "He flaunted his wealth, spent ostentatiously, worked the media to keep himself on the gossip pages and the business pages and the sports pages and the front pages," wrote *The Washington Post*'s Michael Kranish and Marc Fisher in *Trump Revealed: An American Journey of Ambition, Ego, Money, and Power.* [44] The billionaire, global brand and former reality-television star owns

Trump Taj Mahal casino in Atlantic City, N.J. – Trump's largest – closed on Oct. 10 despite a creditor bailout and other efforts to save it. Trump presides over a global business empire that includes hotels, golf courses and a vineyard, as well as numerous licensing deals. Some of his earlier ventures, such as Trump University and the Trump Shuttle, are defunct. His net worth is estimated at more than $3 billion.

homes from California to Virginia but spends the most time at his three-level penthouse in Trump Tower on Manhattan's tony Fifth Avenue. [45] The 58-story skyscraper is also headquarters for the Trump Organization, his family's privately owned international conglomerate.

But Trump's roots are in the far less glamorous, predominantly working- and middle-class New York City borough of Queens. Trump was born there on June 14, 1946, the fourth child of Mary and Frederick (Fred) Trump. His mother, a stay-at-home mom, was a Scottish emigre from a modest farming family, his father a residential real estate developer and first-generation German-American. [46]

Fred Trump was a workaholic and a tough disciplinarian, according to his children. "My father never had any hobbies," Donald's older sister Maryanne Trump Barry told journalist Gwenda Blair, author of *The Trumps: Three Generations That Built An Empire.* Weekends were spent inspecting his buildings, children in tow.

"Dad would take the elevator to the top floor and then walk down. He would look at each landing and the incinerator and boiler room," recalled Robert Trump, Donald's younger brother. [47]

Fred Trump started out building single-family homes in Queens in the 1920s. The Great Depression interrupted his real estate career, but he soon began anew, this time with the help of the federal government. In 1934, President Franklin D. Roosevelt's administration created the Federal Housing Administration (FHA) to jump-start home construction by insuring mortgages that followed certain federal rules. Over the next two decades, Trump would get rich building homes whose owners had secured government-insured loans and helping to create a "quasi-suburban way of life in the outer boroughs," wrote Blair. [48]

But in 1954, Fred Trump and other developers were called before Congress to answer accusations that they were making windfall profits by exploiting loopholes in an FHA program to encourage the building of affordable apartments for World War II veterans. "Although Fred Trump had clearly violated the spirit of the FHA program, he had not been caught in any criminal act," wrote journalist Michael D'Antonio in *Never Enough: Donald Trump and the Pursuit of Success.* [49]

Trump's wealth allowed his children to attend private schools. In 1959, in response to Donald's rebelliousness in class, Fred Trump sent the 13-year-old away to New York Military Academy, 55 miles north of the city. "For the first time, Donald was in a place that encouraged and channeled competitiveness and aggression instead of tamping it down," wrote Blair. [50]

In 1968, Trump graduated with a BA in economics from Wharton, the University of Pennsylvania's business school. His student deferment during the Vietnam War expired upon graduation, but bone spurs in his heels made him ineligible for military service. And so, at

Continued on p. 12

Chronology

1940s-1970s
Trump learns the family business.

1946
Donald John Trump is born June 14 in Queens, N.Y., to Fred Trump, a real estate developer, and Mary Trump, a stay-at-home mom.

1964
Trump graduates from New York Military Academy.

1968
He receives an undergraduate degree from Wharton, University of Pennsylvania's business school, and begins working for his father's business. In 1971 he becomes president of the firm.

1973
U.S. Justice Department accuses the Trumps of refusing to rent apartments to minorities; Donald Trump denies the charge but eventually settles lawsuit and agrees to remove barriers to minority applicants.

1977
Trump marries model Ivana Winklmayr. Before divorcing in 1992, they have three children: Donald Jr., Ivanka and Eric.

— • —

1980s-1990s
Trump's business expands, then nears collapse.

1980
Trump's first major project, the Grand Hyatt hotel, opens next to Manhattan's Grand Central Station, helping to rejuvenate the blighted area.

1983
Trump Tower opens.

1984
Trump opens his first casino, Harrah's at Trump Plaza, in Atlantic City, later renamed Trump Plaza Hotel & Casino.

1987
Trump publishes his first book, the bestselling *The Art of the Deal.*

1988
Trump buys Manhattan's Plaza Hotel; his third casino, the Taj Mahal in Atlantic City; and Eastern Airlines Northeast shuttle, renaming it Trump Shuttle.

1990
Trump Organization's debts hit $9 billion as casino profits dwindle; creditors devise bailout. In 1991 the Taj Mahal files for bankruptcy protection.

1992
Trump Plaza Hotel & Casino files for Chapter 11 protection.

1993
Trump marries model Marla Maples a few months after daughter Tiffany is born. The marriage lasts six years.

1995
Trump forms publicly traded Trump Plaza Hotel & Casino Inc.; the money raised is used to pay down debt, and its stock price soars.

1996
Trump Plaza Hotel & Casino Inc. purchases the failing Taj Mahal and Castle Hotel casinos from Trump for more than they are worth; the company's stock price plunges.

1999
Trump considers seeking Reform Party nomination for president before withdrawing. . . . Fred Trump dies, leaving a large estate to his children.

2000s-Present
Trump becomes reality-TV star and president-elect.

2004
Trump Plaza Hotel & Casino Inc. files for Chapter 11 protection. . . . Trump stars in NBC's "The Apprentice," which becomes an immediate hit.

2005
Trump marries model Melania Knauss; son Barron is born the next year.

2009
Trump Entertainment Resorts, forged from the 2004 Chapter 11 reorganization, files for bankruptcy protection; Trump steps down as chairman.

2011
Trump joins the "birther" movement, questioning whether President Obama was born in the United States.

2014
Trump Plaza Hotel & Casino closes.

2015
Trump announces his presidential candidacy on June 16.

2016
Trump wins the Republican nomination to run against Democratic presidential candidate Hillary Clinton (July). . . . Trump Taj Mahal closes (October). . . . Trump is elected 45th president despite losing popular vote by nearly 3 million votes (November). . . . Trump selects wealthy businessmen, retired military brass and conservative politicians for Cabinet (November-December). . . . CIA suspects Russian President Vladimir Putin approved release of hacked Democratic emails during presidential campaign (December).

Foreign Policy to Test Trump From the Get-Go

Experts say his advisers lack diplomatic experience.

Headlines from mid-December hint at the many foreign policy challenges Donald Trump will face as president. A gunman shouting "God is great" and "Don't forget Aleppo" assassinates Russia's ambassador to Turkey. A truck plows into a Christmas market in Germany, killing 12 and wounding dozens of others, in an attack for which the Islamic State claimed credit. China seizes a U.S. Navy underwater drone in the contested South China Sea. [1]

Experts agree Trump will have his hands full, and many worry his foreign policy team lacks diplomatic experience — a potentially serious problem given that Trump has no background in diplomacy.

A president needs experienced advisers who can frame choices and help their boss avoid a quick rush to judgment, says Michael O'Hanlon, a senior foreign policy fellow at the Washington-based Brookings Institution, a centrist research organization. Trump's picks are talented individuals, but "I don't see that kind of diplomatic experience on the team, and that is a serious shortcoming," he says.

Exxon Mobil CEO Rex Tillerson, selected for secretary of State, has negotiated numerous international business deals but has no formal foreign policy experience. Neither does Nikki Haley, South Carolina's Republican governor, who was tapped to be the U.S. ambassador to the United Nations. Trump turned to two retired generals for secretary of Defense (James Mattis) and national security adviser (Michael Flynn).

"It will be argued that those from the military do have foreign policy experience, but that experience is necessarily geared more toward operations than more conceptual and abstract questions of foreign policy," said James Mann, a resident fellow at the Johns Hopkins School of Advanced International Studies. [2]

Some veterans of the national security establishment disagree. Robert Gates, who served as Defense secretary for Presidents Obama and George W. Bush, said Tillerson possesses "vast knowledge, experience and success in dealing with dozens of governments and leaders in every corner of the world." Sen. John McCain, R-Ariz., praised Mattis as a "forthright strategic thinker." [3]

Here are some likely flashpoints for Trump and his foreign policy team.

Syria and ISIS

In a possible turning point in Syria's civil war, Syria and its primary backers Russia and Iran signed a cease-fire agreement in late December with Turkey and Syrian rebels, excluding jihadists such as the Islamic State (ISIS). One week earlier, Syrian President Bashar al-Assad, with help from Russia, regained control over Aleppo, the last major city with a rebel stronghold.

The costs of the nearly six-year war have been high. Syria and its allies have leveled Aleppo and other cities, killed hundreds of thousands and driven millions from their homes. [4]

The Obama administration wants Assad gone and has provided support for some rebel groups while working to defeat the Islamic State. Trump has signaled that he is prepared to change U.S. strategy by striking a deal to leave Assad in power and make crushing the Islamic State his top priority.

But even Russian President Vladimir Putin called the cease-fire "fragile." [5] And O'Hanlon says the best hope for Syrian long-term peace is for Assad to control only those regions of Syria populated by Christians and his fellow Alawites while allowing some form of autonomy for Sunni and Kurdish regions.

Iran Nuclear Deal

Trump's foreign policy team is divided over the Obama administration's nuclear agreement with Iran. Mattis has said there is no going back while Flynn has attacked the deal. During the campaign Trump called it "the worst deal ever negotiated" and vowed to dismantle it. [6]

The 2015 agreement involving Iran, the United States and five other nations restricts Iran's ability to develop a nuclear weapon, while allowing the country to continue to enrich uranium for civilian purposes. In exchange, the world powers agreed to lift United Nations sanctions against Iran.

Critics said the agreement should have completely dismantled

Continued from p. 10

age 22, he began his full-time apprenticeship with his father. [51]

Learning the Business

Fred Trump's office left much to be desired, wrote D'Antonio. Located in a working-class Brooklyn neighborhood, the "claustrophobic space" had a drop ceiling, fluorescent lights and battered

furniture. "Given the setting, young Donald Trump could be forgiven for letting his mind wander to Manhattan," said D'Antonio. "Keenly aware of the value locked up in his father's eighty-or-so buildings, which were worth well over $100 million, Donald urged him to refinance and create a pool of cash for new endeavors." But Fred Trump was reluctant to venture across the East River to Manhattan, where development was more costly and he had no political connections. [52]

By 1973, Donald Trump was president of Elizabeth Trump & Son, the family business; his father was chairman. [53] (Fred Trump died in 1999.) His first test as the family's public face came in January 1974, when he called a press conference after the U.S. Department of Justice sued the Trumps' property management arm over allegations that it was refusing to rent apartments to minorities. Unlike other developers who quickly settled such charges, the Trumps decided to fight. At

Iran's nuclear program. Supporters say the agreement significantly lengthens the time it would take for Iran to develop a nuclear weapon. [7]

Trump can "swiftly deliver a death blow" to the agreement by demanding it be renegotiated, said Ellie Geranmayeh, policy fellow at the European Council on Foreign Relations, a pan-European think tank. Or he could seek to provoke Iran into abandoning the deal by signing legislation that imposes "fresh sanctions," said Geranmayeh. [8]

China

Trump has threatened to impose trade sanctions against China and defied decades of U.S.-China diplomacy by taking a congratulatory postelection phone call from Taiwan President Tsai Ing-wen.

"At first I thought Trump's China bashing was for the campaign, but now I am not so sure," says Edward Goldberg, an international trade consultant. "It is extremely dangerous. . . . The China-U.S. geopolitical and economic relationship is the key to global stability."

Trump has also vowed to abandon the Trans-Pacific Partnership (TPP), a 12-nation trade deal that aims to deepen economic ties among Pacific Rim countries, excepting China, by slashing tariffs and increasing trade. Trump says it will cause U.S. companies to move production abroad.

No matter its economic merits, the TPP has diplomatic value, and by withdrawing from it, the United States is "leaving a vacuum for China to fill," says Waheguru Pal Singh Sidhu, a visiting professor at New York University's Center for Global Affairs.

China is planning a far-reaching infrastructure project dubbed "One Belt, One Road," a network of roads, rail and oil and gas pipelines that will extend south into Thailand and Myanmar and west into Central Asia and beyond. Ports are to dot the Indian Ocean, South China Sea and the East African coast.

"The Chinese say this is all for economics and business," says Sidhu. "But it's quite possible that China could turn all of these assets into military assets very quickly as well."

— *Barbara Mantel*

Police patrol the Breitscheidplatz Christmas market in Berlin after a truck plowed into holiday shoppers in a terrorist attack on Dec. 19, killing 12 people and injuring dozens. Terrorism is among the key foreign policy challenges facing President-elect Trump.

[1] David Filipov, Kareem Fahim and Liz Sly, "Turkish police officer, invoking Aleppo, guns down Russian ambassador in Ankara," *The Washington Post*, Dec. 19, 2016, http://tinyurl.com/zeat9j4; David Rising and Frank Jordans, "Islamic State Claims Berlin Christmas Market Attack," The Associated Press, *The Washington Post*, Dec. 20, 2016, http://tinyurl.com/hz9sodq; Lolita C. Baldor, "US says Chinese warship seized Navy underwater drone," The Associated Press, *The Washington Post*, Dec. 16, 2016, http://tinyurl.com/hvau9y5.

[2] James Mann, "Donald Trump's Foreign Policy Team: Built to Fail," *The New York Times*, Dec. 17, 2016, http://tinyurl.com/jknyowg.

[3] Jake Sherman and Matthew Nussbaum, "Gates, Rice Praise Tillerson for secretary of state," *Politico*, Dec. 13, 2016, http://tinyurl.com/hg42z4a; Paul Szoldra, "Sen. John McCain endorses Gen. Mattis for Defense Secretary," *Business Insider*, Nov. 21, 2016, http://tinyurl.com/hb3q8v7.

[4] "Confronting Fragmentation! Impact of Syrian Crisis Report," Syrian Center for Policy Research, February 2016, pp. 41, 61, http://tinyurl.com/j2jebeo; "The Six Main Parties that Kill Civilians in Syria and the Death Toll Percentage Distribution among them," Syrian Network for Human Rights, Nov. 14, 2016, p. 4, http://tinyurl.com/zwl5omd.

[5] Louisa Loveluck and Andrew Roth, "Cease-fire to begin across Syria starting at midnight, Syrian army says," *The Washington Post*, Dec. 29, 2016, http://tinyurl.com/hgw939h.

[6] Yeganeh Torbati, "Trump election puts Iran nuclear deal on shaky ground," Reuters, Nov. 9, 2016, http://tinyurl.com/ownjjeo.

[7] Eyder Peralta, "6 Things You Should Know About The Iran Nuclear Deal," NPR, July 14, 2016, http://tinyurl.com/o92ts32.

[8] Ellie Geranmayeh, "Will Trump Destroy the Iran Deal?" *The New York Times*, Nov. 25, 2016, http://tinyurl.com/jjkfb2h.

Donald Trump's side was his newly hired attorney Roy Cohn, who defended organized crime figures and had worked with Sen. Joseph McCarthy, R-Wis., the notorious 1950s anti-communist crusader who sparked a "Red Scare." Cohn announced a countersuit seeking $100 million in damages suffered from the "irresponsible and baseless" claims. [54]

Cohn eventually reached a settlement that required the Trumps to remove barriers to minority applicants.

But, under Cohn's tutelage, Donald Trump's lifelong approach to legal disputes was forged. "He would admit no wrongdoing and define a conflict to insist that he was the victim and not the perpetrator of some immoral or illegal act," D'Antonio wrote. [55]

In 1976, Trump, who had renamed the family business the Trump Organization, arranged his first major real estate deal, in Manhattan. Trump partnered with Hyatt Hotels Corp. to take control

of and rebuild the historic but crumbling Commodore Hotel, located next to 42nd Street's Grand Central Station in then-downtrodden midtown Manhattan. Like his father, he depended on government largess, persuading financially strapped New York City to give the partners a property tax break worth $4 million a year. He also persuaded his father to help guarantee a $70 million construction loan, the first of many instances of paternal financial help over the years. In

Supreme Court an Early Battleground

Stakes high as Trump prepares to nominate a new justice.

On the campaign trail, Donald Trump vowed to appoint a Supreme Court justice who "will protect our liberty with the highest regard for the Constitution." He will soon get his chance — and Democrats are worried about the prospect.

After taking office on Jan. 20, Trump will name a successor to Justice Antonin Scalia. Scalia, who died suddenly last February, anchored the high court's conservative 5-4 majority. He believed that judges should interpret the Constitution and statutes based on their original meaning and not on evolving norms.

Scalia's replacement could tilt the Supreme Court — currently divided 4-4 between liberal and conservative justices — in a conservative direction for decades to come, especially if the new justice is on the younger side.

In March, President Obama nominated Merrick Garland to fill Scalia's seat. Garland is chief judge of the U.S. Court of Appeals for the District of Columbia Circuit and is considered a moderate. But Senate Republicans refused to even hold confirmation hearings. "The American people should have a voice in the selection of their next Supreme Court Justice," said Senate Majority Leader Mitch McConnell, R-Ky., in a statement after Scalia's death. "Therefore, this vacancy should not be filled until we have a new president." [1]

In September, Trump released the final names in a list of 21 potential candidates (not including Garland) for the job, adding that his list was "definitive." [2] The odds are high that he will dip into it more than once. On Inauguration Day, Justice Ruth Bader Ginsburg will be 83 years old, Anthony Kennedy 80 and Stephen Breyer 78. Ginsburg and Breyer are part of the court's liberal wing, while Kennedy is often the swing vote.

The stakes are high, said John G. Malcolm, director of the Edwin Meese III Center for Legal and Judicial Studies at the Heritage Foundation, a conservative think tank in Washington. The court is closely divided on a number of contentious issues, including gun rights, religious liberty, voting laws and the death penalty, said Malcolm, and with Scalia's death, the court's conservatives lost a decisive vote. The justices are also divided on the appropriate reach of executive regulations. For example, just before his death Scalia cast one of five votes to stay enforcement of Obama's Clean Power Plan, which would regulate carbon emissions from electric power plants. Malcolm called Trump's list "excellent." [3]

But Nan Aron, president of the Washington-based Alliance for Justice, a liberal judicial advocacy group, said Trump's prospective justices "would roll back a century of economic and social progress." Candidates on the list, Aron said, have upheld discriminatory voter ID laws; supported the death penalty; questioned the Miranda warning, which advises people of their rights when arrested; and set back women's health by exempting private corporations, in the name of religious freedom, from the Affordable Care Act mandate that company health plans cover certain kinds of contraception. [4]

Presidential candidates typically describe their ideal Supreme Court justice in general terms. But Trump's release of actual names suggested he wanted to reassure conservatives of his bona fides. Carrie Severino of the Washington-based Judicial Crisis Network, a conservative judicial advocacy group, praised the Trump list as "unprecedented" and said it should "please conservatives." [5]

1980, the newly completed, 30-story Grand Hyatt towered over the stone edifices of Park Avenue. [56]

In 1977 Trump married the model Ivana Winklmayr, with whom he had three children before they divorced nearly 15 years later: Donald Trump Jr., born in 1977; Ivanka in 1981; and Eric in 1984.

Even before ground was broken on the Grand Hyatt, Trump was negotiating his second mega-project. In 1979, Trump and his partner, the Equitable Life Assurance Society, began to raze the historic Fifth Avenue building that housed department store Bonwit Teller. Trump Tower would be its replacement.

But Trump used an inexperienced demolition contractor, who could afford to accept a "rock-bottom fee" by hiring undocumented Polish laborers

for less than half the union rate, wrote Blair. They worked 12-to-18-hour shifts seven days a week. [57]

The "honeymoon he had enjoyed in the New York press was over," Blair said. Trump may have helped rescue 42nd Street, but now "he was also a breaker of promises and an art vandal, an anti-tenant landlord and an exploiter of immigrant labor." [58] Nevertheless, Trump Tower was a success; its condos sold quickly. [59]

"As Trump Tower reached for the sky, so, too, did the Trump mythos," wrote Kranish and Fisher. In 1982, *Forbes* estimated Trump's worth at $100 million and placed him on its list of America's 400 wealthiest people. Four years later, Trump generated further publicity — and regained some of the city's goodwill

— when he repaired Central Park's shuttered Wollman Skating Rink under budget and ahead of schedule. [60]

Betting on Atlantic City

In 1981, Trump applied for a license to operate casinos in Atlantic City, N.J. The application asked whether Trump had ever been the subject of any government investigations, but Trump made no mention of the federal discrimination lawsuit, wrote Pulitzer Prize-winning journalist David Cay Johnston in *The Making of Donald Trump*. Nor, according to Johnston, did Trump mention three other federal investigations, including one into his dealings with a mob associate who controlled the flow

Conservatives are intent on avoiding a disappointment like Justice David Souter, who retired in 2009, said Malcolm. Republican President George H.W. Bush appointed Souter in 1990, but Souter's judicial record turned out to be decidedly liberal, Malcolm said. [6]

Lawyer William M. Jay, a former law clerk for Scalia, said his first choice from Trump's list is Judge William H. Pryor Jr. of the U.S. Court of Appeals for the 11th Circuit in Atlanta. Pryor once ended a speech by saying, "Please, God, no more Souters," and he has called the Supreme Court's landmark 1973 *Roe v. Wade* decision establishing a woman's right to abortion "the worst abomination of constitutional law in our history." [7]

"There is a broad consensus that Bill Pryor is a smart, intellectual and fair judge who most conservatives would happily see on a Supreme Court shortlist," said Jay.

But incoming Senate Minority Leader Chuck Schumer, D-N.Y., told NBC's "Meet the Press" that Trump needs to pick a "mainstream candidate, . . . someone you may not agree with on every issue, but basically believes in precedent and basically believes in following the law." If Trump doesn't, "we're going to go at him with everything we have," Schumer said. Democrats, who will control 48 seats in the new Senate, will have some leverage because under current rules 41 senators can filibuster a Supreme Court nomination. [8]

— *Barbara Mantel*

Judge Merrick Garland, a moderate, was nominated by President Obama to fill the late Antonin Scalia's Supreme Court seat, but Senate Republicans refused to hold confirmation hearings. Trump's list of 21 conservative candidates for the job does not include Garland.

Getty Images/Alex Wong

[1] "After Scalia's death, Obama has opening to shift Supreme Court balance," Fox News, Feb. 13, 2016, http://tinyurl.com/hpvb2a7.

[2] "Donald J. Trump Finalizes List of Potential Supreme Court Justice Picks," Trump-Pence Make America Great Again, Sept. 23, 2016, http://tinyurl.com/zu4jcb9.

[3] John G. Malcolm, "With Trump's Election, the Future of the Courts Looks Brighter," *The Daily Signal*, Nov. 15, 2016, http://tinyurl.com/j9w3nnq; John G. Malcolm, "On the Line on Election Day: Eight Key Issues Decided by Next US President — The Supreme Court," Heritage Foundation, Nov. 30, 2016, http://tinyurl.com/zslvzvk.

[4] Nan Aron, "Trump's Supreme Court Justices Would Roll Back A Century Of Progress," *The Huffington Post*, Oct. 7, 2016, http://tinyurl.com/hc6a2j5.

[5] Nina Totenberg, "Donald Trump Unveils New, More Diverse Supreme Court Short List," NPR, Sept. 23, 2016, http://tinyurl.com/hahwbw4.

[6] Adam Liptak, "Trump's Supreme Court List: Ivy League? Out. The Heartland? In," *The New York Times*, Nov. 14, 2016, http://tinyurl.com/hx27v8q.

[7] *Ibid*.

[8] Kevin Daley, "Schumer Warns Trump: Pick A Mainstream Supreme Court Nominee," The Daily Caller News Foundation, Nov. 20, 2016, http://tinyurl.com/hujtvfq.

of concrete to Trump Tower during its construction. No charges were filed. [61]

Trump got his casino license but "continued to have relationships that should have prompted inquiries by the casino investigators," Johnston said. These included a 1988 contract to put the Trump name on a line of customized limousines produced by Dillinger Coach Works, owned by convicted extortionist Jack Schwartz and Colombo crime family soldier and convicted thief John Staluppi. [62]

Trump built and opened his first casino, Harrah's at Trump Plaza, in 1984, later renamed Trump Plaza Hotel & Casino after he bought the gambling company Harrah's' 50 percent stake. In 1985, Trump bought his second casino-hotel, a nearly completed tower owned by the Hilton

Corp., which had to sell when New Jersey denied the company a casino license because of ties to a reputed mob lawyer. Trump named it Trump Castle Hotel & Casino. [63]

Eventually, Trump brought in Stephen Hyde, an experienced gambling executive, to manage his Atlantic City business. "Hyde's colleagues marveled at his ability to anticipate Trump's moods and protect midlevel staff from outbursts," wrote Kranish and Fisher. [64]

In 1988 Trump went on a spending spree. Using mostly borrowed money, Trump paid $365 million for Eastern Airlines' northeastern routes and planes, renaming it the Trump Shuttle, and spent $407 million to purchase Manhattan's iconic Plaza Hotel. Trump went further into debt to complete his biggest casino-

hotel, the Trump Taj Mahal. But as Atlantic City became overbuilt and casino profits dwindled, Trump had trouble securing a bank loan. Instead, his newly formed Trump Taj Mahal Funding Inc. was forced to issue $675 million in high-interest-rate junk bonds. [65]

By 1990, Trump's marriage was publicly unraveling as newspapers wrote of his affair with a model and actress named Marla Maples, and his business empire was collapsing. The Trump Organization and its subsidiaries had accumulated $9 billion in debt. Trump had missed a payment on a Trump Castle loan, his airline was running out of cash and unpaid vendors were filing liens against his casinos. [66]

Hoping to minimize their losses, dozens of creditors reached a deal in

1990 to keep Trump's empire afloat: They reduced what he owed them and advanced him $60 million, at the same time cutting his salary and putting him on a monthly, albeit generous, personal allowance. The Trump Shuttle was closed. The Casino Control Commission approved the bailout, deeming Trump's Atlantic City businesses too big to fail. [67] Nevertheless, in 1991 and 1992, first the Trump Taj Mahal and then Trump Plaza Hotel & Casino filed for Chapter 11 bankruptcy protection, and Trump was forced to turn over nearly half of his hotel stakes to creditors in exchange for more-lenient debt terms. [68]

In December 1993, Trump married Maples, who a few months earlier had given birth to daughter Tiffany. Their marriage lasted six years.

Reinvention

In 1995, Trump formed a publicly traded company around the Trump Plaza Hotel & Casino and raised $140 million at its initial public offering, which he used to pay down debts. The stock price soared, and Trump's stake became worth nearly $300 million by 1996. Later that year, Trump Plaza Hotel & Casino Inc. bought the deeply indebted Trump Taj Mahal and the Trump Castle — one Trump business sold to another — for more than analysts said they were worth, and its share price plunged. [69]

In 2004, Trump Plaza Hotel & Casino Inc. filed for bankruptcy protection and Trump's more than 50 percent stake was cut in half. "While Trump was chairman [from 1995 to 2005], the publicly traded company lost more than $1 billion," according to Kranish and Fisher. Meanwhile, Trump, who also served as CEO for five years, was paid more than $44 million during his 10 years as chairman. [70]

The same year as the bankruptcy filing, Trump became the star of The Apprentice, a TV reality show in which contestants competed to become Trump's business apprentice. The NBC show's premise was his superior business acumen. It was an immediate hit, and Trump's "You're fired!" announcing the banishment of a contestant became its signature slogan. The show's success allowed Trump to license his name to clothing, fragrance and furniture and to hotels around the world. In 2005, he married his current wife, model Melania Knauss from Slovenia, who gave birth to their son Barron in 2006.

In 2009, publicly traded Trump Entertainment Resorts, which had been forged out of the 2004 bankruptcy, also filed for bankruptcy protection and Trump stepped down as chairman. Trump Plaza Hotel & Casino closed in 2014 and Trump Taj Mahal in 2016. [71]

Trump starred in the reality show until declaring his presidential bid on June 16, 2015. He faced off in the primaries against 16 GOP opponents, including such experienced politicians as former Florida Gov. Jeb Bush, Ohio Gov. John Kasich and Sen. Ted Cruz of Texas. By March 2016, Trump was far ahead, and on July 21, he formally accepted the nomination at the Republican convention in Cleveland.

During the campaign, Trump acknowledged the role the TV show played in his popularity. It "was a different level of adulation, or respect or celebrity" than he had previously experienced, he said. [72] But despite his celebrity, Trump might not have won the presidency without the rise of white working-class populism, a mood fueled by fear of social change. [73]

Trump tapped into and fanned this fear even before his campaign. In 2011, he joined the "birther movement" that questioned President Obama's U.S. birthplace, repeatedly calling for Obama to release his long-form Hawaiian birth certificate and, when he did, questioning its validity. During the campaign, Trump called for a halt to Muslim immigration and inaccurately said that homicides were at a record rate. ■

CURRENT SITUATION

Cabinet Controversies

Unlike previous presidents, Trump has never held elective office, been a military commander or served as a Cabinet secretary. To make up for his lack of governing experience, he may rely heavily on his vice president, Indiana Gov. Mike Pence, and his top appointees. So far, the latter are a mix of billionaire businessmen, well-connected corporate executives, retired military brass and conservative politicians. (*See box, p. 4.*)

After weeks of speculation about numerous potential candidates to be secretary of State, Trump picked Rex Tillerson, the chief executive of Exxon Mobil, generating both praise and concern for Tillerson's decades of experience guiding the company's oil and gas projects in Eurasia and the Middle East.

Tillerson has publicly questioned European and U.S. sanctions against Russia after its invasion of Ukraine; these sanctions have halted some of Exxon Mobil's oil exploration projects in Russia, potentially worth billions of dollars. [74] As secretary of State, Tillerson would have to either sell his Exxon Mobil stock or recuse himself from decisions that could affect his financial interests, said Richard W. Painter, a University of Minnesota corporate law professor and former chief ethics lawyer for President George W. Bush. [75]

Other wealthy nominees include Trump's pick for Commerce secretary, Ross, the chairman of a private-equity firm with close ties to Wall Street; Steven Mnuchin, a hedge fund founder and former Goldman Sachs banker, chosen as Treasury secretary; and Michi-

Continued on p. 18

At Issue:

Will Donald Trump be able to unify the country?

FRANCIS H. BUCKLEY
PROFESSOR, ANTONIN SCALIA LAW SCHOOL, GEORGE MASON UNIVERSITY

WRITTEN FOR *CQ RESEARCHER*, JANUARY 2017

*w*hile it might look like a tall order, I believe President-elect Donald Trump will unify the country, and in a way that his Democratic challenger, Hillary Clinton, could never have done.

That Clinton could never have united the country becomes clear when one recognizes that the Democrats have become the party of division and rancor, of race against race, gender against gender, ethnic group against ethnic group.

Recall the 2015 debate in Arizona where the Democratic presidential candidates were asked to choose between "Black Lives Matter" and "All Lives Matter." Only Jim Webb chose the latter, and he withdrew from the race shortly thereafter.

Trump by contrast ran as a unifier, and that message so threatened the Democrats that they saw covert racism in an appeal to American nationalism.

In his Cincinnati speech after the election, Trump called them on this. "Washington's politicians have spent so long appealing to competing interests they've forgotten how to appeal to the national interests, combining the skills and talents of our people in a common cause," he said. "Our goal is to strengthen the bonds of trust between citizens, to restore our sense of membership in a shared national community."

Trump has been faulted for his comments about illegal aliens and about trade issues with China. But a nationalist agenda is necessarily one that prefers Americans to non-Americans, and that asks how a trade deal benefits our people.

In the Cincinnati speech he declared that "from now on it's going to be America First. . . . We're going to put ourselves first." America will seek peace and harmony with other countries, but each country must first look after its own people.

"You hear a lot of talk about how we're becoming a globalized world," Trump said. "But the relationships people in this country value are local — family, cities, state, country. . . . There is no global anthem, no global currency, no certificate of global citizenship. We pledge allegiance to one flag, and that flag is the American flag."

That was evidently a message that many Americans were yearning to hear, and it's a message of unity, one that doesn't prefer one race or group to another. Is Trump a unifier? Of course. That's precisely why he is hated by the Left.

WENDY L. WALL
ASSOCIATE PROFESSOR OF HISTORY, BINGHAMTON UNIVERSITY, SUNY

WRITTEN FOR *CQ RESEARCHER*, JANUARY 2017

*t*he 2016 presidential election was the most divisive in recent memory. In its wake, Donald Trump called on Americans to "come together as one united people." This would be a tall order for even the most skilled politician. Unfortunately, the president-elect has paired such calls with the same kind of incendiary rhetoric and discordant policy prescriptions that he deployed throughout the campaign. Not only will Trump fail to unify the nation, he is likely to further entrench existing divisions.

If national unity could be forged through policymaking alone, there would seem to be room for hope. Trump favors massive infrastructure spending, a rare policy initiative that could garner support from both sides of the aisle. A former Democrat, Trump has in the past praised single-payer health care and supported an assault weapons ban and a woman's right to choose. While Trump's position on these and other issues "evolved" before or during the campaign, his opportunistic approach to politics might make him more willing to compromise than would a fiercely ideological president.

Unfortunately, Trump's political style is also demagogic and vindictive. During the campaign, he attacked religious and racial minorities, mocked a disabled reporter, disparaged women and appeared to celebrate sexual assault. He threatened to jail his opponent, Hillary Clinton, and was slow to repudiate the support of white supremacists. Not surprisingly, many Americans feel a deep sense of trauma that will be almost impossible for Trump to overcome.

Trump's actions since the election have only exacerbated such fears. The president-elect appointed Stephen Bannon, a leading proponent of the so-called "alt-right," chief White House strategist. Trump's Cabinet appointments also suggest he has abandoned a conciliatory approach. In a postelection rally, Trump called for unity — then reiterated promises to build a wall on the Mexican border and restrict Muslim immigration. Hate crimes and episodes of harassment have soared around the country. Meanwhile, cities ranging from Los Angeles to Minneapolis have vowed to limit their cooperation with federal immigration authorities.

Republicans, astonished by their surprise victory, have mostly rallied to the president-elect. Yet Trump's embrace of Russian President Vladimir Putin, despite compelling intelligence reports that the Russians meddled in the U.S. election, has put him on a collision course with powerful members of his own party. Far from unifying the country, Trump could well fracture it further.

Continued from p. 16

gan philanthropist Betsy DeVos, an advocate of giving students the choice to attend non-public schools, slated to head the Education Department.

These selections by a populist president-elect who has vowed to drain the Washington swamp have raised eyebrows for the large number of billionaires and multimillionaires; analysts say it's the wealthiest Cabinet in U.S. history, with the nominees having combined assets of close to $10 billion as of late December, according to *The Wall Street Journal.* [76]

"I'm not shocked by this," said Sen. Sherrod Brown, D-Ohio. "It's a billionaire president being surrounded by a billionaire and millionaire Cabinet, with a billionaire agenda." [77]

Trump and his defenders, however, say he's picking smart, savvy people who know how to fix a broken economic system. "If people in the United States have lived the American dream and have been able to amass that kind of wealth, well certainly they're super talented, or in what the president-elect says, they're actually 'killers,' " said top Trump aid Anthony Scaramucci. [78]

New Senate Minority Leader Schumer has promised a "very thorough and tough vetting" of Trump's nominees, including one of his earliest, Sen. Sessions for attorney general, the nation's top law enforcement officer. In 1986, the Senate failed to confirm Sessions as a federal judge after he was accused of making racially insensitive remarks. [79]

Several Trump appointees have been vocal opponents of the departments they would lead. For example, Trump tapped Rick Perry, former governor of energy-rich Texas, to head the Department of Energy, whose mandate includes funding energy research, supporting alternative-energy efforts and securing the safety of nuclear weapons. While running for president in 2011, Perry advocated abolishing the department — even as he forgot its name during a debate. [80]

The ACA

Trump chose Rep. Tom Price, R-Ga., an orthopedic surgeon and outspoken critic of the Affordable Care Act, to head the Department of Health and Human Services, which issued the law's regulations and oversees their implementation. "He is exceptionally qualified to shepherd our commitment to repeal and replace Obamacare and bring affordable and accessible health care to every American," Trump said in announcing the appointment. [81]

To get a "true" repeal-and-replace law, Trump must go through Congress, and that could be a problem in the Senate where 60 votes are needed to overcome a filibuster, said Jack Hoadley, a research professor at Georgetown University's Health Policy Institute. [82]

But there's plenty that Trump can do to change the Affordable Care Act to his liking without Congress. "The act itself does permit a fair amount of leeway already to the secretary to make changes that could be done through executive action versus through legislative action," says Peter Claude, a partner at PwC Consulting, part of Pricewaterhouse Coopers, a global tax and advisory firm. But Claude says he doubts Congress will stay on the sidelines. It could amend the law or pass a replacement, he says.

Trump's proposed health care policies include expanding the use of tax-free health savings accounts to encourage individuals covered by high-deductible health insurance plans to save money for medical expenses; allowing people to deduct insurance premium costs on their income tax returns; permitting companies to sell health insurance across state lines to encourage competition and lower costs; removing the ACA requirement that individuals must purchase health insurance or face a financial penalty; and converting Medicaid to a block grant that would give states a fixed amount of funding each year and greater freedom in how to spend it. [83]

Some 20 million uninsured people gained health insurance coverage under the Affordable Care Act through its insurance exchanges and its expansion of Medicaid. [84] The Washington-based Commonwealth Fund, a private foundation supporting independent research on health care issues, estimated that repealing the ACA and replacing it with Trump's alternatives would increase the number of uninsured individuals by as many as 25 million and raise the federal deficit by as much as $41 billion. [85]

The Environment

Trump has appointed a politician from another energy-rich state to head the Environmental Protection Agency. Oklahoma Attorney General Scott Pruitt, along with a coalition of conservative state attorneys general, has twice sued the agency he has been chosen to lead. One suit aims to stop the implementation of the EPA's Clean Power Plan, an Obama-era rule designed to reduce electric power plants' emissions of carbon dioxide, a greenhouse gas. [86]

The Clean Power Plan is in legal limbo as both sides wait for the U.S. Court of Appeals for the District of Columbia Circuit to rule on its fate. The second lawsuit is over recent EPA regulations to curtail the oil and gas sector's emissions of methane, another greenhouse gas.

"No state should comply with the Clean Power Plan if it means surrendering decision-making authority to the EPA," Pruitt told a Senate committee in 2015. [87]

Environmental groups are alarmed. "You couldn't pick a better fossil fuel industry puppet," said May Boeve, executive director of the environmental group 350.org. [88]

But undoing the Obama's environmental legacy won't be easy, says Nathan Hultman, director of University of Maryland's Center for Global Sustainability. "Obama has not been out there recklessly issuing executive orders that can be reversed by the next president," he says.

Instead, most of Obama's environmental policies are regulations and rules that took years to develop and finalize and were subject to public review and comment and often court review. Vehicle fuel economy standards and appliance and equipment efficiency standards are prime examples, and undoing them would require the same regulatory process, he says.

In addition, industry might object to rolling back some of the regulations. "Industry has already adapted and retooled, for instance, under the efficiency standards," says Hultman. "Even the industry might complain: 'Hey, we invested all this money making these changes and now you're changing the standards on us?' "

Because the courts have blocked implementation of the Clean Power Plan, analysts say one way Pruitt could pull the plug is to have the EPA stop defending it in court, although the agency would have to explain its about-face. However, others parties affected by the plan could step in to defend it. New York Attorney General Eric Schneiderman said he is "leading a coalition of states that is already aggressively fighting back against efforts to reverse the progress this country has made in combating climate change over the past eight years." [89] ■

OUTLOOK

Hopes and Fears

Given Trump's unpredictability and free-wheeling style, observers agree that forecasting the outcome of a Trump presidency is a perilous business.

Trump has rightly focused attention on those hurt by globalization and on wage stagnation and inequality, says international economic law expert Gadbaw. He says he hopes the new ad-

ministration will renegotiate trade agreements to "deal with widely recognized problems like currency manipulation, abuse of state-owned enterprises and worker rights."

But adjusting the U.S. trade strategy requires "diplomatic finesse," Gadbaw says. "A bad strategy, poorly executed," he says, "could trigger a spiral of retaliation and counter-retaliation that would unravel the fabric sustaining international markets and global supply chains," leading to a global recession.

Noland of the Peterson Institute for International Economics says he expects Trump's policies to temporarily accelerate economic growth and increase the trade deficit — and that could lead the administration to "reach for managed trade protectionism in a quixotic attempt to deal with the growing trade gap."

Civil libertarians, immigrant advocates and others are worried about Trump's harsh rhetoric on illegal immigration, but Cardinal Brown of the Bipartisan Policy Center says compromise might be possible. "My biggest hope is that Donald Trump, in making immigration such a key component of his campaign, will take the opportunity of his election to work on bipartisan immigration solutions with Congress," she says.

Executive actions, by any administration, are not a long-term solution, she says. "We hope that Republicans in Congress, with a president of their own party, will be willing to lead an effort, and Democrats, in the interest of getting some status and stability for the immigrants in our country, will come to the table." Her biggest fear, she says, is that positions will harden on both sides, "pushing any real change in the status quo indefinitely into the future."

The Migration Policy Institute's Capps would like to see Trump adjust immigration admissions "up or down depending on economic conditions and workforce needs — particularly for high-skilled workers — while retaining America's historic commitment" to humanitarianism and to keeping families together.

On balance, Trump's supporters are optimistic he will shake up the status quo and boost economic growth, restoring hope in forgotten places. Trump himself reached for the grand on the night he won the election.

"Ours was not a campaign but rather an incredible and great movement, made up of millions of hardworking men and women who love their country and want a better, brighter future for themselves and for their family," he declared in his victory speech. "The forgotten men and women of our country will be forgotten no longer." [90]

Trump's critics, however, worry the new president represents something dark and dangerous. Many find it difficult to look ahead to the next four years.

"No one should pretend that Trump will be a normal president," wrote *Washington Post* columnist Eugene Robinson in November. "No one should forget the bigotry and racism of his campaign, the naked appeals to white grievance, the stigmatizing of Mexicans and Muslims. . . . No one should forget the vile misogyny. No one should forget the mendacity, the vulgarity, the ugliness, the insanity. None of this should ever be normalized in our politics." [91] ■

Notes

[1] Jeremy Herb, "Trump drops Twitter bomb on Lockheed Martin's F-35 fighter jet," *Politico*, Dec. 22, 2016, http://tinyurl.com/jg2kgge; Scott Calvert and John W. Miller, "State Officials and Companies See Pluses, Minuses of Trump's Carrier Deal," *The Wall Street Journal*, Dec. 2, 2016, http://tinyurl.com/jodak5c.

[2] "Trump takes battleground states in astonishing presidential victory," The Associated Press, Nov. 9, 2016, http://tinyurl.com/h4ezc6w.

[3] "Low Approval of Trump's Transition but Outlook for His Presidency Improves," Pew Research Center, Dec. 8, 2016, http://tinyurl.com/hb8loqs.

[4] Brian Naylor, "Trump Relives Campaign Victory During Thank-You Tour Rally," NPR, Dec. 1, 2016, http://tinyurl.com/j9hlbpy.

[5] "Positions," Trump-Pence: Make America Great Again, http://tinyurl.com/hqabp99.

[6] Binyamin Appelbaum, "Fed Raises Key Interest Rate, Citing Strengthening Economy," *The New York Times*, Dec. 14, 2016, http://tinyurl.com/zpj6nln.

[7] "2016 election results," CNN, http://tinyurl.com/pt27ryx; Philip Bump, "There's no problem with the size of Donald Trump's mandate, believe me," *The Washington Post*, Dec. 12, 2016, http://tinyurl.com/gv6p4vm.

[8] Scott Clement and Dan Balz, "Poll finds tempered optimism after Trump victory, but doubts about mandate," *The Washington Post*, Nov. 16, 2016, http://tinyurl.com/je5ptay.

[9] Jim Malone, "Trump Eager to Act, But With What Kind of Mandate?" VOA News, Nov. 17, 2016, http://tinyurl.com/z3qstkb.

[10] Carl Hulse, "In a Trump Era, Schumer Declares, Democrats are 'the Barrier,' " *The New York Times*, Nov. 19, 2016, http://tinyurl.com/gwta2u4.

[11] Ed O'Keefe and Paul Kane, "McConnell announces Senate probe of suspected Russian interference: 'The Russians are not our friends,' " *The Washington Post*, Dec. 12, 2016, http://tinyurl.com/zvq4czq.

[12] U.S. Office of Government Ethics, Twitter post, Nov. 30, 2016, http://tinyurl.com/j22x3tg; "Trump moves to cancel business deals in Azerbaijan, Georgia," The Associated Press, PBS NewsHour, Dec. 16, 2016, http://tinyurl.com/hu6poan.

[13] " 'Not My President' Anti-Trump Protests Continue Across US," VOA News, Nov. 12, 2016, http://tinyurl.com/za94a5f.

[14] "Ten Days After: Harassment and Intimidation in the Aftermath of the Election," Southern Poverty Law Center, Nov. 29, 2016, http://tinyurl.com/gopqrju; "Donald Trump has a lot to learn from Loretta Lynch," *The Washington Post*, Dec. 13, 2016, http://tinyurl.com/h2tr2dd.

[15] "Transcript: Donald Trump's Victory Speech," *The New York Times*, Nov. 9, 2016, http://tinyurl.com/jelwa8j.

[16] Reid J. Epstein and Colleen McCain Nelson, "Donald Trump Lays Out Protectionist Views in Trade Speech," *The Wall Street Journal*, June 28, 2016, http://tinyurl.com/juovoul.

[17] Andrea Wong and Ye Xie, "Trump to Brand China Currency Manipulator, Ex-Treasury Aide Says," Bloomberg News, Nov. 9, 2016, http://tinyurl.com/jfn6yep.

[18] Billy Melo Araujo, "What Trump means for US trade and globalization," *The Conversation*, Nov. 14, 2016, http://tinyurl.com/jyhp4od.

[19] Peter Navarro and Wilbur Ross, "Scoring the Trump Economic Plan: Trade, Regulatory, & Energy Policy Impacts," Sept. 29, 2016, p. 17, http://tinyurl.com/j7wsenc.

[20] James McBride and Mohammed Aly Sergie, "NAFTA's Economic Impact," Council on Foreign Relations, July 26, 2016, http://tinyurl.com/k2t56fv.

[21] Patrick Gillespie, " 'Without NAFTA, we would be out of business,' " CNN Money, July 22, 2016, http://tinyurl.com/zst8gtj.

[22] *Ibid.*

[23] *Ibid.*

[24] "Full Text: Donald Trump announces a presidential bid," *The Washington Post*, June 16, 2015, http://tinyurl.com/zfqnjr7; Tom LoBianco, "Donald Trump promises 'deportation force' to remove 11 million," CNN, Nov. 12, 2015, http://tinyurl.com/omgs8da.

[25] Muzaffar Chishti and Michelle Mittelstadt, "Unauthorized Immigrants with Criminal Convictions: Who Might Be a Priority for Removal," Migration Policy Institute, November 2016, http://tinyurl.com/z5sqo7r.

[26] "Donald J. Trump: Address on Immigration," Trump Pence: Make America Great Again, Aug. 31, 2016, http://tinyurl.com/hnjfl9v.

[27] "Defending American Workers," Sen. Jeff Sessions, http://tinyurl.com/gtb8el4.

[28] "Immigrants as Share of the U.S. Population and Civilian Labor Force, 1980-2015," Migration Policy Institute, http://tinyurl.com/zp5vmx2; Jeffrey S. Passel and D'Vera Cohn, "Size of U.S. Unauthorized Immigrant Workforce Stable After the Great Recession," Pew Research Center, Nov. 3, 2016, http://tinyurl.com/jr982dp.

[29] Undocumented workers held 26 percent of farming jobs and 15 percent of construction jobs in 2014, according to the Pew Research Center. The center did not calculate the share of documented immigrants in those jobs. See Passel and Cohn, *ibid*.

[30] Miriam Jordan and Santiago Pérez, "Small Businesses Lament There Are Too Few Mexicans in U.S., Not too Many," *The Wall Street Journal*, Nov. 28, 2016, http://tinyurl.com/ze6xxt4.

[31] *Ibid.*

[32] Heather Long, "No way Trump will cause a recession, adviser says," CNN Money, June 27, 2016, http://tinyurl.com/zv2uew8.

[33] Kenneth Megan and Theresa Cardinal Brown, "Culprit or Scapegoat? Immigration's Effect on Employment and Wages," Bipartisan Policy Center, June 2016, p. 4, http://tinyurl.com/z6lvybf.

[34] Daniel Costa, "Testimony before the Indiana Senate, Select Committee on Immigration Issues," Economic Policy Institute, Sept. 21, 2016, http://tinyurl.com/zld7kxo.

[35] Francine D. Blau and Christopher Mackie, eds., "The Economic and Fiscal Consequences of Immigration," National Academies Press, Sept. 22, 2016, http://tinyurl.com/hjtqjdc.

[36] *Ibid.*, p. 180.

[37] John Paul Tasker, "A Trump presidency could add pressure on Canada's defense spending," CBC News, April 27, 2016, http://tinyurl.com/hvy5hgg; David E. Sanger and Maggie Haberman, "Donald Trump Sets Conditions for Defending NATO Allies Against Attack," *The New York Times*, July 20, 2016, http://tinyurl.com/zfs7ean.

[38] "What Is NATO?" NATO, http://tinyurl.com/cwshna.

[39] "Defence Expenditures of NATO Countries (2009-2016)," NATO, July 4, 2016, http://tinyurl.com/z55dc8m.

[40] Stephen Sestanovich, "What Trump Doesn't Know About Allies," *The New York Times*, July 29, 2016, http://tinyurl.com/jptslts.

[41] David E. Sanger and Maggie Haberman, "In Donald Trump's Worldview, America Comes First, and Everybody Else Pays," *The New York Times*, March 26, 2016, http://tinyurl.com/gnrp2lr.

[42] Ryan Browne, "Top general: Cheaper to keep troops in South Korea than U.S.," CNN, April 21, 2016, http://tinyurl.com/z2rzrkd.

[43] *Ibid.*

[44] Michael Kranish and Marc Fisher, *Trump Revealed: An American Journey of Ambition, Ego, Money, and Power* (2016), p. 3.

[45] Alexandra Suarez, "Where Does Donald Trump

About the Author

Barbara Mantel is a freelance writer in New York City. She was a 2012 Kiplinger Fellow and has won several journalism awards, including the National Press Club's Best Consumer Journalism Award and the Front Page Award. She was a correspondent for NPR and the founding senior editor and producer for public radio's "Science Friday." She holds a B.A. in history and economics from the University of Virginia and an M.A. in economics from Northwestern University.

Live? Inside His New York Homes And Other Luxurious Mansions," *International Business Times*, Sept. 27, 2016, http://tinyurl.com/glbrytu.

[46] Gwenda Blair, *The Trumps: Three Generations That Built An Empire* (2000), pp. 23, 29, 147, 223, 225, 227.

[47] *Ibid.*, pp. 226-227.

[48] *Ibid.*, pp. 120-121, 136-137, 141.

[49] Michael D'Antonio, *Never Enough: Donald Trump and the Pursuit of Success* (2015), pp. 15-18.

[50] Blair, *op. cit.*, pp. 236-237.

[51] D'Antonio, *op. cit.*, pp. 66, 69-70.

[52] *Ibid.*, pp. 55-56.

[53] Blair, *op. cit.*, p. 250.

[54] D'Antonio, *op. cit.*, pp. 78-80.

[55] *Ibid.*, pp. 82-84.

[56] *Ibid.*, pp. 98, 100, 105, 109-110; Alexandra Berzon and Richard Rubin, "Trump's Father Helped GOP Candidate With Numerous Loans," *The Wall Street Journal*, Sept. 23, 2016, http://tinyurl.com/zwmsgd6.

[57] Blair, *op. cit.*, pp. 314-316.

[58] *Ibid.*, p. 329.

[59] Kranish and Fisher, *op. cit.*, pp. 94-95.

[60] *Ibid.*, pp. 95, 98.

[61] David Cay Johnston, *The Making of Donald Trump* (2016), pp. 43-44.

[62] *Ibid.*, pp. 48-49, 60.

[63] Kranish and Fisher, *op. cit.*, pp. 127-129.

[64] *Ibid.*, p. 130.

[65] *Ibid.*, pp. 133, 138.

[66] Johnston, *op. cit.*, pp. 85-87; Amy Bingham, "Donald Trump's Companies Filed for Bankruptcy 4 Times," ABC News, April 21, 2011, http://tinyurl.com/3es3h36.

[67] Johnston, *ibid.*, pp. 88, 92-93.

[68] Bingham, *op. cit.*

[69] Kranish and Fisher, *op. cit.*, pp. 206-209.

[70] *Ibid.*

[71] Catherine Clifford, "Trump casino group in bankruptcy," CNN Money, Feb. 17, 2009, http://tinyurl.com/auk4wc; Jonathan Berr, "Trump Entertainment Resorts files for bankruptcy," CBS News, Sept. 9, 2014, http://tinyurl.com/zjupcvx.

[72] Kranish and Fisher, *op. cit.*, p. 219.

[73] Amanda Taub, "Trump's Victory and the Rise of White Populism," *The New York Times*, Nov. 9, 2016, http://tinyurl.com/opa3s4t.

[74] Patrick Reevell, "Russian Officials and Analysts Think Tillerson as Secretary of State Could End Sanctions," ABC News, Dec. 14, 2016, http://tinyurl.com/zz9eer3.

[75] David Koenig, "Trump's Pick for Top US Diplomat Has Close Ties to Russia," NBC News, Dec. 13, 2016, http://tinyurl.com/h8ador4.

FOR MORE INFORMATION

American Enterprise Institute, 1789 Massachusetts Ave., N.W., Washington, DC 20036; 202-862-5800; aei.org. Conservative think tank that researches international and domestic affairs.

Atlantic Council, 1030 15th St., N.W., 12th Floor, Washington, DC 20005; 202-778-4952; atlanticcouncil.org. Centrist research organization focusing on international affairs.

Bipartisan Policy Center, 1225 I St., N.W., Suite 1000, Washington, DC 20005; 202-204-2400; bipartisanpolicy.org. Think tank that promotes bipartisan policy solutions.

Brookings Institution, 1775 Massachusetts Ave., N.W., Washington, DC 20036; 202-797-6000; brookings.edu. Nonpartisan public policy research organization.

Carnegie Endowment for International Peace, 1779 Massachusetts Ave., N.W., Washington, DC 20036; 202-483-7600; carnegieendowment.org. Global network of policy research centers that seeks to advance cooperation among nations.

Cato Institute, 1000 Massachusetts Ave., N.W., Washington, DC 20001; 202-842-0200; cato.org. Libertarian organization that researches public policy.

Migration Policy Institute, 1400 16th St., N.W., Suite 300, Washington, DC 20036; 202-266-1940; migrationpolicy.org. Nonpartisan think tank that analyzes worldwide migration and refugee policies."

Peterson Institute for International Economics, 1750 Massachusetts Ave., N.W., Washington, DC 20036; 202-328-9000; piie.com. Centrist research institution.

[76] Rebecca Ballhaus, "Financial Holdings of Some Donald Trump Nominees Complicates Approval Process," *The Wall Street Journal*, Dec. 27, 2016, http://tinyurl.com/gl6ne8f.

[77] Jim Tankersley and Ana Swanson, "Donald Trump's Cabinet could be wealthiest in modern history," *Chicago Tribune*, Nov. 30, 2016, http://tinyurl.com/h2k8m2w.

[78] Ben Kamisar, "Trump aide defends wealthy Cabinet appointees," *The Hill*, Dec. 2, 2016, http://tinyurl.com/z2d295m.

[79] Byron Tau, "Schumer Promises Close Vetting of Sessions, Wants Explanation From Flynn," *The Wall Street Journal*, Nov. 18, 2016, http://tinyurl.com/jafvuzw.

[80] Scott Detrow, "Donald Trump Taps Rick Perry To Head Agency He Once Forgot," NPR, Dec. 13, 2016, http://tinyurl.com/jz4mkd7; Juliet Eilperin and Steven Mufson, "Trump taps former Texas Gov. Rick Perry to head Energy Department he once vowed to abolish," *The Washington Post*, Dec. 14, 2016, http://tinyurl.com/zfrjedt.

[81] Hallie Jackson and Alexandra Jaffe, "Donald Trump Picks Rep. Tom Price to Lead Department of Health and Human Services," NBC News, Nov. 29, 2016, http://tinyurl.com/zsmf25d.

[82] Alison Kodjak, "Trump Can Kill Obamacare With Or Without Help From Congress," NPR, Nov. 9, 2016, http://tinyurl.com/nkwtqxp.

[83] "Healthcare Reform," Trump-Pence: Make America Great Again, http://tinyurl.com/zne7txc.

[84] "New Report Details Impact of the Affordable Care Act," Department of Health and Human Services, Dec. 13, 2016, http://tinyurl.com/jblgwoc.

[85] "Donald Trump's Health Care Reform Proposals: Anticipated Effects on Insurance Coverage, Out-of-Pocket Costs, and the Federal Deficit," The Commonwealth Fund, Sept. 23, 2016, http://tinyurl.com/j8x7ude.

[86] Chris Mooney, Brady Dennis and Steven Mufson, "Trump names Scott Pruitt, Oklahoma attorney general suing EPA on climate change, to head the EPA," *The Washington Post*, Dec. 8, 2016, http://tinyurl.com/htvekpv.

[87] Alan Neuhauser, "Trump Taps Oklahoma AG, Climate Change Doubter to Lead EPA," *U.S. News & World Report*, Dec. 7, 2016, http://tinyurl.com/jddsoqc.

[88] *Ibid.*

[89] Valerie Volcovici and David Shepardson, "Trump's EPA pick may struggle to dismantle Obama's environmental legacy," Reuters, Dec. 9, 2016, http://tinyurl.com/zfcclz7.

[90] "Here's the Full Text of Donald Trump's Victory Speech," CNN, Nov. 9, 2016, http://tinyurl.com/ntgnyo7.

[91] Eugene Robinson, "Where I wish Donald Trump failure," *The Washington Post*, Nov. 14, 2016, http://tinyurl.com/goj99l5.

Bibliography

Selected Sources

Books

Blair, Gwenda, *The Trumps: Three Generations That Built An Empire*, **Simon & Shuster, 2000.**
A journalist recounts how three generations of Trump businessmen, beginning with Donald Trump's immigrant grandfather, amassed their wealth.

D'Antonio, Michael, *Never Enough: Donald Trump and the Pursuit of Success*, **Thomas Dunne Books, 2015.**
The president-elect's life and career from teenager to successful presidential candidate is recounted in a biography based on interviews with Trump and his associates.

Kranish, Michael, and Marc Fisher, *Trump Revealed: An American Journey of Ambition, Ego, Money, and Power*, **Scribner, 2016.**
Two journalists trace Trump's business record and look at the influence of his father.

Articles

Ballhaus, Rebecca, "Trump's Wealthy Appointments Contrast With Populist Campaign Tone," *The Wall Street Journal*, **Dec. 1, 2016, http://tinyurl.com/h3g7vja.**
The net worth of Trump appointees far exceeds that of Cabinet secretaries of previous administrations.

Calvert, Scott, and John W. Miller, "State Officials and Companies See Pluses, Minuses of Trump's Carrier Deal," *The Wall Street Journal*, **Dec. 2, 2016, http://tinyurl.com/jodak5c.**
After Trump arranged tax breaks for Carrier Corp to keep 800 jobs in Indiana, other state officials worry they would face similar pressures to make financial concessions when companies threaten to move plants from the United States.

Clement, Scott, and Dan Balz, "Poll finds tempered optimism after Trump victory, but doubts about mandate," *The Washington Post*, **Nov. 16, 2016, http://tinyurl.com/je5ptay.**
After Trump wins the Electoral College but loses the popular vote, only three in 10 Americans tell pollsters that the president-elect has a mandate to carry out his agenda.

Gillespie, Patrick, " 'Without NAFTA, we would be out of business,' " CNN Money, July 22, 2016, http://tinyurl.com/zst8gtj.
Business owners who export to Mexico praise the North American Trade Agreement (NAFTA), which Trump says he wants to renegotiate or renounce.

Kodjak, Alison, "Trump Can Kill Obamacare With Or Without Help From Congress," NPR, Nov. 9, 2016, http://tinyurl.com/nkwtqxp.
A Trump administration could change the rules of the Affordable Care Act without congressional action.

Koenig, David, "Trump's Pick for Top US Diplomat Has Close Ties to Russia," ABC News, Dec. 13, 2016, http://tinyurl.com/j5tzrfm.
Exxon Mobil CEO Rex Tillerson, Trump's pick for secretary of State, spent decades guiding the company's Russian projects.

Sanger, David E., and Maggie Haberman, "Donald Trump Sets Conditions for Defending NATO Allies Against Attack," *The New York Times*, **July 20, 2016, http://tinyurl.com/zfs7ean.**
Trump says the United States will defend NATO allies only if they spend enough on defense.

Wong, Andrea, and Ye Xie, "Trump to Brand China Currency Manipulator, Ex-Treasury Aide Says," Bloomberg News, Nov. 9, 2016, http://tinyurl.com/jfn6yep.
The president-elect might label China a currency manipulator, which would trigger an investigation of unfair trading practices.

Reports and Studies

"Donald Trump's Health Care Reform Proposals: Anticipated Effects on Insurance Coverage, Out-of-Pocket Costs, and the Federal Deficit," The Commonwealth Fund, Sept. 23, 2016, http://tinyurl.com/j8x7ude.
A private research foundation says Trump's health care proposals would increase the number of uninsured.

Blau, Francine D., and Christopher Mackie, eds., "The Economic and Fiscal Consequences of Immigration," National Academy of Sciences, Engineering and Medicine, Sept. 22, 2016, http://tinyurl.com/hjtqjdc.
A panel of independent researchers says immigration benefits the economy but harms the wages of a small number of Americans.

Chishti, Muzaffar, and Michelle Mittelstadt, "Unauthorized Immigrants with Criminal Convictions: Who Might Be a Priority for Removal," Migration Policy Institute, November 2016, http://tinyurl.com/z5sqo7r.
Trump overestimates the number of undocumented immigrants with criminal records, says a nonpartisan migration research organization.

Navarro, Peter, and Wilbur Ross, "Scoring the Trump Economic Plan: Trade, Regulatory, & Energy Policy Impacts," Sept. 29, 2016, http://tinyurl.com/j7wsenc.
Trump's nominee for Commerce secretary (Ross) and his director of trade and industrial policy (Navarro) say his plan will accelerate economic growth and create millions of jobs.

The Next Step:

Additional Articles from Current Periodicals

Environmental Issues

"Al Gore meets Donald Trump and Ivanka for climate talks," BBC News, Dec. 5, 2016, http://tinyurl.com/hael4jz.

Donald Trump, a climate change skeptic, and his daughter Ivanka met with former Vice President Al Gore, who urged the president-elect to take a strong stance on the environment.

Bradner, Eric, "Trump picks Scott Pruitt to head EPA," CNN, Dec. 8, 2016, http://tinyurl.com/ht9cszm.

President-elect Trump selected Oklahoma Attorney General Scott Pruitt, a fierce critic of the Environmental Protection Agency, to head the agency.

Mufson, Steven, and Juliet Eilperin, "Trump transition team for Energy Department seeks names of employees involved in climate meetings," _The Washington Post_, Dec. 9, 2016, http://tinyurl.com/z9ttahn.

Trump's transition team asked the Energy Department to provide a list of employees who participated in climate talks — a request critics feared was an attempt to target those officials who helped implement environmental regulations.

Foreign Policy

Lee, Carol E., and Peter Nicholas, "Donald Trump's Forays Into Foreign Policy Strain Transition," _The Wall Street Journal_, Dec. 23, 2016, http://tinyurl.com/hpd79o8.

Donald Trump's foreign policy pronouncements on China, nuclear weapons and the Israeli-Palestinian peace talks challenge President Obama's policies.

Marans, Daniel, "Newt Gingrich: Donald Trump's Twitter Foreign Policy Is 'Brilliant,' " _The Huffington Post_, Dec. 25, 2016, http://tinyurl.com/jz29zne.

Following Donald Trump's tweets about potentially starting a new nuclear arms race, former House Speaker Newt Gingrich called the president-elect's use of Twitter to make policy announcements "brilliant."

Sarlin, Benjy, "Trump's Take on Foreign Policy Breaks Transition Taboo," NBC News, Dec. 22, 2016, http://tiny url.com/jqf4wdq.

Trump critics say he's breaking tradition by commenting on foreign policy issues during the presidential transition.

Future of Health Care

"Donald Trump's repeal of Obamacare could cut Planned Parenthood's federal funds," _Chicago Tribune_, Dec. 18, 2016, http://tinyurl.com/zp9986s.

Part of the GOP-led legislation to repeal President Obama's health care law in early 2017 would cut off federal funding for Planned Parenthood.

Edwards, Haley Sweetland, "What Donald Trump's Cabinet Pick Means for the Future of Obamacare," _Time_, Nov. 29, 2016, http://tinyurl.com/hg45nzk.

President-elect Trump appointed Rep. Tom Price, R-Ga., a critic of the Affordable Care Act (ACA), to head the Department of Health and Human Services.

Kliff, Sarah, "Why Obamacare enrollees voted for Trump," _Vox_, Dec. 13, 2016, http://tinyurl.com/zvfxdm4.

Some Kentuckians who rely on the ACA for health insurance say they voted for Donald Trump because they expect him to improve the program and not rescind it.

Trade Policy

Fares, Melissa, and David Lawder, "In Trump cabinet, Commerce Secretary will run trade policy," Reuters, Dec. 20, 2016, http://tinyurl.com/z2bsxgs.

Billionaire investor Wilbur Ross, who made his fortune by investing in steel companies, is slated to steer U.S. trade policy as Commerce secretary.

Palmer, Doug, "Trump poised to weaken trade agency," _Politico_, Dec. 20, 2016, http://tinyurl.com/j3zusar.

The person chosen to head the Office of the U.S. Trade Representative will likely play a supporting role in the president-elect's vision for trade under Commerce pick Wilbur Ross.

Paquette, Danielle, "How Donald Trump's trade tariffs could hurt his daughter's business," _The Washington Post_, Dec. 6, 2016, http://tinyurl.com/h4cq66w.

Donald Trump's plans to institute a 35 percent tariff on businesses with supply chains largely based overseas could harm his daughter's clothing line.

CITING _CQ RESEARCHER_

Sample formats for citing these reports in a bibliography include the ones listed below. Preferred styles and formats vary, so please check with your instructor or professor.

MLA STYLE

Jost, Kenneth. "Remembering 9/11." CQ Researcher 2 Sept. 2011: 701-732.

APA STYLE

Jost, K. (2011, September 2). Remembering 9/11. _CQ Researcher, 9,_ 701-732.

CHICAGO STYLE

Jost, Kenneth. "Remembering 9/11." _CQ Researcher_, September 2, 2011, 701-32.

In-depth Reports on Issues in the News

Are you writing a paper?

Need backup for a debate?

Want to become an expert on an issue?

For 90 years, students have turned to *CQ Researcher* for in-depth reporting on issues in the news. Reports on a full range of political and social issues are now available. Following is a selection of recent reports:

Civil Liberties
Privacy and the Internet, 12/15
Intelligence Reform, 5/15
Religion and Law, 11/14

Crime/Law
Jailing Debtors, 9/16
Decriminalizing Prostitution, 4/16
Restorative Justice, 2/16
The Dark Web, 1/16
Immigrant Detention, 10/15
Fighting Gangs, 10/15
Reforming Juvenile Justice, 9/15

Education
Student Debt, 11/16
Apprenticeships, 10/16
Free Speech on Campus, 5/15
Teaching Critical Thinking, 4/15

Environment/Society
Mass Transit, 12/16
Arctic Development, 12/16
Protecting the Power Grid, 11/16
Pornography, 10/16
Women in Leadership, 9/16
Child Welfare, 8/16

Health/Safety
Opioid Crisis, 10/16
Mosquito-Borne Disease, 7/16
Drinking Water Safety, 7/16
Virtual Reality, 2/16

Politics/Economy
European Union's Future, 12/16
The Obama Legacy, 11/16
Populism and Party Politics, 9/16
U.S.-Mexico Relations, 9/16
Modernizing the Nuclear Arsenal, 7/16
Reforming the U.N., 6/16

Upcoming Reports

U.S.-Russia Relations, 1/13/17   China and the South China Sea, 1/20/17   Guns on Campus, 1/27/17

ACCESS

CQ Researcher is available in print and online. For access, visit your library or www.cqresearcher.com.

STAY CURRENT

For notice of upcoming *CQ Researcher* reports or to learn more about *CQ Researcher* products, subscribe to the free email newsletters, *CQ Researcher Alert!* and *CQ Researcher News*: http://cqpress.com/newsletters.

PURCHASE

To purchase a *CQ Researcher* report in print or electronic format (PDF), visit www.cqpress.com or call 866-427-7737. Single reports start at $15. Bulk purchase discounts and electronic-rights licensing are also available.

SUBSCRIBE

Annual full-service *CQ Researcher* subscriptions—including 44 reports a year, monthly index updates, and a bound volume—start at $1,131. Add $25 for domestic postage.

CQ Researcher Online offers a backfile from 1991 and a number of tools to simplify research. For pricing information, call 800-818-7243 or 805-499-9774 or email librarysales@sagepub.com.

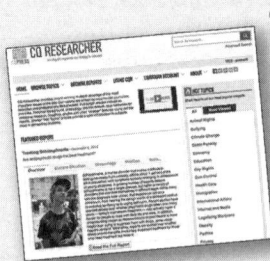

Published by CQ Press, an Imprint of SAGE Publications, Inc.

www.cqresearcher.com

U.S.-Russia Relations

Is a new cold war emerging?

President-elect Donald Trump and Russian President Vladimir Putin appear on a billboard in Montenegro, placed there by a pro-Serbian group sympathetic to Russia, a week after Trump's victory. U.S. intelligence officials say Putin directed Russian hackers to try to tilt the U.S. election in Trump's favor. Trump's disparagement of U.S. intelligence gathering and previous praise of Putin have raised widespread concern.

With Donald Trump's inauguration only days away, U.S. intelligence officials have raised new concerns about relations between the United States and Russia. A report released on Jan. 6 concluded that "an influence campaign" ordered by Russian President Vladimir Putin was designed to damage Hillary Clinton and help elect Trump. The president-elect, who has had long-standing business ties with Russian investors, has angered leaders in both parties by praising Putin's leadership skills and downplaying U.S. intelligence officials' claims that Russian hackers tried to influence the 2016 election. Trump also has stirred controversy by nominating an oil executive with previous business dealings in Russia to head the State Department. Meanwhile, Putin has aggressively pushed to re-establish the country's geopolitical importance by annexing part of Ukraine, joining Iran in supporting Syrian strongman Bashar al-Assad and using hackers and fake news to promote populist candidates and discredit democracy in Europe. In response, the United States and European Union have imposed economic sanctions and bolstered NATO defenses in Central Europe.

CQ Researcher • Jan. 13, 2017 • www.cqresearcher.com
Volume 27, Number 2 • Pages 25-48

THIS REPORT

THE ISSUES	27
BACKGROUND	33
CHRONOLOGY	35
CURRENT SITUATION	38
AT ISSUE	41
OUTLOOK	42
BIBLIOGRAPHY	46
THE NEXT STEP	47

THE ISSUES

27 • Is the West engaged in a new cold war with Russia?
• Should the U.S. try to forge a working relationship with Russian President Putin?
• Can Putin maintain his power in Russia?

BACKGROUND

33 **USSR Emerges**
Vladimir Lenin organized a communist state.

33 **Cold War**
Josef Stalin's expansionism locked the Soviets and the West in a standoff.

34 **USSR Collapses**
All Soviet republics became independent on Dec. 31, 1991.

34 **Putin and New Tensions**
The Russian president sees NATO's expansion as a threat.

CURRENT SITUATION

38 **Confirmation Controversies**
Rex Tillerson faced tough questions during his confirmation for secretary of State.

40 **Russian Hacking**
Intelligence officials say Russia tried to influence the U.S. election.

40 **International Tensions**
Trump's comments about Putin are raising eyebrows.

OUTLOOK

42 **Economic and Political Challenges**
Domestic problems could derail Putin's plans.

SIDEBARS AND GRAPHICS

28 **Tensions Rise Among Russia's Neighbors**
Putin's actions have heightened regional fears.

29 **U.S. Economy Dwarfs Russia's**
Russian gross domestic product declined to $1.36 trillion in 2015.

32 **Americans Sharply Divided Over Putin**
Supporters of Trump and Hillary Clinton had different views on the Russian president.

35 **Chronology**
Key events since 1917.

36 **Facts and Free Expression Become Russian Casualties**
"Putin has seized upon information as a key weapon."

38 **Russian Economy Struggles With Sanctions, Falling Oil Prices**
"It's a highly industrial economy that . . . has to be re-tooled top to bottom."

41 **At Issue:**
Should the Trump administration engage with Russia?

FOR FURTHER RESEARCH

45 **For More Information**
Organizations to contact.

46 **Bibliography**
Selected sources used.

47 **The Next Step**
Additional articles.

47 **Citing CQ Researcher**
Sample bibliography formats.

Cover: AFP/Getty Images/Savo Prelevic

CQ RESEARCHER

Jan. 13, 2017
Volume 27, Number 2

EXECUTIVE EDITOR: Thomas J. Billitteri
tjb@sagepub.com

ASSISTANT MANAGING EDITORS: Kenneth Fireman, kenneth.fireman@sagepub.com, Kathy Koch, kathy.koch@sagepub.com, Scott Rohrer, scott.rohrer@sagepub.com

SENIOR CONTRIBUTING EDITOR:
Thomas J. Colin
tom.colin@sagepub.com

CONTRIBUTING WRITERS: Marcia Clemmitt, Sarah Glazer, Reed Karaim, Peter Katel, Barbara Mantel, Chuck McCutcheon, Tom Price

SENIOR PROJECT EDITOR: Olu B. Davis

EDITORIAL ASSISTANT: Anika Reed

FACT CHECKERS: Eva P. Dasher, Michelle Harris, Betsy Towner Levine, Robin Palmer

SAGE Publishing | CQPRESS

Los Angeles | London | New Delhi
Singapore | Washington DC | Melbourne

An Imprint of SAGE Publications, Inc.

SENIOR VICE PRESIDENT, GLOBAL LEARNING RESOURCES:
Karen Phillips

EXECUTIVE DIRECTOR, ONLINE LIBRARY AND REFERENCE PUBLISHING:
Todd Baldwin

CQ Researcher (ISSN 1056-2036) is printed on acid-free paper. Published weekly, except: (March wk. 4) (May wk. 4) (July wks. 1, 2) (Aug. wks. 2, 3) (Nov. wk. 4) and (Dec. wks. 3, 4). Published by SAGE Publications, Inc., 2455 Teller Rd., Thousand Oaks, CA 91320. Annual full-service subscriptions start at $1,131. For pricing, call 1-800-818-7243. To purchase a CQ Researcher report in print or electronic format (PDF), visit www.cqpress.com or call 866-427-7737. Single reports start at $15. Bulk purchase discounts and electronic-rights licensing are also available. Periodicals postage paid at Thousand Oaks, California, and at additional mailing offices. POSTMASTER: Send address changes to CQ Researcher, 2600 Virginia Ave., N.W., Suite 600, Washington, DC 20037.

U.S.-Russia Relations

BY SUZANNE SATALINE

THE ISSUES

As Donald Trump prepares to assume the presidency on Jan. 20, he faces a series of national security controversies that have raised deep concerns about the future of U.S.-Russia relations.

Front and center is a U.S. intelligence report concluding that Russian President Vladimir Putin oversaw a hacking and disinformation campaign designed "to undermine public faith" in the U.S. election and "denigrate" Trump's Democratic opponent, Hillary Clinton, which eventually became an effort to help Trump get elected. [1] Heightening concerns over the hacking were news articles on Jan. 10 claiming the intelligence report included unsubstantiated allegations that the Russians collected compromising information on Trump's personal life and finances. [2]

In a press conference the next day, Trump called the existence of purported compromising information "nonsense," "fake news" and "phony stuff." He said if the Russians had embarrassing information about him they would have released it. [3]

Trump, whose son said in 2008 that the family's real estate enterprise relied heavily on Russian investors, has disturbed leaders in both parties by repeatedly praising Russian President Vladimir Putin's leadership skills, downplaying the intelligence report on Russian hacking and nominating an oil executive with previous business dealings in Russia to head the State Department.

When questioned at the Jan. 11 press conference about the report that Putin tried to influence the election in his favor, Trump conceded that Russia was likely responsible. But he added: "If

Russian President Vladimir Putin awards the Order of Friendship to then-Exxon Mobil Chairman Rex W. Tillerson, President-elect Trump's pick for secretary of State, in St. Petersburg on June 21, 2013. Some prominent Republicans worry that Tillerson's previous dealings with the Russian oil industry and warm relations with Putin might, Sen. John McCain, R-Ariz., said, "color his approach to . . . Putin and the Russian threat."

Putin likes Donald Trump, guess what, folks, that's called an asset, not a liability. We have a horrible relationship with Putin. I don't know if we will get along. There's a good chance I won't." Still, he said, "Russia will have much greater respect for our country when I'm leading the country" than in the past.

Nevertheless, some Republican leaders have said they are worried about Putin's motives, Trump's praise of Putin and Trump's nomination of Rex W. Tillerson, who conducted several large business agreements in Russia as CEO of Exxon Mobil, to be secretary of State.

"It is a matter of concern to me that [Trump] has such a close personal relationship with Vladimir Putin," Sen. John McCain, R-Ariz., had said last month, after calling Putin "a thug and

a murderer and a killer." [4] And because Tillerson has "done enormous deals" with the Russians, McCain also said, it "would color his approach to . . . Putin and the Russian threat." [5]

The controversies erupted as relations between the United States and Russia — the world's biggest nuclear powers — are more strained than at any time since the Soviet Union collapsed in 1991. Russia has re-emerged as an authoritarian state, with Putin aggressively pushing to re-establish his nation's geopolitical importance. He has strengthened Russia's military, annexed Crimea, supported the regime of Syrian strongman Bashar al-Assad, boosted right-wing nationalists in Europe and tried to influence pending elections in European democracies. (See sidebar, p. 36.) The West has responded by imposing tough economic sanctions on Russia and increasing NATO defenses in central Europe and the Baltic states.

During Senate confirmation hearings on Jan. 11, Tillerson said Putin poses a "danger," but declined to call him a war criminal despite intense pressure from Sen. Marco Rubio, R-Fla., to do so. And Sen. Ben Cardin, a Maryland Democrat, forcefully told Tillerson: "We need to stand up to this bully in Moscow and increase the cost for his behavior." [6]

But Tillerson's nomination also has received bipartisan support. As to whether Tillerson would face a conflict of interest regarding Exxon's business interests in Russia, former Democratic Sen. Sam Nunn told the Senate Foreign Relations Committee that "if confirmed, . . . Tillerson will take off his corporate hat — but use his vast experience to devote 100 percent of his considerable

Tensions Rise Among Russia's Neighbors

A quarter-century after the Soviet Union collapsed, Russian President Vladimir Putin is aggressively pushing to re-establish his nation's geopolitical importance. He has strengthened Russia's military, annexed Crimea, supported separatists in Ukraine and joined Iran in supporting Syrian strongman Bashar al-Assad. Putin's actions have heightened fears among Russia's neighbors, especially former Soviet states in the Baltics, and exacerbated tensions between Russia and the United States and its European allies.

* Crimea was annexed by Russia in 2014 but the action was not recognized by the United Nations. Abkhazia and South Ossetia are Russian-controlled separatist states in Georgia.

intellect, energy and experience to protecting America's interests in this troubled world." [7]

To address potential conflict-of-interest concerns, Tillerson, who retired from Exxon Jan. 1, has agreed, if confirmed, to sell his Exxon stock and allow any additional stock he would receive at retirement to be placed in a trust that could not be invested in the oil giant. [8]

The claims by U.S. intelligence agencies about Russian interference in the U.S. election led President Obama to expel 35 Russian diplomats suspected

of being intelligence operatives and to sanction Moscow's intelligence services. In addition, a bipartisan group of senators is preparing legislation imposing even tougher sanctions on Russia. [9]

Concerns about Trump's potential business ties to Russian investors stem from a 2008 statement by his son Donald Trump Jr., who said, "Russians make up a pretty disproportionate cross-section of a lot of our assets." [10] Trump stressed at his Jan. 11 press conference that he has no business dealings inside Russia, but it remains unclear whether

Russians have invested heavily in his businesses.

Putin's goal is to dismantle the post-Cold War, NATO-European Union order in Europe, argues Fiona Hill, director of the Center on the United States and Europe at the Brookings Institution think tank in Washington. "Putin wants to turn the clock back 70 years to the old 'Yalta agreement' of 1945," Hill wrote in 2015, referring to the agreement among the United States, Great Britain and the Soviet Union giving the Soviets control of Eastern Europe after World War II. Putin wants "a new division of spheres of influence" corresponding "with the historic boundaries of the Russian Empire and the USSR," Hill said. [11]

A former KGB agent, Putin has solidified control over Russian politics and society by using Soviet control tactics — propaganda and repression. He has created a vast state information machine, with state-owned TV stations and digital sites that spin events to burnish the image of Putin and his government and criticize Western democracies. [12] His state security services have investigated, imprisoned and been implicated in the killings of critics and potential challengers. [13]

Putin also has overseen the largest Russian arms buildup since the Soviet Union's demise. Russia has retained its nuclear warheads and is amassing next-generation weapons, including tanks, helicopters, planes and submarines. [14] Internationally, according to the Finnish Institute of International Affairs, a research institute in Helsinki, Putin has sought to reinforce Russia's image as a powerful global actor, raising concerns in the West that his military "poses a serious threat to its neighbors, the whole of Europe and global peace." [15]

In 2014, Russia supported antigovernment rebels in the former Soviet state of Ukraine. After Putin's protégé, Ukrainian President Viktor Yanukovich, was forced from office, Russia invaded and annexed Ukraine's southern province of Crimea, claiming it was an "integral part of Russia" stolen from the country 60 years earlier. [16] The move proved popular at home: Many Russians consider the Black Sea peninsula, which Catherine the Great annexed in 1783, part of the motherland. [17]

But the annexation was widely condemned elsewhere. The United States, the European Union and Australia froze the assets of Russians implicated in the invasion and imposed travel bans and other sanctions on them. [18] NATO, a Western military alliance with 28 member countries, said it would reinforce its forces in Eastern Europe, prompting Russian threats to retaliate if the United States placed missiles near its borders, such as along Romania or Poland. [19]

Putin then challenged U.S. methods for combating Islamic terrorism in Syria, a longtime Russian ally. Addressing the United Nations in September 2015, he called for "a genuinely broad international coalition" to fight the Islamic State (ISIS) and soon began airstrikes in Syria. [20] Putin's critics said he was seeking to build support at home, where Western sanctions had battered the Russian economy. [21] The Syrian campaign brought international anger, however, after it became clear the Russian airstrikes were targeting anti-Assad rebels rather than ISIS, while also destroying humanitarian convoys and civilian hospitals. [22]

Putin has felt threatened by NATO's expansion — former Soviet-controlled Bulgaria, Estonia, Latvia, Lithuania, Romania, Slovakia and Slovenia joined the alliance in 2004 — and has sought to establish a firm line the West should not cross.

"The Ukraine crisis is not just about Eastern Europe; it is also about the world order," said Dmitri Trenin, director of the Carnegie Endowment Moscow Center, the Russian affiliate of the Washington-based international-affairs research organization. "The Kremlin is seeking Washington's recognition of what it regards as its core national security interest: keeping Ukraine as a buffer

U.S. Economy Dwarfs Russia's

Russia's gross domestic product (GDP), a measure of a nation's total economic activity, fell sharply in 2015 to $1.3 trillion because of falling oil prices, while U.S. GDP rose to $18 trillion. The Russian economy, which relies heavily on sales of oil, gas and weapons, has struggled since the demise of the Soviet Union in 1991.

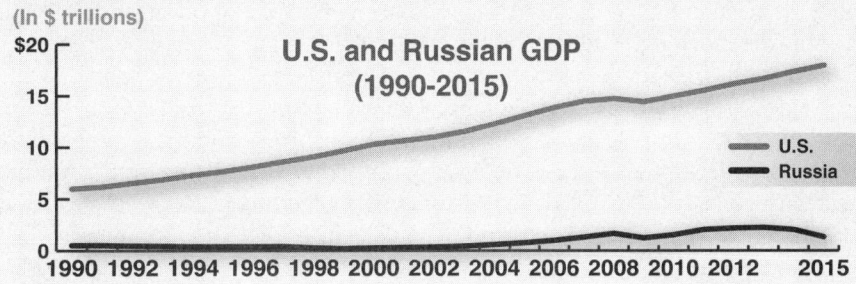

(In $ trillions)

U.S. and Russian GDP (1990-2015)

Source: "Gross Domestic Product," World Bank, Oct. 7, 2016, http://tinyurl.com/jbdsyla

zone between Russia and the West, particularly NATO." [23]

Some Western leaders fear that at a moment of volatility in the Middle East, the Russian president has ignited a new cold war, one more dangerous and volatile than the last, with more nuclear-armed actors than just the United States and Soviet Union. The heightened tensions pose a particular challenge for the Trump administration.

Trump has frequently praised Putin's leadership and said better relations with Moscow would benefit the United States. "Wouldn't it be nice if we actually got along, as an example, with Russia?" he said during the campaign, in more than one iteration. "I'm all for it." [24]

Trump has not said what those warmer relations might look like.

Some foreign policy experts worry that those investments could persuade Trump to help Putin, perhaps by lifting the sanctions, which have harmed Russia's economy and damaged the business interests of Russian oligarchs. [25] Besides the damage from the sanctions, Russia's centralized, oil-dependent economy has been hamstrung by slumping oil prices and outdated manufacturing in a country steeped in corruption. [26] (*See sidebar, p. 38.*)

Since the United States joined other countries in imposing the sanctions, it won't be easy for Trump to cancel them unilaterally, some experts say. Given the Russian economy's weaknesses, several analysts say, the only way Putin would retain his popularity at home in the face of continued sanctions would be to project Russia's power abroad. [27]

As Trump prepares to take office, here are some questions that lawmakers, academics and foreign policy experts are debating:

Is the West engaged in a new cold war with Russia?

Some scholars believe the United States and Russia have entered a new cold war similar to the tense communism-versus-capitalism political and nuclear standoff that defined the period between the end of World War II and the Soviet Union's collapse in 1991.

Today, key flash points between Washington and Moscow include Syria, where Russia's military has intervened to save the Assad regime opposed by the United States, and Ukraine, which has lost two swaths of territory to Russia despite Western protests.

Robert Legvold, a professor emeritus of political science at Columbia University, views tensions between the two nations as a new cold war. "Russia and the West are now adversaries," he wrote. But unlike during the 1980s, the last decade of the post-Cold War period, "when each party viewed the other as neither friend nor foe," the crisis in Ukraine has created a new, less ambiguous relationship, he said. [28]

This deteriorating relationship is reflected in the language used by the two sides, he said, with Putin faulting Washington's "rule of the gun" and Alexander Vershbow, former deputy secretary-general of NATO, saying Russia should now be considered "more of an adversary than a partner." [29]

Just as worries about European stability initially defined the central tension of the original Cold War, in which Moscow and Washington presided over rival alliances, uncertainty over security in Central and Eastern Europe drives the newest crisis. For instance, Russia's annexation of Crimea and invasion of eastern Ukraine triggered fears of similar Russian action in Poland and the Baltic states, which Moscow controlled for more than 40 years after World War II.

Rising tensions between Russia and the Baltics prompted NATO to undertake its biggest military buildup since the Cold War. The alliance, announced in October that it was stationing 4,000 troops on the border between Russia and the Baltic states and in November, the Western alliance put up to 300,000 troops on high alert. [30]

"We have seen a more assertive Russia implementing a substantial military build-up over many years — tripling defense spending since 2000, in real terms; developing new military capabilities; exercising their forces and using military force against neighbors." NATO Secretary-General Jens Stoltenberg told *The Times* of London. [31] Claiming Russia had used propaganda among NATO allies in Europe, he added, "That is exactly the reason why NATO is responding . . . with the biggest rein-

forcement of our collective defense since the end of the Cold War." [32] A 2016 RAND Corp. report had warned earlier in the year that Russia, with its heavier weaponry and larger ground forces, could overrun the Baltics within 60 hours. [33]

The United States and Russia also have supported opposing sides in the conflict in Syria. Washington urged Syrian President Assad to step down, while Russia backed his regime with air and artillery strikes. Putin has vehemently opposed U.S. efforts to restructure the Syrian government, Legvold says, and has refused to join an international effort to allow such a change. Russia has had long-standing ties with Syria, which allowed the Soviet Union to build a resupply station at Tartus, which remains Russia's sole naval base in the Mediterranean region. [34]

In both Syria and Ukraine, U.S.-Russian tensions have peaked at levels similar to those in the original Cold War, said Stephen F. Cohen, a professor emeritus of Russian studies at New York University and Princeton. "We're approaching a Cuban Missile Crisis nuclear confrontation with Russia, both along Russia's borders and possibly over Syria," he said in July, referring to the 1962 standoff between the United States and the USSR over the Soviet placement of nuclear-armed missiles 90 miles from the U.S. mainland. [35] Even if the outcome is a nonmilitary move to isolate Russia, the consequences will be dire, he said.

"Moscow will not bow but will turn, politically and economically, to the East, as it has done before, above all to fuller alliance with China," Cohen wrote in *The Nation*. [36] As a result, "the United States will risk losing an essential partner in vital areas of its own national security, from Iran, Syria and Afghanistan to threats of a new arms race, nuclear proliferation and more terrorism. And — no small matter — prospects for a resumption of Russia's democratization will be terminated for at least a generation." [37]

Cohen argued that the seeds of the current conflict were sown after the Soviet Union collapsed, years before Putin came to power, by NATO's eastward expansion. [38] If the West continues to reject Putin's argument that Russia's perceived boundaries must be respected, "then war is possible, if not now, eventually," Cohen continued. [39]

However, Thomas Graham, managing director at Kissinger Associates, an international consulting firm, says the new cold war rubric is inaccurate because the motivations for the old rivalry no longer exist. "Every time a serious problem emerges in U.S.-Russian relations, someone reaches for the Cold War trope. It is time to put it to rest," says Graham, a former special assistant on Russia during the George W. Bush administration. "The Cold War rivalry resulted from a set of circumstances — ideological and geopolitical — that no longer exist today. What is taking place between Russia and the United States is a not-so-unusual rivalry between great powers."

Mark Kramer, program director for Russian and Eurasian studies at Harvard University's Davis Center, also dismisses a cold war framework. "There's a difference between having acrimonious relations and having a new cold war," he says. "The Cold War was a very bleak period."

Putin's instincts are authoritarian, but post-Soviet Russia is far weaker than the Soviet Union was and does not command global superpower reach, Kramer says. For instance, the Russian army is only about one-fifth the size of the Soviet army, and Russia does not have the Soviet Union's Marxist ideological appeal, because communism has been discredited, he says. Analysts say Putin's political ideology is a mixture of Russian ultra-nationalism, Orthodox Christian fundamentalism and a rejection of liberal Western democracy. [40]

Thus, Kramer concludes, Russia is not the mighty adversary it once was. "It's not even the United States' most powerful rival. I would put China there," Kramer says, adding that while Russia is the larger nuclear rival, "China is the main rival of the United States looking over the next 20 to 30 years."

Should the United States try to forge a working relationship with Russian President Vladimir Putin?

The United States and Russia disagree on numerous issues: Ukraine, Syria, NATO's reach and authority, U.S. activities in the Middle East and the role of democracy and civil liberties in Russia. Yet, the two share some common goals: ending the war in Syria, albeit with differing outcomes; controlling the spread of nuclear weapons; stopping the spread of Islamic terrorism; solving environmental problems; and halting human trafficking and the trade in illegal arms. [41]

Scholars, government officials and even the U.S. presidential candidates have debated whether the United States should put aside its differences with Putin and build a working partnership to tackle more international issues. "I think he respects me," candidate Trump said in July. "I think it would be great to get along with him." [42]

The debate is unfolding in Washington amid questions about how best to punish suspected Russian interference in the presidential election and as the Senate prepares for potentially controversial confirmation hearings on Tillerson.

Columbia's Legvold says that if Russia and the United States continue to view each other as adversaries, it could warp both countries' foreign policies, damage important components of international politics and divert attention and resources from major security issues. "In general, it's a deteriorating situation, because of the unknown crises — the potential crisis around Ukraine, or because of . . . arms racing or militarization of the Central European front," he says.

And with Russia patrolling near the Baltics with ships and aircraft, if NATO takes a step Russia sees as aggressive, "you get a situation that's heating up," Legvold says. The best way to ratchet down the tension, he says, is for the

two sides to talk to each other, at the highest levels, and without preconditions. [43] The Russians are most concerned that "their national interests are respected and not directly assaulted" in the former Soviet countries.

The two nations have a common enemy in ISIS, Legvold points out.

Graham of Kissinger Associates says that nuclear nonproliferation is another topic that has historically been "a good place to start" discussions with the Russians, since "we are the two critical countries dealing with that." But such cooperation has deteriorated due to tensions created by the expansion of NATO and Russia's annexation of Crimea in 2014. [44]

At Tillerson's confirmation hearing, after saying that "the risk of an accidental, unauthorized, or mistaken launch of a nuclear ballistic missile is unnecessarily high — particularly in our world of increasing cyber vulnerability," former Sen. Nunn added, "it is dangerous for the United States, for Russia and for the world when we have virtually no dialogue on reducing nuclear risks and very little military to military communication. If this continues and we are guided by zero-sum logic — we and Russia may be rewarded at some point with catastrophe." [45]

Some U.S. hardliners doubt that establishing a Moscow-Washington partnership is possible. Russia "is undermining the principles of European order and is seeking to rally countries against U.S. leadership," Thomas Graham, a former senior director for Russia at the National Security Council now managing director at Kissinger Associates, an international consulting group, said at a debate just before the election. "We cannot ignore these challenges." [46]

Rather, he continued, "in an interconnected world we need to engage Russia [but] keep in mind the proper balance between cooperation and competition." [47]

Graham would like for Trump to ramp up sanctions and provide weapons to Ukraine, but he realizes that is unlikely.

He also says the new administration needs to reassure its NATO allies that the United States will defend and support the "sovereignty and territorial integrity of Russia's neighbors who seek to join NATO or the European Union." [48] Four more former Soviet-sphere countries have asked to join the alliance: Bosnia and Herzegovina, Georgia, Montenegro and the former Yugoslav Republic of Macedonia. [49]

Citing Russia's annexation of Crimea, Alina Polyakova, deputy director of the Dinu Patriciu Eurasia Center at the Atlantic Council, a research center in Washington, D.C., said, "This is a pattern. A pattern of complete disregard for international law, which Russia signs and then willingly breaks, a pattern of no respect for sovereignty of independent states, and, of course, a brutal disregard for basic human rights. This pattern clearly shows us that Russia is not a trustworthy partner." [50]

Speaking at the McCain Institute debate, Polyakova warned, "Many administrations, both Republican and Democratic, have tried to engage with Russia, and they have failed." She urged the next American president not to "fall" for Russia's claims of a fresh start. [51]

Can Putin maintain his power in Russia?

Putin was an unlikely person to lead the post-Soviet nation. A former KGB colonel, he served as deputy mayor of St. Petersburg and became a Kremlin aide before President Boris Yeltsin named him first prime minister and then acting president in 1999.

Constitutionally barred from serving more than two consecutive terms, Putin stepped aside after his second presidential term ended in 2008 to serve as prime minister under handpicked successor Dmitri Medvedev. Then Putin was re-elected president in the summer of 2012. [52]

Putin has faced daunting challenges in his current term, including plummeting oil and gas prices, international condemnation of Russia's air war against Assad's opponents in Syria and pressures from NATO and Western sanctions after Russia invade Ukraine.

Under the Russian constitution, Putin can serve until 2024 — a total of 12 years if he is re-elected in 2018, bringing to 24 the number of years he will have led Russia either as president or prime minister. Many Russia observers think he will likely serve that full tenure.

Although Russia faces economic struggles, Clifford Gaddy, a senior fellow with the Brookings Institution, says he does not see any domestic political threats to Putin because "they are nonexistent in Russia," because most dissenters have fled to the West. "And the idea that there'd be a palace coup, an internal revolt? I see no evidence for that. I'm convinced he has full control of security," Gaddy says. "So yeah, he'll be in power."

Harvard's Kramer says Putin does not appear to be grooming a successor. In the meantime, he remains popular, although some signs indicate his domestic support is flagging. For instance, 55 percent of Russians told the Levada Center, a Moscow research group, in October that the country is headed in the right direction, but that was down 6 percentage points from a year earlier. [53]

Putin's earlier high popularity numbers were attributed to perceptions about the economy's robust health. During his first two terms, Russians lauded him for their rising standard of living. But in 2011, after Putin announced he would again seek the presidency, Russians balked. In massive demonstrations and rallies, citizens demanded democratic change. Their hopes soured in 2012 after Putin returned to the presidency and the government enacted stiff fines on demonstrators while some opposition leaders were charged with a variety of offenses, seemingly to neuter their power. [54] One of the most prominent, former Deputy Prime Minister Boris Nemtsov, was shot to death near the Kremlin. [55] Five Chechen men are being tried in the killing, but Nemtsov's family believes there is little evidence tying these individuals to the crime. [56]

Americans Sharply Divided Over Putin

Only 8 percent of voters who supported Democratic presidential candidate Hillary Clinton viewed Russian President Vladimir Putin favorably, compared to 35 percent of supporters of Republican winner Donald Trump.

U.S. Voters' Views of Vladimir Putin, 2016

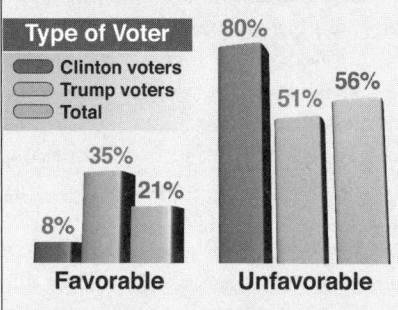

Type of Voter		
▬ Clinton voters		
▬ Trump voters		
▬ Total		

Favorable: 8%, 35%, 21%
Unfavorable: 80%, 51%, 56%

Source: Kathy Frankovic, "Americans and Trump part ways over Russia," YouGov, Dec. 14, 2016, http://tinyurl.com/jtw6fnb

After the United States and the European Union sanctioned Russia in 2014 for its Ukraine invasion, most Russians supported Putin for defying the West and seizing territory they considered part of Russia. They believed Putin was "protecting them from external threats and has made Russia into a great power again," said Jensen. [57]

But some evidence indicates Putin's support may be shallower and more volatile than the numbers indicate. Many poll respondents who said they supported Putin may have feared repercussions if they criticized him, Jensen said. [58] Serious challengers to Putin's power have been sentenced, imprisoned or end up dead, experts say. [59]

Yet an opposition movement survives. Lawyer Alexei Nalvany, a leader of the anti-Putin protests in 2012 and whose nonprofit exposes government corruption, says he plans to oppose Putin in the March 2018 election. [60]

Russia's oligarchs — insiders and friends who managed to buy state-owned enterprises, often at deeply discounted prices, after the USSR dissolved — are no doubt furious that Western sanctions and lower oil prices have dented their wealth. "These critics do not want Putin's personal ambitions to destroy their fortunes, but believe that if they openly opposed him they would be crushed," Jensen said. Putin is vulnerable, he said, and a single event could tip into social unrest, buoy a new opponent and split the elite. [61]

Signs have emerged that Putin may be, once again, eliminating disloyal figures. In November, the nation's economic development minister, Aleksei Ulyukayev, was detained on charges of soliciting a $2 million bribe, which some saw as punishment for contradicting Putin's wishes over a merger of two state-owned energy companies. [62]

To the McCain Institute's Kramer, the arrest is "a sign the element of predictability is starting to erode." Future leaders, he says, likely will come from the state security sphere: Defense Minister Sergei Shoigu; Alexander Bortnikov, director of the Federal Security Service, one of the KGB successor agencies; Nikolai Patrushev, secretary of the security council; and the longtime aide, Igor Sechin, CEO of the state-owned oil giant Rosneft.

Even so, Kramer says he assumes Putin will survive in office. "If change comes it will be through a coup or a forced resignation," he says, adding, however, that such a scenario is unlikely.

"He's become a hostage of his own system, through corruption and self-enrichment. He cannot afford to leave," says Kramer. Some Kremlin watchers have estimated that the president is worth $200 billion. [63]

"He's the only one who can preserve the system and protect himself." If he stepped down, "either he'll be killed, or investigated and arrested, thrown in jail [or have his] money taken away," Kramer says.

BACKGROUND

USSR Emerges

Strikes and protests surged in the early years of the 20th century as Russian workers pushed against a hobbled monarchy that used martial law and prison camps to maintain control. The 1914 decision by Czar Nicholas II (reigned 1894-1917) to enter World War I on the side of France and the United Kingdom against Germany and Austro-Hungary triggered economic and political chaos. [64]

By 1917 a popular uprising forced Nicholas to abdicate. A provisional government was created, but it was toppled later that year by the Bolshevik Party and its leader, Vladimir Lenin. In service of their ideological goal to create a workers' state, the Bolsheviks established a "dictatorship of the proletariat," as defined by German philosopher and socialist revolutionary Karl Marx. Lenin withdrew Russia from the war and initiated broad social and cultural changes under a centralized government that other governments treated as a rogue state.

In 1922, the Bolsheviks organized their nation into the Union of the Soviet Socialist Republics (USSR). When Lenin died two years later, a Georgia-born communist revolutionary Josef Stalin succeeded him. Stalin began a crash industrialization program, forcing farmers into collectives and drawing factory workers from the countryside.

To forestall potential rivals, Stalin ordered a series of purges in the 1930s that began with party officials and eventually included artists, clerics, government officials and army generals. [65] Millions of people were rounded up and shot or exiled to prison camps, or gulags, in the far north and east. [66]

The purges hampered Soviet readiness for the next war against the Germans, which began with a powerful German invasion in June 1941. Nevertheless, despite suffering extreme privation and losses of life, the Soviets repelled the Germans and helped the United States and Great Britain win World War II.

But the victory in what Russians still call their "Great Patriotic War" came at a great cost: An estimated 26 million Soviet soldiers and civilians were killed, leaving the country shattered, with a large population of widows, orphans and maimed veterans. [67]

Cold War

The Soviets' sacrifices were rewarded. Before the war even ended, Stalin had persuaded Allies meeting in 1945 in Yalta (in Crimea) to ratify his seizure of the Baltic nations of Estonia, Latvia and Lithuania, and the return of most of the vast territory Russia had lost in World War I. He orchestrated takeovers of Central and Eastern Europe and pushed those nations, including what became East Germany, into an economic union. British Prime Minister Winston Churchill in 1946 said an "iron curtain" had descended across the continent. [68]

In little more than three decades, the Soviet state had achieved world-power stature. But Stalin's brutal methods — mass detentions and executions and reliance on slave labor — and his expansionist policies repulsed Western leaders. [69] The resultant Cold War locked the Soviet Union and the West in an intense geopolitical battle, usually with the capitalist West trying to stem communism's spread. In 1949, the United States, Canada and several Western European countries created the North Atlantic Treaty Organization (NATO), a military alliance to protect against Soviet expansion. [70] In response, the Soviet Union and seven Eastern European countries in 1955 formed the Warsaw Pact, a military alliance to counter NATO. [71]

In the next decades, the Soviets pushed their security zone beyond Eastern Europe to encompass North Korea, Central Asia and the Middle East. The United States tried to influence nations in Latin America, Western Europe, Southeast Asia and Japan. [72] But the political standoff sometimes erupted into armed conflicts.

Among the tensest Cold War moments was a 1948-49 Soviet blockade of West Berlin designed to force Western powers to withdraw from the city. The United States responded by airlifting supplies into Berlin. In a dangerous nuclear stand-off in 1962, the United States vowed to blockade Cuba if the Soviets did not remove nuclear missiles placed there secretly and threatened to use nuclear weapons against the Soviets if they used them against the United States.

Proxy Cold War conflicts ignited in Korea, Vietnam, Central America, southern Africa, the Middle East and Afghanistan, sometimes with the Soviet Union aided by communist-led China. [73] In the 1960s and '70s, the Soviets tried to use left-wing terrorist groups to destabilize Italy and Germany and break up NATO. [74]

After Stalin died in 1953, his successor, Nikita Khrushchev, denounced his predecessor's repression and violence and sought to reform the economy. He began releasing millions of citizens from labor camps. Residents of some Eastern bloc states began to agitate for change: Poles struck against the government in 1953, and Hungarians demanded greater sovereignty three years later. [75] Khrushchev sent tanks to quell an anti-communist uprising in Budapest in 1956. In 1961 the communist government of the German Democratic Republic raised a concrete barricade knows as the Berlin Wall to seal off that city's eastern, communist-controlled sector.

In 1968 Leonid Brezhnev, who ousted Khrushchev in 1964, deployed troops to Czechoslovakia to suppress a movement seeking democracy and personal freedoms.

In the 1970s, high oil prices helped prop up the Soviet economy, even as consumer goods, priced artificially low, constrained how much money state-owned factories made. [76]

The USSR devoted a large portion of its budget to maintaining military parity with the United States. Moscow's 1979 decision to intervene militarily in Afghanistan to support a shaky communist regime enmeshed the Soviets in a losing, decade-long war. Soviet troubles deepened in 1980 when a Polish trade union, Solidarity, staged mass strikes.

USSR Collapses

After coming to power in 1985, Soviet President Mikhail Gorbachev began to overhaul his country's relations with the West. The nation signed major disarmament treaties with U.S. President Ronald Reagan.

The pace of change accelerated in 1986 after a nuclear reactor exploded in Chernobyl, Ukraine, ultimately caus-

James Clapper, director of National Intelligence, center, tells a Senate Armed Services Committee hearing on Jan. 5 that election-year hacking by Russia could not have occurred without approval at the "highest levels" of the Russian government. Clapper is flanked by Adm. Michael Rogers, director of the National Security Agency, right, and Marcel Lettre II, under-secretary of Defense for intelligence.

ing thousands of deaths. The Soviet government waited days to disclose the disaster, likely increasing injuries and the body count. Buffeted by intense criticism over this decision, Gorbachev realized the government needed to reform quickly if it was to survive. [77]

He instituted policies of glasnost (openness) and perestroika (restructuring), which relaxed some controls on the economy and permitted greater freedoms. He spoke of "common human values," but the Soviet economy still stagnated. [78] Gorbachev began to suggest that citizens of Warsaw Pact countries should be free to select their own governments. [79]

In mostly free elections in June 1989 Poland chose a non-communist government — the first since World War II ended. The Baltic states began agitating for independence, and East Germany's Communist Party boss was ousted. When a new East German government said citizens could cross into the West, residents massed at the Berlin Wall and were allowed to walk through, ending their imprisonment. The sledge hammers used to destroy the hated barrier sounded the death knell of the Cold War.

Other Eastern-bloc countries soon joined Poland in determining their governments. Lithuania's declaration of independence from the Soviet Union in March 1990 signified the start of the union's demise, which accelerated in 1991 after a hardline coup failed and Ukrainians overwhelmingly voted for independence. On New Year's Eve of that year, all 15 Soviet republics officially became independent countries.

Putin and New Tensions

As the Soviet Union crumbled, so did the Russian economy. Industry nearly collapsed, inflation soared and the nation had to import grain. Boris Yeltsin's presidency (1991-99) was rocked by accusations of corruption after the government sold off state-owned oil, gas, minerals, banks and communications entities to a handful of cronies who became very wealthy.

Ethnic tensions that the Soviet Union had kept in check ignited throughout the region. Russian troops brutally suppressed secessionist uprisings — twice — in Chechnya, a republic in the Caucasus. In the mid-1990s, Ukraine agreed to rid itself of nuclear weapons in return for U.S. and Russian guarantees of its territorial integrity.

Putin, whom Yeltsin tapped as his successor, became president in 2000. Rising oil prices boosted the country's GDP and gave Putin a strong mandate. But he was less friendly to the West than Yeltsin had been. Although Putin supported the initial U.S. response to the Sept. 11 terrorist attacks, he opposed the U.S.-led Iraq War in 2003, the NATO-sponsored secession of Kosovo from Serbia in 2008 and the U.S. plan to install a missile defense system in Eastern Europe in the mid-2000s.

As Eastern European countries sought to join NATO, Putin considered the alliance a provocative intrusion on Russia's sphere of interest. [80] He was especially angered in 2004 when former Soviet republics Estonia, Latvia and Lithuania joined the alliance. The Russian government also blamed the CIA and American officials for encouraging anti-Russian revolts that fed the so-called 2003 Rose Revolution in Georgia and the 2004 Orange Revolution in Ukraine.

Putin's handpicked successor Medvedev was elected in 2008, with Putin serving as his prime minister. Eight months later Obama won the

Continued on p. 36

Chronology

1917-1991
Soviet Union rises and falls.

1917
A socialist revolution in Russia overthrows the Romanov dynasty and brings Vladimir Lenin's Bolsheviks to power.

1922
Union of Soviet Socialist Republics (USSR) is formed as a multi-ethnic, atheistic state and embarks on a massive plan to build a modern industrial nation.

1928
Soviet leader Josef Stalin launches the first of several five-year plans, pushing the USSR from its agrarian past to an industrial economy. He will cement control through massive surveillance, arrests and murder.

1945
USSR helps Allies win World War II. Concerns about Stalin's quest to control Eastern Europe lead to the Cold War, a global rivalry between the United States and USSR.

1955
Eight communist countries in Central and Eastern Europe sign the Warsaw Pact military alliance with USSR.

1989
After Communist Party leader Mikhail Gorbachev promotes openness in the Soviet state, anti-communist activism flares in the Soviet bloc. The Berlin Wall separating East and West Germany falls.

1991
The USSR is dissolved; 15 republics emerge. Russia joins the North Atlantic Cooperation Council (1991) and the Partnership for Peace program (1994).

1990s-Present
After turmoil, Russian economy stabilizes. Putin accused of trying to influence U.S. presidential election.

1992
Russian lawmakers privatize state-owned enterprises in effort to rapidly transform from communism to capitalism.

1999
Russian President Boris Yeltsin names Prime Minister Vladimir Putin as acting president; Putin, a former KGB agent, quickly begins consolidating his power.

2003
Rose revolution in Georgia and Orange revolution the next year in Ukraine demand democratic reforms. Worried Russian officials clamp down on civic freedoms.

2004
European Union (EU) and the North Atlantic Treaty Organization (NATO) expand to Russia's western border.

2008
Dmitri Medvedev wins presidency and appoints Putin as prime minister. . . . Russia's demand that Georgia end its bid to join NATO ends with Russia occupying Georgian territory.

2011
Activists assert that Russia's legislative election was marred by fraud. Massive protests erupt, but die out after government crackdown.

2012
Russia joins World Trade Organization. . . . Putin easily wins a new term as president.

2013
EU-Russia relations weaken after the Union announces plans for free-trade pacts with several former Soviet republics, including Ukraine. EU-Ukraine deal falls apart amid accusations of Russian intimidation (November).

2014
More than 100 people are killed in Ukrainian protests over the rejected EU deal, forcing President Viktor Yanukovych to resign. . . . Russia annexes Crimea; U.S. and NATO impose economic sanctions on Russia.

2015
Putin sends tanks, artillery and planes to Syria to defend President Bashar al-Assad, triggering international outrage.

2016
A secret CIA report in October says hackers connected with the Russian government stole information from the Democratic National Committee and leaked embarrassing details about presidential candidate Hillary Clinton in an effort to help businessman Donald Trump win the election. Trump dismisses the allegations. President Obama demands full report on the hacking, expels 35 Russian diplomats and sanctions Moscow's intelligence services.

2017
Intelligence officials release unclassified portion of report on Russian election-year hacking. . . . President-elect Trump is briefed on evidence of hacking and later says he believes the Russians were involved. Trump vows Russia will "have much greater respect" for the U.S. under his leadership.

Facts and Free Expression Become Russian Casualties

"Putin has seized upon information as a key weapon."

On the eighth floor of a nondescript building in southwest Moscow, the successor agency to the KGB employs what researchers call the world's most intrusive listening tool. Referred to by its Russian acronym SORM, the machine scours e-mails and internet searches and scoops up data from Skype and social media networks used in Russia, according to Russian investigative journalists Andrei Soldatov and Irina Borogan. [1]

SORM is the tip of an iceberg, a central component in a vast Russian effort to weaponize information as an instrument of state policy. The effort peers both inward and outward — monitoring and controlling information created by and about Russian citizens in order to prevent challenges to Russian President Vladimir Putin and to burnish his image and advance his geopolitical goals by spreading disinformation. [2]

"Since Putin's return to the presidency [in 2012], the government has successfully pushed for legislative changes to establish stronger state control over all kinds of civic expression and introduced disproportionately harsh sanctions for violating such restrictions," says a report by PEN America, a free speech advocacy group based in New York. "Putin has seized upon information as a key weapon in his fight to promote Russia's resurgence in the world." [3]

A major part of the domestic program is what Soldatov and Borogan call "the Red Web," an effort — patterned on China's "Great Firewall" censorship machine — to sift and control all the online information accessed by Russian citizens. [4] Russia's compliant parliament enacted a series of laws that enable the information collection. One, a 2014 law requiring websites that store data on citizens to use only Russian servers, was used in 2016 to block citizens from accessing the social networking site LinkedIn. [5]

Another, enacted in 2016, gave the Kremlin broad tools to monitor cyberspace, including a provision requiring communication companies to retain users' cellphone, text and internet records for at least six months and to make that information accessible to Russian security services. The government also gained the right to demand the keys to encrypted electronic traffic. The so-called "Yarovaya law" of 2016 was needed to fight terrorism, the government said. [6]

But human rights groups called it an attack on fundamental rights and freedoms and said it was really aimed at limiting internet use by the opposition. [7]

Russia's disinformation campaign has two goals. One is to feed fake news and false information to the Russian public in an effort to deflect attention from internal problems. The program also aims to make the government's foreign policy efforts seem necessary by sowing confusion and falsehoods, a program that the West has used as well, according to a study by journalists Michael Weiss and Peter Pomerantsev. "The aim of this new propaganda is not to convince or persuade, but to keep the viewer hooked and distracted, passive and paranoid, rather than agitated to action," they wrote. [8]

The government-run RT channel (formerly Russia Today) broadcasts conspiracy theories — such as claims that the 9/11 attack was a hoax or intimations that there's a "hidden hand" behind the Syrian conflict. RT and Voice of Russia also republished dubious stories that Syrian rebels engaged in sarin attacks in Damascus. [9] The Kremlin employs an army of "trolls" who inundate Western media companies' comment sections and Twitter feeds with provocative comments, tying up newsroom staff who must clear out the specious comments, according to Weiss and Pomerantsev. [10]

The disinformation program also promotes foreign politicians sympathetic to Putin, such as French ultra-nationalist leader Marine Le Pen, whose party sought a $28 million loan from Russia last year 2016. [11] In 2014, the far right leader had received a loan of 11 million euros from a bank with Russian ties. [12]

The program also strives to undermine foreign leaders whose views are antithetical to the Russian president. After the U.S. presidential election, CIA and FBI officials announced that Russian hackers had broken into Democratic Party servers and stolen information embarrassing to the party, with the aim of helping Donald Trump win the presidency. Russia denied involvement, and Trump said he doubted the truth of the intelligence. [13]

Continued from p. 34

U.S. presidency and vowed to "reset" U.S.-Russian relations.

Medvedev made clear Russia's goal would be to limit U.S. power. "The world should be multipolar," he said. "We cannot accept a world order in which all decisions are taken by one country, even such a serious and authoritative country as the United States of America. This kind of world is unstable and fraught with conflict." He added: "Russia, just like other countries in the world, has regions where it has its privileged interests." [81]

The two nations cooperated on combating militant Islamic fighters in Afghanistan. During the Arab Spring uprisings in 2011, Russia did not veto a U.N. Security Council move to deploy a NATO military mission in Libya, where Libyan leader Moammar Gadhafi was toppled that year. And the United States backed Russia's bid to join the World Trade Organization, allowing greater access to global markets.

Tensions flared, though, when Georgia and Ukraine sought to join NATO, which the United States supported but Russia firmly opposed. [82] The Russia-Georgia war that erupted in 2008 ended with Russia tightening its control over Georgia's two secessionist regions, Abkhazia and South Ossetia. [83]

When he was reelected president in May 2012, Putin faced mounting po-

Putin's drive to control the news media began early in his presidency. In 2000, once-independent TV networks criticized him and the government after an explosion sank the nuclear-powered submarine Kursk. [14] A year later a state gas company took over one network. [15] By 2004, when more than 300 school children being held captive by terrorists were killed during a raid by special forces, Russian TV stations cut away from the event and broadcast movies and TV shows. [16]

After that, Putin "realized that people would not revolt for freedom of the press and would support some quelling of journalism," says Vasily Gatov, a visiting fellow at the University of Southern California's Annenberg Center on Communication Leadership and Policy and a former journalist for Russian and Western media companies. "He started to believe that journalists by definition are traitors of the state," Gatov says. In time, the Russian press code dictating what cannot be covered grew from a few paragraphs to several pages, he says.

In addition, Federal Law No. 398, which Putin signed in 2013, allowed prosecutors to order a state carrier to block websites that call for mass riots, "extremist" activities and participation in illegal assemblies. In early 2014, Roskomnadzor, Russia's communications regulatory agency, blocked more than 85 websites for "extremist content." [17]

During the 2013-14 revolution in Ukraine and Russia's annexation of Crimea in 2014, the Kremlin disseminated fake and misleading news via the state-owned news organizations RT and Sputnik, Gatov says. After Russia invaded Georgia in 2008 the mission of RT — started in 2005 to burnish Russia's image abroad — had changed to one of disseminating disinformation. While RT covered some news accurately, Gatov says, it also has broadcast conspiracy theories, including stories that the United States started the Ebola crisis. [18]

Russian TV and internet sites also have asserted that the conflict in eastern Ukraine was a popular uprising against local rule and that Russia had to intervene to protect the rebels. [19] Western governments say forces that opposed the new government in Kiev were aided and directed by Russia, and in some cases were disguised Russian soldiers. [20]

— Suzanne Sataline

[1] Andrei Soldatov and Irina Borogan, "The Red Web: The Struggle Between Russia's Digital Dictators and the New Online Revolutionaries," PublicAffairs, 2015, http://tinyurl.com/gudemdr.

[2] Peter Pomerantsev and Michael Weiss, "The Menace of Unreality: How the Kremlin Weaponizes Information, Culture and Money," The Interpreter, Institute of Modern Russia, November 2014, http://tinyurl.com/khfg2rp.

[3] "Discourse in Danger: Attacks on Free Expression in Putin's Russia," PEN America, Jan. 25, 2016, http://tinyurl.com/jx8qj8n.

[4] Andrei Soldatov and Irina Borogan, "Putin brings China's Great Firewall to Russia in cybersecurity pact," The Guardian, Nov. 29, 2016, http://tinyurl.com/js3pd69.

[5] Maria Tsvetkova and Andrew Osborn, "Russia starts blocking LinkedIn website after court ruling," Reuters, Nov. 17, 2016, http://tinyurl.com/j58r9nx.

[6] Ksenia Koroleva, "Yarovaya" Law — New Data Retention Obligations for Telecom Providers and Arrangers in Russia," Latham & Watkins LLP, July 29, 2016, http://tinyurl.com/hz64bkr.

[7] Ivan Nechepurenko, "Russia Moves to Tighten Counterterror Law; Rights Activists See Threat to Freedoms," The New York Times, June 24, 2016, http://tinyurl.com/hvrv9xw.

[8] Pomerantsev and Weiss, *op. cit.*

[9] *Ibid.*

[10] *Ibid.*

[11] Ivo Oliveira, "National Front Seeks Russian cash for election fight," Politico, Feb. 19, 2016, http://tinyurl.com/h3uozkn.

[12] *Ibid.*

[13] Adam Entous and Ellen Nakashima, "FBI in agreement with CIA that Russia aimed to help Trump win White House," The Washington Post, Dec. 16, 2016, http://tinyurl.com/gl7k53v.

[14] Robert Service, A History of Modern Russia (2009), p. 549.

[15] "Gazprom completes NTV takeover," Committee to Protect Journalists, April 3, 2001, http://tinyurl.com/hnubfta.

[16] Arkady Ostrovsky, The Invention of Russia: The Journey from Gorbachev's Freedom to Putin's War (2015), pp. 295-296.

[17] Jennifer Dunham, Bret Nelson and Elen Aghekyan, "Freedom of the Press 2015: Russia," Freedom House, 2015, http://tinyurl.com/gu2v67b.

[18] *Ibid.*

[19] Ostrovsky, *op. cit.*

[20] Vincent L. Morelli, "Ukraine: Current Issues and U.S. Policy," Congressional Research Service, Jan. 3, 2017, http://tinyurl.com/gr879w4.

litical problems. At home, near-monthly civic protests grew larger. Initially concerned with accusations of voting fraud in the 2011 legislative elections, protesters eventually turned on Putin and government corruption. In 2012, Putin's party passed a law imposing heavy fines on people who joined unapproved demonstrations. [84] Russian law enforcement also raided the homes of several leading activists, chilling the growing democracy movement. [85]

Russia then annexed Crimea from Ukraine in 2014 and stoked separatist forces in eastern Ukraine. [86] President Yanukovych was overthrown in a popular revolt that February after renouncing a pledge to sign an agreement with the European Union (EU).

Some analysts have said the crisis was triggered by the EU's ultimatum for the divided country to choose between the West and Russia. [87] Others say Yanukovych faced heavy pressure from Moscow — including threats and gas cuts — to renounce the EU deal. [88]

The leaders of what had been the Group of 8 nations announced they would meet as the Group of 7, excluding Russia from a club that it was once desperate to join. [89] After Putin annexed Crimea, the United States, the EU and Australia in July 2014 imposed travel and financial sanctions on Russia and later strengthened them. [90] ∎

Russian Economy Hit by Sanctions, Falling Oil Prices

"It's a highly industrial economy that . . . has to be retooled top to bottom."

At a cement plant in Pikalevo, Russia, 150 miles east of St. Petersburg, employee Nina Suslova learned firsthand about the Russian economy's weaknesses. Her job was to be split among three people, cutting her work hours to just a few each day, with a corresponding reduction in wages, but keeping everyone employed.

"We need to eat. We need to pay our bills. We can only think about surviving now, not about the future," Suslova said. [1]

Once the Texas of Europe, Russia has seen its oil boom go bust. As one of the world's top three oil producers (along with the United States and Saudi Arabia), Russia was battered during the global recession and is slowly emerging from a contraction that lasted about two years. Oil and gas prices began sliding in recent years because of greater competition with alternative energy sources and a global glut, which lowered the country's growth rate.

Sanctions imposed by Western nations after Russia invaded Ukraine in 2014 worsened Russia's problems. As real incomes have fallen, two decades of achievements brought about by the resource-rich economy could be erased, according to some economists. [2] In 2015, Russian GDP shrank by close to 4 percent. [3] The World Bank predicted last spring that the nation's poverty rate would increase in 2016 to 14.2 percent of the population, "undoing nearly a decade's worth of gains." [4]

The economic contraction has highlighted an underlying problem with the Russian economy: Decisions made during the Soviet era — including an overdependence on natural resources, heavy state control of the economy, widespread corruption and an inability to innovate — are hampering the nation, say economists, including Robert Orttung, assistant director of the Institute for European, Russian and Eurasian Studies at George Washington University.

In addition, despite Russia having a well-educated citizenry, small business — which fosters innovation — represents a tinier share of the economy than in Western Europe and the United States, Orttung says.

"The main reason the Russian economy is collapsing is because of its overall structure — its dependence on oil and natural gas and a lack of innovative technologies," Orttung says. "Russia doesn't really export anything besides energy and weapons. You have incredible amounts of innovation in Russia, but it doesn't turn it into product. There's not an economic system that can take advantage of all that talent and commercially use it."

Economist Clifford Gaddy of the Brookings Institution in Washington says Russian President Vladimir Putin has no viable plan to solve the economy's ills. Gaddy expects Putin to continue to rely on megaprojects and spend tens of trillions of rubles to update the defense industry and factories in Russia's bleak eastern regions. But Putin has no clear recognition of what should be done to fix the economy, Gaddy says.

"It's a highly industrial economy that's completely wrong and has to be retooled top to bottom," Gaddy says.

Russian scientists and engineers invented the laser, incandescent bulbs and hydraulic fracking, and its people are renowned in physics and mathematics. Yet the new Russian economy has failed to benefit from scientific breakthroughs. [5] The nation churns out a great deal of heavy machinery and military equipment as in Soviet times, but it struggles to make telecommunications and consumer electronics and appliances that the public wants to buy. [6]

Barry Ickes, chairman of the economics department at Pennsylvania State University, likens Russia's economy to a cockroach, primitive and inelegant in many respects but possessing a remarkable ability to survive in the most adverse and varying

CURRENT SITUATION

Confirmation Controversies

Energy executive Tillerson faced vigorous grilling during his confirmation hearings for secretary of State, with several senators saying they want to know more about Tillerson's relationship — and Exxon's dealings — with Putin.

After Trump announced his pick,

several Republican senators expressed doubts about Tillerson's business connections with Russia, led by Sens. McCain, Rubio and Lindsey Graham of South Carolina. [91] They questioned how Tillerson could represent the United States' best interests when the company he led made a $500 billion Arctic oil drilling deal — presided over by Putin — with the state-owned Rosneft. [92] That agreement has been on ice since the West imposed sanctions on Russia in 2014, raising questions about whether Tillerson, who had publicly opposed sanctions, might push for lifting them in order to revive the Arctic deal. [93]

"If [someone doesn't] believe sanctions are appropriate, given what Putin has been doing all over the world, including in our backyard, then I don't think they have the judgment to be secretary of state," Graham said. "Because if you don't go after Russia, you're inviting the other bad actors on the planet to come after you." [94]

In early January Tillerson said that, if confirmed, he would sell and restructure his assets and had already resigned from organizations that might pose a conflict of interest, such as the American Petroleum Institute trade group. "I am committed to the highest standards of ethical conduct," Tillerson

conditions. The country will continue to lose its most talented people, he says, if it does not improve education and allow those people to thrive.

"They were way ahead in the Soviet period, in the sciences," he says. "Many of the universities have not modernized much in the region. . . . They lose a lot of their people."

Rosstat, the Russian state statistics agency, reported that 350,000 people left Russia in 2015, the most in decades. [7] Lauren Goodrich, a senior Eurasia analyst at research firm Stratfor says the brain drain could hurt the country's competitiveness. "Russia already has a problem funding research and development," she said. "If the people who work in them are also leaving, progress will stagnate across the board," she says.

In recent years, Russian and international investors have moved their money to places considered safer for investments, said Sergei Guriev, a professor of economics at Sciences Po, an international research university in Paris. Since 2011, four to eight percent of Russian GDP has been lost annually in capital outflow. That's a large amount, he said, considering that total capital investment in Russia makes up 20 percent of GDP. [8]

The government faces three choices: imposing steep budget cuts, asking the West to lift sanctions or instituting structural reforms, said Guriev, who fled Russia in 2013. Changes in such areas as ease of starting a business and adopting a floating exchange rate have improved the climate, he said, but state-owned companies and politically connected businesses continue to benefit from the status quo. [9]

Long-lasting growth, he said, can come through the protection of property rights, a stronger rule of law, more competition, an end to corruption and integration into the global economy. [10]

— *Suzanne Sataline*

Russian coal miners head home after work in the Kemerovo region. The nation's faltering economy worsened after Russia invaded Ukraine in 2014, prompting Western nations to impose economic sanctions. Many experts say Russia's industrial economy must be radically retooled.

Getty Images/Bloomberg/Andrey Rudakov

[1] Andrew Higgins, "Putin Took Credit for the Boom. Now There's a Bust," *The New York Times*, May 2, 2016, http://tinyurl.com/zkmf2vh.

[2] "Russian Federation Overview," World Bank, 2015, http://tinyurl.com/blgs8zg; "Russia Economic Report," The World Bank, Nov. 9, 2016, http://tinyurl.com/hcxwq2e.

[3] Sergei Guriev, "Russia's Constrained Economy," *Foreign Affairs*, May/June 2016, http://tinyurl.com/hrptzb8.

[4] Higgins, *op. cit.*

[5] "Milk Without the Cow," *The Economist*, Oct. 22, 2016, http://tinyurl.com/z2alld6; Pavel Koshkin, "How Russia can overcome its innovation challenges," *Russia Direct*, Nov. 11, 2015, http://tinyurl.com/ztm762j.

[6] "Russia: sales of technical consumer goods decreased by 14.4% in 2015 compared to 2014," Household Appliances Parts and Components, March 11, 2016, http://tinyurl.com/zfmm5sp.

[7] Deidre McPhillips, "Russia's 'Slow Bleeding' Brain Drain," *U.S. News & World Report*, Oct. 6, 2016, http://tinyurl.com/hg7y7my.

[8] Guriev, *op. cit.*

[9] *Ibid.*

[10] *Ibid.*

wrote in a letter to the State Department's ethics lawyer. "If confirmed as secretary of State, I will not participate personally and substantially in any particular matter in which I know I have a financial interest directly and predictably affected by the matter." [95]

Others worry that Tillerson's world experience does not include international diplomacy. "Can he step out of the Exxon Mobil persona and then pursue a whole bunch of interests with interlocutors who don't share our interests?" asked Steven Pifer, a retired foreign service officer who served as U.S. ambassador to Ukraine. [96]

Senate Foreign Relations Committee Chairman Bob Corker, R-Tenn., called Tillerson's nomination "an inspired choice." Corker said he was confident in Tillerson's ability to offer advice to Trump because he had led a global enterprise with 70,000 employees and had met world leaders and "knows them up close and personally. You're going to be able to take the years of accomplishment in relationships and . . . translate it into a foreign policy that benefits U.S. national interests. [97]

In his opening statement, Tillerson assured the committee: "We must also be clear-eyed about our relationship with Russia. Russia today poses a danger, but it is not unpredictable." He vowed to cooperate with Russia "based on common interests if possible, such as reducing the global threat of terrorism." But, "we should be steadfast in defending the interests of America and her allies." [98]

Several committee members asked Tillerson if he would support tougher sanctions on Russia for its election-year hacking. Tillerson said he would support such legislation but hoped it would be flexible enough to give the administration room to negotiate with Russia. [99]

Jan. 13, 2017   **39**

Russian Hacking

The portion of the intelligence community report released to the public on Jan. 6 concluded that Russian President Putin "ordered an influence campaign" in 2016 aimed at the U.S. presidential election, in an effort to "undermine public faith in the U.S. democratic process, denigrate Secretary Clinton and harm her electability and potential presidency." The report said the intelligence agencies had "high confidence" that Putin and the Russian government had "a clear preference for President-elect Trump." [100]

Moscow's campaign followed a "Russian messaging strategy that blends covert intelligence operations — such as cyber activity — with overt efforts by Russian government agencies, state-funded media, third-party intermediaries and paid social media users or 'trolls,' " the report said, predicting that Moscow would "apply lessons learned from its Putin-ordered campaign" to influence elections worldwide, including against U.S. allies. [101]

While the report said the hacking did not compromise U.S. vote-tallying systems, the analysis did not address whether the Russian activities overall had changed the election outcome. [102] Nevertheless, President-elect Trump, after being briefed on the intelligence report on Jan. 6, released a statement asserting the Russian campaign had "absolutely no effect on the outcome of the election." Just hours before the briefing he had called the furor over Russian hacking "a political witch hunt." [103]

Besides demanding the intelligence report on the hacking, President Obama had ordered the Russian diplomats and sanctioned Moscow's intelligence services.

Putin, who has denied involvement in the hacking, declined to retaliate against U.S. diplomats in Russia and said he was looking forward to working with the incoming Trump administration to put the two countries "on the way toward the restoration of Russia-United States relations." Trump promptly tweeted that Putin's restraint was "very smart." [104]

Two days after the report's release, Rep. Devin Nunes, R-Calif., chairman of the House Intelligence Committee, told "Fox News Sunday" that he has warned Trump that Putin "is a bad actor," and said, "It is true we'd like to be friends with Russia, but I'm just not sure it's possible." [105]

The same day, Sen. McConnell, R-Ky., compared Trump's desire to "want to get along with the Russians" with similar hopes of his predecessors. "My suspicion is these hopes will be dashed pretty quickly. The Russians are clearly a big adversary, and they demonstrated it by trying to mess around in our election," he said, adding, that the Russians "naively, in my view, thought that somehow they'd be advantaged if Donald Trump were to be elected." [106]

In strongly worded remarks the same day on "Meet the Press," Sen. McCain said the Russians "have slaughtered Ukrainians. They have dismembered a country, and I don't think they are through. . . . And they're putting strains on the post-World War II new world order, the likes of which we've never seen." [107]

On Jan. 5, McCain had convened the Senate Armed Services Committee, which he chairs, in the first of several hearings on cybersecurity, particularly any foreign efforts to influence U.S. elections, which he equated to "an act of war." [108]

At the hearing, lawmakers on both sides of the aisle expressed concern about Trump's disparagement of U.S. intelligence community's claims. And Director of National Intelligence James R. Clapper Jr. reiterated his contention that Russia was behind the election-year hacking and that it could not have occurred without approval at the "highest levels" of the Russian government. The hacking was part of an aggressive, multifaceted "information war" being waged by Russia, designed to, among other things, "drive wedges between us and Western Europe," Clapper said. [109]

Trump was briefed the next day by intelligence officials on the Russian hacking, and appeared to concede that the Russians might have been among those responsible for the election hacking. [110]

Members of Congress on both sides of the aisle have called for a bipartisan select committee to investigate Russian interference in the election, but it is unclear whether that will proceed; the Senate Republican Conference reportedly does not back the idea. [111]

During the election, the anti-government-secrecy site, Wikileaks, published reams of stolen emails from the Democratic National Committee and Democratic nominee Hillary Clinton's campaign manager. The move, according to people who viewed a secret intelligence brief, was designed to strengthen Trump's candidacy and sink Clinton's. [112] Analysts say Moscow also has used false news to create doubt about liberal parties and to support right-wing candidates in Europe. [113]

To be sure, fake news during the presidential election originated in many countries, including the United States, often by writers seeking to make money from online ads. After the election, Obama decried the spread of falsehoods posing as news stories, and Facebook said it was considering ways to stop the trend. [114]

International Tensions

Concerns about President-elect Trump's comments praising Putin worry many hawks in Congress and in the foreign policy and intelligence communities, some of whom view Putin's aggressive moves in Syria and Eastern Europe as dangerous to international peace and cooperation.

With war still smoldering in eastern Ukraine, the International Criminal Court said in November stating that it is investigating the killings of more than 9,500 people in the region since February 2014, the disappearance of more

Continued on p. 42

Should the Trump administration engage with Russia?

JACK F. MATLOCK JR.
U.S. AMBASSADOR TO THE SOVIET UNION, 1987-1991

EXCERPTED FROM "ADVICE TO PRESIDENT TRUMP ON U.S.-RUSSIA POLICY," AN ONLINE SYMPOSIUM COMMISSIONED BY THE NATIONAL INTEREST AND CARNEGIE CORPORATION OF NEW YORK

*t*he most important foreign policy task President-elect Donald Trump will face . . . will be to restore cooperation with Russia to reduce the danger to the world posed by nuclear weapons. The only truly existential threat to the United States today is that of nuclear war.

President Ronald Reagan and [Soviet] General Secretary Mikhail Gorbachev recognized this danger in their 1985 Geneva Summit when they agreed that "a nuclear war cannot be won and must never be fought," and concluded therefore that there could be no war between the United States and the Soviet Union. Their agreement on this point underlay the subsequent mutual steps that ended the arms race and, in remarkably short time, the Cold War itself. By the end of 1991, Europe was whole and free and at peace.

Over the past two decades, American and Russian leaders have allowed the truism recognized by Reagan and Gorbachev to slip from their attention. The recent presidents of both countries, through a series of misconceived actions and emotional reactions, have created an atmosphere of hostility and confrontation that damages both countries and militates against cooperation even when their interests are in harmony. That has brought us to the brink of another senseless nuclear arms race along with the danger that militarized competition over territory could escalate into actual war. . . .

Restoring cooperation with Russia on nuclear issues will be possible only if we overcome the confrontational mentality that pervades much interaction between the United States and Russia today. In fact, the most fundamental interests of both countries are not in conflict: whether it be avoiding a nuclear arms race, combating terrorism, coping with the effects of global warming, building mutually beneficial economic ties or managing the many problems stemming from failed states, cooperation between the United States and Russia — along with the European Union, China and India — is essential.

The Obama administration attempted a "reset" that had some important positive results, notably the New START treaty, but eventually failed following the developing civil war in Syria and, above all, the shock of the Maidan revolution and its aftermath in Ukraine. President Trump's challenge will be to work with [Russian] President [Vladimir] Putin to transcend differences over these issues so that both countries, along with the European Union, can concentrate on dealing with the global challenges that face us all.

MARK KRAMER
PROGRAM DIRECTOR, RUSSIAN AND EURASIAN STUDIES, HARVARD UNIVERSITY

WRITTEN FOR *CQ RESEARCHER*, JANUARY 2017

*d*onald Trump will have many tasks facing him when he takes office on Jan. 20. One thing he must decide promptly is how to counter the Russian government's use of cyberwarfare against the United States and other Western countries. Instead of responding to U.S. intelligence reports about this matter with childish petulance, Trump should take the issue seriously and decide how he can best protect U.S. national interests against Russian encroachments.

But instead of doing this, Trump seems determined to establish a friendly relationship with the authoritarian government of Vladimir Putin, no matter what the cost to U.S. interests and values. Putin has demonstrated his antipathy toward the United States and his willingness to challenge U.S. interests. Yet Trump throughout the presidential campaign expressed fondness for Putin and a desire to have a friendly relationship with him. Trump did this even as he made clear that he had no particular desire to maintain good relations with long-standing U.S. allies. Trump's sense of priorities is so skewed that one wonders what could be behind it.

Most likely what is motivating Trump is a shared desire with Putin to upend the international order that U.S. leaders helped create after World War II. That international order, resting on a global free trade regime and U.S. security commitments to key allies, has immensely benefited U.S. interests and security. Trump and Putin share the goal of reconfiguring this international order, even though they do so for opposite reasons.

Putin has long been seeking to undermine U.S. preeminence in the world, and he is going all-out to see the U.S.-led international order overturned.

Trump, by contrast, mistakenly believes that the U.S.-led international order is detrimental to American interests. This position is baffling, but it is characteristic of Trump. It is leading him to endorse positions that will be hugely damaging to the United States and greatly beneficial to Russia and other tyrannical regimes such as China.

Instead of providing succor to hostile authoritarian states, Trump should be giving top priority to solidifying ties with U.S. allies and reassuring them that he has no intention of abandoning them. He should be going to Ottawa and London and Berlin and Tokyo and Canberra. But I fear his priorities are so warped that he instead will be going to Moscow soon after taking office.

Continued from p. 40

than 400 people and more than 800 crimes. [115] Russia immediately announced it would withdraw from the organization, saying it no longer met the criteria of being "a truly independent, authoritative international tribunal." [116]

Putin's invasion of Ukraine was wildly popular with the Russian public, says James Collins, U.S. ambassador to the Russian federation from 1997 to 2001. "He is seen as the stalwart defender of what Russia is against assaults by the global Americanizer," Collins says.

It's unclear what Trump will do about Ukraine or rising tensions in the Baltics. But some Ukrainian officials fear that the new American president will build closer ties to Putin at Kiev's expense. "Donald Trump's election is a strong signal that Ukraine should be ready to carry out reforms and resist Russian aggression without U.S. and Western support," said Alyona Getmanchuk, director of the Institute of World Policy, a nongovernmental think tank in Kiev. [117]

International resentment lingers about Russia's intervention in Syria, where anti-Assad rebels suffered grave losses against the Assad regime, thanks in part to Russian air support. In early January Russia announced it was reducing its military forces in Syria, under the terms of a ceasefire brokered between opposition groups and the Syrian government. [118]

In Europe, Russia is considering how to respond to a plan to station a multinational force in Eastern Europe by May, which some U.S. analysts say could provoke Moscow. [119] Putin has warned that he might target NATO sites if he sees them as a threat to Russia. "We are forced to take countermeasures — that is, to aim our missile systems at those facilities which we think pose a threat to us," Putin told American filmmaker Oliver Stone in an interview. [120]

Putin's government has been trying to counter U.S. and European political and economic decisions that he sees as weakening Russian interests. In particular, he has been unhappy with Western entreaties to former Eastern bloc countries to trade primarily with the West, as well as decisions to base NATO forces close to the Russian border. "The Russians were always concerned that they were seen by the West as inferior," says the William Courtney, the former U.S. ambassador to Russia. "The notion that the West was double-dealing against the Russian empire, they [the Soviets] played up on that."

The West should realize that Putin has not backed Assad just to oppose the United States, says Paul Saunders, the executive director of the Center for National Interest and a former state department official. About 2,000 Russian-speaking people are fighting for ISIS in Syria, and Putin does not want them returning to Russia. If the Assad government fell, "a lot of those people might flood back to Russia," he says.

Putin also has been upset over U.S. democracy-building efforts in Russia's backyard, says Saunders, such as support for the so-called color revolutions in Georgia in 2003, in Ukraine in 2004 and Kyrgyzstan in 2005. "In most cases, these protests led to a government being ousted," Saunders points out.

Putin's international interventions have been designed not just to garner support at home, but to make the global community realize that Russia is no longer the weak, defeated nation that emerged from the 1990s, many experts say. Putin said as much after annexing Crimea, when he said the world needed to take his country's global concerns seriously. [121]

Russia now faces defiance from many Western governments for its actions in Syria and for creating what could become a frozen conflict in Ukraine. "They're stuck in a simmering war in Ukraine," says Courtney, the former ambassador to Russia who now serves as executive director of the RAND Business Leaders Forum. And Crimea, he says is "an economic burden." ■

OUTLOOK

Economic and Political Challenges

As President Putin tries to buff Russia's global image and demand international respect, some domestic challenges could tarnish his leadership, experts say.

Putin faces some domestic dissent. But while activist Nalvany has vowed to run against Putin in 2018, he may not be eligible. Shortly after he led the 2012 anti-Putin demonstrations, Navalny was charged and convicted of embezzling timber from a state-owned company — a verdict many say was politically motivated due to his support for the protests. Although that verdict recently was overturned, another conviction — which many expect — could make him ineligible for office. [122]

"No one has the potential to challenge Putin," Harvard's Kramer says. "Perhaps Putin, at some point, seven to eight years from now, will designate a successor, but that's long in the future."

Meanwhile, Russia's ossified economy limps along, but some economists and political observers do not expect Putin to restructure the economy, because the political and social costs would be too great. "For Mr. Putin to modernize the economy, he has to change the system, and if does, his popularity is in jeopardy," says former ambassador to Russia Collins.

If Putin were to address corruption, for instance, he would alienate his powerful, wealthy supporters, analysts say. And closing down inefficient production centers would cause huge job losses, potentially sparking labor unrest, says Gaddy of Brookings. Russia already saw several walkouts in 2015, when some teachers and factory workers complained they had gone months without pay. [123] A major strike "might be the end of everything in Russia," he says. "He's doing everything to preserve those jobs, as bad as the products may be, they have to continue."

The quickest way for Putin to gain economic relief would be to pull out of Ukraine, which has been a costly drain on the Russian economy, says Courtney of the RAND Corp.

Experts say it is unknown what Trump might do or what moves Putin might make. But one thing is sure, says Gaddy: "Putin is going to be testing Trump" to see what actions might provoke him. And it is "very naïve," he says, to think that Trump is "Putin's man."

Sen. Tom Cotton, R-Ark., made a similar point during the McCain hearings on the Russian hacking. "Donald Trump has proposed to increase our defense budget, to accelerate nuclear modernization, to accelerate ballistic missile defenses and to expand and accelerate oil and gas production, which would obviously harm Russia's economy," Cotton said. [124]

Russia, some analysts argue, does not aspire to emulate the West or match its strength. Rather, Putin seeks a weaker, more fractured NATO and America, so Russia can claim superiority. [125] To do that, Putin aims to undermine Western institutions while "solving" crises the West cannot, such as in Syria, writes Molly K. McKew, once an adviser to Mikheil Saakashvili, the former president of Georgia. [126]

Jeffrey Gedmin, a senior fellow at the Atlantic Council's Future Europe Initiative, said Putin is working to divide Europe into two spheres of influence and to weaken and fragment the European Union, "rendering NATO, our key alliance, obsolete," while working with Iran to push the United States out of the Middle East. "If that is the world that emerges in three, or five or 10 years," he said, "does that help American security? I say no." [127]

The West's best move might be to disrupt the Kremlin's plans by exposing the tactics and wealth of Putin and his cronies, said Stephen Sestanovich, a professor in the international diplomatic practice at Columbia University. That would create instability in Moscow and show that the West will not back down when it comes to the Kremlin, he said. [128] ■

Notes

[1] Assessing Russian Activities and Intentions in Recent US Elections," Office of the Director of National Intelligence, Jan. 6, 2017, http://tinyurl.com/hye8jnl.

[2] Greg Miller *et al.*, "Classified Russian report targets Trump," *The Washington Post*, Jan. 11, 2017, http://tinyurl.com/jjgwho8.

[3] "Trump acknowledges Russian involvement in meddling in U.S. elections," *The Washington Post*, Jan. 11, 2017, http://tinyurl.com/gw3fumh.

[4] "Face the Nation," CBS News, transcript, Dec. 11, 2016, http://tinyurl.com/gksea69.

[5] "Transcript Dec. 11, 2016: McCain, Conway, Sanders," "Face the Nation," CBS News, http://tinyurl.com/gksea69.

[6] "Secretary of State Confirmation Hearing," CSPAN, Jan. 11, 2017, http://tinyurl.com/zmr3yr5.

[7] *Ibid.*

[8] Daniel J. Graeber, "Exxon, Tillerson address conflict of interest concerns," UPI, Jan. 4, 2017, http://tinyurl.com/gtleoo7. Also see Anne Gearan, "Trump's pick to lead State Dept. discloses wealth approaching $400 million," *The Washington Post*, Jan. 5, 2017, http://tinyurl.com/j7p4hhe.

[9] David E. Sanger, "Obama Strikes Back at Russia for Election Hacking," *The New York Times*, Dec. 29, 2016, http://tinyurl.com/z3zh3ue. Neil MacFarquhar, "Vladimir Putin Won't Expel U.S. Diplomats as Russian Foreign Minister Urged," *The New York Times*, Dec. 30, 2016, http://tinyurl.com/hl755mq.

[10] Rosalind S. Helderman, "Here's what we know about Donald Trump and his ties to Russia," *The Washington Post*, July 29, 2016, http://tinyurl.com/htmledj.

[11] Fiona Hill, "This is what Putin really wants," Brookings Institution, Feb. 24, 2015, http://tinyurl.com/zt3hxs8.

[12] "The fog of wars," *The Economist*, Oct. 22, 2016, http://tinyurl.com/zteevls.

[13] Peter Baker, "Russian Dissident Opens New Chapter in His Anti-Putin Movement," *The New York Times*, Oct. 2, 2014, http://tinyurl.com/jq44h6r. Also see Alexis Flynn, "Putin 'Probably' Approved Litvinenko Poisoning, U.K. Inquiry Says," *The Wall Street Journal*, Jan. 21, 2016, http://tinyurl.com/hspuaj6.

[14] Nikolas K. Gvosdev, "The Bear Awakens: Russia's Military is Back," *The National Interest*, Nov. 12, 2014, http://tinyurl.com/paqkunz.

[15] "European Security: Russia's Actions and Possible Responses," The Finnish Institute of International Affairs, Oct. 5, 2016, http://tinyurl.com/h2b7fa9.

[16] Hill, *op. cit.*

[17] Carolyn Harris, "When Catherine the Great Invaded the Crimea and Put the Rest of the World on Edge," Smithsonian.com, March 4, 2014, http://tinyurl.com/zqfaart.

[18] Steve Holland and Jeff Mason, "Obama warns on Crimea, orders sanctions over Russian moves in Ukraine," Reuters, March 6, 2014, http://tinyurl.com/glm9jlr.

[19] Stephen Cohen, " 'We are not beginning a new cold war, we are well into it,' " Democracy Now! April 17, 2014, http://tinyurl.com/jhksyb7. Also see Denis Dyomkin, "Putin says Romania, Poland may now be in Russia's cross-hairs," Reuters, May 27, 2016, http://tinyurl.com/j9623l7.

[20] Somini Sengupta and Neil MacFarquhar, "Vladimir Putin of Russia Calls for Coalition to Fight ISIS," *The New York Times*, Sept. 27, 2015, http://tinyurl.com/oy4kttu.

[21] Neil MacFarquhar, "On Syria, Putin is Catering to an Audience at Home," *The New York Times*, Sept. 26, 2015, http://tinyurl.com/hn7esyd.

[22] Jonathan Marcus, "Syria war: How Moscow's bombing campaign has paid off for Putin," BBC News, Sept. 30, 2016, http://tinyurl.com/zl8b5og. Adam Entous *et al.*, "U.S. Believes Russia Bombed Syrian Aid Convoy," *The Wall Street Journal*, Sept. 20, 2016, http://tinyurl.com/jq4fa3u. Ellen Francis and Tom Perry, "Warplanes knock out Aleppo hospitals as Russian-backed assault intensifies," Reuters, Sept. 29, 2016, http://tinyurl.com/zclown9.

[23] Dmitri Trenin, "From cooperation to competition — Russia and the West," Carnegie Endowment for International Peace," Jan. 21, 2015, http://tinyurl.com/zclgwbp.

[24] Jeremy Diamond, "Timeline: Donald Trump's praise for Vladimir Putin," CNN, July 29, 2016, http://tinyurl.com/jsrw3p5. Also see "What Donald Trump Said About Russian Hacking and Hillary Clinton's Emails," *The New York Times*, July 27, 2016, http://tinyurl.com/jcn9lbk.

[25] Peter Feaver and Eric Lorber, "Understanding the limits of sanctions," *Lawfare*, July 26, 2015, http://tinyurl.com/gp83jck.

[26] Anna Andrianova, "Russian economy edges near end of recession as contraction eases," Bloomberg, July 28, 2016, http://tinyurl.com/zogwkbe.

[27] MacFarquhar, "On Syria . . .," *op. cit.*

[28] Robert Legvold, "Managing the New Cold War," *Foreign Affairs*, July/August 2014, http://tinyurl.com/o9sscg9.

[29] *Ibid.*

[30] Gabriel Samuels, "NATO puts 300,000 ground troops on 'high alert' as tensions with Russia mount," *The Independent*, Nov. 7, 2016,

http://tinyurl.com/jfv5rk6.

[31] *Ibid*.

[32] *Ibid*.

[33] See David A. Shlapak and Michael W. Johnson, "Reinforcing Deterrence on NATO's Eastern Flank: Wargaming the Defense of the Baltics," RAND Corp., 2016, http://tinyurl.com/zl95hm7.

[34] "Why Russia is an ally of Assad," *The Economist*, Sept. 30, 2015, http://tinyurl.com/nm2qxyv.

[35] Tim Hains, "Trump Wants to Stop the New Cold War, but the American Media Just Doesn't Understand," *RealClear Politics*, July 30, 2016, http://tinyurl.com/hk8qkg8.

[36] Stephen F. Cohen, "Why Cold War Again?" *The Nation*, April 2, 2014, http://tinyurl.com/jdwr3ds.

[37] *Ibid*.

[38] *Ibid*.

[39] Stephen F. Cohen, "Cold War Again: Who's Responsible?" *The Nation*, April 1, 2014, http://tinyurl.com/hu6bl99.

[40] Timothy Snyder, "How a Russian Fascist is Meddling in America's Election," *The New York Times*, Sept. 20, 2016, http://tinyurl.com/jmf7dde. Also see Masha Gessen, "Russia is remaking itself as the leader of the anti-Western world," *The Washington Post*, March 30, 2014.

[41] Bryony Jones and Nic Robertson, "Syria talks: What Russia and the U.S. agree and disagree on," CNN, Sept. 8, 2016, http://tinyurl.com/jue8u3v. Also see: Brad Plumer, "A short timeline of deteriorating U.S.-Russia relations," *The Washington Post*, Aug. 8, 2013, http://tinyurl.com/huf6e2j.

[42] Diamond, *op. cit*.

[43] *Ibid*.

[44] Robert Einhorn, "Prospects for U.S.-Russian nonproliferation cooperation," Brookings Institution, Feb. 26, 2016, http://tinyurl.com/jz8sxo6.

[45] C-Span, *op. cit*.

[46] "After the U.S. Election: Time to Re-Engage Russia?" McCain Institute, October 2016, http://tinyurl.com/hn9egh7.

[47] *Ibid*.

[48] *Ibid*.

[49] "Enlargement," North Atlantic Treaty Organization, Dec. 2, 2015, http://tinyurl.com/j4h8kel.

[50] "After the U.S. Election: Time to Re-Engage Russia? *op. cit*.

[51] *Ibid*.

[52] Ben Judah, "The ruthlessness of Vladimir Putin," *New Statesman*, Oct. 7, 2015, http://tinyurl.com/j6bco8n.

[53] "Approval Ratings," Levada Center, Dec. 2, 2016, http://tinyurl.com/zks9q8q.

[54] Donald N. Jensen, "The Myth of Putin's 89%," Institute of Modern Russia, June 25, 2015, http://tinyurl.com/jyhuxjh.

[55] Andrew Kramer, "Fear Envelops Russia After Killing of Putin Critic Boris Nemtsov," *The New York Times*, Feb. 28, 2015, http://tinyurl.com/p5pqfk2.

[56] Carter Stoddard, "Boris Nemtsov murder trial begins in Moscow," *Politico*, Oct. 3, 2016, http://tinyurl.com/zrno4of.

[57] Jensen, *op. cit*.

[58] *Ibid*.

[59] "Boris Nemtsov murder trial begins at Moscow military court," BBC News, Oct. 3, 2016, http://tinyurl.com/gshk89p. Also see Jeremy Wilson, "Here's a list of Putin critics who've ended up dead," *Business Insider*, March 11, 2016, http://tinyurl.com/znjzn8q.

[60] Ivan Nechepurenko, "Aleksei Navalny, Putin Critic, Says He'll Run for President of Russia," *The New York Times*, Dec. 13, 2016, http://tinyurl.com/hqyjjd8.

[61] Jensen, *op. cit*.

[62] Neil MacFarquhar, "In a Late-Night Move, Russia Arrests a Top Economic Official in a Bribery Case," *The New York Times*, Nov. 15, 2016, http://tinyurl.com/haxebhm.

[63] Adam Taylor, "Is Vladimir Putin hiding a $200 billion fortune?" *The Washington Post*, Feb. 20, 2015, http://tinyurl.com/jmgktwt.

[64] Robert Service, *A History of Modern Russia*, Third Edition (2009), p. 25.

[65] Alexander N. Yakovlev, *A Century of Violence in Soviet Russia* (2002), p. 21.

[66] *Ibid*., pp. 234-235.

[67] Mark Harrison, "Counting Soviet Deaths in the Great Patriotic War: Comment," *Europe-Asia Studies*, Vol. 55, 2003, pp. 939-944, http://tinyurl.com/gu9sdfo.

[68] Anne Applebaum, *Iron Curtain: The Crushing of Eastern Europe* (2012), pp. 192-193.

[69] Service, *op. cit*., p. 294.

[70] "North Atlantic Treaty Organization (NATO), 1949," Department of State, Office of the Historian, accessed on Dec. 21, 2016, http://tinyurl.com/h2oqj3a.

[71] "The Warsaw Treaty Organization, 1955," Department of State, Office of the Historian, accessed on Dec. 21, 2016, http://tinyurl.com/jpbbq83.

[72] "Cold War," The Eleanor Roosevelt Papers Project," accessed Dec. 21, 2016, http://tinyurl.com/zdlhjtz.

[73] Mark Kramer, "Five myths about the Cold War," *The Washington Post*, March 13, 2014, http://tinyurl.com/jastj6o.

[74] Nick Lockwood, "How the Soviet Union Transformed Terrorism," *The Atlantic*, Dec. 23, 2011, http://tinyurl.com/7ndpmwa.

[75] Service, *op. cit*., pp. 342-343.

[76] *Ibid*., p. 410.

[77] *Ibid*., p. 446.

[78] *Ibid*., pp. 454-455.

[79] *Ibid*., p. 483.

[80] Mark Mazzetti and Eric Lichtblau, "CIA Judgment on Russia Built on Swell of Evidence," *The New York Times*, Dec. 11, 2016, http://tinyurl.com/hnx7sza.

[81] "Medvedev on Russia's interests," *The Economist*, Sept. 1, 2008, http://tinyurl.com/zfgwgy5.

[82] Adam Taylor, "That Time Ukraine tried to join NATO — and NATO said no," *The Washington Post*, Sept. 4, 2014, http://tinyurl.com/hxxjwpa.

[83] For background, see Brian Beary, "Separatist Movements," *CQ Global Researcher*, April 1, 2008, pp. 85-114.

[84] David M. Herszenhorn, "New Russian Law Assesses Heavy Fines on Protesters," *The New York Times*, June 8, 2012, http://tinyurl.com/6vgzwvr.

[85] Ellen Barry, "Raids Target Putin's Critics Before Protest," *The New York Times*, June 11, 2012, http://tinyurl.com/74vd3xk.

[86] Yasmeen Serhan, "The Separatists' Cease-Fire in Ukraine," *The Atlantic*, Sept. 13, 2016, http://tinyurl.com/jbs5jab.

[87] Cohen, *op. cit*.

[88] Will Englund and Kathy Lally, "Ukraine, under pressure from Russia, puts brakes on E.U. Deal," *The Washington Post*, Nov. 21, 2013, http://tinyurl.com/gt65gvw.

[89] Steven Lee Myers and Ellen Barry, "Putin Reclaims Crimea for Russia and Bitterly Denounces

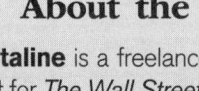

About the Author

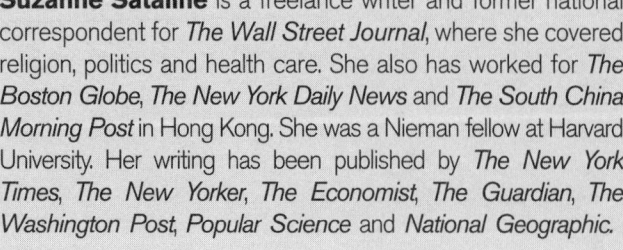

Suzanne Sataline is a freelance writer and former national correspondent for *The Wall Street Journal*, where she covered religion, politics and health care. She also has worked for *The Boston Globe*, *The New York Daily News* and *The South China Morning Post* in Hong Kong. She was a Nieman fellow at Harvard University. Her writing has been published by *The New York Times*, *The New Yorker*, *The Economist*, *The Guardian*, *The Washington Post*, *Popular Science* and *National Geographic*.

the West," *The New York Times*, March 18, 2014, http://tinyurl.com/ledcxy5.

[90] James Kanter, "E.U. to Extend Sanctions Against Russia, but Divisions Show," *The New York Times*, Dec. 18, 2015, http://tinyurl.com/j4xwzeg.

[91] *Ibid.*

[92] Kristina Peterson *et al.*, "Exxon CEO Rex Tillerson Faces Senate Dissent as Potential State Pick," *The Wall Street Journal*, Dec. 13, 2016, http://tinyurl.com/jg42orb. Also see Nataliya Vasilyeva, "Exxon Mobil will look for oil in Russian Arctic and Black Sea," The Associated Press, April 18, 2012, http://tinyurl.com/z4jxgdy.

[93] Andrew E. Kramer and Clifford Krauss, "Rex Tillerson's Company, Exxon, Has Billions at Stake Over Sanctions on Russia," *The New York Times*, Dec. 12, 2016, http://tinyurl.com/gqarcxc.

[94] "Stephen Collinson, "GOP on brink of new Cold War over whether to work with Russia," CNN, Dec. 16, 2016, http://tinyurl.com/jln682o.

[95] Gearan, *op. cit.*

[96] Scheck *et al.*, *ibid.*

[97] CSPAN, *op. cit.*

[98] *Ibid.*

[99] *Ibid.*

[100] Burgess Everett, "George W. Bush called Corker to lobby for Tillerson," *Politico*, Dec. 16, 2016, http://tinyurl.com/h9ragtr.

[101] Scheck *et al.*, *op. cit.*

[102] "Assessing Russian Activities and Intentions in Recent US Elections," *op. cit.*

[103] *Ibid.*

[104] *Ibid.*

[105] "Donald Trump's Statement After Intelligence Briefing on Hacking," *The New York Times*, Jan. 6, 2017, http://tinyurl.com/zfkc5v2. Also see Michael D. Shear and David E. Sanger, "Putin Led a Complex Cyberattack Scheme to Aid Trump, Report Finds," *The New York Times*, Jan. 6, 2017, http://tinyurl.com/jtsgas5.

[106] Neil MacFarquhar, "Vladimir Putin Won't Expel U.S. Diplomats as Russian Foreign Minister Urged," *The New York Times*, Dec. 30, 2016, http://tinyurl.com/hl755mq. "Trump praises Putin over response to US sanctions, calls him 'very smart,' " Fox News, Dec. 30. 2016, http://tinyurl.com/ztyobyj.

[107] "Face the Nation, transcript, Jan. 8, 2017," CBS News, Jan. 8, 2017, http://tinyurl.com/z5ap2oj.

[108] "Meet the Press: January 8, 2017," NBC News, Jan. 8, 2017, http://tinyurl.com/h35ha5e.

[109] Matt Flegenheimer and Scott Shane, "Russia Looms Large as Senate Committee Is Set to Discuss Hacking," *The New York Times*, Jan. 5, 2017, http://tinyurl.com/hyvg3r8.

[110] "Watch: Full Senate hearing on Russian hacking and US cybersecurity," PRI's The World, Jan. 5, 2017, http://tinyurl.com/z93avn9.

FOR MORE INFORMATION

American Enterprise Institute, 1150 17th St., N.W., Washington, DC 20036; 202-862-5800; www.aei.org. Think tank that studies a wide range of policy issues.

Brookings Institution, 1775 Massachusetts Ave., N.W., Washington, DC 20036; 202-797-6000; www.brookings.edu. Think tank that conducts research on domestic and international issues.

Carnegie Endowment for International Peace, 1779 Massachusetts Ave., N.W., Washington, DC 20036; 202-483-7600; www.ceip.org. International-affairs research organization with an affiliate in Moscow.

Center for Strategic and International Studies, 1800 K St., N.W., Suite 400, Washington, DC 20006; 202-887-0200; www.csis.org. Nonpartisan think tank.

Council on Foreign Relations, The Harold Pratt House, 58 East 68th St., New York, NY 10065; 212-434-9400; www.cfr.org. Nonpartisan membership organization that conducts research, sponsors discussions and publishes the journal *Foreign Affairs*.

Eurasia Foundation, 1350 Connecticut Ave., N.W., Suite 1000, Washington, DC 20036; 202-234-7370; www.eurasia.org. Funds programs seeking to build democratic and free-market institutions in Russia and other former Soviet republics.

German Marshall Fund of the United States, 1744 R St., N.W., Washington, DC 20009; 202-683-2650; www.gmfus.org. Foundation that promotes trans-Atlantic relations; has several Russia-specialist scholars.

Rand Corp., 1776 Main St., Santa Monica, CA 90401; 310-393-0411; www.rand.org. Think tank that studies domestic and international issues.

---

[111] Burgess Everett, "Senate push for new Russia hacking probe fizzles," *Politico*, Jan. 3, 2017, http://tinyurl.com/gtqpsbx.

[112] Adam Entous *et al.*, "Secret CIA assessment says Russia was trying to help Trump win White House," *The Washington Post*, Dec. 9, 2016, http://tinyurl.com/h9mxpr3.

[113] Nadine Schmidt and Tim Hume, "Berlin teen admits fabricating migrant gang-rape story, official says," CNN, Feb. 1, 2016, http://tinyurl.com/hcpjesk.

[114] Mike Isaac, "Facebook Considering Ways to Combat Fake News, Mark Zuckerberg Says," *The New York Times*, Nov. 19, 2016, http://tinyurl.com/j35j5tb.

[115] "Report on Preliminary Examination Activities," The Office of the Prosecutor, International Criminal Court, Nov. 14, 2016, http://tinyurl.com/jsbwvfj.

[116] Sheena McKenzie, "Russia quits International Criminal Court, Philippines may follow," CNN, Nov. 17, 2016, http://tinyurl.com/hvfgvdx.

[117] David Stern, "Donald Trump's win shakes Ukraine," *Politico*, Nov. 9, 2016, http://tinyurl.com/zx3mmzk.

[118] "Russia says has begun reducing forces in Syria," Reuters, Jan. 6, 2017, http://tinyurl.com/jrgl9du.

[119] Nathan Hodge, "Russia's Buildup in Kaliningrad to Test Donald Trump on NATO," *The Wall Street Journal*, Dec. 9, 2016, http://tinyurl.com/h9tqm5r.

[120] David Filipov, "Putin says Russia planning 'countermeasures' to NATO expansion," *The Wall Street Journal*, Nov. 21, 2016, http://tinyurl.com/z2hn7vp.

[121] Steven Lee Myers and Ellen Barry, "Putin Reclaims Crimea for Russia and Bitterly Denounces the West," *The New York Times*, March 18, 2014, http://tinyurl.com/hxrxmqb.

[122] Nechepurenko, *op. cit.* Also see Ellen Barry, "Rousing Russia with a Phrase," *The New York Times*, Dec. 2, 2011, http://tinyurl.com/jl4sp6w.

[123] Andrew E. Kramer, "Unpaid Russian Workers Unite in Protest Against Putin," *The New York Times*, April 21, 2015, http://tinyurl.com/mwtfbje.

[124] Ellen Nakashima, Karoun Demirjian and Philip Rucker, "Top U.S. intelligence official: Russia meddled in election by hacking, spreading of propaganda," *The Washington Post*, Jan. 5, 2017, http://tinyurl.com/jd4gg5u.

[125] Molly K. McKew, "Putin's Real Long Game," *Politico Magazine*, Jan. 1, 2017, http://tinyurl.com/zh7rpx9.

[126] *Ibid.*

[127] "US-Russia Relations in the Trump Era," America Abroad, Dec. 14, 2016, http://tinyurl.com/j6exbqr.

[128] Stephen Sestanovich, "Why Exposing Putin's Wealth Would Be Obama's Best Revenge," *The Wall Street Journal*, Dec. 23, 2016, http://tinyurl.com/h4j87d3.

Bibliography

Selected Sources

Books

Hill, Fiona, and Clifford G. Gaddy, *Mr. Putin: Operative in the Kremlin*, Brookings, 2013.
Two senior fellows at the Brookings Institution think tank assess Russian President Vladimir Putin's leadership.

Hosking, Geoffrey, *Russian History: A Very Short Introduction*, Oxford University Press, 2012.
An emeritus professor of Russian history at University College London provides a succinct history of Russia, from its medieval origins to contemporary events.

Judah, Ben, *Fragile Empire: How Russia Fell In and Out of Love with Vladimir Putin*, Yale University Press, 2013.
An associate fellow at the European Council on Foreign Relations sketches a revealing portrait of the Russian leader.

Myers, Steven Lee, *The New Tsar: The Rise and Reign of Vladimir Putin*, Knopf, 2015.
A longtime *New York Times* foreign correspondent argues that the Russian president is a flawed individual swinging between crises rather than an example of an historic Russian leader.

Ostrovsky, Arkady, *The Invention of Russia: The Journey from Gorbachev's Freedom to Putin's War*, Atlantic Books, 2015.
A correspondent for *The Economist* describes how Putin solidified his control, in part, by restricting the mass media.

Pomerantsev, Peter, *Nothing Is True and Everything Is Possible: The Surreal Heart of the New Russia*, Public Affairs, 2015.
A Ukrainian-born media consultant heads to the new Russia and witnesses the creation of an empire empowered by propaganda.

Service, Robert, *A History of Modern Russia, Third Edition*, Harvard University Press, 2009.
A British historian traces Russia's seismic shifts from Nicholas II through Vladimir Putin.

Stent, Angela E., *The Limits of Partnership: US-Russian Relations in the Twenty-First Century*, Princeton University Press, 2014.
The director of the Center for Eurasian, Russian and East European Studies at Georgetown University describes U.S.-Russian relations since the collapse of the Soviet Union.

Articles

Cohen, Stephen F., "Cold War Again: Who's Responsible?" *The Nation*, April 1, 2014, http://tinyurl.com/hu6bl99.
The Russian studies scholar observes how degraded relations between the United States and Russia shaped a new cold war.

Graham, Thomas E., "The Sources of Russian Conduct," *National Interest*, Aug. 24, 2016, http://tinyurl.com/jajp7up.
A Russian scholar and former White House adviser offers strategic advice as to how to deal with a military-minded Russian leader.

Jensen, Donald N., "The Myth of Putin's 89%," Institute of Modern Russia, June 25, 2015, http://tinyurl.com/jyhuxjh.
A resident fellow at the Center for Transatlantic Relations in the Nitze School of International Studies at Johns Hopkins University analyzes what the Russian leader's high popularity statistics might mean.

Plumer, Brad, "A short timeline of deteriorating U.S.-Russia relations," *The Washington Post*, Aug. 8, 2013, http://tinyurl.com/huf6e2j.
The newspaper provides a snapshot of the grudges and missed connections between two of the world's great rivals.

Roth, Kenneth, "What Trump Should Do in Syria," *New York Review of Books*, Dec. 22, 2016, http://tinyurl.com/hbn8n9c.
The executive director of Human Rights Watch, a nongovernmental organization dedicated to ensuring civil rights, analyzes the great powers and how they could end the Syrian civil war.

Reports and Studies

"Inside the bear," *The Economist*, Oct. 22, 2016, http://tinyurl.com/zlvsaa5.
In a special section, the British publication traces the economic stagnation and political dysfunction that threatens Putin's hold on his people.

Pomerantsev, Peter, and Michael Weiss, "The Menace of Unreality: How the Kremlin Weaponizes Information, Culture and Money," The Interpreter, Institute of Modern Russia, November 2014, http://tinyurl.com/khfg2rp.
Journalists assess how state-sponsored hacking and disinformation create scandal and sow doubts about politics.

Rumer, Eugene, "Russia and the Security of Europe," Carnegie Endowment for International Peace, June 30, 2016, http://tinyurl.com/jsfh2mw.
The director of Carnegie's Russia and Eurasia Program suggests a Western strategy in the wake of Russia's annexation of Crimea, which he argues was the latest step in Moscow's rejection of the post-Cold War Euro-Atlantic security order.

The Next Step:

Additional Articles from Current Periodicals

Economy

Afanasieva, Dasha, "Russia's economic woes, sanctions, limit recovery for investment banking," *Reuters*, Dec. 23, 2016, http://tinyurl.com/hjrj4e3.

Despite a 50 percent increase in the value of investment banking deal volumes in Russia during 2016, the industry's rebound growth has been hindered by sanctions and the economy.

Hille, Kathrin, "Substantial recovery still elusive for Russia economy," *Financial Times*, Dec. 19, 2016, http://tinyurl.com/h8uuu3h.

The governor of Russia's central bank predicted "slight positive growth in GDP" for the fourth quarter of 2016.

Rapoza, Kenneth, "Russia's Economy Goes Out With A 'Bang,' " *Forbes*, Dec. 26, 2016, http://tinyurl.com/j5rldg2.

Russia's finance minister expects economic growth of 1.5 percent in 2017, and Morgan Stanley analysts expect a positive U.S.-Russia relationship to bolster the economy.

Foreign Tensions

Golding, Bruce, "How assassination adds to history of Russia-Turkey tension," *New York Post*, Dec. 19, 2016, http://tinyurl.com/zykcsh7.

The up-and-down relationship between Turkey and Russia could again be strained following the assassination of Russia's ambassador to Turkey.

Ingram, David, "Russia asks U.N. Security Council to endorse Syria ceasefire," *Reuters*, Dec. 30, 2016, http://tinyurl.com/jekt4op.

Russia advocated a ceasefire in Syria before the U.N. Security Council, partnering with Turkey to seek an end to the six-year civil war in Syria.

Sharkov, Damien, "Ukraine Launches Black Sea Drill Despite Tension With Russia," *Newsweek*, Dec. 1, 2016, http://tinyurl.com/zfra9tr.

Ukraine fueled tensions by launching a missile drill near the geopolitically contested Crimea after Russian state media issued warnings of retaliation from Moscow.

Putin's Leadership

Dougherty, Jill, "What millennials think of Putin's Russia," *CNN*, Dec. 22, 2016, http://tinyurl.com/hc7lu79.

Some Russian millennials, most of whom were raised under President Vladimir Putin's leadership, have a different view of the country's politics from their parents and grandparents.

Feuer, Alan, and Andrew Higgins, "Extremists Turn to a Leader to Protect Western Values: Vladimir Putin," *The*

New York Times, Dec. 3, 2016, http://tinyurl.com/jzwxdh4.

Praise for Putin has increased among some far-right extremist groups, including the Traditionalist Worker Party.

Kozlowska, Hanna, "When John McCain calls Putin a 'thug and a murderer' this is what he's talking about," *Quartz*, Dec. 16, 2016, http://tinyurl.com/zawjh7x.

Comments by Sen. John McCain, R-Ariz., reignited speculation about murders, suppression of rights and imprisonment of opponents allegedly orchestrated by Russian President Vladimir Putin.

U.S. Presidential Election

Arkin, William M., Ken Dilanian and Cynthia McFadden, "U.S. Officials: Putin Personally Involved in U.S. Election Hack," *NBC News*, Dec. 15, 2016, http://tinyurl.com/zqyojb4.

Intelligence officials said they have "a high level of confidence" that President Vladimir Putin was personally linked to the Russian hacking that occurred during the 2016 presidential election.

Hagen, Lisa, "Kerry: Russian interference had 'profound impact' on election," *The Hill*, Dec. 28, 2016, http://tinyurl.com/z4ueaah.

Secretary of State John Kerry said he believes Russia's email hacking had a "profound impact" on the political process.

Ryan, Missy, Ellen Nakashima and Karen DeYoung, "Obama administration announces measures to punish Russia for 2016 election interference," *The Washington Post*, Dec. 29, 2016, http://tinyurl.com/h7jw6uo.

The Obama administration responded to alleged Russian election interference by expelling Russian officials from the United States and imposing sanctions on Russian intelligence agencies and those suspected of the hacks, among other steps.

CITING *CQ RESEARCHER*

Sample formats for citing these reports in a bibliography include the ones listed below. Preferred styles and formats vary, so please check with your instructor or professor.

MLA STYLE

Jost, Kenneth. "Remembering 9/11." CQ Researcher 2 Sept. 2011: 701-732.

APA STYLE

Jost, K. (2011, September 2). Remembering 9/11. *CQ Researcher, 9,* 701-732.

CHICAGO STYLE

Jost, Kenneth. "Remembering 9/11." *CQ Researcher,* September 2, 2011, 701-32.

In-depth Reports on Issues in the News

Are you writing a paper?

Need backup for a debate?

Want to become an expert on an issue?

For 90 years, students have turned to *CQ Researcher* for in-depth reporting on issues in the news. Reports on a full range of political and social issues are now available. Following is a selection of recent reports:

Civil Liberties
Privacy and the Internet, 12/15
Intelligence Reform, 5/15
Religion and Law, 11/14

Crime/Law
Jailing Debtors, 9/16
Decriminalizing Prostitution, 4/16
Restorative Justice, 2/16
The Dark Web, 1/16
Immigrant Detention, 10/15
Fighting Gangs, 10/15
Reforming Juvenile Justice, 9/15

Education
Student Debt, 11/16
Apprenticeships, 10/16
Free Speech on Campus, 5/15
Teaching Critical Thinking, 4/15

Environment/Society
Mass Transit, 12/16
Arctic Development, 12/16
Protecting the Power Grid, 11/16
Pornography, 10/16
Women in Leadership, 9/16
Child Welfare, 8/16

Health/Safety
Opioid Crisis, 10/16
Mosquito-Borne Disease, 7/16
Drinking Water Safety, 7/16
Virtual Reality, 2/16

Politics/Economy
Trump Presidency, 1/17
European Union's Future, 12/16
The Obama Legacy, 11/16
Populism and Party Politics, 9/16
U.S.-Mexico Relations, 9/16
Modernizing the Nuclear Arsenal, 7/16

Upcoming Reports

China and the South China Sea, 1/20/17   Guns on Campus, 1/27/17   Civics Education, 2/3/17

ACCESS

CQ Researcher is available in print and online. For access, visit your library or www.cqresearcher.com.

STAY CURRENT

For notice of upcoming *CQ Researcher* reports or to learn more about *CQ Researcher* products, subscribe to the free email newsletters, *CQ Researcher Alert!* and *CQ Researcher News*: http://cqpress.com/newsletters.

PURCHASE

To purchase a *CQ Researcher* report in print or electronic format (PDF), visit www.cqpress.com or call 866-427-7737. Single reports start at $15. Bulk purchase discounts and electronic-rights licensing are also available.

SUBSCRIBE

Annual full-service *CQ Researcher* subscriptions—including 44 reports a year, monthly index updates, and a bound volume—start at $1,131. Add $25 for domestic postage.

CQ Researcher Online offers a backfile from 1991 and a number of tools to simplify research. For pricing information, call 800-818-7243 or 805-499-9774 or email librarysales@sagepub.com.

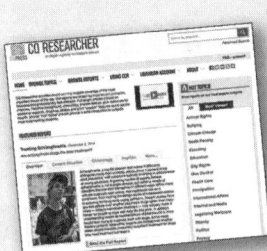

CQ RESEARCHER

CQ PRESS

In-depth reports on today's issues

Published by CQ Press, an Imprint of SAGE Publications, Inc.

www.cqresearcher.com

China and the South China Sea

Can the U.S. stop Chinese expansion?

China has been increasingly aggressive in the strategically vital South China Sea, establishing naval and air bases — and installing weapons — on islands it is constructing atop environmentally sensitive reefs. Tensions in the vast region, heavily patrolled by the U.S. Navy, have risen sharply in recent months. Surrounding nations, including the Philippines, a major U.S. ally, want access to the sea's wealth of natural resources — primarily oil, natural gas and fisheries — and its busy commercial shipping lanes. Responding to China, former President Barack Obama sought to shift more U.S. military resources to the region, but critics say his "pivot" was inadequate. President Trump's nominee for secretary of State, former Exxon Mobil CEO Rex Tillerson, told Congress the United States should forcefully confront China in the South China Sea and possibly deny it access to the islands it has built. Meanwhile, the Philippines' mercurial new president has voiced hostility toward the United States and a desire for closer relations with China, injecting further uncertainty into the region.

Chinese and Russian naval vessels hold a joint exercise in the South China Sea on Sept. 19, 2016. China's aggressive military activities in the region, including building military bases in the contested Spratly Islands and sending an aircraft carrier into the Taiwan Strait, worry many of China's neighbors. Rex Tillerson, President Trump's pick for secretary of State, also denounced China's actions.

INSIDE THIS REPORT

THE ISSUES	.....................**51**
BACKGROUND	.................**57**
CHRONOLOGY	.................**59**
CURRENT SITUATION	..........**64**
AT ISSUE	........................**65**
OUTLOOK	.....................**67**
BIBLIOGRAPHY	................**70**
THE NEXT STEP	...............**71**

CQ Researcher • Jan. 20, 2017 • www.cqresearcher.com
Volume 27, Number 3 • Pages 49-72

RECIPIENT OF SOCIETY OF PROFESSIONAL JOURNALISTS AWARD FOR EXCELLENCE ◆ AMERICAN BAR ASSOCIATION SILVER GAVEL AWARD

Los Angeles | London | New Delhi
Singapore | Washington DC | Melbourne

CHINA AND THE SOUTH CHINA SEA

THE ISSUES

51
- Is China seeking to dominate the South China Sea?
- Should America's regional allies pay more for U.S. protection?
- Is the Trans-Pacific Partnership trade agreement important to maintaining U.S. regional alliances?

BACKGROUND

57 **Colonization and Resistance**
European powers faced opposition as they sought to colonize the South China Sea region in pursuit of trade.

58 **World War II**
With Japan's defeat, communist China began a slow rise.

63 **Post-9/11**
President Obama promised "a new era of engagement" in Asia.

CURRENT SITUATION

64 **Rising Tensions**
A Trump nominee's comments could spark backlash.

66 **Troubled TPP**
Supporters are trying to save the trade pact.

66 **Military Rebalance**
Critics say the U.S. needs a bigger naval presence.

OUTLOOK

67 **Trump's Impact**
Experts are uncertain what the new administration will do.

SIDEBARS AND GRAPHICS

52 **Asian Nations Clash Over South China Sea**
The pursuit of oil, natural gas and other resources is spurring regional tensions.

53 **Asians Back Greater U.S. Military Presence**
A majority backs U.S. "pivot" to South China Sea region.

56 **Malaysia Tops Oil, Gas Reserves**
The South China Sea's reserves are largely unexplored.

59 **Chronology**
Key events since 1511.

60 **U.S.-Philippine Relationship Grows Rockier**
Mercurial leader "just does not want to work with the United States."

62 **China Reaching for Superpower Status**
But analysts see huge obstacles to its bid for global supremacy.

65 **At Issue:**
Does China's military buildup in the South China Sea threaten U.S. security?

FOR FURTHER RESEARCH

69 **For More Information**
Organizations to contact.

70 **Bibliography**
Selected sources used.

71 **The Next Step**
Additional articles.

71 **Citing CQ Researcher**
Sample bibliography formats.

Cover: Getty Images/Xinhua/Zha Chunming

CQ RESEARCHER

Jan. 20, 2017
Volume 27, Number 3

EXECUTIVE EDITOR: Thomas J. Billitteri
tjb@sagepub.com

ASSISTANT MANAGING EDITORS: Kenneth Fireman, kenneth.fireman@sagepub.com, Kathy Koch, kathy.koch@sagepub.com, Scott Rohrer, scott.rohrer@sagepub.com

SENIOR CONTRIBUTING EDITOR:
Thomas J. Colin
tom.colin@sagepub.com

CONTRIBUTING WRITERS: Marcia Clemmitt, Sarah Glazer, Reed Karaim, Peter Katel, Barbara Mantel, Chuck McCutcheon, Tom Price

SENIOR PROJECT EDITOR: Olu B. Davis

EDITORIAL ASSISTANT: Anika Reed

FACT CHECKERS: Eva P. Dasher, Michelle Harris, Betsy Towner Levine, Robin Palmer

Los Angeles I London I New Delhi
Singapore I Washington DC I Melbourne

An Imprint of SAGE Publications, Inc.

SENIOR VICE PRESIDENT, GLOBAL LEARNING RESOURCES:
Karen Phillips

EXECUTIVE DIRECTOR, ONLINE LIBRARY AND REFERENCE PUBLISHING:
Todd Baldwin

CQ Press is a registered trademark of Congressional Quarterly Inc.

CQ Researcher (ISSN 1056-2036) is printed on acid-free paper. Published weekly, except: (March wk. 4) (May wk. 4) (July wks. 1, 2) (Aug. wks. 2, 3) (Nov. wk. 4) and (Dec. wks. 3, 4). Published by SAGE Publications, Inc., 2455 Teller Rd., Thousand Oaks, CA 91320. Annual full-service subscriptions start at $1,131. For pricing, call 1-800-818-7243. To purchase a CQ Researcher report in print or electronic format (PDF), visit www.cqpress.com or call 866-427-7737. Single reports start at $15. Bulk purchase discounts and electronic-rights licensing are also available. Periodicals postage paid at Thousand Oaks, California, and at additional mailing offices. POSTMASTER: Send address changes to CQ Researcher, 2600 Virginia Ave., N.W., Suite 600, Washington, DC 20037.

China and the South China Sea

BY PATRICK MARSHALL

THE ISSUES

The Spratly Islands have long been celebrated for their exotic marine life, including more than 1,000 species of birds, fish, turtles and sea grasses.

Lately, however, the remote collection of coral reefs and small islands in the South China Sea has become a source of ominous political and military tension.

Since 2013, China has been using sand dredged from the seafloor to turn coral reefs in the Spratlys into seven artificial islands covering more than 3,200 acres, complete with harbors, runways and hangars for military bases. [1] China's intentions are benign, a government spokesman said in 2015: "The construction activities . . . fall within the scope of China's sovereignty, and are lawful, reasonable and justified. They are not targeted at any other country." [2]

But last month the Chinese Defense Ministry conceded that China has placed weapons, including anti-aircraft missiles, on the man-made islands, saying "they are primarily for defense and self-protection, and this is proper and legitimate." [3]

China's neighbors, along with many U.S. foreign policy experts and at least one likely key member of President Trump's administration, disagree.

Secretary of State nominee Rex Tillerson said at his Jan. 12 confirmation hearing that China's activities are "extremely worrisome." "Building islands and then putting military assets on those islands is akin to Russia's taking of Crimea. It's taking of territory that others lay claim to," Tillerson said. "We're going to have to send China a clear signal

Protesters from Vietnam and the Philippines demonstrate at China's consular office in Manila on Aug. 3, 2016, to demand that China respect their countries' rights to harvest fish and other resources in the South China Sea. Several Asian nations have overlapping claims to islands, reefs and shoals in the vast sea, which also holds large untapped quantities of oil and natural gas.

AFP/Getty Images/Ted Aljibe

that first, the island-building stops, and second, your access to those islands is also not going to be allowed." [4]

International tensions over China's buildup are only the latest in a decade-long dispute with Beijing over the strategically important South China Sea, which stretches from Brunei in the south to Taiwan in the north and the Philippines in the east. (*See map, p. 52.*) M. Taylor Fravel, an associate professor of political science at the Massachusetts Institute of Technology, says the South China Sea is at the heart of "the world's most complicated territorial dispute," one with military, economic and ecological dimensions.

Six countries — China, Brunei, Malaysia, the Philippines, Taiwan and Vietnam — have overlapping claims to waters, islands, and reefs in the South China Sea. China claims four-fifths of the sea — a claim an international tribunal rejected in July. The most hotly contested areas are the Paracel Islands (occupied by China but also claimed by Vietnam and Taiwan); the Spratly Islands (claimed by Brunei, China, Malaysia, the Philippines, Taiwan and Vietnam); and the Scarborough Shoal, a chain of reefs and rocks about 100 miles west of the Philippines claimed by China, Taiwan and the Philippines.

All but Taiwan have signed the United Nations Convention on the Law of the Sea (UNCLOS) under which a country's territory extends 12 nautical miles from its shoreline. In addition, the treaty gives nations the right to drill, fish or pursue other economic activities 200 miles from its shores in an area known as an Exclusive Economic Zone. In the South China Sea, the 200-nautical-mile zones result in multiple overlapping claims, especially because some countries have occupied — and in some cases created — small islands within the Exclusive Economic Zone of other nations.

For China, the South China Sea is of huge strategic importance. China's naval expansion and its construction of artificial islands, some analysts say, demonstrate that the Chinese want to control navigation throughout the sea and dominate the region militarily. In early January, for example, China sent its lone aircraft carrier into the Taiwan

Asian Nations Clash Over South China Sea

China, the Philippines, Vietnam and other Asian nations have overlapping claims to islands, reefs and shoals in the 1.4 million-square-mile South China Sea. The stakes include the rights to oil, natural gas, fisheries and other natural resources. China is also constructing controversial military outposts in the disputed Spratly Islands in an attempt to tighten its control over the region.

Claims to the South China Sea

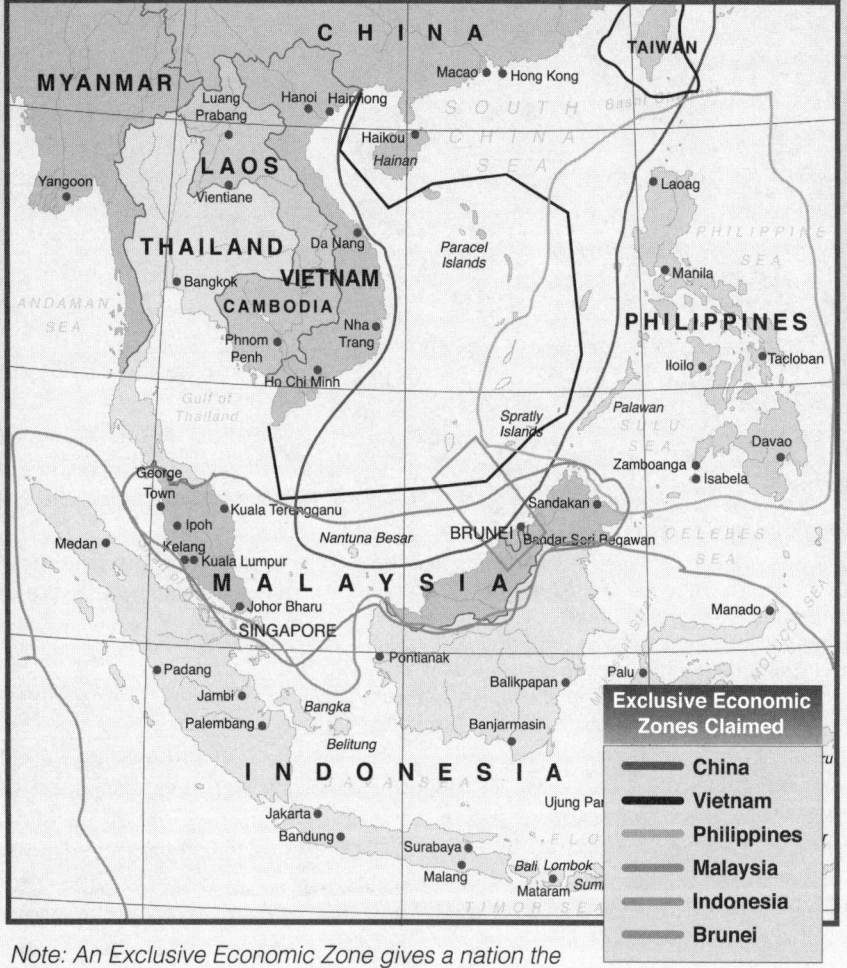

Note: An Exclusive Economic Zone gives a nation the right to drill for oil and gas, fish or pursue other economic activities 200 miles from its shores. In the South China Sea, the zones have resulted in overlapping claims.

Source: Beina Xu, "South China Sea Tensions," Council on Foreign Relations, May 14, 2014, http://tinyurl.com/ckfsb9k

Sen. John McCain, R-Ariz., chairman of the Senate Armed Services Committee, put it more harshly in December: "China is militarizing the South China Sea, its leaders continue to lie about that fact, and Beijing is paying little to no price for its behavior." [6]

China has been beefing up its navy in recent years. After launching more ships than any other country in 2013 and 2014, the Chinese navy had more than 300 vessels, including submarines, amphibious ships and missile-armed patrol craft as of 2015, and the trend is expected to continue, according to the U.S. Office of Naval Intelligence. [7]

China's rapid naval expansion makes some policymakers nervous, especially in light of the amount of shipping that moves through the South China Sea.

"The importance of the South China Sea to global commerce and regional stability cannot be overstated, with estimates of more than half the world's merchant fleet tonnage passing through these waters," Colin Willett, deputy assistant secretary of State for multilateral affairs, told Congress last July. "The South China Sea also serves as an important transit route and operational theater for the U.S. and other regional militaries, including those of our allies and partners. It allows us to shift military assets between the Pacific to the Indian Ocean regions." [8]

In addition, control of the region's natural resources — oil and natural gas reserves and rich commercial fishing grounds — is at stake. By some estimates, the South China Sea may contain more oil than any other area of the planet except Saudi Arabia. And according to some estimates, the region has 60 percent of Asia's hydrocarbon resources. [9] The most significant tensions over oil and gas fields have involved China's clashes with Vietnam and the Philippines over their searches for hydrocarbons in fields claimed by China. [10]

Conflicts over fishing rights are also heated. The South China Sea provides 12 percent of the global fish catch, and countries with territorial claims

Strait in what one analyst called a show of force "intended in part to intimidate" Trump and Taiwan. [5]

"They have nationalistic goals," says former Republican Sen. James Talent, a member of the U.S.-China Economic and Security Review Commission, which Congress created to monitor trade between the two countries. The Chinese, he says, see themselves as "rightfully the dominant power in Asia." (*See sidebar, p. 62.*)

in the region have strongly contested access to fisheries. Competition has led to serious overfishing. Fully half of the fisheries in the South China Sea are either over-exploited or have collapsed, according to experts. [11]

As tensions rose in the past year, critics charged that former President Barack Obama made inadequate attempts to counter growing Chinese influence in the region. Meanwhile, Donald Trump's ascension to the presidency has generated anxiety among many U.S. and Asian experts and policymakers because of his threats to upend alliances and what many see as his unpredictability.

Trump repeatedly has criticized China over trade policy, saying the country unfairly closes its domestic market to imports while flooding the United States with cheap exports. And on Dec. 2, Trump broke decades of diplomatic tradition by taking a congratulatory call from Taiwan's president. Since 1972, despite its close ties to Taiwan, the United States has adhered to a "One China" policy, under which China asserts that Taiwan is a Chinese province and not an independent country.

"I don't know why we have to be bound by a One China policy unless we make a deal with China having to do with other things, including trade," Trump told Fox News on Dec. 11. "We're being hurt very badly by China with [currency] devaluation, with taxing us heavy at the borders when we don't tax them, with building a massive fortress in the middle of the South China Sea, which they shouldn't be doing." [12]

Some argue that China's aggressiveness has actually strengthened the U.S. position in Asia. Citing China's military buildup, retired Adm. Dennis Blair, a former commander of the U.S. Pacific Command and former director of National Intelligence, told Congress last July that other countries were looking to the United States for help in countering an increasingly hard-line China. "China has paid a heavy price for its aggressive

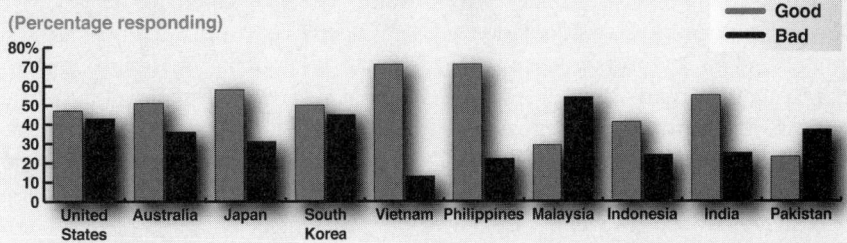

Asians Back Greater U.S. Military Presence

Asians, with the exception of Malaysians and Pakistanis, generally say more U.S. military resources in the Asia-Pacific region would reduce the chances for conflict with China.

Would more U.S. military resources in the Asia-Pacific area be good or bad for peace in the region?

(Percentage responding)

Source: "U.S. Defense Pivot to Asia Welcomed, for the Most Part — But Chinese See U.S. as Trying to Limit China's Power," Pew Research Center, June 22, 2015, http://tinyurl.com/huxa67y

activities in the hostility of the other claimant states," he said. [13]

The Obama administration moved to strengthen the U.S. position by undertaking a "pivot" or "rebalance" of American political, economic and military resources toward Asia and away from the Middle East.

The two most important legs of Obama's strategy were a commitment to increase U.S. naval assets in Asia and the negotiation of the Trans-Pacific Partnership (TPP), a trade pact between the United States and 11 Pacific Rim countries finalized in February 2016 but awaiting congressional approval. TPP backers see it as an attempt to strengthen the economies of regional allies, but many think the Republican-controlled Congress is unlikely to ratify the pact after Trump heavily criticized it during the presidential campaign.

As for the other leg of Obama's "pivot" strategy, the United States pledged in 2012 to deploy 60 percent of its naval assets, including warships and submarines, in the Pacific by 2020, up from the current 50 percent. [14]

Despite those efforts, some experts argue the strategy is failing, "primarily for want of power," Talent says. The U.S. Pacific Fleet, which had 192 ves-

sels two decades ago, had 182 as of January 2016. [15]

Congress has failed to fund a larger Navy due to budget constraints, according to Robert D. Kaplan, a senior fellow at the Center for a New American Security, a bipartisan think tank in Washington focused on security policy. "You can have all of the great concepts of an Asia pivot you want," Kaplan says. "It's not going to matter much" without ships.

Further complicating the situation has been last year's election of Rodrigo Duterte as president of the Philippines, historically America's strongest regional ally. Duterte has been a strident critic of U.S. policy and has reached out to China and Russia. (*See sidebar, p. 60.*)

As policymakers assess the future of international relations in the South China Sea, here are some of the questions they are asking:

Is China seeking to dominate the South China Sea?

It's not just China's growing navy that worries some analysts. China also has been expanding its footprint in the South China Sea by occupying contested islands and building artificial islands for use as military bases.

"China has continued to build harbors, communications and surveillance systems, logistical facilities and three military-grade airfields on many of the features it occupies," Abraham M. Denmark, deputy assistant secretary of Defense for East Asia, told Congress in July. "In the past year, China also has deployed radar systems, anti-ship cruise missiles, surface-to-air missiles, and has rotated fighter jets through features it claims in the South China Sea." [16]

China's construction of hangars and underground storage facilities for fuel and water would support extended deployments of aircraft and ships, he said, as would its installation of anti-aircraft weapons.

China's leaders previously promised they would not militarize the South China Sea. During his state visit to the United States in September, in fact, Chinese President Xi Jinping said, "China does not intend to pursue militarization" on the disputed Spratly Islands in the South China Sea. [17]

While some skeptics scoff at those promises, other experts, noting that the weapons systems placed on the Spratly Islands are limited in range, say China is simply positioning itself to defend its territory and trade routes against the United States and others. [18]

"Since around 2010, China's security policy has evolved from a focus on homeland defense to one . . . best characterized as 'peaceful expansion,' " Timothy Heath, a senior international defense research analyst at RAND Corp., a research organization based in California, told the U.S.-China Economic and Security Review Commission last January. Since China's commercial and military interests have expanded geographically, Heath said, its ability to protect those interests also had to expand. [19]

As a result, he said, China has shown a greater willingness to involve itself in mediating disputes in regions far from its own shores.

MIT's Fravel agrees China's military posture is more defensive than aggressive in nature. "I think they want to ensure that they are in a position not to be dominated," he says. "I think they would like to weaken the influence of the United States, but that paradoxically may mean that they are more willing to cooperate with their neighbors on the things that their neighbors value, like investment projects."

Other experts, however, argue that China's intentions are not so benign. China is patiently building toward the day when it can militarily and economically dominate not just the South China Sea but all of Asia, they claim.

President Xi Jinping has "an empire-building intention," says Ming Xia, a professor of political science at the College of Staten Island in New York. "In foreign affairs, China wants to be respected and feared by countries in both the East China Sea and the South China Sea and India. I think the appropriate comparison is to Japan in the 1930s," when the Japanese invaded Manchuria, a region of China, in 1931.

China's need to dominate the region, says former Sen. Talent, is particularly acute because the country's leaders don't have the legitimacy that comes with democratic elections. "They have to be able to show to their people that they have produced success as rulers," he says. "Part of that is quality of life at home and part of that is prestige in Asia. That is what is driving them to assert sovereignty over the seas, including the South China Sea."

Frank Gaffney, president of the Center for Security Policy, a conservative think tank in Washington, agrees that China wants to expand its control. "This is a moment when I think the China dream, as Xi Jinping calls it, is to be realized at the expense of everybody else in that part of the world, and it will return China to what it considers to be its rightful place as the world's preeminent power," says Gaffney, an adviser to Trump.

At the same time, some analysts say China's aggressiveness may reflect tension between its civilian and military leaders.

During a recent fact-finding trip to China, James Clad, senior adviser for Asia at the Center for Naval Analyses, a federally funded research and development organization in Arlington, Va., serving the Navy and other defense agencies, and a former deputy assistant secretary of Defense for Asia, says he got the impression the political leadership "needs to continue to placate the military, with goodies, acquisitions and with rhetoric that approaches hyper-nationalistic sensitivities."

Some analysts say China is only doing what most rising regional powers do. "An increasingly powerful China is likely to try to push the U.S. out of Asia, much the way the U.S. pushed the European powers out of the Western Hemisphere" in the 19th century, writes John J. Mearsheimer, a professor of political science at the University of Chicago. "Why should we expect China to act any differently than the United States did? Are they more principled than we are? Or ethical? Less nationalistic?" [20]

Bonner R. Cohen, a senior fellow at the National Center for Public Policy Research, a conservative think tank in Washington, agrees. "These people are not reckless," he says. "They make their geostrategic moves in a very calculating way.

"If they see opportunities, they will take advantage of those opportunities," he continues. "They have always considered areas immediately adjacent to China — and that includes bodies of water — as being essentially a part of China."

Should America's regional allies pay more for U.S. protection?

In his first major foreign policy speech during the presidential campaign last April, Trump complained that the United States was paying far too much to protect other countries. "We have spent trillions of dollars over time on planes, missiles, ships, equipment — building up our military to provide a strong defense for Europe and Asia," Trump said. "The countries we are defending must pay for the cost of this defense, and if not, the U.S. must be prepared to let these countries defend themselves. We have no choice." [21]

Trump has also suggested that the United States should end its decades-long policy against nuclear proliferation and encourage South Korea and Japan to acquire nuclear weapons with which to defend themselves. [22]

While most analysts and policymakers reject Trump's position on nuclear proliferation, some observers welcomed his call for greater burden-sharing by Asian allies.

"In every case the allies should be shouldering more of their share of the common defense," says Gaffney of the Center for Security Policy, adding that he found Trump's call for allies to pony up "bracing."

Cohen of the National Center for Public Policy Research agrees. "We don't have the resources that we once did. So it is much better for us to encourage other people to look after their own interests," he says. "There are things that they can do for themselves, and if we don't show them how . . . and encourage them to do it themselves, they will simply rely on us to do it."

Cohen says the United States has no territorial claims at stake in the South China Sea so "it is ultimately incumbent upon those countries . . . to do as much as they possibly can for themselves while at the same time leaning on the U.S. Navy as kind of an ultimate plan B."

Others, however, argue that while wealthier allies, most notably Japan, should be prodded to contribute more, the United States shouldn't be just a backup. Elbridge Colby, a senior fellow at the Center for a New American Security, a liberal-leaning Washington think tank, told Congress in September that "because China is so powerful, we do need to take the lead, but actually that leadership role will be more likely to catalyze that burden sharing." [23]

In September, Japanese Defense Minister Tomomi Inada announced that his nation would increase its presence in the South China Sea and would provide more aid to countries in the region, including the Philippines and Vietnam. The moves, he said, "underline my government's resolve to protect our territorial integrity and sovereignty." Inada, however, did not provide details. [24]

Some policy analysts say Trump's push to get allies to pay more will be counterproductive.

Getty Images/DigitalGlobe

Fiery Cross Reef, in the western Spratly Islands, is among the reefs that China has turned into man-made islands housing army and navy bases and airstrips. In an effort to stem China's regional expansion, the United States deployed warships within 12 nautical miles of Fiery Cross Reef in 2015.

"President Trump will need to stop focusing on burden sharing and focus on security relationships," wrote Anthony Cordesman, a national security analyst at the Center for Strategic and International Studies, a nonpartisan Washington think tank. Trump shouldn't ask allies to contribute more than they can afford and should refrain from giving allies and potential foes the impression that the United States is disengaging, Cordesman said. [25]

Although a discussion of burden sharing can be useful, wrote Robert E. Kelly, an associate professor of international relations at Pusan National University in South Korea, "Trump to date has cast the debate in a bean-counting light: How much do allies pay for this or that American capability?" [26]

Rather than getting allies to pay more for protection, Kelly said, the United States should help allies build their own defensive capabilities and coordinate defense efforts with them. "Multilateral operations carry greater international credibility, relieve [the burden] on the U.S. military and signal to opponents that they face a full-bodied international coalition of serious, committed democracies — not just the Americans yet again," he said.

But others warn that calling on Asian allies to build up their own defense capabilities poses its own dangers. "The Chinese would interpret a buildup of allied military, and they say so, as a hostile act," says former Sen. Talent. "So you don't want to do that unless you're certain that the Americans are going to be there backing them up."

Talent also warns of complications

Malaysia Tops Oil, Gas Reserves

Malaysia has the most known oil and natural gas reserves in the South China Sea, according to the latest available estimates. The sea's vast reserves are largely unexplored and may contain more oil than any other region except Saudi Arabia.

Estimated Oil and Gas Reserves in the South China Sea, 2012

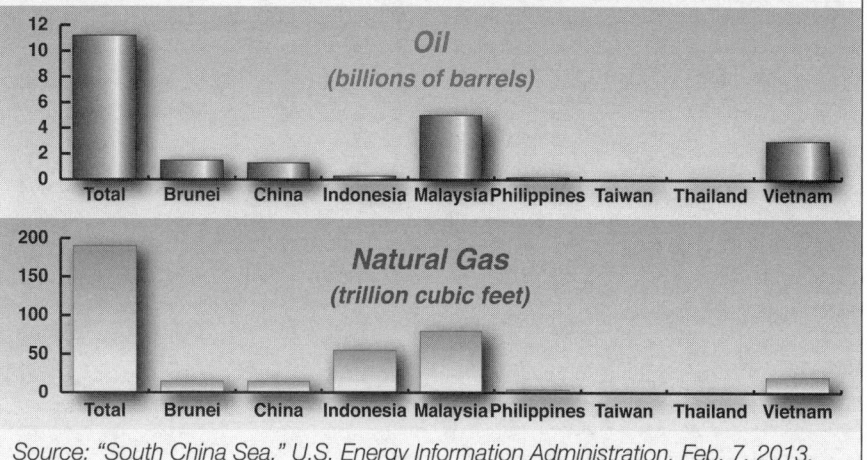

Source: "South China Sea," U.S. Energy Information Administration, Feb. 7, 2013, http://tinyurl.com/znusb9c

in having Japan assume a higher military profile because of the notorious behavior of its soldiers before and during World War II. "For obvious reasons, historical reasons," Talent says, "this needs to be seen in the region as firmly under the umbrella of American leadership."

Oriana Skylar Mastro, an assistant professor of security studies at Georgetown University and a nuclear security fellow at the Council on Foreign Relations, says U.S. alliances in Asia have delivered benefits that are impossible to measure in dollars.

"They allow us access and influence, and access and influence allow us to promote and protect our foreign policy interests," Mastro says. "Outsourcing our national security interests, even to those that we like and trust, is never a good idea."

Is the Trans-Pacific Partnership trade agreement important to maintaining U.S. regional alliances?

One of Trump's most frequent targets on the campaign trail was the Trans-

Pacific Partnership (TPP). At a campaign rally last June, he characterized the trade pact as "a continuing rape of our country" because of its potential to harm the middle class. [27]

Congress has yet to approve the TPP. To take effect, six countries that account for 85 percent of the group's economic output must ratify the pact by February 2018. That means both Japan and the United States must ratify the agreement. In December, Japan became the first, and so far only, signatory to do so. [28]

When the TPP was finalized in 2015, it did not include China, which chose not to participate, according to Thomas J. Christensen, a professor of international relations at Princeton University and former deputy assistant secretary of State for East Asian and Pacific affairs. "The U.S. goal in relation to Beijing was not to exclude China from the TPP," he wrote, "but to . . . catalyze China to compete by further opening its own domestic markets and providing protection for intellectual property rights for the first time." [29]

While China has not actively opposed the pact, its "One Belt, One Road" infrastructure project, which is aimed at strengthening China's economic links to countries in Eurasia by building roads and ports, would likely benefit from the TPP's collapse. That is because more countries in Southeast Asia would look to China rather than to Western countries for increased trade and aid. [30]

Trump's adamant opposition to the pact is "clearly going to ruffle feathers" among the TPP's signatories, says Cohen of the National Center for Public Policy Research. Because China is not a party to the TPP, he says, other nations see the pact as having a "not-too-subtle anti-Chinese bent to it." It was, accordingly, viewed positively by American allies in Asia who hoped the creation of a free-trade zone would be a counterweight to an economically powerful China. Nevertheless, Cohen says the new president will likely reject the TPP. "I think the pact is effectively dead," he says.

While the domestic effects of the TPP were debated during the presidential campaign, the foreign policy implications received scant mention, even though the Obama administration pushed the deal as part of its Asian pivot.

"TPP would've anchored the Asian pivot for us," says Kaplan of the Center for a New American Security. "If you have a free-trade zone that you are the head of, you're in a very strong position in Asia." Kaplan says the Trump administration should push a version of TPP through Congress "by calling it something else."

Georgetown University's Mastro says the Asian pivot got lost during the presidential campaign as the candidates from both political parties focused on jobs and American competitiveness. "I'm not surprised that people in the Rust Belt weren't thinking about the primacy of the United States in the Asia-Pacific when they voted," she says. "You don't realize how much you need it until you lose it."

Asian countries, according to Mastro, saw the TPP as an indication that the United States was going to be more focused on its strategic interests in the South China Sea. With Trump's election, she says, "a lot of the optimism has been thrown out the window along with TPP. It was a big component of maintaining U.S. leadership in the region."

Publicly, Asian leaders say they hope Trump will reverse course. "I am a strong supporter of developing trade and open regionalism in Asia Pacific," said Malaysian Prime Minister Najib Razak in November. "It is key to benefiting our peoples. I look forward to working with President-elect Trump on our shared goals of strengthening security and ensuring growth that is inclusive, sustainable and fair to all." [31]

Some experts say the Trump administration can accomplish many of the TPP's goals through bilateral trade agreements with friendly countries in the region. "If we're not going to go forward with the TPP, it's important to have a substitute . . ., which could be vigorously pursued through bilateral agreements," says former Sen. Talent.

But other analysts say even if the Trump administration successfully negotiates such agreements, the United States will have lost credibility by not ratifying the pact. TPP's failure "will raise very significant questions about our credibility and about our political will," says Gregory B. Poling, director of the Asia Maritime Transparency Initiative at the Center for Strategic and International Studies. "It will tell Asian states that we are engaged militarily but not necessarily in any other way, whereas China is playing on all fronts. That's damage we're going to have a hard time undoing."

Even if Trump reverses course and the TPP is ratified, America's image has already been damaged, says Mira Rapp-Hooper, a senior fellow with the Asia-Pacific security program at the Center for a New American Security. "It has been deeply concerning to our partners

A Chinese coast guard ship patrols near the Scarborough Shoal in the South China Sea on Dec.13 as a Philippine fisherman watches. The shoal, lying within the Philippines' Exclusive Economic Zone, is claimed by not only the Philippines but also China and Taiwan. In July, the Permanent Court of Arbitration, in The Hague, ruled China was infringing on the Philippines' fishing rights.

in East Asia broadly to see how trade has been discussed in the U.S. election," she says. "They are keenly aware that this is not just a partisan issue, but that on both the left and the right there was a really strong anti-free trade sentiment in the United States." ■

BACKGROUND

Colonization and Resistance

Since the early 16th century, European colonization has shaped the countries bordering the South China Sea.

The first sustained Western colonization, driven by commercial and religious motives, began with the Portuguese capture of the city of Malacca on Malaysia's southwestern coast in 1511, a feat that required 1,200 men and more than a dozen warships. [32]

Portugal's occupation of Malacca, where it built a fortress to protect its shipping, was followed by similar oc-

cupations elsewhere in Southeast Asia by the Netherlands, England, France and Spain. Eventually, those five powers controlled nearly all of Southeast Asia. Britain came to occupy "Burma, Malaya and Borneo; France controlled Indochina; the Dutch ruled Indonesia; and the United States had replaced Spain as the colonial master of the Philippines," wrote Asia expert Mark J. Valencia, an associate at the Nautilus Institute for Security and Sustainability, a think tank in Berkeley, Calif. [33]

The experiences of the various Asian countries — and, in some cases, even their borders — depended to a large degree upon the colonizing country and on events in Europe.

"The frontiers were drawn so as to avoid disputes among the European powers," wrote Nicholas Tarling, an economist and historian at Australia's University of Auckland. "As a result, especially at the margins, they bore no firm relation to economic, social, cultural, ethnic or even geographical realities." [34]

Changes in borders, governments and policies — from taxation to land ownership — "did not merely, nor even primarily, result from the changes in tensions within Southeast Asia," Tarling said. Instead, events in Europe drove many of the changes. [35]

For example, as a result of the Napoleonic Wars (1803-15), the French gained dominance over the Dutch Republic and its colonies in Southeast Asia. At the same time, the British took possession of Dutch colonies in India, Ceylon and Java.

The European powers were generally more interested in commerce and protection of their shipping lanes than they were about control of land and populations.

"The changing spirit of the times was most closely captured by Britain's establishment of trading centers at Penang (1786), Malacca (1824) and especially Singapore (1819), occasioning the Dutch to establish similar ports within their sphere of influence," said Robert E. Elson, an emeritus professor of history at Griffith University in Queensland, Australia. "This was the beginning of the age of 'free-trade imperialism,' founded on the belief that 'free trade,' commerce unhindered by protection and undiverted by the demands of territorial administration, inevitably meant Britain's economic success as well as greater prosperity for those peoples with which it traded." [36]

China also had significant influence over the region. Like the Europeans, the Chinese were not interested in controlling lands or peoples in Southeast Asia. China was "content with the confession of vassalage" that would ensure profits for the government and protection for Chinese traders, according to Tarling. When they were challenged, China intervened ruthlessly. [37]

Meanwhile, the Chinese dynasties faced increasing domestic difficulties and became increasingly vulnerable to European encroachment. Two conflicts with Great Britain weakened China's last dynasty, the Qing, which ruled from 1644 to 1911.

The first Opium War (1839-42) broke out when China attempted to prevent British traders from selling opium from India in China. "The resulting widespread addiction in China was causing serious social and economic disruption there," wrote Asia historian Kenneth Pletcher. In March 1839, the Chinese government confiscated and destroyed more than 20,000 chests of opium warehoused at Canton by British merchants.

"The antagonism between the two sides increased a few days later when some drunken British sailors killed a Chinese villager," Pletcher said. "The British government, which did not wish its subjects to be tried in the Chinese legal system, refused to turn the accused men over to the Chinese courts." [38]

Hostilities broke out several months later. British forces captured Nanjing in 1842, leading the Chinese government to capitulate. Besides forcing China to pay a large indemnity, the Treaty of Nanjing required China to increase from one to five the number of "treaty ports" where British merchants could trade and to cede the island of Hong Kong to the British. [39]

The Second Opium War erupted in 1857 as China was attempting to put down the Taiping Rebellion (1850-64), a political and religious upheaval that cost an estimated 20 million lives. British forces, joined by French troops, prevailed, resulting in further Chinese concessions, including legalization of the opium trade.

"In the 19th century, as the Qing dynasty became the sick man of East Asia, China lost much of its territory — the southern tributaries of Nepal and Burma to Great Britain; Indochina to France; Taiwan and the tributaries of Korea and Sakhalin to Japan; and Mongolia, Amuria and Ussuria to Russia," wrote the Center for a New American Security's Kaplan. [40]

The growing reach of European colonizers brought resistance from native populations.

Between the mid-19th century and the 1930s, "European governments found themselves engaged in 'pacification' campaigns against traditional states and popular rebellions," said Carl A. Trocki, an Asia historian at Queensland University of Technology. [41]

At the end of the 19th century, a new global power entered the political maelstrom of the South China Sea: the United States. At war with Spain in the Spanish colony of Cuba in 1898, the United States joined forces with Philippine resistance forces to drive the Spanish out of the Philippines.

The rise of nationalist and communist movements in Southeast Asia was encouraged not only by local conditions but, once again, by events in Europe. The onset of World War I in 1914 pitted the colonial powers against each other. The resulting bloodbath demonstrated two things to resistance movements in Southeast Asia.

"The unprecedented scale and carnage of the hostilities served to undermine any pretensions that Western civilization possessed inherent moral superiority, while on a more concrete level, Britain and France, despite emerging as victors, both suffered a serious (and, it would prove, irreversible) erosion of economic and military power," wrote historians Paul Kratoska and Ben Batson of the National University of Singapore. [42]

By 1920, the confluence of domestic conditions and events in Europe enabled nationalist movements to challenge colonial regimes throughout the region.

World War II

These nationalist movements stalled in the 1930s because of a new Asian occupier, Japan, which began invading its neighbors in the lead-up to World War II.

The Japanese empire — in an attempt to secure resources, especially oil and

Continued on p. 60

Chronology

1500-1898
Outsiders colonize Asia.

1511
Portuguese warships capture Malacca in Malaysia, marking the beginning of 400 years of European colonization in Southeast Asia.

1839
First Opium War begins after China tries to prevent British traders from importing opium into China; with British victory in 1842, Treaty of Nanjing requires China to increase to five the number of ports open to British traders.

1895
Japan occupies Taiwan.

1898
After the Spanish-American War, the United States colonizes the Philippines.

———— • ————

1914-1945
Nationalist movements challenge colonial regimes throughout the South China Sea.

1914
World War I erodes ability of colonial powers to maintain control in Southeast Asia.

1940
With the onset of World War II, Japan — having already occupied Korea in 1910 and Manchuria in 1931 — captures nearly every country in South China Sea region.

1945
Japan surrenders; United States becomes dominant power in western Pacific.

1946-1988
U.S. Navy dominates the western Pacific.

1946
French forces battle Vietnamese nationalists backed by China and Russia; French withdraw in 1954 and Vietnam is partitioned.

1947
China publishes map of the South China Sea outlining its claims to nearly all of the sea.

1949
Communist Chinese forces defeat Nationalist Chinese, who flee to Taiwan.

1964
Gulf of Tonkin incident — a reported clash between a U.S. destroyer and North Vietnamese forces — sparks a major increase in U.S. involvement in Vietnam War.

1974
South Vietnam falls to North Vietnam; China seizes the Paracel Islands, which had been claimed by the South Vietnamese government.

1988
Chinese and Vietnamese forces battle at Johnson South Reef in Spratly Islands, claimed by both countries; 64 Vietnamese soldiers reportedly are killed.

———— • ————

2001-Present
Chinese influence in South China Sea grows.

2001
U.S. reconnaissance aircraft flying near China's Hainan Island collides with a Chinese fighter.

2009
Barack Obama, describing himself as "America's first Pacific president," promises Asian countries "a new era of engagement."

2011
Obama announces a "pivot" to Asia, including a bigger naval presence in the region.

2012
China declares an "air defense identification zone" covering a large maritime area separating China from Japan.

2014
China moves oil exploration gear into the Paracel Islands, renewing tensions with Vietnam. . . . Satellite images show China building an island at Fiery Cross Reef in the Spratlys large enough for an airstrip.

2015
U.S. deploys warships within 12 nautical miles of Chinese-occupied Fiery Cross Reef.

2016
U.S. deploys more ships near Triton Island in the Paracels to reassert its "freedom of navigation" rights (January). . . . International tribunal rules in favor of the Philippines and against Chinese in dispute over ownership of the Spratly Islands (July). . . . Philippine President Rodrigo Duterte visits China and returns with billions of dollars in aid and trade deals after telling the Chinese that "America has lost now" (October). . . . China acknowledges that it has installed weapons on disputed islands in the Spratlys (December). . . . President-elect Donald Trump causes a diplomatic kerfuffle by taking a congratulatory phone call from Taiwanese president; a Chinese warship seizes a U.S. research drone in South China Sea (December).

U.S.-Philippine Relationship Grows Rockier

Mercurial leader "just does not want to work with the United States."

With last year's election of Rodrigo Duterte as Philippine president, the United States' relationship with the Asian island nation — historically America's strongest ally in the South China Sea region — has grown a lot more complicated.

Since taking office in June, Duterte called President Obama a "son of a bitch," threatened to expel U.S. Special Forces from training grounds on the southern Philippine island of Mindanao, announced the end of joint U.S.-Philippine patrols in the South China Sea and suggested he was open to alliances with Russia and China. [1]

The mercurial Duterte visited China in October and came home with billions of dollars in aid after telling the Chinese: "America has lost now. I've realigned myself in your ideological flow. And maybe I will also go to Russia to talk to [President Vladimir] Putin and tell him that there are three of us against the world: China, Philippines and Russia." [2] A few days later, Duterte issued a clarification, saying he did not intend to split from the United States. He said he was calling for a "separation of foreign policy" rather than "a severance of ties." [3]

Then in late October, the Philippine government announced that it had reached an agreement with China on the disputed Scarborough Shoal, an undersea ridge approximately 100 miles west of the Philippines. While details of the agreement were not revealed, a Philippines government spokesman said Chinese ships were no longer blocking Philippine vessels in the area. [4]

Most recently, Duterte, who is scheduled to visit Moscow in April, told Rear Adm. Eduard Mikhailov, head of Russia's Pacific fleet, that he was welcome in the Philippines "anytime you want to dock here for anything, for play, for replenish[ing] supplies or maybe [to be] our ally to protect us." [5]

Some experts have attributed Duterte's antipathy toward the United States to the Obama administration's criticism of Duterte's anti-drug campaign, which the administration said has involved widespread extrajudicial killings and tactics that are "entirely inconsistent with universal human rights." [6] Others see Duterte's outreach to China as evidence of his long-standing hostility to the United States. Duterte, who previously was mayor of Davao City, is "reflexively anti-American," says Gregory B. Poling, director of the Asia Maritime Transparency Initiative at the Center for Strategic and International Studies, a bipartisan policy research organization in Washington. "He just does not want to work with the United States."

Despite Duterte's anti-American rhetoric, many experts say the United States remains popular in its former colony, which it controlled from 1898 to 1946, when the Philippines gained independence. "The United States is quite popular in the Philippines, and the alliance [between the two countries specifically] is quite popular in the Philippines," says Mira Rapp-Hooper, a senior fellow at the Center for a New American Security, a think tank in Washington. Noting that the United States is a top importer of Philippine goods, such as machinery, Rapp-Hooper says the U.S.-Philippines relationship is broader than just security.

"While Duterte may be deriving some personal satisfaction and perhaps some political points from seeming to push back on a longtime patron, I think his true alignment will ultimately be determined by his interests," she says. "It is pretty clear that his interests are not as black-and-white as his rhetoric would suggest."

The foundation of the nations' security relationship is a 1951 mutual-defense treaty that requires each nation to come to the aid of the other in the event of conflict or a threat to national security. In exchange for providing protection to the Philippines, the United States was allowed to maintain large military facilities in the Philippines, most notably a naval base in Subic Bay and Clark Air Base north of Manila.

In 1991, the Philippine Senate, citing the U.S. military presence as a vestige of colonialism, voted to expel U.S. forces from Subic Bay and Clark Air Base. [7]

Continued from p. 58

rubber, that were scarce within its territory — expanded into the Asia mainland with its occupations of Korea in 1910 and Manchuria in northeast China in 1931. It also occupied the island of Taiwan from 1895 until World War II ended in 1945.

With the onset of World War II, Japan quickly moved to take control of nearly all the countries in the South China Sea region. Between 1940 and 1942, Japan invaded Hong Kong, Vietnam, Laos, Thailand, the Philippines, Singapore, Cambodia, Malaysia and

Burma and occupied all of them until the war's end. Its troops in China and elsewhere were accused of committing war crimes, including mass killings and rapes of civilians.

Although the Japanese occupations had stalled nationalist movements in the region, after Japan's defeat these movements "resurfaced and finally succeeded in throwing off the colonial political yoke," wrote Valencia of the Nautilus Institute for Security and Sustainability. [43]

In China, the end of the war — and the end of fighting against the Japanese — meant a return to internal struggles,

primarily between communist forces led by Mao Zedong and nationalist forces led by Chiang Kai-shek. That struggle was settled, at least for mainland China, when Mao triumphed and Chiang and his followers fled in 1949 to Taiwan, which the People's Republic of China still considers its province.

Two years earlier, in the midst of its civil war, China issued a map detailing its South China Sea claims known as the "nine-dash line" — a territory extending hundreds of miles south and east from its southern province of Hainan. China argued that the Paracel

In the years just before Duterte's election, the Philippines had been cooperating more with the U.S. military because of rising South China Sea tensions. In 2014 the Philippines approved a 10-year agreement giving U.S. forces greater access to Philippine bases. [8] And last March the two countries signed an agreement providing for a new permanent U.S. military presence at five Philippine air bases under the recently negotiated Enhanced Defense Cooperation Agreement. [9]

After assuming office Duterte benefited from a July ruling by an international tribunal that sided with the Philippines over China in a dispute involving the Spratly Islands. [10]

The tribunal's ruling, rather than increasing tensions between the two nations, seems to have given Duterte an opportunity to move closer to China. Rapp-Hooper calls Duterte's decision not to press Philippine claims to the disputed islands and waters after the ruling a diplomatic turning point.

"Without the ruling, it would be very hard to see this bilateral diplomatic opening between China and the Philippines taking place," she says.

It is unclear how Donald Trump's election will affect U.S.-Philippines relations. Trump and Duterte spoke by phone in early December when, according to Duterte, Trump endorsed Duterte's controversial anti-drug campaign, calling it "the right way" to deal with the problem. [11] The Trump transition team has not confirmed Duterte's account.

"Duterte is wildly popular in the Philippines as someone who is standing up to the rest of the world, and that also means the United States," says Bonner R. Cohen, a senior fellow at the National Center for Public Policy Research. "I fully expect the Trump administration will try to reach out to him. Duterte clearly has no use for Obama, but Obama will be gone."

— *Patrick Marshall*

Chinese President Xi Jinping greets Philippine President Rodrigo Duterte in Beijing, on Oct. 20. Duterte was on a four-day state visit to China aimed at improving relations between the two South China Sea rivals.

[1] "President Duterte, the Wild Card in U.S.-Filipino Relations," *The New York Times*, Oct. 4, 2016, http://tinyurl.com/zpzhxoy.

[2] Katie Hunt, Matt Rivers and Catherine E. Shoichet, "In China, Duterte announces split with US: 'America has lost,' " CNN, Oct. 20, 2016, http://tinyurl.com/hrvlp8q.

[3] James Griffiths, Matt Rivers and Pamela Boykoff, "Philippines not really severing ties with US, Duterte says," CNN, Oct. 22, 2016, http://tinyurl.com/hc6g8am.

[4] Richard C. Paddock, "Chinese Vessels Leave Disputed Fishing Grounds in South China Sea," *The New York Times*, Oct. 28, 2016, http://tinyurl.com/grn94m2.

[5] "Duterte hopes Russia will become Philippines' ally and protector," Reuters, Jan. 6, 2017, http://tinyurl.com/jjqgum3.

[6] Jim Gomez, "Duterte tells Obama 'you can go to hell,' warns of breakup," The Associated Press, Oct. 4, 2016, http://tinyurl.com/hs99v6n.

[7] David E. Sanger, "Philippines Orders U.S. to Leave Strategic Navy Base at Subic Bay," *The New York Times*, Dec. 28, 1991, http://tinyurl.com/z7jpmce.

[8] Mark Landler, "U.S. and Philippines Agree to a 10-Year Pact on the Use of Military Bases," *The New York Times*, April 27, 2014, http://tinyurl.com/hur8vsq.

[9] Andrew Tilghman, "The U.S. military is moving into these 5 bases in the Philippines," *Military Times*, March 21, 2016, http://tinyurl.com/hhmt2so.

[10] Siegfrid Alegado and Ceclia Yap, "Philippines Posts Strongest Economic Growth in Asia at 7.1%," Bloomberg, Nov. 16, 2016, http://tinyurl.com/janttcd.

[11] Felipe Villamordec, "Rodrigo Duterte Says Donald Trump Endorses His Violent Antidrug Campaign," *The New York Times*, Dec. 3, 2016, http://tinyurl.com/zpddqjl.

and Spratley islands had been integral parts of China for centuries. [44]

The region also became "the cockpit of a contest between Western capitalism and Soviet and Chinese communist ideology," Valencia wrote. "The West, led by the United States, propped up dictators with force to prevent the spread of communism (resulting in the suppression of people's movements in Malaysia and the Philippines) as well as mass humanitarian tragedies in Vietnam and Indonesia." [45]

When French forces withdrew from Vietnam in 1954, the Geneva Accords partitioned the country, with South Vietnam (the Republic of Vietnam) backed by the United States and North Vietnam backed by the Soviet Union and China. Beginning in 1960, American military involvement in Vietnam grew rapidly, especially after the 1964 Gulf of Tonkin incident, in which a U.S. destroyer reportedly clashed with a North Vietnamese fast-attack craft.

With Saigon's fall to North Vietnamese troops in 1974, remaining American forces left Vietnam. China seized the Paracel Islands, which had been occupied by South Vietnam. China and the government of the newly unified Vietnam resolved territorial disputes in the Gulf of Tonkin but not elsewhere in the South China Sea; the two sides are still dueling over the Paracel and Spratley islands. [46] In 1988, Vietnamese and Chinese military forces clashed at Johnson South Reef in the Spratlys, with each country trading accusations of illegally occupying territory in the chain.

The retreat from Vietnam did not mean a U.S. withdrawal from the South China Sea. Since 1979 the United States has carried out a freedom of navigation program, with two goals: preserving freedom of the seas and demonstrating

China Reaching for Superpower Status

But analysts see huge obstacles to its bid for global supremacy.

From China's perspective, it's only a matter of time before it surpasses the United States as the world's premier economic and military power, analysts say. But many say the Asian nation of 1.4 billion people would have to surmount steep economic and military hurdles before it could rival the United States as a global superpower.

"China's leaders believe China represents the future, not just in hard power but also in economy, culture and values," said Mark Valencia, an associate at the Nautilus Institute for Security and Sustainability, a public policy think tank in Berkeley, Calif. "Indeed, China's leaders believe it is China's destiny to regain its prominence, if not preeminence, in the region and perhaps eventually the world." [1]

But Gordon G. Chang, an American author and China specialist, says China's optimism is unwarranted. "The regime that was supposed to own the century may not survive the decade," he said. "The People's Republic of China is now trapped in slow-burning economic and financial crises that are shaking the country." [2]

According to Thomas J. Christensen, former deputy assistant secretary of State for East Asian and Pacific affairs, there is a growing sense among the Chinese that their country is on the rise while the United States is in decline.

"Many in China believe China is significantly stronger and the United States weaker after the [2008] financial crisis," wrote Christensen. That belief, he said, has led to calls within China to become more aggressive in geopolitics. But, he said, "domestic voices calling for a more muscular Chinese foreign policy have created a heated political environment." [3]

Others say China's military leaders already are responding to hawkish voices. "China's military is sending strong signals that it's gearing up to compete with the U.S. as a global superpower, engaging in a multifaceted reform effort to modernize

and professionalize its military," said Yvonne Chiu, an assistant professor of politics at the University of Hong Kong. [4]

The government is streamlining China's military, making the army smaller while expanding the navy and air force, analysts say. Chinese aviation technology, according to a recent Pentagon report, is "rapidly" closing the gap with Western air forces. "At the same time," wrote Paul McLeary, Pentagon reporter for *Foreign Policy* magazine, "China's nuclear and missile forces have been reorganized as an independent service and have been bolstered with a new array of weapons that push China's potential reach farther out into the Pacific." [5]

Yet, many experts are not convinced that China's rise as a global superpower is inevitable.

China's days of "heady" economic growth are over, according to Chang. Growth hasn't been in double digits since 2010, he said, and its gross domestic product (GDP) grew 6.9 percent last year, down slightly from 2015. While that's a rate the United States would welcome, Chang said those figures are possibly inflated. "In the middle of last year, a well-known China analyst was privately noting that [analysts] in Beijing were talking 2.2 percent [growth], and there are indications the economy grew at an even slower pace, perhaps 1 percent," Chang wrote. [6]

China's economy has two long-term vulnerabilities, according to Loren B. Thompson, chief operating officer of the Lexington Institute, a national policy think tank in Arlington, Va.: Its pool of low-cost labor is drying up because of China's growing middle class and urbanization, and China is overly dependent on manufacturing exports for growth.

Even if its labor problem could be solved, Thompson said, "the reliance of an export-driven economy on foreign markets makes China's prosperity — per capita [gross domestic product] is below $10,000 — much more vulnerable than America's." [7]

---

a "non-acquiescence" to coastal states that make "excessive" maritime claims. The centerpiece is regular naval deployments in international waters throughout the region. [47]

The U.S. Navy's primary base of operations in the Western Pacific after World War II was Subic Bay in the Philippines. In 1991, however, negotiations to remain at Subic and Clark Air Base broke down because, in the account of one reporter, the Philippines viewed the Americans' presence "as a vestige of colonialism and an affront to Philippine sovereignty." [48] The U.S. military left the two bases in 1992.

While China has generally avoided conflict with U.S. forces in the South China Sea, the Chinese government passed legislation in 1992 laying claim to four-fifths of the sea. [49] Perhaps emboldened by the expulsion of U.S. forces from the Philippines, China backed up this claim with a series of armed skirmishes with the Vietnamese and Philippine navies in the 1990s.

Only two years after the U.S. departure, wrote Kaplan, "China would move to occupy Philippine-controlled reefs in the Spratlys, and from the mid-1990s forward China would undergo a vast expansion of its air and sea forces, ac-

companied by a more aggressive posture in the South China Sea." [50]

Part of China's increasingly aggressive posture was shadowing and challenging the presence of other forces, even in international waters and airspace. In early April 2001, a U.S. reconnaissance aircraft flying 70 miles from China's Hainan Island collided with a Chinese fighter that had scrambled to intercept it. The collision killed the Chinese pilot, and the American aircraft was forced to land on Hainan. The Chinese later released the American crew of 24 and returned the damaged aircraft to the United States. [51]

Per capita GDP in the United States — the country's total economic output divided by the population — was $56,116 in 2015. [8]

Others point to fundamental problems in China's military, which lags the U.S. military in hardware. China has 1,230 fighter aircraft to the United States' 2,308. China's navy, with an estimated 714 vessels, is larger than the 415 vessels in the U.S. Navy, but China has only one aircraft carrier to the United States' 19. [9]

China has about 260 nuclear warheads, far fewer than the 7,100 in the U.S. arsenal. [10]

Adding missiles and other hardware isn't the only challenge for the Chinese, some experts say. "The Chinese defense industry management is so corrupt, [it's] like a black hole," says Ming Xia, a professor of political science at the College of Staten Island in New York. "And training is horrible."

Even within Asia, China's ability to project its military power is limited now and for the foreseeable future, says Stephen G. Brooks, an associate professor of government at Dartmouth College. China can project power against the Philippines and other rivals in the South China Sea, says Brooks, "but if the United States says, 'No, we don't want you to project power,' China doesn't have, and won't for a long time have, much ability to get around that."

Regardless of its limitations, China appears intent on asserting itself as a regional power.

And whether China is able to gain dominance in the western Pacific or beyond is not solely up to China, says Frank Gaffney, president of the Center for Security Policy, a conservative think tank in Washington.

"It is a question in part of what they do, obviously, but it's also a question of what we do," he says. "If we persist in the trajectory we have been on [with slowing defense budgets],

Chinese marines train with their Russian counterparts in a drill in the South China Sea on Sept. 19. China's military is sending strong signals that it is gearing up to compete with the U.S. as a global superpower, according to one analyst.

there is very little doubt in my mind that they will surpass us at some point. In some respects, I think they already have."

— Patrick Marshall

[1] Mark J. Valencia, "The South China Sea and the 'Thucydides Trap,' " in *The South China Sea: A Crucible of Regional Cooperation or Conflict-Making Sovereignty Claims?* (2016), p. 60.

[2] Gordan G. Chang, "A Turbulent China Shakes the World," in *Warning Order: China Prepares for Conflict and Why We Must Do the Same* (2016), p. 40.

[3] Thomas J. Christensen, *The China Challenge: Shaping the Choices of a Rising Power* (2015), p. 260.

[4] Yvonne Chiu, "China's military is gearing up to compete with the U.S.," CNN, March 9, 2016, http://tinyurl.com/zhwq28w.

[5] Paul McLeary, "Pentagon: Chinese Military Modernization Enters 'New Phase,' " *Foreign Policy*, May 13, 2016, http://tinyurl.com/z9fkdhb.

[6] Chang, *op. cit.*, p. 40; 2015 growth rate is from "China GDP Annual Growth Rate," *Trading Economics*, http://tinyurl.com/pzthrrq.

[7] Loren Thompson, "Five Reasons China Won't Be A Big Threat To America's Global Power," *Forbes*, June 6, 2014, http://tinyurl.com/hgtlrru.

[8] "GDP growth (annual%)," the World Bank, http://tinyurl.com/y3vaz2u.

[9] "Global Firepower," GFP, Jan. 21, 2016, http://tinyurl.com/bgsc8df.

[10] "Nuclear Weapons: Who Has What at a Glance," Arms Control Association, October 2016, http://tinyurl.com/6ovpr2v.

Post-9/11

The Sept. 11, 2001, attacks on the United States by the Qaeda terrorist organization marked a turning point in American foreign policy, with the George W. Bush administration launching invasions of Afghanistan and Iraq.

These wars diverted "the United States away from the rapidly changing strategic landscape of Asia precisely at a time when China [was] making enormous strides in military modernization, commercial conquests, diplomatic inroads, and application of soft power,"

wrote Kurt Campbell, the assistant secretary of State for East Asian and Pacific Affairs from 2009 to 2013. The Americans' preoccupation with the Middle East greatly benefited China, Campbell said: "Rarely in history has a rising power made such prominent gains in the international system largely as a consequence of the actions and inattentiveness of the dominant power." [52]

In 2009, however, newly elected Obama, describing himself as "America's first Pacific president," promised the countries of Asia "a new era of engagement with the world based on mutual interests and mutual respect." [53]

Two years later, Obama defined his "pivot" to Asia as securing adoption of the Trans-Pacific Partnership and a bigger U.S. naval presence in the region. [54]

China took notice of Obama's plans. It had been debating whether supposedly declining powers like the United States would fall away peacefully or launch preemptive wars against the rising powers, says Georgetown University's Mastro. "That debate came to an end with the rebalancing. The rebalancing was seen as a sign that, no, the United States will not go quietly into the night."

In 2012, in Xi's first year as president, China declared an air defense identification zone that covered an expansive maritime area separating China from Japan. It included a contested group of tiny islands, known as the Senkakus (Japanese) or Diaoyu (Chinese), which have been under Japanese control since 1895.

"China followed up on this action almost immediately with a series of gestures that seemed designed to demonstrate its restored strength to its southern neighbors," wrote Howard W. French, a Columbia University journalism professor who focuses on Asia and whose book on East Asian geopolitics, *Everything Under the Heavens: How the Past Helps Shape China's Push for Global Power*, is scheduled for publication in March. "In Xi's early days in office, the country's first aircraft carrier, the *Liaoning*, which was acquired several years ago from Ukraine and then extensively refurbished, was sent with a full battle group of other warships

described as "a deliberate challenge to Beijing's self-declared sovereignty."[57]

Afterward, then-Defense Secretary Ashton Carter told Congress, "We will fly, sail and operate wherever international law permits and whenever our operational needs require."[58] ■

CURRENT SITUATION

Rising Tensions

Secretary of State nominee Tillerson's explosive testimony at his confirmation hearing on the South China Sea is setting off alarms throughout the region.

> "We will fly, sail and operate wherever international law permits and whenever our operational needs require."
>
> — *Ashton Carter,*
> *then-Defense Secretary*

on a maiden cruise straight into many of the most fiercely disputed areas of the South China Sea."[55]

China then blocked the Philippines from delivering supplies and fresh troops to a Philippine navy ship grounded on the disputed Second Thomas Shoal in March 2014. China also sent a large oil rig in May 2014 to disputed waters near the Paracel Islands.[56]

In October 2015, the U.S. Navy sent ships inside the 12-nautical-mile limit that China claims as territory around its artificial islands in the Spratly archipelago in what author James Bamford

China's *Global Times* newspaper said the United States could be forced to fight a war if it tried to block China from its islands. "China has enough determination and strength to make sure that [Tillerson's] rabble-rousing will not succeed," the paper said.

Carlyle A. Thayer, an emeritus professor of politics at the University of New South Wales in Australia, told *The New York Times*: "Tillerson's proposal would provoke a serious confrontation that could quickly develop into armed conflict."[59]

Other experts expressed confusion about the intentions of the Trump ad-

ministration, which did not comment on Tillerson's remarks. "Is this a warning? Or will this be a policy option?" said Zhu Feng, executive director of the China Center for Collaborative Studies of the South China Sea at Nanjing University. "If this is a policy option, this will not be able to block China's access to these constructed islands. There is no legal basis."[60]

China faces troubles on other fronts. The Permanent Court of Arbitration at the Hague, Netherlands, in July rejected China's claims to all waters within its "nine-dash" line, saying they were incompatible with the United Nations Convention on the Law of the Sea. The tribunal also said China cannot claim an Exclusive Economic Zone (EEZ) in the Spratlys. Instead, it said Chinese-built islands remain within the EEZ of the Philippines, which had brought the dispute to the arbitration court.[61]

Having sided with the Philippines, the tribunal then ruled that China had violated the Philippines' sovereign rights by interfering with Philippine fishing and petroleum exploration. China refused to take part in the arbitration proceedings and said it would not "accept, recognize or execute" the verdict.[62]

Some observers criticized the tribunal for provoking China. Rather than resolving tensions, *The Economist* warned that "the sweeping condemnation of [China's] activities by the court could raise tensions in the South China Sea further, embolden other countries to launch copy-cat court actions and possibly lead China to react strongly."

China's island building in the South China Sea is also drawing criticism for another reason: Environmentalists say it is badly damaging one of the world's most important coral reef systems, which provide habitats and food for hundreds of marine species. China's construction of bases atop delicate reefs, wrote John McManus, a University of Miami marine biologist, "constitutes the most rapid rate

Continued on p. 66

At Issue:

Does China's military buildup in the South China Sea threaten U.S. security?

JAMES CLAD
SENIOR ADVISER FOR ASIA, CNA CORP.; FORMER DEPUTY ASSISTANT SECRETARY OF DEFENSE FOR ASIA

WRITTEN FOR *CQ RESEARCHER*, JANUARY 2017

yes

China has made rapid changes to marine topography in the South China Sea in the past few years to create mini-islands or to augment existing islets occupied by Chinese personnel. In addition, China has installed airfields, portable air defense systems and military radars. Chinese President Xi Jinping's assurances that this type of activity wouldn't occur have proved worthless.

Unilaterally raising new land features in contested areas doesn't directly threaten American security. Nor does militarizing these features. But the buildup nonetheless threatens U.S. security because it comes accompanied by assertive, often reckless Chinese tactics.

Preoccupied by placating China's security establishment, Xi and his Communist Party allies underappreciate how unfettered freedom of navigation has totemic importance to the American security establishment. The United States insists on unimpeded access to all international waters lying 12 nautical miles beyond sovereign territory. Phrased rather brusquely as "we go anywhere we want," the ability to enter international waters at pleasure mirrors other navies' expectations of access, even China's.

But China claims sovereignty over myriad shoals and sandbars as well as over adjoining seas enclosed by a "nine-dash line," which first appeared in Chinese maps in the 1930s. During the 1970-80s, Beijing preemptively seized shoals and atolls from South and North Vietnamese garrisons alike. The new buildup affects the Philippines most directly: China occupied and then built structures on top of various shoals beginning in the 1990s.

Beyond that, China has refused to abide by an international tribunal's July ruling that said many of the country's actions in the South China Sea, including its construction of artificial islands and its expansive claims to sovereignty over the waters around them, violated the U.N. Convention on the Law of the Sea treaty (UNCLOS) to which China is a signatory.

Much of this resembles the push-and-parry tactics of past decades. But China's dramatically increased maritime and aerial power has changed the calculation. Its navy selectively informs non-Chinese ships that they're "trespassing." Those hailed — naval vessels, petroleum survey ships or fishing vessels — counter that they're in international waters. Ramming and other tactics have ensued.

Much of the undersea and aerial encounters between Chinese and other navies never makes the news. But harassment of foreign naval ships, including U.S. Navy vessels, has increased. The risk of a shooting incident has steadily risen.

ZHU FENG
EXECUTIVE DIRECTOR, CHINA CENTER FOR COLLABORATIVE STUDIES OF SOUTH CHINA SEA, NANJING UNIVERSITY

WRITTEN FOR *CQ RESEARCHER*, JANUARY 2017

no

According to media coverage, China is speeding up the militarization of the South China Sea by deploying hundreds of missiles in the reclaimed maritime territories, and this supposedly poses a threat to U.S. security in the region. But few people would find such an idea convincing upon closer examination.

China's military buildup in the reclaimed islands in the Spratlys is quite limited but necessary. All the weapon systems are short-range and defensive in nature. Considering the billions of dollars spent on island reclamation and construction, Beijing is legally justified in building military defenses to protect its huge investment.

Second, it is unlikely these weapons would be used to attack nearby American ships and jet fighters. The reason is that any retaliation would put these islands at risk of being fully destroyed. I don't think that Beijing will risk a huge retaliation by using these island-based light weapons — rifle, guns and short-range missiles.

Third, China's limited weapon systems, along with airstrips in those constructed islands, do not forcefully change the military postures of China and the United States in the western Pacific. China's reclaimed islands, even with military facilities there, are more like "sitting ducks" than islands bases, as China's land-based firepower is too far away to defend them. Even a couple of U.S. destroyers could easily paralyze these islands.

China's activities in the Spratly Islands arise from political, not military, motivations. What's more, it's not China that initiated the reclamation and military buildup. Ironically, it's Vietnam and the Philippines, and they have never terminated their projects in their illegally occupied Spratly assets.

Beijing never disavows its promise of peaceful settlement of any maritime disputes in the South China Sea.

China's island construction and military buildup in the Spratlys might complicate U.S. security strategy in the South China Sea as China emerges as a new competitor in the western Pacific. But China's navy and air force remain far behind those of the United States, and it's unimaginable that China's newly claimed islands, even with a number of short-range missiles, could put the United States in jeopardy.

Beijing should be prudently and transparently handling its military buildup in the Spratlys while seeking to ensure the United States does not overreact. No one in the region seeks an escalation of military tension between the two powers.

Continued from p. 64

of permanent loss of coral reef area in human history." [63]

Troubled TPP

With Trump in the White House, most experts see little hope of Congress ratifying the Trans-Pacific Partnership. According to a transition-team memo obtained by *Politico* in mid-November, Trump plans to pull the United States out of the TPP within his first 100 days in office. [64]

An oil production platform lies off the coast of Brunei in the South China Sea, which by some estimates may contain more oil than any other area of the planet except Saudi Arabia. China's claim to four-fifths of the South China Sea was rejected by the Permanent Court of Arbitration in July.

Senate Majority Leader Mitch McConnell, R-Ky., and Minority Leader Chuck Schumer, D-N.Y., told reporters after the election that the pact will likely not receive congressional approval. [65]

Still, a high-profile Republican in Congress and others have suggested TPP could be salvaged. Rep. Kevin Brady, R-Texas, chairman of the House Ways and Means Committee, said on Nov. 15 that Republicans should defend free trade, including the TPP, in the new Congress. "Republicans are going to continue to support the freedom to trade," Brady told a panel of *The Wall Street Journal* CEO Council. "Don't with-

draw, renegotiate. Fix the problems that exist today." [66]

Judging from Trump's appointment of free-trade foe Peter Navarro to lead a new White House office overseeing U.S. trade and industrial policy, Republican free-traders in Congress face an uphill battle.

Navarro, who favors higher tariffs on imports, is a staunch critic of China and other low-cost exporting nations. "Trump will never again sacrifice the U.S. economy on the altar of foreign policy by entering into bad trade deals like the North American Free Trade Agreement, allowing China into the World Trade Organization and passing the proposed TPP," wrote Navarro and a co-author in an article in *Foreign Policy* in November. "These deals only weaken our manufacturing base and ability to defend ourselves and our allies." [67]

Military Rebalance

The other critical component of Obama's pivot to Asia is increasing the U.S. naval presence in the region and the amount of military assistance to allies.

The Pentagon took an initial step in April, when it announced funding for the Maritime Security Initiative (MSI), a five-year, $425 million aid program that seeks to help South China Sea countries improve their ability to monitor activities in their territorial waters and air space. [68]

The Philippines, which remains a U.S. ally despite Duterte's ascension, is receiving the lion's share of the first-year funding, taking in $42 million of the first $50 million. Vietnam, Malaysia, Indonesia and Thailand are getting money to increase maritime security, and Brunei, Singapore and Taiwan for training and headquarter-level integration.

"Countries across the Asia-Pacific are voicing concern with China's land reclamation, which stands out in size and scope, as well as its militarization in the South China Sea," Defense Secretary Carter said last April. "We're standing with these countries. We're helping them build capacity. We're affirming our commitment to their and the region's security with increased posture." [69]

Critics, however, say the Maritime Security Initiative is inadequate. "The problem with MSI is that it's 'budget dust' in Pentagon-speak," Van Jackson, a former Pentagon official who served in the Obama administration, said. "You can't do much with $425 million." [70]

The Pentagon responded that the MSI is not the only increase directed at the South China Sea.

"From a multitude of exercises across the region, to freedom of navigation operations and presence operations, the Department of Defense continues to fly, sail and operate wherever international law allows so that others can do the same," Assistant Secretary of Defense Denmark told Congress in July, citing carrier operations in the Philippine Sea, exercises conducted with Japan and India and other "enhanced tempo" activities. [71]

But former Sen. Talent says U.S. naval power in the region is inadequate, especially given the logistical advantage the Chinese have in being so close to the theater of operations. "Because it is in their near seas, the Chinese can focus their power very quickly," says Talent. "It takes several weeks for us to steam ships from the West Coast to the region."

Others say U.S. forces are up to the challenge. "Certainly, U.S. assets in the Pacific are sufficient to the task now, and if we follow through on pledges to ship further [naval] assets to the Pacific . . ., they should be up to the challenge of the future," says Poling of the Center for Strategic and International Studies.

Some in Congress urged the Obama White House to increase naval patrols near disputed islands in the South China Sea. The proposed Asia-Pacific Maritime Security Initiative Act of 2016, which did not survive last year's Congress, would have required the administration to report to Congress on its China activities and on U.S. plans for freedom of navigation operations in the region. Additionally, the bill called for delivering more sophisticated military hardware to the Philippines. [72] It is unclear whether similar legislation will be introduced in the current Congress.

A few analysts say the United States may already have too big of a military presence in the region and should work toward sharing power with China rather than trying to contain it.

"As the United States military doubles down in Asia, the chances increase that one side will cross a red line," wrote strategic-intelligence consultant Nicholas Borroz and Southeast Asia analyst Hunter Marston in October. "That does not mean Washington should abandon its allies. But it should avoid creating extensive, untenable defense agreements. Washington should maintain a manageable number of security commitments and take steps toward balancing power with China in the Western Pacific — and it should do so while it has the power to shape that balance in its favor." [73] ■

OUTLOOK

Trump's Impact

One of the biggest uncertainties regarding the South China Sea, especially in light of secretary of State nominee Tillerson's confirmation hearing testimony, is what Trump will do as president. Trump's transition team had no immediate reaction to Tillerson's comments, but earlier it said the new administration "will take a hawkish view of China, focus on bolstering regional alliances, have a renewed interest in Taiwan, be skeptical of engagement with North Korea and bolster the U.S. Navy's fleet presence in the Pacific." [74]

Some observers hope Trump will take a measured and balanced approach to China and the South China Sea.

"Trump made it abundantly clear during the campaign that he is no friend of open-ended military interventions [and] nation-building exercises such as what we have experienced in Iraq and Afghanistan," says the Public Policy Research Center's Cohen. "At the same time, he has called for restoring U.S. military might and has deplored what he sees as the deteriorated state of the U.S. Navy. In other words, he appears to see a strengthened United States as deterring potential adversaries from engaging in reckless geopolitical behavior."

Cohen adds that Trump's appointments also indicate that he will follow a policy of deterrence grounded on a stronger military. "Having retired General James Mattis as Defense secretary, a man known to friend and foe alike as 'Mad Dog,' only underscores what I see as a 21st-century version of the older, Cold War-era doctrine of deterrence," says Cohen. In the South China Sea, where the United States wants free navigation and secure shipping routes but where it has no

direct territorial interests, "what we could see is renewed respect for the United States."

Others point to inconsistencies in Trump's appointments. The selection of Iowa Gov. Terry Branstad, a longtime acquaintance of Chinese President Xi, as U.S. ambassador to China may indicate that Trump's approach to China will be more constructive than his comments on the One China policy indicated.

Of course, the future of the South China Sea depends at least as much on China as it does on the Trump administration. According to many experts, China will continue to expand its influence in the region.

"The fundamental problem is that China is not stable [due to potential challenges to its leadership from the military], so its leaders, for various reasons, are in no position, in no mood, to deal with their counterparts in other capitals on a good-faith basis," wrote Gordon G. Chang, a China specialist and *Forbes* magazine contributor. [75]

The Center for Security Policy's Gaffney agrees, pointing to the growing importance of China's military. "The military there is becoming sort of the key powerbroker, and everybody is trying to accommodate them," he says. "It's a worrying thing that the Chinese military is clearly feeling its oats."

According to the Center for a New American Security's Kaplan, the situation in the South China Sea is, indeed, at a "contradictory, unstable inflection point," although he says China's growing influence is not unexpected.

"Nothing we can do will deter China from gradually, inexorably trying to [extend its influence] in the South China Sea, because it is in their demonstrable self-interest to do so," says Kaplan.

His advice for Trump is to resist the temptation for surprises. "Surprises may work from time to time, but, generally, diplomacy requires predictability," he says. "We should establish a predictable relationship with China." ■

Notes

[1] "China's New Spratly Island Defenses," Asia Maritime Transparency Initiative, Dec. 13, 2016, http://tinyurl.com/jofu276.

[2] "Foreign Ministry Spokesperson Lu Kang's Remarks on Issues Relating to China's Construction Activities on the Nansha Islands and Reefs," Ministry of Foreign Affairs of the People's Republic of China, June 16, 2015, http://tinyurl.com/zeer2sw; "Country: China," Asia Maritime Transparency Initiative, http://tinyurl.com/hv3fd8g.

[3] Chris Buckley, "China Suggests It Has Placed Weapons on Disputed Spratly Islands in South China Sea," *The New York Times*, Dec. 15, 2016, http://tinyurl.com/z3ofp2g.

[4] Katie Hunt, "Tillerson sets stage for showdown with Beijing over South China Sea," CNN, Jan. 12, 2017, China's New Spratly Island Defenses," http://tinyurl.com/jdzdfru.

[5] Michael Forsythe and Chris Buckley, "Taiwan Responds After China Sends Carrier to Taiwan Strait," *The New York Times*, Jan. 10, 2017, http://tinyurl.com/zzjafe9.

[6] Buckley, *op. cit.*

[7] Christopher P. Cavas, "China's Navy Makes Strides, Work Remains To Be Done," *Defense News*, May 24, 2015, http://tinyurl.com/ov2mvmq; See also Ronald O'Rourke, "China Naval Modernization: Implications for U.S. Navy Capabilities — Background and Issues for Congress," Congressional Research Service, June 17, 2016, http://tinyurl.com/h83nt3k.

[8] Testimony of Colin Willett, deputy assistant secretary of State for multilateral affairs, Bureau of East Asian and Pacific Affairs, U.S. Department of State, before the House Armed Services Committee, Seapower and Projection Forces Subcommittee, and House Foreign Affairs Committee Subcommittee on Asia and the Pacific, July 7, 2016, http://tinyurl.com/hdz7ymp.

[9] Robert D. Kaplan, *Asia's Cauldron: The South China Sea and the End of a Stable Pacific* (2015), p. 10; Tim Daiss, "Why the South China Sea has More Oil Than You Think," *Forbes*, May 22, 2016, http://tinyurl.com/z9qokas.

[10] Bonnie S. Glaser, "Armed Clash in the South China Sea, Contingency Planning Memorandum No. 14, Council on Foreign Relations, April 2012, http://tinyurl.com/zf4u4ws.

[11] Adam Greer, "The South China Sea Is Really a Fishery Dispute," *The Diplomat*, July 20, 2016, http://tinyurl.com/hur9mcz; Trefor Moss, "Five Things About Fishing in the South China Sea," *The Wall Street Journal*, "July 19, 2016, http://tinyurl.com/zrgw334.

[12] Caren Bohan and David Brunnstrom, "Trump says U.S. not necessarily bound by 'one China' policy," Reuters, Dec. 12, 2016, http://tinyurl.com/zb3b84g.

[13] Dennis C. Blair, written testimony before the Senate Foreign Relations Subcommittee on East Asia, the Pacific, and International Cybersecurity Policy, July 13, 2016, http://tinyurl.com/jzzw32b.

[14] Demetri Sevastopulo and Ben Bland, "US plans to boost Pacific naval forces," *Financial Times*, June 2, 2012, http://tinyurl.com/hcds9xo.

[15] Audrey McAvoy, "U.S. Pacific Fleet shrinks even as China grows more aggressive," *U.S. News & World Report*, Jan. 5, 2016, http://tinyurl.com/zpodvbb.

[16] Abraham M. Denmark, testimony before the House Committee on Armed Services Subcommittee on Seapower and Projection Forces and the House Committee on Foreign Affairs Subcommittee on Asia and the Pacific, July 7, 2016, http://tinyurl.com/guq2wn6.

[17] Shannon Tiezzi, "China Won't 'Militarize' the South China Sea — But It Will Build Military Facilities There," *The Diplomat*, Oct. 16, 2015, http://tinyurl.com/z3dlaqc.

[18] Jeremy Page, Carol E. Lee and Gordon Lubold, "China's President Pledges No Militarization in Disputed Islands," *The Wall Street Journal*, Sept. 25, 2015, http://tinyurl.com/oeayky3; Buckley, *op. cit.*

[19] Timothy Heath, testimony before the U.S.-China Economic and Security Review Commission, Jan. 21, 2016, http://tinyurl.com/hk9c274.

[20] Quoted in Kaplan, *op. cit.*, p. 44.

[21] "Transcript: Donald Trump's Foreign Policy Speech," *The New York Times*, April 27, 2016, http://tinyurl.com/hdfurda.

[22] Stephanie Condon, "Donald Trump: Japan, South Korea might need nuclear weapons," CBS News, March 29, 2016, http://tinyurl.com/jp3qzuk.

[23] Elbridge Colby, testimony before the House Foreign Affairs Committee, Sept. 22, 2016, http://tinyurl.com/gtd8oev.

[24] Emiko Jozuka, "Japan to join US in South China Sea patrols," CNN Wire, Sept. 16, 2016, http://tinyurl.com/gnk98ed.

[25] Anthony H. Cordesman, "Trump Takes Office: The National Security Agenda He Must Address by the End of the Coming Spring," Center for Strategic and International Studies, Nov. 14, 2016, http://tinyurl.com/zzjmplc.

[26] Robert E. Kelly, "The Misplaced Burden-Sharing Fight," *The National Interest*, Dec. 4, 2016, http://tinyurl.com/j7twtns.

[27] Cristiano Lima, "Trump calls trade deal 'a rape of our country,' " *Politico*, June 28, 2016, http://tinyurl.com/jautjrd.

[28] Mitsuru Obe, "Japan Ratifies Trans-Pacific Partnership, Which Trump Has Promised to Leave," *The Wall Street Journal*, Dec. 9, 2016, http://tinyurl.com/hkeuz6u.

[29] Thomas J. Christensen, *The China Challenge: Shaping the Choices of a Rising Power* (2015), p. 250.

[30] "TPP: What is it and why does it matter?" BBC, Nov. 22, 2016, http://tinyurl.com/psjahsa.

[31] "Trump to dump TPP trade deal: World Leaders React," BBC, Nov. 22, 2016, http://tinyurl.com/zbrbxdb.

[32] Constanca, "Portuguese Malacca, 1511-1641," Portuguese World Heritage, June 21, 2015, http://tinyurl.com/j72jceu.

[33] Mark J. Valencia, "The South China Sea and the 'Thucydides Trap,' " in *The South China Sea: A Crucible of Regional Cooperation or Conflict-Making Sovereignty Claims?* (2016), p. 56.

[34] Nicholas Tarling, ed., "The Establishment of the Colonial Regimes," in *The Cambridge History of Southeast Asia*, vol. 2, part 1, (1999), p. 4.

[35] *Ibid.*, p. 7.

[36] "International Commerce, the State and Society: Economic and Social Change," in *The Cambridge History of Southeast Asia*, vol. 2, part 1 (1999), p. 135.

[37] Tarling, *op. cit.*, p. 61.

[38] Kenneth Pletcher, "Opium Wars," *Encyclopaedia Britannica*, last updated April 17, 2015, http://tinyurl.com/jxw9hus.

[39] *Ibid.*

[40] Kaplan, *op. cit.*, p. 21.

About the Author

Patrick Marshall, a freelance policy and technology writer in Seattle, is a technology columnist for *The Seattle Times* and *Government Computer News.* He has a bachelor's degree in anthropology from the University of California, Santa Cruz, and a master's degree in international studies from the Fletcher School of Law and Diplomacy at Tufts University.

[41] "Political Structures in the Nineteenth and Early Twentieth Centuries," in *The Cambridge History of Southeast Asia*, vol. 2, part 1, p. 77, p. 100.

[42] Paul Kratoska and Ben Batson, "Nationalism and Modernist Reform," in *ibid.*, p. 249.

[43] Valencia, *op. cit.*, p. 60.

[44] "Why is the South China Sea contentious?" BBC, July 12, 2016, http://tinyurl.com/m2tfywy.

[45] Valencia, *op. cit.*, p. 60.

[46] Kaplan, *op. cit.*, p. 171.

[47] U.S. Department of Defense, Freedom of Navigation Program Fact Sheet, March 2015, http://tinyurl.com/jvblqfc.

[48] David E. Sanger, "Philippines Orders U.S. to Leave Strategic Navy Base at Subic Bay," *The New York Times*, Dec. 28, 1991, http://tinyurl.com/z7jpmce.

[49] Mohan Malik, "Historical Fiction: China's South China Sea Claims," *World Affairs Journal*, May/June 2013, http://tinyurl.com/zv94bff.

[50] Kaplan, *op. cit.*, p. 126.

[51] Rodolfo C. Severino, "Global Issues and National Interests in the South China Sea," in *The South China Sea: A Crucible of Regional Cooperation or Conflict-Making Sovereignty Claims?* (2016), p. 39.

[52] Richard Baum *et al.*, "Whither U.S.-China Relations?" NBR Analysis, vol. 16, no. 4, December 2005, p. 25, http://tinyurl.com/j3abrs5.

[53] Mike Allen, "America's first Pacific president," *Politico*, Nov. 13, 2009, http://tinyurl.com/hw7l8b7.

[54] Kenneth Lieberthal, "The American Pivot to Asia: Why President Obama's turn to the East is easier said than done," *Foreign Policy*, Dec. 21, 2011, http://tinyurl.com/zubnx9c; Elisabeth Bumiller, "Words and Deeds Show Focus of the American Military on Asia," *The New York Times*, Nov. 10, 2012, http://tinyurl.com/j46hnt5.

[55] Howard W. French, "What's behind Beijing's drive to control the South China Sea?" *The Guardian*, July 28, 2015, http://tinyurl.com/go8nr8t.

[56] Christensen, *op. cit.*, p. 265.

[57] James Bamford, "Could American Spooks Provoke War with Beijing?" *Foreign Policy*, Dec. 8, 2015, http://tinyurl.com/z7bz7td.

[58] *Ibid.*

[59] Javier C. Hernández, "Chinese State Media Denounce Rex Tillerson's Call to Block Island Access," *The New York Times*, Jan. 13, 2017, http://tinyurl.com/jhb3wxl.

[60] Michael Forsythe, "Rex Tillerson's South China Sea Remarks Foreshadow Possible Foreign Policy Crisis," *The New York Times*, Jan. 12, 2017, http://tinyurl.com/hwe5ej2.

[61] "The South China Sea Arbitration (The Republic of the Philippines v. the People's Republic of China," press release, The Hague, July 12, 2016, http://tinyurl.com/h7wpv9e.

[62] "Why a tribunal has ruled against China on the South China Sea," *The Economist*, July 13, 2016, http://tinyurl.com/jmqgafr.

[63] Greg Torode, "'Paving paradise': Scientists alarmed over China island building in disputed sea," Reuters, June 25, 2015, http://tinyurl.com/hfz46bw.

[64] Adam Behsudi and Nancy Cook, "Trump will quit TPP in first days," *Politico*, Nov. 10, 2016, http://tinyurl.com/zjnl4zk.

[65] Jackie Calmes, "What Is Lost by Burying the Trans-Pacific Partnership?" *The New York Times*, Nov. 11, 2016, http://tinyurl.com/h9a3mcu.

[66] Patrick Rucker and Howard Schneider, "Top tax-writing Republican says TPP trade deal not dead in Congress," Reuters, Nov. 15, 2016, http://tinyurl.com/je8efs5.

[67] Alexander Gray and Peter Navarro, "Donald Trump's Peace Through Strength Vision for the Asia-Pacific," *Foreign Policy*, Nov. 7, 2016, http://tinyurl.com/hhqj3ps.

[68] Megan Eckstein, "The Philippines at Forefront of New Pentagon Maritime Security Initiative," USNI News, April 18, 2016, http://tinyurl.com/hbnmnzl.

[69] *Ibid.*

[70] Prashanth Parameswaran, "America's New Maritime Security Initiative for South-east Asia: A look at the Southeast Asia Maritime Security Initiative as it gets underway," *The Diplomat*, April 2, 2016, http://tinyurl.com/j689647.

[71] Denmark, *op. cit.*

[72] Dan De Luce, "Lawmakers to White House: Get Tough With Beijing Over South China Sea," *Foreign Policy*, April 27, 2016, http://tinyurl.com/zz3xy9m.

[73] Nicholas Borroz and Hunter Marston, "Washington Should Stop Militarizing the Pacific," *The New York Times*, Oct. 9, 2016, http://tinyurl.com/hjabnvo.

[74] Forsythe, *op. cit.*; Josh Rogen, "Trump could make Obama's pivot to Asia a reality," *The Washington Post*, Jan. 8, 2017, http://tinyurl.com/hpnma6w.

[75] Gordan G. Chang, "A Turbulent China Shakes the World," in *Warning Order: China Prepares for Conflict and Why We Must Do the Same* (2016), p. 56.

FOR MORE INFORMATION

American Enterprise Institute, 1789 Massachusetts Ave., N.W., Washington, DC 20036; 202-862-5800; www.aei.org. Conservative think tank that focuses on an array of public policy issues, with a special emphasis on foreign and defense policy.

Center for Naval Analyses, 3003 Washington Blvd., Arlington, VA 22201; 703-824-2000, www.cna.org. Nonprofit research organization that produces analysis on foreign policy and other issues.

Center for Security Policy, 1901 Pennsylvania Ave., N.W., DC 20006; 202-835-9077; www.centerforsecuritypolicy.org. Public policy research organization focused on national security issues.

Center for Strategic and International Studies, 1800 K St., N.W., Washington, DC 20006; 202-887-0200; www.csis.org. Centrist think tank that offers bipartisan proposals on U.S. security issues.

Greenpeace Southeast Asia, Room 201 JGS Building, #30 Scout Tuazon St., 1103 Quezon City, the Philippines; +63-2-3321807; www.greenpeace.org/seasia/ph/. Branch of the Greenpeace environmental advocacy organization that monitors environmental issues in Southeast Asia, including the South China Sea.

Lexington Institute, 1600 Wilson Blvd., Suite 203, Arlington, VA 22209; 703-522-5828; www.lexingtoninstitute.org. Conservative think tank that studies national security issues.

U.S.-China Economic and Security Review Commission, 444 N. Capitol St., N.W., Suite 602, Washington, DC 20001; 202-624-1407; www.uscc.gov. Created by Congress to monitor the national security implications of the bilateral trade and economic relationship between the United States and the People's Republic of China.

U.S. Naval War College, 686 Cushing Road, Newport, RI 02841-1207; 401-841-1310; www.usnwc.edu. Navy's staff college supports research on strategy, maritime and security issues.

Bibliography

Selected Sources

Books

Christensen, Thomas J., *The China Challenge: Shaping the Choices of a Rising Power*, W.W. Norton & Co., 2015.

A former deputy assistant secretary of State for East Asian and Pacific affairs argues that the United States should focus on deterring Chinese aggression in Asia while encouraging its cooperation in global economic and security efforts.

Fleitz, Fred, ed., *Warning Order: China Prepares for Conflict and Why We Must Do the Same*, Center for Security Policy Press, 2016.

A collection of essays urges a strong military response to China's attempts to displace the "post-World War II Pax Americana with a new order" that would make China the pre-eminent global power.

Jenner, C. J., and Tran Truong Thuy, eds., *The South China Sea: A Crucible of Regional Cooperation or Conflict-Making Sovereignty Claims?* Cambridge University Press, 2016.

Jenner, a research fellow at Kings College in London, and Thuy, deputy director of the Bien Dong Institute in Vietnam, compile a primer on issues surrounding the ongoing conflicts over the South China Sea.

Kaplan, Robert D., *Asia's Cauldron: The South China Sea and the End of a Stable Pacific*, Random House, 2014.

A senior fellow at the Center for a New American Security, a liberal-leaning Washington think tank, writes that a fundamental change in the balance of power in the western Pacific has taken place, and the change is leading to rising tensions, and the potential for major conflict, in the South China Sea region.

Articles

Gray, Alexander, and Peter Navarro, "Donald Trump's Peace Through Strength Vision for the Asia-Pacific," *Foreign Policy*, Nov. 7, 2016, http://tinyurl.com/hhqj3ps.

Gray, a senior adviser to the Trump campaign, and Navarro, tapped as President Trump's chief trade adviser, offer an insiders' view of the new administration's Asia policies. They predict Trump will bring stability to the region.

Lieberthal, Kenneth, "The American Pivot to Asia: Why President Obama's turn to the East is easier said than done," *Foreign Policy*, Dec. 21, 2011, http://tinyurl.com/zubnx9c.

A senior fellow at the centrist Brookings Institution assesses the Obama administration's evolving policies in Asia and concludes that both the United States and China "must keep in mind that they are best served by adopting positions that engender a healthy respect in the other capital concerning capabilities and goals so that neither acts rashly."

Thompson, Loren, "Five Reasons China Won't Be A Big Threat To America's Global Power," *Forbes*, June 6, 2014, http://tinyurl.com/hgtlrru.

The head of the Lexington Institute, a conservative think tank focused on national security, spells out the reasons he believes China is incapable of challenging the United States; the two primary ones, he says, are China's overreliance on exports and its aging population.

Reports and Studies

"Annual Report to Congress: Military and Security Developments Involving the People's Republic of China 2015," Office of the Secretary of Defense, 2015, http://tinyurl.com/j8fkvbv.

In its annual assessment of China's military power, the Department of Defense concludes that the country is rapidly modernizing its forces, although it still lacks the ability to project significant power far from its own shores.

"Asian Views on America's Role in Asia: The Future of the Rebalance," Asia Foundation, 2016, http://tinyurl.com/ztqmjx5.

Specialists from Asian countries offer strategic recommendations to the incoming U.S. president regarding foreign policy toward Asia; the report stemmed from a series of meetings held by this nonpartisan international development organization.

"Asia-Pacific Rebalance 2025: Capabilities, Presence, and Partnerships," Center for Strategic and International Studies, January 2016, http://tinyurl.com/gpqktxj.

This report by a bipartisan think tank, commissioned by the Department of Defense, finds that the Obama administration's efforts to rebalance U.S. strategic resources in Asia may be insufficient to protect American interests in the region.

"The PLA Navy: New Capabilities and Missions for the 21st Century," U.S. Office of Naval Intelligence, April 2015, http://tinyurl.com/hvf63on.

This report by the U.S. Navy's intelligence service details China's recent efforts to modernize its navy, and finds that while East Asia remains China's primary focus, it is seeking to build a navy capable of deploying beyond that region.

Rinehart, Ian E., "The Chinese Military: Overview and Issues for Congress," Congressional Research Service, March 24, 2016, http://tinyurl.com/ju29zdc.

A report by the research arm of Congress examines in detail China's efforts to modernize its military and finds that it is building "a modern and regionally powerful military with a limited but growing capability for conducting operations away from China's immediate periphery."

The Next Step:

Additional Articles from Current Periodicals

Environmental Issues

"China sets up South China Sea environment protection fund," Reuters, July 25, 2016, http://tinyurl.com/hgdbghd.

China established a $2.25 million fund in an effort to support environmental protection in the South China Sea.

Beech, Hannah, "The Environment Is the Silent Casualty of Beijing's Ambitions in the South China Sea," *Time*, June 1, 2016, http://tinyurl.com/jmqxhwf.

Some biologists say that China's construction of islands atop coral reefs in the South China Sea could lead to ecocide.

Makinen, Julie, "China has been killing turtles, coral and giant clams in the South China Sea, tribunal finds," *Los Angeles Times*, July 13, 2016, http://tinyurl.com/hhyfggy.

Chinese activity in the South China Sea "caused devastating and long-lasting damage to the environment," a tribunal found, and added that China failed to prevent its fishing boats from harvesting endangered species, including sea turtles.

Military Rivalries

Belot, Henry, "South China Sea: Paul Keating says Rex Tillerson threatening to involve Australia in war," Australia Broadcasting Corp., Jan. 13, 2017, http://tinyurl.com/hypa3a5.

Former Australian Prime Minister Paul Keating accused Secretary of State nominee Rex Tillerson of threatening to involve Australia in war following his inflammatory statements about the South China Sea.

Campbell, Charlie, "Chinese Media Has Told Rex Tillerson to 'Prepare for a Military Clash,' " *Time*, Jan. 12, 2017, http://tinyurl.com/hpdg69h.

Chinese state media warned that any American attempts to bar the building of artificial islands in the South China Sea would force a "devastating confrontation" with the United States.

Huang, Kristin, "China's aircraft carrier 'will push range far into Pacific,' " *South China Morning Post*, Jan. 9, 2017, http://tinyurl.com/jnt25j6.

China exacerbated tensions with Japan when it stated that its sole aircraft carrier would carry out its training drills far into the eastern Pacific.

South China Sea Tensions

Forsythe, Michael, "Rex Tillerson's South China Sea Remarks Foreshadow Possible Foreign Policy Crisis," *The New York Times*, Jan. 12, 2017, http://tinyurl.com/hwe5ej2.

Rex Tillerson's comments about possibly blocking China's island building in the South China Sea had experts wondering if he was issuing a warning or a policy option.

Jiao, Claire, "Duterte vows to act if China 'siphons minerals' from South China Sea," CNN Philippines, Dec. 30, 2016, http://tinyurl.com/zh7u2ys.

Philippine President Rodrigo Duterte said the Philippines would stand firm if China attempted to mine mineral resources where his country has economic rights.

McLaughlin, Elizabeth, "What You Need to Know About the Tensions in the South China Sea," ABC News, Dec. 20, 2016, http://tinyurl.com/gmmo469.

China's activities in the South China Sea are raising tensions with other Pacific nations and the United States, experts say.

Mogato, Manuel, "Avoiding China's wrath, Philippines puts off upgrades to South China Sea isles," Reuters, Jan. 12, 2017, http://tinyurl.com/hm6mrnz.

In a move to avoid provoking China, the Philippines deferred repairs on islands it occupies in the South China Sea.

Trade Agreements

Mourdoukoutas, Panos, "Is McDonald's A Victim Of South China Sea Disputes?" *Forbes*, Jan. 11, 2017, http://tinyurl.com/h6gpnuz.

South China Sea disputes have reignited Chinese nationalism, and that may have contributed to McDonald's decision to sell its mainland China and Hong Kong businesses.

Phillips, Tom, "China says Trump's pick of hostile trade adviser is 'no laughing matter,' " *The Guardian*, Dec. 22, 2016, http://tinyurl.com/jgmfweh.

A Chinese newspaper blasted Donald Trump's choice for trade adviser as "another sign of the confrontational approach the incoming Trump administration seems intent on taking."

CITING *CQ RESEARCHER*

Sample formats for citing these reports in a bibliography include the ones listed below. Preferred styles and formats vary, so please check with your instructor or professor.

MLA STYLE

Jost, Kenneth. "Remembering 9/11." CQ Researcher 2 Sept. 2011: 701-732.

APA STYLE

Jost, K. (2011, September 2). Remembering 9/11. *CQ Researcher*, 9, 701-732.

CHICAGO STYLE

Jost, Kenneth. "Remembering 9/11." *CQ Researcher*, September 2, 2011, 701-32.

In-depth Reports on Issues in the News

Are you writing a paper?

Need backup for a debate?

Want to become an expert on an issue?

For 90 years, students have turned to *CQ Researcher* for in-depth reporting on issues in the news. Reports on a full range of political and social issues are now available. Following is a selection of recent reports:

Civil Liberties
Privacy and the Internet, 12/15
Intelligence Reform, 5/15
Religion and Law, 11/14

Crime/Law
Jailing Debtors, 9/16
Decriminalizing Prostitution, 4/16
Restorative Justice, 2/16
The Dark Web, 1/16
Immigrant Detention, 10/15
Fighting Gangs, 10/15
Reforming Juvenile Justice, 9/15

Education
Student Debt, 11/16
Apprenticeships, 10/16
Free Speech on Campus, 5/15
Teaching Critical Thinking, 4/15

Environment/Society
Mass Transit, 12/16
Arctic Development, 12/16
Protecting the Power Grid, 11/16
Pornography, 10/16
Women in Leadership, 9/16
Child Welfare, 8/16

Health/Safety
Opioid Crisis, 10/16
Mosquito-Borne Disease, 7/16
Drinking Water Safety, 7/16
Virtual Reality, 2/16

Politics/Economy
Trump Presidency, 1/17
European Union's Future, 12/16
The Obama Legacy, 11/16
Populism and Party Politics, 9/16
U.S.-Mexico Relations, 9/16
Modernizing the Nuclear Arsenal, 7/16

Upcoming Reports

Guns on Campus, 1/27/17

Civics Education, 2/3/17

Forensic Science, 2/10/17

ACCESS

CQ Researcher is available in print and online. For access, visit your library or www.cqresearcher.com.

STAY CURRENT

For notice of upcoming *CQ Researcher* reports or to learn more about *CQ Researcher* products, subscribe to the free email newsletters, *CQ Researcher Alert!* and *CQ Researcher News*: http://cqpress.com/newsletters.

PURCHASE

To purchase a *CQ Researcher* report in print or electronic format (PDF), visit www.cqpress.com or call 866-427-7737. Single reports start at $15. Bulk purchase discounts and electronic-rights licensing are also available.

SUBSCRIBE

Annual full-service *CQ Researcher* subscriptions—including 44 reports a year, monthly index updates, and a bound volume—start at $1,131. Add $25 for domestic postage.

CQ Researcher Online offers a backfile from 1991 and a number of tools to simplify research. For pricing information, call 800-818-7243 or 805-499-9774 or email librarysales@sagepub.com.

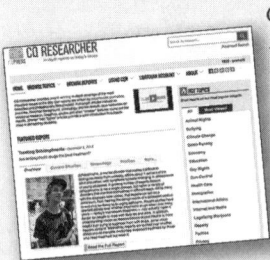

CQ RESEARCHER

CQ PRESS

In-depth reports on today's issues

Published by CQ Press, an Imprint of SAGE Publications, Inc. **www.cqresearcher.com**

Guns on Campus

Would they make colleges safer?

Anthropology professor Pauline Strong posts a sign prohibiting guns in her office at the University of Texas, Austin, on Aug. 1, 2016, the first day of the state's new campus-carry law. Texas is among eight states that allow concealed firearms on campus in certain circumstances. Seventeen states and the District of Columbia ban guns on campuses.

Mass shootings at colleges and universities are spurring lawmakers in a growing number of states to consider allowing students, faculty and others to carry concealed firearms on campus. The American public is evenly split on the issue. Gun-rights supporters say shooters specifically target gun-free spaces such as college campuses. And many students say their constitutional right to bear arms shouldn't end when they walk on campus. But those opposing guns on campus say students with gun permits are not necessarily trained to stop violent crimes. They also note the unique nature of students on college campuses: Young adults' self-control brain functions are not yet fully developed, students often engage in heavy drinking and an increasing number of students are reporting anxiety and other mental health problems. All of this, say foes of guns on campuses, means firearms will make campuses less safe. Debate is also fierce over whether campus security forces should be armed and how colleges and universities can improve counseling services to identify potentially violent students.

CQ Researcher • Jan. 27, 2017 • www.cqresearcher.com
Volume 27, Number 4 • Pages 73-96

I N S I D E THIS REPORT

THE ISSUES **75**

BACKGROUND **81**

CHRONOLOGY **83**

CURRENT SITUATION **87**

AT ISSUE **89**

OUTLOOK **90**

BIBLIOGRAPHY **94**

THE NEXT STEP **95**

THE ISSUES

75
• Would legalizing guns on campuses make colleges and universities safer?
• Should only faculty be allowed to carry guns?
• Would guns on campus threaten free speech?

BACKGROUND

81 **Colonial Policies**
In early America, authorities encouraged young people to arm.

81 **Campus Protests**
Colleges cracked down on firearms on campus after 1960s clashes.

82 **Campus Violence**
Studies on gun ownership divided gun-control advocates and opponents.

85 **Campus-Carry Laws**
Virginia Tech shooting reignited debate about firearms at colleges.

CURRENT SITUATION

87 **States Act**
Some lawmakers seek to eliminate gun-free zones on campuses.

88 **Courts Act**
Some University of Texas professors want firearms barred from classrooms.

88 **Shooting Clubs**
Gun-control advocates worry about a recent surge in interest in collegiate shooting teams.

90 **Limiting Research**
Despite funding restrictions, some studies of gun violence continue.

OUTLOOK

90 **Complicated Issue**
Trump's win could mean end to gun-free zones.

SIDEBARS AND GRAPHICS

76 **Many States Allow Colleges to Set Firearm Rules**
Nearly half of states allow institutions to decide their policies.

77 **Americans Divided Over Guns on Campus**
High-profile shootings heightened concerns about campus safety.

80 **Mass Shootings on College Campuses**
Sixty-nine died in seven incidents.

83 **Chronology**
Key events since 1966.

84 **Arming Campus Cops Spurs Controversy**
"We don't support the 'militarization' of campus security."

86 **Officials Struggle to Prevent Campus Massacres**
Privacy and concealed-carry laws make the job harder.

89 **At Issue:**
Would legalizing guns on campus make colleges safer?

FOR FURTHER RESEARCH

93 **For More Information**
Organizations to contact.

94 **Bibliography**
Selected sources used.

95 **The Next Step**
Additional articles.

95 **Citing CQ Researcher**
Sample bibliography formats.

Cover: AP Photo/*Austin American-Statesman*/Jay Jenner

Jan. 27, 2017
Volume 27, Number 4

EXECUTIVE EDITOR: Thomas J. Billitteri
tjb@sagepub.com

ASSISTANT MANAGING EDITORS: Kenneth Fireman, kenneth.fireman@sagepub.com, Kathy Koch, kathy.koch@sagepub.com, Scott Rohrer, scott.rohrer@sagepub.com

SENIOR CONTRIBUTING EDITOR:
Thomas J. Colin
tom.colin@sagepub.com

CONTRIBUTING WRITERS: Marcia Clemmitt, Sarah Glazer, Reed Karaim, Peter Katel, Barbara Mantel, Chuck McCutcheon, Tom Price

SENIOR PROJECT EDITOR: Olu B. Davis

EDITORIAL ASSISTANT: Anika Reed

FACT CHECKERS: Eva P. Dasher, Michelle Harris, Betsy Towner Levine, Robin Palmer

SAGE Publishing | **CQPRESS**

Los Angeles I London I New Delhi
Singapore I Washington DC I Melbourne

An Imprint of SAGE Publications, Inc.

SENIOR VICE PRESIDENT,
GLOBAL LEARNING RESOURCES:
Karen Phillips

EXECUTIVE DIRECTOR, ONLINE LIBRARY AND
REFERENCE PUBLISHING:
Todd Baldwin

CQ Press is a registered trademark of Congressional Quarterly Inc.

CQ Researcher (ISSN 1056-2036) is printed on acid-free paper. Published weekly, except: (March wk. 4) (May wk. 4) (July wks. 1, 2) (Aug. wks. 2, 3) (Nov. wk. 4) and (Dec. wks. 3, 4). Published by SAGE Publications, Inc., 2455 Teller Rd., Thousand Oaks, CA 91320. Annual full-service subscriptions start at $1,131. For pricing, call 1-800-818-7243. To purchase a *CQ Researcher* report in print or electronic format (PDF), visit www.cqpress.com or call 866-427-7737. Single reports start at $15. Bulk purchase discounts and electronic-rights licensing are also available. Periodicals postage paid at Thousand Oaks, California, and at additional mailing offices. POSTMASTER: Send address changes to *CQ Researcher*, 2600 Virginia Ave., N.W., Suite 600, Washington, DC 20037.

Guns on Campus

BY CHRISTINA L. LYONS

THE ISSUES

As students and faculty walked across the Ohio State University campus in Columbus on Nov. 28, third-year student Abdul Razak Ali Artan suddenly plowed his car onto a busy sidewalk, got out and lunged at bystanders with a butcher knife. In less than two minutes he had wounded 11 people before a university police officer arrived and fatally shot him. [1]

The incident sparked a campus alert message to "Run Hide Fight" and a 90-minute campus lockdown. It also prompted the Ohio Senate to pass a bill to allow the state's public colleges and universities to allow licensed individuals to carry concealed handguns on campus.

"I can legally carry a firearm in my home, at the grocery store, when I take a walk through my neighborhood. Yet when I am at Ohio State, I cannot keep myself safe," law student Jonathan Beshears, who is licensed to carry a concealed weapon, told a prescheduled Senate hearing the day after the attack. "If someone attacks me with a butcher knife or an AK-47, I'm supposed to run away, throw things at them or maybe hide under a desk and pray." [2]

But some students say allowing anyone other than law enforcement to carry concealed weapons on campuses could make them less safe. "A student militia — a student police force — is something I think we should be very wary of," says Kaitlyn Hamby, a senior at Florida State University who has battled a similar measure in her state since another student opened fire in a campus library in 2014, injuring three students before campus police shot him. [3]

A mock shooting victim is helped to a triage area during a shooter-on-campus drill at Illinois State University in Normal in March 2015. Mass shootings in recent years have prompted several states to consider allowing concealed firearms on college campuses. The American public is divided over the question.

AP Photo/The Pantagraph/Steve Smedley

In response to several high-profile shootings on college campuses in recent years, dozens of state legislatures are considering relaxing their 1990s-era "gun-free zone" designations for public college and university campuses, allowing individuals with so-called concealed-carry permits to bring their handguns onto campus. Gun-rights advocates, conservative lawmakers and some faculty and students believe no-guns-on-campus laws infringe on their Second Amendment right to bear arms and hamper their ability to stop violent criminals before police arrive. But gun-control advocates, liberal lawmakers and many campus officials, faculty and students say college campuses are inappropriate — and unsafe — environments for handguns.

"There's a lot of alcohol binge drinking . . . on college campuses [that results in] a lot of spontaneous altercations," says Daniel Webster, a professor of health policy and management at the Bloomberg School of Public Health at Johns Hopkins University in Baltimore. Further, due to their undeveloped prefrontal cortex, young people are "compromised in their ability to think through what they're doing and what the consequences are," he continues. "You add firearms to that type of environment, and you have life-changing, life-ending kinds of consequences." [4]

But Michael Newbern, assistant director of public relations for Students for Concealed Carry, says, "The question here is: Do you want the only guns on campus to be the ones that are carried there illegally?"

President Trump vowed repeatedly during his campaign to eliminate gun-free zones at schools and military bases. "My first day. There's no more gun-free zones," Trump said in January 2016. He has been unclear, however, on whether he wants to lift the bans on guns at K-12 schools as well as college campuses. [5]

While every state permits some form of concealed carry, until recently most of those laws exempted day care centers, government buildings, military bases and schools. Most states barred guns on public college and university campuses after a federal law in the early 1990s designated public primary and secondary schools as gun-free zones.

State laws regarding concealed-carry at higher education institutions now vary widely (*see map, p. 76*): 17 states ban concealed weapons on campus; 23 states (including Ohio) allow each institution to decide whether to allow firearms, and eight states — either by law or court ruling — mandate that in-

Many States Allow Colleges to Set Firearm Rules

Twenty-three states allow public colleges and universities to decide their own gun policies, while 17 states and the District of Columbia prohibit concealed weapons on campus. Eight states have provisions allowing the concealed carry of firearms by all permitted individuals on campus. Two other states — Arkansas and Tennessee — have laws allowing only faculty and other employees to carry concealed firearms.

Where Guns Are Allowed on College Campuses

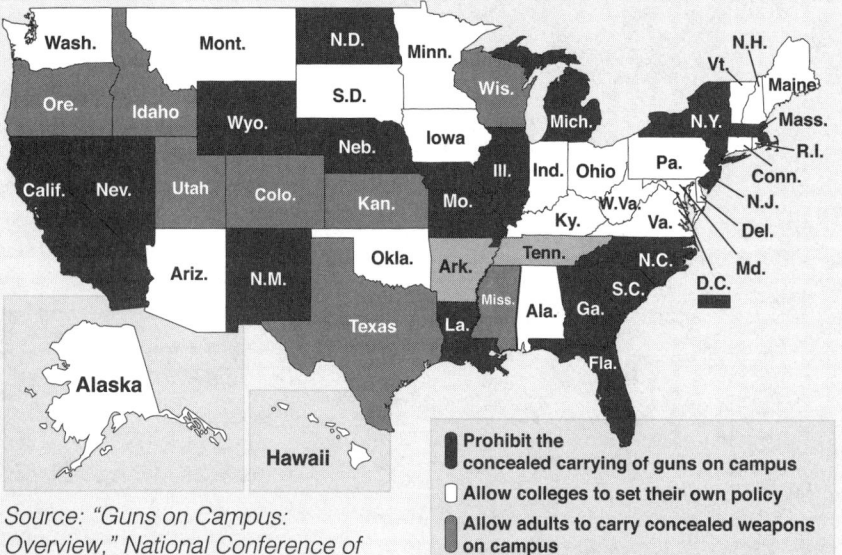

■ **Prohibit the concealed carrying of guns on campus**
□ **Allow colleges to set their own policy**
▨ **Allow adults to carry concealed weapons on campus**
▨ **Allow faculty members and employees to carry concealed weapons**

Source: "Guns on Campus: Overview," National Conference of State Legislatures, Jan. 24, 2017, http://tinyurl.com/p5oey34

dividuals with concealed weapon permits be allowed to carry handguns on all public campuses. [6] Tennessee and Arkansas allow only licensed faculty members to carry weapons on campus. [7]

However, only Tennessee requires faculty who carry a weapon onto campus to register with campus or local law enforcement. In other places, only state agencies maintain registries of permit holders — databases that are not available to the public — so no one knows who or how many people can legally carry concealed weapons on U.S. campuses. [8]

Private colleges typically set their own firearms policies or are allowed to opt in or out of state laws. For instance, private schools in Texas can opt out of a new state law that mandates

colleges and universities allow licensed individuals over 21 to carry concealed firearms on campus. So far, only Amberton University, in Garland, has chosen to allow firearms. [9]

Liberty University, a private Christian school in Lynchburg, Va., permits students and staff to carry concealed firearms anywhere on campus. Chancellor Jerry Falwell in 2013 announced that guns — previously allowed only outside of campus buildings — would be allowed inside of buildings as well, saying the change would "create a higher level of security on campus than what was found at Virginia Tech." [10]

On April 16, 2007, Virginia Polytechnic University senior Seung-Hui Cho, 23, went on a shooting rampage at the Blacksburg campus, killing 32

people before committing suicide. [11] Less than a year later, on Feb. 14, 2008, 27-year-old Northern Illinois University student Stephen Kazmierczak opened fire in a lecture hall, killing five students and wounding 21 others before killing himself. [12]

The incidents prompted Students for Concealed Carry and the National Rifle Association (NRA) to push states to loosen campus gun restrictions. Such efforts gained steam after the 2012 massacre of 20 schoolchildren and six staff members at Sandy Hook Elementary in Newtown, Conn., by Adam Lanza. [13] "The only way to stop a bad guy with a gun is with a good guy with a gun," NRA Executive Vice President Wayne LaPierre said at the time, arguing for eliminating gun-free zones and arming K-12 security personnel. [14]

Gun-rights advocates made similar statements in October 2015, after Christopher Harper-Mercer, a 26-year-old student at Umpqua Community College in Roseburg, Ore., brought five handguns and a semi-automatic rifle into a classroom and killed nine students before police shot and wounded him. He then fatally shot himself. [15]

Estimates vary of how many gun-related incidents have occurred on college campuses. The FBI counted 12 "active shooter incidents" — resulting in 60 deaths — at institutions of higher education between 2000 and 2013. [16] Everytown for Gun Safety, a gun-control advocacy group, says there were 76 accidental and intentional shooting incidents on college campuses from 2013 to 2015. [17]

While campus-carry advocates say students should be able to carry guns under the Second Amendment of the Constitution, opponents note that when the U.S. Supreme Court in 2008 struck down a Washington, D.C., law barring civilians from keeping handguns in their homes, the court said the right to bear arms is "not unlimited" and "should not be taken to cast doubt on . . . laws forbidding the carrying of firearms in sensitive places such as schools and government buildings." [18]

Surveys show most students, professors and administrators oppose having concealed firearms on campus. At the start of the 2016-17 school year, hundreds of University of Texas students protested implementation of the state's new concealed-carry law. [19]

Opponents of guns on campus worry that gun-related accidental discharges, suicides and violent altercations could increase the number of campus fatalities. But Dave Kopel, research director of the Independence Institute, a Denver-based conservative think tank, says none of those fears has played out in Utah, which enacted campus carry in 2004 or Colorado which enacted a concealed-carry law in 2003 that did not exempt college campuses. [20]

Lucinda Roy, an English professor at Virginia Tech, says she would rather not legalize firearms on campus but is sympathetic to students who support such a policy because "we're not really doing anything" to directly address issues that can lead people to violence, such as increasing access to mental health care. "So we're leaving young people vulnerable, and that is inexcusable." (*See sidebar, p. 86.*)

Sue Riseling, executive director of the International Association of Campus Law Enforcement Administrators, based in West Hartford, Conn., worries, among other things, that free speech will be chilled on campus, especially if professors begin to fear challenging potentially armed students "to change their understanding of the world and . . . of themselves."

Republican Georgia Gov. Nathan Deal last year vetoed his state's permissive campus-carry measure, saying "colleges have been treated as sanctuaries of learning where firearms have not been allowed." As a compromise, he signed a measure allowing anyone over 18 to carry stun guns — commercially available "electroshock weapons" — on campus for self-defense. [21]

Americans Divided Over Guns on Campus

Survey respondents were evenly split in 2013 about whether concealed guns should be allowed on college campuses.

Should gun owners with proper permits be allowed to carry concealed weapons on college campuses?

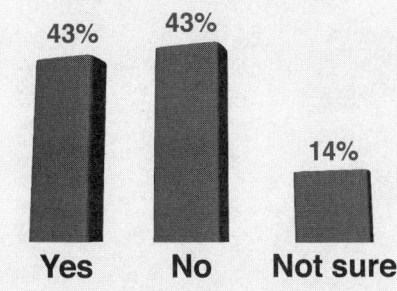

43% Yes 43% No 14% Not sure

Source: "Omnibus Poll," YouGov, The Huffington Post, Jan. 3-4, 2013, http://tinyurl.com/bzze4pp

As more states and universities consider legalizing concealed weapons on campuses, these are some of the questions being debated:

Would legalizing guns on campuses make colleges and universities safer?

Alex Stewart, state director of Florida Students for Concealed Carry, says concealed handguns on campus would "change the gamble" that a criminal is taking. "Before, you were gambling that .001 percent [of the population] wouldn't bother to violate the prohibition on concealed carry. Now you're gambling that if [they do], there will be a good citizen there who can attack . . . them."

Stewart and other campus-carry supporters cite studies by gun-rights advocate and academic John Lott Jr., author of *More Guns, Less Crime* and founder of the nonprofit Crime Prevention Research

Center, in Swarthmore, Pa., to try to prove that relaxing gun restrictions can reduce crime. Lott found in one study that murder rates fell about 16 percent and violent crime by 18 percent between 2007 and 2015 — a period when the number of concealed-handgun permits more than doubled, to more than 14.5 million. [22]

Stewart contends there hasn't been "a single case where a permit holder on a college campus . . . has committed a crime." He also says, "Concealed carriers are abnormally law-abiding citizens; we are almost never convicted of weapons crimes."

Gun-rights advocates also cite research by Florida State University criminal justice professor Gary Kleck showing that permit holders commit fewer crimes than unlicensed holders and that many victims successfully defend themselves with a gun. "If carry permit holders never commit gun violence," Kleck asked, "why are [opponents] worried about them being allowed to carry on college campuses?" [23]

But other researchers refute such correlations between the growing number of gun permits and the falling rate of violent crime. Three researchers, two from Stanford and one from Johns Hopkins, said other factors, such as increased incarceration rates, also must be examined. [24]

In fact, said David Hemenway, director of the Harvard Injury Control Research Center in Boston, which provides research on training to prevent violence, most firearms researchers agree that having "more guns and weaker gun laws have created a serious public health problem." [25]

Already, Hemenway says, we know "for sure that the presence of a gun in the home in the U.S. increases the risk for suicide." And a dozen studies comparing demographic differences in suicide rates have shown that "the overwhelming factor is guns," he says, adding that when trying to stop a shooter, gun holders might shoot innocent bystanders or even undercover police responding to an incident. Others worry that police officers might mistake an armed law-abiding student as the shooter.

Drawing on data from the National Crime Victimization Surveys from 2007 to 2011, Hemenway also said that few people actually use their guns in self-defense during a violent crime. [26]

Little research has focused on the effects of campus-carry laws on campus crime rates. However a forthcoming 2017 report by Julie Gavran, the Southwestern director of the Campaign to Keep Guns Off Campus, concludes that such laws have not

them. However, he also agrees with several points in a 2016 report by the Johns Hopkins Bloomberg School of Public Health that warned various factors of college life make concealed-carry laws more dangerous, including:

• binge drinking, drug abuse and other risky student behaviors;

• ongoing brain development among young adults;

• stress, depression or mental illness, which are increasingly being reported among students. [28]

Jenkins and others also question the value of relying on state permitting

"Even drawing that weapon takes practice to do effectively."

Florida State's Hamby, a member of the Campaign to Keep Guns Off Campus, says, "What if there's more than one student carrying and more than one student who thinks that they can handle the situation? . . . The situation gets very chaotic and very messy quickly."

More recently, the debate has focused on protection for sexual assault victims — a growing problem on college campuses. FSU student Shayna Lopez-Rivas told Florida lawmakers she had been sexually assaulted twice, once on campus, and wants the right "to legally carry a weapon" at all times. "Criminals are already armed, and a gun-free zone sign doesn't change that." [29]

But Andy Pelosi, executive director of the Campaign to Keep Guns Off Campus, says most sexual assault victims on campuses know their attackers, so the woman is unlikely to be carrying her gun. And he warns, "If we start arming people, we may be arming the attacker."

Florida State University students attend a candlelight vigil on Nov. 20, 2014, after three FSU students were shot and wounded in the library earlier in the day. Gun-rights supporters say their Second Amendment rights shouldn't end when they walk on campus. Opponents say guns make campuses less safe.

Getty Images/Mark Wallheiser

reduced violent crime rates on campuses, particularly sexual assaults. [27]

Campus-carry opponents also warn of accidental shootings. A University of Colorado staff member in 2012 accidentally discharged her firearm, injuring herself and another woman, while removing it from her purse to show co-workers. She was fired and faced criminal prosecution, says Patrick O'Rourke, a university vice president.

Rob Jenkins, an associate professor of English at Georgia State University's Perimeter College, sees both sides in the debate. He agrees that gun-free college campuses might attract criminals who want to "shoot as many people as possible before someone shoots"

laws, which vary widely across the nation and often have lax or limited requirements. State concealed-carry permitting requirements do not require the same level of training as that required for police officers, says Gene Deisinger, former deputy chief of police and director of threat management services at Virginia Tech after the 2007 shooting rampage.

"Many people who express an interest in concealed carry have not put themselves through that level of training," says Deisinger, who is now managing partner and co-founder of SIGMA Threat Management Associates, an Alexandria, Va., firm that provides training for colleges on threat assessment.

Should only faculty be allowed to carry guns?

"Let me tell you, if you had a couple teachers with guns in that room, you would have been a hell of a lot better off," then-presidential candidate Trump said after the Umpqua Community College shooting in 2015 while attending a campaign rally in Franklin, Tenn. [30]

The following year, Tennessee Republicans pushed through their measure allowing full-time employees of public colleges and universities to carry licensed concealed handguns on campus. The bill excluded stadiums, gymnasiums, hospitals and disciplinary or tenure meetings. [31]

Republican Gov. Bill Haslam allowed the measure to become law without his signature, saying he preferred that schools set their own rules. The bill's sponsors chose not to include an opt-out provision after learning most campuses would opt out. [32]

The NRA opposed any opt-out provision. "College campuses as gun-free zones present an environment where murderers, rapists and other criminals may commit crimes without fear of being harmed by their victims," NRA lobbyist Erin Luper said. [33]

Since the Virginia Tech shooting, many states have considered proposals to arm college faculty and administrators. Supporters say staff could provide a layer of protection for students if police cannot respond quickly. Policies restricting firearms on campus invite "the wolves to go after the sheep," Virginia GOP Del. Bob Marshall said in 2012. [34]

Before the Tennessee Legislature passed its bill, University of Tennessee President Joe DiPietro said he opposed increasing the number of guns on college campuses, as did a majority of University of Tennessee employees in a survey. One responder said: "If this passes, expect an exodus-like event of your top scholars." [35]

University employee Kristina Robinette said, "Any time that you bring a gun into any place, you're going to bring awareness to yourself and make people feel on edge, but it's our constitutional right to, and I believe in that." Some students also said they would feel safer knowing there was added protection. [36]

Nate Kreuter, an associate professor of rhetoric at West Carolina University in Cullowhee, N.C., says the state's permitting process for carrying a concealed firearm entails only a criminal background check and a class "in how not to get afoul of the law." And any gun holder who "fancies themselves a hero" during a violent incident would not be in uniform, so how would police know they weren't an assailant? he asks.

Maria Gonzalez, an associate professor of English at the University of Houston, says she's concerned about depressed students hurting themselves with guns. Other faculty and students say they fear accidental shootings, such as occurred at Idaho State University in 2014. Just

months after the state's campus-carry law took effect, a professor with a concealed carry permit accidentally shot himself in the foot while in a classroom full of students. [37]

Timothy Furnish, a history professor at Reinhardt University, a private school in Waleska, Ga., says, "A vast majority of college faculty are liberals and are scared of guns," so most probably would not carry a gun. He supports requiring concealed carriers to undergo rigorous training.

Some faculty and administrators believe a faculty-only policy would solve the potential risks associated with allowing young people to carry concealed weapons described in the Bloomberg School of Public Health report.

"This . . . would greatly lessen the risk of allowing students to have and carry guns on campuses, and there are a lot more students than there are faculty," says Webster, of Johns Hopkins. But if faculty and staff "were permitted to bring guns onto college campuses, there should be . . . strict rules and protocols" for securing the firearms and specific training requirements to "ensure that legal gun carriers know how to be safe with guns and know when and how to use them when necessary."

Jenkins, of Georgia State University, says, "I don't like the thought of professors packing," but that "responsible staff members who wish to carry, who qualify for the appropriate permits, and who are willing to undergo special training" should be allowed to carry.

Newbern, of Students for Concealed Carry, says his organization understands many people find legalizing weapons on campuses "a very new and radical idea." So he sees a concealed-carry policy for faculty and staff as an appropriate temporary compromise.

Some professors, however, warn about liability if they carry or use a weapon. Most university policies hold gun permit owners liable for their actions, rather than the university, unless they carry a firearm to fulfill their job duties.

Would guns on campus threaten free speech?

Many administrators and faculty members worry that having concealed weapons on campus could discourage free speech.

"College campuses are marketplaces of ideas, and a rigorous academic exchange of ideas may be chilled by the presence of weapons," wrote several educational associations, including the American Association of University Professors and the American Federation of Teachers, in November 2015. [38]

In a poll of more than 20,000 Kansas public college employees, two-thirds said guns on campus would "limit their freedom to teach the material and engage with students in a way that optimizes learning." [39]

A prominent University of Texas scholar resigned after the Texas Legislature passed the campus-carry measure in 2015, saying it would impede schools' obligations to provide a safe learning environment. Several professors at other universities severed ties with the University of Texas, and three professors sued the university, seeking permission to bar guns from their classrooms. They said they feared the presence of weapons would "chill their First Amendment rights to academic freedom," which involve a "robust exchange of ideas." [40]

During a University of Houston Faculty Senate meeting on guns on campus on Feb. 15, 2016, a PowerPoint presentation stated: "You may want to: Be careful discussing sensitive topics; Drop certain topics from your curriculum; Not 'go there' if you sense anger." [41]

Gonzalez, at the University of Houston, often focuses on hot button issues like the history of racism, sexuality and feminism. She says she hasn't modified her teaching since the campus-carry policy took effect but is constantly aware that any student could be carrying a weapon.

Gonzalez says she is particularly concerned about weapons on the multicultural Texas campus amid heightened tensions after the election of

Mass Shootings on College Campuses

At least 64 people, not counting the shooters, have been killed in seven mass shootings on college and university campuses since 2002. Five of the shooters either killed themselves or were shot by police. Congress defined a "mass killing" in 2013 as an incident in which three or more people are killed in a single incident.

University of Arizona, October 2002 (3 killed, 1 suicide)
Student Robert S. Flores, 41, killed three instructors at the university's nursing school before turning the gun on himself. One victim told her husband she felt threatened by Flores before the shooting.

Virginia Tech, April 2007 (32 killed, 1 suicide)
On April 16, 2007, student Seung-Hui Cho, 23, killed 32 people at the university in the deadliest college campus shooting in the 21st century. After shooting students and professors in a dorm and an academic building, Cho took his own life.

Northern Illinois University, February 2008 (5 killed, 1 suicide)
Former graduate student Stephen Kazmierczak opened fire in an auditorium using at least two legally purchased firearms, shooting 25 people and killing five. The gunman died of a self-inflicted gunshot.

University of Alabama in Huntsville, February 2010 (3 killed)
Three faculty members were shot to death by biology professor Amy Bishop, who had been denied tenure for the second time the day of the shooting. Bishop pleaded guilty to capital murder and is serving a life sentence.

Oikos University, April 2012 (7 killed)
Former student One Goh fatally shot seven people because the private nursing college in Oakland, Calif., refused to refund his tuition, police said. A grand jury indicted Goh, who was said to be suffering from paranoid schizophrenia, on seven counts of murder in 2014.

Santa Monica College, June 2013 (5 killed, 1 shooter killed)
John Zawahri, 23, shot and killed his father and brother before going on a shooting rampage across Santa Monica, fatally shooting three others. He was armed with multiple guns when police shot him to death on the campus.

Umpqua Community College, October 2015 (9 killed, 1 suicide)
Christopher Harper-Mercer, 26, fatally shot nine people in a Roseburg, Ore., classroom before killing himself in front of students.

Sources: Various news reports; compiled by Anika Reed

Trump, who vowed to deport illegal immigrants. "There's a certain heightened awareness now" about the potential presence of firearms and students' emotional state, she says.

Some Houston students who identify as LGBT feared expressing themselves freely. Robyn Foley, 22, a transgender student, said, "I can't stand up for my transgender friends, because if I do, and someone gets pissed off, all they have to do is pull out a gun." [42]

Hamby at FSU says, "A lot of my classes are discussion-based classes where we share perspectives. And I don't agree with a lot of people, and we sometimes have heated debates. And that's OK because we're in an environment that encourages that." As an activist on women's issues, cyberbullying and gun control, she says, "I would be less inclined to be as outspoken about my views" if campus carry was legal.

However, Newbern, of Students for Concealed Carry, says, in states where concealed weapons are permitted, "we are not hearing about people not being able to engage in healthy debate. We are not hearing about licensees threatening other students with their handguns because they don't agree with their position."

The Independence Institute's Kopel also thinks evidence already shows that "people aren't going to pull out their guns when there's a heated debate over Hamlet."

But some faculty and students worry because they don't know who is carrying. Tennessee is the only state that requires local law enforcement to maintain a registry of concealed-carry permit holders who plan to carry on campus. But nationwide only law enforcement officers are allowed to check the state registry or ask if a person carries a concealed weapon.

"There's no more reason to out people who are carrying on campus versus outing those who are carrying in a restaurant," says Jenkins from Georgia State.

Stewart of Florida Students for Concealed Carry says nobody knows who is carrying a concealed weapon — regardless of whether they are on or off campus. "Have you ever walked off campus and suddenly felt the weight of fear of freedom of expression?" he asks. "The answer is no."

Those carrying concealed firearms fear a backlash if it were revealed that they were carrying weapons, including possibly even from instructors at grading time, Newbern says. College campuses "are hostile toward firearms and individual liberties in general," and have limited the free-speech rights of those carrying firearms, he says.

Robert Shibley, executive director of the Foundation for Individual Rights in Education (FIRE), says some colleges — such as Tarrant County College in Fort Worth, Texas, and Santa Fe College in Florida — have shut down or tried to block protests by Students for Concealed Carry in which members wear empty holsters, seen as threatening by some students or administrators.

"So any kind of firearm discussion on campuses can be radioactive because of the perceived threat that comes with it," Shibley says. "Because people seem to be threatening isn't a reason to cut off controversial expression. Campus is the place you have to have that discussion."

Virginia Tech's Roy says she believes both sides of the debate over concealed carry on campus should be heard. Academics often disregard "as right-wing loonies" people who want to be armed in order to defend themselves, she says. "And I think that's unfair." ■

BACKGROUND

Colonial Policies

Authorities during the colonial and revolutionary eras encouraged young people to be armed and ready for militia duty, and colleges did not specifically ban students from carrying firearms for self-defense. [43]

Harvard, for instance, barred hunting but did not explicitly prohibit all firearms. On April 7, 1759, the faculty voted to allow students to use their firearms only in certain areas, " 'at convenient Hours,' and . . . after Evening Prayers.' " [44]

The Second Amendment, contained in the Constitution's Bill of Rights adopted in 1791, states: "A well regulated Militia, being necessary to the security of a free State, the right of the people to keep and bear Arms, shall not be infringed."

Several states adopted similar constitutional amendments. But in 1813, Kentucky and Louisiana outlawed carrying concealed weapons for personal defense, and several states followed suit. However, Mississippi, Missouri and other states affirmed individuals' rights to carry arms for self-defense. [45]

Some colleges also began prohibiting firearms on campus. College students often exhibited unruly behavior, even rioting, to protest certain rules or punishments. For instance, students at the College of William and Mary rioted in 1807 after professors punished two students for dueling. The University of Virginia board on Oct. 4, 1824, ruled that students would not be allowed to "keep or use weapons or arms of any kind." [46]

Other schools established similar rules. In 1868, Yale University barred students from keeping "any kind of firearms, fireworks or gunpowder" or firing "in or near the College yard, or near the dwelling-house or person of any member of the Faculty." [47]

The rules did not always temper students' behavior. At Virginia, students each November celebrated the so-called 1836 military company riot, which they interpreted as "a victory over professorial authority," by firing their pistols, setting off firecrackers, lighting fires and in general "caterwauling." During the celebration in 1840, law professor John A.G. Davis was fatally shot when he tried to quell the ruckus. [48]

In the mid-1800s, many colleges sought to control student behavior under a doctrine, upheld by the courts, known as *in loco parentis* — or "in the parents' place" — based on a British common law granting a tutor or schoolmaster parental authority over a child. [49] Schools began monitoring student adherence to curfews, church attendance, dress codes and other principles to uphold the "university's moral atmosphere."

Still, not all universities barred firearms. During the 1880s, the University of Kentucky in Lexington had 176 rules governing student behavior, ranging from mandating that students walk in a soldier-like manner to barring them from visiting a saloon. However, students could have guns in their rooms and occasionally "the relative tranquility of the campus was broken by the sound of gun shots originating from the windows of the men's dormitory," according to a history of the university. [50]

The National Rifle Association, formed in 1871 to improve the marksmanship of citizens who might serve in the military, began holding target shooting competitions and sponsoring gun clubs and shooting ranges, including on college campuses. [51] And in 1926 it helped devise a model Uniform Firearms Act to encourage states to license citizens wanting to carry a concealed handgun. [52]

Through the early 20th century, colleges and universities grew in size and number, and drunken carousing became an ever more common part of campus life as rules on social decorum eased. Social historian David O. Levine wrote, "The American public expected a new elite of college students to prove their status by misbehaving in ritualized ways." [53]

Campus Protests

In the 1960s, students pushed for additional freedoms on campus, but the period also saw a widespread crackdown on the possession of firearms on college campuses.

Political fervor opposing the Vietnam War and favoring civil rights spread across campuses nationwide, and a growing number of violent incidents began to occur — some related to the protests and some not.

At the University of Texas on Aug. 1, 1966, Charles Whitman, 25, an engineering student and ex-Marine, carried three rifles, two pistols and a sawed-off shotgun to the top of a tower and "launched an orgy of sniping," in the words of the *New York Daily News*, in which 14 died and 32 were wounded. Students, professors and visitors sought cover behind trees, in stairwells and under desks until "police burst into the sniper's 28th-story eyrie and shot him dead after a brief gun duel." [54]

An autopsy revealed that Whitman suffered from a glioblastoma brain tumor. The previous March he had sought psychiatric treatment at the student health center, where he received an hour's session and was told to return within a week and to call if he had concerns in the meantime. He never returned or called.

After an investigation, a medical panel recommended the university implement a mental health program and counseling service for students because the college years are "one of the most stressful periods" in a student's life. [55]

Two years later, the assassinations of civil rights leader Martin Luther King Jr. and Democratic senator and presidential candidate Robert F. Kennedy in 1968 spurred passage of the Gun Control Act, barring individuals who have been "adjudicated as a mental defective" or "committed to a mental institution" from buying or possessing firearms. [56]

In April 1969, more than 80 members of the Afro-American Society at Cornell University occupied the student union, demanding improved mental-health services for minority students and more minority faculty and professors sensitive to black perspectives. Fearing for their safety, they subsequently snuck 15 firearms into the building. Administrators agreed to negotiate with the protesters and allowed them to leave the building armed to ensure their safety — a move some later criticized as an embarrassing capitulation to physical intimidation. Soon after the incident, the New York State Legislature banned guns on campuses. [57]

As student protests spread around the nation, courts began to recognize the constitutional rights of university students, "sounding the death knell for *in loco parentis*," said Philip Lee, an associate

law professor at the University of the District of Columbia. [58] Even so, colleges began to restrict guns on campus. [59]

In 1970, the University of Colorado banned guns on campus, allowing students to store their hunting rifles in lockers with the campus police. Generally only a handful of students did so. [60] The same year, National Guardsmen in Ohio who were called to quell an anti-war protest shot and killed four students at Kent State University.

Many students subsequently began protesting the presence of armed officers on campuses, and at the University of Kentucky, faculty and students unsuccessfully demanded that police and guardsmen, called to calm riots after the Kent State shootings, not carry "weapons of violence" while on campus. [61]

Nationwide, campus safety became a growing concern, particularly after Jeanne Ann Clery, a 19-year-old freshman asleep in her dorm room at Lehigh University in Bethlehem, Pa., was beaten, raped and strangled by a fellow student in 1986. When Clery's parents discovered that 38 violent crimes had occurred at the university in the previous three years, they successfully sued Lehigh for not disclosing details about campus crime to prospective students.

Congress passed the Student Right-to-Know and Campus Security Act in 1990 (later renamed the Jeanne Clery Act), which requires colleges and universities to maintain a public crime log. Congress amended the law in 2008, in part to require schools to provide details about crimes adjacent to campus. [62]

Also in 1990, Congress passed the Gun-Free School Zones Act, barring any individual from knowingly carrying or discharging a firearm near a primary or secondary school. The law primarily was a reaction to several mass shootings at schools, including one at Cleveland Elementary School in Stockton, Calif., which left five children dead and another 30 students and teachers wounded. [63]

The law later was challenged in court for exceeding its constitutional powers under the Commerce Clause. By the time the Supreme Court struck it down in 1995, Congress had replaced it in 1994 with the Gun-Free Schools Act, which called on states receiving federal education funds to adopt "zero-tolerance" policies regarding weapons in schools. [64]

Although the 1994 law did not apply to college and universities, states subsequently passed similar legislation making higher-ed campuses gun-free zones.

Campus Violence

The late 1990s was a particularly violent time at colleges and universities as well as at lower-level schools and across the nation in general. Gun-control advocates and their opponents, led by the NRA, had been arguing about whether restricting firearms would improve or worsen crime statistics.

When a 1993 study published in *The New England Journal of Medicine* concluded that keeping a gun in the home increased the risk of homicide, gun-rights advocates campaigned to eliminate federal funding for such studies. [65]

Ultimately, Congress included a provision — written by then-Rep. Jay Dickey, R-Ark. — in the Omnibus Consolidated Appropriations Act of 1997 prohibiting the Centers for Disease Control and Prevention (CDC) from using funds earmarked for injury prevention and control to be used "to advocate or promote gun control." This was interpreted to mean that the CDC was prohibited from issuing grants for studies about gun violence. [66]

Subsequent studies were largely based on data collected by the FBI and reports issued pursuant to the Clery Act. In 1998, according to one study, 20 murders, 1,240 rapes and 2,267 aggravated assaults were reported on the campuses of four-year higher education institutions. [67]

Continued on p. 84

Chronology

1960s-1990s
Violence on and off campus leads to new gun restrictions.

1966
Sniper at University of Texas kills 14, injures 32.

1968
Congress passes Gun Control Act that regulates interstate commerce of firearms.

1969
Armed members of the Afro-American Society at Cornell University occupying the student union force university to negotiate demands of minority students. . . . New York Legislature bans guns on college campuses.

1970
University of Colorado bans guns on campuses, allows hunting rifles to be stored in lockers with campus police.

1990
Congress adopts so-called Clery Act, which mandates that colleges report campus crimes. . . . Gun-Free School Zones Act designates primary and secondary schools as "gun-free zones." States later adopt similar legislation for their public colleges and universities.

1999
Two students at Columbine High School in Colorado shoot and kill 12 classmates and a teacher before committing suicide, triggering crackdowns on guns on campuses.

———— • ————

2000s-Present
High-profile mass shootings spark new strategies on campus firearms.

2003
Colorado allows concealed weapons statewide, including on college campuses, but not K-12 schools.

2004
Utah becomes first state to allow licensed adult students and employees to carry guns on campus.

2006
Utah Supreme Court strikes down University of Utah ban on guns on campus.

2007
Gunman at Virginia Tech kills 32 before committing suicide. . . . Students for Concealed Carry founded.

2008
Student at Northern Illinois University shoots and kills five people and wounds 21 before committing suicide. . . . The Campaign to Keep Guns Off Campus forms to fight campus-carry laws. . . . U.S. Supreme Court rules unconstitutional District of Columbia law barring residents from keeping guns in homes, but says right to bear arms is not unlimited.

2009
Arizona allows concealed guns on campus if stored in cars. . . . Michigan State University permits concealed guns on campus but not inside buildings.

2011
Mississippi and Wisconsin pass campus concealed-carry laws. . . . Virginia Supreme Court upholds George Mason University's ban on firearms.

2012
Colorado Supreme Court strikes down University of Colorado's ban on firearms. . . . Shooter kills 26 people at Sandy Hook Elementary in Newtown, Conn., triggering calls for more guns on campuses.

2013
Kansas allows concealed guns at public universities and colleges, effective summer 2017. . . . Arkansas follows suit but allows full-time employees at universities to carry concealed weapons but schools can opt out.

2014
Idaho allows concealed weapons on campus. . . . Student opens fire at Florida State University library, injuring three students before being shot by campus police.

2015
Texas says public universities and colleges must allow concealed firearms on campus. . . . Student at an Oregon community college shoots nine people before committing suicide, prompting then-GOP presidential candidate Donald Trump to advocate arming college faculty. . . . California reaffirms ban on concealed weapons at public colleges.

2016
Knife and car attack at Ohio State University injures 11 before campus police kill perpetrator. . . . Ohio allows concealed firearms at colleges, day-care centers, public areas of airports and some government buildings. . . . Tennessee allows public colleges and universities to permit faculty and staff to carry concealed handguns. . . . Florida Senate leader blocks bill to allow concealed weapons on campuses. . . . Georgia Gov. Nathan Deal vetoes campus-carry bill. . . . Liberty University in Lynchburg, Va., permits concealed firearms in residence halls. . . . Three University of Texas professors sue university and the state for right to bar firearms from classrooms. . . . Missouri takes up broad gun legislation, ultimately removes provision that would have allowed full-time employees on college campuses to carry guns.

Arming Campus Cops Spurs Controversy

"We don't support the militarization of campus security."

With high-profile shootings occurring more frequently on college campuses and gun ownership in the United States rising, more universities and colleges are arming campus police with handguns, rifles and, in some places, semi-automatic weapons.

"The more the public gets to arm, the more an institution has to come to grips with upgrading to an armed force," says Sue Riseling, executive director of the International Association of Campus Law Enforcement Administrators, a West Hartford, Conn.-based trade group representing officers at about 1,105 colleges in 10 countries.

Not everyone, however, agrees with arming campus police, particularly with semi-automatic rifles or what some call "military-grade" weaponry. "If law enforcement is armed on campus, we [believe] the training they receive should be commensurate with municipal law enforcement," says Andy Pelosi, executive director of Campaign to Keep Guns Off Campus, a national organization that works with colleges and universities to oppose new so-called campus-carry laws, which allow students to carry concealed weapons on campus. But "we don't support the militarization of campus security."

Educational institutions vary widely on whether to have "security officers" or sworn law enforcement personnel with the same training and authority as municipal police, says Gene Deisinger, managing partner and co-founder of SIGMA Threat Management Associates, an Alexandria, Va., firm that advises colleges and universities on security. Some state laws restrict whether police on public campuses can be armed.

After the 2007 Virginia Tech shooting in which 32 people died, a national organization of city police chiefs and the U.S. Bureau of Justice Statistics devised guidelines for better coordinating campus security and local law enforcement. The guidelines didn't mention arming campus security, but by 2012, as campus enrollments increased and fears about crime and mass shootings rose, many more higher education institutions had taken that route, according to the Justice Department.

During the 2011-12 school year about 75 percent of public, four-year institutions with more than 2,500 students were using armed officers — up from 68 percent in the 2004-05 school year. Most campus officers were conducting joint patrols with local law enforcement. [1]

And universities have continued to arm campus police despite student protests. At Oregon's Portland State University, students have protested a 2014 decision by the Board of Trustees to arm campus police. [2] "It doesn't make me feel any safer knowing that there are more guns on a massively populated campus," said 23-year-old sociology major Cody Shotola. [3]

The next year, Princeton University, responding to a series of deadly shootings around the country, said its public safety officers would have access to rifles — a move the university's student government had battled since 2008. [4]

Local, state and university law enforcement agencies can purchase excess military weaponry from the Defense Department. Between 2006 and April 2014, the Pentagon distributed 79,288 assault rifles, 11,959 bayonets and hundreds of helicopters and mine-resistant vehicles to local police departments across the United States, a portion of which went to colleges. More than 100 colleges have participated in the program in recent years. [5]

City police sometimes object to arming campus officers, particularly with semi-automatic rifles. For instance, the Boston Police Department condemned a decision by Northeastern University to arm campus police with such weapons.

"I can remember having a dialogue not long ago about whether [college police officers] should be carrying handguns," Boston Police Commissioner Bill Evans said. "Now we're talking

Continued from p. 82

In 2003, the Colorado Legislature enacted the Concealed Carry Act, which allowed permitted gun owners to carry their weapons throughout the state except in government buildings, in K-12 schools (except in locked cars) and on private property where owners had barred weapons. Although House lawmakers had defeated an amendment to exempt higher education institutions, Colorado Attorney General Ken Salazar said at the time the University of Colorado could retain its weapons ban based on a Board of Regents policy that guns are "offensive" to the university's "values." [68]

The University of Utah continued to prohibit concealed carry until the Legislature in 2004 clarified that a 1995 statute authorizing anyone with a concealed-carry permit to carry at any public "school" applied to public higher-education. [69] In September 2006, the state Supreme Court struck down the university's ban. [70]

In states that continued to prohibit weapons on campus, it was unclear how many students abided by the restrictions. Researchers at the Harvard School of Public Health reported in 2002 that 4.3 percent of the more than 10,000 undergraduate students at 119 four-year colleges reported having a firearm at school. And the gun carriers were more likely, the report said, to be males, living off campus and who binge drink and "engage in risky and aggressive behavior after drinking." [71]

In November 2006, while investigating the shooting of a homeless man in an alley behind several fraternity houses at Oregon State University in Corvallis, police found more than two dozen guns — .22-caliber rifles and 12- and 20-gauge shotguns — at the Alpha Gamma Rho house and in members' cars — including the weapon used to shoot the homeless man. [72]

about . . . whether they should have patrol rifles. Obviously, I don't think they're necessary. We can be on those campuses within five or six minutes. We're highly trained."

But Northeastern spokesman Matthew McDonald said the vast majority of active shooter situations are over in less than five minutes, and "a quarter of them in less than two minutes. Proximity — with our department and officers being located on campus — is critical to response time." [6]

Deisinger defends military-grade equipment for campus cops. "We're talking about front-line officers and detectives being able to respond and neutralize threats," such as the incident at Ohio State in November when campus police killed the suspect in a knife attack. "So the best weapon [to do that] changes with the scenario. In some scenarios, it might be a handgun at close range. But for down the hallway or across an open campus yard, a rifle is a much better weapon."

Besides, he says, civilians can obtain military-grade weapons at their local sporting goods store. "So if civilians, including the potential perpetrators, can have access to those weapons," he says, it would be "foolish" to prevent campus police officers from having those same weapons.

With many students living off campus in nearby communities, jurisdictional issues can further complicate campus policing. "It's very challenging," for campus police officers, said Robin Hattersley, executive editor of *Campus Safety* magazine. "I don't think it's straightforward at all." [7]

As of 2010-11, most campuses officers were conducting joint patrols with local law enforcement, according to the Department of Justice, and 70 percent of campus security agencies have written agreements on coordinating with city law enforcement in handling off-campus threats and crime. [8] The Major City Police Chiefs Association and the Bureau of Justice encourage such coordination. [9]

However, some off-campus actions by campus police have led to community tensions. Protests erupted, for instance, after a white University of Cincinnati police officer in July 2015 fatally shot an unarmed black man after a traffic stop about a half-mile from campus. The officer, Ray Tensing, was fired and charged with homicide for killing Samuel DuBose, 43, whom Tensing had pulled over for missing a front license plate. Tensing's trial last November ended in a mistrial, but the prosecutor has said he will retry the former officer. [10]

— Christina L. Lyons

[1] Brian A. Reaves, "Campus Law Enforcement, 2011-12," U.S. Department of Justice, January 2015,http://tinyurl.com/hs7ul3d.

[2] "Despite 'die-in' protest, PSU approves arming campus police," Fox 12 Oregon, Dec. 11, 2014, http://tinyurl.com/hmr2vv5.

[3] Andrew Theen, " 'Disarm PSU' group stages walkout, protest at Portland State University," *The Oregonian*, May 10, 2016, http://tinyurl.com/jzpzn8k.

[4] Anna Merriman, "Princeton Univ. officers to get access to guns for active shooter emergencies," NJ.com, Oct. 13, 2015, http://tinyurl.com/jm6gne3.

[5] Kay Brian Melear and Mark St. Louis, "Concealed Carry Legislation and Changing Campus Policies," in *College in the Crosshairs: An Administrative Perspective on Prevention of Gun Violence* (2015), pp. 70-71.

[6] Jake New, "Big(ger) Guns on Campus," *Inside Higher Ed*, Dec. 10, 2015, http://tinyurl.com/hqlcmv4.

[7] Susan Svrluga, Nick Anderson and Mark Berman, "Should college police officers be armed and challenging people off campus?" *The Washington Post*, July 29, 2015, http://tinyurl.com/hretajj.

[8] Reaves, *op. cit.*, p. 1.

[9] William J. Bratton and James H. Burch II, "Campus Security Guidelines: Recommended Operational Policies for Local and Campus Law Enforcement Agencies," Bureau of Justice Assistance, Office of Justice Programs, U.S. Department of Justice, September, 2009, p. 71, http://tinyurl.com/hh45a7b.

[10] Kevin Williams, Wesley Lowery and Mark Berman, "University of Cincinnati police officer who shot man during traffic stop charged with murder," *The Washington Post*, July 29, 2015, http://tinyurl.com/h8o22d5; "Sam DuBose shooting: Cincinnati prosecutor to retry Ray Tensing," CBS News, Nov. 22, 2016, http://tinyurl.com/jk6a73q.

Campus-Carry Laws

The April 2007 shooting at Virginia Tech reignited the debate about firearms on campus. [73]

The night after the shooting, Chris Brown, a political science student at the University of North Texas, formed Students for Concealed Carry on Campus to push for relaxing the rules against concealed weapons on campus. Gun-rights organizations such as Gun Owners of America also urged universities to change their policies. [74]

"No one can say for sure if allowing students and faculty members to carry arms would have prevented the rampage on Monday," said Philip Van Cleave, president of the pro-gun Virginia Citizens Defense League. "But they wouldn't die like sheep, at least, but more like a wolf with some fangs, able to fight back." [75]

The Brady Center to Prevent Gun Violence, a nonprofit group that advocates for gun control, responded: "If the educational community does not respond, this type of legislation may well be enacted in more and more states." [76]

The following November, Students for Concealed Carry sponsored 110 "empty holster" demonstrations on public campuses nationwide. "Historically speaking, there hasn't been a single no-gun sign, law or campus policy that has saved a single life," said a press release announcing the protests. [77]

The group's efforts gained momentum after the 2008 shooting at Northern Illinois University by Kazmierczak, who had bought two empty magazines and a holster through the website of the same company where Cho had bought one of his guns. The owner later offered student discounts on more than 5,400 kinds of firearms. [78]

After the Illinois shooting, the NRA adopted model campus-carry legislation,

Officials Struggle to Prevent Campus Massacres

Privacy and concealed-carry laws make the job harder.

Those on all sides of the debate on whether to allow concealed firearms on campus agree on one thing: They want to prevent another shooting like the 2007 massacre of 32 people at Virginia Tech University in Blacksburg, Va., by a student with a history of depression.

But threat assessment experts, college counselors and many professors say legalizing firearms isn't the solution. They say it only diverts attention from the more complicated factors involved in keeping students safe during a time when more and more college students are reporting mental health concerns.

"I never believed the status for or against concealed carry would make that much of a difference" in deterring threats, says Gene Deisinger, managing partner and co-founder of SIGMA Threat Management Associates, an Alexandria, Va., firm that provides training on violence prevention. He says it doesn't matter in general whether any individual can carry a gun legally. "My question is, does *this* person pose a threat?"

Still, as James DiTulio, director of Western Illinois University's counseling center, says, "Predicting someone is going to become violent, that is very hard to do."

Both he and Deisinger, who also is a mental health expert, worry about making firearms more available on campus without improving mental health services.

A 2015 survey of college counseling centers found that 47.3 percent of students seeking counseling are diagnosed with anxiety, 40.1 percent suffer from depression and 26.1 percent were already taking psychotropic medications.[1] Those percentages were up from 2007, when 36.7 percent of students were diagnosed with anxiety, 39.4 percent with depression and 24 percent were taking medications.[2]

Christopher Corbett, president of the American College Counseling Association, warns that research does not show a direct connection between mental illness and gun violence. He says he is far more concerned about the "huge number of people" on campus who are stressed and depressed and "thinking about hurting themselves all the time."

Lucinda Roy, who was chair of the Virginia Tech English Department before the massacre, warns that while professors see increasing despair among students, "mental illness of itself is not aggressive," and all people with mental illnesses are not "homicidal maniacs."

Other counselors and safety experts agree, and note that those assessing a potential threat must examine behavior that might indicate an individual is troubled and needs attention — either from mental health counselors or law enforcement officials — in order to prevent the person from harming himself or others.

The Virginia Tech shooter, Seung-Hui Cho, had written "dark, very threatening" material in his creative writing classes, sometimes had exhibited "bizarre" behavior and had a history of depression before enrolling at the university, according to Dr. Bella Sood, a psychiatrist at Virginia Commonwealth University who was appointed by then Gov. Tim Kaine to assess what happened prior to the shooting.[3] Before the shooting, Roy had recommended that Cho seek counseling, and she reached out to various campus administrators. Other students and teachers also had expressed concerns about his behavior, she recalled in her 2009 book, *No Right to Remain Silent*. But communication among campus officials was uncoordinated, and the university had no procedures for reporting concerns to one centralized resource. A misunderstanding of privacy laws also interfered with information sharing, Deisinger says.

Further, disability and privacy laws barred Roy from forcing Cho to seek counseling. And while later reports revealed his history of depression, institutions are barred from taking action against a student based *only* on a known or perceived mental health issue.[4]

called the Campus Personal Protection Act.[79] That year students opposed to loosening restrictions formed the Campaign to Keep Guns off Campus. The Association of State Colleges and Universities and the International Association of Campus Law Enforcement also opposed campus-carry policies.[80]

Between 2008 and 2010, more than a dozen states introduced campus-carry bills.[81] Most were defeated, but several states began to reconsider as courts began to favor gun rights. The Supreme Court's 2008 ruling in *D.C. v. Heller* striking down Washington, D.C.'s law barring gun ownership, for instance, overturned the high

court's 1939 ruling in *U.S. v. Miller*, that the Second Amendment referred only to militia members.[82]

In 2011, the Virginia Supreme Court upheld George Mason University's gun ban, while the Oregon Court of Appeals overturned the Oregon University System's ban on guns. In March 2012, the Colorado Supreme Court ruled that the University of Colorado's policy banning guns from campus violated the state's concealed-carry law.[83] More recently, a Florida district court of appeals in 2015 upheld the University of Florida's ban on guns on its campus and in dorm rooms.[84]

After the 2012 massacre at the Sandy Hook Elementary School, both sides of the gun control debate ramped up their lobbying efforts, and President Barack Obama in 2013 ordered that the Centers for Disease Control and Prevention resume research on the causes of gun violence. But Congress repeatedly rejected his request for funds for such research.[85]

In 2013 at least 19 states considered legislation to allow concealed carry on college and university campuses. By then, 35 states had adopted "shall issue" laws, requiring states to grant concealed-carry permits to gun owners who meet minimum qualifications. Almost all those

Roy believes communication on the Virginia Tech campus has been much improved since then.

"The support services [today] are much more visible and much more explicit," Roy says. "You know when you need to go to someone, and if you're sensible you know when you are out of your depth, and you try to get people in to help."

Universities and colleges began improving threat assessment processes after a 2010 federal study concluded that between 1900 and 2008, 272 violent incidents were reported on or near college campuses, and the perpetrators had "demonstrated behaviors and/or communicated information to others that indicated that they were on a pathway toward violence." But, in many cases, no one observing the behaviors knew whom they could or should tell, according to the report. [5]

Now, "it is highly likely that a centralized process would enable the gathering of much of the available information" about an individual, such as reports from other students, colleagues, professors or other administrators, says Deisinger, who was hired as deputy chief of police and director of threat management services for Virginia Tech after the shooting. He also helped develop guidelines for other colleges on how to devise threat assessment plans and teams, which include representatives from various departments and designate a single person to collect information, alerts and reports about troubled students.

New concealed-carry laws specifically bar universities from knowing the identities of gun owners who are legally bringing weapons onto campus. In Colorado, for instance, only a law enforcement officer or judge, if they have a reason to be concerned about an individual's behavior, can access that information, says Pat O'Rourke, vice president and university counsel at the University of Colorado.

Sue Riseling, executive director of the International Association

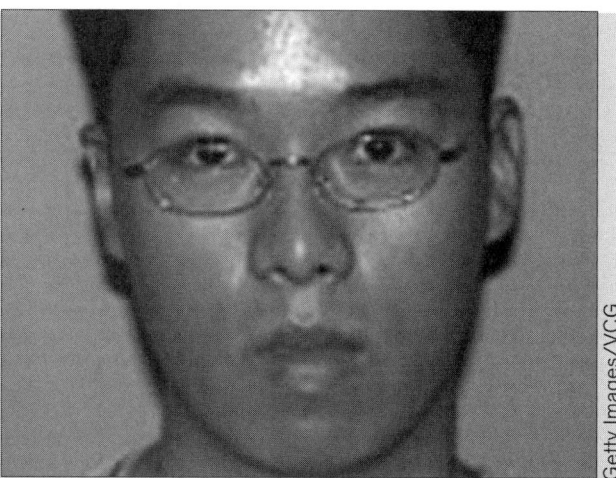

Seung-Hui Cho, 23, an undergraduate at Virginia Tech, killed 32 students and professors at the school on April 16, 2007, before turning his gun on himself.

of Campus Law Enforcement Administrators, says concealed-carry laws make safety officers' jobs even harder. She warns: "What you need in order to carry" out a shooting is an ability and an opportunity. Campus-carry laws now provide individuals with the ability, she says.

— *Christina L. Lyons*

[1] David R. Reetz *et al.*, "Annual Survey," Association for University and College Counseling Center Directors, 2015, p. 14, http://tinyurl.com/zxa437t.

[2] Robert Rando, Victor Barr and Chuy Jesse Aros, "Annual Survey," Association for University and College Counseling Center Directors, 2007, p. 31, http://tinyurl.com/grhk38s.

[3] See Sandy Hausman, "Lessons Learned at Virginia Tech: What Went Wrong?" WVTF Public Radio, April 13, 2015, http://tinyurl.com/hhcy2qs.

[4] Tim Weldon, "Campus Violence and Mental Health: Protecting Students and Students' Rights a Delicate Issue," The Council of State Governments, Oct. 20, 2009, http://tinyurl.com/j5aozml.

[5] John H. Dunkle and Brian J. Mistler, "Risk and Threat Assessment," in *College in the Crosshairs: An Administrative Perspective on Prevention of Gun Violence* (2015), pp. 123-141.

laws exempted schools, colleges and public buildings from places where a concealed firearm could be carried. But that was about to change in some states. [86]

In 2013, Kansas legalized concealed carry on campuses but allowed colleges and universities to prohibit firearms in buildings with "adequate security measures." That law is scheduled to take effect this July. Arkansas also enacted a law in 2013 allowing faculty to carry firearms unless an institution's governing board specifically bars it. [87] In 2015, California reaffirmed its ban on concealed weapons at public colleges and universities.

In 2016, Liberty University expanded its concealed-carry firearms policy to allow handguns to be kept in safes inside dormitories. [88] ∎

CURRENT SITUATION

States Act

As the spring legislative season ramps up, lawmakers and university officials

are again preparing to consider whether to permit concealed firearms on campus. Several measures are expected to be more likely to be adopted in light of GOP election victories in 2016.

In Florida, for example, voters elected nine House members to the state Senate who support loosening gun restrictions, and voted out Republican Sen. Miguel de La Portilla, the Senate Judiciary Committee chairman, who blocked a campus-carry measure last year. The new chairman, Republican Sen. Greg Steube, had sponsored last session's bill as a House member. [89]

And in states where legislatures have

begun to loosen laws, lawmakers hope to go further. For example, Tennessee state Rep. Andy Holt, who sponsored the law that allows faculty to carry guns, said — echoing Trump — "ultimately, I would like to see 100 percent removal of all gun-free zones in public places." [90]

Members of the Campaign to Keep Guns off Campus say some legislatures have limited their involvement in the debate. In Florida House hearings last year, for instance, witnesses were limited to one minute each, says Kathryn Grant, director of state affairs for the Campaign to Keep Guns Off Campus. "Without fully vetting a policy like this, how can anyone come to a conclusion responsibly?" she asks.

More than 420 colleges and universities in 42 states have joined the Campaign to Keep Guns Off Campus. Parents also have begun to make their wishes known. The Texas chapter of Moms Demand Action for Gun Sense in America, lobbied against that state's campus-carry law, saying, "College life is already rife with academic pressures, alcohol and drug abuse; forcing schools to introduce guns into the mix is dangerous and doesn't make sense." [91]

Meanwhile, a fight is expected in Kansas over the 2013 law colleges are expected to implement in July. Many opponents contend the expense of installing metal detectors and security guards at every entrance — which the law requires in order for a gun to be barred from a building — is prohibitive. One community college estimated that would cost $20 million. [92]

Yet, given the long-held Republican majorities in the state Legislature, the policy is unlikely to change. Bob Beatty, a political science professor at Washburn University, said Kansas lawmakers support the idea of "allow guns everywhere, and if somebody does start shooting the place up, hopefully someone will have a gun and shoot them." [93]

But Newbern, of Students for Concealed Carry, says, "Lawmakers are seeing that campus concealed carry isn't

causing blood to flow in the street the way the opposition makes it sound. And so they're like, why are we telling these young adults they can't do what they're allowed to do off campus?"

Nevertheless, he says he doubts many Ohio universities will opt into that state's new law. Ohio State University President Michael Drake has said only trained professionals should carry firearms on campus. [94]

The OSU attack last fall prompted gun-rights supporters to raise concerns about terrorism, since the White House announced that the attacker, a Somali refugee, may have been motivated "by a desire to carry out an act of terrorism." [95]

Shortly afterward, an essay on the NRA website *Bearing Arms* said, "Islamic terrorist groups, most notably ISIS, have called upon Muslims in the West to carry out terrorist attacks against soft targets using knives and vehicles. School and college campuses are among the easiest targets available, as they contain high concentrations of people made unarmed and defenseless because of shortsighted state laws that have made most campuses 'gun-free zones.' " [96]

Courts Act

The lawsuit by three University of Texas professors against the state and university is pending, although a federal judge in August rejected their plea to temporarily block the law. The professors said they fear "robust academic debate" won't happen for fear it could erupt into "gun violence." [97]

The Texas law directs institutions to devise "reasonable rules" to implement the law without actually prohibiting campus carry, says Jeffery L. Graves, associate vice president for legal affairs at the university's Austin campus. Balancing the law's directives with a low desire on campus for handguns, the university barred guns in laboratories with hazardous chemicals due to safety concerns, he says. As in many other states, Texas law

allows the university to bar firearms from sporting events and buildings hosting pre-K-12 programs.

But the university did not bar firearms from classrooms. "That would prohibit the biggest demographic — students — from carrying on campus," Graves says, noting that most students commute to campus and take public transportation because parking is limited. Without a car to store their weapon in while in class, he says, barring guns from the classroom would mean barring them from campus.

Newbern, of Students for Concealed Carry, says logistics make it difficult to permit guns in some areas on a campus and not in others. For instance, several states require concealed firearms to be stored in locked vehicles while on campus, he says, making them unavailable for self-protection.

Some professors are concerned that students visiting their offices might be armed. Gonzalez at the University of Houston says some students tend to get angry during advisory sessions with a professor — sometimes to the point where the professor is tempted to call security. "Students are under a lot of stress, and especially when they are being advised," she says.

The University of Texas permits faculty and staff with "sole occupant offices" to bar concealed firearms provided they give "oral notice" and arrange to meet gun-carrying students elsewhere. The policy also bans weapons during formal student or faculty disciplinary hearings. [98]

But Newbern says his group will file a complaint if any Texas professor otherwise bars firearms from their offices. "Professors can't willy nilly ban firearms in their offices," he says. "Professors don't own their offices. The state owns that property."

Shooting Clubs

Some gun-control advocates worry about a recent surge in interest in

Continued on p. 90

At Issue:

Would legalizing guns on campus make colleges safer?

MICHAEL NEWBERN
*ASSISTANT DIRECTOR OF PUBLIC RELATIONS,
STUDENTS FOR CONCEALED CARRY*

WRITTEN FOR *CQ RESEARCHER*, JANUARY 2017

O ur best and brightest congregate on college campuses
to solve some of the world's most pressing problems
and to prepare to do the same after they leave school. We
want them to be able to focus on their work free of worry for
their safety.

College campuses generally are safer than the areas surrounding them. Campus crime rates are extremely low, and
not just when compared to the general population. But this
isn't just about college campuses.

We don't spend all of our day on campus. We spend part
of the day, including early mornings and late nights, off campus, where criminals have the upper hand. That's why any
college safety program encourages students to travel in numbers at those times. And when we ban concealed guns on
campus, we disarm lawfully licensed students, faculty or staff
members from the time they leave home until they return.

The question for us isn't whether legalizing guns on campus would make campus safer; it's answering why we're treated differently on college campuses? If we're lawfully permitted
to carry our licensed, concealed handgun to the movie theater
on Friday night, why are we not allowed to carry it to class
on Friday before the movie? If we're lawfully permitted to
carry our handgun to the public municipal library, why are
we not allowed to do so at the public university library? If
we're lawfully permitted to carry our licensed, concealed
handgun to the mall food court, why are we not permitted to
do so in the campus dining hall? Why are we treated differently on campus? Is it because we're students?

Research conducted by economist John Lott Jr., author of
More Guns, Less Crime, a has found that gun licensees 21 to
25 years of age do not commit weapons crimes at higher
rates than the general population. That can't be it.

Is it because we're somehow more prone to violence on
campus? The University of Texas at Austin's campus-carry
working group published a report showing that not a single
intentional act of violence has ever been carried out by a
licensee with a firearm on a college campus. That can't be
it either.

So, if campus carry may or may not make a campus safer,
but definitely won't make it less safe, what justification is
there to ban it?

ANDY PELOSI
*EXECUTIVE DIRECTOR, CAMPAIGN TO
KEEP GUNS OFF CAMPUS*

WRITTEN FOR *CQ RESEARCHER*, JANUARY 2017

t he vast majority of colleges want to keep campuses gun
free for good reason, yet we are witnessing a pro-gun
movement that promotes legislation to force colleges and
universities to allow loaded, concealed guns on campus.

Our postsecondary institutions are some of the safest places
in the country. For example, a 2001 U.S. Department of Education study found that the overall homicide rate at postsecondary
education institutions was less than 1 person per 100,000 students. By comparison, the homicide rate in the United States
overall was 5.7 people per 100,000 persons, and 14.1 per
100,000 for persons ages 17 to 29. A 2005 Department of Justice study found that 93 percent of violent crimes that victim-
ize college students occur off campus.

The early-adult years are among the most unstable periods
in a person's life. Several circumstances coalesce to create
high-stress situations for college and university students. These
situations are far likelier to become dangerous, and even fatal,
when firearms are present. Among 18- to 24-year-olds, suicide
is the second-leading cause of death, according to the Centers
for Disease Control and Prevention. Other factors characteristic
of college students — such as increasing rates of sexual assault,
drug and alcohol abuse, impulsivity and mental health problems
— are widely recognized vulnerabilities that, combined with
an increased presence of firearms, could increase the risk of
violence.

Allowing concealed weapons on campus would not only
increase the risk of violence but also impose an unfunded
mandate on colleges, which would need to purchase new
equipment, hire more security and provide training. In addition,
campus law enforcement opposes campus-carry laws, and
most permit holders lack the frequent and ongoing tactical
training needed to use deadly force in the event of an active
shooter. And legislators are not in the best position to assess
the health and safety needs of every campus community.

Finally, supporters of guns on campus often cite the Second
Amendment as the cornerstone for their right to carry concealed
weapons on campus. The late U.S. Supreme Court Justice
Antonin Scalia, in writing the opinion for *District of Columbia
v. Heller*, which backed the right to possess firearms in the
home for self-defense, went out of his way to reaffirm the
legality of laws restricting carrying weapons in sensitive places
such as schools.

Continued from p. 88

collegiate shooting teams. "We literally have way more students interested than we can handle," said Steve Goldstein, one of MIT's pistol coaches.

According to the NRA, nearly 300 U.S. colleges and universities have shooting programs. The National Shooting Sports Foundation, a firearms lobbying group, has awarded more than $1 million in grants since 2009 to start about 80 programs. [99]

Meanwhile, Liberty University plans to open a shooting range on campus next fall as part of its "commitment to promote gun ownership and firearm sports." [100]

One University of Delaware student told FoxNews.com that classmates think club members are "crazy gun kids" who intend to "shoot up the school." [101]

Stewart of Florida Students for Campus Carry is on the University of Florida Action Shooting Team, whose membership fluctuates from about eight to 20. As a team member, he says, he trains regularly and feels he is better trained in firearm tactics than most citizens and thus could handle a violent situation.

"So I see it as my duty" to carry in areas where it is permitted, he says.

Limiting Research

Hemenway of the Harvard Injury Control Research Center says the 1997 law that clamped down on CDC research on gun violence continues to limit research on the topic.

The American Medical Association urged Congress last year to resume gun research funding, but House Republicans rebuffed Democrats' efforts to remove the budget amendment that has frozen most research into gun violence since 1997. [102]

Nevertheless, the Harvard center, with limited funds, is analyzing the level of gun training needed to get a concealed carry permit; when, how and where gun holders' weapons are stolen; and

the connection, if any, between the number of guns, gun laws and killings of and by police.

Since May 2015, Garen Wintemute, a professor at the University of California, Davis, has been leading a study on whether gun owners with a history of alcohol and drug convictions are more likely to commit violence than gun owners without such a history. Funding for that research, provided by the National Institutes of Health, continues through April. [103]

California has appropriated $5 million over five years for a new firearm violence research center at UC Davis. The center, announced by UC President Janet Napolitano in August, plans to offer grants for research projects and increase philanthropic support for such research. [104] ■

OUTLOOK

Complicated Issue

Gun rights supporters hailed Trump's election as a victory for measures to loosen restrictions on guns.

For instance, Trump has said he supports a national right to carry concealed firearms, enabling those with concealed-handgun permits in one state to be able to carry firearms in all other states, potentially enabling more students and visitors at university campuses eligible to carry. [105]

Trump supports allowing adults at elementary and secondary schools to carry guns. But he cannot unilaterally dismantle all gun-free zones, said George Washington University law professor Robert Cottrol, because the zones were established by various federal, state and local laws. "School gun-free zones would have to be changed by an act of Congress," Cottrol said. [106]

Still, others believe much more research needs to be done on the effect of campus-carry laws. "What you need is

a lot of studies looking at the issue from different angles," says Hemenway, of the Harvard Injury Control Research Center.

"We need to bring in experts" in education, campus security and mental health, along with students and parents, to thoroughly review the effect of campus-carry policies, says Grant, of the Campaign to Keep Guns Off Campus.

It is unclear what effect campus carry will have on the ability of public universities to retain faculty, as well as students, Grant says. Some students might want to switch to a private campus that does not allow guns, she says, but for many students a public university is the most affordable.

"This year and next year these campuses will go to conceal carry [rules] . . . and I really hope it keeps people safe. But in the next five to seven years, the buildup of [firearms] will be there," says Riseling of the International Association of Campus Law Enforcement Administrators. She fears an increase in both suicides and homicides.

"This is a multilayered issue and it's complicated," she says. "Campuses have these unique environments" with a higher concentration of young people than are typically found in other communities.

Deisinger, the former director of threat management at Virginia Tech, says he has seen the debate over gun control fluctuate over the years, and even the debate over campus carry, which arose 20 years ago but was drowned out by other issues. "We'll continue to talk about these issues . . . but . . . it will continue to be largely unresolved just because there are competing goals, and what satisfies one interest compromises another."

Lott, of the Crime Prevention Research Center, says, "As more states adopt these laws, . . . people are going to see that the concerns are not that credible. Gradually more and more states will adopt them and the arguments will become weaker."

Kreuter of North Carolina says he has seen mass shootings become "more inevitable" than he would like, but says instead of focusing on guns, greater attention should be paid to mental health care, both on campuses and in the general population.

"I don't want to work at a place where students are carrying guns," he says. Nevertheless, "if students are potentially armed, then I'll be armed as well. That's my resignation, in part, to where this has gone." ■

Notes

[1] Emanuella Grinberg, Shimon Prokupecz and Holly Yan, "Ohio State University: Attacker killed, 11 hospitalized after campus attack," CNN.com, Nov. 28, 2016, http://tinyurl.com/z739xgz/.

[2] Jessie Balmert, "After OSU attack, should Ohio allowed concealed carry on campus?" *The Cincinnati Enquirer*, Nov. 30, 2016, http://tinyurl.com/hzrreu2.

[3] Faith Karimi and Jethro Mullen, "3 shot at Florida State University before gunman killed by police," CNN.com, Nov. 20, 2014, http://tinyurl.com/kl2eh88.

[4] For more information, see Christina L. Lyons, "Reforming Juvenile Justice," *CQ Researcher*, Sept. 11, 2015, pp. 745-768.

[5] Lauren Carroll, "Trump said he would require schools to allow guns, Clinton says," *Politifact.com*, Nov. 1, 2016, http://tinyurl.com/zbmd6ot.

[6] "Guns on Campus: Overview," National Conference of State Legislatures, May 31, 2016, http://tinyurl.com/p5oey34; Jackie Borchardt, "Gov. John Kasich signs bill to allow concealed carry at colleges, daycares, plus 16 other bills," Cleveland.com, Dec. 19, 2016, http://tinyurl.com/gorwtep.

[7] "Guns on Campus: Overview," *op. cit.*; Mark Abadi, "Professors at Tennessee public colleges will soon be able to carry guns on campus," *Business Insider*, May 2, 2016, http://tinyurl.com/hjzn7jw.

[8] Adam Tamburin, "Tennessee colleges scramble as law allowing guns on campus nears," *The Tennessean*, June 17, 2016, http://tinyurl.com/hhr6c7d.

[9] Matthew Watkins and Madeline Conway, "Only One Private Texas University Adopting Campus Carry," *The Texas Tribune*, July 29, 2016, http://tinyurl.com/gqt6wfb.

[10] "LU changes concealed weapons rules for permitted people," *The News and Advance*

(Lynchburg, Va.), April 3, 2013, http://tinyurl.com/d2d9qxo.

[11] Christine Hauser, "Virginia Gunman Identified as a Student," *The New York Times*, April 17, 2007, http://tinyurl.com/jtzpwqz.

[12] "Report of the February 14, 2008 Shootings at Northern Illinois University," Northern Illinois University, undated, p. xv, http://tinyurl.com/gwwjaag.

[13] "Sandy Hook shooting: What happened?" CNN, December 2014, http://tinyurl.com/nmsmygs.

[14] "NRA: 'Only Way To Stop A Bad Guy With A Gun Is With A Good Guy With A Gun,' " CBS DC, Dec. 21, 2012, http://tinyurl.com/lx5bde8.

[15] Julie Turkewitz, "Oregon Gunman Smiled, Then Fired, Student Says," *The New York Times*, Oct. 9, 2015, http://tinyurl.com/hdlvqrx.

[16] J. Pete Blair and Katherine W. Schweit, "A Study of Active Shooter Incidents in the United States Between 2000 and 2013," Texas State University and Federal Bureau of Investigation, U.S. Department of Justice, 2014, pp. 5, 13-15, http://tinyurl.com/gll8qpz.

[17] "Analysis of School Shootings — Appendix: School Shootings in America 2013-2015," Everytown for Gun Safety, 2016, http://tinyurl.com/hsu24vn.

[18] *District of Columbia v. Dick Anthony Heller*, 554 U.S. __(2008), http://tinyurl.com/gtmtd8x.

[19] See Justin Doubleday, "Students Oppose Concealed-Carry Gun Policy on Campuses, Survey Finds," *The Chronicle of Higher Education*, Sept. 11, 2013, http://tinyurl.com/j6eoded; Ryan Patten, Matthew O. Thomas, James C. Wada, "Packing Heat: Attitudes Regarding Concealed Weapons on College Campuses," *American Journal of Criminal Justice*, December 2013, http://tinyurl.com/zmv6uj9; Aaron Bartula and Kendra Bowen, "University and College Officials' Perceptions of Open Carry on College Campus," *Justice Policy Journal*, Fall 2015, http://tinyurl.com/h9osowy.

[20] Utah Code Ann. Section 53-5A-102(2); Colo. Rev. Stat. §18-72 203(1).

[21] Bill Chappell, " 'Campus Carry' Gun Bill Is Vetoed in Georgia, With A Lengthy Explanation," NPR, May 4, 2016, http://tinyurl.com/gqzpdl6; "New stun gun law in Georgia electrifies concealed-carry debate," FoxNews.com, Aug. 15, 2016, http://tinyurl.com/hu8gal5.

[22] John R. Lott Jr., "Concealed Carry Permit Holders Across the United States: 2016," available at SSRN: https://ssrn.com/abstract=2814691.

[23] Danny McAuliffe and Joseph Zeballos, "Professors weigh in on campus carry legislation," FSUNews.com, Oct. 28, 2015, http://tinyurl.com/glyrtva.

[24] Abhay Aneja, John J. Donohue III, Alexandra Zhang, "The Impact of Right to Carry Laws and the NRC Report: The Latest Lessons for the Empirical Evaluation of Law and Policy," National Bureau of Economic Research, Dec. 1, 2014, http://tinyurl.com/hh9r4tg.

[25] David Hemenway and Elizabeth P. Nolan, "The scientific agreement on firearm issues," Injury Prevention, Oct. 6, 2016, http://tinyurl.com/hgu3qcv.

[26] David Hemenway and Sara J. Solnick, "The epidemiology of self-defense gun use: Evidence from the National Crime Victimization Surveys 2007-2011," *Preventive Medicine*, April 21, 2015, http://tinyurl.com/hlk2k52.

[27] Julie A. Gavran, "Concealed Handguns on Campus: A Multi-Year Crime Study," *Visions: The Journal of Applied Research for the Association of Florida Colleges*, 2017.

[28] Daniel W. Webster, John J. Donohue III, Louis Klarevas *et al.*, "Firearms on College Campuses: Research Evidence and Policy Implications," Johns Hopkins Bloomberg School of Public Health, Oct. 15, 2016, http://tinyurl.com/jtqnumz.

[29] For more information, see Barbara Mantel, "Campus Sexual Assault," *CQ Researcher*, Oct. 31, 2014, pp. 913-936; Lloyd Dunkelberger, "Campus gun bill advances in Senate," *Herald-Tribune*, Oct. 20, 2015, http://tinyurl.com/gqvt3pl.

[30] Eugene Scott, "Trump: Armed teachers could have stopped Oregon massacre," CNN.com, Oct. 4, 2015, http://tinyurl.com/ncnswvk.

[31] Joel Ebert, "Bill to allow guns on Tennessee college campuses heads to Haslam," *The Tennessean*, April 20, 2016, http://tinyurl.com/h8yrp3m.

[32] Richard Locker and Joel Ebert, "Haslam allows controversial guns on campus to become law," *The Tennessean*, May 2, 2016, http://tinyurl.com/jrm62hw.

[33] Joel Ebert, "Bill to allow guns on college campuses advances," *The Tennessean*, March 29, 2016, http://tinyurl.com/zjs4zoo.

[34] Amanda Iacone, "Va. bill would allow college faculty to carry guns, negating UVa regulation," *The Daily Progress*, Jan. 12, 2012, http://tinyurl.com/z83qpk3.

[35] Dorman, *op. cit.*

[36] Halley Holloway, "University of Tennessee staff mixed about guns on campus," ABC Wate.com, May 3, 2016, http://tinyurl.com/gtg5cxp; Tamburin, *op. cit.*

[37] Nick DeSantis, "Idaho State University Professor Accidentally Shoots Self in Foot in Class," *The Chronicle of Higher Education*, Sept. 4, 2014, http://tinyurl.com/zsvcll4.

[38] "Joint Statement Opposing 'Campus Carry' Laws," Academe Blog, Nov. 12, 2015, http://tinyurl.com/hcxu7nu.

[39] Sam Zeff, "Kansas Campuses Prepare For Guns In Classrooms," National Public Radio, March 22, 2016, http://tinyurl.com/jzd8snw.

[40] Andrew Kreighbaum, "Harry Edwards Cuts Texas Ties Over Campus Carry," Inside Higher Ed, Aug. 29, 2016, http://tinyurl.com/z6had34; Minkah Makalani, "The Many Costs of Campus Carry," The New Yorker, Oct. 15, 2016, http://tinyurl.com/gmn5bom; Glass, Moore, and Carter v. UT, Texas, July 7, 2016, http://tinyurl.com/h5sbxoz.

[41] Elliot Hannon, "University of Houston Faculty Devises Pointers on How to Avoid Getting shot by Armed Students," The Slatest, Feb. 23, 2016, http://tinyurl.com/zb824oz.

[42] Ema O'Connor, "Texas LGBT Students Say They Don't Feel Safe Now That People Can Carry Guns On Campus," BuzzFeed, Aug. 29, 2016, http://tinyurl.com/jo3up2x.

[43] Clayton E. Cramer, "Guns on Campus: A History," Academic Questions, December 2014, http://tinyurl.com/hzhqphf.

[44] "Signs of the Times," Harvard Magazine, January-February 2017, http://tinyurl.com/hqv7xsa.

[45] Clayton E. Cramer, Concealed Weapon Laws of The Early Republic: Dueling, Southern Violence, and Moral Reform (1999), pp. 2-3, http://tinyurl.com/hxpydfw; Saul Cornell, A Well-Regulated Militia: The Founding Fathers and the Origins of Gun Control in America (2006), pp. 142-143, http://tinyurl.com/z65dm6y.

[46] "Meeting Minutes of University of Virginia Board of Visitors, 4-5 Oct. 1824, 4 October 1824," in "Papers of Thomas Jefferson: Early Access," http://tinyurl.com/jom4od3.

[47] "The Laws of Yale College in New Haven, Connecticut, for the Undergraduate Students of the Academical Department," Yale College, 1868, p. 13, http://tinyurl.com/jj4ux8n.

[48] Carlos Santos, "Bad Boys: Tales of the University's tumultuous early years," UVA Magazine, Winter 2013, http://uvamagazine.org/articles/bad_boys.

[49] Philip Lee, "The Curious Life of In Loco Parentis at American Universities," Higher Education in Review, 8, 2011, p. 67.

[50] Weston T. Thompson and Terry L. Birdwhistell, "The University of Kentucky: A Look Back," University of Kentucky Library, 1998, http://tinyurl.com/zsahcb7.

[51] Barbara Mantel, "Gun Control," CQ Researcher, March 8, 2013, p. 13.

[52] Adam Winkler, "When the NRA Promoted Gun Control," The Huffington Post, Dec. 3, 2011, http://tinyurl.com/cexveaz.

[53] For background, see Peter Katel, "Crime on Campus," CQ Researcher, Feb. 4, 2011, pp. 97-120.

[54] "Ex-marine Charles Whitman shoots at victims from the University of Texas tower in 1966," Daily News, reprinted Aug. 1, 2016, http://tinyurl.com/jl5pa8f; "Press Conference: Report to the Governor Medical Aspects Charles J. Whitman Catastrophe," Sept. 8, 1966, p. 4, http://tinyurl.com/ham5dt7.

[55] "Press Conference," ibid., p. 4; David Eagleman, "The Brain on Trial," The Atlantic, July/August 2011, http://tinyurl.com/cync42y.

[56] The Gun Control Act of 1968, Public Law 90-618, http://tinyurl.com/jenkjuq.

[57] Ian Wilhelm, "Ripples From a Protest Past," The Chronicle of Higher Education, April 17, 2016, http://tinyurl.com/jn8rb87.

[58] Lee, op. cit., p. 70; Katel, op. cit.

[59] "Constructive Changes to Ease Campus Tensions," National Association of State Universities and Land-Grant Colleges, 1970, pp. 50-54, http://eric.ed.gov/?id=ED035384.

[60] Carlos Illescas, "Court tosses CU gun ban," The Denver Post, April 15, 2010, http://tinyurl.com/zldlk64.

[61] Joe LaPage, "Nunn Sued on UK Defense," The Lexington Herald, May 7, 1970.

[62] "Our History," Clery Center for Security on Campus, undated, http://clerycenter.org/our-history.

[63] Josh Richman and Mark Emmons, "Stockton shooting: 25 years later, city can't forget its worst day," The Mercury News, Jan. 16, 2014, http://tinyurl.com/jkq8gn7.

[64] For background, see Kathy Koch, "School Violence," CQ Researcher, Oct. 9, 1998, pp. 881-904; and "Zero Tolerance for School Violence, CQ Researcher, March 10, 2000, pp. 185-208.

[65] Christine Jamieson, "Gun Violence research: History of the federal funding freeze," Psychological Science Agenda, February 2013, http://tinyurl.com/pvcut6f.

[66] Ibid.

[67] "A look at campus crime," The Chronicle of Higher Education, June 9, 2000, http://tinyurl.com/zvlcbvr.

[68] Carlos Illescas and Monte Whaley, "Court tosses CU gun ban," The Denver Post, April 15, 2010, http://tinyurl.com/zldlk64; David Kopel, "Guns on university campuses: The Colorado experience," The Washington Post, April 20, 2015, http://tinyurl.com/jkkx65y.

[69] David B. Kopel, "Pretend 'Gun-Free' School Zones: A Deadly Legal Fiction," Connecticut Law Review, December 2009, http://tinyurl.com/h928tbr.

[70] University of Utah v. Shurtleff, Sept. 8, 2006, http://tinyurl.com/h2emkxs.

[71] Mathew Miller, David Hemenway and Henry Wechsler, "Guns and Gun Threats at College," Journal of American College Health, September 2002, http://tinyurl.com/glcq9sn.

[72] "Frat house arsenal: Police find more than two dozen weapons, and resentment toward transients," Corvallis Gazette-Times, Dec. 10, 2006, http://tinyurl.com/z93jhmf.

[73] Hauser, op. cit.

[74] "FAQ: How was Students for Concealed Carry started?" Students for Concealed Carry, concealedcampus.org/faq/; Brian J. Siebel and Allen K. Rostron, "No Gun Left Behind: The Gun Lobby's Campaign to Push Guns Into Colleges and Schools," Brady Center to Prevent Gun Violence, May 2007, pp. 33-34, footnote 1, http://tinyurl.com/zx2nqnb.

[75] Leslie Eaton and Michael Luo, "Shooting Rekindles Issues of Gun Rights and Restrictions," The New York Times, April 18, 2007, http://tinyurl.com/zdmf66n.

[76] Siebel and Rostron, op. cit., p. 1.

[77] See The Associated Press, "Members of Student group push for the right to carry concealed

About the Author

Christina L. Lyons, a freelance journalist in the Washington, D.C., area, writes primarily about U.S. government and politics. She is a contributing author for CQ Press reference books, including *CQ's Guide to Congress*, and was a contributing editor for Bloomberg BNA's *International Trade Daily*. A former editor for Congressional Quarterly, she also was co-author of CQ's *Politics in America 2010*. Lyons began her career as a newspaper reporter in Maryland and then covered environment and health care policy on Capitol Hill. She has a master's degree in political science from American University.

weapons on college campuses," *Arkansas Online*, Nov. 21, 2007, http://tinyurl.com/za9ocge; "SCCC empty holster protest," Students for Concealed Carry, Sept. 24, 2007.

[78] "6 shot dead, including gunman, at Northern Illinois University," CNN, Feb. 14, 2008, http://tinyurl.com/yjjzdnf; The Associated Press, "Gun dealer linked to 3 mass shootings closes," CBS News, June 20, 2012, http://tinyurl.com/zxbn946.

[79] "ALEC Task Force Adopts Model 'Campus Personal Protection Act,'" NRA-ILA Institute for Legislative Action, May 23, 2008, http://tinyurl.com/ho5e5cq.

[80] Lisa A. Sprague, "IACLEA Position Statement Concealed Carrying of Firearms Proposals on College Campuses," Aug. 12, 2008, http://tinyurl.com/4rt6nzh.

[81] "Guns on Campus," Everytown for Gun Safety, July 9, 2015, http://tinyurl.com/jjry6o7

[82] Kay Brian Melear and Mark St. Louis, "Concealed Carry Legislation and Changing Campus Policies," in Brandi Kephner LaBane and Brian O. Hemphill, eds., *College in the Crosshairs: An Administrative Perspective on Prevention of Gun Violence* (2015), p. 60.

[83] *DiGiacinto v. The Rector and Visitors of the George Mason University*, 704 S.E. 2d 365 (Virginia, 2011), http://tinyurl.com/48ogbtk; "Gun on Campus: Campus Action," National Conference of State Legislatures, March 2012, http://tinyurl.com/p2v6qcg;

[84] *Florida Carry, Inc. v. University of Florida, Bernie Machen*, Case No. 1D14-4614, http://tinyurl.com/jrc8qet.

[85] Alexei Koseff, "California bans concealed handguns on college, school campuses," *The Sacramento Bee*, Oct. 10, 2015, http://tinyurl.com/ppjmuvh; Todd C. Frankel, "Why the CDC still isn't researching gun violence, despite the ban being lifted two years ago," *The Washington Post*, Jan. 14, 2015, http://tinyurl.com/hb6w65a.

[86] Osnos, *op. cit.*

[87] Melear and St. Louis, *op. cit.*, p. 61.

[88] Jessie Pounds, "Liberty University to allow handguns in residence halls next fall," *The News & Advance*, April 26, 2016, http://tinyurl.com/jrno3w7.

[89] James Call, "Election fires up campus carry forces," *Tallahassee Democrat*, Nov. 19, 2016, http://tinyurl.com/goj938c; Editor, "Campus Carry Bill Filed in Florida House," WGCU, Dec. 9, 2016, http://tinyurl.com/hgoq6mo.

[90] Blake Stevens and Randall Barnes, "More guns on Tennessee college campuses beginning July 1," May 5, 2016, http://tinyurl.com/jjlj4e7.

[91] "Texas Moms Demand Action Statement on Guns on Campus," Everytown for Gun Safety, Jan. 29, 2015, http://tinyurl.com/jaru5ws.

[92] Sam Zeff, "Kansas Campuses Prepare For Guns In Classrooms," National Public Radio, March 22, 2016, http://tinyurl.com/jzd8snw.

[93] Dion Lefler, "Kansas regents prepare to open universities to guns under new law," *The Wichita Eagle*, Oct. 5, 2015, http://tinyurl.com/psdhlfz.

[94] Jessica Chasmar, "OSU President Michael Drake still opposed to campus carry after knife attack," *The Washington Times*, Dec. 1, 2016, http://tinyurl.com/jz2p93r.

[95] Madeline Conway and Yousef Saba, "White House: Ohio State attack may have been terrorism," *Politico*, Nov. 29, 2016, http://tinyurl.com/hp98pxj.

[96] Scott Jaschik, "Ohio Showdown on Campus Carry," *Inside Higher Ed*, Dec. 9, 2016, http://tinyurl.com/za44hoq.

[97] Tom Benning, "Federal judge denies UT professors' request to block implementation of campus carry," *The Dallas Morning News*, Aug. 22, 2016, http://tinyurl.com/howjoc7; *Glass, Moore and Carter v. UT, Texas*, July 7, 2016, http://tinyurl.com/h5sbxoz.

[98] "Handbook of Operating Procedures 8-1060: Campus Concealed Carry," The University of Texas at Austin University Policy Office, http://tinyurl.com/zjs445p.

[99] Michael S. Rosenwald, "Gun industry's helping hand triggers a surge in college shooting teams," *The Washington Post*, March 15, 2015, http://tinyurl.com/glcuowx.

[100] T. Rees Shapiro, "Gun-friendly Liberty University to open on-campus shooting range," *The Washington Post*, Dec. 15, 2016, http://tinyurl.com/z4eed8w.

[101] Michelle Leibowitz, "College rifle, pistol-shooting clubs under fire, underfunded amid gun debate," FoxNews.com, July 22, 2016, http://tinyurl.com/hqg2uox.

[102] Sarah Ferris, "GOP blocks Dem attempts to allow federal gun research," *The Hill*, July 7, 2016, http://tinyurl.com/h3vo99a.

[103] Rita Rubin, "Tale of 2 Agencies: CDC Avoids Gun Violence Research But NIH Funds It," The JAMA Network, April 26, 2016, http://tinyurl.com/h667z2f.

[104] "Nation's first state-funded firearm violence research center to be established at UC Davis," UCDavis Health System, Aug. 29, 2016, http://tinyurl.com/jsuxklh.

[105] Manny Fernandez and Mitch Smith, "Gun Owners 'Can Breathe Again,' Trump's Win Emboldens Advocates," *The New York Times*, Nov. 22, 2016, http://tinyurl.com/hpe97or.

[106] Claire Caulfield, "Trump talk of eliminating gun-free schools a long shot, experts say," *The Arizona Republic*, Dec. 30, 2016, http://tinyurl.com/zawk5hh.

FOR MORE INFORMATION

American College Counseling Association, 1101 N. Delaware St., Indianapolis, IN 46202; 855-220-8760; collegecounseling.org. Trade association for mental health professionals and students who work in counseling.

Crime Prevention Research Center, 212 Lafayette Ave.; Swarthmore, PA 19081; 484-802-5373, crimeresearch.org. Nonprofit research organization that argues having more guns on campuses would make them safer.

Everytown for Gun Safety, 646-324-8250; everytown.org. National nonprofit that advocates for gun control; provides research on gun violence.

Harvard Injury Control Research Center, Harvard T.H. Chan School of Public Health, 677 Huntington Ave., Boston, MA 02115; 617-495-1000. Education and research center that provides research on firearms, youth violence and suicide.

International Association of Campus Law Enforcement Administrators, 342 N. Main St., West Hartford, CT 06117-2507; 860-586-7517; www.iaclea.org. International trade association representing law enforcement officers at colleges and universities; provides research and advocacy on campus public safety.

Students for Concealed Carry, concealedcampus.org. Nonprofit advocacy group of students and faculty who support concealed firearms on campuses.

The Campaign to Keep Guns Off Campus, PO Box 658, Croton Falls, NY 10519; 914-629-6726; keepgunsoffcampus.org. Tracks state laws and court cases.

Bibliography

Selected Sources

Books

Klarevas, Louis, *Rampage Nation: Securing America From Mass Shootings*, Prometheus Books, 2016.

A professor in the global affairs department at the University of Massachusetts, Boston, analyzes the link between gun violence — particularly mass shootings — and campus gun regulations.

LaBanc, Brandi Hephner, and Brian O. Hemphill, eds., *College in the Crosshairs: An Administrative Perspective on Prevention of Gun Violence*, Stylus Publishing LLC, College Student Educators International, and Students Affairs Administrators in Higher Education, 2015.

A vice chancellor of student affairs at the University of Mississippi (LaBanc) and the former president of West Virginia State University (Hemphill) compile essays on the history of campus violence and firearms legislation, plus strategies for colleges and universities to prevent violence on campus.

Spitzer, Robert J., *Guns Across America: Reconciling Gun Rules and Rights*, Oxford University Press, 2015.

A political science professor at the State University of New York, Cortland, explores the history of gun regulation in the United States.

Articles

Arrigo, Bruce A., and Austin Acheson, "Concealed carry bans and the American college campus: a law, social sciences, and policy perspective," *Contemporary Justice Review*, Dec. 1, 2015, http://tinyurl.com/zw3yrj3.

Two criminal justice professors review case law, social science findings and public policy perspectives relevant to the debate on whether concealed firearms should be allowed on college campuses.

Bogost, Ian, "The Armed Campus in the Anxiety Age," *The Atlantic*, March 9, 2016, http://tinyurl.com/j2yfoqm.

A Georgia Tech professor says many university administrators and staff worry that allowing firearms on campuses will add to the stresses of college life.

Caputo, Marc, "Lawmakers debate guns as Florida leads nation in mass shootings," *Politico*, Jan. 18, 2017, http://tinyurl.com/hjg8z54.

Lawmakers are debating a bill that would give concealed-weapons permit holders the right to carry their guns on college campuses in Florida, which saw the deadliest mass shooting in U.S. history at an Orlando nightclub in 2016.

New, Jake, "Campus police use of semiautomatic rifles increasingly common at colleges," *Inside Higher Ed*, Dec. 10, 2015, http://tinyurl.com/hqlcmv4.

A reporter examines a growing trend of campus police departments: obtaining semiautomatic rifles through a U.S. Department of Defense program that distributes excess military equipment.

Phillips, Dave, "What University of Texas Campus Is Saying About Concealed Carry," *The New York Times*, Aug. 27, 2016, http://tinyurl.com/h28lxmy.

A reporter profiles University of Texas students from both sides of the debate regarding the state law permitting concealed firearms on campus.

Sandoval, Gabriel, "The Students Behind 'Students for Concealed Carry,' " *The Chronicle of Higher Education*, Aug. 17, 2016, http://tinyurl.com/gldgtsc.

A journalist examines the rise of Students for Concealed Carry, a nationwide organization pushing for laws and policies to permit concealed carry of firearms on college campuses.

Silverman, Lauren, "Gun Violence and Mental Health Laws, 50 Years After Texas Tower Sniper," NPR, July 29, 2016, http://tinyurl.com/j2xbe8t.

Mental health experts discuss the potential link between mental illness and gun violence.

Reports and Studies

Dahl, Patricia P., Gene Bonham Jr. and Frances P. Reddington, "Community College Faculty: Attitudes Toward Guns on Campus," *Community College Journal of Research and Practice*, Feb. 17, 2016, http://tinyurl.com/hwcf9f3.

Three criminal justice professors survey 1,889 community college faculty from 18 states and find that the majority do not support allowing students, faculty or visitors to carry concealed firearms on their campus.

Morse, Andrew, *et al.*, "Guns on Campus: The Architecture and Momentum of State Policy Action," NASPA and Education Commission of the States, January 2016, http://tiny url.com/holkddb.

Policy analysts detail state legislative actions and policy decisions of higher education institutions related to firearms on campus.

Webster, Daniel W., *et al.*, "Firearms on College Campuses: Research Evidence and Policy Implications," Bloomberg School of Public Health, Johns Hopkins University, Oct. 15, 2016, http://tinyurl.com/jtqnumz.

Eights Johns Hopkins University professors and others summarize research and data on gun violence, gun regulations and mental health and behavior of college-age students. Their conclusion: Allowing concealed firearms makes college and university campuses less safe.

The Next Step:

Additional Articles from Current Periodicals

Arming Campus Security

Analco, Michael, "FIU's department a militarized police," **FIU Student Media, Aug. 31, 2016, http://tinyurl.com/jug6c4x.**

Florida International University's police department acquired M16 rifles, a mine-resistant, ambush-protected vehicle and other military-grade weaponry through the Pentagon.

Binkley, Collin, "More campus security forces adding rifles to their arsenals," Portland Press Herald, April 8, 2016, http://tinyurl.com/z6pw7p6.

At least 100 college police forces have added rifles to their arsenals in the past decade, according to federal data and Associated Press interviews and records requests.

Meyer, Gage, "ASM passes legislation requesting transparency on UWPD equipment," The Daily Cardinal, Sept. 7, 2016, http://tinyurl.com/gld74rv.

The University of Wisconsin-Madison student council passed legislation urging transparency and asking the campus police department to annually update a list of its equipment.

Campus-Carry Activism

"Group holds open-carry gun walk in response to attack at OSU," WCMH-TV Columbus, Dec. 5, 2016, http://tinyurl.com/jnxeqrq.

Gun-rights advocates openly carried their guns in a walk across Ohio State University's campus after a stabbing that the activists said was stopped only because an armed police officer was on the scene.

Call, James, "Gun advocates rally troops for open carry fight," Tallahassee Democrat, Jan. 6, 2017, http://tinyurl.com/jxa627b.

The gun-advocacy group Florida Open Carry rallied behind SB-140, a bill that would repeal laws forbidding guns on college campuses, in airports and at government meetings.

Prabhu, Maya T., "S.C. lawmakers look at arming public schools' staff to deter shootings," The Post and Courier, Dec. 25, 2016, http://tinyurl.com/jbyfd2q.

Three South Carolina lawmakers, arguing that gun-free zones attract mass shooters, announced bills that would allow concealed firearms on college campuses.

Protesting Guns on Campus

Dorman, Travis, "Poll: UT faculty oppose campus gun carry bill," Knoxville News Sentinel, April 29, 2016,

A University of Tennessee poll found that its faculty opposed allowing guns on campus, with 87 percent saying guns would not be in the campus community's best interest.

Guarecuco, Lyanne A., "Moms Protest Bill That Would Remove Licensing for Handguns, Allow Them in Schools, Bars, Churches," The Texas Observer, Jan. 17, 2017, http://tinyurl.com/hmbw2hz.

More than 100 activists from Moms Demand Action marched at the Texas Capitol to lobby against a bill that would allow guns on university campuses, among other places, and one that would remove a state-licensing requirement for guns.

White, Laurel, "UW-Madison Students To Carry Sex Toys To Protest Campus Carry Bill," Wisconsin Public Radio, Dec. 26, 2016, http://tinyurl.com/jxsypug.

Drawing on tactics used at University of Texas protests in August, University of Wisconsin-Madison students plan to carry sex toys on campus to protest a bill that would allow concealed firearms on college campuses.

State Legislation

Chappell, Bill, "Ohio's Kasich Signs Gun Law Expanding Concealed Carry In Day Cares, Colleges," NPR, Dec. 21, 2016, http://tinyurl.com/hhkoyh7.

Republican Ohio Gov. John Kasich signed a bill that makes it legal to carry a concealed weapon on college campuses, but college boards of trustees would have to vote to allow guns at their schools.

Woodall, Hunter, "Legislation would allow Kansas colleges to keep guns off campus," The Kansas City Star, Jan. 17, 2017, http://tinyurl.com/h7ojzfj.

A Kansas state lawmaker introduced legislation that would allow state college and universities to opt out of mandates that they allow weapons on their campuses.

CITING CQ RESEARCHER

Sample formats for citing these reports in a bibliography include the ones listed below. Preferred styles and formats vary, so please check with your instructor or professor.

MLA STYLE
Jost, Kenneth. "Remembering 9/11." CQ Researcher 2 Sept. 2011: 701-732.

APA STYLE
Jost, K. (2011, September 2). Remembering 9/11. CQ Researcher, 9, 701-732.

CHICAGO STYLE
Jost, Kenneth. "Remembering 9/11." CQ Researcher, September 2, 2011, 701-32.

In-depth Reports on Issues in the News

Are you writing a paper?

Need backup for a debate?

Want to become an expert on an issue?

For 90 years, students have turned to *CQ Researcher* for in-depth reporting on issues in the news. Reports on a full range of political and social issues are now available. Following is a selection of recent reports:

Civil Liberties
Privacy and the Internet, 12/15
Intelligence Reform, 5/15
Religion and Law, 11/14

Crime/Law
Jailing Debtors, 9/16
Decriminalizing Prostitution, 4/16
Restorative Justice, 2/16
The Dark Web, 1/16
Immigrant Detention, 10/15
Fighting Gangs, 10/15
Reforming Juvenile Justice, 9/15

Education
Student Debt, 11/16
Apprenticeships, 10/16
Free Speech on Campus, 5/15
Teaching Critical Thinking, 4/15

Environment/Society
Mass Transit, 12/16
Arctic Development, 12/16
Protecting the Power Grid, 11/16
Pornography, 10/16
Women in Leadership, 9/16
Child Welfare, 8/16

Health/Safety
Opioid Crisis, 10/16
Mosquito-Borne Disease, 7/16
Drinking Water Safety, 7/16
Virtual Reality, 2/16

Politics/Economy
China and the South China Sea, 1/17
Trump Presidency, 1/17
European Union's Future, 12/16
The Obama Legacy, 11/16
Populism and Party Politics, 9/16
U.S.-Mexico Relations, 9/16

Upcoming Reports

Civics Education, 2/3/17   Forensic Science, 2/10/17   Immigrants and the Economy, 2/17/17

ACCESS

CQ Researcher is available in print and online. For access, visit your library or www.cqresearcher.com.

STAY CURRENT

For notice of upcoming *CQ Researcher* reports or to learn more about *CQ Researcher* products, subscribe to the free email newsletters, *CQ Researcher Alert!* and *CQ Researcher News*: http://cqpress.com/newsletters.

PURCHASE

To purchase a *CQ Researcher* report in print or electronic format (PDF), visit www.cqpress.com or call 866-427-7737. Single reports start at $15. Bulk purchase discounts and electronic-rights licensing are also available.

SUBSCRIBE

Annual full-service *CQ Researcher* subscriptions—including 44 reports a year, monthly index updates, and a bound volume—start at $1,131. Add $25 for domestic postage.

CQ Researcher Online offers a backfile from 1991 and a number of tools to simplify research. For pricing information, call 800-818-7243 or 805-499-9774 or email librarysales@sagepub.com.

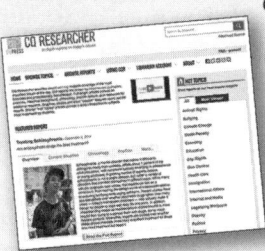

CQ RESEARCHER

CQ PRESS

In-depth reports on today's issues

Published by CQ Press, an Imprint of SAGE Publications, Inc.

www.cqresearcher.com

Civic Education

Are students learning how to be good citizens?

F or years, voter turnout has been dropping, political polarization has been rising and the art of compromise has been waning. Then came the bitter 2016 presidential campaign and its aftermath. The new lows in nastiness, civic education proponents say, have helped demonstrate the need for schools to do a better job teaching youngsters good citizenship in the hopes that they will improve civic discourse as they become adults. Some schools, state governments and private groups are experimenting with programs to build citizenship skills, including a comprehensive approach known as "action civics" that sends students on community improvement projects. However, conservative and liberal advocates of civic education hold different visions for civic learning. Experts also disagree on the internet's impact on civic engagement. But they agree on the importance of helping students navigate the increasingly complex landscape of internet information and social media to sort accurate information from false stories.

Students from Democracy Prep Charter School in East Harlem, N.Y., conduct a voter registration drive before the November election. Proponents of civic education say teaching young people about good citizenship is more vital than ever today, given low voter turnout, poor knowledge of the Constitution and rising concern about the vitriol in politics.

THIS REPORT

THE ISSUES	**99**
BACKGROUND	**105**
CHRONOLOGY	**107**
CURRENT SITUATION	**111**
AT ISSUE	**113**
OUTLOOK	**115**
BIBLIOGRAPHY	**118**
THE NEXT STEP	**119**

CQ Researcher • Feb. 3, 2017 • www.cqresearcher.com
Volume 27, Number 5 • Pages 97-120

RECIPIENT OF SOCIETY OF PROFESSIONAL JOURNALISTS AWARD FOR EXCELLENCE ◆ AMERICAN BAR ASSOCIATION SILVER GAVEL AWARD

Los Angeles | London | New Delhi
Singapore | Washington DC | Melbourne

CIVIC EDUCATION

THE ISSUES

99 • Can education increase civic participation?
• Are young Americans less civically engaged than earlier generations?
• Should students be required to pass the U.S. citizenship test to graduate from high school?

BACKGROUND

105 **Fragile Democracy**
The new American government gained strength from civic participation.

106 **Schools' Civic Mission**
Early Americans disagreed on what should be taught.

108 **Civic Mission Fades**
The space race spurred greater attention on math and science.

109 **Public and Private Initiatives**
Groups collaborated with schools to implement "action civics."

CURRENT SITUATION

111 **Renewed Activism**
Post-inauguration women's marches drew more than 1 million people.

112 **Civic Education Needed**
Experts say holding the government accountable is vital.

114 **Reviving Civic Groups**
Social media may be changing political engagement.

OUTLOOK

115 **Civic Surge?**
The election may be reigniting activism.

SIDEBARS AND GRAPHICS

100 **Civics Test Adopted by 15 States**
The exam consists of questions from the U.S. citizenship test.

101 **Eighth-Graders Lacking in Civics Knowledge**
They continue to score below proficiency level.

104 **Half of Young Adults Didn't Vote in 2016**
Turnout peaked when Barack Obama was elected in 2008.

107 **Chronology**
Key events since 1787.

108 **Media Literacy Called Vital to Citizenship**
"Facts . . . are the medium in which democracy lives and thrives."

110 **'Action Civics' Students Tackle Real Problems**
Participants "begin to actually feel like they have a voice."

113 **At Issue:**
Should states make the U.S. citizenship test a graduation requirement?

FOR FURTHER RESEARCH

117 **For More Information**
Organizations to contact.

118 **Bibliography**
Selected sources used.

119 **The Next Step**
Additional articles.

119 **Citing CQ Researcher**
Sample bibliography formats.

 **CQ RESEARCHER**

Feb. 3, 2017
Volume 27, Number 5

EXECUTIVE EDITOR: Thomas J. Billitteri
tjb@sagepub.com

ASSISTANT MANAGING EDITORS: Kenneth Fireman, kenneth.fireman@sagepub.com, Kathy Koch, kathy.koch@sagepub.com, Scott Rohrer, scott.rohrer@sagepub.com

SENIOR CONTRIBUTING EDITOR:
Thomas J. Colin
tom.colin@sagepub.com

CONTRIBUTING WRITERS: Marcia Clemmitt, Sarah Glazer, Reed Karaim, Peter Katel, Barbara Mantel, Chuck McCutcheon, Tom Price

SENIOR PROJECT EDITOR: Olu B. Davis

EDITORIAL ASSISTANT: Anika Reed

FACT CHECKERS: Eva P. Dasher, Michelle Harris, Betsy Towner Levine, Robin Palmer

SAGE Publishing | CQPRESS

Los Angeles I London I New Delhi
Singapore I Washington DC I Melbourne

An Imprint of SAGE Publications, Inc.

SENIOR VICE PRESIDENT, GLOBAL LEARNING RESOURCES:
Karen Phillips

EXECUTIVE DIRECTOR, ONLINE LIBRARY AND REFERENCE PUBLISHING:
Todd Baldwin

CQ Researcher (ISSN 1056-2036) is printed on acid-free paper. Published weekly, except: (March wk. 4) (May wk. 4) (July wks. 1, 2) (Aug. wks. 2, 3) (Nov. wk. 4) and (Dec. wks. 3, 4). Published by SAGE Publications, Inc., 2455 Teller Rd., Thousand Oaks, CA 91320. Annual full-service subscriptions start at $1,131. For pricing, call 1-800-818-7243. To purchase a CQ Researcher report in print or electronic format (PDF), visit www.cqpress.com or call 866-427-7737. Single reports start at $15. Bulk purchase discounts and electronic-rights licensing are also available. Periodicals postage paid at Thousand Oaks, California, and at additional mailing offices. POSTMASTER: Send address changes to CQ Researcher, 2600 Virginia Ave., N.W., Suite 600, Washington, DC 20037.

Cover: AP Photo/Rainmaker Photo/MediaPunch

Civic Education

BY MARCIA CLEMMITT

THE ISSUES

American democracy got some help on Election Day from 1,670 Chicago high school students. Before dawn, the civic-minded juniors and seniors reported to polling places to work a 15-hour day as election judges. For the 17th year, the Chicago nonprofit group Mikva Challenge and the Chicago Board of Elections trained students for the job, which involved setting up equipment, checking in voters, answering questions and helping citizens vote. [1]

"Seeing a bunch of people cast a ballot and making their voices heard was really exciting," said Lincoln Park High School senior Sharon Alvarado, who also worked during the primary elections in March.

"It's rare that students are given an opportunity for leadership on this scale," said Meghan Goldenstein, director of Mikva's Elections in Action program. "They are protecting and empowering people to cast real votes." [2]

High school student Navil Babonoyaba, 16, attends a civics class in Yuma, Colo., home to many Hispanic immigrants. Experts disagree on what good civic education should encompass. Some say conservatives tend to focus on the responsibilities of American citizens, while liberals emphasize teaching about rights-based movements. With many schools emphasizing college preparation and career readiness, advocates fear civic education is getting less attention.

Such real-world learning about civic duties and rights helps build the knowledge, skills and attitudes students need to become active and informed citizens, many civic-education experts say.

The election-judge program is part of a campaign by private and public organizations to improve civic education in Illinois. [3] Other states also are trying to improve civic learning as concerns mount about record-low voter turnout among Americans under age 30 and about the state of civic discourse in the United States.

For proponents of civic education — teaching young people about government and good citizenship — the problem has been building for years. Besides low voter turnout, experts cite poor knowledge of the Constitution and the government, the breakdown of compromise in the political system and the decline of civility in discussions of race, abortion and other charged issues.

The Nov. 8 election, they add, offered further evidence for why the country needs to improve its civic education. The campaign saw apocalyptic rhetoric on both sides, vilification of the major-party nominees, the spread of "fake" news and rising fears about the survival of civil rights for Muslims, immigrants and others.

With emotions running high, "It is vital that we seize on [the election] to teach our young people valuable lessons about government and democracy," wrote two members of Generation Citizen, a nationwide civic-education group. [4]

At the same time, though, experts disagree on what good civic education should encompass, and high schools strongly emphasize college preparation and career readiness, making it is unclear how far efforts to beef up civic learning will go.

Americans' understanding of civics is not impressive, polls show. In a December 2014 survey, only 37 percent of adults said it was very important to keep informed about public issues, down from 56 percent in 1984. [5] Another poll found Americans' knowledge of government weak, such as knowing how many women serve on the Supreme Court. [6]

Moreover, U.S. voter turnout ranked 27th among industrialized countries, at 53.6 percent in 2012. [7] (Preliminary figures indicate turnout rose in 2016 to nearly 55 percent, but the international ranking remained unchanged. [8])

Millennials — born between 1980 and about 2004 — score lowest on virtually all citizenship measures. The voting rate among Millennials under 25 dropped from 51 percent in 1964 to 38 percent in 2012. [9] And in 2016, only 16 percent of Millennials said they trust government and political institutions such as Congress, and just 18 percent said they trust major news media. [10]

Young and old questioned whether the 2016 Democratic and Republican nominees were trustworthy. In the Democratic primaries and the general

Civics Test Adopted by 15 States

Fifteen states require high school students to take the U.S. citizenship test, and another 17 are considering doing it. The Civics Education Initiative wants to make the citizenship test part of high school graduation requirements in all 50 states by Sept. 17, 2017.

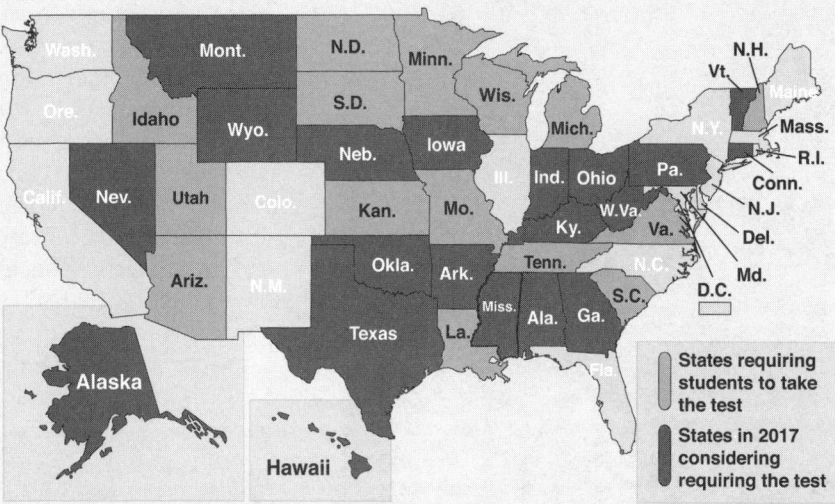

States requiring students to take the test

States in 2017 considering requiring the test

Source: Joe Foss Institute

Sample Test Questions

The U.S. citizenship test consists of 100 questions on American government, history and geography. Here are 10 sample questions from the 2017 test; correct answers are in parentheses.

What does the Constitution do? (sets up the government; defines the government; protects the basic rights of Americans)

How many amendments does the Constitution have? (27)

What is one responsibility that is only for U.S. citizens? (serve on a jury; vote in a federal election)

What do we show loyalty to when we say the Pledge of Allegiance? (the United States and the flag)

Who lived in America before the Europeans arrived? (American Indians; Native Americans)

There were 13 original states. Name three. (NH, MA, RI, CT, NY, NJ, PA, DE, MD, VA, NC, SC, GA)

The Federalist Papers supported passage of the U.S. Constitution. Name one of the writers. (James Madison; Alexander Hamilton; John Jay; Publius)

Who was president during World War I? (Woodrow Wilson)

Who did the United States fight in World War II? (Japan, Germany and Italy)

Name one U.S. territory. (Puerto Rico; U.S. Virgin Islands; American Samoa; Northern Mariana Islands; Guam)

Source: "The Civics Education Initiative 2017," Civics Education Initiative, Jan. 18, 2017, http://tinyurl.com/j85nru7

campaign, news reports about Clinton Foundation fundraising and Hillary Clinton's email use, among other things, had many voters doubting her honesty.

President Trump has his own critics. Some commentators question his knowledge of, and interest in, U.S. governing traditions. The president repeatedly has made false statements, such as claiming he would have won the popular vote if millions of illegal votes hadn't been counted, that "undermined critical democratic norms," said Evan McMullin, chief policy director for the U.S. House Republican Conference, who ran for president as an independent conservative in 2016. Those norms include peaceful debate and transitions of power, commitment to truth, freedom from foreign interference and abstention from the use of executive power for political retribution. [11]

Given what McMullin sees as threats to American democracy, he said, "We need a new era of civic engagement that will reawaken us to the cause of liberty and equality. That engagement must extend to ensuring that our elected representatives uphold the Constitution, in deed and discourse." [12]

To meet this challenge, civic scholars are calling for steps to reverse the decline of civic knowledge, increase voter turnout, improve public knowledge of current events and teach the value of compromise.

Schools must play a leading role, these scholars say, noting that U.S. leaders throughout the nation's history have stressed schools' vital role in teaching citizenship. "That the schools make worthy citizens is the most important responsibility placed on them," said President Franklin D. Roosevelt (1933-45). [13]

Schools, however, are doing a poor job of teaching civics, said David E. Campbell, a professor of American democracy at the University of Notre Dame in Indiana. Most states require a civics course for high school graduation, almost all as part of a multiyear requirement for history and social studies courses. The call for renewed commitment to civics "means doing it better," Campbell said. [14]

But conservative and liberal advocates of improving civics hold different visions for civic learning, says Frederick Hess, director of education policy studies at the conservative American Enterprise Institute (AEI) in Washington. Conservatives generally want courses to "focus on the responsibilities of American citizens," such as obeying laws and voting. "On the other side, the focus is on rights-based movements — what you can demand from the country," such as civil-rights campaigns, he says. "People tend to teach it from one point of view or the other."

Another challenge is the "incontrovertible evidence that poor and non-white students are receiving demonstrably less and worse civic education than middle-class and wealthy white students," said Meira Levinson, a professor at the Harvard Graduate School of Education. This deficiency likely puts already disempowered segments of the population at further disadvantage in political life and may threaten political stability by deepening a sense of alienation in large numbers of Americans, she said. [15]

Much of the push to invigorate civic education has come from proponents of augmenting factual learning with activities, including projects in which students seek policy changes from their school administrations or city councils. (*See sidebar, p. 110.*) "Older students can and should be expected to develop the skills of monitoring and influencing public policy," said a paper by the Communitarian Network, a nonpartisan coalition of scholars interested in ways to create positive social change. [16]

Some conservative groups strongly disagree. A new report on college civic education from the National Association of Scholars, a New York group working for "reasoned scholarship," argues that service- and project-based civics teach-

8th-Graders Lacking in Civics Knowledge

Eighth-grade students continue to score well below proficiency level on an exam that measures "civics knowledge and skills." For example, "they should understand how and why powers are divided and shared between the national and state governments." In 2014, scores averaged 154 out of a possible 300, well below the 178 indicating proficiency.

Average Scores Among Eighth-Graders on the Civics Assessment Exam

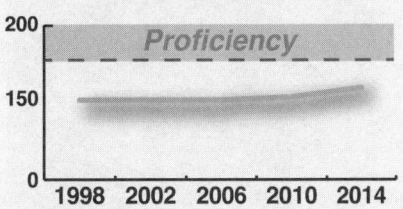

Source: "2014 Civics Assessment," The Nation's Report Card, National Assessment of Educational Progress, National Center for Education Statistics, 2014, http://tinyurl.com/gsn6725

ing is a stealth attempt to turn students into activists for liberal causes such as climate change and wealth redistribution. Condemning what it sees as attempts to teach students "that a good citizen is a radical activist," the group calls for a return to "traditional" civics emphasizing in-class instruction on self-government. [17]

Meanwhile, some state governments, individuals and private organizations want civics to go beyond memorization of facts about government that have formed the core of many courses in the past.

In Illinois, a public-private civics coalition is celebrating a major milestone this school year: The state is beginning to implement a law requiring all high school graduates to complete comprehensive civics training that will include discussion of current and controversial public issues and community service. [18]

The Joe Foss Institute, an Arizona group seeking to improve civic knowledge, is spearheading a multistate Civics Education Initiative to get state lawmakers to require high school graduates to pass the U.S. citizenship test, which immigrants must pass to become citizens. As of January 2017, 15 states have approved some version of the measure. [19] (*See map and sample questions, p. 100.*)

Historically, schools did not carry the full burden of civic education. Americans have had a long tradition of participating in town hall meetings and voluntary associations of all kinds, from sewing circles to labor unions and homeowner associations. Such groups provided opportunities for people to practice leadership skills and cooperate to accomplish community goals, said Robert D. Putnam, a professor of public policy at Harvard University and author of the 2000 best-seller *Bowling Alone*, about the breakdown of community ties. However, membership in voluntary associations has plummeted, with the drop steepest among younger generations, Putnam said. Membership in the Masons fraternal service organization, for example, fell from over 4 million members in 1964 to 1.2 million in 2015. [20]

To encourage civic participation, many high schools and some colleges are requiring or encouraging students to volunteer in the community, such as working in a soup kitchen, says Peter Levine, a professor of citizenship and public affairs at Tufts University in Medford, Mass. Largely because of such programs, volunteerism rates for Millennials have risen to record highs of about 25 percent, up from 20 percent in the 1970s, he says.

That trend raises hopes among civics educators that young people's enthusiasm for community service can spur an interest in voting and other civic activities, but exactly how to make that leap remains unclear, Levine says.

As educators, policymakers and others discuss civic learning and engagement, here are some of the questions they are asking:

Can education increase people's civic participation?

The wide variation in curriculum and approaches, as well as the existence of many additional influences

One review of multiple studies from countries worldwide concluded that civic education has no apparent effect on whether people will vote or register to vote. The study did find that civic education appears to make it more likely that someone will express a political opinion, such as by signing a petition, said authors Nathan Manning, a lecturer in sociology at England's University of York, and Kathy Edwards, a senior lecturer in the School of Global, Urban and Social Studies at RMIT University in Melbourne, Australia. [21]

ier peers, but experts find it harder to judge the effects of civics classes because of the differences in the political engagement levels in students' home environments.

Furthermore, the particulars of a civics-related class make a big difference in whether it builds engagement, Levine says.

In recent decades, one of the most unhelpful changes was "a shift to more academic and college-like courses" in high school, says Levine. "AP [Advanced Placement] American Government is one of the most rapidly growing courses. But it's a full-fledged college-like political science course." Typically, students in such classes no longer learn the basics of how to participate in elections, he says.

AP courses also don't discuss current events enough, Levine adds. By contrast, "in the mid-20th century, 40 percent of kids took a course in current events. If you want engagement, you have to focus on current events and media," including helping students recognize inaccurate or biased information found online, he says.

Some types of civic education may actually drive students away from participating in real-world politics, according to John Hibbing and Elizabeth Theiss-Morse, professors of political science at the University of Nebraska, Lincoln. Classes that avoid "controversial political issues rather than teaching students to be comfortable in dealing with those issues [leave students] more likely to react negatively when in the real world they are exposed to the gritty, barbaric side of politics," they wrote. [22]

Furthermore, "there are still a lot of classes where people are going just for mastery of facts rather than asking a range of critical questions that push for a deeper exploration of citizenship," says AEI's Hess.

"We know that in many places, most of what happens is memorization, fill-in-the-blank [facts]," says Notre Dame's Campbell. "But we know that students learn more when there's discussion in their classes," he says. That's especially

Getty Images/*Detroit Free Press*/Mandi Wright

Michaela Mast, 21, of Harrisonburg, Va., signs a mockup of the U.S. Constitution during the Women's March on Washington on Jan. 21. After that march and others, Barack Obama's spokesman said the former president was "heartened by the level of engagement taking place in communities around the country. Citizens exercising their constitutional right to assemble, organize and have their voices heard . . . is exactly what we expect to see when American values are at stake."

on students' civic behavior, make civic education's long-term effects hard to gauge. Nevertheless, some scholars say recent small studies demonstrate that civics classes in which teachers lead informed and open discussion of public issues improve students' knowledge of civics and their engagement with politics.

Overall, evidence shows that education levels are closely related to voting rates, "but when it comes to whether civics classes matter for [who votes], it's not clear," says AEI's Hess.

A few factors make the effects hard to judge, says Tufts' Levine. Civic education in the United States is unequal, he says. Students from wealthier, better-educated families often take good civics classes because they are in stronger academically performing schools. But they would likely have participated in civic life anyway, Levine says, because they come from families and neighborhoods where people often get politically involved. Poorer students at weaker schools are not only at a disadvantage compared with their wealth-

true in "open classrooms" — learning environments in which students feel "teachers encourage questions and discussion of issues, even controversial ones," Campbell says.

Furthermore, recent research shows that low-income students' knowledge and attitudes toward civic participation improve most in such open classes, Campbell says. "School seems to be compensating for what is not learned at home."

"We know that it makes a critical difference if students have a deep and broad understanding of the issues of the day, of election processes and of how, quite literally, to take part in an election," said Diana Hess, dean of the University of Wisconsin-Madison School of Education. "Recent studies have shown that young people who choose not to participate — especially those who could vote but don't — sit out elections because they are afraid that they don't know enough to make an informed choice or because they are intimidated by the mechanics of voting." [23]

Kahne of the University of California says one study found "that what happens in junior year [of high school] matters for early adulthood. The evidence is reasonably strong. When you discuss political ideas, kids get more interested in politics." [24]

Effective school-based civic education goes beyond the classroom, says Campbell. Adolescents' social environment, including in their schools, educates them about civic participation and influences future political behavior, he said. For example, a school with "strong civic norms" — that is, a school in which many people promote the idea that voting and participating in political life are an important responsibility — will "lead to a greater likelihood of voting well over a decade following high school." [25]

"We do know a lot less about what works in citizenship education than in math and science, for example," Campbell says. "Civics never gets as much research attention as those subjects."

More attention from policymakers would increase progress."

Research on how to implement good civics teaching throughout the nation is needed most, says Levine. "We do know what good teaching looks like," he says. "But we don't know what good policies are to take small examples of good teaching and scale them up" to implement good civic teaching everywhere.

Are young Americans less civically engaged than earlier generations?

On virtually every measure — from voting turnout to civic knowledge — young people seem less civically involved than earlier generations, experts say. However, surveys do find that Millennials express deep concern about many public issues, from the environment to poverty — representing a reservoir of public spiritedness that schools could tap to awaken civic engagement in politics, some analysts say.

When it comes to knowledge and awareness of political issues, younger generations have not always lagged older people, researchers say. In the 1940s and '50s, surveys of political knowledge found no age gap, according to Michael Delli Carpini, dean of the University of Pennsylvania's Annenberg School of Communication in Philadelphia, and Scott Keeter, senior survey adviser at the Pew Research Center, a nonpartisan research organization in Washington.

By 1989, however, "18- to 29-year-olds were considerably less informed than older citizens," they said. [26]

The age-related knowledge gap has widened in the 2000s. Data indicate that the knowledge gap does not exist because older people have lived longer and thus have had time to accumulate more knowledge. Later-born generations are learning less and less about politics, Delli Carpini and Keeter said. [27]

Meanwhile, voter turnout has declined in recent decades among most age groups, most steeply among voters under age 25, whose turnout rate dropped from 51 percent in 1964 to 38 percent in 2012. (In 1972, the voting age dropped to 18.) From 1964 to 2012, turnout for voters age 25 to 44 dropped from 69 percent to 49.5 percent. For voters age 45 to 64, the drop was less steep — from 75.9 percent to 63.4 percent. Among those age 65 and older, turnout actually rose, from 66.3 percent to 69.7 percent. [28]

Other measures of civic engagement include how actively people participate in community groups, such as unions, lodges or political parties, and to what degree they believe the political system can solve problems. Young Americans score lower on both.

The "frightening" declines in civic engagement "do not involve young people's political knowledge but rather their actual experience participating in voluntary groups and deliberating with others who hold different views," said Levine of Tufts. "Membership in groups, attendance at meetings and discussion of issues have fallen badly" among young people, he wrote, for reasons that are unclear. [29]

Furthermore, young Americans "do not see the political system as the best way to enact change," said a white paper by the nonprofit group Generation Citizen, which assists schools with civic education. "Institutions are seen as the problem and not the solution," it said. According to survey data from 1973, a majority of young people said they trusted the government to do the right thing, while today only 20 percent say so. "These attitudes influence behavior, leading to a decrease in youth political involvement," the paper said. [30]

The picture is not entirely bleak, however.

Early data suggest that voter turnout in 2016 for those under 30 may have resembled 2012 — close to 50 percent — and was even higher in 11 battleground states with highly competitive presidential or Senate races, according to the Center for Information and Research on Civic Learning and Engagement (CIRCLE), a research organization at Tufts. [31]

Moreover, some details about young voters' turnout rates could point the way to remedies, according to Levine.

For one thing, he says, today's youngest voting generation is more ethnically and socioeconomically diverse than previous generations. Among those 55 and older, 75 percent are white; the figure for those 35 to 54 is 61.5 percent white. But the 18-to-34-year-old age group is only 55.8 percent white, and under 18 the percentage is 51.5 percent. [32] This means that "the turnout rate for a whole generation in any given election is misleading," because it conceals wide demographic differences among people of the same age, Levine says.

Notably, voter turnout is low and falling among the least educated but is much more stable among the most educated. In the 2004 election, those with a high school education or less made up 31 percent of the electorate; in 2016, they made up only 19 percent. [33] Therefore, effective efforts to raise turnout rates should focus on less educated young people, Levine says.

Research also shows that some political campaigns and other groups have not aggressively targeted young people, compared with outreach efforts for older voters, says Levine. Increasing outreach to younger generations would likely raise their voting rates, he says. Barack Obama's two presidential campaigns was one of the exceptions. It hired young people for important jobs and highlighted issues that mattered to them, Levine said. [34] The Democratic presidential campaign of Sen. Bernie Sanders of Vermont also effectively reached out to Millennials in 2016, analysts say. [35]

Furthermore, while young people generally distrust politics and government, in study after study they say they care about an array of social problems, according to Generation Citizen. Climate change and homelessness concern those on the left while restricting abortion and expanding religious freedom concern those on the right, for example.

Half of Young Adults Didn't Vote in 2016

Only about 50 percent of eligible voters ages 18 to 29 cast ballots in the 2016 presidential election, according to preliminary exit-poll data. Since 2000, turnout among young adults in presidential elections has hovered around 40 to 50 percent. It peaked in 2008 at 52 percent when Barack Obama was elected president.

Turnout Among 18-to-29-Year-Old Voters

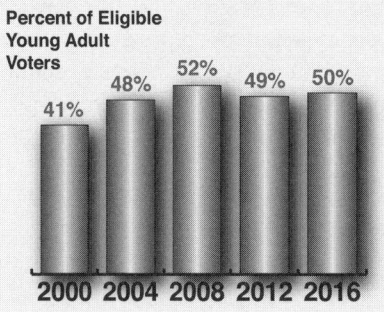

Percent of Eligible Young Adult Voters

2000	2004	2008	2012	2016
41%	48%	52%	49%	50%

Source: Clara Hendrickson and William A. Galston, "How Millennials voted this election," Brookings Institution, Center for Information and Research on Civic Learning and Engagement, Nov. 21, 2016, http://tinyurl.com/hpbvwcn

That's a reservoir of commitment toward the community that could be tapped to increase civic engagement, the group suggests. "Across the board, evidence shows that our youngest generations . . . want to make a positive impact [and] work towards a better and fairer country," Generation Citizen said. [36]

Should students be required to pass the U.S. citizenship test to graduate from high school?

The Civics Education Initiative spearheaded by the Joe Foss Institute is a nationwide campaign to make the U.S. citizenship test a high school graduation requirement. All immigrants applying for citizenship must pass the 100-question, multiple-choice test on U.S. history and basic civics facts.

Skeptics, however, fear that requiring the test would make it too easy for educators and lawmakers to avoid making deeper investments in civic learning.

"It's an empty symbolic effort," said Kahne of the University of California, Riverside. "There's not any evidence base to show that this will be effective. . . . Making the short-answer test a key requirement of civics education is the equivalent of "teaching democracy like a game show." [37]

The Joe Foss Institute disagrees, calling the test a "first step to ensure all students are taught basic civics." [38] Fifteen states now require high school students to take the test.

The test contains such questions as: What is the supreme law of the land? (the Constitution). We elect a U.S. senator for how many years? (six) How many amendments does the Constitution have? (27) [39] Supporters of the test point out that knowing the basics of how government functions is a necessary first step to participating in it.

"I like the idea," says Robert Pondiscio, a senior fellow and vice president for external affairs at the Thomas B. Fordham Institute, an education think tank in Washington that focuses on parental choice and standards-based school reforms. "By no means do I suggest that it's a proxy for a full, rich, robust civics education. But I also think we shouldn't overlook the fact that it does show us something valuable," he says. "If kids who get any kind of civics education at all cannot pass that test, then we'll quickly know that there's something really wrong" with their civics learning.

Pondiscio also said that since the test requires only memorization, it could work as an exit exam for elementary school students. [40]

After a unanimous vote in the Legislature, South Carolina in July 2015 enacted a law requiring the test for all high school students. It will not be a graduation requirement, however. Instead, South Carolina will use the results to gauge the success of the state's civics education. [41]

"It is absolutely critical that all South Carolina students have a sound knowledge of civics," said former South Carolina Gov. Richard Riley, who was U.S. secretary of Education under President Bill Clinton and co-chaired a South Carolina panel that examined the test. "This is not a partisan issue. It is an American issue." [42]

Even the most ardent supporters of using the test nationwide say doing so should be only the beginning of improving civics education.

Implementing the test as a high school graduation requirement is a way of "shining a light on the issue" of America's civic-learning problem, says Lucian Spataro, chief academic officer and vice president of legislative affairs at the Joe Foss Institute. "It's a first step toward minimum competency, like the multiplication table or the periodic table" of the chemical elements, he says.

The idea is to put civics learning "back on the front burner where it belongs by bringing this fun, attractive and important subject" back into every school, Spataro says. The test is a good starting point "because there's very little cost attached to it. A teacher can get the test online, Google 'citizenship,' and find all kinds of free materials to build a free online course."

Campbell of Notre Dame says he worries about the test's lasting value for students' civic education. "I appreciate the spirit behind the initiative. It would be hard for legislators to decline," he says. "But if there's nothing there but the test, then some people will just cram for it short term, which doesn't result in any long-term learning."

Making the test the centerpiece of a state civics program is "the exact opposite of what we want," said Louise Dubé, executive director of iCivics, a Cambridge, Mass., group founded by retired Supreme Court Justice Sandra Day O'Connor that produces interactive online civics games.

Effective civics learning occurs when students actively discuss issues and

Abortion foes rally on the National Mall for the 44th annual March for Life on Jan. 27, the anniversary of the Roe v. Wade decision, which opponents of abortion want to overturn. Some experts on civic education cite such activism as evidence of a growing interest in civic engagement, especially among the nation's youth.

write analytical essays, Dubé said. A short-answer test can't accomplish those things or tell students what they need to hear about government, she said: "that that big machine that seems like it has nothing to do with you matters more than you think." [43] ∎

BACKGROUND

Fragile Democracy

The nation's Founders, who were well versed in classical history, including the fate of the ancient Roman republic, believed democracies were fragile and needed careful tending if they were to survive.

"[History] teaches us that few countries have sustained democratic governments for prolonged periods, a lesson that we Americans are sometimes inclined to forget," wrote Margaret Stimmann Branson, associate director of the Center for Civic Education, an independent nonprofit resource center in Calabasas, Calif. [44]

Government by and for the people survives only when citizens are committed to informed voting, respect the law and demonstrate concern for the common good — habits that no one is born with, Branson said. "Each new generation . . . must acquire the knowledge, learn the skills and develop the . . . traits of private and public character that undergird a constitutional democracy." [45]

Americans in the new nation learned self-government by working together in New England town hall meetings and in churches, fraternal organizations such as Elks Lodges and reform groups such as temperance societies. [46]

American democracy gained its strength from people's widespread participation in voluntary public and private groups, said Alexis de Tocqueville, a French political scientist who traveled throughout the United States in the early 1830s. Public "town-meetings are to liberty what primary schools are to science; they bring it within the people's reach, they teach men how to use and how to enjoy it," he wrote. [47]

"Americans of all ages, all conditions, and all dispositions constantly form associations," de Tocqueville observed. "I have often admired the extreme skill with which the inhabitants of the United States succeed in proposing a common object for the exertions of a great many men and in inducing them voluntarily to pursue it." [48]

For much of U.S. history, such groups were "a civil training ground" for citizenship and public office, says Michael Johanek, a senior fellow at the University of Pennsylvania Graduate School of Education. "People got practice talking about issues with people with different points of view, running for office, using Robert's Rules of Order" — a parliamentary procedure guide on running meetings — and learning skills of group participation and leadership, he says.

Schools' Civic Mission

Only a small fraction of people went to school in the 18th and early 19th centuries, and the few schools that existed were poorly run. Nevertheless, the founding generation hoped schools would play important roles in building the nation. In the Land Ordinance of 1785, Congress dedicated a portion of public land in every township to support schools. [49]

Philadelphian Benjamin Franklin — scientist, inventor, signer of the Declaration of Independence — wrote that schools should lay "such a foundation of knowledge and ability as . . . may qualify [individuals] to . . . execute the several offices of civil life, with advantage and reputation to themselves and country." [50]

Early Americans didn't agree on what schools should emphasize in teaching citizenship. Thomas Jefferson, who in 1779 proposed a taxpayer-funded public school system and later founded the University of Virginia, thought American schools should emphasize critical-thinking skills. He believed such skills would enable people to govern themselves in a democracy and avoid tyrannical rule by helping them think independently and critically. [51]

Others, such as Noah Webster of Connecticut, who compiled a dictionary that bears his name, believed schools should help build a sense of American unity and national identity, distinct from Europe, especially Britain. Webster's view of schools as nurseries of nationalism dominated 19th-century civic education. [52]

Horace Mann (1796-1859), a Massachusetts reformer who became that state's first secretary of education, originated the "common school" tradition in the United States. "Education must be universal," he said. "The qualification of voters is as important as the qualification of governors, and even comes first, in the natural order." [53]

In the mid-to-late 19th century, immigrants streamed into the United States, and Catholic immigration, in particular, grew. "People were wondering how to keep this very diverse set of people together," says Johanek. "Worried about the democratic competencies of new people coming in," schools again wanted civic lessons to build a sense of national identity.

Not until the 1920s did the proportion of Americans graduating from high

school top 20 percent. [54] Nevertheless, the first half of the 20th century saw a growing high school population and a few experiments aimed at broadening schools' citizenship mission.

American education reformer John Dewey (1859-1952) proposed that civic education engage students in "active inquiry and careful deliberation in the significant and vital problems" that crop up in their classrooms, schools and communities. Such lessons would best engage students' interest, said Dewey, a professor of philosophy and psychology who founded the private University of Chicago Lab Schools that still use his "experiential" teaching approach. [55]

In the 1930s and '40s, New York City educator Leonard Covello turned East Harlem's Benjamin Franklin High School, a public boys' school, into a community resource center where students, parents and local citizens researched and implemented programs to improve life in their multiethnic community. The goal, said Covello, was to "make the school the training ground for democratic living." [56]

Few schools attempted anything so ambitious. However, by the mid-20th-century the majority of Americans attended high school, so more people received civic education than ever before. Moreover, many high school students took three civics-related courses: a current-events course; a civics course on the rights and responsibilities of citizenship such as voting; and a government course explaining the structure of local, state and national governments. [57]

Nevertheless, few of the classes were "noted for stimulating student interest," said Charles Quigley, executive director of the Center for Civic Education. "The most common method of teaching was lecture." Skills important for active citizenship, such as discussion and debate, got short shrift. [58]

Continued on p. 108

Chronology

1780s *Founders call citizenship education vital to nation's survival.*

1787
Northwest Ordinance declares that to help promote "good government . . . schools and the means of education shall forever be encouraged."

1789
"[W]herever the people are well informed they can be trusted with their own government," Thomas Jefferson says.

1830s-1930s *Schools teach American citizenship to immigrants and citizens.*

1837
All children, not just the well-off, should attend public "common schools" to learn about freedom, says reformer Horace Mann.

1882
In this peak year for the 19th century, 788,992 immigrants enter the United States.

1900
Philosopher John Dewey warns, "Democracy has to be born anew every generation, and education is its midwife."

1929
Share of 14- to 17-year-olds attending high school passes 50 percent for the first time.

1934
Benjamin Franklin High School in East Harlem, N.Y., is established to build students' citizenship skills.

1950s-1990s *Americans increasingly disengage from civic groups.*

1957
Soviets' launch of *Sputnik* satellite shifts schools' focus toward science and math and away from civics.

1963
Decade's tumults, from Vietnam War protests to civil rights marches, begin making civics courses controversial.

1972
First presidential election is held allowing 18-year-olds to vote.

1983
"A Nation At Risk" report from the National Commission on Excellence in Education urges schools to focus on practical subjects, such as math and science.

1998
Voter turnout for Americans ages 18 to 29 is just 25 percent, down from 58 percent in 1972.

2000s-Present *Young Americans' civic engagement continues to drop.*

2000
Harvard professor Robert Putnam publishes *Bowling Alone*, showing steep decline in Americans' participation in organizations since 1970.

2002
No Child Left Behind Act requires standardized testing in reading and math. Critics say the testing drains resources from civics.

2003
The Home School Legal Defense Association founds Generation Joshua to help Christian teens learn political and leadership skills.

2006
First Democracy Prep charter school opens in Harlem.

2008
Brown University students launch nonprofit Generation Citizen to help schools give students hands-on experience in policy-making.

2009
Retired Supreme Court Justice Sandra Day O'Connor founds iCivics to create interactive online civics games.

2012
U.S. voter turnout rate of 54 percent ranks 27th among industrialized democracies. . . . Tennessee begins assessing civics achievement based on projects in which students choose issues, research them and suggest solutions.

2015
Illinois enacts civics graduation requirement.

2016
Generation Joshua volunteers contact nearly 700,000 registered voters on behalf of Republican Senate candidates. . . . Only 16 percent of 18- to 34-year-olds say they trust Congress.

2017
Donald Trump inaugurated as 45th president amid concerns that he lacks civic knowledge; a day later, more than 1 million participate in rallies for women in Washington, D.C., and across the U.S., plus major cities worldwide. . . . Fifteen states now require high school students to take the U.S. citizenship test.

Media Literacy Called Vital to Citizenship

"Facts . . . are the medium in which democracy lives and thrives."

Learning to be an active citizen means mastering skills and attitudes that don't come naturally to students, civic educators say. Chief among them are the ability to distinguish between reliable and unreliable information sources and discuss controversial issues with people holding different views.

"When we think about civics and news and media literacy, we have to realize that facts held in common are the medium in which democracy lives and thrives," says Peter Adams, senior vice president for literacy programs at The News Literacy Project, a Bethesda, Md., nonprofit that creates media-literacy resources for schools. "If we arrive at a point where we hold no facts in common, there's nothing to sustain our civic dialogue. And then it becomes impossible to create policy."

The way people get information in the internet age is putting commonly agreed-upon facts further out of reach, many educators say.

"People feel today that if news is important, it's going to come to them" through social media such as Facebook, says Shawn Healy, who advocates for civic learning at the Chicago-based Robert R. McCormick Foundation, established by the late Chicago Tribune publisher McCormick to support programs for improving education, journalism and civic knowledge. But most such news is forwarded by like-minded friends or written to persuade readers of a particular point of view rather than to provide facts, says Healy.

Last fall, an analysis by the news website BuzzFeed found that 38 percent of posts by highly partisan conservative websites and Facebook pages were partly or mostly false. For highly partisan left-wing sites, the figure was 19 percent. [1]

False tweets and other statements by prominent people can sow distrust of vital institutions, media analysts say. After his election and again on Jan. 23, President Trump sent a series of tweets charging that voter fraud was rampant, potentially totaling millions of votes, with no evidence. "Simply by raising the question, the president-elect sows the seeds of doubt," which "may yet ripen into an utter lack of faith in the system," said political reporter David Graham of *The Atlantic*. [2]

Former President Barack Obama made similarly questionable statements about his health care plans, such as stating in June 2009 that "no matter how we reform health care, I intend to keep this promise: If you like your doctor, you'll be able to keep your doctor; if you like your health care plan, you'll be able to keep your health care plan." Critics noted this was too sweeping and that the Affordable Care Act would lead to some Americans changing their plans or doctors. [3]

Helping students understand what well sourced and vetted information looks like and how to distinguish it from biased or false material is "not a choice for teachers any more. They have to do it," says Adams.

Another necessary habit for democratic citizenship is the willingness and ability to discuss controversial topics with people who hold different views, said Peter Levine, professor of citizenship and public affairs at Tufts University in Medford, Mass. "Good citizens deliberate," he said. "By talking and listening

Continued from p. 106

Civic Mission Fades

Beginning around the 1960s, civic education began losing ground in the public school system.

To some extent, the courses were a victim of the changing — and more contentious — times. The 1960s brought the Vietnam War and massive campus protests, race riots, marches for civil rights and assassinations, all of which strained the political system and shredded civic discourse. The 1970s brought the Watergate scandal, the unprecedented resignation of a president, a constitutional crisis over that scandal and widespread loss of faith in government.

Current-events courses, in particular, says Tufts' Levine, "may have seemed too hot to handle as the '60s, '70s proceeded. In 1955, you could have a big debate in class on taxes," but when current political events involved controversial issues such as race, war and the Watergate scandal, schools and parents may have become reluctant to encourage students to discuss them.

But the main driving force for civics' loss of place in the schools was almost certainly changing education priorities, Levine and others say.

The Soviet Union's launch in 1957 of the first man-made Earth-orbiting satellite, *Sputnik*, spurred American schools to devote more hours to math and science, says Paul Baumann, director of the National Center for Learning and Civic Engagement at the Denver-based Education Commission of the States, a nonpartisan resource center sponsored by the U.S. states and territories.

Americans now thought of schools as an economic driver for individuals and the country, obscuring the civic mission, Baumann says. And then, beginning in the 1980s, policymakers pushed to make schools more accountable for what students learned, mostly measured through standardized reading and math tests. For many schools, that meant shifting resources from other subjects, including civics. "What's measured is what matters, and other things sort of get pushed aside," he says.

Despite the changing curriculum, most states retained civics as a graduation requirement. As of 2014, all but Alaska, Delaware, Illinois, Montana, Oregon and Rhode Island required a civics course for graduation, according to CIRCLE. [59]

to people who are different from themselves, they . . . build a degree of consensus" that can then be translated into action for the public good.[4]

Diana Hess, dean of the University of Wisconsin-Madison School of Education, says schools play a role in teaching this quality. "We've got, I think, really strong evidence that high quality classroom discussion of political issues is very important and highly effective" in encouraging students to become civically engaged, she says.

A key is "the understanding that we have to live in this world together," says Constance Flanagan, a professor of human ecology at the University of Wisconsin, Madison. Teachers can impart that principle even to fifth-graders by asking students doing a project "to sit at a table with people with whom they don't agree."

By contrast, when adults choose conflict over cooperation, students tend to follow suit, some analysts say. For example, teachers and school administrators in a November survey reported that the presidential campaign had increased fighting, bigotry and threats of violence in their schools. "In over 15 years of teaching high school, this is the first year that swastikas have been appearing all over school furniture," wrote a Washington state teacher, while others said some students who backed Trump were harassed in school.[5]

Some conservative analysts worry that discussion classes can potentially indoctrinate students because of what they call a widespread bias in the civics-teaching community toward liberal rather than conservative views.

"You'll find a lot of civics classes where teachers will ask, 'Is it fair that Johnny's family is poor?' " says Frederick Hess, director of education policy studies at the conservative American Enterprise Institute in Washington. But where is the flip side that questions the fairness of high taxes? he asks.

Other civic-education scholars say research demonstrates most teachers try to avoid such bias.

"There's a popular view that teachers are trying to indoctrinate students and that they're all liberal Democrats," says Healy. But the overwhelming majority of teachers "don't disclose their own views" to students, he says. "And we know that teachers often play the devil's advocate," arguing in class for a position that no one in the class is taking.

— *Marcia Clemmitt*

[1] Craig Silverman *et al.*, "Hyperpartisan Facebook Pages Are Publishing False And Misleading Information At An Alarming Rate," *BuzzFeed*, Oct. 20, 2016, http://tinyurl.com/jny4csw.

[2] David A. Graham, "The Lasting Damage from Trump's False 'Voter Fraud' Allegations," *The Atlantic*, Nov. 28, 2016, http://tinyurl.com/hzkg5xb.

[3] "Obama: 'If you like your health care plan, you'll be able to keep your health care plan,' " *PolitiFact*, http://tinyurl.com/lng93o2.

[4] Peter Levine, *We Are the Ones We Have Been Waiting For: The Promise of Civic Renewal in America* (2013), Kindle edition, location 55.

[5] "The Trump Effect: The Impact of the 2016 Presidential Election on Our Nation's Schools," Southern Poverty Law Center, Nov. 28, 2016, http://tinyurl.com/jlz2xyq.

Around 1970, participation began to plummet in groups of all kinds, from town meetings to labor unions, churches and lodges — even bowling leagues and bridge clubs, Harvard's Putnam wrote. The reasons for the nationwide decline remain little understood but likely include the spread of television, population sprawl into suburbs where distance between neighbors was greater and time stresses on two-earner families, he said.[60]

And along with the groups went many opportunities to learn civic habits such as cooperation, public spiritedness, thoughtful deliberation of issues and opportunities to share political ideas and be recruited to political causes, Putnam said.[61]

The youngest generations experienced the steepest declines in partici-pation, according to Putnam. "The more recent the cohort, the more dramatic its disengagement from community life."[62]

Political activities, including voting, have seen similar declines and also have fallen most among younger voters. In 1972, the first year in which 18- to 20-year-olds could vote, voter turnout for 18 to-29-year-olds was 58 percent. By 2000, turnout had dropped to 46 percent.[63]

Yet this period also saw a few countervailing trends. The religious right in the 1980s mobilized in the political arena to fight for conservative and Christian values. While the effect of the Internet is hotly debated and still largely unknown, some believe that the rise of social media in the 1990s and 2000s may be providing new op-portunities for organizing. And after the election of Barack Obama in 2008, the political world saw the grass-roots conservative movement known as the tea party that successfully pushed the Republican Party further to the right.

Public and Private Initiatives

Throughout these ups and downs, private groups, individuals and some state governments have sought to make civic participation more compelling.

In 2009, retired Justice O'Connor, the first woman to serve on the high court, started iCivics, a nonprofit group that develops free online games. As of 2015, the group had released 19 games

'Action Civics' Students Tackle Real Problems

Participants "begin to actually feel like they have a voice."

Mary Breslin's seventh-grade students in Arlington, Va., are finding solutions to environmental issues in their community, working with politicians and simultaneously meeting state-mandated learning standards.

Breslin's students work with Earth Force, a program that provides training and funding for civic-engagement projects with a focus on the environment, and they have done everything from growing wetland plants as a way to reduce bacteria in the watershed to reducing trash levels in their community.

Earth Force is a member of the National Action Civics Collaborative, a Chicago-based network of civic education reform organizations, educators and researchers. The collaborative is promoting "action civics," a comprehensive approach to civic education that encompasses traditional classroom learning, project-based experiential learning and leadership development.

The goal, says the collaborative, is "to create a world that invites young people to take collective action inside and outside the classroom." [1]

Advocates say this multifaceted approach to civics is the key to greater student engagement.

"We know from the research that [traditional approaches focusing on facts is] a component of an effective civic education, but it's quite limiting," says Shawn Healy, a civic learning scholar at the Robert R. McCormick Foundation, which awards grants to improve civic education and engagement opportunities in the Chicago area. "We want people engaged in our democracy in lots of different ways."

Jan Brennan, a project leader with the National Center for Learning and Civic Engagement, highlights four practices that action civics incorporates: pursuing active student involvement; encouraging diverse viewpoints; seeking real-world interactions with local leaders; and instituting professional development for teachers.

Breslin says these practices are a good start. "What I have the benefit of allowing my students to do is not to just learn these standards but to learn how these standards function within their local government," she says. "Not only are they learning how these learning standards work in their local government, but [they're coming to understand] the complexity of each different topic and how hard it is for communities to actually pass laws."

But critics say it is difficult to measure action civics' impact on student performance, and they worry that taxpayer dollars could end up supporting a political party or partisan viewpoint. [2]

Other critics say civic education should return to knowledge-based classroom instruction and not focus on experiential learning. The Heartland Institute, a conservative organization in Illinois, argues that although school-based projects may be "wholesome," it gives students "little insight into how our system of government works and what roles they must fill as citizens of a democratic republic." [3]

Healy disagrees, stressing that focusing on knowledge is not enough. "Both [approaches] matter," he says. "We need traditional civic education; there's far too many places where we don't even have that, but it has to be paired with these action civics components, where we get young people involved in not just elections but the policy-making process itself."

Healy, though, says he agrees that civics education should be nonpartisan. "We have a responsibility as educators writ

and accompanying teacher lesson plans on topics such as federal budgets and international diplomacy. [64]

Private groups also have worked with public school systems and state and local governments to develop and implement projects.

In 2008 two Brown University students, Scott Warren and Anna Ninan, founded Generation Citizen, a nonprofit that works with schools in six states to implement "action civics" classes in which students research solutions to local problems and approach government officials to seek change. [65]

"Part of the challenge is that young people don't think government institutions matter or represent them," says Warren. That's especially true for "low-income kids who go to dilapidated schools, kids who walk through metal detectors every morning," he says. "But when kids in the Generation Citizen program engage with state reps and city council members and see that people actually are concerned about their issues, they are immediately transformed."

In 2015, after years of advocacy by a public-private coalition including universities, corporations and nonprofit foundations, Illinois lawmakers enacted their new public-school graduation requirement in civics, which is being phased in this school year. Unlike most such laws, the statute spells out that an acceptable class must include instruction "on government institutions, the discussion of current and controversial issues, service learning and simulations of the democratic process." [66]

"Most of the time when we focus on government, it's on what it does to us or for us," says Shawn Healy, who advocates for civic learning at the Robert R. McCormick Foundation in Chicago. But we are civic actors with the responsibility to help shape public policies, he says. "Civics teaching has been mainly 'Washington-centric.' " To foster student engagement, it makes sense to study local and state laws, because they are the ones that usually affect us most closely, he says.

large to create opportunities in our classrooms for students to pursue their own beliefs, their own causes for concern," he says. "We should be pretty agnostic."

Supporters say the most successful action civics projects tap into students' passions.

"The really critical piece to it . . . is student voice," Healy says. "The students are involved from the very beginning in determining whatever work of democracy they're going to do."

Brennan says, "Some of the most powerful action civics experiences are when you ask students, 'What are you concerned about?' "

For Breslin's students, participating in these projects allows them to develop core competency skills, which enables students to take the "next step in their educational learning process."

"The students choose their own topics; they make their own decisions throughout the project [and] they begin to actually feel like they have a voice," Breslin says.

Colleges and universities have also instituted action civics programs in recent years. In 2011, retired Democratic Sen. Bob Graham, who served as Florida's governor from 1979 to 1987, established the Civic Scholars program at the University of Florida in Gainesville. Students selected for the program work together to research solutions for one or more challenging public issues in the state.

To date, Florida's Civic Scholars have issued policy papers on homelessness, water resources, aging infrastructure, school cafeteria nutritional guidelines and mental health services for children, among other topics. [4]

"We need an investment and support for those programs

An Earth Force student works at a local nature center in Texas on a project to protect beavers. Earth Force provides training and funding for civic-engagement projects with a focus on the environment.

Courtesy EarthForce.org

. . . so they can provide a high-quality, nonpartisan civic learning experience," Brennan said.

— Anika Reed

[1] "About Us," National Action Civics Collaborative, http://tinyurl.com/h57bzq3.

[2] Joy Pullmann, "Research & Commentary: Civic Education," The Heartland Institute, Jan. 31, 2012, http://tinyurl.com/zcy8by4.

[3] "A Crisis in Civic Education," The Heartland Institute, Jan. 14, 2016, http://tinyurl.com/zssh7g5.

[4] Graham Civic Scholars, Bob Graham Center, http://tinyurl.com/jpoctbv.

Some other states also have sought new approaches, says Baumann. Alaska, California, Kentucky and Massachusetts, among others, have formed task forces to pursue innovations in civics learning. Arizona and Illinois recognize schools whose civics programs follow best teaching practices. Tennessee now assesses high school students' civic learning based on projects they present, he says.

Two federal funding streams for civic learning, the Learn and Serve America grants for service learning and the California-based Center for Civic Education resource center, have essentially dried up since 2000, says Baumann. However, the federal Every Student Succeeds Act of 2015 gives states more choice about how to use federal funds. It could provide resources for the many local school districts clamoring for more money for subjects other than math and reading, although funds will likely be quite limited.

"We need to get out of the zero-sum" mindset that sees a funding increase for one school subject as a threat to funding for another, Baumann says. With innovative programs, "you can do STEM [science, technology, engineering and math] and the arts and civics all in one fell swoop," he says. "States are beginning to think about this." ∎

CURRENT SITUATION

Renewed Activism?

The Jan. 21 women's marches held in Washington and across the country, which were held in reaction to Trump's election, drew more than 1 million participants, with speaker after speaker urging participants to fight for women's rights and other causes. A week later abortion foes held their annual march on the anniversary of the *Roe v. Wade* decision that legalized abortion. For some analysts, the activism may have signaled greater attention to civic education and engagement.

Former President Obama "is heartened by the level of engagement taking place in communities around the country," according to a Jan. 29 statement from his spokesperson Kevin Lewis. "Citizens exercising their constitutional right to assemble, organize and have their voices heard by their elected officials is exactly what we expect to see when American values are at stake," said the statement. [67]

In the run-up to the election, "[one teacher] told me, 'The elections are such a mess this year — so ugly, so charged — that I think I will give them a pass,' " said the University of Wisconsin's Diana Hess. But "even though this year's contests are undeniably challenging," she said, they should be discussed among K-12 students, because research shows that "the knowledge that young people acquire by learning about campaigns predicts whether they will participate politically." [68]

Several experts say civic knowledge is more important than ever. One rea-

with more civic and policy knowledge than Trump displayed during the final presidential debate." [69]

Trump's defenders dismiss such criticisms, stressing that he was elected as a populist outsider pledged to shake up political norms. In his inaugural address, Trump himself said "today's ceremony . . . has very special meaning, because today we are not merely transferring power from one administration to another, or from one party to another, but we are transferring power from Washington, D.C., and giving it back to you, the people." [70]

Supporters of Democratic presidential hopeful Bernie Sanders rally at the Presidio in San Francisco on June 6, 2016. Contrary to the common belief that young people are politically apathetic, Becky Bond, a coordinator of volunteers for the Vermont senator, said that the under-26 Millennials on the campaign were "incredibly hardworking."

Getty Images/Bloomberg/Andrew Harrer

Normally, says Generation Citizen's Warren, "it's an uphill battle to get people to realize that civics is important, but in the last six months we've seen more interest than ever. People are realizing that we've got to change something. I'm seeing more policymakers talking about it."

Others, however, worry the 2016 presidential campaign demonstrates the United States' low state of civic discourse. The campaign's negativity discouraged some teachers from discussing politics in class.

son, they contend, is the election of President Trump: They question his commitment to U.S. civic traditions and even his knowledge of them.

"When it comes to the issues any American president would face, Trump is a shockingly ignorant man," wrote Michael Gerson, a former Republican Senate aide and speechwriter and senior policy adviser to President George W. Bush. "He bluffs through questions on campaign finance and foreign policy. . . . I have honestly met precocious high school students

Civic Education Needed

Legal experts say strong civics education is vital if the citizenry is to act as a watchdog over government. The need for vigilance transcends any party or president, they say, citing two recent controversies that require watching. One involves presidents' growing use of executive orders. Republicans heavily criticized former President Obama for resorting to these orders to bypass Congress, calling it dictatorial and tyrannical; Democrats are responding in kind, noting that Trump signed numerous executive orders during his first week in office. [71]

The other is the potential conflicts of interest involving Trump's presidency. Critics say Trump's business empire will result in him violating the Constitution's so-called "emolument" clause, which bans a president from receiving payments or favors from foreign governments.

The ban is intended to wall presidents off from situations in which their business interests might expose them to attempts by foreign governments to unduly influence U.S. policy, says Pamela Karlan, a professor of public interest law at Stanford Law School in Palo Alto, Calif. "That's why the president has to take an oath to support the Constitution. If he does something not

Continued on p. 114

At Issue:

Should states make the U.S. citizenship test a graduation requirement?

LUCIAN SPATARO
CHIEF ACADEMIC OFFICER,
JOE FOSS INSTITUTE

WRITTEN FOR *CQ RESEARCHER*, JANUARY 2017

*a*sk 10 adults what citizenship means and you'll probably get 10 different answers. Ask 10 students and you'll get a bewildered look and a shrug of the shoulders. Studies show that a majority of our students and many adults lack a basic understanding of how our country was founded, how it's governed and what it means to be a citizen. Former Supreme Court Justice Sandra Day O'Connor has termed this the "quiet crisis in education." We believe it is the quiet crisis in America.

In 2015, the Joe Foss Institute, dedicated to promoting civics education, set out to change this with the Civics Education Initiative and legislation in Arizona that requires students to pass a civics test before graduating. Since then, 13 other states have enacted this or similar legislation, and another 20 states will consider the legislation in 2017. By the end of this year, we hope to have the bill enacted in over half the country and that long-neglected civics education will be back on the front burner where it belongs.

The proposal requires high school students to score 60 percent or higher on the U.S. citizenship test to earn their diploma, the same test taken by immigrants, 92 percent of whom pass on their first attempt. Compare this to 29,000 eighth-graders who were tested in 2014. A scant 23 percent scored at or above proficiency in civics — an abysmal number by any standards.

States that have adopted the test as a graduation requirement are now engaging students and showing transformative results. For example, in Jamestown, N.D., not one freshman passed the pretest given on the first day of class last year; most were under 45 percent, but 95 percent scored over 70 percent at the end of the semester, using the very same study materials, readily available online, used by immigrants.

As a former professor, I know the one question students will always ask during a lecture is: "Is this going to be on the test?" Answer yes, and students lean forward, take notes and are engaged in the discussion. Answer no, and the entire class leans back, drifts off and disengages. As this relates to America, we must put civics on a test that matters today, so our students will lean forward and engage as active, informed and responsible citizens.

SHAWN HEALY
CIVIC LEARNING SCHOLAR,
ROBERT R. McCORMICK FOUNDATION

WRITTEN FOR *CQ RESEARCHER*, JANUARY 2017

*t*he Joe Foss Institute of Arizona has rightly focused its attention on the marginalization of civic learning in K-12 education throughout the United States. However, its solution — requiring high school students to pass the U.S. citizenship test before graduation — isn't the answer to fostering the knowledge, skills, attitudes and behaviors among young people necessary for informed engagement in our democracy.

The test itself wasn't designed as a summative assessment for students. While many of the questions and answers constitute important factual knowledge that I would hope we all possess as Americans, some of them border on trivia. My fear is that a citizenship test will serve as more of a ceiling than a floor for civic learning in the United States.

Based on my analysis of the results of the last three iterations of the National Assessment of Educational Progress in Civics (1998, 2006 and 2010), instruction in the form of textbook reading, memorization of material and worksheet completion too often constitutes the sum of students' civic learning experience.

Moreover, I tested the link between teaching specific content knowledge, such as the U.S. Constitution or Congress, and student performance by measuring civic knowledge and skills. I found no relationship between these variables.

Instead, students did best when discussing current events in class daily, simulating democratic processes regularly and engaging in community service annually. These practices are too often neglected in content-centered courses, and students depart with a fleeting knowledge base and are poorly prepared for the demands of democratic governance.

Student-centered civic learning practices should lie at the heart of policy efforts to improve youths' civic knowledge. For example, Illinois recently passed a law requiring schools to offer a semester-long course that embeds these practices through discussion, service-learning and simulations.

Assessment is also imperative, and Tennessee opted for a project-based learning requirement in civics, where students demonstrate their civic capacity by doing, the heart of democratic governance.

Instead of a shallow exercise in memorization, let's unite around course requirements, standards and assessments that empower students not only with knowledge, but also skills, attitudes and behaviors requisite for lifelong civic engagement.

Continued from p. 112

because it defends the United States but because it advances his own personal interest, that's a conflict of interest" and citizens need to speak up.

Trump has said he sees no conflict. In a late-November interview with *The New York Times*, he said that while he intends to avoid situations in which personal benefit might cloud his judgment, he disagreed that the law required him to sell any businesses. "The law is totally on my side, meaning, the president can't have a conflict of interest," Trump said. [72]

Many experts disagree with the president's reasoning, and he already is facing a lawsuit arguing that he is violating the Constitution by allowing his hotels and other businesses to accept payments from foreign governments. [73]

"Voters have got to start to focus on this. Voters need to be educated about what's going on," says Richard Painter, professor at the University of Minnesota School of Law, who was chief ethics lawyer to President George W. Bush from 2005 to 2007.

Some polls show voters are paying attention to the controversy. A December survey by the Pew Research Center found that 65 percent of Americans are "very" or "somewhat" concerned that Trump's business and foreign government ties could affect his ability to serve the country. [74]

Yet another December poll, by Bloomberg, 69 percent of respondents said it would "go too far" to require Trump to "sell all his businesses so that neither he nor his family could potentially profit from actions he takes as president." [75]

That kind of thinking alarms some legal scholars.

Ultimately, it is voters and institutions such as courts and the media who must demand that public officials serve the people's interests and not their own, says Neil Siegel, a professor of law and political science at Duke Law School, in North Carolina. This fact

makes better civic education vital, he says. For example, if the public accepts Trump's assertion that he is not required by law to sell any businesses, "it's very important to make clear to people that that's simply not the case."

The public understanding of such issues ranges from excellent to non-existent, Siegel says. "That's why it's critical for our leaders, including our president, to lead by example instead of preying on the worst instincts and the greatest lack of understanding of their supporters."

This is not a liberal-versus-conservative issue, says Karlan. The concerns are "clearly anchored directly in various pieces of constitutional text and constitutional structure" that both liberal and conservative constitutional scholars agree form the bedrock of the American system, she says.

Reviving Civic Groups

The impact of the internet and social media on civic engagement have been mixed, analysts say. Some say the internet age has made it easier for citizens to become civically engaged and for activists to organize. The Jan. 21 women's marches, they note, started out as a Facebook posting in Hawaii and grew into a worldwide event drawing huge crowds that exceeded expectations. [76]

But others say that activism in the Twitter age is superficial and that citizen-run groups of old have been replaced by professionally run organizations that rely on the internet to find members and raise money. The causes remain passionate — the environment, for example — but reliance on the internet limits face-to-face interaction by grass-roots members. "Clicking a check box on a website is a poor substitute for articulating and even defending your views in a public arena," said Notre Dame's Campbell. [77]

William Forbath, a professor and associate dean for research at the University of Texas' School of Law in

Austin, says it's important to rebuild the locally based citizen-run membership organizations that once helped average Americans learn about and exercise their civic duties.

And as civic skills and traditional grass-roots participation have declined, Americans have turned over their power to affect public policy to public officials, professional organizers and wealthy businessmen, Forbath says.

Wealthy activists on both the left and the right are funding political action committees (PAC) that operate independently from the political parties, and critics of money in politics say these "super PACs" are distorting American democracy. Forbath likens the influence of the rich in government to the "moneyed aristocracy" that the Founders feared in the eighteenth century. "From the beginning it was seen as a real peril to the constitutional order," Forbath says, because government will represent the people's interests only if its leaders are "derived from the great body of society, not a portion of it."

The only way to reverse this trend is for average citizens to raise their voices about public policy, as they did historically, he says. "We have to think about rekindling the kinds of organizations [such as unions] that once stemmed the domination of our policymaking by wealth."

Postelection, some civic groups are reporting good news and bad news.

The Service Employees International Union (SEIU), which has been leading campaigns across the country to raise the minimum wage to $15, expects to face severe obstacles with a Trump-led White House, a Republican-controlled Congress and many statehouses and a Supreme Court soon to have a conservative majority.

The union will cut its budget by 30 percent over the next year in the expectation that a conservative-dominated government may push regulations to curb "the ability of working people to join together in unions," thus dampening membership growth, wrote SEIU President Mary Kay Henry in an internal memo. [78]

The minimum-wage campaign will remain active, however, said Henry. "You can't go smaller in this moment. You have to go bigger." [79]

Others activists say young Americans are showing a new interest in civic engagement.

Contrary to the common belief that young people are unengaged, "the under-26 Millennials I found on the campaign were an incredibly practical, incredibly hardworking demographic," said Becky Bond, who coordinated volunteers for the Sanders presidential campaign. "These are young people that came of age during the financial crisis in 2007, 2008. Many of them had been from downwardly mobile middle-class homes. Instead of being tracked to a four-year college, they're being tracked to community college or having to take time off and work instead of going to college at all," she said. [80]

After Sanders' campaign ended last summer, one group renamed itself Millennials for Revolution, said Bond. It started as a Facebook group and then "became this big very active social media group that also pushed people to take action in real life," she said. "They're continuing to organize for their causes that they care about," such as climate change, racism and immigration reform. [81] ■

OUTLOOK

Civic Surge?

Americans' enthusiasm for political engagement seems high following the 2016 campaign and election, but experts are unsure whether it will last.

Normally after an election, things quiet down for a bit, says Carrie Davis, executive director of the Ohio chapter of the League of Women Voters. "This time, from the

very next day, people were wanting to do something," she says. "That's partly because it was the ugliest election we'd seen. No matter what people's politics are, this got under their skins."

Activism appears to be up in Ohio as well, says Davis. The league's Ohio office is across the street from the Statehouse in Columbus, "and in the last two months, I can't count how many rallies, demonstrations and marches I've seen," she says. "You see a lot of young people carrying signs. That's different. You always have winners and losers. You don't always have people taking to the streets." Across the country, for example, "Not My President" protests broke out the day after the election.

"The big question in my mind, though," says Davis, "is, 'Does it last?' This is wonderful. But can we keep people engaged? You can't tell at this point," she says.

One driving factor is that people want a positive experience from the political process, says Chris Carson, president of the League of Women Voters of the United States, a 97-year-old nonpartisan group that works on voter education, voter turnout and defense of voting rights, as well as campaign finance reform. "People want the facts, the information they need to decide how to vote, and they want to debate issues," she says. "But they want something that doesn't include screaming or character assassination."

Big questions remain about how to reignite civic engagement among Americans, experts say, and the schools' role in it.

While the burden of reversing America's civic-engagement decline shouldn't be laid entirely on the schools, schools can help by teaching students to discuss complicated and contentious issues without descending into the personal attacks that are turning off Americans of all ages to politics, wrote Wisconsin's Hess and Paula McAvoy, program director for the Madison Center for Ethics and Education at the University of Wisconsin. [82]

"Learning to talk about political differences is a 'democracy-sustaining' approach to education, because learning to talk about issues of the day is the cornerstone of a healthy and well-functioning democracy," Hess and McAvoy said. [83]

"We're a pretty disempowered people, but I don't think we're apathetic," says Healy of the Illinois civics initiative. "People think the young are too busy playing on their cellphones to care about their communities. But it's not true."

"What I say to people is that being engaged as the league is engaged is a lot of fun," says the League of Women's Voters' Carson. "It's not boring. It's great sport. You meet great people in the community," she says. "And you're doing really important work. And then I say — 'If you don't do it, then what are we left with?' " ■

Notes

[1] Heidi Stevens, "More than 1,600 Chicago high schoolers witnessing history as election judges," *Chicago Tribune*, Nov. 8, 2016, http://tinyurl.com/zwmd68k.

[2] Quoted in *ibid*.

[3] For background, see "The Facts on Civics Education," Illinois Civics, http://tinyurl.com/hznrulf.

[4] Nora Howe and Thomas Kerr-Vanderslice, "Was Nov. 8 a massive failure of civics education?" *The Hechinger Report*, Nov. 17, 2016, http://tinyurl.com/jdv7ypn.

[5] "5 things about Americans' slipping sense of civic duty," The Associated Press, *The New York Post*, Dec. 29, 2014, http://tinyurl.com/glq6uxk.

[6] Nick Gass, "Americans Bomb Pew test of basic political knowledge," *Politico*, April 28, 2015, http://tinyurl.com/zzl9k2v; "What the Public Knows — in Pictures, Words, Maps and Graphs," Pew Research Center, April 28, 2015, http://tinyurl.com/m4dscjc.

[7] Drew DeSilver, "U.S. voter turnout trails most developed countries," Pew Research Center, Aug. 2, 2016, http://tinyurl.com/zcvtlpf.

[8] Gregory Wallace, "Voter turnout at 20-year low in 2016, CNN, Nov. 30, 2016, http://tinyurl.com/jgdtf5q.

[9] Thom File, "Young-Adult Voting: An Analysis of Presidential Elections, 1964-2012," U.S.

Census Bureau, April 2014, http://tinyurl.com/q4jtph2. Preliminary data for 2016 indicate voter turnout rose to 50 percent for 18-to-29-year-olds. See Clara Hendrickson and William A. Galston, "How Millennials voted this election," Brookings Institution, Center for Information and Research on Civic Learning and Engagement, Nov. 21, 2016, http://tinyurl.com/hpbvwcn.

[10] "2016 Millennial Poll Analysis," Center for Information and Research on Civic Learning and Engagement, October 2016, pp. 8-9, http://tinyurl.com/zc4yz2x.

[11] Evan McMullin, "Trump's Threat to the Constitution," The New York Times, Dec. 5, 2016, http://tinyurl.com/z2ym9zh.

[12] Ibid.

[13] Quoted in Jack Crittenden and Peter Levine, "Civic Education," Stanford Encyclopedia of Philosophy, May 30, 2013, http://tinyurl.com/jroulwu.

[14] "State Civic Education at a Glance," op. cit.; David E. Campbell, "Introduction," in Making Civics Count: Citizenship Education for a New Generation (2012), David E. Campbell, Meira Levinson, and Frederick M. Hess, eds., Kindle edition, location 74.

[15] Meira Levinson, No Citizen Left Behind (2012), Kindle edition, locations 741, 805.

[16] Margaret Stimmann Branson, "The Role of Civic Education," Center for Civic Education, September 1998, http://tinyurl.com/jgsgod3.

[17] David Randall, "Making Citizens: How American Universities Teach Civics," National Association of Scholars, January 2017, http://tinyurl.com/hfjw7k9.

[18] "New Illinois law enforces civics requirement for high schoolers," The Associated Press, Sept. 8, 2015, http://tinyurl.com/qcnrwaf; for background, see Civics Course Implementation Blog, IllinoisCivics.org, http://tinyurl.com/z5wspjo.

[19] For background, see "100 Facts Every High School Student Should Know," Civics Education Initiative, http://tinyurl.com/juooaqz.

[20] Robert D. Putnam, Bowling Alone (2000),

pp. 247, 283; "Masonic Membership Statistics, 2014-2015," Masonic Service Association of North America, http://tinyurl.com/6ptene3.

[21] Nathan Manning and Kathy Edwards, "Does civic education for young people increase political participation? A systematic review," Educational Review, March 11, 2013, pp. 22-45, http://tinyurl.com/gmbycbe.

[22] Quoted in Campbell, op. cit., Kindle edition, location 128.

[23] Diana Hess, "No Time to Take a Pass: Why Schools Should Teach Young People About the 2016 Elections," Social Education, October 2016, pp. 252-253, http://tinyurl.com/huosroy.

[24] The study is at Joseph Kahne et al., "Different Pedagogy, Different Politics: High School Learning Opportunities and Youth Political Engagement," Political Psychology, June 2013, http://tinyurl.com/z5ad2gn.

[25] David E. Campbell, Why We Vote: How Schools and Communities Shape Our Civic Life (2008), Kindle edition, location 163.

[26] Quote in Richard G. Niemi, "What Students Know About Civics and Government," in Campbell, Levinson, Hess, op. cit., Kindle edition, location 365.

[27] Ibid.

[28] File, op. cit.

[29] Peter Levine, "Action civics goes mainstream and gets controversial," A Blog for Civic Renewal, Jan. 23, 2012, http://tinyurl.com/j45tny6.

[30] "Returning To Our Roots: Educating For Democracy," Generation Citizen, 2016, p. 5, http://tinyurl.com/hm76pbv.

[31] "Young Voters in the 2016 General Election," Center for Information and Research on Civic Learning and Engagement (CIRCLE), November 2016, http://tinyurl.com/heebgql.

[32] William H. Frey, "Diversity defines the millennial generation," Brookings Institution, June 28, 2016, http://tinyurl.com/hpo8dam.

[33] "More Young White Men, More College Grads Among 2016 Youth Electorate," CIRCLE, Nov. 14, 2016, http://tinyurl.com/jze26az.

[34] Marjorie Howard, "Reaching Young Voters," Tufts Now, Oct. 23, 2012, http://tinyurl.com/hml4anm.

[35] Sophia A. McClennen, "Why millennials love Bernie Sanders: This is what Trump, Hillary — and Chris Matthews don't understand about how politics has changed," Salon, June 3, 2016, http://tinyurl.com/h83oyqk.

[36] "Returning To Our Roots: Educating For Democracy," op. cit.

[37] Quoted in Alia Wong, "Why Civics Is About More Than Citizenship," The Atlantic, Sept. 17, 2015, http://tinyurl.com/zqals4c.

[38] Civics Education Initiative website, http://tinyurl.com/juooaqz.

[39] For background, see "Civics (History and Government) Questions for the Naturalization Test," U.S. Citizenship and Immigration Services, http://tinyurl.com/kmlslwk.

[40] Wong, op. cit.

[41] Stephanie French, "South Carolina Students Required to Take U.S. Citizenship Test," July 22, 2015, WJBF.com, http://tinyurl.com/j5wfjys.

[42] Quoted in "Government, history knowledge lacking; S.C. plan on target," The [Orangeburg, SC] Times and Democrat, Sept. 18, 2014, http://tinyurl.com/zaohpru.

[43] Quoted in Wong, op. cit.

[44] Margaret Stimmann Branson, "Project Citizen: An Introduction," Center for Civic Education, February 1999, http://tinyurl.com/h5byspw.

[45] Ibid.

[46] For background, see Theda Skocpol, Marshall Ganz and Ziad Munson, "A Nation of Organizers: The Institutional Origins of Civic Voluntarism in the United States," American Political Science Review, September 2000, http://tinyurl.com/zjhwqrc.

[47] Alexis de Tocqueville, "Necessity of Examining the Condition of the States — Part 1," Democracy in America, vol. 1, chp. 5, http://tinyurl.com/zzb6q8x.

[48] Alexis de Tocqueville, "On the Use Which the Americans Make of Public Associations in Civil Life," Democracy in America, vol. 2, chp. 5, http://tinyurl.com/gwvbyvt.

[49] Kathleen Hall Jamieson, "The Challenges Facing Civic Education in the 21st Century," Daedalus, Spring 2013, http://tinyurl.com/hrsmytr.

[50] Quoted in ibid.

[51] Crittenden and Levine, op. cit.

[52] Ibid.

[53] Jamieson, op. cit.

[54] "120 Years of American Education: A Statistical Portrait," U.S. Department of Education, January 1993, p. 27, http://tinyurl.com/jk4awr7.

[55] Crittenden and Levine, op. cit.

[56] Quoted in Gerald Meyer, "When Frank Sinatra

About the Author

Marcia Clemmitt is a veteran social-policy reporter who previously served as editor in chief of *Medicine & Health* and staff writer for *The Scientist*. She has also been a high school math and physics teacher. She holds a liberal arts and sciences degree from St. John's College, Annapolis, and a master's degree in English from Georgetown University. Her recent *CQ Researcher* reports include "The Dark Web" and "Teaching Critical Thinking."

Came to Italian Harlem: The 1945 'Race Riot' at Benjamin Franklin High School," *Political Affairs*, May 3, 2010, http://tinyurl.com/jqft7ad; for background, see Shawn Weldon, "Biographical Note," Leonard Covello, Historical Society of Pennsylvania, http://tinyurl.com/zsm2alz; and Michael C. Johanek and John Puckett, "Accounting for Citizenship: Are our expectations for civic education too modest?" *Education Week*, July 14, 2004, http://tinyurl.com/zfxqb5c.

[57] Jamieson, *op. cit.*

[58] Charles N. Quigley, "Civic Education: Recent History, Current Status, and the Future," paper presented to American Bar Association Symposium, Washington, D.C., Feb. 25-26, 1999, http://tinyurl.com/jrlzp9w.

[59] "State Civic Education at a Glance," Center for Information and Research on Civic Learning and Engagement, http://tinyurl.com/govlxcf.

[60] Putnam, *op. cit.*, pp. 247, 283.

[61] *Ibid.*, pp. 338-339.

[62] *Ibid.*, p. 251.

[63] Mark Hugo Lopez and Carrie Donovan, "Youth & Adult Voter Turnout From 1972-2002," CIRCLE, September 2002, http://tinyurl.com/zogmp77.

[64] Natasha Singer, "A Supreme Court Pioneer, Now Making Her Mark on Video Games," *The New York Times*, March 27, 2016, http://tinyurl.com/j6l8e8b; for background, see iCivics, http://tinyurl.com/cu9fell.

[65] "About Us," Generation Citizen, http://tinyurl.com/hssg9qr.

[66] Diane Rado, "Civics class required for high school graduation will push the envelope," *Chicago Tribune*, Sept. 7, 2015, http://tinyurl.com/hmc2jfw.

[67] Quoted in Ben Kamisar, "Obama 'heartened' by protests, spokesman says," *The Hill*, Jan. 30, 2017, http://tinyurl.com/jhfh9vb.

[68] Diana Hess, *op. cit.*, pp. 252-253.

[69] Michael Gerson, "Trump reveals fragility at the heart of American democracy," *The Washington Post*, Oct. 20, 2016, http://tinyurl.com/zhoe932.

[70] "Here's the Full Transcript of Donald Trump's Inaugural Address," Yahoo, Jan. 23, 2017, http://tinyurl.com/zugvvwp.

[71] Carl Hulse, "Trump Follows Obama's Lead in Flexing Executive Muscle," *The New York Times*, Jan. 26, 2017, http://tinyurl.com/zfsagq6.

[72] "Donald Trump's New York Times Interview: Full Transcript," *The New York Times*, Nov. 23, 2016, http://tinyurl.com/zxyc8sk.

[73] Eric Lipton and Adam Liptak, "Foreign Payments to Trump Firms Violate Constitution, Suit Will Claim," *The New York Times*, Jan. 22, 2017, http://tinyurl.com/hyfx44e.

[74] "Views of President-elect Trump and his administration," Pew Research Center, Dec. 8, 2016, http://tinyurl.com/z7rj3tx.

[75] John McCormick, "Majority of Say Trump Can Keep Businesses, Poll Shows," Bloomberg Politics, Dec. 7, 2016, http://tinyurl.com/glhe2kd.

[76] Perry Stein, Steve Hendrix and Abigail Hauslohner, "Women's marches: More than one million protesters vow to resist President Trump," *The Washington Post*, Jan. 22, 2017, http://tinyurl.com/gqc6mpc.

[77] Campbell, in Campbell, Hess, Levinson, *op. cit.*, Kindle edition, location 98.

[78] Josh Eidelson, "Fear of Trump Triggers Deep Spending Cuts by Nation's Second-Largest Union," *Bloomberg Businessweek*, Dec. 27, 2016, http://tinyurl.com/zzm3cwe.

[79] *Ibid.*

[80] Quoted in Don Hazen, Steven Rosenfeld and Ivy Olesen, "Rules for Revolutionaries: How Big Organizing Can Change Everything," *AlterNet*, Dec. 26, 2016, http://tinyurl.com/jyglmtb.

[81] Quoted in *ibid.*

[82] Paula McAvoy and Diana Hess, "Classroom Deliberation in an Era of Political Polarization," *Curriculum Inquiry*, no. 1, 2013, p. 43.

[83] *Ibid.*, p. 17.

FOR MORE INFORMATION

Center for Civic Education, 5115 Douglas Fir Road, Suite J, Calabasas, CA 91302-2590; 818-591-9321; www.civiced.org. Provides civic education resources nationally and internationally.

Center for Information and Research on Civic Learning and Engagement (CIRCLE), Jonathan M. Tisch College of Civic Life, Lincoln Filene Hall, Tufts University, Medford, MA 02155; 617-627-2529; civicyouth.org. Focuses on civic education and youth civic engagement.

Civics Education Initiative, Civics Proficiency Institute, 8925 E. Pima Center Parkway, Suite 100, Scottsdale, AZ 85258; 480-348-0316; civicseducationinitiative.org. National coalition of individuals and groups that urges states to make the U.S. citizenship test a high school graduation requirement.

Civics for All — The Seattle K-12 Initiative, civicsforall.org. Website of a Seattle coalition seeking to expand civic education in Seattle schools.

Generation Citizen, 175 Varick St., 5th Floor, New York, NY 10014; generationcitizen.org. Helps schools implement action-civics education in six states.

Generation Joshua, 1 Patrick Henry Circle, Purcellville, VA 20132; 877-338-8803; www.generationjoshua.org/GenJ. Group established by conservative Christian homeschoolers offers training programs to help conservative Christian families learn and practice civic activism.

iCivics, 1035 Cambridge St., Suite 21B, Cambridge, MA 02141; 617-356-8311; www.iCivics.org. Creates interactive online games and teaching resources; founded by retired U.S. Supreme Court Justice Sandra Day O'Connor.

Illinois Civics, Robert R. McCormick Foundation, Chicago, IL 60601; 312-445-5000; www.illinoiscivics.org. Public-private coalition that provides civic education resources and is helping to implement a new Illinois law expanding civic education.

National Center for Learning & Civic Engagement, Education Commission of the States, 700 Broadway St., #810, Denver, CO 80203; 303-299-3600; www.ecs.org. Resource and research center on civic education sponsored by the 50 state governors and leaders of the U.S. territories and the District of Columbia.

News Literacy Project, 5525 Devon Road, Bethesda, MD; 301-651-7499; www.thenewsliteracyproject.org/contact. Produces resources on media literacy and civic learning.

Bibliography

Selected Sources

Books

Campbell, David E., Meira Levinson and Frederick M. Hess, eds., *Making Civics Count: Citizenship Education for a New Generation*, Harvard Education Press, 2012.

Scholars from the University of Notre Dame (Campbell), Harvard Graduate School of Education (Levinson) and the conservative American Enterprise Institute (Hess) present analyses of major civic-education issues such as teacher education, the civic-education record and the internet's role.

Graham, Bob, and Chris Hand, *America, the Owner's Manual: You Can Fight City Hall and Win*, SAGE/CQ Press, 2017.

Former Democratic U.S. Sen. and Florida Gov. Bob Graham and his former press secretary provide detailed instructions on how citizens can turn ideas into public policy, including case studies of real projects.

Hess, Diana E., and Paula McAvoy, *The Political Classroom: Evidence and Ethics in Democratic Education*, Routledge, 2014.

Civic-education scholars from the University of Wisconsin, Madison, describe how schools can educate students for active citizenship even in today's contentious political climate.

Levine, Peter, *We Are the Ones We Have Been Waiting For: The Promise of Civic Renewal in America*, Oxford University Press, 2013.

A Tufts University professor of citizenship proposes strategies for reawakening Americans' civic engagement.

Levinson, Meira, *No Citizen Left Behind*, Harvard University Press, 2012.

A Harvard Graduate School of Education professor argues that it is crucial to improve civic education and civic opportunities in low-income and minority neighborhoods.

Putnam, Robert D., *Bowling Alone*, Touchstone Books, 2001.

A Harvard professor of public policy details in this classic work how Americans stopped participating in community groups over the past several decades and discusses the consequences for the nation's political life.

Schmitt, Gary J., and Cheryl Miller, eds., *Trendsetting Charter Schools: Raising the Bar for Civic Education*, Rowman & Littlefield, 2015.

Authors assembled by the director of the American Enterprise Institute's Program on American Citizenship (Schmitt) and the program's former manager (Miller) provide analysis of charter-school civics programs around the country.

Articles

Howe, Nora, and Thomas Kerr-Vanderslice, "Was Nov. 8 a massive failure of civics education?" *The Hechinger Report*, Nov. 17, 2016, http://tinyurl.com/j5sf7rz.

Students are surprised to learn that so few adults vote in presidential elections, say staff members at the civic-education group Generation Citizen.

Pullman, Joy, "Report: Schools Are Teaching Kids to Hate America Under the Guise of 'Civics,'" *The Federalist*, Jan. 16, 2017, http://tinyurl.com/j5lcqqa.

Project-based civics courses promote a progressive agenda damaging to the United States rather than teaching students crucial facts about U.S. history and government, the conservative National Association of Scholars argues.

Wong, Alia, "Why Civics Is About More Than Citizenship," *The Atlantic*, Sept. 17, 2015, http://tinyurl.com/zqals4c.

Analysts debate whether states should require high school graduates to pass the U.S. citizenship test, which immigrants must pass to become naturalized citizens.

Reports and Studies

"Young Voices at the Ballot Box: Advancing Efforts to Lower the Voting Age," Generation Citizen, December 2015, http://tinyurl.com/hj8xybv.

A nonprofit group that provides civic education lays out the arguments and evidence for lowering the voting age to 16 or 17 as a way of encouraging civic engagement among young people.

Kahlenberg, Richard D., and Clifford Janey, "Putting Democracy Back into Public Education," The Century Foundation, Nov. 20, 2016, http://tinyurl.com/jgvjoax.

A senior fellow at the left-leaning Century Foundation (Kahlenberg) and a senior researcher at the Boston University School of Education (Janey) recommend public-policy changes to refocus schools on educating for citizenship

Lautzenheiser, Daniel K., Andrew P. Kelly and Cheryl Miller, "The Contested Curriculum: How Teachers and Citizens View Civics Education," Program on American Citizenship, American Enterprise Institute, June 16, 2011, http://tinyurl.com/h2ybljg.

A survey of 1,000 Americans reveals sharp divisions between the kind of civic education teachers support and the kind that other Americans view as appropriate. The survey also points to Republicans' and Democrats' differing preferences for what civics classes should cover.

The Next Step:

Additional Articles from Current Periodicals

Action Civics

"State launches school civic engagement program," *Wilton Bulletin*, July 6, 2016, http://tinyurl.com/jx33yxt.

Connecticut's secretary of state and education commissioner started the Red, White and Blue Schools Initiative, which rewards schools that create and develop programs that encourage students to become civically engaged.

Lambert, Diana, "New social studies guidelines encourage students as young as 5 to do community service," *The Sacramento Bee*, Jan. 7, 2017, http://tinyurl.com/hsy7gku.

California's most recent social studies and history guidelines encourage teachers to promote civic engagement for students as a way to teach them about politics and society.

Smeltz, Adam, "City teen program offering a lesson in civics," *Pittsburgh Post-Gazette*, Jan. 23, 2017, http://tinyurl.com/hc3j2ld.

A new program in Pittsburgh will allow up to 21 young people to work closely with the municipal government and develop a proposal for the 2018 budget.

Stevens, Heidi, "More than 1,600 Chicago high schoolers witnessing history as election judges," *Chicago Tribune*, Nov. 8, 2016, http://tinyurl.com/zwmd68k.

The nonprofit group Mikva Challenge and the Chicago Board of Elections joined forces to recruit and train high school juniors to serve as elections judges at polling stations for the 2016 presidential election.

Postelection Engagement

Fowler, Geoffrey A., "Can Tech Make Democracy Great Again?" *The Wall Street Journal*, Jan. 18, 2016, http://tinyurl.com/jqr4gj8.

Civic technologists and open-data advocates are pushing for increased use of technology and data as tools to better understand government and hold officials accountable.

Rosenbaum, Steven, "Trump Fires Up Civic Tech Startups," *Forbes*, Jan. 18, 2017, http://tinyurl.com/z75ummf.

The 2016 presidential election inspired increased civic engagement through technology from startups such as Act On This and ShiftSpark that seek to solve problems among voters, donors and local governments.

Stein, Perry, Steve Hendrix and Abigail Hauslohner, "Women's marches: More than one million protesters vow to resist President Trump," *The Washington Post*, Jan. 22, 2017, http://tinyurl.com/zc3787w.

More than a million people rallied at the Women's March on Washington and in cities around the country, sparked in part by President Trump's controversial statements about women.

Teehan, Sean, "Massachusetts AG Maura Healey encourages civic engagement at Springfield town hall," *Mass Live*, Jan. 18, 2017, http://tinyurl.com/z5ffjjs.

In her fourth town hall since the presidential election, the Massachusetts attorney general urged greater civic engagement, urging people to run for office or volunteer.

State Legislation

"Missouri Law to Require Civics Test, CPR for High Schoolers," The Associated Press, CBS St. Louis, June 22, 2016, http://tinyurl.com/jdgkm4p.

As part of a national push from the civic group Joe Foss Institute, a new Missouri law will require the state's high school students to pass a civics exam and force public schools to set aside time daily for the Pledge of Allegiance.

Mannion, Annemarie, and Diane Rado, "LT, Nazareth work to fit civics requirement into curriculum," *Chicago Tribune*, Jan. 9, 2017, http://tinyurl.com/hlu2674.

New legislation in Illinois mandates that high school students take two years of social studies, including a semester of civics, in order to graduate.

Sisk, Chas, "Who's George Washington? What's Congress? Now, Tennessee High School Grads Have To Show They Know," Nashville Public Radio, Jan. 6, 2017, http://tinyurl.com/jnlwdbw.

Tennessee school districts now require high school students to pass the U.S. citizenship test under a new law.

CITING *CQ RESEARCHER*

Sample formats for citing these reports in a bibliography include the ones listed below. Preferred styles and formats vary, so please check with your instructor or professor.

MLA STYLE
Jost, Kenneth. "Remembering 9/11." CQ Researcher 2 Sept. 2011: 701-732.

APA STYLE
Jost, K. (2011, September 2). Remembering 9/11. *CQ Researcher*, 9, 701-732.

CHICAGO STYLE
Jost, Kenneth. "Remembering 9/11." *CQ Researcher*, September 2, 2011, 701-32.

In-depth Reports on Issues in the News

Are you writing a paper?

Need backup for a debate?

Want to become an expert on an issue?

For 90 years, students have turned to *CQ Researcher* for in-depth reporting on issues in the news. Reports on a full range of political and social issues are now available. Following is a selection of recent reports:

Civil Liberties
Privacy and the Internet, 12/15
Intelligence Reform, 5/15
Religion and Law, 11/14

Crime/Law
Jailing Debtors, 9/16
Decriminalizing Prostitution, 4/16
Restorative Justice, 2/16
The Dark Web, 1/16
Immigrant Detention, 10/15
Fighting Gangs, 10/15
Reforming Juvenile Justice, 9/15

Education
Student Debt, 11/16
Apprenticeships, 10/16
Free Speech on Campus, 5/15
Teaching Critical Thinking, 4/15

Environment/Society
Guns on Campus, 1/17
Mass Transit, 12/16
Arctic Development, 12/16
Protecting the Power Grid, 11/16
Pornography, 10/16
Women in Leadership, 9/16

Health/Safety
Opioid Crisis, 10/16
Mosquito-Borne Disease, 7/16
Drinking Water Safety, 7/16
Virtual Reality, 2/16

Politics/Economy
Trump Presidency, 1/17
European Union's Future, 12/16
The Obama Legacy, 11/16
Populism and Party Politics, 9/16
U.S.-Mexico Relations, 9/16
Modernizing the Nuclear Arsenal, 7/16

Upcoming Reports

Forensic Science, 2/10/17   Traffic Deaths, 2/17/17   Immigrants and the Economy, 2/24/17

ACCESS

CQ Researcher is available in print and online. For access, visit your library or www.cqresearcher.com.

STAY CURRENT

For notice of upcoming *CQ Researcher* reports or to learn more about *CQ Researcher* products, subscribe to the free email newsletters, *CQ Researcher Alert!* and *CQ Researcher News*: http://cqpress.com/newsletters.

PURCHASE

To purchase a *CQ Researcher* report in print or electronic format (PDF), visit www.cqpress.com or call 866-427-7737. Single reports start at $15. Bulk purchase discounts and electronic-rights licensing are also available.

SUBSCRIBE

Annual full-service *CQ Researcher* subscriptions—including 44 reports a year, monthly index updates, and a bound volume—start at $1,131. Add $25 for domestic postage.

CQ Researcher Online offers a backfile from 1991 and a number of tools to simplify research. For pricing information, call 800-818-7243 or 805-499-9774 or email librarysales@sagepub.com.

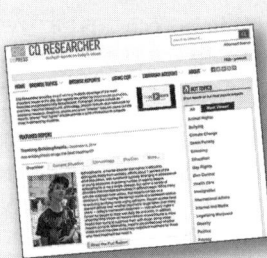

CQPRESS

CQ RESEARCHER

In-depth reports on today's issues

Published by CQ Press, an Imprint of SAGE Publications, Inc. **www.cqresearcher.com**

Forensic Science Controversies

Are courts relying too much on "junk science"?

The criminal justice system often relies on forensic evidence to convict or acquit the accused, but some legal experts say many forensic techniques, including bite-mark, ballistic and hair analysis, lack scientific credibility. Even when forensic methods, such as DNA analysis, are scientifically valid, they often have error rates far higher than juries are led to believe. Prosecutors, however, defend forensic methods as reliable and proven by long-standing practice. They worry that if forensics is undermined, convicting criminals will be much harder. Still, both sides agree that the methodology behind many forensic tools can be strengthened by improving the underlying science. In Texas, which was once heavily criticized for weak oversight of forensic practices, a newly reorganized commission is working to improve forensic science in the state. Meanwhile, the FBI is reconsidering its hair-analysis standards following a scandal that triggered a massive post-conviction review of 2,500 cases in which the agency's lab provided sometimes flawed hair-matching evidence.

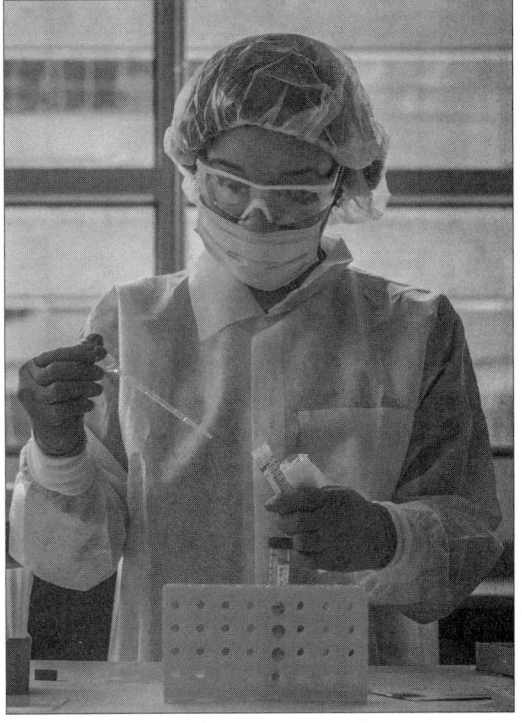

A technician works at the District of Columbia crime lab. Scientists say many forensic techniques, such as bite mark and hair analysis, lack scientific credibility. But prosecutors contend most forensic evidence is reliable and that questioning established methods will make convicting criminals harder.

I N S I D E — THIS REPORT

THE ISSUES **123**

BACKGROUND **130**

CHRONOLOGY **131**

CURRENT SITUATION **136**

AT ISSUE **137**

OUTLOOK **139**

BIBLIOGRAPHY **142**

THE NEXT STEP **143**

CQ Researcher • Feb. 10, 2017 • www.cqresearcher.com
Volume 27, Number 6 • Pages 121-144

SAGE
Publishing

CQPRESS
Los Angeles | London | New Delhi
Singapore | Washington DC | Melbourne

RECIPIENT OF SOCIETY OF PROFESSIONAL JOURNALISTS AWARD FOR
EXCELLENCE ◆ AMERICAN BAR ASSOCIATION SILVER GAVEL AWARD

THE ISSUES

123
- Are forensic sciences reliable?
- Do current legal standards prevent "junk science" from being used in the courtroom?
- Should defendants convicted of serious crimes have a right to DNA testing?

BACKGROUND

130 **Policing's Golden Age**
Investigators began using fingerprinting and other forensic sciences in the early 20th century.

130 **Discredited Techniques**
Polygraph testing, voice printing and bullet-lead analysis faded from use.

132 **DNA Evidence**
DNA was critical in several trials in the 1980s and '90s.

134 **DNA's Shortcomings**
Samples with DNA from multiple sources complicated findings.

135 **Forensic Scandals**
Reform advocates complained about a lack of lab oversight.

CURRENT SITUATION

136 **Policy Shifts**
The Trump administration could have little effect on forensics.

138 **Scandals and Reviews**
The FBI plans to review forensic techniques.

138 **New Research**
Reformers are seeking stronger statistical foundations for forensics.

OUTLOOK

139 **Slow Progress**
Better fingerprint analysis is in the works.

SIDEBARS AND GRAPHICS

124 **State Laws Vary on DNA Testing**
Twenty-two states allow anyone convicted of a crime to seek testing.

125 **DNA Exonerations Remain Low**
The number hovers around 20 per year.

128 **Key Rulings on the Use of Forensic Evidence**
Key cases cover post-conviction DNA testing.

131 **Chronology**
Key events since 1900.

132 **Hair Analysis Remains Subjective, Experts Say**
FBI agrees but says it is still a "valid scientific technique."

134 **Once Weak, Texas Panel Becomes a Watchdog**
Chairman sees "ethical duty" to review forensic evidence.

137 **At Issue:**
Should forensic techniques require federal approval for use in court?

FOR FURTHER RESEARCH

141 **For More Information**
Organizations to contact.

142 **Bibliography**
Selected sources used.

143 **The Next Step**
Additional articles.

143 **Citing *CQ Researcher***
Sample bibliography formats.

 **CQ RESEARCHER**

Feb. 10, 2017
Volume 27, Number 6

EXECUTIVE EDITOR: Thomas J. Billitteri
tjb@sagepub.com

ASSISTANT MANAGING EDITORS: Kenneth Fireman, kenneth.fireman@sagepub.com, Kathy Koch, kathy.koch@sagepub.com, Scott Rohrer, scott.rohrer@sagepub.com

SENIOR CONTRIBUTING EDITOR:
Thomas J. Colin
tom.colin@sagepub.com

CONTRIBUTING WRITERS: Marcia Clemmitt, Sarah Glazer, Reed Karaim, Peter Katel, Barbara Mantel, Chuck McCutcheon, Tom Price

SENIOR PROJECT EDITOR: Olu B. Davis

EDITORIAL ASSISTANT: Anika Reed

FACT CHECKERS: Eva P. Dasher, Michelle Harris, Betsy Towner Levine, Robin Palmer

SAGE Publishing | **CQPRESS**

Los Angeles I London I New Delhi
Singapore I Washington DC I Melbourne

An Imprint of SAGE Publications, Inc.

SENIOR VICE PRESIDENT, GLOBAL LEARNING RESOURCES:
Karen Phillips

EXECUTIVE DIRECTOR, ONLINE LIBRARY AND REFERENCE PUBLISHING:
Todd Baldwin

CQ Press is a registered trademark of Congressional Quarterly Inc.

CQ Researcher (ISSN 1056-2036) is printed on acid-free paper. Published weekly, except: (March wk. 4) (May wk. 4) (July wks. 1, 2) (Aug. wks. 2, 3) (Nov. wk. 4) and (Dec. wks. 3, 4). Published by SAGE Publications, Inc., 2455 Teller Rd., Thousand Oaks, CA 91320. Annual full-service subscriptions start at $1,131. For pricing, call 1-800-818-7243. To purchase a *CQ Researcher* report in print or electronic format (PDF), visit www.cqpress. com or call 866-427-7737. Single reports start at $15. Bulk purchase discounts and electronic-rights licensing are also available. Periodicals postage paid at Thousand Oaks, California, and at additional mailing offices. POSTMASTER: Send address changes to *CQ Researcher*, 2600 Virginia Ave., N.W., Suite 600, Washington, DC 20037.

Cover: Getty Images/*The Washington Post*/Bill O'Leary

Forensic Science Controversies

BY RACHEL KAUFMAN

THE ISSUES

Just after midnight on Aug. 11, 1993, Bill Richards, an electrical engineer, arrived at the motor home he shared with his wife, Pamela, in the high California desert near Hesperia, while they built a new house. [1]

It was dark, and the generator they normally used wasn't running. He went to the shed to restart the generator, then started to walk back to their home. Then, he told police, he tripped over Pamela's half-naked body.

Her head had been crushed, presumably by a blood-spattered cinderblock found nearby. [2] Bill called the police, who determined that — since nobody else seemed to have been on the property at the time of Pamela's death — he must have been the killer.

After two trials ended in hung juries, a forensic dentist testified for the first time at a third trial, saying a crescent-shaped mark on Pamela's hand matched her husband's teeth. Because a person's teeth are unique, chances were only "one or two or less" out of 100 that someone else besides Richards left the bite mark on Pamela's hand, the dentist said. [3] The defense had no answer, and Richards was sentenced to life in prison.

In May 2016, after an appeal by California's Innocence Project, the California Supreme Court reversed that conviction, paving the way for his release from prison a month later.

His exoneration followed passage of a California law updating the definition of "false evidence": Individuals could challenge their imprisonment if their conviction was based on evidence that was

A gun that may have been used in a crime is test-fired to obtain slugs to compare with those recovered at a crime scene. Nearly 400 people have been exonerated in the past two decades after the forensic evidence that helped convict them was shown to have been flawed or misleading.

Getty Images/*Los Angeles Times*/Steve Osman

repudiated by the expert who originally testified or if later scientific research or technological advances undermined it. [4]

According to decades of scientific research, bite mark evidence — in which a forensic odontologist matches a suspect's teeth to a mark found on a victim's skin — has little to no scientific legitimacy. Bite mark analysis and certain other forensic techniques are "the kinds of methods that have to be eradicated from forensic science and replaced with those that come directly out of science," Jo Handelsman, a senior Obama administration policy adviser on science issues, said in 2014. [5]

The forensic sciences cover many disciplines, including the examination of firearms and bullets, tool marks, fire debris, blood type, blood-spatter patterns and digital evidence.

Different types of specialists conduct forensics in a variety of settings. Scientists perform DNA analysis in laboratories, while police or technicians do fingerprint analysis within police departments. Forensic pathologists trained in chemistry, medicine or advanced computer technology conduct digital or fire debris analysis, and law enforcement personnel analyze blood spatter.

A recent government report is especially critical of "feature-comparison" forensics, which match crime scene fingerprints, shoeprints, hair, fibers or tire tracks with those of a suspect. And expert witnesses often overstate the reliability of forensic methods, the reports said, even those with rigorous scientific backing such as DNA.

However, prosecutors and others in the criminal justice system insist most forensic evidence is reliable and worry that questioning established methods will make it harder to convict criminals.

One study estimated that up to 5 percent of those convicted of serious crimes such as rape or murder may be innocent. [6] Rebecca Brown, director of policy at the Innocence Project, a New York-based nonprofit that works to overturn wrongful convictions using DNA evidence, says in about half of the over 300 exonerations her group has facilitated in the past two decades, the real perpetrators had committed 75 rapes, 35 murders and other serious violent crimes before they were brought to justice.

Nearly 2,000 people have been exonerated in the past two decades,

State Laws Vary on DNA Testing

Twenty-two states allow anyone convicted of a crime to apply to a court for DNA testing of evidence used to convict them; 17 allow testing for any felony and 11 allow it only for some felonies.

Availability of Post-Conviction DNA Testing, by State

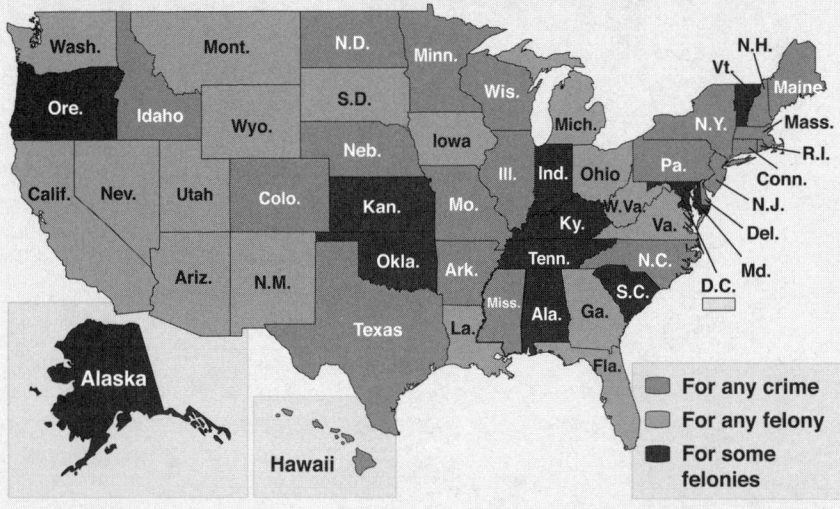

For any crime
For any felony
For some felonies

Source: "Post Conviction DNA Testing," National Conference of State Legislatures, 2013, http://tinyurl.com/j6t3euz

according to the National Registry of Exonerations — a database of all known exonerations since 1989 run by the Newkirk Center for Science and Society at the University of California, Irvine, the University of Michigan Law School and Michigan State University College of Law. And in more than 400 of those cases, flawed or misleading forensic evidence had helped convict them. [7]

"Traditional forensics put these people in prison in the first place," says Brandon Garrett, a University of Virginia law professor and a member of the advisory board of the National Registry of Exonerations who wrote *Convicting the Innocent: Where Criminal Prosecutions Go Wrong*. "People came in and said, 'The evidence absolutely matches the defendant; nobody else could have left that print.' A lot of the science was either exaggerated . . . or inaccurately presented."

A scathing 2009 National Academy of Sciences report on almost all types of forensics said that "with the exception of nuclear DNA analysis, how-ever, no forensic method has been rigorously shown to have the capacity to consistently, and with a high degree of certainty, demonstrate a connection between evidence and a specific individual or source." The President's Council of Advisors on Science and Technology (PCAST) reaffirmed those conclusions in a 2016 report. [8]

Prosecutors and others in the criminal justice field defend forensic science and say proposed reforms would damage the criminal justice system, which they note has its own checks and balances. The National District Attorneys Association (NDAA), the country's largest organization representing prosecuting attorneys, called the PCAST report "scientifically irresponsible." Adopting its recommendations would have a "devastating effect on the ability of law enforcement, prosecutors and the defense bar to fully investigate their cases, exclude innocent suspects, implicate the guilty and achieve true justice at trial," the group said in a statement. [9]

In trials where forensic evidence is introduced, judges act as gatekeepers to determine the reliability and admissibility of forensic evidence, the NDAA said. In addition, it said, "many accrediting bodies consisting of world-renowned scientists and highly skilled experts evaluate forensic labs and practitioners, helping to guarantee that only qualified forensic experts testify to solid forensic facts in our courts." [10]

Association President Mike Ramos added that PCAST members were not "trained or tested for competence in the forensic disciplines," and they "ignored vast bodies of research, validation studies and scientific literature authored by true subject-matter experts." [11]

It's true that there were no forensic scientists in the working group that prepared the 2016 report, but among its members are respected scientists in many disciplines. Eric Lander, the working group chair, was one of the leaders of the Human Genome Project. And he was one of the scientists who wrote, in the PCAST paper, that not even DNA is a bulletproof method.

Some types of DNA analysis are much more complex than others, and only the simplest tests are scientifically valid, said the PCAST report. [12]

Former Attorney General Loretta Lynch said that despite the PCAST report, the Department of Justice (DOJ) remained "confident that, when used properly, forensic science evidence helps juries identify the guilty and clear the innocent." In addition, she said, the department believed current legal standards regarding the admissibility of forensic evidence were "based on sound science and sound legal reasoning." [13]

Garrett says Lynch's response was "dismissive" and "embarrassing." In a later email, he added: "DOJ offered no valid reason for totally ignoring scientific recommendations. The scientists [said] some forensics simply should not be used because there is no evidence of their reliability or validity. The DOJ had no actual response to that."

Nevertheless, he says, the department has made "great efforts" to improve forensics, including — in response to the 2009 National Academy report — creating the National Commission on Forensic Science to promote scientific validity and improve federal coordination on forensics. The commission ramped up its work in 2014 and has issued 10 formal recommendations to the attorney general's office on everything from improving communications between medical examiner and coroners' offices to advancing the interoperability of fingerprint systems. The department has adopted one commission recommendation — on lab accreditation requirements — and has been instructed to take several steps to support some of the other recommendations. [14]

Hard statistics on exactly how important forensics' are in criminal cases are lacking. Evidence is not always available or meaningful, and investigators do not always collect or process it even when available. Prosecutors are unlikely to introduce weak evidence, and defense attorneys may withhold evidence detrimental to their cases.

For some types of crimes, the availability of forensic evidence during the pretrial period makes a suspect more likely to take a plea bargain, according to a report from the National Criminal Justice Reference Center. [15] No one knows, however, whether that is because the suspect was guilty and realized the evidence against him was strong, or because the threat of evidence was enough to prompt a plea or false confession. According to the National Registry of Exonerations, 237 people who have been exonerated had confessed, even though they were innocent.

Because many forensic sciences originated in police departments rather than labs, they lack the kind of peer-reviewed rigor that underlies other sciences, legal and scientific experts say. And while some forensic sciences work — or "have probative value," in the

DNA Exonerations Remain Low

The number of prisoners exonerated based on DNA evidence has remained relatively low, hovering at around 20 per year, despite an overall rise in exonerations. False accusations and official misconduct account for most exonerations, while false or misleading forensic evidence contributes to about a quarter.

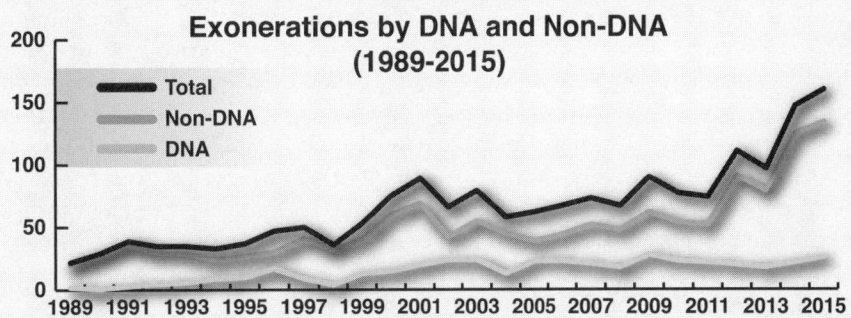

Exonerations by DNA and Non-DNA (1989-2015)

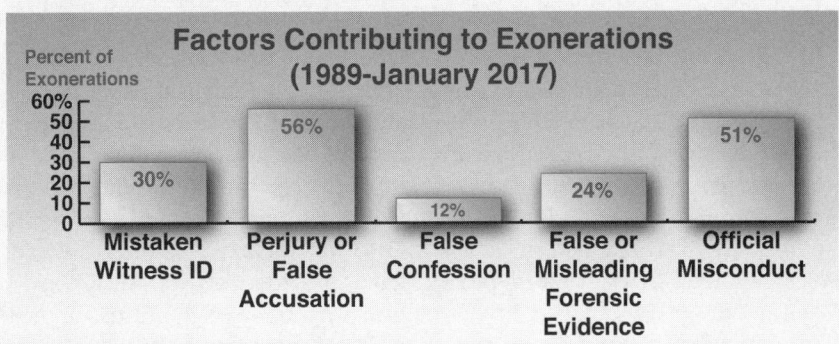

Factors Contributing to Exonerations (1989-January 2017)

Percent of Exonerations

Mistaken Witness ID	Perjury or False Accusation	False Confession	False or Misleading Forensic Evidence	Official Misconduct
30%	56%	12%	24%	51%

Sources: "Exonerations by Year: DNA and Non-DNA," National Registry of Exonerations, Feb. 2, 2017, http://tinyurl.com/lu4kndn; "% Exonerations by Contributing Factor," National Registry of Exonerations, Feb. 2, 2017, http://tinyurl.com/jy6zsal

lingo of lawyers — no one knows how often the results are either wrong or overstated.

Expert witnesses often overstate the reliability of their conclusions, saying they are "100 percent certain" or have "zero," "vanishingly small" or "microscopic" error rates. Even in disciplines with known error rates, the report said, the rates are always higher than "vanishingly small." [16]

For example, ballistics examiners often compare grooves on a spent bullet with those test-fired from a suspected weapon. If they match, the bullets likely came from the same gun. But "we don't have any idea what the

[procedure's] error rates are," says Alicia Carriquiry, director of the Center for Statistics and Applications in Forensic Evidence at Iowa State University.

David Deakin, a prosecutor in Suffolk County, Mass., says proposals for accurately determining error rates are unrealistic. "There's no such thing as a . . . genetics database for guns," says Deakin, who is on the NDAA's forensics science committee, referring to DNA analysis. "You can't test-fire a limited quantity of guns" and use that data to extrapolate to every known gun. That doesn't mean firearms analysis is invalid or unreliable, he says, or that "it shouldn't be used in court."

As for the forensic dentist whose testimony helped convict Bill Richards, he recanted his testimony a decade later, saying he should not have used the "one or two" out of 100 error statistic to back up his belief that Richards' teeth matched Pamela's bite mark. [17] Nevertheless, because Richards' appeal was based on the dentist recanting his testimony — rather than a judge ruling that bite mark evidence is invalid — the Richards case did not set a legal precedent in California for how bite mark evidence could be used.

As experts, prosecutors, defense attorneys and others debate the reliability of forensic evidence, here are some of the questions being raised:

Are forensic sciences reliable?

The report by the President's Council of Advisers on Science and Technology (PCAST) concluded that "there is no science underlying forensic science. It's not a discipline, [but] basically a police-based enterprise being used for prosecutions," says David Faigman, a law professor at the University of California, Hastings College of Law.

Indeed, some high-profile incidents have cast doubt on certain frequently used forensic techniques:

• In 2004, the FBI erroneously matched the fingerprint of a U.S. citizen with prints found at the scene of a train bombing in Madrid, Spain, carried out by Islamic extremists. [18] A government review found that the FBI had allowed its examiners to know personal information about the suspect — that he was Muslim — and to switch back and forth between his print and the print found at the scene in a way that allowed examiners to minimize differences and magnify similarities. [19]

• In 2012, Santae Tribble of Washington, D.C., was exonerated for murder and armed robbery after 28 years in prison. He had been convicted after an FBI examiner said he had microscopically matched Tribble's hair to 13 strands found at the scene. Subsequent DNA testing revealed that none of the hairs were Tribble's and that one belonged to a dog. [20] (*See sidebar, p. 132.*)

• In 2013, David Camm of Georgetown, Ind., was exonerated of murdering his wife and children after DNA found at the scene was linked to the real killer. Blood-spatter experts had disagreed on whether the blood found on Camm's shirt proved he was near his daughter when the gun went off, or were "contact stains" produced when Camm tried to pull his son's body out of the car where he was found. A forensic biologist who testified for the defense said "people who are not scientists" had rendered most of the earlier opinions. [21]

The Tribble case, along with that of Kirk Odom — another D.C. man, who was convicted of rape, sodomy, armed robbery and first-degree burglary, also on hair evidence — triggered a massive post-conviction review of 2,500 cases in which the FBI's lab had provided hair-matching evidence. So far, FBI examiners have been found to have provided flawed testimony in over 95 percent of 268 cases. Of those, 32 defendants had been sentenced to death, 14 of whom were executed or died in prison. [22]

Moreover, the FBI had taught 1,000 state and local crime lab analysts to testify using the same language. Three states are formally reviewing their cases that relied on hair analysis, and informal efforts are underway in another 15. [23]

Experts agree some forensic sciences provide useful information, particularly in excluding a suspect. The markings on a bullet cartridge can be compared with those on a test-fired cartridge from a seized gun; if they don't match, the bullet was not fired from that gun. Other feature-comparison disciplines, such as footwear and tire tread analysis, can also exclude a suspect. The problem arises, reform advocates say, when investigators use these methods to identify a suspect "to the exclusion of all other" suspects.

In addition, the "breathtaking" statistics that forensic examiners use — such as stating that the chances of two shoes sharing three characteristics are 1 in 683 billion — are based on "unsupported assumptions," the PCAST report said. [24]

For example, examiners might match a suspect's shoe based on gouges, cuts, nicks or other types of wear. But no studies have established the accuracy of such matches, said the report, and none has shown how frequently shoes acquire certain wear marks, which could be from a design flaw.

However, the NDAA, the national district attorneys' group, said the forensic disciplines criticized by the PCAST authors are or have been "reliably used every day by investigators, prosecutors and defense attorneys across the United States to aid in both exonerating the innocent and convicting the guilty." [25] Two months later, it released a second statement suggesting that forensic sciences are not actually science, so they do not need to be held to the same standards as science, with its self-correcting peer review and rigorous studies.

Instead, the NDAA said, forensics should be considered "technical" or "specialized" evidence. [26] An example of "specialized" testimony could be a banker testifying on land values or a police officer testifying on the use of code words during drug deals. Under current legal rules, this type of testimony is held to the same admissibility standard as a fingerprint examiner testifying that two prints match exactly. [27]

"The reason the PCAST study chooses to call [forensic sciences] sciences is so they can then hold them to a standard of scientific validity that is difficult, if not impossible, for those disciplines to meet," prosecutor Deakin says. "There is plenty of testimony that has a scientific basis but is not in itself a science and isn't held to the same standards — rather it's held to the same standard of technical validity that the community adheres to."

Some evidence, however, indicates that "the community" — in the case of forensics, the professional associations and boards that self-regulate their practices — are not adhering to a very high standard, legal experts say.

The Association of Firearm and Tool Mark Examiners, the industry body for those who study ballistics markings, has a theory of identification that, PCAST said, uses circular logic. It says an examiner can say that two marks have a "common origin" if there is "sufficient agreement" between their features; it then defines "sufficient agreement" as occurring when the examiner decides that it would be a "practical impossibility" for the marks to have come from different origins. [28]

These things "mean absolutely nothing," says Iowa State's Carriquiry.

A study by the American Board of Forensic Odontology, which oversees bite mark analysts, found false positive rates as high as 63.5 percent. [29] Another study by the board asked 39 examiners if bite mark photos provided enough detail to determine whether the marks were from a human bite and, if so, whether the image had enough distinguishing features to be of value as evidence. The analysts unanimously agreed in only four of 100 cases, and reached 90 percent agreement in only eight. [30]

Critics of forensic science also have noted that many lab workers are not required to have advanced — or any — training in science. [31] Indeed, the definition of a crime lab is wide and fluid; one survey defined a lab as a place that employed a single examiner with a bachelor's degree in science. [32]

Barry Fisher, a former president of the American Academy of Forensic Sciences, says forensics doesn't necessarily need the same scientific grounding as other sciences. Experienced lab workers often draw conclusions "without having numbers to back them up," he says. "Is it really fair to say that if you spent a good portion of your career and you

have some subjective opinions about something [but] you don't have statistics, you shouldn't be using it?"

Nevertheless, Fisher says recent developments — such as the collaboration between the Innocence Project and the FBI to review old hair matching cases — are encouraging. The reviews are "painful, but it's something that has to be done.

Getty Images/*The Denver Post*/Andy Cross

Arson investigators look for clues after a furniture store fire in Denver in 2016. Several years earlier, in a controversial case in Texas, investigators said Cameron Todd Willingham set fire to his house and killed his three young children. He was executed in 2004, despite having proclaimed his innocence. Five years later, the arson science used to convict him was discredited.

If we value our criminal justice system, it's something that has to be seriously looked at and taken care of. Otherwise we're no better than many of the countries that we're out there criticizing."

Do current legal standards prevent "junk science" from being used in the courtroom?

Since 1993, federal and most state courts have used the Daubert Standard to determine whether scientific testimony is admissible as evidence. Under the standard, testimony can be admitted only if the expert can prove that the technique or theory used can be tested; has been peer reviewed; has a known error rate, standards and controls; and

is "generally accepted in the scientific community." (A later addition held that these factors can also be applied to nonscientific expert testimony.) [33]

The rule is intended to make judges responsible for determining what evidence is admissible, says Faigman of the University of California. In fact, when the Supreme Court ruled in 1993 in *Daubert v. Merrell Dow Pharmaceuticals*, observers believed it would result in judges aggressively screening out poorly founded or speculative scientific theories. [34]

Critics say that didn't happen. "*Daubert* doesn't really apply in criminal cases," says Garrett, the UVA law professor. "Judges don't use it. They may use the words of the standard, but they don't really demand that forensic evidence adhere to *Daubert*."

Faigman agrees: "Courts were not applying *Daubert* as rigorously on the criminal side, where prosecutors are introducing arguably the worst forms of junk science." Judges often fear public scrutiny if they don't allow evidence,

Key Rulings on the Use of Forensic Evidence

Several U.S. Supreme Court rulings have helped determine how the courts can use forensics. In the sample of key cases below, the first three deal with admissibility of evidence, and the following three relate to whether criminal defendants, or inmates, have a right to post-conviction DNA testing.

Frye v. United States; Daubert v. Merrell Dow Pharmaceuticals Inc.; and Kumho Tire Company Ltd., v. Carmichael, http://tinyurl.com/hxepomh

These three Supreme Court cases set the legal precedents for what evidence can be admitted in court. *Frye* (1923), determined that expert testimony must be based on "established" science with "general acceptance" in its field. *Daubert* and *Kumho Tire* (1990s) overturned *Frye* and made judges the gatekeepers of both scientific and "technical" testimony.

Brady v. Maryland, http://tinyurl.com/jfemcy4 (1963)

This case determined that prosecutors in criminal trials have an obligation to provide defendants with evidence that might exonerate them. How *Brady* applies to untested DNA evidence has been a question in the courts for years.

Arizona v. Youngblood, http://tinyurl.com/hb2qfuz (1988)

The defendant in this case, who had been convicted of child molestation and sexual assault, argued that he could have been exonerated if the state had properly preserved all forensic evidence related to the crime. The Supreme Court disagreed, saying that "failure to preserve potentially useful evidence," unless as part of a "bad faith" effort, is not a constitutional violation.

District Attorney's Office for the Third Judicial District v. Osborne, http://tinyurl.com/gtqa7al (2009)

This Supreme Court case ended the debate — for now — on whether defendants have a constitutional right to post-conviction DNA testing. The defendant had asked for a more sophisticated test of the genetic evidence than was conducted at the time of the original trial, but the state of Alaska refused to turn over the evidence for retesting; the Supreme Court sided with Alaska, finding that the defendant had no constitutional right to post-conviction testing, even if the test would exonerate him.

he says. "[Judges] aren't trained well enough in science to have the confidence that they're going to get it right."

Disallowing expert testimony, at least in criminal cases, is still the exception rather than the rule. [35] Defense attorneys first challenged fingerprint evidence under *Daubert* in *U.S. v. Byron Mitchell* in 1999, when Mitchell's attorneys argued nobody had satisfactorily proved that fingerprints are unique. [36] But the judge denied the lawyers' request to exclude fingerprint evidence.

In *United States v. Llera Plaza*, however, Judge Louis Pollak of the U.S. District Court for the Eastern District of Pennsylvania ruled in 2002 that fingerprint identification was not a legitimate form of scientific evidence because it flunked all but one of the tests laid out in *Daubert*, that of general acceptance. [37] "[The ruling] was on the front page of *The New York Times*," Faigman says. "An absolute firestorm descended on [Pollak] and on the courts, and he then ordered a rehearing in March of that same year and reversed himself."

Perhaps fingerprints have not been challenged successfully because, in addition to having over 100 years of precedent in U.S. case law, they are reliable — for the most part, fingerprint experts say.

But the scientific community overwhelmingly rejects bite mark evidence. With regard to bite marks, "there's no there there," says attorney Peter Neufeld, co-founder of the Innocence Project.

Yet lawyers and judges have only occasionally challenged the admissibility of bite mark evidence, and courts have always upheld the evidence on appeal, even post-*Daubert*. All 35 appellate courts that have reviewed the issue have found bite marks admissible, Neufeld says, adding: "There's a parallel universe between science on one hand and criminal justice on the other."

Deakin says the prosecutor's association "absolutely agrees" with PCAST that forensic odontology needs further study. But, he adds, "It's one thing to say there's still work to be done, it's another to say it shouldn't be used in court."

Some states require judges to get continuing education, but not necessarily in forensic science. In addition, public defenders are not challenging evidence as often as they should, Faigman says, either because they are overworked or lack the money to hire their own experts.

"The argument that you should just . . . bring in your expert and the jury decides . . . that could be a rule, but that is not the rule" Faigman says. The rule, laid out in *Daubert* and later finalized in the *Federal Rules of Evidence*, is that judges should pre-screen evidence and reject evidence that does not pass muster.

Deakin, speaking on behalf of the NDAA's Forensic Science Committee, says that's what's happening. "In my experience, judges are pretty good at spotting junk science," he says. Junk science may be hard to define, he adds, but "everybody knows it's junk science." Larger cities, including Boston, where Deakin is based, have programs that occasionally review past cases to determine whether convictions were based on reliable evidence.

The PCAST report recommended that judges consider "the appropriate scientific criteria for assessing scientific validity," and disallow expert testimony that describes error rates as "zero," "vanishingly small" or "negligible." [38]

Deakin responds: "We're going to ask judges to be very skeptical of claims by anyone or any scientific group that tell them how they should act in court."

Should defendants convicted of serious crimes have a right to DNA testing?

Garrett of the University of Virginia says, "We have no idea how many innocent people are in prison."

While scholars say it may be impossible to ever know the true wrongful-conviction rate, the rate can be estimated with some degree of reliability by extrapolating from known exonerations, they say. [39] D. Michael Risinger, a law professor at Seton Hall University in South Orange, N.J., has estimated that a minimum of 3.3 percent of capital rape-murder cases end in wrongful convictions. If that floor holds for all death-row crimes, nearly 100 of the 2,905 people being held on death row in the United States as of July 2016 are innocent. [40]

DNA retesting likely could exonerate some of them. But as the 2009 *Osborne* case in Alaska demonstrated, some state officials oppose making DNA testing available to prisoners. (*See box, p. 128.*)

William Osborne was found guilty in 1993 of kidnapping, raping and assaulting

a prostitute in Alaska. At the time, the state crime lab tested sperm found in a condom at the scene using a broad test, which did not exclude Osborne, who is black, but also failed to exclude 16 percent of African-Americans. Osborne wanted a more sophisticated test, but his defense didn't request it, fearing it would harm Osborne's case. Osborne ultimately appealed and asked for the test, but the state refused to turn over the material for testing.

Allowing testing would have superseded established state procedure, says Ken Rosenstein, the assistant attorney general who argued against Osborne's motion. "I view [the case] as one involving state's rights," he says. "The states get to set their own criminal procedure, and the procedure counts for something. . . . You just don't get to ask, 'I want this, I want that.' You have to follow the procedure."

Neufeld, co-founder of the Innocence Project, which supported Osborne's efforts to get the test and even offered to pay for it, said, "We're not talking about vacating a conviction or a retrial or anything like that. We're just talking about a test. What's the big deal? Why can't you give them the test?" [41]

Some in the judicial system fear that giving prisoners the right to test would lead to a flood of lawsuits that would overwhelm already overworked courts and labs. "A blanket right to post-conviction DNA testing would be a dangerous prospect," said Chris Asplen, former director of the National Commission on the Future of DNA Evidence, which was established by the U.S. attorney general to maximize the value of forensic DNA evidence in the criminal justice system. [42]

The Supreme Court in 2009 sided with Alaska, ruling that Osborne was not entitled to circumvent the state's procedures in order to get the test. "A criminal defendant proved guilty after a fair trial does not have the same liberty interests as a free man," Chief Justice John Roberts wrote in the majority decision, and states as a

result have greater flexibility in deciding procedures for post-conviction testing than they do for defendants awaiting trial, he said. [43]

However, Eric Holder, U.S. attorney general at the time, moved quickly to distance the Obama administration from the ruling. "The Court merely spoke about what is constitutional, not what is good policy," Holder said in a statement. "And there is a fundamental difference. Constitutional rights are only one part of a fair and full system of justice." [44]

At the time, Alaska did not have a statute allowing post-conviction testing. Now it does in felony cases involving murder, assault and other offenses "against the person" where the defendant did not plead guilty and where there is a reasonable probability that the test would prove innocence. [45]

Alaska was one of the last states to pass such a law. Every U.S. state currently has a statute allowing some inmates access to DNA testing in certain cases. However, the laws are patchy. (*See map, p. 124.*)

"Some [laws] are limited in substance and scope, or courts interpret the laws poorly," says Brown of the Innocence Project. And many states limit the time frame in which defendants can request a test or limit it to death-row inmates. [46]

Moreover, fewer than half of the states have "robust" laws mandating the preservation of the evidence states say convicts should have access to, Brown adds. "Imagine how screwy that is."

It's often by chance whether the criminal justice system preserves the biological evidence. Kirk Bloodsworth, the first American exonerated from a death-row case, petitioned for a DNA test on the evidence that convicted him of rape and murder in Virginia in 1985. The evidence — traces of semen in the victim's underwear — ultimately was found in a paper bag in the trial judge's closet. [47]

"Whether or not the biology still existed [was] serendipitous," says Neufeld. "Not only did it vary from state to state but county to county. It might have had to do with whether someone had a big enough basement."

Storage capacity is a major obstacle to making evidence available to all convicts. So are the enormous backlogs that exist at most crime labs. By the end of 2009, according to one survey, the nation's public crime labs had more than 1 million backlogged requests for services. [48] ∎

BACKGROUND

Policing's Golden Age

Sherlock Holmes may have been the first forensic investigator. About the time that Sir Arthur Conan Doyle in the late nineteenth century was imagining a detective who collected fingerprints from crime scenes, analyzed handwriting and even determined the origin of a flake of tobacco on a rug, real police officers and scientists were beginning to use fingerprints and other sciences to investigate crimes.

The first true crime lab was established in Lyon, France, in 1910 by Edmond Locard. [49] He believed in the "exchange principle," which asserts that when a perpetrator comes into contact with a crime scene, he or she will invariably leave something and take away something — for example, hair and fibers.

Locard had studied under French police officer and researcher Alphonse Bertillon, who had developed the then-leading "scientific" form of criminal identification, which involved measuring the lengths of various body parts under the theory that no two people's body parts would match exactly. [50] (Bertillon believed, without any proof, that it would be impossible for two people to have

identical measurements of their head, middle finger, left foot and the distance from their elbow to middle finger. [51])

Experts saw "Bertillonage" and other burgeoning disciplines such as fingerprint identification as modernizing and improving the criminal justice system, which had relied on confessions, sometimes forced, and often unreliable eyewitness accounts. [52]

Bertillonage fell out of favor, however, after a 1903 case at Leavenworth Penitentiary in Kansas involving a man named Will West, who was sent to the prison. A filing clerk insisted that West had been to the prison before, based on his Bertillon measurements. West denied it. It turned out that another William West was already serving a life sentence at Leavenworth, and his Bertillon measurements were almost identical to those of the new West. [53] (History is unclear on why: The Wests may have been twins or may have not been related at all. [54])

Nevertheless, sciences' promise in identifying perpetrators seemed to be the dawning of a golden age of policing in the early 20th century, according to Jim Fisher, a former FBI agent. Criminal identification based on eyewitness accounts, including the questionable reliability of mug shot and lineup identifications, would eventually represent "the old-fashioned, unprofessional way of conducting investigations," he writes. [55]

"One of the first things forensic science would replace would be the widespread use of jailhouse informants," he writes, "the most insidious and underhanded tool in the investigator's (and prosecutor's) bag of tricks." New techniques based on science and scientific methodology, he contends, would significantly reduce "the chance of an innocent person being convicted of a crime." [56]

Among these new forensic sciences was fingerprint identification, which had been used in business transactions and official recordkeeping for centuries. A few officials had pushed for the use of fingerprints in law enforcement as early as the mid-1800s, but police departments

generally were uninterested. In 1891, Edward Henry, the British inspector general of police in Nepal (a British protectorate at that time), began examining fingerprints' potential in investigations; by 1897, his system of classification was being used throughout British India and was adopted in England three years later. [57]

In 1906 New York City detective Joseph Faurot became one of the first Americans to use fingerprints to identify a suspect. Faurot, who had been trained in the Henry system now used in London's Scotland Yard, arrested a man leaving a suite in the Waldorf Astoria Hotel. The man, dressed in formal evening wear but not wearing shoes, claimed to be a respectable British citizen named James Jones. Faurot sent the prints to Scotland Yard, where they were matched with those of a known hotel thief named Daniel Nolan. Faced with this evidence, Nolan confessed. [58]

Over the next century, crime labs and police departments devised several techniques now known as forensic sciences. The United States now has about 400 publicly funded forensics labs, fielding millions of analysis requests per year. The vast majority of requests are to analyze and identify seized drugs. [59]

Many of these methods, except for DNA analysis, were "devised as rough [techniques] to aid criminal investigations," not as scientifically validated determiners of one objective truth, according to the PCAST authors. [60] These methods, then, have not been validated in the type of double-blind, black-box studies that the scientific community uses to test its techniques. (In such studies, participants and organizers are blinded to "the right answers," and the results, not procedures, are paramount.)

Discredited Techniques

Many early forensic techniques eventually faded from use, including the polygraph (lie detector) test,

Continued on p. 132

Chronology

1900s-1920s
Forensics, especially fingerprint identification, gains gradual acceptance.

1900
A system of fingerprint identification being used throughout British India is adopted in England.

1906
New York City detective Joseph Faurot uses fingerprints to identify a suspect as a known hotel thief, one of the first — and among the highest-profile — uses of fingerprints in U.S. criminal justice history.

1910
Forensic science pioneer Edmond Locard establishes the first true crime lab in Lyon, France.

1911
In *People v. Jennings*, an Illinois appellate court declares that fingerprint expert testimony is admissible. The first U.S. conviction obtained with fingerprint evidence alone occurs in *People v. Crispi*.

1923
In *Frye v. United States*, the Supreme Court rejects the lie-detector test as junk science in a case involving convicted murderer James Frye.

1960s *Forensic techniques become widespread.*

1963
After the assassination of President John F. Kennedy, FBI investigators try to analyze the chemical composition of the bullets that killed him, in a new technique that will be used for decades despite a shaky scientific foundation.

1980s-1990s
DNA analysis transforms forensics.

1984
British scientist Alec Jeffreys invents the process by which a person's DNA can be analyzed.

1987
Tommie Lee Andrews becomes the first person convicted on DNA evidence in the United States. A semen sample collected at the scene matched Andrews' blood, and he was sentenced to 22 years for rape, aggravated battery and burglary. His lawyers a year later challenged the admissibility of the DNA evidence, but the courts sided with the state of Florida and denied Andrews' request for a rehearing.

1989
New York's Supreme Court rules DNA evidence inadmissible. In response, scientists develop new methods and standards that have enabled DNA analysis to become the gold standard of forensic science.

1993
The Supreme Court, in *Daubert v. Merrell Dow Pharmaceuticals*, makes judges the gatekeepers of scientific evidence and testimony. . . . Kirk Bloodsworth becomes first person on death row to be exonerated by DNA testing.

1995
Former football star O.J. Simpson is acquitted of the 1994 killings of his ex-wife and her friend after a lengthy trial in which the defense team, composed partially of Innocence Project co-founders Barry Scheck and Peter Neufeld, argued that the DNA evidence in question had been so badly contaminated by police that it was too tainted to use.

2000s-Present
Experts begin questioning the validity of forensic science.

2002
Judge Louis Pollak of federal District Court in Philadelphia declares that fingerprints are not scientific; he reverses his decision six weeks later.

2004
National Research Council report finds no probative value in bullet-lead evidence. . . . Cameron Todd Willingham, who was convicted of arson in 1992, is executed in Texas; five years later, a report would strongly condemn the science used in arson investigations that led to his conviction.

2009
National Academy of Sciences report finds concerns with most branches of forensic science.

2013
U.S. District Court Judge Shira Scheindlin declares New York City's "stop-and-frisk" tactics, in which police stop, question and search pedestrians for weapons or contraband, unconstitutional because they disproportionately target black and Latino youths.

2015
The FBI admits that its hair-analysis experts overstated evidence in almost all trials in which they testified over more than a two-decade period before 2000.

2016
President's Council of Advisors on Science and Technology report says many types of forensic evidence are not based on science, and that expert witnesses often overstate the certainty of their conclusions.

Hair Analysis Remains Subjective, Experts Say

FBI agrees but says it is still a "valid scientific technique."

Santae Tribble was 17 in August 1978 when Washington, D.C., police surrounded his mother's house and arrested him. The charge: murder.

The evidence was a stocking mask containing 13 hairs that was found at the scene of the crime. Analysts claimed one hair matched Tribble's "in all microscopic characteristics," the prosecutor told the jury at Tribble's trial, adding, "There is one chance, perhaps for all we know, in 10 million that it could [be] someone else's hair." [1]

And yet, after he spent more than 25 years in prison, court-ordered DNA testing found that none of the hairs matched Tribble's — and one belonged to a dog.

Microscopic hair comparison is part of the branch of forensics known as feature comparison . Such methods involve comparing crime-scene evidence — hairs, fibers, fingerprints or a spent bullet, for example — to a known quantity, such as hair taken from a suspect.

Examiners enlarge the hairs up to 400 times and look for similarities under a microscope. [2] If they match, the suspect is linked to the crime. The FBI provides guidelines for examiners to distinguish between human and animal hair, between the hair of humans of different races and between hair from different parts of the body. [3]

In most cases, however, what constitutes a "match" using the feature-comparison method is entirely subjective, say many scientists. In addition, they say, no one has done a baseline statistical study to determine how often an individual's hair resembles someone else's, or how often the hair from the top of the head differs from that pulled from the nape of their neck.

This issue extends beyond hair comparison. The President's Council of Advisors on Science and Technology (PCAST) has said that the methodology for analyzing fingerprints is "foundationally valid" but is subject to examiners' individual opinions, so fingerprint matches can have a much higher false positive rate than is usually presented to juries. Most other feature-comparison methods also are subject to examiners' subjectivity and lack statistical baselines, the council said.

A 2002 FBI study also highlighted the subjectivity of hair analysis. When the bureau used mitochondrial DNA analysis to re-examine old hair-analysis cases based on microscopic comparisons, it found that in nine out of 80 cases (11 percent) in which an examiner had declared a match, the hairs in fact came from different people. [4]

Nevertheless, when the FBI announced it would review thousands of cases in which FBI hair examiners gave testimony based on microscopic comparisons, it said: "It's important to note that microscopic hair comparison analysis is a valid scientific technique still conducted by the FBI Laboratory." It added: "Cases with hair evidence recovered from a crime scene are examined . . . through a microscope. If these hairs share similar characteristics with a known hair sample, a probative association may be established." [5]

Vanessa Antoun, senior resource counsel with the National Association of Criminal Defense Lawyers, which is assisting the FBI with the review, says the association and other scientists aren't sure whether hair comparison is valid.

The PCAST report argued that the Justice Department faces a small conflict of interest when discussing whether forensics it used might be scientifically invalid. Critical evaluations by the department "might be taken as admissions that could be used

Continued from p. 130

"voice printing," which purported to be able to uniquely identify a person by the sound of his voice, and bullet-lead analysis.

From the 1960s until 2005, the FBI used chemical analysis to try to link bullets found at crime scenes to those found in a suspect's possession. If two bullets were found to have the same chemical composition, they were assumed to have come from the same box. In the 1990s, however, an FBI study discovered that bullets packaged 15 months apart had the same composition, and bullets in a single box often did not match. [61] But the bureau did not stop using bullet-lead methods until a 2004 National Academy of Sciences

report called FBI bullet-lead testimony "unreliable and potentially misleading."

Likewise, other practices remained in use despite growing concern from the scientific community about their value.

Even fingerprints have come under fire. After the FBI mistakenly identified an American as the person who left a partial fingerprint in the Madrid train bombing case, the Office of the Inspector General concluded that "misidentification could have been prevented" if proper procedures had been followed, namely, if the examiner had not been told the suspect was Muslim. "One of the examiners candidly admitted that if the person identified had been someone without these characteristics, like the 'Maytag repairman,' the laboratory might

have revisited the identification with more skepticism and caught the error." [62]

Further, the examiners were allowed to go back and forth between the print found at the scene and the American's print on file, a practice the FBI now discourages. [63] "Having found as many as 10 points of unusual similarity [between the prints], the FBI examiners began to 'find' additional features in [the latent print] that were not really there," the inspector general said. [64]

DNA Evidence

Many agree that the advent of DNA pushed scientists to be more critical of other forensic discito challenge past convictions or current prosecutions," the report's authors wrote. Thus, "it is important for evaluations of scientific validity and reliability to be carried out by a science-based agency that is not itself involved in the application of forensic science within the legal system." [6]

The mistakes in hair analysis result from a series of fallacies, one of the biggest being that many forensic practitioners claim their substantial casework experience is a predictor of accuracy, according to three British scientists. "The statement in court, 'I know this to be true because I have seen hundreds of these cases,' should never be accepted," they wrote in 2015. [7]

Forensic mistakes can have devastating effects on the lives of the wrongly convicted. Tribble was exonerated in 2012 at age 51 after spending more than 26 years in prison, where he contracted hepatitis C and HIV from heroin use. (Tribble and his attorneys said he was clean when he entered the system.) Prison, according to Tribble's lawyers, who sued the District of Columbia for restitution, "ruined his life, leaving him broken in body and spirit and, quite literally, dying." [8]

In 2016, a D.C. Superior Court judge ordered the city to pay Tribble $13.2 million — one of the largest such awards the District of Columbia has been ordered to pay. Tribble's prognosis, however, is not good. Doctors say he may not live past 2019. [9]

— *Rachel Kaufman*

Santae A. Tribble, left, of Washington, D.C., was exonerated after he spent more than 26 years in prison. Faulty FBI hair analysis helped convict him of murder and armed robbery charges.

[3] Douglas W. Deedrick and Sandra L. Koch, "Microscopy of Hair Part 1: A Practical Guide and Manual for Human Hairs," *Forensic Science Communications*, January 2004, http://tinyurl.com/gmmjmjv.

[4] M.M. Houck and B. Budowle, "Correlation of microscopic and mitochondrial DNA hair comparisons," *Journal of Forensic Science*, September 2002, http://tinyurl.com/gw6ldeh.

[5] "FBI/DOJ Microscopic Hair Comparison Analysis Review," FBI, June 10, 2016, http://tinyurl.com/zakkqwp.

[6] "Report to the President: Forensic Science in Criminal Courts: Ensuring Scientific Validity of Feature-Comparison Methods," President's Council of Advisors on Science and Technology, September 2016, http://tinyurl.com/zzz3aso.

[7] Éadaoin O'Brien, Niamh Nic Daeid and Sue Black, "Science in the court: pitfalls, challenges and solutions," *Philosophical Transactions B*, Aug. 5, 2015, http://tinyurl.com/j3hl3m2.

[8] *Tribble v. District of Columbia*, Superior Court of the District of Columbia, 2016, http://tinyurl.com/zw9uvm9.

[9] Spencer S. Hsu, "Judge orders D.C. to pay $13.2 million in wrongful FBI hair conviction case," *The Washington Post*, Feb. 28, 2016, http://tinyurl.com/z78lvjf.

[1] Spencer S. Hsu, "For D.C. man, 28 years lost," *The Washington Post*, April 17, 2012, http://tinyurl.com/z5rlyey.

[2] Douglas W. Deedrick, "Hair Evidence," *Forensic Science Communications*, July 2000, http://tinyurl.com/ho53dbe.

plines, yet DNA has had its own growing pains.

DNA evidence was critical in several high-profile trials in the 1980s and '90s. The first DNA-based conviction in the United States occurred in Florida in 1987, when Tommie Lee Andrews was found guilty of rape after DNA tests matched his genetic material from a blood sample with semen traces in a rape victim. [65]

By the end of 1988, DNA evidence had been admitted in more than 80 trials across the country, and the FBI had opened its own DNA lab. [66]

Alarmed by DNA's rapid ascent and its perception of infallibility, defense lawyers and DNA experts Peter Scheck and Neufeld, who would later co-found

the Innocence Project, also began to argue against DNA's absolute reliability. In one case, they sought to distance DNA typing in a research or medical setting from DNA analysis in criminal justice.

In a research setting, technicians have a practically unlimited supply of material to analyze, because if they run out, they can go back to the patient and draw more blood. In court cases, biological material is often scant, degraded or contaminated. [67]

Scheck and Neufeld also argued that DNA analysis performed by private companies (major players in the field at the time) was suspect, because their methodologies and quality controls were trade secrets protected from scrutiny.

Then, in 1994, the O.J. Simpson case introduced DNA to the American public in a high-profile televised trial. "After watching this trial, people understood that we had this technology [DNA] in forensic matters," Scheck told the *Los Angeles Times*. [68] DNA testing linked Simpson, a former football star, to the killings of his ex-wife and a friend of hers, but the defense team attacked police officers' sloppy handling of the material, arguing their findings were unreliable. Swabs were placed in plastic bags and kept in a hot car for hours, and the analyst who did the testing couldn't remember whether he had changed his gloves between samples. [69]

DNA technology, however, was rapidly advancing. By 1996, the National

Once Weak, Texas Panel Becomes a Watchdog

Chairman sees a "moral and ethical duty" to review forensic evidence.

Among the handful of state commissions dedicated to improving forensic science in their criminal justice systems, Texas' Forensic Science Commission is considered one of the best.

But the Texas commission didn't start out that way. First formed in 2005 after a scandal at the Houston Crime Lab, the commission did not receive any state funding or office space for two years. [1] Then, the panel's first real investigation nearly killed it.

The Innocence Project, a New York-based group working to overturn wrongful convictions using DNA evidence, had asked the commission to look into the case of Cameron Todd Willingham, whom prosecutors said had killed his three young children by setting his house on fire. He steadfastly maintained his innocence, even refusing a plea deal that would have given him life in prison in lieu of a trial possibly ending in the death penalty.

He was convicted in 1992 and executed in 2004. The evidence against him included a jailhouse informant who said Willingham had confessed and arson investigators who said the fire was deliberately set. [2]

While Willingham was on death row, however, the prosecution's case began to crumble. The informant, eventually diagnosed with post-traumatic stress disorder and bipolar disorder, recanted his testimony and then recanted his recantation. The arson investigator's conclusions faced a growing number of questions because they relied on techniques that scientists had disavowed since the 1970s. [3]

The Texas Forensic Science Commission hired fire scientist Craig Beyler to look into the evidence that had sent Willingham to his death. In a 2009 report, Beyler concluded that the views of the investigator who testified against Willingham were "hardly consistent with a scientific mindset." [4]

But before Beyler could officially present his findings to the commission, Republican Gov. Rick Perry, in a decision that made national headlines, abruptly fired commission Chairman Sam Bassett and two other members and brought on three new commission members. [5] The new chairman, John Bradley, who had a reputation as a tough-on-crime district attorney in Williamson County, had told the press Willingham was a "guilty monster." [6]

In 2011, the commission released its own report on the Willingham case. But criminal justice reform advocates who had hoped Texas would be the first state to acknowledge that it had executed an innocent person were disappointed. The commission's report did not comment on innocence or guilt. Instead, it said, the investigators were simply using the methods of the time, even though they had been discredited. It recommended improved fire science be used in future investigations. [7]

The commission soon ran into two more obstacles that limited its effectiveness. In July of that year, the Texas attorney general declared that the commission did not have jurisdiction over cases tried before the commission was created in 2005, nor could it investigate any concerns unless they involved a state-accredited lab. [8] That ruling, said the Innocence Project's policy director, who had encouraged the commission to investigate the Willingham case, "may have largely neutered this commission's potential effectiveness and undermined legislators' clear intent" in creating it. [9]

Then things changed. The chairman chosen by Perry was not reappointed, and — with the help of the state fire marshal — commission members began to review other arson investigations that had occurred since 2005. "There is no legal requirement

Research Council was able to state that "the admissibility of properly collected and analyzed DNA data should not be in doubt." [70] Neufeld and Scheck now call DNA "a gold standard for truth-telling." [71]

DNA, of course, has since played an enormous role in the criminal justice system. In addition to the Simpson case, the so-called Central Park Five case, in which five black and Latino teens had been convicted in 1989 of assault, robbery, riot, rape, sexual abuse and attempted murder of a jogger in Central Park, remained in prison until 2002 when DNA evidence exonerated them.

DNA's Shortcomings

The use of DNA is not infallible, especially when it is found in complex mixtures.

Modern DNA analysis uses a process in which a set of predetermined DNA segments are "amplified," or copied millions of times over, and the relative lengths (called "peak heights") of the segments are measured and compared with those in the DNA from another source. If the DNA is from the same person, the peak heights would match. In a situation in which the DNA of two people end up in one sample,

such as in biological material from a rape kit, the peak heights of the victim can be subtracted, leaving only the DNA of the assailant.

However, analysis is more complicated when a sample has DNA from multiple sources, such as those recovered from, say, a car's steering wheel. It is possible but difficult to obtain useful results from this type of analysis. For instance, Italian scientists reported on two cases in 2015 in which they were able to analyze DNA from multiple sources found on a dead boy's coat and a missing man's boot. By doing so they were able to reopen the murder investigation into the boy's death and

for retroactive review," said the new chair, Nizam Peerwani, who is chief medical examiner for Tarrant County (Fort Worth). "But there is some moral and ethical duty to do that." [10]

Since then, the commission has developed a reputation as one of the nation's most important forensic science policy groups. In 2013, the Legislature doubled the commission's budget and expanded its jurisdiction to any lab in Texas, as well as to any forensic discipline or procedure that had generated a citizen complaint.

The commission is establishing a system for collecting DNA from unidentified bodies found near the Texas border with Mexico, reviewing old hair-comparison cases (part of an FBI nationwide review), and reviewing how slight changes in how DNA matches are calculated might have skewed some results. [11]

Most recently, the commission examined whether flawed bite mark evidence contributed to wrongful convictions in Texas, ultimately recommending a moratorium on the use of such evidence and ordering a review of past cases that used bite mark testimony. [12]

Commission members say their actions are less aimed at assigning blame than at improving forensic sciences.

"If the science was unsupported at the time and could lead to erroneous results [but]a scientist followed [it] in good faith, that's fine," said commission member Lynn Robitaille Garcia, a lawyer. "It's about providing a safe harbor, a place for labs to come and work through these issues in a way no one else around the country is doing." [13]

— *Rachel Kaufman*

[1] Michael Hall, "False Impressions," *Texas Monthly*, January 2016, http://tinyurl.com/zdqc6h9.

Members of the Campaign to End the Death Penalty demonstrate at the Criminal Justice Center in Austin, Texas, on Oct. 6, 2010, during a hearing about controversial arson evidence that had been used to convict Cameron Todd Willingham, who was executed in 2004.

[2] David Grann, "Trial by Fire," *The New Yorker*, Sept. 7, 2009, http://tinyurl.com/kf66qzf.
[3] *Ibid*.
[4] Craig Beyler, "Analysis of the Fire Investigation Methods and Procedures Used in the Criminal Arson Cases Against Ernest Ray Willis and Cameron Todd Willingham," http://tinyurl.com/ztdck6l.
[5] Hilary Hylton, "Why did Texas gut its forensics commission?" *Time*, Oct. 6, 2009, http://tinyurl.com/z968mf9.
[6] Hall, *op. cit*.
[7] Beyler, *op. cit*.
[8] Hall, *op. cit*.
[9] Brandi Grissom, "Forensic panel calls for review of past arson cases," *The Texas Tribune*, Sept. 9, 2011, http://tinyurl.com/jz8edjs.
[10] *Ibid*.
[11] Hall, *op. cit*.
[12] "In a landmark decision, Texas Forensic Science Commission issues moratorium on the use of bite-mark evidence," Innocence Project, Feb. 12, 2016, http://tinyurl.com/hduenca.
[13] Hall, *op. cit*.

solve the case of the missing man. [72]

In most cases, rather than positively identifying a person based on a DNA profile, investigators ask whether a person's DNA could be present within the mixture, and if so, the odds of that observation occurring by chance. [73]

But the formulae for determining those probabilities, called the "combined probability of inclusion" statistic, can be subjective. For example, in the 2003 double-homicide case, *Winston v. Commonwealth*, a prosecutor told the jury the probability that the defendant's DNA appeared on a discarded glove purely by chance was 1 in 1.1 billion. But in 2009, according to the PCAST report, a

paper by criminologist W.C. Thompson made "a reasonable scientific case" that the chance was closer to 1 in 2. [74]

Forensic Scandals

Criminal justice reform advocates complain that oversight of the laboratories where most forensics work is performed is often slipshod and many lab technicians have weak science backgrounds.

The number of scandals associated with crime labs around the country indicates a need for stricter procedural controls, says Garrett of the University

of Virginia. Since 2006, according to the National Association of Criminal Defense Lawyers, more than 30 scandals have erupted in labs, ranging from technicians losing or stealing drug samples to mixing up DNA samples to deliberately falsifying results. [75]

While stricter protocols likely would not stop a deliberate bad actor, according to an article in *Chemical and Engineering News*, they would go a long way toward preventing innocent errors and help management discover dishonest technicians sooner. [76]

In most states, accreditation of crime labs is voluntary. [77] In 2009, the Bureau of Justice Statistics found that 17 percent

The murder trial of former football star O.J. Simpson, right, introduced DNA to the American public in a high-profile televised trial. Simpson was acquitted of the 1994 killings of his ex-wife and a friend after the defense team successfully argued that the DNA evidence was tainted. Scientists say even scientifically valid DNA analysis can have error rates that are higher than juries are led to believe.

of publicly funded labs were unaccredited. [78] Accreditation rates at private labs are thought to be much lower. [79]

In 2015, the Justice Department announced that it would require its prosecutors to use only accredited crime labs "when it is practicable." [80] The National Commission on Forensic Sciences had recommended the requirement, and commission members hailed its adoption. But others say it doesn't go far enough.

"The accreditation requirements are really thin," Garrett says. "Accreditation requires agencies have the right procedures in place, [but] they don't actually do quality control."

In some cases, labs can choose which cases they submit to the accrediting board (often an independent nonprofit or for-profit company) for review, rather than having them selected at random. "What's the chance you'll give them your best-ever casework?" National Commission on Forensic Science Commissioner Paul Giannelli told the news documentary program "Frontline." "It's high. That's what I would do." [81]

Crime labs need to be regulated and required to follow scientific standards, Garrett says. "If clinical labs are doing medical testing in a way that's shoddy, they lose their federal grants and get shut down because lives are at stake. But lives are at stake for forensic science too," he says.

Even the FBI's labs have come under fire. The two most high-profile incidents in the last two decades — the bullet-lead and hair-comparison scandals — have involved the misapplication of discredited forensic techniques by the FBI. ■

CURRENT SITUATION

Policy Shifts

With a new Republican administration and a new attorney general, changes in forensic policies likely are coming at the federal level.

The tough-on-crime stance of Attorney General Jeff Sessions, a former Republican senator from Alabama, is not likely to directly affect the world of forensics, because states handle most criminal prosecutions. However, experts say federal policies can signal shifts in priorities that could trickle down to the states.

In addition, Sessions could influence spending at the Office of Justice Programs, which currently provides $2 billion annually to a wide range of programs. According to a former high-ranking Justice Department official, spending priorities under Sessions could shift away from measures intended to prevent crime, rehabilitate prisoners or reform forensics and toward law enforcement.

Sessions has not said where he stands on forensics reform, but as a member of the Senate Judiciary Committee he has attended hearings on the topic. In a 2009 hearing on scientific issues plaguing forensic science, he complained about the lack of funding dedicated to forensic labs.

"Forensic sciences are being shortchanged financially, and we can do better," he said, adding that justice is delayed when prosecutors cannot get forensic reports in a timely manner. On the other hand, he said, "I don't think we should suggest that those proven scientific principles that we've been using for decades are somehow uncertain and leaving prosecutors having to fend off challenges on the most basic issues in a trial." [82]

President Trump has not spoken about forensic sciences, and his comments on crime policy during the campaign mostly praised "law and order" and "stop-and-frisk" tactics, where police stop pedestrians, question them, then search them for weapons or contraband. (The practice, at least as applied in New York City, was declared unconstitutional in 2013 by U.S. District Court Judge Shira Scheindlin, who found it disproportionately targeted black and Latino youths. [83])

Trump also has doubled down on his claims that the Central Park Five were guilty, despite their 2002 exoneration

Continued on p. 138

Getty Images/Sygma/Ted Soqui

At Issue:

Should forensic techniques require federal approval for use in court?

SARA CHU
SENIOR FORENSIC POLICY ADVOCATE, INNOCENCE PROJECT

WRITTEN FOR *CQ RESEARCHER*, FEBRUARY 2017

u.S. Marine Keith Harward was sentenced to death for a Newport News, Va., rape and murder based largely on the testimony of two forensic dentists who concluded that a bite mark on the victim came from Harward. In fact, seven dentists, including Harward's defense expert, erroneously named him as the source of the bite mark. Harward was spared the death penalty because of an issue regarding how the capital murder statute should be interpreted. But he served 33 years in prison before DNA evidence proved his innocence.

His case isn't unique. At least 25 people have been arrested or convicted based on discredited bite mark evidence. More broadly, the misapplication of forensic science has contributed to nearly half of the nation's 347 wrongful convictions overturned by DNA.

The National Academy of Sciences acknowledged the problems with forensic science in 2009, concluding that "with the exception of DNA, no forensic method has been rigorously shown to have the capacity to consistently, and with a high degree of certainty, demonstrate a connection between evidence and a specific individual or source." The President's Council of Advisors on Science and Technology published similar findings last year. On Feb. 12, 2016, the Texas Forensic Science Commission called for a moratorium on bite mark comparisons until foundational scientific issues are satisfied. If a bite mark is not scientifically sound in Texas, how can it be in any other state?

To prevent further injustice and to ensure that evidence used against all defendants is valid, the federal government should evaluate the validity and reliability of forensic disciplines to ensure consistent application of evidence in courtrooms nationwide. The National Commission on Forensic Science approved a recommendation on this issue last September and named the National Institute of Standards and Technology as the agency responsible for this work.

Just as we expect clinical labs in Detroit and Dallas to arrive at the same result for a strep throat test and to base those results on validated techniques, so too should there be national standards for the results of forensic analysis. For this reason, when addressing fundamental issues in forensic science, a national strategy is needed, and the federal government has an essential leadership role to fulfill. The federal government is also uniquely positioned to fund a forensic science research agenda and to ensure that all states benefit from this work.

BARRY A. J. FISHER
FORMER CRIME LAB DIRECTOR, LOS ANGELES COUNTY SHERIFF'S DEPARTMENT; FORMER PRESIDENT, AMERICAN ACADEMY OF FORENSIC SCIENCES, INTERNATIONAL ASSOCIATION OF FORENSIC SCIENCE AND AMERICAN SOCIETY OF CRIME LABORATORY DIRECTORS

WRITTEN FOR *CQ RESEARCHER*, FEBRUARY 2017

*t*here are several issues wrapped up in this simple question. What are "forensic techniques?" Courts do not differentiate between forensic techniques and any other expert evidence. Expert witnesses are different from ordinary ones and may offer their opinions and conclusions to juries. Expert witnesses afford juries an understanding of technical issues beyond their areas of knowledge.

Judges are the so-called gatekeepers and decide if expert testimony is reliable enough for a jury to hear and consider. Judges are guided by earlier cases ruled on by higher courts, along with Rule 702 of the Federal Rules of Evidence. The cases usually cited are *Frye v. United States*; *Daubert v. Merrell Dow Pharmaceuticals Inc.*, and *Kumho Tire Co. Ltd. v. Carmichael*. These cases and Rule 702 set forth the standards judges are to follow to determine the admissibly of expert evidence.

In 2009, the National Academy of Sciences issued a report on forensic science, "Strengthening Forensic Science in the United States: A Path Forward." It noted shortcomings in certain classifications of forensic science, notably "pattern evidence" — such as fingerprints, firearms evidence, tool-mark evidence, foot wear and tire impression evidence and bite marks — which is evidence based on subjective observations.

As a result of the report and recommendations from criminal-justice experts, the U.S. Department of Justice, in collaboration with the National Institute of Standards and Technology, formed the National Forensic Science Commission and the Organization of Scientific Area Committees for Forensic Science. These bodies are to develop consensus standards for techniques used in public crime labs.

In a sense, a federal body is working to develop reliable standards in crime laboratories. However, under the rules of evidence, it is still within the courts' purview to decide whether forensic evidence is admissible.

Courts do not differentiate between types of expert evidence. If there were a requirement for a federal body to review one category of expert evidence, it would have to review all: social science, engineering, medical, psychiatric, psychological, accounting and any other type of expert evidence presented in courts.

Basically, such review is an impracticable idea.

Continued from p. 136

based on DNA evidence and a detailed confession by a serial rapist named Matias Reyes, who was already serving a life sentence in another case. [84] (The statute of limitations on the Central Park case had run out by this time, anyway.) [85] During their 1989 trial Trump had taken out full-page newspaper ads calling for a return of the death penalty for the five defendants. Last October Trump repeated his claim that they were guilty — more than a decade after their exoneration.

"They admitted they were guilty. The police doing the original investigation say they were guilty," he said. "The fact that that case was settled with so much evidence against them is outrageous." [86]

If anything, the incident shows that "Mr. Trump is apparently ignorant of our country's epidemic of wrongful convictions, which disproportionately affect minorities," wrote Sarah Burns, one of the writers and directors of the 2013 documentary, "The Central Park Five." [87]

Scandals and Reviews

After the FBI hair scandal, then-Deputy Attorney General Sally Yates announced that the department would conduct similar reviews for other forensic disciplines, but it is unclear whether this will still happen under the Trump administration. [88]

The original hair-testimony review was "unprecedented," the Innocence Project's Neufeld says, not only because of how wide-reaching it was but because of the level of transparency the FBI provided; the bureau even collaborated with the Innocence Project and the National Association of Criminal Defense Lawyers.

The new reviews, in which the Innocence Project is also assisting, are in the early stages, Neufeld says. The bureau must first define what constitutes appropriate testimony in other forensic

disciplines. Then the bureau will review transcripts and lab reports to see if statements were made "that exceeded the limits of science."

Meanwhile, the FBI's review of its hair-matching testimony continues. When the bureau released its preliminary results, the agency had examined 342 cases; another 1,200 remain to be analyzed. In 700 of those cases, police or prosecutors have not responded to requests for information, according to the bureau. [89]

New Research

The National Institute of Standards and Technology and other agencies are promising millions of dollars for research on some widely used techniques. Research groups, such as Iowa State's Center for Statistics and Applications in Forensic Evidence, may help develop more robust statistical foundations for forensic techniques. The center is funded for only five years, but that should be enough time "to make good progress," director Carriquiry says.

Other studies also are underway. The FBI, for example, is undertaking a massive initial study on footwear characteristics, studying 700 pairs of identical boots worn by FBI special agent cadets during a 16-week training camp. [90] Studying how the boots change over time could provide an initial dataset for studies that determine the statistical chance of two different shoes leaving the same footprint. [91]

Scientists also may develop new ways to analyze old information. For example, forensic firearms examiners are starting to use 3-D topographic maps of bullets, rather than the old 2-D "comparison microscope" method. According to the National Institute of Standards and Technology, the 3-D maps produce much more detailed data and allow for greater accuracy. [92]

Robert Thompson, senior forensic science research manager at the institute, predicts that within about five

years these tools will be proven "helpful in the courtroom and in the crime laboratory." Then within another five years, he says, "we'll have validated statistical methods to measure the similarity" between one bullet and another.

New techniques also may come into use soon. Future investigators may identify suspects based on their microbiomes — the colonies of microorganisms that live in and on every human being. They also might develop new tools for retrieving and interpreting digital information or to identify a person based on sunscreen or makeup smudges left on a cellphone screen. [93] In addition, researchers are developing ways to help medical examiners determine time of death based on a body's "necrobiome," the bacteria and microorganisms that move in after a person dies. [94]

Scientists also have developed a way to retrieve fingerprints left on metal — even after the prints have been wiped off (sweat corrodes brass, and an electrical charge and carbon powder reveal the hidden prints). The technique has been used in at least one case in court. [95]

A new technology — rapid DNA testing — just making its way into law enforcement allows DNA to be read "in less time than it would take to wait at a typical DMV," according to *The New Republic.* [96] Police departments have begun using the technology, but there is no national database yet to centrally store and search results. Rapid testing would have "profound implications" for criminal justice, said Rep. James Sensenbrenner, R-Wis., who co-sponsored a measure to allow police departments that use rapid DNA testing to upload the results into the national DNA database to search for matches. Exonerations of arrestees could take hours instead of days, he said. [97]

The rapid test, however, has raised concerns among some lawyers and forensic experts over cost and privacy. The test costs more than a regular lab test, and it could increase the potential for abuse by creating a massive database of people who might have done nothing more heinous than be pulled over for a routine traffic stop. [98]

Another emerging DNA technique — familial searching — also raises privacy and fairness concerns. In this technique, officials scan a database looking not for an exact match to a sample of DNA, but for a similar profile — someone who might be related to the unknown offender. Critics say that, because of the makeup of offender databases, these searches disproportionately target blacks and Latinos.

Still, California has solved seven cases using familial searching, and nine other states have used the technique. [99] ■

OUTLOOK

Slow Progress

Advocates for forensics reform say they are making some progress, and individual techniques are being refined and improved, albeit slowly.

Scientist Anil Jain, of Michigan State University, predicts a more reliable system for fingerprint analysis will be ready within a decade, and hopes forensic examiner training will be more rigorous.

He also predicts that experts will be guided to give more nuanced testimony, acknowledging the error rates of a technique or giving a probabilistic assessment "rather than simply a binary presentation." Testimony from experts in other fields will evolve in a similar way, he says, with witnesses moving away from statements such as "100 percent certainty" in favor of statements such as "these features are consistent with each other."

That's also the goal of Carriquiry at the Center for Statistics and Applications in Forensic Evidence at Iowa State. "I hope that [in 10 years] the

courts will have a better grasp of statistics and probability, and the things that one must take into account when deciding whether to admit some evidence in court." Besides studying forensics, her group also is studying how witnesses can best communicate statistics to non-mathematically inclined courts and juries.

New regulations also may be on the horizon. "There's now a widespread understanding that forensic science is flawed, and science and technology keep improving," says Virginia law professor Garrett. "[But] I think we're moving toward having regulations of science in the courtroom."

Garrett also says he hopes President Trump's Justice Department will maintain a commitment to using only the most accurate evidence. "They cannot unring the bell," he wrote in an email. "We now know that many traditional forensics are not sufficiently reliable. Judges increasingly know it, too, and crime labs are working to raise their standards for quality control.

"But until a reliable research foundation exists," he adds, "continuing to use error-prone forensics will just lead to more tragic wrongful convictions and scandalous audits and reversals."

Neufeld predicts there will be "a greater emphasis on having a strong scientific foundation for various disciplines" and that for a new generation of forensic scientists "there will be a change in the culture. It will be less the old guard of those who may have had interest in [working] with law enforcement. It will be the new guard — people who see their role as scientists who only want to get to the truth." ■

Notes

[1] "William Richards," California Innocence Project, http://tinyurl.com/hycwl6u.

[2] Maura Dolan, "Murder conviction reversed in 23-year-old case that turned on a bite mark," Los Angeles Times, May 28, 2016,

http://tinyurl.com/zvu3ob2; California Senate bill 1058, Cal. Penal Code § 1473 (2014).

[3] Jordan Smith, "Junk science on trial in Bill Richards bite mark appeal," The Intercept, May 6, 2016, http://tinyurl.com/hmnjb8j.

[4] Ibid.

[5] Radley Balko, "A high-ranking Obama official just called for the 'eradication' of bite-mark evidence," The Washington Post, July 22, 2015, http://tinyurl.com/jovhudh.

[6] D. Michael Risinger, "Innocents Convicted: An Empirical Justified Factual Wrongful Conviction Rate," Journal of Criminal Law and Criminology, 2007, http://tinyurl.com/hykltfg; Samuel Gross and Barbara O'Brien, "Frequency and Predictors of False Conviction: Why we know so little, and new data on capital cases," Journal of Empirical Legal Studies, December 2008, http://tinyurl.com/hhn5q9m.

[7] "The National Registry of Exonerations," http://tinyurl.com/7x2efzu.

[8] "Strengthening Forensic Science in the United States: A Path Forward," Committee on Identifying the Needs of the Forensic Sciences Community, National Research Council, August 2009, http://tinyurl.com/ykpscj8.

[9] "National District Attorneys Association Slams President's Council of Advisors on Science and Technology report," National District Attorneys Association, Sept. 2, 2016, http://tinyurl.com/j7ppnh3.

[10] Ibid.

[11] Ibid.

[12] "Report to the President: Forensic Science in Criminal Courts: Ensuring Scientific Validity of Feature-Comparison Methods," President's Council of Advisors on Science and Technology, September 2016, http://tinyurl.com/j29c5ua.

[13] Gary Fields, "White House Advisory Council Report Is Critical of Forensics Used in Criminal Trials," The Wall Street Journal, Sept. 20, 2016, http://tinyurl.com/jv8wm9u.

[14] Loretta E. Lynch, "Recommendations of the National Commission on Forensic Science," Department of Justice, March 17, 2016, http://tinyurl.com/z62hmj3.

[15] The National Institute of Justice notes that of 93 robbery cases where physical evidence was collected, 68 percent were resolved through plea bargains. Also see Joseph Peterson et al., "The Role and Impact of Forensic Evidence in the Criminal Justice Process," National Criminal Justice Reference Service, June 2010, http://tinyurl.com/zn23laa.

[16] "Strengthening Forensic Science in the United States," op. cit.

[17] Smith, *op. cit.*

[18] "FBI apologizes to lawyer held in Madrid bombings," The Associated Press, NBC News, May 25, 2004, http://tinyurl.com/j49k8ed.

[19] "A Review of the FBI's Handling of the Brandon Mayfield Case," Oversight and Review Division, Office of the Inspector General, March 2006, http://tinyurl.com/zz9q565.

[20] Spencer S. Hsu, "Judge orders D.C. to pay $13.2 million in wrongful FBI hair conviction case," *The Washington Post*, Feb. 28, 2016, http://tinyurl.com/z78lvjf.

[21] Travis Kircher, "David Camm Blog: 'Our own little experiment . . . ,' " WDRB, Oct. 3, 2013, http://tinyurl.com/jnf87sj.

[22] Spencer S. Hsu, "FBI admits flaws in hair analysis over decades," *The Washington Post*, April 18, 2015, http://tinyurl.com/o2af8wj.

[23] *Ibid.*

[24] "Report to the President: Forensic Science in Criminal Courts: Ensuring Scientific Validity of Feature-Comparison Methods," *op. cit.*

[25] "National District Attorneys Association Slams President's Council of Advisors on Science and Technology report," *op. cit.*

[26] "Forensic Science in Criminal Courts: Ensuring Scientific Validity of Feature-Comparison Methods," letter to President Obama, National District Attorneys Association, Nov. 16, 2016, http://tinyurl.com/hczkt3k.

[27] "Rule 702. Testimony by Expert Witnesses," Federal Rules of Evidence, http://tinyurl.com/cbsoh43.

[28] "AFTE Theory of Identification as it Relates to Toolmarks," Association of Firearm and Tool Mark Examiners, http://tinyurl.com/j9v26mu.

[29] Erica Beecher-Monas, "Reality Bites: The illusion of science in bite-mark evidence," *Cardozo Law Review*, 2009, http://tinyurl.com/hfp6xss.

[30] Radley Balko, "A bite mark matching advocacy group just conducted a study that discredits bite mark evidence," *The Washington Post*, April 8, 2015, http://tinyurl.com/htcakm9.

[31] "Report to the President: Forensic Science in Criminal Courts: Ensuring Scientific Validity of Feature-Comparison Methods," *op. cit.*

[32] "The Role and Impact of Forensic Evidence in the Criminal Justice Process," *op. cit.*

[33] "Rule 702," *op. cit.*

[34] Linda Greenhouse, "Supreme Court Roundup; Justices Put Judges in Charge of Deciding Reliability of Scientific Testimony," *The New York Times*, June 29, 1993, http://tinyurl.com/jzeapfz.

[35] "Rule 702," *op. cit.*

[36] Sharath Pankanti, Salil Prabhakar and Anil Jain, "On the individuality of fingerprints." *IEEE Transactions on Pattern Analysis and Machine Intelligence*, August 2002, http://tinyurl.com/gq5pu6b.

[37] Jennifer L. Mnookin, "Fingerprints: Not a Gold Standard," *Issues in Science and Technology*, Fall 2003, http://tinyurl.com/gm6feom.

[38] "Report to the President: Forensic Science in Criminal Courts: Ensuring Scientific Validity of Feature-Comparison Methods," *op. cit.*

[39] Samuel R. Gross *et al.*, "Rate of false conviction of criminal defendants who are sentenced to death," *Proceedings of the National Academy of Sciences*, May 20, 2014, http://tinyurl.com/mplbvaz.

[40] "Innocents Convicted: An Empirically Justified Factual Wrongful Conviction Rate," *op. cit.*; "Death row inmates by state," Death Penalty Information Center, July 1, 2016, http://tinyurl.com/y8fycq7.

[41] Lisa Demer, "High court to hear Alaska man's DNA appeal," *Anchorage Daily News*, Feb. 7, 2009, http://tinyurl.com/jkjgk9g.

[42] Jerry Markon, "Justices Might Take DNA Evidence Case," *The Washington Post*, Nov. 2, 2008, http://tinyurl.com/z5rt3lg.

[43] *District Attorney's Office for the Third Judicial District et al. v. Osborne*, http://tinyurl.com/gtqa7al.

[44] "Statement from the Attorney General on Today's Decision by the Supreme Court in District Attorney's Office for the Third Judicial District et al. v. Osborne," Department of Justice, June 18, 2009, http://tinyurl.com/zwaf4qe.

[45] "Post-Conviction DNA Testing," National Conference of State Legislatures, 2013, http://tinyurl.com/j6t3euz.

[46] Sue Russell, "The Right and Privilege of Post-Conviction DNA Testing," *Pacific Standard*, Oct. 4, 2012, http://tinyurl.com/j8kymb6.

[47] Earl Lane, "DNA Evidence Was Lifeline for Exonerated Death Row Survivor Kirk Bloodsworth," *AAAS News*, Oct. 29, 2014, http://tinyurl.com/kefcw4p.

[48] Matthew R. Durose, Kelly A. Walsh and Andrea M. Burch, "Census of publicly funded crime laboratories, 2009," Bureau of Justice Statistics, August 2012, http://tinyurl.com/hkzl9w2.

[49] "Locard, Edmond," *Encyclopedia.com*, 2005, http://tinyurl.com/jm4zljg.

[50] *Ibid.*

[51] "The Bertillon System," National Library of Medicine, February 2006, http://tinyurl.com/2mbq3q.

[52] Jim Fisher, "Forensics Under Fire," Jan. 15, 2008, jimfisher.edinboro.edu/forensics/fire/overview.html. Also see Jeffery G. Barnes, "Chapter 1: History," *Fingerprint Sourcebook*, National Institute of Justice, 2011.

[53] "History of the 'West Brothers' Identification . . . Bertillon Measurements Are Not Always A Reliable Means Of Identification," National Law Enforcement Museum, http://tinyurl.com/m2xoqfy.

[54] "Bertillon System of Criminal Identification," National Law Enforcement Museum, November 2011, http://tinyurl.com/kv7cw2e. Also see John Fischer and Joe Nickell, *Crime Science: Methods of Forensic Detection* (2013).

[55] Fisher, *op. cit.*

[56] *Ibid.*

[57] Charles R. Swanson *et al.*, *Criminal Investigation* (2012), p. 11.

[58] Nigel McCrery, *Silent Witnesses: The Often Gruesome but Always Fascinating History of Forensic Science* (2014).

[59] Census of Publicly Funded Forensic Crime Laboratories, 2002, http://tinyurl.com/jmaaaa6.

[60] "Report to the President: Forensic Science in Criminal Courts: Ensuring Scientific Validity of Feature-Comparison Methods," *op. cit.*

[61] John Solomon, "FBI's forensic test full of holes," *The Washington Post*, Nov. 18, 2007, http://tinyurl.com/25tw9g.

[62] "A Review of the FBI's Handling of the Brandon Mayfield Case," Office of the Inspector General, January 2006, http://tinyurl.com/zap2ftk.

[63] "A Review of the FBI's Progress in Responding to the Recommendations in the Office of the Inspector General Report on the Fingerprint Misidentification in the Brandon Mayfield Case," Office of the Inspector General, June 2011, http://tinyurl.com/gss4twe.

[64] *Ibid.*

About the Author

Rachel Kaufman is a freelance writer and editor whose science writing has appeared in *The Washington Post, National Geographic News, Smithsonian.com* and *Scientific American*. She was managing editor of *Elevation DC*, an online publication about Washington, D.C., neighborhoods. She also was co-founder of a daily news blog on jobs in the media.

[65] Lisa Calandro, Dennis J. Reeder and Karen Cormier, "Evolution of DNA evidence for crime solving — a judicial and legislative history," *Forensic Magazine*, Jan. 6, 2005, http://tinyurl.com/gvv8wje.

[66] Michael Newton, *The FBI Encyclopedia* (2003), p. 189.

[67] Jay D. Aronson, *Genetic Witness: Science, Law, and Controversy in the Making of DNA Profiling* (2007), p. 59.

[68] Patt Morrison, "Barry Scheck on the O.J. trial, DNA evidence and the Innocence Project," *Los Angeles Times*, June 17, 2014, http://tinyurl.com/j2o2r2b.

[69] "OJ Simpson: Week-by-week, Week 17," Court TV News, May 15-19, 1995, archived at http://tinyurl.com/jva4ywm.

[70] Edward Connors *et al.*, "Convicted by Juries, Exonerated by Science: Case studies in the use of DNA evidence to establish innocence after trial," National Institute of Justice, June 1996, http://tinyurl.com/aewf67.

[71] Barry Scheck, Peter Neufeld and Jim Dwyer, *Actual Innocence: Five Days to Execution and Other Dispatches From the Wrongly Convicted* (2002).

[72] Giorgia Tasselli *et al.*, "Complex DNA mixture analysis: report of two cases," *Forensic Science International: Genetics Supplement Series*, 2015, http://tinyurl.com/j69vhgl.

[73] "Report to the President: Forensic Science in Criminal Courts: Ensuring Scientific Validity of Feature-Comparison Methods," *op. cit.*

[74] *Ibid.*

[75] "Crime lab and forensic scandals," National Association of Criminal Defense Lawyers, http://tinyurl.com/zpgjpfy.

[76] Carmen Drahl and Andrea Widener, "Forcing change in forensic science," *Chemical & Engineering News*, May 12, 2014, http://tinyurl.com/zsk5egz.

[77] Katie Worth, "Crime lab scandals the focus of new DOJ plan," "Frontline," Dec. 8, 2015, http://tinyurl.com/gvhqxm7.

[78] Matthew R. Durose, Kelly A. Walsh and Andrea M. Burch, "Census of publicly funded forensic crime laboratories, 2009," Bureau of Justice Statistics, August 2012, http://tinyurl.com/hkzl9w2.

[79] Worth, *op. cit.*

[80] "Justice Department Announces New Accreditation Policies to Advance Forensic Science," Department of Justice, Dec. 7, 2015, http://tinyurl.com/zms4rcm.

[81] Worth, *op. cit.*

[82] "Strengthening Forensic Science in the United States," hearing before the Committee on the Judiciary, U.S. Senate, 111th Congress, Sept. 9, 2009, http://tinyurl.com/zghrm6d.

[83] Eugene Kiely, "Is Stop and Frisk Unconstitutional?" FactCheck.org, Sept. 29, 2016, http://tinyurl.com/hllmmc8.

[84] Kevin Flynn, "Suspect in Rape Absorbed Pain and Inflicted It," *The New York Times*, Dec. 7, 2002, http://tinyurl.com/czop2ot.

[85] Edward Conlon, "The myth of the Central Park Five," *The Daily Beast*, Oct. 19, 2014, http://tinyurl.com/mwzxous.

[86] Steven A. Holmes, "Member of 'Central Park 5' blasts Trump," CNN, Oct. 7, 2016, http://tinyurl.com/jt5vr75. Also see Sarah Burns, "Why Trump Doubled Down on the Central Park 5," *The New York Times*, Oct. 17, 2016, http://tinyurl.com/gv3q672.

[87] *Ibid.*

[88] "Innocence Project praises DOJ for undertaking unprecedented review of FBI forensic testimony," The Innocence Project, Feb. 24, 2016, http://tinyurl.com/ja6utj6.

[89] Spencer S. Hsu, "FBI admits flaws in hair analysis over decades," *The Washington Post*, April 18, 2015, http://tinyurl.com/o2af8wj.

[90] "Report to the President: Forensic Science in Criminal Courts: Ensuring Scientific Validity of Feature-Comparison Methods," *op. cit.*

[91] *Ibid.*

[92] "NIST 3D ballistics research database goes live," National Institute of Standards and Technology, July 7, 2016, http://tinyurl.com/j9apxz6.

[93] Robert Lee Hotz, "Cellphone smudges yield a trove of forensic data," *The Wall Street Journal*, Nov. 14, 2016, http://tinyurl.com/jey3ccu.

[94] Sara G. Miller, "Time of Death? Check the Body's 'Necrobiome,' " *LiveScience*, Dec. 22, 2016, http://tinyurl.com/gphzz72.

[95] "Enhanced Fingerprints," in "Best Inventions of 2008," *Time*, 2008, http://tinyurl.com/hkp3mxw.

[96] Ava Kofman, "The troubling rise of rapid DNA testing," *The New Republic*, Feb. 24, 2016, http://tinyurl.com/jyjm3ov.

[97] Aliya Sternstein, "House Committee OKs Bill Letting the FBI Use Rapid DNA Profiling," NextGov, July 8, 2016, http://tinyurl.com/zm2ec4b.

[98] Kofman, *op. cit.*

[99] Eli Rosenberg, "Family DNA Searches Seen as Crime-Solving Tool, and Intrusion on Rights," *The New York Times*, Jan. 27, 2017, http://tinyurl.com/gmy5fws.

FOR MORE INFORMATION

American Academy of Forensic Sciences, 410 N. 21st St., Colorado Springs, CO 80904; 719-636-1100; www.aafs.org/. Professional society dedicated to the application of science to the law.

Center for Statistics and Applications in Forensic Evidence, Iowa State University, Ames, IA 50011; 515-294-3440; http://forensic.stat.iastate.edu/. Studies the statistical foundation of forensics.

The Innocence Project, 40 Worth St., Suite 701, New York, NY 10013; 212-364-5340; www.innocenceproject.org/contact/. Works to exonerate the wrongfully convicted.

National Association of Criminal Defense Lawyers, 1660 L St., N.W., #12, Washington, DC 20005; 202-872-8600; http://nacdl.org. Professional association representing the defense bar.

National Commission on Forensic Science, U.S. Department of Justice, 950 Pennsylvania Ave., N.W., Washington, DC 20530; www.justice.gov/ncfs. Partnership between the Justice Department and the National Institute of Standards and Technology to promote the scientific validity of forensic science.

National District Attorneys Association, 1400 Crystal Drive, Suite 330, Arlington, VA 22202; 703-549-9222; www.ndaa.org. Membership organization that represents prosecutors nationwide.

National Registry of Exonerations, 625 S. State St., Ann Arbor, MI 48109; www.law.umich.edu/special/exoneration/Pages/about.aspx. Provides information about every known exoneration in the United States since 1989, including those that were obtained after forensic evidence was discredited or rejected.

Bibliography

Selected Sources

Books

Aronson, Jay D., *Genetic Witness: Science, Law, and Controversy in the Making of DNA Profiling*, Rutgers University Press, 2007.

A Carnegie Mellon University professor of science, technology and society who founded Carnegie Mellon's Center for Human Rights Science traces the development of forensic DNA analysis in the American legal system.

Dwyer, Jim, Peter Neufeld and Barry Scheck, *Actual Innocence: Five Days to Execution, and Other Dispatches from the Wrongly Convicted*, Doubleday, 2000.

In this book, which has been called the "signature document of the modern innocence movement," Innocence Project co-founders Neufeld and Scheck and *New York Times* columnist Dwyer profile 10 people who were wrongly convicted and then exonerated.

Garrett, Brandon, *Convicting the Innocent: Where Criminal Prosecutions Go Wrong*, Harvard University Press, 2011.

A University of Virginia professor examines, via trial transcripts, the first 250 cases of people exonerated by DNA evidence, in an attempt to determine the root causes for their wrongful convictions — including faulty forensics.

McCrery, Nigel, *Silent Witnesses: The Often Gruesome but Always Fascinating History of Forensic Science*, Chicago Review Press, 2014.

A cop-turned-crime novelist explores the early history and development of forensic science over the past two centuries.

Articles

Hall, Michael, "False Impressions," *Texas Monthly*, January 2016, http://tinyurl.com/zdqc6h9.

The author discusses the Texas Forensic Science Commission's work on bite-mark evidence and in other arenas of forensics.

Hsu, Spencer S., "FBI admits flaws in hair analysis over decades," *The Washington Post*, April 18, 2015, http://tinyurl.com/o2af8wj.

The preliminary results from an unprecedented FBI case review of hair matching testimony showed that in almost all cases government experts had testified in ways that incorrectly favored the prosecution.

Mnookin, Jennifer L., "Fingerprints: Not a Gold Standard," *Issues*, Fall 2003, http://tinyurl.com/gm6feom.

When a judge disallowed fingerprint evidence in court for the first time in decades, then reversed his decision, the event made headlines.

Rosenberg, Eli, "Family DNA Searches Seen as Crime-Solving Tool, and Intrusion on Rights," *The New York Times*, Jan. 27, 2017, http://tinyurl.com/gtosxtp.

Critics of familial searching say it can result in errors and disproportionately affect blacks and Hispanics, who tend to be overrepresented in offender databases.

Smith, Jordan, "Junk science on trial in Bill Richards bite mark appeal," *The Intercept*, May 6. 2016, http://tinyurl.com/hmnjb8j.

This piece by an investigative journalism publication debunks bite-mark evidence for the lay audience.

Reports and Studies

"Report to the President: Forensic Science in Criminal Courts: Ensuring Scientific Validity of Feature-Comparison Methods," President's Council of Advisors on Science and Technology, September 2016, http://tinyurl.com/zzz3aso.

A panel of scientists performs an exhaustive review of scientific studies claiming to prove the validity of many forensic sciences, and determines that many lack scientific rigor.

"Strengthening Forensic Science in the United States: A Path Forward," Committee on Identifying the Needs of the Forensic Science Community, the National Academies, August 2009, http://tinyurl.com/ykpscj8.

This report was one of the first to raise questions about the reliability of forensic evidence; its authors concluded that most forensics, with the exception of DNA, were unreliable.

"A Review of the FBI's Handling of the Brandon Mayfield Case," Office of the Inspector General, Oversight and Review Division, U.S. Department of Justice, March 2006, http://tinyurl.com/zz9q565.

A remarkably candid analysis of what went wrong when the FBI erroneously identified a U.S. citizen as the perpetrator of the Madrid train bombings.

Connors, Edward, *et al.*, "Convicted by Juries, Exonerated by Science," U.S. Department of Justice, June 1996, http://tinyurl.com/aewf67.

Much of modern criminal justice reform efforts can be traced to this 20-year-old pamphlet, called "the green book" because of the color of its cover, which explained how science is being used to exonerate some prisoners.

Gross, Samuel, *et al.*, "Rate of false conviction of criminal defendants who are sentenced to death," Proceedings of the National Academy of Science, May 20, 2014, http://tinyurl.com/hwu63he.

A review finds that among convictions in which the defendant is sentenced to death, a conservative floor for the wrongful conviction rate is 4.1 percent.

The Next Step:

Additional Articles from Current Periodicals

Exonerations

"Illinois man exonerated after 25 years in prison on rape charge," The Associated Press, *New York Daily News*, Jan. 4, 2017, http://tinyurl.com/hfd4vkj.

An Illinois man who spent 25 years in prison was exonerated after forensic testing revealed none of the physical evidence in the rape case matched him.

Luthern, Ashley, "Milwaukee man exonerated by DNA after 24 years in prison," *Milwaukee Journal Sentinel*, Oct. 5, 2016, http://tinyurl.com/h8c3gt2.

DNA evidence in a sexual assault case helped clear a Milwaukee man who served 24 years in prison for the wrongful conviction.

McQuaid, Russ, "Proposed bills seek to pay wrongfully convicted Hoosiers," Fox59, Jan. 23, 2017, http://tinyurl.com/zmqosyx.

Two bipartisan bills in Indiana would allow payment to former prisoners of between $25,000 and $35,000 for each year they served time for a wrongful conviction.

Expanded DNA Testing

DeStefano, Anthony M., "NYPD seeking green light to use DNA technique in jogger case," *Newsday*, Jan. 26, 2017, http://tinyurl.com/zc2ey8w.

The New York Police Department is seeking to help solve a jogger's killing through the use of a new DNA technique known as "familial searching," which uses probability rankings to identify people in state databases who may be relatives of the unknown assailant.

Wang, Amy B., "Police use DNA to solve 1976 murder of Karen Klaas, ex-wife of Righteous Brothers singer," *The Washington Post*, Jan. 30, 2017, http://tinyurl.com/znwcxyy.

Police utilized a familial DNA search to help them solve the notorious 1976 murder of Karen Klaas, ex-wife of Righteous Brothers singer Bill Medley.

New Research

Holtz, Robert Lee, "Cellphone Smudges Yield a Trove of Forensic Data," *The Wall Street Journal*, Nov. 14, 2016, http://tinyurl.com/h4kt4qj.

Although it is not yet admissible in court, a new forensic technique creates a chemical portrait of people by gathering molecular and microbial trace evidence found on their cellphones.

Reagan, Mark, "Texas Forensic Science Commission Asks For AG Opinion on Bite-Mark Evidence," *San Antonio Current*, July 22, 2016, http://tinyurl.com/hjem6oh.

The Texas Forensic Science Commission has sought a mora-torium on bite-mark testimony after a new study revealed forensic dentists could not definitively tell whether injuries were bite marks.

Tolan, Casey, "Prosecutors are ignoring new research debunking popular science used to convict people," *Fusion*, Sept. 23, 2016, http://tinyurl.com/jtojtcj.

Former U.S. Attorney General Loretta Lynch rejected a report that concluded that bite marks, shoe prints, hair samples and other forensic techniques were unreliable and often misrepresented.

Scandals and Reviews

Bobshart, Rod, "Iowa officials to review evidence for potential wrongful convictions," *Cherokee Tribune and Ledger-News*, Jan. 30, 2017, http://tinyurl.com/hyheyt8.

Iowa state officials plan to use federal grant money from the FBI to review Iowa cases that involve hair-comparison testing, a forensic technique that is facing scrutiny.

Iannelli, Jerry, "BSO Crime Lab Could Be Mishandling Crucial DNA Evidence, Whistleblower Says," *New Times Broward-Palm Beach*, June 29, 2016, http://tinyurl.com/jqlc5dn.

A Florida whistleblower filed a complaint about the handling of DNA evidence in a sheriff's crime lab, which had previously faced allegations that a former analyst tainted thousands of cases.

Maciborski, Walt, "Concerns over APD DNA lab raised over 5 years ago," CBS Austin, July 6, 2016, http://tinyurl.com/hj7u8oe.

The Austin Police Department's forensics lab is facing scrutiny by a Texas state commission amid concerns about the lab's handling of DNA.

CITING *CQ RESEARCHER*

Sample formats for citing these reports in a bibliography include the ones listed below. Preferred styles and formats vary, so please check with your instructor or professor.

MLA STYLE
Jost, Kenneth. "Remembering 9/11." CQ Researcher 2 Sept. 2011: 701-732.

APA STYLE
Jost, K. (2011, September 2). Remembering 9/11. *CQ Researcher, 9*, 701-732.

CHICAGO STYLE
Jost, Kenneth. "Remembering 9/11." *CQ Researcher*, September 2, 2011, 701-32.

In-depth Reports on Issues in the News

Are you writing a paper?

Need backup for a debate?

Want to become an expert on an issue?

For 90 years, students have turned to *CQ Researcher* for in-depth reporting on issues in the news. Reports on a full range of political and social issues are now available. Following is a selection of recent reports:

Civil Liberties
Privacy and the Internet, 12/15
Intelligence Reform, 5/15
Religion and Law, 11/14

Crime/Law
Jailing Debtors, 9/16
Decriminalizing Prostitution, 4/16
Restorative Justice, 2/16
The Dark Web, 1/16
Immigrant Detention, 10/15
Fighting Gangs, 10/15
Reforming Juvenile Justice, 9/15

Education
Civic Education, 2/17
Student Debt, 11/16
Apprenticeships, 10/16
Free Speech on Campus, 5/15

Environment/Society
Guns on Campus, 1/17
Mass Transit, 12/16
Arctic Development, 12/16
Protecting the Power Grid, 11/16
Pornography, 10/16
Women in Leadership, 9/16

Health/Safety
Opioid Crisis, 10/16
Mosquito-Borne Disease, 7/16
Drinking Water Safety, 7/16
Virtual Reality, 2/16

Politics/Economy
Trump Presidency, 1/17
European Union's Future, 12/16
The Obama Legacy, 11/16
Populism and Party Politics, 9/16
U.S.-Mexico Relations, 9/16
Modernizing the Nuclear Arsenal, 7/16

Upcoming Reports

Traffic Deaths, 2/17/17   Immigrants and the Economy, 2/24/17   Women in Prison, 3/3/17

ACCESS

CQ Researcher is available in print and online. For access, visit your library or www.cqresearcher.com.

STAY CURRENT

For notice of upcoming *CQ Researcher* reports or to learn more about *CQ Researcher* products, subscribe to the free email newsletters, *CQ Researcher Alert!* and *CQ Researcher News*: http://cqpress.com/newsletters.

PURCHASE

To purchase a *CQ Researcher* report in print or electronic format (PDF), visit www.cqpress.com or call 866-427-7737. Single reports start at $15. Bulk purchase discounts and electronic-rights licensing are also available.

SUBSCRIBE

Annual full-service *CQ Researcher* subscriptions—including 44 reports a year, monthly index updates, and a bound volume—start at $1,131. Add $25 for domestic postage.

CQ Researcher Online offers a backfile from 1991 and a number of tools to simplify research. For pricing information, call 800-818-7243 or 805-499-9774 or email librarysales@sagepub.com.

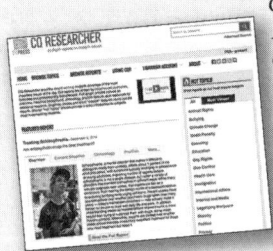

CQPRESS

CQ RESEARCHER

In-depth reports on today's issues

Published by CQ Press, an Imprint of SAGE Publications, Inc.

www.cqresearcher.com

Reducing Traffic Deaths

Can automation and tougher laws save lives?

Behavioral choices — such as speeding, driving while drunk, texting or not buckling up — are fueling a highway death rate that increased more in 2015 than in half a century. After decades of decline, fatalities jumped by more than 7 percent that year, and early figures indicate that 2016 may be an even deadlier year. Nearly half of the 2015 fatalities involved an unbelted passenger or driver and about one-third were alcohol-related. Experts say stronger laws and beefed-up public awareness programs would help. And they say technological developments, including automatic braking and collision avoidance, also will save lives. Distracted driving raises new concerns: As more cars include hands-free capabilities for smartphones as standard equipment, safety experts warn that use of such devices is as dangerous as talking on handheld versions. Self-driving cars are on the road in California, Pennsylvania and elsewhere, potentially adding another dimension to the possible safety solutions but raising new questions around the life-and-death choices the software programs in those vehicles must make.

Jacksonville, Ala., in 2010 became the first city in the state to adopt a "no texting while driving" ordinance. Forty-six states now have anti-texting laws and 14 states ban hand-held cellphone use while driving. But experts say the laws have had little or no effect on traffic deaths.

CQ Researcher • Feb. 17, 2017 • www.cqresearcher.com
Volume 27, Number 7 • Pages 145-168

I N S I D E THIS REPORT

THE ISSUES	147
BACKGROUND	153
CHRONOLOGY	155
CURRENT SITUATION	159
AT ISSUE	161
OUTLOOK	162
BIBLIOGRAPHY	166
THE NEXT STEP	167

CQ RESEARCHER

Feb. 17, 2017
Volume 27, Number 7

EXECUTIVE EDITOR: Thomas J. Billitteri
tjb@sagepub.com

ASSISTANT MANAGING EDITORS: Kenneth
Fireman, kenneth.fireman@sagepub.com,
Kathy Koch, kathy.koch@sagepub.com,
Scott Rohrer, scott.rohrer@sagepub.com

SENIOR CONTRIBUTING EDITOR:
Thomas J. Colin
tom.colin@sagepub.com

CONTRIBUTING WRITERS: Marcia Clemmitt,
Sarah Glazer, Reed Karaim, Peter Katel,
Barbara Mantel, Chuck McCutcheon,
Tom Price

SENIOR PROJECT EDITOR: Olu B. Davis

EDITORIAL ASSISTANT: Anika Reed

FACT CHECKERS: Eva P. Dasher,
Michelle Harris, Betsy Towner Levine,
Robin Palmer

Los Angeles | London | New Delhi
Singapore | Washington DC | Melbourne

An Imprint of SAGE Publications, Inc.

SENIOR VICE PRESIDENT,
GLOBAL LEARNING RESOURCES:
Karen Phillips

EXECUTIVE DIRECTOR, ONLINE LIBRARY AND
REFERENCE PUBLISHING:
Todd Baldwin

CQ Researcher (ISSN 1056-2036) is printed on acid-free
paper. Published weekly, except: (March wk. 4) (May
wk. 4) (July wks. 1, 2) (Aug. wks. 2, 3) (Nov. wk. 4)
and (Dec. wks. 3, 4). Published by SAGE Publications,
Inc., 2455 Teller Rd., Thousand Oaks, CA 91320. Annual
full-service subscriptions start at $1,131. For pricing,
call 1-800-818-7243. To purchase a CQ Researcher report
in print or electronic format (PDF), visit www.cqpress.
com or call 866-427-7737. Single reports start at $15.
Bulk purchase discounts and electronic-rights licensing
are also available. Periodicals postage paid at Thousand
Oaks, California, and at additional mailing offices.
POSTMASTER: Send address changes to CQ Researcher, 2600 Virginia Ave., N.W., Suite 600, Washington,
DC 20037.

THE ISSUES

147
- Are anti-texting laws effective?
- Will automation reduce traffic fatalities?
- Can driving behavior be changed?

BACKGROUND

153 Safety "Not a Luxury"
Federal regulators in the 1960s began demanding safer cars.

156 Seat Belts
By 1996, every state but New Hampshire required seat belts.

157 Alcohol
The portable Breathalyzer was invented in 1953.

158 Speed
Congress repealed the 55 mph speed limit in 1995.

159 Manufacturers' Defects
Recent safety recalls have generated public outcry.

CURRENT SITUATION

159 Safety Measures
States are considering bills to strengthen safe-driving laws.

160 Autonomous Cars
Automatic emergency braking, collision avoidance and self-driving cars are being developed.

OUTLOOK

162 Win-Wins
Experts say new technology, increased public awareness and government safety programs will reduce deaths.

SIDEBARS AND GRAPHICS

148 Driving Deaths Rise to Record Level
Traffic fatalities in 2015 saw the biggest increase in 50 years.

149 Seat-Belt Enforcement Varies Widely
Thirty-four states and Washington, D.C., have "primary" seat-belt laws.

152 Most Traffic Deaths Involve Thirtysomethings
Nearly twice as many males as females died in car crashes in 2015.

155 Chronology
Key events since 1886.

156 Millennials Likely to Embrace Driverless Cars
"The automobile just isn't that important to people's lives anymore."

158 Using Apps to Control Distractions
Parents embrace strategies to fight distracted driving.

161 At Issue:
Will technology reduce roadway fatalities?

FOR FURTHER RESEARCH

165 For More Information
Organizations to contact.

166 Bibliography
Selected sources used.

167 The Next Step
Additional articles.

167 Citing CQ Researcher
Sample bibliography formats.

Cover: AP Photo/*Gadsden Times*/Marc Golden

Reducing Traffic Deaths

BY ELLEN KENNERLY

THE ISSUES

The Snapchat screen read 115.6 mph over the blurry image of the driver as his girlfriend shot a video. Ten minutes later, Pablo Cortes and Jolie Bartoleme were dead, along with a mother and two of her children who were returning from church when Cortes' car slammed into their white minivan. Another daughter and her cousin in the van were critically injured, as was the driver of another vehicle struck by Cortes' car. [1]

"There were no cars around him right where the crash occurred, so racing was not a factor," said Sgt. Steve Gaskins, a Florida Highway Patrol spokesman. "But speed was." [2]

The horrific three-car accident in Tampa, Fla., last October and others are fueling debate over how to stem the rising number of traffic deaths. After decades of decline, car fatalities jumped by more than 7 percent between 2014 and 2015, the biggest annual increase in half a century. The reason? Many experts point to the improving economy. When times are better, and gasoline prices are lower, Americans drive more, and a significant chunk of those motorists are riskier drivers: teens. The rise has spurred a flurry of recommendations, bills and programs aimed at increasing the safety of transportation infrastructure and automobile technology as well as decades-old efforts to change driver behavior. [3]

After dropping to 32,479, in 2011, their lowest point in 60 years, traffic deaths in 2015 spiked to 35,092. And 2016 appears to have followed suit,

Five people in Tampa, Fla., died last October, including a mother returning from church and two of her children, when a car traveling 115 mph lost control and crashed into their minivan. Police later said the passenger in the car had been streaming the driver's speeding on Snapchat just before the accident. U.S. highway deaths increased 7 percent, to 35,092, from 2014 to 2015, the biggest jump in 50 years. Most of the jump was due to risky driver behavior.

AP Photo/Tampa Bay Times/Luis Santana

with the latest data showing that fatalities in the first nine months were up 8 percent over the same period in 2015. In other words, more Americans die on average every month on U.S. roads than were killed in the 9/11 terrorist attacks in 2001. The AAA Foundation for Traffic Safety found 88 percent of drivers ages 19 to 24 acknowledged engaging in risky behavior such as texting while driving, running red lights or speeding during the previous month. [4]

Human factors account for more than 94 percent of fatal crashes, according to the National Highway Traffic Safety Administration (NHTSA). Despite

extensive educational campaigns about wearing seat belts and not driving drunk or distracted, nearly half of the 2015 fatalities involved unbelted drivers or passengers, about a third were alcohol-related and at least 3,000, or about 10 percent, resulted from distracted driving. [5]

"Belts, booze and speed" are the three biggest reasons for most of the fatalities on U.S. roads, says Jonathan Adkins, executive director of the Governors Highway Safety Association, which represents state highway safety offices. And the most frustrating part? "These deaths are completely preventable."

They also are expensive. Traffic fatalities due to human error cost the nation nearly $600 billion in economic loss and harm to quality of life, according to a 2015 NHTSA report analyzing 2010 data: Driving or riding unbelted cost the country $69 billion; distracted driving, $123 billion; drunken driving, $194 billion; and speeding, $203 billion. [6]

"Teens are the riskiest drivers on the road," says Jessica Cicchino, vice president for research at the industry-funded Insurance Institute for Highway Safety (IIHS). Car accidents account for about one-third of all teen deaths — 2,715 in 2015 — making traffic accidents the leading cause of death for teenagers. [7]

"Everything is going in the wrong direction," Adkins says. "The role of alcohol is increasing. We're seeing speed increasing." Thirty-eight states now have speed limits of 70 mph or higher, and speed limits on some stretches of highway are as high as 85 mph. [8] An insurance industry study released last

Driving Deaths Rise to Record Level in 2015

The number of highway deaths in 2015 — 35,092 — jumped by more than 2,000 over 2014. The 7.2 percent increase was the largest since 1966, when the annual rise was 8.1 percent. Preliminary reports indicate that 2016 will end up being even more deadly.

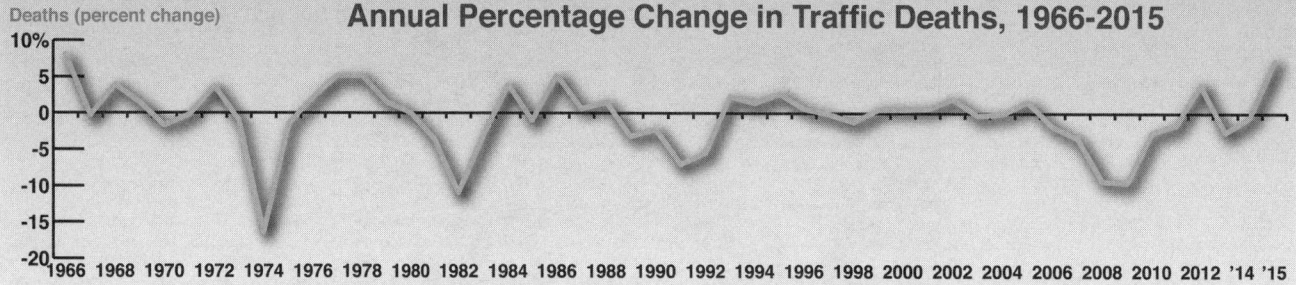

Annual Percentage Change in Traffic Deaths, 1966-2015

Deaths (percent change)

Sources: "2015 Motor Vehicle Crashes: Overview," National Highway Traffic Safety Administration, U.S. Department of Transportation, August 2016, http://tinyurl.com/zj3fxpn; "Motor Vehicle Traffic Fatalities & Fatality Rates," Informed For Life, http://tinyurl.com/j2nke72; "Number of deaths, crashes and motor vehicles in fatal crashes, 1975-2015," Insurance Institute for Highway Safety, November 2016, http://tinyurl.com/j2ourf2

year attributed higher speed limits to an additional 33,000 deaths over the past 20 years. [9]

To reverse the rise in traffic fatalities, government agencies have banded together to encourage placing protective technology, such as automated braking and avoidance features, in cars. Road to Zero, a coalition of top U.S. transportation and health stakeholders, has vowed to eliminate traffic fatalities in the next 30 years. Safety agencies are broadening their focus by adopting a "Safe Systems" approach, examining better ways to change driver behavior while endorsing self-driving cars and safer infrastructure. [10]

"We know that people will make mistakes," says Erin Sauber-Schatz, leader of the Transportation Safety Team at the Division of Unintentional Injury Prevention at the Centers for Disease Control and Prevention (CDC). "How do we create a safe system so if they make a mistake, it won't result in a fatality?"

Agencies have changed how they approach traffic safety, adopting safe systems in an effort to save lives, she says. "It's a different paradigm than we're used to," involving road features

such as roundabouts and other "traffic calming" measures, she says, so that "if and when there is a crash, it's not a head-on collision which may be fatal."

Technology such as automatic braking will cut crash rates by 30 percent, says John D. Lee, an expert in driver distraction at the University of Wisconsin, Madison. "That type of 'guardian angel' technology will have a huge safety benefit."

But there is a potential downside. "Automation may encourage bad behavior," says Lee. Drivers can stop paying as much attention when they feel safe, he says.

The apparent public apathy about the thousands of traffic deaths each year is another part of the problem, says former National Transportation Safety Board chair Deborah Hersman, president and CEO of the National Safety Council (NSC), a nonprofit organization in Itasca, Ill., that promotes health and safety. "Our complacency is killing us. We will sacrifice 4,000 of our teens so they can drive and go to football games," she says. "We're willing to make that trade-off."

Just passing laws prohibiting dangerous behavior such as texting is not

delivering the intended results, she adds. "We try to create laws and rules, but we have got to recognize that human beings aren't always going to make the best decisions," Hersman says. We have texting laws, but texting while driving remains a huge problem."

The nation needs the kind of sweeping cultural shift that occurred when municipalities banned smoking in restaurants, she says. "We have totally changed our culture in my lifetime" regarding smoking in public places, says Hersman. "We reached a tipping point" where such behavior was no longer acceptable. Now, "the U.S. just really has to get serious about roadway fatalities."

Ralph Hingson, director of the Division of Epidemiology and Prevention Research at the National Institute on Alcohol Abuse and Alcoholism, says, "It's a matter of generating public demand." Tough laws that are effective should be applied across the board, he says. For instance, all states have ignition interlock laws, which require drivers convicted of DUI to blow into a Breathalyzer-type device before being able to start a vehicle. But not all states require them after a first drunken driving offense, and enforcement varies. [11] "It's not enough to pass laws. The laws have to be enforced," he says.

Meanwhile, some valuable tools are not being used. "Sobriety checkpoints are effective in reducing drinking and driving if they are publicized," so they can serve as a deterrent, says Hingson.

Russ Rader, senior vice president of communications for IIHS, agrees. Not only are states not using effective tools such as frequent sobriety checkpoints and speed cameras, he says, but some "states are going in the opposite direction on speed by raising speed limits." In 1973 a federal law required states to limit speed limits to 55 mph in order to receive their share of federal highway funds. But Congress repealed the law in 1995, and speed limits have been rising around the country since.

A bill raising Michigan's speed limit to 75 mph on about 600 miles of highway was signed into law earlier this year. "Ensuring that all Michiganders are safe while operating vehicles on our state's roadways is critically important, and these bills allow for appropriately increased speed limits on certain roadways after safety studies are conducted," Republican Gov. Rick Snyder said in a statement. [12]

Seat-belt laws have been passed in every state except New Hampshire, whose motto is "Live Free or Die." (See map, above.) But while the United States reached a historic level of seat-belt use — 90 percent — in 2016, nearly half (48 percent) of traffic deaths in 2015 involved unbelted riding and driving. [13]

Seat-belt laws, and their enforcement, vary by state. Thirty-four states have "primary" seat-belt laws, in which police can ticket a driver or passenger for going unbelted. Other states have secondary seat-belt laws, in which an officer can ticket a passenger for not wearing a belt only if a traffic citation is issued for another violation at the same time. [14]

Seat Belt Enforcement Varies Widely

Thirty-four states and the District of Columbia have "primary" seat-belt laws, which allow an officer to stop and ticket a driver or passenger for not wearing a seat belt. Fifteen states have secondary seat-belt laws, in which police can ticket a passenger for a belt law violation only if another traffic citation is being issued at the same time. New Hampshire, whose motto is "Live Free or Die," is the only state with no seat-belt law.

Seat-Belt Enforcement by State

Source: "Map: enforcement of the safety belt use laws," Insurance Institute for Highway Safety, February 2017, http://tinyurl.com/zn85ed6

As safety experts, lawmakers and insurance industry representatives try to reduce traffic deaths, here are some of the questions being debated:

Are anti-texting laws effective?

It took a few minutes to convince the driver that the construction worker giving him a ticket was a police officer in disguise and that texting while stopped at a red light was indeed illegal in Georgia. Once he received the $150 ticket, which included a point on his license, however, he got the message.

"It doesn't matter if you're stopped at a light," said officer Nick Serkedakis of the Marietta Police Department. "If you're on a public thoroughfare and facing the phone, we're going to have a conversation with you." Police in the

Atlanta suburb had dressed as construction workers at a busy intersection in July 2015 to get a better view into cars, to spot drivers who were texting. [15]

Anti-texting laws have passed in 46 states, and 14 states ban hand-held cellphone use while driving. But such laws have not made a dent in traffic deaths. [16] "We haven't found any evidence that these laws are bringing down crashes," says Cicchino at the IIHS.

Such laws are "difficult for police officers to enforce," says the CDC's Sauber-Schatz.

Despite the preponderance of anti-texting laws, "texting while driving remains a huge problem," says the National Safety Council's Hersman. Not only is there a "highly addictive nature" to such activities, she says, but texting is extremely dangerous.

For instance, in the time it takes to send a text, a driver traveling 55 mph would cover the length of a football field as if blindfolded. And while many activities are defined as "distracted" — including eating, talking and using GPS — texting is the most alarming because it involves cognitive, visual and manual distractions. [17]

"The bottom line is, just because your eyes are on the road, doesn't mean your mind is," says Lee of the University of Wisconsin. "As a driver, you don't even know you're distracted.

A motorist in New York City uses a smartphone while driving. While safety experts agree that automatic braking, collision avoidance and other emerging technologies will save lives, they say driving with a hands-free smartphone is as dangerous as using a hands-on version.

What you miss, you didn't notice."

"Hands-free devices offer no safety benefit when driving," according to a white paper from the safety council. "Driving while talking on cellphones — hand-held and hands-free — increases risk of injury and property damage crashes fourfold," said the safety council paper. [18]

Yet, nearly 70 percent of teens admitted to talking on a cellphone while driving in the previous month, and more than 50 percent said they had read a text or an email while driving during

the same period, according to the American Automobile Association (AAA), a nonprofit member-service organization. Even so, 80 percent of drivers between the ages of 17 and 26 see themselves as safer than average. [19]

Another analysis, by TrueMotion, a technology company with a cellphone app to detect distracted driving, found that 71 percent of drivers text while driving. The analysis involved 18,201 drivers in 49 states who drove more than 22 million hours last fall and reflects data from actual interactions between drivers and their devices, says a spokesman for TrueMotion. Even though enforcement is challenging, anti-texting laws play an important role, says Adkins of the Governors Highway Safety Association. "It does send an awareness message," he says. However, he acknowledges, "the horse is out of the barn. The public wants to use their cellphones while they drive."

But automation expert Costa Samaras of Carnegie Mellon University says just because consumers want to do something doesn't mean they should be al-

lowed to do it. The government regulates "impaired driving," he says, and "you can't drive with your headphones on. [But] staring at your phone is probably worse."

Watching cars come toward you on a freeway at night, with drivers' faces aglow with the cool light of a cellphone screen, is "just terrifying," he says.

Some New York legislators want to resurrect an old idea and use it in a new way. A device called the Textalyzer allows an officer arriving at the scene of the crash to test the phones of those involved to determine whether there was recent cellphone activity. Refusal to hand over one's cellphone for inspection could prompt a license suspension. New York is the first state to propose the idea, which is still under discussion.

One potential hurdle is a concern over privacy, but the sponsor of the bipartisan bill, Democratic Assemblyman Félix W. Ortiz, said police would not have access to any content on the device. It would only offer a way to catch drivers illegally using such devices. "We need something on the books" that will change people's behavior, said Ortiz. If the bill becomes law, he said, "people are going to be more afraid to put their hands on the cellphone." [20]

Other new initiatives have been modeled after anti-drunken driving efforts.

Harvard's School of Public Health, which helped push the effort to get people who are out drinking to name a "designated driver" in the 1980s, is working on a new awareness campaign against distracted driving, fashioned from its previous work. MADD founder Candace Lightner formed the Partnership for Distraction-Free Driving in 2016 to push social media companies to exert the same kind of pressure against the use of distracting devices while driving that liquor companies did to discourage drunken driving. [21]

Twenty-three percent of the drivers who are involved in fatal crashes are

Getty Images/Spencer Platt

in their 20s, an age group that makes up 38 percent of the distracted drivers on their cellphones during fatal accidents, according to the NHTSA. [22]

Will automation reduce traffic fatalities?

The red car is maybe three lengths ahead, traveling at about the speed limit. Suddenly an alert sounds in the vehicle behind it as the red car hits a previously unseen SUV in front of it, careening into the next lane, while the SUV rolls over directly ahead.

The driver behind the red car stops safely, still about three car lengths behind, with everyone safe and sound.

This is not a simulation. It's an actual video shot from the inside of a Tesla car equipped with automated braking capability carrying a family of four last December in the Netherlands. The software started braking before the driver could react to the alert and apply the brakes himself. [23]

By 2022, under an agreement the Obama administration struck with automakers in 2016, automatic emergency braking would be standard equipment on more than 99 percent of new vehicles sold in the United States. "Automated vehicles have the potential to save thousands of lives, driving the single biggest leap in road safety that our country has ever taken," Anthony Foxx, Obama's Transportation secretary, said in announcing the policy. [24]

The Federal Automated Vehicles Policy established guidelines for several levels of automation. At those levels, a car's automated system will be able to:

• Occasionally assist the human driver in some aspects of driving (Level 1);

• Perform some driving tasks (Level 2);

• Perform some driving tasks and monitor the environment in some instances with the human ready to reassume control as needed (Level 3);

• Perform and monitor as above, without the human resuming control, but only under certain conditions (Level 4);

• Perform all aspects of driving under any conditions (Level 5).

Automation will save lives, but it will be years before the impact of these developments is significant, says Adkins of the Governors Highway Safety Association. "It will take 13 to 15 years to be fully integrated."

But "we will make a big step change in the next 15 years, when lots of cars in the fleet will have Level 1 and Level 2 autonomy," says Carnegie Mellon automation expert Samaras. "Even at Level 1 and 2, there's billions of dollars in

A North Miami Beach police officer conducts a sobriety test at a DUI checkpoint. Such checkpoints are effective in reducing drinking and driving, safety experts say, especially if they are well publicized. All states have ignition interlock laws, which require drivers convicted of DUI to blow into a Breathalyzer-type device before being able to start a vehicle. But not all states require such devices after a first drunken-driving offense, and enforcement varies.

social costs that can be saved in crashes," says Samaras. And "we could [prevent] about a third of the fatalities."

Another proposal moving forward would require vehicle-to-vehicle communications systems on new vehicles, a technology that could help drivers avoid or mitigate 70 to 80 percent of vehicle crashes involving unimpaired drivers, a NHTSA spokesman said in an email. Such systems would "sense"

another car in dangerous proximity and either avoid the vehicle or warn the driver or both.

But automation raises other issues. Driving in a partially automated environment can diminish human attention and thus lead to mistakes and crashes. For instance, in 2016 the driver of a Tesla in which the autopilot feature was enabled died after the car drove under an 18-wheeler. The truck driver said he thought the Tesla driver had been watching a movie. Preliminary reports said the car was speeding and

that the autopilot misread the white side of the truck as blank space. [25]

"Keeping human beings in the loop is a challenge," says Hersman of the National Safety Council. "If you condition them not to act, that creates problems."

For instance, when Google set out to create a self-driving car, it began testing with staffers. The company soon found that the employees began to

Most Traffic Deaths Involve Thirtysomethings

More people between the ages of 30 and 39 died in all age groups in traffic accidents in 2015 than in any other age group. Fatalities among males in all age groups (14,724) were nearly double those of females (7,806).

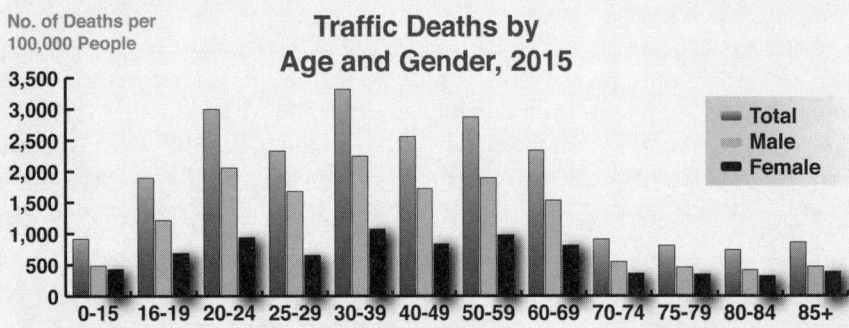

No. of Deaths per 100,000 People

Traffic Deaths by Age and Gender, 2015

Total
Male
Female

Source: "Passenger vehicle occupant deaths per 100,000 people by age and gender, 2015," Insurance Institute for Highway Safety, November 2016, http://tinyurl.com/zv9w3ag

trust the automation and stopped paying full attention to the road, says a spokeswoman. That observation supported the company's decision to build a fully self-driving car, she says.

Autonomous cars will make mistakes. "Accidents will occur," says Timothy Carone, a professor of physics in the Department of IT, Analytics, and Operations in the University of Notre Dame's Mendoza College of Business and the author of *Future Automation: Changes to Lives and to Business*. "People will be killed because of what autonomous vehicles do wrong."

But such "unpredictable failures" are "part and parcel to the maturation process," he says. So, delaying adoption of the new technology and the benefits it offers "would be really tragic. The benefits far outweigh the negatives."

Samaras agrees. "The truth is, this is an area where there's going to be mistakes," he says. "There is a balancing act here."

While automation holds great promise, Adkins advises caution. "[We] don't want policymakers to say 'autonomous vehicles will solve it [traffic fatalities],' " he says. "The driver still needs to be engaged."

Can driving behavior be changed?

Since human error overwhelmingly causes traffic deaths, the goal of reducing traffic deaths to zero is doable, experts say, if human behavior can be changed or the environment around drivers can be made so safe that fatal mistakes are impossible. [26]

Other countries have sparked turnarounds in their fatality rate "through a force of will," says John D. Lee a professor of engineering at the University of Wisconsin, Madison. "From a very high level, they made it a priority."

Lee cites France, Ireland and Israel all as nations in which it was deemed "disgraceful" that so many were dying in traffic accidents, and policy was shifted. Their death rates were "all above the U.S. and now are below," he said.

In Ireland, the decline was linked to changes to the law and enforcement, including the introduction of mandatory sobriety checkpoints, speed-detection cameras, lower legal blood-alcohol limits, expansion of moving violations that rack up penalty points and drug impairment testing. [27]

Mobile speed cameras and lower speed limits are credited with lowering the number of fatalities in France. Interior Minister Manuel Valls had promised to improve the country's traffic safety record when the Socialist government came to power in 2012. [28]

"There's hope for the U.S. to follow a similar path," says Lee. "We shouldn't lose hope on changing the driver."

Such a campaign could be hampered by Americans' cowboy reputation for risk-taking, he says. "People don't want the government constraining them," says Lee. "That general overconfidence in our abilities undermines our ability to deal with traffic safety risk."

Efforts to reduce drunken driving deaths are proceeding on several fronts. About 10,000 people — one every 53 minutes — die due to drunken driving each year. But that number, representing one-third of all traffic deaths, is sharply down from 1982, when nearly half of all fatalities — about 25,000 — were alcohol-related. [29]

MADD was instrumental in bringing those numbers down. "We put a face on the crime," says J.T. Griffin, MADD's chief government affairs officer. "It's not just 10,000 people. It's daughters and sons and moms and dads." And it's about consistency, he says. "Making sure that the public knows that . . . if I break this law, then this is going to happen to me."

It is now a crime to drive with a blood alcohol concentration (BAC) level higher than .08 everywhere in the United States. And ignition locks are required as part of the sentencing structure in every state, although in varying degrees and with varying levels of enforcement.

"We've seen fatality reductions of 30 to 40 percent [with ignition interlock laws]. That's unheard of in traffic safety," Griffin says. "Those are the ways you stop people from dying." One of MADD's goals is to mandate ignition interlocks on first-offense convictions for driving under the influence (DUI) in every state. Currently, 22 states do not require it.

"Society is changing," says Tony Corroto, an Atlanta police veteran and a national expert witness in cases involving DUIs. Corroto has also served as a NHTSA instructor. Back in 1992, "when I first started on the [police department's] DUI task force, every single car I stopped had an impaired driver."

Learning more about the ramifications of drunken driving before getting a license would also help, he says. It will make a difference "if you know you're going to lose your insurance," he says. But even with education and tough laws, he doubts the issue will ever be eliminated. "As long as there's alcohol, there's going to be impaired driving."

The medical community also needs to be more involved if behavioral change is going to happen, according to Hingson of the National Institute on Alcohol Abuse and Alcoholism. "We could make progress in increasing health care awareness of these issues," he says. More doctors need to inquire about drinking and drugging beyond the standard checklist, particularly with younger people, he says.

And some of it may boil down to environment. A *Harvard Business Review* article on changing behavior cites a study from the *American Journal of Public Health* that found if teens live near liquor stores, they are much likelier to binge drink or drive under the influence, even though parents, teachers, TV and ads in liquor stores tell teens about the dangers of drinking and driving. [30]

Griffin sees the goal as attainable. "The future is bright for the elimination of drunk driving," he says. "We have to support our law enforcement."

"It's making sure they know they're going to get caught," he says. And "it's making sure the punishment is swift and certain." ■

BACKGROUND

Safety "Not a Luxury"

The first person to die in a traffic accident in the United States wasn't

Signs alert drivers to a "traffic calming" roundabout in Golden, Colo. Such roadway improvements, known as Safe Systems, are designed to reduce traffic fatalities.

Getty Images/*The Denver Post*/Karl Gehring

even in a car. Henry Bliss was getting off a streetcar and helping a woman step down behind him in New York City on Sept. 13, 1899, when an electric taxi struck him. He died the next morning. The driver was arrested but was not found to be negligent. [31]

That year, 26 traffic deaths were recorded nationwide. Barring a few blips, traffic deaths rose steadily, reaching a record 54,589 — in 1972. [32] They began declining the following year, dropping by about 10,000 in 1974, attributed to the new federal 55-mph speed limit and the fact that fewer miles were being driven as gaso-

line prices rose following the gasoline shortage connected to the Arab oil embargo. [33]

Although traffic deaths rose again, by 2011, they had declined to a record modern-era low of 32,367, chalked up largely to better cars, better roads and public safety programs, such as anti-drunken driving and seat-belt laws. [34]

Now the reverse is true, with an improving economy and the accompanying increase in miles driven. Traffic deaths have risen by the highest percentage since 1966, the year President Lyndon B. Johnson signed the National Traffic Motor Vehicle Safety Act and the Highway Safety Act into law. Under the two laws, the federal government for the first time became responsible for setting standards for traffic safety.

"In this century," said Johnson, "more than 1.5 million of our fellow Americans have died on our streets and highways — nearly three times as many Americans as we have lost in all our wars." However, he continued, "safety is no luxury item. No optional extra; it must be the normal cost of doing business." [35]

Getty Images/Bettmann

A sign on a Ford Pinto warns other drivers to keep their distance. In 1978, all Pintos manufactured between 1971 and 1976 were recalled to install protective shielding to prevent gas tank ruptures and fires in a crash.

The new legislation was sparked by a book written a year earlier by lawyer and consumer activist Ralph Nader, *Unsafe at Any Speed*, which pointed an accusing finger at automakers for purposefully failing to make cars safe. The first line set the tone: "For over half a century the automobile has brought death, injury and the most inestimable sorrow and deprivation to millions of people." [36]

The book is widely known for its examination of the Chevrolet Corvair's dangerous flaws in the first chapter, although most of the book details the

auto industry's consistent disregard for safety in design and technology.

The two 1966 laws required seat belts for everyone in the car, safety steering wheels, better handles so doors didn't fly open in crashes, side mirrors, shatter-resistant windshields, defrosters, lights on the sides of cars and interior padding.

Before this time, planned obsolescence was the economic order of the day for the auto industry, driven by new designs each year with more metal and usually more glitz and glamour. The new economic model was pioneered by Alfred Sloan, president and CEO of General Motors from its early days. It replaced Henry's Ford's inexpensive, cookie-cutter concept with "a visible and easily understood symbol of personal progress," wrote historian Daniel Boorstin. "Sloan's annual model change, and the accompanying ladder of consumption, came closer than any earlier American institution to creating a visible and universal scheme of class distinction in the democratic United States of America." [37]

Drivers traded in their cars long before necessary for new ones that often sported only new sheet metal. The seduction of curvaceous fins and shiny chrome "was carried to its illogical extremes in the 1950s and 1960s," wrote historian James Flink. The Big Three automakers — Ford, GM and Chrysler — "engaged in an orgy of nonfunctional and dysfunctional styling." [38]

However, after the 1966 laws were enacted, federal regulators demanded a new focus on safety rather than panache in car design.

In fact, 1966 was the last year traffic deaths rose as sharply as they did in 2015. [39] While experts blame the 2015 increase — up more than 7 percent to over 35,000 — largely on the improving economy and the accompanying uptick in miles driven — particularly among teens, others cite growing smartphone distractions and a complacent public, willing to accept that more people die on U.S. roads each year than the equivalent of the *Titanic* sinking twice every month. [40]

President Barack Obama in late 2015 signed a five-year transportation law — the Fixing America's Surface Transportation Act (FAST) — the first long-term transportation bill passed by Congress in 10 years. Although it mostly focuses on infrastructure funding, it includes several safety provisions.

FAST increases funding for state safety programs and improves incentives for states to adopt regulations to address impaired and distracted driving and strengthen graduated driver license programs for young drivers. All states have a three-stage licensing systems for young drivers, but provisions and enforcement vary by state. Such programs allow young drivers to gain experience in stages — usually a learning stage, an intermediate stage and a full privilege stage — before getting an adult driver's license.

The law also includes incentives for putting safety technologies in cars — such as so-called vehicle-to-infrastructure

Continued on p. 156

Chronology

1880s-1930s
Safety measures take hold as driving spreads.

1886
German engineer Karl Benz invents first gasoline-powered automobile.

1901
Connecticut sets first speed limits — 12 mph in cities and 15 mph in the country.

1910
New York state adopts first law against drunken driving.

1913
National Safety Council begins compiling traffic safety statistics.

1936
Drunkometer patented to determine a driver's intoxication.

1938
States begin setting intoxication levels as having a blood alcohol concentration (BAC) of 0.15.

1940s-1950s
Companies begin creating auto safety features.

1947
First padded dashboard introduced.

1949
Chrysler introduces standard disc brakes in the Imperial.

1953
Police officer and scientist Robert Borkenstein invents the Breathalyzer. . . . American engineer John Hetrick patents air bag design.

1959
Swedish engineer Nils Bohlin invents three-point lap/shoulder seat belt.

1960s-1980s
Federal government assumes key role in traffic safety.

1965
Lawyer and consumer activist Ralph Nader publishes landmark *Unsafe at Any Speed*, prompting passage of federal auto safety regulations.

1966
Congress enacts National Traffic and Motor Vehicle Safety Act, the first federal auto safety law.

1968
Government requires all cars to have seat belts.

1969
Front seat headrests mandated.

1970
National Highway Transportation Safety Administration established.

1971
Chrysler Imperial is first car to have standard anti-lock brakes.

1972
Traffic fatalities reach record high — 54,589.

1974
Congress sets 55 mph national speed limit.

1980
Mothers Against Drunk Driving formed.

1984
New York is first state to require seat belts.

1984
Congress raises legal drinking age from 18 to 21.

1985
All states require child safety seats.

1990s-Present
Traffic deaths fall to record low and then begin to rise.

1995
Federal speed limit repealed; states begin setting higher limits.

1998
Air bags required in all new cars.

2000
Congress adopts .08 blood alcohol concentration (BAC).

2007
Apple's iPhone revolutionizes cellphone use, leading to rise in distracted driving. . . . Washington state passes first ban on driver texting.

2009
Volvo introduces automatic emergency braking system.

2011
Traffic fatalities fall to record low — 32,479.

2012
Alabama is last state to require ignition interlocks to prevent drunken driving.

2015
Traffic fatalities jump 7 percent, the largest one-year increase in half a century.

2016
In first nine months, traffic deaths rise 8 percent over same period in 2015.

Millennials Likely to Embrace Driverless Cars

"The automobile just isn't that important to people's lives anymore."

The same smartphone whose apps and distractions are partly blamed for the recent uptick in traffic deaths may also be a cultural game-changer, enabling a future with fewer traffic deaths.

The generation that was, in Bruce Springsteen's immortal words, "Born to Run," who saw cars as representing freedom and a way to meet up with friends, have given birth to a generation of Millennials, only half of whom went to the trouble to get a driver's license by the time they turned 18. [1]

Experts in car culture say social media and smartphones have replaced cars as the crucial link to social interaction. Millennials rely on digital connectivity rather than cars for socializing. For them, the decision is not: Ford or Chevy? but iPhone or Android? They also are the likeliest cohort to telecommute and use public transit. [2] In fact, 85 percent of Millennials would prefer to telecommute 100 percent of the time. [3] And they have now surpassed Generation Xers — the generation that preceded them — as the largest peer group in the U.S. workforce. [4]

"The automobile just isn't that important to people's lives anymore," said Mike Berger, a historian who studies the social effects of the car. "The automobile provided the means for teenagers to live their own lives. Social media blows any limits out of the water. You don't need the car to go find friends." [5]

And if Millennials do need a ride, they may soon be able to summon a self-driving car. Google's self-driving car project executed its first driverless ride in 2015 on public roads in Austin, Texas, with a blind "driver." The ride-hailing company Uber introduced its self-driving cars in Pittsburgh late last year — the first time the public has been able to summon an autonomous car. (For now, a human being still sits in the driver's seat in Uber's self-driving cars.) [6]

"I think we're eventually going to go to transportation as a service," says Timothy Carone, an automation expert at the University of Notre Dame. "I fully expect over the next five to 10 years that car ownership will start to decrease, especially in the cities, and people will simply summon a car" when they need a ride.

Driverless cars will "without a doubt" be a disruptive innovation, or a revolutionary change that replaces an industry or technology, says Carone. Costa Samaras, an automation expert at Carnegie Mellon University in Pittsburgh, where Uber is testing its self-driving cars, agrees. "The elephant in the room here is the disappearance of the human grid in transportation," he says, with the impact felt across the board — from the trucking industry to health care.

While driverless cars may be disruptive, they also will save lives: Researchers estimate that by 2050, widespread adoption of

Continued from p. 154

equipment to sense obstacles, funds for drug awareness programs and calls for a study on developing an impairment standard for driving under the influence of marijuana.

Over the decades, three culprits primarily have been responsible for the deaths on American roads — driving while intoxicated, not wearing a seat belt and driving too fast.

Seat Belts

In 1955, neurologist C. Hunter Shelden, frustrated by the "ever-increasing number of fatalities occurring daily" due to auto accidents, proposed a retractable seat belt. [41] Further, he wrote, "the doors, seats, cushions, knobs, steering wheel, and even the overhead structure are so poorly constructed from the safety standpoint that it is

surprising anyone escapes from an automobile accident without serious injury." [42]

One of the most widely reprinted articles in *Reader's Digest* history was about another year when — as in 2015 — there were about 35,000 traffic deaths. It was 1935.

In "— And Sudden Death!" J.C. Furnas writes, "What is needed is a vivid and sustained realization that every time you step on the throttle, death gets in beside you, hopefully waiting for his chance." Given the dangerous car interiors of the day, many believed it was preferable to be thrown out of the car upon impact. [43]

In the 1950s, seat belts that only crossed over the lap, used regularly by race car drivers, were the only option to safeguard drivers. However, the belt's buckle position sometimes caused serious internal injuries in high-speed crashes.

Then in 1959, Swede Nils Bohlin, Volvo's chief safety engineer, designed the three-point belt still widely used today. Its purpose was to secure both the upper and lower body while still being able to be buckled with one hand. The straps joined at the hip, holding the body securely in a crash. Volvo gave the new design to other automakers for free. [44]

In the United States, automakers began installing lap seat belts in all new cars in 1964, with shoulder belts in 1968. The combined three-point belts were not installed until 1974.

But surveys showed that only about 10 percent of Americans were using seat belts, and states did not start requiring drivers and passengers to buckle up until 1984, when New York passed the first state law requiring the use of seat belts. By 1996, every state except New Hampshire required seat belts at least in the front seats. [45]

driverless cars could cut traffic deaths by 90 percent. Based on 2015 numbers, that's more than 31,000 lives per year. [7]

But there will be obstacles, experts agree. Automakers must become as comfortable with software releases as they are with recalls. And technology companies will face decisions about what kind of steel and fiberglass to use in their cars as well as which new software enhancement to put into new models of their driverless cars. [8]

While no one expects self-driving cars to completely replace those on the road today, cultural attitudes in the newest crop of drivers may speed the embrace of autonomous cars.

"All the children see it coming by," says Samaras. "It's normal to them that a car drives itself," he says.

— *Ellen Kennerly*

The ride-hailing company Uber introduced its self-driving cars in Pittsburgh late last year — the first time the public has been able to summon an autonomous car. For now, a human still sits in the driver's seat.

AFP/Getty Images/Angelo Merendino

[1] Marc Fisher, "Cruising Toward Oblivion," *The Washington Post*, Sept. 2, 2015, http://tinyurl.com/pml2o4f.

[2] Marc Fisher, "American car culture hits skids with millennials," *Chicago Tribune*, Sept. 11, 2015, http://tinyurl.com/nbh6gdr.

[3] Jessica Howington, "Survey: Changing Workplace Priorities of Millennials," Flexjobs, Sept. 25, 2015, http://tinyurl.com/za8nbf2

[4] Richard Fry, "Millennials surpass Gen Xers as the largest generation in U.S. labor force," Pew Research Center, May 11, 2015, http://tinyurl.com/mblretz.

[5] *Ibid*.

[6] Ashley Halsey III and Michael Laris, "Blind man sets out alone in Google's driverless car," *The Washington Post*, Dec. 13, 2016, http://tinyurl.com/j9extuz; Jeff Zurschmeide, "Uber's Pittsburgh Robotaxis Amuse Rider Still Struggle with Double Parked Cars," *Digital Trends*, Oct. 18, 2016, http://tinyurl.com/jjrfbn9.

[7] Adrienne LaFrance, "Self-Driving Cars Could Save 300,000 Lives Per Decade in America," *The Atlantic*, Sept. 29, 2015, http://tinyurl.com/z3wqhk3.

[8] Chunka Mui, "31 Primers on Driverless Car Innovation and Disruption," *Forbes*, Feb. 12, 2017, http://tinyurl.com/jed9cyj.

Seat-belt laws vary among the states. Some have so-called primary laws, which allow officers to stop cars solely if passengers are not buckled up. Secondary seat-belt laws only allow officers to cite someone for being unbuckled if they had stopped the vehicle for another traffic infraction.

By 2015, according to the National Highway Traffic Safety Administration, seat belts were saving more than 13,941 lives a year. [46]

Air bags were required beginning Sept. 1, 1998, on both sides of the front seat. According to NHTSA, air bags save about 2,000 lives each year. [47]

Alcohol

New York was the first state to outlaw drunken driving, in 1910, but police officers had to base their decisions on their best judgment of the level of inebriation. In 1938, a biochemistry professor and toxicologist created the Drunkometer, a chemical process that could determine inebriation based on a driver's breath. A collaborator on the Drunkometer, Robert Borkenstein, invented the portable Breathalyzer in 1953. Police began using it to measure the level of blood alcohol concentration based on the amount of alcohol vapors in the driver's exhalation. [48]

In the 1970s alcohol contributed to 60 percent of all traffic fatalities and two-thirds of those involving victims between the ages of 16 and 20. [49] Until then, efforts to prevent drunken driving had been focused on middle-aged drivers.

In 1984, the federal government enacted the National Minimum Drinking Age Act, requiring all states to raise the drinking age to 21 by October 1986, or lose 10 percent of the state's highway funding. Much of the subsequent drop in traffic fatalities among 16-to-20-year-olds was attributed to this change. [50]

But the biggest impact on drunken driving began on May 3, 1980, when 13-year-old Cari Lightner of Fair Oaks, Calif., was walking to a church carnival. The driver who hit and killed Cari had numerous arrests for drunkenness and had been arrested on another hit-and-run drunken driving charge just a week earlier. After being told that such cases were rarely treated harshly, Cari's mother, Candace, started Mothers Against Drunk Driving (MADD) to fight what she called "the only socially accepted form of homicide." [51]

MADD's campaigns focused on getting states to raise the drinking age, passing stiffer penalties for drunken driving and lowering the nation's legal BAC from 0.1 to .08. Since MADD was founded, alcohol-related deaths on U.S. roads have been cut by more than half. [52]

Using Apps to Control Distractions

Parents embrace strategies to fight distracted driving.

Start to write a text or read email while driving, and this app will forcefully tell you to stop. Known as Focus, it is one of many apps being offered by cellphone providers seeking to use technology to combat the growing problem of distracted driving.

The risky lure of a cellphone's games, social media and texting connections while driving has spurred the development of numerous apps to safeguard drivers. Some prevent cellphone users from texting, placing calls or playing games while the vehicle is in motion or when the user turns it on. Others try to "train" drivers to improve their driving over time using incentives such as reward points.

It's difficult to know whether the apps actually reduce deaths due to distracted driving because it's unclear how many fatalities each year are caused by distracted driving: Estimates range from 10 percent to as high as 50 percent. [1] The number of distracted-driving deaths is anyone's guess. It is a self-reported behavior, and at present is not measured by any technology. Estimates range from 10 percent to as high as 50 percent of traffic fatalities. In addition, there are often contributing factors. An intoxicated driver may also be texting, or a speeding driver may be using a smartphone app. [2]

"Teens . . . implicitly believe that using their phone while driving is safe and not a stressor or distraction behind the wheel," said Dr. Gene Beresin in a study on teen driving. Beresin is senior adviser on adolescent psychiatry with Students Against Destructive Decisions (SADD) and executive director of the Clay Center for Young Healthy Minds at Massachusetts General Hospital. [3]

Some of the most popular anti-distraction apps, which hold particular appeal for parents, include:

- **BeeHive:** This app connects drivers to safe-driving sponsors — such as schools, businesses, families and others — who often offer rewards for safe driving.
- **Cellcontrol DriveID:** This device, which works on Android or iPhone devices, mounts on the windshield and can disable all apps and phone and texting functions while the vehicle is in motion unless specifically allowed by the administrator. The unit can also free up zones in the car in which cellphones can be used without restriction, and it can remove restrictions when the car stops. It can also rate driving behaviors.
- **DriveMode:** AT&T's app can be set to start automatically as soon as the car exceeds 15 mph. It silences text alerts and delivers a "busy driving" message. It doesn't disable navigation, music or contacts. And parents can configure the app to send an alert if it is disabled. For Android or iPhone devices.
- **MessageLOUD:** If you can't possibly wait until you reach your destination to find out what is happening in your virtual world, this app will read your texts and emails to you en route. It lets you manage your email without taking your eyes off the road, but new research indicates that hands-free texting is just as distracting as hands-on. For Android.
- **SafeDrive:** One of several apps that make a game out of staying off the phone. The more the driver leaves his phone alone, the more points he earns, redeemable at some retailers, including gas stations. For Android and iPhone.
- **Sprint's Drive First:** The app blocks calls and alerts and automatically sends "can't answer" texts. Users can set a list of numbers to always answer, and 911 calls will override the app.
- **T-Mobile's SyncUP DRIVE:** Monitors driving, communicates location and sends speed alerts. It also analyzes driving behavior.
- **tXtBlocker:** Marketed to parents of teens, this will completely shut the phone down when the car is in motion. A parent may also set up "No-Cell Zones" to block texting in certain places.
- **TrueMotion:** This app rates driving behavior with the goal of improving safe driving over time. It tracks instances in which the driver may have been distracted and can communicate a driver's location in real time as well as trip history. [4]

— Ellen Kennerly

---

[1] "Distracted Driving," AAA, January 2017, http://tinyurl.com/j92tv2r; "Distracted Driving," National Highway Traffic Safety Administration, undated, http://tinyurl.com/hbued5t.

[2] "Distracted Driving," U.S. Centers for Disease Control and Prevention, undated, http://tinyurl.com/hor6x3e.

[3] "Teen Driving Study Reveals 'App and Drive' is New Danger Among Teens, New Worry for Parents," Students Against Destructive Decisions (SADD), Aug. 1, 2016, http://tinyurl.com/hptqfrc.

[4] For more on apps and distracted driving, see Jennifer Jolly, "The best tech to prevent distracted driving," *USA Today*, May 29, 2016, http://tinyurl.com/zkkjc28; "Apps to Fight Distracted Driving," DMV.ORG, http://tinyurl.com/zyl9pdw.

Speed

Connecticut was the first state to pass a speed limit for automobiles. On May 21, 1901, the state set limits of 12 mph in cities and 15 mph in rural areas.

Adoption of such limits varied. By 1930, about a dozen states still had no speed limit. In the 1970s, when gasoline prices rose dramatically following the 1973 Arab oil embargo, Congress enacted a national speed limit of 55 mph, primarily as an effort to conserve gasoline. But the lower limit is credited by some with lowering the death rate per million miles traveled from 4.28 in 1972 to 2.73 in 1983. [53]

However, in 1982 the National Motorists Association was formed to lobby for repeal of the federal speed limit, says Sheila Dunn, the association's communications director. Sometimes driving too slow can be just as dangerous as driving too fast, she says. "Speed limits have to be modern, and they have to reflect the [safer] kinds of roads that we're on."

The federal maximum speed limit was repealed in 1995, part of a federalism movement to returning control over such decisions to the states. [54] Thirty-three states raised their speed limits soon after the repeal, and two years later NHTSA reported that the traffic death rate dropped to a then-record low. "In 1997, the fatality rate per 100 million vehicle miles of travel reached a new historic low of 1.6, down from 1.7, the rate since 1992."

While the death rate per miles traveled fell, overall total deaths, which had fallen to 39,250 in 1992, began rising again as state speed limits rose, reaching a modern-day high of 43,510 in 2005. (*See graph, p. 148.*)

Some experts say it is not speed that kills but the variability of speed — when some are driving fast and others slowly. There is "no statistically discernible relationship between the fatality rate and average speed, though there is a strong relationship to speed variance," said transportation economist Charles A. Lave of the University of California. "When most cars are traveling at about the same speed, whether it is a high speed or a low one, the fatality rate will be low. . . . Variance kills, not speed," he wrote. [55]

Manufacturer's Defects

A component of the government's Road to Zero initiative focuses on "proactive vehicle safety," or working with automakers to help better identify defects before they become a safety risk. Among other things, that includes requiring better communica-

tions about recalls, reviewing lessons learned from past recalls and examining new approaches to emerging safety issues.

One of the most infamous automobile recalls involved the Ford Pinto. In 1978, all Pintos manufactured between 1971 to 1976 were recalled to install protective shielding to prevent gas tank ruptures and fires in a crash. Ford was exposed as having known about the issue but chose to go into production without fixing it. [56]

General Motors issued a recall of 6.7 million vehicles in 1971 after 172 cases of engine-mount failures were blamed for 63 accidents and 18 injuries. [57] An airbag software defect triggered a GM recall involving more than 4 million vehicles involving model years from 2014 to 2017. The defect is linked to at least one death, according to the automaker. [58]

And in 2014, Toyota agreed to pay $1.2 billion to avoid prosecution for covering up problems with "unintended acceleration" and for continuing to manufacture cars with parts it "knew were deadly," according to court documents. [59] The defect was brought to light after a series of accidents involving unintended acceleration, including the death of California Highway Patrolman Mark Saylor and three members of his family. Saylor called 911 while his car was going over 100 mph and was explaining his ordeal right up until the crash that killed him. [60]

Most recently, in what NHTSA has been called "the largest and most complex safety recall in U.S. history," the agency has ordered 19 automakers to recall vehicles manufactured between 2002 through 2015 that contain air bags made by Takata Corp. of Japan. The air bags could deploy explosively, endangering occupants with metal fragments. The recall is expected to affect 42 million U.S. vehicles. Eleven deaths have been attributed to this defect. [61]

CURRENT SITUATION

Safety Measures

Legislatures around the country are considering dozens of bills that would strengthen existing laws on texting, DUI and seat-belt use.

"People know that wearing your seat belt can save your life," says the CDC's Sauber-Schatz. "Primary seat-belt laws have been effective at increasing seat-belt use. That policy does work."

Ohio, meanwhile, enacted a new ignition interlock law for first-time DUI offenders in January. Arizona is discussing what would be its first anti-texting law. [62] Other states are trying new sanctions to deter texting. In Pennsylvania, a bill signed into law late last year could add five years to the prison sentence of a driver found responsible for a fatal crash while texting. [63]

Some states are strengthening the provisions of their graduated licensing systems for young drivers. States with the strongest laws — such as Connecticut and New York — have seen the deepest reductions in teen driver deaths. [64]

Where these laws exist, there has been "a 20 to 40 percent reduction in fatalities among the youngest teens," says Sauber-Schatz, "because it slowly exposes teens to higher risk as they learn to drive."

Legislatures also are enacting laws removing obstacles to testing of driverless cars and automated technologies. States that have put legislation on the books regarding automated vehicle technology include California, Florida, Louisiana, Michigan, Nevada, North Dakota, Tennessee, Utah, Virginia and Washington, D.C. [65]

However, automation technology is changing so fast state regulators often have no idea what future generations of autonomous vehicles will look like.

"The fact that the technology doesn't really exist yet at the deployment scale is what makes it sort of challenging to imagine all the different things that might happen," says Andrew Dick, a policy adviser for the Oregon Department of Transportation. [66]

For instance, Nevada — one of the first states to regulate driverless cars, has already had to amend regulations it enacted in 2008, which required two human operators to remain in the vehicle while it was running. The state

NHTSA issued guidance for states last September encouraging them to allow manufacturers the flexibility to create vehicles that meet safety standards without requiring specific features. State regulators should "stay open-minded" in regulating automated vehicles, said Kevin Biesty, the deputy director for policy at the Arizona Department of Transportation. "Oftentimes, as folks in government, our knee-jerk reaction is to regulate and govern. That's not always the answer, because technologies are going to advance past what we're currently thinking about." [68]

The initiative builds on existing programs, such as the Safe Systems approach to making the infrastructure safer, and assumes the emergence of self-driving cars and more effective programs to address behavioral issues. [69]

Among other things, the initiative calls for a grant program for innovative approaches to "evidence-based highway safety countermeasures," with $1 million awarded each year for three years to successful applicants. The initiative also plans to enlist the RAND Corp. think tank to help develop a roadway system optimized for safety. [70]

Federal and Virginia state officials are spending $5.1 million to help develop a technology to prevent drunken driving, called the Driver Alcohol Detection System for Safety (DADSS). The system would passively detect a driver's blood alcohol concentration and prevent the car from starting if the driver is at or above the legal limit. [71]

The race to get a fully autonomous car on the road is heating up. At least 19 companies are aiming to have driverless technology ready by 2020 – including Google, Tesla, Toyota, Honda, Audi and Nissan – and some carmakers plan to have cars on the road by then. Above, Tesla's self-driving Model S electric automobile.

Getty Images/Bloomberg/Jasper Juinen

Autonomous Cars

Meanwhile, the development of automation is occurring on two tracks.

Automated braking and collision avoidance technologies are both part of the initial stages of the rollout of the Federal Automated Vehicles Policy, which will involve a gradual ratcheting up of automation to Level 5, in which the automated system does all the driving.

Under their agreement with the federal government, car manufacturers are proceeding with standardizing automatic emergency braking by 2022, and vehicle-to-vehicle communication is expected to be standard in all new cars within five years. Almost 1 million crashes could have been prevented in 2014 if every car on the road had forward collision warning with automated emergency braking, according to an IIHS analysis, says the group's vice president for research, Cicchino.

revised those regulations last year after officials decided they were "completely outdated," says April Sanborn, a services manager with the Nevada Department of Motor Vehicles. Nevada is considering removing such traditional terminology as "steering wheels," which could limit future technology that might call for a car to be controlled by a tablet, joystick or some other mechanism, she says. [67]

Meanwhile, the federal government is proceeding with its Road to Zero initiative, aiming to eliminate traffic deaths within 30 years. The initiative is spearheaded by NHTSA, which is partnering with the National Safety Council, the Federal Highway Administration and the Federal Motor Carrier Safety Administration. Nonprofits, health officials and technology companies and automakers also are working toward the goal.

Continued on p. 162

At Issue:

Will technology reduce roadway fatalities?

DEBORAH A.P. HERSMAN
PRESIDENT AND CEO,
NATIONAL SAFETY COUNCIL

WRITTEN FOR *CQ RESEARCHER*, FEBRUARY 2017

*c*ar crashes remain a leading cause of preventable death in the United States. To err is human, so it is no surprise that more than 90 percent of crashes are attributed to human error. As human beings, we are distracted, impaired, fatigued, or we drive too fast and miscalculate stopping distance, among other potentially fatal mistakes.

With automated technology, these errors could be mitigated and even become a thing of the past.

Some car-safety technologies have been around for years, such as anti-lock braking, electronic stability control and air bags. Cars today are built to reduce harm in a collision, and some technology can prevent crashes from occurring in the first place. Automakers have given us drowsiness alerts, obstacle and pedestrian detection, adaptive cruise control, forward collision warning and automatic emergency braking, to name a few.

According to the Insurance Institute for Highway Safety, we could save more than 10,000 lives a year if all vehicles were equipped with just four technologies that are available today — lane departure warning, forward collision warning, blind-spot monitors and adaptive headlights. Ten thousand lives represent nearly a quarter of all fatalities occurring on our roads every year.

Taking automation a step further, self-driving vehicles represent the most promising lifesaving innovation in transportation in our lifetime. Automated cars have already captured the public's imagination, but the path to full automation is far from clear.

As this transformational technology develops, we will need innovation, but we will also need oversight, robust testing and data collection so automakers and regulators have the knowledge and information needed to improve safety. Transparency and data sharing can ensure that technology failures are investigated, explained and prevented.

If we want to get to a tipping point where most cars on the road are self-driving, the public must have confidence that automated technology will work perfectly every time. Before that happens, we will have decades when humans are still calling the shots behind the wheel with a variety of levels of automation interacting on our roadways.

We cannot abdicate our responsibility for safer roads in the interim. Until we get to zero deaths on our nation's highways, we need smarter cars, as well as smarter drivers, to get us home safely.

JOHN D. LEE
ENGINEER AND EXPERT IN DRIVER
DISTRACTION,
UNIVERSITY OF WISCONSIN, MADISON

WRITTEN FOR *CQ RESEARCHER*, FEBRUARY 2017

*t*echnology is not the only solution to traffic fatalities. Other countries, such as Israel, Ireland and France, once had substantially higher fatal crash rates than the United States, but they embraced a safety culture that shifted behavior through public awareness campaigns and rigorous enforcement, and they now have significantly lower rates.

The United States, which was once a leader in driving safety, trails the developed world. One reason? Drivers believe they are safer than they are. This "Lake Woebegone" effect, where we all feel above average, leads us to continue to drive dangerously.

Partially self-driving cars might degrade safety by exacerbating this overconfidence. Automation can give drivers a false sense of security even as they become more distracted and less able to take back control. Similarly, automation can make monotonous drives even more monotonous, leading to more drowsiness-related fatalities.

Automation can also confuse drivers, similar to how automation has confused pilots and contributed to aircraft accidents.

While automation might eliminate many current contributors to crashes, it will be vulnerable to situations that drivers now negotiate with ease, such as work zones. When automation makes "easy" errors — failing at something that people do easily — trust in the automation could drop precipitously.

More generally, people perceive risk as being much greater when they are not in control, even if the objective risk is less. Uncontrolled risk must be 1,000 times lower than controlled risk for people to see them as comparable. Applied to automated vehicles, this means an acceptable annual fatality rate has to be closer to 35, far less than the current 35,092 or even 3,500. Drivers might not accept automation even if it performs very well.

Vehicle automation might affect driving safety the way air bags did. It may hold the allure of a future safety benefit without the corresponding benefit today, leading public policy to neglect the safety benefits that could be had from changing current behavior.

The failure to focus on seat-belt use in the belief that air bags could eventually make crashes survivable contributed to tens of thousands of deaths.

We can only hope the allure of vehicle automation will not do the same.

Continued from p. 160

The second track is development of a fully autonomous car. An "almost" self-driving car isn't enough, said John Krafcik, the CEO of Waymo, the company formed by Google in 2016 to focus on autonomous vehicle technology. "We're mastering the hardware

Sen. Bill Nelson, D-Fla., holds up an exploded Takata air bag during a meeting of the Senate Commerce, Science and Transportation Committee on Nov. 20, 2014. The National Highway Transportation Safety Administration recently ordered 19 automakers to recall up to 42 million U.S. vehicles manufactured between 2002 through 2015 that contain air bags made by the Japanese firm. The bags can explode when deployed, spewing occupants with metal fragments. Eleven deaths have been attributed to the defect.

and software to build a better 'driver' for a fully self-driving car." [72]

The race to ge a fully autonomous car on the road is heating up. At least 19 companies are aiming to have driverless technology ready by 2020 — including Google, Tesla, Toyota, Honda, Audi and Nissan —

and some plan to be on the road by then. [73]

An early obstacle — high costs — is being overcome. For example, LiDAR, which works like radar but uses a laser for sensing its surroundings and is central to self-driving technology, cost $75,000 per car when Google's self-driving project began, said Krafcik. By building the technology in-house, the price tag was cut by 90 percent. [74]

Cost is a big reason for building self-driving cars from the ground up under one roof, he said. Development cycles are also significantly shorter, said a Waymo spokeswoman.

Lee of the University of Wisconsin agrees that end-to-end creation of such products is vital. "There needs to be an intimate connection between the software and the hardware, and getting that right is safety-critical."

To speed up the acceptance of driverless cars, the outgoing Obama administration in January proposed spending $3.9 billion on pilot programs to test "connected cars" that communicate with one another to avoid crashes. The proposal would require congressional approval, and its future is uncertain.

The Department of Transportation's new Advisory Committee on Automation in Transportation, which includes representatives from agencies, technology companies and the automotive industry, met for the first time in January. Its role is to advise the government on how to enable automation, such as lifting certain safety regulations to allow for testing of driverless cars.

"With new technologies and innovative approaches to mobility, we hold the keys to reach a future without transportation fatalities," says the National Safety Council's Hersman, who serves on the new board. ∎

OUTLOOK

Win-Wins

With automatic-braking and forward-collision warning capability on track to become standard within a few years, driverless cars will also become part of the transportation landscape, experts say. [75] It is estimated these technologies could cut traffic fatalities by up to 90 percent by 2050. [76]

However, the fate of federal safety and driverless programs is uncertain under the new Trump administration. An NHTSA spokesman said the agency would not speculate on what sort of policies President Trump would choose to prioritize or pursue.

The Obama administration's proposed pilot program includes aligning state policies to make it legal for automated cars to drive from one state to another. For instance, New York state requires drivers to have their hands on the wheel at all times, which would be impossible in a driverless car.

"If you have a wholly Level 5 vehicle that doesn't require a steering wheel or brake pedals, you'll run afoul of a third of the Federal Motor Vehicle Safety Standards," said Paul Brubaker, president and CEO of the Alliance for Transportation Innovation. [77]

The development of driverless technology will demand engagement from government in unfamiliar ways. While legislatures are clearing the way for testing such vehicles by passing laws defining the cars themselves and their operation, many believe Congress eventually will have to act.

For example, Congress may have to make sure that state laws and regulations are compatible so a driverless car that is legal in one state can drive into another. "I'd be surprised if Congress does not have to act," said Gary Shapiro, the president and CEO of the Consumer Technology Association. [78]

In an effort to clear the way for speedy development of driverless cars, two senators said recently they were exploring legislation to remove regulatory constraints that could slow the deployment of autonomous cars. Current federal rules mandate the existence of brake pedals and steering wheels, for instance, which do not exist in driverless cars. Sens. John Thune, R-S.D., chair of the Senate Commerce, Science and Transportation Committee, and Gary Peters, D-Mich., plan to launch the bipartisan effort. [79]

But for now, testing will continue apace. Driverless cars can be tested and brought to market within a few years without any action from Congress.

"In terms of the ability for manufacturers to thoughtfully test and deploy, you don't need new law" at the moment, said David Strickland, the counsel spokesman for the Self-Driving Coalition for Safer Streets. Many in the industry and the Republican-controlled Congress share that view and do not wish to regulate testing too strictly for fear of losing the technology to overseas companies, observers say. [80]

However, at some point, accidents between driverless vehicles and those driven by a human will occur, likely prompting attention from lawmakers. "Momentum for federal regulation won't start until accidents begin occurring, much like with the automobile 100 years ago," said Adie Tomer, a fellow with the Brookings Institution's Metropolitan Policy Program. [81]

Discussions already are under way about what kind of ethical decisions driverless cars will have to make. For instance, if a driverless car is faced with the choice between driving off a bridge or hitting a vehicle filled with passengers, what will it do? Currently, "their software will do whatever it takes to protect occupants in their car, even if the car kills students in a school bus," says automation expert Carone of the University of Notre Dame. "Software will make decisions that we may not make."

Driverless car developers fear future accidents or incidents involving autonomous cars being hacked will prompt lawmakers to overreact with harsh regulations. Protective technology will be needed to prevent someone from hacking into a vehicle's software and demanding money to release it — and/or the driver or passengers.

"Waiting for the government to approve technology is never a good formula," said Rep. Michael Burgess, R-Texas. "That said, we must remain vigilant in areas like cybersecurity, where industry must be held accountable." [82] While a driverless world could significantly reduce traffic deaths, it could also cut gasoline consumption, threatening federal funding for transportation infrastructure, which depends heavily on an 18.4-cents-per-gallon gasoline tax gasoline taxes.

Rep. Earl Blumenauer, a Democrat from Oregon, says Congress might eventually replace the gas tax with a tax on vehicle miles traveled.

Meanwhile, the DADSS technology to prevent a car from starting if the driver is inebriated — enthusiastically supported by MADD — could appear in cars in five to eight years. [83] Although the technology is being developed as optional equipment, some safety advocates hope it will become a standard safety feature.

However, traffic safety experts say the measures that would make the biggest impact on traffic fatalities are:

• Having all states adopt primary seat-belt laws for front and back seats, making it possible for police to stop a vehicle and issue citations solely for unbelted driving or riding;

• Using DUI checkpoints more often;

• Having all state ignition interlock laws apply to first offenders;

• Adopting more-effective efforts against distracted driving;

• Having all states adopt strong graduated licensing programs.

• Building more Safe Systems — environments that discourage speeding including roundabouts and other features;

But even if all those measures are adopted, sophisticated new cars will still pose dangers. For instance, as more and more cars come outfitted with Wi-Fi, hacking is expected to become a danger.

"Ransomware will be real," says Carone. "It's going to happen."

"One of the riskiest things any of us do is vehicle travel," says automation expert Samaras of Carnegie Mellon University. "This is a huge public health issue."

But technology, public attention and agency safety efforts provide the "opportunity for a lot of win-wins," he says. ■

Notes

1 "Nightly News with Lester Holt," NBC News, Oct. 21, 2016, http://tinyurl.com/h8rlehj.

2 Tony Marrero, Sara DiNatale and Anastasia Dawson, "MLK crash kills five, including two Tampa children ages 9 and 10," *Tampa Bay Times*, Oct. 27, 2016, http://tinyurl.com/zn5vdk9.

3 "2015 Motor Vehicle Crashes: Overview, Traffic Safety Facts, Research Note," National Highway Traffic Safety Administration, August 2016, http://tinyurl.com/zj3fxpn.

4 "9/11 Death Statistics," Statistic Brain, http://tinyurl.com/b3sae36. "Millennial drivers are highway hazards, survey shows," *USA Today*, Feb. 15, 2017, http://tinyurl.com/h4wp4lg.

5 "Yearly Snapshot, 2015," General Statistics, Insurance Institute for Highway Safety, Highway Loss Data Institute, http://tinyurl.com/zy2xnjo.

6 Robert Thomson, "Researchers came up with a price tag for bad driving," *The Washington Post*, Oct. 15, 2016, http://tinyurl.com/jpp4ncb. For full report, see "The Economic and Societal Impact of Motor Vehicle Crashes, 2010 (Revised)," National Highway Traffic Safety Administration, May 2015, http://tinyurl.com/zl6xqtj.

7 "Fatality Facts, Teenagers," Insurance Institute for Highway Safety, http://tinyurl.com/nryku8y.

8 Amanda Essex, Douglas Shinkle and Anne Teigen, "Transportation Review, Speeding and Speed Limits," Jan. 18, 2016, National Conference of State Legislatures, http://tinyurl.com/z4kejpj.

9 "Speeding and Aggressive Driving," Governors Highway Safety Association, http://tinyurl.com/zosplfk. "Speed limit increases cause 33,000 deaths in 20 years," Insurance Institute for Highway Safety, April 12, 2016, http://tinyurl.com/hq7qhwx.

10 "U.S. DOT, National Safety Council Launch 'Road to Zero' Coalition to End Roadway Fatalities," National Highway Traffic Safety Administration, Oct. 3, 2016, http://tinyurl.com/z5oaa3h.

11 "Status of State Ignition Interlock Laws," Mothers Against Drunk Driving, http://tinyurl.com/hf64nmw.

12 Alissa Pietila, "Gov. Snyder signs legislations to raise speed limits on designated roadways following safety studies," FoxUP, Jan. 5, 2017, http://tinyurl.com/h56c7eq.

13 "Seat belt use in U.S. reaches historic 90 percent," National Highway Traffic Safety Administration, Nov. 21, 2016. http://tinyurl.com/z924tj6.

14 "Safety belts: Thousands of people still die because they didn't buckle up," Insurance Institute for Highway Safety, February 2017, http://tinyurl.com/hf7wybg.

15 "Police dress up as construction workers to catch distracted drivers," WSB-TV, Atlanta, Ga. July 29, 2015, http://tinyurl.com/hhzdlbm.

16 "Distracted Driving," Governors Highway Safety Association, http://tinyurl.com/j9fz2bd

17 "Facts and Statistics," Official Government Website of Distracted Driving, distraction.gov, http://tinyurl.com/h38phan.

18 "Understanding the Distracted Brain," National Safety Council, White Paper, April 2012, http://tinyurl.com/px7s7nb.

19 "Teen Driver Safety," AAA Exchange, http://tinyurl.com/hy8q7p3.

20 Matt Richtel, "Texting and Driving? Watch out for Textalyzer," *The New York Times*, April 27, 2016, http://tinyurl.com/gntyzwx.

21 *Ibid.*

22 "Facts and Statistics," *op. cit.*

23 Phil McCausland and Shamar Walters, "Tesla's 'Autopilot' Begins Braking for Wreck Before Driver," NBC News, Dec. 28, 2016, http://tinyurl.com/jrhbora.

24 "U.S. DOT issues Federal Policy for safe testing and deployment of automated vehicles," National Highway Traffic Safety Administration, Sept. 20, 2016, http://tinyurl.com/zccvyve.

25 Jeff Plungis and Dana Hull, "Fatal Tesla Crash Spurs Criticism of On-The-Road Testing," *Bloomberg Technology*, July 1, 2016, http://tinyurl.com/zrxylvl.

26 "Road to Zero," National Safety Council, http://tinyurl.com/gwv43lc.

27 Peter Murtagh, "Road Deaths down 18%," *The Irish Times*, Dec. 23, 2015, http://tinyurl.com/hxtdzm2.

28 Ben McPartland, "France sees record fall in number of road deaths," *The Local*, Jan. 20, 2014, http://tinyurl.com/jkoxjar.

29 "Fatality Facts: Alcohol-impaired driving," IIHS, http://tinyurl.com/hm8cllz.

30 Peter Bregman, "The Easiest Way to Change People's Behavior," *Harvard Business Review*, March 12, 2009, http://tinyurl.com/zqefv69.

31 "Fatally Hurt by Automobile. Vehicle Carrying the Son of ex-Mayor Edson Ran over H.H. Bliss, Who Was Alighting from a Trolley Car," Courtesy NYPL's *New York Times* database, http://tinyurl.com/83xl65b.

32 "An Analysis of the Significant Decline in Motor Vehicle Traffic Fatalities in 2008," NHTSA, DOT, June, 2010, http://tinyurl.com/zw7ljh5.

33 Special to *The New York Times*, "Traffic Death Toll in 1974 18% Lower Than in 1973," *The New York Times*, Oct. 12, 1975, http://tinyurl.com/jc8d9su.

34 Michael Cooper, "Happy Motoring: Traffic Deaths at 61-year-low," *The New York Times*, April 1, 2011, http://tinyurl.com/j389oj5.

35 "1966 President Johnson signs the National Traffic and Motor Vehicle Safety Act," *This Day in History*, http://tinyurl.com/glvagxp.

36 Ralph Nader, *Unsafe at Any Speed* (1965).

37 Daniel J. Boorstin, *The Americans: The Democratic Experience* (1973).

38 "Annual model change was the result of affluence, technology, advertising," *Automotive News*, Sept. 14, 2008. http://tinyurl.com/hs24u24.

39 "The People History," www.thepeoplehistory.com/1966.html.

40 "Titanic Victims," *Titanic Facts*, "The Life & Loss of the RMS Titanic in Numbers," www.titanicfacts.net/titanic-victims.html.

41 C. Hunter Shelden, "Prevention, the only cure for head injuries resulting from automobile accidents," *JAMA*, Nov. 5, 1955, http://tinyurl.com/zcstsr9.

42 *Ibid.*

43 J.C. Furnas, "— And Sudden Death," *A Readers Digest Classic*, August 1935, http://tinyurl.com/zb36ang.

44 "Three-point seatbelt inventor Nils Bohlin born," *This Day in History*, http://tinyurl.com/lfvecnz.

About the Author

Ellen Kennerly has worked as a journalist for more than three decades, mostly with the *Atlanta Journal-Constitution* where she held editing and managerial positions in print and digital. Since then, she worked as professional in residence for the Office of Student Media at Louisiana State University and as an editorial department director for WebMD. She is now a communications consultant in Atlanta.

[45] "Injury Prevention & Control: Motor Vehicle Safety," Centers for Disease Control and Prevention, http://tinyurl.com/hglm79r.

[46] "Seatbelts," Overview, National Highway Traffic Safety Administration, http://tinyurl.com/zo34dwp.

[47] "How many lives do airbags save each year?" Reference.com, http://tinyurl.com/hvmupga.

[48] "1897 First drunk driving arrest," *This Day in History*, http://tinyurl.com/28gx5uh.

[49] Ibid.

[50] "Alcohol-related Traffic Deaths,"NIH Fact Sheets, U.S. Department of Health & Human Services, January 2017, http://tinyurl.com/j6jxlmg.

[51] "1980 — MADD founder's daughter killed by drunk driver," *This Day in History*, http://tinyurl.com/bn55wx5.

[52] "Drunk driving deaths, 1982-2014," MADD.org, http://tinyurl.com/njr5fkd.

[53] "Connecticut enacts first speed-limit law," *This Day in History*, http://tinyurl.com/6434huq.

[54] For background, see Kenneth Jost, "The States and Federalism," *CQ Researcher*, Sept. 13, 1996, pp. 793-816.

[55] Stephen Moore, "Speed Doesn't Kill, The Repeal of the 55-mph Speed Limit," Policy Analysis, The Cato Institute, May 31, 1999, http://tinyurl.com/hwoo2h3.

[56] Ben Wojdyla, "The Top Automotive Engineering Failures: The Ford Pinto Fuel Tanks," *Popular Mechanics*, May 20, 2011, http://tinyurl.com/gsdet8n.

[57] "GM Recall History," GM-Recall.com, http://tinyurl.com/zgbs5y8.

[58] The Associated Press,"General Motors recalls 4 million vehicles after software linked to 1 death," *Los Angeles Times*, Sept. 9, 2016, http://tinyurl.com/zpbzx7s.

[59] Brian Ross *et al.*, "Toyota to Pay $1.2B for Hiding Deadly 'Unintended Acceleration,'" ABC News, March 19, 2014, http://tinyurl.com/jw2x5ke.

[60] Ibid.

[61] "Takata Airbag Recall, Everything You Need to Know," *Consumer Reports*, Jan. 4, 2017, http://tinyurl.com/jzjykbv.

[62] State Traffic Safety Legislation Database, National Conference of State Legislatures, Feb. 8, 2017, http://tinyurl.com/j8gnht7.

[63] House Bill No. 2025, General Assembly of Pennsylvania, http://tinyurl.com/jb8oq2t.

[64] "State Laws: Teenagers," IIHS, http://tinyurl.com/jjh8yov. "States could sharply reduce teen crash deaths by strengthening graduated driver licensing laws," IIHS, May 31, 2012, http://tinyurl.com/j25vetj.

[65] "State Traffic Safety Legislation Database," National Conference of State Legislatures, Feb. 8, 2017, http://tinyurl.com/j8gnht7.

[66] "States Struggle to Steer Driverless Cars," *CQ Magazine*, Oct. 17, 2016.

[67] Ibid.

[68] Ibid.

[69] "Safe System: The key to managing road safety," Road and Traffic Authority of New South Wales, http://tinyurl.com/jcvz4x3.

[70] "Road to Zero Safe System Innovation Grants," http://tinyurl.com/hl5llzg.

[71] "U.S. DOT urges public to 'drive sober or get pulled over, and announces funding for innovative technology to end drunk driving," NHTSA, Dec. 14, 2016, http://tinyurl.com/jjpbowl.

[72] Linda Chiem, "4 Questions Raised by DOT's Connected Car Tech Proposal," *Law 360*, http://tinyurl.com/jmambu5.

[73] Danielle Muoio, "These 19 companies are racing to put driverless cars on the road by 2020," *Business Insider*, Aug. 28, 2016, http://tinyurl.com/jpotb38.

[74] John Krafcik of Waymo, Keynote address, Automobili-D, Detroit, January 2017.

[75] Tim Higgins, Google-Parent Alphabet's Self-Driving Car Testing Far Ahead in California, Reports Show," *The Wall Street Journal*, Feb. 1, 2017, http://tinyurl.com/zrtoyz2.

[76] Adrienne LaFrance, "Self-Driving Cars Could Save 300,000 Lives per Decade in America, Automation on the roads could be the great public-health achievement of the 21st century," *The Atlantic*, Sept. 29, 2015, http://tinyurl.com/z3wqhk3.

[77] See Jacob Fischler, "No One Is Driving," *CQ*, Feb. 6, 2017.

[78] Ibid.

[79] Joan Lowy, "Senators try to speed up deployment of driverless cars," The Associated Press, Feb. 13, 2017, http://tinyurl.com/zrvjapl.

[80] Ibid.

[81] Ibid.

[82] Ibid.

[83] "Frequently Asked Questions," dads, Driver Alcohol Detection System for Safety, http://tinyurl.com/hs2awr3.

FOR MORE INFORMATION

Centers for Disease Control and Prevention, 1600 Clifton Rd., Atlanta, GA 30329; 800-232-4636; www.cdc.gov. Federal agency that seeks to protect the public from health and safety threats.

Governors Highway Safety Association, 444 N. Capitol St., N.W., Suite 722, Washington, DC 20001; 202-789-0942; www.ghsa.org. A nonprofit representing government safety offices that manage federal grant programs on highway safety.

Insurance Institute for Highway Safety, 988 Dairy Road, Ruckersville, VA 22968; 434-985-4600; www.iihs.org. A scientific and educational organization dedicated to reducing deaths, injuries and property damage from car crashes.

Mothers Against Drunk Driving, 511 E. John Carpenter Freeway, Suite 700, Irving, TX 75062; 877-275-6233; www.madd.org. An advocacy group formed to reduce drunk and drugged driving and to help victims and survivors.

National Highway Traffic Safety Administration, 1200 New Jersey Ave., S.E., Washington, DC 20590; 1-888-327-4236; www.nhtsa.gov. Federal agency that seeks to save lives, prevent injuries and reduce traffic crashes through education, research and law enforcement.

National Institute on Alcohol Abuse and Alcoholism, 9000 Rockville Pike, Bethesda, MD 20892; 301-443-2857; www.niaaa.nih.gov. The National Institutes of Health's largest funder of alcohol research on human health and well-being.

National Motorists Association, 402 W. 2nd St., Waunakee, WI 53597; 800-882-2785; www.motorists.org. An organization formed to fight excessive regulation and safeguard drivers' rights.

National Safety Council, 1121 Spring Lake Dr., Itasca, IL 60143; 800-621-7615; www.nsc.org. A congressionally chartered nonprofit that works to eliminate preventable deaths through leadership, research, education and advocacy.

Bibliography

Selected Sources

Books

Boorstin, Daniel J., *The Americans: The Democratic Experience*, Knopf Doubleday Publishing, 1973.

In this Pulitzer Prize-winning book, an historian and former head of the Library of Congress explores the transformation of the U.S. auto industry from Henry Ford's inexpensive production line model to Alfred Sloan's planned obsolescence system, in which General Motors built in yearly design changes incentivizing annual purchases, but with little or no regard for safety.

Christensen, Clayton M., *The Innovator's Dilemma: When New Technologies Cause Great Firms to Fail*, Harvard Business Review Press, 2011.

The author details how innovation, such as driverless cars, can lay waste to standard business beliefs and practices.

Nader, Ralph, *Unsafe at Any Speed: The Designed-In Dangers of the American Automobile*, Richard Grossman, 1965.

This landmark book by a 32-year-old lawyer who later became a famous consumer advocate details how automakers were ignoring life-saving technologies, prompting passage of the National Traffic and Motor Vehicle Safety Act of 1966 and spurring laws requiring the use of seat belts.

Articles

Bregman, Peter, "The Easiest Way to Change People's Behavior," *Harvard Business Review*, March 12, 2009, http://tinyurl.com/zqefv69.

A new study finds that the closer teens live to places where alcohol is sold, the greater likelihood they will binge drink and drive under the influence.

Jensen, Christopher, "Traffic Deaths Drop to Lowest in 60 Years," *The New York Times*, Sept. 10, 2010, http://tinyurl.com/jcly2r5.

Safety efforts, including improvements in vehicle design, have reduced fatalities.

LaFrance, Adrienne, "Self-Driving Cars Could Save 300,000 Lives per Decade in America," *The Atlantic*, Sept. 29, 2015, http://tinyurl.com/z3wqhk3.

Widespread adoption of self-driving cars could have a life-saving potential on a par with that of the introduction of vaccines.

Pogue, David, "Hands-Free Texting Is No Safer to Use While Driving," *Scientific American*, undated, http://tinyurl.com/hh2q3h5.

Studies show reaction time declines the same amount while texting, regardless of whether it is hands-free or hands-on.

Spector, Mike, and Mike Ramsey, "U.S. Proposes Spending $4 Billion to Encourage Driverless Cars," *The Wall Street Journal*, Jan. 14, 2017, http://tinyurl.com/zlb38ec.

The Obama administration proposed spending $4 billion over a 10-year period to establish pilot programs to promote the acceptance of driverless and "connected" cars, which avoid crashes and travel delays by enabling cars to communicate with one another.

Reports and Studies

"Distracted Driving," Governors Highway Safety Administration, January 2017, http://tinyurl.com/j9fz2bd.

The association representing state highway safety officials details state distracted-driving laws, including whether the laws cover all cellphone use or just texting.

"The Economic and Societal Impact of Motor Vehicle Crashes, 2010 (Revised)," National Highway Traffic Safety Administration, May 2015, http://tinyurl.com/zl6xqtj.

The federal traffic safety agency estimates that auto crashes — both fatal and nonfatal — cost society $836 billion in economic losses and harm to quality of life.

"Facts and Statistics," Distraction.Gov, National Highway Traffic Safety Administration, U.S. Department of Transportation, undated, http://tinyurl.com/h38phan.

The federal government website on distracted driving provides facts about distracted driving in the United States. For example, about 660,000 drivers are on a cellphone or other device while driving at any given moment during daylight hours.

"Seat Belts," Governors Highway Safety Administration, undated, http://tinyurl.com/hhd9pnf.

This database provides details on state seat-belt laws by type — primary or secondary — and by the age and seat position of passengers covered, as well as fines.

"Teenagers," Insurance Institute for Highway Safety, undated, http://tinyurl.com/jjh8yov.

A safety group funded by the auto insurance industry gives a breakdown, by state, of graduated license systems — three-stage approaches in which young drivers gain experience in lower-risk conditions before moving into adult driving situations by state.

"Yearly Snapshot, 2015," Insurance Institute for Highway Safety, undated, http://tinyurl.com/zy2xnjo.

The institute breaks down traffic fatalities by year, type, gender, age and more.

The Next Step:

Additional Articles from Current Periodicals

Death Surge

"Are poor driving safety laws responsible for surge in traffic deaths?" CBS News, Jan. 31, 2017, http://tinyurl.com/hmul3m4.

A study shows that "optimal" traffic safety laws can reduce highway deaths, with Rhode Island, Washington and Louisiana ranked as the safest states.

"Dramatic surge in traffic deaths outpaces increase in travel," The Associated Press, *Los Angeles Times*, Jan. 13, 2017, http://tinyurl.com/zfzr3y5.

An 8 percent spike in traffic deaths during 2015 outpaced the increase in vehicle miles traveled, which rose only about 3 percent.

Silverstein, Stuart, "Traffic deaths have red state-blue state divide," *Times Union* [Albany, N.Y.], Feb. 1, 2017, http://tinyurl.com/gwzduaw.

States that voted Democratic in the past two presidential elections had some of the lowest traffic fatality rates in 2015, while states that turned "red" in those elections had the highest death rates

Distracted Driving

Boudette, Neal E., "Biggest Spike in Traffic Deaths in 50 Years? Blame Apps," *The New York Times*, Nov. 15, 2016, http://tinyurl.com/h2cstwv.

The Department of Transportation devised a plan to eliminate traffic fatalities within 30 years in response to an increase in deaths caused by technology-based distracted driving.

Paul, Jesse, "CDOT director blames surge in Colorado roadway fatalities on an 'epidemic of distracted driving,' " *The Denver Post*, Jan. 31, 2017, http://tinyurl.com/jhqxw7z.

The executive director of Colorado's Department of Transportation blamed a surge in the state's 2015 roadway fatalities on distracted driving, calling it an "epidemic."

Stern, Joanna, "The Smartest Ways to Use Your Smartphone in the Car," *The Wall Street Journal*, Feb. 7, 2017, http://tinyurl.com/hwwvem3.

Using voice control and hands-free options is the safest method of utilizing smartphones while driving, according to experts.

State Legislation

Moore, Janet, and Tim Harlow, "Distracted-driving bill aims 'to stop the carnage on our roads today,' " *Star Tribune*, Feb. 8, 2017, http://tinyurl.com/j8cq2qq.

To combat inattentive driving, proposed legislation in Minnesota would ban drivers from using hand-held phones while on the road, for which citations nearly doubled from 2014 to 2016.

Myers, Alexis, "Distracted driving penalties could increase statewide in Wash.," The Associated Press, KIRO7, Feb. 12, 2017, http://tinyurl.com/hlmn8q2.

Proposals in the Washington state Legislature would ban the use of any hand-held devices and double the fine for those caught holding a phone while driving or texting while driving.

Salazar, Daniel, "Kansas measures would crack down on cellphone use while driving," *The Wichita Eagle*, Feb. 8, 2017, http://tinyurl.com/jr3dy9f.

Two Kansas proposals seek to bar drivers from holding a phone up to their ears and would fine motorists for using a cellphone in a school zone or road construction zone.

Technology

Gandel, Stephen, "How Self-Driving Cars Could Actually Make Traffic Worse," *Fortune*, Jan. 24, 2017, http://tinyurl.com/zzhqd4n.

Traffic might increase with the widespread use of self-driving cars, because more people would be able to take to the road.

Murnane, Kevin, "Cyclists May Benefit The Most And Be The Greatest Challenge For Self-Driving Cars," *Forbes*, Feb. 13, 2017, http://tinyurl.com/hje3bqt.

Although self-driving cars could help cyclists by reducing encounters with irate or inattentive human drivers, bicycle recognition could be difficult for the tech-savvy vehicles.

Stewart, Jack, "Self-Driving Cars Won't Just Watch the World — They'll Watch You," *Wired*, Feb. 13, 2017, http://tinyurl.com/zx6vst7.

New technology can allow self-driving vehicles to monitor whether their human counterpart can take over in an emergency.

CITING *CQ RESEARCHER*

Sample formats for citing these reports in a bibliography include the ones listed below. Preferred styles and formats vary, so please check with your instructor or professor.

MLA STYLE

Jost, Kenneth. "Remembering 9/11." CQ Researcher 2 Sept. 2011: 701-732.

APA STYLE

Jost, K. (2011, September 2). Remembering 9/11. *CQ Researcher, 9,* 701-732.

CHICAGO STYLE

Jost, Kenneth. "Remembering 9/11." *CQ Researcher*, September 2, 2011, 701-32.

In-depth Reports on Issues in the News

Are you writing a paper?

Need backup for a debate?

Want to become an expert on an issue?

For 90 years, students have turned to *CQ Researcher* for in-depth reporting on issues in the news. Reports on a full range of political and social issues are now available. Following is a selection of recent reports:

Civil Liberties
Privacy and the Internet, 12/15
Intelligence Reform, 5/15
Religion and Law, 11/14

Crime/Law
Forensic Science Controversies, 2/17
Jailing Debtors, 9/16
Decriminalizing Prostitution, 4/16
Restorative Justice, 2/16
The Dark Web, 1/16
Immigrant Detention, 10/15
Fighting Gangs, 10/15

Education
Civic Education, 2/17
Student Debt, 11/16
Apprenticeships, 10/16
Free Speech on Campus, 5/15

Environment/Society
Guns on Campus, 1/17
Mass Transit, 12/16
Arctic Development, 12/16
Protecting the Power Grid, 11/16
Pornography, 10/16
Women in Leadership, 9/16

Health/Safety
Opioid Crisis, 10/16
Mosquito-Borne Disease, 7/16
Drinking Water Safety, 7/16
Virtual Reality, 2/16

Politics/Economy
Trump Presidency, 1/17
European Union's Future, 12/16
The Obama Legacy, 11/16
Populism and Party Politics, 9/16
U.S.-Mexico Relations, 9/16
Modernizing the Nuclear Arsenal, 7/16

Upcoming Reports

Immigrants and the Economy, 2/24/17   Women in Prison, 3/3/17   Charter Schools, 3/10/17

ACCESS

CQ Researcher is available in print and online. For access, visit your library or www.cqresearcher.com.

STAY CURRENT

For notice of upcoming *CQ Researcher* reports or to learn more about *CQ Researcher* products, subscribe to the free email newsletters, *CQ Researcher Alert!* and *CQ Researcher News*: http://cqpress.com/newsletters.

PURCHASE

To purchase a *CQ Researcher* report in print or electronic format (PDF), visit www.cqpress.com or call 866-427-7737. Single reports start at $15. Bulk purchase discounts and electronic-rights licensing are also available.

SUBSCRIBE

Annual full-service *CQ Researcher* subscriptions—including 44 reports a year, monthly index updates, and a bound volume—start at $1,131. Add $25 for domestic postage.

CQ Researcher Online offers a backfile from 1991 and a number of tools to simplify research. For pricing information, call 800-818-7243 or 805-499-9774 or email librarysales@sagepub.com.

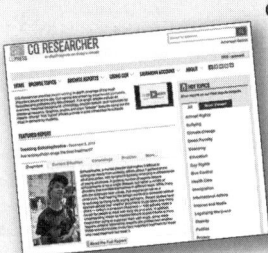

CQPRESS

CQ RESEARCHER

In-depth reports on today's issues

Published by CQ Press, an Imprint of SAGE Publications, Inc.   **www.cqresearcher.com**

Immigrants and the Economy

Do they help spur growth?

President Trump's vows to protect American jobs and improve national security by tightening U.S. borders are intensifying the debate over immigration's impact on the economy. Many politicians and workers argue that immigrants — legal and illegal — undercut wages and take jobs from native-born workers. They also contend undocumented immigrants burden society with welfare, medical and education costs. Immigration advocates respond that newcomers bring badly needed skills to the American economy, especially in the technology sector, where half the leaders of billion-dollar Silicon Valley companies are immigrants. Advocates also say immigrants often fill low-wage jobs short on workers, from home building to landscaping and dishwashing. Many experts fear the heated debate over immigration may cause the world's most talented young people to avoid studying at American universities or moving to the United States. Meanwhile, "Dreamers" — children brought to the United States illegally — are nervously waiting to learn whether the administration will allow them to stay in this country.

Workers at Morning Glory Diner in Philadelphia, many Latino, skipped work on Feb. 16, 2017, to join the nationwide "Day Without Immigrants" campaign dramatizing immigrants' importance to the economy. President Trump's crackdown on immigration, including his proposal to build a wall on the Mexican border and deport undocumented immigrants, spurred the protests.

CQ Researcher • Feb. 24, 2017 • www.cqresearcher.com
Volume 27, Number 8 • Pages 169-192

I N S I D E

THIS REPORT

THE ISSUES **171**

BACKGROUND **177**

CHRONOLOGY **179**

CURRENT SITUATION **184**

AT ISSUE.......................**185**

OUTLOOK **187**

BIBLIOGRAPHY **190**

THE NEXT STEP **191**

CQ RESEARCHER

Feb. 24, 2017
Volume 27, Number 8

EXECUTIVE EDITOR: Thomas J. Billitteri
tjb@sagepub.com

ASSISTANT MANAGING EDITORS: Kenneth
Fireman, kenneth.fireman@sagepub.com,
Kathy Koch, kathy.koch@sagepub.com,
Scott Rohrer, scott.rohrer@sagepub.com

SENIOR CONTRIBUTING EDITOR:
Thomas J. Colin
tom.colin@sagepub.com

CONTRIBUTING WRITERS: Marcia Clemmitt,
Sarah Glazer, Reed Karaim, Peter Katel,
Barbara Mantel, Chuck McCutcheon,
Tom Price

SENIOR PROJECT EDITOR: Olu B. Davis

EDITORIAL ASSISTANT: Anika Reed

FACT CHECKERS: Eva P. Dasher,
Michelle Harris, Betsy Towner Levine,
Robin Palmer

Los Angeles | London | New Delhi
Singapore | Washington DC | Melbourne

An Imprint of SAGE Publications, Inc.

SENIOR VICE PRESIDENT,
GLOBAL LEARNING RESOURCES:
Karen Phillips

EXECUTIVE DIRECTOR, ONLINE LIBRARY AND
REFERENCE PUBLISHING:
Todd Baldwin

THE ISSUES

171 • Are undocumented immigrants good for the U.S. economy?
• Do local economies benefit from the arrival of legal immigrants?
• Should more H-1B visa holders be allowed to remain in the United States?

BACKGROUND

177 **Immigrants Spur Economy**
Early America's economy grew along with immigration.

178 **Great Famine**
Mass starvation led to the 19th-century Irish exodus.

180 **Chinese Contributions**
Immigration from China rose after normalization of Chinese-U.S. relations.

181 **Mexico's Ups, Downs**
The population of undocumented Mexican immigrants rose by 5 million in 30 years.

CURRENT SITUATION

184 **Immigration in Crosshairs**
Immigrant advocates are pushing back against the Trump administration's plans.

184 **Immigration Restrictions**
Tech company executives have denounced President Trump's executive order.

186 **Sanctuary Cities**
Trump threatens to cut funding for cities offering safe havens.

OUTLOOK

187 **Searching for Solutions**
Trump's plan to restrict travel could face Supreme Court review.

Cover: Getty Images/Jessica Kourkounis

SIDEBARS AND GRAPHICS

172 **Asians Are Wealthiest U.S. Immigrants**
Mexicans have the most low-income households.

173 **U.S. Immigrant Count on the Rise**
Almost 13 percent of the U.S. population was foreign-born in 2013.

176 **H-1B Applications Hit New High**
Nearly 350,000 applications were filed in 2015.

179 **Chronology**
Key events since 1607.

180 **A 'Dreamer' Fears for Her Family**
Children who were undocumented when they arrived could face deportation.

182 **Immigrants Help Tech Engine Run**
"I don't know if we can close our borders and be self-sustaining."

185 **At Issue:**
Will limiting illegal immigration protect U.S. economic interests?

FOR FURTHER RESEARCH

189 **For More Information**
Organizations to contact.

190 **Bibliography**
Selected sources used.

191 **The Next Step**
Additional articles.

191 **Citing CQ Researcher**
Sample bibliography formats.

CQ Press is a registered trademark of Congressional Quarterly Inc.

CQ Researcher (ISSN 1056-2036) is printed on acid-free paper. Published weekly, except: (March wk. 4) (May wk. 4) (July wks. 1, 2) (Aug. wks. 2, 3) (Nov. wk. 4) and (Dec. wks. 3, 4). Published by SAGE Publications, Inc., 2455 Teller Rd., Thousand Oaks, CA 91320. Annual full-service subscriptions start at $1,131. For pricing, call 1-800-818-7243. To purchase a CQ Researcher report in print or electronic format (PDF), visit www.cqpress. com or call 866-427-7737. Single reports start at $15. Bulk purchase discounts and electronic-rights licensing are also available. Periodicals postage paid at Thousand Oaks, California, and at additional mailing offices. POSTMASTER: Send address changes to CQ Researcher, 2600 Virginia Ave., N.W., Suite 600, Washington, DC 20037.

Immigrants and the Economy

BY MICHELINE MAYNARD

THE ISSUES

After emigrating from Syria to the United States in 1906, Ed Hyder's grandfather got his start peddling shirt collars and dry goods to men maintaining the Erie Canal and railroads in New York state. Hyder's father and uncles eventually took over the business, opening shops that sold meat and groceries.

The first two generations of Hyders would have been dazzled to see what the third and fourth generations of the family have done with the business. In a converted firehouse in Worcester, Mass., Hyder and his son Gregory run a popular Mediterranean market with a staff of 15 workers, drawing an avid foodie audience with far more upscale tastes than the working-class customers who gave the early Hyders their start. The shelves are filled with big containers of flour and racks of exotic spices, and refrigerator cases contain homemade Middle Eastern specialties and soups.

For Hyder, the heated debate over the Trump administration's hard-nosed immigration plans hits home. Friendly immigration policies allowed his ancestors to immigrate to the United States, he says; restrictive ones would have kept them out. "Limiting immigration limits the possibilities of what we can achieve as Americans," Hyder says. "I don't want to indiscriminately let in people who hate America. But it's a hard call, who's good and who's bad."

Since taking office, President Trump has moved on several fronts to tighten immigration policy. On Jan. 25, he signed an executive order to build a

Syrian-Americans Ed Hyder and his son Gregory operate a popular Mediterranean grocery in Worcester, Mass. Friendly immigration policies enabled Ed's grandfather to immigrate to the United States in 1906, where he got his start peddling dry goods. Americans worried about homeland security and jobs praised President Trump's immigration actions, while potential immigrants and businesses that rely on foreign workers called them harmful to the economy.

wall on the U.S.-Mexico border to keep migrants from Mexico and Central America from crossing into the United States. He then signed a second order on Jan. 27 temporarily blocking immigration from seven predominantly Muslim Middle East countries. And on Feb. 21, the Department of Homeland Security detailed a more aggressive approach to arresting and deporting undocumented immigrants — even those who have committed minor offenses — including enlisting local police as enforcers, building new detention facilities and speeding up deportations. [1]

Reaction was swift on all sides. Supporters of the tough new policies believe they will protect the country's security and provide more jobs to American citizens. But other Americans and businesses that rely on immigrants to spur innovation and keep operations flowing voiced deep reservations.

The furor underscored how deeply conflicted Americans are over the impact of immigration on jobs and the overall U.S. economy. Opponents focus mainly on illegal immigration and say it takes jobs from Americans and costs the treasury billions of dollars. Supporters discount these concerns and say immigration — especially legal immigration of highly educated foreigners — is a boon to the economy.

After a federal judge issued a stay on implementing parts of Trump's executive order on refugees and travel — which the Trump administration appealed — more than 100 chief executives from technology and other companies filed a brief with the Ninth U.S. Circuit Court of Appeals, arguing the President's so-called "Muslim ban" violated the U.S. Constitution and would badly hurt their businesses.

"The backbone of our engineering team is from overseas," said Randy Wootton, CEO of the advertising-technology firm Rocket Fuel, which signed the brief. "Imagine not having access to that talent — it's a real disservice to American business." [2] (See sidebar, p. 182.)

In addition, a coalition of nearly 600 colleges and universities sent a letter to Homeland Security Secretary John Kelly saying the country could

Asians Are Wealthiest U.S. Immigrants

Almost 1.5 million Asian-American households in the United States had annual incomes of $100,000 or more in 2012, the most of any immigrant group.

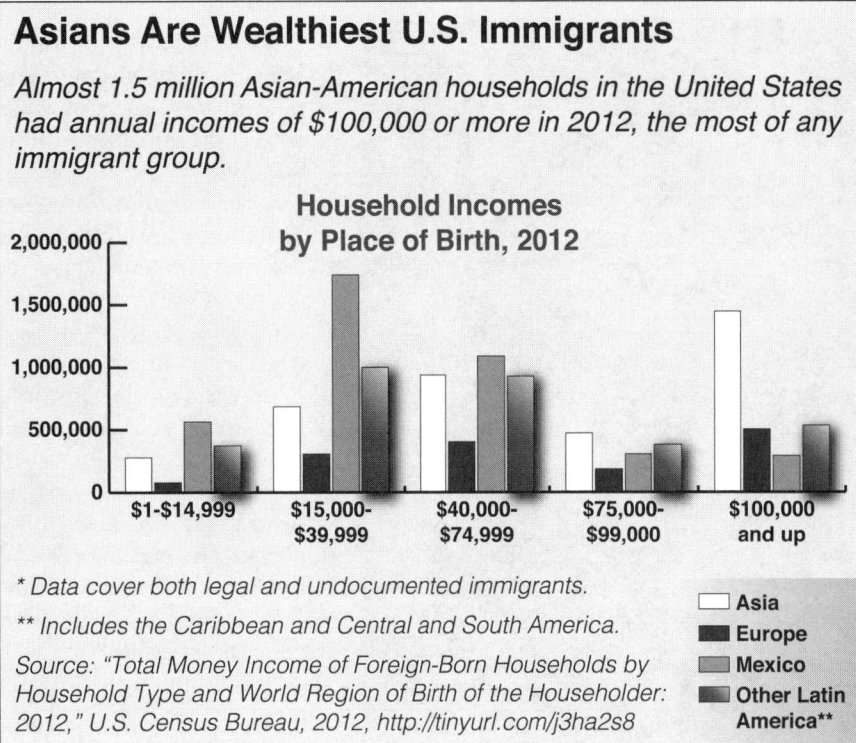

Household Incomes by Place of Birth, 2012

* *Data cover both legal and undocumented immigrants.*

** *Includes the Caribbean and Central and South America.*

Source: "Total Money Income of Foreign-Born Households by Household Type and World Region of Birth of the Householder: 2012," U.S. Census Bureau, 2012, http://tinyurl.com/j3ha2s8

☐ Asia
■ Europe
■ Mexico
■ Other Latin America**

maintain its "global scientific and economic leadership position" only if it encouraged talented people to come to the United States. [3]

A number of experts and others dispute these arguments, saying undocumented workers take jobs from Americans and cost state, local and federal governments billions of dollars in educational, health and welfare benefits. Some also oppose legal immigration. Trump's chief strategist, Stephen Bannon, who is pushing an "America First" agenda, said last March that Asian immigrants have been filling American graduate schools and keeping American students from finding work in Silicon Valley and elsewhere. "Twenty percent of this country is immigrants. Is that not the beating heart of this [unemployment] problem?" he asked. [4]

Boston College political science professor Peter Skerry, who has written extensively on immigration issues, says anti-immigration arguments resonate with Americans who believe globalization and the free movement of workers across borders have hurt

them. "If you're some white American in a disadvantaged situation, you wouldn't have to be a mean-spirited bigot to say, 'Gee, do we really want more of these guys?' " he says.

The stakes in the debate over the impact of immigration on the U.S. economy are high. The 35 million people who identify as Hispanic are a significant economic force in the United States, representing a consumer market of $1.3 trillion. [5]

Close behind in economic importance are the nation's 12.7 million people who identify as being of Asian descent. [6] (*See graphic, above.*) If current population trends continue, Asian immigrants will outnumber Hispanic immigrants by 2055, according to the Pew Research Center, relying on census data. [7]

The nation's 42 million immigrants are more likely to start businesses than native-born Americans. [8] As a result, immigrants represent 18 percent of all small-business owners but only about 13 percent of the population. [9]

Regarding the impact of legal immigrants on the U.S. economy, experts

mostly debate how many additional skilled foreign workers should be encouraged to come to the United States through visas and other means. Richard Florida, a University of Toronto professor of management who coined the phrase "the creative class," warned that Trump's effort to restrict immigration threatens "the very core of America's innovative edge — the ability to attract global talent." [10]

But at the other end of the economic scale, says Skerry, "if you haven't got a high school diploma, you're bound to be competing with immigrants."

Much of the president's focus has been on the nation's 11 million undocumented immigrants, who critics say are more of a drain than a boon to the economy.

The 8 million undocumented immigrants who are working pay about $13 billion a year in state, local and federal taxes, says the Federation for American Immigration Reform (FAIR), a conservative group that wants to restrict immigration. But in a widely quoted 2013 study, the group contended that undocumented immigrants cost the economy $113 billion a year, largely in state and local services — a figure that immigrant advocates dispute. [11]

"Right or wrong, opponents are concerned about the risks of market competition" from immigrant workers who often are willing to work for less, said Cass R. Sunstein, who directs the Program on Behavioral Economics and Public Policy at Harvard Law School. Among the factors he thinks are driving immigrant opponents, he says, "they want native-born Americans to keep their jobs, and they don't want them to face wage cuts." [12]

Because the number of undocumented immigrants equals about 5 percent of the working population, some critics say the nation's unemployment rate could be reduced to zero if authorities expelled as many as 3 million of these people. Others argue they should be allowed to stay legally, which would enable them to earn higher incomes and pay more in taxes.

AnnaLee Saxenian, dean of the University of California, Berkeley School of Information and an expert on Silicon Valley and technology, says much of this discussion misses the point. "The debate over immigration is deteriorating into a conversation over, 'Are they stealing jobs?' " she says.

Undocumented immigrants hold large numbers of jobs in construction, health care and restaurants, especially in Texas, which has the second-largest number of undocumented immigrants behind California. Evicting them, Saxenian says, might mean immediate hardships for the companies that employ them, because of a worker shortage in a tight job market.

Such concerns did not stop Arizona from enacting a series of tough laws between 2000 and 2010 aimed at stemming the flow of illegal immigration.

The state's undocumented immigrant population peaked at about 500,000 in 2007 and has dropped 40 percent since then, in part because the 2008 recession caused construction jobs to dry up. Nationwide, the number of undocumented immigrants has been basically unchanged since 2008, partly because economic opportunities have increased in Mexico due to new investments there, according to the Pew Research Center, a Washington, D.C., polling and research organization. [13]

Saxenian says that although technology and other business sectors highly value immigrants, foreign-born workers look at the controversies over immigration as evidence of an unwelcome American climate. This, she says, could lead some foreign entrepreneurs to establish their companies elsewhere.

"In the 1970s and '80s, everybody felt they were welcome in the U.S.," she says. "And since 9/11, they've encountered a pretty hostile immigration system. Making them feel welcome is important. These are people who would like to stay."

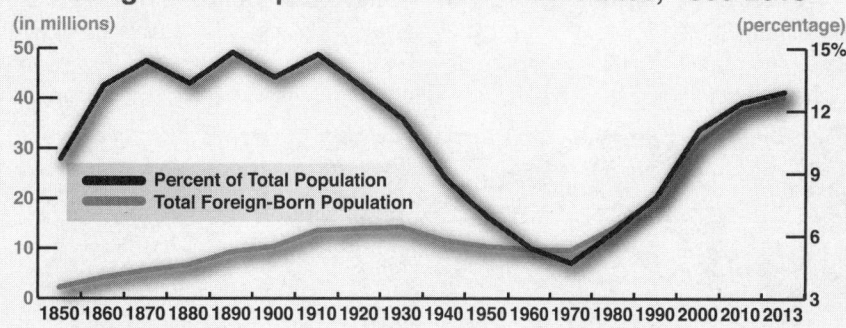

U.S. Immigrant Count on the Rise

The nation's foreign-born population has doubled in the past quarter-century, with more than 40 million legal and undocumented immigrants making up almost 13 percent of the total U.S. population in 2013, the latest tally. The immigrant count dipped in the 1960s and '70s, hitting a low of 4.7 percent of the total, before beginning a sharp increase.

Foreign-Born Population in the United States, 1850-2013

(in millions) / (percentage)

- Percent of Total Population
- Total Foreign-Born Population

1850 1860 1870 1880 1890 1900 1910 1920 1930 1940 1950 1960 1970 1980 1990 2000 2010 2013

Sources: "Nativity of the Population and Place of Birth of the Native Population: 1850 to 2000," U.S. Census Bureau, http://tinyurl.com/h27pl2d; "Population by Sex, Age, Nativity, and U.S. Citizenship Status: 2010," U.S. Census Bureau, http://tinyurl.com/gmjsent; and "Population by Sex, Age, Nativity, and U.S. Citizenship Status: 2013," U.S. Census Bureau, http://tinyurl.com/h6q28yr

As the immigration debate continues among economists, politicians and the public, here are some of the questions they are asking:

Are undocumented immigrants good for the U.S. economy?

As a candidate and now as president, Trump has cited a widely quoted figure from the Federation for American Immigration Reform: Illegal immigration costs U.S. taxpayers about $113 billion a year at the federal, state and local level. [14]

Other conservative think tanks and countless opinion pieces also cite the $113 billion figure as they seek to ban undocumented immigrants or expel them from the country. "Illegal immigration increases income inequality and corrupts our democracy," wrote University of Maryland economics professor Peter Morici in *The Washington Times.* [15]

He added, "When the nation is flooded with immigrants in skill categories without genuine shortages," such as jobs in which employers would have to pay higher wages in order to find qualified applicants, "illegal immigration drives down wages and increases unemployment, especially for America's lowest-paid workers."

That $113 billion figure, according to FAIR, includes federal expenses for education, medical treatment and law enforcement, as well as other expenditures covering undocumented immigrants, who have been blocked from receiving federal welfare since passage of the 1996 welfare reform law. [16] The bulk of the expense, however, is paid by state and local governments, estimated by FAIR at $84 billion.

The American Immigration Council, a pro-immigrant think tank in Washington, said FAIR's report relied "upon flawed and empirically baseless assumptions to inflate its estimate of the costs." It added: "Much of what FAIR counts as the cost of unauthorized immigration is actually the cost of education and health care for U.S. citizen children." PolitiFact, a Pulitzer Prize-winning fact-checking website, said the cost of undocumented immigrants to the country was as low as $1.9 billion, but noted that the estimates vary widely.

"It's uncertain how much immigrants in the United States illegally cost taxpayers," said PolitiFact. [17]

The Center for American Progress, a liberal think tank, argues that undocumented immigrants contribute significantly to the U.S. economy — and that the

Mexican farmworkers harvest lettuce in California's Imperial Valley. Immigration supporters say many industries would suffer without undocumented workers. For example, migrants – most of whom are from Mexico and Puerto Rico – constitute about 50 percent of U.S. farmworkers. A study of undocumented workers in Texas acknowledges they "lubricate" the economy, but on the negative side, the researchers note, many migrant farmworkers live in or near poverty and draw heavily on state social programs.

country is missing an economic opportunity by creating an atmosphere hostile to newcomers. "Immigrants in fact are makers, not takers," wrote three experts on immigration and the economy. [18]

They cited research by Raúl Hinojosa-Ojeda, an immigration expert at the University of California, Los Angeles, concluding that undocumented residents could contribute $1.5 trillion to the U.S. gross domestic product (GDP) over a decade if all 11 million were granted

legal resident status. His reasoning: Legal workers earn higher wages than undocumented workers, and they use those higher wages to buy homes, cars, appliances and electronics. As this money flows into the economy, businesses expand to meet demand, and jobs are added.

James H. Johnson Jr., a professor of strategy and entrepreneurship at the University of North Carolina's Kenan-Flagler Business School, says immigrants have an economic ripple effect that is not widely recognized. "People are not fully accounting for the way that immigrants add value to the economy," Johnson says. "They create additional jobs that would not be there." For instance, undocumented immigrants need attorneys to help them navigate U.S. laws. Or they may need translators or help filing their tax returns.

In addition, some industries might have trouble functioning without undocumented workers. For instance, undocumented immigrants constitute

about 50 percent of hired farmworkers, down about 5 percentage points from the peak in 1999-2001, according to a 2016 report by the U.S. Department of Agriculture. About 69 percent of agricultural employees are from Mexico. The same is true in the construction industry; experts say immigrants are helping to fill labor shortages, and they constitute more than 25 percent of the housing construction workforce. [19]

Even as the number of undocumented workers has fallen in recent years in many places, Texas has continued to see its immigrant population rise. In construction, for example, about 25 percent of jobs go to undocumented workers, according to an in-depth series in *The Texas Tribune*. "There are almost always jobs waiting for them," it said, because of a building boom in the state's biggest cities. [20]

But using undocumented workers carries both benefits and costs, according to a study on immigrants' impact on the Texas economy by two researchers for the Texas Public Policy Foundation, a conservative think tank in Austin. "The peripatetic ways of immigrants, both legal and illegal, serve as an economic lubricant," they said. But on the negative side, the authors continued, 65 percent of the state's illegal immigrants are in or near poverty, and a majority are forced to use a "major [Texas] welfare program." [21]

Restaurant owners are among those concerned about a crackdown on undocumented workers. "If every one of [the undocumented immigrants] working in a restaurant was gone tomorrow, you'd have to close down the entire industry," says Mike Monahan, owner of Monahan's Seafood in Ann Arbor, Mich.

The true cost of undocumented workers to American society may be debatable, but Maria Minniti, a professor of entrepreneurship at the Whitman School of Management at Syracuse University, sees advantages, both to the country and the workers themselves.

Many would not be employable in parts of the job market that require higher skill levels, she says. But working in restaurants or in similar jobs lets the newcomers get their bearings while they learn English and the ways of American society, Minniti says. "It's one of the great diversifying features of the country, the importance of freedom, the stress on the market, the commitment to work that gets you where you are," she says.

Do local economies benefit from the arrival of legal immigrants?

In Durham, N.C., City Council member Steve Schewel says his community's economy needs immigrants to prosper.

"Durham is [experiencing] a construction boom and a cultural renaissance," Schewel says. "None of that would be possible without our immigrant population, both documented and undocumented."

Durham is best known as the home of Duke University and Research Triangle Park, one of the nation's leading centers of biotechnology and life sciences research, with more than 200 companies. The city's restaurant scene is flourishing, and Durham has attracted new residents from around the world. [22]

Durham's population has grown from 149,000 in 1990, when only 4 percent were foreign born, to more than 295,000 in 2016, with 14 percent foreign born, primarily from Latin America and Asia, according to the Census Bureau. [23]

The newcomers help fill both lower-paying jobs and positions at startups, Schewel says. "There is almost nothing that we're doing that doesn't depend on immigrant brain power," he says. "We're very much a foodie town, and immigrants are vital to that. We have a massive cluster of startup companies, and immigrants are vital to that."

Immigration opponents see things differently. Trump adviser Bannon has argued that legal immigration hurts American communities and the fabric of American life. "A country's more than an economy. We're a civic society," Bannon said in 2015. Bannon advocates an economic nationalism that puts native-born Americans first. [24]

Ohio real estate agent Mary Theis backs Trump's proposals to limit immigration and renegotiate trade deals that she said favored other countries. Citing the president's business skills as a deal-maker, Theis said that "with Donald Trump negotiating on trade, maybe we'll get some of these [lost] jobs back." [25]

Schewel says he can understand such frustrations, especially among older, white Americans who have been displaced by economic change. "I think that's real. I acknowledge and affirm that experience," he says. "But keeping immigrants out won't help them. It will hurt them [because limiting immigration will limit economic growth]. We need the kind of economy that can grow and be prosperous."

A number of economists argue that legal immigrants boost local economies in several ways. One is their impact on small businesses — the lifeblood of small towns. According to a 2012 report, 18 percent of small-business owners in the United States are immigrants, employing an estimated 4.7 million people and generating revenue of more than $776 billion annually. They are especially well represented in retail, including restaurants, groceries and dry cleaning. [26]

California and New Jersey benefit the most from immigrant-owned businesses in terms of jobs created, said a 2017 study by the personal finance website WalletHub. [27]

Another benefit of immigration is its ability to help revive struggling rural communities, according to the American Immigration Council. [28]

One example the council cited is Ottumwa, a town of 25,000 in southeastern Iowa. Its Hispanic population rose from 1 percent in 2000 to 11.3 percent in the latest U.S. census, with mostly legal Hispanic workers being drawn by the lure of jobs at a Cargill pork processing plant. As the Hispanic population rose, Latino-owned groceries and restaurants followed. The influx helped spark a downtown revival, city officials said, with new businesses opening, including a home-improvement store and a Kohl's department store. "Hispanics," said loan officer Nicole Banner of U.S Bank, "are pulling this town out of a long recession." [29]

Ottumwa was not alone. The Hispanic population in the Midwest jumped 49 percent between 2000 and 2010, according to the census. [30]

In Michigan, Republican Gov. Rick Snyder said he supports legal immigration because of its potential to boost the state economy. The state's population fell seven years in a row, from 2005 to 2011, reflecting an economy battered by the 2008 recession and job cuts resulting from the auto industry's struggles.

In 2014, Snyder created the Michigan Office for New Americans in an effort to attract foreign entrepreneurs and encourage foreign students to stay in Michigan to get advanced degrees. "We want the world to know Michigan is a welcoming state," Snyder said. [31]

Michigan's efforts to attract more immigrants are paying off in small ways so far. Between 2000 and 2014, Detroit lost 36,000 native-born residents but gained 4,400 immigrants, hardly enough to offset the loss, but at least a sign the city was appealing to newcomers. Statewide, Michigan has gained 50,000 immigrants in the past six years, Snyder said in his most recent state-of-the-state address. [32]

Citing the impact of foreigners in Silicon Valley, the University of California's Saxenian says immigrants bring energy to communities, creating a flow of ideas between their new and old homes — what she calls "brain circulation."

She says she discovered this phenomenon in the 1990s, when she began

H-1B Applications Hit New High

Applications for the H-1B visa program, which allows employers to hire foreign workers in specialty occupations, hit a record 348,699 in 2015, with 257,317 approved.

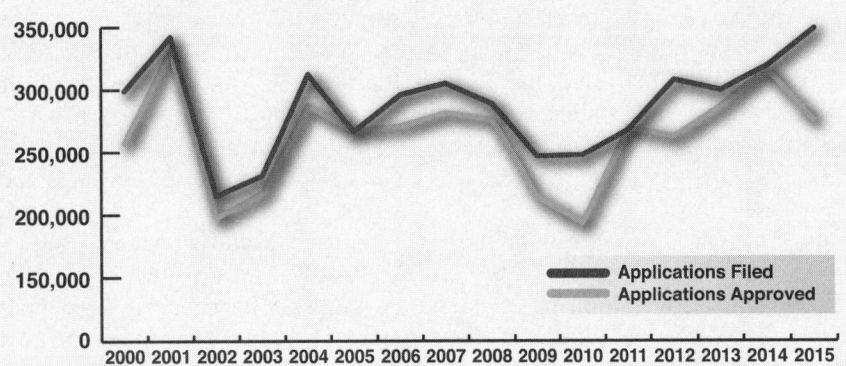

H-1B Visa Requests and Approvals, 2000-2015

Applications Filed
Applications Approved

Source: "Reports and Studies," U.S. Citizenship and Immigration Services, Jan. 10, 2017, http://tinyurl.com/gqrb9hd

studying Silicon Valley's venture capitalists.

These company founders set up satellite offices in their home countries, such as India and Taiwan. The practice has encouraged companies in those countries to invest in the United States, too, Saxenian says. More than 600 Taiwanese companies have operations in the United States, while 100 Indian firms have collectively invested more than $15 billion in American operations. [33]

Says Saxenian: "This circulation has been mutually beneficial. It's clear there's so much opportunity elsewhere in the world. People can move quickly, and communication is much cheaper."

Should more H-1B visa holders be allowed to remain in the United States?

Every April, foreigners from around the world take part in the H-1B lottery to get one of the coveted, special visas that allow a limited number of highly skilled foreigners into the country each year. The winning applicants are allowed to work in the United States for three years, with the possibility of applying for additional time when their visas expire. Competition is stiff: In 2015, a record 348,699 people applied and 257,317 slots were approved. [34]

Each applicant must have a corporate sponsor, who must show that the applicant is earning as much as native-born employees, that the company has unsuccessfully tried to recruit Americans with similar skills and that the applicant's work is essential to the company's operations.

Applicants generally are scientists, engineers or computer programmers working in highly skilled "specialty occupations." A 2014 estimate said 65 percent of H-1B visas went to tech workers, mostly from India. H-1B visas also are available for those with other graduate degrees, such as MBAs. [35]

Critics say companies use the visas to import cheaper labor to suppress wages across the country. They say universities and hospitals also use the visas to hire low-wage teaching assistants and nurses.

Then-Sen. Jeff Sessions, R-Ala., now the U.S. attorney general, said in 2016 Congress should consider eliminating the program.

"We shouldn't be bringing in people where we've got workers," Sessions said in Indianola, Iowa. "There are a number of ways to fix it. I don't think the republic would collapse if it was totally eliminated." [36]

Trump senior policy adviser Stephen Miller has proposed scrapping the lottery system used to award the visas and potentially replacing it with a program that would seek to prevent foreign workers from undercutting domestic salaries. [37]

Yet, Labor Department records showed that Trump's golf club and model management companies had received two dozen H-1B visas for employees in the past five years, and he later said the United States needed to ensure that companies could retain employees brought to the U.S. under the H-1B program. [38]

The month before Trump took office, he convened a group of tech company CEOs, whose top priorities include expanding the H-1B program in order, they say, to recruit the most talented workers. [39] For years, many executives have been urging the White House and Congress to allow more immigration. In 2013, Facebook CEO Mark Zuckerberg co-founded FWD.us, an effort backed by Silicon Valley companies that is pushing for "commonsense" reform solutions that will satisfy both sides in the debate.

However, some startups and other small firms see the H-1B visa program as favoring bigger tech companies. If employees cannot obtain H-1B visas, they must apply for legal residence, which can take years. "Small companies can't afford to put them through the green-card process," says Syracuse University's Minniti, referring to a permit that allows a foreigner to live and work permanently in the United States.

Infosys, an Indian company whose U.S. operations are based in Plano, Texas, is the country's top applicant for H-1B visas, according to MyVisaJobs.com, a website that track companies' applications. Between 2014 and 2016, Infosys filed 82,506 applications for H-1B visas on behalf of its employees. Of that figure, just 57 were denied or withdrawn, said MyVisaJobs.com. Infosys was sued for visa fraud to circumvent the H-1B system. [40]

In addition to Infosys, Tata Consultancy Services and Wipro, a global technology and consulting firm, both based in India, have made heavy use of H-1B visas to staff their U.S. operations. [41]

The government can bar companies from receiving H-1B visas if they're found to be "willful violators" by displacing U.S. workers with foreign-born ones by failing to recruit Americans for the jobs. Sixteen companies are on the Labor Department's banned list, including technology and fashion firms and even a dairy. [42]

Jiangtao Liu, the business development manager for autonomous driving at Intel, who went to the University of Michigan, is among those working in the United States on an H-1B visa, which he obtained in 2015. Says Liu: "The whole U.S. immigration system is a mess."

But Liu says the H-1B lottery is a crapshoot. "There is no guarantee you will win," says Liu, who was sponsored by Intel. At least 10 of his foreign-born Michigan classmates failed to get H-1B visas and had to leave the country — some to the United Kingdom, others to Australia. In a few cases, their companies reassigned them to subsidiaries abroad.

Liu says he received a three-year H-1B visa that will expire in 2019 and is eligible to apply for a three-year extension. But he also is thinking about applying for permanent residency. "It's a painful process," says Liu. ∎

BACKGROUND

Immigrants Spur Economy

In the 13 colonies that became the United States, immigration and economic growth went hand in hand.

At Jamestown, Va., the first permanent English colony in North America, the settlers struggled to survive in the early years until they developed a marketable crop — tobacco. But planters needed a labor force, and they first tried indentured servants, an arrangement in which they paid for an English worker's passage to the colonies in return for several years of servitude — usually seven. When the system did not meet the needs of a growing economy, planters increasingly turned to using slaves, who were first brought to Jamestown from Africa in 1619. [43]

Outside of Virginia, immigration surged, with the Scotch-Irish and Germans making up the two largest groups. Between 1683 and 1775, more than 200,000 Scotch-Irish arrived, followed by some 111,000 Germans. By 1750, the colonial population had reached 1.1 million — a sixfold increase from 1700. The polyglot colonies were peopled by immigrants from across Europe; Pennsylvania alone was believed to be one-third German. The new arrivals built an agriculture-based economy, since most colonists were farmers or planters. The rest were artisans, shopkeepers, merchants or lawyers. [44]

Upon the outbreak of the Revolutionary War in 1775, immigration for the most part ceased and did not resume until after the fighting ended in 1781. In 1789 the U.S. Constitution took effect, and Article 1, Section 8, Clause 4 gave Congress the authority "to establish an uniform Rule of Naturalization." Congress then undertook a long line of legislative efforts to define and regulate immigration in the United States.

The Naturalization Act of 1790 declared that any alien who was a "free white person" was eligible to become a citizen after living in the United States for two years. At the time, about 4,000 white people a year were immigrating to the United States. [45] But that figure was about to swell.

In the 19th century the Irish and Germans were the dominant immigrant groups, along with many Chinese. Then Italian immigration surged with more than 4 million coming between 1880 and 1914, while Caribbean natives and more Chinese arrived later in the 20th century. [46]

One of the most notable British immigrants was William Colgate, who left Kent, England, with his family as a boy in 1795. Colgate settled in New York City in 1803 and soon decided that what New Yorkers needed was soap.

In those days, wrote historian Tyler Anbinder, "manufactured soap was considered a luxury item only the wealthy could afford." Most people either used no soap at all, leading to the term "the unwashed masses," or made a crude version by boiling fat drippings from their food with potash. This homemade soap, according to Anbinder, was "greasy, foul smelling and extremely abrasive." [47]

Colgate discovered that if he could significantly cut the price of soap, New Yorkers would be willing to buy it. By 1817, after much experimentation, Colgate was the leading soap in the New York market. By the 1840s, after he had added scent to his soap, Colgate's Manhattan factory was producing 20 tons of soap a day to keep up with demand.

Colgate later expanded well beyond soap to toothpaste, toothbrushes and mouthwash. Today, Colgate is one of the nation's best-known brands.

Great Famine

Ireland's Great Famine, a period of mass starvation and disease caused by catastrophic failures of the potato crop, killed 1 million people and led to the emigration of possibly 2 million more between 1845 and 1849. Most went to the United States, especially Boston and New York. [48]

Some of the earliest Irish arrivals joined New York City's ranks of pros-

Americans to political office. In 1836, the party ran Samuel F.B. Morse, inventor of the single-wire telegraph system, as its candidate for mayor. However, Morse received only 6 percent of the vote, and the party soon faded. [49]

By 1860, the Irish had become New York's largest ethnic group — and they achieved a milestone of sorts in gender history that year: 35 percent of Irish-born women worked at jobs outside their homes, compared with 18 percent of other immigrant women. [50]

spread far beyond New York to Chicago, Milwaukee, Cincinnati and smaller cities such as Ann Arbor, Mich.

Many German immigrants prospered, including artisans such as cabinetmakers and gilders, shoemakers, bakers, locksmiths, brewers and cigar makers. Germans owned half the grocery stores in New York, even in Irish neighborhoods.

German Levi Strauss arrived in New York just as men and women from all over the country were streaming to California and points west for the 1849 Gold Rush. He followed them to San Francisco in 1853 and by 1860 was selling tents, clothing and other dry goods to stores from Nevada to Hawaii.

After the Civil War, a tailor came to him with an idea for a more rugged pair of overalls with pockets reinforced with metal rivets. Blue jeans were born in 1873. [53]

But by far, German influence was felt most significantly in big business. John Jacob Astor, the country's first multimillionaire, was of German descent. So was Harvey Firestone, the founder of Firestone Tire and Rubber Co. Others included Henry Heinz, the ketchup company founder; Otto Kahn, the investment banker; Conrad Hilton, founder of the hotel chain; and Isaac Singer of the sewing machine company.

Nevertheless, German immigrants endured two waves of anti-German sentiment, one before and during World War I, the other during World War II.

"World War I had a devastating effect on German-Americans and their cultural heritage," wrote Katja Wüstenbecker, a historian of migration at the University of Jena, Germany. [54]

Until the war's outbreak in 1914, she said, German-Americans were viewed mostly as well-integrated and esteemed. "All this changed with the outbreak of the war. At once, German ancestry was a liability." In 1910, German-Americans made up about 10 percent of the U.S. population, and their presence

Mexican visitors enter the United States at a border crossing in Nogales, Ariz. Homeland Security Secretary John Kelly has signed sweeping guidelines that empower federal authorities to more aggressively detain and deport undocumented immigrants. The department also plans to hire thousands of additional enforcement agents and enlist local law enforcement to help make arrests – plans that alarm immigration advocates.

Getty Images/John Moore

perous businessmen, becoming known as "lace curtain Irish" because they took on an air of respectability. Other, less-educated Irish immigrants, known as "shanty Irish," worked on ships and raised pigs in the city's teeming neighborhoods.

Irish immigrants who settled near City Hall in lower Manhattan received an especially hostile reception. A nativist political party that opposed both immigrants and Catholics — the Native American Democratic Association — condemned the appointment of Irish-

The leading jobs were in garment factories, domestic service and needle trades such as sewing; 4 percent of Irish women were listed as business owners, twice as many as other immigrant women. [51]

German immigrants were outnumbered by their Irish counterparts in New York, but they were numerous enough that a swath of the city was called Kleindeutschland — Little Germany. "What multitudes from Germany are in our midst," *The New York Times* wrote in 1855. [52] German influence

Continued on p. 180

Chronology

1600s-1800s
Immigration fuels economy.

1607
Virginia Company founds the first permanent English settlement in North America at Jamestown.

1619
First slaves arrive in Virginia.

1775
Revolutionary War causes a near halt to immigration.

1790
Naturalization Act declares that "any alien, being a free white person, may be admitted to become a citizen."

1820
German immigration expands, peaking with about 1.4 million arriving between 1880-1890.

1845
Ireland's Great Famine prompts migration to the U.S. As many as 4.5 million Irish arrive between 1820 and 1930.

1849
Chinese immigration accelerates.

1882
After riots, Congress passes the Chinese Exclusion Act, virtually halting Chinese immigration.

1900s-1950s
Immigration backlash grows.

1907
Peak year for immigration as 1.3 million enter U.S.

1917
Anti-German sentiment builds with U.S. entry into World War I.

1924
Johnson-Reed Act curtails immigration; Asian immigrants are barred entry.

1930s
During the Depression, hundreds of thousands of Mexican immigrants are deported.

1941
U.S. enters World War II. Tens of thousands of Americans, most of Japanese descent, are declared "enemy aliens."

1942
Bracero Program allows Mexican workers to enter the U.S., easing a wartime labor shortage.

1952
McCarren-Walter Act ends Asian exclusion.

1960s-1990s
Illegal immigrations grows.

1965
Hart-Celler Act removes immigration quotas based on nationality.

1972
President Richard Nixon visits China and begins normalization of relations. The move opens the door to increased Chinese immigration.

1975
Vietnam War ends with fall of Saigon to communist forces; emigration from Vietnam, Thailand and Cambodia picks up.

1986
Immigration Reform and Control Act sets fines for employers who knowingly hire undocumented immigrants and amnesty for some 3.2 million undocumented immigrants.

1990
Congress creates the H-1B visa program for skilled foreign workers, allowing them to work in the U.S. for three years.

1996
Undocumented immigrant population reaches 5 million.

2000s-Present
Presidents Bush, Obama and Trump seek to change immigration policy.

2000
H-1B cap is raised to 195,000; in 2004, Congress lowers it to 65,000.

2006
Number of undocumented immigrants reaches 11.6 million.

2007
Congress rejects George W. Bush administration's attempt to create pathway to citizenship for longtime undocumented immigrants.

2012
President Barack Obama signs an executive order protecting undocumented children, known as "Dreamers." An appeals court blocks his actions; the Supreme Court upheld the ruling in 2016.

2014
Immigration reform efforts fail in Congress.

2017
President Trump tightens immigration policy, signing an executive order blocking refugee immigration and temporarily banning entry by nationals from seven Muslim-majority countries. An appeals court upholds a lower court's stay of the order.

A 'Dreamer' Fears for Her Family

Children who were undocumented when they arrived could face deportation.

Surf through the videos Maria Garcia posts on YouTube and you'll get a joyous picture of a young woman who loves the camera. She posts videos about eye makeup, nail polish, the Halloween costumes she makes and last-minute Christmas shopping. [1]

But one of her videos tells a far less upbeat story. Garcia, 20, of Los Angeles is a "Dreamer" — the child of parents who brought her to the United States as an undocumented immigrant. The name comes from a 2012 executive order, signed by then-President Barack Obama, called the Deferred Action for Childhood Arrivals program (DACA).

Under it, more than 725,000 young people provided personal information such as their passport numbers, school records and travel histories in order to obtain work permits, access to driver's licenses and the ability to get college educations. They received a renewable two-year moratorium on deportation. [2]

But DACA has been hotly debated, with opponents saying it encourages illegal immigration. Throughout his campaign for the White House, Republican candidate Donald Trump vowed to quickly repeal the act as part of his broader plan to expel undocumented immigrants. He has not moved to repeal DACA during his first weeks as president, during which he issued a temporary ban on entry to the United States of all refugees as well as immigrants from seven predominantly Muslim countries. (The ban has been stayed by a federal court.) Asked at a

Feb. 16 news conference whether he will repeal DACA, Trump did not indicate what he will do, saying this "is a very, very difficult subject for me, I will tell you, . . . because you know, I love these kids." [3]

Garcia says she is watching the immigration debate with dread. "I'm scared for everyone in this undocumented situation," she says. "I can already see the number of families who are going to be affected by Trump's actions. I'm put in a situation where I would be very concerned over my family's safety and unity."

In 2014, House Republicans voted to defund DACA, saying it amounted to a temporary legalization program that ran counter to U.S. immigration law. (The vote had no impact on the program, because defunding failed in the Senate.) [4]

Mark Krikorian, executive director of the conservative Center for Immigration Studies, which wants to reduce immigration, derided the Dreamers act as "green-card lite" — a way for children of undocumented immigrants to permanently stay in the United States. [5]

Garcia, a junior at California State University who is majoring in communications, defends DACA. Her goal, she says, is to become an American citizen. She says her parents emigrated from Jalisco, Mexico, when she was a child and that her younger brother and sister — both born after her parents moved to California — are citizens. But she and her parents are undocumented. She says her father is working, but she declines to be

Continued from p. 178

in virtually every major U.S. city made them instant targets.

"The battle against all things German" ran from business to entertainment, Wüstenbecker said. Music halls closed. Teachers had to sign loyalty oaths. By March 1918, the teaching of German in schools had been restricted or ended in 38 of the 48 states, Wüstenbecker wrote.

In 1918, President Woodrow Wilson declared German-Americans to be "alien enemies." About 2,000 people were confined to internment camps in Utah, Georgia and North Carolina. To protect themselves, some German-Americans anglicized their family and business names. (In Britain, the royal family did so as well, changing its name from the House of Saxe-Coburg and Gotha to the House of Windsor.)

German-Americans were barred from living near military facilities and airports, and business owners had to turn over their books to an "alien property custodian."

After the war ended, Congress passed the Quota Act of 1921, which restricted immigration, and the Johnson-Reed Act of 1924, which banned immigration by anyone from Asian countries. The latter act also set quotas on immigrants from other places.

For instance, 34,000 visas were allotted to Great Britain, but just 6,000 to Poland and 100 to Greece. In all, quotas cut immigration to 164,000 annually in the late 1920s. The figures were not revised until after World War II. [55]

German immigrants faced a new round of trouble when the world went to war in 1939 and the United States

entered it in December 1941. Some 11,000 German-Americans were interned during World War II. Ten times that many Japanese-Americans were sent to camps in the United States. [56]

Chinese Contributions

In the nation's early years prejudice stalked another important immigrant group: the Chinese. Migration from China to the United States came in two waves: the 1850s to the 1880s, when Congress halted Chinese migration, and from the 1970s to the present, after U.S.-China relations were normalized in 1972. As a result, Chinese immigrants are now the third-largest ethnic group in the United States, behind natives of Mexico and India. [57]

more specific. Her mother is a homemaker.

Garcia says her parents "didn't see much of a bright future in our native country due to the lack of resources and poverty. This caused them to take the risk and migrate to the U.S. That decision has turned into a greater opportunity in education and well-being for myself and my siblings."

Garcia says she faces obstacles that American-born students do not. Obtaining financial aid in the form of student loans is one difficulty. Undocumented students are not eligible for federal assistance and must turn to private aid. [6]

Although she's been able to get small grants, "it is not enough," she says. "I've paid my taxes since I started working when I was 17. I have had to work a bit harder" than native-born students "for the chance to continue to pursue higher education," Garcia says.

It is also difficult for Garcia to travel outside the United States. Many of her fellow students have spent semesters abroad or have vacationed in other countries. For Dreamers, however, "the opportunity is very rare. You have to go through a lot of paperwork and investigation just to be allowed to go."

Says Garcia, "I yearn to learn and experience other cultures. I've heard from my professors that it is an experience that can open your mind and help you grow."

Garcia says her video about her Dreamer status generated personal stories and messages of support from her YouTube followers, but a number of people posted negative comments expressing opposition to the Dreamers act. "You are an illegal student, draining our resources," wrote one, who called himself Julio Iglesias, the same name as the Spanish singer.

"Dreamer = illegal immigrant. I think it's better you cut the bull and get to the point. You want something. For nothing," wrote another, called Onaturalia. [7]

Garcia calls the comments "very upsetting." But she says she will continue posting YouTube videos and, after graduation, will try to become an entrepreneur and create a scholarship fund for undocumented and low-income students.

Beyond that, she wants to create financial security for her family. That would be "part of achieving the American dream," she says.

— *Micheline Maynard*

[1] Maria Garcia's YouTube videos can be found at http://tinyurl.com/h9uvshj.

[2] Griselda Nevarez, "4 Years Later, Lives Built By DACA at Risk in 2016 Election," NBC News, June 15, 2016, http://tinyurl.com/hxzggkw.

[3] "Full Transcript: President Donald Trump's News Conference," CNN, Feb. 17, 2017, http://tinyurl.com/h2ceucw.

[4] Miriam Jordan, "Immigrants Benefit From White House Initiative," *The Wall Street Journal*, Sept. 5, 2014, http://tinyurl.com/hqa6oy3.

[5] *Ibid.*

[6] Federal Student Aid, U.S. Department of Education, http://tinyurl.com/ho9b48e.

[7] The comments were posted on YouTube at http://tinyurl.com/h73zucx.

In the early years, Chinese immigrants took mostly low-skilled and temporary jobs, working in mining, construction (especially helping build the nation's expanding railroads), manufacturing and service industries such as laundries and restaurants. Immigration records show that as many as 300,000 Chinese entered the United States in the first wave, although many returned to China, especially after Congress passed the Chinese Exclusion Act in 1882. That law barred Chinese immigrants from becoming U.S. citizens, a restriction that was not lifted until 1943.

In the 1950s, Chinese immigrants began to return to the United States. Some were escaping the oppressive policies of Communist leader Mao Zedong, while many came from the then British colony of Hong Kong, some arriving illegally.

However, Chinese immigration did not truly accelerate until President Richard M. Nixon and Mao normalized relations between the two countries in 1972. In 1980, Chinese immigrants in the United States numbered 385,000; by 2013, the figure topped 2 million, according to the U.S. Census Bureau. [58]

Unlike the first wave of Chinese migration, the second, still underway, tends to include immigrants who are well-educated and highly skilled. Most Chinese settle in California and New York; Chicago and Boston also are popular.

Nearly half of Chinese immigrants ages 25 or over hold a bachelor's degree or higher, compared with 28 percent of the total immigrant population and 30 percent of the native-born population. Their professions include management, business, science and the arts. [59]

Mexico's Ups, Downs

Today, Mexican immigrants are greeted warily in some parts of the country. The story was different during World War II.

In 1942, the United States and Mexico agreed on what became known as the Bracero Program, which allowed Mexican "guest workers" to fill agricultural jobs left vacant when American servicemen went to war. The Mexicans signed contracts allowing them to work in the United States, with some people coming back multiple times. In all, 4.6 million contracts were signed under the Mexican Farm Labor Program. [60]

Employers were supposed to hire *braceros* (manual laborers) only for jobs certified to have a domestic labor shortage. They also were barred from using

Immigrants Help Tech Engine Run

"I don't know if we can close our borders and be self-sustaining."

Lesli Ann Mie Agcaoili, an engineer at Tesla Motors in Fremont, Calif., has a front-row seat to the role that immigrants play in the technology sector — and to their fears of the Trump administration's restrictive plans on immigration.

Throughout the day, she says, she interacts with co-workers from Mexico, Canada, Germany and Australia. She socializes with people from India, who shop in their own section of Fremont called Little India.

Agcaoili says it's normal to hear conversations in different languages. Lately, much of the talk has been about President Trump's executive order — which several federal courts have blocked — temporarily barring entry to nationals from seven Muslim-majority countries.

"It has crossed peoples' minds: 'What if I have to go back?' " Agcaoili says. "People who are here legally ought to be fine, but I think there is some fear and apprehension about the [Trump] administration."

Founded by Elon Musk, who was born in South Africa, Tesla sits among a sea of companies started by people from outside the United States. More than half of 87 technology companies individually worth $1 billion or more have at least one foreign-born founder, according to the National Foundation for American Policy, an immigration research group in Arlington, Va. [1]

About two-thirds of people working in computing and mathematics jobs in San Mateo and Santa Clara counties, which comprise Silicon Valley, were born outside the United States, said the Silicon Valley Institute for Regional Studies, the research arm of Joint Venture Silicon Valley, an organization studying the region's economy. Immigrants make up 60 percent of those working in engineering and architectural jobs.

Critics say Silicon Valley recruits cheap labor from overseas. The tech industry, they say, is especially misusing the H-1B program — special visas that allow a limited number of highly skilled foreigners into the country each year. Sixty-five percent of H-1B petitions approved in the 2014 fiscal year went to tech workers, most of whom were from India, according to the U.S. Citizenship and Immigration Services. [2]

Trump senior adviser Stephen Bannon has denounced "progressive plutocrats in Silicon Valley" who want the freedom to bring overseas workers into the United States. American graduates, as a result, can't find work in the tech field, Bannon complained in March 2016. [3]

However, Trump told technology executives in a recent meeting that his immigration order was intended to stop "bad people" from entering the United States, but said he was open to amending the H-1B program so talented workers can come. [4]

To Agcaoili, the thought of a technology sector minus im-

the workers as strike breakers. In practice, employers took full advantage of this cheap labor, paying workers 30 cents an hour, according to government statistics. That was slightly higher than the rate for Texas agricultural workers in 1940 but well below the 81 cents an hour that agricultural workers were earning by the end of the war in 1945. [61]

Despite the low wages, workers routinely overstayed their contracts, prompting the Immigration and Naturalization Service in 1954 to undertake Operation Wetback, a pejoratively named policy in which more than 1 million Mexicans and their children were deported. But some major farmers protested and persuaded Congress to extend the Bracero Program. [62]

In 1980, 2.1 million Mexican immigrants were in the United States, according to the Census Bureau. By 2010, the total number of Mexican immigrants had mushroomed to 11.7 million.

Historians say a search for economic opportunity, political instability in Mexico and fears about crime spurred Mexican immigration to the United States. [63] Also, says Boston College's Skerry, many older Mexican immigrants did not intend to stay; their plan was to earn money and then return home.

Once in the United States, Mexican immigrants tend to achieve less than other immigrants and native-born Americans, according to the Migration Policy Institute, a Washington think tank that researches immigration. Only 6 percent have college degrees, compared with 28 percent of all immigrants. [64]

Mexican immigrants, both legal and undocumented, are more likely to be employed in service occupations, construction and maintenance jobs than other immigrants or the native-born population, the institute said. Their wages are significantly lower than other immigrants', with their average household income in 2014 at $37,390, compared with $49,487 for all immigrants and $54,565 for native-born residents. [65]

But Mexican immigrants' income in the United States is three times the average household income in Mexico, according to the Organisation for Economic Co-operation and Development (OECD), a Paris-based economic research organization, made up of 34 developed nations, that promotes market-based economic policies. About 28 percent of workers in Mexico work more than 10 hours a day, compared with 13 percent of workers in other OECD member countries. [66]

The higher income helps explain why so many Mexicans risk crossing the border illegally, experts say.

migrants makes no sense. "Just in terms of labor, they're vital to the companies and helping make them run," she says. "I just don't think it's going to be good for the economy" if the administration imposes immigration limits. "I don't know if we can close our borders and be self-sustaining."

For Agcaoili, a 45-year-old Asian-American, the issue is personal. Her father is Filipino and her mother's roots are in Japan. Born in Los Angeles, Agcaoili spent her childhood traveling between there and Hawaii, where her ancestors emigrated to work on plantations. Some of her mother's relatives were placed in internment camps during World War II.

Agcaoili, who has also worked for Ford Motor Co. in Dearborn, Mich., and the parent company of BlackBerry in Waterloo, Ontario, says immigration scares have happened before. In the early 2000s, when jobs were scarce, she says foreign-born classmates in business school were worried about whether they would be able to stay in the United States after they earned their degrees.

"It was a huge, huge deal," she says. "'Will you sponsor a visa?' That was the first thing anyone would talk about before figuring out if a job was a good fit."

Agcaoili says the multiculturalism of Silicon Valley is key to its companies' success. Tech CEOs argue much the same. The problem, they say, is not just a shortage of workers but the need to find the best talent possible. Restricting immigration "will make it far more difficult and expensive for U.S. companies to hire some of the world's best talent — and impede them from competing in the global marketplace," the CEOs of 100 tech companies said in a legal filing opposing Trump's executive order. [5]

Executives say this need extends far beyond Silicon Valley. Manufacturers in Columbus, Ind. — the hometown of Vice President Mike Pence — are heavily dependent on skilled immigrants. Dave Glass, CEO of LHP Engineering Solutions, said his company makes hiring American engineers a priority, but he can't find enough of them to fill openings. "In the last few years, we've had, like, three [Americans] apply," he said. So relying solely on domestic labor is "not an option" for his company, he said. [6]

— *Micheline Maynard*

[1] Shira Ovide, "Trump Win Is Silicon Valley's Loss on Immigration," Bloomberg News, Nov. 9, 2016, http://tinyurl.com/hx33jzr.

[2] Mica Rosenberg, Stephen Nellis and Emily Stephenson, "Trump, tech tycoons talk overhaul of H1B visas," Reuters, Jan. 12, 2017, http://tinyurl.com/grtljcr.

[3] Frances Stead Sellers and David A. Fahrenthold, " 'Why even let 'em in?' Understanding Bannon's worldview and the policies that follow," *The Washington Post*, Jan. 31, 2017, http://tinyurl.com/htcvuhf.

[4] Rosenberg, Nellis and Stephenson, *op. cit.*

[5] Elizabeth Dwoskin and Craig Timberg, "How Canada is trying to capitalize on Trump's executive order," *The Washington Post*, Feb. 10, 2017, http://tinyurl.com/hw2cogg.

[6] Annie Ropeik, "Immigration Executive Order Causes Anxiety In VP Mike Pence's Hometown," NPR, Feb. 16, 2017, http://tinyurl.com/hxsa5l6.

The federal government in recent years has attempted to reform immigration policy, with much of the debate focusing on the economic implications of legal and illegal immigration.

In 1986 the Republican-controlled Senate and Democratic-controlled House passed, and Republican President Ronald Reagan signed, the Immigration Reform and Control Act, which among other things required employers to verify that their workers were in the country legally and created fines for businesses that knowingly hired undocumented immigrants. It also awarded "amnesty" to undocumented immigrants who had entered the United States before Jan. 1, 1982 But experts say the act did little to reduce illegal immigration. [67]

Since then, immigration-reform measures have repeatedly failed to pass, regardless of which party controlled the White House or the chambers of Congress. In 2007, Republican President George W. Bush pushed a comprehensive reform that sought to satisfy supporters and foes of immigration by providing legal status to undocumented migrants and giving them a pathway to citizenship while tightening border security.

He also proposed a controversial temporary worker program that he said would help meet the demands of a growing economy. "This program would create a legal way to match willing foreign workers with willing American employers to fill jobs that Americans will not do," Bush said. "Workers would be able to register for legal status for a fixed period of time, and then be required to go home." But critics opposed the temporary worker program, saying it would harm American workers, and they denounced the granting of citizenship to undocumented immigrants as "amnesty" for lawbreakers. The bill passed the House but died in the Senate. (Democrats controlled both chambers.) [68]

Democratic President Obama's administration tried again in 2013, proposing a reform package that went beyond Bush's. Besides giving undocumented workers a chance at citizenship and tightening border security, it included a new visa program for lesser-skilled workers and provisions designed to attract immigrants with needed work skills, such as in technology. Despite having bipartisan support and being passed by the Democratic-controlled Senate, the measure died after House Republicans opposed the citizenship provision as amnesty. [69]

The Obama administration, meanwhile, was aggressively expelling undocumented immigrants. In all, it deported about 3 million people during Obama's eight years in office, earning him the title of "Deporter-in-Chief" from some immigration groups critical of his policies. [70] ■

To dramatize the importance of immigrants to the economy, advocates staged a "Day Without Immigrants" on Feb. 16 in which shops and restaurants nationwide closed for the day. Their

partment also plans to hire thousands of additional enforcement agents and enlist local law enforcement to help make arrests. [72]

During the week of Feb. 5, U.S. Immigration and Customs Enforcement (ICE) agents arrested hundreds of undocumented immigrants in raids in Atlanta, Chicago, Los Angeles, New York and other cities. The raids and roundups created great fear among undocumented immigrants and their defenders. ICE, however, said the raids were not unusual and the alarms raised are greatly exaggerated. "We do not have the personnel, time or resources to go into communities and round up people and do all kinds of mass throwing folks on buses. That's entirely a figment of folks' imagination," a Department of Homeland Security official told reporters on a conference call. "This is not intended to produce mass roundups, mass deportations." [73]

In Durham, N.C., City Council member Schewel says he hopes authorities do not deport undocumented immigrants or restrict legal immigration. "I think this is one world, and to shut off the immigration spigot is to shut off the way this country was built and made great."

Gkrishnan Ganapathy, a Hindu priest from Fremont, Calif., takes part in a ceremony during the grand opening of the Hindu Temple and Cultural Center in Centennial, Colo., on June 7, 2015. Supporters of immigration celebrate the diversity that people from different cultures bring to the American "melting pot." Critics complain that some newcomers take American jobs and are slow to learn English.

Getty Images/The Denver Post/Helen H. Richardson

CURRENT SITUATION

Immigration in Crosshairs

President Trump is moving aggressively against illegal immigration by cracking down on "sanctuary cities" (places that provide haven to undocumented immigrants) and loosening the rules on who can be deported. Businesses and immigrant advocates are warning in response that limiting immigration will hurt the U.S. economy.

goal was to show what would happen if the United States were to lose large numbers of foreign-born residents in a crackdown on illegal immigration.

"From doctors to dishwashers, immigrants are integral to daily life in the U.S.," said Janet Marguía, president and CEO of the National Council of La Raza, a Latino advocacy group. [71]

The protest was spurred by Trump's executive order on immigration, his proposal to build a wall on the Mexican border and his crackdown on sanctuary cities, as well as recent federal raids on workplaces.

Homeland Security Secretary John Kelly has signed sweeping guidelines that empower federal authorities to more aggressively detain and deport undocumented immigrants. The de-

Immigration Restrictions

Tech companies, meanwhile, are campaigning against Trump's plans to tighten immigration controls. Immigration is the lifeblood of the technology sector, they say, with immigrants bringing much innovation to the economy. Half of the technology companies in the United States worth $1 billion or more are headed by chief executives with roots elsewhere, according to a letter signed by more than 200 industry leaders and investors. The roster includes Microsoft and Google, while firms such as Apple have sizable numbers of non-U.S.

Continued on p. 186

At Issue:

Will limiting illegal immigration protect U.S. economic interests?

STEVEN CAMAROTA
RESEARCH DIRECTOR,
CENTER FOR IMMIGRATION STUDIES

WRITTEN FOR *CQ RESEARCHER*, FEBRUARY 2017

*t*he notion that enforcing our immigration laws will harm the economy is not supported by the facts. First, illegal immigration is a trivial share of the United States' $18 trillion economy, accounting for 2 or 3 percent of gross domestic product (GDP), according to Harvard's George Borjas, the nation's top immigration economist. This tiny addition to GDP almost entirely goes to the illegal immigrants themselves as wages and benefits.

Yes, the aggregate size of the U.S. economy would fall a little if these immigrants went home — fewer people means a slightly smaller economy. But what matters is the per capita GDP — the nation's total output, divided by the number of people in the United States — and not aggregate GDP. And there is no indication that reducing illegal immigration would reduce the per capita GDP of natives or legal immigrants.

The best way to think about enforcement is that it creates winners and losers. If more immigrants here illegally went home, low-skilled Americans who compete with them would benefit. Borjas has estimated that by increasing the supply of workers, illegal immigrants may reduce wages by $99 billion to $118 billion a year. Their departure would mean higher wages at the bottom of the labor market. It also would mean that some of the 23 million working-age Americans with no education beyond high school who are not employed might find work.

The other winners from enforcement would be taxpayers. On average, adult illegal immigrants have only about a 10th-grade education. As a result, they tend to earn low wages, and this allows them — or more often their U.S.-born children — to qualify for welfare programs.

My own research indicates that 62 percent of such households use one or more major welfare programs. Consistent with all prior research, a 2016 report by the National Academies of Sciences, Engineering and Medicine found that immigrants with no education beyond high school create significantly more costs for government than they pay in taxes. As a result, the departure of those immigrants in the United States illegally would save taxpayers billions.

It is true that some low-wage employers and the illegal immigrants themselves would lose if we enforced our immigration laws. But the poorest and least-educated Americans would benefit, as would taxpayers. Furthermore, enforcing immigration laws could help reduce crime, enhance national security and restore the rule of law.

EDIBERTO ROMÁN
LAW PROFESSOR; DIRECTOR OF CITIZEN-
SHIP AND NATIONALITY INITIATIVES,
FLORIDA INTERNATIONAL UNIVERSITY

WRITTEN FOR *CQ RESEARCHER*, FEBRUARY 2017

*l*imiting immigration and undertaking mass deportations are not the solutions to the purported immigration crisis. In fact, the leading studies on the subject conclude mass deportation will harm the economy and is an irresponsible policy that will fail, especially if businesses' demands for undocumented labor continue.

The Immigration Policy Center, for instance, said mass deportation would reduce U.S. GDP by 1.46 percent a year. Over 10 years, the cumulative GDP loss would be $2.6 trillion, not including the actual cost of deportation. This approach would lower wages for higher-skilled natives and lead to widespread job loss.

Similarly, the Center for American Progress concluded the "costs of a massive deportation policy would not only be substantial, but in many ways, financially reckless."

A number of prominent Republicans agree. Tom Ridge, former secretary of Homeland Security, for instance, stated: "Attempting to deport everybody is neither feasible nor wise." Sen. John McCain, R-Ariz., said: "I have listened to and understand the concerns of those who simply advocate . . . rounding up and deporting undocumented workers. . . . But that's easier said than done. . . . I have yet to hear a single proponent of this point of view offer one realistic proposal for locating, apprehending and returning to their countries of origin over 11 million people."

Besides the economic costs, mass deportation is simply inhumane. The advocacy group Families for Freedom observed: "Every year, nearly 200,000 non-citizens — many with kids who are U.S. citizens — are deported and torn away from their families . . . resulting in more single-parent households and psychological and financial hardship, or forcing their U.S. citizen children into deportation with them."

It continued: "These American children may have to start over in a country with a new language, fewer resources and an uncertain future. America's immigration laws force American children to lose their parent or their country. Mandatory deportation is a life sentence of exile. Such a severe 'one size fits all' punishment cannot be the basis of our immigration system."

It is thus time to end to baseless assertions that immigration restrictions are a viable option to the immigration debate. We must turn to data, not demagoguery; we must demand facts and not merely accept economically baseless as well as inhumane rhetoric.

Continued from p. 184

natives in their management and staff ranks. [74]

"In my conversations with officials here in Washington this week, I've made it clear that Apple believes deeply in the importance of immigration — both to our company and to our nation's future," Apple CEO Tim Cook said in a memo to staff in late January after Trump's immigration order was announced. "Apple would not exist without immigration, let alone thrive and innovate the way we do." [75]

"The reality is that high-skilled immigrants can choose where to go," said the University of Toronto's Florida. "Countries like Canada and Australia have come to understand the economic advantages of attracting immigrants, and have upped their efforts to attract the top talent from around the globe." [76]

On Feb. 9, Trump suffered another legal setback in his effort to temporarily ban immigrants from seven Middle East countries and halt the flow of refugees for 120 days. The San Francisco-based Ninth U.S. Circuit Court of Appeals refused to lift a lower-court suspension of his executive order, the result of a lawsuit filed by the state of Washington. Trump reacted harshly, saying the judges' motivations were political, the decision was "disgraceful" and the country's security was in peril. [77]

Trump's executive order had caught airports, airlines and immigration officials off guard. *The Washington Post* reported that administration officials were divided over the breadth of the order, especially when it came to holders of green cards, who also were temporarily barred entry back into the United States. [78]

In challenging the order, Washington state's attorney general argued that Trump's actions represented executive overreach and would hurt those who "have, overnight, lost the right to travel, lost the right to visit their families, lost the right to go perform research, lost the right to go speak at conferences around the world." [79]

Throughout the legal wrangling, Trump insisted that the Constitution gives the president wide latitude to set immigration policy, and government lawyers told the appeals court that the president has "unreviewable authority to suspend the admission of any class of aliens" — an assertion the three-judge panel rejected. The Justice Department told the appeals court on Feb. 16 that the administration will rescind the executive order and replace it with a new one. [80]

Sanctuary Cities

Businesses also are worried about the economic impact of Trump's crackdown on sanctuary cities, in which he is threatening to cut off federal funding to any municipality that offers safe haven to undocumented immigrants.

Currently, five states and at least 633 counties have adopted practices meant to shield undocumented residents and refugees from deportation, according to the Immigrant Legal Resource Center in San Francisco. Methods range from declining federal requests to hold arrestees in jail because of their immigration status to limiting police cooperation with federal agents. [81]

Twenty-eight universities also have declared themselves sanctuaries, including Columbia, Wesleyan and all 23 campuses of the California State University system. [82]

University of Michigan President Mark Schlissel said his school would continue to welcome applications from undocumented students and would not disclose information about the immigration status of its international students beyond what was required by law. [83]

But foes of illegal immigration, and some who want legal immigration reduced, say the United States needs to regain control of its borders so it can both keep potential terrorists out and protect American jobs. "Decades of record immigration have produced lower wages and higher unemployment for our citizens, especially for African-American and Latino workers," Trump said in his July acceptance speech at the Republican National Convention. [84]

No matter the outcome of the immigration debate and the court battle over Trump's executive order, Boston College's Skerry says the country is likely to remain divided.

Many Americans, he says, passionately believe immigrants should be allowed to enter the country and undocumented workers should be able to stay, because their own family members had made similar journeys in search of prosperity.

Several advertisements broadcast during this year's Super Bowl made pleas for inclusion and tolerance. An ad by Airbnb, for example, showed a series of people from different races, including a man with a turban. The subtitles read, "We believe no matter who you are, where you're from, who you love, or who you worship, we all belong. The world is more beautiful the more you accept." And in the most-talked about ad, Anheuser-Busch depicted German-born founder Adolphus Busch arriving in America, where he's greeted by people shouting, "Go back home!" [85]

Others, however, feel just as passionately that both legal and illegal immigration harms the economy because foreigners create more competition for jobs that Americans need and are often willing to work for less so they suppress wages.

"When the supply of workers goes up, the price that firms have to pay to hire workers goes down" said George J. Borjas, an economics professor at Harvard University. "Wage trends over the past half-century suggest that a 10 percent increase in the number of workers with a particular set of skills probably lowers the wage of that group by at least 3 percent." [86]

Skerry thinks attitudes on both sides of the debate "are pretty dug in right now. The people who are going to feel sympathetic will feel sympathetic, and those who are angry will be angry, and they're going to feed off each other." ■

OUTLOOK

Searching for Solutions

President Trump remains determined to suspend immigration from seven Muslim-majority countries, and legal experts believe the Supreme Court ultimately may tackle the issue. [87]

In the meantime, Saxenian at Berkeley says immigrant executives and venture capitalists in Silicon Valley are watching closely to gauge whether to invest in the United States or in their overseas operations. She hopes the debate does not scare them — or their potential employees — away.

"To the extent that these ecosystems develop outside the United States, we want to make sure the U.S. remains attractive," Saxenian says. "We're in a space where anxieties over globalization are so strong that we could see a slowing down" of investment.

Minniti at Syracuse University says attracting younger immigrants is critical to keeping the U.S. economy competitive. "There is a strong correlation between age and starting a business," Minniti says, noting many businesses are started by people between the ages of 24 and 35 years old.

"You don't immigrate when you're 70," she says. "You immigrate when you're young." That's equally true for lesser-skilled immigrants, who continue to come to the United States in search of advancement.

"When you come, you want to work," Minniti says. "That is something that's innately entrepreneurial. They don't have the skills that others do in

the workforce. But they are able and willing to do a lot of work, usually work that is physically demanding. These are usually the people who are accused of stealing American labor, but it is not true."

Boston College's Skerry says a compromise on immigration is possible. One solution conservatives could embrace, he says, is to establish a nationwide, government-sponsored effort to teach immigrants to become fluent in English. "It needs the oomph of a national campaign to encourage immigrants to learn English," he says, similar to the way Scottish-American industrialist Andrew Carnegie jumpstarted the library system by building libraries across the United States.

Such a campaign could "placate people who supported Trump who understandably have been concerned about the cultural changes that have been taking place," he says. "You tell all those people, 'English is really important. It's our language, and we want people to learn it.' I've never met many immigrants who don't want to learn English."

In the end, Minniti says immigrants everywhere are an easy target for changes caused by technology and changing consumer tastes. "It's not immigrants' fault. It's not the Chinese's fault. Unfortunately, the marketplace changes and requires readjustment. Who pays the price? People with lower skills."

Trump adviser Bannon would agree that Americans with fewer skills are the ones paying the price for globalization. But more immigration is not the answer, he said. The solution, he argued, is to gain control of national borders and construct an economic nationalism that focuses on the needs of the American economy over internationalism.

"Strong countries and strong nationalist movements in countries make strong neighbors," he said. "And that is really the building blocks that built Western Europe and the United States, and I think it's what can see us forward." [88] ■

Notes

[1] "Full Executive Order Text: Trump's Action Limiting Refugees Into the U.S.," *The New York Times*, Jan. 27, 2017, http://tinyurl.com/huz723.; Michael D. Shear and Ron Nixon, "New Trump Deportation Rules Allow Far More Deportations," *The New York Times*, Feb. 21, 2017, http://tinyurl.com/jtr2qmq.

[2] Greg Bensinger and Rachael King, "Tech CEOs Take a Stand Against Donald Trump's Immigration Order," *The Wall Street Journal*, Feb. 6, 2017, http://tinyurl.com/hh893na.

[3] Letter from the American Council On Education to Homeland Security Secretary John Kelly, Feb. 3, 2017, http://tinyurl.com/zptvsum.

[4] Frances Stead Sellers and David A. Fahrenthold, " 'Why even let 'em in?' Understanding Bannon's worldview and the policies that follow," *The Washington Post*, Jan. 31, 2017, http://tinyurl.com/htcvuhf.

[5] Renee Stepler and Anna Brown, "Statistical Portrait of Hispanics in the United States," Pew Research Center, April 19, 2016, http://tinyurl.com/z7axefn. The definition of "Hispanic" varies by study, and the U.S. census permits people to self-identify as Hispanic or "Latino." See "Hispanic Origin Main," U.S. Census Bureau, http://tinyurl.com/hqbmd2s.

[6] Jie Zong and Jeanne Batalova, "Asian Immigrants in the United States," Migration Policy Institute, Jan. 6, 2016, http://tinyurl.com/gqtyet4; "Asian-Americans Are Expanding Their Footprint in the U.S. and Making an Impact," Nielsen Company, May 19, 2016, http://tinyurl.com/hrq882b.

[7] "Modern Immigration Wave Brings 59 Million to U.S., Driving Population Growth and Change Through 2065," Pew Research Center, Sept. 28, 2015, http://tinyurl.com/qhfo8js.

[8] Jason Furman and Danielle Gray, "10 Ways Immigrants Help Build And Strengthen Our Economy," Obama White House Archives, July 12, 2012, http://tinyurl.com/hto2rum.

[9] "Foreign Born Population," U.S. Census Bureau, 2017, http://tinyurl.com/jsbzqc5.

[10] Richard Florida, "How Trump Threatens America's Talent Edge," *CityLab*, Jan. 31, 2017, http://tinyurl.com/jros2wj.

[11] Alexia Fernández Campbell, "The Truth About Undocumented Immigrants and Taxes," *The Atlantic*, Sept. 12, 2016, http://tinyurl.com/zs9ud27; "The Fiscal Burden of Illegal Immigration on the United States Taxpayer," Federation for American Immigration Reform, 2013, http://tinyurl.com/od66dx3.

[12] Cass R. Sunstein, "The Real Reason So Many Americans Oppose Immigration," *Real Clear Politics*, Sept. 28, 2016, http://tinyurl.com/gs9fa27.

[13] Jeffrey S. Passel and D'Vera Cohn, "Size of U.S. Unauthorized Immigrant Workforce Stable After the Great Recession," Pew Research Center, Nov. 3, 2016, http://tinyurl.com/hvyqz7j; Anthony Cave, "Has Arizona's Economy Improved Because of Its Immigration Laws?" Politifact Arizona, March 3, 2016, http://tinyurl.com/z99ar2c.

[14] "The Fiscal Burden of Illegal Immigration on United States Taxpayers," *op. cit.*

[15] Peter Morici, "The real cost of illegal immigration," *The Washington Times*, Sept. 6, 2016, http://tinyurl.com/hd59gwf.

[16] For background, see Sarah Glazer, "Welfare Reform," *CQ Researcher*, Aug. 3, 2001, pp. 601-632.

[17] "Statistical Hot Air: FAIR's USA Report Lacks Credibility," American Immigration Council, March 29, 2011, http://tinyurl.com/hkdu5gz; Miriam Valverde, "Donald Trump Says Illegal Immigration Costs $113 Billion," PolitiFact, Sept. 1, 2016, http://tinyurl.com/hnuzdsa.

[18] Marshall Fitz, Philip E. Wolgin and Patrick Oakford, "Immigrants Are Makers, Not Takers," Center for American Progress, Feb. 8, 2013, http://tinyurl.com/zlzc585.

[19] Farm Labor Background Report, Economic Research Service, U.S. Department of Agriculture, 2017, pp. 3, 7, http://tinyurl.com/glrf3ar; Kenneth Megan, "Labor Shortages Make the Case for Immigration," Bipartisan Policy Center, Oct. 23, 2015, http://tinyurl.com/zht7oox.

[20] Travis Putnam Hill, "In Texas, Undocumented Immigrants Have No Shortage of Work," *The Texas Tribune*, Dec. 16, 2016, http://tinyurl.com/hhdxy34.

[21] Ike Brannon and Logan Albright, "Immigrations' Impact on the Texas Economy," Texas Public Policy Foundation, March 2016, http://tinyurl.com/jzcffbt.

[22] Economic Profile, Greater Durham Chamber of Commerce, 2017, http://tinyurl.com/gu5t3bp.

[23] Demographics, City of Durham, N.C., 2017, http://tinyurl.com/hdjx4oa; "Durham's Immigrant Communities: Looking to the Future," Latino Migrant Project, 2016, http://tinyurl.com/ztcwpzh.

[24] Benjamin Wallace-Wells, "The Trump Administration's Dark View Of Immigrants," *The New Yorker*, Feb. 2, 2017, http://tinyurl.com/hpuk999.

[25] Farei Chideya, "Trump's Blue Collar Base Wants More Jobs and an America Like the Past," *Five Thirty Eight*, Sept. 13, 2016, http://tinyurl.com/jrsvsas.

[26] "Immigrant Small Business Owners: A Significant and Growing Part of the Economy," Immigration Research Initiative, Fiscal Policy Institute, June 2012, http://tinyurl.com/6vt5fae.

[27] "Economic Impact of Immigration by State," WalletHub, Feb. 14, 2017, http://tinyurl.com/hvpc4yt.

[28] "How States and Local Economies Benefit From Immigrants," American Immigration Council, http://tinyurl.com/goj2sge.

[29] Miriam Jordan, "Heartland Draws Hispanics to Help Revive Small Towns," *The Wall Street Journal*, Nov. 8, 2012, http://tinyurl.com/z2vvqet.

[30] *Ibid.*

[31] Michigan Population Trends, Michigan Department of Health And Human Services, 2017, http://tinyurl.com/jdjdsk7; "Snyder Creates Office for New Americans," press release, Office of Governor Rick Snyder, Jan. 31, 2014, http://tinyurl.com/gu7e5d2.

[32] "How Immigrants Are Helping Detroit's Recovery," *The Economist*, Feb. 16, 2017, http://tinyurl.com/zqjqvbk.

[33] "Taiwanese Companies in the U.S.," U.S.-Taiwan Connect, 2017, http://tinyurl.com/z3l28el; "Indian Companies Invest Billions in the U.S.," *The Wall Street Journal*, July 15, 2015, http://tinyurl.com/z5wsusa.

[34] Sara Ashley O'Brien, "High-Skilled Visa Applications Hit Record High — Again," CNN Money, April 12, 2016, http://tinyurl.com/zs473gb.

[35] Mica Rosenberg, Stephen Nellis and Emily Stephenson, "Trump, tech tycoons talk overhaul of H1B visas," Reuters, Jan. 12, 2017, http://tinyurl.com/grtljcr.

[36] Paige Godden, "Jeff Sessions Considers Eliminating H-1B Program," *Des Moines Register*, Oct. 25, 2016, http://tinyurl.com/zrksa79.

[37] Rosenberg, Nellis and Stephenson, *op. cit.*

[38] *Ibid.*

[39] *Ibid.*

[40] Profile of Infosys, My Visa Jobs, 2017, http://tinyurl.com/jdqut2w, http://tinyurl.com/z7tdykv.

[41] "Fearing Tighter U.S. Visa Regime, Indian IT Firms like Infosys, TCS Rush To Hire, Acquire," Reuters, Nov. 29, 2016, http://tinyurl.com/hoyw9h3.

[42] "H-1B Debarred/Disqualified List of Employers," U.S. Labor Department, 2017, http://tinyurl.com/zhgkvmr.

[43] Edmund S. Morgan, *American Slavery, American Freedom* (reprinted 2003).

[44] Richard Hofstadter, *America at 1750: A Social Portrait* (1971), p. 19; Marianne S. Wokeck, *Trade in Strangers: The Beginnings of Mass Migration to North America* (1999), p. 46.

[45] Naturalization Acts of 1790 And 1795, George Washington's Mount Vernon, http://tinyurl.com/zhc729m.

[46] Tyler Anbinder, *City Of Dreams, The 400-Year Epic History of Immigrant New York* (2016), p. xxv.

[47] *Ibid.*, p. 110.

[48] "Great Famine," *Encyclopedia Britannica*, Jan. 28, 2016, http://tinyurl.com/z7ntujp.

[49] *Ibid.*, p. 124.

[50] *Ibid.*

[51] *Ibid.*, p. 188.

[52] "New-York City: Germans in America," *The New York Times*, June 27, 1855. (URL not available.)

[53] Our History, Levi Strauss & Company, http://tinyurl.com/zujk3n4.

[54] Katja Wüstenbecker, "German-Americans In World War I," *Immigrant Entreprenuership*, Sept. 19, 2014, http://tinyurl.com/jpcxm8y.

[55] "Who Was Shut Out?" *History Matters*, George Mason University, http://tinyurl.com/hzjoutz.

[56] Tetsuden Kashima, *Judgment Without Trial: Japanese American Imprisonment During World War II* (2003), p. 124.

[57] Kate Hooper and Jeanne Batalova, "Chinese Immigrants in the United States," Migration Policy Institute, Jan. 28, 2015, http://tinyurl.com/jqovnxs.

[58] *Ibid.*

[59] *Ibid.*

[60] Bracero History Archive, 2017, http://tinyurl.com/82huf75.

[61] Marilyn Sworzin, "Wartime Wages, Income and Wage Regulation in Agriculture," *Bulletin of the U.S. Bureau of Labor Statistics*, 1946, Federal Reserve, http://tinyurl.com/gvutub4.

[62] *Ibid.*

[63] "Most Mexicans See a Better Life in the U.S.; One-In-Three Would Migrate," Pew Re-

About the Author

Micheline Maynard is a former senior business correspondent and Detroit bureau chief for *The New York Times* and a contributor to *Forbes*. She has reported and written extensively on global manufacturing, among other things. Her books include *Curbing Cars* (2014), *The Selling of the American Economy* (2009) and *The End of Detroit* (2003).

search Center, Sept. 23, 2009, http://tiny url.com/nos7k7c.

[64] Jie Zong and Jeanne Batalova, "Mexican Immigrants in the United States," Migration Policy Institute, March 17, 2016, http://tiny url.com/ln449qb.

[65] *Ibid.*

[66] Mexico, OECD Better Life Index, Organisation for Economic Co-operation and Development, 2017, http://tinyurl.com/3h6oasu.

[67] Caroline Mimbs Nyce and Chris Bodenner, "Looking Back at Amnesty Under Reagan," *The Atlantic*, May 23, 2016, http://tinyurl.com/jn6o627.

[68] Mark Knoller, "The last president who couldn't get Congress to act on immigration," CBS News, Nov. 21, 2014, http://tinyurl.com/hc4qpy2.

[69] Seung Min Kim, "Senate Passes Immigration Bill," *Politico*, June 28, 2013, http://tinyurl.com/hth3g3m.

[70] Serena Marshall, "Obama Has Deported More People Than Any Other President," ABC News, Aug. 29, 2016, http://tinyurl.com/j7y6wy9. For more see, Reed Karaim, "Immigration Detention," *CQ Researcher*, Oct. 23, 2015, pp. 889-912.

[71] Doug Stanglin, "Businesses across U.S. close, students skip school on 'Day Without Immigrants,' " *USA Today*, Feb. 16, 2017, http://tiny url.com/jptxfhe.

[72] David Nakamura, "Memos signed by DHS secretary describe sweeping new guidelines for deporting illegal immigrants," *The Washington Post*, Feb. 18, 2017, http://tinyurl.com/zdg6mln.

[73] Nicholas Kulish, Caitlin Dickerson and Liz Robbins, "Reports of Raids Have Immigrants Bracing for Enforcement Surge," *The New York Times*, Feb. 10, 2017, http://tinyurl.com/hwgbj5j; and Lisa Rein, Abigail Hauslohner and Sandhya Somashekhar, "Federal agents conduct immigration enforcement raids in at least six states," *The Washington Post*, Feb. 11, 2017, http://tiny url.com/jg2wcgm; David Nakamura, "Trump administration issues new immigration enforcement policies, says goal is not 'mass deportations,' " *The Washington Post*, Feb. 21, 2017, http://tinyurl.com/jh7xlk3.

[74] April Glaser, "What Silicon Valley Can Expect Under Trump," *Recode*, Jan. 23, 2017, http://tiny url.com/j5jchlq.

[75] Jonathan Shieber, "Apple CEO Tim Cook Sent a Memo to Employees About the Immigration Ban," *Tech Crunch*, Jan. 28, 2017, http://tinyurl.com/jdrndk4.

[76] Florida, *op. cit.*

[77] Matt Zapotosky, "Federal appeals court rules 3 to 0 against Trump on travel ban," *The*

FOR MORE INFORMATION

American Civil Liberties Union, 125 Broad St., 18th Floor, New York, NY 10004; 212-549-2500; www.aclu.org. Civil rights group that defends immigrants' legal rights.

American Immigrants Lawyers Association, 331 G St., N.W., Suite 300, Washington, DC 20005; 202-507-7600; www.aila.org. Association for immigration lawyers.

Arab-American Institute, 1600 K St., N.W., Suite 601, Washington, DC 20006; 202-429-9210; www.aaiusa.org. Represents Arab-American causes, including discrimination matters and immigration.

Center for Immigration Studies, 1629 K St., N.W., Suite 600, Washington, DC 20006; 202-466-8185; http://cis.org/. Conservative research group whose goal is to restrict illegal and legal immigration.

Federation for American Immigration Reform, 25 Massachusetts Ave., N.W., Suite 330, Washington, DC 20001; 202-328-7004; www.fairus.org. Advocacy group seeking limits on immigration that produced a widely quoted study on undocumented immigration.

Hispanic Federation, 555 Exchange Place, New York, NY 10005; 212-233-8955; http://hispanicfederation.org/. Network of 100 grassroots Hispanic organizations that provides education and job training resources to immigrants and their families.

National Council of Agricultural Employers, 525 9th St., N.W., Suite 800, Washington, DC 20004; 202-629-9320; www.ncaeonline.org. Lobbies on immigration issues and provides guidance to its members on immigration matters.

NumbersUSA, 400 Crystal Drive, Suite 240, Arlington, VA 22202; 703-816-8820; www.numbersusa.com. Advocacy group that wants to reduce legal immigration.

U.S. Border Control, PO Box 97115, Washington, DC 20090; 703-740-8668; www.usbc.org. Federal agency responsible for securing U.S. borders.

Washington Post, Feb. 9, 2017, http://tinyurl.com/hxc6vd8.

[78] Josh Rogin, "Inside the White House-Cabinet battle over Trump's immigration order," *The Washington Post*, Feb. 4, 2017, http://tinyurl.com/gpyx832.

[79] Adam Liptak, "The President Has Much Power Over Immigration, but How Much?" *The New York Times*, Feb. 5, 2017, http://tinyurl.com/zu6rm79.

[80] "The Ninth Circuit makes the right call on Trump's travel ban," *The Washington Post*, Feb. 10, 2017, http://tinyurl.com/j92wj6x; Julie Hirschfeld Davis, "Supreme Court Nominee Calls Trump's Attacks on Judiciary 'Demoralizing,' " *The New York Times*, Feb. 8, 2017, http://tinyurl.com/gs6b8tl; and Brent Kendall and Laura Meckler, "Trump Administration Plans New Executive Order Next Week, Ends Legal Push in Appeals Court," *The Wall Street Journal*, Feb. 16, 2017, http://tinyurl.com/z4g fjvg.

[81] Jasmine C. Lee, Rudy Omri and Julia Preston, "What Are Sanctuary Cities?" *The New York Times*, Feb. 6, 2017, http://tinyurl.com/hyrw4qc.

[82] Yara Simon, "28 Universities That Vow to Offer Sanctuary to their Undocumented Students," *Remezcla*, November 2017, http://tiny url.com/gqx4mor.

[83] Mark Schlissel, "Protecting the Interests of Our International Community of Scholars," University of Michigan, Jan. 28, 2017, http://tiny url.com/z8pgh8r.

[84] "Full Text: Donald Trump 2016 RNC draft speech transcript," *Politico*, July 21, 2016, http://tinyurl.com/gt4clje.

[85] Michelle Castillo, "AirBnb cofounders personally edited the company's controversial Super Bowl Ad," CNBC, Feb. 6, 2017, http://tinyurl.com/hxkethm; Claire Atkinson, "Anheuser-Busch's Super Bowl ad tackles immigration," *New York Post*, Jan. 31, 2017, http://tinyurl.com/z3y6asl.

[86] George J. Borjas, "Yes, Immigration Hurts American Workers," *Politico Magazine*, September/October 2016, http://tinyurl.com/hol5pmp.

[87] Jeff John Roberts, "Trump's Travel Ban: The Supreme Court and What Happens Next," *Fortune*, Feb. 6, 2017, http://tinyurl.com/z9rgmah.

[88] Sellers and Fahrenthold, *op. cit.*

Bibliography

Selected Sources

Books

Anbinder, Tyler, *City of Dreams: The 400-Year Epic History of Immigrant New York*, Houghton Mifflin Harcourt, 2016.

A George Washington University history professor tells the stories of immigrants and the role they played in defining a polyglot New York City.

Hsu, Madeline T., *The Good Immigrants: How the Yellow Peril Became the Model Minority*, Princeton University Press, 2015.

An associate professor of history at the University of Texas, Austin tells the history of Chinese immigrants and their path from a loathed ethnic group to an educated and admired migrant group.

Peralta, Dan-el Padilla, *Undocumented: A Dominican Boy's Odyssey From a Homeless Shelter to the Ivy League*, Penguin Press, 2015.

The author, whose family migrated from the Dominican Republic and became homeless, describes his impoverished childhood — and his rise to salutatorian at Princeton University.

Urrea, Luis Alberto, *The Devil's Highway: A True Story*, Back Bay Books, 2005.

A writer tells the story of a group of 26 Mexican immigrants who got lost in the Arizona desert, of whom just 12 survived.

Articles

Borjas, George J., "Yes, Immigration Hurts American Workers," *Politico Magazine*, September/October 2016, http://tinyurl.com/hol5pmp.

An economics professor at Harvard's Kennedy School of Government argues that during the 2016 presidential campaign, neither Republican Donald Trump nor Democrat Hillary Clinton gave a complete picture of immigration's impact on the United States.

Campbell, Alexia Fernández, "The Truth About Undocumented Immigrants and Taxes," *The Atlantic*, Sept. 12, 2016, http://tinyurl.com/zs9ud27.

A journalist explains how many undocumented immigrants collectively pay millions of dollars annually in Social Security taxes, even though they are ineligible to collect retirement benefits.

Davis, Bob, "The Thorny Economics of Illegal Immigration," *The Wall Street Journal*, Feb. 9, 2016, http://tiny url.com/jo3pfbm.

A journalist explores the steps Arizona took to limit undocumented immigration and how it affected the state's economy, in both negative and positive ways.

Fitz, Marshall, Philip E. Wolgin and Patrick Oakford, "Immigrants Are Makers, Not Takers," Center for American Progress, Feb. 8, 2013, http://tinyurl.com/zlzc585.

Analysts at a liberal public policy think tank look at ways undocumented immigrants contribute to the American economy and their potential for providing more value.

Glaser, April, "What Silicon Valley can expect under Trump," *Recode*, Jan. 23, 2017, http://tinyurl.com/j5jchlq.

Technology industry CEOs discuss their priorities, including immigration reform, during the Trump presidency.

Goodman, H.A., "Illegal immigrants benefit the U.S. economy," *The Hill*, April 23, 2014, http://tinyurl.com/kefo83e.

The author looks at various data about undocumented immigrants, arguing that they make a positive contribution to the U.S. economy.

Koch, Edward, "Why Americans Oppose Amnesty for Illegal Immigrants," *Real Clear Politics*, June 2, 2010, http://tinyurl.com/255ulm3.

The late New York City mayor argued the United States should expand quotas for legal immigrants rather than allow those here illegally to stay.

Reports and Studies

Brannon, Ike, and Logan Albright, "Immigration's Impact on the Texas Economy," Texas Public Policy Foundation, March 2016, http://tinyurl.com/jzcffbt.

Researchers from a conservative think tank look at the impact of legal and undocumented immigration on the economy of Texas, which has the nation's second-largest number of undocumented immigrants.

Cadman, Dan, "President Trump's Immigration-Related Executive Orders," Center for Immigration Studies, February 2017, http://tinyurl.com/z442bxg.

A fellow at the Center for Immigration Studies, which favors limiting legal immigration, analyzes President Trump's actions on immigration.

Dimock, Michael, "How America Changed During Barack Obama's Presidency," Pew Research Center, Jan. 10, 2017, http://tinyurl.com/hwb8kbk.

A political scientist discusses the changes that took place during the Obama years, including the administration's policy moves on immigration.

Krogstad, Jens Manuel, Jeffrey S. Passel and D'Vera Cohn, "Five facts about illegal immigration in the U.S.," Pew Research Center, Nov. 3, 2016, http://tinyurl.com/gtmhrft.

The authors look at the demographics of the undocumented immigrant population and the immigrants' impact on the broader U.S. population.

The Next Step:

Additional Articles from Current Periodicals

H-1B Visas

Bloomfield, Doni, John Lauerman and Matthew Campbell, "Trump's H-1B Visa Crackdown Threatens Cutting-Edge U.S. Medicine," *Bloomberg*, Feb. 7, 2017, http://tinyurl.com/jo66u2w.

President Trump's travel restrictions could slow research and deplete the number of skilled immigrants at U.S. biotech firms, industry experts say.

Bukhari, Jeff, "Why H-1B Visas Aren't So Great for Silicon Valley Workers," *Fortune*, Feb. 15, 2017, http://tinyurl.com/zgoyyz9.

Although hiring foreign-born IT workers raised wages nationwide and lowered costs for computer products, domestic employment could have been 10 percent higher in the computer sector without immigrant labor, the author says.

Iyengar, Rishi, "H-1B debate: Trump is making India's tech industry nervous," CNN, Feb. 15, 2017, http://tinyurl.com/hy8lchb.

India's IT outsourcing industry, which generates about 10 percent of the country's gross domestic product, could suffer if President Trump restricts the available number of H-1B visas.

Immigrant-Owned Businesses

Chou, Elizabeth, "Immigrants fueled LA economy to tune of $232.9 billion in 2014," *Los Angeles Daily News*, Feb. 8, 2017, http://tinyurl.com/gptykm6.

Immigrants in Los Angeles County contributed about 35.7 percent of the region's economic output.

Delikat, Stacey, "Immigrant-owned restaurants host 'food diplomacy' meals," Fox 5 NY, Feb. 6, 2017, http://tinyurl.com/j2rvybs.

New York-based "food tour guides" are looking to create a cultural bridge and foster community by highlighting restaurants with owners who are from countries affected by President Trump's travel restrictions.

Flynn, Kerry, "What the tech industry would look like without immigrants," *Mashable*, Jan. 31, 2017, http://tinyurl.com/jlpfsdu.

Immigrants and first-generation Americans played central roles in creating some of the United States' biggest tech companies, including Sergey Brin of Google and Jerry Yang of Yahoo.

New Legislation

Burnett, John, "Republican Lawmakers Propose New Law To Reduce Legal Immigration," NPR, Feb. 7, 2017, http://tinyurl.com/gnzxr2y.

A bill offered by two Republican senators would limit the number of green cards given to foreign nationals, slash the number of refugees admitted and remove the diversity lottery that gives visas to countries with low rates of immigration.

Carney, Jordain, "Senate Dems move to nix Trump's deportation order," *The Hill*, Feb. 16, 2017, http://tinyurl.com/jymr2fy.

A group of Senate Democrats introduced legislation to roll back President Trump's executive order on deportation.

Turque, Bill, "In era of Trump, CASA pushing for new laws in Maryland suburbs," *The Washington Post*, Feb. 9, 2017, http://tinyurl.com/jx79ue8.

CASA de Maryland, one of Maryland's biggest immigrant advocacy groups, plans to push for legislation in two of the state's counties that would codify longtime unstated protections for undocumented immigrants.

Political Unrest

Knefel, John, "Inside the Huge JFK Airport Protest Over Trump's Muslim Ban," *Rolling Stone*, Jan. 29, 2017, http://tinyurl.com/j5j8ogs.

In response to President Trump's executive order restricting travel from seven majority Muslim countries, thousands of protesters converged on JFK International Airport, setting off a wave of protests around the country, including in Silicon Valley.

Perez-Peña, Richard, and Katie Rogers, "Day Without Immigrants to Hit Washington in the Stomach," *The New York Times*, Feb. 15, 2017, http://tinyurl.com/h68mmwc.

Immigrant restaurant owners in Washington, D.C., including big names such as Zaytinya and Oyamel proprietor José Andrés and Busboys and Poets owner Andy Shallal, participated in the "Day Without Immigrants" campaign.

CITING *CQ RESEARCHER*

Sample formats for citing these reports in a bibliography include the ones listed below. Preferred styles and formats vary, so please check with your instructor or professor.

MLA STYLE
Jost, Kenneth. "Remembering 9/11." <u>CQ Researcher</u> 2 Sept. 2011: 701-732.

APA STYLE
Jost, K. (2011, September 2). Remembering 9/11. *CQ Researcher, 9,* 701-732.

CHICAGO STYLE
Jost, Kenneth. "Remembering 9/11." *CQ Researcher,* September 2, 2011, 701-32.

In-depth Reports on Issues in the News

Are you writing a paper?

Need backup for a debate?

Want to become an expert on an issue?

For 90 years, students have turned to *CQ Researcher* for in-depth reporting on issues in the news. Reports on a full range of political and social issues are now available. Following is a selection of recent reports:

Civil Liberties
Privacy and the Internet, 12/15
Intelligence Reform, 5/15
Religion and Law, 11/14

Crime/Law
Forensic Science Controversies, 2/17
Jailing Debtors, 9/16
Decriminalizing Prostitution, 4/16
Restorative Justice, 2/16
The Dark Web, 1/16
Immigrant Detention, 10/15
Fighting Gangs, 10/15

Education
Civic Education, 2/17
Student Debt, 11/16
Apprenticeships, 10/16
Free Speech on Campus, 5/15

Environment/Society
Guns on Campus, 1/17
Mass Transit, 12/16
Arctic Development, 12/16
Protecting the Power Grid, 11/16
Pornography, 10/16
Women in Leadership, 9/16

Health/Safety
Reducing Traffic Deaths, 2/17
Opioid Crisis, 10/16
Mosquito-Borne Disease, 7/16
Drinking Water Safety, 7/16
Virtual Reality, 2/16

Politics/Economy
Trump Presidency, 1/17
European Union's Future, 12/16
The Obama Legacy, 11/16
Populism and Party Politics, 9/16
U.S.-Mexico Relations, 9/16

Upcoming Reports

Women in Prison, 3/3/17

Charter Schools, 3/10/17

Alt-Right Movement, 3/17/17

ACCESS

CQ Researcher is available in print and online. For access, visit your library or www.cqresearcher.com.

STAY CURRENT

For notice of upcoming *CQ Researcher* reports or to learn more about *CQ Researcher* products, subscribe to the free email newsletters, *CQ Researcher Alert!* and *CQ Researcher News*: http://cqpress.com/newsletters.

PURCHASE

To purchase a *CQ Researcher* report in print or electronic format (PDF), visit www.cqpress.com or call 866-427-7737. Single reports start at $15. Bulk purchase discounts and electronic-rights licensing are also available.

SUBSCRIBE

Annual full-service *CQ Researcher* subscriptions—including 44 reports a year, monthly index updates, and a bound volume—start at $1,131. Add $25 for domestic postage.

CQ Researcher Online offers a backfile from 1991 and a number of tools to simplify research. For pricing information, call 800-818-7243 or 805-499-9774 or email librarysales@sagepub.com.

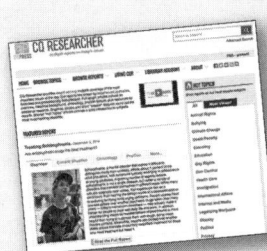

CQ RESEARCHER

CQPRESS

In-depth reports on today's issues

Published by CQ Press, an Imprint of SAGE Publications, Inc.

www.cqresearcher.com

Women in Prison

Should they be treated differently from men?

The number of women in state and federal prisons has surged since 1978 by nearly 800 percent — twice the growth rate for men. Mandatory sentences for drug offenses enacted during the 1980s and 1990s have hit women particularly hard, many experts say. But some prosecutors and Republicans dispute the claim that the so-called war on drugs has disproportionately hurt women. They say mandatory sentencing has reduced crime, helped break up drug rings and ended sentencing disparities. Reformers hope states' recent efforts to reduce prison populations and spend more on drug treatment will help women. But they say women still remain an afterthought in the penal system. For example, reformers say courts and prisons rarely recognize women's responsibility as mothers or the factors underlying their participation in crime, such as domestic abuse. The justice system, women's advocates say, needs to think creatively about how to help female prisoners. Meanwhile, in the juvenile system, girls often receive harsher punishments than boys who commit similar offenses.

Women make up 7 percent of the nation's prison population. Since 1978, the number of women in state and federal prisons has surged by almost 800 percent. Above, women in the Julia Tutwiler Prison for Women in Wetumpka, Ala.

CQ Researcher • March 3, 2017 • www.cqresearcher.com
Volume 27, Number 9 • Pages 193-216

I N S I D E THIS REPORT

THE ISSUES **195**

BACKGROUND **201**

CHRONOLOGY **203**

CURRENT SITUATION **208**

AT ISSUE......................**209**

OUTLOOK **211**

BIBLIOGRAPHY **214**

THE NEXT STEP **215**

WOMEN IN PRISON

CQ RESEARCHER

THE ISSUES

195 • Are harsh drug laws responsible for the high number of women in prison?
• Have mandatory sentences unfairly punished women?
• Should women offenders be treated differently from men?

BACKGROUND

201 **Prison Reform**
Early reformers debated how female prisoners should be treated.

202 **Return to Punishment**
U.S. prisons focused on rehabilitation until the 1970s.

202 **Crack Epidemic**
The "war on drugs" hurt women, some experts say.

205 **Sentencing Reform**
With prisons overflowing, states have begun reducing penalties for drug offenders.

CURRENT SITUATION

208 **Federal Actions**
Sentencing reform remains uncertain under the Trump administration.

211 **State Actions**
States are taking differing approaches to sentencing reform.

OUTLOOK

211 **Crackdown Feared**
Crime rates remain at a 20-year low, yet worries about crime are at a 15-year high.

SIDEBARS AND GRAPHICS

196 **Prison Rates for Females Soared Since 1980s**
The incarceration rate for women rose sixfold from 1978 to 2015.

197 **Minority Girls Over-represented in Juvenile System**
Native American girls have the highest detention rate.

200 **Incarceration of Women Highest in Rural States**
Oklahoma incarcerates women at the highest rate.

203 **Chronology**
Key events since 1873.

204 **Advocates Want Courts to Consider Domestic Violence Evidence**
Many women prisoners were victims of abuse, studies find.

206 **Double Standard Seen for Girls in Juvenile System**
Girls are arrested more often than boys for minor offenses.

209 **At Issue:**
Should mandatory minimum sentences be repealed?

FOR FURTHER RESEARCH

213 **For More Information**
Organizations to contact.

214 **Bibliography**
Selected sources used.

215 **The Next Step**
Additional articles.

215 **Citing CQ Researcher**
Sample bibliography formats.

March 3, 2017
Volume 27, Number 9

EXECUTIVE EDITOR: Thomas J. Billitteri
tjb@sagepub.com

ASSISTANT MANAGING EDITORS: Kenneth Fireman, kenneth.fireman@sagepub.com, Kathy Koch, kathy.koch@sagepub.com, Scott Rohrer, scott.rohrer@sagepub.com

SENIOR CONTRIBUTING EDITOR:
Thomas J. Colin
tom.colin@sagepub.com

CONTRIBUTING WRITERS: Marcia Clemmitt, Sarah Glazer, Reed Karaim, Barbara Mantel, Chuck McCutcheon, Tom Price

SENIOR PROJECT EDITOR: Olu B. Davis

EDITORIAL ASSISTANT: Anika Reed

FACT CHECKERS: Eva P. Dasher, Michelle Harris, Betsy Towner Levine, Robin Palmer

Los Angeles I London I New Delhi
Singapore I Washington DC I Melbourne

An Imprint of SAGE Publications, Inc.

SENIOR VICE PRESIDENT,
GLOBAL LEARNING RESOURCES:
Karen Phillips

EXECUTIVE DIRECTOR, ONLINE LIBRARY AND REFERENCE PUBLISHING:
Todd Baldwin

Copyright © 2017 CQ Press, an Imprint of SAGE Publications, Inc. SAGE reserves all copyright and other rights herein, unless previously specified in writing. No part of this publication may be reproduced electronically or otherwise, without prior written permission. Unauthorized reproduction or transmission of SAGE copyrighted material is a violation of federal law carrying civil fines of up to $100,000.

CQ Press is a registered trademark of Congressional Quarterly Inc.

CQ Researcher (ISSN 1056-2036) is printed on acid-free paper. Published weekly, except: (March wk. 4) (May wk. 4) (July wks. 1, 2) (Aug. wks. 2, 3) (Nov. wk. 4) and (Dec. wks. 3, 4). Published by SAGE Publications, Inc., 2455 Teller Rd., Thousand Oaks, CA 91320. Annual full-service subscriptions start at $1,131. For pricing, call 1-800-818-7243. To purchase a CQ Researcher report in print or electronic format (PDF), visit www.cqpress. com or call 866-427-7737. Single reports start at $15. Bulk purchase discounts and electronic-rights licensing are also available. Periodicals postage paid at Thousand Oaks, California, and at additional mailing offices. POSTMASTER: Send address changes to CQ Researcher, 2600 Virginia Ave., N.W., Suite 600, Washington, DC 20037.

Cover: AP Photo/*The Montgomery Advertiser*/Albert Cesare

Women in Prison

BY SARAH GLAZER

THE ISSUES

In 2015, Ramona Brant had served almost 21 years of a life sentence for conspiracy to distribute crack cocaine, even though she said she was merely a bystander in the dealings of an abusive boyfriend. [1]

Brant said her boyfriend, who authorities alleged had been running a multimillion-dollar interstate drug operation, had beaten Brant so severely that she had landed in the emergency room numerous times. When Brant tried to leave him, she said, he beat up her brother and threatened to kill her mother.

Brant denied dealing drugs. She thought she had a defense: the hospital records and police reports documenting the abuse that forced her to accompany her boyfriend during drug-dealing trips. However, her public defender never presented those records at the trial.

Under mandatory federal sentencing guidelines in force at the time, the judge sent her to prison for life, citing the amount of drugs her boyfriend's drug ring had sold. In December 2015, President Barack Obama granted clemency to Brant, and she was released from prison on Feb. 2, 2016. [2]

"There are a lot of Ramonas" still serving lengthy sentences, says Amy Povah, who served more than nine years of a 24-year sentence in federal prison in connection with the ecstasy-drug-selling activities of her husband before receiving clemency in 2000. [3]

Povah is founder of CAN-DO, a nonprofit in Malibu, Calif., that seeks clemency for prisoners serving long sentences for nonviolent drug offenses. "A lot of [women] are like me," she says. "We

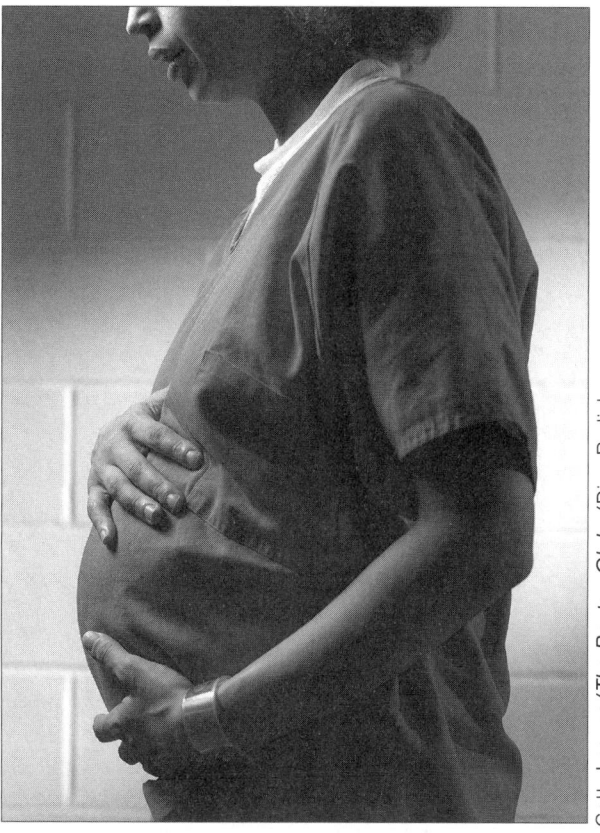

The nation's female prison population has remained stubbornly high, but some researchers say prisons are not meeting the medical and psychological needs of female inmates. "The reproductive issues of women make the provision of health care more complicated for women than for men," said University of Massachusetts human services professor Sylvia Mignon. Above, a pregnant inmate at the Western Massachusetts Regional Women's Correctional Center in Chicopee.

Getty Images/The Boston Globe/Dina Rudick

didn't wake up one day and say, 'I want to sell drugs.' We were in love with a man or we participated in some minor way, but it was the man driving it, and we were held equally culpable for their actions."

Since 1978, the female population in state and federal prisons has surged by almost 800 percent, about twice the growth rate for men, although women are only 7 percent of the nation's prison population. [4]

Brant's case exemplifies many of the forces that experts say have helped drive this rise:

• Ramped-up anti-drug enforcement starting in the mid-1980s;

• State and federal laws imposing lengthy mandatory sentences that don't take into account the personal circumstances of women;

• Increasingly aggressive prosecution, and

• Lack of treatment for the root causes of crime, such as addiction.

The majority of women in prison, according to researchers, have suffered some kind of trauma, such as domestic or sexual violence; many are addicts; and many suffer from serious mental illness. [5] "Prison is a place where those things generally will get worse — for mothers and their children," says Georgia Lerner, executive director of the Women's Prison Association in New York City, which helps women involved in the criminal justice system.

About half of the nation's 222,000 women behind bars are being held in local jails, where the female population has exploded in recent years, jumping fourteenfold since 1970. During that same period, the male jail population increased only fivefold, according to a recent report by the Vera Institute of Justice, a research organization in New York City, and the John D. and Catherine T. MacArthur Foundation in Chicago. Jails detain people who are awaiting trial — often because they cannot afford bail — or for low-level crimes carrying a sentence of a year or less. [6]

Women are the poster child for "what's wrong with America's use and misuse of jails," especially when faced with women's cumulative vulnerabilities, according to Laurie Garduqe, director of justice reform for MacArthur. As low-income, single heads of households, they often end up in jail because they can't afford bail or fines. Then, for many

Prison Rates for Females Soared Since 1980s

The proportion of females serving time in state or federal prisons rose more than sixfold from 1978 to 2015, from 10 to 64 women per 100,000 female U.S. residents.

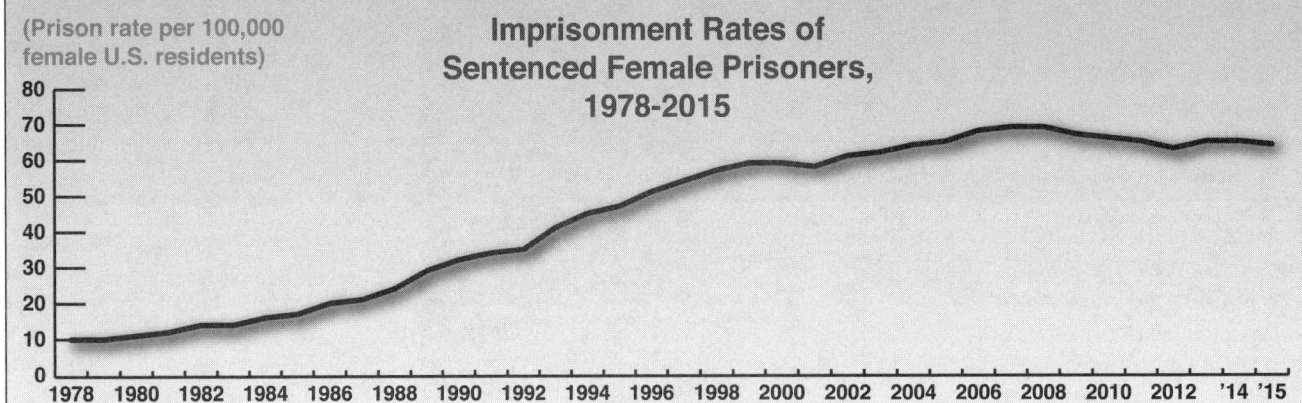

(Prison rate per 100,000 female U.S. residents)

Imprisonment Rates of Sentenced Female Prisoners, 1978-2015

Source: "Imprisonment rate of sentenced female prisoners under the jurisdiction of state or federal correctional authorities per 100,000 female U.S. residents," Bureau of Justice Statistics, Sept. 23, 2016, http://tinyurl.com/hzvfaj9

women, jails become gateways to longer-term incarceration in state prisons. [7]

Experts are still trying to tease out the causes for the dramatic rise in women being incarcerated.

"Even after doing this research we don't have a complete answer to this question," says Elizabeth Swavola, lead author of the Vera report and senior program associate with Vera's Center on Sentencing and Corrections. She cites one factor in particular: an increased focus on arresting people for low-level, quality-of-life offenses, such as public intoxication, disorderly conduct and vagrancy. That approach, plus the escalation in the nation's so-called war on drugs in the 1980s and '90s, targeted low-level activities such as drug possession, in which women are more likely to be involved, according to the Vera Institute. [8]

Nearly 60 percent — 58.6 percent — of the women in federal prisons were convicted of drug offenses. Most women in local jails were arrested for nonviolent offenses, such as drug possession or property offenses like shoplifting, and they were less likely than men to have an extensive criminal history. [9]

It's a different story at the state level, however, where only 25 percent of the women are in state prisons for drug-related crimes. And prosecutors note that more than a third (36 percent) of the 93,536 women in state prisons at the end of 2014 were convicted of violent crimes, including murder. That was up from 28 percent in 1998, according to the Bureau of Justice Statistics. [10]

But Lauren-Brooke Eisen, senior counsel at New York University's Brennan Center for Justice, says more than 40 percent of women in state or federal prison are unnecessarily incarcerated if society's prime concern is whether they pose a threat to public safety. "We need to think more creatively [about] how we punish; prison isn't the only sanction," she says, suggesting alternatives such as court-ordered drug treatment, electronic monitoring and community service. [11]

Women also are especially vulnerable to arrest for technical violations of probation, such as not showing up for a court-ordered appointment or missing a drug test, according to Vera. Nearly 80 percent of women in jail are mothers with mostly younger children, and they often have trouble finding childcare. [12]

"Treating women equally is not necessarily just," says Swavola. "Women are different."

Some researchers also note that jails and prisons are not meeting the special medical and psychological needs of female inmates. Incarcerated women "have significant health problems," said Sylvia Mignon, professor of human services at the University of Massachusetts, Boston. "The reproductive issues of women make the provision of health care more complicated for women than for men and are an additional challenge to health care services within prison walls." [13]

Small, mainly rural counties in the South have some of the nation's highest rates of incarceration, spurring much of the huge growth of the nation's female jail population, according to Christian Henrichson, research director of Vera's Center on Sentencing and Corrections. [14]

The trend is puzzling, experts say, because small counties are not crime centers. "No one's saying this rise is because there's a crime wave among women" either nationally or in rural areas, says Henrichson. However, rural counties have been hit especially hard by a nationwide opioid crisis, he says, and jail is "the landing place where women go if addicted and there's not a treatment or a care facility in that county." [15]

Since peaking in 2008, the female prison population has remained at a stubbornly high level, largely because of the surging imprisonment rate among white women, even as the rate among black women has fallen. Experts suggest white women may have been affected to a greater extent by the methamphetamine and prescription opioid crises.

Growing attention to the condition of women behind bars has raised many of the same questions as the debate surrounding mandatory minimum sentences: Do lengthy mandatory sentences curb crime? Would drug treatment be more effective in preventing crime?

Since 2000, dozens of states, burdened with the cost of overcrowded prisons, have rolled back some of the harshest mandatory minimums and drug penalties enacted over the last 30 years. [16] More than two dozen states — including conservative Southern states such as Mississippi and Alabama — have participated in a Justice Department-funded program since 2007 to reduce prison populations by, among other things, shortening sentences. Participating states use the money saved from lower prison costs for drug treatment and prisoner rehabilitation. [17]

Despite President Trump's tough-on-crime campaign rhetoric, the momentum for this kind of state sentencing reform "is certainly continuing," says Marc Levin, policy director of Right on Crime, an initiative begun by the conservative Texas Public Policy Foundation in Austin that aims to reduce spending on prisons and invest in more treatment for drug offenders.

The outlook for reforming federal mandatory minimum sentencing laws is uncertain, however. A bill to reduce some federal mandatory sentences, sponsored by Senate Judiciary Committee Chairman Chuck Grassley, R-Iowa, won bipartisan majority support in committee last year. But Republican lawmakers were deeply

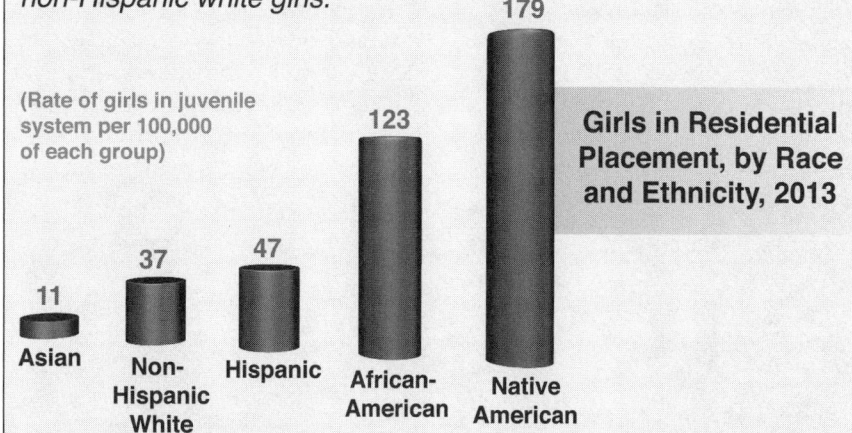

Minority Girls Over-represented in Juvenile System

A far higher proportion of minority girls are placed in juvenile justice residential facilities than white girls. Native American girls were sent to such facilities at a rate of 179 per 100,000, compared with 123 per 100,000 African-American girls and 37 per 100,000 non-Hispanic white girls.

(Rate of girls in juvenile system per 100,000 of each group)

Girls in Residential Placement, by Race and Ethnicity, 2013

Asian 11
Non-Hispanic White 37
Hispanic 47
African-American 123
Native American 179

Source: Malika Saada Saar et al., "The Sexual Abuse To Prison Pipeline: The Girls' Story," Human Rights Project for Girls, Georgetown Law Center on Poverty and Inequality, Ms. Foundation for Women, 2015, http://tinyurl.com/ntnlyxw

divided on the issue during an election year, and the GOP leadership did not bring the measure to the Senate floor. [18]

As prisoners, their advocates, judicial reform proponents and lawmakers discuss the problems of women in prisons, here are some of the questions being debated:

Are harsh drug laws responsible for the high number of women in prison?

During the crack cocaine epidemic in the 1980s and early '90s, the nation's intensified effort to stop the sale and distribution of illegal drugs hit women particularly hard, experts say. As state and federal mandatory minimum sentencing laws were adopted, they say, women increasingly got caught in the criminal justice system's expanding net.

"[T]he war on drugs has been a war on women, particularly women of color," Emily Salisbury, who teaches criminal justice at the University of Nevada, Las Vegas, told a justice conference recently. What has been driving

the spike in women's imprisonment, she said, "is not women becoming more violent or becoming more problematic, but the fact that our sentencing laws have changed." [19] Between 1980 and 2009, the arrest rate among women for drug possession or use tripled, while it doubled for men. [20]

That trend is reflected in the nation's state and federal prisons: The 25 percent of women in state prisons for drug-related offenses is double the 12 percent rate in 1986, at the start of the drug-war era. By comparison only 15 percent of the men currently in state prisons are there for drug offenses, and less than half of the men in federal prisons (compared to the nearly 60 percent of women). [21]

The high percentage of women — compared with men — serving time for drug offenses shows how the war on drugs disproportionately affected women, said Marc Mauer, executive director of the Washington, D.C.-based Sentencing Project, which advocates reforms in sentencing. "Since women have always represented a small share of persons committing violent crimes, their numbers in prison would not have grown as dramatically had it not been for changes in drug enforcement policies and practices," he wrote in an analysis of trends starting in the 1980s. [22]

However, Fordham University law professor John Pfaff contends that reformers have overemphasized the role of the drug crackdown and mandatory sentencing on the prison population increase. In a new book, Pfaff attributed the rise to increasingly aggressive prosecutors.

federal criminal justice system "is working exactly as Congress carefully intended and designed it to work." The association also denies that sentences are overly punitive. Sentencing reform, the association said in a November 2016 letter to candidate Trump, "would seriously undermine our ability to disrupt and dismantle violent gangs and domestic and international drug trafficking organizations." [24]

Surprisingly, the current female prison population "is being maintained by surging imprisonment among

in urban neighborhoods and a shift in big cities' policing away from arrests for possession of small amounts of drugs such as marijuana. [26] Black women are still imprisoned at twice the rate of white women, but that is down dramatically from the early 1990s, when they were imprisoned at six times the rate of whites. [27]

The long-term rise in women prisoners has masked some dramatic decreases in big cities. New York City's prison population — for both men and women — has shrunk by more than 50 percent since the mid-'90s, according to Michael Jacobson, a former New York City correction commissioner who is now executive director of the Institute for State and Local Governance at the City University of New York.

The biggest reason is "huge changes" in police enforcement practices, as police officers cracked down on minor law-breaking, a strategy that coincided with a drop in major crime, says Jacobson. "The admission stream to jail in New York City completely flipped, from overwhelmingly felonies to misdemeanors," he says. The jail population fell sharply "because that mix changed."

However, in rural county jails, the increasing focus on low-level infractions seems to have had the opposite effect — it has sent women to jail for offenses they never got arrested for before, according to the Vera Institute's Henrichson. In 1970, 70 percent of the nation's counties did not have a single woman in jail; now some of those rural counties have the highest rates of jailed women in the country. "It's not as if women were not using drugs or as if no crime was committed by women in the 1970s," he says. "What has changed in America since 1970?"

What's changed, some experts hypothesize, is the "over-criminalization" of small infractions like driving with a broken tail light or the "crime of poverty" — arresting someone for failing to pay fines or keeping them in jail

A female defendant represented by a public defender appears in drug court in Joliet, Ill. Reformers hope states' efforts to reduce prison populations and spend more on drug treatment will help women. But they say women still remain an afterthought in the penal system.

Getty Images/Bloomberg/Daniel Acker

Between 1994 and 2008, he writes, crime was falling and fewer arrests were being made, but those arrested were increasingly being charged with felonies, serious crimes carrying a prison sentence of more than a year. The decision on whether to charge someone with a felony is often up to the prosecutor. In the 1990s and 2000s, Pfaff wrote, "the probability that a prosecutor would file felony charges against an arrestee basically doubled." [23]

The National Association of Assistant U.S. Attorneys denies that prosecutors were overly aggressive and says the

women of a particular race: whites," said Keith Humphreys, a professor of psychiatry and behavioral sciences at Stanford University. Both white and black women had been entering prison in rising numbers since the 1980s, but in 2000 the number and rate of black women being incarcerated began to fall, while white women continued a 30-year rise, possibly because of the methamphetamine and prescription-opioid crises. [25]

The falling incarceration rates among African-American women may be due to the waning of the crack epidemic

because of their inability to afford bail. Many localities have begun using the court system as a way to generate revenue by writing more tickets and jailing more people and charging them for their room and board, experts say. When judges do set bail, women are less able to afford it, according to Vera's report on jails. [28]

In places where low-level crimes are pursued with greater vigor, more cash-strapped women may find themselves behind bars, Henrichson says.

Have mandatory sentences unfairly punished women?

In December 2003, Mandy Martinson, a dental hygienist in rural Mason City, Iowa, started dating a man who sold methamphetamine. He moved in with her and she let him store drugs in her house. Five weeks later, police raided her house and found two pounds of methamphetamine, 10 pounds of marijuana and a gun in a bag containing Martinson's purse.

Martinson said she never sold drugs or carried a gun, but she traveled with her boyfriend when he picked up drugs from his supplier and helped him bundle the cash from his drug profits. [29]

At her trial, the judge said he was forced against his judgment to sentence Martinson to the 15 years mandated by Congress: 10 years for conspiracy to sell 500 grams or more of methamphetamine and marijuana and five additional years for possession of a gun during a trafficking crime. [30]

Noting Martinson's tangential role, the judge expressed dismay that she was getting a longer sentence than her boyfriend's 12 years. As is often the case in women's drug convictions, their trafficking boyfriends can get reduced sentences by giving the prosecutors information on drug rings. Martinson said she couldn't provide information valuable enough to get a similar plea deal.

The mandatory sentence in Martinson's case stems from the Anti-Drug Abuse Act passed by Congress in 1986 at the height of the crack cocaine era. To punish drug-trafficking "kingpins," Congress tied mandatory minimum sentences to the quantity of drugs captured from the entire ring, rather than to the role of an individual in an operation.

Congress also added federal drug conspiracy provisions to the law in 1988, creating an "unjust" system that ends up with women often receiving longer sentences than the men, says Jesselyn McCurdy, deputy director of the American Civil Liberties Union (ACLU) Washington legislative office.

"It doesn't take much to be considered part of a drug conspiracy in the federal system, and that's often how women get caught," she says. "We call it the 'girlfriend problem.' Either the husband or boyfriend is involved in drug dealing and the women take the money to the bank or take a phone call and are considered part of the conspiracy."

Similar "complicity" provisions in state laws recognize no difference between major and minor accomplices, according to the Vera Institute. Women can face the same sentence as ringleaders by taking a phone message or letting a partner keep drugs or firearms at their home. [31]

However, Steve Cook, an assistant U.S. attorney in the Eastern District of Tennessee and the president of the National Association of Assistant U.S. Attorneys, says, "I don't see any statistical support for any conclusion that females are disproportionately impacted by mandatory minimums." For example, female offenders were convicted under federal mandatory minimum sentencing laws at a lower rate (24 percent) than male offenders (27 percent), according to the U.S. Sentencing Commission. [32]

Cook also doubts that a girlfriend typically has little knowledge of her boyfriend's drug ring: "The truth is more often than not they're very close to the offender and they know who their associates are and what role they play." Fear is more of a barrier than ignorance in his experience. "In the vast majority of cases one of the first things they say is, 'He's going to hurt me or my family,' " according to Cook.

Defenders of mandatory sentences say the laws have been responsible for the dramatic drop in the nation's crime rates. Violent crime has fallen by about half since 1991. [33]

"The mandatory minimums are a critical part of our ability to disrupt drug-trafficking organizations," says Cook. "Regardless of [someone's] role in the organization, the ability to use those mandatory minimums," with the threat of a long sentence to encourage cooperation, "is a cornerstone to our ability to fight those crime problems."

Cook and others also credit the 1984 Sentencing Reform Act for bringing consistency to federal sentencing by creating mandatory sentencing guidelines for each crime, including drug trafficking.

"If you give too much discretion to sentencing judges, you get different results depending on which judge a defendant draws, versus what he deserves; that concern remains valid today," says Kent Scheidegger, legal director of the conservative Criminal Justice Legal Foundation, a public interest law firm in Sacramento, Calif. "People who want to go all the way back to before the 1984 Sentencing Reform Act are saying we're going back to the problem we tried to get rid of."

Yet Douglas A. Berman, a law professor at Ohio State University and a long-standing critic of mandatory sentences, says both the sentencing guidelines and the congressionally set mandatory minimums put women at a distinct disadvantage. Historically, he says, judges had exhibited "a soft paternalism" in sentencing women and were allowed to consider their individual circumstances, such as the impact of a long sentence on their children.

In an effort to prevent racial bias, however, the 1984 sentencing guidelines specified that judges could no longer consider factors like gender or race.

Incarceration of Women Highest in Rural States

Largely rural states such as Oklahoma, Kentucky and Idaho had the highest rates of incarcerated women in 2015. Oklahoma's rate was more than 13 times that of Rhode Island, which had the lowest rate.

Imprisonment Rate of Sentenced Female Prisoners by State, 2015
(Per 100,000 women in the adult population)

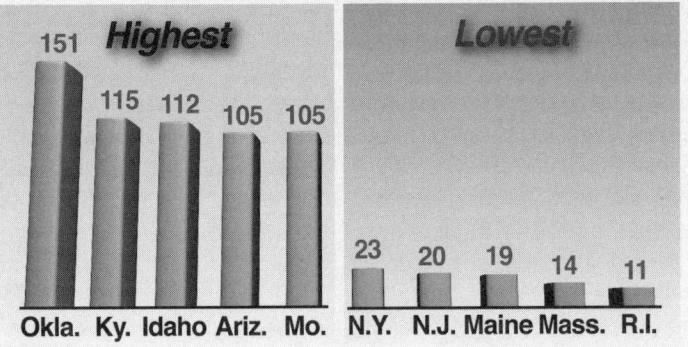

Source: E. Ann Carson and Elizabeth Anderson, "Prisoners in 2015," Bureau of Justice Statistics, December 2016, http://tinyurl.com/gvwp6ds

By taking away judges' discretion, "we formally limited the opportunities . . . that historically benefited female offenders," says Berman, "so over the range of cases women get more time and serve more time."

Cook notes, however, that judges have more discretion today after the Supreme Court in 2005 held that the sentencing guidelines were "advisory" and thus not binding on judges. As a result, some of the harshest sentences mandated by the guidelines, such as Brant's life sentence, would not occur today if the judge considered it inappropriate.

Should women offenders be treated differently from men?

After she got into a street altercation with her partner, Tamika was facing two to four years in prison for first-degree assault and the loss of her two daughters.

Then she learned about a New York City program, JusticeHome, which would allow her to stay at home with her two daughters rather than serve her sentence behind bars. She was able to complete the program in nine

months, and today she lives at home and is in school. [34]

For some time, experts have said most aspects of the criminal justice system — from prison uniforms to rehabilitation programs — have been designed for men, who make up about 93 percent of the nation's prison population. [35]

Cities and counties have been experimenting with diverting criminal offenders into programs that tackle the root causes of their crimes, such as addiction. "But virtually all of these alternative responses stem from research on men in jail," according to a recent report from the Vera Institute of Justice. [36]

Recently, several programs around the country have started to focus on female offenders. Recognizing that women who run afoul of the law are more likely than men to be the primary caretakers of small children and suffer from higher rates of addiction, mental illness and past sexual or physical abuse, these programs aim to help women outside of the prison setting.

For instance, the court can assign women with drug-related offenses in Tulsa, Okla., to the 14- to 18-month

Women in Recovery program, which houses the women in apartments while they receive treatment for addiction and mental health. It also helps them find housing and employment and to reunify with their children. The program was begun in 2009 with money from the George Kaiser Family Foundation after it realized Oklahoma had the nation's highest female incarceration rate.

"It's very easy in Oklahoma to get a felony conviction because we have a lot of mandatory minimums and no well-funded mental health or substance abuse agency," says Amy Santee, senior program officer at Kaiser.

Since its inception, the program has graduated 301 women. In the past three years it has had a recidivism rate of 3.5 percent compared with the state's 13 percent rate for imprisoned women, according to program Director Mimi Tarrasch.

Elizabeth Swavola, co-author of a 2016 Vera Institute of Justice report, says that vocational programs in jail, such as heavy construction, often are inappropriate for women. In addition, the report said, pretrial risk assessment tools used by a growing number of courts to decide if a defendant is a high risk for fleeing or committing another crime often assess women as riskier than they are. That's because many of these tools are based on research about men and don't take into account women's stronger ties to their families and communities. As a result, women who should be released are kept behind bars, said the report's authors. [37]

JusticeHome is based on research that found women are less likely to reoffend when allowed to stay with their children. "There's a spike in women arrested within a couple of months after children are removed; children are the last thing helping women hold everything together," according to Lerner of the Women's Prison Association, which runs the program.

During a six-to-nine-month stay in the program, women receive guidance on parenting, treatment for substance abuse or mental health problems and help with basic needs like housing and employment. Since JusticeHome began in 2013, 36 women with charges ranging from drug possession to robbery have successfully completed the program, and only five have been re-arrested, according to Eric Grossman, JusticeHome's director.

But some prosecutors and judges have been reluctant to refer women to the program if they've committed serious crimes, says Lerner. "There is this idea that it's not hard or we're not punishing people enough," she says. Yet even a short prison stay would defeat the purpose, she says, because the idea is to eliminate some of the "collateral consequences" of imprisonment — losing housing or jobs — that lead to reoffending.

Cook of the National Association of Assistant U.S. Attorneys questions whether it's fair or constitutional to offer such a program for women — and not men — if it could result in a sentencing disparity between the sexes. "We can't not punish prisoners for very serious criminal behavior because it has some collateral consequence," such as an impact on their children, he says.

Diana McHugh, communications director of the Women's Prison Association, responds, "There are plenty of well-funded diversion programs available for men. . . . The Women's Prison Association simply specializes in women as other programs specialize in youth or those with mental illness. Our intervention is designed for women based on women-specific risks."

Former federal Judge Nancy Gertner, who teaches law at Harvard University, has argued, "[W]omen's crime *is* different than men's crime." Family ties play a more important role "in the likelihood that they will recidivate, and in their chances of rehabilitation," she wrote. And because women are more likely to be caretakers, she said, "their im-

prisonment has a disproportionate impact on the children in their care." [38]

Many participants in Tulsa's Women in Recovery have children. Research has shown that once their mothers are imprisoned, children are "more likely to be abused, engage in criminal behavior, experiment with drugs and end up in prison themselves," said a recent press release from the program. Reunifying women with their children once they graduate from the program "helps to break the cycle of incarceration." [39] ∎

BACKGROUND

Prison Reform

Since the early 19th century, reformers have debated whether women prisoners should be treated differently from men.

The earliest Pennsylvania penitentiaries originated as a form of penal reform promoted by the Quakers, who prescribed solitary confinement for both men and women as a way to rebuild the individual through penitence and reflection.

"The idea is that women in theory could be treated the same as men — which is progressive for that time," says Erica Rhodes Hayden, a historian at Trevecca Nazarene University in Nashville, Tenn., and co-editor of the 2017 history, *Incarcerated Women.* [40] The reality, she says, was that women were "outside their cell doing washing and cooking for prison officials" and were often sexually exploited by male guards.

Racial disparities were another problem. Before the Civil War, few black women were imprisoned in the South because owners were responsible for disciplining their slaves. That changed after slavery ended. Under the so-called black codes enacted in the Reconstructionist South, blacks — but not whites — were penalized for

minor infractions such as being out after a certain hour. From 1831 to 1859, only three of Tennessee's women prisoners were black; after the Civil War 100 percent were. [41]

Things were not much better in the North, says Hayden. Before the Civil War, black women were arrested and convicted at high rates in nonslave states, she says, as were Irish and German immigrants.

In 1839, the first facility for women opened its doors — as an annex on the grounds of the male Sing Sing penitentiary in Ossining, N.Y. But women continued to experience high levels of corporal punishment and abuse by male guards.

As the 19th century ended, middle-class female reformers argued that women prisoners should be treated differently than men. They should have their own facilities and the focus should be on rehabilitation over punishment, the reformers said. The Indiana Reformatory Institution for Women and Girls, which opened in 1873, was the first all-female prison of this type. By 1940, nearly two dozen states had similar facilities. [42]

But, although these reformatories at first resembled campus-like settings with quaint cottages where women learned domestic skills, the facilities eventually came to resemble prisons where women who committed felonies were warehoused. [43]

The rehabilitation philosophy was doubled-edged: Women who had "fallen" into immoral ways were seen as both more criminal than men but also more capable of reformation if they were kept long enough in a reformatory.

During the Progressive era (1890s-1920s), concern about promiscuous women, "white slavery" and prostitution channeled many women from the streets into reformatories. During World War I reformatories from Connecticut to Arkansas began receiving women suspected of having venereal disease

— over concern about potential infection of soldiers.

In 1913, Pennsylvania passed the Muncy Act, requiring all women convicted of an offense punishable by more than one year in prison to be given an indefinite, or indeterminate, sentence. Other states passed similar

Prison was "used reluctantly as a punishment of last resort," wrote Todd Clear, a professor of criminal justice at Rutgers University, Newark. The prison population was so stable between the early 1900s and 1972, Clear said, that criminologists suggested it had reached the maximum level society would tolerate. [46]

pushed for passage of the Comprehensive Drug Abuse Prevention and Control Act of 1970, which emphasized treatment and rehabilitation and abolished federal mandatory minimum sentences enacted in the early 1950s for drug crimes. When Nixon left the White House in 1974, drug offenders still made up less than 7 percent of prisoners. [47]

But during the 1970s crime experts began to question the effectiveness of rehabilitation for criminals. An influential 1974 article titled "What Works?" by City University of New York sociologist Robert Martinson, who reviewed more than 200 studies, concluded essentially that "nothing works." [48]

The growing endorsement of "incapacitation" — locking up criminals for many years as the only way to stop crime — influenced state legislatures, starting in New York. Its drug laws came to be known as the Rockefeller drug laws because of enthusiastic support from Republican Gov. Nelson Rockefeller (1959-1973). The laws — which for years remained the nation's toughest — imposed a minimum sentence of 15 years to life for selling 2 ounces of marijuana, among other drugs, and 25 years to life for larger amounts. [49]

Getty Images/Bettmann

Republican President Richard M. Nixon, left, and Gov. Nelson Rockefeller, R-N.Y., pushed for tougher drug penalties in the 1970s. In his 1970 State of the Union address, Nixon announced a "war against the criminal elements." New York state's so-called Rockefeller drug laws imposed a minimum sentence of 15 years to life for selling 2 ounces of marijuana, among other drugs, and 25 years to life for larger amounts.

Crack Epidemic

The war on drugs — and the fallout from the so-called crack epidemic of the 1980s and early '90s — has been described as "a war on women" by several criminal justice experts. [50] In the 1980s, predominantly black neighborhoods in the inner cities faced a new drug — crack cocaine, which was cheap and could be smoked for a quick high. With its appearance came a surge in crack-related crime.

On Oct. 14, 1982, President Ronald Reagan declared his own "war on drugs," saying the use of illegal narcotics was a threat to national security. He later created the Office of National Drug Control Policy to coordinate drug-

Continued on p. 204

laws, and women were often sent to reformatories for longer terms than men were, even for the same offenses. [44] The law was not invalidated as discriminatory until 1968, freeing many women held under its provisions. [45]

Return to Punishment

In the early 20th century, U.S. prisons generally focused on rehabilitation, providing job training, education or psychological treatment for prisoners.

That began to change in the 1970s. In his State of the Union address, President Richard M. Nixon announced a "war against the criminal elements" in society and proposed doubling federal law enforcement spending. In 1971, with large numbers of veterans returning from the Vietnam War addicted to heroin, Nixon declared drug abuse "public enemy No. 1."

Although Nixon's declaration became known as the start of the "war on drugs," he had actually favored "public health responses over punitive ones," wrote Pfaff in *Locked In.* For example, Nixon

Chronology

19th Century
Reformers stress rehabilitation for women in separate reformatories.

1873
First all-female reformatory opens in Indiana.

1960s-1970s
Rehabilitation philosophy governs until drug-related crime wave leads to harsher laws.

1968
President Richard M. Nixon elected on law-and-order plank, soon declares war on drugs.

1973
New York's Rockefeller drug laws mandate long sentences for drugs.

1980s
Crack-related crime spurs Congress, states to pass lengthy mandatory penalties for drug traffickers, leading to rise in women prisoners.

1984
Sentencing Reform Act abolishes parole and creates commission to set mandatory sentencing guidelines.

1986
Congress mandates minimum sentences for drug traffickers, which unfairly impacts women, civil liberties advocates say.

1988
Congress mandates minimum sentence for conspiracy to distribute drugs, blamed for rising convictions of women with minimal roles.

1990s
Number of female inmates rises, as more states pass harsh drug sentences.

1991
Violent crime reaches all-time high.

1994
Violent Crime Control Act provides nearly $10 billion in state prison-building grants. . . . California enacts first "three strikes" law, imposing mandatory life sentence for third offense.

1999
Over half of states have three-strikes laws; 34 percent of women in state prison are there for drug offenses, 72 percent in federal prison.

2000s
Female prison population peaks; number of black women prisoners falls.

2002
Michigan eliminates mandatory sentences for most drug offenses.

2007
Gov. Rick Perry, R-Texas, urges legislative shift to rehabilitation to avoid billions in prison costs.

2008
Women's prison population peaks at 106,358 — up 9-fold from 1978.

2009
Rhode Island repeals mandatory sentences for drug offenses; New York also repeals some.

2010
Fair Sentencing Act cuts sentences for crack cocaine vs. powder cocaine. . . . Conservatives launch Right on Crime sentencing reform campaign; South Carolina eliminates some mandatory minimums.

2012
Violent crime falls to half its 1991 peak; state prison populations decline for third year in row as federal inmate population rises. . . . California relaxes three-strikes law.

2014
More than 30 states have rolled back mandatory minimums. . . . U.S. Sentencing Commission retroactively reduces drug trafficking penalties under federal guidelines.

2015
Bipartisan bill to reduce some drug mandatory minimums dies in Senate.

2016
Republicans blame murder spikes in some cities on early federal prisoner releases under new guidelines. . . . Donald Trump wins presidential election with tough-on-crime rhetoric; some reform prosecutors elected, displacing hardline district attorneys. . . . Oklahoma, with nation's highest rate of female incarceration, reduces some drug sentences and invests in treatment. . . . FBI announces more than 10 percent increase in murder in 2015. . . . Female prison population declines 1 percent in 2015 but remains more than eightfold the 1980 level; women in jail increase fourteenfold since 1970, the Vera Institute of Justice reports.

2017
Obama grants clemency to record number of prisoners, but only 6 percent are women; Sen. Chuck Grassley, R-Iowa, expected to re-introduce bill reducing some mandatory minimums. . . . Missouri considers legislation to repeal some mandatory minimums. . . . Trump announces task force to reduce violent crime (February). . . . Sentence-reform opponent Sen. Jeff Sessions, R-Ala., is sworn in as attorney general, saying America has "a crime problem."

Advocates Want Courts to Consider Abuse Evidence

Many women prisoners were victims of domestic violence.

On the night of Dec. 17, 1991, 25-year-old Kim Dadou was happy to see her boyfriend drive up to her mother's house in Rochester, N.Y., despite their four-year, on-and-off relationship that she said included beatings from him.

She joined him in the car out front and they started kissing, Dadou recalled, but 250-pound Darnell Sanders got angry when she refused his further advances and began to choke her. She said she reached for the gun Sanders kept under the seat and fired. She fled the car, and he drove away, according to Dadou.[1]

The next day, police found Sanders' body in a snow bank. Dadou was convicted of first-degree manslaughter and sentenced to eight to 25 years in prison. She was released in 2008.

At the trial, the judge refused to admit into evidence police reports about Sanders' five arrests for assault, the hospital records of Dadou's treatment for beatings, battered-women shelter records or witness statements attesting to the abuse.[2]

Because judges have broad discretion in determining what evidence is relevant and admissible, "it is not uncommon for judges to exclude evidence of domestic violence," according to Gail T. Smith, director of the Women in Prison Project at the Correctional Association of New York, a nonprofit that advocates for prisoners.

Studies have shown that a large proportion of women in prison have been victims of domestic violence. In New York state, a study by the prison system found that 67 percent of women incarcerated for killing someone close to them in 2005 had been abused by that person.[3] But until the early 1990s, most states did not officially recognize battering as admissible evidence in cases involving murder charges. In 1992, California was among the first to permit evidence of "battered woman syndrome"

to be introduced at trial. (Current law now refers to it as "intimate partner battering," the term victims' advocates prefer.)[4]

A coalition of domestic violence victims' groups supports a bill in the New York Legislature that would allow judges to consider evidence of abuse when sentencing a female or male defendant whose crime was directly related to the abuse — either through self-defense or if the defendant's abuser coerced her into committing a crime.

The bill would allow judges to set shorter sentences than the mandatory minimum required under existing law or to order an alternative to incarceration. It would also allow prisoners whose crime was related to domestic violence to apply to the court for a rehearing on their sentence.

The Correctional Association estimates that at least 357 people in New York state prisons would be eligible under the bill, as would another 483 per year in the court system.[5]

The Assembly passed the bill in the last session, but it did not advance to a floor vote in the Senate. It has since been reintroduced. The main opposition comes from the District Attorneys Association of the State of New York. The bill "ignores the harm caused to the actual crime victim," the association said in a 2012 letter, "and creates a strong incentive for every violent offender to claim that he or she was subjected to some form of domestic abuse in order to receive a more lenient sentence."[6]

California enacted a series of laws between 1992 and 2012 permitting prisoners whose abuse received only a limited hearing at trial to petition for a rehearing on their conviction or sentence. The laws also require the parole board to consider evidence of abuse when making parole decisions.

However, the changes haven't worked as well as advocates had hoped, according to Colby Lenz, legal advocate with the

Continued from p. 202

related legislative, diplomatic, research and health policy throughout the government. The media dubbed the agency's directors "drug czars."[51]

Growing inner-city crime and shootings became a regular feature of nightly news as competing drug gangs fought over turf. Congress passed the Anti-Drug Abuse Act of 1986, establishing mandatory minimum sentences triggered by specific quantities of crack and powder cocaine. Congress singled out crack cocaine for special treatment, penalizing it 100 times more severely than powder cocaine measured by the quantity seized.[52]

Between the late 1970s and early '80s, states began to establish similar "determinate" sentences — a precise sentence length or narrow range with less liberal policies on early release on the grounds that judges had too much discretion to set sentences. Both liberals and conservatives had criticized judicial discretion for leading to racially biased and widely varying sentences for the same crime. During this period, 19 states passed guidelines to reduce disparity in sentencing among judges.[53]

For similar reasons, Congress in 1984 passed the Sentencing Reform Act, replacing the parole system with a system of mandatory sentencing guidelines for

drug offenses and other crimes, to be set by a presidentially appointed U.S. Sentencing Commission. Yet this supposedly neutral system, prescribing a range of sentences starting at a mandatory minimum for each crime, put women defendants in a worse position than the old system, critics said.

And in 1988, Congress added conspiracy to commit a drug offense to the list of crimes subject to a mandatory minimum, a step the ACLU has said pulled many girlfriends and wives of drug dealers into the justice system. Under the law, every participant in a conspiracy can be held liable for the crime of every other participant.[54]

San Francisco-based advocacy group California Coalition for Women Prisoners. About 60 prisoners have been released since 2002, more than half through the parole process, but "so many more are eligible" — potentially hundreds, she says.

Many women filed their petitions over a decade ago and are still awaiting court action, according to Lenz.

The legislation applies only to prisoners convicted before 1996, when the state Supreme Court upheld California's battered-defense law. [7] But Lenz says that cut-off date disqualifies thousands of inmates who should be allowed a rehearing. Even into the late 1990s, she says, women often "weren't allowed to bring evidence or bring expert witnesses or were given expert witnesses who didn't know anything about domestic violence."

In Illinois, a similar law that went into effect in January 2016 adds a history of domestic violence to the list of mitigating factors judges can consider during sentencing. It also creates a process for courts to review petitions for resentencing for certain offenses committed by a victim of domestic violence who was unable to present evidence of domestic violence at trial. [8]

Chicago lawyer Margaret Byrne, co-director of the Illinois Clemency Project for Battered Women, says the law is so narrowly drawn that a woman can't avail herself of it if any evidence of abuse was presented at her court proceeding: "I would say of the hundreds of battered women I've represented in 35 years, probably none of them would have been able to use this law because some evidence comes out at trial, sentencing or plea negotiations."

Nevertheless, Byrne says prisoners' advocates are making progress. Compared to 20 years ago, "it's standard practice for a judge to take a history of abuse when sentencing," she says. "On the other hand, there's a persistent myth of the 'perfect battered woman.' Judges still feel, 'I know a battered woman

Kim Dadou of Rochester, N.Y., served 17 years in prison after being convicted of first-degree manslaughter. The trial judge refused to admit into evidence hospital records of Dadou's treatment for abuse by her boyfriend.

when I see one, and this one isn't, because she is an alcoholic or has previous convictions.' "

— ***Sarah Glazer***

[1] Natalie Pattillo, "She killed her abuser before he could kill her," *Salon*, Jan. 7, 2017, http://tinyurl.com/jgskka6.

[2] *Ibid.*

[3] "Women's Pathways into Crime," Bulletin, Office for the Prevention of Domestic Violence, New York State, Winter 2014, http://tinyurl.com/zmtu2jv.

[4] Jordan Rau, "Battered Women's Law OKd," *Los Angeles Times*, Sept. 18, 2004, http://tinyurl.com/hl7ph8o.

[5] "Justice and Dignity for DV Survivors in the Criminal Justice System," Women in Prison Project/Correctional Association of New York, March 2013, http://tinyurl.com/ja744du.

[6] Letter from Janet DiFiore, then president of the District Attorneys Association of the State of New York, to Assemblyman Jeffrion Aubry and State Sen. Ruth Hassell-Thompson, May 8, 2012, http://tinyurl.com/jpo29pf.

[7] Rau, *op. cit.*

[8] Dennis Robaugh, "New Illinois Laws 2016," *Joliet Patch*, Jan. 1, 2016, http://tinyurl.com/j8hduxx.

By the early 1990s, most states had passed a variety of laws mandating long sentences for drug offenses, violent offenses and career criminals. The trend accelerated after 1994, when Congress passed the Violent Crime Act endorsed by Democratic President Bill Clinton. It provided $30 billion for states in prison-building grants if they passed truth-in-sentencing laws requiring that 85 percent of a prisoner's sentence be served.

The law also mandated life sentences for some offenders convicted of a third offense — a "three strikes and you're out" habitual offender law Clinton had endorsed in his State of the Union address earlier that year. [55] More than half the states enacted similar three strikes laws in the 1990s, mandating minimum sentences of 25 years or longer. [56]

Ironically, crime rates had peaked in 1991 — three years before the federal law was passed. Between 1991 and 2000, homicide rates fell 30 percent, robbery 44 percent and rape 41 percent, the largest drop in crime of the 20th century. [57]

Yet many criminologists say the federal prison-building funds provided during the Clinton administration helped to trigger the largest jump in the federal and state prison population of any administration in U.S. history. Between 1975 and 2005, the nation's prison population exploded by 700 per-

cent and reached a peak of 1.6 million in 2009. [58]

The female state and federal prison population saw an even more dramatic surge, rising from less than 12,000 inmates in the late 1970s to a peak of 106,358 in 2008. [59] By 1999, drug offenses accounted for 72 percent of the female population in federal prison, 34 percent in state prison and 24 percent in local jails. [60]

Sentencing Reform

Over the last 15 years, state and federal governments have been rolling

Double Standard Seen for Girls in Juvenile System

Girls are arrested more often than boys for minor offenses.

When it comes to teens in trouble, not all things are equal, experts say. "National data shows that girls receive harsher punishment than boys for less serious offenses and are often detained to protect their safety rather than to protect the public," according to the Vera Institute of Justice, a research organization in New York City. [1]

For years, experts on adolescence and juvenile justice have been complaining that the juvenile-justice system treats girls differently. That's a particular concern because involvement in the system can easily become a pathway to adult prison. [2]

"Once a child is in the juvenile-justice system, their likelihood of ending up in the adult system is significantly higher," says Mary Marx, CEO of the PACE Center for Girls, a public-private partnership in Jacksonville, Fla., that runs education, counseling and advocacy programs for troubled girls. "For us, it's about shutting the door before they enter the system in the first place."

Girls of color also are more likely than others to be charged. In 2013, black girls were 20 percent more likely to be detained in the juvenile system than white girls. American Indian/Alaska native girls were 50 percent more likely to be detained. [3]

"Black girls are being criminalized in and by the very places that should help them thrive," wrote Monique W. Morris, co-founder of the National Black Women's Justice Institute, a Berkeley, Calif., advocacy group. Teachers viewed black girls as "loud, defiant and precocious," in one study she cites. [4]

In response to gang violence and school shootings in the 1990s, many public schools adopted "zero-tolerance" discipline policies, stationing police officers in hallways to keep order. That trend became the primary driver of school-based arrests, Morris writes. [5]

Girls tend to be arrested more often than boys for "status offenses," such as being truant, running away or drinking alcohol, that would not be crimes if committed by adults, according to a report from the National Crittenton Foundation, a group in Portland, Ore., that aims to help girls thrive. [6] Boys' arrest rates for violent crimes are four times that of girls. [7]

Although the number of juveniles in custody has fallen to half its early-2000s peak, the decline among girls hasn't been as steep as among boys. What's more, the number of girls in custody as a proportion of all juveniles arrested is rising in some regions. Nationally, girls' share of arrests grew from 20 percent in 1992 to 29 percent in 2012, and their share of detentions rose in that period from 15 percent to 21 percent. [8]

Girls are more likely than boys to be locked up for the same behavior. In 2013, 39 percent of girls who faced delinquency charges were detained for status offenses or technical violations, compared with 21 percent of boys. [9]

Arrests of girls for simple assault are frequently connected to their experience with violence and abuse in their homes, according to the Crittenton report. But the arrests can also be a response from desperate parents. Girls who are arrested "often have intense conflicts with their mother or father" in a chaotic family, says Lindsay Rosenthal, senior program associate at the Vera Institute of Justice. "Often it's parents who are at their wits' end and don't want the girls in the house anymore and call police."

Judges' tendency to try to protect girls can also land them in juvenile detention, Rosenthal says. "Often judges will openly admit they detain girls when they run away because they fear

back some of their harshest sentencing policies, in part because of the high cost of incarceration and a swing back toward rehabilitation and drug treatment.

Critics of the nation's drug laws also have long complained that they disproportionately damage black communities, particularly laws targeting crack, which is more popular among blacks, and favor the drug of choice among the white population — powder cocaine. Under the federal drug law passed in 1986, a person convicted of possessing 10 grams of crack would receive a 10-year-mandatory sentence; for powder cocaine, a person had to possess 100 times as much, or 1,000 grams, to be sentenced to 10 years — a 100:1 disparity. These harsh federal penalties,

similar state mandatory sentences and intensified police enforcement in black neighborhoods contributed to a much higher rate of imprisonment for black women than white women — six times higher by 2000, according to the Sentencing Project. [61]

In 2010, President Obama signed the Fair Sentencing Act, which reduced the federal penalties for crack and eliminated the mandatory minimum sentence for simple possession of crack. While the original bill would have eliminated the disparity between crack and powder entirely, a compromise with Senate Republicans legislated an 18:1 ratio. [62]

In 2014, the U.S. Sentencing Commission announced it would reduce penalties for most drug-trafficking of-

fenses, effective in late 2015. Those changes also applied retroactively, to inmates convicted under the guidelines in place before 2005, when they were still mandatory. However, the change has no impact on mandatory minimums set by congressional statute.

Nevertheless, some of sentencing commission's guideline ranges had previously gone far above the congressionally mandated minimums, and the changes in 2014 sought to bring the guidelines closer to congressional statutes. The commission also said the quantity of drugs no longer needed to play as large a role in determining the sentence.

Prisoners convicted under the previous guidelines could petition a court for early release. The commission es-

they will be raped or trafficked on the street, but wouldn't incarcerate a boy for the same reason," she says.

That tendency was one reason Florida began a program in 1985 aimed at preventing at-risk middle- and high-school girls from getting in trouble with the law. Girls referred by schools and judges receive intensive academic help and treatment for sexual abuse and other past trauma over 12 to 24 months at 19 centers around the state, run by the PACE Center. The recidivism rate for PACE graduates is 8 to 9 percent, compared with 45 percent for Florida's juvenile justice system, according to Marx.

New Florida laws that prohibit the arrest of juveniles for misdemeanors and authorize police officers to issue a civil citation instead have helped cut the number of girls' arrests in half over the past six years. The Legislature also directed schools to limit the disciplinary issues they refer to the justice system. [10]

New York City, partnering with the Vera Institute, established a task force in February that will study such approaches as part of an effort to end the detention of girls over the next three years. [11]

"We think there's an opportunity to get to zero girls [in detention] nationally," Rosenthal says. "The idea is by working in New York City and showing it can be done, it can spread around the country."

— Sarah Glazer

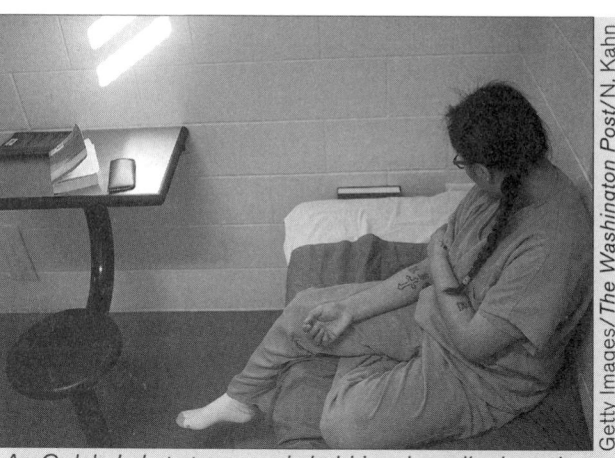

An Oglala Lakota teenager is held in a juvenile detention center in Kyle, S.D. A far higher proportion of Native American girls are held in juvenile justice residential facilities than other girls.

Getty Images/The Washington Post/N. Kahn

[1] "Ending Girls' Incarceration in New York City: Learn More," Vera Institute of Justice, 2017, http://tinyurl.com/jud5o5n.
[2] *Ibid.*

[3] Francine T. Sherman and Annie Balck, "Gender Injustice," National Crittenton Foundation 2015, http://tinyurl.com/h4zrrn3.
[4] Monique W. Morris, *Pushout: The Criminalization of Black Girls in Schools* (2016).
[5] *Ibid.*
[6] Sherman and Balck, *op. cit.* , pp. 4-5.
[7] "Statistical Briefing Book," Office of Juvenile Justice and Delinquency Prevention, U.S. Department of Justice, http://tinyurl.com/jnnrem7.
[8] Francine Sherman and Liz Ryan, "Locking up traumatized girls is no way to help them," *The Huffington Post*, June 2, 2015, http://tinyurl.com/p4y9jee.
[9] Office of Juvenile Justice and Delinquency Prevention, U.S. Department of Justice, "Detailed Offense Profile by Sex for the United States, 2013," http://tinyurl.com/zw462j6.
[10] Florida Statute on Misdemeanors, http://tinyurl.com/jvfp52m; Florida Statute on Civil Citation, http://tinyurl.com/gqkmufm; "Zero Tolerance," Florida Department of Education, http://tinyurl.com/jsex6um.
[11] "Ending Girls' Incarceration Is Goal of New Task Force in New York City," press release, Vera Institute of Justice, Feb. 2, 2017, http://tinyurl.com/ja5sssy.

timated that 46,000 prisoners sentenced between 1991 and 2014 would be eligible for reduced sentences. [63] So far, 67 percent of the motions filed have been granted, and 29,872 prisoners — of whom 7 percent were women — have been released. [64]

Since 2000, at least 30 states have passed legislation to move away from the severe mandatory minimums passed during the past 30 years. States' reconsideration has generally not extended to repeal, according to a recent summary of state trends in 2014 and 2015 from the Vera Institute of Justice. Instead, states have created "safety valves," giving judges the option to ignore a statutory mandatory sentence if certain factual criteria are met or a shorter

sentence is otherwise deemed appropriate. Some states have set a high bar for departing from mandatory sentences, while others have given judges more discretion. [65]

Alabama, Mississippi, Nebraska and Utah have joined the more than two dozen states that have reformed their criminal justice systems under the Justice Reinvestment Initiative. Funded by the Justice Department, the initiative enables states to use savings from reductions in prison populations to invest in drug treatment and other programs. [66]

However, women's experts have long criticized treatment and rehab programs for being mostly tailored to men — although data are scarce on how they affect women versus men. For example,

says Vera's Swavola, drug treatment programs often "do not address women's distinct needs, including high rates of trauma and co-occurring illness," and fail to account for women's child care responsibilities.

A high proportion of women on parole or probation do not successfully complete this supervision — often because they are struggling with child care responsibilities or having difficulties meeting financial obligations, securing jobs or finding safe housing. In a national study of post-prison recidivism, about 60 percent of women released were arrested again, and nearly 30 percent returned to prison within three years of release. [67]

A bipartisan movement evolved around sentencing reform in the previous

Congress, with support from Obama, but no legislation was passed. A bill introduced by Senate Judiciary Committee Chairman Grassley sought to reduce some drug and gun mandatory minimum sentences. Known as the Sentencing Reform and Corrections Act,

year, the GOP leadership did not bring the measure up for a floor vote.

The advocacy group Families Against Mandatory Minimums (FAMM) preferred another bill introduced by Sens. Rand Paul, R-Ky., and Patrick Leahy, D-Vt., that would have given

ident since Harry S. Truman: A total of 1,927 prisoners received clemency; 212 were pardoned (forgiveness for past crimes and had their civil rights restored); and 1,715 had their sentences commuted (completely or partially). [70]

Obama in January called the president's clemency power an "important and underutilized tool for advancing reform." In addition, he said, the "vast majority" of his commutation recipients "had already served far more time than the sentence they would receive today." [71]

However, Povah, whose organization CAN-DO helped women prisoners file clemency petitions, expressed dismay at the small number of women — 106 — who got clemency, just 6 percent of the total granted by Obama.

"The men who drove the drug war are the ones getting clemency, even if they are four-time offenders. How is it that they get it and first-offender women are being denied?" she asked. ▪

On March 30, 2016, then-President Obama met with former prison inmates Serena Nunn, left, and Ramona Brant, to whom he granted clemency. Brant served almost 21 years of a life sentence for conspiracy to distribute crack cocaine, even though she said she was only a bystander in the dealings of an abusive boyfriend. Obama granted clemency to a near-record number of prisoners before his term ended in January, but only 6 percent were women.

AFP/Getty Images/Nicholas Kamm

the measure also made retroactive the reduced crack cocaine penalties under the 2010 Fair Sentencing Act so that they could apply to inmates in federal prison convicted under the older sentencing policy.

Championing reform represented a remarkable turnaround for Grassley, who had vowed to kill any bills weakening mandatory sentences. However, he said in late 2015, "I've learned from what some states have done, [that] changes could be made and money could be saved and not hurt society with people that do harm coming from behind bars." [68]

Grassley's committee approved the bill in October 2015. But with congressional Republicans sharply divided on the issue and law-and-order Republicans opposing it in an election

judges discretion to ignore mandatory minimums in most cases as long as public safety was not harmed. But FAMM quickly threw its support behind Grassley's bill once it became clear it would be the main vehicle. So did liberal groups like the ACLU and the more conservative National District Attorneys Association.

However, the National Association of Assistant U.S. Attorneys strongly opposed legislation to weaken mandatory minimums. The organization pointed to a 10.8 percent spike in homicides in 2015, blaming — in part — the release of thousands of federal prisoners after the U.S. Sentencing Commission changed its guidelines in 2014. [69]

By the time Obama left office in January, he had used his clemency power more often than any other pres-

CURRENT SITUATION

Federal Actions

Despite bipartisan support in the last Congress for federal sentencing reform — which some experts say could dramatically help women — such legislation has uncertain prospects with Trump in the White House.

Sen. Grassley has said he plans to reintroduce his bill, substantially unchanged, to reduce some federal mandatory minimum sentences for drug and gun crimes. But it is unclear whether the bill will encounter the same kind of opposition it met in the last Congress. [72]

Attorney General Jeff Sessions likely will oppose any such legislation, based on his opposition to Grassley's bill last

Continued on p. 210

At Issue:

Should mandatory minimum sentences be repealed?

KEVIN RING
PRESIDENT, FAMILIES AGAINST MANDATORY MINIMUMS

WRITTEN FOR *CQ RESEARCHER*, MARCH 2017

*j*ournalist H.L. Mencken might as well have been discussing crime and mandatory minimum sentencing laws when he wrote in 1917, "For every complex problem, there is an answer that is clear, simple and wrong."

Mandatory sentencing laws have an intuitive, superficial appeal: Isn't it fair to give everyone who commits the same crime the same sentence? Think for just a moment longer, however, and you quickly realize that no two people — and no two crimes — are exactly the same.

Consider 55-year-old Iowa widow Shirley Schmitt. In 2013, she was convicted of conspiracy to distribute methamphetamine and sentenced to 10 years in prison. Her decade-long sentence was based on her part in manufacturing more than 50 grams of methamphetamine, a weight equal to about 20 pennies. Despite the small quantity involved, the law required the 10-year sentence — a prison term Congress thought would target kingpins and major suppliers.

But Schmitt was no kingpin or major dealer. The federal judge who was forced to sentence her to 10 years said, "All matters of methamphetamine manufacturing are serious. The Court's well aware of that. But this case, the evidence was pretty clear, that there wasn't anybody really selling any methamphetamine. There wasn't — nobody had any big cars or stacks of 20s in their pocket or anything like that. It involved a group of addicts who were satisfying their own addiction."

To be cost-efficient, our criminal justice system must operate with precision. Dangerous offenders should be held accountable and spend time in prison. It's obvious that releasing a dangerous offender too early can jeopardize public safety.

But so, too, can holding less-dangerous offenders too long: Prisoners who spend longer in prison than necessary are more likely to reoffend. Additionally, when we spend millions keeping people like Shirley Schmitt behind bars, we divert resources away from better anti-crime uses, like apprehending murderers and rapists.

Over the past few decades, numerous states have repealed or reformed their mandatory sentencing laws and watched their crime rates fall. New York state, for example, dramatically scaled back its infamous Rockefeller drug laws in 2009. Violent and property crime rates tumbled across the state and in New York City.

Treating all offenders and all crimes the same was an approach that proved clear, simple and wrong. To get tough on crime, we must eliminate mandatory minimums.

STEVE COOK
PRESIDENT, NATIONAL ASSOCIATION OF ASSISTANT U.S. ATTORNEYS

WRITTEN FOR *CQ RESEARCHER*, MARCH 2017

*f*ederal mandatory minimum penalties are perhaps the single most important tool available to law enforcement and to federal prosecutors to infiltrate, disrupt and dismantle violent gangs, international drug cartels and other drug-trafficking organizations. Congress should reject any call to weaken or repeal these laws.

In the mid-1980s, we faced a staggering crime wave. Violent crime had more than tripled. Congress responded by enacting mandatory minimum penalties for high-level drug-trafficking and serious firearm offenses. Using those tools, law enforcement targeted the worst of the worst and sent them to federal prison.

By 1991, we began to experience a dramatic reduction in violent crime, including homicides, rapes, robberies and assaults. By 2014, violent crime rates had been cut in half.

Those promoting weakening the federal criminal justice system describe drug traffickers as "nonviolent drug offenders." This is a ridiculously false description. The drug-trafficking business is inherently violent from top to bottom. Street-level dealers have a clientele desperate to get their product. Traffickers up the distribution chain routinely possess tens of thousands of dollars' worth of drugs or cash proceeds. Disputes among drug traffickers are not resolved in court; they are resolved on the streets through violence.

Moreover, even beyond the violence, drug trafficking exacts a high toll in our communities. In 2015 alone, there were over 52,000 overdose deaths in the United States. Sadly, these deaths are only the tip of a pyramid of harm. The pain of addiction, the crime generated, families torn apart, lost productivity and the costs to our health care system are immeasurable.

Changes weakening the federal criminal justice system have already been implemented, including the early release of tens of thousands of drug traffickers from federal prisons, a 27 percent reduction in federal prosecutions and an 11 percent reduction in the federal prison population.

Predictably, violent crime rates are now surging upward. In 2015 homicides increased a staggering 10.8 percent, rapes 6.3 percent and aggravated assaults 4.6 percent. While the official 2016 statistics will not be released for some time, preliminary figures look just as ominous.

In short, we are in the middle of a drug epidemic of historic proportion and face a wave of violent crime. We simply cannot further dismantle the federal criminal justice system by weakening the very laws to bring violent drug traffickers to justice.

Continued from p. 208

year when he was a Republican senator from Alabama and was serving on Grassley's committee. Releasing "thousands of violent criminals is a risky and possibly devastating social experiment in criminal leniency," he said. "The Senate bill would drastically reduce mandatory minimum sentences for all drug traffickers, even those who are armed and traffic in dangerous drugs like heroin, and provide for the early release of dangerous drug felons currently incarcerated in federal prison." [73]

In February, Trump directed the Justice Department to form a task force

declining since the crack epidemic of the 1990s, except for a few upticks. [75]

The number of women prisoners, meanwhile, has held steady in the past six years: About 105,000 women were sentenced to state or federal prisons in 2015, about the same number as in 2010, according to Bureau of Justice figures. [76]

The administration's power over sentencing is limited, because the vast majority of criminal prosecutions take place at the state level. Nonetheless, Trump could reverse a 2013 order from Obama's attorney general, Eric Holder, who directed federal prosecutors not to charge certain low-level nonviolent

Sessions was "an early supporter, and he has experience; Trump seems to like to delegate, so it seems like Sessions will have a strong influence" in opposing legislation to reduce mandatory minimums.

Marc Levin, who heads the conservative Right on Crime initiative, which supports reducing drug penalties, is a little more optimistic, noting that some of the rural areas hit hardest by the opioid crisis went overwhelmingly for Trump in the presidential election. "I don't think Trump ever said, 'We need to put more people in prison who are drug addicts,'" says Levin. "That's an open opportunity as to what his position will be."

However, federal prosecutors represented by the National Association of Assistant U.S. Attorneys strongly oppose any legislation to weaken mandatory minimums. "Letting dealers out of prison early has an impact; there's a reason they're in prison" the association's Cook says. He cites the case of Wendell Callahan, a drug dealer charged with killing his ex-girlfriend and her two daughters last year after he was released early. [78] "We think this notion that drug crime is not a violent crime is crazy talk," says Cook.

The ACLU's McCurdy argues there is "no correlation," between prisoner releases and crime, noting that Washington, D.C.'s crime spike, which occurred before the prisoner release, dropped after the release. Nationwide, the violent crime rate remains at about half its level in the 1990s, despite a 4 percent jump in the number of violent crimes in 2015 from the previous year. Property crimes dropped 2.6 percent in 2015, declining for the thirteenth consecutive year. [79]

Congress also might consider new mandatory minimums in select cases, according to both opponents and advocates. As part of last year's compromise, Grassley's bill added new minimums for domestic violence and terrorism. There also has been some discussion of raising penalties for prescription opioids that have been contributing to the recent wave of overdoses, Ring and Cook note.

> **President Trump could reverse a 2013 order from Obama's attorney general, Eric Holder, who directed federal prosecutors not to charge certain low-level nonviolent drug offenders with the maximum sentence available under law.**

to address violent crime. At his February swearing-in, Sessions said the United States "has a crime problem," prompting experts to point out that violent crime and murder rates are still about half the level they were at their peak in the 1990s. But Sessions said the recent rise in the number of murders by more than 10 percent was not a "blip." [74]

Although the number of murders rose 10.8 percent nationally between 2014 and 2015, experts noted that rise was driven by large increases in seven cities: Baltimore, Chicago, Houston, Kansas City, Mo., Milwaukee, Philadelphia and Washington. However, in late 2016, when the figures were announced, that trend was already shifting, with murders dropping in Baltimore and Washington. In general, the murder rate has been

drug offenders with the maximum sentence available under law. [77]

"I'm sure that's one of the things the incoming administration will want to revisit pretty quickly," says Cook, of the National Association of Assistant U.S. Attorneys, which along with Sessions has criticized the Holder policy for reducing the number of prosecutions and for contributing to rising crime.

Although Sessions supported the Fair Sentencing Act that reduced the disproportionate sentencing for crack cocaine compared to the powder form, he opposed making those reforms retroactive for prisoners convicted under the old rules, as Grassley's bill would do.

Sessions "has a lot of sway with Trump," says Kevin Ring, president of FAMM, which seeks repeal of mandatory minimums.

State Actions

New York state is considering a bill to permit women prisoners to petition a court for early release if their convictions were tied to domestic violence. The measure would allow judges to sentence people for shorter periods than the mandatory sentence if domestic abuse was an important factor in commission of a crime. Similar legislation has passed in California and Illinois. (*See sidebar, p. 204.*)

Given the change of administrations in Washington, reform activists view state legislatures as a more fruitful forum than Congress for rolling back what they see as harsh sentencing policies.

"A lot of us are shifting our assets to the states," says FAMM's Ring. For instance, he says, Missouri is considering legislation proposed by a former sheriff's deputy, Republican state Rep. Galen Higdon, to repeal mandatory minimums for nonviolent or minor crimes. [80]

Despite tough-on-crime talk and the fact that 25 states are now in the hands of both a Republican governor and legislature, the momentum to soften drug sentences "is certainly continuing," says Right on Crime's Levin, as cash-strapped states try to reduce prison populations.

Alaska, Maryland and Oklahoma have undertaken such reforms, he says. Oklahoma, which overwhelmingly voted for Trump, also passed a ballot initiative to reduce some drug possession offenses from a felony to a misdemeanor and to reinvest the savings in drug treatment, Levin points out. [81]

"We always like to say saving money is the appetizer, but the main course is public safety and redeeming people's lives," Levin says, explaining why conservatives are attracted to this movement. "As conservatives, we should be locking up people whom we're afraid of, not people we're mad at. And that means taking a different approach to people with addiction and mental health issues."

Levin's coalition also supports bail reform, which would benefit women prisoners, who are disproportionately impacted by current bail procedures. The ACLU's goal is to eliminate the "money bail system" at the state and local level, says McCurdy. [82]

In January, New Jersey Republican Gov. Chris Christie signed a bipartisan bill containing funds to implement a new law that removes the state's cash bail requirement for pretrial release, allowing defendants to be freed based on whether they pose a risk to the community. New Jersey is one of three states to enact bail reform in the past two years. [83] Texas is considering similar legislation, according to Levin. ■

OUTLOOK

Crackdown Feared

Researchers and policymakers increasingly are focusing on the high number of women entering prisons and jails — once largely overlooked. And even though women make up less than 10 percent of the nation's prison population, their fates are tied to the sentencing reform trends sweeping the nation.

Some worry the nation might be becoming increasingly punitive, judging from recent polls and Trump's vows to crack down on crime. Last April, a Gallup Poll found that Americans' concern about crime had reached a 15-year high, even though violent crime levels nationwide remained at 20-year lows. [84]

A more punitive approach may be reflected in the rural counties where the jail rate for women is rising fastest. The criminalization of poverty and the tendency of towns like Ferguson, Mo., to use the justice system as a cash register are two trends that could continue to send women to jail for minor offenses or for failing to pay bail, fines and fees, experts say. [85]

However, sentencing reform advocates on both the left and the right cite a contrary trend sweeping the states toward reducing severe sentences for drug offenses, and instead investing more in drug treatment, mental health and re-entry programs.

Another encouraging sign for reformers is the unusual number of tough-on-crime prosecutors who lost to reformers in district attorney races in Colorado, Florida and Texas in November. A month after taking office in Chicago, the new Cook County state's attorney, Democrat Kim Foxx, ordered her prosecutors to stop charging low-level shoplifting as a felony. [86]

While most of the action in the next few years is expected to be in the states, some reformers are optimistic about change at the federal level, too. In a recent editorial, former *New York Times* executive editor Bill Keller, now editor-in-chief of the non-profit journalism site The Marshall Project, argued that "prospects of federal reform are actually better in 2017" than in the last Congress in part because it is not an election year. [87]

Sen. Grassley has said his sentencing reform bill could have garnered a veto-proof majority if it had made it to the Senate floor, and Keller said reform continues to have a broad base of support, from libertarians to conservative Christians and fiscal conservatives. [88]

In the waning days of his presidency, Obama wrote an article for the *Harvard Law Review* calling the need for criminal justice reform "urgent."

"How we treat those who have made mistakes speaks to who we are as a society and is a statement about our values," he wrote. [89]

It remains to be seen how the nation will respond to that challenge. ■

Notes

[1] "Life after Prison: Ramona Brant," Medium, The Obama White House, May 5, 2016, http://tinyurl.com/j7p44sx.

[2] Casey Tolan, "How a first time drug charge became this life sentence for a mother of two," *Fusion*, Dec. 10, 2015, http://tinyurl.com/glx3xno. Also see Barack Obama, "The President's Role in Advancing Criminal Justice Reform," *Harvard Law Review*, Jan. 5, 2017, http://tinyurl.com/jkvp3kh.

[3] "CAN-DO's Founder Amy Povah," CAN-DO, http://tinyurl.com/zuahszu. Also see David France, "A Crime against Women," *Glamour*, September 2016, http://tinyurl.com/gt58jtd.

[4] "Quick Tables: Sentenced female prisoners under the jurisdiction of state and federal correctional authorities, 1978-2015," Bureau of Justice Statistics, http://tinyurl.com/z5nawjc.

[5] "Ten Truths That Matter When Working With Justice Involved Women," National Resource Center on Justice Involved Women, April 2012, p. 2, http://tinyurl.com/h5cg26t.

[6] Elizabeth Swavola et al., "Overlooked: Women and Jails in an Era of Reform," Vera Institute of Justice, August 2016, http://tinyurl.com/hd6cklu.

[7] *Ibid.*, p. 6.

[8] *Ibid.*, p. 23.

[9] E. Ann Carson and Elizabeth Anderson, "Prisoners in 2015," Bureau of Justice Statistics, U.S. Department of Justice, December 2016, pp. 14, 15, http://tinyurl.com/gvwp6ds; Allen J. Beck and Paige M. Harrison, "Prisoners in 2000," Bureau of Justice Statistics, U.S. Department of Justice, p. 11, http://tinyurl.com/jzssn9q; Swavola *et al.*

[10] Bureau of Justice Statistics, U.S. Department of Justice, Special Report, "Women Offenders," December 1999, p. 6, http://tinyurl.com/jd7ncol.

[11] See James Austin and Lauren-Brooke Eisen et al., "How Many Americans Are Unnecessarily Incarcerated?" Brennan Center for Justice, Dec. 9, 2016, http://tinyurl.com/gmgp4x4. A Brennan Center estimate for *CQ Researcher* estimated 44,000 women (42 percent of women) in state and federal prisons are imprisoned unnecessarily. February 2017 email from Lauren-Brooke Eisen to author.

[12] Swavola *et al.*, *op. cit.*

[13] Sylvia Mignon, "Health issues of incarcerated women in the United States," Ciência & Saúde Coletiva, July 2016, http://tinyurl.com/z9gonp4.

[14] Timothy Williams, "Number of women in jail has grown far faster than that of men, study says," *The New York Times*, Aug. 17, 2016, http://tinyurl.com/jrffjvp.

[15] See Peter Katel, "Opioid Crisis," *CQ Researcher*, Oct. 7, 2016, pp. 817-840.

[16] See Sarah Glazer, "Sentencing Reform," *CQ Researcher*, Jan. 10, 2014, pp. 25-48.

[17] Rebecca Silber *et al.*, "Justice in Review: New Trends in State Sentencing and Corrections 2014-2015," Vera Institute of Justice, May 2016, p. 34, http://tinyurl.com/jff9k54.

[18] Erin Murphy, "Grassley pitches sentencing reform bill," *The* [Cedar Rapids] *Gazette*, July 20, 2016, http://tinyurl.com/hezht7h.

[19] Whitney M. Woodworth, "Oregon faces skyrocketing female prison population, " *Statesman Journal*, Feb. 16, 2017, http://tinyurl.com/j6w29wj.

[20] Swavola *et al.*, *op. cit.*, p. 23.

[21] "Prisoners in 2015," *op. cit.*, Table 9, p. 14, and Table 10, p. 15.

[22] Marc Mauer, "The Changing Racial Dynamics of Women's Incarceration," The Sentencing Project, Feb. 27, 2013, http://tinyurl.com/hlmo97j.

[23] John Pfaff, *Locked In: The True Causes of Mass Incarceration — and How to Achieve Real Reform* (2017), p. 127.

[24] Letter to President-elect Trump and Vice President-elect Pence, National Association of Assistant U.S. Attorneys and other organizations, Nov. 22, 2016, http://tinyurl.com/glbqkst.

[25] Keith Humphreys, "White women are going to prison at a higher rate than ever before," *The Washington Post*, Jan. 24, 2016, http://tinyurl.com/hk9xvkm.

[26] Mauer, *op. cit.*, Table 4. Between 2000 and 2009, black women's incarceration rate dropped 30.7 percent; while white women experienced a 47 percent rise and Hispanic women a 23 percent rise.

[27] Humphreys, *op. cit.*

[28] Swavola *et al.*, *op. cit.*, p. 30. See Christina Hoag, "Jailing Debtors," *CQ Researcher*, Sept. 16, 2016, pp. 745-768.

[29] John Schuppe, "Inmates hope for last-ditch shot at Obama's clemency program," NBC News, Dec. 17, 2016, http://tinyurl.com/zovfuu3.

[30] *Ibid.* Also see Mandy Martinson, FAMM, http://tinyurl.com/j4p43dj. Mandy Martinson was granted clemency by President Obama in 2016.

[31] Swavola *et al.*, *op. cit.*

[32] "Quick Facts: Women in the Federal Offender Population," U.S. Sentencing Commission, http://tinyurl.com/zfznbuk. Statistics are for fiscal 2013. Federal law also sets mandatory minimum sentences for child pornography and firearms offenses. Women are 13.8 percent of offenders sentenced under federal guidelines and while they are slightly overrepresented in drug trafficking, composing 14.9 percent of all offenders, they are under-represented in the two other major areas that carry mandatory minimums — firearms offenses (3 percent) and child pornography (2 percent). See Sourcebook, Gender of Offenders in Each Primary Offense Category, U.S. Sentencing Commission, Fiscal Year 2015, Table 5, http://tinyurl.com/j3pdgsf.

[33] "Crime in the United States 2010," FBI, http://tinyurl.com/jmehfbl.

[34] Email from Diana McHugh, director of communications, Women's Prison Association. Tamika's last name has been withheld for privacy reasons.

[35] "Prisoners in 2015," *op. cit.*, p. 4.

[36] Swavola, *op. cit.*, "From the Director."

[37] Swavola *et al.*, *op. cit.*

[38] Nancy Gertner, "Women Offenders and the Sentencing Guidelines," *Yale Journal of Law & Feminism*, 2002, pp. 291-305, http://tinyurl.com/jrrdgrm. Gertner was then a judge in the U.S. District Court, Massachusetts, p. 293.

[39] "F&CS Women in Recovery Wins National Addiction Recovery Award," press release, Tulsa Family and Children's Services, Jan. 21, 2016, http://tinyurl.com/j7mrfch.

[40] Erica Rhodes Hayden and Theresa R. Jach, eds., *Incarcerated Women* (2017), p. 38.

[41] Victoria Law, *Resistance Behind Bars* (2012), p. 160.

[42] Stacey L. Mallicoat, *Women and Crime* (2015), pp. 378-379.

[43] Hayden and Jach, *op. cit.*, pp. xiv, 101.

[44] Mallicoat, *op. cit.*, p. 380.

[45] The decision is *Commonwealth of Pennsylvania v. Daniel*. Also see Kathryn Cullen-DuPont, "Muncy Act (1913)," *Encyclopedia of Women's History in America* (2014), pp. 171-172, http://tinyurl.com/grede6t.

About the Author

Sarah Glazer is a London-based freelancer who contributes regularly to *CQ Researcher*. Her articles on health, education and social-policy issues also have appeared in *The New York Times* and *The Washington Post*. Her recent *CQ Researcher* reports include "Privacy and the Internet" and "Decriminalizing Prostitution" She graduated from the University of Chicago with a B.A. in American history.

[46] Todd R. Clear and Natasha A. Frost, *The Punishment Imperative* (2014), pp. 27, 63.

[47] Pfaff, *op. cit.*, p. 27.

[48] Robert Martinson, "What Works? Questions and Answers About Prison Reform," *The Public Interest*, 1974, 35:22-44, http://tinyurl.com/z3zbh3h.

[49] Glazer, *op. cit.*, p. 34.

[50] Woodworth, *op. cit.*

[51] Pfaff, *op. cit.*, p. 22.

[52] "Caught in the Net: The Impact of Drug Policies on Women and Families," ACLU, 2011, http://tinyurl.com/h5r652p.

[53] Glazer, *op. cit.*

[54] ACLU, *op. cit.*, p. 35.

[55] Glazer, *op. cit.*, p. 34.

[56] Jeremy Travis *et al.*, eds. "The Growth of Incarceration in the United States," National Research Council, National Academy of Sciences, 2014, pp. 3-4, http://tinyurl.com/j93hv8w.

[57] Glazer, *op. cit.*, p. 36.

[58] *Ibid.*, p. 34.

[59] "Prisoners in 2015," Table 3, p. 6., *op. cit.*

[60] "Caught in the Net," *op. cit.*

[61] Mauer, 2013, *op. cit.*

[62] Glazer, *op. cit.*, p. 38.

[63] "Frequently Asked Questions: Retroactive Application of the 2014 Drug Guidelines Amendment," U.S. Sentencing Commission, http://tinyurl.com/jqoyzdz.

[64] "2014 Drug Guidelines Amendment Retroactivity Data Report," U.S. Sentencing Commission, http://tinyurl.com/hcs9ex7, Table 1.

[65] Silber, *op. cit.*, p. 27.

[66] *Ibid.*, p. 34.

[67] "Ten Truths that Matter When Working with Justice Involved Women," *op. cit.*

[68] Nick Pinto, "Why Can't We End Mass Incarceration?" *Rolling Stone*, Oct. 26, 2015, http://tinyurl.com/pdpt69u.

[69] Carrie Johnson, "FBI: 'Murders Up Nearly 11 Percent in 2015; Violence Crime Rose Slightly,'" NPR, Sept. 26, 2016, http://tinyurl.com/jdr3mvo; "2014 Drug Guidelines Amendment Retroactivity Data Report," *op. cit.*, Table 1.

[70] "Obama used clemency power more often than any president since Truman," Pew Research Center, Jan. 20, 2017, http://tinyurl.com/zdxqegw. However, only 5 percent of petitions were granted — a much lower proportion than Truman's 41 percent. One reason was Obama's Clemency Initiative in 2014, which encouraged qualified federal inmates to apply — resulting in a flood of more than 36,000 petitions.

[71] Obama, *op. cit.*

[72] Seung Min Kim, "Senators Plan to Revive Sentencing Reform Push," *Politico*, Jan. 4, 2017, http://tinyurl.com/gmgyp6y.

[73] Jacob Sullum, "Opponents Of Sentencing Reform Recklessly Conflate Drug Offenders With Murderers," *Forbes*, Feb. 11, 2016, http://tinyurl.com/h3zgobu; Katie McHugh, "Jeff Sessions: Prison Sentence 'Reform' Grants Early Release 'For All Drug Traffickers,'" *Breitbart*, May 11, 2016, http://tinyurl.com/zxoo3f3.

[74] Matt Zapotosky, "In executive actions, Trump vows crackdown on violent crime," *The Washington Post*, Feb. 9, 2016, http://tinyurl.com/jgtc bgg.

[75] "2015 Crime in the United States," FBI, http://tinyurl.com/zc6pg55; Table 1 (1996-2015) and Table 1a, http://tinyurl.com/zsuree8; and Johnson, *op. cit.*

[76] "Prisoners in 2015," *op. cit.*, Table 3, p. 6.

[77] Glazer, *op. cit.*, p. 28.

[78] "Man charged with killing woman, 2 daughters had early prison release," *Columbus Dispatch*, Jan. 13, 2016, http://tinyurl.com/hn697vo.

[79] See Johnson, *op. cit.*; "FBI Releases 2015 Crime Statistics," FBI, 2016, http://tinyurl.com/hwojky6.

[80] Tom Dempsey, "Missouri bill could get rid of mandatory minimum sentences," KSHB, Jan. 2, 2017, http://tinyurl.com/z6wanzc.

[81] "State Questions 780 and 781," *Ballotpedia*, 2016, http://tinyurl.com/zjm7cnm.

[82] See Christina Hoag, "Jailing Debtors," *CQ Researcher*, Sept. 16, 2016, pp. 745-768.

[83] "Christie signs bill to add 20 judges as part of massive bail overhaul," nj.com, Jan. 9, 2017, http://tinyurl.com/hfluh7c; Silber, *op. cit.*, p. 9.

[84] Alyssa Davis, "In U.S., Concern About Crime Climbs to 15-Year High," Gallup, April 6, 2016, http://tinyurl.com/zy52ujz.

[85] Obama, *op. cit.*

[86] Eli Hager, "Against the Trump tide," The Marshall Project, Jan. 25, 2017, http://tinyurl.com/joj3mt3.

[87] Bill Keller, "Why Congress May Bring Criminal Justice Reform Back to Life," The Marshall Project, Dec. 16, 2016, http://tinyurl.com/zd48thu.

[88] *Ibid.*

[89] Obama, *op. cit.*

FOR MORE INFORMATION

American Civil Liberties Union, 125 Broad St., 18th Floor, New York, NY 10004; 212-549-2500; www.aclu.org. National organization that aims to protect individual civil rights and advocate for sentencing reform.

CAN-DO Foundation, PO Box 6468, Malibu, CA 90264; 310-699-3357; www.cando clemency.com. Nonprofit foundation that seeks clemency for nonviolent drug offenders.

Families Against Mandatory Minimums, 1100 H St., N.W., Suite 1000, Washington, DC 20005; 202-822-6700; http://famm.org. National organization advocating repeal of mandatory minimum sentences and reform of federal and state sentencing.

The Marshall Project, 156 W. 56th St., Suite 701, New York, NY 10019; 212-803-5200; www.themarshallproject.org. Nonprofit news organization that covers the American criminal justice system.

National Association of Assistant U.S. Attorneys, 5868 Mapledale Plaza, Suite 104, Woodbridge, VA 22193; 1-800-455-5661; www.naausa.org. Promotes the interests of assistant U.S. attorneys.

Sentencing Project, 1705 DeSales St., N.W., Eighth Floor, Washington, DC 20036; 202-628-0871; www.sentencingproject.org. Research and advocacy organization working to change sentencing policy and find alternatives to incarceration.

Texas Public Policy Foundation, 901 Congress Ave., #400, Austin, TX 78701; 512-472-2700; www.texaspolicy.com. Research foundation that launched Right on Crime, an initiative making conservatives' case for reform of sentencing and corrections.

Vera Institute of Justice, 233 Broadway, 12th Floor, New York, NY 10279; 212-334-1300; www.vera.org. Research organization that works to build and improve justice systems that ensure fairness.

Bibliography

Selected Sources

Books

Hayden, Erica Rhodes, and Theresa R. Jach, eds., *Incarcerated Women: A History of Struggles, Oppression, and Resistance in American Prisons*, Lexington Books, 2017.

This collection of essays, edited by a historian at Trevecca Nazarene University (Hayden) and a professor of history at Houston Community College (Jach), describes women's experience in American prisons from the 19th century to the 21st.

Law, Victoria, *Resistance behind Bars: The Struggles of Incarcerated Women*, PM Press, 2012.

A journalist recounts the history of women prisoners' resistance movements and civil rights struggles from the 19th century to the present.

Mallicoat, Stacy L., *Women and Crime: A Text/Reader*, 2nd ed., SAGE, 2015.

A professor of criminal justice at California State University, Fullerton, compiles a comprehensive textbook covering the history, sentencing and incarceration of women and girls.

Pfaff, John, *Locked In: The True Causes of Mass Incarceration — and How to Achieve Real Reform*, Basic Books, 2017.

A Fordham law professor argues that increasingly aggressive prosecution played at least as important a role in the rise of incarceration as the so-called war on drugs and draconian sentencing.

Articles

Cook, Steve, "Sentencing Reform Leads to More Crime," *Polizette*, Sept. 9, 2016, http://tinyurl.com/j87pqbn.

The president of the National Association of Assistant U.S. Attorneys says sentencing reforms and the recent early release of federal prisoners under revised sentencing guidelines have led to rising crime.

France, David, "A Crime Against Women," *Glamour*, September 2016, http://tinyurl.com/gt58jtd.

A magazine investigates why thousands of women end up doing more time than men due to federal mandatory sentences.

Humphreys, Keith, "White women are going to prison at a higher rate than ever before," *The Washington Post*, Jan. 24, 2016, http://tinyurl.com/hk9xvkm.

A professor of psychiatry at Stanford University notes that the rising number of white women entering prison is keeping the female prison population high.

Johnson, Carrie, "FBI," NPR, Sept. 26, 2015, http://tinyurl.com/jdr3mvo.

The latest FBI statistics show murders rose nearly 11 percent in 2015, but seven cities were responsible for the increase.

Keller, Bill, "Why Congress May Bring Criminal Justice Reform Back to Life," The Marshall Project, Dec. 16, 2016, http://tinyurl.com/zd48thu.

The editor-in-chief of the journalism site The Marshall Project explains why the chances for sentencing reform in Congress in 2017 may be improving.

Obama, Barack, "The President's Role in Advancing Criminal Justice Reform," *Harvard Law Review*, Jan. 5, 2017, http://tinyurl.com/jkvp3kh.

The former president cites the case of Ramona Brant, sentenced to life for her involvement in her boyfriend's drug trafficking ring, as "emblematic" of the problems with "overly harsh" mandatory sentences.

Zapotosky, Matt, "In executive actions, Trump vows crackdown on violent crime," *The Washington Post*, Feb. 9, 2016, http://tinyurl.com/jgtcbgg.

President Trump's plan to crack down on crime and appoint a new task force comes as crime levels remain at historic lows despite upticks in some cities.

Reports and Studies

Carson, E. Ann, and Elizabeth Anderson, "Prisoners in 2015," *Bureau of Justice Statistics Bulletin*, December 2016, http://tinyurl.com/gvwp6ds.

The government's most recent incarceration statistics show a 1 percent decline in the female prison population from 2014.

Eisen, Lauren-Brooke, *et al.*, "How Many Americans Are Unnecessarily Incarcerated?" Brennan Center for Justice, Dec. 9, 2016, http://tinyurl.com/gmgp4x4.

This much-discussed New York University research center report concludes that 39 percent of the nation's prisoners are incarcerated for nonviolent offenses. Forty-two percent of women are unnecessarily incarcerated, the authors calculated for *CQ Researcher*.

Silber, Rebecca, *et al.*, "Justice in Review: New Trends in State Sentencing and Corrections 2014-2015," Vera Institute of Justice, May 2016, http://tinyurl.com/jff9k54.

A report summarizes recent state trends in sentencing reform, mandatory minimums, reducing prison sizes and bail reform.

Swavola, Elizabeth, *et al.*, "Overlooked: Women and Jails in an Era of Reform," Vera Institute of Justice, August 2016, http://tinyurl.com/hd6cklu.

The number of women in jail has risen 14-fold since 1970, with small rural counties the main engine of the growth, concludes this report by a New York research organization.

The Next Step:

Additional Articles from Current Periodicals

Domestic Violence

Hauser, Christine, "Florida Woman Whose 'Stand Your Ground' Defense Was Rejected Is Released," *The New York Times*, **Feb. 7, 2017, http://tinyurl.com/j82wnob.**

A Florida woman who spent almost six years in prison for firing a "warning shot" after she said her husband abused her says she will fight for domestic abuse victims.

McCrabb, Rick, "Attorney says Middletown woman shot ex-husband in self defense," *Journal-News*, **Feb. 8, 2017, http://tinyurl.com/hgwxrrw.**

The attorney for an Ohio woman charged with murdering her husband said she was "in fear for her life."

Pattillo, Natalie, "She killed her abuser before he could kill her: After 17 years locked up, she's taking on justice system," *Salon*, **Jan. 7, 2017, http://tinyurl.com/j72gcxf.**

A woman, who spent 17 years in prison for killing her abusive boyfriend, is now advocating for legislation that would help protect survivors of domestic violence charged with a crime related to the abuse.

Drug Crimes

Ellis, Randy, "Governor's task force calls for decreasing sentences for drug crimes," *The Oklahoman*, **Feb. 2, 2017, http://tinyurl.com/z6kmckl.**

A task force created by the governor of Oklahoma, where the female incarceration rate is the highest in the country, recommends the state reduce sentences for nonviolent drug offenders.

Lacanlale, Rio, "Woman is arrested after trying to smuggle drugs into Ely State Prison," *Las Vegas Review-Journal*, **Feb. 21, 2017, http://tinyurl.com/htjz9l6.**

Police arrested a visitor after she tried to smuggle drugs into a Las Vegas jail with her three children present.

Yurkanin, Amy, "In an Alabama jail, pregnant addicts find little sympathy, and less treatment," Alabama Media Group, Feb. 21, 2017, http://tinyurl.com/jz96d5h.

More than 500 pregnant women in Alabama have been charged with felony chemical endangerment of a child since 2006, when the state adopted its "meth lab law."

Legal Reforms

Cason, Mike, "Alabama lawmakers taking deeper look at $800 million prison plan," AL.com, Feb. 5, 2017, http://tinyurl.com/jv7476d.

Alabama lawmakers are considering an $800 million plan that would build three prisons, including one for women.

Kim, Seung Min, "Senators plan to revive sentencing reform push," *Politico*, **Jan. 4, 2017, http://tinyurl.com/gmgyp6y.**

A bipartisan sentencing law reform bill, led by Sen. Chuck Grassley, R-Iowa, would loosen some mandatory minimum sentences for nonviolent crimes and seek to reduce recidivism rates.

Metzger, Andy, "Justice reform bill would give prisoners route to shorter sentences," *Mass Live*, **Feb. 21, 2017, http://tinyurl.com/jnzvd4b.**

New Massachusetts legislation would give prisoners a greater chance for early release, even those who received mandatory minimum sentences.

Mental Illness

Brady-Lunny, Edith, "State making progress in overhaul of prison mental health," *Pantagraph*, **Feb. 4, 2017, http://tinyurl.com/jmawdtq.**

The Illinois Department of Corrections is looking to spend about $80 million to improve conditions for 11,000 mentally ill prisoners, including women.

Cramer, Maria and Jenna Russell, "There may be no worse place for mentally ill people to receive treatment than prison," *The Boston Globe*, **Nov. 25, 2016, http://tinyurl.com/hvvm3m9.**

Prisoners who suffer from a mental illness or addiction issues make up a large portion of Massachusetts' criminal justice system, many suffering from substance use disorders.

Mulvaney, Katie, "R.I. prison official: Too few social workers to handle inmates' mental health cases," *Providence Journal*, **Jan. 26, 2017, http://tinyurl.com/zobwdto.**

Despite large numbers of mentally ill inmates, Rhode Island's prison system only has 11 social workers for 3,000 prisoners.

Citing CQ Researcher

Sample formats for citing these reports in a bibliography include the ones listed below. Preferred styles and formats vary, so please check with your instructor or professor.

MLA STYLE

Jost, Kenneth. "Remembering 9/11." CQ Researcher 2 Sept. 2011: 701-732.

APA STYLE

Jost, K. (2011, September 2). Remembering 9/11. *CQ Researcher, 9*, 701-732.

CHICAGO STYLE

Jost, Kenneth. "Remembering 9/11." *CQ Researcher*, September 2, 2011, 701-32.

In-depth Reports on Issues in the News

Are you writing a paper?

Need backup for a debate?

Want to become an expert on an issue?

For 90 years, students have turned to *CQ Researcher* for in-depth reporting on issues in the news. Reports on a full range of political and social issues are now available. Following is a selection of recent reports:

Civil Liberties
Privacy and the Internet, 12/15
Intelligence Reform, 5/15
Religion and Law, 11/14

Crime/Law
Forensic Science Controversies, 2/17
Jailing Debtors, 9/16
Decriminalizing Prostitution, 4/16
Restorative Justice, 2/16
The Dark Web, 1/16
Immigrant Detention, 10/15
Fighting Gangs, 10/15

Education
Civic Education, 2/17
Student Debt, 11/16
Apprenticeships, 10/16
Free Speech on Campus, 5/15

Environment/Society
Guns on Campus, 1/17
Mass Transit, 12/16
Arctic Development, 12/16
Protecting the Power Grid, 11/16
Pornography, 10/16
Women in Leadership, 9/16

Health/Safety
Reducing Traffic Deaths, 2/17
Opioid Crisis, 10/16
Mosquito-Borne Disease, 7/16
Drinking Water Safety, 7/16

Politics/Economy
Immigrants and the Economy, 2/17
Trump Presidency, 1/17
European Union's Future, 12/16
The Obama Legacy, 11/16
Populism and Party Politics, 9/16
U.S.-Mexico Relations, 9/16

Upcoming Reports

Charter Schools, 3/10/17   Alt-Right Movement, 3/17/17   Rural Issues, 3/31/17

ACCESS

CQ Researcher is available in print and online. For access, visit your library or www.cqresearcher.com.

STAY CURRENT

For notice of upcoming *CQ Researcher* reports or to learn more about *CQ Researcher* products, subscribe to the free email newsletters, *CQ Researcher Alert!* and *CQ Researcher News*: http://cqpress.com/newsletters.

PURCHASE

To purchase a *CQ Researcher* report in print or electronic format (PDF), visit www.cqpress.com or call 866-427-7737. Single reports start at $15. Bulk purchase discounts and electronic-rights licensing are also available.

SUBSCRIBE

Annual full-service *CQ Researcher* subscriptions—including 44 reports a year, monthly index updates, and a bound volume—start at $1,131. Add $25 for domestic postage.

CQ Researcher Online offers a backfile from 1991 and a number of tools to simplify research. For pricing information, call 800-818-7243 or 805-499-9774 or email librarysales@sagepub.com.

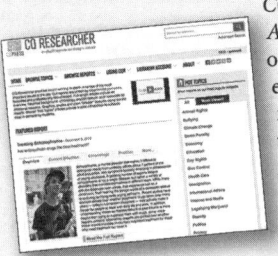

CQPRESS

CQ RESEARCHER

In-depth reports on today's issues

Published by CQ Press, an Imprint of SAGE Publications, Inc.   **www.cqresearcher.com**

Charter Schools

Do they outperform traditional public schools?

C harter schools — public schools with more freedom to innovate than traditional public schools —
have exploded in popularity in the past 25 years.
About 6,800 charters now operate in 43 states
serving 5 percent of the nation's public school students. Advocates
say charter schools provide a superior education, and as proof they
cite studies showing that charters have been particularly successful
in raising student achievement scores in troubled inner-city districts.
Charters do more with less, they say, by eliminating bureaucracy
and allowing teachers to try different educational approaches.
Critics, however, say that while some charters excel, most do no
better than traditional public schools and many do worse. They
also accuse charters of cherry-picking the best students and say
the charter movement is driven, at least partly, by the desire of
for-profit charter operators to make money from public education.
Opposition to charter expansion has grown in some states, but
President Trump and his new Education secretary, Betsy DeVos,
are charter supporters.

*Supporters of charter schools call for New York City
to authorize more of the independently run public
schools at a rally in Brooklyn on Sept. 28, 2016.
A recent study found that, overall, charter schools
mirror the performance of traditional public schools.*

CQ Researcher • March 10, 2017 • www.cqresearcher.com
Volume 27, Number 10 • Pages 217-240

I N S I D E THIS REPORT

THE ISSUES **219**

BACKGROUND **226**

CHRONOLOGY **227**

CURRENT SITUATION **232**

AT ISSUE.......................**233**

OUTLOOK **234**

BIBLIOGRAPHY **238**

THE NEXT STEP **239**

THE ISSUES

219 • Do charter schools provide a better education than traditional public schools?
• Are charter schools publicly accountable?
• Should charter schools be required to follow the same rules as other public schools?

BACKGROUND

226 **Budding Movement**
Concerns about educational bureaucracy sparked the charter school movement.

229 **Charters Catch Fire**
Charter schools expanded rapidly during the Clinton administration.

231 **Backlash**
Opposition to charter schools grew in the past decade.

CURRENT SITUATION

232 **Administration Action**
President Trump plans to increase federal funding for "school choice."

232 **State Action**
Charter school implementation varies at the state level.

234 **NAACP Acts**
The civil rights group is holding public hearings on ways to improve charter schools.

234 **Virtual Charters**
Opponents and backers of charter schools say online charters need reform.

OUTLOOK

234 **Privatization Push**
Experts differ over charters' future under Education Secretary Betsy DeVos.

SIDEBARS AND GRAPHICS

220 **Charters Show Mixed Results**
More than half showed the same level of improvement in reading as traditional public schools.

221 **Most Students Attend Traditional Public Schools**
Sixteen percent attend charter, magnet and other public schools.

222 **New Education Secretary Favors Charters**
"We must revolutionize our education delivery system."

224 **New Orleans Leads Charter Enrollment**
After Hurricane Katrina, the city converted most traditional public schools to charters.

227 **Chronology**
Key events since 1974.

228 **New Orleans Becomes Movement's Poster Child**
The city's experiment illustrates the potential and pitfalls of charter schools.

233 **At Issue:**
Do charter schools hurt traditional public schools?

FOR FURTHER RESEARCH

237 **For More Information**
Organizations to contact.

238 **Bibliography**
Selected sources used.

239 **The Next Step**
Additional articles.

239 **Citing CQ Researcher**
Sample bibliography formats.

Cover: Getty Images/Drew Angerer

CQ RESEARCHER

March 10, 2017
Volume 27, Number 10

EXECUTIVE EDITOR: Thomas J. Billitteri
tjb@sagepub.com

ASSISTANT MANAGING EDITORS: Kenneth Fireman, kenneth.fireman@sagepub.com, Kathy Koch, kathy.koch@sagepub.com, Scott Rohrer, scott.rohrer@sagepub.com

SENIOR CONTRIBUTING EDITOR:
Thomas J. Colin
tom.colin@sagepub.com

CONTRIBUTING WRITERS: Marcia Clemmitt, Sarah Glazer, Reed Karaim, Barbara Mantel, Chuck McCutcheon, Tom Price

SENIOR PROJECT EDITOR: Olu B. Davis

EDITORIAL ASSISTANT: Anika Reed

FACT CHECKERS: Eva P. Dasher, Michelle Harris, Betsy Towner Levine, Robin Palmer

Publishing

Los Angeles I London I New Delhi
Singapore I Washington DC I Melbourne

An Imprint of SAGE Publications, Inc.

**SENIOR VICE PRESIDENT,
GLOBAL LEARNING RESOURCES:**
Karen Phillips

**EXECUTIVE DIRECTOR, ONLINE LIBRARY AND
REFERENCE PUBLISHING:**
Todd Baldwin

CQ Researcher (ISSN 1056-2036) is printed on acid-free paper. Published weekly, except: (March wk. 4) (May wk. 4) (July wks. 1, 2) (Aug. wks. 2, 3) (Nov. wk. 4) and (Dec. wks. 3, 4). Published by SAGE Publications, Inc., 2455 Teller Rd., Thousand Oaks, CA 91320. Annual full-service subscriptions start at $1,131. For pricing, call 1-800-818-7243. To purchase a CQ Researcher report in print or electronic format (PDF), visit www.cqpress. com or call 866-427-7737. Single reports start at $15. Bulk purchase discounts and electronic-rights licensing are also available. Periodicals postage paid at Thousand Oaks, California, and at additional mailing offices. POSTMASTER: Send address changes to CQ Researcher, 2600 Virginia Ave., N.W., Suite 600, Washington, DC 20037.

Charter Schools

BY REED KARAIM

THE ISSUES

The average ninth-grader enters Thurgood Marshall Academy in Washington, D.C.'s impoverished Anacostia neighborhood lagging behind in basic skills by three or more grade levels. [1]

Then the public charter high school's challenging college-prep curriculum kicks in. In addition to an academic summer program, freshmen and sophomores take double-blocks of English and math. Later come AP courses in calculus, literature and other subjects. And every year, a self-assessment program encourages students to examine their academic struggles and achievements and present their plans for the future to a panel of teachers, staff and parents. [2]

Since Thurgood Marshall opened in 2001, every one of its graduates, virtually all of whom are African-American, have been accepted to college, and about two-thirds have graduated — eight times the college-graduation rate for the city's public schools overall. The D.C. board that authorizes and reviews city charter schools called the academy's record of college acceptances "outstanding." [3]

While Thurgood Marshall exemplifies the innovative educational approaches that help some charters succeed, the for-profit Celerity Educational Group, which operates seven charter schools in Southern California, demonstrates the perils. In January, FBI and Homeland Security agents raided Celerity's Los Angeles headquarters, seizing computers and records. The federal government has not disclosed the reason for the raid, but the Los Angeles Unified School District's inspector general has been investigating allegations of fraud and mismanagement by the company. [4]

Anti-charter school activists in Massachusetts celebrate the overwhelming defeat of Question 2, a referendum last Nov. 8 that would have allowed up to 12 new or expanded charter schools a year in the state. About 6,800 charter schools in 43 states serve 5 percent of the nation's public school students.

Getty Images/The Boston Globe/Barry Chin

A former Celerity teacher described the disconnect she felt between conditions at her school — which she said lacked a library, cafeteria, gym or basic supplies — and the spending behavior of administrators, who threw a lavish party for themselves and staff. "I remember being really confused that night," Tien Le said. "When I asked for basic supplies, I couldn't get those things, yet you have money for this expensive party? . . . For a public school it was not normal." [5]

As these sharply differing portraits illustrate, the education community is divided on whether charter schools, which today serve 2.9 million children, or 5 percent of public school students, improve K-12 education. [6]

Charters are tuition-free, taxpayer-supported, independently run public schools that operate under a charter, a kind of contract, often with a particular mission, such as fostering college preparation or educating low-income students. They can be run by nonprofit groups, school districts, for-profit companies or others. Charter students must take all required standardized tests, but teachers can use innovative educational approaches, a fundamental goal of charter schools. Charters are part of the "school choice" movement, which advocates giving parents of K-12 students the option to select from a wide array of alternatives to traditional public schools, plus taxpayer funded vouchers for students to attend private and religious schools.

Charter school critics question their overall academic performance, their accountability and the motives of supporters, such as newly appointed Education Secretary Betsy DeVos, who strongly support for-profit companies running charter schools. The overarching question is whether the dramatic growth of charter schools — from a single school in Minnesota in 1992 to more than 6,800 schools today — has helped or hurt public education. [7]

Because states regulate charters and each state has its own standards and requirements for charter schools, it is difficult to assess their overall performance. States differ on what kind of groups can create a charter school, and the authorizing charters also vary by state. [8]

"When you look at the preambles of all the state charter school laws, every state approached the reason they created a charter school law differently," says Nina Rees, president and CEO of the Washington-based National Alliance for Public Charter Schools.

Much media attention has focused on success stories, particularly in low-

Charters Show Mixed Results

More than half the nation's charter schools showed the same level of improvement in reading as traditional public institutions, and nearly half had the same improvement in math. Students at about a quarter of charter schools showed greater improvement than students at traditional public schools in reading and math in 2013, the latest year for which data are available.

Percentage of Charter Schools Showing Improvement in Reading and Math Versus Traditional Schools, 2013

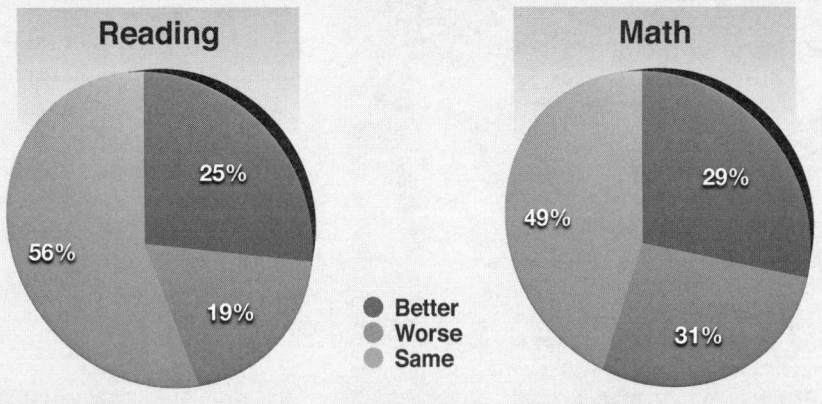

Reading

Math

● Better
● Worse
● Same

Types of Schools

Traditional public: Taxpayer-supported school governed by school district as part of a free public education system for primary and secondary students.

Charter: Tuition-free, taxpayer-supported independently run public school that operates under a charter and can be run by school districts, nonprofit groups, for-profit companies or others.

Magnet: Public school that specializes in a particular field, such as math, science or the arts.

Private: Nonpublic school run by a private organization or individuals and paid for through tuition and fees. Some students use publicly funded vouchers to pay tuition.

Religious: Private school run by religious organization. Some students use publicly funded vouchers to pay tuition.

Source: "National Charter School Study 2013," Center for Research on Education Outcomes, Stanford University, 2013, p. 57, http://tinyurl.com/npr5wq6

income, inner-city neighborhoods where traditional schools have struggled. Some charter schools, including those run by the for-profit BASIS and KIPP charter school chains, which operate in several states, have established a record of aca-demic achievement based on test scores and college acceptance rates.

"Have they done better? Unequivocally, yes," says Jeanne Allen, founder and CEO of the Center for Education Reform, a charter advocacy organization in Washington. "They were intended to create a new path, new opportunities and new patterns of accountability. They have done better in all these areas."

A 2015 study of charter schools in 41 urban school districts by the Center for Research on Education Outcomes (CREDO) at Stanford University supports claims that many urban charters outperform their public school counterparts. [9] Charter supporters also cite studies indicating that traditional schools that convert to charters often improve academic performance while receiving less money per student. [10]

But critics cite an earlier CREDO study that found a large majority of charter schools in 2013 did no better or worse than traditional schools. Even among schools that did better, the authors said other factors, such as the composition of the student body, can explain the differences. [11] They also reject straight spending comparisons, saying most charters do not provide the level of services for physically disabled and special-needs children that traditional public schools are required to provide.

Moreover, the authors said, charters, which are governed by appointed boards in many states, lack the accountability and transparency of traditional schools governed by elected school boards, making it difficult or impossible for taxpayers to determine whether charter schools are using their money wisely.

A study by the Center for Popular Democracy, a liberal advocacy group in Washington, found that at least $216 million has been lost in waste, fraud or abuse in charter schools since 1994, which it said was "just the tip of the iceberg." [12]

"There's definitely a disconnect between what the well-oiled charter PR machine is championing and what is actually happening in the charter sector," says Bob Tate, a senior policy analyst with the National Education Association (NEA), a teachers union based in Washington. "Questions over accountability only scratch the surface." The NEA does not oppose charter schools but is highly skeptical and critical of how they have evolved. The union opposes private, for-profit charters and online charter schools for home schooling, which it believes neglect the socialization aspect of education.

Many critics say some for-profit charter chains appear more interested in making money than in educating students. For-profit companies manage more than 900 charter schools around the United States, according to one study. [13] The charter industry has attracted support among hedge funds and real estate companies, which have sought to take advantage of tax credits tied to locating charter schools in underserved areas. The charter movement also has been promoted by several wealthy private foundations, including the Walton Family Foundation and the Bill & Melinda Gates Foundation. [14]

Other critics question the disciplinary practices and high rates of student suspensions in some charter school chains, such as the Success Academy in New York City and the KIPP network of schools, which have zero-tolerance policies for misbehavior. Last June, then-Secretary of Education John King suggested some charters should rethink their approaches to discipline to make sure students are not being unnecessarily pushed out of school. [15]

Concerns about how charters operate led the National Association for the Advancement of Colored People (NAACP), the nation's oldest civil rights organization, based in Baltimore, to call last fall for a moratorium on charter expansion until questions about accountability and performance could be answered. [16]

Charter school advocates don't claim charters are superior in every case, or that some charters don't have problems. But they say the ability to try alternative approaches to discipline and other facets of schooling are necessary to better serve students with different interests or capabilities. "As a movement,

Most Students Attend Traditional Public Schools

Although school-choice options have increased in the past two decades, 71 percent of school-age children still attend traditional neighborhood public schools. Another 16 percent attend alternative public schools, such as charter (4 percent), magnet (4 percent) or non-neighborhood (8 percent) schools.

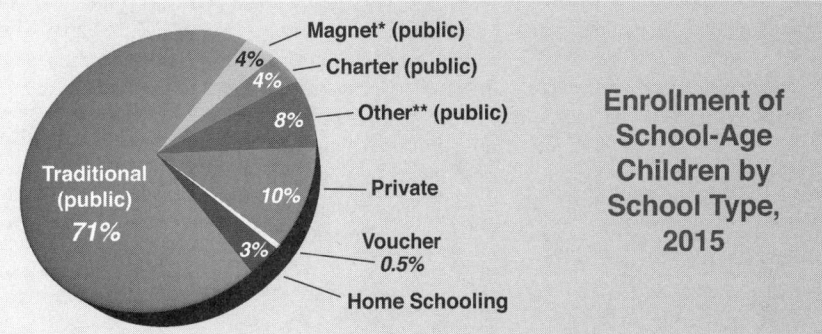

Enrollment of School-Age Children by School Type, 2015

- Magnet* (public) — 4%
- Charter (public) — 4%
- Other** (public) — 8%
- Traditional (public) — 71%
- Private — 10%
- Voucher — 0.5%
- Home Schooling — 3%

Note: Percentages do not add to 100 because of rounding.

* Magnet public schools specialize in a particular field, such as math, science or the arts.

** Covers students who may attend a non-neighborhood public school within or outside their districts if space is available.

Source: "School Choice: What the Research Says," Center for Public Education, October 2015, Updated January 2017, http://tinyurl.com/gl4spl4

a lot of us came to the charter camp because we didn't want to have a one-size-fits-all solution," says Rees.

The debate over charters is likely to intensify as the Trump administration institutes its education policy. President Trump has vowed to spend up to $20 billion to promote school choice, which includes charters as well as vouchers and tax credits for parents to use to send their children to private schools. (*See sidebar, p. 222.*)

As educators, parents and administrators debate the value of charter schools, here are some of the questions central to the debate:

Do charter schools provide a better education than traditional public schools?

The fundamental question for many education analysts and parents is how charter schools stack up academically compared to traditional public schools.

The charter movement was born in the 1990s out of concern that the nation's public school system was failing to provide children with a high-quality education.

Many defenders of traditional schools, which still educate 95 percent of public school students, say the spread of charter schools is built on a false belief that traditional schools are failing. [17]

"It's discouraging to be constantly told that American schools are failing, when by many indicators they're actually improving quite a bit," says Patte Barth, director of the Center for Public Education, a research initiative of the National School Boards Association in Alexandria, Va.

Traditional schools have made significant gains in student performance over the last 20 years, she says. In 1995, for example, U.S. eighth-graders scored below the international average in math, but in 2015 they were well above average, outscored by only six of 33 countries. [18]

New Education Secretary Favors Charters

"We must revolutionize our education delivery system."

President Trump's Cabinet nominees have included several controversial choices, but none has aroused more passionate debate than Secretary of Education Betsy DeVos, who was confirmed by the Senate only after Vice President Mike Pence cast a tie-breaking vote. [1]

DeVos and her husband, Dick, Michigan billionaires and long-time Republican political activists, are fierce advocates for education options outside of traditional public schools, particularly charter schools run by for-profit companies and vouchers that allow children to use public funds to attend private schools. The couple has spent millions of dollars lobbying officials, setting up advocacy groups, backing political candidates and supporting ballot measures to boost charters and "school choice." [2]

Dick DeVos' family fortune comes from the Amway marketing company, which his father co-founded. Betsy also comes from a wealthy, politically conservative family: Her father founded a successful auto parts company and was one of the early financial supporters of the Family Research Council, a conservative Christian organization. [3]

The charter school movement considers Betsy one of its own. "She has been a great supporter of parental choice," says Nina Rees, president and CEO of the National Alliance for Public Charter Schools, in Washington. "She has invested money in elected officials who have supported choice. You have someone [as Education secretary] who truly believes that parents will make better choices than bureaucrats. I know that alarms some people, but I think that's very refreshing."

Indeed, to many supporters of traditional public schools, the DeVoses have placed free-market ideology ahead of concern for children. "The whole DeVos family has used their wealth to drive an agenda that says profits are more important than kids," says Doug Pratt, director of public affairs for the Michigan Education Association, a teachers union. "Michigan has the highest concentration of for-profit charters in the country, and that's a direct result of policies the DeVoses have pushed over the years. This isn't about kids. It's about companies being able to make a profit off of public education."

About 80 percent of Michigan's charter schools are for-profit, the highest ratio in the United States. [4] Michigan schools overall rank near the bottom in national assessments of reading and math skills, and the state's charter schools rank below the state average. [5]

An investigation by the *Detroit Free Press* also found the state's charter schools almost completely lacking in transparency and accountability. Among the abuses the paper found: "Wasteful spending and double-dipping. Board members, school founders and employees steering lucrative deals to themselves or insiders. Schools allowed to operate for years despite poor academic records. No state standards for who operates charter schools or how to oversee them." [6] The investigation also found that a lack of transparency in the state system makes it almost impossible to determine how for-profit charters are spending their money.

Yet the DeVoses have fought state legislative efforts to impose greater oversight of Detroit charter schools, contributing heavily last summer to lawmakers who helped to defeat a bipartisan effort to increase accountability. [7] Betsy DeVos personally holds a range of investments in for-profit enterprises connected to education, according to an analysis of her financial disclosure forms by the Center for American Progress, a liberal think tank and advocacy group in Washington. [8]

DeVos also has been a strong supporter of online charter schools, which even charter advocacy groups say have largely had dismal results. In 2006, *Politico*, the political news website, reported that Dick DeVos had invested in K12 Inc., one of the nation's largest for-profit chains of online schools and one that has been accused of suspect practices in several states, including requiring students to log in for as little as a minute a day to be counted present. [9]

High-school graduation rates also are at historic highs, with 82 percent of seniors graduating on time in 2014, the most recent data available. [19]

"We know we have to continue to do better, but by some measures we're performing better than ever," Barth says.

Priscilla Wohlstetter, an education professor at Columbia University in New York City, says that, overall, charter school performance parallels public school performance. "There are some high performers, many in the middle and some in the lower rank," she says. "It kind of mirrors a bell curve."

The 2013 CREDO study backs those conclusions. It found that while one in four charter schools outperformed a comparable traditional public school in reading, more than half of charters and traditional schools performed about the same. About one in five charters did worse. For mathematics, 29 percent of charters did better, 31 percent did worse and about 40 percent did the same as traditional public schools. [20] (*See graphs, p. 220.*)

Some states' charter schools performed better than others, Wohlstetter says. Ohio's charter schools performed at a subpar level, for instance, with their students lagging behind those in traditional public schools in math and reading. Analysts blame the state's relatively lax charter standards. [21]

But charter supporters cite other studies to bolster the claim that, in many places, charters provide a superior education. In particular, they cite CREDO's 2015 analysis showing that more than half of the charter schools in 41 urban districts outperformed their traditional public school counterparts in math and reading. The gains were larger for black, Hispanic, low-income and special-education students. [22]

DeVos' supporters say she has worked to bring market forces to bear in education and strip away unnecessary regulation, and they hope she takes the same approach as Education secretary. "What she should be doing is working to explore every single rule and regulation and piece of guidance and looking into ways to loosen up those restrictions for all educators and schools," says Jeanne Allen, founder and CEO of the Center for Education Reform, a pro-charter advocacy organization in Washington.

Speaking to an educator's conference in Texas in 2015, DeVos described the American system of education as "antiquated" and "embarrassing" because of what she described as poor performance stretching back half a century — a view that education analysts say ignores recent gains. "We must revolutionize our education delivery system," DeVos said. "That's it — that's all I'm asking for. Open education up; allow for choice, innovation, and freedom." [10]

But to her critics, DeVos's track record in Michigan promoting charters while opposing stronger oversight is the final argument against her approach to public education. Diane Ravitch, a research professor and historian of education at New York University, says, "Detroit, which has one of the highest concentrations of charter schools, is the lowest performing district in the country. Is this supposed to be the model under Betsy DeVos?"

Ravitch, a former assistant secretary of Education and school choice advocate, now takes a negative view of charters, outlined in her 2013 book, *Reign of Error: The Hoax of the Privatization Movement and the Danger to America's Public Schools*.

— *Reed Karaim*

Betsy DeVos, the new secretary of Education, is a strong advocate of charter schools and vouchers, which allow parents to use public funds to send their children to private schools.

[1] Emma Brown, "With historic tiebreaker from Pence, DeVos confirmed as education secretary," *The Washington Post*, Feb. 7, 2017, http://tinyurl.com/jpwtmh7.

[2] Stephen Henderson, "Betsy DeVos and the twilight of public education," *The Detroit Free Press*, Dec. 3, 2016, http://tinyurl.com/gtm242s.

[3] Noam Scheiber, "Betsy DeVos, Trump's Education Pick, Plays Hardball With Her Wealth," *The New York Times*, Jan. 9, 2017, http://tinyurl.com/gr4e9hw.

[4] Zack Stanton, "How Betsy DeVos used God and Amway to take over Michigan Politics," *Politico Magazine*, Jan. 15, 2017, http://tinyurl.com/zltoblr.

[5] Caitlin Emma, Benjamin Wermund and Kimberly Hefling, "DeVos' Michigan schools experiment gets poor grades," *Politico*, Dec. 9, 2016, http://tinyurl.com/hqrw8w9.

[6] Jennifer Dixon, "Michigan spends $1B on charter schools but fails to hold them accountable," *Detroit Free Press*, June 22, 2014, http://tinyurl.com/jpkmp9f.

[7] Henderson, *op. cit.*

[8] Ben Miller and Laura Jimenez, "Inside the Financial Holdings of Billionaire Betsy DeVos," Center for American Progress, Jan. 27, 2017, http://tinyurl.com/jarteyj.

[9] Matt Barnum, "Betsy DeVos, Trump's EdSec Pick, Promoted Virtual Schools Despite Dismal Results," *The 74*, Dec. 1, 2016, http://tinyurl.com/j9urc4z.

[10] Valerie Strauss, "The telling speech Betsy DeVos gave about education — full text," *The Washington Post*, Dec. 21, 2016, http://tinyurl.com/h38ysl9.

"These are communities where students have significant education challenges and are in great need of effective approaches to achieve academic success," CREDO Director Margaret Raymond said. "This research shows that many urban charter schools are providing superior academic learning for their students, in many cases quite dramatically better." [23]

However, charter critics question the fairness of such comparisons because charters' populations are, by definition, mostly self-selected. Although charters are open to all applicants, skeptics note

they often require families to make a substantial commitment in travel or homework time, so only the most motivated families end up in charters.

In addition, critics say, many charter schools focus on high-performing students, who are the least expensive to educate. For instance, because many charter schools lack support programs for children with learning or physical disabilities, fewer of those students apply to charter schools, critics say.

They add that some charters are quick to push out students who can't keep up academically — an option

not available to traditional public schools — resulting in distorted test-score results. One school in the Success Academy chain in New York City reportedly kept a "Got to Go" list of students that administrators wished to see forced out of the school. [24]

"Give me the story of a miracle charter, and I'm almost guaranteed there's going to be some sort of shenanigans about student population — who's let in, who's kicked out, that sort of thing," says Wayne Au, a professor of education at the University of Washington in Seattle.

New Orleans Leads Charter Enrollment

More than half of the public school students in three cities attended charter schools during the 2015-16 academic year, with New Orleans topping the list at 92 percent. After Hurricane Katrina destroyed many of New Orleans' public schools in 2005, the city rebuilt and reopened them as charter schools. Two Michigan school districts each had charter enrollment of 53 percent.

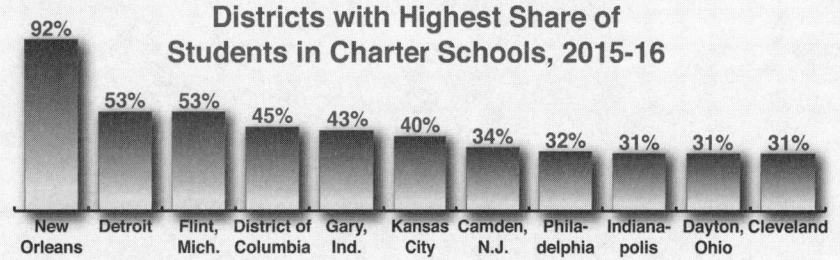

Districts with Highest Share of Students in Charter Schools, 2015-16

92% New Orleans
53% Detroit
53% Flint, Mich.
45% District of Columbia
43% Gary, Ind.
40% Kansas City
34% Camden, N.J.
32% Phila-delphia
31% Indiana-polis
31% Dayton, Ohio
31% Cleveland

Source: "A Growing Movement: America's Largest Charter Public School Communities and Their Impact on Student Outcomes," National Alliance for Public Charter Schools, Nov. 3, 2016, http://tinyurl.com/zdusry2

Susan Aud Pendergrass, vice president of research and evaluation for the National Alliance for Public Charter Schools, acknowledges that research shows charters have a slightly smaller percentage of students with disabilities, differences that increase for students with more severe disabilities. While charters are open to these students, she says, their families may be drawn to traditional schools with programs that can better serve their needs.

But Pendergrass says studies contradict the idea that self-selection of motivated students is responsible for charter performance. "The couple of studies that have been done on that have looked at public schools that were converted to charters. Basically, what they have found is that when the school converted to a charter school, there was a positive academic effect at that school," says Pendergrass "These were kids who are already there, so these aren't cases where students were self-selecting."

Rees, of the National Alliance for Public Charter Schools, notes that many charters have taken steps to ensure students spend more time learning, providing a simple explanation for some of the gains.

"By and large, they do expand the school day, they do expand the school year, they do bring some kids in on Saturday," she says, "so there's more focus on content and an effort to make sure the child is achieving to the best of their potential."

Are charter schools publicly accountable?

One of the sharpest differences between charter proponents and skeptics involves accountability and transparency. Elected school boards govern traditional public schools, and they are generally subject to open-meeting and public-records laws, which means the public can scrutinize spending and budgets.

That is not the case for charters in many states. "Some states have more oversight than others, but, generally, I would say they don't have enough accountability," says the University of Washington's Au. "Basically, charter schools are using public money without actual public oversight. [Individual] charter school boards are appointed, and usually the charter school state authorizing boards are appointed."

Allen, of the Center for Education Reform, sees the charter structure as

making them more accountable than public schools.

"What's wonderful about the non-governmental boards that manage charter schools is that they're not elected. Charter schools take the politics out of schools," she says. "It's the board that files for a charter; it's the board that's accountable for everything. A [traditional public] school board isn't directly responsible for performance. Nobody is going to hold them accountable."

Allen also says charter schools face an ultimate standard: The charters under which they operate can run 100 pages or more. Those charters are in effect only for a certain number of years, often five or 10, and schools that fail to live up to their charter requirements can be closed. An average of about 500 charter schools have closed per year over the last 10 years, although all those closures are not necessarily tied to performance, says Pendergrass, of the National Alliance for Public Charter Schools.

Supporters of traditional schools say school board members are accountable to the voters, who can throw them out of office, and school board meetings are open to the public. Indeed, Julian Vasquez Heilig, a professor of educational leadership and policy studies at California State University Sacramento, says too many underperforming charter schools remain open. Without direct accountability to voters, he says, charter schools should really be considered private schools that receive public money.

"They're not public schools because they're run by private boards," Vasquez Heilig says. "They do get public money, but so do defense contractors. Is anybody going to argue that Grumman or Boeing are public entities? They can say they're public schools until they're blue in the face, but they're privately run."

Rees, of the National Alliance for Public Charter Schools, responds that charters are public schools because they are open to everyone, and they're free. But requiring full transparency of private charter boards could hurt their effectiveness, she says. "I fear that sometimes our opponents use transparency to discourage certain people from joining our boards and turn us into the same inefficient system that existed before," she says.

But Columbia University's Wohlstetter notes that charters vary widely from state to state, although she says there has been a movement toward holding charter schools to more thorough requirements.

In addition, charter critics say, states allow charters to escape public scrutiny in other ways as well. Of the 43 states with charter school laws, "a third do not require that the charters comply with the same open-meeting laws that govern traditional school boards," says the NEA's Tate. [25]

In 35 states, charter school finances are kept from the public through a structure in which a school contracts out control of its operations to a private for-profit company — called an education charter management organization (EMO), which does not have to disclose how the money is spent. EMOs manage between 35 to 40 percent of U.S. charter schools, according to a study by Bruce Baker, an education professor at Rutgers University in New Brunswick, N.J., and Gary Miron, a professor of evaluation, measurement and research at Western Michigan University in Kalamazoo. [26]

"The charter school is a public entity, but what happens is the charter school is run by a private management entity, so all the charter school says is, 'We got a million dollars to educate these kids and we handed this money over to this private company to run his school,' and that's what the public knows," says Doug Pratt, director of public affairs for the Michigan Education Association, the state NEA chapter. So it's "impossible to determine" how much of the money is being used to educate the students, he adds.

The private-management structure also raises potential conflicts-of-interest questions. In 2012, an investigation by *The Arizona Republic* found that 40 nonprofit charter schools paid $70 mil-

Diane Ravitch, a former assistant secretary of Education, says charter schools should not be able to cherry-pick the best students but should be required to have student bodies that reflect the district's overall public school population, with the same proportion of students with disabilities and immigrants with weak English skills. "Absolutely, they should have to follow the same rules," says Ravitch, now an historian of education at New York University.

lion to companies run by the schools' board members, executives or their relatives. Through EMOs, the salaries of top executives in charter chains also can be kept secret. [27]

Baker and Miron said the combination of weak oversight and the financial management structures used by some charter schools makes it likely that improper behavior or wasteful procedures are going undetected. As a result, it is possible that "a substantial share of public expenditure intended for the delivery of direct educational services to children is being extracted inadvertently or intentionally for personal or business financial gain," they wrote. [28]

Should charter schools be required to follow the same rules as other public schools?

Charter school students must take

the same state and federal standardized performance tests as children in traditional public schools. Charters also must abide by federal laws that prohibit discrimination based on race, sex, national origin or disability. [29]

But U.S. public education is largely governed by the states, and state laws and regulations governing charter schools vary widely. For instance, some states, such as Arizona and Wisconsin, exempt charter schools from most state regulations and laws governing public schools. Others, such as Massachusetts and Maryland, require charters to comply with state laws and regulations that apply to traditional public schools, but charters can seek waivers in certain cases. [30]

Even teacher-training requirements differ by state. Some states require charter school teachers to be fully certified in line with teachers at traditional schools, while others require only that a certain percentage of a charter school's teachers be certified. Still other states have no certification requirements for charter teachers. [31]

A number of education experts believe states should require charters to meet the same standards as other public schools in a district, such as those concerning teacher qualifications or student suspensions. Sometimes, critics say, some backers have supported charters — the vast majority of which are not unionized — as a way to undermine teachers unions. (*See background, p. 231.*)

Diane Ravitch, an historian of education at New York University's Steinhardt School of Culture, Education and Human Development, says charter schools should be required to have student bodies that reflect the district's overall public school population, including those who cost the most to educate: students with disabilities and immigrants with weak English skills.

"Absolutely, they should have to follow the same rules. They should also have the same proportion of students with disabilities and the same proportion of kids who don't speak English," says Ravitch, who supported charter schools before becoming one of their foremost critics. She is author of *Reign of Error: The Hoax of the Privatization Movement and the Danger to America's Public Schools.*

Other analysts believe charters should be given more latitude in certain areas. Columbia's Wohlstetter says charters should follow the same health and safety rules as other public schools and continue to give their students "the same tests as other district kids take" so they're being measured by the same achievement standards. But when it comes to regulating classroom work, such as length of the school day or the hours teachers spend in the classroom, she says, "I'm a big proponent of deregulation in terms of the education program. Without the freedom to try new approaches, charters will be failing their essential mission to

find innovative ways to improve school performance."

Charters also should be allowed more latitude with curriculum, she says, noting that charters have embraced a wide variety of teaching approaches beyond the traditional public school template. "Some use project-based learning; some are dual immersion, in which students learn two languages; some are focused on a particular area, such as the arts; some have a team-teaching approach."

Allen, of the Center for Education Reform, says many of the rules and regulations imposed on traditional schools do not correlate with the quality of education. "A charter school [in many states] doesn't have to report how often its teachers show up and their sick days and that sort of thing. Those are inputs. Charter schools are output-driven," or measured by results, she says. "All of the bureaucracy that surrounded public education before charters showed up is the kind of stuff that critics are used to, and they think that if you're not sending those keystrokes into the state [you're not doing your job]."

Rees, of the National Alliance for Public Charter Schools, says "over-regulation" is a danger as states react to the growth of the charter movement. The urge can be toward standardization, she notes, and even though 25 years of charter experience has provided models of what's successful, "we need to be careful because if we want to stay vibrant, we do need to stay open to new ideas and new people."

But charter critics note that some of the concerns about charter schools involve discipline and suspension policies, particularly in regard to minority students and children with disabilities. A 2016 study by the Center for Civil Rights Remedies at the University of California, Los Angeles, found that charter schools suspend black children and children with disabilities at higher rates than other schools do, particularly in high school. [32]

The disciplinary policies at some successful charters, such as the Success Academy chain in New York, have been the subject of public criticism. Teachers from the chain told *The New York Times* that a culture existed of belittling and embarrassing children, including tearing up incorrect homework in front of the class. "It's this culture of, 'If you've made them cry, you've succeeded in getting your point across,' " Jessica Reid Sliwerski, a former Success Academy teacher, said. [33]

Eva Moskowitz, founder and CEO of the chain, said its training materials say teachers should never shame or embarrass students and that the incidents reported were isolated cases of teachers behaving improperly. [34]

Many of the rules and regulations that govern traditional schools are there to protect both teachers and students, says the University of Washington's Au. "The education bureaucracy can be burdensome," he says. "But that same bureaucracy means there is also regulatory oversight to make sure all kids can be served, and we're just not seeing that in charter schools." ∎

BACKGROUND

Budding Movement

The beginnings of the charter school movement can be traced to Ray Budde, a former junior high school administrator who became a professor of education at the University of Massachusetts, Amherst. Budde, who had an interest in organizational theory, presented a paper to a research society in 1974 titled "Education by Charter." [35]

His idea was different from how today's charter schools work, however.

Continued on p. 228

Chronology

1970s-1991
Charter school concept introduced after concern grows about U.S. public education.

1974
Ray Budde, a former junior high school principal, proposes that school districts sign contracts (charters) with teachers to improve educational outcomes; his idea attracts little attention.

1983
National Commission on Excellence in Education's report, "A Nation at Risk," says U.S schools are not adequately educating students and calls for raising educational standards, spurring reform movement.

1988
American Federation of Teachers union president Albert Shanker suggests teachers set up innovative, independent schools within existing schools, which he calls "charter schools." . . . The Citizen's League, a Minnesota think tank, modifies the charter school idea to include entire schools established outside traditional ones, chartered by groups such as universities or the state.

1991
Minnesota is first state to allow school districts to create charters.

1992-2000
Charter movement expands.

1992
City Academy in St. Paul, Minn., opens with 53 students, becoming nation's first charter school.

1994
Improving America's Schools Act, which includes grants to states for establishing charter schools, gets bipartisan support. . . . Two young teachers start Knowledge Is Power Program (KIPP) charter school, which expands into a network of 200 schools serving nearly 80,000 students.

1996
Congress passes D.C. School Reform Act, leading to first charter school in the nation's capital.

2000
U.S. has nearly 2,000 charter schools.

2001-2011
Charter schools proliferate and movement's political power grows, but questions arise about their performance and approaches.

2005
National Alliance for Public Charter Schools, is founded. . . . After Hurricane Katrina devastates New Orleans' public schools, city converts to a largely charter system, which improves performance.

2006
Former New York City Council member Eva Moskowitz opens Success Academy, the first of what will become a controversial 41-school for-profit charter network in the city known for rigorous academics and strict discipline.

2009
Stanford University-based Center for Research on Educational Outcomes (CREDO) finds that 17 percent of charter schools are outperforming comparable public schools, but 37 percent are doing worse.

2011
On the 20th anniversary of the passage of the first state law authorizing charter schools, the nation has more than 5,000 charters, but they enroll only 5 percent of all public school students.

2012-Present
Charter school performance improves, but concern grows about the schools' racial composition, accountability and standards.

2012
Education Department inspector general says the department has not effectively overseen and monitored disbursement of federal charter school grants to states and state oversight has been lax.

2013
CREDO finds charter school performance improving, but unevenly.

2015
Washington's Supreme Court rules the state's charter schools are unconstitutional because they are governed by appointed, rather than elected, boards. Legislature moves to keep charters open.

2016
NAACP calls for moratorium on new charter schools amid concerns they are increasing racial segregation. . . . Massachusetts voters defeat a referendum to allow more charter schools. . . . Number of charter schools nationally tops 6,800.

2017
Longtime charter advocate Betsy DeVos becomes Education secretary after Vice President Mike Pence casts a tie-breaking vote in the Senate.

New Orleans Becomes Movement's Poster Child

City's experiment illustrates potential and pitfalls of charter schools.

Hurricane Katrina, which devastated New Orleans in 2005, led to an unparalleled educational experiment: When the city rebuilt its schools, they reopened as a nearly all-charter school system.

By 2015, 92 percent of New Orleans' 47,880 public school students were attending charter schools, by far the highest percentage in the United States. Detroit and Flint, Mich., tied for having the second-highest charter school attendance rates, at 53 percent. [1]

Under the new system, New Orleans students have shown some significant educational gains, making it a poster child for many in the charter movement. By 2014, 63 percent of elementary and middle schools were proficient on state achievement tests, up from 37 percent the year Katrina struck. [2] High school graduation rates also improved dramatically, with 73 percent of students graduating on time in 2015, compared to 54 percent in 2004. [3]

The gains appeared so impressive that in 2010 U.S. Education Secretary Arne Duncan said, "I think the best thing that happened to the education system in New Orleans was Hurricane Katrina." [4]

But many of those involved in the New Orleans makeover say the truth is far more complicated, and the New Orleans experiment illustrates both the potential and the pitfalls of such an approach.

The academic gains have been real, they say, but at a cost. "We don't want to replicate a lot of the things that took place to get here," said Andre Perry, who was one of the city's few black charter-school CEOs. "There were some pretty nefarious things done in the pursuit of academic gain." [5]

For instance, Perry and others say, in their drive to improve performance, schools sought to skim the best students, counseled

out those who were not keeping up and did not provide enough support for special-needs children. [6] A former state school official said expulsions were "out of control" and that charters used the few remaining traditional public schools as "dumping grounds" for difficult or academically struggling students. [7]

A chaotic admissions system also made it hard for many parents to get their children into the charter schools they wanted. As a result, the average distance children had to travel to attend school rose significantly. [8]

During the reorganization, nearly all 7,000 New Orleans public school system employees were fired, including all 4,600 teachers. [9] Even before the hurricane, state officials had set up a special authority to take control of the district's low-performing schools, and as the system was rebuilt, officials felt they needed a clean slate.

The Louisiana Federation of Teachers, the local educators' union, brought a class-action lawsuit on behalf of the fired teachers, but in 2015 the state Supreme Court declined to hear a final appeal on behalf of the teachers. [10]

The firings were devastating for many of the city's longtime teachers. As they were replaced by a younger group of teachers, the racial composition of the city's teaching staff also changed. Before Katrina, 71 percent of the city's 1,300 public school teachers were black; in 2015, 49 percent were black, with 45 percent white. The student population, however, remains 90 percent African-American. [11]

School leaders have taken several steps to mitigate some of the problems. For instance, the city introduced a centralized application system that makes it easier for parents to enroll

Continued from p. 226

He envisioned charters as a way to cut down on educational bureaucracy within existing school systems. Essentially, teachers would have a contractual relationship through a "charter" agreement with the school board that would give them direct responsibility for effective teaching. [36]

Budde's paper received almost no attention at the time. But in 1983, the National Commission on Excellence in Education created by President Ronald Reagan issued a report, "A Nation at Risk," warning that American schools were declining academically and falling behind internationally.

"If an unfriendly foreign power had attempted to impose on America the

mediocre educational performance that exists today, we might well have viewed it as an act of war," the report said. "As it stands, we have allowed this to happen to ourselves." [37]

The report received national attention and ignited interest in educational reform. When Budde republished his original paper in 1988, it attracted a new audience. Albert Shanker, then head of the American Federation of Teachers, an educators union, expanded on Budde's idea. Speaking at the National Press Club in Washington, Shanker proposed creating separate schools within existing schools to serve as laboratories of innovation. Teachers would have greater autonomy to try different education approaches, such

as team teaching or tailoring educational programs to the different ways children learn. [38]

Such schools-within-schools would operate with a charter outlining their approach and guaranteeing their operation for a certain number of years — Shanker suggested five to 10 years — to give their ideas a fair tryout. The schools would be exempt from many of the rules imposed on traditional schools, which he felt restricted teachers' ability to meet the needs of their students. But Shanker envisioned these schools as unionized parts of the overall school system. [39]

"The school district and the teacher union would develop a procedure that would encourage any group of six or

their students and harder for charters to manipulate the composition of their student bodies. The district also has increased funding for educating special-needs students. [12]

In addition, a citywide code of conduct now bans expulsions for minor offenses and has established a review process for students who are expelled. [13] Some city charter schools that formerly took a zero-tolerance approach to discipline also have shifted to an approach that works individually with students to help resolve behavior that has been getting them into trouble. [14]

New Orleans' educators say efforts to improve the system continue, defying those who want to see the transition to charters as either a simple success or a failure.

"Yes, we've come a long way, and we have a long way left to go," Rahel Wondwossen, the principal of Cohen College Prep charter school, told *Education Week*. "And that's not as clean of an answer as sometimes folks want." [15]

— *Reed Karaim*

Students have shown educational gains since New Orleans converted most of its traditional public schools — many of them rebuilt after being destroyed in 2005 by Hurricane Katrina — to charters. Above, kindergartners line up for class at the Dr. Martin Luther King Jr. Charter School for Science and Technology.

[1] "A Growing Movement: America's Largest Charter Public School Communities and Their Impact on Student Outcomes," 11th Annual Edition, National Alliance for Public Charter Schools, November 2016, http://tinyurl.com/hv7pt28.

[2] Andrea Gabor, "The Myth of the New Orleans School Makeover," *The New York Times*, Aug. 22, 2015, http://tinyurl.com/jpyveo5.

[3] Emma Brown, "Katrina swept away New Orleans' school system, ushering in new era," *The Washington Post*, Sept. 3, 2015, http://tinyurl.com/zp55lev.

[4] Nick Anderson, "Education Secretary Duncan calls Hurricane Katrina good for New Orleans schools," *The Washington Post*, Jan. 30, 2010, http://tiny url.com/ycnbomk.

[5] Gabor, *op. cit.*

[6] *Ibid.*

[7] Thomas Toch, "The Big Easy's Grand Experiment," *U.S. News & World Report*, Aug. 18, 2015, http://tinyurl.com/hfls27t.

[8] Brown, *op. cit.*

[9] Corey Mitchell, " 'Death of My Career' — What happened to New Orleans' veteran black teachers?" *Education Week*, Aug. 19, 2015, http://tinyurl.com/hgkmftw.

[10] *Ibid.*

[11] *Ibid.*

[12] Toch, *op. cit.*

[13] *Ibid.*

[14] Mallory Falk and Eve Troeh, "A 'No Excuses' New Orleans Charter School Has A Change of Heart," WWNO, New Orleans Public Radio, Jan, 23, 3017, http://tinyurl.com/zmmvrbk.

[15] Rahel Wondwossen, "The last Word: Can New Orleans deliver a high quality education for all it's children?" video, *Education Week*, Aug. 19, 2015, http://tinyurl.com/hp5oahl.

more teachers to submit a proposal to create a new school," Shanker told the press club. In Shanker's vision, these charter schools would have to be approved by a special board and accept a student population that reflected the overall district composition — so they could not cherry-pick their students. [40]

He also imagined a central database where the best ideas could be shared, spurring improvement in public schools nationwide. "Other teachers could then dig into that and find the eight or 12 or 15 ways that have been found by other teachers to work, and add their own comments," he said. [41] Shanker would later call the schools-within-schools he envisioned "charter schools." [42]

His ideas were taken up most enthusiastically by the Citizens League, an advocacy and policy group in Minneapolis. The league published a report advocating the establishment of charter schools and worked with Minnesota legislators to pass the first state law enabling charter schools in 1991. [43]

In a key change from Shanker's vision, however, the Minnesota law allowed charter schools to be established outside and independent of traditional public schools. In 1992, a year after the law passed, a small group of teachers set up City Academy in St. Paul, the nation's first publicly funded, privately run charter school. It opened with only 53 students but would become the first of a wave of charters that would spread across the nation. [44]

Charters Catch Fire

That same year, California became the second state with a charter school law. In 1993 five other states passed charter laws, and by 1996, 25 states and the District of Columbia had embraced charters as a way to spur competition and improvement in public education. [45]

The charter movement received a federal boost in 1994 when President Bill Clinton supported including creation of the Charter School Program in a larger education bill signed into law. Under the program, the U.S. Department of Education provided grants to state and local education agencies to support the planning, development and start-up of new charter schools. [46]

Speaking in 1998, Clinton said, "Across our nation, public school choice, and in particular charter schools are renewing public education with their energy and new ideas." He

Students plant a "teaching garden" at the KIPP Infinity Charter School in New York City's Harlem neighborhood. Some charters boast high academic achievement, particularly in low-income, inner-city neighborhoods. But even when charters outperform traditional public schools, critics say other factors, such as cherry-picking applicants, could explain some of the differences.

stressed, however, that charter schools should remain open only so long as they met rigorous standards of accountability. [47]

During Clinton's eight years as president the number of charter schools in the country grew from one to more than 2,000. Federal grants for charters totaled $4.5 million in 1995; in 2016, they were $245 million. [48] Since the beginning of the program, the federal government has invested more than $3 billion in charter school development through an expanded set of grants.

The U.S. Education Department says that in the past decade, those investments have enabled the launch of more than 2,500 charter schools serving approximately 1 million students. [49]

As the movement caught fire in the 1990s, many states wrote laws that made it relatively easy to open charter schools. The goal was to spur growth and allow charters to experiment. But support and training programs for operating schools were often lacking, according to some people involved in the early expansion.

"With the schools that opened in the first two years [of the state charter program], it was basically, 'Here's your charter, and good luck,' " said Cassandra A. Larsen, executive director of the Arizona State Board for Charter Schools in a 2001 interview with *Education Week.* [50]

The combination of minimal state oversight and rapid expansion led to problems in some states. In Arizona, the state auditor in 2002 found that 21 of 43 schools were in financial trouble. Embarrassing cases also surfaced in the press, including one in the Phoenix area, in which the state briefly could not locate a school to which it was sending money. It turned out the school had lost its lease and was meeting under a tree in a city park. [51]

But many new charter schools showed the kind of innovation and results that advocates had hoped to see flower. The Minnesota New Country School, a rural charter created in Henderson in 1994, works with families to devise individualized learning programs for every student. The school has no grades, bells or formal classes and is organized as a cooperative without a principal. The teachers share administrative responsibilities. The school's academic achievements were significant enough that the Bill & Melinda Gates Foundation provided $4 million to help the school replicate its model in other charters. [52]

In Boston, the Academy for the Pacific Rim, founded in 1995, combines Asian and American approaches to learning and cultural practices. Classes begin with students and teachers standing, bowing and thanking one another for their efforts. Each school day starts with an assembly, in which the school regularly hands out its "gambette award." *Gambette* is Japanese for "to persist." The school's academic track record places it among the best in the Boston area. [53]

But as the charter movement expanded, some analysts say its size and scope began to exceed the concept envisioned by its original supporters.

"It was never intended to create a parallel, market-based alternative to the public school system," says Stan Karp, a longtime high school educator who serves on the board of Rethinking Schools, a nonprofit education publisher and advocacy group in Milwaukee. "It was about creating model programs that might have some innovation, which could then generate useful reforms [in] the public school system."

A key part of the original charter idea had been individual schools operating locally. Karp says a fundamental shift came about in the late 1990s or 2000s, with the development of charter chains and for-profit schools. "These charter networks began to develop nationally and began to attract a lot of funding from people whose interests were not education reform," he says. Instead, people began to see charters as a "source of revenue, a way to promote a free-market ideology or undermine teachers unions."

Only about 11 percent of charter teachers belong to unions, according to Pendergrass, from the National Alliance for Public Charter Schools, compared to the 68 percent of public school teachers who were union members as of 2014, according to the National Bureau of Labor Statistics. [54]

A U.S. Department of Education survey for the 2011-12 school year found that charter school teachers' salaries averaged 17 percent less than those of teachers at traditional schools. However, that could be because charter teachers were also younger on average, with fewer years of teaching experience. Teacher turnover at charter schools was higher, the survey found, than at traditional schools, although it had declined significantly since the 2004-05 school year, while turnover rates at traditional schools crept slightly higher. [55]

Charter school growth continued to be strong through the first decade of the 21st century, topping 5,000 in the 2010-11 school year. [56] Charter schools also continued to draw bipartisan political support. In the 2008 presidential campaign, both Republican John McCain and Democrat Barack Obama backed more assistance to charters. [57]

But as charter schools took an expanding share of public education spending, a backlash began to develop in parts of the United States.

Backlash

California, the nation's most populous state, has the largest number of charter schools — 1,234 as of the 2015-16 school year, according to the National Alliance for Public Charter Schools. [58] But in recent years, the state has been the center of a bitter battle over further charter expansion.

In Los Angeles, the teachers union gathered a coalition of other unions and public supporters to oppose a plan led by the Eli and Edythe Broad Foundation to enroll half of the city's public school students in charter schools over the next eight years. [59] The Los Angeles-based foundation, created by billionaire homebuilder Eli Broad and his wife, says it works to promote "entrepreneurship for the public good in education, the science and arts." The plan also has attracted support from the Walton Family Foundation, the founders of the Walmart chain and one of several philanthropic groups that have invested heavily in promoting charters. [60]

Union leaders said the large-scale transfer of the city's education funds to the charter schools created under the plan would devastate the city's traditional public schools.

Resistance to further charter growth has emerged elsewhere in California as well. The City Council of Huntington Park in suburban Los Angeles voted last October to extend a moratorium on charter expansion until September 2017. The city already has 10 charters among its 24 schools, and unionized local teachers and others have opposed further expansion on the grounds that the city has plenty of education options. [61] A citizens group also attempted to get a measure on the state ballot last November that would have repealed the 1992 California law allowing charters, but the organization failed to secure the nearly 400,000 signatures required to get an initiative on the ballot. [62]

Charters did not fare as well in two other states last November. In Massachusetts, voters decisively defeated a measure that would have allowed up to 12 new or expanded charter schools annually beyond a current cap, which limits charter expansion in school districts according to a complex formula based on school enrollment and funding.

Charter opponents prevailed in Massachusetts despite being outspent — $26 million to $15 million — by charter supporters. [63] Opponents argued the measure would undermine traditional public schools. Massachusetts, which regulates its charter schools more tightly than most states, has the nation's best public school system, according to at least one study. [64]

Voters in Georgia also defeated an amendment that would have allowed the state to seize control of the worst-performing public schools and turn them over to charter operators. Polls before the election showed that voters did not like the idea of turning over local control of schools. [65]

"As more communities start to experience the hidden downfalls of charters, that's where we're seeing more pushback," the NEA's Tate says, calling the referendums in Massachusetts and Georgia "examples of growing public concern."

But despite resistance in some states, Pendergrass, of the National Alliance for Public Charter Schools, says charters remain popular with the general public. An alliance survey of 1,000 parents with school-age children, she says, found that "60 percent-plus have a positive opinion of charter schools."

Independent polling also has found majority support for charter schools over the years, although a 2005 Gallup Poll found that only 28 percent of respondents would support a charter school in their community if it meant taking money from traditional public schools. [66] ∎

CURRENT SITUATION

Administration Action

After more than six weeks in office, the Trump administration has yet to formally present its education policy.

However, in an address to Congress on Feb. 28, President Trump labeled education "the civil rights issue of our time," and called on Congress to pass an education bill "that funds school choice for disadvantaged youth, including millions of African-American and Latino children. These families should be free to choose the public, private, charter, magnet, religious or home school that is right for them." [67]

Three days later he visited a Catholic school in Orlando, Fla., to tout the use of vouchers, or public subsidies for children to attend private or religious schools. Teachers unions say Trump's preference for vouchers shows he is hostile toward public schools and that he intends to turn education into a profit-making industry. [68]

During his campaign, Trump promised to spend up to $20 billion to promote school choice, which includes not only charters but also vouchers. [69] If combined with $110 billion in state funding, that money "could provide $12,000 in school choice funds to every single K-12 student who today is living in poverty," Trump said at a campaign event in Cleveland in September. [70]

Analysts point out that such a plan would require each state to dedicate more than $2 billion, which they are not likely to do. More significantly, charter critics ask, if Trump and the Republican-controlled Congress plan to hold the line on federal spending, how would Congress fund the program?

"We think it's a terrible idea," says the NEA's Tate. "Where is the money going to come from?"

Because of the size of Trump's campaign proposal, several education experts say they fear the money would likely come from the budgets for two education programs: the Every Student Succeeds Act and Title I education funding.

The Every Student Succeeds Act, signed into law by President Obama in 2015, replaces the No Child Left Behind Act as the principal federal tool to ensure equal access to education for all students and establishment of achievement standards and annual statewide tests to measure educational progress. [71] Title I of the Elementary and Secondary Education Act provides financial assistance to public schools with large numbers or percentages of low-income children to help all children meet challenging academic content and achievement standards. [72]

"Traditional school districts all across the country benefit from and rely on these [Title I] funds," says Tate. "If they're going to be diverted to pay for this voucher-charter scheme, that's really going to raise a lot of concern."

Charter school supporters, however, say they hope for greater federal attention and financial support. "We are cautiously optimistic," says Rees of the National Alliance for Public Charter Schools. "A lot remains to be seen in what they produce in terms of a budget, and how they use the regulatory and guidance [capabilities] of the Education Department, but we are optimistic."

Part of that optimism, charter supporters say, stems from the fact that Education Secretary DeVos, a longtime advocate of school choice and charter schools, would be charged with implementing Trump's plan. DeVos, whose Senate confirmation was highly contentious and required Vice President Mike Pence to cast a tie-breaking vote, continues to raise the ire of supporters of traditional schools. [73] After visiting a public school in Washington in February, she made what many called disparaging remarks about the teachers at the school. [74]

DeVos also said she has taken the helm of a federal Cabinet agency that she wouldn't mind eliminating. "It would be fine with me if I worked myself out of a job," she said. She added that while the federal government needed to get involved in important educational issues in the past — such as ending school segregation — she said she can't think of any current issues requiring federal intervention. [75]

State Action

Although opponents of charter expansion won victories in Georgia and Massachusetts last fall, proponents of charter schools continue to press their cases in the seven states without charter school laws.

In Kentucky, several bills authorizing charters are pending in the Legislature. One, introduced by Rep. John "Bam" Carney, the Republican chair of the Kentucky House Education Committee, has received the most attention. It would allow only local school districts to review and approve charter schools. Other proposed measures would allow a wider variety of organizations to authorize charters. [76]

In Montana, state Rep. Jonathan Windy Boy, a Democrat, has introduced a bill that would allow the state to authorize charter schools. He said charters would provide additional options for students in school districts with poorer schools. However, opposition to charters remains strong in Montana, with Democratic Gov. Steve Bullock and the executive director of the Board of Public Education both expressing skepticism about the legislation. [77]

In North Dakota, legislation is pending in the Senate that calls for a legislative study of charters and other school choice options, to be conducted during the period between legislative sessions. Initially, the measure — which has passed the House — would have allowed the creation of charter schools and educational savings accounts that could be used for

Continued on p. 234

At Issue:

Do charter schools hurt traditional public schools?

LILY ESKELSEN GARCÍA
PRESIDENT, NATIONAL EDUCATION ASSOCIATION, AND UTAH TEACHER OF THE YEAR, 1989

WRITTEN FOR *CQ RESEARCHER*, MARCH 2017

charter schools have delayed and distracted us from achieving equal access for all students to the same opportunities available to students in our best public schools. Charters dismantle our system of neighborhood public schools and diminish the community's responsibility to fight for all students, turning education into an individual commodity instead of a public good and a civil right. For a century, our system has allowed gross inequities among public schools. What we do for some students, we do not do for all. Charters have only made that problem worse.

Look at the disaster in Michigan — home of unlimited, unregulated and overwhelmingly for-profit charters — and you will see the reality of "school choice" as a magic cure-all. Parents from Detroit came to Washington to speak against the confirmation of Betsy DeVos as Education secretary because they believe charters have devastated their public schools and surrounded them with an illusion of "choice" where none of the options are good.

The fact is, America has the best public schools in the world — but those schools are most often located in affluent communities. Any good reformer would begin with an analysis of what's happening in our best public schools to see if there's something different from what's happening in our struggling schools.

The answer is not a mystery: Resources. Programs. Student supports and services. A good school might have arts programs, a girls' volleyball team, AP courses, a library and a librarian. Wouldn't it be interesting to take an inventory of the programs and services in our best schools and compare that list with what struggling schools have?

I once asked an advocate for charters why we shouldn't give students in poor communities the opportunities that affluent public schools offer. She smiled and said, "Well, that would be nice. But do you know what that would cost to provide?"

Of course we know. Because we provide it for some children. The moral question before us is whether we will provide the same for all children.

This is about more than spending equal dollars; the issue is equity in programs and services to support students. Our most affluent and well-connected parents are able to choose a great, fully resourced neighborhood public school. Why is that the rare choice for parents in poorer communities?

NINA REES
PRESIDENT AND CEO, NATIONAL ALLIANCE FOR PUBLIC CHARTER SCHOOLS

WRITTEN FOR *CQ RESEARCHER*, MARCH 2017

charter public schools do not hurt traditional public schools. In fact, when school districts and charter schools work together, the presence of charter schools enhances the quality of district schools and the overall public school system.

Nowhere is this clearer than in Washington, D.C., where charter schools have been on the public education landscape for about 20 years. Over that time, D.C. public schools have experienced a renaissance, with rising scores on the National Assessment of Educational Progress at both district and charter schools. Perhaps even more encouraging: Washington has seen enrollment in its public schools increase over the past decade. Parents of all backgrounds no longer feel the need to flee to suburban Maryland or Virginia to give their children access to better schools.

The improvement in D.C.'s schools isn't only because of the presence of charter schools. The city has benefited from a procession of big-thinking mayors and education chancellors who took bold steps to make schools safer and more quality-focused. But the presence of charter schools also has helped to drive this improvement. As the percentage of D.C. students attending charter schools climbed to nearly half, the district system has found ways to de-ossify itself and make its own schools better and more appealing to parents.

D.C.'s success is partly due to the almost unparalleled level of cooperation between the city's Public Charter School Board and the district school system. Through combined efforts like annual school quality reports and a common enrollment system, charter and district leaders have improved the quality of education, enhanced equity and reduced discipline rates.

Other cities are working hard to foster cooperation between the public school system and charter schools, with positive results. The Center on Reinventing Public Education found that sustained collaboration between charters and district schools benefits students in both types of school. This may seem obvious. Yet, too many school district leaders and mayors still chafe at the very existence of charter schools. Exhibit A: New York City has some of the nation's best charter schools, but the mayor is intent on preventing more students from gaining access to them.

After 25 years of charter schooling, the evidence shows that charter schools give students and families better options. Nowhere is this greater than in school districts that are willing to see charters as partners rather than adversaries.

Continued from p. 232

private school tuition and home schooling, but that provision was deleted. [78]

Charter school supporters are holding rallies and lobbying public officials in other non-charter states. In Nebraska and Vermont, pro-charter crowds rallied on the state Capitol steps in January as part of School Choice Week, an annual event started in 2011 by supporters of choice. In Nebraska, a group supporting traditional public schools, Nebraska Loves Public Schools, scheduled a counter-campaign the same week that included house parties to view a film supporting traditional schools, a sign of the growing division between those supporting and opposing school choice. [79]

In Washington state, a battle over charter schools is being fought in the courts and the Legislature. In 2015, the state Supreme Court ruled that the funding mechanism for charter schools was unconstitutional because it did not provide for elected oversight. The Legislature then passed a new law in 2016 funding the state's eight charter schools through the state lottery. But a coalition of charter opponents, including parents, civic and education groups, sued again, saying the new bill still did not meet constitutional muster.

On Feb. 17, King County Superior Court Judge John H. Chun ruled against the coalition, saying they had failed to prove their claim that charters were improperly diverting public funds to charter schools. Coalition members say they haven't decided whether to appeal but plan to press the Legislature to fully fund traditional public schools. [80]

NAACP Acts

Charter schools have recorded some of their strongest academic achievements in inner-city neighborhoods with high minority populations, but the NAACP's Board of Directors has called for a moratorium on charter school expansion until schools strengthen governance and performance. [81]

"This came from the bottom up," Cornell William Brooks, NAACP president, says about the moratorium resolution. "It was generated by the consequences and concerns about charter schools our rank-and-file members had."

Those concerns, Brooks says, include "charter schools that open and close in the twinkling of the eye and in a fraction of the school year," leaving families stranded. The NAACP's concerns also include what Brooks says is a lack of accountability and a focus on high-performing students who are the least expensive to educate.

NAACP members also are worried about the overly punitive disciplinary practices of some charters, Brooks says, and the impact that increased state spending on charter schools will have on traditional public schools.

To solicit input about these concerns, the civil rights group is holding a series of public hearings around the country. [82] Brooks says the association is not calling for a permanent ban on charter expansion but a "reasoned pause" to examine the challenges and consequences of charter expansion.

The NAACP president says it's too early to know what the hearings will find, but, "we absolutely know that something must be done to ensure that charter schools operate as public schools, really responsible for educating all the public and that means not manipulating the system so you get a select few, as opposed to the many."

Virtual Charters

Both sides of the charter school debate share concerns about the performance of online or "virtual" charter schools. About 200 such schools are serving 200,000 elementary, middle and high school students across the country, according to the most recent information available. [83] But various studies have shown that students in online charters are not learning at a rate equal to their peers in either traditional schools or other charters.

"Across all grades and subjects, students in online charter schools perform worse on standardized assessments and are significantly less likely to pass Ohio's test for high school graduation than their peers in traditional charter and traditional public schools," said Andrew McEachin, a policy researcher at the RAND Corp. think tank and one of the authors of a New York University study released in February. [84]

A 2015 CREDO study found even bleaker results: Students attending an online charter school fell behind by 72 days' worth of learning in reading and 180 days in math in a single 180-day school year. [85] In other words, said CREDO Director Macke Raymond, when it came to math it was "literally as though the student did not go to school for the entire year." [86]

Charter school advocates acknowledge the problems. Last year the National Alliance for Public Charter Schools and the National Association for Charter School Authorizers issued a joint report on online charters, calling for the closure of poorly performing online charter schools and the establishment of stronger accountability procedures. [87]

"Basically, we challenge [the online charter companies] to create better models because the current ones don't seem to be very effective," says Pendergrass, of the National Alliance for Public Charter Schools. ◾

OUTLOOK

Privatization Push

Some education experts believe the Trump administration, supported by Education Secretary DeVos, could bring the most profound shift in U.S. education policy since compulsory public education began to take hold in the 1850s.

"I expect to see a concerted effort to destroy public education," says New York University's Ravitch. "It will be a push for privatization, and whether it's charters or vouchers, it will be the same thing. . . . We're heading back toward the 19th century before there was public education. People went to church schools; they went to private schools; they were home schooled, and some kids got no education at all. We've had a 200-year battle to try to create a universal public school system, and now that's under assault."

Other charter school critics don't see the future as quite so bleak, but they still expect a dramatic shift of resources away from traditional schools. "I suspect that we're going to see a double-down on private control of schools and finding ways to make schools profit mechanisms for corporations and individuals — so voucher programs and perhaps more for-profit charter schools," says California State University's Vasquez Heilig.

The University of Washington's Au believes the administration's expected retreat from support for traditional public education "means everything will get kicked down to the states. You will have some states with some strong educational systems and some with terrible ones, but no federal watchdog saying you need to take care of stuff like equal treatment for LGBT [lesbian, gay, bisexual and transgender] students or minority students."

In fact, on Feb. 22, the Trump administration announced it was rescinding Obama administration guidelines requiring that transgender students be allowed to use public school bathrooms matching the gender with which they identify, rather than their birth gender. Trump administration officials said the issue is best dealt with at the state and local levels. [88]

Charter advocates see the administration's deemphasis of the federal role as empowering for communities and individual schools. "The school should be the focal point of all efforts. Money should flow to schools. Decision-making should be at schools. Choices of whether or not that's the school for you, parents should make those decisions," says Allen, of the Center for Education Reform.

Rees, of the National Alliance for Public Charter Schools, hopes charter school officials will be "brought to the table" to play a larger role in state education policy. She also wants to see the charter movement, which has been strongest in urban areas, expand to less populated parts of the country. "I think that's been neglected for a long time," she says.

Barth, of the Center for Public Education, believes the number of charters will continue to grow, but increased attention to charter performance by authorizers could slow the movement. That would improve the quality of charters, she says, "but if you're turning down charters at a higher rate, you're not likely to be growing as fast."

Pratt, of the Michigan Education Association, says the wave of public opposition that greeted DeVos' nomination as Education secretary "speaks to the fact that people have wised up and are going to push back" on further expansion of charters and school choice.

But charter school supporters believe their movement has plenty of room for growth, despite opposition in some quarters. "When we asked parents what would be their No. 1 choice for a school, one in 10 said a charter school," says Pendergrass, of the National Alliance for Public Charter Schools. "That's nearly twice the percentage [of public school students] currently in a charter school. . . . I definitely don't feel like we're anywhere near saturation."

Looking further ahead, Pendergrass believes the nation has made a long-term shift toward school choice. "We're not going to turn back the clock and start assigning more kids to school," she says. "Support for charters and school choice actually increases as you get younger. It's highest among Millennials. They fully expect that as they go forward they will get to pick a school for their children. We, as a people, always want more choices, rather than less." ∎

Notes

[1] Debra Bruno, "D.C.'s Education in School Reform," *Politico*, July 16, 2015, http://tinyurl.com/pq98dxk.

[2] "College Preparatory Curriculum," Thurgood Marshall Academy, 2017, http://tinyurl.com/z9o6hxd.

[3] "2015-2016 Renewal Report, Thurgood Marshall Academy Public Charter School," District of Columbia Public Charter School Board, Jan. 27, 2016, p. 3, http://tinyurl.com/zx6e2rk.

[4] Anna M. Phillips, Howard Blume and Matt Hamilton, "Federal agents raid Los Angeles charter school network," *Los Angeles Times*, Jan. 25, 2017, http://tinyurl.com/juoe23r.

[5] Anna M. Phillips, "Few school supplies but a lavish party: At charter school, teachers saw a clash between scarcity and extravagance," *Los Angeles Times*, Jan. 31, 2017, http://tinyurl.com/zd67wte.

[6] "A Closer Look at the Charter School Movement: Charter Schools, Students, and Management Organizations 2015-2016," National Alliance for Public Charter Schools, 2016, http://tinyurl.com/j85ztlh.

[7] *Ibid.*

[8] "Charter School Enrollment," National Center for Education Statistics, April 2016, http://tinyurl.com/hv4bc39. Also see Arianna Prothero, "More States Create Independent Charter-Approval Boards," *Education Week*, Aug. 19, 2014, http://tinyurl.com/z236o9p.

[9] "Urban Charter School Study Report on 41 Regions, 2015," Center for Research on Education Outcomes, Stanford University, 2015, p. v, http://tinyurl.com/q5wmh4v.

[10] Meagan Batdorff *et al.*, "Buckets of Water into the Ocean: Non-Public Revenue in Public Charter and Traditional Public Schools," School Choice Demonstration Project, Department of Education Reform, University of Arkansas, June 2015, http://tinyurl.com/gn33bfg. Also see Atila Abdulkadiroglu *et al.*, "Charters Without Lotteries: Testing Takeovers in New Orleans and Boston," National Bureau of Economic Research, December 2014, http://tinyurl.com/zpcxavn.

[11] "National Charter School Study 2013," Center for Research on Education Outcomes, Stanford University, 2013, p. 57, http://tinyurl.com/npr5wq6.

12 "Charter School Vulnerabilities to Waste, Fraud, and Abuse," Center for Popular Democracy, May 2016, http://tinyurl.com/zkfk9mf.

13 Bruce Baker and Gary Miron, "The Business of Charter Schooling: Understanding the Policies that Charter Operators Use for Financial Benefit," National Education Policy Center, Colorado University, December 2015, http://tinyurl.com/jnludyq.

14 Abby Jackson, "The Walmart family is teaching hedge funds how to profit from publicly funded schools," *Business Insider*, May 17, 2015, http://tinyurl.com/zh8wdwr.

15 Lauren Camera, "Education Secretary to Charter Schools: Rethink School Discipline," *U.S. News & World Report*, June 28, 2016, http://tinyurl.com/grg4pvs.

16 Valerie Strauss, "NAACP ratifies controversial resolution for a moratorium on charter schools," *The Washington Post*, Oct. 15, 2016, http://tinyurl.com/grrr5tk.

17 "Charter School Enrollment," National Center for Education Statistics, April 2016, http://tinyurl.com/hv4bc39.

18 "School Choice: What the Research Says," Center for Public Education, National School Boards Association, January 2017, p. 5, http://tinyurl.com/gl4spl4.

19 "Public High School Graduation Rates," National Center for Education Statistics, May 2016, http://tinyurl.com/j6ubcbu.

20 "National Charter School Study 2013," *op. cit.*

21 Patrick O'Donnell, "Ohio's charter school performance is 'grim' and needs state attention, Stanford researcher tells the City Club," *The Cleveland Plain Dealer*, Dec. 10, 2014, http://tinyurl.com/hujasey.

22 "Urban Charter School Study 2015," *op. cit.*

23 "CREDO Study Finds Urban Charter Schools Outperform Traditional School Peers," Center for Research on Education Outcomes, Stanford University, March 18, 2015, http://tinyurl.com/zgjlpjy.

24 Kate Taylor, "At a Success Academy Charter School, Singling Out Pupils Who Have 'Got

to Go,' " *The New York Times*, Oct. 29, 2015, http://tinyurl.com/z9h7oby.

25 For a list of the seven states without charter school laws, see "Charter Schools — Does the state have a charter school law?" Education Commission of the States, January 2016, http://tinyurl.com/hzldwhy.

26 Baker and Miron, *op. cit.*

27 "Charters, be Transparent," *The Arizona Republic*, Nov. 21, 2012, http://tinyurl.com/gue4sqy.

28 Baker and Miron, *op. cit.*

29 Evie Blad, "Federal Civil Rights Laws Apply Equally to Charter Schools, Guidance Says," *Education Week*, May 14, 2014, http://tinyurl.com/jv6scqt.

30 "Charter Schools — what rules are waived for charter schools?" Education Commission of the States, January 2016, http://tinyurl.com/zqxxabm.

31 "Charter Schools: Do teachers in a charter school have to be certified?" Education Commission of the States, January 2016, http://tinyurl.com/h9u5to5.

32 Daniel J. Losen *et al.*, "Charter Schools, Civil Rights and School Discipline: A Comprehensive Review," The Civil Rights Project, University of California, Los Angeles, March 31, 2016, http://tinyurl.com/j6k5r82.

33 Kate Taylor, "At Success Academy School, a Stumble in Math and a Teacher's Anger on Video," *The New York Times*, Feb. 12, 2016, http://tinyurl.com/hpm84hq.

34 *Ibid.*

35 Ted Kolderie, "Ray Budde and the origins of the 'Charter Concept,' " education/evolving, the Center for Policy Studies and Hamline University, June 2005, http://tinyurl.com/h3g4k4n.

36 *Ibid.*

37 Edward Graham, "'A Nation at Risk' turns 30: Where Did It Take Us?" *NEA Today*, April 25, 2013, http://tinyurl.com/j67vqff.

38 Albert Shanker, "National Press Club Speech," National Press Club, March 31, 1988, http://tinyurl.com/hp9sl7c.

39 *Ibid.*

40 *Ibid.*

41 *Ibid.*

42 Richard D. Kahlenberg and Halley Potter, "Restoring Shanker's Vision for Charter Schools," American Federation of Teachers, 2014, http://tinyurl.com/zvdppjk.

43 Ted Kolderie, "How the idea of 'chartering' schools came about, what role did the Citizen's League play?" *Minnesota Journal*, 2008, http://tinyurl.com/hxkhzxf.

44 Claudio Sanchez, "From a Single Charter School, a Movement Grows," WSIU National Public Broadcasting, Sept. 2, 2012, http://tinyurl.com/z8m3gnt.

45 "Charter School Law Rankings and Scorecard 2015," Center For Education Reform, 2015, http://tinyurl.com/lerk86m.

46 "President Bill Clinton Honored with Lifetime Achievement Award at National Charter Schools Conference," National Alliance for Public Charter Schools, June 13, 2011, http://tinyurl.com/hutlt2n.

47 William J. Clinton, "Remarks to the American Legion Boys Nation," The American Presidency Project, July 24, 1998, http://tinyurl.com/zbuw8yj.

48 "Charter School Law Rankings and Scorecard 2015," *op. cit.*

49 "U.S. Department of Education Awards $245 Million to Support High-Quality Public Charter Schools," U.S. Department of Education, Sept. 28, 2016, http://tinyurl.com/h4fdk8a. Also see "Charter Schools Program State Educational Agencies (SEA) Grant — Funding Status," U.S. Department of Education, Sept. 26, 2016, http://tinyurl.com/glngrwg.

50 "The Charter School Movement: 25 Years in the Making," *Education Week*, 2016, http://tinyurl.com/gsbqy5x.

51 Reed Karaim, "The New School Beat," *The Children's Beat*, Winter 2004, http://tinyurl.com/gr7lz6o.

52 "The Charter School Movement, 25 Years in the Making," *op. cit.*

53 *Ibid.*, p. 27.

54 Rachel M. Cohen, "When Charters go Union," *The American Prospect*, June 18, 2015, http://tinyurl.com/hgngy95.

55 "Who teaches at charter schools, and how do they differ from teachers at traditional public schools?" *Charter Schools in Perspective*, 2013, http://tinyurl.com/zqfld9h.

56 The Hechinger Report, "Number of U.S. Charter Schools Up 7 Percent, Report Shows," *U.S. News & World Report*, Nov. 3, 2014, http://tinyurl.com/nh8hmcn.

57 Shan Carter *et al.*, "On the Issues: Education, Election Guide 2008," *The New York Times*,

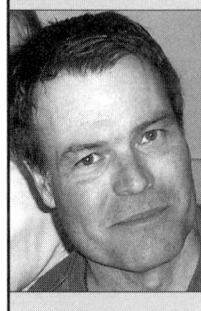

About the Author

Reed Karaim, a freelance writer in Tucson, Ariz., has written for *The Washington Post, U.S. News & World Report, Smithsonian, American Scholar, USA Weekend* and other publications. He is the author of the novel *If Men Were Angels*, which was selected for the Barnes & Noble Discover Great New Writers series. He is also the winner of the Robin Goldstein Award for Outstanding Regional Reporting and other journalism honors. Karaim is a graduate of North Dakota State University in Fargo.

May 23, 2012, http://tinyurl.com/zeh9uvx.

[58] "A Closer Look at the Charter School Movement," op. cit.

[59] Howard Blume, "Unions forge alliance to fight growth of charter schools in L.A.," *Los Angeles Times*, Oct. 13, 2015, http://tinyurl.com/j2b32oq.

[60] The Eli and Edythe Broad Foundation, 2017, http://tinyurl.com/jnr6w93.

[61] Sonali Kohli, "Huntington Park leaders vote to ban new charter schools for a year," *Los Angeles Times*, Oct. 18, 2016, http://tinyurl.com/hpkn2gg.

[62] Maureen Magee, "Inside the fight against California's charter schools," *Los Angeles Times*, Feb. 18, 2016, http://tinyurl.com/z4gdx6u.

[63] Shira Schoenburg, "Massachusetts votes against expanding charter schools, saying no to Question 2," *Masslive*, Nov. 8, 2016, http://tinyurl.com/jop5725.

[64] "2016 Report Ranks States with the Best and Worst School Systems," *Education World*, Aug. 1, 2016, http://tinyurl.com/zab4rwh.

[65] Ty Tagami, "Voters say 'no' to Opportunity School District," *Atlanta Journal-Constitution*, Nov. 9, 2016, http://tinyurl.com/jam2gb7.

[66] "Public Opinion," *Charter Schools in Perspective*, http://tinyurl.com/j3kw7dp.

[67] Jake Miller, "Trump to pitch school vouchers at Orlando Catholic school," CBS News, March 2, 2017, http://tinyurl.com/jrjmy3s.

[68] "Trump to visit Orlando private school today to promote school choice," WESH News, March 3, 2017, http://tinyurl.com/hz6cukg.

[69] Ben Kasimar, "Trump pledges to earmark $20B for school choice," *The Hill*, Sept. 8, 2016, http://tinyurl.com/j8f49p7.

[70] *Ibid*.

[71] "Every Student Succeeds Act (ESSA)," U.S. Department of Education, http://tinyurl.com/hdc62y4.

[72] "Improving Basic Programs Operated by Local Educational Agencies (Title I, Part A)," U.S. Department of Education, http://tinyurl.com/zgt4ysn.

[73] Emma Brown, "With historic tiebreaker from Pence, DeVos confirmed as education secretary," *The Washington Post*, Feb. 7, 2017, http://tinyurl.com/gsuj2bd.

[74] Yamiche Alcindor, "Rough First Week Gives Betsy DeVos a Glimpse of the Fight Ahead," *The New York Times*, Feb. 19, 2017, http://tinyurl.com/h3vrh8g.

[75] *Ibid*.

[76] Ryland Barton, "House Education Chair Files New Charter School Bill," WFPL Kentucky Public Radio, Feb. 20, 2017, http://tinyurl.com/gn2r7zq.

[77] Michael Siebert and Freddy Monares, "Charter schools, non-discrimination laws, wine define legislature's seventh week," *Bozeman Daily Chronicle*, Feb. 20, 2017, http://tinyurl.com/zrkb4y6.

[78] "Bill Actions for HB1382," North Dakota Legislative Branch, 2017, http://tinyurl.com/hhs5pxr.

[79] "Parents, students, and teachers across the state will be joined by Governor Scott and Kevin Chavou," *Business Wire*, Jan. 20, 2017, http://tinyurl.com/hbqbg6w. Also see Joe Dejka, "Charter school debate: Hundreds rally in Lincoln in support school choice," *Omaha World-Herald*, Jan. 28, 2016, http://tinyurl.com/h49pjtg.

[80] Paige Cornwell, "King County judge rules state's charter-school law is constitutional," *The Seattle Times*, Feb. 17, 2017, http://tinyurl.com/h9p4vbm.

[81] "Statement Regarding the NAACP's Resolution on a Moratorium on Charter Schools," NAACP, Oct. 15, 2016, http://tinyurl.com/ho86knp.

[82] "NAACP task force to hold hearing on education quality," NAACP, Dec. 2, 2016, http://tinyurl.com/jdk7eom.

[83] Brian Gill *et al.*, "Inside Online Charter Schools," *Mathematica*, Oct. 27, 2015, http://tinyurl.com/hpckr7b.

[84] "Students in Ohio's Online Charter Schools Perform Worse Than Peers in Traditional Schools," New York University, Feb. 16, 2017, http://tinyurl.com/j9u6sbg.

[85] "Online Charter School Students Falling Behind Their Peers," Center for Research on Education Outcomes (CREDO), Stanford University, Oct. 27, 2015, http://tinyurl.com/zr5a32m.

[86] Benjamin Herold, "Cyber Charters Have 'Overwhelming Negative Impact,' CREDO Study Finds," *Education Week*, Oct. 27, 2017, http://tinyurl.com/zaftmfa.

[87] "A Call to Action to Improve the Quality of Fulltime Virtual Charter Schools," National Alliance for Public Charter Schools, June 16, 2016, http://tinyurl.com/jbzjaes.

[88] Sandhya Somashekhar, Emma Brown and Moriah Balingit, "Trump administration rolls back protections for transgender students," *The Washington Post*, Feb. 22, 2017, http://tinyurl.com/hh5knjz.

Bibliography

Selected Sources

Books

Moskowitz, Eva, and Arin Lavinia, *Mission Possible: How the Secrets of the Success Academies Can Work in Any School*, Jossey-Bass, 2012.

The founder and CEO (Moskowitz) of the Success Charter Network in Harlem, N.Y., and her co-author offer lessons learned at their charter schools that they believe can improve teaching and learning for all students.

Ravitch, Diane, *Reign of Error: The Hoax of the Privatization Movement and the Danger to America's Public Schools*, Knopf, 2013.

A New York University professor and former U.S. assistant secretary of Education says the school charter and privatization movement is an effort to destroy public education, led in part by investors driven by the profit motive.

Russakoff, Dale, *The Prize: Who's in Charge of America's Schools?* Houghton Mifflin Harcourt, 2016.

A veteran journalist examines the challenges that ensued in Newark, N.J., after Republican Gov. Chris Christie and Democratic Mayor Cory Booker — backed by $100 million from Facebook founder Mark Zuckerberg — introduced charter schools and more choice into the Newark school system in 2010.

Wohlstetter, Priscilla, Joanna Smith and Caitlin Farrell, *Choices and Challenges: Charter School Performance in Perspective*, Harvard Education Press, 2013.

Three academic experts on choice in education sift through the main studies on charter school performance to determine how well they are meeting the wide range of goals established for charters across the country.

Articles

Calefati, Jessica, "California Virtual Academies: Is online charter school network cashing in on failure?" *The* [San Jose] *Mercury News*, April 16, 2016, http://tinyurl.com/j49237b.

An investigation of a California online charter school operated by K12, one of the nation's largest online charter companies, finds questionable practices required of teachers and a failure of students to learn.

Mead, Sara, "Charters Score in Cities," *U.S. News & World Report*, March 19, 2015, http://tinyurl.com/nmdne9y.

A study by a Stanford University research center shows charter schools are making a difference in urban areas, with students learning significantly more than their peers in the 41 school districts studied.

Smith, Morgan, "When Private Firms Run Schools, Financial Secrecy Is Allowed," *The New York Times*, Dec. 14, 2013, http://tinyurl.com/zghhfx4.

An examination of charter school applications in Texas finds that charter schools are using private management firms to keep much of their financial records private, allowing them to sidestep public records and transparency laws.

Strauss, Valerie, "Separating fact from fiction in 21 claims about charter schools," *The Washington Post*, Feb. 28, 2015, http://tinyurl.com/hz6mstv.

Academic experts examine some of the key claims and counterclaims made in the debate over charter schools, including whether they receive more or less money than traditional public schools and whether they are sufficiently accountable and transparent.

Zernike, Kate, "Condemnation of Charter Schools Exposes a Rift Over Black Students," *The New York Times*, Aug. 20, 2016, http://tinyurl.com/j5qrorn.

The National Association for the Advancement of Colored People (NAACP.), the civil rights organization, and the Movement for Black Lives, an association of civil rights groups organized by Black Lives Matter, have both called for a moratorium on charter schools, citing various concerns.

Reports and Studies

"Charter School Vulnerabilities to Waste, Fraud, And Abuse," Center for Popular Democracy, May 2016, http://tinyurl.com/zkfk9mf.

A study by a nonprofit group that promotes equity, opportunity and democracy, finds $203 million in financial fraud, waste, abuse and mismanagement in charter schools in 15 states.

"A Growing Movement: America's Largest Charter School Communities and Their Impact on Student Outcomes," National Alliance for Public Charter Schools, November 2016, http://tinyurl.com/zdusry2.

A report by a national charter school group finds that as enrollment continues to grow, school districts with the most charter schools are producing a disproportionate share of students who test as proficient or above in assessment tests.

"School Choice: What the Research Says, Center for Public Education," National School Boards Association, October 2015, http://tinyurl.com/hlmvwbh.

An examination of independent research on charter schools finds that school choice, including charter schools, works for some students, is worse than traditional public schools for some and often is no better or worse.

Candal, Cara, *Just the Facts: Success, Innovation and Opportunity in Charter Schools*, The Center for Education Reform, 2017, http://tinyurl.com/zffnzka.

A pro-charter school group analyzes negative charges about charters and concludes they are more accountable, more efficient and provide better outcomes than traditional public schools.

The Next Step:

Additional Articles from Current Periodicals

Academic Performance

Schulz, Sam, "Milwaukee charter schools performed better than public schools on ACT, report shows," *The Daily Cardinal*, March 1, 2017, http://tinyurl.com/jxsvmyz.

Milwaukee charter schools scored 8 percent better on the ACT than their traditional public counterparts, a study finds.

Taketta, Kristen, "These St. Louis charter schools have struggled for 14 years, but continue to evade closure," *St. Louis Post-Dispatch*, Feb. 26, 2017, http://tinyurl.com/gnejkvs.

Despite lagging behind state averages on standardized testing during their 14-year history, five Missouri charter schools continue to receive funding with no direct oversight.

Vogell, Heather and Hannah Fresques, " 'Alternative' Education: Using Charter Schools to Hide Dropouts and Game the System," *ProPublica*, Feb. 21, 2017, http://tinyurl.com/zwj3vwg.

Some charter schools have attempted to maintain high graduation rates by sending lower-performing students to "alternative" high schools managed by for-profit companies.

Charter Controversies

Laracy, Charlotte, "Why Philadelphia charter schools have sparked recent controversy," *The Daily Pennsylvanian*, Sept. 1, 2016, http://tinyurl.com/zfnptjm.

Experts in Philadelphia disagree about the effectiveness of the city's charter schools, with some arguing that the schools perpetuate racial segregation and others praising the schools' impact on black communities.

Stavely, Zaidee, "Charter School Controversy At Heart of School Board Race," KQED, Oct. 18, 2016, http://tinyurl.com/z9kvqhu.

Investigators said school board officials in a California region favored a charter school over the traditional public school.

Strauss, Valerie, "NAACP ratifies controversial resolution for a moratorium on charter schools," *The Washington Post*, Oct. 15, 2016, http://tinyurl.com/j4zoylx.

NAACP leaders approved a resolution calling for a pause on charter school expansion until the schools receive the same funds as traditional public schools.

Funding

Garcia, Nicholas, "Should Colorado charter schools get a share of local tax increases? Some Colorado lawmakers think so," *The Denver Post*, Feb. 8, 2017, http://tinyurl.com/jhywc9t.

Colorado charter schools are hoping for additional funding under a bill that would require school districts to share tax increases with charters.

Heath, Christopher, "Charter schools poised to get dedicated capital funding," WFTV, Feb. 22, 2017, http://tinyurl.com/z9l492o.

A Florida bill would dedicate a funding source to the state's charter schools, focusing primarily on schools with higher numbers of low-income students or students with disabilities.

McVicar, Brian, "Cyber charter schools could lose $16 million under Gov. Snyder's proposed funding cut," *MLive Michigan*, March 2, 2017, http://tinyurl.com/znenas3.

Michigan lawmakers will decide on a request from Republican Gov. Rick Snyder to cut funding for online charter schools.

State Legislation

Algar, Selim, "De Blasio denies charters space in public schools, flouting state law: report," *New York Post*, March 2, 2017, http://tinyurl.com/grz43c7.

A report says New York Mayor Bill de Blasio is violating a state law that mandates access to public facilities for charters by denying space to charter schools in public buildings.

Joyner, Tammy, "Stovall legislation aimed at helping charter schools, public comment," *Atlanta Journal Constitution*, March 2, 2017, http://tinyurl.com/jr83ly8.

A Georgia bill would allow charter schools to use unoccupied buildings under the jurisdiction of public school districts.

Powell Crain, Trisha, "Lawmakers hear proposed changes to Alabama public charter school law," AL.com, Feb. 22, 2017, http://tinyurl.com/hfz67k4.

Alabama lawmakers reviewed changes to a state charter school law that would clarify the funding mechanism for the schools, which have yet to open.

CITING *CQ RESEARCHER*

Sample formats for citing these reports in a bibliography include the ones listed below. Preferred styles and formats vary, so please check with your instructor or professor.

MLA STYLE

Jost, Kenneth. "Remembering 9/11." CQ Researcher 2 Sept. 2011: 701-732.

APA STYLE

Jost, K. (2011, September 2). Remembering 9/11. *CQ Researcher, 9*, 701-732.

CHICAGO STYLE

Jost, Kenneth. "Remembering 9/11." *CQ Researcher*, September 2, 2011, 701-32.

In-depth Reports on Issues in the News

Are you writing a paper?

Need backup for a debate?

Want to become an expert on an issue?

For 90 years, students have turned to *CQ Researcher* for in-depth reporting on issues in the news. Reports on a full range of political and social issues are now available. Following is a selection of recent reports:

Civil Liberties
Privacy and the Internet, 12/15
Intelligence Reform, 5/15
Religion and Law, 11/14

Crime/Law
Forensic Science Controversies, 2/17
Jailing Debtors, 9/16
Decriminalizing Prostitution, 4/16
Restorative Justice, 2/16
The Dark Web, 1/16
Immigrant Detention, 10/15
Fighting Gangs, 10/15

Education
Civic Education, 2/17
Student Debt, 11/16
Apprenticeships, 10/16
Free Speech on Campus, 5/15

Environment/Society
Women in Prison, 3/17
Guns on Campus, 1/17
Mass Transit, 12/16
Arctic Development, 12/16
Protecting the Power Grid, 11/16
Pornography, 10/16

Health/Safety
Reducing Traffic Deaths, 2/17
Opioid Crisis, 10/16
Mosquito-Borne Disease, 7/16
Drinking Water Safety, 7/16

Politics/Economy
Immigrants and the Economy, 2/17
Trump Presidency, 1/17
European Union's Future, 12/16
The Obama Legacy, 11/16
Populism and Party Politics, 9/16
U.S.-Mexico Relations, 9/16

Upcoming Reports

The 'Alt-Right' Movement, 3/17/17   Rural Issues, 3/31/17   Brazil, 4/7/17

ACCESS

CQ Researcher is available in print and online. For access, visit your library or www.cqresearcher.com.

STAY CURRENT

For notice of upcoming *CQ Researcher* reports or to learn more about *CQ Researcher* products, subscribe to the free email newsletters, *CQ Researcher Alert!* and *CQ Researcher News*: http://cqpress.com/newsletters.

PURCHASE

To purchase a *CQ Researcher* report in print or electronic format (PDF), visit www.cqpress.com or call 866-427-7737. Single reports start at $15. Bulk purchase discounts and electronic-rights licensing are also available.

SUBSCRIBE

Annual full-service *CQ Researcher* subscriptions—including 44 reports a year, monthly index updates, and a bound volume—start at $1,131. Add $25 for domestic postage.

CQ Researcher Online offers a backfile from 1991 and a number of tools to simplify research. For pricing information, call 800-818-7243 or 805-499-9774 or email librarysales@sagepub.com.

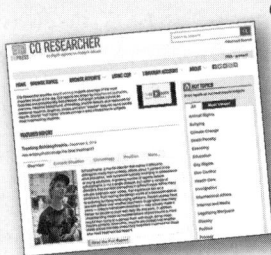

CQ RESEARCHER

CQPRESS

In-depth reports on today's issues

Published by CQ Press, an Imprint of SAGE Publications, Inc.   **www.cqresearcher.com**

'Alt-Right' Movement

Do its white-nationalist views have wide support?

The "alt-right," a loose coalition of white nationalists, white supremacists, anti-Semites and others seeking to preserve what they consider traditional Western civilization, is urging white Americans to band together and fight multiculturalism. The movement has gained more attention than any fringe group in decades because of its role in the 2016 election and its embrace of President Trump's America First agenda. Political observers say the alt-right has tapped into some whites' fears about immigration and the nation's changing demographics, where whites will soon be a minority. The alt-right remains small, but both conservatives and liberals denounce its beliefs as racist. They point with alarm to the alt-right's online use of profane language and images to attack social conventions — moves that are helping it gain followers. The movement's use of identity politics, some say, is reminiscent of how liberals used it to fight for racial and gender equality. A number of analysts note that hate crimes have been increasing since the November election and urge Trump to more forcefully speak out against them.

White nationalist Richard Spencer, unofficial leader of the alt-right movement, talks with reporters after he was ejected from the Conservative Political Action Conference on Feb. 23, 2017, because of his controversial views. But some audience members gave him a warm welcome.

CQ Researcher • March 17, 2017 • www.cqresearcher.com
Volume 27, Number 11 • Pages 241-264

I N S I D E THIS REPORT

THE ISSUES **243**

BACKGROUND **249**

CHRONOLOGY **251**

CURRENT SITUATION **255**

AT ISSUE.......................**257**

OUTLOOK **259**

BIBLIOGRAPHY **262**

THE NEXT STEP **263**

THE ISSUES

243
- Is the alt-right a white-supremacist movement?
- Does the Trump administration support alt-right ideas?
- Does the alt-right promote violence?

BACKGROUND

249 **American Racial Purity**
Pro-white, anti-immigrant sentiments have a long history in the United States.

252 **Far-Right Thinkers**
"Paleoconservatives" embraced a white-nationalist vision in the 1980s.

253 **Europe's New Right**
Globalization and immigration reinvigorated Europe's far right, whose roots lay in 1930s fascism.

CURRENT SITUATION

255 **Campus Outreach**
White nationalists are trying to recruit new members at colleges and universities.

258 **Internet Savvy**
The alt-right uses memes to support Trump's presidency.

258 **International Movement**
The alt-right is finding kindred spirits in Europe.

OUTLOOK

259 **Spreading Influence?**
Gaining off-line followers will be a challenge for the alt-right.

SIDEBARS AND GRAPHICS

244 **Hate Groups Again On the Rise**
The number of hate groups has risen nearly 17 percent in the past three years.

245 **Defining the 'Alt-Right'**
The movement has numerous branches and beliefs.

248 **White Nationalists Gain on Social Media**
The alt-right has gained more than 22,000 Twitter followers since 2012.

251 **Chronology**
Key events since 1995.

252 **Researchers: Alt-Right Uses Internet to Normalize Hate**
"You have all these men who see their role as internet warriors."

254 **Alt-Right Borrows a Page From the Left**
The movement is using identity politics to build a bigger following.

257 **At Issue:**
Should online racist speech be regulated?

FOR FURTHER RESEARCH

261 **For More Information**
Organizations to contact.

262 **Bibliography**
Selected sources used.

263 **The Next Step**
Additional articles.

263 **Citing CQ Researcher**
Sample bibliography formats.

 **CQ RESEARCHER**

March 17, 2017
Volume 27, Number 11

EXECUTIVE EDITOR: Thomas J. Billitteri
tjb@sagepub.com

ASSISTANT MANAGING EDITORS: Kenneth Fireman, kenneth.fireman@sagepub.com, Kathy Koch, kathy.koch@sagepub.com, Scott Rohrer, scott.rohrer@sagepub.com

SENIOR CONTRIBUTING EDITOR:
Thomas J. Colin
tom.colin@sagepub.com

CONTRIBUTING WRITERS: Marcia Clemmitt, Sarah Glazer, Reed Karaim, Barbara Mantel, Chuck McCutcheon, Tom Price

SENIOR PROJECT EDITOR: Olu B. Davis

EDITORIAL ASSISTANT: Anika Reed

FACT CHECKERS: Eva P. Dasher, Michelle Harris, Betsy Towner Levine, Robin Palmer

SAGE Publishing | **CQPRESS**

Los Angeles | London | New Delhi
Singapore | Washington DC | Melbourne

An Imprint of SAGE Publications, Inc.

SENIOR VICE PRESIDENT, GLOBAL LEARNING RESOURCES:
Karen Phillips

EXECUTIVE DIRECTOR, ONLINE LIBRARY AND REFERENCE PUBLISHING:
Todd Baldwin

CQ Researcher (ISSN 1056-2036) is printed on acid-free paper. Published weekly, except: (March wk. 4) (May wk. 4) (July wks. 1, 2) (Aug. wks. 2, 3) (Nov. wk. 4) and (Dec. wks. 3, 4). Published by SAGE Publications, Inc., 2455 Teller Rd., Thousand Oaks, CA 91320. Annual full-service subscriptions start at $1,131. For pricing, call 1-800-818-7243. To purchase a CQ Researcher report in print or electronic format (PDF), visit www.cqpress.com or call 866-427-7737. Single reports start at $15. Bulk purchase discounts and electronic-rights licensing are also available. Periodicals postage paid at Thousand Oaks, California, and at additional mailing offices. POSTMASTER: Send address changes to CQ Researcher, 2600 Virginia Ave., N.W., Suite 600, Washington, DC 20037.

Cover: Getty Images/Chip Somodevilla

'Alt-Right' Movement

BY MARCIA CLEMMITT

THE ISSUES

At the Conservative Political Action Conference (CPAC) in February, where leading conservatives gather annually near Washington for four days of speeches and strategizing, organizers minced no words about one of the attendees and his beliefs.

Richard Spencer, unofficial leader of the white nationalist "alt-right" movement, had bought a ticket to the conference, but was later escorted out by security guards. "He is not welcome here," CPAC Communications Director Ian Walters said. "His views are repugnant and have absolutely nothing to do with what goes on here." [1] And in an address to the conference, organizer Dan Schneider called the alt-right a "sinister organization that is trying to worm its way into our ranks."

But some in the CPAC audience welcomed Spencer and treated him like a celebrity, posing with him for selfies. "Richard Spencer is, like, the coolest guy," said the president of a College Republicans group at a New England state university. [2]

Undaunted by the organizers' harsh words and encouraged by the audience's reception, Spencer said, "What the alt-right is doing is clearly resonating with people. You can call it names, or you can actually ask, why is it resonating? Why does a young white person feel alienated in the modern world?" [3]

White nationalists have long existed in the United States. What's surprising today, historians and political analysts say, is that over the past two years the loose assemblage of white nationalists, white supremacists and others who

Demonstrators protest a speech at Texas A&M University on Dec. 6, 2016, by Richard Spencer, who coined the term "alt-right." Many in the movement hope white Americans eventually will live in a whites-only ethno-state that Spencer has said might be created by some means of "peaceful ethnic cleansing."

AP Photo/David J. Phillip

gather under the alt-right banner have gained more attention than any fringe group in decades because of their ties to a major-party political nominee, Donald Trump, who won the presidency in November. The alt-right's use of internet attacks on Trump's behalf, and Trump's occasional retweeting during the campaign of material posted by white extremists, brought the alt-right waves of media attention and new enthusiasts, such as the Spencer fans at CPAC.

The movement also has sparked criticism and alarm at both ends of the political spectrum. Many on the Left denounce its stances and say the very term "alt-right" is a politically correct mask for

its extremist views. Meanwhile, critics on the Right say the movement is racist and an affront to both conservatism and traditional Republicanism; they also note that most Trump voters reject white extremism. [4]

Political observers say several other factors are spurring interest in the movement, including its ability to tap into some whites' fears about the changing demographics of the nation, where whites will soon be a racial minority, eclipsed by Hispanics and other groups. Another factor is Trump's populist appeals to whites worried about immigration, such as his false suggestion that a high percentage of Mexican immigrants are criminals. [5]

International developments also are propelling the alt-right. In Europe, a backlash against globalization and recent surges in refugees has led to the rise of far-right political parties throughout the Continent. Moreover, some backers of the alt-right make savvy online use of profane, taboo or abusive language and images to attack political correctness and social conventions. Those tactics attract many social media users, especially young men, analysts of extremist groups say.

White nationalism's new prominence is "a reaction against the multicultural explosion in America," says Lawrence Rosenthal, chair of the Center for Right-Wing Studies at the University of California, Berkeley. "We have just had a black president. Even the South is a very different place than it was 50 years ago. California has already turned majority minority."

Whether this primarily internet-based movement can solidify and expand its

Hate Groups Again On the Rise

The number of hate groups in the United States rose nearly 17 percent over the past three years, according to the Southern Poverty Law Center (SPLC), which monitors extremist organizations. Its count of hate group reflects only those that have a website and also undertake on-the-ground operations, such as rallies or leaflet distribution. The number of hate groups rose steadily between 1999 and 2011 before falling over the next three years. The SPLC attributed that decline to the fact that some groups moved exclusively to the Web.

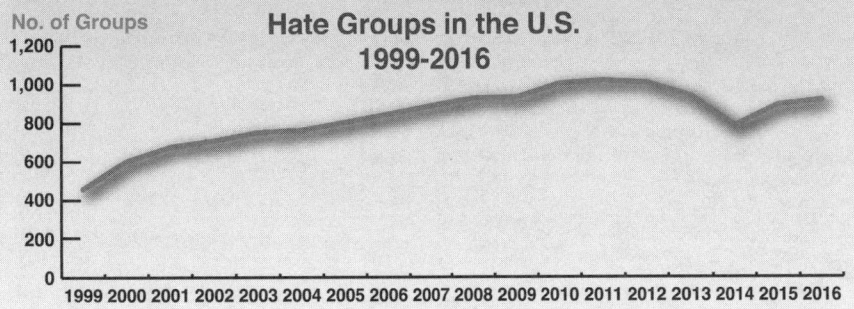

Hate Groups in the U.S.
1999-2016

No. of Groups

Source: Mark Potok, "The Year in Hate and Extremism," Southern Poverty Law Center, Feb. 15, 2017, http://tinyurl.com/hhfvcwj

influence with voters and within the Trump administration remains unclear, observers say.

"We shouldn't exaggerate the alt-right's size and influence," says George Hawley, an assistant professor of political science at the University of Alabama and the author of the 2016 book *Right-Wing Critics of American Conservatism*. In this mostly online movement, it's unknown how many people are core members — defined as those "who are really serious content creators" of, for example, original tweets or message-forum posts, he says. Hawley estimates the core group at a few thousand.

The term "alt-right" was first used in 2010, when Spencer, a writer and activist for a white nationalist think tank, the National Policy Institute (NPI), launched *Alternative Right*, an online publication featuring what were widely viewed as white racist, misogynist and anti-Semitic writings. [6] Spencer holds that alt-right thinking springs mainly from the perception that America's dominant white majority is losing ground to others.

Spencer didn't respond to *CQ Researcher*'s requests for an interview. In November he told the Center for Investigative Reporting, "Yes, white people are generally better off than many other people." But today, institutions such as government and media are acting on nonwhite people's behalf, he said. "And you can talk about this being fair . . . but . . . fairness has never been really a great value in my mind. I like greatness and winning and dominance and beauty." [7]

The Anti-Defamation League (ADL), a U.S.-based advocacy group that opposes anti-Semitism and other bigotry, holds that the alt-right movement is a loose network of people — mostly white males — who believe the United States is a majority white nation that should reject policies that dilute whites' influence and behave in a nationalistic fashion.

Besides fostering white identity, the alt-right also encourages "aggressive anti-feminist and misogynistic politics," says Matthew Lyons, co-author of the 2000 book *Right-Wing Populism in America*. Alt-right groups "say they have no interest

in recruiting women or addressing any of women's concerns," he says.

Still, groups that accept the alt-right label aren't monolithic in their views, says Marilyn Mayo, a director of the ADL's Center on Extremism.

For example, while some are anti-Semitic neo-Nazis, others appear not to be, she says. In fact, because most alt-right activity consists of anonymous online posts, it is not even clear how many alt-right followers are racists, Mayo says. "Some certainly are attracted just because they enjoy the rejection of political correctness. But a lot are really racist," she says.

Further dooming attempts to definitively describe the alt-right are frequent squabbles and defections in the group, for example over such questions as whether gays should be allowed to call themselves "alt-right" or whether Jews can be considered white people. [8]

Alt-right members may differ about the ideal outcome of their activism, but Spencer has made his clear, says Hawley. "He wants to see an all-white ethno-state established in North America," he says.

Spencer, however, has not clarified how the ethno-state would come about, a lack of detail that Hawley says is par for the alt-right course. The movement does not have "a lot in the way of real policy platforms," he says.

The lack of policy specifics springs from necessity, at least in part, says Brian Levin, director of the Center for the Study of Hate and Extremism at California State University, San Bernardino. "Spencer has to maintain credibility with extremists in the alt-right network, while also sending a more amorphous message that might reach mainstream voters" without frightening those voters off, says Levin.

While members of what's now called the alt-right have been active for years, they came to public attention in the last two years after various white nationalists began speaking out in favor of Trump's candidacy, and alt-right online activism caught the media's attention. Trump, who has denounced the movement, is "energizing" white nationalists in the United States, said Spencer, because of his anti-immigration, America First rhetoric. [9]

The movement's profile rose further when candidate Trump retweeted white nationalist and neo-Nazi messages, such as a fictitious crime statistic claiming that 81 percent of 2015 white murder victims were killed by blacks. (The correct figure is about 15 percent.) [10] Democratic presidential nominee Hillary Clinton accused Trump of stoking racism. The alt-right represents "a paranoid fringe in our politics," Clinton said in an August 2016 speech in Reno, Nev., and Trump had invigorated the movement by "stoking it, encouraging it and giving it a national megaphone." [11]

Over the past several years the movement also received exposure from the right-wing Breitbart News Network. Stephen Bannon, who became executive chairman after founder Andrew Breitbart died in 2012, said in August 2016 that *Breitbart News* is "the platform for the alt-right." [12] Trump named Bannon his campaign chief executive in August 2016, and then, post-election, named him chief White House strategist, moves that again raised the movement's public profile and that some observers fear could give the group a say in government policymaking. [13]

Throughout his campaign, Trump won endorsements from extremist groups, such as white supremacists and neo-Nazis, while also winning over tens of millions of mainstream voters, says Levin — something virtually unprecedented in U.S. history. "Far-right extremists have tried for decades to field candidates who could go mainstream, but they haven't ever had a charismatic leader who could do it," he says.

Still unclear, though, is the degree to which the Trump administration can or would act to turn white nationalist ideas into public policies, analysts say.

Defining the 'Alt-Right'

The alt-right movement has gained prominence since white nationalist Richard Spencer coined the term in 2008 in what some analysts call an effort to make its beliefs more acceptable to a broader audience. Believing white interests are under attack from multiculturalism, adherents are using the internet and supporting the Trump administration in an attempt to build a following.

Glossary

Alt-right: An umbrella term for various groups — white supremacists, anti-Semites and others — that espouse far-right ideologies centered on white nationalism. Spencer, its unofficial leader, wants an "ethno-state" — a territory set aside for people of European descent.

European New Right: With roots in 1930s fascism, the movement opposes multiculturalism and espouses isolationist and anti-globalization ideologies; it is a source of ideas for American white nationalists.

Paleoconservatism: An ideology founded in the 1980s that maintains the United States owes its greatness to the Founders' European heritage; it strenuously opposes immigration and other policies that might dilute that heritage.

White nationalism: A belief that the United States was founded as a white nation and whites should band together to keep it that way.

White separatism: A more extreme form of white nationalism and supremacism; its adherents advocate separation from other races in either an ethno-state or a racially segregated society.

White supremacism: The view that whites are superior to all other races and whites should dominate American society.

Sources: "Alternative Right," Southern Poverty Law Center, http://tinyurl.com/gmafta5; Dylan Matthews, "Paleoconservatism, the movement that explains Donald Trump, explained," Vox, May 6, 2016, http://tinyurl.com/hdrh397

In his inaugural address, Trump promised to fight for all Americans. "It is time to remember that old wisdom our soldiers will never forget: that whether we are black or brown or white, we all bleed the same red blood of patriots, we all enjoy the same glorious freedoms, and we all salute the same great American flag," he said. [14]

Advocates of race-based politics say they have only modest hopes. In his inaugural address, Trump served up "egalitarian schmaltz," self-proclaimed "race realist" Jared Taylor, founder of the alt-right American Renaissance website, said with disapproval. However, Trump does seem "to realize that at least some people don't belong [in the United States]," Taylor said, and may learn from some advisers, such as Bannon, to become more race-conscious with time. [15]

As political observers and others speculate on the alt-right's future, here are some of the questions they are asking:

Is the alt-right a white-supremacist movement?

People who identify as "alt-right" view race as central to human identity and consider the mixing of races in one society as a recipe for strife. In the past, many such people professed belief in "white supremacy" — the idea that whites are by nature superior to all other races, such as blacks, and therefore deserve to dominate society. (*See glossary, p. 245.*)

Alt-right groups do not use the term white supremacy to describe their be-

American white-nationalist author Jared Taylor, founder of the alt-right American Renaissance *website, addresses the International Russian Conservative Forum in St. Petersburg, Russia, on, March 22, 2015. Taylor has said the alt-right is "in unanimity" about rejecting "the idea that the races are basically equivalent and interchangeable."*

liefs. Some political analysts, however, argue that many in the alt-right are traditional white supremacists who have dropped the term because it fell out of public favor.

Several terms are routinely used to describe white identity politics, says Rosenthal, of the University of California, Berkeley.

White nationalism is "the idea that this is a white country," Rosenthal says. "Then there's white separatism — the desire to have a literal place, a state,

where white people can live on their own. Then there's white supremacy, which sees white people as having created all of Western civilization and asserts that they should therefore dominate in society. It's difficult to tell who holds which of these ideas, [partly because] people are very likely to say different things depending on who's there," he says. [16]

The alt-right has members with various beliefs. It "is now the main refuge of what previously was a hodgepodge of bigots, including neo-Nazis," says Levin of the Center for the Study of Hate and Extremism. Held in common "is a widespread notion that diversity and internationalism are traitorous," he says.

Many scholars of extremism, including Levin, say that the idea of white supremacy underlies the beliefs of many in the alt-right.

"Alt-right, much like white nationalism, is a rebranding of white supremacy," says Mayo of the ADL. "Some reject the term 'white supremacy,' but when you read their materials, their articles, their

blogs, there's a constant focus on whites being superior," she says.

For example, the *American Renaissance* website posts a series of articles called "How I Saw the Light About Race," collating website readers' comments. One reader who grew up in an all-white area wrote, "When I did finally meet blacks, I found them to be childish, unintelligent, inarticulate, and often immoral and degenerate. That opinion has been confirmed over the decades." [17]

"Biological determinism that argues some races are objectively inferior to others isn't as easy a sell as it once was, neither politically nor scientifically," says Levin. "Most people just don't buy it any longer." As a result, arguments for white separatism or dominance based on white supremacy are seldom used today, at least publicly, he says. White nationalists still do use the biological determinism argument for some audiences, calling it "biological diversity," Levin says.

Today, the alt-right argues that "white Europeans" have singlehandedly created a superior U.S. culture that has gained nothing of value from the presence of other ethnicities, Levin says.

The shift away from the white supremacy term began as early as 1994, when some members of the Ku Klux Klan and others realized that it made many people envision "a certain kind of uncultured bigot," said Michael Waltman, an associate professor of interpersonal and organizational communication at the University of North Carolina, Chapel Hill. Many adopted "white nationalist" as a substitute. But "it is really hard to be a white nationalist and not sort of think of white people as better than other folks," Waltman said. [18]

Taylor, founder of the *American Renaissance* website, said in September that the alt-right is "in unanimity" about rejecting "the idea that the races are basically equivalent and interchangeable." Genetic differences make white people more moral and more intelligent than black people, Taylor claimed. [19]

Nevertheless, Taylor added that he rejects the white supremacist term because "you could very effectively argue that East Asians are objectively superior to whites. Does that make us yellow supremacists? I don't think so." [20]

Many in the alt-right movement hope white Americans eventually will live in a whites-only ethno-state that Spencer has said might be created by some means of "peaceful ethnic cleansing." [21] The ethno-state would not be open to Jews, he said. "Jews are Jews." [22]

In a November 2016 speech to a Washington conference of the alt-right sponsored by the National Policy Institute think tank, which Spencer heads, he laid out many of his ideas.

He did not use the term white supremacy. Nevertheless, he argued that the United States was "great" through the early 1960s, citing its space program and other accomplishments, but has since lost its lead. The cause: "American society was 90 percent European" in the early 1960s, but since then ethnic diversity and racial minorities' influence in society have increased, to the country's detriment, Spencer said. [23] (The Immigration and Nationality Act of 1965, also known as the Hart-Celler Act, abolished immigration quotas based on national origin, and the Civil Rights Act of 1964 outlawed discrimination based on race, color, religion, sex or national origin. [24])

To applause from the nearly 300 people at the conference, Spencer described white Americans as superior people continually under attack by liberals, who he said are allied with blacks and Hispanics. "The American Left is driven by anti-white hatred, full stop," he said, adding that "we have nothing in common with these people." [25]

In a multiethnic society, said Spencer, white Americans who have had their nation's greatness unfairly stripped away are ready to fight back. "We were not meant to beg for moral validation from some of the most despicable creatures to ever populate the planet," he said,

referring to liberals and nonwhite Americans. "We were meant to overcome, overcome all of this, because that is natural and normal for us. Because for us, as Europeans, it is only normal again when we are great again."

Then he concluded by declaring: "Hail Trump. Hail our people. Hail victory." [26]

Does the Trump administration support alt-right ideas?

Political analysts say the alt-right owes its current prominence to the fact that, from the day he announced his presidential campaign on June 16, 2015, President Trump often asserted white nationalist-friendly ideas, such as his calls for a wall between the United States and Mexico and his broad-brush assertions to African-Americans that "you're living in poverty." [27]

White nationalists — who had not openly embraced a Democratic or Republican presidential candidate within living memory — began praising Trump's statements online. And, to some extent, at least, candidate Trump appeared to respond in kind, such as when he retweeted a depiction of his primary opponent Jeb Bush as a beggar that was originally posted by someone with the white nationalist Twitter name @WhiteGenocideTM. [28]

Taking notice of this relationship between a major-party candidate and white nationalists, the media began covering the alt-right, creating a level of public awareness of white nationalism that has not been seen for years.

Trump himself has said he rejects the alt-right, although his critics say he was slow to do so. In a Nov. 22 interview with *The New York Times* the president said of the alt-right: "I don't want to energize the group. I disavow the group." [29]

Nevertheless, two months into his presidency, signs point both for and against the Trump administration pursuing an agenda that parallels certain alt-right beliefs, experts say.

The movement's leaders are clearly supportive of many of the administra-

tion's ideas. For example, Trump's plan to aggressively deport more undocumented immigrants is nothing less than a revolution that might restore a white America, said Kevin MacDonald, editor of the online *Occidental Observer*, a leading white nationalist publication. [30]

Another sign that alt-right-friendly ideas are in play are reports that the Trump administration plans to shift a government program for monitoring violent ideologies to focus on so-called Islamic extremism, says Jasmin Mujanoviĉ, a New York City-based international relations scholar and consultant specializing in Eastern Europe. [31] In the past, the program has also monitored domestic extremists from the right, such as white nationalists, who have been responsible for many U.S. bombings and shootings, Mujanoviĉ says.

The focus on Islamic extremism is a signal the alt-right might welcome, he says.

Writers at some neo-Nazi websites associated with the alt-right have taken it just that way. "This measure would be the first step to us going fully mainstream, and beginning the process of entering the government in full-force without the fear of being attacked, financially assailed, and intimidated into silence by the nefarious Jews," wrote poster Marcus Cicero at the neo-Nazi website *Infostormer.* [32]

Trump's appointment of Bannon as White House chief strategist suggests that white nationalist ideas might get a hearing but not necessarily automatic approval, political observers say.

On the one hand, Bannon has said he has no tolerance for "some racial and anti-Semitic overtones" in alt-right thinking. [33] However, he is also an outspoken critic of immigration, free trade and international alliances and is widely reported to be the moving force behind some hardline actions that the Trump administration has taken against undocumented immigrants, refugees and travelers from several majority Muslim countries. [34]

Those moves are in tune with alt-right views, notes Hussein Ibish, a senior resident scholar and expert on hate crimes and civil liberties at the independent Arab Gulf States Institute, a Washington think tank. Trump himself, however, has taken a more pragmatic view of immigration through the years, raising questions about whether he'll fully support such hardline actions throughout his presidency or eventually move in another direction, Ibish says.

Ibish cites a *Breitbart News Daily* radio interview that Bannon conducted with Trump in 2015, in which Trump "called for using practical economic considerations" to decide which immigrants to admit, saying that "there are advantages to bringing in Indian computer scientists." "But Bannon basically said, 'Absolutely not.' If they weren't white Europeans they weren't wanted in this society," Ibish recalls. [35]

Many Trump supporters don't see his policies as racist but as pro-white, says Carol Swain, a professor of law and politics at Vanderbilt University, in Nashville, and the author of two books about contemporary white nationalism. "White people have real concerns — rising mortality rates in some places with people dying of despair, drug abuse, overdoses," she says. "Naturally when they hear about government addressing the problems of other groups they want to hear about their own problems. And Mr. Trump tapped into that."

"I don't think Donald Trump is a white nationalist," Swain says. "He was tapping into real concerns. And he was steering people toward patriotism — things that unite."

On the whole, the alt-right hopes Trump will be a transitional figure whose ideas can nudge public debate in the direction of their ideology, many analysts say.

Trump can help normalize their ideas by introducing less extreme but related concepts into the discussion as a sort of "gateway drug" to accustom

White Nationalists Gain on Social Media

White-nationalist movements have gained 22,000 Twitter followers since 2012, a more than sevenfold increase but still a minuscule part of social media traffic. Among Twitter accounts of white nationalists, those with pro-Nazi sympathies were more prevalent than those focusing on other alt-right ideologies.

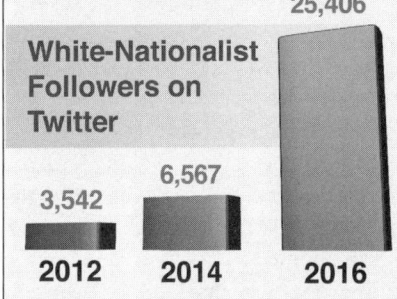

White-Nationalist Followers on Twitter

2012	2014	2016
3,542	6,567	25,406

Source: J.M. Berger, "Nazis vs. ISIS on Twitter: A Comparative Study of White Nationalist and ISIS Online Social Media Networks," September 2016, pp. 3-4, http://tinyurl.com/gpc57jr

people to hearing racist and isolationist views, says Mujanoviĉ. "They've been working on this for years online, and they've been looking for a carrier to bring it to a wider audience."

"They call it shifting the Overton window" — a term invented by a conservative think tank to describe a range of socially acceptable positions, says Lyons, co-author of *Right-Wing Populism in America*. [36] "They were on the verge of saying 'This is hopeless!' Then Trump came along" and showed willingness to try widening the window. His ability to voice previously unacceptable ideas gave the movement new hope for its plan, Lyons says.

Alt-right members see some early presidential actions as less than encouraging, however. For instance, few of Trump's

Cabinet appointees appear to favor a U.S. exit from international alliances. "These are globalists in general. They love free trade, they love immigration — big red flags for us," said MacDonald of the *Occidental Observer*. [37]

Does the alt-right promote violence?

So far, there is no evidence the alt-right has explicitly inspired violent acts, says the University of Alabama's Hawley.

Alt-right leader Spencer said he opposes direct threats of violence but supports the free-speech rights of those who display swastikas or make racist statements. "In terms of self-expression, we're not going to condemn something like [displaying swastikas] wholesale," Spencer said. [38]

Ku Klux Klan members wearing hoods may not be the threats that some perceive them to be, Spencer told NPR. Instead, he said, such apparently provocative actions may just be people's attempt "to get in touch with their identity as a European." [39]

In fact, Spencer contended, the real causes of violence and hatred in society are situations in which people of different races are forced into close interaction. History demonstrates this, he argued. "When you have two really dramatically different cultures, two dramatically different races all being forced together, it's a recipe for turmoil," Spencer said. "I don't know of an historical example that contradicts that." [40]

Some psychologists, however, say that simply identifying oneself as part of a group with common interests and a shared identity — such as race or religion — makes people more likely to express and act on prejudices against non-group members, even to the point of violence.

That's because the more strongly people believe they have a rational reason to harm another person, the more likely they are to feel free to do so, wrote Daniel Effron, an assistant professor of organizational behavior at London Business School in England,

and Eric Knowles, an associate professor of psychology at New York University in New York City. Moreover, people are highly likely to believe that protecting the shared interests of one's group from a suspected threat provides just such a reason, said Effron and Knowles, who conducted several studies of the matter on ordinary people, not extremist groups. [41]

"Our research therefore raises the concern that as the [the United States] continues to diversify, whites not only may develop greater hostility toward other racial groups but also may increasingly regard themselves as possessing a license to express it," Effron and Knowles wrote. [42]

History bears out that connection, says Heidi Beirich, director of the Southern Poverty Law Center's (SPLC) Intelligence Project, which monitors extremist groups. "Historically there's been violent politics when things change culturally," such as in the 1920s when the nation's white Protestant majority felt threatened by a large wave of immigration, and Ku Klux Klan violence escalated, she says.

If a recognized authority figure simply suggests that some demographic group should be feared or disliked, some people may view that statement as permission to commit violence, said Charles Taylor, professor emeritus of philosophy at McGill University in Montreal, who is an expert on xenophobia and the challenges that multicultural societies face. [43]

"Whenever political leaders propose to limit the rights of Muslims," said Taylor, "they encourage Islamophobic sentiment and disinhibit hostile acts," whether they intend to do so or not. "If highly respected leaders share that hostility, why shouldn't people who hold the same views act on them?" Trump's limitations on travel visas from Muslim-majority countries may have had that effect on Alexandre Bissonnette, who killed six Muslim men in a Quebec City, Canada, mosque, Taylor said. [44]

Guatemalan immigrants deported from the United States arrive in Guatemala City on Feb. 9, 2017. Political observers say the alt-right has tapped into some whites' fears about immigration and the nation's changing demographics, where whites will soon be a minority. President Trump's populist appeals to people worried about immigration also have resonated with alt-right supporters.

After Spencer spoke at a Washington conference on Nov. 19, the U.S. Holocaust Memorial Museum issued a statement arguing that the speech could incite violence. Spencer made "several direct and indirect references to Jews and other minorities, often alluding to Nazism," the statement read. "He implied that the media was protecting Jewish interests and said, 'One wonders if these people are people at all?' . . . His statement that white people face a choice of 'conquer or die' closely echoes Adolf Hitler's view of Jews and that history is a racial struggle for survival. . . . [45]

"By the end of World War II," the museum's statement continued, "the Germans and their collaborators had murdered six million Jews and millions of other innocent citizens, many of whom were targeted for racial reasons. The Holocaust did not begin with killing; it began with words."

Words can spark violence and also help keep violence at bay, notes political consultant Mujanović, a Bosnian who in the 1990s was a young refugee from the former Yugoslavia, where ethnic and religious strife helped fuel wars and authoritarian takeover.

"I would really love it if the Republicans and Democrats could release some statement together, saying, 'There are certain things about which we'll likely always disagree, but there are some ways of talking that we all find unacceptable. Here are a handful of things that we do not support.' As a former refugee, I understand the anxiety many people say they feel in this climate. And it means so much for elder statesmen to come out and say, 'This has gone too far,' " he says. ∎

BACKGROUND

American Racial Purity

The alt-right's beliefs are nothing new. Throughout U.S. history, many Americans have held that national greatness rested on maintaining the values of European whites. Likewise, the alt-right idea that the nation should avoid foreign alliances has had many adherents, including President George Washington.

Non-British immigration was unpopular at times during the colonial period. Benjamin Franklin, a philosopher, scientist and apostle of the Enlightenment, worried about the large number of German-speaking immigrants in Pennsylvania.

While these immigrants had "industry and frugality" that would likely be useful to the colony, Franklin wrote in a 1753 letter, it might still be advisable to cap their numbers. "Those who come hither are generally of the most ignorant Stupid Sort." Moreover, he continued, "few of their children in the Country learn English," to the point that "in a few years [interpreters] will be also necessary in the [colony's] Assembly, to tell one half of our Legislators what the other half say," he grumbled. [46]

Once the United States became an independent nation, established under a written Constitution, two competing visions emerged about what nationhood entailed, says Levin of the Center for the Study of Hate and Extremism.

"Some see the nation as having a unifying national creed that includes things such as respect for religious pluralism" and accepting as citizens all people who agree to embrace that creed, Levin says. "But for many of the electorate this is less important than another notion — seeing their nation in racial, ethnic and religious terms." The struggle between those visions persists to this day, he says.

"A foreigner can immigrate to France or Japan but never become truly French or Japanese," said Matthew Spalding, associate vice president of the Washington-based Allan P. Kirby Jr. Center for Constitutional Studies and Citizenship, a project of Michigan's Hillsdale College. [47] "But a foreigner of any ethnic heritage or racial background can immigrate to the United States and become, *in every sense of the term*, an American," he wrote. [48]

"The Founders were not afraid that immigrants, by themselves, would subvert the American republic," so long as, in the words of Founder Alexander Hamilton, the new nation's first Treasury secretary, they would "learn the principles and imbibe the spirit of our government," Spalding said. [49]

But many Americans also have argued strenuously against opening citizenship to all and against the idea that people of different ethnicities are equal. They needed only to look at the Constitution and its "three-fifths" compromise, which counted a slave as three-fifths of a person for the purposes of apportioning taxes and representation.

"Ours is the Government of the white man," and that is the source of its success, contended U.S. Sen. John C. Calhoun of South Carolina in 1848. Some other young countries in the Americas, colonized by Spain, were failing because they had committed the "fatal error of placing the colored race on an equality with the white," said Calhoun, arguing against a call for the United States to annex Mexico after the 1846-1848 Mexican-American War. More than half of Mexico's population were "pure Indians" and many more were of "mixed blood," and Calhoun "[protested] against the incorporation of such a people," he said. [50]

During periods when America's white Protestant majority believed its dominance was threatened, the ethnicity-based vision of nationhood strengthened and produced organizations dedicated to enforcing it, sometimes through acts of terror.

In the 1850s, the nativist party known as the Know-Nothings argued that the country was being overrun by Irish Catholics and other immigrants, and it fought to limit immigration.

With the defeat of the South in the Civil War and the freeing of slaves, the Republican-controlled Congress embarked on a program to "reconstruct" the former Confederate states by creating biracial governments in the South and trying to integrate African-Americans into civic life. But the Ku Klux Klan, which was founded in Tennessee in 1866, fought to maintain white supremacy by using violence to terrorize newly freed slaves and their white supporters. [51]

After about a decade and a half of activity, the Klan and its sympathizers had largely achieved their goal of squelching black freedmen's attempts to exercise their voting rights or otherwise seek social equality. That success and some government action to quell the violence, led to the Klan's virtual (but temporary) disappearance by the 1880s and the rise of Jim Crow laws in the South that legalized racial segregation. [52]

The vision of a nation whose strength derived from a common creed, not a common ethnicity, remained alive for some, however, even in those times. Sen. Charles Sumner of Massachusetts, for example, argued in 1871 for a law to ensure equal civil rights for freedmen. "There is true grandeur in an example of justice, making the rights of all the same as our own, and beating down prejudice, like Satan, under our feet," Sumner said. [53]

As the 20th century began, a massive wave of immigration from across the world once again made white Protestants uneasy. Asians, Eastern Europeans, Catholics, Jews and others arrived in greater numbers. Nearly 1.3 million legal immigrants entered the country in 1907, and more than 1.2 million arrived in 1914 — annual immigration peaks that would not be matched until the 1990s. [54]

In 1915, the Ku Klux Klan announced that it would reassemble, this time establishing itself as both an anti-black and an anti-immigrant organization in the South and the Midwest. [55]

"In the 1920s, one-seventh to one-eighth of the electorate were tied to the Klan," says Levin.

In its successful outreach to middle- and upper-class Americans, the Klan published books and newspapers, ran seminars, and even tried to open its own university, said Kelly J. Baker, author of the *Gospel According to the Klan: The KKK's Appeal to Protestant America, 1915-1930*. The Klan successfully spread the belief that biology proved white people to be the world's "leading race" and that God had ordained it so, Baker said. [56]

Continued on p. 252

Chronology

1990s *White supremacists use the internet to spread racist ideas.*

1995
Don Black of Florida sets up *Stormfront*, believed to be the world's first hate website, for white supremacists and neo-Nazis.

1999
Far-right parties, allies of U.S. white nationalists, win 11 percent of seats in the European Union's Parliament.

— • —

2000s *White nationalists win support by rebranding as an "identity" movement, urging whites to band together to protect common interests.*

2005
Conservative publishing-dynasty heir William Regnery II and other white nationalists open the National Policy Institute (NPI) think tank to promote white people's interests through meetings and publications.

2008
In the title of an article about "paleoconservatives" — members of a far-right group interested in preserving white dominance — *Taki's Magazine* editor Richard Spencer labels them the "alternative right."

— • —

2010s *A loose network of white-identity groups become known as the alt-right.*

2010
Leadership of NPI operations passes to Spencer. . . . He founds the online publication *Alternative Right* to publish essays on race and gender and serve as a gathering place for the alt-right.

2013
Alt-right, anti-Semitic website *Daily Stormer* is founded.

2014
Europe's far-right parties make further gains in the EU Parliament, winning just under 23 percent of the seats. . . . Russian President Vladimir Putin boosts the political fortunes of Marine Le Pen, leader of the French far-right National Front party, with a loan of 9 million euros from a Russian-backed bank.

2015
White supremacist Jared Taylor attends a March conference in Moscow on the denigration of white European traditions. . . . Republican presidential candidate Donald Trump is praised online by several alt-right members when, at his June 16 campaign launch, he labels many Mexican immigrants criminals. . . . Alt-right members use the term #cuckservative — formed from "cuckold," a man who's been cheated on, and "conservative" — to insult conservatives they say have sold out to liberals.

2016
Stephen Bannon, executive chairman of the conservative *Breitbart News*, is appointed chief executive of the Trump presidential campaign and says *Breitbart* has been "the platform for the alt-right." . . . Alt-right members' enthusiasm for candidate Trump grows when he retweets posts from someone using the Twitter name @WhiteGenocideTM. . . . Profile of alt-right rises after Democratic nominee Hillary Clinton calls it a "paranoid fringe." . . . On Nov. 8, Trump wins the presidency. . . . Nearly 300 people attend a Nov. 20 alt-right conference in Washington, up from 172 in 2015; when conference organizer Richard Spencer closes a speech saying "Hail Trump! Hail our people! Hail victory!" some in audience raise their arms in a Nazi salute. . . . After Spencer's speech, the U.S. Holocaust Memorial Museum said in a statement, "The Holocaust did not begin with killing. It began with words." . . . Asked on Nov. 22 about his possible alt-right connections, President-elect Trump says "I disavow the group."

2017
At the February annual meeting of the Conservative Political Action Conference (CPAC), President Trump and Bannon, now White House chief strategist, get enthusiastic welcomes from the event organizer. Self-described alt-right "fellow traveler" Milo Yiannopoulos, a former *Breitbart News* editor, whom Spencer calls an inspiration for his provocative use of hate speech as humor, is scratched from a CPAC speaking spot after a taped interview surfaced in which he appeared to sanction sex between men and underage boys. Spencer buys a ticket to sit in the CPAC audience but is escorted from the venue by hotel security because of his beliefs; some attendees enthusiastically welcome him, however. . . . Anti-Defamation League reports 63 cases of white nationalists distributing fliers on campuses in January and February, a significant increase over 2016. . . . Critics charge that some actions by President Trump tacitly encourage the alt-right; they point to travel bans for citizens of six Muslim-majority countries and a plan to publicize a list of criminal acts committed by undocumented immigrants. . . . IRS suspends the tax-exempt status of Spencer's NPI think tank because the group filed no IRS paperwork since 2013.

Researchers: Alt-Right Uses Internet to Normalize Hate

"You have all these men who see their role as internet warriors."

When David French, a writer for the conservative *National Review*, criticized Donald Trump during the 2016 presidential campaign and questioned his alleged ties to the "alt-right," followers of the movement began to attack him online.

One attack, French said, involved the posting of "images of my daughter's face in gas chambers, with a smiling Trump in a Nazi uniform preparing to press a button and kill her." [1]

The incident, researchers say, is one example of how the alt-right has been using its online skills over the past two years to attack opponents, raise its profile and gain members.

During the 2016 presidential campaign, people identifying themselves as alt-right followers targeted Trump's "critics, among others, with streams and streams of abuse through anonymous Twitter accounts," says Matthew Lyons, a Philadelphia-based researcher and author specializing in right-wing movements.

"It's a devastating tactic," says Lyons. "And you can't even say that anybody in particular is orchestrating it. You have all these men who see their role as internet warriors. And somebody points to a person who's perceived as an enemy, like *National Review* writer David French, who criticized Trump. And someone says, 'Let's go after his family,' " he says.

It's not surprising that the alt-right is skillfully using the Web to win followers and wield political influence, says Jessie Daniels,

a sociology professor at Hunter College in New York City and the author of the 2009 book *Cyber Racism*.

Racist groups were among the earliest organizations to see the internet's potential, she says. In an early-1990s interview, for example, David Duke, founder of the Louisiana-based Knights of the Ku Klux Klan, called the internet the greatest-ever opportunity to spread racist ideologies. "I believe that the Internet will begin a chain reaction of racial enlightenment that will shake the world by the speed of its intellectual conquest," Duke wrote. [2]

Some alt-right websites, such as the anti-Semitic white nationalist site *Daily Stormer*, have been building an online following quickly, says Heidi Beirich, director of the Southern Poverty Law Center's Intelligence Project, which monitors extremist groups.

The center found that the *Daily Stormer*, which was founded in 2013, needed only three years to surpass the Web traffic of the oldest hate sites online, such as *Stormfront*, which debuted in 1995, Beirich says.

Trolling — posting inflammatory messages in an attempt to provoke controversy — is one way the alt-right wins new followers, says George Hawley, an assistant professor of political science at the University of Alabama in Tuscaloosa.

"Trolling isn't done to influence the person being trolled," he says. "Other people are watching, and the trolls know they'll attract some of them if they draw the target into a fight" or

---

Continued from p. 250

Some important government policies reflected those ideas.

For example, in 1924, Congress passed the Johnson-Reed Immigration Act, banning Asian immigration and capping annual immigration of other nationalities at 2 percent of the total number of people of that nationality appearing on the 1890 census. The law's "most basic purpose" was "to preserve the ideal of U.S. homogeneity," according to the U.S. State Department. [57]

During the Great Depression of the 1930s, Klan membership dropped steeply as immigration fell, the group faced some scandals and Americans focused on the economy. White supremacist groups have never regained their 1920s prominence. A resurgence of such groups began in the 1950s, however, as the civil rights movement intensified.

Far-Right Thinkers

The alt-right has roots in racist movements such as the Ku Klux Klan and similar groups that focused on intimidating people who tried to assert minority rights. But it also has roots in another area in which some advocates of white nationalism have worked — conservative political theory.

One such group, called "paleoconservatives," was the early political home of Spencer. [58]

Paleoconservatism — which is considered a far-right political movement — took shape in the 1980s as an effort to dissuade the Republican Party from following the lead of the "neoconservatives," a group of influential formerly liberal scholars and journalists who had joined the Republican ranks around 1970.

By the time President Ronald Reagan took office in 1981, neoconservatives had won significant Republican support for ideas that horrified some traditional conservatives, such as open immigration, embrace of the civil-rights movement and aggressive use of both diplomacy and military might to advance U.S. interests abroad. [59]

Although they did not burn crosses or view race as the sole unifying idea of their philosophy, paleoconservatives nevertheless embraced a white nationalist vision of America. They argued that the United States owed its greatness to the Founders' European heritage, and they strenuously opposed policies that might dilute that heritage, such as open immigration and foreign alliances. [60]

In the 1990s one prominent paleoconservative, Patrick Buchanan, a former adviser to Republican Presidents Richard Nixon, Gerald Ford and Ronald Reagan,

simply troll in an aggressive way that seems "edgy and fun" to some people. "It sends the message that, 'Hey, if you follow us, you too can rile famous people online,' " Hawley says.

During the 2016 campaign, the alt-right also used bots — automated software — to quickly spread political memes, which are images or other material passed around online, says Daniels.

When a topic alt-rightists wanted to target came up in a Twitter feed — such as the #imwithher hashtag connected to the campaign of Democratic presidential nominee Hillary Clinton — a bot would instantly retweet the hashtagged tweet along with the cartoon Pepe the Frog meme that the alt-right adopted as a symbol, Daniels says. "Bots were able to quickly get it into the general online conversation" much faster than humans could, she says.

Extremists also have learned how to gradually shift public discourse in directions they choose, Daniels says.

For example, a website on slavery run by white supremacists can excerpt oral histories found in the public domain and twist their meaning, such as by highlighting innocent-seeming facts about slaves being allowed to grow vegetables for their own use, she says. By savvy use of linking and other methods, they can change search engine results, so that when someone types into Google "was slavery so hard?" sites that give a misleading picture turn up, Daniels says.

"So much of what we know and understand about the world happens through search engines now," and white nationalists are among the internet-savvy people who can shape the public's picture of reality without anyone being aware of the manipulation, Daniels says.

Alt-right followers use similar methods to shift public discourse toward acceptance of once forbidden racist words and images, says Lyons. Some alt-right-related websites go out of their way to use the most shocking images of bigotry possible as a way to gradually make once-shunned speech and imagery seem normal through repetition, he says.

A case in point is some posters' recent heavy use of gas-chamber jokes, Lyons says. "Thousands and thousands of tweets have gone out telling gas-chamber jokes, and even if many people are still horrified," some will begin to view the jokes as normal, which shifts the political and social climate without most people even realizing it, he says.

— *Marcia Clemmitt*

[1] David French, "The Price I've Paid for Opposing Donald Trump," *National Review*, Oct. 21, 2016, http://tinyurl.com/j9ddfrr.

[2] Quoted in Jessie Daniels, Cyber Racism (2009), p. 3; also see Mark Weitzman, " 'The Internet Is Our Sword,' " *Remembering for the Future: The Holocaust in an Age of Genocide* (2001), pp. 911-925, http://tinyurl.com/jn2s4kf.

presented the group's ideas directly to voters with some success, winning more than a fifth of the votes cast in both the 1992 and 1996 Republican presidential primaries. He especially railed against immigration. "If America is to survive as 'one nation, one people,' " Buchanan said in 1994, "we need to call a "time-out" on immigration, to assimilate the tens of millions who have lately arrived." [61]

Despite paleoconservatives' inability to get buy-in from elected officials, such ideas held some public appeal and "continued to attract young intellectuals" into the 2000s, said Lyons. [62]

In 2008, leading paleoconservative Paul Gottfried, a retired professor of humanities at Elizabethtown College in Pennsylvania, said the movement had "youth and exuberance on our side, and a membership that is largely in its twenties and thirties." The young blood might eventually overcome what he

deemed a long-running media and political-establishment collaboration to block far-right challenges to mainstream Republicanism. [63]

Among this younger generation was Spencer, a former graduate student at the University of Chicago and Duke University, in North Carolina, who worked as an editor at two paleoconservative publications before starting his own online publication in 2010. That website, AlternativeRight.org, which Spencer edited until 2012, gathered many far-right voices into what is now known as the alt-right. [64]

Unlike paleoconservatives, "the alt-right is about race per se," says the University of Alabama's Hawley.

Like older paleoconservatives, Spencer wrote journal essays about his political ideas. Unlike them, however, he also argued on social media and reached out to neo-Nazis and other

less staid advocates of white racial politics, who used racist epithets freely and with the intention to shock. [65] The alt-right is "revolutionary," while paleoconservatives are not, Spencer said. "I think we might need a little more chaos in our politics, we might need a bit of that fascist spirit," he said. [66]

Europe's New Right

Another major source of alt-right thinking was the far-right parties that have appeared in virtually all European countries over the past few decades. [67]

Called the European New Right (ENR), the movement has roots in the highly authoritarian, nationalistic fascism that took hold in Germany and Italy in the 1930s and eventually went down to defeat in World War II, says Lyons, the co-author of *Right-Wing Populism in*

Alt-Right Borrows a Page From the Left

The movement is using identity politics to build a bigger following.

Taking its cue from the "identity politics" of the Left — in which people rallied around campaigns for gay rights or black pride — the so-called alt-right is attempting to rally mainstream white Americans to its cause by appealing to white pride, according to researchers Carol Swain of Vanderbilt University and Russ Nieli of Princeton University. [1]

Richard Spencer, the unofficial spokesman of the alt-right — an umbrella group of people with various racist beliefs, including anti-Semites, white supremacists and white nationalists who want whites to live in a separate "ethno-state" — urged white Americans to see themselves as a unified group. Whites, he said, must band together to fight for common interests or watch "European culture" get wiped out in a multicultural United States in which whites are simply one more minority group. [2]

White identity is at the core of the alt-right's appeal to the average white person and to President Trump's supporters, Spencer claimed, even if, he said, most Trump voters "aren't willing to articulate it as such." [3]

Identity language, experts say, clearly resonates with some whites.

J.P. Sheehan, president of a College Republican club, said he was an Obama voter who gradually came to believe that ethnic minorities were moving into the forefront at his expense. He said he latched onto the white-identity language Spencer uses because it gave him a sense of meaning. "People think the alt-right is just simply about being mean to other people," said Sheehan. "It's really not. The alt-right is simply identity politics for white people." [4]

The appeal of identity language for some whites isn't surprising, Swain says.

"White people have real concerns, such as rising mortality rates, with older white people in some communities dying of despair, drug overdoses," she says. "They want those concerns recognized. But in the liberal political language [of the last several decades], they were hearing about everybody else and not about themselves."

For disaffected whites — including those who argue that whites are superior to other races — the "logical next step was to copy that multiculturalist language and use it to talk about themselves," Swain says. It was clear in the early 2000s that white identity would soon become the next rallying cry for disaffected white people, both mainstream whites and white racists, she says.

Swain says she recognized then that identity politics could be an effective tool for the far right to reach mainstream whites and help build opposition to racial inclusiveness.

Walter Benn Michaels, an English professor at the University of Illinois, Chicago, made a similar argument in his 2006 book, *The Trouble With Identity: How We Learned to Love Identity and Ignore Inequality.*

In the book, Michaels argued that identity politics was a dangerous diversion that allowed politicians to ignore the country's real socioeconomic problems, which afflict people from all demographics. Michaels, like Swain, warned that identity politics could backfire by making white people see themselves as an identity group victimized by racism.

In 2006, many liberal critics rejected both those arguments. But "someone told me they'd just discovered the book last week, and now it reads like a prophecy," said Michaels last year. [5]

As identity politics and language come to dominate the public debate, "what you get is an increasing number of white people who are committed and convinced that they're the victims of racism," something that was evident in the 2016 campaign cycle, said Michaels.

America. Beginning in the 1990s, ENR texts were translated from French to English and became a source of ideas for "Americans seeking to develop a white nationalist movement outside of traditional neo-Nazi/Ku Klux Klan circles," he wrote. [68]

After World War II, European far-right politicians had to recast their ideas to win over a wary public, Lyons says. Classical fascism developed in an era when Europeans' imperial conquests in Africa and elsewhere seemed to confirm the idea that Western Europeans were a "master race," as Germany's Nazis had declared, Lyons says.

After independence movements essentially ended colonialism in the 1960s, however, the ENR switched from the vision of a conquering European master race to a "defensive mode," says Lyons. ENR politicians, including Nigel Farage in the United Kingdom, vowed to defend European civilization and a heritage whose greatness they said was under attack, diluted by immigration and by the new mass culture that globalization of economics and media was creating, he said. [69]

The alt-right takes a similar approach, casting the United States' long-dominant white majority as a group under attack who must fight to protect their common interests, say Lyons and others.

In 2005, a small group of white nationalists launched the National Policy Institute (NPI) think tank, mostly online, to host conferences and publish writings about what they called the fast-shrinking influence of white Americans. "Within the first- or secondhand memories of people in this room, the white race may go from master of the universe to an anthropological curiosity," said chief NPI founder William Regnery II, whose father, Henry, founded the conservative publisher Regnery Publishing.

In a 2014 survey by the independent research group Public Religion Research Institute, 52 percent of white Americans, 61 percent of Republicans and 73 percent of people identifying themselves as tea party members said racial discrimination against whites was as big a problem as racial discrimination against minorities. [6]

"White people are indeed victimized — they're the largest group of poor people," Michaels said. "Those people begin to think, yeah, racism is the problem. That's why what we've seen emerge during this Trump campaign is a white identity politics." [7]

To combat this view — and to prevent white nationalists from continuing to use it to build support for racism — "we have to take new approaches to problems like poverty," Swain argues. "Look at socioeconomic problems that affect whites along with other ethnic groups and address them as that — as socioeconomic problems, not as problems of this identity group or that."

Others, however, defend identity politics and warn against abandoning it. The 2016 election did not demonstrate white backlash, said Jacob T. Levy, a professor of political theory at McGill University in Montreal. Trump got a lower share of white votes than Republican nominee Mitt Romney in 2012, 58 percent versus 59 percent. Moreover, in polls white voters expressed reluctance to vote for Trump when he spoke against minorities or showed disrespect for women, Levy said. [8]

Identity politics is necessary, Levy said, because so much injustice is "targeted injustice." He pointed to laws banning gay sexual activity and to policing that leads to the disproportionate arrests of blacks. To progress as a society, "we need to be able to hear each other talking about particularized injustices, and to cheer each other on when we seek to overturn them," he said.

— *Marcia Clemmitt*

A Ku Klux Klan member in Hampton Bays, N.Y., said on Nov. 22, 2016, that his KKK branch has had some 1,000 inquiries from people interested in joining since Donald Trump's election. The alt-right has roots in racist movements such as the Klan.

[1] Carol M. Swain, *The New White Nationalism in America: Its Challenge to Integration* (2002); Carol M. Swain and Russ Nieli, eds., *Contemporary Voices of White Nationalism in America* (2003), p. 5.

[2] Maya Oppenheim, "Alt-right leader Richard Spencer worries getting punched will become the 'meme to end all memes,' " *Independent*, January 2017, http://tinyurl.com/jzmkm5d.

[3] Joseph Goldstein, "Alt-Right Gathering Exults in Trump Election Win With Nazi-Era Salute," *The New York Times*, Nov. 20, 2016, http://tinyurl.com/jauuls5.

[4] Michelle Goldberg, "Alt-Right Facts," *Slate*, Feb. 23, 2017, http://tinyurl.com/jylf6l4.

[5] Ryan Smith, "Walter Benn Michaels on how liberals still love diversity and ignore equality," *Chicago Reader*, Nov. 23, 2016, http://tinyurl.com/zsesmcl.

[6] Robert P. Jones, Daniel Cox and Juhem Navarro-Rivera, "Economic Insecurity, Rising Inequality, And Doubts About The Future," Public Religion Research Institute, Sept. 23, 2014, p. 39, http://tinyurl.com/jajsus9.

[7] *Ibid*.

[8] Jacob T. Levy, "The Defense Of Liberty Can't Do Without Identity Politics," Niskanen Center, Dec. 13, 2016, http://tinyurl.com/jdrmsrv.

In 2010, control of NPI's operations passed to Spencer. [70] For the next several years, NPI and other white nationalist websites, online magazines and membership groups continued trying to promote their ideas but were getting little public or media attention. Members wrote blog posts, journal articles and social-media posts. Spencer, Taylor and others held small conferences for white nationalists. But it wasn't until July 2015 when white nationalists responded enthusiastically to Trump's announcement that he would be a candidate for the presidency, did the groups capture much public attention. ■

CURRENT SITUATION

Campus Outreach

White supremacists and other members of the alt-right are stepping up their efforts to recruit college students, according to the Anti-Defamation League.

The group said it cataloged 63 incidents of movement members distributing fliers on campuses in January and February, a significant increase from 2016. A number of activists also are giving speeches. Spencer, for example, spoke at Texas A&M in College Station in early December. The league said white supremacists are "emboldened by the 2016 elections and the current political climate." [71]

The alt-right's outreach is roiling universities. Appearances by Milo Yiannopoulos, a former *Breitbart* editor who is considered an alt-right ally, have been especially controversial. Three hours before he was scheduled to speak at the University of California, Berkeley, on Feb. 1, students gathered outside the student union to protest his speech. The protests were peaceful, according to authorities, until several dozen protesters wearing black masks arrived and attacked police barricades, threw firecrackers and broke windows. Authorities canceled the speech. A Berkeley student told a reporter, "We won't put up with the violent rhetoric of Milo, Trump or the fascistic alt-right." [72]

On Inauguration Day, a black-clad protester punched Spencer in the face while he was being interviewed by a journalist on a Washington, D.C., street. "There was an actual anti-fascist rally going on, and I walked into it," he said. [73]

Conservative groups are increasingly speaking out against the alt-right. The

"They are not an extension of the conservative movement." [74]

On March 12, though, Rep. Steve King, R-Iowa, drew praise from former Ku Klux Klan grand wizard David Duke after tweeting support for Dutch far-right politician Geert Wilders, who has called for ending Muslim immigration, closing mosques and banning the Koran. Americans from across the political spectrum blasted as racist King's remark that "we can't build our civilization with other people's babies." [75]

Meanwhile, a number of administration critics say President Trump is tacitly encouraging the alt-right with his immigration policies, including the revised travel ban that temporarily bars new visas for citizens of six predomi-

shooting of two Indian immigrants in Kansas by a suspect who reportedly shouted "Get out of my country!" [77]

Many mainstream Republicans defend Trump, and the White House denies the criticisms, saying the president — including in his Feb. 28 speech to Congress — has repeatedly condemned racial and religious attacks as evil. It also dismisses any links between the president's rhetoric and acts of violence. "Any loss of life is tragic," White House press secretary Sean Spicer said on Feb. 24. "To suggest that there's any correlation I think is a bit absurd." [78]

As the debate continues, experts agree that the white nationalist movement thrives on controversy and is enjoying its time in the spotlight. A search of Google's news page turns up hundres of thousands of hits for the term "alt-right."

Nevertheless, most of the public remains unfamiliar with the movement. A December poll by the Pew Research Center in Washington found that 54 percent of the public had heard "nothing at all" about the alt-right, while 28 percent had heard only "a little." [79]

Conferences held under the alt-right banner remain small but have grown recently, at the same time as the movement's press coverage has expanded. After Trump's election, nearly 300 people attended a Nov. 19, 2016, NPI-sponsored conference in Washington, according to one affiliated group, Identity Evropa (IE). [80] That was up from 172 the year before. [81]

IE is led by Nathan Damigo, a former Marine corporal who is a student at California State University, Stanislaus, and formerly headed the National Youth Front, a wing of the Neo-Nazi American Freedom Party. It's one of the few alt-right groups to try offline activism, visiting university campuses to reach out to college Republican clubs and posting signs about the importance of white European identity. [82]

For reasons not yet understood, young people's involvement in white

A flare shows a damaged window at a Wells Fargo Bank in Berkeley, Calif., during protests against a scheduled speech at the University of California by former Breitbart News Network *editor Milo Yiannopoulos, a political provocateur who is considered an alt-right supporter. Authorities canceled the speech after protesters broke windows and threw flares and smoke bombs.*

AFP/Getty Images/Josh Edelson

Tea Party Nation — an affiliate of the tea party movement, which espouses conservative principles — calls the alt-right fake conservatism and warns that it "pits itself against 'establishment' conservatism." At CPAC in February, organizer Schneider, who is executive director of the American Conservative Union, denounced alt-right members' beliefs. "They are anti-Semitic. They are racist. They are sexist," he said.

nantly Muslim countries. They also point to Trump's issuing of an executive order on Jan. 25 for the Department of Homeland Security to make public a list of all criminal acts committed by undocumented immigrants. [76]

And they say he offered delayed responses to an attack on the Canadian mosque that killed six; to some 100 bomb threats to Jewish organizations; to vandalism at Jewish cemeteries; and to the

Continued on p. 258

At Issue:

Should online racist speech be regulated?

JESSIE DANIELS
PROFESSOR OF SOCIOLOGY,
HUNTER COLLEGE

WRITTEN FOR *CQ RESEARCHER*, MARCH 2017

*t*he commonplace view of free speech in the United States is often attributed to this quote, supposedly from the French philosopher Voltaire: "I disapprove of what you say, but I will defend to the death your right to say it." The quote is actually from a Voltaire biographer, and it misleads us about the nature of protected speech.

In 2003, the U.S. Supreme Court ruled that a burning cross is not protected speech, because it is meant to terrorize a group of people. When we think about the hate speech that can be located online today through Google searches, the question becomes: What constitutes a burning cross in the digital era?

Before Dylann Roof decided to kill nine people in a Bible study group in Charleston, S.C., in 2015, he searched online for "black on white crime." In his manifesto, he said that what he learned left him determined "to do something."

One racist site, *Stormfront,* has grown from 124,000 registered users in 2008 to over 320,000 today. And, because the internet is nearly borderless, our homegrown white supremacy is available to a global audience with deadly consequences. The Southern Poverty Law Center has linked that site alone to some 100 hate-crime murders.

The misbegotten notion that white supremacist views deserve First Amendment protection is rooted in another ill-formed idea: that good ideas will rise to the top and bad ideas will sink to the bottom.

But that is not true. When white supremacist ideas have a platform, they thrive, gain legitimacy, grow in popularity and endanger lives.

The Department of Homeland Security should treat white supremacy as a terrorist threat to the government and monitor online sites that promote racial hate. Unfortunately, it gutted its monitoring program for domestic terrorism in 2010, after conservatives objected to a "politically charged" leaked report. It is time to rebuild it, and identify and outlaw the kind of online speech that can cause real harm.

Other democracies do not see free speech as an absolute right; they see it as a right that must be balanced with others, such as the human right to not be the target of violence based on race, ethnicity, religion or sexual identity.

We should refuse to allow the First Amendment to be used to protect the speech of those who wish to use that protection to harm others.

JEFFREY HERBST
PRESIDENT AND CEO, NEWSEUM

WRITTEN FOR *CQ RESEARCHER*, MARCH 2017

*t*he Web and the social media revolution it spawned are in many ways the First Amendment realized. Families have been reconnected, friendships renewed across vast distances and the isolation of some relieved. At the same time, social media, perhaps inevitably, has been the vehicle for the transmission of a tremendous amount of hatred, including numerous examples of racist speech that rightfully anger many.

What to do about the racism polluting parts of the information ecosystem is an important and emotional issue. In its recent survey of high school students — the "digital natives" supposedly at the core of the social media revolution — the Knight Foundation found that only 43 percent agreed people should be allowed to say offensive things on social media.

It is still not understood that the government is not allowed to regulate many instances of racist speech. Indeed, hate speech, except under very narrow exceptions — such as direct encouragement of others to immediately commit violence — is protected speech in the United States.

As private companies, the social media platforms themselves are able to regulate what they present to the public. Although these companies, notably Facebook, initially asserted that they were merely pipes through which others posted, they have become increasingly aggressive in developing and enforcing company-specific community standards, including prohibitions on racist speech.

The challenge is that social media use is evolving quickly, and the sheer volume of posts in almost every language transmitted at great speed makes regulation exceptionally difficult. Racists also continually push to see what they can get through.

In the new information order where the gatekeepers inevitably struggle, perhaps the ultimate form of "regulation" rests with citizens themselves. Racism flourishes online in part because hateful speech is allowed to dominate conversations.

Racism should be identified and countered. However, the ultimate way to do so is for the public to speak up and make persuasive statements through posts, videos, tweets and snaps showing that the only way we will prosper as a society is to figure out how we can live together as individuals.

The power of algorithms used by the social media platforms is that they figure out with great speed the sentiments that are most popular and then distribute them. By guiding searchers to anti-racist speech, algorithms can help counter an age-old evil without violating the First Amendment.

Continued from p. 256

nationalism is rising, says Hawley. At meetings of groups such as American Renaissance, he says, more people under 30 seem to turn up today than did so 10 years ago.

Among Millennials, an October poll by Ipsos Public Affairs, a market research and consulting firm in Washington, found that 34 percent had a favorable view of the alt-right and only 21 percent an unfavorable. (The rest had no opinion.) [83]

Hawley told *The Washington Post* that "the alt-right has been able to successfully brand itself as an edgy and fun and ironic movement that takes pleasure in needling both liberals and conservatives, and it's tongue-in-cheek and rebellious as opposed to just being motivated by genocidal hatred." [84]

Internet Savvy

Individuals and groups have long used the internet to boost their causes, and the alt-right is using it effectively on Trump's behalf, political and technology analysts say.

The alt-right "contributed in a significant way to Trump's victory by their skillful use of online activism," such as by devising internet memes, says Lyons, co-author of *Right-Wing Populism in America.* An internet meme is a catchy phrase, video or image that encapsulates an idea and spreads quickly online, carrying the idea with it. (*See sidebar, p. 252.*)

Two such memes were #cuckservative and #draftourdaughters.

Combining the words "cuckold" — an insulting word for a man whose wife has cheated on him — and "conservative," #cuckservative denigrates traditional Republicans, whom the alt-right sees as selling out to liberal ideas such as allowing large-scale immigration. It was used to boost the image of outsider Republican candidate Trump. For #draftourdaughters, online activists photoshopped authentic-looking fake Clinton campaign materials

stating that as president Clinton would bring more women into the armed services to fight wars she planned, such as a war with Russia. [85]

The alt-right's work with memes "was effective enough that mainstream media took notice. So that's power," says Lyons. "Could Trump have won anyway? Maybe. But this certainly helped him. It made his opponents look ridiculous in the eyes of some voters. And there was no defense."

International Movement

Internet or no, the alt-right wouldn't have risen from obscurity without an international trend that's made many white voters receptive to extremist messages, political scholars say.

Support for far-right political parties has soared across Europe since 1999, according to British investigative journalist Nafeez Ahmed. The parties' voter appeal has recently risen to heights not seen since the 1930s, when Hitler came to power in Germany, he wrote. In the most recent elections, held in 2014, far-right parties won just under 23 percent of the seats in the European Union's legislative body — the European Parliament — up from just 11 percent in 1999. [86]

This spring in France, far-right nationalist anti-immigrant politician Marine Le Pen, leader of the National Front party, has a good chance of winning the presidential election. [87] Germany and the Netherlands also have far-right candidates running strongly in presidential elections this year. [88]

Many European far-right parties have relationships with Russian Federation President Vladmir Putin, who apparently hopes the rise of parties that shun international alliances can weaken the European Union, a top economic and political rival of Russia, political observers say. [89]

It can be said "with a high degree of confidence" that Putin has been

building ties with Europe's far right for a decade, says Alina Polyakova, deputy director of the Dinu Patriciu Eurasia Center at the nonpartisan international affairs think tank Atlantic Council in Washington. Le Pen even received a 9 million euro campaign loan from the Moscow-based First Czech Russian Bank, which has ties to Russia's government, she says.

Putin has given European far-right politicians "a kind of ideological architecture — strongly and consistently arguing against the EU and NATO," says international-affairs consultant Mujanoviĉ. "It's a language that has proven very attractive to many people who feel as if they and their traditions have been left behind" by the newly united EU and has helped the far-right parties gain voters, Mujanoviĉ says.

In recent years, the alt-right and other American far-right groups have been building international connections, both with Europe's far-right parties and with Putin's Russia. Alt-right leaders have praised Putin for his "anti-globalist" stance and for promoting white nationalism. American Renaissance founder and alt-right ally Taylor, for example, attended a 2015 conference on nationalist and ethnic issues in Moscow. Spencer has called Russia "the sole white power in the world." [90] And Trump has repeatedly praised Putin, which critics say has further encouraged the alt-right.

Despite alt-right members' apparent outreach to Putin, the movement's situation is "profoundly different" from that of European far-right parties in ways that make it unlikely that a Putin-alt-right alliance does or even could exist, Polyakova says. For one thing, "while there is overlap in ideas, the alt-right here is very new." Moreover, because the United States has a primarily two-party political system, small interest groups such as the alt-right are in no position to work with Putin "in a strategic way" as Europe's far-right politicians can, she says. ∎

OUTLOOK

Spreading Influence?

Whether the alt-right can expand its online influence to win more real-world support for its views is still unknown. Also unknown — and worrisome to many — is whether the alt-right's race-oriented politics will lead to social disruption or violent pushback from other groups.

"White supremacists in the alt-right are fringe still," says the ADL's Mayo. "A few different groups are trying to meet and do real-world events, but those efforts are mostly just beginning."

The alt-right may pin most hope for expanding its support base on online trolling of people they disagree with and on speeches and writings from provocateurs such as Yiannopoulos, the former *Breitbart* editor who recently resigned over tapes in which he appeared to approve of sex between men and underage boys. [91]

Yiannopoulos and some other provocateurs friendly to the movement "are not white nationalists but try to be outrageous about the same issues to get a rise out of people," Mayo says. "The thought is that if you attract people by criticizing politically correct views, you may be able to gradually nudge them" into adopting more extreme racist and misogynist political views, she says. "I think that would be a small percentage of people, but it could happen."

Unlike the alt-right, advocacy groups with true clout "have think tanks, policy papers [and] people on congressional staffs," says the University of Alabama's Hawley. The alt-right has "already put themselves on the radar in ways that the far right hasn't previously been able to do. But it's not clear how they would get additional resources [and] support. It's possible that they've already accomplished all they're ever going to."

While the alt-right's online presence has gained it some young followers, it's also not clear whether exclusionary, isolationist politics will be as attractive to younger generations as they have sometimes been to older ones, says Levin of the Center for the Study of Hate and Extremism. In general, "Millennials are far more tolerant than their grandparents."

The attempts at relationship building carried out by the alt-right and European far-right parties could be a sign of desperation, says Ibish of the Arab Gulf States Institute. "They all want a movement because they know they're a minority, so if they don't go international, really become a worldwide movement, they're likely to die."

But Ibish says that may be more easily said than done. "How do you make an international movement of nationalists?" he says. And the differences among groups are substantial, in both the European far right and in the U.S. alt-right. "Some are anti-Semitic, some accept Jews but are very anti-Islam; some accept gays and others don't. The differences seem large. And the more they try to work in unison, the more they're likely to find it harder than they imagine," Ibish says.

The threat of violence from extremists on the right and left is real, says Levin. "The progressive left is now out of power, and with the absence of leadership there we have a fringe of the hard left — the anti-fascists, the Marxists — who believe that resistance should be violent" he says. "Will there be a coalescence of the hard violent left in response" to the rise of alt-right ideas or to policies put in place by an alt-right-friendly Trump administration? "We just don't know." ∎

Notes

[1] Alice Ollstein, "CPAC Boots White Nationalist Richard Spencer After He Crashes The Party," *Talking Points Memo*, Feb. 23, 2017, http://tinyurl.com/jrlfgb2.

[2] Quoted in Michelle Goldberg, "Alt-Right Facts," *Slate*, Feb. 23, 2017, http://tinyurl.com/jylf6l4.

[3] Ollstein, *op. cit.*

[4] "The Alt-Right: NOT Right — NOT Conservative," Tea Party Nation, http://tinyurl.com/jo92yg8.

[5] For background, see Reed Karaim, "Immigrant Detention," *CQ Researcher*, Oct. 23, 2015, pp. 889-912.

[6] For background, see Matthew N. Lyons, "Calling them 'alt-right' helps us fight them,' *threewayfight*, Nov. 22, 2016, http://tinyurl.com/zh9s6wy; Christopher Caldwell, "What the Alt-Right Really Means," *The New York Times*, Dec. 2, 2016, http://tinyurl.com/jne5xtd.

[7] Quoted in "A frank conversation with a white nationalist," Reveal, Center for Investigative Reporting, Nov. 10, 2016, http://tinyurl.com/zbkko6c.

[8] For background, see "Queer Fascism: Why White Nationalists Are Trying To Drop Homophobia," *Anti-Fascist News*, Nov. 6, 2015, http://tinyurl.com/jejle6z, and Lukas Mikelionis, "Alt-Right Meltdown After Tweets About the 'Jewish Question,'" *HeatStreet*, Dec. 27, 2016, http://tinyurl.com/grhl4j7.

[9] Quoted in Garrett Haake, "White Nationalist group to hold conference on Trump in DC Saturday," WUSA.com, March 2, 2016, http://tinyurl.com/zsmdl45; "Donald Trump's New York Times Interview: Full Transcript," *The New York Times*, Nov. 23, 2016, http://tinyurl.com/juymes5.

[10] Nicholas Confessore, "For Whites Sensing Decline, Donald Trump Unleashes Words of Resistance," *The New York Times*, July 13, 2016, http://tinyurl.com/jh5nx69.

[11] Abby Ohlheiser and Caitlin Dewey, "Hillary Clinton's alt-right speech, annotated," *The Washington Post*, Aug. 25, 2016, http://tinyurl.com/jksmlan.

[12] Sarah Posner, "How Stephen Bannon Created an Online Haven for White Nationalists," The Investigative Fund, The Nation Institute, Aug. 22, 2016, http://tinyurl.com/z5wm6za.

[13] Jonathan Martin, Jim Rutenberg and Maggie Haberman, "Donald Trump Appoints Media Firebrand to Run Campaign," *The New York Times*, Aug. 17, 2016, http://tinyurl.com/gmav62k; Michael D. Shear, Maggie Haberman and Alan Rappeport, "Donald Trump Picks Reince Priebus as Chief of Staff and Stephen Bannon as Strategist," *The New York Times*, Nov. 13, 2016, http://tinyurl.com/zm3fp44.

[14] "Inaugural address: Trump's full speech," CNN, Jan. 21, 2017, http://tinyurl.com/j6jjkkg.

[15] Jared Taylor, "I Was There," *American Renaissance*, Jan. 21, 2017, http://tinyurl.com/hned8t7.

[16] For background, see Josh Harkinson, "We Talked to Experts About What Terms to Use for Which Group of Racists," *Mother Jones*, Dec. 8, 2016, http://tinyurl.com/h24w9lz.

[17] "How I Saw the Light About Race (Part VIII)," *American Renaissance*, Feb. 27, 2017, http://tinyurl.com/h96tlp4.

[18] Quoted in Harkinson, *op. cit.*

[19] Quoted in Betsy Woodruff, "Alt-Right Leaders: We Aren't Racist, We Just Hate Jews," *The Daily Beast*, Sept. 9, 2016, http://tinyurl.com/zfqh8vo.

[20] Quoted in *ibid.*

[21] Amanda Taub, "'White Nationalism' Explained," *The New York Times*, Nov. 21, 2016, http://tinyurl.com/zxfwxz4.

[22] Woodruff, *op. cit.*

[23] "Richard Spencer — NPI 2016, Full Speech," Red Ice TV, YouTube, Nov. 21, 2016, http://tinyurl.com/hgybpgh.

[24] For background, see "U.S. Immigration Through 1965," History.com, http://tinyurl.com/24hemcb; "Civil Rights Act," History.com, http://tinyurl.com/pp7sa3w.

[25] Spencer, *op. cit.*

[26] *Ibid.*

[27] Richard Fausset, Alan Blinder and John Eligon, "Donald Trump's Description of Black America Is Offending Those Living in It," *The New York Times*, Aug. 24, 2016, http://tinyurl.com/hx7fmb7.

[28] Tal Kopan, "Donald Trump retweets 'White Genocide' Twitter user," CNN.com, Jan. 22, 2016, http://tinyurl.com/gnjvh3g.

[29] "Donald Trump's New York Times Interview: Full Transcript," *op. cit.*

[30] Quoted in Sarah Posner and David Neiwert, "How Trump Took Hate Groups Mainstream," *Mother Jones*, Oct. 14, 2016, http://tinyurl.com/h9kfd6b.

[31] For background, see Julia Edwards Ainsley, Dustin Volz and Kristina Cooke, "Exclusive: Trump to focus counter-extremism program solely on Islam — sources," Reuters, Feb. 2, 2017, http://tinyurl.com/zo9cmv3.

[32] Marcus Cicero, "President Trump Ready To Change Definition Of 'Extremis,' Will Remove White Supremacists From List," *Infostormer*, Feb. 2, 2017, http://tinyurl.com/jl3tg7g.

[33] "Steve Bannon: 'Zero Tolerance' For Anti-Semitic, Racist Elements Of The Alt-Right," *Breitbart*, Nov. 19, 2016, http://tinyurl.com/h4otqxb.

[34] For background, see Evan Perez, Pamela Brown and Kevin Liptak, "Inside the confusion of the Trump executive order and travel ban," CNN Politics, Jan. 30, 2017, http://tinyurl.com/zx4mfk8; John Walcott and Julia Edwards Ainsley, "Trump's go-to man Bannon takes hardline view on immigration," Reuters, Jan. 31, 2017, http://tinyurl.com/zxx95lq.

[35] For background, see David A. Fahrenthold and Frances Stead Sellers, "How Bannon flattered and coaxed Trump on policies key to the alt-right," *The Washington Post*, Nov. 15, 2016, http://tinyurl.com/jbsde9h.

[36] For background, see Nathan J. Russell, "An Introduction to the Overton Window of Political Possibilities," Mackinac Center, Jan. 4, 2006, http://tinyurl.com/hzqlodo.

[37] Frank Morris, "White Nationalists' Enthusiasm for Trump Cools," All Things Considered, NPR, Jan. 13, 2017, http://tinyurl.com/hgvvfna.

[38] Quoted in Laurie Richards, "The alt-right reveals its agenda to influence Trump's presidency," ThinkProgress, Nov. 20, 2016, http://tinyurl.com/zctstqy.

[39] "'We're Not Going Away': Alt-Right Leader On Voice In Trump Administration," All Things Considered, NPR, Nov. 17, 2016, http://tinyurl.com/habljcy.

[40] "A frank conversation," *op. cit.*

[41] Daniel A. Effron and Eric D. Knowles, "Entitativity and Intergroup Bias: How Belonging to a Cohesive Group Allows People to Express Their Prejudices," *Journal of Personality and Social Psychology*, February 2015, pp. 234-253, http://tinyurl.com/gwfqdw9.

[42] *Ibid.*

[43] Nathan Gardels, "Weekly Roundup: When Leaders Disinhibit Acting Out Hate," WorldPost, *The Huffington Post*, Feb. 3, 2017, http://tinyurl.com/hrz8mc7.

[44] Quoted in *ibid.* For background, see Jonathan Montpetit, "Muslim leaders in Quebec City find it difficult to ignore tensions that preceded shooting," CBC News, Jan. 31, 2017, http://tinyurl.com/h6eoq9f; Les Perreaux and Eric Andrew Gee, "Quebec City mosque attack suspect known as online troll inspired by French far right," *The Globe and Mail* (Toronto), Jan. 31, 2017, http://tinyurl.com/zyslahg.

[45] "Museum Condemns Hateful Rhetoric At White Nationalist Conference; Calls On The Nation to Confront Hate Speech," press release, U.S. Holocaust Memorial Museum, Nov. 21, 2016, http://tinyurl.com/zsc3fey.

[46] Benjamin Franklin, "Letter to Peter Collinson," TeachingAmericanHistory.org, May 9, 1753, http://tinyurl.com/jzxxq6a.

[47] Matthew Spalding, "Why Does America Welcome Immigrants?" The Heritage Foundation, June 30, 2011, http://tinyurl.com/zbxqvm3.

[48] *Ibid.*

[49] *Ibid.*

[50] John C. Calhoun, speech on Mexico, Jan. 4, 1848, http://tinyurl.com/hvvupqf.

[51] "Ku Klux Klan," *Encyclopedia Britannica*, Dec. 6, 2016, http://tinyurl.com/h4dwkfa.

[52] *Ibid.*

[53] Quoted in W.E.B. DuBois, *Black Reconstruction in America, 1860-1880* (1998), pp. 592-593.

[54] "Legal Immigration to the United States, 1820 to Present," Migration Policy Institute, http://tinyurl.com/jd8hvym.

[55] "Ku Klux Klan," *op. cit.*

[56] Kelly J. Baker, "White-Collar Supremacy," *The New York Times*, Nov. 25, 2016, http://tinyurl.com/zkku59y.

[57] "The Immigration Act of 1924 (The Johnson-Reed Act)," Office of the Historian, U.S. Department of State, http://tinyurl.com/qe2tnuw.

[58] Jacob Siegel, "The Alt-Right's Jewish Godfather," *Tablet*, Nov. 29, 2016, http://tinyurl.com/hku86bb.

[59] For background, see Matthew N. Lyons, "AlternativeRight.com: Paleoconservatism for the 21st Century," *threewayfight*, Sept. 10, 2010, http://tinyurl.com/goqww49; Euan Hague and Edward H. Sebesta, "Neo-Confederacy and Its Conservative Ancestry," in *Neo-Confederacy: A Critical Introduction*, E. Hague, Heidi Beirich, and E.H. Sebesta, eds. (2008), p. 26; and George Hawley, *Right-Wing Critics of American Conservatism* (2016).

[60] Siegel, *op. cit.*

[61] Patrick J. Buchanan, "Immigration Time-out," Oct. 31, 1994, http://tinyurl.com/hrut4w4; "US

About the Author

Marcia Clemmitt is a veteran social-policy reporter who previously served as editor in chief of *Medicine & Health* and staff writer for *The Scientist*. She has also been a high school math and physics teacher. She holds a liberal arts and sciences degree from St. John's College, Annapolis, and a master's degree in English from Georgetown University. Her recent *CQ Researcher* reports include "The Dark Web" and "Teaching Critical Thinking."

President-R Primaries," 1992, Our Campaigns, http://tinyurl.com/z34em5d; and "US President-R Primaries," Our Campaigns, 1996, http://tinyurl.com/hbzl9fk.

[62] Lyons, "AlternativeRight.com: Paleoconservatism for the 21st Century," op. cit.

[63] Paul Gottfried, "The Decline and Rise of the Alternative Right," Taki's Magazine, Dec. 1, 2008, http://tinyurl.com/j2t4mt6.

[64] Lyons, "AlternativeRight.com: Paleoconservatism for the 21st Century," op. cit.; Richard Spencer, "Am I Not Being Outrageous Enough?" National Policy Institute, Nov. 20, 2014, http://tinyurl.com/jcmots9.

[65] Siegel, op. cit.

[66] Quoted in Siegel, op. cit.

[67] For background, see Margaret Quigley, "Some Notes on the European 'New Right,' " Political Research Associates, Aug. 29, 2016/Jan. 1, 1991, http://tinyurl.com/h46arxf; Zack Beauchamp, "An expert on the European far right explains the influence of anti-immigrant politics," Vox, May 31, 2016, http://tinyurl.com/hbwapt7.

[68] Matthew N. Lyons, "Crl-Alt-Delete," Political Research Associates, January 2017, p. 4, http://tinyurl.com/goay3st.

[69] Ibid.

[70] "The Groups," Southern Poverty Law Center Intelligence Report, Jan, 29, 2010, http://tinyurl.com/hwtd5pm; "About," Radix Journal, http://tinyurl.com/z5u42os.

[71] "ADL: White Supremacists Making Unprecedented Effort on U.S. College Campuses to Spread Their Message, Recruit," Anti-Defamation League, March 6, 2017, http://tinyurl.com/jljmr5u.

[72] Julia Carrie Wong, "UC Berkeley cancels 'alt-right' speaker Milo Yiannopoulos as thousands protest," The Guardian, Feb. 2, 2017, http://tinyurl.com/h2rluvn.

[73] Liam Stack, "Attack on Alt-Right Leader Has Internet Asking: Is It O.K. to Punch a Nazi?" The New York Times, Jan. 21, 2017, http://tinyurl.com/h2avjmz.

[74] Joseph Weber, "CPAC leader blasts 'alt-right,' as conservatives define agenda under Trump," Fox News, Feb. 23, 2017, http://tinyurl.com/zcehd49; Tea Party Nation, op. cit.

[75] Brian Naylor, "Rep. Steve King Stands By Controversial Tweet About 'Somebody Else's Babies,' " NPR, March 13, 2017, http://tinyurl.com/h4frc3y; Matthew Haag, "Steve King Says Civilization Can't Be Restored With 'Somebody Else's Babies,' " The New York Times, March 12, 2017, http://tinyurl.com/hg8o6nh.

[76] Peter Beinart, "Trump Scapegoats Unauthorized Immigrants for Crime," The Atlantic, March 1, 2017, http://tinyurl.com/z84kglx.

FOR MORE INFORMATION

American Renaissance, www.amren.com. Alt-right-affiliated website and organization founded by white nationalist Jared Taylor that argues that race heavily determines traits such as intelligence and morality.

Anti-Defamation League, 605 Third Ave., New York, NY 10158; 212-885-7700; www.adl.org. International Jewish group that researches, monitors and opposes anti-Semitism and other forms of bigotry.

Center for Right-Wing Studies, 2420 Bowditch St., MC5670, University of California, Berkeley, CA 94720-5670; 510-643-7237; crws.berkeley.edu. Research center that studies right-wing movements around the world.

Center for the Study of Hate and Extremism, State University of California, 5500 University Parkway, San Bernardino, CA 92407-2318; 909-537-7711; http://hatemonitor.csusb.edu. Research group that analyzes data and policy on bigotry, terrorism and extremism's effects on civil rights.

National Policy Institute, www.npiamerica.org. Alt-right think tank and publisher of material on white European identity politics.

Occidental Observer, www.theoccidentalobserver.net. Far-right Web publication on white European culture and white identity politics.

Political Research Associates, 1310 Broadway, Suite 201, Somerville, MA 02144; 617-666-5300; www.politicalresearch.org. Think tank that researches and analyzes threats to social justice from the far right.

Southern Poverty Law Center, 400 Washington Ave., Montgomery, AL 36104; 334-956-8200 www.splcenter.org. Monitors domestic hate groups and extremists and provides training and legal advocacy to oppose hate crimes.

[77] Jaweed Kaleem, "Trump speaks out against attacks on Jews and shooting of Indian immigrants," Los Angeles Times, Feb. 28, 2017, http://tinyurl.com/hys2cd6.

[78] Ishaan Tharoor, "An Act of American Terror in Trump's Heartland," The Washington Post, Feb. 27, 2017, http://tinyurl.com/jb3takr.

[79] John Gramlich, "Most Americans haven't heard of the 'alt-right,' " Pew Research Center, Dec. 12, 2016, http://tinyurl.com/hfaqwte.

[80] Karl North, "NPI 2016," Identity Evropa, Nov. 29, 2016, http://tinyurl.com/zt8u54h.

[81] Richard Spencer, "The Rainbow Coalition," America blog, National Policy Institute, Nov. 4, 2015, http://tinyurl.com/ht6r9j4.

[82] "Identity Evropa: Mapping the Alt-Right Cadre," Northern California Anti-Racist Action, ICD, Dec. 9, 2016, http://tinyurl.com/zhvpvto; Hailey Branson-Potts, "In diverse California, a young white supremacist seeks to convert fellow college students," Los Angeles Times, Dec. 7, 2016, http://tinyurl.com/z3q9348.

[83] Susan Page and Karina Shedrofsky, "Poll: How Millennials view BLM and the alt-right," USA Today, Oct. 31, 2016, http://tinyurl.com/j8szksm.

[84] Max Ehrenfreund, "What the alt-right really wants, according to a professor writing a book about them," The Washington Post, Nov. 21,

2016, http://tinyurl.com/hjt4fqy.

[85] For background, see Abby Ohlheiser, "What was fake on the Internet this election: #draftourdaughters, Trump's tax returns," The Washington Post, Oct. 31, 2016, http://tinyurl.com/he4wtfx.

[86] Nafeez Ahmed, "European support for far right extremism reaches 1930s scale," Medium, June 19, 2016, http://tinyurl.com/h9hu84q. Also see Brian Beary, "European Unrest," CQ Researcher, Jan. 9, 2015, pp. 25-48.

[87] Nicole Stinson, "Marine Le Pen defends Putin and attacks Europe for 'carrying out Cold War AGAINST Russia,' " [U.K.] Express, March 6, 2017, http://tinyurl.com/znzlvxw.

[88] Michelle Martin, "Germany's divided anti-immigrant party faces rocky election road," Reuters, March 2, 2017, http://tinyurl.com/gpjmyo4.

[89] For background, see Suzanne Sataline, "U.S.-Russia Relations," CQ Researcher, Jan. 13, 2017, pp. 25-48.

[90] Casey Michel, "Beyond Trump and Putin: The American Alt-Right's Love of the Kremlin's Policies," The Diplomat, Oct. 13, 2016, http://tinyurl.com/zeck4xb.

[91] For background, see Shikha Dalmia, "Conservatives Made Their Bed With Milo, Now They Have to Lie In It," Reason, Feb. 26, 2017, http://tinyurl.com/jtmho62.

Bibliography

Selected Sources

Books

Daniels, Jessie, *Cyber Racism*, Rowman & Littlefield, 2009.
A sociology professor at Hunter College in New York City recounts how white supremacists have used the internet to win followers and spread their message.

Hawley, George, *Right-Wing Critics of American Conservatism*, University Press of Kansas, 2016.
An assistant professor of political science at the University of Alabama describes how far-right thinkers — including white nationalists and "paleoconservatives" — have challenged mainstream conservatives and helped spawn the so-called alt-right.

Swain, Carol M., and Russ Nieli, *Contemporary Voices of White Nationalism in America*, Cambridge University Press, 2003.
A professor of political science and law at Vanderbilt University (Swain) and a lecturer in politics at Princeton University (Nieli) present in-depth interviews with 10 leading white nationalists in the United States, several of whom are members of the loose network that has become the "alt-right."

Articles

Beauchamp, Zack, "White Riot," *Vox*, Jan. 20, 2017, http://tinyurl.com/j57rmcf.
The rising number of minorities in the United States and Europe may have led to a white backlash against increasing ethnic diversity and multiculturalism and contributed to the election of President Trump.

Ehrenfreund, Max, "What the alt-right really wants, according to a professor writing a book about them," *The Washington Post*, Nov. 21, 2016, http://tinyurl.com/hjt4fqy.
A University of Alabama assistant professor of political science, who is interviewing alt-right members for a new book, describes what he has learned about the beliefs and demographics of the movement, saying "it is predominantly an online phenomenon, and amorphous."

Letson, Al, "A frank conversation with a white nationalist," Reveal, The Center for Investigative Reporting, Nov. 10, 2016, http://tinyurl.com/hpm6n2g.
In an interview, alt-right spokesman Richard Spencer describes his hopes that the United States eventually will become a white "ethno-state" — a nation populated entirely by people of white European ancestry.

Ohlheiser, Abby, and Caitlin Dewey, "Hillary Clinton's alt-right speech, annotated," *The Washington Post*, Aug. 25, 2016, http://tinyurl.com/jksmlan.
Democratic presidential nominee Hillary Clinton brought the alt-right heightened publicity when, in a 2016 speech, she sharply criticized the movement and then-candidate Donald Trump's alleged embrace of it.

Penny, Laurie, "On the Milo Bus With the Lost Boys of America's New Right," *Pacific Standard*, Feb. 21, 2017, http://tinyurl.com/hduulp7.
A reporter describes her conversations with young men who worked for alt-right-affiliated provocateur Milo Yiannopoulos during his college lecture tour. These alt-right members were primarily involved with the movement for amusement, not because of the ideology, she says.

Roy, Avik, "Up From White Identity Politics," *National Review*, Aug. 18, 2016, http://tinyurl.com/zg334he.
A conservative columnist explains why he believes white-identity politics are bad for the country, for conservatives and for Republican priorities.

Siegel, Jacob, "The Alt-Right's Jewish Godfather," *Tablet*, Nov. 29, 2016, http://tinyurl.com/hku86bb.
Richard Spencer's alt-right network includes anti-Semites. But Spencer's philosophical mentor is Paul Gottfried, a Jewish professor and a developer of paleoconservatism, which criticizes mainstream conservatives as too friendly to social and political equality.

Tanner, Charles, Jr., "Richard Spencer: Alt-Right, White Nationalist, Anti-Semite," Institute for Research and Education on Human Rights (IREHR), Jan. 5, 2017, http://tinyurl.com/jpuqaje.
A human-rights advocate describes alt-right spokesman Richard Spencer's background in the world of far-right political theory.

Reports and Studies

Berger, J.M., "Nazis vs. ISIS on Twitter: A Comparative Study of White Nationalist and ISIS Online Social Media Networks," George Washington University Program on Extremis, September 2016, http://tinyurl.com/gpc57jr.
A university-based researcher on extremist movements describes how white nationalists and the Islamic State gather followers and communicate their views using social media.

Klapsis, Antonis, "An Unholy Alliance: The European Far Right and Putin's Russia," Wilfried Martens Center for European Studies, 2015, http://tinyurl.com/zryk9oc.
A centrist European think tank examines links between European far-right parties with similarities to the alt-right and Russian President Vladimir Putin and his government.

Lyons, Matthew N., "Ctrl-Alt-Delete: The Origins And Ideology Of The Alternative Right," Political Research Associates, Jan. 20, 2017, http://tinyurl.com/zm7f7cu.
An independent researcher on right-wing extremism traces the origins of the alt-right.

The Next Step:

Additional Articles from Current Periodicals

Controversies

Romano, Aja, "Milo Yiannopoulos still has alt-right fans," ***Vox***, **Feb. 23, 2017, http://tinyurl.com/jmguz6w.**

Despite a video surfacing that seems to show former *Breitbart* editor Milo Yiannopoulos defending pedophilia, his most ardent "alt-right" followers have defended him and argue that the mainstream media is unfairly attacking him.

Weigel, David, and John Wagner, "Alt-right leader expelled from CPAC after organizer denounces 'fascist group,' " ***The Washington Post***, **Feb. 23, 2017, http://tinyurl.com/hqqjd28.**

The Conservative Political Action Conference ejected alt-right founder Richard Spencer from its meeting due to his controversial views on white nationalism.

Yoo, Noah, and Amy Phillips, "Adult Swim Cancels 'Million Dollar Extreme,' Show Accused of Racism and Bigotry," ***Pitchfork***, **Dec. 6, 2016, http://tinyurl.com/gtvs3t7.**

The Adult Swim network canceled the program "Million Dollar Extreme," created by an alt-right supporter, after critics said the show promoted sexist and racist viewpoints.

International Following

"Meet the IB, Europe's version of America's alt-right," ***The Economist***, **Nov. 12, 2016, http://tinyurl.com/hbhthma.**

The "identitarian" movement, which espouses anti-Muslim, anti-media and anti-migrant messages, has become Europe's version of the alt-right.

Mohdin, Aamna, "What's 'alt-right' in German? Breitbart News is expanding in Europe," ***Quartz***, **Nov. 20, 2016, http://tinyurl.com/z7sljwz.**

The conservative website Breitbart News, a platform for the alt-right, is looking to expand to Germany and France to take advantage of anti-immigration fervor in Europe.

Townsend, Mark, "Britain's extremist bloggers helping the 'alt-right' go global, report finds," ***The Guardian***, **Feb. 11, 2017, http://tinyurl.com/jrbxkph.**

The United Kingdom's far right is seeking to build support for the alt-right internationally by using social media and "click-bait" articles and videos that taunt the Left.

Political Backing

Altman, Alex, "How Donald Trump Is Bringing the Alt-Right to the White House," ***Time***, **Nov. 14, 2016, http://tinyurl.com/z5lqmla.**

By appointing former Breitbart Executive Chairman Stephen Bannon to a powerful White House position, critics say President Trump is giving voice to the alt-right and other fringe groups.

Morgan, Jonathon, "How the 'Alt-Right' Came to Dominate the Comments on Trump's Facebook Page," ***The Atlantic***, **Jan. 21, 2017, http://tinyurl.com/zsrjbhn.**

An increasing number of comments reflecting white nationalist sentiments were left on President Trump's Facebook page during 2016, according to a new analysis.

Shelbourne, Mallory, "Conway denies retweeting white nationalist," ***The Hill***, **Feb. 14, 2017, http://tinyurl.com/z4397ew.**

White House adviser Kellyanne Conway came under fire when her Twitter account retweeted a white nationalist account; she denied retweeting it herself and denounced the tweet.

Social Media's Role

Broderick, Ryan, "I Made A Facebook Profile, Started Liking Right-Wing Pages, And Radicalized My News Feed In Four Days," ***Buzzfeed***, **March 8, 2017, http://tiny url.com/hhgun26.**

A *BuzzFeed* experiment found that Facebook's algorithm suggested increasingly far-right accounts and news stories, some of which were fake, once the user began "liking" the pages of conservative politicians and others.

Guyunn, Jessica, "Twitter suspends alt-right accounts," ***USA Today***, **Nov. 15, 2016, http://tinyurl.com/haxgowo.**

In an attempt to crack down on hate speech, Twitter began suspending high-profile accounts linked to the alt-right.

Hanna, Andrew, and Bryan Bender, " 'Alt-right's [sic] favored social network: Fake news welcome here," ***Politico***, **Dec. 8, 2016, http://tinyurl.com/zfavteq.**

A new social media website, Gab, is becoming the platform for members of the alt-right movement.

CITING *CQ RESEARCHER*

Sample formats for citing these reports in a bibliography include the ones listed below. Preferred styles and formats vary, so please check with your instructor or professor.

MLA STYLE

Jost, Kenneth. "Remembering 9/11." CQ Researcher 2 Sept. 2011: 701-732.

APA STYLE

Jost, K. (2011, September 2). Remembering 9/11. *CQ Researcher,* 9, 701-732.

CHICAGO STYLE

Jost, Kenneth. "Remembering 9/11." *CQ Researcher*, September 2, 2011, 701-32.

In-depth Reports on Issues in the News

Are you writing a paper?

Need backup for a debate?

Want to become an expert on an issue?

For 90 years, students have turned to *CQ Researcher* for in-depth reporting on issues in the news. Reports on a full range of political and social issues are now available. Following is a selection of recent reports:

Civil Liberties
Privacy and the Internet, 12/15
Intelligence Reform, 5/15
Religion and Law, 11/14

Crime/Law
Forensic Science Controversies, 2/17
Jailing Debtors, 9/16
Decriminalizing Prostitution, 4/16
Restorative Justice, 2/16
The Dark Web, 1/16
Immigrant Detention, 10/15
Fighting Gangs, 10/15

Education
Charter Schools, 3/17
Civic Education, 2/17
Student Debt, 11/16
Apprenticeships, 10/16

Environment/Society
Women in Prison, 3/17
Guns on Campus, 1/17
Mass Transit, 12/16
Arctic Development, 12/16
Protecting the Power Grid, 11/16
Pornography, 10/16

Health/Safety
Reducing Traffic Deaths, 2/17
Opioid Crisis, 10/16
Mosquito-Borne Disease, 7/16
Drinking Water Safety, 7/16

Politics/Economy
Immigrants and the Economy, 2/17
Trump Presidency, 1/17
European Union's Future, 12/16
The Obama Legacy, 11/16
Populism and Party Politics, 9/16
U.S.-Mexico Relations, 9/16

Upcoming Reports

Reviving Rural Economies, 3/31/17   Troubled Brazil, 4/7/17   Foreign Aid, 4/14/17

ACCESS

CQ Researcher is available in print and online. For access, visit your library or www.cqresearcher.com.

STAY CURRENT

For notice of upcoming *CQ Researcher* reports or to learn more about *CQ Researcher* products, subscribe to the free email newsletters, *CQ Researcher Alert!* and *CQ Researcher News*: http://cqpress.com/newsletters.

PURCHASE

To purchase a *CQ Researcher* report in print or electronic format (PDF), visit www.cqpress.com or call 866-427-7737. Single reports start at $15. Bulk purchase discounts and electronic-rights licensing are also available.

SUBSCRIBE

Annual full-service *CQ Researcher* subscriptions—including 44 reports a year, monthly index updates, and a bound volume—start at $1,131. Add $25 for domestic postage.

CQ Researcher Online offers a backfile from 1991 and a number of tools to simplify research. For pricing information, call 800-818-7243 or 805-499-9774 or email librarysales@sagepub.com.

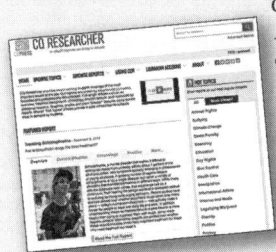

CQ RESEARCHER

CQ PRESS

In-depth reports on today's issues

Published by CQ Press, an Imprint of SAGE Publications, Inc.

www.cqresearcher.com

Reviving Rural Economies

Can they make a comeback?

R ural areas have been shedding jobs and population for decades, but the problems are growing worse. Farm consolidation has reduced the number of agricultural jobs, while thousands of factories in rural areas have closed due to automation and overseas competition. Although some rural communities are doing well, hundreds have high levels of poverty and unemployment. Because of the poor economic prospects, rural counties typically lose up to a third of their high school classes within two years of graduation as young adults flee to metropolitan areas where jobs are more plentiful. Those left behind tend to be older, and many have severe health problems. Addiction and suicide are on the rise, and life expectancy is dropping. During the presidential campaign, Donald Trump pledged to bring manufacturing and mining jobs back to such areas, which voted overwhelmingly for him. But some observers warn that his policies on immigration, trade and health care, as well as his proposed budget cuts, could hurt rural America.

One of the few remaining steelworkers in Braddock, in western Pennsylvania, relaxes after work on Oct. 12, 2016. The once thriving steel town all but collapsed after the demise of the U.S. steel industry in the 1970s and '80s. With only one steel mill remaining, the community is trying to revive its fortunes as a center for the arts.

THIS REPORT

I
N
S
I
D
E

THE ISSUES	**267**
BACKGROUND	**272**
CHRONOLOGY	**275**
CURRENT SITUATION	**279**
AT ISSUE	**281**
OUTLOOK	**282**
BIBLIOGRAPHY	**286**
THE NEXT STEP	**287**

CQ Researcher • March 31, 2017 • www.cqresearcher.com
Volume 27, Number 12 • Pages 265-288

RECIPIENT OF SOCIETY OF PROFESSIONAL JOURNALISTS AWARD FOR
EXCELLENCE ◆ AMERICAN BAR ASSOCIATION SILVER GAVEL AWARD

THE ISSUES

267 • Can rural areas revive their economies?
• Can rural areas retain highly educated workers?
• Do rural voters have disproportionate clout?

BACKGROUND

272 **Agrarian Beginnings**
Southern farming relied on slave labor.

273 **Modern Challenges**
Mechanization increased agricultural efficiency.

274 **War on Poverty**
Congress created programs designed to reduce poverty in Appalachia and other rural areas.

274 **Globalization and Retraining**
As jobs were lost to free trade and automation, worker retraining programs proliferated.

276 **Recession and Bailout**
Many rural regions have not recovered from the financial crisis.

CURRENT SITUATION

279 **Trump's Budget**
Critics say the president's proposal would harm rural areas.

280 **Health Care Costs**
Some experts say the GOP health insurance proposal would have disproportionately hurt rural America.

282 **Restoring Rural Jobs**
President Trump promised to bring back rural jobs.

OUTLOOK

282 **Political Futures**
Experts predict some businesses will move outside of cities and suburbs.

SIDEBARS AND GRAPHICS

268 **Education Gap Plagues Rural Areas**
Urban adults were twice as likely as rural residents to have bachelor's degrees in 2013.

269 **Rural South Is Poorest Region**
Its poverty rate was the nation's highest from 2011 to 2015.

272 **Hispanics Outpace Others in Rural Growth**
Count surged in rural areas during the 1990s.

275 **Chronology**
Key events since 1963.

276 **In Rural America, Immigrants Get Mixed Reception**
"Many of these communities feel completely powerless."

278 **Many Rural Hospitals on Life Support**
Up to 673 facilities could close within 10 years.

281 **At Issue:**
Do rural voters have disproportionate power?

FOR FURTHER RESEARCH

285 **For More Information**
Organizations to contact.

286 **Bibliography**
Selected sources used.

287 **The Next Step**
Additional articles.

287 **Citing CQ Researcher**
Sample bibliography formats.

Cover: Getty Images/Corbis/Andrew Lichtenstein

CQ RESEARCHER

March 31, 2017
Volume 27, Number 12

EXECUTIVE EDITOR: Thomas J. Billitteri
tjb@sagepub.com

ASSISTANT MANAGING EDITORS: Kenneth Fireman, kenneth.fireman@sagepub.com, Kathy Koch, kathy.koch@sagepub.com, Scott Rohrer, scott.rohrer@sagepub.com

SENIOR CONTRIBUTING EDITOR:
Thomas J. Colin
tom.colin@sagepub.com

CONTRIBUTING WRITERS: Marcia Clemmitt, Sarah Glazer, Reed Karaim, Barbara Mantel, Chuck McCutcheon, Tom Price

SENIOR PROJECT EDITOR: Olu B. Davis

EDITORIAL ASSISTANT: Anika Reed

FACT CHECKERS: Eva P. Dasher, Michelle Harris, Betsy Towner Levine, Robin Palmer

SAGE Publishing | **CQPRESS**

Los Angeles I London I New Delhi
Singapore I Washington DC I Melbourne

An Imprint of SAGE Publications, Inc.

SENIOR VICE PRESIDENT, GLOBAL LEARNING RESOURCES:
Karen Phillips

EXECUTIVE DIRECTOR, ONLINE LIBRARY AND REFERENCE PUBLISHING:
Todd Baldwin

CQ Researcher (ISSN 1056-2036) is printed on acid-free paper. Published weekly, except: (March wk. 4) (May wk. 4) (July wks. 1, 2) (Aug. wks. 2, 3) (Nov. wk. 4) and (Dec. wks. 3, 4). Published by SAGE Publications, Inc., 2455 Teller Rd., Thousand Oaks, CA 91320. Annual full-service subscriptions start at $1,131. For pricing, call 1-800-818-7243. To purchase a CQ Researcher report in print or electronic format (PDF), visit www.cqpress.com or call 866-427-7737. Single reports start at $15. Bulk purchase discounts and electronic-rights licensing are also available. Periodicals postage paid at Thousand Oaks, California, and at additional mailing offices. POSTMASTER: Send address changes to CQ Researcher, 2600 Virginia Ave., N.W., Suite 600, Washington, DC 20037.

Reviving Rural Economies

THE ISSUES

Wayne County is struggling. Tennessee's second-largest county is one of its least densely populated, with just 17,000 residents. Over the past quarter century, several factories in the county closed, including those that made shoes, children's clothing and men's pants. And many traditional Main Street stores across the county have shut down.

"With Wayne County being a real rural area, we've lost so many jobs over the last couple decades," said Stephanie Pearson, a clerk for the city of Collinwood. "People are just really . . . disheartened."

Pearson is active in local GOP politics and said it was no surprise that county voters overwhelmingly supported Republican Donald Trump for president last November, giving him a whopping 86 percent of the vote, compared with just 12 percent for Democrat Hillary Clinton. Trump's message resonated with people in Wayne County, who were ready for a different approach to issues such as immigration and trade. [1]

The story was similar across rural America, especially in towns that were economic monocultures, relying for decades on a single industry — such as farming, mining or manufacturing — that has been lost to foreign competition, increased automation or agricultural consolidation. Although rural areas have been shedding jobs and population for decades, the problem is growing worse, leaving behind towns struggling to attract alternative sources of jobs for residents that are older, poorer and sicker than those in urban areas.

Machines milk about 3,000 cows daily at the Joe Fernandes & Sons Dairy near Porterville, Calif. In many rural areas automation and overseas competition have decimated blue-collar jobs in agriculture, coal, timber, mining, textiles and manufacturing. Scarce job prospects across rural America are leading to poor health outcomes and deep political resentment.

AP Photo/The Porterville Record/Chieko Hara

"Many of the places that have relied on a single industry have seen major job losses," says Kathy Nothstine, a former economic development program director for the National Association of Counties, a local-government advocacy group in Washington.

Since the end of the 2007-09 recession, many metropolitan areas have rebounded, with cities such as Seattle, Denver and San Francisco attracting new residents and employers. Between 2010 and 2014, half of the net national increase in business establishments occurred in just 20 urban counties — out of more than 3,100 counties nationwide, accord-

ing to the Economic Innovation Group, a policy and advocacy organization in Washington, D.C. [2]

But rural areas, where about 15 percent of the nation's population lives, have continued to struggle, seemingly unable to bounce back or foster industries that can succeed in the global economy. As a result, rural areas are losing population — particularly young people — to cities, accelerating a downward trend.

Rural areas, defined by the Census Bureau as places that are not part of an urban area with 50,000 or more people, lost 116,000 residents between 2010 and 2014. [3] The typical rural county can lose 25 to 30 percent of its high school classes within a couple of years of graduation, and many lose up to half, according to Kenneth Johnson, a demographer at the University of New Hampshire.

"There's a distinction between urban Americans and rural Americans that's been getting stronger and stronger in the last decade or so," said Eric Schnurer, president of Public Works, a firm in West Chester, Pa., which advises state and local governments on budget and management issues. "The nonurban centers are largely being left out of the global economy. It's not surprising that they feel an extreme antipathy." [4]

That antipathy was expressed most emphatically at the ballot box. Trump carried most rural counties by a landslide and outperformed prior Republican officeholders in declining industrial areas that once swung Democratic. [5] Clinton won less than 25 percent of the vote in many of those counties.

By contrast, she carried 88 of the nation's 100 largest counties. [6]

Trump made a direct appeal to the economic concerns of rural voters, addressing the resentment caused by both the decline in blue-collar employment and clashes over conservative opposition to gun control, abortion and other issues. He spoke repeatedly about restoring jobs in industries such as steel and coal mining and pledged to renegotiate trade deals and change tax laws to discourage the outsourcing of factory jobs overseas. "Trump supporters are more rural than even average Republicans," said Matthew Oczkowski, who led the Trump campaign's digital efforts. [7]

Since taking office Trump has taken some steps he said would help rural economies, such as signing a bill repealing an Obama-era rule preventing companies from dumping coal waste into waterways and an executive order to roll back several anti-global warming rules that limited coal use. Rep. Bill Johnson, R-Ohio, who sponsored the measure to repeal the anti-dumping rule, said the regulation had not been "designed to protect streams [but] was an effort to regulate the coal mining industry right out of business." [8]

But critics say many of Trump's budget proposals could hurt rural constituents, including proposed cuts to federally subsidized health insurance and the elimination of programs that provide funds for economic development and infrastructure in rural areas. "It's very sad to see a budget proposal like this," said former Sen. Max Baucus, D-Mont. "It's red meat on a surface level to Trump's supporters, but it will hurt rural America." [9]

It is too soon to say how Trump's policies will affect rural America — or how many of his budget cuts will be passed by Congress. But it's clear that many rural voters are hoping he can help alter the downward trajectory of their communities.

Today, about 85 percent of the nation's population lives in a metropolitan area,

Education Gap Plagues Rural Areas

Urban adults were much more likely to hold a bachelor's degree than those living in rural areas in 2013. More than one-third of rural adults had only a high school diploma, compared to a quarter of those in cities. High school graduates have a lower lifetime earning potential than college graduates.

Educational Attainment of Adults, 25 or Older, 2013

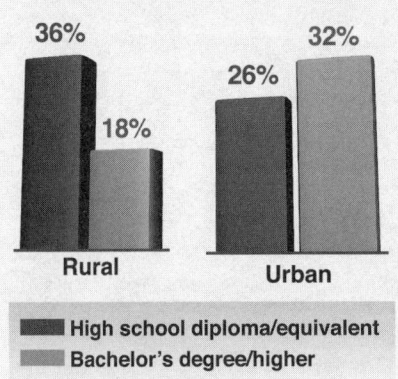

High school diploma/equivalent
Bachelor's degree/higher

Source: "Rural Education," Economic Research Service, U.S. Department of Agriculture, http://tinyurl.com/m49gm7v

up from 80 percent in 1990, and the people left behind are older and poorer than their city counterparts. [10] The average rural resident is older than 50, compared with about 45 for urban residents. [11] And according to the Department of Agriculture (USDA), 353 counties nationwide, or 11 percent of the total, are "persistently poor" — of which 301 are not near metropolitan areas. [12] Persistently poor counties, which are disproportionately in the South, are those where 20 percent or more of the population has lived in poverty for the past 30 years.

Such counties share another char-

acteristic. "If you overlay those persistent poverty maps with places with a high percentage of those over 25 who didn't finish high school, it's a perfect match," says Mil Duncan, a fellow and founding director of the Carsey Institute at the University of New Hampshire. Historically, people in those counties "haven't needed education to get work," she says, because people could get jobs on farms and in factories without attending college. But in today's economy, "I'm personally pessimistic about those places turning things around."

Experts say the lack of a post-high school education in rural families has contributed to their poorer economic outcomes, with only 18 percent of people in rural areas holding bachelor's degrees in 2013, compared with 32 percent in urban counties. [13] (*See graph, left.*) Hourly wages for American men with only a high school diploma dropped 14 percent, in inflation-adjusted terms, between 1973 and 2012. [14]

Inadequate education and employment also have led to poor health outcomes in rural areas, including high rates of addiction and suicide. For each percentage point that joblessness rises in a county, the opioid death rate increases 3.6 percent and emergency room visits 7 percent, according to a new study by the National Bureau of Economic Research. [15]

And research by two Princeton University economists, released on March 23, shows since the late 1990s middle-age white Americans with limited education have been dying younger, on average, than other middle-age adults. Anne Case and Angus Deaton say the loss of steady middle-income jobs for those with high school degrees or less has contributed to the rise in "deaths of despair" — suicides, drug overdoses and alcohol-related deaths such as liver failure. And the problem is not limited to rural areas, they said. [16]

"This is a story of the collapse of the white working class," said Deaton, who won the Nobel Prize in economics in 2015 for his work on solutions to poverty. "The labor market has very much turned against them." It is unclear why these trends have affected whites much more than African-Americans or Hispanics, whose death rates are improving, the study said. [17]

It's not just whites who are struggling in rural communities, of course. About one-fifth of rural residents are African-Americans, nonwhite Hispanics or Native Americans. "This rural America receives even lower pay and fewer [labor] protections than does rural white America," wrote Mara Casey Tieken, an assistant professor of education at Bates College. And their schools "receive far less funding and other resources" than those attended by rural whites. [18] *(See graph, p. 272.)*

Some experts say the plight of rural America can be overstated. Although many counties are struggling, others are not. Rural areas near population centers attract newcomers, while so-called recreation counties — those that offer amenities such as skiing or beaches — continue to draw tourists and retirees. "I wouldn't overstate how far rural America is falling relative to urban America," says Linda Lobao, a sociologist at Ohio State University. "Rural growth in family income and the decrease in poverty, post-recession, is just a little bit less than [in] urban [areas]. The gap wasn't that great."

But the postrecession recovery has not reached rural areas, or even all of the nation's cities. In a study released last year, the National Association of Counties found that more than three-quarters of counties with fewer than 50,000 residents have not returned to their pre-recession economic peaks. [19]

"You see things going well for people in the economic powerhouses, but when you're sitting in a rural place in Iowa or Minnesota or Idaho, you don't see it coming back as fast as what's been reported in urban places," says Eddy Berry, a sociologist at Utah State.

As politicians, residents and economists consider the future of rural

America, here are some of the questions they are debating:

Can rural areas revive their economies?

Eastern Kentucky has lost much of its coal industry due to competition from natural gas and from Western states such as Wyoming, where coal is cheaper to extract. Last year, Kentucky coal jobs fell to their lowest level since the 19th century. [20]

"We have put all our eggs in one basket for decades in this region, and that basket has spilled," said Harlan County Judge Executive Dan Mosley, the county's top administrator. [21] Last fall, Mosley hired the county's first full-time economic development director, charged with bringing in new companies and jobs. The key, Mosley says, is diversifying rather than depending on a single, unreliable industry.

But some of the new companies will hire only a few workers, so progress is slow going. And the new jobs — such as telemarketing — don't pay

nearly as well as, or have the generous benefits of, unionized mining jobs.

Eastern Kentucky's struggles are not unique. Historically, many rural areas relied on a single industry for the bulk of their employment. That's a model that no longer works in today's globalized economy, experts say. A lot of these communities were "rooted in a 19th-century model of dispersed manufacturing or farming," says David Peters, a sociologist at Iowa State University. "It's very hard to maintain or reinvigorate these communities when you have an entirely different economic system than you did over 100 years ago."

Some rural communities are in a vicious cycle: As employment drops, people move away, leaving a diminished tax base to support schools and health services and fewer consumers to patronize local stores. As services decline, more people decide to move away. Many places are then left with a struggling population, with some areas seeing rising rates of obesity, smoking, diabetes, heart disease and prescription drug abuse.

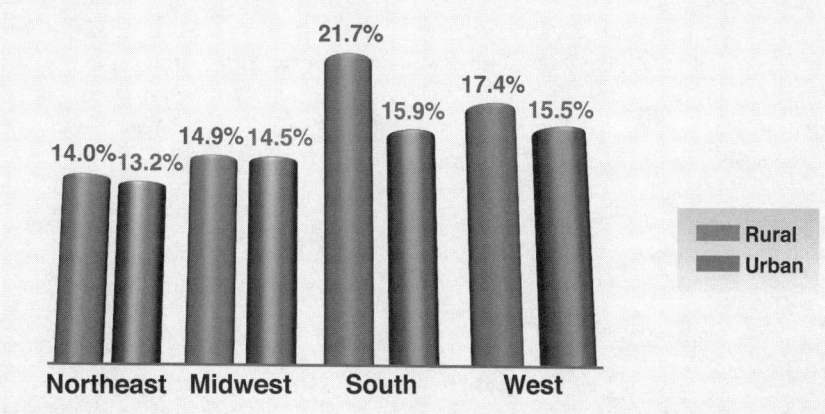

Rural South Is Poorest Region

The rural South had a poverty rate of almost 22 percent from 2011 to 2015, the highest in the nation and nearly 6 percentage points higher than in Southern cities, which also had the highest poverty among the nation's urban areas.

Poverty Rates by Region and Rural/Urban Status, 2011-2015

Northeast: 14.0% 13.2%
Midwest: 14.9% 14.5%
South: 21.7% 15.9%
West: 17.4% 15.5%

■ Rural
■ Urban

Source: "Geography of Poverty," Economic Research Service, U.S. Department of Agriculture, 2015, http://tinyurl.com/j28ph8w

Jeff Skelton, a lumber salesman in Wayne County, Tenn., says his firm could hire more people but can't find enough people with the right work ethic or who "can pass a drug test, honestly. That's the problem rural America is facing," he said. [22]

Other places enjoy certain advantages, such as natural beauty. Recreation counties bring in tourists who support service jobs in the hospitality industry. Rural communities on the fringes of metropolitan areas also can lure newcomers, as people in the cities move

universities nearby tend to fare better than those without them.

New extractive techniques also can provide a boon to rural areas. Fracking, or injecting liquid at high pressure into rock to release oil or gas, for instance, drove rapid employment growth in North Dakota and other states before a downturn hit the energy sector in recent years. "To this day, we see commodity booms," says Lyman Stone, an economist at the Agriculture Department. "When the price of cotton is good, West Texas does better. It's that simple."

Such projects may sound minor, but the population in some rural areas is so small that even a tiny uptick in employment can make a difference. "In a big city, you need a scalable solution, but in rural areas you don't always need a scalable solution," Stone says. "One person doing the legwork to recruit a company, or a few people trying to beautify a community, can really make a difference."

Those who work in rural economic development say leadership is the biggest difference between stagnating and successful communities. Two neighboring areas might have beautiful mountains, but only one might devise a plan to develop a lively tourism sector. "Aggressive leaders have found ways to remain relevant," says Brian Depew, executive director of the Center for Rural Affairs, a research and advocacy group in Lyons, Neb.

For instance, officials in Newport, Ore., built on the local fishing industry, using an Oregon State University facility to create a growing marine-science research sector, attracting both federal agencies and private companies.

"This cluster didn't happen by accident," said Gil Sylvia, an Oregon State University economist. "You start with something small, and you build out the components." [23]

Chris Langdon, a marine scientist at Oregon State University's Hatfield Marine Science Center in Newport, tends barrel-grown dulse, a protein-rich seaweed that tastes like bacon when fried. Some small communities with natural assets, like coastal Newport, are using those resources to attract new or different types of businesses. Building on its fishing industry, the city of 10,000, has created a robust ocean research sector, attracting both federal agencies and private companies.

farther out to find cheaper housing and better quality schools. Although population increases in such rural areas can draw complaints from longtime residents about increased traffic or other community changes, such places at least are drawing in taxpaying residents. And small towns with colleges and

He notes that some areas are using the assets they have to attract new types of business. Farm tourism, for instance, is growing. "It can be a significant employment driver," Stone says. "Don't just buy a carton of milk, meet the cow. We'll charge three times as much for the milk, and you'll pay it."

Can rural areas retain highly educated workers?

Many small towns hope to reverse the perennial "brain drain" that drives rural America's best and brightest young people to big cities.

"In almost all rural counties, there's a net migration out of people in their 20s," says Johnson, the University of New Hampshire demographer. They leave for various reasons: to join the military, attend college, pursue a job. And those who leave are likely to be those with the best prospects.

"The people who grow up in these communities who are most capable of having a strong income trajectory — they leave," says Rolf Pendall, a housing and community development expert at the Urban Institute, a Washington think tank. "It's true in struggling [urban] neighborhoods, and it's true in rural America."

While hundreds of rural counties have had chronic population loss for a long time, growth in other nonmetro counties used to make up for those losses. But the 2010 census showed for the first time that "counties that were growing didn't offset that," says John Cromartie, a geographer with the Department of Agriculture.

The problem hasn't gotten any easier to solve at a time when big companies, many of which used to locate near natural resources, increasingly are moving to urban areas to attract top talent. [24] After fleeing center cities in past decades, corporations such as McDonald's and Motorola have moved headquarters or sizable numbers of workers to large cities over the past few years. [25]

But some rural areas can attract and retain professionals. Most towns with more than 1,000 people have jobs for people with college degrees, such as doctors, pharmacists and business managers, Cromartie says. And some people, whose jobs allow them to telecommute, bring their professional jobs with them from larger cities to live near ski resorts or other amenities.

"That does happen, but it's not happening at a level that transforms communities," Cromartie. "It's not like they're moving big firms out there. It's individuals or consultants."

He and others who study rural populations note that some of those who leave will return in their 30s and 40s to raise their children or to have a cheaper, less stressful lifestyle or to care for an older parent. But the rural rebound isn't enough to offset the loss of younger adults.

That leaves rural officials such as Mosley in Eastern Kentucky facing a chicken-or-egg problem: Do they invest in education and training to create a skilled workforce to attract companies, or do they first try to lure companies that can then attract skilled workers — or train local residents?

"In this region, there's a lot of money being put into education, which is critical," Mosley says. "But a lot of times, we're spending money to train some of these people to do jobs that do not exist here."

Despite millions of dollars spent in recent decades by companies, universities and government programs to retrain displaced workers, not enough high-skilled, high-paying jobs have been created in rural areas, says Stone, the USDA economist. "The problem is not that rural areas lose talented people. It's not the outflows," Stone says. "It's the lack of inflows."

Plenty of skilled workers prefer living in rural places, says Willa Johnson, an education coordinator in the Eastern Kentucky city of Hazard. She's part of a networking group called Stay Together Appalachian Youth, or STAY, which encourages young professionals to remain in the region. "The narrative has always been that if you're staying in Eastern Kentucky, it's because you had to or failed," she says. "The STAY project is about saying you're staying because you want to."

But people who want to live in rural America find it difficult if appropriate jobs are in short supply, says Martha Crowley, a sociologist at North Carolina State University in Raleigh. "Especially after people have gotten a college education, they have debt to pay and they have skills they want to use," she says.

Do rural voters have disproportionate clout?

Because their populations are declining, rural areas are represented by far fewer congressional and state lawmakers than 50 years ago.

Still, when it comes to state and federal funds, rural counties — at least in some states — have powerful advantages, because funding formulas created in earlier eras provide extra education and economic development money to rural areas. Nevada, for example, awards thousands of dollars more per pupil to school districts in low-population areas than to districts in urban areas. [26] And while many rural residents believe that their taxes disproportionately help people living in cities, several studies show that rural residents receive more from federal government on a per capita basis than city residents. [27]

The number of rural lawmakers may have declined, but they have learned to stick together out of necessity. And rural legislators are overwhelmingly Republican — a big advantage at a time when Republicans dominate most state legislatures. Bill sponsors trying to round up GOP votes must get the support of rural lawmakers, who often vote as a bloc, perhaps in exchange for support for their own priority legislation.

Urban delegations, by contrast, often view other cities as economic competitors so they often don't stick together. And even legislators from the same metropolitan region often view colleagues from adjoining jurisdictions as competitors.

This is not a new phenomenon. A 2013 study by political scientists Gerald Gamm and Thad Kousser found that between 1880 and 2000, bills benefiting smaller cities were more likely to pass than measures affecting cities with populations of more than 100,000. "Year after year, while most bills affecting smaller districts pass, most big-city bills fail," they concluded. [28] As urban legislative delegations have gotten bigger, Gamm and Kousser said, they have found it even harder to work together.

Still, in states where metropolitan lawmakers control the legislature, rural legislators complain they have a hard time getting lawmakers to focus on rural issues. They also complain that they are outnumbered by urban counterparts who don't understand rural problems or culture and values. "There is a lack of representation in rural America," says Jerry Sonnenberg, a Republican state senator in Colorado whose district is large and mostly rural.

Hispanics Outpace Others in Rural Growth

Hispanic populations in rural areas surged during the 1990s, growing 64 percent, compared to 7 percent among non-Hispanics.* Hispanics' robust growth continued in the 2000s, though at a slower pace.

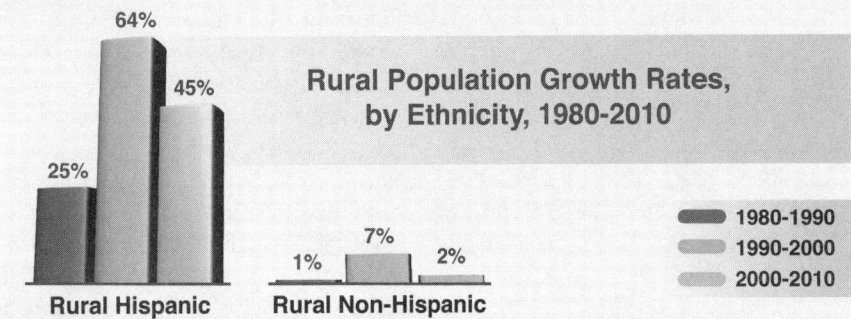

Rural Population Growth Rates, by Ethnicity, 1980-2010

Rural Hispanic: 25%, 64%, 45%
Rural Non-Hispanic: 1%, 7%, 2%

1980-1990
1990-2000
2000-2010

* The U.S. Census Bureau uses the term Hispanic to refer to people "of Cuban, Mexican, Puerto Rican, South or Central American or other Spanish culture or origin regardless of race."

Source: "Immigration and the Rural Workforce," Economic Research Service, U.S. Department of Agriculture, updated Feb. 3, 2017, http://tinyurl.com/hyhoa73

In 2012, for example, voters in 75 of Minnesota's 87 counties voted to block recognition of same-sex marriage. But the other 12 counties, including those in the Minneapolis-St. Paul area, outvoted them. [29]

In Washington state, rural-urban resentment has gotten so bad that some lawmakers have introduced legislation to allow rural eastern counties to form a new breakaway state called Liberty. [30] Its sponsors say the agricultural east has a different economy, climate and values than western population centers such as Seattle.

The bill might not go anywhere, but the idea of rural areas seceding has been floated in several other states, including in Colorado. Voters in 11 Colorado counties considered secession measures in 2013. They passed in five counties, supported by residents angry about state policies regarding gun control and the environment. [31]

Although rural legislators often feel they are being ignored, they can sometimes punch above their weight at the congressional level. Smaller states often keep sending the same politicians back to Washington, allowing them to build seniority and, thus, clout. The 2017 edition of the *Roll Call Clout Index*, the publication's measure of congressional power, finds that mostly rural states — including Alaska, Mississippi and Wyoming — have far more influence on Capitol Hill than their relatively small populations would suggest. [32]

The Constitution's architects designed Congress to give smaller states power. Each state is entitled to two senators, whether it's Wyoming, with fewer than 600,000 people, or California, with some 39 million. "That's been the case since the founding of the nation, that rural areas have had more clout than urban" areas, says Berry, the sociologist at Utah State University.

In the Senate, rural states have enhanced power in electing presidents. In the Electoral College, each state has the same number of electors as the size of its House and Senate delegations, combined. As a result, each of California's 55 electoral votes represented about 714,000 people, while Wyoming's three electoral votes represented only about 195,000 people.

Political analyst Steven Hill once described this effect as "affirmative action for low-population states." [33] It helps explain why Trump was elected president in 2016 despite losing the popular vote — the second time in five elections that the popular vote winner was defeated.

However, rural interests get little attention when it comes to major federal legislation, except from the federal farm bill, which provides billions of dollars in crop and conservation support, says Johnson, the University of New Hampshire demographer.

Although rural residents and officials often complain about their lack of power, they recognize that institutional structures — such as the Senate, the Electoral College and the makeup of congressional and legislative districts — offer them more attention than their 15 percent share of the national population would otherwise command.

"Our forefathers were absolutely brilliant in figuring out how those people in less populated areas would not get run over by the masses," says Sonnenberg. "They did that with the Electoral College." ∎

BACKGROUND

Agrarian Beginnings

Forty years ago, historian Richard Hofstadter wrote: "The United States was born in the country and has moved to the city." [34] During the American Revolution, more than 90 percent of Americans lived in a rural setting, with the vast majority making at least part of their living from farming. [35]

Agriculture helped make the new nation self-sufficient. After the Revolution, farming spread beyond the original 13 colonies as land was added to the nation through expansions such as the 1803 Louisiana Purchase. Federal and state governments helped farmers move into the new areas by extinguishing Indian claims, surveying the land and building the roads and canals needed to bring goods to market.

Farmwork was performed primarily by families, except in the South, where slavery was the primary source of labor for nearly 250 years. "In such locales as the South Carolina rice coast and the Louisiana sugar parishes, [slaves] approached 90 percent of the population," wrote rural historian David B. Danbom. [36]

Because of its slave labor, the South, with its huge tobacco and cotton plantations, was slower to mechanize than the North. The number of slaves grew exponentially in the decades leading up to the Civil War, rising from just under 700,000 in the 1790 census to nearly 4 million by 1860. [37]

But elsewhere the invention of reapers and harvesters and increased settlement in farming regions led to tremendous increases in yield. Wheat exports from Chicago grew from just 80 bushels in 1839 to 2 million bushels 10 years later. [38]

As farming methods improved, farmers could feed more people with less labor. By the 1860s, fueled by the growth of manufacturing jobs and immigration, cities contained nearly 20 percent of the U.S. population — four times their share in the 1790s. [39]

The Civil War created both high crop prices and scarce labor, leading to further mechanization. In 1862, Congress took several steps that further promoted new settlements and farming, including:

• Authorizing construction of a railroad between Iowa and California;

• Passing the Land-Grant College Act, which set aside hundreds of thousands of acres for colleges specializing in agriculture and mechanical arts;

• Enacting the Homestead Act, which allowed settlers to receive 160 acres of public land if they made certain improvements, including building a dwelling and living there for five years. [40]

Between 1862 and 1913, some 4 million settlers filed claims to 270 million acres — 10 percent of America's land

Supporters of Republican presidential candidate Donald Trump await his arrival in Charleston, W. Va., on May 5, 2016. During the campaign, Trump repeatedly addressed concerns of blue-collar Americans, particularly in rural areas, promising to restore steel and coal mining jobs, rewrite trade deals and change tax laws to discourage the outsourcing of factory jobs overseas.

mass at the time. Only 40 percent of these claims were finalized, however, due to drought and low farm prices. [41]

Nevertheless, the final three decades of the 19th century saw a dramatic expansion of rural America, with the number of farms, their total acreage and production of wheat, corn and cattle all roughly doubling. [42]

Modern Challenges

By 1920, the number of Americans living in cities had surpassed the rural population, thanks to the lure of jobs created by industrialization and the influx of European immigrants. [43]

Farmers' incomes and land values continued to grow until the Great Depression. The 1929 stock market crash contributed to falling domestic demand for farm products and a precipitous fall in crop exports. In 1929, Americans spent $19.5 billion on food; three years later, they spent only $11.4 billion. People also cut back on clothes purchases, suppressing cotton and wool prices. Between 1929 and 1932, farm incomes plunged 40 percent. [44]

Despite many crop failures — such as the Dust Bowl disaster of 1934 to

1936, when millions of tons of dry topsoil literally blew away from the Great Plains — rural areas saw a net population increase. [45] Although many small farmers lost their farms, those who remained at least could feed themselves. And President Franklin D. Roosevelt's New Deal programs of the 1930s included extensive assistance for agriculture, including price supports and crop insurance.

The post-World War II years produced a revolution in agricultural productivity, with rural electrification, the increasing use of tractors to replace horse- or mule-drawn plows and the development of hybrid crops. With increased productivity, food prices fell, and the percentage of Americans' incomes spent on food dropped dramatically. [46]

But over the long term, more-efficient agriculture eroded the need for farm labor, contributing to the depopulation of rural America. In 1940, 30.5 million Americans, or 23 percent of the population, lived on farms. By 1970, that had dropped to less than 5 percent.

"In one generation, farmers went from being a major demographic group to being a marginal one," Danbom wrote in *Born in the Country*, his history of rural America. [47]

By 1970, after the Great Migration of African-Americans from the rural South to cities in the Midwest and the North, which began in 1910, nearly half of all African-Americans lived outside the South, compared with 10 percent in 1915. [48] Many rural whites also headed north, seeking factory jobs in the industrial Midwest and elsewhere. By 1960, 10 percent of people living in Ohio had been born in Kentucky, West Virginia or Tennessee. [49]

In *Hillbilly Elegy*, J.D. Vance's 2016 bestselling memoir about growing up in Appalachia, the author recalls his grandfather leaving Kentucky to work

Former coal miner Jim Ratliff was among nearly 1,000 people who responded to ads posted by Bit Source, a software-development startup seeking unemployed coal workers who wanted to be trained as computer programmers. Located in an old Coca-Cola bottling plant in Pikeville, Ky., the company has been able to hire nine programmers.

for the Armco steel company in Ohio. "A special policy encouraged wholesale migration: Applicants with a family member working at Armco would move to the top of the employment list," Vance writes. "Armco didn't just hire the young men of Appalachian Kentucky; they actively encouraged these men to bring their extended families." [50]

War on Poverty

The post-World War II economic boom did not extend nationwide.

The influential 1962 book *The Other America*, by political scientist and socialist activist Michael Harrington, argued that 25 percent of the American population was living in poverty (the actual number was closer to 20 percent), and many of the "invisible" poor lived in the rural South. [51]

In 1964, President Lyndon B. Johnson traveled to Martin County, in central Kentucky, where poverty topped 60 percent, to declare a "war on poverty." [52] He later unveiled several of his signature "Great Society" anti-poverty programs, such as subsidized health insurance for the elderly (Medicare) and for the poor (Medicaid), food stamps and Head Start. Some initiatives, such as the Model Cities program and creation of the Department of Housing and Urban Development, targeted the urban poor. But Johnson also created a Commission on Rural Poverty and other programs designed to stimulate rural economies.

In 1965, Congress expanded the scope of the Appalachian Regional Commission (ARC) to help the 13-state region develop economically. Overseen by both federal and state officials, the commission has dispensed $23 billion over the years in grants for highways and other infrastructure, community health projects and technical education, among other programs. [53] The number of high-poverty counties in the region has dropped from 295 in 1960 to 84 today, according to the ARC, while the overall poverty rate has fallen from 30 percent to 17 percent. [54]

Some conservatives have argued that 1960s-era social-welfare programs created dependency problems that have worked against the original goal of making the poor more self-sufficient. "In fact, a significant portion of the population is now less capable of self-sufficiency than it was when the War on Poverty began," the Heritage Foundation, a conservative think tank, contended in 2014. [55]

At the same time, the private sector has been eliminating jobs across rural America, and agriculture has continued to mechanize and consolidate. During the 1980s, 92 of Iowa's 99 counties lost at least 25 percent of their population, after having already lost considerable residents in previous decades. [56] In some cases, the loss of farm incomes was offset by small factories that grew up in communities near metropolitan areas such as Chicago and Detroit and supplied major manufacturers in the cities.

But with the growth of free-trade pacts over the past 30 or 40 years, globalization disrupted many of those supply chains, and production scattered across the globe to lower-wage countries.

Globalization and Retraining

The postwar focus on free trade helped lower prices for U.S. consumers while lifting millions of workers out of poverty around the world. But it also caused millions of Americans and others in industrialized countries to lose their good-paying manufacturing jobs.

During the 1980s, as factories in big cities and small towns across America shut down and moved abroad, the in-

Continued on p. 276

Chronology

1960s-1970s
Despite federal intervention, rural economies are struggling.

1963
Supreme Court finds that Georgia's system of counting votes by county instead of population gives rural counties disproportionate representation. The decision ends the practice of dividing legislative districts by county, rather than population.

1964
President Lyndon B. Johnson visits rural Kentucky to declare "war on poverty," which leads to new federal programs such as Head Start, Medicaid and food stamps.

1965
The Appalachian Regional Commission, a partnership between the federal government and 13 states, is formed to promote economic development. . . . Cesar Chavez, leader of the National Farm Workers Association, calls for a consumer boycott of grapes to pressure growers to bargain with workers as a group, resulting in the first collective bargaining agreement for farmworkers.

1969
Coal Mine Health and Safety Act requires annual inspections of coal mines and creates penalties for safety violations.

1977
Congress enacts a surface mining law designed to protect rural environments from adverse effects.

1979
Manufacturing jobs, which make up about 20 percent of rural employment, peak in June.

1980s-2000s
Mechanization and falling farm prices result in declining farm populations, and many rural manufacturing plants shut down as companies move jobs to lower-wage countries.

1983
Falling commodity prices leave the average Iowa farm operating at a loss for the year.

1986
Commodity prices fall to a lower level, relative to farming costs, than during the Great Depression of the 1930s.

1990
U.S. Census shows that 92 of Iowa's 99 counties have lost at least a quarter of their population since 1980.

2000
One-fifth of Americans live in rural places.

2003
Medicare Modernization Act increases federal spending on rural health. . . . Child poverty rates in rural America begin a decade-long rise.

2007-2009
Steep recession hits rural America hard, with net farm profits falling 38 percent from 2008 to 2009.

———— • ————

2010s
Rural areas continue to lose population and economic power relative to cities.

2011
President Barack Obama creates the White House Rural Council to foster policies to assist low-income rural residents.

2013
Median income for high school graduates has dropped 27.8 percent in real terms from its 1973 peak.

2014
Congress passes a farm bill authorizing $489 billion over four years for nutrition, agriculture and various other programs.

2015
Eighty-seven percent of the U.S. population lives in metropolitan areas, up from 56 percent in 1950. . . . The number of rural counties losing population reaches 1,320 out of 3,100 counties nationwide — a historic high. . . . Democratic presidential candidate Hillary Clinton proposes a $30 billion plan to aid struggling coal communities.

2016
Since 2010, 80 rural hospitals have closed. . . . Coal production has dropped by 40 percent since 2008. . . . National Association of Counties finds that large counties generate a disproportionate share of new jobs, particularly those paying above-average wages. . . . Donald Trump is elected president, with heavy support from rural counties after promising to bring back jobs in manufacturing, coal and steel.

2017
President Trump signs legislation abolishing a regulation designed to protect streams and waterways from coal mining waste, which he says will save thousands of coal jobs (Feb. 16). . . . Farm incomes are projected to drop 9 percent this year, leading to more farm closures. . . . Trump signs an executive order to allow more federal coal leases and begin rolling back Obama-era environmental regulations that limit coal use. (March 28).

In Rural America, Immigrants Get Mixed Reception

"Many of these communities feel completely powerless."

I n 2000, Faribault, Minn., was 90 percent white. Since then, the black population has tripled, largely due to an influx of Somali refugees seeking low-skilled jobs at local industries, such as a turkey processing plant. [1]

Many longtime residents in the town of 23,000, located 50 miles south of Minneapolis, resent the newcomers, finding their language, culture and even driving habits bewildering. Some have complained that the Somalis are a financial drain, receiving government benefits such as food stamps or welfare.

"I ain't racist, but these Somalis get everything and the vets get nothing," said Kevin Miller, a disabled Faribault resident. "We shouldn't be bringing people over here and supporting them." [2]

In recent decades, immigrants have spread far beyond traditional gateways such as New York and Los Angeles. As they have moved into rural America, some have received hostile receptions. Many small communities aren't used to welcoming strangers, says Martha Crowley, a sociologist at North Carolina State University.

"In rural places, it's not the same as urban places, where you have people moving in and out all the time," she says. "These are places where people have known each other for a long time."

Still, many communities have welcomed immigrants. For rural areas with struggling economies and diminished populations, immigrants can provide a needed influx of workers. Hispanic migrants in particular have helped offset rural population loss in the Midwest and Southeast. Although racial and ethnic minorities make up just over 20 percent of the nation's rural

population, they accounted for 83 percent of rural population growth between 2000 and 2010 — with Hispanics alone making up half of that growth. [3]

"The rural counties that are gaining population, by and large, are ones where there has been an increase in foreign-born residents," says Tim Marema, editor of *The Daily Yonder*, a website focused on rural issues. "Without this influx of new residents, the rural population drop would be even more dramatic."

Immigrants tend to go where the jobs are. In many cases, that means meatpacking plants that now are scattered across rural America. Decades ago, butchers were skilled workers located in population centers, near their customers. That work has largely been consolidated, with much of the nation's meat now processed by large companies that have cut costs by "moving away from urbanized . . . areas, because everything is cheaper" in rural communities, Crowley says.

Nowadays, most meatpacking plants are huge operations, with jobs segmented into discrete, repetitive tasks. Those jobs require less skill, so they pay lower salaries and are less attractive to native-born workers, creating a labor vacuum that immigrants fill.

In addition, immigrants are often willing to do manual labor for less money than native-born Americans, sociologists say. "In the plantation pine sector, virtually every one of those trees has been planted by a migrant worker," says Conner Bailey, a professor emeritus of agricultural economics and rural sociology at Auburn University. "Our forest industry would not survive without migrant workers."

Continued from p. 274

dustrial Midwest became known as the Rust Belt. For example, in the 1960s Galesburg, Ill., a city of 36,000, had 10,275 manufacturing jobs producing appliances. [57] By the 1980s, about 3,000 of those jobs were lost as factories were bought, resold and eventually closed. [58]

But the job loss was not only due to globalized trade. "Thanks to automation, we now make 85 percent more goods than we did in 1987, but with only two-thirds the number of workers," wrote *New York Times* technology columnist Farhad Manjoo, citing figures from the St. Louis Federal Reserve Bank. [59]

To help employees displaced by automation and globalization, state and federal agencies set up countless worker

retraining programs in small towns and rural areas across the country.

Some critics say there are too many retraining programs and excessive bureaucratic overlap. The Workforce Innovation and Opportunity Act of 2014 ordered agencies to streamline dozens of training programs across multiple agencies over the next three to five years.

Others complain that government-funded training too often lifts the burden of retraining workers from the companies seeking qualified personnel.

Nevertheless, many advanced manufacturing enterprises still complain of a shortage of skilled workers, with 70 percent of manufacturing executives in a 2015 study saying they cannot find enough workers with sufficient technical

training. Contributing to the problem, some advanced manufacturing jobs require highly specialized skills that may not be transferable to other employers. [60]

"It's unrealistic today to think of traditional, very idiosyncratic manufacturing jobs where you're going to walk in, get a job, get trained in a bunch of very specific skills, and they'll hold onto you for decades," said Harvard economist Lawrence Katz. "That's just not the trajectory of employment anymore." [61]

Recession and Bailout

A ccording to Arthur Brooks, president of the conservative American Enterprise Institute think tank, rural

In the 1970s, Garden City, Kan., welcomed a meatpacking plant and the immigrants who accompanied it. While many neighboring communities have turned into veritable ghost towns, Garden City is faring well, with a 3 percent unemployment rate, well below the roughly 5 percent national average.

"Our community would be a dying community without the immigrants that have come in to fill in the gaps, and to grow business," said Kevin Bascue, the sheriff in Finney County, which includes Garden City. [4]

Not all went smoothly, however. Tensions arose in southwest Kansas when Vietnamese immigrants — and later Latinos — came to work in the meatpacking plants, a fairly common pattern, says László Kulcsár, a sociologist at Kansas State University. A community might learn to incorporate foreign-born residents but face a renewed period of adjustment when a new group comes in, according to Kulcsár.

Often, groups of immigrants appear to arrive suddenly, drawn by a particular plant, family connections or a refugee-resettlement agency. Such rapid population shifts can make it harder for long-settled residents to adjust. "Many of these communities feel completely powerless against the forces of globalization," Kulcsár says. "They say, 'We have all these people showing up, and we did not invite them.' "

Rural immigrants have lower family incomes and higher poverty rates than their native-born neighbors or their urban immigrant counterparts, according to researchers at the University of New Hampshire. "The rural immigrant population is disproportionately of working age (thus comprising fewer children or seniors), more racially and ethnically diverse, and less educated than the rural native-born population," the researchers wrote. [5]

Ayan Abdi, a Somali immigrant, studies English at her home in North Dakota with Tony Ross, a University of North Dakota graduate student who volunteers with a group that aids refugees and other immigrants. While the newcomers have sometimes received hostile receptions, some struggling communities with diminished populations have welcomed them as providing a needed influx of workers.

— Alan Greenblatt

[1] Matt McKinney, "Some in Faribault see sense, not bias, in an immigration timeout," *Minneapolis Star-Tribune*, Feb. 3, 2017, http://tinyurl.com/jzdlvva.

[2] Alan Greenblatt, "What Trump Means for State and Local Races," *Governing*, July 2016, http://tinyurl.com/zqz5uxe.

[3] Kenneth M. Johnson, "Rural Demographic Change in the New Century," *Issue Brief No. 44*, Carsey Institute, Winter 2012, http://tinyurl.com/ju4vx8j.

[4] Frank Morris, "A Thriving Rural Town's Winning Formula Faces New Threats Under Trump Administration," NPR, Feb. 19, 2017, http://tinyurl.com/glo7nh3.

[5] Andrew Schaefer and Marybeth J. Mattingly, "Demographic and Economic Characteristics of Immigrant and Native-Born Populations in Rural and Urban Places," *Issue Brief No. 106*, Carsey Institute, Fall 2016, http://tinyurl.com/zk6jd3x.

America's problem is its lack of mobility: Not enough people are moving to where the jobs are, mostly in urban centers.

In the past 40 years, "the percentage of American families that move from state to state in a given year has been cut in half," he said. "So this idea of staying where you are, wanting job retraining but not moving to where the jobs are, it's just crazy by the standards of the 1970s in the United States." [62]

Brooks called for a grassroots "cultural change" to get people moving more. "The concept that we've got to stay in a town, even when we don't have any work simply because the family is there or that's where we've always lived, . . . that's sort of anathema to the American experience." [63]

While rural joblessness has fallen somewhat since the recession, employment in urban areas has been growing. [64] In rural areas, 20.3 percent of young people between ages 16 and 24 are neither in school nor working, compared with 14.2 percent in urban areas. [65]

The lack of job prospects has contributed to severe health problems, often linked to depression, in rural America, notably, deaths from suicide and drug overdoses. Roger Winemiller, a corn and soybean farmer in Ohio, wanted his children to inherit the farm. But two have died from heroin overdoses, and his last child is being treated for addiction. Opioid deaths in Winemiller's area have nearly tripled since 1999. [66]

The nationwide opioid epidemic has hit rural areas hard. [67] A recent University of Michigan study found that the rates of babies born with opioid withdrawal symptoms are rising much faster in rural areas than in cities, and a 2015 study found that more rural adolescents abuse opioids than urban teens. [68]

Researchers say economic, environmental and social factors make rural areas particularly fertile ground for the growing opioid problem. For instance, because rural areas have lagged behind urban areas in recovering from the 2007-09 recession, said University of California Davis epidemiologist Magdalena Cerda, "people might be particularly vulnerable to perhaps using prescription

Many Rural Hospitals on Life Support

Up to 673 facilities could close within 10 years.

Despite layoffs and staff pay cuts, the ailing Gulf Coast Medical Center in Wharton, Texas, was forced to close in November. A sign on the door directed patients to a hospital in El Campo, about 20 minutes away.

For a rural town with fewer than 9,000 residents, the loss of the only hospital has been painful. Diverting ambulances to El Campo is costing Wharton about $16,000 a month, and patients are finding it more difficult to get care. [1]

Wharton's story is not unique, experts say. Since 2010, 80 rural hospitals have closed. [2] "We predict as many as 673 rural hospitals have the potential to close over the next 10 years," says Alan Morgan, CEO of the National Rural Health Association. "That's a third of the nation's rural hospitals."

Experts say several factors are causing the closures. Areas with declining populations find it difficult to support a hospital. And due to a 2011 budget law, Medicare has cut reimbursements to health providers by 2 percent. [3] State government resistance to the Affordable Care Act (ACA), particularly in Southern states where 40 percent of rural hospitals are located, has prevented other federal dollars from flowing to those hospitals. [4]

"Half of the nation's rural population lives in states that have not expanded Medicaid" under the ACA, which would have generated additional federal funds for those states, Morgan says. "Enrollment through the health exchanges in rural America hasn't been anywhere near what we expected," he adds, referring to insurance marketplaces set up under the ACA, also known as Obamacare, through which individuals can receive federal subsidies for coverage.

It's not just hospital closures that are limiting rural residents' access to health care. The health care industry has been consolidating in recent years, with smaller clinics and hospitals being bought by large companies. Many seek to funnel patients toward a smaller number of specialists, who generally are located in urban or suburban areas, according to Eddy Berry, a sociologist at Utah State University.

"If you need three or four visits with doctors to schedule a surgery, that's pretty rough when you're driving an hour to get to each place," Berry says.

Rural areas have an average of 68 primary-care physicians per 100,000 residents, compared with 84 for urban areas, according to the American Academy of Family Physicians. [5] Shortages are particularly acute for behavioral health providers, such as mental health physicians.

"I spent a couple of years at the National Alliance on Mental Illness, heading up a state-by-state report card on the mental health system," says Laudy Aron, a senior fellow at the Urban Institute, a Washington think tank. The alliance "would get calls from very rural parts of the country, where you'd have a mental health professional on the verge of retirement. They would have 300 to 400 patients, some driving for hours." Yet, the retiring physicians "had no one to hand their caseloads off to."

The spread of such "medical deserts" across rural America has contributed to increases in mortality rates, experts say. [6] Suicides and deaths from drug overdoses have become a scourge across rural areas, exacerbated by a lack of access to drug treatment and mental health providers. [7] Alcohol-related deaths also are increasing among non-Hispanic whites in small towns and rural areas. [8]

"While life expectancy continues to increase in urban areas, since about 1990 life expectancy has been on a downward trend in rural America," Morgan says. The gap in urban-rural life expectancy is now two full years — five times the difference in the early 1970s. [9] Teen birth rates also are 63 percent higher in rural areas than in big cities. [10]

To address treatment shortages, rural hospitals and other providers increasingly are connecting patients with distant specialists via telemedicine, or computer technology. And many states are trying to encourage more doctors to set up practice in rural settings.

For instance, Arkansas, Georgia and Tennessee are increasing the number of medical residency programs associated with their state university medical schools in hopes that more doctors will stick around where they train. [11] And medical schools in Kansas and Kentucky have opened satellite campuses to train physicians in outlying areas. Other states offer loan forgiveness to physicians who practice for at least two years in underserved areas.

Other hospitals and towns are recruiting foreign doctors under the H-1B and J-1 temporary visa programs, which have recently come under scrutiny and could be curtailed by President Trump's efforts to crack down on immigration.

opioids to self-medicate a lot of symptoms of distress related to sources of chronic stress, chronic economic stress." [69]

In addition, she said, the kind of jobs available in rural areas — such as manufacturing, farming and mining — tend to have higher injury rates, which can lead to the use of potentially addictive painkillers. Because treatment alternatives such as physical therapy are often unavailable in rural areas, opioids have become a key part of a rural doctor's pain management, said Jack Westfall, a family physician and researcher at the University of Colorado. And medication-assisted treatment for drug addiction is also limited in rural areas, he said. [70]

"It's not a fundamentally rural problem," said former Agriculture Secretary Tom Vilsack. "But it's a unique problem in rural America because of the lack of treatment capacity and facilities." [71]

Poor health outcomes, the lack of good-paying jobs and concern about their children's futures are "anxieties that are more deeply felt by rural whites than by whites living in the nation's cities or suburbs," the Pew Research Center concluded after last November's

About one in four practicing physicians in the United States was trained abroad, and that share is even higher in many rural areas. [12] Some were recruited under the H-1B visa program, which offers visas to skilled foreigners when there is a shortage of domestic workers. [13] High-tech companies have been accused of using the program to hire low-wage foreigners to replace American computer programmers and engineers, and the Trump administration in March halted expedited processing of H-1B applications. [14] But the slowdown is affecting rural areas' ability to recruit doctors.

The J-1 visa program allows thousands of foreign medical students to enter the country as long as they practice in rural and other underserved areas for up to seven years. [15] During the presidential campaign, candidate Trump called for the J-1 program to be abolished, and some students have been affected by the administration's temporary travel ban from certain Muslim countries. [16]

The big question facing rural providers is how Congress might change health policy. A bill that would have replaced the Affordable Care Act and turned Medicaid into a block grant program was pulled from the House floor on March 24, due to lack of support among the Republican majority. The bill, known as the American Health Care Act, would have cut funding for groups disproportionately represented among rural residents — Medicaid recipients and those receiving federal subsidies for private insurance. House Speaker Paul Ryan, R-Wis., said Congress would not try again to replace the ACA, but GOP moderates hinted in the following days that they might try to craft a compromise that would attract support from moderate Democrats. Meanwhile, health officials are nervous about possible funding cuts through the budget process. [17]

— *Alan Greenblatt*

People gather in the predawn hours, many after sleeping in their cars, waiting to see a doctor at the Remote Area Medical (RAM) mobile dental and medical clinic on Dec. 4, 2016, in the economically struggling Florida panhandle community of Milton.

Getty Images/Spencer Platt

[1] Laura Garcia, "Wharton's hospital closes," *Victoria Advocate*, Nov. 18, 2016, http://tinyurl.com/jht4sth.

[2] Ayla Ellison, "A state-by-state breakdown of 80 rural hospital closures," Becker's Hospital CFO, Dec. 13, 2016, http://tinyurl.com/lk5943h.

[3] "FAQs on the 2013 Sequestration," American Medical Association, 2013, http://tinyurl.com/hzzgg5l.

[4] Jane Wishner *et al.*, "A Look at Rural Hospital Closures and Implications for Access to Care: Three Case Studies," Kaiser Family Foundation, July 7, 2016, http://tinyurl.com/h3vkco4.

[5] Stephen M. Petterson *et al.*, "Unequal Distribution of the U.S. Primary Care Workforce," *American Family Physician*, June 1, 2013, http://tinyurl.com/zdmxcwe.

[6] Joel Achenbach and Dan Keating, "A new divide in American death," *The Washington Post*, April 10, 2016, http://tinyurl.com/zxmbkbb.

[7] For background, see Peter Katel, "Opioid Crisis," *CQ Researcher*, Oct. 7, 2016, pp. 817-840.

[8] Anne Case and Angus Deaton, "Rising morbidity and mortality in midlife among white non-Hispanic Americans in the 21st century," *Proceedings of the National Academy of Sciences*, Sept. 17, 2015, http://tinyurl.com/j378n6b.

[9] Gopal K. Singh and Mohammad Siahpush, "Widening Rural-Urban Disparities in Life Expectancy, U.S., 1969-2009," *American Journal of Preventive Medicine*, February 2014, http://tinyurl.com/gvb9yte.

[10] Brady E. Hamilton, Lauren M. Rossen and Amy M. Branum, "Teen Birth Rates for Urban and Rural Areas in the United States, 2007-2015," National Center for Health Statistics, November 2016, http://tinyurl.com/jobxh62.

[11] Michael Ollove, "Rural doctor shortage spurs states to act," PBS NewsHour, June 10, 2016, http://tinyurl.com/zyb24jo.

[12] Lauren Silverman, "Trump Travel Ban Spotlights U.S. Dependence On Foreign-Born Doctors," NPR, Feb. 11, 2017, http://tinyurl.com/j57pbum.

[13] Parija Kavilanz, "Visa ban could make doctor shortage in rural America even worse," CNN Money, Feb. 2, 2017, http://tinyurl.com/zo6phky.

[14] Jackie Wattles and Parija Kavilanz, "What Trump's latest H-1B move means for workers and business," CNN Money, March 4, 2017, http://http://tinyurl.com/zpb4yqq.

[15] Silverman, *op. cit.*

[16] Olivia So, "International students fear what will happen when Trump takes office," *USA Today*, Jan. 5, 2017, http://tinyurl.com/h9rwg28.

[17] Fred Bauer, "What Next for Health-Care Reform? Possible Strategies for the GOP," *National Review*, March 25, 2017, http://tinyurl.com/kxaykws.

election. [72] Those anxieties made most rural voters receptive to Trump's message of economic nationalism, including skepticism about immigration and global trade agreements. According to Pew, Trump defeated Hillary Clinton in small towns and rural areas by 62 percent to 34 percent, while winning by only 5 percentage points in suburbs and losing by double digits in urban areas. [73] ■

CURRENT SITUATION

Trump's Budget

Although Donald Trump owed his election victory in large part to rural voters, critics say his budget blueprint released on March 16 would cut or eliminate several programs aimed at helping rural areas. [74]

"If you're in a rural area — and were likely a Trump supporter — you may have some questions about why this is the budget we got," said Johnathan Hladik, policy program director for the Center for Rural Affairs, an advocacy group in Lyons, Neb. [75]

For instance, the Agriculture Department's budget would be slashed by 21 percent — one of the deepest proposed cuts. [76] The Essential Air Service program, which provides federal subsidies for commercial airline services to underserved rural airports, would

Corn farmers Jud Vaught, right, and his brother, Bill Kirklin, set up an irrigation system near Whiteland, Ind., on July 20, 2012, during a severe drought. While drought has always posed an existential threat to the nation's farmers, in recent decades automation and the consolidation of small family farms into so-called industrial farms have reduced the number of farms and the rural workforce.

be eliminated, as would the rural water and sewer loan and grant program. [77]

Funding for the Appalachian Regional Commission, along with two other rural regional development agencies, would also be ended. [78] "Rural America elected Trump," said Dee Davis, founder of the Center for Rural Strategies, an advocacy group in Whitesburg, Ky. "His message to rural America is, 'I don't care.' " [79]

According to the commission's annual report, the ARC pays for such things as sewer renovation, clean water, access to medical care and infrastructure. In 2015, ARC projects created or helped to retain 23,000 jobs, and the commission attracted $8 in private investment for every $1 spent. [80]

But University of Maryland economics professor and conservative commentator Peter Morici said about the ARC cuts: "Heck, we've been pouring

money into Appalachia since the Roosevelt administration. . . . Maybe it's time to say, they don't need special treatment anymore." [81]

David M. Carney, a GOP consultant in Hancock, N.H., thinks Trump's supporters may not be so upset about these cutbacks. "Most of these programs don't touch folks directly," he says. "They affect the poverty special-interest professionals and insiders. Studies, planning, meetings, conferences and the like — not direct aid to folks. It makes Congress look like they're helping and caring by having offices, signs and a 'presence' in these rural areas."

But even Republicans are expected to resist some of the president's proposals. "The president's proposed budget reduction for agriculture does not work," said Sen. John Hoeven, R-N.D. "Given the challenging times in the farm patch . . . we need to prioritize and maintain our agriculture budget." [82]

However, not all of Trump's proposals would hurt rural America. His proposed $54 billion increase in defense spending could help places with military installations, which are disproportionately rural. And administration officials

say that critics are not taking into account the savings rural residents will see through reduced taxes.

"When you start looking at places that we reduce spending, one of the questions we asked was, can we really continue to ask a coal miner in West Virginia or a single mom in Detroit to pay for these programs?" said Mick Mulvaney, director of the Office of Management and Budget. "The answer was no." [83]

Whether rural residents, or other Americans, will see net savings under Trump's budget plan will depend on final congressional action regarding spending and tax policy.

Health Care Costs

Rural lawmakers also worry about proposed changes to health programs such as Medicaid, the program that subsidizes health insurance for the poor. The GOP-sponsored American Health Care Act was designed to offer fewer federal subsidies for insurance and turn Medicaid into a block-grant program for states.

Although repealing the ACA has been a top priority of Republicans for years, the bill was pulled from the House floor on March 24, when it was clear Republicans could not produce a majority for passage. Democrats were united in opposing it; conservatives complained it doesn't go far enough toward abolishing the ACA, and moderate Republicans say too many of their constituents would lose coverage.

Republican Sen. Shelley Moore Capito of West Virginia said she doubted the American Health Care Act would "sufficiently [help] those in the lower-income, rural older population, which is increasingly a large part of my state." [84]

Rural voters have had reason to be dissatisfied with the ACA. Monthly premiums for insurance acquired through the law's health care exchanges jumped an average of 30 percent in rural areas

Continued on p. 282

Getty Images/Scott Olson

At Issue:

Do rural voters have disproportionate power?

NICK LICATA
FORMER MEMBER,
SEATTLE CITY COUNCIL

WRITTEN FOR *CQ RESEARCHER*, MARCH 2017

*d*ata show that rural voters clearly have more political influence than urban voters. Because Republicans control a majority of state governments, most congressional and legislative district boundaries have been gerrymandered to dilute urban Democrats' voting power. As a result, on both the national and state levels, rural voters have greater influence than urban voters. A pure one-person, one-vote distribution of electoral power is modified based on where a voter lives.

The debate on this topic is quickly moving from one based on data to one about political philosophy. Liberals argue the Electoral College and state legislative boundaries over-emphasize rural areas by focusing more on allocating votes by the square mile than by person.

Consequently, those living in cities are at a disadvantage in shaping public policy. They see states spending more money on highways than on subways, rail or bus transportation. At the federal level, they see Congress cutting public funding for urban social services geared to the poorest folks or minority groups.

Those supporting the current bias toward rural areas justify it as necessary to avoid concentrating federal assistance on just a few heavily populated states; they say citizens should be able to live anywhere in the country and be assured that federal money will be available to improve their community.

Donald Trump's presidential campaign and subsequent victory have introduced a second rationale for retaining the current arrangement, as articulated by Fox News host Bill O'Reilly. He says because most rural voters are white, abandoning the Electoral College or redrawing legislative district boundaries would put white voters at a disadvantage.

"The heart of liberalism in America is based on race," O'Reilly asserts, because progressives want "power taken away from the white establishment, and they want a profound change in the way America is run."

Creating equal voting power for rural and urban voters would result in cities holding greater political clout. Because more ethnic minorities live in urban areas than rural areas, political power would be more reflective of cities' greater ethnic diversity.

To achieve a more democratic system, we must avoid implying that racial political motives are behind the pursuit of a fairer rural-urban voting balance.

TIM MAREMA
EDITOR, THE DAILY YONDER;
VICE PRESIDENT,
CENTER FOR RURAL STRATEGIES

WRITTEN FOR *CQ RESEARCHER*, MARCH 2017

*i*n elections decided by razor-thin margins, any bloc of voters can claim they were the deciding factor, either because they voted or because they didn't vote.

On the winning side of the tally, rural voters turned out strongly for the 2016 presidential election. They supported Donald Trump by 2 to 1 — an impressive margin, but not one that was determinative on its own.

There were other factors as well. Urban, African-American, Latino and other traditionally Democratic-leaning voters did not show up at the polls in anticipated numbers. And Democrats underperformed in all but the nation's largest metropolitan areas.

So add it up: To sway the presidential election, rural voters had to vote en masse for one candidate and be part of a larger movement that included suburbs and medium-sized cities. Additionally, there had to be lower turnout among other sets of voters. To me, that sounds like rural voters are an important part of the electorate, but so are other geographic and demographic groups.

The work needed to address the concerns of rural voters is not unduly onerous. Because of their advantage in large urban areas, Democrats don't need outright victories in rural America to win the White House. They simply need to make races in rural precincts more competitive. That's something former President Barack Obama accomplished in his two election wins, but John Kerry in 2004 and Hillary Clinton in 2016 did not.

To perform up to even this unambitious standard would require Democrats to suit up and show up in rural America. White papers and policy platforms, no matter how compelling, are no substitute for the work of retail politics.

Luckily for Democrats, Republicans don't set too high a standard themselves. With Democrats ceding the field, Republicans have been able to dominate rural voting through appeals to cultural-values issues and little else.

This makes it seem as if the real complaint about the power of the rural vote is the Electoral College. The reasoning behind the Electoral College is well documented and, by American standards, ancient.

The Electoral College is not changing any time soon. So it's time to stop acting like our Constitution is some sort of October surprise.

Winning national office requires candidates to muster some kind of appeal among rural voters. So what?

Continued from p. 280

last year, compared to 20 percent in urban areas. [85] Rural residents are less likely to sign up for coverage under the law, making the patient pool smaller and driving costs up further. And 41 percent of the rural population has only one insurance carrier to choose from, while most city residents can choose from at least three. [86]

"Patients in rural areas are facing higher premiums, fewer insurance choices and hospitals are being forced to close," said Sen. John Barrasso, a Wyoming Republican. "We are committed to stabilizing the insurance market and giving states flexibility, so they can design reforms that meet their unique needs." [87]

But critics of the GOP measure said it would have disproportionately hurt rural America. Much of the federal funding for opioid prevention and treatment would have been cut, for instance. And, because rural insurance bills tend to be higher, proposed cuts to ACA subsidies would hit harder. Older rural residents would be particularly affected, since insurance companies would have been allowed to increase premiums for older people. [88]

The measure was clearly unpopular with the public, with a Quinnipiac University poll released on March 23 showing it had support from only 17 percent of those surveyed, compared with 56 percent who disapproved of it. [89] Still, congressional Republicans may press for health policy changes at a later date, with Trump predicting that the ACA would have to be revised once it "explodes." [90]

Restoring Rural Jobs

President Trump depends on rural support, especially in Appalachia, where he carried West Virginia by 42 percentage points and Kentucky by 30. [91] He promised to bring jobs back to rural America. But can he deliver?

Trump has pressured American companies not to ship jobs overseas, although

factcheckers have noted that Trump has claimed credit for plans that were already in the works, at least in some cases. [92] And during a Feb. 28 address to Congress he claimed: "Since my election, Ford, Fiat-Chrysler, General Motors, Sprint, Softbank, Lockheed, Intel, Walmart and many others have announced that they will invest billions and billions of dollars in the United States, and will create tens of thousands of new American jobs." [93]

Trump said his energy policies, such as approval of controversial oil pipelines, allowing more federal coal leases and eliminating rules to curb climate change that discouraged the use of coal would spark "a new energy revolution." Flanked by more than a dozen coal miners on March 28 as he signed the order rolling back anti-climate change rules, Trump said it was all about "bringing back our jobs, bringing back our dreams and making America wealthy again." [94]

Even in coal country, however, some doubt whether Trump can restore jobs. The industry faces competition from cheaper, cleaner natural gas, and machinery has reduced the need for labor, so just changing regulations may not be enough to bring jobs back. [95]

"I would not expect to see a lot of growth because of the Trump presidency," Nick Carter, interim president of the Kentucky Coal Association, an industry group, said shortly after the election. "If there is any growth in Eastern Kentucky, it will be because of an improved economy for coal." [96]

Other Trump proposals may in fact hurt rural businesses. Trump's proposed limits on immigration, for instance, could decimate the agricultural labor pool, driving up growers' costs and Americans' grocery bills.

And Trump's proposed import duties on products made abroad, designed to discourage U.S. manufacturers from outsourcing jobs, may lead to increased automation instead of new hiring. Expect manufacturers "to use robots to keep labor costs down," *Barron's* reported. [97]

Protectionist tariffs also could trigger a trade war, hitting rural areas that ship agricultural products overseas especially hard.

"We're in such a world economy that any other production or any trade issue [affecting] agricultural goods that happens anywhere in the world 100 percent affects my income and my ability to sell my product at its greatest value," said Adam Kirian, a 29-year-old Ohio farmer who voted for Trump. "Any place in the world that we're not able to trade, it has a huge effect on United States agriculture." [98] ■

OUTLOOK

Political Futures

Stone, the Department of Agriculture economist, predicts that rural America will be in better shape five years from now. He foresees a shift in the sort of macroeconomic dynamics that until now have hurt rural areas. Rather than continuing to flock to large metropolitan areas, companies and individuals may realize they can save money if they move to less crowded places, he says.

"We'll see more people exurbanizing," or moving to the exurbs. "More companies will see that agglomeration" — or businesses clustering close together in denser areas — "has its costs," so they may move out to rural quarters. As a result, he says, "I think in five years rural America will be somewhat better off. It won't be rolling in the money, but I think their situation will be somewhat improved."

Exploiting local resources is key, says László Kulcsár, a sociologist at Kansas State University. For instance, sprucing up downtowns could appeal to people, such as retirees, seeking walkable communities, and investing in the area high school could appeal to those who moved away but might want to return to raise their kids. "If there are resources on the ground, those will be magnets for additional resources," he says.

In Eastern Kentucky, county administrator Mosley hopes Harlan County's mountainous beauty, plentiful water and cheap electricity will attract new companies. "The downturn of the coal industry has had an absolutely devastating impact on this economy," Mosley says. "We weren't going to have anything left for my kids and maybe my grandkids if we didn't get to work having a diversified economic development effort." On the political front, the major parties face challenges.

Despite being a billionaire real estate mogul, President Trump won over rural voters in part by speaking their language on immigration, gun owners' rights and cultural issues, and because those voters felt ignored or even denigrated by urban or coastal elites. "For some people, it certainly has been a relief just to hear their concerns addressed at all in a public way," says Crowley, of North Carolina State. "I would imagine they feel validated having someone talk about it in the same way they talk about it. I can understand that, because these are serious problems that people are living with."

Trump has promised to restore industries that once employed rural voters en masse, opening himself up to political risk. If he runs for reelection in 2020 but hasn't convinced Congress to approve his policies, he will have failed in his promise to "drain the swamp" and shake up the status quo in Washington.

Rural resentment toward Washington stems, in part, from the belief that decision-makers there "fail to give rural communities their fair share of resources," wrote Katherine J. Cramer, a public policy professor at the University of Wisconsin, in her 2016 book *The Politics of Resentment*. [99]

But studies consistently show, she noted, that while cities receive more federal and state support, they also pay more in taxes, and rural residents receive more from the federal government per capita. "We help rural Americans get roads and internet access," said Los Angeles Mayor Eric Garcetti. "We subsidize states in the South with job-training dollars to help their economies out. We only get 72 cents back for every dollar we give." [100]

However, Democrats have failed to stress such facts, experts say, and have not fashioned an effective message to appeal to white working-class rural voters. "We've got to speak to the working-class people, the blue-collar people," Democratic Rep. Tim Ryan of Ohio said late last year, as he launched an unsuccessful challenge against Rep. Nancy Pelosi of California as House minority leader. [101]

While Trump's approval ratings have been historically low for a new president, there's no sign yet that he's losing support among more than a small fraction of his supporters. And despite all the criticism that his budget and health policies will hurt rural areas, he continues to have deep residual appeal among rural voters nostalgic for a more prosperous past.

"They look back into the midcentury and they see white working-class communities, people who never finished university degrees or even high school, who were able to get stable 9-to-5 jobs that paid a livable wage and allowed them to support a family of four," said Justin Gest, a public policy assistant professor at George Mason University and the author of the 2016 book *The New Minority: White Working Class Politics in an Age of Immigration and Inequality*. [102]

"From their perspective, they've lost it all," he said. [103] ∎

Notes

[1] Dave Boucher, "Rural America looks to Donald Trump for revival," *The Tennessean*, Nov. 18, 2016, http://tinyurl.com/lfg7b45.

[2] "The New Map of Economic Growth and Recovery," Economic Innovation Group, May 2016, http://tinyurl.com/zffdnfx.

[3] Michael Ratcliffe *et al.*, "Defining Rural at the U.S. Census Bureau," Census Bureau, December 2016, http://tinyurl.com/hnucy6m; Rural America at a Glance, 2015 Edition," Department of Agriculture, January 2016, http://tinyurl.com/mfco6gg.

[4] Alan Greenblatt, "Can Counties Fix Rural America's Endless Recession?" *Governing*, August 2016, http://tinyurl.com/jqt6rco.

[5] Bill Bishop, "Caught in a Landslide — County-Level Voting Shows Increased 'Sorting,' " *Daily Yonder*, Nov. 21, 2016, http://tinyurl.com/hkjgld5.

[6] Rhodes Cook, "The 2016 Presidential Vote: A Look Down in the Weeds," *Sabato's Crystal Ball*, Jan. 26, 2017, http://tinyurl.com/go3tlnr; Ronald Brownstein, "How the Election Revealed the Divide Between City and Country," *The Atlantic*, Nov. 17, 2016, http://tinyurl.com/grkzhdw.

[7] Helena Bottemiller Evich, "Revenge of the Rural Voter," *Politico*, Nov. 13, 2016, http://tiny url.com/h5rtbgz.

[8] "House GOP dismantles Obama regulation protecting streams from coal mining debris," *Chicago Tribune*, Feb. 1, 2017, http://tinyurl.com/hbqrys9.

[9] Rob Chaney, "Baucus warns Trump budget would hurt rural America, world," *Missoulian*, March 17, 2017, http://tinyurl.com/mu53xyz.

[10] Hamilton Lombard, "The metropolitanization of rural America," University of Virginia Demographics Research Group, June 6, 2016, http://tinyurl.com/hjra2aq; Marc J. Perry and Paul J. Mackun, "Population Change and Distribution 1990 to 2000," Census Bureau, April 2001, http://tinyurl.com/or73th3. Alana Semuels, "The Graying of Rural America," *The Atlantic*, June 2, 2016, http://tinyurl.com/jy326a6.

[11] Dante Chinni, "Urban, Rural Divide Growing Deeper Throughout US," NBC News, Nov. 7, 2014, http://tinyurl.com/hmrcwnm.

[12] "Geography of Poverty," Department of Agriculture, March 1, 2017, http://tinyurl.com/htxj626.

[13] "Rural Education," Department of Agriculture, Sept. 20, 2016, http://tinyurl.com/m49gm7v.

[14] Andrew J. Cherlin, "Why Are White Death Rates Rising?" *The New York Times*, Feb. 22, 2016, http://tinyurl.com/jgpaduu.

[15] Alex Hollingsworth, Christopher J. Ruhm and Kosali Simon, "Macroeconomic Conditions and Opioid Abuse," National Bureau of Economic Research Working Paper No. 23192, February 2017, http://tinyurl.com/gq2x2gh.

[16] See Christopher S. Rugaber, "White, working-class, middle-age Americans dying younger than their peers," The Associated Press, March 23, 2017, http://tinyurl.com/leth2k8; Anne Case

and Angus Deaton, "Mortality and morbidity in the 21st century," BPEA Conference Drafts, March 23-24, 2017, http://tinyurl.com/ldve9cb, and Brookings Papers on Economic Activity, March 23, 2017, http://tinyurl.com/lrevt2j.

[17] Rugaber, *ibid.*

[18] Mara Casey Tieken, "The rural America everyone is ignoring," *The Washington Post*, March 26, 2017, http://tinyurl.com/jwrn4x6.

[19] Emilia Istrate and Tadas Pack, "County Economies 2016: Wider Recovery, Slower Growth," National Association of Counties, Feb. 8, 2017, http://tinyurl.com/zlofyp7.

[20] Bill Estep, "Coal jobs in Kentucky fall to lowest level in 118 years," *Lexington Herald-Leader*, May 2, 2016, http://tinyurl.com/hwszvp6.

[21] Alan Greenblatt, "In Life After Coal, Appalachia Attempts to Reinvent Itself," *Governing*, December 2016, http://tinyurl.com/mtv2d68.

[22] Boucher, *op. cit.*

[23] Greenblatt, *op. cit.*

[24] Lauren Weber, "Companies Flock to Cities With Top Talent," *The Wall Street Journal*, April 12, 2016, http://tinyurl.com/zhdpeyn.

[25] Nelson D. Schwartz, "Why Corporate America Is Leaving the Suburbs for the City," *The New York Times*, Aug. 1, 2016, http://tinyurl.com/n5ozb8m.

[26] "Nevada K-12 Education Finance," Guinn Center for Policy Priorities, Feb. 2015, http://tinyurl.com/lyol3re.

[27] Katherine J. Cramer, *The Politics of Resentment: Rural Consciousness in Wisconsin and the Rise of Scott Walker* (2016).

[28] Gerald Gamm and Thad Kousser, "No Strength in Numbers: The Failure of Big-City Bills in American State Legislatures, 1880-2000," *American Political Science Review*, November 2013, http://tinyurl.com/h3wmv7v.

[29] Andy Mannix, "When will gay marriage be legal in Minnesota?" *City Pages*, Jan. 2, 2013, http://tinyurl.com/z4lmajh.

[30] Jim Camden, "Matt Shea, Bob McCaslin propose creating new state called 'Liberty' in

Eastern Washington," *The Spokesman-Review*, Dec. 7, 2016, http://tinyurl.com/jjd9r7h.

[31] Monte Whaley, "51st state question answered 'no' in 6 of 11 counties contemplating secession," *The Denver Post*, Nov. 5, 2013, http://tinyurl.com/hv25g62.

[32] David Hawkings, "Nevada's Hill Sway Sinks While Other Small States Surge," *Roll Call*, Feb. 27, 2017, http://tinyurl.com/jg3e8lu.

[33] Steven Hill, *Fixing Elections: The Failure of American Winner Take All Politics* (2002), p. 119.

[34] Richard Hofstadter, *The Age of Reform: From Bryan to FDR* (1977), p. 23.

[35] David B. Danbom, *Born in the Country: A History of Rural America*, 2nd ed. (2006), p. xiii.

[36] *Ibid.*, p. 100.

[37] Peter Kolchin, *American Slavery 1619-1877* (1993), p. 93.

[38] John Steele Gordon, *An Empire of Wealth: The Epic History of American Economic Power* (2004), p. 175.

[39] Danbom, *op. cit.*, p. 82.

[40] *Ibid.*, p. 112.

[41] Robert J. Gordon, *The Rise and Fall of American Growth* (2016), p. 261.

[42] Danbom, *op. cit.*, p. 131.

[43] Tanvi Misra, "A Complex Portrait of Rural America," *CityLab*, Dec. 8, 2016, http://tinyurl.com/hobznf3.

[44] Danbom, *op. cit.*, p. 198.

[45] *Ibid.*, p. 200.

[46] Eliza Barclay, "Your Grandparents Spent More Of Their Money On Food Than You Do," NPR, March 2, 2015, http://tinyurl.com/pp7hd59.

[47] Danbom, *op. cit.*, p. 245.

[48] Isabel Wilkerson, *The Warmth of Other Suns: The Epic Story of America's Great Migration* (2010), p. 10.

[49] J.D. Vance, *Hillbilly Elegy: A Memoir of a Family and Culture in Crisis* (2016), p. 28.

[50] *Ibid.*, p. 27.

[51] Maurice Isserman, "50 Years Later: Poverty

and The Other America," *Dissent*, Winter 2012, http://tinyurl.com/zcffsys.

[52] Pam Fessler, "Kentucky County That Gave War On Poverty A Face Still Struggles," NPR, Jan. 8, 2014, http://tinyurl.com/k4hkuxp.

[53] Bill Estep, "Trump plan cuts funds for Appalachian agency that helps Eastern Kentucky," *Lexington Herald-Leader*, March 16, 2017, http://tinyurl.com/khu4dk7.

[54] Elaine Godfrey, "Trump's Proposal to Scrap the Agency Devoted to Developing Appalachia," *The Atlantic*, March 16, 2017, http://tinyurl.com/kwpdndh.

[55] Rachel Sheffield and Robert Rector, "The War on Poverty After 50 Years," Heritage Foundation, Sept. 15, 2014, http://tinyurl.com/m2bnwxl.

[56] Richard C. Longworth, *Caught in the Middle: America's Heartland in the Age of Globalism* (2008), p. 89.

[57] Chad Broughton, *Boom, Bust, Exodus* (2015), p. 34.

[58] *Ibid.*, p. 49.

[59] Farhad Manjoo, "How to Make America's Robots Great Again," *The New York Times*, Jan. 25, 2017, http://tinyurl.com/hwmd4p6.

[60] "The skills gap in U.S. manufacturing: 2015 and beyond," Deloitte and The Manufacturing Institute, 2015, http://tinyurl.com/k5fqy7c.

[61] Ruth Graham, "The Retraining Paradox," *The New York Times Magazine*, Feb. 23, 2017, http://tinyurl.com/zp8evxf.

[62] Kai Ryssdal, "What it means to close the 'dignity gap,'" *Marketplace*, March 7, 2017, http://tinyurl.com/m23nwvu.

[63] *Ibid.*

[64] "Rural America at a Glance: 2016 Edition," Department of Agriculture, November 2016, http://tinyurl.com/mxdk36f.

[65] Sarah Burd-Sharps and Kristen Lewis, "Promising Gains, Persistent Gaps: Youth Disconnection in America," Social Science Research Council, March 8, 2017, http://tinyurl.com/kscjdns.

[66] Jack Healy, "2 of a Farmer's 3 Children Overdosed. What of the Third — and the Land?" *The New York Times*, March 12, 2017, http://tinyurl.com/l7az3qq.

[67] For background, see Peter Katel, "Opioid Crisis," *CQ Researcher*, Oct. 7, 2016, pp. 817-840.

[68] Beata Mostafavi, "Study: Rural Communities See Steep Increase in Babies Born with Opioid Withdrawal," M Health Lab, Dec. 12, 2016, http://tinyurl.com/javyheb. Also see Shannon M. Monnat and Khary K. Rigg, "Examining Rural/Urban Differences in Prescription Opioid Misuse Among US Adolescents," *The Journal of Rural Health*, Sept. 6, 2015, http://tinyurl.com/n2v2hx4.

About the Author

Alan Greenblatt is a staff writer at *Governing* magazine. Previously he covered politics and government for NPR and *CQ Weekly*, where he won the National Press Club's Sandy Hume Award for political journalism. He graduated from San Francisco State University in 1986 and received a master's degree in English literature from the University of Virginia in 1988. His *CQ Researcher* reports include "Gentrification," "Future of the GOP," "Immigration Debate," "Media Bias" and "Downtown Revival."

[69] Luke Runyon and Harvest Public Media, "Why Is The Opioid Epidemic Hitting Rural America Particularly Hard?" "All Things Considered," NPR, http://tinyurl.com/gnpzlze.

[70] Ibid.

[71] Ibid.

[72] Rich Morin, "Behind Trump's win in rural white America: Women joined men in backing him," Pew Research Center, Nov. 17, 2017, http://tinyurl.com/l4hqtyd.

[73] Ibid.

[74] Dana Farrington, "Read President Trump's Budget Blueprint," NPR, March 16, 2017, http://tinyurl.com/z5oesz4.

[75] Donnelle Eller, "Trump cuts would hurt Iowans who supported him, critics say," Des Moines Register, March 17, 2017, http://tinyurl.com/n3qopjn.

[76] Ibid.

[77] Scott Lilly, "Thanks, Rural America!!" The Huffington Post, March 16, 2017, http://tinyurl.com/mxkocr6.

[78] Jeff Guo, "President Trump won big in these places. Now he wants to eliminate 3 agencies dedicated to helping them," The Washington Post, March 17, 2017, http://tinyurl.com/kg6ubuu.

[79] Jenny Hopkinson, Catherine Boudreau and Helena Bottemiller Evich, "Rural voters lose in Trump's budget plan," Politico, March 16, 2017, http://tinyurl.com/mftjb78.

[80] Guo, op. cit.

[81] "Two Economists With Opposing Political Views On The Trump Budget," "Morning Edition," NPR, March 17, 2017, http://tinyurl.com/klc6u4z.

[82] April Baumgarten, "Hoeven, Peterson: Trump budget doesn't work for rural communities," Grand Forks Herald, March 16, 2017, http://tinyurl.com/moj3xud.

[83] Louis Nelson, "Mulvaney justifies budget: We can't ask a coal miner to pay for the Corporation for Public Broadcasting," Politico, March 16, 2017, http://tinyurl.com/hyhpvh3.

[84] Astead W. Herndon and Victoria McGrane, "Obamacare repeal could hurt rural areas — a key Trump constituency," The Boston Globe, March 14, 2017, http://tinyurl.com/k7jjouo.

[85] Erin Mershon, "Trumpcare: Big Bills in Small Towns," CQ Magazine, March 13, 2017, http://tinyurl.com/kdjec8p.

[86] Ibid.

[87] Ibid.

[88] Anna Wilde Mathews and Dante Chinni, "GOP Health Plan Would Hit Rural Areas Hard," The Wall Street Journal, March 13, 2017, http://tinyurl.com/j24ua86.

[89] "U.S. Voters Oppose GOP Health Plan 3-1," Quinnipiac University Poll, March 23, 2017, http://tinyurl.com/ny4clb7.

[90] Linda Qiu, "Fact Check: Trump's Misleading Claims on the Health Bill Failure," The New York Times, March 24, 2017, http://tinyurl.com/mxw735a.

[91] "2016 Election Results," CNN, http://tinyurl.com/pt27ryx.

[92] Allison Graves, "Did Donald Trump's Carrier deal actually save 'less than half' of jobs headed to Mexico?" Politifact, Dec. 4, 2016, http://tinyurl.com/gn4syvw; http://tinyurl.com/jwnyxqa.

[93] "Remarks by President Trump in Joint Address to Congress," The White House, Feb. 28, 2017, http://tinyurl.com/ztt7a3f.

[94] Matthew Daly and Jill Colvin, "Trump, in break from other world leaders, digs in on coal," The Associated Press, March 28, 2017, http://tinyurl.com/lwqbl9n.

[95] For background, see Barbara Mantel, "Coal Industry's Future," CQ Researcher, June 17, 2016, pp. 529-552.

[96] Daniel Desrochers, "McConnell: It's 'hard to tell' if ending 'war on coal' will bring back jobs," Lexington Herald-Leader, Nov. 11, 2016, http://tinyurl.com/zrql6gl.

[97] Jack Hough, "Rise of the Robots," Barron's, March 4, 2017, http://tinyurl.com/zgfzweu.

[98] Mary Kilpatrick, "In rural Seneca County, conservative values reign: Ohio Matters," Cleveland Plain Dealer, Feb. 23, 2017, http://tinyurl.com/hbeu54u.

[99] Cramer, op. cit., p. 5.

[100] Daniel C. Vock, "L.A.'s Mayor on Trump, the Irony of Urban Politics and 'Un-American' Ideas," Governing, Jan. 5, 2017, http://tinyurl.com/kcbx72r.

[101] Ian Schwartz, "Rep. Tim Ryan On Pelosi Challenge: We Need A Leader Who Can "Represent Entire Party," Win In OH, WI, MI," Real Clear Politics, Nov. 18, 2016, http://tinyurl.com/jhb2s4a.

[102] Sean Illing, "Why the white working class feels like they've lost it all, according to a political scientist," Vox, Dec. 21, 2016, http://tinyurl.com/jaxkjw3.

[103] Ibid.

FOR MORE INFORMATION

Appalachian Studies Association, West Virginia University, 1 John Marshall Drive, Huntington, WV 25755; 304-696-2904; appalachianstudies.org. Promotes research and education on Appalachia; publishes the Journal of Appalachian Studies.

Center for Rural Affairs, 145 Main St., Lyons, NE 68038; 402-687-2100; www.cfra.org. An advocacy group that works on farming, conservation, health and other issues, while also providing technical support and loans to small, rural businesses.

Center for Rural Strategies, 46 E. Main St., Whitesburg, KY 41858; 606-632-3244; www.ruralstrategies.org. A nonprofit group that aims to improve rural communities by conducting polls and publishing information about life in the countryside, including The Daily Yonder, a news site devoted to rural topics.

Economic Research Service, U.S. Department of Agriculture, 333 E St., S.W., Washington, DC 20024; 202-694-5000; www.ers.usda.gov. A federal agency that tracks farm, food and trade figures and publishes reports about rural economies.

In These Times, 2040 N. Milwaukee Ave., Chicago, IL 60647; 773-772-0100; http://inthesetimes.com/rural-america. A progressive publication that focuses on rural issues, with a blog and in-depth reports.

National Rural Assembly, 865-688-9546; ruralassembly.org. A nonprofit group supported by the W.K. Kellogg Foundation; convenes meetings of groups concerned with rural issues, with a focus on education and the environment.

Opportunity Finance Network, 620 Chestnut St., Suite 572, Philadelphia, PA 19106; 215-923-4754; ofn.org. An association of community development financial institutes that advocates for programs that assist financially stressed areas.

Rural Policy Research Institute, University of Iowa, 145 N. Riverside Drive, Iowa City, IA 52242; 319-384-3857; www.rupri.org. An academic consortium that provides data and analysis about the impact of public policy decisions on rural areas.

Rural Sociological Society, 1 University Circle, Western Illinois University, Macomb, IL 61455; 309-298-3518; www.ruralsociology.org. Promotes the study of rural populations and issues; publishes the Rural Sociology journal.

Bibliography

Selected Sources

Books

Bailey, Conner, Leif Jensen and Elizabeth Ransom, eds., *Rural America in a Globalizing World*, West Virginia University Press, 2014.

The Rural Sociological Society offers dozens of scholarly essays on rural health, demographic changes, agriculture, the economy and the environment.

Cramer, Katherine J., *The Politics of Resentment: Rural Consciousness in Wisconsin and the Rise of Scott Walker*, University of Chicago Press, 2016.

A University of Wisconsin public policy professor interviewed dozens of groups in rural communities around the state and found that residents feel urbanites are taking an unfair share of government resources and not treating rural values with respect.

Danbom, David B., *Born in the Country: A History of Rural America, 2nd ed.*, Johns Hopkins University Press, 2006.

A North Dakota State University historian examines the agricultural economy.

Vance, J.D., *Hillbilly Elegy: A Memoir of a Family and Culture in Crisis*, Harper, 2016.

In this bestseller, a Yale-trained lawyer raised in Ohio and Kentucky examines his family's dysfunction and violence to explain broader problems of the rural, white working class.

Articles

Barrett, Rick, "Dairy farmers fear Trump's immigration policies," *USA Today*, March 6, 2017, http://tinyurl.com/hfoaboa.

Wisconsin dairy farmers, many of whom voted for Donald Trump, worry his immigration policies could put them out of business because they rely on Mexican workers, often undocumented.

Bouie, Jamelle, "Broken Pledge," *Slate*, March 9, 2017, http://tinyurl.com/zjub9f9.

A political reporter contends that President Trump's policies will hurt rural America, particularly proposed cuts to health care.

Cohn, Nate, "Why Trump Won: Working Class Whites," *The New York Times*, Nov. 9, 2016, http://tinyurl.com/h7coo6t.

Trump's victory was due to a swing among working class white voters away from the Democratic Party in the rural countryside and former industrial strongholds in the North and Midwest.

Condon, Patrick, "Urban-rural split in Minnesota grows deeper, wider," *Minneapolis Star-Tribune*, Jan. 25, 2015, http://tinyurl.com/jvxcay6.

Republicans have been able to take advantage of a perception in rural precincts that cities such as Minneapolis and St. Paul —

which have boomed as rural counties have shrunk and grown older — are unfairly hogging jobs and government resources.

Johnson, Kenneth, "Where is rural America, and what does it look like?" *The Conversation*, Feb. 20, 2017, http://tinyurl.com/gu4ebqz.

Rural areas continue to shrink relative to cities, with minorities accounting for any recent upticks in population growth.

Leonard, Robert, "Why Rural America Voted for Trump," *The New York Times*, Jan. 5, 2017, http://tinyurl.com/z8kpxmz.

Rural voters perceive urban areas as receiving the bulk of government spending on services and infrastructure and believe Democrats do not share their cultural values.

Newman, Jesse, and Patrick McGroarty, "The Next American Farm Bust Is Upon Us," *The Wall Street Journal*, Feb. 8, 2017, http://tinyurl.com/jhsouan.

A worldwide grain glut is expected to cause U.S. farm income to drop 9 percent this year, and the number of farms could drop below 2 million — a number not seen since the Louisiana Purchase was made, in the early 19th century.

Semuels, Alana, "America's Great Divergence," *The Atlantic*, Jan. 30, 2017, http://tinyurl.com/jqxj4jx.

As college graduates increasingly are attracted to cities, good-paying jobs that do not require college degrees are disappearing from rural regions due to globalization and automation.

Reports and Studies

"Rural America at a Glance: 2016 Edition," Economic Research Service, U.S. Department of Agriculture, November 2016, http://tinyurl.com/henqroc.

Rural incomes are growing but remain below pre-recession levels, and rural populations are largely stagnant.

Cromartie, John, Christiane von Reichert and Ryan Arthun, "Factors Affecting Former Residents Returning to Rural Communities," Economic Research Service, U.S. Department of Agriculture, May 2015, http://tinyurl.com/zpdy8lp.

Many rural residents who left their hometowns in their early 20s would like to return due to family considerations, but they often find the lack of job opportunities an obstacle.

Wishner, Jane, *et al.*, "A Look at Rural Hospital Closures and Implications for Access to Care: Three Case Studies," Kaiser Family Foundation, July 7, 2016, http://tinyurl.com/h3vkco4.

Foundation researchers found that recently closed hospitals in Kansas, Kentucky and South Carolina were hurt by cuts and freezes in Medicare and Medicaid payment rates and that the few privately insured local patients are seeking care elsewhere.

The Next Step:

Additional Articles from Current Periodicals

Economic Conditions

Hinchliffe, Emma, "FCC follows through on bringing internet to rural America with $2 billion commitment," *Mashable*, **Feb. 23, 2017, http://tinyurl.com/h2uo7r4.**

The Federal Communications Commission committed $2 billion to encourage broadband internet access in rural parts of America in an effort to close the gap with connected urban regions.

Tankersley, Jim, "A very bad sign for all but America's biggest cities," *The Washington Post*, **May 22, 2016, http://tinyurl.com/hu956ue.**

Americans in rural areas and small communities are less likely to create startups, so new businesses increasingly are concentrated in urban centers, according to a new data analysis.

Williams, Dave, "Georgia House launches rural development council," *Atlanta Business Chronicle*, **March 10, 2017, http://tinyurl.com/hgmndc8.**

Georgia's House of Representatives voted to form a council that will focus on boosting the state's rural economy.

Immigrant Communities

Barrett, Rick, "Dairy farmers fear Trump's immigration policies," *USA Today*, **March 6, 2017, http://tinyurl.com/hfoaboa.**

Dairy farms that rely on immigrant labor fear President Trump's immigration policies, which they say could deplete their workforce and raise consumer prices for milk.

Marso, Andy, "Doctors Caught In Middle As Travel Ban Intersects With Rural Recruitment," KCUR, **Feb. 27, 2017, http://tinyurl.com/zq53ezr.**

With American hospitals increasingly relying on highly skilled immigrants, President Trump's attempt to place a temporary ban on immigration from certain countries could block some foreign doctors from working in the rural health system.

Runyon, Luke, "Immigrant Communities Diversify The Face Of A Rural Colorado City," KMUW, **March 14, 2017, http://tinyurl.com/j48m26z.**

Colorado's Fort Morgan, a town of 11,000 residents, is experiencing cultural adjustment and growing pains as immigrants move in, making it a minority-majority community.

Retraining Initiatives

"Work to transform area IT workforce training continues," *Floyd County Times*, **March 14, 2017, http://tinyurl.com/ztao8rr.**

Federal, state and local leaders met in Eastern Kentucky to explore technology opportunities for the region's workforce, including expanding initiatives such as TechHire East Kentucky, which teaches former coal miners how to write computer code.

Carmel, Margaret, "Library partnership brings job counseling to rural areas," *The News & Advance*, **Feb. 26, 2017, http://tinyurl.com/n4gs9la.**

A rural Virginia county's public library has joined forces with a workforce center to offer job counseling to residents who live in remote areas.

McMullen, Maureen, "Businesses seek solutions for aging rural workforce," *DL-Online*, **Feb. 16, 2017, http://tinyurl.com/mvm8udh.**

Minnesota businesses are seeking creative ways to help the state's aging rural workers, including part-time positions and flexible schedules for retirees.

Rural Health

Healy, Jack, "2 of a Farmer's 3 Children Overdosed. What of the Third — and the Land?" *The New York Times*, **March 12, 2017, http://tinyurl.com/mek3875.**

Despite the return of jobs since the recession in one rural Ohio county, opioid addiction continues to increase.

Johnson, Steve, "Tennessee's problems with rural health care linked to poor job prospects, limited education," *Times Free Press*, **March 4, 2017, http://tinyurl.com/ly253ql.**

Poverty and low education levels directly affect rural health care, including access to health professionals, according to experts.

Radcliffe, Shawn, "Rural Hospitals Closing at an Alarming Rate," *The Huffington Post*, **Feb. 24, 2017, http://tinyurl.com/m9q93vb.**

About 80 rural hospitals have closed since 2010, leaving a health care vacuum for people living outside of metropolitan areas, health experts say.

CITING *CQ RESEARCHER*

Sample formats for citing these reports in a bibliography include the ones listed below. Preferred styles and formats vary, so please check with your instructor or professor.

MLA STYLE

Jost, Kenneth. "Remembering 9/11." CQ Researcher 2 Sept. 2011: 701-732.

APA STYLE

Jost, K. (2011, September 2). Remembering 9/11. *CQ Researcher, 9,* 701-732.

CHICAGO STYLE

Jost, Kenneth. "Remembering 9/11." *CQ Researcher*, September 2, 2011, 701-32.

In-depth Reports on Issues in the News

Are you writing a paper?

Need backup for a debate?

Want to become an expert on an issue?

For 90 years, students have turned to *CQ Researcher* for in-depth reporting on issues in the news. Reports on a full range of political and social issues are now available. Following is a selection of recent reports:

Civil Liberties
Privacy and the Internet, 12/15
Intelligence Reform, 5/15
Religion and Law, 11/14

Crime/Law
Forensic Science Controversies, 2/17
Jailing Debtors, 9/16
Decriminalizing Prostitution, 4/16
Restorative Justice, 2/16
The Dark Web, 1/16
Immigrant Detention, 10/15
Fighting Gangs, 10/15

Education
Charter Schools, 3/17
Civic Education, 2/17
Student Debt, 11/16
Apprenticeships, 10/16

Environment/Society
Women in Prison, 3/17
Guns on Campus, 1/17
Mass Transit, 12/16
Arctic Development, 12/16
Protecting the Power Grid, 11/16
Pornography, 10/16

Health/Safety
Reducing Traffic Deaths, 2/17
Opioid Crisis, 10/16
Mosquito-Borne Disease, 7/16
Drinking Water Safety, 7/16

Politics/Economy
'Alt-Right'Movement, 3/17
Immigrants and the Economy, 2/17
Trump Presidency, 1/17
European Union's Future, 12/16
The Obama Legacy, 11/16
Populism and Party Politics, 9/16

Upcoming Reports

Troubled Brazil, 4/7/17   Foreign Aid, 4/14/17   Technology and Policing, 4/21/17

ACCESS

CQ Researcher is available in print and online. For access, visit your library or www.cqresearcher.com.

STAY CURRENT

For notice of upcoming *CQ Researcher* reports or to learn more about *CQ Researcher* products, subscribe to the free email newsletters, *CQ Researcher Alert!* and *CQ Researcher News*: http://cqpress.com/newsletters.

PURCHASE

To purchase a *CQ Researcher* report in print or electronic format (PDF), visit www.cqpress.com or call 866-427-7737. Single reports start at $15. Bulk purchase discounts and electronic-rights licensing are also available.

SUBSCRIBE

Annual full-service *CQ Researcher* subscriptions—including 44 reports a year, monthly index updates, and a bound volume—start at $1,131. Add $25 for domestic postage.

CQ Researcher Online offers a backfile from 1991 and a number of tools to simplify research. For pricing information, call 800-818-7243 or 805-499-9774 or email librarysales@sagepub.com.

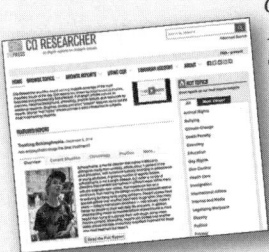

CQ RESEARCHER

CQPRESS

In-depth reports on today's issues

Published by CQ Press, an Imprint of SAGE Publications, Inc.   **www.cqresearcher.com**

Troubled Brazil

Can it overcome corruption, inequality and recession?

O nly a few years ago, Brazil seemed poised to fulfill its potential as a global powerhouse. Almost as big as the continental United States and with a population of nearly 206 million, it boasted the world's eighth-largest economy. Thanks to robust economic growth and spending on social programs, millions had moved out of poverty, and the nation's middle class was growing. But plummeting demand for Brazil's commodity exports and a massive corruption scandal have plunged Brazil into the worst recession in its history. Last summer, just after Brazil hosted the first-ever Olympic Games in South America, an event meant to showcase its progress to the world, President Dilma Rousseff was impeached on charges of political malfeasance. Scores of other politicians and business officials also have been accused or convicted of wrongdoing. Now, analysts say Brazil must pursue major reforms before it can regain its momentum. Meanwhile, government plans to radically expand hydropower along the Amazon River have sparked resistance from environmentalists and indigenous peoples.

Demonstrators in São Paulo in December 2016 protest the widespread corruption that has helped drag down Brazil's once flourishing economy. Experts say a return to prosperity will require overcoming the vast nation's economic and structural problems, including its dilapidated infrastructure, inefficient workforce and high unemployment rate.

CQ Researcher • April 7, 2017 • www.cqresearcher.com
Volume 27, Number 13 • Pages 289-312

THIS REPORT

I N S I D E

THE ISSUES **291**

BACKGROUND **297**

CHRONOLOGY **299**

CURRENT SITUATION **303**

AT ISSUE.....................**305**

OUTLOOK **307**

BIBLIOGRAPHY **310**

THE NEXT STEP **311**

THE ISSUES

291
- Can Brazil eliminate its corruption?
- Can Brazil resolve its social problems?
- Can Brazil be a global economic leader?

BACKGROUND

297 **Portuguese Colonization**
African slaves helped make Brazil a global sugar power.

298 **Brazilian Independence**
Political upheaval led to Brazil's split from Portugal in 1822.

298 **Early Republic**
Brazil became a federation of states after a coup.

301 **Democracy Returns**
Civilians returned to power after 21 years of military rule.

CURRENT SITUATION

303 **Sputtering Economy**
Amid ongoing corruption investigations, the economy remains weak.

304 **Faint Progress**
Rises in commodity prices are sparking hopes for an economic recovery.

306 **Corruption Fallout**
Latin American countries have begun probes into the Odebrecht Group, a Brazilian construction giant.

OUTLOOK

307 **More Political Uncertainty**
No front-runners have emerged in the 2018 presidential race.

SIDEBARS AND GRAPHICS

292 **A Struggling Goliath**
Political scandals and economic woes have set Brazil back.

293 **Hydroelectricity Is Main Power Source**
The government plans to build as many as 100 dams along the Amazon River.

296 **Steep Recession Grips Brazil**
The country's GDP shrank 3.6 percent in 2016.

299 **Chronology**
Key events since 1500.

300 **Hydropower Plans Spark an Amazon Water War**
"We see these projects as a disaster."

302 **Catholics, Evangelical Protestants Battle for Brazilian Souls**
"The days when everybody is born and dies in the Catholic Church are long gone."

305 **At Issue:**
Should Brazil have a permanent seat on the U.N. Security Council?

FOR FURTHER RESEARCH

309 **For More Information**
Organizations to contact.

310 **Bibliography**
Selected sources used.

311 **The Next Step**
Additional articles.

311 **Citing CQ Researcher**
Sample bibliography formats.

 CQ RESEARCHER

April 7, 2017
Volume 27, Number 13

EXECUTIVE EDITOR: Thomas J. Billitteri
tjb@sagepub.com

ASSISTANT MANAGING EDITORS: Kenneth Fireman, kenneth.fireman@sagepub.com, Kathy Koch, kathy.koch@sagepub.com, Scott Rohrer, scott.rohrer@sagepub.com

SENIOR CONTRIBUTING EDITOR:
Thomas J. Colin
tom.colin@sagepub.com

CONTRIBUTING WRITERS: Marcia Clemmitt, Sarah Glazer, Reed Karaim, Barbara Mantel, Chuck McCutcheon, Tom Price

SENIOR PROJECT EDITOR: Olu B. Davis

EDITORIAL ASSISTANT: Anika Reed

FACT CHECKERS: Eva P. Dasher, Michelle Harris, Betsy Towner Levine, Robin Palmer

SAGE Publishing | CQPRESS

Los Angeles | London | New Delhi
Singapore | Washington DC | Melbourne

An Imprint of SAGE Publications, Inc.

SENIOR VICE PRESIDENT, GLOBAL LEARNING RESOURCES:
Karen Phillips

EXECUTIVE DIRECTOR, ONLINE LIBRARY AND REFERENCE PUBLISHING:
Todd Baldwin

CQ Researcher (ISSN 1056-2036) is printed on acid-free paper. Published weekly, except: (March wk. 4) (May wk. 4) (July wks. 1, 2) (Aug. wks. 2, 3) (Nov. wk. 4) and (Dec. wks. 3, 4). Published by SAGE Publications, Inc., 2455 Teller Rd., Thousand Oaks, CA 91320. Annual full-service subscriptions start at $1,131. For pricing, call 1-800-818-7243. To purchase a CQ Researcher report in print or electronic format (PDF), visit www.cqpress.com or call 866-427-7737. Single reports start at $15. Bulk purchase discounts and electronic-rights licensing are also available. Periodicals postage paid at Thousand Oaks, California, and at additional mailing offices. POSTMASTER: Send address changes to CQ Researcher, 2600 Virginia Ave., N.W., Suite 600, Washington, DC 20037.

Cover: AFP/Getty Images/Miguel Schincariol

Troubled Brazil

BY CHRISTINA HOAG

THE ISSUES

In a country where graft seldom is punished, the sentence billionaire businessman Marcelo Odebrecht received was stunning. As CEO of the Odebrecht Group, he presided over a respected global construction conglomerate that symbolized Brazil's ability to compete with more-developed nations.

But the company's sterling reputation collapsed last March when Odebrecht was sentenced to 19 years in prison for corruption, including overseeing an elaborate kickback system that paid $64 million in bribes to secure lucrative contracts from the state oil company, Petrobras. [1]

The sentence has been one of the most resounding outcomes of the sweeping political corruption probe known as Operation Car Wash, which arose from a routine investigation in 2013 into the laundering of drug profits by a gas station owner and an associate in Brasilia, the nation's capital. [2]

In a bid for leniency, the defendants told prosecutors they were laundering much more than drug proceeds. In fact, they said, they were part of a widespread system of corporate kickbacks paid to lawmakers who had power over government contracts.

Three years later, the scandal has implicated more than 230 politicians and business executives, notably in the construction sector, and courts have imposed more than $10 billion in fines. [3]

The scandal comes just a few years after Brazil won acclaim as a model of economic success and social progress in the developing world. "Emerging

Marcelo Odebrecht, head of Brazil's Odebrecht Group, a global construction firm, was sentenced to 19 years in prison in March 2016 after his conviction on charges stemming from Operation Car Wash, a sweeping corruption probe. In the last three years, more than 230 politicians and business executives have been implicated in the bribery and kickback probe that also ensnared then-President Dilma Rousseff and Petrobras, the government-owned oil giant.

AFP/Getty Images/Heuler Andrey

markets have to have an example, and Brazil was that example," says Lourdes S. Casanova, academic director of the Emerging Markets Institute at Cornell University in Ithaca, N.Y. "Brazil became a symbol."

But corruption and a punishing recession — the worst in its history — have kept Brazil from fulfilling its potential and prevented it from exercising a greater role in world affairs, analysts say. At the start of 2017, Brazil's gross domestic product (GDP) — a measure of a country's economic output — was 8 percent smaller than in 2014, and 12.6 percent of the workforce — 13 million Brazilians — were unemployed. January's unemployment rate was double that of late 2013. [4]

Now, analysts see Brazil as a cautionary tale for what can go wrong in a developing nation. The crisis is "pretty disastrous," says Peter Hakim, senior fellow and president emeritus of the Inter-American Dialogue, a think tank in Washington that focuses on the Americas. "For a while, Brazil was looking so promising. That's what's so awful about it."

With a population of nearly 206 million occupying a land mass almost as big as the continental United States, Brazil is the world's sixth-most-populous country and eighth-largest economy. It is also the heavyweight in Latin America, with a gross domestic product of $1.7 trillion in 2015, ahead of Mexico's $1.1 trillion. Nicaragua has the region's smallest economy, with a 2015 GDP of $12.7 billion. [5]

Brazil is rich in raw materials, such as iron ore and timber, and in agricultural products, including coffee, sugar and soybeans. Aircraft and textiles are among its manufacturing exports. [6]

"Brazil has huge potential as a great economic powerhouse," says Monica de Bolle, a senior fellow at the Peterson Institute of International Economics, a think tank in Washington. "It's a huge country with a huge domestic market."

Earlier this century, Brazil seemed to be on track to fulfill its oft-discussed potential. During the presidency of leftist Luiz Inácio Lula da Silva from 2003 to 2010, the economy boomed, thanks to global demand for the country's commodities.

Lula, who left office with an 80 percent approval rating, instituted welfare programs that lifted 36 million people out of poverty. According to the World

A Struggling Goliath

Brazil, the world's sixth-most-populous country, has the largest economy in Latin America and eighth-largest globally. Almost as big as the continental United States, it was seen as an emerging global leader among developing nations in the early 2000s. But a political scandal, a presidential impeachment and the worst recession in its history have set Brazil back in the past four years.

Brazil at a Glance, 2016

Area: 3.2 million square miles

Population: 205,823,665

Labor force: 110.4 million

Unemployment rate: 12.6 percent

GDP: $1.769 trillion, 3.6 percent lower than in 2015

Trade: $190 billion exports (coffee, sugar, beef/poultry, aircraft, textiles); $144 billion imports (oil, autos)

Religions: Catholic (65%); Protestant (22%); Other (5%); None (8%)

Government: Federal republic; president elected to four-year term.

Sources: "The World Factbook," Central Intelligence Agency, http://tinyurl.com/33leeb; "Economic indicators," Banco Central do Brasil, March 15, 2017, http://tinyurl.com/mqv9xpu

Bank, the poverty rate dropped from 22 percent in 2003 to 7 percent in 2009. Officials from developing countries in Africa, the Middle East and Asia flocked to Brazil to learn how to replicate its model. In 2010, Brazil's economy grew 7.5 percent. [7]

The spotlight on Brazil got still brighter. The country was chosen to host the 2014 FIFA World Cup soccer championship and then the 2016 Summer Olympics, a first for South America. Ten times, Brazil has served as a temporary member of the U.N. Security Council — along with Japan, the most of any nation — and has lobbied for a permanent seat to represent emerging economies. (Proposals through the years to enlarge the Security Council have met with resistance from permanent members and others for a variety of reasons.) [8]

But for decades, Brazil has been dogged by income inequality, ranking 16th-worst globally. [9] About 30 percent of Brazilians are functionally illiterate, meaning they can read words and numbers but cannot comprehend sentences. Nevertheless, more than half of Brazil's population qualifies as middle class, and economists have long seen the country as a huge emerging market, comparable to India and Russia. [10]

Corruption, however, has held the economy back. Transparency International, a Swiss organization that monitors corruption around the world, places Brazil above the global average. In a ranking of 176 countries, with 1 as the least corrupt (Denmark), Brazil places 79th, tied with China and India but well above Russia, at 131st. The United States ranks 18th. [11]

Under Operation Car Wash, prosecutors have uncovered a system of kickbacks, the extent of which took even many Brazilians by surprise. "Brazilians always knew corruption existed, but no one ever really understood the magnitude of ties between the state political system and capitalism," says Matthew M. Taylor, an associate professor in the School of International Service at American University in Washington who specializes in Brazil's economy.

Operation Car Wash grew to encompass some of the country's most important companies, including Petrobras, and some of its top politicians. Among them was Lula, who as president survived a 2005 scandal known as the Mensalão, in which his Workers'

Party gave legislators cash payments in return for votes. [12]

The scandals helped plunge Brazil into recession. In 2013, when Operation Car Wash was getting underway, the economy started to slow as world demand for commodities dropped. The investigation slowed it even more. "The major drivers of the economy, the housing and construction sectors, were paralyzed," says Mark S. Langevin, director of the Brazil Initiative at George Washington University in Washington. "Executives were blacklisted from doing business with the government. They couldn't finish projects or start new ones. If [Operation Car Wash] hadn't happened, the economy would have slowed, but it wouldn't have sunk to the depths that it did."

The scandal rocked the political establishment. As public anger grew, Lula's handpicked successor, Dilma Rousseff, was impeached in 2016 for borrowing $11 billion from public banks to cover budget gaps, a move she said her predecessors had done routinely despite it being illegal. Her removal from office spurred many to claim she was a scapegoat for the country's reversal of fortune. [13]

One consequence of the turmoil has been Brazil's embrace of foreign investment as a means to jumpstart the economy. Last fall, the administration of President Michel Temer, who succeeded Rousseff, loosened regulations on foreign and private investment in several key sectors, including oil, aviation and land ownership. [14]

China, a key trading partner during Brazil's commodity boom, has emerged as the country's top foreign investor. Looking favorably at Brazil's growth prospects and sizable consumer market, China invested $4 billion in the country in 2016, well ahead of the United States, which ranked second with $2.5 billion. Among notable Chinese purchases were three ships from the Brazilian mining company Vale. A Chinese consortium bought the vessels for $269 million. Meanwhile, a Chinese utility acquired

a 24 percent stake in an energy company from the ailing Brazilian construction firm Camargo Corrêa. [15]

Analysts hail Brazil's turn to foreign investment but warn that the country is significantly behind others such as Mexico and even tiny Paraguay in adopting more business-friendly laws in areas such as taxes and labor. As an example of Brazil's uncompetitiveness, they point to provisions for the oil and gas industry stipulating that foreign companies must buy equipment from local Brazilian firms. Those rules are scheduled to be rolled back for oilfield bidding later this year. [16]

But protectionist measures have hurt the country's global competitiveness for decades, says Riordan Roett, director of Latin American studies at Johns Hopkins University in Washington.

Brazil is keen to expand its energy sector. The country is the world's 11th-largest oil producer, producing enough heavy crude to meet its domestic demand. [17] However, due to a lack of refining capacity for the heavy oil, Brazil imports light oil to refine into gasoline and other derivatives for domestic consumption. [18]

The government plans to build a series of hydroelectric dams along the Amazon River and its tributaries to provide cheap power, saying the region's vast waterways are an under-tapped resource. (*See sidebar, p. 300.*)

As Brazil struggles to stabilize its economy and government, here are some of the questions being debated:

Can Brazil eliminate its corruption?

It was supposed to be a pioneering anti-corruption law, but during a marathon congressional session that lasted into the wee hours last November, federal lawmakers rewrote and approved a bill that would significantly dilute the power of prosecutors investigating graft.

Among the changes, the lower house watered down provisions allowing prosecutors to reach more plea deals and seize civil servants' assets in corruption cases. Moreover, instead of making it easier to bring graft cases against legislators, the lower house retained statutes of limitations that ruled out many such cases. The revisions came a week after lawmakers tried to give themselves amnesty, a move they canceled after a public outcry. [19]

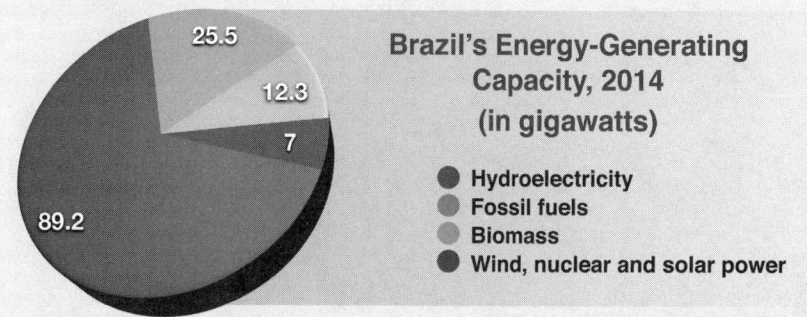

Hydroelectricity Is Main Power Source

Hydroelectricity provided much of Brazil's power in 2014, with fossil fuels a distant second. Despite opposition from environmentalists and other allies of indigenous peoples, the government is pressing ahead with plans to build as many as 100 dams along the Amazon River and its tributaries.

Brazil's Energy-Generating Capacity, 2014 (in gigawatts)

25.5
12.3
7
89.2

● Hydroelectricity
● Fossil fuels
● Biomass
● Wind, nuclear and solar power

Source: "Brazil: Electricity," U.S. Energy Information Administration, U.S. Department of Energy, Dec. 2, 2015, http://tinyurl.com/kkuk7om

The legislators' actions underscore the difficulty of combating corruption in Brazil. Despite the aggressive prosecutions of some of the country's biggest names in business and politics, some experts say Operation Car Wash may not ultimately do much to curb corruption because it is so ingrained in the way transactions are done in Brazil. Others disagree, arguing that Operation Car Wash is holding people of all social strata accountable and showing that the judicial system works.

De Bolle of the Peterson Institute of International Economics says she isn't optimistic that Operation Car Wash is a game-changer. "I don't see that much of a change in mentality," she says.

Experts see several signs that attitudes aren't changing sufficiently to eliminate corruption.

Although public approval of the investigations is generally high, the resulting economic paralysis has caused many Brazilians to wonder whether Operation Car Wash has been worth the effort. Some feel that graft helped grease the wheels and enabled the system to work. "There's a sense of 'could we put the genie back a bit in the bottle?'" says Hakim of the Inter-American Dialogue.

The length of the investigation, which formally started in 2014, is contributing to the public's growing weariness of fighting corruption, says Taylor of American University. "This has been a roiling crisis for three years now. Brazilians are reaching an exhaustion point," he says.

Perhaps most important, the lawmakers' lack of action to support the prosecutions with anti-corruption laws has led some observers to worry about the political will to root out graft.

If Congress were serious about ending kickbacks, a key first step would be a law protecting whistleblowers, says Langevin of George Washington University. "An anti-corruption campaign is not in place," he says. "Everybody's just running for cover."

Moreover, because the investigations have ensnared politicians, some Brazilians say the prosecutions are politically motivated. For instance, former President Lula has been indicted in five corruption cases, the latest in December for allegedly orchestrating a scheme in which Odebrecht paid $22.1 million in kickbacks to secure eight construction contracts with Petrobras. [20]

According to prosecutors, Lula appointed executives to the board of Petrobras who would go along with the scheme and used the money to fund his leftist Workers' Party and its allies. Still Brazil's most popular politician, Lula has said he will run for president in 2018, but a conviction in any of the cases would bar him from the race. [21]

"The cases against him are really weak," Langevin says. "There's no smoking gun, no evidence. They've really targeted Lula, it looks like, more for political reasons."

Judge Sergio Moro, who is handling most of the Operation Car Wash cases, said last fall that there is "just cause" for Lula's indictments, although he added the extent of the former president's involvement in the graft cases was unclear. [22]

The country's electoral system also needs revamping if corruption is to be eliminated, scholars say. Brazil has a federal system with a bicameral Congress consisting of a Senate and a lower house called the Chamber of Deputies. While the president and senators are elected directly, deputy seats are a hybrid where candidates must win votes for themselves and their party against dozens of candidates. Moreover, Brazil's statewide electoral districts are huge, with some containing as many as 32 million voters. Candidates thus often resort to buying votes by slipping bills equivalent to $14 to $28 inside campaign pamphlets. [23]

That leads to a need for huge campaign chests, often more than parties can acquire through legal donations. Brazil also does not have a strong

A worker separates coffee beans during harvest in Brazil's Minas Gerais state. Brazil is rich in raw materials, such as iron ore and timber, and crops including coffee, sugar and soybeans. Aircraft and textiles are among its leading manufacturing exports. Global demand for its commodities helped the economy boom from 2003 to 2010.

Getty Images/Bloomberg/Patricia Monteiro

tradition of individual voters donating to political campaigns. Parties, as a result, rely heavily on corporate funding, although in a bid to wipe out corporate graft, the Supreme Court last year outlawed company donations to parties altogether. [24]

Overall, de Bolle says, Brazil's political system produces a "very cozy relationship between the public and private sector." But others say Operation Car Wash has sent powerful messages that the justice system can punish corrupt officials.

"Brazilians are taking some comfort in that. [Car Wash] is putting some very powerful people behind bars," Taylor says, pointing to former Rio de Janeiro state Gov. Sérgio Cabral and former Chamber of Deputies President Eduardo Cunha. "There's a nervous hope that things will get better."

Some analysts add that while corruption will probably always exist, the well-oiled system of organized kickbacks exposed by Operation Car Wash is likely done.

"The cost-benefit analysis of corruption in Brazil has forever changed because of [Car Wash]," says Brian Winter, vice president for policy at the Council of the Americas, a Washington-based organization that advocates free trade and democracy in the region. "It's not to say corruption will disappear or even be dramatically reduced, but corruption on a massive scale will be ended."

Can Brazil resolve its social problems?

In the 1970s, an economist came up with a term for Brazil's social landscape: "Belíndia," for "Belgium-like bubbles surrounded by destitution worthy of India." [25] The term remains apt, with slums ringing Brazil's cities in belts of misery.

In Rio de Janeiro, nearly a quarter of the city's population, or about 1.5 million people, live in overcrowded, violence-plagued slums, known as favelas, that dot the city's hillsides. [26] Built without planning, the shantytowns feature jerry-built brick houses; most lack running water, trash pickup and sewage lines. Just a few miles away lies one of the world's most famous beaches, Copacabana, lined with luxury apartment towers and trendy boutiques and restaurants.

Social problems resulting from vast income disparities have dogged Brazil for centuries. Ten percent of the population controls 43 percent of the wealth, while the poorest 34 percent owns just over 1 percent, according to 2012 figures. That made Brazil the world's 16th-most inequitable country in 2012, the latest year for which data are available. By comparison, Mexico, Latin America's second-biggest country, ranked 25th, and the United States 43rd, out of 145 countries. [27]

Analysts say the inequity is the result of the government's long-term neglect of the poor in education, small-business development and social services. After courting the poor to get elected, legislators often represent the interests of the middle class and elites since those are the classes that wield the most economic power.

"Congress is organized to benefit 30 million to 50 million Brazilians and manage the rest," says Langevin of George Washington University.

Brazil has had success reducing poverty in recent years. Under Lula's "Brazil without Misery" welfare programs, almost one in four Brazilians, or 50 million people, receive a monthly cash payment averaging $54 a month. (The government-mandated minimum monthly wage in Brazil is about $300. [28]) One program is Bolsa Família (Family Grant), which gives monthly cash stipends in return for families enrolling children in school and taking them for health checkups. The programs are credited with halving Brazil's extreme poverty, those living on less than $1.90 per day, from 9.7 percent of the population in 2003 to 4.3 percent in 2013. "This stipend makes a huge difference in people's lives, and it's rel-

atively cheap for the government," the Peterson Institute's de Bolle says.

But analysts say more needs to be done to create economic opportunity to improve Brazilians' lives without creating a culture of dependency. Just 46 percent of Brazilian adults ages 25 to 64 have completed secondary school. [29] Inadequate public K-12 education is a key area that perpetuates social inequality because impoverished youths lack the skills to attend the best universities or land higher-paying jobs, says Roett of Johns Hopkins University.

Public schools are so shoddy that the middle and upper classes typically send their children to private schools, which better prepare them to enter the country's prestigious public university system, according to experts. The majority of graduates of public schools, who typically have weaker academic skills than their private-school counterparts, cannot get into public universities and often turn to private for-profit colleges. [30]

The government last fall announced a plan to bolster public education, mainly by offering more flexibility to students in their choice of study in a bid to make school more attractive to students and lower the 11.5 percent dropout rate. The government also said it would offer more technical high schools to teach marketable skills. Critics said the plan does not address core issues such as deteriorated school buildings, poor teacher training and methods and overcrowded classrooms. [31]

The poor also suffer from inadequate state-run health care, often waiting months for treatment while those who can afford it go to private doctors. The mosquito-borne Zika virus, which has resulted in some 2,500 babies born over the past year with microcephaly, or undersized heads, and other severe defects, has underscored the health system's inequities. Many of the Zika babies were born to poor mothers in Brazil's impoverished northeast, where the disease was first detected. [32]

Steep Recession Grips Brazil

An economic downturn that began in Brazil in 2012 deepened in 2016, with the country's gross domestic product (GDP) — a measure of total economic output — shrinking by 3.6 percent. Economists blame the recession on falling commodity prices, political corruption and deep structural problems, such as an inefficient workforce and inadequate infrastructure.

Brazilian GDP in
Current U.S. Dollars,
1986-2016

Sources: "Economic indicators," Banco Central do Brasil, March 15, 2017, http://tinyurl.com/mqv9xpu; "GDP (current US$)," World Bank, http://tinyurl.com/krt9esg

Many poor parents are on lengthy waiting lists for treatment and services provided by the public health system. Meanwhile, costs are rising to treat a growing list of Zika-related impairments: breathing problems, trouble swallowing, clubbed feet, seizures, severe muscle weakness that prevents the babies from lifting their heads and behavioral symptoms such as extreme irritability.

The government has given poor families modest disability payments to help them care for affected children and mobilized campaigns to eradicate mosquitoes and raise public awareness about Zika. Meanwhile, researchers continue researching the virus.

Crime, particularly drug trafficking, is another key concern. With high poverty, little economic opportunity and weak security forces, Brazil is becoming a haven for transnational narco-trafficking driven by gangs that have expanded beyond their bases in urban slums, scholars say. "The urban violence of the south has shifted into the north-east and less developed areas," says Taylor of American University.

In January, the government announced a national security plan calling for federal officials to take a bigger role in combating homicides and the narcotics trade. [33] Still, it is unclear what that will entail. "The government hasn't had any serious policy dealing with drug trafficking," says de Bolle.

Roett says opportunity in Brazil comes down to how much money a person is born into, as the system offers little chance of upward social mobility. "If you're wealthy in Brazil, you're fine," he says.

Can Brazil be a global economic leader?

In one of Brazil's most dramatic reversals of fortune, the tycoon who just five years ago was ranked the country's richest man with a $35 billion fortune was jailed in February to await trial on charges that he paid $16.5 million in bribes to the former governor of Rio de Janeiro state in exchange for government contracts. After commodity prices tumbled, Eike Batista said his oil and mining conglomerate is now $1 billion in debt. [34]

For many observers, Batista's rise and fall epitomize Brazil's boom-and-bust story. Just when its economy appears to make progress, Brazil slides backward. One problem, economists say, is its overreliance on commodities, whose prices are subject to the whims of global markets. Another is economic mismanagement and corruption.

"Brazil needs to stop being the land of missed opportunities, because that's what it's been time and time again," the Peterson Institute's de Bolle says.

Experts say economic progress hinges on several reforms that will require significant shifts in policy direction, such as moving away from commodity-driven exports to more finished goods and high-tech products that will enable Brazil to compete globally.

Brazil also needs to shore up its dilapidated infrastructure and improve its workforce, as well as streamline taxes and regulations, says Roett of Johns Hopkins. "Brazil is neither a productive nor a competitive economy," he says. He points to basic improvements that could boost Brazil's competitiveness, such as upgrading highways so that trucks traversing bumpy roads don't spill a portion of their crops. Trucks are the main method of transporting goods across the vast country because railways, ports, airports and waterways remain underdeveloped. [35]

The country's public and private sectors underinvest in capital infrastructure, according to a report by the global business consulting firm Accenture. In 2014, Brazil invested 17 percent of GDP in roads, buildings and machinery, compared with 25 percent for other emerging markets. The government is addressing this problem with a $52.2 billion plan to grant contracts to companies to operate highways, ports, airports and railroads. [36]

The workforce also harms Brazil's competitiveness. Brazilian workers are a quarter as productive as those in the United States. [37] "There's never been a commitment to investing in human capital," Roett says. "The workforce is poorly trained."

The country particularly lacks technical skills and managerial expertise, and labor costs have risen steadily because of government-mandated annual increases in the monthly minimum wage. In 2017, the minimum monthly salary rose 6 percent from 2016. Labor productivity, increased only 12 percent from 2005 to 2014 while labor costs doubled. [38]

Labor laws heavily favor employees. Among the mandates, employers are supposed to provide meals and cover transportation costs, pay a month's bonus salary at year-end, give 30 days' dismissal notice and provide 30 days' vacation per 12 months worked. Because of the extensive rights they are granted under labor laws, Brazilians also have a penchant for suing employers, experts say. [39]

The cost of doing business in Brazil hampers entrepreneurs as well. Due to inefficiencies in the public and private sectors, including excessive red tape, high taxes and chronic underinvestment in infrastructure, it takes 84 days to launch a business in Brazil — compared with just four days in South Korea, 29 in India and 32 in China, all competitors of Brazil, according to Accenture. And the average cost of exporting a shipping container from Brazil is $2,323, compared with $1,332 in India, $1,224 in the United States, $823 in China and $670 in South Korea. [40]

Despite these challenges, Brazil has success stories. São Paulo sandal maker Alpargata turned flip-flops into a worldwide fashion item in the 2000s with its Havaianas brand. [41] Embraer, an aircraft manufacturer based in São José dos Campos, is a top global aviation company; Vale, based in Minas Gerais, is a world name in the mining industry; and Petrobras remains a major state-owned oil company despite its setbacks in the corruption scandal, notes Casanova of Cornell University.

Still, for a country its size, Brazil should have more global companies and a stronger private sector, Casanova says. Only seven Brazilian companies are in the Global Fortune 500, while China, whose economy is five times Brazil's, has 95. [42]

The government particularly needs

The Cantagalo shantytown, or favela, rises above Rio de Janeiro, Brazil's capital. About 1.5 million people, nearly a quarter of the city's population, live in the overcrowded, violence-plagued slums that dot Rio's hillsides. The favelas reflect the income disparity and other social problems that have dogged Brazil for centuries.

Getty Images/Mario Tama

to support small- and medium-sized enterprises so they can grow, Casanova says. The National Bank for Economic Social Development (known by its Portuguese acronym BNDES) typically finances already-large companies and infrastructure projects but should be reoriented to boost smaller companies, especially as recovery from the recession gets underway, she says.

Others agree that Brazil's companies could use help to revive the economy. With labor costs rising annually, credit lacking and consumer demand languishing because of the recession, "the prospects for the private sector really aren't that great at all," says de Bolle of the Peterson Institute of International Economics.

As the economic and political turmoil continues, Brazilian companies are moving to other nations, many to Paraguay, which is striving to become South America's low-cost manufacturing hub. From toy to textile companies, about 80 percent of Paraguay's foreign manufacturers are now Brazilian businesses taking advantage of energy prices that are 60 percent lower and labor costs that are more than 50 percent cheaper than in Brazil. [43]

With unemployment rising, Brazil's Ministry of Industry, Trade and Services says it's trying to keep Brazilian businesses at home. The country has many natural advantages, including its huge population, the absence of internal racial and ethnic strife and good standing with its neighbors, that make it a natural magnet for investors, says Winter of the Council of the Americas. "People ignore Brazil at their own peril," he says. ∎

BACKGROUND

Portuguese Colonization

After Portuguese explorer Vasco da Gama discovered a new route to India by circumnavigating the Cape of Good Hope, the Portuguese crown was eager to capitalize on the trading riches this maritime path promised.

In 1500, the year after da Gama returned from his epic two-year voyage, King Manuel sponsored a fleet of 13 ships and appointed Pedro Alvares

Cabral to lead the expedition. The fleet left Lisbon in March 1500, but just weeks later Cabral's lead ship veered off course to the west and ended up on what is now Porto Seguro in Brazil's central-eastern Bahia state. [44]

Much like Christopher Columbus' accidental discovery of the Caribbean islands in 1492, the Portuguese had stumbled on a vast new territory. Cabral's landing party spent the next nine days observing the natives' hunter-gatherer existence and mapping the coast. Cabral christened the terrain Vera Cruz, or True Cross, and dispatched a ship to Portugal to notify the king of the discovery. [45]

The news did not generate much enthusiasm in Lisbon because the territory was thought to be a large island, devoid of riches. Nevertheless, the Portuguese established trading posts along the coast, soon finding a redwood called the brazil tree, valuable as a dye and timber. The land began to be known as "Brazil" as early as 1503, and trading brazil wood for trinkets formed the main economic activity until 1535. [46]

To solidify its claim on the territory, the crown had to colonize it or risk losing it to other European powers. Sugarcane imported from Africa became the cash crop, and a capital was established at Salvador.

Sugar cultivation generated a high demand for labor. Colonists enslaved Indians, whose populations were being decimated by smallpox, influenza and measles brought by the Europeans. Surviving Indians fled inland and were chased by "bandeirantes," flag-bearing colonists charged with capturing Indians. In the process, these colonists explored much of Brazil's interior and sought gold and other riches.

Facing a decimated Indian population and resistance from Jesuit missionaries trying to help the natives, the Portuguese turned to Africa for labor. By 1580, some 2,000 African slaves a year were arriving in Brazil. Their labor helped make Brazil a world sugar

power from 1600 to 1650. [47] But competition from sugar plantations in Spanish, English and Dutch colonies in the Americas sent Brazil's industry into decline in the late 17th century.

The discovery of gold in 1695 in today's Minas Gerais state boosted Brazil's fortunes, sparking a gold rush and the first major wave of immigration. Over the next six decades, some 600,000 Portuguese and other Europeans settled Brazil's interior. [48]

In a bid to prop up its own ailing economy, Portugal in the late 18th century reasserted control over its colony, which was growing increasingly wealthy due to tobacco, cattle ranching and gold mining. Brazil's colonial elites, however, bristled at Lisbon's moves, including the creation of monopolistic trading companies and an overhaul of the colony's administrative structure that caused Brazilian laws to favor the mother country. [49]

Brazilian Independence

Ironically, Brazil's independence movement was spurred by the monarchy. In 1807, French emperor Napoleon Bonaparte invaded Spain and Portugal, causing the latter's royal family and 10,000 citizens to flee to Brazil. After settling at Rio, Prince regent Dom João VI, ruling in place of his mentally incompetent mother, Queen Maria I, wasted no time in installing European-style amenities, including a theater, orchestra and newspapers. By 1822, Rio's population had doubled to 150,000. [50]

In 1821, political upheaval in Portugal pushed João VI, who had become king after his mother's death, to return to Lisbon and leave his son Pedro as regent in Brazil. The new Portuguese parliament soon returned Brazil to colonial status. In 1822, an angry Pedro declared Brazil's independence and was crowned Dom Pedro I, emperor of Brazil. [51]

His reign lasted just nine years. After a costly war to prevent the secession of present-day Uruguay and growing

political dissension, Pedro abdicated and returned to Portugal, leaving his 5-year-old son, Pedro II, as future emperor. For the next nine years, regents ruled Brazil until Pedro turned 14. [52]

In the following decades, Brazil debated how it was to be governed. Its wealth, meanwhile, was growing from coffee, rubber, and cotton exports, which led to the construction of railroads and other infrastructure. As with sugar, the coffee plantations relied on slave labor. Although British pressure had led Brazil to end the slave trade in 1831, the government did not enforce the law, and an estimated 712,000 slaves arrived during the 1830s and 1840s. Slavery was finally abolished in 1888 after increasing international pressure. [53]

In the wake of abolition, plus a costly five-year war to repel an invasion by Paraguay, Pedro II lost the support of key allies. In 1889, the military staged a bloodless coup and the royal family fled to Portugal. [54]

Early Republic

The military government promulgated a new constitution in 1891 that declared Brazil a federation of states. Over the next four decades, the country's first presidents hailed from powerful coffee oligarchies as a huge influx of immigrants arrived, largely from Portugal, Italy and Spain, but also from Japan, Syria and Lebanon. Drawn by the coffee industry and opportunity in the new republic, some 2.7 million immigrants arrived in Brazil between 1872 and 1910. [55]

This new urban class challenged the domination of the coffee producers, and political unrest followed. In 1937, with a worldwide depression collapsing coffee prices, the military overthrew the elected government and installed Getúlio Vargas as dictator-president. Vargas, an authoritarian populist, implemented protectionist policies and oversaw the

Continued on p. 300

Chronology

1500-1888 Europeans colonize territory that becomes Brazil.

1500
Portuguese nobleman Pedro Álvares Cabral steers off course during a voyage to India and lands at Porto Seguro. He claims the territory for the king of Portugal.

1700s
Discovery of gold spurs large-scale European settlement.

1808
Fleeing Napoleon, Portugal's prince regent, Dom João VI, arrive in Rio de Janeiro, transforming the city with business and culture.

1821
Dom João returns to Lisbon after Napoleon's fall, leaving his son Pedro I as prince regent.

1822
Pedro declares independence from Portugal, forms the Empire of Brazil and rules as emperor for nine years before unrest forces him to abdicate in favor of his 5-year-old son, Pedro II.

1840
Fourteen-year-old Pedro II takes over after nine years of rule by regents.

1888
Brazilian slavery is abolished.

1889-1963 Power swings between civil and military governments.

1889
A republic is formed after a military coup backed by landowners upset about the end of slavery.

1930
Military installs Getúlio Vargas as president in a coup. He retains power until 1945.

1945
Another coup ousts Vargas, leading to a period of democratically elected presidents and economic growth.

1960
President Juscelino Kubitschek moves the capital from Rio de Janeiro to a newly made inland city, Brasilia.

1964-1984 Repressive military dictatorships seize power.

1964
Brazilian military overthrows President João Goulart after he attempts socialist reforms; five generals rule for the next 20 years.

1968
Guerrilla movement starts, causing the government to suppress dissent through arrests, torture, disappearances and killings over the next decade. Future President Dilma Rousseff, a Marxist guerrilla, is arrested and tortured.

1985-Present Democracy takes hold amid economic struggles.

1985
With inflation soaring, the military passes power to Tancredo Neves, a civilian, but he dies days before his inauguration.

1988
Brazil adopts a new constitution.

1990
Fernando Collor de Mello is the first popularly elected president in 30 years.

1992
Collor de Mello, facing impeachment, resigns.

1994
Fernando Henrique Cardoso is elected president and implements an austerity plan to rein in inflation and government spending.

2002
Labor leader Luiz Inácio Lula da Silva, a founding member of the Workers' Party, is elected president. He implements a social program that lifts millions out of poverty and supports big business, sparking economic growth and talk of Brazil rising onto the world stage.

2011
Rousseff, a Lula acolyte, becomes Brazil's first female president.

2014
A probe reveals massive graft between business and politicians; sending the nation's economy into a nosedive.

2015
Rousseff starts second term after narrow re-election victory.

2016
Rio hosts the Olympics Games, a first for South America, as Rousseff is impeached.

2017
Brazil endures its worst recession as interim President Michel Temer tries to jumpstart the economy. . . . Olympic venues deteriorate as nation struggles to find uses for stadiums, athletes' village.

Hydropower Plans Spark an Amazon Water War

"We see these projects as a disaster."

Brazil's environmental and indigenous-rights activists scored a key victory last summer when the government denied permits for the construction of the $9.4 billion São Luiz do Tapajós dam in the Amazon basin, a joint Brazilian-European project slated to have been the world's sixth-largest hydroelectric dam. [1]

In its decision, Brazil's environmental institute ruled that the consortium had not presented enough evidence about the social and ecological effects of the 8,000-megawatt dam, which would have flooded 145 square miles of Munduruku tribal ancestral land. [2]

The win, however, may not amount to much for dam opponents. The Brazilian government has given no indication it is backing off its strategy of harnessing the Amazon's prodigious water resources to meet the country's energy needs. Brazil's National Energy Plan calls for as many as 100 dams mostly along tributaries throughout the world's largest rainforest. [3]

"Let's not forget that in the developed world almost 70 percent of the hydro potential has already been exploited, whereas here in Brazil, 70 percent of our hydro has not been explored yet," said Luiz Augusto Barroso, president of Empresa Pesquisa de Energética, the government's energy-planning agency. "It makes sense for the country, and it's a resource that benefits society." [4]

Activists argue that the government's plan is shortsighted. Not only do the dams wipe out indigenous tribes' habitats and disrupt one of the planet's most diverse biosystems of fish, animals and plants, but deforestation contributes to climate change when forested areas are flooded. Trees absorb carbon dioxide in the atmosphere while rotting vegetation in the dam reservoirs produces methane. Higher levels of both gases are linked to global warming.

Moreover, construction workers' settlements often turn into towns after projects are completed when some workers stay on. And the presence of towns leads to more logging and ranching, which further reduce forests and cause more environmentally harmful emissions from vehicles, activists say.

"We see these projects as a disaster," says Christian Poirier, program director for Amazon Watch, a nonprofit in Oakland, Calif., that monitors issues affecting the Amazon region. "Even small projects have had irreversible impacts."

The most controversial project to date has been the $18 billion Belo Monte megadam, partially completed on the Xingu River, a major Amazon tributary, and slated to be the world's fourth-largest hydroelectric dam in terms of installed capacity (11,000 megawatts) when fully operational in 2019. [5] Last year, Brazil's environmental agency fined dam developer Norte Energie $10.8 million after 16.2 million tons of fish were killed when a river tributary was diverted to fill the dam's reservoir. [6]

The project also has become a national symbol of corruption. Last year, a Brazilian state senator testified that $12 million skimmed from overpriced Belo Monte construction contracts helped pay for former President Dilma Rousseff's 2010 and 2014 election campaigns. [7] Also last year, an appeals court found a conflict of interest because Eletrobras, the state energy utility, had awarded the Belo Monte environmental assessment study without competitive bidding to three of Brazil's largest construction companies. The companies, Odebrecht Group, Andrade Gutierrez and Camargo

Continued from p. 298

modernization of Brazil. But in 1945, with labor unrest and opposition against the dictatorship growing in favor of an elected president, the military again intervened and ousted Vargas to return the nation to an elected presidency. [56]

In the post-World War II years, inflation eroded wages and caused popular discontent. This created a path for Vargas to return to power by winning the 1951 presidential election. During his term, he nationalized the oil industry, creating the state company Petróleos Brasileiros (Petrobras), but industrial strikes, corruption and a decision to double the minimum wage weakened him politically. In 1954, with a military coup looming, Vargas killed himself. [57]

As fertility rates rose (an average 6.28 children per mother by 1960), the 1950s witnessed rapid population growth and rural migration to industrialized urban centers. [58] Faced with a housing shortage, the migrants built shantytowns on city outskirts. The youthful population also outstripped the capacity of public schools and health care, setting the foundation for a vast gap between haves and have-nots.

In the late 1950s, President Juscelino Kubitschek embarked on an ambitious development plan that included creating a national automobile industry and building roads, electricity plants and a new inland city, Brasília, to serve as the nation's capital. Although the plan lifted the economy, Kubitschek's successors

were saddled with the bills for his "Program of Goals." Inflation started climbing in the early 1960s. A bleak economy prompted the military to depose President João Goulart in 1964. [59] Military chiefs also were unhappy with Goulart's leftist measures, such as giving the vote to illiterates, allowing enlisted soldiers to unionize and permitting the expropriation of underused properties.

Unlike its previous takeovers, the military did not immediately relinquish power to civilians. Instead, a succession of five generals ran the country over the next 21 years. By 1969, more than a dozen guerrilla groups — largely Marxists, but also liberation theologists and radical opponents to the dictatorship — had sprung up in opposition.

Corrêa, later formed part of a consortium that built the dam. [8]

Researchers see alternatives to hydropower that are less invasive to the environment and cheaper to produce than building dams. "Brazil has a huge capacity for wind and solar. It's underinvested in these areas," says Eve Bratman, an assistant professor of environmental studies at Franklin & Marshall College in Lancaster, Pa., who specializes in the Brazilian Amazon.

Additionally, shoring up the electricity supply grid would increase the power supply, Poirier says. "[Utilities] lose up to 20 percent of energy in transmission lines," he says. "Just fixing old lines would make them more efficient."

Brazil's 2024 energy plan calls for increasing both hydropower and non-hydro renewable energy sources, plus natural gas and nuclear generation. The country, which currently relies on hydroelectricity for 70 percent of its power, has seen power shortages in recent years because of drought. [9]

With the government reeling from a recession, many dam projects are on hold. Another factor slowing the projects is an ongoing corruption investigation called Operation Car Wash that has implicated scores of politicians and key players in the country's construction industry. But activists fear that once the dust settles, the development floodgates will reopen, especially if the government pursues infrastructure projects to reignite the economy. The Tapajós dam, for instance, can be revived with a new permit application, Poirier notes.

"There's good reason for activists to keep fighting," Bratman says.

— *Christina Hoag*

The Belo Monte dam on the Xingu River, a major Amazon tributary, has been plagued by corruption and environmental problems during its construction. The $18 billion hydroelectric dam will be the world's fourth-largest when completed in 2019.

[1] John Vidal, "Major Amazon dam opposed by tribes fails to get environmental licence," *The Guardian*, Aug. 5, 2016, http://tinyurl.com/mojxtd4.

[2] *Ibid.*

[3] Wyre Davis, "Amazon culture clash over Brazil's dams," BBC News, Jan. 10, 2017, http://tinyurl.com/m9djyfw.

[4] *Ibid.*

[5] *Ibid.*

[6] Sue Branford, "Fish kills at Amazon's Belo Monte Dam point up builder's failures," *Mongabay*, July 13, 2016, http://tinyurl.com/k24pauk.

[7] "Brazil's Rousseff benefited from Belo Monte dam graft," Reuters, March 11, 2016, http://tinyurl.com/kr3rcqs.

[8] Sarah Bardeen and Brent Millikan, "Belo Monte Operating License Suspended," *International Rivers*, Sept. 6, 2016, http://tinyurl.com/mafgj7m.

[9] "Hydroelectric plants account for more than 70 percent of Brazil's power," *Electric Light & Power*, Aug. 17, 2016, http://tinyurl.com/lfychsh.

The government responded with repression, including the arrests and torture of dissenters, press censorship and spying. By 1974 it had defeated the armed groups, including the Comandos of National Liberation and the Revolutionary Armed Vanguard. [60]

The economy flourished under authoritarian rule, as foreign investment, notably in the automotive sector, increased and exports diversified beyond coffee. Inflation dropped from 92 percent in 1964 to 28 percent in 1967, and GDP grew an average of 10.9 percent over the next six years. Much of the economic expansion, however, was contingent on foreign loans and imports such as oil, which made up 43 percent of Brazil's imports by 1980. [61]

In the wake of a 1979 oil price increase and a subsequent rise in interest rates globally, Brazil's foreign debt ballooned to $100 billion, from $3 billion in 1964. Inflation hit triple digits, and Brazil plunged into recession in 1981. [62]

Democracy Returns

The mass urbanization of society, which started in the 1950s and resulted in profound social inequality, coupled with dissatisfaction with the military's handling of the economy, led to political movements that pushed for a return to democracy. In 1985, the military handed control of the country

to a civilian, Tancredo Neves, elected by the electoral college. But he abruptly died and Vice President José Sarney succeeded him. [63]

Sarney unsuccessfully tried to tame inflation with a new currency, price freezes and a minimum wage indexed to inflation, as well as political reform through a new constitution. In 1989 the first free presidential elections were held in three decades. Fernando Collor de Mello, who hailed from a powerful northeastern family, won on a platform of neoliberal economics and anti-corruption. [64]

Collor de Mello's first initiative was to tackle inflation by freezing savings accounts. He then fired thousands of federal workers, slashed tariffs and

Catholics, Evangelical Protestants Battle for Brazilian Souls

"The days when everybody is born and dies in the Catholic Church are long gone."

Brazil has long had the world's largest population of Roman Catholics, but it may not hold that title much longer. Large numbers of Brazilians are turning to evangelical Protestant sects, mainly Pentecostalism, while many others are abandoning organized religion altogether.

"Brazil is on an inexorable march toward no longer being majority Catholic," says R. Andrew Chesnut, a professor of religious studies at Virginia Commonwealth University in Richmond, Va. "The days when everybody is born into the Catholic Church and dies in the Catholic Church are long gone."

According to a survey by São Paulo pollster Datafolha published last December, 50 percent of Brazilians over age 16 identified as Catholic, down from 60 percent in 2014, or about 9 million worshippers. In 1970, 92 percent of Brazilians declared themselves Catholic. [1]

The percentage who said in the Datafolha survey that they followed no religion doubled from 2014 to 2016, from 6 percent to 14 percent. [2] The proportion of Brazilians who identified as evangelical Protestants remained at about 29 percent. Only 1 percent said they were atheists. [3]

Catholicism has been steadily shrinking in Brazil since the late 1960s, when military dictatorships saw Catholic liberation theology, which advocated social justice for the poor, as a threat and sought to repress church teachings, experts say. In addition, Brazil, whose slaves brought their African religions with them in earlier periods, has had a long history of embracing non-Catholic alternatives.

"Brazilians are less afraid of trying new religions. They're very open," says Virginia Garrard-Burnett, director of the Benson Latin American Studies and Collections at the University of Texas, Austin.

While Pentecostalism has become popular in other parts of Latin America, its growth in other nations has not mirrored that in Brazil. Other Protestant sects also have made inroads in Brazil and Latin America, including Mormonism, which has doubled its number of Brazilian congregations since the 1980s and now has 1.3 million adherents. [4]

Brazil's urban poor, with little access to medical care, were the first to turn to Pentecostalism, finding appeal in the movement's emphasis on faith healing. Many Brazilian poor also embraced Pentecostalism's other rituals, including speaking in tongues and exorcism, that had parallels with African-based religions such as candomblé, scholars say.

Moreover, the urban poor felt more affinity with their pastors, many of whom were darker skinned and less educated than Catholic priests, traditionally regarded as part of the elite, who are mostly lighter skinned, Chesnut says.

Pentecostalism has since grown to encompass the middle and upper classes and expanded to rural and suburban areas. Faith leaders have succeeded by conducting marketing surveys to determine people's needs and building programs to address them, establishing media networks to reach more converts and building so-called megachurches.

One such center is the Universal Church of the Kingdom of God's Temple of Solomon in São Paulo, designed to resemble the ancient temple in Jerusalem. It can accommodate 10,000 congregants, says Garrard-Burnett.

---

privatized state assets, all accomplished mainly via decree. By 1992, his backing had dwindled, and he resigned just hours before a Senate vote to impeach him on corruption charges. [65]

Minister of Finance Fernando Henrique Cardoso, an academic who had turned to politics, was elected president in 1994 on the strength of his economic plan that had started to yield results. During his two terms (1995-2002), Cardoso helped stabilize Brazil's economy and eliminate its chronic hyperinflation (from 2,489 percent in 1993 to 4 percent in 1997) through a series of liberal reforms and privatizations. But the changes did little to alleviate poverty, and by the end of his second term his popularity had plummeted amid the onset of re-

cession. [66] That set the stage for the presidential triumph of labor leader Lula, who had run unsuccessfully for president three times as the Workers' Party candidate.

Under Lula, Brazil's economy boomed. Durable consumer goods manufacturing, construction, financial services and consumer credit, and commerce all grew. Exports of agricultural and mineral products, in concert with global demand led by China, increased as well. The expansion led to lower unemployment and social inequality and a rise in internal consumer demand. Inflation was halved, from 12.5 percent in 2002 to just under 6 percent in 2010. [67]

A key part of Lula's economic strategy was "state capitalism," in which

the government took minority stakes in private companies and projects as an economic stimulus. It also expanded social programs such as the Bolsa Familiar cash aid program that bolstered the poor's living standards.

Barred from seeking a third consecutive term under Brazil's constitution, Lula in 2011 passed the presidential baton to his handpicked successor, his chief of staff Rousseff, a former Marxist guerrilla who was tortured while imprisoned under the military dictatorship from 1970 to 1973. [68]

Brazil's first female president, Rousseff continued Lula's policies but increased the government's interventionist role in the economy, which was reeling from the global collapse in commodity

"[Evangelical churches] are really a presence in every level of society in a way that few Brazilian institutions are," says Garrard-Burnett, a history and religious studies professor who specializes in Latin American Protestantism.

The Catholic Church has responded to the membership loss by establishing charismatic churches, which, like Pentecostalism, offer faith healing, prophecy, speaking in tongues and popular music during Mass. It also has endorsed personalities such as Marcelo Rossi, a charismatic-church pop-star priest with a Snapchat account who gives concerts and records albums, experts say. Formally known as the Catholic Charismatic Renewal, the movement originated in the 1960s and has become an accepted part of the Catholic Church with Vatican support.

"There was lightning-speed approval of charismatic churches in all the episcopacies," Chesnut says. "They saw it as the best way to compete."

The choice of Pope Francis, an Argentinian, in 2013 to lead the Catholic Church was widely seen as an effort by the Vatican to stem the exodus of Catholics throughout Latin American. But while Francis is extremely popular in Brazil, experts say the hemorrhaging continues. "He's more likely to stanch the flow of secular conversions rather than conversions to the Pentecostals," Garrard-Burnett says.

In societies with widespread poverty, weak social support from government and little opportunity, evangelical Protestant churches can be hard to beat, scholars say. Besides preaching the prosperity gospel, which holds that faith will be rewarded by material wealth, such churches typically offer life resources, such as literacy skills and instruction about how to open a bank account.

Evangelicals participate in the March for Jesus on June 4, 2015, in São Paulo. Once solidly Roman Catholic, Brazil has seen a steady rise of evangelical Protestant sects in recent years.

"They've sort of understood the culture they're working in, Brazilians' history, their worldview, and they've been incredibly successful," Garrard-Burnett says. "The Catholic Church took Brazil for granted for the longest time."

— *Christina Hoag*

[1] "Brazil: Loss of at least 9 million Catholics in two years," Documentation Information Catholiques Internationales, Feb. 2, 2017, http://tinyurl.com/mc7dos5; "The Catholic Church in Brazil and the evangelical offensive," Documentation Information Catholiques Internationales, Sept. 8, 2013, http://tinyurl.com/myhltrq.

[2] Ana Estela de Sousa Pinto, "At Least Nine Million Brazilians Give Up Catholicism, Shows Datafolha Survey," Folha de S. Paulo, Dec. 26, 2016, http://tinyurl.com/jvqmldb.

[3] "Brazil: Loss of at least 9 million Catholics in two years," *op. cit.*

[4] "Brazil," Church of Jesus Christ of the Latter-day Saints, http://tinyurl.com/ktv3mkz.

demand. She narrowly won a second term in 2015 but soon became enmeshed in Operation Car Wash.

Rousseff denied knowledge of the kickbacks, but because she was chairwoman of the Petrobras board from 2003 to 2010, many doubted her credibility. Rousseff's political support suffered as a result. [69] As more corporate executives and politicians were arrested, the economy became paralyzed and the recession deepened.

In 2016, just after the Summer Olympic Games were held in Rio de Janeiro, Rousseff was impeached in August for procuring loans from public banks to cover budget deficits, and Vice President Michel Temer assumed the presidency until the 2018 election.   ■

CURRENT SITUATION

Sputtering Economy

Although signs of an anemic recovery are emerging, Brazil's deep recession continues. Analysts say economic activity in both the private and public sectors remains weak amid fears of further fallout from Operation Car Wash.

Moreover, unrelated investigations are exposing graft in other places. In March, prosecutors arrested more than two dozen people, alleging officials at Brazil's two

biggest meatpacking companies bribed food sanitation inspectors to approve contaminated meat. Analysts say the scandal could jeopardize Brazil's $12 billion exports of poultry and beef. [70]

The recession is squeezing public coffers, resulting in months-long delays in paying civil servants, including teachers, police officers and firefighters, as well as pensioners. The recession also is contributing to supply shortages in hospitals and affecting other social services.

Many of Brazil's 26 states are in dire fiscal straits due to overspending, high borrowing from federal banks and overly generous tax breaks awarded during the boom years of the early 2000s. [71]

The financial situation in the states of Rio de Janeiro, Minas Gerais and

Rio Grande do Sul is especially serious, with the latter declaring "a state of financial calamity" in November. Despite an $850 million federal emergency loan to stave off bankruptcy last summer, Rio de Janeiro state has money only to cover salaries until mid-2017. [72]

Last year, the state declared a fiscal emergency weeks before the Summer Olympics so it could borrow federal funds. Private companies and the city of Rio de Janeiro, which was in a

Brazilian President Dilma Rousseff delivers her farewell address after her impeachment in August 2016. Handpicked by President Luiz Inácio Lula da Silva as his successor, Rousseff was removed from office for illegally borrowing $11 billion from public banks to cover budget gaps. Vice President Michel Temer, who replaced her, is trying to jumpstart the economy by loosening regulations on foreign and private investment in several key economic sectors.

much better financial position than the state, financed much of the Games' $4.56 billion cost. Many of the Olympic buildings, including athletes' housing, a swimming pool, stadium, handball arena and broadcast center, are boarded up despite officials' promises not to leave any "white elephants." Mayor Marcelo Crivella says the city is on an austerity budget. [73]

Brazil's financial crisis has led to a breakdown in public services. In early February, police demanding higher wages and better working conditions in the southeastern state of Espírito Santo found a way to circumvent a law prohibiting strikes by law enforcement: Their families blockaded police stations, preventing them from leaving to patrol

streets. Looting, street muggings and other types of crime spiked, with homicides rising from four in January to 143 over the nine days of the police work stoppage. [74] The impasse largely ended when President Temer called in troops to patrol the streets, airlifted the officers out of the stations and consented to considering raising their base monthly pay of $850. [75]

The federal government has little choice but to bail out the states, analysts say. In November, Finance Minister Henrique Meirelles said the federal government would use revenue from the repatriation of Brazilians' undeclared foreign income and holdings to help the bankrupt governments. [76]

The debate now focuses on whether the federal government should impose austerity measures on the states. In late December, Temer vetoed a bailout bill after legislators stripped out cost-cutting mandates, such as salary freezes, increased pension contributions and privatizations, in return for debt relief. [77]

However, a month later the federal government reached a deal with the Rio de Janeiro state government, allowing it to suspend its debt payments for three years in exchange for budget cuts and

tax increases. Meirelles said the plan, if approved by federal and state lawmakers, could be a model for other states, although critics warned that it simply postpones Rio's day of reckoning. [78]

Faint Progress

The International Monetary Fund forecasts that Brazil's economy will turn the corner this year, but just barely, growing 0.5 percent. Rises in commodity prices, including iron ore, soybeans, corn and oil, will help. Commodities make up about half of Brazil's exports. [79]

Although analysts stress the economy has a long way to go, signs of recovery are surfacing. Foreign investment surged to $78.9 billion in 2016, up 6 percent from 2015, as investors anticipate a more favorable investment climate under Temer. The Chinese utility State Grid bought a majority stake in the Brazilian utility CPFL Energia, while Britain's Jaguar Land Rover Automotive opened a $296 million factory in Rio de Janeiro state.

Investors say the country is too big a market to discount. "[Brazil] is a strong economy, and once it shakes off its troubles it will go back to having an economic rally again," said Hanno Kirner, executive director of strategy at Jaguar Land Rover. "It has got resources, it has got a young dynamic population. It has got everything in the long term." [80]

In February, Swiss food multinational Nestlé announced plans to build an $86 million Purina dog food plant in São Paulo state, seeing a huge consumer market for 75 percent of the plant's output and an ideal location to export the remainder to surrounding South American countries. [81]

Over the past year, Brazil's currency, the *real*, has strengthened 20 percent against the U.S. dollar, and the stock market has surged 37 percent, buoyed by Temer's more business-friendly government than Rousseff's. Investors have been encouraged by the willingness of

Continued on p. 306

At Issue:

Should Brazil have a permanent U.N. Security Council seat?

MARK S. LANGEVIN
DIRECTOR, BRAZIL INITIATIVE, ELLIOTT SCHOOL OF INTERNATIONAL AFFAIRS, GEORGE WASHINGTON UNIVERSITY

WRITTEN FOR *CQ RESEARCHER*, APRIL 2017

*t*he United Nations Security Council should be expanded, and Brazil should be granted a permanent seat. Brazil was an original member of the first Council of the League of Nations following World War I.

During the establishment of the United Nations, U.S. President Franklin D. Roosevelt pushed for a six-nation U.N. Security Council, including Brazil. Roosevelt's untimely death put Brazilian ambitions on hold.

A permanent Security Council seat remains the holy grail for Brazilian officials, but even temporary membership has played a central role in the formation of the nation's foreign policies. Brazil has served as a frequent rotating member on the Security Council and is well-known in U.N. circles as a constructive voice for moderation and consensus building. Brazil participates in the G-4, along with Germany, India and Japan, to advocate for seats on the Security Council.

Moreover, Brazil's longtime leadership role in the Group of 77 developing nations and its more recent innovative, multilateral engagements with the BRICS nations (an association for five emerging economies) and the IBSA Dialogue Forum (India, Brazil and South Africa) provide a compelling argument that Brazil is one of a handful of member-states that could make the Security Council more representative and effective.

Brazil's notable stature at the United Nations, its demonstrated diplomatic capacity to work with many different member-states to open up lines of dialogue and even forge consensus, and its experience as a rotating member of the council provide ample evidence to make the case that Brazil, along with the other G-4 member-states, should be granted Security Council seats. That would make the institution more representative and better positioned to confront 21st-century collective security challenges.

These impressive credentials, however, are insufficient to move existing council members to agree to expansion. If Brazil wants to realize this national goal, its political leaders must pay more of the costs of collective security and expand the nation's capacity to respond to humanitarian emergencies, such as the Syrian refugee flows.

Brazil must also consider its current political distance from the United States, especially in terms of its General Assembly votes, given the U.S. strategic partnerships with all nations of the G-4 except Brazil. Today, the world needs Brazil's special voice and vote on those multilateral matters at the heart of the struggle for peace and prosperity for all.

RIORDAN ROETT
DIRECTOR, LATIN AMERICAN STUDIES PROGRAM, PAUL H. NITZE SCHOOL OF ADVANCED INTERNATIONAL STUDIES, JOHNS HOPKINS UNIVERSITY

WRITTEN FOR *CQ RESEARCHER*, APRIL 2017

*b*razil has always aspired to greatness but has failed to achieve it. Brazil is a strong advocate of "soft power," such as peacekeeping and transferring agricultural technology to poor countries in Africa.

But "hard power" is not in the Brazilian elites' DNA. Brazil will never commit troops to geopolitical missions such as those in Iraq or Afghanistan. Respecting sovereignty, and not interfering in the internal affairs of its neighbors, is a paramount belief of the foreign policy elites.

Brazil also faces frequent social and economic internal crises. The elites fail to understand that the world powers have reasonably stable political systems — democratic or authoritarian. The G-7 nations also have advanced educational and health standards. Deep disparities in educational levels prevent Brazil from becoming a competitive or productive economy. Its economy is still based on the export of commodities and minerals.

It has never fully industrialized and produces very little that would be attractive on world markets. Therefore, it is always the victim of swings in international prices for iron ore, coffee, sugar, etc. And it remains a closed economy in terms of world trade. Unproductive firms in Brazil are not allowed to fail.

Brazilians were very disappointed when President Barack Obama visited India and publicly endorsed it for a seat on the U.N. Security Council. He did not do so when he visited Brazil. The foreign policy elites in Brazil don't seem to understand that India is an important geopolitical player in Asia. It has difficult neighbors — Pakistan and China — and it is a nuclear power.

That gives India a global status that is very different from that of Brazil. Brazil is not a nuclear power; it does not have any border disputes with its neighbors; it does not have a terrorist threat or jihadists within its national territory. Geographically, it is far removed from the major theaters of world politics.

Brazilian leaders must understand that given the country's relative isolation in world politics, their main challenge is to address inequality and underdevelopment within their own borders. They must improve the conditions needed to be competitive and productive economically, and they must find a formula to achieve political stability. Then, the country might receive the respect it so desperately wants from the global players in world politics.

Continued from p. 304

Temer's administration to tackle some necessary but politically unpopular reforms. The 76-year-old constitutional lawyer has said he is not planning to seek another term and thus is not concerned about currying favor with voters by pursuing "fiscal populism." His public approval rating stands at just 15 percent. [82]

He scored a major victory in December when he pushed through Congress a 20-year cap on public spending, the cornerstone of an austerity program to rein in a growing budget deficit. [83]

A homeless man sleeps outside Maracana Stadium in Rio de Janeiro. Since the iconic soccer venue hosted events at the Summer Olympics and World Cup it has fallen into disrepair along with many other Olympic buildings. Rio de Janeiro state is among several Brazilian states in dire economic straits. Despite an $850 million federal emergency loan to stave off bankruptcy last summer, Rio de Janeiro state has money only to cover salaries until mid-2017.

AFP/Getty Images/Vanderlei Almeida

Next on Temer's agenda are plans to simplify the country's complex tax code, liberalize labor laws that deter hiring, cut pension costs by raising the retirement age for public workers from 54 to 65 and improve the public school system by raising graduation rates to produce a more competitive workforce. [84]

Analysts say getting those reforms through Congress will be an uphill battle. Temer may not be worried about re-election, but legislators are. "I don't know if the government has the legitimacy to do these reforms," says Langevin of George Washington University.

Going forward, the economy also may not get much of a lift from Brazil's sprawling companies, particularly those in construction, that have been significantly weakened by the corruption scandal. The Odebrecht Group has shed nearly 60,000 of its 180,000 employees while its revenues have plummeted 50 percent since the investigation began. [85] "It's been banned from doing government work. It will be a shadow of its former self," Taylor of American University says.

The outlook for Petrobras is a bit more optimistic. The company has a new CEO, Pedro Parente, who has downsized the workforce, revamped its governance and announced the sale of $40 billion in assets over the next decade. Last fall, 11,700 employees agreed to voluntarily leave, and Congress approved allowing foreign companies to take over offshore oil fields. [86]

"Petrobras is a fifth of its size at its peak in 2008-09. It's going to be a very different company," says Taylor.

Corruption Fallout

Brazil's ongoing corruption investigation is turning global as prosecutors in several countries undertake their own probes of the Odebrecht Group's bribery schemes. In February, a Peruvian judge issued an arrest warrant for former President Alejandro Toledo, who is accused of receiving $20 million in bribes from the construction giant for infrastructure contracts, including a highway connecting Peru and Brazil. [87] In Colombia, prosecutors said President Juan Manuel Santos' 2014 campaign may have received a $1 million contribution from a third party linked to Odebrecht, prompting Santos to call for an investigation. [88]

The expanding investigations come on the heels of Odebrecht's agreement in December to pay $3.5 billion in global penalties after the U.S. Department of Justice revealed that the construction multinational had a secret department tasked with funneling bribes totaling $800 million to government officials in 12 countries in Latin America and Africa. [89]

The widening scandal has caused more embarrassment for Brazilians. "Brazil's international prestige has just melted," says Hakim of the Inter-American Dialogue.

Brazil's own investigation is set to expand significantly with the public release of details from a wave of plea bargains reached last year between prosecutors and dozens of Odebrecht executives in which defendants received more lenient sentences in exchange for their testimony. The plea agreements are believed to implicate top politicians in Brazil and other countries, possibly including Temer, who has been mentioned in other plea bargains but never charged. A court could remove him if evidence surfaces of illegal campaign funds that he has long been accused of receiving. Temer has denied any wrongdoing. [90]

"I would say that the new plea agreements could allow the Car Wash operation to double its size in the future," Deltan Dallagnol, the federal prosecutor in charge of the operation, told The Associated Press.

Dallaganol said no end to the investigation is in sight, and he vowed that he and Judge Moro, the other key figure in the investigation, will continue despite significant political pressure from legislators to scale it back or drop it. [91]

In the meantime, the nation waits for further revelations from the plea bargain testimony and the political fallout that will cause, experts say. "People are worrying about the next shoe to drop," says Winter of the Council of the Americas.

Operation Car Wash promises to be front and center for some time because prosecutions will take time, Winter says. "Winding down the investigation will allow some degree of stability to return, but the trials will last years," he says.

The scandals are having a spillover effect on politics. Underscoring public discontent with the political class and system, Brazil's two largest cities inaugurated outsiders as mayors in January: Joao Doria, a São Paulo millionaire businessman, and Crivella, an evangelical Protestant bishop in Rio de Janeiro. Both men had defeated allies of the president, and Doria also defeated the incumbent. [92] ■

OUTLOOK

More Political Uncertainty

The near-term outlook for Brazil pivots on the October 2018 presidential election, analysts agree. So far, no candidates have emerged as overwhelming front-runners, although Lula, 72, has said he will run as the Workers' Party candidate.

Still, even if he avoids conviction on the five corruption indictments pending against him, he may not have the popular support to win. A December poll by São Paulo pollster Datafolha put Lula as the front-runner with just 25 percent support and Marina Silva, his former environmental minister who would run for her newly created party Sustainability Network (REDE), in second place with 15 percent. [93]

A fragmented race could boost Lula into a second-round runoff between the top two vote-getters, but that may not be enough to net him the presidency, says Taylor of American University. (Brazil's presidential election system calls for a second runoff election between the two top contenders if no candidate wins more than 50 percent.)

That could benefit Silva, an Afro-indigenous former rubber tapper from the Amazon who is supported by a strong evangelical movement. (*See sidebar, p. 302.*) The December poll had Silva beating Lula by 9 points in a runoff. [94]

However, experts note that with such scant support for the two leading contenders, the electoral landscape remains an open field. "No one knows who will be the next president," says Hakim of the Inter-American Dialogue.

Full economic recovery and long-term growth, economists say, will depend on whether the new president has the popular support and political will needed to tackle unpopular but necessary reforms, such as restructuring the generous pension system and the byzantine tax code.

Although the Temer government has started to implement some reforms, such as opening Petrobras to more private investment and streamlining business regulations, there is no guarantee the incoming leader will be of the same mind-set.

"I see a very large chance that a new government may not continue these reforms," de Bolle of the Peterson Institute of International Economics says.

Others, however, say Brazil has no choice but to open up its economy. "By 2020, it'll be a more liberal country in the economy," Langevin says.

Casanova of Cornell University says weaknesses in the private sector pose another problem. "The big private-sector companies are dismantled, and there is no strong private sector," she says. "I don't know how the country is going to recover."

As the political landscape evolves, Brazil's economic fortunes will continue to depend on commodities. If world demand and prices recover, that could spur a revival in government spending on public infrastructure projects and thus help restore economic growth. "If the price of oil goes up, everything will be all right again," Johns Hopkins University's Roett says.

Absent that spark, observers note that recovery of Brazil's private sector may lag for some time, as it was never strong to begin with and has been badly harmed by the recession and the weakening of consumer demand.

Experts agree that for the foreseeable future, Brazil will continue to be an underachieving country whose potential will be much talked about but not fulfilled.

"What has happened over the past four years has been a huge blow to Brazil. I'm pretty pessimistic about what's coming," says Winter of the Council of the Americas. "They'll move out of recession soon, but getting back to reducing poverty and to growth of 3 to 5 percent won't be in the short term. Deep structural issues need to be addressed." ■

Notes

[1] Blake Schmidt and Sabrina Valle, "Brazil's Marcelo Odebrecht Gets 19 Years in Jail in Carwash," Bloomberg, March 8, 2016, http://tinyurl.com/mo8t4xo.

[2] Andrew Jacobs and Paula Moura, "At the Birthplace of a Graft Scandal, Brazil's Crisis Is on Full Display," *The New York Times*, June 10, 2016, http://tinyurl.com/llj4q8c.

[3] Brian Winter, "Brazil's Car Wash Probe: Tell Me How This Ends," *Americas Quarterly*, Sept. 28, 2016, http://tinyurl.com/k57fjrz.

[4] Merrit Kennedy, "Brazil's Recession The Longest And Deepest In Its History, New Figures Show," NPR, March 7, 2017, http://tinyurl.com/knbgwjm; "Brazil Unemployment Hit Fresh High of 12.6%," *Trading Economics*, undated, http://tinyurl.com/7rzyjnf.

[5] "Brazil: People & Society" and "Brazil: Economy," *CIA World Factbook*, http://tinyurl.com/kzfjzg5; "Brazil National Economic Profile," United Nations Economic Commission of Latin America and the Caribbean, http://tinyurl.com/kpsko9h; "Mexico National Economic Profile." United Nations Economic Commission of Latin America and the Caribbean, http://tinyurl.com/n5gnm7f; and "Nicaragua National Economic Profile," United

Nations Economic Commission of Latin America and the Caribbean, http://tinyurl.com/lu2p76k.

[6] Ibid., "Brazil: Economy."

[7] "Brazil's Lula to leave office with record-high popularity," Reuters, Dec. 16, 2010, http://tinyurl.com/lo5qq9w.

[8] "Brazil and the United Nations Security Council," Ministry of Foreign Affairs, undated, http://tinyurl.com/m7dkdaq.

[9] "Country Comparison, Distribution of Family Income: GINI Index," CIA World Factbook, http://tinyurl.com/mn8how.

[10] Jessica Brice, Ney Hayashi and David Biller, "Brazil Suffers Slow Growth with Lula China Policy Sowing Doubts," Bloomberg, Sept. 22, 2014, http://tinyurl.com/laex39m.

[11] "Corruption Perceptions Index 2016," Transparency International, http://tinyurl.com/z7bmnu8.

[12] "Brazil starts jailing those convicted in 'Mensalao' trial," Agence France-Presse, The Telegraph, Nov. 16, 2013, http://tinyurl.com/ksahhpq.

[13] Fabiola Moura and Jessica Brice, "Brazil Has a School Problem," Bloomberg News, March 2, 2017, http://tinyurl.com/me96mas; Simon Romero, "Dilma Rousseff Is Ousted as Brazil's President in Impeachment Vote," The New York Times, Aug. 31, 2016, http://tinyurl.com/ko4joz2.

[14] Samy Adghirni, "After Oil Industry Shift, Brazil Seeks to Open Up Defense," Bloomberg, Oct. 25, 2016, http://tinyurl.com/kgmq6wl.

[15] Vinicy Chan, "The Gold Medal for Buying Up Brazilian Assets Goes to China, Inc.," Bloomberg, Aug. 18, 2016, http://tinyurl.com/n733fsx.

[16] "Brazil to ease local content rules in oil industry," Reuters, Oct. 17, 2016, http://tinyurl.com/m92754u.

[17] "Country Comparison Crude Oil Production," CIA World Factbook, http://tinyurl.com/kssswhm.

[18] Rebeca Duran, "Importation of Oil in Brazil," The Brazil Business, Aug. 26, 2013, http://tinyurl.com/meg8o9z.

[19] Simon Romero, "As a Distracted Brazil Mourns, Lawmakers Gut a Corruption Bill," The New York Times, Nov. 30, 2017, http://tinyurl.com/m23pdsz.

[20] Brad Brooks, "Brazil prosecutors hit ex-president Lula with more corruption charges," Reuters, Dec. 15, 2016, http://tinyurl.com/l7x8hyp.

[21] "Lula indictment may affect 2018 race," The Economist, Sept. 22, 2016, http://tinyurl.com/kovbclo.

[22] Mario Sergio Lima, Anna Edgerton and Bruce Douglas, "Lula Faces Trial as Judge Accepts Corruption Charges," Bloomberg, Sept. 20, 2016, http://tinyurl.com/zpwuojn.

[23] Ryan Lloyd and Carlos Oliveira, "How Brazil's electoral system led the country into political crisis," The Washington Post, May 25, 2016, http://tinyurl.com/kw7shgn.

[24] Igor Utsumi, "Funding of Political Parties in Brazil," The Brazil Business, Oct. 3, 2014, http://tinyurl.com/k4s7eeo; Anthony Boadle, "Millionaires, evangelicals benefit from Brazil campaign funds ban," Reuters, Sept. 29, 2016, http://tinyurl.com/lxelz32.

[25] Alex Cuadros, Brazillionaires: Wealth, Power, Decadence, and Hope in an American Country (2016), p. 12.

[26] Erik Ortiz, "What is a favela? 5 Things to Know About Rio's So-Called Shantytowns," NBC News, Aug. 4, 2016, http://tinyurl.com/hp3sssz.

[27] Jing Xu, "Economic Inequality in Brazil," The Borgen Project, July 28, 2014, http://tinyurl.com/krgj9h3; "Country Comparison: Distribution of Family Income, Gini Index," CIA World Factbook, Central Intelligence Agency, http://tinyurl.com/lf7gjwy.

[28] Deborah Wetzel, "Bolsa Família: Brazil's Quiet Revolution," World Bank, Nov. 4, 2013, http://tinyurl.com/mopjhv5; Sarah Illingworth, "Bolsa Família: The Program Helping 50M Brazilians Exit Poverty," The Huffington Post, June 10, 2015 (updated June 9, 2016), http://tinyurl.com/kvbfbov; and Jay Forte, "Brazil Raises 2017 Monthly Minimum Wage to R$937," Rio Times Online, Dec. 30, 2016, http://tinyurl.com/l7t7puo.

[29] "Brazil," Organisation for Economic Co-Operation and Development, http://tinyurl.com/lc2q2de.

[30] Fabiola Moura and Jessica Brice, "Brazil Has a School Problem," Bloomberg, March 2, 2017, http://tinyurl.com/k6wod3d.

[31] Lise Alves, "Brazilian Government Announces New Education Model," Rio Times, Sept 23, 2016, http://tinyurl.com/kbaw8ka.

[32] Pam Bellick and Tania Franco, "For Brazil's Zika Families, a Life of Struggles and Scares," The New York Times, March 11, 2017, http://tinyurl.com/k32waok. Also see Alan Greenblatt, "Mosquito-Borne Disease," CQ Researcher, July 22, 2016, pp. 601-624.

[33] "National Security Plan will rationalise prison system," Brazil Office of the Presidency, Jan. 4, 2017, http://tinyurl.com/k5zm8br.

[34] "Brazil's former richest man Eike Batista sent to prison," BBC, Jan. 31, 2017, http://tinyurl.com/kb53vho; Anderson Antunes, "Former Billionaire Eike Batista Bemoans His Return to the Middle Class," Forbes, Sept. 18, 2014, http://tinyurl.com/nxa34pe.

[35] "Brazil: Transportation," U.S. International Trade Administration, Export.gov, Oct. 14, 2016, http://tinyurl.com/km85no9.

[36] Athena Peppes and Armen Ovanessoff, "What Business Must Do To Reignite Brazil Productivity Growth," Accenture, 2015, p. 17, http://tinyurl.com/mu2z5p9; Ibid., "Brazil: Transportation."

[37] Moura and Brice, op. cit.

[38] Forte, op. cit.; Peppes and Ovanessoff, op. cit., p. 18.

[39] Cynthia Fujikawa Nes, "Brazilian Employment Law in a Nutshell," The Brazil Business, Nov. 20, 2016, http://tinyurl.com/llmftkf.

[40] Peppes and Ovanessoff, op. cit., p. 15.

[41] Luiza Belloni, "Despite Brazil's Financial Crisis, Havaianas Still Has the World at Its Feet," The Huffington Post, Dec. 4, 2015, http://tinyurl.com/me2mqj6.

[42] Lourdes Casanova, "Making the Brazil Dream a Reality," Latin Trade, undated, http://tinyurl.com/m3a85vx.

[43] Bruce Douglas and Matthew Malinowski, "Brazil Worries the 'China of South America' Is Eating Its Lunch," Bloomberg, Jan. 9, 2017, http://tinyurl.com/lbb64yp.

[44] Thomas E. Skidmore, Brazil: Five Centuries of Change (1999), p. 5.

[45] Marshall C. Eakin, Brazil: The Once and Future Country (1997), p. 15.

[46] Boris Fausto, A Concise History of Brazil (1999), pp. 9-11.

[47] Skidmore, op. cit., pp. 17, 19.

[48] Fausto, op. cit., p. 49.

[49] Skidmore op. cit., p. 30.

[50] Eakin, op. cit., p. 27; ibid., Skidmore, p. 36.

[51] Fausto, op. cit., p. 70; ibid., Eakin, pp. 28-29.

[52] José Fonseca, "A Brief History of Brazil," The New York Times, undated, http://tinyurl.com/kx35luw.

About the Author

Christina Hoag is a freelance journalist in Los Angeles. She previously worked for *The Miami Herald* and The Associated Press and was a correspondent in Latin America. She is the co-author of *Peace in the Hood: Working with Gang Members to End the Violence.*

[53] Skidmore, *op. cit.*, pp. 54, 70.

[54] Eakin, *op. cit.*, p. 37.

[55] *Ibid.*, Eakin, p. 34.

[56] *Ibid.*, pp. 43-46.

[57] Skidmore, *op. cit.*, pp. 136-138.

[58] *Ibid.*, p. 139.

[59] Eakin, *op. cit.*, p. 55.

[60] Skidmore, *op. cit.*, pp. 165-166.

[61] *Ibid.*, pp. 177, 181.

[62] Eakin, *op. cit.*, p. 59; Fausto, *op. cit.*, p. 305.

[63] Fonseca, *op. cit.*

[64] Fausto, *op. cit.*, p. 315; Skidmore, *op. cit.*, p. 217.

[65] *Ibid.*, Fausto, p. 319.

[66] Mark S. Langevin and Timothy Stackhouse, "Brazil and Development: Growth, Equity and Sustainability in the 21st Century," Brazil Initiative, George Washington University Elliott School of International Affairs, August 2015, p. 4, http://tinyurl.com/mxo4ppb; Skidmore, *op. cit.*, p. 228.

[67] *Ibid.*, Skidmore; "Historic inflation: Brazil," Inflation.eu, undated, http://tinyurl.com/mpg4dkb.

[68] Walter Brandimarte and Vivianne Rodrigues, "From Guerrilla to Impeachment: The Dilma Rousseff Story," Bloomberg, Aug. 30, 2016, http://tinyurl.com/jauahf6.

[69] *Ibid.*

[70] Brad Haynes and Sergio Spagnuolo, "Brazil police raid BRF and JBS plants in meatpacking probe," Reuters, March 17, 2017, http://tinyurl.com/labmr7d.

[71] Alonso Soto and Reese Ewing, "Brazil's federal, state governments reach accord to balance accounts," Reuters, Nov. 22, 2016, http://tinyurl.com/kgjcrd4.

[72] Mac Margolis, "In Brazil, State Debt Is a Ticking Time Bomb," Bloomberg, Dec. 2, 2016, http://tinyurl.com/mr697fp.

[73] Jonathan Watts, "Rio de Janeiro governor declares financial emergency ahead of Olympics," *The Guardian*, June 17, 2016, http://tinyurl.com/lzdrfxh; "The cost of hosting this year's Olympics in Rio lowest since 2004," *Sports Illustrated*, Aug. 24, 2016, http://tinyurl.com/jk6c6a2; and Anna Jean Kaiser, "Legacy of Rio Olympics Is So Far Series of Unkept Promises," *The New York Times*, Feb. 15, 2017, http://tinyurl.com/lt678fp.

[74] Marina Lopes, "Police went on strike in a Brazilian state. The result was near anarchy," *The Washington Post*, March 1, 2017, http://tinyurl.com/knr7ee6.

[75] "Brazil army takes over state's security as 100 killed amid police strike," *The Guardian*, Feb. 9, 2017, http://tinyurl.com/za7swg8.

[76] Soto and Ewing, *op. cit.*

[77] Rachel Garnarski and Walter Brandimarte,

FOR MORE INFORMATION

Brazilian-American Chamber of Commerce, 509 Madison Ave., New York, NY 10022; 212-751-4691; www.brazilcham.com. Promotes trade and investment and closer business ties between Brazil and the United States.

The Brazil Initiative, George Washington University, 1957 E St., N.W., Suite 501, Washington, DC 20052; 202-994-4060; www.brazil.elliott.gwu.edu. Promotes understanding of Brazilian culture, development, history and foreign policy.

Brazil-U.S. Business Council, 1615 H St., N.W., Washington, DC 20062; 202-463-5729; www.brazilcouncil.org. Promotes policies for increasing cooperation, bilateral trade and investment between the United States and Brazil.

Council of the Americas, Suite 250, 1615 L St., N.W., Washington, DC 20036; 202-659-8989; www.as-coa.org. Business think tank focusing on free trade, open markets and democracy in the Americas.

Embassy of Brazil, 3006 Massachusetts Ave., N.W., Washington, DC 20008; 202-238-2700; www.washington.itamaraty.gov.br/en-us. Official diplomatic mission of Brazil in the United States.

Inter-American Dialogue, 1155 15th St., N.W., Suite 800, Washington, DC 20005; 202-822-9002; www.thedialogue.org. Think tank that works to foster better understanding and mutual cooperation in the Americas.

Lemann Center for Brazilian Studies, Columbia University, 420 W. 118th St., 8th Floor IAB, MC 3339, New York, NY 10027; 212-854-4642; www.ilas.columbia.edu/centers-and-programs/brazil-center. Sponsors lectures and visiting scholars on contemporary and historical aspects of Brazil and funds research grants.

"Brazil's Indebted States Dealt Blow as Temer Vetoes Relief," Bloomberg, Dec. 28, 2016, http://tinyurl.com/kjqecpr.

[78] Rachel Garnarski and Samy Adghirni, "Brazil's Government Deal With Rio Won't Solve Its Debt Crisis," Bloomberg. Jan. 31, 2017, http://tinyurl.com/m8ppwvx.

[79] Mary Sadler, "Is Brazil's Recovery Back on Track for 2017?" *Market Realist*, Feb. 24, 2017, http://tinyurl.com/n9xgss7.

[80] Joe Leahy, "Business bets big on Brazil economic rally," *Financial Times*, Feb. 6, 2017, http://tinyurl.com/ltrpfm4.

[81] Fabiola Moura, "Nestle to Open $86 million Brazil Plant to Tap Dog Food Demand," Bloomberg, Feb. 2, 2017, http://tinyurl.com/lrjggpj.

[82] Joe Leahy, "Temer stays tough on Brazil economic reforms," *Financial Times*, Feb.2, 2017, http://tinyurl.com/mb5qqab.

[83] Anthony Boadle and Marcela Ayres, "Brazil Senate passes spending cap in win for Temer," Reuters, Dec. 13, 2016, http://tinyurl.com/mm5arwp.

[84] Leahy, *op. cit.*

[85] Marina Lopes and Nick Miroff, "How a scandal that started in Brazil is now roiling other Latin American countries," *The Washington Post*, Feb. 22, 2017, http://tinyurl.com/l3yadjc.

[86] Zainab Calcuttawala, "Brazilian Congress Authorizes Sale of Petrobras 'Pre-Salt' Fields," Oilprice.com, Nov. 29, 2016, http://tinyurl.com/jwacxt9.

[87] Andrea Zarate, "Corruption Scandal Ensnares Leaders of Peru and Colombia," *The New York Times*, Feb. 7, 2017, http://tinyurl.com/k7nzcm9.

[88] "Colombia's Santos calls for probe of Odebrecht's role in 2014 campaign," Reuters, Feb. 8, 2017, http://tinyurl.com/ldzko87.

[89] Alexandra Stevenson and Vinod Sreeharsha, "Secret Unit Helped Brazilian Company Bribe Government Officials," *The New York Times*, Dec. 21, 2016, http://tinyurl.com/mmtu77q; Marina Lopes and Nick Miroff, "How a scandal that started in Brazil is now roiling other Latin American countries," *The Washington Post*, Feb. 22, 2017, http://tinyurl.com/l3yadjc.

[90] Peter Prengaman, "Brazil Prosecutor Says Massive Corruption Prosecution Could Double in Size," *Time*, Jan. 26, 2017, http://tinyurl.com/mhoty99.

[91] *Ibid.*

[92] Sarah DiLorenzo and Mauricio Saverese, "Fed up with politics, Brazil cities swear in outsider mayors," The Associated Press, Jan. 1, 2017, http://tinyurl.com/l7xx2nq.

[93] Flavio Ferreira, "Marina Silva is the leader in all second round scenarios, points Datafolha," Folha de S. Paulo, Dec 12, 2016, http://tinyurl.com/kq3wqy3.

[94] *Ibid.*

Bibliography

Selected Sources

Books

Alston, Lee J., et al., Brazil in Transition: Beliefs, Leadership and Institutional Change, Princeton University Press, 2016.
Academics and other experts analyze Brazil's political and economic history over the last 50 years, examining how the nation evolved into a potential world superpower and what remains to be done to achieve that status.

Barbassa, Juliana, Dancing with the Devil in the City of God: Rio de Janeiro and the Olympic Dream, Touchstone, 2015.
A former Associated Press correspondent examines the city of her birth, detailing both its glamour and drawbacks.

Cuadros, Alex, Brazillionaires: Wealth, Power, Decadence, and Hope in an American Country, Spiegel & Grau, 2016.
A journalist chronicles how Brazil's superrich amassed spectacular wealth through political skullduggery, their soap opera lives and their downfalls amid economic collapse.

Mares, David R. and Harold A. Trinkunas, Aspirational Power: Brazil on the Long Road to Global Influence, Brookings Institution Press, 2016.
Scholars at a Washington think tank explain why Brazil, despite its size, has never emerged as a global power.

Reid, Michael, Brazil: The Troubled Rise of a Global Power, Yale University Press, 2016.
The Latin American columnist for *The Economist* explores why Brazil has been overshadowed by other emerging economies such as Russia, China and India, and what the South American nation must do to gain equal status to those nations.

Schneider, Ben Ross, New Order and Progress: Development and Democracy in Brazil, Oxford University Press, 2016.
A professor in the Massachusetts Institute of Technology's Brazil program explains why Brazil has not achieved its potential despite gains in its economic and political stability since the days of military dictatorship.

Articles

DiLorenzo, Sarah, and Mauricio Savarese, "Fed up with politics, Brazil cities swear in outsider mayors," The Associated Press, Jan. 1, 2017, http://tinyurl.com/l7xx2nq.
Sao Paulo and Rio de Janeiro inaugurated political outsiders as mayors, underscoring the public's frustration with politicians and rampant corruption.

Phillips, Dom, "Once underfed, Brazil's poor have a new problem: obesity," The Washington Post, Nov. 21, 2016, http://tinyurl.com/mvxkkqo.
Brazilians' emergence from poverty has led to new diets of junk and processed food, which in turn has caused a sharp rise in obesity.

Rapoza, Kenneth, "Brazil's Sale of the Century," The Boston Globe, June 5, 2016, http://tinyurl.com/ln2uan2.
Brazil's state oil company, Petrobras, can recoup from corruption scandal setbacks by allowing foreign companies full control over deep-water oil wells.

Stevenson, Alexandra, and Vindo Sreemarsha, "Secret Unit Helped Brazilian Company Bribe Government Officials," The New York Times, Dec. 21, 2016, http://tiny url.com/lbtpedu.
Latin America's biggest construction company had a division that coordinated and facilitated bribes and kickbacks.

Watts, Jonathan, "Fresh crisis in Brazil as new president faces corruption allegations," The Guardian, Nov. 25, 2016, http://tinyurl.com/mgjr45z.
A former Cabinet colleague of President Michel Temer alleges he used his influence in a construction project, fueling opposition moves for impeachment.

Reports and Studies

Brasil, P., et al., "Zika Virus Infection in Pregnant Women in Rio de Janeiro," The New England Journal of Medicine, Dec. 15, 2016, http://tinyurl.com/gp5fda9.
Medical experts study the effects of the Zika virus on pregnant women and their newborns.

Moro, Sergio, "Handling Systemic Corruption in Brazil," Wilson Center for International Scholars, Dec. 8, 2016, http://tinyurl.com/ktfn3e7.
A Brazilian judge known for his efforts to reform the judicial system discusses the extent of graft and the partly successful efforts to combat it.

Muggah, Robert, "The State of Security and Justice in Brazil: Reviewing the Evidence," Brazil Initiative, George Washington University, March 2015, http://tinyurl.com/kmedcl9.
A specialist in security and development examines the challenges and reforms in Brazil's public safety and justice systems.

Nobre, Carlos A., et al., "Land-use and climate change risks in the Amazon and the need of a novel sustainable development paradigm," National Academy of Sciences, Aug. 11, 2016, http://tinyurl.com/n3p3svu.
Scientists examine deforestation in the Brazilian Amazon over the past 50 years and say a new sustainable development approach is needed.

The Next Step:

Additional Articles from Current Periodicals

Corruption

Carolina, Maria Marcello, and Brad Brooks, "Brazil's gov't says meat industry may lose 10 pct market share," Reuters, Nasdaq, March 22, 2017, http://tinyurl.com/lo6tfxg.

Allegations of corruption and unsafe meat could hurt Brazil's meatpacking industry.

Trevisani, Paulo, "Brazil Cases Against Politicians Include Corruption, Money Laundering," *The Wall Street Journal*, March 16, 2017, http://tinyurl.com/kk7mlun.

Brazil's prosecutor general requested permission from the country's Supreme Court to investigate senior officials in President Michel Temer's Cabinet as part of a corruption and money laundering probe known as Operation Car Wash.

Woody, Christopher, "Brazil's latest corruption scandal appears to be rotting one of its major exports," *Business Insider*, March 21, 2017, http://tinyurl.com/kscx8xb.

After a two-year investigation, federal police launched almost 200 raids targeting Brazilian food processors, which are accused of bribing government officials to allow the sale of poor-quality meat.

Environmental Challenges

Fadnes, Ingrid, "Brazil's Fundao dam collapse: The silence after the mud," Al Jazeera, June 14, 2016, http://tinyurl.com/hzteypr.

The three companies that operated the Fundao dam in the Brazilian state of Minas Gerais have agreed to spend $5.6 billion to repair damage caused when the dam burst, unleashing a massive mudslide.

Tabuchi, Hiroko, Claire Rigby and Jeremy White, "Amazon Deforestation, Once Tamed, Comes Roaring Back," *The New York Times*, Feb. 24, 2017, http://tinyurl.com/zqs8atw.

A resurgence of deforestation in the Brazilian Amazon is driven by farmers clearing their land to meet demand for soybeans.

Totaro, Paola, "Environmentalists and farmers must unite to save Amazon, says ex Brazilian minister," Reuters, March 23, 2017, http://tinyurl.com/koqnzww.

Brazil's former environmental minister urged environmentalists and the agriculture industry to work together to protect the country's largest tropical rainforest.

Labor Reforms

"Brazil moves to allow outsourcing in labor law modernization," Reuters, March 22, 2017, http://tinyurl.com/my522tz.

Over the fierce objections of labor unions, the Brazilian Congress passed a bill to allow companies to outsource jobs and offer longer temporary work contracts.

Lazzeri, Thais, "Investigations Reveal Slave Labor Conditions in Brazil's Timber Industry," *Pacific Standard*, March 15, 2017, http://tinyurl.com/l4e6g8a.

The Brazilian government played a role in creating the slave labor-like conditions in the logging industry, according to a report by a land commission and a human-rights group.

Taylor, Ed, "Brazil: McDonald's Fined $30 Million for Labor Law Violations," Bloomberg BNA, Dec. 7, 2016, http://tinyurl.com/l45vpeb.

The Brazilian labor ministry fined the country's McDonald's unit $30 million after an investigation found the company was violating labor laws.

Recession

"Brazil's Temer Says Economy Turning Around, Confidence Rising," Reuters, Voice of America, March 17, 2017, http://tinyurl.com/k8jda9x.

Moody's raised its outlook on Brazil's economy from negative to stable amid signs the nation is slowly emerging from the worst recession in its history.

Adghirni, Samy, "Brazil Economy Adds Jobs for First Time in Two Years," Bloomberg, March 16, 2017, http://tinyurl.com/mrkp8ct.

Brazil added more than 35,000 jobs in February after 22 months of job losses, President Michel Temer announced.

Gillespie, Patrick, "Brazil's worst recession: 8 consecutive quarters of contraction," CNN, March 7, 2017, http://tinyurl.com/kebvevm.

Brazil's economy shrank 3.6 percent in 2016, a slight improvement from 2015, when it contracted 3.8 percent.

CITING *CQ RESEARCHER*

Sample formats for citing these reports in a bibliography include the ones listed below. Preferred styles and formats vary, so please check with your instructor or professor.

MLA STYLE
Jost, Kenneth. "Remembering 9/11." CQ Researcher 2 Sept. 2011: 701-732.

APA STYLE
Jost, K. (2011, September 2). Remembering 9/11. *CQ Researcher, 9*, 701-732.

CHICAGO STYLE
Jost, Kenneth. "Remembering 9/11." *CQ Researcher*, September 2, 2011, 701-32.

In-depth Reports on Issues in the News

Are you writing a paper?

Need backup for a debate?

Want to become an expert on an issue?

For 90 years, students have turned to *CQ Researcher* for in-depth reporting on issues in the news. Reports on a full range of political and social issues are now available. Following is a selection of recent reports:

Civil Liberties
Privacy and the Internet, 12/15
Intelligence Reform, 5/15
Religion and Law, 11/14

Crime/Law
Forensic Science Controversies, 2/17
Jailing Debtors, 9/16
Decriminalizing Prostitution, 4/16
Restorative Justice, 2/16
The Dark Web, 1/16
Immigrant Detention, 10/15
Fighting Gangs, 10/15

Education
Charter Schools, 3/17
Civic Education, 2/17
Student Debt, 11/16
Apprenticeships, 10/16

Environment/Society
Women in Prison, 3/17
Guns on Campus, 1/17
Mass Transit, 12/16
Arctic Development, 12/16
Protecting the Power Grid, 11/16
Pornography, 10/16

Health/Safety
Reducing Traffic Deaths, 2/17
Opioid Crisis, 10/16
Mosquito-Borne Disease, 7/16
Drinking Water Safety, 7/16

Politics/Economy
Reviving Rural Economies, 3/17
Immigrants and the Economy, 2/17
Trump Presidency, 1/17
European Union's Future, 12/16
The Obama Legacy, 11/16
Populism and Party Politics, 9/16

Upcoming Reports

Foreign Aid, 4/14/17   Technology and Policing, 4/21/17   Sex Abuse in Sports, 4/28/17

ACCESS

CQ Researcher is available in print and online. For access, visit your library or www.cqresearcher.com.

STAY CURRENT

For notice of upcoming *CQ Researcher* reports or to learn more about *CQ Researcher* products, subscribe to the free email newsletters, *CQ Researcher Alert!* and *CQ Researcher News*: http://cqpress.com/newsletters.

PURCHASE

To purchase a *CQ Researcher* report in print or electronic format (PDF), visit www.cqpress.com or call 866-427-7737. Single reports start at $15. Bulk purchase discounts and electronic-rights licensing are also available.

SUBSCRIBE

Annual full-service *CQ Researcher* subscriptions—including 44 reports a year, monthly index updates, and a bound volume—start at $1,131. Add $25 for domestic postage.

CQ Researcher Online offers a backfile from 1991 and a number of tools to simplify research. For pricing information, call 800-818-7243 or 805-499-9774 or email librarysales@sagepub.com.

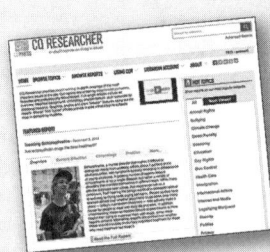

CQ RESEARCHER

CQ PRESS

In-depth reports on today's issues

Published by CQ Press, an Imprint of SAGE Publications, Inc.

www.cqresearcher.com

Rethinking Foreign Aid

Should the U.S. cut back on assistance?

C andidate Donald Trump promised to cut aid to countries that "hate us," and in February, a month after becoming president, he proposed slashing foreign aid by nearly a third. Advocates of a robust aid program point out that foreign military and economic aid represents a mere 1.3 percent of the federal budget and say it is vital in protecting U.S. security interests, spreading democracy and promoting U.S. exports. More than 120 retired military officers wrote to Congress opposing cuts in foreign aid, saying it prevents conflict and helps keep poor countries from breeding terrorism. But critics of U.S. aid policy argue that too much is spent on programs that fail to produce results or winds up funding despotic regimes. With aid programs scattered across two dozen agencies, both critics and advocates of foreign assistance agree the U.S. aid bureaucracy could be more efficient. Some suggest reducing the number of agencies managing aid programs; others want more privatization of U.S. aid efforts.

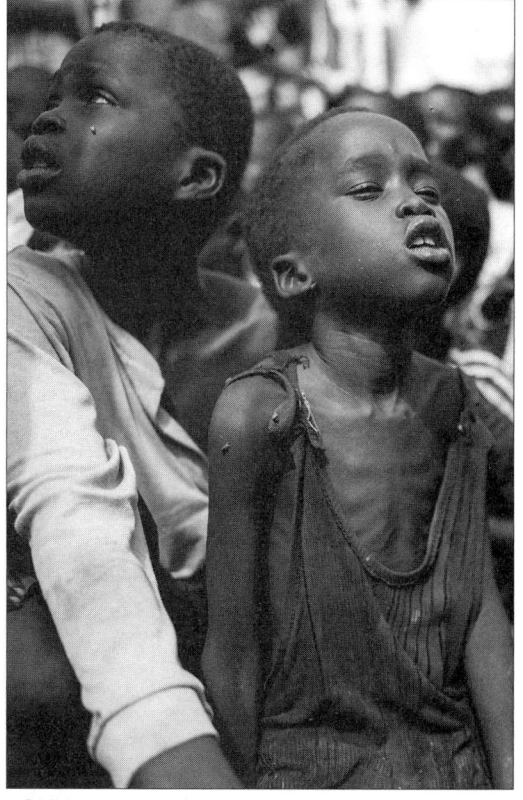

Children wait for food aid during a lull in fighting in famine-plagued South Sudan on March 17, 2016. The United States spent about $48 billion on military, development and humanitarian aid in 2015, or about 1.3 percent of the nation's $3.7 trillion federal budget. A large percentage of Americans think far more is spent on foreign aid.

I N S I D E — THIS REPORT

THE ISSUES	**315**
BACKGROUND	**321**
CHRONOLOGY	**323**
CURRENT SITUATION	**328**
AT ISSUE	**329**
OUTLOOK	**331**
BIBLIOGRAPHY	**334**
THE NEXT STEP	**335**

CQ Researcher • April 14, 2017 • www.cqresearcher.com
Volume 27, Number 14 • Pages 313-336

RECIPIENT OF SOCIETY OF PROFESSIONAL JOURNALISTS AWARD FOR
EXCELLENCE ◆ AMERICAN BAR ASSOCIATION SILVER GAVEL AWARD

Los Angeles | London | New Delhi
Singapore | Washington DC | Melbourne

CQ RESEARCHER

April 14, 2017
Volume 27, Number 14

EXECUTIVE EDITOR: Thomas J. Billitteri
tjb@sagepub.com

ASSISTANT MANAGING EDITORS: Kenneth
Fireman, kenneth.fireman@sagepub.com,
Kathy Koch, kathy.koch@sagepub.com,
Scott Rohrer, scott.rohrer@sagepub.com

ASSOCIATE MANAGING EDITOR: Val Ellicott

SENIOR CONTRIBUTING EDITOR:
Thomas J. Colin
tom.colin@sagepub.com

CONTRIBUTING WRITERS: Marcia Clemmitt,
Sarah Glazer, Reed Karaim, Barbara Mantel,
Chuck McCutcheon, Tom Price

SENIOR PROJECT EDITOR: Olu B. Davis

EDITORIAL ASSISTANT: Anika Reed

FACT CHECKERS: Eva P. Dasher,
Michelle Harris, Betsy Towner Levine,
Robin Palmer

THE ISSUES

315
• Should the United States increase its economic aid to other countries?
• Does the United States attach too many conditions to its foreign aid?
• Are public-private aid partnerships more effective than government-run projects?

BACKGROUND

321 **Ancient Aid**
Nations have dispensed foreign aid since the days of Alexander the Great.

322 **Marshall Plan**
The United States provided $12.5 billion to stabilize Western Europe after World War II.

325 **"Structural Adjustment"**
The World Bank and other donors pushed aid recipients to adopt free-market reforms in the 1980s but later abandoned the policy.

CURRENT SITUATION

328 **Hunger Crisis**
Millions in four countries face famine.

328 **Reform Recommendations**
Some critics say aid distribution should be consolidated under one entity, but others want it privatized.

OUTLOOK

331 **Coming Crisis**
Oxfam International predicts intensifying climate change could worsen the aid crisis in Africa.

SIDEBARS AND GRAPHICS

316 **Where the Money Goes**
The U.S. spent $48.1 billion on aid in 2015, nearly half of it on military assistance.

317 **Top Aid Recipients: Israel, Egypt, Afghanistan**
Israel received the most in military assistance in 2015.

318 **U.S. Ranks 24th in Aid as Share of Wealth**
Donations were less than 0.2 percent of gross national income.

323 **Chronology**
Key events since 1850.

324 **Millennium Challenge Corp. Pushes Countries to Reform**
Agency "only works in a fairly narrow range of countries," critics say.

326 **Corrupt Governments Pose Donor Dilemma**
"Cuts to aid disproportionately hurt people living in poverty."

329 **At Issue:**
Should USAID be the primary manager of U.S. development aid?

FOR FURTHER RESEARCH

333 **For More Information**
Organizations to contact.

334 **Bibliography**
Selected sources used.

335 **The Next Step**
Additional articles.

335 **Citing CQ Researcher**
Sample bibliography formats.

Los Angeles I London I New Delhi
Singapore I Washington DC I Melbourne

An Imprint of SAGE Publications, Inc.

SENIOR VICE PRESIDENT,
GLOBAL LEARNING RESOURCES:
Karen Phillips

EXECUTIVE DIRECTOR, ONLINE LIBRARY AND
REFERENCE PUBLISHING:
Todd Baldwin

CQ Researcher (ISSN 1056-2036) is printed on acid-free paper. Published weekly, except: (March wk. 4) (May wk. 4) (July wks. 1, 2) (Aug. wks. 2, 3) (Nov. wk. 4) and (Dec. wks. 3, 4). Published by SAGE Publications, Inc., 2455 Teller Rd., Thousand Oaks, CA 91320. Annual full-service subscriptions start at $1,131. For pricing, call 1-800-818-7243. To purchase a CQ Researcher report in print or electronic format (PDF), visit www.cqpress. com or call 866-427-7737. Single reports start at $15. Bulk purchase discounts and electronic-rights licensing are also available. Periodicals postage paid at Thousand Oaks, California, and at additional mailing offices. POSTMASTER: Send address changes to CQ Researcher, 2600 Virginia Ave., N.W., Suite 600, Washington, DC 20037.

Cover: Getty Images/Lynsey Addario

Rethinking Foreign Aid

BY PATRICK MARSHALL

THE ISSUES

In announcing his candidacy for president, Donald Trump said the United States should stop spending so much money helping other nations and instead use the funds at home. "It is necessary," he declared, "that we . . . stop sending foreign aid to countries that hate us and use that money to rebuild our tunnels, roads, bridges and schools." [1]

As president, Trump followed through on that idea, proposing a budget in February that would slash funds for the U.S. Agency for International Development (USAID) — the primary conduit for foreign aid — by nearly a third, with the biggest cuts in economic development assistance. [2]

Aid specialists reject the proposal, as do some members of Trump's own Republican Party. "Foreign aid is not charity" but is crucial to national security, Florida Sen. Marco Rubio tweeted. "A disaster," South Carolina Sen. Lindsey Graham said of the plan, which he predicted would be "dead on arrival" in the Senate. [3]

Foreign aid "helps build stable, democratic partners who share our interests and values," says Shannon Green, a senior analyst at the Center for Strategic and International Studies, a think tank in Washington.

While foreign aid may play a central role in national security and U.S. relations abroad, Trump's skepticism about its importance has helped revive several longstanding questions: How effectively is aid dispensed to struggling nations? What are the strategic goals of aid? Does aid to despotic regimes have positive or negative effects?

President Trump has proposed cutting U.S. foreign aid by about a third, saying he wants to spend more money on infrastructure projects at home and to bolster the military. Foreign aid advocates say aid to countries that support the U.S. fight against terrorism is vital to U.S. national security. Critics say aid is often wasted on inefficient programs or stolen by corrupt foreign dictators and officials.

Getty Images/Bloomberg/Aude Guerrucci

"Foreign aid has long been notorious for breeding kleptocracies — governments of thieves," libertarian commentator James Bovard wrote in 2016. [4]

Foreign assistance has always stirred controversy far greater than its share of the federal budget. Americans typically think aid consumes "somewhere between one-fourth and one-third" of the budget, says Lindsay Koshgarian, research director at the National Priorities Project, a nonpartisan research group in Northampton, Mass., that focuses on the federal budget. In fact, the $48.1 billion spent on aid in fiscal 2015 amounted to about 1.3 percent of the $3.7 trillion federal budget, according to the latest available data. [5]

Just over half of that aid went to anti-poverty and humanitarian programs, and nearly half was in the form of military and security-related assistance, much of it going to countries cooperating in the fight against terrorism. [6] (*See graph, p. 316.*)

Despite the minuscule portion of the federal budget consumed by foreign aid, fiscal hawks question whether it is wasted on inefficient programs. Meanwhile, some humanitarian-aid advocates worry about aid falling into the hands of dictators who use it to suppress their own people. And "America First" proponents such as Trump argue that domestic needs should take priority over causes in remote corners of the globe.

Sen. Rand Paul, R-Ky., is on the side of cuts. In 2015 he called for taking a "meat ax to foreign aid, because I think we ought to quit sending it to countries that hate us," Paul said in 2015. [7]

Development aid "for the most part is a waste," echoes Doug Bandow, a senior fellow at the Cato Institute, a libertarian think tank in Washington. "I don't think that economic development aid produces economic growth in poor countries."

However, aid proponents say bipartisan reforms enacted by Congress in the Foreign Aid Transparency and Accountability Act of 2016 have improved how aid projects are evaluated. "There's a great deal of confidence in USAID on the Republican side of the aisle as well as the Democratic side now," says J. Brian Atwood, administrator of USAID during the Clinton administration and now professor emeritus at the Humphrey School of Public Affairs at the University of Minnesota.

Where the Money Goes

The U.S. government spent $26.2 billion on anti-poverty and humanitarian programs in other countries in fiscal 2015, slightly more than half of the $48.1 billion appropriated for foreign aid, according to the latest available data. Military and security-related aid accounted for the rest — $21.9 billion, or 46 percent.

U.S. Foreign Aid, Fiscal 2015

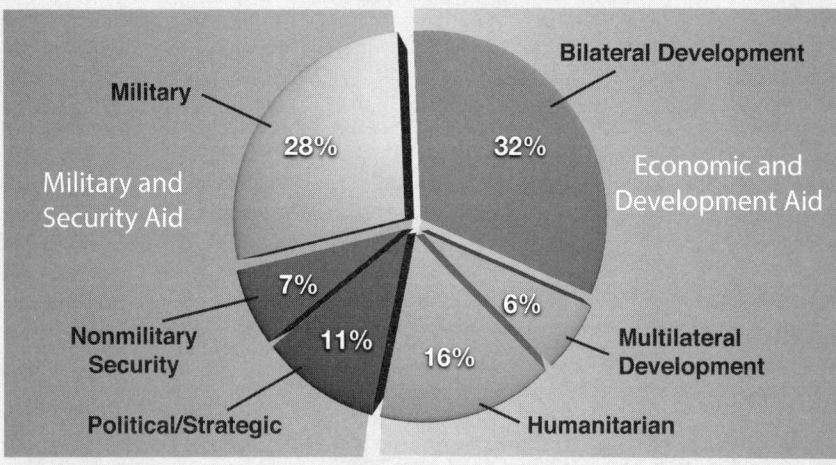

Military and Security Aid
- Military 28%
- Nonmilitary Security 7%
- Political/Strategic 11%

Economic and Development Aid
- Bilateral Development 32%
- Multilateral Development 6%
- Humanitarian 16%

Aid Programs and Amount Allocated in Fiscal 2015

Bilateral development: $15.8 billion. Funds programs promoting poverty reduction, sustainable agriculture, anti-HIV/AIDS efforts, private-sector development and good governance; funds the Peace Corps, Millennium Challenge Corp. and USAID operations.

Multilateral development: $2.8 billion. Funds U.S. share of UNICEF, U.N. Development Fund, World Bank and other multilateral development banks.

Humanitarian assistance: $7.6 billion. Provides disaster assistance and food aid; supports U.N. High Commissioner for Refugees and International Red Cross.

Political/Strategic: $5.4 billion. Promotes economic, political and security interests, particularly in countries important to U.S. counterterrorism strategy. A significant portion — 27 percent — supports Egypt, the West Bank and Jordan as part of the 1979 Middle East peace agreement known as the Camp David Accords.

Nonmilitary security: $3 billion. Supports efforts to counter illicit drugs, crime and weapons proliferation and to detect and dismantle terrorist financial networks.

Military: $13.5 billion. Provides military equipment, training and weapons to U.S. allies, primarily Israel, Egypt, Jordan, Pakistan and Iraq.

Source: Curt Tarnoff and Marian L. Lawson, "Foreign Aid: An Introduction to U.S. Programs and Policy," Congressional Research Service, June 17, 2016, p. 6, http://tinyurl.com/nymlqwz

Nevertheless, even some aid advocates agree a certain amount of assistance is wasted because of inefficiencies or corruption. "In some severe cases of systemic corruption, we have seen substantial portions of country budgets lost to waste, fraud and abuse, stalling and, in some cases, halting development progress altogether," USAID Administrator Gayle E. Smith told the Senate Foreign Relations Committee last June. [8] The solution, she said, is to support local watchdog groups that can hold governments, businesses and citizens accountable by monitoring public spending.

Indeed, according to a 2016 report by the Special Inspector General for Afghanistan Reconstruction, an independent office created by Congress, much of the more than $100 billion in aid provided to Afghanistan after the U.S. invasion of that country in 2001 was "subverted by systemic corruption [which] cut across all aspects of the reconstruction effort, jeopardizing progress made in security, rule of law, governance, and economic growth." [9]

John Sopko, the new agency's inspector general, blamed the flood of foreign assistance since 2001, inadequate oversight and "unsavory" partners for creating "endemic corruption" that posed an "existential threat" to the country. [10]

Both critics and advocates of foreign assistance also say the U.S. aid bureaucracy — with programs scattered across two dozen agencies — could be more efficient, with some suggesting consolidating all aid programs into fewer agencies, and others wanting to see more aid programs privatized.

"You want to have a unified approach to a country or region and not have the sorts of stove-piping and Balkanization that you might have with these independent power bases within the U.S. government," says James M. Roberts, a research fellow at the Heritage Foundation, a conservative think tank in Washington.

In an earlier effort to fight corruption and make foreign aid more efficient,

Republican President George W. Bush in 2004 created an independent agency — the Millennium Challenge Corp. (MCC) — to deliver development aid only to countries that meet stringent economic, political and social standards. That agency has produced mixed results. (*See sidebar, p. 324.*)

Other recent attempts to modernize and reform U.S. aid programs have been insufficient, says Roberts. "We are urging a complete top-down review of all forms of U.S. development assistance," as well as "a frank conversation" about priorities, he says.

Historically, national security has been a major objective of U.S. foreign aid. By supporting economic development in poor countries that might become targets — or breeding grounds — of terrorists, aid agencies "are critical to preventing conflict and reducing the need to put our men and women in uniform in harm's way," according to 121 retired three- and four-star flag and general officers who wrote to Congress protesting Trump's proposed foreign aid cuts. [11]

U.S. military aid since the Sept. 11, 2001, terrorist attacks has gone mostly to allies in the fight against Islamic extremism, such as Jordan, Pakistan and Afghanistan. Israel received the most military assistance in fiscal 2014 ($3.1 billion) and Egypt the second-largest amount ($1.3 billion), but those countries historically have received the bulk of U.S. military aid as a result of the Middle East peace settlement of 1978 known as the Camp David Accords. [12] (*See graph, above.*)

Providing aid to countries accused of suppressing human rights, such as Egypt, presents a moral dilemma for donors. Indeed, human rights advocates were dismayed when Trump welcomed Egyptian President Abdel Fattah el-Sissi to the White House on April 3 and reportedly promised to "maintain a strong and sufficient level of support to Egypt." [13] In 2013, the Obama administration suspended its

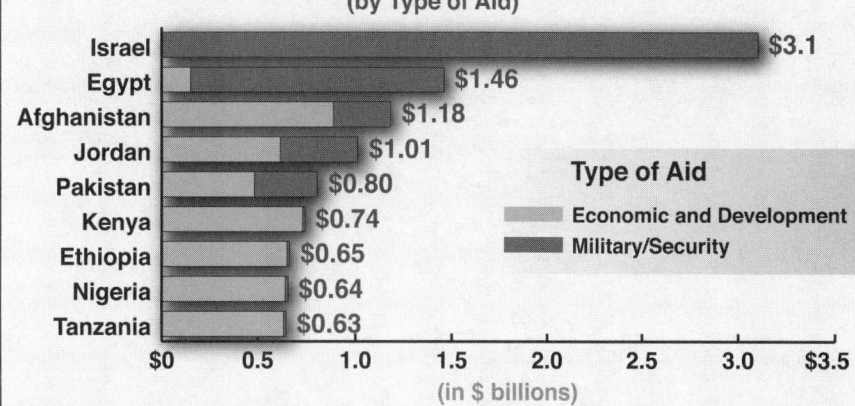

Top Aid Recipients: Israel, Egypt, Afghanistan

Israel received the most U.S. foreign aid, all of it in the form of weapons and military training, in fiscal 2015, according to the latest available data. Egypt, the second-largest aid recipient, received mostly military assistance. Afghanistan received the most economic and development aid.

Top U.S. Foreign Aid Recipients, Fiscal 2015
(by Type of Aid)

Israel	$3.1
Egypt	$1.46
Afghanistan	$1.18
Jordan	$1.01
Pakistan	$0.80
Kenya	$0.74
Ethiopia	$0.65
Nigeria	$0.64
Tanzania	$0.63

Type of Aid
■ Economic and Development
■ Military/Security

(in $ billions)

Source: "Congressional Budget Justification: Foreign Assistance," U.S. Department of State, Fiscal Year 2017, pp. 7-10, http://tinyurl.com/knrn6a2

$1.3 billion aid package after the Egyptian military ousted democratically elected President Mohamed Morsi and the Sissi-led government cracked down on domestic opponents and jailed dozens of Americans who were working at charities in Egypt. [14]

"Inviting [Sissi] for an official visit to Washington as tens of thousands of Egyptians rot in jail and when torture is again the order of the day is a strange way to build a stable strategic relationship," said Sarah Margon, Washington director at Human Rights Watch. [15] (*See sidebar, p. 326.*)

To gain support for foreign aid, proponents have long argued that aid helps expand markets for U.S. exports by improving receiving countries' economies so they can eventually buy U.S. products. In addition, some American aid is required to be in the form of U.S. products and services.

Trump's proposed budget cuts have given new urgency to a longstanding debate about whether attaching such

conditions to U.S. aid is wise. For instance, while a requirement that 50 percent of U.S. food aid be shipped on U.S.-flagged vessels supports the maritime industry, aid advocates say using such vessels is often costly and inefficient.

Others warn that tightening restrictions on aid may push recipients into closer relations with less-demanding donors, including economic rivals such as China. The Chinese, who generally do not require aid recipients to respect human rights or adopt free-market policies, have increased aid to Africa in recent years.

The renewed debate about the appropriate size and nature of U.S. foreign aid is playing out as more than 20 million people in Yemen and three other countries in Africa — South Sudan, Somalia and Nigeria — face starvation and famine. "We are facing the largest humanitarian crisis since the creation of the United Nations," Stephen O'Brien, the U.N.'s top official for humanitarian affairs, said in early March. [16] Others

U.S. Ranks 24th in Aid as Share of Wealth

The United States provided $30.8 billion in nonmilitary foreign aid in 2015, more than any other country. But it ranked 24th in the percentage of national wealth, or gross national income (GNI), allocated for such aid. Top-ranked Sweden donated 1.4 percent of its GNI and was among seven industrialized countries that reached the U.N. goal of donating at least 0.7 percent of GNI. The U.S. spent less than 0.2 percent, its lowest level since 2007.

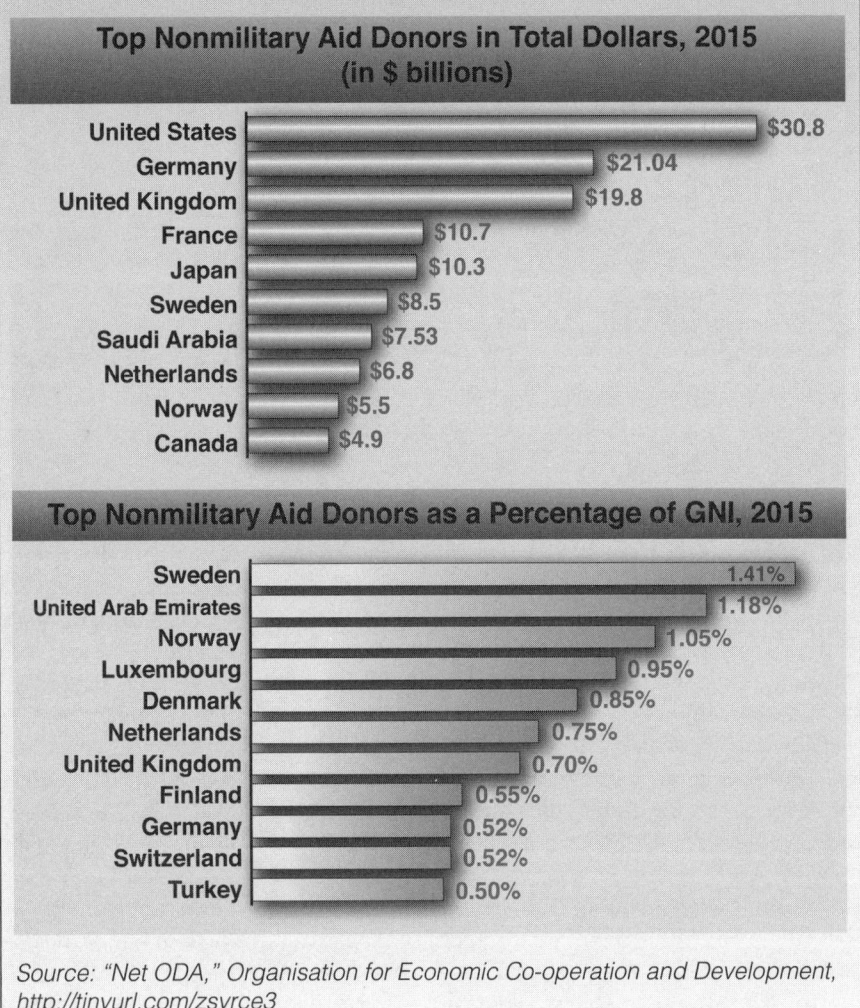

Top Nonmilitary Aid Donors in Total Dollars, 2015 (in $ billions)

- United States — $30.8
- Germany — $21.04
- United Kingdom — $19.8
- France — $10.7
- Japan — $10.3
- Sweden — $8.5
- Saudi Arabia — $7.53
- Netherlands — $6.8
- Norway — $5.5
- Canada — $4.9

Top Nonmilitary Aid Donors as a Percentage of GNI, 2015

- Sweden — 1.41%
- United Arab Emirates — 1.18%
- Norway — 1.05%
- Luxembourg — 0.95%
- Denmark — 0.85%
- Netherlands — 0.75%
- United Kingdom — 0.70%
- Finland — 0.55%
- Germany — 0.52%
- Switzerland — 0.52%
- Turkey — 0.50%

Source: "Net ODA," Organisation for Economic Co-operation and Development, http://tinyurl.com/zsvrce3

warn that in coming decades, as climate change begins to cause drought, floods and other damaging conditions, struggling countries' needs will increase even more.

As policy makers and politicians consider U.S. foreign aid policies, here are some of the questions they are asking:

Should the United States increase its economic aid to other countries?

The more than $30 billion in nonmilitary, or economic, aid contributed by the United States in 2015 was far more in total dollars than any other country donated. [17] But when viewed as a percentage of overall national wealth — or gross national income

(GNI) — the United States ranks 24th among the world's industrialized countries. (*See graph, left.*)

By donating less than 0.2 percent of its GNI in economic aid in 2015, the United States ranked far below the 0.7 percent goal set for wealthy countries by the United Nations in 1970. [18] In 2005, 15 of the 28 European Union countries committed to reaching that goal by 2015, and six succeeded: Luxembourg, Denmark, Norway, the Netherlands, the United Kingdom and Sweden, which donated the highest percentage (1.4 percent). [19] The United States never agreed to the 0.7 percent target but has said that while it did not subscribe to specific targets or timetables, it supported the general aims of the U.N. goal. [20]

"The U.S. does not invest enough in foreign assistance programs that help people living in extreme poverty around the world become self-sufficient," InterAction, an alliance of U.S.-based nongovernmental development organizations, said. "This approach is short-sighted and does not reflect American values." [21]

However, some critics of foreign aid argue that the United States should actually reduce — or even eliminate — its government-to-government development aid, which they say often does not generate economic growth and can hinder local development. "The best solution that I can offer is to move away from the government-to-government transfer model," says Ryan Young, a fellow at the Competitive Enterprise Institute, a free-market think tank in Washington. Young argues that free markets are better at generating economic growth than government-run programs.

Subsidizing governments may discourage them from adopting needed economic reforms, says the Cato Institute's Bandow. Instead of aid, "They need good policies, they need open markets."

Nobel Prize-winning British economist Angus Deaton argued in a 2013 book that development aid works only where it isn't needed. If a country already has the elements needed for development to occur, such as basic infrastructure, financial institutions and effective government, then aid isn't needed because capital will be available from taxes or investors, he wrote. But when poverty is the result of "poor institutions, poor government and toxic politics, giving money to poor countries — particularly giving money to the governments of poor countries — is likely to perpetuate [poverty], not eliminate it," wrote Deaton. [22]

He cited studies showing that when foreign aid to Africa reached its highest point during the Cold War, the economies of recipient countries grew more slowly than before or after the Cold War, when aid dropped. "Growth decreased steadily while aid increased steadily," Deaton wrote. "When aid fell off after the end of the Cold War, growth picked up." [23] The Cold War competition between the United States and the Soviet Union for global influence resulted in massive injections of foreign aid in some regions, especially in Africa and Latin America.

Others, however, say Deaton's arguments are outdated. According to Alex Thier, executive director of the Overseas Development Institute, an anti-poverty think tank in London, aid agencies have invested heavily in recent years in monitoring and evaluating development programs so that now "we actually see what works." Those new tools, he says, are "helping all of us to make sure that we are spending all of these resources better and more effectively."

Green, who worked at USAID for 11 years before joining CSIS, says Deaton's argument is "decades-old and doesn't reflect the sophistication in the science and the norms in the development community these days." While some development projects occasionally may be ineffective or even cause harm, she says, they are not the norm. "USAID and the other major bilateral donors are much more sophisticated, and [perform] an array of analyses to make sure that the project they're going to do will be beneficial in that environment," she says.

A 2016 report by the Congressional Research Service (CRS), the nonpartisan research arm of Congress, found that aid agencies have taken steps in recent years "to improve both the quantity and quality of aid evaluations, and to make better use of the information gleaned from those efforts." However, CRS said, determining the success or failure of previous aid programs "is not entirely clear," in part, because most aid programs in the past were not "evaluated for the purpose of determining their actual impact." [24]

USAID's Smith told Congress that instead of cutting or eliminating aid, the United States could better fight corruption by holding "governments, corporations, organizations and individuals to account through enforcement measures and by other means." [25]

Reducing foreign aid, some contend, also reduces America's economic influence in emerging markets, where other countries, such as China, are investing heavily in infrastructure and other development projects, especially in Africa.

According to Junyi Zhang, a U.S.-China policy exchange fellow at the Brookings Institution think tank in Washington, since launching a "Go Global" strategy of aid to developing countries in 2005, especially those with natural resources critical to China's economy, "China has deepened its financial engagement with the world, and its foreign aid totals have grown at an average rate of 21.8 percent annually." [26]

Does the United States attach too many conditions to its foreign aid?

Three days after his inauguration, President Trump reinstated a prohibition, instituted in 1984 during the administration of Republican Ronald Reagan, on U.S. foreign aid to groups that provide abortions or even discuss them as an option in family planning. [27]

U.S. foreign aid comes with many such conditions. Some ban aid to countries that violate human rights or require recipient countries to enact specific financial or business regulatory reforms. Other conditions, particularly in bilateral aid programs, require that food or other aid be provided by American companies or shipped on U.S.-flag vessels.

The anti-abortion condition is among the most controversial. It has been repeatedly rescinded by Democratic presidents and then reinstated by Republican presidents. (*See background, p. 326.*)

Human rights conditions, first imposed on U.S. aid by the 1961 Foreign Assistance Act, prohibit foreign aid to "the government of any country which engages in a consistent pattern of gross violations of internationally recognized human rights." [28]

But the law allows exceptions for "emergency conditions" and when compliance "would be seriously detrimental to the foreign policy interests of the United States." [29] Some critics have argued that since the Sept. 11, 2001, terrorist attacks on New York City and the Pentagon, the U.S. government has often exempted authoritarian countries, such as Egypt, from the human rights requirement because they cooperate in the U.S. fight against terrorism.

Some experts see little evidence that human rights conditions accomplish anything and argue that aid should be given where it is needed regardless of a government's human rights record. CSIS's Green, for instance, does not think humanitarian or "lifesaving health assistance should be conditioned," but that the United States "should do a better job leveraging assistance" to get recipient governments to honor human rights.

University of Chicago law professor Eric Posner has argued that Western human rights norms are the exception rather than the rule in many developing countries. He wrote that there is no reason to believe "institutionally enforced human rights . . . [are] appropriate for poor countries with different traditions and facing a range of challenges that belong, in the view of Western countries, to the distant past." Developed countries should provide aid, he wrote, "with the understanding that helping other countries is not the same as forcing them to adopt Western institutions, modes of governance, dispute-resolution systems and rights." [30]

Others warn that taking too strong a stance on human rights could make countries more inclined to seek aid

on human rights, it can worsen conditions for citizens in those countries, because of "China's tendency to facilitate authoritarianism and corruption," according to Zhang, at Brookings. [32]

Also controversial are the requirements that some U.S. aid be tied to the use of U.S. food and other products and services. Such conditions are designed to boost domestic support for foreign aid, experts say. They usually involve food aid and include requirements that:

But the U.S. maritime industry defends the so-called cargo preference requirement. "The government has said that cargo preference is key to maintaining and supporting the U.S. Merchant Marine," which provides sealift capability to the government during wartime and other emergencies, says Bryant Gardner, spokesman and counsel for Liberty Maritime Corp., a U.S. shipping company. Previous cuts in cargo preference requirements have led to a dangerous 26 percent decline in the merchant fleet since 2012, according to Gardner.

According to a 2010 study commissioned by USA Maritime, a coalition of cargo carriers, requirements that food aid be grown in the United States and that half must be shipped on U.S. carriers add approximately $2 billion a year to the U.S. economy. Dropping those requirements, according to the study, would cost between 16,000 and 33,000 U.S. jobs in agriculture and shipping. [34]

But two analysts at the American Enterprise Institute (AEI) think tank say vessels used to ship most food aid are too old and slow to be considered critical to the Defense Department. "Over the past five years," AEI researcher Ryan Nabil and visiting scholar Vincent H. Smith, wrote in 2016, "more than 80 percent of U.S. food aid carried under cargo preference has been shipped on vessels that the Department of Defense considers inappropriate for military purposes." [35]

Others say such preference conditions should be eliminated, or at least reduced, in favor of sending money to buy commodities locally, which USAID Administrator Smith says saves time and lives. [36]

"New research suggests that cash grants to the poor are as good as or better than many traditional forms of aid when it comes to reducing poverty," wrote Christopher Blattman, an assistant professor of international affairs at Columbia University, and Paul Niehaus, assistant professor of economics at the University of California, San Diego. Given the growing ease of transferring

Protesters in Washington denounce Egyptian President Abdel Fattah el-Sissi during his meeting with President Trump at the White House on April 3, 2017. Human-rights advocates criticized Trump's decision to continue providing more than $1 billion in mostly military aid to Egypt, which has been accused of suppressing human rights and is the second-largest recipient of U.S. aid. In 2013, the Obama administration temporarily suspended Egypt's aid package after the military ousted democratically elected President Mohamed Morsi and the Sissi-led government cracked down on domestic opponents.

AFP/Getty Images/Nicholas Kamm

from China, which generally does not impose human rights requirements on aid. However, China does tie its aid to the use of Chinese products and services, experts say, even to a much greater extent than the United States does.

"Chinese [aid] projects create access to Africa's natural resources and local markets, business opportunities for Chinese companies and employment for Chinese laborers," wrote Yun Sun, a fellow at the Brookings Institution. [31]

Ironically, when countries turn to China for aid to avoid U.S. demands

• All agricultural commodities come from the United States.

• At least 75 percent of nonemergency in-kind food aid be in processed, fortified or bagged form.

• At least 50 percent of food aid be shipped on U.S.-flag vessels. [33]

The Heritage Foundation's Roberts opposes requiring aid to be shipped on U.S. vessels. "If that sort of conditionality were eliminated, you could deliver a lot more food because you wouldn't waste so much money on logistics," he says.

cash via cellphones, they wrote, donors should view cash payments as "one of the most sensible tools of poverty alleviation." [37]

The tradeoff, some say, is between efficient delivery of aid and maintaining political support at home for foreign aid.

"It's really tricky, because those domestic requirements are the things that garner bipartisan support," says Green. "If you drop them, there's a real possibility that there would be less and less support domestically for international development, and it's already pretty low, to be honest. It's just one of those political trade-offs to maintain bipartisan domestic support."

Are public-private aid partnerships more effective than government-run projects?

U.S. aid agencies increasingly have been partnering with for-profit companies.

"In the late 1990s, we began to more proactively engage the private sector as true partners," Eric G. Postel, associate administrator at USAID, told senators at a hearing in July 2016. "This was an important shift." [38]

Under the Global Development Alliances program, established in 2001 to promote public-private partnerships, he said, the agency began to rely less on traditional client-vendor arrangements, with USAID consultants and contractors designing and implementing projects. Today, private companies increasingly design, manage and fund development projects.

"Today, as we partner more, we are focusing on those instances where business interests and development objectives align," Postel said. "When they don't align, we should not and do not pursue partnerships. And, as always, all of our partnerships adhere to all of the safeguards we have in place to protect against misuse of funds and other challenges." [39]

Over the past 15 years, USAID has created more than 1,500 partnership projects involving more than 3,500 pri-

vate-sector partners, according to Postel. The projects have ranged from the ongoing Advanced Maize Seed Adoption Program in Ethiopia, with a division of DuPont as the partner, to a garment-worker safety program in which two Bangladeshi banks are partnering with the Alliance for Bangladesh Worker Safety, an advocacy group. [40]

Another example, he said: USAID's Power Africa program, aimed at doubling access to electricity in sub-Saharan Africa, has received $7 billion in funds from the U.S. government and $31 billion from private-sector partners. [41]

Some experts agree public-private aid partnerships, which represent a growing part of U.S. foreign assistance, can effectively leverage funding and expertise for development projects. Public-private partnerships, however, give some analysts pause. Thier, of the Overseas Development Institute, sees the advantages of public-private partnerships, but he worries they may sometimes result in the realignment of aid programs in ways that benefit the partnering companies more than the recipients. Such partnerships may pull agencies toward projects that are "the cream of the crop," where the companies see the potential for profits. "What you really need to do is to make sure that your program is targeted toward the people that our aid dollars are intended to help, the poorest of the poor," Thier says. The goal of development, he adds, "is not just to get deals done and to bring in the private sector."

So far, he says, USAID partnerships have appeared to be crafted to minimize such concerns.

According to the Congressional Research Service, the public-private partnership model pioneered by USAID and adopted by the State Department and the Millennium Challenge Corp., the independent aid agency created at the behest of President Bush, involves other risks. Most partnerships require more time and effort to design and implement than traditional contract-

based programs and it is "difficult to judge whether this effort is justified by development impact," CRS said. [42]

In addition, it said, U.S. agencies could be damaged if they partner with disreputable private-sector entities. "Some development professionals are uneasy, for example, about USAID partnering with mining and oil companies in Angola, the Democratic Republic of the Congo and Ghana because of the corruption and exploitation often associated with these industries," according to CRS. It also warned that some public-private partnerships could support the outsourcing of American jobs to developing countries. [43]

However, others say partnerships could help steer aid to needy countries that are not particularly important in the fight against terrorism. Official development aid "tends to be skewed towards big strategic partners, . . . who aren't necessarily among the least developed countries, and [to] basket-case countries on the other," says CSIS's Green. Other countries get left out, she says. "That's where I think the private sector can help fill the gap."

But like Thier, Green warns that using public-private partnerships requires tight oversight. "So long as there really is a shared goal and there is a commitment to advancing that shared goal, they can be terrific," she says. "But you have to be careful." ■

BACKGROUND

Ancient Aid

Nations have employed foreign aid — in the form of economic subsidies, technical assistance and humanitarian aid — as a tool of diplomacy for more than 2,000 years.

As early as 336 B.C., Alexander the Great offered Egypt technical advisers to help build the port city of Alexandria. And the earliest recorded instance of humanitarian assistance took place when nations around the Mediterranean Sea in 226 B.C. sent food and other aid to the earthquake-devastated island of Rhodes. [44]

It wasn't until the mid-19th century, however, during the age of European imperialism, that some nations began systematically offering development aid to encourage economic growth in other countries, typically colonies of the donor

Greek children receive food made from flour distributed after World War II. Postwar concerns about the political stability of war-devastated countries in Europe, along with the threat of an increasingly aggressive Soviet Union, led the United States in 1947 to create the European Recovery Program. Better known as the Marshall Plan, it pumped $12.5 billion into Western Europe and helped put the continent on the road to recovery.

countries. Colonial powers such as Britain, France, Belgium, Holland and Germany provided grants and discounted loans to their colonies, protectorates and dependencies to expand infrastructure, develop health services and fund education, according to Louis A. Picard, a professor of public and international affairs at the University of Pittsburgh, and Terry F. Buss, a professor of public policy at Carnegie Mellon University in Pittsburgh.

In the late 1800s, the United States and other Western countries competed to provide technical advisers to developing countries, especially in Asia. The technical advisers were sent abroad,

Picard and Buss wrote, "as much to promote the donor country's products and equipment or its strategic interests as it was to provide assistance." [45]

Apart from technical support, U.S. aid efforts before the 1930s primarily were focused on humanitarian relief. During World War I, the United States contributed $387 million to the Commission for Relief in Belgium, founded by future President Herbert Hoover. [46] In 1917, as the United States entered the war, Hoover was appointed director of the U.S. Food Administration, an agency tasked with providing food for the U.S. Army and allies in Europe. In 1919, Congress created the American Relief Administration, also directed by Hoover, to coordinate the delivery of relief supplies to war-torn Europe. [47]

Federal humanitarian aid efforts in this period were supplemented — and in some cases dwarfed — by aid from private foundations, notably the Ford, Rockefeller and Carnegie foundations, and from religious organizations, such as the American Friends Service Committee.

Partly to deter growing Nazi influence in the Western Hemisphere, the United

States began to offer development aid in the 1930s, primarily to Latin American countries. [48]

Marshall Plan

Foreign aid became a consistent, ongoing element of U.S. foreign policy beginning with the Lend-Lease Act of 1941, which provided military and other aid to cash-strapped Britain as it struggled to fend off German aggression at the start of World War II. With the British unable to pay for ships and supplies, the United States "lent" them the matériel under the Lend-Lease Act.

It was understood, according to a State Department historian, that eventual repayment would not be in dollars but "would primarily take the form of a 'consideration' granted by Britain to the United States." After many months of negotiation, the two countries agreed that this consideration "would primarily consist of joint action directed towards the creation of a liberalized international economic order in the postwar world." [49] Eventually, Lend-Lease was extended to other allies, including Free France, China and the Soviet Union.

After the war, concerns about the political stability of war-devastated countries in Europe, along with the threat of an increasingly aggressive Soviet Union, led the United States in 1947 to create the European Recovery Program, also known as the Marshall Plan. Named after Secretary of State and former chairman of the Joint Chiefs Gen. George C. Marshall, the plan pumped $12.5 billion into Western Europe to help rebuild the economy and was at that time by far the largest development aid package ever undertaken by the United States. [50]

As the Cold War got underway between the communist Soviet Union and the democracies of the West, the administration of Democratic President Harry S. Truman saw foreign assistance

Continued on p. 324

Chronology

1850-1930s
Foreign aid takes root in the West.

1850
European colonial powers, including Britain, France, Belgium, Holland and Germany, begin to provide financial assistance to their colonies, protectorates and dependencies.

1914-1919
The United States contributes $387 million to the Commission for Relief in Belgium, an aid organization founded by future U.S. president Herbert Hoover to help Belgium and northern France during World War I. After America enters the war, Hoover directs the U.S. Food Administration, which provides food to the U.S. Army and allies in Europe. . . . After the war, Congress creates American Relief Administration, also directed by Hoover, to coordinate the delivery of aid to war-torn Europe.

1930
U.S. begins offering development aid, primarily to Latin American countries, to deter growing Nazi influence in the Western Hemisphere.

1941-1960s
United States uses aid to counter Nazi and, later, Soviet influence.

1941
Under the Lend-Lease Act, a still-neutral United States "lends" military and other supplies to the British during World War II, a program later extended to Free France, China and the Soviet Union.

1947
Concerned about postwar stability in Europe, the United States pumps $12.5 billion into the Western European economy under the Marshall Plan. . . . As part of the Truman Doctrine — an effort to curtail Soviet geopolitical expansion — Congress approves $400 million in aid for Greece and Turkey.

1961
President John F. Kennedy signs the Foreign Assistance Act, which aims to help further economic, political and social development in underdeveloped countries and creates the U.S. Agency for International Development (USAID) to disburse most U.S. aid.

1980s-1990s
U.S. aid focuses on helping developing countries restructure their economies to be more market-oriented.

1981
President Ronald Reagan announces the Private Enterprise Initiative, an aid program that aims to boost private enterprise in developing countries.

1984
Reagan administration halts aid to overseas health providers who discuss or provide abortions as an option in family planning, a controversial condition that will be attached to U.S. aid — or rescinded — by successive administrations.

1993
President Bill Clinton rescinds Reagan ban on aid for abortion providers and counselors.

1997
The Clinton administration responds to congressional calls to restructure or abolish USAID by

requiring the agency's director to report to the secretary of State.

2001-Present
Foreign aid after 9/11 focuses on countries helping to fight the war on terrorism.

2001
President George W. Bush reverses Clinton aid abortion policy . . . . U.S. government increases foreign aid in the aftermath of the Sept. 11 terrorist attacks. Aid to Afghanistan and Pakistan, in particular, soars from $70 million and $45.7 million annually, respectively, to $4.7 billion and $1.9 billion by 2010.

2004
Congress creates the Millennium Challenge Corp., an independent aid agency that awards grants to developing countries that meet economic and political criteria.

2005
The Bush administration begins a series of foreign aid reforms; USAID is required to improve staff training and institute annual evaluations for aid programs.

2006
Secretary of State Condoleezza Rice creates Office of Foreign Assistance Resources within the State Department.

2016
Congress passes the Foreign Aid Transparency and Accountability Act of 2016, which requires stronger monitoring and reporting of foreign aid effectiveness.

2017
President Trump's administration announces plans to cut USAID's budget by nearly 30 percent.

Millennium Challenge Corp. Pushes Countries to Reform

Agency "only works in a fairly narrow range of countries," critics say.

Its admirers call it "the MCC effect" — how the Millennium Challenge Corp. (MCC), a federal agency that distributes anti-poverty aid, pushes recipient countries to govern themselves responsibly and transparently.

On its first bid for aid, Cote d'Ivoire passed only three of 20 MCC "scorecard indicators," or political, economic and social benchmarks showing that a country is committed to "just and democratic governance, investments in its people and economic freedom." [1] But five years later, the West African nation received an MCC grant after meeting 13 indicators.

"MCC's scorecard and global brand have created a powerful incentive for countries to undertake reforms to achieve eligibility," Dana J. Hyde, then MCC's chief executive officer, told Congress in March 2016. [2]

But critics say the agency is underfunded and limited in scope. "MCC only works in a fairly narrow range of countries," says Steven Koltai, former State Department entrepreneurship director, and most of those are not, from a foreign policy standpoint, where U.S. aid can have the most impact.

The MCC has signed 33 compacts with 27 countries, most of them in Africa, worth more than $11 billion, according to Laura M. Allen, press secretary for the MCC Office of Congressional and Public Affairs. Recipient countries must be classified as low income or lower middle income by the World Bank. In fiscal 2017, a country's per capita gross national income must be below $4,035, according to Allen.

Created by Congress in 2004 at the urging of President George W. Bush, the MCC emerged from post-9/11 concerns about terrorist groups forming in Africa. In 2002, Bush announced he wanted to increase U.S. foreign aid by 15 percent a year, with much of the increase directed to Africa. Republican lawmakers, however, worried that corrupt African governments would swallow up much of the money. [3]

Bush responded by creating the MCC, an independent entity operating separate from the traditional foreign aid community, which established a set of "good governance" criteria that countries would have to meet before they would get any grants. "Money will now be given to countries that have shown a willingness to establish an environment where foreign aid will be most effective," Joshua Bolten, director of the Office of Management and Budget under Bush, said at the time. [4]

Governed by a board that includes the secretaries of State and Treasury, the U.S. Trade Representative and the administrator of the U.S. Agency for International Development (USAID), the MCC offers two types of grants: large, five-year grants, called compacts, for countries that meet the MCC's eligibility benchmarks; and smaller grants for countries on the threshold of meeting those criteria.

Besides meeting MCC's eligibility requirements, countries must establish priorities for achieving sustainable economic growth and poverty reduction. [5] Moreover, recipients must demonstrate "rigorous and transparent" monitoring of funds. "Many countries view their ability to perform well on MCC's scorecard as a seal of approval, signaling to their citizens and to the private sector that the country is well-governed and open for business," says Allen.

Still, the MCC has struggled with lower-than-expected funding and questions about its effectiveness.

At its founding, the MCC was expected within a few years to be funded at $5 billion annually, according to the Congressional Research Service (CRS), the nonpartisan research arm of Congress. "For a variety of reasons, not least of which is the limitation on available funding for foreign aid more broadly, the MCC never achieved anywhere near that level of funding," the CRS said. "In fact, in most years since the MCC was established, its enacted appropriation has been below the president's request."

Continued from p. 322

as a tool. "It must be the policy of the United States to support free people who are resisting attempted subjugation by armed minorities or by outside pressures," Truman told Congress on March 12, 1947, when he announced a policy of Soviet "containment" that came to be known as the Truman Doctrine. "I believe that our help should be primarily through economic and financial aid, which is essential to economic stability and orderly political processes." [51]

Meanwhile, at Truman's request Congress provided $400 million in aid for Greece and Turkey, countries with sig-

nificant domestic unrest attributed in part to communist political parties.

During the Cold War, wrote Picard and Buss, foreign aid was "at least nominally premised on the thesis that economic and social development, and democratic government, [were] essential to national security." [52]

On Nov. 3, 1961, at the height of the Cold War, Democratic President John F. Kennedy signed the Foreign Assistance Act, which created an array of programs and long-term goals aimed at the economic, political and social development of underdeveloped countries. "The Congress declares that the individual liberties,

economic prosperity, and security of the people of the United States are best sustained and enhanced in a community of nations which respect individual civil and economic rights and freedoms," the legislation said. [53]

The law also created the U.S. Agency for International Development to oversee most of the country's bilateral development and humanitarian aid programs.

However, during the Vietnam War, some policymakers grew concerned that military priorities were skewing aid priorities. [54] In 1965, approximately 90 percent of USAID's aid budget went to military forces and intelligence ser-

Only $901 million was appropriated in 2016; $1 billion was requested for 2017. [6]

CRS said questions had been raised about the sustainability of some MCC projects. In the West African island nation of Cape Verde, a road project reportedly met only half of its requirements for maintenance funds, and Honduras did not increase its national road maintenance funds sufficiently, CRS said.

The lure of MCC funding apparently was not enough to bring Sierra Leone and Benin in conformance with the agency's anti-corruption requirements. The MCC dropped both countries from consideration for grants in 2013 for failing to satisfy the "control of corruption" indicator. [7]

James Roberts, research fellow at the conservative Heritage Foundation think tank, originally supported the MCC, arguing in 2009 that the federal government should shift aid funds from USAID to the agency. [8] "We were enthusiastic in the beginning," he says, especially because of its anti-corruption standards. "It forced country ownership, country accountability."

But as the MCC has evolved, "it kind of went the way of all flesh," he says. "You ended up with a lot of bureaucrats running it and . . . during the Obama years it kind of morphed into a mini-USAID. That was not what conservative thinkers behind it had in mind."

Alicia Phillips Mandaville, vice president for global development policy and learning at InterAction, an association of U.S.-based nongovernmental aid organizations, disagrees with Roberts' assessment. The MCC model has been and continues to be very effective, she says.

"Countries come in and look at that scorecard and talk with MCC about whether they've met those criteria or not," says Mandaville, a former MCC chief strategy officer. "A number of countries really put in serious policy reforms in an effort to

Jordanian Foreign Minister Nasser Judeh meets with then Secretary of State Hillary Clinton during a signing ceremony for an agreement to fund an anti-poverty program in Jordan through a Millennium Development Corp. grant.

become eligible to work with MCC." In fact, Benin, one of the countries turned away by the MCC in 2013, did subsequently institute reforms that resulted in the MCC awarding a compact to Benin in 2015 with the signing of a $375 million grant to develop its energy sector.

— *Patrick Marshall*

[1] "Who We Fund," Millennium Challenge Corp., http://tinyurl.com/ly9vd4w.
[2] "Testimony of Dana J. Hyde before the House Committee on Foreign Affairs," U.S. House of Representatives, March 15, 2016, http://tinyurl.com/mtp946g.
[3] Elizabeth Becker, "With Record Rise in Foreign Aid Comes Change in How It Is Monitored," *The New York Times*, Dec. 7, 2003, http://tinyurl.com/n2jjchj.
[4] *Ibid.*
[5] "About MCC," Millennium Challenge Corp., http://tinyurl.com/khrkdzs.
[6] Curt Tarnoff, "Millennium Challenge Corporation," Congressional Research Service, Jan. 11, 2017, p. 19, http://tinyurl.com/lfesl39; http://tinyurl.com/k4qxl53.
[7] "MCC Board Selects Countries Eligible for Compacts and Threshold Programs," press release, Millennium Challenge Corp., Dec. 10, 2013, http://tinyurl.com/myu5dog.
[8] James Roberts, "Foreign Aid: Congress Should Shift USAID Funds to the Millennium Challenge Account," The Heritage Foundation, Aug. 4, 2009, http://tinyurl.com/k3oad45.

vices in Vietnam and only a fraction went to Vietnam's industrial or agricultural development. [55]

In December 1962, Kennedy appointed Gen. Lucius D. Clay to lead a committee to assess the effectiveness of U.S. foreign aid programs. The so-called Clay report raised crucial questions about the effectiveness of foreign aid, leading to increased focus on market economics, wrote Picard and Buss. To some observers, the report also created frustration about foreign aid that would later be dubbed "donor fatigue," they added. [56]

Frustrations with aid programs and concerns over the mounting costs of the

Vietnam War made Congress increasingly reluctant to fund aid programs. In 1971, U.S. development aid dropped below $3 billion for the first time since passage of the Foreign Assistance Act in 1961.

The steadily dropping American aid in the 1960s and early '70s troubled many. Unless the United States substantially increased its contribution, its global aid efforts could fail, "triggering a confrontation with poor nations that could make the Cold War pale in comparison," *New York Times* reporter Felix Belair Jr. wrote in 1971. [57]

But the warning went unheeded, and U.S. development and humanitarian

aid dropped further in the 1970s and '80s. USAID funding would not reach its 1965 level of $12.8 billion (in 2015 dollars) again until 2002. [58]

"Structural Adjustment"

In the 1980s, U.S.-led multilateral institutions such as the World Bank and International Monetary Fund pushed policies of "structural adjustment," or requiring aid recipients to adopt market-based economic reforms to enhance the role of private enterprise over that of local governments. The

Corrupt Governments Pose Donor Dilemma

"Cuts to aid disproportionately hurt people living in poverty."

From Nigeria to Syria and beyond, aid donors face an excruciating question: Is their aid helping or hurting people living under corrupt or repressive regimes?

One side argues foreign aid props up corrupt governments and ultimately harms those it is intended to help. Others say cutting off assistance disproportionately hurts those in need.

For instance, in the Syrian civil war, some observers say, the regime of strongman Bashar al Assad has forced aid agencies to choose the lesser of two evils: Don't give any aid, or give it to President Assad, who distributes it to civilians in "friendly" areas rather than to those in besieged rebel areas.

Between Jan. 1 and Aug. 31, 2015, U.N. humanitarian health assistance reached only about 4 percent of Syrian civilians in embattled areas each month, wrote physician and health activist Annie Sparrow, an assistant professor at the Icahn School of Medicine in New York City. The agencies were even less successful in getting food and other items — such as tents, blankets and soap — to those in need, she said. Because the Syrian government controls most aid coming into the country, she wrote, "the main effect is to relieve the government of responsibility for caring for its own citizens, freeing up resources for it to pursue its military strategy of targeting civilians in politically unsympathetic areas." [1]

Sparrow said aid agencies' rationale that any aid delivered through the Assad regime is better than none "has not been weighed against the human and financial cost of bolstering a regime that is deliberately increasing the hardship of people in opposition-held areas." [2]

David Saldivar, a policy and advocacy manager at Oxfam America, an international anti-poverty organization, says it is "a real challenge" to find a proper balance, but his organization comes down on the side of getting aid to those who are suffering. "You can make a morally defensible assessment that [this] is, on balance, doing good for those people versus harming them by propping up a government that's hostile to people's rights," he says.

Like Syria, Nigeria, a nation of about 190 million on Africa's west-central coast, poses great challenges for donors. "Corruption in Nigeria is endemic — from parents bribing teachers to get hold of exam papers for their children through clerks handed 'dash' money to get round the country's stifling bureaucracy to policemen taking money for turning a blind eye," wrote British historian Michael Burleigh. Since gaining independence in 1960, he said, Nigeria has received $400 billion in aid — "six times what the U.S. pumped into reconstructing the whole of Western Europe after World War II." [3]

Meanwhile, nearly the same amount — $380 billion — has been diverted by corruption, according to Burleigh. "Given the appalling levels of corruption in that nation, this largesse is utterly sickening,"

Reagan administration pursued similar policies in American bilateral aid.

The Private Enterprise Initiative, begun under Reagan in 1981, focused on improving the policy environment for private enterprise in developing countries. Beginning in 1989, the initiative established several enterprise funds, which invested USAID money in small and medium-sized private businesses, initially in Central and Eastern Europe. The goal, according to a CRS report, was to spur "private-sector development in countries transitioning toward market-based economies." [59]

The kind of single-minded reliance on structural adjustment popular under the Reagan administration would be abandoned in the 1990s as an increasing number of studies showed that free-market policies were not effective under the conditions present in most developing countries.

Besides pursuing market-based economic reforms, the Reagan administration sought to enforce the values of its conservative and religious supporters. In 1984, the administration announced it would no longer provide aid to overseas groups that performed abortions or that counseled abortion as a method of birth control. The policy became a political football: Democratic President Bill Clinton reversed the policy in 1993; Republican George W. Bush reinstated it in 2001; Democrat Barack Obama reversed it in 2009; and Republican Trump reinstated it in 2017 as one of the first acts of his presidency. [60]

In the 1990s, policymakers increasingly worried that aid was being poorly coordinated and lacked sufficient monitoring. "Many U.S. departments and agencies had adopted their own assistance programs, funded out of their own budgets and commonly in the

form of professional exchanges with counterpart agencies abroad — the Environmental Protection Agency, for example, providing water quality expertise to other governments," wrote Congressional Research Service analysts Curt Tarnoff and Marian Lawson. [61]

USAID came under the most scrutiny. "Many observers believe that, for more than a decade, USAID neglected its evaluation processes and capacities," wrote Tarnoff. In 1995, in an attempt to better focus its monitoring and evaluation resources, the agency decided to permit senior managers to determine which programs needed more oversight, rather than requiring evaluations of all programs. According to Tarnoff, "While the intention was to eliminate pro-forma evaluations, it apparently did not have this effect." [62]

In April 1997 the Clinton administration responded to congressional calls to restructure or abolish USAID by re-he concluded. "Frankly, we might as well flush our cash away or burn it for all the good it's doing for ordinary Nigerians."[4]

Some analysts say critics are vastly exaggerating the amount of aid lost to corruption. According to a United Nations study, only 0.006 percent to 0.16 percent of six donors' aid money (given collectively) was lost to fraud or corruption in 2011.[5]

A 2015 Oxfam report said aid organizations can do several things to reduce losses to corruption, including "nurturing a country's domestic accountability system" and support local approaches that affect "the root causes of corruption."[6] The report also advised donors against automatically cutting off aid in response to corruption.

"There is no evidence that cutting off aid to a country with deteriorating governance conditions has any long-term effect on reducing corruption or increasing accountability," the report said. "Cuts to aid disproportionately hurt people living in poverty, who are already experiencing the brunt of the effects of corruption, while having little impact on the power or comfort of corrupt elites."[7]

— Patrick Marshall

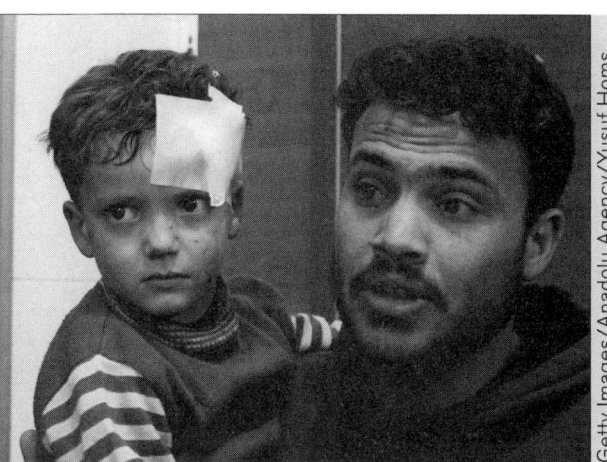

A Syrian child wounded during an air strike is comforted at a Damascus-area hospital on April 4, 2017. The Syrian civil war has forced aid agencies to choose between not giving any aid or giving it to President Bashar al Assad, who distributes it in "friendly" areas rather than in besieged rebel areas.

[1] Annie Sparrow, "Aiding Disaster: How the United Nations' OCHA Helped Assad and Hurt Syrians in Need," *Foreign Affairs*, Feb. 1, 2016, http://tinyurl.com/lgssous.
[2] *Ibid.*
[3] Michael Burleigh, "A country so corrupt is would be better to burn our aid money," *The Daily Mail*, Aug. 8, 2013, http://tinyurl.com/nxfgz8v.
[4] *Ibid.*
[5] Paul Farmer, "Rethinking Foreign Aid: Five Ways to Improve Development Assistance," Foreign Affairs, Dec. 12, 2013, http://tinyurl.com/m6wuh4x. The six donors were Australia, Belgium, Denmark, the European Commission, the United Kingdom and the United States.
[6] Jennifer Lentfer, "4 new ways to think about foreign aid's role in fighting corruption around the world," Oxfam America, March 25, 2015, http://tinyurl.com/lfgpm2a.
[7] *Ibid.*

quiring the agency director to report to the secretary of State, even though USAID would continue to remain an independent agency with its own appropriations.[63]

The terrorist attacks on the World Trade Center and the Pentagon on Sept. 11, 2001, were a turning point for U.S. foreign aid.[64] The United States immediately boosted aid to two countries considered hotspots in what the Bush administration was calling a war on terrorism: Afghanistan and Pakistan.

Economic aid to Pakistan soared from $45.7 million in 2001 to $1.9 billion in 2010.[65] Afghanistan's economic aid jumped from $70 million in 2000 to $4.7 billion in 2010.[66]

With such huge increases, the Bush administration undertook a series of foreign aid reforms, particularly at USAID. In 2005, the agency began an Initiative to Revitalize Evaluation, which included

expanded staff training and requirements for annual evaluations.[67] A year later, Secretary of State Condoleezza Rice brought the agency more firmly under State Department control and made the director of USAID the director of foreign assistance within the State Department.

"The moves eased fears at USAID that the agency, set up in 1961 under President John F. Kennedy, would be merged into the State Department," wrote *The Washington Post*. "But it prompted other worries, . . . that USAID's strategic planning role might end up diminished and that the agency's corps of experienced foreign aid specialists might be superseded by Foreign Service officers."[68]

The Bush administration also undertook two programs that would have a lasting impact on foreign aid. In his 2003 State of the Union address, President Bush called for a five-year, $15 billion

program to combat AIDS in 15 countries, 12 of which were in Africa. Called the President's Emergency Plan for AIDS Relief, or PEPFAR, the project remains the largest-ever global health initiative dedicated to a single disease.[69]

Also at Bush's request, Congress in 2004 created the Millennium Challenge Corp., an independent agency that provides aid only to countries that meet specified economic, political and social conditions. President Obama continued support for PEPFAR and the MCC.

Questions about the massive amounts of aid that went to Afghanistan after 9/11 were raised in 2014, when the Office of the Special Inspector General for Afghanistan Reconstruction charged that USAID had "covered up information" that some aid funds delivered to the Afghan government couldn't be accounted for and may have gone to terrorist groups. USAID denied the charge.[70]

Obama sponsored two major aid efforts. He signed into law the Electrify Africa Act of 2015, a partnership with African governments, multilateral development organizations and private-sector companies that aims to deliver electricity to at least 50 million people by 2020. [71] And in 2016, Obama signed the Global Food Security Act, which allocated more than $7 billion to promote agriculture, small-scale food producers and nutrition for women and children worldwide. [72]

Congress produced a significant piece of bipartisanship foreign aid legislation in 2016. The Foreign Aid Transparency and Accountability Act, sponsored by two Republicans and two Democrats, requires agencies to closely monitor and evaluate the effectiveness of all aid programs and to make that data public. [73] ∎

CURRENT SITUATION

Hunger Crisis

On March 7, while visiting Somalia, U.N. Secretary General António Guterres appealed to the global donor community for $825 million in immediate aid to the East Africa nation, which is on the brink of famine because of drought and an insurgency by Islamic extremists. Guterres said half of Somalia's population of 11 million may not survive six months without the aid. [74]

In addition to Somalia, two other African countries and Yemen are suffering from food shortages stemming from drought and conflict, putting some 20 million people at risk of famine. Those are Nigeria, where the Islamic extremist group Boko Haram has been attacking villages and killing residents for years; South Sudan, struggling with both a drought and civil war; and Yemen, which has been riven by civil war since 2011. [75]

The U.N. requested a total of $4.4 billion in aid for the four countries. [76] Last year, the United States provided approximately 28 percent of that aid. "Nobody can replace the U.S. in terms of funding," Yves Daccord, the director general of the International Committee of the Red Cross (ICRC), told *The Washington Post*. [77]

The Trump administration thus far has not responded publicly to the U.N. request for emergency aid. [78]

Congress also has said little about the hunger crisis, but Sens. Rubio and Graham have criticized Trump's proposal to cut foreign aid, with Graham giving it little chance of passage in the Senate. [79]

"U.S. foreign assistance priorities have been remarkably bipartisan for the last decade, with investments for reducing HIV/AIDS and malaria, increasing food security, energizing Africa and stabilizing Afghanistan getting consistent support on both sides of the aisle," according to the Overseas Development Institute's Thier. "Foreign aid is also something conservatives frequently decry when they don't control it, and see as a vital tool when they do." [80]

Only two foreign aid bills — both of which focus on delivering specific types of aid — passed either chamber of Congress last session. The Digital Gap Act, introduced by Rep. Edward Royce, R-Calif., aims to promote Internet access in developing countries. It passed the House on Sept. 7, 2016, but died in the Senate. It was reintroduced and passed again in January and is pending in the Senate Foreign Relations Committee.

The Reinforcing Education Accountability in Development Act, which passed the House on Jan. 24, is also pending before the Senate Foreign Relations Committee. Sponsored by Rep. Nita Lowey, D-N.Y., it would improve the transparency and reach of basic education programs managed by U.S. aid agencies. No hearings have been scheduled for either bill.

Another bill, the Criminal Alien Deportation Enforcement Act introduced by Rep. Brian Babin, R-Texas, would require the United States to suspend foreign aid and travel visa privileges for countries that refuse to accept their citizens when the United States tries to deport them.

"The problem is hundreds of Americans are being robbed, assaulted, raped or murdered every year by criminal aliens who are then released back onto the streets because their countries of origins refuse to take them back," Babin claimed. "I have personally met with a number of these victims, or if the victim is deceased, I have met with their families. It is heart-wrenching." [81]

However, the bill, which is being reviewed by the House Judiciary Committee, is given only a 4 percent chance of being enacted by GovTrack, an independent company that monitors federal legislation. [82]

Reform Recommendations

Talk of budget cuts and inefficiencies in foreign aid has highlighted proposals for reorganizing how American aid is administered.

Currently, foreign aid is administered through USAID and more than 20 other agencies and departments, including Defense, Energy, Health and Human Services, Interior, State and Treasury. [83]

Thier, of the Overseas Development Institute, says the problem goes beyond the mere number of agencies. "In trying to do a lot of different things we spread ourselves too thinly," he says. "I think that having a focused and strategic program that does fewer things well in a lot of our partner countries is going to yield better outcomes than having a lot of different parts of the government working on a lot of different things."

The Heritage Foundation's Roberts says the scattered nature of the aid bureaucracy has been problematic for years. To "focus and prioritize scarce resources," Roberts favors fully integrating USAID into the State Department, "desk officer

Continued on p. 330

At Issue:

Should USAID be the primary manager of U.S. development aid?

ALEX THIER
EXECUTIVE DIRECTOR,
OVERSEAS DEVELOPMENT INSTITUTE

WRITTEN FOR *CQ RESEARCHER*, APRIL 2017

*t*he U.S. government has 24 departments and agencies that manage foreign assistance. USAID, the largest, with a 54-year track record, has a deep bench of expertise, tools and evidence to guide what it does.

However, other agencies have unique mandates and perspectives that can make them a critical part of the development portfolio. The Overseas Private Investment Corp. for example, provides access to credit and financial analysis for potential investors. The Millennium Challenge Corp. has flexibility to deliver funds for infrastructure and other needs.

When these agencies are aligned around a common agenda and working together, the impact can be powerful. This was true for former President Barack Obama's Power Africa initiative, which brought together many agencies and private-sector partners into a tight circle to get things done.

The various streams of assistance, however, are often not well coordinated. When agencies have separate authorities and budgets, they tend to use them separately. Their leaders have different objectives, and the effort to bring those objectives, timing and systems together in Washington or on the ground can be very challenging.

So how can things be done better? In the last few years, USAID has invested heavily in people, innovation and evidence. Today, it has some of the most creative, rigorous tools to leverage outside resources and deliver results of any aid agency in the world. We know this because USAID subjects its work to intensive evaluation and publishes all the evidence — good, bad and otherwise. This transparency pushes accountability and performance in a virtuous cycle.

We also know this because recent independent assessments from places such as the Organisation for Economic Co-operation and Development and Results for America gave very high ratings to USAID for its evidence-based decision-making. Finally — and most important — we know this because millions of people have demonstrably benefited from the increased access to food, health, education and electricity that USAID programs have supported.

Given this record of success and the level of investment it took to get there, U.S. taxpayers would get even more bang for their buck if more of the foreign assistance and creative financing tools were housed within USAID.

This is especially true since foreign aid work increasingly is taking place in fragile states, where an in-country presence, understanding of political dynamics and long-term relationships can be key to getting things done.

RETIRED ADM. JAMES G. STAVRIDIS
DEAN, FLETCHER SCHOOL,
TUFTS UNIVERSITY; AND
STEVEN R. KOLTAI
FORMER SENIOR ADVISER FOR
ENTREPRENEURSHIP,
U.S. DEPARTMENT OF STATE

WRITTEN FOR *CQ RESEARCHER*, APRIL 2017

*u*SAID and its contractor-centric development projects are not delivering the local jobs needed to deter violent extremism and grow economies. With America's foreign policy — and especially foreign aid as expressed through USAID — seemingly about to go through a "redo," there is an opportunity to reconfigure USAID, the Department of State and some related agencies.

Coincidentally, America has a new "Entrepreneur-in-Chief," President Trump, so this is a doubly auspicious moment to leverage that know-how against the single biggest driver of international instability — joblessness. Nothing creates more jobs than entrepreneurship. We can make entrepreneurship promotion a pillar of U.S. foreign development policy and make America safer.

Supporting entrepreneurship not only uses America's soft power in today's world but also generates economic opportunities for U.S. businesses and investors. Creating consumers for U.S. products and investment opportunities for America's companies are important additional benefits to an entrepreneurship-focused foreign development policy.

The Overseas Private Investment Corp. (OPIC) — the perfect place to house this effort — would not require new federal funding. Here are the key elements of the plan:

• Consolidate people and dollars from the 20-plus offices involved in international entrepreneurship development.

• Coordinate funding for multilateral development agencies, such as the World Bank, to get them to pursue more entrepreneurship development.

• Put OPIC on equal footing with other Western development finance agencies (i.e., trading competitors) and authorize it to take minority, direct equity stakes in equity funds.

• Lastly, create a Peace Corps for Entrepreneurship that attracts experienced American entrepreneurs and early-stage investors, a great many of whom are from some of the very countries in which we need to spur entrepreneurship. This program would be administered by private-sector development organizations but staffed with experienced people working on short-term contracts (six months to two years).

The president sees himself as an "entrepreneur par excellence." As Trump takes the helm, it may be the best chance yet to put entrepreneurship in the service of foreign policy.

Continued from p. 328

by desk officer, really ending the agency's independent role."

USAID was created as fully independent, but in 2006 the Bush administration, seeking to align aid more directly with U.S. foreign policy, brought the agency more firmly under State Department control by having the USAID director report to the secretary of State.

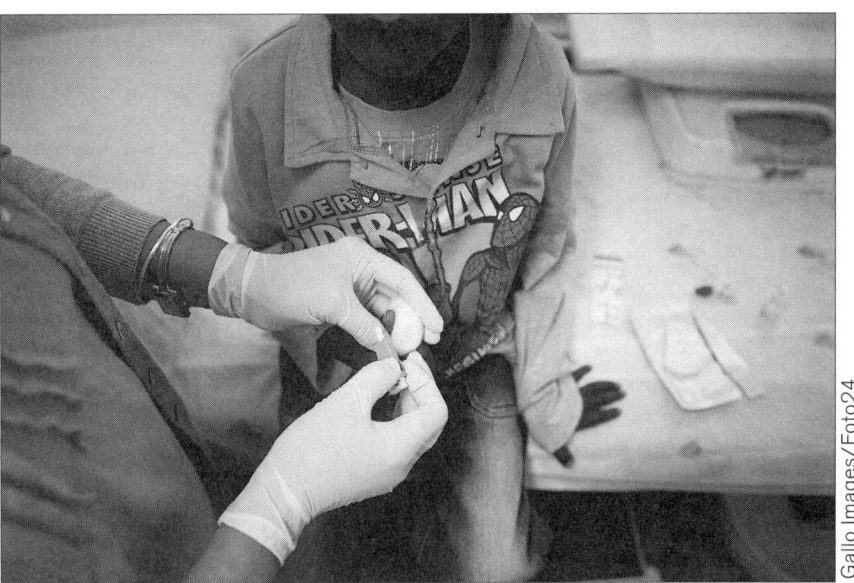

A youngster receives an HIV test at a U.S.-funded AIDS clinic in Johannesburg, South Africa. President George W. Bush's President's Emergency Plan for AIDS Relief, or PEPFAR, called for a $15 billion program to combat AIDS in 15 countries. The project remains the largest-ever global health initiative dedicated to a single disease.

While the idea Roberts favors would consolidate most development and humanitarian aid programs into one agency, other aid programs, such as those administered by the Department of Defense, would remain separate.

Others, such as former State Department entrepreneurship director Steven Koltai and Retired Adm. James G. Stavridis, dean of the Fletcher School of Law and Diplomacy at Tufts University, would like to see development aid coordinated by the Overseas Private Investment Corporation (OPIC), an independent agency that mobilizes private capital for development projects, including promoting entrepreneurship. "There are 60 offices and 12 different departments that are involved in one

way or another with international entrepreneurship development," one type of foreign aid, Koltai says. "You can't do this successfully if it's this disaggregated." (See "At Issue," p. 329.)

But others say charges of poor coordination and inefficiencies are overblown. "I would argue that there has been more progress on that front than perhaps is appreciated during the time of the Obama administration," says Scott Morris, a senior fellow at the Center for Global Development, a pro-aid think tank in Washington. "There was more effective coordination going on, particularly around the big initiatives, such as Power Africa," which aims to bring electricity to much of the continent.

Still, he says, "there probably are some elements of consolidation that make sense. But I don't think it's realistic, or ultimately effective, to collapse everything together in a supersized agency."

Alicia Phillips Mandaville, vice president of global development policy and learning at InterAction, the alliance of U.S.-based nongovernmental aid organizations, echoes that view. "Consolidating all U.S. foreign assistance through

a single point would be counterproductive," she says. Different aid agencies manage different kinds of projects and have different skill sets, she says. For instance, the kind of work OPIC does in encouraging private enterprise requires different skills than the work performed by USAID in delivering health care or education, she says.

Even those who argue for consolidation do not argue for combining all economic aid programs into a single entity. Nonmilitary economic aid managed by the Defense Department, says Roberts, should not be moved to another agency. "One of the things that DoD does well, and we would want them to continue to do well, is to respond to humanitarian crises — tsunamis, earthquakes."

With all the consolidation talk, Mandaville says that without clear policy proposals from the Trump administration, "People are nervous about a merger of things that shouldn't be merged."

Others worry that proposed cuts to foreign aid may leave too much of the development efforts up to the Defense Department, whose funding Trump wants to increase significantly. "If major budget cuts to foreign assistance go through at the same time DoD's budget is increased, the imbalance between DoD and its sister agencies — State and USAID — will continue to grow with devastating effects on our diplomacy and foreign assistance capabilities," says CSIS's Green. Cutting foreign assistance, "especially of the magnitude proposed, will exacerbate the tendency to militarize U.S. foreign policy and to see every problem as a nail."

Morris, of the Center for Global Development, agrees. The proposed budget cuts would "put more pressure on the Defense Department to engage in these activities if . . . they can no longer lean on a USAID to do it," he says. But, he warns, there is "less transparency" at the Defense Department.

Former USAID Administrator Atwood sees another problem in consolidating economic aid under either the State Department or the DoD. "When the State

Department or DoD take over an aid program, as in Afghanistan, they are likely to have 15 short-term projects, whereas they should have one 15-year, effective, sustainable project," Atwood says.

Some experts have recommended encouraging a greater role for the private sector as a way to make foreign aid programs more efficient.

"Step one is to consolidate. Step two is to put it in an agency that is closer to working with the private sector than USAID or the State Department," says Koltai. He advocates creation of an Office of Private Sector Development at OPIC that would make investments in developing countries as a seed investor in projects that are minority-government, majority-private enterprises.

OPIC provides loans and guaranties, political risk insurance and support for American businesses expanding into emerging markets, especially where risks of economic losses through political turmoil or nationalization of industries are high.

"The only reason I hesitate about privatizing OPIC completely is that in many of the places where this work has to happen, the private sector is not going to invest," says Koltai, noting the risks of political and economic uncertainty in many developing countries.

Others, however, have called for full privatization of OPIC, arguing that its involvement in high-risk areas only encourages bad behavior on the part of governments. Countries with favorable investment climates will attract foreign investors without government help, wrote Heritage Foundation analysts Brett Schaefer and Bryan Riley in 2014. But, they argued, "When OPIC guarantees investments in risky foreign environments, those countries have less reason to adopt policies that are friendly to foreign investors." [84]

Young, of the Competitive Enterprise Institute, argues for privatizing OPIC and all aid agencies. Moving all government aid through nongovernmental organizations (NGOs) would be a better model,

he says, "although once they have that kind of guaranteed revenue source, NGOs can become their own special interest. That's something we need to look out for." ■

OUTLOOK

Coming Crisis

Oxfam International, an independent association of antipoverty organizations, predicts that the current aid crisis in eastern Africa and Yemen is only the beginning. When the full impact of climate change kicks in, the group says, conditions will get much worse unless industrialized nations act quickly to limit and remediate the damage.

"Developing countries' economies face being crushed under the double burden of climate change adaptation costs of almost $800 billion and more than twice that in economic losses every year by 2050 if pledges to cut [carbon] emissions are not improved," the organization warned in 2015. "World leaders need to step up. We need further cuts to emissions and more climate funding so vulnerable communities — who are already facing unpredictable floods, droughts and hunger — can adapt to survive." [85]

On March 28, Trump signed an executive order that would unwind most of President Obama's efforts to battle climate change, and he has said he intends to withdraw from a 2015 international agreement to curb carbon emissions. [86] Factions within the administration reportedly are in heated debate over whether to withdraw from the accord. [87]

In addition, most experts expect U.S. foreign aid to decline. "The aid budget is going to shrink," says the Heritage Foundation's Roberts, and it will be "prioritized to match up with the most

immediate and crucial U.S. national security objectives."

But other experts say expanding foreign aid will be essential to protect U.S. national security interests. The administration's proposed budget cuts would signal "U.S. withdrawal from the world, rather than continued leadership and engagement," says Travis Adkins, senior director for public policy and government relations at InterAction.

"Slashing foreign assistance would provide no significant debt relief but would have dire impacts for people in the world's poorest places, as well as U.S. national interests," he says. Global crises today "demand U.S. global engagement, because we as Americans feel the consequences of these global challenges."

Supporting foreign aid is a good way to put "America first," according to Adkins, because it ensures "that our people are safe and secure and that there is stability in the world so that our security interests aren't threatened."

Former USAID administrator Atwood agrees and adds, "I don't know whether I'm terribly confident that the Trump administration is going to think in those terms." Furthermore, he warns, U.S. foreign aid cutbacks could snowball across the globe. "The way the United States goes, the rest of the world goes."

Since Trump released his proposal in late February to slash foreign aid by nearly one-third, the aid community has been anxiously awaiting further details, and some experts say they still hope the administration will recognize the importance of aid to national security.

"With any new administration, and potentially with this one, there's a desire to show that there are things being improved," says InterAction's Mandaville. "That is always a good instinct." ■

Notes

[1] Michael Gerson and Raj Shah, " 'America first' shouldn't mean cutting foreign aid," *The Washington Post*, Feb. 24, 2017, http://tinyurl.com/mgqha7d.

[2] The Associated Press, "Trump's budget entails steep cuts for diplomacy, foreign aid," CNBC, Feb. 28, 2017, http://tinyurl.com/zy9ox8r.

[3] Sylvan Lane and Rebecca Kheel, "Trump's cuts to foreign aid face resistance in Congress," *The Hill*, Feb. 28, 2017, http://tinyurl.com/hnggcjg.

[4] James Bovard, "Obama's global anti-corruption cops should call Internal Affairs," *USA Today*, May 19, 2016, http://tinyurl.com/l2drnfa.

[5] "Final Monthly Treasury Statement of Receipts and Outlays of the United States Government For Fiscal Year 2015 Through September 30, 2015, and Other Periods," U.S. Department of the Treasury, September 2015, http://tinyurl.com/mxr3hfr.

[6] Curt Tarnoff and Marian L. Lawson, "Foreign Aid: An Introduction to U.S. Programs and Policy," Congressional Research Service, June 17, 2016, p. 6, http://tinyurl.com/nymlqwz

[7] "On the Issues," Fox News, http://tinyurl.com/kj6tu7w.

[8] "Testimony of Gayle E. Smith before the Senate Foreign Relations Committee," USAID, June 30, 2016, http://tinyurl.com/mjsp6vc.

[9] "Corruption in Conflict: Lessons from the U.S. Experience in Afghanistan," Special Inspector General for Afghanistan Reconstruction, September 2016, http://tinyurl.com/lpcjdc9.

[10] Geoff Dyer, "US aid fuelled corruption in Afghanistan, watchdog says," *Financial Times*, Sept. 14, 2016, http://tinyurl.com/hz84sma.

[11] Sidney Traynham, "Over 120 Retired Generals, Admirals on State and USAID Budget: 'Now is not the time to retreat,' " U.S. Global Leadership Coalition, Feb. 27, 2017, http://tinyurl.com/k423vg3.

[12] Nick Thompson, "Seventy-five percent of U.S. foreign military financing goes to two countries," CNN, Nov. 11, 2015, http://tinyurl.com/ja3kvse.

[13] Tracy Wilkinson and Noah Bierman, "Egypt's authoritarian-minded president gets a warm White House welcome," *The Chicago Tribune*, April 3, 2017, http://tinyurl.com/krqgqtv.

[14] See "Detained Americans Fast Facts," CNN Library, March 29, 2017, http://tinyurl.com/mgard3k.

[15] *Ibid.*

[16] "Statement of Stephen O'Brien to the United Nations Security Council," United Nations, March 10, 2017, http://tinyurl.com/mcobh7z.

[17] "Net ODA," Organisation for Economic Co-operation and Development, http://tinyurl.com/zsvrce3. This $30 billion figure is for calendar 2015. It differs from the $26.2 billion figure cited elsewhere, which is for fiscal 2015.

[18] *Ibid.*

[19] Naomi Larsson, "Foreign aid: which countries are the most generous?" *The Guardian*, Sept. 9, 2015, http://tinyurl.com/kusonku.

[20] "The 0.7% ODA/GNI target — a history," Organisation for Economic Co-operation and Development, http://tinyurl.com/jo9zl6s.

[21] "Policy Brief: U.S. International Development Funding," InterAction, January 2013, http://tinyurl.com/mgeqn28.

[22] Angus Deaton, *The Great Escape: Health, Wealth, and the Origins of Inequality* (2013), p. 273.

[23] *Ibid.*, p. 285.

[24] Marian L. Lawson, "Does Foreign Aid Work? Efforts to Evaluate U.S. Foreign Assistance," Congressional Research Service, June 23, 2016, p. 4, http://tinyurl.com/lv7lj84.

[25] "Testimony of Gayle E. Smith before the Senate Foreign Relations Committee," *op. cit.*

[26] Junyi Zhang, "Order from Chaos: Chinese foreign assistance, explained," Brookings Institution, July 19, 2016, http://tinyurl.com/kr33vo3.

[27] Somini Sengupta, "Trump Revives Ban on Foreign Aid to Groups That Give Abortion Counseling," *The New York Times*, Jan. 23, 2017, http://tinyurl.com/hr4qkts.

[28] The Foreign Assistance Act of 1961, Section 116, 22 U.S.C. 2151n, http://tinyurl.com/k29bw4y.

[29] *Ibid.*

[30] Eric Posner, "The Case Against Human Rights," *The Guardian*, Dec. 4, 2014, http://tinyurl.com/l8agpzd.

[31] Yun Sun, "China's Aid to Africa: Monster or Messiah?" Brookings Institution, Feb. 7, 2014, http://tinyurl.com/lj6juxg.

[32] Zhang, *op. cit.*

[33] Randy Schnepf, "U.S. International Food Aid Programs: Background and Issues," Congressional Research Service, Sept. 14, 2016, p. 2, http://tinyurl.com/k4wlvw3.

[34] Olga Khazan, "Here Are the U.S. States That Benefit Most From America's Wacky International Food-Aid Program," *The Atlantic*, April 5, 2013, http://tinyurl.com/kurxoxa.

[35] Ryan Nabil and Vincent H. Smith, "U.S. food aid's costly problem," *Foreign Affairs*, Nov. 1, 2016, http://tinyurl.com/hqkf9v5.

[36] "Testimony of Gayle Smith before the House Committee on Foreign Affairs," *op. cit.*

[37] Christopher Blattman and Paul Niehaus, "Show Them the Money: Why Giving Cash Helps Alleviate Poverty," *Foreign Affairs*, May/June 2014, http://tinyurl.com/lobd9lc.

[38] "Testimony of Eric G. Postel before the Senate Foreign Relations Committee Subcommittee on State Department and USAID Management," U.S. Senate, July 12, 2016, http://tinyurl.com/kffr7cf.

[39] *Ibid.*

[40] *Ibid.*

[41] *Ibid.*

[42] Marian L. Lawson, "Foreign Assistance: Public-Private Partnerships," Congressional Research Service, Oct. 28, 2013, p. 14, http://tinyurl.com/kj34mfs.

[43] *Ibid.*, p. 14.

[44] Louis A. Picard and Terry F. Buss, *A Fragile Balance: Re-examining the History of Foreign Aid, Security, and Diplomacy* (2013), p. 14.

[45] *Ibid.*, p. 46.

[46] George I. Gay, "Public Relations of the Commission for the Relief in Belgium, Documents," Stanford University Press, 1929, http://tinyurl.com/kl9w7mw.

[47] C. E. Noyes, "American relief of famine in Europe," *Editorial Research Reports*, (Vol. II), (1940), http://tinyurl.com/m5jye3f.

[48] Picard and Buss, *op. cit.*, p. 21.

[49] "Lend-Lease and Military Aid to the Allies in the Early Years of World War II," Office of the Historian, U.S. Department of State, http://tinyurl.com/ln4d573.

[50] "The Plan: As the Marshall Plan Becomes the Test Between the U.S. and the U.S.S.R, the Main Needs of Europe According to the President," *The New York Times*, Dec. 21, 1947, http://tinyurl.com/kwndcml.

[51] Felix Belair Jr., "President Blunt in Plea to Combat Coercion as World Peril," *The New York Times*, March 13, 1947, http://tinyurl.com/l9rko73.

[52] Picard, *op. cit.*, p. 76.

[53] "Legislation on Foreign Relations Through 2002,"

About the Author

Patrick Marshall, a freelance policy and technology writer in Seattle, is a technology columnist for *The Seattle Times* and *Government Computer News*. He has a bachelor's degree in anthropology from the University of California, Santa Cruz, and a master's degree in international studies from the Fletcher School of Law and Diplomacy at Tufts University.

House and Senate Committees on International Relations and Committees on Foreign Relations, July 2003, http://tinyurl.com/mawldqj.

[54] Charles Mohr, "U.S. Opens Study of Aid in Vietnam," *The New York Times*, Sept. 5, 1966, http://tinyurl.com/k7c2utb.

[55] Picard, *op. cit.*, p. 110.

[56] *Ibid.*, p. 97.

[57] Felix Belair Jr., "Foreign Aid Off as Need Rises," *The New York Times*, Jan. 10, 1971, http://tinyurl.com/k8t8qaa.

[58] "Trends," Foreign Aid Explorer, USAID, undated, http://tinyurl.com/zokmdh9.

[59] Lawson, "Foreign Assistance: Public-Private Partnerships," *op. cit.*

[60] Amanda Terkel and Laura Bassett, "Donald Trump Reinstates Ronald Reagan's Abortion 'Global Gag Rule,' " *The Huffington Post*, Jan. 23, 2017, http://tinyurl.com/z273q3s.

[61] Tarnoff and Lawson, *op. cit.*, p. 2, http://tinyurl.com/nymlqwz.

[62] Curt Tarnoff, "U.S. Agency for International Development (USAID): Background, Operations, and Issues," Congressional Research Service, July 21, 2015, p. 35, http://tinyurl.com/mhbdvxh.

[63] *Ibid.*, p. 53.

[64] Tarnoff and Lawson, *op. cit.*, p. 1.

[65] "Sixty years of US aid to Pakistan: Get the data," *The Guardian*, http://tinyurl.com/k7nqzyg.

[66] Kiran Dhillon, "Afghanistan Is The Big Winner In U.S. Foreign Aid," *Time*, March 31, 2014, http://tinyurl.com/nbamrve.

[67] Tarnoff, *op. cit.*, p. 36.

[68] Bradley Graham and Glenn Kessler, "Rice Explains Aid Restructuring to USAID Employees," *The Washington Post*, Jan. 20, 2006, http://tinyurl.com/l4are3w.

[69] Myra Sessions, "Overview of the President's Emergency Plan for AIDS Relief (PEPFAR)," Center for Global Development, undated, http://tinyurl.com/kgsaaxr.

[70] Tom Vanden Brook, "Aid agency accused of coverup in Afghanistan," *USA Today*, April 2, 2014, http://tinyurl.com/kfovoph.

[71] "Electrify Africa Act of 2015 — Report to Congress," USAID, Aug. 10, 2016, http://tinyurl.com/gn5kqb6.

[72] Fernanda Crescente, "Obama signs Global Food Security Act to end hunger," *USA Today*, July 21, 2016, http://tinyurl.com/jvfjmjm.

[73] Adva Saldinger, "US Congress approves long-sought Foreign Aid Transparency and Accountability Act," Devex, July 7, 2016, http://tinyurl.com/jwjuukp.

[74] Hussein Mohamed and Sewell Chan, "U.N. Chief, Visiting Somalia, Pleads for Aid to Avert Famine," *The New York Times*, March 7, 2017,

FOR MORE INFORMATION

Cato Institute, 1000 Massachusetts Ave., N.W., Washington, DC 20001-5403; 202-842-0200; www.cato.org. Libertarian think tank that opposes most foreign aid spending.

Center for Global Development, 2055 L St., N.W., Fifth Floor, Washington, DC 20036; 202-416-4000; www.cgdev.org. Research and advocacy organization focused on global poverty and inequality.

Center for Strategic and International Studies, 1800 K St., N.W., Washington, DC 20006; 202-887-0200; www.csis.org. Centrist think tank that researches U.S. security issues.

Heritage Foundation, 214 Massachusetts Ave., N.E., Washington, DC 20002; 202-546-4400; www.heritage.org. Conservative think tank that focuses on foreign aid as one of its areas of policy concerns.

InterAction, 1400 16th St., N.W., Suite 210, Washington, DC 20036; 202-667-8227; www.interaction.org. Association of U.S.-based nongovernmental aid organizations.

Millennium Challenge Corp., 1099 14th St., N.W., Suite 700, Washington, DC 20005-3550; 202-521-3600; www.mcc.gov. A federal foreign aid agency.

Overseas Development Institute, 203 Blackfriars Road, London SE1 8NJ, United Kingdom; +44 (0)20 7922 0300; www.odi.org. Independent think tank on international development and humanitarian issues.

Oxfam America, 1101 17th St., N.W., Suite 1300, Washington, DC 20036-4710; 800-862-5800; www.oxfamamerica.org. Nonpartisan advocacy group working to end poverty.

U.S. Agency for International Development, Ronald Reagan Building and International Trade Center, Washington, DC 20523-1000; 202-712-0000; www.usaid.gov. Primary federal agency managing foreign development and humanitarian aid programs.

http://tinyurl.com/lsxg9u7.

[75] For background, see Brian Beary, "Terrorism in Africa," *CQ Researcher*, July 10, 2015, pp. 577-600.

[76] Kevin Sieff, "Trump's plan to slash foreign aid comes as famine threat is surging," *The Washington Post*, March 1, 2017, http://tinyurl.com/n773swb.

[77] *Ibid.*

[78] *Ibid.*

[79] Sylvan Lane, "GOP senator: Trump budget 'dead on arrival,' " *The Hill*, Feb. 28, 2017, http://tinyurl.com/jyx2h79.

[80] Alex Thier, "Foreign aid under Trump's 'America-first' doctrine," Devex, Nov. 11, 2016, http://tinyurl.com/ls2n83q.

[81] Malia Zimmerman, "Law would cut off aid to countries that refuse to accept illegal immigrant criminals," Fox News, Jan. 16, 2017, http://tinyurl.com/jybu3bc.

[82] "H.R. 82: Criminal Alien Deportation Enforcement Act of 2017," Gov.track, http://tinyurl.com/lz2xk3f.

[83] "Total Obligations," Foreign Aid Explorer, USAID, undated, http://tinyurl.com/n6fqfqx.

[84] Brett Schaefer and Bryan Riley, "Time to Privatize OPIC," The Heritage Foundation, May 19, 2014, http://tinyurl.com/k9nnmnn.

[85] "Delays in cutting emissions set to cost developing countries hundreds of billions of dollars more," press release, Oxfam International, Nov. 25, 2015, http://tinyurl.com/lsnybbg.

[86] Coral Davenport and Alissa J. Rubin, "Trump Signs Executive Order Unwinding Obama Climate Policies," *The New York Times*, March 28, 2017, http://tinyurl.com/k7vyjr6. See also Jill U. Adams, "Energy and Climate Change," *CQ Researcher*, June 15, 2016.

[87] Coral Davenport, "Top Trump Advisers Are Split on Paris Agreement on Climate Change," *The New York Times*, March 2, 2017, http://tinyurl.com/jccavzh.

Bibliography

Selected Sources

Books

Deaton, Angus, *The Great Escape: Health, Wealth, and the Origins of Inequality*, Princeton University Press, 2013.

A professor of economics and international affairs at Princeton University and winner of the 2015 Nobel Prize in economics argues that development aid works only where it isn't needed and that it can hinder the conditions that encourage economic growth.

Koltai, Steven R., and Matthew Muspratt, *Peace Through Entrepreneurship: Investing in a Startup Culture for Security and Development*, Brookings Institution Press, 2016.

A former director of the State Department's Global Entrepreneurship Program (Koltai) and a development consultant (Muspratt) say joblessness is the main cause of violent unrest in developing countries and that encouraging entrepreneurship is more effective than traditional development programs at delivering jobs.

Picard, Louis A., and Terry F. Buss, *A Fragile Balance: Re-examining the History of Foreign Aid, Security, and Diplomacy*, Kumarian Press, 2013.

A professor of public and international affairs at the University of Pittsburgh (Picard) and a professor of public policy at Carnegie Mellon University (Buss) present a history of foreign development and humanitarian aid policies.

Articles

De Luce, Dan, David Francis and John Hudson, "Will Foreign Aid Get Cut on Trump's Chopping Block?" *Foreign Policy*, Nov. 23, 2016, http://tinyurl.com/lqelqmd.

Journalists say President Trump brings uncertainty to the foreign-aid community, and they explore the level of Republican support in Congress for aid programs.

Greenberg, Jon, "Most U.S. foreign aid flows through U.S. organizations," *PolitiFact*, March 8, 2017, http://tinyurl.com/l3km9t7.

The Congressional Research Service reported that only about 4 percent of U.S. foreign aid in 2014 went directly to foreign governments; most of the funds were funneled through U.S. private partners.

Miliband, David, and Ravi Gurumurthy, "Improving Humanitarian Aid: How to Make Relief More Efficient and Effective," *Foreign Affairs*, July/August 2015, http://tinyurl.com/nqxsltv.

The president (Miliband) and a vice president (Gurumurthy) of the International Rescue Committee, a global relief organization, say humanitarian aid can be improved through better analysis of program effectiveness.

Posner, Eric, "The Case Against Human Rights," *The Guardian*, Dec. 4, 2014, http://tinyurl.com/l8agpzd.

A University of Chicago law professor says it is misguided to expect developing countries to improve their human rights records in return for foreign aid.

Smith, Vincent H., and Ryan Nabil, "U.S. Food Aid's Costly Problem," *Foreign Affairs*, Nov. 1, 2016, http://tinyurl.com/hqkf9v5.

A visiting scholar at the conservative American Enterprise Institute (AEI) think tank and Montana State University economics professor (Smith) and an AEI researcher (Nabil) say it is time to eliminate requirements that American-flagged ships carry U.S. food aid.

Reports and Studies

"Foreign Assistance Briefing Book 2016: Critical problems, recommendations, and actions for the new administration and the 115th Congress," InterAction, 2016, http://tinyurl.com/l4w4w4e.

An alliance of U.S.-based nongovernmental organizations lists the most critical issues facing the aid community in its attempt to boost economic development and fight poverty and disease in developing countries.

Lawson, Marian L., "Does Foreign Aid Work? Efforts to Evaluate U.S. Foreign Assistance," Congressional Research Service, June 23, 2016, http://tinyurl.com/lv7lj84.

A foreign-assistance analyst for Congress' research arm describes U.S. aid agencies' efforts to evaluate program effectiveness and obstacles faced in making assessments.

Lawson, Marian L., "Foreign Assistance: Public-Private Partnerships (PPPs)," Congressional Research Service, Oct. 28, 2013, http://tinyurl.com/mu9pjw6.

A foreign-assistance analyst traces the evolution of private sector involvement in U.S. foreign assistance programs over recent decades.

Tarnoff, Curt, "Millennium Challenge Corporation," Congressional Research Service, Jan. 11, 2017, http://tinyurl.com/lfesl39.

A specialist in foreign affairs recounts the history of the Millennium Challenge Corp., a U.S. foreign aid agency, and the challenges it faces.

Tarnoff, Curt, and Marian L. Lawson, "Foreign Aid: An Introduction to U.S. Programs and Policy," Congressional Research Service, June 17, 2016, http://tinyurl.com/nymlqwz.

Analysts provide an overview of U.S. foreign-aid policies and programs, discuss recent priorities and trends in the field and explore the growing role of the private sector in aid programs.

The Next Step:

Additional Articles from Current Periodicals

Cutting Spending

Clark, Hilary, Kara Fox, and Richard Allen Greene, "Alarm bells ring for charities as Trump pledges to slash foreign aid budget," CNN, March 1, 2017, http://tinyurl.com/n7rquak.

President Trump says he wants to cut foreign aid to save money and bolster spending on national security, but 121 retired U.S. military officers signed a letter to Congress explaining foreign aid's role in preventing conflict and keeping troops safe.

Cowan, Richard and Roberta Rampton, "Trump's budget cuts to domestic, aid programs draw Republican scorn," Reuters, March 17, 2017, http://tinyurl.com/z65ffwk.

President Trump's first federal budget proposal drew criticism from congressional Republicans, including South Carolina Sen. Lindsey Graham, who said cutting foreign aid would occur "at the expense of national security."

Saine, Cindy, "US Lawmakers Criticize Cuts to Diplomacy, Foreign Aid" Voice of America, March 17, 2017, http://tiny url.com/k4e4qbx.

Democratic and Republican lawmakers alike are hesitant to support President Trump's budget proposal, but House Speaker Paul Ryan, R-Wis., praised Trump for aiming to cut wasteful spending.

Hunger Crisis

Dixon, Robyn, "With 20 million people facing starvation, Trump's foreign aid cuts strike fear," Los Angeles Times, March 19, 2017, http://tinyurl.com/mus8n6q.

Some international humanitarian officials are concerned that proposed U.S. foreign aid cuts would cause famine conditions in South Sudan, Somalia, northeastern Nigeria and Yemen to spiral out of control.

Nichols, Michelle, "U.N. chief warns against abrupt U.S. funding cuts to world body," Reuters, March 16, 2017, http://tinyurl.com/hawu6b5.

With the United States the largest contributor to the United Nations, providing 22 percent of the organization's $5.4 billion core budget, two U.N. officials warned that "abrupt" U.S. foreign aid cuts could lead to global instability.

Sieff, Kevin, "Trump's plan to slash foreign aid comes as famine threat is surging," The Washington Post, March 1, 2017, http://tinyurl.com/lwlvvv8.

Trump's plans to limit foreign aid clash with a U.N. request for $4.4 billion to "avert a catastrophe" and prevent widespread famine across northern Nigeria, South Sudan, Somalia and Yemen.

Privatization

Flows, Daniel, "Reform Bill Trades Foreign Aid For Corporate Welfare," Forbes, March 28, 2017, http://tinyurl.com/me56loj.

Favoring privatization in foreign aid would likely benefit corporations more than needy countries, according to a Washington think tank researcher.

Lyons, Charles, and Richard Stearns, "The U.S. Should Continue Its Fight against AIDS in Children," National Review, April 7, 2017, http://tinyurl.com/n6ntbor.

Two human rights activists say public-private partnerships are essential to efficient foreign aid spending and have saved millions of lives through programs like PEPFAR.

Reforms

Kesten, Rebecca, "Trump's proposed budget seeks major cuts to UN programs," Fox News, March 16, 2017, http://tinyurl.com/kp3eytj.

President Trump, who has often criticized the United Nations, now plans to reduce the organization's funding and change foreign aid strategy through his proposed "America First" budget.

Lederman, Josh, "US cites abortion provision in cutting off UN agency funding," NBC2, April 4, 2017, http://tiny url.com/mijhujh.

The Trump administration will cut $32.5 million from the United Nations Population Fund after alleging that it supported China's "coercive" abortion programs.

Zimmerman, Malia, "Law would cut off aid to countries that refuse to accept illegal immigrant criminals," Fox News, Jan. 16, 2017, http://tinyurl.com/jybu3bc.

In January, Rep. Brian Babin, R-Texas, introduced the Criminal Alien Deportation Enforcement Act, which would cut foreign aid to countries that refuse to take back undocumented immigrants with criminal records who are deported by the United States.

In-depth Reports on Issues in the News

Are you writing a paper?

Need backup for a debate?

Want to become an expert on an issue?

For 90 years, students have turned to *CQ Researcher* for in-depth reporting on issues in the news. Reports on a full range of political and social issues are now available. Following is a selection of recent reports:

Civil Liberties
Privacy and the Internet, 12/15
Intelligence Reform, 5/15
Religion and Law, 11/14

Crime/Law
Forensic Science Controversies, 2/17
Jailing Debtors, 9/16
Decriminalizing Prostitution, 4/16
Restorative Justice, 2/16
The Dark Web, 1/16
Immigrant Detention, 10/15
Fighting Gangs, 10/15

Education
Charter Schools, 3/17
Civic Education, 2/17
Student Debt, 11/16
Apprenticeships, 10/16

Environment/Society
Women in Prison, 3/17
Guns on Campus, 1/17
Mass Transit, 12/16
Arctic Development, 12/16
Protecting the Power Grid, 11/16
Pornography, 10/16

Health/Safety
Reducing Traffic Deaths, 2/17
Opioid Crisis, 10/16
Mosquito-Borne Disease, 7/16

Politics/Economy
Troubled Brazil, 4/17
Reviving Rural Economies, 3/17
Immigrants and the Economy, 2/17
Trump Presidency, 1/17
European Union's Future, 12/16
The Obama Legacy, 11/16
Populism and Party Politics, 9/16

Upcoming Reports

Technology and Policing, 4/21/17   Sex Abuse in Sports, 4/28/17   Native Americans, 5/5/17

ACCESS

CQ Researcher is available in print and online. For access, visit your library or www.cqresearcher.com.

STAY CURRENT

For notice of upcoming *CQ Researcher* reports or to learn more about *CQ Researcher* products, subscribe to the free email newsletters, *CQ Researcher Alert!* and *CQ Researcher News*: http://cqpress.com/newsletters.

PURCHASE

To purchase a *CQ Researcher* report in print or electronic format (PDF), visit www.cqpress.com or call 866-427-7737. Single reports start at $15. Bulk purchase discounts and electronic-rights licensing are also available.

SUBSCRIBE

Annual full-service *CQ Researcher* subscriptions—including 44 reports a year, monthly index updates, and a bound volume—start at $1,131. Add $25 for domestic postage.

CQ Researcher Online offers a backfile from 1991 and a number of tools to simplify research. For pricing information, call 800-818-7243 or 805-499-9774 or email librarysales@sagepub.com.

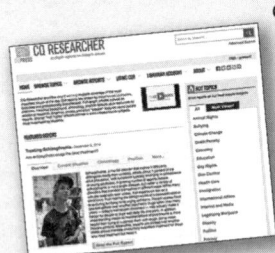

CQ RESEARCHER

CQPRESS

In-depth reports on today's issues

Published by CQ Press, an Imprint of SAGE Publications, Inc.

www.cqresearcher.com

High-Tech Policing

Are new surveillance technologies effective and legal?

Police officer Quinn Gatrell of West Valley City, Utah, makes a traffic stop on March 2, 2015, using a camera attached to his glasses. While police increasingly are using body cameras, basic procedures are hotly debated, such as when footage should be released to the public.

C ontroversial new technologies are transforming how police pursue suspects, monitor suspicious activity and seek to deter crime. Police departments are using computer algorithms to forecast where and when crimes might occur, sophisticated software to monitor social media posts, body cameras to record interactions with civilians, aerial drones to surveil neighborhoods and license-plate readers to find stolen cars and track criminal suspects. Law enforcement officials vigorously defend the technologies' overall effectiveness. But civil liberties groups say such tools raises troubling constitutional and privacy questions and that some police departments are using them without public notice, clear rules or proper oversight. While some cities have restricted the use of certain surveillance methods, others are under pressure to allow the public a greater say in formulating policies governing the technologies' use. Police maintain they are deploying high-tech equipment without violating individuals' rights and that opening its use to public review would play into the hands of criminals and terrorists.

CQ Researcher • April 21, 2017 • www.cqresearcher.com
Volume 27, Number 15 • Pages 337-360

RECIPIENT OF SOCIETY OF PROFESSIONAL JOURNALISTS AWARD FOR EXCELLENCE ◆ AMERICAN BAR ASSOCIATION SILVER GAVEL AWARD

I N S I D E THIS REPORT

THE ISSUES	.................**339**
BACKGROUND	...............**345**
CHRONOLOGY	...............**347**
CURRENT SITUATION	........**352**
AT ISSUE	......................**353**
OUTLOOK	.....................**355**
BIBLIOGRAPHY	...............**358**
THE NEXT STEP	.............**359**

THE ISSUES

339
- Is predictive policing effective and fair?
- Are body cameras an effective policing tool?
- Should police be able to monitor social media?

BACKGROUND

345 **Professional Policing**
Reformers sought to professionalize policing in the early 20th century.

345 **Law-and-Order Campaigns**
Clashes between police and protesters in the 1960s led to changes in police tactics.

349 **Legal Protections**
As new law enforcement technologies arose, questions swirled about how they were used.

CURRENT SITUATION

352 **Legislatures Weigh In**
Some lawmakers want use of police surveillance technology to be more transparent.

352 **Cities Seek Oversight**
Two New York City council members seek to lift the secrecy around surveillance.

354 **Regulating Technologies**
New state laws address the use of license-plate readers.

OUTLOOK

355 **Predictive Policing**
Experts say the software could become commonplace.

SIDEBARS AND GRAPHICS

340 **Body Camera Footage Restricted in 26 States**
All or some footage is blocked from public viewing.

341 **Most Americans Back Police Drones**
More than two-thirds support the use of the aerial craft to help solve crimes.

344 **FBI Casts Wide Facial-Recognition Net**
The agency's database holds images mainly of Americans without criminal records.

347 **Chronology**
Key events since 1845.

348 **Facial Recognition Offers Promise — and Pitfalls**
Civil libertarians worry the technology will lead to mass surveillance.

350 **Security Cameras Stirring Privacy Concerns**
"They are truly a dragnet surveillance."

353 **At Issue:**
Should elected officials decide whether police and prosecutors can use surveillance technologies?

FOR FURTHER RESEARCH

357 **For More Information**
Organizations to contact.

358 **Bibliography**
Selected sources used.

359 **The Next Step**
Additional articles.

359 **Citing CQ Researcher**
Sample bibliography formats.

CQ RESEARCHER

April 21, 2017
Volume 27, Number 15

EXECUTIVE EDITOR: Thomas J. Billitteri
tjb@sagepub.com

ASSISTANT MANAGING EDITORS: Kenneth Fireman, kenneth.fireman@sagepub.com, Kathy Koch, kathy.koch@sagepub.com, Scott Rohrer, scott.rohrer@sagepub.com

ASSOCIATE MANAGING EDITOR: Val Ellicott

SENIOR CONTRIBUTING EDITOR:
Thomas J. Colin
tom.colin@sagepub.com

CONTRIBUTING WRITERS: Marcia Clemmitt, Sarah Glazer, Reed Karaim, Barbara Mantel, Chuck McCutcheon, Tom Price

SENIOR PROJECT EDITOR: Olu B. Davis

EDITORIAL ASSISTANT: Anika Reed

FACT CHECKERS: Eva P. Dasher, Michelle Harris, Betsy Towner Levine, Robin Palmer

Publishing

Los Angeles I London I New Delhi
Singapore I Washington DC I Melbourne

An Imprint of SAGE Publications, Inc.

SENIOR VICE PRESIDENT,
GLOBAL LEARNING RESOURCES:
Karen Phillips

EXECUTIVE DIRECTOR, ONLINE LIBRARY AND
REFERENCE PUBLISHING:
Todd Baldwin

CQ Researcher (ISSN 1056-2036) is printed on acid-free paper. Published weekly, except: (March wk. 4) (May wk. 4) (July wks. 1, 2) (Aug. wks. 2, 3) (Nov. wk. 4) and (Dec. wks. 3, 4). Published by SAGE Publications, Inc., 2455 Teller Rd., Thousand Oaks, CA 91320. Annual full-service subscriptions start at $1,131. For pricing, call 1-800-818-7243. To purchase a CQ Researcher report in print or electronic format (PDF), visit www.cqpress.com or call 866-427-7737. Single reports start at $15. Bulk purchase discounts and electronic-rights licensing are also available. Periodicals postage paid at Thousand Oaks, California, and at additional mailing offices. POSTMASTER: Send address changes to CQ Researcher, 2600 Virginia Ave., N.W., Suite 600, Washington, DC 20037.

Cover: Getty Images/George Frey

High-Tech Policing

BY BARBARA MANTEL

THE ISSUES

Two years ago the Tacoma, Wash., Police Department began an ambitious effort to reduce burglaries, using computer analysis of crime data to tell officers when and where future burglaries might occur.

The results of this "predictive policing" approach, coupled with tactics such as educating residents on how to keep their homes safe, surpassed expectations. Burglaries plunged 22 percent in 2015, said Pete Cribbin, assistant Tacoma police chief. "We've exceeded the two-year goal in the first year by a wide margin," he said. [1]

For Tacoma police, predictive policing deserved much of the credit. But civil libertarians see the practice as a potential tool for racial profiling and a violation of citizens' civil liberties. Predictive policing is "profoundly flawed: It is systematically biased against communities of color and allows unconscionable abuses of police power," 17 civil rights organizations said in a statement last August. [2]

The controversy is emblematic of a larger and rapidly expanding debate over the role of technology in police work. From the use of license-plate readers that can monitor citizens' whereabouts to the deployment of aerial drones over crime-ridden neighborhoods, police departments are spending millions of dollars on high-tech equipment, software and technical support to fight crime, an investment they say is revolutionizing their work and making communities safer.

"We believe that we are the leading department in this country, if not the

Police Sgt. Charles Coleman patrols an area of Los Angeles identified by predictive policing software as a potential crime hotspot. While many police departments say the sophisticated software and other new crime-fighting technologies are effective in fighting crime, civil liberties groups say the tools raise troubling privacy and fairness questions.

Getty Images/The Washington Post/Patrick T. Fallon

world, in our embrace of . . . technology," William Bratton said last September, the day before he retired as New York City police commissioner. "And we are very mindful of the responsibilities that come with that, doing it lawfully, doing it constitutionally." [3]

But civil libertarians say these powerful technologies offer an unprecedented window into people's private lives and may actually hamper police work by adding a new layer of fear and suspicion of the police, especially in neighborhoods already wary of police misconduct. Critics

also note that many police departments are purchasing and using the technologies without public notice, clear rules or judicial oversight. Visible body-worn cameras, which civil rights groups have promoted as a way to hold police officers accountable, may be the exception.

"As of right now, we have only a piecemeal understanding of intrusive technologies, based on investigative reporting or litigation," says Rashida Richardson, legislative counsel for the New York Civil Liberties Union (NYCLU), a civil liberties advocacy organization. As a result, there has been little public discussion about their costs, benefits, proper use and necessary privacy and constitutional protections, she says.

In response to a Freedom of Information request by the NYCLU, the New York City Police Department disclosed last year that between 2008 and 2015 it had been using portable devices known as cell-site simulators in criminal investigations, and did so without obtaining search warrants. Dubbed Stingrays, they act like a commercial cellphone tower and retrieve a cellphone's identifying data, allowing police to pinpoint a person's location — including inside a home, where people reasonably expect privacy.

Instead of getting search warrants, the police were relying on so-called pen register orders, court orders with weaker privacy protections. [4]

In a pilot program in Baltimore, police tested an aerial camera last year for eight months without notifying the public or elected officials, according to a *Bloomberg Businessweek* investigation. A small airplane equipped with

Body Camera Footage Restricted in 26 States

Twenty-six states either bar public disclosure of police body camera footage or make only certain kinds of footage available for public viewing, sometimes only after police or court authorization. Opponents of public access say the footage can be misleading or undermine a defendant's right to a fair trial; proponents say public access helps to keep police honest and improve policing.

States That Restrict Public Access to Body Camera Footage

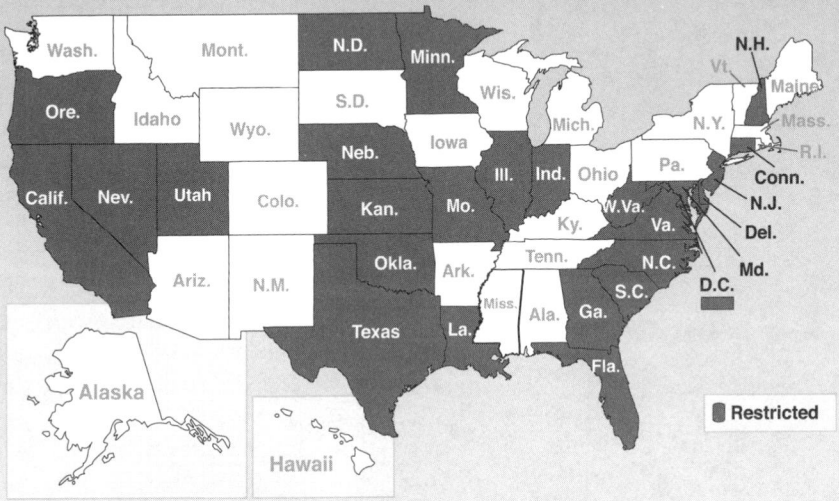

Source: "Police Body-Worn Camera Legislation Tracker," Urban Institute, Jan. 1, 2017, http://tinyurl.com/lc4snrs

wide-angle cameras flew over the city transmitting images to crime analysts for real-time or future review. Jay Stanley, a privacy expert in the Washington, D.C., office of the American Civil Liberties Union, told Bloomberg such surveillance resembled "Big Brother" from George Orwell's dystopian novel *1984,* in which authorities keep constant watch over citizens. [5]

But after the article's August publication, a police department spokesman called the plane a "21st-century investigative tool" that had helped to solve a shooting. Then-Mayor Stephanie Rawlings-Blake, who had been unaware of the test program, defended it as "cutting-edge technology aimed at making Baltimore safer." [6]

In addition to predictive policing software, other advanced policing technologies that raise privacy and constitutional concerns include: [7]

• **Cell-site simulators:** Besides pinpointing an individual's location, they sweep up information from nearby bystanders and in some configurations can intercept voice and text communications.

• **Automatic license-plate readers:** Cameras that photograph license plates, digitize the images and compare them against a license-plate database. The readers can help locate stolen cars, among other uses. But the images can be stored for months or years, making it possible for police to track a car's movements over time.

• **Z Backscatter Vans:** Developed for use in war zones, these mobile X-ray vans see through vehicle exteriors (and sometimes buildings) and are deployed to search for drugs, bombs or people.

• **Closed-circuit television cameras:** Police can monitor 24-hour video feeds from buildings and public spaces in real time, or video can be stored

for future examination.

• **Body cameras:** Officers turn on these audio and video recording devices during encounters with civilians, and they can leave them on when patrolling street demonstrations or their beat.

• **Facial-recognition software:** This technology allows a facial image to be compared against those in city, state or federal databases. When combined with body cameras and closed-circuit television cameras, facial recognition allows police to identify a person in real time or reconstruct a person's movements using stored footage. (*See sidebar, p. 348.*)

• **Social media monitoring software:** By searching usernames, keywords, hashtags or geographic locations, police can quickly collect and analyze public social media posts for potential threats or to gather investigative information.

• **Predictive policing software:** Algorithms that analyze past crime data and other factors to forecast risk of future crime.

As the technology gets more sophisticated, the constitutionality of these devices is unclear, legal experts say. "Under what circumstances does an eye in the sky (or on a pole or inside your phone) constitute a search under the Fourth Amendment — and thus presumptively require a warrant — when it is used for public surveillance?" wrote Rachel Levinson-Waldman, senior counsel for the Liberty and National Security Program at the New York-based Brennan Center for Justice, a public policy and law institute. [8]

The Fourth Amendment guarantees protection against unreasonable government searches and seizures of property. [9]

Another problem is that vendors set the terms for the hardware they are selling, Elizabeth Joh, a law professor at the University of California, Davis, wrote in a forthcoming paper. "These companies act out of private self-interest, but their decisions have considerable public impact," she wrote. For instance, the "terms of use" in some vendors' contracts prohibit police from disclosing information about the technology, which could prevent authorities from providing crucial information that defendants, judges, journalists and the public normally would have, she said. [10]

Harris Corp., a technology company in Melbourne, Fla., that dominates the market for cell-site simulators, requires police departments to abide by nondisclosure agreements, often overseen by the FBI, when using the devices, according to Joh. As a result, the simulators often are referred to in court only cryptically, and police departments typically won't discuss them with the public. Prosecutors reportedly have dropped criminal charges against defendants when it appeared that Stingray details would be revealed during a trial. [11]

Media Sonar, a company in Ontario, Canada, whose software monitors social media posts, specified in a proposal to Fresno, Calif., that the police department "must use all reasonable care" to keep the company's brand and methodology out of the public eye because widespread media attention could decrease the software's "efficacy and [harm] the overall business model." The ACLU of Northern California obtained the document through a Freedom of Information request. [12]

Police technologies aren't inexpensive. Body cameras may cost as little as $400 each, but the annual cost for storing the immense amount of footage they generate runs into the millions of dollars for some large police departments. A car-mounted license-plate reader can top $20,000, not including camera maintenance and data storage fees. One Z Backscatter van costs as much as $825,000. [13]

But local taxpayers often are not footing the entire bill. Police buy surveillance technologies with money from private foundations, property forfeitures from drug busts and state and federal grants.

As law enforcement agencies, elected officials, citizens and community

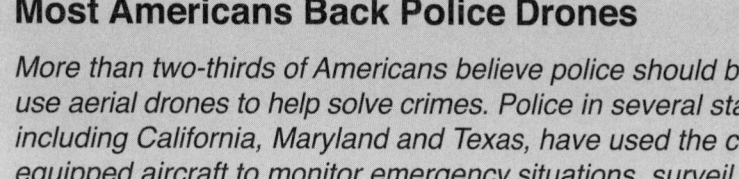

Most Americans Back Police Drones

More than two-thirds of Americans believe police should be able to use aerial drones to help solve crimes. Police in several states, including California, Maryland and Texas, have used the camera-equipped aircraft to monitor emergency situations, surveil crime scenes or assist in search-and-rescue operations.

Should police be allowed to use drones to help solve crimes?

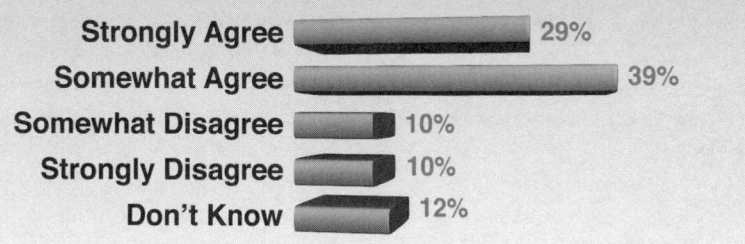

- **Strongly Agree** — 29%
- **Somewhat Agree** — 39%
- **Somewhat Disagree** — 10%
- **Strongly Disagree** — 10%
- **Don't Know** — 12%

Source: "Ipsos Poll Conducted for Reuters," Ipsos/Reuters, Jan. 29, 2015, http://tinyurl.com/mx9z7sr

and civil rights groups debate the use of advanced technology by police, here are some of the questions they are asking:

Is predictive policing effective and fair?

Police departments are increasingly employing so-called predictive policing software that uses mathematical algorithms to try to forecast when and where crimes are likely to occur. The goal is to position police resources in high-risk areas and prevent crime.

But community and civil-rights groups, including the Brennan Center and the ACLU, question predictive policing's efficacy and fairness. [14]

"It's a vicious cycle," said John Chasnoff, program director for the ACLU of Eastern Missouri. Many police departments disproportionately arrest minorities, and historical crime data fed into algorithms reflect that bias, Chasnoff said, leading to "even more arrests, compounding the racial problem." [15]

At least eight vendors offer the software, including IBM and Hitachi. [16] Industry leader PredPol, based in Santa Cruz, Calif., charges annual fees ranging from $10,000 for small police departments

up to $70,000 for the largest, says PredPol co-founder and UCLA anthropology professor Jeff Brantingham.

Some companies, including PredPol, feed only a jurisdiction's historical crime data — crime type; crime location; and crime date and time — into their algorithms. Others, like IBM and Philadelphia-based Azavea, add dozens of other factors, such as weather, school hours or locations of ATMs, vacant lots and liquor stores, depending on the crimes being predicted.

The algorithms forecast when different types of crimes are most likely to occur within areas as small as 500 square feet. They typically show up as colored boxes on digital maps that police officers view on tablets or smartphones as they begin their shifts.

Police crime analysts have always focused resources on high-crime areas, but predictive software crunches more data, uncovers unexpected areas and gives greater detail, say vendors. "We know you know the areas where you need to patrol, but do you know the precise street you need to be on? Well, we can tell you," said Cynthia Fay, IBM's sales manager for crime prevention and prediction. [17]

Police officials from Modesto, Calif., to Reading, Pa., say predictive policing gets results. The PredPol software "forces the officers to go to particular areas, conduct patrol checks and get themselves out there and talking with the people in the different neighborhoods," said Brandon McIntyre, a police officer in Cocoa, Fla. "And that just causes the visibility to go up and less crime all together." [18]

But skeptics say other factors could be at work. "We don't know if the drop in crime in these jurisdictions was because of the predictive technology or because of other environment or economic or social reasons," says Andrew Ferguson, a University of the District of Columbia law professor who studies predictive policing. In addition, crime has been declining across the country, he says.

Randomized controlled trials are widely viewed as the best way to determine whether predictive policing works, but few such studies have been done, in part because they are time consuming. PredPol's founders conducted a 21-month study of property crimes across three Los Angeles police districts in 2011 and 2012. It found the software was twice as successful at predicting crimes as human crime analysts.

"Police are the ones who get out of the car and deal with the challenge that's on the street, and predictive policing provides guidance on where and when that precious resource can have a big impact," says Brantingham.

But David Robinson, a principal at Upturn, a Washington, D.C., consulting group specializing in technology and social issues, finds the Los Angeles study unpersuasive: "The fraction of crime predicted is really small in either case."

Meanwhile, an independent study conducted in 2012 by RAND Corp., a Santa Monica, Calif., think tank, found no statistical evidence that a predictive policing algorithm developed by the Shreveport, La., police reduced crime any more than traditional policing. [19]

"The promise of [predictive policing] is amazing, so I can see why everyone wants to believe in it," said Jessica Saunders, a RAND study co-author. She and her colleagues speculated that perhaps police in Shreveport did not effectively use the algorithm-generated information. [20] Most predictive policing software tells police where to go and when, but not what to do once there.

"Were officers assigned in those locations for the entire shift? Were officers put there for 10 to 15 minutes a few times randomly during the shift?" asks Jeremy Heffner, senior data scientist at Azavea, maker of HunchLab predictive software. "Those things all impact what the outcome would be."

Efficacy is not the only concern about predictive policing. Critics worry that it perpetuates biased policing against poor and minority communities. Historical crime data used to forecast crime risk typically is pulled from reports that police officers file after collecting crime-scene information. It often reflects police decisions about where and when to enforce the law, which can be biased, critics say.

Narcotics is the best example, they say. "The normal way of policing drug crimes is going to be observing transactions in open-air drug markets or by putting your police in observation posts," says Ferguson. "But there's obviously a lot of drug crime that goes on behind closed doors in fancy neighborhoods that isn't going to be policed, and that creates a distorted window into actual crime problems."

That's why Predpol forecasts risk only for aggravated assault, including homicide; burglary; robbery; and car theft, says Brantingham. "We don't do narcotics and traffic moving violations, where the discovery of the crime is primarily at the discretion of the police officer."

Heffner says HunchLab is not typically used to forecast drug-crime risk. But when it is, the company tries to minimize bias by not using historical crime reports,

he says. Instead, it relies on the calls people make to police to report suspicious activity or a crime.

Civil rights groups also worry that predictive policing might encourage officers to be overly vigilant. Officers must have a reasonable suspicion to stop someone, but Ferguson notes that the Supreme Court has said that they can take an area's characteristics into account when determining reasonable suspicion. So an officer following a predictive map into an area marked high risk for robbery may feel justified in stopping anyone carrying a bag. [21]

"And so the Fourth Amendment," which protects against unreasonable searches and seizures, "can be distorted by these predictive technologies," says Ferguson.

Are body cameras an effective policing tool?

Since 2014, high-profile deaths of unarmed black men at the hands of police in New York City, Baltimore, Ferguson, Mo., and elsewhere have led to calls for more law enforcement agencies to use body cameras to record encounters with the public.

For 2016 alone, the Justice Department committed $20 million to help police agencies purchase cameras and train officers in their use, and departments from San Francisco to Atlanta now have officers wearing them. [22] New York City, plans to issue cameras to all 23,000 patrol officers by 2019 — the most ambitious program in the nation. [23]

In a rare instance of agreement, city councils, civil rights groups and police chiefs say the cameras can make police operations more transparent, hold police and civilians accountable for their actions and reduce police-civilian conflict. Yet stakeholders cannot agree on basic procedures such as where and when officers should record and when departments should release footage to the public. And research into body cameras' intended and unintended effects is barely keeping pace with their rapid deployment.

"I can assure you that if [the cameras] didn't provide these agencies a glimmer of improvement on changed behaviors, complaints against police and police use of force, they wouldn't be buying them," says Steve Tuttle, spokesman for Axon, formerly Taser International, a Scottsdale, Ariz., manufacturer that is the market leader. More than one-third of the country's roughly 18,000 law enforcement agencies have purchased the company's body cameras, Tuttle says.

As of two years ago, only eight empirical studies on body camera use in the United States had been completed. [24] Since then, a few more have been published. "The results of the studies are really mixed," says Nancy La Vigne, director of the Justice Policy Center at the Urban Institute, a Washington think tank.

Most studies indicate that formal complaints against police decline when officers wear cameras. "But we don't know why," says Cynthia Lum, director of the Center for Evidence-Based Crime Policy at George Mason University in Fairfax, Va. Individuals may be more satisfied, lodging fewer frivolous complaints or resolving complaints informally in the field as officers show them footage, Lum says.

While some studies show a decrease in police use of force with body cameras, others find no impact, including a study of eight police departments in the United Kingdom and the United States. But when the study's British authors did a deeper analysis, they found that "if officers turned cameras on and off during their shift, then use-of-force increased, whereas if they kept the cameras rolling for their whole shift, use-of-force decreased." Based on these results, the researchers recommended cameras remain on "during each and every interaction with citizens." [25]

However, that's not often the case, according to the Police Executive Research Forum (PERF), a research organization in Washington. "Of the police departments that PERF consulted, very few have adopted the policy of record-ing all encounters with the public," it said in a 2014 report. Instead, most require officers "to activate their cameras when responding to calls for service and during law enforcement-related encounters and activities, such as traffic stops, arrests, searches, interrogations, and pursuits." [26]

Officers need discretion "in sensitive situations, such as encounters with crime victims or witnesses," said PERF. In addition, turning on a body camera when chatting with neighborhood residents can "seem officious and off-putting," it said. [27]

Denver police officer Robert Greaser monitors license plates using an automatic plate reader. The devices can scan up to 1,800 license plates per minute. Typically mounted on light poles or in police cars, they connect to a computer database and can check if a car is stolen, the registration is expired or the owner has an outstanding arrest warrant.

Getty Images/The Denver Post/Brent Lewis

The ACLU agrees that discretion is needed when officers are interviewing witnesses and crime victims, says Chad Marlow, the organization's advocacy and policy counsel, and it adds a third circumstance: Individuals should be able to ask an officer to turn off the camera when they invite police into their homes. [28]

However, many law enforcement agencies allow officers to record inside homes "as long as they have a legal right to be there," said PERF. [29]

No matter a department's body-camera policy, officers don't always turn on cameras when they should. A November audit in Miami revealed that 63 of the 82 officers assigned body cameras had uploaded zero hours of footage over a two-week period. Departmental policy requires the officers to record all civilian encounters and upload the footage at shift's end, and the department is investigating why it's being ignored. [30]

But while body-camera footage can supplement witness accounts, the cameras have limits, say experts. If the point is to see what the police officer saw, then "in some cases the body camera footage might actually be misleading" because the human eye takes in less than the camera, says Seth Stoughton, a University of South Carolina law professor, who studies regulation of the police.

In addition, a camera may provide little useful information during a struggle. "The officer's body is likely to be very close to the suspect and to be moving rapidly and in different directions in a way that's going to jostle the camera," Stoughton says.

Another problem is that most police officers wear body cameras on the

FBI Casts Wide Facial-Recognition Net

A network of FBI databases that stores information gathered by facial-recognition technology is composed largely of images of Americans with no criminal record. The bureau compiled the databases by searching passport photos, visa applications and 16 states' driver's license databases. By contrast, the FBI's DNA database includes information only on Americans with criminal records.

Composition of FBI Databases: Criminal vs. Non-criminal, 2016

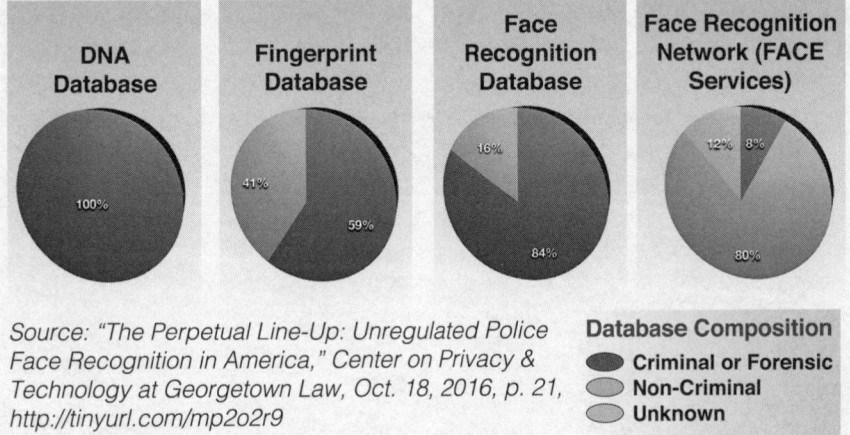

Source: "The Perpetual Line-Up: Unregulated Police Face Recognition in America," Center on Privacy & Technology at Georgetown Law, Oct. 18, 2016, p. 21, http://tinyurl.com/mp2o2r9

Database Composition
● Criminal or Forensic
◐ Non-Criminal
○ Unknown

chest, not at eye level, so the camera's lens is pointed upward. "As a result, people captured on camera, particularly people close to the officer, look taller and broader, and that makes them look more threatening," says Stoughton.

Police departments often struggle with how to respond to public demands for footage. In high-profile police shootings of citizens, "the public wants to see the footage, and they want it yesterday," says La Vigne. "But it's crucial evidence in a criminal case, and most law enforcement agencies and most state statutes say that type of evidence is exempt from public release."

Nevertheless, more departments are releasing the footage because not doing so causes too much community strife, she says.

Educating the public about the cameras' limits is crucial, says Stoughton. Tuttle agrees and says Axon has a toolkit, with sample videos, for that purpose. "You're setting up the community for false expectations if you don't," says Tuttle.

Should police be able to monitor social media?

Most people who use Facebook, Twitter, Instagram, Reddit or other social media platforms know that corporations mine the public data found there. But they may not realize that police departments do the same.

Police look for posts during emergencies from people who might need help, scrutinize the accounts of criminal suspects, track gang activity and search keywords and hashtags for potential threats. In a 2016 survey of 539 law enforcement agencies from 48 states, 70 percent said they used social media for intelligence gathering for investigations. [31]

Some police departments still do it the old-fashioned way — by searching and scrolling themselves. But an increasing number have been using monitoring software, which automates the process and can follow real-time posts and quickly search archived posts of thousands, if not millions, of people at once.

"But the technology can also be used to monitor political and social

justice movements, posing risks to First Amendment-protected activity" on free speech and assembly, according to the Brennan Center for Justice.

Over the past six months, law enforcement agencies that used such software were dealt a blow after civil liberties groups revealed that police were not only monitoring the social media activities of criminal suspects but also of political activists. In response, Twitter in November and Facebook and its Instagram platform in March strengthened their prohibition against vendors mining their data to develop tools for police surveillance. [32]

Others say police have every right to comb through public social media posts. Law enforcement is no different from businesses that gather such information, "except they're using it for public safety, not to market the latest and greatest coffee to somebody," said former police cybercrime officer Ryan Duquette, who heads Hexigent, a cybersecurity firm in Ontario, Canada. [33]

The actions of Facebook and Twitter were precipitated by the ACLU of California. Last September, after making public-records requests, it received thousands of pages of documents about the social media monitoring of dozens of California police departments, sheriffs and district attorneys. Forty percent of the responding agencies, or 20 in total, had acquired social media monitoring tools, many in the past year. [34]

"None of those agencies had engaged in public debate, and none produced any kind of policies about how the systems would be used or how civil rights would be protected," says Nicole Ozer, technology and civil liberties policy director at the Northern California ACLU chapter.

That was particularly worrisome because of the alarming nature of some of the marketing materials that the ACLU discovered, she says. Chicago-based Geofeedia "was marketing its product to monitor protests and activists, and it characterized protests and unions as 'overt threats,' " Ozer says. [35]

In a statement last October, Geofeedia CEO Phil Harris said the firm works to ensure "end-users do not seek to inappropriately identify individuals based on race, ethnicity, religious, sexual orientation or political beliefs, among other factors. That said, we understand . . . that we must continue to work to build on these critical protections of civil rights." [36]

Geofeedia was not the only problem vendor, says Ozer. The year before, Ozer's organization requested records from Fresno police and found marketing materials from Media Sonar containing a list of suggested search terms that included hashtags for activist groups and their slogans, such as #Blacklivesmatter. [37]

Records also show that San Jose police used Geofeedia to monitor South Asian, Muslim and Sikh protesters "only a few days after acquiring it," according to Ozer. [38]

Last fall, the ACLU of Colorado received documents from the Denver Police Department revealing that it briefly used Geofeedia. A media relations official with the Denver police told *CQ Researcher* in an email that the department used the software to monitor large public events, with key words filtering results to identify possible threats of violence, and to identify possible witnesses or suspects after a violent crime. "Thankfully, no such activities or incidents were identified during the time we used it," the official said.

Police do not have to obtain a warrant to monitor public social media posts. But Mark Silverstein, legal director at the ACLU of Colorado, says the monitoring software amasses so much data — or did before the Facebook and Twitter crackdowns — that it allows the police to "track our movements, our associations, our networks, who we know, who we talk to and how often." It is far different from just seeing a few posts online, he says, and has a chilling effect on free speech and association.

"There needs to be very strict safe-

guards and oversight in place to make sure those powers are not misused," says Ozer. The actions of Facebook and Twitter are a start, but now cities need to form oversight committees and pass legislation, she says.

But Detective Chris Adamczyk of the Mesa, Ariz., Police Department calls the Facebook and Twitter actions a "sad state of affairs."

His investigative unit is responsible for covering downtown and had been using Media Sonar software to investigate cyberbullying, human trafficking and some stabbings and drive-by shootings. Adamczyk says the software was used only when officers suspected criminal activity. But the social media platforms' crackdown has rendered the software practically useless, so his unit hasn't used Media Sonar in months, he says.

Denver has asked Geofeedia to cancel its contract after Twitter and Facebook specifically banned it from using their data streams in the fall. Geofeedia, Media Sonar and two other social media tracking companies, Liferaft, in Canada, and San Francisco-based Meltwater, did not respond to requests for interviews. ∎

BACKGROUND

Professional Policing

Before the mid-19th century, full-time police forces did not exist in the United States. The agrarian South had armed slave patrols, which hunted escaped slaves and enforced slave codes; the Northeast relied on nightwatch patrols, which rounded up drunks and focused on petty crime; and frontier areas used vigilantes and private police-for-hire. [39]

But as the country urbanized, cities began organizing formal police departments. New York City was the first,

establishing its department in 1845 with 800 officers. Boston and Philadelphia soon followed.

These early departments quickly became bastions of patronage, however. "The only qualification for becoming a cop was a political connection," wrote journalist Radley Balko in *Rise of The Warrior Cop: The Militarization of America's Police Forces*. "Training was nonexistent, beatings were common, and . . . the system had little effect on crime." [40]

During the first three decades of the 20th century, reformers worked to professionalize policing and distance it from political meddling. August Vollmer, police chief in Berkeley, was the nation's pre-eminent reformer, introducing forensic science in 1907, creating the Berkeley Police School in 1908, helping to establish the School of Criminology at the University of California, Berkeley, in 1916, and using the newly invented lie detector in 1920. [41]

Police departments across the country adopted entry requirements and personnel standards, and crime specialists began using technology — photography and fingerprinting — to investigate crimes and track suspects. [42]

Some police officials and politicians wanted to fingerprint everyone. In a 1936 campaign in Berkeley, Calif., the police chief and local businesses set up fingerprinting stations in public buildings, in shops and on street corners, and merchants offered discounts to citizens if they produced a police-issued "I have been fingerprinted" card, wrote sociologist Christian Parenti in *The Soft Cage: Surveillance in America From Slavery to the War on Terror*. The police had a clear goal: Fingerprinting enabled "us to follow the movement and activities of Communists, Anarchists and Radicals," according to a contemporary account. [43]

Law-and-Order Campaigns

Professionalizing police departments "wasn't easy," wrote New York

University law professor Barry Friedman in *Unwarranted: Policing Without Permission.* Many departments were corrupt, and vigilante justice, especially against African-Americans during the Jim Crow era, continued to pervade the rural South and West. [44]

"The facade of professional policing crumbled entirely during the turbulent 1960s," wrote Friedman. Violent crime

away for numerous "law and order" conservative politicians, including Richard M. Nixon in the 1968 presidential campaign, was a demand for police and courts to crack down on gangs, protesters and drug usage.

The 1970s saw New York and other states pass stringent anti-drug laws and tougher, mandatory sentencing rules for repeat offenders. [46]

cops, turning them into social workers who were expected to help residents with their problems.

Others said community policing and its emphasis on deterrence had a dark side: encouraging police officers to engage in discriminatory practices, such as New York City's stop-question-and-frisk policy. [48] The tactic involved temporarily detaining, questioning and sometimes searching individuals on suspicion of carrying weapons or contraband.

A related strategy — the "broken windows" theory of policing — required officers to show zero tolerance toward minor crimes such as vandalism and public drinking. Defenders of stop-and-frisk and broken-windows strategies said it made New York City safer in the 1990s and early 2000s by creating an atmosphere of order, preventing more serious crimes. But a judge in federal District Court in Manhattan ruled in 2013 that New York's stop-and-frisk violated minorities' constitutional rights. [49]

A demonstrator is arrested during a protest in Ferguson, Mo., on Aug. 10, 2015, marking the one-year anniversary of the controversial shooting of Michael Brown, an unarmed black teenager, by a white police officer. Brown's death in Ferguson ignited street protests around the country and calls by citizens and civil liberties groups for police departments to adopt body cameras to record officers' encounters with the public.

Getty Images/Scott Olson

more than tripled, from 288,000 in 1960 to 1,040,000 in 1975. Riots also engulfed the nation's inner cities over a five-year span in the 1960s. Angry over, among other things, racial prejudice, poverty and the assassination of Martin Luther King Jr., rioters looted stores and burned city blocks. A presidential commission in 1967 blamed the riots, in part, on deep hostility between police and impoverished inner-city communities. [45]

Massive protests against the Vietnam War, meanwhile, swept across the nation. Police in Chicago and other cities reacted harshly to the riots and protests, further raising tensions. But the take-

But by the late 1980s, progressive reformers and some police chiefs were embracing the notion of community policing: getting police officers out of their squad cars and walking neighborhood beats, where they would get to know residents, rebuild trust and devise creative solutions to improve public safety. Today, it is a "key component of policing efforts in most mid- and large-sized law enforcement agencies across the United States," according to an Urban Institute report. [47]

Some law enforcement officials, however, complained that community policing was a vague hodgepodge of policies that asked too much of beat

Despite the criticisms, law enforcement agencies were looking for new, cost-effective tools to enhance community policing efforts, according to the Urban Institute. One such tool was closed-circuit television. [50]

Although businesses began using closed-circuit cameras for security in the 1970s — and in 1973 the New York Police Department installed cameras in Times Square as a crime-fighting tool — law enforcement agencies didn't begin to deploy them widely in public spaces until the 1990s. A 2001 RAND survey found that 41 percent of local police departments and 66 percent of state police departments used "fixed-site video surveillance cameras." In 2002, the District of Columbia started building "a centrally monitored, citywide closed-circuit television surveillance system — the first of its kind in the nation," according to Parenti. [51]

Today, closed-circuit television "has become a ubiquitous tool of policing," according to a report from Data & Society,

Continued on p. 348

Chronology

1840s-1950s
Police departments become more professional.

1845
New York City establishes first police department with 800 officers. Boston and Philadelphia soon follow.

1905
August Vollmer, champion of a movement to professionalize policing, becomes police chief in Berkeley, Calif., and pioneers squad cars, police radios and crime labs.

1929
President Herbert Hoover establishes a national commission on law enforcement; it finds that brutality and corruption pervade Prohibition-era policing.

1950s
Most police now patrol in squad cars.

1960s-1990s
Police adopt community policing.

1965
Race riot erupts in the Watts section of Los Angeles, the first of many inner-city riots over the next four years.

1967
President Lyndon B. Johnson's Crime Commission recommends police improve community relations. . . . His National Advisory Commission on Civil Disorders blames race riots on white racism and hostility between police and inner-city communities. . . . In *United States v. Katz*, U.S. Supreme Court says police need warrants to wiretap public phone booths.

1973
New York City Police Department (NYPD) installs closed-circuit television cameras in Times Square.

1979
Flint, Mich., police officers begin to walk beats; it is part of an emerging community policing movement that seeks to rebuild trust and improve public safety by deemphasizing vehicular patrols.

1983
In *United States v. Knotts*, Supreme Court upholds police's warrantless use of a hidden beeper to track a suspect's car.

1984
Supreme Court rules a warrant is required when police place a beeper inside a home.

1994
President Bill Clinton embraces community policing and vows to put 100,000 new police officers on the street.

2001-Present
Police adopt powerful technologies to deter crime.

2001
Survey finds 41 percent of local police departments and 66 percent of state police use fixed-site closed-circuit cameras. . . . Supreme Court rules police must get a warrant before using thermal-imaging technology to obtain information from inside a home.

2002
Washington, D.C., begins building one of the first centrally monitored, citywide closed-circuit television surveillance systems.

2007
Nineteen percent of surveyed law enforcement agencies report using license-plate readers.

2008
NYPD secretly begin using cell-site simulators — portable devices that allow investigators to locate individuals by capturing signals from their cellphones.

2012
Eighty-five percent of law enforcement agencies say they plan to purchase or expand the use of license-plate readers.

2013
Police in Rialto, Calif., are first to use body cameras. . . . Seattle ordinance requires city council to give police guidance when purchasing surveillance technology.

2014
Darren Wilson, a white police officer in Ferguson, Mo., shoots to death unarmed black teenager Michael Brown and ignites street protests; civil liberties groups and citizens call for police nationwide to adopt body cameras to record encounters with the public.

2015
Ninety-seven percent of surveyed major police and sheriff's departments say they are moving forward with body cameras.

2016
Santa Clara County, Calif., gives elected officials the right to veto law enforcement purchases of surveillance technology.

2017
Several cities, including New York, consider measures to oversee police technology purchases and usage.

Facial Recognition Offers Promise — and Pitfalls

Civil libertarians worry the technology will lead to mass surveillance.

Lt. Dan Zehnder says he looks forward to the day when patrol officers can walk the Las Vegas Strip, use their body cameras to record pedestrians' faces, stream the footage to the cloud and get back an almost instantaneous answer: "Hey, that guy you just passed 20 feet ago has an outstanding warrant." [1]

Zehnder, who runs the Las Vegas Metropolitan Police Department's body-camera program, thinks that day is almost here — and so do civil libertarians, who worry about what this will mean for privacy.

As police increasingly use body cameras on patrol, civil liberties groups fear they will soon pair the cameras with facial-recognition software, turning them into mass-surveillance tools. That ability already exists. A Justice Department-commissioned survey found that 10 of 38 body-camera vendors offer models that allow facial-recognition software to be used with the camera or include an option for the software to be used later. [2]

Facial-recognition software analyzes someone's face and tries to match it against an identified face in a database.

"By combining body cameras with tagging technologies [such as facial recognition], government agencies could take videos of and catalog every individual attending a protest, participating in a religious ceremony, going to a union meeting or entering a health clinic," said a report from The Constitution Project, a bipartisan think tank in Washington.

Or a police department could send someone's facial image to every officer's body camera to track that person's location in real time. "Such a measure could occur on a mass scale, allowing police to place a digital 'tail' on hundreds of individuals without any suspicion of wrongdoing," the think tank warned. [3]

A quarter of state or local police departments already use facial recognition with still photographs, according to a study by Georgetown University's Center on Privacy & Technology. For example, police officers run facial-recognition searches using photographs they have taken with smartphones or tablets of individuals who can't or won't identify themselves. [4]

Utah's Statewide Information & Analysis Center uses facial recognition to conduct about a thousand checks per year, according to Utah Department of Public Safety Director Maj. Brian Redd. "We've helped law enforcement agencies solve frauds and home invasions and bank robberies," he said. [5]

Twenty-nine states allow facial-recognition searches of driver's license photos. More than 125 million American adults, or slightly more than half, are in databases that law enforcement can search with facial-recognition software, according to the Georgetown report. [6]

Utah once used its software to identify a man who was discovered badly injured on the side of a road. "It's very beneficial. It's been a great tool for us," said Redd. [7]

But civil libertarians warn that police officers' motives aren't always so benign. Police in San Diego County have used facial recognition since 2012. In 2014, civil rights attorney Victor Manuel Torres started receiving numerous complaints from residents who had been stopped by police officers and photographed without their permission. The complaints stopped in 2015 after the county police adopted a formal facial-recognition policy to guide its use. [8]

"Changes in technology are likely to make suspicionless searches even more common," Alvaro Bedoya, executive director of the Georgetown center, said in testimony before a congressional subcommittee last month. "The most advanced use of face recognition . . . scans the face of every man, woman or child who passes in front of a surveillance camera in or close to real-time."

Law enforcement agencies in Chicago, Dallas, Los Angeles, New York City and West Virginia "either have bought this technology, have announced plans to use it, or are actively exploring it" for use with closed-circuit television cameras, he said. [9]

But civil liberties groups worry most about pairing facial recognition with body cameras: the video images would be

Continued from p. 346

a think tank in New York City. That's despite studies showing that closed-circuit television may merely displace crime to other areas; has likely had a negligible effect on violent crime; and can even increase petty theft, since cameras give potential victims a false sense of security so they guard their belongings less diligently. [52]

Body cameras began their ascent in 2013, when police in Rialto, Calif., reportedly became the first to outfit all its officers with the cameras. [53] Before taking that step, the department completed a yearlong study in which it randomly assigned the cameras to some of its police shifts. The results were dramatic: "Shifts without cameras experienced twice as many incidents of use of force as shifts with cameras," the researchers reported. [54]

The small study — the department had only 54 frontline officers at the time — generated tremendous attention from police departments interested in reducing police use of force and citizen complaints. In a 2013 survey of 254 police departments, more than three-quarters reported that they were not using body cameras as of July that year. [55]

Public interest in the technology exploded in 2014, after Darren Wilson, a white police officer in Ferguson, Mo., shot to death an unarmed black teenager, Michael Brown. Wilson suspected Brown of shoplifting at a convenience store and stopped him as he walked on a nearby street. Wilson said Brown charged him after a short chase, and he opened fire in what he said was more accurate than those from fixed surveillance cameras because body cameras can be aimed directly at someone's face.

The ACLU recommends that police officers never use body cameras for routine filming of protests and rallies, in part because of the potential of facial recognition, says Chad Marlow, the organization's advocacy and policy counsel. Participants would know that the police could identify them using facial recognition and put them on a list of people to watch, Marlow says. "It would kill free speech."

Civil liberties groups also worry about the use of facial recognition during routine patrols, when officers on the street could stream facial images from body cameras to databases to identify individuals or check for outstanding warrants.

Such outstanding warrant notifications, cautions Jake Laperruque, The Constitution Project's senior counsel, should be given only for serious crimes and not for misdemeanors, such as overdue parking tickets or loitering. "A lot of jurisdictions have a huge number of outstanding warrants for small misdemeanors, sometimes half the population," says Laperruque.

Police officers could use those outstanding warrants as an excuse to arrest people they may not like, possibly including minorities or protesters, or simply to bring in someone who is giving them a hard time, says Laperruque.

"If you're going to give the government increased power that could be used in some ways for surveillance, it's really, really important that we get the policies right and put proper limits in place to make sure it can't be abused," says Laperruque.

But so far, states haven't stepped forward to pass such facial-recognition legislation. "With only a few exceptions, there are no laws governing police use of the technology, no standards ensuring its accuracy and no systems checking for bias," said Clare Garvie, a co-author of the report from Georgetown's Center on Privacy & Technology, where she is an associate. "It's a wild West." [10]

— *Barbara Mantel*

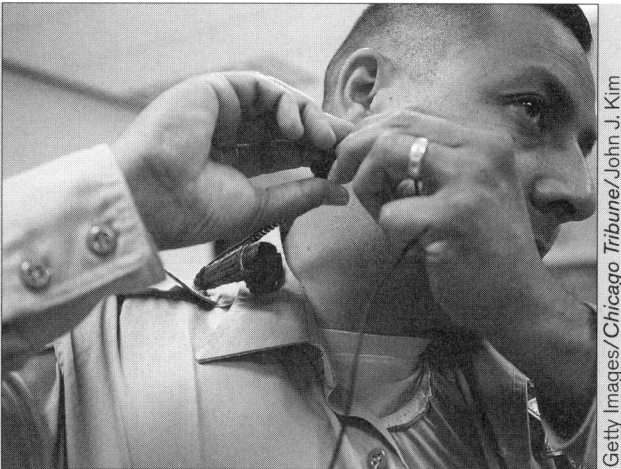

Las Vegas police Sgt. Miguel Garcia attaches a body camera to his shirt collar at the start of his shift on Feb. 17. Civil liberties groups worry that body cameras, increasingly used nationwide, will be linked with facial-recognition software, turning them into mass-surveillance tools.

[1] Karen Weise, "Will a Camera on Every Cop Make Everyone Safer? Taser Thinks So," *Bloomberg Businessweek*, July 12, 2016, http://tinyurl.com/mkytwcr.

[2] Alvaro Bedoya, "Statement of Alvaro Bedoya, Executive Director, Center on Privacy & Technology at Georgetown Law," Committee on Oversight and Government Reform, U.S. House of Representatives, March 22, 2017, p. 7, http://tinyurl.com/n5n9wlu.

[3] "Guidelines For The Use of Body-Worn Cameras By Law Enforcement," The Constitution Project, December 2016, p. 17, http://tinyurl.com/n2hvvsb.

[4] Clare Garvie *et al.*, "The Perpetual Line-Up: Unregulated Police Face Recognition in America," Center on Privacy & Technology, Georgetown Law, Oct. 18, 2016, pp. 2, 10-11, http://tinyurl.com/mp2o2r9.

[5] Andrew Adams, "How facial recognition solves crimes in Utah," KSL.com, Sept. 19, 2016, http://tinyurl.com/l2nh6dt.

[6] Bedoya, *op. cit.*, p. 1.

[7] Adams, *op. cit.*

[8] Garvie, *op. cit.*, p. 58.

[9] Bedoya, *op. cit.*, p. 7.

[10] Ava Kofman, "Study: Face Recognition Systems Threaten The Privacy of Millions," *The Intercept*, Oct. 18, 2016, http://tinyurl.com/koddx63.

self-defense. Some witness accounts supported Wilson's version of events, but others said Brown had his hands raised in surrender. [56]

When a grand jury declined to indict Wilson, Brown's family issued a statement: "Join with us in our campaign, to ensure that every police officer working the streets in this country wears a body camera." [57]

In a 2015 survey of 70 major police and sheriff's departments, 97 percent "indicated that they were moving forward with body camera systems." [58]

Legal Protections

In the past decade, city police and county sheriff departments have adopted a wide range of powerful technologies, from license-plate readers to aerial drones to cell-site simulators. And the spread of these high-tech tools has raised an important question about whether using them would require a warrant under the Fourth Amendment.

The Fourth Amendment to the U.S. Constitution reads in part: "The right of the people to be secure in their persons, houses, papers, and effects, against unreasonable searches and seizures, shall not be violated, and no warrants shall issue, but upon probable cause." [59] The amendment has been interpreted as specifically protecting citizens from unwarranted searches by government agents. It does not guarantee a right to privacy in general — such as protection from corporations spying on one's online purchasing activity.

If something is a "search" within the meaning of the amendment, law en-

Security Cameras Stirring Privacy Concerns

"They are truly a dragnet surveillance."

When two bombs went off at the finish line of the Boston Marathon on April 15, 2013, investigators immediately began screening footage from bystanders' smartphones and government and private surveillance cameras blanketing the area. It took several days, but they found what they were looking for: suspicious images of two men, one with a backpack, captured by a department store camera. [1]

The men were quickly identified as brothers Dzhokhar and Tamerlan Tsarnaev, and over a two-day manhunt, Tamerlan was killed and Dzhokhar captured. Dzhokhar was tried, convicted and sentenced to death in the bombing that killed three and wounded more than 200. [2]

For some, the episode was a powerful example of the potential for public and private surveillance cameras to help law enforcement deter or solve crimes.

"They serve an important function for the city in providing the type of safety on a day-to-day basis — not just for big events like a marathon, but day-to-day purposes," said Mayor Rahm Emanuel, of Chicago, which has the nation's largest surveillance camera network. [3]

Nevertheless, studies of the cameras' impact have shown mixed results. [4] And civil libertarians say street cameras and other surveillance equipment that indiscriminately scoop up broad swaths of information raise privacy concerns because they are trained on the general public as well as crime suspects. This equipment, said Jake Laperruque, senior counsel at The Constitution Project, a think tank in Washington, is "upending how we view surveillance and the limits the Fourth Amendment places on it in maintenance of a democratic society." [5]

The number of closed-circuit television cameras monitored by law enforcement officials in the United States is unknown, but there are scattered reports about their spread. In Detroit, more than 100 businesses have invested in high-definition surveillance cameras since January 2016 and linked them via the Internet to a police command center. [6]

The New York City Police Department reportedly monitors 6,000 street cameras, of which two-thirds are privately owned. [7] Chicago has 22,000 integrated surveillance cameras positioned throughout the city, including on trains and buses. The cameras employ facial recognition and automatic tracking, which means a computer can track an individual from one camera to the next. [8]

State and local police departments, including in Alabama, Arkansas, Florida, Idaho, Texas and Washington state, also are using aerial drones equipped with cameras and sometimes night vision. Police typically use the equipment to document crime scenes, assist SWAT teams and locate suspects in real time. [9]

Automated license-plate readers can scan up to 1,800 license plates per minute. That means in a week, the Los Angeles sheriff's and police departments are able to collect data on about 3 million vehicles, according to the San Francisco-based Electronic Frontier Foundation, a digital-rights organization. [10]

These high-speed cameras, typically mounted on light poles or police cars, connect to a computer database and can check if a car is stolen, the registration is expired or the owner has an outstanding arrest warrant. The collected data are stored.

All these technologies trouble civil libertarians to varying degrees, but license-plate readers are one of the most disturbing "because they are truly a dragnet surveillance," says Rachel Levinson-Waldman, senior counsel to the Liberty and National Security Program at the Brennan Center for Justice, a law and policy institute in New York City. For example, the Virginia State Police used the readers to record the license plates of vehicles arriving from Virginia for the inauguration of former President Barack Obama in 2009, she says.

forcement can do it, "so long as they have probable cause and a warrant," wrote New York University's Friedman. "But if it is not a 'search' within the meaning of the Fourth Amendment, there are no limits on what the government can do. To any of us." [60]

The Supreme Court has been grappling for decades with what constitutes a search. In 1967, the FBI wiretapped a public phone booth to try to catch Charles Katz of Los Angeles, suspected of placing illegal sports bets from the phone. The agent did not get a warrant for the wiretap, reasoning that it was not a search because any member of the public walking by the booth, even with the door closed, might overhear Katz. But in *Katz v. United States*, the Supreme Court disagreed, ruling that the Fourth Amendment protects people, not places. [61]

The decision established what became known as the "Katz test." Whether something is a search or not "depends on whether the government invaded a person's 'reasonable expectation of privacy,' " according to Friedman. At the same time, the court said that "what a person knowingly exposes to the public, even in his own home or office, is not a subject of Fourth Amendment protection."

But place still mattered. In the early 1980s, the Supreme Court ruled that the police were within their rights to attach a beeper — a radio transmitter that acts as a tracking device — to a suspect's car without a warrant, but then ruled a year later that placing a beeper inside a home was a search and required a warrant. [62]

Today's modern technology has advanced far beyond beepers and is "effectively erasing the distinction so critical to *Katz*: between what we knowingly expose to the public and what we seek to keep private," said Friedman. And this presents a challenge to the courts. [63]

Police say the data are useful for finding stolen cars or even kidnapped children. "We've got numerous cases where this is used as an investigative resource," said Sgt. Kyle Hoertsch of the Sacramento County, Calif., Sheriff's Department. "We use it in every aspect of the job." [11]

Public involvement is the key to balancing privacy issues with the technologies' crime-fighting value, says Levinson-Waldman. Local and state officials, with public input, can pass measures about when and how the technologies can be used, how long collected data can be kept and whether search warrants are needed, she says.

Jim Bueermann, president of the Police Foundation, a group in Washington that provides training and technical assistance to law enforcement agencies, agrees and says police should also solicit public opinion directly.

Bueermann was police chief in Redlands, Calif., from 1998 to 2011 and oversaw the installation of a surveillance camera system on poles and buildings throughout the city. "We created a Citizens Privacy Council, which anyone could join," says Bueermann, "and with each successive camera we wanted to install, we went to the council and got them to sign off."

When he wanted to install microphones on some of the cameras, the council told him it was "too creepy, and so we created a policy to never put microphones on these cameras," he says.

Redlands is a small city, with a population of about 71,000. But that doesn't excuse larger cities from doing the same, says Bueermann. "The police departments can hold precinct-level meetings about this stuff, and they can hold meetings in city council districts."

— Barbara Mantel

A New York City Police Department security camera is mounted on a light pole across the street from Trump Tower. The NYPD reportedly monitors 6,000 street cameras, of which two-thirds are privately owned.

[1] Heather Kelly, "After Boston: The pros and cons of surveillance cameras," CNN, April 26, 2013, http://tinyurl.com/d3a6o6h.

[2] Jerry Markon, Sari Horwitz and Jenna Johnson, "Dzhokhar Tsarnaev charged with using 'weapon of mass destruction,' " *The Washington Post*, April 22, 2013, http://tinyurl.com/k8abxvv; Milton J. Valencia, "Dzhokhar Tsarnaev gets death penalty for placing Marathon bomb," *The Boston Globe*, May 15, 2015, http://tinyurl.com/k9m7e33.

[3] Craig Dellimore, "Emanuel Stresses Value of Surveillance Cameras in Probe of Boston Bombings," CBS Chicago, April 17, 2013, http://tinyurl.com/bucpncu.

[4] Max Bauer, "Review of Studies on Surveillance Camera Effectiveness," Privacy SOS, http://tinyurl.com/krqj4vg.

[5] Jake Laperruque, "Preventing an Air Panopticon: A Proposal For Reasonable Legal Restrictions on Aerial Surveillance," *University of Richmond Law Review*, March 24, 2017, p. 705, http://tinyurl.com/kjvgv6k.

[6] Laura Kelly, "Smart cities becoming a reality," *Security Systems News*, April 3, 2017, http://tinyurl.com/k9dwg7e.

[7] Bryan Joshua Schonfeld, "Expand New York City's surveillance camera network," *New York Daily News*, Feb. 16, 2015, http://tinyurl.com/kyzvnnr.

[8] Brendan McQuade, "Surveillance and Policing in Chicago . . . and its Discontents," American Association of Geographers, April 2, 2015, http://tinyurl.com/lpnnfdn.

[9] "Spotlight on Surveillance — October 2014," Electronic Privacy Information Center, October 2014, http://tinyurl.com/k9vg6bz.

[10] "Street Level Surveillance," Electronic Frontier Foundation, http://tinyurl.com/kn696uh.

[11] Raheem F. Hosseini, "Cops' license-plate readers keep their eye on you, Sacramento," *Sacramento News & Review*, April 7, 2016, http://tinyurl.com/jje4sct.

In 2001, the Supreme Court ruled in *Kyllo v. United States* that police must get a search warrant before deploying any kind of "sense-enhancing technology" to obtain information from inside a home. Without a warrant, the police had used a thermal heat detector to measure infrared radiation emitted from a roof, indicating the use of grow lamps inside to cultivate marijuana plants. However, the court said its ban on the warrantless use of such technology holds only as long as "the technology is not in the general use." [64]

"Given the current pace of technology, soon everything law enforcement possesses might be 'in general use,' " wrote Friedman. For example, many hobbyists fly drones. "Does that mean the government is now free to hover them outside our windows and over our backyards?" he asked. [65]

No court has yet ruled on law enforcement's use of drones, said the Brennan Center's Levinson-Waldman. And court rulings on other examples of the latest technology are infrequent. For example, no court has ruled on law enforcement's use of body cameras inside a home.

While the Supreme Court has ruled that drivers cannot expect their license-plate numbers to be private, no case to date has challenged the creation of license-plate databases of presumptively innocent people. At least two courts, however, have said that police need a warrant to use a Stingray device. "Absent a search warrant, the government may not turn a citizen's cellphone into a tracking device," said a federal judge. [66]

Meanwhile, municipalities began taking the matter into their own hands earlier in the decade. After the Seattle police department's controversial acquisition of a drone, the city became the first municipality to adopt an ordinance requiring some kind of oversight before the police or any city department purchases surveillance equipment. The 2013 ordinance requires the Seattle City Council to assess "the technology's impact on privacy and anonymity and propose steps to be taken to mitigate those impacts," wrote the University of California's Joh. [67] ∎

Marchers in Los Angeles' Skid Row area protest police brutality on Oct. 22, 2015, joining other demonstrators in New York City and some 30 other cities. A placard calls for the release of police body camera footage taken during the police shooting death of an unarmed, homeless Cameroonian immigrant, Charly Leundeu Keunang. Los Angeles County's district attorney found that the three officers involved reasonably believed Keunang posed a lethal threat during attempts to arrest him.

CURRENT SITUATION

Legislatures Weigh In

Lawmakers in Maine and California are considering legislation to make the use of surveillance technology more transparent.

Ten Maine legislators, a mix of Democrats and Republicans, introduced a bill in March that would require "a state entity to hold a public hearing and obtain legislative approval prior to engaging in certain activities relating to the acquisition

and use of surveillance technology." [68]

And legislative committees in California are considering a bill — introduced last December by two California Democratic state senators — that would require any city or county public agency to provide, at a public hearing, a proposed plan for "the use of each type of surveillance technology and the information collected." [69]

The California legislation does not give city and county elected officials veto power over equipment purchases. Nevertheless, it has drawn criticism from law enforcement.

"If we put out there the type of surveillance we use, what data we are collecting, how the surveillance technology is monitored for security . . . we're really setting it up to expose the utility and the security of [the technology] to those who would seek to defeat it or manipulate it," said Cory Salzillo, legislative director of the California State Sheriffs' Association. [70]

Shahid Buttar, director of grassroots advocacy at the Electronic Frontier

Foundation, a San Francisco group that champions user privacy and free expression in the digital world, argues the bill would not undermine public safety but instead would provide some transparency. In fact, he says, it doesn't go far enough because it contains too many loopholes.

"If a law enforcement agency wants to propose a new use for an existing technology, it doesn't have to go through the transparency process that the bill requires for new technologies," he says. In addition, the bill's language might permit nondisclosure agreements that allow the secret use of equipment like cell-site simulators.

"It has a lot of holes, so many in fact that we fear it could become a pathway to legitimizing the use of surveillance technology to monitor communities without . . . community control over their police departments," says Buttar.

The Maryland General Assembly is considering creating a taskforce to study how police deploy its surveillance technology. The bill's sponsor, Delegate Charles Sydnor, D-Baltimore, said transparency is important as more departments throughout the state use facial recognition, cell-site simulators and aerial surveillance. ""It seems as if we are moving toward a surveillance state with the type of surveillance used by law enforcement," he said.

The Maryland Image Repository System, for instance, allows investigators to cross-check digitized images against driver's license photos or police booking photos. [71]

Cities Seek Oversight

In early March, New York City Democratic City Council members Dan Garodnick and Vanessa Gibson introduced the Public Oversight of Surveillance Technology Act, or POST Act, that they say would remove the shroud of secrecy under which the New York

Continued on p. 354

At Issue:

Should elected officials decide whether police and prosecutors can use surveillance technologies?

CHAD MARLOW
ADVOCACY AND POLICY COUNSEL,
AMERICAN CIVIL LIBERTIES UNION

WRITTEN FOR *CQ RESEARCHER*, APRIL 2017

*t*hroughout America, police have acquired advanced surveillance technologies and trained them on communities of color and other unjustly targeted groups, from Muslims to political activists.

Not surprisingly then, as the local use of surveillance technologies continues to increase, so have questions about what limits should be placed on their use, or if they should even be used at all.

But in most U.S. cities, when it comes to acquiring and using surveillance technologies, public concern is irrelevant. So are the concerns of elected officials. The only stakeholder with a voice in the matter is the local police department, and when it decides to use surveillance technologies, it generally keeps those decisions secret.

Modern surveillance technologies now enable the police to monitor tens of thousands of people at a time. Considering that these technologies have the broad ability to undermine civil liberties, and have been used to do so in the past, allowing police to secretly make decisions about their use with no public knowledge or input not only is unwise, it also is dangerous to our democracy.

Fortunately, an effort to change that is underway in 17 cities. The effort, called Community Control Over Police Surveillance (CCOPS), seeks to modify local laws to require open hearings and city council approval before any surveillance technologies are used or their data are shared with others entities.

Moreover, when approvals are sought, CCOPS' laws require the public to receive information about how the technologies work and what safeguards will be implemented to protect civil rights and liberties. The laws also include annual reporting requirements, so inappropriate uses can be quickly identified and corrected.

To counter such efforts, law enforcement likes to try to scare the public by creating a false choice between liberty and security. They tell the public that open hearings will let the "bad guys" know how law enforcement is watching them, but in truth, most police surveillance technologies can be purchased or researched online.

They also tell us that secrecy is needed so "terrorists" won't learn about our methods for preventing attacks. In reality, terrorists are well aware we are spying on them.

Surveillance technologies may have some beneficial purposes. Or maybe they don't. Ultimately, it should be up to the people and their elected representatives to make that call.

JOSHUA MARQUIS
BOARD MEMBER, NATIONAL DISTRICT
ATTORNEYS ASSOCIATION

WRITTEN FOR *CQ RESEARCHER*, APRIL 2017

*i*n the past few years some well-meaning, if ill-informed, activists have urged and sometimes persuaded city governments to require that any use of what they call police "surveillance" be approved by the city council or governing municipal board.

The concerns are not entirely unreasonable, given that more than 40 years ago the federal government ran a highly illegal intelligence operation known an COINTELPRO. Its function was to infiltrate and often destabilize groups who strongly disagreed with government policies. But the key word in that description is "illegal," and eventually people were fired and Sen. Frank Church, D-Idaho, presided over extensive hearings on the program.

Local police should not be tapping into people's phones, hacking their computers or using spy-like technology, at least not without a search warrant issued by a judge. But a reality check is necessary.

Police agencies in America simply do not have access to National Security Agency spy technology, nor should they.

Another reasonable question has to be, "What constitutes surveillance?" Is reading a public Facebook page "snooping"? The American Civil Liberties Union (ACLU) has argued, with some success, that using the noses of dogs or even simple binoculars constitutes a "search" under the Fourth Amendment ban on unreasonable searches.

Beyond that, many intelligence agencies are so siloed that it is often impossible for them to share information, as we saw in the wake of 9/11.

But groups like the ACLU have convinced a few cities, such as Portland, Ore., and San Francisco, to drop out entirely of the Joint Terrorism Task Forces that have allowed a few local police to obtain security clearances and share information with their federal counterparts. The tragic murders in San Bernardino, Calif., in 2015 show that there are very real reasons police sometimes need to know about potential terrorist threats.

Those who demand that accountability lie only with a group of city councilors, none of whom likely have any law enforcement background or the interest or capability to get a security clearance, are ignoring an important fact.

The vast majority of chief prosecutors and sheriffs in America are elected, and if voters think they are overstepping the bounds of propriety, recent elections have shown they are not the least bit afraid to throw them out of office.

Continued from p. 352

City Police Department (NYPD) surveils residents.

The bill would require the department to display its surveillance policies on its website, explaining the capabilities, rules and guidelines for the use of various surveillance technologies, how the NYPD would safeguard collected data and whether that data would be shared. The police would not have

these uncertain times, Garodnick says. But decisions to purchase and deploy new and powerful surveillance technologies should not be made in secret, he says. "Even local elected officials, like me, are kept in the dark about what technologies the NYPD is buying and how they're being used."

The bill would allow the public and elected officials to comment on the impact and use policy, and the police

towers. Larry Byrne, NYPD's deputy commissioner for legal affairs, said Garodnick's bill would be a boon to terrorists, who would love to know the NYPD's surveillance technologies. [75]

That latter argument drew a retort from Jim Bueermann, retired police chief in Redlands, Calif., and president of the Police Foundation, a research and police training organization in Washington. "Dude, don't you think terrorists know all about these technologies?" he says. "I don't know why anyone would object to this. Getting community input is one of the underpinnings of community policing."

Seventeen other cities and counties have introduced similar measures, and some give elected officials the right to approve or reject each type of surveillance technology. The cities include Oakland, Palo Alto, Fresno, Santa Rosa and Santa Cruz, all in California, as well as Cambridge, Mass., and Providence, R.I.

Last year, Santa Clara County, Calif., which encompasses Silicon Valley, passed a surveillance oversight ordinance giving the Board of Supervisors veto power over county agencies' surveillance technology purchases. Agencies now must develop board-approved use policies that protect civil rights and civil liberties. Agencies also must send annual reports to the board on how they are using the surveillance equipment.

"The legislative veto is key. It gives legislation some teeth," says Buttar of the Electronic Frontier Foundation. "New York City's POST Act unfortunately does not have a veto, but we do support it." New York state law doesn't permit such a veto, Buttar adds.

Sheriff's deputy Dave Durbin prepares to fly a drone during a demonstration of a search and rescue operation in Dublin, Calif. Police typically use drones, which are equipped with cameras, to document crime scenes, assist SWAT teams and locate suspects. Some cameras also have night vision equipment. More than two-thirds of Americans believe police should be able to use drones to solve crimes.

AP Photo/Noah Berger

to reveal operational details or get permission from the City Council to purchase technology. [72]

The NYPD has "quietly amassed" Stingrays, Z Backscatter vans, license-plate readers and a Domain Awareness System "that integrates data from thousands of security cameras, license-plate readers, E-ZPass readers and MetroCard swipes to track New Yorkers' travels," all without public notice, debate or oversight, the sponsors said. The NYPD shares the data with the FBI-led Joint Terrorism Task Force, which includes representatives from Immigration and Customs Enforcement. [73]

"The NYPD has a strong capability for surveillance, as they should" in

department could take those comments into consideration. [74] Because the policy would include only general information about each technology's capabilities and use, the bill strikes a balance between "significant law enforcement and national security concerns with transparency and democratic accountability," says Garodnick.

But Police Commissioner James O'Neill said the bill overreaches and "would not be helpful to anyone in New York City." Defenders of New York's robust surveillance capabilities also note that the city is a popular terrorist target, most horrifically on Sept. 11, 2001, when terrorists crashed two jetliners into the World Trade Center, destroying the two

Regulating Technologies

A number of states have enacted technology-specific laws, creating a nationwide patchwork of regulations. As of February, at least 13 states have laws regulating the use of license-plate readers or the retention of the data they collect, according to the National Conference of State Legislatures.

The laws typically specify how long the data can be stored — from three minutes in New Hampshire to three years in Colorado; whether it can be shared with the public; which kinds of law enforcement officers can access the data; and how they can use it.

None of the state laws require the kind of public scrutiny and oversight mandated by Santa Clara County's more general measure and others like it, and they don't give local governments veto power over use of the equipment. [76]

Thirty-two states and Washington, D.C., have laws governing body cameras as of August, according to the National Conference of State Legislatures. (*See graphic, p. 340.*) Again, the laws don't give local governments veto power over camera use or require periodic public hearings. Instead, they deal with issues such as where body cameras can be used, whether officers need to notify people that the cameras are turned on and whether the footage is exempt from state laws requiring the release of records to the public, says the Urban Institute's La Vigne. [77]

According to La Vigne, several notable trends are emerging. States have begun to recognize the complex issues around body cameras and several have initiated pilot studies. And while most state laws "dictate when cameras should be turned on, more recent legislation dictates when they should be turned off," she wrote. In addition, some states, such as Oklahoma, are mandating the release of footage in high-profile cases, recognizing the growing public demand to view such video. [78]

Nevertheless, local law enforcement agencies in many of these states still have wiggle room to develop their own body camera policies, says La Vigne. "State laws are not very prescriptive on camera use, with the exception of 'reasonable expectation of privacy' and a few recent state laws that prohibit body camera use in schools and hospital settings," she says. ∎

OUTLOOK

Predictive Policing

The pressure to be smarter in fighting crime will increase the likelihood that predictive policing software will become the norm in American policing within the next 10 years, says Ferguson of the University of the District of Columbia.

But he would like to see cities send in social workers, construction crews and other service providers, and not just police officers, to high-risk areas. For example, if a particular parking lot is experiencing a rash of stolen cars, city workers should figure out the root causes, such as poor lighting, and fix them, he says. "The problem is that all the funding goes through the police, and so we are in this police paradigm."

HunchLab's Heffner says his company is encouraging police departments to do things that might be a bit outside their comfort zone, such as repositioning intervention services in areas flagged as high risk for narcotics crimes.

"Something that we've talked about with Chicago is if we can accurately predict where the shootings may be," Heffner says, "we can reposition ambulances so that we reduce the response time, which increases the likelihood of saving the life of the person who ends up getting shot."

Body cameras also are going to be "increasingly commonplace" in five to 10 years, says the Urban Institute's La Vigne. "This is going to be a standard piece of equipment on sworn officers who interact with the public."

Tuttle of Axon says a growing number of the cameras will be automatic. Axon has just introduced a model that has a side-arm signal. The sensor is mounted to the officer's holster, and all body-worn cameras within 30 feet automatically turn on when that firearm is drawn. The sensor can be used in other ways too, says Tuttle, including "if you turn

your lights on, turn your siren on, open your car door or remove a gun from the car's electronically locked rifle rack."

"It will be really interesting to see how the effectiveness of body-worn cameras changes when agencies start adopting these more higher-tech models that automatically turn on," says La Vigne.

Lum of George Mason University says researchers need to look into the unintended effects of body cameras on police behavior. One study has shown that officers might become more legalistic and choose to "arrest an individual as opposed to use their discretion" and issue a warning, she says.

Studies are also needed on whether the cameras "can reduce implicit or explicit bias and differential treatment based on race, sex, age, ethnicity or other extralegal characteristics," according to Lum. After all, a federal judge ordered New York City to get body cameras as part of a ruling that found the NYPD's stop-and-frisk practices wrongly targeted minorities. [79]

As sophisticated technologies become more common over the next several years, civil liberties and community groups expect greater civilian oversight of the police.

"In this spirit, a powerful coalition of national organizations is launching a multicity legislative initiative, Community Control Over Police Surveillance (CCOPS), to introduce more local laws to bring transparency and community control to the acquisition and use of local police surveillance technologies," the Northern California ACLU chapter's Ozer said in September. [80]

Ferguson proposes that cities and counties hold annual surveillance summits. Residents, technology experts, elected officials and the police would discuss, before a technology is adopted, "how are we going to protect against racial bias, how are we going to address transparency concerns, how are we going to make sure that it works so we're not wasting money that could be used on building better schools," he says. ∎

Notes

1 Stacia Glenn, "Burglaries dropping in Tacoma," *The News Tribune*, Oct. 18, 2015, http://tinyurl.com/k6fu6cm.

2 "Predictive Policing Today: A Shared Statement of Civil Rights Concerns," Joint Statement by 17 Civil Rights Groups, Aug. 31, 2016, http://tinyurl.com/k7stf48.

3 "William Bratton on Tech and the Changing Face of Policing," Brennan Center for Justice, Sept. 15, 2016, http://tinyurl.com/mqhya3w.

4 "NYPD has used Stingrays more than 1,000 times since 2008," New York Civil Liberties Union, Feb. 11, 2016, http://tinyurl.com/knsorab.

5 Monte Reel, "Secret Cameras Record Baltimore's Every Move From Above," *Bloomberg Businessweek*, Aug. 23, 2016, http://tinyurl.com/ln4aoys.

6 "Baltimore Police Respond To Report Of Secret Aerial Surveillance Program," CBS Baltimore, Aug. 24, 2017, http://tinyurl.com/kf3d8um.

7 "Community Control Over Police Surveillance," American Civil Liberties Union, 2017, http://tinyurl.com/mmbpdyh.

8 Rachel Levinson-Waldman, "Hiding in Plain Sight: A Fourth Amendment Framework for Analyzing Government Surveillance in Public," *Emory Law Journal*, March 2017, p. 528, http://tinyurl.com/kuxb2tj.

9 "Fourth Amendment," U.S. Constitution, Legal Information Institute, Cornell University Law School, http://tinyurl.com/k4mvu8r.

10 Elizabeth Joh, "The Undue Influence of Surveillance Technology Companies on Policing," *New York University Law Review*, forthcoming, Abstract, p. 2, http://tinyurl.com/kkrgzjn.

11 *Ibid.*; Cyrus Farivar, "FBI would rather prosecutors drop cases than disclose stingray details," *Ars Technica*, April 7, 2015, http://tinyurl.com/mpc7vxe.

12 "Proposal for Media Sonar: FRESNORTC001,"

Media Sonar, Oct. 22, 2015, http://tinyurl.com/kpm7yw4.

13 Brian Bakst and Ryan J. Foley, "For police body cameras, big costs loom in storage," The Associated Press, Feb. 6, 2015, http://tinyurl.com/lfabkao; "Automated License Plate Readers: Frequently Asked Questions," Electronic Frontier Foundation, http://tinyurl.com/k6dfvfb; and Michael Grabell, "Judge Orders NYPD to Release Records on X-Ray Vans, *ProPublica*, Jan. 9, 2015, http://tinyurl.com/n9frgln.

14 "Predictive Policing Today: A Shared Statement of Civil Rights Concerns," *op. cit.*

15 Maurice Chammah, "Policing the Future," The Marshall Project, Feb. 3, 2016, http://tinyurl.com/hyf3ocd.

16 David Robinson and Logan Koepke, "Stuck in a Pattern: Early evidence on 'predictive policing' and civil rights," *Upturn*, August 2016, pp. 3-4, http://tinyurl.com/kdl8e3w.

17 David Griffith, "Predictive Policing: Seeing the Future," *Police Magazine*, June 30, 2015, http://tinyurl.com/gwllfb7.

18 "Cocoa police use software to thwart crime," WFTV9 (ABC), Oct. 23, 2015, http://tinyurl.com/l49sg2v.

19 Priscilla Hunt *et al.*, "Evaluation of the Shreveport Predictive Policing Experiment," RAND Corp., 2014, pp. xiii, 4, http://tinyurl.com/zm5xtf4.

20 Emily Thomas, "Why Oakland Police Turned Down Predictive Policing," *Motherboard*, Dec. 28, 2016, http://tinyurl.com/nxbaqsd; Hunt *et al.*, *ibid.*, p. xiii.

21 *Illinois v. Wardlow*, 528 U.S. 119, 124 (2000), https://supreme.justia.com/cases/federal/us/528/119/case.html.

22 "Justice Department Announces $20 Million in Funding to Support Body-Worn Camera Pilot Program," U.S. Department of Justice, May 1, 2015, http://tinyurl.com/nyqxec2.

23 Colleen Long, "NYPD plans 23,000 body cams. Number on streets now: 0," The Associated Press, Feb. 11, 2017, http://tinyurl.com/ktvbedp.

24 Cynthia Lum *et al.*, "Existing and Ongoing Body Worn Camera Research: Knowledge Gaps and Opportunities," George Mason University, 2015, pp. 6-7, http://tinyurl.com/kxny5ge.

25 Barak Ariel *et al.*, "Report: increases in police use of force in the presence of body-worn cameras are driven by officer discretion: a protocol-based subgroup analysis of ten randomized experiments," *Journal of Experimental Criminology*, May 17, 2016, p. 461, http://tinyurl.com/m2euptl.

26 "Implementing a Body-Worn Camera Program: Recommendations and Lessons Learned," U.S. Department of Justice, Police Executive Research Forum, 2014, p. 13, http://tinyurl.com/lxdg7ej.

27 *Ibid.*

28 "A model act for regulating the use of wearable body cameras by law enforcement," American Civil Liberties Union, January 2017, http://tinyurl.com/m5q5bqg.

29 "Implementing a Body-Worn Camera Program: Recommendations and Lessons Learned," *op. cit.*

30 Jessica Lipscomb, "Dozens of Miami Cops Aren't Uploading Their Body Cam Footage," *Miami New Times*, Dec. 15, 2016, http://tinyurl.com/zlq4hgy.

31 KiDeuk Kim, Ashlin Oglesby-Neal and Edward Mohr, "2016 Law Enforcement Use of Social Media Survey," International Association of Chiefs of Police and the Urban Institute, February 2017, p. 3, http://tinyurl.com/kd2twc3.

32 "Developer Policies to Protect People's Voices on Twitter," Twitter, Nov. 22, 2016, http://tinyurl.com/l2yv2nv; "Facebook and Privacy," Facebook, March 13, 2017, http://tinyurl.com/mtcmocm.

33 Michelle McQuigge, "Experts divided on social media surveillance after Twitter pulls plug on Media Sonar," The Canadian Press, Jan. 5, 2017, http://tinyurl.com/lcp8jga.

34 Nicole Ozer, "Police use of social media surveillance software is escalating, and activists are in the digital crosshairs," ACLU of Northern California, Sept. 22, 2016, http://tinyurl.com/n5z4p7t.

35 "Usage Overview," Geofeedia, http://tinyurl.com/myrojyh.

36 Craig Timberg and Elizabeth Dwoskin, "Facebook, Twitter and Instagram sent feeds that helped police track minorities in Ferguson and Baltimore, report says," *The Washington Post*, Oct. 11, 2016, http://tinyurl.com/l7hjqto.

37 "Keywords List," *Media Sonar*, http://tinyurl.com/n38uhff.

38 Ozer, *op. cit.*

39 Radley Balko, *Rise of the Warrior Cop: The*

About the Author

Barbara Mantel is a freelance writer in New York City. She was a 2012 Kiplinger Fellow and has won several journalism awards, including the National Press Club's Best Consumer Journalism Award and the Front Page Award. She was a correspondent for NPR and the founding senior editor and producer for public radio's "Science Friday." She holds a B.A. in history and economics from the University of Virginia and an M.A. in economics from Northwestern University.

Militarization of America's Police Forces (2013), pp. 28-29.

[40] *Ibid.*, pp. 30-31.

[41] Charles Bennett, "Legendary Lawman August Vollmer," officer.com, May 27, 2010, http://tinyurl.com/mj2k2pl.

[42] Balko, *op. cit.*, p. 32.

[43] Christian Parenti, *The Soft Cage: Surveillance in America From Slavery to The War on Terror* (2003), pp. 58-59.

[44] Barry Friedman, *Unwarranted: Policing Without Permission* (2017), p. 39.

[45] *Ibid.*, p. 40. Crime statistics are from FBI Uniform Crime Reports, Table Ec1-10 — Estimated crimes known to police, by type of offense: 1960-1997, in Susan Carter, ed., *Historical Statistics of the United States Millennial Edition Online* (2009), http://tinyurl.com/54vmz2.

[46] For more, see Sarah Glazer, "Sentencing Reform," *CQ Researcher*, Jan. 10, 2014, pp. 25-48.

[47] Friedman, *op. cit.*, p. 42; Nancy G. La Vigne *et al.*, "Using Public Surveillance Systems for Crime Control and Prevention: A Practical Guide for Law Enforcement and Their Municipal Partners," Urban Institute, Sept. 19, 2011, p. v, http://tinyurl.com/mzn7jf7.

[48] Friedman, *op. cit.*, p. 44.

[49] "David Floyd, Lalit Clarkson, Deon Dennis, and David Ourlicht v. The City of New York," U.S. District Court Southern District of New York, Aug. 12, 2013, p. 181, http://tinyurl.com/ks85b77.

[50] La Vigne, *op. cit.*

[51] Parenti, *op. cit.*, pp. 116, 109.

[52] Alexandra Mateescu, Alex Rosenblat and Danah Boyd, "Police Body-Worn Cameras," Data & Research Institute, February 2015, p. 4, http://tinyurl.com/l6wh77l.

[53] Dina Demetrius, "Meet the first U.S. police department to deploy body cameras," Al Jazeera America, Dec. 17, 2014, http://tinyurl.com/nrmchje.

[54] "Self-Awareness to Being Watched and Socially-Desirable Behavior: A Field Experiment on the Effect of Body-Worn Cameras on Police Use-of-Force," Bureau of Justice Assistance, U.S. Department of Justice, pp. 4, 8, http://tinyurl.com/kyf2x72.

[55] "Implementing a Body-Worn Camera Program: Recommendations and Lessons Learned," Police Executive Research Forum and U.S. Department of Justice, 2014, p. 2, http://tinyurl.com/lxdg7ej.

[56] "What Happened in Ferguson?" *The New York Times*, Aug. 10, 2015, http://tinyurl.com/htrsxvj.

[57] Demetrius, *op. cit.*

[58] "Major Cities Chiefs and Major County Sheriffs: Technology Needs — Body Worn Cameras" The Lafayette Group, December 2015, p. 2, http://tinyurl.com/mv4ym6p.

[59] "The Fourth Amendment," Legal Information Institute, Cornell University Law School, http://tinyurl.com/k4mvu8r.

[60] Friedman, *op. cit.*, p. 213.

[61] Levinson-Waldman, *op. cit.*, p. 532, http://tinyurl.com/kuxb2tj.

[62] *Ibid.*, p. 533.

[63] Friedman, *op. cit.*, p. 222.

[64] *Ibid.*, p. 223.

[65] *Ibid.*

[66] Levinson-Waldman, *op. cit.*, pp. 539, 544, 546, 547.

[67] Joh, *op. cit.*, p. 28.

[68] "An Act To Promote Transparency with Respect to Surveillance Technology," Maine Legislature, p. 3, http://tinyurl.com/mzs329t; "Actions for LD 823," Maine Legislature, http://tinyurl.com/k6kumnm.

[69] "California Senate Bill 21," http://tinyurl.com/z9tv448.

[70] "California, NYC Lawmakers Seek to Reveal Police Surveillance," *Communications Daily*, March 15, 2017, http://tinyurl.com/kacnksu.

[71] Carrie Snurr, "Legislation creates task force to study surveillance tactics," The Associated Press, *The Washington Post*, April 7, 2017, http://tinyurl.com/m9g9jzz.

[72] "Creating comprehensive reporting and oversight of NYPD surveillance technologies," The New York City Council, Introduced March 1, 2017, http://tinyurl.com/l6m4cdy.

[73] "Public Oversight of Surveillance Technology (POST) Act: Fact Sheet," Brennan Center for Justice, http://tinyurl.com/m2ulvy4.

[74] "Creating comprehensive reporting and oversight of NYPD surveillance technologies," *op. cit.*

[75] Noah Hurowitz, "NYPD Blasts Surveillance Transparency Bill as a Boon to 'Terrorists,' " DNAinfo, March 2, 2017, http://tinyurl.com/l7vluna.

[76] Shahid Buttar, "A California County Breaks New Ground for Surveillance Transparency," Electronic Frontier Foundation, June 15, 2016, http://tinyurl.com/hhq5ycl.

[77] "Automated license plate readers: State statutes regulating their use," National Conference of State Legislatures, Feb. 27, 2017, http://tinyurl.com/lxbxobc.

[78] "Body-worn cameras interactive graphic," National Conference of State Legislatures, Aug. 30, 2016, http://tinyurl.com/kjwnx89.

[79] Nancy G. La Vigne and Margaret Ulle, "Police camera policies: what's in and what's out," Urban Institute, Jan. 12, 2017, http://tinyurl.com/lpy8xea.

[80] Lum *et al.*, *op. cit.*; Long, *op. cit.*

[81] Ozer, *op. cit.*

Bibliography

Selected Sources

Books

Balko, Radley, *Rise of the Warrior Cop: The Militarization of America's Police Forces*, PublicAffairs, 2013.

An investigative journalist examines the militarization of U.S. police agencies' growing reliance on technology.

Friedman, Barry, *Unwarranted: Policing Without Permission*, Farrar, Straus and Giroux, 2017.

A New York University law professor describes how the public can regain control over policing.

Parenti, Christian, *The Soft Cage: Surveillance in America From Slavery to the War on Terror*, Basic Books, 2004.

A sociologist traces the long history of police and corporate surveillance of Americans.

Articles

Beebe, Drew, "Since January, police have been testing an aerial surveillance system adapted from the surge in Iraq. And they neglected to tell the public," *Bloomberg Businessweek*, Aug. 23, 2016, http://tinyurl.com/ln4aoys.

Baltimore police secretly tested aerial surveillance cameras after riots broke out in the Freddie Gray case.

Chammah, Maurice, "Policing the Future," The Marshall Project, Feb. 3, 2016, http://tinyurl.com/hyf3ocd.

A journalist rides along with a police officer who is using software that forecasts crime hot spots.

Hurowitz, Noah, "NYPD Blasts Surveillance Transparency Bill as a Boon to 'Terrorists,' " DNAinfo, March 2, 2017, http://tinyurl.com/l7vluna.

The New York City Police Department says a City Council bill to provide oversight of surveillance technology would play into the hands of terrorists.

Long, Colleen, "NYPD plans 23,000 body cams. Number on streets now: 0," The Associated Press, Feb. 11, 2017, http://tinyurl.com/ktvbedp.

New York City police plan to put a body camera on every patrol officer by 2019.

Timberg, Craig, and Elizabeth Dwoskin, "Facebook, Twitter and Instagram sent feeds that helped police track minorities in Ferguson and Baltimore, report says," *The Washington Post*, Oct. 11, 2016, http://tinyurl.com/l7hjqto.

Police reportedly have used social media-monitoring software to track minorities and activists.

Reports and Studies

"Implementing a Body-Worn Camera Program: Recom-mendations and Lessons Learned," Police Executive Research Forum, U.S. Department of Justice, 2014, http://tiny url.com/lxdg7ej.

A police research organization compiles best practices on police use of body cameras.

Ariel, Barak, *et al.*, "Report: increases in police use of force in the presence of body-worn cameras are driven by officer discretion: a protocol-based subgroup analysis of ten randomized experiments," *Journal of Experimental Criminology*, May 17, 2016, http://tinyurl.com/m2euptl.

British researchers conclude that use of force increases when police are given more discretion over body camera use.

Garvie, Clare, *et al.*, "The Perpetual Line-Up: Unregulated Police Face Recognition in America," Center on Privacy & Technology at Georgetown Law, Oct. 18, 2016, http://tiny url.com/mp2o2r9.

Researchers find that a quarter of police departments use facial-recognition technology and urge Congress to regulate it.

Hunt, Priscilla, *et al.*, "Evaluation of the Shreveport Predictive Policing Experiment," RAND Corp., 2014, http://tinyurl.com/zm5xtf4.

RAND researchers tested predictive policing software in Louisiana and say it comes up short.

Joh, Elizabeth, "The Undue Influence of Surveillance Technology Companies on Policing," *New York University Law Review*, forthcoming, http://tinyurl.com/kkrgzjn.

A University of California, Davis, law professor argues that vendors of surveillance technology exert too much control over policing.

Levinson-Waldman, Rachel, "Hiding in Plain Sight: A Fourth Amendment Framework for Analyzing Government Surveillance in Public," *Emory Law Journal*, March 2017, p. 528, http://tinyurl.com/kuxb2tj.

A civil liberties advocate proposes a framework for protecting privacy rights in an era of public surveillance.

Lum, Cynthia, *et al.*, "Existing and Ongoing Body Worn Camera Research: Knowledge Gaps and Opportunities," George Mason University, 2015, http://tinyurl.com/kxny5ge.

George Mason University researchers review body camera studies and conclude more research is needed.

Ozer, Nicole, "Police use of social media surveillance software is escalating, and activists are in the digital crosshairs," ACLU of Northern CA, Sept. 22, 2016, http://tinyurl.com/n5z4p7t.

The ACLU of Northern California finds that some California police departments are using social media monitoring software without oversight from elected officials.

The Next Step:

Additional Articles from Current Periodicals

Legislation

Goldberg, Ted, "ACLU Slams SFO's New License Plate Reader Policy," KQED News, April 10, 2017, http://tinyurl.com/ml5d4gu.

San Francisco International Airport's surveillance practices came under fire after airport officials adopted a policy propelled by new state legislation requiring data collected by license-plate readers to be safeguarded by its users.

Prabhu, Maya T., "Charleston senator wants to charge police who erase body camera footage," *The Post and Courier*, April 4, 2017, http://tinyurl.com/m3vjvpc.

A South Carolina Democratic state senator introduced a bill that would make it a crime, punishable by up to a year in prison and a fine, for a police officer to delete body camera footage.

Wootson, Cleve Jr., "A body cam captured a cop's violent encounter with a teen — but a new law keeps the video secret," *The Washington Post*, April 6, 2017, https://tinyurl.com/kvd4n9b.

A new North Carolina law requires those who want access to police body camera footage to pay a fee and plead their case to a Superior Court judge.

Racial Disparities

Eckhouse, Laurel, "Big data may be reinforcing racial bias in the criminal justice system," *The Washington Post*, Feb. 10, 2017, https://tinyurl.com/kj8zkl5.

Judges across the country are using data-driven estimates to set prison sentences for defendants based on their risk of recidivism, but opponents argue pre-existing biases in the justice system could skew the data and unfairly harm minorities.

Edwards, Ezekiel, "Predictive Policing Software Is More Accurate At Predicting Policing Than Predicting Crime," *The Huffington Post*, Aug. 31, 2016, http://tinyurl.com/k6ql9hc.

The director of the ACLU Criminal Law Reform Project says predictive policing, which uses algorithms to analyze crime data, can result in racial profiling.

Expanding Technology

Blidner, Rachelle, "Southampton chief Steven Skrynecki plans to use data to help policing," *Newsday*, March 30, 2017, http://tinyurl.com/mc5xm99.

A police chief in a New York town proposed hiring an analyst and using more data to allocate its limited resources.

Kelly, Laura, "Smart cities becoming a reality," *Security Systems News*, April 3, 2017, http://tinyurl.com/k9dwg7e.

Cities nationwide are encouraging police and business owners to coordinate their video surveillance systems.

Rocco, Matthew, "Taser Maker Offers Free Body Cams to Police, NYPD Not Interested," Fox Business, April 6, 2017, http://tinyurl.com/m2djdbv.

A body camera manufacturer is offering police departments free body cameras, but a competing provider said the offer would come with "significant internal implementation costs."

Transparency

Fussell, Sidney, "NYPD's Proposed Body Camera Policies Are a Disaster for Police Accountability," *Gizmodo*, April 10, 2017, http://tinyurl.com/lfpa77q.

The New York Civil Liberties Union says the New York City Police Department's new body camera policies disregard transparency and accountability.

Hansen, Teri L., "Body cameras promote trust, improve transparency for officers," *McPherson Sentinel*, April 7, 2017, http://tinyurl.com/m6px2ny.

Officers in a Kansas county say body cameras can promote transparency and public safety.

McGahan, Jason, "Are Police Body Cameras Pointless If the Public Can't See the Footage?" *L.A. Weekly*, April 7, 2017, https://tinyurl.com/mje74zr.

Critics say plans to equip 7,000 Los Angeles officers with body cameras are useless without improved transparency.

Miller, Ben, "Exclusive: Predictive Policing Startup Publishes Code Online, Seeks to Address Bias," *Government Technology*, March 20, 2017, https://tinyurl.com/kvb8n5d.

CivicScape, a predictive policing company, aims to promote transparency by making its code public and addressing biases in its algorithms.

CITING *CQ RESEARCHER*

Sample formats for citing these reports in a bibliography include the ones listed below. Preferred styles and formats vary, so please check with your instructor or professor.

MLA STYLE
Mantel, Barbara. "Coal Industry's Future." CQ Researcher 17 June 2016: 529-552.

APA STYLE
Mantel, B. (2016, June 17). Coal Industry's Future. *CQ Researcher*, 6, 529-552.

CHICAGO STYLE
Mantel, Barbara. "Coal Industry's Future." *CQ Researcher*, June 17, 2016, 529-52.

In-depth Reports on Issues in the News

Are you writing a paper?

Need backup for a debate?

Want to become an expert on an issue?

For 90 years, students have turned to *CQ Researcher* for in-depth reporting on issues in the news. Reports on a full range of political and social issues are now available. Following is a selection of recent reports:

Civil Liberties
Privacy and the Internet, 12/15
Intelligence Reform, 5/15
Religion and Law, 11/14

Crime/Law
Forensic Science Controversies, 2/17
Jailing Debtors, 9/16
Decriminalizing Prostitution, 4/16
Restorative Justice, 2/16
The Dark Web, 1/16
Immigrant Detention, 10/15
Fighting Gangs, 10/15

Education
Charter Schools, 3/17
Civic Education, 2/17
Student Debt, 11/16
Apprenticeships, 10/16

Environment/Society
Women in Prison, 3/17
Guns on Campus, 1/17
Mass Transit, 12/16
Arctic Development, 12/16
Protecting the Power Grid, 11/16
Pornography, 10/16

Health/Safety
Reducing Traffic Deaths, 2/17
Opioid Crisis, 10/16
Mosquito-Borne Disease, 7/16

Politics/Economy
Rethinking Foreign Aid, 4/17
Troubled Brazil, 4/17
Reviving Rural Economies, 3/17
Immigrants and the Economy, 2/17
Trump Presidency, 1/17
European Union's Future, 12/16
The Obama Legacy, 11/16

Upcoming Reports

Sex Abuse in Sports, 4/28/17   Native Americans, 5/5/17   Anti-Semitism, 5/12/17

ACCESS

CQ Researcher is available in print and online. For access, visit your library or www.cqresearcher.com.

STAY CURRENT

For notice of upcoming *CQ Researcher* reports or to learn more about *CQ Researcher* products, subscribe to the free email newsletters, *CQ Researcher Alert!* and *CQ Researcher News*: http://cqpress.com/newsletters.

PURCHASE

To purchase a *CQ Researcher* report in print or electronic format (PDF), visit www.cqpress.com or call 866-427-7737. Single reports start at $15. Bulk purchase discounts and electronic-rights licensing are also available.

SUBSCRIBE

Annual full-service *CQ Researcher* subscriptions—including 44 reports a year, monthly index updates, and a bound volume—start at $1,131. Add $25 for domestic postage.

CQ Researcher Online offers a backfile from 1991 and a number of tools to simplify research. For pricing information, call 800-818-7243 or 805-499-9774 or email librarysales@sagepub.com.

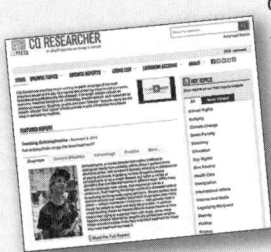

CQPRESS

Published by CQ Press, an Imprint of SAGE Publications, Inc.

www.cqresearcher.com

CQ RESEARCHER

In-depth reports on today's issues

Sports and Sexual Assault

Can colleges and pro leagues curb abuse by athletes?

Hundreds of college and professional athletes, along with some college and Olympic coaches, have been accused of sexual assault in recent years, including gang rape. While athletes have gone to prison for their sex crimes, studies show that relatively few accusations lead to arrest or conviction. Researchers say schools, leagues and Olympic organizations frequently have failed to investigate credible allegations and that sports programs have ignored or covered up sex crimes by star athletes, who often receive preferential treatment from schools, teams and police. While no sport is immune from allegations of sexual abuse, researchers say extremely aggressive sports, such as football, can fuel what they call a culture of rape. Still, some athletes have been falsely accused, and universities are under pressure to improve their methods of distinguishing guilt from innocence. Meanwhile, professional leagues are implementing new policies for dealing with sexual and domestic abuse and are requiring assault-prevention training.

Baylor University President Kenneth Starr, shown at a football game in 2012, was demoted and then resigned in 2016 following criticism that the university had not taken sexual assault allegations against football players seriously. The scandal also claimed Baylor's athletics director and head football coach.

I N S I D E — THIS REPORT

THE ISSUES	363
BACKGROUND	370
CHRONOLOGY	371
CURRENT SITUATION	375
AT ISSUE	377
OUTLOOK	378
BIBLIOGRAPHY	382
THE NEXT STEP	383

CQ Researcher • April 28, 2017 • www.cqresearcher.com
Volume 27, Number 16 • Pages 361-384

RECIPIENT OF SOCIETY OF PROFESSIONAL JOURNALISTS AWARD FOR EXCELLENCE ◆ AMERICAN BAR ASSOCIATION SILVER GAVEL AWARD

SAGE Publishing
Los Angeles | London | New Delhi
Singapore | Washington DC | Melbourne

CQPRESS

THE ISSUES

363
- Are athletes more likely than others to be accused of sexual assault?
- Are athletes in certain sports more likely to commit sexual violence?
- Are universities doing enough to investigate sexual assault allegations against athletes?

BACKGROUND

370 **Dawn of Team Sports**
Collegiate games began in the 1800s.

374 **Sexual Assault**
Universities began working with rape crisis centers in the 1970s.

374 **General Crackdown**
In 2011 the Office for Civil Rights detailed how schools must prevent sexual harrassment.

375 **Pro Sports**
The NFL commissioner required all personnel to complete assault-prevention training.

CURRENT SITUATION

375 **Recruiting Coaches**
"We have to change the culture of sports in youth sports."

376 **Campus Efforts**
Allegations of widespread sexual assault touched off a major investigation at Baylor.

378 **Pro Sports Actions**
Leagues are trying to prevent sexual assault.

OUTLOOK

378 **'So Much Fear'**
Some students worry that the Trump administration will weaken Title IX protections.

SIDEBARS AND GRAPHICS

364 **Charges Valid in Nearly Two-Thirds of Cases**
Sixty-three percent of accused athletes were found responsible in sexual assault claims.

365 **NFL Sex, Assault Arrests Below National Average**
The rate of players arrested for sex offenses was 38 percent of the national average.

368 **Critics Say 'Star-Struck' Officers Jeopardize Assault Cases**
"There are significant odds that work against rape victims."

371 **Chronology**
Key events since 1852.

372 **Abuse Scandals Plague Some Olympic Sports**
Gymnasts, swimmers seen as particularly at risk.

377 **At Issue:**
Can bystander-intervention training prevent sexual assault by college athletes?

FOR FURTHER RESEARCH

381 **For More Information**
Organizations to contact.

382 **Bibliography**
Selected sources used.

383 **The Next Step**
Additional articles.

383 **Citing CQ Researcher**
Sample bibliography formats.

CQ RESEARCHER

April 28, 2017
Volume 27, Number 16

EXECUTIVE EDITOR: Thomas J. Billitteri
tjb@sagepub.com

ASSISTANT MANAGING EDITORS: Kenneth Fireman, kenneth.fireman@sagepub.com, Kathy Koch, kathy.koch@sagepub.com, Scott Rohrer, scott.rohrer@sagepub.com

ASSOCIATE MANAGING EDITOR: Val Ellicott

SENIOR CONTRIBUTING EDITOR:
Thomas J. Colin
tom.colin@sagepub.com

CONTRIBUTING WRITERS: Marcia Clemmitt, Sarah Glazer, Reed Karaim, Barbara Mantel, Chuck McCutcheon, Tom Price

SENIOR PROJECT EDITOR: Olu B. Davis

EDITORIAL ASSISTANT: Anika Reed

FACT CHECKERS: Eva P. Dasher, Michelle Harris, Betsy Towner Levine, Robin Palmer

$SAGE Publishing | **qp CQPRESS**

Los Angeles I London I New Delhi
Singapore I Washington DC I Melbourne

An Imprint of SAGE Publications, Inc.

SENIOR VICE PRESIDENT, GLOBAL LEARNING RESOURCES:
Karen Phillips

EXECUTIVE DIRECTOR, ONLINE LIBRARY AND REFERENCE PUBLISHING:
Todd Baldwin

CQ Researcher (ISSN 1056-2036) is printed on acid-free paper. Published weekly, except: (March wk. 4) (May wk. 4) (July wks. 1, 2) (Aug. wks. 2, 3) (Nov. wk. 4) and (Dec. wks. 3, 4). Published by SAGE Publications, Inc., 2455 Teller Rd., Thousand Oaks, CA 91320. Annual full-service subscriptions start at $1,131. For pricing, call 1-800-818-7243. To purchase a CQ Researcher report in print or electronic format (PDF), visit www.cqpress. com or call 866-427-7737. Single reports start at $15. Bulk purchase discounts and electronic-rights licensing are also available. Periodicals postage paid at Thousand Oaks, California, and at additional mailing offices. POSTMASTER: Send address changes to CQ Researcher, 2600 Virginia Ave., N.W., Suite 600, Washington, DC 20037.

Cover: Getty Images/Cooper Neill

Sports and Sexual Assault

By Susan Ladika

The Issues

Last year was a notorious one for sexual assault cases involving star athletes.

In November, former National Football League (NFL) star and broadcaster Darren Sharper was sentenced to 20 years in prison after pleading guilty or no contest to various charges of drugging and raping nine women in four states. [1]

In December, Tampa Bay Buccaneers quarterback Jameis Winston settled a lawsuit filed by a woman alleging that he had raped her in 2012 when he was at Florida State University (FSU). In a separate settlement, the university agreed to pay $950,000 to Winston's accuser and her attorneys. [2]

Stanford University swimmer Brock Turner was sentenced last June to six months in jail — a punishment widely criticized as too lenient — for sexually assaulting an unconscious woman behind a dumpster on campus. [3]

And despite an increased focus by federal officials and the media on the sexual conduct of professional and college athletes, attacks have continued to make headlines.

A lawsuit filed by a Baylor University graduate alleges she was gang raped by two football players in 2013 and that the school fostered "the most widespread culture of sexual violence and abuse of women ever reported in a collegiate athletic program." [4] The suit alleges that 31 Baylor football players committed 52 acts of rape, including five gang rapes, between 2011 and 2014. It also says Baylor didn't look into the plaintiff's rape claims for more than two years, despite a federal law requiring schools and universities that

The case of Stanford University swimmer Brock Turner sparked national outrage in 2016 after Turner served just three months of his six-month sentence for sexually assaulting an unconscious woman. The sentence spurred California lawmakers to pass a law denying probation for anyone convicted of sexually assaulting a victim who was unconscious or too intoxicated to decide whether to consent.

receive federal funding to investigate sexual assault allegations. [5] The two players named in the 2013 allegation were arrested in March, after the suit was filed. [6]

Baylor now faces federal lawsuits filed by more than 12 women, and school officials have acknowledged that 17 women have reported being sexually assaulted by 19 football players. [7]

One of the most infamous cases of sexual assault involving a university athletic department occurred at Penn State, where former assistant football coach Jerry Sandusky was convicted of sexually abusing 10 boys between 1994 and 2009. Sandusky was sentenced in 2012 to between 30 and 60 years in prison. [8]

For years, college and professional sports have been wracked by allegations of sexual assault committed by athletes. Yet, because many cases go unreported, it is impossible to say exactly how many attacks have been perpetrated by athletes.

Incidents of sexual violence by athletes have been reported even at the high school level. In a recent case in Texas, football, baseball and basketball players at La Vernia High School allegedly took part in team "initiations" involving violent sexual abuse of male team members. The parents of one alleged victim have filed a federal civil rights lawsuit against the local school district for enabling a "persistent rape culture" within the football program. [9]

Some experts say rape is particularly prevalent among those who play aggressive team sports, and that the behavior is driven by a so-called rape culture that normalizes sexual violence against women. They also believe college and professional athletes may feel a sense of entitlement because of their celebrity status, and that teams and schools sometimes minimize or cover up bad behavior to avoid negative publicity that could harm big-money sports programs.

Many high-profile sexual assault cases never result in criminal charges. That includes the Winston case, in which legal experts and the would-be prosecutor in the case have accused the Tallahassee Police Department of conducting a seriously flawed investigation. [10]

To be sure, only a tiny fraction of the more than 493,000 professional and college athletes in the United States are ever accused of sexual misconduct, and an even tinier fraction are convicted

Charges Valid in Nearly Two-Thirds of Cases

A Maryland company that provides liability insurance for colleges and universities reported that 45 of the 305 sexual assault claims it handled at 104 colleges from 2011-2013 involved athletes, and that two-thirds of the athletes were found responsible for the alleged acts (top graph). Of the athletes found responsible, 41 percent were expelled (bottom graph), 24 percent were placed on disciplinary probation and 29 percent were suspended.

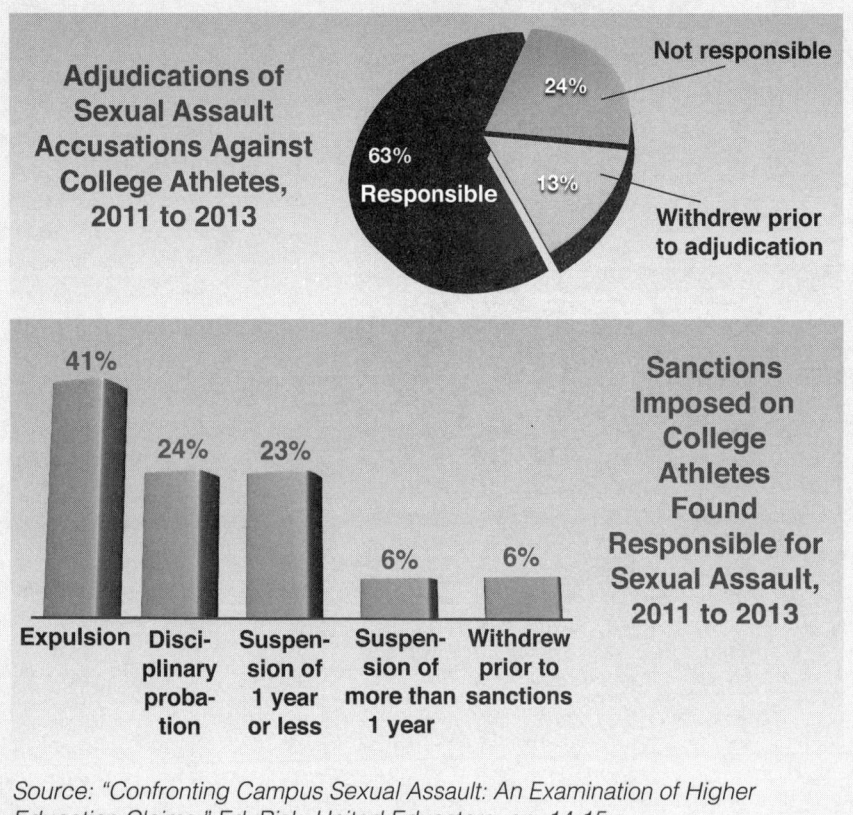

Adjudications of Sexual Assault Accusations Against College Athletes, 2011 to 2013

Not responsible 24%

63% Responsible

13%

Withdrew prior to adjudication

Sanctions Imposed on College Athletes Found Responsible for Sexual Assault, 2011 to 2013

41% Expulsion

24% Disciplinary probation

23% Suspension of 1 year or less

6% Suspension of more than 1 year

6% Withdrew prior to sanctions

Source: "Confronting Campus Sexual Assault: An Examination of Higher Education Claims," EduRisk, United Educators, pp. 14-15

or punished by schools. [11] Many schools are providing sexual assault prevention training to athletes and other students, as well as training on how to safely intervene if they believe a potentially dangerous situation may be brewing. And some college football programs are having team members sign pledges against sexual violence.

But experts say that in some cases, college athletes must take greater responsibility for their behavior.

"Privilege protects [some star college athletes] from consequences, and they can get used to it," says Lisa Wade, an associate professor of sociology at Occidental College and author of *American Hookup: The New Culture of Sex on Campus.* "It doesn't feel like privilege to them at all. It just feels like what their life is like." Colleges, she says, should "start taking power back from these hyperpowerful male student groups on campus."

Conversely, some experts say athletes can be singled out for false accusations or unfair punishment. For instance, prosecutors decided that a woman's 2012 rape allegation against Xavier University basketball player Dez Wells

wasn't worth pursuing. When the Cincinnati school expelled Wells anyway, for violating its student conduct code, Wells sued, later settling the case for undisclosed terms. [12] University spokeswoman Kelly Leon said the suit was resolved "in a manner satisfactory to the parties." [13]

"If he had been a normal, non-athlete student, would Xavier have moved ahead with this?" asks KC Johnson, a history professor at Brooklyn College and co-author of the 2017 book *The Campus Rape Frenzy: The Attack on Due Process at America's Universities.* "I suspect probably not. But in this case, you're dealing with one of the three or four highest-profile athletes on campus."

Statistics from the National Crime Victimization Survey compiled by the U.S. Department of Justice show that from 1995 to 2013, the latest year for which data are available, a total of 37,846 post-secondary school students between ages 18 and 24 — 31,302 females and 6,544 males — were victims of rape, attempted rape, sexual assault or the threat of rape or sexual assault. [14] Of the female victims, just 20 percent reported the rape or sexual assault to police. Eighty percent of all the victims said they knew their attacker. [15]

While the Justice Department report doesn't look at the percentage of rapes or assaults committed by student athletes, other studies have yielded striking results.

A 1996 study found that 35 percent of 90 cases of both sexual assault and battering reported to campus officials involved student athletes, although athletes represented just 3 percent of the student bodies. The study's authors cautioned that the small number of cases likely represented a small number of actual assaults "due to the stigma, fear and negative connotations of reporting crimes as intimate and taboo as sexual assault and battering." [16]

Athletes also appear to be overrepresented in gang-rape allegations.

Journalist Jessica Luther, author of the 2016 book *Unsportsmanlike Con-*

duct: *College Football and the Politics of Rape*, says her research shows college football players were involved in at least 110 sexual assault allegations made since 1974. Forty-nine of those cases involved accusations against multiple players. [17] The prevalence of gang-rape allegations "is the most surprising thing that came out of this," she says.

The federal government has stepped up pressure on colleges to be more aggressive in investigating sexual assault allegations. Between April 2011 and April 2017, the government initiated 389 investigations of colleges accused of failing to do a good job. Just 62 cases have been resolved. [18]

Under Title IX of the Education Amendments of 1972, which bans gender discrimination at schools that receive federal funds, a university can be held legally responsible if it knew — or should have known — about sexual assault or harassment but failed to address it. [19] The law is enforced by the Education Department's Office for Civil Rights (OCR). [20]

Colleges have repeatedly been accused of failing to comply with Title IX, triggering several lawsuits resulting in hefty payouts. In 2016, the University of Tennessee paid almost $2.5 million to settle claims by eight female students that they were sexually assaulted — or otherwise physically abused — by athletes. [21]

Failing to act to stop sexual abuse on college campuses also can lead to criminal consequences. In March, former Penn State University President Graham Spanier was convicted of child endangerment for covering up the allegations against Sandusky. [22]

Dan Schorr, managing director of Kroll Associates, a New York-based firm that provides investigative and other services, says Spanier's conviction could encourage prosecutors in Michigan to consider charges against top officials at Michigan State University (MSU), where Lawrence G. Nassar once worked as a gymnastics team doctor.

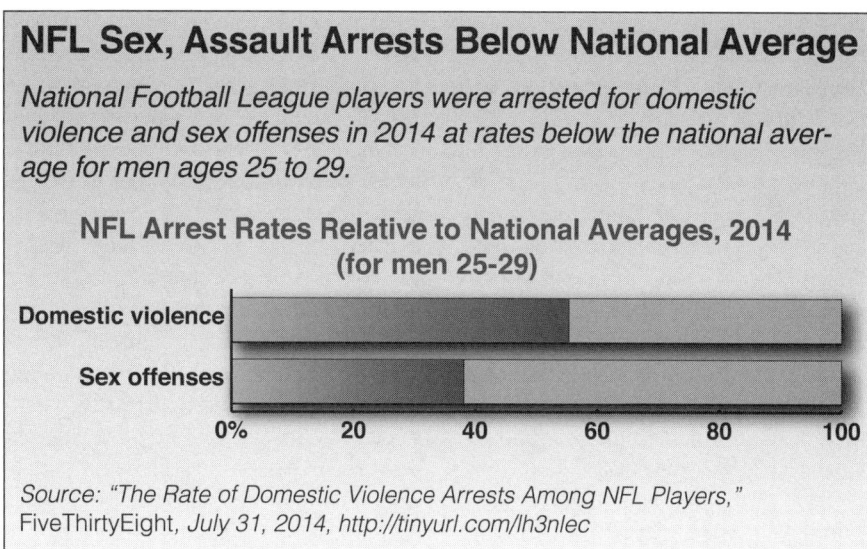

NFL Sex, Assault Arrests Below National Average

National Football League players were arrested for domestic violence and sex offenses in 2014 at rates below the national average for men ages 25 to 29.

NFL Arrest Rates Relative to National Averages, 2014 (for men 25-29)

Domestic violence

Sex offenses

0%   20   40   60   80   100

Source: "The Rate of Domestic Violence Arrests Among NFL Players," FiveThirtyEight, *July 31, 2014, http://tinyurl.com/lh3nlec*

More than 100 girls and women have sued or filed notice of intent to sue Nassar and the university, claiming MSU covered up the assaults. [23] Nassar has been accused of sexually assaulting dozens of athletes during his time at MSU and at USA Gymnastics, which oversees Olympic gymnastics. (*See sidebar, p. 372.*)

"Penn State was an extremely egregious case, but there could be other cases where prosecutors might wish to bring charges," said Schorr. [24]

B. David Ridpath, an associate professor of sports administration at Ohio University, says the United States puts athletes "on a pedestal." But, he adds, "they're also people. They have human failings and flaws, and they also have to be held accountable for their actions."

Sexual assault cases involving professional athletes are less often in the news than cases involving college athletes, which could be due to several factors. The pool of professional sports figures is much smaller, for one thing. More than 480,000 students compete in the National Collegiate Athletic Association (NCAA), while there are only about 13,700 professional athletes. [25] And, as Laura Finley, an associate professor of sociology and criminology at Barry University in Miami Shores, Fla.,

says, most people "age out" of committing crimes.

Victims of professional athletes also might be hesitant to come forward, Finley says, because "if you take on a professional athlete, your name is going to be dragged through the mud."

The spotlight on assaults involving sports figures intensified with the 2014 release of a video showing Ray Rice, then a running back for the Baltimore Ravens, knocking out his then-fiancée, Janay (now his wife), in a casino elevator. Rice was charged with third-degree aggravated assault, but a judge dismissed the charge after Rice paid a $125 fine and completed anger-management counseling. [26]

Rice was cut by the Ravens and indefinitely suspended from football, but he appealed and was reinstated. [27] He has not played for the NFL since.

The Rice video prompted the NFL, followed by the National Hockey League (NHL) and Major League Baseball (MLB), to require players to receive training on what behavior constitutes sexual assault or domestic violence. [28] And both the NFL and MLB have developed procedures for investigating sexual assault and domestic violence allegations. [29]

"We believe that these efforts will foster not only an approach of education and prevention, but also a united stance against these matters throughout our sport and our communities," MLB Commissioner Rob Manfred said in a statement. [30]

The NFL also is financially aiding the fight to prevent sexual assault and domestic violence. Last June, three organizations announced creation of "Raliance," which describes itself as "a collaborative initiative dedicated to ending sexual violence in one generation." The initiative is supported by a $10 million, multiyear commitment from the NFL — the first time a major organization has funded a sexual violence prevention effort. [31]

NFL Commissioner Roger Goodell said sexual assault "is an issue that impacts communities worldwide in staggering numbers, and we share Raliance's belief that we all have a responsibility to help change that." The group brings together the National Sexual Violence Resource Center, the California Coalition Against Sexual Assault-PreventConnect and the National Alliance to End Sexual Violence. [32]

As universities and professional sports organizations seek to deal with sexual assault, here are some of the questions being debated:

Are athletes more likely than others to be accused of sexual assault?

The string of sexual-assault allegations in recent years against college and professional athletes has led to increased debate about whether athletes are more likely to commit sexual violence or are falsely accused of such violence more often than non-athletes.

Also under debate is whether a perceived lack of consequences for some high-profile athletes might encourage them to behave in sexually aggressive ways. For instance, the belated investigation into allegations of sexual assault by football players at Baylor found that university officials had "created a cultural perception that football was above the rules." [33]

As for whether college athletes are more prone to sexual violence than non-

athletes, some early research indicated that intercollegiate athletes are responsible for a disproportionate percentage of sexual violence cases on campus. For instance, 1995 data showed that male athletes accounted for 19 percent of all sexual assault cases at 30 National Collegiate Athletic Association Division 1 institutions but represented only 3 percent of the student populations. [34]

"Male intercollegiate athletes are at particularly high risk for perpetrating sexual violence," said a 2016 study conducted by researchers at four different universities. The study assessed 379 male undergraduate athletes and non-athletes and found "significant differences between . . . athletes and non-athletes" in their attitudes toward women, rape and "prevalence of sexual coercion." [35]

The 2016 study also examined attitudes among intramural and recreational athletes and found that they had similar risk factors for sexual violence as intercollegiate athletes. Some scientists had argued in the past that intercollegiate athletes were at greater risk of sexual violence because they tend to be isolated from the rest of the university community, in separate dorms and classes.

Such isolation, "leads to sexual violence," said Belinda-Rose Young, a research associate with the University of South Florida and lead author of the 2016 study. "And there's that constant reiteration of male superiority and athletes who are rewarded for being aggressive." However, she said, "We saw that that attitude is just a part of the general sporting environment," adding, "I actually was surprised." [36]

Kristy L. McCray, an assistant professor of sport management at Otterbein University in Westerville, Ohio, said, "Sports are a hypermasculine endeavor, and there's a lot that connects hypermasculinity to violence." McCray, who in 2014 conducted a review of previous studies on the topic, said, "Sex segregation . . . makes it easier to de-value women." [37]

In a review of student sexual-violence claims from 104 colleges, United Educators, a college liability insurer, said athletes were accused in 45 of the 305 claims the company received from 2011 through 2013. The report also found that athletes were involved in 12 of the 30 incidents involving multiple perpetrators. [38]

If athletes are overrepresented in sexual assault allegations, Barry University's Finley says that doesn't mean they are convicted at higher rates than others, nor does it mean they are more likely to have been falsely accused. Athletes, especially professional players, "tend to have more resources to navigate the criminal justice system better," she says. And victims know, she says, that "If you take on a professional athlete, your name is going to be dragged through the mud."

As for the argument that athletes are falsely accused of sexual violence more often than non-athletes, journalist Luther, asks, "What would a woman get out of that behavior?" Instead, she says, many of the sexual assault victims she has spoken with have said "they don't report it because he's an athlete or because they knew there would be retaliation for coming forward."

Johnson, the author of *The Campus Rape Frenzy*, says he is unaware of reliable data indicating that student athletes are more likely than others to face false accusations. Rather, there is "a decent amount" of anecdotal evidence, he says, that high-profile athletes in non-revenue-producing sports are more likely to be "subjected to wrongful disciplinary action." The college may want to make "a high-profile example" of the athlete, he says, or fears the "negative publicity if they come back with a not-guilty finding or they don't follow through with the investigation."

To be sure, some athletes have been falsely accused. For instance, the jury in a 2016 civil trial in Los Angeles found NBA star Derrick Rose and two of his friends did not rape a woman, concluding instead that the encounter was consensual. Rose's attorney said the woman was trying to extort money from Rose. No criminal charges were filed against the men. [39]

Mitch Abrams, a sports psychologist and the author of *Anger Management in Sport: Understanding and Controlling Violence in Athletes*, wrote that professional athletes "are no more violent than non-athletes. This is the 'myth of the violent athlete.' Pro-athletes are arrested at a lower rate than their age-based peers." [40]

According to a *USA Today* database of NFL arrests, 2.5 percent of players were arrested every year between 2000 and 2014, which is lower than the national average for men of the same age group. [41] And an analysis by Benjamin Morris at *FiveThirtyEight*, the ESPN-owned blog, showed that NFL stars displayed lower levels of domestic and sexual violence than the national average. [42] (*See graph, p. 365.*)

But when an athlete transgresses, Abrams argued, it makes national news "before the facts are even corroborated," unlike everyday crimes that "generally are not considered newsworthy." [43]

However, he acknowledged, sports present certain risk factors that can contribute to violence, which should be ameliorated.

"If a male athlete is treated like a god from the time he is young and showered with fame, money and female attention, is he at risk to think he has a different set of rules and has the financial resources to . . . afford good representation if arrested? Sadly, yes," Abrams wrote. "And we as a society could do something about that by holding athletes accountable for immoral conduct from the time the players are in youth sport." [44]

Are athletes in certain sports more likely to commit sexual violence?

Research suggests that sexual assault is more prevalent among athletes in "power and performance sports" such as football and basketball, "where

male bonding is encouraged," says Finley of Barry University. "It's rare in cross-country, which is more of an individual sport."

"Groups that are heavily hypermasculine have a hard time trying to know when to turn this off and on," she

Allegations of sexual assault against athletes sometimes involve false accusations or unfair punishment. Xavier University basketball player Dez Wells was accused of rape in 2012 but prosecutors decided not to file charges. When Xavier expelled Wells for violating its student conduct code, he sued the school, later settling the case for undisclosed terms.

says. "They have societal permission to be aggressive and violent."

A 2014 California study found that teenage boys who played certain sports — football, basketball or both — were about twice as likely as other boys to have recently abused their girlfriends. And boys who only played football were about 50 percent more likely to have abused their partners. [45]

"Boys who had hypermasculine attitudes were three times more likely to have recently abused their female dating partners," said Heather McCauley, the researcher who led the study. And football and basketball players were more

likely to have such attitudes than teens who were wrestlers, swimmers or tennis players, the study concluded. [46]

McCauley, a researcher at the University of Pittsburgh's Children's Hospital of Pittsburgh, said the study showed that "something in the environment of these youths . . . is sending the message that it's acceptable to use aggression and violence off the field and in their dating relationships." [47]

Morris, at FiveThirtyEight.com, found that although NFL players' levels of domestic and sexual violence were lower than the national average, their rate of domestic violence was much higher than expected, given their income bracket. [48]

The authors of the United Educators report said their review of the sexual-violence claims received by the company "suggests a subculture within some fraternities and teams that promotes hyper-

Getty Images/Streeter Lecka

Critics Say 'Star-Struck' Officers Jeopardize Assault Cases

"There are significant odds that work against rape victims."

When a Georgia college student said Pittsburgh Steelers quarterback Ben Roethlisberger raped her at a Georgia nightclub in 2010, she was interviewed by a local police officer who seemed to have already made his mind up about the case.

Milledgeville police Sgt. Jerry Blash, who had posed for a photo with the star quarterback earlier that evening, told one of Roethlisberger's bodyguards the 20-year-old accuser was a "drunken bitch," adding that it "pisses me off [that] women can do this." He immediately told Roethlisberger of the accusation. [1]

Blash later resigned as internal investigators examined his behavior. Roethlisberger was never charged in the case, nor in an alleged sexual assault in Nevada in 2008. But NFL Commissioner Roger Goodell suspended him in 2010 for four games for violating the league's personal conduct policy involving consumption of alcohol by minors. [2]

Local law enforcement officers are supposed to handle sexual assault complaints impartially. But critics of police procedures in such cases say officers can be too star-struck by college and professional athletes to do a fair and effective job.

"There are significant odds that work against rape victims, especially those who are raped by professional athletes," attorney Bethany P. Withers, who has written widely on athletes and violence against women, said in a 2015 article. [3]

Conversely, some athletes have been unjustifiably indicted or prosecuted on sexual assault allegations. In 2006, three white Duke University lacrosse players were indicted on charges they had sexually assaulted an exotic dancer at a team party. But DNA evidence proved no assault had occurred, and all charges were dropped.

In many cases, however, women face an "uphill battle . . . in pressing sexual assault charges," especially when the accused is

a professional athlete, Withers wrote. In the 18 allegations she examined, spanning 2010 through 2014, no professional athlete accused of sexual assault was convicted; two pleaded no contest.

Often, accusers must overcome a cozy relationship among law enforcement, team security and players' personal security, Withers wrote.

Such factors may have been at work in the 2012 case against Florida State University quarterback Jameis Winston.

Winston was accused of sexually assaulting fellow student Erica Kinsman after the two met at a Tallahassee bar. Local police officers never asked to see the video from the bar where the two met. They made some attempts to identify the cabbie who drove Winston and Kinsman back to Winston's apartment, but gave up when their initial efforts were unsuccessful. They didn't try to talk to Winston for two weeks. Later, however, police matched his DNA with the DNA in her rape kit. [4]

"A full investigation was never done and the state's attorney was never contacted to look into the case," Jessica Luther, an investigative journalist who has written extensively about college football and sexual assault, wrote in her book, *Unsportsmanlike Conduct: College Football and the Politics of Rape.* [5]

Luther's book says local law enforcement officers and sports teams often develop a close relationship because teams may hire off-duty police to escort players to games or shepherd them on and off the field.

"It's kind of a little plum detail if you're a football fan," said Maj. Cary Sutton of the Alabama State Police. [6]

In Tallahassee, police officers earn an extra $40 to $45 per hour, paid by the university, for handling traffic on game days, an arrangement that critics say can help to cement relationships between the university and police. [7]

masculinity, sexual aggression and excessive alcohol consumption. These sociocultural factors may encourage students within these groups to engage in or excuse sexual violence." [49]

While the report doesn't single out any sport, it cites an incident in which members of an unnamed football team were accused of sexually assaulting a student who was unconscious from drinking, and another case in which basketball team members pursued a student who was shy and lonely and " 'easy' to obtain sex from. . . . In one instance, five players showed up at her residence hall to have sex with her." [50]

Luther, the journalist who listed 49 gang-rape allegations out of more than 110 incidents involving college football players, said her research shows that "it's a bonding experience for people who are perpetrating that kind of violence."

A 2015 study published in Harvard Law School's *Journal of Sports & Entertainment Law* cited 18 allegations of sexual assault in pro sports — 12 against football players, four against baseball players and two against NBA players. [51]

Despite the preponderance of allegations against players in hyper-aggressive sports, athletes in other sports also are accused of sexual assault, such as the Stanford swimmer Turner, who was

found guilty on three felony counts of sexual assault for his attack on an unconscious woman. [52]

That same year, two female former Boise State University track team members sued the school and reached an out-of-court settlement for $800,000, after accusing the university of not stopping a male track star from sexually assaulting them and other female teammates. [53]

Abrams says the issue isn't so much that certain athletes are more likely to be sexually violent, but that "narcissism is a natural consequence of chronic winning."

Athletes can develop "rape supportive attitudes and misogynistic views of the

"The treatment of the Winston complaint was in keeping with the way the police on numerous occasions have soft-pedaled allegations of wrongdoing by Seminoles football players," *The New York Times* wrote of the Winston case. [8]

Such cases have raised new questions about how schools handle sexual assault allegations.

Under Title IX, the federal law that bars sex discrimination at schools receiving federal money, schools are obligated to investigate all reports of sexual assault, but any decision to report an assault to police is up to the accuser. Schools are required only to inform students of their right to file a criminal complaint and to help them contact the authorities if they decide to do so.

Republican Georgia state Rep. Earl Ehrhart introduced legislation this year that would bar schools from investigating sexual assault claims unless local police participate. [9] The bill was spurred by several lawsuits filed by Georgia Tech students who said they were falsely accused of sexual assault and expelled as a result. The legislation, which passed the House but did not come up for a vote in the Senate before the legislature adjourned in March, also would require certain school employees to report possible felonies, such as sexual assault allegations, to law enforcement. [10]

But E. Everett Bartlett, president of SAVE (Stop Abusive and Violent Environments), a nonprofit in Rockville, Md., focused on the rights of sexual assault victims and those falsely accused of sexual assault, says "all felony-level offenses should be handled by [outside] law enforcement and the criminal justice system."

B. David Ridpath, an associate professor of sports administration at Ohio University, agrees. "It's very important when there's a major crime to have some outside eyes looking on it," he says. "That doesn't mean local authorities can't be manipulated. I've seen that happen."

— *Susan Ladika*

Pittsburgh Steelers quarterback Ben Roethlisberger was never charged after two sexual assault allegations but was suspended for four games for violating the NFL's policy invloving consumption of alcohol by minors.

[1] Bethany P. Withers, "Without Consequences: When Professional Athletes Are Violent off the Field," *Journal of Sports & Entertainment Law*, October 2015, p. 13, http://tinyurl.com/lbkem9e.

[2] "Ben Roethlisberger's Ban at 4 Games," ESPN.com, Sept. 4, 2010, http://tinyurl.com/mkocp62.

[3] Withers, *op. cit.*

[4] Walt Bogdanich, "A Star Player Accused, and a Flawed Rape Investigation," *The New York Times*, April 16, 2014, http://tinyurl.com/lw22kgz.

[5] Jessica Luther, *Unsportsmanlike Conduct: College Football and the Politics of Rape* (2016), p. 53.

[6] *Ibid.*, p. 87.

[7] Mike McIntire and Walt Bogdanich, "At Florida State, Football Clouds Justice," *The New York Times*, Oct. 10, 2014, http://tinyurl.com/modh5n7.

[8] *Ibid.*

[9] Shannon McCaffrey and Janel Davis, "Bill Would Restrict Colleges' Response to Sexual Assault Reports," *The Atlanta Journal-Constitution*, Jan. 16, 2017, http://tinyurl.com/j6ltkae.

[10] Emmanuella Grinberg, "This bill could change how colleges handle sexual assault in Georgia," CNN, Feb. 2, 2017, http://tinyurl.com/mz2dhlz.

world — that girls and women are there for the taking, that they do not need to respect women, that one's social worth is based on the number of sexual partners they have," Abrams says.

Are universities doing enough to investigate sexual assault allegations against athletes?

Title IX compels schools to investigate sexual assault complaints. Schools then decide, sometimes after a hearing before a student disciplinary board, whether the accused is "responsible" for sexual misconduct, which can result in expulsion. Accusers also can file a criminal complaint with local police.

Dozens of schools across the country have been hit by Title IX lawsuits claiming officials did not take sexual assault claims seriously. And universities are shelling out big money to settle those claims, including the $950,000 settlement FSU paid in the Winston case and the nearly $2.5 million paid to the eight University of Tennessee female students.

In Baylor's motion to dismiss the lawsuit filed against it in January, the university claimed that "as a general rule, universities do not have a legal duty to protect their students from harm caused by other students." [54] But a 1999 Supreme Court ruling — in *Davis v. Monroe County Board of Education*

— said that under Title IX, schools can be liable for failing to stop student-on-student sexual harassment. [55]

The U.S. Department of Education's Office for Civil Rights sent schools a "Dear Colleague" letter in 2011 providing guidance on how to handle sexual assault allegations. The letter says colleges must, among other things, appoint a Title IX coordinator, develop a clear grievance procedure and train staff — including coaches — on how to identify and report sexual violence complaints. [56]

Each college sets its own policies on who directs Title IX investigations and how they're handled. [57] Schools are obligated to investigate and resolve complaints even if law enforcement officials conduct a criminal probe. Campus officials judge the merits of an allegation based on a less stringent "preponderance of evidence" standard — rather than the "beyond a reasonable doubt" standard used in criminal cases. [58]

Colleges also are urged to coordinate their civil investigations with any criminal inquiries.

"Because the standards for pursuing and completing criminal investigations are different from those used for Title IX investigations, the termination of a criminal investigation without an arrest or conviction does not affect the school's Title IX obligations," according to the Office for Civil Rights. [59]

Still, some experts say coaches and school administrators often cover up allegations of sexual assault targeting athletes, and team members may pressure victims to retract their accusations. "When it comes down to money and winning and prestige and power, rational people do irrational things," says Ridpath, at Ohio University. "A lot of the time, people will look the other way, say it's a boys-will-be-boys type thing or blame the victim."

According to the latest data from the Department of Education, college football generated about $3.4 billion in revenue in 2014. The average school generates nearly $30 million in football revenue each year, while the next largest 25 sports, combined, generate less than $25 million. [60]

"I'm always skeptical when there's a major athlete [involved] and then you hear campus police investigated and found nothing," says Ridpath. "I don't want to impugn the integrity of some campus police departments, but I saw it myself when I worked in college athletics that campus police can be manipulated."

A 2014 study launched by U.S. Sen. Claire McCaskill, D-Mo., a former sex crimes prosecutor, found that of 440 four-year colleges and universities surveyed, more than 20 percent allowed athletic departments to investigate sexual assault allegations involving athletes. [61]

"Athletics should never be investigating itself because it's inherently conflicted," says W. Scott Lewis, a partner with the NCHERM Group, a law firm in Pennsylvania specializing in risk management strategies for schools.

The Philadelphia-based nonprofit FIRE — for Foundation for Individual Rights in Education — argues that police and the judicial system, not campus courts, should investigate and adjudicate all sexual assault cases on college campuses. The organization, which focuses on defending students' rights, also says colleges and campus courts lack the ability to subpoena witnesses, collect forensic evidence or use discovery procedures to uncover key facts.

"Expecting campus courts to consistently deliver justice without these tools is unreasonable," FIRE says on its website. [62]

The issue can become even more complex if athletes are involved. Ridpath says schools "typically follow a protocol" in investigating claims against non-athletes. "But with an athlete, there's always a pause," he says. "You should have a template you can follow on how [to] handle it if it was other students who weren't athletes."

Between April 2011 and April 2017, the Office for Civil Rights launched 389 investigations at colleges accused of mishandling sexual violence reports, according to a *Chronicle of Higher Education* database, of which only 62 have been resolved. But the database did not delineate how many involve athletes. [63]

E. Everett Bartlett, president of Stop Abusive and Violent Environments, based in Rockville, Md., faults universities for siding with accusers too often, rather than for being too lax in investigating sexual assault allegations. Universities too often take the position that "we're going to presume the accuser is telling the truth, and going to assume the accused student is in fact guilty, unless evidence proves otherwise," he says.

Bartlett also notes that on college campuses, the officials who investigate sexual assault allegations also decide the final outcome. "In the criminal justice system, those roles are separate," he says. ∎

BACKGROUND

Dawn of Team Sports

College sports date to the second half of the 1800s. Harvard rowers beat Yale in 1852, and the Harvard-Yale Regatta, held annually since 1864, continues today. [64]

The first intercollegiate baseball game was played in 1859, with Amherst trouncing Williams 73-32 in a game that lasted almost four hours. [65]

A decade later, the first intercollegiate football game pitted Rutgers against Princeton. With 25 men on the field for each side, Rutgers won 6-4. [66]

In 1906, the Intercollegiate Athletic Association of the United States — now the National Collegiate Athletic Association (NCAA) — was formed to establish rules for football and other sports — and to reduce injuries and deaths in college football. [67]

In professional sports, the National League of Professional Baseball Clubs, which became the National League, was founded in 1876, followed by the American League in 1901. [68]

The American Professional Football Association was launched in 1920 and renamed the National Football League two years later. [69] The Basketball Association of America was formed in 1946, with a National League and an American League. In 1949, surviving teams of the National League joined the Basketball Association of America, which was then renamed the National Basketball Association. [70]

Continued on p. 374

Chronology

1850s-1940s
College sports programs begin, and professional sports leagues are created.

1852
Harvard rowers beat Yale.

1876
National League of Professional Baseball Clubs (now the National League) is founded.

1906
Intercollegiate Athletic Association (now the National Collegiate Athletic Association) is formed to set rules for college sports.

1920
American Professional Football Association is created; becomes the National Football League (NFL) two years later.

1949
National Basketball Association is created.

———•———

1970s-2000s
New laws address campus sexual assault.

1972
Title IX of the Education Amendments makes colleges responsible for addressing sexual assault.

1980
Department of Education's Office for Civil Rights (OCR) is authorized to enforce Title IX.

1990
Crime Awareness and Campus Security Act requires colleges to disclose crime statistics and campus safety information.

2006
Three Duke lacrosse players are charged with sexually assaulting an exotic dancer. DNA evidence later clears them.

———•———

2010s-Present
As high-profile sexual-assault allegations emerge, federal officials advise schools on how to handle such cases.

2011
OCR instructs colleges and universities on how to address and prevent sexual assault. . . . Former Penn State assistant football coach Jerry Sandusky is arrested on charges of sexually abusing eight boys over a 15-year period. The number of victims later rises to 10.

2012
A female student at Florida State University accuses quarterback Jameis Winston of rape. Prosecutors later drop case for lack of evidence. . . . Sandusky is convicted and sentenced to 30 to 60 years in prison.

2013
Violence Against Women Reauthorization Act requires colleges to create programs to address sexual assault and domestic violence.

2014
Former Baylor football player Tevin Elliott is sentenced to 20 years in prison for sexually assaulting a former Baylor student. . . . Video shows Baltimore Ravens football player Ray Rice punching and knocking out his fiancée (now his wife) in a hotel elevator, prompting NFL to order sexual and domestic violence prevention training for team personnel. . . .

White House Task Force to Protect Students from Sexual Assault is created to help university officials develop a comprehensive response to sexual assault allegations

2015
Measure introduced in Senate would improve how schools handle sexual assault allegations; bill dies in committee, is reintroduced in House and Senate in April 2017.

2016
Stanford University swimmer Brock Turner is sentenced to six months in jail for sexually assaulting an unconscious woman. . . . USA Gymnastics physician Larry Nassar is arrested on charges of sexually assaulting women and girls. . . . Baylor's president, athletics director and head football coach either resign, quit or are fired following allegations that the university did not take sexual assault allegations seriously. . . . University of Tennessee pays almost $2.5 million to settle claims by eight female students who said they were sexually assaulted or otherwise physically abused by athletes. . . . Former NFL player Darren Sharper is sentenced to 20 years in prison for drugging and raping women in four states.

2017
Former Penn State President Graham Spanier is convicted of endangering the welfare of a child for failing to stop Sandusky's abuse. . . . Baylor graduate who says she was raped by two football players sues the school; her lawsuit alleges 31 Baylor football players committed 52 acts of rape between 2011 and 2014, including five gang rapes. . . . Bipartisan group of U.S. senators introduces legislation aimed at protecting amateur athletes from sexual assault.

Abuse Scandals Plague Some Olympic Sports

Gymnasts, swimmers seen as particularly at risk.

Dozens of women and girls recently have leveled sexual assault charges against Lawrence G. Nassar, the former national medical coordinator for USA Gymnastics and team physician for U.S. gymnasts in three Olympic Games.

They allege that Nassar, whose medical license was revoked in April, sexually abused them during routine exams.[1] One accuser, Jessica Howard, U.S. national champion in rhythmic gymnastics from 1999 to 2001, told CBS News' "60 Minutes" in February that she visited Nassar for a hip problem at age 15.

Jessica Howard, a former U.S. national champion in rhythmic gymnastics, gave graphic testimony to the Senate Judiciary Committee on March 28 alleging that USA Gymnastics team physician Lawrence G. Nassar sexually abused her when she was 15. Nassar has been accused of sexually assaulting dozens of athletes.

Getty Images/Chip Somodevilla

"He started massaging me," said Howard. "And — he had asked me not to wear any underwear — then he just continued to go into more and more intimate places. . . . I didn't feel like I was able to say anything because he was, you know, this very high-profile doctor."[2]

In March, Jamie Dantzscher, 34, tearfully told the Senate Judiciary Committee that she was sexually abused by Nassar "all over the world" when she was a teenage Olympic gymnast. The abuse occurred, "In my own room, in my own bed, in my hotel room in Sydney at the Olympic Games," she said, through tears. "I thought I was the only one."[3] The hearing was to consider a bipartisan bill introduced by Sen. Dianne Feinstein, a California Democrat, that would make it a federal crime for national governing bodies of Olympic sports not to report sexual assault to the police.

Accusations of sex abuse are alarmingly common in gymnastics. The *IndyStar* newspaper in Indianapolis found that 368 gymnasts had alleged sexual abuse by coaches, gym owners or other adults over the past 20 years.[4] But, the sport's governing body — USA Gymnastics — "failed to alert police to many allegations of sexual abuse that occurred on their watch and stashed complaints in files that have been kept secret," the newspaper said. As a result, "Predatory coaches were allowed to move from gym to gym, undetected by a lax system of oversight."[5]

USA Gymnastics says it contacted the FBI about Nassar in 2015, five weeks after the organization's president, Steve Penny, heard about the allegations against the doctor and ordered an internal investigation.[6] The organization fired Nassar the same year, and, after an outcry from former gymnasts over the organization's failure to confront longstanding allegations of abuse, Penny resigned in March at the request of the United States Olympic Committee board.[7] In December, the FBI arrested Nassar on child pornography charges, but charges have not been filed against him in connection with the Olympics investigation.[8]

Nassar also faces multiple charges of criminal sexual conduct in Michigan involving at least seven alleged victims, and prosecutors say they expect additional charges.[9] More than 100 women and girls have filed sexual assault complaints against Nassar. "Based on access he had to young girls over the last 20 years, the numbers are staggering," said Jamie White, a Michigan attorney representing some of the alleged victims.[10]

Dozens of the accusers were gymnasts at Michigan State University (MSU), where Nassar served as team physician. Michigan State, which is facing dozens of lawsuits in connection with the case, knew about allegations against Nassar in 2014 but allowed him to remain on staff until he was fired in 2016, according to *The Washington Post*.[11] Nassar, through his lawyer, has denied that he sexually assaulted anyone and said he was conducting legitimate medical procedures.[12]

USA Swimming, the governing body for Olympic swimming, also has experienced sex-abuse scandals, with more than 100 coaches banned for life as of May 1, 2014.[13] In a 2014 petition opposing the induction of former USA Swimming Executive Director Chuck Wielgus into the International Swimming Hall of Fame, the Women's Sports Foundation said during his 17 years in office, "Many of these coaches had well-known, long histories of sexual abuse, yet Wielgus enabled these men to continue to coach for years." The Hall of Fame rescinded its invitation to Wielgus in June 2014.[14]

In 2013, the Government Accountability Office (GAO), the investigative arm of Congress, was asked to investigate allegations of sex abuse in youth sports. In its 2015 report, it recommended that the U.S. Olympic Committee (USOC) conduct background checks on adults who work with children, educate them to recognize abuse and establish policies to handle sex-abuse complaints. [15]

That same year, three female athletes sued Olympic taekwondo coach Marc Gitelman, claiming he had sexually assaulted them and that USOC and USA Taekwondo, the sport's governing body, had done nothing to protect them. [16] The three eventually filed a criminal complaint against Gitelman, who was found guilty in 2015 and sentenced to at least four years in prison. [17]

"Our Olympic dreams were shattered by the USOC allowing a predator coach to molest us," said Yasmin Brown, one of the three plaintiffs. [18]

"Sexual abuse is obviously a societal issue, not just something happening in the world of youth sports," USOC CEO Scott Blackmun said last September in announcing creation of an independent clearinghouse, the U.S. Center for SafeSport, to investigate sexual abuse in the 47 Olympic sports organizations. "But as leaders in the world of sport, we have to do everything in our power to keep our athletes safe." [19] The center opened in February in Colorado Springs. Within days, it had received nine complaints. [20]

Nancy Hogshead-Makar, an attorney in Jacksonville, Fla., and former Olympic gold medal swimmer, questions whether the center is truly independent from the USOC and whether all employees of a gym that is a member of USA Gymnastics fall under the center's jurisdiction. She also recommends that the center bar juvenile athletes and coaches from being alone together. [21]

"The culture of sport is one of obedience," says Hogshead-Makar, who heads Champion Women, an advocacy group for women in sports. Kids may be reluctant to speak up, thinking that they have "no right to complain about anything," she says. "They're trying so hard to please their coach and achieve their dream. A pedophile can exploit that hunger."

— *Susan Ladika*

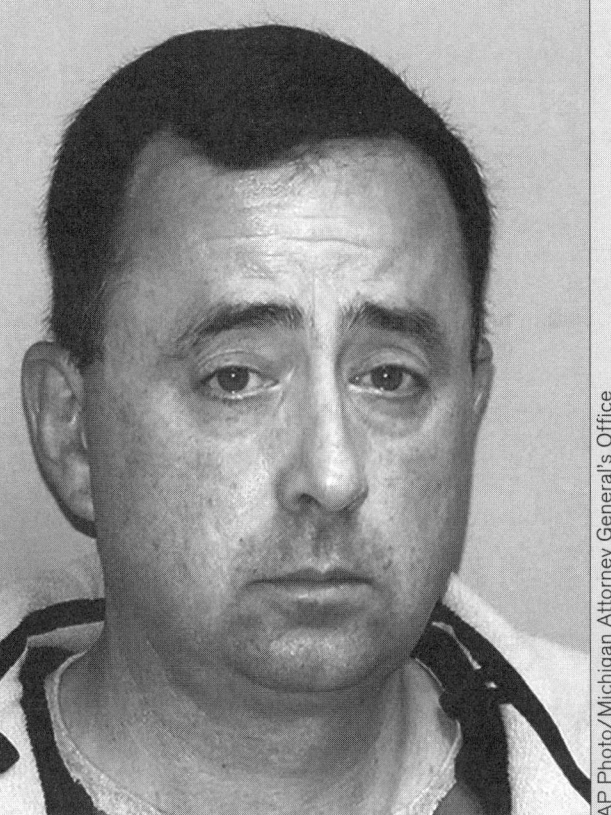

Lawrence G. Nassar is accused of sexually assaulting dozens of women and girls while working as the physician for the U.S. Olympic gymnastics team and for Michigan State University's gymnastics program.

AP Photo/Michigan Attorney General's Office

[1] Dan Murphy, "Former USA Gymnastics Doctor Larry Nassar Has Medical License Revoked," ESPN, April 7, 2017, http://tinyurl.com/lo489tw.

[2] Jonathan LaPook, "Former Team USA Gymnasts Describe Doctor's Alleged Sexual Abuse," "60 Minutes," Feb. 19, 2017, http://tinyurl.com/gve2wwo.

[3] Juliet Macur, "Facing Congress, Some Sports Officials (Not All) Begin to Confront Sexual Abuse," *The New York Times*, March 29, 2017, http://tinyurl.com/mu2scxy.

[4] Mark Alesia, Tim Evans and Marisa Kwiatkowski, "A 20-year Toll: 368 Gymnasts Allege Sexual Exploitation," *IndyStar*, Dec. 15, 2016, http://tinyurl.com/z6w2tyf.

[5] *Ibid*.

[6] Rick Maese and Will Hobson, "USA Gymnastics Says it Alerted FBI to Doctor Accused of Sexual Abuse in 2015," *The Washington Post*, Feb. 16, 2017, http://tinyurl.com/m3fseev.

[7] Mark Alesia, Tim Evans and Marisa Kwiatkowski, "USA Gymnastics President Steve Penny Resigns," *IndyStar*, March 16, 2017, http://tinyurl.com/lzdvnlw; and Tim Evans, Marisa Kwiatkowski and Mark Alesia, "Dominique Moceanu

says USA Gymnastics CEO 'at the forefront' of ignoring abuse," *IndyStar*, Feb. 26, 2017, http://tinyurl.com/zzrq88e.

[8] Matt Mencarini, "Larry Nassar indicted on federal child porn charges," *Lansing State Journal*, Dec. 16, 2016, http://tinyurl.com/mlqmma4.

[9] Victor Mather, "Former USA Gymnastics Doctor Faces New Sexual Assault Charges," *The New York Times*, Feb. 22, 2017, http://tinyurl.com/k2ngqbt.

[10] Tracy Connor, "Former Olympic Gymnastics Doctor Larry Nassar Hit With New Charges," NBC News, Feb. 23, 2017, http://tinyurl.com/hzxhvfl.

[11] Maese and Hobson, *op. cit.*

[12] "MSU pledges further policy review after gymnastics doc," *The Detroit News*, April 13, 2017, http://tinyurl.com/kgkd8uk.

[13] Kelly Whiteside, "Hall of Fame Rescinds Chuck Wielgus' Invite Amid Sexual Abuse Allegations," *USA Today*, June 2, 2014, http://tinyurl.com/la4olrk.

[14] *Ibid*.

[15] Will Hobson, "Government Probe of Sex Abuse Prevention in Olympic Sports Went Nowhere," *The Washington Post*, Feb. 20, 2017, http://tinyurl.com/m62m2ub.

[16] Scott M. Reid, "Three Taekwondo Athletes Sue Coach, USOC over Sexual Assault," *The Orange County Register*, Oct. 29, 2015, http://tinyurl.com/kaxteh5.

[17] Matt Hamilton, "Judge Sends Taekwondo Instructor to Prison for Sexually Abusing Girls," *Los Angeles Times*, Oct. 26, 2015, http://tinyurl.com/khzq356.

[18] Reid, *op. cit.*

[19] Stephen Meyers, "USOC CEO provides details on initiative to protect athletes," *USA Today*, Sept. 22, 2016, http://tinyurl.com/l9ouj2m.

[20] Tim Evans, Marisa Kwiatkowski and Mark Alesia, "SafeSport Center: Is It the Answer to Athlete Sex Abuse?" *IndyStar*, March 8, 2017, http://tinyurl.com/mybk4lg.

[21] *Ibid*.

Continued from p. 370

Sexual Assault

Efforts to address rape on college campuses began in the 1970s, when campus activists began working with community rape crisis centers to provide support services, advocacy and self-defense workshops. One of the first campus rape crisis centers was launched at the University of Maryland in 1972. Campuswide rape prevention programs were launched in the University of California system in 1976. [71]

The federal Title IX law also focused attention on campus sexual assault by requiring colleges to conduct impartial investigations of complaints.

Sexual assault complaints against athletes began gaining attention in the 1970s, and the focus on the problem has intensified in recent years.

Ridpath at Ohio University believes sexual assaults involving athletes "happened a lot before, but we just didn't know about it." He says "it's pretty tough to keep stuff under the rug now" because of the pervasiveness of social media.

Luther, the journalist, said she used Google searches to compile a list of sexual assault allegations dating to 1974. The earliest she found were those that rated coverage in national newspapers such as *The New York Times*. Many smaller newspapers began posting their content online only in the past decade.

Two of the earliest cases on Luther's list involved University of Notre Dame football players. In 1974, an 18-year-old high school student said she was gang raped by six players as other players looked on. The girl spent a month in psychiatric care. She and her parents later requested that no charges be filed. [72]

Two years later, a student at nearby St. Mary's College reportedly was raped by three Notre Dame students, including two of those accused in 1974. The men were caught in the act, but again no charges were filed. [73]

Notre Dame made national news again in 2010, when St. Mary's College student Elizabeth "Lizzy" Seeberg committed suicide after saying she had been sexually assaulted by a Notre Dame football player. [74] The accused continued to play for Notre Dame, and in 2011, the university cleared him of wrongdoing. [75]

On entering the NFL draft three years later, former Notre Dame linebacker Prince Shembo addressed the allegations at a press conference, saying he was the one Seeberg had accused of sexual assault, but that Notre Dame officials had instructed him not to talk about the case. "My name was going to flames, and it just made my name look bad," he said. "I have nothing to hide." [76] Shembo joined the Atlanta Falcons, but was waived in 2015.

The Sandusky case at Penn State represented one of the most shocking examples of inaction by a school in response to clear evidence of sexual abuse. Officials at Penn State, including the school's beloved football coach, Joe Paterno, knew about Sandusky's crimes for years but failed to notify law enforcement, according to grand jury testimony. [77] Sandusky was charged in 2011 with 40 counts of molesting eight boys between 1994 to 2009. Two more boys were later added to the list of victims. [78]

"The most powerful men at Penn State failed to take any steps for 14 years to protect the children who Sandusky victimized," said former FBI Director Louis Freeh, who headed a committee investigating Penn State's handling of the assault allegations. He said Paterno, along with President Spanier, Penn State Athletic Director Tim Curley and the school's vice president, Gary Schultz, "never demonstrated, through actions or words, any concern for the safety and well-being of Sandusky's victims until after Sandusky's arrest." [79]

Paterno was fired after the scandal broke. He died in 2012. Spanier was fired in 2011. Curley was placed on ad-

ministrative leave in 2012 and Penn State opted not to renew his contract. Schultz retired in 2009. Curley and Schultz, who testified for prosecutors at Spanier's trial, pleaded guilty in March to misdemeanor child endangerment for their roles in covering up Sandusky's crimes. [80]

Athletes other than football players also have been accused of sexual assault in high-profile cases, including swimmer Turner at Stanford. After he served only half of his six-month jail sentence, nationwide outrage spurred California to pass a law in 2016 denying probation for anyone convicted of sexually assaulting a victim who was unconscious or too intoxicated to decide whether to consent to sex. [81]

In professional leagues, the *Journal of Sports & Entertainment Law* study found two no-contest pleas among the 18 cases it identified against professional baseball, basketball and football players. [82]

But prosecutors have obtained guilty verdicts against professional athletes. In 2016, for instance, former Dallas Cowboy C.J. Spillman was sentenced to five years in prison after being convicted of sexually assaulting a woman at a hotel. He claimed the sex was consensual. [83]

General Crackdown

In late 2010, federal education officials negotiated agreements with Eastern Michigan University and Notre Dame College in Ohio that required them to improve procedures for dealing with sexual harassment complaints under Title IX.

"Experts read the agreements, which were much more extensive than past ones, as a clear message that the department's Office for Civil Rights was cracking down on Title IX violations," *Inside Higher Ed* said in an April 2011 story. [84] That same year, OCR sent its "Dear Colleague" letter to institutions, detailing specifics on how schools must address and prevent sexual harassment.

The guidance did not outline any special procedures for how schools should deal with allegations involving athletes. It required schools to impartially investigate and resolve alleged sexual assault cases — even if a criminal investigation is not launched or the students or their parents don't want to file a complaint or request action. [85] Each school must have procedures for students to file and present complaints, and accusers have the right to present evidence and witnesses. And each school must distribute its anti-sex discrimination policy and designate an employee to be responsible for Title IX compliance. [86]

Schools must make sure accusers know about resources such as counseling and victim advocacy, and schools must act to protect accusers, and take immediate action if an accuser faces retaliation. [87]

Title IX is not the only federal law related to campus sexual assaults. In 1990, Congress enacted the Crime Awareness and Campus Security Act, which amended the Higher Education Act of 1965. It requires postsecondary institutions receiving federal money to make campus crime statistics and security information public. In 1998 the law was renamed the Jeanne Clery Disclosure of Campus Security Policy and Campus Crime Statistics Act, known as the Clery Act. [88] Clery was a Lehigh University freshman who was raped and murdered in her dorm room in 1986. [89]

The act outlines a bill of rights for sexual assault victims and requires colleges to report crime statistics. [90] A growing number of colleges have faced fines for violating the Clery Act after federal education officials created a special unit in 2010 to enforce the law.

The Violence Against Women Reauthorization Act of 2013 amended the Clery Act to require colleges to disclose statistics on sexual assault, dating violence, domestic violence and stalking and to implement awareness and other programs aimed at preventing such crimes. It also requires institutions to disclose their procedures for disciplining offenders. [91]

From 2011 to 2013, the number of sexual assault claims on campuses increased from 78 to 154, according to the report by liability insurer United Educators. "We likely can attribute this increase to more institutions publicizing their policies and heightened campus awareness of sexual assault — whether from student-led advocacy or other means," the report said. [92]

In 2014, President Obama created the White House Task Force to Protect Students from Sexual Assault, led by Vice President Joe Biden and the White House Council on Women and Girls. [93]

The task force released "A Guide for University and College Presidents, Chancellors, and Senior Administrators" this year to help university officials develop a comprehensive response to sexual assault allegations. [94]

Pro Sports

Professional sports came under intense pressure to address domestic violence and sexual assault after the Ray Rice video was released in 2014. The case followed another major professional sports scandal involving Pittsburgh Steelers quarterback Ben Roethlisberger, who was accused in 2010 of raping a Georgia college student. (*See sidebar, p. 368.*)

NFL Commissioner Goodell came under intense criticism initially for only suspending Rice for two games. But Rice's punishment was strengthened after the video of him punching his fiancée went viral on the Internet. Goodell then sent a letter to all teams, requiring that personnel take part in training to prevent sexual assault and domestic violence. [95] The NHL and MLB followed suit. [96]

Both the NFL and MLB have established procedures for investigating sexual assault and domestic violence allegations. [97] The NFL suspends accused offenders for six games without pay "when there is an incident that requires review." [98]

In January, NBA owners and players reached a contract deal that included creation of a program to focus on preventing sexual assault, domestic violence and child abuse. It would provide players and their families training and counseling, and players accused of an assault would face new investigative and disciplinary procedures. [99]

Abrams, the New Jersey psychologist and author of *Anger Management in Sport*, praises such progress. "People don't appreciate the fact that professional sports are doing more than they have [in the past], and they're trending in the right direction," he says. "There's still more to be done."

Goodell was the first to say he would suspend players, Abrams notes: "He's taking a stand in some places where no one else has the courage to." ∎

CURRENT SITUATION

Recruiting Coaches

In January, Brenda Tracy, who says she was gang-raped by two Oregon State University football players and two other men in 1998, addressed a crowd of at least 3,000 football coaches about how to prevent sexual assault. [100]

"I don't hate football. I don't hate men," Tracy told the coaches gathered in Nashville, Tenn., for the annual conference of the American Football Coaches Association (AFCA), which represents all NFL coaches, most college coaches and a growing number of high school coaches. "It's only 10 percent of the population doing this. Ninety percent of our men in this country would not commit a violent act. So let's get them to start speaking out." [101]

Tracy has spoken to college football programs around the country since going public with her story in 2014. At the AFCA conference, she told coaches that football can help solve the issue of sexual assault, including by adopting a zero-tolerance policy for players to sign.

"I look at sports as a vehicle for change," she says. "You have a big stage. You should be taking this issue on." [101]

Coaches are beginning to take her message to heart. "We've been needing to address these things for a long time," says Todd Berry, executive director of the AFCA.

Some college football programs have had their players sign pledges against sexual violence in which they vow to monitor themselves and others. Berry says he hopes to unveil something similar for AFCA members, and the association is working on a pledge for college players.

"We need to make sure the statements fit on university campuses and from a legal standpoint, so the pledge is something acceptable across the country," Berry says. "This has to be something that has significant buy-in from our players — that they recognize there are going to be consequences if those rules aren't followed."

Berry says the only concern from universities "is that we're invading the Title IX space as we try to take more of this on." He says the association needs to work with universities on that issue, since state, university and Title IX co-ordinators take different approaches in dealing with the law.

"So many of our young people these days are growing up in fatherless homes," Berry says. "A lot of young people may not be talked to the way they should be in relation to this [violence against women]. Many times a coach plays that [father] role. We think we can have a very, very strong impact."

Abrams, the New Jersey psychologist, says the effort should start early.

"We have to change the culture of sports, in youth sports," he says. "When you have a college or pro athlete, you're already talking about young adults who have [had it] reinforced for

[such] a long period of time that they have a different set of rules."

Campus Efforts

Some schools are working to improve their efforts to address sexual assault allegations against athletes.

"If universities do not get ahead of this problem of sexual assault, it is going to bankrupt these schools," Abrams says, referring to potential lawsuits by both the survivors and those falsely accused of assault.

Baylor's sexual assault scandal prompted the Texas Rangers, part of the Texas Department of Public Safety, to begin a preliminary investigation this year into how the university handled the allegations against it. [103]

The Baylor scandal also has prompted Texas lawmakers to demand that colleges toughen up their sexual assault reporting requirements. They have introduced legislation that would require school employees and student leaders to immediately report alleged assaults to school investigators or face criminal charges or expulsion. Schools also would be barred from using conduct code violations to intimidate victims and witnesses, and would have to make it easier to report assault anonymously and online. [104]

In 2016, a Philadelphia law firm produced a report criticizing Baylor's Title IX process. In response, the university fired head football coach Art Briles and demoted university President Kenneth Starr, who then resigned. Athletic Director Ian McCaw also resigned. [105]

In 2014, Sen. McCaskill began focusing on campus sexual assaults in general after championing legislation to reform how the military handles assault cases. In both the military and at colleges, McCaskill said, survivors feel "pressure from peer groups about how they will be perceived in this closed environment if they are willing to publicly talk about what happened."

Institutions have failed to prioritize the rights of the victims and "certainly could be guilty of trying to minimize this problem because of how it reflects on [them]," she said. [106]

A 2014 report by the Senate Subcommittee on Financial and Contracting Oversight at McCaskill's request found that "many institutions are failing to comply with the law and best practices in how they handle sexual violence among students." It specifically criticized the practice of allowing athletic departments to investigate allegations against athletes. [107]

McCaskill used the report to help shape the Campus Accountability and Safety Act. Introduced by a bipartisan coalition of 12 senators in 2015, it was designed to protect both accusers and the accused on college campuses and would have prohibited athletics departments from handling assault complaints. It also would have increased penalties for noncompliance — including a fine of up to 1 percent of an institution's operating budget — and would have increased Clery Act fines from $35,000 to $150,000. [108]

"To truly curb these crimes, we've got to have a road map for colleges and universities to increase responsiveness when crimes occur, better protect and empower students and establish better informed guidelines that actually have some teeth," McCaskill said. [109]

The Senate Health, Education, Labor and Pensions Committee held hearings on the bill in 2015, but the measure died. The bill was reintroduced on April 6, in the House by Reps. Carolyn B. Maloney, D-N.Y., and Pat Meehan, R-Pa., and in the Senate by Sens. McCaskill and Dean Heller, R-Nev. [110]

Meanwhile, in January, the White House Task Force to Protect Students from Sexual Assault launched "It's On Us," a program to get students and communities to work to end sexual assault. The program's main goals are to provide education about sexual con-

Continued on p. 378

At Issue:

Can bystander-intervention training prevent sexual assault by college athletes?

MICHELLE BANGEN
ASSOCIATE DIRECTOR FOR PREVENTION AND WELLNESS, STUDENT HEALTH SERVICES, OREGON STATE UNIVERSITY

WRITTEN FOR *CQ RESEARCHER*, APRIL 2017

*w*hile the issue of sexual assault has been in the national spotlight in recent years, the number of victims is incredibly disheartening. Despite the many ways activists and educators have attempted to reduce these statistics, little seems to have changed over the past few decades. Recently, prevention practitioners and researchers have adopted a more promising approach: bystander intervention.

This approach is recognized as the best primary prevention strategy across the nation, especially following recommendations from the White House Task Force on Campus Sexual Assault. Bystander intervention works partly because it is community-based. Instead of speaking strictly to potential victims or potential perpetrators, bystander intervention makes everyone responsible for preventing sexual violence.

Successful programs produce a population of active bystanders who strive to create a safe community for everyone and take responsibility for their own actions — and reactions to the inappropriate conduct of others. This encourages respect, support and accountability, helps set expectations and reinforce community values and helps shift the culture toward one where sexual violence is not tolerated and where victims/survivors are believed and supported.

Bystander-intervention programs are not one-size-fits-all and must consider the needs, values and preferences of individual communities. One way this has been successful, particularly with athletes, is to make a curriculum's language, examples and scenarios relevant to the athletes' experiences. This is best done in collaboration with the athletes themselves, as well as with athletics administrators, to ensure the relevance and credibility of the messages and to meet the most pressing needs of the community.

Another way to enhance success is to include athletes in delivering these programs, preferably alongside a sexual-violence prevention expert. While community context may dictate how best to pair facilitators with an audience, strong peer leaders can be more compelling in the "how" and "why" — and more convincing with their own anecdotes and advice.

I've seen strong bystander-intervention programs succeed in several communities when athletes were included. Student athletes, often seen as leaders on campus, can help build a positive culture and safe environment as active bystanders. Helping athletes recognize different types of sexual violence and enhancing their skills and confidence to intervene are perhaps some of the first steps in helping them become positive agents of change.

LISA WADE
ASSOCIATE PROFESSOR OF SOCIOLOGY, OCCIDENTAL COLLEGE; AUTHOR, AMERICAN HOOKUP: THE NEW CULTURE OF SEX ON CAMPUS

WRITTEN FOR *CQ RESEARCHER*, APRIL 2017

*b*ystander intervention is a promising strategy for reducing the frequency of college sexual assault. Students who have been trained report lowered tolerance for sexual coercion, less sexual aggression and heightened intention to protect others. Setting a baseline for interpersonal care and responsibility may shift the attitudes of rape-prone students, while sending a strong signal that sexually coercive behaviors will not go unnoticed.

Realizing the potential of bystander intervention, however, requires careful attention to the role status plays in the sociosexual lives of students. In my book, *American Hookup: The New Culture of Sex on Campus*, I found that status — separate from affinity, attraction and even pleasure — is a potent driver of hookup-inclined students' partner choices.

As one female student explained: "The whole point of hookups is to be able to point the person out to your friends and be like, 'Yeah, that guy. That's right. The hot one over there. I got that.' " Another explained: "It's almost bragging rights if you hook up with a guy with a higher social status." One male student wrote that sex is a "commodity," especially valuable if the woman is "blonde" (i.e., highly desirable and elusive).

Social capital translates into sexual access. High-status students — including athletes who play valorized sports and members of elite social fraternities — report enjoying hookup culture more than their peers and hook up more often, with higher-status peers. Social capital also lets them intervene with fewer personal consequences. High-status students may be among the most effective bystanders.

High-status students, however, also are among the most likely to perpetrate sexual assault. And when they do, they may evade intervention more easily than their lower-status peers. It is substantially more difficult to intervene when potential perpetrators are prominent, well-loved and accustomed to getting what they want. Meanwhile, students who do intervene may suffer the same consequences as those who report high-status peers after being assaulted: bullying, abuse and social ostracism. Facing such a possibility, many students may choose to look the other way.

As campuses implement bystander-intervention programs, and as we continue to test their efficacy, it will be important to consider the role status plays in empowering some people to intervene more than others, and in enabling some to act coercively with less risk of intervention.

Continued from p. 376

sent, increase intervention by bystanders and create a supportive environment for survivors. Events have been held on more than 500 college campuses. [111] Partners include the NCAA and the U.S. Olympic Committee.

The task force also is starting a Student Engagement Program, with eight regional teams of student leaders working on coordinated prevention strategies and messages. Another new program will focus on engaging the athletic community. [112]

Concern about assaults involving sports figures intensified with the 2014 release of a video showing Ray Rice, then a Baltimore Ravens running back, knocking out his fiancée Janay (now his wife) in a casino elevator. The video prompted the NFL and other pro leagues to require players to receive training on what behavior constitutes sexual assault and domestic violence.

Oregon State, whose sports teams are called the Beavers, has started a bystander intervention program called "Beavers Give a Dam," says Michelle Bangen, the school's associate director for prevention and wellness. Such programs train students to recognize different types of sexual violence, understand sexual consent and practice intervention methods.

The school's athletics department is a partner in the program, which gives all teams — male and female — "real skills and techniques," Bangen says. "We're talking to everybody as a potential person to intervene and prevent violence."

Pro Sports Actions

This year, former Ravens running back Rice taped an interview for the program the NFL launched in 2014 to train players on how to address sexual assault and domestic violence.

"I just think there's so much more to learn from my situation," Rice told *USA Today*. Anna Isaacson, the NFL's senior vice president of social responsibility, said that in the 2-3 minute interview, Rice "speaks openly about the series of unhealthy choices he made, about how he got to where he was when was in that elevator in 2014." [113]

The NFL also has established critical-response teams to assist anyone, including league spouses and significant others, victimized by abuse. And it laid out policies for responding to abuse allegations, including independent investigative procedures and the baseline six-game suspension without pay for those accused of sexual assault or a similar violation. [114]

The NFL also appointed Lisa Friel, a former sex crimes prosecutor, and B. Todd Jones, former head of the Bureau of Alcohol, Tobacco, Firearms and Explosives, to manage investigative procedures and determine discipline for those who violate the league's personal conduct policy. At the same time that the league created its multimillion-dollar partnerships with organizations to address sexual assault and domestic violence, it also developed a program to help educate young people on those crimes and on character development and healthy relationships. [115]

Other professional leagues have taken similar action. In 2015, Major League Baseball (MLB) began mandatory training in English and Spanish on preventing sexual assault, domestic violence and child abuse, and the baseball commissioner was granted authority to investigate all allegations and discipline players.

Major League Baseball Players Association Executive Director Tony Clark said the MLB hopes its policies "will deter future violence, promote victim safety and serve as a step toward a better understanding of the causes and consequences of domestic violence, sexual assault and child abuse." [116]

Change in professional sports leagues won't happen overnight, psychologist and author Abrams says. "Organizations that size are like aircraft carriers," he says. "You can't [stop] them on a dime. It takes time to navigate where you want to go." ∎

OUTLOOK

'So Much Fear'

Many worry that the Trump administration will roll back protections against sexual assault under Title IX.

"There's so much fear among survivors and marginalized communities about what's going to happen," says Maddy Moore, a Georgetown University senior who serves as a peer educator on sexual assault. [117]

The concern focuses on the protections outlined in the Office of Civil

Rights' letter to colleges and universities in 2011, which are considered merely "guidance." Last year, 21 law professors wrote to federal officials asking them to clarify which department protections qualify as guidance and which qualify as regulations. [118]

In March, more than 90 organizations wrote to Education Secretary Betsy DeVos and Attorney General Jeff Sessions, urging them to enforce Title IX protections. The letter was signed by such groups as Amnesty International at Columbia University and the Alpha Phi Alpha fraternity at Duke University. [119]

DeVos has not indicated whether her agency will continue Obama administration efforts to step up enforcement of Title IX.

There are encouraging signs on other fronts, however.

The NFL "seems to really want to help make a difference over a longer period of time," says Karen Baker, director of the National Sexual Violence Resource Center in Enola, Pa., referring to the league's $10 million partnership with her organization and others. "We're really working to ultimately prevent sexual violence by changing the culture."

Tracy, the accuser in the 1998 gang rape case at Oregon State, also believes prevention efforts will succeed. "If I didn't believe that, I wouldn't do this work," she says.

Athletic departments and coaches must "stay engaged in meaningful ways — such as [providing] ongoing education, raising awareness," and also, she adds, "holding everyone accountable should these things happen."

Sociology professor Wade at Occidental College says colleges need to "stop worshiping athletes and make sports a less important part of what is happening on college campuses."

If nothing else changes college administrators' minds, she says, perhaps financial concerns will do the trick. Under Title IX, colleges "put themselves at risk for a lawsuit from one party or the other" if they fail to properly deal with sexual assault allegations, Wade says.

"Increasingly they're going to be losing money on lawsuits," she says. "I'm hoping the monetary costs start making colleges much, much more serious about preventing assaults than they already are."

In the end, she says, "I think a lot of colleges are going to start thinking it might be a lot cheaper to prevent sexual assault." ■

Notes

[1] Corina Knoll, "Ex-NFL Star Darren Sharper Sentenced to 20 Years in Prison as Rape Victims in L.A. Speak Out," *Los Angeles Times*, Nov. 29, 2016, http://tinyurl.com/jjjeqpd.

[2] Marissa Payne, "Jameis Winston Settles Civil Lawsuit with Accuser in Sexual Assault Case," *The Washington Post*, Dec. 15, 2016, http://tinyurl.com/ky43nqz.

[3] Matt Hamilton, "Brock Turner to be Released from Jail after Serving Half of Six-Month Sentence in Stanford Sexual Assault Case," *Los Angeles Times*, Aug. 30, 2016, http://tinyurl.com/hnonz8q.

[4] See *Elizabeth Doe v. Baylor University*, Civil Action No. 6:17-CV-27, http://tinyurl.com/mvtheb3.

[5] Sarah Mervosh, "New Baylor Lawsuit Alleges 52 Rapes by Football Players in 4 Years, 'Show 'em a Good Time' Culture," *The Dallas Morning News*, Jan. 27, 2017, http://tinyurl.com/z5ybvnu.

[6] Ron Clements, "Former Baylor LB Myke Chatman Arrested on Rape Charges," *SportingNews*, March 24, 2017, http://tinyurl.com/m59hgqx.

[7] The Associated Press, "Baylor Scandal Inspires Flood of Texas Campus Assault Bills," CBS-DFW.com, April 5, 2017, http://tinyurl.com/lsccj9q.

[8] David Wenner, "At a glance: fallout from the Jerry Sandusky case," pennlive.com, March 13, 2017, http://tinyurl.com/kp8gdev.

[9] Katie Mettler, "Alleged 'sadistic hazing rituals' lead to 13 arrests of male student athletes in small Texas town," *The Washington Post*, April 14, 2017, http://tinyurl.com/lbqgt6z.

[10] David Jesse, "Could Michigan State face charges in handling of Larry Nassar case?" *Detroit Free Press*, March 29, 2017, http://tinyurl.com/mxkt6uk.

[11] "Athletes and Sports Competitors," *Occupational Outlook Handbook*, Bureau of Labor Statistics, Dec. 17, 2015, http://tinyurl.com/mcxl38d.

[12] Nicole Auerbach, "Xavier expels Dez Wells for violating student conduct code," *USA Today*, Aug. 21, 2012, http://tinyurl.com/m87bh3r.

[13] Amanda Lee Meyers, "Dez Wells, Xavier settle lawsuit," The Associated Press, April 24, 2014, http://tinyurl.com/qzo9q7w.

[14] Sofi Sinozich and Lynn Langton, "Rape and Sexual Assault Victimization among College-Age Females 1995-2013," U.S Department of Justice, December 2014, http://tinyurl.com/loo4gdx.

[15] *Ibid*.

[16] Kristy L. McCray, "Intercollegiate Athletes and Sexual Violence: A Review of Literature and Recommendations for Future Study," *Trauma, Violence, & Abuse*, October 2015, http://tinyurl.com/mmes47u.

[17] Jessica Luther, *Unsportsmanlike Conduct: College Football and the Politics of Rape* (2016), p. 16.

[18] "Title IX: Tracking Sexual Assault Investigations," accessed April 22, 2017, http://tinyurl.com/lu3djy8.

[19] "Taking Legal Action Under Title IX," "Know Your IX," undated, accessed April 1, 2017, http://tinyurl.com/lw4k3tz.

[20] "Title IX and Sex Discrimination," U.S. Department of Education, April 29, 2015, http://tinyurl.com/86g9tme.

[21] Steve Almasy and Khushbu Shah, "University of Tennessee Settles Title IX Lawsuit with Eight Women," CNN.com, July 15, 2016, http://tinyurl.com/kmjju6b.

[22] Will Hobson, "Former Penn State President Graham Spanier Convicted of Child Endangerment," *The Washington Post*, March 24, 2017, http://tinyurl.com/lzmrdz8.

[23] Julie Mack, "More than 100 patients now claiming sexual assault by ex-MSU Dr. Larry Nassar," *MichiganLive*, March 23, 2017, http://tinyurl.com/kf29k8l.

[24] *Ibid*.

[25] "Athletes and Sports Competitors," *op. cit.*

[26] Elliott C. McLaughlin, "Janay Rice: Ray Rice Was 'Terrified' after Hitting Me," CNN.com, Dec. 1, 2014, http://tinyurl.com/larp6qc; and "Judge Dismisses Domestic Violence Charge against Ray Rice," *USA Today*, May 21, 2015, http://tinyurl.com/n8ltk8z.

[27] Louis Bien, "A Compete Timeline of the Ray Rice Assault Case," *SB Nation*, Nov. 28, 2014, http://tinyurl.com/p5ybyn8.

[28] "The NFL's Response to Domestic Violence and Sexual Assault," NFL.com, Aug. 12, 2015, http://tinyurl.com/q83pegl; Paul Hagen, "MLB, MLBPA Reveal Domestic Violence Policy," MLB.com, Aug. 21, 2015, http://tinyurl.com/kf43aet; Stephen Whyno, "NHL Begins Domestic Violence and Sexual Assault Training," The Associated

Press, Jan. 15, 2016, http://tinyurl.com/llbql2p.

29 "The NFL's Response to Domestic Violence and Sexual Assault," *ibid.*; and Hagen, *ibid.*

30 Hagen, *ibid.*

31 "NFL Commits $10 Million to Sexual Violence Prevention Initiative," NFL.com, June 28, 2016, http://tinyurl.com/l6zo9gy.

32 *Ibid.*

33 Kate Wheeling, "Are Student Athletes More Likely to Commit Sexual Assault?" *Pacific Standard*, May 31, 2016, http://tinyurl.com/kz2kcvo. Also see Baylor University Board of Regents, "Findings of Fact," undated, p. 11, http://tinyurl.com/mcxam4p.

34 Belinda-Rose Young *et al.*, "Sexual Coercion Practices Among Undergraduate Male Recreational Athletes, Intercollegiate Athletes, and Non-Athletes," *Sage Journals*, May 30, 2016, http://tinyurl.com/mfnb8hv.

35 *Ibid.*

36 Amy Ellis Nutt, "A shocking number of college men surveyed admit coercing a partner into sex," *The Washington Post*, June 5, 2016, http://tinyurl.com/ma7vu2p.

37 *Ibid.*; and McCray, *op. cit.*

38 "Confronting Campus Sexual Assault: An Examination of Higher Education Claims," *United Educators*, undated, accessed March 29, 2017, www.ue.org/uploadedfiles/confronting%20campus%20sexual%20assault.pdf, p. 2.

39 Joel Rubin, "Jury Finds Claim that NBA Star Derrick Rose and Two Friends Sexually Assaulted Woman Not Credible," *Los Angeles Times*, Oct. 19, 2016, http://tinyurl.com/h3apja7.

40 Mitch Abrams, "The Problem of Violent Athletes Is Exaggerated," *The New York Times*, July 3, 2013, http://tinyurl.com/mfa2jbg.

41 Lisa Wade, "NFL Players are More Law Abiding than Average Men," *Pacific Standard*, Sept. 22, 2014, http://tinyurl.com/lnw7qzw.

42 Benjamin Morris, "The Rate of Domestic Violence Arrests Among NFL Players," *FiveThirtyEight*, July 31, 2014, http://tinyurl.com/lh3nlec.

43 Abrams, *op. cit.*

44 *Ibid.*

45 Shereen Jegtvig, "Sports aggression may 'spillover' in teen relationships," Reuters, March 25, 2014, http://tinyurl.com/ldrzskx.

46 *Ibid.*

47 *Ibid.*

48 Morris, *op. cit.*

49 "Confronting Campus Sexual Assault: An Examination of Higher Education Claims," *op. cit.*

50 *Ibid.*

51 Bethany P. Withers, "Without Consequences: When Professional Athletes are Violent off the Field," *Journal of Sports & Entertainment Law*, July 12, 2015, p. 6, http://tinyurl.com/lbkem9e.

52 Hamilton, *op. cit.*

53 Katy Moeller, "How much did Boise State pay to settle a sexual misconduct lawsuit?" *Idaho Statesman*, Feb. 11, 2016, http://tinyurl.com/ld83v8b.

54 Matt Young, "Baylor seeks to dismiss lawsuit claiming 52 rapes by football players," *Chron*, March 29, 2017, http://tinyurl.com/ld7a4dr.

55 Todd A. DeMitchell, "Davis v. Monroe County Board of Education," *Encyclopaedia Britannica*, March 18, 2016, http://tinyurl.com/k6m5puj.

56 "Title IX," "Know Your IX, undated, accessed April 14, 2017, http://tinyurl.com/lw2n6ml.

57 "Questions and Answers on Title IX and Sexual Violence," U.S. Department of Education Office for Civil Rights, undated, accessed April 29, 2014, http://tinyurl.com/llx5dnf.

58 "Title IX," *op. cit.*

59 "Questions and Answers on Title IX and Sexual Violence," *op. cit.*

60 Cork Gaines, "The average college football team makes more money than the next 25 college sports combined," *Business Insider*, Oct. 20, 2016, http://tinyurl.com/mxos6a5.

61 "Sexual Violence on Campus: How Too Many Institutions of Higher Education are Failing to Protect Students," Senate Subcommittee on Financial & Contracting Oversight, July 9, 2014, p. 2, http://tinyurl.com/lv5p84k.

62 Joe Cohn, "Law Enforcement Involvement Key to Protecting Students from Sexual Assault," Foundation for Individual Rights in Education,

Jan. 19, 2017, http://tinyurl.com/mz5jx3s.

63 "Title IX: Tracking Sexual Assault Investigations," *Chronicle of Higher Education*, accessed March 30, 2017, http://tinyurl.com/lu3djy8.

64 "Harvard-Yale Regatta — 150 Years of Tradition," *Harvard Athletics*, undated, accessed March 31, 2017, http://tinyurl.com/kp886l7.

65 Michael Beschloss, "The Longest Game: Williams vs. Amherst," *The New York Times*, Sept. 26, 2014, http://tinyurl.com/n4vz2po.

66 "The First Game: Nov. 6, 1869," Rutgers Athletics, undated, accessed March 31, 2017, http://tinyurl.com/pnghcaf.

67 "The 1905 Movement to Reform Football," Library of Congress, undated, accessed March 31, 2017, http://tinyurl.com/3pesphb.

68 "National League of Baseball Is Founded," undated, accessed April 1, 2017, http://tinyurl.com/mvq63ep.

69 "Sept. 17, 1920 — The Founding of the NFL," Pro Football Hall of Fame, undated, accessed April 1, 2017, http://tinyurl.com/k4a8f5y.

70 "A Chronology of the Teams of the NBA," NBA.com, undated, accessed April 1, 2017, http://tinyurl.com/jw9xvpb.

71 Baillee Brown and Caroline Heldman, "A Brief History of Sexual Violence Activism in the U.S.," *Ms. Magazine*, Aug. 8, 2014, http://tinyurl.com/hhfw8wz.

72 Jessica Luther, "A List of College Football Sexual Assault Investigations and Cases," *Jessica W. Luther.com*, Oct. 30, 2016, http://tinyurl.com/mvkloer.

73 *Ibid.* Also see Melinda Henneberger, "Reported Sexual Assault at Notre Dame Campus Leaves More Questions than Answers," *National Catholic Reporter*, March 26, 2012, http://tinyurl.com/mnl5l9q.

74 Stacy St. Clair and Todd Lighty, "Notre Dame Silent on Teen's Death," *The Chicago Tribune*, Nov. 21, 2010, http://tinyurl.com/2dlg3df.

75 "Notre Dame Clears Football Player of Sexual Assault Complaint, Parents Cry Foul," *The Huffington Post*, Nov. 24, 2011, http://tinyurl.com/azwpemq.

76 Chris Hine, "Notre Dame's Prince Shembo Defends His Name," *The Chicago Tribune*, Feb. 22, 2014, http://tinyurl.com/l9f3t4e.

77 Will Hobson and Cindy Boren, "New court documents suggest others at Penn State knew of Jerry Sandusky abuse," *The Washington Post*, July 12, 2016, http://tinyurl.com/lklnbs3.

78 Mark Viera, "Sandusky Arrested on Charges Involving Two New Accusers," *The New York Times*, Dec. 7, 2011, http://tinyurl.com/798vbdy.

79 Eyder Peralta, Mark Memmott and Korva Coleman, "Paterno, Others Slammed In Report

About the Author

Susan Ladika is a freelance writer in Tampa, Fla., whose work has appeared in *HR Magazine*, Workforce, Bankrate.com, CreditCards.com, *Science*, *The Wall Street Journal-Europe* and *International Educator*. She spent a dozen years as a writer and editor for newspapers in the Southeast, including *The Tampa Tribune*, and also reported from Europe for The Associated Press.

For Failing To Protect Sandusky's Victims," NPR, July 12, 2012, http://tinyurl.com/ko63c5p.

[80] Laila Kearney, "Two former Penn State officials cut deal in Sandusky cover-up," Reuters, March 13, 2017, http://tinyurl.com/luxo4a6.

[81] Sarah Larimer, "In Aftermath of Brock Turner Case, California's Governor Signs Sex Crimes Bill," *The Washington Post*, Sept. 30, 2016, http://tinyurl.com/mxph2fe.

[82] Withers, *op. cit.*

[83] "Ex-Cowboy C.J. Spillman Gets 5-Year Prison Term for Sex Assault," The Associated Press, ESPN, July 1, 2016, http://tinyurl.com/k9u8wo4.

[84] Allie Grasgreen, "Call to Action on Sexual Harassment," *Inside Higher Ed*, April 4, 2011, http://tinyurl.com/lrr7h5n.

[85] "Dear Colleague Letter," U.S. Department of Education, Oct. 16, 2015, http://tinyurl.com/k3u5k99.

[86] "Know Your Rights: Title IX Requires Your School to Address Sexual Violence," U.S. Department of Education, undated, accessed April 1, 2017, http://tinyurl.com/k4okjv9.

[87] *Ibid.*

[88] "The Handbook for Campus Safety and Security Reporting, 2016 Edition," U.S. Department of Education, June 2016, http://tinyurl.com/763tbzn.

[89] Margie Peterson, "Murder at Lehigh University Shocked the Nation 25 Years Ago," Patch.com, April 4, 2011, http://tinyurl.com/n2tmlp5.

[90] "The Handbook for Campus Safety and Security Reporting, 2016 Edition," *op. cit.*

[91] *Ibid.*

[92] "Confronting Campus Sexual Assault," *op. cit.*

[93] "Memorandum — Establishing a White House Task Force to Protect Students from Sexual Assault," White House Office of the Press Secretary, Jan. 22, 2014, http://tinyurl.com/n24um4a.

[94] "Preventing and Addressing Campus Sexual Misconduct: A Guide for University and College Presidents, Chancellors, and Senior Administrators," White House Task Force to Protect Students from Sexual Assault," January 2017, http://tinyurl.com/n3ehmtj.

[95] Jane McManus, "NFL Orders Abuse Awareness Training," ESPN.com, Sept. 19, 2014, http://tinyurl.com/ldqvqkm.

[96] Hagen, *op. cit.* Also see Whyno, *op. cit.*

[97] "The NFL's Response to Domestic Violence and Sexual Assault," *op. cit.*; Hagen, *op. cit.*

[98] "The NFL's Response to Domestic Violence and Sexual Assault," *ibid.*

[99] "New NBA Collective Bargaining Agreement signed," NBA, Jan. 19, 2017, http://tinyurl.com/mf4kyhg. See the agreement at http://tinyurl.com/kfjt7pc.

FOR MORE INFORMATION

American Football Coaches Association, 100 Legends Lane, Waco, TX 76706; 254-754-9900; www.afca.com. Supports professional, college and high school coaches.

Champion Women, 3116 St. Johns Ave., Jacksonville, FL 32205; 904-384-8484; championwomen.org. Advocacy group for girls and women in sports.

End Rape on Campus, 811 9th St., Suite 120-140, Durham, NC 27705; 424-777-3762; endrapeoncampus.org. Advocacy group for survivors of sexual violence.

Futures Without Violence, 100 Montgomery St., The Presidio, San Francisco, CA 94129; 415-678-5500; https://www.futureswithoutviolence.org. Develops programs and policies aimed at ending violence worldwide against women.

Know Your IX, https://www.knowyourix.org/college-resources/title-ix/. Organization that aims to end sexual and dating violence at schools.

National Sexual Violence Resource Center, 123 North Enola Drive, Enola, PA 17025; 717-909-0710; www.nsvrc.org. Works to prevent sexual violence.

Office for Civil Rights, 400 Maryland Ave., S.W., Washington, DC 20202-1100; 800-421-3481; www2.ed.gov/about/offices/list/ocr/aboutocr.html. Department of Education office charged with enforcing Title IX compliance.

SAVE (Stop Abusive and Violent Environments), P.O. Box 1221, Rockville, MD 20849; 301-801-0608; www.saveservices.org. Works with survivors and those falsely accused of sexual assault; aims to end sexual assault and domestic violence.

[100] "Brenda Tracy Tells Coaches They Can Help Solve Sexual Assault," The Associated Press, ESPN, Jan. 9, 2017, http://tinyurl.com/mqjjnjv.

[101] *Ibid.*

[102] *Ibid.*

[103] Max Olson and Mark Schlabach, "Texas Rangers Investigating Baylor's Response to Sexual Assault Claims," ESPN.com, March 1, 2017, http://tinyurl.com/hbzh5b8.

[104] The Associated Press, "Baylor Scandal Inspires Flood of Texas Campus Assault Bills," CBSDFW.com, April 5, 2017, http://tinyurl.com/lsccj9q.

[105] "Ousted Baylor President Starr Resigns from Chancellor Role," The Associated Press, June 1, 2016, http://tinyurl.com/jw8w4jd.

[106] Nick Anderson, "Sen. Claire McCaskill Turns Her Focus to Sexual Assaults on College Campuses," *The Washington Post*, June 27, 2014, http://tinyurl.com/m335f3c.

[107] "Expanded Bipartisan Coalition Introduced Legislation to Prevent Sexual Assaults on College and University Campuses," U.S. Sen. Claire McCaskill, Feb. 26, 2015, http://tinyurl.com/n76byb4.

[108] "Expanded Bipartisan Coalition Introduces Legislation to Prevent Sexual Assaults on College and University Campuses," Office of Sen. Claire McCaskill, U.S. Senate, Feb. 26, 2015, http://tinyurl.com/h4yzuwv.

[109] *Ibid.*

[110] "Reps. Maloney and Meehan Introduce Bipartisan Bill to Combat Campus Sexual Assault," Office of Carolyn B. Maloney, House of Representatives, April 6, 2017, http://tinyurl.com/mb3ga7q. "Bipartisan Coalition of Senators Renew Legislation to Combat Sexual Assault on College & University Campuses," Office of Claire McCaskill, U.S. Senate, April 6, 2017, http://tinyurl.com/mxmzxyx.

[111] "Fact Sheet: Final It's On Us Summit and Report of the White House Task Force to Protect Students from Sexual Assault," Office of the Press Secretary, White House, Jan. 5, 2017, http://tinyurl.com/mfp5efv.

[112] *Ibid.*

[113] Christine Brennan, "NFL looks to Ray Rice to help educate players, others," *USA Today*, April 17, 2017, http://tinyurl.com/kedagtp.

[114] "The NFL's Response to Domestic Violence and Sexual Assault," *op. cit.*

[115] *Ibid.*

[116] Hagen, *op. cit.*

[117] Jane McManus, "Incoming Trump Administration Heightens Anxiety about Reversal in Title IX Progress," ESPN, Jan. 17, 2017, http://tinyurl.com/k65pqkp.

[118] Jake New, "Due Process and Sex Assaults," *Inside Higher Ed*, May 17, 2016, http://tinyurl.com/hzakvqt.

[119] Alanna Vagianos, "Over 90 Organizations Demand Trump Administration Enforce Title IX in Powerful Letter," *The Huffington Post*, March 31, 2017, http://tinyurl.com/kw92blw.

Bibliography

Selected Sources

Books

Johnson, KC, and Stuart Taylor Jr., *The Campus Rape Frenzy: The Attack on Due Process at America's Universities*, Encounter Books, 2017.

A professor of history at Brooklyn College (Johnson), and a legal affairs journalist (Taylor) say colleges are too quick to presume the guilt of students accused of sexual assault.

Luther, Jessica, *Unsportsmanlike Conduct: College Football and the Politics of Rape*, Edge of Sports/Akashic Books, 2016.

A journalist examines the prevalence of sexual assault in college football, the response by universities, and changes needed to address the issue.

Wade, Lisa, *American Hookup: The New Culture of Sex on Campus*, W.W. Norton & Co., 2017.

An associate professor of sociology at Occidental College discusses the sexual culture on American college campuses.

Articles

"The NFL's Response to Domestic Violence and Sexual Assault," NFL.com, Aug. 12, 2015, http://tinyurl.com/q83pegl.

The NFL is taking steps to deal with sexual and domestic violence, including mandatory training for all team members.

Alesia, Mark, Tim Evans and Marisa Kwiatkowski, "The 20-year Toll: 368 Gymnasts Allege Sexual Exploitation," *IndyStar*, Dec. 15, 2016, http://tinyurl.com/z6w2tyf.

An in-depth examination of sexual assault allegations involving USA Gymnastics athletes finds 368 cases over 20 years, and says little has been done to address the problem.

Bogdanich, Walt, "A Star Player Accused, and a Flawed Rape Investigation," *The New York Times*, April 16, 2014, http://tinyurl.com/lw22kgz.

The article examines the botched rape investigation by Tallahassee police and Florida State University after football player Jameis Winston is accused of sexual assault.

Hagen, Paul, "MLB, MLBPA Reveal Domestic Violence Policy," MLB.com, Aug. 21, 2015, http://tinyurl.com/kf43aet.

Major League Baseball and the Major League Baseball Players Association announce an agreement regarding new policies on sexual and domestic violence.

Kutner, Max, "Suspended College Athlete Suing U.S. Over Sexual Assault Guidance," *Newsweek*, April 20, 2016, http://tinyurl.com/lovyy7a.

Newsweek looks at the sexual assault accusations against college athlete Grant Neal and his lawsuit against the U.S. Department of Education alleging gender discrimination.

McManus, Jane, "Incoming Trump Administration Heightens Anxiety about Reversal in Title IX Progress," ESPN W, Jan. 17, 2017, http://tinyurl.com/k65pqkp.

The election of Donald Trump has raised concerns his administration will set back efforts to prevent campus sexual assaults.

Mervosh, Sarah, "New Baylor Lawsuit Alleges 52 Rapes by Football Players in 4 Years, 'Show 'em a Good Time' Culture," *The Dallas Morning News*, Jan. 27, 2017, http://tinyurl.com/z5ybvnu.

A Baylor University graduate says in a lawsuit against the school that she was raped by football players there and that 31 Baylor football players committed at least 52 rapes between 2011 and 2014.

Payne, Marissa, "Jameis Winston Settles Civil Lawsuit with Accuser in Sexual Assault Case," *The Washington Post*, Dec. 15, 2016, http://tinyurl.com/ky43nqz.

Erica Kinsman and former Florida State quarterback Jameis Winston settle Kinsman's civil suit accusing Winston of rape.

Reports and Studies

"Confronting Campus Sexual Assault: An Examination of Higher Education Claims," United Educators, 2015, http://tinyurl.com/kz83zuu.

A company that provides liability insurance and risk management services for colleges examines campus sexual assault claims filed between 2011 and 2013.

"Sexual Violence on Campus: How too Many Institutions of Higher Education are Failing to Protect Students," U.S. Senate Subcommittee on Financial & Contracting Oversight, July 9, 2014, http://tinyurl.com/lv5p84k.

A Senate subcommittee survey shows many institutions fail to comply with the law and best practices in handling sexual assault complaints, including those against athletes.

McCray, Kristy L., "Intercollegiate Athletes and Sexual Violence: A Review of Literature and Recommendations for Future Study," *Trauma, Violence, & Abuse*, October 2015, http://tinyurl.com/ko4kpfj.

An Otterbein University assistant professor argues that research on sexual assault by college athletes has stagnated since the 1990s and should be updated.

Withers, Bethany, "Without Consequences: When Professional Athletes Are Violent Off the Field," *Journal of Sports & Entertainment Law*, Harvard Law School, July 12, 2015, http://tinyurl.com/lbkem9e.

An attorney who has studied violence by athletes against women looks at sexual assault and domestic violence accusations targeting pro athletes, and how many escape repercussions.

The Next Step:

Additional Articles from Current Periodicals

College Investigations

Austin, Kyle, "Michigan State football player under investigation in new sexual assault probe," *MLive*, April 13, 2017, https://tinyurl.com/k5mfa34.

  Michigan State suspended a football player and a staff member after a police investigation into a sexual assault complaint.

Fornelli, Tom, "Texas A&M WR charged with indecent exposure, blames 'jock itch,'" *CBS Sports*, April 7, 2017, http://tinyurl.com/mja9amj.

  A Texas A&M student filed a complaint against a football player for indecent exposure, but the athlete rejoined his team without punishment after his lawyer claimed the exposure was due to "a bad case of jock itch."

Lerner, Maura, "University of Minnesota to review its own sex assault investigation of Gophers football players," *Star Tribune*, March 24, 2017, https://tinyurl.com/k3lwukh.

  The University of Minnesota ordered an independent review to quell concerns of how it handled sexual assault allegations.

League Actions

Bromberg, Nick, "Big 12 withholds 25 percent of Baylor's league revenues," *Yahoo Sports*, Feb. 8, 2017, https://tinyurl.com/k5jz3jr.

  The Board of Directors of the Big 12 Conference unanimously voted to withhold 25 percent of Baylor University's share of future revenue it receives from the conference pending a review of athletic operations, after a lawsuit claimed players on the school's football team committed 52 acts of rape over five years.

Pilon, Mary, "Inside the NFL's Domestic Violence Punishment Problem," *Bleacher Report*, Jan. 31, 2017, https://tinyurl.com/hfynaps.

  NFL Commissioner Roger Goodell announced a league policy to suspend first-time offenders for six games without pay and second-time offenders for life.

Puma Mike, "Mets closer Jeurys Familia banned 15 games," *New York Post*, March 29, 2017, https://tinyurl.com/kyvpcg6.

  Major League Baseball suspended New York Mets closer Jeurys Familia for 15 games for violating the league's Joint Domestic Violence, Sexual Assault and Child Abuse Policy.

'Rape Culture' Allegations

Buchsbaum, Shira, "Advocates stress training to address rape culture," *Brown Daily Herald*, April 11, 2017, https://tinyurl.com/l5c5vod.

  Activists at Brown University seeking to end what they see as a rape culture on campus.

Mettler, Katie, "Alleged 'sadistic hazing rituals' lead to 13 arrests of male student athletes in small Texas town," *The Washington Post*, April 14, 2017, https://tinyurl.com/l8lh6jj.

  Police arrested 13 high school students in Texas in connection with accusations of hazing-related sodomy and other sexual abuse; one accuser's parents filed a federal civil rights lawsuit against the school alleging that it had enabled a "persistent 'rape culture.'"

Sokol, Chad, "Gonzaga stops selling 'boys will be boys' T-shirt after complaint that it 'perpetuates rape culture,'" *The Spokesman-Review*, March 31, 2017, https://tinyurl.com/kjwan8v.

  Gonzaga University stopped selling children's T-shirts that promoted men's athletics, featuring the phrase "boys will be boys," after a student tweeted that the slogan "perpetuates rape culture."

Title IX Cases

Budd, Larry, "Feds reach agreement with Wittenberg U. on sexual assault complaints," *Dayton Daily News*, March 25, 2017, https://tinyurl.com/k2zs38w.

  The U.S. Department of Education's Office for Civil Rights agreed to a settlement with Wittenberg University after the office found the university's handling of athlete sexual-assault cases violated Title IX policies.

Mencarini, Matt, "Nassar assaulted 15-year-old girl, MSU Title IX report finds," *Lansing State Journal*, March 21, 2017, https://tinyurl.com/jwsn9ze.

  A Michigan State University Title IX investigator said she found a "preponderance of evidence" that former university doctor Larry Nassar sexually assaulted a 15-year-old girl during medical appointments.

In-depth Reports on Issues in the News

Are you writing a paper?

Need backup for a debate?

Want to become an expert on an issue?

For 90 years, students have turned to *CQ Researcher* for in-depth reporting on issues in the news. Reports on a full range of political and social issues are now available. Following is a selection of recent reports:

Civil Liberties
Privacy and the Internet, 12/15
Intelligence Reform, 5/15
Religion and Law, 11/14

Crime/Law
High-Tech Policing, 4/17
Forensic Science Controversies, 2/17
Jailing Debtors, 9/16
Decriminalizing Prostitution, 4/16
Restorative Justice, 2/16
The Dark Web, 1/16
Immigrant Detention, 10/15

Education
Charter Schools, 3/17
Civic Education, 2/17
Student Debt, 11/16
Apprenticeships, 10/16

Environment/Society
Women in Prison, 3/17
Guns on Campus, 1/17
Mass Transit, 12/16
Arctic Development, 12/16
Protecting the Power Grid, 11/16
Pornography, 10/16

Health/Safety
Reducing Traffic Deaths, 2/17
Opioid Crisis, 10/16
Mosquito-Borne Disease, 7/16

Politics/Economy
Rethinking Foreign Aid, 4/17
Troubled Brazil, 4/17
Reviving Rural Economies, 3/17
Immigrants and the Economy, 2/17
Trump Presidency, 1/17
European Union's Future, 12/16
The Obama Legacy, 11/16

Upcoming Reports

Native Americans, 5/5/17   Anti-Semitism, 5/12/17   Pandemics, 5/19/17

ACCESS

CQ Researcher is available in print and online. For access, visit your library or www.cqresearcher.com.

STAY CURRENT

For notice of upcoming *CQ Researcher* reports or to learn more about *CQ Researcher* products, subscribe to the free email newsletters, *CQ Researcher Alert!* and *CQ Researcher News*: http://cqpress.com/newsletters.

PURCHASE

To purchase a *CQ Researcher* report in print or electronic format (PDF), visit www.cqpress.com or call 866-427-7737. Single reports start at $15. Bulk purchase discounts and electronic-rights licensing are also available.

SUBSCRIBE

Annual full-service *CQ Researcher* subscriptions—including 44 reports a year, monthly index updates, and a bound volume—start at $1,131. Add $25 for domestic postage.

CQ Researcher Online offers a backfile from 1991 and a number of tools to simplify research. For pricing information, call 800-818-7243 or 805-499-9774 or email librarysales@sagepub.com.

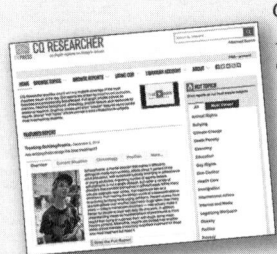

CQ RESEARCHER

CQPRESS

In-depth reports on today's issues

Published by CQ Press, an Imprint of SAGE Publications, Inc.   **www.cqresearcher.com**

Native American Sovereignty

Should Indians have more control over their land?

Native American lands contain $1.5 trillion in untapped coal, oil and other energy resources. The potential bounty is raising hopes among many Indians that energy development can help tribes reduce poverty on their reservations, where unemployment averages 19 percent. But development also is raising fears that it will threaten Indians' traditional way of life and harm the Earth. In addition, the dispute is raising tough questions among Indians, lawmakers and others about energy development and the limits of tribal sovereignty. The Navajo and like-minded tribes want federal regulations relaxed so Indians can develop their energy resources, providing jobs and other benefits. But other tribes argue the federal government remains obligated under treaties to protect Indian land from commercial exploitation. They are further worried about the Trump administration as it relaxes regulations on the energy industry and federal lands. Meanwhile, controversy has arisen over some tribes' disenrolling of members. Critics say the practice is a power grab by tribal leaders, but defenders say tribes have a right to decide who is a member.

Protesters demonstrate in Washington, D.C., on March 10, 2017, against the Dakota Access Pipeline, which runs near the Standing Rock Sioux reservation in North Dakota. Tribal members say the controversial oil project infringes on their sovereignty and will desecrate sacred land and pollute groundwater.

CQ Researcher • May 5, 2017 • www.cqresearcher.com
Volume 27, Number 17 • Pages 385-408

RECIPIENT OF SOCIETY OF PROFESSIONAL JOURNALISTS AWARD FOR EXCELLENCE ◆ AMERICAN BAR ASSOCIATION SILVER GAVEL AWARD

Los Angeles | London | New Delhi
Singapore | Washington DC | Melbourne

I N S I D E THIS REPORT

THE ISSUES 387

BACKGROUND 393

CHRONOLOGY 395

CURRENT SITUATION 400

AT ISSUE 401

OUTLOOK 403

BIBLIOGRAPHY 406

THE NEXT STEP 407

CQ RESEARCHER

May 5, 2017
Volume 27, Number 17

EXECUTIVE EDITOR: Thomas J. Billitteri
tjb@sagepub.com

ASSISTANT MANAGING EDITORS: Kenneth Fireman, kenneth.fireman@sagepub.com, Kathy Koch, kathy.koch@sagepub.com, Scott Rohrer, scott.rohrer@sagepub.com

ASSOCIATE MANAGING EDITOR: Val Ellicott

SENIOR CONTRIBUTING EDITOR:
Thomas J. Colin
tom.colin@sagepub.com

CONTRIBUTING WRITERS: Marcia Clemmitt, Sarah Glazer, Reed Karaim, Barbara Mantel, Chuck McCutcheon, Tom Price

SENIOR PROJECT EDITOR: Olu B. Davis

EDITORIAL ASSISTANT: Anika Reed

FACT CHECKERS: Eva P. Dasher, Michelle Harris, Betsy Towner Levine, Robin Palmer

Los Angeles I London I New Delhi
Singapore I Washington DC I Melbourne

An Imprint of SAGE Publications, Inc.

SENIOR VICE PRESIDENT,
GLOBAL LEARNING RESOURCES:
Karen Phillips

EXECUTIVE DIRECTOR, ONLINE LIBRARY AND
REFERENCE PUBLISHING:
Todd Baldwin

CQ Researcher (ISSN 1056-2036) is printed on acid-free paper. Published weekly, except: (March wk. 4) (May wk. 4) (July wks. 1, 2) (Aug. wks. 2, 3) (Nov. wk. 4) and (Dec. wks. 3, 4). Published by SAGE Publications, Inc., 2455 Teller Rd., Thousand Oaks, CA 91320. Annual full-service subscriptions start at $1,131. For pricing, call 1-800-818-7243. To purchase a *CQ Researcher* report in print or electronic format (PDF), visit www.cqpress.com or call 866-427-7737. Single reports start at $15. Bulk purchase discounts and electronic-rights licensing are also available. Periodicals postage paid at Thousand Oaks, California, and at additional mailing offices. POSTMASTER: Send address changes to *CQ Researcher*, 2600 Virginia Ave., N.W., Suite 600, Washington, DC 20037.

THE ISSUES

387 • Should tribes have full control over their reservations?
• Would energy development improve tribes' economies?
• Should tribes be consulted on projects outside their borders?

BACKGROUND

393 **Allies and Enemies**
European powers were eager to trade with Native Americans during the colonial period.

394 **Forced Assimilation**
The 1887 Dawes Act sought to turn Indians into farmers and landowners.

394 **Termination Period**
Federal officials in the 1960s tried to help tribes by ending trustee protections over reservations.

398 **Rise of Casinos**
A Supreme Court decision in 1987 gave tribes the right to open casinos.

CURRENT SITUATION

400 **Questions About Trump**
Tribal leaders are puzzled over the president's intentions on Indian sovereignty.

402 **In Congress**
Legislators are considering easing energy regulations on tribal lands.

402 **In the Courts**
Many Native Americans praise new Supreme Court Justice Neil Gorsuch.

OUTLOOK

403 **"Backsliding" Feared**
Experts say tribes could lose control over their lands.

SIDEBARS AND GRAPHICS

388 **Navajo Nation Is Biggest U.S. Tribe by Far**
The largest Indian reservations are in the West.

389 **Many Native Homes Lack Phones, Plumbing**
U.S. general population fares better.

392 **Native Lands Hold Vast Resources**
Untapped energy resources on Indian lands are valued at $1.5 trillion.

395 **Chronology**
Key events since 1789.

396 **Climate Change Threatens Tribal Lands**
"It is the federal government's responsibility to protect our fishing rights."

398 **Tribal Councils Increasingly Expel Members**
"Disenrollment is never about who belongs in the tribe."

401 **At Issue:**
Could energy development lift tribes out of poverty?

FOR FURTHER RESEARCH

405 **For More Information**
Organizations to contact.

406 **Bibliography**
Selected sources used.

407 **The Next Step**
Additional articles.

407 **Citing *CQ Researcher***
Sample bibliography formats.

Cover: Getty Images/Justin Sullivan

Native American Sovereignty

BY CHRISTINA L. LYONS

THE ISSUES

On rolling hills in south-central Montana, near where Lt. Col. George Armstrong Custer and his 7th Cavalry made their Last Stand in 1876, the Crow Nation sees the future.

The tribe's 2.2-million-acre reservation is rich in coal, and unlocking its potential is critical to the tribe's economy, tribal leaders say. The Crow's main source of income is the 43-year-old Absaloka Mine in Hardin. The tribe for the past several years has pushed to open a second mine that could produce 1.4 billion tons of coal and generate $10 million for the tribe in five years.

But the tribe's attempts to open the new mine have been stymied in part by federal land-use and environmental rules that the tribal government says tread on its sovereignty. [1]

"I don't want to be dependent on the U.S. government," former Crow tribal Chairman Darrin Old Coyote said. "We have the resources, we have the manpower, we have the capability of being self-sufficient." Noting that the tribe's unemployment rate ranges between 25 percent and 50 percent, he added, "There's no reason why we should be this poor." [2]

But nearby tribes say fossil fuel development threatens the environment and Native Americans' distinct way of life, which they believe the federal government is obligated to protect under centuries-old treaties. Energy development "threatens the cultural heritage of what it means to be Northern Cheyenne," tribal council member Conrad Fisher said. "It has to do with being environmental stewards of the

Former Crow Nation Chairman Darrin Old Coyote says the tribe has the right to develop coal reserves on its vast Montana reservation. Other tribes nearby, however, oppose fossil fuel development as a threat to Native Americans' distinct way of life and want the federal government to protect the land.

AP Photo/The Billings Gazette/Casey Page

land and appreciating this beautiful country we call home." [3]

The tribes' contrasting views highlight a spirited debate among Native Americans, economists, environmentalists, scholars and lawmakers about energy development and tribal sovereignty. Some tribal governments — including the Navajo in the Southwest and the Southern Ute in Colorado — favor authorizing tribes to develop their energy resources or implement their own environmental safeguards without restrictions from the federal government and outsiders.

"It's about sovereignty," said Mark Fox, chairman of the Three Affiliated Tribes of the Mandan, Hidatsa and Arikara Nation, known as MHA Nation,

which has profited from an oil and gas boom on its Fort Berthold reservation in North Dakota. [4]

But other tribal governments, numerous individual natives and environmentalists say the federal government remains obligated to protect Indian land and natural resources from outside commercial exploitation or corrupt tribal governments.

"It's not about business anymore," David Kenny, a member of the Seneca Nation, said as he marched past the White House on March 17 protesting the completion of the Dakota Access Pipeline. The controversial oil pipeline runs under land sacred to Native Americans just outside the Standing Rock Sioux's reservation in North Dakota. "Everybody is going to die if this continues. The Earth is dying." [5]

The debate over energy development has taken on added urgency in recent years because of entrenched poverty on reservations and the growing lure of energy and mineral riches, driven in part by the Trump administration's plans to revitalize the domestic energy industry.

In 2010, 5.2 million people identified as members of one of the nation's 567 American Indian or Alaska Native tribes. About 22 percent of the Native Americans live on one of 334 reservations, which cover 100 million acres scattered across 35 states.

Those reservations contain almost 30 percent of the nation's coal reserves west of the Mississippi River, half of its potential uranium reserves and one-fifth of the known oil and natural gas reserves. Yet the Interior Department in 2008 estimated that 15 million acres

Navajo Nation Is Biggest U.S. Tribe by Far

The five largest Indian reservations in the continental United States are in the West. The Navajo Nation — spanning Arizona, New Mexico and Utah and covering nearly 27,100 square miles — is nearly eight times bigger than the second-largest reservation. It also has the largest population.

Five Largest Native American Reservations

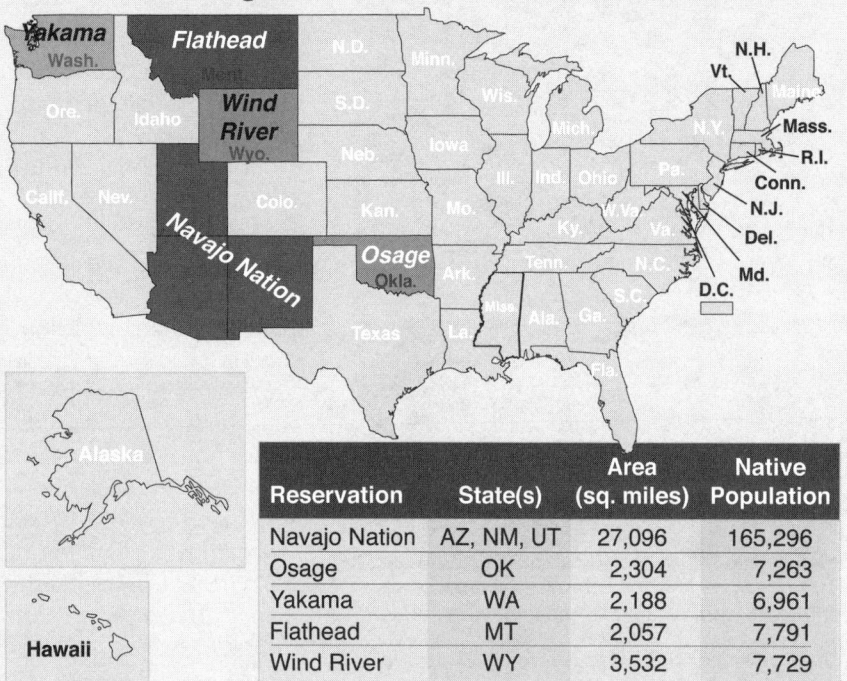

Reservation	State(s)	Area (sq. miles)	Native Population
Navajo Nation	AZ, NM, UT	27,096	165,296
Osage	OK	2,304	7,263
Yakama	WA	2,188	6,961
Flathead	MT	2,057	7,791
Wind River	WY	3,532	7,729

Sources: Amber Pariona, "Biggest Indian Reservations In The United States," World Atlas, July 20, 2016, http://tinyurl.com/lzve6ne; Tina Norris, Paula L. Vines and Elizabeth M. Hoeffel, "My Tribal Area," U.S. Census Bureau, 2011-2015 American Community Survey 5-Year Estimates, http://tinyurl.com/lwavjnn; "Indian Lands of Federally Recognized Tribes of the United States," Bureau of Indian Affairs, http://tinyurl.com/lm2vekh

of reservations' energy rich lands were undeveloped. [6]

Some tribes reside on lands with abundant natural resources for timbering, agriculture or fishing — such as in the Pacific Northwest or Great Lakes areas. Other tribes have rich fossil fuel or mineral reserves, but not all want to harvest them.

The issue of whether to exploit fossil fuel or mineral resources can put tribes at odds with each other or cause divisions within tribes.

"The Navajo Nation has some members who are pro-economic develop-

ment and want to provide jobs [in areas] where there is significant unemployment," says Walter Stern, a lawyer in New Mexico who represents energy companies. "And there are members who are opposed to any kind of disturbance of Mother Earth, so they don't want to see any coal development or anything."

Federal regulations can limit resource development on tribal lands, legal experts say. The regulations are based on the "trustee doctrine," which stems from an 1831 Supreme Court ruling describing tribes as "domestic depen-

dent nations" with a relationship to the U.S. government similar to that of wards to guardians. [7]

Much of the energy development that has occurred on reservations was initiated decades ago, when changing federal policies left reservations with checkerboard land ownership patterns. The Dawes Act of 1887 divvied up native territories and allotted plots to individual Indians, to be held in trust for 25 years or until the United States deemed the individuals competent to be granted ownership. Surplus lands were sold to non-Indians.

When the allotment process ended in 1934, lands remaining in trust were frozen in the trust, while any individuals who had been granted deeds to their lots were free to lease or sell them. According to a 2011 study, about 75 percent of tribal land remains in trust protection for the tribe, 20 percent entail individual lots held in trust (primarily for heirs of the Indians originally granted the lots) and 5 percent is privately owned by Indians or non-Indians. [8]

Before Congress ended the allotment process, it allowed the U.S. government to approve any energy development contracts on tribal trust lands. Many contracts provided only limited royalties to tribes. Tribes regained some authority over development projects on their lands in the 1980s, but the Bureau of Indian Affairs (BIA) retained final approval.

Today, a "complex" regulatory framework governs BIA management of energy development on trust lands, according to the Government Accountability Office (GAO).

"Trusteeship wraps these reservations in red tape," says Terry Anderson, a senior fellow at the Property and Environmental Research Center in Bozeman, Mont., noting that energy development proposals require approval from four federal agencies and compliance with 49 regulations.

He says tribes should have "authority over the land within reservation boundaries. I think from there, tribes can decide what they want to do."

But Jacqueline Pata, executive director of the National Congress of American Indians, a lobbying organization for tribal interests based in Washington, D.C., says the trust status is necessary to prevent exploitation. "The protection of our land is so important to tribes," she says.

At the same time, Pata says, the government must recognize tribes' sovereignty. Various laws, court rulings and treaties pledged the U.S. government to honor tribal self-governance while also providing support for health care, education, housing and economic development. [9]

Yet in 2011 an estimated 40 percent of the American Indians and Alaska Natives on reservations were living in poverty. The unemployment rate averages about 19 percent, nearly a quarter of reservation homes lack plumbing, and health, education and income statistics rank near the bottom of all minority groups nationwide. (*See graph, right.*) Employment options are few. According to the National Congress of American Indians, 4 percent of Indians work in agriculture, forestry, fishing/hunting or mining. About one-third work in education, health care or social services; the rest are in public administration, hold odd jobs or are unemployed. [10]

Because tribes cannot tax property, they must get innovative to generate more revenue, experts say. *

Since the 1970s, many tribes have opened casinos or run bingo games. In 2015, 474 tribal gambling operations generated nearly $30 billion in revenue nationwide. [11] The most successful operations, experts note, are those located near major metropolitan areas.

The Southern Ute tribe now generates about 30 percent of its income from oil and natural gas production.

_____

* Tribes cannot levy property taxes because of the trust status of their land. They can impose sales and excise taxes.

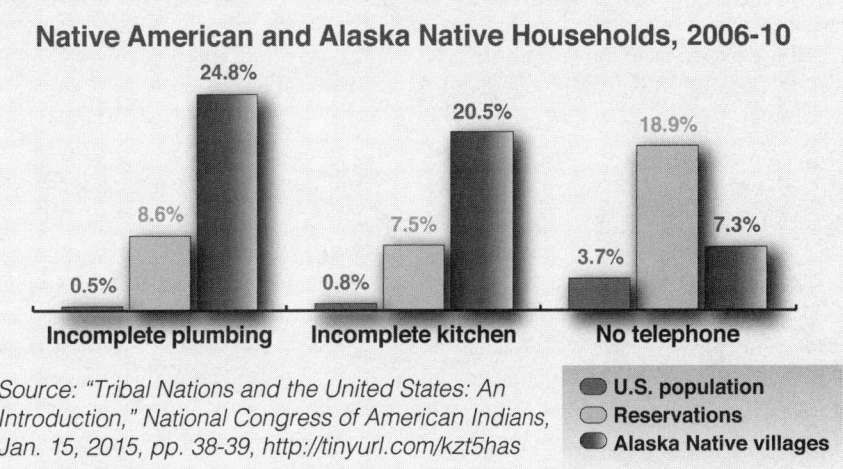

Many Native Homes Lack Phones, Plumbing

Homes on Indian reservations and in Alaska Native villages are in poorer condition than in the general U.S. population, according to the latest census data. Nearly one-fifth of reservation households had no telephone in 2006-10, and a quarter of the homes in Alaska Native villages lacked complete plumbing.

Native American and Alaska Native Households, 2006-10

Incomplete plumbing: 0.5%, 8.6%, 24.8%
Incomplete kitchen: 0.8%, 7.5%, 20.5%
No telephone: 3.7%, 18.9%, 7.3%

- U.S. population
- Reservations
- Alaska Native villages

Source: "Tribal Nations and the United States: An Introduction," National Congress of American Indians, Jan. 15, 2015, pp. 38-39, http://tinyurl.com/kzt5has

But navigating the regulatory process took eight years, during which the tribe lost more than $95 million in potential revenue from permitting fees, oil and gas severance taxes and royalties, according to the GAO. [12]

Matthew Fletcher, a University of Michigan law professor and member of the Grand Traverse Band in Michigan, says the Southern Ute's success is unusual. Energy development often devastates Native American lands. Radioactive material from fracking — the process of injecting high-pressure liquid into underground rock to reach oil or gas — has been dumped on reservation lands, and heavy trucks have damaged roads. In addition, with non-natives entering the reservation to work, crime has risen. [13]

Kevin Washburn, former BIA director for the Obama administration, says Congress needs to alter some outdated, "paternalistic" regulations on Indian lands, but he is wary of too much deregulation.

"All over Indian country are abandoned mines where someone made a lot of money and then left," he says.

"We can't just say we trust the oil and gas companies to do the right thing."

As debate continues, these are some of the questions being considered:

Should tribes have full control over their reservations?

MHA Nation council member Fred Fox said the United States should treat tribes on reservations as sovereign nations. "We have ancestors that owned these lands. . . . Let us collect our own taxes. Let us create economic viability for our people. Let us create the regulatory system." [14]

Former *Wall Street Journal* reporter Naomi Schaefer Riley in her 2016 book, *The New Trail of Tears*, suggests tribes could become more economically self-sufficient if the federal government granted natives private-property rights over the trust lands so they can use it as collateral to start businesses. [15]

Chris Edwards, director of tax policy studies at the Cato Institute, a libertarian think tank in Washington, D.C., agrees. He suggests if the government ended the trustee relationship and created private property, reservations could reach their economic potential.

Most tribal leaders reject any proposals that would move the land out of trust protection and into private ownership. Indeed, many tribes were fearful when they read news accounts in late 2016 indicating that Donald Trump intended to privatize Indian lands after becoming president, accounts the new administration has denied.

Many experts say the current system holds several advantages for tribes, particularily financial. Federal subsidies to Native American tribes total about $20 billion a year, although the level of support varies widely by tribe. [16]

"There are tribes that are worried that if you end the trust responsibility, you will simultaneously end funding" from the federal government, says Joseph Kalt, co-director of the Harvard Project on American Indian Economic Development in Cambridge, Mass.

Furthermore, the trust system gives tribes some political voice, Kalt says. The Indian population is tiny — about 1.5 percent of the U.S. population — "so, a city like Tucson with a million people might be [able to adequately represent itself on a bigger stage, but not] a Potawatomi tribe with just a couple thousand people," he says.

Other experts question tribes' ability to manage their affairs, citing poorly run councils as well as political and regulatory instability that makes companies reluctant to invest in Native American projects. At Fort Berthold, for example, former Chairman Tex Hall lost re-election in 2014 after many tribal members accused him of improperly benefiting from oil business contracts. [17]

Many tribes, however, have successfully exercised their sovereignty and built solid regulatory and economic systems and could thrive outside the trust system, Kalt says. The Confederated Salish and Kootenai Tribes on the Flathead Reservation in Montana oversees everything from road construction and maintenance to schools and natural resources. The tribal nation formed a professional services company, S&K Technologies, in

1999. Since 2002, S&K has obtained federal and commercial contracts, generating more than $25 million — paid in yearly dividends — to run the tribal government and employs about 400 tribal members. [18]

"Tribes are not perfect institutions, nor is the federal government," says Brian Gunn, an attorney in Washington, D.C, who represents tribal groups. "They go through election cycles. Sometimes a tribe will have good leadership, other times not so good."

But the U.S. government should be willing to allow tribes to try and even to fail, suggests Gunn, a member of the Confederated Tribes of the Colville reservation in Washington state.

He says lawmakers are moving in that direction. The Indian Trust Asset Reform Act, passed by Congress last year, allows tribes to manage their assets at a lesser standard than the BIA's standard, but waives the U.S. government's liability if something goes wrong, Gunn says. "So basically it puts the choice in the tribe's hands." [19]

A 2005 law similarly allowed tribes to enter agreements with the BIA to pursue land agreements for energy development on their own. But the law left in place a maze of regulations, which dissuade tribes from pursuing lease agreements, the GAO reported in 2015. [20]

Elizabeth Kronk Warner, director of the Tribal Law and Government Center at the University of Kansas and a member of the Sault Ste. Marie Tribe of Chippewa Indians, criticizes the law because it waives the government's liability if anything goes wrong with the project, even though the government retains supervisory authority. "I think tribes should be . . . fully sovereign and liable, or the federal government [should] maintain its management responsibility" and liability, she says.

Most Native Americans like the idea of federal protection entailed in the government's trust responsibility, "but they don't want the . . . government making decisions," Kalt says.

Kevin Gover, former assistant secretary for Indian affairs under President Bill Clinton and a member of the Pawnee Nation of Oklahoma, has suggested Congress change the trust system by making tribal governments "permanent components of the American federalist system." [21] In other words, tribal reservations would be treated as jurisdictions much like counties or states, he says.

Gover, who now is director of the Smithsonian's National Museum of the American Indian in Washington, says the government could grant tribes the option of managing their own lands — including leveraging them as a capital asset — without federal oversight. If their economic enterprises fail, the land could be foreclosed upon but remain within the tribal jurisdiction.

Fletcher says he can't see how a system outside the trust could work. "The over-arching theory of federal Indian affairs is that the United States has a trust obligation to Indian tribes — that goes back to the original treaties that say the U.S. has a duty of protection to Indian tribes. . . . I do believe that duty of protection is something that can't and should never be given up."

Would energy development improve tribes' economies?

Some economists and legal experts say energy development could help tribes, especially in places like Oklahoma or Wyoming, where large oil reserves are located, or Montana and North Dakota, with their rich coal deposits. "Some reservations have energy resources worth developing, and others [are] less fortunate," attorney Stern says.

In February, Tyson Thompson, a Southern Ute tribal council member, urged Congress to ease federal regulations to encourage more energy development on Indian lands. "Our energy-related economic successes have resulted in a higher standard of living for our [approximately 1,400] tribal members," Thompson told the House Oversight and Government Reform Committee. [22]

In October, Bloomberg News had reported that the tribe "has a higher long-term credit rating than Wells Fargo and Co. and more oil and natural gas wells than it has members." The Ute now control 1,600 wells across four states and are one of the richest tribes in the nation. [23]

Anderson of the Property and Environment Research Center says if federal lawmakers streamline regulations to make it easier for tribes to tap into the energy reserves on their lands, badly needed jobs and royalties would be generated for tribal members.

The Navajo Nation formed the Navajo Transitional Energy Co. in 2013. It purchased a coal mine from BHP Billiton and has signed coal agreements with North American Coal subsidiary Bisti Fuels Co. and the Four Corners Power Plant. It has about 800 employees and announced a year ago it had returned $35 million in royalties to the tribe in 2015. [24]

The Crow government generates 70 percent of its revenue from a coal mining operation on the edge of its reservation, says James Allison, an assistant professor of history at Christopher Newport University in Newport News, Va. The revenue enables it to provide housing, police, water services and more. At the same time, he says, "you wouldn't go onto the Crow reservation and say, look at the prosperity it has produced."

History has proven that energy development is no panacea, he says; successful energy development also depends on timing, Allison warns.

A downturn in oil prices from $100 per barrel in 2013 to $30 per barrel in 2016 particularly hurt the Northern Arapaho and Eastern Shoshone on the Wind River Reservation in central-western Wyoming. Both tribes have long been dependent on oil revenues. Now the Northern Arapaho are investigating solar and wind projects, Allison says. [25]

Many tribes worry a hunger for profit will destroy their culture and ultimately erode their communities.

The Turtle Mountain Band of Chippewa Indians in north-central North Dakota, located about 190 miles from the Fort Berthold reservation, banned fracking because of concerns about its potential to contaminate drinking water and lakes and produce large volumes of waste. [26] Many other tribes also oppose fracking. [27]

In Minnesota, the Fond du Lac Band of the Lake Superior Chippewa Indians sees mining as a threat to its culture. For years the tribe has tried to halt or reverse environmental damage from a century-old iron mine. And it is fighting plans

for a copper mine on land the tribe ceded to the U.S. government in 1854 in exchange for continued rights to its hunting, fishing and gathering resources.

"A hundred years of mining has already left a pretty rugged footprint on the landscape, and it has destroyed wild rice waters," says Nancy Schuldt, water projects coordinator for the Fond du Lac Environmental Program in Cloquet, Minn. "It has exacerbated a problem with mercury in fish, it has destroyed wetlands, it has destroyed headwater streams, destroyed habitat for important species, destroyed cultural resources, sacred sites, all of that." (*See sidebar, p. 396.*)

In the Pacific Northwest, the Lummi Nation, along with other area tribes, has battled the proposed Gateway Pacific Terminal near Bellingham, Wash., that would export coal and other commodities to Asia. The Lummi said spills or maritime accidents could destroy fishing beds and threaten its treaty-protected fishing rights. The Army Corps of Engineers agreed and denied a permit for the project last May. The Crow Nation, however, continues to push for the terminal so it can sell to coal markets in Southeast Asia. [28]

Getty Images/*The Washington Post*/Linda Davidson

An oil and natural gas boom on the MHA Nation's Fort Berthold reservation in North Dakota has been at the center of the ongoing debate over Indian sovereignty versus what some see as the federal government's obligation to protect Indian land and natural resources. Entrenched poverty on reservations and the growing lure of energy and mineral riches have intensified the debate in recent years.

Conservationists at Fort Berthold for years have denounced the tribal council's oversight of energy development, accusing it of choosing monetary profit over the well-being of the land and the people. [29]

At a February hearing in New Mexico before a United Nations representative, Navajo tribal member Leoyla Cowboy said she wanted help for her people to restore sacred lands and build infrastructure for renewable energy. Between 1944 and 1986, uranium extraction on Indian land created hazardous waste sites and contaminated drinking water. "Coal, oil and gas, as well as uranium, have had a huge negative

Native Lands Hold Vast Resources

Untapped energy resources on Indian lands were valued at $1.5 trillion in 2012, the most recent data available. The largest reserves are in coal and natural gas; the Crow reservation alone has 17 billion tons of coal, according to the Department of the Interior.

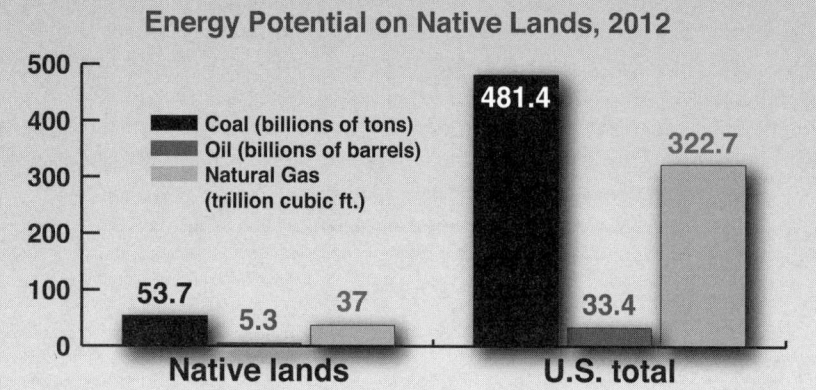

Energy Potential on Native Lands, 2012

Legend:
- Coal (billions of tons)
- Oil (billions of barrels)
- Natural Gas (trillion cubic ft.)

Native lands: 53.7, 5.3, 37
U.S. total: 481.4, 33.4, 322.7

Sources: Shawn Regan and Terry L. Anderson, "The Energy Wealth of Indian Nations," George W. Bush Institute, Property and Environment Research Center, pp. 17, 19, http://tinyurl.com/jwoxgfl; "Annual Coal Report 2012," U.S. Energy Information Administration, December 2013, p. 23, http://tinyurl.com/n5j6gh9; "U.S. Crude Oil and Natural Gas Proved Reserves, Year-end 2015," U.S. Energy Information Administration, December 2016, p. 2, http://tinyurl.com/lzw3579

impact on our lands, and have taken us away from our lands," she said. [30]

Fletcher says energy is not the answer for struggling reservations. "It gives a windfall to political and economic elites in Indian country, just as it does elsewhere in the country. There'll be an influx of cash, and then you'll have a series of tribal governments who fight over that cash, just as the MHA Nation does at Fort Berthold," he says. "That is just going to repeat over and over again if there's a so-called successful influx of cash resources into a tribal community where a tribe is just not used to that sort of thing."

He adds: "What I do see is massive amounts of environmental devastation and cultural devastation too."

Must tribes be consulted on projects outside their borders?

The Standing Rock Sioux tribe and its supporters protesting the completion of the Dakota Access Pipeline said they were demanding their right to "sovereignty" — in this case, their right to protect sacred land and block potential threats to their groundwater from a project that snaked near the reservation boundary.

"It's not that they are against development," says Pata of the National Congress of American Indians, "but they want to make sure the tribe's considerations and concerns are part of the discussion."

In the 18th and 19th centuries, hundreds of tribes signed treaties with the U.S. government where they agreed to smaller territories in return for continued rights to the ceded land for spiritual, cultural or economic purposes. In the case of the Sioux, supporters say the tribe did not legally cede rights to the Missouri River or its shoreline when the government constructed five major dams between the 1930s and 1950s. They say the construction also contravened a 1908 Supreme Court decision, known as the Winters Doctrine, which guaranteed tribes water rights on their reservations. [31]

But disagreements remain about how much say tribes actually have on projects outside their borders, even if the tribes believe the project could affect treaty land or ultimately impede life on their reservations.

In recent years, tribal lawyers have successfully convinced courts of tribes' treaty rights, according to Jan Hasselman, a staff attorney for the nonprofit environmental law firm EarthJustice, based in San Francisco. "Federal court precedent says that where a tribe opposes a project based on its impacts on treaty-reserved fishing, a federal agency cannot authorize anything more than a 'de minis' [minimal] impact," he said. [32]

Kandi Mossett, organizer of the Native Energy and Climate Campaign for the Indigenous Environmental Network, a grassroots organization in Bemidji, Minn., joined thousands of Dakota Access Pipeline protesters who ultimately were removed from their campsites outside the Sioux reservation. "We were forced off of our treaty land again. In 2017," she said. "Because that is what this country was founded upon: the taking, raping and pillaging of Native American land." [33]

Schuldt warns that tribes don't have veto power over land ceded to the government now outside their reservations. "If you go back before 1492, everything was tribal land." She adds that some tribes are looking for a "free prior informed consent right or . . . a veto right as it relates to things even off the reservation. I don't think that, frankly, is workable."

However, many tribes — but not all — do have clearly outlined treaty rights to hunt, fish, collect plants on and off reservation land, she says.

Victoria Tauli-Corpuz, a United Nations special rapporteur, in March faulted the federal government for frequently failing to consult with Native Americans on issues "affecting their land, territory and resources." In a draft report, she said, the Army Corps of Engineers approved an environmental assessment regarding the Dakota Access Pipeline that ignored tribal interests. [34]

Native Americans say the federal government thus violated the 2007 U.N. Declaration on the Rights of Indigenous Peoples, which President Barack Obama in 2010 said the United States would support. The declaration, in part, requires governments to obtain tribes' "free and informed consent" prior to the approval of any project affecting their lands or territories and other resources, particularly in connection with the development, utilization or exploitation of mineral, water or other resources. [35]

Even before adopting that declaration, however, previous administrations had mandated such consultation. Museum Director Gover says that, during the Clinton administration, "our big mantra was consultation." The Bush and Obama administrations adopted the same policy by executive memoranda, although the Trump administration has not reissued the same policy or clearly withdrawn it.

Nevertheless, Gover says the requirement that tribes be consulted is scattered through some federal statutes. 'But it's not thorough going," he says.

Former BIA Director Washburn says the National Historic Preservation Act, a 1966 law that seeks to protect the nation's historical and archaeological sites, clearly states that tribes must be consulted. However, "consultation [is a] word that gets thrown around a lot of different ways," he says. It's unclear how much weight a tribal vote has on a project outside its boundaries. "That's the issue. If it's outside tribal lands, they just don't really have sovereignty," Washburn says. "But it's not a matter of sovereignty; it's a matter of . . . good government relations."

Attorney Stern says various statutes, regulations, executive orders and other policy statements describe the federal government's obligations to consult with tribes.

"It's my view, however, that the consultation obligation that is required under the National Historic Preservation Act is not clear," he says. "For example, that statute and its regulations require that federal agencies exercise 'reasonable good faith' in consulting with the tribes. That term 'reasonable good faith,' to my mind, doesn't really provide clear guidance on the extent of consultation that must be required along the way." ■

BACKGROUND

Allies and Enemies

The treatment of indigenous people in North America by white settlers and later the U.S. government has fluctuated since 1492, when Italian explorer Christopher Columbus stepped foot on what is now the Bahamas.

Many of the earliest Europeans settlers were eager to trade with Native Americans and saw them as allies in their efforts to survive in the New World. However, the European powers also wanted to exploit North America's minerals, furs and fish, while colonists desired land to farm and to establish settlements. [36]

Over time, increasingly violent battles ensued between the settlers and tribes. On March 22, 1622, the Powhatan Confederacy, angry over English expansion in Virginia, launched surprise attacks on settlements along the James River, nearly wiping out the fledgling colony. A few years later, the director of the New Netherland colony, Willem Kieft, tried to tax natives on behalf of the Dutch West India Company. When the Indians refused to pay, Kieft ordered attacks on their villages, prompting the tribes to counterattack. [37]

During the French and Indian War (1754-63), the European combatants wanted the tribes as allies, as did the Americans and British during the American Revolution. Each side attacked tribes that sided with their enemies. After the Revolution, European immigration resumed and settlers pushed farther west, forcing tribes off their lands and leading to more friction. [38]

The Second Continental Congress adopted the Northwest Ordinance in 1787, which allowed new states to be added to the Union but said, "The utmost good faith shall always be observed towards the Indians; their land and property shall never be taken from them without their consent." [39]

Two years later, the U.S. Constitution empowered Congress to "regulate Commerce with . . . the Indian Tribes" and declared treaties to be the "supreme law of the land." And in 1790, Congress barred the purchase of Indian land without federal approval. [40]

But "a relentlessly expansionist white population [drove] the Indians westward without regard to treaty obligations, or . . . even simply humanity," historian Peter Cozzens said. [41]

President James Monroe told Gen. Andrew Jackson in 1817 that "the savage requires a greater extent of territory to sustain it than is compatible with the progress and just claims of civilized life, and must yield to it." [42]

Whites believed they possessed "discoverer rights" to the land — a position upheld by the Supreme Court in 1823, which stated that only the federal government, and not the tribes, could sell land to private interests. [43]

Congress in May 1830 passed the Indian Removal Act, allowing Jackson, who by then was president, to grant Indians lands west of the Mississippi in exchange for their lands within existing state borders. [44] The Cherokee Nation tried to stop the state of Georgia from clearing its members from the land, but in 1831 the Supreme Court refused to hear the case, declaring the tribe a dependent nation under the care of the federal government. [45]

A year later, the court ruled that the federal government, and not states, could regulate Indian affairs and said the Cherokees had rights acknowledged by the U.S. government. Jackson refused to enforce the ruling, however, and Georgia seized the tribe's lands for whites eager to mine newly discovered gold. [46]

About 4,000 out of 15,000 Cherokees died in the 1838-1839 march, known as the Trail of Tears, to lands west of the Mississippi River. [47]

More Indians found themselves in the whites' path after the 1848 Treaty of Guadalupe Hidalgo ended the Mexican-American War, paving the way for U.S. expansion to the Pacific Ocean.

As whites occupied more and more territory, Native Americans lost their traditional hunting grounds and much of their land and way of life. White hunters wiped out the buffalo on the Great Plains, and deadly European diseases for which Native Americans had no immunity decimated many tribes. In 1849 alone, cholera killed half of the native population in the southern plains. [48]

By 1871, when Congress limited the president's power to enter into treaties, the federal government had signed more than 400 treaties, many of which were broken by subsequent waves of settlers, or challenged by tribes throughout the "Indian wars" (about 1860 to 1880). [49]

Forced Assimilation

On July 18, 1885, Republican Sen. Henry Laurens Dawes of Massachusetts wrote to a white-run advocacy group called the Indian Rights Association, lamenting the continued fighting between whites and Indians. He urged work be done with "haste to teach [the Native American] habits of industry, self-reliance, knowledge of property, and a desire for its acquisition." [50]

Two years later, Congress passed the General Allotment Act, or Dawes Act, subdivided reservations into plots and aimed to assimilate Indians into white

society by making them landowners and farmers in the European tradition. Non-native settlers rushed to claim surplus lands not given to Indians. In one day in April 1889, 50,000 prospective settlers raced across Oklahoma and claimed nearl 2 million acres by the end of the day. [51] The allotment process ultimately resulted in more than half of those living on reservations to be non-Indians. [52]

A number of whites cheated Indians out of their land. "Indians were easy marks, especially in a place like Oklahoma, where there was very valuable land, mostly because of oil and gas," Gover of the National Museum of American Indians says.

By the late 1920s, "Indians were poorer than ever," Gover says. "They were still uneducated, and under the thumb of a very oppressive bureaucracy that had told them you may not practice your religion, you may not practice your traditional means of governance, you may not speak your language. Your children will be taken and sent away for education."

The policies "were, in fact, meant to exterminate not the individual Indians but certainly the Indian nations as effective polities and social and cultural institutions," he says.

Many U.S. lawmakers did raise concerns about the natives' plight. In 1921, Congress passed the Snyder Act requiring the federal government to direct money "from time to time" for health care, education, economic development, governing and policing. A 1924 law awarded citizenship to many American Indians and Alaska Natives. [53]

The measures, however, did not reverse the effects of forced assimilation. In 1928, the Institute for Government Research (later renamed the Brookings Institution) reported to the Department of the Interior: "An overwhelming majority of the Indians are poor, even extremely poor, and they are not adjusted to the economic and social system of the dominant white civilization." Among other deficiencies, the report cited the exclusion of Indians from

management of their own affairs and the poor quality of public services. [54]

In the 1930s, Commissioner of Indian Affairs John Collier decried the plight of the estimated 350,000 Native Americans. He created the Emergency Conservation Work program for Indians, focused on training natives to use their own lands and resources. Before its demise in 1943, the program employed 85,349 natives from 71 reservations. [55]

In 1934, the Indian Reorganization Act ended the allotment process and began returning Indian land to the federal trust.

The Supreme Court in 1938 recognized the Native Americans' ownership of minerals and timber on their land, and Congress authorized them to lease their minerals through the Indian Mineral Leasing Act of 1938 with approval from the federal government. And Congress in 1942 passed the Indian Claims Commission Act to allow Native Americans to sue the government for compensation for lands taken from them. [56]

But tribes faced renewed threats as federal policy shifted again.

Termination Period

In 1944, Congress' Pick-Sloan Plan aimed to provide irrigation, generate hydropower and employ World War II veterans by constructing five dams on the Missouri River (including a dam already built at Fort Peck, Mont., in 1937). The Army Corps of Engineers saw condemnation as the best way to acquire Native American lands needed for the project. [57]

The plan reduced the land base of the five Missouri River Sioux reservations by 6 percent and forced the relocation of one-third of the population. The tribes' best land was flooded, and residents were forced to move to land barren of natural resources. [58]

Then, with the BIA under attack and the belief growing that Indians

Continued on p. 396

Chronology

1700s-1850s
Federal government forces tribes from their lands.

1789
Constitution empowers federal government to negotiate with tribes.

1790
Congress enacts the first of six Non-Intercourse Acts, requiring federal approval for any private purchase of Indian land.

1824
Secretary of War John C. Calhoun creates Office of Indian Affairs, which later becomes Bureau of Indian Affairs (BIA).

1838-39
After gold is discovered on Cherokee lands in Georgia, tribe is forced to move west; thousands perish during infamous "Trail of Tears" march.

1831
Supreme Court rules tribes are dependent nations under U.S. guardianship.

1851
Indian Appropriations Act allocates funds to move Western tribes onto reservations.

1880s-1930s
Federal government seeks to force Native Americans to assimilate.

1887
Dawes Act divides Indian lands into parcels to be allotted to Native and non-Native Americans.

1903
Supreme Court says treaties can be modified or terminated without tribes' consent.

1924
Indian Citizenship Act grants constitutional rights to Native Americans.

1934
Indian Reorganization Act ends land allotment process.

1938
Indian Mineral Leasing Act restores tribal control over energy development on reservations.

1970s-1980s
U.S. limits tribes' sovereignty, then promotes self-determination.

1975
Indian Self-Determination and Education Assistance Act funnels federal grants directly to tribes.

1982
Indian Mineral Development Act enables tribes to negotiate energy extraction agreements.

1984
A Reagan administration report assails BIA, says it "thrives on the failure of Indian tribes."

1987
In *California vs. Cabazon Band of Mission Indians*, Supreme Court says tribes can open casinos.

1990s-Present
Federal government increasingly recognizes tribal self-government.

1996
Blackfeet activist Elouise Cobell files class-action suit against federal government for mismanaging trust lands.

2002
U.S. government settles Indian claims over Missouri River dams.

2005
Indian Tribal Energy Development and Self-Determination Act gives tribes greater control over energy development on their lands.

2009
Settlement of Cobell lawsuit awards plaintiffs $3.4 billion.

2010
President Barack Obama signs Tribal Law and Order Act giving tribal courts more authority.

2011
National Wildlife Federation study finds reservations disproportionately suffer more from climate change.

2015
Government Accountability Office concludes BIA mismanagement hinders energy development on Indian lands.

2016
Indian Trust Asset Management Reform Act gives tribes more control over trust lands.

2017
A federal judge refuses request by the Standing Rock Sioux to block Dakota Access Pipeline; Indians march in Washington, D.C., to protest its completion. . . . Trump administration ends moratorium on new coal leasing on federal, including some Indian, lands. Over the objections of Native Americans, the administration also approves completing the 1,179-mile Keystone XL oil pipeline that would cross the land of numerous tribes.

Climate Change Threatens Tribal Lands

"It is the federal government's responsibility to protect our fishing rights."

Ancestors of the Fond du Lac Band of Lake Superior Chippewa settled centuries ago near the headwaters of the St. Louis River in Minnesota, where lush wild rice grasses swayed above wetlands, sustaining the tribe with nutrients and an abundance of wildlife.

White settlers later moved the band to a 100,000-acre reservation off the lake in northeastern Minnesota. Treaties signed in 1837 and 1854 guaranteed tribal members harvesting rights on their original lands crossing into Wisconsin. But years of pollution and climate change-related shifts in weather patterns have diminished the grasses.

"We are doing all we can to restore our wild rice resources," says Nancy Schuldt, water projects coordinator for the tribe. "We're already seeing impacts from climate change. . . . We've had whole years [of harvests] wiped out from big storms."

The Fond du Lac Band and hundreds of other Native American groups say they didn't contribute to the greenhouse gases linked to global warming, and they insist the federal government is duty-bound to protect them.

"Tribes are really contributing very little, if anything, to the [carbon] footprint and are really the ones who are getting" hurt by climate change, says Elizabeth Kronk Warner, director of the Tribal Law and Government Center at the University of Kansas. She says the U.S. government is legally and morally obligated to protect tribes that it forced onto lands now among the most vulnerable to environmental change.

In 2011, the National Wildlife Federation, with several other environmental groups, detailed how climate change disproportionately affects tribal communities because they are more heavily dependent on natural resources for economic, cultural and spiritual purposes. [1]

Many indigenous communities in the United States "are literally on the forefront of losing their land . . . because of climate change," Warner says. Coastal tribal villages in Alaska, Louisiana and South Carolina lose land every year due to rising seas and severe storms, she says.

Fawn Sharp, president of the Quinault Indian Nation in Taholah, Wash., is working with specialists to relocate her tribe's village to higher ground. Rising seas caused by melting glaciers have breached barriers, and storms frequently flood the village. [2]

The Trump administration's stance on climate change has further alarmed Native Americans.

President Trump's fiscal 2018 budget blueprint, submitted to Congress on March 16, would cut $2.6 billion from the Environmental Protection Agency (EPA). Climate change programs would be hit particularly hard. [3]

"We're not spending money on that anymore," Mick Mulvaney, director of the Office of Management and Budget, told reporters. "We consider that to be a waste of your money to go out and do that." [4]

Trump also has ordered the rollback of regulations, including the landmark Clean Power Plan, designed to reduce carbon emissions.

Many tribes fear these actions will hamper their efforts to adjust to climate change.

"The utter disdain for science demonstrated by this administration is insufferable," Sharp wrote in a blog shortly after Trump revealed his budget.

She called the administration's plans unconstitutional and a violation of treaty rights. She said "it is the federal government's responsibility to protect our fishing, hunting and gathering rights, on our ceded areas and in the ocean." [5]

Warner agrees that multiple treaties obligate the government

Continued from p. 394

were ready to assimilate, Congress in 1953 adopted a resolution that Native Americans should no longer be treated as wards of the United States. Between 1953 and 1964, approximately 2.5 million acres of tribal lands were removed from protection under the trust. The losses affected over 100 tribes occupying valuable lands, including the Klamath in Oregon's timber forests. [59]

Gover says federal leaders believed the so-called termination policy was in the best interest of Native Americans, 10 percent of whom served in the

armed forces during World War II. "It occurred to everybody they don't need protection, they're perfectly capable," he says.

But federal lawmakers gradually came to realize the policy wasn't helping Indians and renewed support for tribes.

Presidents John F. Kennedy (1961-63) and Lyndon B. Johnson (1963-68) called for investments in economic development on reservations. The 1968 Indian Civil Rights Act prevented states from assuming jurisdiction over Indian lands without tribal consent and barred Indian tribes from impeding on the constitutional rights of their people. [60]

President Richard M. Nixon (1969-74) formally denounced termination, mandated BIA reform and recognized the rights of tribal governments. On July 8, 1970, he told Congress: "Self-determination among the Indian people can and must be encouraged. . . . This, then, must be the goal of any new national policy toward the Indian people." [61]

Initially, however, internal conflict impeded BIA reform efforts aimed at improving relations with the tribes and led to a series of Native Americans protests. In spring 1973, 200 followers of the militant American Indian Movement occupied the village of Wounded Knee on

to protect tribes and their critical natural resources. The federal government has recognized such obligations in recent years. Since 1980, the EPA has funded 6,179 grants, totaling $1.7 billion, for tribal projects, many of which have supported innovative ways to protect natural resources and respond to climate change. [6]

Trump's budget plan also would cut $6 billion from the U.S. Department of Housing and Urban Development, which awarded the Biloxi-Chitimacha-Choctaw tribe a $48 million natural disaster grant last year to move from its flooding land. [7]

Not all tribes can easily relocate, says Warner, a member of the Sault Ste. Marie Tribe of Chippewa Indians. "While they could theoretically leave, they would lose all their legal protection and legal status," she says. Many tribes also have cultural and spiritual connections to the land. "For a lot of us, our religious practices are land-based, so we're connected to a particular area," Warner says.

The Fond du Lac Band developed air and water quality monitoring programs and pursued alternative and renewable energy sources. In 2007, it adopted the international Kyoto Protocol on climate change and committed to reducing its fossil fuel use by 20 percent by 2020 — a target it hit last year. But the band can't completely avoid the greenhouse gases around it.

The Bureau of Indian Affairs under the Obama administration oversaw a Tribal Climate Resilience Program to provide resources to tribes to help them adapt to changes. But it is unclear how funding for the program will be affected under Trump.

The tribe, however, is bracing for broad federal budget cuts that could affect their local efforts. "We have tried to prepare our tribal leadership to anticipate if all our tribal grants were zeroed out," Schuldt says. "I honestly don't know what is going to happen."

— *Christina L. Lyons*

A Yupik child crosses a boardwalk in Newtok, Alaska. Rising temperatures from global climate change are threatening this and other indigenous villages with flooding.

Getty Images/Andrew Burton

[1] "Facing the Storm: Indian Tribes, Climate-Induced Weather Extremes, and the Future for Indian Country," National Wildlife Federation, 2011, http://tinyurl.com/mcjmprg.

[2] "Climate stressors on the Olympic Peninsula," U.S. Climate Resilience Toolkit, National Oceanic and Atmospheric Administration, accessed April 6, 2017, http://tinyurl.com/ltk3hvm.

[3] Ben Wolfgang, "Trump's EPA budget proposes harshest funding, staffing cuts in agency's history," *The Washington Times*, March 21, 2017, http://tinyurl.com/jvt28j3.

[4] Dan Merica and Rene Marsh, "Trump budget chief on climate change: 'We consider that to be a waste of money,'" CNN, March 16, 2017, http://tinyurl.com/n4jbu3l.

[5] Fawn Sharp, "Trump's utter disdain for science is 'insufferable,'" *The Daily World*, March 31, 2017, http://tinyurl.com/lzhypp4.

[6] Grant Awards Database, Environmental Protection Agency, updated March 17, 2017, http://tinyurl.com/m7oygy8.

[7] Autumn Spanne, "The lucky ones: Native American tribe receives $48m to flee climate change," *The Guardian*, March 23, 2016, http://tinyurl.com/kgn9yax; Jose A. DelReal, "Trump budget asks for $6 billion in HUD cuts, drops development grants," *The Washington Post*, March 16, 2017, http://tinyurl.com/mu9a7yx.

the Pine Ridge Reservation in South Dakota, demanding that the federal government fulfill its treaty obligations. Two Indians died and an FBI agent was critically wounded in a shootout, violence that cost the movement critical support. [62]

Meanwhile, multinational companies began encroaching on tribal lands seeking subbituminous coal found under the Northern Cheyenne and Crow reservations in Montana. "To access this coal, . . . multinational companies exploited a broken and outdated legal regime that sought to promote the development of western resources at the expense of tribal sovereignty, ecological

health, and simple equity," Allison of Christopher Newport University said in his 2015 book, *Sovereignty for Survival: American Energy Development and Indian Self-Determination.* [63]

By 1973, energy companies controlled hundreds of thousands of acres on Indian lands. On Northern Cheyenne and Crow reservations, more than 600,000 acres were opened for mining, causing John Woodenlegs of the Northern Cheyenne to lament, "The impact of uncontrolled coal development could finish us off." [64] He and other natives feared multinationals would destroy their land and way of life.

Other tribes complained the federal bureaucracy barred them from seeking economic self-sufficiency. In October 1973, Navajo Chairman Peter MacDonald told the U.S. Commission on Civil Rights that federal bureaucrats had sabotaged or ignored the council's development programs for its 14-million-acre reservation.

"Most Indian tribes know what they want, where they want programs and in what time frame they want to accomplish these things, but the problem comes at the top," he said. [65]

A series of court rulings and laws gave tribes slightly more control over their affairs. In 1974, the *Boldt* decision,

Tribal Councils Increasingly Expel Members

"Disenrollment is never about who belongs in the tribe."

The U.S. government's growing recognition of tribal sovereignty has correlated with a trend that worries many Indian law experts: tribal councils disenrolling members. From 2009-16, up to 79 tribes in 20 states disenrolled 9,000 tribal members, costing those individuals their cultural identity, civil rights, federal subsidies and — in many cases — royalties from tribal enterprises, says David Wilkins, a professor of American Indian studies at the University of Minnesota Law School.

Gabriel S. Galanda, a Native American attorney who is fighting the disenrollment of more than 300 members of the Nooksack Indian Tribe in northwest Washington state, attributes the trend to "power and greed" sparked by increasing economic capitalism on native lands.

But the Nooksack government said the members it disenrolled lacked proof of ancestry. Most had enrolled in the 1980s, basing their eligibility on an ancestor named Annie George. But George was not in the 1942 census, the tribal government said, and lineage could not be verified. [1]

Other tribal councils said they disenroll members because the individuals did not have sufficient "blood quantum" — the percentage of their tribal blood is too low due to generations of intermarriage with outsiders. Each of the 567 federally recognized tribes sets its own criteria for membership, usually based on a blood quantum or lineal descent from a tribal member. [2]

Wilkins' studies suggest that tribal leaders sometimes seek to disenroll members because of family feuds or to secure political power or limit distribution of royalties.

The first documented case of a tribe disenrolling members involved the Northern Ute in Utah. The disenrollments began in 1951 after the tribe received a $17.5 million federal payout, under the Indian Claims Commission Act, for its claim that the government improperly took its land. [3]

The payout — most of which was to be used for tribal projects, with some of the money distributed as per capita payments to tribal members — widened an existing rift between full-blood Utes and "mixed-blood" Utes, Wilkins says. Full-blood Utes wanted to maintain a relationship with the government and disenrolled the mixed-blood Utes who disagreed, he says.

The government has stayed out of such battles, particularly after the Supreme Court in 1978 affirmed a tribe's right to establish its own membership requirements. [4]

In 2009, the Bureau of Indian Affairs announced it would adhere to a "policy of Indian self-determination and self-government," Galanda says. Based on that decision, the U.S. District Court in *Timbisha Shoshone Tribe v. Kennedy* said in 2009 it would not interfere in disenrollment. [5]

More recently, some groups have pushed for a new policy. In June 2015, the National Native American Bar Association said stripping tribal citizenship without due process was a human rights issue. [6] Later that year, the Association of American Indian Physicians passed a resolution asking tribes to reconsider the disenrollment of members on health grounds, saying the process caused grief and depression for those cast aside. [7]

Galanda says disenrollment is a non-native concept that stems from federal policies that required tribes to determine who belonged.

Wilkins says when tribes began banishing members charged with committing crimes in the 1980s, tribal leaders said it was a tradition to expel members who violated social norms. But he notes that the disenrollments also coincided with increased casino gambling on tribal lands. In California, among 30 tribes that are now disenrolling members, about 23 distribute gambling royalties on a per-capita basis, Wilkins has found. "In some cases, tribes appear to be making rational, economic-based calculations," he says.

---

drafted by George Boldt, the U.S. District judge for the Western District of Washington, granted fishing rights to Indians in the Pacific Northwest. And the Indian Self-Determination and Education Assistance Act of 1975 funneled federal money to tribes through contracts and grants to enable tribal councils — rather than the federal government — to control school, health, housing, law enforcement and other programs. [66]

Rise of Casinos

In the 1980s, President Ronald Reagan (1981-89) reaffirmed support for In-

dian self-determination, but his federal budget cuts sharply reduced funding for tribes, which were struggling with poverty and high unemployment.

Congress, meanwhile, passed the Indian Mineral Development Act of 1982 to allow tribes to enter into energy extraction agreements and set lease terms and royalty amounts. Allison said this gave tribes more control over reservation development. [67]

In 1984, the President's Commission on Indian Reservation Economies assailed the BIA system, saying it "is designed for paternalistic control, and it thrives on the failure of Indian tribes." [68]

Tribal leaders, however, balked at the commission's calls to develop reservations through private ownership and profit models. They rejected recommendations to abolish the bureau and waive the tribes' immunity from lawsuits on some issues, and to subordinate tribal courts to the federal judiciary on certain questions. The commission also proposed forming an Indian Trust Services Administration aimed at protecting oil, gas, minerals, timber, water and agricultural land. [69]

In 1987, the Supreme Court opened the door for a new economic enterprise on reservations: gambling. The court,

In Washington state, meanwhile, the battle over the Nooksack disenrollments continues. Tribal Chairman Bob Kelly said a Nov. 4 referendum — in which those facing disenrollment were barred from voting — showed overwhelming support for disenrollment. [8]

But the Interior Department said the election was illegitimate because the members under a disenrollment cloud were not allowed to vote, and it threatened to withhold federal funds from the Nooksack Tribe until a legitimate vote took place. The department and other agencies did cut off tribal funding earlier this year. [9]

The tribe, in turn, sued the U.S. government, saying it wrongfully denied the Nooksack $13.7 million in federal and state funds. The Nooksack government argued it has the power to disenroll members who had "failed to demonstrate legally sufficient blood connections to the tribe," and it has authority to interpret tribal law and determine the legitimacy of the governing body. [10]

For four years, Galanda has represented Nooksack members facing disenrollment. He says finding proof, such as a birth or death certificate, to confirm proper enrollment of an ancestor — and thereby establish a member's direct lineage to the tribe — can be nearly impossible. "Indians were not [U.S.] citizens until 1924," Galanda says.

But he says he remains hopeful about a possible reversal of the disenrollment trend. The Grand Ronde Tribal Appeals Court in Oregon last year reversed the disenrollment of 66 members who were descended directly from Tumulth, the chief who signed the Willamette Valley Treaty of 1855. [11]

Others, like the Graton Rancheria Tribe in California and the Spokane Tribe in Washington state, have in recent years modified their constitutions to bar disenrollment of tribal members, according to Galanda.

— *Christina L. Lyons*

Native American attorney Gabriel S. Galanda says "power and greed" are behind efforts to disenroll more than 300 members of the Nooksack Indian Tribe in northwest Washington state.

[1] Liz Jones, "Nooksack Tribe Cites 'Missing Ancestor' As Reason to Disenroll 306 Members," KUOW, Dec. 17, 2013, http://tinyurl.com/kcnar8m.

[2] For more on disenrollment, see David E. Wilkins and Shelly Hulse Wilkins, *Dismembered: Native Disenrollment and the Battle for Human Rights* (2017).

[3] *Ibid.*, pp. 60-62. Also see Public Law 671, Chapter 1009, 68 Stat. 868.

[4] The case is *Santa Clara Pueblo v. Martinez*, 436 U.S. 49 (1978), http://tiny url.com/madukjt.

[5] Gabriel S. Galanda, "Obama's Disenrollment Legacy," Indian Country Media Network, Jan. 25, 2017, http://tinyurl.com/m6b2vep.

[6] "Duties of Tribal Court Advocates to Ensure Due Process Afforded to All Individuals Targeted for Disenrollment," National Native American Bar Association, June 26, 2015, http://tinyurl.com/l5jjccn.

[7] "AAIP Resolution on Disenrollment," Association of American Indian Physicians, Oct 22, 2105, http://tinyurl.com/mnsjf22.

[8] Gene Johnson, "Nooksack Tribe says it has booted 289 people off rolls," *The Bellingham Herald*, Nov. 23, 2016, http://tinyurl.com/kb6nqru.

[9] Nina Shapiro, "Feds call Nooksack tribal council 'illegitimate' and 'abusive,'" *The Seattle Times*, April 6, 2017, http://tinyurl.com/m6pje5k.

[10] *Ibid.*

[11] Dean Rhodes, "Tribal Appeals Court reverses disenrollments," The Confederated Tribes of Grand Ronde, Aug. 9, 2016, http://tinyurl.com/l3q6869.

in *California vs. Cabazon Band of Mission Indians*, said tribes could legally engage in gambling not expressly prohibited by the state, and it barred states from regulating tribal gaming. [70]

Complaints about a "wasteful and patriarchal" Bureau of Indian Affairs persisted into the 1990s. Rep. Bill Richardson, D-N.M., chairman of the Subcommittee on Native American Affairs, in 1993 said the bureau "has held back tribes from helping themselves." [71]

Then in 1996, Blackfeet activist Elouise Cobell launched the largest class-action lawsuit ever filed against the federal government. She accused the BIA of mismanaging payments for allotted property and said many allotment landowners lived in poverty despite the drilling of oil and gas on their property under lease arrangements. The lawsuit was settled in 2009 for about $3.4 billion; $1.9 billion went to a Trust Land Consolidation Fund set aside to buy back tribal trust lands, and $1.5 billion was to be disbursed to individual plaintiffs. [72]

President Clinton vowed to change federal attitudes toward tribes. After listening to more than 300 tribal leaders, he issued an executive memorandum mandating federal consultation with tribes "in order to ensure that the rights of the sovereign tribal governments are fully respected." [73]

President George W. Bush continued Clinton's efforts to make amends to tribes and to recognize their sovereignty. He signed a law providing $28 million to the Yankton Sioux of South Dakota and the Santee Sioux of Nebraska for damage caused by the government when the Missouri River, as a result of dams built in the 1950s and 1960s, submerged about 4,000 acres of their land. [74]

Nevertheless, tribes remained poor. The U.S. Commission on Civil Rights

Many tribal leaders view Interior Secretary Ryan Zinke, here testifying before the Senate Indian Affairs Committee on March 8, 2017, as a supporter of Native American interests. "Our sovereign Indian nations and territories must have the respect and freedom they deserve," Zinke said when his nomination was announced.

CURRENT SITUATION

Questions About Trump

Native Americans are uncertain about plans of the Trump administration and the Republican-controlled Congress, but they hope to have a voice in discussions on energy regulation, tax reform and other issues vital to Indians.

When Trump took office, many tribes recalled his 1993 testimony before a House Natural Resources Committee on gambling when he said he thought the Indian Gaming Regulatory Act gave tribes an unfair advantage over his own casinos. "Go up to Connecticut," he said, referring to the Mashantucket Pequot tribe, which owned Foxwoods Resort Casino. "They [the Pequot] don't look like Indians to me." [79] And during the 2016 presidential campaign, he repeatedly called Democratic Sen. Elizabeth Warren of Massachusetts "Pocahontas" after she said she was part Native American.

Trump's decision to create a Native American Coalition during the presidential transition and to appoint Rep. Markwayne Mullin, R-Okla., a Cherokee tribal member, as its chairman, reassured some tribes. [80]

Some Indians believe Trump's attitude toward tribal sovereignty was reflected in his decision to ignore the wishes of the Standing Rock Sioux and allow completion of the Dakota Access Pipeline under Lake Oahe, just north of the tribe's reservation. Over the objections of Native Americans, he also approved Keystone XL, the 1,179-mile oil pipeline that would cross the land of numerous tribes.

But others are not sure where the president stands on Indian sovereignty.

in 2003 reported that federal funding "has not been sufficient to address the basic and very urgent needs of indigenous" people in health care, education, public safety, housing and rural development." [75]

Many tribes also fared poorly when outside companies made deals directly with the government — deals that the Supreme Court upheld in 2003. In *United States v. Navajo Nation*, the court ruled against the tribe, which had sought to negotiate royalties for coal from a mining company. The court said only federal officials could approve the final rate and determine what was in the tribe's best interest. The Navajo Nation later sued the government when it learned the coal company had lobbied the Interior secretary to reject the tribe's higher price and forced it to accept a minimum royalty rate. The Supreme Court, however, ultimately denied the tribe's claim. [76]

In 2005, Congress sought to give tribes more autonomy by passing the Indian Tribal Energy Development

and Self-Determination Act. It allowed tribes to enter agreements with the BIA to pursue lease agreements with energy companies on their own, but the law left in place the thicket of rules and regulations that have discouraged tribes from pursuing such agreements. [77]

During the Obama administration, lawmakers made some progress for self-determination. In 2012, Obama signed the HEARTH Act — Helping Expedite and Advance Responsible Tribal Home Ownership — which aimed to create an alternative process for tribes to lease trust land without further approval of the government. He also signed the Trust Asset Management Reform Act, and during his tenure returned about 542,000 acres to federal trust protection for Native Americans. [78]

Tribes frequently embraced Obama as a strong supporter of sovereignty, although some became disenchanted when his administration waited until December 2016 to halt completion of the Dakota Access Pipeline. ∎

Continued on p. 402

At Issue:

Could energy development lift tribes out of poverty?

TERRY L. ANDERSON
*SENIOR FELLOW, HOOVER INSTITUTION;
SENIOR FELLOW, PROPERTY AND
ENVIRONMENT RESEARCH CENTER*

WRITTEN FOR *CQ RESEARCHER*, MAY 2017

*i*ndian country contains almost 30 percent of the nation's coal reserves west of the Mississippi, as well as significant deposits of oil, natural gas and uranium.

The Council of Energy Resource Tribes, a tribal energy consortium, estimates the value of these resources at nearly $1.5 trillion. Yet these resources remain largely untapped. Developing them could help lift Native Americans out of poverty.

The negative effects of federal regulations can be seen in former President Barack Obama's "war on coal." The Crow tribe has 9 billion tons of coal that could easily be shipped to generating plants anywhere in the United States or exported to Asia. But many cities and towns along rail routes, citing concerns about train safety and the health effects of coal dust, are trying to limit coal-train traffic. And port cities such as Seattle and Portland, Ore., are holding up construction of export terminals on the ground that coal, including that from the Crow reservation, would exacerbate global warming.

Making matters worse, the Bureau of Indian Affairs (BIA) limits energy development on reservations. On the Fort Peck reservation in northeastern Montana, the BIA required an archaeological assessment before a company could begin oil and gas exploration. Fort Peck tribal councilman Stoney Anketell noted the absurdity of this requirement: "We're not short-changing the need for archaeological reviews, but on land that has been farmed for 70 years? It's been tilled, plowed, planted, harvested. There's no teepee rings."

Legislation passed in 1999 for the Fort Berthold reservation in North Dakota reduced from 49 to four the number of regulations from four different federal agencies that must be met before oil and gas can be leased on the reservation. As a result, since the Bakken shale-oil boom started in 2000, hundreds of reservation wells have earned the tribal nation more than $500 million. Still, roughly twice as many oil and gas wells are drilled per acre outside the reservation as inside.

Some bright spots regarding potential development on reservations have come from the Trump administration. For example, the president's executive order "Promoting Energy Independence and Economic Growth" will make it more likely that Indian coal reserves can be developed. In addition, Interior Secretary Ryan Zinke issued a secretarial order to end the coal-leasing moratorium and reinstate the department's royalty advisory committee.

JAMES R. ALLISON III
*ASSISTANT PROFESSOR OF HISTORY,
CHRISTOPHER NEWPORT UNIVERSITY*

WRITTEN FOR *CQ RESEARCHER*, MAY 2017

*n*o population needs economic development more than the first Americans. The poverty rate among Native Americans runs north of 25 percent and unemployment remains mired in double-digits. As recently as November, the U.S. Census Bureau declared American Indians the country's most impoverished racial group. Sadly, this is an annual tradition.

Yet since the 1930s, when federal Indian policy shifted to halt previous attempts at cultural genocide, tribal and federal officials alike have pointed to Native Americans' abundant energy resources as the panacea for Indian poverty. In oft-cited statistics, we are told that reservations contain almost 30 percent of all coal west of the Mississippi, as much as 50 percent of the nation's uranium deposits and upwards of 20 percent of known oil and gas reserves. As LaDonna Harris, a Comanche who founded Americans for Indian Opportunity, once said: "Collectively, [we] are the biggest private owners of energy in the country."

During the 1970s energy crises, Harris and others orchestrated a pan-tribal movement to throw off decades of paternalistic mismanagement by federal officials, who had transferred control over Indian energy to multinational firms for minuscule royalties. By 1982, efforts to undue this injustice had equipped Indians with expertise in managing minerals and produced legal changes that recognized Native American control over tribal resources. It was a remarkable victory.

But then little changed, and herein lies the hard lesson for any group dependent upon a single commodity, such as a fossil fuel, for economic prosperity. After securing the right to manage their own minerals, tribes watched as global events transformed the energy scarcity of the 1970s into the "oil glut" of the 1980s. A world flooded with cheap oil left little room for rural reservation development, and projects were scrapped by the dozens. Meanwhile, intense internal debates raged over the social and environmental costs of reservation mining. All the while poverty deepened.

The lesson here is not that fossil fuel development cannot help tribal communities. It can. But rarely do nations build sustainable prosperity on fossil fuel foundations alone. Those that have — such as in the Middle East — possessed full sovereignty and popular support for such development. They also happened to be on the right side of market trends. Tribal nations do not enjoy such benefits, and so should focus on projects that align better with long-term economic forecasts; federal Indian, environmental and energy policies; and a broader range of communal values. On many reservations, alternative energy presents one such option.

Continued from p. 400

Many tribal leaders see Interior Secretary Ryan Zinke, a former one-term Republican congressman from Montana, as a supporter of Native American interests. When his nomination was announced, Zinke said, "Our sovereign Indian nations and territories must have the respect and freedom they deserve." And during his Senate confirmation hearing, he said he had no intention of selling federal lands. [81] The National Congress of American Indians supported his nomination.

Sen. Maria Cantwell, D-Wash., ranking member of the Senate Energy and Natural Resources Committee, opposed Zinke's confirmation, in part because of his support for the Dakota Access Pipeline and his opposition to Obama's coal-leasing moratorium. And Cantwell worried about Zinke's support for energy development on federal lands, noting it clashes with the government's obligation to protect tribal trust lands. [82]

Zinke also expressed support for the proposed Gateway Pacific Terminal, calling it "literally the gateway to economic prosperity" for the Crow tribe and for blue-collar workers in Washington state. [83]

Meanwhile, Trump's budget blueprint would slash funding for the Environmental Protection Agency by one-third while increasing spending for energy development on federal lands. Under the executive order he issued in March, the president plans to dismantle the Clean Power Plan that would have led to the closure of many coal-fired power plants, halted construction on new plants and replaced them with wind and solar farms. Tribes are split on the power plan. [84]

In Congress

Many tribes are closely watching as Congress considers legislation to ease energy regulations on tribal lands — legislation that failed to move during previous sessions of Congress despite bipartisan support. The Senate Indian Affairs Committee in February approved a bill by its chairman, John Hoeven, R-N.D., that aims to simplify the regulatory process for energy projects on reservations by establishing a pilot program. [85]

Hoeven told the National Congress of American Indians in February that the bill is "a big step toward tribal self-determination in developing its tribal resources."

Other committees are exploring the issue as well. In February, Frank Rusco, the GAO's director of natural resources and environment issues, told a House oversight panel that regulatory uncertainty continues to impede tribal energy projects. [86]

House Natural Resources Committee ranking member Raúl Grijalva, D-Ariz., has long opposed easing regulations for energy development for tribal and other federal lands.

"There's a fundamental lust on the part of industry for the extraction that they want out of the public lands, and there is a fundamental lust by industry for what they see in Indian country on reservations as possibilities as well," Grijalva said. He said he is particularly concerned about a controversial copper mine being reviewed for federal permits, because Congress authorized a land swap allowing the Rio Tinto Group to open the mine on former federal land sacred to Native Americans.

"If the Trump administration and [the Interior Department] go through this whole deregulation agenda that they're on — expediting, streamlining, whatever euphemism they want to use — on the public lands for extraction purposes, then what's happening with Resolution Copper and Oak Flat and those areas is the harbinger of what can happen, across the West," he said. [87]

Grijalva also wants Zinke to testify on Trump's proposed $1.5 billion budget cuts to the Interior Department. He asked how the department would "honor the federal government's trust responsibilities to Native American tribes using $1.5 billion less in funding." [88]

Meanwhile, tribes, including the MHA Nation at Fort Berthold, intend to push Congress and the administration to bar states from taxing non-Native American energy companies that extract resources on tribal lands. They say only tribal governments should be able to levy taxes on those projects. [89]

The GAO in 2015 listed dual taxation of energy projects (by states and tribes) as impediments to Indian energy development, along with tribes' limited access to capital and federal tax credits. [90]

In the Courts

The National Congress of American Indians supported the Supreme Court nomination of U.S. Appeals Judge Neil M. Gorsuch, who was confirmed on April 7.

Gorsuch's "opinions recognize tribes as sovereign governments and address issues of significance to tribes," the group's president, Brian Cladoosby, and Native American Rights Fund Executive Director John Echohawk wrote in a letter. "Judge Gorsuch appears to be both attentive to the details and respectful to the fundamental principles of tribal sovereignty and the federal trust responsibility." [91]

A series of cases regarding tribal sovereignty and land rights is making its way through the courts and could end up before the Supreme Court.

In what some consider a potentially landmark decision, a federal appeals court in Palm Springs, Calif., in March upheld a ruling that the Agua Caliente Band of Cahuilla Indians has federally established rights to groundwater beneath its reservation in Palm Springs and surrounding areas. The appeals court said the creation of the Agua Caliente reservation in the 1870s "carried with it an implied right to use water from the Coachella Valley aquifer." The local water districts could appeal to the U.S. Supreme Court.

Meanwhile, a lawsuit filed by the Standing Rock Sioux and Cheyenne River Sioux tribes accuses the Army Corps of Engineers and the company building the Dakota Access Pipeline of ignoring the risk of oil spills and their potential effects on the tribe. The project, the suit said, violates the 1970 National Environmental Policy Act requiring federal agencies to conduct environmental assessments on projects submitted for federal approval or funding. [92]

The Northern Cheyenne Tribe is suing the Interior Department over the Trump administration's decision to lift the moratorium on coal leasing on federal lands. The tribe said it should have been consulted. Tribe President L. Jace Killsback said he is worried about mining's effect on "our pristine air and water quality . . . [and] sacred cultural properties and traditional spiritual practices." [93] ∎

OUTLOOK

"Backsliding" Feared

Christopher Newport University's Allison says he expects to see tribes gaining more control over their land.

Former Bureau of Indian Affairs Director Washburn, however, warns that federal regulations could tip the other way, as evidenced by Trump's push to complete the Dakota pipeline over tribes' objections. "I hope we don't get backsliding to a federal-control model where tribes are shut out of their own decisions on their land," he says, but adds that "tribes have a lot more clout now. . . . We may see a rolling back of baseline protections of tribal lands, but we may also see tribes creating their own regimes."

Another possibility, Washburn says, is that under the Trump administration's crusade to roll back federal regulations, the president may grant more control to tribes, "so we might see more tribal self-determination and self-governance."

Many legal experts, economists and scholars say the federal government still needs to find a way to resolve the checkerboard pattern of property ownership that remains from the allotment era and complicates tribal governing on reservations.

A "fractionalized" ownership of lots remains an issue that vexes economists and developers, and which the GAO has noted continues to impede energy development on many reservations.

Fractionalized interests refers to lots held in trust by hundreds of individuals. When owners of allotted land died without wills, heirs inherited the property under U.S. law, a process that has continued through the generations with the property divided further among subsequent heirs. Anderson at the Property and Environment Research Center says many of those lots remain undeveloped because of the difficulty in obtaining consensus from all the property owners.

"Every administration since Kennedy has looked at those reservations and said, 'We've got to do something,' including the Obama administration," Gover of the National Museum of American Indians says.

"And everyone walks away saying, 'I don't know what the hell to do.' It's not an absence of caring. It's not an absence of good will," Gover says. "To really turn those reservations around would require an enormous influx of money. Just good-old Yankee dollars that would allow an economy to begin to grow." ∎

Notes

[1] T.J. Raphael, "A Native American tribe in Montana hopes its coal reserves will provide economic opportunity," Public Radio International, Oct. 29, 2015, http://tinyurl.com/lah2eye.

[2] Amy Martin, "Why Montana's Crow Tribe Turns To Coal As Others Turn Away," *Inside Energy*, Oct. 23, 2015, http://tinyurl.com/k5uzequ.

[3] Brittany Patterson, "Tribes divided over unlocking energy wealth," *Climatewire*, Nov. 16, 2016, http://tinyurl.com/m9jh66w.

[4] Julie Turkewitz, "Tribes that Live Off Coal Hold Tight to Trump's Promises," *The New York Times*, April 1, 2017, http://tinyurl.com/kqebzf7.

[5] Baynard Woods, "Out of the Standing Rock, the Birth of a New Environmental Movement," *Nashville Scene*, March 18, 2017, http://tinyurl.com/n8l3ath.

[6] Shawn E. Regan and Terry L. Anderson, "The Energy Wealth of Indian Nations," *Journal of Energy Law and Resources*, Fall 2014, p. 196, http://tinyurl.com/mdo7bpp.

[7] *Cherokee Nation v. Georgia*, 30 U.S. 1 (1831), http://tinyurl.com/kk628sr.

[8] Regan and Anderson, *op. cit.*, pp. 110-111; Terry Anderson and Dominic Parker, "Un-American Reservations," Hoover Institution, Feb. 24, 2011, http://tinyurl.com/l9j6j7u.

[9] "Tribal Nations and the United States: An Introduction," National Congress of American Indians, p. 16, http://tinyurl.com/kdnqsan.

[10] *Ibid.*, pp. 38-41.

[11] "Gaming Revenues by Region," National Indian Gaming Commission, July 2016, http://tinyurl.com/kh7865w.

[12] "Poor Management by BIA Has Hindered Energy Development on Indian Lands," Government Accountability Office, June 2015, p. 22, http://tinyurl.com/mddw2ja.

[13] Sarah van Gelder, "In North Dakota's Booming Oil Patch, One Tribe Beat Back Fracking," *Yes Magazine*, Jan. 21, 2016, http://tinyurl.com/jsc2f8y; "National Drug Control Strategy," Executive Office of the President, 2014, p. 47, http://tinyurl.com/m7zp4kf.

[14] Valerie Volcovici, "Red tape chokes off drilling on Native American reservations," Reuters, Jan. 27, 2017, http://tinyurl.com/mdoywlu.

[15] Naomi Schaefer Riley, *The New Trail of Tears: How Washington Is Destroying American Indians* (2016).

[16] "FY 2017 Federal Funding for Programs Serving Tribes and Native American Communities," Department of the Interior, http://tinyurl.com/lfxg2lk.

[17] Deborah Sontag and Brent McDonald, "In North Dakota, a Tale of Oil, Corruption and Death," *The New York Times*, Dec. 28, 2014, http://tinyurl.com/mvgyhtr; Jodi Rave Spotted Bear, "Tex Hall takes witness stand in murder-for-hire trial," *Native Sun News Today*, March 9, 2016, http://tinyurl.com/m2s9luv; and Josh Wood, "Oil-

rich ND reservation to get new leader," *The Washington Times*, Sept. 17, 2014, http://tinyurl.com/n5lbj88.

[18] Jack McNeel, "S&K Technologies: A Major World Class Enterprise," Indian Country Media Network, March 26, 2017, http://tinyurl.com/kgq8geb.

[19] Indian Trust Asset Reform Act, Public Law 114-178, June 22, 2016, http://tinyurl.com/kmdwtde.

[20] "Poor Management by BIA Has Hindered Energy Development on Indian Lands," *op. cit.*, p. 22.

[21] Kevin Gover, "An Indian Trust for the Twenty-First Century," *Natural Resources Journal*, Spring 2006, http://tinyurl.com/mclxnyx.

[22] "Prepared Statement of Honorable Tyson Thompson, Councilman, Southern Ute Indian Tribal Council, at Hearing: Examining Federal Programs that Service Tribes and Their Members," Subcommittee on the Interior, Energy, and Environment, U.S. House Committee on Oversight and Government Reform, Feb. 15, 2017, http://tinyurl.com/mb77p52.

[23] Catherine Traywick, "A tale of two tribes: Colorado's Southern Utes want to drill while Sioux battle pipeline," Bloomberg News, *The Denver Post*, Oct. 14, 2016, http://tinyurl.com/m2ktd3m.

[24] Joe Cardillo, "New energy player in New Mexico already scoring big firsts," *Albuquerque Business First*, May 4, 2016, http://tinyurl.com/mt24wyl.

[25] Brittany Patterson, "Tribes divided over unlocking energy wealth," *E&E News*, Nov. 16, 2016, http://tinyurl.com/m9jh66w.

[26] Van Gelder, *op. cit.*

[27] Dan Bacher, "Hundreds of Tribal Representatives Join Huge Rally to Oppose Fracking," *Tulalip News*, March 18, 2014, http://tinyurl.com/kg9aexq.

[28] Kirk Johnson, "U.S. Denies Permit for Coal Terminal in Washington State," *The New York Times*, May 9, 2016, http://tinyurl.com/lc9pgws.

[29] Deborah Sontag and Brent McDonald, "In North Dakota, a Tale of Oil, Corruption and Death," *The New York Times*, Dec. 28, 2014, http://tinyurl.com/mvgyhtr.

[30] Celia Raney, "Indigenous people speak out against pollution of tribal lands," *DailyLobo.com*, March 5, 2017, http://tinyurl.com/knwg9kn.

[31] *Winters v. United States*, 207 U.S. 564 (1908), http://tinyurl.com/kovz9tc; Jeffrey Ostler and Nick Estes, "'The Supreme Law of the Land': Standing Rock and the Dakota Access Pipeline," *Indian Country Today*, Jan. 16, 2017, http://tinyurl.com/k8cukxl.

[32] Jan Hasselman, "A New Front in the Battle Against Coal Exports: Treaties," EarthJustice, July 14, 2015, http://tinyurl.com/ks7x59a.

[33] Kandi Mossett, keynote at Local Environmental Action Conference 2017, http://tinyurl.com/mly8ehs.

[34] Joe Helm, "U.N. human rights official criticizes federal relationship with Indian tribes," *The Washington Post*, March 3, 2017, http://tinyurl.com/lfcbo8k.

[35] Valerie Richardson, "Obama adopts U.N. manifesto on rights of indigenous peoples," *The Washington Times*, Dec. 16, 2010, http://tinyurl.com/365ag4f; "United Nations Declaration on the Rights of Indigenous Peoples," United Nations, March 2008, p. 12, http://tinyurl.com/7ans84.

[36] Wilcomb E. Washburn, ed., *Handbook of North American Indians: History of Indian-White Relations* (1988), p. 3.

[37] Tyler Anbinder, *City of Dreams: The 400-Year Epic History of Immigrant New York* (2016), pp. 19-22.

[38] Washburn, *op. cit.*, pp. 3-5.

[39] "History of BIA," Bureau of Indian Affairs, http://tinyurl.com/k4kh6cx.

[40] Peter Cozzens, *The Earth Is Weeping: The Epic Story of the Indian Wars for the American West* (2016), p. 11.

[41] *Ibid.*

[42] *Ibid.*, pp. 11, 14.

[43] *Johnson v. McIntosh*, 21 U.S. 543 (1823), http://tinyurl.com/h8ocs4a.

[44] "Indian Removal Act," Library of Congress, http://tinyurl.com/pgcudn7.

[45] *Cherokee Nation v. Georgia*, 30 U.S. 1 (1831).

[46] *Worcester v. Georgia*, 31 U.S. 515 (1832).

[47] "Primary Documents in American History: Indian Removal Act," Library of Congress, http://tinyurl.com/pgcudn7.

[48] Cozzens, *op. cit.*, pp. 16, 17.

[49] 25 U.S. Code Sec. 71, http://tinyurl.com/nxnrfh6.

[50] "The Indian Problem: Senator Dawes and Gen. Armstrong Give Their Views Regarding It," *The New York Times*, July 22, 1885, http://tinyurl.com/mqz3xfr.

[51] Trevor Hammond, "First Oklahoma Land Rush: April 22, 1889," Newspapers.com, http://tinyurl.com/lrotjf8.

[52] Mary H. Cooper, "Native Americans' Future," *CQ Researcher*, July 12, 1996, pp. 601-624.

[53] "The Indian Citizenship Act," History.com, 2010, http://tinyurl.com/3oprgrk.

[54] "The Problem of Indian Administration," Institute for Government Research, Feb. 21, 1928, p. 3, http://tinyurl.com/m24e7hd; Felix S. Cohen, "The Erosion of Indian Rights," Yale Law School Legal Scholarship Repository, Jan. 1, 1953, http://tinyurl.com/k8gxaj6.

[55] John Collier, "A Life for the Forgotten Red Man Too," May 6, 1934, http://tinyurl.com/lhwatq8; *Encyclopedia of American Indian History*, edited by Bruce E. Johansen and Barry M. Pritzker, pp. 554-555, http://tinyurl.com/mrv43db.

[56] Cohen, *op. cit.* Also see Nancy Oestreich Lurie, "The Indian Claims Commission Act," *The ANNALS of the American Academy of Political Science*, May 1, 1957, http://tinyurl.com/k99axq5.

[57] Judith Graham, "Compensation at last for tribes that lost lands to dams," *Chicago Tribune*, http://tinyurl.com/m92c34r.

[58] Janet McDonnell, "Review of Dammed Indians: The Pick-Sloan Plan and the Missouri River Sioux, 1944-1980," *Great Plains Quarterly*, Spring 1984, pp. 137-38, http://tinyurl.com/mtqt939.

[59] Washburn, *op. cit.*, p. 314; "History and Culture: Termination Policy — 1953-1968," Northern Plains Reservation Aid, http://tinyurl.com/k9m7ers.

[60] Indian Civil Rights Act of 1968, 25 U.S.C. §§ 1301-1304, http://tinyurl.com/ltmlgx2.

[61] Homer Bigart, "American Indian Activists Winning Bureau Reform," *The New York Times*, Jan. 8, 1972, http://tinyurl.com/ld2tkxq; Richard Nixon, "213-Special Message to the Congress on Indian Affairs, July 8, 1970," American Presidency Project, http://tinyurl.com/olxfhhg.

About the Author

Christina L. Lyons, a freelance journalist in the Washington, D.C., area, writes primarily about U.S. government and politics. She is a contributing author for CQ Press reference books, including *CQ's Guide to Congress*, and was a contributing editor for Bloomberg BNA's *International Trade Daily*. A former editor for Congressional Quarterly, she also was co-author of CQ's *Politics in America 2010*. Lyons began her career as a newspaper reporter in Maryland and then covered environment and health care policy on Capitol Hill. She has a master's degree in political science from American University.

[62] Roger L. Nichols, *The American Indian: Past and Present* (2014), pp. 303-305, http://tinyurl.com/m2wllev.

[63] Allison, *op. cit.*, p. 1.

[64] *Ibid.*

[65] James P. Sterba, "Navajo Leader Assails Federal Unit," *The New York Times*, Oct. 23, 1973, http://tinyurl.com/k3dxjz6.

[66] Alex Tizon, "The Boldt Decision / 25 Years — The Fish Tale That Changed History," *The Seattle Times*, Feb. 7, 1999, http://tinyurl.com/kpgrn6d.

[67] Indian Mineral Development Act of 1982, Public Law 97-382, Dec. 22, 1982, http://tinyurl.com/mfyk7lp; Allison, *op. cit.*, p. 6.

[68] "U.S. Indian Bureau Assailed in Report," *The New York Times*, Dec. 1, 1984, http://tinyurl.com/m9twu4h.

[69] Iver Peterson, "Indians Resist Shift in Economic Goals Urged by U.S. Panel," *The New York Times*, Jan. 13, 1985, http://tinyurl.com/k3zmrun.

[70] Cooper, *op. cit.* For more on Indians and casinos, see Peter Katel, "American Indians," *CQ Researcher*, April 28, 2006, pp. 361-384.

[71] Bill Richardson, "More Power to the Tribes," *The New York Times*, July 7, 1993, http://tinyurl.com/lplm8gu.

[72] Shanna Lewis, "American Indian Activist Led A Landmark Suit Against The Federal Government," Colorado Public Radio, Feb. 9, 2017, http://tinyurl.com/kxq8wpw.

[73] "Memorandum for the Heads of Executive Departments and Agencies," The White House, April 29, 1994, available at http://tinyurl.com/l4owjpz.

[74] Graham, *op. cit.*

[75] "A Quiet Crisis: Federal Funding and Unmet Needs in Indian Country," U.S. Commission on Civil Rights, July 2003, p. iii, http://tinyurl.com/lnahf8h.

[76] Kevin K. Washburn, "What the Future Holds: The Changing Landscape of Federal Indian Policy," University of New Mexico Law, forthcoming, p. 18, http://tinyurl.com/kwkbekq.

[77] Regan and Anderson, *op. cit.*, p. 206.

[78] HEARTH ACT of 2012, U.S. Department of the Interior, Indian Affairs, http://tinyurl.com/nyxbrd4; "Obama Administration Exceeds Ambitious Goal to Restore 500,000 Acres of Tribal Homelands," press release, U.S. Department of the Interior, Oct. 12, 2016, http://tinyurl.com/kx466rg.

[79] Bryan Newland, "Donald Trump and Federal Indian Policy: 'They Don't Look Like Indians to Me,' " *Indian Country Today*, July 28, 2016, http://tinyurl.com/lnox8pa.

[80] "Oklahoma representative to chair Donald Trump's Native American Coalition," KOCO News 5, Jan. 4, 2017, http://tinyurl.com/kwth98s; Valerie Volcovici, "Trump advisors aim to privatize oil-rich Indian reservations," Reuters, Dec. 5, 2016, http://tinyurl.com/z9eqace.

[81] Andrew Restuccia and Anna Palmer, "Trump team reaches out to Native Americans," *Politico*, Dec. 16, 2016, http://politi.co/2gPor4o; Darryl Fears, "Ryan Zinke is one step closer to becoming interior secretary," *The Washington Post*, Jan. 31, 2017, http://tinyurl.com/malkhz3.

[82] "Cantwell Details Her Opposition to Zinke's Nomination to be Secretary of the Interior," press release, U.S. Senate Committee on Energy and Natural Resources, Feb. 28, 2017, http://tinyurl.com/mfockuk.

[83] "Staunch supporter of Cherry Point coal project is Trump's Interior secretary," The Associated Press, *The Bellingham Herald*, March 1, 2017, http://tinyurl.com/lbt2dhz.

[84] "White House Budget Increases Funding for Energy Development on Public Lands and Offshore, Continues to Streamline Permitting," *Oil & Gas 360*, March 16, 2017, http://tinyurl.com/mh67tq4; Coral Davenport, "Trump Signs Executive Order Unwinding Obama Climate Policies," *The New York Times*, March 28, 2017, http://tinyurl.com/k5hzovs.

[85] "Committee Passes Nine Bills During Business Meeting," press release, U.S. Senate Committee on Indian Affairs, Feb. 8, 2017, http://tinyurl.com/lhga7rd.

[86] Frank Rusco, "Federal Management Challenges Related to Indian Energy Resources: Testimony Before the Subcommittee on the Interior, Energy, and Environment, Committee on Oversight and Government Reform, House of Representatives," Feb. 15, 2017, http://tinyurl.com/k84xs3x.

[87] Andrew Westney, "House Dem Laments Energy Cos.' 'Lust' For Tribal Lands," *Law360*, March 31, 2017, http://tinyurl.com/maqfzb9.

[88] Charlie Passut, "House Democrat Wants Zinke to Testify on Interior's Budget," *Natural Gas Intelligence*, March 23, 2017, http://tinyurl.com/jvohgpb.

[89] Valeri Volcovici, "Native American tribes decry state taxation of reservation energy projects," Reuters, Jan. 17, 2017, http://tinyurl.com/kv2j3y3.

[90] "Poor Management by BIA Has Hindered Energy Development on Indian Lands," *op. cit.*

[91] Ryan Lovelace, "Support for Gorsuch from Native American groups could put pressure on Western Democrats," *Washington Examiner*, March 27, 2017, http://tinyurl.com/l7bhlgz.

[92] "The Dakota Access Pipeline: Case Overview," EarthJustice, http://tinyurl.com/kkky576.

[93] *Northern Cheyenne Tribe v. Department of the Interior*, March 29, 2017, http://tinyurl.com/ks4vjav; "The Northern Cheyenne Tribe Challenges Trump Administration's Decision to Lift Moratorium on Federal Coal Leases," press release, Northern Cheyenne Tribe Administration, March 29, 2017, http://tinyurl.com/ylog6vm.

FOR MORE INFORMATION

Bureau of Indian Affairs, MS-3658-MIB, 1849 C St., N.W., Washington, DC 20240; 202-208-3710; www.bia.gov. Department of the Interior agency that provides services to Native Americans.

Earth Justice, 50 California St., Suite 500, San Francisco, CA 94111; 800-584-6460; earthjustice.org. Nonprofit environmental law firm that represents several tribes suing the federal government over treaty rights and environmental justice.

Indigenous Environmental Network, PO Box 485, Bemidji, MN 56619; 218-751-4967; www.ienearth.org. Grassroots organization that helps tribes protect natural resources, sacred lands and health.

National Congress of American Indians, 1516 P St., N.W., Washington, DC 20005; 202-466-7767; www.ncai.org. Advocacy group representing tribal governments and communities.

Native American Rights Fund, 1506 Broadway, Boulder, CO 80302-6269; 303-447-8769; www.narf.org. Provides legal assistance to Indian tribes, organizations and individuals.

Property and Environment Research Center, 2048 Analysis Drive, Suite A, Bozeman, MT 59718; 406-587-9591; www.perc.org. Free-market research institute that advocates for property rights to encourage resolution to environmental conflicts.

Bibliography

Selected Sources

Books

Allison, James R., *Sovereignty for Survival: American Energy Development and Indian Self-Determination*, Yale University Press, 2015.
An assistant professor of history at Christopher Newport University in Newport News, Va., explores how tribal resistance to energy development on Indian lands led to increased Native American sovereignty and sparked debate about land management.

Grann, David, *Killers of the Flower Moon: The Osage Murders and the Birth of the FBI*, Doubleday, 2017.
A staff writer for *The New Yorker* examines the 1920s killings of members of Oklahoma's Osage Nation who had become wealthy from oil discovered under their land.

Riley, Naomi Schaefer, *The New Trail of Tears: How Washington Is Destroying American Indians*, Encounter Books, 2016.
A former *Wall Street Journal* reporter concludes that Native Americans' lack of property rights, access to the free market and proper education — combined with continued dependency on federal subsidies — have limited economic growth on reservations.

Wilkins, David E., and Shelly Hulse Wilkins, *Dismembered: Native Disenrollment and the Battle for Human Rights*, University of Washington Press, 2017.
An American Indian studies professor at the University of Minnesota Law School (Wilkins) and a specialist in tribal governmental relations (Hulse Wilkins) analyze an epidemic of disenrollment of members by tribal leaders.

Articles

Mosteller, Kelli, "For Native Americans, Land Is More Than Just the Ground Beneath Their Feet," *The Atlantic*, Sept. 17, 2016, https://tinyurl.com/mfttnl4.
The director of the Citizen Potawatomi Nation Cultural Heritage Center in Oklahoma says proponents of privatization of tribal lands disregard Indian culture and values.

Volcovici, Valerie, "Red tape chokes off drilling on Native American reservations," Reuters, Jan. 27, 2017, https://tinyurl.com/mdoywlu.
Tribes complain that federal energy regulations delay projects on reservations, reduce revenue and undermine tribal sovereignty.

Warner, Elizabeth Ann Kronk, "Everything Old Is New Again: Enforcing Treaty Provisions to Protect Climate Change-Threatened Resources," *Nebraska Law Review*, 2016, http://tinyurl.com/kmglybk.
The director of the Tribal Law and Government Center at the University of Kansas argues that existing treaties could provide useful tools for tribes seeking environmental justice for damage to their land, natural resources and health caused by climate change.

Woodard, Stephanie, "How the U.S. Government Is Helping Corporations Plunder Native Lands," *In These Times*, Sept. 6, 2016, https://tinyurl.com/zmemulc.
The Bureau of Indian Affairs enables outside corporations to profit from energy development and other economic projects on Indian lands, according to a journalist's investigative report.

Reports and Studies

"Improving Tribal Consultation and Tribal Involvement in Federal Infrastructure Decisions," Departments of the Interior, Army and Justice, January 2017, https://tinyurl.com/j5huwe2.
The Obama administration recommended ways that federal decision-making on infrastructure and other projects can include input from Native American tribes.

"Poor Management by BIA Has Hindered Energy Development on Indian Lands," Government Accountability Office, June 15, 2015, p. 22, http://tinyurl.com/mddw2ja.
The Government Accountability Office, the investigative arm of Congress, recommends ways the Bureau of Indian Affairs can enable more energy development on Indians lands and encourage tribes to pursue energy resource agreements with the bureau.

Audio/Video

"How federal policy affects Native Americans: Naomi Schaefer Riley on her book, 'The New Trail of Tears: How Washington Is Destroying American Indians,' " American Enterprise Institute, Jan. 30, 2017, http://tinyurl.com/lknzbjv.
A free-market think tank hosts a forum featuring a former Bureau of Indian Education director, a representative of the libertarian Cato Institute and author Riley discussing impediments to economic improvement on Native American reservations.

"Keynote: Kandi Mossett," Local Environmental Action 2017, March 5, 2017, http://tinyurl.com/mly8ehs.
A member of the Mandan, Hidatsa and Arikara Nation in North Dakota and the lead organizer of the Extreme Energy and Just Transition Campaign for the Indigenous Environmental Network, a Native American grassroots environmental group, discusses the environmental and cultural effects of oil drilling at Fort Berthold, N.D.

The Next Step:

Additional Articles from Current Periodicals

Energy Development

Eilperin, Juliet, and Darryl Fears, "The standoff between Trump and green groups just boiled into war," *The Washington Post*, March 30, 2017, http://tinyurl.com/lbv5drj.

Native Americans are clashing with President Trump over his executive order lifting a coal moratorium on federal land.

Ritter, Ken, "NV Energy pulls plug on coal-fired power plant near Las Vegas," *Las Vegas Sun*, March 16, 2017, http://tinyurl.com/kgezldp.

Nevada's Moapa Band of Paiutes, who blamed power plant emissions for high rates of asthma and heart disease, pressured a coal-fired power plant to shutter.

Siciliano, John, "Native American tribes find it's not always easy being green," *Washington Examiner*, April 3, 2017, http://tinyurl.com/nxtsuuj.

A GOP-backed bill in Congress aims to give tribes more independence to develop their own natural resources.

Environmental Issues

Cwiek, Sarah, "Controversial UP mining project one step closer to reality with new permit," Michigan Radio, April 10, 2017, http://tinyurl.com/ksaveau.

Native Americans in Michigan are concerned about potential sulfuric acid pollution in the Menominee River after a gold mining operation received the third of four permits necessary to open.

Hilleary, Cecily, "Native Americans Most at Risk From Impact of Climate Change," Voice of America, April 19, 2017, http://tinyurl.com/k6ujpk7.

Tribes say climate change threatens their way of life, as many rely on the land for economic and spiritual practices.

Norris, Courtney, "The Rover Pipeline leaked millions of gallons of drilling fluid into Ohio wetlands," PBS Newshour, April 21, 2017, http://tinyurl.com/k6r2w62.

Energy Transfer Partners spilled more than 2 million gallons of drilling fluid into Ohio wetlands.

Federal Regulations

Edwards, Melodie, "New Study Shows Tribes Nationwide Need About 68,000 Homes," Wyoming Public Media, Feb. 2, 2017, http://tinyurl.com/gn4u3gr.

The Department of Housing and Urban Development estimated that tribes need about 68,000 additional housing units due to high unemployment and homelessness.

Marcelo, Philip, "Appeals court reverses ruling blocking tribe's Martha's Vineyard casino bid," *The Boston Globe*, April 11, 2017, http://tinyurl.com/m692d92.

A federal appeals court ruled the Aquinnah Wampanoag tribe may operate a gambling hall in Massachusetts because it exercises sufficient government powers to meet federal gaming requirements.

Mundahl, Erin, "Tribes Divided as Zinke Changes Obama-Era Rule on Mineral Leases," *Value Walk*, April 4, 2017, http://tinyurl.com/mea68f4.

In an effort to stop the "war on coal," Interior Secretary Ryan Zinke announced changes to a rule that defines royalties paid on mineral leases on federal and Native American lands.

Protests

Grueskin, Caroline, "47 DAPL cases closed in March, 33 dismissed," *The Bismarck Tribune*, April 21, 2017, http://tinyurl.com/lwhyekm.

Prosecutors dropped 33 cases against Dakota Access Pipeline protesters, many of whom had criticized the pipeline's path through sacred Native American lands.

Siciliano, John, "Native American groups plan to overrun Trump hotel in Washington," *Washington Examiner*, April 21, 2017, http://tinyurl.com/kntonv9.

Native American groups plan to occupy Trump International Hotel in Washington and are asking Congress to "stop treating indigenous people and lands as America's environmental sacrifice zone."

Volcovici, Valerie, "Last stand: Nebraska farmers still could derail Keystone XL pipeline," Reuters, April 20, 2017, http://tinyurl.com/m6vps87.

Farmers and ranchers who own land in the path of the Keystone XL pipeline have joined Native Americans to protest the project.

CITING *CQ RESEARCHER*

Sample formats for citing these reports in a bibliography include the ones listed below. Preferred styles and formats vary, so please check with your instructor or professor.

MLA STYLE

Mantel, Barbara. "Coal Industry's Future." CQ Researcher 17 June 2016: 529-552.

APA STYLE

Mantel, B. (2016, June 17). Coal Industry's Future. *CQ Researcher, 6,* 529-552.

CHICAGO STYLE

Mantel, Barbara. "Coal Industry's Future." *CQ Researcher,* June 17, 2016, 529-52.

In-depth Reports on Issues in the News

Are you writing a paper?

Need backup for a debate?

Want to become an expert on an issue?

For 90 years, students have turned to *CQ Researcher* for in-depth reporting on issues in the news. Reports on a full range of political and social issues are now available. Following is a selection of recent reports:

Civil Liberties
Privacy and the Internet, 12/15
Intelligence Reform, 5/15
Religion and Law, 11/14

Crime/Law
High-Tech Policing, 4/17
Forensic Science Controversies, 2/17
Jailing Debtors, 9/16
Decriminalizing Prostitution, 4/16
Restorative Justice, 2/16
The Dark Web, 1/16
Immigrant Detention, 10/15

Education
Charter Schools, 3/17
Civic Education, 2/17
Student Debt, 11/16
Apprenticeships, 10/16

Environment/Society
Women in Prison, 3/17
Guns on Campus, 1/17
Mass Transit, 12/16
Arctic Development, 12/16
Protecting the Power Grid, 11/16
Pornography, 10/16

Health/Safety
Sports and Sexual Assault, 4/17
Reducing Traffic Deaths, 2/17
Opioid Crisis, 10/16
Mosquito-Borne Disease, 7/16

Politics/Economy
Rethinking Foreign Aid, 4/17
Troubled Brazil, 4/17
Reviving Rural Economies, 3/17
Immigrants and the Economy, 2/17
Trump Presidency, 1/17
European Union's Future, 12/16

Upcoming Reports

Anti-Semitism, 5/12/17   North Korea, 5/19/17   Pandemics, 6/2/17

ACCESS

CQ Researcher is available in print and online. For access, visit your library or www.cqresearcher.com.

STAY CURRENT

For notice of upcoming *CQ Researcher* reports or to learn more about *CQ Researcher* products, subscribe to the free email newsletters, *CQ Researcher Alert!* and *CQ Researcher News*: http://cqpress.com/newsletters.

PURCHASE

To purchase a *CQ Researcher* report in print or electronic format (PDF), visit www.cqpress.com or call 866-427-7737. Single reports start at $15. Bulk purchase discounts and electronic-rights licensing are also available.

SUBSCRIBE

Annual full-service *CQ Researcher* subscriptions—including 44 reports a year, monthly index updates, and a bound volume—start at $1,131. Add $25 for domestic postage.

CQ Researcher Online offers a backfile from 1991 and a number of tools to simplify research. For pricing information, call 800-818-7243 or 805-499-9774 or email librarysales@sagepub.com.

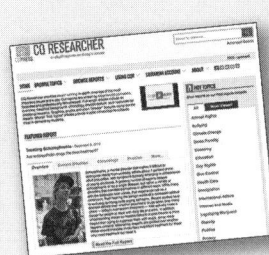

CQ RESEARCHER

In-depth reports on today's issues

Published by CQ Press, an Imprint of SAGE Publications, Inc.   **www.cqresearcher.com**

Anti-Semitism

Is hostility toward Jews on the rise worldwide?

In the run-up to the presidential election and afterward, the United States has experienced disturbing outbreaks of anti-Semitism, including a spate of incidents on more than 100 college campuses, where white supremacists have been distributing anti-Semitic fliers and openly recruiting adherents. Some human rights and Jewish activists say President Trump has emboldened right-wing hostility toward Jews, but others say such charges are unjustified. Defining anti-Semitism is controversial. Members of Congress and state legislators want to codify a definition that would include opposition to Israel's existence. But pro-Palestinian and civil liberties groups say that would violate free-speech rights. A similar debate is playing out in Europe, where some countries have seen a rise in deadly attacks on Jews in recent years, often by radicalized Muslims, such as the 2015 terrorist attack on a kosher grocery in Paris. Paradoxically, growing anti-Muslim attitudes in countries experiencing an influx of refugees have also spurred more prejudice against Jews — the target of history's longest hatred.

In recent months vandals have desecrated Jewish cemeteries in Rochester, N.Y., above, Philadelphia and a St. Louis suburb. Anti-Semitic incidents also have been on the rise on college campuses, and Jewish schools and community centers in the United States have received dozens of hoax bomb threats. Anti-Jewish incidents have risen in some European countries as well.

I N S I D E THIS REPORT

THE ISSUES	**411**
BACKGROUND	**417**
CHRONOLOGY	**419**
CURRENT SITUATION	**424**
AT ISSUE	**425**
OUTLOOK	**427**
BIBLIOGRAPHY	**430**
THE NEXT STEP	**431**

CQ Researcher • May 12, 2017 • www.cqresearcher.com
Volume 27, Number 18 • Pages 409-432

THE ISSUES

411
- Is anti-Semitism on the rise?
- Is opposition to Israel a form of anti-Semitism?
- Should online anti-Semitic speech be further restricted?

BACKGROUND

417 **'Blood Libel'**
False stories about Jews spread in the 12th century.

418 **Fabricated Charge**
A forged document falsely claimed a Jewish plot to take over the world.

421 **Resurging Hostility**
Establishment of the state of Israel sparked new anti-Jewish sentiment.

CURRENT SITUATION

424 **Criticizing Trump**
Some Jewish groups say the president was slow to speak out against anti-Semitism.

426 **International Action**
Britain declared condemnation of Israel a form of anti-Semitism.

426 **BDS Movement**
Governments worldwide and Jewish groups are trying to block the Boycott, Divestment and Sanctions movement's boycott of Israeli products and academic institutions.

OUTLOOK

427 **'New Era'**
Jews say they now must worry about threats from extremists from the right, the left and radicalized Muslims — both online and off.

SIDEBARS AND GRAPHICS

412 **U.S. Colleges Targeted by Anti-Semitism**
More than 100 incidents were reported on campuses in 24 states last year.

413 **Anti-Semitic Incidents Surged in Early 2017**
Harassment and vandalism rose in the first quarter.

416 **Israel, U.S. Have Biggest Jewish Populations**
More than 90 percent of Jews live in five countries.

419 **Chronology**
Key events since 1144.

420 **Anti-Semitism Persists in an Unsettled Poland**
"We didn't resolve the problem of what Poles did to Jews."

422 **Anti-Semitism Charges Roil Britain's Left**
Labour Party suspends a prominent member for controversial remarks.

425 **At Issue:**
Has President Trump spurred anti-Semitism in the U.S.?

FOR FURTHER RESEARCH

429 **For More Information**
Organizations to contact.

430 **Bibliography**
Selected sources used.

431 **The Next Step**
Additional articles.

431 **Citing *CQ Researcher***
Sample bibliography formats.

Cover: AFP/Getty Images/Gretchen Stumme

 **CQ RESEARCHER**

May 12, 2017
Volume 27, Number 18

EXECUTIVE EDITOR: Thomas J. Billitteri
tjb@sagepub.com

ASSISTANT MANAGING EDITORS: Kenneth Fireman, kenneth.fireman@sagepub.com, Kathy Koch, kathy.koch@sagepub.com, Scott Rohrer, scott.rohrer@sagepub.com

ASSOCIATE MANAGING EDITOR: Val Ellicott

SENIOR CONTRIBUTING EDITOR:
Thomas J. Colin
tom.colin@sagepub.com

CONTRIBUTING WRITERS: Marcia Clemmitt, Sarah Glazer, Reed Karaim, Barbara Mantel, Chuck McCutcheon, Tom Price

SENIOR PROJECT EDITOR: Olu B. Davis

EDITORIAL ASSISTANT: Anika Reed

FACT CHECKERS: Eva P. Dasher, Michelle Harris, Betsy Towner Levine, Robin Palmer

SAGE Publishing | **CQ PRESS**

Los Angeles I London I New Delhi
Singapore I Washington DC I Melbourne

An Imprint of SAGE Publications, Inc.

SENIOR VICE PRESIDENT, GLOBAL LEARNING RESOURCES:
Karen Phillips

EXECUTIVE DIRECTOR, ONLINE LIBRARY AND REFERENCE PUBLISHING:
Todd Baldwin

CQ Researcher (ISSN 1056-2036) is printed on acid-free paper. Published weekly, except: (March wk. 4) (May wk. 4) (July wks. 1, 2) (Aug. wks. 2, 3) (Nov. wk. 4) and (Dec. wks. 3, 4). Published by SAGE Publications, Inc., 2455 Teller Rd., Thousand Oaks, CA 91320. Annual full-service subscriptions start at $1,131. For pricing, call 1-800-818-7243. To purchase a *CQ Researcher* report in print or electronic format (PDF), visit www.cqpress. com or call 866-427-7737. Single reports start at $15. Bulk purchase discounts and electronic-rights licensing are also available. Periodicals postage paid at Thousand Oaks, California, and at additional mailing offices. POSTMASTER: Send address changes to *CQ Researcher*, 2600 Virginia Ave., N.W., Suite 600, Washington, DC 20037.

Anti-Semitism

THE ISSUES

"Heil Trump," said an email threatening Jews and African-Americans, received by hundreds of University of Michigan students in February from a forged, or "spoofed," faculty address. The messages, being investigated by the FBI, followed the appearance of racist fliers on campus last fall. [1]

"We've been riding this wave of Donald Trump's election — definitely," said a member of Identity Evropa, a white supremacist group that says it has distributed fliers on more than two dozen campuses. "He's the closest to us we've ever had in recent memory, although we would like to see him go a lot further." [2]

White nationalists "feel emboldened in this current political climate" and are engaged in an "unprecedented" campaign to target college campuses, said Jonathan A. Greenblatt, CEO of the Anti-Defamation League (ADL), a Jewish civil rights group. Extremist anti-Semitic and white supremacist fliers and messages have popped up on more than 100 campuses in 33 states, according to the league, in at least 145 instances since the beginning of the school year. [3] In 2016, the group counted 108 campus incidents specifically targeting Jewish students. [4] (*See graph, p. 412.*)

The Southern Poverty Law Center (SPLC), a liberal hate-watch group based in Montgomery, Ala., has blamed a nationwide "wave of hate speech and harassment" against Jews and others on Trump's election. [5] SPLC senior fellow Mark Potok said such groups were "electrified" by Trump's presidential campaign. [6]

Jewish groups both here and in Eu-

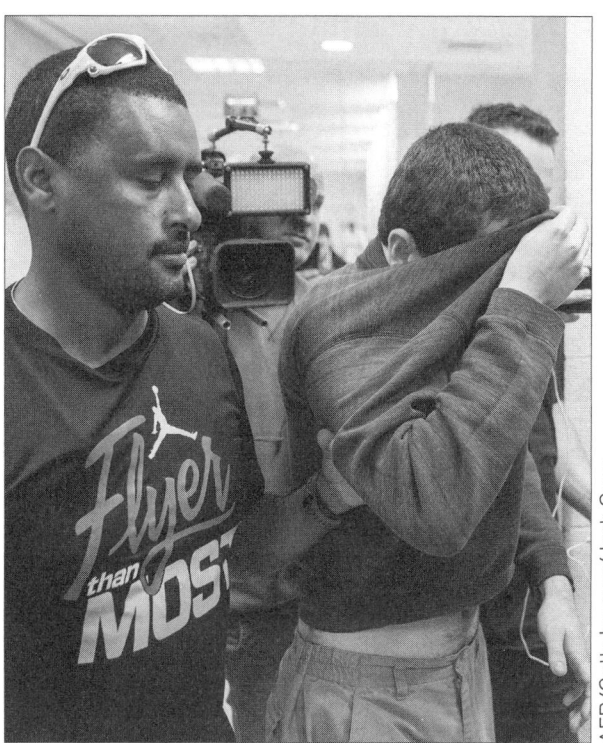

Michael Ron David Kadar, 18, is escorted on March 23 from a courtroom in Israel, where he was charged in connection with hundreds of bomb threats. In April, the U.S. Justice Department charged the Jewish Israeli-American teen in connection with dozens of fake bomb threats in the United States between January and March of this year, many of them targeting Jewish community centers.

AFP/Getty Images/Jack Guez

rope say anti-Semitic incidents are on the rise, and not just on college campuses. Anti-Jewish incidents jumped 34 percent last year to 1,266 — up from to 942 in 2015 — and continued to rise in the first quarter of this year, the ADL said. This year saw disturbing incidents of harassment or vandalism, including more than 100 bomb threats called in to Jewish schools and community centers and the desecration in February of dozens of Jewish graves at cemeteries in Philadelphia and near St. Louis, Mo. [7]

"Over the past six months we've seen a surge of bias incidents and hate crimes we haven't seen before," says Greenblatt. The Trump campaign, he says, legitimized so-called alt-right groups who "brought with them a kind of intolerance that has never before been in the center of the public debate

— not just about Jews but about Mexicans, Muslims and other minorities."

The alt-right, short for "alternative right," refers to a loose amalgam of far-right groups and individuals associated with implicit or explicit racism, anti-Semitism and white supremacy. [8] President Trump's chief strategist Steve Bannon has called the Breitbart News website he headed before joining the Trump campaign "a platform for the alt-right." Rob Eshman, editor-in-chief of the *Jewish Journal*, said the website fomented "a deep antagonism towards Jews," especially in its comments section. [9]

However, some Jewish observers doubt anti-Semitism is any worse under Trump; it just gets more media attention, they say. Others, such as Rep. Chris Smith, R-N.J., who has written legislation to combat anti-Semitism, strongly disagree with the accusation that Trump has inspired anti-Semitism.

"I think it's a very serious diversionary tactic by some," Smith says. "When people make those comments I think it does a disservice to the genuine and systemic causes [of anti-Semitism] we're trying to combat."

Others point out that, historically speaking, anti-Semitic incidents in both the United States and worldwide are substantially lower than they were in the mid-2000s, when Israeli-Arab conflicts were in the news, including the 2006 Israel-Lebanon war — events that experts say helped trigger waves of anti-Semitic sentiment. [10]

Criticism of Trump reached a new peak on April 11, when White House Press Secretary Sean Spicer said Nazi leader Adolf Hitler "didn't even sink to using chemical weapons" like Syrian President Bashar Assad did when he killed dozens of people with deadly

U.S. Colleges Targeted by Anti-Semitism

College campuses in 24 states experienced 108 incidents of anti-Semitism last year, according to data compiled by the Anti-Defamation League. The incidents ranged from threats and slurs to distribution of hate propaganda. California and New Jersey had the highest number of incidents, 19 each.

Number of Incidents Per State, 2016

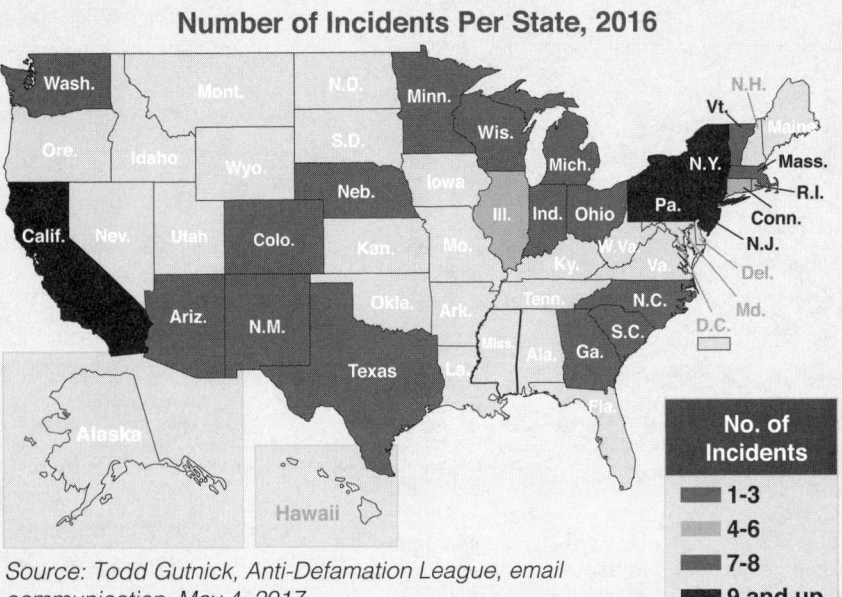

Source: Todd Gutnick, Anti-Defamation League, email communication, May 4, 2017

No. of Incidents

- 1-3
- 4-6
- 7-8
- 9 and up

sarin gas in April. Spicer seemed to have forgotten that the Nazis used poison gas to systematically kill millions of Jews. [11] Although Spicer later apologized, Jewish groups and historians said the administration was either phenomenally insensitive about Jews or verging on the anti-Semitic.

Journalists, Jewish groups and liberal bloggers cited previous occasions when the administration had "sent a clear dog-whistle of approval to anti-Semites," as a blogger from the liberal Center for American Progress in Washington described Spicer's April 11 words. For instance, the administration failed to mention Jews in its International Holocaust Remembrance Day statement and had been slow to denounce the rise in anti-Semitic incidents across the country. Earlier, Trump's campaign had tweeted a white supremacist image showing his opponent Hillary Clinton's face atop $100 bills with a Star of David. [12]

Perhaps to deflect the criticism, Trump recently has condemned anti-Semitism and explicitly mentioned the 6 million Jews killed by Nazis during an April 25 speech at the U.S. Holocaust Memorial Museum. "We will confront anti-Semitism; we will stamp out prejudice, we will condemn hatred and we will act," he told the museum audience, which included Holocaust survivors. [13]

Meanwhile, experts have attributed a rise in anti-Semitism in some parts of Europe to increasingly popular right-wing parties as well as anti-Israel sentiment among Muslims and the political left. Anti-Jewish feeling is linked to hostility toward immigrants and any ethnic group seen as the "other," experts say, such as in the rhetoric of right-wing parties opposed to the influx of more than 2 million immigrants, mostly Muslim, from the Middle East and Africa.

"It's going to be harder and harder for visible Jews to live in France," especially

those who wear religious garb such as a *kippah* (skullcap worn by Orthodox male Jews), says Bruno Chaouat, a professor of French at the University of Minnesota who studies French attitudes towards Jews. "Jews are caught in a vise between the far-right wing and anti-Semitism from Muslim youth and the left."

Hate crimes and anti-Semitic incidents spiked in Britain after the U.K. voted last June to leave the European Union (EU), according to the Community Security Trust, a London-based group that tracks anti-Semitism. Limiting immigration was a central issue in that vote.

In addition, says Mark Gardner, the trust's communications director, Jews have been "the target of jihadi terrorists" in recent years, often exacerbated by the internet. A "widespread increase" in anti-Semitism online has made the internet the main platform for "bigotry and hate," according to Tel Aviv University's Kantor Center, a watchdog group that publishes an annual report on anti-Semitic incidents globally. [14] The increase has stimulated a vigorous debate in Europe about whether to ratchet up penalties against hate speech online.

As for anti-Semitism among young Muslims, Günther Jikeli, a visiting associate professor in Jewish studies at Indiana University in Bloomington, had discovered startling sentiments among young Muslim men in London, Paris and Berlin when he interviewed them in 2007 for a book. They often said they wanted to "kill Jews before they died," Jikeli says. [15] At the time, that was not seen as a realistic possibility. "Now it is," he says, adding, "There are very explicit, detailed instructions on social media by ISIS and others calling for violence against Jews."

Jews are painfully aware of that in cities where deadly Islamist terrorist attacks have occurred at Jewish gathering places in recent years: a Paris kosher grocery and a Copenhagen synagogue in 2015, the Jewish Museum in Brussels in 2014 and a Jewish school in Toulouse in 2012.

The attack on the Paris grocery led to expressions of solidarity with Jews. "France without Jews is not France," said then-French Prime Minister Manuel Valls, promising to protect places of worship. [16] Officials beefed up security at Jewish institutions in Europe, and the number of violent anti-Semitic incidents worldwide fell by 12 percent — from 410 in 2015 to 361 last year. [17] But the brutality of individual events has intensified in recent years, according to the Kantor Center, such as the Paris grocery attack, which left four people dead.

Europe's refugee influx has shifted right-wing animosity more toward Muslims than Jews, according to the center. Still, many of the Muslim refugees come from Syria and Iraq, where anti-Semitic views are widespread, Jikeli points out, adding to nervousness in Europe's Jewish communities.

Some right-wing politicians in Europe have tried to capitalize on that Jewish anxiety. Marine Le Pen, who represents the anti-immigrant National Front, has tried to soften her party's historic anti-Semitism, saying French Jews have more to fear from jihadists than from organizations like hers. However, she recently declared that France was not culpable in rounding up Jews for concentration camps during World War II, which Emory University holocaust historian Deborah Lipstadt calls "soft-core Holocaust denial." [18] (Le Pen was soundly defeated by Emmanuel Macron in the May 7 election to select France's next president.)

Paradoxically, some extreme right-wing groups in Germany blame Europe's refugee influx on an international Jewish conspiracy. Once hatred turns against people seen as alien, experts say, the fallout has historically been bad news for Jews, who have been the target of what some historians call humanity's "longest hatred." [19] (*See sidebar, p. 420.*)

As U.S. and European civil rights groups monitor anti-Semitism, here are

Anti-Semitic Incidents Surged in Early 2017

The number of anti-Semitic incidents in the United States — including vandalism and harassment — jumped to 541 in the first quarter of this year — up from 291 in the same period in 2016. However, many of the 2017 incidents were fake bomb threats allegedly made by two individuals. On an annual basis, assaults declined — from 56 in 2015 to 36 in 2016 — but harassment and vandalism rose, especially in the last quarter of 2016.

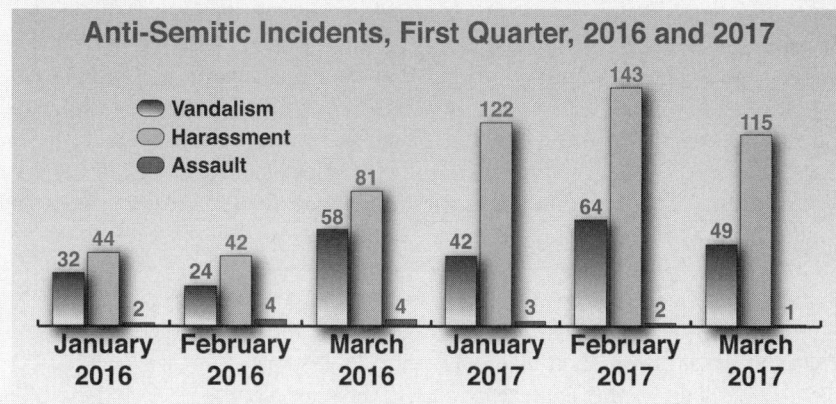

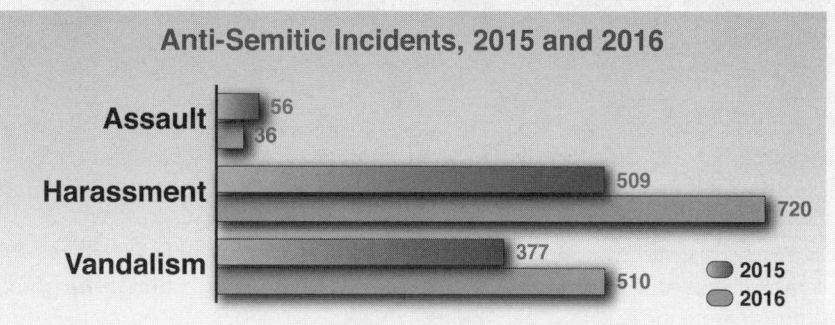

Source: "U.S. Anti-Semitic Incidents Spike 86 Percent So Far in 2017 After Surging Last Year, ADL Finds," Anti-Defamation League, April 24, 2017, http://tinyurl.com/lk2zj2d

some questions being debated in academia, national and state legislatures and the public arena:

Is anti-Semitism on the rise?

Civil rights groups say the United States has experienced an unprecedented number of hate crimes directed at Jews since the Trump presidential campaign. According to the ADL, nearly a third of the 1,266 anti-Semitic incidents last year occurred during the last two months after Trump's election.

As an example of the role the election played, the ADL cited graffiti in

Denver last year that said: "Kill the Jews, Vote Trump." [20]

The surge in incidents continued into the first three months of this year, the league said, spiking 86 percent compared to last year's first quarter. By late March, however, most of that spike was attributed to bomb hoaxes allegedly perpetrated by two disturbed individuals. [21] Israeli authorities charged an Israeli-American teenager, Michael Ron David Kadar, 18, with making hundreds of bomb threats around the world, and a man in St. Louis was charged with making a handful of them. [22]

Nevertheless, says the ADL's Greenblatt, the total number of anti-Semitic incidents spiked, even discounting the fake bomb threats, and the two individuals were not responsible for the cemetery desecrations.

Ryan Lenz, a spokesman for the SPLC, agrees with the charge that Trump's campaign contributed to the rise in anti-Semitism, citing the use of an age-old anti-Semitic stereotype in what he calls Trump's "horrifying final campaign ad, where a series of Jewish financial figures were identified by name as part of a global secret banking cabal."

Lenz adds, "While we're not saying Donald Trump caused this, he is part of a giant mix of racist expression that somehow has been legitimized."

Oren Segal, director of the ADL Center on Extremism, says such incidents "need to be seen in the context of a general resurgence of white supremacist activity in the United States." [23] In the month after the election, more than 1,000 bias crimes were reported, mostly anti-immigrant, anti-black and anti-Muslim in nature. [24]

But U.S. anti-Semitism "may have deeper roots" than Trump-inspired hate, according to Seth Frantzman, a fellow at the Jerusalem Institute for Market Studies and the op-ed editor at *The Jerusalem Post*, both based in Israel. More than 7,000 anti-Semitic incidents occurred during President Obama's eight years in office, he pointed out. [25]

"Every six days, a Jewish person in America was being attacked in 2015, and it went largely ignored," Frantzman wrote in the Jewish newspaper *The Algemeiner* in March, at the height of the bomb scares. "On average, there were threats every day against Jews and Jewish institutions over the last eight years, and most of them did not receive headlines." [26]

Mark Oppenheimer, host of *Tablet* magazine's podcast "Unorthodox," contended that the media have focused more attention on such attacks since

Trump's victory. "My best guess is that we are facing a continued march of the low-level, but ineradicable, Jew hatred that we always live with," he wrote in February. [27]

The arrest of Kadar led George Mason University law professor David Bernstein to repeat an earlier claim that the ADL "chose to hype" the numbers; he said that would worsen racism and anti-Semitism. [28]

"There's no evidence whatsoever that there's a general increase in anti-Semitic attitudes, given the Pew survey that just came out showing Jews are the most popular religious group in the United States," says Bernstein. According to the survey, half of U.S. adults expressed warm feelings towards Jews, rating them at 67 degrees on a 0-to-100 scale, ahead of Catholics and mainline Protestants. [29]

The impact of the 2016 election aside, accurately counting anti-Semitic incidents is a challenge, partly because many police departments do not report hate crimes separately. The latest FBI statistics show that Jews were the targets in more than half of religiously motivated hate crimes in 2014 and 2015. [30]

The SPLC, which monitors hate groups, has never counted hate crimes before, so it has no previous annual statistics to compare them with, according to spokesman Lenz.

Further, methods of gathering statistics on anti-Semitic hate crimes differ around the world, with some countries and organizations showing a decline while others show an uptick.

For instance, the Kantor Center in Tel Aviv, which collects data on anti-Semitism from 40 countries, found violent anti-Semitic incidents worldwide falling 12 percent in 2016 to 361, a 10-year low. And the French government reported a 61 percent plunge in all forms of anti-Semitism last year, which the center largely attributed to increased security after recent terrorist attacks.

However, contrary to claims from right-wing groups, newly arrived Mus-

lim immigrants have not been responsible for rising anti-Semitic incidents, such as a 16 percent uptick in Berlin, said the center. "The perpetrators continue to be the radical circles of the previous Muslim immigrants" including European-born children of Muslim immigrants, and the extreme right, the center said. New immigrants, it said, are "busy surviving," looking for work and learning a new language. [31]

Anti-Semitic hate crimes rose in some countries, including in Austria and Britain, where they reached a record last year, according to London's Community Security Trust. [32] (*See sidebar, p. 422.*)

In addition, the Kantor Center reported "a widespread increase" in anti-Semitism on the web that "cannot be quantified." [33]

In 2016, an anti-Semitic message was posted every 83 seconds in cyberspace, mostly on Twitter, according to the World Jewish Congress. [34]

"Hate against Jews is not really dropping; it has just moved" onto the internet, where enforcement is "less well developed," said European Jewish Congress President Moshe Kantor, after whom the Kantor Center is named. As hate has migrated online, he said, the sense of security in Jewish communities "remains fragile." [35]

Is opposition to Israel a form of anti-Semitism?

Scholars and activists have debated for more than a decade whether opposition to the state of Israel is a new form of anti-Semitism. Bernard Lewis, a professor emeritus of Near Eastern Studies at Princeton University, used the term "the new antisemitism" in a 2004 paper [36]

Since then, the concept has been adopted by the State Department and some prominent scholars, but it remains highly controversial. Natan Sharansky, a Soviet dissident who became an Israeli politician, said the new anti-Semitism could be recognized by using his "three Ds" test: Demonization (comparing the Israelis to Nazis); a double standard (singling Israel out for its alleged human-rights violations when other countries are far worse); and delegitimization (denying Israel's right to exist). [37]

Since then Sharansky's three Ds have been incorporated into the State Department's "working definition" of anti-Semitism. [38] The formulation also was adopted last year as a non-legally binding definition by Britain and by the International Holocaust Remembrance Alliance — 31 nations committed to Holocaust education. [39]

The question of when criticism of Israel becomes anti-Semitism has been at the heart of two recent controversies: proposals to include the State Department definition in federal and state legislation and claims that the Boycott, Divestment and Sanctions (BDS) movement is anti-Semitic.

The movement is a worldwide campaign to get governments, universities and individuals to boycott Israeli products and divest themselves of investments in Israeli holdings as a way to protest Israel's 50-year occupation of the West Bank and Gaza territories. The debate over the boycott centers on whether the movement is just aimed against Israel's treatment of Palestinians living in the territories or is also a protest against Israel's existence.

Last year the Senate passed a bill to require the federal government to use the State Department definition of anti-Semitism when investigating discrimination complaints on college campuses. Known as the Anti-Semitism Awareness Act, the measure died without reaching the House floor but is expected to be reintroduced. Several prominent Jewish groups strongly support it, but the American Civil Liberties Union (ACLU) says it infringes on free speech. [40] Several state legislatures also have considered similar bills.

Kenneth Marcus, president of the Washington-based Louis D. Brandeis Center, which fights anti-Semitism, says the bill is needed because harassment of Jewish students on college campuses has been rising and is often associated with BDS demonstrations.

AMCHA, a college watchdog group named after the Hebrew word for "your people" or "grassroots," reported a 45 percent increase in anti-Semitic incidents on campuses in the first half of 2016, to 287, over the same period the previous year. [41]

Messages of sympathy, "We are all Jews," hang outside a kosher grocery store in Paris where four people were killed in a terrorist attack in 2015. Muslim extremists have been implicated in several deadly terrorist attacks in recent years on Jewish gathering places in Europe, including a Copenhagen synagogue, the Jewish Museum in Brussels and a Jewish school in Toulouse, France.

But according to Mitchell Bard, executive director of the American-Israeli Cooperative Enterprise, a nonprofit that aims to strengthen relations between the two countries, more than a third of the events were lectures, "echo chambers attended by the like-minded," and some were peaceful protests against Israeli policies. "[W]hile some guerrilla theater meant to highlight Israel's alleged abuses is disturbing, it is not de facto anti-Semitic," he wrote. [42]

Marcus says the legislation is needed to deal with "campuses where there's a large amount of severe pervasive hostility to Jews, not just in protest activities but threats, vandalism and physical assaults — where the perpetrators often hide behind the notion that they're merely anti-Zionist." (Historically Zionism referred to the movement to establish a Jewish homeland in Israel; in modern times, it usually refers to support for the modern state of Israel.)

However, Kenneth S. Stern, who helped draft the original definition of anti-Semitism for a European monitoring group, strongly opposes the congressional legislation. The three Ds were intended to help countries collect data on anti-Semitic acts by using a uniform definition, says Stern, who is now executive director of the Justus and Karin Rosenberg Foundation, which combats anti-Semitism. "That's quite different from using it as a way to chill discussion on college campuses," he says.

Some Jewish groups have used the definition to try to stop protests against Israel's treatment of Palestinians, he says, such as the annual "Apartheid Week" held on many campuses or debates over the BDS movement. If the bill becomes law, university administrators would likely shut down such protests and debate to avoid losing federal funding or being sued for discrimination, he says.

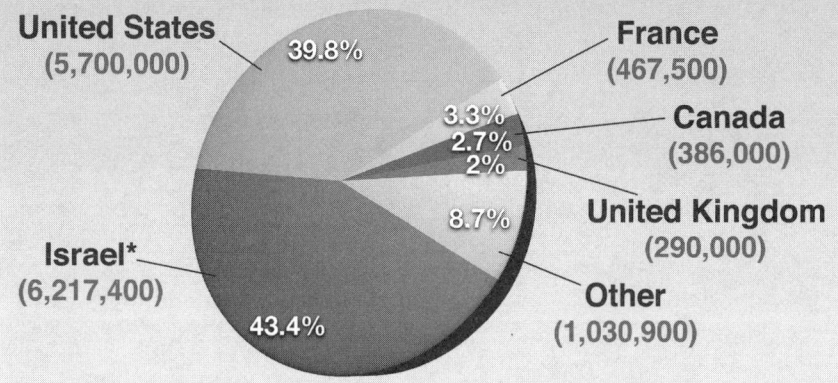

Israel, U.S. Have Biggest Jewish Populations

More than 90 percent of the global Jewish population lives in just five countries, with Israel and the United States home to the largest numbers by far.

Countries With Largest Jewish Populations and Their Percentage of World Jewish Population, 2015

United States (5,700,000) — 39.8%

France (467,500) — 3.3%

Canada (386,000) — 2.7%

United Kingdom (290,000) — 2%

Other (1,030,900) — 8.7%

Israel* (6,217,400) — 43.4%

* Includes Jewish residents in East Jerusalem, the West Bank and the Golan Heights.

Source: "Antisemitism Worldwide 2015," Tel Aviv University Kantor Center, p. 66, http://tinyurl.com/keubxwk

Doing so would shut down a chance to develop a deeper understanding of what actually constitutes anti-Semitism, Stern says.

Yet some who are troubled by the "new anti-Semitism" say they do not oppose criticism of Israeli policies but draw a line when it evolves into opposition to Israel's existence. In a recent essay entitled "Why present-day 'anti-Zionism' is anti-Semitic," Bernard Harrison, emeritus professor of philosophy at the University of Utah, defined anti-Zionism as "political anti-Semitism," because it aims to bring about the destruction of Israel. [43]

The ADL's Greenblatt echoes that view. The BDS movement is "a global effort designed to isolate and punish Israel and end the Jewish state," he says, "denying solely to the Jewish people a universal right of self-determination."

However, Liz Jackson, a staff attorney at Palestine Legal, a group that litigates on behalf of Americans advocating for Palestinian rights, says she does not see opposition to Israel's existence as anti-Semitic. She does not believe in a separate state for Jews, she says, even though she is Jewish.

"Jews have to be safe everywhere in the world; not in just one country," she says. "You can't have a democratic society which privileges one religious group above another; anti-Jewish hatred has nothing to do with that."

In England, a similar debate is raging over the Conservative government's adoption of the State Department definition of anti-Semitism. Jewish groups supporting Palestinian rights say it could chill speech. [44]

The question of whether Israel should exist is a legitimate political argument, says Naomi Wayne, an Executive Committee member of the London-based Jews for Justice for Palestinians. "Was Israel founded in compliance with international law? People have different . . . views. What is wrong with having those debates?" she asks.

Should online anti-Semitic speech be further restricted?

In a YouTube video entitled "Jews Admit Organizing White Genocide," former Ku Klux Klan Imperial Wizard David Duke says "Zionists" are "ethnically cleansing" Israel of Palestinians and planning "to do the same thing" in Europe and America by promoting the immigration of non-whites. [45]

That video triggered controversy in Britain after a Parliamentary committee investigating hate crimes recently flagged it to Google, which owns YouTube. However, Google vice president Peter Barron told the committee his company had not removed the video because it did not meet the company's standards for speech so objectionable it should be blocked. [46]

The committee's chair, Yvette Cooper, was incredulous. "You allow David Duke to upload an entire video which is all about malicious and hateful comments about Jewish people. How on Earth is that not a breach of your own guidelines?" [47]

Cooper's frustration is shared by groups fighting anti-Semitism in Europe and the United States, where online anti-Semitism is becoming increasingly hard to monitor or control. In fact, the Duke video was just one of more than 200 anti-Semitic YouTube videos discovered by a *Times of London* investigation. [48] In the United States, an ADL investigation found more than 2.6 million anti-Semitic tweets between August 2015 and July 2016, many directed at Jewish journalists. [49]

Most of the 28 EU countries ban hate speech, but debate rages over how to apply those laws to the fast-changing world of online interactions. The major hosting companies — Google, Facebook and Twitter — are based in the United States, where hate speech is constitutionally protected except when used to incite imminent violence and in other narrow circumstances. [50]

Thus, regulating the borderless internet requires negotiation between American companies and the European Union or its members. [51] Under a voluntary agreement with the EU, Google and other major media companies have agreed to review and remove illegal hate speech within 24 hours after it has been identified by an internet user. [52]

Critics say Twitter and Facebook have been even less responsive. In Germany, a recent survey by the Justice Ministry found that Twitter deletes only 1 percent of offensive content, and Facebook, about half. [53]

In response, and due to politicians' concerns that "fake news" and hate speech could sway upcoming elections, Germany became the first EU country to impose clear guidelines for penalizing online hate speech in April, when the cabinet approved controversial new fines for such speech. The law imposes fines of up to 50 million euros ($53 million) for social media companies that do not remove hate speech within 24 hours for clearly illegal content, as defined by German law, and within seven days in more ambiguous cases. [54]

The tech industry and civil liberties groups oppose the measure. Human Rights First has called it "a dangerous abridgement of free speech rights" that would embolden authoritarian governments to suppress legitimate speech. Such a broad attempt "tends to drive those sympathetic to such ideas underground, likely reinforcing their ideology," said Erika Asgeirsson, a fellow at Human Rights First. And clamping down on social media "will just change the means of dissemination." [55]

"We don't need more restrictions," says Barbora Bukovská, senior director for law and policy at Article 19, a London-based international group that advocates for free speech. Restricting speech of figures like Duke elevates them "to a pedestal as a hero and gives them exposure they don't deserve," she says.

Bitkom, an association representing digital companies, said the short dead-

lines and high penalties in the German law would seriously curtail free speech by forcing providers to delete doubtful content as a precaution. And the law would make "private companies rather than the courts . . . the judges of what is illegal in Germany," said a Facebook spokesman. [56]

In Britain, it is unclear whether the government will try to penalize Google under existing law or propose legislation similar to Germany's. [57] Either step would likely raise similar objections. Stephen Pollard, the editor of the London-based *Jewish Chronicle*, has said Duke's video should remain online so his assertions can be debated. Exposure of anti-Semites' lies is what "actually defeats them," he wrote. [58]

In the United States, banning online hate speech would run afoul of the First Amendment and Section 230 of the Communications Decency Act, which immunizes internet service providers (ISPs) from prosecution for content created by others. [59]

However, Rep. Smith, a senior member of the House Foreign Relations Committee, says he wants such immunity eliminated so ISPs that host speech inciting people to violence can be penalized. "I love the First Amendment, but it is not absolute," Smith says. Some websites, he says, are getting people "ginned up to commit horrific violence." [60]

Groups such as the ADL and Human Rights First say they will continue working with Google and other media companies on a voluntary basis to help improve their ability to identify hate speech.

But the "haters have honed their skills to skirt the websites' terms of service in a skillful way," says Jonathan Vick, the ADL's associate director for investigative technology and cyber-hate response. Once a Duke video is taken down, supporters repeatedly repost it under different titles, reducing the exercise to a game of "whack-a-mole," he says. ∎

BACKGROUND

'Blood Libel'

Anti-Semitism has endured for centuries and been almost universal — causing Jews to be repeatedly expelled from their home countries and to become the target of unparalleled levels of violence. Anti-Semitism has long been rooted in Christian teachings that Jews killed Jesus Christ, although many Christian leaders, including recent popes, have disavowed that view. [61]

One of the oldest slanders about Jews — that they killed Christian children as part of a ritual murder — originated in 12th-century Europe. The fabricated story that a young Christian boy in Norwich, England, had been killed by Jews for a religious ritual would become one of the most common incitements to anti-Jewish riots and killings during the Middle Ages.

Partly as a result of this "blood libel," Christians increasingly saw Jews as evil; in many countries Jews were forced to live apart and wear special clothing or badges to alert strangers to the dangers they supposedly posed, such as starting plagues or poisoning wells. [62]

In Europe riots against Jews erupted even as they were denied equal rights with Christians. Jews were barred from owning land and from craft guilds, forcing them to depend on money-lending or commerce, leading to the stereotype of the Jew as a greedy money-lender.

In the first large-scale deportation of Jews from a European country, King Edward expelled all Jews from England in 1290, ending their presence there for 400 years. In 1306 and 1394 Jews were expelled from France and over the next 150 years from Hungary, Austria, Lithuania and various German localities. Jews were expelled from Spain in 1492. Jews escaping Catholic persecution in

Brazil in 1654 became the first Jewish settlers in North America. [63]

During the French Revolution in 1791, Jews were granted full equal rights based on the radical idea that citizenship should be granted without regard to religion or ethnicity.

"In the 19th century, France was the one country where Jews faced no legal obstacles to social and economic integration," says Maurice Samuels, director of the Yale Program for the Study of Antisemitism and author of *The Right to Difference: French Universalism and the Jews* (2016). By contrast, he notes, some American states such as New

By the late 19th century, most of continental Europe had enacted full Jewish emancipation, but that roused resentment — most famously in a German journalist and Jew-hater, Wilhelm Marr. In 1879, he coined the term "anti-Semitism" declaring himself a proud "anti-Semite." Like the Nazis later, Marr saw the Jews as a threatening race that had seized control of the German economy and society, and he argued that the only solution was their forced removal from Germany. He used the term "Semite" for Jews, according to historians, because it sounded scientifically neutral and modern. [64]

cities. The so-called Dreyfus Affair became a watershed event for French Jews, who felt increasingly vulnerable. Dreyfus' innocence was not officially recognized until 1906.

Herzl, a secular Jew, decided that if anti-Semitism was so entrenched in the capital of the European Enlightenment, Jews could never assimilate in Europe. In 1907 he organized the First Zionist Congress in Basel, Switzerland, which voted to establish a "publicly and legally secured home" for the Jews in the geographic region between the Mediterranean Sea and the Jordan River known as Palestine. [65]

In Herzl's utopian vision of a Jewish homeland, he imagined that Arabs in Palestine would welcome the gifts of science brought by the Jews. But Arab opposition to the influx of Jews only hardened over time, leading to the development of the Palestine national liberation movement.

Members of Jewish groups and their supporters protest in Beverly Hills, Calif., on Dec. 4, 2016, against President-elect Donald Trump for what they saw as his failure to condemn a spate of anti-Semitic incidents and his hiring of Stephen Bannon as his chief strategist. Bannon, the former head of Breitbart News, has called the website "a platform for the alt-right," referring to the alternative right, which includes anti-Semitic and white nationalist groups.

Hampshire, until 1877, still barred Jews from holding public office, even though the Constitution granted them equal rights at the federal level.

Compared to France, he says, "there was prevailing anti-Semitism in American life that lasted to the 1960s — quotas at universities, de facto exclusion from law firms and corporations, and housing covenants," which barred Jews from buying or renting in certain neighborhoods. They were also excluded from private schools and clubs and hotels.

Some Jewish intellectuals began to wonder if they were welcome in Europe. Theodor Herzl, an Austro-Hungarian Jewish journalist for a Viennese newspaper, covered the notorious 1894 trial of Capt. Alfred Dreyfus, a French Jew falsely accused of spying for the Germans. During the trial Herzl witnessed anti-Jewish demonstrations in Paris, during which cries of "death to the Jews" were common; Jewish businesses, synagogues and homes were attacked and anti-Jewish riots erupted in about 70

Fabricated Charge

The elaborate forgery known as the "Protocols of the Learned Elders of Zion" is the most infamous document to libel the Jews. It purportedly comprised the minutes from a conference of Jewish groups plotting a takeover of the world. It first appeared in Russia between 1903 and 1905, concocted by the Russian secret police as part of a campaign against the Jews. In 1921, the *Times of London* exposed the tract as a fraud, showing how the author had copied fictional works to create it. [66]

However, "The Nazis saw its value immediately," as evidence of an alleged Jewish conspiracy theory, wrote Stephen Eric Bronner, a professor of political science at Rutgers University. "The Jew is not simply a capitalist or a communist revolutionary, but the Jew is now any enemy required by the anti-Semite," Bronner wrote. [67]

In the United States, automobile

Continued on p. 420

Chronology

Middle Ages-19th Century

Ritual-murder rumors incite pogroms; Jews are persecuted during Spanish inquisition.

1144
"Blood libel" claim that Jews murder Christian children for religious ritual emerges in England.

1290
Jews expelled from England.

1492-1498
Jews expelled from Spain, then Portugal and France.

1654
Jewish families arrive in New Amsterdam (later called New York), after fleeing Portuguese persecution in Brazil.

1791
During French Revolution France gives Jews equal rights.

1879
German journalist Wilhelm Marr coins term "anti-Semitism."

1894-99
Capt. Alfred Dreyfus, a French Jew, is falsely accused of treason. Affair radicalizes journalist Theodor Herzl, who later leads Zionist movement.

1900s-1960s

Immigration laws aim to keep Jews out of the United States; Nazis kill 6 million Jews. Holocaust enters public consciousness.

1903
"Protocols of the Learned Elders of Zion," a hoax claiming a Jewish plot for world domination, published in Russia.

1907
First Zionist Congress in Basel, Switzerland, votes to establish Jewish homeland in Palestine, which later becomes Israel.

1920
Industrialist Henry Ford serializes "Protocols of Zion."

1924
National Origins Law closes United States to most Jewish immigrants.

1942
Mass gassings begin at Nazis' Auschwitz-Birkenau camp. Vichy government deports 15,000 French Jews to Auschwitz.

1945
World War II ends. Allied troops liberate German concentration camps. An estimated 6 million Jews have died at Nazi hands. Nuremberg war crimes trials begin.

1948
Jewish community in Palestine proclaims state of Israel.

1962
Israelis find former Nazi official Adolf Eichmann guilty of crimes against the Jewish people; he is hanged.

2000-Present

Jews become targets of terrorist attacks in Europe and rising anti-Semitism in the United States and Britain.

2000
Second Palestinian uprising ("intifada") spurs anti-Semitic crimes in Europe. . . . European Union begins tracking anti-Jewish incidents.

Sept. 11, 2001
Islamist terrorists fly hijacked passenger planes into the World Trade Center in New York and the Pentagon, sparking rumors that Jews knew about it in advance.

2002
Pakistani Islamist terrorists kill *Wall Street Journal* reporter Daniel Pearl.

2012
French Muslim attacks Jewish school in Toulouse, France, killing four.

2014
Four people killed at Jewish Museum of Brussels in Belgium.

2015
Islamist gunman kills four people in kosher grocery in Paris after attack on *Charlie Hebdo* magazine (Jan. 9). . . . Gunman opens fire on Copenhagen synagogue, killing one (Feb. 14).

2016
Record number of anti-Semitic attacks reported in Britain; U.S. Senate passes Anti-Semitism Awareness Act, defining anti-Semitism as including "demonization" of Israel; it dies in House.

2017
More than 100 bomb threats at U.S. Jewish institutions raise fear of growing anti-Semitism; Jewish Israeli-American man arrested, alleged to have made most of the threats. . . . Anti-Defamation League reports spikes in anti-Semitic incidents in United States in 2016 and 2017, citing increases in white supremacist activity by groups following presidential election campaign. . . . Violent attacks on Jews decline worldwide, Tel Aviv University reports, citing beefed-up security.

Anti-Semitism Persists in an Unsettled Poland

"We didn't resolve the problem of what Poles did to Jews."

The image of an ultra-orthodox Jew being burned in effigy at an anti-refugee rally in Poland in 2015 outraged many people around the world — and puzzled them as well. Why were Jews being blamed for the influx of refugees — most of them Muslims — arriving in Europe from Syria and elsewhere?

During his trial last November for inciting hatred by burning the effigy, Polish businessman Piotr Rybak, one of the rally's organizers, explained that his straw man represented billionaire Jewish-American financier George Soros. [1]

Poles with anti-Muslim views "generally blame Jews for being liberals, and there are a lot of conspiracy theories about liberals such as George Soros bringing Muslims to Europe," explains Michal Bilewicz, director of the Center for Research on Prejudice at the University of Warsaw. A survey released by the center in January, he says, showed anti-Semitism rising between 2014 and 2016 "fueled by the anti-Muslim panic that spread towards other religious and ethnic groups — for example Jewish people."

The survey also found that fewer Poles today consider anti-Semitic statements offensive. For example, a media reference to Jews as "scumbags" was offensive to only 43 percent of young people in 2016 — down from 66 percent in 2014. [2]

Bilewicz attributes the rise in anti-Semitism to an increase in anti-Semitic and right-wing rhetoric online. More than 90 percent of young people have daily contact on the internet with hate speech — against Roma (gypsies), Muslims and Jews, he says. And in a survey of 18- to 35-year-olds a week before Poland's October 2015 parliamentary elections, he found that most young voters were supporting "extremely conservative, anti-immigrant and xenophobic" political parties.

It has long been a mystery why anti-Jewish attitudes persist in a country where few Jews remained after World War II. Most of Poland's 3 million Jews were murdered in the Holocaust. [3] About 300,000 Jews survived, but the majority of them left the country after the war or never returned to their homes as word spread of Poles killing returning Jews. Most emigrated to Central Europe, the United States or Israel. [4] According to the last census, only about 10,000 Jews live in Poland, out of a population of 38 million, but there could be up to 20-30,000, says Bilewicz, because "it's a society where not a lot of people are open about their Jewish identity."

Poles have struggled to come to terms with the Holocaust and their role in it. A flare-up arose recently after a 2015 article by Polish-born Princeton historian Jan T. Gross, who wrote that Poles killed more Jews than Germans during the war. [5] The Polish public prosecutor has been investigating whether to charge Gross with "insulting the Polish nation," a crime punishable by up to three years in prison. [6]

In addition, a proposed law would make it a crime, also with a maximum three-year prison sentence, to say Poles were complicit in the murder of Jews during the Holocaust. [7] In his 2001 book *Neighbors*, Gross described how Polish citizens of the town Jedwabne killed their Jewish neighbors in 1941 by corralling up to 1,600 men, women and children into a barn and setting it on fire. And Gross' 2006 book *Fear* described the 1946 massacre by Poles of Jews returning to their homes in the city of Kielce after the war. [8]

Gross told the *Haaretz* newspaper that he would welcome the chance to defend his research in court, but blamed the push to prosecute him on the right-wing conservative government elected in Poland in 2015. "This strange regime works very hard on falsification of history," he said. [9]

These days, Poles are mainly interested in hearing about Polish heroes who risked their lives to save Jews, not those who killed them, says Anna Bikont, a journalist for Poland's largest paper, *Gazeta Wyborcza*. "It's all about the pride of Poland," she says. "You use Jews only to say how we [Poles]

Continued from p. 418

manufacturer Henry Ford was the strongest booster of the "Protocols." In 1920, he began serializing them in his newspaper, *The Dearborn Independent.* American Jews tried to persuade him it was a forgery, and in 1921 President Woodrow Wilson signed a letter denouncing *The Independent* for its anti-Semitic campaign. [68]

But the "Protocols" continued to be popular, contributing to a rise in anti-Semitism in the United States. In May 1924, President Calvin Coolidge signed the National Origins Act, effectively closing the United States to most Jewish immigrants, particularly those from eastern and southern Europe. [69]

The term Holocaust did not come into use until several years after World War II ended. In 1943, Jews were barely mentioned in Allied propaganda. [70]

Soon after the war's end, it was widely known that the Germans had killed 6 million Jews during World War II, and 21 Nazi Party leaders were tried for war crimes in Nuremberg, Germany, in 1945 and 1946. But European Jewry's fate under the Nazis did not enter European public consciousness until the 1960s, when Israel tried Nazi official Adolf Eichmann and Germany tried former Auschwitz guards, said historian Tony Judt in his book *Postwar.* [71]

Then in 1979, the acclaimed 1978 American TV miniseries "Holocaust," starring Meryl Streep, was shown in Germany and watched by half of the German population. During discussion forums following each of the four episodes, some 10,000 phone calls poured in from viewers. For many Germans, the series was

saved them . . ., how we were brave and fantastic. We have such a bad attitude towards immigrants because we didn't resolve the problem of what Poles did to Jews."

The proposed law is aimed at Gross and writers like herself, says Bikont, whose forthcoming book about Irena Sendler, a Pole who saved 2,500 Jewish children from the Warsaw Ghetto, describes those efforts as a lonely struggle amidst Poles who wanted to denounce or kill Jews. [10] "For my new book, I could theoretically be sentenced," Bikont says.

Scholars around the world protested the news that Gross was under prosecutorial investigation. [11] And the proposed legislation, widely condemned as historical censorship, is unlikely to pass, according to Maciej Kozlowski, a former Polish ambassador to Israel who teaches Holocaust history at Collegium Civitas university in Warsaw. But it could discourage writers and scholars from publishing on the controversial topic, Bikont says.

Although Bilewicz's survey has found growing anti-Semitic attitudes, Michael Schudrich, the American-born Chief Rabbi of Poland, says he hasn't sensed any recent upsurge in overt anti-Jewish behavior. Thousands of Jewish visitors come to Poland every year, he says, but "there are almost no acts of anti-Semitism."

Schudrich presides over a small but growing community of about 700 Jewish families in Warsaw, many of them converts from Catholicism. "I have people still coming to me saying, 'I discovered three months ago my grandfather is Jewish. What do I do?' "

Poland's Jewish community has a future, Schudrich maintains, "and that couldn't be said 20 years ago."

— *Sarah Glazer*

Edward Mosberg, a Holocaust survivor from New Jersey, and his granddaughter participate on April 24 in the annual March of the Living between Auschwitz and Birkenau, the sites of two former Nazi death camps in Poland. The Polish people in recent years have struggled to come to terms with their role in the Holocaust.

[1] "Polish man jailed for burning effigy of ultra-Orthodox Jew," *The Times of Israel*, Nov. 21, 2016, http://tinyurl.com/m77zmd6. The effigy-burning occurred in Wroclaw, Poland, in November 2015. The sentence was reduced from 10 months to three months by a district court in April. See "There is a verdict for burning a Jewish puppet on a Wroclaw Market," *Newsweek*, April 13, 2017, http://tinyurl.com/kewgqf4.

[2] Don Snyder, "Anti-Semitism Spikes in Poland — Stoked by Populist Surge against Refugees," Reuters, Jan. 24, 2017, http://tinyurl.com/ml9ygtt.

[3] "Polish Victims," *Holocaust Encyclopedia*, U.S. Holocaust Memorial Museum, http://tinyurl.com/n5dycy8.

[4] Yad Vashem, "Frequently Asked Questions: In what condition were the Jews in Germany and Poland after the liberation?" http://tinyurl.com/l3xnd3x.

[5] Jan T. Gross, "Eastern Europe's Crisis of Shame," Project Syndicate, Sept. 13, 2015, http://tinyurl.com/n55ayro.

[6] Ofer Aderet, "Historian May Face Charges in Poland for Writing that Poles Killed Jews in World War II," *Haaretz*, Oct. 30, 2016, http://tinyurl.com/h7wx5s2.

[7] "Testimony of Mark Weitzman," Simon Wiesenthal Center, Subcommittee on Africa, Global Health, Global Human Rights, and International Organizations, House Committee on Foreign Affairs, March 22, 2017, p. 3, http://tinyurl.com/l4362ut.

[8] Alex Duval Smith, "Polish move to strip Holocaust expert of award sparks protests," *The Observer*, Feb. 14, 2016, http://tinyurl.com/lv6wd6z.

[9] "Historians May Face Charges," *op. cit.*

[10] Anna Bikont, *Sendlerowa: In Hiding* (forthcoming).

[11] "Historian May Face Charges in Poland for Writing that Poles Killed Jews in World War II," *op. cit.*

"an emotional introduction, the first encounter with the almost incomprehensible horrors of the Nazi regime," according to Jewish historian Julius H. Schoeps. [72]

Afterward, the word "Holocaust" entered common usage in Germany, and Germans became "among the best-informed Europeans on the subject of the Shoah [Hebrew for Holocaust] and at the forefront of all efforts to maintain public awareness of their country's singular crime," according to Judt. [73]

Meanwhile, the French did not acknowledge their wartime guilt in sending Jews to their death until 1995, when President Jacques Chirac admitted that the French helped to round up nearly 13,000 Jews — more than 4,000 of them children — for deportation to Auschwitz in July 1942.

Resurging Hostility

Much of the anti-Semitism that emerged in the 1990s and 2000s can be traced to the proclamation establishing the state of Israel by the Jewish community in Palestine on May 14, 1948. The U.N. General Assembly had tried to partition the territory into Jewish and Arab states in 1947, but the Arab League and Palestinian institutions rejected the plan. [74]

Israel's Arab neighbors immediately declared war, resulting in hundreds of thousands of Palestinian refugees fleeing to neighboring Jordan, Lebanon and Syria. An equal number of Jews were driven from their ancestral homes in the region. [75]

The Six-Day War in 1967 led to Israel's occupation of Gaza and the West Bank,

Anti-Semitism Charges Roil Britain's Left

Labour Party suspends a prominent member for controversial remarks.

For the past year, Britain's opposition Labour Party, representing the country's liberal left, has been convulsed by charges of endemic anti-Semitism.

The issue came to a head in April as Labour considered whether to expel former London Mayor Ken Livingstone permanently for bringing disrepute to the party in connection with remarks he made linking Nazi leader Adolf Hitler with Zionism.

On April 4, after an 11-month inquiry, Labour's constitutional committee recommended a one-year suspension, during which Livingstone may not run for office. [1] The sanction followed a one-year suspension already imposed on him.

Livingstone's remarks came last year while defending a Labour member of Parliament, Naz Shah, against charges of anti-Semitism. In 2014 she had shared a post on Facebook proposing to "relocate" Israel to America as a "solution" to the Middle East crisis. [2]

Livingstone called the criticism against Shah "a very well-orchestrated campaign by the Israel lobby to smear anybody who criticizes Israeli policy as anti-Semitic." He told a BBC interviewer that Hitler supported Zionism "before he went mad and ended up killing 6 million Jews." [3] Zionism is the national movement to re-establish a Jewish homeland in the territory now known as Israel; since establishment of Israel in 1948, Zionism has referred to the development and protection of the Jewish nation in Israel. [4]

Livingstone apparently was referring to an agreement Hitler made in 1933 with several German Zionists to allow some Jews to emigrate to Palestine. Nazi regulations prohibited German Jews from taking their savings out of Germany. But under the agreement, the Palestinian Jewish community was allowed to buy German agricultural equipment with some of the funds blocked by the Nazis.

Jews who came to Palestine from Israel were able to "claw back a portion of their funds upon arrival," explains Emory University Holocaust historian Deborah Lipstadt. [5]

But historians dispute the idea that Hitler favored a Jewish homeland. [6] The Nazis' primary motive, it seems, was to break an economic boycott initiated by American Jews a few months' earlier. [7]

David Baddiel, a British Jewish comedian, observed that Livingstone's interpretation showed "no compassion" for this moment when the Nazis were "taking advantage of the terror and despair of fleeing refugees to get more of them to leave the country." That reflects a feeling on the left, Baddiel said, that "Jews don't quite fit into the category of The Oppressed, and so therefore don't deserve the same protections and sympathy as other minorities." [8]

"Livingstone's comments about Zionist-Nazi so-called collaboration are part of a longstanding undercurrent on the British far left of accusing Zionists of being party to the Holocaust," says Paul Bogdanor, a British writer and co-editor of the 2006 book *The Jewish Divide over Israel.*

It's not surprising, he says, that the 2015 election of leftist Jeremy Corbyn as Labour's leader coincided with "a vast outpouring of anti-Semitism among Labour's far left forces," including thousands of anti-Semitic tweets and social-media messages received by Jewish members of Parliament. Corbyn has described Hamas and Hezbollah — labeled as terrorist groups by the United States — as "friends" and argues that Palestinian refugees who left Israel in 1948 and their descendants have the right to return to Israel and reclaim their property. [9]

Last April, Labour suspended Shah for the social-media remarks she made about Israel, for which she apologized. But the media publicity about her suspension was followed by a spike of anti-Semitic incidents in May, reaching a record high for a single month, according to the Community Security Trust (CST), a London-based group that tracks such incidents. [10]

Overall the organization counted a record 1,309 anti-Semitic incidents in 2016, up 36 percent from 2015, including a record 106 violent assaults. [11]

Anti-Semitism has been growing on the right as well. The CST attributed the increase partly to an uptick in xenophobia and racist hate crimes following Brexit — Britain's vote on June 23, 2016, to leave the European Union.

"The debate at the time turned ugly, and it was a debate about who is British and who is not and who belongs . . .," says Mark Gardner, the group's communications director. "When you have that sort of language, Jews don't benefit." Hate crimes rose 41 percent in the first month after the Brexit vote, but they

where more than a million Palestinians still live under Israeli occupation today. In 1987 and 2000, Palestinian resentment erupted into violent so-called *intifadas* ("shaking off" in Arabic). [76] Anti-Semitic incidents surged in Europe after the Second Intifada.

Muslim terrorists' hatred of Jews surfaced in a spectacular way on Sept. 11, 2001, when 19 Islamist radicals flew hijacked planes into the World Trade Center in New York City and into the Pentagon, killing approximately 3,000 people. A former member of the al-Qaeda cell that planned the attack testified that New York City was targeted because it was the "center of world Jewry." A Lebanese TV station falsely claimed the Israeli secret police knew of the impending attack and warned Jews not to go to work at the trade center that day, even though 400 Jews died there. [77]

In 2002, radical Islam's anti-Semitism resurfaced when Pakistani terrorists slit the throat of American *Wall Street Journal* reporter Daniel Pearl on camera, and later decapitated him, after forcing him to say "I am a Jew." [78]

Other deadly attacks on Jews by Muslims include the 2012 attack on a Jewish school in Toulouse, France, killing a rabbi and three children, two of them his own. [79] A French Muslim, Mehdi

weren't all against Jews. News reports also cited the killing of a Polish man, anti-Polish graffiti and anti-Muslim demonstrations. [12]

"The discourse is being allowed to fester in far right, far left and Islamist circles," says Gideon Falter, chairman of the Campaign Against Antisemitism, a British charity that organizes volunteers to counter anti-Semitism through education and alerting law enforcement. "If you allow this kind of hate to fester it becomes acts of hate."

Some pro-Palestinian advocates have called the recent turmoil in the Labour Party a "witch hunt" against party members for their criticism of Israel. [13]

While Livingstone's interpretation that Hitler supported Zionism was wrong, that doesn't make Livingstone anti-Semitic, said Donald Sassoon, emeritus professor of comparative history at Queen Mary University of London, one of 32 Jewish academics and Labour Party members who signed a letter condemning the disciplinary charges. "To be anti-Semitic you have to hate Jews, believe they control the world and so on," he said. "Nothing in [Livingstone's] statement suggests that." [14]

But others say the party has not gone far enough to discipline Livingstone. Nearly half of Labour's 229 members of Parliament signed an open letter protesting the decision not to expel Livingstone from the party. "[W]e will not allow our party to be a home for anti-Semitism and Holocaust revisionism," said the letter. [15]

The controversy seems unlikely to go away. Within hours of the April 4 announcement that he was being suspended, Livingstone was repeating his assertions about Nazi-Zionist collaboration in media interviews in which he appeared far from contrite. [16]

Party leader Corbyn responded by calling for Labour's ruling executive committee to consider further action based on Livingstone's new "offensive" remarks. [17]

— Sarah Glazer

Former London Mayor Ken Livingstone received a one-year suspension from the Labour Party in Britain in connection with remarks — considered anti-Semitic — linking Adolf Hitler with Zionism.

Getty Images/Chris Ratcliffe

[1] Rowena Mason and Jessica Elgot, "Labour suspends Livingstone for another year over Hitler comments," *The Guardian*, April 5, 2017, http://tinyurl.com/kythu9l.

[2] Heather Stewart, "Naz Shah suspended by Labour Party amid anti-Semitism row," *The Guardian*, April 27, 2016, http://tinyurl.com/m9pxrue.

[3] "UK Rabbi: Nothing more offensive than Livingstone's equation of Zionism and Nazism," *Times of Israel*, April 28, 2016, http://tinyurl.com/zy3dxtt.

[4] "Zionism," Jewish Virtual Library, http://tinyurl.com/m8d84qe.

[5] Deborah Lipstadt, "End the Misuse of Holocaust History," *The Atlantic*, April 14, 2017, http://tinyurl.com/krfzvs4.

[6] This was known as the Ha'avara ("transfer") agreement. See Edwin Black, "The Holocaust," Jewish Virtual Library, http://tinyurl.com/kfenpn7.

Also see, Paul Bogdanor, "Ken Livingstone's claims are an insult to the truth," *Jewish Chronicle*, March 31, 2017, http://tinyurl.com/lr7l34c.

[7] Black, *op. cit.*

[8] David Baddiel, "Why Ken Livingstone has it so wrong over Hitler and Zionism," *The Guardian*, April 6, 2017, http://tinyurl.com/khdldo3.

[9] Paul Bogdanor, "Jeremy Corbyn is placing himself at the head of Britain's 'Palestine Solidarity' Lynch Mobs," *The Algemeiner*, Sept. 17, 2015, http://tinyurl.com/lpmbp3k.

[10] Kate McCann, "Labour Party linked to increase in anti-Semitic incidents, according to charity report," *The Telegraph*, Feb. 2, 2017, http://tinyurl.com/j2q6nvc.

[11] Community Security Trust, "Antisemitic Incidents Report 2016," p. 6, http://tinyurl.com/mzvoz3b.

[12] Community Security Trust, *op. cit.*, p. 13.

Also see, Katie Forster, "Hate Crimes Soared by 41 percent after Brexit vote," *The Independent*, Oct. 13, 2016, http://tinyurl.com/hs5wnb7.

Also see, "Brexit: Increase in Racist attacks after EU referendum," Aljazeera, June 28, 2016, http://tinyurl.com/gvxbvbf.

[13] Jonathan Cook, "Labour's witch hunt against Ken Livingstone," Free Speech on Israel, April 2, 2017, http://tinyurl.com/mcg3c9l.

[14] Koos Couve, "Ken Livingstone's comments were not anti-semitic, leading Jewish academics say," *Islington Tribune*, April 14, 2017, http://tinyurl.com/k6zv55a.

[15] Ben Kentish, "Almost half of Labour's MPs sign letter criticizing decision to allow Ken Livingstone to remain in party," *The Independent*, April 5, 2017, http://tinyurl.com/l7o9apv.

[16] See video of Ken Livingstone's remarks here: http://tinyurl.com/khdldo3.

[17] Joe Watts and Jon Stone, "Jeremy Corbyn calls meeting of Labour executive to probe fresh Ken Livingstone Nazi-Zionist comments," *The Independent*, April 5, 2017, http://tinyurl.com/mrkzkoc.

Nemmouche, who had reportedly returned from a stint with ISIS in Syria before killing four people at the Jewish Museum in Brussels in 2014, is awaiting trial in that case. [80]

After the 2015 attack on the Paris office of the satirical magazine *Charlie Hebdo*, a gunman who had pledged his allegiance to the Islamic State killed four people in a kosher grocery in Paris before being killed by police. [81]

A month later, a gunman killed a Jewish security guard at a Copenhagen synagogue during a bat mitzvah celebration. The suspected shooter, who grew up in Denmark and Jordan of Palestinian parentage, was killed during a shootout with police. [82]

The rise of right-wing parties in Europe has driven some of the growth of anti-Semitic crime in Europe, as politicians capitalize on xenophobic fear of

new immigrants. When German hate crimes doubled in 2015, right-wing extremists were responsible for 91 percent of the anti-Jewish incidents, according to the Ministry of the Interior. [83]

In April, the U.S. Justice Department filed 36 charges against David Kadar, 18, the Israeli-American arrested in connection with the recent fake bomb threats, detailing 245 threatening calls, many targeting Jewish community centers, between

January and March. Kadar appears to be linked to more than 240 hoax threats in the United States and Canada between August and December 2015. [84]

A few days later, the Israeli government indicted the teenager, whose name is under a gag order in Israel, for some 2,000 bomb threats over the past two to three years in the United States, Canada and other countries. His lawyer has said he has a brain tumor and suffers from autism. [85]   ■

CURRENT SITUATION

Criticizing Trump

President Trump has been criticized by Jewish groups for being slow to condemn the rise in anti-Semitic incidents, but he recently made two statements sharply denouncing anti-Jewish hatred.

In a video address on April 21, Israel's Holocaust Remembrance Day, Trump called the murder of 6 million Jews by the Nazis the "darkest chapter in human history," adding: "The mind cannot fathom the pain, the horror and the loss" of the Holocaust. [86] Four days later he made his comments during the U.S. Holocaust Memorial Museum's annual days of remembrance.

But those comments followed at least two missteps by his administration — the failure to mention Jews in the International Holocaust Remembrance Day statement and his press secretary Sean Spicer's inaccurate claim that Hitler had never used poison gas on his own people. [87]

More worrying, however, says Susan Corke, director of countering anti-Semitism at Human Rights First, an international human-rights organization based in New York and Washington, are reports that Trump's counterterrorism adviser, Sebas-

tian Gorka, was a sworn member of the anti-Semitic, quasi-Nazi Hungarian nationalist group, Vitezi Rend. Gorka has denied the charge. [88]

Human Rights First has asked Trump to fire him. [89] His status remained unclear at press time. [90]

In April, the State Department announced that it would appoint a special envoy to monitor and counter anti-Semitism, a position created by Congress in 2004 but that has been vacant since January. Several watchdog groups have expressed concern that Trump's proposed budget cuts and a hiring freeze could cripple the office. [91] GOP Rep. Smith, who wrote the 2004 legislation, has introduced a bill to elevate the position to that of ambassador, saying the office must be "adequately staffed and resourced." [92]

In other legislation, opposing sides are gearing up to debate the Anti-Semitism Awareness Act, expected to be re-introduced. It would require the Education Department's Office of Civil Rights (OCR) to use the State Department's definition of anti-Semitism when investigating claims of discrimination and harassment on college campuses. The controversy centers on the State Department explanation of when anti-Israel criticism crosses the line into anti-Semitism — such as "demonizing" Israel by comparing it to Nazi Germany.

Under Title VI of the Civil Rights Act of 1964, the Education Department can withhold federal funding from a university found to have discriminated on the basis of race, color, or national origin. In 2004, the office said Jewish, Sikh and Muslim students also were protected from discrimination under Title VI. [93]

Yet the Brandeis Center's Marcus, who drafted the policy while serving as an official at the OCR, says the department has not found any civil rights violation in any anti-Semitism case it has investigated. "That system just isn't working. And Congress really needs to take action," he says. The proposed law "is the best solution because it gets to the root of OCR's and the universities' problems [about how to define anti-

Semitism], while fully protecting freedom of speech and academic freedom."

Opponents of the measure say the department never found discrimination in any of these cases because there wasn't any. "Exposure to such discordant and robust expressions, even when offensive and hurtful, is a circumstance that a reasonable student in higher education may experience," the OCR said in dismissing a 2012 harassment complaint at the University of California about two anti-Israel speakers. [94]

The ACLU likely will oppose the bill, as it did last year, saying it could infringe on freedom of expression. "You don't want government making decisions about whether people have access to federal programs simply based upon their expression of political beliefs," says Michael W. Macleod-Ball, chief of staff and First Amendment counsel at the ACLU's Washington office. The organization and other opponents have complained the bill was passed without hearings or floor debate under the Senate's expedited unanimous consent procedure.

However, several prominent Jewish groups, including the ADL, strongly support the measure. Jewish students frequently say they feel uncomfortable or ostracized by demonstrations favoring boycotts of Israel or during Apartheid Week, especially if demonstrators use Nazi images or call Israelis "baby-killers" — reminiscent of the historic blood libel against Jews. "The effect is to isolate and to alienate Jews," says the ADL's Greenblatt.

Jackson of Palestine Legal, which opposes the bill, agrees that "criticism of Israeli policy often is vigorous, emotional, passionate, upsetting and uncomfortable for Jewish students; I experienced it as a Jewish student myself." But the goal of a university is "to have your ideas and world views challenged; that discomfort is not something universities should protect students from."

Legislatures in Tennessee, South Carolina and Virginia have been considering bills to require public universities

Continued on p. 426

At Issue:

Has President Trump spurred anti-Semitism in the U.S.?

ROB ESHMAN
PUBLISHER AND EDITOR-IN-CHIEF, JEWISH JOURNAL.COM AND TRIBE MEDIA CORP.

WRITTEN FOR *CQ RESEARCHER*, MAY 2017

*t*here has been an increase in anti-Semitic acts since Donald Trump's presidential campaign got underway. Nonprofit groups have documented an increase, as have government agencies such as the Los Angeles and New York City police departments. The only institution yet to weigh in is the FBI, which won't release its 2016 hate-crime statistics until year-end. Maybe the FBI will give a different picture, but as of now, anti-Semitism is worse.

To argue that Trump bears some responsibility for this is not to accuse him of being anti-Semitic. In fact, the Trump White House may be the most "Jewish" in American history. His two top advisers, daughter Ivanka and son-in-law Jared Kushner, are Jewish, as are senior officials such as Treasury Secretary Steven Mnuchin, National Economic Council Director Gary Cohn, senior adviser Steven Miller and Jason Greenblatt, special representative for international negotiations. If Trump is an anti-Semite, he's really bad at it.

But one doesn't have to be anti-Semitic to give cover to anti-Semites, and here is where Trump's campaign and administration are guilty.

During the campaign Trump refused to reject an endorsement from white supremacist David Duke. He retweeted an image of Hillary Clinton under the influence of stacks of $100 bills and a Star of David. By retweeting several posts from white supremacists, he garnered what the Southern Poverty Law Center called "unprecedented support" from this radical fringe. That support grew when Trump brought on Steve Bannon as a senior adviser. Bannon took over the website Breitbart.com and — in his words — recreated it as a "platform for the alt-right."

And these alt-right trolls unleashed their bile on Trump's Jewish critics. There has been truly unprecedented online harassment of Jewish journalists who dare criticize Trump.

"I've experienced more pure, unadulterated anti-Semitism since coming out against Trump's candidacy than at any other time in my political career," the conservative columnist Ben Shapiro wrote in the *National Review.*

Long after the campaign was over, Trump finally took a stand against this hate in his address to Congress. But he never explained why his administration left the mention of Jews out of its Holocaust Memorial Day announcement. De-Judaizing the Holocaust is a long-term goal of the radical right.

Trump an anti-Semite? No. Trump as someone who out of ignorance, instinct or connivance has used and given cover to anti-Semites? The evidence for that is strong, and unforgiveable.

DAVID E. BERNSTEIN
PROFESSOR, GEORGE MASON UNIVERSITY SCHOOL OF LAW

WRITTEN FOR *CQ RESEARCHER*, MAY 2017

*d*onald Trump has not inspired a new wave of American anti-Semitism. A Pew survey early in 2017 showed that Jews are the most admired religious group in the United States. A March Anti-Defamation League (ADL) survey shows a slight uptick in the percentage of Americans deemed anti-Semitic, but it was still near a historic low at 14 percent.

Nevertheless, some American Jews, especially among those who lean liberal politically, have been in something of an unwarranted panic over a purported surge in American anti-Semitism they attribute to Trump.

Part of this is Trump's fault. Trump has a Jewish daughter and grandchildren and a record of friendship with the Jewish community and has been an outspoken supporter of Israel, but his behavior during the campaign raised concerns that he is at best indifferent to anti-Semitism and at worst was purposely stoking it for political gain. Trump seemed to hesitate to renounce David Duke's support, failed to condemn anti-Semitic Twitter attacks on Jewish reporters and opponents, and retweeted memes with anti-Semitic origins. More generally, Trump's Euro-right style of nationalistic populism and insulting remarks about Muslims and Mexicans have raised concerns about rising intolerance against minorities, from which Jews are unlikely to be immune.

Much of the panic over anti-Semitism, however, ranged from overreaction to outright fantasy. Trump adviser Steve Bannon, for example, was widely but unfairly depicted as an anti-Semitic white nationalist. A few acts of vandalism at Jewish cemeteries, common during the Obama administration, were treated as an unprecedented outgrowth of Trumpism. A handful of alt-right provocateurs meeting in a hotel ballroom near Washington received wildly outsized media attention.

The hysteria reached a fever pitch in early 2017 when a wave of bomb threats against Jewish institutions was widely but prematurely attributed to white supremacists emboldened by the anti-Semitic environment purportedly created by Trump. In fact, the threats were the product of a psychologically disturbed Jewish Israeli and a copycat left-wing journalist angry at his girlfriend.

Unfortunately, the ADL, America's leading anti-Semitism watchdog, has fanned the flames. Leader Jonathan Greenblatt made the absurd claim that anti-Semitic discourse in the United States was at its worst level since the 1930s. Such overheated rhetoric may be good for fundraising, but it stoked unwarranted panic.

Americans, and especially American Jews, should always be vigilant about anti-Semitism. But anti-Semitism didn't disappear during the Obama years, and it hasn't suddenly become a crisis under Trump.

Continued from p. 424

or state agencies to use the State Department definition of anti-Semitism when investigating allegations of discrimination, but states do not have the power to threaten the ultimate penalty — to withdraw federal funding. The South Carolina bill passed the House. [95] A similar measure died in Virginia's short legislative session this spring. [96] Another is pending in Tennessee. [97]

International Action

Britain is one of the first countries to declare sweeping condemnation of Israel a form of anti-Semitism. The Conservative government announced the decision last December after it was agreed upon by the International Holocaust Remembrance Alliance in May 2016.

While the U.S. State Department has a similar definition, it is employed only in diplomatic efforts. The British government has said the new definition should apply to anti-Israel activities at home and was needed to "ensure that culprits will not be able to get away with being anti-Semitic because the term is ill-defined or because different organizations or bodies have different interpretations of it." [98]

Jewish groups in Britain who advocate for Palestinian rights oppose widespread adoption of the definition, citing two universities' decision to cancel their Israel Apartheid Week events in February 2017 as examples of the potential "chilling" effect of the measure. [99] The cancellations followed a letter to universities from government minister Jo Johnson just ahead of Apartheid Week saying they should have "zero tolerance" for anti-Semitism following recent anti-Semitic incidents on British campuses. [100]

While pro-Palestinian groups and some professors condemned the cancellations as suppression of free speech, the British watchdog group Campaign Against Anti-Semitism hailed them as successfully preventing expressions of anti-Jewish hatred. [101]

In April, the Austrian government joined Britain and Israel in defining anti-Semitism as including assaults on Israel's legitimacy, following reports that anti-Jewish incidents had reached a record high last year. [102]

BDS Movement

Local and national governments worldwide are writing legislation and Jewish groups are filing lawsuits aimed at blocking the Boycott, Divestment and Sanctions (BDS) movement to boycott Israeli products and academic institutions. Proponents describe the movement, launched by pro-Palestinian groups in 2005, as a protest against Israel's occupation of Palestinian territories. Opponents call it an effort to bring about the end of Israel as a Jewish state.

In the United States, 17 states have passed laws either barring government contracts with groups that support the boycott or requiring state pension funds to divest themselves of companies that support it. Several states — including Texas, Washington, Nevada and New York — are considering anti-BDS legislation, as are some local governments. [103]

The Palestine Legal group says such laws are unconstitutional, citing legal opinions that boycotts are a form of protected speech. [104] In any case, says Palestine Legal attorney Jackson, the movement is growing in popularity. "People's interest in BDS is growing," especially as the peace process between Israel and Palestine seems perpetually stalled, she says. "There is no alternative to a peaceful solution; this is the only thing out there," Jackson says.

Numerous efforts are underway on campuses to persuade universities to join the boycott, but so far no American university has agreed to divest of its Israeli investments. Since 2012, however, 51 campuses have voted on resolutions urging divestment, mostly by student governments. Slightly fewer than half have passed. [105]

Last December Fordham University in New York City denied a student group's application to form a chapter of Students for Justice in Palestine, which supports the BDS movement. Dean of Students Keith Eldredge said in rejecting the application that the movement "presents a barrier to open dialogue and mutual learning and understanding" and creates the potential for campus "polarization." [106]

Four students, represented by Palestine Legal and the Center for Constitutional Rights, sued Fordham on April 26, saying the rejection represents discrimination based on students' political viewpoint and violates the university's free-speech policies. [107]

In Britain, the government has prohibited local governments from boycotting Israeli products. [108] The Palestine Solidarity Campaign, a British organization that supports Palestinian human rights, is taking the government to court over the prohibition, calling it a threat to freedom of expression.

Campaign Director Ben Jamal says boycotts are "used across the world to oppose human rights violations and in situations where diplomatic routes have failed." He adds, "The line that it's anti-Semitic doesn't hold and is a very dangerous line, because it conflates criticism of Israel with hatred of the Jewish people and by doing so undermines the fight against racism."

U.S. associations representing professors in academic specialties, such as the American Anthropological Association, have been bitterly divided over BDS resolutions, which some critics have said would prevent Israeli scholars from participating in conferences in the United States or other two-country exchanges. Both sides have raised concerns about academic freedom. [109]

After the American Studies Association voted for an academic boycott in 2013, eight academic organizations followed suit, according to Jackson. Four professors have sued the association, saying the boycott violated the association's own rules on how votes should be conducted. [110]

However, several larger academic organizations, including the American Anthropological Association and the Modern Language Association, have rejected the boycott, and numerous university presidents have condemned it. ∎

OUTLOOK

'New Era'

The recent wave of bomb threats and cemetery desecrations created an unusual sense of uncertainty among American Jews, who until now have felt mostly comfortable in their home country compared to Jews in Europe. American Jews have rarely had to ask — as French Jews did after the 2012 attack on a Jewish school in Toulouse — whether they have a future in their own country. Nearly 7,000 Jews left France and immigrated to Israel in 2014. [111]

Perhaps the greatest fear in Europe remains the threat of another terrorist attack by radical Islamists animated by anti-Jewish hatred.

In Germany, young Muslim male refugees often hold "conspiratorial notions of Jewish power," according to Alvin H. Rosenfeld, director of the Institute for the Study of Contemporary Antisemitism at Indiana University in Bloomington, who is interviewing the refugees for a book.

Those underlying views, combined with a conservative religious upbringing, "don't mesh with liberal societies in the democratic West. It will take a generation or two to resolve," Rosenfeld says. "The last thing Germany wants, given its history, is a return of anti-Semitism. But whether Germany is successful remains to be seen."

With anti-Jewish screeds migrating to the internet, some experts fear the impact of thousands of widely shared toxic messages could be enormous.

"One person who was sitting in a basement 10 years ago using a printer to print Nazi leaflets can now reach tens of thousands with a single click," says Paul Goldenberg, national director of the Secure Community Network in New York, which works with law enforcement officials and Jewish communities to provide security against attacks.

Yet French anti-Semitism expert Chaouat predicts that a government clampdown on anti-Semitic expression, online or off, could be "counterproductive." When the French government has banned the shows of anti-Semitic comedian Dieudonné M'Bala M'Bala, it only boosts his popularity, he says. [112] "The more Dieudonné is sued, the more people go to his shows," he says.

Today's anti-Semitism is fundamentally different from that of centuries past, when it was driven by Christian teachings that Jews killed Christ, says Rosenfeld. Instead, he says, Jews now must be aware of threats from all directions — rising populist nationalist movements hostile to minorities, radicalized Muslims, far-left politicians and hate-filled cyberspace.

That increased uncertainty can give Jews an ominous feeling about the future, even in America. Rosenfeld says he was taken aback upon seeing armed security guards inside and outside of a synagogue in Boca Raton, Fla., where he recently attended services. Another worshiper told him it was now normal.

"I wasn't used to that in America," Rosenfeld says. "It told me we've entered a new era." ∎

Notes

[1] Amy Crawford, "White nationalists are targeting college campuses," Southern Poverty Law Center, May 2, 2017, http://tinyurl.com/lu4cc4c.

[2] "Reports of Hate Crimes on the Rise at American Universities," CBS News, May 3, 2017, http://tinyurl.com/m7o2bys.

[3] "ADL: White Supremacists Making Unprecedented Effort on U.S. College Campuses to Spread their Message, Recruit," Anti-Defamation League, April 24, 2017, http://tinyurl.com/jljmr5u.

[4] Todd Gutnick, email communication, Anti-Defamation League, May 4, 2017.

[5] Crawford, op. cit.

[6] Mark Potok, "The Year in Hate and Extremism," Intelligence Report, Spring 2015, Southern Poverty Law Center, http://tinyurl.com/hhfvcwj.

[7] Daniel Victor, "Muslims Give Money to Jewish Institutions that are Attacked," The New York Times, Feb. 27, 2017, http://tinyurl.com/zr5vzrp.

[8] Marcia Clemmitt, "'Alt-Right' Movement," CQ Researcher, March 17, 2017, pp. 241-264.

[9] Rachael Revesz, "Steve Bannon connects network of white nationalists at the White House," The Independent, Feb. 7, 2017, http://tinyurl.com/zwof6m2.

[10] "Study: Anti-Semitic Incidents Worldwide Doubled in 2006," Haaretz, April 15, 2007, http://tinyurl.com/n4ydxca.

[11] "Gassing Operations," Holocaust Encyclopedia, U.S. Holocaust Memorial Museum, http://tinyurl.com/n32az25.

[12] Laurel Raymond, "The Trump Team's history of flirting with Holocaust deniers," Think Progress, April 11, 2017, http://tinyurl.com/ll5cw4w.

[13] "Watch: Trump Remarks at the U.S. Holocaust Memorial Museum's National Days of Remembrance," USA Today, April 25, 2017, http://tinyurl.com/lyobqcx.

[14] "Antisemitism Worldwide 2016," Tel Aviv University Kantor Center for the Study of Contemporary Antisemitism and Racism, April 23, 2017, p. 5, http://tinyurl.com/mhwg98n.

[15] The book was: European Muslim Antisemitism: Why Young Urban Males Say They Don't Like Jews (2015).

[16] " 'France without Jews is not France,' " The New York Times, Jan. 13, 2015, http://tinyurl.com/l78yu4o.

[17] "Antisemitism Worldwide 2016," op. cit. Also see "Antisemitism Worldwide 2015," Kantor Center, May 4, 2016, http://tinyurl.com/keubxwk.

[18] Deborah Lipstadt, "End the Misuse of Holocaust History," The Atlantic, April 14, 2017, http://tinyurl.com/krfzvs4.

[19] Robert S. Wistrich, Antisemitism: The Longest Hatred (1991).

[20] "U.S. Anti-Semitic Incidents Spike 86 Percent So Far in 2017 After Surging Last Year, ADL Finds," Anti-Defamation League, April 24, 2017, http://tinyurl.com/lk2zj2d.

[21] Ibid.

[22] In early March, Juan Thompson, a former reporter was arrested and charged with fewer than a dozen of the bomb threats. See Benjamin Weiser, "Ex-reporter Charged with Making Bomb Threats against Jewish Sites," The New York Times, March 3, 2017, http://tinyurl.com/hcvz7ao.

[23] "U.S. Anti-Semitic Incidents Spike 86 Percent So Far in 2017 After Surging Last Year, ADL Finds," *op. cit.*

[24] "Hatewatch, Update," Southern Poverty Law Center, Dec. 16, 2016, http://tinyurl.com/j8asg8e.

[25] Seth Frantzman, "Why were the 7,000 Incidents under Obama Largely Ignored?" *The Algemeiner*, March 1, 2017, http://tinyurl.com/k69uexw.

[26] *Ibid.*

[27] Mark Oppenheimer, "Is anti-semitism truly on the rise in the U.S.? It's not so clear," *The Washington Post*, Feb. 17, 2017, http://tinyurl.com/kvs4jmj.

[28] David Bernstein, "19-year-old American-Israeli Jew arrested in JCC bomb threats," *The Washington Post*, March 23, 2017, http://tinyurl.com/mgh6dvm.

[29] "Americans Express Increasingly Warm Feelings Toward Religious Groups," Pew Research Center, Feb. 15, 2017, http://tinyurl.com/grkmch5.

[30] "2015 Hate Crime Statistics," FBI, http://tinyurl.com/kl854ot.

[31] "Antisemitism Worldwide 2016," *op. cit.*, pp. 5-8.

[32] Community Security Trust, "Antisemitic Incidents Report 2016," p. 6, http://tinyurl.com/mzvoz3b.

[33] "Antisemitism Worldwide 2016," *op. cit.*, p. 5.

[34] *Ibid.*, p. 8.

[35] See video at "Antisemitism Worldwide 2016," *op. cit.*

[36] Bernard Lewis, "The New Anti-Semitism," *The American Scholar*, Dec. 1, 2005, http://tinyurl.com/mgbx5qf.

[37] Natan Sharansky, "3D Test of Anti-Semitism: Demonization, Double Standards, Delegitimization," *Jewish Political Studies Review*, Fall 2004, http://tinyurl.com/lbep7tk.

[38] "What is Anti-Semitism Relative to Israel?" U.S. Department of State, http://tinyurl.com/ljysro7.

[39] "Working Definition of Anti-Semitism," International Holocaust Remembrance Alliance, Dec. 12, 2016, http://tinyurl.com/lhjxokq.

[40] Tana Ganeva, "How legitimate fear over bias-motivated crimes is generating potentially unconstitutional policies," *The Washington Post*, Dec. 7, 2016, http://tinyurl.com/ltmm98g.

[41] "Study: 45 percent spike in anti-Semitic campus incidents," *The Jewish News of Northern California*, June 29, 2016, http://tinyurl.com/lapeg63.

[42] Mitchell Bard, "Facts vs. Hysteria," *The Times of Israel*, Dec. 1, 2016, http://tinyurl.com/ny7dtnv.

[43] Bernard Harrison, "Why present-day 'anti-Zionism' is anti-Semitic," paper presented at University of Bristol-Sheffield Hallam Colloquium on Contemporary Antisemitism, Sept. 13-15, 2016.

[44] "QC's opinion: major faults with government IHRA anti-Semitism definition," Jews for Justice for Palestinians, March 27, 2017, http://tinyurl.com/kn3fxyy.

[45] "Jews admit organizing white genocide," YouTube, http://tinyurl.com/n5jndln.

[46] "Oral Evidence: Hate Crime and its Violent Consequences," House of Commons Home Affairs Committee, March 21, 2017, http://tinyurl.com/gnflr5w.

[47] Rob Merrick, "Google condemned by MPs after refusing to ban anti-Semitic YouTube video by ex KKK Leader," *The Independent*, March 14, 2017, http://tinyurl.com/mhalv5l.

[48] Mark Bridge, "Google lets anti-Semitic videos stay on YouTube," *The Times* (London), March 18, 2017, http://tinyurl.com/luyb27n.

[49] "ADL Task Force Issues Report Detailing Widespread Anti-Semitic Harassment of Journalists on Twitter during 2016 Campaign," Anti-Defamation League, Oct. 19, 2016, http://tinyurl.com/mssooan.

[50] Eugene Volokh, "No, there's no 'hate speech' exception to the First Amendment," *The Washington Post*, May 7, 2015, http://tinyurl.com/mxoblkt.

[51] "Antisemitism Worldwide 2016," *op. cit.*

[52] "European Commission and IT companies announce code of conduct on illegal online hate speech," press release, European Commission, May 31, 2016, http://tinyurl.com/jlhbcqp.

[53] "Antisemitism Worldwide 2016," *op. cit.*

[54] "German Justice minister calls for hefty fines to combat online hate speech," *DW*, April 6, 2017, http://tinyurl.com/lxe2tef.

[55] Erika Asgeirsson, "German Social Media Law Threatens Free Speech," Human Rights First, April 10, 2017, http://tinyurl.com/ljr7tbd.

[56] Emma Thomasson, "German Cabinet agrees to fine social media over hate speech," Reuters, April 5, 2017, http://tinyurl.com/mevkwy7.

[57] "Seedier Media," *The Times* (London), March 16, 2017, http://tinyurl.com/kv35ctr. Also see, "Clean up YouTube or Face Fines, Bosses Told," *The Times*, March 18, 2017, http://tinyurl.com/l3bfaap.

[58] Stephen Pollard, "Why I, editor of the Jewish Chronicle, think anti-Semites should be allowed on YouTube," *The Telegraph*, March 15, 2017, http://tinyurl.com/homrwyk.

[59] "CDA 230," Electronic Frontier Foundation, http://tinyurl.com/klr7ohb.

[60] Rep. Chris Smith is chairman of the House Foreign Affairs Committee Subcommittee on Africa, Global Health, Global Human Rights, and International Organizations. His subcommittee held a hearing, "Anti-Semitism Across Borders," on March 22, 2017, http://tinyurl.com/n7vocq4.

[61] Dennis Prager and Joseph Telushkin, *Why the Jews?* (2016), p. 3. Also see "Declaration on the Relation of the Church to Non-Christian Religions, Nostra Aetate, Proclaimed by His Holiness Pope Paul VI, on October 28, 1965," Vatican, http://tinyurl.com/k4dj.

[62] Phyllis Goldstein, *A Convenient Hatred* (2012), pp. 75-91.

[63] Prager and Telushkin, *op. cit.*, p. 4. Also see, Nathan Glazer, *American Judaism* (1957), p. 45.

[64] Robert Fine and Philip Spencer, *Antisemitism and the Left* (2017), pp. 3-4. Also see Sarah Glazer, "Anti-Semitism in Europe," *CQ Researcher*, June 1, 2008, pp. 149-181.

[65] *Ibid.*, Glazer, p. 169.

[66] Goldstein, *op cit.*, p. 250.

[67] Sarah Glazer, *op. cit.*, p. 168.

[68] Goldstein, *op. cit.*, p. 252.

[69] *Ibid.*, p. 256.

[70] See Sarah Glazer, *op. cit.*, p. 170.

[71] Tony Judt, *Postwar* (2007), p. 811.

[72] "The Emotional Impact of the Airing of 'Holocaust,' an American TV Miniseries, in the Federal Republic," Two Germanies, 1961-1989 (1979), http://tinyurl.com/kl3qh7y.

[73] Judt, *op. cit.*, p. 811.

[74] "UN Partition Plan," BBC News, http://tinyurl.com/2igr.

[75] Goldstein, *op cit.*, p. 311. Also see "The Six-Day War," Jewish Virtual Library, http://tinyurl.com/m8aqca7. Also see "Six-Day War," *Encyclopedia Britannica*, http://tinyurl.com/lt68lqg.

[76] For background, see David Masci, "Middle East Conflict," *CQ Researcher*, April 6, 2001, pp. 273-296.

About the Author

Sarah Glazer is a London-based freelancer who contributes regularly to *CQ Researcher*. Her articles on health, education and social-policy issues also have appeared in *The New York Times* and *The Washington Post*. Her recent *CQ Researcher* reports include "Privacy and the Internet" and "Decriminalizing Prostitution." She graduated from the University of Chicago with a B.A. in American history.

[77] Goldstein, *op cit.*, p. 343, and p. 3 of Foreword.

[78] "Philosopher on the trail of Daniel Pearl's Killer," *The New York Times*, Aug. 30, 2003, http://tinyurl.com/l5gl54n.

[79] Joseph Strich, "On Two-Year Anniversary of Toulouse shooting, Europe's Jews Still Wary of Terrorism," *The Jerusalem Post*, March 19, 2014, http://tinyurl.com/l57qcbd. Also see Jeffrey Goldberg, "Is it time for the Jews to leave Europe?" *The Atlantic*, April 2015, http://tinyurl.com/ksu3c6s.

[80] Alan Hope, "Jewish Museum shooting investigation complete," *Flanders Today*, April 17, 2017, http://tinyurl.com/kcrudfa.

[81] Julian Borger, "Paris gunman Amedy Coulibaly declared allegiance to Isis," *The Guardian*, Jan. 12, 2015, http://tinyurl.com/kbd5pvm.

[82] "Four charged with helping gunman attack Copenhagen synagogue," The Associated Press, *Times of Israel*, Feb. 3, 2016, http://tinyurl.com/jt3o2og.

[83] "Germany Conflicted," Human Rights First, Feb. 6, 2017, http://tinyurl.com/l8jljcr.

[84] Joseph Ax, "U.S. identifies, charges Israeli teen accused of Jewish threats," Reuters, April 21, 2017, http://tinyurl.com/kq8tm6g.

[85] "Teen accused of JCC bomb threats," *Times of Israel*, April 24, 2017, http://tinyurl.com/ka4kdk8.

[86] "Trump Condemns Anti-Semitism on Israel's Holocaust Remembrance Day," Reuters, April 23, 2017, http://tinyurl.com/mquacfc.

[87] *Ibid.*

[88] David A. Graham, "Sebastian Gorka and the White House's Questionable Vetting," *The Atlantic*, March 16, 2017, http://tinyurl.com/k8lsxfj.

[89] Dora Illei, "Sebastian Gorka's Shady Ties to Racist Groups," Human Rights First, April 11, 2017, http://tinyurl.com/kp7saar.

[90] Vivian Salama, "Trump advisor to leave White House," The Associated Press, *The Washington Post*, April 30, 2017, http://tinyurl.com/kshk7hz.

[91] "Anti-Semitism Envoy Post to be Filled, State Dept. Says," *New York Jewish Week*, April 16, 2017, http://tinyurl.com/m52n5gm.

[92] Rep. Chris Smith, press release: "Smith Introduces Legislation to Help Combat Anti-Semitism," U.S. House of Representatives, April 5, 2017, http://tinyurl.com/myjpx4o.

[93] Kenneth Marcus, "How the Government Can Crack Down on anti-Semitism on college campuses," *Politico*, Jan. 11, 2017, http://tinyurl.com/j3co77f.

[94] "Anti-Semitism complaints against two California universities are dismissed," Jewish Telegraphic Agency, Aug. 28, 2013, http://tinyurl.com/ma2r69j.

[95] Avery G. Wilks, "Anti-Semitism bill passes SC House," *The State*, March 9, 2017, http://tinyurl.com/mnype28.

[96] "Update: Victory!" *Palestine Legal*, Feb. 8, 2017, http://tinyurl.com/kaw87jv. Also see, "Controversial Anti-Semitism Bill dies in House," Jewish Telegraphic Agency, Dec. 10, 2016, http://tinyurl.com/m8hhs8r.

[97] See "Brandeis Center Calls on Tennessee Lawmakers to Combat Rising Anti-Semitism," press release, Louis B. Brandeis Center for Human Rights Under Law, March 29, 2017, http://tinyurl.com/k7vb36h.

[98] Peter Walker, "UK adopts antisemitism definition to combat hate crime against Jews," *The Guardian*, Dec. 12, 2016, http://tinyurl.com/jpdocvb.

[99] "QC's Opinion," Free Speech on Israel, March 27, 2017, http://tinyurl.com/kn3fxyy.

[100] Jasmin Gray, "Universities urged to adopt 'Zero Tolerance' Policy to Anti-Semitism Ahead of Israel Apartheid Week," *The Huffington Post*, Feb. 27, 2017, http://tinyurl.com/mrhe5wa.

[101] "Universities spark free-speech row after halting pro-Palestinian events," *The Guardian*, Feb. 27, 2017, http://tinyurl.com/ztdmn3b.

[102] Tamara Zieve, "Jewish Officials Hail Austria's Decision to Adopt Anti-Semitism Definition," *The Jerusalem Post*, April 28, 2017, http://tinyurl.com/l6xz675.

[103] "What to Know about anti-BDS legislation," Palestine Legal, April 4, 2017, http://tinyurl.com/krgqnfg.

[104] *Ibid.*

[105] "Antisemitic Divestment from Israel Initiatives Scorecard on U.S. Campuses 2012-2016," AMCHA, April 4, 2017, http://tinyurl.com/k8uk3a4.

[106] Elizabeth Redden, "Pro-Palestinian Group Banned on Political Grounds," *Inside Higher Ed*, Jan. 18, 2017, http://tinyurl.com/kdjf3cd.

[107] *Ahmad Awad v. Fordham University*, http://tinyurl.com/mhqxu6q.

[108] "Javid to place Israeli boycott restrictions on legal footing," *Public Finance*, Feb. 15, 2017, http://tinyurl.com/k8uk3a4.

[109] See Sarah Glazer, "Free Speech on Campus," *CQ Researcher*, May 8, 2015, pp. 409-432.

[110] "Federal Judge Advances Lawsuit Challenging Academia Boycotting Israel," Brandeis Center, April 4, 2017, http://tinyurl.com/kedsvun.

[111] "France without Jews is not France," *op. cit.*

[112] See Laurence Dodds, "Who is Dieudonne," *The Telegraph*, Nov. 25, 2015, http://tinyurl.com/lsmj8o5.

FOR MORE INFORMATION

AMCHA (Hebrew for "Your People" or "grassroots") Initiative, P.O. Box 408, Santa Cruz, CA 95061; www.amchainitiative.org. Investigates, documents and combats anti-Semitism on college campuses.

American Jewish Committee, 212-751-4000; www.ajc.org. Global Jewish advocacy organization.

Anti-Defamation League, www.adl.org. International organization fighting anti-Semitism, headquartered in New York City.

Community Security Trust, https://cst.org.uk/about-cst. British charity that seeks to protect British Jews from anti-Semitism; issues annual report on anti-Semitism in Britain.

Human Rights First, 75 Broad St., 31st Floor, New York, NY 10004; 202-370-3323; www.humanrightsfirst.org. International advocacy organization that monitors hate crimes in Germany and France and government policies affecting anti-Semitism.

Jewish Voice for Peace, 1611 Telegraph Ave., Suite 1020, Oakland, CA 94612; 510-465-1777; https://jewishvoiceforpeace.org. Supports Palestinian rights and the boycott against Israel.

Kantor Center for the Study of Contemporary European Jewry, Gilman Building, Room 454 C [454 Gimmel] Tel Aviv University, P.O.B. 39040, Ramat Aviv, Tel Aviv, 6139001, Israel; 972-3-6406073; http://kantorcenter.tau.ac.il. Research center that issues annual report on anti-Semitism worldwide.

Palestine Legal, 637 S. Dearborn St., 3rd Floor, Chicago, IL 60605; 312-212-0448; http://palestinelegal.org. Provides legal advice, advocacy and litigation support to those advocating justice in Palestine.

Southern Poverty Law Center, 400 Washington Ave., Montgomery, AL 36104; 888-414-7752; www.splcenter.org. Litigation and education group aimed at fighting bigotry; tracks hate crimes; has filed landmark suits against racism, anti-Semitism.

Bibliography

Selected Sources

Books

Beller, Steven, *Antisemitism: A Very Short Introduction*, Oxford University Press, 2015.

An independent scholar in Washington, D.C., discusses the history of anti-Semitism from antiquity to today, focusing on schools of philosophical thought, including nationalism and romanticism, that have been marshaled to support it.

Fine, Robert, and Philip Spencer, *Antisemitism and the Left*, Manchester University Press, 2017.

An emeritus professor of sociology at the University of Warwick, England, (Fine) and an emeritus professor in holocaust studies at the University of London (Spencer) analyze anti-Semitism on the left historically from Marxism to today's anti-Zionism.

Goldstein, Phyllis, *A Convenient Hatred: The History of Antisemitism*, Facing History and Ourselves, 2012.

Facing History and Ourselves, an educational organization in Brookline, Mass., that helps students study the Holocaust in order to put today's moral choices in perspective, produced this history from ancient times to the post-Cold War era in Europe, the Middle East and the United States.

Jewish Voice for Peace, ed., *On Anti-Semitism: Solidarity and the Struggle for Justice*, Haymarket Books, 2017.

In a collection of essays edited by a national advocacy group for Palestinian rights, academics and activists argue that criticism of Israel, including the boycott movement, does not constitute anti-Semitism.

Julius, Anthony, *Trials of the Diaspora: A History of Anti-Semitism in England*, Oxford University Press, 2010.

A British lawyer who famously headed the legal team defending historian Deborah Lipstadt against a libel suit brought by Holocaust-denier David Irving provides a comprehensive history of anti-Semitism in England.

Articles

Bikont, Anna, "Jan Gross' Order of Merit," *Tablet*, March 15, 2016, http://tinyurl.com/mnz2ajh.

A Polish journalist describes the controversy over historian Jan Gross' accounts of Poles who killed Jews during World War II.

Hankes, Keegan, "Eye of the Stormer," *Intelligence Report*, Feb. 9, 2017, http://tinyurl.com/mdnzuod.

The magazine of the Southern Poverty Law Center describes how "The Daily Stormer" became the top hate site in America.

Lipstadt, Deborah, "End the Misuse of Holocaust History," *The Atlantic*, April 14, 2017, http://tinyurl.com/krfzvs4.

A professor of modern Jewish history and Holocaust studies at Emory University and author of *Denying the Holocaust*

says politicians who manipulate Nazi history for their own ends are guilty of "soft-core" Holocaust denial — a form of anti-Semitism.

Oppenheimer, Mark, "Is anti-semitism truly on the rise in the U.S.? It's not so clear," *The Washington Post*, Feb. 17, 2017, http://tinyurl.com/kvs4jmj.

The host of *Tablet Magazine*'s podcast "Unorthodox" raises questions about whether hate crimes and anti-Semitic incidents in the United States have been rising, noting the data are often faulty.

Raymond, Laurel, "The Trump Team's history of flirting with Holocaust deniers," Think Progress, April 11, 2017, http://tinyurl.com/mbkwqck.

A blogger for Think Progress, part of the liberal Center for American Progress think tank in Washington, asserts that President Trump and his White House team have a long history of thinly veiled anti-Semitism.

Reports and Studies

"ADL Audit: U.S. Anti-Semitic Incidents Surged in 2016-2017," Anti-Defamation League, April 24, 2017, http://tinyurl.com/mro6ds7.

In its annual report, the Jewish civil rights group finds that anti-Semitic incidents in the United States surged by one-third in 2016 compared to 2015. The report also says anti-Semitic incidents spiked 86 percent in the first three months of 2017, compared to the same period last year, but about two-thirds of that was due to bomb threats attributed to two individuals. "The 2016 presidential election and the heightened political atmosphere played a role in the increase," the report says.

"Antisemitism: Overview of Data Available in the European Union, 2005-2015," European Union Agency for Fundamental Rights, November 2016, http://tinyurl.com/lsl46m9.

The European Union agency that tracks anti-Semitic incidents in each of its 28 member countries reported increased security measures and closed schools in Jewish communities in the wake of terrorist attacks in Europe in 2012, 2014 and 2015.

"Antisemitism Worldwide 2016," Kantor Center for the Study of Contemporary European Jewry, 2017, http://tinyurl.com/mv6x947.

A Tel Aviv University center issues an annual report on the level of anti-Semitism worldwide.

"Special Status Report," Center for the Study of Hate and Extremism, 2017, http://tinyurl.com/lb6dq4u.

A research center at California State University San Bernardino found that hate crimes in New York City doubled in the first four months of this year compared to the same period in 2016, led by a surge in anti-Semitic incidents.

The Next Step:

Additional Articles from Current Periodicals

BDS Movement

Ironmonger, Jon, "Concerns raised over students' unions' anti-Israel stance," BBC, April 27, 2017, https://tinyurl.com/n2mnab4.

Many Jewish students in the U.K. say the rise in support for the Boycott, Divestment and Sanctions (BDS) movement, endorsed by 17 student unions, correlates with a rise in Anti-Semitism on British college campuses. The movement is a campaign to boycott Israeli products and investments.

Turner, Camilla, "Charity Commission probes student unions over calls to boycott Israel," The Telegraph, April 27, 2017, https://tinyurl.com/k2p9jb9.

The Charity Commission, which regulates charities in England and Wales, is probing more than a dozen student unions that have endorsed the BDS movement over potential violations of charity laws.

Legislation

Hatuqa, Dalia, "BDS activists defy US moves to curb Palestine advocacy," Al Jazeera, April 12, 2017, http://tinyurl.com/lblwab5.

U.S. lawmakers introduced at least 26 bills in 2017 that would target supporters of the BDS movement, who say such bills would violate the First Amendment.

Marchant, Bristow, "Today at the SC State House: a hearing on anti-Semitism bill," The State [South Carolina], April 27, 2017, https://tinyurl.com/lvm4rrr.

Proponents of a South Carolina bill that would adopt the State Department's definition of anti-Semitism on college campuses say the measure would combat a rise in anti-Semitic incidents, but opponents say it would curtail free speech rights.

Sisk, Chas, "Tennessee Puts Off Effort To Define 'Anti-Semitism' On Campus After Students Say It's Not A Problem," Nashville Public Radio, April 5, 2017, https://tinyurl.com/m97zosj.

After some University of Tennessee-Knoxville students testified that they haven't experienced anti-Semitism on campus, state lawmakers are postponing until next year a proposal that would define anti-Semitic speech similarly to how the State Department does.

Online Hate Speech

Phillips, Kristine, "The 'hotbed of anti-Semitism' isn't a foreign country. It's U.S. college campuses, a new report says," The Washington Post, April 24, 2017, https://tinyurl.com/n3y5y3r.

Although anti-Semitic violence has been declining over the past decade, a Tel Aviv University report described college campuses across the globe as "hotbed[s] of anti-Semitism,"

with high rates of social media harassment and student protests.

Rudgard, Olivia, "Rising anti-semitism in the UK fueled by social media, report finds," The Telegraph, April 23, 2017, http://tinyurl.com/kucrctt.

A Tel Aviv University study recorded 557 anti-Semitic incidents in the United Kingdom between 2015 and 2016, almost one-fourth of them on social media.

Ziv, Stav, "Jared Kushner Targeted in Anti-Semitic Campaign Online: ADL," Newsweek, April 11, 2017, http://tinyurl.com/l9ogd39.

White nationalists are targeting Jared Kushner, President Trump's son-in-law and head of the White House Office of American Innovation, with anti-Semitic hate speech on Twitter.

Recent Incidents

"Reward Climbs to $74,000 In Philadelphia Jewish Cemetery Vandalism Investigation," 6ABC News, March 7, 2017, https://tinyurl.com/mr39sdp.

The Philadelphia Police Department announced an increased cash reward of $74,000 for information about the hundreds of headstones vandalized at a Jewish cemetery in February.

Johnson, Jenna, and Ashley Parker, "Spicer: Hitler 'didn't even sink to using chemical weapons,' although he sent Jews to 'the Holocaust center,' " The Washington Post, April 11, 2017, https://tinyurl.com/l7nbo27.

Pro-Jewish organizations called for the firing of White House Press Secretary Sean Spicer after he said Adolf Hitler "didn't even sink to using chemical weapons," despite the Nazis' use of poison gas to systematically kill millions of Jews.

In-depth Reports on Issues in the News

Are you writing a paper?

Need backup for a debate?

Want to become an expert on an issue?

For 90 years, students have turned to *CQ Researcher* for in-depth reporting on issues in the news. Reports on a full range of political and social issues are now available. Following is a selection of recent reports:

Civil Liberties
Privacy and the Internet, 12/15
Intelligence Reform, 5/15
Religion and Law, 11/14

Crime/Law
High-Tech Policing, 4/17
Forensic Science Controversies, 2/17
Jailing Debtors, 9/16
Decriminalizing Prostitution, 4/16
Restorative Justice, 2/16
The Dark Web, 1/16
Immigrant Detention, 10/15

Education
Charter Schools, 3/17
Civic Education, 2/17
Student Debt, 11/16
Apprenticeships, 10/16

Environment/Society
Native American Sovereignty, 5/17
Women in Prison, 3/17
Guns on Campus, 1/17
Mass Transit, 12/16
Arctic Development, 12/16
Protecting the Power Grid, 11/16

Health/Safety
Sports and Sexual Assault, 4/17
Reducing Traffic Deaths, 2/17
Opioid Crisis, 10/16
Mosquito-Borne Disease, 7/16

Politics/Economy
Rethinking Foreign Aid, 4/17
Troubled Brazil, 4/17
Reviving Rural Economies, 3/17
Immigrants and the Economy, 2/17
Trump Presidency, 1/17
European Union's Future, 12/16

Upcoming Reports

North Korea, 5/19/17   Pandemics, 6/2/17   Food Labeling, 6/9/17

ACCESS

CQ Researcher is available in print and online. For access, visit your library or www.cqresearcher.com.

STAY CURRENT

For notice of upcoming *CQ Researcher* reports or to learn more about *CQ Researcher* products, subscribe to the free email newsletters, *CQ Researcher Alert!* and *CQ Researcher News*: http://cqpress.com/newsletters.

PURCHASE

To purchase a *CQ Researcher* report in print or electronic format (PDF), visit www.cqpress.com or call 866-427-7737. Single reports start at $15. Bulk purchase discounts and electronic-rights licensing are also available.

SUBSCRIBE

Annual full-service *CQ Researcher* subscriptions—including 44 reports a year, monthly index updates, and a bound volume—start at $1,131. Add $25 for domestic postage.

CQ Researcher Online offers a backfile from 1991 and a number of tools to simplify research. For pricing information, call 800-818-7243 or 805-499-9774 or email librarysales@sagepub.com.

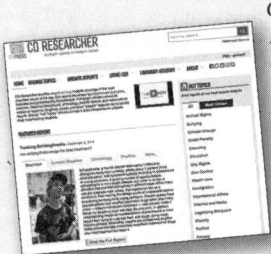

CQPRESS

CQ RESEARCHER

In-depth reports on today's issues

Published by CQ Press, an Imprint of SAGE Publications, Inc.   ***www.cqresearcher.com***

North Korea Showdown

Can a military confrontation be averted?

Tension is running high between the United States and North Korea, a family-run communist dictatorship with a record of horrific human rights abuses. One of the world's most militaristic nations, the "Hermit Kingdom" is testing increasingly powerful nuclear bombs, seeking to develop ballistic missiles capable of reaching the United States and threatening U.S. ally South Korea with a massive arsenal of artillery and other weapons. After years of attempts by U.S. presidents to rein in North Korea's nuclear ambitions through negotiations and ever-more-stringent economic sanctions, the Trump administration is vowing to eliminate the North Korean military threat. President Trump warns of the possibility of a "major, major conflict" with North Korea, and administration officials say they are considering all options. Neighboring China and Japan fear a full-scale regional war, and South Korea's new government — fearing that tens of thousands of its citizens could die in a war with the North — wants a more conciliatory approach in dealing with Pyongyang.

Ballistic missiles dominate a military parade in Pyongyang on April 16. As North Korea seeks to develop ever-more-powerful nuclear bombs and missiles capable of reaching the United States, President Trump has warned of a possible "major, major conflict" with the secretive "Hermit Kingdom."

I N S I D E THIS REPORT

THE ISSUES 435

BACKGROUND 442

CHRONOLOGY 443

CURRENT SITUATION 448

AT ISSUE.....................449

OUTLOOK 451

BIBLIOGRAPHY 454

THE NEXT STEP 455

CQ Researcher • May 19, 2017 • www.cqresearcher.com
Volume 27, Number 19 • Pages 433-456

CQ RESEARCHER

May 19, 2017
Volume 27, Number 19

THE ISSUES

435 • Is there a viable nonmilitary strategy to get North Korea to drop its nuclear weapons program?
• Is military action against North Korea a realistic option?
• Is North Korea at risk of collapse?

BACKGROUND

442 **Early Era**
The Korean Peninsula divided and reunified under multiple dynasties.

442 **Colonial Period**
Korea became more industrialized under Japan's rule.

444 **War and Aftermath**
Almost 1 million people died in the Korean War.

445 **Rising Provocations**
North Korea has periodically provoked the United States and South Korea.

447 **Nuclear Arsenal**
The North tested its first ballistic missile in 1984.

CURRENT SITUATION

448 **Trump Policies**
The administration has signaled a tough approach to North Korea.

450 **Fratricide**
The murder of Kim Jong Un's half-brother sparked questions and worries.

OUTLOOK

451 **Signs of Prosperity**
North Korea's economy seems to be improving.

SIDEBARS AND GRAPHICS

436 **North Korea Worries Its Neighbors**
The communist nation poses a major threat to regional U.S. allies.

437 **North Korea at a Glance**
The nation is barely larger than the state of Virginia.

438 **North Korea Raises Nuclear Stakes**
Nuclear bombs tested by Pyongyang have been increasingly powerful.

440 **North Korea's Economy Dwarfed by South's**
The North's GDP was 1 percent of the South's in 2015.

443 **Chronology**
Key events since 1945.

444 **Personality Cult Makes Kim a God**
"All-encompassing indoctrination" begins in early childhood.

446 **Defectors Risk Death to Escape**
"How could our country lie so completely to us?"

449 **At Issue:**
Should the U.S. tighten penalties on companies dealing with North Korea?

FOR FURTHER RESEARCH

453 **For More Information**
Organizations to contact.

454 **Bibliography**
Selected sources used.

455 **The Next Step**
Additional articles.

455 **Citing CQ Researcher**
Sample bibliography formats.

Cover: AFP/Getty Images/KCNA

EXECUTIVE EDITOR: Thomas J. Billitteri
tjb@sagepub.com

ASSISTANT MANAGING EDITORS: Kenneth Fireman, kenneth.fireman@sagepub.com, Kathy Koch, kathy.koch@sagepub.com, Scott Rohrer, scott.rohrer@sagepub.com

ASSOCIATE MANAGING EDITOR: Val Ellicott

SENIOR CONTRIBUTING EDITOR:
Thomas J. Colin
tom.colin@sagepub.com

CONTRIBUTING WRITERS: Marcia Clemmitt, Sarah Glazer, Reed Karaim, Barbara Mantel, Chuck McCutcheon, Tom Price

SENIOR PROJECT EDITOR: Olu B. Davis

EDITORIAL ASSISTANT: Anika Reed

FACT CHECKERS: Eva P. Dasher, Michelle Harris, Betsy Towner Levine, Robin Palmer

Los Angeles | London | New Delhi
Singapore | Washington DC | Melbourne

An Imprint of SAGE Publications, Inc.

SENIOR VICE PRESIDENT,
GLOBAL LEARNING RESOURCES:
Karen Phillips

EXECUTIVE DIRECTOR, ONLINE LIBRARY AND
REFERENCE PUBLISHING:
Todd Baldwin

CQ Press is a registered trademark of Congressional Quarterly Inc.

CQ Researcher (ISSN 1056-2036) is printed on acid-free paper. Published weekly, except: (March wk. 4) (May wk. 4) (July wks. 1, 2) (Aug. wks. 2, 3) (Nov. wk. 4) and (Dec. wks. 3, 4). Published by SAGE Publications, Inc., 2455 Teller Rd., Thousand Oaks, CA 91320. Annual full-service subscriptions start at $1,131. For pricing, call 1-800-818-7243. To purchase a CQ Researcher report in print or electronic format (PDF), visit www.cqpress.com or call 866-427-7737. Single reports start at $15. Bulk purchase discounts and electronic-rights licensing are also available. Periodicals postage paid at Thousand Oaks, California, and at additional mailing offices. POSTMASTER: Send address changes to CQ Researcher, 2600 Virginia Ave., N.W., Suite 600, Washington, DC 20037.

North Korea Showdown

BY DAVID HOSANSKY

THE ISSUES

When President Obama met with President-elect Donald Trump in the Oval Office after the 2016 election, Obama reportedly warned his successor that North Korea was the nation's most serious foreign policy challenge.

Indeed, Trump had scarcely been sworn in on Jan. 20 when long-simmering tension between the United States and North Korea, a nuclear power with increasingly sophisticated capabilities, threatened to escalate into armed conflict.

Within days, reports surfaced that North Korea had restarted a reactor used to make plutonium for nuclear bombs. In March, after the United States and Japan demonstrated new technology to shoot down incoming ballistic missiles, North Korea test-fired missiles in the Sea of Japan that reached within 200 miles of Japan.

In turn, the United States, South Korea and Japan dispatched high-tech missile defense ships to the region and engaged in large-scale military drills — only to have North Korea conduct additional missile tests. These included, on May 13, an intermediate-range missile that flew more than 430 miles and reached an estimated altitude of more than 1,245 miles, drawing sharp international condemnation and potentially putting U.S. military bases in Guam within range of North Korea's growing arsenal. [1]

With Japan holding evacuation drills to prepare for a North Korean missile attack and U.S. leaders floating the prospect of a pre-emptive military strike, Washington and Pyongyang, North

North Korean leader Kim Jong Un, who was about 27 years old when he succeeded his father in 2011, has accelerated the nation's military buildup. In addition to nuclear arms, North Korea is believed to have vast stockpiles of chemical and biological weapons. The Trump administration has urged China, North Korea's main trading partner, to use its economic leverage to help persuade Kim to abandon his nuclear program.

AFP/Getty Images/Ed Jones

Korea's capital, found themselves agreeing on one thing: the Korean Peninsula potentially faced a catastrophic war.

"[W]e could end up having a major, major conflict with North Korea," Trump said on April 28. "We'd love to solve things diplomatically, but it's very difficult." [2] But every warning by White House officials, including repeated declarations by Secretary of State Rex Tillerson and others that "all options are on the table," only served to stiffen North Korea's resolve.

Assailing the United States for "becoming more vicious and aggressive" under Trump, North Korea's vice foreign minister, Han Song-ryol, said, "We will go to war if they choose." [3] A North Korea army spokesman added, "Nothing will be more foolish if the United States thinks it can deal with us the

way it treated Iraq and Libya, miserable victims of its aggression." [4]

Long known as the "Hermit Kingdom," North Korea is the world's most isolated and secretive country, ruled since the end of World War II by a family dynasty with Stalinist roots that tightly controls information and brutally stamps out dissent. A 2014 U.N. report said the country's human rights abuses were the worst in the world. [5] Thousands of defectors flee every year, including a small but growing number of more-affluent North Koreans, leading some analysts to wonder if the regime of leader Kim Jong Un is becoming unstable. But Kim has shown remarkable resilience. (See sidebar, p. 446.)

U.S.-North Korea animosity dates to 1953, when the Korean War ended with an uneasy armistice and North and South Korea divided by a narrow, 2.5-mile-wide demilitarized zone (DMZ) along the 38th parallel. Washington has never recognized the Democratic People's Republic of Korea — the name North Korea prefers — and Pyongyang repeatedly has launched provocative attacks on South Korea, including a 2010 bombardment of the island of Yeonpyeong that left four South Koreans dead.

The stakes have risen dramatically over the past decade. North Korea has tested five nuclear bombs since 2006 and reportedly is within a few years of developing intercontinental ballistic missiles (ICBMs) capable of reaching America's West Coast — a development U.S. policy makers view as intolerable. [6]

"This is a slow-motion Cuban missile crisis," says Robert Litwak, director of International Security Studies at the

North Korea Worries Its Neighbors

As one of the world's nine nuclear-armed nations, North Korea poses a major threat to regional U.S. allies, South Korea and Japan, and to the United States itself if it develops long-range ballistic missiles capable of reaching the West Coast. The "Hermit Kingdom's" nuclear ambitions also worry its neighbors to the north and west, Russia and China. North Korea's latest launch test put a missile near the Russian coast. Meanwhile, China fears an onslaught of refugees if war breaks out in the region.

North Korea and Its Environs

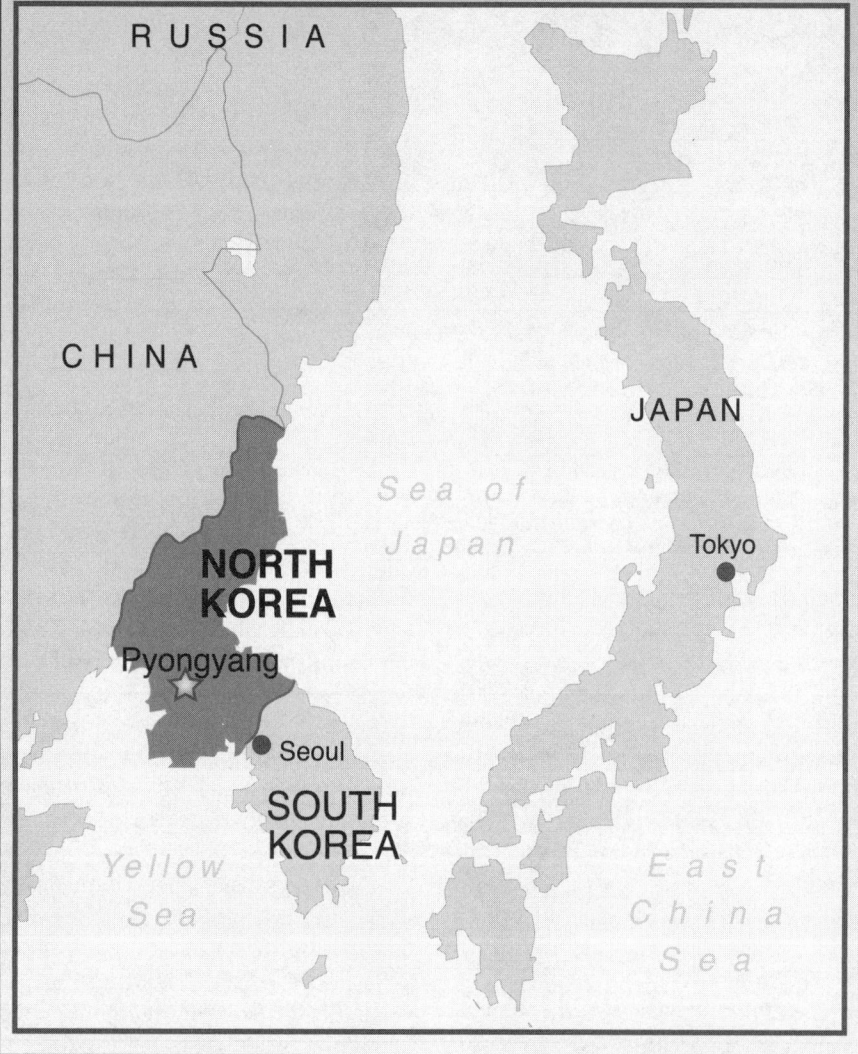

Trump and his foreign policy team have vowed a break from past administration policies, including Obama's "strategic patience" approach of slowly pressuring Pyongyang until it agrees to come to the negotiating table. But it is unclear what course the new administration will take, and foreign policy and military experts warn the crisis will be difficult to resolve.

Kim, who succeeded his father in 2011, has accelerated the nation's push toward greater military capabilities. North Korea has tested three nuclear bombs since the younger Kim took power, including its most powerful yet: an estimated 10-kiloton explosion in 2016, two-thirds the explosive force of the 15-kiloton bomb the United States dropped on Hiroshima during World War II. [7]

North Korea's missiles also are increasingly sophisticated, as shown by a successful February test of its new solid-fuel, intermediate-range missile, the KN-15, which is difficult to detect because it can be fired from a mobile launcher. [8]

In addition, North Korea is believed to have vast stockpiles of chemical and biological weapons. Pyongyang allegedly used a banned chemical agent to kill Kim's estranged half-brother at an airport in Malaysia in February, possibly signaling its willingness to use chemical weapons if provoked. [9]

North Korea also has long-range artillery massed along the DMZ that could destroy much of the South Korean capital of Seoul, one of the world's largest metropolitan areas, and an international center of commerce. [10] For its part, South Korea has a formidable armada of tanks, armored fighting vehicles, fighter jets and attack helicopters. [11]

And this spring the United States, which has more than 60,000 troops stationed in South Korea and nearby Japan, began deploying a powerful antimissile system — the Terminal High Altitude Area Defense, or THAAD — in South Korea, despite strong objections from neighboring China, which views the system as a threat to its own military operations. [12]

Wilson Center, a think tank in Washington chartered by Congress to study global issues. "North Korea is on the verge of a strategic breakout, and their development of multistage ballistic missiles would be a game-changer."

The United States and U.N. Security Council have tried for years to persuade Pyongyang to dismantle its nuclear program, imposing increasingly strict economic sanctions and sharply condemning its nuclear bomb and missile tests.

Washington also is believed to be using cyber and electronic attacks to sabotage North Korea's test missile launches, under a program initiated by President Obama in 2013. Although it is difficult to assess the effectiveness of the strategy, several recent North Korean missiles have blown up almost immediately upon launch. [13]

North Korea itself also has exhibited considerable cyber-prowess. It was blamed for a massive 2014 hack of Sony Pictures Entertainment after the company produced a movie, "The Interview," about a fictional assassination plot against Kim Jong Un. Although Pyongyang denied it was behind the hacking, President Obama in 2015 ordered additional sanctions against North Korea. Cyber-security firms also found evidence potentially linking North Korea with ransomware attacks in mid-May that crippled computer systems worldwide. [14]

With all sides poised for major retaliation if attacked, policy experts say the situation is highly combustible.

"I'm fairly worried," says Jeffrey Lewis, director of the East Asia Nonproliferation Program at the Middlebury Institute for International Studies in Monterey, Calif. "Every party in this conflict sees their forces as defensive. That's the good news. The bad news is that everybody sees everyone else's forces as offensive. In a crisis, that could be an excuse to strike first."

Roiling the waters, South Korea's newly elected president, Moon Jae-in, has embraced a more reconciliatory approach to Pyongyang than the previous government, which could put it at odds with the Trump administration. China, which shares an 880-mile-long border with North Korea and fears a wave of North Korean refugees if war breaks out, wants Washington to set aside its threats and engage in talks with Pyongyang.

"We must stay committed to the path of dialogue and negotiation," said China's foreign minister Wang Yi. "The use of force does not solve differences and will only lead to bigger disasters." [15]

North Korea at a Glance

North Korea is barely larger than Virginia and has a population one-twelfth that of the United States.

Area: 46,540 square miles, slightly larger than Virginia

Geography: Borders China, South Korea and Russia

Natural resources: Include coal, lead, tungsten, zinc, graphite, magnesite, iron ore, copper, gold

Population: 25.1 million (est., July 2016)

Life expectancy: 70.4 years

Religions: Traditionally Buddhist and Confucianist, some Christian and syncretic Chondogyo (Religion of the Heavenly Way)

Government: Communist; ruled by Kim Jong Un since 2011

GDP per capita: $1,013 (est. 2015)

Labor force: 14 million; agriculture, 37 percent; industry, services 63 percent

Unemployment rate: 25.6 percent (est., 2013)

Industries: Military products, machine building, electric power, chemicals, mining, metallurgy, textiles, agriculture

Exports: $4.2 billion (est., 2015); minerals, metallurgical products, manufactured goods, textiles, agricultural and fishery products

Imports: $4.8 billion (est., 2015); petroleum, coking coal, machinery and equipment, textiles, grain

Sources: "Country Comparison: GDP — Per Capita (PPP)," and "East & Southeast Asia: Korea, North," The World Factbook, Central Intelligence Agency, Jan. 12, 2017, http://tinyurl.com/2yckfx and http://tinyurl.com/5sajkr; "North Korea GDP," Trading Economics, 2017, http://tinyurl.com/k5gjulg; "North Korea per capita GDP rises above $1,000, think tank says," United Press International, Sept. 29, 2016, http://tinyurl.com/m8j7say

Still to be determined, however, is the role China will play in bringing Pyongyang to the negotiating table. The Trump administration has urged China, North Korea's main trading partner, to use its economic leverage to help persuade Kim to abandon his nuclear program. Beijing has been reluctant to clash with Pyongyang but has supported U.N. sanctions and agreed to suspend coal imports from North Korea, a major source of cash for the "Hermit Kingdom."

Nor is it clear that China could sway North Korea even if it turned up the economic pressure. When a Chinese-run media outlet called on Pyongyang to end nuclear tests, North Korean state media harshly criticized China for "a string of absurd and reckless remarks" and warned of unspecified "grave" consequences. [16]

Amid the international cross-currents and tensions, long-time observers see no easy solution. "It's an extraordinary problem for which there's no good answer," says Doug Bandow, a senior fellow at the Cato Institute think tank in Washington who has written widely on North Korea. (*See "At Issue," p. 449.*)

As officials on both sides of the Pacific seek to de-escalate the situation, here are key questions they are debating:

Is there a viable nonmilitary strategy to get North Korea to drop its nuclear weapons program?

When fragments from a North Korean rocket fell into the Yellow Sea last year, international weapons experts who examined them made an interesting discovery: Many of the key components came from China. This and other find-

North Korea Raises Nuclear Stakes

Nuclear bombs tested by North Korea have been increasingly powerful, with the latest, in September 2016, generally estimated at 10 kilotons, although some analysts believe it may have been up to 30 kilotons. By comparison, the atomic bomb the United States dropped on Hiroshima, Japan, during World War II was 15 kilotons. North Korea also has tested several ballistic missiles, the most recent of which flew more than 430 miles and demonstrated Pyongyang's increasing military capability.

North Korean Nuclear Bomb Tests, 2006-2016

1 kiloton
October 2006

6-9 kilotons
February 2013

6-9 kilotons
January 2016

More than
10 kilotons
September 2016

2-6 kilotons
May 2009

Source: "A Decade of North Korean Nuclear Tests," Center for Strategic and International Studies, Oct. 17, 2016, http://tinyurl.com/lajcgf2; "North Korea and the History of Underground Nuclear Testing," Atomic Heritage Foundation, Sept. 10, 2016, http://tinyurl.com/k5rhpcl

ings led the United Nations earlier this year to conclude that years of international sanctions have failed to cut off materials and technologies needed by North Korea to keep developing nuclear weapons.

"That case demonstrates the continuing critical importance of high-end, foreign-sourced components" for North Korea's military programs, stated a U.N. report. "The Democratic People's Republic of Korea continues to trade in arms and related materiel, exploiting markets and procurement services in Asia, Africa and the Middle East." [17]

In fact, despite military pressure, global sanctions and on-and-off negotiations, North Korea has continued — and even accelerated — its march toward increasingly powerful nuclear bombs and missiles.

Exasperated, top White House officials say it's time to change strategies.

"[T]he political and diplomatic efforts of the past 20 years to bring North Korea to the point of denuclearization have failed," Secretary of State Rex Tillerson said in March, less than two months after assuming his position. "In the face of this ever-escalating threat, it is clear that a different approach is required." [18]

Policy experts, however, are divided over what, if anything, can stop North Korea from developing an even more potent arsenal.

The two decades of efforts Tillerson referenced began with a 1994 agreement between the United States and North Korea in which Pyongyang agreed to freeze and eventually dismantle its nuclear weapons program in return for U.S. aid and two U.S.-supplied light-water nuclear reactors that could not be used to create weapons. The deal fell apart in 2002,

with each side blaming the other for failing to adhere to its terms.

After North Korea tested its first atomic bomb in 2006, President George W. Bush's administration attempted unsuccessfully to negotiate a new deal. The Obama administration then embarked on its strategic-patience policy, refraining from engaging with North Korea until it ceased its provocative behavior while relying on sanctions to help bring it to the negotiating table.

Meanwhile the United Nations, growing alarmed over North Korea's tests of nuclear bombs and missiles, passed a series of increasingly stringent sanctions between 2006 and 2016. These initially targeted certain military goods and luxury supplies and then were expanded to encourage member states to inspect ships suspected of smuggling military goods to North Korea. The U.N. also restricted money transfers and, last year, banned the export of gold and rare earth metals, which are needed to make high-tech electronics and hybrid car batteries, and capped exports of coal and iron.

Some experts say the ever-tougher sanctions, coupled with stepped-up enforcement and China's cooperation, eventually will make a difference. They cite the example of Iran, which agreed to negotiations over halting its nuclear weapons program after years of crippling sanctions.

"Iran sanctions worked," says Anthony Ruggiero, a senior fellow at the Foundation for Defense of Democracies, a think tank in Washington that focuses on fighting terrorism and promoting democracy. "There's a template there." In addition, he says, even though North Korea is not as integrated into the world economy as Iran was, "there are areas where they can be squeezed."

Ruggiero and other foreign policy experts say the United States should consider so-called "secondary sanctions," or directly targeting companies, including those based in China, that are selling banned goods to North

Korea. Such sanctions could, in theory, choke off the flow of goods and money to North Korea.

"We need to do a much better job of, first, devoting sufficient resources to finding out where North Korea's money laundering is going through, and second, we have to have the political will to sanction, to designate, to freeze the assets of companies and banks in third countries, including China, that are helping North Korea violate the sanctions," said Joshua Stanton, a Washington-based attorney and former U.S. Army judge advocate in South Korea who has advised the House Foreign Affairs Committee on North Korean sanctions. [19]

Other foreign policy experts, however, warn that tougher sanctions could further isolate Pyongyang, leaving it more entrenched than ever. In addition, Beijing might not take kindly to the United States trying to impose financial penalties against some of its companies.

"That's a really indiscriminate set of tools, and it's not clear that the consequences of imposing those kinds of sanctions are well understood," says Toby Dalton, co-director of the nuclear policy program at the Carnegie Endowment for International Peace. "It may make it much harder to get China on our side."

As an alternative, Dalton suggests the United States consider opening talks with North Korea without preconditions. It is worth exploring whether Pyongyang would agree to freeze its nuclear program in exchange for concessions such as sanctions relief and a reduction in U.S.-South Korea military exercises, he says. Even if that is not a satisfactory, long-term solution, it could at least reduce tensions and open the door for ongoing negotiations, he says.

"We think we're being tough by refusing to negotiate, but we need to negotiate to try to get a freeze on their nuclear program," agrees Lewis of the Middlebury Institute for International Studies. "Talking can keep things at a slow boil so you're not getting major

provocations. Generally speaking, I think you have to find a way to get tensions down until whatever is going to happen in North Korea happens — the regime collapses or they moderate some policies."

Daily life for the average citizen is extremely difficult in North Korea, one of the world's poorest nations. But in the capital, Pyongyang, above, more-affluent residents enjoy well-stocked stores, cellphones and other modern luxuries. The economy appears to be in somewhat better shape since Kim Jong Un eased government restrictions on commercial activities. And a booming black market is boosting the importation of consumer goods, largely from China.

Other foreign policy experts, however, doubt that negotiations would do any good. Proponents of such a policy "have provided no rationale for why yet another attempt at negotiations would be any more successful than previous failures," said Bruce Klinger, a North Korea expert with the conservative Heritage Foundation think tank in Washington. Instead, he told a subcommittee of the House Committee on Foreign Affairs in March, sanctions will have an effect — if policymakers give them enough time. [20]

"It is a policy of a slow python constriction," he said, "rather than a rapid cobra strike." [21]

Is military action against North Korea a realistic option?

Battling Islamic State fighters in Afghanistan, the United States this year for the first time deployed its most powerful non-nuclear weapon, known

as the "mother of all bombs," on a cave complex where the fighters were hiding. The unusually aggressive tactic left foreign policy experts wondering if the Trump administration was sending a message to North Korea.

If Pyongyang refuses to change course, the United States should consider a pre-emptive military attack on North Korea as a last-ditch option to keep it from developing missiles that could drop nuclear bombs on U.S. cities, some congressional leaders have said. "[There are] no good choices left, but if there's a war today, it's over there," said Sen. Lindsey Graham, R-S.C., a member of the Armed Services Committee. "In the future, if there's a war and they get a missile, it comes here." [22]

Many foreign policy and military experts, however, warn that even a limited attack on North Korea could trigger a full-scale war with almost unimaginable casualties, especially for two of America's closest allies: South Korea and Japan. North Korea has one of the world's largest armies, a formidable array of artillery and chemical and biological weapons in addition to its nuclear bombs — and appears

North Korea's Economy Dwarfed by South's

The North Korean economy was about 1 percent of South Korea's in 2015. North Korea's GDP — the total market value of its goods and services — in 2015 was $16.1 billion, equal to about half the economic output of Vermont, the lowest of any U.S. state. South Korea's GDP in 2015 was nearly $1.4 trillion.

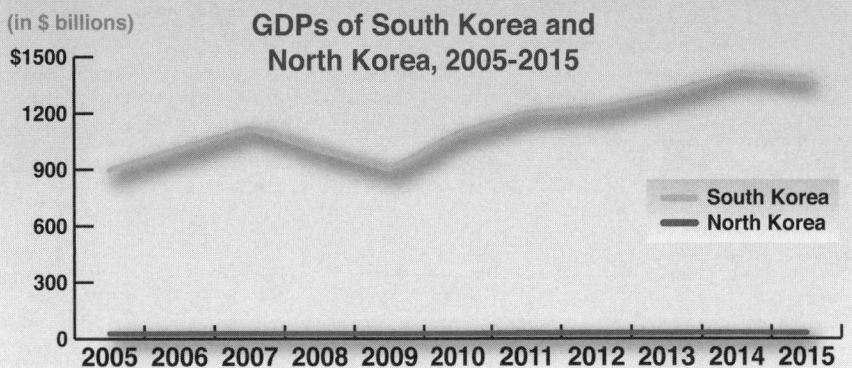

Sources: "GDP (current US$)," World Bank, http://tinyurl.com/k9d6hff; "North Korea GDP," Trading Economics, 2017, http://tinyurl.com/k5gjulg; "Vermont," Bureau of Economic Analysis, March 28, 2017, http://tinyurl.com/l9u9koe

determined to defend itself by any means possible.

"That's a very serious business," says Nicholas Eberstadt, an expert in international security in the Korean Peninsula and Asia at the American Enterprise Institute (AEI), a conservative think tank in Washington. "I would hope that people thinking about a military option would have given a great deal of thought to the risks."

The risks begin with metropolitan Seoul, home to about 25 million people. North Korea has amassed hundreds of long-range artillery pieces near the demilitarized zone that can unleash a catastrophic assault. "They essentially have the equivalent of a nuclear option pointed at Seoul in the form of artillery," says the Wilson Center's Litwak. South Korea, whose army of 655,000 is about half the size of North Korea's, has a modern air force and navy as well as thousands of artillery pieces, but Pyongyang is not within artillery range of the DMZ like Seoul is. [23]

Other risks include the more than 130,000 Americans who live in South Korea and about 28,000 U.S. troops who

are stationed there. [24] "If we had 20,000 troops incinerated, I'm pretty sure we would consider that a war," says Jim Walsh, a senior research associate at the Massachusetts Institute of Technology's Security Studies Program.

North Korean missiles also pose a "grave threat" to Japan, says Japanese Prime Minister Shinzo Abe, who has warned that Pyongyang could strike Japan with missiles loaded with sarin, a highly toxic chemical weapon. [25]

While U.S. leaders hope a pre-emptive strike could disable North Korea, military experts say that is unlikely. North Korea is believed to have many hundreds of missiles, some kept in underground bunkers that would be hard to detect and destroy, as well as 10,000 artillery shells in caves and other hiding places that can reach Seoul within minutes. [26]

But Pyongyang's weapons of mass destruction represent its greatest threat. North Korea has an estimated 2,500 tons of chemical weapons, including the deadly VX nerve agent allegedly used to kill Kim's estranged half-brother in Malaysia in February. It also is believed

to have biological weapons that could spread deadly diseases such as smallpox. And military experts are deeply uncertain whether a U.S. preemptive strike could wipe out North Korea's approximately 20 nuclear bombs. [27]

"Every U.S. administration, as they have looked at this problem, has said that all options are available. But that's not really true," said Carl Baker, a retired Air Force officer with extensive experience in South Korea who is now director of programs at the Pacific Forum of the Center for Strategic and International Studies. "We really don't have a military option." [28]

U.S. politicians have also floated the idea of targeted attacks on North Korea's leaders. Ohio Gov. John Kasich, a Republican presidential candidate in 2016, recently suggested that the United States could "eradicate" the leadership of North Korea. "The North Korean top leadership has to go," he said. "And, you know, I think that is not beyond our capability to achieve that." [29]

Korean experts, however, say that even if such a strike succeeded, it might unleash chaos, with the country potentially splintering into violent factions squaring off with chemical weapons while U.S. and Chinese forces maneuver to take control.

"It's really astonishing to me that people don't think of the consequences of doing that in any serious way," says Joel Wit, co-founder and senior fellow of the U.S.-Korea Institute at the Paul H. Nitze School of Advanced International Studies at Johns Hopkins University. "We would have such a security nightmare that people might yearn for the good old days of a nuclear North Korea with a central government."

Is North Korea at risk of collapse?

In 2013, Kim Jong Un turned his guns on his own family. He arranged for two trusted deputies of his uncle, Jang Song-thaek, to be executed in a particularly gruesome way — with antiaircraft guns. He then ordered that his uncle, widely viewed as the nation's second most powerful official and a voice for reform, be executed in the same way. [30]

Since assuming power at the end of 2011, Kim has moved ruthlessly against potential rivals, executing more than 300 people, including senior government, military and ruling Korean Workers' Party officials, according to a 2016 report by a South Korean think tank, the Institute for National Security Strategy. [31]

U.S. policy makers question whether Kim is tightening his grip on power or if the executions indicate that he is struggling to control growing dissent. "There are people who would say he has consolidated his power with these purges and that may be true, but I can't help but wonder if this stuff also undermines his regime," says the AEI's Eberstadt.

Others cite the gradually rising number of mostly low-level North Korean officials and more affluent residents who are defecting every year. The most senior defector in years — North Korea's former deputy ambassador to the United Kingdom, who defected last summer with his family — said dissent is spreading in North Korea. "Kim Jong Un's days are numbered," the defector, Thae Yong Ho, said earlier this year. "Control over the residents has been collapsing due to information seeping in." [32]

Long-time Korean observers, however, cautioned against assuming the regime will fall any time soon. The Kim family has demonstrated enormous staying power since taking control of the country. They survived war with South Korea and the United States in the early 1950s, a famine in the 1990s that killed up to 2.5 million people and the transition to power of Kim Jong Un, who was only about 27 years old at the time, following the sudden death of his father.

The demise of the regime "has always been more of a hope than a realistic policy outcome," says Carnegie's Dalton. "They have survived all manner of calamities, crises, disasters, tricky political transitions. If you were looking for signs of decay, you would look for loss of government control in border

South Korean activists in Seoul burn images of North Korea's leader Kim Jong Un on Sept. 10, 2016, to protest a North Korean nuclear test. On May 13, 2017, Pyongyang tested an intermediate-range missile that flew more than 430 miles, drawing international condemnation. South Korea's new government — fearing a war with the North — wants to adopt a more conciliatory approach in dealing with Pyongyang.

regions and more high-level defections that might indicate stress in the system. But I don't see it."

Korean experts say the younger Kim relies on a few trusted aides and a network of security services, often pitted against each other, to reduce threats to the leader. Anyone suspected of disloyalty faces death or years of confinement in extremely harsh prison camps.

A devastating 2014 report by a special U.N. investigative commission documented human rights abuses in North Korea, which the panel said exceeded those of any other contemporary dictatorship. "The gravity, scale and nature of these violations reveal a State that does not have any parallel in the contemporary world," concluded the report. Drawing on public testimony and private interviews with hundreds of victims and witnesses, the report accused the government of retaining its hold on power through such tactics as murder, enslavement, torture, sexual violence and prolonged starvation. It estimated that 80,000-120,000 political prisoners were held in four large political prison camps. [33]

"The key to the political system is the vast political and security apparatus

that strategically uses surveillance, coercion, fear and punishment to preclude the expression of any dissent," the report stated. "Public executions and enforced disappearance to political prison camps serve as the ultimate means to terrorize the population into submission." [34]

Daily life is extremely difficult even for average residents. With its GDP per capita ranked 180th out of 193 countries by the United Nations, North Korea is among the world's poorest nations. About half its population is believed to live in "extreme poverty," and 84 percent had "borderline" or "poor" levels of food consumption in 2013, according to the U.N. [35] But the more affluent living in Pyongyang in recent years have enjoyed well-stocked stores, cellphones and other luxuries of modern life.

The combination of brutal repression and extreme poverty might seem a source of substantial discontent among the population. But North Korean experts warn against such a conclusion.

"It's not like you're living in Western Europe and your standard of living has dramatically nosedived," says Wit of Johns Hopkins University. "It's more like you're living in a developing country where you're not used to a very high standard of living, but you can improve your lot.

"There's a lot of nationalism," he adds. "These are not people who grew up in a democracy. It's not as though North Koreans are saying to themselves, 'I wish I lived in the United States.' It's a very different reality there."

In recent years, some central controls have been relaxed, and North Koreans appear to have more economic opportunities. The result has been a slow increase in the buying and selling of goods and services, sometimes under the official aegis of the state and sometimes unofficially tolerated by authorities, who had cracked down more vigorously on the black market under the regime of Kim's father, Kim Jong-Il.

"My perception is at least in Pyongyang things are better than they were 10 years ago," says MIT's Walsh. "The government has clearly recognized that they need to evolve their economy if they are to survive."

That slow marketization, along with an increased awareness of the outside world through cellphone contacts and more access to South Korean media, could nudge the country on a different path, experts say. But it may take time.

"That trend could be five years, it could be 50 years," Walsh says, "before it amounts to something." ∎

BACKGROUND

Early Era

Although North Korea and South Korea emerged as separate nations comparatively recently, the Korean Peninsula has a long history of division and reunification while contending with external threats. From 56 B.C. until 926, the land was divided into three kingdoms, unified under the Silla dy-

nasty and then divided again into three kingdoms.

The peninsula was reunified under the Koryo dynasty, established by a general named Wang Kon, and was first named "Korea." The Koryo royal rulers, who reigned from the 10th to 14th centuries, introduced a civil service, codified a legal system and allowed Buddhism to spread through the peninsula. After the Mongols invaded in 1231, the Koryo family eventually was replaced by the Choson dynasty, started by Gen. Yi Song-gye, in 1391. [36]

The Choson leaders, who would govern Korea as an independent nation for nearly 500 years, depended on China for military protection and borrowed liberally from Chinese society, adopting Confucianism as the official religion. However, after repeated invasions by the Japanese, the Manchu (who ruled China) and others, Korea gradually closed its doors to foreigners in the 18th century, becoming known as the "Hermit Kingdom." Its isolation ended in the mid-19th century, after European and American traders and missionaries moved into the region.

But Koreans remained highly suspicious of Western motives. When the armed merchant vessel *U.S.S. General Sherman* sailed up the Taedon River to Pyongyang in 1866 and became stranded on a sandbar, Koreans attacked it and killed the crew. [37]

Korea remained independent through the late 19th century, but in 1910 Japan annexed the peninsula after victories in both the Sino-Japanese (1894-1895) and Russo-Japanese (1904-1905) wars and claimed Korea as part of its growing empire.

Colonial Period

Under Japan's colonial rule, which lasted until 1945, Korea became more industrialized and began to build a modern infrastructure. But the Japanese repeatedly and savagely crushed

resistance. After unsuccessful attempts to overthrow the Japanese, the Western-educated politician, Syngman Rhee, established a provisional Korean government in Shanghai in 1919.

Meanwhile, a communist-led guerrilla movement soldiered on against the Japanese until 1940, when some of its leaders, including Kim Il Sung, fled to the Soviet Union to avoid capture by the Japanese. Kim became a major in the Soviet Army and did not return to Korea until 1945.

During World War II, the United States, Britain and China agreed at a 1943 conference in Cairo that Korea would return to its independent status after the war. But after the war the peninsula became caught up in a struggle between the United States and the Soviet Union.

The Soviets, who occupied northern Korea and adjoining areas of Manchuria in China, viewed the peninsula as an important buffer zone to protect against attacks from the east. The United States, in turn, viewed it as a bulwark against communist expansion. In August 1945, the United States decided unilaterally to divide Korea at the 38th parallel into Soviet and U.S. zones. Within a month, 25,000 American soldiers occupied South Korea while Soviet forces took over the north, accompanied by Kim Il Sung and other Korean communist leaders. Koreans protested both occupying forces as a continuation of colonialism.

Joint American and Soviet discussions over the future of Korea made little progress, and the country was permanently divided in 1948. The Republic of Korea was established in the South, with Rhee elected as the first president. The Democratic People's Republic of Korea was established in the North, headed by resistance fighter Kim, who became premier.

Kim nationalized industry and became very popular, while the new leaders in the South were seen as "puppets" of their occupiers. Kim's brand of communism was not a carbon copy of the

Continued on p. 444

Chronology

1940s-1950s
Korean Peninsula is divided into North and South, followed by war and a tense standoff.

1945
Korea splits as World War II ends, with the Soviet-backed communist regime ruling the North and a U.S.-backed regime controlling the South in Cold War maneuvering.

1948
As Soviet and U.S. troops begin to withdraw, longtime communist guerrilla fighter Kim Il Sung takes control of the North.

1950
North Korean troops invade the South; U.S. and U.N. troops rapidly enter the war to help the South, and then China enters on the side of the North.

1953
After massive loss of life, armistice divides peninsula at 38th Parallel.

1960s-1980s
Aided by China and Russia, North undergoes industrial growth and escalates provocations against the South.

1965
North's nuclear weapons program begins as the Soviets help build its first nuclear reactor, at Yongbyon.

1968
North seizes U.S. spy ship *U.S.S. Pueblo*, releases crew a year later.

1983
Amid mounting North Korean provocations, Pyongyang tries unsuccessfully to assassinate South Korean president.

1984
North test-fires first SCUD missile.

1985
North agrees to 1968 Nuclear Nonproliferation Treaty.

1990s
North faces famine and a transfer of political leadership from Kim Il Sung to his son but continues military buildup.

1991
North and South begin ministerial talks in Pyongyang. . . . U.S. withdraws nuclear weapons from South.

1994
Kim Jong Il takes control after the death of his father, Kim Il Sung. . . . U.S. and North Korea sign Agreed Framework, with Pyongyang promising to freeze nuclear weapons program in exchange for aid.

1995
Three-year famine leaves up to 2.5 million dead.

1998
North test-fires long-range *Taepodong-1* missile over Japan.

2000s-Present
North develops increasingly powerful nuclear arsenal.

2002
President George W. Bush calls North Korea part of an "axis of evil." . . . U.S. accuses North of starting uranium-enrichment program.

2003
North withdraws from Nuclear Nonproliferation Treaty. . . . Six-party talks begin among U.S., North Korea, China, Japan, Russia and South Korea.

2006
North conducts its first underground nuclear bomb test; U.N. Security Council imposes sanctions.

2007
North agrees to disable its nuclear facilities for economic aid.

2009
North cuts diplomatic ties with South, carries out second underground nuclear test.

2010
North shells South Korean island of Yeonpyeong months after it reportedly sank a South Korean warship, killing 46 sailors.

2011
Kim Jong Un succeeds his father, Kim Jong Il, as North Korea's leader.

2014
U.N. report details massive North Korean human rights violations.

2016
North Korea tests 10-kiloton nuclear bomb, its most powerful to date.

2017
Kim Jong Un's estranged half-brother is killed with a chemical agent in Malaysia; suspicion quickly turns to Pyongyang (Feb. 13). . . . North Korea test-fires four missiles into the Sea of Japan, penetrating Japan's 200-mile economic exclusion zone (March 6). . . . President Trump warns of the potential for "major, major conflict" with North Korea; (April 28). Moon Jae-in wins South Korean presidency, pledges to reach out to North in potential split with Washington.

Personality Cult Makes Kim a God

"All-encompassing indoctrination" begins in early childhood.

North Korea is one of the world's poorest nations, with nearly half its population living in extreme poverty. But that hasn't stopped the ruling regime from erecting massive, 70-foot statues of its leader, Kim Jong Un, in provincial capitals across the country. Residents also can gaze upon miniature statues of Kim's predecessors — his father Kim Jong Il and grandfather Kim Il Sung — at the Pyongyang Folk Park, a theme park that features tiny versions of North Korean landmarks.

From the time the Kim family took power following World War II, the state has attributed godlike powers to them. Now the government is extending this cult of personality to Kim Jong Un, who was just in his late 20s when he took over in 2011 upon his father's death.

From early childhood, North Koreans are bombarded with images of the ruling family. The state requires that portraits of the leaders be cleaned daily with a special cloth and look out at residents in every home, office, classroom and other public spaces, including train cars. Starting in kindergarten, teachers and officials regularly instruct children about the greatness of their leaders.

"The milk would arrive [in kindergarten] and we would go up one by one to fill our cups," a North Korean woman told *The Washington Post.* "The teachers would say: 'Do you know where the milk came from? It came from the Dear Leader. Because of his love and consideration, we are drinking milk today." [1]

Governments, especially those run by dictators, regularly try to instill a sense of respect or even awe toward their rulers. But the Kim dynasty takes this veneration to a different level, using a nonstop barrage of propaganda about the nation's leaders as a way of cementing their grip on power.

"It's clear they have very good control of the country, and part of it is because of this cult of personality which permeates the whole system from when you're in kindergarten to when you're in university," says Joel Wit, a senior fellow at the U.S.-Korea Institute at the Paul H. Nitze School of Advanced International Studies at Johns Hopkins University in Washington.

In addition to the ubiquitous images, Pyongyang cultivates quasi-mystical worship of the Kims. The nation's calendar calculates time from 1912, when Kim Il Sung is said to have descended to Earth from heaven. More than two decades after his death in 1994, he remains the "eternal president" under the North Korean constitution. His son, Kim Jong Il, who ruled from 1994 to 2011, was also said to have extraordinary abilities, such as walking at just three weeks, talking at eight weeks and writing 1,500 books while studying at Kim Il Sung University. [2]

Even as this cult of personality continues to extol the virtues of North Korea's first two rulers, it is now also turning to Kim Jong Un. He is said to have demonstrated pistol marksmanship at age 3. As a youth, he supposedly mastered seven languages, discovered new geographical features and became a scholar of famous generals in world history. [3]

A 2014 United Nations report on human rights violations in North Korea said the propaganda serves as a powerful tool for the government, building up support for the leaders while directing hatred toward other countries, including the United

Continued from p. 442

Soviet model. Rather, he developed a highly nationalistic ideology known as juche, which stressed self-reliance, independence and resistance to foreign influence.

War and Aftermath

After years of border skirmishes, Kim Il Sung — with support from the Soviet Union and the new communist government of China — invaded South Korea on June 25, 1950, quickly taking control of the South except for a small southeastern corner near the port of Pusan. The United States and other allies immediately came to the aid of South Korea.

Before ending in a virtual stalemate, the three-year Korean War produced a massive loss of life: 800,000 Koreans, 115,000 Chinese and 37,000 Americans. An armistice was signed on July 27, 1953, officially splitting the peninsula at the 38th parallel and suspending hostilities, but not technically ending the war. [38]

An uneasy truce prevailed between the two countries throughout the 1950s and '60s. The North, ruled by the autocratic Kim, again became a closed society. A huge personality cult helped lift the "Dear Leader," as Kim was called, to almost godlike status among his people. The communist Korean Workers' Party, the leading political entity in the North, ran the centralized government, the military and the economy.

After the Korean War, Moscow and Beijing helped rebuild the war-torn North, and its industrialized economy surged ahead of the South's. Eventually, however, bolstered by the United States and others, the South developed export-oriented industries and became a growing economic power, surpassing the North in the 1970s. Today it has the world's 15th-largest economy and is home to such industrial giants as Samsung and Hyundai. [39]

By the 1990s, North Korea's sputtering economy and international isolation left it vulnerable to grave crises. Kim Il Sung died of a heart attack in 1994 and was succeeded by his son, Kim Jong Il. After the collapse of the Soviet Union in 1991, the economy went into steep decline because of reduced trade and the loss of subsidized Soviet oil. Economic misman-

States, South Korea and Japan.

"The State operates an all-encompassing indoctrination machine that takes root from childhood to propagate an official personality cult and to manufacture absolute obedience to the Supreme Leader (Suryong), effectively to the exclusion of any thought independent of official ideology and State propaganda," the report said. [4]

The money spent on advancing this personality cult, the report added, comes at the expense of "providing food to the starving general population." [5]

But some Korean experts say the propaganda is becoming less persuasive. Increasing numbers of North Koreans are able to get alternative views from the outside world because of the growing availability of cellphones, homemade radios and the internet, although access is limited.

Doug Bandow, a senior fellow at the Cato Institute, a Washington think tank, and author of *Tripwire: Korea and U.S. Foreign Policy in a Changed World*, says this technology may make it harder to maintain the cult of personality.

"It's increasingly less effective," he says. "It's so much easier now to be aware that you're being lied to."

— *David Hosansky*

AFP/Getty Images/Pedro Ugarte

Kim Jong Un and other North Korean officials attend the unveiling of giant statues of Kim's father, Kim Jong Il, right, and grandfather, Kim Il Sung, left, on April 13, 2012. The state attributes godlike powers to the Kim family.

[1] Anna Fifield, "North Korea begins brainwashing children in cult of the Kims as early as kindergarten," *The Washington Post*, Jan. 16, 2015, https://tinyurl.com/nx2wzwk.

[2] Robert Kiener, "North Korean Menace," *CQ Global Researcher*, July 5, 2011, pp. 315-340.

[3] Christopher Richardson, "North Korea's Kim dynasty: the making of personality cult," *The Guardian*, Feb. 16, 2015, https://tinyurl.com/ldt4tt2.

[4] "Report of the Commission of Inquiry on Human Rights in the Democratic People's Republic of Korea," U.N. Human Rights Council, Feb. 7, 2014, https://tinyurl.com/lbwc8du.

[5] *Ibid.*

agement, coupled with widespread floods in 1995 led to a three-year famine that left an estimated 600,000 to 2.5 million dead. [40] As the younger Kim consolidated his hold on power, he announced small market-oriented measures, such as bonuses to high-performing workers.

Rising Provocations

Even as the North and South created contrasting economic systems in the years after the Korean War, they built up massive armed forces. The United States established military bases after the armistice was signed and stationed some of its nuclear arsenal in the South. The North responded by focusing increasingly on strengthening its military,

while provoking the leaders of South Korea and the United States.

In 1964, Pyongyang took its first steps toward developing nuclear weapons by setting up a nuclear-energy research complex at Yongbyon, where the Soviets had built the North's first nuclear reactor.

In 1968, tensions with the United States flared after the North captured the *USS Pueblo*, an electronic spy ship that was cruising in international waters off the coast of North Korea gathering intelligence. After 11 months of negotiations, Pyongyang agreed to release the 82 crew members — who had been starved and tortured — in exchange for an admission of guilt and an apology, both of which Washington retracted once the crew were safe. The *Pueblo* remains

a "hostage" in North Korea, and the loss of its sensitive surveillance equipment to a communist country during the Cold War is considered one of the greatest intelligence debacles in U.S. history. [41]

Despite ongoing tensions, Koreans on both sides of the border hoped for reconciliation. Many families and friends were separated by the DMZ. But border skirmishes and provocations periodically dashed such dreams.

In 1971 negotiations offered hope for reunifying the two nations, and an agreement on ground rules for unification was reached in 1972. But many of the talks were scuttled by provocative actions by the North, such as alleged assassination attempts on South Korean leaders in 1968 and 1974, a bombing that killed 17 South Korean officials in

Defectors Risk Death to Escape

"How could our country lie so completely to us?"

Thae Yong Ho grew weary of lying to his sons about the greatness of their country. Posted in London as North Korea's deputy ambassador to the United Kingdom, he kept fending off questions from his oldest son, a high school student who wanted to study computer science at a London university, about why North Korea was so different. Why did their native country not permit access to the internet or allow residents to watch foreign films?

"As a father, it was hard for me to tell lies, and it started a debate within the family," Thae said at a Jan. 25 press conference in Seoul, South Korea. "This North Korean system is a really inhuman system. It even abuses the love between parents and their children." [1]

Finally, last summer, Thae defected with his wife and two sons. He made headlines because he was the highest-ranking defector in years. But several thousand North Koreans reportedly flee the country annually. [2]

For North Koreans, the decision to leave is fraught with peril. The most straightforward route is north across the Yalu River into China, but North Korean ruler Kim Jong Un has increased security along the border in recent years. Those who are caught face imprisonment or even execution.

And those who make it into China can face difficulties, such as human trafficking or being arrested by police and sent back to North Korea.

Defectors also must deal with guilt when the regime punishes relatives left behind. Park Sang-hak fled North Korea in 1999 after discovering his family would be punished because his father, who was working in Japan, had decided against coming

back. Park bribed a border guard to cross the Yalu into China with his mother, brother and sister. But the regime exacted retribution after he escaped: His fiancée was beaten so badly she was left unrecognizable; two uncles were tortured to death; and his teenage cousins lost their jobs and had to beg in the streets. [3]

Nowadays, relatives and a black market are helping a small but growing number of more-affluent North Koreans, especially those with family members already living abroad, to find their way to South Korea or other nations.

"There have been shifts in the composition of defectors," says Scott Snyder, a senior fellow for Korea studies and director of the program on U.S.-Korea policy at the Council on Foreign Relations, a think tank in Washington. "It used to be a lot more people living in the border areas who were marginalized individuals." But today, he says, most defectors are elites who rely on family connections and brokers. "Money is paid, arrangements are made," Snyder says. "People are almost pulled out by their relatives and the growing influence of cash."

Although the numbers don't indicate "true internal instability," Snyder says, the defections are nevertheless important "because they open up greater understanding and information for people on the outside about the parts of the regime that really matter."

Thae, who has both spoken privately with South Korean officials and gone public with media interviews, has painted a grim picture of the Kim government. "When Kim Jong Un first came to power I was hopeful that he would make reasonable and rational decisions to save North Korea from poverty," he

---

1983 and the North's continued efforts to develop nuclear weapons. [42]

Nevertheless, in 2000 both nations signed the North-South Declaration, promising to seek peaceful reunification. Over the following decade, the two countries held a series of talks aimed at normalizing relations. The South pursued a so-called Sunshine Policy, which aimed to project diplomatic "warmth" toward the North. But the countries failed to achieve significant breakthroughs. The North's numerous provocations — including an artillery attack on the South Korean island of Yeonpyeong and an apparent torpedo attack on a South Korean warship, both in 2010 — eradicated any chance for reconciliation.

The death of Kim Jong Il in 2011 briefly stirred speculation that the regime might struggle to maintain its hold on power. Kim Jong Un reportedly was his father's favorite, but he was young (about 27 years old, but his exact birth date is unknown). He had been named a four-star general the previous year despite having no military experience and was touted by the state-run media for his alleged high-tech savvy. But outside observers wondered if such a young and inexperienced man would be able to establish his authority, especially in a Confucian society that revered age.

A South Korean journalist said at the time: "The chances of a smooth succession by Kim Jong Un are less

than 10 percent" because of his few supporters. [43]

But the younger Kim was named supreme leader after his father's funeral and assumed his father's posts as leader of the Korean Workers' Party and the highest position in the military.

At the same time, he relentlessly purged potential rivals. After his reform-minded uncle, Jang, was spectacularly executed in 2013, along with his family, a deputy security minister, O Sang-hon, who was accused of conspiring with Jang, reportedly was executed with a flame thrower. [44] Kim also continued his father's military policies and continued to push for his grandfather's dream of developing nuclear weapons.

said. "But I soon fell into despair watching him purging officials for no proper reason." [4]

Despite the difficulties of life in North Korea, defectors have had mixed experiences abroad.

Seoul is home to an estimated 28,000 defectors, most of whom are women, possibly because women have more freedom of movement and can defect more easily than men without being immediately detected. [5]

Among the best known is Hyeonseo Lee, who wrote a bestselling book about her experiences, *The Girl with Seven Names*. While she grew up in a comparatively wealthy family, Lee was traumatized by such experiences as seeing an execution when she was 7. Eventually, after secretly watching Chinese television as a teenager, she crossed an icy river into China. After narrowly avoiding servitude in a brothel and surviving a police interrogation by pretending to be Chinese, she made her way to South Korea and then daringly snuck back into North Korea to guide her mother and brother to China.

These experiences haunt her, Lee said, and she sometimes cries. "When I meet people, I forget the pain," she said in an interview last year. "I want to keep positive and show that North Koreans can be positive people. But when I am on my own, I think about the past and it gives me more trauma." [6]

Some defectors seek to liberate those still in North Korea. Defector Park now uses homemade balloons to send millions of leaflets across the border criticizing the Kim government, along with declarations of human rights and booklets about South Korea. He believes such information is the best way to undermine Pyongyang.

When former North Korean deputy ambassador to Great Britain Thae Yong Ho defected with his wife and two sons last summer, he was the highest-ranking North Korean defector in years. Several thousand North Koreans reportedly flee the country annually.

"All defectors," he said, "ask the same question: How could our country lie so completely to us?" [7]

— *David Hosansky*

[1] Anna Fifield, "Ex-diplomat: 'I've known that there was no future for North Korea for a long time,' " *The Washington Post*, Jan. 25, 2017, https://tinyurl.com/lem3pvb.

[2] Anna Fifield, "Just about the only way to escape North Korea is if a relative has already escaped," *The Washington Post*, March 31, 2016, https://tinyurl.com/kftz6ta; and Kim Tae-woo, "Number of elite North Korean defectors on the rise," *The Diplomat*, Aug. 19, 2016, https://tinyurl.com/ka3nkjw.

[3] Ian Birrell, " 'How could our country lie so completely?': meet the North Korean defectors," *The Guardian*, Aug. 27, 2016, https://tinyurl.com/hh7fmbe.

[4] Mark Hanrahan, "North Korea defector says elite turning their backs on Kim Jong Un," NBC News, Jan. 25, 2017, https://tinyurl.com/gubftg2.

[5] Birrell, *op. cit.*, and Shinui Kim, "Why are the majority of North Korean defectors female?" NK News, July 31, 2013, https://tinyurl.com/kfcf4fe.

[6] Birrell, *ibid*.

[7] *Ibid*.

Nuclear Arsenal

North Korea's interest in nuclear weapons can be traced back to the Korean War, when Kim Il Sung discovered that U.S. Army Gen. Douglas MacArthur had asked to use nuclear weapons against the North. Declassified documents show that during the Korean War Kim asked both Russia and China for help in developing a nuclear arsenal. [45] But the North's nuclear program made its biggest gains after the government obtained centrifuges and nuclear secrets from Pakistani nuclear scientist A. Q. Khan in the 1990s. [46]

The North first tested a ballistic missile in 1984, using Soviet Scud missile technology. Although the North joined the Nuclear Nonproliferation Treaty (NPT) in 1985, international inspections to determine whether the North was abiding by the treaty did not begin until 1992. In 1994, following nearly 18 months of bilateral negotiations, the United States and North Korea signed the so-called Agreed Framework, in which the North Korea agreed to abide by the NPT and both sides agreed to remove barriers to full economic and diplomatic relations. [47]

For halting its nuclear program the North would receive oil and nuclear reactors to generate electric power. At the time, Western intelligence agencies believed the North had enough plutonium for one or two bombs. [48] In 1999, North Korea agreed to suspend missile testing, and the United States eased trade sanctions it had imposed in 1988, for the bombing of a South Korean jetliner in 1987, which killed all 115 passengers. [49]

In 2002 U.S. negotiators accused the North of running a clandestine uranium-enrichment program. The Bush administration immediately stopped oil shipments to the North and persuaded other nations to follow suit. North Korea responded by expelling international monitors and restarting its nuclear reactor and reprocessing plant. [50]

In 2003, North Korea withdrew from the NPT, prompting creation of six-party talks — negotiations among the United States, Japan, China, Russia, and North and South Korea that aimed to push the North to eliminate or reduce its nuclear arsenal. In return, the North sought, among other things, a guarantee of its security, the right to use nuclear energy for peaceful purposes, the normalization of diplomatic relations and the lifting of trade sanctions. The United States and Japan wanted verifiable, irreversible disarmament, while China and Russia wanted a more gradual disarmament process, in which the North is rewarded with some form of aid.

Negotiations broke down, however, and in October 2006 North Korea tested its first nuclear device, becoming the world's eighth atomic power and drawing strong international condemnation. Simultaneously, North Korea was building a rocket delivery system. In April 2009, it failed in an attempt to launch the long-range *Taepodong-2* rocket, designed to travel more than 3,000 miles.

After a second nuclear test in 2009, the U.N. Security Council unanimously tightened sanctions on North Korea and encouraged member nations to inspect airplanes and vessels suspected of transporting weapons and other military materiel to North Korea. Besides developing nuclear weapons, Pyongyang also was accused of exporting nuclear and ballistic technology to other states, including Syria and Iran. [51]

Despite the protests and sanctions, North Korea's nuclear weapons program has expanded. In 2012, the Obama administration agreed to provide North Korea with food aid and nutritional supplements for children in return for Pyongyang imposing a moratorium on long-range missile launches and activity at the nation's main nuclear facility. But less than a year later, North Korea conducted its third nuclear test — the first under Kim Jong Un. North Korea's National Defense Commission said the tests and launches will build to an

"upcoming all-out action" against the United States, "the sworn enemy of the Korean people." [52]

In 2015, North Korea claimed to have a hydrogen bomb and to have successfully miniaturized nuclear warheads to fit on ballistic missiles. Although U.S. officials expressed skepticism about both claims, no one questioned North Korea's growing nuclear capabilities.

Then last Sept. 9, about a month before the U.S. presidential election, North Korea detonated the nuclear warhead estimated to have the explosive power of 10 kilotons or possibly more — its most powerful to date. [53] ■

CURRENT SITUATION

Trump Policies

In its first months in office, the Trump administration has made vague, sometimes conflicting statements about North Korea. The underlying message, though, is clear: the United States will not stand by while Pyongyang develops increasingly advanced nuclear weapons that could eventually target the United States.

"We can't allow it to happen," Trump said in an interview in late April. "We cannot let what's been going on for a long period of years to continue." [54]

But the administration's own approach has yet to come into focus. Officials have suggested that tighter sanctions, coordination with China, talks with North Korea and, if necessary, military action might resolve the crisis.

"All options for responding to future provocation must remain on the table," Secretary of State Tillerson told the UN. Security Council on April 29. "Diplomatic and financial levers of power will be backed up by a willingness to counteract North Korean aggression

with military action if necessary." [55]

Tillerson called for better enforcement of existing sanctions and new international sanctions, such as halting a guest-worker program under which Pyongyang gets hard currency from other countries in exchange for cheap labor.

Underscoring U.S. determination on the issue, Tillerson visited the DMZ in March. A month later, the Trump administration sent Vice President Mike Pence to the border "so they can see our resolve in my face," as he said. The administration also dispatched an aircraft carrier, the *Carl Vinson*, to the Sea of Japan in April to stage drills with the South Korean navy. [56] Also in April, the administration summoned all 100 members of the U.S. Senate to the White House for an emergency briefing on the situation, although officials reportedly said little new. [57] A similar briefing was provided on Capitol Hill for members of the House.

Although Trump's actions on North Korea so far have not differed notably from those of past presidents, the administration's rhetoric has been sharper and more dramatic than that of his predecessors. The "theatrics of the Trump administration can be very useful in sending a message to Pyongyang," said Mark Dubowitz, CEO of the Foundation for Defense of Democracies, a nonpartisan foreign policy think tank in Washington that favors stronger sanctions on North Korea. "So much of this is about psychology." [58]

Other experts, however, worry about administration missteps. For example, the White House for days said the *Carl Vinson* was headed toward the Sea of Japan when, in fact, it was moving in the other direction (it eventually changed course). [59] Trump also angered South Koreans when he said Korea "used to be a part of China" (technically it wasn't) and called on Seoul to pay for the THAAD antimissile system, which was not Seoul's understanding of who was paying for it. [60] Recently,

Continued on p. 450

At Issue:

Should the U.S. tighten penalties on companies dealing with North Korea?

SUE MI TERRY
MANAGING DIRECTOR, KOREA, BOWER GROUP ASIA

EXCERPTED FROM TESTIMONY BEFORE THE HOUSE COMMITTEE ON FOREIGN AFFAIRS, ON FEB. 7, 2017, HTTP://TINYURL.COM/M7SKG3V.

*c*ontrary to what many believe, the U.S. has not yet used every option available at our disposal to ratchet up pressure against the Kim regime. As a near-term solution, there's much more we can still do on sanctions, on human rights, on getting information into the North, as well as on deterrence, defense and on diplomacy. . . .

The first step to raise the cost for North Korea is through stricter sanctions, by adding even more individuals and entities to the sanctions list and by seeking better enforcement of sanctions, including secondary sanctions.

Until February 2016 . . . U.S. sanctions against North Korea were a mere shadow of the sanctions applied to Iran, Syria or Burma, and even narrower than those applicable to countries like Belarus and Zimbabwe. Thankfully, with the bipartisan support of this committee, the North Korea Sanctions and Policy Enhancement Act of 2016 was passed and signed into law, and today we finally have stronger sanctions in place.

A month after its passage, in March, the United Nations Security Council also unanimously passed a resolution, U.N. Security Council (UNSC) Resolution 2270, imposing new sanctions on the Kim regime, including mining exports.

In June, triggered by the requirements of the Sanctions Act, the Obama administration finally designated North Korea as a primary money laundering concern, and in July, the Treasury Department sanctioned Kim Jong Un and 10 other senior North Korean individuals and five organizations for human rights violations.

In late November, the U.N. Security Council also got around to another round of sanctions, adopting UNSC Resolution 2321, which further caps North Korea's coal exports, its chief source of hard currency.

But for sanctions to work, [they] will need to be pursued over the course of several years as we did with Iran, and most importantly, they need to be enforced. Here, the chief problem has been that Beijing is still reluctant to follow through in fully and aggressively implementing the U.N. sanctions. . . .

Secondary sanctions must be placed on Chinese banks that help North Korea launder its money and Chinese entities that trade with North Korea or are involved with North Korea's procurement activities. . . . Even if the U.S. has to endure some ire from Beijing for enforcing secondary sanctions, this is exactly what Washington should do.

DOUG BANDOW
SENIOR FELLOW, CATO INSTITUTE; AUTHOR, TRIPWIRE: KOREA AND U.S. FOREIGN POLICY IN A CHANGED WORLD

WRITTEN FOR *CQ RESEARCHER*, MAY 2017

*n*o one outside of Pyongyang wants the Democratic People's Republic of Korea (DPRK) to have nuclear weapons. But there is no obvious way to stop North Korea's program, and enhancing sanctions likely won't work.

Despite the claim that the DPRK's leader Kim Jong Un is irrational, he, along with his grandfather and father, behaved rationally in developing nuclear weapons. Otherwise, no one would pay attention to the small, impoverished state. Nukes also offer North Korea national prestige and a tool for extortion. Most important, nuclear weapons are the only sure deterrent to U.S. military action. Washington is allied with the South, routinely deploys threatening naval and air forces near the North and imposes regime change in nations whenever the whim strikes American policymakers.

If diplomacy ever was going to dissuade the North from building nukes, that time has passed. Military action would be a wild gamble and likely would trigger the Second Korean War with catastrophic consequences.

Unfortunately, tougher economic penalties likely will be ineffective without China's cooperation. Winning that assistance requires more than offering unspecified trade concessions. The United States must address Beijing's political and security concerns about a failed DPRK and a reunited, U.S.-allied Korea.

Washington could impose secondary sanctions, penalizing Chinese enterprises dealing with the North. But that would likely generate resistance from China, a rising nationalistic power. Economic penalties also would disrupt Washington's relationship with Beijing in several important areas. North Korea also might well refuse to comply even if the United States imposed more sanctions. The Kim dynasty refused to change policy even during the mass starvation of the 1990s — and survived.

It would be better if the United States took a multifaceted approach toward the DPRK. Washington should coordinate with Japan and South Korea, engage the North, develop a comprehensive offer for Pyongyang, forge a deal with China to win the latter's support and only then press sanctions with Beijing's support if the North refuses to negotiate. Finally, to reduce North Korea's insecurity, Washington should back away from the two Koreas' military struggle. Washington should withdraw its forces from the South because Seoul can defend itself from conventional attack.

There is no simple answer for eliminating Pyongyang's nuclear program, and focusing on more sanctions is unlikely to work.

Continued from p. 448

Trump also surprised both U.S. officials and allies by praising Kim Jong Un as a "pretty smart cookie" and saying he would be "honored" to meet with Kim "under the right circumstances." [61]

The abrupt shifts in rhetoric can make the already tense situation more dangerous, Korea experts warn. "When they take position A one day and position B the next, that is inherently destabilizing," says MIT's Walsh. "The chances of misinterpretation are larger than they've been in the past."

Subsequently, North Korea accused U.S. and South Korean intelligence agencies in early May of plotting to assassinate Kim Jong Un with biochemical agents and warned it could counterattack. South Korea's National Intelligence Service dismissed the accusation. [63]

In recent months, North Korea has further raised tensions by detaining two American professors working at the Pyongyang University of Science and Technology, bringing the total of detained U.S. citizens to four. The State Department had little comment

must "embrace the North Korean people to achieve peaceful reunification one day." [65] This position puts him at odds with the United States and could greatly complicate Trump administration efforts to pressure Pyongyang.

Some experts say the growing tensions may provide the catalyst for China to take a harder line with Kim. Although Beijing has been reluctant to pressure him in the past, alarms are rising in Beijing over the prospect of war. "China may finally be persuaded to put pressure on North Korea," says the Wilson Center's Litwak.

Other foreign policy experts, however, warn that even if Beijing wanted to pressure North Korea — which remains uncertain — it may not have as much influence as the Trump administration hopes.

"Those who focus on China suggest that Chinese leaders can snap their fingers and North Korea would come to heel," says Cato's Bandow. "That almost certainly is not the case. North Korea doesn't want to be subject to anyone."

Fratricide

On Feb. 13, the estranged half-brother of North Korea's ruler Kim Jong Un was waiting to catch a flight at Kuala Lumpur International Airport to his home in Macau when two young women walked up to him and touched something to his face. Within moments, he was struggling to breathe. He died on his way to the hospital.

Authorities rapidly determined that the 45-year-old was killed by VX nerve agent, a banned chemical weapon that North Korea is suspected of stockpiling. Suspicion immediately turned to the North Korean government, even though Pyongyang denied any involvement.

South Korea's acting president Hwang Kyo-ahn said the killing "starkly demonstrated the North Korean regime's recklessness and cruelty as well as the fact that it will do anything, everything, in order to maintain its power." [66]

Kim Jong Nam, the estranged half-brother of North Korean ruler Kim Jong Un, was poisoned on Feb.13 with VX nerve agent at Kuala Lumpur International Airport. VX is among the banned chemical weapons North Korea is suspected of stockpiling. Kim Jong Nam, who had questioned his family's right to hereditary rule, had worried for years that his half-brother might try to kill him. Pyongyang has denied any involvement in his death.

AFP/Getty Images/JoongAng Sunday

If Washington expects to intimidate Kim, there is no sign it is succeeding. During the new president's first 100 days in office, North Korea conducted nine missile tests — although not all were successful — and repeatedly threatened overwhelming retaliation to any U.S. military strikes. The *Rodong Sinmun*, official newspaper of the ruling Korean Workers' Party, warned of a "super-mighty preemptive strike" that would reduce American military forces "to ashes." [62]

on the most recent detention, except to say it was "aware of reports" that an American had been detained and was working with the Swedish embassy in Pyongyang. [64]

Further clouding the situation, South Korea on May 9 elected a new president, human rights lawyer Moon Jae-in, who favors a more conciliatory approach with North Korea, emphasizing dialogue instead of sanctions and pressure. He contended that South Korea

Kim Jong Nam had questioned his family's right to heredity rule, and he had worried for years that his half-brother might try to kill him. But he had little interest in politics and was living in Macau, an autonomous administrative district of China, under Beijing's protection, including sometimes a round-the-clock security detail.

Foreign policy analysts question why Pyongyang would go to such lengths to kill Kim Jong Nam, and to do so with a banned chemical agent in a public place. Some observers speculate that a key motive may have been self-preservation. If the United States or other countries wanted to assassinate Kim Jong Un, then eliminating his half-brother would make it harder to find a successor.

"It shouldn't be surprising that, if people are talking about decapitation, the logical counter is to decapitate the prospective successors," says MIT's Walsh. "The prospects of the half-brother really being a leader were limited, but China was protecting him because they wanted an option."

Indeed, Beijing officials were reportedly shocked by the effrontery of the murder. "China's inner circle of government is highly nervous about this," said Wang Weimin, a professor at the School of International Relations and Public Affairs at Fudan University in Shanghai. The assassination, he argued, makes China "more aware of how unpredictable and cruel the current North Korean regime is." [67]

Kim also may have been demonstrating that his arsenal extends beyond nuclear weapons. North Korea, which is not a party to the Chemical Weapons Convention — a 1997 treaty that prohibits the use, development, production and stockpiling of chemical weapons — has produced chemical weapons since the 1980s and is believed to have biological weapons. [68]

In a war, experts say, Pyongyang could use aircraft, missiles, artillery or even grenades to attack South Korea and possibly Japan with chemical and biological weapons.

And deploying VX nerve agent — which forces a victim's muscles to clench uncontrollably, preventing breathing — in a crowded airport may have been intended to send a message about Pyongyang's willingness to expose large populations to lethal chemicals.

"This may have been a timely reminder to adversaries that North Korea has more than one way to strike back," Walsh says. ∎

OUTLOOK

Signs of Prosperity

John Delury, an assistant professor of international studies at Yonsei University in Seoul, says that when he used to travel to North Korea he could easily keep track of how many cars he saw. But when he went in 2013, there were too many cars to count, as well as a surprising number of people with cellphones.

"The crude economic indicators that we get are of steady growth," said Delury. "You can see the emergence of a public-consumer culture." [69]

Delury and other Korea specialists say the North Korean economy, while still lagging far behind most countries, seems to be in somewhat better shape since Kim Jong Un eased government restrictions on commercial activities. A booming black market is boosting the importation of consumer goods, largely from China. Residents, especially in Pyongyang, have more access to South Korean soap operas through cellphones, flash drives and other technologies, many made in China.

Some observers of North Korea say the greater affluence and access to information may lead to an increased openness and perhaps an eventual softening in government policies. "There are more cellphones, more North Koreans doing

business," says MIT's Walsh. "North Koreans are more aware, and you might make an argument that opening up is a first step toward a resolution."

Like Delury, other recent visitors to Pyongyang have been surprised at signs of prosperity despite years of sanctions. Journalist Jean Lee, who opened up an Associated Press bureau in Pyongyang five years ago and then returned to the country this year as a global fellow with the Wilson Center, said nearly everyone in the city had smartphones and plenty of shopping options.

It's "just amazing the kinds of products that they have on the shelves," she said. "I saw so many varieties of potato chips, varieties of canned goods, what would be their equivalent of Spam, for example, but all kinds of things — computers, tablets, PCs — all kinds of things that you might not expect to see in a country that is still very poor." [70]

An increasing number of goods appear to be made locally, reportedly driven by government policies designed to make the country more self-sufficient and to diminish the potential impact of sanctions. "Around 2013, Kim Jong Un started talking about the need for import substitution," said Andray Abrahamian, associate director of research at the Choson Exchange, a Singapore-based group that trains North Koreans in business skills. "There was clearly recognition that too many products were being imported from China." [71]

If sanctions and negotiations don't work, some foreign policy experts wonder if Washington could play for time, in the hopes that North Korea — like the Soviet Union and Maoist China decades ago — will becomes less of a military threat as it moves toward a more market-oriented system.

Some say the consensus in Washington is that the United States must stop North Korea from developing intercontinental missiles, even if that means covert actions to topple the Kim government or a military strike. "Otherwise, we're staring down the barrel of an ICBM," said Sen.

Bob Corker, R-Tenn., chairman of the Senate Foreign Relations Committee. [72]

But some long-time Korean observers say the calculus may not be so clear-cut. "We lived through the Cold War with Soviet missiles aimed at every American city," Walsh says. "It wasn't pretty, but we got through it." ∎

Notes

[1] Choe Sang-Hun, "North Korea launches a missile, its first test after an election in the South," *The New York Times*, May 13, 2017, http://tinyurl.com/kc2bvg3.

[2] Stephen J. Adler, Steve Holland and Jeff Mason, "Exclusive: Trump says 'major, major' conflict with North Korea possible, but seeks diplomacy," Reuters, April 28, 2017, http://tinyurl.com/mmtw3sn.

[3] Gerry Mullany, Chris Buckley and David E. Sanger, "China warns of 'storm clouds gathering' in U.S.-North Korea standoff," *The New York Times*, April 14, 2017, http://tinyurl.com/lbqbf8j.

[4] *Ibid.*

[5] "Report of the Commission of Inquiry on Human Rights in the Democratic People's Republic of Korea," U.N. Commission of Inquiry on Human Rights in the Democratic People's Republic of Korea, U.N. Office of the High Commissioner for Human Rights, Feb. 17, 2014, http://tinyurl.com/nxl2d3e.

[6] Peter Grier, Jack Detsch and Francine Kiefer, "U.S. missile defense: Getting to 'ready' on North Korea threat," *The Christian Science Monitor*, May 3, 2017, http://tinyurl.com/ms7z6kq.

[7] Katie Hunt, K. J. Kwon and Jason Hanna, "North Korea claims successful test of nuclear warhead," CNN, Sept. 10, 2016, http://tinyurl.com/gpnc89e.

[8] Elizabeth McLaughlin and Luis Martinez, "A look at every North Korean missile test this year," ABC News, April 28, 2017, http://tinyurl.com/ny2aydd.

[9] Russell Goldman, "DNA confirms assassination victim was half-brother of Kim Jong-un, Malaysia says," *The New York Times*, March 15, 2017, http://tinyurl.com/l7nk34h.

[10] "South Korea," *The World Fact Book*, https://www.cia.gov/library/publications/the-world-factbook/geos/ks.html.

[11] See Niall McCarthy, "How North and South Korea's armed forces compare (infographic)," *Forbes*, April 11, 2017, http://tinyurl.com/lwmm5xp.

[12] Troop estimates are summarized in Greg Price, "U.S. military presence in Asia: troops stationed in Japan, South Korea and beyond," *Newsweek*, April 26, 2017, http://tinyurl.com/mt7ygf5. China's objections to the THAAD antimissile system are covered in "China presses South Korea on Thaad missile system," BBC News, May 11, 2017, http://tinyurl.com/muorzqc.

[13] Choe Sang-Hun, David E. Sanger and William J. Broad, "North Korean missile launch fails, and a show of strength fizzles," *The New York Times*, April 15, 2017, http://tinyurl.com/mrnyxas.

[14] Zeke J. Miller, "U.S. sanctions North Korea over Sony hack," *Time*, Jan. 2, 2015, http://tinyurl.com/lgae9h8. Melanie Eversley, "Ransomware hack linked to North Korea, researchers say," *USA Today*, May 15, 2017, http://tinyurl.com/lgmtr75.

[15] Robert Delaney, "Tillerson calls for all countries to downgrade ties with North Korea to pressure country," *South China Morning Post*, April 28, 2017, http://tinyurl.com/jvzprbs.

[16] "North Korea threat: Pyongyang directly criticizes China in rare move," Fox News, May 4, 2017, http://tinyurl.com/lee9c9g.

[17] "Report of the Panel of Experts established pursuant to resolution 1874 (2009)," U.N. Security Council, Feb. 27, 2017, http://tinyurl.com/kaurzbb.

[18] Anna Fifield and Anne Gearan, "Tillerson says diplomacy with North Korea has 'failed'; Pyongyang warns of war," *The Washington Post*, March 16, 2017, http://tinyurl.com/kd63h7t.

[19] Jenny Lee, "Sanctions against North Korea: How strong should they be?" Voice of America, Feb. 9, 2017, http://tinyurl.com/mqao2kn.

[20] Testimony by Bruce Klingner, "Sisyphean diplomacy: The dangers of premature negotiations with North Korea," House Subcommittee on Asia and the Pacific, Committee on Foreign Affairs, March 21, 2017, http://tinyurl.com/mte2evf.

[21] *Ibid.*

[22] Ellen Mitchell, "Graham: There are 'no good choices left' with North Korea," *The Hill*, April 25, 2017, http://tinyurl.com/l5d46yd.

[23] McCarthy, *op. cit.*

[24] Kim Chul-soo, "Number of U.S. citizens living in South Korea rises 30 percent in 10 years," *The Korea Times*, July 2, 2015; and Ryan Browne, "Top general: Cheaper to keep troops in South Korea than U.S.," CNN, April 21, 2016, http://tinyurl.com/lo6wo4g.

[25] Yoko Wakatsuki and James Griffiths, "North Korea may be able to arm missiles with sarin, Japan PM says," CNN, April 13, 2017, http://tinyurl.com/maxqjwz.

[26] John M. Donnelly, "Analysis: U.S. Military Options in North Korea — From Bad to Worse," *Roll Call*, April 25, 2017, http://tinyurl.com/lj2mfa6.

[27] *Ibid.*

[28] Anna Fifield, "Twenty-five million reasons the U.S. hasn't struck North Korea," *The Washington Post*, April 21, 2017, http://tinyurl.com/maxmqmp.

[29] Philip Rucker, "Kasich: Trump should 'eradicate' North Korean leadership," *The Washington Post*, April 28, 2017, http://tinyurl.com/k5j5cv3.

[30] Choe Sang-Hun, "In hail of bullets and fire, North Korea killed official who wanted reform," *The New York Times*, March 12, 2016, http://tinyurl.com/kykaxok.

[31] K. J. Kwon and Ben Westcott, "Kim Jong Un has executed over 300 people since coming to power," CNN, Dec. 29, 2016, http://tinyurl.com/lazvyc2.

[32] Mark Hanrahan, "North Korean defector says elite turning their backs on Kim Jong Un," NBC News, Jan. 27, 2017, http://tinyurl.com/gubftg2.

[33] "Report of the Commission of Inquiry on Human Rights in the Democratic People's Republic of Korea," *op. cit.*

[34] *Ibid.* See the press release accompanying the report, which is at http://tinyurl.com/peobg3f.

[35] Joshua Stanton and Sung-Yoon Lee, "Pyongyang's Hunger Games," *The New York Times*, March 7, 2014, http://tinyurl.com/lmkckq6; and Katie McKenna, "North Korea, South Korea: Economic Snapshot," Fox Business, April 28, 2017, http://tinyurl.com/n4j2zfe.

[36] For background, see Robert Kiener, "North Korean Menace," *CQ Researcher*, July 5, 2011, pp. 315-340.

[37] Kim Young-Sik, "The Early US-Korea Relations,"

About the Author

David Hosansky is a freelance writer in the Denver area. He previously was a senior writer at *CQ Weekly* and the *Florida Times-Union* in Jacksonville, where he was twice nominated for a Pulitzer Prize. His previous *CQ Researcher* reports include "Mass Transit" and "Preventing Hazing."

Association for Asian Research, July 25, 2003, http://tinyurl.com/ms8czat.

[38] Mary H. Cooper, "North Korean Crisis," *CQ Researcher*, April 11, 2003, pp. 321-344, http://tinyurl.com/d5wyr7.

[39] See "Republic of Korea," World Bank, April 14, 2017, http://tinyurl.com/nuj33xk.

[40] Stanton and Lee, *op. cit.*

[41] Ray Locker, "Book reveals new details of N. Korea capture of Pueblo," *USA Today*, Jan. 1, 2014, http://tinyurl.com/mfw6ln8.

[42] William Chapman, "North Korean leader's son blamed for Rangoon bombing," *The Washington Post*, Dec. 3, 1983, http://tinyurl.com/lslwjt9.

[43] "Kim Jong-Un's chances of success 'less than 10 percent,' " *Chosunilbo*, Oct. 16, 2010, http://tinyurl.com/kwczsc5.

[44] Terrence McCoy, "North Korean official reportedly executed with a flamethrower," *The Washington Post*, April 8, 2014, http://tinyurl.com/n6j5knv.

[45] Brian Knowlton and David E. Sanger, "N. Korea's first nuclear test draws condemnation," *The New York Times*, Oct. 9, 2006, http://tinyurl.com/lkz2kb3.

[46] David E. Sanger, "North Koreans unveil new plant for nuclear use," *The New York Times*, Nov. 21, 2010, http://tinyurl.com/mbb7rhx.

[47] Kelsey Davenport, "The US-North Korean Agreed Framework at a Glance," The Arms Control Association, Aug. 17, 2004, http://tinyurl.com/zcqnwo4.

[48] Mary Beth Nikitin, "North Korea's Nuclear Weapons: Technical Issues," Congressional Research Service, Jan. 20, 2011, http://tinyurl.com/ke6lfg3.

[49] Rupert Wingfield-Hayes, "The North Korean spy who blew up a plane," BBC News, April 22, 2013, http://tinyurl.com/k4svfbz.

[50] Simon Jeffery, "Expelled UN inspectors leave N. Korea," *The Guardian*, Dec. 31, 2002, http://tinyurl.com/loc2gmu.

[51] Louis Charbonneau, "North Korea, Iran trade missile technology: U.N.," Reuters, May 15, 2011, http://tinyurl.com/lhzg887.

[52] "North Korea nuclear timeline fast facts," CNN, April 6, 2017, http://tinyurl.com/z75fcsz.

[53] Katie Hunt, K. J. Kwon, and Jason Hanna, "North Korea claims successful test of nuclear warhead," CNN, Sept. 10, 2016, http://tinyurl.com/gpnc89e.

[54] Susan Jones, "Trump: North Korean leader 'a pretty smart cookie,' " CBS News, May 1, 2017, http://tinyurl.com/msf4y9g.

[55] Margaret Besheer, "Tillerson urges UN Security Council to take action before N. Korea does," Voice of America, April 29, 2017, http://tinyurl.com/kcz5cxs.

[56] Michael Crowley, "North Korea defies Trump," *Politico*, April 28, 2017, http://tinyurl.com/kx2yybs.

[57] Audie Cornish, "The White House briefs the Senate on North Korea," NPR, April 26, 2017, http://tinyurl.com/mwh2hzj.

[58] Crowley, *op. cit.*

[59] Mark Landler and Eric Schmitt, "Aircraft carrier wasn't sailing to deter North Korea, as U.S. suggested," *The New York Times*, April 18, 2017, http://tinyurl.com/kkenv4v.

[60] Michelle Ye Hee Lee, "Trump's claim that Korea 'actually used to be a part of China,' " *The Washington Post*, April 19, 2017, http://tinyurl.com/mos6zvu. Also see Choe Sang-Hun, "Trump rattles South Korea by saying it should pay for antimissile system," *The New York Times*, April 28, 2017, http://tinyurl.com/m9s8xws.

[61] Ashley Parker and Anne Gearan, "President Trump says he would be 'honored' to meet with North Korean dictator," *The Washington Post*, May 1, 2017, http://tinyurl.com/nxb8p3p.

[62] Doug Stanglin, "North Korea threatens 'super-mighty' strike on U.S.," *USA Today*, April 20, 2017, http://tinyurl.com/kndfrxt.

[63] Choe Sang-Hun, "North Korea accuses South and U.S. of plotting to kill Kim Jong-un," *The New York Times*, May 5, 2017, http://tinyurl.com/n5cxqdg.

[64] Taehoon Lee, "North Korea detains fourth US citizen," CNN, May 8, 2017, http://tinyurl.com/m4x2lrj.

[65] Choe Sang-Hun, "South Korea elects Moon Jae-in, who backs talks with North, as president," *The New York Times*, May 9, 2017, http://tinyurl.com/lw7l86x.

[66] Choe Sang-Hun and Richard C. Paddock, "Kim Jong-nam killing was 'terrorist act' by North Korea, South says," *The New York Times*, Feb. 20, 2017, http://tinyurl.com/ke4wp2u.

[67] Simon Denyer, "In China, a sense of betrayal after the assassination of Kim Jong Nam," *The Washington Post*, Feb. 17, 2017, http://tinyurl.com/mdc3e9m.

[68] Hyung-Jin Kim and Kim Tong-Hyung, "North Korea's chemical weapons," *Real Clear Defense*, Feb. 25, 2017, http://tinyurl.com/jr7oxrf.

[69] Mark Bowden, "Understanding Kim Jong Un, the world's most enigmatic and unpredictable dictator," *Vanity Fair*, Feb. 12, 2015, http://tinyurl.com/q4qczez.

[70] "In North Korea's capital, more abundance than expected in everyday life," NPR, May 5, 2017, http://tinyurl.com/lryqn6n.

[71] Sue-Lin Wang and James Pearson, "Made in North Korea: As tougher sanctions loom, more local goods in stores," Reuters, May 8, 2017, http://tinyurl.com/k96ghk7.

[72] Fifield and Gearan, *op. cit.*

FOR MORE INFORMATION

Carnegie Endowment for International Peace, 1779 Massachusetts Ave., N.W., Washington, DC 20036-2103; 202-483-7600; www.carnegieendownment.org. Global network of policy research centers that favors exploring negotiations with North Korea.

The Committee for Human Rights in North Korea, 1001 Connecticut Ave., N.W., Suite 435, Washington, DC 20036; 202-499-7970; www.hrnk.org. Seeks to raise world awareness about conditions in North Korea, including human rights abuses.

The Council on Foreign Relations, 58 E. 68th St., New York, NY 10065; 212-434-9400; www.cfr.org. Think tank that specializes in U.S. foreign policy and international affairs, including U.S. relations with North Korea.

Foundation for Defense of Democracies, PO Box 33249, Washington, DC 20033; 202-207-0190; www.defenddemocracy.org. Nonpartisan institute focusing on foreign policy and national security that favors imposing stronger sanctions on North Korea.

James Martin Center for Nonproliferation Studies, 460 Pierce St., Monterey, CA 93940; 831-647-4154; www.nonproliferation.org. Affiliated with Middlebury College; conducts policy-oriented research and trains East Asia scholars and government officials.

U.S.-Korea Institute, Paul H. Nitze School of Advanced International Studies, 1740 Massachusetts Ave., N.W., Washington, DC 20036; 202-663-5600; www.sais-jhu.edu. Researches the Korean Peninsula and maintains a website, 38 North, that offers analysis of North Korean issues.

Bibliography

Selected Sources

Books

Demick, Barbara, *Nothing to Envy: Ordinary Lives in North Korea*, Spiegel & Grau, 2009.
A journalist formerly based in South Korea examines the lives of six "ordinary" North Koreans, based on their reports after defecting to the South.

Lankov, Andrei, *The Real North Korea: Life and Politics in the Failed Stalinist Utopia*, Oxford University Press, 2014.
A native of the Soviet Union who has studied North Korea since visiting as an exchange student in the 1980s looks at how its leaders have sustained the regime with limited resources and amid international hostility.

Lee, Hyeonseo, *The Girl with Seven Names: A North Korean Defector's Story*, William Collins, 2015.
This international bestseller tells of Lee's escape from North Korea at age 17, her subsequent struggles in China and her daring trip back to North Korea to bring her mother and brother to South Korea.

Oberdorfer, Don, and Robert Carlin, *The Two Koreas: A Contemporary History*, Basic Books, 2013.
Two Korea experts examine the ongoing conflicts between South and North and show how the once unified nations might achieve reconciliation.

Articles

Birrell, Ian, " 'How could our country lie so completely to us?': meet the North Korean defectors," *The Guardian*, Aug. 27, 2016, http://tinyurl.com/hh7fmbe.
The author interviews defectors in South Korea to learn about their life in the North, their escapes and their struggles to adapt to new lives.

Bowden, Mark, "Understanding Kim Jong Un, the world's most enigmatic and unpredictable dictator," *Vanity Fair*, Feb. 12, 2015, http://tinyurl.com/q4qczez.
Journalist Bowden, author of *Black Hawk Down*, portrays the North Korean leader as clever, ruthless, impetuous and very much in charge.

Crowley, Michael, "North Korea defies Trump," *Politico*, April 28, 2017, http://tinyurl.com/kx2yybs.
A senior correspondent analyzes Pyongyang's responses to the Trump administration's declarations and how President Trump's policies may ultimately resemble those of the previous administration.

Donnelly, John M., "Analysis: U.S. Military Options in
North Korea — From Bad to Worse," *Roll Call*, April 25, 2017, http://tinyurl.com/lj2mfa6.**
This in-depth look at North Korea's military capabilities underscores the challenges the United States would face in a preemptive strike.

Hunt, Katie, K.J. Kwon and Jason Hanna, "North Korea claims successful test of nuclear warhead," CNN, Sept. 10, 2016, http://tinyurl.com/gpnc89e.
The authors cover North Korea's fifth and most powerful nuclear bomb test and provide context on Pyongyang's nuclear program.

Lee, Jenny, "Sanctions Against North Korea: How Strong Should They Be?" Voice of America, Feb. 9, 2017, http://tinyurl.com/mqao2kn.
Several Korean experts analyze how sanctions can be toughened or better enforced to get Pyongyang to stop its nuclear program.

Snyder, Scott, "How North Korea evades UN sanctions through international 'front' companies," *Forbes*, March 3, 2017, http://tinyurl.com/mxjxs7j.
An expert at the Council on Foreign Relations examines North Korean strategies to evade international sanctions.

Reports and Studies

"Report of the Commission of Inquiry on Human Rights in the Democratic People's Republic of Korea," U.N. Commission of Inquiry on Human Rights in the Democratic People's Republic of Korea, Office of the U.N. High Commissioner for Human Rights, Feb. 17, 2014, http://tinyurl.com/nxl2d3e.
A special U.N. commission says North Korea uses murder, torture, starvation, sexual violence and other tactics to maintain political control.

Chanlett-Avery, Emma, Ian E. Rinehart and Mary Beth D. Nikitin, "North Korea: U.S. Relations, Nuclear Diplomacy, and Internal Situation," Congressional Research Service, Jan. 15, 2016, http://tinyurl.com/k7938np.
Congress' bipartisan research arm discusses Pyongyang's nuclear program, economy and human rights record, as well as past U.S. negotiations and the role of China.

Klingner, Bruce, "Sisyphean Diplomacy: The Dangers of Premature Negotiations with North Korea," Heritage Foundation, March 21, 2017, http://tinyurl.com/mte2evf.
A former CIA analyst and now a senior fellow at the conservative think tank examines the crisis with North Korea and says rather than trying to restart failed negotiations the United States should try using tougher sanctions to pressure Pyongyang.

The Next Step:

Additional Articles from Current Periodicals

China's Role

Eleftheriou-Smith, Loulla-Mae, "China 'tells citizens to leave North Korea,' as tensions with US escalate," *The Independent,* **May 3, 2017, https://tinyurl.com/mmbk5js.**

A Chinese man living in North Korea told Radio Free Asia, a U.S. based radio station broadcasting to Asian countries, that China warned its citizens to leave North Korea immediately due to tensions between Pyongyang and the United States.

Feldscher, Kyle, "Trump: If China wanted to end North Korean aggression, it could," *The Washington Examiner,* **April 21, 2017, https://tinyurl.com/lqe3foo.**

President Trump tweeted that China is the "economic lifeline" to North Korea and said China should play a larger role in combatting North Korean aggression.

Griffiths, James, Tim Schwarz and Serenitie Wang, "North Korean ships dock in Chinese port despite coal embargo," CNN, April 21, 2017, https://tinyurl.com/mqfglrx.

Six North Korean ships loaded with coal docked at Chinese ports in April, despite China banning coal imports from North Korea in February.

North Korean Leadership

Brunnstrom, David, "North Korea media issues rare criticism of China over nuclear warnings," Reuters, May 3, 2017, https://tinyurl.com/mvwywkl.

North Korea's state-run media said China worsened international tensions when Chinese state-run media called for tougher sanctions on North Korea's nuclear program.

Jamieson, Alastair, and Stella Kim, "North Korea Detains Fourth American Citizen," NBC News, May 7, 2017, http://tinyurl.com/m7zc2oa.

North Korea detained a fourth American citizen, who was working at a university in the nation's capital, for "hostile acts against the republic," according to a state-run news outlet.

Rucker, Philip, "Kasich: Trump should 'eradicate' North Korean leadership," *The Washington Post,* **April 28, 2017, https://tinyurl.com/m4k6wte.**

Gov. John Kasich, R-Ohio, said President Trump should launch a surgical military and intelligence strike to "eradicate" North Korean leader Kim Jung Un and his top lieutenants but stopped short of calling for assassination.

Nuclear Weapons

The Associated Press, "US test fires ballistic missile from California coastal base," ABC News, May 3 2017, https://tinyurl.com/l4xbrfh.

Amid rising tensions between the United States and North

Korea, the United States fired an unarmed test missile from a California military base after 10 months of planning.

Gaydos, Ryan, "North Korea threat: WH official says Kim could use nuclear weapons as 'blackmail,' " Fox News, May 3, 2017, https://tinyurl.com/n7smz4p.

Matt Pottinger, the Asia director on President Trump's National Security Council, said North Korea could use its nuclear weapons as "blackmail" to force the United States out of the Korean Peninsula and abandon its South Korea ally.

Hjelmgaard, Kim, "North Korea writes rare letter to House protesting new sanctions," *USA Today,* **May, 12, 2017, http://tinyurl.com/k8jvhbl.**

North Korea sent the U.S. House of Representatives a letter protesting new U.S. military sanctions over North Korea's ballistic and nuclear weapons testing.

Trump Strategy

Abraham, Alana, "President Trump and Vladimir Putin Had a 'Very Good' Phone Call," *Time,* **May 2, 2017, https://tinyurl.com/mbh6cut.**

The White House told reporters that President Trump discussed ways to de-escalate tensions with North Korea in a "very good" phone call with Russian President Vladimir Putin.

Jacobs, Jennifer, and Margaret Talev, "Trump Says He'd Meet With Kim Jong Un Under Right Circumstances," Bloomberg, May 2, 2017, https://tinyurl.com/kqs8k5k.

President Trump said he "would be honored" to meet North Korean leader Kim Jung Un under the right conditions, which White House Press Secretary Sean Spicer later clarified "are not there right now."

CITING *CQ* RESEARCHER

Sample formats for citing these reports in a bibliography include the ones listed below. Preferred styles and formats vary, so please check with your instructor or professor.

MLA STYLE

Mantel, Barbara. "Coal Industry's Future." <u>CQ Researcher</u> 17 June 2016: 529-552.

APA STYLE

Mantel, B. (2016, June 17). Coal Industry's Future. *CQ Researcher,* 6, 529-552.

CHICAGO STYLE

Mantel, Barbara. "Coal Industry's Future." *CQ Researcher,* June 17, 2016, 529-52.

In-depth Reports on Issues in the News

Are you writing a paper?

Need backup for a debate?

Want to become an expert on an issue?

For 90 years, students have turned to *CQ Researcher* for in-depth reporting on issues in the news. Reports on a full range of political and social issues are now available. Following is a selection of recent reports:

Civil Liberties
Privacy and the Internet, 12/15
Intelligence Reform, 5/15
Religion and Law, 11/14

Crime/Law
High-Tech Policing, 4/17
Forensic Science Controversies, 2/17
Jailing Debtors, 9/16
Decriminalizing Prostitution, 4/16
Restorative Justice, 2/16
The Dark Web, 1/16
Immigrant Detention, 10/15

Education
Charter Schools, 3/17
Civic Education, 2/17
Student Debt, 11/16
Apprenticeships, 10/16

Environment/Society
Anti-Semitism, 5/17
Native American Sovereignty, 5/17
Women in Prison, 3/17
Guns on Campus, 1/17
Mass Transit, 12/16
Arctic Development, 12/16

Health/Safety
Sports and Sexual Assault, 4/17
Reducing Traffic Deaths, 2/17
Opioid Crisis, 10/16
Mosquito-Borne Disease, 7/16

Politics/Economy
Rethinking Foreign Aid, 4/17
Troubled Brazil, 4/17
Reviving Rural Economies, 3/17
Immigrants and the Economy, 2/17
Trump Presidency, 1/17
European Union's Future, 12/16

Upcoming Reports

Pandemics, 6/2/17   Food Labeling, 6/9/17   Trust in Journalism, 6/16/17

ACCESS

CQ Researcher is available in print and online. For access, visit your library or www.cqresearcher.com.

STAY CURRENT

For notice of upcoming *CQ Researcher* reports or to learn more about *CQ Researcher* products, subscribe to the free email newsletters, *CQ Researcher Alert!* and *CQ Researcher News*: http://cqpress.com/newsletters.

PURCHASE

To purchase a *CQ Researcher* report in print or electronic format (PDF), visit www.cqpress.com or call 866-427-7737. Single reports start at $15. Bulk purchase discounts and electronic-rights licensing are also available.

SUBSCRIBE

Annual full-service *CQ Researcher* subscriptions—including 44 reports a year, monthly index updates, and a bound volume—start at $1,131. Add $25 for domestic postage.

CQ Researcher Online offers a backfile from 1991 and a number of tools to simplify research. For pricing information, call 800-818-7243 or 805-499-9774 or email librarysales@sagepub.com.

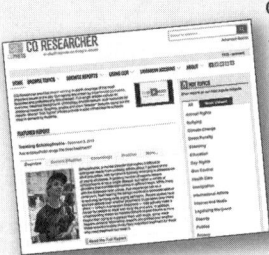

CQ RESEARCHER

CQPRESS

In-depth reports on today's issues

Published by CQ Press, an Imprint of SAGE Publications, Inc.

www.cqresearcher.com

Pandemic Threat

Is the world prepared for the next outbreak?

P ublic health officials say the world is overdue for a pandemic that could kill 30 million people within a year. The possible causes include the expanding and mobile global population, mutating viruses that can outfox vaccine makers, the threat of bioterrorism and accelerating climate change that breeds new diseases. Meanwhile, in the wake of recent outbreaks of the Zika virus in Brazil, Ebola in Africa and a new strain of bird flu in China, many experts say the World Health Organization (WHO) and other agencies charged with protecting against dangerous pathogens are under-resourced and underfunded. But some experts are more optimistic, saying the global health community has taken important steps to prevent and respond to pandemics. For example, the United States has invested in crisis preparation, and WHO set up a global surveillance network and pandemic emergency fund, these experts note. But gaps in funding and leadership remain, and many warn that vaccines exist for just a fraction of the 300 known infectious viruses.

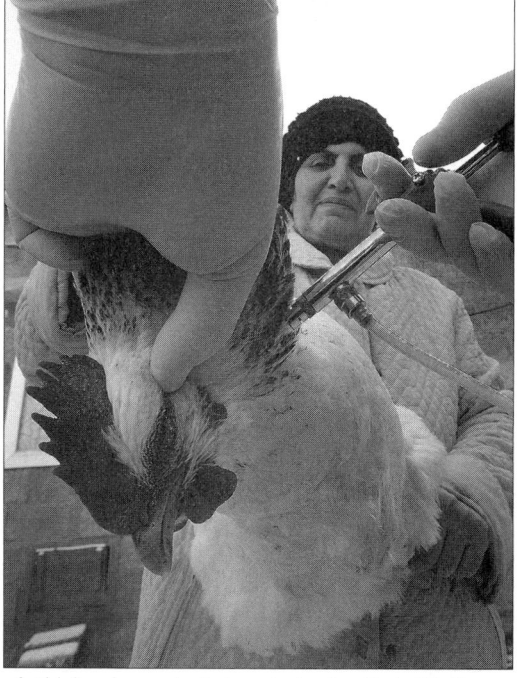

A chicken is vaccinated against avian flu in Chaltyr, a village in Russia's Rostov region, on Feb. 9. The U.S. Agency for International Development is monitoring disease outbreaks in 20 countries for their potential to become the next pandemic. Most infectious diseases that afflicted humans this century originated in animals.

I THIS REPORT

THE ISSUES	**459**
BACKGROUND	**465**
CHRONOLOGY	**467**
CURRENT SITUATION	**470**
AT ISSUE	**473**
OUTLOOK	**474**
BIBLIOGRAPHY	**478**
THE NEXT STEP	**479**

CQ Researcher • June 2, 2017 • www.cqresearcher.com
Volume 27, Number 20 • Pages 457-480

RECIPIENT OF SOCIETY OF PROFESSIONAL JOURNALISTS AWARD FOR EXCELLENCE ◆ AMERICAN BAR ASSOCIATION SILVER GAVEL AWARD

SAGE Publishing · CQPRESS
Los Angeles | London | New Delhi
Singapore | Washington DC | Melbourne

THE ISSUES

459 • Are the World Health Organization and other groups prepared to stop the next pandemic?
• Is the United States spending enough on pandemic preparedness?
• Should governments mandate quarantines and vaccinations to prevent pandemics?

BACKGROUND

465 **First Pandemics**
Disease spread as humans created social and economic networks.

466 **Plague and Quarantines**
The "Black Death" killed up to 200 million.

466 **Vaccines and Antibiotics**
An English doctor invented the first vaccine in 1796.

469 **Bioterror Threats**
Armies used biological agents as early as 184 B.C.

CURRENT SITUATION

470 **Emerging Threats**
Recent disease alerts range from measles to yellow fever.

472 **Leadership Vacuum**
Numerous positions are unfilled in the global health community.

474 **Global Collaboration**
Researchers worry about the Trump administration's commitment to health funding.

OUTLOOK

474 **Preventing Pandemics**
Experts say the world is overdue for one.

SIDEBARS AND GRAPHICS

460 **Predicting the Next Pandemic**
A U.S. agency is monitoring disease outbreaks in 20 countries.

461 **U.S. Is Biggest Donor to WHO**
The World Health Organization relies on donors for 70 percent of its budget.

464 **Ebola Killed Thousands in West Africa**
Guinea, Liberia and Sierra Leone bore the brunt of the crisis.

467 **Chronology**
Key events since 1796.

468 **Waging War on Superbugs**
"In China and India, there are bacteria resistant to all antibiotics."

470 **Experts Warn of Growing Bioterrorism Threat**
"The risk of bioterrorism goes up every day."

473 **At Issue:**
Should governments mandate quarantines?

FOR FURTHER RESEARCH

477 **For More Information**
Organizations to contact.

478 **Bibliography**
Selected sources used.

479 **The Next Step**
Additional articles.

479 **Citing CQ Researcher**
Sample bibliography formats.

Cover: Getty Images/TASS/Valery Matytsin

 CQ RESEARCHER

June 2, 2017
Volume 27, Number 20

EXECUTIVE EDITOR: Thomas J. Billitteri
tjb@sagepub.com

ASSISTANT MANAGING EDITORS: Kenneth Fireman, kenneth.fireman@sagepub.com, Kathy Koch, kathy.koch@sagepub.com, Scott Rohrer, scott.rohrer@sagepub.com

ASSOCIATE MANAGING EDITOR: Val Ellicott

SENIOR CONTRIBUTING EDITOR:
Thomas J. Colin
tom.colin@sagepub.com

CONTRIBUTING WRITERS: Marcia Clemmitt, Sarah Glazer, Reed Karaim, Barbara Mantel, Chuck McCutcheon, Tom Price

SENIOR PROJECT EDITOR: Olu B. Davis

EDITORIAL ASSISTANT: Anika Reed

FACT CHECKERS: Eva P. Dasher, Michelle Harris, Betsy Towner Levine, Robin Palmer

SAGE Publishing | **CQPRESS**

Los Angeles | London | New Delhi
Singapore | Washington DC | Melbourne

An Imprint of SAGE Publications, Inc.

SENIOR VICE PRESIDENT,
GLOBAL LEARNING RESOURCES:
Karen Phillips

EXECUTIVE DIRECTOR, ONLINE LIBRARY AND REFERENCE PUBLISHING:
Todd Baldwin

CQ Researcher (ISSN 1056-2036) is printed on acid-free paper. Published weekly, except: (March wk. 4) (May wk. 4) (July wks. 1, 2) (Aug. wks. 2, 3) (Nov. wk. 4) and (Dec. wks. 3, 4). Published by SAGE Publications, Inc., 2455 Teller Rd., Thousand Oaks, CA 91320. Annual full-service subscriptions start at $1,131. For pricing, call 1-800-818-7243. To purchase a CQ Researcher report in print or electronic format (PDF), visit www.cqpress.com or call 866-427-7737. Single reports start at $15. Bulk purchase discounts and electronic-rights licensing are also available. Periodicals postage paid at Thousand Oaks, California, and at additional mailing offices. POSTMASTER: Send address changes to CQ Researcher, 2600 Virginia Ave., N.W., Suite 600, Washington, DC 20037.

Pandemic Threat

BY BARA VAIDA

THE ISSUES

The killer is small, hidden and elusive. Known by the mundane name of H7N9, the influenza virus has taken hold in China, lurking inside the guts of chickens and other fowl.* It is sickening a growing number of humans, including street-market poultry workers. [1]

The virus causes severe pneumonia in most victims and kills one-third of them, according to public health officials. And it is wily, like other flu viruses. H7N9 mixes with other viruses, swapping genes and circulating among birds. Every 10 to 50 years, influenza viruses mutate so drastically that large numbers of healthy people are vulnerable to contracting the flu. [2]

If H7N9 gains the ability to move more easily between humans, public health experts warn, it could cause a pandemic — a lethal, fast-moving and global infectious disease outbreak. A century ago, an influenza virus caused the 1918 Spanish flu pandemic that killed an estimated 20-50 million people worldwide. [3] Some experts say H7N9 could be equally deadly.

"I think this virus poses the greatest threat to humanity than any other in the past 100 years," said Guan Yi, director of the State Key Laboratory of Emerging Infectious Diseases and the Center of Influenza Research at the University of Hong Kong. [4]

Equally alarming, public health officials say, vaccines exist for just a fraction of the 300 or so known infectious viruses. [5]

* Researchers name influenza viruses by their particular strains, with the "H" and "N" designating the kind of proteins covering the flu virus.

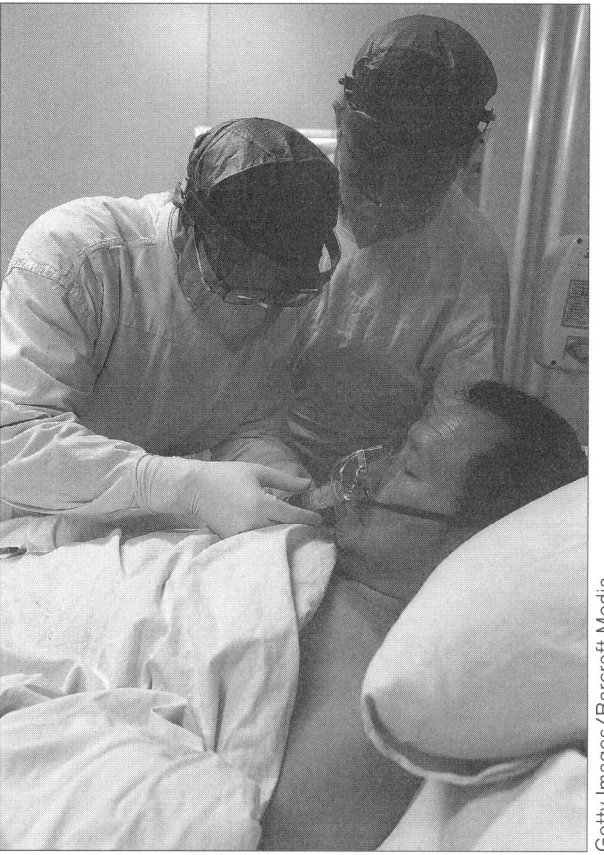

A man in Sichuan province, China, is treated on Feb. 3 after he was infected by the H7N9 virus, or avian flu. Public health experts warn the virus has the potential to become a lethal, fast-moving pandemic on the scale of the 1918 Spanish flu that killed an estimated 50 million people worldwide.

Getty Images/Barcroft Media

Microsoft co-founder Bill Gates, a billionaire philanthropist who is working to eradicate infectious diseases, warns that the global health community must do more to prepare for a pandemic. "Epidemiologists say a fast-moving airborne pathogen could kill more than 30 million people in less than a year," he told an international security conference in Munich in February. "And they say there is a reasonable probability the world will experience such an outbreak in the next 10 to 15 years." [6]

The global health community was slow to respond to two recent disease outbreaks — Ebola in West Africa in 2014 and Zika in Brazil and elsewhere in 2015 and 2016. If officials had responded sooner, the death toll likely would have been lower, experts say. Now they are questioning whether the world will be ready if H7N9 or another infectious disease becomes a pandemic. They attributed the world's poor response to the Ebola and Zika crises to several factors: bureaucratic infighting and insufficient resources at the World Health Organization (WHO); weak public health systems in poor countries; gaps in international and local cooperation; scarcity of vaccines for fast-spreading diseases; and inattention by some in power. [7]

Some experts, however, say health agencies and governments are getting ahead of the pandemic threat.

"I'm optimistic that we are prepared for a pandemic," says Dr. Steven Gordon, chair of the Department of Infectious Disease at the Cleveland Clinic in Ohio. "We have learned so much from past outbreaks [that fell short of a pandemic]. There has been lots of preparation, there have been tremendous advances in the development of vaccines, and the U.S. has [established] lots of surveillance and information-sharing measures."

WHO, the arm of the United Nations charged with coordinating responses to world health emergencies, has a global surveillance network watching for potential pandemics and an emergency fund if a one should arise. [8]

In recent years the United States has made substantial investments of time and money to prepare for a pandemic, and it has shared its expertise worldwide. In 2014, Washington expanded the Global Health Security Agenda, which is helping poor and middle-income countries build stronger public health systems capable of fighting a pandemic. In addition, a

Predicting the Next Pandemic

The U.S. Agency for International Development (USAID) is monitoring disease outbreaks in 20 countries for their potential to become the next pandemic. Nearly 75 percent of infectious diseases that have afflicted humans this century originated in animals. Disease outbreaks have included severe acute respiratory syndrome (SARS), H7N9 avian influenza and the 2009 pandemic known as swine flu.

USAID Monitors Disease Outbreaks in 20 African, Asian Nations

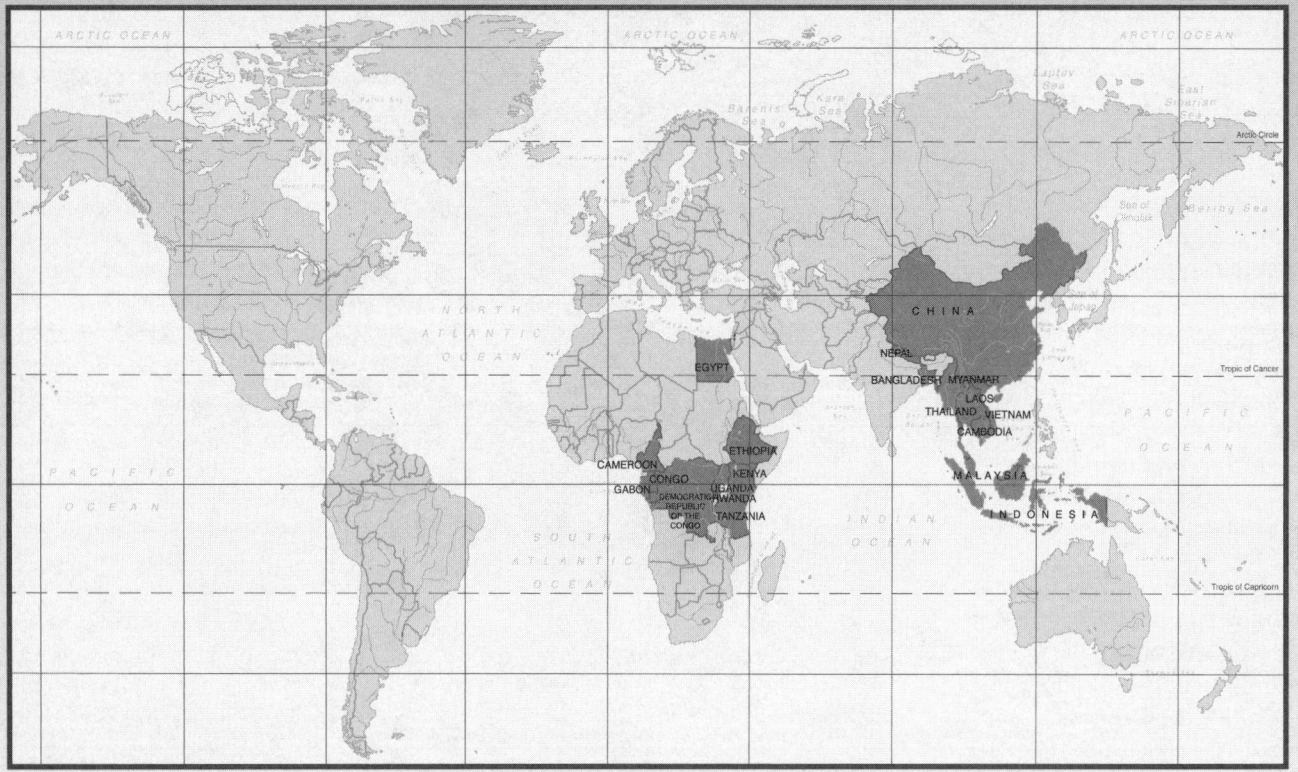

Sources: "Emerging Pandemic Threats Program," U.S. Agency for International Development, Jan. 11, 2016, https://tinyurl.com/ktbf35c; "The Road To EPT-2," U.S. Agency for International Development, undated, p. 5, https://tinyurl.com/k65okjy; and "Emerging Pandemic Threats 2 Program (EPT- 2)," U.S. Agency for International Development, Aug. 1, 2016, https://tinyurl.com/k9rntro

public-private consortium of governments, nonprofits and pharmaceutical companies is aiming to raise $2 billion to create vaccines for infectious diseases. [9]

Further, technological advances have enabled scientists to hasten development of new vaccines, including one for Zika that entered the testing phase within a year of the outbreak in Brazil.

But even the most optimistic observers say crucial gaps remain, ranging from financial to organizational. WHO faces a difficult leadership transition, and President Trump is proposing deep

cuts in foreign aid and domestic programs that could halt or diminish U.S. preparedness, they say. [10]

Further, key leadership posts in U.S. health agencies remain unfilled by the Trump administration. Most poor governments still don't have a functioning public health system, and nationalistic movements in Europe and the United States are threatening the international cooperation necessary to make global health systems work. [11]

"We aren't prepared [for a pandemic]," says Michael Osterholm, director of the

Center for Infectious Disease Research and Policy (CIDRAP) at the University of Minnesota.

Today's planet is a perfect incubator for pandemics, scientists say, due to an expanding global population of 7.3 billion, industrialized farming, destruction of wildlife habitats, easy access to foreign travel that can speed the spread of viruses, unstable governments and climate-change-induced proliferation of disease-carrying mosquitos.

Between January 2016 and May 23, 2017, dozens of disease outbreaks occurred in 55 countries, according to WHO, and a new outbreak of Ebola struck the Democratic Republic of the Congo. The last pandemic was in 2009, when the swine flu, originating in Mexico, killed up to 575,000 people worldwide. [12]

Localized disease outbreaks, which affect fewer people than pandemics, are costly. In 2003, an outbreak of severe acute respiratory syndrome (SARS) cost the global economy $54 billion in lost trade and transportation and health care costs. A flu pandemic, on the other hand, could cost the global economy $4 trillion, according to the World Bank. [13]

Gates advises the world community to treat the pandemic threat as an urgent matter of national security and not just a health issue. "What we need to do is prepare for epidemics the way the military prepares for war," he said. "This includes germ games and other preparedness exercises so we can better understand how diseases will spread, how people will respond in a panic, and how to deal with things like overloaded highways and communications systems." [14]

The threat, public health experts say, is even greater than in 1918 because of the ease of international travel today. A person in China with a flu virus can get on a plane, cough and sneeze on fellow passengers and be in the United States in 13 hours.

Public health officials also worry about the growing antibiotic resistance of microbes. Since the 1940s, when antibiotics came into wide use to treat people and animals, many strains of bacteria, fungi and parasites have evolved into antibiotic-resistant "superbugs."

Currently, 2 million Americans contract antibiotic-resistant bacteria annually, and 23,000 die as a result. In one dramatic example that garnered national headlines, a woman died in Nevada in 2016 because the microbe she contracted was resistant to antibiotics. [15]

If superbugs become more common, it could be the end of much of modern medicine, experts say. Without certainty

U.S. Is Biggest Donor to WHO

The World Health Organization (WHO) relies on donors for 70 percent of its budget. The two largest contributors are the United States and the United Kingdom. WHO's $4.7 billion budget has been flat for decades and is far smaller than the $7 billion budget for the U.S. Centers for Disease Control and Prevention.

Amount (in $ millions)

Top 10 WHO Contributors, 2015

U.S.	U.K.	Bill & Melinda Gates Foundation	Global Alliance for Vaccines and Immunization	National Philanthropic Trust*	Nigeria	Rotary International	U.N. Development Program	Canada	European Commission
$305.8	$195.7	$185.3	$126.4	$86.3	$67.6	$56.3	$47.2	$47.2	$45.6

* A public charity in Pennsylvania.

Sources: "Voluntary contributions by fund and by contributor, 2015," World Health Organization, May 13, 2016, https://tinyurl.com/mekl5a3; Donald G. McNeil Jr., "The Campaign to Lead the World Health Organization," The New York Times, April 3, 2017, http://tinyurl.com/kylbmmu

that antibiotics would work to control infection, any surgery, joint replacement, or cancer chemotherapy would become so dangerous that most hospitals would refuse to perform them, according to Dr. Ali Khan, former director of the Office of Public Health Preparedness and Response at the Centers for Disease Control and Prevention (CDC).

"If this trend continues, eventually we'll reach a new post-antibiotic age in which we slip back a century or more in terms of health care programs" because doctors won't be able to perform surgery, Khan said. [16]

Experts also worry that terrorists could use pathogens as weapons. (*See sidebar, p. 470.*) When someone in 2001 sent weaponized spores of the anthrax bacterium through the mail — the FBI said it was a rogue scientist, but the culprit remains unknown — the United States spent billions to create anti-bioterrorism programs, including a detection system to flag airborne

toxins in major U.S. cities. But funding has fallen, and the aging bioterrorist detection system has "outlived its usefulness," according to former Homeland Security Secretary Tom Ridge. [17]

Meanwhile, technological advances have enabled scientists worldwide to create deadly viruses and bacteria to study how they evolve and to develop potential treatments. Security experts worry that a rogue scientist could launch a bioterrorism attack or share the expertise with terrorists. [18]

"All the know-how needed to create a bioterrorism tool is publicly available," says Tara O'Toole, executive vice president at In-Q-Tel, a nonprofit venture capital firm that invests in security companies. "A bioterrorism attack would be like a flu epidemic on steroids."

As scientists and health agencies prepare for the next pandemic, here are some of the questions being debated:

Are the World Health Organization and other groups prepared to stop the next pandemic?

Three years after the Ebola outbreak, WHO, the United States and other wealthy nations have made progress toward improving global responses to pandemics, many experts say.

The United States, in partnership with WHO, funded the expansion of the Global Health Security Agenda to work with poor and middle-income countries, particularly in Africa, on preventing, detecting and responding to outbreaks before they become pandemics. [19]

Before the Ebola crisis, all 194 member countries of WHO were supposed to adhere to the organization's international health regulations that specify how to report outbreaks and prevent their proliferation. However, most poor and middle-income countries, such as Liberia and Sierra Leone, were not complying with the regulations. They feared reporting on a disease would harm their economies and lacked the resources to bolster their public health systems, according to a report in the journal *Globalization and Health*. [20]

Ebola galvanized the G-7 countries — Canada, France, Germany, Italy, Japan, the United Kingdom and the United States — to make sure poorer nations had the resources needed to adopt the WHO regulations. [21]

The health agenda has served as a roadmap to help nations prevent or mitigate infectious diseases, detect and report outbreaks when they occur and employ a global network that can respond effectively to an outbreak. The United States also has partnered with the African Union Commission, the administrative branch of the African Union, to create the African Centers for Disease Control and Prevention, which is modeled after the U.S. CDC. [22]

And the U.S. Agency for International Development (USAID) expanded its Emerging Pandemic Threats program, in coordination with WHO, to boost surveillance of potential emerging infections in 20 African and Asian countries. Because about 60 to 75 percent of emerging and re-emerging diseases originate in animals, USAID is training local health workers to detect and respond to pathogens that may be jumping from animals to people. [23]

"Outbreaks are like fires," said Eddy Rubin, chief science officer at Metabiota, a San Francisco startup that developed software to predict and prevent outbreaks. "If you're able to understand where there is a greater likelihood of their occurring and detect them early on, you can shift the impact." [24]

Cameroon has developed an emergency operations center able to respond within 24 hours to an avian flu outbreak. Last year the West African country quickly killed 67,000 birds that could have spread the virus to humans. A year before that, Cameroon took two months to respond to a cholera outbreak. [25]

"I feel quite heartened by what is going on," says John Lange, senior fellow of global health diplomacy at the U.N. Foundation and former U.S. ambassador to Botswana in southern Africa. "The world has woken up to the need to improve capabilities to prepare for infectious disease outbreaks. I think the global community is prepared to fight a pandemic."

Still, global health experts say far more needs to be done.

The Commission on a Global Health Risk Framework for the Future — an international panel that gathered the input of 250 global health experts — declared in 2016 that the world needs to invest at least $3.4 billion annually to strengthen national health systems and spend another $1 billion to speed development of new drugs and to stockpile vaccines. WHO and the World Bank should invest up to $155 million in pandemic preparedness funding, it said. [26]

But WHO is underfunded, say global health experts. Its budget of about $2.2 billion is much smaller than the CDC's budget which was over $7 billion in fiscal 2016. [27]

In addition, WHO's operational structure stymies its ability to respond quickly to outbreaks, health experts say. The organization must contend with the competing priorities of the 194 countries who make up its governing body and the priorities of six regional offices. WHO infighting over the economic impact of declaring an emergency was blamed in part for the organization's failure to respond quickly to Ebola, according to a report in *The Lancet* medical journal in November 2015. [28] It also was slow to respond to the Zika outbreak, experts say.

"While WHO should serve as a global front-line defense against pandemics and bioterror attacks, at the moment, it does not look like it's up to the job," wrote Annie Sparrow, assistant professor of global health at Mount Sinai Hospital in New York City. [29]

On May 23, WHO members elected Dr. Tedros Adhanom Ghebreyesus to be director-general, replacing Margaret Chan of China, who has run the organization since 2007. Many experts say Tedros' leadership will be critical to WHO's ability to respond to a pandemic. [30]

In addition, few vaccines are available for the dozens of viruses posing the greatest global health risks. Yet, pharmaceutical companies in recent decades have devoted less than 1 percent of their research and development budgets to vaccines for emerging diseases, judging the profit margin to be too small. [31]

To counteract that trend, an effort to bolster vaccine research was begun in January by the Bill & Melinda Gates Foundation, the European Commission, six vaccine makers and others. Called the Coalition for Epidemic Preparedness Innovations (CEPI), the group is pledging to develop a vaccine for at least three of the 11 viruses identified by WHO as the most contagious and dangerous: Lassa fever, the Nipah virus and Middle East Respiratory Syndrome (MERS).*

CEPI also is supporting the development of technologies to speed up vaccine development. [32]

"The work that CEPI is doing is really important and could be a game changer," says Dr. Rebecca Katz, co-director of the Center for Global Health Science and Security at Georgetown University. "If we had vaccines for these emerging diseases, then we'd have something in our toolkit to confront these threats."

Is the United States spending enough on pandemic preparedness?

The federal government is spending about $13 billion in fiscal 2017 on programs to improve medical and health infrastructure in the United States, address bioterrorism and prevent pandemic influenza. [33]

While that figure may seem large, it is a tiny fraction of the $3.6 trillion federal budget and is spread among at least 10 federal departments, including Commerce, Health and Human Services and Homeland Security. Related programs are in the Environmental Protection Agency, USAID and the National Science Foundation. [34]

The United States is the largest contributor to WHO, providing about $341 million in 2016. [35]

The effectiveness of U.S. anti-bioterrorism programs is hampered by poor interagency coordination, according to the Center for Health Security at Johns Hopkins University in Baltimore. "Currently, there is no systematic accounting by the federal government of those programs that are essential for building health security," said center senior associate Crystal Watson and senior analyst Matthew Watson in a January memo to President Trump on biosecurity. [36]

Many health experts want the Trump administration to appoint a leader to coordinate all the federal health security programs. The Blue Ribbon Study Panel on Biodefense, a bipartisan nonprofit created in 2014 to assess U.S. biodefense readiness, said that person should be in the White House — preferably the vice president. [37]

"We have questions about who is overseeing the $6 [billion] or $7 billion [for biosecurity] in multiple agencies which seemed to be siloed from one another," said panel co-chair Ridge. "Who is coordinating it? We want it to be the vice president." [38]

Health security experts also worry that spending on U.S. preparedness and response has declined. A frugally minded Congress worried about wasteful spending has cut the CDC's budget about 20 percent since 2008 — to $7.3 billion in fiscal 2017. Meanwhile, public health emergency preparedness spending has dropped from a high of $940 million in 2002 (the year after the Sept. 11 terror attacks on the United States) to $660 million in 2017. [39]

"The threat environment isn't dwindling," says James Blumenstock, chief of health security at the Association of State and Territorial Health Officials, representing various public health agencies. "It's getting more intense, more difficult and more challenging, but resources are leveling off or [have] declined. That isn't a healthy situation."

Despite the cuts, Blumenstock and a number of other experts say U.S. pandemic preparedness has improved dramatically since the 2001 anthrax and terrorist attacks. The U.S. government created national strategies to prevent or respond to an infectious disease outbreak or a bioterrorist event. And this year, the National Health Security Preparedness Index, a collaboration of the nation's health security experts, including the Association of State and Territorial Health Officials and the Robert Wood Johnson Foundation, said the U.S. government has made progress in "health security surveillance" and information-sharing systems. [40]

But the index also said work remains to be done, which is why many health security experts worry about the huge budget cuts Trump has proposed for fiscal 2018 to agencies involved in preparedness. They include an 18 percent cut at the Health and Human Services Department, which would mean a $1.2 billion reduction in funds to the CDC; the latter provides grants to hospitals and international infectious disease programs.

Trump also proposed reducing the National Institutes of Health (NIH) budget by $5.8 billion, including $838 million from the NIH's National Institute of Allergy and Infectious Diseases, which oversees flu and Zika vaccine programs. [41]

The "proposed CDC budget [is] unsafe at any level of enactment," said former CDC Director Tom Friedan. "It would increase illness, death, risks to Americans, and health care costs." [42]

Trump has also proposed a 33 percent cut in the State Department budget, which could reduce U.S. funding for WHO and USAID health-related programs. And he has proposed a 21 percent cut in the Agriculture Department's budget, even though the Government Accountability Office (GAO) said in a report in April that the department faces "ongoing challenges" getting poultry farmers to control viruses in birds with pandemic potential. [43] Controlling bird viruses is especially important because eggs are used to produce flu vaccines.

As funding for health security preparedness has declined, Congress has funded the U.S. response to outbreaks disease by disease, after a disease reaches crisis level, health officials say. With the Ebola and Zika outbreaks, the Obama administration had to ask for supplemental money to fight both. "We literally had to rob Peter to pay Paul," said Ron Klain, President Obama's Ebola czar. [44]

Health experts prefer a permanent emergency-response fund for public health threats, similar to that earmarked for natural disasters at the Federal Emergency Management Agency (FEMA). When a hurricane or flood strikes, FEMA can

---

* Lassa, spread by rodents, is a hemorrhagic illness that kills about 1 percent to 15 percent who contract it and is endemic in parts of Africa. Nipah, spread by fruit bats, can cause severe brain inflammation. It can be found in parts of Asia and Australia and has a fatality rate of 40 to 75 percent. MERS, spread through contact with camels, causes severe respiratory disease and has a mortality rate of about 36 percent.

Ebola Killed Thousands in West Africa

The largest outbreak of the Ebola virus in history occurred primarily in three West African countries between 2014 and 2016. Sierra Leone had the most cases and Liberia the most deaths. The World Health Organization declared the virus a "public health emergency of international concern" in August 2014, but the epidemic did not spread widely enough to be classified as a pandemic.

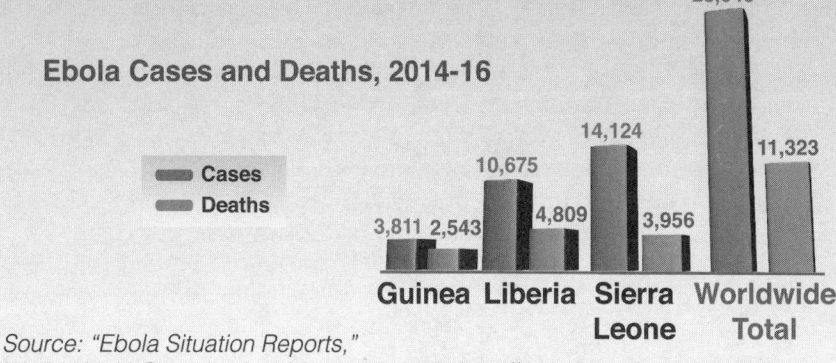

Ebola Cases and Deaths, 2014-16

Cases
Deaths

Guinea	Liberia	Sierra Leone	Worldwide Total
3,811 / 2,543	10,675 / 4,809	14,124 / 3,956	28,646 / 11,323

Source: "Ebola Situation Reports," World HealthOrganization, March 27, 2016, http://tinyurl.com/q4j88p7

tap the fund to help local communities.

"It would be an example of good government if we were able to put something in place to ensure that [health emergency] responses can get dealt with quickly," said Matthew Watson, former managing senior analyst of the Center for Health Security at the University of Pittsburgh Medical Center. Watson is now a senior managing analyst at Johns Hopkins Center for Health Security. [45]

Should governments mandate quarantines and vaccinations to prevent pandemics?

The U.S. government has the authority to restrict the movement of Americans and can block sick people from entering the country. But many public health officials say quarantines can spark panic and worsen an outbreak. [46]

Quarantines involve sequestering individuals who may have been exposed to an infection and monitoring them during the contagious period.

In extreme cases when an epidemic has no known medical treatment, a nation can close its borders to all travelers from a country experiencing an outbreak — something Trump as a

private citizen recommended in 2014 during the Ebola outbreak. [47]

With Ebola spreading that year, Liberia deployed riot police to shut off neighborhoods in the capital after people raided an Ebola center and stole medical equipment. When people tried to flee the quarantine, the government cracked down. Violence followed, and the country had to end the quarantine. In neighboring Sierra Leone, the government imposed a three-day national quarantine, but some people fled instead. [48]

"If you tell people that a deadly disease is afoot and you can't leave, people will always try to leave," says In-Q-Tel's O'Toole.

A WHO task force in 2014 said traveler quarantines are ineffective and recommended nations not impose them during the Ebola crisis. Quarantines on trade and travel bans "can create a false impression of control," it said. "Such measures may also adversely reduce essential trade, including shipments of food, fuel and medical equipment to the affected countries, contributing to their humanitarian and economic hardship." [49]

Quarantines can work if a person with an incubating disease is identified

and complies with the quarantine, said Richard Schabas, former chief of staff at Canada's York Central Hospital in Richmond Hill, Ontario. [50]

To get people to comply, authorities must engage communities and seek their cooperation, says Khan, former director of the CDC's Office of Public Health Preparedness and Response. "Making an effort to understand what people are going through, what they believe, what they fear and then trying to come up with a solution that doesn't push people to hide or flee can solve an outbreak of a magnitude like Ebola," he said.

The 2014 Ebola crisis in Sierra Leone and Guinea was contained after health care workers learned to track patients with potential exposure and got them to agree to limit their exposure to others for 21 days. [51]

In the United States, the CDC has authority to impose a quarantine on people with cholera, diphtheria, tuberculosis plague, smallpox, yellow fever, hemorrhagic illnesses such as Ebola or severe respiratory syndromes like a flu that can cause a pandemic. [52]

The CDC in January issued new guidelines giving it broad authority to quarantine individuals for 72 hours if officials suspect someone poses a risk. [53] The new rules were necessary because the agency "has been operating its infectious disease powers under really antiquated regulations," said Lawrence Gostin, a professor of global health law at Georgetown University. [54]

However, the new powers raise concerns that Americans' civil liberties could be threatened, said Northeastern University health policy law professor Wendy Parmet. [55]

When American nurse Kaci Hickox returned from volunteering in Sierra Leone during the Ebola outbreak, she landed at Newark Liberty International Airport in New Jersey and was flagged for extra screening. Although she had no symptoms, Republican Gov. Chris Christie ordered her quarantined in a tent at the airport; she was released three days later. Hickox sued the state, saying "my liberty, my interests and consequently my civil rights were ignored because some ambitious governors saw an opportunity to use an age-old political tactic: fear." Christie defended his actions, and New Jersey is contesting the suit. [56]

As for mandating vaccinations, public health experts say vaccines are the most effective way to stem the spread of infectious diseases, such as diphtheria and measles. Each year, vaccines for infectious diseases save 3 million lives, and 3 million more children around the world could be saved if they were vaccinated, according to the Children's Hospital of Philadelphia. [57]

"Immunizations are the safest, longest-lasting and most effective way to prevent communicable diseases," said Dr. Ian Gemmill, past chair of the Canadian Coalition for Immunization Awareness and Promotion, a nongovernmental advocacy organization. [58]

In the United States, in the event of a spreading contagion overseas, the federal government could ask immigrants at the border to show proof of vaccination. But inside the country, only the states have the authority to mandate vaccinations.

All 50 states and the District of Columbia require children to be vaccinated — typically for diphtheria, measles, rubella and polio — before they can attend public school, but some states allow exemptions for medical, religious or philosophical reasons. [59]

Since 1998, a small but growing number of parents have been refusing vaccinations for their children due to fears that vaccines cause autism. The fears stem from a now discredited study that a British scientist said demonstrated an association between autism and vaccination. [60]

Countless studies have shown the safety of vaccinations. Nevertheless, childhood vaccination rates have fallen. The decline has caused measles outbreaks to flare, most recently in Minnesota, where 44 unvaccinated children in a Somali community contracted the disease. [61]

Parental fears have been supported by some celebrities and prominent

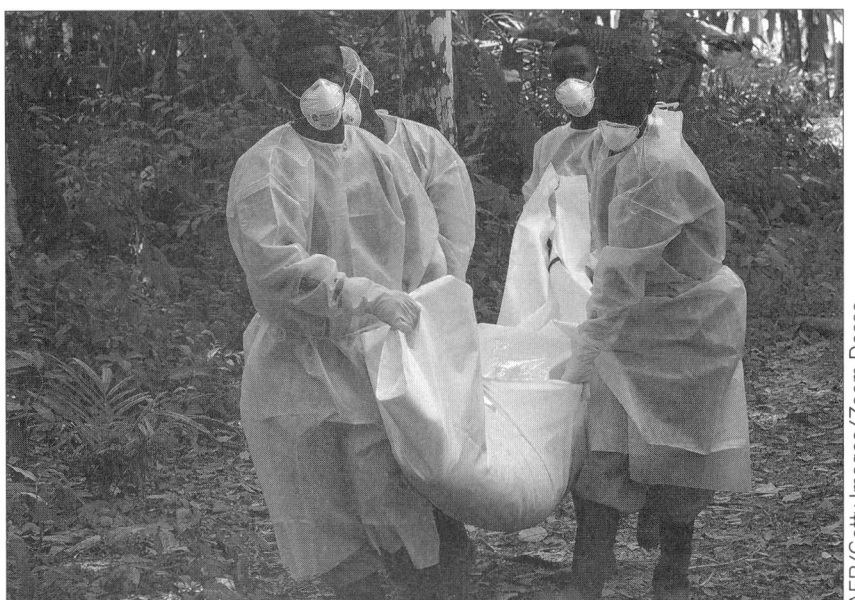

Workers prepare to bury an Ebola victim in Monrovia, Liberia, on Jan. 5, 2015. The largest outbreak of the Ebola virus, spread by bats, monkeys and other animals, occurred primarily in West Africa between 2014 and 2016. More than 11,000 people died. Experts say the toll would have been lower if the global health community had responded more quickly to the crisis.

politicians such as Christie; Housing and Urban Development Secretary Ben Carson, a neurosurgeon; and Sen. Rand Paul, a physician and Kentucky Republican, who say vaccination decisions should be left to parents.

"I think the parent should have input," Paul said. "The state doesn't own your children. You own your children, and it is an issue of freedom." [62]

Trump invigorated the anti-vaccine movement when he said — contradicting the numerous studies — during a 2015 Republican presidential debate: "You take this little beautiful baby, and you pump — I mean, it looks like just it's meant for a horse and not for a child," he said. "We had so many instances . . . a beautiful child, went to have the vaccine and came back and a week later got a tremendous fever, got very, very sick. Now is autistic." He is considering creating a commission to look into vaccine safety. [63]

At least 19 states have passed legislation since 2001 allowing mandated vaccinations during a health emergency, but experts say ongoing doubts about

vaccines' safety could make people resistant to such requirements. Opponents, on the other hand, say the measures "could allow governments to abuse their power," said the American Civil Liberties Union. [64] ∎

BACKGROUND

First Pandemics

Humans have been threatened by pandemics for most of history.

Scientists believe widespread infections began when humans domesticated animals about 10,000 to 15,000 years ago, coming in contact with an army of bacteria, viruses and fungi that could pass to humans. Most of these microbes were harmless, but some evolved to become pathogenic. Throughout history, 60 to 75 percent of emerging infectious diseases can be traced to furred or winged animals. [65]

The animal microbes that became harmful to humans spread by direct person-to-person contact, such as through coughing, sneezing, sweating or sexual interaction. Fleas, mosquitos and other carriers (known as vectors) can spread disease when they bit animals and then humans. From cows came measles and tuberculosis; from pigs and birds, influenza; from primates and mosquitos, malaria; and from bats, Ebola. Rats have been particularly lethal to humans as the source, through fleas, of the bubonic plague of the Middle Ages, which killed an estimated 20-25 million in Europe over five years.

At first, dangerous diseases spread slowly because people lived in small, isolated groups. But as agriculture took hold in about 9,000 B.C., populations grew and humans ventured farther from their homes to trade and wage war. [66]

"Global transportation networks, exploration, conquest and trade" enabled diseases endemic in one region to spread, blossoming into epidemics elsewhere as new populations without immunity were exposed to them, said Peter Daszak, a scientist who is president of the EcoHealth Alliance, a global health research group. [67]

For centuries, people were virtually helpless to stop the spread of disease. People thought diseases were caused by imbalances in the body, evil spirits or the will of God. Living conditions, meanwhile, contributed to the spread of contagions. Many humans lived in houses along with their livestock. Human excrement and garbage were dumped onto streets. One of the few tools societies had to prevent disease was to separate sick people from the healthy. [68]

Plague and Quarantines

Bubonic plague prompted one of the first society-wide responses to a pandemic.

In October 1347, a dozen Genoese trading ships docked in Sicily after journeying to ports along the Black Sea. The ships likely contained rats that harbored *Yersinia pestis*, the bacterium causing bubonic plague. The bacterium lived inside the fleas that fed off the rats. When the rats died, the fleas jumped to the nearest warm mammal, usually humans. Eventually the pathogen became known as "the Black Death" because people would develop skin boils that turned black before they died. [69]

The plague spread throughout Italy, wiping out entire towns. In 1348, Venetian leaders cut off access to outsiders. Boats from areas suspected of having a plague outbreak were kept away. Travelers coming from areas beyond Venice were told to wait up to 40 days before they could enter. "Quarantine" is derived from the Italian words *quarante giorni*, or 40 days. [70]

The containment was effective because symptoms became visible within 40 days and after that people could be considered "medically harmless." Some historians credit the use of quarantines with Europe's ultimate control of the plague, which largely disappeared by the mid-19th century. [71]

Quarantines also were used during the worst pandemic in modern history — the Spanish flu outbreak in 1918. Governments in the United States and Europe closed schools, churches and theaters and banned most public gatherings. However, the CDC said the quarantines and closures were ineffective because "the measures were implemented too late and in an uncoordinated manner." [72]

Modern quarantines face new challenges, as the 2003 SARS outbreak showed. SARS is a respiratory coronavirus that scientists had never seen before. It originated in Guangdong province in China and became a global threat because it spread rapidly along air-travel routes. The illness went from Hong Kong to Southeast Asia, to Canada and then Europe. It sickened more than 8,000 worldwide and killed 774. [73]

China's government quickly imposed quarantines, closing off buildings inhabited by infected individuals and imposing checkpoints. Violators were punished.

SARS died out at the end of 2003. Some public health officials believe the quarantines worked because SARS had an incubation period of two to 10 days, which gave governments time to limit people's interactions. [74]

Vaccines and Antibiotics

As far back as A.D. 1000, the Chinese used an inoculation technique, called variation, against smallpox, a virus that causes fever and disfiguring pustules. Physicians would take ground smallpox scab and insert it in the noses of healthy people, inducing a mild form of the disease and thus creating immunity against smallpox. [75]

Vaccination began in 1796 with English doctor Edward Jenner. He had long heard stories of how milkmaids were immune from smallpox, which according to one estimate was killing 400,000 Europeans a year during the 18th century. Jenner found a milkmaid with fresh lesions from cowpox, a mild virus related to smallpox, and he inserted pus from her cowpox into a cut on an 8-year-old boy's arm. The boy became immune to smallpox, proving a person could be protected from smallpox without being directly exposed to it. [76]

By the end of the 19th century, governments in Egypt, Germany began mandating vaccination against smallpox. Great Britain in 1853 required children to be vaccinated, while in the United States, Massachusetts in 1809 became the first state to mandate smallpox vaccination. In 1813, President James Madison created the National Vaccine Agency to encourage vaccinations. [77]

In the late 1880s, microscopes had improved enough that scientists could see bacteria and viruses, paving the way for medical treatments, the understanding of how disease spreads from animals

Continued on p. 468

Chronology

1300s-1800s
Medical breakthroughs give hope for preventing pandemics.

1347
"The Black Death" — a bubonic plague — travels from Crimea to Europe; 20 to 25 million die over the next five years.

1348
Venice responds to the plague by imposing the world's first quarantine, isolating incoming ships for 40 days.

1796
English physician Edward Jenner inoculates a boy with cowpox, immunizing him against smallpox, ushering in vaccination.

1817
Cholera spreads worldwide from Calcutta, India.

1851
Sanitary conference focusing on cholera meets in Paris, marking the first gathering of international health leaders.

1854
Physician John Snow recognizes dirty water as the source of a cholera outbreak. He hastens end of the outbreak by shutting off a London water pump.

1894
Alexandre Yersin, a French bacteriologist, discovers the bacillus responsible for bubonic plague.

1900s-1940s
Health cooperation expands.

1918
"Spanish flu," the first pandemic involving the H1N1 influenza, kills 20-50 million.

1928
Scottish biologist Alexander Fleming discovers penicillin at a London hospital.

1940
Japan spreads plague-infested fleas over China during World War II; it also is accused of encasing disease-causing microbes in bombs.

1948
United Nations creates the World Health Organization (WHO).

1950s-1970s
As global cooperation ends many diseases, others emerge.

1953
U.S. researcher Jonas Salk creates the polio vaccine.

1967
WHO begins immunization campaign to eliminate smallpox, declaring it eradicated in 1980.

1972
Biological Weapons Convention, the first multilateral disarmament treaty banning development, production and stockpiling of biological weapons, is signed.

1974
WHO launches vaccine campaign to eliminate six diseases — diphtheria, pertussis, tetanus, measles, polio and tuberculosis.

2000s-Present
Antibiotic-resistant microbes fuel pandemic fears.

2001
An American scientist is accused of sending anonymous letters containing anthrax spores to news organizations in two states and to the Washington offices of two Democratic senators, killing five people and infecting 17 others. The attacks spur heavy investment in bioterrorism prevention.

2003
Severe acute respiratory syndrome (SARS), a type of pneumonia, spreads rapidly from China.

2005
U.S. creates the National Strategy for Pandemic Influenza, outlining how the nation would respond to a flu pandemic.

2009
"Swine flu" pandemic spreads worldwide; up to 575,000 die.

2013
The Centers for Disease Control and Prevention issues first-ever report on the threat the U.S. faces from antibiotic-resistant organisms, or "superbugs."

2014
Ebola emerges in three West African countries, killing more than 11,000. . . . U.S. expands the Global Health Security Agenda, an international partnership aimed at bolstering safeguards against infectious disease.

2016
WHO declares Zika a global health emergency as the mosquito-borne virus hits the southern U.S. . . . A Nevada woman dies from an infection resistant to all 26 antibiotics approved for use in the U.S.

2016-2017
China experiences its fifth epidemic of H7N9 influenza, a bird flu virus.

Waging War on Superbugs

"In China and India, there are bacteria resistant to all antibiotics."

Inside the sprawling Walter Reed Army Institute of Research in Silver Spring, Md., microbiologist Patrick McGann spends much of his time growing "superbugs" — antibiotic-resistant strains of bacteria.

A year ago, McGann and his team learned of a Pennsylvania woman infected with a strain of *E. coli* bacteria resistant to colistin, an antibiotic used when all others fail. Other antibiotics were effective against the bug, but public health officials were still alarmed. If the woman's strain combined with other antibiotic-resistant bugs, the world could be on the brink of an unstoppable outbreak. [1]

"In some ways, I think we aren't on the cusp of a post-antibiotic world; we are already there," says McGann, chief of molecular research and diagnostics at Walter Reed's Multidrug Resistant Organism Repository and Surveillance Network (MRSN). "In China and India, there are now bacteria resistant to all antibiotics."

McGann points to a 70-year-old woman who died in September 2016 in Nevada from a bacterium resistant to all approved antibiotics in the United States. The woman had traveled to India and been hospitalized there for a broken leg. [2]

At least 2 million people in the United States contract an antibiotic-resistant bacterium each year and 23,000 die as a result, according to estimates from the Centers for Disease Control and Prevention (CDC). Antibiotic-resistant bugs may kill 700,000 people worldwide annually. [3]

Microbes have mutated to resist human attempts to kill them ever since antibiotics became widely used in the 1940s. Antibiotics have all but eliminated the threat of sepsis, tuberculosis, plague, cholera and other diseases that once killed millions. But antibiotics' overuse on humans and animals has spawned a growing number of resistant superbugs.

The Army created the MRSN in 2009 to monitor potential outbreaks of dangerous pathogens inside the military. Part of McGann's work is to quickly identify superbugs and then seek to keep them from spreading. His lab houses genome-sequencing machines that categorize bacteria and search for pathogens that may have mutated to resist antibiotics.

Such work allowed McGann to discover the Pennsylvania woman's superbug, which carried a colistin-resistant gene called mcr-1. Researchers first found the gene in 2015 in pigs and people in China, where farmers had regularly used colistin in animal feed to promote growth. [4]

The colistin-resistant bacteria has since spread and been found in more than 30 additional countries, including the United States. In response, China has banned the use of colistin in animal feed.

McGann found a second U.S. patient, a former military officer living in Bahrain, with bacteria carrying the mcr-1. His body

Continued from p. 466

to humans and the connection between sanitary conditions and health.

Physicians now understood that contaminated water was making people sick with cholera and that bacterium carried by fleas had caused the bubonic plague. Breakthroughs followed. Researchers developed vaccines for plague (1897), typhoid (1899), cholera (1911), diphtheria (1914) and tuberculosis (1921). Vaccines for polio (1955), measles (1963), mumps (1967) and rubella (1969) came next. [78]

In 1928, Alexander Fleming discovered antibiotics, which came to be widely used to treat soldiers during World War II. Antibiotics changed the course of medicine because they could kill most bacteria that plagued humans at the time. [79]

After World War II, the world community expanded efforts to work together to prevent pandemics. In 1948, the newly founded United Nations created the World Health Organization to coordinate global efforts on health issues, and WHO became the leading global institution on epidemic control.

"The bottom line is, readiness for a pandemic is connected to our world solidarity," Laurie Garrett, a senior fellow at the Council on Foreign Relations think tank, says of WHO's importance.

Scientists, meanwhile, continued reducing the death toll from infectious diseases. With dozens of vaccines and antibiotics to use, average life expectancy in the United States rose to 78.8 by 2015, up from 48.3 for women and 46.3 for men in 1900. [80]

But nature had some surprises. Flu viruses can't be contained. Although flu virus was discovered in 1933 and the first vaccine produced in 1942, scientists learned that flu viruses constantly mutate. Frequent vaccinations are necessary to prevent flu. Because flu changes so quickly, drug companies don't always make a vaccine that is an exact match for a virus.

Since 1500, 14 or more flu pandemics have been recorded, with six occurring in the past 140 years — in 1889, 1918, 1957, 1968, 1977 and 2009, according to a 2010 report in the journal *Public Health*. [81]

The 2009 outbreak of H1N1, or swine flu, moved from birds to pigs and then to humans. It was first reported as a cluster of cases in Mexico. Initially, death rates were said to be 8 percent, making it almost as deadly as the 2003 SARS outbreak. The CDC then began receiving reports of swine flu spreading in the United States and five other countries. [82]

Hospitals, at the beginning, were overwhelmed with patients. It took more than six months for drug companies to

fought the bacteria on its own and he recovered, says McGann. The woman who died in Nevada didn't have a bacterium with the mcr-1 gene, and scientists are still working on understanding how her bacteria became resistant.

McGann's lab is part of the CDC's National Action Plan for Combating Antibiotic Resistant Bacteria, which coordinates efforts across federal agencies and sets goals for reducing the spread of antibiotic-resistant bugs and inappropriate use of antibiotics in medicine and agriculture. [5]

In April, the CDC tapped state health department laboratories in Maryland, Minnesota, New York, Tennessee, Texas and Washington to help with testing for antibiotic-resistant bugs, according to McGann. The CDC chose these labs for strategic regional reasons. Before this, state and local labs weren't equipped to perform such tests, so it is unclear how many superbugs may be circulating in the United States.

"The more we watch for these bugs, the faster we will pick up on this," McGann says of the fight to prevent a pandemic of antibiotic-resistant disease.

— Bara Vaida

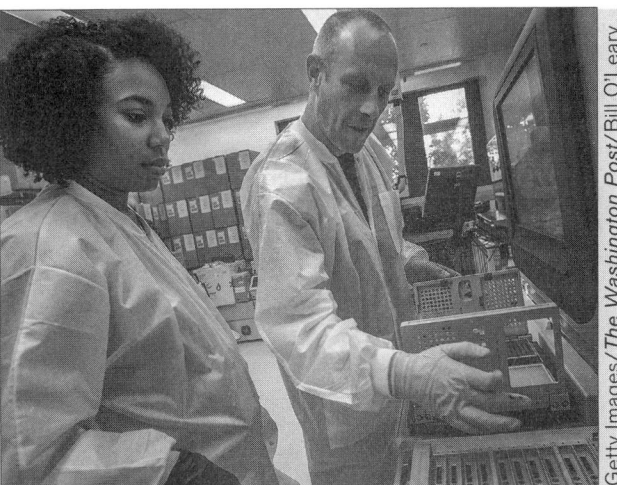

Microbiologist Patrick McGann, with research scientist Rosslyn Maybank, studies "superbugs" at the Walter Reed Army Institute of Research in Silver Spring, Md.

[1] Lena H. Sun and Brady Dennis, "The superbug that doctors have been dreading just reached the U.S.," *The Washington Post*, May 27, 2016, http://tinyurl.com/mmsqnhl.

[2] Lei Chan *et al.*, "Notes from the Field: Pan-Resistant New Delhi Metallo-Beta-Lactamase-Producing Klebsiella Pneumonia — Washoe County, Nevada, 2016," Centers for Disease Control and Prevention, Jan. 13, 2017, http://tiny url.com/zklmrwb.

[3] "Antibiotic/Antimicrobial Resistance," Centers for Disease Control and Prevention, http://tinyurl.com/la3tgtj; Maryn McKenna, "The Coming Cost of Superbugs: 10 Million Deaths per Year," *Wired*, Dec. 15, 2014, http://tinyurl.com/m7prunp.

[4] Sun and Dennis, *op. cit.*; Chris Dall, "Studies show spread of MCR-1 gene in China," Center for Infectious Disease Research and Policy, Jan. 27, 2017, http://tinyurl.com/mkw2t8e.

[5] "National Action Plan for Combating Antibiotic-Resistant Bacteria," The White House, March 2015, http://tinyurl.com/nylq9ey.

create an H1N1 vaccine. Fortunately, the flu proved not to be as lethal as the first reports from Mexico. Within the year, about 24 percent of the world was infected with the swine flu, showing how quickly a flu can spread, but the death rate was just 0.02 percent. Approximately 24,000 Americans die annually from the flu, but only about 17,000 Americans died from the swine flu. [83]

"With H1N1, we got lucky," says Dr. Stacey Schultz-Cherry, deputy director of St. Jude Children's Research Hospital's Center of Excellence in Influenza Research and Surveillance.

Bioterror Threats

On many occasions during the past 2,000 years, military leaders have used biological agents in the form of disease, human cadavers and animals.

In preparing for a naval battle against King Eumenes of Pergamum (modern-day Turkey) in 184 B.C., Hannibal, the leader of Carthage (Tunisia), directed his sailors to fill earthen pots filled with "serpents of every kind" and launch them at enemy ships.

During the French and Indian War (1754-63), Sir Jeffrey Amherst, commander of the British forces in North America, devised a plan to send blankets infected with smallpox to Indians hostile to the British. The move triggered an epidemic among tribes in the Ohio River Valley.

Biological warfare efforts accelerated during the two world wars. In World War I, vials of anthrax were found in the luggage of a captured German spy, intended to infect animals used by the Allies. During World War II, Japan unleashed plague-infested fleas and contaminated rice in China, causing 10,000 casualties.

By the 1960s, the U.S. military had developed a biological arsenal that included numerous weaponized pathogens. Canada, France, Britain and the Soviet Union also had germ-warfare research programs. [84]

During the late 1960s, international concerns arose about the risks such programs posed to society. In 1972 a U.N. convention prohibited the development, production and stockpiling of infectious diseases. The agreement was signed by 103 countries, and since then the United States and most other countries have engaged only in biodefense research. The Soviet Union, however, continued its biological weapons program, called Biopreparat. During the late 1990s, the United States learned that before its demise, the Soviet Union had been developing dangerous pathogens, including anthrax, plague, smallpox and toxic bugs.

Experts Warn of Growing Bioterrorism Threat

"The risk of bioterrorism goes up every day."

In 2014, a laptop belonging to an Islamic State fighter fell into the hands of Syrian rebels. Its contents raised fresh alarms about the jihadist group's plans. The ISIS fighter, a chemist and physicist identified as Muhammad S., had been teaching himself to develop biological weapons and, most alarmingly, to weaponize the bubonic plague.

"The advantage of biological weapons is that they do not cost a lot of money, while the human casualties can be huge," said a document found on the laptop. [1]

Just how close ISIS and other jihadist groups are to developing such a weapon is unknown, but U.S. intelligence sources believe "there are a lot of terrorists that keep working on it," says Jeff Schlegelmilch, deputy director of the National Center for Disaster Preparedness at Columbia University's Earth Institute.

Under the 1972 Biological Weapons Convention, all United Nations member countries pledged not to develop or stockpile weaponized biological and toxic agents. [2] But the convention had no enforcement mechanism, and states like North Korea, China, Iran and Israel are believed to have developed weapons. Syria violated the accord by using chemical weapons on at least four occasions since December 2016, including one in April on a rebel-held town, which prompted the Trump administration to order a U.S. missile attack on a Syrian air base in April. [3]

The Soviet Union developed a program called Biopreparat that produced tons of anthrax and smallpox virus, some for use in intercontinental ballistic missiles. After the Soviet Union collapsed in 1991, the United States worked with the Russians to dismantle the Biopreparat lab. [4]

Accessing pathogens and turning them into a biological weapon doesn't require the backing of a nation-state, experts say. Only determination and access to medical supplies or a laboratory are required, as the Oregon town of The Dalles discovered in 1984. A religious sect called the Rajneeshees obtained a bacterial strain of salmonella from a commercial medical supply company and spread it on salad bars to try to disrupt a local election. More than 750 in the town of 10,000 were sickened. At the time, this was the largest bioterrorist attack in the country.

Then in 2001, someone created a blend of anthrax spores and weaponized them. According to investigators, Army scientist Bruce Ivins sent the spores to the media and members of Congress in the mail, killing five people in what remains the nation's worst bioterrorist attack. Some scientists, however, questioned the investigation's findings and doubts remain whether Ivins was the culprit. He killed himself before he was charged in the case. [5]

Many security experts today remain worried that another rogue scientist or an individual with some laboratory skills could wreak havoc. New technology can alter viruses and bacteria and make them more infectious or impervious to current treatments. These tools are widely available on the internet.

"Technology gets simpler and easier every day, and the risk of bioterrorism goes up every day," says Dr. Ali Khan, former director of the CDC's Office of Public Health Preparedness and Response.

Tara O'Toole, executive vice president at In-Q-Tel, a venture capital firm in Arlington, Va., specializing in security technology, says even nonscientists could use gene-editing tools available on the internet to develop dangerous biological agents and devise ways to disperse them.

All were ready to be deployed via a missile. [85]

In 2001, just weeks after the Sept. 11 terrorist attacks on New York City and the Pentagon, letters filled with anthrax were sent to some news media and members of Congress. A massive investigation concluded that a mentally ill biodefense researcher was the source of the letters, which infected 22 people and killed five. The suspect killed himself before he was charged, and some experts doubt he was the culprit. [86]

The government by some estimates spent as much as $1 billion testing and cleaning up the contaminated government buildings and the mail-sorting centers that handled the letters. The incident awoke many Americans to the possibility that the country was vulnerable to bioterrorism attack, not only from a terrorist organization but also from a deranged scientist. [87]

With advances in genetic engineering, a skilled scientist could alter a virus or bacterium in a lab and design it to be impervious to vaccines and antibiotics. "We no longer can concern ourselves just with highly funded national and international defense labs," wrote Michael Osterholm and Mark Olshaker in their 2017 book, *Deadliest Enemy: Our War Against Killer Germs*. "Information on how to gin up a potential killer microbe with new lab technology tools is readily available on the Internet." [88] ∎

CURRENT SITUATION

Emerging Threats

Hundreds of infections are constantly emerging around the world and spreading among and between animals and humans.

During one week at the beginning of May, there were 847 alerts about a patient or group of patients with potentially dangerous infectious diseases ranging from

In the bioterror version of a suicide bombing, a terrorist group also could infect people with a contagious respiratory disease and send them on multiple airline flights to spread the virus worldwide, along the lines of the 1995 movie "12 Monkeys."

"Bioterrorism remains one of the top two threats to the country, the other one being a nuclear attack," says O'Toole.

After the anthrax attacks in 2001, the United States spent more than $30 billion on programs to respond to a potential biological attack. For example, Project BioShield directs the federal government to stockpile medical countermeasures in case of a chemical, biological or nuclear attack. [6] Another program, BioWatch, is designed to detect airborne disease in major U.S. cities. [7]

"Those systems proved to be extremely valuable for the whole of the U.S. health system," says Schlegelmilch.

But Congress has cut spending on bioterrorism response by hundreds of millions of dollars in recent years. Further, BioWatch's systems for detecting airborne pathogens are old and unreliable, former Homeland Security Secretary Tom Ridge told a National Association of County and City Health Officials (NACCHO) conference on April 25. [8]

"We need a better disease and surveillance system to replace BioWatch," he said. Ridge, the nation's first Homeland Security secretary, co-chairs the Blue Ribbon Study Panel on Biodefense, created in 2014 to address gaps in the nation's biodefenses. The organization has made 33 recommendations to Congress including designating the vice president to be the lead federal coordinator in the event of a bio emergency.

"We have a lot in place to respond to and prevent biological and pandemics and biological terrorist attack, but the programs have atrophied," former Sen. Joseph Lieberman, an independent from Connecticut who is co-chair of the Blue Ribbon panel, said at the April NACCHO conference. "You get less focused on a problem that hasn't occurred lately. That makes you unprepared for when it does happen. So God forbid there should be another bioterrorism attack or infectious disease outbreak." [9]

— *Bara Vaida*

[1] Harald Doornbos and Jenan Moussa, "Found: The Islamic State's Terror Laptop of Doom," *ForeignPolicy.com*, Aug. 28, 2014, http://tinyurl.com/kqjkxes.

[2] "Convention on the Prohibition of the Development, Production and Stockpiling of Bacteriological (Biological) and Toxin Weapons and on their Destruction (BWC)," U.S. Department of State, March 26, 1975, http://tinyurl.com/m9ywuje.

[3] "North Korea's Biological Weapon Program," *Biological Warfare Blog*, April 2, 2014, http://tinyurl.com/kcel9jw; Missy Ryan, "Chemical attack in Syria that drew U.S. response was just one in a series, rights group alleges," *The Washington Post*, May 1, 2017, http://tinyurl.com/mh63voo.

[4] Michael T. Osterholm and Mark Olshaker, *Deadliest Enemy: Our War Against Killer Germs* (2017).

[5] Mara Bovsun, "750 sickened in Oregon restaurants as cult known as the Rajneeshees spread salmonella in town of The Dalles," *N.Y. Daily News*, June 15, 2013, http://tinyurl.com/karkvvk; Joby Warrick, "FBI investigation of 2001 anthrax attacks concluded; U.S. releases details," *The Washington Post*, Feb. 20, 2010, http://tinyurl.com/ybgtvr2.

[6] Milton Leitenberg, "Assessing the Biological Weapons and Bioterrorism Threat," Strategic Studies Institute, December 2005, http://tinyurl.com/k34nbv3.

[7] Frank Gottron, "Science and Technology Issues in the 115th Congress," Congressional Research Service, March 14, 2017, http://tinyurl.com/k6fzook.

[8] Tom Ridge remarks via webcast of Preparedness Summit, National Association of County and City Health Officials conference, April 25-28, 2017, http://tinyurl.com/lbhfd5d. For more on the conference, see Preparedness Summit, http://tinyurl.com/ozfwfb5, and "Biodefense advocates take on U.S. preparedness funding fight," *Homeland Preparedness News*, April 25, 2017, http://tinyurl.com/lkk637z.

[9] *Ibid.*, webcast of the April 25-28 conference.

Zika, Ebola and measles to yellow fever. Poultry, swine and cow illnesses were reported, too, according to HealthMap, a website that tracks infectious disease outbreaks worldwide. [89]

"Are we sitting on the edge of the next pandemic? I hope not," says Osterholm of the Center for Infectious Disease Research and Policy. "But could it happen tomorrow? Yes."

WHO is tracking these outbreaks through its Global Outbreak Alert and Response Network, which links local, regional, national and international networks of laboratories and medical centers. The organization also monitors flu outbreaks through its Global Influenza Surveillance and Response System, which is connected to hundreds of laboratories around the world. [90]

The most worrisome potential outbreak could be in China. A growing market for poultry in that nation has led to an explosion in chicken farming. In Shanghai alone, farmers hatch 100 million chickens a month, increasing the opportunity for novel influenza viruses to thrive.

One of those, the H7N9 virus, has been circulating among birds for years but has mutated to become more dangerous for both birds and humans handling the birds. The virus' changes are raising worries that it might lead to a pandemic, according to *Eurosurveillance*, Europe's journal of infectious disease epidemiology. [91]

China has reported more than 700 cases of H7N9 in humans and 203 deaths since October 2016. Nearly every victim was exposed to poultry, although a few cases may have been transmitted between individuals. [92]

Other outbreaks at the end of April included measles in Italy and Romania and yellow fever in Brazil. There also were outbreaks of MERS and three viruses — Lassa fever, Nipah and Crimean-Congo hemorrhagic fever. In early May, WHO reported an outbreak of Ebola in the Democratic Republic of Congo; by mid-May, four people had died and the number of cases had risen to 37. [93]

Experts say climate change increases the pandemic risk because certain diseases, such as Zika, thrive in hot and humid regions. Warming temperatures also increase the populations of disease carriers — mosquitos and parasites — making disease transmission easier. [94]

Leadership Vacuum

During this time of global risk, health policy experts are particularly worried about leadership gaps in the health community. [95]

Within the White House, the Trump administration's National Security Council (NSC) doesn't have a point person

One-year-old twins Heloisa and Heloa Barbosa of Areia, Brazil, were born with microcephaly after their mother was bitten by a mosquito with the Zika virus. Although technological advances have enabled scientists to develop new vaccines faster, including one for Zika, vaccines exist for only a fraction of the 300 or so known infectious diseases.

on global health security, although the White House told *The Washington Post* that Trump's homeland security adviser at the NSC, Thomas Bossert, has global health in his overall portfolio. Both Presidents George W. Bush and Obama dedicated one person solely to global health security.

At the Health and Human Services Department, Trump has yet to nominate anyone to serve as assistant secretary for preparedness and response. [96]

The president also has not named

a permanent director at the CDC. Dr. Anne Schuchat, a respected CDC veteran, is running the agency, but because she's only acting director, her ability to mobilize resources during an emergency could be stymied, experts say. [97]

At the Defense Department, the administration has not nominated an assistant secretary for nuclear, chemical and biological defense, who would oversee the global emerging infectious disease surveillance and response programs, as well as the National Center for Medical Intelligence. [98]

"No one is in charge" of bioterrorism strategy, says In-Q-Tel's O'Toole, which

is worrisome because "this is a national security issue. As Bill Gates says, the only thing that can kill millions of people is a bioterrorist attack or a pandemic."

Many health security experts were pleased when the Trump administration in early May nominated former Rep. Mark Green, R-Wis., to run USAID. Green was an ambassador to Tanzania under President George W. Bush and worked on his global AIDS initiative. Many health experts see him as an advocate for international aid programs.

"Mark Green is a really strong choice to head USAID," Jeremy Konyndyk, former head of the agency's Office of U.S. Foreign Disaster Assistance, told NPR. [99]

The U.N. Foundation's Lange says he is not too worried about the lack of nominees. Most of the positions are filled by experienced acting caretakers such as Schuchat at the CDC, he says. "The people that are there are of very high caliber and in a real emergency, their expertise [would] prevail," Lange says.

Health and Human Services Secretary Tom Price assured Congress in March that health security is a top priority for the administration and that it would provide resources to fund preparedness.

"This is an absolute priority," Price testified at a March 29 hearing of the House Appropriations Subcommittee on Labor, Health and Human Services, Education and Related Agencies. When asked if HHS would have the money it needs to fund public health emergency preparedness, he said: "The American people expect us to be prepared and to be able to respond in the event of a challenge, especially in a bioterror area." [100]

WHO, too, is in the middle of a leadership transition as Tedros readies to become director-general. His election came as the organization struggles with financial challenges and an ongoing restructuring to better respond to emergency health outbreaks like Ebola. In May, The Associated Press published a scathing report criticizing WHO's $200 million travel budget, which is more than the agency devotes to AIDS, malaria and tuberculosis combined. [101]

Although WHO began a capital drive in 2015 for an emergency contingency fund for pandemics, some experts say that without decisive leadership the organization has been unable to reach its goal of $100 million. Tedros is a malaria expert who will have his work cut out for him. He is best known for drastically reducing deaths from malaria, AIDS, tuberculosis and neonatal problems when he was Ethiopia's health minister. [102]

Continued on p. 474

At Issue:

Should governments mandate quarantines?

CENTERS FOR DISEASE CONTROL AND PREVENTION (CDC)

EXCERPTED FROM CDC WEBSITE

*i*solation and quarantine help protect the public by preventing exposure to people who have or may have a contagious disease. Isolation involves separating sick people with a contagious disease from people who are not sick. . . .

The duration and scope of quarantine measures would vary, depending on their purpose and what is known about the incubation period (how long it takes for symptoms to develop after exposure) of the disease-causing agent.

If people in a certain area were potentially exposed to a contagious disease, this is what would happen: State and local health authorities would let people know that they may have been exposed and would direct them to get medical attention, undergo diagnostic tests, and stay at home, limiting their contact with people who have not been exposed to the disease. Only rarely would federal, state, or local health authorities issue an "order" for quarantine and isolation.

However, both quarantine and isolation may be compelled on a mandatory basis through legal authority as well as conducted on a voluntary basis. States have the authority to declare and enforce quarantine and isolation within their borders. This authority varies widely, depending on state laws. It derives from the authority of state governments granted by the U.S. Constitution to enact laws and promote regulations to safeguard the health and welfare of people within state borders.

Further, at the national level, the CDC may detain, medically examine or conditionally release persons suspected of having certain contagious diseases. This authority applies to individuals arriving from foreign countries, including Canada and Mexico, on airplanes, trains, automobiles, boats or by foot. It also applies to individuals traveling from one state to another or in the event of "inadequate local control."

The CDC regularly uses its authority to monitor passengers arriving in the United States for contagious diseases. In modern times, most quarantine measures have been imposed on a small scale, typically involving small numbers of travelers (airline or cruise ship passengers) who have curable diseases, such as infectious tuberculosis or cholera. No instances of large-scale quarantine have occurred in the U.S. since the "Spanish Flu" pandemic of 1918-1919.

Based on years of experience working with state and local partners, the CDC anticipates that the need to use its federal authority to involuntarily quarantine a person would occur only in rare situations — for example, if a person posed a threat to public health and refused to cooperate with a voluntary request.

JEFFREY A. TUCKER
DIRECTOR OF CONTENT, FOUNDATION FOR ECONOMIC EDUCATION; POLICY ADVISER, HEARTLAND INSTITUTE

EXCERPTED FROM FOUNDATION FOR ECONOMIC EDUCATION WEBSITE

*t*he government already has the power to create sick camps, kidnap and intern people upon suspicion that they are diseased, and keep people in camps for an undetermined amount of time. Anyone concerned about human freedom should be uncomfortable with this policy, especially given the hysteria that surrounds the issue of communicable diseases. It is easy to imagine a scenario in which such powers end up exposing undiseased people rather than protecting people from the disease.

Quarantine powers have been around since the ancient world and have been invoked through U.S. history since colonial times. But government can use those powers any way it wants. In World War I, prostitutes were routinely arrested and quarantined in the name of preventing the spread of diseases.

In the 1892 typhus outbreak, it became common to arrest and quarantine any immigrant from Russia, Italy or Ireland, even without any evidence of disease. In 1900, the San Francisco Board of Health quarantined 25,000 Chinese residents and gave them a dangerous injection to prevent the spread of bubonic plague (it turned out later to have been entirely pointless). In more recent times, fears of AIDS have led to calls for arresting Mexican immigrants. And it's not just about disease. The quarantine power has been used by despotic governments worldwide to round up political enemies.

Does the government really need quarantine power? Let's think rationally and normally about this. Government power is not necessary, nor is it likely to be effective. And when it is not effective, the tendency is to overreact, clamping down and abusing, as we've seen with the war on terror. People assume government is doing its job, but government fails and then government gets more power and does awful things with it.

Remember, it is not government that discovers the disease, treats it, keeps diseased patients from wandering around or otherwise compels sick people to stay in their sick beds. Institutions do this, institutions that are part of the social order and not exogenous to it.

Individuals don't like to get others sick. People don't like to get sick. Given this, we have a mechanism that actually works. Society has an ability and power of its own to bring about quarantine-like results without introducing the risk that the state's quarantine power will be used and abused for political purposes.

Continued from p. 472

Meanwhile, the Global Fund to Fight AIDs, Tuberculosis and Malaria also is seeking a new leader. The organization gets one-third of its money from the United States and estimates that it saves 2 million lives a year worldwide. It is unclear whether the United States will continue providing money under Trump and whether a new leader can fulfill the organization's goals without U.S. aid. [103]

Global Collaboration

The uncertainty surrounding the Trump administration's commitment to international health funding has created anxiety among global researchers who have been working together on vaccines and other medical countermeasures for a potential pandemic.

The first successful Ebola vaccine, which is awaiting regulatory approval in the United States, demonstrates the importance of global collaboration, experts say. The vaccine was developed in conjunction with WHO and companies, governments and universities from the United States, Canada, Europe and West Africa. Brazilian and European researchers collaborated with U.S. researchers to produce a Zika vaccine. [104]

But Trump's proposed temporary ban on travel from six Muslim countries alarmed researchers, who say the ban, although on hold, has slowed collaboration on tropical-disease vaccines and other emerging infectious-disease treatments. It also leaves international researchers wary of working with Americans and could place the United States at risk over the long term, said infectious disease expert Peter Hotez at the Baylor College of Medicine in Houston.

"Scientific communities across the world need collaborators in these countries who can combat epidemics before they arrive in the U.S.," said Hotez. [105]

The United States also needs to continue working with international researchers on influenza vaccines, because

the flu spreads so quickly between borders, global health experts say. WHO maintains centers in Australia, the United States, China, Japan and the United Kingdom for collaborating on influenza vaccine research. The CDC developed three vaccines for H7N9 and stockpiled 12 million doses. Officials say, however, that virus has mutated, making the stockpiled vaccine less effective against the current H7N9 strain. [106]

To create another vaccine to match the version of H7N9 that is circulating now, the United States needs to keep working with China and other international colleagues, says Richard Webby, director of WHO's Collaborating Center for Studies on the Ecology of Influenza in Animals in Memphis, Tenn.

Further, the United States needs international partners when it comes to manufacturing vaccines. Companies produce a flu vaccine by growing it in fertilized eggs. The United States relies on four pharmaceutical companies for flu vaccines, but only one has a manufacturing facility in the U.S. If a flu pandemic struck and killed the chickens needed to produce eggs, the United States might have trouble getting enough vaccine produced, because the three non-U.S. companies may decide to withhold the vaccines for their own populations, the Government Accountability Office said. [107]

If the United States can develop technologies that do not use eggs to produce vaccines, it would be less vulnerable, said Osterholm of the Center for Infectious Disease Research and Policy. "It would be the single most important thing we can do in public health today," he said. [108]

Researchers are making progress toward that goal. University of Georgia scientists are working to create a vaccine with genetic sequences of flu strains that have circulated over the past century. At Mount Sinai Hospital researchers are using genome sequencing to help the immune system better target a flu virus. [109]

OUTLOOK

Preventing Pandemics

Public health leaders agree that, statistically, the world is overdue for a lethal pandemic. They don't know whether it would begin with a rapidly evolving regional outbreak such as occurred with Ebola and Zika or a flu virus that has mutated to a point that no vaccine is effective; or a bioterrorist attack.

Preventing massive loss of life will require the world to continue working together to help poor and middle-income countries bolster their health systems, public health officials say, adding that the United States must maintain its investments in vaccine research and emergency preparedness.

"We should always have a good, high guard and never be complacent," said David Nabarro, an international health expert from Great Britain who was a candidate to lead WHO. [110]

Global health experts are optimistic that the Ebola and Zika crises have awakened leaders to the potential threats and that countries are on guard. They say the Global Health Security Agenda, the G-20 countries and individual nations are laying the groundwork to fight a pandemic. Further, advances in computing power and genetic engineering could bolster scientists' efforts to develop vaccines to fight the flu and other diseases.

Possibly as soon as the end of 2017, a total of 68 countries are expected to be evaluated by a multilateral body associated with WHO. The G-20 and World Bank have pledged funding to help them close preparedness gaps. The efforts involve wide swaths of governments — from the health ministries to environmental agencies to agriculture departments. The private sector also is stepping up.

"I am encouraged about the future," says Georgetown's Katz. "There are some smart people who have awakened to this threat."

Efforts by vaccine researchers and the Coalition for Epidemic Preparedness Innovations are expected to bear fruit within the decade, says John-Arne Rottingen, chief executive of the Research Council of Norway.

"We will probably have developed six to 10 vaccines for what we believe will be the most likely threats," he says of the next 10 years. "Hopefully we will have a couple of technology platforms based on [genetic engineering] techniques, so we can fast-track new vaccines for new, emerging pathogens, and that will increase our capacities to prevent and stop a new epidemic."

Microsoft's Gates and former Harvard University President Lawrence Summers are among the private-sector leaders whom Katz says are aggressively pushing leaders worldwide to see pandemic preparedness as a matter of national security and economics — and not just of health. Ebola cost the world economy about $32 billion, and Zika could cost North and South America and the Caribbean up to $18 billion by the end of 2017. [111]

"This is a big deal," Katz says. "Public health experts can bang the drums all day about pandemic threats, but ministers of health tend not to be politically important. Gates, Sands and Summers, however, are able to make strong arguments to ministers of finance to encourage their governments that investing in this [affects business]," she says, "and they are changing the framework of this discussion." ∎

Notes

[1] "Human infection with avian influenza A(H7N9) virus — China," World Health Organization, April 20, 2017, http://tinyurl.com/mrwycej.

[2] Lisa Schnirring, "China reports 23 more H7N9 cases, 7 fatal," Center for Infectious Disease Research and Policy, May 12, 2017, http://tinyurl.com/kutlvk8; Jeffrey K. Tauben-

berger and David M. Morens, "Influenza: The Once and Future Pandemic," Public Health Reports, U.S. National Library of Medicine, 2010, http://tinyurl.com/ldh4rfu.

[3] Dan Vergano, "Mystery of 1918 Flu That Killed 50 Million Solved?" National Geographic, April 29 2014, http://tinyurl.com/moxx767.

[4] Rob Schmitz, "Why Chinese Scientists Are More Worried Than Ever About Bird Flu," Goats and Soda blog, NPR, April 11, 2017, http://tinyurl.com/mjnk6yk.

[5] James Joyce, "Why the nation must prepare for future pandemic threats," San Diego Union-Tribune, Nov. 24, 2016, http://tinyurl.com/morjhhy.

[6] Bill Gates, "A new kind of terrorism could wipe out 30 million people in less than a year and we are not prepared," Business Insider, Feb. 18, 2017, http://tinyurl.com/z5pc9rn.

[7] Annie Sparrow, "Who isn't equipped for a pandemic or a bioterror attack? The WHO," Bulletin of the Atomic Scientists, June 20, 2016, http://tinyurl.com/msrpmy2; Sheri Fink, "Cuts at W.H.O. Hurt Response to Ebola Crises," The New York Times, Sept. 3, 2014, http://tinyurl.com/m4ppmys.

[8] "The WHO Contingency Fund for Emergencies," World Health Organization, November 2015, http://tinyurl.com/k7xdkbo.

[9] "Fact Sheet: The Global Health Security Agenda," Office of the Press Secretary, The White House, July 28, 2015, http://tinyurl.com/m6ybyd9; "The Global Health Security Agenda," http://tinyurl.com/m8wjl5k; "Coalition for Epidemic Preparedness Innovations (CEPI) Presentation to the WHO," World Health Organization, July 21, 2017, http://tinyurl.com/l3msobz.

[10] Donald G. McNeil Jr., "The Campaign to Lead the World Health Organization," The New York Times, April 3, 2017, http://tinyurl.com/kylbmmu; Julia Belluz, "Trump has set the US up to botch a global health crises," Vox.com, April 3, 2017, http://tinyurl.com/ksvb83q.

[11] Lena H. Sun, "The Trump administration is ill-prepared for a global pandemic," The Washington Post, April 18, 2017, http://tinyurl.com/n3ocur8; Lawrence Gostin and Eric Friedman, "Global Health: A Pivotal Moment of Opportunity and Peril," Health Affairs, Feb. 28, 2017, http://tinyurl.com/mf6gmht.

[12] "Emergency Preparedness and Response 2016," World Health Organization, http://tinyurl.com/l25xwpa; "First Global Estimates of 2009 H1N1 Pandemic Mortality Released by CDC-Led Collaboration," Centers for Disease Control and Prevention, June 25, 2012, http://tinyurl.com/lunzuhk; Denise Grady, "Suspected Cases of Ebola Rise to 29 in Democratic

Republic of Congo," The New York Times, May 18, 2017, http://tinyurl.com/l4kw7ya.

[13] Anmar Frangoul, "Counting the costs of a global epidemic," CNBC.com, Feb. 5, 2014, http://tinyurl.com/kkh8nep; "World Bank Group Launches Groundbreaking Financing Facility to Protect Poorest Countries Against Pandemics," World Bank, May 21, 2016, http://tinyurl.com/mwtgsjd.

[14] Gates, op. cit.

[15] "Antibiotic/Antimicrobial Resistance," Centers for Disease Control and Prevention, April 27, 2017, http://tinyurl.com/la3tgtj; Helen Branswell, "A Nevada woman dies of a superbug resistant to every available antibiotic in the US," STAT, Jan. 12, 2017, http://tinyurl.com/hdxdcmq.

[16] Ali S. Khan with William Patrick, "The Next Pandemic: On the Front Lines Against Humankind's Gravest Dangers," PublicAffairs, 2016, p. 250, http://tinyurl.com/mk8gneo.

[17] Tom Ridge remarks via webcast of Preparedness Summit, National Association of County and City Health Officials conference, April 25-28, 2017, http://tinyurl.com/lbhfd5d.

[18] Michael Osterholm and Mark Olshaker, Deadlist Enemy: Our War Against Killer Germs (2017), chap. 11, http://tinyurl.com/myacoga.

[19] "Fact Sheet: The Global Health Security Agenda," op. cit.

[20] "International Health Regulations," World Health Organization, 2005, http://tinyurl.com/n5lv3qz; Haitham Shoman, "The link between the West African Ebola outbreak and health systems in Guinea, Liberia, and Sierra Leone: A systematic review," Globalization and Health, Oct. 17, 2016, http://tinyurl.com/mqqmphl.

[21] "U.S. Launches Global Health Security Agenda, Partners With 26 Countries," Henry J. Kaiser Family Foundation, Feb. 14, 2014, http://tinyurl.com/lkfn745.

[22] "African Union launches Africa CDC, a continent-wide public health agency," ReliefWeb, Feb. 2, 2017, http://tinyurl.com/mpbv5yx.

[23] "USAID announces second phase of Predict project with global partners," EcoHealth Alliance, Nov. 21, 2014, http://tinyurl.com/lyt2zk4; "Factsheet: Emerging Pandemic Threats," USAID, http://tinyurl.com/n86geuu.

[24] Bryan Walsh, "The World Is Not Ready for the Next Pandemic," Time, May 3, 2017, http://tinyurl.com/mopxrys.

[25] Sun, op. cit.

[26] Peter Sands et al., "The Neglected Dimension of Global Security — A Framework for Countering Infectious-Disease Crises," The New England Journal of Medicine, March 31, 2016, http://tinyurl.com/lfqkub4.

[27] McNeil Jr., op. cit.; "Budget Fact Sheets,"

Centers for Disease Control and Prevention, http://tinyurl.com/mw9ox53.

[28] Suerie Moon *et al.*, "Will Ebola Change the Game? Ten Essential Reforms Before the Next Pandemic," *The Lancet*, Nov. 22, 2015, http://tinyurl.com/lyq6o89.

[29] Sparrow, *op. cit.*

[30] "World Health Assembly elects Dr. Tedros Adhanom Ghebreyesus as new WHO Director-General," World Health Organization, May 23, 2017, http://tinyurl.com/lhj7yn7; McNeil Jr., *op. cit.*

[31] Helen Branswell, "Finding the World's Unknown Viruses — Before They Find Us," *STAT*, Dec. 13, 2016, http://tinyurl.com/keruja7.

[32] "What is CEPI?" Center for Epidemic Preparedness Innovations, http://tinyurl.com/m29tyam.

[33] Crystal Watson and Matthew Watson, "Funding and Organization of US Federal Biosecurity Security Programs," Johns Hopkins Bloomberg School of Public Health Center for Health Security, January/February 2017, http://tinyurl.com/mu3lwf4.

[34] "2017 United States Budget Estimate," *Inside Gov*, http://tinyurl.com/mtc2fc3.

[35] "The U.S. Government and the World Health Organization," Henry J. Kaiser Family Foundation, March 16, 2017, http://tinyurl.com/mcoswva.

[36] Watson and Watson, *op. cit.*

[37] "Biodefense Indicators: One Year Later, Events Outpacing Federal Efforts to Defend the Nation," Blue Ribbon Study Panel on Defense, December 2016, http://tinyurl.com/y97jvw3q.

[38] Ridge, *op. cit.*

[39] "FY2010 Budget Overview," CDC Coalition, http://tinyurl.com/k64o4v6; "Division H — Departments of Labor, Health and Human Services, and Education and Related Agencies Appropriations Act 2017," House of Representatives, May 2017, http://tinyurl.com/lao845n.

[40] "Prepared, National Health Security Preparedness Index," Robert Wood Johnson Foundation, http://tinyurl.com/ltj8wyh.

[41] Ilene MacDonald, "Trump budget proposal cuts billions and would 'devastate' healthcare programs," *FierceHealthcare*, May 23, 2017, http://tinyurl.com/lkeauwx.

[42] Tom Friedan tweet by Friedan, May 23, 2017.

[43] Donovan Slack and Gregory Korte, "Trump's first budget slashes education, health spending to make way for military buildup," *USA Today*, March 16, 2017, http://tinyurl.com/kw8c977; "Avian Influenza: USDA Has Taken Actions to Reduce Risks but Needs a Plan to Evaluate Its Efforts," U.S. Government Accountability Office, April 2017, http://tinyurl.com/mcptyjj.

[44] Walsh, *op. cit.*

[45] Zoë Carpenter, "The United States Has an Emergency Fund for Natural Disasters. Why Not for Pandemics?" *The Nation*, Aug. 25, 2016, http://tinyurl.com/k4q2lh5.

[46] "Specific Laws and Regulations Governing the Control of Communicable Diseases," Centers for Disease Control and Prevention, March 21, 2017, http://tinyurl.com/mkbzxbd.

[47] Lenny Bernstein, "Trump wanted to keep Americans critically ill with Ebola out of the U.S.," *The Washington Post*, Aug. 24, 2016, http://tinyurl.com/mhyzqdu.

[48] Norimitsu Onishi, "Clashes Erupt as Liberia Sets an Ebola Quarantine," *The New York Times*, Aug. 20, 2014, http://tinyurl.com/k2d5ggn; Adam Nassiter, "Sierra Leone to Impose 3-Day Ebola Quarantine," *The New York Times*, Sept. 6, 2014, http://tinyurl.com/lnh7dgu.

[49] "Statement from the Travel and Transport Task Force on Ebola virus disease outbreak in West Africa," World Health Organization, Nov. 7, 2014, http://tinyurl.com/lprlxaz.

[50] Richard Schabas, "Severe Acute Respiratory Syndrome: Did Quarantine Help?" *Canadian Journal of Infectious Diseases and Medical Microbiology*, July/August 2004, http://tinyurl.com/krr8jbf.

[51] Shoman, *op. cit.*

[52] "Legal Authorities for Isolation and Quarantine," Centers for Disease Control and Prevention, Oct. 8, 2014, http://tinyurl.com/n8xx33a.

[53] Kyle Edwards, Wendy Parmet and Scott Burris, "Why the C.D.C.'s Power to Quarantine Should Worry Us," *The New York Times*, Jan. 23, 2017, http://tinyurl.com/l3bsrhk.

[54] Rob Stein, "CDC Seeks Controversial New Quarantine Powers to Stope Outbreaks," *Shots blog*, NPR, Feb. 2, 2017, http://tinyurl.com/zm6azve.

[55] *Ibid.*

[56] Matt Arco, "Ebola Nurse Lawsuit Against Christie Continues Despite Judge Tossing Federal Claims," NJ.com, Sept. 9, 2016, http://tinyurl.com/kus22dx.

[57] "Global Immunization: Worldwide Disease Incidence," Children's Hospital of Philadelphia, December 2014, http://tinyurl.com/jktr3ot.

[58] Erin Walkinshaw, "Mandatory Vaccinations: No Middle Ground," *Canadian Medical Association Journal*, Nov. 8, 2011, http://tinyurl.com/lfynf5f.

[59] Kathleen S. Swendiman, "Mandatory Vaccinations: Precedent and Current Laws," Congressional Research Service, March 10, 2011.

[60] "Background of the Issue" ProCon.org, March 22, 2016, http://tinyurl.com/zmqo9xq.

[61] "Health, United States, 2015," Department of Health and Human Services, 2016, http://tinyurl.com/m8uz5gs; Lena H. Sun, "Anti-vaccine activists spark a state's worst measles outbreak in decades," *The Washington Post*, May 5, 2017, http://tinyurl.com/l9wjpto.

[62] "Hardball with Chris Matthews," NBCNews.com, Feb. 3, 2015, http://tinyurl.com/ko2bwrb.

[63] Lena H. Sun, "Trump energizes the anti-vaccine movement in Texas," *The Washington Post*, Feb. 20, 2017, http://tinyurl.com/n5cnzom; Dylan Scott, "Robert K. Kennedy Jr. Says He Expects Trump Vaccine Panel Will Move Forward," *STAT*, Feb. 16, 2012, http://tinyurl.com/jhor5gb.

[64] "The Model State Emergency Health Powers Act," Network for Public Health Law, Aug. 1, 2011, http://tinyurl.com/l2shxah; "Q&A Model State Emergency Health Powers Act," American Civil Liberties Union, http://tinyurl.com/mzutrgh.

[65] Sonia Shah, *Pandemic: Tracking Contagions, from Cholera to Ebola and Beyond* (2016), chap. 1.

[66] *Ibid.*

[67] Marcia Clemmitt, "Emerging Infectious Diseases," *CQ Researcher*, Feb. 13, 2015, pp. 145-168.

[68] "Black Death," History.com, http://tinyurl.com/bk3z46l.

[69] *Ibid.*; Eugenia Tognotti, "Lessons from the History of Quarantine, From Plague to Influenza A," Centers for Disease Control and Prevention, February 2013, http://tinyurl.com/lmd34wx.

[70] Shah, *op. cit.*

[71] *Ibid.*; Tognotti, *op. cit.*

[72] *Ibid.*, Tognotti.

[73] For background see Mary H. Cooper, "Fighting SARS," *CQ Researcher*, June 20, 2003, pp. 569-592.

[74] "Lessons from the History of Quarantine, From Plague to Influenza A," *op. cit.*

About the Author

Bara Vaida is a Washington-based freelancer with more than 25 years' experience as a journalist, covering primarily health care policy issues. She has worked for Agence France-Presse, Bloomberg News, *National Journal* and *Kaiser Health News.* She also has published articles in, among others, *Cancer Today, Stateline, WebMD* and *Washingtonian* magazines.

[75] "Background of the Issue," *op. cit.*

[76] "Edward Jenner," Science Museum, http://tinyurl.com/my93qbn; Max Roser, "Eradication of Diseases," *Our World in Data*, http://tinyurl.com/n42crl6.

[77] "Background of the Issue," *op. cit.*; Cole and Swendiman, *op. cit.*

[78] *Ibid.*, Swendiman.

[79] Rustam I. Aminov, "A Brief History of the Antibiotic Era: Lessons Learned and Challenges for the Future," *Frontiers in Microbiology*, Oct. 29, 2010, http://tinyurl.com/lv4elnd.

[80] "Life Expectancy in the USA," University of California, Berkeley, http://tinyurl.com/l3qzudg; Rob Stein, "Life Expectancy in U.S. Drops For First Time In Decades, Report Finds," NPR, Dec. 6, 2016, http://tinyurl.com/grf86xv.

[81] Taubenberger and Morens, *op. cit.*

[82] James A. Wilde, "A(H1N1) 'Swine Flu' 2009/2010: Where We've Been, What We Know, Where We May Be Heading," AHC Media, March 1, 2010, http://tinyurl.com/kgoafgq.

[83] Robert Roos, "Study Puts Global 2009 Pandemic H1N1 Infection Rate at 24%," Center for Infectious Disease Research and Policy, Jan. 24, 2013, http://tinyurl.com/k2sa5r3; Joe Neel, "How Many People Die From Flu Each Year? Depends On How You Slice The Data," *Shots blog*, NPR, Aug. 26, 2010, http://tinyurl.com/jlo9wtd.

[84] Osterholm and Olshaker, *op. cit.*, chap. 11.

[85] *Ibid.*

[86] Joby Warrick, "FBI investigation of 2001 anthrax attacks concluded; U.S. releases details," *The Washington Post*, Feb. 20, 2010, http://tinyurl.com/ybgtvr2.

[87] Khan and Patrick, *op. cit.*, chap. 5.

[88] Osterholm and Olshaker, *op. cit.*

[89] "Alerts for the Week," *HealthMap*, May 14, 2017, http://tinyurl.com/24eyvvh.

[90] "Global Influenza Surveillance and Response System," World Health Organization, http://tinyurl.com/72ex3oa; "Global Outbreak Alert and Response Network," World Health Organization, http://tinyurl.com/hpblh9j.

[91] "Eurosurveillance: Preliminary Epidemiology and Analysis of Jiangsu's 5th H7N9 Wave," *Avian Flu Diary*, March 30, 2017, http://tinyurl.com/kb9sbyv.

[92] Schnirring, *op. cit.*

[93] Stephanie Soucheray, "WHO: 37 Ebola cases in the DRC, 4 Deaths" Center for Infectious Disease Research and Policy, May 22, 2017, http://tinyurl.com/mwlbvkm.

[94] "Climate Change and Infectious Diseases," World Health Organization, http://tinyurl.com/o9ylyme.

[95] Belluz, *op. cit.*

[96] "Political Appointee Trackers," Partnership for Public Service, May 23, 2017, http://tinyurl.com/lxxhv6k.

[97] Sun, "The Trump administration is ill-prepared for a global pandemic," *op. cit.*

[98] "Political Appointee Tracker," *op. cit.*

[99] Jason Beaubien, "Trump's Proposed USAID Head Knows Aid — And Politics," *Goats and Soda blog*, NPR, May 11, 2017, http://tinyurl.com/k7d8k6l.

[100] Testimony of Tom Price, Budget Hearing, Department of Health and Human Services, March 29, 2017, http://tinyurl.com/mvvc85z.

[101] "AP Exclusive: UN Health Agency Slammed for High Travel Costs," The Associated Press, *The New York Times*, May 22, 2017, http://tinyurl.com/n5ezobw.

[102] McNeil Jr., *op. cit.*; Donald G. McNeil Jr. and Nick Cumming-Bruce, "WHO Elects Ethopia's Tedros as First Director General from Africa," *The New York Times*, May 23, 2017, http://tinyurl.com/lx6gw7d.

[103] Jeremy Youde, "Wanted: A New Executive Director for the Global Fund," *Duck of Minerva*, March 4, 2017, http://tinyurl.com/mjmdl8m.

[104] Belluz, *op. cit.*

[105] Amy Maxmen, "Trump immigration ban upends international work on disease," *Nature*, Feb. 1, 2017, http://tinyurl.com/l7afwuc.

[106] "Asian Lineage Avian Influenza A (H7N9)," Centers for Disease Control and Prevention, May 9, 2017, http://tinyurl.com/l7qd6ou.

[107] "Avian Influenza: USDA Has Taken Actions to Reduce Risks but Needs a Plan to Evaluate Its Efforts," *op. cit.*

[108] Marlene Cimons, "There may someday be a way to avoid the yearly flu shot," *The Washington Post*, Jan. 7, 2017, http://tinyurl.com/k4g3gy3.

[109] *Ibid.*

[110] Stephanie Nebehay, "World must not miss early signals of any flu pandemic: WHO," Reuters, Jan. 23, 2017, http://tinyurl.com/kkf2mb5.

[111] Deb Reichmann, "World Bank: Economic impact of Ebola epidemic could top $32.6 billion by end of year," The Associated Press, *USA Today*, Oct. 8, 2014, http://tinyurl.com/lqkp5ff; "Report says cost of Zika estimated at up to $18 billion," The Associated Press, WTOP.com, April 6, 2017, http://tinyurl.com/mc5kf7e.

FOR MORE INFORMATION

Association of State and Territorial Health Officials, 2231 Crystal Drive, Suite 450, Arlington, VA 22202; 202-371-9090; www.astho.org. Represents public health agencies and professionals.

Center for Global Health Science and Security, Georgetown University Medical Center, N.W., 306, Medical-Dental Building, 3900 Reservoir Rd., N.W., Washington, DC 20007; 202-687-9823; https://ghss.georgetown.edu/. Works on global health security with policy leaders worldwide.

Center for Infectious Disease Research and Policy, University of Minnesota, Academic Health Center, 420 Delaware St., S.E., MMC 263, C315 Mayo, Minneapolis, MN 55455; 612-626-6770; www.cidrap.umn.edu/. Provides research and news on infectious-disease outbreaks and policy response.

Centers for Disease Control and Prevention, Division of Global Health Protection and Security, 1600 Clifton Rd., Atlanta, GA 30329-4027; 800-232-4636; www.cdc.gov/globalhealth/healthprotection/index.html. Federal agency that works with international partners on global health and infectious-disease surveillance and response.

HealthMap, Boston Children's Hospital, Computational Epidemiology Lab, Landmark Center, Seventh Floor, 401 Park Drive, Boston, MA 02215; 617-355-6000; www.healthmap.org/en/. Internet-based reporting system.

International Society for Infectious Disease, 9 Babcock St., Unit 3, Brookline MA 02446; 617-277-0551; www.isid.org. Membership organization for professionals specializing in infectious diseases.

Trust for America's Health, 1730 M St., N.W., Suite 900, Washington, DC 20036; 202-223-9870; http://healthyamericans.org/. Public health advocacy group.

World Health Organization, Regional Office for the Americas, 525 23rd St., N.W., Washington, DC 20037; 202-974-3000; www.who.int/about/regions/amro/en/. United Nations agency that helps shape global policy and research.

Bibliography

Selected Sources

Books

Khan, Ali S., *The Next Pandemic: On the Front Lines Against Humankind's Gravest Dangers*, PublicAffairs, 2016.

The former head of the Office of Public Health Preparedness and Response at the Centers for Disease Control and Prevention (CDC) recalls investigating frightening disease outbreaks and offers advice on how to prevent pandemics.

Osterholm, Michael T., and Mark Olshaker, *Deadliest Enemy: Our War Against Killer Germs*, Little Brown & Company, 2017.

The founder of the University of Minnesota's Center for Infectious Disease Research and Policy recounts the history of pandemics and explains how political leaders can implement policy initiatives to prevent them.

Shah, Sonia, *Pandemic: Tracking Contagions from Cholera to Ebola and Beyond*, Picador USA, 2016.

A science journalist summarizes past pandemics and explains how dealing with cholera helped prepare the world to prevent future pandemics.

Articles

"AP Exclusive: UN Health Agency Slammed for High Travel Costs," The Associated Press, *The New York Times*, May 22, 2017, http://tinyurl.com/n5ezobw.

The World Health Organization is spending $200 million a year on travel expenses, more than what it spends fighting AIDS, malaria and tuberculosis combined, according to an Associated Press investigation.

"Lessons from the History of Quarantine, from Plague to Influenza A," Centers for Disease Control and Prevention, February 2013, http://tinyurl.com/lmd34wx.

The federal agency in charge of preventing the spread of infectious diseases reflects on lessons learned from quarantines imposed during pandemics and how quarantines can be used to safeguard public health without violating civil rights.

Boyce, Nell Greenfield, "Inside a Secret Government Warehouse Prepped for Health Catastrophes," NPR, June 27, 2016, http://tinyurl.com/jyxgply.

The CDC is stockpiling drugs, vaccines and medical equipment in preparation for potential health emergencies.

Gostin, Lawrence, and Eric Friedman, "Global Health: A Pivotal Moment of Opportunity and Peril," *Health Affairs*, January 2017, http://tinyurl.com/lyvxkac.

Two Georgetown University researchers highlight policies they say are needed to strengthen global health security.

McNeil, Donald G. Jr., "Turning the Tide Against Cholera," *The New York Times Magazine*, Feb. 6, 2017, http://tinyurl.

com/hzlx7uq.

A journalist examines efforts to eliminate cholera, an infectious disease that can be contracted from contaminated water or food.

Rull, Monica, Ilona Kickbusch and Helen Lauer, "Policy Debate: International Responses to Global Epidemics: Ebola and Beyond," International Development Policy, February 2015, http://tinyurl.com/kuo6l6k.

Researchers look at a policy debate about the World Health Organization's response to Ebola.

Saunders-Hastings, Patrick R., and Daniel Krewski, "Reviewing the History of Pandemic Influenza: Understanding Patterns of Emergence and Transmission," *Pathogens*, Dec. 6, 2016, http://tinyurl.com/n5fqu7l.

Researchers from the University of Ottawa offer a historical primer on influenza pandemics.

Reports and Studies

"Avian Influenza: USDA Has Taken Actions to Reduce Risks but Needs a Plan to Evaluate Its Efforts," Government Accountability Office, April 2017, http://tinyurl.com/mcptyjj.

A government report outlines steps the Agriculture Department has taken to protect the country from an avian pandemic and raises questions about whether the nation is too reliant on a single U.S.-based egg producer for the manufacturing of influenza vaccines.

"Biodefense Indicators: One Year Later, Events Outpacing Federal Efforts to Defend the Nation," Blue Ribbon Study Panel on Biodefense, December 2016, http://tinyurl.com/m9lsq3z.

A bipartisan group, created in 2014 to assess the nation's biodefense readiness, updates efforts to encourage Congress to devote more attention and funding to preparing for health emergencies.

"Ready or Not? Protecting the Public's Health From Diseases, Disasters and Bioterrorism," Trust for America's Health, December 2016, http://tinyurl.com/mafd4gf.

A public health advocacy group provides a snapshot of federal and state investment in emergency health preparedness.

"Tackling Drug Resistant Infections Globally: Final Report and Recommendations," Review on Antimicrobial Resistance, Wellcome Trust, May 2016, http://tinyurl.com/zxxjmww.

A report funded by the British government focuses on the growing number of antibiotic-resistant bacterial infections and discusses policy recommendations for halting their spread.

Gottron, Frank, "The Project BioShield Act: Issues for the 113th Congress," Congressional Research Service, June 18, 2014, http://tinyurl.com/mreoqgu.

Congress' nonpartisan research arm updates the status of U.S. spending on bio-preparedness.

The Next Step:

Additional Articles from Current Periodicals

Bioterrorism

Fox, Maggie, "Worse Than Ebola: U.S. Not Preparing for the Next Bio-Threat," NBC News, May 1, 2017, https://tiny url.com/mlfuzky.

Disease experts, who have urged the United States to prepare for potential outbreaks or bioterrorist strikes, say little planning or funding has been implemented to protect against pandemics.

Selk, Avi, "Bill Gates: Bioterrorism could kill more than nuclear war — but no one is ready to deal with it," The Washington Post, Feb. 18, 2017, https://tinyurl.com/mdrvqog.

Microsoft co-Founder Bill Gates warned world leaders in February to prepare for bioterror attacks, which he said are easier to execute than nuclear weapons and could trigger pandemics that could kill more people.

International Agencies

Disparte, Dante, and Tom Ridge, "The World Needs a DARPA-Style Project to Prevent Pandemics," Harvard Business Review, April 24, 2017, https://tinyurl.com/k3z8wkq.

Two experts say world governments should prepare for pandemics through transnational, cross-sector coordination, similar to how the Defense Advanced Research Projects Agency, the Defense Department's research arm, collaborates with academia, industry and other government agencies to help develop emerging technologies.

Levey, Noam N., "Trump pushes historic cuts in global health aid, stoking fears of new disease outbreaks and diminished U.S. clout," Los Angeles Times, April 10, 2017, https://tinyurl.com/kt9pjst.

International aid groups said President Trump's proposed cuts to U.S. foreign aid in the health field could cause higher levels of disease outbreaks around the world.

Sun, Lena H., "New global coalition launched to create vaccines, prevent epidemics," The Washington Post, Jan. 18, 2017, https://tinyurl.com/lozb8dx.

The Bill & Melinda Gates Foundation, Britain's Wellcome Trust and the Japanese, Norwegian and German governments have formed an international coalition to create vaccines to stop future pandemics.

New Diseases

Klint, Chris, "Alaskan gets infected with Zika virus in Central America," Alaska Dispatch News, April 28, 2017, https://tinyurl.com/mdca5xy.

An Alaskan resident returning from Central America contracted the state's third recorded Zika virus infection.

MacMillan, Amanda, "Powassan Virus Is the Scary New

Reason to Avoid Ticks," Time, May 4, 2017, https://tiny url.com/llthyjj.**

The Powassan virus, a rare contagious disease that causes brain swelling and is transmitted mostly by ticks, is reportedly becoming more common in the Northeast.

Walsh, Bryan, "The World Is Not Ready for the Next Pandemic," Time, May 4, 2017, https://tinyurl.com/mopxrys.

A new bird flu called H7N9 circulating across China is mostly infecting poultry, but humans who have contracted the disease during a recent spike have a 41 percent mortality rate.

Vaccination Controversies

Sepic, Matt, "Public health workers push back against anti-vaccine claims at Somali community meeting," Minnesota Public Radio News, May 1, 2017, https://tinyurl.com/mz8gj84.

Anti-vaccination groups gathered in Minnesota to discuss their beliefs that measles vaccinations can and have caused autism in children, but pediatricians in the audience refuted the claims.

Sisson, Paul, "Tougher law is indeed getting more students vaccinated in San Diego and statewide," The San Diego Union-Tribune, April 17, 2017, https://tinyurl.com/n3jpsja.

The California Department of Public Health announced the immunization rate for San Diego County kindergarteners is up to 94.7 percent after a new law banned personal-belief exemptions for vaccinations.

Tracy, Abigail, "Donald Trump Taps Anti-Vaccine Activist To Investigate Vaccine Science," Vanity Fair, Jan. 10, 2017, http://tinyurl.com/hvlx6bh.

President Trump appointed a noted vaccine skeptic to chair a vaccination safety commission.

CITING *CQ RESEARCHER*

Sample formats for citing these reports in a bibliography include the ones listed below. Preferred styles and formats vary, so please check with your instructor or professor.

MLA STYLE

Mantel, Barbara. "Coal Industry's Future." CQ Researcher 17 June 2016: 529-552.

APA STYLE

Mantel, B. (2016, June 17). Coal Industry's Future. CQ Researcher, 6, 529-552.

CHICAGO STYLE

Mantel, Barbara. "Coal Industry's Future." CQ Researcher, June 17, 2016, 529-52.

In-depth Reports on Issues in the News

Are you writing a paper?

Need backup for a debate?

Want to become an expert on an issue?

For 90 years, students have turned to *CQ Researcher* for in-depth reporting on issues in the news. Reports on a full range of political and social issues are now available. Following is a selection of recent reports:

Civil Liberties
Privacy and the Internet, 12/15
Intelligence Reform, 5/15
Religion and Law, 11/14

Crime/Law
High-Tech Policing, 4/17
Forensic Science Controversies, 2/17
Jailing Debtors, 9/16
Decriminalizing Prostitution, 4/16
Restorative Justice, 2/16
The Dark Web, 1/16
Immigrant Detention, 10/15

Education
Charter Schools, 3/17
Civic Education, 2/17
Student Debt, 11/16
Apprenticeships, 10/16

Environment/Society
Anti-Semitism, 5/17
Native American Sovereignty, 5/17
Women in Prison, 3/17
Guns on Campus, 1/17
Mass Transit, 12/16
Arctic Development, 12/16

Health/Safety
Sports and Sexual Assault, 4/17
Reducing Traffic Deaths, 2/17
Opioid Crisis, 10/16
Mosquito-Borne Disease, 7/16

Politics/Economy
North Korea Showdown, 5/17
Rethinking Foreign Aid, 4/17
Troubled Brazil, 4/17
Reviving Rural Economies, 3/17
Immigrants and the Economy, 2/17
Trump Presidency, 1/17

Upcoming Reports

Trust in Journalism, 6/9/17   Food Labeling, 6/16/17   Christian Right, 6/23/17

ACCESS

CQ Researcher is available in print and online. For access, visit your library or www.cqresearcher.com.

STAY CURRENT

For notice of upcoming *CQ Researcher* reports or to learn more about *CQ Researcher* products, subscribe to the free email newsletters, *CQ Researcher Alert!* and *CQ Researcher News*: http://cqpress.com/newsletters.

PURCHASE

To purchase a *CQ Researcher* report in print or electronic format (PDF), visit www.cqpress.com or call 866-427-7737. Single reports start at $15. Bulk purchase discounts and electronic-rights licensing are also available.

SUBSCRIBE

Annual full-service *CQ Researcher* subscriptions—including 44 reports a year, monthly index updates, and a bound volume—start at $1,131. Add $25 for domestic postage.

CQ Researcher Online offers a backfile from 1991 and a number of tools to simplify research. For pricing information, call 800-818-7243 or 805-499-9774 or email librarysales@sagepub.com.

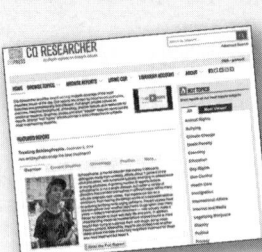

CQPRESS

CQ RESEARCHER

In-depth reports on today's issues

Published by CQ Press, an Imprint of SAGE Publications, Inc.   **www.cqresearcher.com**

Trust in Media

Can news outlets regain the public's confidence?

J ournalism is facing a credibility crisis. Declining faith in government and other institutions and a decades-long assault by conservatives have hurt mainstream news outlets. And President Trump has called journalists "the enemy of the American people." Recent incidents involving public figures, including a Montana congressional candidate's alleged assault on a reporter, have underscored the hostility that journalists face. Some traditional media also have suffered from self-inflicted wounds by blurring the lines between news and commentary and ignoring the interests of rural readers to focus on well-off urbanites. Ad revenue and subscriptions at newspapers have plummeted, in part due to the rise of the internet and changing consumer habits. Meanwhile, social media have fostered "echo chambers" in which people seek out news that affirms their beliefs. Journalists and those studying the news business say mainstream outlets must be more transparent about how they do their jobs and more skillful at explaining events to survive.

Supporters of then-presidential candidate Donald Trump protest alleged bias by CNN at the cable network's offices in Hollywood, Calif., on Oct. 22, 2016. As president, Trump frequently criticizes the media. "If the media's job is to . . . tell the truth, the media deserves a very, very big fat failing grade," he said at a rally marking his 100th day in office.

I
N
S
I
D
E

THIS REPORT

THE ISSUES 483

BACKGROUND 490

CHRONOLOGY 491

CURRENT SITUATION 497

AT ISSUE......................499

OUTLOOK 501

BIBLIOGRAPHY 505

THE NEXT STEP 506

CQ Researcher • June 9, 2017 • www.cqresearcher.com
Volume 27, Number 21 • Pages 481-508

RECIPIENT OF SOCIETY OF PROFESSIONAL JOURNALISTS AWARD FOR
EXCELLENCE ◆ AMERICAN BAR ASSOCIATION SILVER GAVEL AWARD

TRUST IN MEDIA

THE ISSUES

483
- Are traditional standards of objective journalism outdated?
- Are the national news media out of touch with ordinary Americans?
- Does the use of anonymous sources erode trust in journalism?

BACKGROUND

490 **Early Press Coverage**
Newspapers in the 19th century were mouthpieces for political parties.

493 **Vietnam and Watergate**
Coverage of war and scandal hardened partisan attitudes toward the media.

494 **Media Scandals**
Several journalists were found to have fabricated or embellished their work.

495 **Social Media**
Politicians began appealing directly to mass audiences via social media.

CURRENT SITUATION

497 **Trump and the Media**
Reporters are aggressively covering Trump's presidency.

500 **Trust-Related Projects**
Several nonprofit groups are funding projects to develop trust in media.

500 **Facebook and Google**
The influential internet companies want to bolster confidence in the media and stop the spread of so-called fake news.

OUTLOOK

501 **Unpleasant Truths**
Experts predict mistrust of journalists will continue.

SIDEBARS AND GRAPHICS

484 **Views of Media's Performance Show Partisan Divide**
More Democrats than Republicans say the media do a good job of informing people.

485 **Newspapers Slashing Editorial Staffs**
Newsroom jobs fell 37 percent between 2004 and 2015.

488 **People Most Trust Media They Use**
But they distrust "the news media" in general.

491 **Chronology**
Key events since 1919.

492 **Catching Politicians With Their 'Pants on Fire'**
Fact-checking sites perform "very important journalism."

496 **Falling Newsroom Employment Erodes Trust**
Reporters are "stretched thinner. That hurts trust."

499 **At Issue:**
Should journalists try to be objective?

FOR FURTHER RESEARCH

504 **For More Information**
Organizations to contact.

505 **Bibliography**
Selected sources used.

506 **The Next Step**
Additional articles.

507 **Citing CQ Researcher**
Sample bibliography formats.

Cover: AFP/Getty Images/Mark Ralston

 **CQ RESEARCHER**

June 9, 2017
Volume 27, Number 21

EXECUTIVE EDITOR: Thomas J. Billitteri
tjb@sagepub.com

ASSISTANT MANAGING EDITORS: Kenneth Fireman, kenneth.fireman@sagepub.com, Kathy Koch, kathy.koch@sagepub.com, Scott Rohrer, scott.rohrer@sagepub.com

ASSOCIATE MANAGING EDITOR: Val Ellicott

SENIOR CONTRIBUTING EDITOR:
Thomas J. Colin
tom.colin@sagepub.com

CONTRIBUTING WRITERS: Marcia Clemmitt, Sarah Glazer, Reed Karaim, Barbara Mantel, Chuck McCutcheon, Tom Price

SENIOR PROJECT EDITOR: Olu B. Davis

INTERN: Robert DePaolo

FACT CHECKERS: Eva P. Dasher, Michelle Harris, Betsy Towner Levine, Robin Palmer

SAGE Publishing | **CQPRESS**

Los Angeles | London | New Delhi
Singapore | Washington DC | Melbourne

An Imprint of SAGE Publications, Inc.

SENIOR VICE PRESIDENT, GLOBAL LEARNING RESOURCES:
Karen Phillips

EXECUTIVE DIRECTOR, ONLINE LIBRARY AND REFERENCE PUBLISHING:
Todd Baldwin

CQ Researcher (ISSN 1056-2036) is printed on acid-free paper. Published weekly, except: (March wk. 4) (May wk. 4) (July wks. 1, 2) (Aug. wks. 2, 3) (Nov. wk. 4) and (Dec. wks. 3, 4). Published by SAGE Publications, Inc., 2455 Teller Rd., Thousand Oaks, CA 91320. Annual full-service subscriptions start at $1,131. For pricing, call 1-800-818-7243. To purchase a CQ Researcher report in print or electronic format (PDF), visit www.cqpress.com or call 866-427-7737. Single reports start at $15. Bulk purchase discounts and electronic-rights licensing are also available. Periodicals postage paid at Thousand Oaks, California, and at additional mailing offices. POSTMASTER: Send address changes to CQ Researcher, 2600 Virginia Ave., N.W., Suite 600, Washington, DC 20037.

Trust in Media

BY CHUCK MCCUTCHEON

THE ISSUES

The annual White House Correspondents' Dinner is known for its movie stars and not-so-gentle ribbing of the president. But this year's event was different. For the first time in 36 years, the president didn't attend. And one of journalism's legendary figures offset the glamour and jokes with a sober assertion countering criticism of the mainstream media as biased.

"Journalists should not have a dog in the political fight except to find that best obtainable version of the truth," *Washington Post* reporter Bob Woodward, whose work uncovering the Watergate scandal in the 1970s helped spur President Richard M. Nixon's resignation, said in a speech at the April gala. [1]

That same night, 95 miles away, at a rally in Harrisburg, Pa., to mark his 100th day in office, President Trump delivered a different message about journalists. "Their priorities are not my priorities, and not your priorities," Trump told a cheering, partisan crowd. "If the media's job is to be honest and tell the truth, the media deserves a very, very big fat failing grade." [2]

Woodward's and Trump's remarks illustrate the conflicting views that confront traditional news outlets as they try to rebuild public trust in the media that polls show has hit bottom. Those outlets — newspapers, magazines, websites and broadcast networks with professional, nonpartisan staffs — are victims of an overall decline of faith in government and nongovernmental institutions, as well as constant assaults from politicians that have put them in the crosshairs of today's polarized po-

Fox News proclaims its clout at its New York studios. Attitudes about media outlets, particularly Fox and The New York Times, *reflect partisan views. According to a recent poll, 73 percent of Republicans found Fox credible – compared to 45 percent of Democrats.* The Times *drew a 76 percent credibility rating from Democrats versus 52 percent from Republicans.*

Getty Images/Drew Angerer

litical climate. Trump is the latest leader of the assaults, labeling journalists "the enemy of the American people" and dismissing unfavorable coverage of him as "fake news." * [3]

The media also have deeply fragmented as the internet has given rise to a cacophony of voices casting doubt on traditional-media staples — notably the use of anonymous sources and the concepts of neutrality and dispassionate reporting. Facebook and other social media have fostered that ca-

---

* While Trump defines unfavorable coverage as "fake news," the accepted definition is fabricated stories, posted on obscure websites, intended to disparage politicians and generate ad revenue through clicks after readers share them.

cophony by creating "echo chambers" that affirm people's beliefs and enable them to spread information — accurate and inaccurate — faster than ever.

But trust in the media also has been hurt by self-inflicted wounds, including blurred lines between news and commentary; fabricated stories written by rogue reporters; a focus on well-off urbanites while giving less attention to rural Americans; and the post-9/11 failure to aggressively challenge the unfounded claim that Iraq had weapons of mass destruction. In addition, competition for readers has led some outlets to focus on "clickbait" — frivolous and incendiary stories, some untrue — at the expense of substantive topics.

Journalists and those studying the news business say mainstream media outlets must rise to the challenge by performing skillfully in the face of greater outside pressure and shrinking resources. They also must devote more energy to educating readers, listeners and viewers about how they operate.

"Journalism has a trust problem. . . . There's a growing rift between news organizations and the consumers they exist to serve," said Benjamin Mullin, managing editor of Poynter.org, the website for the Poynter Institute, a journalism-training center in St. Petersburg, Fla. [4]

Recent Gallup polls suggest the rift is wide:

• Just 32 percent of Americans trust the media, the lowest level recorded since Gallup began asking the question in 1972. [5]

• Forty-one percent of the respondents to another survey asking about the honesty and ethical standards of

Views of Media's Performance Show Partisan Divide

Democrats are more likely than Republicans to say the national news media do a very good job of keeping people informed. The percentage of Republicans with that view dropped 6 points over the last year, while the percentage of Democrats who feel that way increased by 5 points.

Percentages of U.S. adults who say national news media do "very well" or "fairly well" at keeping them informed:

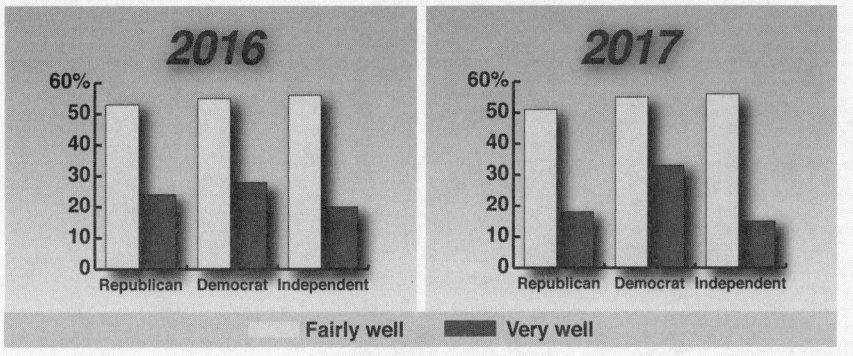

Source: Surveys conducted March 13-27, 2017, and Jan. 12-Feb. 8, 2016, "Americans' Attitudes About the News Media Deeply Divided Along Partisan Lines," Pew Research Center, May 10, 2017, https://tinyurl.com/lwvktsu

22 professions ranked journalists "low" or "very low." Only members of Congress and car salespeople scored lower. [6]

• Sixty-two percent of Americans said the media favor one political party over the other, compared with 50 percent in past years. [7]

News organizations' failure to engender trust could cause society to splinter even further, warns Tom Rosenstiel, executive director of the American Press Institute and a senior fellow at the Brookings Institution, a centrist Washington, D.C., think tank.

"The press needs to rebuild its trust with the public," Rosenstiel says. "We've got to create [news stories] in such a way that people will say, 'I don't like the tone of that, but yeah, I'll accept it, because it's probably true.' "

The two biggest reasons people do not trust news are that they consider it one-sided or inaccurate, according to a 2016 poll by the Press Institute — a nonpartisan media-research organization in Arlington, Va. [8]

Yet the entire notion of "wrong" has become politicized. Trump made so many assertions judged false that the Oxford Dictionaries named "post-truth" its 2016 word of the year. [9] One of his advisers, Kellyanne Conway, caused an uproar in January when she described a questionable assertion about the size of Trump's inauguration crowd as an "alternative fact." [10] Another aide defended giving Trump a false magazine cover warning of a forthcoming ice age instead of global warming at a briefing by contending the information it contained was "fake but accurate." [11]

But more than most issues, Gallup and other polls show, media mistrust reflects the country's entrenched political divide.

A Pew Research Center poll in May found a 47 percentage-point gap between Democrats and Republicans over whether criticism from the media helps keep politicians honest — the largest gap since Pew began asking the question in 1985. [12] And according to a Morn-

ing Consult poll in December, 73 percent of Republicans found GOP-leaning Fox News credible — compared to 45 percent of Democrats. *The New York Times* drew a credibility rating of 76 percent from Democrats versus 52 percent from Republicans. [13]

Mistrust of the media is not a strictly partisan issue. African-Americans have accused the media of failing to recognize the Black Lives Matter movement as well as the importance of events fueling its rise.

Media scholars say some outlets have fueled the divide by coarsening discourse and lambasting news organizations whose politics differ from theirs. They also say the growth of watchdog groups, such as Media Matters and the Media Research Center, has added to the divide. Wealthy partisans finance many of those groups, which track inaccurate reporting, media bias and political gaffes.

Journalists of late have had to endure additional abuse. Four incidents occurred in May:

• A Federal Communications Commission (FCC) guard allegedly pinned a reporter for *CQ Roll Call* against a wall as he sought to ask commissioners a question at FCC headquarters in Washington, then forced him to leave a public meeting. An FCC commissioner apologized for the incident.

• In Montana, Republican congressional candidate Greg Gianforte was charged with misdemeanor assault after he allegedly threw a reporter to the ground who asked him a question. After winning the special election for the state's at-large House seat, Gianforte apologized for his conduct.

• Dan Heyman, a Public News Service reporter in West Virginia, was arrested after trying to question Health and Human Services Secretary Tom Price in a state Capitol hallway. Heyman said he was holding his phone toward Price to record him; police said he was trying to bypass Price's security detail.

• Reporter Nathanial Herz of the *Alaska Dispatch News* said state Sen. David

Wilson (R-Wasilla) slapped him across the face after he asked the senator a question. Herz filed a police report, and the case has been turned over to the state's Office of Special Prosecution. [14]

Also in May, several windows were shattered at the offices of Kentucky's *Lexington Herald-Leader*, with investigators attributing the damage to small-caliber bullets, or possibly a BB gun. Newspaper publisher Rufus M. Friday cited a rise in hostile rhetoric toward journalists. [15]

For some media veterans, the media's role in uncovering inaccurate statements by Trump and other politicians while serving as the public's government watchdog is the biggest barometer of the media's future credibility.

"If the media for whatever reason fails to meet this challenge, then democracy as we have known it will slowly die," longtime television network correspondent Marvin Kalb, a professor emeritus at Harvard University's Kennedy School of Government and founding director of its Shorenstein Center on the Press, Politics and Public Policy, said in March. [16]

Those on the political right, however, see the mainstream media — or what they call the "legacy media" — as facing an insurmountable obstacle to rebuilding public trust. Above all, perhaps, they consider the media guilty of hypocrisy for its perceived bias against Republicans while insisting it favors neither party.

"The biggest challenge facing journalists today is a self-inflicted problem: too many activists with bylines posing as neutral observers, and they've been found out," says John Bicknell, executive editor of Watchdog.org, a network of websites covering local and state government funded by the Franklin Center for Government & Public Integrity, a news organization based in Alexandria, Va., with a free-market, limited-government perspective. "Once you've destroyed your own credibility, it's very difficult to get it back — and

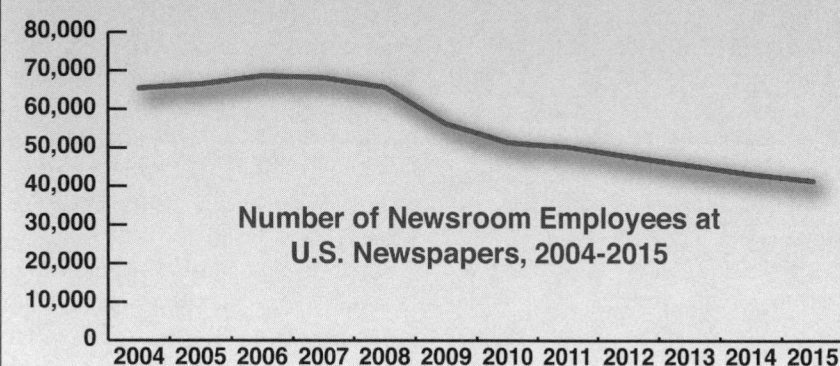

Newspapers Slashing Editorial Staffs

Newspapers in the United States cut more than 24,000 newsroom jobs — a decline of 37 percent — between 2004 and 2015, the most recent year data were available. Layoffs and buyouts among reporters and editors are expected to continue as newspapers struggle with falling circulation and ad revenue.

Number of Newsroom Employees at U.S. Newspapers, 2004-2015

Source: "Newspapers Fact Sheet," Pew Research Center, June 1, 2017, p. 8, https://tinyurl.com/yb8g77ht

we see that in many, if not most, legacy newsrooms." [17]

Both conservative and liberal journalism observers say generalizing about "the media" is difficult, in large part because it encompasses an ever-growing array of news and information sources, each with its own mission and leanings.

"Lumping these disparate entities under the same single, bland label is like describing the denizens of the ocean as 'the fish,' " wrote *Washington Post* media reporter Paul Farhi. [18]

Despite such media diversity, the public tends to focus on national — not local — outlets when expressing mistrust. Joy Mayer, a consulting fellow at the University of Missouri's Donald W. Reynolds Journalism Institute, says she noticed this when speaking with readers and viewers around the country for a project she leads on media trust-building.

"I couldn't believe how quickly, in most people's minds, 'the media' jumps to national political coverage," Mayer says. "I tell them, 'The media are people who cover your local school board and high school sports.' "

The notion of "journalist" also is being expanded with the phenomenon of cellphone video capturing news incidents and social media's ability to give members of the general public the power to give direct on-the-scene reports while sharing information among friends.

Social media have created what Rosenstiel calls the "atomization of the news," in which people place more trust in who shared information with them than in the quality of news brands. That phenomenon, he says, helped fuel the "fake news" phenomenon.

As journalists, academics and others debate trust in the news media, here are some of the questions being raised:

Are traditional standards of objective journalism outdated?

One of the bedrock principles of traditional journalism is objectivity, generally defined as not playing favorites despite one's personal views. But the notion of objectivity has come under attack from critics of President Trump, who say his unfitness for the presidency demands the media take up an advocacy role to portray the truth more directly and accurately.

Many veteran journalists say objectivity is essential to developing trust. Media outlets, they say, have an obligation never to identify with any side in a conflict or other issue.

"Journalists in this tradition [of objectivity] have plenty of opinions, but by setting them aside to follow the facts — as a judge in court is supposed to set aside prejudices to follow the law and the evidence — they can often produce results that are more substantial and more credible," former *Times* executive editor Bill Keller said. [19]

In January, Lewis Wallace was fired from his job a reporter for the syndicated business radio show "Marketplace" after publishing an article on the website *Medium*. [20] Journalists, Wallace wrote, "need to become more shameless, more raw, more honest with ourselves and our audiences" instead of simply reacting passively to what he predicted would be arrests and other attempts to curtail media freedom of speech under Trump. [21]

Among the most vocal critics of objectivity is American journalist Glenn Greenwald, whose articles in London's *Guardian* contained classified information on U.S. government surveillance in 2013 released by former national-security contractor Edward Snowden. "This voice that people at NPR and PBS and CNN are required to assume, where they're supposed to display this kind of non-human neutrality about the world in which they're reporting, is a deceitful, artificial one," said Greenwald, editor of the national-security website *The Intercept*. [22]

Kerry Lauerman, executive editor of the liberal-leaning news and commentary website *Mic*, which targets Millennials, encourages reporters not to hide their views. "We're stronger by having people with different points of view approach things with those points of view," Lauerman said. "It probably does further erode the sort of old-fashioned

notion of objectivity. But I think that's better for journalism, too." [23]

Some critics of traditional media point to earlier eras to argue that mainstream journalism never has been truly objective — and should stop pretending it is.

Objectivity "has seldom existed in American history, and has especially been scarce since the 1960s, when activist journalism came out of the closet with its ideological coverage of Vietnam and then Watergate, all perfumed with the spurious claim to journalistic integrity and public service," said Bruce Thornton, a fellow at Stanford University's Hoover Institution. [24]

Other critics fault the language of objectivity. *National Review* columnist Jonah Goldberg pointed to The Associated Press stylebook's barring the use of "illegal immigrants," though "illegal immigration" is still permitted. Instead, The AP and other outlets have recommended terms such as "unauthorized" and "undocumented" for immigrants.

That usage, Goldberg said, is part of left-wing pro-immigration activists' agenda "to blur the distinctions between legal and illegal immigration. . . . As a matter of fact and logic, the difference between an 'unauthorized immigrant' and an 'illegal immigrant' is nonexistent." [25]

Many journalists say absolute objectivity is impossible, given the inherent subjective nature of choosing one fact over another in telling a story.

But they say that something close to it can be achieved by doing rigorous reporting offering deep insights. That includes weeding out extremist voices and specious claims in favor of provable facts.

"Objectivity is all about doing your job well as a journalist," says Ken Paulson, a former editor of *USA Today* who is president of the First Amendment Center, which studies free-expression issues. He also is dean of Middle Tennessee State University's College of Media and Entertainment. "The question is, can you get up every morning and write what you

find out — accurately write about what you've discovered?"

Paulson and many journalists say objectivity is rooted in fairness — conveying the arguments of all sides of an issue. But, they add, fairness does not mean "he said, she said" reporting — the oft-criticized practice of unquestioningly giving both sides equal weight.

"Good journalism doesn't require perfect balance," said Michael Kinsley, founding editor of *Slate* magazine. "In fact, perfect balance may be a distortion of reality. But journalism gains credibility when it gives all sides their due." [26]

The American Press Institute's Rosenstiel says one means of bolstering media trust — greater transparency — is enhancing objectivity by borrowing the methods of science and demonstrating to readers and viewers how news outlets arrive at their conclusions.

The Post, in publishing an e-book biography of Trump last year, put online an archive of most of its research materials, including thousands of pages of interview transcripts, court filings, financial reports, immigration records and other material. [27]

"There's this discipline of verifying — making sure you have enough sources and describing as much as can about your sources, like showing your math in a school assignment that proves to the teacher that you did the work yourself," Rosenstiel says. "That's what the idea of an objective method of journalism is about."

Are the national news media out of touch with ordinary Americans?

Critics of mainstream journalism question whether staffers at national outlets are disconnected from people in blue-collar jobs who often live outside of the metropolises of the East or West coasts. But journalists at those outlets dispute the charge.

The debate is an old one. In a 1996 article, "Why Americans Hate the Media," *Atlantic* national correspondent James Fallows said national political journalists fixate on tactical matters at the expense of issues that the public cares about more deeply.

"When ordinary citizens have a chance to pose questions to political leaders, they rarely ask about the game of politics," Fallows wrote. "They want to know how the reality of politics will affect them — through taxes, programs, scholarship funds, wars." [28]

Those tendencies have only worsened over the last two decades with the explosion of the internet and interest in polls and celebrity at the expense of more time-consuming, deeply reported pieces, media observers say. As the news business has shrunk, it has concentrated in New York, Washington and California.

The result, those observers say, helps explain the traditional media's failure to anticipate the outcome of 2016's election, in which Trump defied almost all polls and pundits to win the Electoral College despite losing the popular vote.

"Much of the East Coast-based media establishment is arguably out of touch with the largely rural population that voted for Trump," said Mathew Ingram, a *Fortune* senior writer covering the media. [29]

Dean Baquet, the *Times'* executive editor, said he is proud of his paper's campaign coverage. But he said after the election: "The New York-based and Washington-based media powerhouses . . . don't get the role of religion in people's lives." [30]

Veteran reporter and author David Cay Johnston, former board president of the group Investigative Reporters and Editors, said today's journalists no longer closely share their audience's concerns.

"There's been a tendency in the news to focus very much on, 'What's going on with the internet? What's going on with these exciting new gizmos?' As opposed to, 'What's happening to people who work in factories in Iowa and Michigan and their concerns?'" Johnston said.

Johnston attributed the shift to changing demographics. In 1960, nearly one-third of reporters and editors had never attended a single year of college; in 2015, that figure was down to 8 percent — 38 percentage points below the number of adults 25 and older nationwide. [31]

College-educated journalists "began making newspapers move up the income ladder and the wealth ladder in terms of readership and lost sight of this mass audience they used to have," he said. "And a result, the coverage and what newspapers defined as important tended to be the concerns of the upper-middle class." [32]

Too many of the journalists are liberal, putting them further out of touch, says Watchdog.org's Bicknell. "If mainstream news organizations want to regain credibility with the public, they should begin by hiring young conservative journalists," he says.

The White House Correspondents' Dinner, which has evolved from an intimate gathering in 1921 into a tele-

vised gala of hundreds of journalists and politicians — and the celebrities they invite — often is cited as symbolizing the gulf between the national media and public. *The Times* stopped attending the dinner in 2008, saying it sent a misleading signal that the paper was too chummy with politicians. [33]

Criticism of the national media's aloofness from America extends beyond economic class and politics into race.

African-American talk show host Tavis Smiley cited the Trayvon Martin case as evidence that newsrooms have "the same unconscious bias that exists in police departments" because they lack staffers who understand black America. Martin, an unarmed 17-year-old African-American, was shot and killed in 2012 by neighborhood-watch volunteer George Zimmerman in a gated Florida community. Zimmerman, who is white, pleaded self-defense and was acquitted of second-degree murder. [34]

"The reality is that that story would never have made it to the front pages

Edgar Maddison Welch surrenders to police in Washington, D.C., on Dec. 4, 2016. Armed with an assault rifle, the Salisbury, N.C., man drove to Washington to try to stop what online conspiracy theories falsely said was a child sex ring being run by Democratic presidential candidate Hillary Clinton out of a local pizza restaurant. Media experts and scholars say many voters were swayed during the presidential campaign by the proliferation of so-called fake news spread by alternative news websites and social media.

AP Photo/Sathi Soma

People Most Trust Media They Use

Americans tend to trust the news sources they rely on but distrust "the news media" as an abstract concept. For example, just over half of those surveyed viewed the news sources they consult as moral, but only 24 percent said that about the media in general.

Percent who said the following about each type of media:

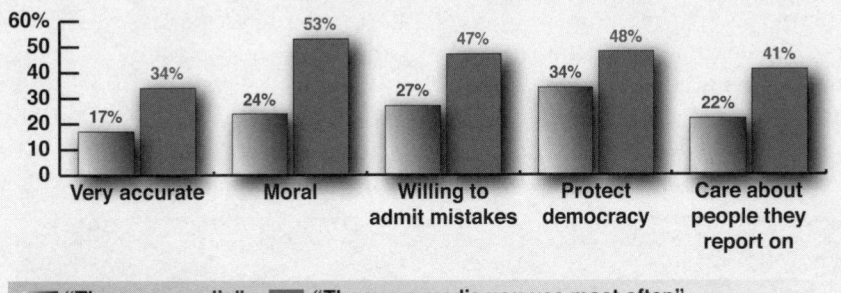

Source: " 'My' media versus 'the' media: Trust in news depends on which news media you mean," American Press Institute, May 24, 2017, p. 2, https://tinyurl.com/ya32z2za

were it not for black media," Smiley said. "Oftentimes the mainstream media — particularly where people of color are concerned — is on the late freight." [35]

However, a number of academics and journalists say major news outlets are responding to such criticisms.

"That is something that needs a correction, and the correction has begun," former *Post* executive editor Leonard Downie, now a professor of journalism at Arizona State University, says of the accusation of being out of touch.

Downie and other media observers cite *The Times*' and other newspapers' detailed stories explaining the impacts of Trump's policies. That includes the White House's proposed budget, which calls for slashing or eliminating federal programs important to small communities and rural areas that backed Trump.

They also note that while the number of minorities at media outlets is still too low, it is on the rise. An American Society of News Editors survey found the minority workforce rose

5.6 percent from 2015 to 2016 among the 433 news organizations that took part in both years' surveys. Overall, minorities made up 17 percent of workers at daily print newspapers and 23 percent of employees at digital-only publications. [36]

Media observers are encouraged by journalists' willingness to "crowd-source" reporting — asking the public directly for help, expanding their networks and building credibility. *Post* reporter David Fahrenthold won a Pulitzer Prize in April for his work investigating Trump's charitable contributions, in part by soliciting information from readers about whether they belonged to organizations that had been promised or received contributions.

When looking into whether Trump used $10,000 of charitable money to buy a portrait of himself, Fahrenthold recalled, "I asked my readers and Twitter followers for help, and they amazed me with their ingenuity. They found things that I never would have thought to find on my own." [37]

Times domestic-affairs correspondent Sheryl Gay Stolberg also cites

"Anxious in America," a 2016 series to which she contributed, as another example of reporting about everyday Americans. It explored economic and social concerns in rural Appalachia, among African-Americans at a Philadelphia food pantry and evangelical Christians in small-town Iowa as well as other places. [38]

While acknowledging that the national media focuses too much on polls and "horse-race" journalism, Stolberg says of her paper, "I disagree that we don't reflect America."

Does the use of anonymous sources erode trust in journalism?

Critics of the use of anonymous sources call it a significant contributor to the erosion of trust in the media, while the practice's defenders say that — when done judiciously — it gets closer to the truth than quoting people only by name.

The use of such sources requires the public to place considerable faith in journalists, said Mary Louise Kelly, who covers intelligence agencies for NPR. "If I am using an anonymous source, I have given my word that I will not reveal their identity," Kelly said. "But I am asking you, the listener, to trust me that I have done everything in my power to make sure this person is who they say they are, that they have access to the information and also to weigh what's their motive." [39]

A Morning Consult/*Politico* poll in March found that 44 percent of those surveyed said it is likely reporters make up unnamed sources. As with other polls involving media trust, the poll showed a deep partisan split: 65 percent of Republicans said journalists made up sources, while just 24 percent of Democrats agreed.

The poll also showed that half of those surveyed didn't consider it appropriate for the media to use anonymous sources when reporting on government business. That issue also broke along partisan lines: 66 percent of Republicans considered it inappropriate compared to only 36 percent of Democrats. [40]

Trump has fed public mistrust about the practice. Reporters "have no sources; they just make them up when there are none," he said in February. [41]

The Times tightened its requirements for the use of unnamed sources in 2016 in response to two erroneous articles. One was based on unnamed officials who said inspectors general asked the Justice Department to open a criminal investigation into whether Hillary Clinton had mishandled sensitive information on a private email account she used as secretary of State. *The Times* later clarified that the referral was not criminal and did not name Clinton as a focus. [42]

Nevertheless, when *The Times* this year published a string of exclusive stories about Trump, the paper drew a warning from Liz Spayd, the paper's public editor.* She noted the articles relied heavily — some entirely — on unnamed sources. "The descriptions [of sources' identities] generally tilt far more toward protecting the sources than giving readers confidence in what they said," Spayd wrote. [43]

Conservative political commentator Mollie Hemingway, a senior editor at the *Federalist* magazine, responded to a slew of critical articles about Trump in May with a sarcastic tweet: "I didn't go to journalism school, but should our media really privilege unaccountable, anonymous sources to on-the-record accountable ones?" [44]

However, many in the news business say mainstream media outlets do a largely successful job in drawing a distinction between unnamed sources with a partisan ax to grind and those wanting

Comedian Melissa McCarthy parodies White House press secretary Sean Spicer on "Saturday Night Live" on May 13, 2017. In recent weeks, assistant press secretary Sarah Huckabee Sanders has been giving press briefings instead of Spicer, who has had a rocky relationship with the press. Spicer faced withering criticism after President Trump pulled out of the Paris climate accord, telling reporters he did not know whether Trump accepted climate change science.

Getty Images/NBC/NBCU/Will Heath

to provide helpful information without risking their jobs.

Of those in the latter camp, "These are not people who pull us aside because they want to screw Donald Trump," *The Times'* Baquet said. "These are people who are worried about the direction of government." [45]

Reporters who make the most frequent use of anonymous sources have accumulated considerable trust with those sources, which should persuade the public to have confidence in those reporters, said Dana Priest, a Pulitzer Prize-winning national security reporter at *The Post*.

Those reporters "are pretty good at judging the character of somebody that they actually quote without their name," Priest said. "And that's how we do that business. It would not happen without it, because they're really not supposed to be talking to us." [46]

The use of anonymous sources declined in the half-century between 1958 and 2008, reaching its peak in the 1970s, according to a 2011 study.

The study found journalists increasingly described the backgrounds of anonymous sources in some way rather than simply identifying them as "reliable sources." In 1958, 34 percent of stories with unnamed sources used that type of vague language, but that figure fell below 3 percent in 2008. It also found reporters more frequently explained the reasons why they grant anonymity. [47]

Paulson of the First Amendment Center says procedures to discourage reliance on anonymous sources — including having reporters share the names of sources with senior editors — led to a 70-percent reduction in their usage during his stint as *USA Today's* editor from 2004 to 2009.

Relying on unnamed sources while sustaining trust is "a balancing act," he says. "It has to be offset by the importance of the story. We were not going to use anonymous sources to find out the name of the new Taylor Swift album — only to reveal important information about national security." ∎

---

* *The Times* announced on May 31 that it was eliminating the public editor position, and Spayd resigned. The paper has recently created the Reader Center, which it described as a way to "build even stronger bonds with our readers."

BACKGROUND

Early Press Coverage

The First Amendment's guarantee of press freedom makes the news media "the only business in America specifically protected by the Constitution," as President John F. Kennedy once observed. [48] Nonetheless, journalists seldom have been held in high public regard.

Thomas Jefferson famously championed free expression: "Were it left to me to decide whether we should have a government without newspapers or newspapers without a government, I should not hesitate a moment to prefer the latter," the author of the

CBS News anchor Walter Cronkite, considered the country's most trusted figure during his long tenure, helped change public perception of the Vietnam War when he declared in a 1968 commentary that it was destined "to end in a stalemate."

Declaration of Independence and the nation's third president once said. Yet he griped about how those papers covered him.

"Nothing can now be believed which is seen in a newspaper," Jefferson wrote in 1787. "Truth itself becomes suspicious by being put into that polluted vehicle." [49]

For much of the 19th century, journalists stressed sensationalism over accuracy, with papers serving as mouthpieces for political parties. "He lies like a newspaper" became a common criticism. [50]

"Editors ran their own candidates — in fact they ran for office themselves, and often continued in their post at the paper while holding office," historian Garry Wills wrote. "Politicians, knowing this, cultivated their own party's papers, both the owners and the editors, shared staff with them, released news to them early or exclusively to keep them loyal, rewarded them with state or federal appointments when they won." [51]

Ulysses S. Grant, the commanding Union general during the Civil War, later served two scandal-filled presidential terms. During his second inaugural address in 1873, Grant railed against reporters, saying he had been "the subject of abuse and slander scarcely ever equaled in political history." [52]

The New York Press in 1897 coined the term "yellow journalism" to describe the fiercely competitive and sensationalistic New York newspapers owned by titans Joseph Pulitzer and William Randolph Hearst. The term

came from the comic strip "The Yellow Kid," about a mischievous boy in a yellow nightshirt. [53]

The splashy reporting of Hearst's and Pulitzer's papers was offset by *The New York Times*. Tennessee publisher Adolph S. Ochs acquired the paper in 1896 and vowed "to give the news impartially, without fear or favor, regardless of party, sect or interests involved." [54]

The emergence of investigative journalists — muckrakers — in the early 20th century helped boost trust. The best known was Upton Sinclair, whose 1906 novel *The Jungle* exposed labor and sanitary abuses in the meat-packing industry. Thirteen years later, Sinclair's *The Brass Check*, a work of nonfiction, compared the brass token used by patrons of prostitutes to wealthy newspaper owners' buying off journalists' credibility. [55] It sold more than 150,000 copies. [56]

Legendary journalist Walter Lippmann helped found *The New Republic* magazine in 1914 and became one of the world's most widely respected columnists. [57] Lippmann warned in a 1920 book that without a "steady supply of trustworthy and relevant news," then "all that the sharpest critics of democracy have alleged is true." [58]

During the 1920s, radio became common in American households. In 1934, President Franklin D. Roosevelt signed a bill into law stipulating that stations could lose their licenses if their broadcasts were considered too controversial. It required stations to offer equal time for political candidates. [59]

With the advent of television after World War II, the federal government again became involved in regulating journalistic content. Lawmakers became concerned that the three TV networks of the era — NBC, ABC and CBS — could misuse their broadcast licenses to advance a biased agenda. The Federal Communications Commission issued the Fairness Doctrine in 1949 requiring radio and TV stations to devote

Continued on p. 492

Chronology

1900s-1950s
Newspapers draw competition from radio, television.

1919
Celebrated muckraker Upton Sinclair, known for attacking his era's social and economic institutions, publishes *The Brass Check*, a nonfiction book equating the brass tokens that brothel patrons used to buy prostitutes' services with the money that newspaper owners paid journalists to influence their reporting.

1949
Federal Communications Commission (FCC) issues "Fairness Doctrine" requiring radio and TV stations to devote some programming to controversial issues and the airing of opposing views.

1954
CBS News correspondent Edward R. Murrow wins praise for commentary highly critical of Wisconsin Sen. Joseph McCarthy's "Red Scare" investigation of suspected communists in the United States.

1956
Two-thirds of Americans say in polls that newspapers are fair, more than twice the percentage as those who consider them unfair.

—————•—————

1960s-1980s
Partisan attitudes harden toward media.

1968
CBS News anchor Walter Cronkite helps turn public opinion against the Vietnam War by predicting it will end in a stalemate. . . . Republican Richard M. Nixon is elected president and attacks the media's credibility.

1969
Conservative media critic Reed Irvine starts Accuracy in Media to provide what he calls a check against liberal media excesses.

1972
After a break-in at Democratic National Committee offices at Washington's Watergate complex, *Washington Post* reporters Bob Woodward and Carl Bernstein write numerous articles tying Nixon and his aides to the break-in, a subsequent cover-up and other misdeeds, all leading to Nixon's resignation.

1976
Gallup Poll shows public confidence in the media at an all-time peak of 72 percent.

1980
Republican Ronald Reagan is elected president, serving two terms during which his aides sought to aggressively shape media coverage through staged events and other means. . . . Business tycoon Ted Turner launches CNN, the first TV channel providing 24-hour news coverage.

1981
Washington Post reporter Janet Cook wins Pulitzer Prize for "Jimmy's World," an article about an 8-year-old heroin addict that is later exposed as a fabrication.

1987
FCC abolishes "Fairness Doctrine," paving the way for talk radio to become a platform for conservatives and others to regularly attack perceived media bias.

1990s-Present
Internet reshapes public's perception of the media.

1994
Matt Drudge, an unknown political commentator, starts the news-aggregation website *Drudge Report*, among the first of a number of conservative-leaning media outlets.

1996
Fox News launched; within six years it is the most-watched cable network.

2003
Critics of the Iraq War bash news outlets, saying they didn't aggressively challenge President George W. Bush's assertions that Iraq possessed weapons of mass destruction.

2004
Facebook social network launched; it quickly becomes a massively popular alternative to news outlets by taking their content and tailoring it to users' preferences.

2008
Alaska Gov. Sarah Palin, the GOP vice presidential nominee, lambastes what she calls "the lamestream media."

2016
During the presidential campaign, conservatives accuse mainstream media of under-covering Hillary Clinton's perceived misdeeds and Democrats accuse them of over-covering Donald Trump's rallies in order to boost ratings and online traffic. Some Democrats also accuse Fox News of pro-Trump bias.

2017
President Trump calls the media "the enemy of the American people" amid constant clashes with reporters.

Catching Politicians With Their 'Pants on Fire'

Fact-checking sites perform "very important journalism."

In the media-trust debate, two phrases have become part of the lexicon: "Pants on Fire" and "Pinocchios." The colorful expressions are used, respectively, on the fact-checking websites PolitiFact and Fact Checker, which evaluate the truth of government officials' statements. The sites' popularity has both irked their targets and raised questions about how the administrators of the sites choose which statements to parse.

The two sites are far from alone. U.S. news outlets had 52 separate fact-checking operations in 2016, up by 15 from 2015. [1] The biggest is PolitiFact (www.politifact.com), launched by the *Tampa Bay Times* in 2007, which won a Pulitzer Prize two years later and now has affiliations with news outlets in 18 states, public radio and the Scripps chain of television stations.* [2]

The Washington Post also started its fact-checking site, Fact Checker (https://www.washingtonpost.com/news/fact-checker/), in 2007. Another well-known site, FactCheck.org, was launched in 2003 by the University of Pennsylvania's Annenberg Public Policy Center. [3] On the political right, the website Conservapedia (www.conservapedia.com) — a conservative version of the online dictionary Wikipedia — aims to debunk what it considers overly liberal claims. [4]

At PolitiFact, claims are rated — as shown on an accompanying "Truth-O-Meter" — on a scale from "True" to "Pants on Fire," while Fact Checker assesses the degree of truth of a statement on a scale of zero to four "Pinocchios."

A Fact Checker column on May 18 assigned three Pinocchios to the assertion by House Minority Leader Nancy Pelosi, D-Calif., that 7 million veterans would definitely lose tax credits under the House Republicans' bill to repeal former President Obama's health-care overhaul, the Affordable Care Act. "In reality, it's not so certain," Fact Checker said. [5]

On May 12 PolitiFact gave a "Pants on Fire" rating to President Trump's assertion that allegations that his campaign may have colluded with Russia was a "made-up story" that Democrats used as an excuse for his victory. "Democrats did not create the story, nor do they

---

* PolitiFact won the Pulitzer Prize for National Reporting for its coverage of the 2008 election, including its use of "probing reporters and the power of the World Wide Web to examine more than 750 political claims, separating rhetoric from truth to enlighten voters."

control the agenda of the House and Senate committees, which are conducting their own investigations," the column declared. [6]

Fact-checking has evolved beyond its origins in the 1990s, when news outlets occasionally assessed claims in campaign advertisements, journalism scholars say. Today, TV networks such as CNN also do on-screen fact-checking during debates.

"It is very important journalism, and it's here to stay," says former *Post* executive editor Leonard Downie, now a professor of journalism at Arizona State University. (As a young deputy metropolitan editor of *The Post*, Downie supervised much of the paper's Watergate coverage by Bob Woodward and Carl Bernstein.)

A Pew Research Center survey last fall found 83 percent of voters consider it the media's responsibility to check the statements of candidates and campaigns. And 77 percent of those who said they planned to vote for Trump saw it as either a major or minor responsibility, compared with 89 percent of Hillary Clinton's supporters. [7]

Politicians have noticed. In a 2015 interview, then-Gov. Rick Perry, R-Texas, — now U.S. Energy secretary — said his state had reduced nitrogen-oxide emissions levels by 63.5 percent. Then he added, "Say 63 percent — that way, we won't get PolitiFacted." (The actual figure was 62.5 percent, the site noted.) [8]

But conservatives have criticized such sites because, they say, no public mechanism exists to show which assertions are fact-checked and which aren't, opening the selection process to bias. "When you're only advocating a political agenda, like PolitiFact, I understand, guys, where you're coming from," Fox News commentator Sean Hannity said in 2015 while disputing a "Pants on Fire" rating for an earlier assertion about Syrian refugees. [9]

In a 2016 study, political scientists Stephen Farnsworth of the University of Mary Washington and Robert Lichter of George Mason University examined hundreds of PolitiFact and Fact Checker evaluations and found that PolitiFact's selections were more critical of Republicans than Democrats "to a statistically significant degree." Fact Checker also was more critical of GOP politicians, they found, but not to as significant a degree.

Farnsworth and Lichter said the sites should better explain how they choose claims to evaluate. "The lack of transparency from the organizations regarding their selection procedures, and the practical difficulties of content analyzing every controversial statement by every lawmaker, make it difficult to untangle the central question

---

Continued from p. 490

some of their programming to controversial issues and allow the airing of opposing views. [60]

During the 1930s and '40s, polls showed "at best only modest levels of trust in the news media," according to

Georgetown University public policy professor Jonathan M. Ladd. [61]

But around midcentury, competition from television led newspapers to expand coverage and offer more deeply sourced and interpretative reporting. Papers also developed, along with magazines, a com-

mercial model that led many of them to be hugely profitable through classified and display advertising.

It was during this period that a few newspapers, including the *Milwaukee Journal* and *Washington Post*, questioned accusations by Wisconsin GOP

of whether partisan differences in fact-checking reflect the values of the fact-checkers or the behavior of their targets," they said. [10]

PolitiFact creator Bill Adair, now a journalism professor at Duke University who remains a contributing editor at the site, says PolitiFact vigorously tries to avoid bias by examining the most significant or newsworthy statements, regardless of political affiliation.

The Fact Checker's Glenn Kessler responded to complaints about Trump getting more fact-checks in 2016 than Clinton by saying the GOP nominee talked more. "We would have liked to publish a lot more fact-checks of Hillary than we did, but she didn't give many interviews, her speeches were rigidly vetted and didn't vary that much," Kessler said. "Meanwhile, Trump would call in to four to five TV shows and go off the script in rallies." [11]

Tom Rosenstiel, executive director of the American Press Institute, a nonpartisan media-research organization, encourages fact-checking that goes beyond cataloguing assertions. "We've heard fact-checking is more effective if it's viewed as 'Help me understand this issue' rather than just right and wrong," Rosenstiel says. "The idea we have is, let's fact-check a broader issue rather than a specific claim. You would pick issues based on how important they are. Like transportation — what are the key facts? Or water — how clean is the water?"

Several efforts are underway to incorporate new technologies into fact-checking and to present the results in various formats. Studies show that charts and other graphical information can make information stick better in readers' minds, Adair says.

"We need to develop different ways of presenting accurate information," he says.

— Chuck McCutcheon

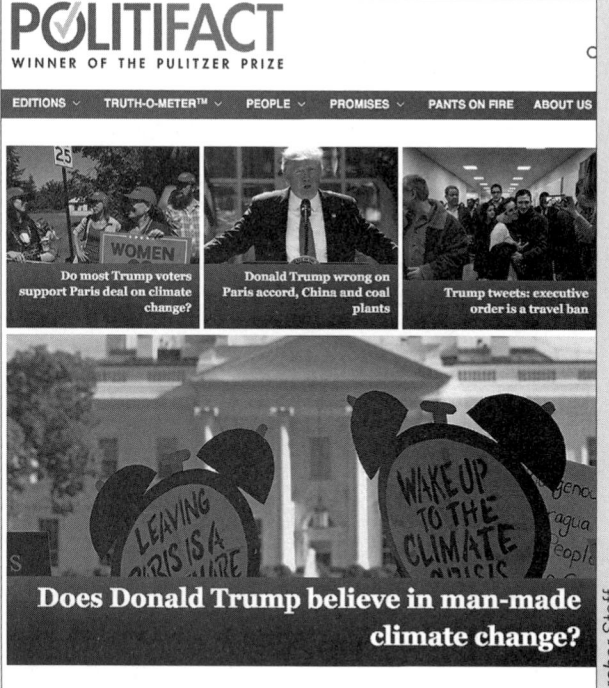

Screenshot/CQ Researcher Staff

The online fact-checking site PolitiFact has made "Pants on Fire" part of the media-trust lexicon. Fact Checker, with its "Pinocchio" rating, is another popular site that evaluates the truth of government officials' statements.

[1] Bill Adair, "Keep on Fact-Checking!" *The New York Times*, Nov. 8, 2016, http://tinyurl.com/l9kwxqj.

[2] Mark Stencel, "The facts about fact-checking across America," ReportersLab.org, Aug. 3, 2016, http://tinyurl.com/ya6fqb4n.

[3] Brooks Jackson, "Is This a Great Job or What?" FactCheck.org, Dec. 5, 2003, http://tinyurl.com/ya4w9btx; Glenn Kessler, "About the Fact Checker," *The Washington Post*, Sept. 11, 2013, http://tinyurl.com/ybsf4v9t; The PolitiFact Staff, PolitiFact.com, http://tinyurl.com/yck9q3pw.

[4] "Conservapedia.com," undated, http://tinyurl.com/2ppol7.

[5] Michele Ye Hee Lee, "Nancy Pelosi's claim that 'seven million veterans will lose their tax credit' under the GOP health bill," *The Washington Post* Fact Checker, May 18, 2017, http://tinyurl.com/ybqrlm2z.

[6] Jon Greenberg, "Donald Trump's Pants on Fire claim Russia story 'made-up' by Democrats," PolitiFact.com, May 12, 2017, http://tinyurl.com/yaktmejd.

[7] Michael Barthel, Jeffrey Gottfried and Kristine Lu, "Trump, Clinton Supporters Differ on How Media Should Cover Controversial Statements," Pew Research Center, Oct. 17, 2016, http://tinyurl.com/ybhyyf3f.

[8] W. Gardner Selby, "Rick Perry gets a laugh out of Texas Truth-O-Meter," PolitiFact Texas, Jan. 15, 2015, http://tinyurl.com/y7stbhgj.

[9] Alex Griswold, "Hannity Blasts 'Left-Wing Website' Politifact For Giving Him 'Pants on Fire' Rating,' " *Mediaite*, Oct. 28, 2015, http://tinyurl.com/oncqu6g.

[10] Stephen J. Farnsworth and S. Robert Lichter, "A Comparative Analysis of the Partisan Targets of Media Fact-checking: Examining President Obama and the 113th Congress," paper presented at the American Political Science Association convention, September 2016, http://tinyurl.com/yabwrdx2.

[11] Alexios Mantzarlis, "Fact-checking under President Trump," Poynter.org, Nov. 10, 2016, http://tinyurl.com/jmbg4sn.

Sen. Joseph McCarthy, who led the "Red Scare" investigations of alleged communists in the United States during the 1950s. CBS News reporter Edward R. Murrow, in a 1954 special report, said of the senator: "He didn't create this situation of fear — he merely exploited it, and rather successfully." [62]

By 1956, two-thirds of Americans said in polls that newspapers were fair. Of those charging unfairness, most thought they were too favorable toward President Dwight D. Eisenhower (1953-61) and other Republicans. [63]

Vietnam and Watergate

The Vietnam War hardened partisan attitudes toward the media. Reporters found struggles on the battlefront at odds with the upbeat assessments of military leaders, while TV news broadcast vivid combat images directly into American homes. CBS News anchor Walter Cronkite, considered the country's most trusted figure, changed the public perception of the war when he declared in a 1968 commentary that the war was destined "to end in a stalemate." [64]

Republican Nixon (1969-74) and his first vice president, Spiro T. Agnew, often accused reporters of untrustworthiness. On Vietnam, Nixon said "our worst enemy seems to be the press," while Agnew blasted "the tiny, enclosed fraternity of privileged men elected by no one." [65]

Reed Irvine, a Republican journalist and press critic, in 1969 founded the conservative watchdog group Accuracy in Media to provide what he saw as a check against the media's liberal excesses. It grew within two decades into a 30,000-member organization with a $1.5 million annual budget, drawing praise from GOP lawmakers for its work exposing alleged biases, errors and distortion. [66]

Journalists played the central role in the era's other most significant controversy — the 1972 break-in at Democratic National Committee headquarters in Washington's Watergate office building and subsequent events that culminated in Nixon's resignation in 1974.

Relying on anonymous sources, *Post* reporters Woodward and Carl Bernstein uncovered many of the developments tying Nixon and top aides to the break-in, a cover-up and other misdeeds. A 1976 movie portrayed the pair as dogged investigators, and a Gallup poll that year showed public confidence in the media at an all-time peak of 72 percent. [67]

But Republican Ronald Reagan's presidency (1981-89) ushered in greater public skepticism. Some Democrats accused reporters of being reluctant to criticize him out of fear of being cut off from the flow of White House information. They also said reporters were too willing to take part in stage-managed events crafted by Reagan aides with an eye toward enhancing the president's popularity. [68]

In 1987, during Reagan's second term, the FCC abolished the Fairness Doctrine, paving the way for talk radio. [69] Rush Limbaugh, a conservative political commentator and host of a talk show in Sacramento, Calif., made perceived liberal bias one of his signature issues and saw his program become nationally syndicated in 1988 and the nation's most popular radio show. [70]

The Reagan era also saw competitive constraints and government regulation of cable channels relaxed by the Cable Communications Policy Act of 1984. The industry boomed, as all-news "24/7" cable channels such as CNN changed the face of television journalism by reaching a wide audience and offering coverage for longer periods than the TV networks. [71]

Media Scandals

Cable increased pressure on print media, which in the post-Watergate era had boosted in-depth reporting. *The Post*'s Janet Cooke won a Pulitzer Prize in 1981 for "Jimmy's World," a lengthy article about an 8-year-old heroin addict that the paper retracted when she admitted the boy was fictitious. [72]

The Cooke controversy was followed by scandals involving other journalists found to have fabricated or embellished their work:

• *The New Republic*'s Stephen Glass, who wrote articles in the 1990s about young conservatives, Wall Street traders and Silicon Valley technology entrepreneurs that were found to be entirely or partially false. [73]

• *USA Today*'s Jack Kelley, who wrote dispatches from Serbia and other war-torn countries in the 1990s and early 2000s that the newspaper found were substantially inaccurate. Editor Karen Jurgensen resigned in 2004 over her failure to detect the fabrications. [74]

• *The Times*' Jayson Blair, who was found in 2003 to have copied material from other publications as well as devising fake quotations, then lying about

it. The paper's two top editors subsequently stepped down. [75]

• NBC News anchor Brian Williams, who was suspended without pay for six months in 2015 — and eventually lost his anchor post — following a segment in which he exaggerated details of his travels in a military helicopter during the Iraq War. The story opened a controversy involving other instances in which Williams exaggerated or invented dangers he faced. [76]

• Sabrina Rubin Erdely, a journalist for *Rolling Stone*, the magazine and its parent company were found guilty of defamation of a former University of Virginia administrator in a 2014 magazine article about sexual assault on campus that included a debunked account of a fraternity gang rape. [77]

Media trust levels, as measured by Gallup, fell to just over 50 percent of Americans polled through the late 1990s and into the early 2000s. Media credibility has consistently been below 50 percent since 2007. [78]

Democratic President Bill Clinton was a polarizing figure, especially after his sexual relationship with White House intern Monica Lewinsky led to his impeachment and subsequent acquittal. "The Drudge Report," a conservative news-aggregation website launched in 1994, led the charge against Clinton and other Democrats.

Other right-wing outlets that followed in its wake, such as Breitbart News, were aggressively skeptical of President Barack Obama. The outlets gave voice to the "alt-right," a loose coalition of white nationalists, white supremacists, anti-Semites and others seeking to preserve what they consider traditional Western civilization. [79]

Such outlets "were preaching this is the only place you can get news — this is the only place you can trust," said Ted Newton, president of a Washington political communications firm and an adviser to Republican Mitt Romney's 2012 presidential campaign. "All other media outlets are lying to you [they said], so you need to come to us. And so in an attempt to capture an audience, they almost made them slaves to those news outlets." [80]

Cable news discovered that many viewers were hungry for partisanship. Fox News launched in 1996 with a motto to be "fair and balanced," combining straight news reporting with pro-Republican commentary.

Though critics labeled Fox a GOP soapbox for bigotry and propaganda, it struck a chord with viewers who believed the rest of media displayed an overly liberal tilt to become the most-watched cable channel in 2002. [81] Rival cable channel MSNBC, created in 1996 as a partnership between NBC and Microsoft, sought starting in 2007 to become Fox's liberal counterweight. [82]

Critics of the Iraq War blasted Fox and the rest of the media for not more aggressively investigating GOP President George W. Bush's justification of the 2003 invasion — that Iraq possessed nuclear, chemical or other so-called weapons of mass destruction. One *Times* reporter, Judith Miller, came under criticism for writing articles giving credence to Iraqi and U.S. officials who made that claim. [83]

Some journalists said deep public support for Bush after the Sept. 11, 2001, terrorist attacks influenced how aggressively they challenged his claims.

In the run-up to the war, "There wasn't any reporting in the rest of the press corps, there was stenography," recalled John Walcott, Washington bureau chief for McClatchy Newspapers, which published some of the most skeptical coverage about the decision to invade. "The administration would make an assertion, people would make an assertion, people would write it down as if it were true, and put it in the newspaper or on television." [84]

Social Media

Facebook, Twitter and other social-media sites further lessened the need

for Americans to rely on newspapers, TV or other news outlets. Facebook's algorithms assessed what people clicked on and then fed them similar content, a development that many experts say further lessened trust in mainstream outlets.

Politicians began recognizing the power of social media in appealing directly to a mass audience. Alaska

Craigslist founder Craig Newmark, whose website has attracted millions of dollars' worth of ads away from local newspaper classified advertising, has joined several private and nonprofit groups and media organizations in supporting projects aimed at developing faith in the media. "As a news consumer, like most folks, I want news we can trust," Newmark said. "That means standing up for trustworthy news media and learning how to spot clickbait and deceptive news."

Gov. Sarah Palin, the 2008 GOP vice-presidential nominee, inveighed against "the lamestream media." [85]

At the same time, media watchdog groups formed across the ideological spectrum. On the political right, hedge fund executive Robert Mercer and his daughter Rebecca gave $13.5 million between 2008 and 2014 to the Media Research Center, whose projects include a website (CNSNews.com) that publishes stories it says the mainstream media overlooks. [86] On the left, liberal business magnate George Soros gave at least $1 million to Media Matters for America, which also has obtained funding from or formed partnerships with several groups that Soros funds or has funded. [87]

In the 2016 presidential race, tradi-

tional media came under attack from all sides. Hillary Clinton's campaign castigated journalists for lavishing too much uncritical attention on Trump, whose colorful candidacy drew far more coverage than any of his Republican primary rivals. [88] Supporters of Vermont Sen. Bernie Sanders, Clinton's main primary opponent, accused the

media of not taking him seriously and undermining his campaign. [89]

Neither Trump nor Sanders, however, made media criticism as central to their races as Trump. Three months before the election, Trump named Steve Bannon, a founding member of the board of Breitbart, as head of his campaign. He later tapped the controversial Bannon as his chief strategist in the White House.

Trump made, and continues to make, near-daily use of Twitter as a weapon to bypass and attack traditional media. [90] House Majority Leader Kevin McCarthy, R-Calif., a Trump supporter, said the president's deployment of Twitter is "like owning newspapers." [91]

Facebook came under heavy criticism during the campaign for tailoring stories

Falling Newsroom Employment Erodes Trust

Reporters are "stretched thinner. That hurts trust."

Journalists are having a tough time building trust, in part because there are fewer of them and those who remain are stretched thin.

Declining circulation and falling advertising revenue have led to dramatic downsizing at print, broadcast and digital outfits. Newspapers, for instance, shed more than 24,000 reporting and editing jobs — a 37 percent drop — between 2004 and 2015, the latest year for which figures exist. [1] And the remaining reporters must not only gather the news and write stories but also shoot videos and constantly update their stories in real time using Twitter, Facebook and other social media.

"As newsrooms shrink, there's less time to do stories and they're doing shorter, more incomplete stories," says Tom Rosenstiel, executive director of the American Press Institute, a nonpartisan media research group in Arlington, Va. "As a consumer, you say, 'This is paper is thinner,' " he says, while journalists are having to "write a tweet and do a video [so] they're stretched thinner. That hurts trust. You don't have as much time to do everything."

Facing plummeting ad income, Gannett Co., the country's largest newspaper chain and owner of *USA Today* and more than 100 other dailies, reduced its workforce about 2 percent last October. [2] The company also cut staff at its Tennessee and New Jersey papers this year, but has refused to publicize recent cuts, according to the *Columbia Journalism Review*. [3] BH Media Group, a subsidiary of Berkshire Hathaway, the conglomerate headed by Nebraska investor Warren Buffett, announced in April it was cutting 289 jobs at its 31 dailies and nearly 50 weeklies. [4]

And the future economic climate for newspapers could get even worse, said Nicco Mele, former *Los Angeles Times* senior vice president. "If the next three years look like the last three years," he predicted in 2016, "somewhere between a third to a half" of the 50 largest metropolitan papers in the country could go out of business. Mele is now director of the Shorenstein Center on Media, Politics and Public Policy at Harvard University. [5]

Staff cuts have decimated coverage of state legislative news. Between 2005 and 2014, investigative and in-depth reporting on state government declined 30 percent at six major papers,

according to a 2016 study by a George Washington University graduate student. [6]

Downsizing local and state government coverage means greater secrecy — and potentially increased corruption — because fewer media outlets are holding state and local institutions accountable, several watchdog groups have warned. "The traditional media, particularly newspapers, have always led the open-government charges if the school board is closing a meeting illegally or the city is denying records or a judge is kicking a reporter out," said Jeffrey Hunt, a media lawyer in Salt Lake City. He sees the media "leaving the field in terms of fighting these battles." [7]

Not all of the economic news is bad — especially for the big media outlets such as *The New York Times*, *The Washington Post* and cable network MSNBC that have devoted substantial resources to the unfolding controversy over Russia's alleged involvement in the U.S. presidential election and ties to President Trump's administration.

In January *The Post* generated more new subscriptions than in any other month, beating what had been a record-setting November. [8] The paper has hired hundreds of reporters and editors since Amazon's Jeff Bezos bought the paper a few years ago, and Jed Hartman, chief revenue officer, predicted that 2017 would be its third year of double-digit revenue growth. [9] And during the first three months of this year *The Times* added 308,000 net digital-only news subscriptions — more than in any quarter in its history. [10] First-quarter revenues increased 5.1 percent over the first quarter of 2016, and circulation revenues jumped 11.2 percent. [11]

Stephen Farnsworth, a professor of political science and international affairs at the University of Mary Washington in Fredericksburg, Va., said the two papers are benefiting from a jump in the number of serious news consumers because of Trump. Those people "are appreciating the media more than they did last year at this time," says Fransworth, who directs Mary Washington's Center for Leadership and Media Studies. [12]

Despite those numbers, *The Times* in late May announced a round of newsroom buyouts aimed primarily at editors. The

in users' online feeds to what those users had previously read. That included a substantial amount of fake news, which made the network "a sewer of misinformation," according to Joshua Benton, director of Harvard's Nieman Journalism Lab. [92]

As polls showed trust in the media plummeting, news organizations and outside groups ramped up efforts to rebuild it.

One effort was the Reynolds Institute's Trusting News project, launched in January 2016 to look at how news outlets could rebuild trust through social media. The project found successful social-media posts shared several traits: They were about familiar topics that people were inclined to interact with; they gave people something specific to react to; and they used informal language to be relatable. [93]

A participant, the *Standard-Examiner* in Ogden, Utah, developed a video for Facebook and its website in which local African-Americans and law enforcement officials met to discuss Black Lives Matter. [94] The project "was a new way for us to see the importance of having a conversation with the readers and being transparent," says Ann Elise Taylor, the paper's news editor.

paper also announced it was abolishing the "public editor," or ombudsman, position held by Liz Spayd. Publisher Arthur Sulzberger said the paper would create a "Reader Center" to interact with the public. [13]

Meanwhile, the left-leaning MSNBC was the second-most-watched cable network during prime time during the week of May 15 — behind TNT, which carried several NBA playoff games. MSNBC's weekday prime-time shows averaged 2.44 million, eclipsing Fox News' 2.40 million for the first time ever. [14] Fox has devoted less coverage to the Russia controversy, and its commentary has been solidly pro-Trump. Some industry analysts wonder if its approach will hurt both its credibility and financial situation. [15]

Numerous advertisers backed away from Fox after commentator Bill O'Reilly was forced out in April amid allegations of sexual harassment and popular Fox commentator Sean Hannity had to apologize for advancing a discredited rumor that a murdered Democratic National Committee staffer was targeted for death by Hillary Clinton and liberal philanthropist George Soros. [16]

No one in the industry, however, has an easy solution for how news organizations can boost revenues while maintaining trust. Some foundations are financing investigative reporting, and some wealthy donors are providing millions of dollars to fight fake news and support in-depth reporting.

Another experiment is emulating the Netherlands' *De Correspondent* (*The Correspondent*), which recently announced a U.S. prototype. The online news site is funded by 56,000 members, who each pay about $63 a year for work done by its 21 full-time staff and 75 freelancers. The site aims to do in-depth, unique articles without competing against other media for breaking news, said Jay Rosen, a New York University professor of journalism who is helping with the U.S. version's launch. [17]

At journalism conferences, Rosen wrote, he has heard "a very good question: What if news organizations optimized every part of the operation for trust? Not for speed, traffic, profits, headlines or prizes . . . but for trust. What would that even look like? My

answer: It would look a lot like *De Correspondent*." [18]

— *Chuck McCutcheon*

[1] "Newspapers Fact Sheet," Pew Research Center, p. 8, June 1, 2017, https://tinyurl.com/yb8g77ht.

[2] Philana A. Patterson, "Gannett to reduce workforce by about 2% to help manage costs," *USA Today*, Oct. 24, 2016, http://tinyurl.com/yaknjj3y.

[3] Steve Cavendish, "Gannett Slashes Staffs at Tennessee Papers," *Nashville Scene*, March 28, 2017, http://tinyurl.com/ydff4nfa; Benjamin Mullin, "Layoffs hit North Jersey Media Group, again," Poynter.org, http://tinyurl.com/h8erxqr. Also see David Uberti, "Gannett newspapers are hiding an important local story," *Columbia Journalism Review*, May 5, 2017, http://tinyurl.com/y97jnu7w.

[4] Paul Fletcher, "Berkshire Hathaway's Media Group Cuts 289 Newspaper Jobs Nationwide," *Forbes*, April 4, 2017, http://tinyurl.com/ybwl52l3.

[5] "Nicco Mele — In Search of a Business Model: The Future of Journalism in an Age of Social Media and Dramatic Declines in Print Revenue," Shorenstein Center on Media, Politics and Policy, Harvard University, Feb. 18, 2016, http://tinyurl.com/ya3qes95.

[6] Lauren A. Dickinson, "The Strength of State Government Reporting: How In-Depth News and Investigative Coverage by Six U.S. Newspapers Fared from 2005 Through 2014," master of arts thesis, George Washington University, May 15, 2016, http://tinyurl.com/yb6ajwsl.

[7] Miranda S. Spivack, "Public contracts shrouded in secrecy," "Reveal" (Center for Investigative Reporting), Nov. 16, 2016, http://tinyurl.com/y9jvtrue.

[8] Ken Doctor, "Trump Bump Grows Into Subscription Surge — and Not Just for the New York Times," *TheStreet.com*, March 3, 2017, http://tinyurl.com/y7hu29ff.

[9] James B. Stewart, "Washington Post, Breaking News, Is Also Breaking New Ground," *The New York Times*, May 19, 2017, http://tinyurl.com/y8cs94x2.

[10] Sydney Ember, "New York Times Co. Reports Rising Digital Profit as Print Advertising Falls," *The New York Times*, May 3, 2017, http://tinyurl.com/m72ezr5.

[11] "The New York Times Company Reports 2017 First-Quarter Results," *Business Wire*, May 3, 2017, http://tinyurl.com/y8mr6d8b.

[12] Natalia Wojcik, "Trump has been 'rocket fuel' for NYT digital subscriptions, CEO says," CNBC.com, May 3, 2017, http://tinyurl.com/kyp6y46.

[13] Tali Arbel, "Among the job cuts at The New York Times, the public editor," *Boston.com* (The Associated Press), May 31, 2017, http://tinyurl.com/y88zmdz8.

[14] James Hibberd, "MSNBC weekly ratings beat Fox News, CNN for first time ever," *Entertainment Weekly.com*, May 22, 2017, http://tinyurl.com/m2sntup.

[15] Stephen Battaglio, "Trump-Russia story is a threat to Fox News' ratings dominance," *Los Angeles Times*, May 23, 2017, http://tinyurl.com/y9l5msgq.

[16] Simon Dumenco, "Is the Sean Hannity Advertiser Revolt Bill O'Reilly All Over Again?" *Advertising Age*, May 25, 2017, http://tinyurl.com/ybpayo4k.

[17] Jay Rosen, "Jay Rosen: This is what a news organization built on reader trust looks like," NiemanLab, March 28, 2017, http://tinyurl.com/ktkmpgb.

[18] *Ibid.*

The Coloradoan newspaper in Fort Collins, Colo., used a hit-and-run bicycle accident as a way to explain how — contrary to some readers' beliefs — journalists regret having to cover bad news. The Facebook post generated more than 3,500 link clicks — far more than expected. [95]

The Cincinnati television station WCPO-TV also took part, using Facebook to explain its commitment to covering child poverty while acknowledging the challenges in exploring the topic because it cannot show children's faces or use their voices on camera. [96]

"With the state of media and the way people think about media, it's crazy not to get involved with a project like this to win their trust," says Mike Canan, WCPO.com's editor.

CURRENT SITUATION

Trump and the Media

The early months of Trump's presidency have been marked by aggressive news coverage — led by *The Times* and *Post* — about whether Russia's government worked behind the scenes to help his campaign and influence his new administration.

A Quinnipiac University poll in early May indicates the media covering Trump may have gained some ground in winning the public's confidence. But it also showed skepticism of journalists remains entrenched.

When asked whom people trusted more to tell the truth about important

Rachel Maddow, host of the "Rachel Maddow Show" on MSNBC, is celebrated by liberals – and reviled by conservatives – for her partisan commentary. In today's highly polarized political and media climate, 62 percent of Americans say the media favor one political party over the other, compared with 50 percent in past years.

issues, 31 percent picked Trump and 57 percent cited the media, a rise of 5 percentage points from mid-February, when the president denounced the media as "the enemy of the American people" in a tweet. [97]

However, the poll also showed that voters disapproved, 58 percent to 37 percent, of the way the media cover the president. [98]

Such a split in attitudes reflects the harm inflicted from Trump's attacks, says Bill Adair, a former *Tampa Bay*

Times reporter and founder of the fact-checking site *PolitiFact* who is now a professor of journalism at Duke University.

"Clearly there's been a hunger for accurate, objective news lately — that's been encouraging," Adair says. "But Trump has said some incredibly damaging things about the media."

Both *The New York Times* and *Post* have seen financial gains that media analysts say reflect increased trust. (*See sidebar, p. 494.*) [99]

Barton Swaim, a conservative *Post* columnist, said he expected the mainstream media to aggressively cover Trump's presidency after being demonized during the election. "Even so, the sheer visceral animosity from the media, together with the aggressively insurgent opposition by [Democratic] holdovers from within the government, has shocked me as much as the election itself," Swaim said. [100]

Media scholars and journalists say Trump tacitly understands traditional

media's importance. They note that when the initial attempt to overturn Obama's Affordable Care Act could not win enough GOP supporters to be brought up for a House vote in March, the first reporters Trump notified were not from a conservative outlet, but *The Times* and *Post*. [101]

Commentators at Fox News, like other GOP-leaning outlets, have remained supportive of Trump, devoting less airtime to the ongoing investigation's into the Trump campaign's possible collusion with Russia than other outlets. Fox's opinion-givers and other conservatives have echoed the president in arguing that the leaking of classified information to the media is far more serious than speculation of any administration wrongdoing. [102]

William Kristol, a conservative pundit and former Fox commentator, criticized the conservative media, particularly Fox News, for "rationalizing everything" Trump does. [103]

The nonprofit investigative website *ProPublica*, founded in 2008, recently has expanded on its collaborations with other outlets, pairing with *The Times* and The Associated Press in March to rapidly collect White House staffers' financial-disclosure forms. [104] *ProPublica* opened a bureau in Chicago this spring, its first outside Washington and New York. [105]

In the Midwest, Cleveland's *Plain Dealer* and *Cleveland.com* launched the reporting collaboration "Ohio Matters," which has sent reporters to six rural, suburban and urban parts of the crucial swing state to hear concerns. Trump carried Ohio by 8 percentage points in 2016, far above most polls' earlier projections. [106]

To try to show its commitment to watchdog journalism, *The Post* in February put the motto "Democracy Dies in Darkness" below its front-page nameplate. The move led the conservative *Washington Times* to launch its own slogan — "Real News for Real Americans." [107]

Continued on p. 500

At Issue:

Should journalists try to be objective?

THOMAS KENT
*PRESIDENT AND CEO, RADIO FREE EUROPE/
RADIO LIBERTY; FORMER STANDARDS
EDITOR, THE ASSOCIATED PRESS*

WRITTEN FOR *CQ RESEARCHER*, JUNE 2017

*n*ot every journalist needs to be objective. But if sources of objective journalism disappear, society will suffer a tragic loss.

Some claim it's impossible for journalists to be objective; no one, they say, can report the news without a shade of personal opinion.

This might be true if a journalist's job were simply to provide one version of reality. That would open the way for journalists to impose their views on others. But the real goal of objectivity isn't so much about controlling the information available as about making sure readers get all the facts and interpretations they need to make up their own minds.

Smart journalists draw these facts and interpretations not only from their own investigations but also from reporting and reasonable opinions on social networks — making a well-done objective news story deeply democratic, reflecting input from many places. Objectivity demands only that journalists keep their personal views out of their stories. Personal opinions should be saved for opinion columns, where people expect writers to advocate for their points of view.

Critics sometimes claim objective journalism is a robotic, mindless craft of simply writing down what everyone says. It is nothing of the sort. So-called fake news and fantasy narratives have no place in an objective news article. Some things happened; others didn't. A newsmaker spoke in one context; to put his or her words in another is a lie. Journalists remain responsible for the truth of what they publish.

Some critics also accuse objective journalists of scrubbing humanity and emotion out of stories in a bid to avoid any opinion. But objectivity doesn't mean rejection of human feeling. The slaying of children by a gunman at a school can be fairly referred to as horrific; there is no need for a paragraph saying "on the other hand." A photographer covering a war or disaster can put aside his camera when he has a chance to save a life.

The world will be far poorer if journalism is allowed to become nothing but a stream of opinion pieces, which by their nature shortchange some points of view in order to advance the author's argument.

Society must have a place where thoughtful readers without the time to do extensive personal research can find fair, accurate accounts of events as well as a variety of responsible opinion to put them into context. Objective journalism fills this need.

BRUCE THORNTON
*RESEARCH FELLOW, HOOVER INSTITUTION;
PROFESSOR OF CLASSICS AND HUMANITIES,
FRESNO STATE UNIVERSITY*

WRITTEN FOR *CQ RESEARCHER*, JUNE 2017

*s*o-called objective journalism is another progressive idea based on scientism, the notion that human behavior and action can be as predictable and reliable as science. In earlier times, media reported obvious facts, but the political interpretation of those facts reflected what James Madison called the "passions and interests" of the competing political factions in a diverse country. The numerous newspapers across the country reflected this diversity, which is why they often had the word "Democrat" or "Republican" in their titles.

After World War II, journalism was professionalized and training happened in "J schools" at liberal universities, which biased much reporting toward liberal and urban sensibilities. The advent of television reduced the number of newspapers that once provided diversity, allowing the liberal interpretation to dominate far beyond the media centers in New York, Washington, Chicago and Los Angeles.

In the 1960s journalism became an activist and advocacy business. Coverage of the Vietnam War and the Watergate scandal interpreted events from a partisan and left-wing perspective that saw U.S. intervention as neocolonial adventurism and President Richard Nixon as a budding tyrant out to destroy the Constitution. As a consequence, South Vietnam was abandoned to the communist North, and Nixon was forced to resign, paving the way for Jimmy Carter's disastrous foreign policy of retreat and appeasement.

The repeal of the Federal Communications Commission's Fairness Doctrine in 1987 was followed by the advent of talk radio, which began to erode the monopoly of the big-three television networks and dominant newspapers like *The New York Times* and *The Washington Post*. Then came cable news with shows like Fox News, and the internet. Now thousands of outlets reflect the diversity of opinion that the First Amendment was written to protect. Where once maybe 50 opinion makers dominated political discourse, now there are hundreds of thousands. Their impact became clear when in 2004 CBS icon Dan Rather was brought down by internet sleuths for reporting "fake news" about George W. Bush's National Guard service.

Today we've returned to a true "marketplace of ideas" in which diverse political perspectives can compete, and ideological biases pretending to be "objective" can be exposed within hours. Once more it is up to the citizens to be informed and use their critical judgment rather than taking on faith the reporting of a handful of media outlets. If they misuse that freedom, that's the price always to be paid when people are free.

Continued from p. 498

Trust-Related Projects

Several private and nonprofit groups have joined media organizations on projects aimed at developing trust.

A global coalition of technology leaders, academic institutions and others announced a $14 million undertaking in April, The News Integrity Initiative, to combat declining trust in media and advance news literacy. Supporters include Craig Newmark, founder of the online classified-ad site Craigslist, which,

Pierre Omidyar, founder of eBay, launched a $100 million global project in April aimed at restoring trust in the media and other institutions. The focus will be on strengthening independent media and investigative journalism, confronting misinformation and hate speech and enabling citizens to better engage with government.

ironically, has severely crippled newspapers' classified revenues.

"As a news consumer, like most folks, I want news we can trust," Newmark said. "That means standing up for trustworthy news media and learning how to spot clickbait and deceptive news." [108]

The program will be administered by the CUNY Graduate School of Journalism. It will focus in part on helping readers better spot fake news and frivolous "clickbait" disguised as news articles. [109]

The philanthropic investment firm Omidyar Network, the brainchild of eBay founder Pierre Omidyar, in April launched a $100 million project over the next three years aimed at restoring trust in the media and other institutions globally. The funding will focus on strengthening independent media and investigative journalism, tackling misinformation and hate speech, and enabling citizens to better engage with government. [110]

The Reynolds Institute recently wrapped up the second phase of its "Trusting News" project with 30 media outlets around the country. That phase — which will conclude with a report this fall — invited local readers and viewers to describe how news outlets can win their confidence, Mayer says.

In Cincinnati, WCPO.com's invitation for readers to take part drew 463 responses in less than a day — a sign Canan says people care about the issue.

"One of the biggest takeaways is, there's a lot of guilt by association," he says. "As I delved into conversations with people, they said, 'I don't trust the media,' but it was really, 'I don't when comes to politics.' Or they don't trust the national media."

Canan says he has started collaborating with the *Cincinnati Enquirer*, a journalistic competitor, on ways to build trust. Peter Bhatia, the newspaper's editor and vice president for audience development, said he and other editors have been trying to "demystify our process" by explaining how the newsroom operates in talks to tea party as well as progressive groups and when publishing investigative projects or deeply reported work.

Transparency "becomes more of an imperative as we work hard to restore trust lost in the last election cycle, regardless of how fair the charges against us may be," Bhatia said. [111]

The *Standard-Examiner*'s Taylor, who also took part in the Reynolds Institute project, agrees on the need for increased transparency. She says a surprising number of readers do not make the distinction between news and commentary, with separate staffs handling each as at most outlets.

"That's knowledge a lot of journalists take for granted," she says. "One thing I'd like to address in being more transparent is explain what is an editorial, what is an opinion piece, how do they differ from a news story and how are all these things connected? That would be a valuable tool people could use as they consume news for the rest of their lives."

Facebook and Google

The twin colossi of the information world are trying to bolster confidence in the media in the face of criticism that they have enabled the spread of fake news and profited from sharing journalism content without paying its producers for it.

Facebook has put out new tools to stem the spread of fake news. If users click on a news story, they now have the option of reporting it as being false. If enough users flag such stories, Facebook will send the article to a fact-checking organization such as Snopes.com or PolitiFact — and if those outlets agree, the article will appear on Facebook with a red banner that says "Disputed by third-party fact checkers" and include a link to the explanation.

In addition, Facebook has promised to employ software to help identify fake news stories and has its engineers working on finding websites that impersonate actual news sites. [112]

Founder Mark Zuckerberg published a manifesto in February outlining how the social-media giant can contribute to restoring trust in news and information. One of his aims is to encourage the growth of local news and improve the range of business models on which news organizations rely. [113]

Google's News Lab, launched in 2015, seeks to connect journalists with programs, data and other resources to use in their reporting. It started the First Draft coalition to create standards and best practices for verifying eye-witness media content and combating fake news. The coalition expanded last year to include 80 partners, including Facebook and Twitter, and is working with universities and other organizations around the world. [114]

Critics of Google's and Facebook's efforts, however, say their continued dependence on incorporating news articles in their content compels them to do far more to help the media regain trust.

Steven Waldman, founder of Life-Posts.com, where people share personal stories online, said Facebook and Google should devote 1 percent of their profits for five years to create a $4.4 billion permanent endowment to transform local journalism.

"These companies are among the biggest beneficiaries of the digital disruption that has, among other things, caused the crisis in American journalism," Waldman said. "It's time for the disrupters to solve the problems." [115] ∎

OUTLOOK

Unpleasant Truths

With political polarization deeply rooted in society, journalism scholars and those in the news media predict mistrust of journalists will continue — the question is to what degree.

"The media will never be all that popular; it's in the business of telling unpleasant truths," says Stephen Farnsworth, a professor of political science and international affairs at the University of Mary Washington in Fredericksburg, Va., who directs its Center for Leadership and Media Studies.

The American Press Institute's Rosenstiel says trust levels "are going to continue to slip, because we're in a more polarized world, and I don't see a solution to that on the horizon." Part of the problem, he adds, is the inability of the Democratic and Republican parties to produce leaders who are considered trustworthy to a broad bipartisan audience.

"It's ironic that when he left office, Barack Obama had much higher approval ratings than Trump or any politician has now," he says. "I think there's a sort of nostalgia — we can, in retrospect, appreciate people, but when we're on the field of battle, we retreat to our team."

More conservatives need to have their voices heard in traditional media, said former Wisconsin right-wing talk-radio host Charlie Sykes. If that does not happen, he said, those conservatives will continue putting their faith in outlets that mirror their preconceived views.

"You can do the best reporting in the world, but unless you can find a way to restore that credibility . . . it won't even register," said Sykes, now a contributing New York Times columnist. [116]

Benton, of Harvard's Nieman Lab, is particularly interested in seeing whether online outlets such as BuzzFeed and Mic that have marketed themselves to younger, urban readers will start courting conservative readers.

"Do they double down on identity-driven stories embracing the values of diversity and multiculturalism?" he asked. "Or — at a time when many are under their own revenue strains . . . do any of them see a market opportunity in the Trump voter?" [117]

Finding ways to finance quality journalism at larger-scale mainstream outlets will be critical, says Arizona State's Downie, the former Post editor.

"I'm pleased to see that audiences are beginning to find ways to pay more for digital subscriptions to the Times, support events produced by other news organizations and increase membership in public radio," he says. "Foundations are stepping up and philanthropists are stepping up. But whether that's sufficient five or 10 years from now, I can't say."

The Reynolds Institute's Mayer, who leads the Trusting News project, predicts a split between news organizations catering to polarization and those willing to earn more trust. Of the latter group, she expects an increased effort to listen more closely to readers.

"There's no room in journalism any more for people who don't see customer service and understanding the audience as part of the job," she says. "People in journalism have to have an entrepreneurial mindset and a customer-service mindset with a focus on, 'Here's what we do.' "

Duke University's Adair, the PolitiFact creator, estimates that if trust levels do pick up, it will take 10 or 15 years. The media "will do better at labeling types of articles and being more transparent," he says. "There's likely to be a renewed effort to invest in news literacy so that people, particularly young people, have a better understanding of the news ecosystem."

Until then, said Post media columnist Margaret Sullivan, a former Times public editor, young people going into journalism must accept being mistrusted.

"You have to understand there's a mission attached to our job and that we need to do it well," Sullivan told a student audience at the University of Wisconsin-Madison, "and put on our big-boy and big-girl pants and not worry that we're under attack — because it's going to continue." [118] ■

Notes

[1] Jennifer Calfas, "Read the Advice Bob Woodward and Carl Bernstein Gave at the White House Correspondents' Dinner," *Time*, April 30, 2017, http://tinyurl.com/n7qvosk.

[2] Mark Landler, "Trump Savages News Media at Rally to Mark His 100th Day," *The New York Times*, April 29, 2016, https://tinyurl.com/ycvcq7u9.

[3] See Chuck McCutcheon, "Populism and Political Parties," *CQ Researcher*, Sept. 9, 2016, pp. 721-744.

[4] Benjamin Mullin, " 'I want to see us take journalism to people where they are': A Q-&-A with Jeff Jarvis about restoring trust in journalism," Poynter.org, April 3, 2017, https://tinyurl.com/y6uugszv.

[5] Art Swift, "Americans' Trust in Mass Media Sinks to New Low," Gallup, Sept. 14, 2016, https://tinyurl.com/hda5s4u.

[6] "Honesty/ethics in professions," Gallup, Dec. 7-11, 2016, https://tinyurl.com/lcer8a.

[7] Art Swift, "Six in 10 in US See Partisan Bias in News Media," Gallup, April 5, 2017, https://tinyurl.com/metlvk6.

[8] "How trust can be broken, and the decline of confidence in the press," American Press Institute, April 17, 2016, https://tinyurl.com/yadwe7or.

[9] "Oxford Dictionaries Word of the Year 2016 is . . . Post-Truth," Oxford Dictionaries.com, Dec. 12, 2016, https://tinyurl.com/kdgknmd.

[10] "Meet The Press 01/22/17," NBC News, Jan. 22, 2017, https://tinyurl.com/y7fuxnjy.

[11] Shane Goldmacher, "How Trump gets his fake news," *Politico*, May 15, 2017, https://tinyurl.com/kwlt3yl.

[12] Michael Barthel and Amy Mitchell, "Americans' Attitudes About the News Media Deeply Divided Along Partisan Lines," Pew Research Center, May 10, 2017, https://tinyurl.com/ydgclyxx.

[13] Laura Nichols, "Poll: Majority Find Major Media Outlets Credible," Morning Consult, Dec. 7, 2016, https://tinyurl.com/ya59mcra.

[14] Paul Farhi, "Reporters say they are being roughed up. Observers point to Trump," *The Washington Post*, May 26, 2017, https://tinyurl.com/ycfzvlbj.

[15] "Windows shattered at Herald-Leader building; suspected bullet damage found," *Lexington Herald-Leader* (Ky.), May 29, 2017, https://tinyurl.com/ycp3c2ds.

[16] "Marvin Kalb on Current Challenges to the Freedom of the Press," National Press Club Journalism Institute speech, YouTube.com, posted April 1, 2017, http://tinyurl.com/ycxubgdd.

[17] Andrew Collins, "Meet Watchdog editor John Bicknell: journalist, author, history buff," Franklin Center for Government & Public Integrity, Nov. 3, 2015, https://tinyurl.com/y9pwrkyd.

[18] Paul Farhi, "Dear readers: Please stop calling us 'the media.' There is no such thing," *The Washington Post*, Sept. 23, 2016, https://tinyurl.com/y9v84hfb.

[19] Mathew Ingram, "Glenn Greenwald vs. the NYT's Bill Keller on objectivity and the future of journalism," *Gigaom*, Oct. 28, 2013, https://tinyurl.com/yd76vw7v.

[20] Margaret Sullivan, "How one reporter's rejection of objectivity got him fired," *The Washington Post*, Feb. 1, 2017, https://tinyurl.com/y7e98afx.

[21] Lewis Wallace, "Objectivity is dead, and I'm okay with it," Medium.com, Jan. 27, 2017, https://tinyurl.com/y8k56rtw.

[22] Adam Ragusea, "Glenn Greenwald on the 'adversarial force' of a free press," *Current*,

March 29, 2016, http://tinyurl.com/y8zokx8h.

[23] "Objectivity: What Is It Good For?" WNYC-FM's "On the Media" transcript, Feb. 3, 2017, https://tinyurl.com/ybg5hlbe.

[24] Bruce Thornton, "We Citizens Have to Guard the Media 'Guardians,' " *FrontPageMag*, Sept. 2, 2016, https://tinyurl.com/ya368tpe.

[25] Jonah Goldberg, "The Press Is Not the Enemy," *National Review*, Feb. 24, 2017, https://tinyurl.com/yaox2yj7.

[26] Michael Kinsley, "Is It Possible There Is Nothing Nice to Say?" *The New York Times*, May 13, 2017, https://tinyurl.com/ybrufzqw.

[27] " 'Trump Revealed': The reporting archive," *The Washington Post*, Aug. 30, 2016, https://tinyurl.com/h9g6rgg.

[28] James Fallows, "Why Americans Hate the Media," *The Atlantic*, February 1996, https://tinyurl.com/y8y9h3st.

[29] Mathew Ingram, "Here's Why the Media Failed to Predict a Donald Trump Victory," *Fortune*, Nov. 9, 2016, https://tinyurl.com/z8db88p.

[30] " 'New York Times' Executive Editor On The New Terrain Of Covering Trump," "Fresh Air," NPR, Dec. 8, 2016, https://tinyurl.com/jdo6pxg.

[31] Andrew McGill, "U.S. Media's Real Elitism Problem," *The Atlantic*, Nov. 19, 2016, https://tinyurl.com/y9jd3fu6.

[32] Carrie Sheffield, "WATCH: Journalism used to fight for the working man, now it's a bastion of 'trust fund kids,' " *Salon.com*, March 19, 2017, https://tinyurl.com/yd8esfe3.

[33] "History of the WHCA," White House Correspondents' Association, https://tinyurl.com/csdr45h; Jim Romenesko, "Why NYT doesn't attend White House Correspondents' Association Dinner," Poynter.org, May 4, 2011, https://tinyurl.com/yawpvrp9.

[34] See Peter Katel, "Racial Conflict," *CQ Researcher*, Jan. 8, 2016, pp. 25-48.

[35] Nick Tabor, "PBS?'s Tavis Smiley on What's Wrong (and Right) With the Media," *New York*, July 24, 2016, https://tinyurl.com/yabdclp3.

[36] Shan Wang, "U.S. newsrooms seem to be getting a little more diverse. But minority journalists are still, well, a minority," NiemanLab.org, Sept. 9, 2016, https://tinyurl.com/zqkx9zg.

[37] "The President and the Press: The First Amendment in the First 100 Days," Newseum.org event transcript, April 12, 2017, https://tinyurl.com/y8yn3o4w.

[38] "Anxious in America," *The New York Times*, 2016, https://tinyurl.com/y8dx7ucp.

[39] "Why The Media Use Anonymous Sources," "Morning Edition," NPR, Dec. 16, 2016, https://tinyurl.com/hs9a4v4.

[40] Eli Yokley, "Voters Skeptical of Anonymous Sourcing, but Still Trust Political Reporting,"

About the Author

Chuck McCutcheon is a former assistant managing editor of *CQ Researcher*. He has been a reporter and editor for *Congressional Quarterly* and Newhouse News Service and is co-author of the 2012 and 2014 editions of *The Almanac of American Politics* and *Dog Whistles, Walk-Backs and Washington Handshakes: Decoding the Jargon, Slang and Bluster of American Political Speech*. He also has written books on climate change and nuclear waste.

Morning Consult, March 8, 2017, https://tinyurl.com/y7m6dryj; "Morning Consult National Tracking Poll #170301," *Morning Consult*, March 2-6, 2017, p. 265, https://tinyurl.com/ycvdgy5h.

[41] Tara Golshan, "Full transcript: President Trump's CPAC speech," *Vox.com*, Feb. 24, 2017, https://tinyurl.com/ybescrr8.

[42] "Following Multiple Debacles, NY Times Is 'Cracking Down On The Use Of Anonymous Sources,' " Media Matters for America, March 15, 2016, https://tinyurl.com/yamapyfc.

[43] Liz Spayd, "The Risk of Unnamed Sources? Unconvinced Readers," *The New York Times*, Feb. 18, 2017, https://tinyurl.com/yb2wmu3r.

[44] Mollie Hemingway, tweet, May 15, 2017, https://tinyurl.com/y9z4rmgv.

[45] Jill Disis, "New York Times editor: Why journalists need to use anonymous sources," CNN.com, Feb. 26, 2017, https://tinyurl.com/ycuvz6hd.

[46] "Why The Media Use Anonymous Sources," *op. cit.*

[47] Steve Myers, "Study: Use of anonymous sources peaked in 1970s, dropped by 2008," Poynter.org, Aug. 9, 2011, https://tinyurl.com/y98utmk9. The study was by Matt J. Duffy, a professor of international media law at Zayed University in Abu Dhabi, and Ann E. Williams, a professor of communication at Georgia State University.

[48] "John F. Kennedy Speeches/The President and the Press: Address before the American Newspaper Publishers Association, April 27, 1961," John F. Kennedy Presidential Library and Museum, https://tinyurl.com/zuxwmen.

[49] Lindsey Bever, "Memo to Donald Trump: Thomas Jefferson invented hating the media," *The Washington Post*, Feb. 18, 2017, https://tinyurl.com/ybh5hqro; Daniel Lattier, "Thomas Jefferson Had Some Issues With Newspapers," *Intellectual Takeout*, Aug. 28, 2015, https://tinyurl.com/y76v92bt.

[50] Ryan Holiday, "Abraham Lincoln as Media Manipulator-in-Chief: The 150 Year History of Corrupt Press," *The Observer*, Nov. 5, 2014, https://tinyurl.com/ycq45rf6.

[51] Garry Wills, "How Lincoln Played the Press," *New York Review of Books*, Nov. 6, 2014, https://tinyurl.com/yaoc27mz.

[52] "Second Inaugural Address of Ulysses S. Grant," Yale University Law School, Lillian Goldman Law Library, https://tinyurl.com/yb9okf5b.

[53] "Yellow journalism," *New World Encyclopedia*, https://tinyurl.com/yagthwpu.

[54] "Our History," New York Times Company, https://tinyurl.com/y7hxev7j; "Without Fear or Favor," *The New York Times*, Aug. 19, 1996, https://tinyurl.com/ybtored9.

[55] Upton Sinclair, *The Brass Check: A Study of American Journalism* (1919), https://tinyurl.com/y7zsf7um.

[56] "Upton Sinclair," https://tinyurl.com/yc2574cl.

[57] "Walter Lippmann," *Encyclopaedia Brittanica*, https://tinyurl.com/y93ffgw5.

[58] Walter Lippmann, *Liberty and the News* (1920), p. 11.

[59] Stuart N. Brotman, "Revisiting the broadcast public interest standard in communications law and regulation," Brookings Institution, March 23, 2017, https://tinyurl.com/kpugnbz.

[60] Dan Fletcher, "A Brief History of the Fairness Doctrine," *Time*, Feb. 20, 2009, https://tinyurl.com/yawejko8.

[61] Jonathan M. Ladd, *Why Americans Hate the Media and How It Matters* (2013), p. 62, http://tinyurl.com/mljy8vp.

[62] "Joseph R. McCarthy," History.com, https://tinyurl.com/o724hco; David Mindich, "For journalists covering Trump, a Murrow moment," *Columbia Journalism Review*, July 15, 2016, http://tinyurl.com/ybhfryk4.

[63] Ladd, *op. cit.*

[64] "Final Words: Cronkite's Vietnam Commentary," NPR, July 18, 2009, https://tinyurl.com/3wncqv3.

[65] Chester Pach, "Public Learned Less After Media Was Blamed for Failure in Vietnam," *The New York Times*, April 29, 2015, https://tinyurl.com/ycult2yx; Christopher Cimaglio, " 'A Tiny and Closed Fraternity of Privileged Men': The Nixon-Agnew Antimedia Campaign and the Liberal Roots of the U.S. Conservative 'Liberal Media' Critique," *International Journal of Communication 10* (2016), https://tinyurl.com/y86wosuv.

[66] "The Retromingent Vigilantes Revel," Accuracy in Media Report, October 1989, https://tinyurl.com/y8h26snb.

[67] Swift, "Americans' Trust in Mass Media Sinks to New Low," *op. cit.*

[68] Mark Hertsgaard, *On Bended Knee: The Press and the Reagan Presidency* (1988).

[69] Fletcher, *op. cit.*

[70] "Rush Limbaugh," Biography.com, https://tinyurl.com/ce2e5qh.

[71] Michael I. Meyerson, "The Cable Communications Policy Act of 1984: A Balancing Act on the Coaxial Wires," *Georgia Law Review 19*, Spring 1985, https://tinyurl.com/y8kfytwm.

[72] Mike Sager, "The fabulist who changed journalism," *Columbia Journalism Review*, Spring 2016, https://tinyurl.com/y7rmfgnh.

[73] Michael Hiltzik, "Stephen Glass is still retracting his fabricated stories — 18 years later," *Los Angeles Times*, Dec. 15, 2015, https://tinyurl.com/yb3ryk6r.

[74] Jacques Steinberg, "Editor of USA Today Resigns; Cites Failure Over Fabrications," *The New York Times*, April 21, 2004, https://tinyurl.com/y8gdzx53.

[75] Isabella Kwai, "Why he did it: Jayson Blair opens up about his plagiarism and fabrication at the New York Times," ReportersLab.org, April 12, 2016, https://tinyurl.com/y8msdlel.

[76] Paul Farhi, "At long last, Brian Williams is back — humbled and demoted to MSNBC," *The Washington Post*, Sept. 21, 2015, http://tinyurl.com/y7gnkb6c.

[77] T. Rees Shapiro, "Jury finds reporter, Rolling Stone responsible for defaming U-Va. dean with gang rape story," *The Washington Post*, Nov. 4, 2016, http://tinyurl.com/ybhzols8.

[78] Swift, *op. cit.*

[79] See Marcia Clemmitt, " 'Alt-Right' Movement," *CQ Researcher*, March 17, 2017, pp. 241-264.

[80] Oliver Darcy, "Donald Trump broke the conservative media," *Business Insider*, Aug. 26, 2016, https://tinyurl.com/j8qprjf.

[81] "Roger Ailes Looks Back on 15 Years of Fox News," The Associated Press, Fox News.com, Oct. 5, 2011, https://tinyurl.com/y9anos9o.

[82] Alex Weprin, "A Brief History Of MSNBC.com And NBCNews.com," *AdWeek*, July 16, 2012, https://tinyurl.com/ydz8jpqz.

[83] Erik Wemple, "Judith Miller tries, and ultimately fails, to defend her flawed Iraq reporting," *The Washington Post*, April 9, 2015, https://tinyurl.com/y8occ74s.

[84] Max Follmer, "The Reporting Team That Got Iraq Right," *The Huffington Post*, May 25, 2011, https://tinyurl.com/yo99zz.

[85] Andy Barr, "Palin trashes 'lamestream media,' " *Politico*, Nov. 18, 2009, https://tinyurl.com/yc9g7ok7.

[86] Matea Gold, "The Mercers and Stephen Bannon: How a populist power base was funded and built," *The Washington Post*, March 17, 2017, https://tinyurl.com/m8gctl3.

[87] Keach Hagey, "Soros gives $1 million to Media Matters," *Politico*, Oct. 20, 2010, https://tinyurl.com/29da5l3.

[88] Nicholas Confessore and Karen Yourish, "$2 Billion Worth of Free Media for Donald Trump," *The New York Times*, March 15, 2016, https://tinyurl.com/z9jkzcn.

[89] Nicole Fisher, "Sanders' Supporters: Why Some Won't Back Clinton," *Forbes*, Aug. 17, 2016, https://tinyurl.com/y7kt698g.

[90] Robert Draper, "Trump vs. Congress: Now What?" *The New York Times Magazine*, March 26, 2017, https://tinyurl.com/mxl7vvv.

[91] *Ibid.*

[92] Joshua Benton, "The forces that drove this election's media failure are likely to get worse," NiemanLab, Nov. 9, 2017, https://tinyurl.com/nrccvms.

[93] "Trusting News," Donald W. Reynolds Journalism Institute, February 2017, https://tinyurl.com/kbsgehl.

[94] "VIDEO: Discussing race and policing in Northern Utah," *Standard-Examiner* (Ogden, Utah), July 27, 2016, https://tinyurl.com/ybpdzlqd.

[95] "Newsrooms Partners: The Coloradoan," Trusting News website, undated, http://tinyurl.com/ycyyjwxu/.

[96] "WCPO — 9 On Your Side," Facebook post, Sept. 23, 2016, https://tinyurl.com/yb926w5u.

[97] Michael M. Grynbaum, "Trump Calls the News Media the 'Enemy of the American People,' " *The New York Times*, Feb. 17, 2017, https://tinyurl.com/js4uyw5.

[98] "May 10, 2017 — U.S. Voters Send Trump Approval To Near Record Low; Quinnipiac University National Poll Finds; No Winner In Media War, But Voters Trust Media More," Quinnipiac University, May 10, 2017, https://tinyurl.com/kebfbpv.

[99] Sydney Ember, "New York Times Co. Reports Rising Digital Profit as Print Advertising Falls," *The New York Times*, May 3, 2017, https://tinyurl.com/m72ezr5.

[100] Barton Swaim, We're not learning from the Trump story — because we've peeked at the last page," *The Washington Post*, May 18, 2017, https://tinyurl.com/y9pj3tbv.

[101] Jackie Strause, "After 'Fake News' Claims, Trump's First Calls After Health-Care Defeat Were to N.Y. Times, Washington Post," *Hollywood Reporter*, March 24, 2017, http://tinyurl.com/kxenhcp.

[102] Maxwell Tani, "Here's how Fox News responded to reports Trump leaked classified information to Russian officials," *Business Insider*, May 16, 2017, https://tinyurl.com/ycbbmkor.

[103] Aidan McLaughlin, "Bill Kristol: Most of Fox News Has Become 'Ridiculous,' " *Mediaite*, May 15, 2017, https://tinyurl.com/mb87gr4.

[104] Eric Umansky, "How We're Learning To Do Journalism Differently in the Age of Trump," *ProPublica*, May 8, 2017, https://tinyurl.com/mk2lvhe.

[105] Jackie Spinner, "Q&A: Louise Kiernan says ProPublica Illinois will 'find areas where we can have impact,' " *Columbia Journalism Review*, March 6, 2017, https://tinyurl.com/ybj3zgbh.

[106] "Ohio Matters: Redesigning Political Coverage in Ohio," *Cleveland.com*, http://tinyurl.com/mvecskx; "Ohio: Trump vs. Clinton," *Real ClearPolitics.com*, http://tinyurl.com/y923vh3u

[107] Rachel Stoltzfoos, "The Washington Times Adopts A New Slogan For Trump Era," *The Daily Caller*, March 13, 2017, https://tinyurl.com/y8etm5nq.

[108] Benjamin Mullin, "Can trust in the news be repaired? Facebook, Craig Newmark, Mozilla and others are spending $14 million to try," Poynter.org, April 3, 2017, http://tinyurl.com/nyfkvh4.

[109] *Ibid.*

[110] Margaret Sullivan, "Omidyar network gives $100 million to boost journalism and fight hate speech," *The Washington Post*, April 4, 2017, https://tinyurl.com/y9a84mes.

[111] Peter Bhatia, "To Restore Trust, Enhance Transparency," *Nieman Reports*, Feb. 15, 2017, https://tinyurl.com/yb8jh224.

[112] David Pogue, "What Facebook Is Doing to Combat Fake News," *Scientific American*, Feb. 1, 2017, https://tinyurl.com/h26du9a.

[113] Mark Zuckerberg, "Building Global Community," Facebook, Feb. 16, 2017, https://tinyurl.com/myq4nkf.

[114] Steve Grove, "The Google News Lab in 2016, and where we're headed," *Medium.com*, Dec. 6, 2016, https://tinyurl.com/y747x5bt.

[115] Steven Waldman, "What Facebook Owes to Journalism," *The New York Times*, Feb. 21, 2017, https://tinyurl.com/y9kjtyf2.

[116] Cadence Bambenek, "Recap: Trust, Truth and the Future of Journalism," Center for Journalism Ethics, University of Wisconsin-Madison, April 13, 2017, https://tinyurl.com/ycdxnwxf.

[117] Benton, *op. cit.*

[118] "Truth, Trust & the Future of Journalism: Keynote Conversation with Margaret Sullivan," Center for Journalism Ethics, University of Wisconsin-Madison, YouTube video, posted April 5, 2017, https://tinyurl.com/y8dpw97y.

FOR MORE INFORMATION

Accuracy in Media, 4350 East West Highway, Suite 555, Bethesda, MD 20814; 202-364-4401; www.aim.org. Conservative media watchdog organization that searches for potential liberal bias in news reporting.

American Press Institute, 401 N. Fairfax Drive, Suite 300, Arlington, VA 22203; 571-366-1200; www.americanpressinstitute.org. A nonprofit group that researches journalism trends.

American Society of News Editors, 209 Reynolds Journalism Institute, Missouri School of Journalism, University of Missouri, Columbia, MO 65211; 573-884-2430; www.asne.org. Promotes ethical journalism, supports First Amendment rights and defends freedom of information and open government.

Fairness & Accuracy in Reporting, 124 W. 30th St., Suite 201, New York, NY 10001; 212-633-6700; www.fair.org. Liberal media watchdog organization that monitors bias and censorship in news reporting.

Media Matters for America, P.O. Box 52155, Washington, DC 20091; 202-756-4100; www.mediamatters.org. Liberal media watchdog group that looks for potential conservative bias in news reporting.

Media Research Center, 325 S. Patrick St., Alexandria, VA 22314; 703-683-9733; www.mrc.org. Conservative media watchdog group that searches for potential liberal bias in news reporting.

Nieman Journalism Lab, Harvard University, 1 Francis Ave., Cambridge, MA 02138; 617-495-2237; www.niemanlab.org. Analyzes the news media's future in the internet age.

Pew Research Center for the People & the Press, 1615 L St., N.W., Suite 700, Washington, DC 20036; 202-419-4300; www.people-press.org. Nonpartisan media research organization funded by the Pew Charitable Trusts.

Poynter Institute for Media Studies, 801 Third St. South, St. Petersburg, FL 33701; 727-821-9494; www.poynter.org. Journalism education and research organization and owner of the *Tampa Bay Times*; ethics section of its website includes articles, discussions, tips and case studies.

Bibliography

Selected Sources

Books

Anderson, C.W., Leonard Downie and Michael Schudson, *The News Media: What Everyone Needs to Know*, Oxford University Press, 2016.

A media culture professor at the College of Staten Island (Anderson), a former *Washington Post* executive editor (Downie) and a Columbia University journalism professor (Schudson) explain the economic, technological and societal forces that have helped erode trust in journalism.

Carlson, Matt, *Journalistic Authority: Legitimating News in the Digital Era*, Columbia University Press, 2017.

A St. Louis University communications professor examines the cultural, structural and technological factors that prompt readers to accept or reject a journalist's version of events.

Graves, Lucas, *Deciding What's True: The Rise of Political Fact-Checking in American Journalism*, Columbia University Press, 2016.

A University of Wisconsin professor of journalism and mass communication chronicles the evolution of fact-checking websites and their importance in assessing assertions by government officials.

Stone, Roger, *The Making of the President 2016: How Donald Trump Orchestrated a Revolution*, Skyhorse Publishing, 2017.

A political adviser and friend of Donald Trump details how Trump's strategy of castigating mainstream news outlets helped him win the presidency.

Articles

"The Case Against the Media. By the Media," *New York*, July 25, 2016, https://tinyurl.com/zm2sn6g.

The weekly magazine interviews dozens of print, broadcast and online journalists about what they see as their profession's biggest flaws.

Benton, Joshua, "The forces that drove this election's media failure are likely to get worse," NiemanLab, Nov. 9, 2017, https://tinyurl.com/nrccvms.

The director of Harvard University's media-research center says the problems that led the media to be blindsided by Trump's victory must be corrected.

Rosenstiel, Tom, "What the post-Trump debate over journalism gets wrong," Brookings Institution, Dec. 20, 2016, https://tinyurl.com/h6pgke5.

A senior fellow at the centrist think tank and executive director of the American Press Institute says journalists must embrace new methods to earn trust, such as making documents and other reporting research available for readers to see firsthand.

Shafer, Jack, "How Trump Took Over the Media By Fighting It," *Politico Magazine*, Nov. 5, 2016, https://tinyurl.com/jqnhfwn.

The political website's media writer says Donald Trump went far beyond any other presidential candidate in condemning reporters.

Thornton, Bruce, "We Citizens Have to Guard the Media 'Guardians,' " *Frontpage Mag*, Sept. 2, 2016, https://tinyurl.com/n86nge5.

A fellow at Stanford University's Hoover Institution says negative coverage of Trump's presidential campaign reflects the mainstream media's longtime bias against Republicans.

Toffel, Richard J., "The Country Doesn't Trust Us — But They Do Believe Us," NiemanLab, Dec. 12, 2016, https://tinyurl.com/n2vjyzy.

The president of the investigative website *ProPublica* highlights the importance of trust in an essay accompanying interviews with several dozen journalists, academics and others predicting future media trends.

Umansky, Eric, "How We're Learning To Do Journalism Differently in the Age of Trump," *ProPublica*, May 8, 2017, https://tinyurl.com/mk2lvhe.

ProPublica, a nonprofit online news organization, says it will cover the Trump administration by digging deeper, collaborating, being transparent and being comfortable with uncertainty.

Reports and Studies

"State of the News Media 2016," Pew Research Center, June 15, 2016, https://tinyurl.com/zh7vqdj.

The nonprofit research group says the economic pressures facing the news media intensified in 2015, with average weekday newspaper circulation seeing its biggest drop since 2010.

"Trusting News," Donald W. Reynolds Journalism Institute, February 2017, https://tinyurl.com/kbsgehl.

A research project of the University of Missouri's journalism think tank says news outlets can employ Facebook and other social media to effectively build trust with audiences.

" 'Who Shared It?': How Americans decide what news to trust on social media," American Press Institute, March 20, 2017, https://tinyurl.com/leh49n7.

A collaboration between the American Press Institute and The Associated Press-NORC Center for Public Affairs Research finds that when Americans read news on social media, how much they trust the content is determined less by who creates the news than by who shares it.

Swift, Art, "Americans' Trust in Mass Media Sinks to New Low," Gallup, Sept. 14, 2016, https://tinyurl.com/hda5s4u.

The polling company finds trust in the media at its lowest level since Gallup began asking the question in 1972.

The Next Step:

Additional Articles from Current Periodicals

Alternative-Media Outlets

Benkler, Yochai, et al., "Study: Breitbart-led right-wing media ecosystem altered broader media agenda," Columbia Journalism Review, March 3, 2017, https://tinyurl.com/y7vga6be.

A study of more than 1 million online news stories shows how the Breitbart News site used social media "to transmit a hyper-partisan perspective to the world" during the 2016 election, influencing how other media covered the election.

Chang, Alvin, "We tracked the Trump scandals on right-wing news sites. Here's how they covered it," Vox, May 18, 2017, https://tinyurl.com/k9xr5hh.

According to Vox, a news and opinion website founded by former Washington Post columnist Ezra Klein, Breitbart and Fox News covered the firing of FBI Director James Comey very differently than The New York Times, primarily by removing context and blaming the "liberal" media for spreading false information to take down President Trump.

Manjoo, Farhad, "How Twitter Is Being Gamed to Feed Misinformation," The New York Times, May 31, 2017, https://tinyurl.com/yb82rr5f.

Fake news, misinformation and propaganda are shared so often on Twitter that mainstream journalists feel compelled to cover the stories to explain what is true and false.

Plunkett, Chuck, "In so many ways, users of social media improve our journalism," The Denver Post, March 26, 2017, https://tinyurl.com/kk3trtf.

Although social media can spread misinformation, says an editorial writer, it also can benefit journalism by allowing citizens to shine a spotlight on stories that are not being covered and enabling journalists to quickly solicit information from readers with knowledge about a topic or a different perspective.

Future of Local News

Ali, Chrisopher, and Damian Radcliffe, "Life at small-market newspapers: A survey of over 400 journalists," Columbia Journalism Review, May 10, 2017, https://tinyurl.com/y87n5hq9.

An online survey found that journalists working at newspapers with circulations under 50,000 are surprisingly upbeat about their future and eager to take on new challenges, despite a standard 50-hour work week, low pay and the threat of layoffs.

Edge, Sami, "Demystifying Media: What's the Future of Local Newspapers?" MediaShift, March 31, 2017, https://tinyurl.com/lvfameu.

An assistant professor of media studies at the University of Virginia and a professor at the University of Oregon School of Journalism and Communication discuss the challenges and opportunities facing newspapers with circulations under 50,000.

Griggs, Tim, "Hands across America: How to make local/national journalism collaborations work," NiemanLab, May 4, 2017, https://tinyurl.com/y7krhxdb.

The former publisher of The Texas Tribune, a digital-first, nonprofit news organization, looks at how national and local media operations can benefit from collaborating more with each other.

Heintz, Paul, "Can a Retired Judge Save Southern Vermont's Newspapers?" Seven Days, March 29, 2017, https://tinyurl.com/y9e7vo9y.

A Vermont weekly says a small group of investors, led by retired Judge Frederic Rutberg, is trying to reinvigorate local daily newspapers in northern Massachusetts and southern Vermont.

Lee, Deron, "The pleasure and pain of going nonprofit," Columbia Journalism Review, May 8, 2017, https://tinyurl.com/ycqezepz.

By becoming nonprofits, some local news websites have increased readership, expanded their staffs and seen their donations exceed the revenue they generated as for-profit papers. However, local sites are still having problems expanding and obtaining funding.

Uberti, David, "Gannett and the last great local hope," Columbia Journalism Review, spring 2017, https://tinyurl.com/y7x9udoc.

A media analyst says Gannett's national reach can help the company's 109 local newspapers do more with less, but he notes that the push to share content online may make it harder for those papers to retain their local flavor.

Warren, James, "New York Times editor: Local news is the biggest 'crisis' in journalism," Poynter, May 31, 2017, https://tinyurl.com/yaw9wj7z.

New York Times Executive Editor Dean Baquet discusses why it is important to sustain and invigorate local and regional journalism.

Trump Effect

Ingram, Mathew, "Trump's Victory Has People Signing up For News Like It's Going Out of Style," Fortune, March 7, 2017, https://tinyurl.com/z9yvyzy.

The New York Times, The Washington Post, Mother Jones and other publications have seen increased subscriptions or donations this year, thanks to a renewed interest in public service journalism apparently linked to the election of Donald Trump.

Scutari, Mike, "We Knew Trump Was Good For Nonprofit Journalism, But This Is Getting Ridiculous," *Inside Philanthropy*, April 17, 2017, https://tinyurl.com/ya2dloh8.

Donations and grants to nonprofit journalism organizations have risen sharply since Donald Trump was elected president.

Schreckinger, Ben, and Hadas Gold, "Trump's fake war on the fake news," *Politico Magazine*, May/June 2017, https://tinyurl.com/yb6q7wgt.

Although the president has used alarming rhetoric to denigrate the press, the relationship between the White House and news outlets is much more complex than the one of deep hostility that the public perceives.

Swaim, Barton, "We're not learning from the Trump story — because we've peeked at the last page," *The Washington Post*, May 18, 2017, http://tinyurl.com/ybsvlp29.

The writer says journalists covering the Trump administration must be aware of how their own expectations of a Trump presidency could affect their work.

Trust in the Media

Baker, Mitchell, "Restoring the Public's Trust in American Journalism," *The Atlantic*, May 11, 2017, https://tinyurl.com/y77zmhwo.

The internet has helped make politicians more accountable and the public more informed, but it also has aided the spread of fake news, eroding trust in democratic institutions.

Barthel, Michael, and Amy Mitchell, "Americans' Attitudes About the News Media Deeply Divided Along Partisan Lines," Pew Research Center, May 10, 2017, https://tinyurl.com/lwhqwt2.

Republicans and Democrats disagree more than ever about the media's watchdog role, with many Democrats saying the media's criticism helps keep political leaders in line and many Republicans saying such criticism keeps leaders from doing their jobs.

Blake, Aaron, "Trump's media coverage has been 4-to-1 negative — but that isn't really the point," *The Washington Post*, May 19, 2017, https://tinyurl.com/y8qetsvn.

The Washington Post's political analysis blog says a study showing that President Trump received strongly negative news coverage during his first 100 days doesn't mean the media is out to get him.

Mullin, Benjamin, "Can trust in the news be repaired? Facebook, Craig Newmark, Mozilla and others are spending $14 million to try," Poynter, April 3, 2017, http://tinyurl.com/nyfkvh4.

Working with the City University of New York Graduate School of Journalism, the newly launched News Integrity Initiative — funded by organizations such as Facebook, Mozilla and the Ford Initiative — is seeking to help the public and news organizations deal with mistrust and misinformation.

Pogue, David, "What Facebook Is Doing to Combat Fake News," *Scientific American*, Feb. 1, 2017, http://tinyurl.com/h26du9a.

Facebook is taking steps to stop the spread of fake news and is giving users tools to help in the fight.

Shafer, Jack, and Tucker Doherty, "The Media Bubble Is Worse Than You Think," *Politico Magazine*, May/June 2017, https://tinyurl.com/mhs2emm.

The decline of print journalism and the rise of online media have redistributed journalists, putting most of them in extremely liberal areas of the country where their reporting reflects their readers' political views.

Stanley, Timothy, "Trump is right about media bias," CNN, April 30, 2017, https://tinyurl.com/khw5axb.

A historian and columnist for Britain's *Daily Telegraph* says reporters are just as guided by their personal biases and "tribal passions" as are most Americans, and journalists in the age of Donald Trump increasingly see themselves as participants in a resistance movement.

Sullivan, Margaret, "Omidyar network gives $100 million to boost journalism and fight hate speech," *The Washington Post*, April 4, 2017, http://tinyurl.com/ycpnpdn6.

A nonprofit foundation and investment firm created by eBay founder Pierre Omidyar is donating $100 million to organizations such as The International Consortium of Investigative Journalists, the Anti-Defamation League and the Latin American Alliance for Civic Technology to help fight fake news, corruption, hate and mistrust.

CITING *CQ RESEARCHER*

Sample formats for citing these reports in a bibliography include the ones listed below. Preferred styles and formats vary, so please check with your instructor or professor.

MLA STYLE

Mantel, Barbara. "Coal Industry's Future." CQ Researcher 17 June 2016: 529-552.

APA STYLE

Mantel, B. (2016, June 17). Coal Industry's Future. *CQ Researcher, 6*, 529-552.

CHICAGO STYLE

Mantel, Barbara. "Coal Industry's Future." *CQ Researcher*, June 17, 2016, 529-52.

In-depth Reports on Issues in the News

Are you writing a paper?

Need backup for a debate?

Want to become an expert on an issue?

For 90 years, students have turned to *CQ Researcher* for in-depth reporting on issues in the news. Reports on a full range of political and social issues are now available. Following is a selection of recent reports:

Civil Liberties
Privacy and the Internet, 12/15
Intelligence Reform, 5/15
Religion and Law, 11/14

Crime/Law
High-Tech Policing, 4/17
Forensic Science Controversies, 2/17
Jailing Debtors, 9/16
Decriminalizing Prostitution, 4/16
Restorative Justice, 2/16
The Dark Web, 1/16
Immigrant Detention, 10/15

Education
Charter Schools, 3/17
Civic Education, 2/17
Student Debt, 11/16
Apprenticeships, 10/16

Environment/Society
Anti-Semitism, 5/17
Native American Sovereignty, 5/17
Women in Prison, 3/17
Guns on Campus, 1/17
Mass Transit, 12/16
Arctic Development, 12/16

Health/Safety
Pandemic Threat, 6/17
Sports and Sexual Assault, 4/17
Reducing Traffic Deaths, 2/17
Opioid Crisis, 10/16
Mosquito-Borne Disease, 7/16

Politics/Economy
North Korea Showdown, 5/17
Rethinking Foreign Aid, 4/17
Reviving Rural Economies, 3/17
Immigrants and the Economy, 2/17
Trump Presidency, 1/17

Upcoming Reports

Food Labeling, 6/16/17   Christian Right, 6/23/17   Hunger in America, 7/7/17

ACCESS

CQ Researcher is available in print and online. For access, visit your library or www.cqresearcher.com.

STAY CURRENT

For notice of upcoming *CQ Researcher* reports or to learn more about *CQ Researcher* products, subscribe to the free email newsletters, *CQ Researcher Alert!* and *CQ Researcher News*: http://cqpress.com/newsletters.

PURCHASE

To purchase a *CQ Researcher* report in print or electronic format (PDF), visit www.cqpress.com or call 866-427-7737. Single reports start at $15. Bulk purchase discounts and electronic-rights licensing are also available.

SUBSCRIBE

Annual full-service *CQ Researcher* subscriptions—including 44 reports a year, monthly index updates, and a bound volume—start at $1,131. Add $25 for domestic postage.

CQ Researcher Online offers a backfile from 1991 and a number of tools to simplify research. For pricing information, call 800-818-7243 or 805-499-9774 or email librarysales@sagepub.com.

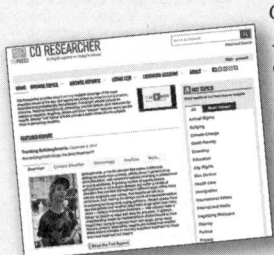

CQ RESEARCHER

In-depth reports on today's issues

Published by CQ Press, an Imprint of SAGE Publications, Inc.

www.cqresearcher.com

Food Labeling

Should the government require clearer packaging?

C onsumer advocates want the food industry to put clearer nutrition information on food labels, contending that manufacturers often mislead consumers by proclaiming products are "healthy" or "natural." The critics are pressing the Food and Drug Administration (FDA) to define such terms and require labels to make nutrition information easier to find and comprehend. Some consumer advocates argue that a symbol such as a stoplight should be used on labels to rate food simply as "healthy" or "unhealthy." But the food industry says it already has taken steps to give consumers more useful and understandable nutrition information, pointing to growing adoption of its Facts Up Front labeling, which lists fat, salt, sugar and calorie content on package fronts. Both sides are watching the Trump administration closely, as it already has delayed a key labeling regulation, and many observers predict more rule delays are to come. Meanwhile, critics are questioning the validity of industry-backed food research and the safety of artificial food dyes in cereal, candy and other foods.

A shopper in Irvine, Calif., learns about healthy food ingredients as part of the "Shop with Your Doc" program sponsored by the St. Joseph Hoag Health hospital group. Consumer advocates want to make nutrition information on labels easier to understand, but some in the food industry says its Facts Up Front labeling already does that.

CQ Researcher • June 16, 2017 • www.cqresearcher.com
Volume 27, Number 22 • Pages 509-532

I N S I D E — THIS REPORT

THE ISSUES **511**

BACKGROUND **517**

CHRONOLOGY **519**

CURRENT SITUATION **523**

AT ISSUE......................**525**

OUTLOOK **526**

BIBLIOGRAPHY **530**

THE NEXT STEP **531**

THE ISSUES

511   • Does the food industry have too much influence over food labeling?
• Do food packaging labels influence consumer behavior?
• Should the government adopt a system that rates foods as good or bad?

BACKGROUND

517   **Secret Ingredients**
Early manufacturers used to conceal problems in foods.

517   **Dietary Evolution**
Knowledge of healthy eating was poor in the early 1900s.

518   **Health Claims Grow**
In the 1980s, regulators loosened rules on claims that an ingredient could help reduce disease.

520   **Labeling Transfats**
The controversial ingredients came to be seen as dangerous in the 1990s.

CURRENT SITUATION

523   **New Labels**
A new rule for disclosing genetically modified organisms (GMOs) is in the offing.

524   **State Efforts**
Food companies oppose patchwork labeling laws.

524   **Defining Healthy**
The FDA seeks to define commonly used words.

OUTLOOK

526   **Anti-Regulatory Fervor**
Analysts predict the campaign to improve labeling will stall.

SIDEBARS AND GRAPHICS

512   **Nutrition Facts Label to Get a Makeover**
Changes are aimed at presenting more-accurate information.

513   **Most Consumers Read Nutrition Information**
Only 9 percent say they never consult the Nutrition Facts label.

516   **Americans Retain Love of Meat**
Consumers are eating more fruit, vegetables — and meat.

519   **Chronology**
Key events since 1902.

520   **Critics Say Some Food Studies Are Tainted**
"Industry funding only has one purpose, and that is to sell food products."

522   **Food Dyes Scrutinized for Impact on Children**
Calls are growing for manufactures to add warning labels.

525   **At Issue:**
Should food labels feature "healthy" or "unhealthy" ratings?

FOR FURTHER RESEARCH

529   **For More Information**
Organizations to contact.

530   **Bibliography**
Selected sources used.

531   **The Next Step**
Additional articles.

531   **Citing _CQ Researcher_**
Sample bibliography formats.

Cover: AFP/Getty Images/Robyn Beck

CQ RESEARCHER

June 16, 2017
Volume 27, Number 22

EXECUTIVE EDITOR: Thomas J. Billitteri
tjb@sagepub.com

ASSISTANT MANAGING EDITORS: Kenneth Fireman, kenneth.fireman@sagepub.com, Kathy Koch, kathy.koch@sagepub.com, Scott Rohrer, scott.rohrer@sagepub.com

ASSOCIATE MANAGING EDITOR: Val Ellicott

SENIOR CONTRIBUTING EDITOR:
Thomas J. Colin
tom.colin@sagepub.com

CONTRIBUTING WRITERS: Marcia Clemmitt, Sarah Glazer, Reed Karaim, Barbara Mantel, Chuck McCutcheon, Tom Price

SENIOR PROJECT EDITOR: Olu B. Davis

INTERN: Robert DePaolo

FACT CHECKERS: Eva P. Dasher, Michelle Harris, Betsy Towner Levine, Robin Palmer

SAGE Publishing | **CQPRESS**

Los Angeles I London I New Delhi
Singapore I Washington DC I Melbourne

An Imprint of SAGE Publications, Inc.

SENIOR VICE PRESIDENT, GLOBAL LEARNING RESOURCES:
Karen Phillips

EXECUTIVE DIRECTOR, ONLINE LIBRARY AND REFERENCE PUBLISHING:
Todd Baldwin

CQ Researcher (ISSN 1056-2036) is printed on acid-free paper. Published weekly, except: (March wk. 4) (May wk. 4) (July wks. 1, 2) (Aug. wks. 2, 3) (Nov. wk. 4) and (Dec. wks. 3, 4). Published by SAGE Publications, Inc., 2455 Teller Rd., Thousand Oaks, CA 91320. Annual full-service subscriptions start at $1,131. For pricing, call 1-800-818-7243. To purchase a CQ Researcher report in print or electronic format (PDF), visit www.cqpress. com or call 866-427-7737. Single reports start at $15. Bulk purchase discounts and electronic-rights licensing are also available. Periodicals postage paid at Thousand Oaks, California, and at additional mailing offices. POSTMASTER: Send address changes to CQ Researcher, 2600 Virginia Ave., N.W., Suite 600, Washington, DC 20037.

Food Labeling

BY RACHEL KAUFMAN

THE ISSUES

With a bright, sun-splashed design, Nature Valley touts its granola bars by proclaiming on the package's front: "Made with 100% NATURAL whole grain oats."

Consumer health advocates beg to differ. The granola bars, they contend, are not "natural" because they contain the pesticide glyphosate, a carcinogen they say is potentially harmful to humans. A Brooklyn, N.Y., law firm filed four class-action lawsuits on consumers' behalf in August 2016 accusing General Mills, maker of Nature Valley granola bars, of deceptive packaging.

One of the suits, filed in the U.S. District Court in the Eastern District of New York, claims General Mills is misleading consumers "concerned about the potential health risks and environmental damage caused by artificial-chemical-laden foods, especially packaged foods." The suit demands that the company remove the word "natural" from its label and pay back buyers of the granola bars.

But General Mills rejects the consumer claim, saying "We stand behind our products and the accuracy of our labels." [1]

The skirmish is the latest in an expanding battle over what information packaged-food labels should contain, at a time when most Americans' calories come from processed food. [2] Food industry groups are hopeful that Scott Gottlieb, President Trump's new Food and Drug Administration (FDA) commissioner, will be hostile to regulations, while consumer groups worry that their campaign to force companies to

Scott Gottlieb, President Trump's new Food and Drug Administration commissioner, testified in April that he supported delaying the rollout of the new Nutrition Facts label until 2021. His overall views drew the praise of many in the food industry and the concern of consumer groups, which fear regulatory changes will slow.

more accurately label foods as "natural," "healthy" or "organic" will falter.

The battleground in this dispute is a small patch of turf — the food package and what should be on it. Currently, federal regulations permit front-of-package labeling to contain health claims, logos certifying that a product meets certain standards and other badges, marks and rating systems. The Nutrition Facts label on the back provides details, including serving sizes, calories and the amount of sodium, protein and carbohydrates.

Consumer advocates want both labels to be not only more accurate but simpler, saying the various numbers specifying grams, percent of daily values and calories from fat can be confusing.

They also are bringing more class-action suits against food manufacturers, whom they accuse of boosting sales by falsely claiming their products are healthy.

"The Nutrition Facts labels are tough for people who are not fairly knowledgeable," says Michael Jacobson, co-founder of the Center for Science in the Public Interest (CSPI), a food-safety and nutrition advocacy group in Washington. "If you think of somebody with a high school education, those [panels] are hard. All those numbers."

Industry groups and some experts say food manufacturers also want better labels. This isn't "a story of 'big bad food companies are evil and do evil things and [are] in cahoots with the government in trying to kill us,' " says David Schleifer, an expert on transfats at the nonpartisan think tank Public Agenda. Food companies "capitalize on trends," he says. "So whether the trend is pie, barbecue or low sodium or organic . . . industry capitalizes on whatever they can, and that includes health trends."

But despite general agreement on the need for more accurate and clearer labeling, the details are proving elusive and controversial, experts lament.

After decades of lobbying by public-interest groups, the FDA last year finalized changes to the Nutrition Facts label, which looks largely the same as it did in 1994 when it was introduced. [3]

The most important changes included an update to serving sizes, a larger font for "total calories" and, perhaps most controversially, a new listing for "added sugars" showing how much

Nutrition Facts Label to Get a Makeover

After decades of lobbying by public-interest groups, the Food and Drug Administration (FDA) finalized changes to the Nutrition Facts label last year. The new label, which had been scheduled to take effect July 26, 2018, but which has been delayed, was designed to present more-accurate nutrition information by, among other things, updating recommended serving sizes and displaying calorie counts more prominently. Some food manufacturers have already introduced the new label on their products, and they may be hurt if their competitors do not make the same change.

Old Label Versus the New

Source: "Side-by-Side Comparison," Food and Drug Administration, http://tinyurl.com/y7bu3gsx

sugar the manufacturer has added to the product. [4] *

The new Nutrition Facts label was scheduled to be required beginning July 26, 2018, but the FDA on June 13

announced it is indefinitely delaying implementation. [5]

Another contentious issue in recent years has been front-of-package claims.

For years, the Institute of Medicine (IOM), part of the National Academies, has recommended that the FDA adopt a unified, mandatory system that would assign ratings to packaged foods — up to three stars or checkmarks on the front label — based on whether the food has "acceptable" levels of saturated and transfats, sodium and added

sugars. The agency most recently studied the issue in 2010 and 2012, releasing two reports considered the gold standard in the field by both food labeling reform advocates and industry. [6]

But shortly before the institute released its second report, the Grocery Manufacturers Association and the Food Marketing Institute, two large industry associations, unveiled their own front-of-package system. Their "Facts Up Front" label, designed to be simple to grasp, lists calories, saturated fat, sodium and sugar counts. Consumer groups including the CSPI and scientists such as Marion Nestle, a nutrition professor at New York University, called it an "end run" around potential FDA rulemaking. [7]

The FDA held off issuing new rules, saying it wanted to monitor the Facts Up Front approach. If the system were adopted widely, the agency said, it "may contribute to FDA's public health goals" and would "provide consumers more ready access to information about the nutrient content of packaged foods, without compromising consumer protection." [8]

Despite an aggressive effort to improve food labeling by former first lady Michelle Obama and her Let's Move! anti-obesity campaign, the FDA never took additional steps. With Trump in the White House, consumer advocates worry further delays will result because he has condemned what he calls excessive federal regulation.

During the 2016 presidential campaign, Trump promised in a fact sheet to eliminate the "FDA Food Police" who he said "govern the soil farmers use, farm and food production hygiene, food packaging, food temperatures, and even what animals may roam which fields and when." (The campaign later took down the fact sheet and replaced it with one that didn't mention the FDA. [9]) After his inauguration, Trump pledged to reduce FDA regulations by 75 percent. [10]

Industry groups, as a result, are hopeful they will get a sympathetic hearing, especially after the Senate confirmed Gottlieb on May 9.

---

* Added sugars come in a variety of forms, some of which are not obvious, such as anhydrous dextrose, high-fructose corn syrup, maltose and sucrose. Distinguishing the relative proportions of those sugars in a food can be difficult because of the presence of naturally occurring sugars, such as milk sugar in plain yogurt.

"Scott Gottlieb is an excellent choice to lead FDA," the Grocery Manufacturers Association said in a statement. [11] Likewise, the president of the Independent Bakers Association (IBA), a Washington-based trade association representing 200 wholesale bakeries, said, "Dr. Gottlieb doesn't have preconceived notions about food policy. This should allow IBA and its allies to drive policy in coordination with FDA leaders, rather than having to play defense for years at a time." [12]

At least 64 countries require foods with GMO ingredients to be labeled, and Congress last July mandated such labels in the United States, after dozens of states had considered similar measures. [13] GMOs are ingredients made from crops whose DNA has been altered in the lab, usually to resist pesticides and herbicides. Although the FDA considers genetically modified foods safe, some consumer groups have fought for years to get them labeled, despite strong opposition from the food and biotechnology industries. [14]

Debra Eschmeyer, who was executive director of Obama's Let's Move! initiative, says American diets need to change and that packaged food and its messaging must change as well. "[But] we have to be realistic. People are busy," she says, and are going to eat packaged foods. The trick is giving them "the most scientifically relevant information . . . so they can make the right choice for their families."

As industry, government and consumer groups wrestle over these issues, here are some of the questions they are debating:

Does the food industry have too much influence over food labeling?

The requirement for an "added sugars" line on the new Nutrition Facts panel was the product of decades of lobbying by public-interest groups, which squared off against industry groups arguing the information was unnecessary and potentially inaccurate.

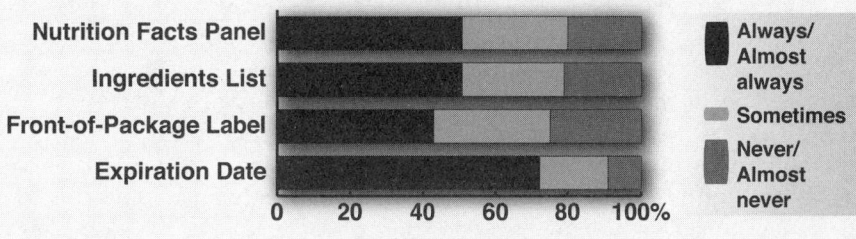

Most Consumers Read Nutrition Information

A majority of consumers consult the Nutrition Facts panel on the back of food packages, according to a 2017 survey by the International Food Information Council Foundation, an industry-backed group that studies food safety and nutrition. Majorities also read the ingredients list and expiration date. But many experts question how much of the information on labels consumers understand.

Packaging Information Consulted During Purchase, 2017

Source: "2017 Food & Health Survey," International Food Information Council Foundation, 2017, p. 45, http://tinyurl.com/y9oxeqz4

"Industry has tremendous influence," says the CSPI's Jacobson. "It blocks just about anything."

The Sugar Association, which represents sugar growers and refiners, was initially among the most vocal opponents of the rule. It argued the line doesn't make sense scientifically because "metabolically, your cells don't know if the sugar came from an apple or a gummy bear, says association President Courtney Gaine, who is a dietitian and has a Ph.D. in nutrition science.

(Many nutritionists reject this claim as a half-truth: While the Sugar Association's statement is true, they say, the point is that apples have vitamins and fiber, while a gummy bear has neither.)

Gaine says that as a representative of growers and refiners, the Sugar Association has to oppose such policies as the added sugars line. The possibility the food industry will have to reformulate products so they contain less sugar "is real; we're seeing it in the U.K.," she says. "When you look at it that way, from a business perspective, there's a concern" the same thing will happen in the United States.

When the FDA proposes a new rule, it takes comments from the public and

industry, "This is a democracy," says Eschmeyer of the Let's Move! campaign. "Of course industry is going to contribute to the process, as they should."

However, regulators sometimes give the industry's comments greater weight than it should, says Jacobson. "In terms of numbers, the consumer comments [which typically support regulations] generally outweigh the industry comments [which typically oppose regulation]," he says. "But in terms of substance and impact, industry comments count for a whole lot more. Because FDA knows that companies are powerful and they could sue the agency if they don't like the outcome. They could go to Congress and try to get regulations overturned or derailed."

Traditional food and beverage industry groups outspend consumer watchdogs and producers of so-called good — healthy — food. Companies such as Coca Cola, PepsiCo, Kellogg's and Kraft spent more than $36 million on lobbying in 2014, according to records examined by *Politico*, whereas the producers of "good food" spent little. For example, the Organic Trade Association, which represents farmers, manufacturers and retailers of organic foods, spent about $190,000 on lobbying that year, and a spokesperson for organic meat producer Applegate said the company has "never considered hiring a lobbyist," preferring instead to focus on changing "voter sentiment." [15]

An analysis by the Environmental Working Group, an advocacy group that opposes GMOs, found that food and biotechnology industries spent $51.6 million in the first half of 2015 fighting mandatory GMO labeling laws in the United States, in contrast to the $2.5 million spent by advocates of GMO labeling. [16]

The balance of power may change as "good food" producers realize the gains to be had with a presence on Capitol Hill, some analysts say. The Plant Based Foods Association, founded by food lawyer Michele Simon, promotes veggie-friendly initiatives in Congress. Yogurt-maker Chobani, known for its simple ingredients, donates yogurt to congressional offices, and Ben & Jerry's served ice cream to congressional staff to encourage mandatory GMO labeling. The company began phasing out GMO ingredients from its ice cream in 2013. [17]

What appears on packaged food, on both the front and the back, reflects the complex interplay between lobbying groups, scientists and government agencies.

When KIND, a maker of popular granola bars, began calling its foods "healthy" on labels, the FDA sent the company a warning letter saying its products did not meet the legal definition of healthy, because it was not low in fat. [18] Under regulations last updated in 1993, a "healthy" food had to be low in fat.

KIND CEO Daniel Lubetzky pointed out that that definition excluded many foods now generally considered healthy by the public, such as nuts, avocados and olives. [19] The company requested that the FDA reevaluate its criteria, and the agency reversed itself, allowing

KIND to include "healthy" on its labels. It also promised to take a look at redefining the term.

Lubetzky later said that, based on his years of observing industry lobbying practices, he concluded his industry had too much power in food policy. In February 2017, he pledged $25 million to create a public advocacy organization, Feed the Truth, to counteract that influence. [20] To avoid any potential conflicts of interest, he said he will "cut the cord" from Feed the Truth after supplying the initial grant money.

"In establishing Feed the Truth," Lubetzky said, "my intent is to elevate reputable science, bolster the voices of the nutrition community and improve the guidance and information offered to Americans." [21]

Do food packaging labels influence consumer behavior?

When the Nutrition Facts panel was introduced in 1994, Australian researchers estimated that Americans would collectively gain up to 2.1 million years of life over 20 years due to better health. [22] Those estimates were not accurate, although experts say it is hard to disentangle the effects of the label from other factors that might affect diet and health.

Studies indicate that most Americans claiming they read the Nutrition Facts panel may not understand the information presented. Several studies show a correlation between reading Nutrition Facts and eating healthier, but it is unclear whether Nutrition Facts is the reason for better diets. [23]

However, in the decades since the Nutrition Facts panel debuted, obesity has increased dramatically in the United States. "Nutrition Facts haven't been as effective as we had hoped," the CPSI's Jacobson says.

Other information on food packages apparently doesn't have much effect, either.

What people say they do (read nutrition labels and health claims, and

make purchasing decisions accordingly) might be different from what they actually do (purchase unhealthy foods, because they taste good or are familiar, or are inexpensive or convenient).

Numerous studies have looked at what consumers say they do in the grocery store, but few have examined what they actually do, so there is a dearth of information on how labeling really affects behavior. When the Institute of Medicine compiled its two reports on front-of-package labeling, the researchers found only a few studies over the past three decades on consumers' grocery purchasing behavior. [24]

In a 1985 study, researchers placed signs on shelves for products that had "low sodium" or "reduced fat" and compared their sales to those in control stores selling the same products but without the signs. On average, sales of the labeled products were 4 to 8 percent higher than sales of unlabeled products. [25]

More recent studies in the 2000s and 2010s were inconclusive as to whether labels encouraged consumers to buy healthier products. In many cases, when a company actively markets its foods as healthier, sales decrease; one example was Campbell's use of lower sodium in its "Select Harvest" line of soups. In 2011, the company announced it was putting some of the salt back. "Not everyone is willing to make a taste trade-off; not everyone is looking for low sodium," a Campbell's spokesperson said. [26]

Transfat expert Schleifer says this incident may have inspired companies to reformulate their products to be healthier without advertising it. "If it was advertised, people would start thinking about the fact that it tasted less salty," he says. "People are so sensitive to [the taste of salt]."

In addition, statements on food packages can be confusing or misleading, causing even the best-intentioned consumers to make errors.

In a workshop hosted by the FDA in March 2017, Linda Verrill, a sociologist at the agency's Center for Food Safety and Applied Nutrition, said marketing messages cause much consumer confusion. "We hear a lot that consumers think that whatever is sold in the marketplace or put on the label is approved by someone," she said. That is not entirely true. [27]

The FDA strictly regulates some statements on food packages but not others:

• To be labeled "reduced-calorie," a food must have at least 25 percent fewer calories per serving than a comparable food. Similar regulations apply to foods labeled "lite" or "low in fat."

• "Natural" does not have a legal definition, so manufacturers can use it on anything.

• The "healthy" label is allowed if the food meets certain nutritional requirements.

• Smart" or "fit": These two terms are unregulated.

Producers also can highlight nutrients and their link to preventing certain diseases. Examples include "good source of protein" and "diets rich in whole grain foods and other plant foods, and low in total fat, saturated fat, and cholesterol may help reduce the risk of heart disease." [28]

Food makers are free to do whatever they want with the rest of their package design.

"When you look at the front of a package, there's so many things trying to grab your attention and maybe trying to distract you from certain things," Jacobson says. Examples include high sodium or fat content or the presence of artificial colors or transfats.

The packaged food industry says it wants "smart consumers who can make intelligent choices, but they don't mind if you remain ignorant either," wrote Hank Cardello, a former food industry executive, in his book *Stuffed: An Insider's Look at Who's (Really) Making America Fat and How the Food Industry Can Fix It*. "They're not consciously trying to confuse you; they're merely trying

Major supermarket chains in the United Kingdom adopted a "traffic light" label, similar to this one at Sainsbury's, for their made-in-store and house-brand foods. Instead of only listing the fat, sugar, salt and calories in a food, the label grades those numbers and assigns them a rating of red, orange or green, depending on their healthiness.

to sell you, or more subtly, lull you into just giving up and buying," he wrote. "They take out the transfats, but they are still peddling saturated fats. They say they take away the carbs, but there weren't any to begin with." [29]

Grocery Manufacturers Association spokesman Roger Lowe said in an email that such a view is outdated. "The fact is that [the Grocery Manufacturers Association] and its members are working to give consumers tools and information to make informed decisions about the products they buy and consume," he said, pointing to Facts Up Front and a barcode system called SmartLabel, which allows consumers to get more nutrition information on their smartphones.

Cardello acknowledges that he's seen positive changes in the industry since writing his book in 2009, due in large part to consumer pressure. "Consumers are demanding transparency now," he says.

He says he still sees some misleading or inaccurate labels, and blames a lack of communication between company

leadership and the marketing department. "You might have the CEO and the president saying, 'I'm all with you' [on transparency], but when it comes down to the marketing director level, they're charged with growing their business. That's part of the problem, but I think it's getting better."

Today, with many consumers adopting gluten-free diets (thanks in part to debunked books such as *Wheat Belly*), the label "gluten-free" is appearing on foods and beverages, such as tea, that never had gluten in the first place. [30]

Such claims could be made with the best of intentions, says Sally Greenberg, president of the National Consumers League, a consumer advocacy group in Washington. "Maybe [a consumer doesn't] understand what gluten is. I imagine there might be a parent who has a kid with celiac," an autoimmune disorder that can damage the small intestine if gluten is ingested, Greenberg says. The parent "might say, 'Maybe there's something gluten-related, some wheat product, I don't know about that might be in here.' "

Americans Retain Love of Meat

Americans ate more fruits and vegetables in 2014 than in 1970, but not enough to meet levels recommended under the government's 2015-20 Dietary Guidelines. But they did eat above the recommended levels for meat, eggs, nuts and grains.

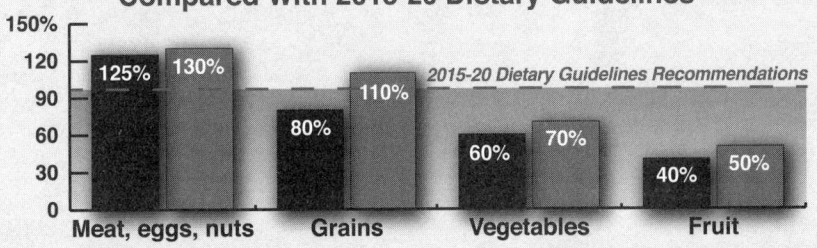

Estimated Average U.S. Consumption in 1970 and 2014, Compared With 2015-20 Dietary Guidelines

2015-20 Dietary Guidelines Recommendations

Meat, eggs, nuts: 125%, 130%
Grains: 80%, 110%
Vegetables: 60%, 70%
Fruit: 40%, 50%

■ % of Guidelines, 1970
■ % of Guidelines, 2014

Source: "Estimated average U.S. consumption compared to recommendations, 1970 and 2014," Economic Research Service, U.S. Department of Agriculture, http://tinyurl.com/ya6zhkyn

Should the government adopt a system that rates foods as good or bad?

Some retailers and food makers in the United Kingdom use "traffic-light" labeling, a voluntary system recommended by the U.K.'s Food Standards Agency. [31]

The front-of-package system, adopted in 2006, is called a traffic light because instead of simply listing the fat, sugar, salt and calories in a food, it grades those numbers and assigns them a rating of red, orange or green, depending on whether the amounts are considered healthy or not. Each product participating in the system has five colored icons on the front of the package, rating the food for calories, fat, total sugar, saturated fat and salt.

The system, while optional for manufacturers, is polarizing. Major supermarket chains adopted the approach only for their made-in-store and house-brand foods. And Mars U.K., Nestlé U.K., PepsiCo U.K. and other major manufacturers, which account for about 60 percent of food sales in the U.K., also use traffic lights. But Coca-Cola, Kellogg's and Mondelez — the maker of Oreo, Chips Ahoy!, Cadbury and other popular products — do not. [32]

Critics of such a rating system say no food is inherently unhealthy or healthy, because only diets can be healthy or unhealthy. "Classification of specific foods as good or bad is overly simplistic and can foster unhealthy eating behaviors" by encouraging people to eat unbalanced diets, the Academy of Nutrition and Dietetics, a Chicago-based organization representing food and nutrition professionals, said. [33]

In addition, according to at least one study, the new system confuses some consumers, who are unsure whether it's better to eat a food with two reds and three greens or five oranges. Nevertheless, France, Ecuador, Chile and other countries have adopted similar systems. [34]

Several U.S. food industry groups say a traffic-light system would be unworkable in this country because of the difficulty in getting the industry, the FDA and consumer advocates to agree on which foods are healthy. Instead, they favor a rating system that presents nutrition data on the package front, as Facts Up Front does.

"When we looked at developing Facts Up Front, we looked at the other systems. And the research at the time

— and I think it bears true today — is that all of these systems are only as useful as the consumer education effort behind them," says Mary Sophos, the Grocery Manufacturers Association's executive vice president for policy and strategic planning.

"We think that Facts Up Front, because it reports the facts and doesn't try and add a lot of interpretation, probably serves the consumer best," she says. "What we hear from consumers is, they want the facts, and they can make up their own mind."

CSPI's Jacobson, who favors a traffic-light-type system, disagrees. "I think one of the things that's really needed is a mandatory symbol of some sort on the front of the package that would convey to the consumer the overall nutritional value," he says. "Is it good, is it bad, is it somewhere in between?"

He calls Facts Up Front "totally worthless." All it does, Jacobson says, is "drag . . . some of the information from the nutrition label and puts it on the [front]." He argues that because the nutrition label is hard for many Americans to use, simply putting the same information on the front doesn't help them make a better decision. Jacobson adds that the food industry's system is "designed to occupy the field and say, 'We don't need a different system.' "

But the Grocery Manufacturers Association and the Food Marketing Institute say their system is working. They cite research commissioned by the grocers group showing that nine in 10 shoppers "agree that Facts Up Front makes nutrition information easy to find and use . . . and that it is simple to understand." [35]

Sophos says the two industry groups worked closely with the FDA and other government agencies to develop Facts Up Front. "We felt on solid ground in terms of the nutrients we selected," she says. "If you ask consumers who read labels, those are the nutrients they would look for when shopping." The system is "widely adopted," Sophos says.

NYU's Nestle scoffed at industry claims about the usefulness of Facts Up Front and noted that the grocery association was behind the survey. "Facts Up Front is a tool for selling, not buying," Nestle wrote. "Its purpose is to make highly processed foods look healthier, whether or not they really are." [36]

Eschmeyer, the "Let's Move!" ex-director, says studies are needed to determine whether "traffic lights" would work in the United States. "Why not just educate folks about the label so they can quickly make the decision?" she asks. "To me that would be the best and most empowering . . . to actually educate people."

The 28-member European Union (EU) is considering traffic-light labeling similar to the British version. But countries that produce "Protected Designation of Origin" foods, which cannot be reformulated by law, oppose it. [37]

For example, the manufacturer of an unprotected lunchmeat could tweak its recipe to lower the amount of fat in its product. But the maker of a traditional salami like Ciauscolo, whose "protected designation of origin" means it must be made the same way it was hundreds of years ago, could not. EU countries that oppose the labeling argue that their traditional foods would look less healthy in comparison.

The Brussels-based lobbying group Liaison Centre for the Meat Processing Industry in the European Union said 99 percent of meat products could receive red labels because of their fat content. But, in practice, because the system is voluntary it would be closer to 50 to 60 percent, based on data from the U.K. The lobbying group also warned of 20 percent reductions in meat sales, citing its data from the U.K., although independent studies have not noted such drastic effects. [38]

"So many other countries are beginning to implement these labeling schemes," the CSPI's Jacobson said "If Ecuador and Chile are doing it, why not the United States?" ∎

BACKGROUND

Secret Ingredients

The early 20th century was a veritable wild west of foods and drugs. Patent medicines whose ingredients were secret, but were often just vegetable extracts mixed with alcohol and morphine, were popular. Milk was sometimes watered down and colored with chalk, coffee could be mixed with dirt and rotten meat's taste was at times concealed with boric acid. [39]

Concerns about misleading food labels at the time centered on whether manufacturers used a chemical to conceal a problem in the food. The industry could make butter look fresher by adding turmeric or annatto, or brighten ketchup made from spoiled tomatoes with a little cochineal dye, while a little copper would make poorly canned peas look better. [40] But soon attention turned to those additives and how they might affect health.

In the early 1900s, Congress awarded chemist Harvey Wiley at the U.S. Department of Agriculture $5,000 to investigate the preservatives commonly used in foods — borax, salicylic acid and formaldehyde among them. He paid volunteers, dubbed the "Poison Squad," to ingest foods laced with these contaminants, then recorded the effects of the chemicals on their health. [41]

Although not very scientific, his studies drew widespread attention to the issue and led to the passage of the Pure Food and Drug Act in 1906. [42] The law required food manufacturers to accurately label a food's ingredients and banned interstate trafficking in adulterated foods.

In an essay in *The World's Work* magazine in 1907, Edward Ayers, a medical doctor, praised the changes. "The national Pure Food Law is a fairly complete enactment. It marks a vast improvement over previous conditions," Ayers wrote, noting that misleading labels would be banned. [43]

With the 1906 act, the FDA's modern role was born, although the agency would not receive its name until 1930. The agency's roots reach back to the Lincoln administration, when the Bureau of Chemistry was formed inside the Department of Agriculture. In 1927 the bureau was split up, with one entity becoming the Food, Drug and Insecticide Administration, which became the Food and Drug Administration three years later. [44]

Diet's Evolution

The American diet has evolved over the past century. An American of 1906 would hardly recognize a dinner table in 2017, nor understand the obsession with vitamins, transfats, sodium or GMOs.

When Congress passed the Pure Food and Drug Act, most Americans believed a good diet meant good health, but that was the extent of their knowledge. [45] Advertisements and food labels generally pointed to a food's "purity" or its "easy digestibility," but they rarely made specific claims.

Polish chemist Casimir Funk discovered vitamins in 1912, and the United States soon went "vitamin crazy" — fruit, milk and vegetables became much more popular. [46]

In the mid-20th century, "convenience foods" became more popular because of improvements in taste, the growing popularity of TV and the increase in women working outside the home having less time to prepare labor-intensive meals. At the same time, Americans' interest in diet shifted from seeking out "good" foods to avoiding "bad" foods. The discovery in 1961 that saturated fat was linked to cardiovascular disease kicked off decades of "avoidance" diets structured around avoiding foods with specific bad elements. [47]

By the 1960s, the organic movement was in full swing, pushed by health reformers and "hippies" who argued that food grown without chemicals was better for the Earth and for consumers. Many foods, such as granola, kombucha and tofu, that are now popular first reached Americans' consciousness through '60s-era co-ops. [48]

Nutrition went mainstream in the late 1970s and early '80s. [49] The Senate Nutrition Committee issued dietary goals in 1977, urging consumers to cut back on cholesterol, saturated fat, salt and sugar; the departments of Agriculture and Health and Human Services released dietary guidelines in 1980; and the National Research Council published a report in 1982 linking cured meats to cancer.

In the 1980s, "The word 'nutrition' was launched into the headlines more than in any previous decade," wrote Elaine McIntosh, a nutritionist. [50]

The interest in nutrition has only risen since then. Blueberries were the "granddad of the superfood trend" in the '90s, according to Barbara Brueckner, a food-trend consultant in San Francisco. [51]

Then came acai, kale, chia and quinoa. Polls of Millennials and Generation Z (those born after Millennials) show that younger Americans are looking for "better-for-you" products, food policy expert Eschmeyer says, driving more companies to produce foods that are at least marginally healthier.

Yet obesity is still rising, with 30.4 percent of Americans 20 and older reporting in 2015 they were obese, up from 19.4 percent in 1997, according to the CDC's National Health Interview Survey. Globally, more than 10 percent of the world's population is obese, a study in *The New England Journal of Medicine* reported. [52]

The word "obesity" entered the public consciousness only in the past 15 years, according to *The New York Times*, which tracks the percentage of stories it publishes that use the word. Before 2000, the word almost never appeared, *The Times* said. After that, "obesity" began to be mentioned in about one in 1,000 stories; the rate skyrocketed to four in 1,000 a decade later. That may not sound like a lot in absolute terms, but the paper publishes more than 200 pieces of content per day, which would mean obesity is mentioned in an average of one story per week. [53]

Now, 95 percent of Americans believe it is important to prevent obesity, according to a 2015 poll for the Robert Wood Johnson Foundation. [54]

Experts believe two of the biggest causes of the obesity epidemic are the proliferation of fast food and the large amount of food consumed away from home. [55] Whether labeling food will help reverse the trend remains to be seen.

Health Claims Grow

Before the mid-1980s, the FDA had banned food companies from making any packaging statement that an ingredient could help reduce disease. The agency had argued that making such a claim would mean the food needed to be regulated as a drug. [56]

But in 1984, based on research from the National Cancer Institute, Kellogg's labels on All-Bran cereal began saying high-fiber diets can reduce the risk of colon cancer. The company did not consult with the FDA before putting the claim on its cereal boxes. [57]

Although Kellogg's had worked with the cancer institute and felt its claim was on solid scientific footing, the FDA was concerned about what would happen if it allowed similar claims. "You open the door to all types of medical claims being made for food products," an FDA spokesman said at the time. "You then get the people who will sell bees' knees and other crazy foods." [58]

But the incident ultimately forced the FDA to reevaluate its stance. "The statement was truthful, not misleading, and provided a significant public health benefit," wrote food scientist Clare Hasler of the University of California, Davis, in a study on health claims. Millions of people, in fact, began buying high-fiber cereals as a result of this and similar fiber claims. [59]

The FDA's decision not to fine Kellogg's opened the floodgates to other health claims. By 1986, *The New York Times* was decrying a label on a package of Land O'Lakes butter touting its vitamin A benefits.

"[To] obtain just half the recommended daily allowance for vitamin A from butter, it would be necessary to consume more than 6 tablespoons, which contains 66 grams of fat and 600 calories," *The Times* wrote. [60] Clearly, the effects of those calories and fat would outweigh any possible improvements to eye health from vitamin A, it said.

In 1990, Congress passed the Nutrition Labeling and Education Act, which mandated the Nutrition Facts panel on all packaged foods, beginning in 1994. It also standardized and regulated claims like Kellogg's linking fiber to cancer, as well as standardized terms such as "low fat" and "lite."

The FDA now calls the Nutrition Facts panel "one of the most recognized graphics in the world," and food policy expert Eschmeyer says it is found on 800,000 products. [61]

In 2004, the agency began considering changes to the panel, but the label was still being studied when Barack Obama became president in 2009. A year later, first lady Obama took up the label-reform cause as part of her Let's Move! campaign. She said she was "driven by a simple belief: that parents deserve to have the information they need to make healthy choices for their kids." In 2014, after lobbying by the first lady's staff and consumer advocates and years of study, the FDA proposed changes to the label and finalized them in 2016. [62]

With regard to front-of-package claims, consumer advocates say some statements

Continued on p. 520

Chronology

1900s-1930s
As packaged food grows in popularity, food labeling is reformed.

1902
To investigate preservatives used in foods, government chemist Harvey Wiley conducts his "Poison Squad" tests, in which volunteers eat large quantities of borax, salicylic acid and formaldehyde.

1906
Upton Sinclair's *The Jungle* highlights the unsanitary practices of Chicago's meatpacking industry, leading to passage of the Pure Food and Drug Act, which disallows the sale of "mislabeled adulterated or misbranded or poisonous or deleterious foods." The act also gives birth to the agency that in 1930 becomes known as the Food and Drug Administration (FDA).

1912
Polish chemist Casimir Funk discovers vitamin B1 and proposes the existence of vitamins B2, C and D, leading to a vitamin craze in the U.S.

1924
Supreme Court rules that the Pure Food and Drug Act bans misleading statements on product packaging, even if they are technically true.

1933
The book *100,000,000 Guinea Pigs* argues the FDA is not protecting consumers from adulterated foods. The immensely popular book helps pave the way in 1938 for the Food, Drug and Cosmetic Act, expanding the FDA's authority. The act also defined food additives and mandated that producers of such additives demonstrate to a reasonable certainty that the additive is not harmful.

1938
The Food, Drug and Cosmetic Act replaces the Pure Food and Drug Act, expanding the FDA's authority.

1939
The FDA issues the first "food standards," defining what a product can contain before it can be legally sold.

1960s-1990s
A better understanding of nutrition and a growing reliance on convenience foods transform the American diet.

1961
Research links saturated fat to cardiovascular disease, launching decades of diets aimed at avoiding fat.

1962
In an address to Congress, President John F. Kennedy proclaims a Consumer Bill of Rights, including the right to safety and the right to be informed, leading to a number of food labeling regulations.

1980
U.S. Department of Agriculture issues first dietary guidelines, urging Americans to eat a variety of foods and avoid excessive sugar and sodium.

1984
Kellogg prints a claim, contrary to FDA policy at the time, on All-Bran cereal boxes that high-fiber diets can help reduce the risk of colon cancer. It opened the door to numerous health claims on foods.

1990
The Nutrition Labeling and Education Act makes the Nutrition Facts panel — which debuts four years later and lists the number of calories and amount of fat, carbohydrates, protein and some nutrients — mandatory on packaged foods and standardizes health claims like the one introduced by Kellogg.

2000s-Present
Consumers demand more information about the food they eat.

2003
In the first update to the Nutrition Facts panel, the FDA requires that food labels list the amount of transfat the foods contain.

2004
The Food Allergy Labeling and Consumer Protection Act requires foods containing any of the eight most common allergens to be labeled.

2006
The British government recommends a "traffic light" system to rate the healthiness of foods; many major supermarket chains as well as food manufacturers selling products in the U.K. adopt it.

2011
The food industry unveils Facts Up Front, the first standardized front-of-package labeling system in the U.S.

2016
The FDA finalizes rules that will overhaul the Nutrition Facts panel; changes include specifying how much added sugars a food has and displaying calories more prominently.

2017
President Trump taps physician Scott Gottlieb as head of the FDA; the agency announces in June it is delaying the implementation of the Nutrition Facts label.

Critics Say Some Food Studies Are Tainted

"Industry funding only has one purpose, and that is to sell food products."

Impartiality has long been a pillar of science, but many consumer health advocates question whether research funded by the food industry can meet that objective.

Marion Nestle, a nutritionist and food studies professor at New York University, examined 168 industry-funded studies published in the 12 months ending in March 2016. In all but 12, results favored the sponsors, she told "Nutrition Action," a health newsletter. [1]

And a 2013 article in *PLoS Medicine* — a peer-reviewed medical journal — looked at studies on the science of sugar-sweetened beverages. Ten of the 12 studies funded independently of the sugar industry found that drinking sugary beverages could cause weight gain. Five of the six industry-funded studies found no association between sugary drinks and weight gain. [2]

"[Industry] funding only has one purpose, and that is to sell food products," Nestle said. [3]

But the food industry — and many nutrition scientists — defend the integrity of industry-funded studies, saying industry financing makes research possible that would not otherwise get done because of budgetary pressures.

"My personal experience makes me reluctant to support a blanket condemnation of industry-supported research," wrote Dutch researcher Martijn B. Katan, who has received funding from food companies such as Nestlé, the European coffee industry and others. "Collaboration with industry has allowed me to discover things that I could not have found otherwise. [4]

"But," he acknowledged, "researchers dealing with industry may be subjected to pressure."

Industry has supported research for decades. The Sugar Research Foundation, a sugar producers' group now known as the Sugar Association, in 1965 funded the work of three Harvard scientists on the causes of heart disease, which was published in *The New England Journal of Medicine*. "The [sugar foundation] set the review's objective, contributed articles for inclusion and reviewed drafts," said a 2016 article in *JAMA Internal Medicine*, a journal of the American Medical Association. "The [foundation]'s role was not disclosed." [5]

That study, one of the *JAMA* authors said, was "very influential" and helped divert the medical community's focus from sugar to fat. [6] The industry then funded decades of research that downplayed the funding and role of sugar in coronary heart disease and played up the role of fat, the *JAMA* authors said. [7]

"We acknowledge that the Sugar Research Foundation should have exercised greater transparency in all of its research activities; however, when the studies in question were published, funding disclosures and transparency standards were not the norm they are today," the Sugar Association said in a statement. "Generally speaking, it is not only unfortunate but a disservice that industry-funded research is branded as tainted. What is often missing from the dialogue is that industry-funded research has been informative in addressing key issues." [8]

But some researchers maintain that even when industry is a hands-off funder it can influence study results in subtle ways, and scientists are not always aware of the effect. For example, researchers studying funding bias have found that industry funders can influence how studies are designed and whether they get published. [9]

Michele Simon, a food policy lawyer who also founded a trade association for makers of plant-based foods, studied the links between industry funding and the American Society for Nutrition, one of the most prestigious nutrition-science organizations in the country. She found that the society's "Sustaining Partners" — those who donate at least $10,000 per year to the organization — included the Sugar Association, PepsiCo,

Continued from p. 518

remain misleading. For one, numerous studies show that foods bearing claims such as "low in fat" or "high in fiber" have, at best, marginally better nutrition profiles than similar foods that do not carry the claims. [63] For another, consumer advocates say some food companies use claims deceptively to encourage people to purchase their products.

"[There] are food companies that will take advantage of any type of dietary advice that we can give," Lindsay Moyer, a senior nutritionist for the Center for Science in the Public Interest, said at the March FDA workshop. "Whether it's to eat more fruits and vegetables, eat more whole grains or choose healthier fats, they can find fruit snacks, vegetable chips, vegetable pasta, cookies, even chocolate milk, that are appealing to these claims." [64]

An FDA study found that snack foods with vitamins were more attractive to consumers, despite the fact that they weren't much healthier than nonfortified snack foods. If a snack food touted its added-vitamin benefits, the FDA said, consumers were less likely to read the Nutrition Facts label, were more likely to buy the food and were less likely to identify which of two foods were healthier. [65]

Labeling Transfats

By the mid-1990s, scientists were beginning to understand that transfats, once heralded as a replacement for artery-clogging lard and butter, may be more harmful than the saturated fats they replaced. Transfats, the Mayo Clinic says, are a cholesterol double whammy, because unlike other fats, they raise

Monsanto, the National Cattlemen's Beef Association and many other industry voices.

This support, she argues, raises questions. "It's not to say [the society] is totally bought, but . . . science has already told us that there's an inherent bias in that situation," she says, because of funders' ability to influence the direction studies take.

The American Society for Nutrition was one of the only mainstream scientific organizations to oppose placing a line on the new Nutrition Facts panel about "added sugars" — the amount of sugar the manufacturer added to the product — saying there was a "lack of consensus in the scientific evidence" on sugar's health effects. [10] The American Heart Association, the American Cancer Society and the American Diabetes Association all supported the inclusion of added sugars on labels.

"The Sugar Association is always seeking to further understand the role of sugar and health, but we rely on quality science and facts to drive our assertions," the association said. [11]

— Rachel Kaufman

Marion Nestle, a prominent nutrition expert at New York University, has challenged studies funded by the food industry, saying most of the 168 studies she examined favored the industry sponsors.

Getty Images/The New York Times/Neilson Barnard

[1] Caitlin Dow, "How industry influences nutrition science," *Nutrition Action*, March 15, 2017, http://tinyurl.com/y96cubz9.

[2] Maira Bes-Rastrollo *et al.*, "Financial Conflicts of Interest and Reporting Bias Regarding the Association between Sugar-Sweetened Beverages and Weight Gain: A Systematic Review of Systematic Reviews," *PLoS Medicine*, Dec. 31, 2013, http://tinyurl.com/y8hm9ez7.

[3] Dow, *op. cit.*

[4] Martijn B. Katan, "Does Industry Sponsorship Undermine the Integrity of Nutrition Research?" *PLoS Medicine*, Jan. 9, 2007, http://tinyurl.com/yclaybkk.

[5] Cristin E. Kearns, Laura A. Schmidt and Stanton A. Glantz, "Sugar Industry and Coronary Heart Disease Research: A Historical Analysis of Internal Industry Documents," *JAMA Internal Medicine*, Nov. 1, 2016, http://tinyurl.com/hoxgxao; Robert B. McGandy, D.M. Hegsted and F.J. Stare, "Dietary Fats, Carbohydrates and Atherosclerotic Vascular Disease," *The New England Journal of Medicine*, July 27, 1967, http://tinyurl.com/ycjuv8p2.

[6] Kelly McEvers, "Sugar Industry Manipulated Research About Health Effects,

Study Finds," *All Things Considered*, Sept. 13, 2016, http://tinyurl.com/zbjjjz3.

[7] Kearns, Schmidt and Glantz, *op. cit.*

[8] "The Sugar Association Statement on Kearns JAMA Study," Sugar Association, Sept. 12, 2016, http://tinyurl.com/y9utm8ja.

[9] David Michaels, "It's not the answers that are biased, it's the questions," *The Washington Post*, July 15, 2008, http://tinyurl.com/yb6cd2c7.

[10] Patrick Mustain, "Science for Sale: Big Food's Influence on Top Nutrition Research Org," *Scientific American*, June 15, 2015, http://tinyurl.com/onnzd7z.

[11] "The Sugar Association Statement on Kearns JAMA Study," *op. cit.*

so-called bad cholesterol and lower good cholesterol. [66]

In 2003, after campaigns by public health advocates, the FDA finalized rules that required food companies to show the amount of transfats on food labels by 2006. By the time the change took effect, manufacturers had voluntarily removed nearly all transfats from the food supply. [67]

Food manufacturers, says transfat expert Schleifer, were " 'pilloried' for using saturated fats and they said, 'we can't have that happen to us again.' " Companies acted quickly to remove transfats from

their products so that when the labeling measure took effect, their products would not bear the stigma of containing a controversial ingredient.

This reaction was to be expected, Schleifer says. He wrote in a study of transfat that "American food labeling . . . has historically aimed to shame corporations into manufacturing products differently by defining certain ingredients as adulterants." [68]

At first, companies understood that having to declare the presence of an unwanted and previously hidden ingredient would hurt sales, Schleifer said in

his study, and they dropped transfat from their production lines. But then companies saw a marketing opportunity if they let consumers know a product did not contain an unwanted ingredient.

"I suspect that most consumers did not know about transfats until manufacturers started marketing products to them labeled '0 g transfats,' " he wrote. But regulators, industry and academic scientists agreed that manufacturers would reformulate a product if they could market it as healthier. "Companies that replaced transfats could frame cookies, chips, donuts and other prod-

Food Dyes Scrutinized for Impact on Children

Calls are growing for manufactures to add warning labels.

Trix may still be for kids, but it isn't quite so colorful anymore. The venerable breakfast cereal stopped using food dyes in January 2016 because of concerns the additives can cause hyperactivity in children. It now relies on natural colors that are less bright than their laboratory cousins, and the cereal is minus blue and green pellets because those colors are hard to replicate naturally.

General Mills' decision to go natural is part of a growing movement by food manufacturers to stop using artificial dyes in some or all of their products in response to these safety fears. [1]

Seven artificial dyes to turn food blue, green, red or yellow are approved for use in the United States. In 2007, British researchers linked three of the seven to "hyperactive behavior" among children. [2]

Since that widely cited study by the University of Southampton in England, advocates on both sides of the Atlantic have demanded that producers place warning labels on foods containing artificial dyes or ban the additives outright. But some scientists have questioned the British conclusions, saying the study was poorly designed because it examined the effects of dyes in mixtures, rather than individually, and because it relied on a small sample size of about 300 children. [3]

Britain's Food Standards Agency recommended banning the six dyes cited in the study (three from the United States and three from the United Kingdom). Instead of a ban, however, products in the U.K. containing the dyes have had to carry a label since 2009 alerting consumers to a link between dyes and childhood hyperactivity. [4]

The 28-member European Union (EU) adopted a similar labeling law. [5] As a result, multinational companies sell one form of, say, candy, in Europe and another in the United States. Orange M&Ms available in the U.K. are colored with carotene, derived from sweet potatoes, while orange M&Ms in the United States are colored with artificial dyes. But Mars Inc., one of the nation's largest candy and food makers, pledged last year to remove all artificial food colorings by 2021. [6] "That came from consumers wanting more natural colors," says Kelly Horton, Mars' North America policy director.

Some other U.S. companies also are voluntarily removing dyes from their products. Kraft's macaroni and cheese, for example, is now colored with paprika, turmeric and annatto, which is extracted from tree seeds. [7]

In the meantime, consumers' calls to ban artificial food dye or add warning labels in the United States are growing louder.

When a food contains an artificial dye, it must be listed in the ingredients panel with its name, such as FD&C Yellow No. 5. Groups like the Center for Science in the Public Interest, (CSPI), a food-safety advocate in Washington, have asked the Food and Drug Administration (FDA) to mandate the addition of a warning label, such as: "May have an adverse effect on activity and attention in children."

In 2011, in response to a petition from the CSPI, the FDA convened a panel to review food dyes and possibly recommend warning labels. [8]

"Many parents . . . would assume that the food that they're giving their children and the additives that have been approved by the FDA, of course, it must be safe," panelist Lisa Lefferts, an environmental health consultant, said. "It doesn't even occur to them that there could be any link between these color additives and the very serious behavioral problems that some of them observe in their children." [9]

But other panelists questioned whether the science was firmly established and worried that a warning label for every ingredient with potential safety concerns would lead to information overload. "If we put a label that long or a statement that long on every chemical and ingredient," said panelist Tim Jones, deputy state epidemiologist for the Tennessee Department of Health, "you wouldn't see the package anymore." [10]

ucts as healthier and could therefore frame themselves as doing the right thing," Schleifer said. [69]

Whatever the motivation, mandating the labeling of transfats "essentially got it out of the food supply," food policy expert Nestle wrote in an email.

The transfat experience, consumer health advocates say, could be repeated when the latest update to the Nutrition Facts panel goes into effect mandating the disclosure of added sugars. Companies could reformulate their products to avoid the stigma of a "bad" ingredient on the label — which would lead to healthier products.

But reformulating food is hard, health experts say: Frito-Lay, for example, spent $22 million a decade ago removing transfats from Doritos, Tostitos and Cheetos. [70]

"There are all sorts of properties that food scientists have to pay attention to, and one of those physical properties when it comes to sugar and salt is that they tend to hold things together," obesity researcher William Dietz told *The Washington Post.* [71]

The CSPI's Jacobson concurs. "There is no really good replacement for sugar like there was for transfat," he says. "But I think the labeling would be an incentive to use less."

Most likely, new products will enter the market with less sugar. It's hard to convince people that their favorite candy bar tastes just as good with less sugar, but it's usually possible to get consumers to try something new, says Schleifer. ∎

The panel voted 8-6 that warning labels were unneeded. [11]

The debate has been simmering since 1973, when Dr. Benjamin Feingold presented a paper to the American Medical Association (AMA) linking artificial dyes to hyperactivity or ADHD. A 2010 review of 35 years of literature on the subject concluded that a diet free from dyes could improve the symptoms of children who already have ADHD, but that artificial colors and dyes do not cause hyperactivity in children who are not already susceptible to attention problems or hyperactivity. [12]

In February, California state Sen. Bob Wieckowski, D-Fremont, co-sponsored a bill with support from the CSPI that would have required food sold in California containing synthetic dyes to bear a warning label — the first such labeling requirement in the United States. [13]

But the Committee on Health amended the bill so it will only direct the state's Office of Environmental Health Hazard Assessment to review the scientific literature and issue a report by 2019 on the possible risks of food dyes to children.

CSPI plans to lobby other states on the issue. "We are laying the groundwork for a full-fledged effort to get warning notices on dyed foods in a couple of years," CSPI co-founder Michael Jacobson said by email. "We plan to look for other jurisdictions that would consider some kind of warnings about dyed foods."

— *Rachel Kaufman*

Because candy makers face different food-dye rules in different countries, M&Ms in the United States do not have the same coloring as those in Europe. Mars, the popular candy's maker, has pledged to remove all artificial food coloring from its products by 2021.

[1] Malia Wollan, "Brand New Hue: The Quest to Make a True Blue M&M," *The New York Times*, Oct. 5, 2016, http://tinyurl.com/gphurx8; "Trix cereal looks a whole lot different — here's why," Fox News, Jan. 21, 2016, http://tinyurl.com/ybgfmst6.

[2] Donna McCann *et al.*, "Food additives and hyperactive behaviour in 3-year-old and 8/9-year-old children in the community: a randomised, double-blinded, placebo-controlled trial," *Lancet*, Nov. 3, 2007, http://tinyurl.com/777ay9n.

[3] Phillip Button, "Monday's medical myth: food additives cause childhood behavioural disorders," *The Conversation*, June 4, 2012, http://tinyurl.com/ya7whflp;

"Hyperactivity and colours: advice to parents," U.K. Food Standards Agency, Sept. 7, 2007, http://tinyurl.com/al9goc3.

[4] Martin Hickman, "Food agency calls for ban on six artificial colours," *The Independent*, April 10, 2008, http://tinyurl.com/5757tm; "Ministers agree food colour ban," BBC, Nov. 12, 2008, http://tinyurl.com/yb8txsg3; and "Colourings," Action on Additives, http://tinyurl.com/y9b4amv8.

[5] Sacha Pfeiffer, "Why M&M's Are Made With Natural Coloring In The EU And Not The U.S.," *Here and Now*, March 28, 2014, http://tinyurl.com/y7fgmtkz.

[6] Wollan, *op. cit.*

[7] *Ibid.*

[8] Gardiner Harris, "F.D.A. Panel to Consider Warnings for Artificial Food Colorings," *The New York Times*, March 29, 2011, http://tinyurl.com/62bqddl.

[9] "2011 Food Advisory Committee Meeting Materials," Food and Drug Administration, Sept. 30, 2015, http://tinyurl.com/ybq5wmyu.

[10] *Ibid.*

[11] Gardiner Harris, "Artificial Dye Safe to Eat, Panel Says," *The New York Times*, April 1, 2011, http://tinyurl.com/ydbaxkho.

[12] Laura J. Stevens *et al.*, "Dietary Sensitivities and ADHD Symptoms: Thirty-five Years of Research," *Clinical Pediatrics*, 2011, http://tinyurl.com/yc8xrcdn.

[13] "Wieckowski introduces warning label bill on synthetic food dyes in children," press release, Office of Sen. Bob Wieckowski, Feb. 16, 2017, http://tinyurl.com/y8hvfkfl; Elizabeth Grossman, "New California Bill Could Be First in Nation to Require Food Dye Labeling," *Civil Eats*, March 16, 2017, http://tinyurl.com/mpqe4vl.

CURRENT SITUATION

New Labels

The Agriculture Department is crafting a rule to implement the 2016 GMO labeling law.

Under a compromise in the legislation, the final rule will likely require companies to use one of several ways to disclose whether a product contains GMOs: through text on the package; through a not-yet-designed icon on the package; by having a consumer call a 1-800 number or access a website; or by a consumer scanning a Quick Response (QR) code on the package using a smartphone. [72]

Labeling reform advocates say the latter two methods are a cop-out because the poor, elderly and others who lack cellphones or computers might be unable to access the information. But the Grocery Manufacturers Association, which introduced the digital barcode system SmartLabel in 2015, and other industry groups say technology is the only way to give consumers all the information they want. [73]

"You have to set reasonable expectations, particularly [on] a product label where you have limited space," says the association's Sophos. "[Labeling will] be more digital. That's where

SmartLabel comes into play, because of its ability to answer all the questions consumers have in a more in-depth way and far beyond the capability of a label."

"We think it is the modern way that people are shopping," association spokesman Lowe added.

Already, thousands of products are using SmartLabel, and the Grocery Manufacturers Association predicts that number will grow to 34,000 by the end of 2017. [74]

Consumer advocates remain skeptical. "I don't think that many people are going to use their smartphones to check out the UPC label or the QR code"

considered requiring packaged foods to declare whether they contain GMOs. If adopted, such laws could have created a patchwork of state rules for food manufacturers.

Then, after Vermont became the first state to enact such a law in 2014, Congress responded by passing the bipartisan GMO labeling law, which overrode the Vermont law and any other measure a state might pass. [76] Food companies said it was nearly impossible for them to produce different labels for different states.

California legislators, meanwhile, are considering SB 300, which would require drinks containing more than 75

In Baltimore, the Health Department is leading a campaign for a law requiring soda warning labels on restaurant menus and vending machines. The legislation was last introduced in 2016 and has not been reintroduced this year. [79]

Defining Healthy

The FDA is pursuing a number of initiatives to better define commonly used words. The agency solicited comments last year on what the word "natural" should mean in food labeling. It does not yet have a definition, according to the FDA website.

"From a food science perspective, it is difficult to define a food product that is 'natural' because the food has probably been processed and is no longer the product of the earth," the FDA said. "However, the agency has not objected to the use of the term if the food does not contain added color, artificial flavors, or synthetic substances." [80]

This definition is not legally binding and is open to creative interpretation, with the makers of lemonade mix, chicken nuggets and fruit snacks labeling these products as natural. [81]

But a 2016 survey by Consumers Union, a Washington consumer advocacy group seeking better labels, found that consumers confused the term "natural" with "organic." Many believed "natural" meant that a food was made without pesticides, artificial ingredients or colors, or GMOs, and that manufacturers used no chemicals during processing — which is the legal definition of organic. But public health advocates note that none of those statements are actually true in reference to so-called natural foods. [82]

The same survey found that nearly two-thirds of consumers "usually" buy foods with the natural label, but most held mistaken beliefs about what the label meant, and half incorrectly believed that claims about natural have been independently verified.

Farmer Carl Russell produces organic milk and other products in Bethel, Vt. After Vermont in 2014 became the first state to require packaged foods to list genetically modified organisms, Congress passed the bipartisan GMO labeling law, which overrode the Vermont law and any other similar future state laws.

Getty Images/The Christian Science Monitor/M. Freeman

to find out if a product has GMOs, CSPI's Jacobson said at the 2017 National Food Policy Conference, hosted by the Consumer Federation of America in Washington in April. [75] "It's just too much of a nuisance."

State Efforts

State food labeling initiatives often have effects far beyond their borders. In recent years, dozens of states have

calories per 12 fluid ounces to carry a label warning consumers about the role added sugars play in obesity, diabetes and tooth decay. Similar bills were introduced in 2013 and 2014, but neither passed. [77]

"Certainly the victories in local communities show a growing awareness of the health risk posed by these drinks," the bill's sponsor, Democratic Sen. Bill Monning, told Reuters, referring to soda taxes passed by three Bay Area cities in November 2016. [78]

Continued on p. 526

At Issue:

Should food labels feature 'healthy' or 'unhealthy' ratings?

MICHAEL F. JACOBSON
PRESIDENT, CENTER FOR SCIENCE IN THE PUBLIC INTEREST

WRITTEN FOR *CQ RESEARCHER*, JUNE 2017

*W*hy can't every American see what Chileans see on the front of food packages? Or even what some shoppers see at certain American supermarkets?

In Chile, a shopper will see a stop sign-shaped image on the label front saying a product is "high" in calories, saturated fat, sugar or sodium. In the United States, some stores use the "NuVal" rating system, which provides a 1-to-100 nutritional rating for products: the higher the NuVal score, the more nutritious the product.

But to hear American food manufacturers talk, such labels would confuse consumers and destroy the industry. The experiences of some companies and their customers indicate otherwise. Consumers love simple, easy-to-understand labels, and they use them to protect their health.

The whole debate about front-of-package labeling is whether it should be easy for consumers to know how healthy a packaged food is. Does it have too much of nutrients that, if a regular part of their diet, increase consumers' risk of a chronic disease such as obesity, heart disease or Type 2 diabetes? Front-of-pack labeling is risk communication done in a consumer-friendly manner.

Today in the United States, we have the Nutrition Facts label. Now mind you, the label is a huge win for consumers that the Center for Science in the Public Interest and other advocates fought long and hard to obtain. Many young consumers don't know that before the early 1990s, the Nutrition Facts label didn't exist, and health-conscious consumers could only guess at the nutritional quality of most foods.

However, consumers need to know a fair amount about the relationship between nutrients and health to really understand the mass of numbers on Nutrition Facts. It can be especially hard for low-literacy populations to use the Nutrition Facts label in a way that benefits their health.

We should be learning from the experiences of countries like Chile and the United Kingdom, and from supermarkets like Hy-Vee, Hannaford Bros. and Walmart, which have different forms of front-of-pack labeling to determine which approach works best with consumers.

In fact, multinational companies already are coming to terms with the reality that front-of-pack labeling is in their future. That's why a group of large companies recently announced its support for a front-of-pack labeling initiative in the European Union.

If we want to Make America Great Again, shouldn't the United States be leading instead of following?

MARY SOPHOS
EXECUTIVE VICE PRESIDENT, POLICY AND STRATEGIC PLANNING, GROCERY MANUFACTURERS ASSOCIATION

WRITTEN FOR *CQ RESEARCH*, JUNE 2017

*C*onsumers want tools and information so they can make informed choices about the foods and beverages they buy for their families. They do not want judgments made for them about which foods are good or bad.

Facts Up Front, an unprecedented, voluntary front-of-pack nutrition label, was launched in 2011 by the Grocery Manufacturers Association and the Food Marketing Institute. Facts Up Front takes key nutrition information from the Food and Drug Administration-mandated Nutrition Facts panel on the back of food packages and beverage products and moves it to the front where busy consumers are more likely to notice and use that information.

When Facts Up Front was being designed, we paid a lot of attention to what consumers were saying: They wanted the basic facts so they could decide for themselves what the right choice might be.

According to recent research by the International Food Information Council, 70 percent of consumers reported using the Nutrition Facts panel when deciding to purchase a food or beverage and 58 percent reported using calorie and other nutrition information on front of pack via an icon or graphic. Other surveys show that label readers are most often interested in key nutrients — calories, fats, sugars and sodium — all of which are provided on the Facts Up Front label.

Moms in particular often look for different product characteristics — calories, sodium — for different members of their families. What these shoppers typically do not ask for at the grocery store is to be directed to the "good" food or the "bad" food.

An important principle for Facts Up Front is that the label can be applied to all products, not just a select few.

When label information becomes too complicated or tries to convey too many messages, it can become less useful to consumers. This can be the case with some consumers when nutrition facts and nutrition information are overlaid with "colors" — such as "stoplights" — whose meaning is implied but far from clear.

Facts Up Front continues to grow, with 120 companies participating and food and beverage products carrying the label in every eligible product category. In product categories such as cereals, snacks and beverages, Facts Up Front has a significant presence. This voluntary front-of-pack label is becoming a familiar "staple" in the shopping experience.

Continued from p. 524

The line between artificial and non-artificial ingredients, experts say, is more porous than many consumers think. *Consumer Reports*, for example, derided xanthan gum — a thickening agent — as "an ingredient extracted from a 'slime' (we're not making that up!) produced from bacteria." But that process is not necessarily "unnatural," and the FDA said xanthan gum is a safe additive. Arsenic is a naturally occurring element, too, but experts say it doesn't belong in food. [83]

Despite the difficulties of defining natural, consumers believe the government should regulate the term, according to surveys. [84]

The FDA also is soliciting comments on the definition of "healthy." Currently, food companies wishing to call their products healthy must meet defined targets for fat, sodium and cholesterol. A product that doesn't meet those targets can be labeled "smart" or "fit," as those words are unregulated.

At a public meeting in March on the definition of healthy, some consumers and public health advocates argued that the FDA should take a holistic approach, allowing manufacturers to say, for example, that a product "provides 2 of the recommended five to nine daily servings of fruit and vegetables." Others argued that "healthy" is such a subjective term that the food industry should not use it at all. Yet others said that if the term were banned, claims like "fit" and "smart" would proliferate, causing more confusion.

No final decision is forthcoming, and what direction the agency will go is unclear. [85]

Meanwhile, General Mills is defending itself against the lawsuit challenging its statement that its Nature Valley granola bars are "made with 100% NATURAL whole grain oats." It is the second lawsuit on the granola bars in five years; in 2014, the company settled a suit and agreed not to call the products "100% natural" because they are made with high-fructose corn syrup. [86]

In 2015, Coca-Cola settled a six-year lawsuit against its Vitaminwater brand, removing claims that said Vitaminwater could reduce the risk of eye disease or improve metabolic function. [87]

Recent investigations have found that fraud is present in the organic world. For example, for milk to be labeled organic, the cows it comes from must be allowed to graze daily throughout the growing season.

The Washington Post investigated Aurora Organic Dairy, a large producer in Colorado, visiting it multiple times over a week and studying high-resolution satellite imagery. It found no more than a handful of cows out of the herd of 15,000 outside at any time. Aurora dismissed the visits as "anomalies" and "drive-bys," and CEO Marc Peperzak said, "Aurora Organic Dairy's cows graze on pasture, and we meet and exceed the organic pasture standards." But chemical testing showed that Aurora milk was almost identical to non-organic milk. [88]

In another recent example, documents obtained by *The Post* showed that 36 million pounds of soybeans left Ukraine as a non-organic product; by the time the shipment arrived in California, the soybeans were bearing the "USDA Organic" label. The new designation boosted the soybeans' value by $4 million, according to *The Post*. The USDA maintains that its processes for detecting fraud are robust, but critics disagree. With organic food costing an average of 47 percent more than its conventional counterparts, consumers are being scammed out of potentially billions of dollars a year, they allege. [89] ■

OUTLOOK

Anti-Regulatory Fervor

New FDA Commissioner Gottlieb already has shifted the agency's priorities. On June 13, the agency announced that implementation of the new Nutrition Facts label was being delayed indefinitely, to the frustration of public health advocates — as well as those food companies that had already updated their labels.

Kelly Horton, North America policy director for candy-maker Mars, criticized the delay. "We have been planning to meet the compliance deadline of July 2018, and we believe that if we do that and other folks don't, there will be confusion in the marketplace," she says.

Nabisco/Mondelez has already started putting the new labels on its Wheat Thins crackers, PepsiCo has added the labels to a number of chips and snack foods, and KIND has updated the labels on its granola bars. Industry players fear that if they update their labels but their competitors do not, consumers will be confused about which products really are healthier.

"The fact that we'll have the added sugar declaration and the percent daily value, but our competitors won't? That just ends up confusing consumers," Brad Figel, vice president of public affairs for Mars in North America, told *The Washington Post*. [90]

The FDA's actions should have been expected, industry watchers said.

"The pendulum's going to swing back to the right whether we like it or not," attorney Richard Frank, who represents the food industry, said at the Food Policy Conference. [91]

Delaying the new Nutrition Facts label was "reasonable and inevitable," food and nutrition science consultant Susan Pitman said at the same conference (before the announcement), arguing that a label redesign is too expensive for companies to do twice in a decade.

Mars and other manufacturers had already been working toward reducing the amount of sugar in their products.

"We know, and FDA even said it, this [rule] is so food manufacturers will reformulate," says the Sugar Association's Gaine. "If you are now above 20 percent of the daily value [for added sugars], you're now [considered] 'high in added sugars.' I think we're going to find there aren't going to be a lot of products with more than 10 grams of added sugars" going forward.

Many companies are thinking about ways to reduce sugar, and some will likely move forward with those plans. Nestlé has come up with sugar crystals that are essentially hollow, allowing the company to reduce the sugar in its candy by as much as 40 percent without affecting the taste, it said. Conference agendas for the industry are packed with panels and workshops related to reformulating products and identifying new sweeteners with names like allulose, galactooligosaccharides, monatin and brazzein. [92]

"It's definitely a conversation that has got to be happening" within the industry, transfat expert Schleifer says.

With an "abdication" of responsibility from Washington, Frank says, "there is definitely going to be an increase in state and local activity." More states and cities will introduce or pass laws related to labeling, and some of those laws may spur activity on the national level, as Vermont's GMO bill did.

More class-action suits are likely, the CSPI's Jacobson says. "When the federal government doesn't enforce — doesn't keep the food industry under control — they're going to do everything they can to trick us into buying their products. Class actions are at least part of the answer." ∎

Notes

[1] *Yesenia Nuez v. General Mills Inc.*, U.S. District Court, Eastern District of New York, 2016, pp. 1, 4, http://tinyurl.com/ya66fmx4; Mary Beth Quirk, "Lawsuits Claim '100% Natural' Label On Nature Valley Granola Bars Is Deceptive," *Consumerist*, Aug. 25, 2016, http://tinyurl.com/yda32q54.

[2] "Highly processed foods dominate U.S. grocery purchases," Federation of American Societies for Experimental Biology, March 29, 2015, http://tinyurl.com/ncsk3s4.

[3] "FDA modernizes Nutrition Facts label for packaged foods," Food and Drug Administration, May 20, 2016, http://tinyurl.com/znre926.

[4] *Ibid.*

[5] "FDA modernizes Nutrition Facts label for packaged foods," *op. cit.*

[6] Ellen A. Wartella, Alice H. Lichtenstein and Caitlin S. Boon, eds., "Front-of-Package Nutrition Rating Systems and Symbols: Phase I Report," Institute of Medicine, 2010, http://tinyurl.com/ydbgamnx; Ellen A. Wartella *et al.*, "Front-of-Package Nutrition Rating Systems and Symbols: Promoting Healthier Choices (Phase II Report)," Institute of Medicine, 2012, http://tinyurl.com/yazzmcey.

[7] Marion Nestle, "Food industry puts $50 million into another end run around the FDA," *Food Politics*, March 4, 2014, http://tinyurl.com/y8mh2mm2.

[8] "Letter of Enforcement Discretion to GMA/FMI re 'Facts Up Front,' " Food and Drug Administration, Dec. 13, 2011, http://tinyurl.com/y8mbpkct.

[9] Lydia Wheeler, "Trump floats rolling back food safety regulations," *The Hill*, Sept. 15, 2016, http://tinyurl.com/hd24wv8.

[10] Zachary Brennan, "Trump to Pharma CEOs: 75% to 80% of FDA Regulations Will be Eliminated," Regulatory Affairs Professionals Society, Jan. 31, 2017, http://tinyurl.com/y73xobjv.

[11] "GMA Praises Scott Gottlieb as Excellent Choice to Lead FDA," Grocery Manufacturers Association, March 11, 2017, http://tinyurl.com/y8kgzxwy.

[12] Mike Pomranz, "FDA Nominee Wants to Delay Changes to Nutrition Labels," *Food & Wine*, April 6, 2017, http://tinyurl.com/yd62pnbf; "Food Industry Urges Delay of Nutrition Facts Label," Center for Science in the Public Interest, April 5, 2017, http://tinyurl.com/y9ohlls7.

[13] "International Labeling Laws," Center for Food Safety, undated, http://tinyurl.com/y949g53h. Also see Norma Volkmer, "Congress Passes GMO Labeling Bill," E-Newsletter, Council of State Governments, July 29, 2016, http://tinyurl.com/ybmdrkcm.

[14] "Letter to Secretary Price expressing concern with the current compliance deadline," March 14, 2017, http://tinyurl.com/y97s2s3z. For background, see Jason McLure, "Genetically Modified Food," *CQ Researcher*, Aug. 31, 2012, pp. 717-740.

[15] Helena Bottemiller Evich, " 'Good Food' vs 'Big Food,' " *Politico*, Aug. 1, 2015, http://tinyurl.com/ydejde7f.

[16] Libby Foley, "Big Food Companies Spend Millions to Defeat GMO Labeling," Environmental Working Group, Aug. 4, 2015, http://tinyurl.com/y9xkh746.

[17] Evich, *op. cit.*; Hunter Stuart, "Ben & Jerry's Will Stop Using Genetically-Modified Ingredients, Company Says," *The Huffington Post*, June 2, 2013, http://tinyurl.com/lexr58l.

[18] "Warning Letter," Food and Drug Administration, March 17, 2015, http://tinyurl.com/y7os2elv.

[19] Roberto Ferdman, "Why you can't call nuts, avocados, olives, or salmon 'healthy,' " *The Washington Post*, Dec. 11, 2015, http://tinyurl.com/yd2gkjcd.

[20] Caitlin Dewey, "Why one food executive is pledging $25 million to fight his own industry," *The Washington Post*, Feb. 15, 2017, http://tinyurl.com/y8wobb36.

[21] "KIND Snacks Founder & CEO Creates New Organization to Promote Public Health Over Special Interests," PR Newswire, Feb. 15, 2017, http://tinyurl.com/yd25orxo.

[22] P.G. Williams, "Consumer understanding and use of health claims for foods," *Nutrition Reviews*, 2005, 256-64, http://tinyurl.com/ydzbqecy.

[23] Wartella *et al.*, eds. "Front-of-Package Nutrition Rating Systems and Symbols: Phase I Report," Institute of Medicine, 2010, *op. cit.*; M.W. Kreuter *et al.*, "Do nutrition label readers eat healthier diets? Behavioral correlates of adults' use of food labels," *American Journal of Preventive Medicine*, 1997, http://tinyurl.com/y6vc93q8.

[24] Wartella *et al.*, "Front-of-Package Nutrition Rating Systems and Symbols: Promoting Healthier Choices (Phase II Report)," *op. cit.*

[25] *Ibid.*

[26] Katie Moisse, "Campbell's Panned for Adding Salt to Soups," ABC News, July 14, 2011, http://tinyurl.com/5rg2kbo.

[27] Transcript of "Public meeting: Use of the term 'healthy' in the labeling of human food products," Food and Drug Administration, March 9, 2017, http://tinyurl.com/ya5wqx7f.

[28] "A food labeling guide: Guidance for Industry," Food and Drug Administration, January 2013, http://tinyurl.com/ybzu9dyd.

[29] Hank Cardello, *Stuffed: An Insider's Look at Who's (Really) Making America Fat and How the Food Industry Can Fix It* (2007), p. 46.

[30] Julia Belluz, "The gluten-free craze is out of hand. Here are 8 facts to counter the madness," *Vox*, June 8, 2015, http://tinyurl.com/y7jej3an; Ilan Brat, "Food Goes 'GMO Free' With Same Ingredients," *The Wall Street Journal*, Aug. 20, 2015, http://tinyurl.com/y9etf7un.

[31] Gary Sacks, Mike Rayner and Boyd Swinburn, "Impact of front-of-pack 'traffic-light' nu-

trition labelling on consumer food purchases in the UK," *Health Promotion International*, 2009, http://tinyurl.com/y8d2tq6b.

[32] Emma Hall, "Why Some U.K. Marketers Are Flashing Caution Over 'Traffic Light' Food Labels," *Ad Age*, July 12, 2013, http://tinyurl.com/ydfaq5h9.

[33] J.H. Freeland-Graves and S. Nitzke, "Position of the Academy of Nutrition and Dietics: Total Diet Approach to Healthy Eating," *Journal of the Academy of Nutrition and Dietics*, February 2013, http://tinyurl.com/y9slr3at.

[34] "Shoppers confused by 'traffic light' food labels, says study," University of Birmingham, July 3, 2015, http://tinyurl.com/y8y4rgkj; "Ecuador, Chile and Bolivia defend labeling of processed foods at PAHO meeting," Pan American Health Organization, Sept. 29, 2016, http://tinyurl.com/ydcdxhau. See also Emmet Livingstone, "French food labels: Salt, fat, sugar, controversy," *Politico*, Sept. 22, 2016, http://tinyurl.com/yd7qryto; and Eileen Smith, "Chile Battles Obesity With Stop Signs On Packaged Foods," *The Salt*, Aug. 12, 2016, http://tinyurl.com/hs8oto9.

[35] "Facts Up Front Launches Consumer Education Campaign to Drive Awareness and Increase Nutrition Knowledge," "MarketWatch," March 3, 2014, http://tinyurl.com/ybor2pbr.

[36] Nestle, *op. cit.*

[37] Liz Newmark, "Seven EU states oppose British traffic light labeling," *Global Meat News*, March 21, 2016, http://tinyurl.com/y89pp5k3.

[38] *Ibid.*; Stefan Storcksdieck, genannt Bonsmann and Josephine M. Wills, "Nutrition Labeling to Prevent Obesity: Reviewing the Evidence from Europe," *Current Obesity Reports*, Sept. 1, 2012, http://tinyurl.com/ydxc7r22.

[39] "History of Patent Medicine," Hagley Museum and Library, http://tinyurl.com/yb38hku6; Andrew F. Smith, *Food In America* (2017), p. 25. Also see Laura Schumm, "Food Fraud: A Brief History of the Adulteration of Food," History.com, Aug. 1, 2014, http://tinyurl.com/yayx939v.

[40] Edward Ayers, "What the Food Law Saves Us From," *The World's Work*, 1907, pp. 9317-18, http://tinyurl.com/yaabeceo.

[41] Smith, *op. cit.*, p. 25; "Harvey W. Wiley," *FDA Consumer Magazine*, January-February 2006, http://tinyurl.com/y725enby.

[42] "Significant Dates in U.S. Food and Drug Law History," Food and Drug Administration, last updated Dec 19, 2014, http://tinyurl.com/7mav93o.

[43] Ayers, *op. cit.*

[44] "History," Food and Drug Administration, http://tinyurl.com/y8rgajfx.

[45] "How America's Eating Has Changed," *LifeSkills*, Summer 2001, http://tinyurl.com/y7eswoou.

[46] *Ibid.*

[47] Lowell K. Dyson, "American Cuisine in the 20th Century," *Food Review*, January-April 2000, http://tinyurl.com/y8qz37p8.

[48] Christine Muhlke, "The Hippies Have Won," *The New York Times*, April 4, 2017, http://tinyurl.com/y98r2q6h.

[49] Dyson, *op. cit.*

[50] Elaine McIntosh, *American Food Habits in Historical Perspective* (1995), p. 136.

[51] Whitney Kimball, "The rise and fall of superfoods," *Hopes&Fears*, June 11, 2015, http://tinyurl.com/yb986dgx.

[52] "National Health Interview Survey," Centers for Disease Control and Prevention, 2015, http://tinyurl.com/ybrjp5v9. Matt Richtel, "More Than 10 Percent of World's Population Is Obese, Study Finds," *The New York Times*, June 12, 2017, http://tinyurl.com/y7c7fv5z.

[53] Robinson Meyer, "How Many Stories Do Newspapers Publish Per Day?" *The Atlantic*, May 26, 2016, http://tinyurl.com/ya2ny4tq; Margot Sanger-Katz, "How Changing Attitudes Went Along With a Drop in Calories," *The New York Times*, July 28, 2015, http://tinyurl.com/ya62ejok.

[54] "New Report Finds 23 of 25 States with Highest Rates of Obesity are in the South and Midwest," Robert Wood Johnson Foundation, Sept. 21, 2015, http://tinyurl.com/yblxmuwb; Margot Sanger-Katz, "How Changing Attitudes Went Along With a Drop in Calories," *The New York Times*, July 28, 2015, http://tinyurl.com/ya62ejok.

[55] Joanne E. Arsenault, "Can Nutrition Labeling Affect Obesity?" *Choices*, 2010, http://tinyurl.com/7uqgppp.

[56] Marian Burros, "Health claims on food put FDA in a corner," *The New York Times*, Feb. 19, 1986, http://tinyurl.com/ycbw57ee.

[57] Clare Hasler, " Health Claims in the United States: An Aid to the Public or a Source of Confusion?" *Journal of Nutrition*, June 2008, http://tinyurl.com/y7uw7bua; Caroline Mayer, "FDA Studies Advertising For Kellogg's All-Bran," *The Washington Post*, Nov. 6, 1984, http://tinyurl.com/yakkpl4r.

[58] Mayer, *ibid.*

[59] Hasler, *op. cit.*

[60] Burros, *op. cit.*

[61] "Nutrition Facts Label Better Informs Your Food Choices," Food and Drug Administration, updated Aug. 18, 2016, http://tinyurl.com/kff6a82.

[62] "FLOTUS remarks on nutrition facts label announcement, transcript," *Politico*, Feb. 27, 2014, http://tinyurl.com/ydauatpa.

[63] Wartella *et al.*, "Front-of-Package Nutrition Rating Systems and Symbols: Promoting Healthier Choices (Phase II Report)," *op. cit.*; Asha Kaur *et al.*, "The nutritional quality of foods carrying health-related claims in Germany, The Netherlands, Spain, Slovenia and the United Kingdom," *European Journal of Clinical Nutrition*, 2016, http://tinyurl.com/ybrcff69.

[64] Transcript of "Public meeting: Use of the term 'healthy' in the labeling of human food products," *op. cit.*

[65] Linda Verrill *et al.*, "Vitamin-Fortified Snack Food May Lead Consumers to Make Poor Dietary Decisions," *Journal of the Academy of Nutrition and Dietetics*, March 2017, http://tinyurl.com/y9hsu3eq.

[66] "Trans fat is double trouble for your heart health," Mayo Clinic, March 1, 2017, http://tinyurl.com/mp7e2a4.

[67] Dan Charles, "FDA Moves to Phase Out Remaining Trans Fats in Food Supply," *The Salt*, Nov. 7, 2013, http://tinyurl.com/y85m9hcm; David Schleifer, "Categories count: Trans fat labeling as a technique of corporate governance," *Social Studies of Science*, 2013, http://tinyurl.com/y72gkwpp.

[68] Schleifer, *ibid.*

[69] David Schleifer, "We Spent a Million Bucks and Then We Had To Do Something: The Unexpected Implications of Industry Involvement in Trans Fat Research," *Bulletin of Science, Technology & Society*, 2011, http://tinyurl.com/y8rdjazx.

About the Author

Rachel Kaufman is a freelance writer and editor in Washington whose science writing has appeared in *The Washington Post*, *National Geographic News*, *Smithsonian.com* and *Scientific American*. She was managing editor of *Elevation DC*, an online publication about Washington, D.C., neighborhoods, and co-founded a daily news blog on jobs in the media.

[70] David Schleifer, "Fear of Frying: A brief history of trans fats," *N+1*, May 21, 2011, http://tinyurl.com/y8kgfbj6.

[71] Ariana Eunjung Cha, " A first look at the FDA's new nutrition label — and 10 reasons it's different from the old one," *The Washington Post*, May 20, 2016, http://tinyurl.com/y7qrn29y.

[72] Andrew Amelinckx, "What you need to know about the new GMO labeling law," *Modern Farmer*, Aug. 8, 2016, http://tinyurl.com/j3l6jsn.

[73] "New SmartLabel™ Initiative Gives Consumers Easy Access to Detailed Product Ingredient Information," Grocery Manufacturers Association, Dec. 2, 2015, http://tinyurl.com/pr9ksqu.

[74] "Frequently Asked Questions," Smart Label.org, http://tinyurl.com/yd56scvx.

[75] "The New Administration's Food Policy Agenda: Panel," National Food Policy Conference, http://tinyurl.com/y887257q.

[76] Chris Morran, "Vermont's GMO Labeling Law Is Now In Effect. Here Are The Labels The Senate Is Trying To Get Rid Of," *Consumerist*, July 1, 2016, http://tinyurl.com/y8ez24uj.

[77] "SB-300 Sugar-sweetened beverages: health warnings," http://tinyurl.com/y8esm9fv; Kendra Lounsberry, "Warning: California takes aim at food and beverage industry," *National Law Review*, April 3, 2017, http://tinyurl.com/ybvfyuhm.

[78] Chris Prentice, "California lawmaker makes push for health warning labels on soda," Reuters, Feb. 13, 2017, http://tinyurl.com/hahu7u8.

[79] "Baltimore Health Officials Call on City Council to Pass Legislation to Educate Residents about the Dangers of Sugary Drinks," Baltimore City Health Department, June 7, 2016, http://tinyurl.com/ydcqdow7.

[80] "What is the meaning of 'natural' on the label of food?" Food and Drug Administration, updated April 28, 2017, http://tinyurl.com/3stepla.

[81] Deena Shanker, "After more than 30 years, the US government may finally define 'natural' food," *Quartz*, Nov. 10, 2015, http://tinyurl.com/qdtwdjl.

[82] Andrea Rock, "Peeling Back the Natural Food Label," *Consumer Reports*, March 2016, http://tinyurl.com/ydcvtlto. For background, see Kathy Koch, "Food Safety Battle: Organic vs. Biotech," *CQ Researcher*, Sept. 4, 1998, pp. 761-84.

[83] "Peeling Back the Natural Food Label," *ibid.*; Code of Federal Regulations Title 21, Food and Drug Administration, http://tinyurl.com/nxck4tm; and "Arsenic," Centers for Disease Control and Prevention, http://tinyurl.com/y9rjp4du.

FOR MORE INFORMATION

Center for Science in the Public Interest, 1220 L St., N.W., Suite 300, Washington, DC 20005; 202-332-9110; cspinet.org. Consumer organization that focuses on nutrition, food safety and health.

Consumers Union, 101 Truman Ave., Yonkers, NY 10703; 914-378-2000; consumersunion.org. Policy arm of *Consumer Reports*, the nonprofit products-rating magazine.

Environmental Working Group, 1436 U St., N.W., #100, Washington, DC 20009; 202-667-6982; ewg.org. Environmental organization that researches chemicals in the environment, including in foods, and pushes for their labeling or removal.

Grocery Manufacturers Association, 1350 I St., N.W., Washington, DC 20005; 202-639-5900; gmaonline.org. Trade association representing major food brands.

Institute of Food Technologists, 1025 Connecticut Ave., N.W., # 503, Washington, DC 20036; 202-466-5980; ift.org. Trade association for food science professionals.

National Cattlemen's Beef Association, 9110 E. Nichols Ave., #300, Centennial, CO 80112; 303-694-0305; beef.org. Association for beef producers nationwide.

National Consumers League, 1701 K St., N.W., Suite 1200, Washington, DC 20006; 202-835-3323; nclnet.org. Consumer advocacy organization that works on food safety and labeling initiatives.

Sugar Association, 1300 L St., N.W., Suite 1001, Washington, DC 20005; 202-785-1122; sugar.org. Lobbying and policy arm for U.S. sugar growers and refiners.

U.S. Food and Drug Administration, 10903 New Hampshire Ave., Silver Spring, MD 20993; 1-888-INFO-FDA; fda.gov. Government agency responsible for regulating food, ingredients and food packaging.

[84] "Re: Citizen Petition re Definition of the term 'Natural' for making claims on foods and beverages regulated by the Food and Drug Administration," Sugar Association, Feb. 28, 2006, http://tinyurl.com/yc2yagmw.

[85] "Summary of Themes Heard from Stakeholders during Breakout Sessions at the Public Meeting on Use of the Term 'Healthy' in the Labeling of Human Food Products," Food and Drug Administration, 2017, http://tinyurl.com/yb5pvdjn.

[86] Quirk, *op. cit.*; Deena Shanker, "Is a Granola Bar 'Natural' If There's a Pesticide in It?" Bloomberg News, Aug. 25, 2016, http://tinyurl.com/jbebchn.

[87] Jonathan Stempel, "Coke to change Vitaminwater labels to settle U.S. consumer lawsuit," Reuters, Oct 1, 2015, http://tinyurl.com/ybzvhfw3.

[88] Peter Whoriskey, "Why your 'organic' milk may not be organic," *The Washington Post*, May 1, 2017, http://tinyurl.com/ybzaw3xl; "We Are 100% Organic — A Letter from Our Founder," Aurora Organic Dairy, 2017, http://tinyurl.com/ycx5qqce.

[89] Peter Whoriskey, "The labels said 'organic.' But these massive imports of corn and soybeans weren't," *The Washington Post*, May 12, 2017, http://tinyurl.com/y76l2z54; "Organic Market Overview," Economic Research Service, U.S. Department of Agriculture, updated April 4, 2017, http://tinyurl.com/yafgqss4; and "The cost of organic food," *Consumer Reports*, March 19, 2015, http://tinyurl.com/ochxt9e.

[90] Caitlin Dewey, "Trump's FDA just took another swipe at Michelle Obama's food legacy," Wonkblog, *The Washington Post*, June 13, 2017, http://tinyurl.com/y735ndcw.

[91] "The New Administration's Food Policy Agenda: Panel," *op. cit.*

[92] Stephanie Strom, "Nestlé Reformulates Sugar and Says It Will Use Less in Its Candy," *The New York Times*, Nov. 30, 2016, http://tinyurl.com/y8b9qrmo; "Emerging Sweeteners for a Changing Market," Institute of Food Technologists conference agenda, http://tinyurl.com/m4p69ol.

Bibliography

Selected Sources

Books

Cardello, Hank, *Stuffed: An Insider's Look at Who's (Really) Making America Fat and How the Food Industry Can Fix It*, Ecco, 2007.

A former food executive argues that market forces make it hard for the industry to produce healthy food.

Jenkins, McCay, *Food Fight: GMOs and the Future of the American Diet*, Avery, 2017.

An environmental journalist gives a balanced portrait of the controversies over genetically modified foods in the United States.

Nestle, Marion, *Food Politics: How the Food Industry Influences Nutrition and Health*, University of California Press, 2007.

A renowned nutritionist at New York University examines how industry marketing practices affect what consumers eat.

Ruhlman, Michael, *Grocery: The Buying and Selling of Food in America*, Abrams Press, 2017.

A food writer spends a year in a store cataloguing how supermarkets affect the American diet.

Articles

"A food label that gets right to the point," *The New York Times*, May 25, 2016, http://tinyurl.com/y9a9w5ge.

The Times' Editorial Board praises the new Nutrition Facts label but argues that a front-of-package system is needed.

"Peeling Back the Natural Label," *Consumer Reports*, March 2016, http://tinyurl.com/ydcvtlto.

The magazine surveyed consumers about what they believed "natural" should mean.

Belluz, Julia, "The FDA just made the most significant changes to the nutrition label in years," *Vox*, May 20, 2016, http://tinyurl.com/hlq54qw.

A journalist summarizes the changes to the revamped nutrition label.

Ferdman, Roberto A., "Why you can't call nuts, avocados, olives, or salmon 'healthy,'" *The Washington Post*, Dec. 11, 2015, http://tinyurl.com/yd2gkjcd.

When KIND Bars asked the Food and Drug Administration for permission to use the word "healthy" on its label, the request sparked debate about what, exactly, healthy means.

Strom, Stephanie, "Nestle Reformulates Sugar and Says It Will Use Less in Its Candy," *The New York Times*, Nov. 30, 2016, http://tinyurl.com/y8b9qrmo.

A new type of sugar allows candy-makers to use less of the sweetener while retaining the taste. Many companies will likely be embracing sugar substitutes or reformulations once the requirement to list added sugars on the nutrition label goes into effect.

Wollan, Malia, "Brand New Hue: The Quest to Make a True Blue M&M," *The New York Times*, Oct. 9, 2016, http://tinyurl.com/gphurx8.

A journalist describes the challenges in removing artificial dyes from food.

Reports and Studies

"Front of Labeling Consumer Research Project," International Food Information Council Foundation, http://tinyurl.com/yce8s2xv.

A nonprofit that studies food safety surveyed 7,363 consumers about front-of-package labels and found that "increasing the amount of nutrition information . . . served to strengthen consumers' comprehension."

Lefferts, Lisa, "Seeing Red: Time for Action on Food Dyes," Center for Science in the Public Interest, 2016, http://tinyurl.com/yakk37x3.

A public-interest group in Washington lays out the case against artificial food dyes and recommends that the Food and Drug Administration ban them or require warning labels on packages.

Simon, Michele, "Nutrition Scientists on the Take from Big Food," Eat Drink Politics, 2015, http://tinyurl.com/y86ju66k.

A food policy attorney finds that a large nutrition association receives tens of thousands of dollars in sponsorship money from major food-industry groups.

Wartella, Ellen, Alice Lichtenstein and Caitlin Boon, eds., "Front-of-Package Nutrition Rating Systems and Symbols: Phase I Report," Institute of Medicine, 2010, http://tinyurl.com/ydbgamnx.

This landmark report from the Institute of Medicine (now the Health and Medicine Division), part of the National Academy of Sciences, focuses on existing front-of-package symbols and systems to determine which approach might work best in the United States.

Wartella, Ellen, *et al.*, "Front-of-Package Nutrition Rating Systems and Symbols: Promoting Healthier Choices (Phase II Report)," Institute of Medicine, 2012, http://tinyurl.com/yazzmcey.

The second half of this influential report recommended that all U.S. packaged foods rate their healthiness by using up to three stars or checks on labels. The report's recommendations have not been implemented.

The Next Step:

Additional Articles from Current Periodicals

Consumer Lawsuits

Miculka, Cameron, "Second lawsuit filed against Kona Brewing parent company," *Hawaii Tribune-Herald*, March 10, 2017, http://tinyurl.com/m8evg9r.

A San Francisco resident sued Craft Brew Alliance in March over its beverage labels that imply the company's beer is brewed in Hawaii.

Steinberg, Julie, "Dannon 'Natural' Yogurt Label Tricks Consumers, Suit Says," Bloomberg BNA, Feb. 13, 2017, http://tinyurl.com/nyqzg4.

A Minnesota woman sued Dannon in February, arguing the company's "all natural" yogurt label is deceiving because the product uses milk from cows that allegedly eat food with GMOs.

Victor, Daniel, "Butter or Margarine? In Dunkin' Donuts Lawsuit, Man Accepts No Substitutes," *The New York Times*, April 4, 2017, http://tinyurl.com/llassf4.

A Massachusetts resident sued 23 Dunkin' Donuts locations in March for serving him a butter substitute with his bagels when the menus said he was supposed to get real butter.

Deregulation

Aubrey, Allison, "More Salt In School Lunch, Less Nutrition Info On Menus: Trump Rolls Back Food Rules," NPR, May 2, 2017, http://tinyurl.com/lgh4xdo.

Agriculture Secretary Sonny Perdue plans to give schools more flexibility on nutrition standards and restaurants more leeway on calorie labeling.

Bomkamp, Samantha, "Calorie labeling rule delayed by FDA until next year," *Chicago Tribune*, May, 1, 2017, http://tinyurl.com/n6u9wrw.

A federal rule requiring food sellers to post calorie counts on their menus was set to take effect in May, but the FDA pushed the deadline back a year.

Toutant, Charles, "Trump's Anti-Regulation Edict Bogs 'Natural' Food-Label Fight," *New Jersey Law Journal*, May 5, 2017, http://tinyurl.com/mtnegf8.

A food law expert says President Trump's executive order requiring the elimination of two older regulations for each new one adapted could affect the fight over the use of "natural" on food labels: Courts that had been waiting for guidance from the Food and Drug Administration (FDA) will now lift stays on lawsuits challenging manufacturers' use of natural on labels.

Health Trends

Bottemiller Evich, Helena, "Michelle Obama's nutrition message to Trump: 'Don't play with our children," *Politico*, May 12, 2017, http://tinyurl.com/k3ctfmq.

Michelle Obama, who as first lady pushed for better food labeling to improve eating habits and reduce childhood obesity, criticized the Trump administration's decision to roll back school nutrition standards that supported her "Let's Move!" campaign.

Marini, Richard, "As organics become more mainstream, offerings in S.A. keep blooming," *San Antonio Express-News*, April 28, 2017, http://tinyurl.com/lunujpb.

With food labels and signage, more grocery stores are seeking to tap into the growing popularity of organic foods.

Peterson, Hayley, "Millions of shoppers are abandoning Whole Foods — and it's not just because of high prices," *Business Insider*, May 11, 2017, http://tinyurl.com/kx8yowa.

A competitor's "Simple Truth" line of organic foods is contributing to the struggles of the Whole Foods chain.

Industry Influence

Dewey, Caitlin, "Industry is counting on Trump to back off rules that tell you what's in your food," *The Washington Post*, April 27, 2017, http://tinyurl.com/lve9pcf.

Multiple food industry groups have cited President Trump's anti-regulatory stances as reason to roll back Obama-era nutritional regulations, including font size on labels, calorie disclosure on menus and label definitions.

Thomas, Katie, "Senate Confirms Scott Gottlieb to Head F.D.A.," *The New York Times*, May 10, 2017, http://tinyurl.com/lxhzkf4.

Newly confirmed FDA Commissioner Scott Gottlieb drew praise from business executives, but consumer advocates fear he is too closely tied to industry and will be hostile to regulatory changes.

CITING *CQ RESEARCHER*

Sample formats for citing these reports in a bibliography include the ones listed below. Preferred styles and formats vary, so please check with your instructor or professor.

MLA STYLE

Mantel, Barbara. "Coal Industry's Future." CQ Researcher 17 June 2016: 529-552.

APA STYLE

Mantel, B. (2016, June 17). Coal Industry's Future. *CQ Researcher*, 6, 529-552.

CHICAGO STYLE

Mantel, Barbara. "Coal Industry's Future." *CQ Researcher*, June 17, 2016, 529-52.

In-depth Reports on Issues in the News

Are you writing a paper?

Need backup for a debate?

Want to become an expert on an issue?

For 90 years, students have turned to *CQ Researcher* for in-depth reporting on issues in the news. Reports on a full range of political and social issues are now available. Following is a selection of recent reports:

Civil Liberties
Privacy and the Internet, 12/15
Intelligence Reform, 5/15
Religion and Law, 11/14

Crime/Law
High-Tech Policing, 4/17
Forensic Science Controversies, 2/17
Jailing Debtors, 9/16
Decriminalizing Prostitution, 4/16
Restorative Justice, 2/16
The Dark Web, 1/16
Immigrant Detention, 10/15

Education
Charter Schools, 3/17
Civic Education, 2/17
Student Debt, 11/16
Apprenticeships, 10/16

Environment/Society
Trust in Media, 6/17
Anti-Semitism, 5/17
Native American Sovereignty, 5/17
Women in Prison, 3/17
Guns on Campus, 1/17
Mass Transit, 12/16

Health/Safety
Sports and Sexual Assault, 4/17
Reducing Traffic Deaths, 2/17
Opioid Crisis, 10/16
Mosquito-Borne Disease, 7/16

Politics/Economy
North Korea Showdown, 5/17
Rethinking Foreign Aid, 4/17
Troubled Brazil, 4/17
Reviving Rural Economies, 3/17
Immigrants and the Economy, 2/17
Trump Presidency, 1/17

Upcoming Reports

The Christian Right, 6/23/17   Hunger in America, 7/7/17   Medical Marijuana, 7/14/17

ACCESS

CQ Researcher is available in print and online. For access, visit your library or www.cqresearcher.com.

STAY CURRENT

For notice of upcoming *CQ Researcher* reports or to learn more about *CQ Researcher* products, subscribe to the free email newsletters, *CQ Researcher Alert!* and *CQ Researcher News*: http://cqpress.com/newsletters.

PURCHASE

To purchase a *CQ Researcher* report in print or electronic format (PDF), visit www.cqpress.com or call 866-427-7737. Single reports start at $15. Bulk purchase discounts and electronic-rights licensing are also available.

SUBSCRIBE

Annual full-service *CQ Researcher* subscriptions—including 44 reports a year, monthly index updates, and a bound volume—start at $1,131. Add $25 for domestic postage.

CQ Researcher Online offers a backfile from 1991 and a number of tools to simplify research. For pricing information, call 800-818-7243 or 805-499-9774 or email librarysales@sagepub.com.

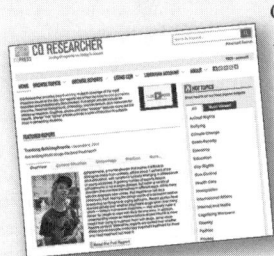

Future of the Christian Right

Are evangelicals losing their political clout?

Conservative white Christian voters — mostly evangelical Protestants, Mormons and Catholics — carried President Trump to victory last November. Many members of this group, known as the Christian Right, argue that while he may be flawed — Trump is twice divorced and has sparked concerns about his personal morality — his opposition to abortion rights and other liberal policy priorities made him the best option. But some evangelicals question whether the Christian Right betrayed Christian principles in backing Trump and whether it will benefit from his administration. The controversy points to a larger debate over the future of the movement as a national political force. Nearly four decades after evangelical leaders joined with Republicans to elect conservatives to office, many experts see little progress on many Christian Right priorities, such as restoring prayer in public schools and banning gay marriage, which is now legal nationwide. Moreover, the share of the population identifying as conservative Christian is declining, potentially weakening the Christian Right's influence.

Anti-abortion activists rally at the Washington Monument on Jan. 27, 2017, for the March for Life, featuring a speech by Vice President Mike Pence. The former Indiana governor is among several conservative Christians in key leadership positions in the Trump administration.

CQ Researcher • June 23, 2017 • www.cqresearcher.com
Volume 27, Number 23 • Pages 533-556

THIS REPORT

INSIDE

THE ISSUES 535

BACKGROUND 541

CHRONOLOGY 543

CURRENT SITUATION 548

AT ISSUE.......................549

OUTLOOK 550

BIBLIOGRAPHY 554

THE NEXT STEP 555

THE ISSUES

535
- Is the Christian Right shrinking in size and influence?
- Will the Trump administration support Christian Right priorities?
- Has the Christian Right reshaped the Republican Party?

BACKGROUND

541 **Early Evangelicals**
White Protestants have dominated American culture since colonial times.

542 **Political Sorting**
Mormons and Catholics joined conservative Protestants on the political right.

544 **Emerging Social Issues**
Efforts to legalize abortion troubled conservative Christians.

547 **Gay Rights Tidal Wave**
The Christian Right lost its battle against gay marriage.

CURRENT SITUATION

548 **Trump Administration**
The president's Cabinet appointments have cheered the Christian Right.

550 **Trump Policies**
The new president has signaled his loyalty to conservative Christians.

OUTLOOK

550 **Cautious Optimism**
Trump's victory may help turn the country from "increasing immorality," says an evangelical leader.

SIDEBARS AND GRAPHICS

536 **Evangelicals Strongly Backed Trump**
The president won 81 percent of the white evangelical Christian vote.

537 **Evangelical Count Dips**
Membership in conservative Christian churches declined for the first time between 2007 and 2014.

540 **Some Issues Divide Evangelical Generations**
Many Millennial and older Christian conservatives differ on issues such as gay marriage.

543 **Chronology**
Key events since 1925.

544 **Evangelical Support for Free Markets Has Long History**
"Freedom is a big concept for the Christian Right."

546 **Finding a Kindred Spirit in Russia**
Some evangelicals applaud Vladimir Putin's social conservatism.

549 **At Issue:**
Will its support of President Trump hurt the Christian Right?

FOR FURTHER RESEARCH

553 **For More Information**
Organizations to contact.

554 **Bibliography**
Selected sources used.

555 **The Next Step**
Additional articles.

555 **Citing CQ Researcher**
Sample bibliography formats.

Cover: AFP/Getty Images/Tasos Katopodis

CQ RESEARCHER

June 23, 2017
Volume 27, Number 23

EXECUTIVE EDITOR: Thomas J. Billitteri
tjb@sagepub.com

ASSISTANT MANAGING EDITORS: Kenneth Fireman, kenneth.fireman@sagepub.com, Kathy Koch, kathy.koch@sagepub.com, Scott Rohrer, scott.rohrer@sagepub.com

ASSOCIATE MANAGING EDITOR: Val Ellicott

SENIOR CONTRIBUTING EDITOR:
Thomas J. Colin
tom.colin@sagepub.com

CONTRIBUTING WRITERS: Marcia Clemmitt, Sarah Glazer, Reed Karaim, Barbara Mantel, Chuck McCutcheon, Tom Price

SENIOR PROJECT EDITOR: Olu B. Davis

INTERN: Robert DePaolo

FACT CHECKERS: Eva P. Dasher, Michelle Harris, Betsy Towner Levine, Robin Palmer

SAGE Publishing | CQPRESS

Los Angeles I London I New Delhi
Singapore I Washington DC I Melbourne

An Imprint of SAGE Publications, Inc.

SENIOR VICE PRESIDENT, GLOBAL LEARNING RESOURCES:
Karen Phillips

EXECUTIVE DIRECTOR, ONLINE LIBRARY AND REFERENCE PUBLISHING:
Todd Baldwin

CQ Researcher (ISSN 1056-2036) is printed on acid-free paper. Published weekly, except: (March wk. 4) (May wk. 4) (July wks. 1, 2) (Aug. wks. 2, 3) (Nov. wk. 4) and (Dec. wks. 3, 4). Published by SAGE Publications, Inc., 2455 Teller Rd., Thousand Oaks, CA 91320. Annual full-service subscriptions start at $1,131. For pricing, call 1-800-818-7243. To purchase a CQ Researcher report in print or electronic format (PDF), visit www.cqpress. com or call 866-427-7737. Single reports start at $15. Bulk purchase discounts and electronic-rights licensing are also available. Periodicals postage paid at Thousand Oaks, California, and at additional mailing offices. POSTMASTER: Send address changes to CQ Researcher, 2600 Virginia Ave., N.W., Suite 600, Washington, DC 20037.

Future of the Christian Right

BY MARCIA CLEMMITT

THE ISSUES

The 40 or so Christian leaders who dined with President Trump on May 3 got what was no doubt an unexpectedly warm welcome.

"It was a fantastic night," said Greg Laurie, senior pastor at Harvest Christian Fellowship in Riverside, Calif., and a member of a panel that advises Trump on evangelical concerns. The president ended up "hanging out with us for like three hours. It just went on and on. I think he was having a good time." [1]

Trump's hospitality shown to evangelicals that night came as no surprise to many political observers. About 45 million white Christians with conservative theological, social and political views — evangelical Protestants, Roman Catholics and Mormons — cast 70 percent of the votes that put Trump in the White House. [2]

In addition to Trump's warm embrace, evangelicals expect the president to help further their social agenda, such as by opposing abortion and expanded rights for gay and transgender people. Evangelicals' hopefulness is based in part on the fact that Trump has selected several conservative Christians for key leadership positions, such as former Indiana Gov. Mike Pence as his running mate, Central Intelligence Agency Director Mike Pompeo, the secretaries of Education, Energy, Agriculture and Health and Human Services (HHS), and the heads of the Environmental Protection Agency (EPA) and the Justice Department.

"I was really surprised to find how many members of this administration were overt Christians, and many of them meet for Bible study every week," Laurie said. [3]

Then-Republican presidential candidate Donald Trump delivers the convocation at evangelical Liberty University, in Lynchburg, Va., on Jan. 18, 2016. Although conservative Christians backed Trump's campaign, some experts question whether the Christian Right will benefit from the Trump administration.

But while many evangelicals are celebrating Trump's election, it remains unclear how Christian Right policy preferences will fare during his administration. President Ronald Reagan, for example, elected with a similar level of conservative Christian support, abandoned rather quickly an attempt to put prayer back in public schools. And President George W. Bush failed in his effort to push a gay marriage ban through Congress.

In addition, Trump has come to power at a crossroads for the movement, when membership in evangelical churches is falling for the first time. Millennials are the largest group leaving, and even some who remain disagree with traditional conservative Christian priorities such as curtailing gay rights. If the decline in membership continues, the movement's influence could wane in coming decades, scholars of religion and politics say.

However, the Christian Right also has seen policy victories, especially at the state level. From 2010 through 2014, for example, states put 231 new abortion limits in place, including restricting the gestational stage at which the procedure can be performed and limiting insurance coverage for abortion. [4] In addition, in 2014 the Supreme Court ruled in favor of private companies owned by conservative Christians when it said President Obama's Affordable Care Act could not require such companies to pay for workers' insurance coverage for contraceptives, which many company owners object to on religious grounds. [5]

Those developments largely are the result of years of political advocacy by the Christian Right, a network of politically active organizations and individuals who consistently support certain conservative policies and aspire to "reassert the public moral authority of Christianity," says Molly Worthen, an assistant professor of history at the University of North Carolina, Chapel Hill (UNC), who studies evangelicalism.

Christian Right voters come mainly from Catholicism, the Church of Latter-day Saints (Mormonism) and the evangelical branch of Protestantism, which believes salvation depends wholly on personal conversion to belief in Jesus Christ; that the Bible is factually true and that every Christian has a duty to convert others. Most Christian Right voters are white. About 6.5 percent of Americans belong to theologically conservative black evangelical congregations, but most black evangelicals embrace more liberal policies and politics. [6]

Religious leaders and scholars offer a variety of reasons why Trump captured

Evangelicals Strongly Backed Trump

Republican presidential candidate Donald Trump won 81 percent of the white, born-again evangelical vote in 2016, a much larger share than he won from any other religious group. White Catholics also voted strongly for Trump, but Hispanic Catholics favored Democratic nominee Hillary Clinton. Mormons and non-evangelical Christians also supported Trump over Clinton.

2016 U.S. Presidential Vote, by Religious Affiliation and Race

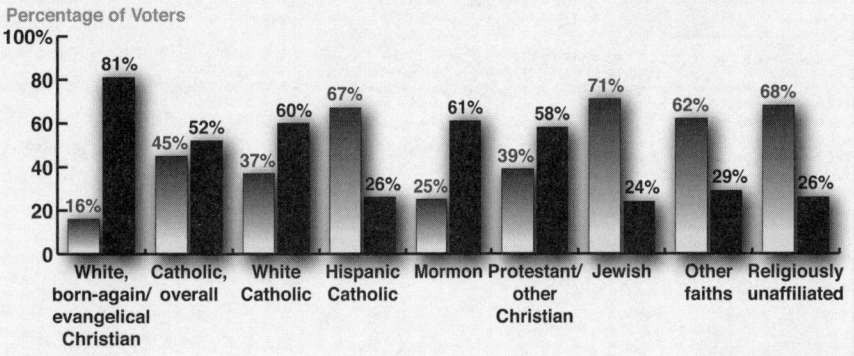

Source: "How the faithful voted: A preliminary 2016 analysis," Pew Research Center, Nov. 9, 2016, https://tinyurl.com/h5zd2fl

81 percent of the white evangelical vote, slightly more than Republican presidential candidates have won since 1980, when the GOP and some Christian leaders first worked together to back conservative candidates. (*See graph, above.*)

Some scholars say deep concern over social issues likely spurred many conservative Christians to vote for Trump. During his campaign, the president promised to promote several key Christian Right priorities including appointing anti-abortion judges, defunding Planned Parenthood, protecting religious liberty and, to the extent possible, rolling back federal legalization of same-sex marriage. [7]

Such social issues spurred many Christian conservatives to support a candidate who came across on the stump as a pugnacious fighter, says Seth Dowland, an associate professor of religion at Pacific Lutheran University in Tacoma, Wash. "This is a war for your culture. So you need a fighter," he says.

Jerry Falwell Jr., president of evangelical Liberty University, in Lynchburg,

Va., however, said that for many conservative Christian voters, Trump's perceived potential to address dire economic and security problems mattered most in 2016, such as his promise to restrict immigration and create jobs. "Social issues come at the bottom of the list after saving our country," said Falwell. "After securing our borders. After stopping terrorism. After . . . getting the debt under control and saving our economy." [8]

Then there were evangelicals like Richard Land, president of the Southern Evangelical Seminary, in Charlotte, N.C., who said last year that he would reluctantly vote for Trump, only because he distrusted Hillary Clinton far more. "Out of the 17 Republican primary candidates, Mr. Trump was my 18th choice," Land said. "However, I cannot vote for Hillary Clinton. . . . [She] is the most pro-abortion presidential candidate ever nominated by a major party." In addition, he continued, the "financial corruption of the Clintons is a truly lethal threat to American democratic government." [9]

But some conservative Christians doubt Trump will push for their priorities. On gay and transgender rights, the administration has sent mixed signals, they say. For example, it has extended an Obama order requiring federal contractors to have LGBT nondiscrimination policies. And in February, the State Department announced that Randy Berry would remain special envoy for the human rights of LGBTI persons, a diplomatic post created by the Obama administration to promote the rights of lesbian, gay, bisexual, transgender and intersex people worldwide. [10] *

Berry's reappointment was a "blow to pro-family advocates who oppose the LGBT agenda and are counting on Trump to root out homosexual and abortion activists" from government, said a commentary in LifeSite, an anti-abortion website. [11]

Meanwhile, demographic issues threaten to weaken the Christian Right's influence. For decades, the percentage of Americans claiming a religious affiliation has been declining. [12] Until recently, white evangelical churches — most but not all of which are politically conservative — were an exception to that rule. But in the last decade, they too have seen their numbers decline.

The largest drops continue among the more liberal, mainline Protestant churches and in the Roman Catholic Church, each of which saw its share of the U.S. population drop by about 3 percentage points between 2007 and 2014. White evangelical Protestantisms' share of the population also fell during that period, but by only about 1 percentage point — from 26.3 percent to 25.4 percent. (*See graph, p. 537.*)

Conservative Christian church membership is declining in part, some religion scholars say, because young adults are more liberal on some cultural issues. For instance, only 23 percent of older evangelical Protestants (born before

_____

* Intersex individuals have both male and female sexual characteristics and organs.

1981) favor same-sex marriage, compared with 45 percent of Millennials, born between 1981 and 1996. [13] (*See graph, p. 540.*)

Millennials also hold liberal attitudes on other policy issues, according to a poll by the Pew Research Center, a nonpartisan think tank in Washington that collects and analyzes social trends data. Among older evangelical Protestants, only 13 percent view the nation's growing immigrant population as a good thing, and only 27 percent say it is good for government to provide more services. But among Millennials, 27 percent view immigration as positive, and 41 percent approve of government-provided services. [14]

The declining numbers and shifting views raise questions about the Christian Right's future strategies and priorities.

At present, at least, softening the Christian Right's stance on hot-button moral issues such as gay marriage just to appeal to younger members appears out of the question for many. "If we have to choose between Jesus and Millennials, we choose Jesus," said Russell Moore, president of the Southern Baptist Convention's Ethics and Religious Liberty Commission. [15]

As the Christian Right, its critics and conservative Republican lawmakers ponder the movement's future, here are some questions they are asking:

Is the Christian Right shrinking in size and influence?

Since the 1960s, the percentage of Americans affiliated with any religious group has declined, with most religiously unaffiliated people saying they no longer believe in churches' teachings, such as that religion is necessary to give children good morals and values. [16]

After bucking this trend for many years, churches whose members make up the Christian Right have seen similar drop-offs over the last decade. Nevertheless, some analysts argue that other trends — such as the fact that many people continue to identify as evangelical Christians even

---

Evangelical Count Dips

Membership in the country's evangelical churches declined for the first time — by just under 1 percentage point — between 2007 and 2014, the most recent year for which data are available. During the same period, membership in mainline Protestant churches and the Roman Catholic Church continued a decades-long fall, each declining by more than 3 points.

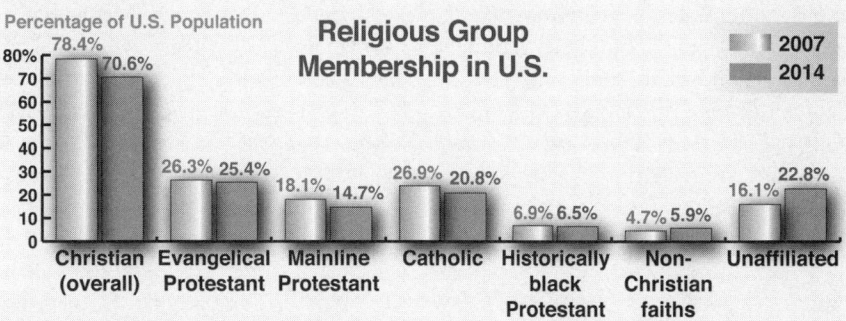

Religious Group Membership in U.S.

Percentage of U.S. Population

2007 / 2014

Christian (overall): 78.4% / 70.6%
Evangelical Protestant: 26.3% / 25.4%
Mainline Protestant: 18.1% / 14.7%
Catholic: 26.9% / 20.8%
Historically black Protestant: 6.9% / 6.5%
Non-Christian faiths: 4.7% / 5.9%
Unaffiliated: 16.1% / 22.8%

Source: "Christians Decline as Share of U.S. Population; Other Faiths and the Unaffiliated Are Growing," Pew Research Center, May 7, 2015, https://tinyurl.com/ohg333s

---

after leaving their churches — make it unlikely that Christian Right numbers and voting power will soon wane.

In the second half of the 20th century, mainline Protestant churches lost members steadily while many white evangelical churches saw strong growth. Between 1960 and 2000, the Episcopal Church lost 900,000 members and the United Methodist Church more than 2 million. On the evangelical side, however, the Church of the Nazarene grew by 300,000 members and the Assemblies of God by at least 2 million during the same period. [17]

More recently, though, the numbers of white evangelicals have declined as well, and steeply, said Robert P. Jones, founder of PRRI (Public Religion Research Institute), a nonpartisan research organization in Washington that studies religion and public life. According to PRRI analyses, mainline Protestants had dropped from 24 percent of the population in 1988 to 14 percent in 2012, at which point their share seems to have stabilized. Meanwhile, white evangelical Protestants made up 22 percent of the population as recently as 2008

but by 2014 accounted for only 18 percent, he wrote. [18]

In 2015, the country's largest primarily white evangelical denomination, the Southern Baptist Convention, saw its membership decline for the ninth straight year. [19] Birth rates for evangelical families also have dropped, says UNC's Worthen, "barely holding steady or declining for decades."

The two other churches that make up most of the Christian Right reflect a similar story. In 2015 the Church of Jesus Christ of Latter-day Saints — the Mormons — whose members strongly identify with Republicans, recorded its lowest annual growth rate — 1.7 percent — since 1937. [20]

The number of white Catholics — the most likely Catholics to identify with the Christian Right in polling — is also falling, wrote Jones. In 1990, they made up 22 percent of the U.S. population. By 2014, their share had dropped to 13 percent, in part a reflection of the fact that the nation is growing less white overall. [21]

The past decade also saw the apparent weakening of the Christian Right's longtime institutions, Jones said. In 2007, two of the Christian Right's most stalwart voices died — evangelist Jerry Falwell Sr. and influential Florida-based televangelist D. James Kennedy. Falwell had created the Moral Majority in 1979 as the first large organization to facilitate the Christian Right-GOP alliance.

And beginning in 2007, the policy and communications organization Focus on the Family laid off hundreds of staffers as it faced budget shortfalls and a dwindling radio audience. By 2011 it operated with half the staff it had in 2002, and it has since remained about this size. [22]

Moreover, many younger evangelicals are becoming alienated because they have more liberal views than their parents, says UNC's Worthen. "They have gay friends. So whatever homophobia they maintain, it has lost the dehumanizing 'ick' factor that continues to make their parents' homophobia so powerful," Worthen says. Thirty-one percent of Millennials who left their childhood churches say negative teachings about gays were a factor. [23]

Nevertheless, it would be a mistake to underestimate the Christian Right's potential for continued influence, many analysts say.

For instance, in the early days of Trump's presidential campaign, his poll numbers among Mormons and Catholics "were terrible," says Neil J. Young, an independent scholar of history and religion who specializes in interfaith relations. "People were writing, 'This is the coming apart of the Religious Right.' But in November, all three groups voted about the same as they have for decades."

Moreover, "the solidification of these groups as Republican has become clear," Young says. "For a long time, they portrayed themselves as outsiders to the party, saying, 'If you don't do certain things, we'll walk away.' But with Trump, they didn't even threaten," he says. "They can't go over to the party that supports gay marriage."

Some scholars also say that falling church affiliations do not necessarily

mean people are abandoning Christian Right ideas. This dynamic played out in the 2016 election, says Pacific Lutheran University's Dowland, in the apparent emergence of a new class of Republican-aligned evangelicals that some call "cultural evangelicals," he says.

"These people say, 'I don't know [evangelist] Billy Graham. I don't know [evangelist] Jerry Falwell. But I'm an evangelical,' " Dowland says. How many people fall into this so-far little studied category is unknown, but most likely live in communities with a long conservative evangelical history, primarily in the South, he says.

And they were the first to support Trump in the Republican primary contests, CNN reported in January 2016. At the time, Trump had low approval among churchgoing evangelicals, although churchgoers ultimately supported him strongly. [24]

Some conservative Christians point out that most conservative Protestant denominations grew so much from the mid-1960s into the 2000s that recent declines hardly dent the overall numbers. The Southern Baptist Convention (SBC), for example, had nearly 11 million members in 1965 but close to 16 million in 2013, even after several years of membership drops, said Joe Carter, an editor at *The Gospel Coalition*, a publication of the evangelical Reformed churches. [25]

Other leaders, however, view the declines as serious and blame them partly on contemporary evangelicals' neglect of their duty to convert others.

"God help us all!" said Frank Page, president and CEO of the SBC Executive Committee. "In a world that is desperate for the message of Christ, we continue to be less diligent in sharing the Good News." [26]

Will the Trump administration support Christian Right priorities?

Ever since conservative Christian leaders such as Jerry Falwell Sr. committed themselves to helping Republicans gain Christian votes nearly 40 years ago, some leaders have com-

plained that the party generally fails to deliver on conservative Christian Right priorities.

Today observers are divided on how top Christian Right goals will fare under a Trump administration.

Some analysts say Trump has already demonstrated his loyalty to Christian Right priorities. "Donald Trump didn't walk around pretending to be a paragon of Christian virtue" during his campaign, said J. Hogan Gidley, a Republican strategist who has worked for conservative Christian policymakers, including former Arkansas Gov. Mike Huckabee. "What he did say was that he'd protect your right to be one." [27]

Trump established an advisory board of conservative evangelicals and repeatedly asked them for recommendations about possible staff appointees, said the Southern Evangelical Seminary's Land, initially a reluctant Trump supporter. Trump's requests were so unusual for a politician that Land said he asked himself, "Are we hallucinating, or is this actually happening?" [28]

Trump delivered on some top priorities early, many observers say. Just a few days after his inauguration, he named a Christian conservative favorite, Neil Gorsuch, a federal judge in Denver, as his nominee for a vacant Supreme Court seat.

"As a family ministry concerned with the sanctity of life, marriage and religious freedom, we are optimistic that Judge Gorsuch will continue to protect our cherished liberties," said Jim Daly, president of Focus on the Family, a Christian conservative advocacy organization in Colorado Springs. [29] The Senate confirmed Gorsuch's nomination on April 7.

On May 15, Trump addressed a policy issue that has long been a Christian Right priority, dramatically expanding the so-called "global gag rule" or "Mexico City Policy" — a funding ban intended to stamp out abortion worldwide. First announced in 1984 by President Reagan and temporarily rescinded by Democratic presidents Bill Clinton and Barack Obama, the ban has been in effect for about 17 of the past 37 years. [30]

In the past, groups that provide abortions, mention abortion to clients or argue for looser abortion restrictions in their countries were barred from receiving any of the approximately $600 million a year in family-planning funds that the U.S. Agency for International Development (USAID) disburses. Under the new rule, the penalty is much harsher. Groups found in violation are barred from receiving not just family-planning funds but any of the $8.8 billion in global health funds dispensed annually by USAID, the U.S. global AIDS coordinator, the State Department or the Department of Defense. [31]

Those early actions indicate Trump is going to be loyal to Christian Right voters, says Mark Rozell, dean of George Mason University's Schar School of Policy and Government in Fairfax, Va.

Many supporters remain hopeful, even after a recent disappointment. Candidate Trump promised to quickly relocate the United States' embassy from Tel Aviv to Jerusalem, which the Bible describes as Israel's most important city. Congress called for the relocation in 1995, but successive presidents have delayed the move, which is politically difficult because Palestinians also claim Jerusalem as their capital. On June 1, Trump signed another six-month postponement.

Nevertheless, "I trust the Trump administration to eventually fulfill their commitment to move our embassy to Jerusalem at the most opportune time," said Robert Jeffress, pastor of the First Baptist Church in Dallas. "'Not now' does not mean 'never.' " [32]

So far, the new president "seems willing to support the Christian Right agenda in ways that previous presidents haven't," says Christopher Stroop, a commentator on evangelical religion and a historian at the University of South Florida in Tampa. The administration may be more in tune with conservative evangelicals than most people realize, he says. Proposed policies to restrict Muslim immigration, for

example, are in line with "a lot of anti-Islam polemics" published by evangelicals, Stroop says.

However, many scholars of religion and politics note that, historically, Republican presidents have opted to spend their political capital on matters favored by other constituencies, such as businesses. For that reason, some are skeptical that Trump will ultimately do more to advance major conservative Christian goals than his predecessors.

Evangelicals' support of Trump "was very utilitarian. They said, 'We know

he's not great, but we also know he'll get us the Supreme Court,' " says Melissa Deckman, a professor of public affairs at Washington College in Chestertown, Md., who studies religion, gender and politics. But it's unlikely that he or his appointees will accomplish the Christian Right's most cherished social-policy goals, she says. "What Trump will do is tax cuts. I guarantee that abortion is still going to be legal."

History suggests that the Christian Right's high hopes are misplaced, said David Gushee, distinguished university professor of Christian ethics at Georgia's Mercer University. "The fact that GOP

presidents of much more serious conservative conviction than Trump routinely have failed to deliver on their promises to the Christian Right seems to be forgotten rather conveniently every four years," Gushee said. [33] (President George W. Bush, himself a conservative evangelical, for example, was unable to push a ban on gay marriage through Congress. [34])

Some observers even warn that the Christian Right might do itself harm by supporting the Trump administration, since the public might view that support as extending to the questionable views

President Trump demonstrated his support of Christian Right priorities early on by picking Neil Gorsuch, a Christian conservative federal judge in Denver, to fill the seat of the late Supreme Court Justice Antonin Scalia. Gorsuch, here testifying during his confirmation hearing before the Senate Judiciary Committee, was confirmed by the Senate on April 7.

of other Trump-supporting groups. The new president most likely regards his white nationalist supporters as his most important constituency, said Rob Schenck, an evangelical minister and activist on homelessness and abortion. (White nationalists, many of whom now dub themselves the "alt-right," support policies such as banning immigration in order to limit the numbers and influence of non-white Americans. [35])

Trump "has no facility in the language of faith" and is likely to simply use Christians' support to push through a potentially white-supremacist agenda that runs contrary to Christ's commandments,

Some Issues Divide Evangelical Generations

Younger evangelical Protestants often hold sharply different views than older evangelicals, a 2014 Pew Research Center poll found. The biggest difference was on same-sex marriage, with 45 percent of younger evangelicals — Millennials, born between 1981 and 1996 — favoring it, versus only 23 percent of older evangelicals.

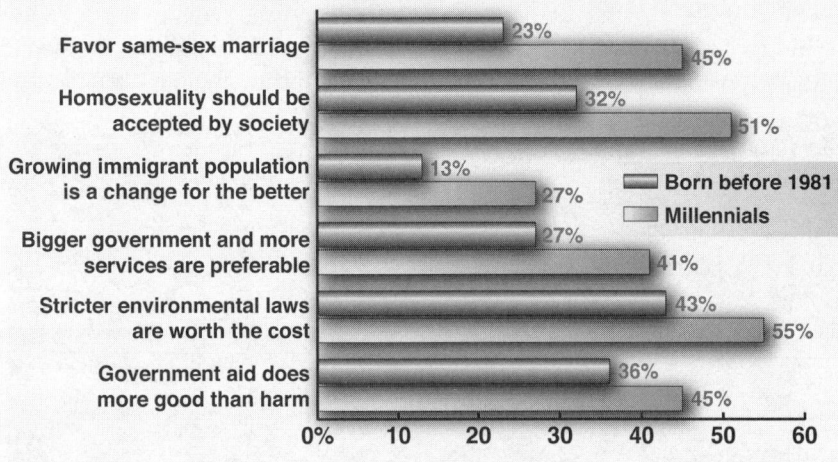

Evangelical Protestants' Views on Social Issues, by Generation, 2014

Favor same-sex marriage — 23% / 45%
Homosexuality should be accepted by society — 32% / 51%
Growing immigrant population is a change for the better — 13% / 27%
Bigger government and more services are preferable — 27% / 41%
Stricter environmental laws are worth the cost — 43% / 55%
Government aid does more good than harm — 36% / 45%

Born before 1981
Millennials

Source: "Evangelical Millennials' views on some issues differ from those of their elders," Pew Research Center, May 3, 2017, https://tinyurl.com/yan6lthl

Schenck said. "Evangelicals are a tool of Donald Trump. This could be the undoing of American evangelicalism." [36]

On June 13, the SBC's annual convention of denomination leaders voted to condemn the alt-right and all racism as "of the devil." [37]

Has the Christian Right reshaped the Republican Party?

Some analysts say conservative Christians have a great deal of influence on the Republican Party, citing substantial changes in party policy positions as a direct result of Christian Right advocacy. Others, however, point out that while the GOP has shifted its platform from socially liberal to socially conservative, conservative policies often are shoved aside.

Republicans' alliance with conservative Christians brought about "real change in issue composition for the GOP," says Daniel Schlozman, an assistant professor

of political science at Johns Hopkins University in Baltimore. The party's central focus has become "social conservatism lashed together with economic conservatism based on low taxes," he says. (*See sidebar, p. 544.*)

Before the alliance, Republican leaders took a generally liberal approach to abortion, gender equality and other social issues, Schlozman and others say. For example, "in the '70s, even among GOP conservatives, there was not much support for squelching abortion rights," says Daniel K. Williams, an associate professor of history at the University of West Georgia in Carrollton. By 1980, though, when the Christian Right and the GOP solidified their union, opposition to abortion entered the Republican slate of issues "and there it's stayed," says Schlozman.

To put an anti-abortion plank in their platform, GOP leaders had to persuade the party's "pro-choice majority" to accept it, which was not easy, according to

Williams. In 1976, the first year the debate surfaced, 28 female delegates to the Republican presidential-nominating convention signed a "minority report urging the Republican Party not to take a position on abortion," he says.

Realizing that GOP leaders were determined to win votes with an anti-abortion stance, however, the women consented to the plank in exchange for a 1976 platform endorsement of the Equal Rights Amendment (ERA) — a constitutional amendment proposed in the 1940s to guarantee that "equality of rights under the law shall not be denied or abridged by the United States or by any state on account of sex." [38] (All Republican platforms had endorsed the ERA, beginning in 1952, and Congress approved it in 1972. Only 35 of the required 38 states had ratified it by the 1982 deadline, however.)

Activists led by the late Phyllis Schlafly, a conservative Catholic and the founder of the Eagle Forum, strenuously opposed the ERA, however. Many viewed it as a threat to the family structure they preferred, in which men were the sole breadwinners. [39] And by the time the 1980 platform appeared, GOP leaders had backed off their support, stating only that "we acknowledge the legitimate efforts of those who support or oppose ratification of the Equal Rights Amendment." [40]

Not only has the GOP-Christian Right alliance moved the party away from long-held liberal social positions, it has also helped lead to polarized politics across the board, some scholars contend. The alliance "has influenced the evolution of the Democratic Party as well," said Clyde Wilcox, a professor of government at Georgetown University.

With high-profile evangelists such as Falwell strongly identifying as Republicans, Democrats changed their campaign strategy in some parts of the country, Wilcox said. In some regions, a Democratic ad linking a televangelist such as Falwell to a Republican candidate could rally voters who feared

Falwell's socially conservative views on issues such as gay rights and birth control. "This inevitably attracted more secular activists to the Democratic Party, which in [turn] pushed more observant Christians to the Republicans." [41]

With only two major parties, the U.S. system is likely to have some liberal-conservative polarization, no matter what, wrote PRRI's Jones. But with religious whites giving a strong majority of their votes to Republicans year after year, while racial minorities and non-religious whites repeatedly vote mostly for Democrats, the political "polarization we are currently witnessing is turbocharged by the racial and religious divisions." When riling up a single demographic group can win an election as effectively as reaching out to a variety of voters, parties have little reason to seek compromise, he wrote. [42]

Despite these changes to the GOP image and the nation's political climate, however, the Republican Party wages fewer all-out battles to enact Christian Right priorities than might be expected, some scholars say. The only marked exception was the fight to increasingly restrict access to abortion, which has been done mainly at the state level, says Williams.

When the 1980s policy achievements of the Christian Right-Republican alliance are tallied up, the Moral Majority turns out to have been "more significant as a way to rebrand the GOP to evangelicals" to win votes than as a way to focus political attention on conservative Christian policy ideas, Williams says.

Today, many Christian conservatives "portray Reagan as having been this perfect president, godlike," but during Reagan's presidency (1981-89), many conservatives complained, " 'You promised us all these things, and then they all went onto the back burner,' " says independent religion scholar Young.

Christian Right disappointments began early, said Graham Dodds, an associate professor of political science at Montreal's Concordia University. When Reagan's term began in 1981, for example,

evangelical Bob Jones University, in Greenville, S.C., was facing the loss of its tax-exempt status because it practiced racial discrimination. To fulfill a promise to evangelical voters, Reagan planned to order the Internal Revenue Service to grant tax-exempt status to schools that refused to desegregate on religious grounds, but he dropped the idea after a public outcry. [43]

And during the 12 years from 1994 through 2006, when the GOP mostly controlled Congress, "only limited symbolic legislation on abortion made it through," said Wilcox. "The attempt to amend the national Constitution to bar same-sex marriage was given less attention than tax cuts and deregulation." The party has mainly used the clout it's gained from having a large and dedicated Christian Right voter pool to enact the priorities of its business wing, Wilcox argued. [44] ∎

BACKGROUND

Early Evangelicals

From America's earliest days, white Protestants have dominated American culture. Puritans and other religious radicals fled Europe in the 17th and 18th centuries seeking freedom of conscience, and the country became a refuge for sects and churches holding vastly different views on Protestantism and politics. [45]

Christians in the 19th century pursued a host of social reforms ranging from abolition of slavery to temperance. People did not separate faith from politics or from their daily lives, says Matthew Sutton, a professor of history at Washington State University in Pullman. In 1845, for example, Baptists split into Southern and Northern branches over the issue of slavery. [46]

Around 1900, a series of bitter debates emerged over such issues as evolution and how to combat poverty. These dis-

putes split nearly all of America's white Christians into opposing groups. One camp with conservative political and theological views was dedicated to maintaining traditional mores. The other group was more open to a modernizing world, where a truth might arise from science as easily as from the Bible.

This division sharpened over the decades as traditionalists grew increasingly unhappy with laws and customs that often moved in a modernist direction. To hold back that tide, some conservative Christian leaders around 1980 allied with the Republican Party, offering to deliver votes in return for the party's support for Christian priorities such as banning abortion. Thus was born the Christian Right, an alliance between a political party and a single demographic group that continues to influence America's religious and political life today. [47]

Until the late 19th century, almost all Protestants called themselves "evangelicals," from the Greek and Latin words for "good news." They proclaimed a faith at whose center was each individual's conversion to Christianity, which often came in the form of a "sudden, overwhelming experience of God's grace," explained historian Frances FitzGerald in her 2017 book, *The Evangelicals*. With conversion came a primary duty: to spread the good news to others, or to evangelize. [48]

However, some Christians wondered whether reason, scientific findings and historical evidence should replace faith and the Bible as standards of truth in some matters. Others struggled to reconcile the belief that theirs was the one true faith with the desire to live peaceably in a religiously diverse society.

Perhaps the most famous example of that struggle was the so-called Scopes "monkey" trial. In July 1925 the state of Tennessee charged substitute high school teacher John Scopes with violating a new law barring the teaching of evolution in state-funded schools. Conservatives — who said evolution contradicted the Bible's version of creation — saw Scopes' conviction as a win, but it was overturned later on a technicality. [49]

The evolution debate was only one of many that arose. "Critical studies of the Bible questioned its divine origins" based on discoveries in fields such as archaeology and linguistics, wrote Darren Grem, an assistant professor of history and Southern studies at the University of Mississippi. "Historical study upended long-held beliefs about the birth, life and death of Christ, as well as about His divinity." [50]

The tension extended into missionary work, says UNC's Worthen. With Protestant conversion rooted in personal emotional experience, some missionaries grew wary of insisting that others embrace a faith they could not logically prove, she says. Modernist missionaries argued that "we shouldn't push our ideas on this Buddhist culture," for example. "We should build hospitals to help people instead," Worthen says. "But conservatives continued to say, 'No. We must preach' " and win converts.

Christians also split bitterly over the Social Gospel — a movement in which modernist Protestants sought to improve the conditions of America's poorest by reforming the economic system, said Michael McVicar, an assistant professor of religion at Florida State University in Tallahassee. [51] Social Gospel clergy preached that a Christian life required efforts to remedy systemic evils, he said.

Some 19th-century clergy had made similar arguments against slavery. Alarmed over poverty in a rapidly industrializing America, Social Gospel advocates made equally controversial proposals, such as allowing workers to unionize and strike and banning child labor and enacting factory safety standards. [52]

Conservative clergy pushed back, wrote Kevin Kruse, a professor of history at Princeton University in New Jersey. They argued that clergy who attributed problems of the poor to bad systems had abandoned Protestantism's central tenet: that helping individuals find a personal relationship with Christ should be a Christian's only spiritual concern. [53]

Political Sorting

Conservative and modernist Protestants also battled to control the network of Protestant institutions around the country, says Worthen, but since leading intellectuals were part of the modernist faction, which wanted to adapt Protestantism to modern conditions, modernists won control.

Meanwhile, conservative Protestants also had been building institutions. In 1887, for example, famed evangelist Dwight Moody had opened the Chicago Evangelization Society to tackle urban problems through evangelical — rather than Social Gospel — means. Society-trained missionaries would help the poor find peace through Christian conversion, not by striking against their employers, said Moody. [54]

Eventually, a network of conservative Protestant colleges, publishing houses and Bible institutes spread through the South and West, said McVicar. This "evangelical subculture largely insulated from broader secular trends" ultimately developed and disseminated the ideas that shaped the Christian Right. [55]

Denominations that leaned modernist, such as the Episcopal and Presbyterian churches, became known as "mainline Protestant," possibly after the wealthy "Main Line" area of Philadelphia where many lived. [56] Conservative Protestants were first called "fundamentalists" but eventually claimed the old name "evangelical." [57]

In the 1930s and early '40s, Democratic President Franklin D. Roosevelt's plan for government safety nets to ease Depression-era poverty presented a defining moment for evangelicals, scholars say. Roosevelt used some of the hated Social Gospel language to describe how New Deal programs would use government systems to help the unemployed and the elderly, says Kruse.

Many Catholic and mainline Protestants praised the plan as "the Christian thing to do," Kruse says. But although numerous Southern Baptists appreciated the promise of economic relief and sup-

ported Roosevelt, many evangelicals viewed his plans with alarm. They argued, for example, that the New Deal was a government ploy to take over religion's place as the supplier of "daily bread" to people in need, says Kruse. [58]

The New Deal era proved an especially powerful spur for 20th-century evangelicals "to look at things politically and adversarially and [try] to gather power unto themselves" to fight changes they opposed, says Darren Dochuk, an associate professor of history at the University of Notre Dame in Indiana.

Also beginning around the 1930s, migration of Southern evangelicals into the Sun Belt regions of Arizona and Southern California accelerated the link between evangelicalism and conservative politics. Northern evangelical churches had long been heavily Republican while Southern evangelicals had voted Democratic, along with other Southern whites, says Dochuk.

But an economic boom in the West, driven by a growing defense industry, made many evangelicals wealthier and more skeptical of tax-funded anti-poverty programs. (*See sidebar, p. 544.*) "In California there was already a strong constituency for free enterprise" that influenced the newcomers, Dochuk says.

In the mid-20th century, the Mormons and white Catholics also shifted toward the political right. Earlier, many Catholics were recent immigrants and urban dwellers, 80 to 90 percent of whom voted Democratic, says independent scholar Young. In midcentury, though, more Catholics moved into all-white-Protestant suburbs and grew more conservative. Eventually, Catholics split their votes roughly 50-50 between the two parties, as they do today, he says.

Mormons, who historically had divided their votes about evenly between the parties, followed the political lead of a church leader, Ezra Taft Benson. Benson, who was Agriculture secretary (1953-61) under Republican President Dwight D. Eisenhower, called for a strenuous fight against socialism at home

Continued on p. 544

Chronology

1920s-1940s
White Protestants split over politics and theology and form mainline and conservative evangelical wings.

1925
Christian conservatives hail the conviction of teacher John Scopes, charged with violating a Tennessee law against teaching evolution.

1940
Conservative Los Angeles pastor James Fifield argues that President Franklin D. Roosevelt's New Deal violates Christ's teachings by elevating group actions over individual freedom.

1960s-1970s
Conservative Christians feel increasingly at odds with a liberalizing society.

1960
Mainline Protestant churches begin losing members while evangelical ones see substantial growth. . . . Evangelist Bob Jones Sr. criticizes civil rights movement.

1962
Supreme Court bans nondenominational prayer in public schools.

1964
After the Civil Rights Act passes, IRS moves to end tax-exempt status for segregated Christian schools and colleges.

1972
Congress approves the Equal Rights Amendment (ERA) to ensure equal treatment under law for women, but it fails to get the 38 states needed for ratification.

1973
Supreme Court's *Roe v. Wade* ruling legalizes abortion.

1974
Republican Party is in disarray after President Richard M. Nixon resigns in Watergate scandal.

1976
To win conservative Christian votes, Republicans add anti-abortion plank to platform but keep a pro-ERA plank. . . . Democrat Jimmy Carter, a former Georgia governor and a Southern Baptist Sunday school teacher, wins presidency with help from conservative Christian voters.

1979
Frustrated with Carter's overtures to gays, feminists and other liberals, conservative Christian groups ally with Republican Party. . . . Christian Right forms after evangelist Jerry Falwell Sr. creates the voter-outreach group Moral Majority to help the GOP.

1980s-1990s
Conservative white evangelicals, Mormons and conservative Catholics become solid Republican voting bloc.

1980
Activists led by conservative Catholic Phyllis Schlafly persuade GOP to drop support for the ERA.

1985
Cartoonist Vic Lockman publishes "Biblical Economics," a comic book for teaching conservative economics to home-schooled children.

1988
Televangelist Pat Robertson loses Republican presidential nomination.

1989
Moral Majority shuts down. . . . Robertson creates the Christian Coalition to continue Christian voter outreach with a greater emphasis on local politics.

1997
Conservative Christian Allan Carlson founds World Congress of Families to host international discussions about stopping the spread of liberal laws on gay marriage and other issues.

2000s-Present
Christian Right voters become a large faction of GOP base.

2004
Massachusetts is first state to legalize same-sex marriages.

2015
Southern Baptist Convention, the country's largest Protestant evangelical denomination, sees ninth year of membership decline. . . . Mormon church records lowest annual growth rate — 1.7 percent — since 1937.

2016
Republican Donald Trump receives strong backing from Christian Right voters and is elected president.

2017
Trump appoints Christian conservative Neil Gorsuch to Supreme Court and numerous conservative Christians to top posts, including attorney general. . . . Trump signs legislation aimed at halting federal funding to Planned Parenthood, a move long sought by conservative Christians who oppose the group's support of abortion. (April)

Evangelical Support for Free Markets Has Long History

"Freedom is a big concept for the Christian Right."

Long before the coalition between the Christian Right and Republican Party emerged in the 1980s, conservative Republican economic policies — low taxes, lightly regulated markets and strict limits on welfare benefits — enjoyed widespread support among evangelicals, historians say.

Theology-based arguments in favor of free-market economics were common at least as early as the 1930s, say scholars. An early example occurred during the Great Depression when President Franklin D. Roosevelt pursued his New Deal reforms, including creation of public works programs for the unemployed and Social Security for the elderly, says Kevin Kruse, a professor of history at Princeton University.

Noting the role that individual freedom played in Protestant theology and conservative economics, some business leaders opposed to the reforms enlisted clergy to counter Roosevelt, says Kruse.

The theological campaign against the New Deal was developed largely by James Fifield, pastor of Los Angeles' First Congregational Church. According to Kruse, Fifield argued that the central tenet of Protestant belief was that each individual was free and empowered to choose personal salvation through Christ; thus, only an individualistic economic system based on free choice — with as little government involvement as possible — could exemplify Christ's teachings. These arguments helped reshape the national debate about the relationship between government and the economy, Kruse said. [1]

But scholars note that evangelicals draw different political conclusions from different biblical teachings, such as verses on charity and helping the poor.

Many members and clergy of black evangelical churches, for example, embrace "liberal" politics that emphasize an activist government, says Melissa Deckman, professor of public affairs at Washington College in Chestertown, Md.

Meanwhile, a 2014 book by Lydia Bean, a Texas-based sociologist who writes about religion in public life, looked at the political beliefs of four theologically similar evangelical congregations — two in northern New York state and two just across the border in Canada — and found they were near polar opposites. [2]

On the question of whether government should support individuals' health and welfare, the U.S. evangelicals took the conservative view that allowing the state to help people represents the failure of churches, which should provide such help themselves, says Deckman, while the Canadian evangelicals took the liberal view that taxpayer-provided support is fine.

Through the decades, many U.S. evangelical leaders made a concerted effort to promote free-market capitalism, says Seth Dowland, an associate professor of religion at Pacific Lutheran University in Tacoma, Wash. The late Jerry Falwell Sr., an evangelist who founded the Christian Right organization Moral Majority, defended free-market capitalism in sermons beginning in the 1950s, says Dowland.

Evangelicals' belief in traditional families with a working father and stay-at-home mother often drove their support of conservative economics, says Dowland. In the 1980s, Falwell supported tax cuts because they would help women stay home, Dowland says.

Around 1980, conservative Christian home schooling took off and provided a powerful new vehicle for conservative economic ideas, says Michael McVicar, an assistant professor of religion at Florida State University in Tallahassee. For example, Vic Lockman, a cartoonist who created many of the Donald Duck characters, wrote *Biblical Economics in Comics*, which laid out the libertarian free-market views of Rousas Rushdoony, an evangelical Calvinist theologian and home-schooling pioneer, McVicar says.

Continued from p. 542

and abroad during the post-World War II Cold War period. Benson's lasting influence encouraged many Mormons to become conservative Republicans, Young says.

Emerging Social Issues

Beginning in the 1960s, new social issues emerged that troubled conservative Christians and caused some clergy to seek political allies.

In its 1962 *Engel v. Vitale* decision, for example, the Supreme Court declared

that a school-sponsored, voluntary, nondenominational prayer recited in a public school violated the constitutional ban on government-established religion. [59] "The school prayer issue was very galvanizing" for white evangelical Protestants, as well as for conservative Catholics and Mormons, Young says.

The three groups worked to bring school-sponsored prayer back into the schools. And although their efforts failed, the process taught them that they had more in common than with liberal Catholics and mainline Protestants, an insight that paved the way for the Christian Right to emerge, he says. [60]

The civil rights movement further politicized white evangelicals. High-profile evangelists preached against civil-rights protests and racial integration. On Easter Sunday in 1960, Bob Jones Sr., founder of Bob Jones University, told his congregation that "for a man to stand up and preach pious sermons in this country . . . about rubbing out the line between the races — I say it makes me sick." [61]

After the federal Civil Rights Act passed in 1964, the IRS withdrew tax-exempt status from some evangelical schools and colleges, including Bob Jones University, because they practiced racial discrimina-

"These folks may never have heard a political message from the pulpit, just hellfire and brimstone. But they home-schooled their kids and got strong political messages without realizing it" through such home-schooling materials, says McVicar.

The political organization Christian Coalition, founded in 1989, rallied voters around conservative economics, says Mark Rozell, dean of George Mason University's Schar School of Policy and Government in Fairfax, Va.

In voter guides, the Christian Coalition listed numerous policy issues that affected families, Rozell says. But they put economics and taxes atop the list to "show voters the connection between government economic policy" and evangelical beliefs, he says.

Stephanie A. Martin, an assistant professor of corporate communication and public affairs at Southern Methodist University in Dallas, examined more than 100 sermons by evangelical pastors putting the 2008 recession into a faith context. As in the arguments made against Roosevelt's New Deal, the pastors focused on the primacy of individual choice in shaping the economy, she says. [3]

In all realms of life, the sermons indicated, "individual, internal failings can lead to massive calamities" such as a recession, Martin says. For example, pastors generally did not mention how banks or lax government regulation allowed risky mortgages that helped trigger the recession. Instead, they stressed "that individuals failed to do the right thing in their finances because of personal failings," Martin says.

White evangelical Christians are the Americans most likely to embrace conservative economic principles, researchers say. In one survey, 74 percent of white evangelical Protestants preferred lower taxes and fewer government services, compared

In a case closely watched by evangelicals, members of the Little Sisters of the Poor and others celebrate May 16, 2016, after the Supreme Court suspended a requirement in the Affordable Care Act that religious organizations cover contraception in their employee health plans. The justices ordered the government and religious employers to come up with a new plan for contraception coverage that doesn't require the employers' direct participation.

with 65 percent of white Catholics and 58 percent of all Americans. [4]

— *Marcia Clemmitt*

[1] Kevin Kruse, *One Nation Under God: How Corporate America Invented Christian America* (2015), Kindle edition, location 414.

[2] Lydia Bean, *The Politics of Evangelical Identity: Local Churches and Partisan Divides in the United States and Canada* (2014).

[3] Stephanie A. Martin, "Recession Resonance: How Evangelical Megachurch Pastors Promoted Fiscal Conservatism in the Aftermath of the 2008 Financial Crash," *Rhetoric & Public Affairs*, Spring 2015, http://tinyurl.com/yao7lef4.

[4] Melissa Deckman, "Faith and the Free Market: Are Evangelicals Economic Conservatives Too?" Religion in Public, Feb. 14, 2017, http://tinyurl.com/ya68sojw.

tion. Evangelicals disputed the rulings based on the idea that individual freedom is Protestant theology's highest value.

Other emerging social issues troubled conservative Christians. The 1973 Supreme Court ruling in *Roe v. Wade*, legalizing abortion nationwide, distressed conservative Catholics, for example. Many evangelical leaders initially supported it, however. [62]

"I have always felt that it was only after a child was born and had a life separate from its mother that it became an individual person and it has always, therefore, seemed to me that what is best for the mother and for the future

should be allowed," wrote W.A. Criswell, pastor of Dallas's First Baptist Church, in response to the court's ruling. [63] By the late 1970s, however, in an effort that helped to create the Christian Right, some Republican operatives and influential evangelists persuaded most evangelicals that their theology supported an anti-abortion position. [64]

Throughout the 1970s, growing fear that many social trends threatened families and faith sent conservative Christian leaders looking for political champions, historians say.

In the 1976 presidential election, former Georgia Gov. Jimmy Carter, a South-

ern Baptist Sunday school teacher and a Democrat, faced off against incumbent Gerald R. Ford. [65] Carter was a devout evangelical who, for example, considered homosexuality and abortion "inherently sinful," said J. Brooks Flippen, a history professor at Southeastern Oklahoma State University in Durant. That raised hopes he might be the champion conservative Christians had sought.

But Carter, who had a modernist bent, soon disappointed many conservative Christians, said Flippen. His administration consulted with the gay community, appointed a divorced single mother to lead a White House conference

Finding a Kindred Spirit in Russia

Some evangelicals applaud Vladimir Putin's social conservatism.

For allies in its fight to defend traditional values, many in the Christian Right are looking to a seemingly unusual place: the Russia of President Vladimir Putin.

"Isn't it sad . . . that America's own morality has fallen so far that on this issue — protecting children from any homosexual agenda or propaganda — Russia's standard is higher than our own?" wrote evangelist Franklin Graham, president of the Billy Graham Evangelistic Association. He was referring to a 2013 Russian law, signed by Putin, that bans distribution of any material to minors that casts "nontraditional sexual relations" in a positive light or depicts "traditional" and "nontraditional" sexual relations as equivalent in social value. [1]

Graham's frustration echoes that of many conservative Christians in Western democracies, who see both law and public opinion increasingly embracing the once unthinkable — allowing gay marriage or adoption by gay families. By contrast, Russia and some of the former communist — and atheist — Soviet-bloc countries have returned to their religiously conservative Russian Orthodox roots and are banning what they view as threats to the "natural family." [2]

In 2011, Russia enacted its first abortion restrictions in decades, allowing the procedure only through the 12th week of pregnancy except in some special circumstances. [3] Two years later, it banned adoption of Russian children by any country in which gay marriage was recognized. [4]

"Many Euro-Atlantic countries have moved away from their roots, including Christian values," Putin said in a December 2013 speech. "Policies are being pursued that place on the same level a multi-child family and a same-sex partnership. . . . This is the path to degradation." [5]

Partnering with the Russian Orthodox Church, Putin's government is attempting to influence social conservatives around the world, including in Western democracies, by tapping into their anxiety over the loss of traditional mores.

Some say the effort is succeeding. A Russian Orthodox cathedral that recently opened in Paris "is an outpost of the other Europe — ultraconservative and anti-modern — in the heart of the country of libertinism and secularism," wrote Michel Eltchaninoff, a Russian-French philosopher and author of the 2015 book *The Putin Doctrine.* [6]

"Having swept all before them in the aimless societies of the West, the LGBTIQ [Lesbian, Gay, Bisexual, Transgender, Intersex and Questioning] crowd is in a howling fury with Russia's pro-family movement for its refusal to capitulate to their gay-marriage agenda," said Janice Shaw Crouse, a senior fellow at the Beverly LaHaye Institute, a conservative Christian think tank in Washington. But Russia will hold firm, she said. "Whatever critiques of Putin's foreign policy you may have, the pro-family movement in Russia is a genuine and deep phenomenon, unrelated to foreign affairs."

Russians who have clear memories of their recent past under atheist communist rule are embracing their Orthodox heritage and will fight threats to the traditional family from modern trends such as feminism, Crouse said. [7]

Historian Christopher Stroop, a Russia specialist at the University of South Florida in Tampa, says many Russians believe "the West has become too godless, and that Russia has a divine calling to reverse this."

Scholars also point out, however, that the Russian campaign is about driving a wedge between conservative Christians and the secular Left in Western nations.

on family issues and campaigned for the Equal Rights Amendment. [66]

Conservative Christians "believed that he was, at best, ineffective at stopping" social trends they abhorred and "at worst a wolf in sheep's clothing," says the University of West Georgia's Williams.

At around the same time, the Republican Party was scrambling to find a new identity after the Watergate scandal that led to the resignation of President Richard M. Nixon. "There was a lot of GOP soul searching about what could define the party, how they might unify it," says Williams. The party was willing to listen to conservative Christian leaders, who had long hoped to gain

politicians' support for their concerns, Williams says. [67]

Conservative Christians around the country constituted "a moral majority" of people who agreed on many issues but were "separated by geographical and denominational differences that have caused them to vote differently," Republican operative Paul Weyrich said at a meeting about the potential alliance. Falwell seized on "Moral Majority" for the name of his new organization to link evangelicals with the party. [68]

In 1980, with the support of conservative Christians and their TV and radio broadcast ministries, Republican presidential nominee Reagan won an impressive victory over Carter. [69] "One of the

things that drove fundamentalists to get involved was the feeling that they were a disenfranchised people," said top Falwell aide Ed Dobson. "The 1980 election affirmed us as more than an inconsequential splinter group in American culture." [70]

It was unclear, however, whether Christian leaders had actually brought in new voters. "They at least did increase the turnout level [of evangelicals] in the 1980s and 1990s compared to the 1940s and 1950s," says Corwin Smidt, a professor emeritus of political science at Calvin College in Grand Rapids, Mich. "If you increase evangelical turnout by just 2 percent, then you win," he says.

For its part, the GOP proposed a constitutional amendment to outlaw

Russian advocates of traditional values are "very good at pushing a narrative that's seductive to the Religious Right" as well as to white nationalist groups and other ultra-conservatives to whom Putin has reached out in the past few years, says Stroop. "They say, 'We Russians have already defeated communism and so we know how to win in this new fight' " against the West's rising secularism and liberalism, he says.

The endgame of Putin's fledgling alliances with Western conservatives — and, especially, how they relate to Western conservatives' own political goals — isn't clear, Stroop and other analysts say. "Putin is not a complete cynic," Stroop says. "He does believe that Russia should be a great state," an aspiration in tune with the Russian sense of its historical destiny.

Under Putin, there's "also a broader attempt to drive Western instability and undermine faith in democratic institutions" in order to give Russia the upper hand in foreign affairs, Stroop says. For some members of the Christian Right and other disgruntled Westerners to admire Russia more than their own governments "shows them that there are alternatives to liberal democracy," an idea that Putin wants to foster, he says.

"Russia has long wanted to weaken its perceived rivals in the West and would work with the Left or the Right to weaken them," says Stroop. "With Putin now, it's the Right."

— *Marcia Clemmitt*

Russian President Vladimir Putin, at a church in Pskov, Russia, is an unlikely ally of conservative Christians. His government is partnering with the Russian Orthodox Church to support social conservatives worldwide.

[1] Franklin Graham, "Putin's Olympic Controversy," Billy Graham Evangelistic Association, Feb. 28, 2014, http://tinyurl.com/y8pc8vqh; Innokenty (Kes) Grekov, "Russia's Anti-Gay Law, Spelled Out in Plain English," *Mic*, Aug. 8, 2013, http://tinyurl.com/y8shjwk3.

[2] For background, see Casey Michel, "How Russia Became the Leader of the Global Christian Right," *Politico*, Feb. 9, 2017, http://tinyurl.com/gvsmvz5; Masha Gessen, "Family Values," *Harper's*, March 2017, http://tinyurl.com/y8gxmppv; and Christopher Stroop, "Russian Social Conservatism, the U.S.-based WCF, & the Global Culture Wars in Historical Context," Political Research Associates, Feb. 16, 2016, http://tinyurl.com/y9yqv8tn.

[3] "Russia: Abortion Restrictions Adopted," The Associated Press, *The New York Times*, Oct. 21, 2011, http://tinyurl.com/y7983psf.

[4] "Russia's Putin signs law limiting adoption by gays," The Associated Press, *USA Today*, July 3, 2013, http://tinyurl.com/ycs3tvae.

[5] Patrick Buchanan, "Whose Side Is God on Now?" *Creators*, April 14, 2014, http://tinyurl.com/ydxowxxq.

[6] Andrew Higgins, "In Expanding Influence, Faith Combines With Firepower," *The New York Times*, Sept. 13, 2016, http://tinyurl.com/hlgk9db.

[7] Janice Shaw Crouse, "Learning from Russia's Return to Its Historical Roots," *The American Thinker*, Sept. 19, 2014, http://tinyurl.com/y8mbdpsk.

abortion in its 1980 political platform. And Reagan himself campaigned that year on the promise to push an amendment allowing school prayer. [71] Neither measure advanced, but in 1984 Reagan easily won a second term.

The Moral Majority disbanded in 1989, declaring its mission accomplished. [72] Falwell and some other Christian Right leaders of the 1980s had "become disillusioned with the task of trying to fight America's cultural shifts" toward diversity and sexual openness, says Williams. In addition, by the second half of the 1980s, "public opinion polls repeatedly indicated that a substantial majority of the population held negative views of Falwell and his organization," said William Martin, a professor emeritus of religion and public policy at Rice University in Houston. [73]

Also in 1989, Virginia-based televangelist Pat Robertson, who had unsuccessfully sought the Republican presidential nomination in 1988, formed a new group, the Christian Coalition. Republican activist Ralph Reed served as executive director. The Christian Coalition targeted local, state and national races in an effort to integrate conservative Christians into party operations at every level. [74]

"In terms of mobilizing voters, Reed probably had far more impact than Falwell had," says Pacific Lutheran University's Dowland. The Christian Coalition said "we need school boards, not a president. It was an effective strategy and a new one," he says, that achieved some long-held conservative Christian goals, such as restricting the teaching of evolution in some schools.

Gay Rights Tidal Wave

In 2000 and 2004, Christian conservatives won a long-awaited victory when evangelical Republican George W. Bush was elected and then re-elected president. While his administration was largely defined by the Sept. 11, 2001, terrorist attack on the United States and the controversial wars in Iraq and Afghanistan that ensued, he appointed two conservative Catholics to the Supreme Court — Chief Justice John Roberts and Justice Samuel Alito. He also banned a particular second- and third-trimester abortion procedure that abortion opponents call especially brutal, and he sought — unsuccessfully — to get national and international bans on human cloning. [75]

The culture at large continued to move in a liberal social direction in many ways, however, said PRRI's Jones. "No issue captures white Christian America's loss of the culture better than the rapid rise in public support for same-sex marriage" beginning in the

that resembled Roosevelt's New Deal, many scholars say. [77]

"Although President Obama is not the Antichrist, he is certainly paving the way for the Antichrist," by flouting God's laws while still enjoying public support, said Jeffress, of Dallas. [78]

In the 21st century, the Christian Coalition and other Christian Right organizations continue to operate, but with little fanfare, since the job they were created for is largely completed, says Johns Hopkins' Schlozman. The goal of the Christian Right "was to transform conservative Christians into loyal Republican voters, and it has,"

CURRENT SITUATION

Trump Administration

Thirty-six years after the Christian Right hailed the inauguration of Reagan, its first presidential choice, questions remain about whether the controversial new president — who was once a Democrat who declared "I'm very pro-choice" — will champion conservative Christian interests. [81] By appointing staunch Christian conservatives to his administration and to the Supreme Court, however, Trump has given many in the Christian Right the first real hope they've had in years for more federal action to restrict abortion, according to some of Trump's supporters. But with Christian conservatives slowly dwindling as a share of the population, the way forward for the Christian Right seems less clear than ever.

In its staffing, "the administration has been way over the top in giving [conservative Christians] visibility and recognition," said Ronnie Floyd, pastor of Cross Church in northwest Arkansas and a past president of the Southern Baptist Convention. Among "followers of Christ" appointed to top posts are HHS Secretary Tom Price, EPA chief Scott Pruitt, Agriculture Secretary Sonny Perdue, Energy Secretary Rick Perry and Attorney General Jeff Sessions. [82]

An early pick was Pence as vice president. As governor of Indiana, Pence had drawn cheers from conservative Christians and howls from civil-rights groups when he signed the state's 2015 Religious Freedom Restoration Act. The law required the government to allow individuals to act in accord with their religious principles unless the government had a compelling interest in stopping them. Gay-rights groups and others said

Evangelical Christians attend a service at the First Baptist North Church in Spartanburg, S.C. President Trump won 81 percent of the white, born-again evangelical vote in 2016, which is largely concentrated in the South. The share of the nation's population identifying as conservative Christian is declining, potentially weakening the Christian Right's influence.

AFP/Getty Images/Nicholas Kamm

mid-2000s, he said. In 2006, New Jersey had authorized civil unions for gay and lesbian couples. In 2007, New Hampshire legalized civil unions, and Washington state and Oregon approved same-sex domestic partnerships. In 2009, Iowa, Vermont and the District of Columbia approved same-sex marriage, and the trend of acceptance accelerated from there. [76]

For much of the Christian Right, the 2008 election of Democrat Barack Obama represented a horror, as he embraced same-sex marriage and created a government-run health care program

he says. That fact became clear in the outcome of the 2016 presidential contest.

As the 2016 primary season began, polling suggested that Trump might struggle to win enough Christian Right votes to become the party's nominee, let alone win the general election. Soon, however, non-churchgoing evangelicals were telling pollsters that they supported the controversial businessman and reality-TV star. [79] And once he gained the nomination, Trump won over conservative churchgoers as well, with about four of every five white evangelical votes going for Trump. [80]

Continued on p. 550

At Issue:

Will its support of President Trump hurt the Christian Right?

JOSEPH LOCONTE
*ASSOCIATE PROFESSOR OF HISTORY,
KING'S COLLEGE, NEW YORK CITY*

WRITTEN FOR *CQ RESEARCHER*, JUNE 2017

*i*f the conservative Christians who endorsed Donald Trump for president are having qualms, there isn't much evidence. Trump delivered his first commencement speech as president at evangelical Liberty University in Lynchburg, Va.

Liberty President Jerry Falwell Jr. delighted the audience with this hymn of praise: "I do not believe any president in our lifetimes has done so much that has benefited the Christian community in such a short time span as Donald Trump."

Whatever the imagined benefits, the costs of enthusiasm for this presidency are likely to be severe.

First, the notion that character is irrelevant to political leadership is becoming normalized. For all the effort the Founders invested in designing a constitution, they never imagined that republican government could be preserved without virtue. George Washington, in his Farewell Address, deemed religion and morality "indispensable supports" to political prosperity, calling them the "firmest props of the duties of Men and citizens" and essential to patriots.

By embracing Trump, conservative Christians have validated a secular mythology about America's experiment in self-government: no need for faith or morals. They have forgotten that history is littered with the tragic mistakes of leaders blinded by ambition, hubris, lust, racism and greed.

Second, we are likely to see a continued deterioration of trust in our political institutions. Conservatives complain that the political Left, by using executive orders and federal courts to impose a social agenda, has subverted the democratic process.

They have a point. But Trump is unlikely to reverse this trend. His personal attacks on public servants and government agencies — he has compared CIA officers to Nazis — make the problem worse. We can expect more cries to simply "blow up the system."

Finally, there is the cancer of identity politics — an obsession with "rights" based on group identity, regardless of any obligations to the common good. This brand of tribalism, pioneered by liberals, now threatens to infect conservative Christianity. Hence the message of Trump supporters: The president can play the bully, as long as he is *our* bully. By endorsing a politics of grievance, Christians will further weaken and marginalize their influence in public life.

Is this the new face of Christians in politics? Maybe we need a little more of that old-time religion: the gospel of grace that rescues the poor in spirit and breaks the backs of the proud.

JOSHUA C. WILSON
*ASSOCIATE PROFESSOR OF
POLITICAL SCIENCE, UNIVERSITY
OF DENVER; AND*
AMANDA HOLLIS-BRUSKY
*ASSOCIATE PROFESSOR OF
POLITICS, POMONA COLLEGE*

WRITTEN FOR *CQ RESEARCHER*, JUNE 2017

*i*n 2016, the Christian Right seemed headed for a walk in the political wilderness. The Supreme Court had ruled against a promising means of restricting abortion access, and Hillary Clinton's anticipated election would allow Democrats to fill a vacant Supreme Court seat. The fight against gay marriage appeared lost, and the emerging battle against the transgender community had met potent resistance.

The November election changed everything. And while some argue that support of President Trump could harm conservative Christians, it already has produced benefits, redirecting the movement from the margins to the center of power. The appointments of Justice Neil Gorsuch to the Supreme Court, Betsy DeVos as Education secretary, and Jerry Falwell Jr., president of Liberty University, to head a higher education task force show what the Christian Right can gain.

Gorsuch is hailed as a natural successor to the late Antonin Scalia. He favors states' rights and is deeply skeptical of the regulatory state. But whereas Scalia demonstrated hesitance to elevate religious liberty concerns over health, safety and welfare regulations, Gorsuch has favored a muscular interpretation of religious liberty, deriving from a commitment to natural law — the belief that specific, God-given rights form the basis of law.

This commitment forms the heart of the Christian Right's legal movement and has implications for reproductive rights, physician-assisted suicide and, perhaps, the death penalty.

DeVos' interest in school vouchers that could be used at religious schools, and how the Christian Right stands to benefit from them, is clear. While the details regarding the higher education task force are unknown, Falwell's selection suggests intent in part to open up accreditation standards and federal qualifications for higher education institutions such as religious universities and religious law schools that have had problems in the past.

Christian leaders have long faced questions about how to preserve their educational institutions' unique character in the face of accreditation standards and federal rules regarding non-discrimination. Some schools faced internal battles over allowing students to accept federal financial aid, since doing so might threaten a school's ability to control its mission. As task force head, Falwell stands to lower the costs of creating such schools and to strengthen their abilities to control their Christian character.

As with the Christian Right generally, these schools' prospects of reaching their goals was in question half a year ago. The elevation of Gorsuch, DeVos and Falwell demonstrate Trump's recognition of the importance of empowering the Christian Right.

Continued from p. 548

the measure could lead to rampant discrimination. [83] Later that year, Pence approved legislative changes intended to liberalize the law, but that pleased neither its supporters nor its opponents. [84]

As vice president, Pence, of course, casts tie-breaking votes in the Senate if it deadlocks, which he did on March 30, ending an Obama administration rule that forbade states from withholding federal grants for women's health clinics as a way to stop them from providing abortions and contraceptives. [85]

The CIA's Pompeo, also an evangelical Christian, stresses that the small Muslim minority who are terrorists will "press against us until we . . . make sure that we know that Jesus Christ our Savior is truly the only solution for our world." [86]

Education Secretary Betsy DeVos is a Michigan philanthropist who has said she wants the administration to channel more government money to parents for tuition at private schools, including religious schools. DeVos has called her long-time fight for such "school choice" policies a way to "advance God's kingdom." [87]

Among conservative Christians deeper in the bureaucracy is longtime leading abortion opponent Charmaine Yoest, a former staff member at the Family Research Council, a conservative Christian lobbying group, and former president of the anti-abortion group Americans United for Life. As the assistant secretary for public affairs, Yoest will direct communication policies for the Department of Health and Human Services. [88]

Of Yoest's appointment, Marjorie Dannenfelser, president of the anti-abortion group Susan B. Anthony List, said, "This is a new era for the pro-life movement and our fight to protect unborn children and their mothers from the horror of abortion." [89]

Trump Policies

While the Trump administration is still in its early days, the new president has sent some strong signals of loyalty to the Christian Right.

Perhaps the most significant was his Jan. 31 nomination of Gorsuch to the Supreme Court. Gorsuch was confirmed to take the seat of Justice Antonin Scalia, which had stood vacant since Scalia's death on Feb. 13, 2016. [90]

Americans can count on Gorsuch to recognize "the human rights of the pre-born" and "to protect the rights of conscience for all people and to embrace the role of religion in serving the public good," said Mike Norton, senior counsel for the conservative Christian legal non-profit Alliance Defending Freedom. [91]

In addition, on May 4, the president issued an executive order expanding the right of nonprofits such as churches and charities to participate in political campaigns by donating money and publicly endorsing or opposing candidates, while remaining tax-exempt. Such activity was banned under the 1954 "Johnson Amendment." The May 4 action orders the IRS to stop enforcing that amendment against churches and other religious organizations. [92]

Some conservative Christians applaud the step. "We should not be muzzled on political issues just because we're people of faith," said Franklin Graham, son of famed evangelist Billy Graham and president of the Billy Graham Evangelistic Association. The order shows that Trump will be loyal to supporters, he said. [93]

Some critics, however, note that the IRS has rarely penalized churches for political speech by clergy. Moreover, they argue that the order would allow political donors to funnel large amounts of cash into political campaigns through existing religious nonprofits without transparency about the money's source. [94]

In earlier days, Christian Right groups had organized conservative Christians as Republican voters and party workers in return for, they hoped, the GOP's commitment to prioritize Christian Right issues. Today, though, the Christian Right's organizational side has "slowly declined in strength [and] relevance" as the Republican Party has funneled the movement's member lists into their own voter rolls and "avoids depending on the work of organizations they can't control," says Calvin College's Smidt.

Once outsiders, Christian conservatives are now firmly inside the party, and some Christian Right leaders are looking to President Trump, himself once a Republican outsider, to embrace conservative Christians' most cherished goals. "I predict [Trump will] be the most faith-friendly president in our nation's history," Jeffress, of Dallas's First Baptist Church, tweeted Jan. 3. [95] ∎

OUTLOOK

Cautious Optimism

Since the Christian Right-GOP alliance began around 1980, some analysts have declared that it wouldn't last. Such pronouncements have been overblown, and similar predictions are likely wrong today, some religion scholars say.

"People keep on predicting the end of the Religious Right," says Young, the independent researcher who specializes in the movement's interfaith aspect. "But I think it's important to emphasize the consistent presence of religious conservatives in Republican Party politics. They're the most deeply engaged segment of the electorate. Religious conservativism continues to shift and evolve, but it persists."

The white evangelical Protestant population is highly concentrated in some regions, mainly in the South, so the Christian Right likely will continue to be the dominant political players there, said PRRI's Jones. In addition, winning some states decisively gives a voting demographic national influence, especially when hot-button issues such as gay marriage are in play, he noted. [96]

Jones said even as their percentage of the population declines, the Christian Right will continue to decide many congressional, state and local races if historical voting patterns persist. In non-presidential-election years, older white voters — many of them conservative Christians — vote, while others stay home, he said. [97]

How their strong support for President Trump will affect their future remains to be seen, however. "If over time it continues to look like the administration's a disaster, then the Christian Right is going to own it, because their support legitimized it," says George Mason University's Rozell. But if the Trump administration is ultimately deemed a success, then the Christian Right's support will be vindicated, he says.

Joseph Loconte, an associate professor of history at King's College, in New York City, warned that to trust a leader with Trump's "unabashedly crude, proudly manipulative" character just to obtain policy concessions, such as restrictions on Muslim immigration, is a dangerous mistake. "A government that can shut down a mosque can shut down a church," he wrote. "A president who insults entire categories of human beings with impunity will not hesitate to attack any religious community that dares to criticize him." [98] (*See "At Issue," p. 549.*)

But Dean Nelson, national outreach director of the anti-abortion group the Human Coalition, said his group is "cautiously optimistic," largely because, "For the first time, really, we are able to interface with the federal government to achieve our goals." [99]

Conservative Christians helping to propel Trump to victory may be part of God's plan to turn the country back from its "increasing immorality," said Land, of the Southern Evangelical Seminary, a sign that "accounts of the death of the Christian evangelical right are premature." [100]

But questions remain about the clear trend of younger conservative Christians expressing skepticism about some Christian Right views, religion scholars

say. "Conservative religious groups' very future hinges on how willing they are to navigate . . . toward the new mainstream" on cultural matters, especially gay rights, but the issue presents a tough dilemma, wrote Jones. [101]

"To move away from strong opposition" would lose the support of churches' base of older conservatives, he said. Unwillingness to bend, however, could relegate Christian Right groups "to cultural irrelevancy and continued decline, as more and more young people leave church behind." [102] ∎

Notes

[1] Quoted in Samuel Smith, "Greg Laurie Details White House Dinner With Evangelicals, Trump Breaking Protocol," *The Christian Post*, May 8, 2017, https://tinyurl.com/y9jmlgrd.

[2] Gregory A. Smith and Jessica Martinez, "How the faithful voted: a preliminary 2016 analysis," Pew Research Center, Nov. 9, 2016, https://tinyurl.com/h5zd2fl. Kate Shellnutt, "Trump Elected President, Thanks to 4 in 5 White Evangelicals," *Christianity Today*, Nov. 9, 2016, https://tinyurl.com/y9e3h54b. "2016 November General Election Turnout Rates," United States Elections Project, https://tinyurl.com/oc646v8.

[3] Quoted in Smith, *op. cit.*

[4] Elizabeth Nash and Rachel Benson Gold, "In Just the Last Four Years, States Have Enacted 231 Abortion Restrictions," Guttmacher Institute, Jan. 15, 2015, https://tinyurl.com/y73wwzap.

[5] *Burwell v. Hobby Lobby Stores*, 573 US (2014), Oyez, https://tinyurl.com/y8z48vo2.

[6] "Religious Landscape Study," Pew Research Center, https://tinyurl.com/ov8z97d; Michael O. Emerson, "A New Day for Multiracial Congregations," *Reflections*, Spring 2013, https://tinyurl.com/y9sucy87.

[7] Pete Baklinski, "President Trump takes office: Here are six key promises he made on abortion, marriage and liberty," LifeSite, Jan. 20, 2017, https://tinyurl.com/yaoooooqr.

[8] Laura Vozzella, "Falwell on evangelicals' support for Trump: 'They're voting as Americans this time,' " *The Washington Post*, July 20, 2016, https://tinyurl.com/y7h4bgog.

[9] Quoted in Bob Eschliman, "Dr. Richard Land Makes a Surprising Statement About Donald Trump," *Charisma News*, Aug. 24, 2016,

https://tinyurl.com/z5wv2yz.

[10] Samantha Allen, "Why President Trump Isn't Anti-Gay Enough for the Religious Right," *The Daily Beast*, Feb. 17, 2017, https://tinyurl.com/yb428dpx.

[11] Quoted in Peter LaBarbera, "Meet the Trump official paid to promote LGBT 'rights' around the world," LifeSite, Feb. 15, 2017, https://tinyurl.com/y73cpeoa.

[12] Betsy Cooper, Daniel Cox, Rachel Lienesch and Robert P. Jones, "Exodus: Why Americans are Leaving Religion — and Why They're Unlikely to Come Back," PRRI, Sept. 22, 2016, https://tinyurl.com/yc7btjju.

[13] Jeff Diamant and Becka A. Alper, "Though still conservative, young evangelicals are more liberal than their elders on some issues," Pew Research Center, May 4, 2017, https://tinyurl.com/n8mxo2g.

[14] *Ibid.*

[15] Quoted in Robert P. Jones, *The End of White Christian America* (2015), Kindle edition, location 1899.

[16] Cooper *et al.*, *op. cit.*

[17] Angela Lahr, *Millennial Dreams and Apocalyptic Nightmares* (2007), p. 14.

[18] Jones, *op. cit.*, location 692.

[19] Travis Loller, "Southern Baptists see 9th year of membership decline," The Associated Press, June 7, 2016, https://tinyurl.com/y9j339d7.

[20] Jana Riess, "Mormon growth slows to its lowest level since 1937," *Religion News*, April 19, 2016, https://tinyurl.com/jhzuwsd.

[21] Jones, *op. cit.*, location 888.

[22] Sarah Pulliam Bailey, "Refocusing on the Family," *Christianity Today*, July 1, 2011, https://tinyurl.com/5sxc4vy. Jones, *op. cit.*, location 1233; "Focus on the Family," Nonprofit Organization Information, Economic Research Institute, http://tinyurl.com/ydd75qzd.

[23] *Ibid.* (Jones), location 1766.

[24] Quote in Daniel Burke, "7 types of evangelicals — and how they'll affect the presidential race," CNN Politics, Jan. 25, 2016, https://tinyurl.com/htovlqy.

[25] Joe Carter, "Factchecker: Are All Christian Denominations in Decline?" *The Gospel Coalition*, March 17, 2015, https://tinyurl.com/kv7frxz.

[26] Quoted in Bob Allen, "Freefall continues in SBC membership, baptism stats," *Baptist News*, June 8, 2016, https://tinyurl.com/y7yjoqhy.

[27] Quoted in Jeremy W. Peters, "For Religious Conservatives, Success and Access at the Trump White House," *The New York Times*, Feb. 13, 2017, https://tinyurl.com/y9s4o7xn.

[28] Quoted in *ibid.*

[29] Quoted in Kate Shellnutt, "Trump's Supreme

Court Pick: Religious Freedom Defender Neil Gorsuch," *Christianity Today*, Jan. 31, 2017, https://tinyurl.com/y9eme5vw.

[30] See "The Mexico City Policy: An Explainer," Kaiser Family Foundation, June 1, 2017, https://tinyurl.com/zcw6fem.

[31] Laura Bassett, "Donald Trump Drastically Expands "Global Gag Rule" On Abortion," *The Huffington Post*, May 15, 2017, https://tinyurl.com/ma4qry5; Alexandra DeSanctis, "Trump Administration Expands Pro-Life Mexico City Policy," *National Review*, May 16, 2017, https://tinyurl.com/yb5vr3pp.

[32] Quoted in Adelle M. Banks and Emily McFarlan Miller, "Trump's evangelical supporters disappointed about Israel embassy decision," Religion New Service, June 1, 2017, https://tinyurl.com/yaal7puo.

[33] David Gushee, "Why the Christian right still supports Trump," Religion News Service, Oct. 15, 2016, https://tinyurl.com/ycfsdc69.

[34] Garance Franke-Ruta, "George W. Bush's Forgotten Gay-Rights History," *The Atlantic*, July 8, 2013, https://tinyurl.com/ybc75zrf.

[35] For background see Marcia Clemmitt, " 'Alt-Right' Movement," *CQ Researcher*, March 17, 2017, pp. 241-264.

[36] Quoted in Sarah Posner, "Amazing Disgrace," *The New Republic*, March 20, 2017, https://tinyurl.com/ka8wf7j.

[37] Kate Shellnutt, "Southern Baptists Approve Alternate Resolution Against the Alt-Right," *Christianity Today*, June 14, 2017, https://tinyurl.com/yderh2wm.

[38] Quoted in Sarah Kliff, "How the Republican party became pro-life," *The Washington Post*, March 10, 2012, https://tinyurl.com/y6u8d9l8.

[39] See "The Equal Rights Amendment," https://tinyurl.com/hncl2tf; J.B. Haws, "Three Decades after the Equal Rights Amendment: Mormon Women and American Public Perception," Religious Studies Center, Brigham Young University, Winter 2015, https://tinyurl.com/ybgv7h3a; Amanda Terkel, "GOP Platform in Years Past

Supported Equal Rights, Higher Wages, Funding For The Arts," *The Huffington Post*, Sept. 4, 2012, https://tinyurl.com/9tv6mny.

[40] "End of an Era," *New York*, March 25, 2012, https://tinyurl.com/y8tcdrpd.

[41] Clyde Wilcox, "Of Movements and Metaphors: The Co-Evolution of the Christian Right and the GOP," paper prepared for Christian Conservative Movement and American Democracy conference, April 2007, Researchgate, January 2009, https://tinyurl.com/ybxldth4.

[42] Jones, *op. cit.*, location 3230.

[43] Graham G. Dodds, "Crusade or Charade?: The Religious Right and the Culture Wars," *Canadian Review of American Studies*, 2012 (Issue 3), pp. 274-300; see Howell Raines, "President Shifts View On Tax Rule In Race Bias Cases," *The New York Times*, Jan. 13, 1982, https://tinyurl.com/y8xgulkx.

[44] Wilcox, *op. cit.*

[45] For background on this period and the influence of evangelical religion on society, see Nathan O. Hatch, *The Democratization of American Christianity* (1989).

[46] "Abolition and the Splintering of the Church," This Far by Faith, PBS.org, https://tinyurl.com/ybjbj8z9.

[47] See Jones, *op. cit.*

[48] Frances FitzGerald, *The Evangelicals* (2017), kindle edition, locations 82 and 258.

[49] See "Scopes Trial," Evolution, PBS, https://tinyurl.com/bjfr6m.

[50] Darren E. Grem, *The Blessings of Business: How Corporations Shaped Conservative Christianity* (2016), kindle edition, location 450.

[51] Michael J. McVicar, "The Libertarian Theocrats: The Long Strange History of R.J. Rushdoony and Christian Reconstructionism," Political Research Associations, Sept. 1, 2007, https://tinyurl.com/y87usx9d.

[52] Bradley W. Bateman, "The Social Gospel and the Progressive Era," Divining America, TeacherServe, National Humanities Center, May 2009, http://tinyurl.com/o2qzxoq; "Social

Gospel," *Encyclopaedia Britannica*, https://tinyurl.com/y83apbw6.

[53] Kevin Kruse, *One Nation Under God: How Corporate America Invented Christian America* (2015), Kindle edition, location 414.

[54] Grem, *op. cit.*, location 459; Dan Graves, "Evangelization Society to Storm Chicago," Church History Timeline, Christianity.com, https://tinyurl.com/yafredgw.

[55] Michael J. McVicar, "The Religious Right in America," Religion, *Oxford Research Encyclopedias*, March 2016, https://tinyurl.com/y9qq6bvz.

[56] William B. Bradshaw, "Mainline Churches: Past, Present Future," *The Huffington Post*, Jan. 23, 2014, https://tinyurl.com/ya8yj4vm.

[57] FitzGerald, *op. cit.*, location 132.

[58] Daniel K. Williams, "The Christian Right's Partisan Commitment," *Historically Speaking*, April 2011, pp. 7-9.

[59] See *Engel v. Vitale*, 370 US 431 (1962), Oyez, https://tinyurl.com/y8sb565w.

[60] See Becker Amendment, Civil Liberties, Nov. 22, 2011, https://tinyurl.com/y7axyqlu; Neil J. Young, *We Gather Together: The Religious Right and the Problem of Interfaith Politics* (2015), p. 78.

[61] Quoted in "Is Segregation Scriptural? A Radio Address From Bob Jones On Easter Of 1960," Evangelical History, *The Gospel Coalition*, July 26, 2016, https://tinyurl.com/y82qhcr3.

[62] See *Roe v. Wade*, 410 US 113 (1973), Body Politic, Oyez, https://tinyurl.com/y9vxxb2a; Terkel, *op. cit.*; Kliff, *op .cit.*

[63] Quoted in Randall Balmer, "The Real Origins of the Religious Right," *Politico*, May 27, 2014, https://tinyurl.com/y9m8p89e.

[64] Jonathan Dudley, "The Not-So-Lofty Origins Of The Evangelical Pro-Life Movement," *Religion Dispatches*, Feb. 5, 2013, https://tinyurl.com/ya8wms9z.

[65] See "Election Polls — Vote by Groups, 1976-1980," Gallup, https://tinyurl.com/o7rff7a; J. Brooks Flippen, "Carter, Catholics, and the Politics of Family," *American Catholic Studies*, Fall 2012, pp. 27-51.

[66] *Ibid.* (Flippen).

[67] See Williams, *op. cit.*, p. 88ff and p. 171ff.

[68] Quoted in Flippen, *op. cit.*

[69] William Martin, *With God on Our Side* (1996), p. 271; see Neil J. Young, "The Origins of the Religious Right: A Q&A With Neil Young," *OUPblog*, Nov. 18, 2015, https://tinyurl.com/y7vh7bk2.

[70] *Ibid.* (Martin), p. 225.

[71] Quoted in *ibid.*, p. 213.

[72] Jones, *op. cit.*, location 1201.

[73] Martin, *op. cit.*, p. 213.

About the Author

Marcia Clemmitt is a veteran social-policy reporter who previously served as editor in chief of *Medicine & Health* and staff writer for *The Scientist.* She has also been a high school math and physics teacher. She holds a liberal arts and sciences degree from St. John's College, Annapolis, and a master's degree in English from Georgetown University. Her recent *CQ Researcher* reports include "The Dark Web" and " 'Alt-Right' Movement."

[74] FitzGerald, *op. cit.*, location 191.

[75] Steven Ertelt, "President Bush Will Leave Strong Pro-Life Legacy on Abortion, Biethics Issues," LifeNews.com, Jan. 16, 2009, https://tinyurl.com/ya7lfvay.

[76] "Gay Marriage Timeline," Pew Research Center, April 1, 2008, https://tinyurl.com/yaa2v5bq; Richard Wolf, "Timeline: Same-sex marriage through the years," *USA Today*, June 24, 2015, https://tinyurl.com/yahnyp6d.

[77] Jones, *op. cit.*, location 1125.

[78] Quoted in Andre Mitchell, "President Obama the Antichrist? Not really, but he's 'paving the way,' evangelists say," *Christian Today*, Aug. 11, 2015, https://tinyurl.com/n9nlg3z.

[79] See Burke, *op. cit.*

[80] Shellnutt, "Trump Elected President, Thanks to 4 in 5 White Evangelicals," *op. cit.* Michael J. O'Loughlin, "New data suggest Clinton, not Trump, won Catholic vote," *America*, April, 6, 2017, https://tinyurl.com/yc3rmg3c; Jana Riess, "Most Mormons planned NOT to vote for Trump. What the heck happened?" Religion News Service, Nov. 15, 2016, https://tinyurl.com/y8puay3z.

[81] Philip Bump, "Donald Trump took 5 different positions on abortion in 3 days," *The Washington Post*, April 3, 2016, http://tinyurl.com/yazdlxna.

[82] Quoted in Alex Kotch, "When God steps in: Why the Christian Right is rejoicing under Trump's presidency," *Salon*, Feb. 25, 2017, https://tinyurl.com/yalasddx.

[83] Brian Eason, "Trump's VP: 10 things to know about Mike Pence," *Indianapolis Star*, July 7, 2016, https://tinyurl.com/gpmlw6p.

[84] Katie Glueck, "Evangelicals still peeved over Pence's religious freedom flip act," *Politico*, July 15, 2016, https://tinyurl.com/j77r7fy.

[85] Lisa Lambert, "Senate kills family-planning rule; Pence breaks tie," Reuters, March 30, 2017, https://tinyurl.com/y9v7mr2t.

[86] Quoted in Michael W. Chapman, "CIA Dir. Pompeo: 'Jesus Christ Our Savior Is Truly the Only Solution For Our World,'" CNSNews.com, Jan. 25, 2017, https://tinyurl.com/zy2gebp.

[87] Quoted in Benjamin Wermund, "Trump's education pick says reform can 'advance God's kingdom,'" *Politico*, Dec. 2, 2016, https://tinyurl.com/zjjgrbp.

[88] Rachana Pradhan, "Trump names anti-abortion leader Yoest to top HHS post," *Politico*, April 28, 2017, https://tinyurl.com/kyxjmu3; Caitlin MacNeal, "Trump To Appoint Anti-Abortion Leader Charmaine Yoest To Post At HHS," *TPM*, April 28, 2017, https://tinyurl.com/ycb4khr4.

[89] Quoted in *ibid.* (Pradhan).

FOR MORE INFORMATION

Alliance Defending Freedom, 15100 N. 90th St., Scottsdale, AZ 82560; 480-444-0020; www.adflegal.org. Provides legal assistance in religious-freedom cases and advocates for legislative change to advance religious liberty.

Christian Coalition of America, PO Box 37030, Washington, DC 20013; 202-479-6900; www.cc.org/our_agenda. Political organization established in the 1990s with offices around the country to help link conservative Christians with election issues and candidates.

Concerned Women for America, 1015 15th St., N.W., Suite 1100, Washington, DC 20005; 202-488-7000; concernedwomen.org. Women's public policy group that develops policy positions and assists conservative Christian grassroots activists around the country.

Council for National Policy, 444 N. Capitol St., N.W., Suite 830, Washington, DC 20001; 202-207-0165; www.cfnp.org. Organization of influential conservatives that develops policy proposals supported by the Christian Right.

Family Research Council, 801 G St., N.W., Washington, DC 20001; 202-393-2100; www.frc.org. Christian conservative think tank and advocacy group on social issues.

Pew Research Center — Religion and Public Life, 1615 L St., N.W., #700, Washington, DC 20036; 202-419-4550; www.pewforum.org. Nonpartisan research, data and analysis group specializing in the role of religion in public life.

Public Religion Research Institute (PRRI), 27 Massachusetts Ave., N.W., Floor 3, Washington, DC 20036; 202-238-9424; www.prri.org. Nonpartisan research, data and analysis group that examines the links between religion and public life.

World Congress of Families, 815-997-7106; https://wcf11.org. U.S.-based Christian Right group that convenes international conferences to promote policies abroad dealing with gay marriage, abortion and other issues.

[90] See Karoun Demirjian, "Republicans refuse to budge following Garland nomination to Supreme Court," *The Washington Post*, March 16, 2016, https://tinyurl.com/ydelz34m. President Obama had nominated U.S. Court of Appeals Judge Merrick Garland to the seat in 2016, but the GOP-led Senate refused to consider the nomination, arguing that since Obama had under a year left in his term, the next president should fill the vacancy.

[91] Mike Norton, "Gorsuch is a solid conservative pick for the Supreme Court," *The Hill*, Jan. 31, 2017, https://tinyurl.com/ya22q6yg.

[92] Blake Seitz, "Unmuzzling the Pastors," *The American Interest*, May 5, 2017, https://tinyurl.com/y7bwspxo.

[93] Quoted in Sarah Pulliam Bailey, "Many religious freedom advocates are disappointed with Trump's executive order," *The Washington Post*, May 5, 2017, https://tinyurl.com/ybkgz36l.

[94] Dahlia Lithwick, "Trump's Churches Order Is a Nonsolution to a Nonproblem — With a Dangerous Side Effect," *Slate*, May 4, 2017, https://tinyurl.com/l67c9ua.

[95] Daniel Burke, "Inflammatory pastor preached to Trump before inauguration," CNN Politics, Jan. 22, 2017, https://tinyurl.com/zo7zofd.

[96] Jones, *op. cit.*, location 1729.

[97] *Ibid.*, location 141.

[98] Joseph Loconte, "Before Donald Trump, the sad history of when Christians anointed another political bully," *The Washington Post*, Feb. 22, 2016, https://tinyurl.com/y7lrqoac.

[99] Quoted in Jeremy W. Peters, "Trump on Their Side, Conservatives See Hope in Lengthy Abortion Fight," *The New York Times*, Jan. 26, 2017, https://tinyurl.com/ycr87u83.

[100] Carol Kuruvilla, "After Trump's Win, White Evangelical Christians Face a Reckoning," *The Huffington Post*, Nov. 9, 2016, https://tinyurl.com/za8tzrd.

[101] Jones, *op. cit.*, location 1766ff.

[102] *Ibid.*

Bibliography

Selected Sources

Books

Dochuk, Darren, *From Bible Belt to Sun Belt: Plain-Folk Religion, Grassroots Politics, and the Rise of Evangelical Conservatism*, W.W. Norton & Company, 2012.

An associate professor of history at the University of Notre Dame argues that a migration of Southern evangelicals to California and Arizona in the 1930s helped shape evangelicals' politics.

Dowland, Seth, *Family Values and the Rise of the Christian Right*, University of Pennsylvania Press, 2015.

An associate professor of religion at Pacific Lutheran University describes the origins of the Christian Right's family-values policy agenda.

FitzGerald, Frances, *The Evangelicals: The Struggle to Shape America*, Simon & Schuster, 2017.

A Pulitzer Prize-winning journalist recounts the history of evangelicals in America and the many political and cultural debates that split the faithful.

Jones, Robert P., *The End of White Christian America*, Simon & Schuster, 2016.

The founder of the Public Religion Research Institute, a polling and research organization in Washington, provides statistics to argue that white Christians' responses to their waning influence in the United States is the cause of many current cultural and political battles.

Kruse, Kevin, *One Nation Under God: How Corporate America Invented Christian America*, Basic Books, 2015.

A Princeton University professor of history says that in the mid-20th century, corporate leaders promoted a vision of the United States as a Christian nation to strengthen public belief in free-market economics.

Young, Neil J., *We Gather Together: The Religious Right and the Problem of Interfaith Politics*, Oxford University Press, 2016.

An independent scholar of religious history describes the separate paths that led white evangelical Protestants, conservative Catholics and Mormons to form the Christian Right political coalition and the lasting divisions among them.

Articles

Balmer, Randall, "The Real Origins of the Religious Right," *Politico*, May 27, 2014, http://tinyurl.com/j77hvkg.

The John Phillips chair in religion at Dartmouth College explains how disputes over the tax-exempt status of segregated Christian schools helped lead to the Christian Right's creation.

Burke, Daniel, "7 types of evangelicals — and how they'll affect the presidential race," CNN, Jan. 25, 2016, http://tinyurl.com/ydyd2ycl.

The world of politically engaged evangelicals includes liberals and conservatives, as well as an influential evangelical demographic that doesn't attend church at all.

Dias, Elizabeth, "Inside Evangelical Leaders' Private White House Dinner," *Time*, May 3, 2017, http://tinyurl.com/yc94gahr.

Carried into office with help from Christian Right voters, President Trump returned the favor by asking evangelical leaders for advice.

Higgins, Andrew, "In Expanding Influence, Faith Combines With Firepower," *The New York Times*, Sept. 13, 2016, http://tinyurl.com/hlgk9db.

The Russian government and Russian Orthodox Church hope to rebuild their nation's prestige by reaching out to Christian conservatives who distrust Western Europe's liberalizing views of sexuality.

Marcotte, Amanda, "Abstinence only, rebranded: Failed right-wing sex-ed policy returns as 'sexual risk avoidance,' " *Salon*, June 12, 2017, https://tinyurl.com/ybmebnyd.

The Trump administration signals it might aid in the push for more abstinence-only sex-education programs in school districts, a cause championed by the Christian Right.

Reports and Studies

"Presidential vote by religious affiliation and race," Pew Research Center, Nov. 9, 2016, http://tinyurl.com/y9hydhqc.

The largest sector of the Christian Right — white born-again and evangelical Christians — voted overwhelmingly for the Republican nominee in the 2012 and 2016 elections, according to the nonpartisan Pew Research Center in Washington.

Flippen, J. Brooks, "Carter, Catholics, and the Politics of Family," *American Catholic Studies*, Fall 2012, http://tinyurl.com/yag3vokn.

Conservative Catholics hoped that President Jimmy Carter, an evangelical, would champion social-conservative causes, but he quickly disappointed them, according to a professor of history at Southeastern Oklahoma State University.

Martin, Stephanie A., "Recession Resonance: How Evangelical Megachurch Pastors Promoted Fiscal Conservatism in the Aftermath of the 2008 Financial Crash," *Rhetoric & Public Affairs*, Spring 2015, http://tinyurl.com/yao7lef4.

In sermons preached during and soon after the 2008 recession, evangelical pastors stressed that individuals and their personal decisions about money shaped not just families' welfare but also the nation's economic welfare, according to a Southern Methodist University assistant professor of communications studies.

The Next Step:

Additional Articles from Current Periodicals

Christian Right Divisions

"Why do Christian evangelicals have faith in Trump?" Al Jazeera, April 22, 2017, https://tinyurl.com/mjux4b9.

Jim Wallis, a former spiritual adviser to President Obama, and prolific evangelical writer and radio host Eric Metaxas debate the racial divide among black, white and Hispanic evangelicals and why so many support President Trump.

Goodstein, Laurie, "Religious Liberals Sat Out of Politics for 40 Years. Now They Want in the Game," The New York Times, June 10, 2017, https://tinyurl.com/y8dbjaek.

Liberal Christian leaders are mounting what some call a "religious resistance" as they seek to weaken the Christian Right by preaching an agenda of caring for the poor, the planet and refugees.

Lovett, Ian, "Russell Moore, Baptist Leader Who Shunned Trump, Splits the Faithful," The Wall Street Journal, June 9, 2017, https://tinyurl.com/yalu95lv.

Rifts may be developing in the Southern Baptist Convention as one of its leaders seeks to push the nation's largest Protestant denomination leftward.

Evangelical Millennials

Jacobson, Susan, "Church forum seeks to build bridge with LGBT community," Orlando Sentinel, May 12, 2017, https://tinyurl.com/ycuvtmpa.

A church near Orlando, Fla., invited Matthew Vines, a gay, evangelical Millennial who founded the Reformation Project, a Christian grassroots organization created to work toward the inclusion of LGBT people in the church, to host a public forum to help increase understanding of the LGBT community.

Turrentine, Jeff, "These Christians Are on a Climate Mission — and Winning Converts," OnEarth, May 5, 2017, https://tinyurl.com/ya5eobdz.

Evangelical Millennials are more willing than earlier generations to fight climate change, a columnist argues.

Wicker, Molly, "A Conservative Christian College Protest of Mike Pence," The New York Times, May 19, 2017, https://tinyurl.com/knh23eg.

Students at Grove City College, a conservative Christian college in Pennsylvania, who are upset about President Trump's morals protested the decision to invite Vice President Mike Pence to speak at commencement.

Russia Connections

Altman, Alex, and Elizabeth Dias, "Moscow Cozies Up to the Right," Time, March 10, 2017, https://tinyurl.com/h6xblny.

Russian officials are trying to cultivate relationships with Republican members of Congress and other GOP officials by stressing common values with the Christian Right.

Michel, Casey, "How Russia Became the Leader of the Global Christian Right," Politico Magazine, Feb. 9, 2017, https://tinyurl.com/gvsmvz5.

Under President Vladimir Putin, Russia has emerged as a leader of an international Christian Right, and some U.S. Christian leaders are strengthening their ties to Russia to get support and ideas.

Stroop, Christopher, "Russian Social Conservatism, the U.S.-based WCF [World Congress of Families], & the Global Culture Wars in Historical Context," Political Research Associates, Feb. 16, 2016, https://tinyurl.com/y997sy45.

A scholar of Russian history says the Russian government's embrace of Christian "family values" as a means of gaining international influence has deep historical roots.

Trump Administration

Green, Emma, "Why Trump's Executive Order on Religious Liberty Left Many Conservatives Dissatisfied," The Atlantic, May 4, 2017, https://tinyurl.com/yaame6s5.

Some on the Christian Right criticized President Trump's May 4 executive order on religious liberty as "woefully inadequate."

Kilgore, Ed, "The More Trump Struggles, the More the Christian Right Loves Him," New York Magazine, June 13, 2017, https://tinyurl.com/ycrcmupv.

A number of conservatives on the Christian Right say they feel a kinship with President Trump because they have the same enemies.

CITING CQ RESEARCHER

Sample formats for citing these reports in a bibliography include the ones listed below. Preferred styles and formats vary, so please check with your instructor or professor.

MLA STYLE
Mantel, Barbara. "Coal Industry's Future." CQ Researcher 17 June 2016: 529-552.

APA STYLE
Mantel, B. (2016, June 17). Coal Industry's Future. CQ Researcher, 6, 529-552.

CHICAGO STYLE
Mantel, Barbara. "Coal Industry's Future." CQ Researcher, June 17, 2016, 529-52.

In-depth Reports on Issues in the News

Are you writing a paper?

Need backup for a debate?

Want to become an expert on an issue?

For 90 years, students have turned to *CQ Researcher* for in-depth reporting on issues in the news. Reports on a full range of political and social issues are now available. Following is a selection of recent reports:

Civil Liberties
Privacy and the Internet, 12/15
Intelligence Reform, 5/15
Religion and Law, 11/14

Crime/Law
High-Tech Policing, 4/17
Forensic Science Controversies, 2/17
Jailing Debtors, 9/16
Decriminalizing Prostitution, 4/16
Restorative Justice, 2/16
The Dark Web, 1/16
Immigrant Detention, 10/15

Education
Charter Schools, 3/17
Civic Education, 2/17
Student Debt, 11/16
Apprenticeships, 10/16

Environment/Society
Trust in Media, 6/17
Anti-Semitism, 5/17
Native American Sovereignty, 5/17
Women in Prison, 3/17
Guns on Campus, 1/17
Mass Transit, 12/16

Health/Safety
Food Labeling, 6/17
Sports and Sexual Assault, 4/17
Reducing Traffic Deaths, 2/17
Opioid Crisis, 10/16
Mosquito-Borne Disease, 7/16

Politics/Economy
North Korea Showdown, 5/17
Rethinking Foreign Aid, 4/17
Troubled Brazil, 4/17
Reviving Rural Economies, 3/17
Immigrants and the Economy, 2/17

Upcoming Reports

Hunger in America, 7/7/17   Medical Marijuana, 7/14/17   Arts Funding, 7/21/17

ACCESS

CQ Researcher is available in print and online. For access, visit your library or www.cqresearcher.com.

STAY CURRENT

For notice of upcoming *CQ Researcher* reports or to learn more about *CQ Researcher* products, subscribe to the free email newsletters, *CQ Researcher Alert!* and *CQ Researcher News*: http://cqpress.com/newsletters.

PURCHASE

To purchase a *CQ Researcher* report in print or electronic format (PDF), visit www.cqpress.com or call 866-427-7737. Single reports start at $15. Bulk purchase discounts and electronic-rights licensing are also available.

SUBSCRIBE

Annual full-service *CQ Researcher* subscriptions—including 44 reports a year, monthly index updates, and a bound volume—start at $1,131. Add $25 for domestic postage.

CQ Researcher Online offers a backfile from 1991 and a number of tools to simplify research. For pricing information, call 800-818-7243 or 805-499-9774 or email librarysales@sagepub.com.

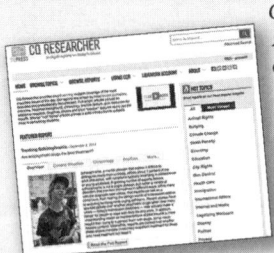

CQ RESEARCHER

CQPRESS

In-depth reports on today's issues

Published by CQ Press, an Imprint of SAGE Publications, Inc.   *www.cqresearcher.com*

Hunger in America

Should the government spend more on food aid?

More than 40 million Americans need government help to keep from going hungry, and some 6 million households lack adequate food or nutrition at least occasionally. While hunger has abated since the 2007-09 recession, advocates for the poor say the federal government still needs to do much more to provide food aid and access to healthy food for the needy. But many conservatives say food-aid programs are rife with waste and fraud and need major reforms. They want to stiffen work requirements for able-bodied recipients, and some conservatives and liberals argue that food stamps should not be used to buy junk foods lacking in nutritional value. President Trump wants to slash federal spending on food aid and scientific research into nutrition. But some of his budget proposals — described as draconian by critics — face an uphill battle in Congress. Advocates for the poor, meanwhile, are expanding innovative programs that bring healthy foods to low-income areas, and celebrity chefs are joining the fight against hunger.

Demonstrators in New York on May 24, 2017, urge Mayor Bill de Blasio to increase the city's food aid to compensate for President Trump's proposed food stamp cuts. Advocates for the poor say the cuts would worsen the nation's hunger problem. Many conservatives say food-aid programs are rife with waste and fraud and need reform.

CQ Researcher • July 7, 2017 • www.cqresearcher.com
Volume 27, Number 24 • Pages 557-580

THIS REPORT

THE ISSUES	.................**559**
BACKGROUND	...............**565**
CHRONOLOGY	...............**567**
CURRENT SITUATION	........**571**
AT ISSUE	.....................**573**
OUTLOOK	....................**574**
BIBLIOGRAPHY	..............**578**
THE NEXT STEP	.............**579**

CQ RESEARCHER

July 7, 2017
Volume 27, Number 24

EXECUTIVE EDITOR: Thomas J. Billitteri
tjb@sagepub.com

ASSISTANT MANAGING EDITORS: Kenneth
Fireman, kenneth.fireman@sagepub.com,
Kathy Koch, kathy.koch@sagepub.com,
Scott Rohrer, scott.rohrer@sagepub.com

ASSOCIATE MANAGING EDITOR: Val Ellicott

SENIOR CONTRIBUTING EDITOR:
Thomas J. Colin
tom.colin@sagepub.com

CONTRIBUTING WRITERS: Marcia Clemmitt,
Sarah Glazer, Reed Karaim, Barbara Mantel,
Chuck McCutcheon, Tom Price

SENIOR PROJECT EDITOR: Olu B. Davis

INTERN: Robert DePaolo

FACT CHECKERS: Eva P. Dasher,
Michelle Harris, Betsy Towner Levine,
Robin Palmer

SAGE Publishing | **CQ PRESS**

Los Angeles I London I New Delhi
Singapore I Washington DC I Melbourne

An Imprint of SAGE Publications, Inc.

SENIOR VICE PRESIDENT,
GLOBAL LEARNING RESOURCES:
Karen Phillips

EXECUTIVE DIRECTOR, ONLINE LIBRARY AND
REFERENCE PUBLISHING:
Todd Baldwin

CQ Researcher (ISSN 1056-2036) is printed on acid-free
paper. Published weekly, except: (March wk. 4) (May
wk. 4) (July wks. 1, 2) (Aug. wks. 2, 3) (Nov. wk. 4)
and (Dec. wks. 3, 4). Published by SAGE Publications,
Inc., 2455 Teller Rd., Thousand Oaks, CA 91320. Annual
full-service subscriptions start at $1,131. For pricing,
call 1-800-818-7243. To purchase a CQ Researcher report
in print or electronic format (PDF), visit www.cqpress.
com or call 866-427-7737. Single reports start at $15.
Bulk purchase discounts and electronic-rights licensing
are also available. Periodicals postage paid at Thousand
Oaks, California, and at additional mailing offices.
POSTMASTER: Send address changes to CQ Researcher, 2600 Virginia Ave., N.W., Suite 600, Washington,
DC 20037.

THE ISSUES

559 • Should the federal government spend more on anti-
hunger programs?
• Would better nutrition
education decrease hunger?
• Should federal aid programs
stop paying for junk food?

BACKGROUND

565 **Early Aid**
With hunger widespread,
the government issued food
stamps during the Depression.

566 **'Great Society' Era**
The food stamp program
became permanent in 1964.

568 **Republican Cuts**
After the GOP took control of
Congress in 1995, it reduced
spending on anti-hunger
programs.

569 **School Nutrition**
The Obama administration
strengthened requirements
for school lunches in 2010.

CURRENT SITUATION

571 **Rules Delayed**
The Trump administration has
begun reversing Obama-era
nutrition rules aimed at
reducing hunger.

572 **Budget Cuts**
Defenders say proposed
reductions in anti-hunger
programs would improve
efficiency.

OUTLOOK

574 **Continued Decline?**
Experts see a stronger economy as crucial to reducing
hunger.

SIDEBARS AND GRAPHICS

560 **Food Insecurity Is
Highest in South**
A dozen states have above-
average hunger or dietary
deficiencies.

561 **44 Million Americans
Used Food Stamps in
2016**
The number has fallen 10 percent since 2013.

564 **Hunger Falling in U.S.**
Food insecurity has been
declining since 2011.

567 **Chronology**
Key events since 1918.

568 **Offering Fresh Produce to
the Poor**
Programs bring healthy foods
to low-income areas and
"food deserts."

570 **Celebrity Chefs Fight
Hunger**
"We feed the few, but we
need to be taking care of
feeding the many."

573 **At Issue:**
Should the federal government
stop funding free school
lunches for students who
aren't poor?

FOR FURTHER RESEARCH

577 **For More Information**
Organizations to contact.

578 **Bibliography**
Selected sources used.

579 **The Next Step**
Additional articles.

579 **Citing CQ Researcher**
Sample bibliography formats.

Cover: Getty Images/Spencer Platt

Hunger in America

BY TOM PRICE

THE ISSUES

Johnnie Lindsey, a 72-year-old grandmother, said she never turned to welfare while working and raising a family in Alabama. Now, she lives on Social Security, food-pantry donations and $66 a month in food stamps.

"I can eat for a month on $66, as long as my grandkids don't come over," she said jokingly. But she worries how she will eat if her benefits are reduced. "It's a struggle, for real," she said. "You've got to be penny-pinching to survive, and it's still hard to survive. I would hate for them to cut mine off." [1]

Lindsey is unlikely to see her food stamps totally disappear. But President Trump has proposed slashing federal food stamp spending by $193 billion over 10 years, and advocates for the poor say such a deep cut would worsen a serious problem: hunger in America.

At stake is the well-being of more than 11 million Americans who live in households that experience hunger from time to time, and the more than 40 million who fend off hunger with federal assistance. Also at stake is the health of some half-million children who occasionally go hungry — a crisis that experts warn is a demographic time bomb because today's hungry youths could become tomorrow's poor and hungry adults. [2]

The bipartisan National Commission on Hunger, appointed by Congress in 2014, defines two categories of hunger in America:

• "Very low food security" — households that had to eat less at times during the previous year because they didn't have enough food.

The food pantry at the Victory Dream Center, a church in Carbondale, Ill., serves some 200 families each week. More than 40 million Americans a year fend off hunger with federal assistance. The president has proposed cutting the federal food stamp program by $193 billion over 10 years, but experts say Congress is unlikely to approve the cuts.

AP Photo/The Southern/Byron Hetzler

• "Low-food-security" — households that sometimes face a diet of reduced quality, variety or desirability but don't have to reduce their eating. Thirty-one million people, including nearly 6 million children, are in this category. [3]

American hunger is dropping because of an improving economy, according to the Agriculture Department, but it is still higher than before the severe 2007-09 recession because of the uneven economic recovery and other factors.

Most of the hungry are non-elderly adults, although the National Foundation to End Senior Hunger, an anti-hunger group in Alexandria, Va., reported that the number of elderly facing the threat of hunger exceeded 10 million last year for the first time. Households below the poverty line are more than three

times as likely to experience very low food security than average households. Other groups with higher-than-average hunger are single parents, women living alone, blacks, Hispanics and people living outside metropolitan areas. The South and Midwest had slightly higher levels of hunger than the Northeast and West because of regional economic differences. [4] (*See map, p. 560.*)

Besides cutting food stamp spending by $193 billion over 10 years, Trump's 2018 budget proposes enacting stricter work requirements for able-bodied food-aid recipients, cutting federal programs that help finance Meals on Wheels and implementing tougher rules about who qualifies for food assistance and how long they can receive the help.

The cuts would be "cataclysmic," said James Weill, president of the Food Research and Action Center, a research and advocacy organization in Washington, although congressional observers say Trump's budget cuts face stiff opposition. [5] Many anti-hunger activists say federal spending on food aid already is too low. Mariana Chilton, a professor of health management at Drexel University and co-chair of the National Commission on Hunger, proposes a 30 percent increase in food stamp benefits. Many food stamp recipients "just can't make it" on existing benefits, she says.

White House Management and Budget Director Mick Mulvaney, however, said the proposed cuts are necessary because some spending is going to people who don't need help, and some of the programs don't work. [6]

"You're only focusing on half of the equation, right?" Mulvaney said to re-

Food Insecurity Is Highest in South

Households in 12 states, mainly in the South, have above average "food insecurity," which means they sometimes go hungry. Mississippi has the nation's highest rate, at 21 percent, and North Dakota the lowest, at 8.5 percent. According to the U.S. Agriculture Department, 16 million U.S. households are food insecure.

Food Insecurity by State, 2013-15

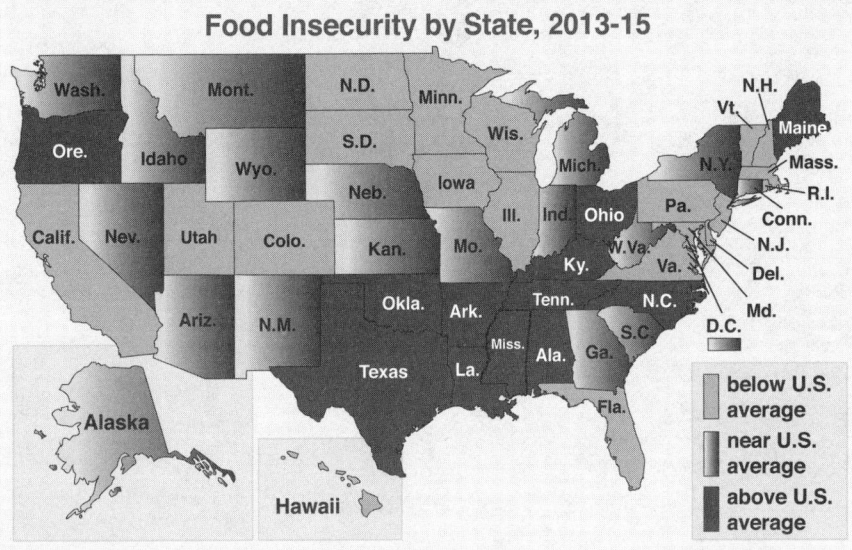

Source: "Prevalence of food insecurity, average 2013-15," Economic Research Service, U.S. Department of Agriculture, http://tinyurl.com/yavkdvuo

porters as he unveiled the budget in March. "You're focusing on recipients of the money. We're trying to focus on both the recipients of the money and the folks who give us the money in the first place. And I think it's fairly compassionate to go to them and say, 'Look, we're not going to ask you for your hard-earned money anymore, unless we can guarantee to you that that money is actually going to be used in a proper function." [7]

Robert Rector, a senior research fellow in domestic policy at the conservative Heritage Foundation think tank, says it is important that capable recipients work for their benefits. "Food assistance for able-bodied adults should not be a one-way handout," Rector says. "It's reasonable to expect recipients to engage in constructive activities for the aid."

Chilton disagrees, calling food "a basic human right" and saying food stamps should not contain work requirements.

Current federal rules require able-bodied adults between the ages of 18 and 49 with no dependents to work at least 80 hours per month, participate in an educational or training activity or comply with a workfare program. [8]

Conservatives want to give states more responsibility for anti-hunger programs, while liberals fear that states' pockets are not deep enough to handle activities funded by the federal government.

Many food-aid recipients worry about potential cuts.

Barbara Makris, 94, said "the only way I can stay in my home" is with the six Meals on Wheels deliveries she receives weekly. The Georgia retiree is blind and can't cook, and "if you can't cook, you can't stay at home" without help, she said. [9]

Tim Keefe, a 49-year-old Navy veteran, lost his job at a plow factory in Rockland, Maine, after a wrist injury left him unable to lift more than 25

pounds. When Maine toughened its work requirements in 2015, Keefe also lost his food stamps and turned to catching, skinning and roasting squirrels over an open fire beside his tent in Augusta. "I hope they understand that people fall through the cracks," he said of government policymakers. [10]

A study published this year by the University of Wisconsin found surprisingly high levels of hunger among community college students, and there were anecdotal reports of student hunger at Ivy League schools. The Wisconsin HOPE Lab, a research organization that focuses on reducing inequality in education, surveyed 33,000 students at 70 community colleges in 24 states and said a third had experienced very low food security. [11]

While the proportion of hungry students may seem high, many community college students come from lower-income families, says Sara Goldrick-Rab, who founded the lab and now teaches in the Temple University College of Education in Philadelphia. "Adding in college tuition and housing prices, it is possible they run out of money for food at a higher rate" than the general population, she says.

Many studies have found that hunger, particularly in childhood, leads to physical, mental, behavioral and financial problems.

Experts of all political persuasions agree that poverty is the top cause of hunger and that an improving economy can reduce it. Federal food aid has declined steadily in recent years because of the economic rebound. In 2013, 47.6 million people received food stamps at a cost of $76 billion. Those figures dropped in March to 42 million people at an annualized cost of about $63 billion. [12]

"A good-paying job is the best anti-hunger program," says Rebecca Middleton, executive director of the Alliance to End Hunger, an association of more than 90 service and advocacy organizations that work for food security in the United States and abroad.

Other factors contributing to hunger include lack of access to healthful food, ignorance of good nutrition practices and unwise behavior. Malnutrition — not consuming the proper amount of nutrients — is widespread in the United States, usually the result of individuals eating too much or eating the wrong things rather than eating too little. More than two-thirds of American adults and nearly one-third of children are overweight or obese. About 85 percent of Americans' diets do not meet U.S. Food and Drug Administration recommendations for the most important vitamins and minerals. [13]

Obesity among the poor, which can lead to diabetes and other ailments, stems from "famine-or-feast" eating practices, unhealthy diets and the stresses of poverty and food scarcity, experts say.

Noting that the poor often live in areas that lack well-stocked grocery stores, Middleton says that "if an individual cannot get somewhere to buy fresh produce, it makes it impossible to provide a healthy balanced diet." (See sidebar, p. 568.)

Many poor people don't understand the components of a nutritious diet and don't know how to shop efficiently, Rector says. Adults with very low food security drink an average of nearly two cans of soda each day, and more than 40 percent of them smoke 19 packs of cigarettes a month, which threatens their health and wastes money that could go toward more and better food, says Rector, who got his data from the Centers for Disease Control and Prevention. [14]

Cultural heritage also can steer people to unhealthy diets.

"Cultural tradition and the preferences of family members influence food stamp participants to continue serving high-fat meat products and other traditional foods," according to an Agriculture Department survey of food stamp recipients that was published last year. [15]

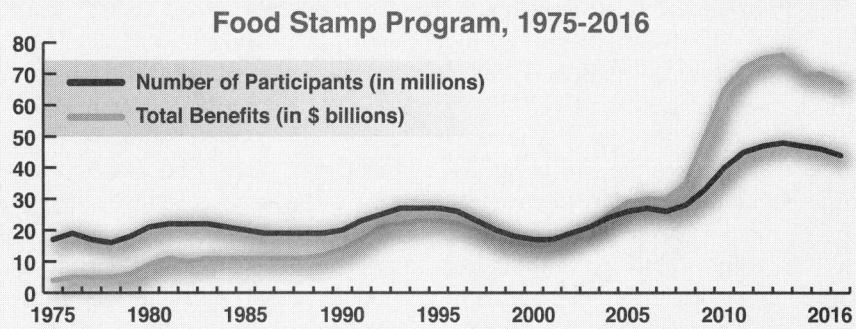

44 Million Americans Used Food Stamps in 2016

The number of people using food stamps dropped about 10 percent since 2013, to 44 million, but that figure remains far higher than in the years before the 2007-09 recession because of the slow recovery. In 2007, 26 million Americans were relying on food stamps.

Food Stamp Program, 1975-2016

Source: "Supplemental Nutrition Assistance Program Participation and Costs," Federal Nutrition Service, Department of Agriculture, http://tinyurl.com/m5o2r78

As government officials debate making changes to America's anti-hunger programs, here are some of the questions they are considering:

Should the federal government spend more on anti-hunger programs?

Health care providers, educators and grocers have noticed trends among beneficiaries of the food stamp program, formally known as the Supplemental Nutrition Assistance Program (SNAP): Life seems better shortly after recipients receive their monthly allowance than it does near the end of the monthly cycle when their benefits may have run out. [16]

Comparing the last week of the month with the first week, California hospitals reported that 27 percent more poor people sought treatment for hypoglycemia, a low-blood-sugar condition related to diabetes that can be caused by lack of food, according to research at the University of California, San Francisco. [17]

Third- through eighth-grade students in North Carolina whose parents received food stamps scored best on math and English tests between the 15th and 24th day of the monthly food stamp cycle, when they likely would have benefited from having the most food in the home, Duke University researchers reported. And grocers in poor neighborhoods commonly report higher sales when food stamps are distributed than at the end of the cycle. [18]

For advocates of the poor, this is prima facie evidence that food aid is inadequate. Others, however, say recipients don't manage their benefits wisely.

The formula used to calculate food-stamp benefits — called the Thrifty Food Plan — is "wildly insufficient and outdated," says Drexel's Chilton, and fails to account for regional differences in food, housing and other costs.

Last revised in 2006, the plan is based on the Agriculture Department's dietary guidelines and federal surveys of what low-income families pay for the food they purchase. The plan follows a benefit level established in 1999 for "a nutritious, minimal-cost diet" and is adjusted for inflation. It assumes all food is prepared at home. [19]

Diane Whitmore Schanzenbach, a professor of human development and social policy at Northwestern University who studies the long-term effects of child poverty, notes the formula assumes a family can spend 15 hours a week preparing meals from scratch. While food prepared this way tends to be healthier and less costly, "no one spends that kind of time cooking anymore," Schanzenbach says, "and I don't think it's reasonable to expect low-income families to spend that amount of time cooking while they're also working."

Far more mothers work outside the home — and thus have less time to cook — than when the Agriculture Department devised the formula in 1999, said economist James Ziliak, director of the Center for Poverty Research and of the Kentucky Research Data Center, both at the University of Kentucky. Time pressures are heavier for food-stamp families because they are more likely to be headed by a single mother, he said. Elderly recipients also face difficulty preparing meals from scratch.

The formula doesn't consider advances in nutrition research, Ziliak said. And it doesn't recognize that teenagers need more food than younger children. [20] A family with two teenage boys would need $50 a month more than the current benefit, the Agriculture Department calculated, he said. [21]

Schanzenbach says the federal government could improve recipients' well-being by basing the SNAP formula on the Agriculture Department's Low Cost Food Plan, which would be about 25 percent more expensive. While a Thrifty Plan dinner might include baked beans and hotdogs, the Low Cost dinner could allow for roast beef.

SNAP is not meant to cover a family's total food costs, says Robert Doar, who studies poverty at the American Enterprise Institute (AEI), a conservative think tank in Washington, D.C., and was co-chair of the hunger commission. "It's always been intended to be a supplement to other forms of income," he says. "Viewed that way, I think the benefit amounts are adequate."

Angela Rachidi, an AEI research fellow in poverty studies, says recipients may run out of benefits before the end of the month because of "short-term impatience" rather than inadequate benefits. They might spend their allotment when they get it, rather than parcel it out throughout the month, she says. She and Doar suggest SNAP distribute the benefits more frequently rather than raising them. [22]

Rachidi says federal food aid is meeting most people's needs. She pointed to a 2015 study that looked at regional variations in food prices and found that 70 percent of SNAP households received sufficient benefits to provide a diet determined adequate by the Agriculture Department.

Some conservatives also argue that eliminating fraud and waste could cut food-aid costs.

Ohio state auditor David Yost released a report last year that concluded "there are likely millions of dollars in fraud" in his state's $2.5 billion SNAP program. "I do not believe fraud is rampant in Ohio," Yost said, "but it does exist and it is significant." [23]

Yost said he found 1,800 instances of dead people receiving benefits, including 36 who died before 2014 and remained on the rolls in 2015. Suspicious transactions during the first six months of 2015 included more than 96,000 instances of the entire monthly benefit spent at once and more than $28.5 million in even-dollar sales, which he said are uncommon for food purchases. [24]

Nationally, the U.S. Agriculture Department reported the program had a fraud rate of 1.3 percent in 2014, down from 4 percent 15 years earlier when paper food stamps were still used. In contrast, the Government Accountability Office estimated Medicare and Medicaid programs have a fraud rate at nearly 10 percent. [25]

Would better nutrition education decrease hunger?

Tammy Whitmire of Rabun Gap, Ga., described herself as "a good Southern girl" whose family diet was limited because "the only way we knew how to eat vegetables was fried." Since taking cooking classes at the Food Bank of Northeast George in Clayton, however, she has learned how to prepare a variety of foods and has lost 84 pounds. She also has changed her husband's habits "from everything fried to, 'Oh, this [non-fried food] is really pretty good,' " she said. [26]

Education plays an important part in reducing hunger and malnutrition by helping low-income families learn how to "maximize their food budget and make healthier food choices," said Billy Shore, founder and chief executive officer of Share Our Strength, a Washington-based anti-hunger organization that sponsors cooking classes nationwide. [27]

David Ludwig, director of the New Balance Foundation Obesity Prevention Center at Boston Children's Hospital, says lack of knowledge has created "a generation that for the first time in human history has largely not learned how to cook and has become dependent on the food industry, not just to provide the food but to cook it for us. One can't get the same nutritional quality [from processed foods]," says Ludwig, who also teaches at Harvard Medical School and its School of Public Health.

Since 1993, Share Our Strength has provided cooking, nutrition and shopping education to more than 265,000 low-income families. Typically the program, "Cooking Matters," is staffed by volunteers, including chefs, and offers one-day-a-week cooking classes for six weeks, a field trip to a grocery store to learn effective shopping techniques and nutrition education.

The shopping trip teaches such skills as reading nutrition labels, comparing unit prices and identifying whole grains. Participants take home groceries after each class to practice at home. After the last class, they receive a booklet with recipes and shopping tips, a reusable grocery bag and $10 worth of grocery coupons. [28]

"Instead of just heating up pizzas and Hot Pockets," Cara-Lee Langston, who teaches Cooking Matters classes in

Georgia, "helped the guys understand what goes into preparing a meal, how to eat on a budget and how to eat nutritious food," said Shane Pauley, ministry facilitator at Pilgrim Ministries, a faith-based organization in Georgia that works with troubled men. "All guys like meat and potatoes, but she made us throw some greens and yellows and oranges in there." [29]

But given the many challenges facing the poor, others say, education can't make a significant dent in hunger.

"No amount of nutrition education by itself is going to help anybody," Drexel's Chilton says. "You can have a family who knows that white bread is bad. But when the cost of white bread is half that of whole grain, they're going to go for the white bread. From my perspective, that's not an unwise choice given your economic situation."

Northwestern's Schanzenbach says of SNAP's education component: "There's not a lot of evidence that it works," but it may be possible to make it work better.

An evaluation of Cooking Matters found real but modest improvements in participants' behavior. Six months after completing the course, according to a survey by the Altarum Institute, a nonprofit health research and consulting organization in Ann Arbor, Mich., participants were 8 to 11 percent more likely to reduce salt consumption and to increase consumption of low-fat dairy products, lean protein and whole grains. [30]

In a paper last year for the Heritage Foundation, Rector said evaluations have found that federal programs are as effective as Cooking Matters. One evaluation compared low-income women who participated in the Agriculture Department's Expanded Food and Nutrition Education Program with a control group who did not participate. The program participants reduced their food spending by $10 to $20 a month while improving the quality of their diet, he wrote. A study of the Food Stamp Nutrition Education Program in Indiana found "modest but significant

reductions in food insecurity among participants," he said. [31]

Rector said the government could improve its education programs by using interactive computer technology where people apply for food stamps. All recipients should be required to complete a course covering such topics as the cost-effectiveness of different kinds of food and the importance of buying non-perishable staples in bulk, he said. Educational materials — including recipes for preparing food quickly — should be distributed to recipients and made available at food banks, he said. [32]

According to *Washington Post* food columnist Tamar Haspel, peanut butter, whole-grain pasta, whole-wheat flour, eggs, pearled barley, corn flour, brown rice and dried black beans are among cheap, nutritious foods that can be turned into healthy meals.

A person can "eat pretty well for under $4 per day (about the average food stamp benefit) by combining those

foods with somewhat more expensive chicken thighs, sweet potatoes, carrots, frozen corn, walnuts, yogurt or frozen broccoli, Haspel said. But, she said, that requires time and skill, which many food stamp recipients don't have. [33]

Some experts suggest that physicians should play a bigger role in nutrition education for the poor. New treatment guidelines from the American Diabetes Association, for instance, urge clinicians

White House Management and Budget Director Mick Mulvaney defended the Trump administration's proposed food-aid cuts. "We're trying to focus on both the recipients of the money and the folks who give us the money in the first place," he said. "And I think it's fairly compassionate to go to them and say, 'Look, we're not going to ask you for your hard-earned money anymore . . . unless we can guarantee to you that that money is actually going to be used in a proper function."

to ask patients about food insecurity. And doctors began setting up tables at the Houston Food Bank and offered blood-sugar tests, enrollment in a blood-sugar reduction program and bags of healthy food.

A study of such programs in Texas, California and Ohio found modest improvements in participants with the worst blood sugar readings. But behavior of some participants also illustrated the hurdles education efforts can face.

At a Corpus Christi, Texas, food bank, for example, 61-year-old Bruce

Hunger Falling in U.S.

Food insecurity among U.S. households has been declining since 2011 after jumping in 2008 during the height of the 2007-09 recession. In 2015, 12.5 percent of the nation's households suffered from food insecurity, or went hungry at times, and 5 percent had very low food security, or reduced food intake at times during the year.

Percentage of U.S. Households With Food Insecurity or Very Low Food Security, 1995-2015

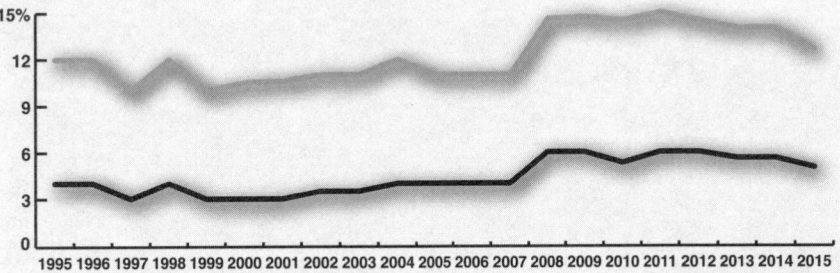

Source: "Trends in prevalence rates of food insecurity and very low food security in U.S. households, 1995-2015," Economic Research Service, U.S. Department of Agriculture, http://tinyurl.com/y7nnawkc

Food Insecurity (includes low and very low food security)

Very Low Food Security

Cook enrolled in the anti-diabetes program and picked up his bag of healthy vegetables. The next day, however, he returned to pick up a dozen chocolate-chip-and-M&M cookies. "I know what I'm supposed to eat and not supposed to eat,' " he said. "'But I still eat what I want." [34]

Should federal aid programs stop paying for junk food?

Running late for a medical checkup, the Salas family scoured their kitchen for a quick breakfast. The 9-year-old picked sweetened cereal and chocolate milk, the 4-year-old cheddar potato chips and a granola bar. For the 40-year-old single mother, it was an insulin injection to treat her diabetes.

Living on food stamps in southernmost Texas, Blanca Salas was feeding her children the way she herself ate, and she was passing on the expected health consequences, her doctor said. A 13-year-old-daughter showed the symptoms of early-onset diabetes, while the 9-year-old was taking cholesterol medicine.

Their doctor gave them a stark warning about the need to change their diets: "Either you address this now or it will be too late. I can give you medicine, but that's not the permanent solution." [35]

The Salas family's eating habits mirror those of many other food stamp recipients. Overall, recipients spend 20 percent of their food budgets on junk, according to a 2016 Agriculture Department study of purchases at a nationwide grocery chain. Soft drinks alone account for 5 percent of their purchases. Another 5 percent goes for other sweetened beverages, such as energy drinks, sweetened teas and fruit juice, which health experts say is not a healthy alternative to the other sweet drinks. The remaining 10 percent buys desserts, salty snacks and candy. [36]

Another study, published last year in the *Journal of the American Medical Association*, found that 61 percent of low-income Americans had unhealthy diets during 2012-13, compared with 36 percent of affluent Americans. Americans are eating more whole grains, fruits, nuts and seeds, while consuming fewer

white potatoes and sugary beverages, the researchers said. But the improvement is greater among the affluent than among those living in or near poverty. [37]

Health advocates say such findings demonstrate that food stamps, the nation's largest nutrition program, support unhealthy eating by the nation's poor, which contributes to obesity, diabetes and other diet-related illnesses among low-income Americans. Those advocates want to restrict food stamps, school lunches and other federally funded food aid to healthy foods.

Nutrition standards already apply in the $17.8 billion-a-year school feeding programs and the $6 billion Special Supplemental Nutrition Program for Women, Infants, and Children, which is known as WIC. But the Trump administration has delayed the implementation of stricter school-meal standards, and food stamps can buy anything that can be consumed except alcoholic beverages, nonfood items and food prepared in restaurants and other businesses. [38]

Opponents of tougher restrictions say the poor should be able to purchase whatever foods they want. Besides, some opponents say, restrictions wouldn't prevent the poor from continuing unhealthy eating habits.

"As an economist I can tell you that, if I say you can't purchase sugar-sweetened beverages with your food stamp money, people still will likely purchase sugar-sweetened beverages with their own cash," Schanzenbach says. "We should focus on policies that are likely to change behavior, not on symbolic actions that are not likely to change behavior."

The debate has spawned unlikely alliances, with liberals and conservatives found on both sides of the dispute.

The food and beverage industries, not surprisingly, have spent millions of dollars to lobby against restrictions. But the Obama administration's Agriculture Department also opposed food stamp standards, insisting that states and cities prove that nutrition requirements would work before imposing them. (No state has done so to the department's satisfaction.) Department officials have said the proposed restrictions would be unfair to food stamp recipients by limiting their choices and would be too complex to administer.

At the same time, though, the Obama administration imposed requirements on school meal programs, which feed more than 31 million children, and proposed raising the number of healthy foods that stores accepting food stamps must carry. [39]

Among those who have called for food stamp standards are mayors of 18 major cities, members of at least 14 state legislatures, the American Medical Association and the Center for Science in the Public Interest, a liberal consumer organization in Washington that focuses on nutrition and health. Two U.S. senators — conservative Republican Tom Coburn of Oklahoma and liberal Democrat Tom Harkin of Iowa — offered an unsuccessful amendment to the 2013 farm bill that would have allowed states to test junk-food restrictions. [40]

Federal food programs should follow the Agriculture Department's healthy-diet guidelines, which are updated every five years, the Obesity Prevention Center's Ludwig says. Because food stamps can buy unhealthy foods, he says, "the public winds up paying twice — once purchasing sugary beverages and the second time for diet-related diseases and higher Medicare and Medicaid and insurance costs for everybody." If government food programs promoted nutritious eating, he adds, "it would pay back the whole society in a healthier, more productive work force and lower food related diseases."

In addition to opposing SNAP standards and stiffer school-lunch requirements, food industry organizations fought proposed regulations to increase the variety of fruits, vegetables and other healthy food that would have to be stocked by stores that accept food stamps. While supermarkets could have met the requirements proposed by the department early last year, the National Association of Convenience Stores said, more than 90,000 smaller markets would not have enough shelf and refrigeration space to comply. [41]

Small grocers were able to meet WIC's nutrition requirements and could meet new food stamp standards as well, the Center for Science in the Public Interest argued. Foods stamps currently perpetuate "food deserts" — areas without easy access to fresh, healthy, affordable food — by "paying retailers for stocking junk foods," the group said. "A healthier SNAP would help communities overcome the food-desert problem by creating demand for healthy foods." [42]

Congress in 2014 told the administration to promulgate grocery standards, but this year lawmakers said the requirements were too strict. The Agriculture Department then delayed implementing the new standards, which would have required stores to carry 84 healthy-food items, up from the current 12 but half of the 168 the department initially proposed in February 2016. [43]

Volunteers deliver Christmas dinner to a home in Westbrook, Maine, as part of a Meals on Wheels program in the state. The Trump administration wants to reduce spending on federal programs that help finance Meals on Wheels, as well as impose tougher eligibility rules for food assistance.

Getty Images/*Portland Press Herald*/Gabe Souza

BACKGROUND

Early Aid

When Mabel McFiggan walked into Joseph Mutolo's store in Rochester, N.Y., on May 16, 1939, she became the first person to use a food stamp. At that time, recipients purchased the stamps at a discount. They came in two colors — orange for buying any food, and blue for buying food that the Agriculture Department designated as surplus. The stamps were intended not only to feed the hungry during the Great Depression but also to boost the sale of food that farmers couldn't sell in an economy reeling from 25 percent unemployment, low wages and other problems. [44]

As Milo Perkins, the first food stamp administrator, put it: "We got a picture of a gorge, with farm surpluses on one cliff and undernourished city folks with outstretched hands on the other.

We set out to find a practical way to build a bridge across that chasm." [45]

While the food stamps of 1939 were the precursor of today's largest food-aid program — renamed the Supplemental Nutrition Assistance Program (SNAP) in 2008, but still commonly called food stamps — they were far from the earliest American attempts to feed the hungry.

The federal government's first forays into food and nutrition sought to encourage and improve food production.

In 1862, the Agriculture Department was created. The Homestead Act that year gave away 160-acre plots to applicants who agreed to live on and farm the land for five years, and Congress passed the Morrill Act to support land-grant colleges, which would research and teach "agriculture and the mechanic arts."

The land-grant system eventually grew to encompass more than 100 state colleges and universities, as well as the Cooperative State Research, Education and Extension Service, which distributes the findings of agricultural research to farmers and others interested in the topic. The Agriculture Department itself began conducting research in 1883. [46]

Early feeding programs were aimed at children. In 1853, the Children's Aid Society of New York was serving meals to vocational school students. Around the beginning of the 20th century, school meal programs were begun in Philadelphia and Boston, and by 1918 schools were serving lunch in at least 86 cities, according to a survey by the New York Bureau of Municipal Research. [47]

Only five cities aimed the programs at the needy, however. Instead, most of the programs were begun because school executives had concluded that many high school students lived too far from school to go home for lunch. By 1937, 15 states authorized public schools to serve lunch, but just four made special provisions for the poor.

By then, the Depression had drawn the federal government into action. In 1932 it began making loans to pay school lunch employees in a few com-munities and expanded the lending to 39 states two years later. In 1933, the Federal Surplus Relief Corp. began buying surplus commodities from struggling farmers and distributing the food to hunger relief agencies around the country. In 1936 the corporation began giving surplus food to school lunch programs.

It also used funding from the Works Progress Administration — the federal agency that put the unemployed to work on public works projects — to pay lunch workers in almost every community in the country, and it supplied part-time lunch workers through the National Youth Administration. [48]

To encourage Americans to eat healthy, the Agriculture Department released its first dietary recommendations in 1941. They urged Americans to eat meals that met specific targets for calories, protein, iron, calcium and several major vitamins. The 1940s also saw the birth of the Green Revolution of scientifically based agriculture improvements that greatly increased production and dealt major blows to hunger around the world. [49]

Federal school lunch participation peaked at 6.2 million children in 93,000 schools in the 1941-42 academic year, during which the United States entered World War II and food and money were diverted to the military. The food stamp program ended in 1943, when the government determined that "the conditions that brought the program into being — unmarketable food surpluses and widespread unemployment — no longer existed."

Congress authorized $60 million to feed 1.5 million children in 1943-44, support that grew to a new high of 6.7 million students two years later. Schools participating — more than 45,000 — remained below the 1941-42 rate, however. In 1946, Congress required that the meals meet "minimum nutritional requirements." [50]

Congress authorized creation of a new food stamp program in 1959, but President Dwight D. Eisenhower's administration didn't follow through.

Shortly after his inauguration in 1961, President John F. Kennedy announced a pilot program for food stamps that sold the stamps at a discount. These stamps could purchase all items intended for human consumption except alcoholic beverages and imported food.

The Agriculture Department — which recorded Mabel McFiggan's first purchase of the original food stamp program — also recorded Mr. and Mrs. Alderson Muncy's purchase of a can of pork and beans with discounted stamps at Henderson's Supermarket in Paynesville, W.Va., on May 29, 1961. [51]

'Great Society' Era

Just as the Depression spurred creation of food programs in the 1930s, President Lyndon B. Johnson's Great Society, which aimed to eliminate racial injustice and poverty, increased government food aid in the 1960s and made food stamps permanent in 1964. "In a land rich in harvest, children just must not go hungry," Johnson said in his 1965 inaugural address. [52]

The actions were inspired in part by journalistic and congressional exposés of significant hunger in impoverished urban and rural areas. Among the most famous was a description of then-Sen. Robert F. Kennedy of New York crying as he rubbed the distended belly of a hungry child who sat on his lap in the Mississippi Delta region in 1967. Also influential were reports from doctors about "Third World diseases and hunger in the South," according to Weill, of the Food Research and Action Center. [53]

The government began to issue food stamps for free in 1979 to those who qualified. By 2004, all states had replaced stamps with plastic cards similar to debit cards. In addition to being less cumbersome to manage than stamps, they were expected to reduce theft and fraud because they required use of a personal identification number and created a record of all transactions, making it possible to

Continued on p. 568

Chronology

1900s-1940s
Government action to alleviate hunger waxes and wanes.

1918
School lunches served in at least 86 cities.

1932
Federal government makes loans to schools to pay their lunch employees.

1933
U.S. government buys surplus commodities from farmers, redistributes the food to hunger relief agencies.

1936
School lunch programs receive federal surplus food.

1939
First food stamps issued.

1941
Agriculture Department releases its first dietary guidelines.

1943
First food stamp program ends.

1960s-1993
President Lyndon B. Johnson's anti-poverty programs expand efforts to relieve hunger.

1961
Modern food stamps distributed in pilot program; becomes permanent in 1964.

1966
Federally funded school breakfast program begins as pilot project; becomes permanent in 1975.

1968
Federally funded summer meals program for children begins.

1972
Special Supplemental Nutrition Program for Women, Infants and Children (WIC) created.

1981
Federal Temporary Emergency Food Assistance Program distributes surplus commodities to the needy.

1993
Share Our Strength anti-hunger organization begins nutrition-focused cooking and shopping classes for low-income families.

1995-Present
Republicans and Democrats battle over anti-hunger policies, and major recession worsens the hunger problem.

1995
Republican-controlled Congress begins cutting funds for food stamps, school breakfasts and summer feeding programs for children. Food charities report jump in requests for emergency assistance.

2004
Food stamps replaced with electronic cards.

2007
Deep recession begins; ends in 2009.

2008
Hunger rises sharply. . . . Food-stamp program renamed Supplemental Nutrition Assistance Program (SNAP).

2009
First lady Michelle Obama plants White House garden.

2010
Congress allows high-poverty school districts to serve free meals to all students, requires chain-restaurant menus to list calories by 2017, calls for phase-in of stricter nutrition rules for school meals starting in 2012-13.

2014
President Barack Obama and Republican-led Congress agree to 10-year, $8.7 billion cut in food stamps. . . . Government reports food stamp fraud rate of 1.3 percent, down from 4 percent 15 years earlier.

2015
Hunger declines as nation continues economic recovery.

2016
Pilot program allows Medicaid-eligible children to automatically qualify for school meals. . . . Food and Drug Administration mandates more informative nutrition panels for packaged foods by 2018. . . . Federal study finds food stamp recipients spend one-fifth of their food budgets on junk food. . . . *Journal of the American Medical Association* reports 61 percent of low-income Americans have unhealthy diets compared with 36 percent of the affluent.

2017
President Trump begins to reverse Obama-era hunger and nutrition initiatives, including postponing implementation of the 2018 nutrition-label mandate, the requirement that restaurant menus show calorie counts and stricter school lunch nutrition rules. Trump also proposes deep cuts in anti-hunger programs, including SNAP, Meals on Wheels and nutrition research. . . . Study shows that one-third of community college students go hungry at times. . . . U.S. counts 60,000 private, nonprofit anti-hunger organizations serving 46 million people.

Offering Fresh Produce to the Poor

Programs bring healthy foods to low-income areas and "food deserts."

The Dollar Fifty Plus convenience store in a low-income neighborhood in Toledo, Ohio, used to be a fresh-produce-free zone. Now the store carries fresh fruits and vegetables, whole grain bread and healthy snacks such as baked chips and nuts.

"It's something new for me and for my customers because we're so used to having unhealthy food," owner Erma Blakely said about a year after she began offering the healthy items in August 2015. "I enjoy it because I've dropped some pounds myself."

Blakely is offering healthy foods with help from the Toledo-Lucas County Healthy Corner Store Initiative, part of a nationwide campaign begun by The Food Trust, a Philadelphia-based organization that works to increase access to nutritious food. The initiative is part of an effort to bring healthy foods to "food deserts," which the Agriculture Department defines as areas without easy access to fresh, healthy, affordable food. Stores in those areas typically do not stock many, if any, healthy groceries.

The department estimates that 23.5 million Americans live in food deserts and that the lack of access to produce contributes to poor diet and higher levels of obesity and other food-related ailments, such as diabetes and heart disease.

When small stores in Lucas County join the initiative, they receive a wooden produce stand, access to a wholesale distributor of fresh foods, free marketing assistance and a kickoff event that includes tastings of fresh-food dishes, recipes and nutritional advice from dietitians of the Toledo-Lucas County Health Department.

Seventeen stores in the Toledo-area have joined the project, [1] and about 700 are participating in New Jersey, Delaware and Pennsylvania, according to Candace Young, the Food Trusts' associate director for research and evaluation. Because the project is decentralized, the trust doesn't know how many stores participate nationwide, but there is "quite a number," says Karen Shore, the organization's director of consulting and technical assistance.

The Food Trust has evaluated the project's effectiveness in the Philadelphia area, finding that produce sales increased more than 60 percent at two stores studied and that produce sales more than doubled at a store on days when cooking classes and other programs were offered.

Shore says the trust has not attempted to determine the projects' impact on customers' health because "we would not look to a healthy corner store program alone to improve diet quality. But we also want to improve access to supermarkets, help farmers' markets flourish, connect our farmers, ranchers, and fishermen with our schools, help food pantries stock delicious fresh foods, and so on."

Studies say poverty and crime make low-income neighborhoods less attractive to supermarket chains. Other studies have shown that small stores are less likely than larger markets to stock healthy foods, in part because of limited space on shelves and in refrigerated compartments.

Low-income families also may eat poorly because they lack knowledge of good nutrition.

Researchers say that families with higher levels of income and education tend to eat healthier. After a 17,000-square-foot supermarket opened in a Bronx, N.Y., food desert in 2011, residents didn't change their diets. Food experts say healthy diets don't have to cost more than unhealthy ones, but low-

---

Continued from p. 566

flag nonfood purchases. [54]

Congress created a pilot school-breakfast program in 1966 to help schools with "nutritionally needy" children and permanently authorized it in 1975. Schools with "severe need" received extra aid. [55] The Summer Food Service Program was established in 1968 to feed children when school is not in session.

WIC was created in 1972 to improve the nutrition of pregnant women, new mothers and their young children. The Temporary Emergency Food Assistance Program was started in 1981 to distribute surplus commodities to the needy. [56]

Under pressure from health organizations and the Clinton Foundation — founded in 1997 by then-President Bill Clinton — the soft-drink industry in 2005 and 2006 agreed to severely limit the sale of its products in schools, beginning a process that now sees few soft-drink sales there. [57]

Republican Cuts

The robustness of federal food aid rose and fell over the years depending on economic conditions and whether liberals or conservatives held Congress and the White House. After Republicans took control of Congress in 1995, for example, they cut spending on food stamps, school breakfasts and summer feeding programs for children. Food charities subsequently reported a jump in requests for emergency assistance. [58]

Food aid increased significantly during the 2007-09 recession, and SNAP work requirements were waived across the country until last year, when 22 states either lost their waivers due to an improving economy or voluntarily gave them up. [59]

President Obama sought major reforms of both hunger and nutrition programs during his time in the White House (2009-2017). Much of the effort was led by first lady Michelle Obama, who planted a White House garden to encourage Americans to grow and eat fresh produce, promoted exercise and advocated for healthier school meals.

income families may not have the knowledge, facilities and time to cook well from scratch.

To address some of these issues, the corner store initiative offers in-store nutrition education, cooking demonstrations and blood-pressure checks. It also teaches nutrition at nearby schools. [2]

To help food stamp recipients prepare healthy meals, the Arlington Food Assistance Center in Virginia demonstrates how to cook foods that are being distributed at the time, says Rebecca Middleton, executive director of the Alliance to End Hunger, an association of more than 90 service and advocacy organizations that work for food security in the United States and abroad. "Folks can taste it and get advice," she says.

The Agriculture Department early next year plans to roll out a two-year pilot project to test using food stamps, formally known as the Supplemental Nutrition Assistance Program (SNAP), to purchase groceries online. The test will occur in urban and rural parts of Maryland, New Jersey, New York, Oregon, Pennsylvania, Iowa, Alabama and Washington state.

"Online purchasing is a potential lifeline for SNAP participants living in urban neighborhoods and rural communities where access to healthy food choices can be limited," outgoing Agriculture Secretary Tom Vilsack said when announcing the project in January.

The department already has tested online ordering, but payment had to be made in person upon delivery. In the new test, payment can be made when the order is placed. [3]

In the Boston area, "food rescue" organizations get fresh produce to 85 food programs by collecting unsold items from grocery stores, wholesalers and farmers. Regular contributors include Whole Foods, Trader Joe's, Costco and smaller grocers.

A customer learns about the nutritional advantages of whole grain tortillas at the Indiana Food Market in Philadelphia, one of hundreds of small grocery stores nationwide that bring fresh produce to so-called food deserts in poor neighborhoods.

"The same way recycling has become second nature, so should food rescue," said Ashley Stanley, founder of Lovin' Spoonfuls, one of the rescue organizations. [4]

— Tom Price

[1] Michelle Liu, "Store expands selection through health-food initiative," *Toledo Blade*, June 22, 2016, http://tinyurl.com/yboyctvj; Jillian Kravatz, "Fresh food closer to home," *Toledo Blade*, Aug. 10, 2015, http://tinyurl.com/y8h6s43t.

[2] "What We Do: In Corner Stores," The Food Trust, http://tinyurl.com/chgaj2b.

[3] "USDA Announces Retailer Volunteers for SNAP Online Purchasing Pilot," U.S. Department of Agriculture, Jan. 5, 2017, http://tinyurl.com/yajb7jm7.

[4] Lisa Zwirn, "Recovering wholesome food and getting it to those in need," *The Boston Globe*, Feb. 5, 2014, http://tinyurl.com/khk4lfb.

The 2,800-square-foot garden — planted where Eleanor Roosevelt tended a Victory Garden during World War II — fed the Obama family, guests at White House dinners and clients of Miriam's Kitchen, which provides food and shelter to the homeless about a mile from the White House. [60]

For his part, the president appointed a national task force on childhood obesity; established pilot programs to provide electronic cards to buy food during the summer for children eligible for free and reduced-price school meals; started an experimental program to streamline eligibility for school meals by allowing states to automatically enroll students for free and reduced price lunches if

they qualify for Medicaid; allowed schools in high-poverty areas to provide free meals to all students without collecting eligibility documents from each family; and added a cash benefit to WIC for purchase of fruits and vegetables.

Obama's Food and Drug Administration approved a revised Nutrition Facts panel on packaged foods that would have, among other things, displayed calories more prominently. The agency also required calorie counts on vending machines and chain-restaurant menus by mid-2018. The Centers for Disease Control and Prevention increased its promotion of breast feeding to improve the nutrition of young children. [61]

Obama compromised with the

Republican-controlled House to pass the 2014 farm bill, which included an $8.7 billion cut in food stamps over the following decade — a reduction that some on the left harshly criticized. [62] But the administration's most controversial action — promoted by the first lady — was strengthening nutrition requirements for food sold in schools.

School Nutrition

Initially not contentious, the requirements passed the Senate unanimously in 2010. The provisions doubled the amount of fruits and vegetables that had to be served at lunch, required

Celebrity Chefs Fight Hunger

"We feed the few, but we need to be taking care of feeding the many."

Early in his working life, Michael Babin was a congressional aide and a lobbyist. Later, after he entered the restaurant business, he maintained his interest in public policy. Still later as a business success — 2014 "Restaurateur of the Year" and owner of 11 Washington-area restaurants, a wine shop, a bakery, a butcher shop and a catering service — Babin found himself able to act on that interest.

In 2010, he founded the Arcadia Center for Sustainable Food and Agriculture, which delivers fresh food to low-income neighborhoods and operates a farm. The effort is one of the many ways American restaurateurs are fighting hunger, from raising money for food charities to running food-service operations in low-income schools. [1]

"Every responsible business tries to do something positive in its community," Babin says. "We decided we could have the biggest impact in the food system. You just open your eyes, and you see all of the issues and problems."

Arcadia is based at Woodlawn Plantation in Alexandria, Va., once part of George Washington's Mount Vernon estate, where Martha Washington's granddaughter Nelly and her husband, Lawrence Lewis, built a Georgian/Federal-style house. In 1952 the house became the first site operated by the National Trust for Historic Preservation. [2]

On the plantation, Arcadia tends a garden that doubles as a teaching tool for children. It also runs a farm at Woodlawn that demonstrates sustainable agricultural techniques and produces food for two "mobile markets" — converted buses that sell affordable food in low-income areas.

At mobile market stops and in schools, Arcadia teaches people how to prepare the food in inexpensive and nutritious ways.

Another restaurateur from the Washington area, chef Daniel Giusti, is trying to improve school lunches, beginning in New London, Conn., where 91 percent of the students qualify for free and reduced-price meals. Giusti said he went to New London because of the district's small size, which would make it easier to implement change, and the partnership he could forge with schools Superintendent Manuel Rivera. [3]

Giusti, who was executive chef at 1789, one of Washington's most prominent restaurants, had been the No. 2 chef at Noma in Copenhagen, a two-star Michelin awardee that is listed as one of the top dining spots in the world and where a couple can drop $1,000 on food and drink. [4]

"I got into cooking because I come from a big Italian family," Giusti said. "I like the idea of feeding people," but he became weary of the high-pressure world of fine dining. [5]

Giusti and two other chefs prepared the meals at New London High School and a local elementary school in the just-completed academic year. He is planning to run the kitchens at four other schools in the fall.

Students have been treated to chicken curry; roasted sweet potatoes; spiced chicken tacos; pizza with barbecue chicken; and apples or pears poached in green tea for dessert.

The challenge is to make healthy food that children will eat, Giusti said. He tells his chefs that "it's not about you, it's about the kids. . . . You need to just make food that they like."

The kids give most of Giusti's meals a thumbs-up.

"The food didn't taste this good last year," 11-year-old Fortune Adekoya said. "The old cheese was like plastic," seventh-grader Mallory Suprenant said of the pizza. "Now it tastes real." [6]

Not all of Giusti's offerings hit the spot, however. Of his butternut squash soup, he said: "They hated it — thought it was revolting," so it's not on the menu anymore.

---

use of whole grains and cut the amount of salt, sugar and fat that could be offered. The new rules covered not just lunches but all food offered at schools, including in vending machines.

The School Nutrition Association, which represents school food managers and vendors, initially supported but then turned against the legislation, complaining that it was unpopular with students and cost too much. The association asked the Agriculture Department to allow more salt and less whole grains, saying students would find that tastier. [63]

When the regulations began to take effect during the 2012-13 academic year, some schools said some students — especially those who pay for their food — were not buying school meals. Some schools reported significant revenue declines because of lower consumption.

Missouri reported that the number of lunches served statewide dropped 11 percent from 2009-10 to 2013-14. In Georgia, the Gwinnett County school district reported the percentage of students eating lunch regularly fell from 81 percent in 2010 to 69 percent in 2016. [64]

Some students started posting online photos of food they didn't like with the hashtag "ThanksMichelleObama." The first lady dismissed the students' complaints, saying, "You know what? Kids don't like math either. What are we gonna do, stop teaching math?" [65]

The rules came under ideological attack as well, with Daren Bakst, a research fellow at the conservative Heritage Foundation, declaring that "it's not up to the government to dictate the personal dietary choices of individuals." [66]

There were signs, however, that time might change the students' tastes.

"The little guys are eating more fruits and vegetables than they were three years ago," Marlene Pfeiffer, director of food services for Missouri's Parkway School District, west of St. Louis, said

Because cooking from scratch is more labor-intensive and can use more-expensive ingredients than cooking with canned or processed food, Giusti and Rivera need private donations. So far, Target has kicked in $100,000.

Giusti's newly formed company Brigaid has a $130,000-a-year contract to feed the students. In addition, each chef costs the district about $60,000 annually. [7]

Superstar chef José Andrés — with 26 restaurants from South Beach, Fla., to Hollywood, Calif., to Mexico City — has been a leader in the chefs-against-hunger movement, raising funds for local food programs and heading anti-hunger efforts in Haiti and other poor nations.

"We feed the few, but we need to be taking care of feeding the many," he said. [8]

Andrés began his anti-hunger work with DC Central Kitchen, which prepares 3 million meals a year for homeless shelters, public and private schools that serve low-income children and other nonprofit organizations. The kitchen also trains homeless and low-income people for careers in the food industry. [9] Andrés said he was drawn to the organization because "it does more than feed people — it employs and trains people to put them on a new path in life." [10]

Andrés founded World Central Kitchen, a global network of 60 chefs who promote health, education, employment, food safety and healthy school meals, as well as distribute clean cookstoves to replace indoor cooking fires, and train low-income people for jobs in the hospitality industry. They are active in Brazil, Cambodia, Cuba, Dominican Republic, Haiti, Nicaragua, Zambia and the United States. [11]

— *Tom Price*

Renowned chef José Andrés, left, has been a leader in the chefs-against-hunger movement, raising funds for local food programs in the United States as well as in Haiti and other poor nations.

[1] "Our Programs," Arcadia Center for Sustainable Food & Agriculture, http://tinyurl.com/yazp5k7a.

[2] "Explore Woodlawn," Woodlawn and Pope-Leighey House, http://tinyurl.com/yaeady69.

[3] Sophie Haigney, "Why is a chef from one of the world's top restaurants cooking in public school kitchens?" *The Boston Globe*, Oct. 25, 2016, http://tinyurl.com/y8d84tp8.

[4] Tim Carman, "Noma chef Daniel Giusti keeps the world's top restaurant running," *The Washington Post*, May 27, 2014, http://tinyurl.com/y7x6mo4w.

[5] Haigney, *op. cit.*

[6] *Ibid.*; Greg Smith, "Chefs transforming New London school lunches," *The* (New London, Conn.) *Day*, Sept. 23, 2016, http://tinyurl.com/ybkz5r59.

[7] *Ibid.*

[8] Tim Carman, "José Andrés gets political at food conference in D.C.," *The Washington Post*, March 28, 2015, http://tinyurl.com/yb6b3qfn.

[9] "About Us," DC Central Kitchen, http://tinyurl.com/yd8c26yl.

[10] Tovin Lapan, "With citizenship in hand, chef now ready to focus on SLS Las Vegas opening," *Las Vegas Sun*, Dec. 30, 2013, http://tinyurl.com/ya3e2ovb.

[11] "About," World Central Kitchen, http://tinyurl.com/yc7rnwqw.

in 2014. "It takes a few years to get the palate turned around, and that's harder for older students." [67] ∎

CURRENT SITUATION

Rules Delayed

Critics of the Obama nutrition requirements are encouraged by the steps the Trump administration is taking to reverse those rules.

Earlier this year, the administration delayed the menu rules until next May and the new Nutrition Facts label indefinitely.

Nutrition and consumer advocates condemned the delays, while industry groups gave mixed reactions to the labels decisions.

"We're very pleased that our voices have been heard" on the menu rules, said Tim McIntyre, chairman of the American Pizza Community trade group. But Cicely Simpson, executive vice president of the National Restaurant Association, said the delays leave the industry under a "patchwork" of state and local regulations that is "even more burdensome for restaurants to implement." [68]

"To ease the regulatory burden on the economy," a coalition of 17 food industry organizations had asked the administration to postpone implementation of the new Nutrition Facts panel. But some companies — including Mars Inc., known for its candies — had begun producing the new label and said the delay would harm them. [69]

"The fact that we'll have the added-sugar declaration and the percent daily value, but our competitors won't? That just ends up confusing consumers," said Brad Figel, vice president of public affairs for Mars in North America. [70]

Jim O'Hara, director of health promotion policy at the Center for Science in the Public Interest, noted the industry divisions over nutrition reforms. "Just like with the menu-labeling delay, this [Trump] administration is denying consumers critical information they need to make decisions, and [delaying the new Nutrition Facts panel] is throwing the food industry into disarray." [71]

First lady Michelle Obama tends the White House garden with Florida fifth-grader Emilo Vega in 2013. President Obama sought to reform food programs during his eight years in office, including improving nutrition for schoolchildren and offering more free and reduced-price school meals. Many of the president's efforts were led by the first lady, who first planted the garden in 2009.

Schools can request exemption from the whole-grain requirements and can wait until 2020 to resume implementing the rules on salt.

School Nutrition Association Chief Executive Patricia Montague praised the administration for giving schools needed flexibility. But Margo Wootan, director of nutrition policy at the Center for Science in the Public Interest, said the postponement will be "locking in dangerously high sodium levels" in school meals. Wootan also worried that Trump might turn school-meals programs into block grants to the states

with little federal regulation, further weakening them. [72]

Budget Cuts

The president has not moved to create block grants, but his proposed 2018 budget seeks cuts to food-related programs, with some conservatives joining liberals in supporting the programs. Because food aid is in the same legislation that funds farm subsidies, Congress is unlikely to make big reductions, Doar of the American Enterprise Institute says. "By being combined, it buys off urban support for expensive subsidies for the agriculture industry and it gets rural, conservative support for a very expensive safety net."

The biggest proposed cut in federal food stamp spending would come from requiring states to cover a quarter of the costs by 2023. Other reductions would come from decreasing the time unemployed able-bodied adults without minor children can collect benefits; prohibiting states from providing federal

food aid to families earning more than 130 percent of the federal poverty threshold, which for a family of four is $32,319; charging fees to stores that accept food stamps; capping aid to large families at the level received by a family of six; and slashing funding for scientific research. [73]

"Requiring states to have "skin in the game" will improve efficiency because "red states and blue states manage their own money better than they do federal money," the Heritage Foundation's Rector says of shifting food-stamp costs.

Budget Director Mulvaney said Meals on Wheels is among "programs that don't work." "Meals on Wheels sounds great," he said, but "we're not going to spend on programs that cannot show that they actually deliver the promises that we've made to people." [74]

Mulvaney said the administration proposes cutting research funding at the National Institutes of Health [NIH] because "we think there's been mission creep. We think they do things that are outside their core functions." [75]

Noting that food stamp rolls remain substantially above prerecession levels, Mulvaney asked whether "there [are] folks on SNAP who shouldn't be." [76]

Some say this is because the recovery has been slow. Those who say "yes" point to Maine, where a tougher work requirement in 2015 led 80 percent of those affected by the requirement to drop out of the program. Rector says that indicates a significant number of able-bodied adult recipients "had an off-the-books job" or "other resources the government doesn't know about."

Among those arguing against the proposed cuts is the Obesity Prevention Center's Ludwig. The NIH budget should not be reduced, he says, because it is "the main sponsor of nutrition and obesity research," and obesity is "the No. 1 nutritional problem and the most important medical problem in the United States, now exceeding tobacco as a cause of death and disability."

Continued on p. 574

At Issue:

Should the federal government stop funding free school lunches for students who aren't poor?

DAREN BAKST
RESEARCH FELLOW, AGRICULTURAL POLICY, HERITAGE FOUNDATION

WRITTEN FOR *CQ RESEARCHER*, JULY 2017

*t*he federal welfare system is being turned on its head. American taxpayers are now being forced to provide welfare to wealthy families.

Through the Community Eligibility Provision of the Healthy, Hunger-Free Kids Act of 2010, students from middle-class and wealthy families can receive free school meals courtesy of taxpayers, as long as 40 percent of students within a school, group of schools or school district are deemed eligible for free meals.

The system is so extreme that it is possible that a school could provide free meals to all its students without having a single low-income student enrolled. In fact, all the students could come from wealthy families.

Congress needs to eliminate the Community Eligibility Provision immediately.

There's really only one critical point for policymakers and the public to remember: eliminating the Community Eligibility Provision wouldn't change the fact that all students who are eligible for free or reduced-priced meals would remain eligible.

Admittedly, such a change would mean free meals wouldn't go to those who aren't in need, but that's the entire point. Usually, when welfare benefits are going to those who are not in need, this draws serious concern over mismanagement of taxpayer dollars. Just because the federal government has given its blessing to handing out free meals regardless of need doesn't change the fact that this is still waste and abuse, and it undermines the legitimacy of the school meal programs.

Proponents of the Community Eligibility Provision claim it will reduce the administrative burden on schools. This is a worthy goal. However, it's amusing that these proponents are generally the same individuals who want to maintain the biggest school meal-related burden on schools: the federal school meal standards.

Further, while reducing administrative burden is important, it doesn't justify ignoring the necessary requirements of operating a means-tested welfare system. For any such system, the government must determine the means of potential welfare recipients.

Congress is taking taxpayer dollars from lower-income households to funnel welfare benefits to higher-income households, creating a "reverse Robin Hood" policy. This inexcusable wealth transfer is creating even greater dependence on government.

The federal school meal program, which is designed to help those in need, should help only those in need. It's sad that such an obvious and common-sense point even has to be made.

MARIANA CHILTON
PROFESSOR OF HEALTH MANAGEMENT AND POLICY AND DIRECTOR, CENTER FOR HUNGER-FREE COMMUNITIES, DREXEL UNIVERSITY

WRITTEN FOR *CQ RESEARCHER*, JULY 2017

*a*ll of us, in good conscience, know that everyone deserves to have adequate nutrition. So this question is a little problematic: It implies a judgment of who is "deserving," especially when not everyone agrees on who is "poor."

Food hardships go far beyond the federal poverty line, which is just $24,600 for a family of four. Poverty is not a static condition. Income volatility among low-wage earners living close to the poverty line can lead to food insecurity. Almost half of food-insecure households have incomes between 130 and 200 percent of the poverty line. Food insecurity accounts for poor health, truncated child development, poor school performance and suicidal ideation among teenagers. On top of that, school breakfasts and lunches reduce absenteeism and improve cognitive performance, grades and standardized-test scores.

At the core is the Community Eligibility Provision. It allows schools with more than 40 percent of students eligible for other public assistance programs to apply to provide free meals to all students. The provision reduces administrative costs and helps buoy communities with concentrated poverty through hard times.

Children in high-poverty areas are hit hard by exposure to violence, stress and environmental hazards that affect everyone who lives there, not just those classified as poor. Remember, a few hungry kids can disrupt an entire classroom.

Because of Philadelphia's high concentrated poverty, categorical eligibility was in place years before the Healthy, Hunger-Free Kids Act of 2010 implemented a more efficient way of funding school meals. The Agriculture Department found that before 2010, when the Philadelphia School District was piloting community eligibility, the district had saved 20,480 hours of staff time, an average 19 cents per meal, in a single year. That's a great return on investment: more-effective administrators, less red tape, less hunger, smarter kids.

The provision has been adopted in every state, with high take-up rates in Kentucky, Georgia, Tennessee, North Dakota and Wisconsin. Across America, school districts are taking more control over how they choose to nourish their kids; they are investing in America's brain trust.

Still can't see the wisdom? Go to a high-poverty area and stand in the cafeteria. Stare down those hungry kids whose parents are doing their best — often working multiple jobs — but can't get ahead and otherwise wouldn't qualify for a free lunch. Pulling their meals away from them would be shortsighted.

Continued from p. 572

Drexel's Chilton says she is especially worried about making states shoulder more of the food stamp burden because "I'm not sure state legislators are protective of the most vulnerable people."

"The federal nutrition programs are set up to be countercyclical," said Duke Storen, senior director for research, advocacy and partnership development at Share Our Strength. "They expand to meet increased need during down times and contract when the economy and the economic profile of Americans improves." States — most of which are constitutionally required to balance their budgets every year — can't run deficits when their tax revenues decline. [77]

"If you look at what happened during the Great Recession, SNAP responded to meet the need and TANF didn't," Middleton of the Alliance to End Hunger says, referring to Temporary Assistance for Needy Families, a block-grant program that provides aid to needy pregnant women and to families with one or more dependent children.

Capping aid to large families is "totally inconsistent with the goals of SNAP as an anti-hunger program," said Craig Gundersen, an agricultural economist at the University of Illinois who studies food stamps. "This all derives from that old canard that people have more children to get more welfare benefits." [78]

Weill at the Food Research and Action Center said he worries that participation fees would cause small retailers in poor communities to stop accepting food stamps. [79]

Among the conservative Republicans opposing some of the cuts is Agriculture Secretary Sonny Perdue, the former Georgia governor. Perdue told the House Agriculture Committee that SNAP is "a very important, effective program" and that "you don't try to fix things that aren't broken." [80] He reaffirmed that position after the White House released the budget, which was prepared before he assumed his administration post. [81]

Rep. Mark Meadows, R-N.C., chairman of the conservative House Freedom Caucus, defended Meals on Wheels, saying "I've delivered meals to a lot of people [for whom] perhaps it's their only hot meal of the day." [82]

The federal government provides 35 percent of the funding for locally operated Meals on Wheels programs. Other support comes from private contributions and state and local governments. Some of the local organizations get all of their money from Washington; some get none. The program serves 2.4 million seniors a year, and the volunteer visits provide social interaction as well as nutrition. [83]

"With volunteers going to the senior's house several times a week, this means someone is putting eyes on them," said Jason Tucker, director of meal services for the program in Atlanta. "They can tell if there's a decline in their health or if something else is wrong." [84]

Many private organizations provide food aid that supplements federal assistance. And some are applying new tactics to increase the amount of aid they give, to improve the quality of the food they deliver or to serve new kinds of clients. Examples include efforts to make more fresh produce available in poor neighborhoods in cities and isolated rural communities, tapping the expertise of professional chefs and turning college campuses into sources of aid for the nearby poor and for needy college students themselves. (*See sidebar, p. 568.*)

Move for Hunger, a nonprofit based in New Jersey, has enlisted 750 moving companies throughout the United States and Canada to retrieve nonperishable foods that their clients otherwise would throw away. Facebook, Google, Hewlett-Packard, Bridgestone and Sodexo have agreed to incorporate Move for Hunger into their employee-relocation processes. The organization has delivered more than 8 million pounds of food to food banks and other programs since 2009. [85]

The Campus Kitchen Project — an offspring of the DC Central Kitchen food program in Washington — retrieves unused food from college and high school dining halls on more than 60 campuses, prepares meals and distributes them to the needy near campus. Some of the student volunteers also garden and teach nutrition in the community around their campus. During the last academic year, nearly 29,000 volunteers salvaged 1.3 million pounds of food and prepared 350,000 meals. Students at one secondary school in the coalition — Gonzaga College High School in Washington — volunteer at a homeless shelter on campus. [86]

Swipe Out Hunger, another campus-based program, collects unused meals from dining-hall cards and converts them into groceries for nearby food programs or into free meals for needy students. The College and University Food Bank Alliance has members serving hungry students on more than 450 campuses. [87] In Massachusetts, 25 of the 29 public college campuses have a food assistance program for students. In Ohio, eight colleges and four community colleges host food pantries. [88] ■

OUTLOOK

Continued Decline?

B oth liberals and conservatives agree that hunger will continue to diminish if the economy keeps strengthening. Many on both sides of the political spectrum also see employment as the key to reducing hunger. As a family's income increases, so does its ability to purchase food.

"Ultimately, I think we're going to revamp the welfare system to make it much more supportive of work and marriage, and that will be an effective policy for increasing income," which will cause hunger to fall, the Heritage Foundation's Rector says.

In addition to holding jobs, people need their workplace to pay a living wage, Drexel's Chilton says. "I'm deeply concerned that wages will not increase and living costs will continue to increase and people will not keep up with that, and we will see more homeless and more suffering," she says. For that reason, the poor need "a really good safety net that focuses on their health and well-being."

Schanzenbach, of Northwestern University, says she is "gravely worried about the future of the safety net in this country" because of President Trump's proposed cuts. On the other hand, she says, Congress did a reasonable job of passing food-stamp legislation for the current budget year, although "I would argue it's underfunded."

Like Rector, Doar of the American Enterprise Institute expects "a little more focus on work" in federal food programs, and "that will lead to reductions in food insecurity and poverty. I think people will still use food stamps as a supplement to their earnings to make work pay more, and I think that will be good."

Calling herself "an eternal optimist," Middleton of the Alliance to End Hunger expects that as Americans "become more aware that food fuels people's potential — that children learn more on a full stomach, that seniors stay healthy longer when they have access to good meals — we're going to make this a national priority and we're going to hold our elected officials accountable."

Similarly, Goldrick-Rab of Temple University says awareness probably will lead to extension of school meals to community college students.

"I harbor no illusion that this is going to happen in this [Trump] administration," she says. "But I think the move to making community college free is going to help establish it as the next level of schooling" and that it logically should be the next level of school meals. "The college-affordability challenge is getting greater and it will become more visible

and it is clear to me that when confronted with these challenges there's more likely to be action."

Michael Babin, a Washington-area restaurateur, also doesn't expect the Trump administration to increase federal anti-hunger efforts. But he is optimistic about broader society.

"If the forces that have animated Trump's rise are in ascendance, I don't see the political will to deal with these issues," he says. But, he adds, "I don't think those forces are ascendant. There are so many people activated on these issues — so much more awareness now — I don't think you can put that genie back in the bottle." ■

Notes

[1] Connor Sheets, " 'I've got to make $15 stretch': Food stamp cuts hit Alabama's Black Belt hard," *Birmingham News*, June 10, 2017, https://tinyurl.com/y7jb8gnb.

[2] "Key Statistics & Graphics," Economic Research Service, U.S. Department of Agriculture, Oct. 11, 2016, https://tinyurl.com/y8jhrwuq.

[3] *Ibid.*

[4] *Ibid.*; James P. Ziliak and Craig Gundersen, "The State of Senior Hunger in America 2014: An Annual Report," National Foundation to End Senior Hunger, June 2016, http://tinyurl.com/z3qtg43.

[5] James D. Weill, "President's Brutal Budget Will Cause a Spike in Hunger and Poverty for Millions," Food Research & Action Center, May 23, 2017, http://tinyurl.com/y9x4k5px.

[6] Christopher Ingraham, "Meals on Wheels is 'not showing any results' only if you ignore all these results," *The Washington Post*, March 16 2017, https://tinyurl.com/y9thhkpa; Caitlin Dewey and Tracy Jan, "Trump to poor Americans: Get to work or lose your benefits," *The Washington Post*, May 22, 2017, https://tiny url.com/y9dyw34y.

[7] Louis Nelson, "Mulvaney: Proposed cuts to Meals on Wheels are compassionate to taxpayers," *Politico*, March 16, 2017, https://tinyurl.com/myruee3.

[8] "Supplemental Nutrition Assistance Program: Able-Bodied Adults Without Dependents," Food and Nutrition Service, U.S. Department of Agriculture, April 24, 2017, http://tinyurl.com/yd9odcae.

[9] Shelia M. Poole, "Trump's proposed cuts make Meals on Wheels groups worry about

seniors," *The Atlanta Journal-Constitution*, March 18, 2017, https://tinyurl.com/y8w9ggvf.

[10] Dewey and Jan, *op. cit.*

[11] Sara Goldrick-Rab, Jed Richardson and Anthony Hernandez, "Hungry and Homeless in College," Wisconsin Hope Lab, University of Wisconsin, March 2017, https://tinyurl.com/y7qy5g62.

[12] Supplemental Nutrition Assistance Program Participation and Costs," Federal Nutrition Service, U.S. Department of Agriculture, June 9, 2017, https://tinyurl.com/o28odbs; "Supplemental Nutrition Assistance Program (data)," Federal Nutrition Service, U.S. Department of Agriculture, June 9, 2017, https://tinyurl.com/yc5cntjr.

[13] "Food Insecurity and Hunger in the United States: An Assessment of the Measure," National Academies, 2006, https://tinyurl.com/yc4q8w85; Jessica Fanzo, "Malnutrition in the United States and the UK," Global Nutrition Report, https://tinyurl.com/y7f4ozj8; Barbara Bush and Hugh Welsh, "Hidden hunger: America's growing malnutrition epidemic," *The Guardian*, Feb. 10, 2015, http://tinyurl.com/jncby2h.

[14] "National Health and Nutrition Examination Survey, 2009-2010," National Center for Health Statistics, Centers for Disease Control and Prevention, http://tinyurl.com/y7usgzuu.

[15] Robert Rector, "Reducing Hunger and Very Low Food Security," The Heritage Foundation, Feb. 11, 2016, https://tinyurl.com/y8lxn3y7.

[16] Emily Badger, "What happens when a family runs out of food stamps," *The Washington Post*, Dec. 9, 2015, http://tinyurl.com/y7576axs.

[17] *Ibid.*

[18] *Ibid.*

[19] "Thrifty Food Plan 2006," Center for Nutrition Policy and Promotion, U.S. Department of Agriculture, April 2007, https://tinyurl.com/yawpk4v5.

[20] James Ziliak, "Modernizing SNAP Benefits," The Hamilton Project, Brookings Institution, May 2016, https://tinyurl.com/y9m84zgz.

[21] "Policy Brief 2016-06, Modernizing SNAP Benefits," The Hamilton Project, Brookings Institution, May 2016, https://tinyurl.com/ydghoswt.

[22] Angela Rachidi, "Are SNAP benefits really too low?" *The Hill*, Jan. 20, 2016, https://tiny url.com/y92kfz3s.

[23] Jack Torry, "Auditor grilled over food stamp probe," *Dayton Daily News*, July 6, 2016, https://tinyurl.com/yb864eqq.

[24] Brian Kollars, "Dead people got food stamps in Ohio, audit shows," *Dayton Daily News*, June 29, 2016, https://tinyurl.com/y7rzxdhd; Jim Otte, "Plan announced to put photos on food stamp cards," *Dayton Daily News*, Feb. 8, 2017, https://tinyurl.com/y7l2y9l2; "Auditor Yost Releases Report on Supplemental Nutrition

Assistance Program," Ohio Auditor of State, June 28, 2016, http://tinyurl.com/sqbptub.

[25] "SNAP Integrity Efforts Reduce Fraud," Food and Nutrition Service, U.S. Department of Agriculture, March 25, 2014, https://tinyurl.com/pwjbjku; Kim Severson, "Food Stamp Fraud, Rare but Troubling," *The New York Times*, Dec. 19, 2013, https://tinyurl.com/mhm35u9.

[26] C.W. Cameron, "Food bank's fresh approach goes far beyond distribution," *The Atlanta Journal-Constitution*, April 6, 2017, https://tinyurl.com/ybehfcj7.

[27] "Walmart Foundation Gives $2.5 Million to Share Our Strength to Increase the Availability of Nutrition Education Programs for Families," Walmart Foundation, Oct. 24, 2013, https://tinyurl.com/y8fp27hl.

[28] "What We Do," Share Our Strength's Cooking Matters, https://tinyurl.com/yb543rqj; "Cooking Matters at the Store," Share Our Strength's Cooking Matters, https://tinyurl.com/y7nmxsmp.

[29] Cameron, *op. cit.*

[30] "Cooking Matters: A Long-Term Impact Evaluation," Share Our Strength's Cooking Matters, https://tinyurl.com/yawhp6cp.

[31] See Janie Burney and Betsey Haughton, "EFNEP: A Nutrition Education Program that Demonstrates Cost-Benefit," *Journal of the American Dietetic Association*, http://tinyurl.com/y9n8c3hn; Heather A. Eicher-Miller *et al.*, "The Effect of Food Stamp Nutrition Education on the Food Insecurity of Low-income Women Participants," *Journal of Nutrition Education and Behavior*, http://tinyurl.com/y9zkd9bf.

[32] Rector, *op. cit.*

[33] Tamar Haspel, "Is nutritious food really pricier, and, if so, is that really the problem?" *The Washington Post*, Nov. 25, 2016, https://tinyurl.com/y8dcusco.

[34] Catherine Saint Louis, "Food Banks Take On a Contributor to Diabetes: Themselves,"

The New York Times, June 17, 2016, http://tinyurl.com/h2mxnzh.

[35] Eli Saslow, "Too much of too little," *The Washington Post*, Nov. 9, 2013, https://tinyurl.com/yak82t4m.

[36] Anahad O'Connor, "In the Shopping Cart of a Food Stamp Household: Lots of Soda," *The New York Times*, Jan. 13, 2017, https://tinyurl.com/j3ehdnu; "Sugary Drinks," The Nutrition Source, Harvard University School of Public Health, https://tinyurl.com/ya5gptax.

[37] Max Ehrenfreund, "The difference between what rich and poor Americans eat is getting bigger," *The Washington Post*, June 23, 2016, https://tinyurl.com/yaefwjx5.

[38] "Federal Cost of School Food Programs," Food and Nutrition Service, U.S. Department of Agriculture, June 9, 2017, https://tinyurl.com/yd5xgehu; "WIC Program Participation and Costs," Food and Nutrition Service, U.S. Department of Agriculture, June 9, 2017, https://tinyurl.com/yc5gwaf5; and Supplemental Nutrition Assistance Program, "Eligible Food Items," Food and Nutrition Service, U.S. Department of Agriculture, March 22, 2017, https://tinyurl.com/mxq4n6y.

[39] O'Connor, *op. cit.*; Caitlin Dewey and Moriah Balingit, "Trump official freezes Michelle Obama's plan to fight childhood obesity," *The Washington Post*, May 1, 2017, https://tinyurl.com/y8h76k9s.

[40] "Seeds of Change: Growing Momentum for a Healthier SNAP," Physicians Committee for Responsible Medicine, https://tinyurl.com/lxg85yc; "Update: SNAP Momentum," Physicians Committee for Responsible Medicine, https://tinyurl.com/y846qvrp.

[41] Greg Trotter, "Healthy food rules amended for SNAP," *op. cit.*

[42] "Seeds of Change: Growing Momentum for a Healthier SNAP," *op. cit.*

[43] Trotter, *op. cit.*

[44] Jessica Shahin, "Commemorating the History of SNAP," Food and Nutrition Service, U.S. Department of Agriculture, Oct. 15, 2014, https://tinyurl.com/yanaee7h.

[45] "Supplemental Nutrition Assistance Program," Food and Nutrition Service, U.S. Department of Agriculture, http://tinyurl.com/p2o5hmf.

[46] Jennifer Weeks, "Farm Policy," *CQ Researcher*, Aug. 10, 2012, pp. 693-716; Tom Price, "Science in America," *CQ Researcher*, Jan. 11, 2008, pp. 25-48.

[47] Gordon W. Gunderson, "National School Lunch Program (NSLP)," Food and Nutrition Service, U.S. Department of Agriculture, June 17, 2014, https://tinyurl.com/y78nwl7t.

[48] *Ibid.*; "The History of SNAP," New America, https://tinyurl.com/y7x6w6mm.

[49] Jennifer Weeks, "Farm Policy: Does U.S. farm policy promote unhealthy eating?" *CQ Researcher*, Aug. 10, 2012; Tom Price, "Global Hunger," *CQ Researcher*, Aug. 8, 2014, pp. 673-696.

[50] Gunderson, *op. cit.*; "Supplemental Nutrition Assistance Program," *op. cit.*

[51] "Supplemental Nutrition Assistance Program," Food and Nutrition Service, U.S. Department of Agriculture, *op. cit.*

[52] Evie Blad, "School Meal Programs Extend Their Reach," *Education Week*, Aug. 5, 2014, https://tinyurl.com/ydg3ugvz.

[53] *Ibid.*

[54] "Supplemental Nutrition Assistance Program," *op. cit.*

[55] Gunderson, *op. cit.*

[56] Kathy Koch, "Hunger in America," *CQ Researcher*, Dec. 22, 2000, pp. 1033-1056.

[57] Tom Price, "Activists in the Boardroom," Foundation for Public Affairs, 2006.

[58] Koch, *op. cit.*

[59] Dewey and Jan, *op. cit.*

[60] Par Meghan Werft, "Food & Hunger: 7 Ways the Obamas Worked to Keep People Fed," *Global Citizen*, https://tinyurl.com/ybsms7r4.

[61] Helena Bottemiller Evich and Darren Samuelsohn, "The great FLOTUS food fight," *Politico*, March 17, 2016, https://tinyurl.com/hwehn33; Olivia Barrow, "Fighting Child Hunger in the Obama Administration's Final Year," *New America*, Feb. 8, 2016, https://tinyurl.com/y9c3bh47; Caitlin Dewey, "Trump doesn't threaten only President Obama's legacy. He could ruin Michelle Obama's, too," *The Washington Post*, Dec. 14, 2016, https://tinyurl.com/ybogfs4t; and Caitlin Dewey, "A record number of poor kids

About the Author

Tom Price, a contributing writer for *CQ Researcher*, is a Washington-based freelance journalist who previously was a correspondent in the Cox Newspapers Washington Bureau and chief politics writer for *The Dayton Daily News* and *The (Dayton) Journal Herald*. He is author or co-author of five books including, with former U.S. Rep. Tony Hall (D-Ohio), *Changing The Face of Hunger: One Man's Story of How Liberals, Conservatives, Democrats, Republicans and People of Faith Are Joining Forces to Help the Hungry, the Poor and the Oppressed*. His previous *CQ Researcher* reports include an examination of hunger in the developing world.

are eating breakfast — thanks to a program many conservatives hate," *The Washington Post*, Feb. 14, 2017, https://tinyurl.com/yd69snhv.

[62] Ned Resnikoff, "President Obama signs $8.7 billion food stamp cut into law," MSNBC, Feb. 7, 2014, https://tinyurl.com/ljht9x3.

[63] Dewey, *op. cit.*; "Lobbyists want to reverse Michelle Obama's healthy school lunch program," *The Grio*, March 15, 2017, https://tiny url.com/y7gjfoyd.

[64] Michele Munz, "Food sales drop in schools, but changes have kids eating more fruits, veggies," *St. Louis Post-Dispatch*, Dec. 6, 2014, https://tinyurl.com/yd2457xw; Eric Stirgus, "Hold the flavor: Georgia students eating fewer school lunches," *The Atlanta Journal-Constitution*, Dec. 22, 2016, https://tinyurl.com/y8sfg5z5.

[65] "Lobbyists want to reverse Michelle Obama's healthy school lunch program," *op. cit.*; Caitlin Dewey, "Michelle Obama on Trump rollback: 'Think about why someone is okay with your kids eating crap,' " *The Washington Post*, May 12, 2017, https://tinyurl.com/yavxzsua.

[66] Dewey, *op. cit.*

[67] Munz, *op. cit.*

[68] Samantha Bomkamp, "Calorie labeling rule delayed by FDA until next year," *Chicago Tribune*, May 1, 2017, https://tinyurl.com/n6u9wrw; Dan Orlando, "FDA delays menu labeling rule," *Supermarket News*, April 27, 2017, https://tiny url.com/ybllsk8z.

[69] Caitlin Dewey, "Industry is counting on Trump to back off rules that tell you what's in your food," *The Washington Post*, April 27, 2017, https://tinyurl.com/y8dht96d.

[70] Caitlin Dewey, "Trump's FDA just took another swipe at Michelle Obama's food legacy," *The Washington Post*, June 13, 2017, https://tiny url.com/ybmxbumv.

[71] *Ibid.*

[72] Erica L. Green and Julie Hirschfeld Davis, "President Takes Aim at Lunch Guidelines and a Girls' Education Program," *The New York Times*, May 2, 2017, https://tinyurl.com/y7wjtbxt; "Schools get a pass on serving more healthful lunches next fall," *The Washington Post*, May 1, 2017, https://tinyurl.com/y88j3xoy; Allison Aubrey and Dan Charles, "Big Battles Over Farm And Food Policies May Be Brewing As Trump Era Begins," NPR, Dec. 28, 2016, https://tinyurl.com/z3ugseq.

[73] *Ibid.*, Weill, *op. cit.*; Caitlin Dewey, "Trump's budget would cut off food for poor people if they have too many kids," *The Washington Post*, May 24, 2017, https://tinyurl.com/yb2cfkjg. Ingraham, *op. cit.*

[74] Nelson, *op. cit.*

FOR MORE INFORMATION

Alliance to End Hunger, 425 3rd St., S.W., Suite 1200, Washington, DC 20024; 202-688-1157; http://alliancetoendhunger.org/. Association of more than 90 service and advocacy organizations that works for food security in the United States and abroad.

American Enterprise Institute, 1789 Massachusetts Ave., N.W., Washington, DC 20036; 202-862-5800; www.aei.org. Conservative think tank whose focus includes poverty and hunger.

Arcadia Center for Sustainable Food and Agriculture, 9000 Richmond Highway, Alexandria, VA 22309; 571-384-8845; http://arcadiafood.org. Nonprofit whose nutrition programs in the Washington area include a farm and children's garden, mobile food markets, nutrition-education programs for children and low-income adults.

Bread for the World, 425 3rd St., S.W., Suite 1200, Washington, DC 20024; 800-822-7323; www.bread.org. Christian organization that lobbies for the United States to take action against hunger at home and abroad.

Campus Kitchens Project, 19 I St., N.W., Washington, DC 20001; 202-234-0707; www.campuskitchens.org. Nonprofit organization that coordinates more than 60 student-run chapters on college and high school campuses that retrieve unused food from school dining halls, prepare meals and distribute them to the needy.

Food Research & Action Center, 1200 18th St., N.W., Suite 400, Washington, DC 20036; 202-986-2200; www.frac.org. Nonprofit organization that researches hunger in America and advocates at the federal, state and local levels.

Share Our Strength, 1030 15th St., N.W., Suite 1100 W, Washington, DC 20005; 800-969-4767; www.nokidhungry.org. Education and advocacy group that teaches low-income families to cook nutritiously and efficiently and campaigns for action against child hunger.

[75] "Mick Mulvaney's Epic Description Of Climate Science Was A Really Big Hit With The Media," *Red State*, March 17, 2017, https://tinyurl.com/ya6js8pv.

[76] Dewey and Jan, *op. cit.*

[77] Duke Storen, "New Report Released by the National Commission on Hunger," Share Our Strength, Jan. 4, 2016, https://tinyurl.com/yd3qw2qp.

[78] Dewey, "Trump's budget would cut off food for poor people if they have too many kids," *op. cit.*

[79] Weill, *op. cit.*

[80] Dewey and Jan, *op. cit.*

[81] Caitlin Dewey, "Trump official in charge of food stamps departs from Trump's plan to gut the program," *The Washington Post*, May 24, 2017, https://tinyurl.com/y8jvjkn7.

[82] Damian Paletta and Robert Costa, "Trump's budget proposal slashes spending by $3.6 trillion over 10 years," *The Washington Post*, May 22, 2017, https://tinyurl.com/y94nqova.

[83] Poole, *op. cit.*

[84] Laura Berrios, "Meals on Wheels helps seniors age in place," *The Atlanta Journal-Constitution*, Feb. 7, 2017, https://tinyurl.com/hj8qsxl.

[85] Daniel Beam, "Move For Hunger Integrating Food Recovery Into Employee Relocation Process," Alliance to End Hunger, May 16, 2017, http://tinyurl.com/st69geq.

[86] Matt Schnarr, "The Campus Kitchens Project: Student-Powered Hunger Relief," Alliance to End Hunger, Sept. 12, 2014, https://tinyurl.com/y9zjrylx; "Student-Powered Hunger Relief," The Campus Kitchens Project, https://tinyurl.com/ydfmctkg; "CKP by the Numbers," The Campus Kitchens Project, https://tinyurl.com/y8gqn6b5; and Eliza McGraw, "With a homeless center on campus, students have an unusual chance to serve," *The Washington Post*, April 4, 2017, https://tinyurl.com/ycwezuh4.

[87] "Our Programs," Swipe out hunger, https://tinyurl.com/y7c7673l; "Our Members," College and University Food Bank Alliance, June 27, 2017, https://tinyurl.com/y7ljljx8.

[88] Kirk Carapezza, "National Survey Shows High Rates Of Hungry And Homeless Community Students," March 15, 2017, WGBH Radio, Boston, https://tinyurl.com/gnj9oum; Laura A. Bischoff and Max Filby, "Wright State among colleges with food pantries," *Dayton Daily News*, March 23, 2017, https://tinyurl.com/y97ebyh4.

Bibliography

Selected Sources

Books

Bartfeld, Judith, et al., eds, SNAP Matters: How Food Stamps Affect Health and Well-Being, Stanford University Press, 2015.

In this collection of essays, scholars address key questions regarding food stamps, including whether they reduce poverty or contribute to obesity and how they work with other food programs.

Baylen, J. Linnekin, Biting the Hands That Feed Us: How Fewer, Smarter Laws Would Make Our Food System More Sustainable, Island Press, 2016.

An attorney who specializes in food law and writes a column for libertarian Reason magazine argues that government overregulation is an obstacle to the development of sustainable agriculture.

Fisher, Andrew, Big Hunger: The Unholy Alliance Between Corporate America and Anti-Hunger Groups, MIT Press, 2017.

A sustainable-food activist acknowledges anti-hunger organizations' success in feeding the poor but argues that many have become too close to their corporate funders and should more strongly oppose business actions that hurt low-income people.

Norwood, F. Bailey, et al., Agricultural and Food Controversies: What Everyone Needs to Know, Oxford University Press, 2014.

Sarah Lancaster, a scientist, and three agriculture professors explore key food debates, such as whether modern farming threatens the welfare of future generations.

Articles

Evich, Helena Bottemiller, and Darren Samuelsohn, "The great FLOTUS food fight," Politico, March 17, 2016, http://tinyurl.com/hwehn33.

Politico reporters take a comprehensive look at former first lady Michelle Obama's crusade to improve nutrition in America, from planting a White House garden to campaigning for healthier school meals.

Haspel, Tamar, "Is nutritious food really pricier, and, if so, is that really the problem?" The Washington Post, Nov. 25, 2016, http://tinyurl.com/y8dcusco.

A Washington Post food columnist shows how it is possible to eat "pretty well" on a food-stamp budget.

Ingraham, Christopher, "Meals on Wheels is 'not showing any results' only if you ignore all these results," The Washington Post, March 16, 2017, http://tinyurl.com/y9thhkpa.

A journalist reviews the accomplishments of the nutrition service for seniors, which U.S. Office of Management and Budget Director Mick Mulvaney had included among "programs that don't work."

Reports and Studies

"Freedom from Hunger," National Commission on Hunger, 2015, http://tinyurl.com/yb73luk3.

A bipartisan commission draws up a blueprint for reducing hunger, issuing recommendations ranging from providing more employment assistance to food stamp recipients to improving child nutrition programs.

"Nutrition Standards in the National School Lunch and School Breakfast Programs Final Rule," Food and Nutrition Service, U.S. Department of Agriculture, Jan. 26, 2012, http://tinyurl.com/7dovzfx.

In 2012, the Agriculture Department issued the final rules for school meals and began to implement them incrementally; the Trump administration, however, has postponed them.

Garasky, Steven, et al., "Foods Typically Purchased by Supplemental Nutrition Assistance Program (SNAP) Households," Food and Nutrition Service, U.S. Department of Agriculture, November 2016, http://tinyurl.com/y8soq85s.

An analysis of sales records from a leading grocery retailer concludes that food stamp recipients spend a fifth of their grocery budgets — including government aid and other income — on soft drinks, other sweetened beverages, desserts, salty snacks, candy and other junk food.

Goldrick-Rab, Sara, Jed Richardson and Anthony Hernandez, "Hungry and Homeless in College," Wisconsin HOPE Lab, University of Wisconsin, March 2017, http://tinyurl.com/y9kcbwkn.

A survey of community college students finds that a third sometimes go hungry.

Gunderson, Gordon W., "National School Lunch Program (NSLP)," Food and Nutrition Service, U.S. Department of Agriculture, 1971, http://tinyurl.com/y78nwl7t.

A longtime manager of government food programs recounts the history of school lunch programs from the 18th century into the 20th.

Hartline-Grafton, Heather, "Understanding the Connections: Food Insecurity and Obesity," Food Research & Action Center, October 2015, http://tinyurl.com/ybvuhbha.

A senior nutrition policy and research analyst for a major hunger research and advocacy organization explores the apparent irony of obesity among people who have difficulty getting enough to eat.

The Next Step:

Additional Articles from Current Periodicals

Anti-Hunger Programs

Gilmer, Maureen, "Farm on wheels will deliver fresh produce to Indy food deserts," *The Indianapolis Star*, June 30, 2017, https://tinyurl.com/y729b8rv.

An Indiana resident who started a farm in 2016 to grow food for the hungry is now planning to take fresh produce into "food deserts," areas without access to healthy, affordable food.

Pathi, Krutika, "The Food Bank of the Future Could Be in a Post Office," *CityLab*, Feb. 8, 2017, https://tinyurl.com/ybryqg95.

Washington University students are proposing to repurpose post offices in Los Angeles to store food and use postal trucks to deliver it to needy residents.

Wahlberg, David, "UW Health to screen for hunger, provide free meals for children," *Wisconsin State Journal*, June 7, 2017, https://tinyurl.com/ya95jj8p.

University of Wisconsin's medical center has begun screening patients for hunger and directing those who need help to food pantries.

Childhood Hunger

Balingit, Moriah, "To reach hungry children in the summer, these school cafeterias moved outside," *The Washington Post*, June 29, 2017, https://tinyurl.com/ycs5hal2.

Fairfax County, Va., is hosting outdoor barbecues at 11 schools, four apartment complexes and one community center almost every day during the summer to provide free meals to kids.

Brody, Jane E., "Feeding Young Minds: The Importance of School Lunches," *The New York Times*, June 5, 2017, https://tinyurl.com/ycd3z485.

Ensuring students eat healthy meals can improve their academic performance, experts say.

Martinez, Alessandra, "New Amherst school policy prevents 'lunch shaming' students," WWLP-22News, June 20, 2017, https://tinyurl.com/y73zo3lj.

A Massachusetts school district has implemented a policy ensuring each student will receive lunch every day regardless of any overdue lunch payments.

Food Stamp Funding

Luna, Jenny, "Trump Takes a Big Bite out of His Voters' Food Stamps," *Mother Jones*, May 23, 2017, https://tinyurl.com/yajnaq34.

Seven of the 10 states with the highest food stamp use by population voted Republican in the 2016 presidential election.

Schanzenbach, Diane Whitmore, Robert E. Rector and Robert Gebelhoff, "Are the Trump administration's pro-

posed food stamp cuts justified?" *The Washington Post*, June 16, 2017, https://tinyurl.com/y82kk9kg.

Experts debate the merits and potential consequences of President Trump's proposed budget cuts to food stamps.

Thomas, Lauren, "Trump's plan to slash food stamp assistance could be a major setback for these retailers," CNBC, June 2, 2017, https://tinyurl.com/ybqer2sj.

President Trump's plan to reduce food stamp benefits could affect Walmart and other retailers by limiting their low-income customers' spending power.

Food Waste

Kowitt, Beth, "A Grocery Store for All, Powered By Wasted Food," *Fortune*, June 5, 2017, https://tinyurl.com/yaecya88.

The nonprofit store Daily Table in Dorchester, Mass., sells at steeply discounted prices donated food from grocery stores and food purchased from manufacturers that has passed or is near its sell-by date.

Petronzio, Matt, "Feeding America wants to wipe out hunger and food waste with the power of a single app," *Mashable*, April 24, 2017, https://tinyurl.com/y9pfatsb.

A food bank network launched MealConnect, a Web-based app that stores and farmers' markets wanting to donate excess food can use to find food pantries or programs.

Rossman, Sean, "Here's how many people America's wasted food could feed," *USA Today*, May 16, 2017, https://tinyurl.com/y95pbovm.

A study found that 31 percent to 40 percent of food in America is thrown away after it is harvested, and much of it contains nutrients that most Americans need more of.

In-depth Reports on Issues in the News

Are you writing a paper?

Need backup for a debate?

Want to become an expert on an issue?

For 90 years, students have turned to *CQ Researcher* for in-depth reporting on issues in the news. Reports on a full range of political and social issues are now available. Following is a selection of recent reports:

Civil Liberties
Privacy and the Internet, 12/15
Intelligence Reform, 5/15
Religion and Law, 11/14

Crime/Law
High-Tech Policing, 4/17
Forensic Science Controversies, 2/17
Jailing Debtors, 9/16
Decriminalizing Prostitution, 4/16
Restorative Justice, 2/16
The Dark Web, 1/16
Immigrant Detention, 10/15

Education
Charter Schools, 3/17
Civic Education, 2/17
Student Debt, 11/16
Apprenticeships, 10/16

Environment/Society
Future of the Christian Right, 6/17
Trust in Media, 6/17
Anti-Semitism, 5/17
Native American Sovereignty, 5/17
Women in Prison, 3/17
Guns on Campus, 1/17

Health/Safety
Food Labeling, 6/17
Sports and Sexual Assault, 4/17
Reducing Traffic Deaths, 2/17
Opioid Crisis, 10/16
Mosquito-Borne Disease, 7/16

Politics/Economy
North Korea Showdown, 5/17
Rethinking Foreign Aid, 4/17
Troubled Brazil, 4/17
Reviving Rural Economies, 3/17
Immigrants and the Economy, 2/17

Upcoming Reports

Arts Funding, 7/14/17   Medical Marijuana, 7/21/17   Muslims in America, 7/28/17

ACCESS

CQ Researcher is available in print and online. For access, visit your library or www.cqresearcher.com.

STAY CURRENT

For notice of upcoming *CQ Researcher* reports or to learn more about *CQ Researcher* products, subscribe to the free email newsletters, *CQ Researcher Alert!* and *CQ Researcher News*: http://cqpress.com/newsletters.

PURCHASE

To purchase a *CQ Researcher* report in print or electronic format (PDF), visit www.cqpress.com or call 866-427-7737. Single reports start at $15. Bulk purchase discounts and electronic-rights licensing are also available.

SUBSCRIBE

Annual full-service *CQ Researcher* subscriptions—including 44 reports a year, monthly index updates, and a bound volume—start at $1,131. Add $25 for domestic postage.

CQ Researcher Online offers a backfile from 1991 and a number of tools to simplify research. For pricing information, call 800-818-7243 or 805-499-9774 or email librarysales@sagepub.com.

CQ RESEARCHER

CQ PRESS

In-depth reports on today's issues

Published by CQ Press, an Imprint of SAGE Publications, Inc.

www.cqresearcher.com

Funding the Arts

Should government support artistic and cultural expression?

The Trump administration wants to end federal funding for the National Endowment for the Arts, the Corporation for Public Broadcasting and other cultural agencies. While those agencies receive only a fraction of the federal budget, the administration says other needs are more pressing and that government arts spending represents a wealth transfer from poorer to richer citizens. The proposal has revived an argument that raged during the "culture wars" of the 1980s and '90s, when conservatives and liberals sparred over whether the government has a role in supporting the arts and whether federal money should help pay for art that some deem offensive. Funding advocates say exposure to the arts helps students perform better in school and that theaters, symphonies and museums help bolster local economies. The arts continue to have powerful supporters, including local politicians and civic leaders who serve on arts boards in nearly every congressional district. Nonetheless, some cash-strapped state and local governments are cutting school and public arts programs.

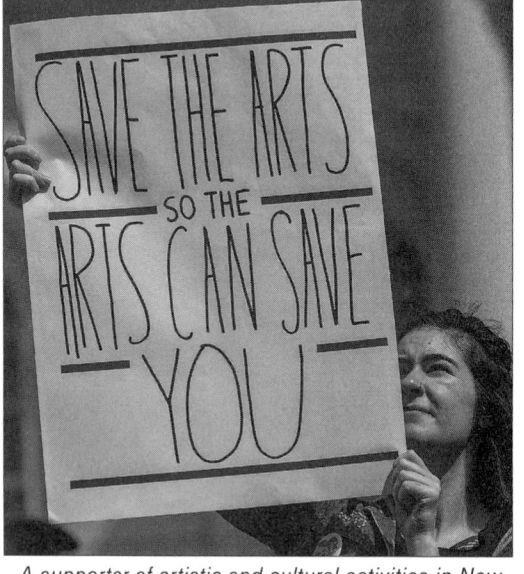

A supporter of artistic and cultural activities in New York City protests on April 3, 2017, against a Trump administration proposal to eliminate federal funding for cultural agencies such as the National Endowment for the Arts and the Corporation for Public Broadcasting, which helps fund NPR.

I N S I D E THIS REPORT

THE ISSUES **583**

BACKGROUND **590**

CHRONOLOGY **591**

CURRENT SITUATION **596**

AT ISSUE **597**

OUTLOOK **599**

BIBLIOGRAPHY **602**

THE NEXT STEP **603**

CQ Researcher • July 14, 2017 • www.cqresearcher.com
Volume 27, Number 25 • Pages 581-604

$SAGE Publishing | CQ PRESS
Los Angeles | London | New Delhi
Singapore | Washington DC | Melbourne

RECIPIENT OF SOCIETY OF PROFESSIONAL JOURNALISTS AWARD FOR EXCELLENCE ◆ AMERICAN BAR ASSOCIATION SILVER GAVEL AWARD

The Issues

583
- Should the government subsidize the arts?
- Should arts education be restored?
- Do the arts promote economic growth?

Background

590 **Arts Ambivalence**
Americans often prized practicality over beauty for public spaces.

590 **Birth of the NEA**
President Lyndon B. Johnson created the National Endowment for the Arts and National Endowment for the Humanities in 1965.

592 **Growth and Criticism**
Disputes began to plague the NEA in the 1970s.

594 **Rising Controversy**
Republican efforts to defund the NEA continued through the mid-1990s.

Current Situation

596 **Strong Support**
No one expects Congress to eliminate arts programs this year.

598 **Local Projects**
Some cities are seeking ways to support local artists.

Outlook

599 **Unending Debate**
Squabbles over arts funding seem destined to return periodically.

Sidebars and Graphics

584 **Arts Studies Required in Half of States**
Twenty-five states and the District of Columbia require high school students to take at least one arts class to graduate.

585 **Arts Funding a Sliver of Federal Budget**
The arts receive a fraction of 1 percent of federal spending.

588 **More Americans Oppose Cutting Arts Spending**
Fewer than a third of Americans favor cutting federal support for the arts, while 44 percent oppose cuts.

591 **Chronology**
Key events since 1943.

592 **Agencies Seek Community Input for Public Art**
Collaboration is key to preventing controversy.

594 **Arts Requirements Draw Controversy**
"While the goals are admirable, the costs are unreasonable."

597 **At Issue:**
Should the National Endowment for the Arts be abolished?

For Further Research

601 **For More Information**
Organizations to contact.

602 **Bibliography**
Selected sources used.

603 **The Next Step**
Additional articles.

603 **Citing CQ Researcher**
Sample bibliography formats.

Cover: AP Photo/Sipa/Albin Lohr-Jones

 **CQ RESEARCHER**
CQ PRESS

July 14, 2017
Volume 27, Number 25

EXECUTIVE EDITOR: Thomas J. Billitteri
tjb@sagepub.com

ASSISTANT MANAGING EDITORS: Kenneth Fireman, kenneth.fireman@sagepub.com, Kathy Koch, kathy.koch@sagepub.com, Scott Rohrer, scott.rohrer@sagepub.com

ASSOCIATE MANAGING EDITOR: Val Ellicott

SENIOR CONTRIBUTING EDITOR:
Thomas J. Colin
tom.colin@sagepub.com

CONTRIBUTING WRITERS: Marcia Clemmitt, Sarah Glazer, Reed Karaim, Barbara Mantel, Chuck McCutcheon, Tom Price

SENIOR PROJECT EDITOR: Olu B. Davis

INTERN: Robert DePaolo

FACT CHECKERS: Eva P. Dasher, Michelle Harris, Betsy Towner Levine, Robin Palmer

SAGE Publishing | CQ PRESS

Los Angeles | London | New Delhi
Singapore | Washington DC | Melbourne

An Imprint of SAGE Publications, Inc.

SENIOR VICE PRESIDENT, GLOBAL LEARNING RESOURCES:
Karen Phillips

EXECUTIVE DIRECTOR, ONLINE LIBRARY AND REFERENCE PUBLISHING:
Todd Baldwin

CQ Researcher (ISSN 1056-2036) is printed on acid-free paper. Published weekly, except: (March wk. 4) (May wk. 4) (July wks. 1, 2) (Aug. wks. 2, 3) (Nov. wk. 4) and (Dec. wks. 3, 4). Published by SAGE Publications, Inc., 2455 Teller Rd., Thousand Oaks, CA 91320. Annual full-service subscriptions start at $1,131. For pricing, call 1-800-818-7243. To purchase a CQ Researcher report in print or electronic format (PDF), visit www.cqpress.com or call 866-427-7737. Single reports start at $15. Bulk purchase discounts and electronic-rights licensing are also available. Periodicals postage paid at Thousand Oaks, California, and at additional mailing offices. POSTMASTER: Send address changes to CQ Researcher, 2600 Virginia Ave., N.W., Suite 600, Washington, DC 20037.

Funding the Arts

BY ALAN GREENBLATT

THE ISSUES

The Public Theater has been presenting free Shakespeare plays in New York's Central Park for 60 years, but its latest production, this summer, may be its most controversial. [1] A staging of *Julius Caesar* recasts the dictator to resemble President Trump, complete with golden hair and a red tie. There's even an added reference to killing people on Fifth Avenue, as Trump once said he could do without losing popularity. [2]

Some conservatives complained that because Caesar is killed in the play, the production could be seen as fomenting violence against Trump. Dan Bongino, a former Secret Service agent, warned that the play conceivably could lead someone who is mentally ill to try to kill the president. [3]

Liberals scoffed, noting that a 2012 production that toured nationally and featured a Caesar modeled after President Barack Obama prompted no such outcry. [4]

"If you read the play, Shakespeare's against assassination," says Michael Bronski, a media studies professor at Harvard University. "To have a kneejerk reaction that this is defaming the president or it can lead to violence against the president seems to me to be too much."

Nevertheless, amid the controversy, Delta Air Lines and Bank of America announced they were pulling their financial support from the production. On June 11, the president's son, Donald Trump Jr., tweeted, "I wonder how much of this 'art' is funded by taxpayers?" [5] The National Endowment for the Arts (NEA), the lead federal agency providing support for arts organizations throughout the nation, rushed out a state-

Critics of federal arts funding say it is not government's role to subsidize the arts, especially controversial artworks like sculptor Tony Matelli's "Sleepwalker," displayed along Manhattan's High Line, a popular pedestrian space. The Trump administration insists the federal government can no longer afford to fund arts programs, but arts backers say federal funding amounts to a tiny fraction of 1 percent of the federal government's annual budget.

Getty Images/Spencer Platt

ment the same day — and posted a pop-up notice on its Web page — making clear that "no taxpayer dollars" paid for the production. [6]

The NEA might have been feeling skittish because the president's proposed 2018 budget calls for eliminating funding for the NEA and other cultural agencies, including the National Endowment for the Humanities (NEH), the Institute of Museum and Library Services and the Corporation for Public Broadcasting (CPB), arguing that they represent an unnecessary expense. [7]

Although some lawmakers have said that much of Trump's budget is dead on arrival on Capitol Hill, arts agencies and their supporters worry that his proposal to eliminate arts funding could

revive battles fought in the 1980s and '90s over government support for the arts. At the time, critics sought to strip federal arts agencies of their funding, saying it was not the government's role to subsidize art and that some agencies were funding artworks of dubious value. Although those efforts largely failed, the NEA has changed some of its policies to address critics' concerns. Federal arts agencies again find their existence under attack, however, and some cash-strapped state and local governments are cutting school and public arts programs.

The administration insists the federal government can no longer afford to fund arts programs, which it sees as a so-called wealth transfer from poorer to wealthier citizens.

"I put myself in the shoes of that steelworker in Ohio, the coal-mining family in West Virginia, the mother of two in Detroit," Budget Director Mick Mulvaney said at a White House news conference in March, when asked about the proposed cuts. "Can I really go to those folks, look them in the eye and say: 'Look, I want to take money from you, and I want to give it to the Corporation for Public Broadcasting?' That is a really hard sell, and in fact, it's something we don't think we can defend anymore." [8]

Arts advocates say federal spending for the NEA amounts to only 45 cents per capita annually. Theaters, symphonies and museums help bolster local economies, and student exposure to the arts improves academic performance, they say. According to Americans for the Arts, a Washington-based arts advocacy group, local, state and federal governments spend a total of

Arts Studies Required in Half of States

Half the states and the District of Columbia require high school students to take at least one arts class to graduate. Depending on the school or school district, classes may include fine arts, visual or performing arts or other forms of creative expression.

States Requiring High School Students to Take an Arts Class to Graduate, 2017

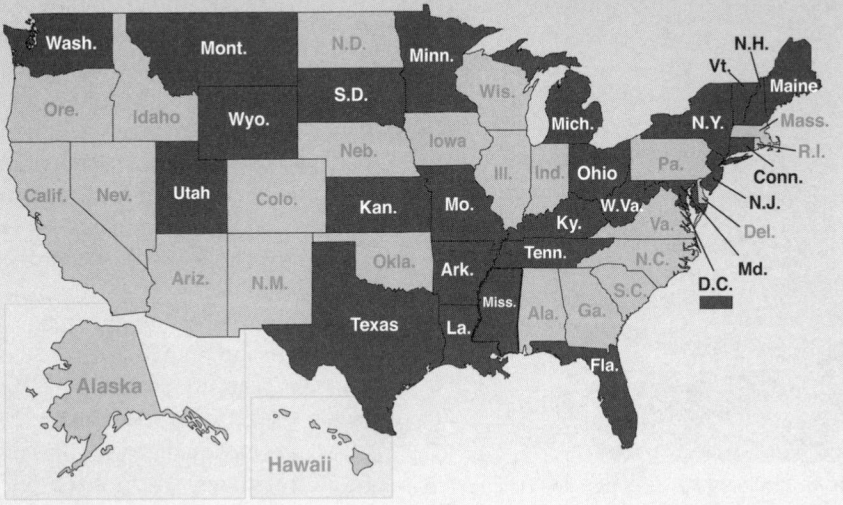

Source: "ArtScan at a Glance," Arts Education Partnership, Education Commission of the States, updated, March 2017, http://tinyurl.com/ybcykop2

$5 billion on the arts per year, while arts programs generate $27.5 billion in tax revenue annually in return and support $166.3 billion worth of economic activity each year. [9] Advocates also point out that, compared to European governments, American taxpayers contribute only a fraction of U.S. arts funding. The Paris Opera alone receives the equivalent of more than $100 million in government support. [10] In addition, state and local support for the arts dwarfs the NEA's contributions. The New York City Department of Cultural Affairs alone has a bigger budget than the NEA. [11]

The National Endowment for the Arts promotes citizen access to the arts — performing arts such as theater and visual arts such as works that might be seen at a museum. It provides grants to arts organizations and state and regional arts agencies to encourage attendance at arts events. The National Endowment for the Humanities performs a similar function

with a somewhat overlapping mission. NEH grants generally go to cultural institutions, such as museums, colleges and libraries, as well as public broadcasting and individual scholars, to promote scholarship and learning about the humanities, particularly history. It also supports publication of literary classics through the Library of America and some forms of music such as jazz and folk.

Congress created the NEA and NEH in 1965, after decades of debate about whether the federal government should support nonprofit arts organizations. After social conservatives failed to shut down the NEA in the 1980s and '90s, the issue had lain mostly dormant until Trump revived it.

"Private individuals and organizations should be able to donate at their own discretion to humanities organizations and programs as they wish," the Heritage Foundation, a conservative Washington think tank that has long called

for the NEA's and NEH's elimination, argued in a "budget blueprint" that served as an influential framework during the Trump administration's budget deliberations. "Government should not use its coercive power of taxation to compel taxpayers to support cultural organizations and activities." [12]

Art may be a good thing, but it doesn't follow that government subsidies for it are also good, conservative columnist George F. Will wrote in March. "Attempting to abolish the NEA is a fight worth having," he wrote, arguing that the agency has dispensed grants of questionable value and that the private sector can and does do a better job of funding the arts. [13]

Will conceded almost immediately, however, that the fight would be futile because the NEA spreads its grant money around to every state and because people who sit on nonprofit arts boards tend to be powerful and well-connected. Echoing Will, Michael Tanner, who favors abolishing the NEA, says: "It's very popular. In each district, there's a little money spread around. Its beneficiaries are very vocal." Tanner is a senior fellow at the libertarian Cato Institute think tank in Washington.

The arts community, of course, views the broad dispersal of funds around the country as a plus. The NEA, in particular, has been conscious about earlier complaints that its grants mainly benefited big coastal cities such as New York. "We see our funding actively making a difference with individuals of all ages in thousands of communities, large, small, urban and rural, and in every congressional district in the nation," said Jane Chu, who chairs the NEA. [14]

Trump's desire to kill the agency might get no further than earlier attempts have. Shortly after the president announced his intention to eliminate the federal culture agencies, Congress in May increased funding for the NEA and NEH, from $148 million to $150 million each, as part of its budget for the rest of fiscal 2017. [15]

Those were not huge increases, but they signaled continuing support in Congress for the arts, with arts programs seen as benefiting communities both in terms of individual enrichment and as a tool for driving economic development.

What's more, arts funding is not a huge part of the overall federal budget. Funding for the NEA, NEH and the Corporation for Public Broadcasting, which subsidizes National Public Radio (NPR) and the Public Broadcasting Service (PBS), amounts to less than $750 million per year, or a fraction of 1 percent of the budget, arts advocates point out. [16] (*See graph, right.*)

But the agencies' funding fight for fiscal 2018 will be more intense than it was in fiscal 2017, they believe. Negotiations over next year's budget are expected to stretch at least into the fall. "We remain very, very wary and cautious about the prospects for the fiscal year 2018 budget," says Robert Lynch, president of Americans for the Arts, an advocacy group for arts organizations.

In the meantime, arts organizations — museums, theater companies, symphony orchestras — are urging subscribers and patrons to contact their members of Congress and encourage them to maintain arts and culture funding.

The Trump administration believes that "if NEA funding gets cut, that [money] will be made up by the private sector," says Susan Baley, executive director of the Swope Art Museum in Terre Haute, Ind. But "it's hard to see that happening."

Arts advocates say federal funding is crucial because arts organizations often tout those grants as a way to attract other donors. "Eliminating these agencies is not going to make a difference to the [federal] deficit, but it makes a tremendous difference to these organizations that rely on them," Baley says.

To make the case for continuing support, advocates attribute a variety of benefits to the arts, from improving educational outcomes to drawing people to cities with vibrant arts scenes

Arts Funding a Sliver of Federal Budget

The arts and public broadcasting received a razor-thin slice of the fiscal 2016 federal budget — $741 million, or less than 1 percent of the total $3.9 trillion outlay. The Corporation for Public Broadcasting, which helps to fund National Public Radio and the Public Broadcasting Service, received $445 million. The National Endowment for the Arts and National Endowment for the Humanities each received $148 million.

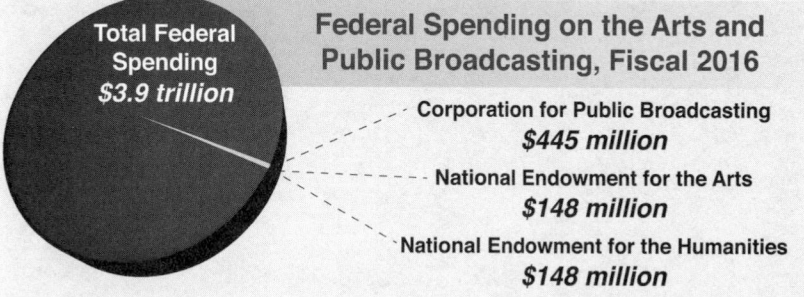

Total Federal Spending $3.9 trillion

Federal Spending on the Arts and Public Broadcasting, Fiscal 2016

Corporation for Public Broadcasting
$445 million

National Endowment for the Arts
$148 million

National Endowment for the Humanities
$148 million

Sources: "CPB's Past Appropriations," Corporation for Public Broadcasting, undated, http://tinyurl.com/yaf2fobz; "National Endowment for the Arts Appropriations History," National Endowment for the Arts, undated, http://tinyurl.com/jreutxx; "Appropriations Request For Fiscal Year 2016," National Endowment for the Humanities, undated, http://tinyurl.com/yawyk3l8; "Budget," Congressional Budget Office, undated, http://tinyurl.com/zvsl2eh

and promoting economic development in specific neighborhoods in those cities. "To make a city, you can't just have housing," says Todd Schliemann, a New York-based architect who designs science museums. "You have to have a mixed-use component that includes cultural things such as museums and performing arts."

As the arts funding debate plays out in Washington, here are some of the questions policymakers are asking:

Should the government subsidize the arts?

Terell Stafford, a prominent jazz trumpet player, runs the Jazz Orchestra of Philadelphia, a big band that features local musicians and presents concerts celebrating musicians with ties to the city. The nonprofit orchestra relies on government grants to cover some of its costs.

"Music is not an easy thing to make a living by, and we need all the support

possible," Stafford says. "The only way we can survive is through arts funding."

Artists such as Stafford have been making the case to their audiences that governments should continue supporting the arts. "As our elected officials in Washington work on the federal budget . . . the survival of funding for the arts hangs in the balance," the San Francisco Symphony wrote in an email to audience members in April, providing them with the phone numbers of members of the Bay area congressional delegation. "We need your help to advocate for the arts TODAY!" [17]

Supporters say arts organizations boost local economies by providing jobs, bringing in tourists and attracting local visitors who spend money on things like meals and parking. "The economic footprint of the arts is so much bigger than anyone actually realizes," says Lynch, the Americans for the Arts president.

The NEA provides funds to support those local and regional arts organizations. But federal funds account for only a portion of the amount contributed by local and state arts agencies as a whole. And it accounts for a smaller share than individual donations — or even the amount raised through crowdfunding sites such as Kickstarter, according to a study by Ramana Nanda,

Lin-Manuel Miranda, center, creator and star of the popular musical Hamilton, said that when he was growing up, his family rarely had money to see Broadway shows. "But because of PBS' 'Great Performances,' I saw Into the Woods. And it changed my life," he said. Critics say arts funding largely benefits wealthy Americans who are most likely to patronize the arts, but supporters say people at all income levels can enjoy the arts through free museums and public radio and television programs.

a Harvard professor of business administration. "Crowdfunding has enabled a democratization of access" to the arts, Nanda said. [18] In 2016, while the federal government devoted less than $1 billion to arts agencies, individual Americans gave $18 billion to arts and culture nonprofits. [19]

"This seems like the quintessential thing the private sector should do, and certainly does to a far greater degree," says Cato's Tanner.

In 2013, when the House Budget Committee unsuccessfully proposed eliminating funding for arts and cultural agencies, the panel said such activities

are "generally enjoyed by people of higher-income levels, making them a wealth transfer from poorer to wealthier citizens." [20]

But supporters of the arts say people at all income levels, including those who cannot afford to attend live performances, enjoy the arts through public radio and television programs. "I grew up loving musicals," said Lin-Manuel Miranda, creator of the hit Broadway musical *Hamilton*, but he added that because his family rarely "had money to go see Broadway shows. I think I saw three, maybe, before I was an adult. But because of PBS' 'Great Performances,' I saw *Into the Woods*. And it changed my life." [21]

Some conservatives argue that government-subsidized art does not have to respond to market demands, giving recipients of those funds an unfair edge over their unsubsidized competitors. "This means that the real way to succeed as an arts organization is not to create a product that attracts

new audiences, but to create a product that pleases those who dole out the free cash," wrote David Marcus, director of a New York theater company that does not receive government subsidies. "The [arts] industry receives more free money than it did a decade ago, and has fewer attendees." [22]

Too much of the money dispensed by NEA or NEH is still being sent to organizations concentrated in coastal states such as New York and California, the cultural critic and editor Roger Kimball complained, including money devoted to large institutions capable of massive private fundraising, such as the Metropolitan Museum. "Doubtless many initiatives could be worthy, but a lot of the funded projects are inane, repellent or both," he wrote. [23]

However, these days few arts nonprofits rely heavily on federal funds for ongoing expenses but use grants to fund specific projects, such as museum exhibitions. "The number of arts organizations that count on NEA dollars for regular maintenance of their programming is declining," says Roland Kushner, who teaches arts administration at Muhlenberg College in Pennsylvania. "It's more likely to be connected with issues such as access and education."

While both sides agree arts and culture spending makes up a microscopic portion of the federal budget, supporters and critics disagree over whether that is an argument for keeping or killing agencies such as the NEA and NEH. Those who favor abolishing them say if Congress cannot eliminate such relatively small programs, it will never get serious about cutting spending. Arts supporters maintain that spending on arts and culture offers needed support, not only for arts organizations but for state and regional arts councils and commissions.

For example, say NEA supporters, the agencies' support often serves as a seal of approval on projects, helping to attract other donors. Last year, every $1 of NEA funding was matched by up

Getty Images/FilmMagic/Bruce Glikas

to $9 in support from other entities, according to Aaron Knochel, an art education professor at Penn State University. [24]

"It's an incentives system," Lynch says about NEA funding. "It should be a conservative's delight. It's something they should hold up as a model."

But Tanner says the federal government should not be acting as a sort of venture capital fund, offering seed money that helps attract other support. "I don't think government should be picking and choosing winners when it comes to art," he says.

Should arts education be restored?

The Crystal Bridges Museum of American Art in Bentonville, Ark., was founded and has been richly supported by Alice Walton, an heir to the Walmart fortune. As part of its educational mission, the museum sponsors free field trips for school groups — not just waiving admission fees but reimbursing schools for transportation and teachers' time.

Despite the free ride, some Arkansas schools — particularly schools that serve lower-income students — have stopped taking trips to the museum, says Jay P. Greene, an education professor at the University of Arkansas. "The museum analyzed its own data and found that the more wealthy the school kids are, the more likely they are to take them up on free field trips," Greene says. "It's a cruel irony, because poor and rural kids were the most enriched from those trips," gaining not just subject knowledge but skills such as the ability to draw inferences.

In addition, the amount of classroom time and other resources devoted to arts education have been declining for years, especially during lean times such as the 2007-09 recession. A 2012 study by the Department of Education found that although math and visual arts programs were still widely offered, the percentage of elementary schools offering dance or theater instruction had declined from 20 percent at the start of the 21st century to 3 or 4 percent,

respectively, by 2009. And more than 40 percent of secondary schools no longer required courses in the arts for graduation, according to the Education Department study. [25] (See graph, p. 588.)

While schools are cutting arts education, Greene's research and other scholarly studies suggest that art education programs, including field trips to museum or theaters or in-class work

The Crystal Bridges Museum of American Art in Bentonville, Ark., founded by Alice Walton, an heir to the Walmart fortune, sponsors free field trips for school groups as part of its educational mission. Although scholarly studies suggest that arts education offers many benefits to students, some schools have stopped taking advantage of such free museum visits and are cutting arts programs to focus on core subjects such as reading and math.

on painting or music, offer many benefits to students. [26]

"There is some evidence that music education, for instance, can actually boost IQ," says Steven Holochwost, a research scientist at the Science of Learning Institute at Johns Hopkins University. "The arts yield benefits in terms of improvement in academic education and also executive function."

Holochwost and other education scholars say the arts offer a wealth of skills that transfer to other subjects, such as mastering self-directed learning (when working on individual projects) and collaboration (when students play in bands or are parts of other groups). [27]

Art "inspires critical thinking," says Kim Huyler Defibaugh, president of the National Art Education Association,

a membership organization for visual arts instructors. "It's not like chemistry. Art has multiple answers."

Some academic researchers are skeptical of such studies. Most studies that show arts education leading to improved performance in other areas measure correlation, not causation, they say. In other words, the researchers say, the type of students who partic-

ipate in arts programs may be those who are going to succeed anyway, thanks to their own initiative, parental involvement or the overall quality of the schools they attend.

"There's plenty of correlational evidence — smart kids take piano lessons, for example," says Ellen Winner, a psychologist at Boston College who studies the effects of the arts on development. "Kids who take lots of art in high school have higher SAT scores than those who don't, but that is not causal."

However, a widely cited 2009 study by James Catterall, a University of California, Los Angeles education professor, found that lower-income students who attended schools with rich arts programming tended to perform better in terms of grades in school and future college attendance. [28]

More Americans Oppose Cutting Arts Spending

More American adults — 44 percent — oppose reducing federal support for the arts and public broadcasting than favor such cuts (32 percent), according to a March poll. A majority of Republicans (56 percent) favor such cuts, compared with only 15 percent of Democrats.

Percentage Who Favor or Oppose Cutting Federal Support for the Arts and Public Broadcasting

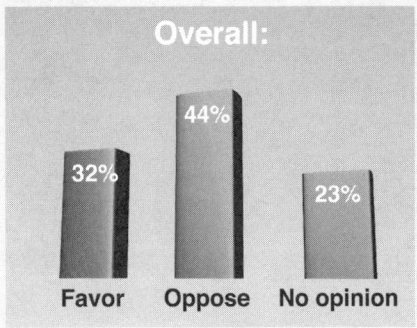

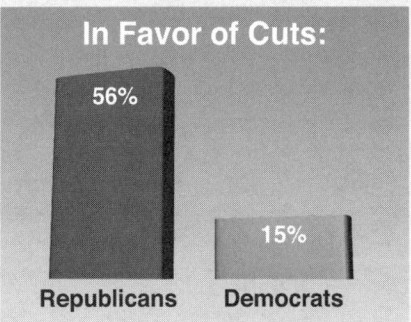

Sources: "The March 2017 AP-NORC Center Poll," http://tinyurl.com/y95dn9t7, and "Taxes and the Budget," http://tinyurl.com/y7fx9kvd, The Associated Press-NORC Center for Public Affairs Research, April 2017

Many districts have continued to cut back on fine arts education even after the economy began to recover from the recession. Prompted by an $18 million budget shortfall, the school district in Charleston County, S.C., last year overhauled its arts curriculum, laid off teachers and eliminated drama and dance programs. [29] It simply wasn't possible to keep a full slate of full-time arts teachers, according to district administrators. "When a principal has to decide between courses for core content and electives such as world languages or fine arts, principals tend to fund core content-area teachers first," says Kathleen Magliacane, the district's human resources director.

Such decisions are common. "Due to budget constraints, things need to be prioritized," says Steven Geis, president of the National Association of Elementary School Principals, explaining the rationale behind such cuts. "Approximately 85 percent of a district's budget is (salaries for) teachers. What are you going to cut, a [regular] classroom teacher or one of the specialist classes?"

In addition to budget constraints, arts programming often is cut due to classroom time pressures. Given federal and state mandates for annual testing in core academic subjects such as reading and math, other subjects often are as lower priorities. "Many schools have responded to those pressures by narrowing their efforts significantly and cutting the amount of time devoted to non-tested subjects," Greene says.

In addition, according to the Education Department study, an "equity gap" now exists in arts education, with schools serving lower-income students less likely to offer substantial arts programming than more affluent schools.

Under the No Child Left Behind Act — a 2002 federal law that mandated annual testing in math and language skills between grades 3 and 8 — "the poorest schools were the hardest pressed," says Dennie Palmer Wolf, a principal researcher at WolfBrown, an arts research and consulting firm in Cambridge, Mass. "To the extent principals had discretionary money, they

often used it for things like extra tutoring. They did not spend it on arts education or debate or chess."

Although this dynamic is frequently decried by arts education advocates, Winner says it makes sense. "Maybe they recognize that if your aim is to improve performance in math and reading and writing, the best route is a direct one: more time on these subjects, rather than the claimed indirect route through the arts," she says.

But Greene, the Arkansas professor, notes that arts instruction remains popular with parents, particularly in upper middle class communities. Schools may have cut back, but most still offer art classes of one form or other

"The pendulum has got about as far as it can go squeezing the arts," Greene says. "These programs are inherently popular. Parents want their kids to play in bands, they want their kids to learn the arts."

Do the arts promote economic growth?

In recent years, a majority of states have enacted tax incentives to attract film and television productions. Georgia, for instance, offers film producers tax rebates worth 20 percent of their costs. [30] Republican Gov. Nathan Deal says the incentives helped bring 245 productions to the state in 2016 with spending totaling $2 billion. [31]

In May, Georgia doubled down on its investments in the arts as an economic development strategy, enacting new tax credits for the music industry. Sponsors claim the credits, which will apply to recordings made in Georgia and to large-scale tours that rehearse and start in Georgia, will create 10,000 jobs. [32]

However, a study last year from the University of Southern California found that such incentive credits for film and TV companies had no measurable effect on job growth in 26 states that had implemented them. [33] And a recent report from the Pew Charitable Trusts lists Georgia among 23 states that do not evaluate whether their investment is paying off.

"Despite the significance of the program, Georgia lacks a process for evaluating the film tax credit and other incentives," according to the report. "Evaluations could help lawmakers determine how well these policies are working for the state's budget and economy and for businesses too." [34]

"The research on this . . . is not particularly favorable to the states that are putting out benefits," says Douglas Noonan, an economist at Indiana University-Purdue University Indianapolis. "They're boondoggles for large producers that have mobile productions. It's hard [for states] to recoup the positive side of things."

There is no question that the arts contribute to the economy. In 2014, arts and cultural production amounted to $729.6 billion worth of economic activity according to the U.S. Bureau of Economic Analysis, or 4.2 percent of overall GDP. [35] "There's a lot of great research showing that arts provide not only a great cultural asset, but support 4.6 million jobs," says Randy Cohen, vice president of research and policy for Americans for the Arts.

His organization's surveys have found that the average patron spends $31.47 on top of any admission price when attending a cultural event. [36] "It's a huge economic force," says Phil Dunlap, director of education for Jazz St. Louis, a nonprofit performing arts presenter. "If arts and culture events went away, tens of thousands of jobs would be lost."

Many arts organizations such as Dunlap's tell stories about how their presence helped turn around struggling communities. What were once nearly abandoned neighborhoods or small downtowns are now thriving, with patrons coming in and spending money, followed by other businesses drawn to such areas.

"We're finding that arts and culture are an important part of any economic development strategy," says Jennifer Henaghan, deputy research director for the American Planning Association. "It's becoming more and more important to get those elements for communities of all sizes."

Indeed, a federal arts grant helped to trigger an economic comeback in Whitesburg, Ky., devastated by downturns in coal mining. "We have 18 full-time employees and five part-time employees," said Ada Smith, a program director and fundraiser for a film workshop that has received NEA funding. "We have over a million-dollar payroll annually." [37]

But for every popular venue that helps revitalize an area, how many arts organizations fail to boost the local economy or go out of business? No one seems to know, says Stephen Sheppard, an urban economist at Williams College in Williamstown, Mass.

"You hear about the success stories, but the problem is you never hear about the failure stories," he says. "When a nonprofit museum goes out of existence, its records are completely lost. No one is collecting that data."

Noonan says it is difficult to know whether arts organizations help attract investment, or whether a rising economic tide in an area naturally lead to more support for such nonprofit entities. It is unclear whether arts- and culture-driven investments are going to "have a bigger bang" than bringing in auto dealerships or any other type of investment, Noonan says.

"The arts can be a useful part of the mix, but they are not going to save your town, if you think that's the one thing you need to do," says Michael Rushton, a professor of arts administration at Indiana University at Bloomington, citing other factors such as schools, public safety and infrastructure.

However, arts organizations, more than other types of businesses, can increase the quality of life in an area, helping to attract highly mobile knowledge workers in sectors such as technology and finance, says Kushner, of Muhlenberg College in Pennsylvania. "The arts make tremendous contributions to community development," he says. "Some of those benefits are economic. In Bethlehem, former steel companies have been repurposed as arts spaces. It's played a significant role in the revitalization of Bethlehem from its industrial past. And Bethlehem is not alone."

Since undergoing a $5.5 million renovation 20 years ago, the Newberry Opera House in South Carolina has hosted performances by such name acts as Willie Nelson and Olivia Newton-John. Such performances may attract an older crowd to Newberry, but they've also helped increase occupancy rates in nearby housing developments and drawn companies such as M.M. Technics, a German metal supply company, and ThermaFlo Engineering Co., a water heater manufacturer, according to Molly Fortune, the opera house's executive director. "When companies are looking to move to the Upstate (region), state or county officials point out there's a huge quality of life here for your workers," she says.

Positive effects may occur within some localities, Noonan says, but he's not convinced the same strategy can work everywhere. And, while some places may draw a crowd for a time, fashions inevitably change and an initial boost from a cultural organization may not sustain itself for more than a few years. "There's a lot of good anecdotal evidence about the success stories, but when you start averaging things out, it becomes a very diluted story," he says.

However, Sheppard, the Williams economist, examined the effects of cultural nonprofits in 300 metropolitan areas. [38] Overall, he says, they had a net positive impact on income "that doesn't fade away over time. That's a positive message to support the assertion that there should be some policy to support these organizations," he says.

■

BACKGROUND

Arts Ambivalence

Americans have had ambivalent feelings about the arts nearly since the arrival of the first European settlers. During colonial times and the early years of the republic, preachers and politicians worried that the arts could serve as a distraction from more practical endeavors.

Controversy over sexually explicit photographs by Robert Mapplethorpe, who had received funding from the National Endowment for the Arts, prompted the Corcoran Gallery of Art in Washington to cancel a planned exhibit of his works in 1989. In protest, other artists projected Mapplethorpe's images onto the Corcoran's façade, and several galleries showed the photographs, attracting large crowds.

"Until the 20th century, the United States government possessed no official arts policy," wrote historian Donna Binkiewicz. [39] Congress was reluctant to discuss arts funding or policy, and even avoided discussions about installing art works in the Capitol. [40]

In 1835, when James Smithson, an English chemist, offered to donate roughly the equivalent of $15.5 million today to create what eventually would become the Smithsonian Institution, several senators denounced the idea as unconstitutional, and it took Congress 10 years to accept the gift. [41] In his influential 1835 study *Democracy in America*, the French observer Alexis de Tocqueville wrote that Americans "habitually prefer the useful to the beautiful, and they will require the beautiful should be useful." [42]

In the 1930s, during the Great Depression, the federal Works Progress Administration, which put jobless Americans to work building roads, bridges and dams, also employed thousands of writers and artists. Four federal arts projects encompassed theater, music, the visual arts and writing. [43] Among the celebrated federally subsidized theatrical productions was the 1935 "voodoo" *Macbeth*, set in Haiti and directed by a 20-year-old Orson Welles, who went on to direct *Citizen Kane* and other classic films. [44] The play was a critical and popular success and was performed before 150,000 people around the country. [45]

Congressional efforts to create a permanent federal arts agency never got far during the first half of the 20th century. That was due partly to opposition from fiscal conservatives, but also to concerns by some in the artistic community that they could lose artistic freedom by producing works under the shackle of bureaucratic regulation. In 1953, the American Symphony Orchestra League released a poll of its members showing that 91 percent opposed federal subsidies. [46]

But during the Cold War the U.S. government became a major funder of the arts after they began to be viewed as a weapon in the U.S.-Soviet competition for influence around the globe. The arts could be used to promote democratic values such as openness and tolerance. The State Department sponsored overseas tours featuring symphony orchestras and jazz musicians, while the CIA underwrote performers, artists and writers, often through foundations.

"I remember the enormous joy I got when the Boston Symphony Orchestra won more acclaim for the U.S. in Paris than [Secretary of State] John Foster Dulles or Dwight D. Eisenhower could have bought with a hundred speeches," one CIA operative recalled. [47]

Meanwhile, interest in the arts was growing rapidly at home. Sales in musical instruments increased fivefold between 1940 and 1960. [48] Thanks in part to the so-called GI bill, which provided college scholarships to military veterans, university attendance also skyrocketed, including a huge increase in students majoring in the arts.

Universities, which built museums on campus and began presenting major performances, were becoming "the new Medicis," as an American Council for the Arts in Education report called them, referring to the art patrons of Renaissance Florence, in Italy. [49]

Birth of the NEA

President John F. Kennedy, who made the arts a symbol of his administration, had praised their value during his 1960 campaign, saying "the encouragement of art in the broadest sense is indeed a function of government." [50] Kennedy invited 155 prominent artists and scientists to his inauguration, which featured a reading by

Continued on p. 592

Chronology

1940s-1950s
State Department and CIA fund the arts as a diplomatic tool.

1943
With unemployment below 2 percent, Congress kills the Works Progress Administration, which included the first major government effort to put artists to work.

1948
Smith-Mundt Act authorizes use of culture as Cold War propaganda tool.

1959
Philadelphia establishes the first local percent-for-art program to fund public art.

1960s-1970s
First federal agencies devoted to the arts are established.

1963
President John F. Kennedy creates the President's Advisory Council on the Arts.

1965
Congress establishes the National Endowment for the Arts (NEA) and the National Endowment for the Humanities.

1974
President Richard M. Nixon increases NEA funding to $64 million, eight times the amount when he took office in 1969.

1976
Some 10,000 artists are working under the auspices of a federal program known as the Comprehensive Employment and Training Act.

1980s-1990s
Controversial grants spark increased opposition to NEA.

1985
President Ronald Reagan begins annual granting of the National Medal of Arts to outstanding artists.

1986
NEA creates an arts-in-education program for elementary and secondary schools.

1989
Exhibitions involving controversial photographs by Andres Serrano and Robert Mapplethorpe stir nationwide debate over arts funding. . . .

1990
An amendment to abolish the NEA fails in the House. . . . Congress bars federal funding for art deemed obscene.

1992
NEA funding peaks at $176 million.

1994
GOP's Contract With America calls for abolishing the NEA.

1996
NEA funding drops below $100 million for the first time since 1977.

1997
Congress eliminates NEA grants to individual artists.

1998
Supreme Court rules that the NEA decision to deny funds to artists for failing to maintain standards of values and decency is constitutional.

1999
Offended by an exhibit featuring a portrait of the Virgin Mary decorated with dung, New York City Mayor Rudy Giuliani attempts to evict the Brooklyn Museum of Art.

2000s-Present
NEA budget again grows.

2000
NEA receives $105 million in funding, its first increase in eight years.

2007
Congress approves largest percentage increase in NEA funding in 28 years.

2009
Federal stimulus law includes $50 million for NEA to distribute to preserve nonprofit arts jobs threatened by recession.

2011
House votes to strip federal funding from National Public Radio, but the Senate doesn't act on the proposal.

2013
House proposal would eliminate NEA funding, but it fails to pass.

2015
The Every Student Succeeds Act urges states to offer arts education as part of a "well-rounded" education.

2017
An appropriations bill to fund the government through September increases NEA funding slightly (May 5). . . . President Trump's budget calls for eliminating funding for the NEA and other cultural agencies (May 22). . . . Delta Air Lines and Bank of America pull funding from a controversial Public Theater production of *Julius Caesar* that some saw as a portrayal of Trump (June 11).

Agencies Seek Community Input for Public Art

Collaboration is key to preventing controversy.

The controversy dragged on for eight years. The federal General Services Administration (GSA) paid $175,000 for a sculpture by Richard Serra, a 120-foot-long, 12-foot-high metal wall called "Tilted Arc," which was placed in a Manhattan plaza. Hundreds of local workers, many of whom used the plaza as a lunch spot, signed petitions to get rid of the installation. When the GSA agreed, Serra sued, saying it had been constructed for that specific site and should not be moved. He eventually lost, and the by-then rusted piece was put in storage. [1]

That was back in the 1980s when such battles were common. Monumental sculptures drew complaints in dozens of communities. [2] Huge, abstract works dropped into public plazas were derided as "plop art."

"You almost never hear members of the public saying, 'Hey, let's all voluntarily chip in and pay a sculptor $100,000 to fill this public space with what appears to be the rusted remnants of a helicopter crash!" columnist Dave Barry wrote as Serra's case was coming to a close. "It takes concerted government action to erect one of those babies." [3]

A lot has changed since then. In response to criticism, arts agencies began incorporating artists' input in the landscape-design process for public spaces, in an effort to reach broad agreement from the start on how works of art could best fit within a particular site.

"Artists started to sit down with planners and architects to figure out how really to create an artwork that is specific to that building," says Patricia Walsh, manager of public art programs for Americans for the Arts, an advocacy group in Washington. "That became the norm, particularly for a lot of major cities."

Consultation has become a mantra in public art circles, in part to avoid the mistakes of the past. It's common to see close coordination between public works departments, publicly owned utilities, developers and a city's arts program. "What we're seeing is that there is a high demand from private developers, city agencies and social services to work with artists," says Jennifer Cole, executive director of the Metro Nashville Arts Commission.

Many cities are trying to make sure not only that artists are talking with design professionals but that the public is heard

Continued from p. 590

the celebrated poet Robert Frost. Early in his term, Kennedy hosted cellist Pablo Casals for a well-received recital at the White House. [51]

John Crosby, a columnist for the *New York Herald Tribune*, gushed, "President Kennedy is the best friend culture . . . has had in the White House since Jefferson." [52]

In 1963, Kennedy created the President's Advisory Council on the Arts. "For the first time, the arts will have some formal government body which will be specifically concerned with all aspects of the arts," the president's statement declared. [53] Following Kennedy's assassination that year, his successor, Vice President Lyndon B. Johnson, promoted arts policy as part of Kennedy's legacy.

Arts organizations, which had once been skeptical about federal involvement in the field, by then largely had decided they could use a champion in Washington. And Johnson's landslide re-election in 1964 helped sweep out members of Congress who had long opposed creation

of a federal arts agency. In his 1965 State of the Union address, Johnson called for a national foundation for the arts.

Rep. Harold Gross, an Iowa Republican, mocked the idea, offering an amendment to expand the definition of artistic pursuits to include belly dancing, baseball, football, golf, tennis, squash, pinochle and poker. [54] He also complained that taxpayers' pockets were being picked, sending the president a telegram requesting that he veto the bill.

"Let's . . . balance the budget before subsidizing the longhairs and the little twinkletoes," Gross wrote. [55]

Such arguments had prevailed in Congress for nearly 20 years, but in 1965, Johnson signed the bill creating the National Endowment for the Arts and the National Endowment for the Humanities. [56]

Growth and Criticism

Private foundations remained the primary patrons of the arts. In

1966, the Ford Foundation, the nation's biggest arts funder, was planning to give 61 orchestras $80 million dollars. A foundation executive reached out to the NEA to make sure this wouldn't duplicate any of the new agency's plans. But since the NEA had only $2.5 million to distribute during its first nine months across all the arts, Roger Stevens, the agency's first chair, assured Ford it could go ahead. [57]

The NEA would soon receive a significant boost. President Richard M. Nixon, who had been elected in 1968, decided significant arts funding would improve his image among the sort of Eastern elites who were active on arts organization boards. "Support for the arts is, increasingly, good politics," presidential aide Leonard Garment informed Nixon. "You will gain support from groups who have hitherto not been favorable to this administration." [58] Over the course of his presidency Nixon boosted the NEA's budget nearly eight-fold — from $8.5 million in 1969 to $64 million in 1974. [59]

in the process, through open meetings or neighborhood outreach. In San Francisco, the Municipal Transportation Agency asked the public to vote this spring via the Web on poetry and visual art pieces that would adorn a hundred of its buses over the summer.

As its name suggests, the point of public art is to connect the public with art — making institutional settings more pleasant and welcoming, as well as providing members of the public with more exposure to art. "Having a gallery experience on a bus democratizes the experience of the gallery," says Darcy Brown, executive director of SF Beautiful, a nonprofit that works with the transportation agency on its art program.

That doesn't mean everyone ends up happy with the final result. Maybe it's the nature of public art that it will inevitably be contentious, because no piece is going to satisfy everyone's taste. And even when people don't find a work offensive or ugly, some still complain that the government has wasted money on what they consider frills.

"There's a lot of pushback, of course," Kristen Ramirez, public

Sculptor Richard Serra sued the General Services Administration (GSA) in the 1980s when it decided to remove his installation, "Tilted Arc," from Federal Plaza in New York City. He lost his suit, and the GSA removed the controversial work, which it had purchased.

art manager for the city of Seattle, says. "Not everybody is excited about spending public money for art."

— *Alan Greenblatt*

[1] Alice Goldfarb Marquis, *Art Lessons: Learning From the Rise and Fall of Public Arts Funding* (1995), p. 197.
[2] *Ibid.*, p. 198.
[3] Dave Barry, "The Naked Truth," *The Washington Post*, Dec. 19, 1990, http://tinyurl.com/y9e6mtno.

Nancy Hanks, Nixon's first NEA chair, proved to be an effective lobbyist for the organization, building coalitions with groups such as the 4-H and the Boy Scouts, which helped show that arts are part of the wider community. [60] Only a few states had their own arts councils or commissions when the NEA was founded. However, the agency gave grants to promote state groups, which helped build support for the arts beyond New York City, which had received a disproportionate share of early NEA funding.

In lean budget times, such as during and after the recession that ended in 2009, states have cut back support for arts agencies. In 2011, Republican Kansas Gov. Sam Brownback eliminated the Kansas Arts Commission, costing the state $800,000 in matching NEA grants. [61] But the following year he created a new commission, and the state is receiving federal arts dollars again. [62]

"Kansas tried to abolish its arts agency, throwing away federal matching dollars, but still failed because con-

stituents were able to push back," says Noonan, of Indiana University-Purdue University Indianapolis. "At the state level, the arts are incredibly resilient."

During the Jimmy Carter administration of the late 1970s, Joan Mondale, Vice President Walter Mondale's wife, became such a strong advocate for federal art support that the press dubbed her "Joan of Art." [63] She helped persuade Congress to increase the percentage of federal construction funds devoted to public art from 0.375 percent to 0.5 percent. [64] Vice President Mondale called up the White House budget director to reverse a $5 million cut to the NEA's budget, saying "my wife would divorce me" if it went through. [65]

But the NEA was becoming hard to manage. Grants were extended to artists and organizations based on the recommendations of panels of experts and artists, but each discipline had become its own fiefdom, with little overarching strategic vision. Myriad conflicts of interests emerged, as panel members found ways to reward their friends. [66]

During the Carter administration, a majority of visual arts grants went to abstract artists, something Republicans began to criticize. [67] Works of dubious merit frequently drew congressional criticism, such as a 1977 project by an "anti-object" artist named Le Ann Wilchusky, who tossed crepe paper streamers from a small plane as an exercise in "sculpting in space." The project had cost taxpayers $6,000. [68]

A 1978 study commissioned by the NEA found that arts consumers remained disproportionately well-educated, with teachers and other professionals making up the bulk of audiences. "We could find no evidence that audiences were becoming more democratic," the study concluded. [69] And Ronald Berman, a former NEA chair under Nixon, complained in 1979 that the NEA had yet to fund a single work of art worth remembering, despite having spent almost $1 billion. [70]

When Republican Ronald Reagan became president in 1981, he sought to cut the endowment's funding by

Arts Requirements Draw Controversy

"While the goals are admirable, the costs are unreasonable."

More than 50 years ago, Philadelphia adopted an ordinance setting aside a small percentage of the cost of government capital projects for art — the nation's first such requirement. Now, hundreds of cities and counties, and about half the states, have followed suit, even including Guam, a tiny U.S. territory in the middle of the Pacific Ocean.

Most so-called percent-for-art programs apply only to government-funded projects. The idea is that having a small percentage of construction funds — typically ranging from 0.5 percent to 2 percent — set aside for art will help spruce up highways, bridges and the like and make them more inviting.

"Why do we have parks all over the place? Why do we care about our environment?" says Erika Lindsay, communications manager for the Office of Arts and Culture in Seattle, which has one of the nation's oldest percent-for-art programs. "We want places where we feel comfortable, where we enjoy ourselves."

The federal government has had percent-for-art programs, off and on, since the 1930s.[1] For the last four decades, the General Services Administration has set aside half of a percent of the projected cost of each new federal building to commission works from artists.[2] The requirement also is increasingly common on college campuses.

Supporters of the percent-for-art concept say it makes public spaces more beautiful and welcoming. Since the terrorist attacks of 2001, airports, which have large capital budgets, have invested heavily in public art in hopes of brightening up terminals to please frazzled travelers.[3] "Public art is very popular for airports," says Robert Lynch, president of Americans for the Arts, an advocacy group in Washington. "You almost have to have public art in airports to be competitive."

Even 1 percent of a multibillion project such as an airport expansion can add up to a lot of money. Some places cap the overall amount that can be collected while others limit the size of projects covered by the requirement, such as not requiring the set-aside if a project costs less than $5 million.

In February, Democratic New York Mayor Bill de Blasio signed legislation increasing the scope of that city's percent-for-art program for the first time since it was created in 1982. Rather than applying only to the first $20 million of a project, the law now applies to the first $50 million.[4] It also stipulated that more funds should be directed toward local artists.

"Public art plays a crucial role in capturing the extraordinary energy and diversity of this city," de Blasio said.

But some taxpayer groups argue percent-for-art requirements subsidize a lot of bad art and divert money that could be better spent on roads and sewers. In 2011, Wisconsin suspended its three-decade old percent-for-art program, as part of a large cut to its overall budget for arts spending. When the city council in Madison considered creating its own percent-for-art requirement this spring, Christian Britschgi, an assistant editor at the libertarian-leaning *Reason* magazine, complained: "Madison, Wis., might become the next town to subsidize godawful sculptures."[5]

And in 2015, Massachusetts Republican Gov. Charlie Baker vetoed percent-for-art legislation, saying, "While the goals of this program are admirable, the costs and structure are unrea-

---

more than half, from $175 million to $85 million.[71] He appointed a task force to come up with ways to justify the cut, but the effort did not pay off, with appointees — including Reagan's friend from Hollywood, actor Charlton Heston — defending the agency.[72]

Rising Controversy

If Nixon found the arts a useful bridge to elite opinion makers, the NEA became a useful target for conservatives under Reagan's successor, Republican George H.W. Bush.

"It was a way for social conservatives within the Republican Party who didn't like Bush . . . to embarrass the president," say Paul DiMaggio, a New York University sociologist who has studied arts policy.

A pair of controversies in 1989 thrust the NEA into the national spotlight. The NEA had given financial support to the Southeastern Center for Contemporary Art in Winston-Salem, N.C., which hosted a traveling exhibit of works by photographer Andres Serrano.[73] One image, entitled "Piss Christ," showed a crucifix submerged in urine. North Carolina GOP Sen. Jesse Helms complained, "He is not an artist. He is a jerk. And he is taunting the American people, and I resent it."[74] Sen. Al D'Amato, a Republican from New York, tore up a copy of the photo on the Senate floor.[75]

That summer, the Corcoran Gallery of Art in Washington decided to cancel its plans to show a traveling solo exhibit of photographs by Robert Mapplethorpe, who had received NEA funds prior to his death earlier in the year. Some of the photographs were sexually explicit, including portrayals of sadomasochism. As a protest, other artists projected Mapplethorpe's images onto the Corcoran's facade. The Washington Project for the Arts displayed the show in its galleries, attracting large crowds.[76] The next year, as soon as the show opened at the Cincinnati Contemporary Arts Center, the museum and its director were cited on obscenity charges — the first and only time in U.S. history such charges had been brought against an

sonable in light of the many legitimate demands and constraints on the Commonwealth's capital investment plan." [6]

But support remains firm for percent-for-art programs in most communities that have had them for a long time. And other communities that feel they cannot afford to devote 1 percent of their capital funding to art have been exploring alternative ways to promote public art. Last year, for instance, Indianapolis began requiring that developers who receive tax incentives from the city devote 1 percent of their project budgets to art. [7]

Other communities are seeking ways to support public art, short of redirecting a set percentage of their capital budgets. Greensboro, N.C., for example, has created a Public Art Endowment to pay for permanent installations. In Buffalo, the Albright-Knox Art Gallery runs a public art initiative in collaboration with the city and Erie County to commission works of art to place around the area. [8]

"Certainly not every community, and probably most communities, don't have $100,000 to drop on a big name artist's piece," says Jennifer Henaghan, deputy research director for the American Planning Association, a city planners' trade association. "But art can involve a range of skills and a range of costs. Doing a community mural, you're still getting that sense of local identity, without a big price tag."

— Alan Greenblatt

The mural *Children of the World Dream Peace* is part of an installation at the Denver International Airport. Communities fund public art in a variety of ways, including by requiring developers to spend a percentage of their capital budget on art.

[1] Alan J. Stein, "Seattle's 1 Percent for Art Program," HistoryLink.org, Oct. 18, 2013, http://tinyurl.com/yaapub63.

[2] "Art in Architecture Program," General Services Administration, http://tinyurl.com/y8rjz7yf.

[3] Scott McCartney, "Airport for Art Lovers," *The Wall Street Journal*, Sept. 18, 2013, http://tinyurl.com/ybopb8oo.

[4] Lauren Lloyd, "NYC increases Percent for Art program funding for the first time in 35 years," *The Architect's Newspaper*, Feb. 20, 2017, http://tinyurl.com/ycx46s76.

[5] Christian Britschgi, "Wisconsin Ordinance Would Waste Tax Dollars on Public Art," *Reason*, May 31, 2017, http://tinyurl.com/y9alfgqu.

[6] Shira Schoenberg, "Gov. Charlie Baker vetoes 'percent for art' program," *Springfield Republican*, Nov. 6, 2015, http://tinyurl.com/y7h5nwfs.

[7] Brian Eason, "Indianapolis Mayor Joe Hogsett signs 'percent for art' into law," *Indianapolis Star*, May 9, 2016, http://tinyurl.com/ybp3vmfk.

[8] "The Public Art Endowment, Community Foundation of Greensboro, http://tinyurl.com/ydafs8mv. "About the Public Art Initiative, Albright-Knox Art Gallery, http://http://tinyurl.com/ydfclsmg.

art gallery. [77] A jury found them not guilty on all charges. [78]

Socially conservative groups such as the American Family Association focused their ire on the NEA, complaining that it supported works that debased values. Congressional Republicans also took up the cause, with Rep. Dick Armey, R-Texas, complaining that the agency sponsored "artists whose forte is ridiculing the values of Americans who are paying for it." [79]

The NEA reacted by imposing stricter standards on artists, denying funding to artists who smeared chocolate on their bodies or urinated onstage. [80] But that wasn't enough to satisfy congressional critics. In 1989 and 1990, Helms succeeded in passing amendments barring the NEA from funding works deemed as obscene and mandating that the agency uphold "general standards of decency and respect." [81]

A group of avant-garde artists who became known as the NEA Four (Holly Hughes, Karen Finley, John Fleck and Tim Miller) sued the agency, arguing it had violated their constitutional right to free expression by denying them grant money. [82] But the Supreme Court ruled in 1998 that the NEA's denial of funds had not amounted to censorship. [83]

During the 1990s, Congress was unable to abolish the NEA, but it clipped the agency's wings by blocking it from dispensing grants to individuals and requiring that 40 percent of its funds be sent to state and regional arts agencies. [84] (The 1965 law creating the agency had required that at least 20 percent be passed through to such agencies.) [85] In 1996, Congress cut NEA funding from $162 million to $99 million.

Although an amendment to abolish the NEA in 1990 had been defeated on a lopsided 64-361 vote, conservative groups continued to call for the NEA's abolition. But congressional leaders realized they could not overcome NEA support among movers and shakers who served on arts organization boards and who hailed from every state. [86]

"After Republicans couldn't eliminate it in 1996, they just gave up," DiMaggio says. "The flow of anti-NEA press releases basically just stopped in the 1990s."

There were occasional arts controversies involving public officials, including Republican New York Mayor Rudolph Giuliani's threat in 1999 to evict the Brooklyn Museum of Art over an exhibit that contained a work he considered sacrilegious. [87] And House Republicans occasionally pushed the idea of defunding the NEA during the presidency of Barack Obama, but the idea never got very far.

The debate about art and arts funding seemed to have died down. The NEA now devotes much of its attention to audience development, with more policies in place designed to filter out potentially controversial grants. It also has lost relative importance as a patron, with its funding dwarfed

Marc Broussard, right, performs at the New Orleans Jazz & Heritage Festival on April 29, 2017. Arts supporters say art and culture are good for business. Arts programs generate $27.5 billion in tax revenue annually and support $166.3 billion in economic activity per year, according to Americans for the Arts, a Washington-based arts advocacy group.

by the amount given by individual donors and state arts commissions and councils. [88]

"So we coasted," Mark Swed, classical music critic for the *Los Angeles Times*, wrote earlier this year, arguing that Obama had appointed "caretakers" to run the agency. "The president had to pick his

fights, and the NEA, it turned out, was never to be one of them." [89]

CURRENT SITUATION

Strong Support

President Trump's call to eliminate funding for the National Endowment for the Arts has made the agency a front-burner issue for the first time in more than 20 years. When Kevin Kline received the Tony Award for best leading actor in a Broadway play ("Present Laughter") on June 11, he thanked "a couple of organizations without whom half the people in this room wouldn't be here — and that would be the National Endowment for the Arts and the National Endowment for the Humanities." [90]

Earlier that day, Delta Airlines and Bank of America had withdrawn their support from of the controversial Julius Caesar production, with Fox News calling it a "disgusting New York City play [that depicts] the president brutally assassinated." [91]

But even critics of the NEA and NEH do not expect Trump to succeed in eliminating the agencies this year, especially since the short-term appropriations bill enacted in May provided them with a slight increase. However, it is unclear how the debate over future spending levels will play out. Even if they remain intact, the agencies could suffer some cutbacks. Still, even if the NEA and NEH were eliminated, that wouldn't get the federal government out of the business of supporting arts and culture. Arts money is sprinkled throughout numerous agencies.

For instance, cultural institutions in Washington such as the Kennedy Center, the National Gallery of Art and the Smithsonian receive direct federal support. The Indian Arts and Crafts Board, run by the Interior Department, operates three regional museums and offers assistance to federally recognized tribes. [92] The Forest Service supports folk arts and craft demonstrations and artists' residency programs. [93] The Department of Defense spends more than $400 million annually supporting military bands. [94] In fact, NEA supporters have long pointed out that the agency receives far less financial support than military bands.

Most states are still in the process of drafting education plans to meet the latest federal requirements. "They're game, but they really don't know what it will look like," Lynn Tuttle, director of arts education policy and professional development for the Arizona Department of Education. "You have state boards and state educational leadership that for 15 years have had only one version of accountability. If you're

Continued on p. 598

Getty Images/Wirelmage/Tim Mosenfelder

At Issue:

Should the National Endowment for the Arts be abolished?

MICHAEL D. TANNER
SENIOR FELLOW, CATO INSTITUTE

WRITTEN FOR *CQ RESEARCHER*, JULY 2017

*e*liminating the National Endowment for the Arts (NEA) is not going to help balance the federal budget. We are talking about a minuscule amount of money by Washington standards — a paltry $150 million. Yet, by the same logic, eliminating the NEA is hardly going to mean the end of art in America.

After all, private philanthropy contributes more than $17 billion annually to the arts. Ticket and merchandise sales bring in another $12.7 billion. In fact, government sources at all levels contribute less than 4 percent of arts funding.

Art would continue to do just fine without a dime of government money.

But doesn't government funding provide an imprimatur of approval that can be leveraged for additional support? Perhaps. But that's exactly why the government should not be in the art-funding business. The government shouldn't be approving or disapproving any type of expression.

It is true that the NEA's ability to withhold funding based on content has been limited since the Supreme Court's 1998 decision in *NEA v. Finley*. But that doesn't mean the NEA doesn't pick and choose guided by prejudices and preconceived notions.

Even when its decisions don't reflect politics or a particular worldview, its funding can be determined by the artistic vogue of the day — abstract or avant-garde art, performance, minimalist, you name it, rather than figurative art or realism in general — as has been the trend over the last few decades. Like other viewers and consumers, I have my own preferences and biases about the types of art I like. The government shouldn't signal its own likes and dislikes.

Nor should we count on the NEA to nourish new artists or those trying to challenge the art establishment. Following a series of embarrassments in the 1990s, the NEA stopped funding individual artists. Today, its money goes to arts organizations and educational programs that have their own built-in rigidities. In many ways, the NEA simply rubber-stamps the artistic status quo. That is ultimately bad for the arts and artists.

The fight to defund the NEA shouldn't be about money. The NEA is little more than a drop in an ocean of red ink. It is hardly the most egregious use of taxpayer money. But it is a prime example of how government intrudes into areas where it does not belong. If we truly care about art, we should want the government to keep its hands off.

ROBERT B. EKELUND JR.
PROFESSOR EMERITUS OF ECONOMICS, AUBURN UNIVERSITY

WRITTEN FOR *CQ RESEARCHER*, JULY 2017

*c*onservatives have long advocated the elimination of the half-century-old National Endowment for the Arts (NEA), whose budget of $150 million is only a minuscule fraction of government spending. This, in a nation where the ever-growing contribution of the arts to gross domestic product (GDP) is now above 4 percent of GDP.

The Trump administration proposes totally eliminating funds shared by 19 different art forms (opera, dance, music, museums, and others). Small grants from the agency — most of which are under $20,000 — are used primarily to educate Americans in all aspects of their culture.

What is the fundamental objection to the NEA? Opponents argue it is an elitist, non-market organization that taxes all to support the interests of the wealthy few. That view is simply incorrect.

First, the NEA is not allowed to subsidize individual artists, so it spreads around small grants to various projects. NEA grants are imprimaturs of quality for projects originating in every congressional district in the United States. A quarter of its grants go to rural areas. As such, the NEA is a goad to private enterprise, employment and GDP in the most underserved areas.

By my calculation, matching grants to museums alone ($4.25 million for 125 grants in 2016) produced an estimated $17 million to $20 million in private funds. By comparison, the Small Business Administration (SBA), with a budget of $719 million in 2017, performs similar functions by helping business projects. It would make just as much sense to eliminate the SBA!

Elitism is a charge without merit. Put aside the fact that most NEA grants focus on neglected arts and supporting ongoing cultural projects. Consider, instead, evidence that arts attendance is countercyclical: In periods of high unemployment, arts participation rises, and vice versa.

This means that it is the poorer, younger and minority segments of society, not the wealthy, who benefit most from programs supported by the NEA both in ordinary times and in economic downturns.

Finally, opposition to the NEA is misplaced. The Marine Band, the National Gallery of Art and the Smithsonian all receive government support and, I dare say, will continue to receive it.

American culture promulgated by the NEA is for all Americans, because culture and education change lives, and our country, for the better.

Continued from p. 596

used to doing it one way, it's hard to do it another way."

Local Projects

Most cities of any size run a public art program, commissioning works to augment or decorate schools and roadsides. (*See sidebar, p. 592.*) Many mayors are convinced the arts are a key part of economic development strategies. Some cities are looking for innovative

A poster advertises The Public Theater's production of Shakespeare's *Julius Caesar, which recasts the dictator to resemble President Trump. When the president's son, Donald Trump Jr., tweeted, "I wonder how much of this 'art' is funded by taxpayers?" the NEA rushed out a statement saying it had not funded the controversial production.*

ways to support and retain local artists.

Cities that rely heavily on the arts such as Austin, Texas, Nashville, Tenn., and New York have plans to subsidize housing for artists. Mitch Landrieu, the Democratic mayor of culture-rich New Orleans, announced a five-year housing plan last year to provide housing support for "artists and culture bearers." Construction is underway on a $37 million

campus in the city's Tremé neighborhood that will provide a place for musicians and artists to live and work. [95]

In December, 36 people were killed in a fire at an Oakland warehouse that had been turned into an artists' collective known as the Ghost Ship. [96] In response, California launched a pilot program to identify communities for designation as culture districts, where housing and workspaces could be provided for artists. The state is considering subsidizing loans to renovate such live-work spaces. [97]

With the growth of the so-called makers movement, with people making crafts in small batches by hand, development agencies in cities such as Baltimore and Indianapolis are sponsoring large workspaces as incubators for artists' and handicraft businesses. [98]

"Cities are changing zoning rules for some types of artisan-focused manufacturing uses," says Jennifer Henaghan,

deputy research director for the American Planning Association. "Someone who produces pottery doesn't have to be relegated to an industrial district. They can be downtown, or downtown-adjacent."

Most major cities have a variety of programs in place to encourage or directly support the arts, including artist-in-residence programs in municipal agencies or commissions for works of art to adorn public spaces.

Lately, even one of the most traditional kinds of public art — statues of war heroes sitting on horses — have become highly controversial. Cities including New Orleans, St. Louis and Richmond and Charlottesville, Va., have held contentious debates this year over the question of removing Confederate monuments, which some view as important recognitions of history but others see as endorsements of the racist history of slavery.

Nationwide, dozens of Confederate symbols have been removed from public spaces, an effort prompted by the shooting of nine African-Americans by a white supremacist at a Charleston, S.C., church in 2015. [99] The effort has gathered renewed momentum this year, thanks in part to a widely replayed and reprinted speech by Landrieu on May 19, in which he laid out his reasons for removing four statues that celebrated the Confederacy.

"The movement which became known as The Cult of the Lost Cause . . . had one goal — through monuments and through other means — to rewrite history to hide the truth, which is that the Confederacy was on the wrong side of humanity," Landrieu said. [100]

The decisions to remove Confederate monuments have sparked protests. Alabama passed a state law in May barring local governments from removing historical monuments or markers that have been in place for 40 years or more. [101]

"When you look at history, every region of the country has different stories to tell about the formation of the state and what took place," says Republican state Sen. Gerald Allen, who sponsored the prohibition. "When you start removing monuments and statues and portraits or buildings, then in a sense you lose history." ■

OUTLOOK

Unending Debate

Advocates for the arts say they not only help boost today's economy but can help young people prepare for jobs in the future. With jobs increasingly being automated, especially those that do not require much analysis or thinking, Kai-Fu Lee, a former Google and Microsoft executive, says perhaps more people should focus on careers in the arts.

"Art and beauty [are] very hard to replicate with AI (artificial intelligence)," Lee said. [102]

While millions more people may not be able to earn living wages at art, the kind of skills used in the arts, such as creativity, are exactly "what business is looking for," National Art Education Association president Defibaugh says. "They want people who can think creatively and critically for jobs that don't even exist yet."

People who lobby for government arts funding have learned that they often can be most effective by highlighting the practical benefits of promoting the arts or arts education. "We realized a long time ago that we needed to show not only that the arts are good for the soul, but that they have an economic impact," says Lynch, president of Americans for the Arts.

Of course, people also make the "soul" argument. Arts lovers say art can raise the spirits and help society grapple with its deepest concerns. "The

arts community . . . adds immeasurably to the stability, cohesion, intelligence, beauty and resilience of the nation," Philip Kennicott, art and architecture critic for *The Washington Post*, wrote in March. [103]

Advocates say that since the combined NEA and NEH budgets cost less than $1 per person per year, and given how states, cities and nonprofit arts organizations leverage their dollars, the country should be able to afford to keep the arts alive. [104]

"There's a philosophical question, whether you care about society producing art, which is how most people judge societies," says Holochwost, the Johns Hopkins researcher. "Do we want to be the most affluent society in history that also produced no art?"

But given the practical nature of the American psyche, many people consider art a luxury, and even if they value it, they don't think the government should pay for it. "Art is really important to who we are — as important in some ways as education and religion in forming character," says Tanner, the Cato Institute fellow. "But it's not what government should do. It's something propaganda societies do, like the Soviets and the Nazis."

This debate appears unending. If art is good for society, then the government should help support it, arts advocates contend. But if the government is picking up the tab, it might make the art so sanitized or safe that it hardly pleases anybody.

That debate preceded the creation of the National Endowment for the Arts, helped fuel the so-called culture wars of the 1980s and '90s and has returned with President Trump's proposal to eliminate funding.

It is an argument that seems destined to recur periodically. "I don't anticipate the argument about support for the arts to go away," Lynch says. "We have an almost 400-year history of taking steps forward, and then taking steps backward." ■

Notes

[1] Haley Richardson, "Joseph Papp and Shakespeare in the Park, 1962 and 1965," WNYC, July 31, 2011, http://tinyurl.com/ybmslbzg.

[2] Ty Burr, "'Julius Caesar' controversy isn't a tempest in a teapot," *The Boston Globe*, June 12, 2017, http://tinyurl.com/y9v6sue9.

[3] Osita Nwanevu, "Today in Conservative Media: The Play's the Thing," *Slate*, June 12, 2017, http://tinyurl.com/yaf6et5g.

[4] Rohan Preston, "Uproar over Trump-themed 'Julius Caesar,' but none for Obama version at Guthrie 5 years ago," *Minneapolis Star Tribune*, June 12, 2017, http://tinyurl.com/y85qjz4f.

[5] Twitter feed of Donald Trump Jr., June 11, 2017, http://tinyurl.com/ybabgsxj.

[6] "National Endowment for the Arts' Statement on the Shakespeare in the Park by the Public Theater's Production of 'Julius Caesar,' " National Endowment for the Arts, June 11, 2017, http://tinyurl.com/yd34dp32.

[7] David Montgomery, "Trump wants to kill federal arts funding. What difference would that make?" *The Washington Post*, June 8, 2017, http://tinyurl.com/y8vx4sow.

[8] "White House Press Briefing; President Trump Releases Budget Plan," CNN, March 16, 2017, http://tinyurl.com/yc8kbpkv.

[9] "Arts and Economic Prosperity 5: The Economic Impact of Nonprofit Arts & Cultural Organizations & Their Audiences," Americans for the Arts, June 17, 2017, http://tinyurl.com/ycqmhrbc.

[10] Frank Cadenhead, "A Healthy Paris Opera," *Musical America*, Dec. 6, 2016, http://tinyurl.com/yccheq2c.

[11] Robin Pogrebin, "Arts Groups on Edge as New York City Re-evaluates Cultural Funding," *The New York Times*, May 8, 2017, http://tinyurl.com/k433zno.

[12] Romina Boccia *et al.*, "Blueprint for Balance: A Federal Budget for Fiscal Year 2018," The Heritage Foundation, March 28, 2017, http://tinyurl.com/ycwu8zbg.

[13] George F. Will, "Abolish the National Endowment for the Arts," *The Washington Post*, March 15, 2017, http://tinyurl.com/yb4vqy6g.

[14] Jane Chu, "Statement from National Endowment for the Arts Chairman Jane Chu on the FY 18 Budget," National Endowment for the Arts, March 16, 2017, http://tinyurl.com/mhm3r9b.

[15] Ted Johnson, "Budget Bill Retains Funding for Arts Agencies, Public Broadcasting," *Variety*, May 1, 2017, http://tinyurl.com/y8y6yzl8.

[16] Philip Bump, "Trump reportedly wants to

cut cultural programs that make up 0.02 percent of federal spending," *The Washington Post*, Jan. 19, 2017, http://tinyurl.com/yb8w2oms.

[17] "Join the San Francisco Symphony in supporting the NEA!" San Francisco Symphony, April 26, 2017, http://tinyurl.com/ydz87hxw.

[18] Katherine Boyle, "Yes, Kickstarter raises more money for artists than the NEA. Here's why that's not really surprising," *The Washington Post*, July 7, 2013, http://tinyurl.com/y7gcgm2k. Also see Christian Camerota, "How Crowdfunding Kick Starts the Arts," Harvard Business School, May 7, 2015, http://tinyurl.com/y83fd3g5.

[19] "Total Charitable Donations Rise to New High of $390.05 Billion," Giving USA, June 12, 2017, http://tinyurl.com/yaz298xg.

[20] Patricia Cohen, "N.E.A. Funds Benefit Both Rich and Poor, Study Finds," *The New York Times*, Feb. 4, 2014, http://tinyurl.com/y7gvvje9.

[21] Erin Moriarty, "For arts' sake: When funding the NEA is in jeopardy," CBS News, April 23, 2017, http://tinyurl.com/kzarvrq.

[22] David Marcus, "Ending Federal Funds Will Be The Best Thing For The Arts In Decades," *The Federalist*, Feb. 8, 2017, http://tinyurl.com/ybyy8eaz.

[23] Roger Kimball, "It Costs Taxpayers a Bundle, but Is It Art?," *The Wall Street Journal*, July 10, 2017, http://tinyurl.com/y9usf2hq.

[24] Alyssa Robinson, "Why Conservatives Want To Defund Federal Arts Funding," Utah Public Radio, June 5, 2017, http://tinyurl.com/ydg3yyvu.

[25] Basmat Parsad, Maura Spiegelman and Jared Coopersmith, "Arts Education in Public Elementary and Secondary Schools: 1999-2000 and 2009-10," U.S. Department of Education, April 2012, http://tinyurl.com/yaj79trq.

[26] For background, see Beth Baker, "Arts Education," *CQ Researcher*, March 16, 2012, pp. 253-276.

[27] Steven J. Holochwost *et al.*, "The Socioemotional Benefits of the Arts: A New Mandate for Arts Education," William Penn Foundation,

Dec. 15, 2016, http://tinyurl.com/y9yc5psf.

[28] James Catterall, *Doing Well and Doing Good by Doing Art: A 12-year Longitudinal Study of Arts Education — Effects on the Achievements and Values of Young Adults* (2009).

[29] Adam Parker, "Budget Cuts Taking Toll on Arts in School," *The Post and Courier*, July 30, 2016, http://tinyurl.com/ya5ltonf.

[30] Bryn Elise Sandberg, "Film and TV Tax Incentives: A State-by-State Guide," *The Hollywood Reporter*, April 21, 2016, http://tinyurl.com/yatwuxxq.

[31] Dave Williams, "Film industry impact in Georgia passes $7 billion," *Atlanta Business Chronicle*, Aug. 2, 2016, http://tinyurl.com/ybygeuqt.

[32] Michelle Baruchman, "Georgia Music Investment Act Becomes Law," *The Atlanta Journal-Constitution*, May 9, 2017, http://tinyurl.com/yb2f9bfw. Gail Mitchell, "Georgia Music Investment Act Passes State Legislature, Aims to Create 10,000 New Jobs and Boost Economy," *Billboard*, March 31, 2017, http://tinyurl.com/ybe6zcq8.

[33] Michael Thom, "Lights, Camera, but No Action? Tax and Economic Development Lessons From State Motion Picture Incentive Programs," *The American Review of Public Administration*, June 15, 2016, http://tinyurl.com/y8bclau3.

[34] "How States Are Improving Tax Incentives for Jobs and Growth," Pew Charitable Trusts, May 2017, http://tinyurl.com/ybbtmpl8.

[35] "Arts and Culture Grow for Third Straight Year," Bureau of Economic Analysis, April 19, 2017, http://tinyurl.com/yckdovgb.

[36] "Arts and Economic Prosperity 5," *op. cit.*

[37] Moriarty, *op. cit.*

[38] Peter Pedroni and Stephen Sheppard, "The Economic Consequences of Cultural Spending," in Michael Rushton, ed., *Creative Communities: Art Works in Economic Development* (2013), p. 166.

[39] Donna M. Binkiewicz, *Federalizing the Muse:*

United States Arts Policy & the National Endowment for the Arts 1965-1980 (2004), p. 11.

[40] Stephen Benedict, ed., *Public Money and the Muse: Essays on Government Funding for the Arts* (1991), p. 33.

[41] *Ibid.*, p. 39.

[42] Alexis de Tocqueville, *Democracy in America* (1835), Chapter XI, available at http://tinyurl.com/y7gn995q.

[43] Nick Taylor, *American-Made: The Enduring Legacy of the WPA* (2008), p. 248.

[44] *Ibid.*, p. 104.

[45] *Ibid.*

[46] Gary O. Larson, *The Reluctant Patron: The United States Government and the Arts, 1943-1965* (1983).

[47] *Ibid.*, p. 57.

[48] Alice Goldfarb Marquis, *Art Lessons: Learning From the Rise and Fall of Public Arts Funding* (1995), p. 25.

[49] *Ibid.*, p. 26.

[50] *Ibid.*, p. 52.

[51] Benedict, *op. cit.*, p. 47.

[52] *Ibid.*, p. 48.

[53] Larson, *op. cit.*, p. 178.

[54] Tyler Cowen, *Good and Plenty: The Creative Successes of American Arts Funding* (2006), p. 140.

[55] Larson, *op. cit.*, p. 216.

[56] Lyndon B. Johnson, "Remarks at the Signing of the Arts and Humanities Bill," The American Presidency Project, Sept. 29, 1965, http://tinyurl.com/yc8dx7nx.

[57] Marquis, *op. cit.*, p. 64.

[58] *Ibid.*, p. 93.

[59] "National Endowment for the Arts Appropriation History," National Endowment for the Arts, http://tinyurl.com/jreutxx.

[60] Marquis, *op. cit.*, p. 98.

[61] Elizabeth Blair, "Kansas Cuts Public Funding For The Arts," NPR, June 13, 2011, http://tinyurl.com/68atchc.

[62] "Kansas receiving arts funds, for now," *Wichita Eagle*, April 19, 2017, http://tinyurl.com/y7b44ufo.

[63] Kevin Duchschere, " 'Joan of Art,' wife of former VP Walter Mondale, dies at 83," *Minneapolis Star Tribune*, Feb. 4, 2014, http://tinyurl.com/yabl7vey.

[64] Marquis, *op. cit.*, p. 137.

[65] *Ibid.*

[66] Allan Parachini, "Conflict of Interest Issue in NEA Grants?" *Los Angeles Times*, July 27, 1990, http://tinyurl.com/ybd2sg8h.

[67] Binkiewicz, *op. cit.*, p. 195.

[68] Michael Straight, "Reflections on a Golden Fleecing at the Arts Endowment," *The Washington Post*, Oct. 16, 1977, http://tinyurl.

About the Author

Alan Greenblatt is a staff writer at *Governing* magazine. Previously he covered politics and government for NPR and *CQ Weekly*, where he won the National Press Club's Sandy Hume Award for political journalism. He graduated from San Francisco State University in 1986 and received a master's degree in English literature from the University of Virginia in 1988. His *CQ Researcher* reports include "Gentrification," "Future of the GOP," "Immigration Debate," "Media Bias" and "Downtown Revival."

com/y7bnr4z5.

[69] Marquis, *op. cit.*, p. 142.

[70] *Ibid.*, p. 139.

[71] *Ibid.*, p. 163.

[72] Benedict, *op. cit.*, p. 58.

[73] *Ibid.*, p. 63.

[74] Andrew Hartman, *A War for the Soul of America: A History of the Culture Wars* (2015), p. 192.

[75] Marquis, *op. cit.*, p. 209.

[76] Hartman, *op. cit.*, p. 193.

[77] Benedict, *op. cit.*, p. 71.

[78] Grace Dobush, "25 years later: Cincinnati and the obscenity trial over Mapplethorpe art," *The Washington Post*, Oct. 24, 2015, http://tinyurl.com/hvlmyzd.

[79] Hartman, *op. cit.*, p. 196.

[80] Eric Pianin, "Helms Wins Senate Vote to Restrict NEA Funds," *The Washington Post*, Sept. 20, 1991, http://tinyurl.com/y7hp6qug.

[81] Courtney Randolph Nea, "Content Restrictions and National Endowment for the Arts Funding: An Analysis from the Artist's Perspective," *William & Mary Bill of Rights Journal*, 1993, http://tinyurl.com/yb8ms9xh.

[82] Hartman, *op. cit.*, p. 197.

[83] Mel Gussow, "Artists See No Decency In Ruling On Grants," *The New York Times*, July 2, 1998, http://tinyurl.com/y9yp39fy. The case is *National Endowment for the Arts v. Finley*, 524 U.S. 569.

[84] Paul DiMaggio and Becky Pettit, "Public Opinion and Political Vulnerability: Why Has the National Endowment for the Arts Been Such an Attractive Target?" Princeton University Center for Arts and Cultural Policy Studies Working Paper, January 1999, http://tinyurl.com/yaojojp6.

[85] Cowen, *op. cit.*, p. 88.

[86] Benedict, *op. cit.*, p. 17.

[87] Isaac Kaplan, "Censorship, 'Sick Stuff,' and Rudy Giuliani's Fight to Shut Down the Brooklyn Museum," *Artsy*, Dec. 23, 2016, http://tinyurl.com/ybaaq4mc.

[88] "How the United States Funds the Arts," National Endowment for the Arts, November 2012, http://tinyurl.com/zdlztvd.

[89] Mark Swed, "Obama left the NEA vulnerable. Could Sylvester Stallone save it?" *Los Angeles Times*, Jan. 7, 2017, http://tinyurl.com/yaf6dywz.

[90] Jessica Gelt, "Kevin Kline gives a shout-out to the NEA and NEH," *Los Angeles Times*, June 11, 2017, http://tinyurl.com/ybsox8ae.

[91] Ian Millhiser, "Fox News upset Shakespeare in the Park isn't a safe space for Trump supporters," ThinkProgress, June 11, 2017, http://tinyurl.com/y7tavg7r.

FOR MORE INFORMATION

Americans for the Arts, 1000 Vermont Ave., N.W., 6th Floor, Washington, DC 20005; 202-371-2830; www.americansforthearts.org. Membership organization representing and advocating for arts organizations.

Fractured Atlas, 248 W. 35th St., 10th Floor, New York, NY 10001; 888-692-7878; www.fracturedatlas.org. Nonprofit that provides logistical services to artists and arts organizations.

Heritage Foundation, 214 Massachusetts Ave., N.E., Washington, DC 20002; 202-546-4400; www.heritage.org. Conservative think tank that helped shape the Trump administration's budget; opposes public arts programs as a waste tax dollars.

National Art Education Association, 901 Prince St., Alexandria, VA 22314; 703-860-8000; www.arteducators.org. Research and advocacy organization representing visual arts instructors.

National Assembly of State Art Agencies, 1200 18th St., N.W., Suite 1100, Washington, DC 20036; 202-347-6352; nasaa-arts.org. Professional association of state and territorial arts agencies that promotes public support for the arts.

National Center for Arts Research, Southern Methodist University, PO Box 750356, Dallas, TX 75275; 214-768-4498; http://mcs.smu.edu/artsresearch2014/. Collects and disseminates data and research that help arts and cultural organizations assess challenges and increase their impact.

National Endowment for the Arts, 400 7th St., S.W., Washington, DC 20506; 202-682-5400; www.arts.gov. Independent agency that is the primary federal funder of the arts.

William Penn Foundation, 2 Logan Square, 100 N. 18th St., 11th Floor, Philadelphia, PA 19103; 215-988-1830; www.williampennfoundation.org. Seeks to improve education for low-income children in the Philadelphia area and sponsors research on the benefits of arts education.

[92] "Our Mission," Indian Arts and Crafts Board, http://tinyurl.com/y7da6v5n.

[93] "Becoming an Artist in Residence," Forest Service, http://tinyurl.com/zm5fvgc.

[94] Leo Shane III, "Latest budget plan won't stop the music for military bands," *Military Times*, March 6, 2017, http://tinyurl.com/yact4ek6.

[95] Teresa Wiltz, "To Keep Their Artists, Cities Explore Affordable Housing," *Stateline*, Feb. 1, 2017, http://tinyurl.com/y9eqy5nh.

[96] Sam Levin, "Oakland warehouse fire is product of housing crisis, say artists and advocates," *The Guardian*, Dec. 5, 2016, http://tinyurl.com/j4danp9.

[97] Guy Marzorati, "State Weighs Funding Artist Housing Improvements in Wake of Ghost Ship Fire," KQED, May 25, 2017, http://tinyurl.com/y7qqd53f.

[98] Consuelo Poland, "Meet the Artist-Run Incubator Empowering Makers in Indiana," *Creators*, Feb 24, 2017, http://tinyurl.com/zqhvjzm.

[99] Alan Greenblatt, "The Next Cities That Might Remove Confederate Monuments," *Governing*, June 1, 2017, http://tinyurl.com/y8nwszqo.

[100] "Transcript of New Orleans Mayor Landrieu's Address on Confederate Monuments," *The Pulse*, May 19, 2017, http://tinyurl.com/y8nwszqo.

[101] Joe Sterling, "A new Alabama law makes sure Confederate monuments are here to stay," CNN, May 26, 2017, http://tinyurl.com/yd8stkhc

[102] Dave Gershgorn, "Your art degree might save you from automation, an AI expert says," *Quartz*, May 16, 2017, http://tinyurl.com/yaovf6ub.

[103] Philip Kennicott, "It's not an attack on the arts, it's an attack on communities," *The Washington Post*, March 16, 2017, http://tinyurl.com/y86qnwck.

[104] Carolina A. Miranda, "What does the NEA's $148-million budget buy? 7,789,473 taco bowls but not even one mile of the 405 Freeway," *Los Angeles Times*, March 18, 2017, http://tinyurl.com/y6v4agry.

Bibliography

Selected Sources

Books

Cowen, Tyler, *Good and Plenty: The Creative Successes of American Art Funding*, Princeton University Press, 2006.

A George Mason University economist says the U.S. government acts as a venture capitalist for arts funding by directly supporting arts projects and helping to attract other donors by offering a sort of federal seal of approval.

Hartman, Andrew, *A War for the Soul of America: A History of the Culture Wars*, University of Chicago Press, 2015.

An historian puts national debates over arts and humanities in the context of broader arguments about social change during the closing decades of the 20th century.

Articles

Huckabee, Mike, "Mike Huckabee: A conservative plea for the National Endowment for the Arts," *The Washington Post*, March 22, 2017, http://tinyurl.com/mu5bbze.

The former Arkansas governor and GOP presidential candidate says the National Endowment for the Arts (NEA) funds necessary education programs for children.

Kimball, Roger, "It Costs Taxpayers a Bundle, but Is It Art?," *The Wall Street Journal*, July 10, 2017, http://tinyurl.com/y9usf2hq.

A new report from a watchdog group finds that 48 percent of the funds granted by federal arts agencies in 2016 went to recipients in 10 mostly coastal states. Those groups in turn have funded artists who have produced work that some would find objectionable or offensive.

Knochel, Aaron D., "Why do conservatives want the government to defund the arts?" *The Conversation*, Feb. 5, 2017, http://tinyurl.com/ycv7ps5j.

Conservatives who want to eliminate the NEA might think they are dismantling a centralized bureaucracy but such action would affect local arts providers the most, an assistant professor of art education says.

Mack, Earle I., Randall Bourscheidt and Robert L. Lynch, "Funding the arts is more than preserving culture. It's big business," *The Hill*, Feb. 19, 2017, http://tinyurl.com/kgvgygb.

Three arts advocates argue that the NEA pays economic dividends by supporting trade and an industry that represents 4.2 percent of the nation's gross domestic product.

Marcus, David, "Ending Federal Funds Will Be The Best Thing For The Arts In Decades," *The Federalist*, Feb. 8, 2017, http://tinyurl.com/ybyy8eaz.

If arts organizations did not receive government subsidies, they would do a better job of attracting audiences because they would have to compete in the marketplace, says the artistic director of a Brooklyn, N.Y., theater project.

Swed, Mark, "Obama left the NEA vulnerable. Could Sylvester Stallone save it?" *Los Angeles Times*, Jan. 7, 2017, http://tinyurl.com/yaf6dywz.

Former President Barack Obama made symbolic gestures in favor of the arts, but did little to build the NEA or an infrastructure to support the arts, argues a classical music critic.

Timberg, Scott, "How Mapplethorpe won: The Jesse Helms art world culture wars are over," *Salon*, April 5, 2016, http://tinyurl.com/zfnls7d.

Since the big cultural battles 25 years ago, the internet has made sexual images less shocking, while the NEA has largely avoided making controversial grants, a journalist says.

Will, George F., "Abolish the National Endowment for the Arts," *The Washington Post*, March 15, 2017, http://tinyurl.com/yb4vqy6g.

A cottage industry has grown up around the NEA and lobbies for its funding, but it would be better if individual patrons funded the arts, says a conservative syndicated columnist.

Wiltz, Teresa, "To Keep Their Artists, Cities Explore Affordable Housing," *Stateline*, Feb. 1, 2017, http://tinyurl.com/y9eqy5nh.

Cities where culture is a big business such as New York, Austin, Texas, and New Orleans are stepping up efforts to provide affordable housing to artists and musicians.

Reports and Studies

"Arts and Economic Prosperity 5: The Economic Impact of Nonprofit Arts & Cultural Organizations & Their Audiences," Americans for the Arts, June 17, 2017, http://tinyurl.com/ycqmhrbc.

The nonprofit arts and culture industry generated $166.3 billion worth of economic activity in 2015, helped support 4.6 million jobs and provided local, state and federal governments with a better than 5-to-1 return on their arts subsidies, according to the advocacy organization.

"State Arts Agencies Revenue: Fiscal Year 2017," National Assembly of State Arts Agencies, February 2017, http://tinyurl.com/yb6kte5a.

State and regional arts agencies received $368.2 million from their state legislatures, with a small number of states accounting for an overall 8 percent increase in funding, according to the association.

Holochwost, Steven J., *et al.*, "The Socioemotional Benefits of the Arts: A New Mandate for Arts Education," William Penn Foundation, April 2017, http://tinyurl.com/y9yc5psf.

Arts education not only helps foster interest in the arts but increases interest in school among the young, according to a report for a Philadelphia civic group.

The Next Step:

Additional Articles from Current Periodicals

Benefits of the Arts

"Struggling schools benefit from adding arts to learning," PBS, Jan. 10, 2017, https://tinyurl.com/y7p7fk7e.

Schools are seeing benefits from Turnaround Arts, a federal program created by the President's Committee on the Arts and Humanities that uses music, theater and other arts to help students in low-achieving schools.

Arndt, Jordyn, "Are the arts valuable? More like invaluable, especially now," *Star Tribune*, May 5, 2017, https://tinyurl.com/l8wx6az.

A graduate of the Perpich Center for Arts Education in Golden Valley, Minn., a Minneapolis suburb, says the arts have helped people communicate better, relate to others and appreciate other cultures.

Taylor, Anna, "Public art aims to drive future economy in historic Elk City," *Charleston Gazette-Mail*, July 7, 2017, https://tinyurl.com/y8owr22x.

Officials in Charleston, W. Va., hope encouraging the installation of public art in the city's historic West Side will attract people and businesses to the area.

Federal Funding

Allen, Brian T., "Don't Eliminate Federal Arts Funding, Redirect It," *National Review*, May 1, 2017, https://tinyurl.com/ydx9lykv.

The former director of the New York Historical Society Museum argues for changes in how federal arts funding is spent, such as increasing support for smaller institutions.

Bowley, Graham, "What if Trump Really Does End Money for the Arts?" *The New York Times*, March 16, 2017, https://tinyurl.com/h7ndt5p.

The newspaper explores questions surrounding federal arts funding, such as whether such funding wastes money and whether arts agencies are too liberal.

Kaine, Tim, and Drue Kataoka, "Tim Kaine: People like Condi Rice and Albert Einstein Show Why We Need the Arts," *Time*, July 7, 2017, https://tinyurl.com/y9nokqdc.

A Democratic senator from Virginia and visual artist Kataoka argue in favor of federal arts funding, saying the arts benefit the United States.

State and Local Cutbacks

Clark, Kristen M., and Kyra Gurney, "After outcry, lawmakers scrap plans to fully slash grant aid to 'Moonlight' alumni's school," *The Miami Herald*, April 29, 2017, https://tinyurl.com/yauglvf4.

Florida state legislators reversed a decision to eliminate a state grant for the New World Schools of the Arts in Miami.

Einhorn, Erin, "No music, art in many Detroit schools: 'A tragic situation' to be addressed," *Detroit Free Press*, July 4, 2017, https://tinyurl.com/y9bmaext.

More than half of Detroit's public schools offer no music or arts classes because most arts programs were eliminated in 2009 by state-appointed emergency managers, but a new school board has allocated $500,000 to hire 15 arts teachers.

Supporting the Arts

Boccella, Kathy, "Schools mixing art and science to create STEAM," philly.com, July 2, 2017, https://tinyurl.com/ycsfjctc.

Public, private and charter schools in Philadelphia are integrating components of the STEAM education movement into their classrooms and curricula, which blends the arts into science, technology, engineering and math education.

Diehl, Phil, "Oceanside looks for ways to boost arts spending," *The San Diego Union-Tribune*, July 1, 2017, https://tinyurl.com/y9lo8cg5.

The City Council and Arts Commission of Oceanside, Calif., near San Diego, recently began a series of community meetings and studies to devise an arts master plan for the city over the next year.

Murphy, T. Michelle, "Supporting and Mentoring the Next Generation of Musicians and Performers with Mentor-Linc," *Playbill*, June 29, 2017, https://tinyurl.com/yaxssr8q.

Lincoln Center Education has begun Mentor-Linc, a program to support high school students who have graduated from the Middle Schools Arts Audition Boot Camp, launched by the New York City department of education in 2014.

CITING *CQ RESEARCHER*

Sample formats for citing these reports in a bibliography include the ones listed below. Preferred styles and formats vary, so please check with your instructor or professor.

MLA STYLE

Mantel, Barbara. "Coal Industry's Future." CQ Researcher 17 June 2016: 529-552.

APA STYLE

Mantel, B. (2016, June 17). Coal Industry's Future. *CQ Researcher*, 6, 529-552.

CHICAGO STYLE

Mantel, Barbara. "Coal Industry's Future." *CQ Researcher*, June 17, 2016, 529-52.

In-depth Reports on Issues in the News

Are you writing a paper?

Need backup for a debate?

Want to become an expert on an issue?

For 90 years, students have turned to *CQ Researcher* for in-depth reporting on issues in the news. Reports on a full range of political and social issues are now available. Following is a selection of recent reports:

Civil Liberties
Privacy and the Internet, 12/15
Intelligence Reform, 5/15
Religion and Law, 11/14

Crime/Law
High-Tech Policing, 4/17
Forensic Science Controversies, 2/17
Jailing Debtors, 9/16
Decriminalizing Prostitution, 4/16
Restorative Justice, 2/16
The Dark Web, 1/16
Immigrant Detention, 10/15

Education
Charter Schools, 3/17
Civic Education, 2/17
Student Debt, 11/16
Apprenticeships, 10/16

Environment/Society
Hunger in America, 7/17
Future of the Christian Right, 6/17
Trust in Media, 6/17
Anti-Semitism, 5/17
Native American Sovereignty, 5/17
Women in Prison, 3/17

Health/Safety
Food Labeling, 6/17
Sports and Sexual Assault, 4/17
Reducing Traffic Deaths, 2/17
Opioid Crisis, 10/16
Mosquito-Borne Disease, 7/16

Politics/Economy
North Korea Showdown, 5/17
Rethinking Foreign Aid, 4/17
Troubled Brazil, 4/17
Reviving Rural Economies, 3/17
Immigrants and the Economy, 2/17

Upcoming Reports

Medical Marijuana, 7/21/17   Muslims in America, 7/28/17   Space Race, 8/4/17

ACCESS

CQ Researcher is available in print and online. For access, visit your library or www.cqresearcher.com.

STAY CURRENT

For notice of upcoming *CQ Researcher* reports or to learn more about *CQ Researcher* products, subscribe to the free email newsletters, *CQ Researcher Alert!* and *CQ Researcher News*: http://cqpress.com/newsletters.

PURCHASE

To purchase a *CQ Researcher* report in print or electronic format (PDF), visit www.cqpress.com or call 866-427-7737. Single reports start at $15. Bulk purchase discounts and electronic-rights licensing are also available.

SUBSCRIBE

Annual full-service *CQ Researcher* subscriptions—including 44 reports a year, monthly index updates, and a bound volume—start at $1,131. Add $25 for domestic postage.

CQ Researcher Online offers a backfile from 1991 and a number of tools to simplify research. For pricing information, call 800-818-7243 or 805-499-9774 or email librarysales@sagepub.com.

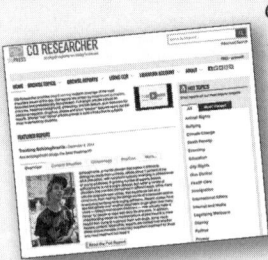

CQ RESEARCHER

CQ PRESS

In-depth reports on today's issues

Published by CQ Press, an Imprint of SAGE Publications, Inc.   **www.cqresearcher.com**

Medical Marijuana

Does cannabis offer health benefits?

A mericans overwhelmingly approve of medical marijuana, and 29 states and the District of Columbia have legalized it, allowing doctors to recommend marijuana products to registered patients. Research shows some forms of marijuana, including a synthetic drug, help treat a few conditions, including chronic pain and chemotherapy-induced nausea. But solid research is limited for other forms, such as smoked or vaped marijuana, and for conditions such as post-traumatic stress disorder, for which states have approved marijuana use. Nevertheless, medical marijuana advocates want all states to legalize it, while opponents say only the Food and Drug Administration should approve drugs for medical use. Yet, federal rules make the studies the FDA relies on difficult to undertake. Complicating the situation are Trump administration efforts to end Obama-era policies curtailing prosecution of medical marijuana in states where it is allowed. Caught in the middle are doctors, who worry they can land in legal trouble if they discuss marijuana with patients, and patients, who must rely on advice from cannabis dispensaries.

A conventiongoer visits a booth at the fourth annual Cannabis World Congress and Business Exposition in New York City on June 16, 2017. The trade show attracts growers, dispensaries, doctors and others involved in the use of legal recreational and medical marijuana. Medical marijuana's effectiveness remains hotly debated.

CQ Researcher • July 21, 2017 • www.cqresearcher.com
Volume 27, Number 26 • Pages 605-628

I N S I D E **THIS REPORT**

THE ISSUES **607**

BACKGROUND **613**

CHRONOLOGY **615**

CURRENT SITUATION **620**

AT ISSUE......................**621**

OUTLOOK **623**

BIBLIOGRAPHY **626**

THE NEXT STEP **627**

MEDICAL MARIJUANA

THE ISSUES

607
- Does marijuana provide clear-cut medical benefits?
- Do state medical marijuana laws lead to increased cannabis use or abuse?
- Should patients rely on dispensary staff to recommend marijuana products and strains?

BACKGROUND

613 **Early Medicinal Use**
Marijuana spread from Asia to Europe.

614 **Public Opinion Sours**
Marijuana's popularity waned in the early 1900s.

614 **War on Drugs**
Cannabis was classified as a dangerous drug in 1970.

620 **Changing Federal Posture**
The Obama administration scaled back medical marijuana prosecutions.

CURRENT SITUATION

620 **Action in Congress**
A bill would let states set their own medical marijuana policies.

622 **State Actions**
States are expanding the medical conditions covered under their cannabis laws.

623 **Not in My Backyard**
Municipalities are restricting cannabis dispensaries.

OUTLOOK

623 **Strong Growth Predicted**
Use of medical marijuana is expected to increase.

SIDEBARS AND GRAPHICS

608 **Medical Marijuana Legal in Majority of States**
Patients have access to it in 29 states and the District of Columbia.

609 **Support for Medical Use Strong Nationwide**
More than 90 percent of Americans back medical marijuana.

612 **Medical Marijuana Sales Expected to Soar**
Sales are projected to reach $13.2 billion by 2025.

615 **Chronology**
Key events since 1842.

616 **Bureaucratic Hurdles Slow Marijuana Research**
"We have major delays in getting done what we need to get done."

618 **Medical Marijuana Laws Perplex Employers**
Companies are struggling to reconcile state, federal laws over use of the drug.

621 **At Issue:**
Should the U.S. reclassify cannabis from a Schedule I drug?

FOR FURTHER RESEARCH

625 **For More Information**
Organizations to contact.

626 **Bibliography**
Selected sources used.

627 **The Next Step**
Additional articles.

627 **Citing CQ Researcher**
Sample bibliography formats.

CQ RESEARCHER

July 21, 2017
Volume 27, Number 26

EXECUTIVE EDITOR: Thomas J. Billitteri
tjb@sagepub.com

ASSISTANT MANAGING EDITORS: Kenneth Fireman, kenneth.fireman@sagepub.com, Kathy Koch, kathy.koch@sagepub.com, Scott Rohrer, scott.rohrer@sagepub.com

ASSOCIATE MANAGING EDITOR: Val Ellicott

SENIOR CONTRIBUTING EDITOR:
Thomas J. Colin
tom.colin@sagepub.com

CONTRIBUTING WRITERS: Marcia Clemmitt, Sarah Glazer, Reed Karaim, Barbara Mantel, Chuck McCutcheon, Tom Price

SENIOR PROJECT EDITOR: Olu B. Davis

EDITORIAL ASSISTANT: Natalia Gurevich

INTERN: Robert DePaolo

FACT CHECKERS: Eva P. Dasher, Michelle Harris, Betsy Towner Levine, Robin Palmer

SAGE Publishing | **CQPRESS**

Los Angeles | London | New Delhi
Singapore | Washington DC | Melbourne

An Imprint of SAGE Publications, Inc.

SENIOR VICE PRESIDENT,
GLOBAL LEARNING RESOURCES:
Karen Phillips

EXECUTIVE DIRECTOR, ONLINE LIBRARY AND
REFERENCE PUBLISHING:
Todd Baldwin

CQ Researcher (ISSN 1056-2036) is printed on acid-free paper. Published weekly, except: (March wk. 4) (May wk. 4) (July wks. 1, 2) (Aug. wks. 2, 3) (Nov. wk. 4) and (Dec. wks. 3, 4). Published by SAGE Publications, Inc., 2455 Teller Rd., Thousand Oaks, CA 91320. Annual full-service subscriptions start at $1,131. For pricing, call 1-800-818-7243. To purchase a *CQ Researcher* report in print or electronic format (PDF), visit www.cqpress. com or call 866-427-7737. Single reports start at $15. Bulk purchase discounts and electronic-rights licensing are also available. Periodicals postage paid at Thousand Oaks, California, and at additional mailing offices. POSTMASTER: Send address changes to *CQ Researcher*, 2600 Virginia Ave., N.W., Suite 600, Washington, DC 20037.

Cover: Getty Images/Spencer Platt

Medical Marijuana

BY BARBARA MANTEL

THE ISSUES

In May 2016, soon after Elizabeth Crewe was diagnosed with cancer in both breasts, she underwent two lumpectomies. But just as her follow-up radiation treatments were winding down, she found her anxiety levels were rising.

"Any time you're facing cancer, you're staring at your own death," says Crewe, 53, who lives in La Grange, Ill., with her husband and three teenagers.

Between anxiety, insomnia and chronic ankle pain from an old injury, Crewe decided she needed help coping. But she is allergic to opioid-based painkillers and wanted to avoid an anti-anxiety drug she would have to take daily.

So in February, Crewe turned to marijuana. *

Now she applies a topical cream to her aching ankle and vapes marijuana when her anxiety is high and before bed when she can't sleep. "It just brings me down a notch," Crewe says. "If I'm not feeling particularly on edge, I don't use it. Whereas, if I had gotten a prescription for anti-anxiety medicine, I'd be on that all the time."

Illinois and 28 other states, along with the District of Columbia, have legalized medical marijuana over the past 21 years, most in the last eight years. Fifteen other states allow only a marijuana extract composed mostly of cannabidiol, a compound that shows

Meredith Bower checks out a cannabis sample at the Takoma Wellness Center, a medical marijuana dispensary in Washington, D.C. Bower lost a leg below the knee after a car accident and treats her phantom limb pain with cannabis. Medical marijuana is legal in 29 states and the District of Columbia.

Getty Images/CQ Roll Call/Tom Williams

promise in treating severe epilepsy and does not produce a high. (*See graphic, p. 608.*) Since 2012, eight states and the District of Columbia have made adult recreational marijuana use legal. [1]

These laws reflect, and possibly affect, the growing acceptance in the United States of the use of marijuana for both recreational and medical purposes. An April poll by Quinnipiac University found that 94 percent of American voters support "allowing adults to legally use marijuana for medical purposes" if their doctor recommends it, the highest level of support to date in national Quinnipiac polls. Sixty percent favored legalizing recreational marijuana, also a record. [2]

Each state law allowing doctors to "recommend" — but not "prescribe"

— marijuana is unique. For example, California allows physicians to recommend cannabis to registered medical marijuana patients as they see fit, but most states have a list of qualifying conditions. For example, Nevada currently allows physicians to recommend marijuana to treat symptoms for nine conditions, including AIDS, cancer and severe pain, while Washington state allows using it to treat 12 conditions, including seizures, Crohn's disease and Hepatitis C. A few states, such as Florida and New York, allow only smoke-free forms of marijuana, such as capsules, liquids and oils. [3]

Yet rigorous research into the potential health benefits of marijuana and its various forms lags behind these evolving mores and laws, in large part because scientists find it so daunting to get government approval — and the marijuana — needed to conduct studies. (*See sidebar, p. 616.*) The lack of a broad base of high quality scientific data means it has been difficult to settle the long-running debate about marijuana's therapeutic value. Meanwhile, many states have stepped in and approved medical marijuana rather than wait for action by the U.S. Food and Drug Administration (FDA), which relies on such research studies when approving drugs.

"We want safe, reliable access for people who are using marijuana for medical purposes," says Morgan Fox, communications manager at the Marijuana Policy Project, an advocacy group in Washington that wants every state to adopt a medical marijuana program and for recreational marijuana to be regulated like alcohol. "The FDA has just been far too slow to act. And

---

* Marijuana and cannabis are often used interchangeably to refer to dried or concentrated material from the cannabis plant that can be delivered through smoking or vaping, liquid tinctures, edibles, capsules, dermal patches, oral sprays or topical creams.

Medical Marijuana Legal in Most States

Twenty-nine states and the District of Columbia have legalized medical marijuana, while 15 other states only allow the medical use of a marijuana extract composed largely of cannabidiol, a compound that shows promise in treating severe epilepsy. California in 1996 became the first state to allow medical marijuana.

States Where Medical Marijuana and Cannabidiol Are Legal

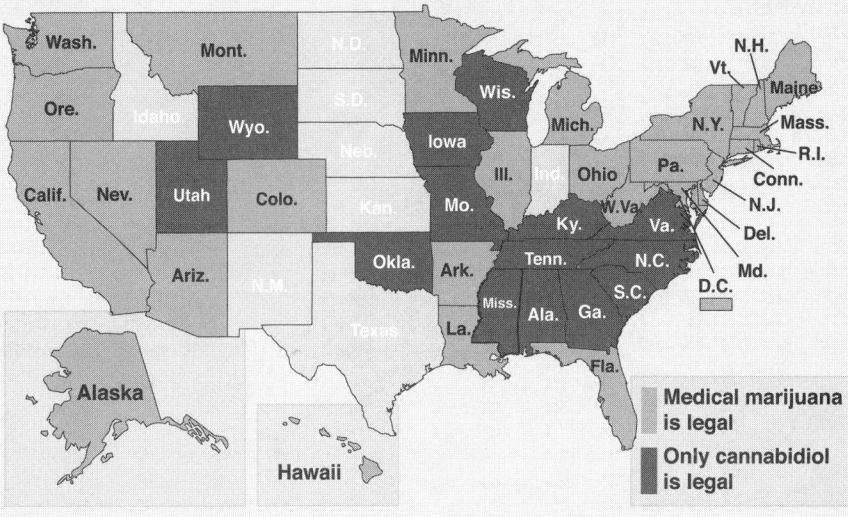

Medical marijuana is legal

Only cannabidiol is legal

Source: "United States," National Organization for the Reform of Marijuana Laws, http://tinyurl.com/yasqlhst

there's no reason for us to wait around for the FDA when we can have a viable alternative in bringing this medicine to patients."

But critics say states are jumping the gun by approving medical marijuana. States are "taking a very well defined and accomplished system that we've used for years to protect Americans from quackery and throwing it out" and replacing it with an approval process conducted by unqualified politicians rather than scientists, says Rhode Island physician Stuart Gitlow, a past president of the American Society of Addiction Medicine. The Rockville, Md.-based group of more than 4,600 physicians, clinicians and associated professionals opposes state laws legalizing medical marijuana.

Because of incomplete state record-keeping, no one knows the number of legal medical marijuana users. But based on available state data, the Mari-

juana Policy Project estimated more than 2.3 million users in 2016.[4] Although the group did not break down that figure by age, the numbers skewed older in at least three states.

In Montana, the 51-to-60-year-old age bracket had the most registered medical marijuana users when compared with other 10-year age brackets. The same was true in New Hampshire. In Oregon, 60-to-69-year-olds outnumbered all other age groups. In all three states, as in most others, severe pain was the most-cited reason users turned to marijuana.[5]

"I would be in a lot worse shape if I wasn't using cannabis, both physically and mentally," said Anita Mataraso, 72, who takes marijuana daily for arthritis and nerve pain and manages a medical marijuana club at her retirement community in San Francisco.[6]

Overall sales of legal medical marijuana totaled $4.7 billion last year, according to New Frontier Data, a market

research firm in San Francisco. An increasing share of those sales is from edibles and from concentrates that can be swallowed, vaped or placed under the tongue. Demand for traditional dried marijuana, which can be smoked, vaped or baked into edibles, fell from 87 percent of sales to 65 percent in 2016.[7]

Meanwhile, state medical marijuana laws and federal law on marijuana clash. The 1970 Controlled Substances Act prohibits the cultivation, processing, distribution and use of marijuana, which the Drug Enforcement Administration (DEA) classifies under the law as a Schedule I substance, a category reserved for drugs such as heroin and LSD that are considered highly addictive with no acceptable medical use. Physicians cannot legally prescribe it.

The Trump administration is signaling that it wants to enforce the federal law and get tougher on medical marijuana businesses, a change in policy from the administration of President Barack Obama.

Under Obama, the Justice Department advised federal prosecutors to conserve their resources and stop prosecuting medical marijuana patients and businesses as long as they were in compliance with state medical marijuana laws. And in 2014, Congress cut off funding for Justice Department medical marijuana investigations in states where it was legal.

But in May, Attorney General Jeff Sessions asked congressional leaders to restore funding for investigations. Sessions called marijuana a harmful drug ripe for abuse with no accepted medical value and state medical marijuana programs a cloak for criminal enterprises.

"In particular, Cuban, Asian, Caucasian and Eurasian criminal organizations have established marijuana operations in state-approved marijuana markets," Sessions said.[8]

But Alex Kreit, a professor at Thomas Jefferson School of Law in San Diego and a leading expert on drug laws, says

Sessions will face political blowback from his own party if federal prosecutors start getting tough. "Among the states that have legalized marijuana for adult use," he says, several have "Republican governors or senators who have been, by and large, pretty united in saying that if the federal government cracks down, they're going to be pretty vocal in calling out the Trump administration."

As the debate about medical marijuana continues, here are some of the questions that physicians, patients, medical marijuana advocates and opponents are asking:

Does marijuana provide clear-cut medical benefits?

The perception is growing among Americans that marijuana has an array of proven health benefits. But marijuana's advocates and detractors have been arguing this point for decades, and the debate shows no signs of resolution.

"There is a mountain of scientific evidence that demonstrates marijuana is a safe and effective medicine for people suffering from a variety of debilitating medical conditions," according to the Marijuana Policy Project. [9]

"The reality is that for a whole host of conditions that advocates claim marijuana helps, there is no evidence," says Kevin Sabet, president of Smart Approaches to Marijuana (SAM), a group in Alexandria, Va., that opposes the legalization of either medical or recreational marijuana.

The marijuana plant contains approximately 100 molecules called cannabinoids, which bind to receptors throughout the human body. These receptors, plus the cannabinoids produced by the human body itself, are known collectively as the endocannabinoid system, which is believed to help regulate gastrointestinal and cardiovascular activity, pain perception, hormone regulation, immune function and more. [10]

Cannibidiol (CBD) is a cannabinoid, and so is Delta-9-tetrahydrocannabinol,

Support for Medical Use Strong Nationwide

A record 94 percent of American voters back the legalization of medical marijuana, including 90 percent of Republicans and 96 percent of Democrats, according to a 2017 Quinnipiac University poll. Support exceeds 90 percent among all age segments of the adult population.

Percentage Who Support or Oppose Medical Marijuana if a Doctor Says a Patient Needs It

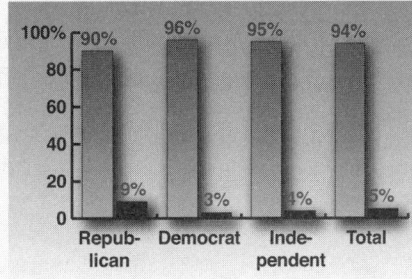
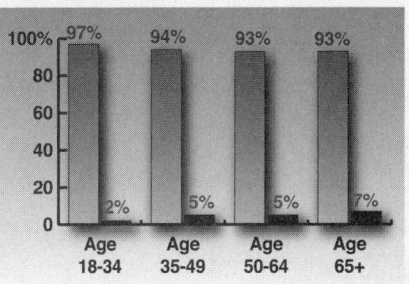

Source: "U.S. Voter Support For Marijuana Hits New High," Quinnipiac University Poll, April 20, 2017, http://tinyurl.com/y93bnkhc

■ Support
■ Oppose

or THC, which is largely responsible for marijuana's mind-altering affects. Their concentrations can vary based upon the marijuana strain and how plants are cultivated.

But experts say not enough high-quality studies exist exploring marijuana's impact on the body to put the debate about marijuana's health benefits to rest.

"[Research] has been limited in the United States, leaving patients, health care professionals, and policy makers without the evidence they need to make sound decisions regarding the use of cannabis and cannabinoids," a committee of the independent National Academies of Sciences, Engineering, and Medicine said in a January report. [11]

The amount of research on the health impact of cannabis and cannabinoids has been growing steadily over the past decade, with thousands of papers published in the United States and elsewhere. But most of them have been based on animal experiments or are not randomized control trials, which scientists consider the gold standard for medical research. The Na-

tional Academies committee combed through the papers, winnowing them by relevance and quality until it had a list of just under 300. [12] Its report assessed that evidence and inched the debate forward.

The committee found conclusive or substantial evidence that cannabis or cannabinoids are effective in treating chronic pain, muscle spasticity in multiple sclerosis sufferers and chemotherapy-induced nausea and vomiting. And it found moderate evidence that cannabis or cannabinoids are effective in treating some forms of insomnia.

But the committee found only limited or no evidence of their effectiveness for treating the symptoms of post-traumatic stress disorder (PTSD), anxiety, irritable bowel syndrome, epilepsy or other conditions for which some states have approved marijuana. (In May, too late for inclusion in the committee's report, American and British researchers published the results of a randomized, controlled trial of Epidiolex, a pharmaceutical-grade cannabidiol extract not yet approved for use, that showed it reduced seizure frequency in children with intractable epilepsy far better than a placebo.) [13]

Jahan Marcu, chief scientific officer at Americans for Safe Access, which advocates for the acceptance of cannabis as medicine, says the committee left out basic animal research, much of it positive. "I know we're not rats and mice," says Marcu, "but all mammals share this endocannabinoid system, and its mechanistic activities have been studied in great detail."

Fox of the Marijuana Policy Project says the committee's report did not consider patients' success stories. "It does leave out a lot of the anecdotal evidence that we've been able to gather from the medical marijuana states that have changed their laws so far," says Fox.

But Deepak D'Souza, a psychiatry professor at the Yale University School of Medicine who does not believe states should decide what substances constitute a medicine, says the National Academies committee was right to be so selective. "Imagine if pharmaceutical companies produced drugs based on anecdotal reports. There would be mayhem," he says. "The FDA process is in place because, for the most part, it has served the public well."

In addition, the majority of studies on the National Academies committee's final list did not involve smoked or vaped whole-plant marijuana, but instead, looked at prescription drugs. One is FDA-approved dronabinol, a synthetic THC that has been available as a capsule since 1985 under the brand name Marinol to treat chemotherapy-induced nausea and vomiting and appetite loss in people with AIDS. Another is nabiximols, a whole-plant marijuana extract with a consistent ratio of THC and cannabidiol. It is widely available as a prescription mouth spray called

Sativex in Europe and Canada to treat spasticity in multiple sclerosis and cancer pain. It is undergoing clinical trials in the United States and is not yet FDA-approved. *

"People are using marijuana in forms for which the research doesn't support it," says Sean Hennessy, a committee member and a professor of epidemiology and pharmacology at the University of Pennsylvania's Perelman School of Medicine. However, that doesn't mean those forms are not effective, but rather that they haven't been sufficiently studied, he says.

Nearly everyone on all sides of the debate agrees that more research is needed, but they differ markedly about what should be available to patients now.

"My dear hope is that there are dozens of marijuana-based medications that find their way to market," Sabet says. "I just want them to find their way to market like every other medicine does, and that is through the FDA."

But Fox says whole-plant marijuana, whether as dried flowers, edibles, oils and other forms, should be available to the public through dispensaries with a doctor's recommendation because they are less expensive than prescriptions, and many patients find they work better.

"Many of the compounds in marijuana work together in what's called the 'entourage effect,' but [the three] FDA-approved cannabinoid drugs are one compound in isolation," says Fox.

Fox, Marcu and other proponents of medical marijuana point out that other drugs used to treat pain are more dangerous than cannabis. "More people die from Tylenol every year than have ever died from marijuana," says Fox.

Marijuana is not entirely benign, however. "There are certainly populations for whom smoking or ingesting marijuana is not a good idea," says Hennessy. The committee found that smoking marijuana in pregnancy is linked to low birth weight in babies and smoking it can lead to frequent chronic bronchitis. And for adolescents, "early cannabis use increases the like-

lihood of problematic cannabis use later in life," says Hennessy.

In addition, "cannabis is likely to increase the risk of developing schizophrenia and other psychoses; the higher the use, the greater the risk," the committee said. [14]

Do state medical marijuana laws lead to increased cannabis use or abuse?

As more states have begun to legalize medical marijuana, skeptics worry that the drug's increased availability will send a message to teens and adults alike that cannabis is acceptable, causing increased recreational usage. But researchers say that has not been the case among teenagers, while for adults the evidence is mixed.

Most studies on the impact of medical marijuana laws on teens have concluded that the passage and enactment of state laws have not led to "increased use of marijuana by young people or increased access to marijuana by young people," says Paul Armentano, deputy director of the National Organization for the Reform of Marijuana Laws (NORML), a Washington group that has advocated for the legalization of adult marijuana use since the group was formed in 1970.

Deborah Hasin, a professor of epidemiology at Columbia University Medical Center in New York, and several colleagues conducted the largest study confirming this result. [15] Relying on survey data on more than 1 million students between 1991 and 2014, the researchers looked at teens' marijuana use in the past month, the past year and their frequency of use. They considered whether states allowed dispensaries, and they accounted for lags in implementation of the laws. Each time the result was the same, says Hasin: Teens' use of marijuana did not increase after passage of a state medical marijuana law.

But Rosalie Pacula, one of Hasin's co-authors and the co-director of the Drug Policy Research Center at the

---

* The FDA has approved three single-cannabinoid synthetic drugs. They are the capsule Marinol and liquid Syndros, brand names for dronabinol; and Cesamet, the brand name for nabilone, a synthetic compound that mimics THC and is also prescribed for chemotherapy-induced nausea and vomiting.

RAND Corp., a think tank in Santa Monica, Calif., added a caveat. The number of marijuana dispensaries can influence teens' attitudes. A study in Colorado before and after 2009, when the U.S Justice Department advised federal attorneys to halt prosecution of medical marijuana patients, found that as dispensaries subsequently proliferated teenagers' perceived risk of marijuana dropped and their abuse of marijuana increased, compared with teens in states without medical marijuana laws. [16]

"We know from alcohol, higher density [of retail outlets] is associated with higher use, even among kids. We know this for tobacco as well," says Pacula. "It's not at all surprising that preliminary studies are suggesting the same thing for marijuana." The implication for states considering legalizing medical marijuana is that making medical marijuana available to patients, in and of itself, is not harmful to youths, but how a state implements the law can have an impact, she says.

The research on adults' illicit use or abuse of marijuana is more mixed. Several studies show no impact when a state implements a medical marijuana law, while a few others, including a new study by Hasin, have found an increase in use. The study Hasin conducted with colleagues looked at three surveys conducted between 1991, when no state had yet legalized medical marijuana, and 2013, when about 25 percent of states had these laws. [17]

"Overall, states that passed these laws had greater increased use of cannabis and of cannabis-use disorders than other states," Hasin says. However, she says, the reasons are speculative. The laws might be promoting the idea that marijuana use is safe or acceptable, or it could be that some growers or dispensaries are diverting medical marijuana to the illicit market, she says.

But Armentano was critical of the adult study and the dataset Hasin chose to use, which varied from the one used in many other studies.

"Her papers have been outliers on this issue for the last few years," says Armentano.

Hasin counters that another group of university researchers came to the same conclusion using the dataset that Armentano prefers. [18]

Marijuana advocates also say doctors are over-diagnosing "marijuana use disorder." According to the National Institute on Drug Abuse (NIDA), which conducts research on drug use, those

Teri Robnett inhales cannabis with a vape pen to deal with fibromyalgia, a chronic pain condition; her husband, left, grinds marijuana. An April poll by Quinnipiac University found that 94 percent of American voters support "allowing adults to legally use marijuana for medical purposes" if their doctor recommends it.

who become dependent on marijuana often report suffering from irritability, mood swings, sleep difficulties, cravings and other physical discomfort within the first week of trying to stop using it. In more extreme cases, NIDA says, marijuana use disorder can become addiction if a person cannot stop using marijuana even when it interferes with quality of life. Studies suggest that 9 percent of people who use marijuana will become dependent, rising to about 17 percent of those who started using the substance as teenagers. [19]

"Marijuana is an objectively less harmful substance than alcohol, and the scientific community generally agrees that marijuana is less addictive than alcohol and other drugs," Mason Tvert, communications director for the Marijuana Policy Project, said in an email. "Unfortunately, the [psychiatric profession] and our government consider even non-problematic marijuana use to be a 'disorder,' whereas they acknowledge that adults can frequently

consume alcohol without it being considered a disorder."

Meanwhile, two studies have shown lower spending on prescription drugs by Medicaid and Medicare patients in states that have legalized medical marijuana. [20] A few studies also have shown a beneficial impact on the overuse of prescription painkillers known as opioids. "We see lower use of opioids overall, fewer reported incidences of opioid abuse, fewer instances of opioid-related hospitalizations . . . and most importantly, we see a reduction in

Getty Images/*The Denver Post*/Andy Cross

Medical Marijuana Sales Expected to Soar

The U.S. market for legal cannabis is projected to more than triple between 2016 and 2025, with medical marijuana sales jumping from $4.7 billion to $13.2 billion during that period. In 2016, medical marijuana sales accounted for 71 percent of the cannabis market, but that share is expected to decline to 55 percent as the number of recreational users grows.

U.S. Legal Cannabis Market, 2016 and 2025

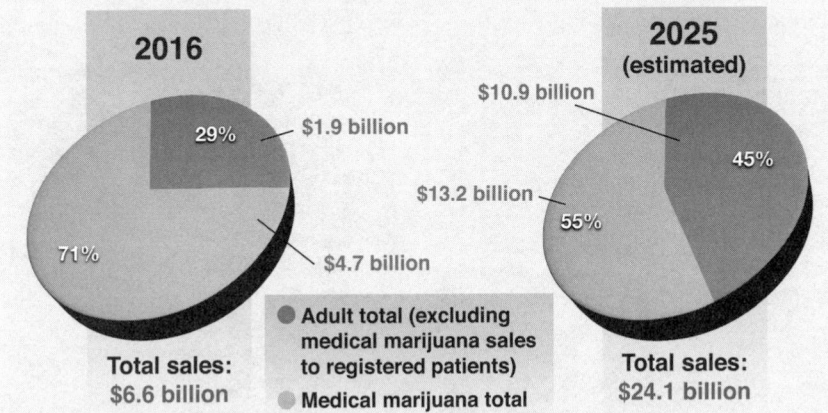

2016

29% $1.9 billion
71% $4.7 billion

Total sales: $6.6 billion

● Adult total (excluding medical marijuana sales to registered patients)
● Medical marijuana total

2025 (estimated)

$10.9 billion 45%
$13.2 billion 55%

Total sales: $24.1 billion

Source: "The Cannabis Industry Annual Report, 2017 Legal Marijuana Outlook Executive Summary," New Frontier Data, 2017, http://tinyurl.com/ybsszfrw

opioid-related mortality," says Armentano.

Pacula says researchers don't know the mechanism behind that mortality drop. People could be switching to marijuana to treat chronic pain instead of using opioids at fatal dosages. In that case, the implication for a state with a serious opioid problem might be to "medicalize marijuana quickly," says Pacula.

However, it may be that people are substituting marijuana for the sedative benzodiazepine, which is commonly misused when taken with opioids. "The likelihood of an opioid fatality when opioids are taken with marijuana is substantially less than when opioids are used with benzodiazepine," says Pacula.

That's good news, she says, but opioid use has not dropped. In this scenario, rather than make medical marijuana available, states might be better off handing out nalaxone, a medication used to block the effects of opioids, especially in overdoses, Pacula says.

Should patients rely on dispensary staff to recommend marijuana products and strains?

Beth Collins' 17-year-old daughter has epilepsy. Several years ago, Collins wanted her to try cannabis to reduce the frequency of her seizures, but it would have been illegal in her home state of Virginia. So in December 2013, she and her daughter relocated to Colorado. However, their doctor's advice was severely circumscribed.

"We had a neurologist who signed her recommendation form but then would not talk with us again about it. He said he couldn't," says Collins, who, after her daughter's illness, became senior director of government relations and external affairs for Americans for Safe Access. Doctors worry that discussions about marijuana strains and the dosing of THC and CBD cannabinoids may seem too close to prescribing, which is illegal under federal law, she says. So with the help of other parents on social media

Collins figured out what product to try.

In 2015, Collins returned to Virginia after the state passed a law allowing the use of certain cannabis extracts to treat severe, debilitating epileptic conditions. But her daughter's Virginia doctor is not allowed to discuss cannabis with them. "The children's hospital has told her not to," says Collins. "She'll refer to it as 'the other treatment.' " Collins says her daughter is now off all epilepsy prescription drugs and has not had a grand mal seizure in years.

Collins' experience with doctors is not unusual for medical marijuana patients, she says. And fear of violating federal law is not the only reason physicians and hospitals are reluctant to have detailed discussions about marijuana. Clear dosing guidelines do not exist. Unlike for FDA-approved drugs, the *Physician's Desk Reference*, the textbook on prescribing information, says nothing about cannabis indications or dosage.

The lack of a standard dosing schedule for cannabis is due to several factors, according to The Answer Page, a Foxboro, Mass., company that provides online continuing education classes to physicians. They include the significant variation in active ingredients of medical cannabis products; the limited cannabis research in humans; the wide variety of cannabis dosages and products used in human studies; the differences in cannabinoid metabolism among patients; and the fact that patients develop tolerance to cannabis over time. [21]

As a result, patients are often on their own, experimenting with different cannabis strains, products and ratios of THC and CBD.

Many turn to dispensary staff for help figuring out which marijuana strains and products to try and how often to consume them. But while most states that allow medical marijuana require dispensary staff to receive some training, it is unclear how often it goes beyond storage and handling requirements and into medical and scientific knowledge.

A survey of dispensary staff in eight states and the District of Columbia published last year in the peer-reviewed journal *Cannabis and Cannabinoid Research* found that only 20 percent of respondents reported having medical or scientific training. Yet 94 percent said they provided cannabis advice to patients. In addition, the study found that some staff were recommending cannabis strains and cannabinoid concentrations that have "either not been shown effective for, or could exacerbate, a patient's condition." [22]

Washington state has one of the strictest training requirements. Jackson Holder, 27, a buyer for Dockside Cannabis in the Seattle metro area and is certified by the state Department of Health as a medical marijuana consultant. Marijuana consultants are the only dispensary staff approved to discuss medical marijuana with customers holding state-issued medical cannabis patient cards. To be certified, one must be 21 or older, complete a health department-approved 20-hour training program and complete CPR training.

"Medical marijuana consultants are not medical professionals or doctors, and they cannot make any statements to a patient about curative properties or claims about treatment potential," says Holder. "Their role, legally, is to route patients to the appropriate products for their given condition."

Dispensary managers must impress on staff that their advice to patients "should not be considered medical advice but rather their opinion based on their knowledge of the product and anecdotal evidence from their customers," says Morgan Fox of the Marijuana Policy Project. Fox also says all states should have minimum training requirements for dispensary staff, including a knowledge of the products available and their sourcing.

The National Cannabis Industry Association has not taken a position on whether training should be mandatory. But Taylor West, the group's deputy director, says competition between dispensaries might be the best way to

raise staff standards. "What we're seeing in really competitive markets, like Colorado, is that dispensaries are having to provide more training for their employees because it is a significant factor in customers choosing one dispensary over another," says West.

Some experts say patients, perhaps with help from dispensary staff, are capable of deciding dosages themselves.

The amount of THC and CBD is usually labeled on edible products, such as capsules, and so people can know how many milligrams of the cannabinoids they're ingesting, says Richard D. Richins, a staff scientist at New Mexico State University in Las Cruces and co-owner of Rio Grande Analytics, a laboratory that tests cannabis products for purity and contamination by bacteria and toxins.

That's not the case when people smoke or vape marijuana because of variations in how deep a breath they take, their lung volume and how long they hold it, he says. "However, the effect is felt fully within 10 minutes and partially within seconds. So somebody who is using it for anxiety, for example, can take a puff and see how that works for them," says Richins.

Letting patients and dispensary staff decide dosages makes physicians uncomfortable, says Yale's D'Souza. "And when you have a drug that is potentially addictive, one has to worry about how much responsibility one gives to the person who is using it," he says. People could become dependent if they overuse marijuana, says D'Souza. ∎

BACKGROUND

Early Medicinal Use

Chinese Emperor Shen Nung, who lived in the third millennium B.C., is credited with the first scientific investigations of cannabis. He advised

drinking marijuana tea to treat ailments ranging from gout to malaria. [23]

At about the same time, nomadic tribes from Central Asia spread word of marijuana to the Indian subcontinent, and its medicinal use expanded across the Middle East into Europe and along the coasts of sub-Saharan Africa. [24] During the 15th century, African slaves brought marijuana seeds to the Western Hemisphere, where the plant was incorporated into folk medicine to treat maladies such as rheumatism and toothaches. [25]

The French were the first Europeans to experiment with marijuana on a large scale. In the 1830s, psychiatrist Jacques-Joseph Moreau de Tours brought hashish, the compressed resin of the cannabis plant, from Egypt to Paris. He fed a resin-based paste to psychiatric patients and observed a calming effect. Moreau de Tours urged other psychiatrists to treat patients with the substance and introduced hashish to French artists and writers for its mind-altering effects. [26]

Historians credit Irish surgeon William O'Shaughnessy with the widespread introduction of marijuana into Western medicine. As a professor at the Medical College of Calcutta in the 1830s, he observed its use in India. O'Shaughnessy gave an orally administered marijuana solution to patients and reported that it reduced the pain of rheumatism, stilled seizures and eased the muscle spasms of tetanus and rabies. When he returned to England in 1842, O'Shaughnessy provided marijuana to pharmacists, and doctors in Europe and the United States began prescribing tinctures and extracts for a variety of conditions. [27]

Within a few decades, patent medicines containing marijuana were readily available at British and American pharmacies and grocery stores, without prescription. So were hashish pills coated with sugar, which were sold as common painkillers. [28]

From 1840 to 1900, "more than one hundred papers were published in

Western medical literature recommending [marijuana] for various illnesses and discomforts," wrote psychiatrist Lester Grinspoon and attorney James B. Bakalar in *Marihuana: The Forbidden Medicine.* [29] In 1851, cannabis was mentioned for the first time in the *U.S. Pharmacopeia*, which identified and standardized the mostly botanical drugs then in medical use. [30]

"Nevertheless, American doctors were never very excited by cannabis for drug therapy. It had too many short-

jectable opiates such as morphine. In addition, over-the-counter opium-based elixirs, nasal sprays and cough medicines were widely available. [32]

By 1900, according to historians, an estimated 3 percent of the U.S. population was addicted to medicinal opiates, raising public alarm. In response, the Harrison Narcotic Act of 1914 required doctors and pharmacists to record narcotic drug transactions and to pay a stamp tax on them. [33]

successful, and by 1934, 33 states had passed laws that made recreational, but not medical, marijuana illegal. [35]

Anslinger persisted. He spearheaded an anti-marijuana campaign, fabricating "lurid and sensational stories of assault, rape, murder, and mayhem allegedly perpetrated by marijuana smokers," wrote Wendy Chapkis and Richard J. Webb in *Dying to Get High: Marijuana as Medicine.* [36] For example, a 1936 government-commissioned film *Reefer Madness* featured marijuana-smoking high school students going insane and killing their parents.

In 1937, Anslinger persuaded Congress to pass the Marijuana Tax Act, which taxed medical, industrial and recreational use of the plant and its extracts. Anslinger also continued his public campaign to discredit marijuana, and, in 1941, all mention of cannabis was removed from the U.S. Pharmacopeia. In addition, Anslinger systematically blocked marijuana research in the United States for the 30 years he led the bureau. [37]

Getty Images/The Washington Post/Matt McClain

People line up to attend the confirmation hearing for Sen. Jeff Sessions as U.S. attorney general outside the Russell Senate Office Building in Washington on Jan. 10, 2017; he was confirmed, 52-47, in February. In May, Sessions called marijuana a harmful drug ripe for abuse with no accepted medical value and state medical marijuana programs a cloak for criminal enterprises.

comings," wrote psychologist Ernest L. Abel in *Marihuana: The First Twelve Thousand Years.* The potency of its preparations varied from pharmacy to pharmacy, its effect on patients was unpredictable, and it was slow to act because it was taken orally. [31]

Public Opinion Sours

In 1895, British chemists isolated a cannabinoid from the marijuana plant for the first time. But by then, chemists had created synthetic painkillers and sedatives, such as aspirin, chloral hydrate and barbiturates. Marijuana had trouble competing with these standardized drugs, as well as with fast-acting in-

The law excluded marijuana. However, marijuana's image began to shift in the century's first three decades as the number of migrant workers from Mexico grew. The public began to associate smoking marijuana with migrant workers, and marijuana became seen as "an alien drug; the fact that it . . . had been an ingredient of patent medicines for decades was conveniently overlooked," wrote historian Martin Booth in *Cannabis: A History.* [34]

In 1930, Harry Anslinger, the head of the Federal Bureau of Narcotics, proposed including medical and recreational marijuana in the Harrison Act. Pharmaceutical manufactures successfully pushed back. Anti-marijuana legislators on the state level were more

War on Drugs

During the cultural upheavals of the 1960s, recreational use of marijuana skyrocketed. Anxious to learn more about the drug, the National Institutes of Health sponsored the research of Israeli scientist Raphael Mechoulam. In 1965, Mechoulam announced that he had isolated THC, marijuana's principal psychoactive cannabinoid, and he conducted clinical trials that showed THC's promise in treating neuropathic pain, hypertension and other conditions. [38]

In 1970, Republican President Richard M. Nixon successfully pressed for passage of the Controlled Substances Act. The law created five "schedules," or categories, to rank drugs according to their acceptable medical use, safety profile and potential for abuse. Marijuana, along with heroin and LSD, was assigned to Schedule I, the category reserved for the most

Continued on p. 616

Chronology

1840s-1890s
Marijuana is introduced to Western medicine.

1842
Irish surgeon William O'Shaughnessy introduces marijuana to Western medicine.

1851
Cannabis is mentioned for the first time in the *U.S. Pharmacopeia*; patent medicines containing marijuana are readily available in Britain and the U.S.

1895
British chemists isolate a cannabinoid from the marijuana plant.

1900s-1940s
The public turns to opiates and synthetic painkillers.

1900
Three percent of the U.S. population is addicted to medicinal opiates.

1934
Thirty-three states outlaw marijuana except as medicine.

1937
Marijuana prescriptions plunge after the government begins taxing all uses of marijuana.

1941
U.S. Pharmacopeia drops all mention of marijuana.

1960s-1990s
Recreational marijuana use skyrockets.

1965
Israeli scientist Raphael Mechoulam announces isolation of THC, marijuana's principal psychoactive cannabinoid.

1970
Controlled Substances Act creates five schedules, or categories, and Justice Department classifies marijuana in Schedule I, reserved for the most dangerous drugs with no accepted medical use; it cannot be grown, distributed or prescribed.

1972
National Organization for Reform of Marijuana Laws (NORML) petitions the government to reschedule marijuana so doctors can prescribe it.

1985
The government classifies synthetic THC as a Schedule II drug, allowing doctors to prescribe it for chemotherapy-induced nausea and vomiting and AIDS-related appetite loss.

1988
Drug Enforcement Administration (DEA) rejects NORML's petition, and marijuana remains in Schedule I.

1990
National Institute of Mental Health researchers discover the cannabinoid receptor system in the human brain.

1992
After a rise in applications from AIDS patients, the George H.W. Bush administration discontinues a "compassionate use" program that had supplied a small number of seriously ill patients with government-grown marijuana.

1996
California becomes the first state to legalize medical marijuana. . . . U.S. threatens to revoke the licenses of physicians who recommend cannabis.

1999
Institute of Medicine says marijuana might provide relief to patients simultaneously suffering severe pain, nausea and appetite loss.

2000-Present
Medical marijuana becomes more widely accepted.

2005
Supreme Court rules the Controlled Substances Act is constitutional.

2010
Obama administration tells U.S. Attorneys to no longer prosecute seriously ill patients using cannabis if they are in compliance with state medical marijuana laws.

2014
Obama administration makes it easier for banks to do business with medical marijuana dispensaries. . . . Congress blocks the Justice Department from spending money on medical marijuana prosecutions.

2016
DEA again keeps marijuana a Schedule I drug but begins accepting applications for more government-registered growers in order to increase the amount of cannabis available for research.

2017
National Academies of Sciences, Engineering, and Medicine concludes marijuana and cannabinoids are helpful in treating chronic pain, muscle spasms in multiple sclerosis and chemotherapy-induced nausea and vomiting but that evidence is lacking for many others. . . . In April, West Virginia becomes 29th state to legalize medical marijuana.

Bureaucratic Hurdles Slow Marijuana Research

"We have major delays in getting done what we need to get done."

It took Ryan Vandrey, a psychiatry professor at the Johns Hopkins University School of Medicine in Baltimore, 18 months to get regulatory approval to study the health impact of marijuana on 76 people. The problem, he said, is that the federal government considers marijuana a Schedule I drug — a classification that places cannabis alongside heroin and other illegal drugs that are considered highly addictive and of no redeeming medical value.

"Every research protocol we design and want to do has to go through a number of extra regulatory approvals before we can do them," Vandrey told the website Live Science last year. "The consequence of that is, we have major delays in getting done what we need to get done." [1]

A committee of the National Academies of Sciences, Engineering, and Medicine, an independent producer of expert policy reports in Washington, faulted the federal government for making it hard for scientists to study marijuana's potential therapeutic effects. The lack of studies due to the restrictions, the committee said in a report in January, is creating a knowledge gap that is placing public health at risk. [2]

Researchers wishing to study marijuana and its compounds must be specially licensed, and they have to apply to both the Drug Enforcement Administration (DEA) and the Food and Drug Administration (FDA) for approvals.

If the agencies give the green light, researchers must then contact the National Institute of Drug Abuse, a federal agency that studies addiction, for further approval and to place an order for marijuana with the specific concentrations of cannabinoids they wish to study. [3] The institute is the sole supplier of marijuana for government-approved research, which it gets under contract from one sanctioned producer: the University of Mississippi.

In addition, researchers often need to submit their marijuana research proposals for review to state government agencies, a state board of medical examiners and the researchers' home institution.

The National Academies called the entire process "daunting" and said it has discouraged a number of scientists from pursuing cannabis research. [4]

Former President Barack Obama's administration took two steps to lower those hurdles. In 2015, the government no longer required the Public Health Service to approve marijuana research protocols, trimming the number of steps in the review process. And in August 2016, the DEA announced it would explore expanding the number of official producers of research marijuana beyond the University of Mississippi. It is considering 25 applications so far, Melvin Patterson, a DEA spokesman, said in an email.

"This change should provide researchers with a more varied and robust supply of marijuana," Patterson said.

All sides on the marijuana debate applaud the moves but say more can be done. However, they disagree on potential next steps.

"The biggest research barrier is that marijuana is a Schedule I agent," says Sean Hennessy, a member of the National Academies committee and a professor of epidemiology and pharmacology at the University of Pennsylvania Perelman School of Medicine.

But last August, the DEA denied the latest petition to reclassify marijuana, relying on the FDA's assessment that it still belongs in the Schedule I category.

Continued from p. 614

dangerous drugs with no currently accepted medical use. Physicians were forbidden to prescribe them. [39]

The law also created a National Commission on Marihuana and Drug Abuse, and Nixon selected members he hoped would spotlight the drug's dangers. However, after two years of study, the commission concluded that marijuana did not seriously impair health, lead to harder drugs or turn users into criminals. Nixon, who had declared a "war on drugs" in 1971, rejected the commission's conclusions. [40]

By the early 1970s, an increasing number of cancer patients were telling doctors that marijuana was helping with chemotherapy's side effects, and in May 1972, the National Organization for the Reform of Marijuana Laws (NORML), which had been founded two years earlier, petitioned the federal government to reschedule marijuana in order "to make the drug available for medical applications." The government rejected the petition and repeatedly defied court orders to hold public hearings. [41]

In 1985, the FDA approved Marinol, a synthetic form of THC, to treat chemotherapy-induced nausea and vomiting, and later for appetite loss in AIDS patients. The DEA classified it a Schedule II drug. Finally, in the summer of 1986, the agency began the long-delayed public hearings on the rescheduling of marijuana.

After two years of testimony and evidence, DEA Administrative Law Judge Francis J. Young ruled that a sizable minority of physicians approved of marijuana's medical use and recommended that the DEA administrator transfer marijuana to Schedule II. Administrator John Lawn refused and instead created stricter criteria for acceptable medical use of a drug. [42]

States were more responsive to patients' demands for marijuana. Between 1978 and 1983, 34 states enacted laws expressing support of medical marijuana. Six also authorized research programs to dispense marijuana to patients with cancer and other serious conditions. But the programs foundered when the federal government refused to supply marijuana. [43]

Up to this point, scientists did not understand how marijuana worked in people. Then in 1990, researchers at the U.S. National Institute of Mental Health

Jahan Marcu, the chief scientific officer at Americans for Safe Access, a Washington group that advocates for the acceptance of cannabis as medicine, says he hopes the National Academies' January report will finally lead to a reclassification: The committee found either conclusive or substantial evidence that cannabis or cannabinoids can effectively treat chronic pain, muscle spasticity in multiple sclerosis patients and chemotherapy-induced nausea and vomiting.

"The National Academies is saying there is evidence that marijuana has therapeutic value, which is not the definition of a Schedule I drug," says Marcu.

Jeffrey Zinsmeister, director of government relations at Smart Approaches to Marijuana, an Alexandria, Va., group that opposes the legalization of medical and recreational marijuana, disagrees. "There are definitely bureaucratic stumbling blocks to research of both the plant and its compounds," he says. "But to say that you have to reschedule the drug to get appropriate levels of research is incorrect."

Instead, his organization wants to make it easier for researchers to amend a research protocol without having to reapply for government approval; allow researchers to store marijuana in locked cabinets rather than in a bolted safe, as some local DEA offices require; and permit researchers to cultivate their own marijuana for their studies.

"All that can be done without removing the product from Schedule I," says Zinsmeister. "Reclassification is supposed to be done as a consequence of the research, not as something that would come before."

— *Barbara Mantel*

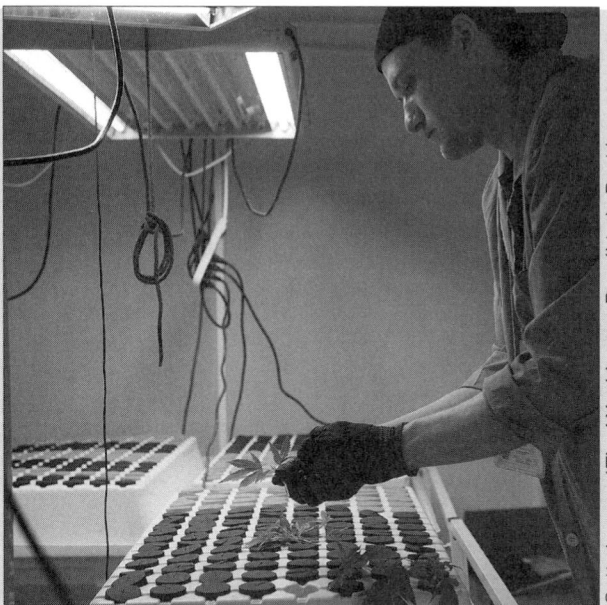

Zachary Lowe clones marijuana plants at Holistic Remedies and Organic Wellness, a licensed medical marijuana growing and processing firm in Washington, D.C., on Sept. 7, 2016.

Getty Images/The Washington Post/Linda Davidson

[1] Rachael Rettner, "New Medical Marijuana Policy Is a Catch-22, Researchers Say," *Live Science*, Aug. 15, 2016, http://tinyurl.com/ybjwtvv6.

[2] "The Health Effects of Cannabis and Cannabinoids: The Current State of Evidence and Recommendations for Research," National Academies of Sciences, Engineering, and Medicine, Jan. 12, 2017, pp. 1, 378, http://tinyurl.com/ya4pzskm.

[3] "NIDA's Role in Providing Marijuana for Research," National Institute on Drug Abuse, revised March 2017, http://tinyurl.com/ya2cfm3v.

[4] "The Health Effects of Cannabis and Cannabinoids: The Current State of Evidence and Recommendations for Research," *op. cit.*, pp. 378, 381.

discovered the cannabinoid receptor system in the human brain. (Later, receptors were discovered throughout the body.) Cannabinoids, such as marijuana's THC, stimulate these receptors. And in 1992, researchers identified an endocannabinoid, produced by the human body. [44]

Since the late 1970s, a small number of patients had been receiving medical marijuana directly from the federal government through the FDA's Compassionate Investigational New Drug Program. In the early 1990s, applications surged as AIDS patients struggling with the debilitating side effects of their prescription drugs turned to the government for help.

The administration of President George H.W. Bush responded in 1992 by terminating the investigational program for marijuana, except for the 13 patients already participating. The Department of Health and Human Services considered "widespread use of marijuana for medical purposes, especially where alternative medications are available . . . bad public policy and bad medical practice." [45]

But the decision "only served to further fuel an explosion of popular interest and political activism," Chapkis and Webb wrote. [46]

In 1996, California voters passed Proposition 215, making California the first state to allow people with a doctor's recommendation to possess and cultivate marijuana for personal use. By using the word "recommend" rather than "prescribe," Proposition 215 made an end run around the Controlled Substance Act, which "said nothing about recommending cannabis for therapeutic use," wrote author Martin A. Lee in *Smoke Signals: A Social History of Marijuana — Medical, Recreational, and Scientific.* [47]

The backlash was immediate. The federal government threatened to revoke the license of any physician who recommended marijuana. A group of California physicians sued "drug czar" Barry McCaffrey and other federal officials for violating their First Amendment right to free speech. Courts issued a temporary and then a permanent injunction against federal interference in physician-patient conversations about marijuana. [48]

Nevertheless, most physicians remained reluctant to recommend marijuana. In addition, the California law did not exempt patients and caregivers from laws against growing marijuana or the sale or transportation of the

Medical Marijuana Laws Perplex Employers

Companies are struggling to reconcile state, federal laws over use of the drug.

Kathryn Russo is an attorney with Jackson Lewis, a nationwide workplace law firm based in White Plains, N.Y. In this interview with CQ Researcher, she explains the complexities of states' medical marijuana laws. In mid-July, a Massachusetts court issued a decision on medical marijuana when Russo was unavailable for a follow-up question on that case; attorney Matthew Nieman of Jackson Lewis answered that question in her stead. The interviews have been edited for space and clarity.

CQR: Currently, 29 states and the District of Columbia have medical marijuana laws. In all of these places, employers can test for marijuana use. But how common is workplace drug testing?

K.R.: It's pretty common. Most employers who conduct drug testing do so for safety reasons. For example, employers in the construction industry and the health care industry.

Have you seen employers stop testing for marijuana in states allowing medical marijuana?

I haven't seen a lot of employers eliminating marijuana from their drug-testing panels.

How long do traces of marijuana linger in the body?

Alcohol is processed through the kidneys and is basically flushed out of your system pretty quickly, within hours, whereas drugs go into the fatty tissues of the body and stay there. That's why you can test positive on a workplace drug test days or even weeks after you use the drugs.

So someone testing positive for marijuana may not necessarily be under the influence or be impaired at work?

That is really the whole controversy, right there. Drug tests can't tell an employer exactly when or where a person used drugs.

How many states offer strong workplace protections for certified medical marijuana users?

There are about 12 states where the medical marijuana law has anti-discrimination language of some type. It will say

something like, "An employer cannot discriminate against a person on the basis that he or she is a qualified medical marijuana patient." The states are Arizona, Arkansas, Connecticut, Delaware, Illinois, Maine, Minnesota, New York, Nevada, Pennsylvania, Rhode Island and West Virginia.

Do these states allow an employee to be fired if he or she is obviously impaired on the job or using marijuana on the premises?

Almost every state with a medical marijuana law has a provision saying that employers don't have to allow people to use marijuana at work or to be under the influence of marijuana at work. So even if you have a medical marijuana user who is protected by these anti-discrimination provisions in certain states, if they are using at work, the employer can fire them. The problem is, what if you are not certain they are using at work but they are acting as if they are under the influence? If you send them for a drug test and the test is positive, we're back to the dilemma of a positive test result that doesn't prove when the person used it.

How many qualified medical marijuana users in any of these 12 states have challenged their firing because of a positive drug test?

The only case is in Rhode Island.

In that case, Darlington Fabrics refused to hire someone for a paid internship because she disclosed she was a certified medical marijuana user and would fail a drug test. She sued, and the state court sided with her.

This is the first employment discrimination case where the court ruled in favor of the medical marijuana user. There had been previous cases in other states — not these 12 states — and employers always won.

What was the court's reasoning?

The court didn't seem to think there was a conflict between federal law, which says marijuana is illegal, and state law. What the court zeroed in on is that Rhode Island state law regulates

drug, according to Lee. California and federal law enforcement officers began arresting growers, dispensary owners and even patients with valid doctor recommendations. [49]

In 1998, citizens of Alaska, Oregon and Washington state voted to legalize medical marijuana. But unlike California, which allowed doctors to recommend

marijuana as they saw fit, these states allowed recommendations only for a small number of medical conditions. [50]

The next year, the National Institute of Medicine, part of the nonprofit National Academy of Sciences, issued a review of the scientific evidence and assessed the potential health benefits and risks of marijuana and its constituent cannabinoids.

The report provided ammunition for both sides of the medical marijuana debate.

"For patients who suffer simultaneously from severe pain, nausea, and appetite loss, such as those with AIDS or who are undergoing chemotherapy, cannabinoid drugs might offer broad-spectrum relief not found in any other single medication," it said.

only workplace conduct. So an employer can regulate only what an employee does in the workplace and not what an employee or applicant does outside.

Darlington Fabrics said it would appeal. But in the meantime, are there implications for Rhode Island employers?

It would seem to me that an employer would have to hire an applicant who is using medical marijuana even if they say, as this applicant did, "I'm going to fail the drug test because I use medical marijuana." Most employers in this situation are looking at how dangerous is the person's job, and [asking] if that person is using medical marijuana, "Am I confident that they're going to be able to do their job safely?" So this ruling is troubling to Rhode Island employers who have people in dangerous jobs.

Are there implications for employers outside of Rhode Island?

No, this was a state court ruling. But I suspect we're going to start seeing other state courts follow suit.

Certified medical marijuana users have lost workplace anti-discrimination cases in other states. I think the courts followed federal law, which says marijuana is illegal.

Some of the older medical marijuana statutes have been tested in court, in California, Colorado, Michigan, Montana and a few other states. And those are the states where employers have prevailed in litigation. One of the reasons employers prevailed there is that those laws did not contain any protections for employees. The newer medical marijuana laws include this anti-discrimination language.

The Massachusetts Supreme Judicial Court ruled on July 17 that an employee who used medical marijuana for Crohn's disease can proceed with her lawsuit challenging her firing after failing a drug test. Is this ruling a big deal?

Yes, it's significant. The court rejected the idea that just because marijuana is illegal under federal law, employers can refuse to accommodate a medical marijuana user who is considered disabled under state disability law. The court expressly noted that the employee could lose at trial. But it said that because the employee shared information about her Crohn's disease, the employer was required to determine if they could accommodate her — even if her request was to use an illegal federal drug. It remains to be seen how the case develops, but, at a minimum, Massachusetts employers need to reflect before terminating someone for a failed drug test when presented with a medical marijuana card.

Do any states expressly allow employers to fire certified medical marijuana users who test positive for marijuana?

Ohio law does permit employers to establish zero-tolerance drug policies. It also has some language that prohibits employees from suing employers who take action against them because they use medical marijuana. And Florida's recently signed medical marijuana law also has some language prohibiting claims against employers for discrimination or wrongful discharge.

To add to the confusion, companies that contract with the federal government are required to have drug-free workplaces. Does the federal Drug Free Workplace Act conflict with state medical marijuana laws?

It does. If you are a federal contractor, you don't have to do drug testing but you do have to have a drug policy that prohibits the employees working under that contract from using illegal drugs. But the question is, is it illegal? Marijuana is illegal under federal law but not under certain state laws. The way most federal contractors look at it is, marijuana is illegal under federal law, so if we're going to comply with the Drug Free Workplace Act, we need to prohibit it.

Have any court cases dealt with this contradiction?

Not yet. I'm waiting to see that case.

— Barbara Mantel

The report dismissed the notion that marijuana leads to the use of harder drugs. But it said that smoked marijuana delivers most of the same harmful substances found in tobacco smoke and that variability of the mix of compounds in each plant makes it difficult to predict marijuana's precise effect. [51]

As a result, the report concluded, "the future of cannabinoid drugs lies not in smoked marijuana but in chemically defined drugs that act on the cannabinoid systems that are a natural component of human physiology. Until such drugs can be developed and made available for medical use, the report recommends interim solutions." These included limited use of smoked marijuana for patients suffering debilitating pain for whom all other medicines had failed. [52]

In 1999, Maine became the fifth state to legalize medical marijuana, and the next year, Hawaii, Colorado and Nevada followed. In 2002, the 9th U.S. Court of Appeals prohibited the federal government from revoking a physician's license solely for recommending medical marijuana. The U.S. Supreme Court denied an appeal. [53]

Changing Federal Posture

Also in 2002, a group of medical marijuana users sued the DEA and Attorney General John Ashcroft, arguing that the Controlled Substances Act violated the Constitution's Commerce Clause, which gives Congress authority to regulate interstate but not intrastate commerce. The federal government argued that local cultivation and use of marijuana affected interstate commerce in the drug, and in 2005, the Supreme Court agreed. *Gonzalez v. Raich* allowed the federal government to continue prosecuting those who cultivate marijuana, distribute it and use it in states with medical marijuana laws. [54]

But in October 2009, the Justice Department under President Obama issued a path-breaking memorandum. It instructed the Justice Department's U.S. Attorneys not to focus limited federal resources on prosecuting seriously ill patients and their caregivers who were complying with state medical marijuana laws, although large-scale, for-profit commercial enterprises remained a potential target. [55]

"While the memorandum was not intended to impact the behavior of states, cities or individuals, there was huge growth in the medical marijuana industry after it was issued," wrote then-Yale law student Samuel Kleiner in *Yale Law & Policy Review.* [56]

In 2010, Arizona became the 15th state to legalize medical marijuana. In 2011, the DEA once again refused to reclassify marijuana as a Schedule II drug. [57]

The Justice Department further restricted prosecutions in 2013. In a memorandum, it advised federal prosecutors to no longer "consider the size or commercial nature of a marijuana operation alone" in determining whether to investigate it for selling to minors or violating other priorities of the federal government. And in 2014,

the Obama administration gave banks guidance on conducting transactions with marijuana dispensaries. Because marijuana is illegal under federal law, banks had refused to deal with dispensaries, and dispensaries were forced to operate as all-cash businesses. [58]

That same year, Congress blocked the Justice Department from allocating funds to prosecute the cultivation, sale or use of medical marijuana in states where it was legal. Rep. Dana Rohrabacher, R-Calif., co-sponsor of the measure, known as the Rohrabacher-Farr amendment, told conservatives that it would force the federal government to respect states' rights. [59] Congress has continued to extend the amendment, most recently in May as part of the Consolidated Appropriations Act of 2017. [60]

In 2016, the DEA once again rejected petitions to reschedule marijuana, but it announced a policy change to make marijuana research easier: It would expand the number of DEA-registered manufacturers of experimental marijuana from its single supplier at the University of Mississippi. The agency is considering 25 applications so far, according to DEA spokesman Melvin Patterson.

As of July 2017, 29 states and the District of Columbia had legalized medical marijuana. ∎

CURRENT SITUATION

Action in Congress

Eight Republican and Democratic members of Congress are pushing a bill that would prohibit federal law enforcement officials from prosecuting the manufacture, distribution, possession or use of medical marijuana in states where it is legal. The Compassionate Access, Research Expansion and Respect States Act

would not legalize medical marijuana in all 50 states but would amend the Controlled Substances Act to allow states to set their own medical marijuana policies.

If it becomes law, patients, caregivers, doctors and businesses, including banks, participating in state medical marijuana programs would no longer be in violation of federal law.

"Federal marijuana policy has long overstepped the boundaries of common sense, fiscal prudence and compassion," said Sen. Cory Booker, D-N.J., a co-sponsor. "This bill will help ensure that people who can benefit from medical marijuana — from children suffering from chronic illnesses to veterans battling PTSD — can do so without worrying about the federal government standing in the way." [61]

The bill also would lift a prohibition against doctors in the Department of Veterans Affairs from recommending marijuana for certain conditions, such as PTSD and chronic pain, in states where it is legal. And it would remove cannabidiol from the Controlled Substances Act's schedules, thus expanding its availability to patients in states without medical marijuana laws. [62]

Sens. Booker, Kirsten Gillibrand, D-N.Y., Rand Paul, R-Ky., Lisa Murkowski, R-Alaska, Al Franken, D-Minn., and Mike Lee, R-Utah, along with Reps. Steve Cohen, D-Tenn., and Don Young, R-Alaska, introduced the bill on June 15. Booker, Gillibrand and Paul had introduced a version in the Senate in 2015, but the bill never got out of committee. Supporters are hoping this year will be different.

"The addition of Sens. Lee and Murkowski as original co-sponsors should inspire other Republicans to seriously consider this legislation and the absurd federal overreach that it seeks to correct," said Don Murphy, director of conservative outreach at the Marijuana Policy Project. [63]

But Sabet of Smart Approaches to Marijuana opposes the legislation. "This bill would completely undermine the FDA approval process and encourage

Continued on p. 622

At Issue:

Should the U.S. reclassify cannabis from a Schedule I drug?

DR. DONALD O. LYMAN, M.D.
CHAIR, COUNCIL ON SCIENCE AND PUBLIC HEALTH, CALIFORNIA MEDICAL ASSOCIATION

WRITTEN FOR *CQ RESEARCHER*, JULY 2017

*t*he federal criminalization of cannabis has failed, and 29 states and the District of Columbia have legalized cannabis for medical use, while eight states have legalized it for adult use. These actions recognize both the clinical utility of cannabis and the failure of the policy of criminalization to control access to it.

The California Medical Association (CMA), which represents 43,000 physicians, believes the United States needs a federal framework with robust regulations, patient safety standards and legally sanctioned research to support regulatory agencies and to document the benefits and risks of medical and nonmedical use.

This belief is why CMA endorsed Proposition 64 (Adult Use of Marijuana Act, 2016) to support universal adult access within a tightly controlled regulatory system, and why it wrote a 2011 white paper which, in part, argued for the reclassification of cannabis.

When California approved Proposition 215 in 1996, the cultivation and use of cannabis was decriminalized for seriously ill individuals who obtained a physician's recommendation. However, because the drug is still criminalized federally, physicians recommending cannabis are in an untenable position. We are the gatekeepers to a medically beneficial substance, but there is no normal regulatory system allowing access to it.

Literature on medical cannabis is sufficiently convincing to recommend it for treating some illnesses and conditions, including pain, nausea and anorexia. Yet, the literature on medical cannabis is not comprehensive, cannabis dosage is not well standardized and little information exists about its side effects. The current Schedule 1 classification prevents the very research needed to regulate cannabis appropriately.

Schedule 1 is defined as drugs, such as cocaine and LSD, with no currently accepted medical use and a high potential for abuse. As such, this definition does not reasonably apply to cannabis.

Without cannabis policy rooted in evidence-based science, our patients and neighbors will continue to access cannabis, possibly without discussing it with their physician, that has not been tested for purity, standardized for dosage or tempered by safeguards to protect all users.

Until the system is changed, physicians will continue to be in an unsustainable position. The U.S. government should invest in researching the benefits and risks of cannabis and in developing evidence-based regulations and quality controls that protect the public and help patients.

JEFFREY ZINSMEISTER
EXECUTIVE VICE PRESIDENT AND DIRECTOR OF GOVERNMENT RELATIONS, SMART APPROACHES TO MARIJUANA

WRITTEN FOR *CQ RESEARCHER*, JULY 2017

*i*f a pharmaceutical giant asked the government to reclassify a prescription drug, skipping Food and Drug Administration (FDA) trials, we would be outraged. Why should marijuana be any different?

Raw, "whole plant" marijuana is in Schedule I with drugs like heroin not because it is just as dangerous but because FDA scientists found just last year that it is addictive and has no accepted medical use, unlike drugs in other schedules.

Additionally, marijuana differs from approved medications in two critical ways. FDA-approved medicine is dosed and standardized. The pill you buy in Boston is the same as the one you buy in Seattle. Not so with marijuana. And since when did we smoke medications?

In contrast to raw marijuana, specific compounds derived from marijuana can be in other schedules. Some of them have been sold legally for decades, such as a pure form of THC, the plant's psychoactive ingredient. Similarly, a pure form of cannabidiol, or CBD, a compound derived from marijuana that helps certain cases of childhood epilepsy, is in the final phases of FDA approval.

But huge for-profit marijuana special interests are spending millions lobbying Congress to blur this distinction and undermine the FDA process. They argue that their product is somehow different from other medicines.

As evidence, these pot lobbyists use very sick people, often children, who have seen some benefits from using medications derived from marijuana (such as cannabidiol). But therein lies the crucial distinction. Those medications — specific compounds derived from the marijuana plant — differ from smoking or eating the plant itself, just as using morphine differs from smoking opium. Precious little evidence shows that smoking or eating marijuana has medical benefits. But the pot industry has glommed on to a handful of small observational studies and distorted them into a narrative of peer-reviewed scientific proof.

Finally, even if Congress bowed to lobbyists and rescheduled marijuana by fiat, it would still only be for sale when incorporated into an FDA-approved, standardized product that can pass clinical trials. There is no scientific evidence today that this is possible with the raw marijuana plant.

The "medical marijuana" debate is just another attempt to undermine the FDA system for money. Like an unscrupulous Big Pharma company, pot businesses see easy money in selling an unapproved, unregulated product. Compassion has nothing to do with it.

Continued from p. 620
the use of marijuana and marijuana products that have not been proven either safe or effective," he said. [64]

The bill's introduction in June came just two days after Attorney General Sessions' letter to congressional leaders became public asking Congress to undo the Rohrabacher-Farr amendment, which must be renewed annually. "I believe it would be unwise for Congress to restrict the discretion of the Department to fund particular prosecutions," Sessions wrote, "particularly in the midst of an

or to committee chairs in Congress in ways that could threaten the future of this Amendment." [67]

State Actions

Medical marijuana enjoys bipartisan support on the state level, as recent legislative activity shows.

When West Virginia legalized medical marijuana in April, its bill was passed by a Republican-controlled Legislature. The same was true in Pennsylvania

that are renewed every year or two. That revenue covers the cost of state oversight. Some states, such as Arizona, Michigan and Oregon, generate a surplus, according to the Marijuana Policy Project. In addition, most states impose a sales tax on dispensary sales. [69]

Several states are expanding the list of medical conditions covered by existing laws. In June alone, New Hampshire added moderate-to-severe chronic pain to the list of serious conditions that can be treated with cannabis; Vermont added post-traumatic stress disorder (PTSD), Parkinson's disease and Crohn's disease; and Colorado added PTSD. The New York legislature passed a bill adding PTSD, and it awaits Gov. Andrew Cuomo's signature. [70]

In fact, 26 states now include PTSD as a qualifying condition. "Veterans with PTSD should not have to choose between FDA-approved medications that carry a blackbox suicide warning and off-label drugs with no clinical efficacy and horrible side effects," said Michael Krawitz, executive director of Veterans for Medical Cannabis Access, as New York debated the change to its law. "There is another way: Medical marijuana has helped veterans have a restful night's sleep instead of night terrors, and thus experience a better quality of life." [71]

Military veterans have been lobbying states for years to add PTSD to their list of conditions treatable with cannabis, despite the lack of randomized controlled studies evaluating marijuana's effectiveness for the condition. According to scientists at the U.S. Department of Veterans Affairs, "there is no evidence at this time that marijuana is an effective treatment for PTSD. In fact, research suggests that marijuana can be harmful to individuals with PTSD." These individuals, the scientists said, "have particular difficulty stopping their use of marijuana and responding to treatment for marijuana addiction." [72]

But the research drought could soon become at least a trickle. In 2016, the DEA and the FDA approved the first-ever randomized controlled trial of

U.S. Sen. Cory Booker, D-N.J., visits with 4-year-old Morgan Hintz, who has epilepsy, during a Capitol Hill news conference on medical marijuana on March 10, 2015. Her mother wants her to be able to use cannabidiol to control her seizures. Eight members of Congress are pushing legislation that would, among other things, expand its availability to patients in states without medical marijuana laws.

historic drug epidemic and potentially long-term uptick in violent crime." [65]

However, the drug epidemic Sessions referred to involves opioids and heroin, not marijuana, and some research has shown that in states with medical marijuana programs, opioid-related deaths and overdoses have fallen. [66]

John Hudak, deputy director of the Center for Effective Public Management at the Brookings Institution, a centrist think tank in Washington, called Sessions' arguments a "scare tactic" that "could appeal to rank-and-file members

and Ohio, which passed medical marijuana laws in 2016. In Arkansas, Florida and North Dakota, whose legislatures are Democratic-controlled, the issue went straight to citizens, who voted to legalize medical marijuana last November while also helping put Donald Trump in the White House. [68]

States are breaking even, and in some cases, making money on their medical marijuana programs. States require medical marijuana dispensaries to pay annual licensing fees, and individuals to purchase registration cards

marijuana to treat PTSD in U.S. veterans. The Multidisciplinary Association for Psychedelic Studies, a nonprofit in Santa Cruz, Calif., that promotes research on psychedelics and marijuana, is overseeing the study, funded by a grant from the state of Colorado. The study is testing the safety and efficacy of smoked marijuana with varying ratios of THC and cannabidiol in 76 military veterans who have not responded to traditional treatment of PTSD. [73]

Not every state is expanding its medical marijuana laws. Citing a lack of supporting scientific research, New Mexico Health Secretary Lynn Gallagher in June rejected the state's Medical Cannabis Advisory Board's recommendation to add Alzheimer's disease and opioid addiction to the list of conditions suitable for marijuana treatment. [74]

Not in My Backyard

Under local zoning rules, municipalities decide such things as where marijuana businesses can locate, their hours of operation and their size. But some states allow local officials to go further and ban marijuana businesses. In June, for example, Marshall, Mich., voted to allow growers but not dispensaries. Fife, Wash., bans both medical and recreational marijuana sales. And dozens of California cities prohibit some or all types of marijuana operations. [75]

After Ohio passed a medical marijuana law in September, Ohio state Sen. Kenny Yuko, a Democrat, pleaded with municipalities to "keep an open mind." In a letter to towns, Yuko wrote, "Please consider all the good that this medicine can do for the citizens of your communities." [76]

But at least two dozen municipalities have ignored Yuko and banned or imposed a moratorium on growers, processors or dispensaries, even though medical marijuana won't become available to Ohio residents until 2018 as the state develops rules for its use. [77]

Sidney, Ohio, is one such munici-

pality. In May, the City Council told its law director to draft legislation to ban the cultivation, processing and dispensing of medical marijuana within city limits. Council member Janet Born said three doctors had told her that effective alternative medications to marijuana exist. "Also, marijuana, no matter how mild or ineffectual it seems, still impairs the brain . . . and many of those people will try driving," Born said. "And that's why I think we should not have it." [78]

Residents of towns that have banned dispensaries can still use medical marijuana if recommended by a doctor, but they will have to buy it elsewhere. ■

OUTLOOK

Strong Growth Predicted

The New Frontier Data research firm predicts that U.S. medical marijuana sales will grow at a compound annual rate of 12 percent in the next nine years, from $4.7 billion in 2016 to $13.2 billion in 2025. Those projections assume marijuana remains a Schedule I substance and that no more states pass legalization measures. [79]

But the status quo, at least among states, is unlikely to remain, say advocates on both sides of the medical marijuana debate.

"There definitely will be more states working toward passing medical marijuana bills, as well as others improving their existing programs" by, for example, adding qualifying medical conditions and allowing more kinds of cannabis products to be sold, says Fox of the Marijuana Policy Project.

Sabet of Smart Approaches to Marijuana agrees that more states are likely to adopt medical marijuana programs, an outcome he opposes, and he blames a well-funded public relations campaign by the cannabis industry.

"Under the guise of compassion, for-profit businesses are bypassing the FDA and instead funding political advocacy to gain legitimacy," says Sabet.

Fox responds that people directly involved in the legal marijuana industry are a small part of the Marijuana Policy Project's donor base — only about 10 percent. "The rest comes from regular donors and philanthropists who recognize that sick people deserve safe, reliable access to medical marijuana," he says, "and that responsible adults should not be criminalized for using a substance that is safer than alcohol."

Both Fox and Sabet expect the DEA under the Trump administration to continue to refuse to reschedule marijuana from the Schedule I category.

Gitlow, the past president of the American Society of Addiction Medicine, says the DEA could fashion a compromise. It could create a Schedule I-A for drugs with an 'unknown medical application,' implement rules to encourage well-designed clinical research for such drugs and place marijuana in that category, he says.

The American Medical Association recommends the government review marijuana's status as a Schedule I drug and make the rules for its research easier. But the nation's largest association of physicians is quick to add that its recommendation is not an endorsement of state-based medical cannabis programs or the legalization of marijuana. [80]

After the 2020 presidential election, federal policy may change, but the details are difficult to predict, according to New Frontier Data.

"It remains possible that there will be sweeping changes to federal cannabis laws within the next decade, including the rescheduling of cannabis from its current status as a Schedule I substance — included in the ranks of the most dangerous drugs — to Schedule II or III status," the research firm said, "or potentially a complete de-scheduling, which would bring cannabis regulations closer to those for alcohol." [81] ■

Notes

1 "United States," National Organization for the Reform of Marijuana Laws, http://tinyurl.com/yasqlhst.

2 "U.S. Voter Support For Marijuana Hits New High," Quinnipiac University Poll, April 20, 2017, http://tinyurl.com/y93bnkhc.

3 Medical Marijuana Patient Cardholder Registry, Nevada Division of Public and Behavioral Health, last updated March 15, 2017, http://tinyurl.com/yaqgmoq3; "United States," *op. cit.*

4 Medical Marijuana Patient Numbers, Marijuana Policy Project, last updated June 23, 2017, https://tinyurl.com/y7mmxj5k.

5 "Montana Marijuana Program (MMP): May 2017 Registry Information," Montana Department of Public Health and Human Services, May 2017, https://tinyurl.com/yarosg3j; "Therapeutic Cannabis Program 2016 Data Report," New Hampshire Department of Health and Human Services, pp. 7, 17, https://tinyurl.com/yae93skb; and "Oregon Medical Marijuana Program Statistical Snapshot: April, 2017," Oregon Health Authority, April 2017, pp. 3-4, https://tinyurl.com/ycgnauco.

6 Winnie Hu, "When Retirement Comes With a Daily Dose of Cannabis," *The New York Times*, Feb. 19, 2017, https://tinyurl.com/gnem38y.

7 "The Cannabis Industry Annual Report: 2017 Legal Marijuana Outlook," New Frontier Data, 2017, p. 2, https://tinyurl.com/y9u3qwgb; Alex Pasquariello and Alicia Wallace, "New studies shine light on cannabis consumers' spending habits," *The Cannabist*, April 26, 2017, https://tinyurl.com/y8u7tkp8.

8 Jeff Sessions' letter, May 1, 2017, https://tinyurl.com/y7ghdkj3.

9 "Effective Arguments for Medical Marijuana Advocates," Marijuana Policy Project, updated April 28, 2017, p. 2, https://tinyurl.com/ycpdj5un.

10 "Endocannabinoid Basics," *Medical Genomics*, https://tinyurl.com/ycyxwyd4.

11 "The Health Effects of Cannabis and Cannabinoids: The Current State of Evidence and Recommendations for Research," National Academies of Sciences, Engineering, and Medicine, Jan. 12, 2017, p. 378, https://tinyurl.com/yc3gx7j6.

12 *Ibid.*, p. 416.

13 *Ibid.*; Orrin Devinsky, "Trial of Cannabidiol for Drug-Resistant Seizures in the Dravet Syndrome," *The New England Journal of Medicine*, May 25, 2017, http://tinyurl.com/yahg3egj.

14 *Ibid.*, p. 289.

15 Deborah S. Hasin *et al.*, "Medical marijuana laws and adolescent marijuana use in the USA from 1991 to 2014: results from annual, repeated cross-sectional surveys," *The Lancet Psychiatry*, June 15, 2015, https://tinyurl.com/yc2fod7m.

16 Joseph Schuermeyer *et al.*, "Temporal trends in marijuana attitudes, availability and use in Colorado compared to non-medical marijuana states: 2003-2011," *Drug and Alcohol Dependence*, 2014, https://tinyurl.com/y7fg5fpc.

17 Deborah S. Hasin *et al.*, "US Adult Illicit Cannabis Use, Cannabis Use Disorder, and Medical Marijuana Laws: 1991-1992 to 2012-2013," *JAMA Psychiatry*, June 2017, https://tinyurl.com/yatp2vyt.

18 Hefei Wen *et al.*, "The effect of medical marijuana laws on adolescent and adult use of marijuana, alcohol, and other substances," *Journal of Health Economics*, July 2015, https://tinyurl.com/ybcz2ejj.

19 "Is Marijuana Addictive?" National Institute on Drug Abuse, updated April 2017, https://tinyurl.com/oksoklx.

20 Ashley C. Bradford and W. David Bradford, "Medical Marijuana Laws May Be Associated with a Decline In The Number Of Prescriptions for Medicaid Enrollees," *Health Affairs*, April 19, 2017, https://tinyurl.com/mtvxd6q; Ashley C. Bradford and W. David Bradford, "Medical Marijuana Laws Reduce Prescription Medication Use in Medicare Part D," *Health Affairs*, July 2016, https://tinyurl.com/zmb4pbo.

21 "New York State Practitioner Education — Medical Use of Marijuana Course," The Answer Page, https://tinyurl.com/y7wzk8se.

22 Nancy A. Haug *et al.*, "Training and Practices of Cannabis Dispensary Staff," *Cannabis and Cannabinoid Research*, December 2016, https://tinyurl.com/yaf2a8uk.

23 Martin Booth, *Cannabis: A History* (2003), p. 19.

24 Barney Warf, "High Points: An Historical Geography of Cannabis," *Geographical Review*, October 2014, https://tinyurl.com/y8njo2vk.

25 Ethan B. Russo, "History of Cannabis and Its Preparations in Saga, Science, and Sobriquet," *Chemistry & Biodiversity*, 2007, p. 1637, https://tinyurl.com/ybe2u65r.

26 Martin A. Lee, *Smoke Signals: A Social History of Marijuana — Medicinal, Recreational and Scientific* (2012), pp. 26-28.

27 Lester Grinspoon and James B. Bakalar, *Marihuana: The Forbidden Medicine* (1993), p. 4; Tod H. Mikuriya, "Marijuana in Medicine, Past, Present and Future," *California Medicine*, January 1969, p. 34, https://tinyurl.com/y853l4vn.

28 Booth, *op. cit.*, pp. 94, 95.

29 Grinspoon and Bakalar, *op. cit.*, p. 4.

30 "The Antique Cannabis Book," May 2016, Appendix C, https://tinyurl.com/yconewk2.

31 Ernest L. Abel, *Marihuana: The First Twelve Thousand Years* (1980), pp. 183-184.

32 Booth, *op. cit.*, pp. 96-97; See Kathy Koch, "Medical Marijuana: Should doctors be able to prescribe the drug?" *CQ Researcher*, April 20, 1999, pp. 705-728.

33 Booth, *ibid.*, pp. 127, 134.

34 *Ibid.*, pp. 132-133.

35 Wendy Chapkis and Richard J. Webb, *Dying to Get High: Marijuana as Medicine* (2008), p. 23.

36 *Ibid.*, p. 24.

37 *Ibid.*, pp. 24, 25, 26.

38 Lee, *op. cit.*, pp. 80-82.

39 *Ibid.*, pp. 118-119.

40 Chapkis and Webb, *op. cit.*, pp. 28-29.

41 *Ibid.*, pp. 29-30.

42 Grinspoon and Bakalar, *op. cit.*, pp. 14-17.

43 Lee, *op. cit.*, p. 166.

44 "Historical Timeline: History of Marijuana as Medicine — 2900 BC to Present," ProCon.org, last updated Jan. 30, 2017, https://tinyurl.com/h6n7e46; Dustin Sulak, "Introduction to the Endocannabinoid System," National Organization for the Reform of Marijuana Laws, https://tinyurl.com/bhj3dsg.

45 *Ibid.*, "Historical Timeline: History of Marijuana as medicine — 2900 BC to Present"; "Kiyoshi Kuromiya *et al.*, Plaintiffs, v. The United States of America, Defendant," U.S. District Court

About the Author

Barbara Mantel is a freelance writer in New York City. She has been a Kiplinger Fellow and has won several journalism awards, including the National Press Club's Best Consumer Journalism Award and the Front Page Award. She was a correspondent for NPR and the founding senior editor and producer for public radio's "Science Friday." She holds a B.A. in history and economics from the University of Virginia and an M.A. in economics from Northwestern University.

for the Eastern District of Pennsylvania, p. 4, https://tinyurl.com/yauauw69.

[46] Chapkis and Webb, *op. cit.*, p. 32.

[47] Lee, *op. cit.*, p. 251.

[48] Chapkis and Webb, *op. cit.*, p. 253.

[49] Lee, *op. cit.*, pp. 253-54, 256-58, 264.

[50] *Ibid.*, p. 275.

[51] Janet E. Joy, John A. Benson Jr. and Stanley J. Watson Jr., eds., "Marijuana and Medicine: Assessing the Science Base," Institute of Medicine, 1999, pp. viii-ix, https://tinyurl.com/y9j7zn6d.

[52] *Ibid.*, p. ix, https://tinyurl.com/y9j7zn6d.

[53] "Historical Timeline: History of Marijuana as Medicine — 2900 BC to Present," *op. cit.*

[54] *Ibid.*; the Supreme Court case can be found at https://tinyurl.com/y95vtgod.

[55] "The Ogden Memorandum," U.S. Department of Justice, Oct. 19, 2009, https://tinyurl.com/ybgd8hr3.

[56] Samuel Kleiner, "The Limits of Pledging Prosecutorial Discretion: The Ogden Memorandum's Failure to Create an Entrapment by Estoppel Defense," *Yale Law & Policy Review*, 2014, https://tinyurl.com/y9j3qmvh.

[57] "Historical Timeline: History of Marijuana as Medicine — 2900 BC to Present," *op. cit.*

[58] "Cole Memorandum," U.S. Department of Justice, Aug. 29, 2013, https://tinyurl.com/y7ggddxu.

[59] "Historical Timeline: History of Marijuana as Medicine — 2900 BC to Present," *op. cit.*

[60] Mary Beth Quirk, "Medical Marijuana Safe From DOJ Prosecution — For Now," *Consumerist*, May 10, 2017, https://tinyurl.com/yar3elkx.

[61] "Lawmakers Reintroduce Bipartisan, Bicameral Medical Marijuana Bill," press release, Office of U.S. Sen. Cory Booker, June 15, 2017, https://tinyurl.com/yb3eotfv.

[62] *Ibid.*

[63] "Bipartisan Bill to End Federal Prohibition of Medical Marijuana Reintroduced in U.S. Senate," Marijuana Policy Project, June 15, 2017, https://tinyurl.com/ybbgxbdy.

[64] Anisha Gianchandani, "Statement from SAM President Kevin Sabet on Senators Booker and Gillibrand's Marijuana Legislation to Bypass FDA," Smart Approaches to Marijuana, June 15, 2016, http://tinyurl.com/ycmjtv3b.

[65] Letter from Jeff Sessions, Office of the Attorney General, May 1, 2017, https://tinyurl.com/y7ghdkj3.

[66] Marcus A. Bachhuber *et al.*, "Medical Cannabis Laws and Opioid Analgesic Overdose Mortality in the United States, 1999-2010," *JAMA Internal Medicine*, Aug. 25, 2014, https://tinyurl.com/luohzzf.

[67] Christopher Ingraham, "Jeff Sessions personally asked Congress to let him prosecute medical-marijuana providers," *The Washington Post*, June 13, 2017, https://tinyurl.com/yamubcrf.

[68] "West Virginia Becomes 29th Medical Marijuana State as Gov. Jim Justice Signs SB 386 Into Law," Marijuana Policy Project, April 19, 2017, https://tinyurl.com/ybebvbju.

[69] "State Medical Marijuana Programs' Financial Information," Marijuana Policy Project, https://tinyurl.com/y7rnpd8o.

[70] "N.Y.: Legislature passes bill to add PTSD to medical marijuana program," Marijuana Policy Project, June 20, 2017, https://tinyurl.com/y9vx9563.

[71] Debra Borchardt, "New York State Adds PTSD To Medical Marijuana Program, Will Menstrual Cramps Be Next?" *Forbes*, May 11, 2017, https://tinyurl.com/y7fguf75.

[72] Marcel O. Bonn-Miller and Glenna S. Rousseau, "Marijuana Use and PTSD among Veterans," U.S. Department of Veterans Affairs, last updated May 10, 2017, https://tinyurl.com/ycr38g8l.

[73] "DEA Approves First-Ever Trial of Medical Marijuana for PTSD in Veterans," Multidisciplinary Association for Psychedelic Studies, April 21, 2016, https://tinyurl.com/j4sfcbq.

[74] "Medical Marijuana for New Mexico Opiate Addicts Rejected," The Associated Press, *U.S. News & World Report*, June 15, 2017, https://tinyurl.com/y7c6clfm.

[75] "Washington Marijuana Business to Open in City With Ban," Cannabis Law Group, March 15, 2017, https://tinyurl.com/ybsbuv88, Allison Edrington, "List of Cities, Counties Banning Commercial Cannabis in California," *The Ganjier*, Jan. 25, 2016, https://tinyurl.com/y7hq5tbx.

[76] Jackie Borchardt, "Ohio lawmaker urges cities not to ban medical marijuana before state sets rules," Cleveland.com, Sept. 8, 2016, https://tinyurl.com/yashnd8s.

[77] Tom Knox, "4 Greater Cincinnati cities among those banning medical marijuana businesses, May 24, 2017, *Cincinnati Business Courier*, https://tinyurl.com/ybnf4b8n.

[78] Sheryl Roadcap, "Council pursues ban on medical marijuana," *Sidney Daily News*, May 10, 2017, https://tinyurl.com/y8bom4ag.

[79] "The Cannabis Industry Annual Report: 2017 Legal Marijuana Outlook," New Frontier Data, 2017, p. 3, https://tinyurl.com/y9u3qwgb.

[80] "AMA Policy: Medical Marijuana," American Medical Association, https://tinyurl.com/y6wzolo2.

[81] "The Cannabis Industry Annual Report," *op. cit.*

FOR MORE INFORMATION

American Society of Addiction Medicine, 11400 Rockville Pike, Suite 200, Rockville, MD 20852; 301-656-3920; www.asam.org. Organization representing physicians, clinicians and associated professionals that opposes marijuana legalization.

Americans for Safe Access, 1624 U St., N.W., Suite 200, Washington, DC 20009; 202-857-4272; www.safeaccessnow.org. Advocacy group seeking legal access to cannabis for therapeutic use and research.

Drug Enforcement Administration, 700 Army Navy Drive, Arlington, VA 22202; 202-307-1000; www.dea.gov. Federal agency combating drug use and smuggling.

Marijuana Policy Project, PO Box 77492, Capitol Hill, Washington, DC 20013; 202-462-5747; www.mpp.org. Advocacy group that lobbies to remove criminal penalties for marijuana use, particularly for medical use.

National Academies of Sciences, Engineering, and Medicine, 500 5th St., N.W., Washington, DC 20001; 202-334-2000; www.nationalacademies.org. Private, non-profit institutions providing expert advice to the government and public.

NORML (National Organization for the Reform of Marijuana Laws), 1100 H St., N.W., Suite 830, Washington, DC 20005; 202-483-5500; www.norml.org. Advocacy group that lobbies for the legalization of adult use of marijuana.

RAND Drug Policy Research Center, RAND Corp., 1776 Main St., Santa Monica, CA 90407; 301-393-0411; www.rand.org/multi/dprc.html. Think tank that conducts research into issues involving alcohol and other drugs.

Smart Approaches to Marijuana, 1001 N. Fairfax St., Suite 201, Alexandria, VA 22314; www.learnaboutsam.org. Advocacy group that opposes marijuana legalization and favors medical research of marijuana-derived compounds.

Bibliography

Selected Sources

Books

Chapkis, Wendy, and Richard J. Webb, *Dying to Get High: Marijuana as Medicine*, NYU Press, 2008.
A sociologist (Chapkis) and an educator (Webb) explore some of the complex issues surrounding medical marijuana, including patient rights and barriers to research.

Grinspoon, Lester, and James B. Bakalar, *Marihuana: The Forbidden Medicine*, Yale University Press, 1997.
A psychiatrist (Grinspoon) and a lawyer (Bakalar) discuss the history of marijuana, including social attitudes toward the drug, and argue for its legalization.

Lee, Martin A., *Smoke Signals: A Social History of Marijuana — Medicinal, Recreational and Scientific*, Simon and Schuster, 2012.
A journalist and activist examines the medical, recreational, scientific and economic dimensions of marijuana.

Articles

Borchardt, Debra, "New York State Adds PTSD To Medical Marijuana Program, Will Menstrual Cramps Be Next?" *Forbes*, May 11, 2017, http://tinyurl.com/y7fguf75.
The New York legislature has placed post-traumatic stress disorder on its list of conditions for which physicians may recommend marijuana.

Borchardt, Jackie, "Ohio lawmaker urges cities not to ban medical marijuana before state sets rules," Cleveland.com, Sept. 8, 2016, http://tinyurl.com/yashnd8s.
A Democratic legislator is asking Ohio municipalities to not ban medical marijuana.

Hu, Winnie, "When Older Age Comes With a Daily Dose of Cannabis," *The New York Times*, Feb. 19, 2017, http://tinyurl.com/gnem38y.
Older Americans are increasingly using marijuana to treat aches and pains.

Ingraham, Christopher, "Jeff Sessions personally asked Congress to let him prosecute medical-marijuana providers," *The Washington Post*, June 13, 2017, http://tinyurl.com/yamubcrf.
U.S. Attorney General Jeff Sessions is seeking congressional funding to investigate medical marijuana providers.

Quirk, Mary Beth, "Medical Marijuana Safe From DOJ Prosecution — For Now," *Consumerist*, May 10, 2017, http://tinyurl.com/yar3elkx.
Congress renewed a prohibition against U.S. Justice Department interference in state medical marijuana programs.

Rettner, Rachael, "New Medical Marijuana Policy Is a Catch-22, Researchers Say," *Live Science*, Aug. 15, 2017, http://tinyurl.com/ybjwtvv6.
Federal regulations place barriers to marijuana research, but the U.S. government will not relax regulations without more research into marijuana's health benefits.

Rubin, Rita, "Medical Marijuana Is Legal in Most States, but Physicians Have Little Evidence to Guide Them," *JAMA*, April 25, 2017, http://tinyurl.com/y8noglpa.
Little research is available to guide doctors on what dose and strain of marijuana to recommend to patients.

Reports and Studies

"The Cannabis Industry Annual Report: 2017 Legal Marijuana Outlook," New Frontier Data, 2017, http://tinyurl.com/y9u3qwgb.
A firm providing data analytics to the cannabis industry predicts continuing growth in sales for legal medical and recreational marijuana.

"The Health Effects of Cannabis and Cannabinoids: The Current State of Evidence and Recommendations for Research," National Academies of Sciences, Engineering, and Medicine, Jan. 12, 2017, http://tinyurl.com/yc3gx7j6.
An independent, expert panel concludes that scientific research supports marijuana's health benefits for three medical conditions — chronic pain, muscle spasticity in multiple sclerosis and chemotherapy-induced nausea and vomiting — but that there's scant or no research to support its use for many other conditions.

Bradford, Ashley C., and W. David Bradford, "Medical Marijuana Laws May Be Associated with a Decline In The Number Of Prescriptions for Medicaid Enrollees," *Health Affairs*, April 19, 2017, http://tinyurl.com/mtvxd6q.
Researchers say that states with medical marijuana laws saw a decline in prescriptions for medications among Medicaid enrollees.

Hasin, Deborah S., *et al.*, "Medical marijuana laws and adolescent marijuana use in the USA from 1991 to 2014: results from annual, repeated cross-sectional surveys," *The Lancet Psychiatry*, June 15, 2015, http://tinyurl.com/yc2fod7m.
Medical marijuana laws had no impact on teen use of marijuana, university researchers say.

Hasin, Deborah S., *et al.*, "US Adult Illicit Cannabis Use, Cannabis Use Disorder, and Medical Marijuana Laws: 1991-1992 to 2012-2013," *JAMA Psychiatry*, June 2017, http://tinyurl.com/yatp2vyt.
University researchers find that medical marijuana laws are associated with an increase in illicit marijuana use and dependence in adults.

The Next Step:

Additional Articles from Current Periodicals

Legalization Drive

Laslo, Matt, "Medical Marijuana: How Six Senators Are Leading Fight for Federally Legal Weed," *Rolling Stone*, June 22, 2017, https://tinyurl.com/ydb7xxgg.

A bipartisan group of six senators has introduced a bill that would allow states' medical marijuana laws to supersede the federal prohibition on cannabis.

Robinson, Grant, "Task force to examine medical marijuana in Tennessee," WBIR, June 16, 2017, https://tinyurl.com/yb6323oe.

Tennessee is creating a task force of state senators and representatives to explore legalizing medical marijuana in the state.

Smith, Aaron, "Vermont expands medical marijuana plan," CNN, June 12, 2017, https://tinyurl.com/y872kkgm.

Vermont's governor has signed a bill adding Parkinson's disease, Crohn's disease and post-traumatic stress disorder to the list of conditions that can be treated with medical marijuana.

Therapeutic Value

Grover, Natalie, "High hopes ride on marijuana painkillers amid opioid crisis," Reuters, June 23, 2017, https://tinyurl.com/yasqqgg5.

In the battle against opioid abuse, some drugmakers are developing marijuana-based painkillers.

Kramer, Molly, "My aging parents smuggle medical marijuana," *Salon*, July 8, 2017, https://tinyurl.com/ybvwo4wp.

A daughter recounts how her parents decided to smuggle marijuana from California to help her father deal with painful side effects of cancer and chemotherapy.

Scutti, Susan, "New potential for marijuana: Treating drug addiction," CNN, May 17, 2017, https://tinyurl.com/ybfjt7gu.

Some addiction specialists have turned to marijuana to help people with severe addictions.

State Implementation

Cox, Erin, "Maryland approves first medical marijuana dispensary," *The Baltimore Sun*, July 5, 2017, https://tinyurl.com/y93jl3pf.

The state's first medical marijuana dispensary opened in Frederick, but the one company authorized to grow cannabis in the state will not have its first complete batch until after Labor Day.

Dixon, Lance, "After new state limitations, Coral Gables will ban medical marijuana dispensaries," *The Miami Herald*, July 11, 2017, https://tinyurl.com/y7gdfkcc.

Florida law allows municipalities to ban marijuana dispensaries, and Coral Gables became the first major city in Miami-Dade County to do so, citing federal law prohibiting the cultivation, processing, distribution and use of marijuana as its justification.

Nicholson, Blake, "State sets tentative timeline for medical marijuana system," The Associated Press, *The Bismarck Tribune*, July 11, 2017, https://tinyurl.com/y9tycs88.

The North Dakota Health Department has asked companies to send letters of intent by July 28 if they want to manufacture or distribute medical marijuana.

Trump Administration

Sherer, Stephen, "Medical marijuana patients need an antidote for Jeff Sessions," *The Hill*, July 10, 2017, https://tinyurl.com/y9ekbw27.

The executive director of Americans for Safe Access, which advocates for safe and equal access to medical marijuana, is urging Congress to renew the Rohrabacher-Farr amendment to ensure the Justice Department does not start prosecutions in states with legalized medical or recreational marijuana.

Ventura, Jesse, "Trump will cripple states if he reverses marijuana legalization," CNBC, July 11, 2017, https://tinyurl.com/yc5k5cnz.

A former Minnesota governor argues that if the Trump administration forces states to reverse their laws legalizing recreational and medical marijuana, it could hurt those states' economies because of the amount of money the industry is generating.

In-depth Reports on Issues in the News

Are you writing a paper?

Need backup for a debate?

Want to become an expert on an issue?

For 90 years, students have turned to *CQ Researcher* for in-depth reporting on issues in the news. Reports on a full range of political and social issues are now available. Following is a selection of recent reports:

Civil Liberties
Privacy and the Internet, 12/15
Intelligence Reform, 5/15
Religion and Law, 11/14

Crime/Law
High-Tech Policing, 4/17
Forensic Science Controversies, 2/17
Jailing Debtors, 9/16
Decriminalizing Prostitution, 4/16
Restorative Justice, 2/16
The Dark Web, 1/16
Immigrant Detention, 10/15

Education
Charter Schools, 3/17
Civic Education, 2/17
Student Debt, 11/16
Apprenticeships, 10/16

Environment/Society
Funding the Arts, 7/17
Hunger in America, 7/17
Future of the Christian Right, 6/17
Trust in Media, 6/17
Anti-Semitism, 5/17
Native American Sovereignty, 5/17

Health/Safety
Food Labeling, 6/17
Sports and Sexual Assault, 4/17
Reducing Traffic Deaths, 2/17
Opioid Crisis, 10/16
Mosquito-Borne Disease, 7/16

Politics/Economy
North Korea Showdown, 5/17
Rethinking Foreign Aid, 4/17
Troubled Brazil, 4/17
Reviving Rural Economies, 3/17
Immigrants and the Economy, 2/17

Upcoming Reports

Muslims in America, 7/28/17   Space Race, 8/4/17   Redistricting, 8/25/17

ACCESS

CQ Researcher is available in print and online. For access, visit your library or www.cqresearcher.com.

STAY CURRENT

For notice of upcoming *CQ Researcher* reports or to learn more about *CQ Researcher* products, subscribe to the free email newsletters, *CQ Researcher Alert!* and *CQ Researcher News*: http://cqpress.com/newsletters.

PURCHASE

To purchase a *CQ Researcher* report in print or electronic format (PDF), visit www.cqpress.com or call 866-427-7737. Single reports start at $15. Bulk purchase discounts and electronic-rights licensing are also available.

SUBSCRIBE

Annual full-service *CQ Researcher* subscriptions—including 44 reports a year, monthly index updates, and a bound volume—start at $1,131. Add $25 for domestic postage.

CQ Researcher Online offers a backfile from 1991 and a number of tools to simplify research. For pricing information, call 800-818-7243 or 805-499-9774 or email librarysales@sagepub.com.

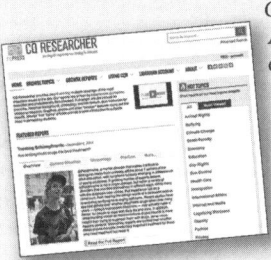

CQ RESEARCHER

In-depth reports on today's issues

Published by CQ Press, an Imprint of SAGE Publications, Inc.

www.cqresearcher.com

Muslims in America

Do Islamic beliefs conflict with American values?

H ate crimes against Muslims have been on the rise in recent years. A string of attacks by Islamist extremists has terrorized the United States and Europe, and anti-Muslim rhetoric during the 2016 presidential campaign by then-candidate Donald Trump and some of his supporters has helped create an anti-Muslim climate in the United States. Polls indicate that Americans have growing concerns about Muslim values and Islamist extremism, although surveys show that U.S. Muslims are a diverse community with values generally in line with those of most Americans. The nation's 3.3 million Muslim population is expected to grow to 8 million by 2050, and Islam will have surpassed Judaism as America's largest non-Christian faith. But most Americans say they know little about Islam and haven't had much contact with Muslims. Meanwhile, protests have erupted over a temporary ban ordered by Trump on travelers from six predominantly Muslim countries, and anti-Muslim groups have staged rallies — met with counter-protests — alleging that Muslims want to impose Islamic law in the United States.

Demonstrators at Los Angeles International Airport on Jan. 28, 2017, protest a temporary ban on Muslim immigration. Polls show Americans increasingly are concerned about terrorism committed in the name of Islam and question whether Muslim values conflict with U.S. values. But surveys indicate that more than half of Americans know little about Islam.

CQ Researcher • July 28, 2017 • www.cqresearcher.com
Volume 27, Number 27 • Pages 629-652

THIS REPORT

THE ISSUES	**631**
BACKGROUND	**637**
CHRONOLOGY	**639**
CURRENT SITUATION	**643**
AT ISSUE	**645**
OUTLOOK	**646**
BIBLIOGRAPHY	**650**
THE NEXT STEP	**651**

CQ RESEARCHER

July 28, 2017
Volume 27, Number 27

EXECUTIVE EDITOR: Thomas J. Billitteri
tjb@sagepub.com

ASSISTANT MANAGING EDITORS: Kenneth Fireman, kenneth.fireman@sagepub.com, Kathy Koch, kathy.koch@sagepub.com, Scott Rohrer, scott.rohrer@sagepub.com

ASSOCIATE MANAGING EDITOR: Val Ellicott

SENIOR CONTRIBUTING EDITOR:
Thomas J. Colin
tom.colin@sagepub.com

CONTRIBUTING WRITERS: Marcia Clemmitt, Sarah Glazer, Reed Karaim, Barbara Mantel, Chuck McCutcheon, Tom Price

SENIOR PROJECT EDITOR: Olu B. Davis

EDITORIAL ASSISTANT: Natalia Gurevich

INTERN: Robert DePaolo

FACT CHECKERS: Eva P. Dasher, Michelle Harris, Betsy Towner Levine, Robin Palmer

Los Angeles I London I New Delhi
Singapore I Washington DC I Melbourne

An Imprint of SAGE Publications, Inc.

SENIOR VICE PRESIDENT,
GLOBAL LEARNING RESOURCES:
Karen Phillips

EXECUTIVE DIRECTOR, ONLINE LIBRARY AND
REFERENCE PUBLISHING:
Todd Baldwin

THE ISSUES

631 • Are Islamic beliefs at odds with American values?
• Are Muslim-Americans doing enough to discourage home-grown Islamic extremism?
• Should the United States restrict immigration and travel from Muslim countries?

BACKGROUND

637 **Long Presence**
Some American slaves were Muslim.

637 **20th-Century Life**
Many African-Americans embraced Islam.

640 **Impact of 9/11**
Anti-Muslim hate crimes surged after Sept. 11 attacks.

641 **American Muslims Today**
Muslims share common values with other Americans.

CURRENT SITUATION

643 **Trump Policies**
Supreme Court backs Trump travel ban from six predominantly Muslim countries.

644 **Banning Sharia**
Some states have banned foreign laws from being used in U.S. courts.

OUTLOOK

646 **Projections Differ**
Some observers fear anti-Muslim tensions will rise, while others see them waning.

SIDEBARS AND GRAPHICS

632 **Muslims Live in All States**
Every state hosts a Muslim population.

633 **Half of Americans Know a Muslim**
Younger Americans and those with college degrees are most likely to personally know someone who is Muslim.

636 **Muslim Share of Population to Double by 2050**
Muslims are expected to rise from 1 percent of the U.S. population to more than 2 percent.

639 **Chronology**
Key events since 1777.

640 **Muslims Work to Refute Anti-Muslim Sentiment**
"It is our responsibility . . . to reach out."

642 **Islam on Track to Become World's Largest Religion**
Muslims already make up nearly a quarter of the planet's population.

645 **At Issue:**
Does Islam need a reformation?

FOR FURTHER RESEARCH

649 **For More Information**
Organizations to contact.

650 **Bibliography**
Selected sources used.

651 **The Next Step**
Additional articles.

651 **Citing CQ Researcher**
Sample bibliography formats.

CQ Press is a registered trademark of Congressional Quarterly Inc.

CQ Researcher (ISSN 1056-2036) is printed on acid-free paper. Published weekly, except: (March wk. 4) (May wk. 4) (July wks. 1, 2) (Aug. wks. 2, 3) (Nov. wk. 4) and (Dec. wks. 3, 4). Published by SAGE Publications, Inc., 2455 Teller Rd., Thousand Oaks, CA 91320. Annual full-service subscriptions start at $1,131. For pricing, call 1-800-818-7243. To purchase a CQ Researcher report in print or electronic format (PDF), visit www.cqpress.com or call 866-427-7737. Single reports start at $15. Bulk purchase discounts and electronic-rights licensing are also available. Periodicals postage paid at Thousand Oaks, California, and at additional mailing offices. POSTMASTER: Send address changes to CQ Researcher, 2600 Virginia Ave., N.W., Suite 600, Washington, DC 20037.

Cover: Getty Images/Anadolu Agecny/Aydin Palabiyikoglu

Muslims in America

THE ISSUES

Jeremy Christian, of Portland, Ore., had a history of making hateful comments online about Muslims and other religious groups. But last May, according to police, he took his hatred to a lethal level.

On a train in Portland, Christian began screaming insults at two young women, one wearing a hijab, or Muslim head covering. When three men intervened, Christian fatally stabbed two of them and wounded the third, police said. He has been charged in their deaths. [1]

"He was saying that Muslims should die," said Dyjuana Hudson, the mother of one of the two girls who were verbally assaulted in what Oregon Democratic Gov. Kate Brown later called "a crime of hate." [2]

Elsewhere, Muslims in recent years have been shot, stabbed, punched while pushing a child in a stroller and beaten outside of their homes and mosques in what authorities consider racially or religiously motivated attacks. Mosques have been firebombed, defaced and otherwise vandalized. [3]

Such incidents, and especially the Portland attack, have helped focus national attention on a rise in anti-Muslim rhetoric and violence in the United States. Polls show that Americans increasingly are concerned about terrorism committed in the name of Islam and question whether Muslim beliefs conflict with American values. At the same time, surveys indicate that more than half of Americans know little about Islam or the roughly 3.3 million Muslims living in the United States. [4]

Such a lack of familiarity provides "fertile ground for misconceptions and

Myhanh Best clutches the flag that draped the casket of her husband, Ricky, a 53-year-old Army veteran, during services on June 5, 2017, in Portland, Ore. Best was stabbed to death on a commuter train on May 26, along with Taliesin Namkai-Meche, 23, after trying to stop Jeremy Christian from taunting two teenage girls, one of whom was wearing a Muslim head covering. Christian was charged in the attack, which also injured Micah Fletcher, 21.

Getty Images/Scott Olson

stereotypes," says Ihsan Bagby, an associate professor of Islamic studies at the University of Kentucky in Lexington.

According to the FBI, the number of hate crimes against Muslims in the United States surged 67 percent in 2015, the latest year for which data is available, to 257 incidents — a level not seen since immediately after the Sept. 11, 2001, terrorist attacks in New York and at the Pentagon. According to the Council on American-Islamic Relations (CAIR), a national Muslim advocacy group in Washington that tracks such incidents, the spike continued in 2016 and in early 2017. [5]

The rise in violence cited by the FBI comes at a time when anti-Muslim rhetoric online has been on the rise and the number of anti-Muslim groups

in the United States has tripled, growing from 34 to 101 between 2015 and 2016, according to the Southern Poverty Law Center, a civil rights advocacy organization in Montgomery, Ala., that tracks such groups. [6]

Meanwhile, a 2015 poll found that 56 percent of Americans believe Islamic beliefs are at odds with American values and way of life, up from 47 percent in 2011. And a 2017 Pew Research Center poll found that 72 percent of Americans are either somewhat or very concerned about Islamist extremism. [7]

Analysts cite several reasons for Americans' increasing suspicions about Islam. The United States' 16-year involvement in conflicts in predominantly Muslim countries in the Middle East has played a role, they say, as have multiple violent terrorist incidents in Europe and the Middle East tied to radical Islamist groups such as the Islamic State, or ISIS, and al Qaeda. Americans acting in the name of ISIS also have been responsible for attacks in the United States, including the 2015 killings in San Bernardino, Calif., that left 14 dead, and a mass shooting in 2016 at a nightclub in Orlando, Fla., that claimed 49 lives. [8]

Many experts also say President Trump's anti-Muslim rhetoric during his presidential campaign helped to create an anti-Muslim climate. Among other comments, Trump said Muslims were "sick people," that "Islam hates us" and called for surveillance of mosques. [9]

In fact, surveys of attitudes and beliefs of U.S. Muslims reveal a far more complex picture than most Americans appear to realize. For example, because of the versions of the faith that dominate in conservative Middle Eastern societies

Muslims Live in All States

All 50 states have Muslim residents. Most American Muslims live in Illinois, Michigan and New York, with heavy concentrations in Chicago, Dearborn and New York City. Significant numbers of Muslims also live in Texas, Florida and California. Because the information was gathered by surveying mosques, Muslims in counties without mosques might not have been counted.

Share of Muslim Population by County

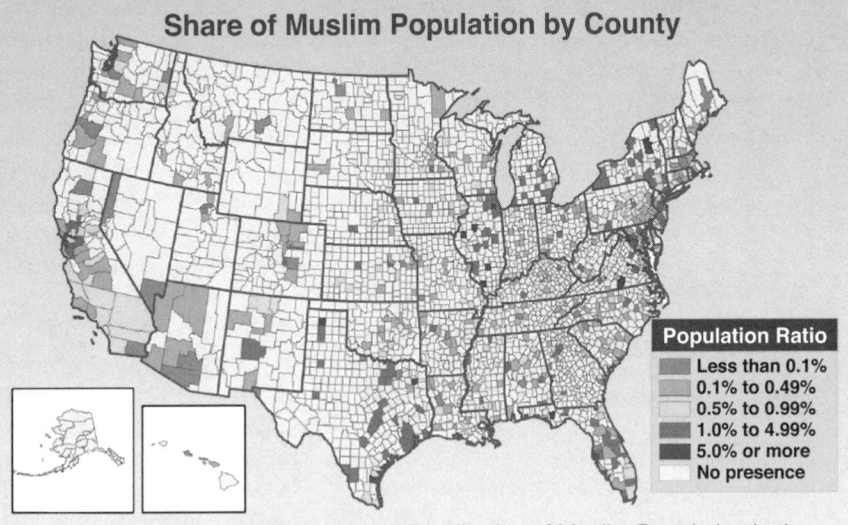

Population Ratio
- Less than 0.1%
- 0.1% to 0.49%
- 0.5% to 0.99%
- 1.0% to 4.99%
- 5.0% or more
- No presence

Source: "Muslim Journeys, Item #169: Distribution of Muslim Population in the United States, 2010," National Endowment for the Humanities, July 20, 2017, https://tinyurl.com/qx5y4dl

such as Saudi Arabia, Islam is widely portrayed as hostile to the rights of women. But 90 percent of American Muslims believe women should be able to work outside the home, and nearly seven in 10 see no difference between male and female political leaders. [10]

American Muslims' attitudes toward homosexuality also have been rapidly growing more tolerant, with 45 percent saying in 2015 that homosexuality should be accepted by society, 9 percentage points more than among evangelical Christians. [11]

Several polls also have found that American Muslims overwhelmingly reject extremist violence. A 2011 Gallup poll found Muslims were "the least likely major religious group in the U.S. to say there is ever a justification for individuals or small groups to attack civilians." [12]

American Muslims are also no more likely than Christians to say religion is

important in their lives. [13] Finally, a 2017 poll found that American Muslims are more likely than any other faith group to say they are satisfied with the overall direction of the country. [14]

"The single most dangerous stereotype is that Muslims do not like American society, do not buy into the American dream, are not integrating in the American society," says Bagby.

Such stereotyping resembles past American attitudes toward other immigrant groups, including Irish Catholics and Eastern Europeans, says Zareena Grewal, an associate professor of religious studies and American studies at Yale University in New Haven, Conn. "There's always that bogeyman, this one population that [some people say] can't really be assimilated," she says. "There's nothing new about this."

Still, some observers of the Muslim community say that even if the majority

fit into the national mosaic of religious and ethnic groups, a significant portion of American Muslims follows a dangerous political ideology they term "Islamism" — the belief all people should eventually come under the rule of a "caliphate," or a fundamentalist Islamic state.

"What extremism exists is very dangerous and should not be underestimated," says Sam Westrop, director of Islamist Watch, a project of the Middle East Forum, a conservative think tank and advocacy group in Washington that works to counter Islamism. Westrop believes Islamism is disproportionately represented in American Muslim leadership, although he said there is no accurate measure of how prevalent the ideology is. Muslim institutions from schools to mosques to advocacy groups "have been infiltrated by these people," he contends.

However, the public perception that radical Islamists are behind most terrorist acts in the United States is in error. In the nearly 16 years since the 9/11 attacks, 73 percent of the violent extremist incidents in the United States were perpetrated by members of non-Muslim groups espousing far right political beliefs, according to data compiled by the U.S. Government Accountability Office (GAO). Islamist extremists were responsible for the other 27 percent. [15]

Trump has accused the press of covering up terrorist attacks perpetrated by Muslims around the world. "It's gotten to the point where it's not even being reported," he said. "And in many cases the very, very dishonest press doesn't want to report it." [16]

But Georgia State University researchers found the opposite is true: A terrorist incident committed by a Muslim gets, on average, about 4.5 times as much coverage in the U.S. press as a terrorist act committed by a non-Muslim. The authors of the study concluded this contributes to the American public's exaggerated sense of the threat of Muslim terrorism. [17]

Observers say groups such as ACT for America in Washington, which fights what it describes as the "threat of radical Islam," have further stirred anti-Muslim sentiment by raising the specter that American Muslims seek to impose Sharia, or Islamic law, across the United States.

Muslims seem likely to remain at the center of an American political debate for the near future, at least. Trump has proposed temporarily banning immigration and visitors from six primarily Muslim countries, saying the move is necessary to protect Americans. The U.S. Supreme Court on June 26 overturned lower court rulings that the ban was discriminatory and allowed a limited version of it to go into effect. The administration also has not ruled out the possibility of requiring American Muslims to register with the federal government, something Trump mentioned during the campaign. [18]

As the United States wrestles with these and other issues concerning Muslim Americans, here are some of the fundamental questions being debated:

Are Islamic beliefs at odds with American values?

Islam's harshest critics characterize the religion as intrinsically violent and totalitarian in nature. They cite passages in the Quran, Islam's holy book, and the Hadiths, which contain accounts of the Prophet Muhammad's life and sayings, that they say require submission to Sharia and call Muslims to jihad, which they define as a holy war against nonbelievers. [19]

Islam, they say, does not recognize the separation of church and state, a bedrock value of secular Western democracies. Virulently anti-Islamic websites such as Jihad Watch paint a picture of Islam that is fundamentally at odds with American beliefs in individual and minority rights, peaceful disagreement and compromise. [20]

American attitudes about Islam also may be influenced by the attention given to the ultra-conservative and intolerant version of the faith, Wahhabism, practiced in Saudi Arabia, where

women's rights are sharply curtailed and the legal system is based on harsh interpretations of Sharia that call for chopping off hands, stoning, flogging and beheading. Although the country's leaders condemn the terrorist acts of groups such as ISIS and have collaborated with the United States and other Western nations in battling jihadists, Saudis also support mosques and religious schools around the world that teach Wahhabi doctrine. [21]

But Wahhabism, also called Salafism, is not the dominant strain of Islam across much of the Islamic world. And all but a handful of Muslim-majority countries modernized and secularized their criminal codes decades ago, according to Mustafa Akyol, a visiting fellow at the Freedom Project at Wellesley College. [22]

Most Islamic scholars and members of the Muslim community flatly reject the view of their faith promoted by Islam's

U.S. critics, saying it selectively picks and distorts passages from the Quran and the Hadiths to stir up "Islamophobia," or fear and hostility toward Muslims.

Corey Saylor, director of CAIR's Department to Monitor and Combat Islamophobia, says it misrepresents Islam to say the faith is hostile to people with different beliefs. "The Quran very clearly says that if God wanted to make everybody in the world Muslim he would have, and he chose not to," he says, "and so Muslims know through our holy book that we're meant to live alongside others."

Sharia is not meant to replace American law, he continues, but to guide Muslims in their personal lives and practices. "It's very clear that Muslims are expected to obey the laws of the land in which they live," Saylor says. "I've been a Muslim for a long time, and there's no conflict in my mind to being a Muslim man in America."

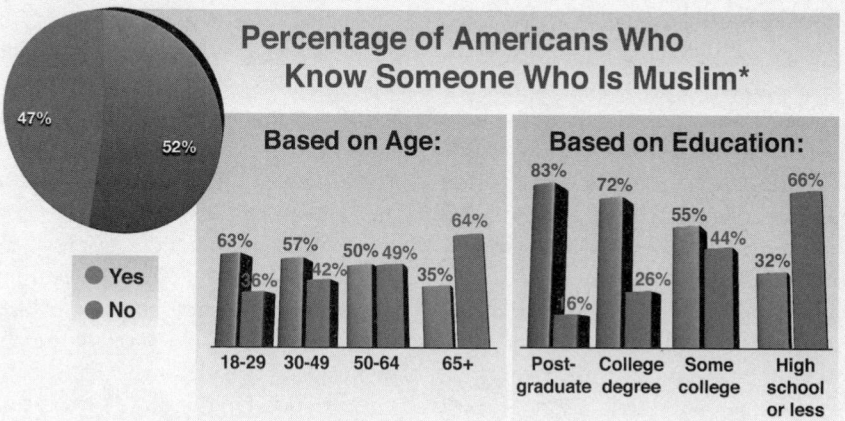

Half of Americans Know a Muslim

Just over half of American adults said they personally know someone who is Muslim, according to a 2016 Pew Research Center poll. Respondents ages 18 through 29 and those with college degrees were more likely to know a Muslim than older Americans or those with only a high school education.

Percentage of Americans Who Know Someone Who Is Muslim*

52% / 47%

● Yes   ● No

Based on Age:

	18-29	30-49	50-64	65+
Yes	63%	57%	50%	35%
No	36%	42%	49%	64%

Based on Education:

	Post-graduate	College degree	Some college	High school or less
Yes	83%	72%	55%	32%
No	16%	26%	44%	66%

* Figures do not add to 100 because up to 2 percent either did not know or refused to answer.

Source: "Republicans Prefer Blunt Talk About Islamic Extremism, Democrats Favor Caution," Pew Research Center poll, Feb. 3, 2016, https://tinyurl.com/znnmxyu

But Hillel Fradkin, who directs the Center on Islam, Democracy and the Future of the Muslim World at the Hudson Institute, a conservative think tank in Washington, says the idea of an Islamic state is a fundamental part of the religion. "It's not a misrepresentation of the faith to say that Islam is political and that the political part is terribly important in the original conception of Islam," he says. "There's a very famous slogan within Muslim discourse: 'There's no religion and there's no state in Islam, they're just one.' "

Akyol also points out that Islamist movements across the Muslim world seek to reorder government and society in accordance with Islamic laws, some vowing to do so through peaceful political means and others through violence. [23] In addition, a 2013 Pew poll of Muslims worldwide found that a majority of them want Sharia to be the "law of the land" where they live, although interpretations differed on what living under Sharia would mean. [24] (*See sidebar, p. 642.*)

Fradkin says American Muslims are not necessarily motivated by the idea of an Islamic political system. "There are a lot of Muslims who might accept the general statement that Islam is political without embracing a political [effort], either because they think it's not appropriate today, or they don't like the [particular] effort."

Fradkin says is he is not surprised by poll results that show a majority of U.S. Muslims are satisfied with the American political system. "Muslims are a minority within this country, and they have every reason within the American context to be supportive of rights that protect them," he says.

The University of Kentucky's Bagby says the American Muslim community in the 1980s, especially the newest immigrants and college students who had come from the Middle East, was inwardly focused. This was partly because of the religious traditions in their home countries, he says, and partly the influence of the Nation of Islam, an African-American offshoot of traditional Islam that supported black separatism.

"In the 1980s, there was a debate whether Muslims could really endorse a truly democratic system which allowed the ultimate authority to lie with people as opposed to God. There was a debate whether Muslims should really participate in the American system," Bagby says. But by the late 1980s and into the 1990s, "the pendulum had swung towards a full embrace of principles of democracy and an embrace of the agenda of involvement in the American political system."

However, Dr. Zuhdi Jasser, president of American Islamic Forum for Democracy, a small think tank in Phoenix that advocates for the separation of church and state, says U.S. Muslim leaders remain largely wedded to a vision of Islam that includes an Islamic state and does not embrace modern ideas involving individual rights and freedoms.

"I believe that 80 percent of American Muslims have values that are in line with American values. [But] they have had to find their way on their own. They have done so despite their leadership," Jasser says. He asserts that the majority of mosques and Muslim activist groups are led by Islamists, still wedded to a political vision for Islam that is antithetical to modern democracy.

However, Patrick Eddington, a policy analyst in homeland security and civil liberties at the Cato Institute, a libertarian think tank in Washington, says the leadership record of Muslims in many walks of American life, including politics and the military — where nearly 5,900 Muslims were serving in 2015 — should answer any question about whether their beliefs conflict with American values. [25]

"We've had Muslim Americans living in this country since the founding, and there's not one instance that I'm aware of where a Muslim American who has run for office has advocated replacing the Constitution with Sharia," he says.

"The public record shows that Arab-Americans and Muslim Americans who have been elected to Congress have served with distinction and honor, so their very presence and commitment to our democratic institutions is a complete refutation of this nonsense."

Are Muslim-Americans doing enough to discourage home-grown Islamist extremism?

After every significant terrorist attack in the name of Islam, either in the United States or abroad, the question arises in the media of whether American Muslims are doing enough to stop the radicalization of Muslims in their communities.

"Absolutely not," says Jasser of the American Islamic Forum for Democracy. "They really are not. If you look at the resources — the bandwidth — that the community is spending on anything related to Islam, they are wasting resources on a focus on bigotry against Muslims," Jasser says. "Yes, we should spend some resources on this, but the best use of our resources to counter bigotry is to lead a reform in our faith." That reform, he continues, must include focusing on defeating political extremism among Muslims.

The Hudson Institute's Fradkin agrees. "The default position of many public Muslims has been to protest against Islamophobia rather than say that we have a problem here and we have to address it," says Fradkin. "This is problematic because it discourages people from speaking out [in] their own community."

But CAIR's Saylor says Muslims face a double standard: "I'm a white male, and nobody called on me to condemn the shooting yesterday," referring to a June shooting at a baseball practice for Republican lawmakers and staff members in Alexandria, Va. "I'm also a Muslim, and if a Muslim had done that, my phone would not have stopped ringing."

He also says the question ignores the reality of the responses from the leadership of CAIR and other Muslim organizations to terrorism. "The executive director of my organization was included on a short list of Western Muslims ISIS wanted to see assassinated," Saylor says. "That is the result of us condemning them repeatedly. You've got to be doing something right if you're being condemned by ISIS."

But even if they denounce terrorism and terrorists, Islamist Watch's Westrop says too many Muslim leaders and imams preaching in mosques support a rigid version of Islamism. "They may be genuinely opposed to terrorism, but the hatred they preach, the rhetoric they preach, they provide the ideological momentum to inspire these kids to pick up a knife," Westrop says.

However, the CATO Institute's Eddington says that Muslim community leaders have cooperated with law enforcement officials to identify potentially dangerous individuals, earning praise from the Department of Homeland Security for their effort. [26] Many also have worked to steer young Muslims away from the lure of extremist beliefs. Minnesota Somalis, for example, have made a dedicated effort to reach out to alienated Somali youths. [27]

"I don't think there's any question that folks within the community have done and will do an enormous amount," Eddington says. But "there's no amount of denunciation of ISIS by the American Muslim community that would ever satisfy some of these critics."

The constant need to defend Islam while denouncing jihadist groups has taken a toll on the psyche of American Muslims, says Haroon Moghul, author of *How to be a Muslim: An American Story.* "For Muslims, we continue to live in a permanent state of anxiety, of being blamed," he says. "It's very hard for a community to mature and develop when it's under permanent scrutiny."

Moghul, who says he was not particularly devout as a teenager, was an undergraduate leader at New York University's Islamic Center when the 9/11 terrorist attack thrust him into the spotlight as an explainer of his faith. His book is an account of his struggle to forge a unique Muslim identity while serving in the role, as he puts it, of "professional Muslim," expected to publicly represent Islam.

Muslim-American billionaire Hamdi Ulukaya, founder and CEO of the Chobani yogurt company, has received death threats for employing refugees. Calling for a boycott of the company, one critic tweeted: "That Muzzie that owns it is hell bent on filling Idaho with Muslims." Ulukaya, who came to the United States from Turkey 23 years ago, employs both local residents and refugees in his yogurt plants in Idaho and upstate New York.

He finds it frustrating that Muslims are constantly asked to define themselves in relation to terrorism. "As dangerous as ISIS is, as vile as al Qaeda is, these are not existential threats to America," he says. "As a Muslim, it kind of feels like you're going crazy because you're trying to explain to people that this is a problem, but not the only problem."

Islam includes people with a wide range of beliefs and personal experiences and different levels of devotion, Moghul continues. "There's not one Islam," he says. Those who hold all Muslims responsible for speaking out against terrorism, he says, reduce the complexity of Muslim identity while simultaneously elevating its significance.

"It becomes this perverse feeling when you realize that your country is obsessed with you, and not in a healthy way," Moghul says. "It's a really strange place to be when your [religious] identity becomes a kind of litmus test on where people stand politically."

Should the United States restrict immigration and travel from Muslim countries?

A centerpiece of President Trump's anti-terrorism agenda has been a 90-day ban on immigration and visitors from six predominantly Muslim countries: Syria, Iran, Libya, Somalia, Sudan and Yemen.

Shortly after taking office, Trump issued an executive order blocking travel from those nations and Iraq until more stringent screening procedures could be

Getty Images/Anadolu Agency/Dursun Aydemir

Muslim Share of Population to Double by 2050

The 3.3 million Muslims living in the United States in 2015 represented about 1 percent of the U.S. population. By 2050, the number of Muslims is expected to grow to 8.1 million, or about 2.1 percent of the population, making them the second-largest religious group behind Christians, who made up nearly 71 percent of the population as of 2014.

Growth in Minority Religious Group Shares of the U.S. Population

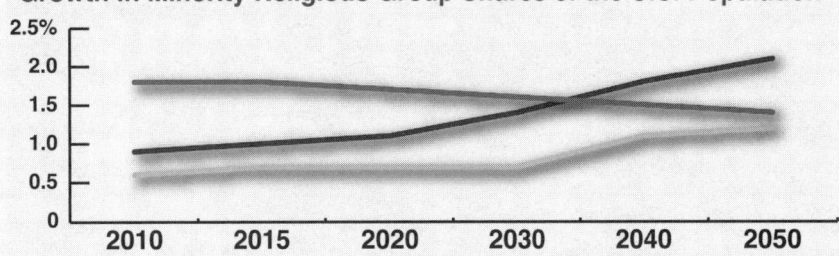

Sources: Besheer Mohamed, "A new estimate of the U.S. Muslim population," Pew Research Center, Jan. 6, 2016, https://tinyurl.com/jg89vsu; "Religious Landscape Study," Pew Research Center, 2014, http://tinyurl.com/ov8z97d

implemented. The order sparked mass protests and widespread confusion at airports about whether legal, green-card-holding residents would be allowed to re-enter the United States. [28]

Federal courts halted the order on the grounds that it unconstitutionally discriminated against a specific religion. The administration responded by issuing a revised order in March, removing Iraq, a U.S. ally in the fight against ISIS, and making other changes designed to help it withstand legal challenges. [29] The new order also no longer gave preference to Middle Eastern religious minorities for refugee resettlement, a provision viewed as anti-Muslim and pro-Christian, and clarified that legal U.S. residents would not be affected. [30]

However, federal judges in Hawaii and Maryland issued injunctions against implementing the revised order, saying it was still discriminatory. But this June, the U.S. Supreme Court ruled that a limited version of Trump's ban could go into effect, pending a hearing on the full proposal this fall. [31]

When announcing the revised order, Cabinet members described it as essential to national safety. "The Executive Order . . . will make America safer, and address long-overdue concerns about the security of our immigration system," said Homeland Security Secretary John Kelly. "We must undertake a rigorous review of our visa and refugee vetting programs to increase our confidence in the entry decisions we make for visitors and immigrants. . . . We cannot risk the prospect of malevolent actors using our immigration system to take American lives." [32]

But critics of the ban say it makes little sense as a security effort. Notably, "it doesn't actually target the countries that have been the primary exporters of terrorism," says the Cato Institute's Eddington. "The two countries at the top of the list for that are Saudi Arabia and Pakistan, and they're not even on the president's list." Fifteen of the 19 attackers on 9/11 and mastermind Osama bin Laden were from Saudi Arabia. [33]

"To me, that alone illustrates that this is about politics, and essentially throwing red political meat at [Trump's] base, and not a serious attempt to address a problem," Eddington continues.

Attorney General Jeff Sessions defended the choice of countries on the list. "Three of these nations are state sponsors of terrorism. The other three have served as safe havens for terrorists — countries where the government has lost control of territory to terrorist groups like ISIL [another name for ISIS] or al Qaeda and its affiliates. This increases the risk that people admitted here from these countries may belong to terrorist groups or may have been radicalized by them," Sessions said. [34]

But Eddington contends the ban would deprive the United States of valuable intelligence about terrorists that could be obtained from refugees as well as voices that could speak out against Islamist extremism.

"Who are the best witnesses we have to the horrors of ISIS?" Eddington asks. "The people who have fled from ISIS, and the vast majority of those folks have been . . . from Syria and Iraq." Those are the very people who could "help to refute the ISIS narrative that they're building a Muslim paradise."

The other key issue in the debate surrounding the executive order is whether it amounts to a de facto Muslim ban. Supporters of the ban contend the order's limited nature indicates it does not single out Muslims. "The seven affected countries represent 12.5 percent of all Muslim-majority states, a mere 8.2 percent of the world's Muslims. Because we Muslims make our homes in more than 183 nations around the world, these orders are neither global nor anti-Muslim," Qanta A. Ahmed, a member of the Council on Foreign Relations, an international affairs think tank in New York, said about the original proposal. [35]

Former White House Press Secretary Sean Spicer was among several administration officials who insisted at the time that the order did not target people of any religion. "It's not a Muslim ban," he said. [36]

But in a ruling halting the ban, U.S. District Judge Derrick Watson in Hawaii cited the president's own words as contradicting that position. Watson referred to campaign statements in which Trump said Muslims were a national threat and that he planned to bar them from entering the United States. [37] The most direct statement, in which Trump called for a "complete and total shutdown of Muslims entering the United States," was still on the campaign's website in May until reporters pointed it out to the White House. [38]

CAIR's Saylor says targeting Muslims undermines the United States in its battle against extremist groups by betraying the American principle of equal treatment for people of all religions. "Our war with ISIS is a battle of ideals, and I think we should be projecting our ideals because our American ideals are great, particularly in reaction to the devil-inspired ideals of these groups," Saylor says.

But Jasser of the American Islamic Forum for Democracy believes an expanded list of nations could be in order. "As we develop our vetting system," he says, "I hope that we start to include our so-called allies," even those that come from a country with an Islamist ideology. ■

BACKGROUND

Long Presence

Muslims have been part of the American landscape since before the country existed. Early records indicate that some of the first Spanish explorers to arrive in the New World in the 15th century were of Arab ancestry and Muslim. [39] Spain, at the time, had only recently become a nation ruled by Christian nobles after several centuries in which North African Muslims, known as Moors, had governed much of the country. [40]

Flanked by his wife, Muslim-American lawyer Khizr Khan brandishes his copy of the U.S. Constitution while speaking at the Democratic National Convention on July 28, 2016, in Philadelphia. Khan, the father of an American soldier killed in action in Iraq, offered to let Donald Trump borrow his copy of the Constitution and said the GOP nominee's promises to ban Muslims violated the document's Equal Protection Clause.

In the original 13 colonies, historians say, Muslims first arrived in significant numbers as early as the 17th century, brought as slaves from West Africa, where Islam had spread from the Middle East in the seventh century. Estimates of the number of Muslim slaves in early America range from a few thousand to a million or more. [41]

Although many Muslim slaves lost their faith or converted to Christianity over time, ethnographers in the 1930s recorded that some Islamic religious practices persisted for generations, including praying several times a day in the direction of Mecca. Islam appears to have been particularly strong among African-American families along the Georgia coast, according to historian Edward Curtis IV. [42]

Thomas Jefferson was one of several of the nation's founders who said the idea of religious freedom in the new nation was intended to include Muslims, referred to at the time as "Mahometans." In his autobiography, Jefferson noted that Virginia's Bill for Establishing Religious Freedom, the forerunner of the religious freedom guarantee in the First

Amendment to the U.S. Constitution, was meant to embrace "within the mantle of its protection, the Jew and the Gentile, the Christian and the Mahometan." [43]

In the 19th century, immigrants from the Middle East, particularly Syria and Lebanon, brought their faith to the heartland of America, settling in Ohio, Michigan, Iowa and North Dakota. [44] Muslim missionaries, many from Asia, also began traveling across the country seeking converts. As the 20th century got underway, they would find their most receptive audience within the African-American community.

20th-Century Life

In 1913, Timothy Drew, whose origins are obscure, founded a temple of worship for African-Americans in New Jersey that drew heavily on Islamic practices. In 1925, Drew founded the larger Moorish Science Temple in Chicago. Drew, known to his followers as Noble Drew Ali, taught that blacks were actually Moors whose Muslim identity had been taken away from them through slavery.

Ali called for African-Americans to reclaim their Islamic identity, although his teachings differed from traditional Islam in several ways. [45]

Also in the 1920s, missionaries from the Muslim Ahmadiyya movement in India established their mission headquarters in Chicago, gathering adherents within the African-American community by teaching that Islam treated all followers equally and preaching against racial inequality in the United States.

of Islam, by Wallace Fard, whose past is also a mystery. The Nation of Islam combined Islamic practices and beliefs with a message that emphasized African-American self-sufficiency and black separatism. [47]

After Fard mysteriously disappeared in 1934, his follower Elijah Muhammad assumed leadership of the Nation of Islam, and by the 1960s it became the largest of many African-American Islamic groups in the United States, with more

Americans make up about 40 percent of native-born Muslims in the United States. [49]

While the African-American Muslim population was growing, immigration from largely Muslim countries in the Middle East had been severely curtailed by the 1924 National Origins Act. The law established quotas for immigrants from different countries and strongly favored Western European white nations. Syria, Turkey and Egypt, for example, initially were each limited to 100 immigrants a year, while Germany was allowed more than 51,000. [50]

Over the next several decades the U.S. government repeatedly tinkered with its immigration laws, but quotas were not formally abolished until the Immigration and Reform Act of 1965, leading to a wave of immigrants from around the world.

From 1966 to 1997, about 2.8 million people from predominantly Muslim countries immigrated to the United States. [51] Because immigration officials and the U.S. Census do not generally ask about religious preference, it is impossible to know exactly how many were Muslims, but one estimate places the number at more than a million. [52] Students from Middle Eastern countries also began studying at U.S. universities.

The last decades of the 20th century saw a growing interest in religious study and devotion among the Muslim population, along with the growth of Islamic institutions across the country, according to historian Curtis. He estimated that perhaps more than 1,000 mosques and Islamic centers were established in the United States during the last three decades of the 20th century.

"They appeared wherever groups of Muslims lived — in small college towns, suburbs and inner cities," Curtis wrote. "By 2000, there was no region of the country without some kind of Muslim mosque." [53]

The influx of Muslim immigrants did not come without tensions, Curtis

Getty Images/Win McNamee

Rep. Keith Ellison, a Minnesota Democrat, became the first Muslim elected to Congress in 2007. In the wake of the anti-Muslim incident on a Portland train in May that resulted in the deaths of two passengers, Ellison accused President Trump of implicitly encouraging anti-Muslim acts. "This kind of thing is green-lighted by the president's rhetoric," Ellison said.

"The Ahmadiyya newspaper, the *Moslem Sunrise*, regularly featured articles critical of Christian racism — an easy target to prove in the 1920s, as the Ku Klux Klan rose to prominence based partly on its appeal to a white Protestant version of Christianity," wrote Curtis. [46]

These movements provided the roots of an enduring connection to Islam within the African-American community that would grow further in the 1930s with the establishment of the Nation

than 100,000 members. [48] Among its most famous members were Muhammad Ali, the heavyweight boxing champion, and Malcolm X, an activist and writer who later embraced traditional Islam following a pilgrimage to the Middle East in 1964. Eventually, the Nation of Islam fractured into two different groups, one pursuing a more traditional version of Islam.

Other Islamic groups also attracted significant numbers of African-Americans during the 20th century. Today, African-

Continued on p. 640

Chronology

16th Century–18th Century

Slave trade brings up to 1 million Muslims from West Africa to the United States.

1777
Thomas Jefferson writes the Virginia Statute for Establishing Religious Freedom, an early model of the first amendment of the U.S. Constitution; he later clarifies it was meant to include Muslims.

· •

1907-1929

Muslim immigrants from Eastern Europe and the Middle East establish a presence in the United States.

1907
Tartar immigrants from Poland, Russia and Lithuania start the American Mohammedan Society in Brooklyn, N.Y., the nation's first Muslim organization.

1921
The Ahmadiyya movement, started by an Indian Islamic sect, begins converting African-Americans to Islam in Chicago.

1929
Muslim immigrants build one of the first mosques in the United States in Ross, N.D.

· •

1930-1965

African-Americans mix a message of black pride and nationalism with Islam to create indigenous Islamic movements.

1930
Wallace Fard Muhammad, whose ori-

gins are obscure, founds the Nation of Islam in Detroit, combining Islamic beliefs with black separatism.

1963
Muslim Students' Association is formed on college campuses, fostering a generation of young leaders who will become influential in national Muslim organizations.

1964
Heavyweight boxing champion Cassius Clay converts to Islam; changes his name to Muhammad Ali.

1965
Malcolm X, a former Nation of Islam leader, is assassinated by the group's supporters. . . . The Immigration and Naturalization Act eliminates entry quotas that favored European immigrants, allowing a surge in Muslim immigration.

· •

1982-1995

Muslim organizations and individuals gain greater prominence and influence in U.S. society.

1982
Islamic students, leaders and professionals establish Islamic Society of North America, an umbrella organization for U.S. Muslim groups, in Plainfield, Ind.

1991
Charles Bilal becomes the first Muslim elected mayor of a U.S. city — Kountze, Texas.

1993
Islamist militants bomb the World Trade Center in New York City, killing six and injuring more than 1,000.

2000
Islamist militants attack the *USS Cole* in Aden, Yemen, killing 17 seamen.

2001-Present

Concern about Islamist jihadism grows in the United States, especially after high-profile terrorist attacks. Donald Trump is elected president after saying Muslims should be banned from entering the country.

2001
On Sept. 11, members of the radical Islamist group al Qaeda use hijacked planes to attack the World Trade Center and the Pentagon, killing nearly 3,000 people.

2007
Rep. Keith Ellison, a Minnesota Democrat, becomes the first Muslim elected to Congress.

2010
Oklahoma bans Sharia, or Islamic law, from state courts. A court overturns the measure as unconstitutional, but more than a dozen other states later consider similar measures.

2015
U.S. Muslim population reaches 3.3 million.

2016
Muslim American Omar Mateen kills 49 people at a gay nightclub in Orlando, Fla., claiming he is acting on behalf of the jihadist Islamic State. . . . GOP presidential candidate Donald Trump calls for surveillance of mosques.

2017
President Trump issues an executive order temporarily banning foreign nationals from certain predominantly Muslim countries from entering the U.S. After lower courts block the order, the Supreme Court rules it can take effect regarding non-citizens without strong ties to the United States.

Muslims Work to Refute Anti-Muslim Sentiment

"It is our responsibility . . . to reach out."

In his years working to educate the public about Islam, Irfan Sheikh has been insulted and threatened. He has heard his faith disparaged repeatedly and has been told, via email, that someone was coming to shoot him.

His response has been to contact, whenever possible, the people insulting or threatening him. "I try to talk to them," he says. "My hope is to be the messenger to tell people how much we have in common."

Sheikh is the Arizona representative of GainPeace, a Chicago-based nonprofit that is part of an effort by Muslim groups, community centers, schools and mosques around the nation to foster understanding of their faith in the face of rising anti-Muslim rhetoric and hate crimes.

For Muslim immigrants who come from countries that are less open than the United States and who are not yet at ease with U.S. customs, such outreach does not come easy, Sheikh says. But he believes Muslims need to step up to help explain their religion to others.

"We have to realize that it's not one person, or two persons, who can do this. We have to realize it is all our responsibility," he says. "We have to reach out."

In Tucson, where Sheikh lives, the Islamic Center of Tucson invited people of all faiths to gather at the center last December to support peace and unity following one of the most divisive presidential elections in history. More than 200 people crowded into the center's prayer hall to hear Islamic, Jewish and Christian speakers resolve not to be divided by prejudice. The event was representative of an interfaith dialogue involving national Muslim organizations and individual mosques around the country. [1]

GainPeace plans to use billboards, ads on buses and fliers distributed at shopping malls and other venues to spread the message that Islam is not at odds with Christianity, Judaism or democratic principles. Sheikh says the materials will excerpt verses from the Quran that speak to shared values among different faiths.

Muslim schools also are reaching out. The Council of Islamic Schools in North America, the national accrediting agency for Muslim schools, has asked its 78 member schools to set up gatherings between their students and students at non-Muslim schools. For instance, in May on Long Island, N.Y., students at MDQ Academy, an Islamic school in Brentwood, visited a nearby Catholic high school, Saint Anthony's. [2]

Continued from p. 638

noted. Some of the students who arrived were supporters of the Muslim Brotherhood, who believe the world would be better off living under Islamic codes. [54] U.S. support for Israel was unpopular with members of the Palestinian immigrant community. [55] Other Muslim immigrants supported the Iranian Revolution of 1979, in which 66 Americans were taken hostage in Tehran and held for more than a year. [56] The U.S. war in Iraq in 1991 also increased tensions with parts of the Muslim world and the American Muslim community.

Between 1993 and 2000, Islamist militants attacked the United States on three occasions: in 1993, when they detonated a truck bomb in the World Trade Center, killing six people; in 1998, when they bombed U.S. embassies in Kenya and Tanzania, killing 226; and in 2000, when suicide bombers attacked the *USS Cole* in Aden, Yemen, killing 17 American sailors. [57]

But historians and analysts largely agree that the most significant shift in American attitudes toward Muslims occurred on Sept. 11, 2001, when members of al Qaeda hijacked four jet airliners and crashed three into the World Trade Center in New York and the Pentagon in Arlington, Va. [58] A fourth plane was overtaken by passengers and forced to crash into the ground in Pennsylvania.

Impact of 9/11

The 9/11 attacks, which claimed nearly 3,000 lives and remains the deadliest terrorist incident in modern history, was perpetrated by 19 supporters of the Qaeda terrorist network, an extremist Islamic group dedicated to purging the Middle East of non-Muslims and establishing a caliphate across the region and, eventually, the world. [59]

In the aftermath, President George W. Bush made repeated public statements indicating the United States did not blame Islam for the attack and did not see itself at war with Muslims. "The face of terror is not the true faith of Islam. That's not what Islam is all about. Islam is peace," Bush said in a speech at the Islamic Center of Washington, D.C., six days after 9/11. "These terrorists don't represent peace. They represent evil and war." [60]

All the major U.S. Muslim organizations publicly denounced the 9/11 attacks. "American Muslims utterly condemn what are apparently vicious and cowardly acts of terrorism against innocent civilians," the American Muslim Public Coordination Council, which included the largest Islamic groups, said in a press release after the attacks. "We join with all Americans in calling for the swift apprehension and punishment of the perpetrators. No political cause could ever be assisted by such immoral acts." [61]

Despite these proclamations, a surge in hate crimes against Muslims — and dark-skinned people of other faiths —

"I hadn't really interacted with many Muslims before," Chris Beirne, a St. Anthony's senior said while eating lunch with the visiting Muslim students. Beirne said such interaction is key to dispelling a misperception held by some Americans of Muslims as extremists. [3]

The Islamic schools council also asks its member schools to undertake volunteer efforts outside the Muslim community and to participate in local government.

A February poll by the Pew Research Center backs up the value of outreach. It found that 60 percent of Americans who know a Muslim personally believe there is little or no support for extremism among U.S. Muslims. Among Americans who don't know a Muslim, that falls to 48 percent. [4]

Some Muslims take an informal approach to encouraging dialogue. Members of the Ahmadiyya, an Islamic sect, with U.S headquarters in Silver Spring, Md., hold Coffee, Cake and True Islam events around the country in which members invite non-Muslims to stop by a local coffee shop for free pastry and coffee, courtesy of the Ahmadiyya members, who then offer to answer questions about Islam. [5]

Sheikh agrees that direct conversation forges the strongest connections. After the 9/11 attacks on New York and the Pentagon in 2001, he says he went to a Muslim bookstore in Chicago, where he was then living, to talk to friends who were feeling as distressed as he was.

While he was there, "a hostile guy" came in and started to insult Muslims and their faith, Sheikh recalled. But as the Muslims explained their own feelings of pain and anger, the visitor calmed down, and they were able to talk.

"I thought, 'There are reasonable people,' " Sheikh says. "We will go on."

— *Reed Karaim*

[1] "Interfaith Relations," Muslim Public Affairs Council, http://tinyurl.com/yb8n7h6n.

[2] Laila Kearney, "To ease fears, U.S. Muslim schools reach out to neighbors," Reuters, May 12, 2917, http://tinyurl.com/y9wojgj8.

[3] *Ibid.*

[4] "Views of Islam and extremism in the U.S. and abroad," Pew Research Center, Feb. 16, 2017, http://tinyurl.com/ybxefyqs.

[5] Dania Sohail, "Coffee, cake and Islam: U.S. Muslims reach out to explain faith," *The San Francisco Chronicle*, June 14, 2017, http://tinyurl.com/y8esvof7. Also see "Meet a Muslim," TrueIslam.com, 2017, http://tinyurl.com/y8o8e3br.

ensued. The FBI reported 481 anti-Islamic incidents in 2002, up from the 28 the previous year and the highest number ever recorded. [62]

In one of the most highly publicized crimes, on Sept. 15, 2001, Frank Roque, a 42-year-old airplane mechanic in Mesa, Ariz., murdered Balbir Singh Sodhi, a Sikh of Indian ancestry who owned a gas station in Mesa. Roque evidently thought Sodhi was a Muslim because he was wearing a turban. He also fired shots at the home of an Afghan-American family and the Lebanese-American owner of another gas station. On the night of 9/11, Roque had told patrons at a bar, "I'm going to go out and shoot some towel-heads." When arrested by police he proclaimed himself "a patriot and an American." [63]

The years after 9/11 were marked by increased tensions between the Muslim community, the U.S. government and some conservative Americans. Following the attacks, the U.S. government increased surveillance of Arab-Americans and vis-

itors, a move that angered many Muslims. The U.S. invasion of Iraq in 2003 in response to claims, later disproved, that Iraq was harboring weapons of mass destruction, was also unpopular with much of the American Muslim population, which felt it was unjustified. [64]

Continued terrorist attacks made in the name of Islam, along with the rise of groups sharply critical of Islam as a faith, also contributed to rising suspicion about Islam in the United States, particularly among Republicans. [65]

The power of 9/11 to arouse strong emotions more than 14 years after the event was illustrated during the presidential campaign, when then-candidate Trump made the widely debunked claim that Muslims in New Jersey cheered when the Twin Towers in Manhattan collapsed after the attack. [66]

Author and former Islamic student leader Moghul believes 9/11 started a chain of events — the Iraq War, which led to the rise of ISIS, which led to increased concern about terrorism —

that has contributed to public fears and insecurity, or "a sense of being unmoored," which resulted in the election of Trump, he says.

"In many respects, we in America continue to live in September 11 even now," Moghul says.

American Muslims Today

Because the U.S. Census does not ask respondents to identify their religious faith, figures about the U.S. Muslim population are based on polling data. In 2015, the Pew Research Center estimated the American Muslim population at 3.3 million, or about 1 percent of the overall U.S. population. [67] About 63 percent of Muslims living in the United States are immigrants, according to Pew. [68]

Christians made up nearly 71 percent of the U.S. population, distantly followed by Jews at slightly less than 2 percent, according to a 2014 Pew study. [69] But

Islam on Track to Become World's Largest Religion

Muslims already make up nearly a quarter of the planet's population.

Muslims make up only slightly more than 1 percent of the U.S. population, with an estimated 3.3 million followers of Islam living in the United States. But globally, Islam is a proportionately much larger and more significant faith — one analysts expect to surpass Christianity to become the world's largest religion by the end of the century. [1]

There were about 1.8 billion Muslims in 2015, representing roughly 24 percent of the planet's population, according to an estimate by Pew Research Center. But Muslims have more children, on average, than members of other faiths. In addition, the Muslim population is young, with many just reaching child-bearing years, leading analysts to predict rapid population growth. [2]

In addition, contrary to popular perceptions, only about one-fifth of the world's Muslims live in the Middle East, where Islam originated in the 7th century. Muslims make up a majority of the population in 49 countries globally, according to Pew Research. [3] Indonesia has the largest Muslim population — 205 million; Pakistan is second with 178 million, and predominantly Hindu India trails slightly with 174 million. [4]

Islam has many smaller sects but two main traditional branches: Sunni and Shiite. The divide between the two branches dates back to a dispute over who should succeed the Prophet Muhammad as leader of the Muslim community following his death in 632. About 10-13 percent of the world's Muslims are Shiites, while the remaining 87-90 percent are Sunnis. Most Shiites live in just four countries, Iran, Pakistan, India and Iraq. [5]

Most Muslim nations in the Middle East are governed by authoritarian regimes. Saudi Arabia, a religiously conservative theocracy and one of America's closest Arab allies, is one of the world's worst human rights abusers, according to the nonpartisan Freedom House, based in New York and Washington, D.C., which tracks global democracy. [6]

Outside of the Middle East, several Muslim-majority countries, such as Indonesia, Mali and Tunisia, are democracies. India is the world's largest democracy. [7] But extremist groups are pressuring the more-tolerant and pluralistic versions of Islam that prevail in Indonesia and Mali. [8] In addition, predominantly Muslim Turkey — historically a secular, democratic society — has adopted increasingly conservative religious policies in recent years and curtailed the rights of dissidents and journalists under President Recep Tayyip Erdogan. [9]

A survey by Pew Research published in 2013 found that most of the world's Muslims prefer a democratic to an authoritarian leader. The survey also found that overwhelming majorities of Muslims — more than 90 percent in most regions — say "religious freedom is a good thing." [10]

Muslims also strongly reject violence against civilians in the name of Islam. "In most countries, the prevailing view is that such acts are never justified as a means of defending Islam from its enemies," Pew concluded. However, in a handful of countries, a substantial minority of Muslims say violent acts against civilians are sometimes justified. That opinion is strongest in the Palestinian territories (40 percent) and Afghanistan (39 percent), two areas long wracked by violence. [11]

the U.S. Muslim population is growing faster than that of most religious minorities. Before 2040, Muslims will overtake Jews as the largest non-Christian religious minority, according to Pew. By 2050, the American Muslim population is expected to reach 8.1 million, or 2.1 percent of the overall population. [70]

Based on earlier Pew research, the Muslim population has much in common with the rest of the American population. "Comparable percentages say they watch entertainment television, follow professional or college sports, recycle household materials and play video games," Pew reported in an extensive 2011 survey of U.S Muslim attitudes. The survey also found that about 33 percent of American Muslims

say they have worked with other people from their neighborhood to fix a problem or improve a condition in the past year, compared to 38 percent of the general public. [71]

Pew also found that American Muslims were about as religious as Christians. The majority are not dogmatic about their religious faith: 57 percent said there is more than one way to interpret the teachings of Islam, while 37 percent said there is only one true interpretation of Islam. [72]

Most also are more tolerant of other religions than evangelical Christians are: Only 35 percent of American Muslims say Islam is the one true faith that leads to eternal life, while 51 percent of U.S. evangelical Christians believe theirs is the one true faith. [73]

Muslim-Americans, however, are much more likely to support the Democratic Party than other Americans. They also are younger, with very diverse origins. Foreign-born Muslims come from 77 countries, with no single nation accounting for more than 14 percent. [74]

Eboo Patel, the founder of Interfaith Youth Core, a Chicago group that promotes dialogue and shared community efforts among college students of different faiths, says he believes the diversity and generally tolerant attitudes of Muslim Americans do not get recognized because they don't fit the narratives of either U.S. Islamic leaders or those who fear Islam.

"Part of what Islamophobes want to do is convince people that Muslims are monolithic and that they're all extremist," he says, "and part of what

A majority of Muslims globally say they want Sharia — or Islamic law — to be "the law of the land" where they live, but many say Sharia should apply only to Muslims. Support for Sharia is highest in South Asia, sub-Saharan Africa, the Middle East-North Africa and Southeast Asia, the 2013 survey found. [12] Currently, only about a dozen Muslim countries have criminal codes based on Sharia. [13]

The survey also shows a wide divergence of opinion on how Muslims interpret Sharia and considerably less support for the most punitive aspects of Islamic law imposed in some strict Muslim countries such as Saudi Arabia, where stoning is a legal punishment for adultery and where the government executed at least 157 people in 2015, most by beheading, according to Amnesty International. [14]

The majority also think "Western music, movies and television pose a threat to morality in their country," Pew reported. But at the same time, many Muslims around the world say they enjoy Western entertainment on a personal level. [15]

— *Reed Karaim*

During the hajj, or annual pilgrimage to the holy city of Mecca in Saudi Arabia, Muslims pray while circling the Kaaba, a building that contains a sacred black stone, located in the courtyard of the Great Mosque.

[1] Michael Lipka, "Muslims and Islam: Key finding in the U.S. and around the world," Pew Research Center, May 26, 2017, https://tinyurl.com/y825pyca.

[2] *Ibid.*

[3] Drew Desilver and David Masci, "World's Muslim population more widespread than you might think," Pew Research Center, Jan. 31, 2017, https://tinyurl.com/hhfxhf6.

[4] "Muslim populations by country: how big will each Muslim population be by 2030?" *The Guardian*, 2016, https://tinyurl.com/ybrwx7rn.

[5] "Sunni and Shia Muslims," Pew Research Center, Jan. 27, 2011, https://tinyurl.com/y9757vjh.

[6] "Freedom in the World 2016," Freedom House, 2016, https://tinyurl.com/jjawg7m.

[7] *Ibid.*

[8] Krithika Varagur, "Indonesia's Moderate Islam Is Slowly Crumbling," *Foreign Policy*, Feb. 14, 2017, https://tinyurl.com/y6wnmjaf.

[9] For background, see Brian Beary, "Unrest in Turkey," *CQ Researcher*, Jan. 29, 2016, pp. 97-120.

[10] "The World's Muslims: Religion, Politics and Society," Pew Research Center, April 30, 2013, https://tinyurl.com/mheey6u.

[11] *Ibid.*

[12] *Ibid.*

[13] Mustafa Akyol, "Shariah's Winding Path Into Modernity," *The New York Times*, July 13, 2017, https://tinyurl.com/y9qt29mu.

[14] "Saudi Arabia: beheadings reach highest level in two decades," *The Guardian*, Jan. 1, 2016, https://tinyurl.com/le7cnzw.

[15] "The World's Muslims: Religion, Politics and Society," *op. cit.*

Muslim religious leaders want to do is convince people that Muslims are monolithic and they're all observant." In truth, Patel says, his experiences working with young Muslims and the larger Muslim American community have taught him they are neither. ■

CURRENT SITUATION

Trump Policies

The Supreme Court's June 26 decision on Trump's travel ban has rekindled the debate over the president's authority to control immigration.

It also has reignited fears among some U.S. Muslims about the intentions of the administration. Nihad Awad, CAIR's executive director, said the ruling "ignores the anti-Muslim bigotry that is at the heart of the travel ban executive orders and will inevitably embolden Islamophobes in the administration." [75]

The president had sought broad authority to block people from Syria, Iran, Libya, Somalia, Sudan and Yemen from entering the United States for 90 days while the administration developed stricter screening procedures. It also wanted to halt refugee resettlement from all countries for 120 days while it conducted a review of screening policies. [76]

The lower courts had said the executive order discriminated against people of a particular religion, based on Trump's own prior statements about Muslims. But pending a full hearing on the order this fall, the Supreme Court said the administration can temporarily block the entry of people from the six countries, unless individuals have "a credible claim of a bona fide relationship with a person or entity in the United States." [77] In explaining its ruling, the court said the president's powers to control entry into the United States "are undoubtedly at their peak when there is no tie between the foreign national and the United States." [78]

Legal analysts were unsure what constitutes a "bona fide relationship," but some experts felt the decision would include a large number of individuals seeking to enter the country, including relatives of people in the United States, students accepted at a university and those coming for a job or to deliver a lecture. [79]

Despite the limited nature of the ruling, Trump hailed the decision as a "clear victory for our national security" in a White House statement. "My number one responsibility as commander in chief is to keep the American people

may be unnecessary because the administration's 90-day review of screening policies probably will have expired by the time the court hears the case. [82]

While the ban was attracting attention, Trump made another decision in June that some Muslims see as evidence of the administration's negative attitude toward them. For the first time in 20 years, the White House did not host a dinner to mark the end of Ramadan, the Islamic holy month in

Banning Sharia

In early June, ACT for America, the group that says it is fighting the "threat of radical Islam," organized protests in about two dozen cities across the country against the potential imposition of Sharia in U.S. courts. David White, a spokesman for the group, described Sharia as a "barbaric code that executes LGBTQ people for their orientation, mutilates children and subjugates individual rights." [85]

Opponents of Sharia believe some Muslims want to impose Islamic rule in the United States. They also say it violates the U.S. Constitution in its view of human rights. During the campaign, Trump seemingly endorsed the view that Muslims wish to follow their own laws, saying, Muslims "are not assimilating . . . don't want the law we have. They want Sharia law," referring to the religious law imposed in some Muslim countries such as Saudi Arabia, Pakistan and Iran. [86]

The anti-Sharia movement, however, predates the election. It began seven years ago in this country, when Oklahoma in 2010 passed a law banning Sharia from state courts. But a court later tossed it out for discriminating against a particular religion.

Since then nine states have passed similar laws, but to avoid the discrimination problem the subsequent bills did not identify Sharia by name. Instead they prohibited judges from applying any foreign law in a state court. Thirteen states, including Montana, considered similar laws this spring. Only Montana's law made it through the legislature, but the governor vetoed it. [87]

Muslim leaders and many scholars of Islam say the views of groups such as ACT for America represent a fundamental misrepresentation of Sharia, which Muslims interpret in various ways. Most do not see it as superseding the laws of the state.

AFP/Getty Images/Sandy Huffaker

Demonstrators, including some Trump supporters, march along the beach in Oceanside, Calif., one of about two dozen protests on June 10, 2017, opposing what they fear could become the imposition of Sharia – or Islamic law – in U.S. courts. Many protesters were met by counter demonstrations in support of Muslims. Legal and Islamic scholars say there is no chance Islamic law will be imposed in U.S. courts.

safe. Today's ruling allows me to use an important tool for protecting our nation's homeland." [80]

The court's decision was unanimous, but Justices Clarence Thomas, Samuel A. Alito Jr. and Neil M. Gorsuch said they would have allowed the entire ban to go into effect. Thomas also predicted the partial ban will result in a flood of litigation by people claiming they were improperly denied entry. "I fear the court's remedy will prove unworkable," Thomas wrote in his dissent. [81]

Although the court scheduled a full hearing on the executive order for its next term, beginning in October, it

which Muslims fast from sunrise to sunset. When asked why Trump had canceled the dinner, White House press secretary Spicer responded, "I don't know." [83]

But several Muslim leaders expressed their disappointment at the decision. It "doesn't send a good message," said Talib Shareef, imam of Masjid Muhammad, known as the Nation's Mosque in Washington. "You get the chance to go golfing and all this other kind of stuff. How come you don't have time for a population of your society that needs some assistance? The message that it sends is that we're not that important." [84]

Continued on p. 646

At Issue:

Does Islam need a reformation?

M. ZUHDI JASSER
PRESIDENT, AMERICAN ISLAMIC FORUM FOR DEMOCRACY; CO-FOUNDER, MUSLIM REFORM MOVEMENT

WRITTEN FOR *CQ RESEARCHER*, JULY 2017

devout Muslims living happily in America have already modernized and reformed our faith interpretations. On a daily basis, when we autonomously choose to accept the elements of personal Islamic Sharia (jurisprudence) that are compatible with American law and reject the incompatible elements, we have "reformed" our own personal faith interpretations and practice. But that is an artificial construct — a bubble created by an enlightened, free society that allows us that choice.

But Islam is not simply what a handful of Americanized Muslims may choose to do. Islam's legacy is more realistically defined by the dominant schools of thought of the world's 1.8 billion Muslims. And polls show that a majority of Muslims believe Sharia — Islamic law — should be imposed in Muslim-majority societies and the vast majority of the ideas and legalisms taught by the dominant thought leaders of Islam's establishment are Islamist, promoting a Muslim theocracy. These are incompatible with modernity.

With only minor differences, the dominant Sunni and Shia schools of thought worldwide emanate from similar, ultra-conservative Salafi-jihadi (extremist Islamist) interpretations of Islamic jurisprudence. From the Sunni madrassas of Pakistan (Deobandi) to Saudi Arabia (Wahhabi and Salafi), Qatar (Muslim Brotherhood), Egypt (Muslim Brotherhood and Salafi) and to the Shia schools of Iran and Iraq (Jaafari), this theological juristic establishment has fossilized and monopolized the overwhelming majority of what defines "normative" Islam across the planet. Muslims living in freedom undeniably have left these forces unchecked.

In a two-page "Declaration of our Muslim Reform Movement," 14 Western Muslim thought leaders laid out core principles in desperate need of reform. For example, Islam will not be legitimately compatible with modernity until a majority of Muslims and their leadership believe in equal rights for women and minorities; free speech and the end of blasphemy and apostasy laws; the end of all violent jihad; the end of institutionalized "sharia;" politicized Islam and the idea of an Islamic state and caliphate. Legitimate Islamic reform will be realized only when mosque and state are separated in the minds of the majority of Muslims, when Muslims affirm the right of every individual to participate in reform and when we redefine and expand our *ummah* (community) to include all of humanity that accepts the "Universal Declaration of Human Rights" adopted by the United Nations in 1948, while rejecting the draconian, Sharia-based "Cairo Declaration of Human Rights in Islam."

ZAINAB ARAIN
COORDINATOR, DEPARTMENT TO MONITOR AND COMBAT ISLAMOPHOBIA, COUNCIL ON AMERICAN-ISLAMIC RELATIONS

WRITTEN FOR *CQ RESEARCHER*, JULY 2017

does Islam need reform? Absolutely not. Do some members of the faith community need to reform? Absolutely yes.

A verse in the Quran states, "This day I [God] have perfected your religion for you." For Muslims, this is a testament to the perfection and infallibility of Islam as a divinely revealed religion. Muslims also believe that though the religion itself is flawless, human beings are not.

Islam's fundamental principles include justice, freedom, respect for life and the dignity of all people. The application of these ideals has varied across the social, political and geographical context at any given time, thus giving rise to enormous diversity within Islam. It is the drive to live by these religious ideals that animates American Muslim achievements today.

Inspired by the faith they believe is perfected, American Muslims form an integral part of the nation, whether as entrepreneurs like the CEO of the yogurt company Chobani or comedians such as Dave Chapelle. The approximately 50,000 American Muslim medical doctors save lives every day. American Muslims include prominent athletes such as the late boxer Muhammad Ali and Olympian Ibtihaj Muhammad. At a local level, Umma Clinic in Los Angeles provides free quality health care to the underserved. The Inner-city Muslim Action Network works to lift people out of poverty in Chicago. In 2016, Muslims donated 30,000 bottles of water to Flint, Mich., during the peak of its water crises.

The call for a reformation of Islam is often riddled with ill-defined and agenda-driven catchphrases such as "Islamism" and "Islamists," which have become shorthand for "Muslims we don't like" and are used almost exclusively in a pejorative context.

No religion is inherently prone to violence. Rather, it is people in differing social, economic and political conditions who can be violent. For example, the actions of Fred Phelps and the Westboro Baptist Church, Eric Robert Rudolph and the Army of God and the cross-burning racists of the Ku Klux Klan are anomalous to the Christian faith. Rightfully, there has been no outcry or call for a reformation of Christianity because of these twisted uses of the religion. Some Christians need reform, not Christianity itself. This same standard holds true for all religions, including Islam.

Ultimately, it is not religion that needs reformation, but the external conditions and internal problems of people that require positive transformation.

Continued from p. 644

"Sharia is not law in the sense that we understand it. Most Muslims who think about Sharia don't think of it as a book of statutes," says Yale's Grewal. "It's really a body of Quran-based guidance that points Muslims toward living an Islamic, ethical life. When Muslims think of the question of how to be good, Sharia is the answer. "In other words," she says, "it's the Muslim equivalent of 'What would Jesus do?' "

Retired engineer John Wider welcomes Muslims in the arrival hall at Los Angeles International Airport on June 29, 2017, the first day of the partial reinstatement of President Trump's controversial temporary ban on travelers from six Muslim-majority nations. Under a June 26 Supreme Court ruling, travelers from Iran, Libya, Somalia, Sudan, Syria and Yemen who lack a "bona fide relationship" with a person or entity in the United States are prevented from entering the country for 90 days.

Within that context, she says, many Muslims wish to be able to follow Sharia in their personal lives in the same manner that Jews or Catholics would follow the dictates of their faith.

Some conservative Muslims do want voluntary Sharia courts to arbitrate on issues such as marriage, divorce and inheritance, but that desire "should not be confused with making Shariah's harsh penal code the law of the land," said Akyol, of Wellesley's Freedom Project. [88] Such systems are similar to those established by other conservative U.S. religious communities — including evangelical Christians, Catholics, Orthodox

Jews and Muslims — who have formed private networks of arbitration tribunals in recent decades to voluntarily resolve disputes within their communities, particularly relating to family law. [89]

Some anti-Sharia activists have conflated such religious tribunals run by mosques with "Sharia courts," even though their rulings are nonbinding and work within the guidelines of U.S. law. In 2015 armed protesters showed up outside of a mosque in Irving, Texas, after rumors spread online that the city had imposed Sharia. But the *Houston Chronicle* tagged the rumor the "2015 Hoax of the Year," pointing out that it was only a religious tribunal similar to those run by other faiths. [90]

Both legal and Islamic scholars dismiss the threat of Sharia being imposed in American civil courts as a manufactured concern. "There is no evidence that Islamic law is encroaching on our courts," said a report by the American Civil Liberties Union. "Courts treat lawsuits that are brought by Muslims or that address the Islamic faith in the same way that they deal with similar

claims brought by people of other faiths or that involve no religion at all." [91]

Islamist Watch's Westrop believes some conservatives' obsession with Sharia serves as a distraction from the real threat of Islamist political ideology. "Sharia law has never been [fully] implemented anywhere in the history of the world. It's unworkable in modern society," he says. The American political right "is more interested in Sharia than the Islamists are."

This June's anti-Sharia protests were met in many cities by counter demonstrations in support of Muslims, which were often larger than the anti-Sharia gatherings. [92] And anti-Sharia legislation has faced opposition among some politicians.

When Montana's Democratic Gov. Steve Bullock vetoed such legislation in April, he said, "There is absolutely no need for this bill," adding that the intent of such bills "is to target a particular religion and group of people for disfavored treatment." [93] ∎

OUTLOOK

Projections Differ

Most analysts agree the present political environment in the United States is as difficult for Muslim Americans as it has been since 9/11. The experts, however, are divided over whether anti-Islamic sentiment will peak or grow stronger.

The Cato Institute's Eddington believes the next five years could lead to increased government harassment and oppression of American Muslims. He cites the presence within the Trump administration's national security team of Sebastian Gorka, a Hungarian academic who has argued that violence is an intrinsic part of Islam's political ideology, and White House strategist Steve Bannon, who as a filmmaker in

2007 outlined a documentary-style film about radical Muslims taking over the country and remaking it into the "Islamic States of America." [94]

With men such as Bannon and Gorka leading the effort, Eddington says, the Trump administration could use the fear of terrorism and the idea that Muslims are trying to establish Sharia in the United States to marginalize and systematically crack down on Muslim-Americans.

"People say there's no way that can happen again here," Eddington says. "I point them to Manzanar [a U.S. internment camp for Japanese Americans during World War II]. A return to that kind of level of oppression is exactly what I'm really fearful of. Those who value the Bill of Rights and want to avoid the kind of oppression that we saw then need to be very vigilant."

Islamist Watch's Westrop also takes a dark view of the future, but for completely different reasons. "The only future I currently see is increased violence and radicalization of the Muslim community," he says. "If the current level of Islamists in control of the U.S. Muslim community continues, we are simply going to see a greater number of American Muslims fall under the influence of Islamists, see more terror," he says.

Westrop thinks that could lead to greater anti-Islamic sentiment. "If anything, we're going to see a reaction by certain sections of the American society angry that their politicians aren't doing anything," he says. "And we're going to see increased acts [of violence against Muslims]."

But several Muslim analysts say the extreme nature of the anti-Islamic forces in the United States was likely to spur a backlash. "I think the tide has turned. I think this is the last hurrah for this Islamophobic sentiment. I think it will lead to a decisive counter-reaction against this narrative of hate and America will swing toward an embrace of the Muslim community," says the University of Kentucky's Bagby.

Moghul, the author and activist, says the strength of the Muslim community should help it persevere. "There are a lot of reasons to be optimistic if you're an American Muslim — the talent in the community, the energy. There are a lot of good things happening, he says, "and when you add to that the fact that a lot of our most fervent critics are racist, I think it helps. I would much rather have a dumb neo-Nazi as my principal opponent than face a critical,

reasoned critique of my religion."

Yale University's Grewal believes the upcoming generation of Muslims will play a role in reshaping perception. "The Muslim Millennials are a really fascinating and important demographic that the American Muslim community has failed to take seriously enough," she says. "They act and think much more like Millennials in general than they do like previous generations of Muslims, and they're really going to profoundly shape the future." In their economic concerns and aspirations and their attitudes toward LGBTQ individuals and justice "they're just culturally, socially and politically much more similar to their generation than they are to their parents," Grewal concludes.

Patel, founder of Interfaith Youth Core, says he has noticed that the average young person in America today

is much more likely to know a Muslim than older generations. As the Muslim population continues to grow, he believes increased interaction will reduce the hostility toward Muslims.

"When people develop meaningful relationships with members of groups that they have generalized ideas about, their attitudes change. This is already happening in our public schools," Patel says. "It's not just diversity, it's interaction that [enriches] American society." ∎

> "The single most dangerous stereotype is that Muslims do not like American society, do not buy into the American dream, are not integrating in the American society."
>
> — *Ishan Bagby,*
> *Associate Professor of Islamic Studies,*
> *University of Kentucky in Lexington*

Notes

[1] Matthew Haag and Jacey Fortin, "Two Killed in Portland While Trying to Stop Anti-Muslim Rant, Police Say," *The New York Times*, May 27, 2017, https://tinyurl.com/yal9zndy.

[2] Maxine Bernstein, "MAX attack unfolded quickly: Extremist cut three in neck, police say," *The Oregonian/OregonLive*, June 2, 2017, https://tinyurl.com/yagdsrr6.

[3] Daniel Burke, "Anti-Muslim hate crimes: Ignorance in action?" CNN, Jan. 30, 2017, https://tinyurl.com/ztc5efq.

[4] Besheer Mohamed, "A new estimate of the U.S. Muslim population," Pew Research Center, Jan. 6, 2016, https://tinyurl.com/jg89vsu. Michael Lipka, "Muslims and Islam: Key findings in the U.S. and around the world," Pew Research Center, May 26, 2017, https://tinyurl.com/y825pyca.

[5] Azadeh Ansari, "FBI: Hate crimes spike, most sharply against Muslims," CNN, Nov. 15, 2016, https://tinyurl.com/h8zw7kl. Also see "CAIR

Report Shows 2017 on Track to Becoming One of Worst Years Ever for Anti-Muslim Hate Crimes," Council on American-Islamic Relations, July 17, 2017, https://tinyurl.com/ya39rn5z.

[6] Melanie Eversley, "Report: Anti-Muslim groups triple in U.S. amid Trump hate rhetoric," *USA Today*, Feb. 15, 2017, https://tinyurl.com/yaa8oxte.

[7] Betsy Cooper *et al.*, "Anxiety, Nostalgia, and Mistrust: Findings from the 2015 American Values Survey," Public Religion Research Institute, Nov. 17, 2015, https://tinyurl.com/y8afrag9. Jacob Poushter, "Majorities in Europe, North America worried about Islamic extremism," Pew Research Center, May 24, 2017, https://tinyurl.com/yd8eevsj.

[8] Kurtis Lee, "Islamist terrorists have struck the U.S. 10 times since 9/11. This is where they were born," *Los Angeles Times*, Feb. 7, 2017, https://tinyurl.com/yal8tvo4.

[9] Jenna Johnson and Abigail Hauslohner, "'I think Islam hates us': A timeline of Trump's comments about Islam and Muslims," *The Washington Post*, May 20, 2017, https://tinyurl.com/y9ylcxwk.

[10] "Muslim Americans: No Signs of Growth in Alienation or Support for Extremism," Pew Research Center, Aug. 30, 2011, https://tinyurl.com/yc6r2p9e.

[11] "U.S. Public Becoming Less Religious, Chapter 4: Social and Political Attitudes," Pew Research Center, Nov. 3, 2015, https://tinyurl.com/jbscyry.

[12] "Muslim Americans: Faith, Freedom, and the Future," Abu Dhabi Gallup Center, August 2011, https://tinyurl.com/y6vg95fd.

[13] Lipka, *op. cit.*

[14] Dalia Mogahed and Youssef Chouhoud, "American Muslim Poll 2017: Muslims at the Crossroads," Institute for Social Policy and Understanding, https://tinyurl.com/ya4rtofz.

[15] Diana Maurer, "Countering Violent Extremism: Actions Needed to Define Strategy and Assess Progress of Federal Efforts," Government Accountability Office, April 2017, p. 4, https://tinyurl.com/lpbzakm/.

[16] Philip Bump, "President Trump is now

speculating that the media is covering up terrorist attacks," *The Washington Post*, Feb. 6, 2017, https://tinyurl.com/yajj6oa7.

[17] Erin M. Kearns, Allison Betus and Anthony Lemieux, "Yes, the media do underreport some terrorist attacks. Just not the ones most people think of," *The Washington Post*, March 13, 2017, https://tinyurl.com/y9z5tvpa.

[18] Ben Kamisar, "Tillerson won't rule out Muslim registry," *The Hill*, Jan. 11, 2017, https://tinyurl.com/y7d7j5a2.

[19] Gregory M. Davis, "Islam 101," Jihad Watch, https://tinyurl.com/zn7zwlc.

[20] *Ibid.*

[21] Scott Shane, "Saudis and Extremism: 'Both the Arsonists and the Firefighters,' " *The New York Times*, Aug. 25, 2016, http://tinyurl.com/lje96m4.

[22] Mustafa Akyol, "Shariah's Winding Path Into Modernity," *The New York Times*, July 13, 2017, https://tinyurl.com/ya3lzaan.

[23] *Ibid.*

[24] "The World's Muslims: Religion, Politics and Society," Pew Research Center, April 30, 2013, https://tinyurl.com/mheey6u.

[25] Mariam Khan and Luis Martinez, "More than 5,000 Muslims Serving in US Military, Pentagon Says," ABC News, Dec. 8, 2015, https://tinyurl.com/hmc6z7y.

[26] Michael Hirsh, "Inside the FBI's Secret Muslim Network," *Politico*, March 24, 2016, https://tinyurl.com/zcjaupr.

[27] Amy Forliti, "Advocates vow to continue work in Minnesota Somali community," The Associated Press, Dec. 24, 2016, https://tinyurl.com/ydemxtd4.

[28] Dan Merica, "How Trump's travel ban affects green card holders and dual citizens," CNN, Jan. 29, 2017, http://tinyurl.com/jc6kj83.

[29] Steve Almasy and Darran Simon, "A timeline of President Trump's travel bans," CNN, March 30, 2017, https://tinyurl.com/y72r2ehq.

[30] Katie Bo Williams and Jordan Fabian, "Trump signs revised travel ban that excludes Iraq," *The*

Hill, March 6, 2017, https://tinyurl.com/jgpc4bo.

[31] Michael D. Shear and Adam Liptak, "Supreme Court to Hear Travel Ban Case," *The New York Times*, June 26, 2016, https://tinyurl.com/y7jprgt4.

[32] "Statement by Secretary of Homeland Security John Kelly on President's Executive Order Signed Today," U.S. Department of Homeland Security, March 6, 2017, https://tinyurl.com/y8vvgkj2.

[33] "September 11th Hijackers Fast Facts," CNN, Sept. 15, 2016, https://tinyurl.com/y8rzgda3.

[34] "Attorney General Jeff Sessions Delivers Remarks on Revised Executive Order Protecting the Nation from Foreign Terrorist Entry," U.S Department of Justice, March 6, 2017, https://tinyurl.com/y8skshga.

[35] Qanta A. Ahmed, "Donald Trump's travel ban makes sense," *Newsday*, Feb. 1, 2017, https://tinyurl.com/y7bkwyvp.

[36] Peter W. Stevenson, "Trump says it's a travel 'ban.' His staff insisted it wasn't," *The Washington Post*, June 5, 2017, https://tinyurl.com/yb2f2qhm.

[37] "Ruling on Trump's second travel ban," *The New York Times*, March 15, 2017, https://tinyurl.com/ya5xld68.

[38] Christine Wang, "Trump website takes down Muslim ban statement after reporter grills Spicer in briefing," CNBC, May 8, 2017, https://tinyurl.com/lfe5ar3.

[39] Edward E. Curtis IV, *Muslims in America: A Short History* (2009), p. 5.

[40] "Muslim Spain (711-1492)," BBC, Sept. 4, 2009, https://tinyurl.com/6xq73x.

[41] Curtis, *op. cit.*, p. 4.

[42] *Ibid.*, p. 17.

[43] James H. Hutson, "The Founding Fathers and Islam, Library Papers Show Early Tolerance for Muslim Faith," The Library of Congress, May 2002, https://tinyurl.com/zjro465.

[44] "Islam in America," *The History Detectives*, PBS, https://tinyurl.com/pgsol5q.

[45] "Moorish Science Temple of America, Religious Movement," Brittanica.com, https://tinyurl.com/y7x5sohe.

[46] Curtis, *op. cit.*, p. 32.

[47] "A History of African American Muslims," *The Washington Post*, Nov. 5, 2011, https://tinyurl.com/y9m5hsfv.

[48] *Ibid.*

[49] "Muslim Americans: No Sign of growth in Alienation or Support for Extremism, Section 1: A Demographic Portrait of Muslim Americans," Pew Research Center, Aug. 30, 2011, https://tinyurl.com/o4hee8d.

[50] "Who Was Shut Out? Immigration Quotas, 1925-1927," History Matters, A U.S. Survey Course on the Web, Jan. 3, 2017, https://tiny

About the Author

Reed Karaim, a freelance writer in Tucson, Ariz., has written for *The Washington Post, U.S. News & World Report, Smithsonian, American Scholar, USA Weekend* and other publications. He is the author of the novel *If Men Were Angels*, which was selected for the Barnes & Noble Discover Great New Writers series. He is also the winner of the Robin Goldstein Award for Outstanding Regional Reporting and other journalism honors. Karaim is a graduate of North Dakota State University in Fargo.

url.com/hzjoutz.

[51] Curtis, *op. cit.*, p. 73.

[52] *Ibid.*

[53] *Ibid.*, p. 91.

[54] Bryony Jones and Susannah Cullinane, "What is the Muslim Brotherhood?" CNN, July 3, 2013, https://tinyurl.com/ybpzjaue.

[55] Curtis, *op. cit.*, p. 63.

[56] Janet Afary, "Iranian Revolution of 1978-79," *Encyclopedia Britannica*, May 31, 2013, https://tinyurl.com/zzq87vf.

[57] For background, see Peter Katel, "Global Jihad," *CQ Researcher*, Oct. 14, 2005, pp. 857-880.

[58] "9/11 Attacks," History.com, 2010, https://tinyurl.com/3c8jypf.

[59] "Worst Terrorist Attacks In World History," Worldatlas.com, April 18, 2017, https://tinyurl.com/kh6tqq3; Mary Habeck, "What does Al Qaeda want?" *Foreign Policy*, March 6, 2012, https://tinyurl.com/gveq3d6.

[60] "Backgrounder: The President's Quotes on Islam," The White House, https://tinyurl.com/y84ghuvl.

[61] "Muslim Americans Condemn Attack," *Islamicity*, Sept. 11, 2001, http://tinyurl.com/y7fkxxlx.

[62] Tanya Schevitz, "FBI sees leap in anti-Muslim hate crimes; 9/11 attacks blamed for bias — blacks still most frequent victims," *San Francisco Chronicle*, Nov. 26, 2002, https://tinyurl.com/pgkeh6q.

[63] Simran Jeet Singh, "A Unique Perspective on Hate-Crimes: The Story of a Convicted Killer," *The Huffington Post*, Sept. 19, 2012, https://tinyurl.com/y9cbyfkr.

[64] David A. Graham, "How Republicans Won and Then Lost the Muslim Vote," *The Atlantic*, Dec. 9, 2015, https://tinyurl.com/y9cgbhux.

[65] "Republicans Prefer Blunt Talk About Islamic Extremism, Democrats Favor Caution," Pew Research Center, Feb. 3, 2016, https://tinyurl.com/yanedokn.

[66] Glenn Kessler, "Trump's outrageous claim that 'thousands' of New Jersey Muslims celebrated the 9/11 attacks," *The Washington Post*, Nov. 22, 2015, https://tinyurl.com/yaons9s5.

[67] Mohamed, *op. cit.*

[68] Lipka, *op. cit.*

[69] "America's Changing Religious Landscape," Pew Research Center, May 12, 2015, https://tinyurl.com/ldnxabw.

[70] Mohamed, *op. cit.*

[71] "Muslim Americans: No Signs of Growth in Alienation or Support for Extremism," *op. cit.*

[72] *Ibid.*

[73] *Ibid.*

[74] *Ibid.*

[75] David G. Savage, Laura King and Noah Bier-

man, "Supreme Court finds a compromise in reviving Trump's travel ban," *Los Angeles Times*, June 26, 2016, https://tinyurl.com/ydezr3vl.

[76] Shear and Liptak, *op. cit.*

[77] *Ibid.*

[78] *Ibid.*

[79] *Ibid.*

[80] "Statement from President Donald J. Trump," The White House, June 26, 2017, https://tinyurl.com/y86kb7vc.

[81] Savage, King and Bierman, *op. cit.*

[82] *Ibid.*

[83] Elle Hunt and David Smith, "Donald Trump abandons traditional White House Ramadan celebration," *The Guardian*, June 26, 2017, https://tinyurl.com/yb3b5ekv.

[84] *Ibid.*

[85] Amy Brittain and Abigail Hauslohner, "Anti-sharia group offers donors a private tour and cocktails at Trump hotel," *The Washington Post*, June 20, 2017, https://tinyurl.com/y7tba62u.

[86] Johnson and Hauslohner, *op. cit.*

[87] Matt Volz, "Montana Lawmakers Poised to Pass Anti-Sharia Law Measure," *U.S. News & World Report*, March 20, 2017, https://tinyurl.com/y8xh7wal. Bobby Caina Calvin, "Montana Governor Rejects Bill Banning Sharia Law in

Courts," *U.S. News & World Report*, April 20, 2017, https://tinyurl.com/y758q7se.

[88] Akyol, *op. cit.*

[89] Michael Broyde, "The rise and rise of religious arbitration," *The New York Times*, June 26, 2017, http://tinyurl.com/y8ugyvjm. Broyde's book, *Sharia Tribunals, Rabbinical Courts, and Christian Panels: Religious Arbitration in America and the West*, was published on May 31, 2017.

[90] Matt Levin, "The 2015 Texas Hoax of the Year: Rumors about Sharia courts," *Houston Chronicle*, Dec. 23, 2015, https://tinyurl.com/zfd73al.

[91] "Nothing to Fear, Debunking the Mythical 'Sharia Threat' to Our Judicial System," The American Civil Liberties Union, May 2011, https://tinyurl.com/y7hnzs9p.

[92] James Doubek, " 'Anti-Sharia' Marchers Met With Counter-Protests Around The Country," NPR, June 11, 2017, https://tinyurl.com/y8tm7vl9.

[93] Calvin, *op. cit.*

[94] Tina Nguyen, "5 Things to Know About Sebastian Gorka, Trump's Jihad Whisperer," *Vanity Fair*, Feb. 21, 2017, https://tinyurl.com/zxmlul7. Matea Gold, "Bannon film outline warned U.S. could turn into 'Islamic States of America,' " *The Washington Post*, Feb. 3, 2017, https://tinyurl.com/y9gabe8r.

FOR MORE INFORMATION

American Islamic Forum for Democracy, PO Box 1832, Phoenix, AZ 85001; 480-225-7473; aifdemocracy.org. Founded in 2003 by Dr. Zuhdi Jasser, a former U.S. naval officer, to confront what it describes as "political Islam," an ideology that rejects church-state separation and fundamental human rights.

Council on American-Islamic Relations (CAIR), 453 New Jersey Ave., S.E., Washington, DC 20003; 202-488-8787; www.cair.com. Muslim civil rights and advocacy group with regional offices nationwide whose mission includes enhancing understanding of Islam, protecting civil liberties and empowering Muslims.

Institute for Social Policy and Understanding, 6 Parklane Blvd., Suite 510, Dearborn, MI 48126; 313-436-0523; www.ispu.org. Provides research on Muslim life in America and develops policy recommendations.

Interfaith Youth Core, 141 W. Jackson Blvd., Suite 3200, Chicago, IL 60604; 312-573-8825; www.ifyc.org. Promotes cooperation and understanding between people of different religions, faiths and secular communities, focusing primarily on college campuses.

Islamic Society of North America, 6555 S. County Road, 750 E. Plainfield, IN 46168; 317-839-8157, www.isna.net. An umbrella organization for Muslim individuals and groups around the nation; promotes public education on Islam and inter-faith dialogue between Muslims, Christians and Jews.

Middle Eastern Forum, 500 Walnut St., No. 1050, Philadelphia, PA 19201; 215-546-5406; www.meforum.org. Works to define and promote Western values in the Middle East and opposes efforts to bring the world under the control of Islamic law.

Bibliography

Selected Sources

Books

Curtis, Edward, *Muslims in America: A Short History (Religion in American Life)*, Oxford University Press, 2009.
A professor of religious studies charts the story of Muslims in North America since the arrival of slaves from West Africa to the British colonies.

Grewal, Zareena, *Islam Is a Foreign Country: American Muslims and the Global Crisis of Authority*, NYU Press, 2013.
A professor of American and religious studies explores the struggles of young Muslim-Americans as they seek to balance their national identity and their faith.

Moghul, Haroon, *How to be a Muslim: An American Story*, Beacon Press, 2017.
A Muslim student leader at New York University who unexpectedly found himself a spokesman for his faith following the 9/11 terrorist attacks explores his struggles to forge a unique Muslim-American identity.

Patel, Eboo, *Acts of Faith: The Story of an American Muslim, in the Struggle for the Soul of a Generation*, Beacon Press, 2010.
The founder of Interfaith Youth Core, a national group that works to bring together young people of different religions, relates his personal journey of faith, which led him to embrace Islam.

Pipes, Daniel, *Militant Islam Reaches America*, W. W. Norton & Co.; Reprint edition, 2003.
A historian and activist explains the distinction between Islam, the religious faith and the political ideology of militant Islamism, which he considers a significant threat to America.

Articles

Beinart, Peter, "The Denationalization of American Muslims," *The Atlantic*, March 19, 2017, https://tinyurl.com/y8caplzy.
The anti-Islamic views once considered extreme even within conservative circles have gained currency within the Trump administration.

Burke, Daniel, "Anti-Muslim hate crimes: Ignorance in Action?" CNN, Jan. 30, 2017, https://tinyurl.com/ycxdn7cs.
Anti-Muslim crimes surged 67 percent last year, with mosques and individual Muslims the target of abuse and violence, even as more than eight in 10 Americans say they know little or nothing about Islam.

Ellis, Burke, and Tony Marco, "Group against Islamic law clashes with counterprotesters," CNN, June 11, 2017, https://tinyurl.com/yantvyo9.
A series of nationwide protests against Sharia, or Islamic law, which organizers describe as incompatible with the U.S.

Constitution, was met by counter-protesters who felt the protests unfairly targeted Muslim-Americans.

Muaddi, Nadeem, "The Bush-era Muslim registry failed. Yet the US could be trying it again," CNN, Dec. 22, 2016, http://tinyurl.com/jqgwgfv.
President Trump's proposal for more stringent screening procedures for visitors from six predominantly Muslim nations resembles a program initiated under President George W. Bush shortly after the 9/11 terrorist attacks that required males over 16 entering the United States from 25 countries to register and be fingerprinted, photographed and interviewed by government officials. Suspended in 2011, the program never identified a single terrorist and was blamed for harming relations with the Muslim community.

Shear, Michael, and Adam Liptak, "Supreme Court Takes Up Travel Ban Case, and Allows Parts to Go Ahead," *The New York Times*, June 26, 2017, https://tinyurl.com/y8sekamp.
The Supreme Court allowed part of President Trump's temporary ban on travel from six predominantly Muslim countries to proceed, pending a full hearing by the court this fall.

Reports and Studies

Lipka, Michael, "Muslims and Islam: Key findings in the U.S. and around the world," Pew Research Center, May 26, 2017, https://tinyurl.com/y825pyca.
This compendium of data from reports by the nonpartisan research center provides a wealth of information on the global and U.S. Muslim populations.

Maurer, Diane, *et al.*, "Countering Violent Extremism: Actions Needed to Define Strategy and Assess Progress of Federal Efforts," U.S. Government Accountability Office, April 2017, https://tinyurl.com/lpbzakm.
The federal agency charged with auditing government programs says the nation has failed to develop a cohesive strategy to counter violent extremism.

Mogahed, Dalia, and Youssef Chouhoud, "American Muslim Poll 2017: Muslims at the Crossroads," Institute for Social Policy and Understanding, March 2017, https://tinyurl.com/y7jwpmpt.
A Michigan-based research and policy institute polled Muslims and Americans of other faiths to determine how Muslim-American attitudes and beliefs compared to those of the overall population on a range of issues. They found U.S. Muslims satisfied with the overall direction of the United States.

Telhami, Shibley, "What Americans really think about Muslims and Islam," Brookings Institution, Dec. 9, 2015, https://tinyurl.com/y9dorvk3.
A study of several polls finds Americans have a generally unfavorable opinion of Muslims, although those who know a Muslim have a much more favorable opinion.

The Next Step:

Additional Articles from Current Periodicals

Homegrown Extremism

Pelley, Scott, "How an American became the leader of an ISIS cell," CBS News, July 2, 2017, https://tinyurl.com/ya33jzwa.

The account of how a U.S. teenager from Minneapolis was exposed to the radicalization of Islam perpetuated by the Islamic State, or ISIS, and eventually joined the terrorist group.

Rich, Maxine, "The US cannot arrest its way out of violent extremism," The Hill, July 2, 2017, https://tinyurl.com/ycq2ga5o.

After detainment and arrest, authorities must evaluate the dedication of potential homegrown Islamist extremists to determine whether they can be de-radicalized.

Ruiz-Grossman, Sarah, "Most Of America's Terrorists Are White, And Not Muslim," The Huffington Post, June 24, 2017, https://tinyurl.com/ydd7y4n2.

Right-wing extremists are found to be twice more likely to commit acts of domestic terrorism in the United States than Islamist extremists.

Misperceptions

Bade, Rachael, and John Bresnahan, "House rejects controversial study of Islam," Politico, July 14, 2017, http://tinyurl.com/ybd8qkls.

The House rejected, 208-217, a controversial bill that aimed to better identify potential extremist material, including "Islamic religious doctrines, concepts or schools of thought." Critics said it would unfairly target Muslims.

Vedantam, Shankar, et al., "When Is It 'Terrorism'? How The Media Cover Attacks By Muslim Perpetrators," NPR, June 19, 2017, https://tinyurl.com/yaf8y2ed.

New research shows that the media labels violent acts by Muslim perpetrators as "terrorism" more often than violent acts committed by non-Muslims.

White, Abbey, "Conservatives claim Linda Sarsour called for holy war against Trump. Here's what she really said," Vox, July 12, 2017, https://tinyurl.com/yc75g7zu.

Critics misquoted Muslim-American activist Linda Sarsour when they accused her of calling for a "holy war" in a recent speech.

Sharia Bans

Akyol, Mustafa, "Shariah's Winding Path Into Modernity," The New York Times, July 13, 2017, https://tinyurl.com/y9qt29mu.

A visiting fellow at the Freedom Project at Wellesley College says some parts of Sharia conflict with Western values, but says American Muslims are not calling for Sharia to be imposed in this country.

Caina Calvan, Bobby, "Montana Governor Rejects Bill Banning Shariah Law in Courts," The Associated Press, U.S. News & World Report, April 6, 2017, https://tinyurl.com/y758q7se.

The governor of Montana vetoed a bill that would have banned Sharia and other foreign laws from the state's courts.

Samee Ali, Safia, Ali Gostanian, and Daniella Silva, "ACT for America Stages Marches Against 'Sharia Law' Nationwide, Arrests Made," NBC News, June 10, 2017, https://tinyurl.com/y8pom2ew.

An anti-Sharia group led several marches against Islamic law and were met with large numbers of counter-demonstrators supporting Muslims, leading to various confrontations nationwide.

Travel Bans

Dixon, Lance, "A Muslim and a Jew urge the Supreme Court to strike down the Muslim ban," Los Angeles Times, July 10, 2017, https://tinyurl.com/yabd433j.

In a joint op-ed, two individuals from different religious backgrounds draw on their shared religious roots and history to argue against the administration's travel ban.

Manchester, Julia, "Hawaii judge weakens Trump travel ban," The Hill, July 14, 2017, https://tinyurl.com/y9bdrpmk.

A federal judge has ruled that the government cannot enforce the temporary ban on travel from six majority-Muslim nations on extended family members of U.S. residents.

Ngai, Mae, "Why Trump is making Muslims the new Chinese," CNN, Jan 30, 2017, https://tinyurl.com/gok23rr.

The author compares the administration's travel ban on six Muslim dominated countries to another immigration order from U.S. history, the Chinese Exclusion Act of 1882.

CITING CQ RESEARCHER

Sample formats for citing these reports in a bibliography include the ones listed below. Preferred styles and formats vary, so please check with your instructor or professor.

MLA STYLE
Mantel, Barbara. "Coal Industry's Future." CQ Researcher 17 June 2016: 529-552.

APA STYLE
Mantel, B. (2016, June 17). Coal Industry's Future. CQ Researcher, 6, 529-552.

CHICAGO STYLE
Mantel, Barbara. "Coal Industry's Future." CQ Researcher, June 17, 2016, 529-52.

In-depth Reports on Issues in the News

Are you writing a paper?

Need backup for a debate?

Want to become an expert on an issue?

For 90 years, students have turned to *CQ Researcher* for in-depth reporting on issues in the news. Reports on a full range of political and social issues are now available. Following is a selection of recent reports:

Civil Liberties
Privacy and the Internet, 12/15
Intelligence Reform, 5/15
Religion and Law, 11/14

Crime/Law
High-Tech Policing, 4/17
Forensic Science Controversies, 2/17
Jailing Debtors, 9/16
Decriminalizing Prostitution, 4/16
Restorative Justice, 2/16
The Dark Web, 1/16
Immigrant Detention, 10/15

Education
Charter Schools, 3/17
Civic Education, 2/17
Student Debt, 11/16
Apprenticeships, 10/16

Environment/Society
Funding the Arts, 7/17
Hunger in America, 7/17
Future of the Christian Right, 6/17
Trust in Media, 6/17
Anti-Semitism, 5/17
Native American Sovereignty, 5/17

Health/Safety
Medical Marijuana, 7/17
Food Labeling, 6/17
Sports and Sexual Assault, 4/17
Reducing Traffic Deaths, 2/17
Opioid Crisis, 10/16

Politics/Economy
North Korea Showdown, 5/17
Rethinking Foreign Aid, 4/17
Troubled Brazil, 4/17
Reviving Rural Economies, 3/17
Immigrants and the Economy, 2/17

Upcoming Reports

Space Race, 8/4/17   Redistricting, 8/25/17   Medical Advances, 9/1/17

ACCESS

CQ Researcher is available in print and online. For access, visit your library or www.cqresearcher.com.

STAY CURRENT

For notice of upcoming *CQ Researcher* reports or to learn more about *CQ Researcher* products, subscribe to the free email newsletters, *CQ Researcher Alert!* and *CQ Researcher News*: http://cqpress.com/newsletters.

PURCHASE

To purchase a *CQ Researcher* report in print or electronic format (PDF), visit www.cqpress.com or call 866-427-7737. Single reports start at $15. Bulk purchase discounts and electronic-rights licensing are also available.

SUBSCRIBE

Annual full-service *CQ Researcher* subscriptions—including 44 reports a year, monthly index updates, and a bound volume—start at $1,131. Add $25 for domestic postage.

CQ Researcher Online offers a backfile from 1991 and a number of tools to simplify research. For pricing information, call 800-818-7243 or 805-499-9774 or email librarysales@sagepub.com.

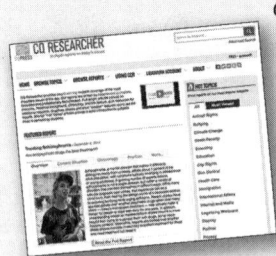

In-depth reports on today's issues

Published by CQ Press, an Imprint of SAGE Publications, Inc.   www.cqresearcher.com

New Space Race

Is the U.S. falling behind Russia and China?

U.S. astronaut Randy Bresnik, top, and fellow crew members from Russia and the European Space Agency depart for the International Space Station from a Russian-operated launch facility in Baikonur, Kazakhstan, on July 28. The U.S. space program has depended heavily on Russian assistance since the space shuttle program ended in 2011.

When Neil Armstrong stepped onto the moon in 1969, the United States was widely proclaimed the victor in the space race with the Soviet Union. Today, however, with the U.S. space shuttle program no longer in operation, NASA pays Russia to transport U.S. crews to the International Space Station and the Pentagon depends on Russian rocket engines to launch its military satellites into orbit. In addition, China's space program is growing rapidly, and U.S. officials worry it threatens American space assets, including military satellites. Policymakers also fear that U.S. satellites are at risk from accidental collisions. Meanwhile, NASA is planning for deep-space missions, even as some experts say these missions cost too much and the agency should rely more on private spaceflight companies. Other debates focus on whether the United States should return astronauts to the moon, as President Trump wants NASA to do in the next two years, and whether humans or robots should take the lead in exploring space.

CQ Researcher • Aug. 4, 2017 • www.cqresearcher.com
Volume 27, Number 28 • Pages 653-676

RECIPIENT OF SOCIETY OF PROFESSIONAL JOURNALISTS AWARD FOR EXCELLENCE ◆ AMERICAN BAR ASSOCIATION SILVER GAVEL AWARD

Los Angeles I London I New Delhi
Singapore I Washington DC I Melbourne

THIS REPORT

I N S I D E

THE ISSUES **655**

BACKGROUND **661**

CHRONOLOGY **663**

CURRENT SITUATION **667**

AT ISSUE.......................**669**

OUTLOOK **670**

BIBLIOGRAPHY **674**

THE NEXT STEP **675**

The Issues

655
- Are U.S. satellites adequately protected?
- Should the private sector play a greater role in space exploration?
- Should the United States establish a moon base?

Background

661 **First Space Race**
Early Soviet successes alarmed U.S. policymakers.

662 **Détente in Space**
NASA's budget declined under President Richard M. Nixon.

665 **Space Shuttle Era**
The first space shuttle flights transfixed the nation in the 1980s.

666 **New Space Competition**
Aerospace companies developed launch capabilities in the 2000s.

Current Situation

667 **Regulatory Debate**
Some experts say the U.S. is lax in overseeing private-sector activities in space.

668 **National Space Council**
The revived council will oversee U.S. activities and policies in space.

Outlook

670 **New Challenges**
Experts say the U.S. must do more to protect satellites.

Sidebars and Graphics

656 **NASA's Budget Fell After Moon Race**
It has not topped 1 percent of federal spending since 1993.

657 **Companies Receive Millions to Develop New Space Vehicle With NASA**
Since 2010, NASA has awarded six aerospace firms more than $300 million to help the space agency develop a replacement for the space shuttle.

658 **Earth Orbit Is Getting Crowded**
The number of satellites orbiting the Earth has increased sharply.

660 **Space Junk Prompts Fear of Collisions**
Fast-moving debris circling the Earth threatens satellites and other spacecraft.

663 **Chronology**
Key events since 1957.

664 **China Challenges U.S. Dominance in Space**
"China arguably has become a space superpower."

666 **Orbiting Debris Poses a Growing Threat**
Experts say global cooperation is needed to avoid spacecraft damage.

669 **At Issue:**
Should the private sector take over the design and management of U.S. space exploration from NASA?

For Further Research

673 **For More Information**
Organizations to contact.

674 **Bibliography**
Selected sources used.

675 **The Next Step**
Additional articles.

675 **Citing CQ Researcher**
Sample bibliography formats.

Cover: AFP/Getty Images/Dmitri Lovetsky

 **CQ RESEARCHER**

Aug. 4, 2017
Volume 27, Number 28

EXECUTIVE EDITOR: Thomas J. Billitteri
tjb@sagepub.com

ASSISTANT MANAGING EDITORS: Kenneth Fireman, kenneth.fireman@sagepub.com, Kathy Koch, kathy.koch@sagepub.com, Scott Rohrer, scott.rohrer@sagepub.com

ASSOCIATE MANAGING EDITOR: Val Ellicott

SENIOR CONTRIBUTING EDITOR:
Thomas J. Colin
tom.colin@sagepub.com

CONTRIBUTING WRITERS: Marcia Clemmitt, Sarah Glazer, Reed Karaim, Barbara Mantel, Chuck McCutcheon, Tom Price

SENIOR PROJECT EDITOR: Olu B. Davis

EDITORIAL ASSISTANT: Natalia Gurevich

INTERN: Robert DePaolo

FACT CHECKERS: Eva P. Dasher, Michelle Harris, Betsy Towner Levine, Robin Palmer

SAGE Publishing | CQPRESS

Los Angeles I London I New Delhi
Singapore I Washington DC I Melbourne

An Imprint of SAGE Publications, Inc.

SENIOR VICE PRESIDENT,
GLOBAL LEARNING RESOURCES:
Karen Phillips

EXECUTIVE DIRECTOR, ONLINE LIBRARY AND
REFERENCE PUBLISHING:
Todd Baldwin

CQ Researcher (ISSN 1056-2036) is printed on acid-free paper. Published weekly, except: (March wk. 4) (May wk. 4) (July wks. 1, 2) (Aug. wks. 2, 3) (Nov. wk. 4) and (Dec. wks. 3, 4). Published by SAGE Publications, Inc., 2455 Teller Rd., Thousand Oaks, CA 91320. Annual full-service subscriptions start at $1,131. For pricing, call 1-800-818-7243. To purchase a CQ Researcher report in print or electronic format (PDF), visit www.cqpress.com or call 866-427-7737. Single reports start at $15. Bulk purchase discounts and electronic-rights licensing are also available. Periodicals postage paid at Thousand Oaks, California, and at additional mailing offices. POSTMASTER: Send address changes to CQ Researcher, 2600 Virginia Ave., N.W., Suite 600, Washington, DC 20037.

New Space Race

THE ISSUES

On July 28, U.S. astronaut Randy Bresnik wedged himself into a seat custom-molded to his body and braced himself to hurtle into the sky at about 17 times the speed of sound on his second trip to the International Space Station. But the retired Marine colonel from Santa Monica, Calif., wasn't aboard a U.S.-made rocket, nor was he lifting off from iconic Cape Canaveral in Florida.

Instead, he and his fellow crew members — a Russian cosmonaut and an astronaut with the European Space Agency — arrived at the space station aboard a Russian-made *Soyuz* spacecraft about six hours after launching from Kazakhstan.[1]

Since 2011, when the U.S. space shuttle program ended, the United States has paid hundreds of millions of dollars to Russia to ferry U.S. astronauts to the space station.[2]

America's dependence on the *Soyuz* is just one of the many ways international activities in space have changed in the 48 years since the United States won the space race with the Soviet Union by landing humans on the moon.

Today, space is a much more crowded, complicated and strategically important arena, not only for the United States but for its adversaries. U.S. officials are working to determine how to protect vital satellites and other space hardware from sabotage and accidental collisions, how much of a role the aerospace industry should play in space exploration and how to prioritize space missions in an era of competing visions and tight budgets.

China's Hard X-ray Modulation Telescope, known as Insight, is lifted onto a Long March-4B rocket at the Jiuquan Satellite Launch Center in the Gobi Desert. The telescope was launched on June 15 to observe black holes, neutron stars and other phenomena. China is now the third major space power, after Russia and the U.S. Since launching its first astronaut into space in 2003, China has landed a rover on the moon, placed its own space lab into orbit and boosted its space spending to an estimated $110 million in 2015. U.S. officials worry that China's rapidly growing space program could threaten American space assets, including military satellites.

AFP/Getty Images/STR

"Our adversaries have seen what a significant advantage space provides the U.S. and have responded by looking for ways to neutralize or destroy our space capabilities," said Republican Rep. Doug Lamborn of Colorado, a member of the House Armed Services Committee's Subcommittee on Emerging Threats and Capabilities. "The U.S. is in the unique position of having the most to gain and most to lose in space."[3]

The flurry of new activity in space has produced "a new space race" involving "a crowd of new actors, from developing countries to small startups," according to Dave Baiocchi and William Welser IV, engineering professors at the Pardee RAND Graduate School in Santa Monica, Calif.

"Unlike in the first space race, the challenge in this one will not be technical," they said. "It will be figuring out how to regulate this welter of new activity."[4]

The United States owes much of its military dominance on the ground to its satellites. It has 576 working satellites in orbit — more than twice as many as any other country — providing communications, weapons guidance, navigation and other services.[5]

"We can attack any target on the planet, anytime, anywhere, in any weather," Gen. John Hyten, commander of the U.S. Air Force Space Command, said recently.[6]

But those satellites are increasingly vulnerable to attack themselves.

Lt. Gen. John W. Raymond, commander of the Joint Functional Component Command for Space, an arm of the U.S. Strategic Command tasked with securing U.S. military satellites, told Congress in 2015 that Russia and China have successfully tested anti-satellite weapons (ASATs).

"We are quickly approaching the point where every satellite and every orbit can be threatened," he said.[7]

The U.S. space programs' dependence on Russia also poses a potential national security concern, experts say. Besides paying Moscow for rides to the International Space Station — the price is now $74.7 million per seat — the United States also relies on Russian-made rockets to launch American military satellites into space.[8]

NASA's Budget Fell After Moon Race

The nation's civilian space agency received almost 4.5 percent of the federal budget in 1966 as the United States raced to beat the Soviet Union to the moon. But NASA's share of overall federal spending declined after that and has not topped 1 percent since 1993. Still, the United States led Russia and China on spending on space programs in 2013, the most recent year for which data were available for all three nations. U.S. space-related spending totaled $39.3 billion that year, compared to $6.1 billion in China and $5.3 billion in Russia.

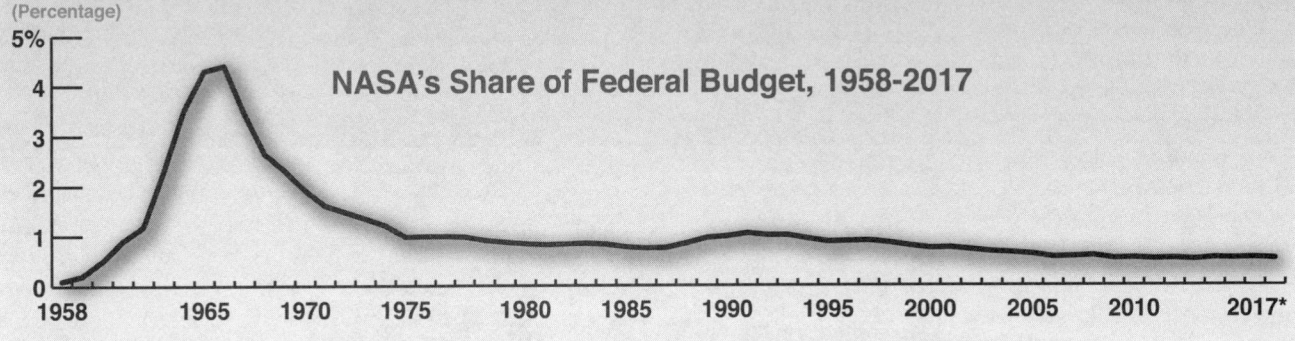

NASA's Share of Federal Budget, 1958-2017

(Percentage)

* Estimated.

Sources: Kimberly Amadeo, "NASA Budget: Current Funding and History," The Balance, May 25, 2017, https://tinyurl.com/y95uksdm; "The U.S. Federal Budget," Inside Gov, undated, http://tinyurl.com/y7ck77gq; "Nasa budgets: US spending on space travel since 1958 UPDATED," The Guardian, 2010, https://tinyurl.com/m72mnb8; and "Which countries spend the most on space exploration?" World Economic Forum, Jan. 11, 2016, https://tinyurl.com/y7fofo73

"Today, Russia holds many of our most precious national security satellites at risk before they ever get off the ground," Republican Sen. John McCain of Arizona, chairman of the Senate Armed Services Committee, said during a hearing in January 2016. [9]

Even apart from national security concerns, "it is embarrassing that the U.S. has not for years had the ability to put a human in orbit and must rely on Russia," James A. Lewis, a senior vice president at the Center for Strategic and International Studies (CSIS), a Washington think tank, told Congress last year. [10]

Further complicating U.S. space strategy is China's rapid rise as the third major space power. China launched its first astronaut into space in 2003. Since then, it has landed a rover on the moon, placed its own space lab into orbit and boosted its space spending to an estimated $110 million in 2015. [11] In January, Wu Yanhua, deputy chief of China's National Space Administration, an-

nounced that the country plans to launch its first Mars rover around 2020. [12]

Chinese officials have made clear they plan to rapidly develop offensive capabilities in space. In a 2014 speech at China's air force headquarters, President Xi Jinping told officers "to speed up air and space integration and sharpen their offensive and defensive capabilities." In 2007, the country caused an international furor when it destroyed one of its own satellites to test an anti-satellite missile. [13]

Other countries also pose potential threats to U.S. satellites, according to a recent report by the National Academy of Sciences. India, Iran, South Korea, North Korea and the 22 member states of the European Space Agency are capable of launching their own satellites into orbit, increasing the likelihood of accidental or deliberate collisions. At the end of 2016, there were 1,459 active satellites in orbit. [14]

Meanwhile, the National Aeronautics and Space Administration (NASA), con-

tinues to suffer from shifting political winds and frequent funding shortfalls. The space agency typically cannot complete major projects during the four or eight years a president holds office, so those projects are subject to cancellation or redirection by an incoming administration. [15]

In May, NASA announced it would delay the first test flight of its deep-space *Orion* capsule, originally scheduled for November 2018, until 2019 at the earliest, because of budgetary pressures.

President Trump's proposed fiscal 2018 budget would cut funding for another major NASA program designed to move an asteroid into lunar orbit and use it to test technologies critical for a crewed mission to Mars. [16]

Support for U.S. space programs is flagging among the American public and members of Congress, and that concerns some lawmakers. Republican Rep. Lamar Smith of Texas, chairman of the House Science, Space, and Technology Committee, called for boosting budgets for space initiatives at a May 2016 hearing.

"America leads the world in space exploration, but that is a leadership role we cannot take for granted," Smith said. "It has been over 40 years since astronaut Gene Cernan became the last man to walk on the moon. It is time to press forward. It is time to take longer strides." [17]

American aerospace companies hope to take some of those strides. Companies such as SpaceX, Boeing and Blue Origin are playing an increasingly vital role in U.S. space programs, sparking debate about how the government should regulate them.

On June 3, SpaceX, a Hawthorne, Calif., company started by Tesla founder Elon Musk, launched a *Falcon 9* rocket carrying supplies to the space station. The rocket's first stage then returned to the launch site for reuse. It was the 39th launch by SpaceX since 2006. In February, the company announced plans to send two space tourists on a trip around the moon in 2018. [18]

As a privately owned company, SpaceX does not have to report its profits, but documents obtained by *The Wall Street Journal* indicate the company expected to make a profit of $55 million in 2016 on revenues of $1.8 billion from launches. The documents also revealed that the company expects to earn between $15 billion and $20 billion by 2025 delivering internet services using its own satellites. [19]

Eight new space-related companies have opened their doors, on average, each year since 2010, according to a recent Congressional Research Service report. And the commercial launch industry booked $2.6 billion in revenues in 2015, up from about $307 million in 2010 and nothing at all in 2011. [20]

"We are on the verge of surpassing NASA," says Rick Tumlinson, co-founder and chairman of the board of Deep Space Industries, which develops technologies to mine asteroids. "I have predicted that the first human spacecraft to land on Mars is probably going to be a private-sector spacecraft, not NASA."

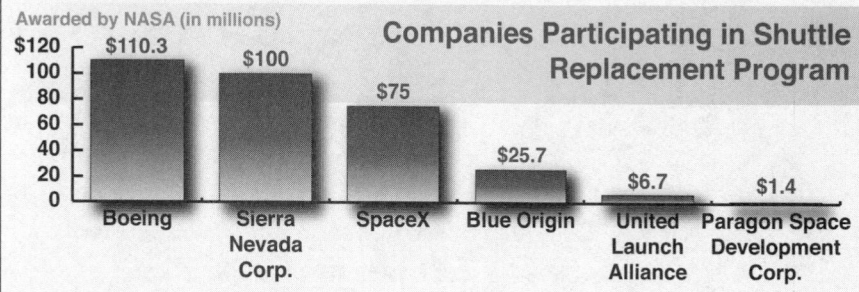

Companies Receive Millions to Develop New Space Vehicle with NASA

Since 2010, NASA has given six aerospace companies more than $300 million to help the space agency develop a replacement for the space shuttle.

Awarded by NASA (in millions)

Companies Participating in Shuttle Replacement Program

Boeing	Sierra Nevada Corp.	SpaceX	Blue Origin	United Launch Alliance	Paragon Space Development Corp.
$110.3	$100	$75	$25.7	$6.7	$1.4

Source: "Commercial Crew Program — The Essentials," NASA, undated, https://tinyurl.com/ybvr96oj

Landing astronauts on the Red Planet, however, remains one of NASA's top goals. The agency is moving ahead with its Space Launch System designed to carry the *Orion* capsule into Martian orbit with a crew of up to six astronauts.

Some experts wonder whether manned deep-space missions even make sense, given the dangers of space travel, rapid advances in robotics and the fact that robots also are much less expensive to send into space than humans. Another debate focuses on the pros and cons of sending astronauts back to the moon, as Trump wants NASA to do by 2019. The space agency has said that deadline is unrealistic. [21]

As experts and policymakers consider the future of U.S. space programs, here are some of the questions they are asking:

Are U.S. satellites adequately protected?

U.S. military officials are taking steps — somewhat belatedly, some experts say — to protect their satellites.

"The . . . bureaucratic and procurement wheels have begun to move, albeit very slowly," said Elbridge Colby, a senior fellow at the Center for a New American Security, a Washington think tank. [22]

Satellites, including those intended for civilian use, are vulnerable not only to collisions with space debris but also to sabotage by anti-satellite weapons. (*See sidebar, p. 666.*) All three major space powers — the United States, Russia and China — can disable or destroy satellites. The 1967 Outer Space Treaty, signed by those three countries and about 100 others, prohibits participants from deploying weapons of mass destruction in space. However, it does not address devices that can disable or destroy satellites. [23]

The major space powers already have tested ASATs, including ballistic missiles capable of hitting satellites in low-Earth orbit (about 500 miles from the surface) and those as high as 22,000 miles from Earth, which are in geosynchronous orbit, meaning they remain in the same position relative to a location on Earth. Ground-based lasers also can blind orbiting cameras and damage fragile satellites. [24]

A satellite can also be destroyed by simply maneuvering another satellite into its path. "It's ugly," says Dean Cheng, a senior research fellow at the Heritage Foundation, a conservative think tank in Washington. "It's a kamikaze, and you lose a satellite in the process, but you can collide satellites."

Earth Orbit Is Getting Crowded

The global community had 1,381 operational satellites orbiting the planet as of Dec. 31, 2015, a 39 percent increase from 2011. The United States currently has about 576 satellites, more than twice as many as any other country. These satellites provide communications, guidance, navigation and other services.

Active Satellites, by Function (as of Dec. 31, 2015)

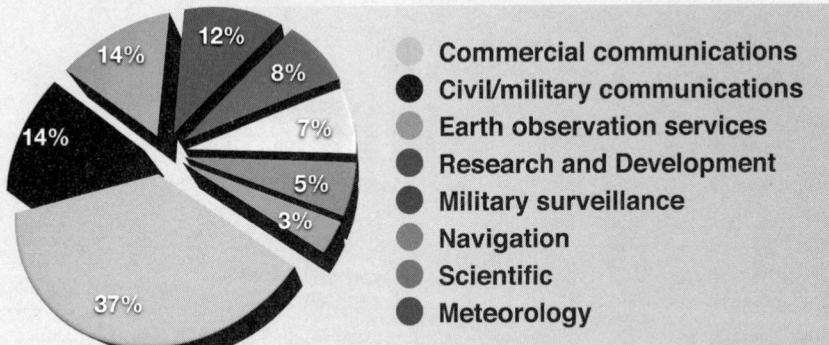

- Commercial communications
- Civil/military communications
- Earth observation services
- Research and Development
- Military surveillance
- Navigation
- Scientific
- Meteorology

Sources: Peter B. de Selding, "The state of the satellite industry in 5 charts," SpaceNews, June 20, 2016, https://tinyurl.com/j5hxmpb; Bill Canis, "Commercial Space Industry Launches a New Phase," Congressional Research Service, Dec. 12, 2016, p. 1, https://tinyurl.com/y7kw5lxa

Any satellite equipped with a robotic arm, including those designed to make repairs, also can be used to "rip a solar panel off or pull other sensitive parts apart," Cheng says.

Satellites are just one point of vulnerability for U.S. space programs.

"Space is not just about what is in orbit," Cheng says. "You also have terrestrial facilities, mission control facilities, tracking facilities." Even if the United States could turn its critical satellites into "armored death stars," he says, an enemy could still target ground-based assets to disable control over satellites.

"Space is actually a giant integrated system," Cheng says. "Integrated systems have advantages, but they are also extremely vulnerable."

Colby said the Pentagon is working to make its satellites maneuverable enough to evade attacks and be more resistant to electronic jamming. In addition, it has deployed two satellites to monitor other countries' activities in space.

He called these actions "encouraging," but said it could be years before their benefits are apparent. He also said it is unlikely the United States will ever completely solve the problem of how to protect its satellites. [25]

U.S. satellites are a particularly tempting target, some experts say, because the military depends so heavily on them for intelligence gathering, communications, navigation and weapons guidance. "Foreign military leaders understand the unique advantages that space-based systems provide to the United States," James R. Clapper, then-director of national intelligence, warned in February 2016. [26]

Peter W. Singer, a national security analyst at New America, a nonpartisan, public policy think tank in Washington, agrees. "It is woven into Chinese and Russian plans to try to take away U.S. space capabilities," Singer says. "What is a strength for us they would like to turn into a weakness."

He says the United States depends more on its space assets — including

satellites, satellite tracking facilities, rockets, launch vehicles and space stations — than either China or Russia.

Cheng is not sure this country's adversaries will ever depend as much on space as the United States does.

"The only reason they would look like us is if they were going to do expeditionary warfare — warfare on the other side of the globe from where they are," he says. "There is just no evidence that China intends to spend a lot of time operating in the Western Hemisphere or that Russia is going to do more than fly a few bombers to be obnoxious up and down the East or West Coast of the United States. We are not talking about far-flung global capabilities except for the United States."

Many experts say the United States should deploy larger numbers of small satellites, seeking protection in redundancy. "We are still overly dependent on a few large, expensive platforms, which are easy targets for the Russians and the Chinese," says Lewis of CSIS. "We would be much better off moving toward smaller satellites. There is general acceptance of that now, I think, in the space community, but we haven't yet started to do it."

Brian G. Chow, a physicist and adjunct physical scientist at the RAND Corp. think tank in Santa Monica, Calif., says one way for the United States to protect its satellites is for the country to make clear it will destroy any other satellite that displays "stalking" behavior indicating a threat. Only that, he says, "can prevent a space Pearl Harbor."

Should the private sector play a greater role in space exploration?

The United States has long encouraged private contractors to participate in space programs, developing products according to NASA specifications. Increasingly, however, the country is depending on aerospace companies to launch satellites and eventually use their own rockets to send humans into space.

During his presidential campaign, Trump said he wanted to let private companies operate the International Space Station, ferry astronauts to the space station within two years and handle other low-Earth orbit tasks. [27]

SpaceX, which has been carrying supplies to the space station since 2012, is not the only private spaceflight company launching satellites and delivering cargo. On April 22, Orbital ATK, based in Dulles, Va., outside Washington, launched its seventh supply mission to the space station. Another company — Blue Origin in Kent, Wash., owned by Amazon founder Jeff Bezos — said in April it will offer space tourism flights by the end of 2018. [28]

Some analysts and industry leaders say private-sector companies — rather than NASA — also should handle deep-space exploration.

"People in the industry are pretty confident that deep-space programs can be done more efficiently and for a lot less money," says an industry spokesperson who spoke anonymously for fear of compromising his relationship with NASA. He described the agency's deep-space plans as "an incredibly large, expensive program that doesn't have a really clear vision."

Historically, NASA has tightly controlled project designs and contractors' work, which some experts say impedes innovation and cost efficiency. James Muncy, founder of PoliSpace, a consultancy in Alexandria, Va., specializing in space entrepreneurship, says contractors are not motivated to save money.

Those who win a contract to deliver a product to the government "are not rewarded . . . the way the competitive marketplace works — [for] innovation, improvement of quality, reduction of price and delivering new capabilities that don't exist anywhere in the marketplace," Muncy says.

NASA's relationship with private spaceflight companies is changing, largely because of the agency's Commercial Crew Program, a partnership between NASA and the private sector to build a replacement for the space shuttle to transport supplies and eventually crew to the International Space Station. Under the program, NASA's private-sector partners will develop the spacecraft and other equipment themselves, with full ownership of the final product. [29]

That is how NASA should handle all work done by private companies, says space historian and author Robert Zimmerman.

"The government should leave the design work and ownership of the product to the private sector," Zimmerman wrote in a January report that generated heated debate in the space community. "The private companies know best how to build their own products to maximize performance while lowering cost, especially because it is in their own self-interest to do this well, as an unreliable rocket will not attract many customers." [30]

Zimmerman cites NASA's Space Launch System as an example of the agency's inefficiencies. The system "is not tied to any results, their work is vague, it takes forever, and the costs balloon," he says. "That has structurally been the problem with how things have been done at NASA and in the space program now for pretty much a half-century."

Tumlinson of Deep Space Industries says NASA's role should involve supporting basic research and serving as a customer of services delivered by private companies.

Other experts are less impressed by the private sector's accomplishments in space.

"Elon Musk sat in my office in 2002 and told me he'd have 10 launches a year by 2006," says Scott Pace, director of the Space Policy Institute at George Washington University. "I'm still looking at my watch."

Pace also says commercial firms usually are more efficient than government agencies because the private sector "doesn't have the same kind of [bureaucratic] shackles and responsibilities that governments have." Those companies largely operate under strict NASA oversight, but some experts worry their performance will suffer when that oversight is gone or reduced.

Loren Thompson, chief operating officer of the Lexington Institute, a libertarian think tank in Arlington, Va., that advocates for smaller government, said SpaceX, despite offering launches at lower cost than NASA, "isn't the model of market-driven responsiveness that Zimmerman would have you believe."

"On average, its launches are over two years late, and the unlaunched missions it is carrying in its backlog on average are nearly three years late," Thompson wrote. "You can see where that might be a problem for the Air Force if the payload being launched was a high priority such as a missile-warning or spy satellite." [31]

Three of the 86 launches attempted by private companies in 2015 failed, destroying launch vehicles and payloads, according to a Congressional Research Service report. [32] In September 2016, a SpaceX rocket exploded on the launch pad at Cape Canaveral.

Pace says NASA clearly has a role to play in conducting scientific missions in space and in exploring beyond Earth orbit. The agency has landed a man on the moon, sent rovers to Mars and achieved other feats that private companies have yet to match. Pace also says that while such missions eventually may pay off commercially, they probably would not have attracted private-sector investment initially.

"Some people argue that NASA ought to be just a conduit of money and not try to do anything," Pace says. "I believe that's incorrect. That's because there are activities that make no commercial sense."

He wrote in April that the United States does not face a stark choice between government and private efforts in space but should pursue "a mixed strategy, using a variety of tools, to serve national interests. It would be

Space Junk Prompts Fear of Collisions

Tens of thousands of man-made objects orbit the Earth, including active and defunct satellites, pieces of spent rockets and fragments created by collisions. Experts warn that these fast-moving pieces of space junk could seriously damage working satellites and other spacecraft, including the International Space Station — and that as more debris accumulates, these risks will grow.

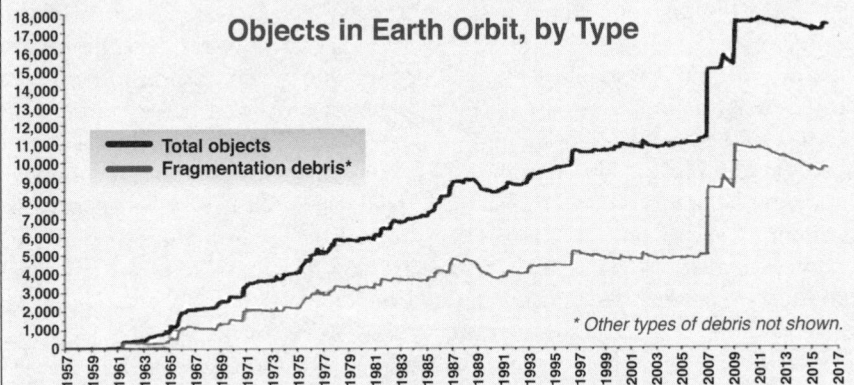

Objects in Earth Orbit, by Type

— Total objects
— Fragmentation debris*

* Other types of debris not shown.

Sources: "STO AVT-262 Lecture series and VKI workshop on Space debris reentry and mitigation," NATO Science and Technology Organization, https://tinyurl.com/yaayjd55; "Space Surveillance," U.S. Space Command, undated, https://tinyurl.com/m5upk3

wise to mistrust any purist strategy, that is, one which is all-government or all-private, where taxpayer dollars are needed." [33]

Should the United States establish a moon base?

On June 20, British theoretical physicist Stephen Hawking called for countries to collaborate on constructing a moon colony within 30 years and then to send a manned mission to Mars.

"We are running out of space [on Earth], and the only place we can go to are other worlds," he said via video link to a conference in Trondheim, Norway. "It is time to explore other solar systems. Spreading out may be the only thing that saves us from ourselves. I am convinced that humans need to leave Earth." [34]

President Trump made similar comments when he signed legislation on March 21 giving NASA $19.5 billion for the current fiscal year, $200 million more than the agency received last year. "Almost half a

century ago our brave astronauts first planted the American flag on the moon," he said. "That was a big moment in our history. Now this nation is ready to be the first in space once again." [35]

Former President Barack Obama wanted to send a manned mission to Mars, but Trump has prioritized returning astronauts to the moon and perhaps establishing a permanent base there. [36]

Blue Origin's Bezos supports the same plan. In March, he circulated a white paper to NASA leadership indicating his interest in developing a lunar lander and establishing a base on the moon. "It is time for America to return to the moon — this time to stay," Bezos said. "A permanently inhabited lunar settlement is a difficult and worthy objective. I sense a lot of people are excited about this." [37]

Rep. Bill Posey, R-Fla., has introduced legislation that would direct NASA to build a base on the lunar surface. He and other policymakers say the need is urgent because Russia and China have announced plans to do the same. [38]

Those countries "don't colonize places just for scientific study; they generally militarize their colonizations," Posey, a member of the House Science, Space and Technology Committee, told a reporter in February. "So if we want to remain the leader in space, we obviously need to at least keep pace with the Russians and Chinese." [39]

Some experts see the moon as a potential staging area for missions to Mars and other deep-space destinations.

"Perhaps one of the greatest practical discoveries of our generation is the presence of vast quantities of water on the moon, verified by NASA in 2009," Robert Richards, CEO of Moon Express, a Mountain View, Calif., company that plans to mine lunar resources, told Congress in May. "The discovery of water on the moon is a game changer, not just for the economic viability of lunar resources, but for the economics of reaching Mars and other deep-space destinations." [40]

William Gerstenmaier, NASA's chief of human exploration, said in 2015 that large amounts of ice at the lunar poles could provide the oxygen and hydrogen needed to fuel a spacecraft for a journey from the moon to Mars.

"If propellant was available from the moon, this could dramatically lower the [amount of fuel] needed from the Earth for a NASA Mars mission," he said. [41]

Other experts warn that a moon mission could set back the Mars program.

"The moon could be a useful test bed for human exploration of Mars, part of a staged campaign of exploration," says Lewis of the Center for Strategic and International Studies. "But there is a concern that lunar missions would divert resources away from the Mars programs."

According to NASA scientists, establishing a moon base would cost $10 billion, a little more than half the agency's current annual budget. [42]

Tom Young, former director of NASA's Goddard Space Flight Center, says the United States lacks the wherewithal to build a base on the moon and also plan a manned mission to Mars. "There is a need to focus our attention, capability and resources on one option," he said. [43]

The moon-or-Mars debate has also revived discussion about whether NASA should focus on human or robotic missions.

Cambridge University astrophysicist Martin Rees famously predicted in 2010 that manned missions to space would soon be a thing of the past.

"The moon landings were an important impetus to technology, but you have to ask the question, what is the case for sending people back into space?" he said. "The practical case gets weaker and weaker with every advance in robotics and miniaturization. It's hard to see any particular reason or purpose in going back to the moon or indeed sending people into space at all." [44]

Sending humans into space is also dangerous. Accidents involving the space shuttles *Challenger* (1986) and *Columbia* (2003) killed 14 astronauts, and three *Apollo 1* astronauts were killed in 1967 during a preflight test when their capsule caught on fire. [45]

Former shuttle astronaut Rick Hauck noted that about 4 percent of humans who made it into space were killed during their missions. "Would I have flown if I had known there was a 4 percent chance of death?" Hauck said in 2003. "No, I don't think I would have flown." [46]

NASA's robotic exploration program, meanwhile, has scored impressive successes, landing three rovers — *Spirit*, *Opportunity* and *Curiosity* — on Mars. *Spirit* and *Opportunity* landed in 2004. Each was expected to last about three months, but *Spirit* worked for six years and *Opportunity* is still active. [47] The two-year mission for *Curiosity*, which landed in 2012, has been extended. [48]

Lewis called NASA's robotics work "the coolest space program in the world." Still, he favors sending astronauts back to the moon "and creating some sort of semipermanent presence, just because I think it's easy." Giving up

Amazon CEO Jeff Bezos, founder of the Blue Origin aerospace firm, unveils the company's reusable New Shepard launch system at the 33rd annual Space Symposium, in Colorado Springs, Colo., on April 5. Blue Origin plans to offer space tourism flights by the end of 2018. Bezos circulated a white paper to NASA leaders in March indicating his interest in developing a lunar lander and establishing a base on the moon.

on manned spaceflight would be "a hard blow" for NASA, he says.

Other experts argue that manned missions help boost public support for space exploration. "Human exploration gets people excited about space, and the private sector can increase how much exploration the government gets for its money," says Tumlinson. "The more you can provide of that excitement, the more public support you're going to get, the more taxpayer dollars you're going to get." ∎

BACKGROUND

First Space Race

Most historians mark Oct. 4, 1957 — the date the Soviet Union launched *Sputnik*, the first satellite, into Earth orbit — as the beginning of the first space race. The next day, President Dwight D. Eisenhower's press secretary called the Russian launch "no surprise" and said the United States was "not in a race with the Soviets."

"Both of the statements were naïve at best," wrote space historian Ted Spitzmiller. [49]

The Soviets' success in making it into space first stunned the American public, but the nation's policymakers also focused on *Sputnik*'s weight, Spitzmiller wrote in *The History of Human Spaceflight*. At 184 pounds, the satellite offered "convincing evidence that the Russians did have the power, the guidance, and the ability to launch ICBMs," or intercontinental ballistic missiles, he wrote. "This was seen as a threat to the very existence of the free world." [50]

The Eisenhower administration and Congress moved quickly to expand U.S. space programs. In signing the 1958 National Aeronautics and Space Act, Eisenhower commended Congress for acting quickly to approve the legislation, which he said equipped the United States "for leadership in the space age." [51]

Besides creating NASA, the act specified that the Defense Department would manage U.S. military activities in space. Eisenhower initially wanted the Pentagon to direct all U.S. space efforts, according to John Logsdon, a historian at the Smithsonian Institution's Air and Space Museum.

But his science adviser, James Killian, and Vice President Richard M. Nixon convinced him that it made more sense to create a separate civilian space agency "to carry out an open program of scientific activities and to engage in international cooperation," wrote Logsdon. "This would provide a contrast to the closed and secretive Soviet space effort." [52]

Apollo 11 *astronaut Edwin E. "Buzz" Aldrin Jr. walks on the moon on July 20, 1969. When the Trump administration said in June it would resurrect the National Space Council to oversee all U.S. activities and policies in space, Aldrin said the council would be "absolutely critical in ensuring that the president's space priorities are clearly articulated and effectively executed." Trump has said he wants NASA to send astronauts back to the moon by 2019.*

NASA did not have to start from scratch. It absorbed the earlier National Advisory Committee for Aeronautics, with its 8,000 employees, an annual budget of $100 million and three major research laboratories — the Langley Aeronautical Laboratory in Virginia, the Ames Aeronautical Laboratory in California and the Lewis Flight Propulsion Laboratory in Ohio. [53]

The new space agency immediately undertook its first manned space program — Project Mercury, with the goal of putting a U.S. astronaut into Earth orbit and returning him safely to Earth. But a month before Project Mercury's first launch in 1961, Soviet cosmonaut Yuri Gagarin became the first human

to orbit the Earth. The next year, on Feb. 20, 1962, U.S. astronaut John Glenn circled the planet three times before splashing down in the Atlantic Ocean near Bermuda. [54]

Eisenhower's proposed fiscal 1961 budget called for reducing NASA's budget. He warned John F. Kennedy's incoming administration that "further tests and experiments will be necessary to establish if there are any valid scientific reasons for extending manned spaceflight beyond the Mercury program." [55]

But in 1961, while Project Mercury was still active, NASA started Project Gemini. The new program involved 10 launches of two-man crews performing the first spacewalks and other tasks, and testing technologies for the upcoming Apollo Program, which aimed to land astronauts on the moon. [56]

According to Logsdon, Kennedy began his presidency with a "complex" attitude toward space. He initially viewed space exploration as a way to ease relations with the Soviet Union, but before the end of 1961 he would commit to

sending U.S. astronauts to the moon by the end of the decade. [57]

Eight days after the Soviet Union sent Gagarin into orbit on April 12, 1961, Kennedy called on his administration to identify a "space program which promises dramatic results in which we could win." On May 25, he told a joint session of Congress of his plan to send astronauts to the moon and backed up that commitment by increasing NASA's budget 89 percent. [58]

On July 20, 1969, *Apollo 11* astronaut Neil Armstrong became the first human to walk on the lunar surface. By the time the Apollo program ended in 1972, 12 astronauts — all Americans — had set foot on the moon. No humans have been there since. [59]

As the United States and Soviet Union expanded their investments in the space race, they also began developing anti-satellite weapons. As early as 1959, the United States attempted to hit one of its own aging satellites with a missile. The Soviets began developing anti-satellite capabilities as early as 1960 and in 1967 successfully used a satellite to intercept another in the same orbit. In the late 1950s and early '60s, the United States and the Soviet Union even tested nuclear bombs in space. [60]

In 1967, the two space superpowers signed the Outer Space Treaty, which bans weapons of mass destruction in space, limits use of the moon and other celestial bodies to peaceful purposes and prohibits countries from claiming sovereignty over space or celestial bodies. [61]

Détente in Space

The tremendous feeling of national triumph following the first moon landings was fleeting," wrote Logsdon. He said Nixon, who began his first term as president six months before the 1969 moon landing, rejected NASA's ambitious post-*Apollo* plans. Those plans included a series of large space stations,

Continued on p. 664

Chronology

1957-1969
United States, Soviet Union compete for space firsts.

1957
Soviet Union launches unmanned *Sputnik* satellite into orbit, fueling urgency of U.S. space program development.

1958
National Aeronautics and Space Act creates NASA and directs the Pentagon to manage military space activities.

1961
President John F. Kennedy announces plan to send astronauts to the moon before the end of the decade and increases NASA's budget request by 89 percent.

1962
U.S. launches its first astronaut, Marine Lt. Col. John Glenn, into orbit.

1967
U.N. Outer Space Treaty bans weapons of mass destruction in space and limits use of the moon and other celestial bodies to peaceful purposes.

1969
U.S. astronaut Neil Armstrong walks on the moon.

1970-1980
U.S. pares space budgets.

1970
President Richard M. Nixon sharply reduces NASA's budget.

1972
Nixon announces development of a new reusable space vehicle, the space shuttle, to deliver astronauts and satellites into orbit for less money.

1972
U.S. launches the Apollo program's final human mission to the moon.

1973
First crewmembers arrive at *SkyLab*, America's first space station.

1981-2010
The space shuttle era brings successes, tragedies.

1981
U.S. launches *Columbia*, the first space shuttle, into orbit.

1984
The Commercial Space Launch Act aims to increase the private sector's role in space programs.

1986
Space shuttle *Challenger* explodes shortly after liftoff, killing all seven crewmembers.

1988
Commercial Space Launch Amendments Act requires companies to buy commercial insurance for launches.

1998
Congress requires NASA to take steps to commercialize space activities. . . . First pieces of International Space Station are launched into orbit.

2003
Space shuttle *Columbia* disintegrates during re-entry, killing all seven crew members.

2004
President George W. Bush unveils Constellation Program — to take humans back to the moon and to Mars.

2007
China destroys one of its own weather satellites to test an anti-satellite weapon.

2008-Present
Private sector's role in space grows.

2008
On its fourth try, SpaceX launches a rocket into orbit. The company's first successful launch of a commercial payload follows in July 2009.

2010
President Barack Obama cancels the Constellation Program and directs NASA to plan for sending astronauts to an asteroid by 2015 and into Mars orbit by the mid-2030s. . . . NASA awards almost $50 million to five U.S. companies working with the agency to develop a replacement for the space shuttle as part of the Commercial Crew Program.

2015
Aerospace companies book $2.6 billion in revenues, launching 83 payloads into orbit.

2016
NASA's *Juno* probe reaches Jupiter. . . . SpaceX's reusable *Falcon 9* rocket lands upright on a drone ship in the Atlantic Ocean.

2017
President Trump proposes reducing NASA's budget 3 percent, with the largest cuts coming from programs that study the Earth's surface and climate.

China Challenges U.S. Dominance in Space

"China arguably has become a space superpower."

When the Chinese blew up one of their own weather satellites a decade ago to test an anti-satellite missile, sending thousands of pieces of debris potentially into the path of other countries' spacecraft, U.S. scientists and officials reacted with shock and alarm.

Harvard astrophysicist Jonathan McDowell accused the Chinese of escalating the "weaponization of space," and a White House official derided them for violating a "spirit of cooperation" between the United States and China in the use of space. [1]

Since then, China has made rapid advances in its space program. Western observers say Beijing's top goal in space is national security, followed by international prestige, projection of power and competition for space-related business.

"Chinese military writings emphasize the importance of establishing space dominance . . . as the key to winning future local wars," says Dean Cheng, a senior research fellow at the Heritage Foundation, a conservative think tank in Washington. He says the People's Liberation Army "pretty much" runs China's space program.

Adds Peter Singer, a national security analyst at New America, a nonpartisan think tank in Washington, "China arguably has become a space superpower."

China did not send its first astronaut into space until 2003. Five years later, a Chinese astronaut took the country's first spacewalk, and in 2011 China launched a small space station. The country has conducted multiple unmanned lunar exploration missions and, according to one report, has studied the feasibility of sending a manned mission to the moon. [2]

In November 2016, representatives of China and the European Space Agency discussed collaborating on establishing a human outpost on the moon. [3] And last year for the first time, China surpassed Russia in successful space launches and matched the 22 by NASA and U.S. aerospace companies. [4]

China spent about $6.1 billion on all space-related programs in 2013, the most recent year for which figures are available. The United States spent about $39.3 billion (including about $18 billion at NASA), and Russia spent about $5.3 billion. [5]

However, figures for China's spending on space are misleading, said James A. Lewis, senior vice president at the Center for Strategic and International Studies, a think tank in Washington.

"Chinese budget figures are opaque, disguise some sources of funding, and do not reflect differences in purchasing power," Lewis told a congressional hearing last September. [6]

Some Chinese officials reportedly are pushing the government to triple spending on the country's space programs. [7]

Rep. Brian Babin, R-Texas, chairman of the House Science, Space and Technology Subcommittee on Space, said the United States isn't taking China seriously enough as a potential threat in space.

"The strategic choices we make clearly impact China's space capabilities — something that we should all pay attention to given that China's civil space activities are inseparable from their military," he said at the same congressional hearing where Lewis testified. [8]

China's expanding space program also may mean increasing competition for U.S. aerospace companies such as SpaceX, Blue Origin and Sierra Nevada. "They're looking for business around the world," Singer says of the Chinese. "There is going to be competition even in the private space realm."

China has built and launched satellites for Nigeria, Venezuela, Pakistan and Bolivia, signed contracts for satellites with Belarus, Laos and Sri Lanka and agreed to build and launch a satellite for Venezuela, according to a U.S.-China Economic and Security Review Commission report. The report says Chinese satellites are cheaper than those sold by other countries, and "China offers a competitive package that includes launch services, training for local operators and low-cost loans through its export-import bank." [9]

Lewis says the United States, which has relied on Russia for access to the International Space Station since the retirement of the space shuttle program in 2011, is falling behind in what some experts say is a "new space race."

"We are sitting on our laurels," he says. "We are the rabbit and China is the tortoise."

— *Patrick Marshall*

[1] Marc Kaufman and Dafna Linzer, "China Criticized for Anti-Satellite Missile Test," *The Washington Post*, Jan. 19, 2007, https://tinyurl.com/33w2dr; William J. Broad and David E. Sanger, "China Tests Anti-Satellite Weapon, Unnerving U.S.," *The New York Times*, Jan. 18, 2007, https://tinyurl.com/y9lf3hjb.

[2] Kevin Pollpeter, Eric Anderson, Jordan Wilson, Fan Yang, "China Dream, Space Dream: China's Progress in Space Technologies and Implications for the United States," report prepared for the U.S.-China Economic and Security Review Commission, March 2, 2015, https://tinyurl.com/yb8nsoej.

[3] Matthew Brown, "China talking with European Space Agency about moon outpost," Phys.org, April 26, 2016, https://tinyurl.com/k7hqmy2.

[4] Clay Dillow, "China's secret plan to crush SpaceX and the US space program," CNBC.com, March 28, 2017, https://tinyurl.com/lhupsrr.

[5] Joe Myers, "The rise and rise of China's space programme — in numbers," World Economic Forum, Oct. 24, 2016, https://tinyurl.com/yaa5voa5.

[6] Testimony of James Lewis before the House Science, Space and Technology Subcommittee on Space, Sept. 27, 2016, https://tinyurl.com/yaqdpndh.pdf.

[7] Dillow, *op. cit.*

[8] Statement of Rep. Brian Babin before the House Science, Space and Technology Subcommittee on Space, Sept. 27, 2016, https://tinyurl.com/yc3mof4f.

[9] *Ibid.*

Continued from p. 662

continued missions to the moon and a mission to Mars in the 1980s. [62]

"We must think of [space activities] as part of a continuing process and not as a series of separate leaps, each requiring a massive concentration of energy," Nixon said in announcing a new U.S. space policy on March 7, 1970. "Space expenditures must take their proper place within a rigorous system of national priorities." [63]

NASA's resources dropped sharply during the Nixon administration. The agency's budget, which peaked in 1966 at 4.4 percent of federal spending, had fallen to less than 1 percent by the time Nixon left office in 1974, when the agency received $3.3 billion. [64]

Public support for lunar missions declined after *Apollo 14*, the third mission to land astronauts on the moon, in part due to a sense that the United States had won the space race, according to Spitzmiller. [65]

NASA would send three more Apollo missions to the moon, the last one launching on Dec. 7, 1972. [66] Earlier that year, despite cutting NASA's budget, Nixon had approved development of a reusable space vehicle — the space shuttle.

"The new system will differ radically from all existing booster systems, in that most of this new system will be recovered and used again and again — up to 100 times," he said in announcing the project on Jan. 5. "The resulting economies may bring operating costs down as low as one-tenth of those present launch vehicles." [67]

However, it took nine years before NASA sent the first shuttle into space. During that time, the agency also turned its attention to building the first space station, called *Skylab*. Working with constrained budgets, NASA engineers designed the station using the third stage of a Saturn heavy-lift rocket designed to reach the moon, adding adapters that allowed two Apollo spacecraft to dock at the station. [68]

Skylab's first crew arrived at the station on May 25, 1973. Over the next six years, it would be occupied for only 171 days, with the last crew logging the longest stay, 84 days. [69] *Skylab* delivered valuable information about the long-term effects of space on the human body of living without gravity, according to Spitzmiller. "It was obvious that a flight to Mars was feasible except for the possible problem with bone loss, which continued to plague the crews," he wrote. [70]

Space Shuttle Era

NASA's space shuttle program flew 135 missions — delivering and repairing satellites and performing scientific experiments — before ending in 2011 because of ongoing safety concerns. [71] It sent the first American woman into space — Sally Ride — helped build the International Space Station and deployed the Hubble Telescope high above the atmosphere to study the universe beyond our solar system. [72]

"It was the first launch vehicle to lift off like a rocket, orbit the Earth as a spacecraft and then land as a glider," space historian Robert Pearlman said of the shuttle. [73]

As the first reusable spacecraft, the shuttles were supposed to provide reliable access to space at a lower cost. However, significant cost reductions did not materialize, according to Steven Dick, a former NASA chief historian. [74]

As the first shuttle flights transfixed the nation during the early 1980s, President Ronald Reagan's administration worked to give private companies a greater role in space beyond that of traditional contractors.

"One of the important objectives of my administration has been, and will continue to be, the encouragement of the private sector in commercial space endeavors," Reagan said in signing the 1984 Commercial Space Launch Act. The law required the government to "encourage private-sector launches, reentries and associated services." [75] That same year, NASA created an Office of Commercial Programs to encourage private-sector involvement in space activities — such as making launch vehicles and satellites — and help commercialize NASA-developed technologies. [76]

However, progress in the shuttle program stalled after Jan. 28, 1986, when leaks in the rocket boosters attached to the space shuttle *Challenger* caused it to explode about one minute after launch, killing all seven astronauts, in-

cluding New Hampshire school teacher Christa McAuliffe. The other shuttles remained grounded until September 1988.

"As a result, many questioned the role of NASA as the primary satellite delivery route to space," the space agency said in a report. [77]

In addition to the *Challenger* disaster, Titan rocket launch failures in 1993 caused military satellite launches to be suspended for a year. [78]

"The period spanning the late 1980s to the early 1990s was a particularly difficult era for spaceflight in the United States," according to a report by CSIS' Aerospace Security Project. "The United States needed a new launch vehicle that could provide assured access to space . . . and stay cost competitive over time." [79]

In 1988, Congress required companies involved in space launch activities to buy commercial insurance or demonstrate the ability to cover any third-party losses. [80]

Congress followed up in 1998 with the Commercial Space Act, which required NASA to encourage commercialization of space services. [81]

That same year, Russia launched the first module of the International Space Station into orbit. The $100 billion station took more than 10 years and 30 missions to build and was the joint project of five space agencies representing 15 countries, with the United States, Russia, the European Union, Canada and Japan having the greatest involvement. [82] Those five agencies — NASA, Russia's Roscosmos State Corporation for Space Activities, the European Space Agency, the Canadian Space Agency and the Japan Aerospace Exploration Agency — continue to operate the station today. [83]

By the early 1980s, the U.S. military was becoming increasingly dependent on its satellites for reconnaissance, communications and navigation, and more and more concerned about keeping them safe as the Soviet Union worked to improve its anti-satellite weapons. [84]

Orbiting Debris Poses a Growing Threat

Experts say global cooperation is needed to avoid spacecraft damage.

An estimated 150 million pieces of space debris whiz constantly around the Earth. Moving at about 5 miles per second, this "space junk" — ranging from tiny flecks of paint to bulky stages of discarded launch vehicles — poses a growing threat to satellites. [1]

"In orbit, these objects . . . [are] faster than a bullet and can damage or destroy functioning space infrastructure, like economically vital telecom, weather, navigation, broadcast and climate-monitoring satellites," Holger Krag, head of the European Space Agency's (ESA) debris office, told a conference on space debris in April. [2]

About 5,000 pieces of space debris are more than three feet long, according to one expert. And about 20,000 measure more than four inches. [3]

So far, the debris has caused only minor damage, including a 16-inch gash that a piece of orbiting junk punched in the solar panel of an ESA satellite last August. [4]

But scientists say more-serious strikes are inevitable. As early as 1978, NASA astrophysicists warned that as space debris accumulates, more collisions will occur, spawning still more collisions in a cascading effect that will be impossible to halt. [5]

Two agencies — NASA and the Defense Department's Space Command — track satellites and space debris using ground-based radar and telescopes on land and in space.

But that equipment only tracks objects at least four inches long, and scientists say fragments as small as 0.04 of an inch can cause significant damage. [6]

The problem became more severe after Jan. 11, 2007, when China tested an anti-satellite weapon by firing an unarmed missile at one of its own defunct weather satellites orbiting at an altitude of 534 miles. The collision created more than 3,000 pieces of debris that still threaten other objects in orbit. One analyst called the test "the most prolific and severe fragmentation in the course of five decades of space operations." [7]

By 1987, U.S. and European space agencies had begun work on what would eventually become the Interagency Space Debris Coordination Committee. The committee is made up of government officials from 13 countries, including the United States, Russia and China. The countries are responsible not only for their own governments' satellites but also for satellites owned by private companies within their borders.

The committee issued space debris mitigation guidelines in 2007, but member countries are not implementing them, according to Krag and other experts. Krag says only 60 percent of satellites are disposed of as the committee recommends. [8]

The committee's guidelines say satellites nearing the end of their useful life should be parked out of orbit or burned up in Earth's atmosphere to keep them from colliding with other satellites and creating debris, says Michael Krepon, co-founder of the Stimson Center, a think tank in Washington focused on security issues. But he says satellite operators prefer to keep dying satellites in service until they use up every last bit of their expensive fuel.

"If you put a satellite up and that satellite is a revenue generator, you want to extract the most money from that investment," Krepon says. He warns that unless countries agree to enforce the guidelines, "we will lose space like we're losing fisheries in the ocean."

The United States conducted its first anti-satellite test in 1985, when an Air Force F-15 fighter flying at 38,000 feet launched a missile that destroyed a failing U.S. satellite. [85]

Another space shuttle tragedy occurred on Feb. 1, 2003, when the space shuttle *Columbia* disintegrated during re-entry, killing all seven astronauts aboard. Investigators determined that a piece of insulating foam from the shuttle's external fuel tank had come loose during launch, striking the spacecraft's wing and damaging its heat shield. [86]

In January 2004, President George W. Bush called for returning astronauts to the moon by 2020 and sending a manned mission to Mars. The result was NASA's Constellation Program. [87]

New Competition

Two years after taking office in 2008, President Obama canceled the Constellation Program, calling it "over budget, behind schedule and lacking in innovation due to a failure to invest in critical new technologies." [88]

His decision effectively eliminated any chance the United States would send astronauts to the moon during his administration. Instead, Obama called for NASA to send astronauts to an asteroid by 2025 and into orbit around Mars by the mid-2030s. But Congress had other ideas and funded NASA to proceed with a program essentially equivalent to the Constellation Program. [89]

Meanwhile, private-sector spaceflight companies were working to develop their own launch capabilities. SpaceX's first three launches failed, but its fourth, in 2008, was a success, as was a 2009 launch that sent the company's first commercial payload, a Malaysian satellite, into orbit. [90]

Zimmerman said SpaceX's fortunes improved from that point on. "SpaceX quickly signed up a large number of customers, even though the company was barely half a decade old," he wrote. "By 2012 . . . the company possessed launch contracts with private satellite companies valued at more than $1 billion. SpaceX's biggest new customer, however, was not a private company; it was NASA." [91]

Private companies' role in space also got a boost from NASA's Commercial

Rolf Densing, the ESA's director of operations, told a recent conference, "This problem can only be solved globally." [9]

Some economists suggest imposing a user fee on space launches to pay for debris mitigation. [10] A British company has proposed a system — called Necropolis — that would collect defunct satellites and move them into an orbit that active satellites don't use. And researchers at the University of Colorado at Boulder have proposed pushing pieces of space junk into higher orbit by firing beams of electrons at them. [11]

The ESA plans a RemoveDEBRIS mission this year to test a net that could be used to drag pieces of space junk into the atmosphere to burn up. It also will test a "dragsail" — like the sail on a boat but pushed by photons of light from the sun instead of wind — to accomplish the same objective. [12]

James A. Lewis, senior vice president at the Center for Strategic and International Studies, a think tank in Washington, says dealing with space debris is the most obvious starting point for international cooperation in space. He calls it one of the few issues where "we can possibly get some utility out of a new agreement."

— *Patrick Marshall*

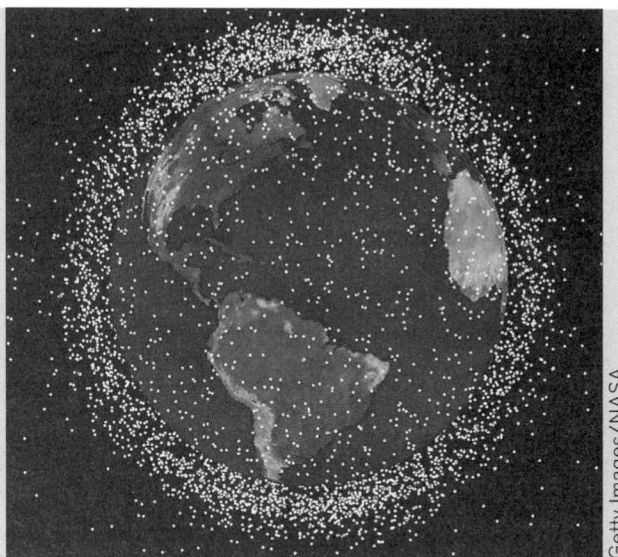

An illustration of Earth created by the National Aeronautics and Space Administration (NASA) in 1989 graphically shows space debris in low-Earth orbit.

[1] "Frequently Asked Questions: Orbital Debris," NASA, undated, https://tinyurl.com/yag6tr7w. Richard Ingham, "Space debris problem getting worse, say scientists," Phys.org, April 18, 2017, https://tinyurl.com/y8xnajhz.

[2] Sarah Knapton, "750,000 pieces of debris orbiting Earth threaten future of spaceflight, warn experts," *The Telegraph*, April 21, 2017, https://tinyurl.com/y9x9cftl.

[3] Ingham, *op. cit.*

[4] Tereza Pultarova, "Experts Call for Legislation and Improved Tracking to Deal with Orbital Debris," *Space News*, April 25, 2017, https://tinyurl.com/y9rral7q.

[5] Brad Plumer, "Space trash is a big problem. These economists have a solution," *The Washington Post*, Oct. 24, 2013, https://tinyurl.com/ycvhs5jf.

[6] Pultarova, *op. cit.*

[7] Brian Weeden, "2007 Chinese Anti-Satellite Test Fact Sheet," Secure World Foundation, updated Nov. 23, 2010, https://tinyurl.com/ya63f4fa.

[8] *Ibid.*

[9] Ingham, *op. cit.*

[10] Plumer, *op. cit.*

[11] Pultarova, *op. cit.*

[12] Tereza Pultarova, "Meet the Space Custodians: Debris Cleanup Plans Emerge," Space.com, April 26, 2017, https://tinyurl.com/ybrvypu2.

Crew Program, created to help the space agency build a replacement for the space shuttle.

Previously, NASA had provided private contractors with detailed specifications for the equipment it wanted them to build, and once it was built, NASA owned it. The plan under the Commercial Crew Program was for contractors to develop the spacecraft and other equipment themselves, with full ownership of the final product. [92]

Congress also acted to boost private-sector activities in space with the U.S. Commercial Space Launch Competitiveness Act of 2015.

Although the 1967 Outer Space Treaty prohibits countries from claiming sovereignty over space or celestial bodies, the act grants rights to resources extracted by companies from asteroids, the moon and other celestial bodies. [93]

CURRENT SITUATION

Regulatory Debate

The United States is the only country where private aerospace companies play a significant role in space, and that role is expanding rapidly. Perhaps not surprisingly, a vigorous debate is unfolding about how much the government should regulate these companies' activities in space.

Article 6 of the 1967 Outer Space Treaty requires that participating countries provide "continuing supervision" of private space-related activities. [94] Some experts say the U.S. government regulates those activities so weakly that it may be violating the treaty.

"The United States has clear rules controlling the export of sensitive space technologies on Earth, but lacks clear rules for private-sector operations in space," wrote Pace, of the Space Policy Institute. "This has caused some countries, such as Russia, to question whether private U.S. space companies are being supervised properly as required by international law. The United States can and should create a supportive regulatory regime for commercial space activities, but at present there is no clear, central authority for doing so." [95]

Matthew P. Schaefer, co-director of the Space, Cyber and Telecommunications Law Program at the University of Nebraska, warned a Senate subcommittee in May that unless the United States takes "minimal steps" to comply with Article 6, U.S. aerospace companies "may face foreign retaliation in the form of denying access to customers or partners, and investors from abroad may shy away as well." [96]

In addition, he said, the United States could not then insist that foreign governments "not harmfully interfere with U.S. commercial activities" in space. [97]

Other experts, however, say the treaty leaves it up to each country to define "continuing supervision."

"How a country chooses to assure that its citizens do not violate these provisions is completely up to that country," James E. Dunstan, a senior adjunct fellow at TechFreedom, a technology policy think tank in Washington, and Berin Szoka, TechFreedom's president, told the same Senate panel where Schaefer testified. [98]

While the Outer Space Treaty does not specify the type or degree of oversight countries should exercise over private-sector activities, industry leaders say uncertainty about the regulatory environment is bad for business. "Internal and external investors, as well as insurers, need to know what, if any, regulatory risks a particular project will face before financing an initiative," Michael Gold, vice president of Space Systems Loral, a Palo Alto, Calif., company that designs and builds satellite and spacecraft systems, said at the hearing. [99]

U.S. regulatory responsibilities are clearly defined. The Federal Aviation Administration oversees launches and re-entries of spacecraft, the Commerce Department licenses commercial satellites, and the Commerce, State and Defense departments oversee export controls and licensing of strategic technologies. [100]

Some industry advocates call that arrangement complex and unpredictable. "The problem . . . is not a 'regulatory gap' for current space activities, but rather a patchwork regulatory system that is complex, nontransparent and extremely expensive to navigate," Dunstan and Szoka told Congress. "Before we start overlaying a whole new 'Mission Authorization' regulatory regime on innovative space activities, we must first streamline the existing regime to reduce cost, redundancy and most of all, opaqueness, where bureaucrats can still pick winners and losers with impunity." [101]

Several free-market advocates want "permissionless approval" for commercial space activities.

"I urge the Congress to consider blanket authorization for all nongovernmental operations in space that do not cause tangible harm to other parties, whether foreign or domestic, in their peaceful exploration and use of outer space," Eli Dourado, director of the Technology Policy Program at George Mason University, said at a House committee hearing in March. "Such an approach would meet our treaty obligations while maximizing the scope for innovation and experimentation in space." [102]

But aerospace firms are not equipped to know whether their space activities might cause harm, other experts say.

"Few if any individual operators have the ability to either assess the risk their activities may pose to other space flight missions, especially U.S. or other government missions, nor the resources or ability to ameliorate the damages their actions might have on those missions," Douglas L. Loverro, former deputy assistant secretary of Defense for space policy, said at the House hearing. "And to ask them to try to develop those capabilities would be a greater constraint to their entrepreneurial activities than some well-designed government-sponsored measures." [103]

Some policymakers have called for amending the Outer Space Treaty to clarify regulatory responsibilities in space and better support the activities of private companies. Sen. Ted Cruz, R-Texas, said in April that 1967 was "a different time and era" and called on Congress to evaluate how a treaty enacted 50 years ago "will impact new and innovative activity within space." [104]

Most experts, however, see little chance the treaty will be modified or replaced. Even if U.S. policymakers agreed to amend the treaty, other space powers would be suspicious of their motives, said CSIS' Lewis. "People always think that it is the United States in some way trying to create opportunity for itself," he says.

Muncy of PoliSpace says the pact does not need to be changed. Instead, he says, the State Department needs to ensure the treaty's provisions are implemented in ways that benefit the United States.

National Space Council

The Trump administration's announcement in June that it will resurrect the National Space Council — with Vice President Mike Pence in charge — to oversee all U.S. activities and policies in space has also stirred controversy. The original council, established in 1958, was disbanded in 1973, revived in 1989 and disbanded again in 1993. [105]

Muncy of PoliSpace says the new council will give President Trump the information he needs to tell individual agencies overseeing space-related activities "whether or not they are actually holding up their end of the bargain to serve the national interest beyond their institutional interest."

When the idea of reviving the council was floated in December, *Apollo 11* astronaut Edwin E. "Buzz" Aldrin Jr. told a reporter it would be "absolutely critical in ensuring that the president's

Continued on p. 670

At Issue:

Should the private sector take over the management and design of U.S. space exploration from NASA?

RICK TUMLINSON
CHAIRMAN, DEEP SPACE INDUSTRIES, AND FOUNDER, NEW WORLDS INSTITUTE

WRITTEN FOR *CQ RESEARCHER*, AUGUST 2017

*e*xploring and opening space should no longer be something exclusive to the government — that it does for the people — rather it should answer the needs of government, and support those who want to go there themselves, to explore and create new homes.

To put the issue in context, let us separate science from exploration, settlement and development. In the first, the customer is the scientist. In the others, the customer is the people. A scientist wants data and information. If the private sector can provide the data cheaper, better and faster, it should get the job — and in most cases it can.

In exploration, the payoff can be science, strategic power, prestige or information that supports the nation or its people's ability to utilize or live in the places explored. Explorers on Earth have always been funded through a mix of sources. In the past, many were employed by government, as were Lewis and Clark. Today, some explorers are government employees, but many operate on grants from the government or private sources.

Settlement and development in space must be initiated by citizens but should be supported by the government. By being so, every other aspect of national interest is satisfied. To the extent that NASA funds can be allocated in ways that enhance human development and settlement of areas of space where people want to go, the agency should be allowed and encouraged to play a role. Yet it need not lead, and it definitely should not plan or control the pace of these activities.

In areas where the interest is purely scientific or at a stage where scientific return is the primary driver, NASA and other science-oriented elements of the government, working with academia, should continue to lead the way. However, funds spent on science and exploration should leverage citizen activities, especially activities that lead enable government-funded scientists and explorers to do more, and more cheaply.

The private sector is will quickly become more efficient than government agencies in gathering data and building infrastructure in space as it already is here on Earth. The government can lease or purchase from businesses, stimulating the economy and lowering taxpayer costs.

NASA should carefully pick science and exploration missions that are not best accomplished by and for the private sector itself, and when possible invest taxpayer funds back into the people, support institutional exploration and help solve the technical challenges we all face as we begin to settle the frontier.

SCOTT PACE
DIRECTOR, SPACE POLICY INSTITUTE, GEORGE WASHINGTON UNIVERSITY

WRITTEN FOR *CQ RESEARCHER*, JUNE 2017

*t*his is a simple question that obscures a deeper public policy question about how governments and markets create public goods, such as scientific knowledge, in the course of space exploration. To answer the question simply: no. Rather, the question should be how to use government to provide appropriate structures and incentives for the private sector, so as to obtain the greatest national good from space explorations.

Governments are responsible for providing public goods — among them national security, basic scientific research and exploration — for which no commercial market exists or is likely to exist.

There are fundamental differences between a publicly funded and directed enterprise chartered to define, explore and exploit a new frontier, and enterprises founded and directed for the purpose of creating wealth and providing shareholder returns. Private philanthropy can and does support science and exploration, but these are, in general, noncommercial, nonmarket activities even if they use private goods, services and capital.

In using the private sector in missions of exploration, the question is, who reports to whom? Is the goal the creation of public goods or the private success of companies? If a private actor who is providing a public good or service fails, changes priorities or slips schedule, the loss cannot always be made whole merely by paying monetary damages. Money is not a substitute for public-good failures in the way it is for commercial failures. Not everything which matters to our society will necessarily look good on a corporate balance sheet.

NASA is responsible for determining when and how it explores space using public funds. It cannot and should not be merely a passive buyer of just those exploration-related goods and services that contractors find it profitable to sell at a particular time. This means that NASA must be a "smart customer" — a role that would be undermined if it outsourced its design and management capabilities to a private contractor.

We do not really know what the human future in space will be. That is a question that exploration is intended to answer. In exploring space, we necessarily employ imperfect options, markets and governments in our portfolio of tools. The most effective exploration strategy will be a mixed one of government initiative and private innovation, not one entirely driven by NASA or left to the uncertainty of dynamic markets. There is room and need for both.

NASA/Mark Garcia

A resupply ship operated by Orbital ATK, an aerospace firm in Virginia, prepares to dock with the International Space Station on April 22. Some analysts and industry leaders say the nation's growing number of private-sector companies – rather than NASA – should handle deep-space exploration.

OUTLOOK

New Challenges

Policymakers and analysts fear that failing to fund U.S. space programs at sufficient levels could have serious implications for U.S. national security. U.S. satellites must be better protected soon or the country could lose strategic advantages in communication, guidance, intelligence gathering and other areas important to the military, they say.

"The era of unchallenged U.S. dominance of space is over," said Colby at the Center for a New American Security. The United States, he said, must "induce, convince, coerce, deter, dissuade, coax, incentivize or otherwise persuade" other countries not to exploit the vulnerabilities of U.S. satellites or the country's other space assets. [109]

Military officials are working to make U.S. satellites more maneuverable and resistant to jamming, but it is unclear whether Trump administration members understand why such steps are necessary, says Singer, of the New America think tank.

He also says competing interests in space among countries such as the United States, China and Russia make war on Earth more likely. "For most of the 20th century, the idea of great state powers going to war against each other was thinkable," he says. "It is thinkable once more."

Some policymakers say the United States must do more to assert its leadership over activities in Earth's orbit. Otherwise, they say, U.S. officials will treat China's progress in space as a potential military threat and will not want aerospace companies involved in space after all.

"China already has demonstrated a strong disregard for interests of other countries in outer space through its anti-satellite tests," Rep. Smith said at a hearing before his House committee in September. "Here on Earth, illegal incursions into the South China Sea represent a

Continued from p. 668
space priorities are clearly articulated and effectively executed." [106]

James Reuter, deputy associate administrator at NASA's Space Technology Mission Directorate, said in May that a new National Space Council might improve communication between the White House and Congress. "There's a lot of congressional guidance on the programs [that members of Congress] fund, and they don't always align with the administration's viewpoints," he said. "Perhaps a space council could help us." [107]

Air and Space Museum historian Logsdon said earlier versions of the council failed to prove "its superiority as an organizational approach to developing a space strategy or coordinating the space activities of executive agencies." After it was revived in 1989, he wrote, the council "managed to alienate most executive agencies." [108]

Aaron Oesterle, project manager at the Space Frontier Foundation, which supports rapid action to colonize other planets, also is skeptical. "Taking all of the various space stuff and putting it under a single regulatory authority is not viable in the long term, and in the short term it is so disruptive," he says. ∎

blatant disregard for the international rule of law. Will their disregard of international law continue to extend into outer space?" [110]

Some experts warn of potential trouble in space from rogue organizations or even individuals.

"Given the revolution in [private space flight], it's possible to imagine other non-state actors having a go at space as well," wrote Baiocchi and Welser. "Non-governmental organizations may start pursuing missions that undermine governments' objectives. An activist billionaire wanting to promote transparency could deploy a constellation of satellites to monitor and then tweet the movements of troops worldwide. Criminal syndicates could use satellites to monitor the patterns of law enforcement in order [to] elude capture, or a junta could use them to track rivals after a coup." [111]

Pace of the Space Policy Institute recommends that the United States work not only with private companies but with other countries as well in planning and conducting space programs.

"In the Cold War, space leadership was about, 'Look what I can do by myself that nobody else can do? I can land on the moon and nobody else can,' " Pace says. "Today, when there are many more state and nonstate actors in space — a lot more players — leadership is about, 'What can I get others to do with me?' " ∎

Notes

[1] Ben Evans, "Soyuz TMA-12M Crew Ready for Six-Hour Fast Ride to Space Station," *America Space*, undated, https://tinyurl.com/ycuxmtek; The Soyuz Experience in Photos," Canadian Space Agency, undated, https://tinyurl.com/q8ykklx; "NASA Astronaut Randy Bresnik Available for Interviews Before Space Station Mission," media advisory, NASA, July 17, 2017, https://tinyurl.com/y99o9lwn.

[2] Sean O'Kane, "NASA buys two more seats to the International Space Station on Russia's Soyuz rocket," *The Verge*, Feb. 28, 2017, https://tinyurl.com/y7ox8uh9.

[3] Doug Lamborn, "Time to get serious about space threats," *The Hill*, May 14, 2015, https://tinyurl.com/ya5osknh.

[4] Dave Baiocchi and William Welser IV, "The Democratization of Space New Actors Need New Rules," *Foreign Affairs*, May/June 2015, p. 98, https://tinyurl.com/ycspycls.

[5] Bill Canis, "Commercial Space Industry Launches a New Phase," Congressional Research Service, Dec. 12, 2016, p. 1, https://tinyurl.com/y7kw5lxa.

[6] Elbridge Colby, "From Sanctuary to Battlefield: A Framework for a U.S. Defense and Deterrence Strategy for Space," Center for a New American Security, January 2017, https://tinyurl.com/ya6wx3a2.

[7] Testimony of Lt. Gen. John W. Raymond before the House Armed Services Subcommittee on Strategic Forces, March 25, 2015, https://tinyurl.com/yd8sv7nh.

[8] "U.S. Should Stop Relying on Russian Rockets," editorial board, *Observer*, May 17, 2016, https://tinyurl.com/ybmw93nr; O'Kane, *op. cit.*

[9] Anthony Cave, "John McCain on target about American reliance on Russian rocket engines," *PolitiFact Arizona*, Jan. 29, 2016, https://tinyurl.com/y733n7z2.

[10] Testimony of James A. Lewis before the House Science, Space, and Technology Subcommittee on Space, "Are We Losing the Space Race to China?" Sept. 27, 2016, https://tinyurl.com/yb3q6hs4.

[11] "China's Secretive Space Program Threatens NASA's dominance," Bloomberg News, Nov. 28, 2016, https://tinyurl.com/hlf6wnl.

[12] Steven Jiang, "China: We will be on Mars by the end of 2020," CNN, Jan. 5, 2017, https://tinyurl.com/z7czqwm.

[13] Leonard David, "China's Anti-Satellite Test: Worrisome Debris Cloud Circles Earth," Space.com, Feb. 2, 2007, https://tinyurl.com/yasn5o5w; "China's President Urges Militarization of Space," Fox News, April 15, 2014, https://tinyurl.com/yde5q75p.

[14] "National Security Space Defense and Protection," National Academies Press, 2016, https://tinyurl.com/y8hpetr7; "UCS Satellite Database," Union of Concerned Scientists, April 11, 2017, https://tinyurl.com/y9pjvegd.

[15] John Logsdon, "Ten Presidents and NASA," *50th Magazine*, NASA, undated, https://tinyurl.com/y8jao7rw.

[16] Kerry Sheridan, "NASA delays deep-space Orion test to 2019 due to costs," Phys.org, May 12, 2017, https://tinyurl.com/y7yruzft; Loren Grush, "Trump's NASA budget cancels Europa lander and Asteroid Redirect Mission," *The Verge*, March 16, 2017, https://tinyurl.com/ybq3gluk.

[17] Statement of Chairman Lamar Smith, R-Texas, "Next Steps to Mars: Deep Space Habitats," House Science, Space and Technology Committee, May 18, 2016, https://tinyurl.com/yckrl2dw.

[18] "SpaceX blasts off cargo using recycled spaceship," Phys.org, June 3, 2017, https://tinyurl.com/y7qs7lzk; "Completed Missions," SpaceX, https://tinyurl.com/mngp9rq; "SpaceX To Send Privately Crewed Dragon Spacecraft Beyond The Moon Next Year," *SpaceX News*, Feb. 27, 2017, https://tinyurl.com/hbrjw2b.

[19] Rolfe Winkler and Andy Pasztor, "Exclusive Peek at SpaceX Data Shows Loss in 2015, Heavy Expectations for Nascent Internet Service," *The Wall Street Journal*, Jan. 13, 2017, https://tinyurl.com/zskb2ua.

[20] Canis, *op. cit.*, pp. 4, 10; "The Commercial Space Industry and Launch Market," everyCRSReport.com, April 20, 2012, https://tinyurl.com/y7dls4e8.

[21] Robin McKie, "Astronauts lift our spirits. But can we afford to send humans into space?" *The Guardian*, Dec. 6, 2014, https://tinyurl.com/y9qc5xzp; Andrew Follett, "NASA Vetoes Trump's Plan To Return Astronauts To Moon In 2019," *The Daily Caller*, May 14, 2017, https://tinyurl.com/lrvlw9z.

[22] Colby, *op. cit.*, p. 10.

[23] "Treaty on Principles Governing the Activities of States in the Exploration and Use of Outer Space, Including the Moon and Other Celestial Bodies," U.S. Department of State, undated, https://tinyurl.com/yanl9blx.

[24] Jonathan Broder, "Why the Next Pearl Harbor Could Happen in Space," *Newsweek*, May 4, 2016, https://tinyurl.com/ybex9noe.

[25] *Ibid.*

[26] James R. Clapper, "Statement for the Record: Worldwide Threat Assessment of the US Intelligence Community," Senate Armed Services Committee, Feb. 9, 2016, https://tinyurl.com/y8hhynfe.

[27] Calla Cofield, "What President Trump Means for NASA," Space.com, Nov. 10, 2016, https://tinyurl.com/hxb8hlh.

[28] "NASA Space Station Cargo Launches aboard Orbital ATK Resupply Mission," news release, NASA, April 18, 2017, https://tinyurl.com/y73w77dq; Jeff Foust, "Blue Origin still planning commercial suborbital flights in 2018," *Space News*, April 5, 2017, https://tinyurl.com/yccqr6vd.

[29] "Commercial Crew Program — The Essentials," NASA, undated, https://tinyurl.com/ybvr96oj.

[30] Robert Zimmerman, "Capitalism in Space: Private Enterprise and Competition Reshape the Global Aerospace Launch Industry," Center for a New American Security, January 2017, p. 27, https://tinyurl.com/ycrgydsu.

[31] Loren Thompson, "Capitalism In Space: The Beguiling Myth Market Forces Can Fix Everything," *Forbes*, March 16, 2017, https://tinyurl.com/y7rc7umm.

[32] Canis, *op. cit.*, p. 8.

[33] Scott Pace, "Wishful thinking collides with policy, economic realities in 'Capitalism in Space,' " *Space News*, April 4, 2017, https://tinyurl.com/y8t3tt2r.

[34] Ben Guarino, "Stephen Hawking calls for a return to the moon as Earth's clock runs out," *The Washington Post*, June 21, 2017, https://tinyurl.com/y7cjukcr.

[35] Darlene Superville, "Trump Wants to Send Humans to Mars," The Associated Press, *U.S. News & World Report*, March 21, 2017, https://tinyurl.com/y9m7yjy4; S.A. Miller, "Trump renews NASA mission for human space travel, deep space exploration," *The Washington Times*, March 21, 2017, https://tinyurl.com/y927gglo.

[36] Marina Koren, "Trump's Advisers Want to Return Humans to the Moon in Three Years," *The Atlantic*, Feb. 9, 2017, https://tinyurl.com/y9aq3zch.

[37] Christian Davenport, "An exclusive look at Jeff Bezos's plan to set up Amazon-like delivery for 'future human settlement' of the moon," *The Washington Post*, March 2, 2017, https://tinyurl.com/y779sb6r.

[38] Text of H.R.870 — REAL Space Act, Congress.gov, undated, https://tinyurl.com/yc2dp3au; Damien Sharkov, "Russia Plans New Rocket For Future Moon Base," *Newsweek*, Nov. 11, 2016, https://tinyurl.com/hjbwyz5; and Andrew Griffin, "China and Europe to build a base on the moon and launch other projects into space," *The Independent*, April 26, 2017, https://tinyurl.com/y8lwng2p.

[39] Shannon Stirone, "Meet the Republican Congressman Obsessed With Sending America Back to the Moon," *Motherboard*, Feb. 27, 2017, https://tinyurl.com/zm9c2j5.

[40] Testimony of Robert Richards before the Senate Commerce, Science, and Transportation Subcommittee on Science, Space, and Competitiveness, May 23, 2017, https://tinyurl.com/yb34ad9d.

[41] Eric Berger, "Quietly, NASA is reconsidering the moon as a destination," *The Houston Chronicle*, April 3, 2015, https://tinyurl.com/qbzk2zf.

[42] Richard Gray, " 'We could be living on the moon by 2022': Nasa claims a 'cheap' $10 billion lunar base will be ready for humans in just six years," *The Daily Mail*, March 24, 2016, https://tinyurl.com/h9hhc6v.

[43] Calla Cofield, "The Moon or Mars? NASA Must Pick 1 Goal for Astronauts, Experts Tell Congress," Space.com, Feb. 4, 2016, https://tinyurl.com/y9hdrheu.

[44] Cian O'Luanaigh, "No need for manned spaceflight, says astronomer royal Martin Rees," *The Guardian*, July 26, 2010, https://tinyurl.com/y8cc9h8t.

[45] Hanneke Weitering, "50th Anniversary of Apollo 1 Fire: What NASA Learned from the Tragic Accident," Space.com, Jan. 27, 2017, https://tinyurl.com/ycsaaqzn.

[46] Jeff Foust, "Weighing the risks of human spaceflight," *The Space Review*, July 21, 2003, https://tinyurl.com/29o7o6r.

[47] "Spirit and Opportunity," NASA, undated, https://tinyurl.com/y9w87lc6.

[48] Davod Szondy, "NASA works to wake up Curiosity as mission gets two-year extension," *New Atlas*, July 7, 2016, https://tinyurl.com/y74j3ou8.

[49] Ted Spitzmiller, *The History Of Human Space Flight* (2017), p. 128.

[50] *Ibid.*, p. 129.

[51] Statement by the President Upon Signing the National Aeronautics and Space Act of 1958, July 29, 1958, The American Presidency Project, University of California, Santa Barbara, http://tinyurl.com/y7oyql3d.

[52] Logsdon, *op. cit.*

[53] Steven J. Dick, "50 Years of NASA History," *50th Magazine*, NASA, undated, http://tinyurl.com/yc4g5p4t.

[54] "Glenn Orbits the Earth," NASA, Feb. 16, 2012, http://tinyurl.com/pb399qr.

[55] Spitzmiller, *op. cit.*, p. 226.

[56] "What Was the Gemini Program?" NASA, March 16, 2011, http://tinyurl.com/y9azc8t9.

[57] Logsdon, *op. cit.*

[58] *Ibid.*; William Harwood, "JFK legacy: Setting America on course for the moon," CBS News, Nov. 21, 2013, http://tinyurl.com/y99qk98e.

[59] "What Was the Apollo Program?" NASA, July 19, 2017, http://tinyurl.com/y98jr8m2; Rochelle Oliver and Amisha Padnani, "They Walked on the Moon," *The New York Times*, Jan. 17, 2017, http://tinyurl.com/ycwdvx7w.

[60] "National Security Space Defense and Protection," Committee on National Security Space Defense and Protection, Division on Engineering and Physical Sciences, National Academy of Sciences, 2016, p. 9, http://tinyurl.com/y8hpetr7; Lee Billings, "War in Space May Be Closer Than Ever," *Scientific American*, Aug. 10, 2015, http://tinyurl.com/ycrzxj4f.

[61] "Treaty on Principles Governing the Activities of States in the Exploration and Use of Outer Space, including the Moon and Other Celestial Bodies," Office for Outer Space Affairs, United Nations, undated, http://tinyurl.com/oxpq3qp.

[62] Logsdon, *op. cit.*

[63] *Ibid.*

[64] "Nasa budgets: US spending on space travel since 1958," DataBlog, *The Guardian*, undated, http://tinyurl.com/m72mnb8.

[65] Spitzmiller, *op. cit.*, p. 429.

[66] "What Was the Apollo Program?" *op. cit.*

[67] "President Nixon's 1972 Announcement on the Space Shuttle," NASA, undated, http://tinyurl.com/yc6e95uj.

[68] Spitzmiller, *op. cit.*, p. 460.

[69] "The Skylab Crewed Missions," NASA, May 6, 2013, http://tinyurl.com/y74m8n5q.

[70] Spitzmiller, *op. cit.*, p. 464.

[71] "Why Did NASA End the Space Shuttle Program?" *Forbes*, Feb. 2, 2017, http://tinyurl.com/y8c6539k.

[72] "Space Shuttle Era," NASA, undated, https://www.nasa.gov/mission_pages/shuttle/flyout/index.html; "First American Woman in Space," NASA, updated July 31, 2015, http://tinyurl.com/y8vh27ux; Clara Moskowitz, "Space Shuttle's Lasting Legacy: 30 Years of Historic Feats," Space.com, April 6, 2011, http://tinyurl.com/ybjowc7m.

[73] Moskowitz, *op. cit.*

[74] Dick, *op. cit.*

[75] Canis, *op. cit.*, p. 1; President Ronald Reagan, "Statement on Signing the Commercial Space Launch Act," The American Presidency Project, University of California, Santa Barbara, Oct. 30, 1984, http://tinyurl.com/kjf6q2a.

[76] "Commercial Orbital Transportation Service: A New Era in Space," NASA, February 2014, p. 10, http://tinyurl.com/ybdg2mcj.

About the Author

Patrick Marshall, a freelance policy and technology writer in Seattle, is a technology columnist for *The Seattle Times* and *Government Computer News*. He has a bachelor's degree in anthropology from the University of California, Santa Cruz, and a master's degree in international studies from the Fletcher School of Law and Diplomacy at Tufts University.

[77] *Ibid.*, p. 3.

[78] Tim Weiner, "Titan Lost Payload: Spy-Satellite System Worth $800 Million," *The New York Times*, Aug. 4, 1993, http://tinyurl.com/y8nvnwrf.

[79] Todd Harrison *et al.*, "Beyond the RD-180," Center for Strategic and International Studies, March 2017, p. 1, http://tinyurl.com/y8gmtdng.

[80] "H.R. 4399 (100th): Commercial Space Launch Act Amendments of 1988," govtrack, Nov. 15, 1988, http://tinyurl.com/y9lktncd.

[81] "Commercial Space Act of 1998, Title II — P.L. 105-303," Office of the General Counsel, NASA, undated, http://tinyurl.com/y9dqnmgz.

[82] "History and Timeline of the ISS," Center for the Advancement of Science in Space, undated, http://tinyurl.com/y78e8xvr; Tim Sharp, "International Space Station: Facts, History & Tracking," Space.com, April 5, 2016, http://tinyurl.com/y73suodm.

[83] "International Space Station Legal Framework," European Space Agency, undated, http://tinyurl.com/y92k46pt.

[84] Anatoly Zak, "The Hidden History of the Soviet Satellite-Killer," *Popular Mechanics*, Nov. 1, 2013, http://tinyurl.com/ycbs8xqa.

[85] Broder, *op. cit.*

[86] Karl Tate, "Columbia Space Shuttle Disaster Explained (Infographic)," Space.com, Feb. 1, 2013, http://tinyurl.com/y9a77qkg.

[87] "President Bush Offers New Vision For NASA," NASA, Jan. 14, 2004, http://tinyurl.com/yd3ra2mz.

[88] Ker Than, "Obama Scrubs NASA's Manned Moon Missions," *National Geographic News*, Feb. 1, 2010, http://tinyurl.com/y72woscm; Clara Moskowitz, "NASA Stuck in Limbo as New Congress Takes Over," Space.com, Jan. 7, 2011, http://tinyurl.com/ydcmwysj; Zimmerman, *op. cit.*, p. 10.

[89] Zimmerman, *op. cit.*, p. 6.

[90] *Ibid.*

[91] *Ibid.*, p. 15.

[92] "Commercial Crew Program — The Essentials," *op. cit.*

[93] "H.R.2262 — U.S. Commercial Space Launch Competitiveness Act," Congress.gov, undated, http://tinyurl.com/o7j7grl.

[94] "Treaty on Principles Governing the Activities of States in the Exploration and Use of Outer Space, Including the Moon and Other Celestial Bodies," *op. cit.*

[95] Scott Pace, "Regulating Outer Space: Making Space Commerce a Priority," *Foreign Affairs*, May 12, 2016, http://tinyurl.com/yd75n9dp.

[96] Testimony of Matthew P. Schaefer before the Senate Commerce, Science, and Transportation Subcommittee on Space, Science,

FOR MORE INFORMATION

Center for a New American Security, 1152 15th St., N.W., Suite 950, Washington, DC 20005; 202-457-9400; www.cnas.org. Nonpartisan think tank that analyzes and proposes national security and defense policies.

Center for Strategic and International Studies, 1800 K St., N.W., Washington, DC 20006; 202-887-0200; www.csis.org. Centrist think tank that has analyzed space-related national security concerns for the United States, including the risks involved in depending on Russia for launches to the International Space Station.

The Heritage Foundation, 214 Massachusetts Ave., N.E., Washington, DC 20002; 202-546-4400; www.heritage.org. Conservative public policy think tank that reports on space-related security issues and other topics.

National Aeronautics and Space Administration, 300 E St., S.W., Suite 5R30, Washington, DC 20546; 202-358-0001; www.nasa.gov. The primary federal agency responsible for civilian space programs.

New America, 740 15th St., N.W., Suite 900, Washington, DC 20005; 202-986-2700; www.newamerica.org. Centrist think tank focused primarily on technology and public policy.

Space Frontier Foundation, 4539 Seminary Road, Alexandria, VA 22304; info@spacefrontier.org; www.spacefrontier.org. Nonprofit group that advocates for settling other planets.

Space Policy Institute, Elliott School of International Affairs, George Washington University, 1957 E St., N.W., Suite 403, Washington, DC 20052; 202-994-1592; https://spi.elliott.gwu.edu/. Conducts research and organizes conferences on domestic and international space policy.

Stimson Center, 1211 Connecticut Ave., N.W., 8th Floor, Washington, DC 20036; 202-223-5956; www.stimson.org. Think tank focused on issues that include space-related global security and prosperity.

and Competitiveness, May 23, 2017, http://tinyurl.com/yb34ad9d.

[97] *Ibid.*

[98] Testimony of James E. Dunstan and Berin Szoka before the Senate Commerce, Science, and Transportation Subcommittee on Space, Science, and Competitiveness, May 23, 2017, http://tinyurl.com/yb34ad9d.

[99] Testimony of Michael Gold before the Senate Commerce, Science and Transportation Subcommittee on Space, Science and Competitiveness, May 23, 2017, http://tinyurl.com/yb34ad9d.

[100] Canis, *op. cit.*, p. 14.

[101] Testimony of James E. Dunstan and Berin Szoka, *op. cit.*

[102] Testimony of Eli Dourado before the House Science, Space, and Technology Subcommittee on Space, "Creating an Environment of Permissionless Innovation in Outer Space," March 8, 2017, http://tinyurl.com/y7rdmp7q.

[103] Testimony of Douglas L. Loverro before the House Science, Space, and Technology Subcommittee on Space, March 8, 2017, http://tinyurl.com/yc4abc59.

[104] Jeff Foust, "Cruz interested in updating Outer Space Treaty to support commercial space activities," *Space News*, April 26, 2017, http://tinyurl.com/ybmu33ag.

[105] Sarah Schlieder, "Trump Is Bringing Back The National Space Council . . . What's That?" abc2news.com, June 7, 2017, http://tinyurl.com/ycsufh5k; "NASA Statement on National Space Council," news release, NASA, June 30, 2017, http://tinyurl.com/yb2w8hqv.

[106] Leonard David, "Playing the Space Trump Card: Relaunching a National Space Council," Space.com, Dec. 29, 2016, http://tinyurl.com/y9p2h3dq.

[107] Jeff Foust, "Executive order creating National Space Council expected soon," *Space News*, May 2, 2017, http://tinyurl.com/n7bz6dh.

[108] John Logsdon, "Is creating a National Space Council the best choice?" *The Space Review*, Jan. 3, 2017, http://tinyurl.com/jc5odex.

[109] Colby, *op. cit.*, p. 17.

[110] Statement of Rep. Lamar Smith, House Science, Space, and Technology Committee, Sept. 27, 2016, http://tinyurl.com/y7h5un67.

[111] Baiocchi and Welser, *op. cit.*, p. 100.

Bibliography

Selected Sources

Books

Spitzmiller, Ted, *The History of Human Spaceflight*, University Press of Florida, 2017.
An aviation historian and pilot delivers a colorful history of human space flight, beginning in 1783 with balloonists and ending with the debate over returning humans to the moon and colonizing other planets.

MacDonald, Alexander, *The Long Space Age: The Economic Origins of Space Exploration from Colonial America to the Cold War*, Yale University Press, 2017.
An economist with NASA's Jet Propulsion Laboratory says philanthropists and private companies historically have provided crucial financing for space programs.

Sivolella, Davide, *The Space Shuttle Program: Technologies and Accomplishments*, Springer Praxis Books, 2017.
An aerospace engineer offers a detailed history of the space shuttle program.

Articles

Baiocchi, Dave, and William Welser IV, "The Democratization of Space: New Actors Need New Rules," *Foreign Affairs*, May/June 2015, https://tinyurl.com/ycspycls.
Two engineers with the RAND Corp. think tank argue that governments need to develop a new legal framework to accommodate the growing role of private companies in space.

Chow, Brian G., "Stalkers in Space: Defeating the Threat," *Strategic Studies Quarterly*, Summer 2017, https://tinyurl.com/y8mk5ntk.
An adjunct physical scientist at the RAND Corp. says the best way to defend U.S. satellite systems against anti-satellite weapons is to announce a policy of pre-emptive strikes against potential adversaries who behave suspiciously.

Pace, Scott, "Regulating Outer Space: Making Space Commerce a Priority," *Foreign Affairs*, May 12, 2016, https://tinyurl.com/yd75n9dp.
The director of the Space Policy Institute at George Washington University says the Outer Space Treaty of 1967 does not adequately cover the activities of private aerospace companies and that the United States needs to take the lead in setting international norms for using space.

Thompson, Loren, "Capitalism In Space: The Beguiling Myth Market Forces Can Fix Everything," *Forbes*, March 16, 2017, https://tinyurl.com/y7rc7umm.
A public-policy analyst challenges the argument that the private sector is better suited than NASA to manage space programs, saying private efforts have regularly run behind schedule, and concern for profits may cause companies to skimp on safety.

Reports and Studies

"National Security Space Defense and Protection: Public Report," Committee on National Security Space Defense and Protection; Division on Engineering and Physical Sciences, National Academies of Sciences, Engineering, and Medicine, National Academies Press, 2016.
A panel of military, academic and private-sector experts assesses the risks to U.S. national security presented by other countries' space capabilities as well as potential measures for countering those risks.

Canis, Bill, "Commercial Space Industry Launches a New Phase," Congressional Research Service, Dec. 12, 2016, https://tinyurl.com/y7kw5lxa.
An analyst for the research arm of Congress describes the growing role of private companies in space, their relationship with NASA and federal regulation of private-sector activities in space.

Colby, Elbridge, "From Sanctuary to Battlefield: A Framework for a U.S. Defense and Deterrence Strategy for Space," Center for a New American Security, January 2017, https://tinyurl.com/ya6wx3a2.
A senior fellow at a national security think tank assesses the vulnerability of U.S. satellite systems and other space-related technology, details the limited steps taken to mitigate those vulnerabilities and explores potential ways to deter attacks by other countries.

Harrison, Todd, Andrew Hunter, Kaitlyn Johnson, Evan Linck and Thomas Roberts, "Beyond the RD-180," Center for Strategic and International Studies, March 2017, https://tinyurl.com/ydgcdwjm.
Analysts at a centrist think tank explore how the U.S. government came to depend on Russian rockets for trips to the International Space Station and options for ending that dependence.

Pollpeter, Kevin, Eric Anderson, Jordan Wilson and Fan Yang, "China Dream, Space Dream: China's Progress in Space Technologies and Implications for the United States," prepared for the U.S.-China Economic and Security Review Commission, March 2, 2015, https://tinyurl.com/yb8nsoej.
Scholars from the University of California's Institute on Global Conflict and Cooperation say China's space program poses challenges for the United States but also may present opportunities for scientific collaboration.

Zimmerman, Robert, "Capitalism in Space: Private Enterprise and Competition Reshape the Global Aerospace Launch Industry," Center for a New American Security, January 2017, https://tinyurl.com/ycrgydsu.
In a report that prompted heated debate among space analysts, a space historian argues that private-sector companies are more efficient than NASA at designing and managing space programs.

The Next Step:

Additional Articles from Current Periodicals

Deep Space Travel

Baggaley, Kate, " 'Cryosleep' May Open the Door to Deep Space. Here's How," NBC News, June 12, 2017, https://tiny url.com/y7djawex.

Scientists are working to develop technology that would put astronauts into a hibernation-like state called "torpor" for long space trips.

Berger, Eric, "Finally, some details about how NASA actually plans to get to Mars," Ars Technica, March 28, 2017, https://tinyurl.com/mn9ep4e.

William Gerstenmaier, NASA's head of human exploration, said the agency will build a "gateway" orbiting the moon as one of its first steps in preparing for a manned mission to Mars in 2033.

Hobson, Katherine, "What Going to Mars Will Do To Our Minds," FiveThirtyEight, March 6, 2017, https://tiny url.com/zbjv3r2.

Astronauts traveling to Mars will experience boredom, isolation and other psychological stressors at levels never before experienced in space travel.

Foreign Space Activity

Grush, Loren, "China's most powerful rocket failed yesterday. What does that mean for the country's space plans?" The Verge, July 3, 2017, https://tinyurl.com/y7vlhtd9.

China's second launch of one of the world's most powerful rockets, the Long March 5, failed on July 2.

Kramer, Mirian, "Here's why you should pay close attention to India's space program," Mashable, June 9, 2017, https://tinyurl.com/y9cxspba.

India tested its biggest rocket in June and simultaneously launched 104 satellites in February.

Scoles, Sarah, "Russia's Quest to Build a Space Empire — Or Go Broke Trying," Wired, April 9, 2017, https://tiny url.com/msue9rd.

Officials with Russia's struggling state-run space program, Roscosmos, sound altruistic when they talk of working with emerging space programs in other countries, but their primary goal is to make money.

Private Sector

Brinkmann, Paul, "Video shows Blue Origin plans Eutelsat launch from Florida," Orlando Sentinel, March 7, 2017, https://tinyurl.com/ycegfecc.

Spaceflight company Blue Origin, run by Amazon founder Jeff Bezos, reached a deal with European satellite company Eutelsat to send a satellite into orbit.

Burton, Charlie, "After the crash: Inside Richard Branson's $600m space mission," GQ, July 5, 2017, https://tiny url.com/y78zr6ch.

Virgin Galactic will conduct rocket-powered test flights on its reusable spaceplane, VSS Unity, this fall, three years after the plane's predecessor exploded and killed one pilot.

Chang, Kenneth, "Moon Express Set Its Sight on Deliveries to the Moon and Beyond," The New York Times, July 12, 2017, https://tinyurl.com/y6uvccs8.

Moon Express, a startup in Florida, says it is on track to put its MX-1E lander on the moon by the end of the year.

U.S. Space Policy

Gaffey, Conor, "NASA Can't Afford to Put Humans on Mars," Newsweek, July 14, 2017, https://tinyurl.com/y9pgog7u.

NASA's head of human exploration, William Gerstenmaier, said the space agency's current budget is not large enough to pay for a manned mission to Mars.

Kaplan, Sarah, "President Trump relaunches the National Space Council," The Washington Post, June 30, 2017, https://tinyurl.com/y7pyoasx.

Promising to restore the United States' global leadership in space, President Trump re-established the National Space Council to oversee the country's activities beyond Earth.

Kheel, Rebecca, "Top general opposes Space Corps plan," The Hill, July 18, 2017, https://tinyurl.com/y7yhw48q.

Gen. Paul Selva, vice chairman of the Joint Chiefs of Staff, told a Senate committee he opposes a plan to create a branch of the military that would address the threats that Russia and China pose to U.S. satellites.

CITING CQ RESEARCHER

Sample formats for citing these reports in a bibliography include the ones listed below. Preferred styles and formats vary, so please check with your instructor or professor.

MLA STYLE

Mantel, Barbara. "Coal Industry's Future." CQ Researcher 17 June 2016: 529-552.

APA STYLE

Mantel, B. (2016, June 17). Coal Industry's Future. CQ Researcher, 6, 529-552.

CHICAGO STYLE

Mantel, Barbara. "Coal Industry's Future." CQ Researcher, June 17, 2016, 529-52.

In-depth Reports on Issues in the News

Are you writing a paper?

Need backup for a debate?

Want to become an expert on an issue?

For 90 years, students have turned to *CQ Researcher* for in-depth reporting on issues in the news. Reports on a full range of political and social issues are now available. Following is a selection of recent reports:

Civil Liberties
Privacy and the Internet, 12/15
Intelligence Reform, 5/15
Religion and Law, 11/14

Crime/Law
High-Tech Policing, 4/17
Forensic Science Controversies, 2/17
Jailing Debtors, 9/16
Decriminalizing Prostitution, 4/16
Restorative Justice, 2/16
The Dark Web, 1/16
Immigrant Detention, 10/15

Education
Charter Schools, 3/17
Civic Education, 2/17
Student Debt, 11/16
Apprenticeships, 10/16

Environment/Society
Muslims in America, 7/17
Funding the Arts, 7/17
Hunger in America, 7/17
Future of the Christian Right, 6/17
Trust in Media, 6/17
Anti-Semitism, 5/17

Health/Safety
Medical Marijuana, 7/17
Food Labeling, 6/17
Sports and Sexual Assault, 4/17
Reducing Traffic Deaths, 2/17
Opioid Crisis, 10/16

Politics/Economy
North Korea Showdown, 5/17
Rethinking Foreign Aid, 4/17
Troubled Brazil, 4/17
Reviving Rural Economies, 3/17
Immigrants and the Economy, 2/17

Upcoming Reports

Redistricting, 8/25/17   Medical Advances, 9/1/17   National Debt, 9/8/17

ACCESS

CQ Researcher is available in print and online. For access, visit your library or www.cqresearcher.com.

STAY CURRENT

For notice of upcoming *CQ Researcher* reports or to learn more about *CQ Researcher* products, subscribe to the free email newsletters, *CQ Researcher Alert!* and *CQ Researcher News*: http://cqpress.com/newsletters.

PURCHASE

To purchase a *CQ Researcher* report in print or electronic format (PDF), visit www.cqpress.com or call 866-427-7737. Single reports start at $15. Bulk purchase discounts and electronic-rights licensing are also available.

SUBSCRIBE

Annual full-service *CQ Researcher* subscriptions—including 44 reports a year, monthly index updates, and a bound volume—start at $1,131. Add $25 for domestic postage.

CQ Researcher Online offers a backfile from 1991 and a number of tools to simplify research. For pricing information, call 800-818-7243 or 805-499-9774 or email librarysales@sagepub.com.

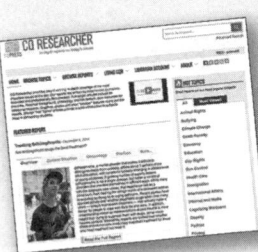

CQ RESEARCHER

CQPRESS

In-depth reports on today's issues

Published by CQ Press, an Imprint of SAGE Publications, Inc.   ***www.cqresearcher.com***

Redistricting Showdown

Should partisan gerrymandering be eliminated?

T he Supreme Court has long rejected legislative districts drawn to give one racial or ethnic group an advantage in state and federal elections. But the court has never set standards for deciding when districts drawn explicitly for partisan political purposes are unconstitutional. That could soon change as the court prepares to hear a potentially landmark Wisconsin redistricting case this fall. At stake is the balance of power in state legislatures and the right to draw the next set of congressional boundaries, based on the 2020 census. Redistricting abuses — known pejoratively as gerrymandering — have sparked outrage for disenfranchising voters and unfairly helping political parties maintain power. Some districts redrawn into contorted shapes — such as Pennsylvania's "Upside-Down Chinese Dragon" and Illinois' "Rabbit on a Skateboard" — have provoked particular scorn. Experts say Democrats had the upper hand in gerrymandering for years but that Republicans have had the edge since 2010. Meanwhile, the Census Bureau is struggling with funding, untested technology and political pressure as it prepares for the 2020 count.

Former lobbyist Russ Tidwell is helping minority-rights groups sue Texas lawmakers over Republican-drawn voting maps that the groups say illegally disadvantage Hispanic and black voters. A potentially landmark Supreme Court case this fall could rewrite the rules on how legislative districts are drawn.

CQ Researcher • Aug. 25, 2017 • www.cqresearcher.com
Volume 27, Number 29 • Pages 677-700

SSAGE Publishing | **CQPRESS**
Los Angeles I London I New Delhi
Singapore I Washington DC I Melbourne

RECIPIENT OF SOCIETY OF PROFESSIONAL JOURNALISTS AWARD FOR EXCELLENCE ◆ AMERICAN BAR ASSOCIATION SILVER GAVEL AWARD

I
N
S
I
D
E

THIS REPORT

THE ISSUES **679**

BACKGROUND **685**

CHRONOLOGY **687**

CURRENT SITUATION **690**

AT ISSUE......................**693**

OUTLOOK **694**

BIBLIOGRAPHY **698**

THE NEXT STEP **699**

CQ RESEARCHER

Aug. 25, 2017
Volume 27, Number 29

EXECUTIVE EDITOR: Thomas J. Billitteri
tjb@sagepub.com

ASSISTANT MANAGING EDITORS: Kenneth Fireman, kenneth.fireman@sagepub.com, Kathy Koch, kathy.koch@sagepub.com, Scott Rohrer, scott.rohrer@sagepub.com

ASSOCIATE MANAGING EDITOR: Val Ellicott

SENIOR CONTRIBUTING EDITOR:
Thomas J. Colin
tom.colin@sagepub.com

CONTRIBUTING WRITERS: Marcia Clemmitt, Sarah Glazer, Reed Karaim, Barbara Mantel, Chuck McCutcheon, Tom Price

SENIOR PROJECT EDITOR: Olu B. Davis

EDITORIAL ASSISTANT: Natalia Gurevich

INTERN: Robert DePaolo

FACT CHECKERS: Eva P. Dasher, Michelle Harris, Betsy Towner Levine, Robin Palmer

Los Angeles | London | New Delhi
Singapore | Washington DC | Melbourne

An Imprint of SAGE Publications, Inc.

SENIOR VICE PRESIDENT, GLOBAL LEARNING RESOURCES:
Karen Phillips

EXECUTIVE DIRECTOR, ONLINE LIBRARY AND REFERENCE PUBLISHING:
Todd Baldwin

CQ Researcher (ISSN 1056-2036) is printed on acid-free paper. Published weekly, except: (March wk. 4) (May wk. 4) (July wks. 1, 2) (Aug. wks. 2, 3) (Nov. wk. 4) and (Dec. wks. 3, 4). Published by SAGE Publications, Inc., 2455 Teller Rd., Thousand Oaks, CA 91320. Annual full-service subscriptions start at $1,131. For pricing, call 1-800-818-7243. To purchase a *CQ Researcher* report in print or electronic format (PDF), visit www.cqpress.com or call 866-427-7737. Single reports start at $15. Bulk purchase discounts and electronic-rights licensing are also available. Periodicals postage paid at Thousand Oaks, California, and at additional mailing offices. POSTMASTER: Send address changes to *CQ Researcher*, 2600 Virginia Ave., N.W., Suite 600, Washington, DC 20037.

THE ISSUES

679
• Is gerrymandering to blame for the nation's political polarization?
• Can a legal standard for partisan gerrymandering be devised?
• Should politics be removed from the redistricting process?

BACKGROUND

685 **Constitutional Roots**
Manipulating legislative boundaries for political gain began with the first congressional election in 1788.

686 **Court Rulings**
Supreme Court Justice Felix Frankfurter said in 1946 that the "courts ought not to enter this [redistricting] political thicket."

689 **No Clear Guidance**
In 1986, the Supreme Court said partisan gerrymandering might violate the Constitution's Equal Protection Clause.

CURRENT SITUATION

690 **Legal Battles**
Fifteen cases from nine states are pending this year involving partisan and racial gerrymandering.

691 **Obama Presses for Reform**
The former president is making redistricting reform a top priority.

692 **Action in the States**
As the 2020 census approaches, interest in redistricting reform is heating up.

692 **Citizen Action**
Some states have created commissions to draw voting maps.

OUTLOOK

694 **Winners, Losers**
More than a dozen states could gain or lose U.S. House seats in the next round of reapportionment.

SIDEBARS AND GRAPHICS

680 **GOP Controls Over Half of State Governments**
The governorship and both legislative branches are in Republican hands in 26 states.

681 **Administration Seeks to Curb Census Funding**
As the 2020 count nears, the Trump administration proposes keeping census spending flat.

684 **Republicans Dominate State Races**
Democrats have lost one-fourth of their state legislative seats since 2009.

687 **Chronology**
Key events since 1787.

688 **Census Faces Funding, Technology Challenges**
"It's going to cost some money to catch up."

690 **Iowa's Nonpartisan Approach Wins Praise**
The state represents "the first and best model," redistricting expert says.

693 **At Issue:**
Can partisan gerrymandering be eliminated?

FOR FURTHER RESEARCH

697 **For More Information**
Organizations to contact.

698 **Bibliography**
Selected sources used.

699 **The Next Step**
Additional articles.

699 **Citing *CQ Researcher***
Sample bibliography formats.

Cover: AP Photo/Eric Gay

Redistricting Showdown

BY JANE FULLERTON LEMONS

THE ISSUES

The question has befuddled courts for decades: When is it unconstitutional for a political party to redraw legislative boundaries for strictly partisan advantage?

The Supreme Court has said repeatedly that manipulating legislative districts by artificially grouping voters by race or ethnicity is illegal. But the court has never established rules on drawing legislative maps to give one political party — whether Republican or Democratic — an edge.

That could be about to change, however. On Oct. 3, the court will hear arguments in *Gill v. Whitford*, a potentially landmark Wisconsin case that could radically reshape the balance of power in state legislatures and Congress and rewrite the rules on what is known as redistricting.

"This is a blockbuster," said Joshua Douglas, a law professor at the University of Kentucky who has written extensively on election law procedures. "This could become the most important election law case in years, if not decades." [1]

The review comes at a critical juncture, when voters and their representatives are becoming more polarized and the federal government is ramping up for the 2020 census. The Supreme Court ruling, expected by next June, will take effect after that census, whose population counts will be the basis on which legislatures will draw new voting maps detailing legislative boundaries. The ruling also will come a few months before the 2018 midterm elections. Justice Ruth Bader Ginsburg said recently the case is "perhaps the most important" of those the Supreme Court has agreed to hear next term. [2]

Redistricting helped defeat then-Rep. Renee Ellmers, R-N.C., in a special primary election last year. When the state's congressional districts were redrawn under federal court order, Ellmers and another incumbent, George Holding, R-N.C., wound up in the same district, forcing them into a primary runoff that she lost.

Getty Images/CQ Roll Call/Al Drago

Throughout the nation's history, political parties have used redistricting to tip the electoral scales their way in states where their members control the legislature. That process, known as gerrymandering, takes a variety of forms. For instance, a Republican-controlled state legislature might "pack" as many Democratic voters as possible into a single district, giving GOP candidates the edge in the remaining districts. A Democratic legislature might "crack" the votes by splitting Republican voters among multiple districts, diluting their voting power in each one. [3]

Debate has intensified over whether partisan gerrymandering has helped produce today's politically polarized electorate, or whether the nation's deeply partisan atmosphere reflects long-term political shifts compounded by increasing numbers of people choosing to live near others with the same political views.

A 2014 survey by the Pew Research Center in Washington concluded that "Republicans and Democrats are more divided along ideological lines — and partisan antipathy is deeper and more extensive — than at any point in the last two decades." The survey also found that the percentage of Americans expressing consistently conservative or liberal opinions had doubled over the previous two decades — from 10 percent to 21 percent. [4]

Courts have had little trouble deciding when legislative boundaries unconstitutionally diluted the voting power of minority voters through racial gerrymandering. But defining a standard for partisan gerrymandering has eluded them. In the most recent such case to come before the Supreme Court, in 2004, four justices said the court had no business even trying to define the practice. [5]

Justices have "recognized that partisan gerrymandering is a problem; they've recognized that it's harmful to our democracy," said Michael Li, an expert on redistricting at the Brennan Center for Justice, a nonpartisan law and policy institute at New York University's School of Law. "But they haven't agreed upon a standard for when partisan gerrymandering goes too far." [6]

Some experts say that coming up with such a standard is impossible. Others disagree, saying mathematical formulas can be used to detect when state lawmakers have used redistricting to unconstitutionally help or hurt a

GOP Controls Over Half of State Governments

Republicans control the governorship and both legislative branches in 26 states, and Democrats in six. Governance in the remaining 18 states is divided between the parties. West Virginia became the most recent state to come under full GOP control when Gov. Jim Justice said on Aug. 4 he was switching to the Republican Party.

State Government by Party Control, 2017*

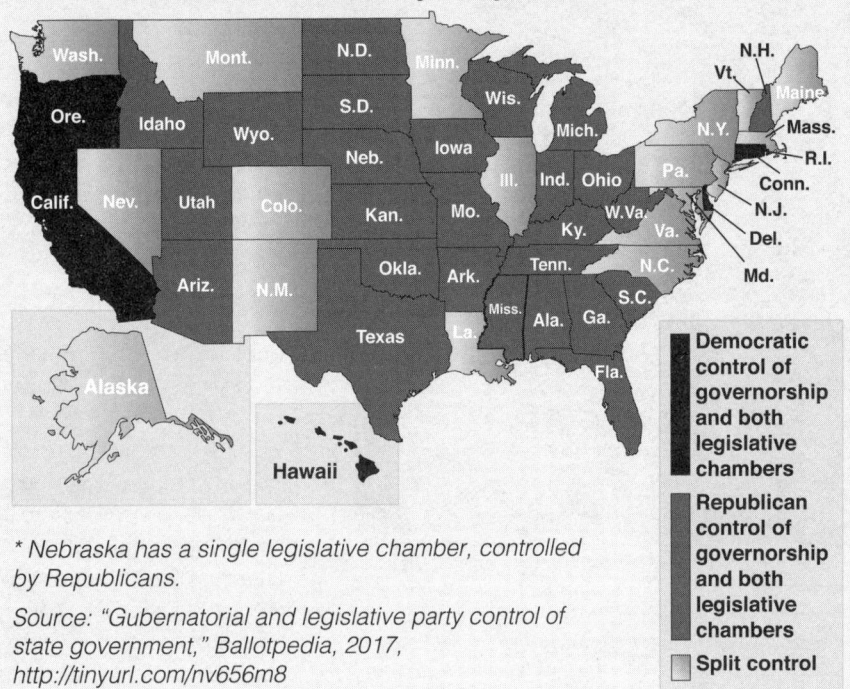

Democratic control of governorship and both legislative chambers

Republican control of governorship and both legislative chambers

Split control

* Nebraska has a single legislative chamber, controlled by Republicans.

Source: "Gubernatorial and legislative party control of state government," Ballotpedia, 2017, http://tinyurl.com/nv656m8

political party, an individual officeholder or a specific candidate.

They point to Wisconsin, where next term's Supreme Court case was born. In 2012, Wisconsin Democrats won 51 percent of the statewide vote but received only 39 percent of Assembly seats. Republicans also won five of the state's eight U.S. House seats in that election. The lawsuit, argues the GOP's electoral map minimized Democrats' voting power, violating the First Amendment right of free association and the 14th Amendment guarantee of equal protection. [7]

Wisconsin Republicans deny that they drew their electoral maps to harm Democrats. They say they enjoy a natural advantage because GOP voters are spread more evenly throughout the state than Democrats, who are concentrated in cities. [8]

In November 2016, a federal District Court sided with the challengers, saying the GOP maps had the intent and effect of diluting Democratic votes, marking the first federal court ruling in more than 30 years against partisan gerrymandering. [9]

"All the data shows that gerrymandering is only getting worse, by both sides," said retired University of Wisconsin law professor William Whitford, one of the 12 plaintiffs in the case. "This is a real problem for democracy, and an increasing number of people seem to understand that." [10] In May, the Brennan Center for Justice released a study saying that "extreme partisan bias" in congressional maps drawn after

the 2010 census helped elect at least 16 Republicans to the U.S. House. That is about two-thirds of the 24 seats Democrats would need to regain control of the chamber. [11]

"There is clear evidence that aggressive gerrymandering is distorting the nation's congressional maps, resulting in both large and remarkably durable levels of partisan bias," the report concluded. "The threat to democracy is both real and alarming." [12]

Gerrymandering tactics have led to voting maps so eccentrically shaped that they have earned nicknames such as "Rabbit on a Skateboard" (Illinois), "Upside-Down Chinese Dragon" (Pennsylvania) and "Praying Mantis" (Maryland). [13]

Analysts often point to North Carolina's 12th Congressional District as the most gerrymandered in the nation. A long, thin district, it snakes southward from Greensboro's northern environs in central North Carolina to the South Carolina border south of Charlotte more than 100 miles away. It was one of two North Carolina districts rejected earlier this year by the Supreme Court as having been racially gerrymandered by the Republican-led Legislature. [14]

Both parties resort to gerrymandering. In 2013, former Maryland Gov. Martin O'Malley acknowledged that Democrats aimed to oust a longtime Republican incumbent from the state's congressional delegation when they redrew Maryland's congressional map in 2011. Testifying in a lawsuit challenging the map, O'Malley said it was his intent "to create . . . a district where the people would be more likely to elect a Democrat than a Republican." [15]

The GOP, however, has made particularly effective use of gerrymandering. Republicans control state legislatures in 32 states compared with 14 controlled by Democrats. The other state legislatures either are split by party or are nonpartisan. [16] (*See map, above.*)

Those GOP gains are partly the result of REDMAP (Redistricting Majority Project), a Republican plan implemented after the 2010 census to focus party resources on state and local legislative seats as a way to lock in the party's political advantage for the remainder of the decade. Republicans were eager to reclaim political ground after losing the 2008 presidential election to Democrat Barack Obama. They realized that the key to controlling more state redistricting efforts was to control more state legislatures.

GOP strategist Karl Rove announced the plan in a *Wall Street Journal* column headlined, "The GOP Targets State Legislatures: He who controls redistricting can control Congress." The column listed the states and races Republicans planned to target in the 2010 elections and how much money the party would save by focusing on smaller races. Rove predicted the strategy "could end up costing Democrats congressional seats for a decade to come." [17]

That is precisely what happened. In the 2010 election, Republicans won control of 25 state legislatures and 29 governorships — with the corresponding control over the redistricting process that followed the 2010 census. Since then, Republicans have continued to make electoral gains. The party now controls 32 legislatures and 34 governorships as well as the U.S. House and Senate. [18]

The next redistricting process will take place after the 2020 census. But plans for that decennial population count remain in peril because of budget constraints, untested technology and the May resignation of the Census Bureau's director. [19] (*See sidebar, p. 688.*)

Meanwhile, the technology used to create the district maps has continued to evolve. The use of "big data" — computer programs and algorithms that enable researchers to uncover household voting patterns — has allowed the parties to pick their voters by giving the parties the ability to draw more-precise district maps, critics say. But big data's advocates say the technology also can be used to reduce partisanship

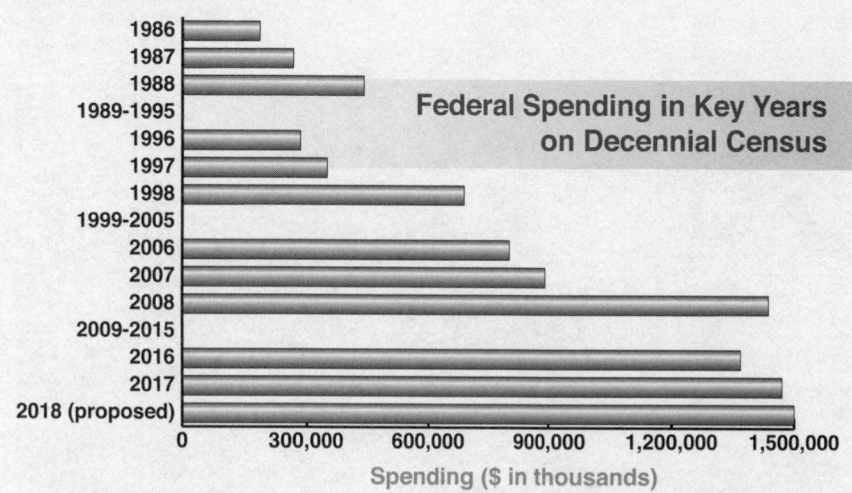

Administration Seeks to Curb Census Funding

Funding for the census has grown sharply in the key years leading up to each of the past three decennial population counts. But increases for the current stage of the 2020 census cycle are far smaller than in comparable periods. Citing the need to control costs in the 2020 census, the Trump administration proposes keeping spending flat, at about $1.5 billion, in year eight of the 10-year budget cycle. But critics fear underfunding will lead to an undercount of minorities.

Federal Spending in Key Years on Decennial Census

Sources: "Public Budget Database, Budget Authority" Office of Management and Budget, Obama White House Archives, undated, https://tinyurl.com/y843vsnu; "April 2017 Update," The Census Project, 2017, https://tinyurl.com/yakaz3p9

by putting the redistricting process into the hands of computers rather than biased humans. [20]

Some states have turned redistricting duties over to independent commissions as a way to reduce partisanship. Meanwhile, Iowa has adopted a system that it says removes virtually all partisanship from the legislative mapmaking process. [21] (*See sidebar, p. 690.*)

Polls show support for such changes. A 2016 national survey of 1,000 Republican and independent voters found that 66 percent backed the concept of requiring impartial commissions to draw congressional districts. [22] And more than 70 percent of people surveyed in a 2013 Harris poll said lawmakers who stand to benefit from redrawn congressional districts "should not have a say in how they are redrawn." [23]

Money also plays a role in redistricting, due partly to a landmark 2010 decision by the Federal Election Commission that allows individuals, corporations, unions and others to donate unlimited amounts of money to political parties and politicians to cover redistricting costs. [24]

Such donations "can provide the cash for voter data, mapping consultants and lobbyists to influence state legislators, who are in charge of redistricting in most states," according to ProPublica, a New York nonprofit that conducts independent investigative journalism. The donations also allow outside interests to finance inevitable lawsuits claiming that redrawn electoral maps treat one party's voters unfairly. [25]

As the debate over redistricting continues, here are some of the questions that Republicans, Democrats, political scientists and voters are asking:

Is gerrymandering to blame for the nation's political polarization?

Gerrymandering is easy to blame for the country's polarized politics and congressional gridlock. But experts disagree about how much it contributes to those conditions.

Wyatt Durrette, a former Republican candidate for Virginia governor who works with OneVirginia2021, a group that advocates redistricting reform, says gerrymandering has contributed to an atmosphere defined by such vitriol that

deadlock have steadily risen over the past half-century," at times encompassing 75 percent of key issues. That gridlock has been costly, both in actual dollars and citizen trust in government.

"The distance between the parties ideologically has all but returned to heights not seen since the end of the 19th century," wrote Binder. "Partisan polarization appears to be on the verge of passing historical levels in the Senate and has surpassed House records stemming from the turn of the century." [28]

blue in the urban areas. In the 2016 election, for instance, Missouri was solid red, with three blue zones — in St. Louis, Kansas City and the college town of Columbia. Such results led to postelection discussions about how many Americans live in "bubbles" with limited exposure to people with different ideas. [30]

Because people increasingly prefer to live near others who share their cultural and political preferences, Brookings senior fellows William A. Galston and Thomas E. Mann contend, "they are voting with their feet and sorting themselves geographically." As a result, they said, reducing gerrymandering would make "only a small dent" in the problem of political polarization. In addition, the situation "not only reflects polarization but also intensifies it" because polarization reinforces the views that led people to sort themselves in the first place, Galston and Mann said. [31]

That view is widely shared by scholars who study the issue. "There is little systematic evidence to support the claim that gerrymandering has had a substantial effect on polarization." wrote Nolan McCarty, a political science professor at Princeton University. "In fact, there is considerable evidence that it has played at most a tiny role." [32]

In discussing his research, McCarty says those trends have developed over several decades, beginning before political polarization was widespread and happening regardless of how districts were drawn.

"Districts matter a little bit, but not very much," McCarty says. "It's really that Democrats and Republicans have just gotten more different in the way they represent districts regardless of what types of districts there are." In other words, political polarization has increased because Democrats and Republicans are representing their districts in increasingly extreme and partisan ways, due to political pressures and the need to fend off challengers in primary elections.

Steffen W. Schmidt, a political science professor at Iowa State University,

New York City voters wait to cast their ballots in the Nov. 8 election. For years, political parties have drawn district lines with an eye toward gaining an edge over their rivals. Both Democrats and Republicans have employed tactics that might "pack" as many opposing voters as possible into one district or "crack" those voters among multiple districts, two commonly used methods for diluting the voting power of the opposite party.

partisan success has become more important than good government. [26]

Tom Davis, former Republican U.S. representative from Virginia, has a similar view.

"Gerrymandering has created many safe seats," he said. "This increases partisanship and makes compromise more difficult. It also amounts to a cynical manipulation of the electoral process." [27]

Few dispute that political polarization has contributed to gridlock in Congress. In a study for the Brookings Institution, a liberal think tank in Washington, senior fellow Sarah A. Binder, a political science professor at George Washington University, found that "levels of legislative

But political scientists say determining gerrymandering's role in polarization is tricky. Many argue that it is not a primary factor behind the current political climate. Rather, they say, people have chosen to sort themselves into like-minded communities, both on social media and geographically. And they point to the U.S. Senate, where seats cannot be gerrymandered because races are statewide, and to states with only one House seat. In both situations, partisanship still rages. [29]

The trend toward geographical self-segregation can be seen in maps of election returns, where a wide swath of red Republican votes across a state will be broken by smaller dots of Democratic

disagrees. In "safe" districts where politicians command large majorities of voters, he says, they feel no need to win over voters from the opposing party — or to even compromise on issues, because partisan voters often see compromise as caving to the opposition.

"Gerrymandering alone does not [account] for the GOP or Democratic victories in gerrymandered districts, but it sure helps in many places," he says. "Do we think Democrat and GOP strategists would use it if it was not helpful?"

David Daley, a senior fellow at Fair-Vote, an organization that supports electoral reforms, and the author of a book detailing how Republicans used redistricting to expand their legislative power, believes political scientists have "a blind spot" when it comes to how the GOP employed gerrymandering to transform the political playing field after 2010.

Norman Ornstein, a resident scholar at the conservative American Enterprise Institute think tank in Washington, says gerrymandering adds to partisanship by creating politically homogenous legislative districts.

"It's one of many things that amplify the polarization," he says. "Redistricting distorts public desires in elections. It can move us away from a representative democracy where voters choose the people that majorities, or in some cases pluralities, want."

Can a legal standard for partisan gerrymandering be devised?

It is not so difficult to determine whether a voting map is unconstitutionally partisan, says Sachin Chheda, a Democratic political consultant in Wisconsin and part of the group behind the original *Gill v. Whitford* suit. It is "a mathematical question that can be answered in any number of different ways," he says.

But others disagree, and they note that developing a legal definition for partisan gerrymandering continues to flummox the courts, including the Supreme Court. The nation's highest court has, in the words of Justice Anthony Kennedy,

sought a "workable standard" for defining when partisan gerrymandering is unconstitutional but has never found it.

"If workable standards do emerge," Kennedy wrote in a 2004 Pennsylvania case, courts should be prepared to strike down voting maps that violate them. [33]

Kennedy's opinion sent "all sorts of democracy nerds and stats geeks and poli sci professors on a quest for redistricting's holy grail, a theorem that would appeal to Justice Kennedy," says Daley of FairVote.

Nicholas Stephanopoulos was among the seekers of mathematical clarity. The University of Chicago law professor and a lawyer for the plaintiffs in the *Gill v. Whitford* case says a gerrymandered legislative district is one that "deliberately and severely and unjustifiably benefits one party over the other."

To gauge whether redistricting crosses into partisan gerrymandering, Stephanopoulos developed a way to measure what he calls the "efficiency gap" in voting outcomes. His formula calculates which party had more "wasted" votes — surplus votes cast for the winner or votes cast for the loser — in an election. He subtracts one party's wasted votes from the other party's wasted votes, then divides by all of the votes cast in the election. The higher the resulting "efficiency gap," the more that party is disadvantaged.

"When a party gerrymanders a state, it tries to maximize the wasted votes for the opposing party while minimizing its own, thus producing a large efficiency gap," Stephanopoulos said in article explaining the concept. "In a state with perfect partisan symmetry, both parties would have the same number of wasted votes." [34]

In Wisconsin — the state at the heart of the *Gill v. Whitford* case — the efficiency gap has been as high as 13 percent, a figure that Stephanopoulos' formula says is clear evidence of a legislative map gerrymandered for partisan advantage. Plaintiffs in the case cited this "efficiency gap" in arguing that Wisconsin Repub-

licans crossed a constitutional line in drawing their 2011 voting map. [35]

Republicans, however, reject the efficiency gap concept. "Even a cursory inspection of this so-called methodology reveals analytical flaws and partisan skullduggery too blatant to pass constitutional muster or stand up to common sense," wrote Chris Winkelman and Phillip Gordon, among the attorneys who filed a Supreme Court brief on behalf of the National Republican Congressional Committee. [36]

One flaw is that the formula "treats voters as monolithic blocs who vote party above all else," they wrote. "This assumption is contrary to reality." A second problem, Winkelman and Gordon said, is that the efficiency gap is based on the results of one statewide election and assumes that voters will continue to vote as they did previously. The efficiency gap, in other words, does not account for changes in voting behavior by those voters who, say, voted Republican before but decide to vote Democratic in the next election.

Because of these flaws, Winkelman and Gordon wrote, "we can only hope that, after 30 years of uncertainty, the court will finally decide what the Constitution has always demanded: In a constitutional republic, it must be the people's representatives who draw districts, not the courts and certainly not unelected academics promoting flawed and biased notions like the 'efficiency gap.' " [37]

Gill v. Whitford could finally settle the debate and establish a legal standard for defining partisan gerrymandering, analysts say. The case landed at the Supreme Court after a U.S. District Court panel ruled 2-1 in 2016 against the map that Wisconsin's Republican state lawmakers drew in 2011 for state Assembly districts. Judge Kenneth F. Ripple said the map aimed to deny Democratic voters the ability "to translate their votes into legislative seats." [38]

The panel, according to an analysis in the *Harvard Law Review*, agreed with plaintiffs that Republicans unfairly drew maps to increase their hold on

Republicans Dominate State Races

Democrats have lost one-fourth of their state legislative seats since 2009. Republicans now hold 4,156 seats to the Democrats' 3,112. One reason for the increase was the Republicans' aggressive campaign, known as REDMAP (Redistricting Majority Project), to win state races so the GOP could control state legislatures and thus the redistricting process for the U.S. House.

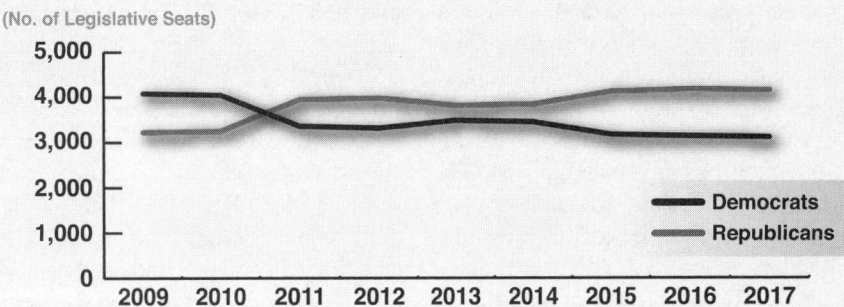

(No. of Legislative Seats)

Note: Totals do not include Nebraska, which has a nonpartisan unicameral legislature.

Source: "State Partisan Composition," National Conference of State Legislatures, Aug. 1, 2017, http://tinyurl.com/guos34u

the state Assembly: They both spread Democratic voters out so they could not achieve a district majority and "packed" Democratic voters into a small number of districts to limit the number of seats that the Democratic Party could win, the District panel said. The judges relied partly on Stephanopoulos' efficiency gap to determine that Wisconsin Republicans engaged in partisan gerrymandering.

In the end, the panel defined partisan gerrymandering as "a rational dividing line between legal partisan considerations and invidious partisan gerrymandering" — that is, between partisanship that could be expected and is constitutionally protected in redistricting and partisanship that crosses the line into unconstitutional territory. [39]

The key for the lower court, according to the law review analysis, was "the harm associated with unconstitutional partisan gerrymanders: entrenchment of power." The panel found the gerrymandered maps made the GOP and the state government "impervious to the interests of citizens affiliated with other political parties." [40]

Can politics be removed from the redistricting process?

Not everyone agrees that politics should play no role in redistricting.

Matt Walter, president of the Republican State Leadership Committee, which works to elect Republicans to state offices, sees a reason the Constitution made state lawmakers responsible for drawing legislative boundary lines.

"The framers . . . could have vested that power in courts or unelected commissions, but they didn't," he said. "Instead, they entrusted it to elected officials whom voters can hold accountable." He added that having the courts adopt "an ad hoc test to determine whether legislators are 'too partisan' in exercising a constitutionally prescribed function would raise serious separation-of-powers issues." [41]

Ornstein, of the American Enterprise Institute, and Daley, of FairVote, say it would be almost impossible to make redistricting completely nonpartisan. "All districting is political," says Daley. "It's extraordinarily difficult to remove politics from districting."

"The standard here ought to be

making sure that you don't have it tilted too far in one of two directions," Ornstein says, where one party holds all the power, or where both parties conspire to protect incumbents.

Brian Cannon, executive director of OneVirginia2021, agrees. "We don't have to take all the politics out of this situation to make it better," he says. Pointing to his own state, he says any change would help because Virginia's districts are so gerrymandered. Reformers do not have to find a perfect solution, he says.

But Schmidt, of Iowa State University, says revamping redistricting procedures could help reduce partisanship. "Redistricting should be done strictly by population," he says, giving districts an equal number of voters to comply with the one-person, one-vote principle.

Republican strategist Chris Jankowski, who helped lead the GOP's successful efforts after 2010 to gain electoral power through redistricting, concedes the process could be improved to lessen politics' impact on the line drawing. He points to the continuing advances in mapmaking as evidence of the need for restraint: "The technology, and the data, in 10 years has grown in its ability to be precise in drawing these districts at a relatively low cost," he says.

He advocates instituting "guardrails" to limit partisanship. "I do not believe you can take the politics out of redistricting," he says. "But I do believe that through state constitutions and state laws you can restrict the amount of partisan impact."

Chuck Todd, NBC News' political director and host of "Meet the Press," says big data could lessen partisanship if used correctly. It all depends on how mapping technology is employed. Currently, mapmakers are using it to reduce the number of swing districts and to keep more districts safely in one party's hands.

"If we decide we want our congressional districts to be more competitive, this is where you could use 'big data,' " Todd says. Todd discussed the issue in March, saying misuse of big data "has accelerated the polarization." Carefully drawn maps could increase balance between the major political parties and thus lead to more-competitive races. [42]

McCarty, the Princeton political scientist, is skeptical that computer technology can completely remove political considerations from redistricting because of built-in assumptions that carry political implications.

"Any procedure you come up with that looks apolitical has to have had a bunch of political decisions made in order to come up with the procedure," he says. Redistricting necessarily involves political tradeoffs, he says, that people can account for better than computers.

Supreme Court Justice Kennedy also recognized the conflict inherent in big data when he called technology's use in redistricting "both a threat and a promise." [43]

Hena Naghmi, a University of Virginia student who participated in a 2011 Virginia Redistricting Competition, said it is not always possible to draw compact, neatly configured legislative districts that don't have any odd shapes. "Virginia's not a square — it's just not," Naghmi said. [44]

Daley believes technology can help make the process of drawing electoral maps more equitable. But he says the process will remain partisan as long as politicians are involved.

"All districting is gerrymandering in some ways," he says. "You will never have a perfect distribution of seats to votes. It's impossible. . . . The question is whether voters have some kind of meaningful say to impact change."

Iowa has tried taking politics out of redistricting by having the state's Legislative Services Agency, which provides nonpartisan services to the General Assembly, draw the voting maps for the state House and Senate and for Iowa's four districts in the U.S. House of Representatives. The agency can only use population and census data, and it must create districts with approximately the same number of people.

"This puts the voter as the primary consideration," said Ed Cook, the agency's legal counsel. "The basic concept is, if it's a blind process the result will be fair." [45] ∎

BACKGROUND

Constitutional Roots

Manipulating legislative boundaries for political gain began with the first congressional election, in 1788, when Patrick Henry configured Virginia's 5th Congressional District in an unsuccessful effort to prevent his political adversary, James Madison, from winning election to the U.S. House. [46]

The redistricting process is rooted in the Constitution, which specifies that each House member must represent approximately the same number of people, a concept known as apportionment. That number has increased from about 30,000 in the first Congress to about 710,000 today. [47]

The Constitution, however, does not say how to achieve apportionment, and this omission led to congressional debates about the best method for apportioning representation that began in 1790 and stretched into the 20th century as the country and its population grew.

The Founders wanted House districts to be small enough that members could accurately represent their constituents' views, yet they needed a way to divide seats fairly among big and small states so the former would not dominate the latter. As Benjamin Franklin put it, "If a proportional representation takes place, the small States contend that their liberties will be in danger. If an equality of votes is to be put in its place, the large States say their money will be in danger." Seeking a solution, several Founders, including Thomas Jefferson and Alexander Hamilton, devised complex mathematical formulas for determining how many House members each state should have. [48]

The first Congress adopted Hamilton's formula, but in 1792, President George Washington vetoed it on constitutional grounds. Washington then signed a new apportionment bill based on Jefferson's formula, which increased the ratio from one House member for every 30,000 residents to one for every 33,000 residents. Jefferson's formula remained in use until 1842, when Congress approved a method by Sen. Daniel Webster of Massachusetts. [49]

Meanwhile, the federal government in 1790 conducted the first census, which counted 3.9 million people and boosted the number of House members from 65 to 105. Since then, the census has provided the official figures used every 10 years to determine the number of congressional representatives apportioned to each state. [50]

In 1812, the salamander-shaped district that Gov. Elbridge Gerry crafted for a state legislative election in Massachusetts led to the term "gerrymander" as a synonym for mapmakers who draw eccentric voting districts for partisan advantage. [51]

Even a few state boundaries are something of a gerrymander — such as when the Dakota Territory was admitted as two states rather than one, thereby doubling that region's representation in Congress and the umber of electors in the Electoral College who vote by state for president based on the popular vote. [52]

Developments after the Civil War, when African-American males received full voting rights, also affected apportionment. The 14th Amendment rectified the "original sin" of slavery, whereby the Northern states had agreed at the 1787 constitutional convention to count a slave as three-fifths of a person when determining a state's population for apportionment and taxation purposes. With the amendment's passage, the census was to count African-Americans as full individuals; the 15th Amendment, ratified in 1870, gave black men the right to vote. [53]

Apportionment and congressional redistricting affect presidential elections, because each state's Electoral College votes are allocated based on the number of senators and representatives in its congressional delegation. In 1872, Congress approved an apportionment plan that resulted in Republican Rutherford B. Hayes winning the 1876 presidential election by one electoral vote over Democrat Samuel J. Tilden, who had won the popular vote. [54]

Congress switched apportionment methods again in 1901, returning to Webster's system with a House size of 386 members. The following year, it enacted legislation to create a permanent census office within the Interior Department to oversee the increasingly complex process of counting the population every 10 years. [55]

Congress failed to pass a new apportionment act after the 1920 census, as required by the Constitution, because some members feared the House was getting too big. They, instead, left the previous law in place. [56]

As a result of that inaction, the 1929 Permanent Apportionment Act created a procedure for automatically reapportioning House seats after each census. The law also capped House membership at 435, where it remains. In addition, the House has five delegates representing the District of Columbia and the territories of American Samoa, Guam, the Northern Mariana Islands and the U.S. Virgin Islands. Puerto Rico, an unincorporated U.S. territory, elects a resident commissioner every four years. [57]

In 1941, Congress switched apportionment methods yet again, to one still in effect today, known as the Huntington-Hill method of equal proportions. Its goal was to keep the ratio of one state's "people per Representative" to that of another as close to 1-to-1 as possible. [58]

Court Rulings

As Congress grappled with apportionment, the Supreme Court expressed reluctance to weigh in on the politics of redistricting. A 1946 case alleged that unfairly drawn districts violated the 14th Amendment's guarantee of equal protection. In rejecting this argument, Justice Felix Frankfurter wrote the majority opinion that redistricting is "peculiarly political" and judicial review "would cut very deep into the very being of Congress." He added words that continue to reverberate: "Courts ought not to enter this political thicket." [59]

The first case of racial gerrymandering to reach the Supreme Court originated after the Alabama Legislature redrew the previously square electoral district boundaries of Tuskegee into a district with 28 sides designed to exclude black voters. In 1960, the court ruled unanimously in *Gomillion v. Lightfoot* that district lines drawn to disenfranchise black voters violated the 15th Amendment. [60]

Five years later, Congress enacted the Voting Rights Act to protect minorities' rights by barring practices, such as gerrymandering, aimed at keeping them from having an effective vote. In 2013, the Supreme Court effectively eliminated a key provision of that law, however: one that had required jurisdictions with a history of discrimination at the ballot box to seek advance approval from the Justice Department before making any changes in their voting procedures. The majority opinion, written by Chief Justice John Roberts Jr., said the law imposed burdens on some states that no longer represented current conditions. [61]

Meanwhile, the Supreme Court's reluctance to get involved in partisan gerrymandering cases changed under Chief Justice Earl Warren. [62]

In *Baker v. Carr*, the court said in 1962 that voters could challenge apportionment issues in federal court under the 14th Amendment's Equal Protection Clause. The first of several significant rulings involving apportionment issues, Baker sparked dozens of redistricting lawsuits in the states. [63]

In 1963, the high court rejected a Georgia redistricting plan in *Gray v. Sanders*. "The conception of political equality from the Declaration of Independence, to Lincoln's Gettysburg Address, to the 15th, 17th, and 19th Amendments can mean only one thing — one person, one vote," Justice William O. Douglas wrote for the court. [64]

In 1964, the Supreme Court applied that principle to congressional districts in another Georgia case, *Wesberry v. Sanders*. Under the Constitution, "one man's vote in a congressional election is to be worth as much as another's," Justice Hugo Black declared. [65]

That same year, the court ruled in *Reynolds v. Sims* that state legislative districts, like congressional districts, must be equal in population. [66]

Warren regarded redistricting cases as the most significant to come before the court during his nearly 16 years as chief justice, a time of liberal, judicial activism that included landmark rulings on desegregation and religious freedom — rulings that many conservatives denounced.

"If everyone in this country has an opportunity to participate in his government on equal terms with everyone else, and can share in electing representatives who will be truly representative of the entire community and not some special interest," he said, "then most of the problems that we are confronted with would be solved through the political process rather than through the courts," [67]

During this era, presidents began to weigh in on the need for redistricting reform, beginning with Democrat John F. Kennedy, who had represented a heavily Democratic Massachusetts district in the U.S. House for six years before moving on to the Senate and the presidency.

"I do think it is difficult for us to try to draw these lines," Kennedy said when asked about gerrymandering during a 1961 news conference. "There isn't any doubt that they are unsatis-

Continued on p. 688

Chronology

1780s-1940s
Congress wrestles with apportionment.

1787
Newly drafted Constitution requires House of Representatives to reapportion seats following decennial census.

1790
Government conducts first census.

1812
Gov. Elbridge Gerry backs salamander-shaped district in Massachusetts, leading to use of the term "gerrymandering."

1902
Congress creates a Census Office within the Department of the Interior.

1911
House passes Apportionment Act of 1911 to keep membership from increasing beyond its 435 seats.

1920
Following the 1920 census, Congress does not carry out 10-year apportionment as required by the Constitution because doing so would have increased the membership total while potentially shifting power to more urbanized states.

1929
House passes Permanent Apportionment Act, capping the number of representatives at 435, where it remains.

1941
Congress adopts the Huntington-Hill method of equal proportions, a formula for determining apportionment still used today.

1946
Supreme Court rejects arguments in *Colegrove v. Green* case alleging that unfairly drawn districts violate equal protection under the Constitution."

1960s-1970s
Supreme Court implements one-person, one-vote standard.

1962
In landmark *Baker v. Carr*, Supreme Court says citizens can challenge apportionment in federal court.

1965
Voting Rights Act becomes law, further protecting against tactics, such as gerrymandering, aimed at keeping minorities from having an effective vote.

1970
Census Bureau develops technology that lays the groundwork for modern computerized systems that map and analyze data.

---·---

1980s-1990s
Supreme Court provides unclear guidance on redistricting.

1980
Iowa General Assembly adopts plan putting nonpartisan legislative staff in charge of congressional and state redistricting.

1986
Partisan gerrymandering can be unconstitutional, the Supreme Court rules, but justices are unable to agree on what constitutes the practice.

1993
A district racially gerrymandered to comply with the Voting Rights Act can be unconstitutional and exacerbate the situation it seeks to offset, the Supreme Court says.

2000s-Present
Republicans gain upper hand in redistricting.

2000
Arizona voters create independent commission to draw congressional and state legislative district lines.

2004
Four Supreme Court justices argue that partisan gerrymandering cannot be defined, but Justice Anthony Kennedy leaves the door open for finding a "workable solution" to identify when the practice becomes unconstitutional.

2008
California voters narrowly approve citizens' commission to redraw state legislative districts.

2010
California voters add congressional redistricting to commission's responsibility. . . . Republican electoral victories allow the party to make inroads in subsequent redistricting.

2013
Supreme Court invalidates key provisions of the Voting Rights Act.

2016
Federal court strikes down Wisconsin redistricting plan as partisan gerrymander. . . . President Barack Obama indicates reforming the redistricting process will be a top priority after he leaves office.

2017
Census Bureau Director John H. Thompson departs earlier than expected, as budget constraints threaten the upcoming 2020 census. . . . Supreme Court agrees to hear potentially landmark partisan gerrymandering case of *Gill v. Whitford*, with arguments set for Oct. 3.

Census Faces Funding, Technology Challenges

"It's going to cost some money to catch up."

As the 2020 count of the U.S. population draws nearer, the Census Bureau is confronting budget constraints, untested technology and the unexpected resignation of Census Director John H. Thompson, all of which has put the census at "high risk," according to government auditors. [1]

At stake in the decennial count mandated under the U.S. Constitution is political representation — the balance of power in Congress and the Electoral College — and the distribution of more than $400 billion in federal funding based on population. The makeup of elected bodies, from school districts to county commissions to state legislatures, also relies on an accurate count. [2]

"The Founding Fathers understood that the census was a cornerstone of American democracy," says Phil Sparks, co-director of the Census Project, a network of nonpartisan organizations whose goal is to ensure an accurate count. "The efficacy and credibility of the American political system is based on fair and equal representation, and it starts with the taking of a fair and accurate census."

Counting the country's population is the government's largest and most expensive civilian undertaking. But the task has become more difficult as the percentage of people who return the initial census forms has been decreasing, from 78 percent in 1970 to 63 percent in 2010. Experts attribute the drop to such factors as a growing number of immigrants who distrust the government and to difficulties reaching people who are struggling financially. [3]

Although some conservative politicians have long criticized the census as an intrusion on privacy rights, polls found no partisan difference in 2010 participation rates. Instead, age, education and income had a larger impact on whether people filled out their forms. [4]

When the response rate drops, the cost of conducting the census goes up because the government must send out workers — 635,000 in 2010 — to find the people who did not mail back their forms. Those people typically are the ones most likely to be undercounted — such as minorities, immigrants, people in low-income and homeless communities, and those who distrust the government or just do not want to be counted. [5]

When people are undercounted, "you impact their political power," says former Census Director Steve Murdock, now a sociology professor at Rice University. "Census data is the key to distribution of our representative government."

Congress has directed that the 2020 census cost no more than the 2010 count, which had a 10-year price tag of $12.3 billion — the most expensive census to date. But analysts say that without adjusting for inflation, this ceiling amounts to a budget cut.

They also note that the census receives funding in a 10-year cycle, and that large increases are needed as the census draws nearer. But the increases for this stage of the cycle are far smaller than in comparable periods in the three previous censuses of 1990, 2000 and 2010. (*See graphic, p. 681.*) Currently, the 2018 funding proposed by the Trump administration and House committees is less than 10 percent above 2016 levels, whereas in 2008 it was 79 percent higher than it had been two years earlier. [6]

In 2013, when he became director, Thompson proposed upgrading several key systems and operations, such as using mapping technology to identify housing units, estimating that would save $5.2 billion. The upcoming census also will mark the first time people can respond via the internet. [7]

But money became an issue. With Republicans arguing the census has become too expensive, Congress since 2015 has appropriated about $170 million less than the bureau has said it needs to carry out the 2020 census. At the same time, the cost of a new electronic data collection system ballooned to $965 million, 67 percent higher than initial estimates. [8]

With his retirement scheduled for the end of the year, Thompson decided to leave early, hinting at frustration with the bureau's setbacks. "We had reached a point where I just could not do any more," he said. "I had done all I could." [9]

The situation surrounding the 2020 census led the Government Accountability Office (GAO) earlier this year to add it to the biannual list of federal agencies and programs it deems "high risk" because of their vulnerabilities to fraud, waste, abuse and mismanagement, or that are most in need of transformation.

Continued from p. 686

factorily drawn, not only for the Congress, which is not the worst offender, but the state legislatures, where we have had for many years notorious examples of gerrymandering." [68]

In 1987, Republican President Ronald Reagan used even stronger language than Kennedy, characterizing congressional district maps as "a horror show of grotesque, contorted shapes." At the

time, his party was on the losing end of the redistricting battle, and his complaints echoed those of Democrats today.

"Gerrymandering has become a national scandal," Reagan told the Republican Governors Club Annual Dinner in 1987. "The Democratic-controlled state legislatures have so rigged the electoral process that the will of the people cannot be heard. They vote Republican but elect Democrats." [69]

As judicial guidance on redistricting changed, so did the technology used to make the voting maps.

In the 1970s, the Census Bureau developed an encoding system for storing geographical data. The bureau added formatting for land features in the 1980s, helping lay the groundwork for today's $8.4 billion geographic information system (GIS) industry. The global positioning systems widely used

The GAO report noted it had made 30 recommendations "to help the Bureau design and implement a more cost-effective census" but that only six of those had been adopted. [10]

Comptroller General Gene L. Dodaro testified Feb. 15 before the House Committee on Oversight and Government Reform, explaining that GAO put the 2020 census on its "high risk" list because of concerns about the cost and testing of new technology being implemented. "We think there's much more needs to be done to manage that risk so we have a cost-effective, and an effective, census, which is very important," he said. [11]

Meanwhile, the Trump administration has not yet selected a permanent replacement as Census Bureau head, who will continue to face budget questions. In June, leaders of the Senate committees that oversee the bureau urged President Trump to make fully staffing it "a priority." One day later, leaders on the House Oversight and Government Reform Committee asked the bureau to provide "a credible and defensible cost estimate" for the upcoming census. [12]

After leaving the bureau in July, Thompson pressed Congress to adequately fund the census. "There is still time, but it's going to cost some money to catch up," he said at the National Press Club. [13]

Both House and Senate appropriations committees approved fiscal 2018 budgets in July with approximately $1.5 billion for the Census Bureau. When Congress returns in September, it will take up the spending measures. The Census Bureau's advocates, meanwhile, have called for $1.8 billion in funding. [14]

"Without an accurate count in this country, basically every fact we have about this country's population is suspect," says Jay Zagorsky, an economist at Ohio State University. "And it's not just about congressional representation."

— *Jane Fullerton Lemons*

In 2010, these "cultural facilitators" worked with census takers to find and count homeless people in California.

[1] Shereen Marisol Meraji, "Could A Census Without A Leader Spell Trouble In 2020?" Code Switch, NPR, July 15, 2017, https://tinyurl.com/y8msmxsj; "2020 Decennial Census," 2017 High Risk Report, U.S. Government Accountability Office, https://tinyurl.com/ybknbalv.

[2] Andrew D. Reamer, "Counting for Dollars: The Role of the Decennial Census in the Geographic Distribution of Federal Funds," Brookings Institution, March 2010, https://tinyurl.com/yajhppgf; Meraji, *ibid.*

[3] "2020 Decennial Census," *op. cit.*; Tara Bahrampour, "U.S. Census director resigns amid turmoil over funding of 2020 count," *The Washington Post*, May 9, 2017, https://tinyurl.com/y8vuaya5.

[4] "With Growing Awareness of Census, Most Ready to Fill Out Forms," Pew Research Center, March 16, 2010, https://tinyurl.com/ycfsd6mv. For background, see Thomas J. Billitteri, "Census Controversy," *CQ Researcher*, May 14, 2010, pp. 433-456.

[5] Mike Miciag, "Without More Census Funding, Disadvantaged Communities Risk Being Overlooked Most," *Governing*, May 15, 2017, https://tinyurl.com/yd53yq4b; "How many census takers are needed to conduct the census?" U.S. Census Bureau, http://tinyurl.com/y77qleu6.

[6] Arloc Sherman, "Census Funding in Crisis," Center on Budget and Policy Priorities, June 28, 2015, https://tinyurl.com/y729vzk8.

[7] Jeffrey Mervis, "Money, politics, and abandoned homes: Why the 2020 Census might be in jeopardy," *Science*, July 24, 2017, https://tinyurl.com/yase3nls.

[8] *Ibid.*; Bahrampour, *op. cit.*

[9] Meraji, *op. cit.*

[10] "2020 Decennial Census," *op. cit.*

[11] "GAO's 2017 High Risk Report: 34 Programs In Peril," House Committee on Oversight and Government Reform, Feb. 15, 2017, https://tinyurl.com/y9m4fbek.

[12] Eric Katz, "Budget and Leadership Problems Plague 2020 Census, Raising Concern on Capitol Hill," *Government Executive*, July 7, 2017, https://tinyurl.com/y7rmnt4f.

[13] Chase Gunter, "Thompson dishes on Census concerns, needs for catch-up," *Federal Computer Week*, July 26, 2017, https://tinyurl.com/y7f4yaz8.

[14] "July 2017 Update," The Census Project, https://tinyurl.com/ycs6bf2l.

in cars and cellphones today, as well as internet mapping providers, owe their existence to the Census Bureau's innovations. [70]

That same GIS software — used to gather, store, manipulate, present and analyze geospatial data — is widely used to make legislative district maps, and cases challenging how the technology is used in redistricting continue to come before the courts. [71]

No Clear Guidance

The 1980s brought more attention to partisan gerrymandering. The Supreme Court in 1986 ruled in *Davis v. Bandemer* that partisan gerrymandering could be unconstitutional if it violates the Constitution's Equal Protection Clause. Democrats in Indiana had challenged the state's 1981 apportionment plan, arguing it amounted to political gerrymandering because the new districts diluted their votes and thus violated their rights. A three-judge federal District Court panel agreed.

But the Supreme Court said the Indiana plan was not unconstitutional, ruling the harm to Democrats from the redrawn maps was not "sufficiently adverse" to violate the Equal Protection Clause. Nevertheless, the case marked

Iowa's Nonpartisan Approach Wins Praise

The state represents "the first and best model," redistricting expert says.

Iowa's approach to redistricting is like no other state's. Iowa does not allow its Legislature to redraw legislative boundaries, nor does it use an outside commission to do so. Instead, the state's Legislative Services Agency, which provides nonpartisan services to the General Assembly, creates the voting maps for the state House and Senate and for Iowa's four districts in the U.S. House of Representatives. [1]

"Iowa does represent the first and best model," says Norman Ornstein, resident scholar at the American Enterprise Institute, a conservative think tank in Washington.

In 1980, the Legislature put its nonpartisan advisory agency in charge of redistricting at a time when both Republicans and Democrats wanted to protect the interest of whichever party was in the minority. [2]

Then-Gov. Terry Branstad, a Republican, noted that history when he signed the most recent redistricting plan into law in 2011. "We can have some pride in the fact that Iowa has a system for reapportionment that is fair," he said, and does not skew "in favor of one party or the other." [3]

In an attempt to keep politics out of the process, Iowa's agency cannot use political or election data, or even the addresses of incumbents, when drawing maps. [4]

Iowa's disregard for partisanship and incumbency when drawing maps makes its approach unique, says Tim Storey, a redistricting expert with the National Conference of State Legislatures. The staff of the Legislative Services Agency is "not

allowed to use political data to draw the plan. They have to only use population and census data."

Steffen Schmidt, a political science professor at Iowa State University, says the Legislative Services Agency is required to draw "normal-shaped" districts, ensuring each of the four districts has roughly the same number of people. "The goal is for compact, contiguous districts that respect county lines," he says. The agency "works in secrecy, and neither the governor nor any other political person is allowed to interfere."

Ed Cook, legal counsel for the Legislative Services Agency, described the mapmakers' task as a juggling act. "You want to get as close on population [as possible] without the districts looking too bad," he said. [5]

Here's how it works: The agency submits a redistricting plan to the Legislature by April 1; an advisory commission then solicits feedback at public meetings and submits a report within two weeks. The Legislature at that point votes on the plan. If it votes no, the agency submits a second plan; if it votes yes, the plan goes to the governor for approval or veto. If the Legislature has not approved maps by Sept. 1, the state Supreme Court steps in to devise a plan.

The Legislature, however, has passed a redistricting plan after each census, and no plan has faced a veto or a court challenge. [6]

So far, the system has avoided the kind of partisanship that has plagued some other states. "Every system, when stretched

---

the first time the high court agreed that partisan gerrymandering could cross the line into unconstitutional territory — if a standard for evaluating such claims could be devised. [72]

In 2004, the high court revisited the issue of partisan gerrymandering in *Vieth v. Jubelirer*, with four justices saying the court should not intervene in cases of partisan gerrymandering and Justice Kennedy urging a definition partisan gerrymandering to be found. [73]

Last year, the District Court panel considering the case, then known as *Gill v. Whitford*, said the state legislative maps that Republican state lawmakers in Wisconsin crafted after the 2010 census amounted to a partisan gerrymander. That marked the first time since *Davis v. Bandemer* that a federal court has ruled in a case alleging partisan gerrymandering. [74]

CURRENT SITUATION

Legal Battles

As the political parties prepare for the redistricting fight that will follow the 2020 census, the court battles continue. Fifteen cases from nine states are pending this year. They fall roughly into three categories — partisan gerrymandering cases, racial gerrymandering cases and cases combining those or other issues. [75]

The case grabbing the most attention remains *Gill v. Whitford*. The Supreme Court is scheduled to hear it on Oct. 3 — the second day of its 2017 term.

Oral arguments are the latest step in a process that began with a handful of Wisconsin Democrats meeting after the 2010 election to discuss what they could do about a situation they viewed as partisan gerrymandering. [76]

"We understood it was a quixotic adventure," recounts Chheda, the Wisconsin consultant who was a member of the group behind the original suit. "It was very ambitious to think we want to solve a problem that hasn't been able to be solved in 30-plus years of Supreme Court litigation."

The case, says retired University of Wisconsin law professor Whitford, is "about as good a case to give the Supreme Court another chance to tackle this issue of partisan gerrymandering as the proponents of our point of view were going to find."

to the breaking point, has weaknesses," Schmidt says. "It would be very politically risky for a highly partisan governor to interfere with a system that has deep bipartisan support. Iowa leaders are very proud that the Iowa model is always cited as the model for nonpartisan redistricting."

In his 2016 book about redistricting, journalist David Daley devoted a chapter to Iowa, which he characterized as "the redistricting unicorn." [7]

"The Iowa model is terrific," Daley says, "but I'm not sure it's easy to export." Storey agrees: "The Iowa system works for Iowa."

Part of what makes the approach hard to use in other states, especially larger and more diverse ones, is that Iowa is geographically simple: fairly square, with no features such as coastlines or mountain ranges to deal with. The state also has a relatively homogenous population — 87 percent of voters are white — which means it doesn't have to configure districts to meet the needs of minority voters under the Voting Rights Act.

Moreover, Iowa, a small Midwestern state of 3.1 million, has an especially engaged citizenry, according to analysts. During presidential campaigns, the state holds the first-in-the-nation caucus, with candidates from both major parties blanketing Iowa as they seek to gain momentum before the primary season gets underway. [8]

Daley says that in other states politicians get away with gerrymandering because voters do not understand the process or pay little attention to it. So passing along Iowans' civic-mindedness about elections would be a good start for reforming the redistricting process elsewhere, Daley says.

"If we could export that attitude elsewhere, we would go a long way toward having a more small 'd' democratic system," he says, because Iowa voters understand "district lines are really the building blocks of our democracy and [that] when they get twisted for partisan purposes it can change the essence of the results."

Schmidt calls the Iowa model "a great example of fairness in designing districts. It makes politics actually look fair — [and that is] remarkable."

— Jane Fullerton Lemons

[1] "Legislative Services Agency (LSA)," Iowa Legislature, https://tinyurl.com/y9e9wpqc; Ed Cook, "Legislative Guide To Redistricting In Iowa," Legislative Services Agency, Iowa Legislature, https://tinyurl.com/ybt6bmks.

[2] Tracy Jan, "Iowa keeping partisanship off the map," *The Boston Globe*, Dec. 8, 2013, https://tinyurl.com/y9g6pe8h.

[3] James Q. Lynch, "Branstad signs redistricting plan into law," *Mason City Globe Gazette*, April 19, 2011, https://tinyurl.com/y76n4b84.

[4] "Redistricting Commissions: State Legislative Plans," National Conference of State Legislatures, Dec. 7, 2015, https://tinyurl.com/y9sh936n ; "Redistricting in Iowa," *Ballotpedia*, https://tinyurl.com/y9pbv2d4.

[5] Linda Wertheimer, "Political Districting the Iowa Way," NPR News, April 21, 2007, www.npr.org/templates/story/story.php?storyId=9750943.

[6] Edith Munro, "Gerrymandering? Not in Iowa," *Albany Times Union*, April 14, 2011, https://tinyurl.com/y9v2nk73.

[7] David Daley, *Rat^{f**}ked: The True Story Behind the Secret Plan to Steal America's Democracy* (2016).

[8] "Redistricting in Iowa," *op. cit.*

While *Gill v. Whitford* blames Republicans for partisan gerrymandering, a case from Maryland, *Benisek v. Lamone*, alleges Democrats manipulated the redistricting process to get their party another congressional seat.

The Maryland case, now before a three-judge U.S. District Court panel, might reach the Supreme Court, but the outcome of the *Whitford* case could affect both the timing and outcome of the Maryland case. [77]

Three other cases alleging partisan gerrymandering come from North Carolina. Each claims maps of congressional districts drawn by Republican state legislators in 2016 amount to partisan gerrymandering. The new maps replaced earlier ones that the Supreme Court and other courts struck down because of racial gerrymandering. The legislators drawing the new maps said they were using political criteria "to gain partisan advantage." As in the Maryland case, these cases could be affected by the *Gill v. Whitford* decision. [78]

An additional three North Carolina cases argue the state's 2011 map of congressional districts constitutes a racial gerrymander. In one case, *Cooper v. Harris*, the Supreme Court in May struck down two district maps as unconstitutional, saying legislators had packed black voters into a few districts, diluting their voting power. The other two cases are pending. [79]

Obama Presses for Reform

Former President Obama is making redistricting reform a top priority. In his final White House press conference, he said he planned to focus on issues where "our core values may be at stake," including "explicit or functional obstacles" to voting rights. [80]

And in his first speech after leaving office in January, he told University of Chicago students that gerrymandering is a key obstacle to addressing national problems.

"What is preventing us from tackling them and making more progress really has to do with our politics and our civic life," he said. "It has to do with the fact that because of things like political gerrymandering, our parties have moved further and further apart and it's harder and harder to find common ground because of money and politics." [81]

Obama raised the issue often during his eight years in the presidency, saying in his 2016 State of the Union address, "I think we've got to end the practice of drawing our congressional districts so that politicians can pick their voters, and not the other way around." [82]

With the next census less than three years away, both parties are raising money and creating organizations to oversee the redistricting efforts that will follow. [83]

"The stakes are high in the 2020 census," says Ornstein of the American Enterprise Institute.

Democrats, who lost considerable electoral ground to Republicans in Congress and state legislatures after the last round of redistricting, have formed the National Democratic Redistricting Committee to counter the Republican State

In his first public appearance since leaving office, former President Barack Obama told University of Chicago students on April 24 that gerrymandering is a key obstacle to addressing national problems: "Because of things like political gerrymandering, our parties have moved further and further apart, and it's harder and harder to find common ground."

Leadership Committee, which oversaw the REDMAP redistricting effort.

Eric Holder, who served as Obama's attorney general, is overseeing the Democratic effort. He said the committee's goal is to get states to redraw the districts that helped solidify the GOP's grip on the U.S. House and state legislatures. It also will pursue court challenges to Republican-drawn maps and campaign for ballot referendums approving new procedures for legislative apportionment.

Republicans, meanwhile, believe the 2020 census will allow to them to expand on the electoral gains they made after the 2010 count. [84]

"What we did in 2010 will be dwarfed by what's going to take place in 2020," says Jankowski, the political consultant behind REDMAP. "Obama has guaranteed that by launching what we presume will be a well-funded, multifront effort."

Action in the States

With the 2020 census on the horizon, interest in redistricting reform is increasing in statehouses around the country. Nearly 150 state bills have been introduced this year addressing redistricting procedures. [85] They include at least 42 bills in 22 states that aim to create independent or advisory redistricting commissions. [86]

"There's a lot of talk about reform," says Tim Storey, a redistricting expert with the National Conference of State Legislatures. But most state legislatures have adjourned for the year, and none passed a redistricting bill.

While state legislatures have most of the power when it comes to drawing House district maps, Congress determines the requirements, such as the mandate that only one lawmaker can represent each congressional district.

Ten reform-related bills are pending in the U.S. House. In February, 47 House Democrats, backed by Common Cause, a public-interest advocacy organization in Washington, introduced a bill that would require states to establish independent, multiparty citizen redistricting commissions to draw congressional maps.

"Gerrymandering districts erodes the trust of the people and undermines democratic principles," said Rep. Julia Brownley, D-Calif., one of the bill's sponsors. "Utilizing independent citizen redistricting commissions will result in a more transparent election process and more accountable representation." [87]

Rep. Don Beyer, D-Va., wants to go even further. To end one party's domination of a district, he would create larger districts that would be represented by three to five lawmakers. Independent commissions under his proposal would draw the maps for these bigger districts. States with five or fewer House members would elect all their representatives at large, while states with six or more members would elect representatives in multimember districts. On Election Day, voters would rank their district's candidates in order of preference, a system that some cities already use. [88]

"This is going to be a paradigm shift in the way we elect members of the House," says Beyer, whose 8th Congressional District in the Washington suburbs is among Virginia's most gerrymandered and most reliably Democratic. "What you're doing is elevating every voter to make sure they're important."

Citizen Action

Some states have taken redistricting reform into their own hands, creating commissions to draw voting maps or proposing such commissions in ballot initiatives.

Continued on p. 694

At Issue:

Can partisan gerrymandering be eliminated?

DAN VICUNA
NATIONAL REDISTRICTING MANAGER,
COMMON CAUSE

WRITTEN FOR *CQ RESEARCHER*, AUGUST 2017

*u*sing big data and voting histories, partisan elected officials and consultants can slice and dice communities to preordain the vote in districts for an entire decade. This partisan system can persist only if we allow politicians to draw districts without rules that prevent them from prioritizing political self-interest over the public's right to fair representation.

In several states with ballot initiatives, voters have shown that they will not accept the manipulation of our elections as an inevitable feature of democracy. In fact, Americans have decided the opposite: It is not a democracy if politicians are choosing their voters instead of the other way around.

Using two ballot initiatives, California voters stripped legislators of the power to draw districts and created a Citizens Redistricting Commission with balanced partisanship, a ban on gerrymandering and strict conflict-of-interest rules. In a 2010 ballot initiative, Floridians added an explicit ban on partisan gerrymandering to their state constitution. This reform led to new congressional and state Senate maps after a lawsuit challenging the districts uncovered the extent to which state legislators schemed to secretly break the rules.

Unfortunately, fewer than half of all states have a robust ballot initiative option; few legislators are interested in voluntarily giving up this power; and voters cannot punish legislators for gerrymandering when districts are drawn to prevent accountability.

Therefore, a judicially mandated limit on extreme gerrymandering is the surest way to make redistricting work for all Americans. This is the responsibility of the courts because extreme partisan gerrymandering is not just wrong, it is unconstitutional. That is why Common Cause is organizing amicus briefs in support of the plaintiffs in *Gill v. Whitford* — the case before the Supreme Court involving Wisconsin's 2011 redistricting plan — and challenging North Carolina's congressional map in *Common Cause v. Rucho*.

The Supreme Court recently ruled that "partisan gerrymanders are incompatible with democratic principles" and that plaintiffs challenging partisan gerrymanders must get their day in court.

We hope the Supreme Court recognizes itself as the best hope to defend the Constitution and the American ideal that voters must have the power to hold their elected officials accountable on Election Day. The states have shown us that extreme partisan gerrymandering can be eliminated, so the Supreme Court now has the proof it needs to limit the practice nationwide.

MATT WALTER
PRESIDENT, REPUBLICAN STATE
LEADERSHIP COMMITTEE

WRITTEN FOR *CQ RESEARCHER*, AUGUST 2017

*r*edistricting is an inherently political process. The Constitution gives the power to draw district lines to state legislatures. The framers could have vested that power in the courts or unelected commissions, but they entrusted it to elected officials whom voters can hold accountable. This is a feature of the system, not some kind of unforeseen aberration.

All human beings have political opinions, so there is no such thing as an "independent" commission, as some have called for. An individual who knows enough about the inner workings of redistricting is almost certainly someone with political opinions.

The facts confirm this. A May 2017 study by UCLA and Yale researchers found that "independent commissions do not draw House maps that encourage greater electoral competition any more than partisan legislatures do." Overall, they wrote, "our results suggest caution in overhauling state redistricting institutions to increase electoral competition: independent commissions may not be as politically neutral as theorized."

Numerous "partisan gerrymander" plans have failed to fulfill their designed goal. For 40 years, Democrats drew boundary lines to their benefit at every turn. Yet in 2010, Republicans had more success than either party has seen in modern history, gaining nearly 700 seats and taking control of 20 legislative bodies in many districts drawn by Democrats. State-level success isn't isolated to Republican-wave elections. In 2012, Republicans secured 410 state legislative districts won by President Obama at the top of the ticket. Voters continued to choose state-level Republican leadership in the same district boundaries that preferred a Democrat in the White House. We overcame their lines because we ran better candidates and campaigns, period.

The most partisan of gerrymanders cannot guarantee a party will win an election. People aren't commodities who always vote for the same party. Candidates and circumstances matter, and upsets happen in every election cycle. We've continued to win because we understand that and fight every day to earn votes.

If the Supreme Court rules that courts can find redistricting plans "too partisan," it would raise serious separation-of-powers issues. All maps will then be open to challenge by whatever party happens to lose the most elections that year. Courts will be flooded with lawsuits by political actors trying to game the system for selfish partisan advantage.

That's bad for the courts and even worse for our elections.

Continued from p. 692

For state legislative districts, 13 states have a commission with the primary responsibility for drawing redistricting plans. Another five states have an advisory commission that can assist the legislature, while another five states have a backup commission to make decisions if the legislature cannot do so. The composition of the commissions varies widely; some members are citizens and some are elected officials. [89]

For congressional districts, six states have a citizen commission that has the primary responsibility for creating the maps. Another five states have an advisory commission, while another two have a backup commission. [90]

In California, the 14-member Citizens Redistricting Commission, selected from a pool of registered voters, chooses the boundaries for state legislative districts and congressional districts. In 2008, voters established the commission to draw state legislative districts, and in 2010 gave it authority over congressional districts.

The results have been mixed, experts say. The commission's maps undercut the safe seats of many incumbents by putting them in districts with other incumbents or by creating open seats. As a result, more than a dozen incumbents retired or were defeated in 2012. On the other hand, interparty competitiveness did not increase, as the new districts overwhelmingly retained the political affiliation of the old. [91]

The problem, according to some experts, is that people sort themselves into like-minded neighborhoods. "California's citizens have taken away from the politicians the power to choose their voters, and that was reflected in the high incumbent turnover in 2012," election reform group the FairVote said. "But no matter who is drawing the lines, the polarization of the American electorate makes achieving competitive single-member districts effectively impossible on a large scale." [92]

Still, Harvard University gave the California Citizens Redistricting Commission high marks for trying. In July, it awarded the commission a $100,000 prize for public engagement in government. The commission "shows how citizens can take the lead in redistricting efforts to construct maps that respect communities and citizens and are fair to political parties," said Archon Fung, a professor of democracy and citizenship at Harvard's John F. Kennedy School of Government. "It is an innovation that other states should consider emulating." [93]

Former Republican California Gov. Arnold Schwarzenegger pushed for creating the commission while in office and remains committed to redistricting reform. He has launched a "Terminate Gerrymandering" crowdfunding effort, recorded a video explaining gerrymandering and plans to speak out on the issue prior to the Oct. 3 oral arguments in the gerrymandering case before the Supreme Court. [94]

Experts also point to Arizona's five-member Independent Redistricting Commission, approved by voters in 2000. An Associated Press analysis earlier this year found the state has one of the lowest levels of unequal representation in the country, meaning the partisan split between officeholders is similar to that of the votes cast in an election. [95]

Michigan, Missouri, Ohio and Oregon are considering possible ballot initiatives to create redistricting commissions. [96]

OneVirginia2021 is seeking an amendment to Virginia's state constitution to "establish an independent, impartial commission to apply a fair and transparent process in drawing political districts after the 2020 census." [97]

Cannon, the group's executive director, says gerrymandering by both parties has created a "bipartisan incumbent protection plan" in the state. The group has made a documentary, "Gerryrigged: Turning Democracy On Its Head," featuring former Virginia congressmen George Allen, a Republican, and Ward Armstrong, a Democrat. Each was redistricted out of his seat when the opposing party controlled the process.

"We've got to end gerrymandering to have better politics in Virginia and in our country," Cannon says. ∎

OUTLOOK

Winners, Losers

When the next round of reapportionment takes place after the 2020 census, states in the South and West with growing populations likely will gain seats in the U.S. House, while those in the Northeast and Midwest probably will lose some.

Projections based on 2016 census data indicate more than a dozen states could gain or lose House seats in the next reapportionment. Texas could net three or four more seats, followed by Florida, which could pick up two seats to become the third-largest congressional delegation in the country, behind California and Texas.

Others likely to gain seats are Arizona, Colorado, Montana, North Carolina and Oregon. Most likely to lose seats are Alabama, Illinois, Michigan, Minnesota, New York, Ohio, Pennsylvania, Rhode Island and West Virginia. The 2020 population count also could increase the number of states with a single House member. There are now seven. [98]

Outside factors — including the results of the 2020 presidential election — might affect the next census figures, said Kimball Brace, president of Election Data Services, a political consulting firm in Manassas, Va., which analyzes census data. Hurricane Katrina in 2005 and the 2007-09 recession, for example, caused population shifts that affected apportionment after the 2010 census. [99]

"The change in administration could have a profound impact on population change and growth in this nation," Brace said.

Coupled with the census data are predictions of landmark demographic changes to the U.S. population that will likely affect how mapmakers draw district lines. Americans are more racially and ethnically diverse than at any point in the nation's history. By 2055, minorities will make up a majority of the country's population. Nearly 59 million immigrants have arrived in the past 50 years, and 14 percent of the population is foreign-born. [100]

The 2016 electorate also was the most diverse in history, mostly due to higher numbers of Hispanic voters. Taken together, blacks, Hispanics, Asians and other racial or ethnic minorities accounted for 26.7 percent of voters.

At the same time, the 2016 presidential election saw more young voters cast ballots than older voters. Turnout among Millennials and their younger Generation X counterparts surpassed that of Baby Boomers and other older Americans. "The ascendance of the Millennial vote is noteworthy because Millennials are more likely to be self-described independents, but they also are more Democratic than older generations in their political preferences," the Pew survey said. [101]

These changes should benefit Democrats, but Republicans' success with redistricting after the 2010 census shows it is possible to overcome that advantage in individual races.

Both political parties remain aware of the population and demographic changes — and the impact they will have on voting patterns and on congressional and legislative districts. These changes are "going to overwhelm this debate," says Republican strategist Jankowski.

A lot, as a result, is riding on an accurate 2020 count of the U.S. population. As the Census Bureau struggles with tight funding and technological challenges, a number of observers say they fear minorities and immigrants will be undercounted. An inaccurate count would have consequences for the subsequent apportionment process and the resulting balance of power.

"As a nation," says Jay Zagorsky, an economist and research scientist at Ohio State University, "this is something we should be concerned about." ∎

Notes

[1] Patrick Marley, "U.S. Supreme Court to hear Wisconsin's redistricting case but blocks redrawing of maps," *Milwaukee Journal Sentinel*, June 19, 2017, https://tinyurl.com/ya32ujdz.

[2] Sam Levine, "Ruth Bader Ginsburg: Gerrymandering Case May Be Most Important Decision SCOTUS Faces," *The Huffington Post*, July 22, 2017, https://tinyurl.com/yckrnhmm.

[3] "Redistricting the Nation," glossary, redistricting thenation.com, https://tinyurl.com/zanghh2.

[4] "Political Polarization in the American Public," Pew Research Center, June 12, 2014, https://tinyurl.com/p4scahz.

[5] Robert Barnes, "Supreme Court to hear potentially landmark case on partisan gerrymandering," *The Washington Post*, June 19, 2017, http://tinyurl.com/y75cfype.

[6] Emma Sarran Webster, "Everything You Need to Know About Gerrymandering," *Teen Vogue*, March 31, 2017, https://tinyurl.com/le35l69.

[7] Michael Li and Thomas Wolf, "5 Things to Know About the Wisconsin Partisan Gerrymandering Case," Brennan Center for Justice, New York University Law School, June 19, 2017, https://tinyurl.com/ybr7gadr; Mark Joseph Stern, "Is Anthony Kennedy Ready to Put an End to Partisan Gerrymandering?" *Slate*, May 23, 2017, https://tinyurl.com/ybx3nx55; https://tinyurl.com/y7en689c.

[8] Michael Li, Thomas Wolf and Alexis Farmer, "The State of Redistricting Litigation (April 2017 edition)," Brennan Center for Justice, May 23, 2017, https://tinyurl.com/ya3xou84.

[9] *William Whitford et al. v. Gerald C. Nichol et al.*, U.S. District Court for the Western District of Wisconsin, https://tinyurl.com/ybsx4fun; "Gill vs. Whitford," Brennan Center for Justice, July 28, 2017, https://tinyurl.com/y7en689c.

[10] David Daley, "Meet the man who may end gerrymandering: A retired Wisconsin law professor's Supreme Court case could save democracy," *Salon*, March 26, 2017, https://tinyurl.com/k69ldwa.

[11] Laura Royden and Michael Li, "Extreme Maps," Brennan Center for Justice at New York University Law School, May 9, 2017, https://tinyurl.com/lecs4b5.

[12] *Ibid.*

[13] Patrick McGreevy, "New redistricting panel takes aim at bizarre political boundaries," *Los Angeles Times*, Dec. 19, 2010, https://tinyurl.com/y7m76oyc.

[14] Adam Liptak, "Justices Reject 2 Gerrymandered North Carolina Districts, Citing Racial Bias," *The New York Times*, May 22, 2017, https://tinyurl.com/lvavnxb; Ingraham, *ibid.*

[15] John Fritze, "Lawsuit forces Maryland Democrats to acknowledge the obvious: Redistricting was motivated by politics," *The Baltimore Sun*, June 1, 2017, https://tinyurl.com/ycm2kxsr; Dave Daley, "How Democrats Gerrymandered Their Way to Victory in Maryland," *The Atlantic*, June 25, 2017, https://tinyurl.com/yc9lm9pd.

[16] "State Partisan Composition," National Conference of State Legislatures, March 2, 2017, https://tinyurl.com/ycm6fmfj.

[17] Karl Rove, "The GOP Targets State Legislatures," Karl Rove website, March 3, 2010, https://tinyurl.com/ybatxwef.

[18] Amber Phillips, "These 3 maps show just how dominant Republicans are in America after Tuesday," *The Washington Post*, Nov. 12, 2016, https://tinyurl.com/y8puspah; Kurtis Lee, "With party switch in West Virginia, Republicans now have matched record number of governors' seats. Will it last?" *Los Angeles Times*, Aug. 4, 2017, https://tinyurl.com/y8mk7m7p.

[19] Henry Farrell, "The U.S. census is in trouble. This is why it's crucial to what the nation knows about itself," *The Washington Post*, May 15, 2017, https://tinyurl.com/ybvfvwup.

[20] Joseph P. Williams, "The Downside of Data," *U.S. News & World Report*, July 28, 2017, http://tinyurl.com/y7k5x7z6; Rosie Cima, "Can an Algorithm Eliminate the Unfairness of Gerrymandering?" *Priceonomics*, Jan. 22, 2016, https://tinyurl.com/y9w8do9g.

[21] Tracy Jan, "Iowa keeping partisanship off the map," *The Boston Globe*, Dec. 8, 2013, https://tinyurl.com/y9g6pe8h.

[22] "The 2016 Presidential Election and Electoral Reform: How Better Polling Tells Us What Republican Voters Really Think," FairVote, Feb. 18, 2016, https://tinyurl.com/yctdp6z8.

[23] Larry Shannon-Missal, "Americans Across Party Lines Oppose Common Gerrymandering Practices," Harris Poll, Nov. 7, 2013, https://tinyurl.com/y8srqjpa; "Who draws the lines?" All About Redistricting: Professor Justin Levitt's guide to drawing the electoral lines, Loyola Law School, https://tinyurl.com/7zoqogl.

[24] Advisory Opinion 2010-03, National Democratic Redistricting Trust, Federal Election Commission, May 7, 2010, https://tinyurl.com/y87yoeru; Steve Spires, "Federal Election Commission Opens the Door for Unlimited Contributions in Redistricting Fights," Open Secrets.org, Center for Responsive Politics, May 11, 2010, https://tinyurl.com/y7mc5s7u.

[25] Olga Pierce, Jeff Larson and Lois Beckett, "The Hidden Hands in Redistricting: Corporations and Other Powerful Interests," ProPublica, Sept. 23, 2011, https://tinyurl.com/3kuu2sa.

[26] "Gerryrigged: Turning Democracy On Its Head,"

OneVirginia2021, https://tinyurl.com/y72g3lge.

[27] "Rep. Tom Davis on His Retirement," transcript, *The Washington Post*, Feb. 1, 2008, https://tinyurl.com/yah5nl3x.

[28] Sarah A. Binder, "Polarized We Govern?" Brookings Institution, May 27, 2014, http://tinyurl.com/yahj9ywn.

[29] Jowei Chen and Jonathan Rodden, "Don't Blame the Maps," *The New York Times*, Jan. 24, 2014, https://tinyurl.com/yccj9xcf; John Sides, "Gerrymandering is not what's wrong with American politics," *The Washington Post*, Feb. 3, 2013, https://tinyurl.com/y9lnndrr.

[30] Derek Thompson, "Everybody's in a Bubble, and That's a Problem," *The Atlantic*, Jan. 25, 2017, https://tinyurl.com/y9zd2ap2; "Presidential Election Results: Donald J. Trump Wins," *The New York Times*, last updated Aug. 9, 2017, https://tinyurl.com/kvkqlfq.

[31] Fred Dews, "A primer on gerrymandering and political polarization," Brookings Institution, July 6, 2017, https://tinyurl.com/yd62vtc2; William A. Galston and Thomas E. Mann, "Republicans Slide Right: The Parties Aren't Equally To Blame for Washington's Schism," Brookings Institution, May 16, 2010, http://tinyurl.com/ybklct2g.

[32] Nolan McCarty, "Hate our polarized politics? Why you can't blame gerrymandering." *The Washington Post*, Oct. 26, 2012, https://tinyurl.com/y8m5sheh.

[33] Justice Anthony Kennedy, concurrence, *Vieth v. Jubelirer*, Cornell University Law School, April 28, 2004, https://tinyurl.com/yb963f9q.

[34] Eric Petry, "How the Efficiency Gap Works," Brennan Center for Justice, undated, https://tinyurl.com/ycnlxx8f; Nicholas Stephanopoulos, "Here's How We Can End Gerrymandering Once and for All," *The New Republic*, July 2, 2014, https://tinyurl.com/y9kgfqqv.

[35] "Is partisan gerrymandering unconstitutional?" *The Economist*, June 22, 2017, https://tinyurl.com/ybhh6uzs.

[36] Chris Winkelman and Phillip Gordon, "Symposium: Mind the gap? The efficiency gap, its failures and the 'problem' of geography and choice in redistricting," SCOTUSblog, Aug. 8, 2017, https://tinyurl.com/ybd493z5.

[37] *Ibid.*

[38] *Whitford v. Gill*, Kenneth F. Ripple opinion, U.S. District Court for the Western District of Wisconsin, Nov. 21, 2016, https://tinyurl.com/ybuht6ms.

[39] "Whitford v. Gill: District Court Offers New Standard to Hold Wisconsin Redistricting Scheme Unconstitutional." *Harvard Law Review*, May 10, 2017, https://tinyurl.com/yc22u6du.

[40] *Ibid.*

[41] Matt Walter, "In Gerrymandering Case, SCOTUS Should Reverse," RealClear Policy, June 8, 2017, https://tinyurl.com/yae8shu4.

[42] Lori Hawkins, "SXSW: Is Big Data destroying the U.S. political system? NBC's Chuck Todd says yes," *Austin American-Statesman*, March 15, 2017, https://tinyurl.com/yck7q3qh; Chuck Todd and Carrie Dann, "How Big Data Broke American Politics," NBC News, March 14, 2017, https://tinyurl.com/y6v4txbe.

[43] Justice Anthony Kennedy, concurrence, *op. cit.*

[44] Rosalind S. Helderman, "Student winners named in college redistricting competition," *The Washington Post*, March 22, 2011, https://tinyurl.com/y7gfocw5.

[45] Jan, *op. cit.*

[46] "Madison's Election to the First Federal Congress, October 1788 — February 1789 (Editorial Note)," Founders Online, National Archives, https://tinyurl.com/yby68gw5.

[47] "History and Organization," Factfinder for the Nation, U.S. Census Bureau, May 2000, https://tinyurl.com/y8jsfbka; "Members of Congress," GovTrack, https://tinyurl.com/ksl6mzp.

[48] "Proportional Representation," History, Art & Archives, U.S. House of Representative, https://tinyurl.com/yah28lrq. The formulas are at https://tinyurl.com/ycoakpvl.

[49] "Methods of Apportionment," History, U.S. Census Bureau, https://tinyurl.com/y82387c7; "Apportionment," History, U.S. Census Bureau, https://tinyurl.com/yabzprpr.

[50] "History and Organization," *op. cit.*

[51] Jennifer Davis, "Elbridge Gerry and the Monstrous Gerrymander," In Custodia Legis: Law Librarians of Congress, Library of Congress, Feb. 10, 2017, https://tinyurl.com/y899ss9k.

[52] Emily Barasch, "The Twisted History of Gerrymandering in American Politics," *The Atlantic*, Sept. 19, 2012, https://tinyurl.com/y94ao7fa.

[53] "Proportional Representation," *op. cit.*

[54] Michael J. Caulfield, "Apportioning Representatives in the United States Congress — Apportionment and Presidential Elections," Convergence, Mathematical Association of America, November 2010, https://tinyurl.com/y93btqq7.

[55] "A Little History," University of Alabama, https://tinyurl.com/y9q8t4v4; "Agency History," History, U.S. Census Bureau, https://tinyurl.com/yfc95tn.

[56] "The 1911 House Reapportionment," History, Art & Archives, U.S. House of Representatives, https://tinyurl.com/htadc7l.

[57] "The Permanent Apportionment Act of 1929," History, Art & Archives, U.S. House of Representatives, https://tinyurl.com/ya2hqqak.

[58] Michael J. Caulfield, "Apportioning Representatives in the United States Congress — Hill's Method of Apportionment," Convergence, Mathematical Association of America, November 2010, https://tinyurl.com/y7dnx56p.

[59] "Colegrove v. Green," Oyez, https://tinyurl.com/y7h7nmap.

[60] "Gomillion v. Lightfoot," Oyez, https://tinyurl.com/ydfvdr48.

[61] "Where are the lines drawn?" All About Redistricting: Professor Justin Levitt's guide to drawing the electoral lines, https://tinyurl.com/7hs3tgk; "Shelby County v. Holder," Oyez, https://tinyurl.com/y97r5qen.

[62] "One Person, One Vote," The Constitution Project, https://tinyurl.com/yb7zwy82; "The Warren Court, 1953-1969," The Supreme Court Historical Society, https://tinyurl.com/yc2awkkf.

[63] "Baker v. Carr," Oyez, https://tinyurl.com/yb6d26ho.

[64] "Gray v. Sanders," Oyez, https://tinyurl.com/yaghs74t; "One Person, One Vote," *op. cit.*

[65] "Wesberry v. Sanders," Oyez, https://tinyurl.com/ybsxjwf6.

[66] "Reynolds v. Sims," Oyez, https://tinyurl.com/y8qlez2m.

[67] Alden Whitman, "Earl Warren, 83, Who Led High Court in Time of Vast Social Change, Is Dead," *The New York Times*, July 10, 1974, https://tinyurl.com/2do87tp.

[68] "President Kennedy's News Conferences, News Conference 3, February 8, 1961," John F. Kennedy Presidential Library and Museum, https://tinyurl.com/ya2b7ptr.

About the Author

Jane Fullerton Lemons is a freelance writer from Northern Virginia with more than 25 years of journalism experience. A former Washington bureau chief for the *Arkansas Democrat-Gazette* and *Farm Journal* magazine, she has covered the White House, Congress, food policy and health care. She is currently seeking a master's degree in creative nonfiction from Goucher College in Towson, Md.

[69] "Remarks at the Republican Governors Club Annual Dinner, October 15, 1987," Ronald Reagan Presidential Library and Museum, https://tinyurl.com/yd37qvhe.

[70] "Technology," History, U.S. Census Bureau, https://tinyurl.com/y8hlmkj4. News Desk, "Credence Research estimates 12.7% CAGR in GIS market by 2024," Geospatial World, June 20, 2017, https://tinyurl.com/y87ohn2u.

[71] Joe Francica, "Political Redistricting With Transparency," Directions Magazine, Aug. 22, 2011, https://tinyurl.com/y7dvbhck.

[72] "Davis v. Bandemer," Oyez, https://tinyurl.com/ybrqsggj.

[73] "Vieth v. Jubelirer," Oyez, https://tinyurl.com/y6v939ot.

[74] "Gill v. Whitford," SCOTUSblog, https://tinyurl.com/y9arhnyo.

[75] "Current Partisan Gerrymandering Cases," Brennan Center for Justice at New York University School of Law, April 26, 2017, http://tinyurl.com/ya5p7rmf.

[76] Gill v. Whitford, Campaign Legal Center, http://tinyurl.com/y744kdjc.

[77] Ann E. Marimow and Josh Hicks, "Judges in Md. redistricting case decry politically motivated electoral map," The Washington Post, July 14, 2017, https://tinyurl.com/yctm6axx.

[78] Robert Joyce, "North Carolina and the Specter of Partisan Gerrymandering," Coates' Canons: NC Local Government Law, University of North Carolina School of Government, June 29, 2017, http://tinyurl.com/ycayb96u; Jim Morrill, "Common Cause challenges partisan gerrymandering in NC," The Charlotte Observer, Aug. 5, 2016, http://tinyurl.com/y7ryw7jz.

[79] Adam Liptak, "Justices Reject 2 Gerrymandered North Carolina Districts, Citing Racial Bias," The New York Times, May 22, 2017, https://tinyurl.com/ybwsw5pa.

[80] "Obama's Last News Conference: Full Transcript and Video," The New York Times, Jan. 18, 2017, http://tinyurl.com/z25of6h.

[81] "Former President Obama at the University of Chicago," C-SPAN, April 24, 2017, https://tinyurl.com/y9ce4qdy.

[82] "Remarks of President Barack Obama — State of the Union Address As Delivered, Jan. 13, 2016," archived Obama White House website, National Archives, https://tinyurl.com/y9u783h5.

[83] Amber Phillips, "The 2020 redistricting war is (already) on," The Washington Post, July 16, 2015, https://tinyurl.com/y9qmhjd5.

[84] Alexander Burns and Jonathan Martin, "Eric Holder to Lead Democrats' Attack on Republican Gerrymandering," The New York Times, Jan. 11, 2017, https://tinyurl.com/hdy6fzy; Bill McCollum and Matt Walter, "Republican state strength will withstand Democrat lawsuits," The Hill, March 9, 2017, https://tinyurl.com/j8snzhu.

[85] "Redistricting Reform Tracker (State Bills)," Brennan Center for Justice, New York University School of Law, https://tinyurl.com/y8feoex4.

[86] "Redistricting Commission Bills," National Conference on State Legislatures, July 24, 2017, https://tinyurl.com/y8gh3z6b.

[87] "House Democrats introduce redistricting reform legislation to end partisan gerrymandering," press release, Rep. Julia Brownley, Feb. 16, 2017, https://tinyurl.com/y8srrgs9.

[88] Don Beyer, "Let's change how we elect the House of Representatives," The Washington Post, June 27, 2017, https://tinyurl.com/yax9ujml; David Daley, "Make democracy great again: Rep. Don Beyer's revolutionary bill could transform how we elect Congress," Salon, June 27, 2017, https://tinyurl.com/yd9y55l9.

[89] "Redistricting Commissions: State Legislative Plans," National Conference of State Legislatures, Dec. 7, 2015, https://tinyurl.com/ycut6ka4.

[90] "Redistricting Commissions: Congressional Plans," National Conference of State Legislatures, Dec. 8, 2015, https://tinyurl.com/y7e7djtm.

[91] Aaron Blake, "California just proved how cracking down on gerrymandering isn't all it's cracked up to be," The Washington Post, Dec. 1, 2016, https://tinyurl.com/yd7lyfh5.

[92] "Did the California Citizens Redistricting Commission Really Create More Competitive Districts?" FairVote, Nov. 26, 2013, https://tinyurl.com/ybmwunst.

[93] "California's Citizens Redistricting Commission Awarded Top 2017 Harvard Public Engagement in Government Award," press release, July 6, 2017, Ash Center for Democratic Governance and Innovation, John F. Kennedy School of Government at Harvard University, https://tinyurl.com/y9m7hnlc.

[94] "Fed Up With Gerrymandering: Action on Redistricting," University of Southern California Schwarzenegger Institute, https://tinyurl.com/ycruyrlp; "Arnie lends some muscle to the campaign against gerrymandering," The Economist, July 22, 2017, https://tinyurl.com/ycf8noef.

[95] Bob Christie, "Analysis: Arizona Mostly Cut Politics From Drawing Districts," The Associated Press, U.S. News & World Report, June 25, 2017, http://tinyurl.com/yderez8h.

[96] Alexis Farmer, "Current Citizen Efforts to Reform Redistricting," Brennan Center for Justice, New York University School of Law, May 19, 2017, https://tinyurl.com/y8akcyuu.

[97] "About Us," OneVirginia2021: Virginians For Fair Redistricting, https://tinyurl.com/yavcbwey.

[98] Sean Trende, "Census Data Shed Light on 2020 Redistricting," Real Clear Politics, Dec. 22, 2016, https://tinyurl.com/y9m2m7qn.

[99] Kimball W. Brace, "No Change in Apportionment Allocations With New 2016 Census Estimates; But Greater Change Likely by 2020," Election Data Services, Dec. 20, 2016, https://tinyurl.com/y7fh9ozl.

[100] D'Vera Cohn and Andrea Caumont, "10 demographic trends that are shaping the U.S. and the world," Pew Research Center, March 31, 2016, https://tinyurl.com/h4c473e.

[101] Jens Manuel Krogstad and Mark Hugo Lopez, "Black voter turnout fell in 2016, even as a record number of Americans cast ballots," Pew Research Center, May 12, 2017, http://tinyurl.com/ya4sm2ja.

FOR MORE INFORMATION

Brennan Center for Justice, New York University Law School, 161 Sixth Ave., 12th Floor, New York, NY 10013; 646-292-8310; www.brennancenter.org. Public policy and law institute that looks at voting rights and election reform.

Campaign Legal Center, 1411 K St., N.W., Suite 1400, Washington, DC 20005; 202-736-2200; www.campaignlegalcenter.org. Litigates cases and develops policy nationwide on campaign finance, elections and ethics laws.

Common Cause, 1250 Connecticut Ave., N.W., #600, Washington, DC 20036; 202-833-1200; www.commoncause.org. Public-interest advocacy organization that has filed lawsuits and supported citizen initiatives to reform redistricting.

FairVote, 6930 Carroll Ave., Suite 240, Takoma Park, MD 20912; 301-270-4616; www.fairvote.org/. Advocate for electoral reform.

League of Women Voters, 1730 M St., N.W., Suite 1000, Washington, DC 20036-4508; 202-429-1965; www.lwv.org. Promotes government reform.

National Conference of State Legislatures, 7700 E. First Place, Denver, CO 80230; 303-364-7700; www.ncsl.org. Bipartisan organization that provides research, technical assistance and other support for legislators and legislative staff.

Bibliography

Selected Sources

Books

Bishop, Bill, *The Big Sort: Why the Clustering of Like-Minded America Is Tearing Us Apart*, Mariner Books, 2009.

A journalist analyzes demographic data to explain how Americans have sorted themselves by jobs and neighborhoods in recent decades — and how that segregation has contributed to a more polarized nation.

Daley, David, *Ratf**ked: The True Story Behind the Secret Plan to Steal America's Democracy*, Liveright Publishing, 2016.

A former editor-in-chief of *Salon* argues that Republicans' successes in state legislative and congressional elections in 2010 enabled them to control redistricting.

Davis, Tom, Martin Frost and Richard Cohen, *The Partisan Divide: Congress in Crisis*, FastPencil Premiere, 2014.

Two former members of Congress (Davis and Frost) and a veteran Washington journalist discuss gerrymandering and other causes of the partisan atmosphere in Congress.

Mann, Thomas E., and Norman J. Ornstein, *It's Even Worse Than It Looks: How the American Constitutional System Collided with the New Politics of Extremism*, Basic Books, 2016.

Longtime congressional scholars update their analysis of the causes of polarization and dysfunction in Washington, critiquing the role of a changing Republican Party and offering potential solutions, including redistricting reform.

Articles

"Whitford v. Gill: District Court Offers New Standard to Hold Wisconsin Redistricting Scheme Unconstitutional," *Harvard Law Review*, May 10, 2017, https://tinyurl.com/yc22u6du.

The Harvard law journal analyzes the Wisconsin gerrymandering case headed to the Supreme Court.

Draper, Robert, "The League of Dangerous Mapmakers," *The Atlantic*, October 2012, https://tinyurl.com/ybguecwc.

A journalist offers a behind-the-scenes look at how voting maps are drawn during redistricting.

Ingraham, Christopher, "This is actually what America would look like without gerrymandering," *The Washington Post*, Jan. 13, 2016, https://tinyurl.com/ybt59h9f.

A journalist discusses the differences between maps created by an algorithm and those drawn by people.

Ingraham, Christopher, "This is the best explanation of gerrymandering you will ever see," *The Washington Post*, March 1, 2015, https://tinyurl.com/y9mjuyyd.

A journalist presents a primer on how gerrymandering works, with graphics illustrating the different ways it can be carried out.

Mervis, Jeffery, "Money, politics, and abandoned homes: Why the 2020 Census might be in jeopardy," *Science*, July 24, 2017, https://tinyurl.com/yase3nls.

The 2020 census faces technical, political and budgetary problems, experts warn.

Najmabadi, Shannon, "Meet the Math Professor Who's Fighting Gerrymandering With Geometry," *The Chronicle of Higher Education*, Feb. 22, 2017, https://tinyurl.com/y7pgleby.

A mathematician explains how math research applies to gerrymandering.

Prokop, Andrew, "Gerrymandering, Explained," *Vox*, undated, https://tinyurl.com/y9mkq6ue.

A journalist illuminates the gerrymandering process.

Reports and Studies

"GAO's 2017 High Risk Report: 2020 Decennial Census," U.S. Government Accountability Office, 2017, https://tinyurl.com/ydf78nzb.

The nonpartisan congressional agency examines federal programs and operations, including the 2020 census, that it considers especially vulnerable to waste, fraud, abuse and mismanagement, or that need transformative change.

McCary, Nolan, Keith T. Poole and Howard Rosenthal, "Does Gerrymandering Cause Polarization?" *American Journal of Political Science*, June 23, 2009, https://tinyurl.com/ya6xflsf.

Political scientists contend that gerrymandering is not a key cause of political polarization.

Stephanopoulos, Nick, and Eric McGhee, "Partisan Gerrymandering and the Efficiency Gap," *University of Chicago Law Review*, Oct. 1, 2014, https://tinyurl.com/yd2j82d6.

Researchers explain the efficiency gap, a mathematical formula designed to quantify partisan gerrymandering.

Williams, Jennifer D., "The Decennial Census: Issues for 2020," Congressional Research Service, 2017, https://tinyurl.com/y93gydc9.

Congress' research arm explores the tension between funding the census and controlling its costs.

Videos

Greer, Christina, "Gerrymandering: How drawing jagged lines can impact an election," TED-Ed Original, undated, https://tinyurl.com/yastzr4b.

A political science professor explains gerrymandering.

Klein, Ezra, "Gerrymandering: How politicians rig elections," *Vox*, Sept. 23, 2015, https://tinyurl.com/ybj459rk.

A Washington journalist delves into gerrymandering.

The Next Step:

Additional Articles from Current Periodicals

Big Data

Daley, David, "How will Big Data change gerrymandering? Both parties are eager to know what you do online," *Salon*, **April 15, 2017, https://tinyurl.com/y7zvjsuq.**

The repeal of a rule requiring internet service providers to get permission from consumers before selling their data means legislators will have access to even more information when they design partisan districts.

Williams, Joseph P., "Big Data and the Gerrymandering of America," USNEWS.com, July 28, 2017, http://tiny url.com/y7k5x7z6.

The use of big data has put gerrymandering on steroids, according to a Silicon Valley data scientist, by enabling redistricting officials to identify and categorize voters and their preferences with near-surgical precision.

Partisan Polarization

Blake, Aaron, "Why you should stop blaming gerrymandering so much. Really," *The Washington Post*, **April 8, 2017, https://tinyurl.com/y86yh97f.**

A political reporter argues that the sorting of Democrats into urban areas and Republicans into rural regions is more responsible for the Republicans' House majority and for political polarization than gerrymandering.

Chapman, Steve, "How to bring moderation back to American politics," *Chicago Tribune*, **July 5, 2017, https://tinyurl.com/y7rbkrdm.**

Ending gerrymandering, revising campaign finance laws and eliminating party primaries could lead to the return of moderation in politics, a columnist says.

Friedersdorf, Conor, "How People Like You Fuel Extremism," *The Atlantic*, **June 27, 2017, https://tinyurl.com/y8t6rwz7.**

A social-science experiment found that when people gathered in a group of like-minded individuals to discuss controversial topics such as gay rights, more-extreme views resulted.

Recent Redistricting Events

Allen, Keith, and Madison Park, "North Carolina given September deadline to draw new maps in gerrymandering case," CNN, Aug. 1, 2017, https://tinyurl.com/yak6pkht.

A federal judicial panel set a Sept. 1 deadline for North Carolina legislators to redraw state legislative districts that it found to be unconstitutional racial gerrymanders.

Dovere, Edward-Isaac, "Dem redistricting group clocks $10.8 million in first 6 months," *Politico*, **July 31, 2017, https://tinyurl.com/yank9hwg.**

Fueled by donations from large donors, the National Democratic Redistricting Committee, which aims to coordinate Democratic efforts in redistricting and upcoming state legislative and gubernatorial races, raised $10.8 million in the first six months of 2017.

Treleven, Ed, "State files first brief to U.S. Supreme Court in gerrymandering case," *Wisconsin State Journal*, **July 28, 2017, https://tinyurl.com/yb73cky9.**

The attorneys defending Wisconsin's 2011 redistricting plan have urged the Supreme Court to throw out a Democratic lawsuit against the plan.

U.S. Census

Leslie, Jacques, "California would be the primary victim in a GOP war on the census," *Los Angeles Times*, **July 16, 2017, https://tinyurl.com/y9rc5lmv.**

A columnist argues that if an underfunded 2020 census results in a high undercount, California would stand to lose more politically and economically than any other state.

Mervis, Jeffrey, "Researchers think they've found a much better way to conduct the 2030 census," *Science*, **July 25, 2017, https://tinyurl.com/y89t2se5.**

The independent federal science advisory group JASON proposes a new method of counting for the 2030 census that could identify as many as 90 percent of Americans through digital records.

Moreau, Julie, "New Bill Seeks to Mandate LGBTQ Inclusion in Federal Surveys," NBC News, July 21, 2017, https://tinyurl.com/ybqbzxn6.

Two House and Senate members reintroduced a bill in July requiring the census and other federal surveys to collect data on sexual orientation and gender identity to ensure these groups are not marginalized in Washington.

CITING *CQ RESEARCHER*

Sample formats for citing these reports in a bibliography include the ones listed below. Preferred styles and formats vary, so please check with your instructor or professor.

MLA STYLE

Mantel, Barbara. "Coal Industry's Future." CQ Researcher 17 June 2016: 529-552.

APA STYLE

Mantel, B. (2016, June 17). Coal Industry's Future. *CQ Researcher, 6*, 529-552.

CHICAGO STYLE

Mantel, Barbara. "Coal Industry's Future." *CQ Researcher*, June 17, 2016, 529-52.

In-depth Reports on Issues in the News

Are you writing a paper?

Need backup for a debate?

Want to become an expert on an issue?

For 90 years, students have turned to *CQ Researcher* for in-depth reporting on issues in the news. Reports on a full range of political and social issues are now available. Following is a selection of recent reports:

Civil Liberties
Privacy and the Internet, 12/15
Intelligence Reform, 5/15
Religion and Law, 11/14

Crime/Law
High-Tech Policing, 4/17
Forensic Science Controversies, 2/17
Jailing Debtors, 9/16
Decriminalizing Prostitution, 4/16
Restorative Justice, 2/16
The Dark Web, 1/16
Immigrant Detention, 10/15

Education
Charter Schools, 3/17
Civic Education, 2/17
Student Debt, 11/16
Apprenticeships, 10/16

Environment/Society
Muslims in America, 7/17
Funding the Arts, 7/17
Hunger in America, 7/17
Future of the Christian Right, 6/17
Trust in Media, 6/17
Anti-Semitism, 5/17

Health/Safety
Medical Marijuana, 7/17
Food Labeling, 6/17
Sports and Sexual Assault, 4/17
Reducing Traffic Deaths, 2/17
Opioid Crisis, 10/16

Politics/Economy
North Korea Showdown, 5/17
Rethinking Foreign Aid, 4/17
Troubled Brazil, 4/17
Reviving Rural Economies, 3/17
Immigrants and the Economy, 2/17

Upcoming Reports

National Debt, 9/1/17   Guaranteed Income, 9/8/17   Medical Advances, 9/15/17

ACCESS

CQ Researcher is available in print and online. For access, visit your library or www.cqresearcher.com.

STAY CURRENT

For notice of upcoming *CQ Researcher* reports or to learn more about *CQ Researcher* products, subscribe to the free email newsletters, *CQ Researcher Alert!* and *CQ Researcher News*: http://cqpress.com/newsletters.

PURCHASE

To purchase a *CQ Researcher* report in print or electronic format (PDF), visit www.cqpress.com or call 866-427-7737. Single reports start at $15. Bulk purchase discounts and electronic-rights licensing are also available.

SUBSCRIBE

Annual full-service *CQ Researcher* subscriptions—including 44 reports a year, monthly index updates, and a bound volume—start at $1,131. Add $25 for domestic postage.

CQ Researcher Online offers a backfile from 1991 and a number of tools to simplify research. For pricing information, call 800-818-7243 or 805-499-9774 or email librarysales@sagepub.com.

![CQ Researcher logo] **CQ RESEARCHER**

CQPRESS

In-depth reports on today's issues

Published by CQ Press, an Imprint of SAGE Publications, Inc.

www.cqresearcher.com

National Debt

Do rising annual deficits threaten the U.S. economy?

T he clock is ticking, so-called budget hawks warn about the nation's growing national debt: Public debt has soared from $925 billion in 1982 to almost $14.4 trillion in 2017. If debt keeps piling up at this rate, by 2032 the federal government will owe an amount larger than the U.S. economy — an outcome that could be disastrous, many economists say. Republicans and Democrats agree that Washington needs to act, but they are far apart on how to lower the debt. One problem is the growth in Medicare and other entitlement programs. With the massive Baby Boom Generation retiring, entitlements are consuming a larger and larger proportion of the budget. Another problem is a tax code that is failing to bring in sufficient revenue. Some economists say the threat of financial catastrophe is overblown. They note the dollar remains the dominant global currency and that foreign investors continue to flock to U.S. markets, meaning the government will be able to continue borrowing for the foreseeable future.

A "United States Official Taxpayer" protests at the Trump International Hotel in Washington before Donald Trump's inauguration on Jan. 20, 2016. Critics say Trump's budget proposals, including tax cuts and a costly border wall with Mexico, are economically unsustainable.

CQ Researcher • Sept. 1, 2017 • www.cqresearcher.com
Volume 27, Number 30 • Pages 701-724

I N S I D E **THIS REPORT**

THE ISSUES 703

BACKGROUND 710

CHRONOLOGY 711

CURRENT SITUATION 716

AT ISSUE.....................717

OUTLOOK 719

BIBLIOGRAPHY 722

THE NEXT STEP 723

THE ISSUES

703   • Could a rising national debt lead to a financial crisis in the near future?
      • Can higher taxes solve the debt problem?
      • Is Washington capable of solving the debt problem?

BACKGROUND

710   **Aversion to Taxes**
      Tariffs and taxes were unpopular after the American Revolution.

713   **Keynesian Economics**
      The Great Depression spawned the theory that government must spend more during downturns.

714   **Short-Lived Restraints**
      The 1990 Budget Enforcement Act tried to limit government spending.

CURRENT SITUATION

716   **Looming Shutdown**
      The government will partially shut down if Congress doesn't pass a spending bill by Oct. 1.

718   **Border Wall**
      President Trump's proposal to stem illegal immigration could stymie congressional debt talks.

719   **Tax Reform**
      House Republicans want to draft a bill in September.

OUTLOOK

719   **Cloudy Forecast**
      Experts predict a surging deficit if spending isn't curbed or new taxes aren't levied.

SIDEBARS AND GRAPHICS

704   **Key Budget, Debt and Currency Terms**
      Explaining the debt ceiling and more.

706   **National Debt Continues to Soar**
      It now tops $14 trillion, equaling 77 percent of the nation's gross domestic product.

708   **Deficit Projected to Explode**
      The gap between spending and revenue could triple between 2017 and 2045.

711   **Chronology**
      Key events since the1780s.

712   **Health Care Spending Fuels Federal Deficits**
      The problem of rising costs extends beyond Medicare and Medicaid.

714   **Tax Reform Could Help Raise Revenue**
      But familiar foes remain: an army of lobbyists and congressional gridlock.

717   **At Issue:**
      Should Congress make deficit reduction a top priority?

FOR FURTHER RESEARCH

721   **For More Information**
      Organizations to contact.

722   **Bibliography**
      Selected sources used.

723   **The Next Step**
      Additional articles.

723   **Citing CQ Researcher**
      Sample bibliography formats.

Cover: Getty Images/Mark Makela

 **CQ RESEARCHER**

Sept. 1, 2017
Volume 27, Number 30

EXECUTIVE EDITOR: Thomas J. Billitteri
tjb@sagepub.com

ASSISTANT MANAGING EDITORS: Kenneth Fireman, kenneth.fireman@sagepub.com, Kathy Koch, kathy.koch@sagepub.com, Scott Rohrer, scott.rohrer@sagepub.com

ASSOCIATE MANAGING EDITOR: Val Ellicott

SENIOR CONTRIBUTING EDITOR:
Thomas J. Colin
tom.colin@sagepub.com

CONTRIBUTING WRITERS: Marcia Clemmitt, Sarah Glazer, Reed Karaim, Barbara Mantel, Chuck McCutcheon, Tom Price

SENIOR PROJECT EDITOR: Olu B. Davis

EDITORIAL ASSISTANT: Natalia Gurevich

INTERN: Robert DePaolo

FACT CHECKERS: Eva P. Dasher, Michelle Harris, Betsy Towner Levine, Robin Palmer

SAGE Publishing | **CQPRESS**

Los Angeles | London | New Delhi
Singapore | Washington DC | Melbourne

An Imprint of SAGE Publications, Inc.

SENIOR VICE PRESIDENT,
GLOBAL LEARNING RESOURCES:
Karen Phillips

EXECUTIVE DIRECTOR, ONLINE LIBRARY AND
REFERENCE PUBLISHING:
Todd Baldwin

CQ Press is a registered trademark of Congressional Quarterly Inc.

CQ Researcher (ISSN 1056-2036) is printed on acid-free paper. Published weekly, except: (March wk. 4) (May wk. 4) (July wks. 1, 2) (Aug. wks. 2, 3) (Nov. wk. 4) and (Dec. wks. 3, 4). Published by SAGE Publications, Inc., 2455 Teller Rd., Thousand Oaks, CA 91320. Annual full-service subscriptions start at $1,131. For pricing, call 1-800-818-7243. To purchase a CQ Researcher report in print or electronic format (PDF), visit www.cqpress.com or call 866-427-7737. Single reports start at $15. Bulk purchase discounts and electronic-rights licensing are also available. Periodicals postage paid at Thousand Oaks, California, and at additional mailing offices. POSTMASTER: Send address changes to CQ Researcher, 2600 Virginia Ave., N.W., Suite 600, Washington, DC 20037.

National Debt

BY MATTHEW K. BENJAMIN

THE ISSUES

The founders of the Concord Coalition joked in 1992, the Washington advocacy organization's first year, that "putting ourselves out of business was the original goal," recalls Executive Director Bob Bixby.

But before the group could close up shop, the federal government would have to balance its budgets and put the national debt on a fiscally sustainable course. Twenty-five years later, Bixby and his staff are still employed, and business is booming.

"I thought things were bad in 1992," says Bixby. "But it's a lot worse now. The political establishment has wasted a lot of time and opportunities to address this."

The national debt has grown from $925 billion in 1982 to almost $14.4 trillion today, or from about 28 percent of the nation's gross domestic product (GDP) to 77 percent. [1] Going forward, the picture looks to get worse, not better. The Congressional Budget Office, the bipartisan congressional agency that evaluates budget matters on Capitol Hill, projects that deficits will only get bigger over the next two decades. The reason: The large demographic cohort known as the Baby Boomers has begun to retire and receive costly Social Security and Medicare benefits. [2]

If nothing changes in how the government raises and spends money, annual shortfalls will continue to pile up until the amount the government owes — the sum of all U.S. annual deficits — is larger than the U.S. economy within 15 years. That would approach debt levels that many experts agree

The total national debt looms on a screen above Federal Reserve Chair Janet Yellen as she testifies before the House Financial Services Committee. She warned the committee the federal government faces an "unsustainable debt situation" if the national debt continues to rise at its current rate.

The Current United States National Debt

$19,006,586,360,812

could invite a financial catastrophe.

The United States has more debt than any other nation, although a more important measure of a nation's debt is how big it is compared to the nation's economy. By that measure, several nations have bigger debt loads, among them Portugal, Italy and Japan. [3] In addition, most U.S. debt, which is issued in the form of U.S. government bonds, is held by U.S. citizens and U.S. entities such as mutual funds and the Federal Reserve. [4] And so far, because of the vast size of the U.S. economy, its record of growth and its centrality to the global economy, investors, including individual foreign investors and sovereign nations, have been willing to continue to lend to the U.S. government through purchases of Treasury securities.

China, for example, holds about $1.1 trillion of U.S. debt, or about 28 percent of the debt that is held by foreign countries. [5]

The crux of the debate over U.S. debt is how much is too much — that is, when does the debt pose a threat to the economy, if not to the nation itself? Some budget analysts and economists have pointed to the 100 percent level: when the debt becomes as big or bigger than the size of the economy. If nothing changes in terms of spending and tax policies, that level will be reached by 2033, although the high cost of another war or recession could move the date closer.

At that point, investors may fear that the federal government will no longer be able to pay interest and principle on its bonds, and may refuse to lend the government additional money at normal interest rates. A financial crisis would quickly follow investors' refusal to buy more U.S. bonds. "The problems we're talking about get really serious in the 2030 to 2040 time frame," says James Kwak, a professor at the University of Connecticut School of Law and co-author of *White House Burning: Our National Debt and Why it Matters to You.*

Or, as interest on the debt begins to consume more and more of the government's budget, spending on key programs — education, infrastructure, defense and everything else the government funds — would continue to

Key Budget, Debt and Currency Terms

Budget — Annual plan for taxes and spending by the federal government that represents the priorities of the president, who submits a budget proposal to Congress each February. Congress also creates its own budget resolution each year as a detailed guide to spending levels in appropriations bills. Congress often disregards the president's budget to create its own.

Appropriations bill — A bill that, if passed by both houses of Congress and enacted, allows Congress to spend money. There are 12 appropriations bills to fund different areas of the federal government, such as agriculture and transportation.

National debt — Total amount that the federal government owes, including debt to U.S. citizens, foreign investors and other governments. The government issues debt through Treasury securities such as bonds, notes and bills.

Debt ceiling — Legal limit imposed by Congress on the maximum amount of debt that the Treasury Department can issue to the public and to other federal agencies. Treasury can borrow funds from other parts of the government — for example the Social Security Trust Fund — and issues a special Treasury security to do so. This borrowing limit has been raised 78 times since 1960. Total borrowing (including debt held by the public and debt held by government accounts such as the trust fund) is now near the current limit of $19.9 trillion, so Congress must raise the ceiling by October for Treasury to continue to meet all of its obligations.

Deficit — Annual gap that results if expenditures by the federal government exceed revenues it raises through taxes. The deficit is often expressed as a percentage of the nation's gross domestic product (GDP), the total value of goods and services the nation produces in a year.

Surplus — Opposite of the deficit, resulting when revenues exceed spending. The last time this occurred in recent years was 2001.

Entitlements — Guaranteed benefits provided by the federal government, including, most prominently, Social Security, Medicare and Medicaid. Unlike other items Congress pays for, it does not set spending levels for entitlement programs but rather sets eligibility requirements, such as age or income level. Any citizen who meets these requirements is "entitled" to benefits under the program, as are some noncitizens who qualify.

Washington needs to avoid such possibilities. Yet few agree on how to put the government back on a sustainable fiscal policy, one where it spends only what it collects in revenue.

First, though, it is worth looking closely at the drivers of growth in the national debt. Why, every year, does the government spend more than it takes in, forcing it to borrow to meet its many financial obligations?

The national debt can be measured several ways. Typically, the measurement is of "debt held by the public," and that stands at about 77 percent of GDP, or $14.4 trillion. However, there also is so-called "intragovernmental debt," or funds borrowed by the government from another part of the government, such as the Social Security Trust Fund. This debt stands at around $5.5 trillion, but many financial analysts looking at the government's accounts don't include it because it is essentially the government borrowing from itself. Still, it too will need to be paid when, for example, Social Security needs to tap its trust fund to pay benefits to all those retired Baby Boomers. For this report, the focus will be debt held by the public.

That debt more than doubled over the past decade, rising from about $5.8 trillion in 2008 to more than $14 trillion today. [6] What happened? In a few words, financial crisis, demographics and policy choices.

The financial crisis a decade ago threw 8.8 million Americans out of work, sending the unemployment rate from 4.6 percent in early 2007 to 10 percent in late 2009. [7] Such a spike in joblessness harms government finances in two ways: Tax revenues decline because so many people lose their incomes (and many more accept smaller paychecks), and safety-net programs such as unemployment insurance and food stamps must expand.

The financial crisis also prompted the Democratic-controlled Congress to pass the 2009 economic stimulus package, known as the American Recovery and

fall, leading to "a slow slide into a lower standard of living due to an economy burdened by debt, higher taxes and less investment," says Bixby.

The two resulting scenarios — a gradually diminished nation or a global financial crisis — are both grim, and the two political parties agree that

Reinvestment Act. Whether it was substantial enough or effective in juicing the economy and putting people back to work is still debated, but the price tag is not: At $831 billion, it was not cheap. [8]

Policy choices can have a big impact on deficits and the national debt. When George W. Bush became president in 2001, he inherited a budget surplus, but it quickly dissipated due to two tax cuts, a brief recession, an expensive drug benefit added to Medicare, and wars in Afghanistan and Iraq. After a few years of big-ticket decisions, the expenses began to add up. Other factors include the unwillingness of Congress in recent years to raise taxes to pay for higher spending.

Finally, and inevitably, demographics had, and will continue to have, an unavoidable, long-term impact on the debt level. The first Baby Boomers, the generation born between 1946 and 1964, reached age 65 in 2011, the start of a massive retirement wave. Today, about 10,000 Boomers retire each day. [9] This demographic boom can't be legislated away or escaped, and it will last until a significant number of that generation passes away.

As Boomers retire, most of them become eligible to receive benefits from Medicare, a federal government health insurance plan for older people, and Social Security, an old-age pension plan. Such programs are known as "entitlement programs" or "mandatory spending." Unlike for other parts of the budget, such as defense and education, Congress does not set spending levels for these programs every year. Instead, it creates eligibility requirements, such as age or income level. Those who meet them are "entitled" to benefits. So the programs shrink or expand according to demographics. The Baby Boom demographic, as it retires, is expanding spending on these entitlements rapidly.

And these programs, or more accurately their future growth, will be the biggest drivers of deficits going forward. Medicare and other mandatory

Key Budget, Debt and Currency Terms *(Cont.)*

Mandatory spending — Spending authorized by Congress outside of normal appropriations bills; the entitlements Medicare and Social Security are the two biggest programs in this category. It also includes programs such as federal civilian and military retirement programs, a tax credit for low-income workers and food stamp programs.

Discretionary spending — Spending that Congress sets every year in appropriations bills, such as for education, transportation or most defense programs.

Treasury securities — Federal government debt instruments issued by the U.S. Treasury include T-bills (short-term), Treasury notes (medium term) and bonds (long term). When citizens, investors or other governments buy such securities, they are in effect lending money to the government, receiving interest payments in return. When the security reaches maturity, the investor's principal is returned. Because Treasury debt is considered the world's safest investment, the market for Treasuries is enormous — about $14 trillion at last count — and undergirds the global financial system.

Interest on the debt — In 2016 interest payments the federal government made on all the bonds and other debt it has issued totaled $241 billion, or about 1.3 percent of GDP. If interest rates rise, as expected, the government's interest payments will rise significantly.

Reserve currency — Bonds issued by many nations are held in central banks and financial institutions around the world for use in times of crisis, for international transactions, or to influence the value of their own currency. For example, if a nation's economy collapses and its own currency loses most of its value, it wants to have dollars (or U.S. Treasury securities that are easily converted to dollars) in reserve to spend on necessities, like oil or food. Also, if a nation wants to decrease the value of its currency to boost exports, it can print more of its currency and use it to buy dollars. Doing so increases the amount of the nation's currency in circulation and makes it less expensive on world markets. The Japanese yen, euro, British pound, Swiss franc and Chinese renminbi are all considered reserve currencies. But the U.S. dollar is the world's preeminent reserve currency.

health programs now represent about 5.5 percent of GDP, but that is expected to grow to 6.9 percent over the next decade. Social Security will increase from 4.9 percent of GDP to 6 percent.

At the same time, interest that the government pays on its debt also is expected to rise, from 1.4 percent of

National Debt Continues to Soar

The national debt has ballooned from $925 billion in 1982 to almost $14.4 trillion in 2017. It now equals 77 percent of the nation's gross domestic product (GDP), up from 28 percent 35 years ago. The debt could reach 150 percent of GDP in the next 30 years, according to the Congressional Budget Office, because of the rising costs of Social Security, Medicare and other entitlement programs as the Baby Boom Generation retires.

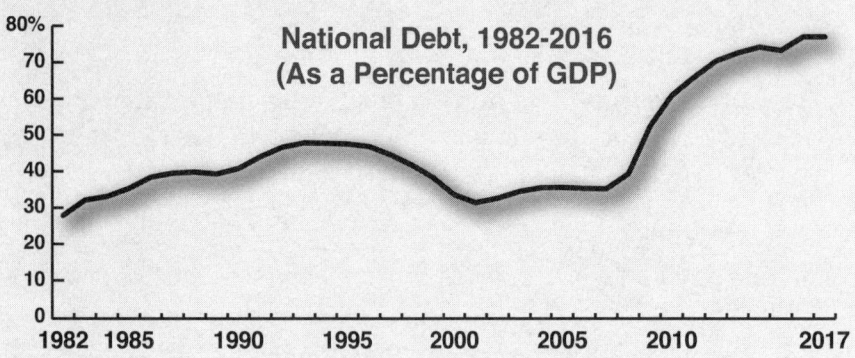

National Debt, 1982-2016 (As a Percentage of GDP)

Source: "The 2017 Long-Term Budget Outlook," Congressional Budget Office, 2017, https://tinyurl.com/mubxx97

GDP to 2.7 percent. The entire rest of the budget, including defense and all nondefense spending, will shrink from about 3.1 percent to 2.6 percent of GDP. [10] The joke among budget wonks in Washington is that, in 10 years, the U.S. budget will look like that of a health care company with a military and a lot of credit card debt.

And polls show that providing generous entitlement programs is what the public wants. A large majority of Americans call Medicare and Social Security among the most important government programs. [11] In comparison, many nations — Sweden is a good example — have pension and health care programs that are much more generous. But they need to be paid for, and in the United States, Republican and many Democratic politicians have balked at higher taxes. "We've had a major shift in this country toward the position that you can never raise taxes," says Kwak.

Moreover, some economists believe deficit reduction should not be a priority

right now. Most prominent among this group is Lawrence Summers, a former Treasury secretary and top economic adviser to former President Barack Obama. Summers has argued for several years that inflation, economic growth and interest rates are too low and the solution is an expansionary fiscal policy — that is, a policy of using deficit spending on education and infrastructure and other programs to boost growth and to invest in the future. [12]

"Borrowing to make investments when interest rates are so low would make a whole lot of sense if we hadn't already borrowed trillions of dollars for consumption when interest rates weren't as low," says Maya MacGuineas, president of the Committee for a Responsible Federal Budget, a nonpartisan advocacy group that seeks to slow the growth of the national debt.

In fact, the Republican Congress and the Trump administration are not interested in borrowing to invest in infrastructure or education but instead are gearing up to pass legislation that

would cut taxes. Many economists hope this can be done by eliminating loopholes and so-called carveouts in the tax code — tax advantages for certain activities such as charitable giving or borrowing to buy a home — and thus pay for lower rates. But changing the tax code is a very difficult thing to do in Washington, where nearly every budget loophole is jealously guarded by a powerful lobbying group. And so the Republican Party is considering pushing for straight tax cuts rather than overhauling the tax code. [13]

It remains unclear what Republicans, who control both Congress and the White House, will propose on tax reform. But the tax plan that President Trump campaigned on would increase the federal debt by $7.2 trillion over the next decade, according to the Tax Policy Center, a nonpartisan think tank. [14]

"Trump campaigned on promises not to touch entitlements and to cut taxes," says the Concord Coalition's Bixby. "That is not a recipe for long-term fiscal sustainability."

No matter what happens in the long term, economists and financial analysts agree that Congress needs to raise the debt ceiling in the fall, which means passing legislation to allow Treasury to borrow more money. Failure to do so could trigger a financial crisis and significantly damage the United States' reputation among investors worldwide.

As policymakers debate the national debt, here are some of the key questions being discussed:

If the U.S. national debt continues to rise, will it lead to a financial crisis in the near future?

In the past, many economists felt that a debt-to-GDP ratio above a certain level would either slow an economy significantly or trigger a financial crisis. Famously, a 2010 paper by Harvard economists Kenneth Rogoff and Carmen Reinhart found that "across both advanced countries and emerging markets, high debt/GDP levels (90 percent and above) are associated with notably lower growth outcomes." [15]

That paper was referring to gross, or total, central government debt (not just debt held by the public), and since its publication the United States has exceeded that level of gross debt to well above 100 percent of GDP. Several other countries, such as Portugal, Italy and Japan, have even higher ratios. [16] Yet investors continue to lend the U.S. money, and economic growth has recovered since the recession.

In recent years, however "the economics profession has grown very skeptical about magic numbers," such as the debt-to-GDP ratio, says Barry Eichengreen, a professor of economics and political science at the University of California, Berkeley, and the author of *Exorbitant Privilege: The Rise and Fall of the Dollar and the Future of the International Monetary System*. Instead of focusing on the debt-to-GDP ratio and making it sacrosanct, investors are looking at the U.S. government's ability to pay its debt as a product of multiple factors, including economic and productivity growth, demography and politics, among other things, he says.

And the United States is a special case because of its currency. The dollar is "far and away the most important currency for invoicing and settling international transactions," even transactions that don't involve the United States. [17] Oil, for example, is bought with dollars worldwide. So if a Russian company pumps and sells oil to a European firm, the transaction occurs in dollars.

Foreign central banks also hold trillions of dollars in bonds from the U.S. Treasury and quasi-U.S. government agencies for various reasons, including insurance in case of an internal crisis. They also might use U.S. bond purchases to manipulate the value of their own currency. Central banks around the world have stashed away some $11 trillion in other nations' currencies (in the form of government bonds,

which are generally easy to convert into currency), according to the International Monetary Fund. More than

Workers restore a vacant building in Newburgh, N.Y., on May 30. The economic crisis of 2007-09 battered the Hudson Valley city, but it is on the road to recovery. Some budget analysts and economists say the nation's economy could be threatened if the national debt becomes as big or bigger than the size of the U.S. economy, a level that could be reached by 2033.

half of that, some $5.7 trillion, is in dollar assets such as Treasury securities; the next closest currency is euros and euro-related assets, at $1.7 trillion. [18]

Clearly, governments and investors around the world want to hold U.S. bonds because they are useful for several purposes. Not only are they seen as the best safe haven in a crisis, but they also are needed for various economic and trade purposes. And every time a U.S. government bond is purchased, the buyer is making a loan to the U.S. government.

The dollar's special status, which an envious French finance minister once called the United States' "exorbitant privilege," should continue in the near term, says Eichengreen. [19] For a few years over the past two decades, it looked as if either the euro, the common currency of 19 member states of the European Union (EU), or China's currency, the renminbi, might challenge the dollar's status as the world's reserve currency. But both China and the EU have had

economic problems in recent years that made that less likely, or at least a prospect more distant in the future.

"There has to be an alternative reserve currency before investors balk at U.S. debt and a crisis unfolds," says Charles Seville, a senior director at Fitch Ratings, a major U.S. credit rating firm.

So while U.S. debt continues to pile up, "it's not yet a problem for sovereign rating [the credit rating of a sovereign nation] because the U.S. remains the issuer of the world's premier reserve currency, and there is demand there for that debt," says Seville. If Fitch, or one of the other major companies that rate the ability of borrowers to pay back loans, downgraded the U.S. credit rating, it would drive up interest rates and hurt economic growth, and it might even cause some investors to sell U.S. bonds. But Fitch currently has no plans to downgrade U.S. debt, continuing to assign it its best rating, "AAA."

Still, "international reserve currency status is not a natural monopoly," Eichengreen points out, and a rival currency that has the dollar's attractive attributes will eventually emerge, he says.

Deficit Projected to Explode

The government's annual deficit, or the gap between federal spending and revenue, is projected to triple between 2017 and 2045. The annual deficit could reach 9 percent of gross domestic product (GDP) in 2045, up from 3 percent in 2017, as interest on the national debt consumes more of the federal budget and the costs of Medicare, Social Security and other entitlement programs keep rising.

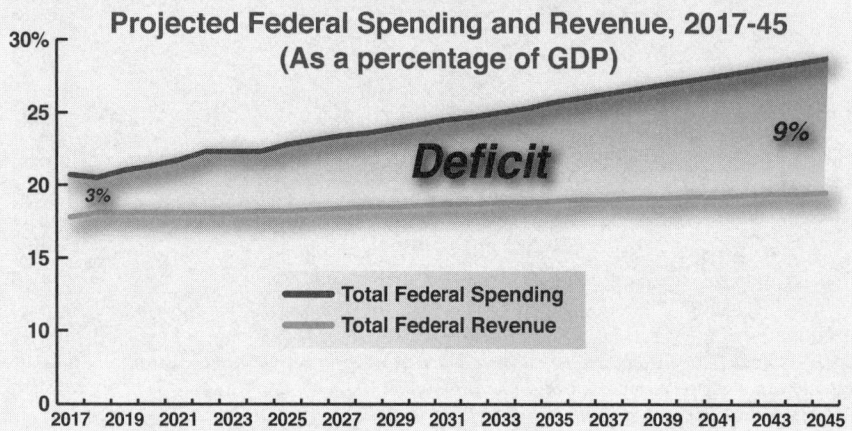

Projected Federal Spending and Revenue, 2017-45
(As a percentage of GDP)

Source: "The 2017 Long-Term Budget Outlook," Congressional Budget Office, 2017, https://tinyurl.com/mubxx97

A more immediate danger is the nation's debt ceiling, which, according to Treasury, has to be raised by Sept. 29 to allow Treasury to borrow more money. [20] Congressional Republicans are divided on just how to deal with the debt ceiling, and if they fail to act in time and the United States misses a single payment, significant, lasting damage could be done to America's pristine credit reputation and sovereign rating.

Barring Congress' failure to act, U.S. borrowing can continue for the foreseeable future. So the question is, when will the United States have borrowed so much that investors decide to look elsewhere, triggering a crisis? "I don't have a tipping point level in mind," says the Concord Coalition's Bixby. "But why try to find out?"

Are higher taxes the answer to the debt problem?

Higher taxes could be a big part of a solution to the nation's debt problem, to be sure.

Entitlement programs such as Social Security and Medicare will be the biggest growers in coming decades, yet they are also enormously popular. Discretionary spending, which includes defense spending and all the other nonmandatory programs the federal government funds, has fallen to just 6.4 percent of GDP (from 10 percent in 1983), and Republicans, who control Congress and the White House, are against cuts to defense. [21] Overall, outlays by the government in 2017 are estimated to be 20.7 percent of GDP. [22]

Revenues flowing into Treasury, which include personal and corporate income taxes, payroll taxes and excise taxes, are only 17.8 percent of GDP, by contrast. The difference, — 20.7 minus 17.8, or 2.9 percent of GDP — is the projected deficit for this year, or $693 billion, according to the Concord Coalition.

That gap looks to grow, as the CBO projects spending to rise to 24.9 percent of GDP, in the 2028-37 period (on average), while tax revenues will rise less than 1 percentage point, to 18.7 per-

cent. As a result, annual deficits in that future period will average 6.2 percent of GDP. [23]

And while both Democrats and Republicans talk about the danger of rising debt, they disagree about how to address it. In general, Democrats want to maintain or even raise government spending and boost taxes to match, while Republicans prefer to cut spending and lower taxes, arguing this would stimulate the economy and lead to higher tax revenues.

Yet the University of Connecticut's Kwak and some other budget analysts have concluded that once Americans get used to a new spending program, such as the Affordable Care Act, they are unwilling to give it up. Republicans vowed to repeal the health care act, dubbed Obamacare, for years after it was passed, but in recent months they have been unable to pass any legislation eliminating it or reducing its benefits.

The same inability to enact cuts goes for Medicare and Social Security. So higher taxes may be the primary way to close the big and growing gap between revenues flowing into Treasury and spending going out, a number of analysts say. "Because the debt problem is driven mainly by demographics, revenue policy is the answer; we have a lot of room on the revenue side," says Diane Lim, a principal economist at the Conference Board, a business membership and research organization, and former chief economist at the Concord Coalition.

Kwak says the nation's credit rating may depend on demonstrating the ability to raise new revenue. "The country's credit is good as long as it's clear you can raise taxes to pay our debt," says Kwak.

In December 2016 the CBO, which is nonpartisan, published "Options for Reducing the Deficit: 2017 to 2026." [24] The long report outlines myriad ways to begin bringing down the national debt, including both spending cuts and increased tax revenues. Raising the tax rates that ordinary Americans pay on their income is one of those ways, but far from the only one.

Taxes could also be raised on capital gains from sales of stocks and other assets, on the profits companies and banks make or on gasoline or alcohol sales, and on many other items. Similarly, tax deductions — a popular one permits homeowners to deduct from their taxes the interest they pay on their mortgages — could be eliminated or capped.

Many Republicans, however, dislike most of those tax hikes, viewing them as just a way to enable the federal government to spend more money. In fact, a prominent anti-tax group in Washington, Americans for Tax Reform, opposes all tax increases as a matter of principle, seeing lower taxes as a way to minimize government control of people's lives. [25] The group's "Taxpayer Protection Pledge," created in 1986, asks lawmakers to promise never to raise taxes above current levels. More than 200 Republican members of the House and 45 Republican senators have signed the pledge, but no current Democratic senator or representative has.

Yet many economists see other, perhaps more compelling reasons to avoid higher taxes. Above a certain level, they say, taxes discourage people from working and earning money, thus suppressing economic activity and therefore holding down tax revenues (which rise and fall with economic growth).

A related theory, developed by economist Arthur Laffer in 1974 and known as the Laffer curve, says that cutting taxes deeply will generate so much economic activity that tax revenues will in fact rise. Many economists doubt this, but Trump has embraced Laffer's theory more than his recent Oval Office predecessors, so many political experts believe that taxes are unlikely to rise while he remains in office. [26]

Is Washington capable of solving the debt problem?

"I believe we will have a budget deal within five to 10 years that addresses

President Trump addresses supporters at a rally in Phoenix on Aug. 22. The tax reform plan that Trump campaigned on would increase the federal debt by $7.2 trillion over the next decade, according to the Tax Policy Center, a nonpartisan think tank. "Trump campaigned on promises not to touch entitlements and to cut taxes," says Bob Bixby, executive director of the Concord Coalition, a nonpartisan group advocating fiscal responsibility. "That is not a recipe for long-term fiscal sustainability."

Getty Images/Ralph Freso

this [debt] problem," says MacGuineas of the Committee for a Responsible Federal Budget. "But it's not going to be this year, even though it should be."

Other advocates for deficit reduction also are cautiously optimistic, believing progress on debt will happen eventually. After all, in 2011 President Barack Obama and Republican Speaker John Boehner, R-Ohio, came very close to a "grand bargain" to reduce deficits by $4 trillion over 10 years with a package of spending cuts — to both discretionary spending and entitlement programs — and new revenues. The deal eventually collapsed, however, over the size of the tax increase. [27]

But many analysts believe the current partisanship and gridlock in Washington will make it difficult to lower deficits and, eventually, the national debt.

Yet there is no shortage of ways to address the rising national debt. In December 2016, a 316-page CBO report detailed 54 non-health spending cut

options, 18 changes to health programs and 43 ways to raise revenue. [28] MacGuineas and other analysts say it is entirely conceivable that a bipartisan compromise can be found that includes a combination of those options.

"A reasonable policy would be to cut back on Social Security and Medicare, raise taxes modestly, look for some inefficiencies in discretionary spending and hope for some economic growth to drive higher tax revenues flowing into Treasury," says Martin Sullivan, chief economist at Tax Analysts, a Falls Church, Va., publisher of tax information and analysis, and former economist at the U.S. Treasury Department and the Congressional Joint Committee on Taxes. Cutting entitlement programs might mean raising the eligibility age gradually, trimming benefits or undertaking similar modest changes.

Where budget analysts disagree is the triggering action or event that will force the two parties to come to the table and negotiate a deal to put balancing the budget — and eventually reducing the debt — back on course.

A crisis of some sort may be needed to force the parties to the table and act, says the Conference Board's Lim. Two possible triggers could be investors balking at further purchases of U.S. debt, or Congress failing to raise the debt ceiling. The latter might happen

Everglades National Park in Florida and other national parks around the country were shut down on Oct. 7, 2013, when Congress was unable to pass a bill funding the U.S. government. This year, If Congress fails to pass a spending bill by Oct. 1, the government will partially shut down, forcing many noncritical governmental functions to close and hundreds of thousands of federal employees to be placed on unpaid leave. No matter what happens in the long term, economists and financial analysts agree that Congress needs to raise the U.S. debt ceiling in the fall, which means passing legislation to allow Treasury to borrow more money.

in the fall, but at the moment, things are relatively placid, she says, "and that's both a blessing and a curse."

The emergence of a competing world reserve currency, perhaps the euro, could force action, says Eichengreen at the University of California. "If international investors have somewhere else to go, that could concentrate the minds of U.S. policymakers on addressing the growth of the debt problem."

MacGuineas says an answer may be closer than that. The current situation in Washington, with Congress unable

to pass any major legislation, is just adding to Americans' frustration with the political system, she says. And the large and growing level of U.S. debt in many ways reflects that dysfunction. MacGuineas says the nation could see a presidential election in the near future in which one candidate focuses on the debt, with the other candidates forced to respond. Such a thing happened in the 1992 campaign when Texas businessman Ross Perot ran on a platform of fiscal responsibility.

"Once one candidate starts talking about debt, it starts to make the free-lunch candidates [those who oppose cuts to programs that are not fully paid for through taxes] look really irresponsible," says MacGuineas. "So I think there is a chance that, if you had a Perot-like candidate, that could change the whole tone in Washington. I'm not an immediate optimist, but I am optimistic." ■

BACKGROUND

Aversion to Taxes

Debt has been with the nation since the beginning. The Revolutionary War cost millions to wage and sent Benjamin Franklin, Thomas Jefferson and John Adams to Europe, hats in hands, to borrow money from France, Spain and the Netherlands. After the war, the first task for Alexander Hamilton, the nation's first Treasury secretary, was to find a way to pay back the $54 million in debt that the new republic had racked up. [29]

Hamilton took to the task eagerly, as he was schooled in the British notion that a nation's power and stability depended on good credit. [30] He also saw it as an opportunity to create a stronger central government, a vibrant bond market and banking system, and taxing powers. [31] "'Tis by introducing order into our finances — by restoreing [sic] public credit — not by gaining battles, that we are finally to gain our object," wrote Hamilton. [32]

A public aversion to taxes is not a new development, either. Tariffs on traded goods, which consumers eventually paid for through higher prices, became the principle way to raise money to pay the national debt. Yet they were highly unpopular, as was the first excise tax imposed on a domestic product. In 1791 farmers in western Pennsylvania and Virginia took up arms to try to keep officials from collecting a tax on corn used to make whiskey. George Washington led a militia to suppress the Whiskey Rebellion. [33]

Crucially, Hamilton succeeded in getting the federal government to assume the states' war debts and thus increase the federal government's influence. He saw assuming debts from the war as "the price of liberty. The faith of America has been repeatedly

Continued on p. 712

Getty Images/Joe Raedle

Chronology

1780s-1790s
Treasury Secretary Alexander Hamilton helps the fledgling republic cope with crushing Revolutionary War debt.

1780-1790s
The nation's first Treasury secretary assumes the states' war debts, issues federal government bonds and implements tariffs to raise money to pay off the bonds.

1791
The Whiskey Rebellion rises in the country's western frontier when farmers revolt against a federal tax on corn to make whiskey.

* * *

1890s-1960s
The modern fiscal system evolves out of post-Civil War troubles.

1890s-1913
Civil War debts and a poor economy plague government finances, leading to a federal income tax. Supreme Court strikes down the tax as unconstitutional, but it is finally implemented in 1913 through the 16th Amendment.

1930s
Democratic President Franklin D. Roosevelt uses massive deficit spending to relieve effects of Great Depression. . . . Social Security Act creates first major entitlement program, a federal pension plan for the elderly.

1945
World War II ends with unprecedented deficits and debt.

1962-1963
Democratic President John F. Kennedy supports Revenue Act, a deficit-increasing tax cut to stimulate the economy; it becomes law in 1964.

1965
Medicare and Medicaid are created.

* * *

1980s *The dollar takes center stage in the international monetary system.*

1980s
Republican President Ronald Reagan pushes through large, permanent tax cuts and a significant increase in defense spending, raising debt level. . . . "Supply side" theory emerges, calling for tax cuts to drive economic growth and tax revenues.

1985
Congress attempts to decrease deficits through Gramm-Rudman-Hollings Act but eventually overrides most of its provisions.

* * *

1990-Present
After fiscal restraint leads to surpluses, lawmakers return to budget deficits.

1990
Budget Enforcement Act, signed by President George H. W. Bush, caps spending and establishes new rules about paying for tax cuts and spending programs.

1992
Independent presidential candidate Ross Perot campaigns on the dangers of growing national debt, forcing other candidates to address the issue.

1993
Democratic President Bill Clinton signs Deficit Reduction Act, raising taxes and cutting spending.

1998-2001
Several years of budget surpluses result from deficit reduction laws and a booming economy.

2001
Republican President George W. Bush and congressional Republicans pass the first of two major tax reduction laws.

2003
Bush pushes a Medicare prescription drug program through Congress, the first major entitlement since Johnson administration.

2007
Major recession sends tax revenues plummeting and expands safety net spending. . . . Congress passes two stimulus bills in response, increasing national debt.

2008-2010
Growing deficits spark rise of the tea party, helping Republicans win control of House.

2011
Spending showdown between congressional Republicans and the Democratic Barack Obama administration results in Budget Control Act, which introduces caps to some spending programs.

2016
Republican Donald Trump is elected president on promises to cut taxes, raise defense spending and protect Medicare and Social Security.

2017
Treasury Secretary Steven Mnuchin informs Congress that the debt ceiling needs to be raised by the end of September.

Health Care Spending Fuels Federal Deficits

The problem of rising costs extends beyond Medicare and Medicaid.

For budget hawks worried about the nation's growing debt, the two biggest causes of federal spending growth are not hard to find.

Medicare and Medicaid are projected to rise from 5.5 percent of the nation's gross domestic product (GDP) today to 8.8 percent in the 2030s. The steep increase will be due largely to the influx of aging Baby Boomers into Medicare, and to rising per person health care costs. Medicaid coverage, meanwhile, is greatly expanding under the Affordable Care Act, as is the Children's Health Insurance Program, which provides coverage to children in low-income families. [1]

But the causes of rising health care spending run deeper than these two federal programs, experts say. One problem is that health spending is a victim of its own success. Improved health care is allowing people to live longer and survive illnesses that in the past they would have succumbed to.

And per person health care spending rises with age. Americans normally become eligible for Medicare at 65 and remain eligible until they die. Medicare spending for those in the 65-to-84 age group was about $9,870 per person in 2012, the most recent year for which data are available. For individuals 85 years and older that amount nearly doubled, to $17,267. [2]

A deeper problem, experts say, is the U.S. health system's expensive ways. The United States in 2015 spent more on health care per person than other advanced-economy nations, including Japan, most of Western Europe, Canada and Australia. The share of U.S. GDP that goes to health spending — all health spending, both government-provided and private — was 16.4 percent, while countries such as Switzerland, Germany, Canada and France were closer to 11 percent, and Great Britain was 8.5 percent. [3]

Yet health outcomes for Americans consistently rank behind many of those same nations by many measures, such as obesity and infant mortality. [4]

"The U.S. spends more on health care than any other country, but what we get for these significant resources falls short in terms of access to care, affordability and coordination," said David Blumenthal, president of the Commonwealth Fund, a foundation that supports improved health care. [5] Why does U.S. health care, despite its high expense, deliver results at or below the average results for similar industrialized nations? Stuart Butler, an expert on health care policy at the Brookings Institution, a centrist think tank in Washington, blames the high cost of training doctors and running hospitals and clinics. "If you actually look at the unit prices in health care, they've been steadily going up," he says.

In addition, says Butler, the U.S. health care system tends to "over-medicalize" many issues by waiting to treat problems when they happen instead of trying to prevent them — for example, treating a broken hip rather than improving living spaces for elderly people to prevent catastrophic falls. Many other wealthy nations, by contrast, stress prevention. "There are a lot of things we don't do here that other countries do that would help reduce demand for medical services," says Butler.

Treatment of the very sick elderly is also different in the United States. Many very old patients are treated in intensive care units, which are costly, when similar patients in other countries typically receive less expensive palliative care, which seeks to improve the quality of life rather than prolong it. [6]

Moreover, the fee-for-service model, an à la carte system in which every service and procedure and doctor visit is billed

Continued from p. 710

pledged for it, and with solemnities that give peculiar force to the obligation." [34] Debt and the methods of paying it back, as a result, helped shape the young nation, creating a new level of centralized federal power.

A century later, war was again instrumental in changing how the United States spent and raised money. The Civil War drove the public debt from about $65 million to $2.76 billion in the 1860s. [35] Decades later, with the nation still burdened by that debt as well as by a poor economy, President Grover Cleveland and Congress in 1894 passed a federal income tax. The

Supreme Court struck down the tax a year later, but it was finally codified into the Constitution in 1913 when the 16th Amendment came into force. [36]

The amendment reads: "The Congress shall have power to lay and collect taxes on incomes, from whatever source derived, without apportionment among the several States, and without regard to any census or enumeration."

The new power to tax brought about a sea change in the country's finances and allowed the United States to play a key role in the First World War. It also gave the federal government more power "to raise revenue and regulate the economy, planting the seeds of

government's dramatic growth in ensuing decades," according to *Dead Men Ruling: How to Restore Fiscal Freedom and Rescue our Future*, by C. Eugene Steuerle, a fellow at the Urban Institute think tank in Washington and former deputy assistant Treasury secretary for tax analysis. [37]

And then came World War II, which drove debt to its highest level in history — 119 percent of GDP in 1946. [38] That debt-to-GDP ratio shrank over the next decades as the economy boomed.

More important than the war debt was the expanded role of the federal government under Democratic President Franklin D. Roosevelt, mostly through

separately, encourages more tests, procedures and visits. [7] That tends to increase health care providers' profits but drives up overall spending.

Reformers cannot wave a magic wand to slow health care spending in the United States, says Butler, but many of the factors driving growth can be improved incrementally. Steps include increasing the use of managed care, in which preventive care such as screenings and periodic checkups are encouraged, and placing some limits on expensive treatments and specialists. Butler also calls for a more candid national conversation about providing expensive life-prolonging treatments to patients with little prospect of recovery.

Meanwhile, some experts say Medicare and Medicaid could be put on a long-term budget and, if they grow too fast, Congress could take remedial actions, such as reducing payments to doctors and hospitals. In fact, the Affordable Care Act has such a requirement that may be triggered this year, although it remains far from certain that lawmakers and the White House will comply with it. [8]

— *Matthew K. Benjamin*

A demonstrator in New York City on July 24 calls for an expansion of Medicare. The federal health care program for the elderly is one of the biggest causes of federal spending growth.

Getty Images/Pacific Press/LightRocket/Erik McGregor

[1] "The 2017 Long-Term Budget Outlook," Congressional Budget Office, March 2017, Table 1, pp. 4, 15, https://tinyurl.com/mubxx97.

[2] "National Health Expenditures by Ages and Gender," Centers for Medicare and Medicaid Services, August 2016, Table 26, https://tinyurl.com/y8c7nwp4.

[3] "Health at a Glance 2015: How Does the United States Compare," Organisation for Economic Co-operation and Development, November 2015, https://tinyurl.com/ycalvb5l.

[4] Maggie Fox, "United States Comes in Last Again on Health, Compared to Other Countries," NBC News, Nov. 16, 2016, https://tinyurl.com/z5eyz2y.

[5] "New 11-Country Health Care Survey: U.S. Adults Skip Care Due to Costs, Struggle Financially, And Have The Worst Health," Commonwealth Fund, Nov. 6, 2016, https://tinyurl.com/hbebnye.

[6] Victor R. Fuchs, "Why Do Other Rich Nations Spend So Much Less on Healthcare?" *The Atlantic*, July 13, 2014, https://tinyurl.com/zxb5qp2.

[7] Rushika Fernandopulle, "Breaking the Fee-For-Service Addiction: Let's Move To A Comprehensive Primary Care Payment Model," *Health Affairs Blog*, Aug. 17, 2015, https://tinyurl.com/nhtz8lt.

[8] "Report: IPAB likely will be triggered in 2017; Medicare trust fund will remain solvent until 2028," Advisory Board, June 23, 2016, https://tinyurl.com/y9potjlg.

the creation of Social Security, the first large "entitlement" that would eventually lead to others, including Medicare and Medicaid in 1965. Through those programs spawned by the Great Depression, the federal government took on the role of providing pensions to older Americans as well as funding health care for the elderly and the poor.

Keynesian Economics

In addition to spawning Social Security, the Depression brought a monumental new economic theory, the brainchild of British economist John Maynard Keynes. Keynesian economics held that governments should pursue deficit spending — borrowing to create jobs and stimulate the economy — during economic downturns. The idea "began to break the balanced budget shackle" that had kept deficits in check to date, according to *Dead Men Ruling*. [39]

The application of Keynes' famous theory grew to include deficit-funded tax cuts in the 1960s, when Democratic President John F. Kennedy pushed for a program of lower taxes in order to boost economic growth. Conservatives were initially hostile to Keynesianism, but in time they, too, succumbed to the lure of deficit spending. In 1971, Republican President Richard M. Nixon declared that "we're all Keynesians now." [40]

Nixon, some say, also created the seemingly limitless credit line that the U.S. government enjoys to this day. In 1971 he formally abandoned the post-World War II system of exchange rates that fixed the price of gold to the dollar and other nations' currencies. [41] As a result, U.S. government debt largely supplanted gold as the main store of value in the international economic system, and made the United States "the world's preeminent economic power while creating the biggest credit line ever," according to *White House Burning*. "Once politicians began accessing this

Tax Reform Could Help Raise Revenue

But familiar foes remain: an army of lobbyists and congressional gridlock.

The nation hasn't seen major tax reform in three decades, and for good reason. "Tax reform is hard," says Martin Sullivan, chief economist at Tax Analysts, a Falls Church, Va., publisher of tax information and analysis, and former economist at the U.S. Treasury Department.

The tax code is more than just a way to raise revenue. The government uses tax deductions and other features in the code to pursue economic or social priorities such as encouraging home-ownership and charitable giving by individuals or, say, research and development by businesses. Changing the code in a fundamental way, as Congress last did in 1986, means some groups will lose their preferences and others may gain some. Lobbyists have long fought to protect existing tax breaks and fight for new ones. [1]

Despite the obstacles to true reform, lawmakers in both parties want to try again this year. The benefits of sweeping tax reform can be large and lasting by boosting both tax revenues and economic growth. Of course, as with just about everything in Washington, lawmakers differ on how to achieve it.

But with tax reform, at least, Republicans and Democrats agree on the need to "broaden the base and lower the rates." That is, they want to cut out some of the so-called loopholes in the code and use the money raised by closing them to pay for lower tax rates and a simpler code for everyone.

Such reform holds manifold benefits, economists say. Every new Congress fiddles with the tax code to add new preferences or deductions, and after many years the code becomes a kind of Frankenstein's monster that is utterly complex, difficult to comply with and often unfair. A tax code riddled with loopholes also is less efficient in collecting revenue — think of all the ways that people and companies can avoid paying their fair share of taxes.

And giving tax preferences to different groups also is bad for the economy, in that it creates distorted incentives for people and businesses to make economic decisions, economists say. Should you stretch your finances and buy a house and get the tax deduction for your mortgage interest payments, or keep renting? Should you buy that new car or save for retirement in a tax-free account? If you are a business, should you raise money by issuing stock or borrow the money instead? The tax code heavily influences all those decisions — and countless others. Ideally, such decisions should be made on their own merits, not because of how they are treated by the tax code.

In addition, the top tax rate that U.S. businesses pay, at 38.9 percent, is the highest of all advanced economies. Yet because of so-called carveouts in the corporate code — tax advantages for income earned abroad or for purchases of factories or machinery or other physical assets — few companies actually pay that rate. Instead, the effective rate they pay is much lower, around 19 percent on average by one calculation. [2]

So, in essence, the high corporate rate may be discouraging companies from locating in the United States, and yet the government does not collect tax revenue commensurate with what the rate suggests. Eliminating some carveouts and lowering the rate could attract companies and jobs, the argument goes, and allow markets — not lawmakers — to decide which companies succeed or fail.

"It is possible to use tax reform to stimulate growth," says Sullivan. "The reason that broadening the base and lowering the rates improves

line of credit, it made possible a historic increase in the national debt." [42]

Succeeding presidents weren't afraid to tap the new credit line. Ronald Reagan, whom Republicans hold up today as a model of fiscal conservatism, was among the most prodigal of them. Reagan pushed dramatically lower tax rates, especially in the top tier, through Congress, at the same time that he was dramatically boosting defense spending to rebuild the military. Spending on social programs ballooned as well because of the deep 1981-82 recession. During the decade before Reagan, the debt-to-GDP level remained relatively constant, about 26 percent to 27 percent. Reagan's policies, along with the recession, drove that to nearly 40 percent. [43]

Reagan also encouraged "supply side" economics, the theory that lower taxes would incentivize businesses to invest more and people to work and save more, all of which would combine to stimulate the economy and drive tax revenues higher. As a result, the two predominant theories informing budget and economic policies were Keynesianism, which Democrats liked, and supply side economics, popular with Republicans. Politicians of both parties exploited the two theories, according to Steuerle, and "invoked them to justify almost any spending or tax giveaway, and fought . . . over whose giveaway was better." [44]

In 1985, Congress attempted to control deficits when it passed the Gramm-Rudman-Hollings Act. The legislation set new deficit goals and mandated automatic spending cuts if those goals were exceeded, but Congress found multiple ways around the law, and ultimately it did little to rein in deficit spending. [45]

Short-Lived Restraints

After the growth of the national debt during the 1980s, the 1990s saw several successful efforts to lessen deficits. The 1990 Budget Enforcement Act, passed with help from Republican President George H.W. Bush, put caps on discretionary spending and created "pay as you go" rules mandating that

economic growth is it makes the tax system more neutral across the board, so you have a more efficient allocation of capital and other resources in the economy and across industries."

Getting those benefits, however, means eliminating loopholes, which are also called "tax expenditures," because they essentially spend money through the tax code. Those expenditures totaled $1.2 trillion in 2015, or more than the cost of Medicare and Medicaid combined. [3] Total taxes collected that year were about $3.3 trillion. [4] (*See graphic, p. 708.*)

Also, consider that the tax preferences — the mortgage interest deduction or the exclusion of employer health insurance contributions, for example — are skewed toward wealthier Americans, those who carry larger mortgages or enjoy more generous health benefits from their employers. The top 1 percent of taxpayers receive 17 percent of the total value of tax expenditures in the individual code. [5]

In the final analysis, it may not be differences between Democrats and Republicans that make fundamental tax reform so difficult. Instead, the vast army of Washington lobbyists protecting provisions in the tax code that benefit their clients, from the housing and real estate lobbies to the health insurance firms, is potentially much more formidable.

— *Matthew K. Benjamin*

In May the White House proposed a 2018 budget with $3.6 trillion in spending cuts, many of them to programs for low-income Americans.

See "Twenty Years Later: The Tax Reform Act of 1986," Tax Foundation, Oct. 23, 2006, https://tinyurl.com/kk6dxkx.

[2] Danielle Kurtzleben, "FACT CHECK: Does the U.S. Have the Highest Corporate Tax Rate in the World?" NPR, Aug. 7, 2017, https://tinyurl.com/y7gk6hfe.

[3] "Policy Basics: Federal Tax Expenditures," Center on Budget and Policy Priorities, Feb. 23, 2016, https://tinyurl.com/yao2khcq.

[4] "An Update to the Budget and Economic Outlook: 2017 to 2027," Congressional Budget Office, June 29, 2017, table 1, https://tinyurl.com/yccmzwzd.

[5] "Selected Charts on the Long-Term Fiscal Challenges of the United States," Peter G. Peterson Foundation, August 2017, slide 24, https://tinyurl.com/ybeb35w3.

[1] In 1986, during President Ronald Reagan's administration, Congress produced a simplified code with fewer tax breaks and significantly lower rates. Since then, Congress has amended the code with thousands of changes, bringing back many of the loopholes that had been eliminated in the reform bill.

any change to taxes and some entitlements that cost money would have to be offset with savings elsewhere. The law remained in effect until 2002, and many credit it for helping improve the nation's finances in the 1990s. [46]

In the 1992 presidential election, independent candidate Perot, who campaigned against rising debt, received nearly 19 percent of the popular vote. The other candidates took notice, and in 1993 newly elected Democratic President Bill Clinton pushed through Congress the Deficit Reduction Act, which raised taxes and cut spending.

"They passed those two major deficit reduction laws because everybody was so concerned about the debt, which was minuscule compared to today," says Sullivan at Tax Analysts. Those laws (and another in 1997) helped push spending down, from 21.7 percent of GDP in 1991 to below 18 percent in 1999. And the booming economy of the late 1990s drove tax revenues from less than 18 percent of GDP in 1995 to 20 percent in 2000. The result was four years of government surpluses, beginning in 1998 and ending in 2001. [47]

The surpluses have yet to return, however. Republican President George W. Bush campaigned in 2000 on a promise to return much of the surpluses to taxpayers through tax cuts. And he delivered, steering two major tax cuts through Congress in three years. Those, along with a stock market collapse in 2000 and a recession in 2001, sent tax revenues plummeting.

Government spending also rose when the United States went to war in Iraq and Afghanistan after the Sept. 11, 2001, terrorist attacks and the Bush administration added a prescription drug program to Medicare. Government outlays as a percentage of the economy grew during the Bush years from 17.6 percent to 20.2 percent. [48]

The financial crisis of 2007-09 was even worse for deficits than Bush's policies. The deep recession — the most severe downturn since the Depression — sent tax revenues below 15 percent of GDP, while raising spending on safety net programs such as unemployment insurance, food stamps and Medicaid. Congress reacted by passing two economic stimulus plans, one pushed by Bush in 2008 ($150 billion in tax cuts) and another by Obama a year later ($288 billion in tax cuts and $500 billion in spending increases; the act was later revised to $831 billion). [49] Debt held by the public jumped from 39.3 percent of GDP in 2008 to 77 percent today. [50]

to the Budget Control Act of 2011, which raised the debt ceiling and introduced several complex mechanisms designed to force Congress to take deficit reduction measures, including spending caps on certain spending categories. [51] Congress subsequently raised those limits. [52]

Since Trump's election in November 2016, the tea party, which clearly was

CURRENT SITUATION

Looming Shutdown

Despite Trump's claims to the contrary, the first 200-plus days of his presidency have brought scant legislative achievement. [54]

The House and Senate spent months attempting to repeal and replace — or at least significantly alter — the Affordable Care Act. The House passed a bill in May, but the Senate was unable to find a compromise that could attract enough moderate and conservative lawmakers to get 50 votes. While some Republicans have called for renewed efforts to resurrect and pass a health bill replacing Obamacare when Congress returns to work after Labor Day, the consensus in Washington is that lawmakers need to move on to priorities that have a better chance of passing this year.

The federal government's fiscal year ends Sept. 30, and with it the government's ability to spend money under its current spending authority. If Congress fails to pass a spending bill by Oct. 1, the government will partially shut down, which means that many noncritical governmental functions will be shuttered — national parks and NASA, for example — and hundreds of thousands of federal employees placed on unpaid leave until a bill is passed that allows government agencies to be funded.

Critical functions such as air traffic control and the military would remain in operation during a shutdown, and furloughed government workers would likely eventually get paid, but such an occurrence has the potential to rattle financial markets' and investors' confidence in the U.S. government's ability to manage its affairs. The last time

Workers repair a sewer pipe in Brooklyn on July 28. As the national debt rises, causing interest on the debt to consume more and more of the federal government's budget, spending on key programs – such as education, infrastructure and defense – and everything else the government funds would continue to fall. That would lead, some experts say, to a nationwide economic decline and a lower standard of living for many Americans.

Opposition to Obama's stimulus plan, as well as deficits that exceeded $1 trillion each year of his first term, helped give birth to the conservative tea party movement and also contributed to the Republican Party's takeover of the House of Representatives in the 2010 midterm elections. In 2011 a showdown between House Republicans and the Obama administration prompted Republicans to refuse to raise the debt ceiling without a deal to address spending. This led

a force in 2009-10 for spending restraint, has quieted. [53] Some say the movement was a relatively brief chapter in the conservative movement. "The anti-debt argument was a manifestation of the "America is in decline" sentiment," says the University of Connecticut's Kwak. "That was a very popular sentiment in the last election. Now that sentiment is being expressed differently, as 'Make America Great Again,' " President Trump's signature campaign slogan. ■

Continued on p. 718

At Issue:

Should Congress make deficit reduction a top priority?

MARC GOLDWEIN
SENIOR VICE PRESIDENT AND SENIOR POLICY DIRECTOR, COMMITTEE FOR A RESPONSIBLE FEDERAL BUDGET

WRITTEN FOR *CQ RESEARCHER*, SEPTEMBER 2017

*t*he national debt today is higher as a share of the economy than at any time in U.S. history aside from the aftermath of World War II. And the debt is projected to rise indefinitely and unsustainably in the coming years. Annual deficits need not be sharply reduced immediately, but with trillion-dollar deficits slated to return in only a few years, policymakers must enact a long-term debt-reduction plan sooner rather than later.

The long-term consequences of high and rising debt are numerous. Ultimately, the U.S. debt load will reduce private investment, slow wage growth, raise interest rates, shrink the economy and increase the likelihood of an eventual fiscal crisis. High debt levels also force the government to spend more on debt service — the interest owed to domestic and foreign bondholders — leaving fewer dollars available to finance new investments, national defense, anti-poverty programs or tax relief. Perhaps most significantly, debt cannot forever rise faster than the economy; and with debt growing unsustainably, the country is making promises we simply cannot keep.

The nation does not need to balance the budget, and deficit reduction must not happen immediately. Indeed, if deficit reduction occurs too rapidly it could temporarily hurt economic growth. But changes should be enacted today that gradually slow the rapid growth of health and retirement spending, raise new revenue through a more efficient and pro-growth tax code and reprioritize government spending from consumption toward investment.

A combination of thoughtful entitlement reform, tax reform, immigration reform, regulatory reform and deficit reduction will put the country on a more sustainable path and at the same time grow the economy and increase wages and income.

Advocates of higher deficits will marshal one argument after another against cutting even a dollar of spending or raising even a dollar of taxes. Pretending deficits don't matter may allow special interests to get new tax cuts and new entitlement programs from Congress, but it imposes a large implicit tax on future generations.

If something sounds too good to be true, it probably is. The United States can't forever spend far more than it brings in, and we can't indefinitely borrow our way to prosperity. A smart, gradual and significant long-term deficit-reduction plan is the best way forward for our debt-burdened nation.

DEAN BAKER
CO-DIRECTOR, CENTER FOR ECONOMIC AND POLICY RESEARCH

WRITTEN FOR *CQ RESEARCHER*, SEPTEMBER 2017

*d*eficit fears are impoverishing our kids. The people complaining about budget deficits fundamentally misrepresent how the economy works and the problems it faces. A deficit is a problem when it creates too much demand, exceeding the economy's ability to supply goods and services. In this situation, a deficit is likely to lead to higher interest rates and inflation, which reduce investment. Less investment means less productivity growth, which means we will be less wealthy in the future.

Ever since the 2007-09 recession, the problem has been the opposite: too little demand. Millions of workers have gone unemployed because there was not enough demand for their labor. In a weak economy, companies invest less.

In a period of weak demand, it is virtually costless for the government to spend in areas that will not only employ people but also increase long-term productivity and spending on infrastructure, research and development and such areas as quality preschool, which pays enormous long-term dividends.

Deficit fears prevented the government from spending the money needed to bring the economy back to full employment. That was costly in the short term because it meant millions of workers went unemployed, but it was also very costly in the long term.

According to the Congressional Budget Office (CBO), the economy's potential output has been permanently stunted by this prolonged period of high unemployment. CBO's most recent estimates of potential GDP are more than 10 percent lower than what was projected for 2017 before the recession. This gap of nearly $2 trillion a year (almost $6,000 per person) can be thought of as an "austerity tax." This is the lost wages and profits each year due to slower post-recession growth.

Debt is meaningless as a measure of generational burdens, in spite of deficit hawks' portrayal of it as such. They have never even tried to calculate the cost borne by the public due to government-granted patent monopolies. These raise the price of drugs and other protected items by several thousand percent above the free market price.

These are effectively privately collected taxes. Anyone honestly concerned about burdens imposed on the young would be hugely concerned about these monopolies, which cost close to $400 billion a year in prescription drugs alone. The complete lack of interest in patent monopolies shows the deficit hawks are not motivated by issues of generational fairness.

Continued from p. 716

Congress was unable to agree on a spending bill, in 2013, the government closed for 16 days. Some 800,000 federal workers were furloughed and the shutdown cost the government $24 billion in lost revenues and productivity, according to the Standard & Poor's rating agency. [55]

Technically, Congress is supposed to pass a budget and then 12 appropriations bills that detail new spending levels for the new fiscal year, and it is to do all of that by the end of September. But that has not been the case in recent years, and Congress often resorts to passing a "continuing resolution" that essentially funds government agencies at current levels for a set amount of time, typically three or six months.

Many lawmakers expect a stopgap spending bill will be necessary in late September to keep the government open while Congress continues to debate the fiscal 2018 budget.

"The [2018] process will be extremely difficult and truncated, and it will make work harder, and we may well find ourselves back here in a matter of months asking for some kind of brief extension," Rep. Tom Cole, R-Okla., chairman of the House Appropriations Committee's Labor, Health and Human Services and Education Subcommittee, said in May. [56]

In May the White House proposed a 2018 budget with $3.6 trillion in spending cuts, many of them to programs for low-income Americans. A president's budget proposal, however, is mostly a statement of priorities that Congress often disregards, and that seems to be the case this year too. [57] Given the limited number of days Congress will be in session in September — just 12 for the House — a continuing resolution is probable. [58]

> ## "The [2018 budget] process will be extremely difficult and truncated, and it will make work harder, and we may well find ourselves back here in a matter of months asking for some kind of brief extension."
>
> — *Rep. Tom Cole, R-Okla.,*
>
> *Chairman, House Appropriations Committee's Labor,*
>
> *Human Services and Education Subcommittee*

Border Wall

Another potential stumbling block to keeping the government's lights on is Trump's proposed border wall with Mexico. Congressional Democrats steadfastly oppose funding the wall, but the president and his budget director, Mick Mulvaney, are determined to include money for it in any spending bill for the new fiscal year and say they may shut down the government if that is what it takes to force Democrats to comply. Sixty votes are required in the Senate to pass a spending bill, and the chamber has only 52 Republicans, so eight Democratic votes are needed.

Conservative Republicans in the House say they may support a government shutdown to get the wall funding through. [59]

More worrisome to financial markets will be the debt ceiling. The national debt is now bumping up against the current limit on borrowing imposed by Congress, so the Treasury Department since March has been resorting to so-called "extraordinary measures," which give it a small amount of extra borrowing capacity while it awaits a legislative increase to the debt ceiling (or a suspension of the limit for a set amount of months). [60] But Treasury is expected to exhaust those measures sometime in October. [61]

The debt ceiling issue will dominate political headlines in coming weeks as Congress nears the so-called "X" date when Treasury runs completely out of borrowing capacity and can no longer meet all of its obligations. Failing to increase the debt limit by that date could create an international financial crisis because of the central place U.S. government debt holds in the global economy. On July 28 Treasury Secretary Steven Mnuchin informed House Speaker Paul Ryan, R-Wis., that the limit needs to be raised by Sept. 29. [62]

The problem with raising the borrowing limit is that many conservative Republican lawmakers want to attach new spending cuts or restraints to any bill that raises borrowing limits, and that may scuttle any such legislation.

Shutting down the government or allowing some kind of government default would be a disaster for the White House and congressional Republicans, who, after failing to pass a health care bill this year, are desperate to show they can govern effectively, says Pete Davis, a Washington-based economic consultant and longtime budget analyst. In early August Rep. Mark Meadows, R-N.C., leader of the conservative Freedom Caucus in the House, eased some anxieties surrounding the issue. "I don't believe we should play around with the full faith and credit of our country," said Meadows. "I'm bullish on getting it done." [63]

Most Republicans in Congress want to avoid both a shutdown and a default on government debt, says Davis. "Congress won't have an easy time funding the government or suspending or increasing the debt limit, but it will get done by midnight on Sept. 30."

Tax Reform

In the best-case scenario, after dealing with the budget and debt limit, congressional leaders will get to work on tax reform. The Republican strategy on taxes has evolved over the course of the year, but as of early August the plan seemed to be to complete and pass a bill by the end of this year. To do that, the House will act first, taking up a tax bill when it returns from the August recess (while also working on the budget and the debt ceiling).

According to this ambitious schedule, House lawmakers will use September to write, debate and pass a tax reform bill. Then the Senate in October will take up the House bill, debate it, make changes and pass it in November. [64] After that, the two chambers would have to reconcile their two bills, which means a small group of lawmakers from each chamber would meet and work out the differences, and then take a compromise bill back to each chamber for a last vote. If a final bill is agreed upon, President Trump is expected to quickly sign it.

But many analysts doubt Congress can pass fundamental tax reform in that abbreviated time frame, if at all. Davis says passage of a tax bill this year is unlikely "because potential losers have enough political power to kill it." They include small businesses and partnerships that file taxes through the individual tax code but will demand the same tax rate as corporations.

They also include farmers and real estate executives, both of whom rely on debt to stay in business. They will likely fight any bill that eliminates the deduction for interest payments on business expenses. And many lawmakers in both parties will oppose any bill that adds significantly to deficits or cuts taxes for the rich, says Davis. "Any one of these issues could kill the bill, particularly in the Senate," he says.

Tax Analysts' Sullivan predicts Congress will act on a bill that merely cuts taxes without changing the code in any significant way. Republicans will find it difficult to offset those cuts, he says, and so will resort to accounting smoke and mirrors to make the bill appear less damaging in terms of deficits. Those maneuvers would probably include overly optimistic assumptions about future economic growth, which could increase tax revenue assumptions, and so-called dynamic scoring, which assumes that tax cuts pay for themselves by juicing the economy, as well as various accounting tricks, Sullivan says.

"The path of least resistance to passing a tax cut bill is to use some sort of gimmicks, and there are four or five pretty good ones" that can make a tax cut bill look much less costly in terms of deficits, says Sullivan. "They wouldn't pass the smell test with tax analysts like me, but they are good enough to get you through the 6 o'clock news."

Meanwhile, the Federal Reserve is on a course of raising interest rates, which eventually will push up interest rates on government bonds. The Congressional Budget Office projects net interest costs will more than double over the next 10 years, from $269 billion this year to $818 billion in 2027. [65]

Interest costs are expected to continue climbing, according to the Peterson Foundation, a New York organization that advocates for a sustainable long-term fiscal path, and are projected

to be the third-largest category in the federal budget by 2028 (after Social Security and Medicare), the second-largest category in 2046 and the single largest in 2050. [66]

"Ballooning interest costs threaten to crowd out important public investments that can fuel economic growth in the future," according to Peterson. "By 2046, interest costs are projected to be more than double what the federal government has historically spent on research and development, nondefense infrastructure, and education, combined." ∎

OUTLOOK

Cloudy Forecast

If little changes in terms of spending and revenue policies and economic growth, the CBO projections are a probably a good estimation of what will happen to the budget over the next decade, says the Concord Coalition's Bixby. The deficit in 2027 would be 5 percent of GDP and the debt held by the public at almost 90 percent — on a course to exceed 100 percent of GDP six years later. And interest paid on the debt will nearly double as a percentage of the economy, from 1.4 percent to 2.7 percent. [67]

"In five to 10 years, I suspect we will still be in the same place we are in today," says the University of Connecticut's Kwak. He predicts the long-term debt outlook will worsen due to unfunded tax cuts Congress may pass and per capita health care costs that will continue to rise. "The two parties will each have their reasons for ignoring the issue — Republicans because they want to keep taxes low, Democrats because they do not want to reduce the size of government," he says.

There are, however, a few positive trends that, if allowed to play out, may deliver more control over rising health care costs, says budget expert Steuerle at the Urban Institute.

For example, the Independent Payment Advisory Board, a panel of health care experts established by the Affordable Care Act, could make a difference. If the growth of per capita spending in Medicare exceeds a certain level — and it is expected to do so this year — the board is supposed to make cost-cutting recommendations to Congress, and those recommendations will automatically take effect unless Congress makes alternative and equal savings elsewhere. [68] Because Congress has been unable to pass legislation to roll back any of Obama's health care law, the board remains in place and Trump may be legally obligated to appoint members to it. [69] Conservatives have been particularly hostile to the board, however, labeling it a "death panel" that seeks to ration — and therefore potentially deny some people — health care. [70]

Also, Congress may take small measures to cut deficits, such as trimming Medicare modestly in various ways and continuing to nip at domestic discretionary spending, says Steuerle.

It's also possible that the economy will exceed expectations, which would help reduce the ratio of deficits and the debt to GDP. Right now the Congressional Budget Office expects GDP growth on average to be about 1.9 percent from 2018 to 2027, while the Trump administration assumes a far higher rate of growth, at 3 percent. [71]

Forecasting the economy's performance that many years in the future is notoriously difficult, so both estimates may be wildly wrong. But many economists say multiple constraints on the economy make the White House outlook appear far too optimistic. [72]

According to CBO estimates cited by Tax Analysts economist Sullivan, every additional 0.1 percentage point of GDP growth brings $280 billion in extra deficit reduction over 10 years. "The administration's emphasis on growth is correct," says Sullivan. "If you can get to 3 percent growth, your problems get a lot easier, but I'm not expecting it." ∎

Notes

[1] "The Debt to the Penny and Who Holds It," TreasuryDirect, Aug. 1, 2017, https://tinyurl.com/z5tz3ux; "An Update to the Budget and Economic Outlook: 2017 to 2027," Congressional Budget Office, June 29, 2017, Table 1, https://tinyurl.com/ya2xwnzq.

[2] "The 2017 Long-Term Budget Outlook," Congressional Budget Office, March 30, 2017, https://tinyurl.com/mubxx97.

[3] Alex Planes, "Is the United States the World's Most Indebted Country? Not Even Close," *Motley Fool*, March 15, 2014, https://tinyurl.com/yahhynya.

[4] "Monthly Statement of the Public Debt of the United States," U.S. Treasury, June 20, 2017, https://tinyurl.com/y9rlrnlf.

[5] Kimberly Amadeo, "U.S. Debt to China: How Much Does It Own?" TheBalance.com, July 20, 2017, http://tinyurl.com/jj4wjax.

[6] "An Update to the Budget and Economic Outlook: 2017 to 2027," *op. cit.*

[7] Christopher J. Goodman and Steven M. Mance, "Employment loss and the 2007-09 recession: an overview," Bureau of Labor Statistics, April 2011, https://tinyurl.com/y8jpzr77; "Labor Force

Statistics from the Current Population Survey: Unemployment Rate," Bureau of Labor Statistics, July 31, 2017, https://tinyurl.com/zyq5xlx.

[8] Kimberly Amadeo, "What Was Obama's Stimulus Package?" *The Balance*, July 1, 2017, https://tinyurl.com/jule7xw.

[9] Barbara A. Friedberg, "Are We in a Baby Boomer Retirement Crisis?" *Investopedia*, June 7, 2017, https://tinyurl.com/k9v7uzc.

[10] "The 2017 Budget and Economic Outlook: Presentation by Keith Hall, CBO Director, to the Prosperity Caucus," Congressional Budget Office, May 30, 2017, https://tinyurl.com/y8efyvjn.

[11] Mira Norton *et al.*, "Medicare and Medicaid at 50," Henry J. Kaiser Family Foundation, July 17, 2015, https://tinyurl.com/ybksetbu.

[12] David Wessel, "Secular Stagnation even truer today, Larry Summers says," Brookings Institution, May 30, 2017, https://tinyurl.com/ydblyef4.

[13] Alexander Bolton, "GOP debates tax cuts vs. tax reform," *The Hill*, Aug. 9, 2017, https://tinyurl.com/y9j3b9j9.

[14] James R. Nunns *et al.*, "An Analysis of Donald Trump's Revised Tax Plan," Tax Policy Center, Oct. 18, 2016, https://tinyurl.com/zdyvudh.

[15] Carmen M. Reinhart and Kenneth S. Rogoff, "Growth in a Time of Debt," Working Paper 15639, National Bureau of Economic Research, January 2010, https://tinyurl.com/d54yyov.

[16] "General government debt," Organisation of Economic Co-operation and Development, 2015, https://tinyurl.com/pk86w59.

[17] Barry Eichengreen, *Exorbitant Privilege: The Rise and Fall of the Dollar and the Future of the International Monetary System* (2011), p. 4.

[18] "Currency Composition of Official Foreign Exchange Reserves," International Monetary Fund, March 31, 2017, https://tinyurl.com/h94udm8.

[19] Eichengreen, *op. cit.*, p. 4.

[20] Letter from the Secretary of the Treasury to Speaker Ryan, July 28, 2017, https://tinyurl.com/yb7xlnkt.

[21] "An Update to the Budget and Economic Outlook: 2017 to 2027," *op. cit.*

[22] "The 2017 Long-Term Budget Outlook," *op. cit.*, Table 1.

[23] *Ibid.*

[24] "Options for Reducing the Deficit: 2017 to 2026," CBO, December 2016, https://tinyurl.com/y9nc8zho.

[25] "About Americans for Tax Reform," Americans for Tax Reform, https://tinyurl.com/capmyju.

[26] Peter Baker, "Arthur Laffer's Theory on Tax Cuts Comes to Life Once More," *The New York Times*, April 25, 2017, https://tinyurl.com/y9cb6v2o.

[27] Lori Montgomery and Paul Kane, "Debt ne-

About the Author

Matthew K. Benjamin is a freelance journalist covering economic, fiscal and trade policy. He also is an editorial consultant at the World Bank and the International Monetary Fund. He lives in the Washington, D.C., area with his wife and two sons.

gotiations collapse between Obama, Boehner," *The Washington Post*, July 23, 2011, https://tinyurl.com/y9snlky9.

[28] "Options for Reducing the Deficit: 2017 to 2026," Table 1.1., *op. cit.*

[29] C. Eugene Steuerle, *Dead Men Ruling: How to Restore Fiscal Freedom and Rescue Our Future* (2014).

[30] Simon Johnson and James Kwak, *White House Burning: Our National Debt and Why It Matters to You* (2013).

[31] Steuerle, *op. cit.*, p. 28.

[32] "From Alexander Hamilton to Robert Morris, [30 April 1781]," Founders Online, https://tinyurl.com/y8scnvmj.

[33] "So, What Was the Whiskey Rebellion, Anyway?" George Washington's Mount Vernon, https://tinyurl.com/yaugastk.

[34] "1790: Hamilton, First Report on Public Credit," Online Library of Liberty, https://tinyurl.com/y829hds2.

[35] Matt Phillips, "The Long Story of U.S. Debt, from 1700 to 2011, in 1 Little Chart," *The Atlantic*, Nov. 13, 2012, https://tinyurl.com/y73vu4fl.

[36] Steuerle, *op. cit.*, p. 26.

[37] *Ibid.*, p. 28.

[38] "Debt and deficit facts," Usgovernmentspending.com, https://tinyurl.com/yarvavao.

[39] Steuerle, *op. cit.*, p. 38.

[40] "We're All Keynesians Now," *The Wall Street Journal*, Jan. 18, 2008, https://tinyurl.com/y7ucnqsh.

[41] "Nixon and the End of the Bretton Woods System, 1971-1973," Office of the Historian, U.S. Department of State, https://tinyurl.com/par9qz7.

[42] Johnson and Kwak, *op. cit.*, p. 42.

[43] "An Update to the Budget and Economic Outlook: 2017 to 2027," Table 1, *op. cit.*

[44] Steuerle, *op. cit.*, p. 46.

[45] Johnson and Kwak, *op. cit.*, p. 64.

[46] "1990 Budget Enforcement Act," Slaying the Dragon of Debt, Bancroft Library, University of California, Berkeley, https://tinyurl.com/ycy4maka.

[47] "An Update to the Budget and Economic Outlook: 2017 to 2027," Table 1, *op. cit.*

[48] *Ibid.*

[49] Johnson and Kwak, *op. cit.*, p. 98.

[50] "An Update to the Budget and Economic Outlook: 2017 to 2027," Table 1, *op. cit.*

[51] "The Budget Control Act of 2011," Congressional Research Service, Aug. 19, 2011, https://tinyurl.com/y92uruyc.

[52] "Bipartisan Budget Act of 2013," Congressional Budget Office, Dec. 10, 2013, https://tinyurl.com/yc5rdgzk.

[53] Jim Geraghty, "The Death of the Tea Party,"

National Review, Jan. 19, 2016, https://tinyurl.com/yahv428n.

[54] Jonathan Easley, "Trump fumes as presidency hits 200 days," TheHill.com, Aug. 7, 2017, https://tinyurl.com/ybmonb22.

[55] Kirsten Appleton and Veronica Stracqualursi, "Here's What Happened the Last Time the Government Shut Down," ABC News, Nov. 18, 2014, https://tinyurl.com/zbsf3hf.

[56] Nancy Ognanovich, "FY 2018 Starts Now, With 10 Takeaways From Omnibus Spending Deal," Bloomberg BNA, May 8, 2017, https://tinyurl.com/ya42og7g.

[57] Erik Wasson *et al.*, "Trump's Budget Bites Deeply Into Programs Benefiting His Voters," Bloomberg News, May 22, 2017, https://tinyurl.com/ybtlzw8o.

[58] Ognanovich, *op. cit.*

[59] Seung Min Kim, Rachael Bade and John Bresnahan, "White House pitches deal for wall money — and no shutdown," *Politico*, Aug. 9, 2017, https://tinyurl.com/y896wqrj.

[60] Shai Akabas *et al.*, "BPC Narrows 'X-Date' Forecast to Early to Mid-October," Bipartisan Policy Center, July 12, 2017, https://tinyurl.com/ycnog3lc.

[61] *Ibid.*

[62] Letter from the Secretary of the Treasury to Speaker Ryan, *op. cit.*

[63] Anna Edgerton and Erik Wasson, "Debt-Limit Battle Eases on Reassurances From House Conservative," Bloomberg News, Aug.

2, 2017, https://tinyurl.com/ycpe5taw.

[64] Lisa Desjardins, "A (quick) guide to the upcoming battle over tax reform," PBS NewsHour, Aug. 1, 2017, https://tinyurl.com/y9rrnxoy.

[65] "An Update to the Budget and Economic Outlook: 2017 to 2027," Table 1, *op. cit.*

[66] "Higher Interest Rates Will Raise Interest Costs on the National Debt," Peter G. Peterson Foundation, Dec. 14, 2016, https://tinyurl.com/h4t74h9.

[67] "An Update to the Budget and Economic Outlook: 2017 to 2027," Table 1, *op. cit.*

[68] "Report: IPAB likely will be triggered in 2017; Medicare trust fund will remain solvent until 2028," Advisory Board, June 23, 2016, https://tinyurl.com/y9potjlg.

[69] Erin Mershon, "Trump administration may have to convene board that inspired 'death panel' fears," *Stat News*, July 12, 2017, https://tinyurl.com/ycxqvf47.

[70] Edward Woodson, "Death Panels: Obamacare IPAB Repeal Can't Wait Three Years," *The American Spectator*, Dec. 9, 2016, https://tinyurl.com/ycple7lb.

[71] Damian Paletta *et al.*, "Forecast of weak economic growth raises big questions about Trump's populist agenda," *The Washington Post*, July 13, 2017, https://tinyurl.com/yd6kw7s5.

[72] Chris Isidore, "Reality check on Trump's economic growth forecasts," CNN Money, May 24, 2017, https://tinyurl.com/ybmms42m.

Bibliography

Selected Sources

Books

Eichengreen, Barry, *Exorbitant Privilege: The Rise and Fall of the Dollar and the Future of the International Monetary System*, Oxford University Press, 2011.
A University of California, Berkeley professor traces the rise of the dollar in the international economy and the challenges to the U.S. currency's dominant global role.

Johnson, Simon, and James Kwak, *White House Burning: Our National Debt and Why It Matters to You*, Vintage Books, 2013.
An MIT business professor (Johnson) and a University of Connecticut law school professor examine the national debt from the Revolutionary War through the Obama administration.

Steuerle, C. Eugene, *Dead Men Walking: How to Restore Fiscal Freedom and Rescue Our Future*, The Century Foundation Press, 2014.
An economist and fellow at the Urban Institute think tank in Washington takes a unique look at the debt and the constraints it imposes on the nation's fiscal choices.

Wessel, David, *Red Ink: Inside the High-Stakes Politics of the Federal Budget*, Crown Business, 2012.
The director of the Hutchins Center on Fiscal and Monetary Policy at the Brookings Institution think tank and former economics editor at *The Wall Street Journal* provides an insightful look at the budget process and the causes of annual deficits.

Articles

Baker, Peter, "Arthur Laffer's Theory on Tax Cuts Comes to Life Once More," *The New York Times*, April 25, 2017, https://tinyurl.com/y76r3pm5.
The 1970s idea that tax cuts pay for themselves by stimulating economic growth and thus tax revenues has reemerged among Trump administration officials.

Paletta, Damian, and Kelsey Snell, "Action on Trump's tax cut plan could be delayed until next year," *The Washington Post*, Aug. 1, 2017, https://tinyurl.com/y7x29swh.
The Trump White House hopes to push major tax reform legislation through Congress this year, but the need to pass a spending bill to keep the government funded and legislation to raise the amount of debt the Treasury can issue may push the process into 2018 or beyond.

Paletta, Damian, "Debt-Ceiling talks between White House, Senate break up with no progress," *The Washington Post*, Aug. 1, 2017, https://tinyurl.com/ybs4e9bz.
Congress must pass legislation to raise the debt ceiling by the end of September, but at the moment there is no consensus in Washington on how to do it.

Kim, Seung Min, and Rachael Bade, "GOP clash looms over raising the debt ceiling," *Politico*, Aug. 3, 2017, https://tinyurl.com/yacc434z.
Conservative Republicans demand that any debt ceiling bill must have accompanying spending cuts, yet Republican leaders believe that agreement on cuts may not be possible, adding to the legislation's difficulties.

Geraghty, Jim, "The Death of the Tea Party," *National Review*, Jan. 19, 2016, https://tinyurl.com/yahv428n.
The Tea Party, vocal and powerful in the Republican Party in 2009-2010, has since quieted. It is unclear why, but the author presents several possible reasons.

Reports and Studies

"An Update to the Budget and Economic Outlook: 2017 to 2027," Congressional Budget Office, June 29, 2017, https://tinyurl.com/yccmzwzd.
The CBO takes one of its periodic looks at the nation's finances, including budget deficits and the projections for economic growth, and the interaction between the two key economic indicators.

"Federal Debt and the Statutory Limit, June 2017," Congressional Budget Office, June 2017, https://tinyurl.com/y8b8amkg.
The nonpartisan federal agency provides an update plus some history of the legislative limit on Treasury borrowing.

"Fitch: Debt Limit, Government Funding to Test US Policy Makers," Fitch Ratings, United States of America, Aug. 23, 2017, http://tinyurl.com/ya29pdkx.
The ratings agency offers its most recent opinion about what may happen this year when Congress faces deadlines to address the debt ceiling and agree to new spending levels for fiscal 2018.

"Options for Reducing the Deficit: 2017 to 2026," Congressional Budget Office, December 2016, https://tinyurl.com/y87pch8z.
The CBO presents many options, including multiple types of spending cuts and tax increases, that it says could help reduce future budget deficits.

Austin, D. Andrew, "The Debt Limit: History and Recent Increases," Congressional Research Service, Nov. 2, 2015, http://tinyurl.com/yc4rh5th.
The Congressional Research Service provides a comprehensive history of the federal debt limit and recent episodes when Congress struggled to raise it.

Reinhart, Carmen M., and Kenneth S. Rogoff, "Growth in a Time of Debt," NBER Working Paper 15639, https://tinyurl.com/d54yyov.
Two prominent economists look into the relationship between government debt and economic growth.

The Next Step:

Additional Articles from Current Periodicals

Medicare Reform

Metz, Cade, "A Bipartisan Plan For Modest, But Important, Long-Term Care Financing Reform," *Forbes,* July 12, 2017, https://tinyurl.com/yc8yo5ve.

With Medicare and other entitlement programs driving up the national debt, the Bipartisan Policy Center, a Washington think tank, is advocating a series of reforms of Medicare.

Miller, Mark, "Republicans' next health reform act targets Medicare," Reuters, July 27, 2017, https://tinyurl.com/yawyckos.

To control costs and slow the rise in the national debt, House Republicans are considering making Medicare an annual voucher that people would use to buy health insurance.

Stein, Jeff, "Inside Bernie Sanders's campaign to save Obamacare," *Vox,* Aug. 7, 2017, https://tinyurl.com/y7r9l8wn.

While conservatives want to cut entitlement programs to lower annual deficits, Sen. Bernie Sanders, an independent from Vermont, proposes something different: creating universal health insurance by making Medicare available to all.

Partisan Divisions

Parkinson, John, and Miriam Khan, "Debt limit may be biggest test for House Speaker Paul Ryan's leadership," ABC News, Aug. 8, 2017, https://tinyurl.com/y8wq4t6m.

Because of internal party divisions, Republicans who want to raise the $19.8 trillion debt limit will likely have to work with congressional Democrats to get the increase passed.

Stein, Harry, "Congress must repeal the debt limit so no party can take it hostage," *The Hill,* July 25, 2017, https://tinyurl.com/ybnw3azu.

The brinkmanship over the debt ceiling should end once and for all, argues the director of fiscal policy at the Center for American Progress, a liberal policy group in Washington.

Yglesias, Matthew, "The looming debt ceiling fight, explained," *Vox,* Aug. 9, 2017, https://tinyurl.com/y79nlkb4.

With the deadline nearing to raise the debt ceiling, both parties in Congress are facing tough choices.

Reform Ideas

Cantow, Caroline, "Voices: College students should be very worried about the national debt. Here's why," *USA Today,* March 20, 2017, https://tinyurl.com/y7qf6ptj.

Millennials have the most to lose from national debt and must get to work finding solutions, a college student argues.

Rendell, Ed, and Judd Gregg, "Opinion: How to Fix the Debt Once and for All," *Roll Call,* March 10, 2017, https://tinyurl.com/yb63zsbz.

A former Democratic governor of Pennsylvania (Rendell) and former Republican U.S. senator from New Hampshire (Gregg) urge establishing a commission to forge a bipartisan solution to the national debt problem.

Tisch, Andrew, "The debt ceiling is dumb — and dangerous," CNN, July 20, 2017, https://tinyurl.com/ydy3aal5.

To end the grandstanding surrounding the debt ceiling, Congress should pursue a "grand fiscal bargain," says the co-chairman of Loews Corp., who is a co-founder of No Labels, a political reform group seeking bipartisan solutions to national problems.

Tax Reform

Gleckman, Howard, "The Deep Gulf Between Democrats and Republicans Over Tax Legislation," *Forbes,* Aug. 1, 2017, https://tinyurl.com/y8k5c3js.

Despite Democrats' signals that they are willing to work with Republicans on tax reform, both sides remain far apart.

Killough, Ashley, "Four big things that could stand in the way of tax reform," CNN, Aug. 8, 2017, https://tinyurl.com/y7dpk6ea.

Passing a fiscal 2018 budget, raising the debt ceiling and negotiating how to offset revenue losses from tax cuts could inhibit Republicans from passing a tax reform bill this year.

Watson, Kathryn, "Conservative group launches $2.5 million ad campaign pushing GOP on tax reform," CBS News, Aug. 9, 2017, https://tinyurl.com/yc4dkc2x.

The conservative American Action Network is running advertisements in 24 congressional districts urging Congress to overhaul the tax code.

CITING *CQ* RESEARCHER

Sample formats for citing these reports in a bibliography include the ones listed below. Preferred styles and formats vary, so please check with your instructor or professor.

MLA STYLE

Mantel, Barbara. "Coal Industry's Future." CQ Researcher 17 June 2016: 529-552.

APA STYLE

Mantel, B. (2016, June 17). Coal Industry's Future. *CQ Researcher,* 6, 529-552.

CHICAGO STYLE

Mantel, Barbara. "Coal Industry's Future." *CQ Researcher,* June 17, 2016, 529-52.

In-depth Reports on Issues in the News

Are you writing a paper?

Need backup for a debate?

Want to become an expert on an issue?

For 90 years, students have turned to *CQ Researcher* for in-depth reporting on issues in the news. Reports on a full range of political and social issues are now available. Following is a selection of recent reports:

Civil Liberties
Privacy and the Internet, 12/15
Intelligence Reform, 5/15
Religion and Law, 11/14

Crime/Law
High-Tech Policing, 4/17
Forensic Science Controversies, 2/17
Jailing Debtors, 9/16
Decriminalizing Prostitution, 4/16
Restorative Justice, 2/16
The Dark Web, 1/16
Immigrant Detention, 10/15

Education
Charter Schools, 3/17
Civic Education, 2/17
Student Debt, 11/16
Apprenticeships, 10/16

Environment/Society
Muslims in America, 7/17
Funding the Arts, 7/17
Hunger in America, 7/17
Future of the Christian Right, 6/17
Trust in Media, 6/17
Anti-Semitism, 5/17

Health/Safety
Medical Marijuana, 7/17
Food Labeling, 6/17
Sports and Sexual Assault, 4/17
Reducing Traffic Deaths, 2/17
Opioid Crisis, 10/16

Politics/Economy
Redistricting Showdown, 8/17
North Korea Showdown, 5/17
Rethinking Foreign Aid, 4/17
Troubled Brazil, 4/17
Immigrants and the Economy, 2/17

Upcoming Reports

Universal Basic Income, 9/8/17   Medical Advances, 9/15/17   Climate Change and National Security, 9/22/17

ACCESS

CQ Researcher is available in print and online. For access, visit your library or www.cqresearcher.com.

STAY CURRENT

For notice of upcoming *CQ Researcher* reports or to learn more about *CQ Researcher* products, subscribe to the free email newsletters, *CQ Researcher Alert!* and *CQ Researcher News*: http://cqpress.com/newsletters.

PURCHASE

To purchase a *CQ Researcher* report in print or electronic format (PDF), visit www.cqpress.com or call 866-427-7737. Single reports start at $15. Bulk purchase discounts and electronic-rights licensing are also available.

SUBSCRIBE

Annual full-service *CQ Researcher* subscriptions—including 44 reports a year, monthly index updates, and a bound volume—start at $1,131. Add $25 for domestic postage.

CQ Researcher Online offers a backfile from 1991 and a number of tools to simplify research. For pricing information, call 800-818-7243 or 805-499-9774 or email librarysales@sagepub.com.

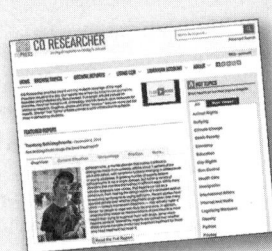

CQ RESEARCHER

CQPRESS

In-depth reports on today's issues

Published by CQ Press, an Imprint of SAGE Publications, Inc.   **www.cqresearcher.com**

Universal Basic Income

Would cash payments relieve job losses due to automation?

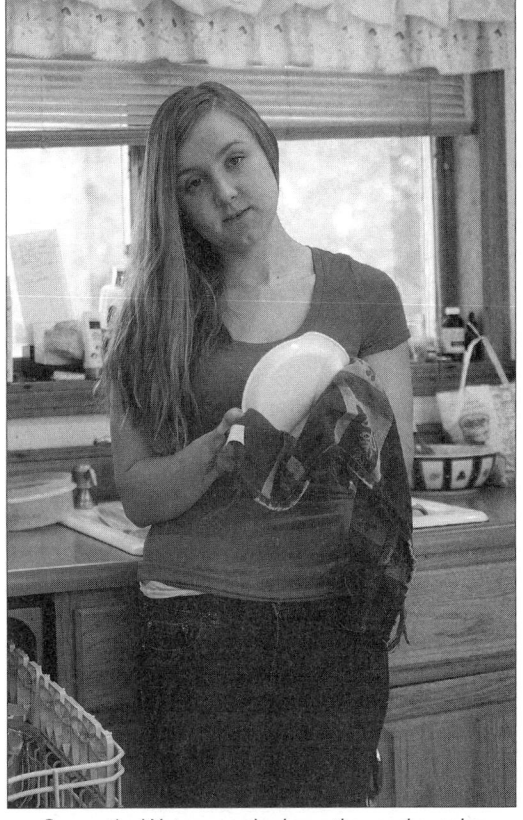

Samantha Watson, a single mother and nursing student in Parsonsfield, Maine, has received benefits from the nation's primary welfare program for low-income families, Temporary Assistance for Needy Families (TANF). Unlike TANF, which requires recipients to prove they are poor enough to qualify, the universal basic income envisioned by some proponents would provide all citizens with a fixed stipend, regardless of income.

T
he prospect of automation replacing workers has helped to revive an old idea: a government check covering basic expenses paid to everyone. Silicon Valley proponents say a guaranteed income — or universal basic income (UBI) — could be crucial in a future with less work to go around. The idea has won enthusiasts among libertarian conservatives who see it as a less bureaucratic alternative to welfare, and liberals who say it could combat inequality and wage stagnation. But UBI supporters on the right and left differ over whether to pay for it by diverting money spent on existing welfare programs or raising taxes. Others dismiss the idea outright, saying it would bust the budget and breed laziness. Still, trial efforts are underway in California, Finland and Canada to investigate whether free cash encourages idleness or, alternatively, boosts education and health — benefits found in 1970s-era American and Canadian experiments and among Alaskans and Native Americans sharing community wealth.

I N S I D E THIS REPORT

THE ISSUES **727**

BACKGROUND **734**

CHRONOLOGY **735**

CURRENT SITUATION **740**

AT ISSUE.....................**741**

OUTLOOK **743**

BIBLIOGRAPHY **746**

THE NEXT STEP **747**

CQ Researcher • Sept. 8, 2017 • www.cqresearcher.com
Volume 27, Number 31 • Pages 725-748

SAGE Publishing   CQPRESS
Los Angeles | London | New Delhi
Singapore | Washington DC | Melbourne

RECIPIENT OF SOCIETY OF PROFESSIONAL JOURNALISTS AWARD FOR EXCELLENCE ◆ AMERICAN BAR ASSOCIATION SILVER GAVEL AWARD

THE ISSUES

727 • Is a universal basic income with no conditions a good idea?
• Would a universal basic income improve quality of life?
• Can governments afford a universal basic income?

BACKGROUND

734 **Founding Ideas**
Thomas Paine proposed a guaranteed payment in 1797.

736 **War on Poverty**
Many economists recommended a basic income to help the poor.

738 **Early Experiments**
Between 1968 and 1980, the federal government tried a universal basic income (UBI) in selected states and cities.

CURRENT SITUATION

740 **New Interest**
Versions of a UBI are gaining support globally.

742 **State and Local Efforts**
Some states are debating distributing carbon-emission tax revenues.

742 **Modern Experiments**
Basic income trials are underway in a handful of countries.

OUTLOOK

743 **Basic Bootstraps**
Automation concerns have contributed to support for a basic income.

SIDEBARS AND GRAPHICS

728 **Automation Threatens Jobs Worldwide**
Most positions in developing nations are vulnerable.

729 **Europeans Back Basic Income — But Few Fully Grasp It**
Only one-fourth say they fully understand the concept.

732 **Most Alaskans Approve of Oil Profit Dividends**
Residents say the payments have improved their quality of life.

735 **Chronology**
Key events since 1797.

736 **Testing a Basic Income in Canada — Again**
A new effort is expected to produce results similar to those from a '70s-era trial.

738 **Finland Tests Basic Income for the Unemployed**
Critics call it a "publicity stunt" to get people to accept low-wage jobs.

741 **At Issue:**
Should the United States adopt a universal basic income?

FOR FURTHER RESEARCH

745 **For More Information**
Organizations to contact.

746 **Bibliography**
Selected sources used.

747 **The Next Step**
Additional articles.

747 **Citing CQ Researcher**
Sample bibliography formats.

Cover: Getty Images/*Portland Express Herald*/Brianna Soukup

Sept. 8, 2017
Volume 27, Number 31

EXECUTIVE EDITOR: Thomas J. Billitteri
tjb@sagepub.com

ASSISTANT MANAGING EDITORS: Kenneth Fireman, kenneth.fireman@sagepub.com, Kathy Koch, kathy.koch@sagepub.com, Scott Rohrer, scott.rohrer@sagepub.com

ASSOCIATE MANAGING EDITOR: Val Ellicott

SENIOR CONTRIBUTING EDITOR:
Thomas J. Colin
tom.colin@sagepub.com

CONTRIBUTING WRITERS: Marcia Clemmitt, Sarah Glazer, Reed Karaim, Barbara Mantel, Chuck McCutcheon, Tom Price

SENIOR PROJECT EDITOR: Olu B. Davis

EDITORIAL ASSISTANT: Natalia Gurevich

FACT CHECKERS: Eva P. Dasher, Michelle Harris, Betsy Towner Levine, Robin Palmer

SAGE Publishing | CQPRESS

Los Angeles | London | New Delhi
Singapore | Washington DC | Melbourne

An Imprint of SAGE Publications, Inc.

SENIOR VICE PRESIDENT, GLOBAL LEARNING RESOURCES:
Karen Phillips

EXECUTIVE DIRECTOR, ONLINE LIBRARY AND REFERENCE PUBLISHING:
Todd Baldwin

CQ Researcher (ISSN 1056-2036) is printed on acid-free paper. Published weekly, except: (March wk. 4) (May wk. 4) (July wks. 1, 2) (Aug. wks. 2, 3) (Nov. wk. 4) and (Dec. wks. 3, 4). Published by SAGE Publications, Inc., 2455 Teller Rd., Thousand Oaks, CA 91320. Annual full-service subscriptions start at $1,131. For pricing, call 1-800-818-7243. To purchase a *CQ Researcher* report in print or electronic format (PDF), visit www.cqpress.com or call 866-427-7737. Single reports start at $15. Bulk purchase discounts and electronic-rights licensing are also available. Periodicals postage paid at Thousand Oaks, California, and at additional mailing offices. POSTMASTER: Send address changes to *CQ Researcher*, 2600 Virginia Ave., N.W., Suite 600, Washington, DC 20037.

Universal Basic Income

BY SARAH GLAZER

THE ISSUES

Scott Santens, a freelance writer in New Orleans, is living a life some social reformers only dream about. Since last year he has been receiving $1,000 a month, no strings attached, from over 300 contributors via the crowdfunding website Patreon, which supports artists, musicians and bloggers.

"I'm able to focus on what I most want to do," Santens says, which is writing and advocating for an unconditional basic income, like the one he receives, for everyone. That financial freedom, he says, is possible because of the knowledge that he won't go hungry or homeless if no work comes his way.

As a longtime freelancer who started in Web design, the 40-year-old says, "I feel like I've been living the 'future of work' for my entire adult life," referring to the trend of people increasingly relying on part-time, short-term jobs with no benefits. "I don't have health care, I don't have unemployment insurance; I'm doing what I can to earn money each month. That's really the direction we're headed — alternative forms of work where people don't have these classical jobs for 40 hours a week."

The idea of a universal basic income (UBI) is gaining renewed attention from governments and Silicon Valley's tech industry, with experiments planned or ongoing in California, Canada, Finland, the Netherlands, Spain and Kenya. With advocates on both the right and left, support for a UBI springs from concerns that increasing automation and the growing gig economy could leave a

Facebook co-founder and CEO Mark Zuckerberg told the Harvard graduating class on May 25 that a universal basic income (UBI) should be explored "to make sure everyone has a cushion to try new ideas." Some Silicon Valley leaders advocate a UBI as a spur to entrepreneurship and as a solution to job instability, which they expect growing automation to exacerbate.

huge number of Americans without permanent jobs, as well as worries about growing income inequality, stagnating wages and rising welfare costs.

Others oppose the whole concept, saying it would cost too much and encourage idleness. And even supporters say a UBI is unlikely to be implemented anytime soon, in part because proponents disagree on how to pay for it.

The idea of a universal basic income is not new. Republican President Richard M. Nixon proposed a guaranteed income in the 1970s, but the idea died in Congress. Two long-standing unconditional

cash payment programs already exist in the United States, although neither is sufficient to cover living expenses. For the past 35 years, every Alaskan has received an annual dividend, ranging in recent years from about $1,000 to $2,000, derived from the state's oil revenues. And since 1997, every member of the Eastern Band of the Cherokee Nation has gotten a yearly cash dividend, ranging from $4,000 to $6,000, as their share of the tribe's casino profits. [1]

Ideally, according to proponents, a UBI is a periodic cash payment covering essential needs, paid to everyone, rich or poor, without any conditions attached. Advocates usually propose pegging it at or above the U.S. poverty level of about $12,000 a year for each individual. [2]

A variation that guarantees a minimum income, known as the negative income tax, was tested in government-run experiments in the United States and Canada in the 1970s. Under this approach, low-income individuals receive payments totaling the difference between their income and a basic income established for the experiment. Benefits are phased out as earned income rises.

Studies predicting that robots, artificial intelligence and new technologies — such as self-driving cars — will soon eliminate jobs involving cognition and judgment have intensified worries over the impact of automation on workers. A widely cited Oxford University study estimated that automation could replace 47 percent of U.S. jobs, although other analyses put the proportion far lower. [3] For instance, the Organisation for Economic Co-operation and Development

Getty Images/Paul Marotta

Automation Threatens Jobs Worldwide

The majority of jobs in developing nations such as China, Ethiopia and India are vulnerable to automation. Technological advances, such as the use of robots in manufacturing, are more likely to affect low- or semi-skilled workers than high-skilled ones, but they are putting high-skilled jobs at risk as well. As jobs disappear, advocates contend that governments should provide people with a basic income to keep them out of poverty.

Percentage of Workforce Potentially Affected by Automation, by Country

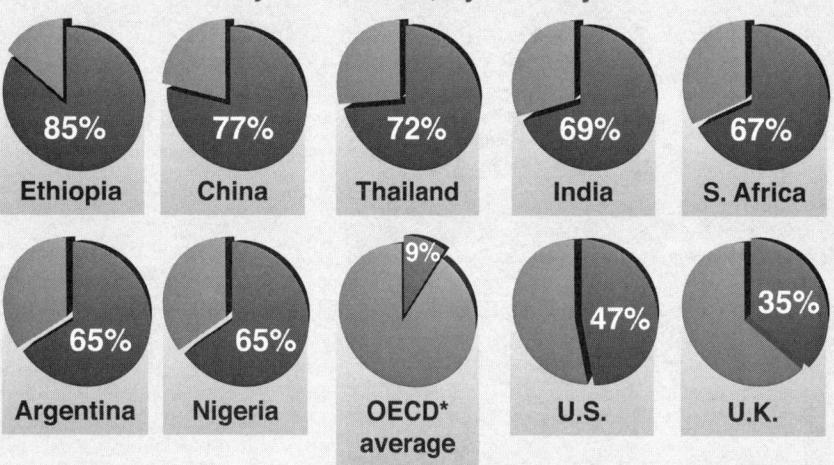

* Twenty-one nations belonging to the OECD (Organisation for Economic Co-operation and Development) were included in the average.

Sources: "Fear thy Robot: Chances of Workers Being Replaced by Automation Vary by Country," Statista, 2016, https://tinyurl.com/y8mrafgd; "The Risk of Automation for Jobs in OECD Countries," Organisation for Economic Co-operation and Development, May 14, 2016, http://tinyurl.com/zdbzkhz

(OECD), an economic research organization in Paris made up of 35 member countries, predicted that automation might replace only 9 percent of U.S. jobs, and the McKinsey Global Institute think tank, looking at the question globally, put the figure at less than 5 percent. [4]

Even without robots, the rapid growth of the so-called gig economy — based on temporary or part-time, nontraditional jobs that typically provide no benefits — is raising similar concerns. [5] Already, 40 percent of American workers are engaged in such "contingent" jobs, including standard part-time jobs and alternative work arrangements, according to the U.S. Government Accountability Office (GAO). [6] Some Silicon Valley leaders advocate a basic income as a solution to such job instability, which they expect growing automation to exacerbate, and as a spur to entrepreneurship. Facebook co-founder Mark Zuckerberg told the Harvard graduating class in May that a UBI should be explored "to make sure everyone has a cushion to try new ideas." [7]

Some in the tech industry think a free check could provide an unprecedented degree of creative and entrepreneurial freedom. Sam Altman, president of Y Combinator, a Mountain View, Calif., company that helps tech startups, is planning to test how people would use their time by giving $1,000

a month, no strings attached, to up to 3,000 individuals, starting next year.

"Fifty years from now . . . it will seem ridiculous that we used fear of not being able to eat as a way to motivate people," Altman said. [8]

Silicon Valley's interest is "one part optimism and one part guilt," for the jobs being eliminated by new technology and automation, says Natalie Foster, co-founder along with Facebook co-founder Chris Hughes of the Economic Security Project, a $10 million, two-year initiative to explore the feasibility of a universal basic income.

Former labor leader Andy Stern, who built the Service Employees International Union (SEIU) into the nation's second largest union before retiring from the union presidency in 2010, says a UBI could return to workers some of the bargaining power lost as labor unions have declined. And some libertarians are pushing for a basic income as an alternative to current welfare programs. Welfare degrades "the traditions of work, thrift and neighborliness," according to Charles Murray, a libertarian political scientist at the conservative American Enterprise Institute (AEI) think tank in Washington. [9]

Despite the unusual coalition of liberal and conservative supporters of a basic income, doubts remain that a UBI could ever be adopted, partly because advocates differ widely on how to fund it and whether it should replace all, some or no existing welfare programs. Others, also on both the right and left, oppose it outright.

Some opponents say a UBI would bust the federal budget. A UBI financed entirely by tax increases "would require the American people to accept a level of taxation that vastly exceeds anything in U.S. history," according to Robert Greenstein, president of the Center on Budget and Policy Priorities, a liberal anti-poverty think tank in Washington. [10] Paying every American $10,000 a year would cost more than $3 trillion — three-quarters of the entire federal

Europeans Back Basic Income — But Few Fully Grasp It

A majority of residents of the 28-nation European Union would support a referendum calling for a universal basic income (UBI) policy, but only about one in four say they fully understand the concept, according to a 2016 poll by Berlin-based Dalia Research. Countries such as Finland and the Netherlands already are considering some form of universal basic income.

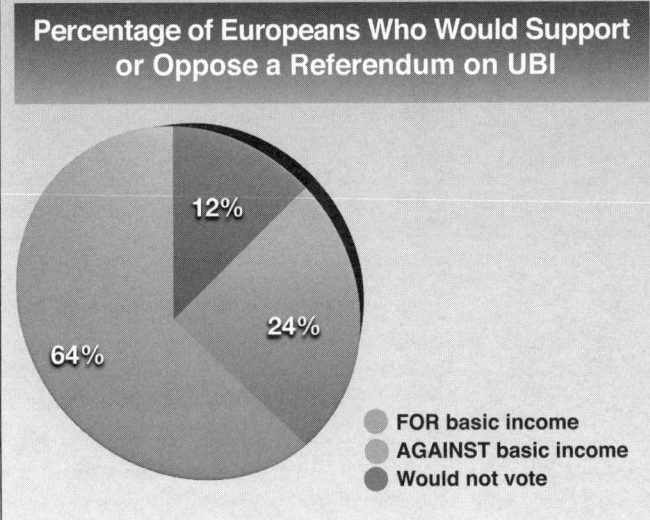

Percentage of Europeans Who Would Support or Oppose a Referendum on UBI

12%

24%

64%

- ● FOR basic income
- ● AGAINST basic income
- ● Would not vote

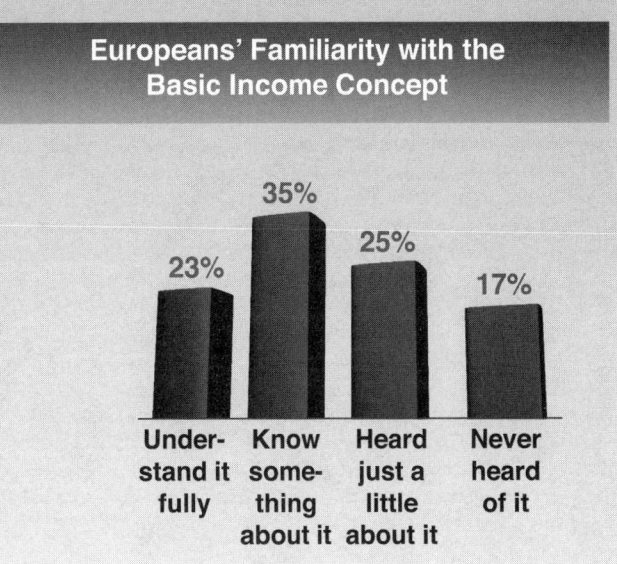

Europeans' Familiarity with the Basic Income Concept

23% — Understand it fully

35% — Know something about it

25% — Heard just a little about it

17% — Never heard of it

Source: "Europe: 64% of People in Favour of Basic Income, Poll Finds," Basic Income News, *May 22, 2016,* https://tinyurl.com/ybx4rppj

budget and equal to all current federal tax revenue, according to the center.

Providing a limited sum to all Americans, rich and poor, would likely increase political pressure to reduce current levels of welfare assistance and eliminate Social Security and other bedrock social programs, Greenstein has warned.

Pavlina Tcherneva, an economist at Bard College, in Annandale-on-Hudson, N.Y., says UBI money would be better spent on a guaranteed-job program, which could be reduced as unemployment falls. A UBI providing everyone a living wage would cost 20-35 percent of GDP, she says, but a program guaranteeing the unemployed a job would cost only 2-4 percent. (*See "At Issue," p. 741.*)

In addition, joblessness "affects one's psyche and well-being," she says, citing research linking stretches of unemployment to ill health.

Others say a UBI would encourage laziness. "We already know that unemployment benefits discourage people from working," wrote Daniel Mitchell, a senior fellow at the Cato Institute, a libertarian think tank in Washington that promotes a free-market ideology. "Why would anyone think we'll get better results if we give generous handouts to everyone?" [11]

However, a recent review of research on what people do with unconditional cash payouts — such as the Alaska and Cherokee dividends — found that, on average, recipients reduce the number of hours they work only slightly, if at all. The extra income also leads to improvements in education and health, according to the review, released by the Roosevelt Institute, a liberal think tank in New York City. [12]

Given such improvements in well-being, "If people choose to work a little less, then it's not clear you should

judge a decrease in work as a bad thing," says Ioana Marinescu, an economist at the University of Pennsylvania and author of the review.

Foster concedes that the idea of a universal basic income is "far off politically." Interim steps might get more political traction, she says, such as imposing a carbon tax on industrial polluters and returning the revenue to citizens, an idea favored by some environmentalists and some conservatives.

The conservative Niskanen Center think tank in Washington has proposed a universal annual federal benefit of $2,000 per child. [13] As a step toward that goal, the center supports an expanded child tax credit proposed by Sen. Marco Rubio, R-Fla. And Rep. Ro Khanna, a California Democrat who represents Silicon Valley, has suggested doubling the existing Earned Income Tax Credit, which reduces the amount of tax owed by low- and moderate-income workers. Workers whose credits exceed their tax liability receive a refund for the difference. [14]

As the nature of work changes radically, both work and welfare will need to be overhauled, say UBI proponents. "Ultimately we have to rewrite the social contract for the 21st century for the way people work today," says Foster.

As government officials, legislators, scholars and advocates for the poor

Michael Bohmeyer, an entrepreneur in Berlin, is conducting an experiment to explore whether a universal basic income (UBI) would be workable. In 2014 he founded Mein Grundeinkommen (My Basic Income), funded by crowd sourcing, which raffles off a one-year basic income of 1,000 euros a month to random individuals. A majority of residents of the 28-nation European Union would support a referendum calling for a UBI. Countries such as Finland and the Netherlands already are studying some form of UBI.

consider evolving U.S. economic and social trends, here are some of the questions being debated:

Is a universal basic income with no conditions a good idea?

The most radical feature of a universal basic income as envisioned by some proponents would be the absence of conditions on recipients. In contrast, most welfare programs today are "means-tested," requiring recipients to prove they are poor enough to qualify. And in-kind welfare, such as food stamps, can be exchanged only for specific types of groceries. [15]

Such conditions are paternalistic and invasive, UBI advocates say. Already, some welfare recipients trade food stamps for rent, indicating that current restrictions do not provide what people need, says Diane Pagen, a New York City social worker and co-founder of Basic Income Action, a national organization that advocates for a UBI. "I have thousands of stories where people could have solved their problem if someone [in the welfare system] had just handed them money," she says.

Under the nation's primary welfare program for low-income families, Temporary Assistance for Needy Families (TANF), states can spend their federal funds to promote a range of other goals such as encouraging marriage, instead of providing cash assistance. [16] "Poor people cannot eat these services," Pagen has objected. [17]

That trend has been increasing since Congress rewrote the nation's welfare law in 1996, turning it into a block grant program in which states had more

freedom in how they spend their TANF funds. Since then, the percentage of TANF funds distributed as cash assistance has dropped from 70 percent in 1997 to less than a quarter in 2015. [18]

In defense of imposing conditions on welfare recipients, AEI resident scholar Michael Strain wrote: "We need a little paternalism. If we take money from John to give to Matthew . . . then we owe it to John" to make sure the money is spent on food and shelter, "not on Matthew's alcohol and gambling." [19]

However, research on how members of the Eastern Band of the Cherokee Nation spend their casino dividends showed teen substance abuse and drug dealing declining among recipient families. [20] "You don't need to resort to those things" if you have economic security, researcher Marinescu says.

Some anti-poverty advocates say a UBI would increase both poverty and inequality by using welfare funds now spent on the poorest two-fifths of the population to provide cash to people of all income levels. The payments would have to be smaller than current welfare benefits, according to Greenstein, of the Center on Budget and Policy Priorities, if spread so widely. [21]

Komal Sri-Kumar, a senior fellow at the Milken Institute, a nonpartisan economic think tank in Santa Monica, Calif., has argued that a UBI could help alleviate stagnating low-income wages. And if everyone received a government check, it would reduce the "shame at receiving handouts," he wrote. [22]

That hypothesis was supported by a basic-income experiment known as MINCOME, conducted in Dauphin, a rural town in Canada's Manitoba Province, in the 1970s, according to a recent analysis of recipient surveys conducted at the time. The government automatically supplemented residents' income when it fell below a certain level, which happened periodically in a farming town subject to crop failures. Participants reported their income by mail monthly, without being subjected to "invasive and degrading caseworker discretion," writes David Calnitsky, a sociologist at the University of Manitoba. [23] (*See sidebar, p. 736.*)

Only 6 percent of MINCOME participants said they would accept welfare, which most viewed negatively. One resident thought welfare was for people "too lazy to work" but viewed MINCOME as a stopgap for when he was "short of money." Participation in MINCOME "did not produce social stigma," Calnitsky concludes, theorizing that occurred because the program was offered to all without distinguishing between the "deserving" and "undeserving" poor. [24]

Oren Cass, a senior fellow at the conservative Manhattan Institute think tank in New York City, rejects the whole UBI concept. "A UBI that reduces the perceived importance of work while putting cash in [young people's] pockets can only reduce the likelihood of their making the daily trek to low-wage jobs" — the first rung on the ladder to upward mobility, he wrote. [25]

The current conditions attached to government aid are rooted in widely shared American values about who deserves help, critics of an unconditional UBI maintain. "We had a problem of children who didn't have enough food to eat, so we started food stamps," says Strain. "We had elderly Americans dying in tenement houses, so we started Social Security."

Once lawmakers face large numbers of constituents with such problems, he predicts, "It wouldn't take long for a universal basic income to turn into our current safety net."

Would a universal basic income improve quality of life?

When the United States and Canada conducted the first guaranteed income experiments in the 1970s, politicians wanted to know if a basic stipend could be structured to encourage more welfare recipients to work. The experiments paid stipends only to low-income individuals and families, so the pay-

ments were not the population-wide, universal basic income favored by many advocates today.

Conventional wisdom held that welfare recipients were reluctant to take jobs because for every dollar they earned the government would reduce their welfare benefits by the same amount. To reduce that work disincentive, both governments created a variation of the so-called negative income

Former President Barack Obama said that the rise of technology and artificial intelligence has made consideration of a universal basic income inevitable. "Whether a universal income is the right model – is it gonna be accepted by a broad base of people? – that's a debate that we'll be having over the next 10 or 20 years," Obama told Wired magazine.

tax, generally deducting only 50 cents in benefits for every dollar earned. Benefits would be phased out once a recipient's income reached a specific level. [26] However, when the initial results of the largest portion of the U.S. experiment — in Seattle and Denver — were reported in the 1970s, congressional lawmakers were dismayed to learn that recipients apparently had worked less — not more.

Yet recent analyses of those results showed that recipients did not stop working in droves but simply reduced the number of hours they worked. And more recently, researchers have found that the extra income and freedom to work fewer hours may have improved

recipient families' quality of life.

In the U.S. experiments, which provided a family of four up to $25,900 a year in today's dollars, households reduced their work hours by about 13 percent across the programs in four states — New Jersey, Pennsylvania, Iowa, North Carolina — and in Seattle, Denver and Gary, Ind. [27] But male heads of households reduced their work hours by only about 7 percent.

The biggest reductions (17 percent) occurred among wives and single mothers. Teens also delayed entering the workforce and stayed in high school longer. [28]

Similarly, in the Canadian experiment in Dauphin, many women used the stipend to take longer maternity leaves, which "was also happening in the United States," says Evelyn Forget, a University of Manitoba economist whose influential 2011 analysis concluded the extra income improved quality of life in Dauphin. While it had been common for teenage boys from low-income families in Dauphin to drop out of high school to work, during the experiment they were more likely to graduate, For-

Most Alaskans Approve of Oil Profit Dividends

The majority of Alaska residents say an annual dividend they receive from the state has had a positive impact on their quality of life (top). The Permanent Fund Dividend (PFD), instituted in 1982 and ranging from about $1,000 to $2,000 per person, comes from profits from the state's oil revenues. Thirty percent of residents say they use the money — a low-pay variant of a basic income — to pay off credit card or other debt (bottom).

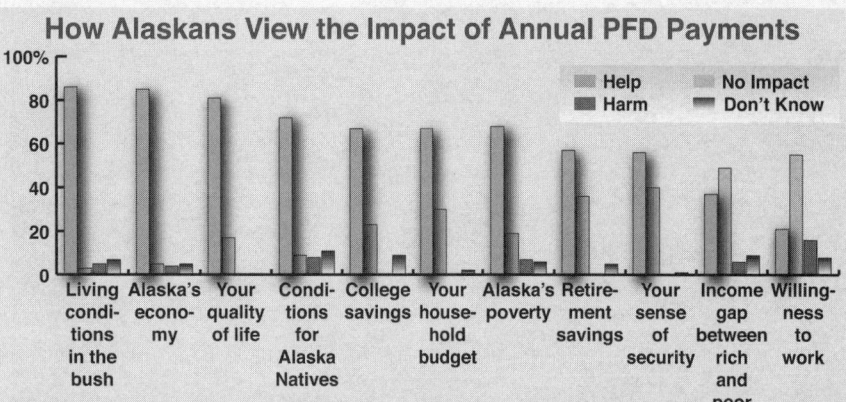

How Alaskans View the Impact of Annual PFD Payments

Source: "The 2017 Long-Term Budget Outlook," Congressional Budget Office, 2017, https://tinyurl.com/mubxx97

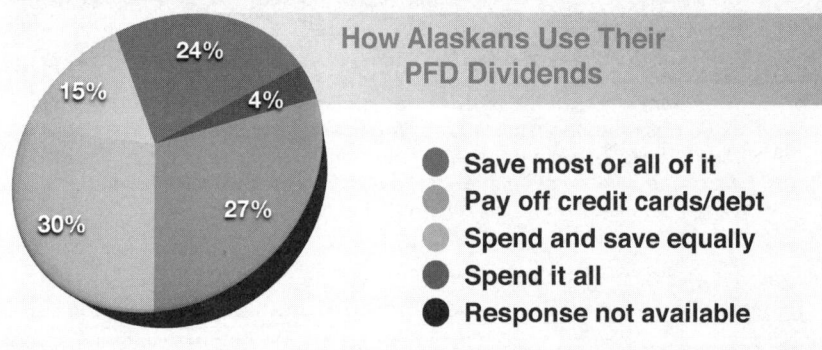

How Alaskans Use Their PFD Dividends

- Save most or all of it
- Pay off credit cards/debt
- Spend and save equally
- Spend it all
- Response not available

Source: "What a New Survey from Alaska Can Teach Us about Public Support for Basic Income," Economic Security Project, 2017, https://tinyurl.com/y9qlm8g9

get found. Families invested in their sons' education "to prepare for better lives going forward," she says.

A recent Roosevelt Institute study examining the 1970s experiments and the cash dividends paid to Alaskans and Cherokee tribal members concluded that the programs either had no impact on the number of hours recipients worked or resulted in only a moderate decrease. In Alaska, the study found, about 2 percent of recipients shifted to part-time work.

Overall, there was "a significant increase in other quality-of-life benefits," such as improved mental and physical health, increased education, better parenting and reduced criminal activity. [29]

Likewise, casino revenue payments to Cherokees improved mental health among tribal members, according to the study. The additional income for the poorest households led to an extra year of schooling.

And for the children of negative income tax recipients in the United States and Canada, school attendance, grades and test scores typically were higher than for similar families, especially among younger and poorer children. Child nutrition also improved in two rural states where residents received the extra income. [30]

While the early Canadian and U.S. experiments involved only low-income individuals and families, Bard economist Tcherneva warns that a truly universal stipend could spur "very disruptive" inflation. For example, if large numbers of workers were to quit their low-paid McDonald's job in response to more money in their pockets, McDonald's would have to raise wages to attract workers and raise hamburger prices to cover the higher labor costs. "Now their burger is three times more expensive, and the value of their basic income is eroded," she says.

Michael Howard, co-editor of the journal *Basic Income Studies* and a professor of philosophy at the University of Maine, counters that a guaranteed basic income would remunerate those who do a large amount of unpaid, socially valuable work, such as childcare and elder care. "Basic income is a way to address that without surveillance from the welfare state," says Howard.

But Philip Harvey, a professor of law and economics at Rutgers Law School in Camden, N.J., co-author of *America's Misunderstood Welfare State*, and an advocate of a job guarantee, says paid parental leave and a benefit check for every child would be more effective in allowing women to stay home with their children.

Many question what life would be like if it were no longer centered around paid work. But some UBI advocates say the stipend they're proposing, typically $1,000 a month, would only help cover essential needs and not be enough to provide a comfortable life.

American society is already shifting away from older generations' "work-centric" worldview, says former labor union leader Stern, now a senior fellow with the Economic Security Project, which funds research on UBI approaches. Younger people, who are having a hard time finding a stable job, "are not as impressed with the value of work," he says. "They work so they can do other things."

Middle-class parents already provide a form of basic income to their grown children — subsidizing their rent or covering emergency expenses, Stern points out. But poor people don't have that opportunity. "Having a regular monthly check . . . allows a woman in an abusive relationship to walk away," he says. And it "allows workers to walk away from a bad job."

Some advocates of a basic income, such as Stern, also point out that the tax code is rife with deductions that disproportionately benefit higher earners. Some of those loopholes could be plugged to finance a UBI. [31]

Can governments afford a universal basic income?

Estimates vary enormously on how much a UBI would cost, depending on how much recipients would receive, how it would be funded and — often — the ideological viewpoints of the proponents.

"A lot people on the left see UBI as an add-on to existing welfare programs; they don't want to cut any existing programs; they want to raise taxes. Folks on the libertarian, conservative end, say, 'Cash out existing programs and replace them,' " observes Michael Tanner, a senior fellow at the Cato Institute. Like many libertarians, Tanner says he could not support a UBI that required raising taxes.

At the far right end of the political spectrum, AEI scholar Murray proposes eliminating all federal and state welfare and social insurance programs, including Social Security and Medicare, as well as federal transfers — or subsidies — to "favored groups" such as farmers. That would save more than $2 trillion

Shianne Bowlang and her mother wait for groceries at a food bank in Welch, W. Va., on May 20. Some advocates for the needy say the nation's poorest would be worse off with a universal basic income (UBI) than under current safety net programs. The Center on Budget and Policy Priorities says that replacing food stamps, TANF, the earned income tax credit and Social Security with a UBI would plunge the poor deeper into poverty.

a year, he says, which he would then divide equally among all U.S. citizens ages 21 and up. That would provide enough to pay every adult an annual guaranteed income of $13,000, he calculates. [32] If such a UBI program had begun in 2014, it would have cost $212 billion a year less than existing income redistribution programs, Murray concludes. [33]

Many liberals dismiss Murray's proposal as impractical, largely because of the enormous popularity of Social Security. The scheme is more attractive to conservative libertarians, who share his view that, given all the millions spent on anti-poverty programs and the millions who are still in poverty, "Only a government can spend so much money so ineffectually." [34]

Sharing some of the same frustrations, former labor leader Stern has proposed eliminating some of the same welfare programs as has Murray. However, he would pay all 18- to 64-year-olds $12,000 a year while retaining Social Security, Medicare and Medicaid but scrapping food stamps, housing

assistance and the Earned Income Tax Credit. [35] To help pay for his program, costing up to $2.5 trillion per year, Stern proposes introducing new taxes, including a tax on financial transactions. [36]

Recently, basic income proponents have been eying other revenue sources that could help pay for a UBI, such as a carbon tax on air polluters, with some of the proceeds going to residents as rebates. [37] Such a tax could provide a rebate of about $160 a month — or $1,920 a year — for a family of four by 2032, according to a new study cited by an environmentalist-labor coalition pushing for a carbon tax in Washington, D.C. [38]

Although that amount would not cover essentials, it could help lower the cost of a basic income, say proponents. Boosting taxes on high-income Americans could help raise the rest, they say. [39]

Many experts doubt that even wealthy countries could afford a basic income. A recent OECD report found that in most rich countries, converting existing cash welfare programs to a universal income for everyone under 65 and leaving Social Security in place would only provide a stipend below the poverty level. Poverty rates would grow, the authors concluded, particularly among the unemployed and single parents, who now receive more in welfare than a UBI would provide. [40]

Some U.S. advocates for the poor agree that the very poorest would be worse off under a UBI than under current welfare programs. The Center on Budget and Policy Priorities estimates that more than 42 percent of Americans are lifted out of poverty by food stamps, TANF, the Earned Income Tax Credit and Social Security. [41] Replacing all or most of those safety-net programs would plunge the poor deeper into poverty, according to Greenstein, the center's president.

Alternatively, raising the basic income to the same level provided by most national welfare payments would require substantial tax increases, according to economist James Browne, who co-authored the OECD report. "The prospect of having to very significantly increase taxes would make it difficult for a government to introduce," he says.

In an editorial, the free-market *Economist* magazine condemned the UBI idea as "fantastically costly." The United States could afford to pay a basic income of $10,000 a year, the editorial said, only if it raised taxes to the same level as Germany's — equal to 35 percent of GDP instead of the current U.S. level of 26 percent — and replaced all existing welfare programs and Social Security. In addition, the editorial said, if wealthy countries adopted such a UBI, they would have to either close their borders to immigrants or create a second-class citizenry excluded from the benefits. [42]

"It just doesn't work," said Jason Furman, former chief economic adviser to President Barack Obama and now a professor at Harvard's Kennedy School of Government. "You would need to double the current income tax to make it work." [43]

Tanner, who calls himself a "sympathetic skeptic" when it comes to a UBI, says he hasn't figured out how it could be financed without raising taxes. For example, Tanner says Murray's basic income would pay for itself, but only because Murray would gradually tax back the stipend as a person's earned income rose above $30,000. By the time a recipient's outside earnings reached $60,000, the basic income would be slashed in half under Murray's approach. [44]

"If you do that you begin to create work disincentives," much like existing welfare programs, Tanner says. A 2013 Cato Institute study found that in 35 states a mother with two children participating in seven common welfare programs could receive more than what she would earn from a minimum-wage job. [45]

"Right now we do a reasonable job of taking care of material poverty but a poor job of making people masters of their own lives," says Tanner. "A UBI could potentially do both of those, but the devil is in the details." ∎

BACKGROUND

Founding Ideas

English radical Thomas Paine, who emigrated to America in 1774 and ardently supported the American Revolution, argued in a 1797 pamphlet, "Agrarian Justice," that each U.S. citizen should receive a basic financial stake upon reaching age 21 and an old-age pension upon reaching 50. Arguing that the Earth was "the common property of the human race," Paine proposed that every owner of cultivated lands be charged rent, which would fund the stipends and compensate citizens for the loss of their "natural inheritance." [46]

Although his proposal was never adopted, it has inspired advocates of a basic income for more than 200 years.

In 1848, German philosopher Karl Marx, in his *Manifesto of the Communist Party*, advocated the redistribution of wealth, an idea that would later become a tenet of communist governments and influence socialist movements worldwide.

To undermine support for socialism and build workers' support for the German empire, Chancellor Otto von Bismarck between 1883 and 1889 set up the first comprehensive system of compulsory workers' insurance, covering illness and old age. His approach helped lay the theoretical basis for programs, such as Social Security in the United States, typically funded by contributions from workers. [47]

By the 1920s, worries about accelerating technology led British engineer C. H. Douglas to propose a government-paid "social credit" to make up the difference between wages and the rising cost of goods. But such notions, tied to national wealth, would play little part in the rise of social security, the minimum wage and welfare programs in Europe and the United States, which were generally tied to work. [48]

As Europe was recovering from World War I, the idea of a basic income gained popularity among some European philosophers and politicians. In 1918 British philosopher Bertrand Russell wrote in *Roads to Freedom* that human beings have a fundamental right to a basic income "sufficient for necessaries . . . whether they work or not." [49]

That same year, British Quaker political leader and Labor Party member Dennis Milner argued for a weekly "state bonus" to end widespread poverty in postwar Britain. Economist James Meade endorsed Milner's idea, saying publicly owned assets should finance a "social dividend." [50]

In the United States, the basic income idea gained currency during the Depression in the 1930s, especially among citizens impatient with Democratic President

Continued on p. 736

Chronology

18th-19th Centuries
Proposals emerge for a form of universal basic income (UBI).

1797
Thomas Paine proposes giving every citizen 15 pounds at age 21, funded by a land tax.

1883
Germany establishes first social insurance program.

1900s-1930s
Philosophers and politicians propose various types of basic income to combat poverty.

1918
In Britain, philosopher Bertrand Russell says people have a right to basic income whether they work or not; Quaker leader Dennis Milner proposes a weekly "state bonus" and economist James Meade suggests financing it with public assets.

1934
Populist U.S. Sen. Huey Long, D-La., proposes taxing the rich to give each "deserving" family a guaranteed income.

1935
President Franklin D. Roosevelt proposes Social Security for seniors.

1938
U.S. enacts first minimum wage.

1960s-1970s
A guaranteed minimum income is proposed to fight poverty.

1962
Conservative economist Milton Friedman proposes a negative income tax — a supplemental income for those earning below a certain amount.

1964
Democratic President Lyndon B. Johnson creates food stamp program.

1967
Civil rights activist Rev. Martin Luther King Jr. supports guaranteed income as an alternative to welfare.

1968
Federal government tests a negative income tax, with pilot programs in four states, Seattle, Denver and Gary, Ind.

1969
Republican President Richard M. Nixon proposes guaranteed income.

1970
U.S. House passes Nixon plan, but Senate rejects it.

1972
Democratic presidential candidate George McGovern proposes a guaranteed minimum income.

1974
Canadian government tests guaranteed income in Dauphin, Manitoba.

1975
Congress passes Earned Income Tax Credit to supplement working people's income.

1977
Democratic President Jimmy Carter proposes guaranteed income.

1978
Experiments in Denver and Seattle find recipients of a negative income tax work less and divorce more often, spurring objections to Carter's plan.

1979
House passes Carter's revised minimum income plan, but it dies in Senate.

1980s-2000s
Alaska, Cherokees establish basic income-style payments to residents and tribal members; new studies revive interest in basic guaranteed income.

1982
Alaska begins sending each resident an annual dividend from oil revenues.

1996
Eastern Band of Cherokee Indians begins sharing casino profits with tribal members in an annual payment; research finds health, education benefits.

2011
New research finds Canada's 1970s basic income in Dauphin improved health, education.

2016
Swiss voters reject UBI in referendum. . . . Washington state rejects carbon tax-rebate ballot initiative. . . . Gov. Bill Walker, R-Alaska, slashes state dividend by half amid falling oil prices.

2017
Finland and Ontario, Canada, begin two-year basic income experiments. . . . California business incubator Y Combinator starts pre-pilot UBI project. . . . Washington, D.C., and five states propose a carbon emissions tax and using the revenues to help finance a UBI.

2018
Y Combinator scheduled to begin UBI experiment in two states.

Testing Basic Income in Canada — Again

New effort expected to produce similar results to '70s-era trial.

In the 1970s, the small prairie farm town of Dauphin, Canada, became the site of an almost forgotten experiment to guarantee all inhabitants a minimum income that would keep them from falling into poverty. During the years the program was in effect (1974-1979), about 20 percent of the town's residents received the basic-income stipend, equivalent to 60 percent of Canada's poverty threshold at the time. [1]

The government-funded experiment, known as MINCOME, has recently drawn renewed attention, with Ontario running experiments with a basic income beginning this fall. Lawmakers in British Columbia and Quebec also have expressed interest but those provinces have no definite plans to initiate a similar project.

Initially funded by the liberal government of Pierre Trudeau, the Dauphin pilot was widely viewed as a prelude to the establishment of a government-guaranteed basic income. But by 1979, a conservative government was in power, and MINCOME was shut down. No analysis of the experiment was done in the years immediately following the end of the project. [2]

However, almost 30 years later, University of Manitoba economist Evelyn Forget delved into 1,800 dusty boxes of data and obsolete tapes left over from the experiment, as well as local hospital records. In an influential analysis published in 2011, she found that hospitalizations dropped significantly while the program was in effect, especially for mental health problems, accidents and injuries. [3]

"The mental health findings are pointing toward tensions that accompany low income and that make your life that much harder," she says.

Within families receiving the stipends, Forget found, women reduced the number of hours they worked, mainly using the extra income to stay home longer with newborns before going back to work, while male heads of households reduced their work hours only minimally. Doreen Henderson, now 70, who participated in the experiment, stayed home with her two kids and helped grow a lot of the family's food while her husband worked as a janitor. "They should have kept it," she said of the minimum income program. "It made a real difference." [4]

Teenage boys also reduced their work hours dramatically or delayed entering the labor force, raising high school graduation rates. During the experiment, an 11th-grader from a low-income family was more likely to have friends continuing on to 12th grade than before the experiment began, an important peer influence in deciding whether to stay in school, Forget has written. [5]

The positive results Forget uncovered have been influential in reviving interest in trying out a basic income in Canada, according to Canadian advocates. Ontario is initiating an experiment that will send a basic income to 4,000 low-income residents in three regions of the province starting this fall. [6] The stipend will be higher than it was in the 1970s: about 75 percent of Canada's poverty threshold.

Like the earlier experiment, benefits will phase out as a recipient's earnings rise. For each dollar earned, benefits will drop by 50 cents — the equivalent of being "taxed back" at 50 percent. That could pose a disincentive to working, but without that feature the program would "cost a lot of money," Forget says.

To make the experiment politically feasible in Canada, Forget says, the stipend will go only to those in the lower-income brackets. By contrast, leading proponents of a universal basic income say it should go to everyone regardless of income.

"I can't imagine a universal basic income taking hold in Canada where everyone, rich and poor, would receive the same amount of money," she says. Forget predicts the latest experiment will have the same impact on families as the Dauphin project did in the 1970s, "but in different ways."

Continued from p. 734

Franklin D. Roosevelt's (1933-45) failure to end the Depression in his first 100 days in office. In 1934, Louisiana's populist Democratic Sen. Huey Long proposed a Share Our Wealth program, to tax the rich and give every "deserving family" a stake equaling "one third of the average wealth" — enough to own a comfortable home, car and radio — coupled with a guaranteed annual income. [51]

Long's program was soon overshadowed by Roosevelt's New Deal programs, which Roosevelt privately admitted to an adviser was his attempt to "steal Long's thunder." [52] In 1935, FDR proposed his Second New Deal, including Social Security pensions for the aged, although it excluded domestic and farm workers, among the poorest working Americans. [53] Included in the Second New Deal was Aid to Dependent Children, which provided minimum income assistance to fatherless families with children. It was renamed in 1962 Aid to Families with Dependent Children (AFDC) and in 1996 became Temporary Assistance to Needy Families. The 1996 welfare reform act, which imposed work requirements and a five-year lifetime limit on benefits, remains the principal welfare program for poor families today. [54]

In 1938, Congress enacted the first minimum hourly wage, set at 25 cents, under the Fair Labor Standards Act. It also required overtime pay for hours worked over a set number of weekly hours. [55]

War on Poverty

In the 1960s, poverty was still pervasive in the United States, even though the nation had emerged from World

For instance, she says, "We'll see fewer people showing up at their doctor's office complaining of depression or anxiety — as we did in the '70s." But since today's mental health treatment relies heavily on psychotropic medications, it will likely show up in fewer prescriptions, she says. And because most school-age children today finish high school, the extra income might lead instead to higher community college attendance. For those already in the work force, it might lead them to seek training to qualify for a different job, she adds.

However, Forget cautions, "We won't answer the big questions about political acceptability among people who might see their taxes increase" or who worry recipients will quit their jobs. "I think we'll see a very small effect, if any," on people significantly reducing their work hours, she says. "But that's something you have to show people over and over again before it convinces anybody."

Ontario provincial elections are scheduled for June 2018. Many political observers predict the province's current Liberal government, which initiated the experiments, will not survive the three-year pilot program. Sid Frankel, associate professor of social work at the University of Manitoba in Winnipeg, questions whether participating families will make a long-term investment in something such as education knowing the pilot program is sponsored "by a not-very-popular government that might not be around at the end of the trial."

Moreover, the Canadian government seems lukewarm about the concept. The federal government is planning to roll out a new poverty-reduction strategy this fall, but "the whole idea of a basic income has been completely absent from any of the federal government consultation documents," according to Frankel.

Yet basic income may be just the tonic needed for Ontario cities hit hard by the loss of jobs, according to Rob Rainer, chairman of the Ontario Basic Income Network, a basic-income advocacy

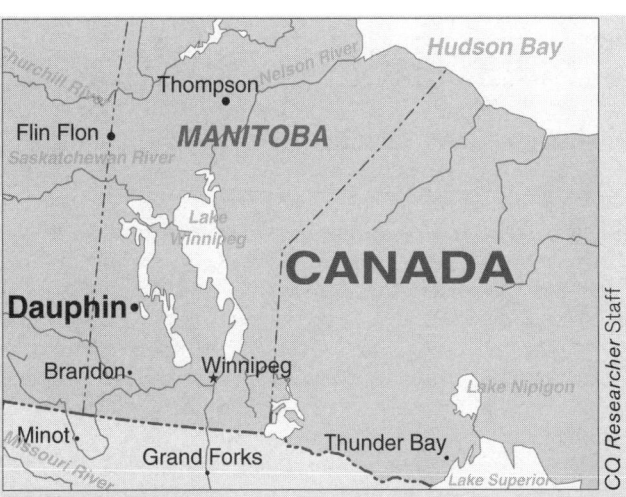

In the mid-1970s, the Canadian government gave a basic income stipend to residents in Dauphin, a small farm town.

group in Ottawa. For instance, residents of Thunder Bay, one of the cities chosen for the experiment, have suffered devastating job losses because of the decline of the local forestry industry.

It will be interesting to see, he says, whether "even a modest influx" of income for those jobless residents "can act as an economic stimulus in some fashion."

— *Sarah Glazer*

[1] David Calnitsky, "More Normal than Welfare: The Mincome Experiment, Stigma, and Community Experience," Canadian Sociological Association, 2016, http://tinyurl.com/y8sjw4tn.

[2] Sarah Gardner, "On the Canadian prairie, a basic income experiment," "Marketplace," NPR, Dec. 20, 2016, https://tinyurl.com/ycokedza.

[3] Evelyn L. Forget, "The Town with No Poverty," University of Manitoba, February 2011, https://tinyurl.com/ov4zukq.

[4] Whitney, Mallett,"The Town Where Everyone Got Free Money," *Motherboard*, Feb. 4, 2015, http://tinyurl.com/ycckglxu.

[5] Forget, *op. cit.*

[6] "Ontario's Basic Income Pilot," Canada Ministry of Community and Social Services, April 24, 2017, https://tinyurl.com/ycyq3kyg.

War II as the world's richest country and was experiencing generally high employment and economic growth. [56]

In 1964, Democratic President Lyndon B. Johnson proposed his Great Society programs, also known as the War on Poverty. One was the food stamp program, now known as the Supplemental Nutrition Assistance Program (SNAP), which provides food vouchers for low-income people. [57]

But even liberals were skeptical that Johnson's programs could eradicate poverty. In 1964, more than 1,000 economists signed a document urging Congress to adopt a system of income

guarantees — "a decent basic income," in the words of signatory and Harvard economist John Kenneth Galbraith. [58]

In his 1967 book *Where Do We Go From Here: Chaos or Community?*, the Rev. Martin Luther King Jr. delivered a withering critique of welfare. Instead of a patchwork of programs aimed at individual needs like housing or hunger, "the solution to poverty is to abolish it directly by a now widely discussed measure: the guaranteed income," the civil rights leader wrote. [59]

Conservatives also disliked welfare programs, but for different reasons. Wel-

fare rolls were rising rapidly despite high employment, as were rates of fathers deserting children and out-of-wedlock births. The female-headed family had become "the symbol of welfare dependency," according to Harvard sociologist Daniel P. Moynihan, who as an adviser to Republican President Nixon championed a guaranteed national income. [60]

Some conservatives said the AFDC program had a built-in work disincentive: For every dollar earned, a welfare recipient lost a dollar in benefits. Originally designed for widowed mothers, the program could withdraw assistance

Finland Tests Basic Income for the Unemployed

Critics call it a "publicity stunt" to get people to accept low-wage jobs.

Finland's northern city of Oulu was once a busy hub for mobile phone developer Nokia. Yet the company's decline in the face of fierce competition in recent years put thousands of software engineers out of work, halving local Nokia jobs.

That makes Oulu fertile ground for start-ups looking for talent among former Nokia workers. But hiring them can be difficult. One Oulu entrepreneur said he offered a part-time job to an ex-Nokia employee for 2,000 euros (about $2,240) a month, but the prospective hire already received more than that in unemployment benefits.

"It's more profitable for him to just wait at home for some ideal job," said the entrepreneur, Asmo Saloranta. [1]

Under Finland's generous welfare state, going back to work part-time can mean losing not only unemployment benefits but other assistance as well, such as housing subsidies and grants for study. Thus, jobless Finns say it is often not worth it to take a part-time job because it will not pay significantly more than benefits they will lose by taking the job. [2]

The solution may be for the government to pay jobless people a basic stipend whether they work or not, which some see as a limited test of the universal basic income (UBI) concept.

To test the hypothesis that such an approach would encourage more unemployed citizens to work, the Finnish government in January began paying a monthly stipend of 560 euros ($657) to 2,000 randomly selected jobless Finns, promising them that during the two-year experiment they will not forfeit monthly benefits, even if they start working at a new job. [3]

Olli Kärkkäinen, an economist with the Nordea bank in Helsinki, said the experiment is unrealistic because it does not include higher taxes that would have to be levied if everyone in Finland were to receive a monthly check under a pure UBI. "There are no losers in this experiment," he said. "The results are bound to be positive. [4]

Government officials also hope the monthly check, which they're calling a "basic income" will encourage people "to take extra risk and build their own business," according to Markus Kanerva, a government adviser who helped design the experiment. Already, some participants have told the Finnish press they will use the cushion to do that or to take part-time work. [5]

International interest in Finland's pilot is intense. Although it applies only to jobless citizens and thus is not quite universal, it has been hailed by some UBI advocates as the largest nationwide test of the approach in a wealthy country.

So far, most opposition to the concept has come from taxpayers concerned that a guaranteed income would raise their taxes, and from labor unions. Unions say the concept is too expensive, but some proponents say Finnish unions, who play a major role in wage negotiations and control large union unemployment funds, really fear losing bargaining power. [6]

Seventy percent of Finnish citizens like the idea of a basic income, but that drops to 35 percent once they learn that their already high taxes could rise even higher to pay for it, according to polls cited by Kanerva.

The experiment also has drawn harsh criticism from Finns who say it should apply to everyone, not just the unemployed. Otto Lehto, former chairman of Finland's Basic Income Network, an advocacy group, calls the experiment a "half-hearted" and "badly mangled" effort by a coalition government dominated by conservatives.

---

if a father was in the household, which critics said encouraged desertion, divorce and unwed motherhood. [61]

As an alternative, conservative economist Milton Friedman had proposed a negative income tax in his 1962 book, *Capitalism and Freedom*, which Moynihan called a "spanking good idea." The tax would give poor people the cash difference between what they earned and the income necessary for a decent standard of living. Friedman's approach "would give less as earnings increased but never to the point of canceling all advantage of increased earnings," Moynihan explained. [62]

A presidential commission had recommended a guaranteed income funded by a version of Friedman's negative income tax in 1969. That same year, Nixon proposed a basic federal payment of $1,600 for a family of four (about $10,881 in today's dollars) as an improvement over services from a bureaucracy. "The best judge of each family's priorities is that family itself," Nixon said. [63]

Although passed by the House in 1970, Nixon's Family Assistance Plan died in the Senate, due to "an unlikely combination of liberals and conservatives," says Leslie Lenkowsky, a professor emeritus of public affairs and philanthropic studies at Indiana University, Bloomington, who helped staff hearings for Moynihan when he was a Democratic senator from New York (1977-2001). Conservatives opposed Nixon's

plan as too costly and a disincentive for work, according to Lenkowsky. Moynihan blamed the defeat equally, if not more so, on liberals "who wanted more, not less than it provided." [64]

The idea was taken up again during the 1972 presidential campaign, when unsuccessful Democratic nominee George McGovern, a U.S. senator from South Dakota, proposed a $1,000 "demogrant" devised by economist James Tobin.

Early Experiments

Between 1968 and 1980, the federal government tested the impact of providing a guaranteed monthly income

By limiting the experiment just to the unemployed, critics say, the trial is too narrow to test advocates' theory that free money would liberate everyone — including workers in low-paying jobs — to engage in charity, stay home to care for children, find a better job or create their own business.

Antti Jauhiainen and Joona-Hermanni Mäkinen, co-directors of the liberal Parecon Finland economic think tank, called the project "a "publicity stunt" by Finland's austerity-minded government to get jobless people "to accept low-paying and low-productivity jobs." [7]

Preliminary results from the experiment should be available early next year, according to Kanerva, but final results are expected to coincide with 2019 parliamentary elections, which Finland's fragile coalition government is unlikely to survive, according to some observers.

"In all likelihood it will be a different coalition, and then basic income could be off the map," says Jurgen De Wispelaere, who helped design the experiment and is now a policy research fellow at the Institute of Policy Research, at the University of Bath in England. Many people in the Finnish government "are very worried about the unconditional side of basic income," such as the lack of work requirements, he says.

But the point of the experiment is to find out if giving out free money has the pernicious effects some people fear, such as creating a nation of loafers on the dole.

"Everyone who disagrees does it for political, ideological or moral reasons but not because of any evidence," says Wispelaere, "because we don't have any evidence."

— *Sarah Glazer*

A homeless woman seeks help in Helsinki, Finland. To encourage unemployed Finns to work, the government in January began a two-year experiment, paying a monthly stipend of 560 euros ($657) to 2,000 randomly selected jobless citizens.

[1] Peter S. Goodman, "Free Cash in Finland. Must be Jobless," *The New York Times*, Dec. 17, 2016, https://tinyurl.com/y8ggsway.

[2] "Worldhacks: Does universal basic income work?" BBC, Aug. 8, 2017, http://tinyurl.com/y7o9cpmc.

[3] "Basic Income Experiment: 2017-2018," Kela, http://tinyurl.com/ybgo5rn5. "How basic income affect the other social security benefits," Kela, http://tinyurl.com/yd9fzv3m.

[4] Sarah Gardner, "Finland to test a basic income for the unemployed," "Marketplace," NPR, Dec. 12, 2016, http://tinyurl.com/ybymh8d7.

[5] "Six months on: Feedback on Finland's basic income trial," *Yle*, July 26, 2017, https://tinyurl.com/y7benmzw.

[6] Raine Tiessalo, "Universal basic income 'useless,' says Finland's biggest union," *The Independent*, Feb. 9, 2017, https://tinyurl.com/he3lr23.

[7] Antti Jauhiainen and Joona-Hermanni Mäkinen, "Why Finland's Basic Income Experiment Isn't Working," *The New York Times*, July 20, 2017, https://tinyurl.com/ya8g2kda.

to low-income families in experiments in New Jersey, Pennsylvania, Iowa, North Carolina and in Gary, Ind.; Seattle and Denver. The largest, conducted in Seattle and Denver, became the center of attention when Congress again debated a version of a basic income in 1977-78.

In 1977, Democratic President Jimmy Carter proposed an anti-poverty scheme — the Program for Better Jobs and Income — that included a jobs program and a form of the negative income tax. The administration requested a basic annual payment of $4,200 ($16,449 in today's dollars) for a family of four, with each dollar earned reducing the benefit by 50 cents. The payments would be eliminated when outside income reached $8,400. [65]

Moynihan, by then a senator holding hearings on Carter's proposal, turned against the idea, citing results from the Seattle and Denver experiments that appeared to show recipients working less and divorcing more often. [66] In a letter to the conservative *National Review*, Moynihan wrote: "But were we wrong about a guaranteed Income! Seemingly it is calamitous. It increases family dissolution by some 70 percent, decreases work, etc." [67]

Headlines such as "Income Plan Linked to Less Work," and "Guaranteed Income Against Work Ethic" appeared in newspapers after the hearings. Carl Rowan, a *Washington Star* columnist and a former official in the Kennedy and

Johnson administrations, was among the few journalists who said it might be acceptable for people working in bad jobs to work less. [68]

Over the past decade, however, researchers re-examining the evidence from those experiments have pointed out that most of the cutback in working hours occurred among wives, single mothers or teen family members — not heads of households. Primary earners reduced their work hours by only about 7 percent, on average, while wives cut theirs by 27 percent and single mothers by 15 to 30 percent. Younger earners cut their work hours and some stayed in school longer. Some analysts said earlier findings of increased divorce rates were erroneous. [69]

Other scholars have suggested that some recipients, fearing they could lose welfare benefits, may not have reported all of their earnings, according to researcher Marinescu, so they may have been working more hours than was reported.

The Carter administration's plan fared no better than Nixon's. It passed the House in 1979 but died in the Senate. The government jobs proposed by Carter raised the cost of the program and led to opposition from conservatives worried about both costs and work disincentives.

Just as the U.S. experiments were winding down, similar experiments were starting in Canada. However, the data from those experiments was not analyzed until 2011, when economist Forget published her findings that the Dauphin experiment had led to higher graduation rates, more women staying home and reduced hospitalizations.

After Carter's failure, discussion of a guaranteed income died in the U.S. political arena. Politicians preferred benefits tied to work, such as the Earned Income Tax Credit, which had been enacted in 1975 and which subsidized the income of low-wage workers, supplying about $3,400 for a family with one child today.

However, the payments to two communities that shared the wealth of unexpected windfalls — Alaskans and the North Carolina Cherokees — are often cited as a form of universal basic income.

In 1976, as the Trans-Alaska pipeline project neared completion, Alaskan voters passed an amendment to the state constitution mandating that at least 25 percent of the money earned from the state's oil revenues, including income from mineral leases and royalties, be placed into a permanent fund, so the state could share its oil profits with future generations. Since 1982, the state has distributed annual dividends, ranging in recent years from about $1,000 to a peak of $2,072 per person in 2015, to all permanent residents, including children. [70] However, that dividend has been imperiled as the price of oil has fallen in recent years.

In 1996, North Carolina's Eastern Band of Cherokee Indians opened its first casino and began sharing profits with tribal members — an annual dividend of up to $6,000 per person. Within five years, the dividend had halved the number of Cherokees living below poverty. Researchers also attributed other benefits to the dividend: a decline in crime, rising high school graduation rates and a lower likelihood of children and teens suffering from drug or alcohol abuse. [71] ∎

CURRENT SITUATION

New Interest

While no nation has implemented an unconditional UBI, the idea is gaining international attention. Several governments and nonprofit groups are studying the concept, usually through small-scale pilot projects as possible precursors to legislative action.

However, in a recent expression of negative sentiment, Swiss voters last year overwhelmingly rejected an initiative that would have required the government to move toward an unconditional monthly UBI of about $2,500. The Swiss government had opposed the move as "ruinously expensive and morally corrosive," *The Economist* reported, because officials believed it would encourage recipients to stop working. [72]

In the United States, some UBI advocates view several legislative proposals to provide rebates or tax credits to Americans as an interim step to a UBI. Foremost among those is a proposal to expand the child tax credit, which currently is pegged at up to $1,000 for each child under 17. [73] An expanded credit could become part of a tax reform package being discussed on Capitol Hill.

Sam Hammond, a poverty and welfare analyst for the Niskanen Center, says a bipartisan coalition is forming to lobby for an increase in the child tax credit, proposed by Sen. Rubio. Rubio has recommended boosting the credit from $1,000 to $2,500 per child and making it refundable, meaning that workers earning an income too low to pay taxes could still receive the credit in the form of a refund from the federal government. Rubio met with President Trump's daughter Ivanka in June, which led to a White House statement of support for the idea. [74]

Hammond had co-authored a paper last year proposing a monthly universal "guaranteed minimum income for kids," a child allowance similar to those offered in Canada and Europe. [75] But expanding the child tax credit looks more politically feasible, he says, and could be an interim step to a universal child allowance.

Hammond cites Canada's experience with a child allowance. Canada pays a family with two children under age 6 $12,800 a year ($10,000 in U.S. dollars) — the equivalent of a basic income. [76] "It's dramatically cut child poverty," says Hammond. "You can't point to any other country where you're sending households this amount of cash unconditionally with no work requirement."

However, the average Canadian family now spends 42.5 percent of its income on federal, provincial and local taxes — up more than 2,000 percent since 1961 and more than the average amount spent on basic necessities such as housing, food and clothing combined, according to a study released in August by the Fraser Institute, a Canadian think tank. [77]

It is uncertain whether an expanded child tax credit will be included in a tax reform proposal expected to be drafted by congressional leaders and the White House this fall, and, if so, at what level. It will be a "tug of war" between expanding the child tax credit and lowering corporate tax rates, as Trump has vowed to do, Hammond says.

Continued on p. 742

At Issue:

Should the United States adopt a universal basic income?

KARL WIDERQUIST
ASSOCIATE PROFESSOR OF POLITICAL PHILOSOPHY, GEORGETOWN UNIVERSITY, SCHOOL OF FOREIGN SERVICE — QATAR; FOUNDING EDITOR, BASIC INCOME STUDIES

WRITTEN FOR *CQ RESEARCHER*, SEPTEMBER 2017

*t*he United States should adopt a universal basic income (UBI) because it's wrong for anyone to come between people and the resources they need to survive, or to put conditions on access to those resources. And that is what we do. We threaten almost every worker with poverty, destitution and extreme economic uncertainty because we think it's a good way to motivate them to work. But we can motivate people with positive rewards, such as good pay and working conditions.

People don't need bosses to work. People can hunt, gather, fish, farm, build their own shelter and start their own business or cooperative enterprise without a boss. People only need bosses because they control resources. There is nothing wrong with working for someone else, as long as you do so voluntarily, but there is something wrong with working for someone else solely because the law makes it impossible for you to work for yourself.

A UBI system would let everyone — not just a controlling elite — benefit from scarce natural resources, which we all need to survive and that were here long before any of us. Under a UBI system, we would all pay taxes for the resources we own and receive a UBI as compensation for the resources that others own. The UBI must be high enough to meet people's basic needs so no one has to take a job under threat of deprivation. That way, a UBI creates a voluntary-participation economy instead of the current forced-participation economy.

We like to think the poor are lazy if they do not take jobs, but we never ask ourselves if employers who do not offer better jobs are cheap. If we have to threaten people with homelessness to get them to take the jobs we offer, maybe we who endorse a forced-participation economy are the cheap ones.

And maybe our cheapness is self-defeating for all but the wealthy. Average workers have not gotten a significant increase in pay since the 1970s — even though our economy has grown enormously since then. Automation has made it possible for every American to work less and consume more, but the benefit of that growth has gone almost entirely to the wealthiest 1 percent. A UBI can give all workers the power to command better wages and working conditions. It's not just for the poor — it's for everyone who works for a living. And it's long overdue.

PAVLINA TCHERNEVA
ASSOCIATE PROFESSOR OF ECONOMICS AND DIRECTOR OF THE ECONOMICS PROGRAM, BARD COLLEGE

WRITTEN FOR *CQ RESEARCHER*, SEPTEMBER, 2017

*i*n 2005, Federal Reserve Chairman Alan Greenspan schooled Rep. Paul Ryan, R-Wis., on Social Security. Solvency, he said, was not the problem, since "there's nothing to prevent the federal government from creating as much money as it wants and paying it to somebody. The question is, how [to] assure that the real assets are created which those benefits are employed to purchase?"

This is the problem with the UBI. Mailing checks is easy. Guaranteeing that every recipient can acquire the real goods and services needed for a basic living standard is not. The market already fails to provide affordable health care, education or housing to many income-earning individuals.

The problem is not the payment but the inequitable production process, which the UBI further undermines. While recipients can purchase part of the nation's GDP, they are not expected or required to contribute to its production. This ability to opt out of one's job (whether it is "good" or "bad") is considered a key "benefit" of the policy.

The solution to "bad" jobs, of course, is to guarantee access to "good" jobs — which my alternative proposal, the Job Guarantee (JG), does. It offers a voluntary job opportunity to the unemployed to work in the public or nonprofit sectors, helping fill the care or environmental needs gaps. It stabilizes the economy, raises incomes at the bottom and reduces the large social costs of joblessness.

A UBI above poverty or at a living-wage level would cost 20-35 percent of GDP. The JG would cost 2-4 percent. A permanent UBI has no counter-cyclical stabilization feature, while the JG expands in recessions and shrinks in expansions, eliminating involuntary unemployment.

UBI experiments show that recipients still desire scarce jobs, a problem the JG solves by guaranteeing a decent job to anyone who wants one. UBI is a giant voucher program — a firm subsidy that removes employers' incentive to pay above-poverty wages while accelerating the "Uberization" of work. The JG, by contrast, obliges firms to match or exceed the JG wage-benefit package. Worse, UBI is often advocated as a replacement for crucial government programs. Why provide Social Security, Medicare or public education if people can buy them with their UBI?

In sum, UBI is a Trojan horse and a false promise. Sending everyone a check is trivial. It takes work to ensure a decent standard of living for all. For that, we'd do much better with a Job Guarantee.

Continued from p. 740

Another potential stepping-stone to universal basic income is Rep. Khanna's proposal — a response to slow wage growth — to double the Earned Income Tax Credit, to $12,000 for families with three or more children. [78] "We would give a 20 percent raise to the bottom 20 percent of the income distribution to compensate them for the stagnancy of wages since 1979," he told *The Atlantic*. [79]

Hammond, who helped draft Khanna's plan, concedes it has zero chance of passage. With an estimated cost of more than $1.3 trillion over 10 years, he calls it a "thought experiment." But if Congress is contemplating Trump's tax reform proposal of up to $6 trillion in tax cuts as estimated by the Congressional Budget Office, he asks, "why not use one-sixth of that to bring people's wages back to what they would be with robust growth?" [80]

A group of conservatives, called the Climate Leadership Council, which includes Cabinet members from the Reagan, Bush and Nixon administrations, has proposed taxing oil refineries and coal mines for their carbon dioxide emissions and distributing the proceeds — $2,000 for a family of four — to all Americans. The proposal should appeal to President Trump, they said, because it's "pro-growth" and "pro-working class" and an alternative to some pollution regulations. [81]

However, the White House announced in April that it was not considering a carbon tax as part of tax reform. [82] But the carbon tax has enough bipartisan support that it could be discussed in the future, says Jason Albritton, director of climate and energy policy for The Nature Conservancy, a founding member of the Climate Leadership Council.

State and Local Efforts

Most discussion over a potential carbon-tax rebate is occurring at the local and state level, but so far proposed carbon-tax rebates do not approach the levels that UBI advocates generally propose.

For example, a coalition of environmentalists and labor union representatives supports a carbon-tax rebate proposal they hope will be introduced in the Council of the District of Columbia this fall, but the tax would generate only a $160 monthly rebate for the average family of four and $277 for a low-income family of four by 2032, according to a recent analysis. [83]

"We're hoping to send the maximum share of that revenue back to D.C. residents," says Camila Thorndike, carbon pricing coordinator for Chesapeake Climate Action Network, a regional nonprofit that works on climate and energy issues in the District, Maryland and Virginia. Low-income users would receive a higher payment because "energy constitutes a greater fraction of their budget," says Thorndike. Some of the revenues, according to Thorndike, would also go to small businesses and be used for building environmentally friendly infrastructure.

In November, Washington state voters rejected the nation's first carbon tax state ballot initiative, which would have raised $2 billion, with proceeds going to rebates for residents, businesses and a tax break for manufacturers. However, many environmental advocates opposed the initiative, preferring that the revenue be spent on green infrastructure projects. Social-justice advocates also wanted the money spent in communities most affected by pollution. [84]

That tussle over how to spend carbon tax revenues is a "perennial" issue when such measures are debated, according to The Nature Conservancy's Albritton. Legislators in five states — Connecticut, Massachusetts, Rhode Island, Vermont and Washington — recently introduced proposals to tax carbon, but none has been enacted. [85]

In May, Hawaii became the first state to commission a study of a universal basic income, among other approaches, to tackle globalization and automation. [86]

Facebook co-founder Zuckerberg recently praised Alaska's 35-year record of sending oil revenue dividends to residents as a "bipartisan idea" and a potential UBI model. [87] But last year, facing declining oil prices, Gov. Bill Walker slashed the individual dividends to $1,022, half the previous level. [88] This year, the Republican-led Alaska Senate beat back efforts by the Democratic majority in the House to restore the dividend to historic levels and introduce a state income tax to help fill the state's coffers. The final budget set the 2017 dividend at $1,100 — half of its historical formula. [89]

Nevertheless, support for the dividend "is very, very high," says Foster, of the Economic Security Project, citing a recent poll showing that 60 percent of Alaskans prefer initiating an income or sales tax — Alaska has neither — to halving the dividend. [90]

Modern Experiments

Versions of a universal basic income are being tested over the next few years in small-scale experiments in Finland, the Canadian province of Ontario, Spain and the Netherlands and in a much larger pilot in Kenya. [91] (*See sidebars, pp. 736 and 738.*)

In the United States, the only experiment underway is privately funded. Altman, at Y Combinator, the Silicon Valley tech incubator, has begun a small experiment to give up to 50 individuals a monthly basic income of $1,000 per month, along with a control group, to guide a larger experiment he plans next year.

"I'm fairly confident that at some point in the future, as technology continues to eliminate traditional jobs and massive new wealth gets created, we're going to see some version of this [UBI] at a national scale," Altman has said. [92] "We hope basic income promotes freedom, and we want to see how people experience that freedom." [93]

Starting early next year, Y Combinator Research, the company's nonprofit research arm, plans to begin a pilot study on the effects of a $1,000 unconditional monthly stipend provided to up to 3,000 people over three to five years in two states yet to be named, according to Elizabeth Rhodes, research director for the basic income pilot.

In the largest basic income experiment to date, GiveDirectly, a charity in New York City, will test cash payments to 200 villages in Kenya as an alternative to in-kind foreign aid, starting this month. [94]

To those who question whether results from a study in a developing country like Kenya could be relevant in the United States, GiveDirectly chief financial officer Joe Huston says the questions being studied, such as — "Will people stop working? Can humans be trusted to spend money or will they buy tobacco and alcohol?" — have universal application because they relate to human nature.

In India, where a small experiment in 2010 debunked the idea that a basic income would be wasted on alcohol and tobacco, the government's chief economic adviser, Arvind Subramanian, has proposed giving all adult Indians $113 a year to cut poverty from 22 percent to 0.5 percent. In a recent editorial, *The Economist* endorsed the idea as an improvement over India's "inefficient and corrupt" welfare programs that put beneficiaries "at the mercy of venal officials." [95] ∎

OUTLOOK

Basic Bootstraps

Concern that automation will displace humans from their jobs in coming years has given the UBI idea new currency, especially in Silicon Valley.

"The beautiful thing about a universal basic income is it solves a lot of problems at the same time" — automation, economic uncertainty created by gig economy jobs, poverty, low wages and the need to remunerate child and elder care, says Stern, of the Economic Security Project.

But it is still unclear how many jobs artificial intelligence will actually replace. Previous industrial revolutions, such as the advent of automated looms in the 19th century, raised similar fears but ended up creating more jobs than they displaced. And when ATMs first appeared 50 years ago, rather than eliminating bank teller jobs as feared, the ATMs saved banks enough money to open more branches. The number of teller jobs has increased faster since 2000 than other jobs in the labor market. [96]

While the concept of a basic income is drawing some enthusiasts from both liberal and conservative quarters, their fundamental differences about which welfare programs should be eliminated to fund it are likely to be exacerbated when it comes to designing an actual program.

"There's a bit of a myth that basic income is really simple to implement," says Jurgen De Wispelaere, a policy research fellow at the Institute for Policy Research at the University of Bath in England who has advised governments in Finland and elsewhere on how to design UBI pilot programs. "The moment you get into the nitty-gritty of design and implementation you have to deal with a huge amount of issues," he says, because the program must interact with other programs such as welfare and Social Security.

In addition, no one knows how a UBI would affect the foundations of society. While proponents cite improvements in the quality of life, *The Economist* recently suggested tensions may develop "between those who continue to work and pay taxes and those opting out" of the workforce. Those tensions could rip a society apart, the magazine editorialized. [97]

In many ways the UBI debate is experiencing growing pains as it moves from a "utopian project in the clouds," to a serious policy, De Wispelaere says.

Yet, while he criticizes some of the more unrealistic visions of UBI, a cash payment can eliminate "the stigmatizing, undignified ways we treat people" in the welfare system, he argues.

Countries testing a basic income, such as Finland and Canada, already have much more generous social insurance programs than the United States. So it is unclear how much the United States, with its tradition of self-sufficiency and individualism, can learn from those experiments. But advocates like De Wispelaere say Americans have the same need as other countries for a basic guaranteed income to prevent a descent into poverty.

"Americans like to talk about how people should pull themselves up by their bootstraps," he says. "Basic income is your bootstraps." ∎

Notes

[1] Ioana Marinescu, "No Strings Attached: The Behavioral Effects of U.S. Unconditional Cash Transfer Programs," Roosevelt Institute, May 11, 2017, https://tinyurl.com/y94u8msa.

[2] The 2017 poverty guideline for a single person household is $12,060. See "Federal Poverty Guidelines," FamiliesUSA, February 2017, https://tinyurl.com/ppxkgkz.

[3] Carl Benedikt Frey and Michael A. Osborne, "The Future of Employment: How Susceptible Are Jobs to Computerisation," Oxford Martin School, University of Oxford, Sept. 17, 2013, https://tinyurl.com/oj67kae.

[4] Melanie Arntz, Terry Gregory and Ulrich Zierahn, "The Risk of Automation for Jobs in OECD Countries," Organisation for Economic Co-operation and Development, June 16, 2016, https://tinyurl.com/y7s5wgnw. James Manyika *et al.*, "Harnessing automation for a future that works," McKinsey Global Institute, January 2017, https://tinyurl.com/hzn5l7c.

[5] For background, see Eugene L. Meyer, "The Gig Economy," *CQ Researcher*, March 18, 2016, pp. 265-288.

[6] Natalie Foster *et al.*, "Portable Benefits Resource Guide," Aspen Institute, 2016, p. 5, https://tinyurl.com/y7f58u68. Also see "Contingent Workforce: Size, Characteristics, Earnings, and Benefits," Government Accountability Office, April 20, 2015, https://tinyurl.com/jq3sta2.

[7] Patrick Gillespie, "Mark Zuckerberg supports universal basic income. What is it?," *CNN Money*, May 26, 2017, https://tinyurl.com/y9j2lyoj.

[8] Sam Altman, "Basic Income," Y Combinator, Jan. 27, 2016, https://tinyurl.com/z7na9xk.

[9] Charles Murray, *In Our Hand: A Plan to Replace the Welfare State* (2016), p. 2.

[10] Robert Greenstein, "Commentary: Universal Basic Income May Sound Attractive But, If It Occurred, Would Likelier Increase Poverty Than Reduce It," Center on Budget and Policy Priorities, May 31, 2016, https://tinyurl.com/y6uwv9ob.

[11] Daniel Mitchell, "Universal Basic Income Experiment in Finland Not Looking Good," CNS News, Aug. 1, 2017, https://tinyurl.com/yaek73m3.

[12] Marinescu, *op. cit.*

[13] Samuel Hammond and Robert Orr, "Niskanen Report: Toward a universal child benefit," Niskanen Center, Oct. 25, 2016, https://tinyurl.com/y9ro4tuk.

[14] Josh Harkinson, "Can this Berniecrat Congressman Win Silicon Valley over to his Progressive Agenda?" *Mother Jones*, June 29, 2017, https://tinyurl.com/y92b3fgn.

[15] "Supplemental Nutrition Assistance Program, Eligible Food Items," USDA, https://tinyurl.com/jktdzos.

[16] "About TANF," Office of Family Assistance, U.S. Department of Health and Human Services, June 28, 2017, http://tinyurl.com/ybdzd8yf. U.S. Department of Health and Human Services, AFDC and TANF Overview, https://tinyurl.com/ya68gwof.

[17] Diane Pagen, "America's Grenfell," *New York Daily News*, July 8, 2017, https://tinyurl.com/ybpgxxxr.

[18] "State TANF Spending in FY 2015: Fact Sheet," Office of Family Assistance, Department of Health and Human Services, Aug. 15, 2016, https://tinyurl.com/y8epuqpf.

[19] Michael R. Strain, "Universal Basic Income Won't Make America Great Again, Either," *The Washington Post*, April 4, 2016, https://tinyurl.com/yc9dqjww.

[20] Marinescu, *op. cit.*, pp. 5, 16.

[21] Greenstein, *op. cit.*

[22] Komal Sri-Kumar and Masood Sohaili, "An Economic Case for Universal Basic Income," *The Milken Institute Review*, Aug. 4, 2017, p. 43, https://tinyurl.com/ybo2qwhv.

[23] David Calnitsky, "More Normal than Welfare: The Mincome Experiment, Stigma, and Community Experience," Canadian Sociological Association, 2016, https://tinyurl.com/y8sjw4tn.

[24] *Ibid.*

[25] Oren Cass, "Why a Universal Basic Income Is a Terrible Idea," *National Review*, June 15, 2016, https://tinyurl.com/y83v97un.

[26] Marinescu, *op. cit.*

[27] Evelyn L. Forget, "The Town with No Poverty," University of Manitoba, February 2011, https://tinyurl.com/yczgpruf.

[28] Michael Tanner, "The Pros and Cons of a Guaranteed National Income," Cato Institute, May 12, 2015, p. 21, http://tinyurl.com/ycxys9n6. Also see Forget, *op. cit.*

[29] Marinescu, *op. cit.*, p. 5.

[30] *Ibid.*

[31] Andy Stern, *Raising the Floor: How a Universal Basic Income Can Renew our Economy and Rebuild the American Dream* (2016), p. 212.

[32] Murray, *op. cit.*, p. 11.

[33] *Ibid.*

[34] *Ibid.*, p. 1.

[35] Stern, *op. cit.*

[36] *Ibid.*, pp. 212-214.

[37] Scott Santens, "How to Reform Welfare and Taxes to Provide Every Citizen with a Basic Income," Economic Security Project, June 5, 2017, https://tinyurl.com/ybofaapw.

[38] "DC Carbon Fee-and-Rebate Policy," The Center for Climate Strategies, 2017, https://tinyurl.com/yajl5g53.

[39] Scott Santens, "The Cost of Universal Basic Income Is the Net Transfer Amount, Not the Gross Price Tag," ScottSantens.com blog, July 7, 2017, https://tinyurl.com/yd6ztgfu.

[40] "Basic income as a policy option: Can it add up?" Policy Brief on the Future of Work, Organisation for Economic Co-operation and Development, May 2017, https://tinyurl.com/y9fk78d7.

[41] Greenstein, *op. cit.*

[42] "Basically Flawed," *The Economist*, June 4, 2016, https://tinyurl.com/ycgayv27.

[43] Trent Gillies, "Money for Nothing," CNBC, July 30, 2017, https://tinyurl.com/y7nw6vj9.

[44] Murray, *op. cit.*, p. 8.

[45] Tanner, *op. cit.*, p. 11.

[46] Stern, *op. cit.*, p. 172.

[47] "Universal Basic Incomes: Sighing for Paradise to Come," *op. cit.* Also see Philippe Van Parijs, "Why Surfers Should be Fed: The Liberal Case for an Unconditional Basic Income," *Philosophy and Public Affairs*, Spring 1991, pp. 65-67, https://tinyurl.com/y7h5hewj.

[48] "Universal Basic Incomes: Sighing for Paradise to Come," *ibid.*

[49] Stern, *op. cit.*, p. 173.

[50] *Ibid.*

[51] "Huey Long — Every Man a King," PBS, https://tinyurl.com/hff9hqg.

[52] Edwin Amenta, Kathleen Dunleavy and Mary Bernstein, "Stolen Thunder: Huey Long's 'Share Our Wealth' Political Mediation, and the Second New Deal," *American Sociological Review*, October 1994, pp. 678-702, https://tinyurl.com/ya2qm9wa.

[53] Larry DeWitt, "The Decision to Exclude Agricultural and Domestic Workers from the 1935 Social Security Act," *Social Security Bulletin*, 2010, https://tinyurl.com/jocovwl.

[54] Parijs, *op. cit.*, p. 67.

[55] "What is the history of the minimum wage?" Center for Poverty Research, University of California, Davis, https://tinyurl.com/yargtj28.

[56] Daniel P. Moynihan, *The Politics of a Guaranteed Income* (1973), p. 29.

[57] Parijs, *op. cit.*, p. 67.

[58] Stern, *op. cit.*, pp. 174-175.

[59] *Ibid.*, p. 175. Also See Martin Luther King Jr., "Where We Are Going?" LoveEarth Network, https://tinyurl.com/y8n38b6k.

[60] Moynihan, *op. cit.* Welfare spending rose sixfold between 1960 and 1970.

[61] Shoshana Grossbard-Shechtman, ed., *Marriage and the Economy: Theory and Evidence from Advanced Industrial Societies* (2003), p. 77.

[62] Moynihan, *op. cit.*, p. 50.

[63] *Ibid.*, p. 223; For today's dollars calculation, see: https://tinyurl.com/y7f3x4qo. See also Livia Gershon, "When 'Welfare Reform' Meant Expanding Benefits," *Jstor Daily*, July 12, 2017, https://tinyurl.com/yb9nm69v.

[64] Moynihan, *op. cit.*, p. 15.

[65] "Moynihan Says Recent Studies Raise Doubts about 'Negative Income Tax' Proposals," *The New*

About the Author

Sarah Glazer is a London-based freelancer who contributes regularly to *CQ Researcher*. Her articles on health, education and social-policy issues also have appeared in *The New York Times* and *The Washington Post*. Her recent *CQ Researcher* reports include "Privacy and the Internet" and "Decriminalizing Prostitution." She graduated from the University of Chicago with a B.A. in American history.

York Times, Nov. 16, 1978, https://tinyurl.com/y7 7s5cum. For conversion to 2017 dollars, see CPI inflation calculator at https://tinyurl.com/k64mxte.

[66] *Ibid.*

[67] Karl Widerquist, "A Failure to Communicate," *Journal of Socio-Economics*, January 2005, pp. 49-81, https://tinyurl.com/ybn9rsve.

[68] *Ibid.*

[69] Forget, *op. cit.*; also see Tanner, *op. cit.*

[70] Historical Timeline, Alaska Department of Revenue, https://tinyurl.com/y8cnh4vg.

[71] Marinescu, *op. cit.*

[72] R.A., "Universal Basic Incomes," *The Economist*, June 6, 2016, https://tinyurl.com/jyc5oy5.

[73] The credit is available to single parents earning up $75,000 yearly, married filing jointly earning up to $110,000 and married filing separately up to $55,000. See Child Tax Credit, Internal Revenue Service, https://tinyurl.com/y95m2gm3.

[74] Nikki Schwab and Frances Chambers, "Ivanka Returns to Capitol Hill to Talk Workforce Issues with Republican Lawmakers," *The Daily Mail*, June 22, 2017, https://tinyurl.com/yca qxt6s.

[75] Hammond and Orr, *op. cit.*

[76] *Ibid.*

[77] Erica Alini, "Average Canadians pay 42.5% of their income in taxes," *Global News*, Aug. 24, 2017, https://tinyurl.com/y8fv3p8l. Also see "Taxes vs. the Necessities of Life," Fraser Institute, August 2017, https://tinyurl.com/yd47nofp.

[78] Annie Lowrey, "Ro Khanna Wants to Give Working-Class Households $1 Trillion," *The Atlantic*, April 28, 2017, https://tinyurl.com/y7d6uxfo.

[79] *Ibid.*

[80] Graham Lanktree, "Trump's Proposed Tax Plan Could Cost the Government $6 Trillion," *Newsweek*, April 26, 2017, https://tinyurl.com/jvz8x5e.

[81] Martin S. Feldstein, Ted Halstead and N. Gregory Mankiw, "A Conservative Case for Climate Action," *The New York Times*, Feb. 8, 2017, https://tiny url.com/y8yw5wu3. Also see "The Four Pillars of our Carbon Dividends Plan," Climate Leadership Council, https://tinyurl.com/ycxyuxt7.

[82] Damian Paletta and Max Ehrenfreund, "White House disavows two controversial tax ideas hours after officials say they're under consideration," *The Washington Post*, April 4, 2017, https://tinyurl.com/y9eooazc.

[83] "DC Carbon Fee-and-Rebate Policy," *op. cit.*

[84] Marianne Lavelle, "Washington State voters reject nation's first carbon tax," *Inside Climate News*, Nov. 9, 2016, https://tinyurl.com/ovpfpbo.

[85] Chelsea Harvey, "Defying Trump, these state leaders are trying to impose their own carbon taxes," *The Washington Post*, May 12, 2017, https://tinyurl.com/y9mftqmk.

[86] Dan Galeon, "Hawaii just became the first

U.S. state to pass a bill supporting basic income," *Business Insider*, June 15, 2017, https:// tinyurl.com/y7zac88w.

[87] Maya Kosoff, "Mark Zuckerberg suggests the Government should give everyone free cash," *Vanity Fair*, July 6, 2017, https://tinyurl.com/ y85789km.

[88] Kate McFarland, "Alaska, U.S.: Amount of 2016 Permanent Fund Dividend divided to be $1022," *Basic Income News*, Sept. 29, 2016, https://tinyurl.com/ydybor5u.

[89] Nathaniel Herz, "Alaska Gov. Walker Signs Budget, leaves dividends at amount set by lawmakers," *Alaska Dispatch News*, June 30, 2017, https://tinyurl.com/y94hj5z7. Also see, "Budget standoff continues as House votes to double Permanent Fund dividends," *Alaska Dispatch News*, June 15, 2017, https://tinyurl.com/ y79p82cg.

[90] "Survey of the Alaska Voters on the PFD, Executive Summary," Harstad Strategic Research, June 26, 2017, p. 6, https://tinyurl.com/y86l3o89.

[91] See Kate McFarland, "Barcelona, Spain, Design

of Minimum Income Experiment Finalized," *Basic Income News*, Aug. 12, 2017, https://tiny url.com/y8htfzox. Also see Tracy Brown Hamilton, "The Netherlands' Upcoming Money-for-Nothing Experiment," *The Atlantic*, June 21, 2016, https://tinyurl.com/yc5panhj.

[92] Altman, *op. cit.*

[93] Sam Altman, "Moving Forward on Basic Income," Y Combinator, May 31, 2016, https:// tinyurl.com/yatdsk56.

[94] Nurith Aizenman, "How to Fix Poverty: Why Not Just Give People Money?" NPR, Aug. 7, 2017, https://tinyurl.com/y8v8s8bh. Also See, GiveDirectly, https://tinyurl.com/zlud7rn.

[95] "India debates the case for a universal basic income," *The Economist*, Feb. 4, 2017, https://tiny url.com/hmsoazw. Also see, Guy Standing, "Unconditional Basic Income: Two Pilot Studies in Madhya Pradesh," https://tinyurl.com/ych2tg6t.

[96] John Detrixhe, "Lesson from the Cupcake ATM: Better to be a baker than a seller," *Quartz*, July 4, 2017, https://tinyurl.com/y7rn6sb9.

[97] "Basically Flawed," *op. cit.*

FOR MORE INFORMATION

American Enterprise Institute, 1789 Massachusetts Ave., N.W., Washington, DC 20036; 202-862-5800; www.aei.org. A nonpartisan public policy think tank that skews conservative, with some scholars supporting a universal income and some criticizing it.

Basic Income Earth Network, c/o Chaire Hoover d'éthique économique et sociale, Université catholique de Louvain Place Montesquieu, 3, B-1348 Louvain-la-Neuve, Belgium; http://basicincome.org. An international nonprofit network of basic-income advocates that organizes an international conference and publishes the online newsletter *Basic Income News* (http://basicincome.org/news).

Cato Institute, 1000 Massachusetts Ave., N.W., Washington, DC 20001; 202-842-0200; www.cato.org. Libertarian think tank dedicated to individual liberty and limited government that has issued discussion papers on universal basic income.

Center on Budget and Policy Priorities, 820 First St. N.E., Suite 510, Washington, DC 20002; 202-408-1080; www.cbpp.org. Nonpartisan think tank that advocates progressive policies to reduce poverty and inequality and has criticized the universal basic income concept.

Economic Security Project, http://economicsecurityproject.org. A two-year fund that supports research and experimentation with unconditional cash stipends; created by, among others, Facebook co-founder Chris Hughes.

Roosevelt Institute, 570 Lexington Ave., 5th Floor, New York, NY 10022; 212-444-9130; http://rooseveltinstitute.org. Nonprofit think tank and partner to the Franklin D. Roosevelt Presidential Library and Museum that focuses on economic and social policy and has published research on basic income.

U.S. Basic Income Guarantee Network, www.usbig.net/index.php. Informal network promoting discussion of a basic income guarantee in the United States; organizes an annual conference and discussion papers.

Bibliography
Selected Sources

Books

Moynihan, Daniel P., *The Politics of a Guaranteed Income: The Nixon Administration and the Family Assistance Plan*, Vintage Books, 1973.

The late Moynihan, the White House adviser behind President Richard M. Nixon's proposed guaranteed income and later a Democratic senator from New York (1976-1995), discusses why he believed the proposal failed in Congress in 1970.

Murray, Charles, *In Our Hands: A Plan to Replace the Welfare State*, AEI Press, 2016.

A libertarian scholar at the conservative American Enterprise Institute says the United States can afford to pay every American adult $13,000 a year if it scraps all existing welfare programs, including Social Security and Medicare.

Stern, Andy, *Raising the Floor: How a Universal Basic Income Can Renew our Economy and Rebuild the American Dream*, Public Affairs, 2016.

A former labor union leader argues that replacing some government programs with a universal basic income is the best response to a globalizing gig economy.

Van Parijs, Philippe, and Yannick Vanderborght, *Basic Income: A Radical Proposal for a Free Society and a Sane Economy*, Harvard University Press, 2017.

Belgian political philosopher (Van Parijs) and political scientist (Vanderborght), both professors at the University of Louvain, Belgium, say a basic income for all would permit "real freedom to flourish."

Articles

"Universal Basic Income: Sighing for Paradise to Come," *The Economist*, June 4, 2016, https://tinyurl.com/ya5tb85b.

A universal basic income would be costly, and many worry it could lead to "a general disengagement from work," says *The Economist* magazine.

Goodman, Peter S., "Free Cash in Finland. Must be Jobless," *The New York Times*, Dec. 17, 2016, https://tinyurl.com/y8ggsway.

A reporter describes the economic and political trends that led Finland to test a basic income for its unemployed.

Lowrey, Annie, "Ro Khanna Wants to Give Working-Class Households $1 Trillion," *The Atlantic*, April 28, 2017, https://tinyurl.com/y7d6uxfo.

A Democratic California congressman describes his proposal to double the Earned Income Tax Credit for low-income working people, which some herald as a move toward a universal basic income.

Morris, David Z., "Universal Basic Income Could Grow the U.S. Economy by an Extra 12.5 percent," *Fortune*, Sept. 3, 2017, http://tinyurl.com/y7wrka2d.

A contributing writer says the claim that a guaranteed income could accelerate U.S. economic growth, published in August by the liberal Roosevelt Institute, would be rejected by conservative economists, who think rising taxes and increased government debt to pay for it would slow the economy.

Pagen, Diane, "America's Grenfell," *New York Daily News*, July 8, 2017, https://tinyurl.com/ybpgxxxr.

A New York City social worker and co-founder of the Basic Income Action advocacy group says a basic income would be a better way to help poor people than America's failing welfare system.

Strain, Michael R., "Universal basic income won't make America great again, either," *The Washington Post*, April 4, 2016, http://tinyurl.com/yamfcdqd.

The director of economic policy studies at the conservative American Enterprise Institute argues a universal basic income that gives the same amount of money to both the disabled and those more capable would be unfair.

Reports and Studies

"Basic income as a policy option: Can it add up?" Organisation for Economic Co-operation and Development, May 2017, https://tinyurl.com/ycc82tqm.

An organization representing 35 member countries, including the United States, finds that an unconditional payment to everyone would require large tax increases or cuts in welfare benefits, increasing poverty rates in some countries.

Forget, Evelyn L., "The Town with No Poverty," University of Manitoba, February 2011, https://tinyurl.com/ov4zukq.

This influential analysis by a University of Manitoba economist of a long-forgotten experiment in Canada found that a guaranteed income led to a higher high-school graduation rate and fewer hospitalizations.

Marinescu, Ioana, "No Strings Attached: The Behavioral Effects of U.S. Unconditional Cash Transfer Programs," Roosevelt Institute, May 2017, https://tinyurl.com/y6wekz2j.

A University of Pennsylvania economist finds improvements in health and education — but only a minimal reduction in work hours — among recipients of cash stipends in Alaska, the Cherokee tribe and U.S. government experiments in the 1970s.

Tanner, Michael, "The Pros and Cons of a Guaranteed National Income," Cato Institute, May 12, 2017, https://tinyurl.com/ycrv7aae.

A senior fellow at the free-market think tank weighs the benefits and drawbacks of a guaranteed income, including the costs and the effects on work incentive.

The Next Step:

Additional Articles from Current Periodicals

Carbon Tax

Kim, Queena, "As Our Jobs Are Automated, Some Say We'll Need A Guaranteed Basic Income," NPR, Sept. 24, 2016, https://tinyurl.com/zq7lgqp.

Due to rising concerns about automation replacing workers, some reformers propose levying carbon emission taxes to pay for a universal basic income (UBI).

Levitan, Dave, "Republicans Offer to Tax Carbon Emissions," Scientific American, Feb. 8, 2017, https://tinyurl.com/z55oe2j.

Republicans released a plan this year to institute a carbon tax and use the revenues to send quarterly checks to every U.S. household.

Paletta, Damian and Max Ehrenfreund, "White House disavows two controversial tax ideas hours after officials say they're under consideration," The Washington Post, April 4, 2017, http://tinyurl.com/y9eooazc.

The Trump administration struck down a value-added tax and a carbon tax proposal that would have gone toward reducing top tax rates on individual and corporate income.

Child Tax Credit

Ellis, Ryan, "Top Marginal Tax Rates, Child Tax Credits, And Tax Reform In The Trump Era," Forbes, July 10, 2017, https://tinyurl.com/y7j6ebmx.

Ivanka Trump and Sen. Marco Rubio, R-Fla., seek common ground on a higher child tax credit, which some UBI advocates see as an interim step to a universal basic income, says a Forbes contributor.

Jagoda, Naomi, "Rubio hosting events to build support for child tax credit proposal," The Hill, Aug. 11, 2017, https://tinyurl.com/yadds582.

Republican Sen. Marco Rubio of Florida has begun hosting tax reform roundtables to discuss his proposal to boost the child tax credit from $1,000 for each child under age 17 to $2,500.

Maag, Elaine, "Simplifying And Targeting Tax Subsidies For Child Care," Forbes, March 23, 2017, https://tinyurl.com/ycpdmpkq.

A Forbes contributor proposes reducing restrictions on the child and dependent care tax credit to better support low-income families.

Earned Income Tax Credit

Fichtner, Jason, and Indivar Dutta-Gupta, "Reforming the earned income tax credit could be a bipartisan victory for Trump," The Hill, April 8, 2017, https://tinyurl.com/y7uvgpnb.

Two researchers say that to raise wages, liberals and conservatives alike would support raising the Earned Income Tax Credit.

Yamachika, Tom, "On the new earned income tax credit, the devil is in the details," Maui News, July 26, 2017, https://tinyurl.com/y8b2h3fn.

Democratic Gov. David Ige of Hawaii signed a bill establishing a state Earned Income Tax Credit, entitling lower-income families to claim a monthly tax refund.

UBI Experiments

Alini, Erica, "What you need to know about Ontario's basic income plan," Global News, April 24, 2017, https://tinyurl.com/n5kve9p.

Ontario enacted a basic income plan this spring, allotting a guaranteed minimum income to those living below the poverty line, regardless of whether they are employed.

Harkinson, Josh, "Hawaii Considers Radical Idea to Make Life in Paradise a Little Easier," Mother Jones, June 15, 2017, https://tinyurl.com/yaw8mz5w.

Hawaii has directed state agencies to study a guaranteed income, making it the first state to consider offering residents "basic financial security."

Weller, Chris, "Finland's basic income experiment is already lowering stress levels — and it's only 4 months old," Business Insider, May 10, 2017, https://tinyurl.com/ycrb4ejo.

Four months after Finland undertook a two-year experiment guaranteeing residents a basic income of $600 a month, 2,000 recipients have reported lower stress and anxiety levels.

CITING CQ RESEARCHER

Sample formats for citing these reports in a bibliography include the ones listed below. Preferred styles and formats vary, so please check with your instructor or professor.

MLA STYLE

Mantel, Barbara. "Coal Industry's Future." CQ Researcher 17 June 2016: 529-552.

APA STYLE

Mantel, B. (2016, June 17). Coal Industry's Future. CQ Researcher, 6, 529-552.

CHICAGO STYLE

Mantel, Barbara. "Coal Industry's Future." CQ Researcher, June 17, 2016, 529-52.

In-depth Reports on Issues in the News

Are you writing a paper?

Need backup for a debate?

Want to become an expert on an issue?

For 90 years, students have turned to *CQ Researcher* for in-depth reporting on issues in the news. Reports on a full range of political and social issues are now available. Following is a selection of recent reports:

Civil Liberties
Privacy and the Internet, 12/15
Intelligence Reform, 5/15
Religion and Law, 11/14

Crime/Law
High-Tech Policing, 4/17
Forensic Science Controversies, 2/17
Jailing Debtors, 9/16
Decriminalizing Prostitution, 4/16
Restorative Justice, 2/16
The Dark Web, 1/16
Immigrant Detention, 10/15

Education
Charter Schools, 3/17
Civic Education, 2/17
Student Debt, 11/16
Apprenticeships, 10/16

Environment/Society
Muslims in America, 7/17
Funding the Arts, 7/17
Hunger in America, 7/17
Future of the Christian Right, 6/17
Trust in Media, 6/17
Anti-Semitism, 5/17

Health/Safety
Medical Marijuana, 7/17
Food Labeling, 6/17
Sports and Sexual Assault, 4/17
Reducing Traffic Deaths, 2/17

Politics/Economy
National Debt, 9/17
North Korea Showdown, 5/17
Rethinking Foreign Aid, 4/17
Troubled Brazil, 4/17
Reviving Rural Economies, 3/17
Immigrants and the Economy, 2/17

Upcoming Reports

Medical Breakthroughs, 9/15/17   Climate Change and National Security, 9/22/17   Democracies, 9/29/17

ACCESS

CQ Researcher is available in print and online. For access, visit your library or www.cqresearcher.com.

STAY CURRENT

For notice of upcoming *CQ Researcher* reports or to learn more about *CQ Researcher* products, subscribe to the free email newsletters, *CQ Researcher Alert!* and *CQ Researcher News*: http://cqpress.com/newsletters.

PURCHASE

To purchase a *CQ Researcher* report in print or electronic format (PDF), visit www.cqpress.com or call 866-427-7737. Single reports start at $15. Bulk purchase discounts and electronic-rights licensing are also available.

SUBSCRIBE

Annual full-service *CQ Researcher* subscriptions—including 44 reports a year, monthly index updates, and a bound volume—start at $1,131. Add $25 for domestic postage.

CQ Researcher Online offers a backfile from 1991 and a number of tools to simplify research. For pricing information, call 800-818-7243 or 805-499-9774 or email librarysales@sagepub.com.

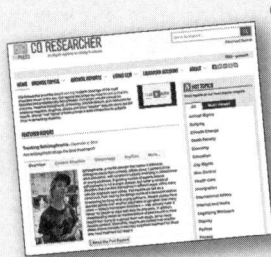

CQ RESEARCHER

CQPRESS

In-depth reports on today's issues

Published by CQ Press, an Imprint of SAGE Publications, Inc.

www.cqresearcher.com

Medical Breakthroughs

Can regulators and ethicists keep up with advances?

The breakthroughs seem like science fiction: editing genes of human embryos to erase disease; controlling a computer cursor with one's thoughts; enabling paralyzed people to walk by fitting them with a robotic "exoskeleton"; using the body's immune system to cure cancer. As fantastic as such advances may seem, however, they are rapidly becoming reality. Yet, medical advances face big hurdles, including steep development costs. President Trump has proposed a 22 percent cut in the National Institutes of Health budget, which funds basic medical research, though Congress wants an increase. Congress also wants the Food and Drug Administration to speed up its regulatory review of new drugs and devices, but some consumer advocates worry that could result in unsafe products. Meanwhile, safety and ethical concerns about certain procedures, especially genetic editing of human embryos to prevent diseases from passing to new generations, are prompting calls for an urgent national discussion on how such technologies should be regulated.

Jennifer Doudna, a professor of biochemistry and molecular biology at the University of California, Berkeley, helped create CRISPR, a gene-editing technique that can remove defective or unwanted genes from a genome. CRISPR may help prevent diseases, but ethicists worry that it could be used in humans to create "designer" babies.

I N S I D E — THIS REPORT

THE ISSUES	**751**
BACKGROUND	**758**
CHRONOLOGY	**759**
CURRENT SITUATION	**763**
AT ISSUE	**765**
OUTLOOK	**766**
BIBLIOGRAPHY	**770**
THE NEXT STEP	**771**

CQ Researcher • Sept. 15, 2017 • www.cqresearcher.com
Volume 27, Number 32 • Pages 749-772

MEDICAL BREAKTHROUGHS

CQ RESEARCHER

THE ISSUES

751
- Should the federal government do more to support medical research?
- Is the FDA's regulatory process adequate for today's cutting-edge medical research?
- Should the federal government do more to address ethical concerns about new medical advances?

BACKGROUND

758 **Early Breakthroughs**
The oldest prosthetic was found on an Egyptian mummy.

761 **New Treatments**
Therapies are being tested to combat cancer.

762 **CRISPR Technology**
The gene-editing technique could cure diseases.

CURRENT SITUATION

763 **Pushing the Limits**
Gene editing is highly controversial when used in human embryos.

766 **Funding Issues**
Experts worry that industry money influences clinical trials.

OUTLOOK

766 **More Cures**
Researchers hope innovations will shift medicine's focus from treatment to cures.

SIDEBARS AND GRAPHICS

752 **Many Americans Do Not Want Certain Enhancements**
At least half of survey respondents do not want certain medical advances.

753 **Industry Spends the Most on Medical R&D**
Private companies fund 65 percent of medical research and development.

754 **Key Medical, Technology and Biology Terms**
From CRISPR to T cells, complex concepts are defined.

756 **Most Back Small Tax Hike for Research**
A majority of survey respondents support paying an extra $1 in taxes.

759 **Chronology**
Key events since 1906.

760 **Woodworking Accident Sparks Worldwide Aid**
"Cool tech like this makes children smile, parents weep and nerds rejoice."

762 **Military Innovations Offer Hope to Injured Veterans**
New prosthetics turn science fiction into reality.

765 **At Issue:**
Should Americans fear genetic engineering of human embryos?

FOR FURTHER RESEARCH

769 **For More Information**
Organizations to contact.

770 **Bibliography**
Selected sources used.

771 **The Next Step**
Additional articles.

771 **Citing CQ Researcher**
Sample bibliography formats.

Cover: Getty Images/*The Washington Post*/Nick Otto

Sept. 15, 2017
Volume 27, Number 32

EXECUTIVE EDITOR: Thomas J. Billitteri
tjb@sagepub.com

ASSISTANT MANAGING EDITORS: Kenneth Fireman, kenneth.fireman@sagepub.com, Kathy Koch, kathy.koch@sagepub.com, Scott Rohrer, scott.rohrer@sagepub.com

ASSOCIATE MANAGING EDITOR: Val Ellicott

SENIOR CONTRIBUTING EDITOR:
Thomas J. Colin
tom.colin@sagepub.com

CONTRIBUTING WRITERS: Marcia Clemmitt, Sarah Glazer, Reed Karaim, Barbara Mantel, Chuck McCutcheon, Tom Price

SENIOR PROJECT EDITOR: Olu B. Davis

EDITORIAL ASSISTANT: Natalia Gurevich

FACT CHECKERS: Eva P. Dasher, Michelle Harris, Betsy Towner Levine, Robin Palmer

Los Angeles I London I New Delhi
Singapore I Washington DC I Melbourne

An Imprint of SAGE Publications, Inc.

SENIOR VICE PRESIDENT, GLOBAL LEARNING RESOURCES:
Karen Phillips

EXECUTIVE DIRECTOR, ONLINE LIBRARY AND REFERENCE PUBLISHING:
Todd Baldwin

CQ Researcher (ISSN 1056-2036) is printed on acid-free paper. Published weekly, except: (March wk. 4) (May wk. 4) (July wks. 1, 2) (Aug. wks. 2, 3) (Nov. wk. 4) and (Dec. wks. 3, 4). Published by SAGE Publications, Inc., 2455 Teller Rd., Thousand Oaks, CA 91320. Annual full-service subscriptions start at $1,131. For pricing, call 1-800-818-7243. To purchase a *CQ Researcher* report in print or electronic format (PDF), visit www.cqpress. com or call 866-427-7737. Single reports start at $15. Bulk purchase discounts and electronic-rights licensing are also available. Periodicals postage paid at Thousand Oaks, California, and at additional mailing offices. POSTMASTER: Send address changes to *CQ Researcher*, 2600 Virginia Ave., N.W., Suite 600, Washington, DC 20037.

Medical Breakthroughs

BY SUSAN LADIKA

THE ISSUES

Steven Sanchez was 17 when a BMX biking accident in 2004 left him paralyzed from the waist down. Now, using a robotic exoskeleton — dubbed the Phoenix, after the mythical bird that rises from its ashes — he's able to stand and walk slowly. "I feel much more myself and humanlike being in this device, being able to stand up eye to eye with somebody," said Sanchez, a machinist, who now demonstrates the Phoenix around the world. "It's strange that this robot helps me feel more a part of this planet than the wheelchair does." [1]

The wearable exoskeleton was developed by SuitX, a startup founded in 2012 by Homayoon Kazerooni, a University of California, Berkeley, mechanical engineering professor, and some of his graduate students. The Phoenix costs about $40,000 and weighs 27 pounds, making it lighter and less expensive than some of its competitors. It is one of many breakthrough technologies changing modern medicine and bringing hope to millions.

Many of the advances sound like science fiction. Besides enabling paraplegics to walk again, cutting-edge devices allow quadraplegics to type using only their thoughts. Scientists also are learning how to correct flawed, disease-causing genes in human embryos, use the body's immune system to fight cancer and build replacement organs using 3D printers. [2]

Yet, while such advances are providing new hope for those dealing with significant disabilities or diseases, ethical concerns, funding challenges and regulatory hurdles are slowing the introduction of some breakthroughs, making

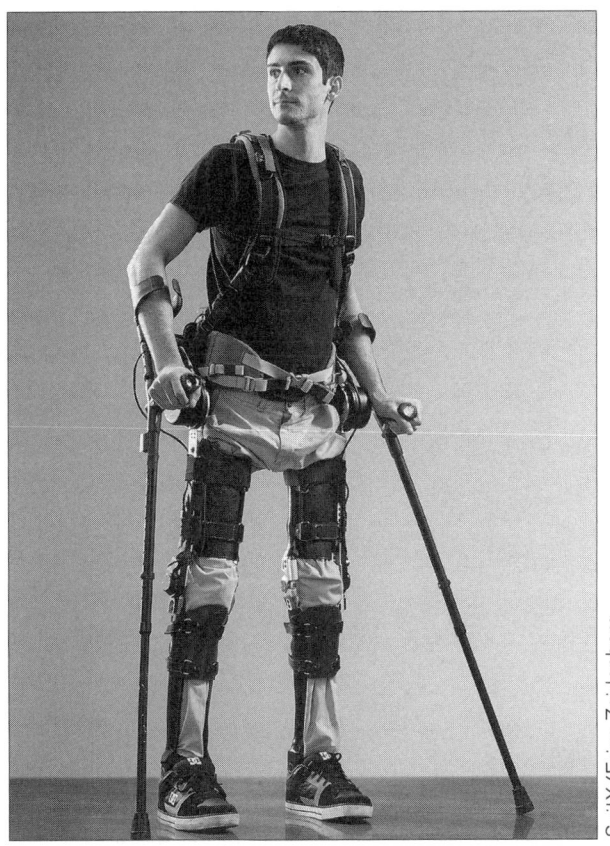

Steven Sanchez, 29, wears a robotic exoskeleton that enables him to stand and walk slowly. Paralyzed from the waist down after a BMX biking accident when he was 17, he now demonstrates the $40,000, 27-pound device, dubbed Phoenix, around the world on behalf of SuitX, its Berkeley, Calif., manufacturer. Such innovations are changing modern medicine and bringing hope to millions.

SuitX/Erica Zeidenberg

it unclear when they might be widely available or affordable.

"The capacity for scientific discovery is growing exponentially," says Dr. Atta Behfar, a director in the Mayo Clinic's Center for Regenerative Medicine, which uses tissue engineering and fortified natural healing processes to heal or replace damaged tissues and organs. [3] "The tools we have in our tool box today, we couldn't imagine in the year 2000." As medical progress continues, doctors will be able to provide "less palliative care and more cures," he predicts.

"We're in the golden age of understanding many of these diseases and disabilities," says William Chin, former executive dean for research at Harvard

Medical School and now chief medical officer and executive vice president of the Pharmaceutical Research and Manufacturers of America (PhRMA), a Washington-based trade association for drug firms.

In late August, the U.S. Food and Drug Administration (FDA) for the first time approved a cancer treatment that uses the genetically modified immune cells of extremely ill children and young adults to help fight acute lymphoblastic leukemia. "We're entering a new frontier in medical innovation with the ability to reprogram a patient's own cells to attack a deadly cancer," said FDA Commissioner Scott Gottlieb. [4] The new treatment, called CAR-T therapy, is the "most exciting thing I've seen in my lifetime," said Dr. Timothy Cripe, an oncologist at Nationwide Children's Hospital in Columbus, Ohio, and a member of the FDA panel that recommended the treatment, which costs $475,000 per patient. [5]

In perhaps the most controversial recent advance, scientists at Oregon Health and Science University this summer announced they had genetically engineered human embryos to correct a mutation that can cause sudden death from heart disease. [6] Scientists say that if the technique proves safe and effective, it could ultimately prevent people from being born with many diseases they might have otherwise inherited. "Potentially, we're talking about thousands of genes and thousands of patients," said Paula Amato, an associate professor of obstetrics and gynecology at the university in Portland, who co-authored the study. [7]

But the procedure has raised safety and ethical concerns. Paul Knoepfler, a

Many Americans Do Not Want Certain Enhancements

At least half of the Americans responding to a Pew survey do not favor medical advances that could reduce babies' disease risk or enhance cognitive or physical capabilities.

Percentage of U.S. Adults Who Want or Do Not Want Medical Advances for Themselves or Their Children

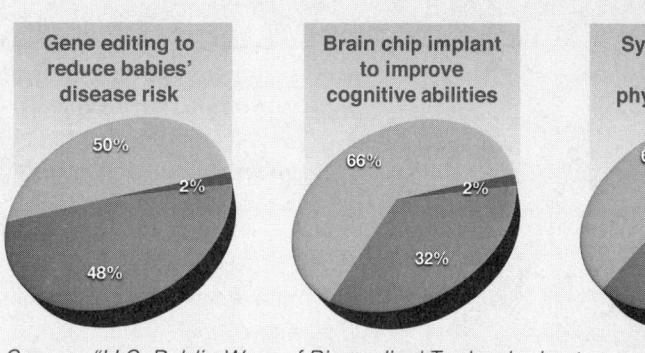

Gene editing to reduce babies' disease risk
50%
2%
48%

Brain chip implant to improve cognitive abilities
66%
2%
32%

Synthetic blood to improve physical abilities
63%
2%
35%

● Would Want
● Would Not Want
● No Response

Source: "U.S. Public Wary of Biomedical Technologies to 'Enhance' Human Abilities," Pew Research Center, 2016, https://tinyurl.com/yccsjweq

professor in the Department of Cell Biology and Human Anatomy at the University of California, Davis School of Medicine, said patient safety cannot yet be guaranteed. "The bottom line is that we'll never really know until someone tries it," because harm might not be apparent until the person reaches adulthood or has children. He also has concerns about the technology potentially being used to manipulate embryos to produce so-called designer babies. "I am not really convinced we can draw a clear line between doing this for only medical purposes versus [cosmetic] traits," Knoepfler said. [8]

George Daley, dean of Harvard Medical School, said that while the research "establishes that we can do embryo gene editing," the question is, "should we, and . . . should there be certain applications that are allowed and others that are prohibited?" [9]

In 2015 researchers at China's Sun Yat-sen University edited the genomes of 86 human embryos, causing an international uproar due to safety and ethical concerns, since any new traits inserted into the genome are passed on to future generations. Forty countries, including the United States, voluntarily imposed a moratorium on government funding to develop such technologies. [10]

Since the 2015 controversy, however, scientists have been perfecting the gene-editing technology called CRISPR, which is now "accessible to people around the globe," said Jennifer Doudna, a professor of biochemistry and molecular biology at the University of California, Berkeley, and one of the creators of the technology. "That's what's wonderful about it, but also one of the real challenges. How do you control something like that?" [11]

In 2016, the United Kingdom became the world's first government to authorize research on genetic editing of human embryos, but the embryos cannot be implanted. [12]

Genetic editing also could pave the way for transplanting pig organs into humans. A recent experiment, led by George Church, a Harvard geneticist, edited out genes carrying pig viruses that could be harmful to humans. [13] If using pig hearts, livers and other organs proved safe, it "could be a real game changer" in addressing the nation's chronic organ shortage, said David Klassen,

chief medical officer at the United Network for Organ Sharing, a nonprofit in Richmond, Va., that manages the country's transplant system. About 117,000 Americans are waiting for organ transplants; 33,600 transplants were done last year. Pig heart valves already are often transplanted into humans. [14]

Meanwhile, more than 53 million Americans have a physical disability, and nearly 50 million suffer from heart disease or cancer, the leading causes of death in the United States. Another 6.5 million have had a stroke, and more than 5 million have been diagnosed with Alzheimer's disease. [15] The prevalence of diseases and disabilities is projected to increase as the nation's population ages: By 2030, about one-fifth of Americans will be 65 or older. [16]

Yet, even as scientific breakthroughs create new hope for millions of people, the Trump administration wants to cut 22 percent from the fiscal 2018 budget of the National Institutes of Health (NIH), the main agency that helps finance U.S. medical and health research. [17] The NIH spends more than $32 billion on medical research each year, most of it going to more than 2,500 universities and research institutes around the globe. [18]

However, both the House and Senate appropriations committees overseeing the NIH budget have pushed back hard on Trump's request, proposing instead to increase NIH funding for fiscal 2018. [19]

Public and private funding on medical and health research and development totaled $158.7 billion in 2015, up 13.3 percent from 2013, according to a 2016 report by Research!America, a nonprofit in Arlington, Va., that advocates for health research. [20]

NIH mostly funds basic research at academic institutions, and the private sector typically "takes ideas from academia and makes them real," Chin says. But "without university work, the initial ideas could never come to light."

In addition to potential funding cutbacks, the length of time and high cost of winning government approval to market a new device or drug also create obstacles for medical breakthroughs. It can take more than a decade and billions of dollars — $2.6 billion, on average — to develop and gain approval for a new drug, according to a study by Tufts University's Center for the Study of Drug Development. The study, which examined 106 drugs developed by 10 companies, found that fewer than 12 percent of drugs make it from clinical trial to approval by the FDA, which regulates drugs and medical devices. [21]

"The FDA is put in a very tough spot," Behfar says. "They need to make sure people are safe. They're the first ones blamed if something is not safe."

However, PhRMA's Chin says the FDA should be better "prepared to guide companies developing the next generation of therapies." His organization has called for modernizing the agency's review process, such as using real-world evidence rather than just results from traditional studies or consulting with outside experts when approving new drugs.

In July FDA Commissioner Gottlieb announced a new program, the Innovation Initiative, to speed up the regulatory approval process using computer models and virtual patients as test subjects. [22] The changes are part of the 21st Century Cures Act enacted last December, which boosted medical research funding and aimed to speed the development and approval of experimental treatments. [23] However, consumer health advocacy groups opposed the new law, which they saw as weakening FDA standards. [24]

The price tags on medical advances also present hurdles. Although the Phoenix is cheaper than other exoskeletons, it still costs around $40,000. And insurers are not keen on paying for expensive new medical breakthroughs. A Florida court in July ordered Blue Cross Blue Shield of Florida to cover the cost of an exoskeleton for a patient after the insurer initially refused to pay for it. [25]

As experts, patients and policymakers consider the future of medical ad-

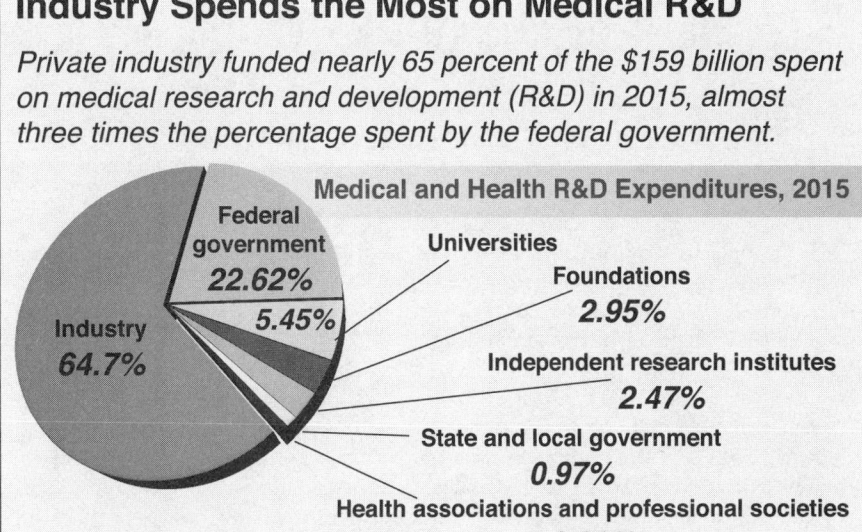

Industry Spends the Most on Medical R&D

Private industry funded nearly 65 percent of the $159 billion spent on medical research and development (R&D) in 2015, almost three times the percentage spent by the federal government.

Medical and Health R&D Expenditures, 2015

Federal government **22.62%**
5.45%
Industry **64.7%**
Universities
Foundations **2.95%**
Independent research institutes **2.47%**
State and local government **0.97%**
Health associations and professional societies **0.83%**

* Figures do not add to 100 because of rounding.

Source: "U.S. Investments in Medical and Health Research and Development 2013-2105," Research!America, 2016, https://tinyurl.com/y8pptynw

vances, here are some of the questions they are asking:

Should the federal government do more to support medical research?

Under President Trump's budget proposal, the NIH budget would drop from $34.6 billion in fiscal 2017 to $26.9 billion next year. [26]

The NIH budget could be cut by identifying "inefficiencies," Health and Human Services Secretary Tom Price, a physician, told a March budget hearing of the House Appropriations Subcommittee for Labor, Health and Human Services. For example, he said, about 30 percent of the NIH's research money is used for indirect — or overhead — expenses, or "for something other than the research." [27]

But universities and research institutions say the amount of government money they receive does not cover the overhead costs for facilities that are required to conduct federal research or the personnel needed to manage the grants. About $4.6 billion is spent each year on meeting federal regulations and maintaining laboratories, according to the administration. [28]

Cutting overhead money would "literally turn out the lights in labs where universities have no other funding to pay for essential research infrastructure and operating expenses," said Mary Sue Coleman, president of the Association of American Universities, which represents 60 major U.S. universities. [29]

The proposed cuts would "cripple our nation's scientific efforts, undermining our economic growth, public health and national security" and "hobble our ability to provide tomorrow's cures and technologies," she said. [30]

"These diseases affect everyone," says Dr. Gary Goldstein, president and CEO of the Kennedy Krieger Institute in Baltimore, which primarily treats children and young adults with developmental diseases or disabilities. "It just is beyond belief that they could cut the NIH budget. In addition to hindering medical research, he says, the cutbacks "would discourage young people thinking about careers" in the field.

As it is, he pointed out, the NIH funds only about 18 percent of the projects proposed each year, and the NIH budget represents only 1 percent

Key Medical, Technology and Biology Terms

CAR-T therapy — Recently approved by the U.S. Food and Drug Administration (FDA) as a treatment for childhood leukemia; first cancer treatment that uses patients' genetically modified immune cells. The process involves removing T cells from a patient, modifying them to attack and kill cancer cells, then re-implanting the cells in the patient. CAR-T therapy is also being reviewed as a new treatment for adult lymphoma; a decision is expected in late 2017. [1]

Cas9 — Enzyme that can cut strands of DNA, like a pair of scissors. The key component of CRISPR gene-editing technology, which scientists say is the most precise, cheapest and easiest means available to remove, add or alter parts of a DNA sequence. It could potentially be used to treat or cure diseases such as muscular dystrophy and sickle cell anemia.

CRISPR (clustered regularly interspaced short palindromic repeats) — Bacterial immune system repurposed as a gene-editing technique that allows scientists to remove defective or unwanted genes from a genome. When used in humans, it could potentially cure or prevent disease, but some worry the technology could also be used to create "designer babies" with preferred traits such as enhanced athleticism or intelligence.

DNA (deoxyribonucleic acid) — Hereditary material in humans and all other organisms; determines the genetic information for creating and maintaining organisms; replicates and is copied when cells divide. [2]

Exoskeleton — Wearable, usually sensor-equipped, device of metal, carbon fiber or elastic that can amplify, augment, reinforce or restore a user's function or performance; can be rigid or flexible and cover all or part of the body. [3]

Gene therapy — Technique in which a gene is inserted into a patient's cells; being tested as treatment for inherited disorders and some cancers and viral infections. Scientists are researching using the process to replace mutated genes with healthy ones, deactivate mutated genes and introduce new genes to help fight a disease. [4]

Germline editing — Also known as germline modification; alters genes in sperm, eggs or embryos. Because altered genes will be passed on to future generations and the technology is not yet advanced enough to guarantee safety or efficacy, more than 40 governments have banned human germline editing, and the National Institutes of Health does not fund such research. [5]

Genome — An organism's complete set of DNA, or genetic information. The human genome contains more than 3 billion DNA letters. [6][7]

Immunotherapy — Treatment using a person's immune system to help fight disease, most commonly cancer. [8]

Stem cells — A type of "master cell" that can divide and renew itself as well as differentiate into specialized cell types; under certain conditions can be induced to become tissue- or organ-specific cells with special functions. In certain organs, such as the intestines and bone marrow, stem cells divide to repair or replace old or damaged tissues. [9]

Targeted therapy — Type of cancer treatment that uses drugs or other substances that precisely identify and attack malignant cells, sparing healthy ones. [10]

T cells — Type of white blood cells that are part of the immune system; protect the body from infection. [11]

— *Susan Ladika*

[1] Rob Stein, "FDA Approves First Gene Therapy For Leukemia," NPR, Aug. 30, 2017, https://tinyurl.com/y9yhetfq.

[2] "What is DNA?" Your Guide to Understanding Genetic Conditions, Genetics Home Reference, U.S. National Library of Medicine, Aug. 29, 2017, https://tinyurl.com/huy4pd3.

[3] "What is an exoskeleton?" *Exoskeleton Report*, https://tinyurl.com/yct5r2gk.

[4] "What is gene therapy?" Your Guide to Understanding Genetic Conditions, Genetics Home Reference, U.S. National Library of Medicine, Aug. 29, 2017, https://tinyurl.com/ze9ykcj.

[5] "About Human Germline Gene Editing," Center for Genetics and Society, July 9, 2015, https://tinyurl.com/yb9l5huz.

[6] "What is a genome?" *Your Genome*, Jan. 6, 2017, https://tinyurl.com/y7p3bguj.

[7] "What is a genome?" Your Guide to Understanding Genetic Conditions, Genetics Home Reference, U.S. National Library of Medicine, Aug. 29, 2017, https://tinyurl.com/hqmzz4e.

[8] "Cancer Immunotherapy," American Cancer Society, https://tinyurl.com/yawkylp2.

[9] "Stem Cell Basics I." Stem Cell Information, National Institutes of Health, https://tinyurl.com/he2ffbd.

[10] "Targeted Cancer Therapy," American Cancer Society, https://tinyurl.com/ya4dxye5.

[11] "NCI Dictionary of Cancer Terms," National Cancer Institute, https://tinyurl.com/y927fwa4.

of the more than $3 trillion spent on health care each year. [31]

The federal government primarily funds basic research, which establishes the foundation for later drug or device development and "wouldn't be covered by industry because it couldn't be commercialized," says Eleanor Dehoney, vice president of policy and advocacy for Research!America. And while industry funds the lion's share of research in the United States, federal funding "fills the gap," she says.

The House Appropriations Committee rebuffed the president, proposing a $1.1 billion increase for the NIH instead. [32] "This bill reflects Republican priorities to cut spending and focus investments in programs our people need the most — public health and medical research," said House Appropriations Chair Rodney Frelinghuysen, a New Jersey Republican. [33] The measure now goes to the full House. In September, the Senate's Labor, Health and Human Services and Education Appropriations Subcommittee voted to boost the NIH's budget by $2 billion — nearly double the House proposal. [34]

Of the $159 billion spent on research and development in 2015, the federal government funded just under 23 percent, while nearly two-thirds of it came from industry and the rest from universities and other sources. [35] In the 1960s and '70s, the federal government funded most basic research in the United States. But by 2013, the government's share had fallen below 50 percent, as corporate funding — primarily by the pharmaceutical industry — rose, according to a National Science Foundation survey. [36]

"The assumption seems to be that the root of all medical innovation is university research, primarily funded by federal grants," wrote Thomas Peter Stossel, a professor emeritus of medicine at Harvard Medical School. "This is mistaken. The private economy, not the government, actually discovers and develops most of the insights and products that advance health." [37]

Nevertheless, says Dr. Jaimie Henderson, a professor of neurology at Stanford University Medical Center, federal funding "has been absolutely vital," and thinking about it being threatened "is a really terrifying proposition." Henderson is part of BrainGate, a national team working on brain-computer interface technologies designed to restore independence, communication and mobility for those with neurologic disorders, injuries or loss of limbs. Without federal funding, he says, "the field wouldn't exist."

Federal funding represents about two-thirds of universities' science and engineering research budgets. Discoveries and insights produced by this research "not only push the limits of our understanding, they also have a clear and direct impact on our daily lives," wrote Deepti Pradhan, a senior research analyst at Yale University. Estimates indicate that U.S. academic research has led to "somewhere between one-quarter and one-half of the drugs on the market today," she added. [38]

Yet, according to a series of articles in *The Lancet*, a British medical journal, up to 85 percent of all research funding may be "avoidably wasted," in part because researchers often do not publish negative findings. Publishing such information would save "resources by alerting other scientists about what might

Twelve-year-old Emma Whitehead of Philipsburg, Pa., was 6 in 2012 when she became the first patient to receive the experimental CAR-T cancer treatment for advanced chronic lymphocytic leukemia. She is now cancer free.

Courtesy Children's Hospital of Philadelphia

not work and allowing them to avoid the same mistakes," Pradhan wrote. [39]

"There's a big move in the private and public sector to make all research transparent," Dehoney says.

Stossel said that while basic academic research advances human knowledge, helps to train scientists and contributes to medical advances, the nation's research system does so "uncommonly and inefficiently" and "is unsustainable," he says. He encouraged academics to join with industry, "where the financial resources and drive to innovate reside." [40]

The vast majority of biomedical research might be wasteful and inefficient, Dr. Michael Bracken, a professor of epidemiology at Yale University School of Public Health told a group at the NIH. "Waste is more than just a waste of money and resources. It can actually be harmful to people's health." For instance, he said, in some cases it might not be necessary to replicate studies. If research shows a treatment is effective, repeating it "means patients are being submitted to [a] placebo when they can receive active therapy," Bracken said. [41]

Moreover, he pointed out, of every 100 research projects, only half result

in published findings, of which half have major design flaws so their results are unreliable. Of the remainder, half are redundant or unneeded because of prior research, Bracken said. [42]

Is the FDA's regulatory process adequate for today's cutting-edge medical research?

The FDA is under pressure to keep up with the rapid pace of medical breakthroughs.

To explain how he feels FDA regulations hamper medical advances, Carl June, a professor of immunotherapy at the University of Pennsylvania who led development of the groundbreaking CAR-T cancer treatment, cited the case of 6-year-old Emma Whitehead. In 2012 Whitehead, who had advanced chronic lymphocytic leukemia, became the first patient to receive the experimental CAR-T (chimeric antigen receptor T-cell) treatment.

Following the treatment, Whitehead developed a 106-degree fever, had multiple organ failure and went into a coma. Doctors feared she would die. They treated her reaction with a medication typically used to treat arthritis. Within hours, Whitehead awoke from

Most Back Small Tax Hike for Research

A majority of Americans say they would pay an extra $1 per week in taxes to fund more federal investment in health research.

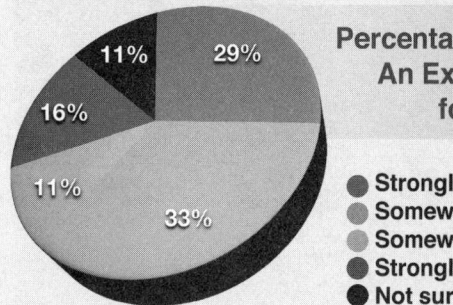

Percentage Who Approve or Oppose An Extra $1 Per Week in Taxes for Medical Research

- Strongly support
- Somewhat support
- Somewhat oppose
- Strongly oppose
- Not sure

29%
11%
16%
11%
33%

Source: "U.S. Investments in Medical and Health Research and Development 2013-2105," Research!America, 2016, https://tinyurl.com/y8pptynw

the coma. "It was literally one of those Lazarus conditions," June said. Two weeks later, she was cancer free.

Since then researchers have found that about one-third of patients who undergo CAR-T treatment experience a violent immune system reaction like Whitehead did.

However, explained June, FDA regulators "err on the side of caution," and "if the first patient dies on a protocol and nobody's been cured, you're over." [43]

FDA regulations are made "so that you can never have more than about 30 percent of people get sick with serious side effects," but patients who receive CAR-T treatment would probably die without it, he said. "We don't have enough leeway for side effects when you have a potential curative therapy." [44]

Henderson of Stanford University says although the FDA has become "more responsive and agile" in recent years, it "needs to streamline to get advances out more quickly, without compromising safety."

But Behfar of the Mayo Clinic says the FDA staff is "reasonably efficient and not obstructionist."

Susan Howley, executive vice president for research at the Christopher & Dana Reeve Foundation, which seeks a cure for spinal cord injuries, also praised the agency. The foundation is supporting

epidural stimulation research to help those with spinal cord injuries recover voluntary movements and stand again. With epidural stimulation, a stimulator is put inside a person's body and wired to their spinal cord. With the stimulator, commands such as "move my right leg" prompt movement. [45]

Epidural stimulation also has improved other areas of the body, such as cardio-vascular and bowel and bladder functions, Howley says. "Our experience with epidural stimulation has been phenomenal," she says. The FDA sees it as "something changing lives right now."

The role of the FDA has evolved over the years, says Chin of PhRMA. "In their old role, they were basically a traffic cop," he says. Now the agency needs to "understand the barriers for discovery and development of these new medications and know how to break down those barriers."

For instance, PhRMA wants the FDA to use cutting-edge tools for drug review and approval. "New and powerful tools emphasize individual patient characteristics and include innovative clinical trial design, advanced statistical methods and use of real-world evidence," says the PhRMA website. The organization also has called on the FDA to increase its staff and tap into the expertise of

outside organizations, such as the NIH and academia. [46]

A study by Ariel Dora Stern, an assistant professor of business administration at Harvard University, found that while the FDA has sped up approvals for innovative drugs, procedures for approving innovative medical devices remain bogged down. [47]

For instance, for the first maker of a new medical device in a particular category, approval takes 7.2 months longer than for subsequent manufacturers of the same type of device, Stern found. In comparison, the first manufacturer of a drug spends just one-third of a month longer in the approval process than the next manufacturer of that drug.

"I kept hearing how frustrating and non-transparent the process was for getting a novel medical device approved," Stern said. [48]

The FDA categorizes devices based on their function rather than on the technology they use. Stern found that devices based on technologies in an existing category are often approved faster than devices using the same technology but classified in a different category, potentially delaying advances using already-approved technologies. Streamlined procedures and product guidelines could help reduce approval times, Stern said. [49]

Another study found that devices that pose the highest potential risk, such as pacemakers, are more highly regulated in the United States than in Europe. Due to the slowness of the U.S. regulatory process, the study said, such devices typically are available in the European Union three years sooner than in the United States. [50]

The FDA's new Innovation Initiative is aimed "at making sure our regulatory processes are modern and efficient . . . and informed by the most up-to-date science," Commissioner Gottlieb said. "We don't want to present regulatory barriers to beneficial new medical innovations . . . if they don't add to our understanding of the product's safety and benefits." [51]

The 21st Century Cures Act, which authorized the initiative, is a "milestone" in improving medical technology innovation and in "ensuring the availability of new lifesaving, life-enhancing devices and diagnostics for patients," said Scott Whitaker, president of the Advanced Medical Technology Association, which represents 300 medical device companies. [52]

But the law has its critics. Michael Carome, director of the Health Research Group at Public Citizen, an advocacy nonprofit founded by consumer advocate Ralph Nader, said the law "continues a trend" that began in the 1990s of eroding FDA standards. "We don't think there should be any further erosion." [53] The law pressures the FDA to rush approval for new treatments, such as cell therapies and medical devices, "based on weaker evidence of safety and efficacy," according to the group. [54]

The "breakthrough" designation for medical devices is too broad, the group said, and by relying on real-world evidence and summaries of study data rather than the complete records of clinical trials, the FDA might approve devices that are not ready for marketing.

"Summary data could hide important information about the safety and effectiveness from the FDA scientists," said Carome. "I'm disappointed to see this." [55]

Should the federal government do more to address ethical concerns about new medical advances?

Certain medical breakthroughs, especially genetic engineering to correct mutations in human embryos, have caused alarm among some ethicists and legal experts.

Scientists say the genetic editing technique known as CRISPR-Cas9 could potentially be used to treat or cure diseases such as breast and ovarian cancer and sickle cell anemia. But scientists also worry about potential unintended consequences on a human's genetic makeup, affecting future generations or society in general. Others worry that CRISPR could be used to create "designer babies"

Food and Drug Administration Commissioner Scott Gottlieb said scientific advances have led to new treatments, including a recently approved therapy for childhood leukemia that targets the underlying mechanisms causing different diseases. "We're entering a new frontier in medical innovation with the ability to reprogram a patient's own cells to attack a deadly cancer," Gottlieb said.

with desirable traits such as enhanced athleticism or intelligence. [56]

"I think it's extraordinarily disturbing," said Marcy Darnovsky, executive director of the Berkeley, Calif.-based Center for Genetics and Society, which opposes heritable genetic modifications. "We'll see fertility clinics advertising gene editing for enhancement purposes. We'll see children being born who are said to be biologically superior." [57]

But Arthur Caplan, a professor of bioethics at New York University School of Medicine, doubts that will happen anytime soon. "Researchers will need to show they can safely repair inherited genetic diseases before putting a toe into the enhancement waters," he wrote. "There are too many genes and too many gene-environment interactions to make the creation of geniuses or music prodigies likely anytime soon." (See "At Issue," p. 765.)

Mark Kay, a professor of pediatrics and genetics at Stanford University, does not oppose genetic editing to cure "horrific human diseases," but says he "would want to make sure there were no off-targeting, since the changes will be heritable." Off-targeting occurs when genetic editing affects nontargeted parts of the

genome, causing unintended mutations. In addition, he says, "applying it to embryos and bringing them to birth is a little more controversial."

To study the ethics of human genome editing, the National Academy of Sciences and the National Academies of Medicine convened a 22-member committee of international experts, which released its final recommendations in February on how the technology should be regulated. The committee supported modification of embryos in clinical trials to fix mutations, but only in rare situations and to fix genes that would cause serious diseases or conditions. The panel's 328-page report recommended that all nations ensure that any potential clinical applications of human genome engineering "reflect societal values and be subject to appropriate oversight" based on seven guiding principles and 10 specific criteria. For example, it said, governments should strictly monitor trials to prevent germline editing for nondisease purposes, such as to give a baby desirable traits. [58]

"We've always said in the past gene editing shouldn't be done, mostly because it couldn't be done safely," said committee co-leader Richard Hynes, a professor of cancer research at the Massachusetts Institute of Technology. "That's still true, but now it looks like it's going to be done safely soon. What our report said was, once the technical hurdles are cleared, then there will be societal issues that have to be considered and discussions that are going to have to happen. Now's the time." [59]

The U.S. government has two policies — both adopted in 2015 — regarding genetic engineering of human embryos. Congress prohibited the FDA from approving clinical trials in which a human embryo "is intentionally created or modified to include a heritable genetic modification," and the NIH has refused to fund any research that edits the genes of human embryos. [60] (The scientists at Oregon Health and Sciences University who used the procedure to correct a heart disease mutation received no federal funds; they also destroyed all of the embryos used in the experiment.) [61]

However, as in most countries, the federal government has no control over what type of research is done in laboratories or experiments that do not receive federal funds.

One federal agency — the Defense Advanced Research Projects Agency (DARPA), the research arm of the U.S. Department of Defense — recently granted $65 million to seven research partners at universities and institutes to develop ways to safely, responsibly and predictably use gene editing to benefit society and address health and security concerns about possible accidental or intentional misuse of the technology. [62]

"With all the power of technology goes ethical, legal and social implications," says Justin Sanchez, director of DARPA's Biological Technologies Office, speaking generally about concerns raised by medical advances. Scientists can get "wrapped up in the science itself and don't think of the broader implications of what they're doing."

In August, the American Society for Human Genetics issued a position paper saying that while it is "inappropriate

to perform germline gene editing that culminates in human pregnancy," research using in vitro human germline editing should be allowed as long as there is "appropriate oversight and consent from [the embryo] donors." The paper also called for public funding for such research. [63]

Some conservative Christian groups, which believe life begins at conception, adamantly oppose research using human embryos — which are fertilized eggs — because embryos are destroyed in the process. "At the outset, it was known that the embryos would not be given a chance to grow and develop," the Rev. Tad Pacholczyk, director of education at the National Catholic Bioethics Center, said in August. "We should never use our fellow human beings as a means" to an end. [64]

Such objections led the George W. Bush administration in 2001 to prohibit federal funding of most stem cell research that used human embryos, but President Barack Obama reversed that policy in 2009. [65] Stem cells are "master cells" capable of being turned into different types of tissue.

Knoepfler, at the University of California, fears a similar backlash against human germline editing. "This stuff is moving at warp speed, and we need to get our act together on establishing guidelines that are much clearer about what is OK and what isn't," he said. [66]

Doudna, the co-developer of CRISPR-Cas9, said, "I'm not categorically against all human germline editing, but I think there would need to be a reason to do it that would justify the risks and costs. This is a harbinger of what's to come." [67] Doudna, who helped organize the 2015 moratorium on human germline editing, has traveled around the world this year to bring attention to the need to build a "global consensus" on how to responsibly use the technology. [68]

The Alliance for Regenerative Medicine, which supports regenerative medicine and gene therapy to treat diseases, opposes editing human embryonic genes.

"You are talking about permanently changing the genome of a person without their consent. That's an ethical question even if the technical challenges and safety get worked out," said Michael Werner, executive director of the Washington, D.C.-based group. [69]

Susan Peschin, president and CEO of the Alliance for Aging Research, a nonprofit in Washington that advocates for research on aging, points out that while the National Academies committee's guiding principles are a good first step, no international organization coordinates how countries regulate human germline editing. And even within each country, no single agency typically regulates both public and private research.

"That is the dilemma we all face," she said. "Many of our concerns about gene editing technologies are 'out of bounds' for the institutions we rely on to regulate those technologies," she said. And public views on human embryonic genome editing vary "among and within countries and reflect both religious and secular influences," she said. "The result has been public policies ranging from permissive, to regulated, to prohibitionist." [70] ∎

BACKGROUND

Early Breakthroughs

People have always sought ways to compensate for disabilities and to combat debilitating diseases. The first known prosthetic — a toe — was found with a mummy in Egypt. A bronze and iron artificial leg with a wooden core, dating to 300 B.C., was discovered in Italy, and a Roman general had an iron hand created in 200 B.C. so he could hold his shield and return to the battlefield. [71]

The first record of a disabled person using a self-propelled wheelchair in Europe dates to the 1600s, when German me-

Continued on p. 760

Chronology

1900s-1980s
Medical regulatory processes are established in the United States.

1906
Pure Food and Drug Act creates the U.S. Food and Drug Administration (FDA), which bans interstate commerce of adulterated or misbranded food and drugs.

1938
Food, Drug and Cosmetic Act increases the FDA's authority to regulate drugs.

1946
Yale pharmacologists Alfred Gilman and Louis Goodman develop the first effective cancer chemotherapy drug.

1958
Defense Department creates Defense Advanced Research Projects Agency in response to technological advances by the Soviet Union.

1962
Congress requires drug manufacturers to use controlled studies to show their products are effective.

1967
South African surgeon Christiaan Barnard performs first successful human heart transplant.

1976
Medical Device Regulation Act creates three classes of devices subject to FDA regulation.

1983
Orphan Drug Act creates financial incentives for drug companies to develop drugs to treat rare diseases.

1987
Japanese researchers discover odd, repeat DNA sequences in bacteria, eventually leading to development of the CRISPR gene-editing tool.

1990s-2000s
Scientists make advances in stem cell and human genome research.

1998
American biologist James Alexander Thomson derives the first human embryonic stem cell line.

2001
Responding to conservative Christian opposition to research using human embryos, President George W. Bush prohibits federal funding of most embryonic stem cell research.

2003
Human Genome Project publishes complete human genome sequence.

2006
Researchers discover that some adult cells can be reprogramed to become a type of stem cell.

2009
President Barack Obama reinstates federal funding of human embryonic stem cell research.

2010s-Present
Medical advances occur at unprecedented pace.

2011
Two patients with advanced leukemia experience "miraculous" recoveries after University of Pennsylvania researchers treat them with a type of immunotherapy called CAR-T.

2012
Jennifer Doudna, a professor of biochemistry and molecular biology at the University of California, Berkeley, and microbiologist and French biochemist Emmanuelle Charpentier develop CRISPR technique that can be used to cut into any DNA sequence, enabling scientists to edit genes from the human genome.

2015
Chinese researchers attempt to use CRISPR to edit human embryos, prompting many scientists to call the effort unsafe, premature and unethical and to call for a moratorium on editing human embryos.

2016
United Kingdom becomes first country to license genetic editing of human embryos for research. . . . Congress approves 21st Century Cures Act, which increases funding for medical research and aims to speed development of new treatments.

2017
National Academy of Sciences committee says modifying embryos to fix genetic mutations that cause serious diseases or conditions is acceptable if no "reasonable alternatives exist." . . . President Trump proposes cutting the NIH's fiscal 2018 budget 22 percent, but House Appropriations Committee later recommends a 3.2 percent increase. . . . FDA approves CAR-T therapy to treat cancer using a patient's genetically modified immune cells. . . . Researchers at Oregon Health and Science University edit human embryos to correct a genetic mutation that can cause sudden heart stoppage. . . . FDA announces Innovation Initiative, designed to speed the regulatory approval process for medical innovations.

Woodworking Accident Sparks Worldwide Aid

"Cool tech like this makes children smile, parents weep and nerds rejoice."

Medical advances do not come cheap, especially prosthetics. An exoskeleton — a wearable robotic suit to help a paralyzed person walk again — can cost $40,000 or more. [1] But thousands of volunteers around the world are using 3D printers to help bring down the cost of new hands.

A collaborative online community called e-NABLE is creating prosthetic hands for less than $50 each and giving them away to people in more than 90 countries who were born with missing fingers or who lost them due to war, disease or natural disaster. Using open-source 3D printable designs, e-NABLE volunteers have produced and distributed about 3,000 hands. [2]

The project began in 2011 when Ivan Owen, of Arlington, Wash., who used to make mechanical props for science fiction productions, created a functional metal puppet hand to wear at a steampunk convention. Steampunk combines science fiction and aesthetics inspired by 19th-century steam-powered machinery. After Owen posted a video of the hand on YouTube, South African carpenter Richard Van As, who had lost his fingers on one hand in a woodworking accident, contacted Owen. The two paired up and created a metal finger for him. [3]

The mother of a 5-year-old South African boy saw information about the project on Facebook and asked them to help her son, Liam, who was born with no fingers on his right hand. Realizing

the boy would soon outgrow any hand made for him, Owen and Van As designed a device that could be created — and reproduced economically in ever-larger sizes — using liquefied plastic and a 3D printer. It was the first 3D-printed mechanical hand for a child, according to e-NABLE. [4] In 3D printing, a blueprint of an object is created using computer-assisted design. Then, the design is printed out in thin layers of liquefied plastic filament, which are then bonded together to create the object. [5]

Using an Indiegogo campaign, Owen and Van As initially raised more than $10,000 to create hands for Liam and other children. [6] Owen and Van As made the design available online for free.

Aided by Jon Schull, a former research scientist at the Rochester (N.Y.) Institute of Technology, the project evolved into the e-NABLE Community, which has attracted nearly 7,000 volunteers worldwide. [7]

Finding prosthetics for children is a particular challenge because they quickly outgrow the devices, which normally cost up to $10,000 each. [8]

E-NABLE volunteer Maria Esquela of Columbia, Md., founded the Alliance for Project Based Learning Solutions, a nonprofit that helps create prosthetics for e-NABLE as part of youth service learning projects. A volunteer Scout chaplain, Esquela has helped

Continued from p. 758

chanic Johann Hautsch developed several rolling chairs. German watchmaker Stephan Farfler built a three-wheeled chair that used a rotary handle on the front wheel to propel the chair. [72]

Humans also have tried to treat diseases since earliest times. In the 5th century B.C., the Greek physician Hippocrates, considered the father of Western medicine, developed ethical standards for treating patients. [73]

The first European medical school was founded in Salerno, Italy, in the 10th century. In the 1200s, the Roman emperor Frederick II decreed that no one could practice medicine unless approved by the teachers in Salerno. The ensuing centuries saw increasing insight and expertise in areas such as anatomy and surgery. In the 1700s, the practice of inoculation against disease was brought from the Middle East to Europe. Vaccination against smallpox became widespread. [74]

In the second half of the 19th century, medical breakthroughs accompanied the economic progress triggered by the Industrial Revolution, including the first laboratory-developed vaccine, produced by French chemist Louis Pasteur in 1879. German physicist Wilhelm Conrad Röntgen developed the first X-rays in 1895. [75]

In the early 20th century, concerns over adulterated and misbranded food and drugs led to passage of the Pure Food and Drug Act of 1906, which established the FDA. [76] Initially, drugs had to meet only strength and purity standards, and the federal government had to show that a drug's label was false and misleading to take it off the market. But the 1938 Food, Drug and Cosmetic Act required manufacturers to show that a drug was safe before it could be marketed. In 1962, Congress required manufacturers to prove that a drug was not only safe but also effective, based on controlled studies. [77]

Meanwhile, medical advances continued to emerge. In 1946, Yale pharmacologists Alfred Gilman and Louis Goodman developed nitrogen mustard, the first effective cancer chemotherapy drug. South African surgeon Christiaan Barnard performed the first successful human heart transplant in 1967. And in 1998, American developmental biologist James Alexander Thomson derived the first human embryonic stem cell line. [78]

The 2000s brought rapid medical advancements, including the first mapping of the human genome; using targeted cancer treatments to block tumor growth or kill cancer cells; and successfully turning adult cells into stem cells. [79]

The Human Genome Project was a collaborative international effort to map and understand human genes, providing detailed information about the structure, organization and function of all 20,500 human genes, known as a genome. The full sequence of the

spread the project to Boy and Girl Scout troops around the world and has set up community events where volunteers form assembly lines to put together the prosthetic hands. There are jobs for everyone, she says, from young kids to older adults.

One Boy Scout who needed a hand joined a project, she recalls, and "literally printed his own hand." His family helped put it together and then created hands for three more people.

Hands made by e-NABLE, which can sometimes include part of a forearm, have gone to wounded U.S. military veterans and children around the globe, Esquela says. "Anyone, anywhere can request a device and not pay for it," she says.

The e-NABLE community's website, enablingthefuture.org, provides several hand models to choose from, with details on how to print and assemble them. The site includes links that allow someone to print a hand for themselves or connect with other people who can print and assemble one for them. [8] Materials for a new hand cost about $50 and come in a range of colors — including gray, pink and turquoise.

"Some people want to use [the hand] to use an iPad," Esquela says. "Some people want to be able to use a broom and a machete."

The e-NABLE volunteer community has more than 100 chapters worldwide, in libraries, schools and other locations on every continent, Esquela says. Members create individualized hands rather than one-size-fits-all devices.

"The hands can have a magical ability to make a kid feel good about his or her special hand or arm, and give them some confidence," Schull said. "The other kids at school think they're really lucky. It turns out to be as important psychosocially as it is mechanically. Cool tech like this makes children smile, parents weep and nerds rejoice." [9]

— *Susan Ladika*

[1] Laurie McGinley, "Novel Cancer Treatment Wins Endorsement of FDA Advisers," *The Washington Post*, July 12, 2017, https://tinyurl.com/y88bljnl.

[2] "About Us," Enabling the Future, undated, https://tinyurl.com/y8ky598s.

[3] Dean Kahn, "Bellingham Man's Work on Low-Cost Prosthetics Becomes International Effort," *The Bellingham Herald*, Sept. 1, 2014, https://tinyurl.com/y8xts257; "About Us," *ibid.*

[4] "About Us," *ibid.*

[5] "How 3D Printers Work," U.S. Department of Energy, June 19, 2014, https://tinyurl.com/ycfayjsq.

[6] "Robohand," Indiegogo, undated, https://tinyurl.com/ybkzyxgd.

[7] "About Us," *op. cit.*

[8] "Need a Hand," Enabling the Future, undated, https://tinyurl.com/yday6xc5.

[9] *Ibid.*; Celena Chong, "This Google-Funded Startup Prints 3D Hands for Disabled Kids So They Can Feel Like 'Superheroes,'" *Business Insider*, Aug. 10, 2015, https://tinyurl.com/omohsn7.

human genome was published in 2003 by the International Human Genome Sequencing Consortium. [80]

The project has helped propel genomic medicine, which uses genetic information about an individual for therapeutic or diagnostic decision-making. Genetic medicine is used in oncology and pharmacology and to treat infectious and rare diseases. [81]

New Treatments

In the past two decades, targeted therapies have become common in cancer treatment, which has long relied on surgery, radiation and chemotherapy. Such therapies use new drugs to zero in on cancer cells by focusing on certain molecular changes seen in those cells. [82] Some treatments work against specific types of cancers, such as breast, colorectal and lung cancer. [83]

A type of targeted therapy called immunotherapy boosts the body's own immune system to fight cancer, using substances made in a person's body or in a laboratory. [84] The CAR-T process extracts T cells, immune cells from the patient's blood, and genetically modifies them to attack the cancer and transfers them back into the patient. [85] Unlike some gene therapy, however, this technology does not affect the patient's genetics or germline. It only reprograms the immune cells to attack the cancer.

The treatment gained attention in 2011 when University of Pennsylvania researchers treated three patients with advanced chronic lymphocytic leukemia, which affects white blood cells. The patients had not responded to other treatments, but two of the three experienced "miraculous recoveries" after T cell treatment. [86]

"It was a tipping point. There was an amazing outpouring because we showed for the first time that it could work," said June, the University of Pennsylvania professor who helped develop the treatment. [87] In further clinical trials, more than 90 percent of pediatric patients with acute lymphoblastic leukemia went into remission after CAR-T treatment. [88]

Progress also is being seen with stem cell treatments used in regenerative medicine, which aims to replace damaged tissue or organs, rather than just treating the symptoms. For example, at Stanford University stem cells harvested from the bone marrow of adult donors were injected into the brains of stroke patients in a clinical trial, according to results published in 2016. Several patients experienced great improvements, including a 71-year-old wheelchair-bound patient who was able to walk again. [89]

Some scientists say stem cell treatments could be the key to cures for conditions such as Parkinson's disease, heart disease and diabetes. [90] The treatment was discovered in 1998, when scientists discov-

Military Innovations Offer Hope to Injured Veterans

New prosthetics turn science fiction into reality.

The U.S. military spends millions of dollars each year to develop prosthetics for wounded soldiers as well as for aging veterans who have lost limbs to diabetes and other diseases. The devices are developed under the auspices of the Defense Advanced Research Projects Agency (DARPA), the research arm of the U.S. military, and the Department of Veterans Affairs (VA). DARPA and VA funding also support, among other things, projects aiming to link brains and computers, make gene editing safer and more effective, test robotic hands for patients recovering from spinal cord injuries and study the benefits of exoskeletons, wearable robotic devices that help paralyzed individuals walk or move their limbs. [1]

"A lot of people may say this is science fiction," Justin Sanchez, director of DARPA's Biological Technologies Office in Arlington, Va., says about the agency's research. "It may be inspired by science fiction. It's actual technology we're making real."

Sanchez says the agency "leads the vision" but that the devices are developed by researchers at universities and other institutions, small and large businesses and national laboratories. Many of the devices later are also used by civilians because the developers retain the intellectual property rights for the devices, which can then be commercialized. "It's a natural secondary consequence of technology," says Sanchez.

The Defense Department created DARPA after the Soviet Union sent the first artificial satellite into orbit in 1957. The agency was designed to keep the United States ahead of other countries in scientific and technological advances and to "develop breakthrough technology for national security," Sanchez says.

Recently, DARPA allocated $65 million for the Safe Genes project, focused on the safe use of genetic engineering, and the same amount for the Neural Engineering System Design program, which is developing a brain-computer interface that ultimately could benefit veterans and others with sensory deficits. [2]

According to the U.S. Census Bureau, 3.9 million veterans have a service-related disability. [3] Many have lost limbs or suffered traumatic brain injuries in Iraq or Afghanistan. Between 2001 and 2015 about 1,650 soldiers lost a limb, and more than 361,000 active duty service members suffered traumatic brain injuries from 2000 to 2016 — about 9,000 of which were "penetrating" or "severe." [4]

VA researchers are working on a robotic glove that combines electrical stimulation with biomechanical movement to help veterans dealing with spinal cord injuries, says Dr. Kevin White, chief of spinal cord injury at James A. Haley Veterans' Hospital in Tampa, Fla. The device, called the Functional Electrical Stimulation Hand Glove 200, was designed by robotics engineer Randy Simmons, who previously created animatronics for "Jurassic Park" and other movies.

"For people who are quadriplegic, their No. 1 goal is to improve their hand function" so they can eat, brush their teeth and perform other daily tasks, White says. The glove can improve mobility for both recently injured veterans and for those injured years ago, he says.

Dr. Steven Scott, co-director of the Center of Innovation on Disability and Rehabilitation Research at the Tampa VA hospital, says, "If you fought for this country, we ought to give you the best of the best."

ered a way to derive stem cells from human embryos, created through in vitro fertilization. When the embryos were no longer needed for reproduction, they were donated for research. [91]

However, conservative Christian opposition to the use of embryos in stem cell research led to President Bush's 2001 ban on federal funding of embryonic stem cell research on cell lines derived after Aug. 9, 2001. But his policy did not affect private-sector research, studies funded by states or research using adult stem cells. [92] In 2009, when President Obama reversed Bush's policy, he allowed the NIH to fund embryonic stem cell research only if federal money was not used to create the stem cells. [93]

In 2006, researchers found that some specialized adult cells could be repro-

grammed to resemble embryonic stem cells. These are called induced pluripotent stem cells (iPSCs). Since then, stem cell advances are taking place in a wide range of fields, from stem cell transplants to treat cancer to restoration or regeneration of tissues and organs. [94]

CRISPR Technology

The roots of the CRISPR gene editing technique stretch back 30 years, when scientists at Osaka University in Japan were studying E. coli bacteria. [95] They found unusual, repeated DNA sequences next to the gene they were studying but did not understand their biological significance. [96]

At the time, scientists had rudimentary techniques to decode DNA. As researchers learned to sequence the entire genomes of bacteria, they found many had the repeated DNA sequences and dubbed them "clustered regularly interspaced short palindromic repeats," or CRISPR. In the mid-2000s, scientists realized the bacteria were using CRISPR to fight viruses. [97]

Cas9 is an enzyme that, like a pair of scissors, can cut strands of DNA. Using CRISPR-Cas9 technology, scientists can remove, add or alter parts of a DNA sequence. Scientists say it is the most precise, cheapest and easiest means available to edit the genome. [98]

In 2012, a team led by the University of California's Doudna and French researcher Emmanuelle Charpentier, who was then at Umea University in Sweden,

VA doctors hope to make the glove less bulky and ultimately win Food and Drug Administration approval to make it available for widespread use. Military research "contributes to all society," Scott says. The Tampa hospital also is testing how three types of exoskeletons affect veterans' cardiovascular systems, bone health and quality of life, White says.

Military advances in prosthetics also include a high-tech arm for amputees, developed with DARPA funds. Electrodes on the prosthetic, known as LUKE, pick up electrical signals from a patient's muscles. As the muscles flex, the prosthetic arm changes position and grip. [5] As the technology for the arm advances, Scott says, "eventually you'll be able to feel with it."

Several research institutions are working to develop "soft robots" — called exosuits — that can be worn as clothing and are designed to help stroke victims recover their normal gait. [6]

Donald Ingber, director of the Wyss Institute for Biologically Inspired Engineering at Harvard University, said exosuits look more like sports clothing than C-3PO, the robot of "Star Wars" movie fame. Yet it is "equally programmable . . . and individualizes itself for each patient." [7]

— *Susan Ladika*

Kapil Katyal, a senior engineer at Johns Hopkins University's Applied Physics Laboratory, demonstrates a robotic hand and arm that responds to brain impulses; he wears a sensor glove on his other hand.

[1] Taylor Hatmaker, "DARPA Awards $65 million to Develop the Perfect, Tiny Two-Way Brain-Computer Interface," *TechCrunch*, July 10, 2017, https://tinyurl.com/y9jrbuvw; "Building the Safe Genes Toolkit," Defense Advanced Research Projects Agency, July 19, 2017, https://tinyurl.com/y8cspwy5; Ed Drohan, "Staff Trains for Exoskeleton Research Project," U.S. Department of Veterans Affairs, July 14, 2016, https://tinyurl.com/y9s6sdxr.

[2] "Building the Safe Genes Toolkit," ibid.; "Towards a High-Resolution, Implantable Neural Interface," Defense Advanced Research Projects Agency, July 10, 2017, https://tinyurl.com/y7xjgsav.

[3] "FFF: Veterans Day 2016: Nov. 11," U.S. Census Bureau, Oct. 25, 2016, https://tinyurl.com/y8rdxhrj.

[4] Nancy Montgomery, "2016 marks first year without combat amputation since Afghan, Iraq wars began," *Stars and Stripes*, March 18, 2017, https://tinyurl.com/yc4v7q7o. Also see "DoD Numbers for Traumatic Brain Injury Worldwide — Totals," Defense and Veterans Brain Injury Center, Feb. 17, 2017, https://tinyurl.com/y72jjujf.

[5] James Vincent, "DARPA-Funded Prosthetic Arm Set to Go on Sale Later this Year," *The Verge*, July 11, 2016, https://tinyurl.com/yapty3zp; Tracey Romero, "Two LUKE Prosthetic Arms now Available to Veterans," *This Week Orthopedics*, July 31, 2017, https://tinyurl.com/y7fs94yf.

[6] Benjamin Boettner, "Robotic Suit Promotes Normal Walking in Stroke Patients," *Harvard Gazette*, July 27, 2017, https://tinyurl.com/yd8a2zws.

[7] Ibid.

showed that the CRISPR-Cas9 technique could be used to cut into any DNA sequence. When a cell tries to repair a cut, the repair is often imperfect, which can disable a gene. Scientists then usually can insert a patch with the genetic change they desire, which is then incorporated into the DNA when the cell fixes the break. [99]

The attempt by Chinese researchers to edit a gene that causes beta thalassemia, a sometimes fatal blood disorder, announced in May 2015, was the first time scientists had edited DNA in human embryos, a highly controversial step that had long been considered off limits. Critics called the experiment unsafe and premature. Only 28 of the 86 embryos used were edited successfully, leading the researchers to

conclude: "Our data . . . support the notion that clinical applications of the CRISPR system may be premature at this stage." [100]

By December of that year a group of international scientists met in Washington and called for a moratorium on germline editing, saying it would be "irresponsible to proceed" until the risks could be better assessed and consensus reached on the appropriate use of the technology. The meeting was convened by the National Academy of Sciences, the Institute of Medicine, the Chinese Academy of Sciences and the Royal Society of London. [101]

Despite the concerns raised by some governments and scientists, Chinese researchers again reported using CRISPR technology on human embryos — in 2016 and 2017. In 2016, they made

four of 26 embryos resistant to HIV infection. In 2017, they corrected mutations in three embryos — two had a mutation that could destroy red blood cells and the other corrected a mutation for the blood disorder beta thalassemia. [102] ∎

CURRENT SITUATION

Pushing the Limits

When scientists at Oregon Health and Science University this summer announced their success using

CRISPR-Cas9 to fix a mutation that can cause sudden death from heart disease, it was the first time the technology had been tried on human embryos in the United States. [103]

The procedure was used to treat hypertrophic cardiomyopathy, or thickening of the heart muscle. It affects about one in 500 people — many of whom are

President Trump wants to cut 22 percent from the fiscal 2018 budget of the National Institutes of Health (NIH), the main agency that helps finance U.S. medical and health research. The NIH spends more than $32 billion on medical research each year, most of it going to universities and research institutes. Both the House and Senate appropriations committees overseeing the NIH budget have pushed back hard on Trump's request, proposing instead to increase NIH funding for next year.

young athletes — and can cause sudden heart failure. The mutant gene was corrected in nearly three-quarters of the embryos, which were destroyed after a few days to address concerns about the ethics of gene editing. [104]

As some scientists debate ethical issues, others are battling over patents for the CRISPR technology. The U.S. Patent and Trademark Office in February upheld patents for the technology, granted to the Broad Institute of Massachusetts Institute of Technology and Harvard University. Although the institute received its patents first, the University of California, which said its researchers invented the technique, had been the first to apply for a patent. [105]

In July, the University of California appealed the patent office decision with the U.S. Court of Appeals for the Federal Circuit in Washington, D.C. [106] The Broad Institute must file its opening brief by Oct. 25, but the case could take "years to resolve," said Robin Feldman, a law professor at the University of California Hastings College of the Law in San Francisco. [107]

In another development, in February researchers at Stanford University announced that paralyzed patients were able to use a brain-computer interface to move a cursor on a screen — just by imagining their own hand movements. One participant typed 39 characters in a minute — the fastest, most accurate typing in such studies to date. [108]

"We continue to push the limits of communications performance," says Stanford's Henderson. "We hope to make it faster, more accurate and easier to use."

Currently, the system must be wired through a patient's skull, but researchers want to make it wireless. Henderson hopes the interface will be available to patients within a decade.

Meanwhile, some scientists are concerned about the growth of commercial stem cell clinics, which are using cells isolated from a patient's fat to treat a variety of conditions, ranging from arthritis to Alzheimer's disease. There are more than 500 such clinics in the United States, and others operate offshore. Small studies indicate that certain types of stem cell injections may help treat patients with conditions such as stroke, but the clinics may not use the same type of stem cells used in those studies. Some patients have developed tumors or gone blind after treatment at unregulated clinics. [109]

The clinics, which charge up to $20,000 for treatment, "promise to cure everything," says Howley of the Reeve Foundation. "Patients and families who are desperate feel they have no option." Until now, however, the FDA "has not really provided a lot of clarity when autologous cells [the person's own stem cells] are involved," Howley says. "It's a little bit of the Wild West out there now."

Until now the FDA has not regulated stem cell clinics, in part because the cells are only minimally manipulated. But the agency has proposed regulating them as drugs, which would require the clinics to go through a tough approval process. [110]

In August, the FDA announced a crackdown on stem cell clinics offering "unapproved and potentially dangerous" treatments, and U.S. marshals recently raided San Diego-based StemImmune Inc. and seized smallpox vaccines that the FDA said had been combined with stem cells derived from fat to create an unapproved product that was injected intravenously and directly into patients' cancer tumors. The FDA "will not allow deceitful actors to take advantage of vulnerable patients by purporting to have treatments or cures for serious diseases without any proof that they actually work," Gottlieb said. [111]

Knoepfler, the University of California stem cell researcher, has harshly criticized clinics that are conducting "an unap-

Continued on p. 766

(AFP/Getty Images/Saul Loeb)

At Issue:

Should Americans fear genetic engineering of human embryos?

AMY WEBB
CEO, THE FUTURE TODAY INSTITUTE

WRITTEN FOR *CQ RESEARCHER*, SEPTEMBER 2017

CRISPR-Cas9 — a process that allows scientists to remove, add or alter a genetic sequence — promises exciting new ways to treat diseases such as muscular dystrophy and HIV. But it also means scientists will be able to remove genetic diseases from human embryos. Soon, we will be able to alter the human germline, influencing our collective gene pool for generations to come.

CRISPR is the most powerful tool scientists have ever developed, and it has the potential to both enhance and harm all life on Earth. Along with other forms of synthetic biology and artificial intelligence, it could soon render Darwin obsolete. It is fine if we toss natural selection out the window, as long as we think through the implications and scenarios for our future.

Currently, not only is the U.S. government not modeling out the future but it also is not working toward a cohesive national biology strategy. Without leadership in this area, much of the debate around CRISPR's future is relegated to the ownership of intellectual property. The existing instruments of change in our country — regulation, patents and lawsuits — are sealing the fate of the commercial and societal effects of this technology.

Meanwhile, our American ideals and values do not necessarily align with the goals of other governments — China, for instance — that also are pushing the frontiers of genetic editing. Hackers and terrorists view gene editing as a viable weapon of mass destruction. The very same technique that can produce malaria-resistant mosquitoes could be used to create mosquitoes that carry a lethal pathogen. If you think it is difficult to contain your backyard mosquitoes during the summer, imagine a massive swarm of weaponized, nearly invisible bugs descending on North America.

Scientists should continue their work, but we must also recognize that CRISPR and other synthetic biology techniques are developing faster than our government's ability to regulate them. As of now, the government employs relatively few researchers and policymakers devoted to the future of CRISPR, and the field is crippled by the nation's existing methods for regulating innovation: patents, regulation and lawsuits.

At the same time, sweeping reforms or bloated legislation could doom CRISPR from its potential to save and enhance human lives. Our future depends on a more sophisticated approach to dealing with this technology — and fast.

ARTHUR L. CAPLAN
PROFESSOR OF BIOETHICS AND FOUNDING DIRECTOR, DIVISION OF MEDICAL ETHICS, NEW YORK UNIVERSITY SCHOOL OF MEDICINE

WRITTEN FOR *CQ RESEARCHER*, SEPTEMBER 2017

recent human germline editing experiments in China and the United States have renewed calls to prohibit any attempt to modify heritable traits in human beings. In fact, governments already prohibit this. The National Institutes of Health will not fund research using human embryonic gene-editing technologies, nearly all European nations adopted the Oviedo Convention in 1997 prohibiting germline engineering and UNESCO's Universal Declaration on the Human Genome and Human Rights says germline interventions "could be contrary to human dignity."

These prohibitions are needed for four reasons: safety, human dignity, worries about eugenics and concerns about fair access. None of them is persuasive. Much needs to be learned about the safety of modifying the genes of human eggs, embryos and sperm, but that means doing more research in animals and on embryo models in the lab.

Such work raises the issue of human dignity: Can human embryos be experimented upon without violating core human values? If an embryo — or more accurately, a pre-embryo — is in a dish and not a uterus, it cannot become a human being. There is more to life than conception — environment counts, too. So, as long as work is done on embryos in dishes, researchers are not violating human dignity.

This takes the discussion to questions of eugenics and access. Could germline editing be used to make superbabies? Yes. Will that happen anytime soon? No.

Researchers first need to show they can safely repair inherited genetic diseases before they can put a toe into the enhancement waters. There are too many genes and too many gene/environment interactions to make the creation of geniuses or music prodigies likely anytime soon. If we think enhancement is always bad — and I, for one, do not — it can be prohibited when that technique is perfected rather than holding an elegant way to eliminate hereditary diseases hostage to a distant future some find frightening.

As for access, if only the rich can use germline editing to eliminate diseases, that is fundamentally unjust. However, inequity in access has never blocked innovative medical technologies before, and it should not stop this one.

We need to regulate human germline editing experimentation more tightly. Journals and the media should condemn, rather than publish, renegade science by incompetent experimenters. We must shape the future of editing the genes of our descendants with oversight, transparency and accountability — not bans.

Continued from p. 764

proved and for-profit gigantic human experiment." [112]

But California plastic surgeon Mark Berman, who owns a chain of stem cell clinics, said academics and giant pharmaceutical firms want to control and profit from the stem cell business because the clinics' success "hurts their business plan." [113]

Funding Issues

Progress requires a continued infusion of federal funding, scientists say. "Funding is key," says PhRMA's Chin. "The work that needs to be done is extensive and also very costly."

Some experts are concerned about the amount of money that drug and device makers spend on clinical trials. Industry funds six times more clinical trials than the federal government does, according to a study by Johns Hopkins University researchers. The number of clinical trials paid for by industry climbed more than 40 percent from 2006 to 2014, to 6,550, the study found. During that same time period, as the NIH's budget fell 14 percent, the number of trials funded by the NIH fell by one-quarter, to 1,048. [114]

However, said study leader Stephan Ehrhardt, an associate professor of epidemiology at Johns Hopkins, industry does not fund trials that are important for public health "because they have no incentive to do that." For instance, the NIH might test a new blood pressure medication against a placebo and against other drugs as well as diet and exercise. But a drug manufacturer may only test it against a placebo, Ehrhardt said. [115]

By funding clinical trials, companies have more control over what patients and physicians learn about new treatments. "Conflicts of interest can also have a pervasive influence on the research questions that are asked, the ways the studies are designed, the framing of the analyses and results and the decision to disseminate the findings," said Dr. Reshma

Jagsi, director of the Center for Bioethics and Social Sciences in Medicine at the University of Michigan. [116]

Meanwhile, funding for medical device development has lagged behind the more lucrative drug development. During the 2007-09 recession, venture capitalists pulled back from funding device research and have not returned. Funding fell from $356 billion in 2006 to $308 billion in 2015. [117]

Even when medical advances win FDA approval, it can be challenging to get insurers to cover the treatments. But the Florida court that ordered Blue Cross and Blue Shield to cover an exoskeleton, said exoskeletons "are no longer experimental or investigational." [118] By the end of the first quarter of 2017, at least 86 paralyzed individuals had received insurance coverage for the devices. [119]

The Reeve Foundation is pushing for research on locomotor training, a common therapy in some European countries, in which a person with a spinal cord injury is suspended in a harness over a treadmill and a therapist helps them move. Besides helping people stand or take steps again, the training improves the cardiovascular system, pulmonary function, bone density and other areas, the foundation's Howley says.

In the United States, health insurance typically covers 30 to 40 rehabilitation sessions "for a sprained ankle or spinal cord injury," she says. But it could take 180 locomotor training sessions for a patient "to plateau."

To get Medicare and Medicaid to cover such nontraditional treatments, the Centers for Medicare & Medicaid Services must hear that paying for the treatment will save money later on medication, equipment and rehospitalization. "You have to show that the payers are going to save money," she says.

On other fronts, the 21st Century Cures Act adopted last December gave the NIH $4.8 billion in new funding. At least $1.8 billion of that was earmarked over the next seven years for the so-called Cancer Moonshot, a program an-

nounced by former President Obama in his final State of the Union address to accelerate cancer research by making a decade's worth of advances in cancer prevention, diagnosis and treatment within five years. [120] The total also included $1.6 billion to find cures for brain diseases, such as Alzheimer's. [121]

OUTLOOK

More Cures

Medical advances occurring in research centers today are spurring hope that in the future physicians will be able to shift their focus from treatment to cures.

"We're moving in the direction of meaningful prevention . . . and cures," says the Kennedy Krieger Institute's Goldstein.

The breakthroughs with CAR-T therapy, for example, could lead to cures for every cancer of the blood and bone marrow, said June, of the University of Pennsylvania. [122]

But such advanced treatments can be extremely expensive — CAR-T is expected to cost patients up to $475,000 — and it's unclear whether health insurance companies will cover it. "While CAR-T is a promising new type of immunotherapy, it is not commercially available, and we have yet to complete our evaluation," Aetna spokesman T.J. Crawford said. [123]

However, the advances are spurring competition, and 40 companies are now making CAR-T cells, June said, adding, "They are incentivized to make [the cells] more cheaply." [124]

The Mayo Clinic's Behfar also sees big advances ahead in stem cell treatments. While patients today use their own stem cells for treatments, he foresees "off-the-shelf" stem cell therapies eventually being available for just a few dollars a dose.

Others expect treatment options to continue to be personalized. For the treatment of spinal cord injuries, for example, "the collective wisdom seems to be that at the end of the day people will be given a cocktail of interventions" based on their age, type of injury and other factors, says Howley of the Reeve Foundation.

Advances also may come from new ventures. Elon Musk, co-founder of the Tesla auto company, recently announced establishment of a new company, Neuralink, which will make devices for treating or diagnosing neurological problems. [125] The California start-up Paradromics is working to develop a small chip that can be inserted into a person's brain that could read nerve signals and restore senses and abilities that have been lost because of disease or injury. [126]

Goldstein would like to see more of a focus on treating brain disorders. "I feel like we're following cancer, but we're decades behind [with] the brain. Work with the brain is more complicated." But because NIH funding is limited and the agency is "somewhat conservative" when choosing which research projects to fund, "we need seed money from someone else," such as individual donors or foundations, he says. New treatments in the pipeline "still aren't what we want in neurological disorders," he adds.

For instance, promising treatments for Alzheimer's disease still are lacking, even though the number of sufferers is projected to jump from 5 million today to up to 16 million in 2050, according to the Alzheimer's Association.

According to FDA chief Gottlieb, scientific advances have helped researchers understand the genetic and protein bases of disease, leading to new treatments that target the underlying mechanisms causing different diseases. "These advances hold out the promise of arresting and even curing a growing number of diseases," he wrote. [127]

At the same time, he added, "the price of new technology affects the ability of people to access these new treatments. We therefore need to be mindful of the costs of our regulatory processes to the degree that these costs also affect the avail-

ability of new innovations, and the way that they are ultimately priced." [128] ■

Notes

[1] Victoria Colliver, "SuitX's Robot Suit Lets Paralyzed People Walk Again," *The San Francisco Chronicle*, April 1, 2016, https://tinyurl.com/y7gq7op6; "UC Berkeley Exoskeleton Soccer," *SuitX*, July 10, 2014, https://tinyurl.com/y7gofdx4.

[2] Pam Belluck, "In Breakthrough, Scientists Edit a Dangerous Mutation from Genes in Human Embryos," *The New York Times*, Aug. 2, 2017, https://tinyurl.com/yc5qu9l8; "What is Cancer Immunotherapy," American Cancer Society, July 23, 2015, https://tinyurl.com/j5b4we2; Bruce Goldman, "Brain-Computer Interface Advance Allows Fast, Accurate Typing by People with Paralysis," Stanford Medicine News Center," Feb. 1, 2017, https://tinyurl.com/y8gbnqyq.

[3] "About regenerative medicine," Mayo Clinic, undated, https://tinyurl.com/zbszb7g.

[4] "FDA Approval Brings First Gene Therapy to the United States," U.S. Food and Drug Administration, Aug. 30, 2017, https://tinyurl.com/y8xku8ol.

[5] Laurie McGinley, "Novel Cancer Treatment Wins Endorsement of FDA Advisers," *The Washington Post*, July 12, 2017, https://tinyurl.com/y9dtgbfz. Denise Grady, "FDA Approves First Gene-Altering Leukemia Treatment, Costing $475,000," *The New York Times*, Aug. 30, 2017, http://tinyurl.com/yacsof4z. See also Gina Kolata, "New Gene-Therapy Treatments Will Carry Whopping Price Tags," *The New York Times*, Sept. 11, 2017, http://tinyurl.com/y85zg6ga.

[6] Belluck, *op. cit.*

[7] "Scientists Precisely Edit DNA in Human Embryos to Fix a Disease Gene," NPR, Aug. 2, 2017, https://tinyurl.com/y9c8z5xb.

[8] Bradley J. Fikes, "Controversial Milestone: Scientists Genetically Modify Human Embryos for First Time, Reports Say," *The San Diego Union-Tribune*, July 27, 2017, https://tinyurl.com/ycy6trem.

[9] Dina Fine Maron, "Embryo Gene-Editing Experiment Reignites Ethical Debate," *Scientific American*, Aug. 2, 2017, https://tinyurl.com/y8p6v47e.

[10] Rob Stein, "Critics Lash Out at Chinese Scientists who Edited DNA in Human Embryos," NPR, April 23, 2015, https://tinyurl.com/ybvyzql3.

[11] Michael Hiltzik, "CRISPR Pioneer Jennifer Doudna Struggles with the Ethical Implications of What She Has Wrought," *Los Angeles Times*, July 21, 2017, https://tinyurl.com/y8zeunlt.

[12] Madhumita Murgia, "How Scientists in Britain Are Deciding the Future of Humanity," *Newsweek*, Dec. 28, 2016, https://tinyurl.com/y828t3aj.

[13] Gina Kolata, "Gene Editing Spurs Hope for Transplanting Pig Organs into Humans," *The New York Times*, Aug. 10, 2017, https://tinyurl.com/yce8gjse.

[14] *Ibid.*

[15] "CDC: 54 Million Adults in the U.S. Live with a Disability," Centers for Disease Control and Prevention, July 30, 2015, https://tinyurl.com/y9pmwawd. "Diseases and Conditions," Centers for Disease Control and Prevention, July 6, 2016, https://tinyurl.com/y99dzflq; "2017 Alzheimer's Disease Facts and Figures," Alzheimer's Association, undated, https://tinyurl.com/yb588nxo.

[16] "Health and Aging Policy," Health and Aging Policy Fellows, undated, https://tinyurl.com/y7t5ev9g.

[17] "What's in Trump's 2018 Budget Request for Science?" *Science*, May 23, 2017, https://tinyurl.com/ka88mut.

[18] "Budget," National Institutes of Health, March 6, 2017, https://tinyurl.com/ma3kvpw.

[19] Jocelyn Kaiser, "House Bill Gives NIH 3% Raise, Blocks Cuts to Overhead Payments," *Science*, July 12, 2017, https://tinyurl.com/ycprdcg6. Jocelyn Kaiser, "Senate Spending Panel Approves $2 Billion Raise for NIH in 2018," *Science*, Sept. 6, 2017, https://tinyurl.com/yc2xjlcd.

20 "U.S. Investments in Medical and Health Research and Development," Research!America, Fall 2016, https://tinyurl.com/y8pptynw.

[21] "Cost of Developing a Drug," Tufts Center for the Study of Drug Development, Nov. 18, 2014, https://tinyurl.com/q5kn8wn.

[22] Evan Sweeney, "FDA Plans to Use Computer Modeling to Speed up Drug, Device Evaluations," FierceHealthcare, July 10, 2017, https://tinyurl.com/ychdbmwk; Scott Gottlieb, "How FDA Plans to Help Consumers Capitalize on Advances in Science," *FDA Voice*, July 7, 2017, https://tinyurl.com/yb6j7v23.

[23] Mike DeBonis, "Congress Passes 21st Century Cures Act, Boosting Research and Easing Drug Approvals," *The Washington Post*, Dec. 7, 2016, https://tinyurl.com/ybcr8fy5.

[24] Sheila Kaplan, "Winners and Losers of the 21st Century Cures Act," STAT, Dec. 5, 2016, https://tinyurl.com/y85op296.

[25] "Florida Blue Cross Blue Shield to Cover ReWalk Exoskeleton for Paralyzed Plan Member Following Court Decision Deeming the Device Medically Necessary," *ReWalk*, June 12, 2017, https://tinyurl.com/yalzs9dc.

[26] "What's in Trump's 2018 Budget Request for Science?" *op. cit.*

27 Jocelyn Kaiser, "Trump Wants 2018 NIH Cut to Come from Overhead Payments," *Science*, March 29, 2017, https://tinyurl.com/ydc3qocl.

28 Jocelyn Kaiser, "NIH Plan to Reduce Overhead Payments Draws Fire," *Science*, June 2, 2017, https://tinyurl.com/y86lg4y7.

29 *Ibid.*

30 Alison Kodjak, "Medical Research, Health Care Face Deep Cuts in Trump Budget," NPR, May 23, 2017, https://tinyurl.com/y8pmcn9c.

31 Kendall Powell, "The Best-Kept Secrets to Winning Grants," *Nature*, May 24, 2017, https://tinyurl.com/y6wampxg.

32 "Appropriations Committee Releases the Fiscal Year 2018 Labor, Health and Human Services, Education Funding Bill," Committee on Appropriations, U.S. House of Representatives, July 12, 2017, https://tinyurl.com/ybfq543v.

33 Jamie Dupree, "House GOP Brushes Aside Trump Plans for Cuts at NIH, CDC," AJC.com, July 12, 2017, https://tinyurl.com/yb7xroqg.

34 Kaiser, "Senate Spending Panel Approves $2 Billion Raise for NIH in 2018," *op. cit.*

35 Ibid. Other sources of funding include voluntary health associations and professional societies, state and local government, independent research institutes and foundations.

36 Jeffrey Mervis, "Data Check: U.S. Government Share of Basic Research Funding Falls Below 50 Percent," *Science*, March 9, 2017, https://tinyurl.com/y8wc6vg6.

37 Thomas Peter Stossel, "Don't Thank Big Government for Medical Breakthroughs," American Enterprise Institute, Jan. 6, 2017, https://tinyurl.com/yd9mx7xs.

38 Deepti Pradhan, "Scientific Research Needs More Funding, but also Smarter Spending," *Footnote*, Jan. 26, 2016, https://tinyurl.com/y9sn9y63.

39 *Ibid.*

40 Stossel, *op. cit.*

41 Eric Bock, "Much Biomedical Research Is Wasted, Argues Bracken," *NIH Record*, National Institutes of Health, July 1, 2016, https://tinyurl.com/y8bm5qu9.

42 *Ibid.*

43 Allysia Finley, "How HIV Became a Cancer Cure," *The Wall Street Journal*, Aug. 18, 2017, https://tinyurl.com/yacugxwb.

44 *Ibid.*

45 "An Unprecedented Breakthrough," Christopher & Dana Reeve Foundation, undated, https://tinyurl.com/yau5tpgs.

46 "Modernizing Drug Discovery, Development and Approval," PhRMA, March 31, 2016, http://tinyurl.com/y9dk9geu.

47 Michael Blanding, "New Medical Devices Get to Patients too Slowly," *Working Knowledge*, Aug. 10, 2015, https://tinyurl.com/y8mw9kum.

48 *Ibid.*

49 *Ibid.*

50 Iris Huang, "Medical Device Startups and the FDA," McNair Center for Entrepreneurship & Innovation, April 11, 2017, https://tinyurl.com/y8t2xerv.

51 Gottlieb, *op. cit.*

52 Sheila Kaplan, *op. cit.*

53 Michael Hiltzik, "The 21st Century Cures Act: A Huge Handout to the Drug Industry Disguised as a Pro-Research Bounty," *Los Angeles Times*, Dec. 5, 2016, https://tinyurl.com/zguy2kg.

54 "Stop The 21st Century Cures Bill," Public Citizen, undated, http://tinyurl.com/y7lbgusu.

55 Sheila Kaplan, "House Approves the 21st Century Cures Act, Sending the Landmark Bill to Senate," STAT, Nov. 30, 2016, https://tinyurl.com/y9rvhdpl.

56 Belluck, *op. cit.* For background, see David Masci, "Designer Humans," *CQ Researcher*, May 18, 2001, pp. 425-440. Ariana Eunjung Cha, "First Human Embryo Editing Experiment in U.S. 'Corrects' Gene for Heart Condition," *The Washington Post*, Aug. 2, 2017, https://tinyurl.com/y8q5s4ua.

57 Rob Stein, "Exclusive: Inside the Lab Where Scientists are Editing DNA in Human Embryos," NPR, Aug. 18, 2017, https://tinyurl.com/ybqro3xk.

58 Jocelyn Kaiser, "U.S. panel gives yellow light to human embryo editing," *Science*, Feb. 14, 2017, https://tinyurl.com/gsdq9d6. See also "Criteria for heritable germline editing," "Human

Genome Editing: Science, Ethics, and Governance," National Academies of Science, https://tinyurl.com/yb39rb5d. Also Susan Pescin, "How should we regulate genome editing?" World Economic Forum, May 4, 2017, https://tinyurl.com/y8sm2no4.

59 Belluck, *op. cit.*

60 For background, see Jill U. Adams, "Manipulating the Human Genome," *CQ Researcher*, June 19, 2015, pp. 529-552.

61 Belluck, *op. cit.*; Robert Cook-Deegan and Jane Maienschein, "Listening for the Public Voice," *Slate*, Aug. 16, 2017, https://tinyurl.com/y8nbzs3k.

62 "Building the Safe Genes Toolkit," Defense Advanced Projects Research Agency, July 19, 2017, https://tinyurl.com/y8cspwy5.

63 Cook-Deegan and Maienschein, *op. cit.*

64 "Gene Editing: Unmoored Science," *The National Catholic Register*, Aug. 11, 2017, https://tinyurl.com/yajwqdsf.

65 "Timeline of Major Events in Stem Cell Research Policy," Research!America, undated, https://tinyurl.com/jwvcgrm.

66 Megan Molteni, "Scientists CRISPR the First Human Embryos in the U.S. (Maybe)," *Wired*, July 27, 2017, https://tinyurl.com/yc3mvunm.

67 Maron, *op. cit.*

68 Megan Molteni, "CRISPR May Cure All Genetic Disease — One Day," *Wired*, June 7, 2017, https://tinyurl.com/ya9bm4bs.

69 Kim Painter, "U.S. Scientists Fix Disease Genes in Human Embryos for First Time," *USA Today*, Aug. 2, 2017, https://tinyurl.com/y8qoyxs8.

70 Pescin, *op. cit.*

71 Kim M. Norton, "A Brief History of Prosthetics," Amputee Coalition, November/December, 2007, https://tinyurl.com/y8rr7kxm.

72 Nick Watson and Brian Woods, "History of the Wheelchair," *Encyclopaedia Britannica*, undated, https://tinyurl.com/ybb53rly.

73 Wesley D. Smith, "Hippocrates," *Encyclopaedia Britannica*, June 29, 2017, https://tinyurl.com/yasd72c7.

74 William Archibald Robson Thomson *et al.*, "History of Medicine," *Encyclopaedia Britannica*, June 14, 2017, https://tinyurl.com/yc6pe45d.

75 "What is Modern Medicine?" *Medical News Today*, Jan. 5, 2016, https://tinyurl.com/ycm4vd3q.

76 Michelle Meadows, "Promoting Safe and Effective Drugs for 100 Years," U.S. Food and Drug Administration, January/February 2006, https://tinyurl.com/ybdm7jat.

77 *Ibid.*

78 "What is Modern Medicine," *op. cit.*

79 "10 Medical Advances in the Last 10 Years," CNN.com, June 5, 2013, https://tinyurl.com/oz2b76k.

About the Author

Susan Ladika is a freelance writer in Tampa, Fla., whose work has appeared in *HR Magazine*, Workforce, Bankrate.com, CreditCards.com, *Science*, *The Wall Street Journal-Europe* and *International Educator*. She previously worked as a writer and editor for newspapers in the Southeast, including *The Tampa Tribune*, and also reported from Europe for The Associated Press.

[80] "An Overview of the Human Genome Project," National Human Genome Research Institute, May 11, 2016, https://tinyurl.com/y9wg5r5h.

[81] "What is Genomic Medicine?" National Human Genome Research Institute, July 21, 2016, https://tinyurl.com/y72zbcch.

[82] "CAR T Cells: Engineering Patients' Immune Cells to Treat Their Cancers," National Cancer Institute, Aug. 7, 2017, https://tinyurl.com/hn6dh4n.

[83] "Understanding Targeted Therapy," Cancer.net, May 2017, https://tinyurl.com/y92femf2.

[84] "Understanding Immunotherapy," Cancer.net, April 2017, https://tinyurl.com/qaetk7k. "What is Cancer Immunotherapy?" American Cancer Society, July 23, 2015, https://tinyurl.com/j5b4we2.

[85] McGinley, op. cit.

[86] Finley, op. cit.

[87] Ibid.

[88] Ibid.

[89] Ariana Eunjung Cha, "Stanford Researchers 'Stunned' by Stem Cell Experiment that Helped Stroke Patient Walk," The Washington Post, June 2, 2016, https://tinyurl.com/y7a9ssk9.

[90] "Stem Cell Basics," National Institutes of Health," undated, https://tinyurl.com/he2ffbd.

[91] Ibid.

[92] "Timeline of Major Events in Stem Cell Research Policy," op. cit.

[93] Maggie Fox, "Conservative Reps Urge Trump to Fire NIH Chief Francis Collins over Stem Cells," NBC News, May 22, 2017, https://tinyurl.com/yb7jvo2h.

[94] "Stem Cell Transplants," National Cancer Institute," April 29, 2015, https://tinyurl.com/y77t9rez; Megan McKenzie, "Renaissance in Medicine," Discovery's Edge, March 24, 2017, https://tinyurl.com/yakngmr9.

[95] Carl Zimmer, "Breakthrough DNA Editor Born of Bacteria," Quanta Magazine, Feb. 6, 2015, https://tinyurl.com/ya4yvcnu.

[96] Andrew Pollack, "A Powerful New Way to Edit DNA," The New York Times, March 3, 2014, https://tinyurl.com/y9fcl8yd.

[97] Zimmer, op. cit.

[98] "What is CRISPR-Cas 9?" Yourgenome.org, undated, https://tinyurl.com/ybhqdnc9.

[99] Pollack, op. cit.

[100] Stein, "Critics Lash out at Chinese Scientists Who Edited DNA in Human Embryos," op. cit.

[101] Nicholas Wade, "Scientists Seek Moratorium on Edits to Human Genome that Could be Inherited," The New York Times, Dec. 3, 2015, https://tinyurl.com/yahmzgyr.

[102] Ewen Callaway, "Second Chinese Team Reports Gene Editing in Human Embryos," Nature, April 8, 2016, https://tinyurl.com/zk5yynp; Michael Le Page, "First Results of CRISPR Gene Editing of Normal Embryos Released," New Scientist, March 9, 2017, https://tinyurl.com/zvfjtal.

[103] Belluck, op. cit.

[104] Eunjung Cha, op. cit.

[105] Heidi Ledford, "Why the CRISPR Patent Verdict Isn't the End of the Story," Nature, Feb. 17, 2017, https://tinyurl.com/y9f7pp6o.

[106] "UC Files Appeal to Revive CRISPR Patent Interference," Berkeley News, July 26, 2017, https://tinyurl.com/y7o3mtm4.

[107] Christine Giuliano, "UC Files Opening Brief to Appeal CRISPR-Cas9 Patent Decision," The Daily Californian, July 30, 2017, https://tinyurl.com/y83g6734.

[108] Goldman, op. cit.

[109] Usha Lee McFarling, "FDA Weighs Crackdown that Could Shut Hundreds of Stem Cell Clinics," STAT, Sept. 9, 2016, https://tinyurl.com/me3roqb.

[110] Ibid.

[111] Laurie McGinley, "FDA Cracks Down on Stem-Cell Clinics, Including One Using Smallpox Vaccine in Cancer Patients," The Washington Post, Aug. 28, 2017, https://tinyurl.com/y7n3pxd8.

[112] Kelly Servick, "Texas has Sanctioned Unapproved Stem Cell Therapies. Will it Change Anything?" Science, June 15, 2017, https://tinyurl.com/y9sg7luw.

[113] McFarling, op. cit.

[114] Meredith Cohn, "Industry Funds Six Times More Clinical Trials than Feds," The Baltimore Sun, Dec. 15, 2015, https://tinyurl.com/hnmr7zj.

[115] Ibid.

[116] Ibid.

[117] Aaron Gregg, "As Venture Investment in Medical Devices Stalls, Companies Get Creative," The Washington Post, Feb. 14, 2016, https://tinyurl.com/y7kjl8nd.

[118] "Florida Blue Cross Blue Shield to Cover ReWalk Exoskeleton for Paralyzed Plan Member Following Court Decision Deeming the Device Medically Necessary," op. cit.

[119] Ibid.

[120] See "Cancer Moonshot," The Obama White House Archives, https://tinyurl.com/ycvy9vxr.

[121] DeBonis, op. cit.; Kaplan, "Winners and Losers of the 21st Century Cures Act," op. cit.

[122] Finley, op. cit.

[123] Deena Beasley, "T Cell Cancer Therapy Holds Promise, Longer-Term Results Await," Reuters, July 13, 2017, https://tinyurl.com/y8fbls2q.

[124] Finley, op. cit.

[125] "Elon Musk Enters the World of Brain-Computer Interfaces," The Economist, March 30, 2017, https://tinyurl.com/mxypyq4.

[126] Charles Piller, "Silicon Valley's Ambitious New Bet: Brain 'Modems' that Restore Sight, Hearing and Speech," STAT, Aug. 17, 2017, https://tinyurl.com/ybme57rp.

[127] Gottlieb, op. cit.

[128] Ibid.

FOR MORE INFORMATION

Advanced Medical Technology Association, 701 Pennsylvania Ave., N.W., Suite 800, Washington, DC 20004-2654; 202-783-8700; www.advamed.org. Trade association with almost 300 members that aims to advance medical technology.

American Association for the Advancement of Science, 1200 New York Ave., N.W., Washington, DC 20005; 202-326-6400; www.aaas.org. Nonprofit devoted to advancing science, engineering and innovation around the world.

Christopher & Dana Reeve Foundation, 636 Morris Turnpike, Suite 3A, Short Hills, NJ 07078; 800-225-0292; www.christopherreeve.org. Works to improve quality of life for victims of spinal cord injuries and to find cures for such injuries.

Defense Advanced Research Projects Agency, 675 N. Randolph St., Arlington, VA 22203; 703-526-6630; www.darpa.mil. The research arm of the Defense Department; invests in research on national security and medical and other technology.

National Institutes of Health, 9000 Rockville Pike, Bethesda, MD 20892; 301-496-4000; www.nih.gov. A Health and Human Services agency that funds medical research projects at thousands of universities and institutes around the country.

Pharmaceutical Research and Manufacturers of America (PhRMA), 950 F St., N.W., Suite 300, Washington, DC 20004; 202-835-3400; www.phrma.org. Trade group representing biopharmaceutical companies.

Research!America, 241 18th St. S., Suite 501, Arlington, VA 22202; 703-739-2577; www.researchamerica.org. Nonprofit that advocates for making health-related research a higher national priority.

Bibliography

Selected Sources

Books

Armstrong, Sue, *P53: The Gene that Cracked the Cancer Code*, Bloomsbury Publishing, 2014.

An international science writer examines researchers' attempts to understand the gene known as p53 — the most studied gene in history — which protects people from cancer.

Doudna, Jennifer A., and Samuel H. Sternberg, *A Crack in Creation: Gene Editing and the Unthinkable Power to Control Evolution*, Houghton Mifflin Harcourt, 2017.

A University of California, Berkeley, professor (Doudna), who helped create the gene-editing technique known as CRISPR, and a scientist at Caribou Biosciences Inc. (Sternberg) trace the discovery of CRISPR.

Mukherjee, Siddhartha, *The Gene: An Intimate History*, Simon & Schuster, May 2016.

A Pulitzer Prize-winning author examines the millennia-long search for the gene and what manipulation of the human genome might mean for the future of humanity.

Articles

"FDA Approval Brings First Gene Therapy to the United States," U.S. Food and Drug Administration, Aug. 30, 2017, https://tinyurl.com/y8xku8ol.

The regulatory agency announces its approval of CAR-T therapy to treat young patients with a certain type of leukemia.

Belluck, Pam, "In Breakthrough, Scientists Edit a Dangerous Mutation from Genes in Human Embryos," *The New York Times*, Aug. 2, 2017, https://tinyurl.com/yc5qu9l8.

For the first time, U.S. scientists use genetic editing to correct a heart defect in human embryos.

Blanding, Michael, "New Medical Devices Get To Patients Too Slowly," *Working Knowledge*, Aug. 10, 2015, https://tinyurl.com/y8mw9kum.

A professor of business administration says it takes longer to gain Food and Drug Administration (FDA) approval for a new medical device that it does to get a new drug approved.

DeBonis, Mike, "Congress passes 21st Century Cures Act, boosting research and easing drug approvals," *The Washington Post*, Dec. 7, 2016, https://tinyurl.com/ybcr8fy5.

Congress boosts funding for medical research and authorizes the FDA to make it easier to develop and win approval for experimental treatments.

Goldman, Bruce, "Brain-computer interface advance allows fast, accurate typing by people with paralysis," Stanford Medicine News Center, Feb. 1, 2017, https://tinyurl.com/y8gbnqyq.

A brain-to-computer hookup allowed paralyzed individuals to control a cursor by envisioning hand movements, scientists say.

Gottlieb, Scott, "How FDA Plans to Help Consumers Capitalize on Advances in Science," *FDA Voice*, July 7, 2017, https://tinyurl.com/yb6j7v23.

The FDA commissioner discusses how the agency plans to speed up approval of medical advances.

Kaiser, Jocelyn, "House bill gives NIH 3% raise, blocks cuts to overhead payments," *Science*, July 12, 2017, https://tinyurl.com/ycprdcg6.

A House committee rejects President Trump's proposed cuts to the National Institutes of Health (NIH) budget.

Kaplan, Sheila, "Winners and losers of the 21st Century Cures Act," *STAT*, Dec. 5, 2016, https://tinyurl.com/y85op296.

Some agencies and industries benefited from the 21st Century Cures Act, while others did not.

Pradhan, Deepti, "Scientific Research Needs More Funding, But Also Smarter Spending," *Footnote*, Jan. 26, 2016, https://tinyurl.com/y9sn9y63.

A Yale University senior research analyst argues the NIH needs to spend its money more wisely.

Stossel, Thomas Peter, "Don't Thank Big Government for Medical Breakthroughs," American Enterprise Institute, Jan. 6, 2017, https://tinyurl.com/yd9mx7xs.

A Harvard medical school professor emeritus credits industry, not the government, with medical advances.

Reports and Studies

"Human Genome Editing — Science, Ethics and Governance," National Academies of Sciences, Engineering, Medicine, 2017, https://tinyurl.com/y8gj9wp2.

A committee of the National Academies issues a detailed report and recommendations on the regulation of human genome editing.

"U.S. Investments in Medical and Health Research and Development 2013-2015," Research!America, Fall 2016, https://tinyurl.com/y8pptynw.

Industry invested far more in medical research in 2015 than did government, according to a nonprofit that advocates for health-related research.

DiMasi, Joseph, Henry G. Grabowski and Ronald W. Hansen, "Cost of Developing a Drug," Tufts Center for the Study of Drug Development, Nov. 18, 2014, https://tinyurl.com/q5kn8wn.

Researchers from Tufts University examine the costs and time involved in developing new drugs for market.

The Next Step:

Additional Articles from Current Periodicals

Genetics

Ling, Geoffrey, "Genomic Vaccines Fight Disease in Ways Not Possible Before," *Scientific American*, **June 26, 2017, https://tinyurl.com/y77bwg4z.**

Dozens of new vaccines made by injecting genes into a person's body to combat a new virus have begun entering clinical trials and could offer a faster and more efficient preventative than conventional vaccines, researchers say.

Mullin, Emily, "Drug Is First to Treat Cancer Based on Genetics, Not Location," *MIT Technology Review*, **May 24, 2017, https://tinyurl.com/mcocpma.**

A new drug for cancer based on "precision medicine" — treatments devised for an individual — will target tumors' genetic characteristics.

Stein, Rob, "Scientists Precisely Edit DNA In Human Embryos To Fix A Disease Gene," *NPR*, **Aug. 2, 2017, https://tinyurl.com/y9c8z5xb.**

Scientists for the first time have successfully edited DNA in human embryos to correct a genetic defect responsible for a heart disorder.

Government Funding

Achenbach, Joel, and Lena H. Sun, "Trump budget seeks huge cuts to science and medical research, disease prevention," *The Washington Post*, **May 23, 2017, https://tiny url.com/yapbo56e.**

President Trump's fiscal 2018 budget proposes large cuts to scientific and medical research and disease-prevention programs.

Bates, Paula J., et al., "NIH program strives to turn more lab discoveries into real-world treatments," *Stat*, **April 17, 2017, https://tinyurl.com/ychk3w74.**

A National Institutes of Health network is offering funding and advice to researchers seeking to turn their discoveries into tangible treatments.

Oatman, Maddie, "Super Gonorrhea Is About to Get the Trump Bump," *Mother Jones*, **July 12, 2017, http://tiny url.com/ycjwpp5p.**

The Trump administration wants to cut or end funding for government programs that fight antibiotic-resistant infections.

Technological Devices

Choi, Charles Q., "These Unbelievably Tiny Tags Promise Big Advances in Medical Care," *NBC News*, **Aug. 1, 2017, https://tinyurl.com/yc4g4zho.**

Scientists hope to monitor the behavior of individual cells by using an antenna connected to a microchip — both small enough to fit inside cells.

Metz, Cade, "A New Way for Therapists to Get Inside Heads: Virtual Reality," *The New York Times*, **July 30, 2017, https://tinyurl.com/yc6k24pq.**

Some psychologists are using Google headsets and a virtual reality program to treat patients struggling with acute anxiety.

Yi, Hannah, "This prosthetic extra thumb might be just the upgrade humans need," *Quartz*, **July 26, 2017, https://tinyurl.com/y9db7pjb.**

A product designer developed a 3-D printed thumb that acts as an extra finger to give humans better dexterity.

Treatments and Tests

Beck, Julie, "The Case for Testing Zika Vaccines on Pregnant Women," *The Atlantic*, **July 6, 2017, https://tinyurl.com/ y9vrsvcl.**

Pregnant women, who usually are excluded from medical research due to risks of complications, are being recommended as test subjects for Zika vaccines so that researchers can better understand the disease, which can cause brain damage in babies.

Belluz, Julia, "There's a promising new HIV vaccine candidate in the pipeline," *Vox*, **July 24, 2017, https://tinyurl.com/y7 y7b74q.**

Researchers say they are getting closer to developing a "mosaic vaccine" that can target all the many strains of HIV.

Wang, Shirley S., "Scientists Aim For Better, Cheaper Tests For Alzheimer's," *NPR*, **Aug. 4, 2017, https://tinyurl.com/ yajk6acz.**

Scientists are striving to create less invasive, more accurate and much cheaper tests to identify people at high risk of developing Alzheimer's.

CITING CQ RESEARCHER

Sample formats for citing these reports in a bibliography include the ones listed below. Preferred styles and formats vary, so please check with your instructor or professor.

MLA STYLE

Mantel, Barbara. "Coal Industry's Future." CQ Researcher 17 June 2016: 529-552.

APA STYLE

Mantel, B. (2016, June 17). Coal Industry's Future. CQ Researcher, 6, 529-552.

CHICAGO STYLE

Mantel, Barbara. "Coal Industry's Future." CQ Researcher, June 17, 2016, 529-52.

In-depth Reports on Issues in the News

Are you writing a paper?

Need backup for a debate?

Want to become an expert on an issue?

For 90 years, students have turned to *CQ Researcher* for in-depth reporting on issues in the news. Reports on a full range of political and social issues are now available. Following is a selection of recent reports:

Civil Liberties
Privacy and the Internet, 12/15
Intelligence Reform, 5/15
Religion and Law, 11/14

Crime/Law
High-Tech Policing, 4/17
Forensic Science Controversies, 2/17
Jailing Debtors, 9/16
Decriminalizing Prostitution, 4/16
Restorative Justice, 2/16
The Dark Web, 1/16
Immigrant Detention, 10/15

Education
Charter Schools, 3/17
Civic Education, 2/17
Student Debt, 11/16
Apprenticeships, 10/16

Environment/Society
Muslims in America, 7/17
Funding the Arts, 7/17
Hunger in America, 7/17
Future of the Christian Right, 6/17
Trust in Media, 6/17
Anti-Semitism, 5/17

Health/Safety
Medical Marijuana, 7/17
Food Labeling, 6/17
Sports and Sexual Assault, 4/17
Reducing Traffic Deaths, 2/17

Politics/Economy
Universal Basic Income, 9/17
National Debt, 9/17
North Korea Showdown, 5/17
Rethinking Foreign Aid, 4/17
Troubled Brazil, 4/17
Immigrants and the Economy, 2/17

Upcoming Reports

Climate Change and National Security, 9/22/17   Think Tanks, 9/29/17   Cyber Warfare, 10/6/17

ACCESS

CQ Researcher is available in print and online. For access, visit your library or www.cqresearcher.com.

STAY CURRENT

For notice of upcoming *CQ Researcher* reports or to learn more about *CQ Researcher* products, subscribe to the free email newsletters, *CQ Researcher Alert!* and *CQ Researcher News*: http://cqpress.com/newsletters.

PURCHASE

To purchase a *CQ Researcher* report in print or electronic format (PDF), visit www.cqpress.com or call 866-427-7737. Single reports start at $15. Bulk purchase discounts and electronic-rights licensing are also available.

SUBSCRIBE

Annual full-service *CQ Researcher* subscriptions—including 44 reports a year, monthly index updates, and a bound volume—start at $1,131. Add $25 for domestic postage.

CQ Researcher Online offers a backfile from 1991 and a number of tools to simplify research. For pricing information, call 800-818-7243 or 805-499-9774 or email librarysales@sagepub.com.

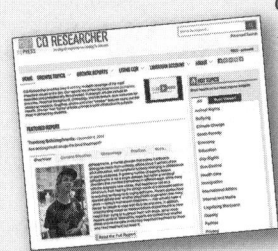

CQ RESEARCHER

CQPRESS

In-depth reports on today's issues

Published by CQ Press, an Imprint of SAGE Publications, Inc.

www.cqresearcher.com

Climate Change and National Security

Will extreme weather lead to more global conflict?

U.S. military officials increasingly view climate change as a "threat multiplier," a factor that can aggravate poverty, political instability and social tensions. That, in turn, could foster terrorism and other forms of global violence while impairing America's military effectiveness. Rising seas, due mainly to Arctic ice melting, already threaten Naval Station Norfolk in Virginia, the world's largest naval base; dozens of other coastal installations also are at risk. Meanwhile, drought in some regions and record rainfall in others have forced millions of people to migrate across borders, adding to tensions in northern Africa, the Middle East and Southeast Asia. Defense Secretary James Mattis said climate change is affecting the stability of areas where U.S. troops are operating. President Trump, who has labeled climate change a "hoax," now says he has an "open mind" on the issue. Some politicians and economists argue that the real danger to U.S. security lies in the erosion of jobs, trade and industrial productivity caused by the costs of unnecessary federal environmental regulations.

A woman wades through floodwaters to a shelter in Dhaka, Bangladesh, on Aug. 16. The U.S. Department of Defense considers climate change a factor that can aggravate other conditions, such as poverty and political or social instability, and create security or geopolitical risks for the United States or its allies. As ice melts and oceans rise, the potential for violent conflict increases.

CQ Researcher • Sept. 22, 2017 • www.cqresearcher.com
Volume 27, Number 33 • Pages 773-796

I N S I D E THIS REPORT

THE ISSUES 775

BACKGROUND 781

CHRONOLOGY 783

CURRENT SITUATION 787

AT ISSUE 789

OUTLOOK 791

BIBLIOGRAPHY 794

THE NEXT STEP 795

CLIMATE CHANGE AND NATIONAL SECURITY

THE ISSUES

775
- Does a weakened commitment to slowing climate change make the United States less secure?
- Does climate change affect U.S. military preparedness?
- Does climate change pose a global economic threat?

BACKGROUND

781 **Weaponizing the Weather**
In the 1940s, scientists pondered changing the weather to gain a military advantage.

782 **Fears Gain Momentum**
The threat of global warming entered the public consciousness in the 1980s.

784 **Security Concerns**
In 2003, the military began focusing on climate change.

CURRENT SITUATION

787 **Military Leaders See Risks**
Pentagon officials are pressing ahead on the climate threat.

788 **A Worrisome Arctic**
The Navy's role in U.S. security is expected to grow as the ice recedes.

790 **Emerging Bipartisanship?**
Congress backs defense and climate change funding.

OUTLOOK

791 **More People, Higher Temperatures**
As warming proceeds, societies will face greater disruption.

SIDEBARS AND GRAPHICS

776 **Coastal Bases Vulnerable to Climate Change**
More than 125 U.S. military installations are at risk of flooding.

777 **Natural Disasters Force Millions from Homes**
More than a quarter-billion people were displaced from 2008-16.

780 **Asia at Highest Risk of Rising Seas**
The land where 145 million Chinese live might one day be under water.

783 **Chronology**
Key events since 1946.

784 **Climate Change Stoking Fear of Migration, Conflict**
Weather events could result in up to 1 billion refugees.

786 **Rising Sea Levels Threaten a Nation's Future**
Climate change could displace millions of Bangladeshis.

789 **At Issue:**
Should climate change be a national security priority?

FOR FURTHER RESEARCH

793 **For More Information**
Organizations to contact.

794 **Bibliography**
Selected sources used.

795 **The Next Step**
Additional articles.

795 **Citing CQ Researcher**
Sample bibliography formats.

 **CQ RESEARCHER**

Sept. 22, 2017
Volume 27, Number 33

EXECUTIVE EDITOR: Thomas J. Billitteri
tjb@sagepub.com

ASSISTANT MANAGING EDITORS: Kenneth Fireman, kenneth.fireman@sagepub.com, Kathy Koch, kathy.koch@sagepub.com, Scott Rohrer, scott.rohrer@sagepub.com

ASSOCIATE MANAGING EDITOR: Val Ellicott

SENIOR CONTRIBUTING EDITOR:
Thomas J. Colin
tom.colin@sagepub.com

CONTRIBUTING WRITERS: Marcia Clemmitt, Sarah Glazer, Reed Karaim, Barbara Mantel, Chuck McCutcheon, Tom Price

SENIOR PROJECT EDITOR: Olu B. Davis

EDITORIAL ASSISTANT: Natalia Gurevich

FACT CHECKERS: Eva P. Dasher, Michelle Harris, Betsy Towner Levine, Robin Palmer

SAGE Publishing | **CQPRESS**

Los Angeles I London I New Delhi
Singapore I Washington DC I Melbourne

An Imprint of SAGE Publications, Inc.

SENIOR VICE PRESIDENT, GLOBAL LEARNING RESOURCES:
Karen Phillips

EXECUTIVE DIRECTOR, ONLINE LIBRARY AND REFERENCE PUBLISHING:
Todd Baldwin

CQ Researcher (ISSN 1056-2036) is printed on acid-free paper. Published weekly, except: (March wk. 4) (May wk. 4) (July wks. 1, 2) (Aug. wks. 2, 3) (Nov. wk. 4) and (Dec. wks. 3, 4). Published by SAGE Publications, Inc., 2455 Teller Rd., Thousand Oaks, CA 91320. Annual full-service subscriptions start at $1,131. For pricing, call 1-800-818-7243. To purchase a CQ Researcher report in print or electronic format (PDF), visit www.cqpress.com or call 866-427-7737. Single reports start at $15. Bulk purchase discounts and electronic-rights licensing are also available. Periodicals postage paid at Thousand Oaks, California, and at additional mailing offices. POSTMASTER: Send address changes to CQ Researcher, 2600 Virginia Ave., N.W., Suite 600, Washington, DC 20037.

Cover: Getty Images/Barcroft Media/Rehman Asad

Climate Change and National Security

BY WILLIAM WANLUND

THE ISSUES

The deadly six-year civil war in Syria has many causes, including brutal government repression, economic mismanagement and ethnic and religious tensions. But a less obvious force may have helped fuel what has become one of the most violent conflagrations in recent history: climate change.

Environmental scientists, military officials and others say an unprecedented drought in Syria from 2006 to 2009 and torrid temperatures led to soaring food prices and mass migration, which in turn sparked civil unrest, a government crackdown and, finally, a war that has killed nearly a half-million people, displaced millions more and unleashed new waves of terrorism. [1]

"First, brutally hot temperatures and drought in western Russia fed fires which reduced the wheat crop," causing Russia — a major supplier of wheat to Syria — to stop exporting the grain, says retired U.S. Marine Brig. Gen. Stephen Cheney. "Then, a four-year drought in Syria caused crop failures there, leading to massive internal migration and social unrest." The chaos and instability that followed made Syria fertile ground for terrorists, he says.

Cheney, now head of the American Security Project (ASP), a defense policy think tank in Washington, says the Syrian crisis arose out of a series of 2011 civil uprisings in the Middle East known as the Arab Spring. Nonetheless, he says, "climate change was a contributor. . . . Syria's civil war is a poster child for climate change as a national security threat."

Many other analysts trace some of the impetus for other Arab Spring uprisings — in Egypt, Tunisia, Yemen and Libya — to soaring global food

Fourteen-year-old Achwaq and her family fled warfare in western Yemen to seek shelter in Khamir in May. The civil uprisings that began in 2011 in Yemen and other countries in the Middle East, known as the Arab Spring, can be blamed in part on drought and heavy rains caused by climate change, many analysts say.

Getty Images/ UN Ocha/Giles Clarke

prices resulting from drought in some agricultural exporting regions and to ruinously heavy rains in others. [2]

"No one would say that climate change caused the Arab Spring or the conflicts in those countries," says Francesco Femia, president of the Center for Climate and Security, a Washington think tank. "You can't distinguish it in isolation from other threats and risks." Still, Femia says, climate change "exacerbated conditions in those countries and helped precipitate those conflicts."

Not everyone is ready to accept the link between climate change and the Syrian conflict. In September, a multidisciplinary group of researchers led by Jan Selby, an international relations professor at the University of Sussex in England, cast doubt on the theory that Syria's drought caused large-scale internal migration and that the migrants were a major cause of the unrest that sparked the civil war. [3]

But researchers and military officials generally agree that climate change represents an international security concern. The U.S. Department of Defense (DOD) considers climate change a "threat multiplier" — a factor that can aggravate other conditions, such as poverty and political or social instability, and create security or geopolitical risks for the United States or its allies. [4]

"By increasing the intensity, frequency and severity of extreme weather events, climate change can make states more unstable, which can lead to increased power of terrorist organizations," Femia says. "It can affect the geostrategic environment in areas that are important to the United States, like the Arctic, Asia and the Middle East."

Drought is not the only potential manifestation of climate change that concerns Pentagon leaders. Another is sea-level rise, stemming largely from the melting of glaciers in Greenland and Antarctica.

In addition, melting Arctic sea ice has unlocked icebound areas, opening them to shipping, oil and gas drilling, mining and even tourism and leading to intensified economic competition for access rights. Russia has increased its military presence in the region, a buildup that Russian officials say is intended to strengthen homeland defense and protect commercial interests. Some U.S. military observers, however, worry that Russia's actions may signal future aggression, such as efforts to take control of shipping lanes at the top of the globe.

Military planners also fear that rising coastal waters could harm the readiness of U.S. forces. A report by the Union of Concerned Scientists said a "roughly three-foot increase in sea level would

Coastal Bases Vulnerable to Climate Change

A three-foot sea level rise could damage 128 U.S. coastal military installations, nearly half of them naval bases, according to the Union of Concerned Scientists. Eighteen installations along the East and Gulf coasts are at highest risk of flooding that could damage roads and other infrastructure. Even under conservative climate change estimates, nine installations would lose at least one-fourth of their land area by the end of the century.

Key Military Bases on East and Gulf Coasts

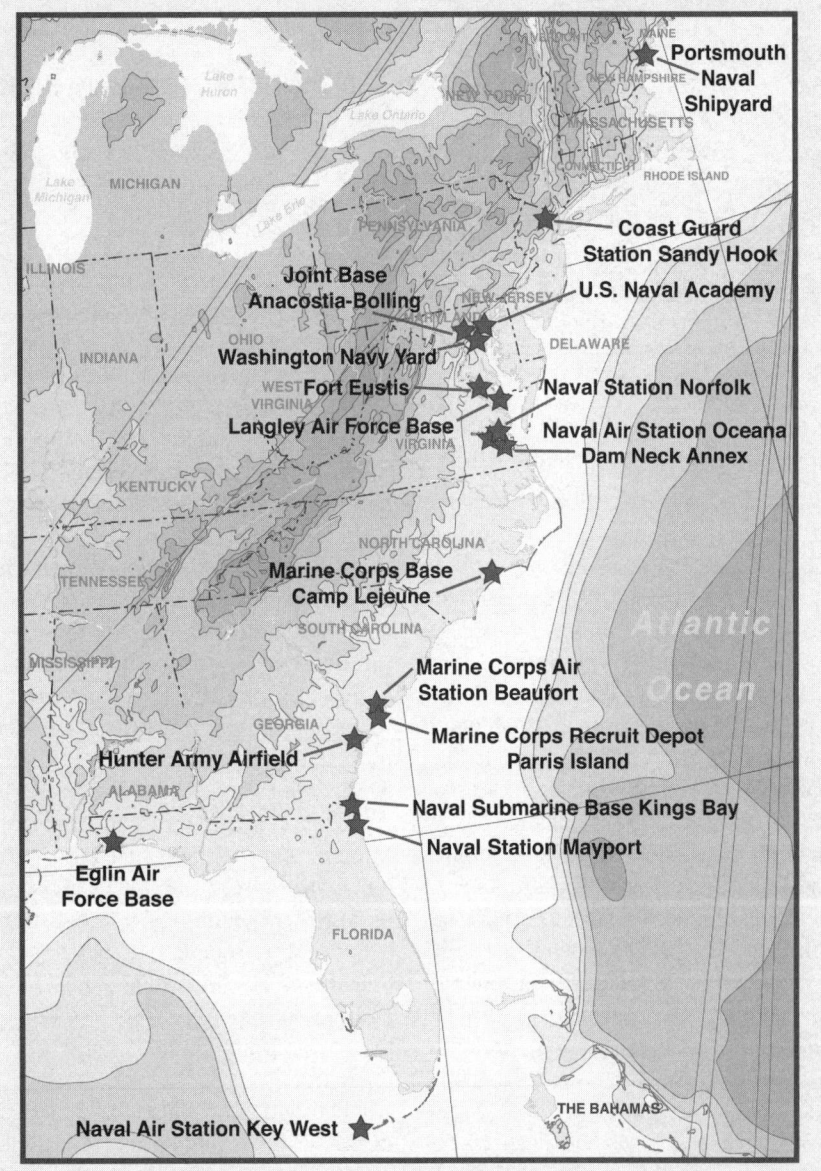

Source: "The US Military on the Front Lines of Rising Seas," Union of Concerned Scientists, July 2016, https://tinyurl.com/hq9u2zd

threaten 128 coastal DOD installations in the United States." [5]

Global warming is expected to raise sea levels between 0.3 meters (1 foot) and 2.5 meters (8.2 feet) by 2100, according to a January report from the National Oceanic and Atmospheric Administration. [6] The report identifies a rise of 1 meter as an "intermediate" projected increase. That, say Navy veterans, could result in troop-deployment delays and reduced access to docking and repair facilities.

Naval Station Norfolk in Virginia, the world's largest naval base and the headquarters of the Navy's Atlantic Fleet, is among the threatened facilities. Parts of the base already flood 10 times a year during extreme high tides. [7] "If you can't get ships underway with a crew intact out of Norfolk, you're going to delay the application of military force or humanitarian assistance somewhere else where they are called upon to go," says retired Navy Vice Adm. Dennis McGinn, president of the American Council on Renewable Energy.

But Dakota Wood, a former Marine officer who is a senior research fellow for defense programs at the Heritage Foundation, a conservative think tank in Washington, says the military's options are limited. "If you accept that sea levels are rising and you expect more localized flooding of coastal areas with major naval bases like San Diego or Norfolk, what is the military supposed to do?" he asks. "Preemptively move a major naval base 50 miles upriver? Where's the funding for that?"

The Navy is already taking steps to fortify its facilities against the effects of climate change, for example by strengthening piers and erecting structures on higher ground, according to Todd Lyman, a spokesman for the Navy Facilities Engineering Command for the mid-Atlantic region. [8]

Former President Barack Obama believed climate change constituted an economic and security threat to the nation. In 2015 he signed the Paris climate agreement, which pledged its nearly 200 participants to work to stem global warming. Without such a worldwide effort, Obama said, "we are going to have to devote more and more and more of our economic and military resources not to growing opportunity for our people, but to adapting to the various consequences of a changing planet." [9]

On Sept. 21, 2016, he instructed federal agencies to consider climate change when drawing up their national security plans. [10] The same day, the National Intelligence Council (NIC), which performs analytical work for the 16 U.S. intelligence agencies, backed Obama with a report saying climate change is "almost certain to have significant direct and indirect social, economic, political, and security implications [and] pose significant national security challenges for the United States over the next two decades." [11]

But President Trump, who succeeded Obama in January, once tweeted that climate change was "a total, and very expensive, hoax." [12] He later said he was keeping an "open mind" on the subject. [13] Nevertheless, on March 28, he declared the costs of complying with government regulations designed to limit climate change pose a greater threat to national security than do the changes themselves, and he rescinded Obama's 2016 national security memorandum and many of Obama's other climate-related directives. Trump said his aim was to end "regulatory burdens that unnecessarily encumber energy production, constrain economic growth and prevent job creation." [14] On June 1, he made similar comments in announcing the United States would withdraw from the Paris agreement. [15]

James Taylor, a senior fellow for environment and energy policy at the Heartland Institute, a libertarian think tank in Arlington Heights, Ill., agrees with Trump. "Climate change certainly isn't a national security threat the way the Obama administration said it was, whereby global warming is causing catastrophes and migrations of people

Natural Disasters Force Millions from Homes

From 2008 to 2016, 227.6 million people were displaced worldwide, most of them within their own country's borders, by weather-related or geophysical disasters, such as earthquakes. Weather-related disasters were responsible for 86 percent of the displacements. In the first half of 2017, disasters in 76 countries and territories uprooted another 4.5 million people.

Displacements by Weather or Geophysical Disasters, 2008-16

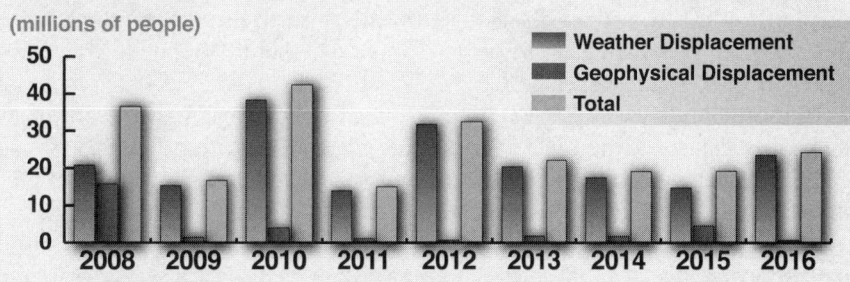

Sources: "Global Report on Internal Displacement," May 22, 2017, https://tinyurl.com/y8dvj789; "Provisional Mid-year Figures, Internal Displacement in 2017," Aug. 16, 2017, https://tinyurl.com/ybhc676k, Norwegian Refugee Council and Internal Displacement Monitoring Centre

and scarce resources and food and water shortages, which they said would be threat multipliers," Taylor says. "You're not seeing any of these. The greater threat to national security would be forcing our economy onto an expensive renewable-power trajectory."

However, Trump's Defense secretary, James Mattis, said in written responses to questions at his Senate confirmation hearing in January that "climate change is impacting stability in areas of the world where our troops are operating today. It is appropriate for [military commanders] to incorporate drivers of instability that impact the security environment in their areas into their planning." [16]

Some observers see signs that the political split over climate change may be narrowing. The House of Representatives has established a bipartisan Climate Solutions Caucus to explore approaches to dealing with a changing climate. The caucus was instrumental in the House's July passage of legislation declaring climate change to be "a direct threat" to U.S. national security and requiring the

Pentagon to report on how climate change affects military operations and readiness. (The legislation has not yet reached the Senate floor.) [17]

In late summer, back-to-back hurricanes caused devastating flooding in Texas and Louisiana and widespread destruction in Florida and other Southeastern states, raising new worries about potential links between climate change and extreme weather. Scientists did not attribute the hurricanes to climate change, but a number said warming ocean temperatures increase the intensity and frequency of such storms. At the same time, the hurricanes tested the military's ability to both protect its assets and contribute to relief efforts.

As Americans debate possible effects of global climate change on national security, here are some key questions they are asking:

Does a weakened commitment to slowing climate change make the United States less secure?

President Trump's announcement on June 1 that the United States would withdraw from the Paris agreement on climate change pleased some members of his administration and GOP lawmakers but dismayed many world leaders who had counted on participation by the planet's second-largest polluter. [18]

The agreement, adopted in 2015 and signed by 196 nations, aims to limit global temperature increases and encourages adoption of renewable-energy resources. [19] British Prime Minister Theresa May called it "the right global framework for protecting the prosperity and security of future generations." [20]

Trump's critics say withdrawing from the accord will isolate the United States and diminish its global influence. But others say the decision will help the country negotiate better trade and other international deals.

"Both the diplomatic costs of leaving and the benefits of staying have been exaggerated," said Nicolas Loris, an economist with the Heritage Foundation. [21] Withdrawing from the accord could help the United States negotiate future agreements by showing other governments "the U.S. is willing and able to resist diplomatic pressure in order to protect American interests," he said. [22]

Peter Engelke, a senior fellow with the Strategic Foresight Initiative at the Atlantic Council think tank in Washington, says Trump's decision will have the opposite effect and will make it "a real challenge . . . to craft complex international agreements in the future."

"There's a real risk that we could have harmed our position as the world's foremost power," says Engelke, whose group works to help international decision-makers by identifying global trends.

In addition to withdrawing from the Paris agreement, Trump appointed a climate change skeptic, former Oklahoma Attorney General Scott Pruitt, to head the Environmental Protection Agency (EPA). Trump has reversed Obama administration policies aimed at addressing climate change and recently disbanded the federal advisory panel for the National Climate Assessment, which helps policymakers and private-sector officials incorporate the government's climate analysis into long-term planning. [23]

Nigel Purvis, who participated in climate change negotiations as a State Department official in the Clinton and George W. Bush administrations, says most other countries view climate change as their biggest threat. The U.S. withdrawal from the Paris agreement means "foreign leaders will think twice about whether to cooperate with President Trump in trade, security and other foreign policy areas," says Purvis, now president of Climate Advisers, a Washington consulting firm that advocates for a low-carbon economy.

Roger Pielke, a political scientist and environmental studies professor at the University of Colorado, says withdrawing from the agreement made little sense, because its goals are voluntary. Trump's decision, he says, "is not a meaningful action unless you want to stick your finger in someone's eye."

Opponents of the Paris agreement say the United States plays too important a role in the world for Trump's decision to jeopardize national security.

"Other countries have a multitude of security, economic, and diplomatic reasons to work with America to address issues of mutual concern," Loris wrote. "Withdrawal from the agreement will not change that."

Under the terms of the Paris agreement, no country can withdraw from it before Nov. 4, 2020 — by chance, the day after the next U.S. presidential election. [24]

Much of the debate over U.S. security and action on climate change focuses on China, the world's biggest polluter, and whether Beijing wants to use the Trump administration's skepticism of climate change to gain political and economic leverage.

"China is stepping up to say, 'We are going to be a leader' in green technology innovation and development while the U.S. is appearing to retreat," Engelke says. "This is an important geopolitical question, because it speaks to who can develop the technology and be a step ahead of the other in seizing the commercial high ground for trade, for seizing military advantages, for having the best technology, etc."

Five of the world's top six solar panel manufacturers and five of the top 10 wind turbine makers are in China. The country invested $88 billion in renewable energy in 2016, more than any other country. [25] In January, China's National Energy Administration announced plans to invest another $360 billion in renewable-power generation by 2020. [26]

Kelly Sims Gallagher, a China specialist and energy and environmental policy professor at the Fletcher School of Law and Diplomacy at Tufts University in Medford, Mass., says Chinese officials see green-energy investments as "key to their own economic development during the 21st century" — and a chance to gain a competitive advantage over the United States. "That's what's at risk: technological leadership and the socioeconomic consequences of ceding this market to the Chinese," she says.

Yale University researchers Angel Hsu and Carlin Rosengarten doubt China will assume the climate change leadership mantle. "Despite China's massive investments in renewable energy, the country is still investing in coal and exporting it," they wrote. China cannot develop as quickly as it wants to "while simultaneously filling a climate leadership vacuum," they said. [27]

But even if that is true, China still stands to gain diplomatically from Trump's decision to leave the Paris climate deal, says David Livingston, an associate fellow in the Energy and Climate Program at the Carnegie Endowment for International Peace. "Headlines like, 'China steps in to help climate adaptation in Africa because the U.S. will no longer fund the Green Climate fund' — this is partially reality, partially rhetoric, but it's a powerful source of leverage for China," he says.

Does climate change affect U.S. military preparedness?

Naval Station Norfolk occupies about 3,400 acres on the Atlantic Coast of southeastern Virginia. The base is home to 75 ships, 134 aircraft and about 70,000 military and civilian employees. [28]

It also is highly vulnerable to the effects of climate change. Ocean levels around Norfolk could rise 4.5 to 6.9 feet by the end of the century, largely because of melting polar ice, according to the Union of Concerned Scientists, a research and advocacy group in Cambridge, Mass. The group says that at the upper end of its estimate, about 20 percent of the base would flood every day by the year 2100, with storm surges creating even more severe problems. [29]

Flooding already is disrupting operations at the base. At least 10 times a year, personnel cut power to the piers that service ships because strong winds or unusually high tides threaten to submerge electrical cables. "It's more than an inconvenience," said retired Navy Capt. Joseph Bouchard, the base's former commander and an expert on the national security aspects of climate change policy. "A ship is on a tight timeline to do all the training and maintenance that's required to be combat ready for deployment. If you interrupt that . . . they have a hard time being ready for deployment." [30]

Climate change raises the possibility that U.S. military assets may not always be available when needed, says retired Vice Adm. McGinn, of the American Council on Renewable Energy. "If you can't get ships underway with a crew intact out of [Norfolk], you're going to delay the application of military force or humanitarian assistance somewhere else," he says.

Fifty-six naval installations around the country could be affected by a sea-level rise of at least 3.3 feet. Such a rise would damage piers and repair facilities, electrical and communications equipment and sewage treatment fa-cilities, according to a 2011 book published by the National Academy of Sciences. [31]

U.S. military bases overseas also are facing climate change challenges, according to a report by the American Security Project. It rated the naval facility on the Indian Ocean island of Diego Garcia as the military's most climate change-vulnerable installation — the island, with a mean elevation of four feet above sea level, is at risk from coastal erosion and flooding, the report said, noting "A sea-level rise of . . . several feet would force the U.S. military to undertake a costly and difficult military relocation process." [32]

Another American Security Project study noted that the U.S. base on the Pacific island of Guam, while not unusually threatened by rising sea levels, could suffer diminished combat readiness. "Because of a changing climate, the joint military base on Guam could lose access to essentials like food and water and will be increasingly threated by extreme weather events" such as extreme storms and erosion, senior fellow for energy and climate Andrew Holland wrote in August. [33]

Michael Werz, a senior fellow at the Center for American Progress, a liberal think tank in Washington, says that in times of global emergency, the U.S. Navy "becomes the 911 number."

Adds Werz, whose work focuses on the intersection of climate change, migration and security, "If friendly neighbors or partners have a climate-related crisis and need a tent city and medical supplies for 40,000 refugees, only the Navy has the capacity to provide it quickly. It would be impossible just to say, 'Sorry, you're on your own.'"

Russia has established a military base on Alexandra Land island in the Arctic. Russia says it has increased its military presence in the region to strengthen homeland defense and protect commercial interests. Some U.S. military observers, however, worry that Russia's actions may signal future aggression.

Langley Air Force Base, about 21 miles from Norfolk, is home to nearly 12,000 military and civilian personnel. Retired Gen. Ronald Keys, former commander of the Air Force's Air Combat Command, headquartered at Langley, said the base is only 7 feet above sea level. In about 15 years, he said, the base could experience 100 days of tidal flooding a year due to climate change, meaning "we [would] lose access to certain parts of our base" at high tide. [34]

Sea-level rise is not the military's only climate concern. Prolonged droughts have disrupted artillery practice because of wildfire risks, and flash flooding in

Asia at Highest Risk of Rising Seas

If the planet warms by 4 degrees Celsius, which scientists expect to happen unless nations act aggressively to stem greenhouse gas emissions, seas would eventually submerge land that currently is home to 145 million Chinese, 55 million Indians and millions of others worldwide, according to Climate Central. If warming rises a less drastic 2 degrees Celsius, the current goal of the Paris climate agreement, the number of people threatened in China and India by rising seas would drop by more than half.

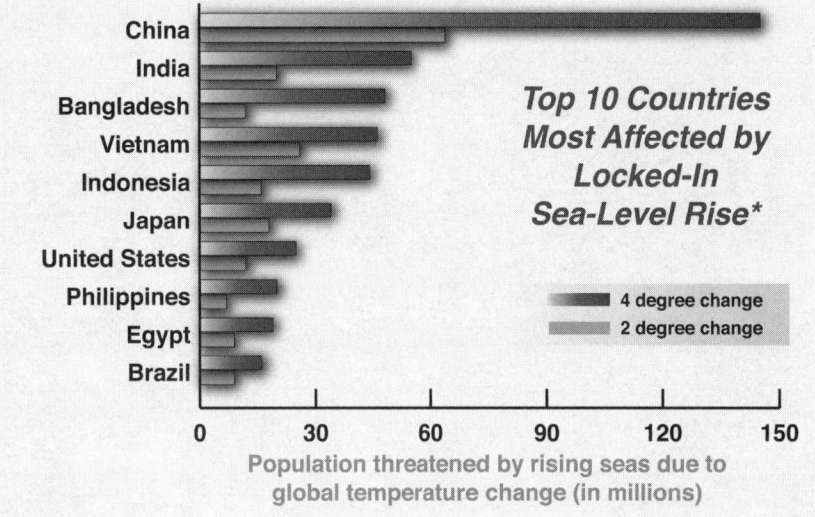

Top 10 Countries Most Affected by Locked-In Sea-Level Rise*

■ 4 degree change
■ 2 degree change

Population threatened by rising seas due to global temperature change (in millions)

* Figures based on 2015 projections of 2010 population data.

Source: "Mapping Choices, Carbon Climate, and Rising Seas, Our Global Legacy," Climate Central, November 2015, https://tinyurl.com/yd9u7p2p

the Southwestern desert forced the closure of an emergency runway for training and testing aircraft for about eight months, according to the Government Accountability Office (GAO), the investigative arm of Congress. The GAO also said rising temperatures at one Army installation halted training for three weeks because the thawed ground was too soft to traverse and made airborne training areas unsafe. [35]

But a 2015 report by the libertarian Heartland Institute challenged the GAO's findings, concluding that reports of climate change's negative effects on military infrastructure are overblown and unsupported by scientific evidence. "Requiring DOD to invest in mitigation or adaptation to address phantom risks could divert resources from other more urgent needs, reducing military preparedness," the think tank said. [36]

In 2014, the Pentagon said climate change will create conditions that make terrorist activity and humanitarian crises more likely — for example by causing or exacerbating food and water shortages and degrading the environment. Such stressors aggravate social tensions and political and social instability — while making U.S. military intervention more difficult. [37]

But the Heritage Foundation's Wood says typhoons and other major storms are nothing new and occur every year. "Are we proposing then that the U.S. Navy or Marine Corps should push more forces into the Western Pacific, and be poised in the event that some major series of storms comes through the region?" he asks. "That's deploy time, it's increased manpower costs, you're tying your ships up on a 'be prepared to' mission rather than being off doing other sorts of things."

Femia of the Center for Climate and Security says the U.S. military already understands the challenge posed by climate change. "It's part of the culture of security institutions, the U.S. military in particular, to plan for long-term risks," he says. "It has to take into account a lot of scenarios, and in a lot of cases plan for the worst."

Does climate change pose a global economic threat?

The World Bank says climate change threatens its "core mission" of supporting economic growth and reducing poverty around the globe.

"Current weather extremes already affect millions of people, putting food and water security at risk and threatening agricultural supply chains and many coastal cities," the bank reported in 2016. "Without further action to reduce extreme poverty, provide access to basic services and strengthen resilience, climate impacts could push an additional 100 million people into poverty by 2030." [38]

Many parts of the business world also see climate change as a compelling danger. Mars, the U.S. candy company, remains committed to achieving "the carbon reduction targets the planet needs," said CEO Grant Reid. Mars is among dozens of firms that recently announced they will submit a plan to the United Nations for meeting U.S. emissions targets under the Paris agreement, even though Trump has pulled the country out of the accord. [39]

The World Economic Forum (WEF) — a Swiss nonprofit that promotes business involvement in global economic, political and social issues — ranks climate change along with cultural polarization and wealth and income disparities as "one of the truly existential risks to our world." [40]

Others who have studied climate change, however, say accurately predicting its economic effects is virtually impossible. Such forecasts fall into a range, and at the low end of that range "are some fairly benign outcomes with which we could probably muddle along without terrible consequence," says the University of Colorado's Pielke. "It's a risk-management problem, like buying insurance," he says. "How much do you need to be covered, and how much is too much?"

Scientists at Stanford University and the University of California, Berkeley, said in 2015 that if climate change is not mitigated, the global economy could be more than 20 percent smaller by 2100. [41] That does not mean the world will be poorer in 2100 than it is today, however, because other factors will cause economies to grow, said the study's lead author, Marshall Burke, an assistant professor in Stanford's Department of Earth System Science.

"Instead, it means that the world will be substantially less rich than it would have been had temperatures not warmed," Burke said. [42]

The study also concluded that not all countries will suffer equally from global warming. About 20 percent — including countries in cooler climates such as Northern Europe and much of Russia — may benefit from rising temperatures, thanks largely to a longer growing season. Warmer countries, including those in Africa and South America, will suffer lower crop yields and drops in labor productivity, the study said. This will result in "a huge redistribution of wealth from the global poor to the wealthy," said study co-author Solomon Hsiang, a professor in the Goldman School of Public Policy at UC-Berkeley. [43]

Poor people also will suffer if countries curtail the use of fossil fuels in response to global warming, said Iain Murray, vice president for strategy at the libertarian Competitive Enterprise Institute, a think tank in Washington. [44]

The Texas National Guard helps rescue people in Orange, Texas, on Aug. 31 from floods caused by Hurricane Harvey. The havoc caused by that disaster and Hurricane Irma raised new concerns about potential links between climate change and extreme weather.

Pielke says that while climate change threatens the economy over the long term, "there's an ignorance factor, too. We just don't know how things are going to turn out. We're not good at predicting the future 100 years from now."

William Nordhaus, an economics professor at Yale University, agrees, saying human ingenuity and advances in technology add to the uncertainty surrounding the economic impact of climate change. "We don't actually have a good handle on when the impacts will become dangerous," he said. "We're taking something that might happen 50 years from now and addressing aspects of economy and human life that will change in unknown ways." [45]

Some believe a warming climate can, at least in the near term, be beneficial. Matthew Ridley, a Conservative Party member in the British House of Lords, cites a study that indicates adding carbon dioxide, a primary culprit in global warming, to the atmosphere has actually contributed to a greener planet. In the last three decades, he wrote, data showed that worldwide plant growth has increased dramatically thanks to the increasing presence of atmospheric carbon dioxide. Another

study noted by Ridley found that global economic output has been rising, thanks to climate change, and will continue to do so until around 2080.

Ridley said the real problem stems from government policies designed to fight climate change. These, he said, "have had negligible effects on carbon dioxide emissions" but they have caused food and fuel prices to go up, made industries uncompetitive, hastened destruction of forestland, killed rare birds of prey and divided communities. Strategies to mitigate climate change, he said, are [impeding] "a change that will produce net benefits for 70 years." [46] ■

BACKGROUND

Weaponizing the Weather

In 1824, French physicist Joseph Fourier theorized that gases in the Earth's atmosphere keep the planet warm by trapping heat from the sun — a phenomenon now known as the greenhouse effect. [47]

Swedish scientist Svante Arrhenius advanced the theory in 1896 by demonstrating that the heat trapped by carbon dioxide (CO_2) increases as concentrations of the gas increase in the atmosphere. Eight years later, he concluded that human use of fossil fuels was causing carbon dioxide to build up in the atmosphere, but he considered this a benefit, reasoning that a warming atmosphere would help the world grow crops and feed its growing population. [48]

Most scientists dismissed or ignored Arrhenius' work, but in 1938 British engineer Guy S. Callendar confirmed that historically, higher concentrations of CO_2 in the atmosphere raised global temperatures. [49]

Beginning in the late 1940s, scientists started studying the possibility of changing the weather to gain a military advantage, by creating a drought that would ruin an enemy's agricultural harvest, or producing other catastrophic weather events.

By the 1950s, Pentagon planners were investigating whether "seeding" clouds with silver iodide crystals would produce rain. That led to Operation Popeye, a 1967 project (motto: "Make mud, not war") designed to create heavy rainfall over enemy communication lines during the Vietnam War "to interdict or at least interfere with truck traffic between North and South Vietnam." [50]

Public opinion turned against Operation Popeye after *The New York Times* disclosed details of the program in July 1972. It was quickly shut down — after 2,602 cloud-seeding flights over North and South Vietnam, Laos and Cambodia — without its having achieved evidence of success. [51]

The following year, the Senate approved a resolution calling for an international treaty to ban "environmental or geophysical modification activity as a weapon of war," and in 1976 the U.N. General Assembly approved a treaty banning environmental modification techniques for hostile purposes. [52]

CIA officials had begun studying climate change by 1974, when the agency's Office of Political Research said that climate change's potential effect on global food supplies "could have an enormous impact, not only on the food-population balance, but also on the world balance of power." [53]

The 1974 CIA report said wealthier countries, including the United States, probably would escape the worst effects of a cooling climate, while U.S. foes such as the Soviet Union and China likely would suffer. It also said, however, that if climate change caused severe food shortages, potential risks to the United States would rise as other, militarily powerful nations made "increasingly desperate attempts" to get food. "Massive migration backed by force would become a very live issue," the report said. "Nuclear blackmail is not inconceivable." [54]

Fears Gain Momentum

Public awareness of climate change's dangers began increasing in the 1980s. The topic first made the front page of *The New York Times* on Aug. 22, 1981, in a story about a NASA report tracing evidence of a global warming trend back to 1880 and predicting global warming of "almost unprecedented magnitude" in the next century. [55]

In 1989, Al Gore, then a Democratic senator from Tennessee, said in a *Washington Post* op-ed that "America's future is inextricably tied to the fate of the globe."

"In effect, the environment is becoming a matter of national security — an issue that directly and imminently menaces the interests of the state or the welfare of the people," wrote Gore, who became President Bill Clinton's vice president in 1993 and shared the 2007 Nobel Peace Prize with the Intergovernmental Panel on Climate Change (IPCC) for his efforts to raise awareness of global warming. [56]

Meanwhile, scientists were becoming increasingly convinced that human activity was causing climate change. In 1990, the IPCC, established by the United Nations to study climate change and develop strategies to counter it, asserted in its first report that the greenhouse effect was real, human activity contributed to it, and global temperatures and sea levels would continue to rise. [57]

Republican President George H.W. Bush acknowledged in a 1990 speech that "human activities are changing the atmosphere in unexpected and in unprecedented ways," but stopped short of committing the United States to strong measures to curb greenhouse gas emissions. [58]

His secretary of State, James Baker, however, told an IPCC conference the world needed to address climate change immediately rather than waiting "until all the uncertainties have been resolved." [59] In 1990, Baker linked environmental protection to national security, saying, "Traditional concepts of what constitutes a threat to national and global security need to be updated and extended to such divergent concerns as environmental degradation, narcotics trafficking, and terrorism." [60]

In 1997, President Bill Clinton signed the Kyoto Protocol, a U.N. treaty requiring developed countries to reduce greenhouse gas emissions to below-1990 levels by 2012. However, U.S. auto and steel manufacturers, oil and gas companies and other industries lobbied against the treaty, saying it would drive up fuel prices and destroy jobs. [61] In addition, the Senate unanimously passed a resolution saying no climate treaty was acceptable that did not require developing countries to reduce their emissions as well. Clinton never submitted the Kyoto Protocol to the Senate for ratification. [62]

Many experts regard the Kyoto debate as the point when U.S. attitudes regarding climate change began to form along partisan lines. Edward Maibach, director of the Center for Climate Change Communication at George Mason University in Virginia, notes that congressional Republicans deeply disliked Clinton, "and when he asked Congress to ratify the Kyoto Protocol . . . they essentially said, 'Screw you,' and that really started the differential trajectory of public understanding of climate change."

Continued on p. 784

Chronology

1940s-1970s
Climate becomes a tool of war.

1946
American scientist Bernard Vonnegut discovers that seeding clouds with silver iodide crystals can produce rain.

1967
U.S. military's Operation Popeye seeds clouds over Southeast Asia to interfere with enemy logistics during the Vietnam War. . . . National Oceanic and Atmospheric Administration scientists Syukuro Manabe and Richard T. Wetherald publish a paper widely considered the first to accurately model climate change.

1972
In response to public pressure, U.S. military officials end Operation Popeye without evidence of success. . . . U.N. Environmental Program is founded to promote sound global environmental practices.

1974
CIA report warns that climate change could alter "the world balance of power" by affecting food supplies.

1980s-1990s
World confronts climate change.

1981
NASA scientists predict global warming "of almost unprecedented magnitude" over the next century.

1988
United Nations Intergovernmental Panel on Climate Change (IPCC) is formed to monitor the effects of climate change and develop strategies to cope with them.

1990
IPCC says human activity contributes to climate change and the resulting rise in global temperatures.

1992
U.N.'s Framework Convention on Climate Change is signed by the U.S. and 191 other nations seeking to stabilize greenhouse gas emissions.

1997
Kyoto Protocol commits participating countries to establishing targets for reducing greenhouse gas emissions; Democratic President Bill Clinton signs the agreement, but opposition from industry groups and Republican senators keeps it from being ratified.

1998
Gallup Poll finds Republicans and Democrats share similar views on the effects of climate change, with roughly half of respondents saying those effects are already evident.

2000s
Climate change becomes a security issue.

2003
Defense Department report says abrupt climate change could "destabilize the geopolitical environment" and recommends elevating the issue "beyond a scientific debate to a U.S. national security concern."

2006
Former Democratic Vice President Al Gore releases "An Inconvenient Truth," a documentary about the dangers of global warming.

2007
Gore and the IPCC share the Nobel Peace Prize for their efforts to educate the public about human-caused climate change.

2008
Pentagon calls climate change a "national security challenge." . . . Gallup Poll shows partisan divide on climate change, with 76 percent of Democrats saying the effects "have already begun" and 41 percent of Republicans agreeing.

2011
Climate change-related drought from 2006 to 2009 is cited as one cause of Syria's civil war.

2014
Defense Department says the effects of climate change could "enable terrorist activity and other forms of violence." . . . United States and China agree to reduce greenhouse gas emissions.

2015
Obama administration calls climate change a national security priority. . . . President Obama signs Paris climate change agreement, a global pact signed by more than 190 countries to reduce carbon emissions.

2016
Obama directs federal agencies to take climate change into account in national security plans.

2017
President Trump signs executive order reversing Obama administration actions on climate change, including the directive on climate change and national security. . . . Trump announces United States will withdraw from Paris climate change agreement. . . . Hurricane Harvey slams Houston with record-breaking rainfall and flooding, and Hurricane Irma causes widespread devastation in the Caribbean and Florida, raising new concerns about potential links between climate change and extreme weather.

Climate Change Stoking Fear of Migration, Conflict

Weather events could result in up to 1 billion refugees.

I t's only a tiny island amid the vast Louisiana bayous, but it could foreshadow what is ahead for tens of millions of people living in small island countries and coastal communities around the world.

Isle de Jean Charles, located in the Gulf of Mexico about 80 miles from New Orleans, has lost 98 percent of its land since 1955 to coastal erosion and rising sea levels attributed to climate change. The Department of Housing and Urban Development (HUD) and the Rockefeller Foundation, a private philanthropy, have provided $48 million in grant money to relocate people living on the island's remaining 320 acres, making them the country's first official climate refugees. [1] By some estimates, the island will disappear completely by 2055. [2]

Around the world, rising sea levels, droughts, intense storms, floods and other extreme conditions caused by climate change could lead to mass migrations to higher ground, competition for scarce resources, political instability and conflict, experts say. "The impacts of climate change combine to make it a clear threat to collective security and global order in the first half of the 21st Century," the International Institute for Strategic Studies, a London security policy think tank, said in a 2011 report. [3]

The report said that "in areas with weak or brittle states, climate change will increase the risks of resource shortages, mass migrations, and civil conflict. These could lead to failed states, which threaten global stability and security." [4]

As climate change worsens, seas could rise one meter — 3.3 feet — by 2100, displacing up to 2 billion people. [5] According to regional studies, 5 million to 10 million people in the Philippines and 10 million in Vietnam would be displaced. Seventy percent of the Nigerian coast would be swamped, displacing 4 million people, and 5 million people would be forced to leave areas in the South Pacific. In the United States, a sea level rise of 2.95 feet

could inundate the homes of 4.2 million people. [6]

By 2050, between 25 million and 1 billion "environmental migrants" will move within their own countries or across borders, with 200 million being the most widely cited estimate, according to the International Organization for Migration in Switzerland, which works for international cooperation on migration issues. "It is evident that gradual and sudden environmental changes are already resulting in substantial population movements," the group said. [7]

Koko Warner at the United Nations University in Bonn, Germany, wrote in a blog post that people displaced by climate change will move to areas "they hope will provide safe and sustainable livelihoods."

"All countries and governments will be affected by people on the move whether those countries are areas of origin, transit or destination," wrote Warner, who runs the university's Environmental Migration, Social Vulnerability and Adaptation section." [8]

Environmental migration on such a large scale is frequently cited as a major security threat. The Pentagon's 2014 "Climate Change Adaptation Roadmap" said it could affect the deployment of U.S forces and test the Defense Department's "capability to provide logistical material and security assistance on a massive scale or in rapid fashion." [9]

Some experts say climate-driven migration is a factor behind the vicious ethnic conflict that has been underway in Darfur in western Sudan since 2003. "[A] decade of drought in the 1970s and 1980s . . . prompted large movements of people within the region of Darfur as well as into it from neighboring areas seeking more fertile land," said a report by the Woodrow Wilson International Center for Scholars, a think tank in Washington. "The new arrivals' need for land — both for agriculture and grazing — caused tension, which slowly escalated into outright hostility and eventually the explosive violence." [10] The

---

Continued from p. 782

In a 1997 Gallup Poll, 46 percent of Democrats and 47 percent of Republicans said they believed "the effects of global warming have already begun." Ten years later, 76 percent of Democrats told Gallup they held that view, but only 41 percent of Republicans said the same. [63]

In 2001, Republican President George W. Bush announced the United States would not adhere to the Kyoto Protocol, saying the treaty's emission reduction targets "were arbitrary and not based upon science." He also noted that China and India, the world's No. 2 and No. 3 polluters, were exempt from Kyoto's mandates. [64]

Security Concerns

After the Sept. 11, 2001, terrorist attacks on the United States, U.S. defense officials began paying more attention to the effects of climate change on military operations. In 2003, a report prepared for the Pentagon predicted that abrupt climate change could "destabilize the geopolitical environment, leading to skirmishes, battles, and even war" due to food and water shortages and disrupted access to energy. The report recommended elevating the possibility of abrupt climate change "beyond a

scientific debate to a U.S. national security concern." [65]

In 2008, the Pentagon said in its "National Defense Strategy" report that climate change would affect "existing security concerns such as international terrorism and weapons proliferation," marking defense officials' first major public statement that they would factor climate change into planning. [66]

Two years later, the Pentagon warned that "climate change will shape the operating environment, roles and missions that we undertake." It noted that rising sea levels would threaten coastal military bases, saying defense officials "will need to adjust to

---

conflict had killed as many as 300,000 people as of 2008, when the U.N. released its last estimate of casualty figures. [11]

Some experts attribute the Darfur migration mainly to forces other than climate change. Most migrants into Darfur's pastoral areas were "Arab nomadic groups who had been squeezed out of Chad" by a civil war there and competed with "pastoral groups whose animals were dying and needed land to cultivate," says Alex de Waal, executive director of the World Peace Foundation at the Fletcher School of Law and Diplomacy at Tufts University. "You can see a little climatic factor in there, but it wasn't a big one," he says.

Experts acknowledge that it is difficult to gauge the effects of climate change, migration and other factors in causing conflict or instability, but they say climate change is an increasingly important factor to consider.

"Climate change and large movements of people clearly present major societal and governance challenges," the Woodrow Wilson center report said. "Governments, international organizations and civil society are being asked to respond, whether they are prepared or not." [12]

In a 2016 report, the National Intelligence Council, composed of intelligence experts from government, academia, and the private sector who aid the U.S. director of national intelligence, said that "even if climate-induced environmental stresses do not lead to conflict, they are likely to contribute to migrations that exacerbate social and political tensions, some of which could overwhelm host governments and populations."

— *William Wanlund*

Isle De Jean Charles, an island off the Louisiana coast, has lost 98 percent of its land to coastal erosion and rising sea levels attributed to climate change.

[3] "The IISS Transatlantic Dialogue on Climate Change and Security," International Institute for Strategic Studies, January 2011, https://tinyurl.com/y9j3wu3f.

[4] *Ibid.*

[5] Ariel Scotti, "Two billion people may become refugees from climate change by the end of the century," *New York Daily News*, June 27, 2017, https://tinyurl.com/yauqr3fx.

[6] "Living with the oceans. — A report on the state of the world's oceans," *World Ocean Review*, undated, https://tinyurl.com/jgogzjr; Don Hinrichsen, "The Oceans Are Coming Ashore," *World Watch*, November/December 2000, https://tinyurl.com/ya2uckmf; and Matthew E. Hauer, Jason M. Evans and Deepak R. Mishra, "Millions projected to be at risk from sea-level rise in the continental United States," *Nature Climate Change*, March 14, 2016, https://tinyurl.com/ya8xcfr7.

[7] "Migration, Climate Change and the Environment," International Organization for Migration, undated, https://tinyurl.com/y88vzstl.

[8] Koko Warner, "Climate Change and Migration: The World Must Be Prepared," *The Huffington Post*, Dec. 1, 2015, https://tinyurl.com/y7bospoo; updated Nov. 20, 2016.

[9] "2014 Climate Change Adaptation Roadmap," U.S. Department of Defense, June 2014, https://tinyurl.com/y9kxrm9o.

[10] Schuyler Null and Heather Herzer Risi, "Navigating Complexity: Climate, Migration, and Conflict in a Changing World," Woodrow Wilson International Center for Scholars, Nov. 22, 2016, https://tinyurl.com/yd8arm5q.

[11] "Darfur death toll could be as high as 300,000: UN official," CBC News, April 22, 2008, https://tinyurl.com/yah2tjao.

[12] Null and Risi, *op. cit.*

[1] Laura Small, "Government Awards $48 Million to Help Climate Change-Impacted Tribe Relocate," Environmental and Energy Study Institute, Feb. 24, 2016, https://tinyurl.com/yacvvezr.

[2] Katy Reckdahl, "Losing Louisiana," Weather.com, undated, https://tinyurl.com/moufhny.

the impacts of climate change on our facilities and military capabilities." [67]

Climate change gained new attention during Obama's second term. "We will respond to the threat of climate change," Obama said in his 2013 inaugural address. "Some may still deny the overwhelming judgment of science, but none can avoid the devastating impact of raging fires and crippling drought and more powerful storms." [68]

In 2014, defense officials described the effects of climate change as potential "threat multipliers that will aggravate stressors abroad such as poverty, environmental degradation, political instability,

and social tensions — conditions that can enable terrorist activity and other forms of violence." [69] Later that year, the Defense Department released a "Climate Change Adaptation Roadmap" outlining the steps it would take to confront such conditions, such as upgrading construction standards to provide better protection from severe storms and reviewing weapons systems to ensure they can operate under extreme weather conditions such as excessive heat or rainfall. [70]

In November 2014, Obama and Chinese President Xi Jinping agreed to cooperate on climate change abatement and reduce their countries' greenhouse gas emissions,

which account for an estimated 38 percent of emissions worldwide. They also said they would work to persuade other countries to limit their emissions. [71]

The United States and 195 other countries on Dec. 12, 2015, signed the Paris Agreement on climate change, which aims to limit global temperature increases through use of renewable energy resources. It also calls on developed countries to contribute $100 billion a year to a fund created to help developing countries switch to renewable energy sources. [72]

The Obama administration's 2015 National Security Strategy identified climate change as a major national security priority,

Rising Sea Levels Threaten a Nation's Future

Climate change could displace millions of Bangladeshis.

Countries around the world view climate change as a national security threat, but for some, the threat is potentially existential.

Bangladesh, an impoverished nation of 158 million on the Bay of Bengal, is among them.

Global warming is expected to raise sea levels between 0.3 meters (1 foot) and 2.5 meters (8.2 feet) by 2100, according to a January report from the National Oceanic and Atmospheric Administration. [1] An "intermediate" increase of 1 meter (3.3 feet) could cost Bangladesh 20 percent of its land mass and force 30 million people to move elsewhere inside the country, says ANM Muniruzzaman, founder and president of the Bangladesh Institute of Peace and Security Studies, a research group focused on South and Southeast Asia.

"My country is on the front lines of the climate change crisis," says Muniruzzaman, who is a retired major general in the Bangladeshi army. "In Bangladesh, climate change is not a theory or a concept — it is a way of life."

Bangladesh is emblematic of nations with limited resources confronting potentially catastrophic climate change challenges. Rising sea levels also threaten to permanently inundate low-lying island states in the Pacific Ocean (the Marshall Islands, Kiribati, Tuvalu, Tonga, the Federated States of Micronesia and the Cook Islands), the Caribbean Sea (Antigua and Nevis) and the Indian Ocean (the Maldives). [2]

Worldwide, rising ocean water will increase the potential for violent conflict by wiping out supplies of fresh water and creating "economic turmoil, migration, and social instability," said Aubrey Paris, a senior fellow at the Institute on Science for Global Policy,

a science and technology think tank in Tucson, Ariz. [3]

"The impact of rising seas . . . is severe enough to threaten the national security of the United States and nearly all other countries, Paris said. [4]

In 2010, the United Nations established the Green Climate Fund, financed by industrialized nations, to help poorer countries limit their greenhouse gas emissions and take other steps to mitigate and adapt to climate change. The fund aims to raise $100 billion a year by 2020. So far, it has collected $10.3 billion in pledges. [5]

In Bangladesh, the fund has approved $40 million — to be matched by contributions from Bangladesh and Germany — for a six-year project to build cyclone shelters, protect access to critical roads and make urban infrastructure more climate-resistant. [6]

"Bangladesh is one of the worst victims of climate change," Prime Minister Sheikh Hasina said. "We need the developed countries to keep their promise and help us." [7]

Other South Asian countries also face severe climate-change threats, with potentially serious consequences for security, according to the Global Military Advisory Council on Climate Change, a network of active and retired military officers concerned about the potential security implications of climate change. The council describes the region as "already politically unstable and particularly vulnerable to further impacts." [8]

Pakistan, for example, has a weak government, terrorist groups operating inside its borders and a black market in nuclear weapons, says Francesco Femia, co-founder and president of the Center for Climate and Security, a policy group in Washington. Global warming is melting Pakistan's glaciers, leading to flooding and shrinking water supplies for drinking and farming. [9] "Climate

drawing ridicule from some Republicans. Then-GOP presidential candidate Jeb Bush told Fox News that "perhaps the most ludicrous comment I've ever heard [is] that climate change is a bigger threat to our country than radical Islamic terrorism. It's baffling to me that the leader of the free world, the commander-in-chief of the greatest armed forces ever created, would state that." [73]

Obama was undeterred. In a 2016 interview with *The Atlantic*, he said climate change represented a more serious threat than the jihadist Islamic State.

"Climate change is a potential existential threat to the entire world if we don't do something about it," he said. "It involves every single country, and it is a comparatively slow-moving emer-

gency, so there is always something seemingly more urgent on the agenda." [74]

On Sept 21 last year, Obama directed federal agencies to identify climate change-related risks that affect national security objectives and develop plans to address them. [75]

Trump issued an executive order in March rescinding the Sept. 21 directive and other Obama administration energy- and climate-related regulatory actions, including the recommendations for action in the military's 2014 "Climate Change Adaptation Roadmap." [76] Trump's order said the move was "in the national interest, to promote clean and safe development of our Nation's vast energy resources, while . . . avoiding regulatory burdens that unnecessarily encumber energy pro-

duction, constrain economic growth, and prevent job creation." [77]

The White House later announced the United States would withdraw from the Paris Agreement, saying the accord worked against U.S. economic interests. [78] He added, however, that the country would continue to participate in international climate change negotiations and meetings "to protect U.S. interests and ensure all future policy options remain open to the administration." [79]

A Pew Research Center survey conducted in 37 countries before Trump announced his decision on the Paris accord found 71 percent disapproval for withdrawal, with 19 percent voicing approval. [80] In a U.S. poll taken the week after Trump's announcement by

change can exacerbate Pakistan's political instability, with global repercussions," Femia says.

In Bangladesh, people displaced by rising sea levels will have few options to leave the country. The country is bordered by India on three sides (except for a 169-mile border with Myanmar), and India protects that border with fencing and armed guards, Muniruzzaman says. "If large numbers of climate migrants try to cross over into India, it will certainly result in a human catastrophe of unknown proportion," he says.

Bangladesh has developed a climate change action plan that addresses food security, public health, national infrastructure and other issues. [10] Muniruzzaman says the plan includes "technical" steps such as planting grains that can tolerate higher salinity, raising the foundations of houses and building cyclone shelters. "Beyond that, I don't think there's much that can be done," he says. "The government hasn't been able to implement the adaptation strategies for lack of funds."

Benjamin Strauss, a vice president at Climate Central, a New Jersey organization composed of scientists who study climate change, said Bangladesh's future beyond 2100 depends on whether global greenhouse gas emissions drop. "It is very plausible that the amount of carbon we put in the atmosphere between today and 2050 will determine whether Bangladesh can even exist in the far future," he said." [11]

— *William Wanlund*

A monitoring station measures melting at the Passu glacier in Pakistan's Gojal Valley. Global warming is melting Pakistan's glaciers, leading to flooding and shrinking water supplies.

[1] "Global And Regional Sea Level Rise Scenarios For The United States," National Oceanic and Atmospheric Administration, January 2017, p. 23, https://tinyurl.com/zvn25ua.

[2] "Working Group II: Impacts, Adaptation and Vulnerability," Intergovernmental Panel on Climate Change, undated, https://tinyurl.com/yd8h7n47.

[3] Aubrey Paris, "Sea Level Rise: Sink or Swim," War Room, U.S. Army War College, July 21, 2017, https://tinyurl.com/y7tkrda5.

[4] *Ibid.*

[5] "Resource Mobilization," Green Climate Fund, undated, https://tinyurl.com/yd5fecrp.

[6] "Project FP004 — Climate-Resilient Infrastructure Mainstreaming in Bangladesh," Green Climate Fund, June 14, 2017, https://tinyurl.com/ybju8j9f.

[7] Anup Kaphle, "An interview with Bangladeshi Prime Minister Sheikh Hasina," *The Washington Post*, Oct. 11, 2011, https://tinyurl.com/yaoxxycx.

[8] Tariq Waseem Ghazi, A.N.M. Muniruzzaman and A.K. Singh," Climate Change and Security in South Asia," Global Military Advisory Council on Climate Change, May 2016, https://tinyurl.com/z856o2s.

[9] "Pakistan seeks to track flood risk from melting glaciers," Climate Himalaya, Sept. 20, 2011, https://tinyurl.com/yd9gnwvj.

[10] "Bangladesh Climate Change Strategy and Action Plan 2009," Bangladesh Ministry of Environment and Forests, September 2009, https://tinyurl.com/ybl5pfhy.

[11] Megan Darby, "What will become of Bangladesh's climate migrants?" *Climate Change News*, Aug. 14, 2017, https://tinyurl.com/yb8vddpa.

The Associated Press and University of Chicago, 46 percent of those surveyed said they opposed the withdrawal, with 29 percent saying they supported it. In that poll, 51 percent of Republicans supported the withdrawal and 69 percent of Democrats opposed it. [81] ∎

CURRENT SITUATION

Military Leaders See Risks

Although President Trump has made clear he wants to roll back many Obama-era environmental initiatives, Pentagon leaders apparently plan to continue factoring climate change into their strategic and operational planning. [82]

Air Force Gen. Paul Selva, vice chairman of the Joint Chiefs of Staff, told the Senate Armed Services Committee on July 18 that "the dynamics that are happening in our climate will drive uncertainty and will drive conflict."

"If we see tidal rises, if we see increasing weather patterns of drought and flood and forest fires and other natural events . . . then we're gonna have to be prepared for what that means in terms of the potential for instability," Selva said. [83]

Geoffrey Dabelko, director of environmental studies at the George V. Voinovich School of Leadership and Public Affairs at Ohio University, believes the military needs to stay above the partisan fray over climate change.

"The military is rightly agnostic in terms of threats and opportunities," he says. "They can't afford to ignore any of them just because they may be out of fashion with whoever's in power. Environment and climate change are among the appropriate issues to track."

Other experts are skeptical that the military needs to deal with climate change now. "There's a temporal component here — how urgent is the issue?" says Wood of the Heritage Foundation. "If it's urgent, then funding should go along with that — so where's the funding? If it's not going to happen for 40 or 50 years, well, the nation has problems we need to deal with today."

A Worrisome Arctic

" Arctic amplification" is the top climate-related concern for David Titley, director of the Center for Solutions to Weather and Climate Risk at Pennsylvania State University. The term refers to the process that causes temperatures to increase faster at the poles than else-

The Chinese aircraft carrier Liaoning steams past a wind turbine as it approaches Hong Kong on July 7, 2017. Much of the debate over U.S. security and action on climate change focuses on China, and whether Beijing wants to use the Trump administration's skepticism of climate change to gain political and economic leverage, in part by embracing green technology.

where. That causes the Arctic ice cap to melt, warming the surrounding water and leading to still more melting.

Diminished sea ice enables more human activity, including "energy and mineral exploitation, fishing, tourism, even celebrity cruises," says Titley, a retired rear admiral who established the Navy's climate change task force in 2009.

That means a bigger job for the Navy, he says. "One of the duties of the Navy is to protect the sea lines of communication" — the maritime routes between ports, which are becoming more extensive as Arctic sea ice melts. "We want

to be able to do that, especially when the U.S. has sovereign territory — Alaska — in that Arctic region," Titley says.

Fran Ulmer, chair of the U.S. Arctic Research Commission, an independent federal agency that advises the president and Congress on Arctic policy, says Arctic temperatures are increasing two to three times faster than temperatures around the world. Since the 1970s, she says, the volume of sea ice has declined 75 percent and the area it covers has declined 50 percent.

"That is a very dramatic change for a place that has been covered with ice for a very, very long time," Ulmer says.

This year, the area covered by Arctic winter ice reached a record low, continuing a decades-long trend toward diminished ice coverage. [84] The melting polar ice cap, along with rising ocean temperatures and thawing glaciers, has contributed to an average sea-level rise of 3 inches since 1992, according to satellite data. Seas could rise between 1 and 3 feet by the end of the century, NASA has reported. [85]

The Arctic warming trend has made Russian officials "particularly enthusiastic

about their northern sea routes that connect eastern Russia and Europe across the Arctic," Ulmer says. "Russia has a lot of oil and gas resources, and they are developing them in the Yamal region [in northern Siberia]," she says. "Less ice means easier access in and out of their northern ports."

In late August, the *Christophe de Margerie*, a modified 984-foot Russian tanker, became the first merchant vessel without an icebreaker escort to pass through the Northern Sea Route, which runs through the Arctic waters connecting the Atlantic and Pacific oceans along the Siberian coast. The ship, carrying liquefied natural gas from Norway to South Korea, made the trip via the Arctic Ocean in 19 days, about 30 percent faster than the conventional route through the Suez Canal, according to the ship's owner, Sovcomflot. The ship, which is designed to break through ice 7 feet thick, is the first of a reported 15 ships constructed by Russia to take advantage of diminishing Arctic sea ice and allow faster and cheaper shipment of goods between European and Asian ports. [86]

Sherri Goodman, a public policy fellow at the Woodrow Wilson International Center for Scholars, says the United States should not underestimate the economic significance of climate change's effects on the Arctic. "With economic opportunity comes political influence," she says. "That's why U.S. global leadership in [the Arctic] is so important, and we ignore the Arctic at our peril. We'd wake up to find this great land mass right off Canada that isn't too far from the U.S., [and] is no longer under friendly leadership."

The melting ice also has military implications. Reuters has reported that Russia also plans to open or reopen six Arctic military facilities "as it pushes ahead with a claim to almost half a million square miles" there. Some of the facilities are equipped with air defense and anti-ship missiles, and possibly military fighters and bombers, the news agency said. [87]

Continued on p. 790

At Issue:

Should climate change be a national security priority?

REP. JIM LANGEVIN, D-R.I.
MEMBER, HOUSE COMMITTEE ON ARMED SERVICES

WRITTEN FOR *CQ RESEARCHER*, SEPTEMBER 2017

*t*here is widespread consensus that the effects of climate change threaten not only our environment and our economy, but also our national security. In fact, the Pentagon's top military and civilian officials have repeatedly stated that climate change poses a direct threat to the national security of the United States, an assessment echoed and amplified by leaders in the intelligence community. Defense Secretary James Mattis understands the risks, as evidenced by testimony given at his confirmation hearing: "The effects of a changing climate — such as increased maritime access to the Arctic, rising sea levels, desertification, among others — will impact our security situation."

We are already feeling those effects. Mission-critical assets like Naval Station Norfolk, home of the Atlantic Fleet, are experiencing "nuisance flooding," and the storm surges are only expected to get worse. Warmer temperatures and more volatile weather could affect training operations at inland bases, reducing readiness capabilities. Moreover, the changing global climate is expected to lead to increased instability due to migration, competition over resources and possibly more failed states, which we know to be breeding grounds for extremism and terrorism.

Policymakers cannot turn a blind eye to the changing environment, because doing so places our troops at risk. Unfortunately, President Trump and his administration seem to be doing just that, withdrawing the United States from the Paris climate accord and rescinding executive actions supporting climate research.

Congress must support our servicemen and women and address the concerns raised by our military leaders about global warming, which is why I amended the fiscal 2018 National Defense Authorization Act to ensure that climate change is properly incorporated into our national security strategy. Specifically, the provision acknowledges that climate change is a direct threat to the national security of the United States and requires the secretary of Defense to provide an assessment of — and recommendations to mitigate vulnerabilities to — the top 10 most threatened military installations in each service branch. It also requires the Department of Defense to address how combatant commander requirements will change as a result of this threat.

Climate change is real, and the threat it poses to our national security is imminent. Congress is listening to the warnings of our military and intelligence leaders. It's time the president does the same.

MARLO LEWIS
*SENIOR FELLOW,
COMPETITIVE ENTERPRISE INSTITUTE*

WRITTEN FOR *CQ RESEARCHER*, SEPTEMBER 2017

*c*limate change should not be a national security priority. Directing the Pentagon to focus on it will actually make America less secure. Generals know how to fight and win wars. They know little about nation building and even less about "sustainable development." Compelling the Department of Defense (DOD) to incorporate climate assessments and strategies in scores of programs, as the Obama administration did, can only promote groupthink, wasteful mission creep and inattention to bona fide security threats.

Climate change would indeed be a security issue if, as is often claimed, it were an existential threat. However, the latest U.N. climate report poured cold water on global warming doomsday scenarios. In the 21st century, Atlantic Ocean circulation collapse is "very unlikely," ice sheet crackup is "exceptionally unlikely" and catastrophic release of methane from melting permafrost is "very unlikely."

The Obama DOD defined climate change as a "threat multiplier," exacerbating conditions like poverty and political stability that "enable" terrorism and violence. However, the research linking climate change to conflict is highly dubious. For example, warming will supposedly exacerbate drought, leading to "water wars." However, studies repeatedly find that water scarcity promotes cooperation rather than conflict.

Climate campaigners have long sought military leaders as spokespersons, hoping to split conservatives on energy policy. But preaching climate peril and carbon taxes would ill-serve both DOD and U.S. national security.

President Trump seeks to secure an era of U.S. "energy dominance" as part of a strategy to achieve 3 percent annual GDP growth. A return to carbon-suppression policies would chill growth, forcing painful tradeoffs between guns and butter.

As an analysis by the Institute for 21st Century Energy shows, if we assume the validity of "consensus" climatology, the world cannot achieve the Paris agreement's goal of limiting global warming to 2 degrees Celsius unless developing countries dramatically reduce their current consumption of fossil fuels. Yet more than 1 billion people in those countries have no access to electricity, and billions more have too little to support development.

Putting energy-poor people on an energy diet would be a cure worse than the alleged disease. It would not promote stability or peace.

Continued from p. 788

A 2015 Russian military exercise involved 45,000 personnel, 15 submarines and 41 warships, and "practiced full combat readiness," according to a report by the Center for Strategic and International Studies, a Washington think tank. [88] Russian military incursions into other countries' airspace also have picked up, according to the Henry Jackson Society, a conservative British think tank, which said that in 2016, the Norwegian air force intercepted 74 Russian warplanes patrolling its coast, up from 58 in 2015.

Nikolay Lakhonin, press secretary at the Russian Embassy in Washington, says Russia's Arctic policy is "very transparent and predictable." He cites a Russian policy document that says the country's Arctic interests include tapping oil, gas and other strategic raw materials, maintaining a military force to protect Russia's borders and conducting environmental and scientific research. [89]

But Penn State's Titley says Russia's intentions in the Arctic aren't clear. "They talk about having search-and-rescue bases, but these bases have missiles on them," he says. "It's more than search-and-rescue, it's more than constabulary — it's real military capability."

U.S. military officials have taken notice. "What concerns me about Russia is . . . the offensive military capability that they are adding to their force that's Arctic-capable," said Air Force Lt. Gen. Kenneth Wilsbach, the senior U.S. military officer in Alaska. "If you really want to keep the Arctic a peaceful place . . . then why are you building offensive capabilities?" [90]

The two massive storms that struck the United States in late summer — Hurricane Harvey wreaking havoc mainly in Texas and Louisiana, and Hurricane Irma in Florida — showed how weather can affect military operations, causing some military bases to curtail or suspend operations.

The military moved aircraft, ships and thousands of civilian and military workers ahead of the storms from Army, Navy and Air Force bases in Texas and Florida. [91] "Local training and work

schedules were affected by the storms, but it did not impact military readiness," DOD spokesperson Heather Babb told *CQ Researcher* in an e-mail.

The storms also highlighted the military's humanitarian responsibilities: Thousands of state and U.S. military personnel were deployed to help with law enforcement and rescue efforts. Republican Texas Gov. Greg Abbott mobilized all 12,000 members of the Texas National Guard, and Republican Florida Gov. Rick Scott called up nearly 8,000 of his state's Guard to help with law enforcement and search and rescue efforts. Guard units from other states also contributed equipment and personnel. [92]

Some climate scientists believe climate change affected the severity of the storm. Michael Mann, a professor of atmospheric science at Pennsylvania State University, said rising sea levels caused by global warming made Hurricane Harvey's storm surge — the sea water driven inland by the hurricane's winds — considerably higher than would have occurred a few decades ago, causing "far more flooding and destruction." [93]

Mann also said warmer water temperatures brought on by global warming put more moisture into the atmosphere, causing greater rainfalls and coastal flooding. Over six days, Harvey dumped an estimated 27 trillion gallons of rain over Texas and Louisiana, according to meteorologist Ryan Maue of WeatherBELL, a meteorology consulting firm. [94]

But Clifford Mass, a University of Washington professor of atmospheric sciences, said climate change can't be blamed for the enormity of Harvey. "You really can't pin global warming on something this extreme. It has to be natural variability. It may juice it up slightly but not create this phenomenal anomaly." [95]

A 2014 government national climate assessment said North Atlantic hurricanes have all increased in intensity, frequency and duration since the 1980s. "Hurricane-associated storm intensity and rainfall rates are projected to increase as the climate continues to warm," it said. [96]

Emerging Bipartisanship?

In July, the House approved an amendment to the fiscal 2018 defense authorization bill calling climate change "a direct threat to the national security of the United States." The amendment, sponsored by Rep. Jim Langevin, D-R.I., would require the secretary of Defense to submit to Congress within one year "a report on vulnerabilities to military installations and combatant commander requirements resulting from climate change over the next 20 years." [97] Forty-six Republicans joined 188 Democrats in voting for the amendment. All 185 "no" votes came from Republicans.

Femia, of the Center for Climate Change and Security, calls the vote "the most significant climate security action in many years."

"Most of those 46 Republicans belong to the Climate Solutions Caucus, and a lot of them are in coastal districts and/or in districts that have been affected by climate and/or have military bases that are vulnerable," he says.

As of mid-September, the Senate had not acted on the defense authorization legislation.

The Climate Solutions Caucus was set up in 2016 by two House members from Florida "to educate members on economically viable options to reduce climate risk and protect our nation's economy, security, infrastructure, agriculture, water supply and public safety." Caucus membership is equally divided between the parties, currently with 28 Republicans and 28 Democrats. [98]

Mark Reynolds, executive director of the Citizens' Climate Lobby, a nonprofit in California that advocates for national policies to address climate change, said it is only a matter of time before caucus members take steps to produce "meaningful legislation to combat climate change."

"At a time when the Trump administration has turned its back on the Paris agreement and partisanship plagues Washington, a bipartisan effort of this size shows the tide is turning on the climate issue," he said. [99]

Some climate change experts say the vote on Langevin's amendment could signal that partisanship on climate change is moderating.

"We have to wait and see, but it's certainly a positive step," says Dabelko of Ohio University. "The true test of whether a reemerging bipartisan approach to climate change is actually taking hold in Congress will be when it comes to budgets and allocating money." ■

OUTLOOK

More People, Higher Temperatures

In January, the National Intelligence Council predicted that "more extreme weather, water and soil stress, and food insecurity will disrupt societies. Sea-level rise, ocean acidification, glacial melt and pollution will change living patterns." The threat "will require collective action to address — even as cooperation becomes harder," the council said. [100]

But whether climate change is accepted by Americans as a national security concern that must be addressed is another question.

Some experts believe that evidence that the climate is changing is too distant in time and space for many Americans to fully absorb its significance.

Veteran environmental journalist Andrew Revkin of the nonprofit investigative news organization ProPublica says environmental policies implemented today won't show any effect for many years. "Our vulnerability to floods and wildfire and agricultural destruction will get worse, and nothing we do right now will have any effect for decades to come," he says. "Global population is heading for 9 billion by 2050 or 2060, and that vulnerability is built in until at least then."

Engelke of the Atlantic Council says there is no question climate change is a national security concern but that more Americans need to understand "it's not just happening to people living in low-lying island states or in the Sahel [in Africa]. And not only is it going to happen to us, it already is."

In June, 13 federal agencies released a report saying average annual temperatures in the United States have risen 1.5 degrees Fahrenheit since 1901 and will increase another 5 to 7.5 degrees by the end of the century. It is "extremely likely" that human activity has caused most of the global temperature increase since 1951, it said. [101]

Engelke believes such evidence will help end the rancorous partisan debate over climate change within 20 years. "There will no longer be a debate about whether climate change is occurring, but rather about how to mitigate it and how to adapt to its effects," he says.

Femia at the Center for Climate and Security says dealing with climate change as a national security issue "will take more than just technical solutions like putting more money into drought-resistant crops or building a seawall — it's going to take a large-scale national and international approach."

He also says technology will allow researchers to be increasingly accurate in predicting the effects of a warming climate. "Climate change is an unprecedented security risk," Femia says. "But we also have unprecedented foresight." ■

Notes

[1] "Syrian war monitor says 465,000 killed in six years of fighting," Reuters, March 13, 2017, https://tinyurl.com/y7qktus3.

[2] Caitlin E. Werrell and Francesco Femia, eds., "The Arab Spring and Climate Change," Center for American Progress, February 2013, https://tinyurl.com/ovlsq4j.

[3] Jan Selby et al., "Climate change and the Syrian civil war revisited," Political Geography, September 2017, https://tinyurl.com/ybr3ppe6.

[4] "Quadrennial Defense Review 2014," U.S.

Department of Defense, March 4, 2014, https://tinyurl.com/j9yf7l3.

[5] Spanger-Siegfried et al., "The US Military on the Front Lines of Rising Seas," Union of Concerned Scientists, 2016, https://tinyurl.com/hq9u2zd.

[6] "Global And Regional Sea Level Rise Scenarios For The United States," National Oceanic and Atmospheric Administration, January 2017, p. 23, https://tinyurl.com/zvn25ua.

[7] Laura Parker, "Who's Still Fighting Climate Change? The U.S. Military," National Geographic, Feb. 7, 2017, https://tinyurl.com/jppz85j.

[8] Tara Copp, "Pentagon is still preparing for global warming even though Trump said to stop," Military Times, Sept. 12, 2017, https://tinyurl.com/y7dz6mrz.

[9] "Press Conference by President Obama," The White House, Dec. 1, 2015, https://tinyurl.com/yd3l6fc9.

[10] "Presidential Memorandum — Climate Change and National Security," The White House, Sept. 21, 2016, https://tinyurl.com/ychwqf36.

[11] "Implications for US National Security of Anticipated Climate Change," National Intelligence Council, Sept. 21, 2016, https://tinyurl.com/hp9arwj.

[12] Donald J. Trump, Twitter post, Dec. 6, 2013, https://tinyurl.com/jaelpj7.

[13] Transcript, Donald J. Trump interview with The New York Times, Nov. 23, 2016, https://tinyurl.com/juymes5.

[14] "Presidential Executive Order on Promoting Energy Independence and Economic Growth," The White House, March 28, 2017, https://tinyurl.com/ny2k4wt.

[15] "Statement by President Trump on the Paris Climate Accord," The White House, June 1, 2017, https://tinyurl.com/ydaz28yb.

[16] "Secretary of Defense James Mattis's Views on Climate, Energy and More," document obtained by Pro Publica journalist Andrew Revkin, March 14, 2017, https://tinyurl.com/yd9obggm.

[17] Mark Hand, "46 Republicans buck party to help Democrats take down anti-climate action amendment," Think Progress Blog, July 14, 2017, https://tinyurl.com/yc8bynvp.

[18] Michael D. Shear, "Trump Will Withdraw U.S. From Paris Climate Agreement," The New York Times, June 1, 2017, https://tinyurl.com/y7hj9x7k.

[19] "Paris Agreement," United Nations, 2015, https://tinyurl.com/y75g5pqb.

[20] Anushka Asthana, "No 10 defends May not signing letter opposing US on Paris climate deal," The Guardian, June 2, 2017, https://tinyurl.com/ya47xdp4.

[21] Nicolas Loris, "Trump's Decision to Ditch the Climate Agreement Will Help America Negotiate Better Deals," Heritage Foundation,

June 7, 2017, https://tinyurl.com/yahurm5w.

[22] Loris, *op. cit.*

[23] Juliet Eilperin, "The Trump administration just disbanded a federal advisory committee on climate change," *The Washington Post*, Aug. 20, 2017, https://tinyurl.com/ydbtvup4.

[24] Brad Plumer, "The U.S. Won't Actually Leave the Paris Deal Anytime Soon," *The New York Times*, June 7, 2017, https://tinyurl.com/yb4bcagv.

[25] Nicholas Stern, "China is shaping up to be a world leader on climate change," *Financial Times*, Jan. 20, 2017, https://tinyurl.com/y8amfz24.

[26] "Here's How Much Money China Is Throwing at Renewable Energy," *Fortune*, Jan. 5, 2017, https://tinyurl.com/jxcne9q.

[27] Angel Hsu and Carlin Rosengarten, "The leadership void on climate change," *China Dialogue*, April 21, 2017, https://tinyurl.com/y8jfqumn.

[28] "Naval Station Norfolk: Welcome to the World's Largest Naval Station," Military.com, https://tinyurl.com/y9hgn8cq.

[29] "On the Front Lines of Rising Seas: Naval Station Norfolk, Virginia," Union of Concerned Scientists, July 27, 2016, https://tinyurl.com/y9fspcnv.

[30] Evan Lehmann, "Inside one naval base's battle with sea-level rise," *E&E News*, Oct. 27, 2016, https://tinyurl.com/je482eq.

[31] *National Security Implications of Climate Change for U.S. Naval Forces* (2011), National Academies Press, https://tinyurl.com/y9c3wezn.

[32] Catherine Foley, "Military Basing and Climate Change," American Security Project, November 2012, https://tinyurl.com/y99p5p5y.

[33] Andrew Holland, "North Korea Threatens Guam Today; Climate Change Threatens it in the Long Term," American Security Project, Aug. 10, 2017, https://tinyurl.com/y8ndq4x5.

[34] Caitlin Werrell and Francesco Femia, "General Keys: The military thinks climate change is serious," Center for Climate and Security, June 2016, https://tinyurl.com/y8na8dgy.

[35] "Climate Change Adaptation: DOD Can Improve Infrastructure Planning and Processes to Better Account for Potential Impacts," U.S. Government Accountability Office, May 2014, https://tinyurl.com/ya6x8obk.

[36] Taylor Smith, "Critique of 'Climate Change Adaptation: DOD Can Improve Infrastructure Planning and Processes to Better Account for Potential Impacts," Heartland Institute, Feb. 5, 2015, https://tinyurl.com/ya97c3u8.

[37] "Quadrennial Defense Review 2014," U.S. Department of Defense, March 4, 2014, https://tinyurl.com/j9yf7l3.

[38] "Climate Change Action Plan 2016-2020," World Bank Group, 2016, https://tinyurl.com/yc7kveo3.

[39] Hiroko Tabuchi and Henry Fountain, "Bucking Trump, These Cities, States and Companies Commit to Paris Accord," *The New York Times*, June 1, 2017, https://tinyurl.com/y9wkrawd.

[40] Cecilia Reyes, "Four key areas for global risks in 2017," World Economic Forum, Jan. 11, 2017, http://tinyurl.com/y889qp8r.

[41] Marshall Burke, Solomon M. Hsiang and Edward Miguel, "Global non-linear effect of temperature on economic production," stanford.edu, Oct. 21, 2015, https://tinyurl.com/y9n3ytqk. Originally published in *Nature*, Nov. 12, 2013, pp. 235-239.

[42] Marshall Burke, "The global economic costs from climate change may be worse than expected," Brookings Institution, Dec. 9, 2015, https://tinyurl.com/ycg7phd5.

[43] David Rotman, "Hotter Days Will Drive Global Inequality," *MIT Technology Review*, Dec. 20, 2016, https://tinyurl.com/jxshnb5.

[44] Iain Murray, "An Issue of Science and Economics," Competitive Enterprise Institute, 2008, https://tinyurl.com/y73hrwts.

[45] "The Economics of Climate Change: Cocktails and Conversation with William Nordhaus," Becker Friedman Institute for Research in Economics, University of Chicago, April 16, 2014, https://tinyurl.com/yby4eham.

[46] Matt Ridley, "Why climate change is good for the world," *The Spectator*, Oct. 19, 2013, https://tinyurl.com/yanh9vvm.

[47] David Wogan, "Why we know about the greenhouse gas effect," *Scientific American*, May 16, 2013, https://tinyurl.com/y8fehazt.

[48] Steve Graham, "Svante Arrhenius (1859-1927)," NASA, Jan. 18, 2000, https://tinyurl.com/y9vhbo6d.

[49] "The Carbon Dioxide Greenhouse Effect," American Institute of Physics, January 2017, https://tinyurl.com/yaqnh5l9.

[50] Edward C. Keefer, ed., "Foreign Relations of the United States, 1964-1968, Vol. XXVIII, Laos," Office of the Historian, U.S. State Department, https://tinyurl.com/y7laoxa7.

[51] "Memorandum From the Deputy Under Secretary of State for Political Affairs (Kohler) to Secretary of State Rusk," Office of the Historian, U.S. Department of State, http://tinyurl.com/yccsgu49.

[52] "Convention on the Prohibition of Military or Any Other Hostile Use of Environmental Modification Techniques," U.S. State Department, undated, https://tinyurl.com/ydxoqsnt.

[53] "Potential Implications of Trends in World Population, Food Production, and Climate," CIA, made available through The Black Vault, August 1974, https://tinyurl.com/yc36rosb.

[54] "Potential Implications of Trends in World Population, Food Production, and Climate," *op. cit.*

[55] Walter Sullivan, "Study Finds Warming Trend That Could Raise Sea Levels," *The New York Times*, Aug. 22, 1981, https://tinyurl.com/ycc88cp2.

[56] Al Gore, "Earth's Fate Is the No. 1 National Security Issue," *The Washington Post*, Oct. 12, 2007, https://tinyurl.com/y6vqzou8.

[57] J.T. Houghton, G.J. Jenkins and J.J. Ephraums, eds., "Climate Change: The IPCC Scientific Assessment," U.N. International Panel on Climate Change, Cambridge University Press, 1990, https://tinyurl.com/n7r4lyj.

[58] President George H.W. Bush, "Remarks to the Intergovernmental Panel on Climate Change," American Presidency Project, Feb. 5, 1990, https://tinyurl.com/yakl8acu.

[59] John H. Goshko, "Baker Urges Steps on Global Warming," *The Washington Post*, Jan. 31, 1989, https://tinyurl.com/yd5ewl3n.

[60] "U.S. Foreign Policy Priorities and FY 1991 Budget Request," Secretary of State James Baker's statement to the Senate Foreign Relations Committee, Feb. 1, 1990, https://tinyurl.com/y8k2uo6l.

[61] John H. Cushman Jr., "Intense Lobbying Against Global Warming Treaty," *The New York Times*, Dec. 7, 1997, https://tinyurl.com/ybbkjpoy.

[62] Amy Royden, "U.S. Climate Change Policy Under President Clinton: A Look Back," *Golden Gate University Law Review*, January 2002, https://tinyurl.com/yapzyucf.

[63] Riley E. Dunlap, "Partisan Gap on Global Warming Grows," Gallup, May 29, 2008, https://tinyurl.com/y7toqhw8.

[64] "President Bush Discusses Global Climate Change," The White House, June 11, 2001, https://tinyurl.com/y6tvzksb.

About the Author

Bill Wanlund is a freelance writer in the Washington, D.C., area. He is a former Foreign Service officer, with service in Europe, Asia, Africa and South America. He holds a journalism degree from The George Washington University and has written for *CQ Researcher* on abortion, intelligence reform and the marijuana industry.

[65] Peter Schwartz and Doug Randall, "An Abrupt Climate Change Scenario and Its Implications for United States National Security," report for the Department of Defense, October 2003, https://tinyurl.com/ybd2bzss.

[66] "National Defense Strategy," Department of Defense, June 2008, https://tinyurl.com/jcvrjnk.

[67] "Quadrennial Defense Review Report," Department of Defense, February 2010, https://tinyurl.com/yd5enopn.

[68] "Inaugural Address by President Barack Obama," The White House, Jan. 21, 2013, https://tinyurl.com/y9lhewr7.

[69] "Quadrennial Defense Review 2014," op. cit.

[70] "2014 Climate Change Adaptation Roadmap," op. cit.

[71] "U.S.-China Joint Announcement on Climate Change," The White House, Nov. 11, 2014, https://tinyurl.com/yd6kxfj6.

[72] "Paris Agreement," United Nations, 2015, https://tinyurl.com/y75g5pqb.

[73] "National Security Strategy," The White House, February 2015, https://tinyurl.com/y9nj6jx3; Colin Campbell, "Jeb Bush is spitting fire at Obama for touting climate-change efforts after Paris attacks," Business Insider, Nov. 25, 2015, https://tinyurl.com/y7l6oswp.

[74] Jeffrey Goldberg, "The Obama Doctrine," The Atlantic, April 2016, https://tinyurl.com/zfzlg5g.

[75] "Presidential Memorandum — Climate Change and National Security," The White House, Sept. 21, 2016, https://tinyurl.com/hj6c6fw.

[76] Copp, op. cit.

[77] "Presidential Executive Order on Promoting Energy Independence and Economic Growth," The White House, March 28, 2017, https://tinyurl.com/ny2k4wt.

[78] "Statement by President Trump on the Paris Climate Accord," The White House, June 1, 2017, https://tinyurl.com/ydaz28yb.

[79] "Communication Regarding Intent To Withdraw From Paris Agreement," Office of the Spokesperson, State Department, Aug. 4, 2017, https://tinyurl.com/ybyk5ury.

[80] Richard Wike et al., "U.S. Image Suffers as Publics Around World Question Trump's Leadership," Pew Research Center, June 26, 2017, https://tinyurl.com/ya65l6js.

[81] "Views on the Paris Climate Agreement," AP-NORC poll, June 2017, https://tinyurl.com/y9os6hqy.

[82] "Secretary of Defense James Mattis's Views on Climate, Energy and More," op. cit.

[83] "Vice Chairman of the Joint Chiefs on Climate Instability and Political Instability," Center for Climate and Security, July 25, 2017, https://tinyurl.com/y7x63jsg.

[84] "Sea Ice Extent Sinks to Record Lows at Both Poles," NASA, March 22, 2017, https://tinyurl.com/k96bsdo.

[85] "NASA Science Zeros in on Ocean Rise: How Much? How Soon?" press release, NASA, Aug. 26, 2015, https://tinyurl.com/yd87goqh.

[86] Patrick Barkham, "Russian tanker sails through Arctic without icebreaker for first time," The Guardian, Aug. 24, 2017, https://tinyurl.com/ybqgo9ru; "Sovcomflot's unique LNG carrier sets new record with Northern Sea Route transit of just 6.5 days," press release, Sovcomflot, Aug. 23, 2017, https://tinyurl.com/ybyfyrh7.

[87] Andrew Osborn, "Putin's Russia in biggest Arctic military push since Soviet fall," Reuters, Jan. 30, 2017, https://tinyurl.com/jpheshv.

[88] Heather A. Conley and Caroline Rohloff, "The New Ice Curtain," Center for Strategic & International Studies, August 2015, https://tinyurl.com/ycuyqevt.

[89] "Russian Federation Policy for the Arctic to 2020," Arctis Knowledge Hub, undated, https://tinyurl.com/y7wcxjct.

[90] "U.S. General Concerned About Russia's Arctic Military Buildup," Radio Free Europe/Radio Liberty, May 26, 2017, https://tinyurl.com/ya6zkbom.

[91] Ellen Mitchell, "Governor activates entire Texas National Guard in response to Harvey," The Hill, Aug. 28, 2017, https://tinyurl.com/yaac5llw; Melissa Nelson Gabriel, "Military bases in Hurricane Irma's path assess storm damage," Pensacola News Journal, Sept. 11, 2017, https://tinyurl.com/y7f8tu4z.

[92] Ibid.

[93] Michael E. Mann, "It's a fact: climate change made Hurricane Harvey more deadly," The Guardian, Aug. 28, 2017, https://tinyurl.com/ycamv4bl.

[94] Ibid., Ellen Mitchell, http://tinyurl.com/yaac5llw.

[95] Seth Borenstein, "Is there a connection between Harvey and global warming?" The Associated Press, Aug. 28, 2017, https://tinyurl.com/y7x2bjkk.

[96] "Climate Change Impacts in the United States," U.S. Global Change Research Program, October 2014, https://tinyurl.com/jfruuux.

[97] "Amendment to H.R. 2810 Offered by Mr. Langevin of Rhode Island," House.gov, June 21, 2017, https://tinyurl.com/ybrjqedy.

[98] "What is the Climate Solutions Caucus?" Citizens' Climate Lobby, https://tinyurl.com/yd26bc4v.

[99] Steve Valk, "25 Republicans And 25 Democrats Now Belong To The Climate Solutions Caucus," Ecosystem Marketplace, July 29, 2017, https://tinyurl.com/ycnd9w2k.

[100] "Paradox of Progress: Trends Transforming the Global Landscape," National Intelligence Council, Jan. 9, 2017, https://tinyurl.com/yagksyqa.

[101] "U.S. Global Change Research Program Climate Science Special Report (CSSR)," DocumentCloud.org, June 28, 2017, https://tinyurl.com/y9fvnjs2.

FOR MORE INFORMATION

American Security Project, 1100 New York Ave., N.W., Suite 710W, Washington, DC 20005; 202-347-4267; www.americansecurityproject.org. Public policy organization focused on national security issues, including climate change.

Center for American Progress, 1333 H St., N.W., Washington, DC 20005; 202-682-1611; www.americanprogress.org. Progressive think tank that addresses a range of social, economic and political issues, including climate change and security.

Center for Climate and Security, 1025 Connecticut Ave., N.W., Suite 1000, Washington, DC 20036; 202-246-8612; climateandsecurity.org. Organization that researches and disseminates information about the impact of climate.

Competitive Enterprise Institute, 1310 L St., N.W., 7th Floor, Washington, DC 20005; 202-331-1010; https://cei.org/. Libertarian think tank that questions concerns about global warming and advocates access to affordable energy.

Heritage Foundation, 214 Massachusetts Ave., N.E., Washington DC 20002-4999; 202-546-4400; www.heritage.org. Conservative think tank that researches and disseminates information about climate change, national security and other issues.

Intergovernmental Panel on Climate Change, c/o World Meteorological Organization, 7bis Avenue de la Paix, C.P. 2300, CH- 1211 Geneva 2, Switzerland; +41-22-730-8208/54/84; www.ipcc.ch. Group set up under the United Nations that regularly updates policymakers on the scientific evidence of climate change.

NASA Global Climate Change, 300 E St., S.W., Washington, DC 20546; 202-358-0000; climate.nasa.gov. Provides information on the effects of global warming.

Bibliography

Selected Sources

Books

Campbell, Kurt M., ed., *Climatic Cataclysm: The Foreign Policy and National Security Implications of Climate Change*, Brookings Institution Press, 2008.
Experts discuss climate-change scenarios and their effects on science, politics, foreign policy and national security.

Miller, Todd, *Storming the Wall: Climate Change, Migration, and Homeland Security*, City Lights Books, 2017.
A journalist predicts border battles as more climate change-displaced migrants seek refuge in developed countries; he chronicles examples of recent climate-induced struggles and forecasts where future clashes might occur.

Moran, Daniel, ed., *Climate Change and National Security: A Country-Level Analysis*, Georgetown University Press, 2011.
An international collection of scholars analyzes the security risks posed by climate change in 19 countries and regions.

Articles

Bromund, Theodore R., "Climate change is not a national security threat," Heritage Foundation Commentary, June 4, 2015, https://tinyurl.com/y7rdm3jk.
A senior research fellow at a conservative think tank argues that ideology, not climate, endangers national security.

Busby, Joshua W., "Climate and Security," *Duck of Minerva* (blog), Oct. 17, 2014, https://tinyurl.com/y8gcn6vf.
An associate professor of public affairs wonders if the climate change-security link might be "a finding in need of a theory" and questions framing the climate change debate in national security terms.

Epstein, Richard A., "Containing Climate Change Hysteria," Hoover Institution, June 5, 2017, https://tinyurl.com/y7sotxj4.
A law professor says American withdrawal from the Paris climate agreement isn't the threat to U.S. security and economic prosperity that President Trump's critics claim.

Lehmann, Evan, "Inside one naval base's battle with sea-level rise," Climatewire, E&E News, Oct. 27, 2016, https://tinyurl.com/je482eq.
A journalist examines the threat that rising sea levels pose to Naval Station Norfolk in Virginia.

Werrell, Caitlin, and Francesco Femia, "Climate Change and Security," *Crisis-Response*, April 2017, https://tinyurl.com/ycwwdbqh.
The co-presidents of the Center for Climate Change and Security, a Washington think tank, discuss how and why the U.S. military views climate change as a "threat multiplier."

Reports and Studies

"Implications for US National Security of Anticipated Climate Change," National Intelligence Council, Sept. 21, 2016, https://tinyurl.com/hp9arwj.
The 16 agencies of the National Intelligence Community look at how climate change could affect global social, economic, political and security conditions in the next 20 years.

"National Security Implications of Climate-Related Risks and a Changing Climate," U.S. Department of Defense, July 23, 2015, https://tinyurl.com/p5qlyz9.
A Pentagon report to the Senate Appropriations Committee outlines the climate-related security risks for each geographic military command and how the commands intend to mitigate those risks.

"Quarterly Defense Review 2014," U.S. Department of Defense, March 14, 2014, https://tinyurl.com/j9yf7l3.
The most recent edition of the Defense Department's quadrennial outline of security issues and strategies identifies climate change as a "threat multiplier" and a "significant challenge for the U.S. and the world at large."

Dellink, Rob and Elisa Lanzi, "TheEconomic Consequences of Climate Change," Organisation for Economic Co-operation and Development, Nov. 3, 2015, https://tinyurl.com/y7dwmrse.
An intergovernmental organization predicts the possible geographic and sectoral consequences of climate change.

Idso, Craig D., Robert M. Carter and S. Fred Singer, "Why Scientists Disagree About Global Warming: The NIPCC Report on Scientific Consensus, (Second Ed.)" The Heartland Institute, 2016, https://tinyurl.com/y8jhjcaa.
The Nongovernmental International Panel on Climate Change argues against the claim that scientists are virtually unanimous in acknowledging the dangers of climate change.

Pezard, Stephanie, et al., "Maintaining Arctic Cooperation With Russia: Planning for Regional Change in the Far North," RAND Corp., March 7, 2017, https://tinyurl.com/ybpnqgmk.
Researchers consider the effects of climate change, along with a host of geopolitical issues, in analyzing Russian-U.S. tensions in the Arctic.

Selby, Jan, et al., "Climate Change and the Syrian civil war revisited," *Political Geography*, September 2017, https://tinyurl.com/ybr3ppe6.
Researchers from the United Kingdom, United States and Germany conclude that, so far, there is "no convincing evidence" linking climate change to the Syrian civil war, and further investigation is required.

The Next Step:

Additional Articles from Current Periodicals

Congressional Debates

"Congress Declares Climate Change a National Security Threat," The Associated Press, July 14, 2017, https://tiny url.com/yaszr6dp.

The Republican-led House of Representatives approved a defense policy bill that declares climate change a national security threat and authorizes $696 billion in defense spending for fiscal 2018.

Siders, David, "More Republican lawmakers bucking their party on climate change," *Politico*, Aug. 23, 2017, https://tinyurl.com/yb2vv8df.

The House Climate Solutions Caucus has tripled in size since January after a surge of congressional Republicans began supporting climate change policy.

Tritten, Travis J., "After fiery debate, House lawmakers back military study on climate change," *Washington Examiner*, June 28, 2017, https://tinyurl.com/ycrjxrh9.

Congress approved an amendment to a defense bill that will require the military to study and report back to Congress on the 10 facilities in each branch most susceptible to climate change.

Global Security

Arraf, Jane, "In Egypt, A Rising Sea — And Growing Worries About Climate Change's Effects," NPR, Aug. 13, 2017, https://tinyurl.com/y753j99r.

Egypt is among the most vulnerable countries to the effects of climate change because rising sea levels can overflow the Nile River Delta and affect crops, according to the World Bank.

Ijaz, Aymen, "Climate Change and Migration in Pakistan," *The Diplomat*, Aug. 22, 2017, https://tinyurl.com/ybtzxmr4.

Heat waves, natural disasters and other effects of climate change could force more and more people to migrate, says the International Panel on Climate Change (IPCC).

Ives, Mike, "North Korea Aside, Guam Faces Another Threat: Climate Change," *The New York Times*, Aug. 11, 2017, https://tinyurl.com/y7glz49k.

Guam is concerned that climate change will cause extensive reef damage, seriously affecting tourism.

Military Preparedness

Bergengruen, Vera, "Trump May Doubt Climate Change, Pentagon Sees It as Threat Multiplier," Military.com, June 2, 2017, https://tinyurl.com/y9dtv3wa.

Climate change threatens at least 128 U.S. military bases with flooding.

Parker, Laura, "Who's Still Fighting Climate Change? The U.S. Military," *National Geographic*, Feb. 7, 2017,

https://tinyurl.com/jppz85j.

Despite congressional efforts to divert resources to other uses, the Defense Department has devoted funding and time to adapt facilities at risk from climate change.

Ryan, Joe, and Jennifer A. Dlouhy, "Ex-Military Brass Back Tillerson, Mattis in Climate Fight," Bloomberg, May 9, 2017, https://tinyurl.com/mtundhp.

President Trump withdrew the U.S. from the Paris climate accord to the dismay of a group of retired senior military officers.

Repercussions

Balaraman, Kavya, "U.S. Crop Harvests Could Suffer with Climate Change," *Scientific American*, Jan. 20, 2017, https://tinyurl.com/zlr2rox.

Hotter temperatures could cause future U.S. harvests to drop by 22 to 49 percent.

Bryan, Bob, "Trump's pulling the US out of the Paris climate agreement could be disastrous for the economy," *Business Insider*, June 1, 2017, https://tinyurl.com/ya2m7nt2.

A recent paper in *Nature* projects that unmitigated warming is expected to reduce average global incomes by roughly 23 percent by the end of the century.

Coffel, Ethan, and Radley Horton, "Climate Change Could Impact The Way We Fly," *Newsweek, The Conversation*, Aug. 15, 2017, https://tinyurl.com/y95gv8yp.

Flights have been grounded this summer due to hotter temperatures, and concerns are growing about how changes in weather patterns might affect the infrastructure of airports and aircraft.

In-depth Reports on Issues in the News

Are you writing a paper?

Need backup for a debate?

Want to become an expert on an issue?

For 90 years, students have turned to *CQ Researcher* for in-depth reporting on issues in the news. Reports on a full range of political and social issues are now available. Following is a selection of recent reports:

Civil Liberties
Privacy and the Internet, 12/15
Intelligence Reform, 5/15
Religion and Law, 11/14

Crime/Law
High-Tech Policing, 4/17
Forensic Science Controversies, 2/17
Jailing Debtors, 9/16
Decriminalizing Prostitution, 4/16
Restorative Justice, 2/16
The Dark Web, 1/16
Immigrant Detention, 10/15

Education
Charter Schools, 3/17
Civic Education, 2/17
Student Debt, 11/16
Apprenticeships, 10/16

Environment/Society
Muslims in America, 7/17
Funding the Arts, 7/17
Hunger in America, 7/17
Future of the Christian Right, 6/17
Trust in Media, 6/17
Anti-Semitism, 5/17

Health/Safety
Medical Breakthroughs, 9/17
Medical Marijuana, 7/17
Food Labeling, 6/17
Sports and Sexual Assault, 4/17
Reducing Traffic Deaths, 2/17

Politics/Economy
Universal Basic Income, 9/17
National Debt, 9/17
North Korea Showdown, 5/17
Rethinking Foreign Aid, 4/17
Immigrants and the Economy, 2/17

Upcoming Reports

Think Tanks, 9/29/17   Cyber Warfare, 10/6/17   Democracies, 10/13/17

ACCESS
CQ Researcher is available in print and online. For access, visit your library or www.cqresearcher.com.

STAY CURRENT
For notice of upcoming *CQ Researcher* reports or to learn more about *CQ Researcher* products, subscribe to the free email newsletters, *CQ Researcher Alert!* and *CQ Researcher News*: http://cqpress.com/newsletters.

PURCHASE
To purchase a *CQ Researcher* report in print or electronic format (PDF), visit www.cqpress.com or call 866-427-7737. Single reports start at $15. Bulk purchase discounts and electronic-rights licensing are also available.

SUBSCRIBE
Annual full-service *CQ Researcher* subscriptions—including 44 reports a year, monthly index updates, and a bound volume—start at $1,131. Add $25 for domestic postage.

CQ Researcher Online offers a backfile from 1991 and a number of tools to simplify research. For pricing information, call 800-818-7243 or 805-499-9774 or email librarysales@sagepub.com.

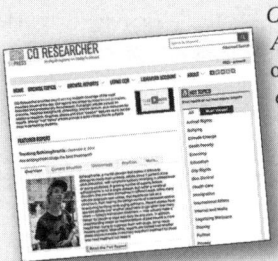

CQ RESEARCHER

CQPRESS

In-depth reports on today's issues

Published by CQ Press, an Imprint of SAGE Publications, Inc.   **www.cqresearcher.com**

Think Tanks in Transition

Do their donors exert too much influence?

Once viewed as independent producers of innovative policy solutions, think tanks are facing new questions about donor influence over their work. Critics argue that wealthy benefactors or corporate interests are unduly influencing some think tanks' policy positions. Think tanks deny the charge and say their relationships with donors are appropriate and help them advance their mission. Meanwhile, the marketplace for new ideas is growing, with consultants, advocacy groups, charities and bloggers all turning out policy positions. The increasing competition is forcing think tanks to move beyond their traditional role as cloistered hives of intellectual activity into functions more akin to public relations and advocacy. They also are adopting digital-age tools such as podcasts and interactive maps to improve the chances that busy policymakers with shrinking attention spans will notice their work. Through all the challenges, the sector is growing: Think tanks, until recently rare outside of North America and Western Europe, now number more than 6,800 worldwide and operate in almost every country.

Myron Ebell, director of the Competitive Enterprise Institute's Center for Energy and Environment, heads a coalition of think tanks, advocacy groups and others that lobbies aggressively against government efforts to limit climate change. Critics say the lobbying effort is an example of how the lines between think tank work and advocacy can blur – a charge that Ebell denies.

CQ Researcher • Sept. 29, 2017 • www.cqresearcher.com
Volume 27, Number 34 • Pages 797-820

ᴵ THIS REPORT
ᴺ
ˢ
THE ISSUES **799**

BACKGROUND **805**

CHRONOLOGY **807**

CURRENT SITUATION **812**

AT ISSUE......................**813**

OUTLOOK **815**

BIBLIOGRAPHY **818**

THE NEXT STEP **819**

Think Tanks in Transition

CQ RESEARCHER

The Issues

799
- Do wealthy donors have too much influence over think tanks?
- Are think tanks still credible sources of data-supported analysis?
- Can think tanks be influential in the 21st century?

Background

805 **Modern Problems**
The earliest think tanks tackled social ills arising from an industrial age.

806 **The First Wave**
In 1910, industrialist Andrew Carnegie sought to eliminate wars.

811 **Advocacy Think Tanks**
In the 1970s, the Heritage Foundation helped spur other think tanks to pursue ideological causes.

Current Situation

812 **Trump Administration**
Some Republicans say think tanks are outdated.

814 **Advocacy Shake-Up**
The Heritage Foundation ousted its president, Jim DeMint, citing management problems.

815 **Foreign Growth**
Think tanks have spread to more than 182 countries.

Outlook

815 **Return of Honest Brokers?**
Growing political polarization might make think tanks more relevant.

Sidebars and Graphics

800 **U.S. Dominates Think Tank Sector**
Think tanks total more than 6,800 worldwide.

801 **Think Tanks Increasingly Open About Donors**
Transparency is improving, a watchdog group says.

804 **Think Tanks by the Numbers**
Larger organizations have annual revenues topping $90 million.

807 **Chronology**
Key events since 1907.

808 **Think Tanks Join the Digital Revolution**
Scholars are using podcasts to buttress their print-based pronouncements.

810 **Government Think Tanks in Critics' Crosshairs**
Trump, congressional Republicans question their usefulness.

813 **At Issue:**
Should think tanks receiving tax-exempt donations promote a political philosophy?

For Further Research

817 **For More Information**
Organizations to contact.

818 **Bibliography**
Selected sources used.

819 **The Next Step**
Additional articles.

819 **Citing CQ Researcher**
Sample bibliography formats.

Cover: Getty Images/*The Washington Post*/Bill O'Leary

Sept. 29, 2017
Volume 27, Number 34

EXECUTIVE EDITOR: Thomas J. Billitteri
tjb@sagepub.com

ASSISTANT MANAGING EDITORS: Kenneth Fireman, kenneth.fireman@sagepub.com, Kathy Koch, kathy.koch@sagepub.com, Scott Rohrer, scott.rohrer@sagepub.com

ASSOCIATE MANAGING EDITOR: Val Ellicott

SENIOR CONTRIBUTING EDITOR:
Thomas J. Colin
tom.colin@sagepub.com

CONTRIBUTING WRITERS: Marcia Clemmitt, Sarah Glazer, Reed Karaim, Barbara Mantel, Chuck McCutcheon, Tom Price

SENIOR PROJECT EDITOR: Olu B. Davis

EDITORIAL ASSISTANT: Natalia Gurevich

FACT CHECKERS: Eva P. Dasher, Michelle Harris, Betsy Towner Levine, Robin Palmer

Publishing

Los Angeles I London I New Delhi
Singapore I Washington DC I Melbourne

An Imprint of SAGE Publications, Inc.

SENIOR VICE PRESIDENT, GLOBAL LEARNING RESOURCES:
Karen Phillips

EXECUTIVE DIRECTOR, ONLINE LIBRARY AND REFERENCE PUBLISHING:
Todd Baldwin

CQ Researcher (ISSN 1056-2036) is printed on acid-free paper. Published weekly, except: (March wk. 4) (May wk. 4) (July wks. 1, 2) (Aug. wks. 2, 3) (Nov. wk. 4) and (Dec. wks. 3, 4). Published by SAGE Publications, Inc., 2455 Teller Rd., Thousand Oaks, CA 91320. Annual full-service subscriptions start at $1,131. For pricing, call 1-800-818-7243. To purchase a *CQ Researcher* report in print or electronic format (PDF), visit www.cqpress.com or call 866-427-7737. Single reports start at $15. Bulk purchase discounts and electronic-rights licensing are also available. Periodicals postage paid at Thousand Oaks, California, and at additional mailing offices. POSTMASTER: Send address changes to *CQ Researcher*, 2600 Virginia Ave., N.W., Suite 600, Washington, DC 20037.

Think Tanks in Transition

BY MARCIA CLEMMITT

THE ISSUES

When Barry Lynn, a prominent scholar at the New America think tank in Washington, read in June that the European Union (EU) had fined Google for anti-competitive practices, he posted a statement praising the EU's actions.

A few hours later he learned that his job, along with about 10 others in his Open Markets program at New America, was on the line.

CEO Anne-Marie Slaughter told Lynn that she "just got off the phone with [Google CEO] Eric Schmidt and he is pulling all of his money" from New America, according to published accounts.

"We are in the process of trying to expand our relationship with Google," Slaughter said in an email to Lynn. "Just THINK about how you are imperiling funding for others." Two months later, Slaughter ended Lynn's program, which opposed the market dominance of tech and telecom giants. She also ousted Lynn in what he said was retribution for his anti-Google stance, which Slaughter denied. [1]

New America criticized Lynn's "repeated refusal to adhere to New America's standards of openness and institutional collegiality." A Google spokesperson also denied his accusation, saying the company respects think tanks' "independence, personnel decisions and policy perspectives." [2]

The argument over donor influence is among the latest signs of a think-tank industry struggling with funding issues and a difficult policy climate. Long known for offering detailed policy positions on a wide range of public issues, think tanks are facing battles on multiple fronts:

Anne-Marie Slaughter, CEO of the New America think tank, fired a prominent scholar at the liberal organization over the summer after he supported a fine against Google, one of the group's major funders. Both Google and New America denied the ouster of Barry Lynn was retribution for his comments, but ethics watchdogs say the incident underscores questions about donors' influence over think tanks.

• Many think tanks' endowments fell in the wake of the 2008 financial crisis, said Daniel Drezner, a professor of international politics at Tufts University in Medford, Mass., and the author of the 2017 book, *The Ideas Industry*. The income drop, in turn, forced think tanks to seek new funding sources, especially annual charitable donations, which left some organizations under pressure from donors to support the donors' short-term priorities, he said. [3]

• Many donors are seeking control over research they fund, according to think-tank leaders, a departure from the days when an ultra-wealthy contributor promised think tank scholars independence of thought. As a result, "think tanks own their agenda less than they used to," said Ellen Laipson,

a distinguished fellow and president emeritus of the Stimson Center, a Washington think tank that focuses on global security issues. [4]

• Think tanks' traditional approach — synthesizing mounds of information into detailed, well-documented policy proposals — is crashing into internet-age realities. Legislators "only read 30 minutes a day, so that means no detailed white papers," forcing think tanks to reach decision-makers through podcasts, interactive graphics and other less traditional means, says James G. McGann, a senior lecturer in international studies and the director of the Think Tanks and Civil Societies Program at the University of Pennsylvania in Philadelphia.

• Think tanks face new competition from business and professional associations, large management consultancies and many other organizations with units that produce detailed research on policy issues.

Yet, for all its challenges, the think-tank world is on the upswing, both in the United States and internationally. The number of U.S. think tanks has more than doubled since 1980 to 1,835 in 2017, with 397 in Washington. Think tanks total more than 6,846 worldwide and exist in almost every country. (*See map, p. 800.*) Most think tanks created in recent decades focus on a limited number of issues or on issues affecting a single region, compared with earlier ones that had broad mandates on a range of issues. [5]

What, exactly, defines a think tank is surprisingly complicated. At their most basic, think tanks are private, nonprofit organizations that are exempt from federal and property taxes, with a few being taxpayer-funded government agencies, such as the Congres-

U.S. Dominates Think Tank Sector

The United States is home to 1,835 think tanks — 27 percent of the 6,846 think tanks worldwide — followed by China at 435 and the United Kingdom at 288. The number of U.S. think tanks has more than doubled since 1980.

No. of Think Tanks, by Country, 2015

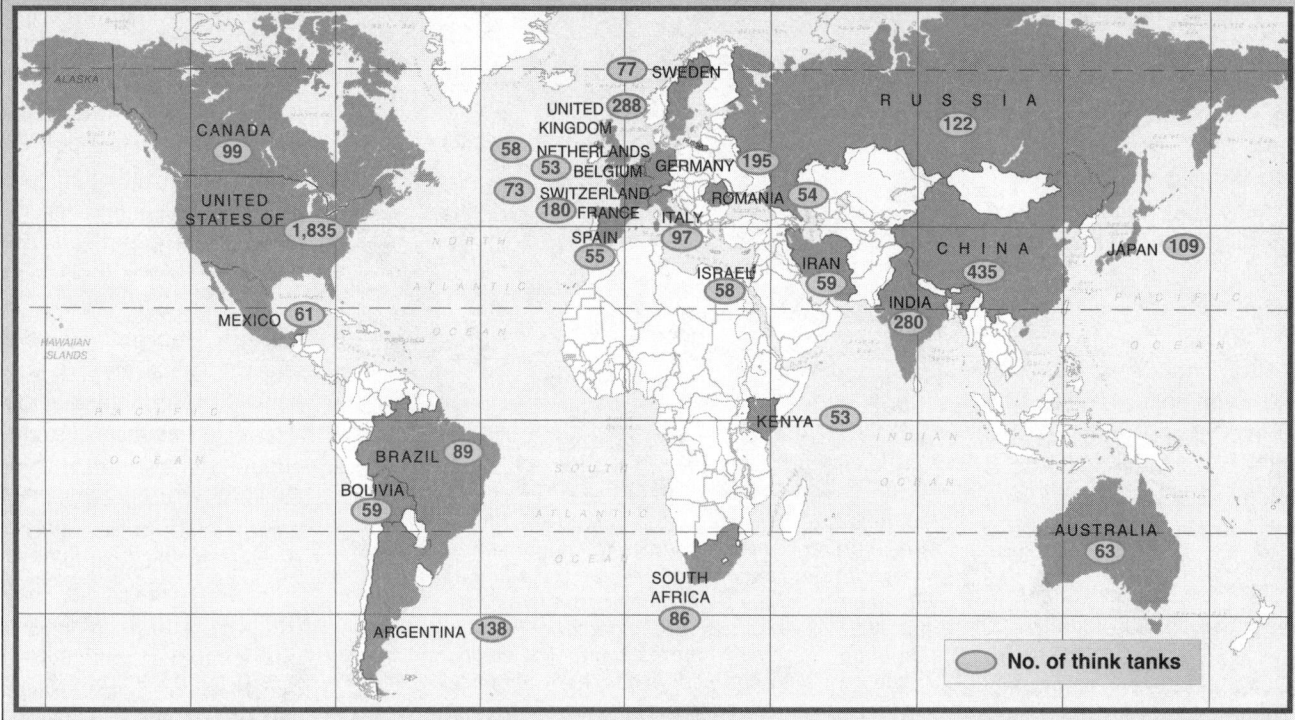

Source: James G. McGann, "2016 Global Go To Think Tank Index Report," University of Pennsylvania Scholarly Commons, Jan. 26, 2017, pp. 26-27, https://tinyurl.com/y8zdj6pm

sional Budget Office and Congressional Research Service.* (*See sidebar, p. 810.*)

Scholars at think tanks examine theories and data in an effort to determine which are relevant to challenges facing a nation or a region, and they develop policy proposals based on their research. Examples of such proposals include an international scheme to rebuild a country destroyed in war, changes to the tax code that allow businesses to keep more of their profits,

---

* Most U.S. think tanks are registered as nonprofit organizations under section 501(c)3 of the federal tax code, which limits their political activities. Some think tanks have formed allied groups under section 501(c)(4), which governs "social welfare or community benefit organizations" and permits participation in political campaigns.

or a program to make health care more affordable for poor people.

By developing policy ideas based on evidence and debating alternative solutions with an eye to the big picture — society overall — think tanks, ideally at least, are "optimizers," said Hans Gutbrod, coordinator of Transparify, a nonprofit group in Tbilisi, Georgia, that urges think tanks to disclose their funding sources so the public can gauge contributors' influence. "They seek to improve everybody's lives." This focus on the big picture sets think tanks apart from political parties or partisan pressure groups, he said. [6]

Nevertheless, the core mission of think tanks has been evolving in recent decades for a variety of reasons, experts say.

While early think tanks mostly employed scholars with a range of ideological views, some organizations on the left and right in recent times declared they would promote only ideas representing a particular political philosophy. These think tanks include the conservative Heritage Foundation, the libertarian Cato Institute and the liberal Center for American Progress (CAP).

Critics, however, say ideology-based think tanks simply cannot pursue independent research and analysis or provide an open forum for a range of potential policies — both vital and valuable hallmarks of traditional think tanks.

Think tanks that align themselves closely with standard political philosophies merely reinforce current views instead of introducing new ideas to move a debate forward, said Thomas Medvetz, an associate professor of sociology at the University of California, San Diego, and author of the 2012 book *Think Tanks in America*. Aligning think tanks with ideologies already in the political mainstream "doesn't seem like a sincere effort to promote intellectual discussion," Medvetz said. [7]

Others argue that a battle of competing ideologies is a perfectly appropriate way of developing policy, so long as the combatants make their premises clear.

"Effective, competitive, credible research" does not need to be nonideological, wrote James Jay Carafano, a vice president at the Heritage Foundation who deals with national security and foreign policy. "Though often used as a pejorative, an 'ideology' is simply an orienting perspective," he said. "What matters is the rigor and credibility of the research, not the ideology. . . . What makes the marketplace of ideas work best is the competition of ideas." [8]

CAP was created to help liberals regain ground in the "competition of ideas" that American conservatives — with Heritage's help — mostly won in the 1980s to the early 2000s period. Founded in 2005 by former Clinton White House Chief of Staff John Podesta, CAP would be a "think tank on steroids" that would help liberal ideas regain their influence, Podesta said. [9]

Some analysts say think tanks' ability to turn ideas into public programs depends at least as much on political climates as on think tanks' own actions.

Getting things done in Washington is extremely hard because of polarization and Washington's many power centers, say Raymond Struyk, a housing and social-assistance policy expert, and Andrew Rich, an associate professor of political science at the City College of New York and the author of *Think Tanks, Public Policy, and the Politics of Expertise*. By contrast, "in many of the developing countries today, the policy-making process is relatively simple,"

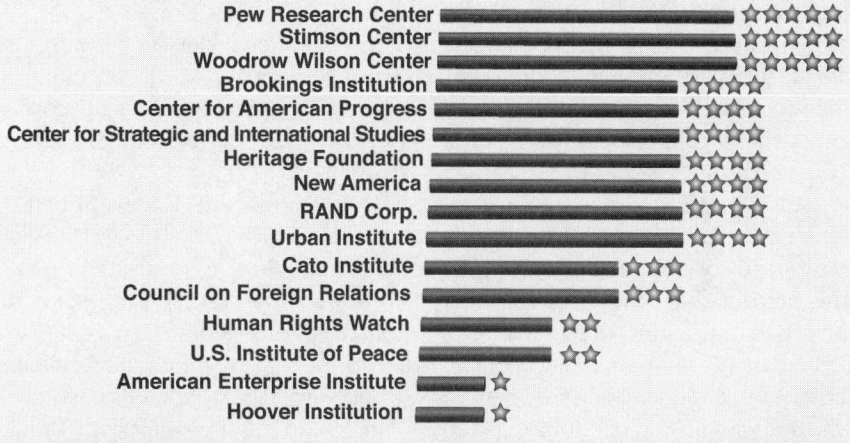

Think Tanks Increasingly Open About Donors

U.S. think tanks are becoming more transparent about identifying their donors, according to Transparify, a nonprofit in Tbilisi, Georgia, that rates global think tanks' openness about their funding. Ethics watchdogs believe that when think tanks disclose their donors and the amounts given, the public can determine whether contributors have too much influence over an organization's research.

U.S. Think Tanks, by Level of Transparency, 2016

Pew Research Center	★★★★★
Stimson Center	★★★★★
Woodrow Wilson Center	★★★★★
Brookings Institution	★★★★
Center for American Progress	★★★★
Center for Strategic and International Studies	★★★★
Heritage Foundation	★★★★
New America	★★★★
RAND Corp.	★★★★
Urban Institute	★★★★
Cato Institute	★★★
Council on Foreign Relations	★★★
Human Rights Watch	★★
U.S. Institute of Peace	★★
American Enterprise Institute	★
Hoover Institution	★

5 stars: "highly transparent"; all donors listed, clearly identifying funding amounts for, and the sources of, particular projects

4 stars: "broadly transparent"; all donations above $5,000 listed

3 stars: all or most donors listed in 2 or 3 broad contribution brackets

2 stars: all or many donors listed, but little or no financial information given

1 star: "highly opaque"; some donors listed, but the list is not exhaustive or systematic

Source: "How Transparent are Think Tanks about Who Funds Them 2016?" Transparify, June 29, 2016, https://tinyurl.com/hu7ncgu

says Struyk, who has advised think tanks in some 25 countries over the past three decades. "You make the sale, and it's done. Here it takes decades, even if it's a really good idea."

Some ethics watchdogs say the lines between think tanks, public charities and political advocacy groups are blurring. They note that both charities and think tanks can organize under the same 501(c)3 section of the tax code. IRS rules bar such entities from devoting a "substantial" portion of their work to lobbying, but critics say the rules are vague and difficult to enforce.

A recent *New York Times* examination of 75 think tanks found that numerous researchers simultaneously worked as

registered lobbyists, members of corporate boards or outside consultants in litigation and regulatory disputes, with infrequent disclosure of their dual roles. [10]

Watchdogs point to the Cooler Heads Coalition, made up of charities and think tanks, as a further example of how the lines among nonprofit groups can blur. The coalition has been producing studies and ad campaigns rejecting climate change and government attempts to control it.

"Public charities serve as so-called independent think tanks, providing analysis to create the appearance they are independent third-party voices," Robert Brulle, a professor of sociology and environmental science at Drexel

University in Philadelphia, told *The Washington Post.* "It becomes so complicated and sophisticated. This is how modern politics operates." [11]

Myron Ebell, who leads the Cooler Heads Coalition and is director of the Center for Energy and Environment at the libertarian Competitive Enterprise Institute (CEI) in Washington. He defended the coalition's lobbying activities and CEI's participation, saying the lobbying did not constitute a substantial part of CEI's work. Ebell labeled climate change an ideological issue, arguing that efforts to slow it would lead to a "regulatory onslaught" and damage the U.S. economy. [12]

Laipson said donors are pushing think tanks to show quick, quantifiable results for the work their dollars support. This expectation often forces think tanks to work on tiny, practical aspects of an issue, rather than engaging in big-picture thinking. She cited Stimson, which studies how to control the spread of nuclear weapons. Because of the pressure to show results, Stimson researchers decided to focus on how insurance coverage could be structured to incentivize manufacturers to better safeguard weaponry components. "It's micro stuff, several steps away from the big idea," she said. [13]

Nevertheless, a recent worldwide push for think tanks to reveal their funding sources is helping the public gauge for itself whether a powerful donor might have too much influence over a think tank's work, some policymaking experts say. [14] (*See graphic, p. 801.*)

As think tank researchers and lawmakers ponder the future role of research-based policymaking, here are some questions they are asking:

Do wealthy donors have too much influence over think tanks?

With hundreds of nonprofits clamoring for support, charitable donors can threaten to take their dollars elsewhere if a think tank does not give them what they want.

According to a *New York Times* investigation, the Brookings Institution promised "donation benefits" to key donors, including Microsoft and JPMorgan Chase, that ran the gamut from pushing donors' agendas to setting up events for corporate executives and government officials. In one instance, *The Times* said, the think tank supported an $8 billion redevelopment project in San Francisco headed by Lennar Corp., a homebuilder and key Brookings donor.

The think tank denied it is a tool of corporate donors. "We do not compromise our integrity," Brookings Executive Vice President Martin S. Indyk told *The Times.* [15]

Many think-tank leaders say they have safeguards in place to fend off donor influence.

At Brookings, its staff can seek input from anyone, including donors, according to the organization's "Research Independence Policy," but the conclusions of their work must be their own. Brookings generally accepts donors' requests to research particular topics as long as the topic is one "where our scholars have expertise," wrote Brookings President Strobe Talbott and former Managing Director Kimberly Churches, now CEO of the American Association of University Women. "The door shuts when it becomes apparent that the contributor [is essentially saying,] 'Here's the answer we want, and we expect you to pose the question accordingly.' " [16]

Donald Abelson, a professor of political science at Western University in London, Ontario, and the author of several books on think tanks, said, "Some former think tankers with whom I corresponded . . . told me that they were often asked to manipulate data, or massage their findings to appease donors supporting their research." He added, "I have no doubt that this happens more often than we think." [17]

Think tanks have no legal responsibility to disclose their donors, and many do not, said Ken Silverstein, an American journalist who has written widely on the

think tank sector. "That makes it impossible for the public and lawmakers to know if a think tank is putting out an impartial study or one that's been shaped by a donor's political agenda." [18]

In recent years, more foreign governments have joined the ranks of think tank donors, according to a 2014 investigation by *The New York Times.* Countries such as Norway, Japan and Qatar have teamed on projects with big-name Washington think tanks such as the Center for Global Development, hoping to use those think tanks' clout to get issues the nations care about onto the Washington agenda, the paper reported. [19]

"I am surprised, quite frankly, at how explicit the relationship is between money paid, papers published and policymakers and politicians influenced," lawyer Amos Jones said. He was referring to agreements he reviewed between the government of Norway and several think tanks, including the Brookings Institution and the Center for Global Development.

The United Arab Emirates, a major Center for Strategic and International Studies (CSIS) supporter, donated more than $1 million to help build the think tank's Washington headquarters near the White House, according to *The Times.* Qatar agreed to make a $14.8 million, four-year donation to Brookings; the Middle East nation has helped fund a Brookings affiliate in Qatar and a project on U.S. relations with the Islamic world. [20]

Many observers say transparency in disclosing a think tank's donors may be the best way to fend off undue influence or perceptions of it. Moreover, they say, think tanks are becoming more open about their contributors. Transparify reported "a strong and sustained global movement toward greater transparency" in 2016. In its first study, in 2013, the group found that of 169 think tanks it reviewed worldwide, only 25 earned its four- or five-star rating for transparency. Today, among the same organizations, 67 are transparent about donors and of those 41 are rated " 'highly transparent,' meaning that they disclose the precise sum that each donor provides." [21]

Think tanks are not "mere puppets of their paymasters," said Till Bruckner, advocacy manager of Transparify. When donors push for influence, larger and more established "institutions can and do push back, difficult as that may be at times," he said. As a result, donors who are most determined to control a message usually "turn to smaller opaque outfits with no reputation to lose, or even set up 'fake tanks' of their own" to push a cause. [22]

After several years of media reports on donor influence at think tanks, "there's now a hypersensitivity about that relationship," says Abelson. "It's becoming a hot-button topic, and things are getting a little better."

But the University of Pennsylvania's McGann says donors' increasing demand to see quick, tangible proof that their money is achieving results can force think tanks to abandon the big-picture thinking they were once known for.

"Beginning in the '80s, donors began supporting individual programs at institutions rather than whole institutions," says McGann. "Then they moved to supporting a single project rather than a program." Today, he says, "donors say things like, 'We'll support the publication of a book about this subject or a conference on it, but we won't support any research.' "

Trouble is, research — as well as think tanks' day-to-day operations, such as keeping the lights on — must be paid for. "This creates a chase for money," McGann says, and situations in which a think tank may see no option besides abandoning a long-term project of high importance in favor of a less-significant one that can show a quick result.

Are think tanks still credible sources of data-supported analysis?

"I work at a think tank. I don't have time to think."

That quip by a think tank staffer captures a key challenge the sector faces in an era of fierce partisanship, a 24/7 media cycle and hundreds of organizations vying for influence. Conducting original, in-depth research is becoming harder to do because of the many demands on a scholar's time, from writing blogs to lobbying policy-makers. Some critics say many think tanks skimp on research because they are spending so much time publicizing and arguing for their proposals. Other observers, however, point out that the sector still includes many organizations focused on research.

Demonstrators on June 21 protest a planned speech by Scott Pruitt, administrator of the Environmental Protection Agency, to the conservative Manhattan Institute think tank in New York City; Pruitt, who questions climate change, canceled the speech. Through research and the hosting of conferences, think tanks play an important role in debate over leading issues such as global warming and health care.

In the education field, state and national think tanks publish many school-improvement proposals that amount to "little more than junk science," often because they cherry-pick evidence to back predetermined conclusions, according to Kevin Welner, an associate professor of education policy at the University of Colorado in Boulder, and Alex Molnar, a professor of education policy at Arizona State University in Tempe.

Few think tank papers on education are based on original research, use rigorous statistical methods or comprehensively review existing research, which puts their conclusions on shaky ground, argue Welner and Molnar. But thanks to think tanks' efforts to publicize their work, flawed reports often are widely disseminated through media outlets and passed on to lawmakers without being reviewed for rigor, said the scholars, who have led a nationwide group of university researchers in reviewing think-tank education proposals since 2006. [23]

Some observers worry that new communications tasks imposed on think-tank scholars by a 24/7 media cycle and more competition from other think tanks may simply leave them with too little energy for thinking. Today's analysts "are expected to pen op-ed articles for newspapers, appear as talking heads on major television networks, testify before congressional committees" and much more, Western University's Abelson said. [24] (See sidebar, p. 808.)

In addition, unlike in science, law and other fields, the think tank sector has no accreditation certification system and has not instituted sector-wide peer review of scholarly writings, Abelson says. "Nobody's actually regulating any of this; I can go home and create my own think tank."

Think Tanks by the Numbers

Think tanks come in many sizes. The largest is RAND Corp., which pursues research under government contracts and employs more than 2,000, while smaller ones have staffs under 50.

U.S. Think Tanks, by Revenue and Employment, 2015

Think Tank	Total Revenue	Number of Employees	Founded
RAND Corp.	$332.2 million	2,137	1948
Urban Institute	$108 million	543	1968
Brookings Institution	$106 million	629	1916
Council on Foreign Relations	$101.5 million	597	1921
Heritage Foundation	$92 million	572	1973
American Enterprise Institute	$60 million	253	1938
Center for American Progress	$50 million	418	2003
Pew Research Center	$38.4 million	170	2004
Cato Institute	$36 million	248	1977
New America	$33.5 million	222	1999
Economic Policy Institute	$6.6 million	43	1986

Source: "Nonprofit Explorer: Research Tax-Exempt Organizations," ProPublica, 2016, http://tinyurl.com/ybhsj52t

Nevertheless, a few think tanks do send their work out for scholarly reviews, and many have internal review processes, say Abelson and international think tank adviser Struyk. But think tanks tend to work on tighter — and more unyielding — deadlines than academics typically do, and that fact can make even good review processes ineffective, says Struyk. "The reality often is that the draft gets done 48 hours before the deadline, somebody gives it a lick and a promise and out the door it goes," he says.

Struyk and others also say critics must remember that think tank work differs from academic ivory-tower thinking. In the think tank world, communication and outreach are crucial for effective policy development, they say. Policymaking is about relationships — finding out who are the necessary players and potential allies, and knowing how to reach and communicate with those people, Struyk says. In fact, think tank staff are more likely to lack that vital skill than to lack analytical and research ability, he says.

Moreover, data-based research still happens at think tanks, including in projects conducted by scholars across ideological lines, sector insiders say. Karlyn Bowman, a senior fellow at the conservative American Enterprise Institute (AEI), which studies international markets and public policy issues, says she has long worked with scholars at liberal CAP and centrist Brookings on demographic analyses of issues such as changing voting patterns. "There's still enormous collegiality in the think tank world," she says. [25]

Some experts on policymaking caution against blaming think tanks for problems that may have more to do with the culture at large, especially the nation's highly charged political polarization, than with the sector.

Think tanks today must scramble "for the attention of an increasingly polarized audience," making it potentially riskier than in the past to behave like true scholars debating a broad range of ideas in search of the best one, said former Rep. Jane Harman,

D-Calif., who is president and CEO of the congressionally chartered Woodrow Wilson International Center for Scholars, a Washington think tank that brings together scholars of many backgrounds to study international issues. [26]

Ideally, think tanks should be "safe political spaces" in which a range of controversial ideas is aired before conclusions are arrived at, said Harman. But for "many think tanks, open discussions are just bad business. How can you afford to challenge members of your audience if they might take their ears and eyeballs elsewhere?" [27]

In recent decades, more think tanks have allied themselves with one party or the other, said Tevi Troy, CEO of the American Health Policy Institute, a Washington think tank that examines health care issues from the perspective of employers who provide employee health coverage. That raises the risk of think tanks "becoming both more conventional and less valuable," he said.

While there is nothing wrong with think tanks helping the parties to hone their messages, independent voices are required, said Troy. There is "a real need for original thinking that can break the mold of some familiar debates," he said, "and propose plausible solutions to the enormous policy problems that now confront us." [28]

Can think tanks be influential in the 21st century?

Think tanks today face stiffer competition in the ideas-and-influence game than they did years ago.

Computerized data-analysis capabilities, plus the ease of publishing on the internet, allow organizations of all sizes, and even individuals, to conduct sophisticated research and put policy ideas into the public debate, observers of the policymaking process say.

Advocacy groups such as Amnesty International, business and professional associations, large management consultancies such as PricewaterhouseCoopers, large banks and many other institutions have established internal research units similar to those at traditional think tanks. [29] Newspapers such as *The Guardian*, based in the United Kingdom, analyze and interpret huge datasets on subjects ranging from health care and air pollution to voter-turnout patterns, work that think-tank researchers have long done. [30]

Moreover, policy influence can come from even more unexpected places as media habits shift. For example, the online audience for TED talks — 18-minute talks billed as "ideas worth spreading" — numbers in the millions, not the mere thousands or even hundreds of people who regularly read think tanks' websites, says the University of Pennsylvania's McGann.

A February 2012 TED talk by Bryan Stevenson, a lawyer who founded the fair-sentencing group Equal Justice Initiative, had been viewed more than 3.6 million times as of July. Moreover, his talk is influencing policy, McGann says. [31]

In part, that is because TED talks' brevity and celebrity atmosphere are designed to attract, among others, wealthy people looking for causes to support, according to Drezner at Tufts. TED talks are short sales pitches for ideas, with no follow-up questions or debate, and may therefore make ideas seem more impressive than they are, said Drezner. [32]

The 21st century's goldfish-style attention spans pose another problem for policy thinkers. Books and papers that lay out the data and analysis that underlie serious policy ideas are long. Historically, one of think tanks' unique strengths has been their ability to "look to the horizon and generate smart ideas that may not be embraced instantly but have long-term merit," said former Stimson Center CEO Laipson. [33] A case in point was the Patient Protection and Affordable Care Act, often called Obamacare, which, ironically, had its roots in a 1989 proposal by the conservative Heritage Foundation. (The proposal, which Heritage has since disavowed, did not pass Congress until 2010.)

Today, "even the intended audiences for [think tanks'] work won't read longer pieces," says CCNY's Rich.

But despite the numerous challenges, think tanks can — and must — find a way to survive, many scholars of policymaking say. "It is impossible to keep a modern society running . . . without experts and expertise," said Bruckner of Transparify. [34]

Some think tanks are already adapting to today's vastly different information environment, scholars say.

"Some think tanks in Canada are trying to fill the information vacuum that's left with newspapers closing by producing more media themselves," says Western University's Abelson. "There's a big investment being made into media infrastructure" — mostly video and social media to attract young audiences — by think tanks such as the Fraser Institute, a free-market advocacy group in Vancouver, British Columbia, he says.

Others are making strategic use of Facebook, LinkedIn and infographics to catch policymakers' attention "so they direct their staff to read the 300-page book or report," McGann said. [35]

Ultimately, think tanks need to carve out a valuable new role as guides through what some describe as the "firehose" of unfiltered information that policymakers and voters today must deal with, says McGann. "The coin of the realm is the fact that they produce high-quality information and analysis. They could have a unique role to play, helping to separate the wheat from the chaff."

New media allow online users to find and forward work they like — whether it is produced by a think tank with a decades-old reputation or by a newcomer. In fact, such a process is bringing the best think tank work to the attention of more people, said Jessica Mathews, president emeritus of the Carnegie Endowment for International Peace.

"In the old days, an institution's reputation lagged its reality for a frustratingly long time, both on the way up, as the quality of its work was improving

but the outside world hadn't yet caught on, and on the way down, when for many years it could enjoy a much better reputation than its current work deserved," Mathews said. Today, "against all expectation, the massive proliferation of largely unedited new media has made it easier to locate top-quality work and to identify the individuals and institutions that are consistently producing it," she said. [36] ∎

BACKGROUND

Modern Problems

The first U.S. think tanks arose during the closing decades of the 19th century and the opening decades of the 20th, scholars say, when the nation was undergoing the so-called Second Industrial Revolution. During that time, inventions such as the electric generator, the internal combustion engine, structural steel and vastly improved processes for steel production, to name just a few, came quickly into broad use. [37]

The emerging technologies generated huge profits for a small group of industrialists and financiers such as steel and railroad magnate Andrew Carnegie.

And with industrial jobs concentrated in cities, millions of Americans left rural areas to find work. This mass migration, along with increased immigration from overseas, led to new social problems.

Urban infrastructure such as sewers and public institutions such as fire protection were stretched beyond their capacity. Infectious disease spread easily through crowded tenements. With their huge furnaces and heavy machinery on crowded factory floors, the new industrial job sites put workers at high risk of injury and death. The supercharged economy also was prone to devastating crashes, causing massive job losses. Depressions struck in the 1870s and the 1890s.

Worse, the sudden onset of these challenges meant that government officials had developed few policies to counter them.

At the turn of the 20th century, two groups tried to fill the policy void.

The first was a new breed of thinkers: the nation's first generation of graduate-trained economists, sociologists and political scientists who were the world's first social scientists, wrote philanthropy historian James A.

and national governments to consider.

The business leaders hoped such private efforts could boost governments' capabilities for "both addressing the social problems that accompanied industrialization and easing the growing discontent [of the business moguls' own] workers," which often boiled over into riots and unionization drives, wrote the University of Pennsylvania's McGann. "Big business, in other words, had its own agenda," he said. [39]

to act. Between 1906 and her death in 1918, Sage gave $35 million — the equivalent of about $850 million today — to social causes, including $10 million to start the think tank.

In 1910, Carnegie gave $10 million from his vast fortune to found the Carnegie Endowment for International Peace in Washington; it also remains in operation.

Carnegie wanted the institution, which became the first U.S. think tank to address foreign affairs, to study the causes of war and devise measures "to hasten" its abolition. One proposal he favored: persuading all national governments to turn international disagreements over to a court of arbitration and abide by its decision rather than fighting, Carnegie wrote to the think tank's trustees in his commissioning letter. [40]

Beginning in 1914, the federal government also established several think tanks as taxpayer-funded independent agencies that would examine various issues free of political interference. Congress created the first, the Congressional Research Service (originally the Legislative Reference Service), as a separate department within the Library of Congress that still operates today. Members of Congress may ask the research service to analyze any topic that bears on federal policymaking, and its reports are frequently cited by the media and those engaged in policy debates.

Other government think tanks include the Government Accountability Office, founded as the General Accounting Office in 1921, and charged with analyzing any activity funded with federal taxes, and the Congressional Budget Office, opened in 1975, which studies the financial implications of federal legislation. [41]

Another first-wave think tank still in operation is the Brookings Institution, opened as the Institute for Government Research in 1916. In 1927, the institute and two affiliated groups — all founded

Gov. Bill Clinton, D-Ark., makes a stop in Texas during the 1992 presidential campaign. The Progressive Policy Institute, the policy arm of the Democratic Leadership Council, is widely credited with helping Clinton win the presidency. The PPI developed policies that could win over voters distrustful of traditional liberal Democratic priorities, such as establishing work requirements for welfare recipients.

Smith, director of research and education at the Rockefeller Archive Center in Sleepy Hollow, N.Y. These new scholarly disciplines were the fruit of a "long quest to devise an empirical science of society and politics [that could serve as] a practical tool of social improvement," said Smith. The center holds the Rockefeller family papers. [38]

The second group of aspiring social improvers were the era's super-wealthy, some of whom hit upon the idea of funding independent nonprofit institutions, staffed by social scientists, to develop policy ideas to attack the root causes of social ills such as urban poverty, substandard housing and crime for local, state

The First Wave

When Wall Street financier Russell Sage died in 1906, his widow, Margaret, became one of the world's wealthiest women. In 1907, she founded one of the first think tanks, the Russell Sage Foundation, which still operates today.

The foundation served as a new national arena for discussing policies on such topics as child welfare, industrial working conditions, infectious diseases, loan sharking and juvenile justice. Its staff collected and published copious data on community problems and used it to urge local governments

Continued on p. 808

Chronology

1900s-1920s
Philanthropists fund research organizations they hope can find solutions for emerging industrial-age problems.

1907
Margaret Sage, widow of financier and railroad magnate Russell Sage, establishes the Russell Sage Foundation to collect data about child welfare, factory working conditions and other issues.

1910
Steel and railroad magnate Andrew Carnegie creates the Carnegie Endowment for International Peace to study wars and devise a plan to prevent them.

1914
Congress establishes the first taxpayer-funded think tank, the Congressional Research Service.

1916
Robert S. Brookings and other business executives form the Institute for Government Research to streamline federal budgeting and other government processes.

1927
The Institute for Government Research is combined with two other Brookings research groups and renamed the Brookings Institution.

* · *

1940s-1960s
Think tanks help develop anti-poverty programs during the Depression, as well as programs to rebuild devastated Europe after World War II.

1946
The Project RAND think tank, established in Santa Monica, Calif., to work under contract to the Air Force, releases its first report, a design for an orbiting spacecraft; two years later RAND is rechartered as an independent nonprofit to be funded by government research projects.

1948-51
Marshall Plan, based on ideas developed by the Brookings Institution, funnels aid to war-ravaged Europe.

1968
Democratic President Lyndon B. Johnson creates the private, nonprofit Urban Institute to help improve government anti-poverty programs.

* · *

1970s-1980s
The number of ideological, advocacy-oriented think tanks increases, and donors begin demanding more input into research agendas.

1973
The conservative Heritage Foundation opens, with a focus on communicating cogent policy statements to politicians and the media.

1977
The libertarian Cato Institute debuts, advocating policies that promote individual liberty, free markets and international peace.

1989
The Progressive Policy Institute forms to develop policy for the Democratic Leadership Council.

* · *

1990s-Present
Think tanks proliferate globally; critics say donors gain excessive influence in U.S. sector.

1996
Democratic President Bill Clinton signs welfare reform legislation developed by several conservative and centrist think tanks.

2003
With Republicans controlling Congress and the White House, Democrats form the Center for American Progress to promote liberal ideas, using the Heritage Foundation as a model of an ideological think tank.

2013
Transparify, a nonprofit in Tbilisi, Georgia, reports that only 25 of 169 top think tanks worldwide fully disclose funding sources.

2014
Spurt of growth brings number of countries with think tanks to at least 182.

2016
The number of think tanks worldwide exceeds 6,800, with 1,835 in the United States. . . . Transparify says 67 of the top 169 think tanks now fully disclose their donors.

2017
Members of President-elect Donald Trump's transition team say Trump and his aides have little regard for think tanks and will rely more on the business world and the military than did earlier administrations. . . . The Heritage Foundation provides the Trump administration with budget ideas. . . . Rep. Mark Meadows, R-N.C., chairman of the House Freedom Caucus, proposes directing the taxpayer-funded Congressional Budget Office to stop estimating the cost of legislation; the change would leave such analysis to private think tanks.

Think Tanks Join the Digital Revolution

Scholars get creative in the internet age.

The Council on Foreign Relations (CFR), founded in 1921 to foster discussion among government leaders and international-affairs experts, won its first Emmy in 2008. But though it may have taken the Council nearly a century to get into the media game, it's wasted no time since. The think tank has won two more Emmys for its multimedia web presentations and is nominated again this year.

In the "New Approaches" news programming category, CFR has defeated big-name competitors such as cable-TV giant MSNBC and *The Washington Post* with presentations such as its "Crisis Guide: Darfur," which uses video, interactive maps and audio commentary to inform online visitors about the long-running conflict between government forces and rebel groups in the Darfur region of Sudan in North Africa. [1]

Communication has long been vital to the work of think tanks, which is to develop ideas into public policies. But in the internet age, think tanks are seeking more innovative communication strategies. "When I first started at [the Center for Strategic and International Studies] in 2005, books had become paperweights on policymakers' desks," says H. Andrew Schwartz, the center's chief communications officer.

Think tanks quickly learned that new media can broaden their audiences and more effectively publicize their work.

"Back in the day, we communicated through media outlets," with scholars publishing newspaper op-eds or giving interviews to reporters, says Lisa Shields, vice president for global communications and media relations at the Council on Foreign Relations. "We still do, but now we also talk directly to the public."

In April, the Center for Strategic and International Studies (CSIS), which focuses on economic and international issues, took home a 2017 Shorty Award — honoring the best social-media content — for its data visualizations. CSIS has pioneered the use of interactive maps with which website visitors can explore topics such as terrorism and China's efforts to stake a claim to disputed territory in the South China Sea by building artificial islands there. [2]

Shorty nominees have included NBC News and internet-search giant Google, heady company for "a think tank in Washington that doesn't have nearly as many resources," Schwartz says. Debuting in 2012, CSIS' South China Sea visualization using satellite imagery also has had important policy consequences, he says. When the visualization went online, only a few experts knew about the territorial-claims disputes between China and other Asian nations, he says. Now, CSIS' website "has actually made it possible for the U.S. and China to have a more open public discussion about it."

An early adopter of online communication, the Council on Foreign Relations introduced its first subject-specific single-issue website in 1999, on how foreign policy played into the 2000 U.S. presidential election. After the Sept. 11, 2001, terrorist attacks in the United States, the think tank followed up with what CFR said was the first online encyclopedia on terrorism and saw "demand increasing dramatically and from a much broader constituency," Shields says.

Building new-media operations is a gradual process, think-tank staff say.

At the Urban Institute in Washington, "we just allowed young researchers to play with technology," creating computer visualizations of their own data, for example, says Bridget Lowell, vice president for strategic communications and outreach. The Urban Institute's data-visualization efforts began with one young scholar who, on a snow day, built an interactive map through which people could explore his research findings on poverty data, she says. "Then he handed it off to a young designer who styled it."

Continued from p. 806

by philanthropist Robert S. Brookings and his associates — united as the Brookings Institution.

Brookings was a fatherless 17-year-old office clerk at a St. Louis wholesaler of household goods when he began his rapid rise as a businessman who gained renown for innovations to enhance efficiency. For example, he redesigned St. Louis' shipping infrastructure to save shippers time and money by relocating the city's warehouse district next to the railroad tracks, in a plan that became a model for other cities.

In line with its founder's interests, the Brookings Institution was the first private think tank created to improve federal government practices in matters including budgeting and economic affairs. The institute's work also extended into many other areas, such as developing the Marshall Plan to rebuild a devastated Europe after World War II.

As at many early think tanks, Brookings emphasized finding pragmatic solutions to problems and included a range of ideological viewpoints among its staff. For example, several Brookings scholars contributed to Democratic President Franklin D. Roosevelt's New Deal policies aimed at pulling the United States out of the Great Depression at the same time as Brookings' president and chief economist, Harold Moulton, remained one of the New Deal's staunchest opponents. [42]

By the 1940s, these and other research organizations were established players in Washington policymaking. The name "think tanks," though, came into use only after World War II popularized the term — military slang for places where it was safe to discuss war strategy.

After the war, Gen. H.H. "Hap" Arnold, commanding general of the Army Air Corps, and engineers from Douglas Air-

"You always start with people being skeptical that the work will be oversimplified" when presentations go beyond traditional spreadsheets and text, Lowell says. But research institutions' traditional rigor needn't be sacrificed, she says. "Ultimately our online tools are not simple. They are for people who have some economic knowledge."

At CSIS, full collaboration between technical staff and scholars who research and develop the policy knowledge is vital, Schwartz says. "It takes a while to prove to everyone that this is a successful model, so we started with things we could achieve" — recorded audio and video of some of CSIS' many live public events.

Now 97 percent of the nearly 500 events CSIS hosts annually with its scholars and invited experts are live webcasts.

Digital communication is coming more naturally to think-tank fellows than some imagine, says James Lindsay, CFR senior vice president and director of studies. "People with deep knowledge of their fields love to talk about their subjects; they want to share," he says. "And sometimes text is the most powerful way to talk about an idea. But sometimes photos and graphics are more powerful."

With the digital revolution, "fellows find they can rely less on others [such as the media] to get their ideas out," Lindsay says. But becoming adept at media such as Twitter, Facebook Live and podcasts requires "an awful lot of experimentation and learning." A top-notch communications and technical staff is needed "to help scholars master the tools," he says.

— *Marcia Clemmitt*

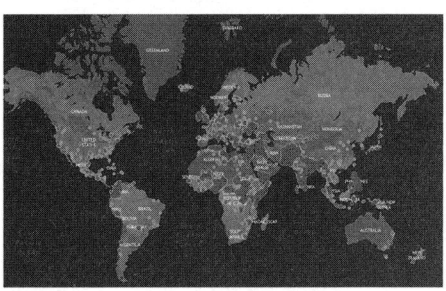

Mapping global terrorist incidents since 2012 as part of the CSIS Commission on Countering Violent Extremism (CVE) .

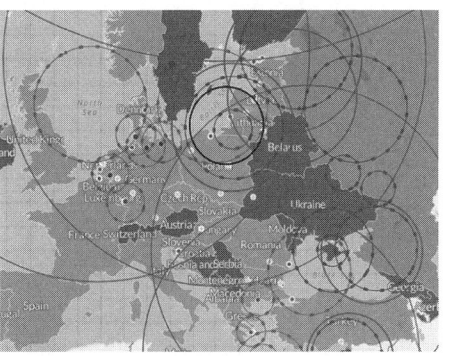

The overlapping missile systems in place in Europe the CSIS Missile Defense Project .

CQ Researcher/Screen shot

The Center for Strategic and International Studies has pioneered the use of interactive maps with which website visitors can explore topics such as terrorism and missile systems.

[1] "CFR.org's Darfur Crisis Guide Wins Emmy Award," Council on Foreign Relations, Sept. 26, 2008, https://tinyurl.com/yax2lt89; "Nominees for the 29th Annual News & Documentary Emmy Awards Announced By The National Academy Of Television Arts And Sciences," emmyonline.com, https://tiny url.com/ydetmp8x; and "Nominees For The 38th Annual News & Documentary Emmy Awards Announced," emmyonline.com, Sept. 8, 2017.

[2] "CSIS wins Shorty Award for Data Visualization," Center for Strategic and International Studies, April 20, 2017, https://tinyurl.com/y7od7xq2.

craft Co. in Santa Monica, Calif., proposed that the federal government contract with Douglas to establish a think tank with technical and engineering expertise to develop ideas mainly related to military policy. The first report under the contract for Project RAND — short for "research and development" — was released in May 1946. Titled "Preliminary Design of an Experimental World-Circling Spaceship," it laid the groundwork for the U.S. space program. [43]

The possibility of conflicts of interest for a think tank run by a for-profit company concerned some Air Force leaders, however. In 1948, Project RAND

was chartered as an independent nonprofit organization to pursue research under government contracts. Today, RAND, with more than 2,000 employees, has the largest staff of any American think tank and counts U.S. cities, nongovernmental organizations and foreign governments among its clients. Its slate of projects includes government operations, education, the environment, justice systems and more. [44]

Social programs were not high on the agenda in the immediate years after World War II, when an economic boom was expected to lift all Americans' incomes. By the 1960s, however, many

communities remained mired in poverty, and the federal government was struggling to implement anti-poverty programs that Democratic President Lyndon B. Johnson had shepherded through Congress in 1964 and '65 as part of his Great Society plan to attack economic and racial inequality. [45]

The Johnson administration proposed creating a think tank that would study poverty and other domestic social issues and that, like RAND, would be a private organization working mainly on government contracts. In 1968 the Urban Institute opened with initial financial support from about

Government Think Tanks in Critics' Crosshairs

Trump, congressional Republicans question their usefulness.

White House Budget Director Mick Mulvaney minced no words. The Congressional Budget Office's time "has come and gone," said Mulvaney, a former Republican congressman from South Carolina. "You can have a government without a Congressional Budget Office." [1]

Mulvaney's criticism of the Congressional Budget Office (CBO), which studies the financial and budgetary impact of proposed legislation, is part of a broader assault on government-based think tanks that produce research reports for Congress. Their defenders say their mission remains vital to good government; their detractors say private think tanks can do the job better and at less cost.

CBO analysts concluded earlier this year that replacing former President Barack Obama's 2010 health care law with a Republican plan would increase the number of people without health insurance by more than 20 million by 2026. In response, many congressional Republicans accused the agency of partisan bias and of bad math.

In the wake of the CBO projections on health care, Rep. Mark Meadows, R-N.C., chair of the conservative House Freedom Caucus, proposed giving much of the CBO's job to private-sector think tanks. Henceforth, CBO would estimate the financial costs and other consequences of bills "solely by facilitating and assimilating scoring data compiled by the Heritage Foundation, the American Enterprise Institute, the Brookings Institution and the Urban Institute," according to Meadows' proposal, which was offered as an amendment to a security-related spending bill but voted down. [2]

During the annual government-funding debate, the House considered multiple proposals to slash CBO's approximately $50 million annual budget, but bipartisan House majorities rejected the cuts. [3]

The Government Accountability Office (GAO), which ferrets out inefficiencies and misconduct in federal programs, also is in House appropriators' crosshairs. For the fiscal 2018 budget, they are seeking to eliminate 200 of the GAO's approximately 3,000 jobs — cuts that Democrats say could reduce the agency's staff to its lowest level since the 1930s. [4]

Staffing cuts, however, are nothing new for public think tanks, which Congress established between 1914 and 1975 to support its work. The three institutions still operating — CBO, GAO and the Congressional Research Service — lost 45 percent of their staff to budget cuts between 1975 and 2015, with most of the losses coming in the late 1990s when Republicans controlled both houses of Congress. [5]

Congress shut down its fourth think tank, the Office of Technology Assessment (OTA), in 1995. The OTA was established in 1972 to evaluate scientific data, but in the 1990s it ran afoul of then-House Speaker Newt Gingrich, R-Ga., and some other leading Republicans after it questioned some proposals lawmakers favored, such as President Ronald Reagan's proposed "Star Wars" missile-defense plan, which survived into the 1990s. [6]

The OTA's closing remains controversial. In late 2016, a bipartisan group of 14 House members petitioned House Speaker Paul Ryan to begin discussion of renewing the OTA. Its expertise saved taxpayers billions of dollars by distinguishing promising scientific projects from nonstarters, said the group. Ryan has not acted, however. [7]

Critics, meanwhile, say President Trump is denigrating expert advice by leaving advisory positions unfilled and by nominating people with no science background for science-policy jobs.

More than eight months into his first term, Trump has not yet nominated a director for the White House Office of Science and Technology Policy (OSTP), which offers policy advice to the administration, and has left most of its other top spots open as well. The office director is the highest-profile science appointee in the executive branch.

Under Obama, the OSTP had 135 staffers, the most in its history. Ultimately, the office under Trump will have a staff of six federal agencies and $1 million ($7 million today) from McGeorge Bundy, former national security adviser to Democratic Presidents John F. Kennedy and Johnson, who became institute president. [46]

Many think tanks in the 1960s continued to operate according to the principle that had animated early think-tank founders and scholars: that research by independent experts could help government and others solve problems as serious as infectious disease, poverty and war. Andrew Carnegie, in fact, had presumed that the Carnegie Endowment for International Peace might persuade the world to abandon warfare within decades.

But beginning around the 1960s, think tanks became the focus of "a contest between two ways of understanding the world," according to historian Smith. One argued for the superiority of practical, data-driven solutions to national problems, while the other argued that political philosophy was the best source of policy ideas. [47]

"Throughout much of our history, American politics has appeared to all the world" as an arena where combatants eventually agreed on practical compromises, Smith said. Accordingly, most early think tanks, too, had aimed at researching and developing policies that would work, with practicality usually edging out ideology in scholars' thinking.

By the 1960s, though, and intensifying thereafter, some political thinkers fought back against the pragmatic view — at first mostly conservatives, who felt that their political principles had been shortchanged throughout the "pragmatic" era, said Smith. A new breed of political activists, including

about 50, in line with the president's view that "government should be looking for ways to do more with less," a White House official told the journal *Science*. [8]

The administration also has shut down some federal science research and policy-advisory programs.

On Aug. 18, Commerce Department officials announced they would disband the Federal Advisory Committee for the Sustained National Climate Assessment, whose initial charter was set to expire Aug. 20. Created two years ago to offer advice to federal officials, states, cities and the private sector, the group examined the federal government's scientific reports on climate-change trends to determine their potential consequences for agriculture, land use, water resources and other systems and translate the information into useful guidelines for managing infrastructure as environmental conditions change. [9]

Trump has nominated some people with no science or engineering background to posts with substantial science- and technology-policy responsibilities. His nominee to head NASA is Rep. Jim Bridenstine, R-Okla., who holds degrees in economics, psychology and business. [10]

"The head of NASA ought to be a space professional, not a politician," Sen. Bill Nelson, D-Fla., said of Bridenstine. [11]

But administration officials defend the choices and the administration's commitment to science. Bridenstine is a fervent backer of space exploration and has the political skills to get funding for it, his defenders say. [12]

— *Marcia Clemmitt*

Rep. Mark Meadows, R-N.C., and other congressional Republicans want private think tanks and not the taxpayer-funded Congressional Budget Office to estimate the cost of legislation; earlier this year CBO said eliminating Obamacare would increase the number of uninsured Americans by more than 20 million by 2026.

Getty Images/NurPhoto/Cheriss May

[1] Michelle Cottle, "The Congressional War on Expertise," *The Atlantic*, July 9, 2017, https://tinyurl.com/yb9hnhao.

[2] Niv Elis, "Meadows: CBO should downsize, aggregate think-tank reports," *The Hill*, July 24, 2017, https://tinyurl.com/yc2gfc33; Mark Barrett, "Meadows tries to cut funds for congressional budget referee," *Citizen-Times* (Asheville, N.C.), Aug. 5, 2017, https://tinyurl.com/yd6j6p9y.

[3] Niv Elis, "CBO survives two House amendments targeting funding," *The Hill*, July 26, 2017, https://tinyurl.com/yclwvkhq.

[4] Niv Elis, "GAO could lose 200 staff under proposed spending levels, say Dems," *The Hill*, June 23, 2017, https://tinyurl.com/y8xfpvfh.

[5] Cottle, *op. cit.*; Curtlyn Kramer, "Vital Stats: Congress has a staffing problem too," Brookings Institution, May 24, 2017, https://tinyurl.com/ycl6lhq8.

[6] Kim Zetter, "Of Course Congress Is Clueless About Tech — It Killed Its Tutor," *Wired*, April 21, 2016, https://tinyurl.com/h2wtar8.

[7] Charles S. Clark, "Still Alive: The Movement to Unshutter the Office of Technology Assessment," Government Executive, Oct. 21, 2016, https://tinyurl.com/y8tbgebm.

[8] Jeffrey Mervis, "Trump's science office is still small and waiting for leadership," *Science*, July 11, 2017, https://tinyurl.com/y9xvj2lt.

[9] Eric Holthaus, "Trump axed a federal climate panel, turning a blind eye to public safety," *Grist*, Aug. 22, 2017, https://tinyurl.com/y9r8syhl; Rene Marsh, "Trump administration dismisses climate change advisory panel," CNN, Aug. 21, 2017, https://tinyurl.com/y7uwww37.

[10] Sofia Lotto Persio, "Why Donald Trump's NASA Chief Pick Is a Controversial Choice," *Newsweek*, Sept. 2, 2017, https://tinyurl.com/ybv6hb3x.

[11] *Ibid.*

[12] Mark R. Whittington, "Jim Bridenstine for NASA administrator," *The Hill*, Feb. 2, 2017, https://tinyurl.com/yc6jaru7.

some think-tank scholars, "had come to see themselves as being consciously engaged in a war of ideas, with Washington as the main battlefield," and they cast aside the pragmatic philosophical assumptions that sustained the social-science approach.

Advocacy Think Tanks

The conservative Heritage Foundation, opened in 1973, was not quite the first think tank with a strongly ideological cast, but it was among the first, and it quickly became the largest, most active and most influential, historians say.

"Heritage made a splash doing two things: being very clear about the values that lay behind its work, and investing a very significant part of its budget into marketing," says City College of New York's Rich.

While earlier think tanks generally developed their own policy ideas, Heritage gathered conservative ideas from many sources, including its own staff. To maximize its impact, Heritage focused on packaging ideas concisely and clearly and distributing them when audiences would be most receptive, such as just before a key congressional vote. "They knew you couldn't take the naïve view that people were just sitting around waiting for think tanks to finish a study," says Rich. "Heritage was very attuned to the fact that they didn't get to set the legislative calendar."

In line with its ideological character, Heritage has focused on advancing conservatism as an overall governing philosophy rather than on promoting specific policies, as more pragmatism-oriented think tanks have done, historians say. Heritage's goal has been "to advance the principles of free enterprise, limited government, individual freedom, traditional American values, and a strong national defense," says the foundation website. "Our hard work has paid off. . . . [We] have seen substantial gains for the conservative agenda." [48]

More ideologically focused think tanks have sprung up in the wake of Heritage's success.

In 1989, the Progressive Policy Institute (PPI) was formed as the policy arm of the Democratic Leadership Council (DLC). The DLC aimed at moving the Democratic Party's agenda from left-liberal to centrist. PPI's role was to develop policies that could win over voters distrustful of traditional liberal Democratic priorities, such as strengthening labor unions. It helped develop centrist policies, including work requirements for welfare recipients, and is widely credited with helping DLC member Bill Clinton win the presidency in 1992. [49]

In 2003, when Republicans controlled both Congress and the White House, Democrats formed another ideological and activist think tank, the Center for American Progress (CAP).

The center has worked on liberal ideas such as universal health care and renewable-energy development. As the Heritage Foundation did for conservatism in the early 1970s when Democrats controlled Congress, CAP has aimed to keep liberal thought in the national consciousness even when its political champions are out of power. [50]

Unlike most other think tanks, Heritage and CAP have created affiliated 501(c)(4) organizations — political advocacy arms that may participate in election campaigns, including running advertising in support of candidates, as long as less than half their spending is directly political. [51]

Pairing a think tank with an advocacy group frees up both organizations to specialize — one on developing the ideas and the other on doing what is required to see them implemented, said Heritage Foundation's Carafano. "In the future,

highly competitive and effective think tanks are more likely to be paired with [such] sister organizations," he said. [52]

Others are skeptical about the merits of think tanks creating 501(c)(4) organizations. "The politicization of think tanks is really working against them," says international think-tank expert Struyk. "They blossomed by being well-informed honest brokers. If they lose that, there's no need for them" in a world with many partisan voices.

At think tanks that focus on issues rather than ideology, people with a range of political views often sit on governing boards. At the Urban Institute, former Indiana Gov. Mitch Daniels, a Republican, is on the Board of Trustees alongside Democrats such as Erskine Bowles, who was Clinton's chief of staff in the White House. The Council on Foreign Relations' global advisory board includes former Danish Prime Minister Helle Thorning-Schmidt, a Social Democrat, and former United Kingdom Prime Minister David Cameron, a conservative. [53]

"The majority of think tanks work very hard on not being ideological," says housing and social-assistance policy expert Struyk. "And many have people from both parties on their boards." ■

CURRENT SITUATION

Trump Administration

With President Trump proudly wearing the "Washington outsider" label, think tanks are coming in for some bashing as a potentially outdated part of the policy process. Nevertheless, despite rumblings about the sector during the administration's early days, think tanks are still playing a role in the executive branch, as they have in most recent administrations.

From the start, because of skepticism about think tanks' usefulness and their independence, Trump indicated after his 2016 election that he intended to rely mostly on business executives and former military officers rather than public-policy experts when staffing his administration, sources in his presidential transition team told *Washington Post* columnist Josh Rogin. The administration will usher in "the death of think tanks as we know them in D.C.," one person on the team declared. It has "empowered whole other centers of gravity for staffing this administration." [54]

By contrast, other incoming administrations relied on think tanks for policy consultation and as sources for staff with policy-development and federal government experience, says Abelson of Western University. Former Georgia Democratic Gov. Jimmy Carter sought input from more than 100 think tank-affiliated analysts after the 1976 election as he assumed the presidency. He hired more than a dozen think tank scholars for federal posts.

Likewise, staff from the generally conservative Hoover Institution organized nearly 50 task forces to advise former California Republican Gov. Ronald Reagan on domestic and foreign-policy issues after he won the presidency in 1980, Abelson wrote. [55]

Ultimately, though, think tanks are assisting Trump and his administration.

The Trump White House drew much of its first budget from documents written at the Heritage Foundation, according to Heritage senior economic policy analyst Stephen Moore. [56]

The administration drew heavily from another think tank's work for one of its most controversial policies — withdrawing the United States from the international Paris agreement to combat climate change.

Ebell, at the Competitive Enterprise Institute's Center for Energy and Environment, led the team that helped the incoming administration prepare for running the

Continued on p. 814

At Issue:

Should think tanks receiving tax-exempt donations promote a political philosophy?

JAMES JAY CARAFANO
VICE PRESIDENT OF FOREIGN AND DEFENSE POLICY STUDIES, HERITAGE FOUNDATION

WRITTEN FOR *CQ RESEARCHER*, SEPTEMBER 2017

Should think tanks be ideological? Sure, as long as they think. Nonpartisan think tanks unaffiliated with academic institutions are almost uniquely American. Other countries have a sprinkling of them; the United States has hundreds. These institutions are rooted in America's philanthropic tradition. Private giving for public good is ingrained in the national character.

But the notion of building and supporting research institutions outside of academia really took off during the Gilded Age. Wealthy industrialists, such as Andrew Carnegie, saw idea factories as a way to tackle global issues — from fostering world peace to fighting poverty.

Later, the creation of special categories of tax-exempt giving expanded the base of think tanks' private support beyond the wealthy elite.

The term "think tank" was first associated with RAND, a federally funded research and development center established after World War II to help the military with research.

Today, the term is widely applied to nongovernmental research institutions. These vary from mom-and-pop shops with few employees that focus on a few issues, to large research centers with hundreds of analysts and multimillion-dollar budgets covering a range of domestic and global issues.

Think tanks registered under the tax code as 501c(3)-qualified institutions are required to be nonpartisan. They cannot affiliate with a political party, conduct grassroots organizing or engage in lobbying activities. Beyond these rules, though, they face few restrictions on how they conduct or promote their research. While they must be nonpartisan, think tanks are allowed to have a point of view.

Some think tanks are dedicated to one cause, such as nuclear nonproliferation. Others have a philosophical or ideological foundation. Still others offer an admixture of scholarly viewpoints. Some think tanks take institutional positions. In others, scholars function independently.

As far as organization and perspective go, there is no single "best" way for a think tank to operate. Analysts can conduct rigorous, valuable research even when they — and their institutions — approach their work with a sense of mission, a point of view or even a full-throated ideology.

A think tank can advocate for policies informed by its research, but a responsible think tank is not just an advocacy organization. The quality of research is what matters, and it is the standard by which a think tank should be judged. Great ideas can come from any end of the ideological spectrum.

DAVID CALLAHAN
FOUNDER AND EDITOR,
INSIDE PHILANTHROPY

WRITTEN FOR *CQ RESEARCHER*, SEPTEMBER 2017

Over the past few decades, philanthropic giving has become an increasingly powerful way to shape the workings of government. By influencing which ideas public officials consider and ultimately turn into law, donations to think tanks can have an even greater impact over policy outcomes than lobbying or contributing to political campaigns. Policy groups on both the right and left — such as the Heritage Foundation and the Center for American Progress — have a long history of working closely with elected officials to shape the agenda.

For donors, an added benefit of using "charitable" gifts to sway policy is that they are tax-deductible.

That's problematic. Through savvy and politicized giving, the wealthy donor class has found yet another way to speak more loudly than citizens of lesser means — while sticking those same citizens with part of the tab, thanks to the charitable tax break. Gifts for policy and advocacy have swelled dramatically in the past decade, even as many Americans report feeling that their voices don't count because the wealthy wield too much clout.

Organized philanthropy, subsidized by government, has rightly been called one of America's greatest inventions. But it has become increasingly distorted in a new Gilded Age and is helping fuel civic inequality in society.

Charitable giving's growing role in public policy reflects an outdated tax code that is overly permissive about what kinds of nonprofits can receive deductible gifts. The charitable tax deduction was created in 1917 to encourage donations to organizations "operated exclusively for religious, charitable, scientific, or educational purposes." The language has changed little since then, and Congress hasn't revisited this area of law in a major way since 1969.

Meanwhile, though, the nonprofit sector has been transformed since the 1970s by an explosion of ideological policy groups financed by a swelling river of philanthropic dollars. That trend has accelerated lately as ever more wealth has piled up at the top of the income ladder — and as more billionaires have looked to influence public policy outcomes.

Anyone who is worried about money in politics has to pay attention to the growing role that philanthropy plays in public life. As the original intent of the charitable tax deduction is increasingly perverted for ideological gain, it is time for Congress to take a critical look at what kinds of charitable gifts are allowable under the law.

Continued from p. 812

Environmental Protection Agency. The center, which opposes most environmental and other business regulation, has for years challenged the idea of climate change and urged the United States to withdraw from the Paris climate pact through which nations have committed to reducing their greenhouse-gas emissions.

Ebell derides climate science as a "scam" pushed by researchers seeking

on the White House National Security Council as senior director for Europe and Russia. [59]

Trump's surprise election is affecting the think tank sector in another way: collaboration between ideological rivals.

Leading conservative William Kristol, founder and editor at large of the *Weekly Standard*, and centrist William Galston of the Brookings Institution are teaming up to start a think tank called the New

Advocacy Shake-Up

In April, the Heritage Foundation announced the sudden ousting of former Sen. Jim DeMint, R-S.C., who had been its president since 2013. His unexpected departure caused head scratching all over Washington.

DeMint's strong conservative principles and willingness to fight hard for his ideas had seemed to many like a good fit with Heritage. In the wake of his firing, though, some wondered whether his approach may have been too aggressively political for a think tank president, even at an institution known for strong advocacy and its formation of an affiliated 501(c)(4) organization. [61]

However, Heritage Board of Trustees Chairman Thomas A. Saunders III said in a statement: "After a comprehensive and independent review of the entire Heritage organization, the Board determined there were significant and worsening management issues that led to a breakdown of internal communications and cooperation. While the organization has seen many successes, Jim DeMint and a handful of his closest advisers failed to resolve these problems." [62]

Heritage co-founder Ed Feulner, now serving as interim president, suggested that the think tank would not be backing off advocacy activity after DeMint's departure, saying that the relationship between Heritage and its advocacy wing "will be closer than it has been in the past." [63]

Meanwhile, with Republicans controlling both the White House and Congress, taxpayer-funded think tanks are facing fresh scrutiny from conservatives who want to cut federal spending and are suspicious of government agencies. The Congressional Budget Office is one such target. This summer, congressional Republicans and the White House hotly disputed CBO estimates of how many people would become uninsured under various proposed repeals of President Obama's Affordable Care Act. [64]

The ousting of Heritage Foundation President Jim DeMint in April led some observers to wonder whether the former Republican senator from South Carolina may have been too aggressively political for a think tank president, even at an institution known for strong advocacy. However, the foundation's board chair said DeMint's management was at issue and that the conservative foundation would not back off from its advocacy activities.

Getty Images/Alex Wong

government grants. He has been leading a public campaign to undercut the science. On June 1, Trump withdrew the United States from the Paris agreement. [57]

Numerous think tank scholars now hold administration jobs, although generally as midlevel policy staff rather than as Cabinet members or top advisers.

Heritage Foundation budget specialist Paul Winfree is the deputy director of the Domestic Policy Council. James Sherk, formerly a Heritage fellow on labor policy, advises the White House on employment issues. [58] Fiona Hill, a senior fellow from the center-left Brookings Institution, has taken a leave of absence from that position to serve

Center Project that will seek to offer an alternative to the policies of the left and the right. Both said the extent of voter discontent with the two political parties in the 2016 election left them shaken. Kristol said, "There was more being missed by Republican politicians and think tanks than I realized," while Galston said, "There's been far more sclerosis than we wanted to admit."

In a 70-page pamphlet, they offered seven goals to "re-center" the United States on a more productive course, including crafting a grand bargain to overhaul the tax code and rebuild the nation's infrastructure and finding ways to encourage more people to start new businesses. [60]

Trump's first budget proposal issued in March would cut funding for the taxpayer-funded International Woodrow Wilson Center for Scholars in Washington by eliminating the one-third of the center's annual budget that the federal government supplies annually. (The rest of the center's funding comes from trust funds.) [65] Established in 1968 as a memorial to President Woodrow Wilson, the think tank convenes scholars from across the political spectrum to discuss global issues. Center officials said they are "concerned but also confident" they will receive funding in the end. [66]

Foreign Growth

Think tanks are enjoying a worldwide boom. Until recently almost nonexistent outside North America and Western Europe, think tanks now number nearly 7,000 and operate in more than 182 countries, ranging from the tiny East African archipelago of Seychelles, with three think tanks, to the breakaway southeastern European state of Kosovo, which has struggled for independence from Serbia since 2008 and also has three think tanks. [67]

The global boom reflects developing countries' interest in evidence-based policymaking to solve social problems, says policy analyst Struyk, who since the 1980s has worked with think tanks in approximately 25 countries, including Japan, Russia, Hungary, Bosnia, Azerbaijan, Myanmar and China.

According to the University of Pennsylvania's McGann, 55 percent of all think tanks are in North America and Europe, but Asia, Latin America and the Middle East are seeing "an expansion in the number and type of think tanks established." Two reasons why, McGann wrote in a 2017 report, are globalization and the growing complexity of policy problems. "Increasingly, think tanks are a global phenomenon because they play a critical role for governments and civil societies around the world by acting as bridges between knowledge (academia) and power (politicians and policymakers)," he said. [68]

Most foreign think tanks are created for the same reason as their U.S. counterparts, says Struyk. "Individuals see that certain issues are being neglected, and they want to start a better policy discussion to address them." Key issues he has observed range from addressing China's food-safety problems to creating a housing finance system in a formerly communist Eastern European country, and many of these projects are now working programs. The common motivation for think-tank founders, says Struyk, is that they "want to do some good." ∎

OUTLOOK

Return of Honest Brokers?

Today's polarized politics have put something of a damper on think tanks' role as developers of pragmatic policy options based on solid research, big-picture thinking and honest debate of options. But many scholars of the policymaking progress hope think tank leaders can find a way to reclaim that role.

"Congress would once have been part of the solution" to national problems such as expanding health care access and overhauling the tax code in ways that are fair to everyone, says Evert Lindquist, a scholar of U.S. and Canadian policymaking and professor of public administration at the University of Victoria in British Columbia, Canada.

But when political parties are polarized and seldom can find a compromise, "someone else needs to ask, 'What can we do that's best for all concerned?' " Lindquist says. "The think tank community is a possible answer to the question of where to have discussions like that."

The University of Pennsylvania's McGann says, "There's a real need to move the country away from polarization and toward consensus" on a range of issues. By trading on their old reputation as honest brokers of ideas, think tanks have an opportunity "to float trial balloons on policies that may be able to bridge some gaps."

More big-picture analysis is needed, says policy analyst Struyk. "There's a real need for the kind issue-defining stuff that Brookings once did — the over-the-horizon stuff," which involves laying out issues "that are likely to bubble up 18 months or two years from now" but aren't yet on people's radar screens, he says. "This kind of work can define the debate space in a way that focuses people on problems that will need attention."

But one important key to keeping the think-tank sector useful and credible lies not with think tanks, or even with government policymakers, but with citizen watchdogs, says Western University's Abelson.

"There are organizations out there who engage in questionable science and questionable research, so it becomes incumbent on the public and the media to critique them," he says.

Under Section 501(c)3 of the tax code, think tanks are exempt from most taxes on the grounds that they serve the general good by informing the public, Abelson says, but no rules defining a think tank exist. This means that even groups pursuing extremist agendas, such as ethnic cleansing or violent revolution, might claim think tank status, he says. So, there is "a very dark side to this," Abelson says. "What happens when you have these fringe movements, pursuing nefarious causes, getting tax breaks as educational institutions?"

Moreover, "other than the [Internal Revenue Service], which has many duties, where is the body dedicated to ensuring that think tanks use their tax-exempt status to educate rather than lobby?" Abelson asks. In a democracy, "the answer has to be that we are all regulators. So as these organizations proliferate around the world, we have to be more vigilant." ∎

Notes

[1] "Open Markets Applauds the European Commission's Finding Against Google for Abuse of Dominance," New America, June 27, 2017, https://tinyurl.com/yb28mjwh; Kenneth P. Vogel, "Google Critic Ousted From Think Tank Funded by the Tech Giant," *The New York Times*, Aug. 30, 2017, https://tinyurl.com/yacg457p; Brody Mullins and John D. McKinnon, "Think Tank Fires Scholar Who Praised Large Antitrust Fine Against Google," *The Wall Street Journal*, Aug. 30, 2017, https://tinyurl.com/ydyfq969; and "New America's Response to the New York Times," New America, Aug. 30, 2017, https://tinyurl.com/y8w2nzj9.

[2] Vogel, *ibid*.

[3] Daniel Drezner, *The Ideas Industry* (2017), Kindle edition, location 2579.

[4] Quoted in Amanda Bennett, "Are think tanks obsolete?" *The Washington Post*, Oct. 5, 2015, http://tinyurl.com/y7c5em5e.

[5] James G. McGann, "2016 Global Go To Think Tank Index Report," University of Pennsylvania Think Tanks and Civil Societies Program, March 1, 2017, pp. 5, 8, https://tinyurl.com/kk5levw.

[6] Hans Gutbrod, "Optimizers: How Hearts, Kidneys and Pareto Help Define Think Tanks," *On Think Tanks*, Sept. 23, 2013, http://tinyurl.com/yd6jahxe.

[7] Till Bruckner, "The Think Tank Scholar: Tom Medvetz," *On Think Tanks*, July 29, 2015, https://tinyurl.com/y7a2fpz2.

[8] James Jay Carafano, "Think Tanks Aren't Going Extinct. But They Have to Evolve," *The National Interest*, Oct. 21, 2015, https://tinyurl.com/ybaebv9p.

[9] Michael Scherer, "Inside Obama's Idea Factory in Washington," *Time*, Nov. 21, 2008, https://tinyurl.com/y84692qo.

[10] Eric Lipton, Nicholas Confessore and Brooke Williams, "Think Tank Scholar or Corporate Consultant? It Depends on the Day," *The New York Times*, Aug. 8, 2016, https://tinyurl.com/yachxb3q.

[11] Robert O'Harrow Jr., "A two-decade crusade by conservative charities fueled Trump's exit from Paris climate accord," *The Washington Post*, Sept. 5, 2017, http://tinyurl.com/y8vynneb.

[12] *Ibid.*

[13] Quoted in Amanda Bennett, "Are think tanks obsolete?" *The Washington Post*, Oct. 5, 2015, https://tinyurl.com/y7c5em5e; "Industry Backgrounders: Insurance," Stimson, Nov. 6, 2012, https://tinyurl.com/ydya8u6b.

[14] "How Transparent are Think Tanks about Who Funds Them 2016?" Transparify, June 29, 2016, https://tinyurl.com/hu7ncgu.

[15] Eric Lipton and Brooke Williams, "How Think Tanks Amplify Corporate America's Influence," *The New York Times*, Aug. 7, 2016, https://tinyurl.com/ycwerrkb.

[16] Strobe Talbott and Kimberly Churches, "Safeguarding independence in an era of restricted giving," Brookings/*Chronicle of Philanthropy*, Feb. 3, 2016, https://tinyurl.com/y855pcl3; "Research Independence Policy," Brookings Institution, Feb. 13, 2015, https://tinyurl.com/ybyxq3qc.

[17] Quoted in Till Bruckner, "Donald Abelson, Professor at Western University," *On Think Tanks*, July 15, 2015, https://tinyurl.com/y8t2fab4.

[18] Ken Silverstein, "The Secret Donors Behind the Center for American Progress and Other Think Tanks," *The Nation*, May 24, 2013, https://tinyurl.com/ybde5k3d.

[19] Eric Lipton, Brooke Williams and Nicholas Confessore, "Foreign Powers Buy Influence at Think Tanks," *The New York Times*, Sept. 6, 2014, https://tinyurl.com/y7xadkk9.

[20] *Ibid.*

[21] "How Transparent are Think Tanks about Who Funds Them 2016?" *op. cit.*

[22] Till Bruckner, "Think tank or fake tank? Seven common misperceptions about think tanks," *On Think Tanks*, May 25, 2017, http://tinyurl.com/ycqt72y2.

[23] Kevin Welner and Alex Molnar, "Truthiness in Education," *Education Week*, Feb. 28, 2007, p. 32, https://tinyurl.com/yce4foph; "Bunkum Award 2016," National Education Policy Center, https://tinyurl.com/ybtqs2ye; and "2017 Think Twice Reviews," Great Lakes Center, https://tinyurl.com/yax3s4hh.

[24] Donald Abelson, "Think tanks must think more about issues of national interest, not self-interest," *LSE Impact blog*, London School of Economics, Oct. 11, 2011, https://tinyurl.com/ycs73tyv.

[25] For background, see "New Simulations Consider Effect of Changing Demographics on Future Presidential Elections," Center for American Progress, Feb. 25, 2016, https://tinyurl.com/y7qrae2p.

[26] Jane Harman, "Are think tanks too partisan?" *The Washington Post*, Oct. 7, 2015, https://tinyurl.com/yabhhy9e.

[27] *Ibid.*

[28] Tevi Troy, "Devaluing the Think Tank," *National Affairs*, Winter 2012, https://tinyurl.com/74xxfxu.

[29] Marcos Gonzalez Hernando, Diane Stone and Hartwig Pautz, "Think tanks can transform into the standard-setters and arbiters of quality of 21st century policy analysis," *LSE Impact blog*, London School of Economics, Feb. 20, 2017, https://tinyurl.com/ycbdo5fv.

[30] Enrique Mendizabal, "On the origin of think tanks — newspapers," *On Think Tanks*, July 28, 2010, https://tinyurl.com/ybtme5l9. For the datasets, see "datablog," *The Guardian*, https://tinyurl.com/phpln5w.

[31] Quoted in Bennett, *op. cit.*

[32] Drezner, *op. cit.*, locations 209, 312.

[33] Ellen Laipson, "Why our demand for instant results hurts think tanks," *The Washington Post*, Oct. 9, 2015, https://tinyurl.com/yahbcn6x.

[34] Bruckner, *op. cit.*

[35] James G. McGann, "For think tanks, it's either innovate or die," *The Washington Post*, Oct. 6, 2015, https://tinyurl.com/yb3x3lho.

[36] Jessica Mathews, "Why think tanks should embrace 'new media,' " *The Washington Post*, Oct. 8, 2015, https://tinyurl.com/y94u4f98.

[37] For background, see James A. Smith, *The Idea Brokers: Think Tanks and the Rise of the New Policy Elite* (1991); Ryan Engelman, "The Second Industrial Revolution, 1870-1914," *U.S. History Scene*, https://tinyurl.com/nwa8aeg; and James G. McGann, *The Fifth Estate: Think Tanks, Public Policy, and Governance* (2016).

[38] Smith, *op. cit.*, pp. xiii and 14.

[39] McGann, *The Fifth Estate, op. cit.*, p. 24.

[40] Andrew Carnegie, "Mr. Carnegie's Letter to

About the Author

Marcia Clemmitt is a veteran social-policy reporter who previously served as editor in chief of *Medicine & Health* and staff writer for *The Scientist*. She has also been a high school math and physics teacher. She holds a liberal arts and sciences degree from St. John's College, Annapolis, and a master's degree in English from Georgetown University. Her recent *CQ Researcher* reports include "The Dark Web" and " 'Alt-Right' Movement."

the Trustees," Carnegie Endowment for International Peace, Dec. 14, 1910, https://tiny url.com/ycppwk2r.

41 "History," Congressional Research Service, https://tinyurl.com/6rpb337; "History," Congressional Budget Office, https://tinyurl.com/y82nabbe; and "The History of GAO — GAO's Start," Government Accountability Office, https://tinyurl.com/y7cb9w8x.

42 Troy, *op. cit.*; "A Century of Ideas," Brookings Institution, https://tinyurl.com/y8dgl4sl.

43 Donald Abelson, *Do Think Tanks Matter?* (2009), Kindle edition, location 848; David Boorstin, "Directions of policy research," *Editorial Research Reports*, 1975, https://tinyurl. com/yb4rmbqa.

44 "Capabilities," RAND Corp., https://tinyurl. com/ybhysjv4.

45 "Our History," Urban Institute, https://tinyurl. com/y9pbarys.

46 Smith, *op. cit.*, p. 152.

47 *Ibid.*, pp. 21-22.

48 "About Heritage," Heritage Foundation, https://tinyurl.com/ya7zzxo2.

49 Abelson, *Do Think Tanks Matter?, op. cit.*, location 2627.

50 McGann, The Fifth Estate, *op. cit.*, p. 28.

51 For background, see Sean Sullivan, "What is a 501(c)(4) anyway?" *The Washington Post*, May 13, 2013, https://tinyurl.com/y8tgv3g8; "About the Center for American Progress Action Fund," Center for American Progress, https://tinyurl.com/y9hjqar3; and Heritage Action for America, https://tinyurl.com/83yeomc.

52 James Jay Carafano, "Think Tanks Aren't Going Extinct, But They Have to Evolve," *The National Interest*, Oct. 21, 2015, https://tinyurl. com/ybaebv9p.

53 Board of Trustees, Urban Institute, https:// tinyurl.com/y9gq8we6; Global Board of Advisors, Council on Foreign Relations, https:// tinyurl.com/yc5favrb.

54 Josh Rogin, "Trump could cause 'the death of think tanks as we know them,' " *The Washington Post*, Jan. 15, 2017, https://tinyurl.com/ y8yyyncy.

55 Abelson, *Do Think Tanks Matter?, op. cit.*, locations 1373, 2436, 2777.

56 Steven Mufson, "Trump's budget owes a huge debt to this right-wing Washington think tank," *The Washington Post*, March 27, 2017, https://tinyurl.com/yaxs962o.

57 Robert O'Harrow Jr., "A two-decade crusade by conservative charities fueled Trump's exit from Paris climate accord," *The Washington Post*, Sept. 5, 2017, http://tinyurl.com/y8vynneb; "The Think Tank That Destroyed the Paris Climate

FOR MORE INFORMATION

American Enterprise Institute, 1789 Massachusetts Ave., N.W., Washington, DC 20036; 202-862-5800; www.aei.org. Conservative think tank founded by New York business executives in 1938 that studies international markets and public policy issues.

Cato Institute, 1000 Massachusetts Ave., N.W., Washington, DC 20001; 202-842-0200; www.cato.org. Libertarian think tank founded in 1974 that promotes individual liberty and free markets.

Council on Foreign Relations, 58 E. 68th St., New York, NY 10065; 212-434-9400; www.cfr.org. Studies international relations from various ideological perspectives; founded in 1921.

Heritage Foundation, 214 Massachusetts Ave., N.E., Washington, DC 20002; 202-546-4400; www.heritage.org/. Influential conservative think tank that promotes limited government and individual freedom.

Institute for Policy Studies, 1301 Connecticut Ave., N.W., Suite 600, Washington, DC 20036; 202-234-9382; www.ips-dc.org. Participated in the anti-Vietnam War and civil-rights movements of the 1960s; studies social equity and environmental sustainability.

Joint Center for Political and Economic Studies, 633 Pennsylvania Ave., N.W., Washington, DC 20004; 202-789-3500; jointcenter.org. Studies issues that affect minorities; founded in 1970 to assist black officials elected to office after the 1960s civil rights movement.

On Think Tanks, https://onthinktanks.org. Website and blog of an international nonprofit group that studies and assists think tanks internationally.

Resources for the Future, 1616 P St., N.W., Washington, DC 20036; 202-328-5000; www.rff.org. The first think tank to focus on the environment and natural resources, founded in 1952.

Think Tank Watch, www.thinktankwatch.com. Website that posts news items about U.S. think tanks.

Transparify, www.transparify.org. A nonprofit in Tbilisi, Georgia, that reports on think tanks' degree of transparency about charitable donations they receive.

Agreement," *Think Tank Watch*, June 2, 2017, https://tinyurl.com/yalhso74.

58 Mufson, *op. cit.*

59 "Fiona Hill," Brookings Institution, https://tiny url.com/y8fo87ju.

60 James Hohmann, "The Daily 202: Trumpism makes strange bedfellows," *The Washington Post*, Sept. 12, 2017, http://tinyurl.com/yaxyksso.

61 Philip Wegmann, "After Jim DeMint, Heritage will develop 'a much closer and tighter relationship' with lobbying arm," *Washington Examiner*, May 5, 2017, https://tinyurl.com/ybe dwsxd.

62 "Statement From the Chairman of Heritage's Board of Trustees," Heritage Foundation, May 2, 2017, https://tinyurl.com/mhdx6fm; Eliana Johnson and Nancy Cook, "The real reason Jim DeMint got the boot," *Politico*, May 2, 2017, https://tinyurl.com/mlpse6b.

63 Wegmann, *op. cit.*

64 Niv Ellis, "Meadows: CBO should downsize, aggregate think-tank reports," *The Hill*, July 24, 2017, https://tinyurl.com/yc2gfc33.

65 "Plan For Federal Funding Hiatus," Woodrow Wilson International Center for Scholars, revised August 2015, https://tinyurl.com/yd9jjkcj.

66 "Wilson Center Statement on FY2018 Budget Plan," Woodrow Wilson International Center for Scholars, March 16, 2017, https://tinyurl.com/ yc6qaj33.

67 McGann, "2016 Global Go To Think Tank Index Report," *op. cit.*; James G. McGann, "2014 Global Go To Think Tank Index Report," University of Pennsylvania Think Tanks and Civil Societies Program, https://tinyurl.com/yc5f3m3j.

68 *Ibid.*, "2016 Global Go To Think Tank Index Report," pp. 8, 9.

Bibliography

Selected Sources

Books

Drezner, Daniel, *The Ideas Industry: How Pessimists, Partisans, and Plutocrats Are Transforming the Marketplace of Ideas*, Oxford University Press, 2017.

A professor of international politics at Tufts University argues that contemporary culture is pushing aside debate, critiques and development of ideas — think tanks' traditional functions — in favor of idea-marketing via celebrity-oriented events such as TED talks.

McGann, James G., *The Fifth Estate: Think Tanks, Public Policy, and Governance*, Brookings Institution Press, 2016.

The head of a University of Pennsylvania center that studies think tanks discusses new challenges posed by the internet and social media while describing typical roles the sector plays in policymaking, such as evaluating government programs and providing a training ground for young policy analysts.

Smith, James A., *The Idea Brokers: Think Tanks and the Rise of the New Policy Elite*, Free Press, 1993.

This classic by a historian of philanthropy and policymaking is the first full-scale analysis of think tanks and remains an important reference for scholars. The author places think tanks in historical context dating to the ancient Greeks.

Struyk, Raymond, *Improving Think Tank Management: Practical Guidance for Think Tanks, Research Advocacy NGOs, and Their Funders*, Results for Development Institute, 2015.

A policy expert in housing and social assistance who has worked with think tanks in 25 countries provides guidance on what it takes to develop and implement evidence-based policy recommendations.

Articles

Arnsdorf, Isaac, "Gramm's border-tax crusade would help his firm," *Politico*, March 8, 2017, https://tinyurl.com/j4pqdqu.

Former Republican Sen. Phil Gramm of Texas is one of many part-time staff at think tanks who sometimes use their credentials as researchers to gain credibility for work on behalf of another employer or business, ethics watchdogs say.

Bordewich, Jean Parvin, "Q&A with Stuart Butler: What does it take to turn ideas into government action?" William and Flora Hewlett Foundation, March 1, 2017, https://tinyurl.com/y9rlgjkv.

A longtime think tank scholar who developed policies on health care access and welfare reform describes how to turn ideas into law.

Burgat, Casey, and C. Jarrett Dieterle, "Don't Gut the CBO," *National Review*, July 27, 2017, https://tinyurl.com/y745agdo.

Fellows from a free-market-oriented think tank argue that congressional proposals to strip the Congressional Budget Office, a taxpayer-funded think tank, of its authority would hurt members of Congress more than anyone.

Cameron, Dell, "Jeff Sessions Was Lobbied to Exclude Democrats From Trump's Election Fraud Panel," *Gizmodo*, Sept. 12, 2017, http://tinyurl.com/y8mrbwgr.

A staff member at the conservative Heritage Foundation demonstrated the strong partisan approach of some think tank scholars when he urged the Department of Justice to staff President Trump's election-fraud panel with conservative Republicans only, denying seats to Democrats and moderate Republicans.

Lipton, Eric, and Brooke Williams, "How Think Tanks Amplify Corporate America's Influence," *The New York Times*, Aug. 7, 2016, https://tinyurl.com/ycwerrkb.

Corporate donors are gaining influence over think tanks' research agendas and using it to advance business interests, critics say.

Norton, Ben, "NYT Lets Huge Think Tank Funded by Gov't and Arms Industry Claim Huge U.S. Military Budget Isn't Huge Enough," FAIR, Sept. 21, 2017, http://tinyurl.com/yasjky5s.

In a story on the federal defense budget, *The New York Times* included commentary from only one think tank, the Washington-based Center for Strategic and International Studies (CSIS). Moreover, the paper failed to explain that CSIS receives substantial funding from defense-industry giants such as the Chicago-based Boeing Co., which could bias CSIS scholars in favor of higher defense spending, reports the left-leaning media-criticism group FAIR.

Reports and Studies

"How Transparent are Think Tanks about Who Funds Them 2016?" Transparify, June 2016, https://tinyurl.com/hu7ncgu.

An international nonprofit in Tbilisi, Georgia, that urges think tanks to publicly divulge their funding sources says the think tanks it tracks became significantly more transparent last year.

"The Oil Tanks," Public Accountability Initiative, December 2015, https://tinyurl.com/y9ucmpcy.

A watchdog group on corporate and government accountability tracks links between oil and gas companies and nine major think tanks that advocated lifting an oil-export ban, a move that would benefit the companies.

McGann, James G., "2016 Global Go To Think Tank Index Report," University of Pennsylvania Think Tanks and Civil Societies Program, Jan. 26, 2017, https://tinyurl.com/kk5levw.

The newest annual report from a university-based center studying think tanks ranks institutions worldwide on qualities such as policy impact and use of social media. Rankings are based on votes by experts in the field.

The Next Step:

Additional Articles from Current Periodicals

Donor Influence

Fung, Brian, and Hamza Shaban, "Want to understand how dominant tech companies have become? Look at the number of issues they lobby on," *The Washington Post*, Aug. 31, 2017, https://tinyurl.com/yd359t7d.

Tech companies have strategically contributed money to think tanks as part of an increasing effort to influence policy.

O'Harrow, Robert Jr., "A two-decade crusade by conservative charities fueled Trump's exit from Paris climate accord," *The Washington Post*, Sept. 5, 2017, https://tiny url.com/ydck6gyb.

The Cooler Heads Coalition, an umbrella group of charities and think tanks that has fought efforts to address climate change, was a factor behind President Trump's decision to withdraw the United States from the Paris agreement.

Vogel, Kenneth P., "Google Critic Ousted From Think Tank Funded by the Tech Giant," *The New York Times*, Aug. 30, 2017, https://tinyurl.com/y96b7svj.

The New America Foundation, a Washington think tank that has received millions in funding from Google, dismissed one of its scholars who had posted a statement on the think tank's website criticizing the tech giant.

Influence Abroad

Dorsey, James M., "Food for thought: UAE ambassador's hacked mails feed crucial policy debates," *The Huffington Post*, Aug. 20, 2017, https://tinyurl.com/yd7c4r2e.

The hacked email account of United Arab Emirates Ambassador Yousef al-Otaiba revealed the UAE's influence over several U.S. think tanks through donations.

Xiangwei, Wang, "China's Think Tanks Overflow, But Most Still Think What They're Told To Think," *South China Morning Post*, Feb. 12, 2017, https://tinyurl.com/zcvpts8.

The growing number of Chinese think tanks face challenges from government officials, especially when articulating ideas that contradict Beijing's agenda.

Yan Oo, Nay, "Why Myanmar needs foreign-policy think tanks," *Asia Times*, July 31, 2017, https://tinyurl.com/y9o92l3b.

Policymakers in Myanmar, a former dictatorship now facing internal conflict, would benefit from guidance by foreign-policy think tanks, an *Asia Times* contributor says.

Relevancy

Drezner, Daniel W., "Are Think Tanks Doomed?" *Politico*, Aug. 30, 2017, https://tinyurl.com/ycx5kxrf.

Think tanks face significant challenges in trying to remain nonpartisan but are still essential for disseminating information and research on policy, says a Tufts University professor.

Drezner, Daniel W., "The traditional think tank is withering. In its place? Bankers and consultants," *The Washington Post*, April 6, 2017, https://tinyurl.com/yaq49a8c.

Private consulting and banking firms are supplanting think tanks as authorities on foreign policy.

Judis, John B., "The Credible Think Tank Is Dead," New Republic, Sept. 15, 2017, https://tinyurl.com/yaanthwm.

The New America Foundation's decision to fire a scholar who criticized its major contributor, Google, is just one example of how think tanks are beholden to their donors, a journalist says.

Trump Administration and Congress

Ruoff, Alex, "Centrist Think Tanks Want GOP to Abandon Obamacare Repeal," Bloomberg BNA, April 12, 2017, https://tinyurl.com/y9lkrag8.

Two centrist think tanks support a bipartisan solution to congressional gridlock on health care and seek a stronger focus on improving Medicaid.

Waldman, Scott, "Climate Skeptics Could Snag EPA Science Adviser Slots," *Scientific American*, Sept. 14, 2017, https://tinyurl.com/ybx3acpz.

The Heartland Institute, a think tank known for supporting "alternative climate science," nominated many of the candidates for the Environmental Protection Agency's Science Advisory Board.

Wilson, Reid, "State think tanks issue stark warnings about GOP healthcare bill," *The Hill*, March 21, 2017, https://tinyurl.com/mt5gge9.

Days before the House planned to vote on legislation repealing the Affordable Care Act in March, think tanks in different states warned that the legislation would eliminate health coverage for thousands nationwide.

CITING *CQ RESEARCHER*

Sample formats for citing these reports in a bibliography include the ones listed below. Preferred styles and formats vary, so please check with your instructor or professor.

MLA STYLE

Mantel, Barbara. "Coal Industry's Future." CQ Researcher 17 June 2016: 529-552.

APA STYLE

Mantel, B. (2016, June 17). Coal Industry's Future. *CQ Researcher*, 6, 529-552.

CHICAGO STYLE

Mantel, Barbara. "Coal Industry's Future." *CQ Researcher*, June 17, 2016, 529-52.

In-depth Reports on Issues in the News

Are you writing a paper?

Need backup for a debate?

Want to become an expert on an issue?

For 90 years, students have turned to *CQ Researcher* for in-depth reporting on issues in the news. Reports on a full range of political and social issues are now available. Following is a selection of recent reports:

Civil Liberties
Privacy and the Internet, 12/15
Intelligence Reform, 5/15
Religion and Law, 11/14

Crime/Law
High-Tech Policing, 4/17
Forensic Science Controversies, 2/17
Jailing Debtors, 9/16
Decriminalizing Prostitution, 4/16
Restorative Justice, 2/16
The Dark Web, 1/16
Immigrant Detention, 10/15

Education
Charter Schools, 3/17
Civic Education, 2/17
Student Debt, 11/16
Apprenticeships, 10/16

Environment/Society
Climate Change and National Security, 9/17
Muslims in America, 7/17
Funding the Arts, 7/17
Hunger in America, 7/17
Future of the Christian Right, 6/17
Trust in Media, 6/17

Health/Safety
Medical Breakthroughs, 9/17
Medical Marijuana, 7/17
Food Labeling, 6/17
Sports and Sexual Assault, 4/17
Reducing Traffic Deaths, 2/17

Politics/Economy
Universal Basic Income, 9/17
National Debt, 9/17
North Korea Showdown, 5/17
Rethinking Foreign Aid, 4/17
Immigrants and the Economy, 2/17

Upcoming Reports

Cyber Warfare, 10/6/17   Democracies, 10/13/17   Future of the Democratic Party, 10/20/17

ACCESS

CQ Researcher is available in print and online. For access, visit your library or www.cqresearcher.com.

STAY CURRENT

For notice of upcoming *CQ Researcher* reports or to learn more about *CQ Researcher* products, subscribe to the free email newsletters, *CQ Researcher Alert!* and *CQ Researcher News*: http://cqpress.com/newsletters.

PURCHASE

To purchase a *CQ Researcher* report in print or electronic format (PDF), visit www.cqpress.com or call 866-427-7737. Single reports start at $15. Bulk purchase discounts and electronic-rights licensing are also available.

SUBSCRIBE

Annual full-service *CQ Researcher* subscriptions—including 44 reports a year, monthly index updates, and a bound volume—start at $1,131. Add $25 for domestic postage.

CQ Researcher Online offers a backfile from 1991 and a number of tools to simplify research. For pricing information, call 800-818-7243 or 805-499-9774 or email librarysales@sagepub.com.

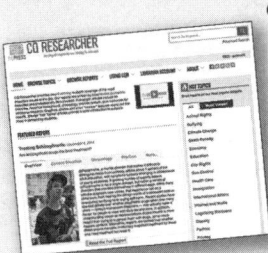

CQPRESS

Published by CQ Press, an Imprint of SAGE Publications, Inc.

www.cqresearcher.com

Cyberwarfare Threat

Do hackers pose a danger to national security?

The next major conflict between world powers may not begin at sea or along a disputed border, but in cyberspace. In the past decade, hackers have targeted voting systems in the United States, electrical grids in Ukraine, uranium enrichment facilities in Iran and hospitals, universities and major corporations around the world. The attacks have focused new attention on whether the United States is acting quickly enough to protect computer networks serving critical infrastructure, from military bases to power plants. Cybersecurity experts say companies holding sensitive data are particularly vulnerable to digital attacks, such as the recent hack of the Equifax credit reporting agency that potentially affects 145.5 million U.S. consumers. The United Nations is working to develop international rules for cyberwarfare, but the effort faces major hurdles, including deciding how even to define a cyberweapon. Allegations that Russia used social media to disrupt last year's presidential election are another focus of concern as the United States prepares for the 2018 congressional elections.

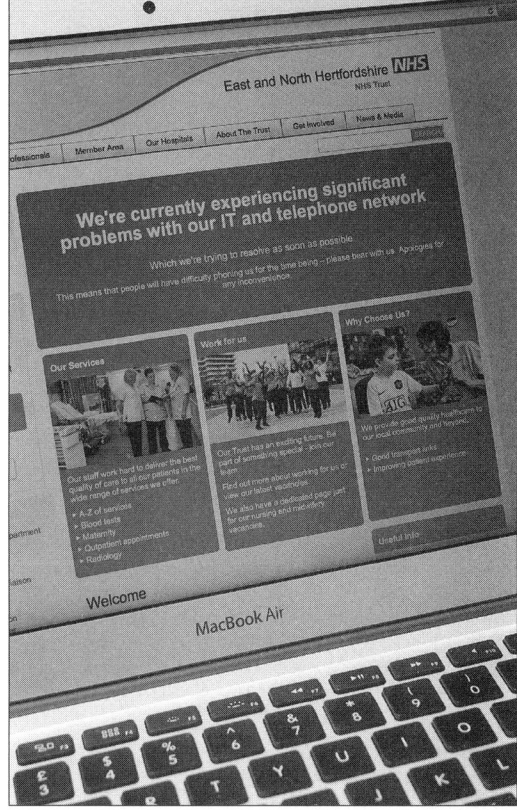

The website of Britain's National Health Service notifies users of online problems caused by a global cyberattack that originated in Ukraine earlier this year. The attack hit more than 65 countries, raising new concerns about whether the United States should act more aggressively against cyberattacks that could change election tallies or disable power grids and key military infrastructure.

CQ Researcher • Oct. 6, 2017 • www.cqresearcher.com
Volume 27, Number 35 • Pages 821-844

THIS REPORT

I
N THE ISSUES **823**
S BACKGROUND **829**
I CHRONOLOGY **831**
D CURRENT SITUATION **835**
E AT ISSUE......................**837**
OUTLOOK **838**
BIBLIOGRAPHY **842**
THE NEXT STEP **843**

THE ISSUES

823 • Does cyberwarfare pose an existential threat to the United States?
• Should the U.S. government regulate private-sector cybersecurity?
• Should the international community pursue agreements governing cyberwarfare?

BACKGROUND

829 **Pre-Internet Attacks**
Spies linked to Russia hacked U.S. government computers in 1986.

830 **Cyberattacks on the Rise**
Russia launched a cyberattack on Georgia before invading with conventional arms in 2008.

832 **Government Action**
In 2013, the National Security Agency received authorization to break into computer systems around the world.

CURRENT SITUATION

835 **Trump Administration**
The president said in August he would elevate the status of the U.S. Cyber Command.

836 **NSA Under Scrutiny**
The National Security Agency often does not tell companies about flaws in their computer networks.

838 **Internet of Things**
The number of internet-connected devices is increasing.

OUTLOOK

838 **Securing State Elections**
Officials are working to protect voting systems from cyberattacks.

SIDEBARS AND GRAPHICS

824 **Most See Russian Hacking as Election Threat**
Sixty-seven percent of Americans say Russia poses a threat to future U.S. elections.

825 **Cyberattacks Target Industrial Computers**
Networks around the world were targeted in digital attacks this year.

831 **Chronology**
Key events since 1986.

832 **Digital Attacks Spur Calls for Cyberalliance**
Some experts want NATO to take the offensive in cyberspace.

834 **Cyberthreats a Growing Concern for 2018 Elections**
Bots and trolls are "an existential threat to U.S. democracy."

837 **At Issue:**
Should the government regulate private-sector cybersecurity?

FOR FURTHER RESEARCH

841 **For More Information**
Organizations to contact.

842 **Bibliography**
Selected sources used.

843 **The Next Step**
Additional articles.

843 **Citing CQ Researcher**
Sample bibliography formats.

Cover: AFP/Getty Images/Daniel Leal-Olivas

CQ RESEARCHER

Oct. 6, 2017
Volume 27, Number 35

EXECUTIVE EDITOR: Thomas J. Billitteri
tjb@sagepub.com

ASSISTANT MANAGING EDITORS: Kenneth Fireman, kenneth.fireman@sagepub.com, Kathy Koch, kathy.koch@sagepub.com, Scott Rohrer, scott.rohrer@sagepub.com

ASSOCIATE MANAGING EDITOR: Val Ellicott

SENIOR CONTRIBUTING EDITOR:
Thomas J. Colin
tom.colin@sagepub.com

CONTRIBUTING WRITERS: Marcia Clemmitt, Sarah Glazer, Reed Karaim, Barbara Mantel, Patrick Marshall, Tom Price

SENIOR PROJECT EDITOR: Olu B. Davis

EDITORIAL ASSISTANT: Natalia Gurevich

FACT CHECKERS: Eva P. Dasher, Michelle Harris, Betsy Towner Levine, Robin Palmer

Los Angeles I London I New Delhi
Singapore I Washington DC I Melbourne

An Imprint of SAGE Publications, Inc.

SENIOR VICE PRESIDENT, GLOBAL LEARNING RESOURCES:
Karen Phillips

EXECUTIVE DIRECTOR, ONLINE LIBRARY AND REFERENCE PUBLISHING:
Todd Baldwin

CQ Researcher (ISSN 1056-2036) is printed on acid-free paper. Published weekly, except: (March wk. 4) (May wk. 4) (July wks. 1, 2) (Aug. wks. 2, 3) (Nov. wk. 4) and (Dec. wks. 3, 4). Published by SAGE Publications, Inc., 2455 Teller Rd., Thousand Oaks, CA 91320. Annual full-service subscriptions start at $1,131. For pricing, call 1-800-818-7243. To purchase a CQ Researcher report in print or electronic format (PDF), visit www.cqpress.com or call 866-427-7737. Single reports start at $15. Bulk purchase discounts and electronic-rights licensing are also available. Periodicals postage paid at Thousand Oaks, California, and at additional mailing offices. POSTMASTER: Send address changes to CQ Researcher, 2600 Virginia Ave., N.W., Suite 600, Washington, DC 20037.

Cyberwarfare Threat

BY PATRICK MARSHALL

THE ISSUES

O n June 27, technicians at the defunct Chernobyl nuclear power plant in Ukraine noticed that the computers monitoring lingering radiation at the plant, destroyed in 1986 by a massive reactor explosion, had stopped working. The same day, ATMs shut down in Ukraine's capital city, Kiev. More than 4,000 miles away in the United States, workers at pharmaceutical giant Merck and Co. found themselves unable to make important vaccines. [1]

The disruptions had a common source — a computer virus that began in Ukraine and spread around the world, crippling more than 12,000 networks and devices in 65 countries. The cyberattack initially appeared to be ransomware, which encrypts digital data and demands payment for decrypting it. But researchers affiliated with NATO said the attack was primarily a "declaration of power" designed to destroy information, not extract ransom. [2]

They also said the attack likely was launched by a government or with backing from a government, raising the possibility that it could be considered an act of war. Ukraine has blamed Russia, but the Kremlin has denied involvement. [3]

Cybersecurity experts point to such attacks as evidence that future wars likely won't begin on land, at sea or in the air but instead in cyberspace. [4]

The rise of digital weapons as a major geopolitical threat raises new concerns about whether the United States should act more aggressively to protect itself from cyberweapons that could change election tallies, shut down

President Trump has proposed several actions to bolster the country's cyber capabilities, including giving increased independence to the U.S. Cyber Command and ordering strengthened cybersecurity for federal networks and critical infrastructure. "The elevation of United States Cyber Command demonstrates our increased resolve against cyberspace threats and will help reassure our allies and partners and deter our adversaries," Trump said.

Getty Images/Chip Somodevilla

power grids or disable key military infrastructure. The United States has powerful digital weapons that some cybersecurity experts say will deter attacks by other countries. U.S. intelligence officials, however, say cyberattacks pose more of a threat to the country than terrorism.

"In 2013, 'cyber' bumped 'terrorism' out of the top spot on our list of national threats," then-Director of National Intelligence James Clapper said last year. "And cyber has led our report every year since then." [5]

Protecting computer networks also is important at companies that make weapons systems or other products and services important to national security. But those companies oppose proposals to make their computers more secure through government regulation. Some cite prior bad experiences working with the government on cybersecurity. Others cite a desire to avoid red tape.

Recent cyberattacks have also inspired calls for international agreements to limit the militarization of cyberspace, but critics of the idea say limiting the use of cyberweapons is virtually impossible because computer code cannot be monitored the same way conventional weapons are.

Some cyberattacks target democratic institutions, mounting "influence campaigns" that exploit social media to spread fabricated information disguised as news, says Herbert Lin, a senior research scholar for cyber policy and security at the Hoover Institution, a conservative think tank at Stanford University.

"Cyber-enabled information warfare is an existential threat to society as we know it," says Lin. "It is people trying to advance the idea that there is no such thing as truth — that truth doesn't matter. There is no shared basis for understanding anymore. Is that a threat to society? You bet it is."

The cyberattack that started in Ukraine in June was just one of a number of such incidents in recent years:

• In May, a ransomware attack disabled hundreds of thousands of computers in more than 150 countries, disrupting operations at hospitals, universities, manufacturers and government agencies. The attack apparently used information stolen from the supersecret U.S. National Security Agency (NSA). FBI officials have noted that such attacks can disrupt the manufacture of electrical components, computer chips and other products important to national security. [6]

Most See Russian Hacking as Election Threat

A majority of Americans believe Russian hacking in the 2016 presidential election means Russia poses a threat to future U.S. elections, though fewer than half view the threat as major.

Percentage of Americans Who View Russian Hacking as a Threat to Future U.S. Elections

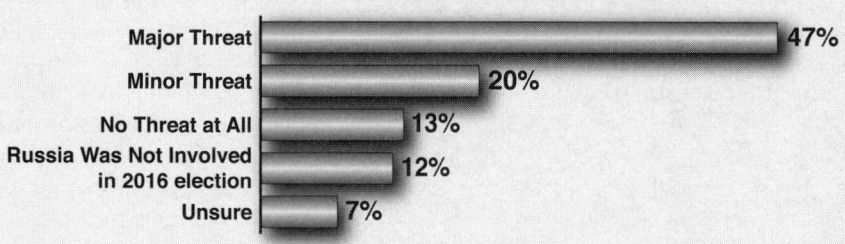

Major Threat	47%
Minor Threat	20%
No Threat at All	13%
Russia Was Not Involved in 2016 election	12%
Unsure	7%

Sources: Laura Santhanam, "New poll: 54% of Americans think Trump's dealings with Russia were unethical or illegal," PBS News Hour, July 6, 2017, https://tinyurl.com/y9wu4vto

• In December, a cyberattack cut about 20 percent of Kiev's electricity supply. Ukraine blamed Russia, saying the Kremlin has waged a "cyber war" against Ukraine since Russia annexed Crimea in 2014 and fighting broke out between Ukrainian forces and pro-Russian separatists in eastern Ukraine. "You can't really find a space in Ukraine where there hasn't been an attack," said Kenneth Geers, a NATO ambassador who focuses on cybersecurity. [7]

• In the United States last year, "Russian government cyber actors," tried to hack into voting systems in 21 states ahead of the presidential election, according to Department of Homeland Security officials. Officials say Russia also used social media, including Twitter accounts and $100,000 in Facebook ads, to distribute propaganda aimed at widening political divisions in the United States as part of a larger campaign to promote Donald Trump's presidential candidacy. And intelligence officials say hackers linked to Russia stole emails from the Democratic National Committee (DNC) and others that they later released in hopes of damaging the candidacy of Trump's opponent, Hillary Clinton. [8]

• In 2014, hackers broke into computers at Sony Pictures, stealing unreleased movies and making them publicly available. U.S. officials blamed North Korea, saying Pyongyang was retaliating for a Sony comedy, "The Interview," that depicted the assassination of the country's leader, Kim Jong-un. A year earlier, South Korean media reported that Kim had called cyberattacks a "magic weapon." [9]

• In 2014, hackers broke into the computer network for South Korea's nuclear power plants, stealing what government officials said was "non-critical" data. And in April 2016, computers at a nuclear power plant in Germany were found to be infected with viruses. [10]

• A 2015 report by Chatham House, a think tank in London, said cybersecurity risks at nuclear power plants are increasing as the plants "become increasingly reliant on digital systems and make increasing use of commercial 'off-the-shelf' software." [11]

• Western military officials said recently that Russia has been hacking into the personal smartphones used by NATO soldiers to gain operational information, assess troop strength and intimidate the soldiers. Some officials worried that compromised cellphones could be used to create confusion and slow NATO's response to Russian military action in a crisis. [12]

Intelligence officials warn that the stakes in cyberwarfare are high.

"The breadth of cyberthreats posed to U.S. national and economic security has become increasingly diverse, sophisticated and serious, leading to physical, security, economic, and psychological consequences," Clapper, then-Undersecretary of Defense for Intelligence Marcel Lettre and Navy Admiral Michael Rogers, director of the NSA, said in a rare joint statement to Congress in January." [13]

Cyberthreats are as varied as the devices connected to computer networks, and cybersecurity experts say the most important weapons systems in the U.S. military's arsenal could be at risk. In 2010, for example, after President Barack Obama ordered his administration to find out if there were security flaws in the systems that manage U.S. nuclear missiles, investigators found deficiencies that could have allowed hackers to shut down the missiles' flight guidance systems. [14]

In June, captains of commercial ships in the Black Sea reported that their GPS navigation systems were incorrect by about 20 miles. Navigation experts later concluded the systems were being "spoofed," or fed false signals, and some experts attributed the incidents to Russian hackers. [15]

Federal computer networks were accessed by hackers or infected with malware — software intended to damage or disable computer networks — about 30,000 times between Oct. 1, 2015 and Sept. 30, 2016, the Government Accountability Office (GAO), the investigative arm of Congress, reported in June. The agency also said the vulnerability of Defense Department computer networks "has grown significantly." [16]

On Sept. 20, the Securities and Exchange Commission, an independent federal agency that regulates Wall Street, revealed that hackers exploited a software vulnerability last year to breach agency computers. And in February 2016, a hacker released online the names and contact information of 29,000 Department of Homeland Security and FBI employees. [17]

Computers at other federal agencies also have been targeted by cyberweapons. A 2016 GAO survey of 24 federal agencies found that 18 with "high-impact" computer systems — those containing information that, if lost, could cause "catastrophic harm" — identified cyberattacks by foreign nations "as the most serious and most frequently occurring threat to the security of their systems." [18] Such attacks may seek to gather information on weapons systems, political strategies or economic plans.

Concerns over private companies' digital security focuses on those serving critical sectors such as banking, utilities and government contracting. Potential threats include ransomware that can shut down computer networks or destroy their data, and computer viruses that can shut down power grids.

"The private sector has been really slow to adopt basic cyber hygiene practices," says Ryan Maness, an assistant professor in the Defense Analysis Department at the Naval Postgraduate School in Monterey, Calif. Fifty-seven percent of companies surveyed by the insurance industry said they were targeted in a cyberattack in the past year, and 42 percent reported at least two attacks. [19]

Such findings have prompted demands for federal regulations to improve cybersecurity in the private sector. "There is clearly a bigger role for government," says Peter W. Singer, a strategist and senior fellow at the left-of-center New America think tank in Washington. Government requirements, he says, would ensure that private companies achieve "more than just aspirational goals" in protecting their networks.

President Trump has issued a strong call for building up the country's cyber capabilities. On Aug. 18, he said he would make the U.S. Cyber Command, the Pentagon's offensive cyberwar unit, a "Unified Combatant Command," a plan originally proposed by the Obama administration. The move will not be final until the Senate confirms someone

Cyberattacks Target Industrial Computers

Vietnam had the highest percentage of industrial control system computers hit by cyberattacks during the first half of 2017, according to a survey of the computers the cybersecurity company Kaspersky Lab has been hired to protect.

Top 10 Countries by Percentage of Industrial Computers Attacked

Vietnam	71%
Algeria	67.1%
Morocco	65.4%
Indonesia	58.7%
China	57.1%
India	56%
Iran	55.3%
Saudi Arabia	51.8%
Egypt	51.6%
Peru	50.8%

Source: "Threat Landscape for Industrial Automation Systems in H1 2017," Kaspersky Lab, Sept. 28, 2017, https://tinyurl.com/y9hgwq83

to run the Cyber Command, which is currently headed by Rogers at the NSA.

Trump's decision will give Cyber Command the same status as organizations that oversee military operations in the Middle East, Europe and the Pacific. Cyber Command is currently under the U.S. Strategic Command, one of the military's nine unified commands. [20]

"The elevation of United States Cyber Command demonstrates our increased resolve against cyberspace threats and will help reassure our allies and partners and deter our adversaries," Trump said in a statement. [21]

Some of Trump's other actions on cybersecurity have been more ambiguous. He has, for example, repeatedly questioned reports by his own intelligence agencies that Russia used cyberweapons to influence the presidential election. [22] And former FBI Director James Comey, whom Trump fired in May, testified in June that Trump showed no interest in preventing future election interference by Russia. [23]

As experts and policymakers consider the threat of cyberattacks, here are some of the questions they are asking:

Does cyberwarfare pose an existential threat to the United States?

Sen. John McCain, R-Ariz., chairman of the Senate Armed Services Committee, warned in May that "glaring gaps in our national cyber policy, strategy and organization undermine our ability to defend the homeland and deter those seeking to undermine our national security in cyberspace." [24]

Intelligence officials have made similar comments. In their joint statement to Congress in January, Clapper, Lettre and Rogers warned that more than 30 nations are developing offensive cyberattack capabilities and that "the proliferation of cyber capabilities coupled with new warfighting technologies" will increase the incidence of cyberattacks.

What's more, they said, a cyberattack targeting the private sector or U.S. infrastructure could escalate quickly and involve not just national security and military officials but corporations, "blurring the distinction between state and non-state action. Protecting critical infrastructure, such as crucial energy, financial, manufacturing, transportation, communication, and health systems, will become an increasingly complex national security challenge," they said. [25]

Hackers linked to Russia already have created a cyberweapon that can bring down power grids. The malware, called "CrashOverride," was used in the December cyberattack that shut down one-fifth of the electric power in Kiev. [26]

Kaspersky Lab, a global cybersecurity company in Moscow that makes anti-virus software and defends computers against digital attacks, said that during the first six months of 2017, it blocked attempted attacks on 37.6 percent of customers' computers operating machinery at plants providing water, power, gas and other critical services. [27] (*See chart, p. 825.*)

Kaspersky itself is controversial. On Sept. 14, the Trump administration ordered federal agencies to remove the company's products from their networks based on concerns that the firm has close ties to the Kremlin and that using its software could jeopardize national security. The company has rejected those assertions. [28]

Singer says that while a cyberattack targeting infrastructure could paralyze the U.S. military and economy, "for it to be a Pearl Harbor equivalent as opposed to a 9/11 shock" would require an enemy to follow it up with an invasion using conventional arms.

Such a scenario unfolded in 2008 when computer networks in Georgia were hit with cyberattacks weeks before Russia invaded the country by land, air and sea. Cyberwarfare experts say the incident marked the first time a known cyberattack was followed by a war using conventional arms. Georgia blamed Russia for the cyberattacks, but Russian officials denied responsibility. [29]

Maness at the Naval Postgraduate School said it is unlikely Russia would target the U.S. power grid the same way it did in Ukraine in December. "I think they would think twice about that because of our own power," he says. "There are these kind of red lines not to be crossed, at least among the major powers."

However, some countries — North Korea, for example — are less likely to be intimidated by U.S. cyberweapons. "North Korea knows it can target the information architecture that developed economies rely on without fearing any direct, symmetrical response," Brian R. Moore, then a resident fellow at the Center for Strategic and International Studies, a bipartisan Washington think tank, and Jonathan R. Corrado, an Asia analyst at McLarty Associates, an international strategic advisory firm in Washington, wrote in June. "The isolated nation already suffers regular blackouts, nearly nonexistent internet access, and a disconnected, cash-based financial system. It thus stands to lose much less in cyberwarfare, increasing the regime's appetite for online conflicts." [30]

Michael Sulmeyer, director of the Cyber Security Project at Harvard University's Belfer Center for Science and International Affairs, says U.S. policy on cyberwar should not rely on deterrence — the belief that other countries are so afraid of the United States' arsenal of cyberweapons that they would never target U.S. military or national security networks in a cyberattack. Instead, he says, "we need to focus much more on making ourselves harder to hack."

Jason Healey, a senior research scholar at Columbia University's School of International and Public Affairs, warned Congress in March that "there is actually very little evidence of adversaries being deterred by an opponent's fearsome cyber capabilities. But there are many examples, especially between the United States and Iran, where capabilities and operations have led to escalation."

An example of such escalation occurred in 2012, when a group backed by Iran disabled websites at U.S. financial institutions. That cyberattack was viewed as retaliation for a 2010 attack by the "Stuxnet" computer virus — thought to have been developed by the United States and Israel — that damaged Iranian centrifuges used to enrich uranium. [31]

Other cybersecurity experts say deterrence is still important even if it is not the sole answer to cyberthreats. "When we try to deter crime with locks on our doors or signs in the window that say, 'Protected by alarms,' or by police cruisers that go by, it doesn't stop all crime, but without it you would have a lot more," says Joseph Nye, a former assistant secretary of Defense for international security affairs. "That's true with cyber actors as well."

John Arquilla, who teaches defense analysis at the Naval Postgraduate School, said cyberattacks by themselves are not an effective strategy in war. "Think about aerial bombing," he said. "Societies have been standing up to it for the better part of a century, and almost all such campaigns have failed . . . If highly destructive bombing hasn't been able to break the human will, disruptive computer pinging surely won't." [32]

Should the U.S. government regulate private-sector cybersecurity?

Private companies own and operate more than 90 percent of U.S. cyberspace infrastructure and would be "the first line of defense" in a cyberwar, according to the Defense Department's 2015 cyber-strategy report. [33]

However, federal officials have largely avoided issuing regulations to make private-sector computer networks more secure. Exceptions include a 1996 law that imposes requirements on the handling of health care data and a 1999 law that does the same for financial data.

Instead, the government has encouraged private companies to voluntarily improve their cybersecurity practices. "The majority of intrusions can be stopped through relatively basic cybersecurity investments that companies can and must make themselves," the Defense Department's 2015 report states. [34]

Since then, however, private companies and organizations have been hit with major hacking and malware attacks.

• Equifax, the credit reporting agency, said in September that hackers had taken advantage of a flaw in its software to steal personal information on up to 145.5 million people, including names, Social Security numbers and birth dates. The source of the hack is still unknown. Equifax knew two months before its network was hacked that a patch was available to fix the software flaw, but the company did not install it, according to the industry group that discovered the flaw. [35]

• Last year's hack at the SEC targeted the agency's system for storing documents filed by publicly traded companies. SEC Chairman Jay Clayton issued a statement saying the breach "may have provided the basis for illicit gain through trading." He also said the agency acted quickly to patch the software vulnerability that the hackers exploited. [36]

• In June 2016, a cybersecurity firm hired by the Democratic National Committee said DNC computers had been hacked by groups linked to Russian intelligence. A blogger called Guccifer 2.0 responded by saying he alone was behind the hack and claimed to have passed along thousands of files to WikiLeaks. [37]

• On Oct. 3, Verizon Communications said a previously disclosed digital attack on Yahoo that took place in 2013 affected all 3 billion of Yahoo's user accounts, making it the biggest known breach of a company's computer network. Verizon acquired Yahoo earlier this year. In September 2016, before the acquisition, Yahoo disclosed a separate attack in 2014 in which "state-sponsored" hackers stole personal data on more than 500 million of the internet company's users. [38]

In March, U.S. law enforcement authorities charged two Russian intelligence officers with running the 2014 operation. Federal prosecutors said the Russian government used the stolen data to spy on White House and military officials, bank executives, Russian government officials and others. Investigators believe the attackers behind the 2013 attack were also Russian and possibly linked to the Russian government. [39]

Last year, the Commission on Enhancing National Cybersecurity, created by President Obama to tighten cybersecurity in government, business and society, called for the "public and private sectors to collaborate on cybersecurity activities." [40]

Singer of New America and other cybersecurity experts say that's not enough. The proposed "code of conduct" that federal officials have proposed to improve private-sector cyber-security has "less power than a code of conduct at a country club," Singer says. "What we have right now is a series of aspirational standards but not enough to backstop them."

Arquilla at the Naval Postgraduate School says the government should regulate how private companies protect their computer networks the same way it regulates how they protect workers from on-the-job injuries. "The government is involved in so many areas of physical safety, it takes just a small leap to understand that

Demonstrators at the 2016 Democratic National Convention in Philadelphia on July 25, 2016, protest the hacking of Democratic National Committee emails. U.S. intelligence officials say hackers linked to Russia stole the emails and later released them in hopes of damaging the election chances of Democratic presidential candidate Hillary Clinton.

the government should also have a role in cybersecurity," he says.

Lin of the Hoover Institution, who served on Obama's cybersecurity commission, disagrees. He says the commission was "very, very wary of explicit regulation" of the private sector, although it never ruled out the possibility. "The market has failed to provide the U.S. with the cybersecurity that it needs," says Lin. "But there are many steps to be tried before imposing regulations." He specifically suggests voluntary programs to help companies improve cybersecurity, as well as holding companies liable for damages resulting from improper security practices.

Not surprisingly, companies generally oppose government regulation of their computer networks. Ann M. Beauchesne, vice president of national security and emergency preparedness at the U.S. Chamber of Commerce, said private companies should spend their money protecting their computer networks "instead of dedicating those resources to dealing with red tape." [41]

Many companies say their experience with federal agencies has taught them to distrust government "cooperation" with the private sector. That's especially true of tech companies that have been pressured by the NSA to equip their products with "backdoors" — hidden openings in encrypted software that allow investigators to monitor data for activity that might threaten national security. Critics of the practice say it is an invasion of privacy and undermines public confidence that encrypted data is secure. [42]

Companies and consumer groups also have criticized the NSA's practice of collecting vulnerabilities in commercial software that the agency might someday want to use to access users' data — without telling companies about those vulnerabilities so they can be fixed. "If the government does not disclose to software companies the vulnerabilities that it obtains, then both public and private systems will be put at risk," according to the Electronic Privacy Information Center, a public-interest research group in Washington. [43]

Insurance companies also play a role in cybersecurity by setting minimum standards that private companies must meet to qualify for coverage against network breaches. But half of companies in the United States are not insured against hacking, and 27 percent of executives

Sulmeyer, at Harvard's Cyber Security Project, agrees, saying software and hardware makers have never been held accountable for data security during the 30 years they have been doing business.

Microsoft security architect Roger A. Grimes, however, says that is the wrong approach. "All software has bugs and all software has security flaws," he wrote recently. Such potentially huge liability would scare off potential investors in software and hardware firms, he said, and "you'd end up with fewer corporations, fewer jobs, and less innovation." [45]

Smith said such a convention should ban countries from launching cyberattacks against tech companies, the private sector or critical infrastructure. "Even in a world of growing nationalism, when it comes to cybersecurity the global tech sector needs to operate as a neutral Digital Switzerland," Smith wrote. "We will assist and protect customers everywhere. We will not aid in attacking customers anywhere. We need to retain the world's trust." [47]

Lin at the Hoover Institution applauds Smith's proposal. "It adds a private-sector voice to this and it's a good thing to have that in the debate," he says. "I'm afraid that in the merits of it, I think that it's going to be really, really hard to do, and actually probably impossible. But that doesn't mean it shouldn't be discussed."

James Carlini, a cybersecurity consultant in Illinois, agrees the chances for an effective cyberwarfare treaty are slim. "Cyber weapons are not part of the Geneva Convention, and the way they are used now, I highly doubt there will ever be a consensus to sign away their latest capabilities," he wrote in August. "To think everyone is going to come to a consensus to limit them or restrict them to only certain areas is ludicrous." [48]

Even advocates for a treaty agree that cyberwar can't be managed like conventional warfare or nuclear weapons.

"You can't outlaw a cyberweapon because you don't know what is a weapon," says Nye, the former Defense official. "It depends on the intention of the user. So you really can't prohibit cyberweapons in a verifiable way."

Arquilla of the Naval Postgraduate School agrees. "Information technology is all dual use, so you can't keep the ability to engage in cyber warfare out of people's hands," he says.

Existing international laws apply to cyberspace, but it's unclear which cyber activities would qualify as military attacks or use of force. "There is a gray area since a cyberattack can cause disruption without causing destruction or

Acting Assistant Attorney General for National Security Mary McCord announces the filing on March 15, 2017, of criminal charges in the 2014 theft of personal data on more than 500 million Yahoo users. Federal prosecutors charged two Russian intelligence officers with running the operation and said the Russian government used the hacked data to spy on White House and military officials, bank executives, Russian officials and others.

AFP/Getty Images/Brendan Smialowski

at those companies say they have no plans to buy such insurance. [44]

Singer says Congress could help lessen the risk by developing standards and requiring federal agencies to share cyberattack data with insurers. "One of the challenges for the cybersecurity insurance industry is that things are defined in and interpreted in different ways in different locales," Singer says.

He also says companies should hold software and hardware vendors accountable — through litigation — for losses stemming from vulnerabilities in their products.

Should the international community pursue agreements governing cyberwarfare?

In February, Microsoft President Brad Smith noted an alarming increase in cyberattacks around the world and called for a "Digital Geneva Convention" — an international treaty that would establish rules for what targets and retaliatory actions would be considered legitimate in a cyberwar. "The time has arrived," Smith wrote, "to call on the world's governments to implement international rules to protect the civilian use of the internet." [46]

casualties," James Lewis, a senior vice president at the Center for Strategic and International Studies think tank, told Congress in 2015. [49]

Michael N. Schmitt, an international law professor at the Naval War College in Rhode Island, says countries "are seemingly hesitant to state where the legal lines in the sand are" regarding cyberwarfare. "It hurts deterrence," he says. "It encourages states to exploit gray areas. We should be really nervous, because as we develop these capabilities we don't know the rules of the game."

Congress is also apparently nervous about the legal status of cyberwarfare. It approved legislation last year that requires the Trump administration to spell out within a year which cyberspace activities would qualify as acts of war against the United States. [50]

Schmitt says reaching consensus won't be easy. "When does a remotely conducted cyberoperation into a country violate that country's sovereignty?" he says. "The lawyers are all over the map on that."

His own view, he says, is that any action that damages a country's cyber infrastructure — including government computer networks and private-sector networks — is a violation of sovereignty. Schmitt says that the hackers who stole and released Democratic National Committee emails, for example, violated international law because they "manipulated our election process." Cyber espionage cases such as the hack that stole data from the SEC, however, are not barred under international law, he said. [51]

Nye says the lack of legal clarity makes it harder to prevent attacks. "One of the things that I worry about is, how do you deter states from creeping up to this threshold," he says.

Because the United States has targeted other countries with aggressive cyberattacks — the 2010 Stuxnet virus that damaged Iranian centrifuges is just one example — some cybersecurity experts say U.S. officials have little credibility to demand that other countries stop such attacks.

Kalev Leetaru, a senior fellow at George Washington University's Center for Cyber and Homeland Security, said it was "somewhat hypocritical" for U.S. officials to file criminal charges against the two Russian intelligence officers who allegedly masterminded the 2014 breach at Yahoo. The charges outline "precisely the same activities the U.S. government itself engages in every day," Leetaru wrote in *Forbes*. [52]

The United Nations has worked to develop cyberwarfare rules through its Group of Governmental Experts on Information Security (GGE), first convened in 2004. (*See sidebar, p. 832.*) The group's latest round of talks stalled without producing consensus, but Nye says he expects some countries to work together on agreements like the one Obama and Chinese President Xi Jinping reached in 2015.

In that deal, China agreed not to conduct commercial cyberespionage to avoid U.S. sanctions against Chinese companies accused of stealing trade secrets. [53] But Clapper noted last year that "China continues to have success in cyber espionage against the U.S. government, our allies, and U.S. companies." [54]

Before the 2015 deal was signed, a spokesman for China's defense ministry accused U.S. officials of conducting their own cyber spying operations. U.S. criticism of cyber espionage by China, he said, was a case of "a thief yelling 'Stop, thief!' " [55]

Paul Rosenzweig, a former Homeland Security deputy assistant secretary for policy who lectures on law at George Washington University, says international adoption of standard practices on cyberattacks is more feasible than a treaty like the one proposed by Microsoft's Smith. He notes that countries already have begun to agree not to target other countries' electricity grids. In 2015, for example, countries participating in that year's round of GGE talks pledged not to target other countries' critical infrastructure in peacetime. "It is not a mandate, but it seems moderately effective," Rosenzweig says. ∎

BACKGROUND

Pre-Internet Attacks

In 1986, Clifford Stoll, a computer analyst at Lawrence Berkeley National Laboratory in California, discovered while investigating a 75-cent accounting anomaly that the lab's network and other high-security government networks had been hacked. Eventually, Stoll tracked the intrusion to a group of West German spies working for the KGB, the Soviet Union's main security agency. [56] The incident — known as the "The Cuckoo's Egg," after the title of Stoll's 1989 book — was the first publicly documented cyberattack by another country on U.S. government computers.

Two years later, on Nov. 3, 1988, about 8,800 computers connected to ARPANET, the forerunner of the internet, were hit by the world's first computer worm and slowed to a crawl or crashed. Robert Morris, a Cornell University graduate student, had released the worm not to cause damage, he said, but to gauge ARPANET's reach. Still, he was convicted under the Computer Fraud and Abuse Act and sentenced to three years of probation. [57]

"Before Morris unleashed his worm, the internet was like a small town where people thought little of leaving their doors unlocked," technology journalist Timothy B. Lee wrote about the incident. "Internet security was seen as a mostly theoretical problem, and software vendors treated security flaws as a low priority. The Morris Worm destroyed that complacency." [58]

In response to the Morris Worm, the Defense Advanced Research Projects Agency (DARPA), a research arm of the Defense Department, contracted with Carnegie Mellon University to create the Computer Emergency Response Team (CERT), a research center focused on software flaws and internet security. [59]

Cyberattacks on the Rise

Increasing use of the internet by government, academia and the private sector prompted the United States and Russia to meet in secret in Moscow in 1996 to talk about a cyberspace disarmament agreement. U.S. officials were focused primarily on protecting data and infrastructure, but the Russians wanted any treaty to cover what they called 'information terrorism,' which referred to "any use of the internet that might

"What Eligible Receiver really demonstrated was the real lack of consciousness about cyber warfare," said John Hamre, deputy secretary of Defense at the time. "The first three days of Eligible Receiver, nobody believed we were under cyberattack." [62]

The March 1998 discovery of a two-year pattern of intrusions on government computer networks — later dubbed "Moonlight Maze" — confirmed the security gaps uncovered by Eligible Receiver. Intelligence officials are still investigating the intrusions, which originated in Russia

picious attempts to access the city's website and called the FBI. Analysts at the bureau found that the probes — which sought information about utilities and emergency systems — had originated in the Middle East and South Asia. That information acquired new significance when U.S. intelligence officials discovered that computers seized from al Qaeda operatives after the 9/11 attacks showed evidence that the terrorist group had engaged in widespread surveillance of U.S. infrastructure. [65]

Two years later, the Bush administration ordered the Homeland Security Department to establish a National Cyber Security Division to develop new technologies, tools and techniques to defend against cyberattacks. Also in 2003, Homeland Security officials issued the National Strategy to Secure Cyberspace, a roadmap for federal agencies and private companies to voluntarily cooperate on cyber security. [66]

The 2007 "surge" in U.S. forces fighting in Iraq marked the first time that defense and intelligence agencies tested cyberwar theories on the battlefield. [67] As part of those tests, U.S. agents sent fake text messages to insurgents in Iraq to entice them to specific locations, where they were then targeted by U.S. troops or drone-fired missiles. [68]

The first known cyberattack targeting an entire country took place in April that same year, when Russian hackers defaced Estonian government websites, posted fake documents and shut down email accounts. The attack was in retaliation for Estonia's decision to remove a statue of a Soviet soldier commemorating World War II. [69]

A year later, Russia launched a more serious cyberattack against Georgia in preparation for a conventional military assault, knocking out commercial banking and media outlets. [70]

In early 2009, almost immediately after winning election, Obama called for a thorough review of federal measures to defend U.S. cyberspace. In June, his

Continued on p. 832

A cyberattack this year on the defunct nuclear plant in Chernobyl, Ukraine, disabled the computers monitoring radiation left over from a massive 1986 explosion at the plant. Ukraine has blamed Russia, but the Kremlin has denied involvement. Cybersecurity experts say such attacks suggest that future wars likely will begin in cyberspace, not at sea, on land or in the air.

Getty Images/Sean Gallup

threaten domestic stability," wrote Adam Segal, director of the Program on Digital and Cyberspace Policy at the Council on Foreign Relations think tank. [60]

In 1997, U.S. defense officials launched an internal exercise dubbed "Eligible Receiver" in response to evidence that military networks were being probed by unknown sources. NSA hackers were assigned to break into Defense Department networks using only publicly available computer hardware and software to test the networks' security. The NSA hackers were able to take control of Pentagon computers as well as power grids and 911 systems in nine major U.S. cities. [61]

and compromised tens of thousands of files — including maps of military installations and military hardware designs. [63]

Weaknesses in U.S. military and civilian computer networks prompted President Bill Clinton in 1998 to issue the first national cybersecurity strategy. His directive said that "non-traditional attacks on our infrastructure and information systems may be capable of significantly harming both our military power and our economy" and ordered federal agencies to secure their networks within five years. [64]

In 2001, a city network administrator in Mountain View, Calif., noticed sus-

Chronology

1980s Pre-internet attacks focus on hacking into networks.

1986
An analyst discovers that the computer network at Lawrence Berkeley National Laboratory in California and other high-security government networks have been hacked by West German spies who sold the information to the Soviet Union.

1988
Thousands of computers in the United States are hit with the first computer worm, called the "Morris Worm," alerting federal agencies to the dangers posed by software and network vulnerability.

—————•—————

1990s-2000s Internet use expands and cyber-attacks increase.

1997
The Defense Department's "Eligible Receiver" exercise lets the National Security Agency (NSA) hack into department networks to test for vulnerabilities. The NSA team finds it can take control of Pentagon computers and civilian power grids.

1998
U.S. officials discover a pattern of computer intrusions — later dubbed "Moonlight Maze" — that had originated in Russia and had compromised maps of military installations and other sensitive files. . . . President Bill Clinton issues the first national cybersecurity strategy, which directs the federal government to secure its computer networks within five years.

2002
Following the 9/11 terrorist attacks on the United States, Congress increases penalties for several computer crimes, requires federal agencies to better protect their networks and provides $900 million to research cybersecurity improvements.

2003
George W. Bush administration releases the National Strategy to Secure Cyberspace, setting priorities for agencies with responsibility for cybersecurity. . . . Bush makes the Homeland Security Department responsible for protecting the country's non-military cyberspace infrastructure.

2007
Estonia accuses Russia of attacking its government computers.

2008
President George W. Bush calls for a Comprehensive National Cybersecurity Initiative to establish cybersecurity requirements for government agencies. . . . Russian agents hack into Georgian government websites before launching a conventional military attack.

2009
North Korea is suspected in cyber-attacks on U.S. and South Korean government, media and financial computer systems.

—————•—————

2010-Present Governments go on the cyber offensive.

2010
Google says its servers were hacked, apparently from China, and Secretary of State Hillary Clinton warns the United States will retaliate after such attacks. . . . The Stuxnet cyber-weapon, used to destroy centrifuges at an Iranian nuclear facility and attributed to the United States and Israel, is publicly identified.

2012
Iran launches a cyberattack on the Saudi Arabian national oil company. . . . Researchers identify a digital worm called "Flame" that deleted information from computers in Iran, Sudan and the Middle East.

2013
U.S. discloses that hackers, later determined to be Chinese, stole data on the F-35 fighter aircraft. . . . President Obama issues an executive order making it easier for companies and government agencies to share cyberthreat information.

2014
The FBI says North Korea was behind a cyberattack that released confidential data from Sony Pictures. The attack followed North Korean outrage over a Sony comedy film, "The Interview," about a plot to assassinate the country's leader, Kim Jong-un.

2015
Cybersecurity Information Sharing Act allows government agencies and the private sector to share data about cyberattacks and cyberthreats, including data on private citizens.

2016
Intelligence officials say Russia hacked and released Democratic National Committee emails to influence the U.S. presidential election. . . . In December, Russian hackers disable part of Ukraine's power grid.

2017
A computer virus originating in Ukraine disrupts computer networks around the world. . . . Facebook says it sold $100,000 in ads to Russian operatives hoping to influence the 2016 presidential election.

Digital Attacks Spur Calls for Cyberalliance

Some experts want NATO to take offensive in cyberspace.

With 4.7 billion people expected to be online by 2025, cyber officials are expressing growing fears about digital security and urging countries to work together to protect cyberspace. [1]

The question is how best to foster such international collaboration.

The United States already participates in cyberdefense exercises with NATO, a U.S.-European military alliance that says it must defend itself in cyberspace "as effectively as it does in the air, on land and at sea." Under Article 5 of its charter, NATO would treat a cyberattack against one of its members as an attack against all members, according to the alliance's secretary general, Jens Stoltenberg. [2]

NATO has not made clear, however, what type of cyberattack would trigger Article 5, or how it would decide on a proportional response. [3] One challenge is that it is often difficult to say for sure whether a particular cyberattack was launched by a government agency or a private group. [4]

The alliance's policy on cyberwarfare — as in conventional warfare — is to act only in self-defense, which some cybersecurity experts believe is misguided. "Can any military force credibly claim to have advanced capabilities if it does not include offensive cyber operations in its arsenal?" James Lewis, a senior vice president at the Center for Strategic and International Studies, a bipartisan think tank in Washington, wrote in 2015. [5]

A NATO spokesperson said in July the alliance warded off 500 cyberattacks each month in 2016. "Foreign governments, criminals and terrorists can all be the source of cyberattacks, and attribution can be difficult," Oana Lungescu said. "But of course, nations have the largest resources in the cyber field, and they are responsible for the majority of targeted attacks against NATO networks." [6]

One such attack occurred in June, when computers at government offices, financial firms, utilities and industries around the world were wiped clean in a digital attack that a NATO-affiliated research firm said was likely caused by a "state actor" or by someone with state backing. Researcher Tomáš Minárik at NATO's Cooperative Cyber Defense Centre of Excellence said the attack "could count as a violation of sovereignty" that would justify countermeasures by the targeted countries. Ukraine, where the attack started, has blamed Russia. The Kremlin has denied involvement. [7]

Former NATO Supreme Commander Philip M. Breedlove argued in May that NATO should develop offensive cyberweapons, specifically to deter Russia from launching digital attacks. "We in NATO have incredible cyber capability," he said. "But we in NATO do not have an incredible cyber policy. In fact, our policy is quite limiting. It really does not allow us to consider offensive operatives as an alliance in cyber." [8]

The United Nations also is working to come up with international standards for responding to hostile acts in cyberspace. In June, the U.N.'s fifth Group of Governmental Experts on Information Security (GGE) disbanded, reportedly over disagreements about whether its final report should deal with the use

Continued from p. 830

administration announced the creation of the U.S. Cyber Command within the Defense Department to defend department networks. [71]

China began to attract attention from U.S. cybersecurity officials in 2010, after Google said Chinese hackers stole intellectual property from the company and broke into the email accounts of human-rights activists. [72] The attack — dubbed Operation Aurora — also targeted dozens of other companies. [73]

As federal agencies worked to strengthen their cyberdefenses, defense officials prepared offensive cyberweapons.

In 2010, a cyberweapon called Stuxnet was accidentally discovered to have migrated from an Iranian nuclear facility to computer networks around the world. The virus, thought to have been created by the NSA and Israel, was designed to undermine Iran's nuclear weapons program by causing centrifuges that enrich uranium to spin out of control. [74]

One participant in the operation said the aim was not to cause immediate, extensive damage but to make the Iranians think their engineers were incompetent. "The idea was to string it out as long as possible," the person said. "If you had wholesale destruction right away, then they generally can figure out what happened, and it doesn't look like incompetence." [75]

Two years later, researchers identified "Flame," a digital worm that had deleted information from computers in Iran, Sudan and the Middle East. The worm consisted of different modules, including one called "Shredder" that instructed breached computers to remove all traces of the infection. Other modules stole documents, recorded keystrokes and screenshots or lifted data and audio from smartphones or other Bluetooth devices near the targeted computer. [76]

Flame may have been first used in 2004. In 2012, it was considered possibly the most complex piece of malware ever discovered. Some analysts suspect it was created by the United States and Israel. It also was the first identified virus that used Bluetooth wireless technology to send and receive commands and data. [77]

Government Action

On Nov. 17, 2010, Dean Turner, director of the Global Intelligence Network at Symantec, a private security firm, called Stuxnet "a wake-up call to critical infrastructure systems around the world."

of countermeasures after a cyberattack. (The first GGE group formed in 2004 to examine potential cyberthreats and possible cooperative measures to address them.) [9]

Advocates for cyberdefense cooperation viewed the disbanding as a major setback, saying it leaves the future of international cooperation on cyberspace up in the air. [10] Paul Rosenzweig, a former Department of Homeland Security deputy assistant secretary and a law lecturer at George Washington University, said the GGE's deadlock shows how difficult it will be for countries to agree even on basic standards of behavior in cyberspace.

Some experts say the only way to counter cyberchallenges from Russia, China, North Korea and other authoritarian governments is to form a "cyberalliance" of democratic countries, separate from NATO.

"The alliance will need a common perception that it matters to each of us and each nation to defend the democratic civil societies against the economic losses and political intrusions" of China and other authoritarian countries, Chris C. Demchak, who teaches cybersecurity at the U.S. Naval War College, said in May. She said such an alliance would consist of up to 40 countries containing 900 million people who would have "the economic market weight and the technological talent pool to face China as a peer." [11]

U.S. defense officials have not advocated for a formal cyberalliance, according to Masao Doi, acting deputy chief of public affairs at the U.S. Cyber Command. But, he added, "cooperation and partnership are vital to the success of U.S. Cyber Command's missions."

— *Patrick Marshall*

[1] David Burt *et al.*, "Cyberspace 2025: Today's Decisions, Tomorrow's Terrain," Microsoft, June 2014, https://tinyurl.com/y9ql3vrq.

[2] Roland Oliphant and Cara McGoogan, "Nato warns cyber attacks 'could trigger Article 5' as world reels from Ukraine hack," *The Telegraph*, June 28, 2017, https://tinyurl.com/y9qdxbaq.

[3] "NATO Cyber Defence," NATO fact sheet, April 2017, https://tinyurl.com/y7cnlkee; Oliphant and McGoogan, *ibid.*

[4] "Massive cyber attack could trigger NATO response: Stoltenberg," Reuters, June 15, 2016, https://tinyurl.com/ydaycggb.

[5] James A. Lewis, "The Role Of Offensive Cyber Operations In NATO's Collective Defence," The Tallinn Papers, NATO Cooperative Cyber Defence Centre of Excellence Tallinn Estonia, 2015, https://tinyurl.com/y7zbby5q.

[6] Ryan Browne, "NATO: We ward off 500 cyberattacks each month," CNN, July 18, 2017, https://tinyurl.com/y83sa5yo.

[7] Luke Graham, "NATO think-tank says a 'state actor' was behind the massive ransomware attack and could trigger military response," CNBC, June 30, 2017, https://tinyurl.com/y73vhbph; Thomas Fox Brewster, "NotPetya Ransomware Hackers 'Took Down Ukraine Power Grid,'" *Forbes*, July 3, 2017, https://tinyurl.com/ya4bscfv.

[8] Patrick Tucker, "Former NATO Commander: Alliance Needs to Take Cyber Fight to Russia's Door," *Defense One*, July 6, 2017, https://tinyurl.com/y8bdld49.

[9] "Developments in the Field of Information and Telecommunications in the Context of International Security," fact sheet, United Nations Office for Disarmament Affairs, April 2017, https://tinyurl.com/yaeaplo7; Elaine Korzak, "UN GGE on Cybersecurity: The End of an Era?" *The Diplomat*, July 31, 2017, https://tinyurl.com/ybpa5kpf.

[10] *Ibid.*, Korzak.

[11] "Key Trends across a Maturing Cyberspace affecting U.S. and China Future Influences in a Rising deeply Cybered, Conflictual, and Post-Western World," testimony of Chris C. Demchak before the U.S. China Economic and Security Review Commission, May 4, 2017, https://tinyurl.com/ya6hud5u.

"This is the first publicly known threat to target industrial control systems and grants hackers vital control of critical infrastructures such as power plants, dams and chemical facilities," Turner told a Senate committee. [78]

In retaliation for Stuxnet, an activist group backed by Iran launched about 200 "denial of service" attacks aimed at disabling websites at nearly 50 U.S. financial institutions. [79]

Iran also was reportedly behind a 2012 cyberattack on Saudi Aramco, the Saudi Arabian national oil company and the world's largest oil exporter, using a virus called Shamoon. The attack wiped data from 30,000 computers.

"The Shamoon attack in Saudi Arabia seriously spooked the U.S. government," the Council on Foreign Relations' Segal wrote. Later that year, Defense Secretary Leon Panetta warned of a potential "cyber Pearl Harbor" in which hackers would derail passenger trains or trains loaded with lethal chemicals. [80]

U.S. cybersecurity officials were further shaken by the disclosure in June 2013 that hackers had stolen technical and design data for the F-35, America's next-generation fighter aircraft. [81] China was eventually identified as the culprit. "The Chinese might never have to fight the jet if it didn't get off the ground," Shane Harris wrote in his 2014 book *@War: The Rise of the Military-Internet Complex.* [82]

U.S. officials, however, were making progress themselves on offensive cyber capabilities. By 2013, the NSA had implanted malware in an estimated 85,000 computer systems in 89 countries to allow them to access those networks should they need to in the future. [83] That same year, the NSA's Remote Operations Center received authorization to spend $651.7 million breaking into computer systems around the world — twice the amount the entire intelligence community spent that year defending classified U.S. military networks from attack. [84]

The Obama administration also was focused on securing critical infrastructure. On Feb. 12, 2013, Obama signed an executive order telling federal agencies to start sharing more cyberthreat information with private companies and directing the Homeland Security Department to identify infrastructure elements "where a cybersecurity incident could reasonably result in catastrophic regional or national effects." [85]

The hacking attack targeting Sony Pictures took place a year later when hackers

Cyberthreats a Growing Concern for 2018 Elections

Bots and trolls are "an existential threat to U.S. democracy."

Securing the nation's voting systems has taken on new urgency ahead of next year's midterm congressional elections, as evidence mounts that Russia used hacking and bogus social media accounts to interfere in last year's presidential race.

But many election officials say they still feel vulnerable to cyberthreats, and security officials are scrambling to find solutions.

In July, officials from the Homeland Security Department, FBI and the Election Assistance Commission — the only federal agency that works exclusively to make sure voting systems are secure — met with state election officials to explain the department's plan to protect voting systems. The plan focuses on sharing information with election officials regarding potential threats, analyzing risks to individual voting systems and ensuring election officials have the tools to support cybersecurity. [1]

On Sept. 22, the Homeland Security Department contacted election officials in 21 states and told them hackers linked to the Russian government attempted to hack their voting systems last year. State election officials and congressional lawmakers earlier had expressed frustration with the department's unwillingness to share information on which states were targeted.

"We heard feedback from the secretaries of state that this was an important piece of information," said Bob Kolasky, acting deputy undersecretary for DHS's National Protection and Programs Directorate. "We agreed that this information would help election officials make security decisions."

He said Homeland Security officials recognized the need for states to strengthen their voting systems now "rather than a few weeks before" the 2018 elections. Department officials left it to individual states to decide whether to publicly reveal they had been targeted. [2]

Even with the new information on which states were targeted, many states say they do not have enough money to secure their voting systems. Of 33 states surveyed by the news organization *Politico*, officials in at least 10 said they had asked state lawmakers this year for more money for election cybersecurity. But officials in only six states said they either received the money or expected to get it. [3]

Officials in 21 states said the federal government should provide money to help states strengthen election security or replace voting machines.

Not all states agree. "The last thing we need to do is create more government bureaucracy and throw federal money at a problem when the states can devise a solution," Georgia Secretary of State Brian Kemp said. [4]

Russia's hacking attempts last year apparently did not affect voting tallies. [5] "What this boils down to is that someone tried the door knob and it was locked," said Reid Magney, a spokesman for the Wisconsin Elections Commission.

Even so, Congress has been trying to find ways to prevent election interference. In January, Rep. Eliot Engel, D-N.Y., introduced legislation that would freeze the assets of foreigners who meddle in U.S. elections and deny them entry visas. In July, six Democratic House members led by Rep. Jim Langevin of Rhode Island announced they had formed a task force that aims to give members of Congress and cybersecurity experts a forum to discuss threats to voting systems. So far, however, no Republicans have joined the group. [6]

Hacking of voting systems is just one source of concern. Some cybersecurity experts say "influence campaigns," conducted through social media to disrupt democratic institutions and processes, are even more dangerous. [7]

Such campaigns, including the one Russia is accused of pursuing last year, may pose "an existential threat to U.S. democracy," says Peter W. Singer, a strategist and senior fellow at New America, a left-leaning think tank in Washington.

operating under the name "Guardians of Peace" made five unreleased Sony films publicly available. [86]

In 2015, Congress passed the Cybersecurity Information Sharing Act, which allows federal agencies and private companies to share data about cyberattacks and threats, including data on private citizens.

Civil liberties groups say the law threatens individual privacy rights. "It was billed as a cybersecurity bill but it seemed more like a surveillance bill," says Neema Singh Giuliani, legislative counsel with the American Civil Liberties Union (ACLU).

Cybersecurity experts also say the 2015 law is already out of date. They say computer attackers around the world have grown so sophisticated — often with state sponsorship — that the concept of allowing companies and the government to share cyber information seems antique. [87]

In December 2016, nearly 250,000 people in Ukraine lost electricity as the result of a suspected Russian cyberattack that came just six months before the June attack that began in Ukraine and spread around the world. The December attack was linked to the war in eastern Ukraine, where Russian-backed separatists are fighting Ukrainian government forces. [88]

Russia's multipronged campaign to influence the 2016 presidential election has continued to generate headlines since U.S. officials said last October they were confident the Kremlin was behind the hacking and release of Democratic National Committee emails. (*See sidebar, above.*)

"Such activity is not new to Moscow — the Russians have used similar tactics and techniques across Europe and Eurasia, for example, to influence public opinion there," the Department of Homeland Security and Office of the

Intelligence officials say influence campaigns played a key role in Russia's attempts to interfere in last year's election through the use of "state-funded media, third-party intermediaries, and paid social media users or 'trolls.' " [8]

Special counsel Robert Mueller, the former FBI director investigating Russia's activities before the election, is looking at whether $100,000 of Facebook ads bought by a Russian "troll farm" may have influenced voters. On Sept. 21, Facebook said it would turn over more than 3,000 of the ads to congressional panels probing Russia's election meddling. [9]

The same Russian operatives linked to the Facebook ads also used Twitter accounts, the company told congressional investigators in September. The investigators are probing how Russia used both social media platforms as part of an effort to influence the results of the election by spreading misleading propaganda. [10]

Even before the ad sale, Russian agents had posed as Americans on social media to encourage people to visit sites containing false or derogatory stories about Democratic presidential nominee Hillary Clinton, according to *The New York Times*. [11]

Election-related cyberthreats tend to divide members of Congress along party lines. In early February, Republicans on the House Administration Committee voted to shut down the Election Assistance Commission (EAC). The full House has not taken up the measure.

"If we're looking at reducing the size of government, this is a perfect example of something that can be eliminated," committee Chairman Gregg Harper, R-Miss., said after the vote. He said the EAC has outlived its usefulness and that the Federal Election Commission should take over its functions. [12]

Two experts on election security — Dan S. Wallach, a computer science professor at Rice University, and political consultant Justin Talbot-Zorn — disagree. They wrote in February that the vote to eliminate EAC funding reflects "a radical disconnect between a handful of influential House Republicans and nearly everyone else." [13]

— Patrick Marshall

[1] Erica Orden and Byron Tau, "GOP Seeks to Close Federal Election Agency," *The Wall Street Journal*, July 17, 2017, https://tinyurl.com/ya4vc3dm; Tim Starks, "DHS accelerates work to protect 2018 elections under 'critical infrastructure' tag," *Politico*, July 11, 2017, https://tinyurl.com/y6udbaho.

[2] Sari Horwitz, Ellen Nakashima and Matea Gold, "DHS tells states about Russian hacking during 2016 election," *The Washington Post*, Sept. 22, 2017, https://tinyurl.com/ycnmxy3z.

[3] Cory Bennett *et al.*, "Cash-strapped states brace for Russian hacking fight," *Politico*, Sept. 3, 2017, https://tinyurl.com/ybttxsom.

[4] *Ibid.*

[5] Tal Kopan, "DHS officials: 21 states potentially targeted by Russia hackers pre-election," CNN, July 18, 2017, https://tinyurl.com/y7bfyn33.

[6] "H.R.530 — Secure Our Democracy Act," Congress.gov, Feb. 8, 2017, https://tinyurl.com/yc7mmuzw; Rachael Kalinyak, "Task force focused on securing election systems crystallizes," *Federal Times*, July 27, 2017, https://tinyurl.com/yajamdlg.

[7] Massimo Calabresi, "Inside Russia's Social Media War on America," *Time*, May 18, 2017, https://tinyurl.com/lctxsar.

[8] "Assessing Russian Activities and Intentions in Recent US Elections," Office of the Director of National Intelligence, Jan. 6, 2017, https://tinyurl.com/hye8jnl.

[9] Dylan Byers, "Facebook handed Russia-linked ads over to Mueller under search warrant," CNN, Sept. 17, 2017, https://tinyurl.com/ydyd7zl6; Scott Shane and Mike Isaac, "Facebook to Turn Over Russian-Linked Ads to Congress," *The New York Times*, Sept. 21, 2017, https://tinyurl.com/y9vjagpy.

[10] Elizabeth Dwoskin, Adam Entous and Karoun Demirjian "Twitter finds hundreds of accounts tied to Russian operatives," *The Washington Post*, Sept. 28, 2017, https://tinyurl.com/y7bkjzhj.

[11] Scott Shane, "The Fake Americans Russia Created to Influence the Election," *The New York Times*, Sept. 7, 2017, https://tinyurl.com/ybf6rfw5.

[12] "As Trump fears fraud, GOP eliminates election commission," The Associated Press, Feb. 7, 2017, https://tinyurl.com/ybnzn2ek; "Harper: Time to Eliminate Obsolete Election Assistance Commission & Presidential Election Campaign Fund," press release, Rep. Gregg Harper, Feb. 8, 2017, https://tinyurl.com/y8k47kkx.

[13] Dan S. Wallach and Justin Talbot Zorn, "Want Secure Elections? Then Maybe Don't Cut Security Funding," *Wired*, Feb. 14, 2017, https://tinyurl.com/y7jc545r.

Director of National Intelligence said in a joint statement last year. [89]

In September, Facebook said it would turn over more than 3,000 Russia-linked ads to congressional committees investigating the Kremlin's influence operation prior to the election. Facebook also has given information on the ads to Robert Mueller, the special counsel investigating Russia's activities linked to the election. [90]

Also in September, Department of Homeland Security officials contacted election officials in 21 states and told them Russia had tried to hack into their voting systems before the 2016 presidential election. [91] ∎

CURRENT SITUATION

Trump Administration

On May 11, President Trump issued an executive order aimed at strengthening cybersecurity for federal networks and critical infrastructure. The order identifies three priorities: protecting federal networks, updating antiquated systems, and directing all department and agency heads to work together "so that we view our federal [internet technology] as one enterprise network," said Tom Bossert, Trump's homeland security adviser. [92]

The order also specifically makes agency heads responsible for cybersecurity at their departments, a job that Lin at the Hoover Institution says typically fell to chief information officers or chief security officers. Lin also says requiring interagency cooperation is important because "what happens at the Department of Treasury matters to the Department of Agriculture."

Trump's executive order was in addition to his decision to make U.S. Cyber Command — the Department of Defense's offensive cyber force — its own unified military command. [93]

New America's Singer, who supports the move, says "the battleground and the organization have become more operational since Cyber Command was formed, and this is a natural evolution."

Even as the Cyber Command assumes a higher-profile role, Congress is looking to exercise tighter oversight over cyber

A billboard promotes the Sony Pictures comedy "The Interview," in Venice, Calif., on Dec. 19, 2014. Earlier that year, hackers broke into Sony computers, stealing unreleased movies and making them publicly available. U.S. officials said North Korea launched the attack in retaliation for the film, which depicts a plot to assassinate the country's leader, Kim Jong-un.

operations. In July, the House approved legislation that would require Defense officials to notify Congress within 48 hours of any "sensitive military cyber operation" undertaken by the United States. The measure is part of the 2018 National Defense Authorization Act, which has passed the House and is pending before the Senate. It would apply to both offensive and defensive operations, but exempts covert actions. [94]

NSA Under Scrutiny

NSA officials have made it a practice to identify "zero-day" vulnerabil-

ities in software used by private companies. The term refers to major coding flaws that hackers could exploit and that the companies do not know exist.

The NSA collects such flaws in case it might someday want to use them to launch a cyberattack or extract information from a computer network. But the agency has opted not to tell companies about those vulnerabilities, drawing criticism from companies and consumer groups. [95]

The risks linked to that policy came to light in August 2016, when Cisco and Fortinet, which make networking equipment, alerted their customers that a hacking group called Shadow Brokers had made certain data available for sale on the Web. The data included hacking software that could be used to target networking appliances made by Cisco, Fortinet and other companies.

Shadow Brokers said they had stolen the data from a group linked to the NSA, and analysts concluded that the data consisted of zero-day vulnerabilities the agency had collected without telling the companies. [96]

The incident took place two years after the Obama administration, in a break with the policy in effect during

the George W. Bush administration, directed the NSA to reveal any vulnerabilities it discovered in companies' software, but made an exception for vulnerabilities that could serve "a clear national security or law enforcement need." [97] One former government official said that by 2014 the NSA had stored more than 2,000 zero-day vulnerabilities for potential use against Chinese systems alone. [98]

Security flaws in software and hardware have spawned an entire industry, with private companies finding the holes and then turning them into hacking weapons — known as "zero-day exploits" — that they sell to the NSA and other agencies and companies.

"This gray market is not precisely illegal, but it operates on the fringes of the Internet," Harris wrote in his 2014 book. [99] He said zero-day exploits in software go for $50,000 to $100,000, while exploits based on flaws in computer hardware can earn their creators millions of dollars. [100]

Giuliani at the ACLU says the NSA's handling of zero-day vulnerabilities needs to be more transparent. "It should be written in the law instead of being subject to change every time there's a change of political leadership," she says.

Such transparency was a top priority for Democratic and Republican lawmakers in Congress who introduced legislation on May 17 spelling out criteria for how the NSA and other agencies decide whether to tell companies about software and hardware vulnerabilities the agency has discovered. [101]

"Hoarding technological vulnerabilities to develop offensive weapons comes with significant risks to our own economy and national security," Rep. Ted Lieu, D-Calif., said in introducing the bill. [102]

White House officials say the current process is transparent enough. Michael Anton, a spokesman for the National Security Council, described it as "a disciplined, high-level interagency decision-making process for disclosure of known vulnerabilities." [103]

Continued on p. 838

Getty Images/Christopher Polk

At Issue:

Should the government regulate private-sector cybersecurity?

JOHN ARQUILLA
*PROFESSOR AND CHAIR OF DEFENSE
ANALYSIS,
U.S. NAVAL POSTGRADUATE SCHOOL*

WRITTEN FOR *CQ RESEARCHER*, OCTOBER 2017

*i*n 2003, President George W. Bush issued his "National Strategy to Secure Cyberspace," an attempt to guide — but not to regulate — efforts to protect commercial, infrastructural and personal information systems. Congress soon allocated about $5 billion in support of such efforts, and the public and private resources expended trying to improve cybersecurity have dwarfed that amount since — to little effect.

The list of costly hacks and massive data breaches has only lengthened over time, as major retail firms, leading social media sites and even some of the most sensitive, classified government databases have been penetrated. Add hundreds of billions of dollars' worth of intellectual property raided by hackers each year, and the cyber-cataclysm underway can no longer be denied or ignored.

The fault lies in the choice initially made by Bush — and reaffirmed since — to make government's role informational rather than regulatory. By doing so, government has granted the commercial sector the "freedom to innovate," as the Information Technology Association of America put it. And privacy concerns about government intrusiveness also have been kept at politically acceptable levels. The result: precious little innovation in cybersecurity has come from the business sector, and privacy has been shredded — not by Big Brother, but by a host of Little Brother hacking cliques.

Clearly, this is a case of what economists call "market failure." Consumers continue to purchase insecure products in ever-increasing quantities, so there has been no invisible hand to drive producers toward better cybersecurity. Given that the paths to improvement have been perceptible for some time — cloud computing, block chains and the ubiquitous use of strong encryption — government is now well positioned to require producers to employ such means, and to use its bully pulpit to nudge consumers to make informed purchases.

For the past two decades, government steered by the guardrails when it came to cybersecurity. First it lurched toward reliance on market mechanisms that have failed; then it went in the other direction with the misguided effort to obtain "backdoors" into commercial products that would allow government surveillance of anyone, at any time. The more sensible path is simply to regulate the adoption of the best cybersecurity technologies and practices.

The issue is not one of Right or Left. It has always been a matter of distinguishing right from wrong. If we fail, ruin lies ahead.

HERBERT LIN
*SENIOR RESEARCH SCHOLAR FOR
CYBER POLICY AND SECURITY,
HOOVER INSTITUTION*

WRITTEN FOR *CQ RESEARCHER*, OCTOBER 2017

*r*egulation should be a tool of last resort that directs private firms to take actions for enhancing the nation's cybersecurity that they would not otherwise take.

Market failure in cybersecurity is apparent in two ways. First, individual entities do not do all they should to provide for their own cybersecurity needs. Providing these entities with the information they need to take cybersecurity-enhancing actions in their own self-interest may be a partial solution to this kind of market failure, and providing information is obviously not a regulatory activity.

Second, even if these individual entities did all that could reasonably be expected, the national cybersecurity posture would still be inadequate because of the interdependencies between private and government entities. This aspect of market failure is much harder to address because it is not in any entity's self-interest to do for the nation more than it needs to do for itself. Here, regulation should be considered only when the risks to public safety and security are material and other approaches fail.

As an example of a nonregulatory approach, the NIST Cybersecurity Framework was designed to provide a systematic and voluntary way for private firms to assess their cybersecurity risks and take corrective action commensurate with them. Broader use of that framework would improve the nation's cybersecurity.

A more controversial — but still nonregulatory — approach would be to subject private vendors of IT products and services to tort liability for security lapses and inadequacies. Vendors say such liability would stifle innovation. But today's market environment has few incentives to attend to security while innovating. Tort liability — with appropriate carve-outs and limits — would help to redress that balance.

In any event, the liability question is likely to be moot with the advent of the Internet of Things (IOT). A robust liability regime already exists for "things"; the manufacturer of a faulty toaster that burns down your house is liable for damages. Adding an IOT dimension to the toaster will not change that; it is inconceivable that the manufacturer will be able to escape liability by denying the toaster's IOT parts caused the fire.

We have not yet exhausted the potential of such measures to improve the nation's cybersecurity posture. If and when we do, regulation may need to be considered as the only way to improve the nation's cybersecurity.

Continued from p. 836

Internet of Things

Internet security has increasingly become a challenge as more and more everyday devices and machines — driverless cars, pacemakers, refrigerators, virtual personal assistants — send and collect data via computer networks, a phenomenon known as "the internet of things." By 2020, an estimated 34 billion devices will be connected to the internet, up from 10 billion in 2015. [104]

"The 'attack surface' in which anybody — a state or a nonstate actor — can do damage will enormously increase," says former Defense official Nye. Many of the billions of devices connected to the internet "are built not for security but for efficiency," he says.

And while internet-connected devices may not be a security hazard in themselves, they often offer hackers an unprotected entry point. "For a cyberdefender, this means that hackers will not only have three times as many targets — they will also have three times as many vectors from which to attack any given target," James Stavridis, a retired Navy admiral and dean of the Fletcher School of Law and Diplomacy at Tufts University, and Dave Weinstein, New Jersey's chief technology officer, wrote last year. "This creates vast new challenges for network security and complicates the already murky legal and technical landscape for attributing who is responsible for an attack." [105]

In August, Sens. Mark R. Warner, D-Va., Cory Gardner, R-Col., Ron Wyden, D-Ore., and Steve Daines, R-Mont., introduced legislation that would require vendors who supply the U.S. government with internet-connected devices to ensure that their software can be patched if vulnerabilities are found, that the devices do not include passwords that can't be changed, and that they are free of security flaws. The bill was referred to the Senate Homeland Security and Governmental Affairs Committee on Aug. 1. It had not signed up additional cosponsors as of Sept. 29. [106]

Nicholas Weaver, a lecturer in computer science at the University of California, Berkeley, said the bill ideally will create standards that all internet-connected devices — not just those used by the government — will follow. [107]

Stavridis and Weinstein say much more needs to be done, such as requiring that internet-connected devices automatically update their security software. "First, we need to require higher levels of security in any device that will be connected to the Web," they wrote. "Second, we need better technology to manage in real time the vulnerability of Internet of Things devices." [108]

The two said consumers need to play a role. "[W]e all have to recognize that we have a broad responsibility to protect the internet as consumers of it. While it's easy to place blame on device manufacturers, in the end, perhaps the more appropriate culprit is the user." [109] ∎

OUTLOOK

Securing State Elections

Russia's meddling in last year's presidential election has focused the attention of state election officials and congressional lawmakers on making sure voting systems are secure in time for next year's elections.

Officials in many states say the federal government should provide money to help states strengthen election security or replace voting machines. "If we want to enhance people's confidence in our elections, Congress absolutely should secure funding for the modernization and securing of voting systems," said Nicole Lagace, communications director for Rhode Island's Department of State.

But officials in other states say they don't need federal help to solve their voting problems, citing a desire to avoid government bureaucracy. [110]

As cyberattacks by other nations, rogue states and criminals increase, cybersecurity experts say private-sector computer networks must be protected, but many say legislation is not the answer.

"Cyber changes so quickly that if we can actually get a bill passed in Congress and signed by the president, it will be outdated by the time it goes into effect," says Maness at the Naval Postgraduate School. "The private sector taking care of its own will probably be the faster and more efficient way."

Some legislators have proposed allowing companies to "hack back" against attackers to deter future attacks. More than one-third of companies said in a survey that they responded in kind to hacking attacks, even though doing so is illegal in the United States. [111]

In 2013, Microsoft and several other major corporations joined forces, with court approval, to disable a large cluster of hijacked computers being used for online crime. [112]

Jeremy Rabkin, a law professor at George Mason University in Fairfax, Va., has argued for letting federal officials approve a list of cybersecurity firms that private companies could hire to retaliate for hacking attacks. [113]

"That's a bit too much of the Wild West for me," says Arquilla of the Naval Postgraduate School. "We don't want to start a whole business of privateering in cyberspace. Things are already close to out of hand."

Other cybersecurity experts say the government needs to force companies, through regulation, to secure their computer networks. "The United States should continue to improve its regulation and oversight of the development and adoption of new software and technologies," political scientists Chad C. Serena and Colin P. Clarke at the RAND Corp. think tank wrote last year. "Networks and many of their components are inherently and increasingly insecure." [114]

Arquilla disagrees with proposals to impose government regulation on private-sector cybersecurity, saying encryption is the key to security in cyberspace. "Creating Maginot Lines around the military information infrastructure is not the answer," he says. "Expect bad guys to get into systems but make sure they can't do much damage once they are in."

He also advocates storing critical data in the cloud, or remote computer servers that are accessed online. That way, he says, the data is scattered among different servers rather than sitting in one location that hackers can target.

"We are married to a paradigm of cybersecurity based on [antivirus software] and firewalls," Arquilla says. "The problem, of course, is that antivirus programs only recognize what they already know, and good hackers just walk right through firewalls. I think we need a paradigm shift." ■

Notes

[1] Nicole Perlroth, Mark Scott and Sheera Frenkel, "Cyberattack Hits Ukraine Then Spreads Internationally," *The New York Times*, June 27, 2017, https://tinyurl.com/y7kyr2wm; M. Deleon, "NotPetya Ransomware Disrupts Merck Vaccine Production," University of Hawai'i West O'ahu Cyber Security Coordination Center, Aug. 4, 2017, https://tinyurl.com/y8o7674n.

[2] Luke Graham, "NATO think-tank says a 'state actor' was behind the massive ransomware attack and could trigger military response," CNBC, July 7, 2017, https://tinyurl.com/y73vhbph.

[3] *Ibid.*; Jack Stubbs, Matthias Williams, "Ukraine scrambles to contain new cyber threat after 'NotPetya' attack," Reuters, July 5, 2017, https://tinyurl.com/ycbzwx8u.

[4] Andy Greenberg, "'Crash Override': The Malware That Took Down a Power Grid," *Wired*, June 12, 2017, https://tinyurl.com/y7qdudt9; Lorenzo Franceschi-Bicchierai, "The History of Stuxnet: The World's First True Cyberweapon," *Motherboard*, Aug. 9, 2016, https://tinyurl.com/y7wk224c.

[5] Aaron Boyd, "DNI Clapper: Cyber bigger threat than terrorism," *Federal Times*, Feb. 4, 2016, https://tinyurl.com/ycqh5qm3.

[6] Ian Sherr, "WannaCry ransomware: Everything you need to know," CNET, May 19, 2017, https://tinyurl.com/mmlznxl; Testimony of Gordon M. Snow before the Senate Judiciary Subcommittee on Crime and Terrorism, April 12, 2011, https://tinyurl.com/y8rky8ey.

[7] "Ukraine power cut 'was cyber-attack,'" BBC, Jan. 11, 2017, https://tinyurl.com/ycmo9cu2; Jackie Wattles and Jill Disis, "Ransomware attack: Who's been hit," CNN, May 15, 2017, https://tinyurl.com/y9sgabhk; Andy Greenberg, "How An Entire Nation Became Russia's Test Lab For Cyberwar," *Wired*, June 20, 2017, https://tinyurl.com/y9gx5thj; Natalia Zinets, "Ukraine hit by 6,500 hack attacks, sees Russian 'cyberwar,'" Reuters, Dec. 29, 2016, https://tinyurl.com/ya5onol4.

[8] Elizabeth Dwoskin, Adam Entous and Karoun Demirjian, "Twitter finds hundreds of accounts tied to Russian operatives," *The Washington Post*, Sept. 28, 2017, https://tinyurl.com/y7bkjzhj; Adam Entous, Craig Timberg and Elizabeth Dwoskin, "Russian operatives used Facebook ads to exploit America's racial and religious divisions," *The Washington Post*, Sept. 25, 2017, https://tinyurl.com/ybf22uh2; Adam Entous, Ellen Nakashima and Greg Miller, "Secret CIA assessment says Russia was trying to help Trump win White House," *The Washington Post*, Dec. 9, 2016, https://tinyurl.com/yc27tzml; Scott Shane, "The Fake Americans Russia Created to Influence the Election," *The New York Times*, Sept. 7, 2017, https://tinyurl.com/ybqc4ecx.

[9] Victor Luckerson, "Everything We Know About the Massive Sony Hack," *Time*, Dec. 4, 2014, https://tinyurl.com/lvy3j5m.

[10] Reuters and Libby Plummer, "Nuclear power plants are at risk of Militant Attacks: UN says recent cyber hacks are the 'tip of the iceberg,'" *Daily Mail*, Oct. 10, 2016, https://tinyurl.com/y9lqwsut.

[11] David Livingstone, "Cyber Security at Civil Nuclear Facilities: Understanding the Risks," Chatham House, Oct. 5, 2015, https://tinyurl.com/pj5cds3.

[12] Thomas Grove, Julian E. Barnes and Drew Hinshaw, "Russia Targets NATO Soldier Smartphones, Western Officials Say," *The Wall Street Journal*, Oct. 4, 2017, https://tinyurl.com/y82qpbcr.

[13] James R. Clapper, Marcel Lettre, Michael S. Rogers, "Joint Statement for the Record to the Senate Armed Services Committee: Foreign Cyber Threats to the United States," Jan. 5, 2017, http://tinyurl.com/ycemrq46.

[14] Bruce G. Blair, "Why Our Nuclear Weapons Can Be Hacked," *The New York Times*, March 14, 2017, https://tinyurl.com/y9n8bc6a.

[15] David Hambling, "Ships fooled in GPS spoofing attack suggest Russian cyberweapon," *New Scientist*, Aug. 10, 2017, https://tinyurl.com/ycuzl3pz; Mark L. Psiaki and Todd E. Humphreys, "Protecting GPS From Spoofers Is Critical to the Future of Navigation," *IEEE Spectrum*, July 29, 2016, https://tinyurl.com/y97z6vmz.

[16] "Department of Defense: Actions Needed to Address Five Key Mission Challenges," Government Accountability Office, June 2017, p. 2, https://tinyurl.com/y7jep8rb.

[17] Renae Merle, "SEC reveals it was hacked, information may have been used for illegal stock trades," *The Washington Post*, Sept. 20, 2017, https://tinyurl.com/ydarfzaz; Riley Walters, "Cyber Attacks on U.S. Companies in 2016," The Heritage Foundation, Dec. 2, 2016, https://tinyurl.com/ybnf5kv6.

[18] "Information Security: Agencies Need to Improve Controls over Selected High-Impact Systems," Government Accountability Office, May 2016, https://tinyurl.com/ya5xycwj.

[19] "The Hiscox Cyber Readiness Report 2017," Hiscox Insurance Company, undated, https://tinyurl.com/yc43xxws.

[20] Martin Matishak, "Trump elevates U.S. Cyber Command, vows 'increased resolve' against threats," *Politico*, Aug. 18, 2017, https://tinyurl.com/y9b3ene5.

[21] Thomas Gibbons-Neff and Ellen Nakashima, "President Trump announces move to elevate Cyber Command," *The Washington Post*, Aug. 18, 2017, https://tinyurl.com/y7cxtj57.

[22] Saba Hamedy, "Trump: Russian meddling story an 'excuse' for why Democrats lost," CNN, May 12, 2017, https://tinyurl.com/ycyzt9ax.

[23] Ken Dilanian, Hallie Jackson, Likhitha Butchireddygari and Gabriela Martinez, "Trump White House Has Taken Little Action To Stop Next Election Hack," NBC News, June 24, 2017, https://tinyurl.com/ybwop5fv.

[24] Sean D. Carberry, "I think we need to throw a few stones," Federal Computer Week, May 12, 2017, https://tinyurl.com/yakjtv5t.

[25] Clapper, Lettre and Rogers, *op. cit.*

[26] Ellen Nakashima, "Russia has developed a cyberweapon that can disrupt power grids, according to new research," *The Washington Post*, June 12, 2017, https://tinyurl.com/yb8r6ytt.

[27] "Industrial cybersecurity treat landscape in H1 2017: Every third ICS computer under attack was from manufacturing sector," Kaspersky Lab, Sept. 28, 2017, https://tinyurl.com/y9fmc678.

[28] Dustin Volz, "Trump bars US government from using Russian cybersecurity firm Kaspersky," Reuters, Sept. 14, 2017, https://tinyurl.com/ybegkrda.

[29] John Markoff, "Before the Gunfire, Cyber-attacks," *The New York Times*, Aug. 12, 2008, https://tinyurl.com/yblvebvo.

[30] Brian R. Moore and Jonathan R. Corrado, "North Korea Proves You Barely Need Computers to Win a Cyberwar," *Foreign Policy*, June 5, 2017, https://tinyurl.com/ybgzlt4c.

[31] "Cyber Warfare in the 21st Century: Threats, Challenges, and Opportunities," testimony of Jason Healey before the House Armed Services Committee, March 1, 2017, https://tinyurl.com/yamylzmh; Nicole Perlroth and Quentin Hardy, "Bank Hacking Was the Work of Iranians, Officials Say," *The New York Times*, Jan. 8, 2013, https://tinyurl.com/y9z3qfx8.

[32] John Arquilla, "Cyberwar Is Already Upon Us," *Foreign Policy*, Feb. 27, 2012, https://tinyurl.com/ycwlwz6m.

[33] "2015 DoD Cyber Strategy," Defense Department, April 2015, p. 5, https://tinyurl.com/ya42y7g7.

[34] *Ibid.*

[35] Ron Lieber and Stacy Cowley, "Trying to Stem Fallout From Breach, Equifax Replaces C.E.O.," *The New York Times*, Sept. 26, 2017, https://tinyurl.com/yck7cvtx; Elizabeth Weise and Nathan Bomey,"Equifax had patch 2 months before hack and didn't install it, security group says," *USA Today*, Sept. 14, 2017, https://tinyurl.com/y7t54ywy; Elizabeth Weise and Nathan Bomey, "Equifax breach hit 2.5 million more Americans than first believed," *USA Today*, Oct. 2, 2017, https://tinyurl.com/yaosx287.

[36] Brittany De Lea, "SEC breach can jeopardize trillions of dollars of wealth, cybersecurity expert warns," Fox Business, Sept. 21, 2017, https://tinyurl.com/yckyhksd; Jay Clayton, "Statement on Cybersecurity," Securities and Exchange Commission, Sept. 20, 2017, https://tinyurl.com/y7gtcdr7.

[37] "2016 Presidential Campaign Hacking Fast Facts," CNN, Aug. 6, 2017, https://tinyurl.com/had4auj.

[38] Nicole Perlroth, "All 3 Billion Yahoo Accounts Were Affected by 2013 Attack," *The New York Times*, Oct. 3, 2017, https://tinyurl.com/yd79ymcf; Robert McMillan, "Yahoo Says Information on

at Least 500 Million User Accounts Was Stolen," *The Wall Street Journal*, Sept. 22, 2016, https://tinyurl.com/y7fxhacz.

[39] Vindu Goel and Eric Lichtblau, "Russian Agents were Behind Yahoo Hack, U.S. Says," *The New York Times*, March 15, 2017, https://tinyurl.com/yawv3sdq; Perlroth, *op. cit.*

[40] "Report on Securing and Growing the Digital Economy," Commission on Enhancing National Cybersecurity, Dec. 1, 2016, p. 7, https://tinyurl.com/y8rl9oh5.

[41] Ann M. Beauchesne, "More Regulation Isn't the Answer," *The New York Times*, Oct. 18, 2012, https://tinyurl.com/y7emxwv5.

[42] Shane Harris, @*War: The Rise of the Military-Internet Complex* (2014), p. xxi; Tom McCarthy, "NSA director defends plan to maintain 'backdoors' into technology companies," *The Guardian*, Feb. 23, 2015, https://tinyurl.com/ybctd7y6.

[43] "Vulnerabilities Equities Process," Electronic Privacy Information Center, undated, https://tinyurl.com/y8qq7b2v.

[44] "Why 27% of U.S. Firms Have No Plans to Buy Cyber Insurance," *Insurance Journal*, May 31, 2017, https://tinyurl.com/y7zhzvb9.

[45] Roger A. Grimes, "Vendors should not be liable for their security flaws," CSO, July 12, 2012, https://tinyurl.com/y8tyg9wg.

[46] Brad Smith, "The need for a Digital Geneva Convention," Microsoft blog, Feb. 14, 2017, https://tinyurl.com/hxg3w8b.

[47] *Ibid.*

[48] James Carlini, "Geneva Convention in Cyberwarfare? Don't Count on It," *International Policy Digest*, Aug. 6, 2017, https://tinyurl.com/yd2pqt3d.

[49] "Cyber War: Definitions, Deterrence and Foreign Policy," testimony of James A. Lewis before the House Foreign Affairs Committee, Sept. 30, 2015, https://tinyurl.com/ycs97wpu.

[50] Morgan Chalfant, "Legislators grapple with cyber war rules," *The Hill*, March 1, 2017, https://tinyurl.com/yanglsyc.

[51] Michael N. Schmitt and Liis Vihul, "Respect for Sovereignty in Cyberspace," *Texas Law Review*, Aug. 12, 2017, https://tinyurl.com/y9vcrvmb.

[52] Kalev Leetaru, "Is It Hypocritical To Charge

Russia For Hacking Yahoo When The US Does The Same Thing?" *Forbes*, March 16, 2017, https://tinyurl.com/y7y4rvpg.

[53] Everett Rosenfeld, "US-China agree to not conduct cybertheft of intellectual property," CNBC, Sept. 25, 2015, https://tinyurl.com/y8b77n2l.

[54] Franz-Stefan Gady, "Top US Spy Chief: China Still Successful in Cyber Espionage Against US," *The Diplomat*, Feb. 16, 2016, https://tinyurl.com/yctttoz2.

[55] Shannon Tiezzi, "China Decries US 'Hypocrisy' on Cyber-Espionage," *The Diplomat*, March 28, 2014, https://tinyurl.com/yalsx9ya.

[56] Clifford Stoll, *The Cuckoo's Egg* (1989), p. 3.

[57] Timothy B. Lee, "How a grad student trying to build the first botnet brought the Internet to its knees," *The Washington Post*, Nov. 1, 2013, https://tinyurl.com/yb24zlcb.

[58] *Ibid.*

[59] "30 years of risky business: A cybersecurity timeline," *Government Computer News*, June 3, 2013, https://tinyurl.com/ycj2pgdo.

[60] Adam Segal, *The Hacked World Order: How Nations Fight, Trade, Maneuver, and Manipulate in the Digital Age* (2016), p. 95.

[61] Frontline, "The Warnings?" PBS, April 24, 2003, https://tinyurl.com/2oy2g.

[62] *Ibid.*

[63] *Ibid.*

[64] "The Clinton Administration's Policy on Critical Infrastructure Protection: Presidential Decision Directive 63," The White House, May 22, 1998, https://tinyurl.com/ybrb9pdf.

[65] Frontline, *op. cit.*

[66] "The National Strategy to Secure Cyberspace," Department of Homeland Security, February 2003, https://tinyurl.com/hzplmb3.

[67] Harris, *op. cit.*, p. 25.

[68] *Ibid.*, Segal, p. 18.

[69] Damien McGuinness, "How a cyber attack transformed Estonia," BBC, April 27, 2017, https://tinyurl.com/y7fen2zx; Segal, *op. cit.*, p. 60.

[70] *Ibid.*, Segal, p. 67.

[71] "U.S. Cyber Command (USCYBERCOM)," U.S. Strategic Command, Sept. 30, 2016, https://tinyurl.com/ycaf244w.

[72] Kim Zetter, "Google Hack Attack Was Ultra Sophisticated, New Details Show," *Wired*, Jan. 14, 2010, https://tinyurl.com/y7ykf4kc.

[73] Alina Selyukh, "Long Before 'WannaCry' Ransomware, Decades Of Cyber 'Wake-Up Calls,' " NPR, May 16, 2017, https://tinyurl.com/ybe5lcks.

[74] Ellen Nakashima and Joby Warrick, "Stuxnet was work of U.S. and Israeli experts, officials say," *The Washington Post*, June 2, 2012, https://tinyurl.com/ybnndqql.

[75] *Ibid.*

About the Author

Patrick Marshall, a freelance policy and technology writer in Seattle, is a technology columnist for *The Seattle Times* and *Government Computer News*. He has a bachelor's degree in anthropology from the University of California, Santa Cruz, and a master's degree in international studies from the Fletcher School of Law and Diplomacy at Tufts University.

[76] Segal, *op. cit.*, p. 124.

[77] Ellen Nakashima, "Newly identified computer virus, used for spying, is 20 times size of Stuxnet," *The Washington Post*, May 28, 2012, https://tinyurl.com/yaf9fbpq.

[78] Testimony of Dean Turner before the Senate Committee on Homeland Security and Governmental Affairs, Symantec, Nov. 17, 2010, https://tinyurl.com/yb3k96xu.

[79] Segal, *op. cit.*, p. 5.

[80] *Ibid.*, p. 6.

[81] Sydney J. Freedberg Jr., "Top Official Admits F-35 Stealth Fighter Secrets Stolen," *Breaking Defense*, June 20, 2013, https://tinyurl.com/m3z9opn.

[82] Harris, *op. cit.*, p. xv.

[83] *Ibid.*, p. 70.

[84] *Ibid.*, p. 74.

[85] *Ibid.*, p. 54.

[86] Segal, *op. cit.*, p. 51.

[87] David E. Sanger and Nicole Perlroth, "Senate Approves a Cybersecurity Bill Long in the Works and Largely Dated," *The New York Times*, Oct. 27, 2015, https://tinyurl.com/y83kldvf.

[88] Holly Williams, "Russian hacks into Ukraine power grids a sign of things to come for U.S.?," CBS, Dec. 21, 2016, https://tinyurl.com/y9uhmqw7.

[89] Evan Perez and Theodore Schleifer, "US accuses Russia of trying to interfere with 2016 election," CNN, Oct. 18, 2016, https://tinyurl.com/zlurum7.

[90] Scott Shane and Mike Isaac, "Facebook to Turn Over Russian-Linked Ads to Congress," *The New York Times*, Sept. 21, 2017, https://tinyurl.com/yb8ttspd.

[91] Sari Horwitz, Ellen Nakashima and Matea Gold, "DHS tells states about Russian hacking during 2016 election," *The Washington Post*, Sept. 22, 2017, https://tinyurl.com/ydx9rh3a.

[92] David Jackson and Elizabeth Weise, "President Trump signs cybersecurity executive order," *USA Today*, May 11, 2017, https://tinyurl.com/y94xbe27.

[93] Gibbons-Neff and Nakashima, *op. cit.*

[94] Richard Lardner, "Defense Bill Calls Climate Change a National Security Threat," *US News and World Report*, July 14, 2017, https://tinyurl.com/y9lc9t3s.

[95] Henry Farrell, "Hackers have just dumped a treasure trove of NSA data. Here's what it means," *The Washington Post*, April 15, 2017, https://tinyurl.com/ycofutmb; Andy Greenberg, "The Shadow Brokers Mess Is What Happens When the NSA Hoards Zero-Days," *Wired*, Aug. 17, 2016, https://tinyurl.com/gv8ebm5.

[96] *Ibid.*

[97] David E. Sanger, "Obama Lets N.S.A. Exploit Some Internet Flaws, Officials Say," *The New York Times*, April 12, 2014, https://tinyurl.com/ybuj7xeu.

[98] Harris, *op. cit.*, p. 96.

[99] *Ibid.*, p. 94.

[100] *Ibid.*, p. 95.

[101] Sean D. Carberry, "What the PATCH Act doesn't do," *Federal Computer Week*, May 26, 2017, https://tinyurl.com/ybhmy4ea.

[102] Chris Bing, "Lawmakers introduce bill to shine spotlight on government hacking stockpile," *Cyberscoop*, May 18, 2017, https://tinyurl.com/y7dpeezk.

[103] Nicole Perlroth and David E. Sanger, "Hacks Raise Fear Over N.S.A.'s Hold on Cyberweapons," *The New York Times*, June 28, 2017, https://tinyurl.com/ybkt4gwv.

[104] "Here's how the Internet of Things will explode by 2020," *Business Insider*, Aug. 31, 2016, https://tinyurl.com/z3q7ow7.

[105] James Stavridis and Dave Weinstein, "The Internet of Things Is a Cyberwar Nightmare," *Foreign Policy*, Nov. 3, 2016, https://tinyurl.com/y9pvcdab.

[106] Bruce Sterling, "Spime Watch: The Fact Sheet For The Internet Of Things Cybersecurity Improvement Act Of 2017," *Wired*, Aug. 11, 2017, https://tinyurl.com/ycanztel; "S.1691 — Internet of Things (IoT) Cybersecurity Improvement Act of 2017," congress.gov, undated, https://tinyurl.com/ybxxof8l.

[107] Nicholas Weaver, "The Internet of Things Cybersecurity Improvement Act: A Good Start on IoT Security," *Lawfare*, Aug. 2, 2017, https://tinyurl.com/ya6exmah.

[108] Stavridis and Weinstein, *op. cit.*

[109] *Ibid.*

[110] Cory Bennett *et al.*, "Cash-strapped states brace for Russian hacking fight," *Politico*, Sept. 3, 2017, https://tinyurl.com/ybttxsom.

[111] Segal, *op. cit.*, p. 17.

[112] Harris, *op. cit.*, p. 118.

[113] Josephine Wolff, "When Companies Get Hacked, Should They Be Allowed to Hack Back?" *The Atlantic*, July 14, 2017, https://tinyurl.com/yau2ubeu.

[114] Chad C. Serena and Colin P. Clarke, "America's Cyber Security Dilemma — and a Way Out," *Defense One*, Dec. 22, 2016, https://tinyurl.com/zdtnpsv.

FOR MORE INFORMATION

Alliance for Securing Democracy, 1744 R St., N.W., Washington, DC 20009; 202-683-2650; securingdemocracy.gmfus.org. Bipartisan, transatlantic group that works to expose Russia's "ongoing efforts to subvert democracy in the United States and Europe."

American Civil Liberties Union, 125 Broad St., 18th Floor, New York, NY 10004; 212-549-2500; www.aclu.org. Nonprofit organization that defends individual rights and civil liberties guaranteed by the Constitution and U.S. law.

Council on Foreign Relations, 58 East 68th St., New York, NY 10065; 212-434-9400; www.cfr.org. Nonpartisan think tank focused on foreign policy choices facing the United States and other countries.

Cyber Security Division (Department of Homeland Security), 3801 Nebraska Ave., N.W., Washington, DC 20016; 202-282-8000; www.dhs.gov/science-and-technology/cyber-security-division. Formed in 2010 to defend U.S. computer networks against cyber-attacks.

Electronic Privacy Information Center, 1718 Connecticut Ave., N.W., Suite 200, Washington, DC 20009; 202-483-1140; www.epic.org. Public interest research center that works to protect individuals' privacy rights and civil liberties in the internet age.

New America, 740 15th St., N.W., Suite 900, Washington, DC 20005; 202-986-2700; www.newamerica.org. Left-of-center think tank focused on technology and public policy.

Office of Cyber and Infrastructure Analysis (Department of Homeland Security), 300 7th St., S.W., Washington, DC 20024; 202-282-8000; www.dhs.gov/office-cyber-infrastructure-analysis. Responsible for providing analysis to help U.S. officials protect critical infrastructure from cyberattacks.

U.S. Naval War College, 686 Cushing Road, Newport, RI 02841-1207; 401-841-1310; www.usnwc.edu. Simulates cyberwar to build analytical, strategic and decision-making skills and prepare military leaders for disaster scenarios.

Bibliography

Selected Sources

Books

Harris, Shane, @War: The Rise of the Military Internet Program, Mariner Books, 2014.

A senior writer at *The Wall Street Journal* recounts the development of America's cyber weapons and defenses, and explains the close ties between government and the private sector on cybersecurity issues.

Mazanec, Brian M., *The Evolution of Cyber War: International Norms for Emerging-Technology Weapons*, University of Nebraska Press, 2015.

A George Mason University adjunct professor of policy and government examines global norms for cyberwar and recommends that the United States not pursue practices that limit its development of cyberweapons.

Segal, Adam, *The Hacked World Order: How Nations Fight, Trade, Maneuver, and Manipulate in the Digital Age*, PublicAffairs, 2016.

The director of the Digital and Cyberspace Policy Program at the Council on Foreign Relations think tank argues that because it is difficult to pinpoint where digital attacks originate and to measure their impact, international rules of engagement in cyberspace must be reworked.

Articles

Jensen, Benjamin, Brandon Valeriano and Ryan C. Maness, "Cyberwarfare has taken a new turn. Yes, it's time to worry," *The Washington Post*, July 13, 2017, https://tinyurl.com/yd8247wd.

Three cybersecurity professors at military universities, two of whom have previously described cyberthreats as overblown, explain why they are now worried about these threats.

Moore, Brian R., and Jonathan R. Corrado, "North Korea Proves You Barely Need Computers to Win a Cyberwar," *Foreign Policy*, June 5, 2017, https://tinyurl.com/ybgzlt4c.

Two Asia specialists argue that the relative ease of developing cyberweapons gives outsized power to underdeveloped, isolated nations such as North Korea that have few cybertargets to defend.

Riley, Michael, Jordan Robertson and Anita Sharpe, "The Equifax Hack Has the Hallmarks of State-Sponsored Pros," *Bloomberg*, Sept. 29, 2017, https://tinyurl.com/yakbka44.

The hackers who stole massive amounts of data from the Equifax credit reporting agency showed a level of sophistication that suggests they were sponsored by a foreign government, but investigators are divided on whether China is the most likely culprit.

Serena, Chad C., and Colin P. Clarke, "America's Cyber Security Dilemma — and a Way Out," *Defense One*, Dec. 22, 2016, https://tinyurl.com/zdtnpsv.

Two RAND Corp. analysts say the United States should lead the way in forging international cybersecurity practices and find ways to rapidly determine the source of cyberattacks.

Stavridis, James, and Dave Weinstein, "The Internet of Things Is a Cyberwar Nightmare," *Foreign Policy*, Nov. 3, 2016, https://tinyurl.com/y9pvcdab.

A retired admiral and dean of the Fletcher School of Law and Diplomacy at Tufts University (Stavridis) and New Jersey's chief technology officer (Weinstein) argue that the emerging network of internet-connected devices will lead to unprecedented cybersecurity challenges.

Wolff, Josephine, "When Companies Get Hacked, Should They Be Allowed to Hack Back?" *The Atlantic*, July 14, 2017, https://tinyurl.com/yau2ubeu.

An assistant professor public policy at the Rochester Institute of Technology says that allowing companies targeted by hackers to respond in kind would make it harder to tell good actors from bad on the internet.

Reports and Studies

"Critical Infrastructure Protection: Sector-Specific Agencies Need to Better Measure Cybersecurity Progress," U.S. Government Accountability Office, November 2015, https://tinyurl.com/yasqdqbt.

The investigative arm of Congress says it found significant cyber-related risks at 11 of 15 federal agencies it audited between June 2014 and November 2015.

"Department of Defense: Actions Needed to Address Five Key Mission Challenges," U.S. Government Accountability Office, June 2017, https://tinyurl.com/y7jep8rb.

The GAO says the vulnerability of Defense Department computer networks has grown "significantly" as the department has become more dependent on the internet.

"The Department of Defense Cyber Strategy," U.S. Department of Defense, April 2015, https://tinyurl.com/ya42y7g7.

The Defense Department's most recent explanation of its strategy for strengthening cyber defenses discusses three primary missions: defending military networks and information, defending the country against cyberattacks and developing offensive cyber capabilities.

Davis, John S. II, *et al.*, "Stateless Attribution: Toward International Accountability in Cyberspace," RAND Corp., 2017, https://tinyurl.com/y9axtesl.

Analysts at the nonpartisan think tank evaluate options for attributing cyberattacks to specific individuals or groups in a "standardized and transparent" way that make the attribution credible to the public.

The Next Step:

Additional Articles from Current Periodicals

Digital Security

Hay Newman, Lily, "The U.S. Give Cyber Command the Status It Deserves," *Wired*, Aug. 19, 2017, https://tinyurl.com/yb3pd97b.

To strengthen the nation's cybersecurity, a Trump administration directive elevated the U.S. Cyber Command, a division of the National Security Agency, to a unified military command.

Sebenius, Alyza, "Writing the Rules of Cyberwar," *The Atlantic*, June 28, 2017, https://tinyurl.com/yb62jkc9.

The distinction between offensive and defensive measures is hard to define when it comes to cybersecurity, says a postdoctoral Harvard fellow in his book, *The Cybersecurity Dilemma*.

Tucker, Patrick, "For the US Army, 'Cyber War' Is Quickly Becoming Just 'War,' " *Defense One*, Feb. 9, 2017, https://tinyurl.com/yay4als5.

By the end of the year the Army aims to have 41 cyber teams fully operational to help soldiers on the battlefield and disrupt enemy operations.

Foreign Threats

Bing, Chris, "Why the U.S. is struggling with the digital war on ISIS," *CyberScoop*, June 14, 2017, https://tinyurl.com/yczwsnff.

The Islamic State is proving to be an elusive cyber foe for the U.S. military because it uses computers not for weapons systems but to recruit, coordinate and raise money, experts say.

Delcker, Janosch, "A hacked-off Germany hacks back," *Politico*, May 23, 2017, https://tinyurl.com/y9ze3w3w.

Germany embraced an aggressive, combative approach to cyberattacks after hackers infiltrated its parliamentary computer network for several weeks in 2015.

Greenberg, Andy, "How an Entire Nation Became Russia's Test Lab for Cyberwar," *Wired*, June 20, 2017, https://tinyurl.com/y9gx5thj.

In 2015 Russia demonstrated it could cut off electricity for almost a quarter-million Ukrainians by hacking into their power grid.

International Cooperation

"EU Defense Ministers Hold Cyberwar Game In Tallinn," *Radio Free Europe, Radio Liberty*, Sept. 7, 2017, https://tinyurl.com/y9dzosyz.

European Union defense ministers participated in a simulated exercise to counter hackers who had crippled the command of a naval mission.

Cohen, Jared, "How to Prevent a Cyberwar," *The New York Times*, Aug. 11, 2017, https://tinyurl.com/yd3hryyh.

World leaders need to establish laws against cyberattacks, says an adjunct senior fellow at the Council on Foreign Relations.

Simonite, Tom, "Do We Need a Digital Geneva Convention?" *MIT Technology Review*, Feb. 15, 2017, https://tinyurl.com/zv6wg3d.

Microsoft President Brad Smith argues an international digital treaty is needed to protect citizens and private companies from hacking by nation-states.

Private-Sector Security

Chertoff, Philip, "Why the U.S. Government Shouldn't Ban Kapersky Security Software," *Wired*, Sept. 4, 2017, https://tinyurl.com/y7foabcx.

A cybersecurity analyst says barring U.S. government agencies from using software produced by Kapersky Lab, a Russia-based security vendor, would have a chilling effect on government contractors and consumers.

Schwartz, Mattathias, "Cyberwar for Sale," *The New York Times Magazine*, Jan. 4, 2017, https://tinyurl.com/yah9cuxy.

Private surveillance firms face few trade controls, and their software is available not only to large governments but also to any party with the money to buy it.

Uchill, Joe, "White House advisory group raises cybersecurity concerns," *The Hill*, Aug. 22, 2017, https://tinyurl.com/yatmr7gx.

The National Infrastructure Advisory Council said federal agencies and private-sector firms are collectively capable of protecting government infrastructure from hacking but are hindered by bureaucratic hurdles.

In-depth Reports on Issues in the News

Are you writing a paper?

Need backup for a debate?

Want to become an expert on an issue?

For 90 years, students have turned to *CQ Researcher* for in-depth reporting on issues in the news. Reports on a full range of political and social issues are now available. Following is a selection of recent reports:

Civil Liberties
Privacy and the Internet, 12/15
Intelligence Reform, 5/15
Religion and Law, 11/14

Crime/Law
High-Tech Policing, 4/17
Forensic Science Controversies, 2/17
Jailing Debtors, 9/16
Decriminalizing Prostitution, 4/16
Restorative Justice, 2/16
The Dark Web, 1/16
Immigrant Detention, 10/15

Education
Charter Schools, 3/17
Civic Education, 2/17
Student Debt, 11/16
Apprenticeships, 10/16

Environment/Society
Climate Change and National Security, 9/17
Muslims in America, 7/17
Funding the Arts, 7/17
Hunger in America, 7/17
Future of the Christian Right, 6/17
Trust in Media, 6/17

Health/Safety
Medical Breakthroughs, 9/17
Medical Marijuana, 7/17
Food Labeling, 6/17
Sports and Sexual Assault, 4/17

Politics/Economy
Think Tanks in Transition, 9/17
Universal Basic Income, 9/17
National Debt, 9/17
North Korea Showdown, 5/17
Rethinking Foreign Aid, 4/17
Immigrants and the Economy, 2/17

Upcoming Reports

Future of the Democratic Party, 10/13/17   Democracies, 10/20/17   Sexual Harrassment, 10/27/17

ACCESS

CQ Researcher is available in print and online. For access, visit your library or www.cqresearcher.com.

STAY CURRENT

For notice of upcoming *CQ Researcher* reports or to learn more about *CQ Researcher* products, subscribe to the free email newsletters, *CQ Researcher Alert!* and *CQ Researcher News*: http://cqpress.com/newsletters.

PURCHASE

To purchase a *CQ Researcher* report in print or electronic format (PDF), visit www.cqpress.com or call 866-427-7737. Single reports start at $15. Bulk purchase discounts and electronic-rights licensing are also available.

SUBSCRIBE

Annual full-service *CQ Researcher* subscriptions—including 44 reports a year, monthly index updates, and a bound volume—start at $1,131. Add $25 for domestic postage.

CQ Researcher Online offers a backfile from 1991 and a number of tools to simplify research. For pricing information, call 800-818-7243 or 805-499-9774 or email librarysales@sagepub.com.

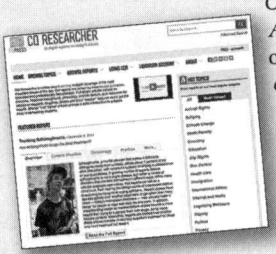

CQ RESEARCHER

CQPRESS

In-depth reports on today's issues

Published by CQ Press, an Imprint of SAGE Publications, Inc.   **www.cqresearcher.com**

Future of the Democratic Party

Can it stage a comeback?

After disastrous losses in the 2016 elections, Democrats are shut out of power in Congress, the White House and 23 states, and party strategists are locked in a fierce debate over how to reverse those defeats. The party's most liberal wing says Democrats must energize their base by moving further left and embracing universal health care and other ideas that Sen. Bernie Sanders, a self-described democratic socialist, proposed during his strong 2016 run for the presidential nomination. But moderate Democrats counter that the party must broaden its support by attracting white working-class voters who helped elect President Trump. Yet others, pointing to weaknesses in Hillary Clinton's presidential campaign, argue the party lacks a compelling vision for the United States and cannot win by simply opposing Trump. Meanwhile, as a raft of liberal groups work to elect Democrats on the state and federal levels, party officials are debating whether support for abortion rights should be required of Democratic candidates seeking party endorsement.

Hillary Clinton concedes the presidential election in New York City on Nov. 9, 2016, after her surprising defeat by Republican nominee Donald Trump. To regain power, liberals say Democrats must move further to the left. But moderates say the party must do more to attract white working-class voters who backed Trump.

I N S I D E THIS REPORT

THE ISSUES 847

BACKGROUND 853

CHRONOLOGY 855

CURRENT SITUATION 859

AT ISSUE......................861

OUTLOOK 862

BIBLIOGRAPHY 866

THE NEXT STEP 867

CQ Researcher • Oct. 13, 2017 • www.cqresearcher.com
Volume 27, Number 36 • Pages 845-868

CQ RESEARCHER

Oct. 13, 2017
Volume 27, Number 36

EXECUTIVE EDITOR: Thomas J. Billitteri
tjb@sagepub.com

ASSISTANT MANAGING EDITORS: Kenneth Fireman, kenneth.fireman@sagepub.com, Kathy Koch, kathy.koch@sagepub.com, Scott Rohrer, scott.rohrer@sagepub.com

ASSOCIATE MANAGING EDITOR: Val Ellicott

SENIOR CONTRIBUTING EDITOR:
Thomas J. Colin
tom.colin@sagepub.com

CONTRIBUTING WRITERS: Marcia Clemmitt, Sarah Glazer, Alan Greenblatt, Reed Karaim, Barbara Mantel, Patrick Marshall, Tom Price

SENIOR PROJECT EDITOR: Olu B. Davis

EDITORIAL ASSISTANT: Natalia Gurevich

FACT CHECKERS: Eva P. Dasher, Michelle Harris, Betsy Towner Levine, Robin Palmer

SAGE Publishing | CQ PRESS

Los Angeles | London | New Delhi
Singapore | Washington DC | Melbourne

An Imprint of SAGE Publications, Inc.

SENIOR VICE PRESIDENT, GLOBAL LEARNING RESOURCES:
Karen Phillips

EXECUTIVE DIRECTOR, ONLINE LIBRARY AND REFERENCE PUBLISHING:
Todd Baldwin

CQ Researcher (ISSN 1056-2036) is printed on acid-free paper. Published weekly, except: (March wk. 4) (May wk. 4) (July wks. 1, 2) (Aug. wks. 2, 3) (Nov. wk. 4) and (Dec. wks. 3, 4). Published by SAGE Publications, Inc., 2455 Teller Rd., Thousand Oaks, CA 91320. Annual full-service subscriptions start at $1,131. For pricing, call 1-800-818-7243. To purchase a CQ Researcher report in print or electronic format (PDF), visit www.cqpress.com or call 866-427-7737. Single reports start at $15. Bulk purchase discounts and electronic-rights licensing are also available. Periodicals postage paid at Thousand Oaks, California, and at additional mailing offices. POSTMASTER: Send address changes to CQ Research-er, 2600 Virginia Ave., N.W., Suite 600, Washington, DC 20037.

THE ISSUES

847
- Are Democrats moving too far to the left?
- Do Democrats need new leaders?
- Can Democrats win back white working-class voters?

BACKGROUND

853 **Jeffersonian Origins**
The two-party system emerged in the 1790s.

854 **GOP's Electoral "Lock"**
President Ronald Reagan's 1984 re-election sparked discussion of the GOP's Electoral College advantage.

857 **Clinton's Second Defeat**
In 2016 Hillary Clinton won the popular vote but lost the Electoral College.

CURRENT SITUATION

859 **Improving Prospects**
Democrats are pouring money into congressional races.

860 **The 2018 Map**
To regain the House, Democrats must overcome GOP-drawn congressional districts.

860 **Efforts in the States**
Many governorships occupied by Republicans will be up for grabs next year.

OUTLOOK

862 **Culture War?**
Political polarization is not the only obstacle Democrats face.

SIDEBARS AND GRAPHICS

848 **Democrats Suffer Steep Losses in States**
The Democratic Party lost 968 legislative seats during Barack Obama's two presidential terms.

849 **Five Democrats to Watch in the Run-Up to 2020**
Cory Booker and Kamala Harris are among possible White House contenders.

852 **Democrats Struggled in Electoral College**
The geographic distribution of voters presents challenges for Democratic candidates.

855 **Chronology**
Key events since 1964.

856 **Democrats Debate a Litmus Test on Abortion**
"Every Democrat . . . should support a woman's right to make her own choices."

858 **Activists Go to Battle for the Democratic Party**
Some party officials worry they could undercut efforts to regain power.

861 **At Issue:**
Can Democrats win back white working-class voters?

FOR FURTHER RESEARCH

865 **For More Information**
Organizations to contact.

866 **Bibliography**
Selected sources used.

867 **The Next Step**
Additional articles.

867 **Citing CQ Researcher**
Sample bibliography formats.

Cover: Getty Images/Brooks Kraft

Future of the Democratic Party

BY ALAN GREENBLATT

THE ISSUES

Many Democrats believe their time in the wilderness will be short.

Come 2020, a number are hopeful, confident even, that a Democrat can win back the White House, thanks to President Trump's historically low approval ratings and the unending controversies surrounding his presidency. "When Trump got elected, I said, 'For God's sake, take away his phone so he'll stop tweeting,' " says Democratic Connecticut Gov. Dannel Malloy. "Now I say, 'Let's give him more accounts.' "

But some Democratic strategists say such optimism is misguided and stress that the party's problems run much deeper than the losses it suffered in the 2016 elections. "The party needs to get back to the basics of the question, what does it mean to be a Democrat?" says Mo Elleithee, former communications director for the Democratic National Committee (DNC), which supports candidates and formulates strategy.

Shut out from power at the White House, Congress and a majority of states, the Democratic Party is in its worst shape in years. Even if presidential nominee Hillary Clinton had defeated Trump last November, the party would have had to find a way to regain other offices. Yet it is unclear whether Democrats have a clear strategy, beyond opposing Trump, for rebuilding their party, political analysts say.

Democrats, according to party strategists and others, have a number of challenges, including:

• Overcoming internal divisions between liberals and moderates;

Democratic supporter Laura Henderson attends a rally with House and Senate Democrats in Berryville, Va., on July 24, 2017, after party leaders announced "A Better Deal," their plan to increase Americans' wages and create jobs by investing in infrastructure. Through a carefully tailored economic pitch, Democrats hope to regain the votes of blue-collar whites.

Getty Images/CQ Roll Call/Tom Williams

• Broadening their base beyond college-educated whites and racial and ethnic minorities;

• Finding ways to overcome their weaknesses in the Electoral College by attracting support outside the cities and the coasts; and

• Developing a compelling vision for American society.

Democrats must confront "both a messaging and a policy problem," says Lanae Erickson Hatalsky, vice president for the social policy and politics program at Third Way, a centrist Democratic think tank in Washington. "When you talk to people about what Democrats stand for on the economy, they think that their entire program is anti-business

and minimum wage. Raising the minimum wage is popular, but almost no one thinks it will change their lives."

The party is widely perceived as simply anti-Trump. A *Washington Post*/ABC News poll in July found that a majority of people believe the Democratic Party "just stands against Trump," compared with 37 percent who believe the party actually stands for something. [1] Only 28 percent of those surveyed in an April *Washington Post*/ABC News poll thought the party was in touch with the concerns of most Americans. [2]

Of course, the Democrats' plight is not terribly unusual for the party out of power. The Republicans went through much the same thing during Democrat Barack Obama's presidency. With no standard-bearer in the White House, a party often is rudderless, with competing wings debating about who is to blame for electoral setbacks and how to regain voters' favor. [3]

History is repeating itself in 2017 as the Democratic Party struggles to revive its fortunes. Many liberals — or "progressives" as they often prefer to be called — say the party must lay out an agenda that defines Democratic differences with Republicans. For a majority of Democratic senators, that includes supporting a universal health care plan. Others are touting the idea of providing a basic income, guaranteeing all Americans cash support. [4] They also would expand on Clinton's agenda, which included greater rights for immigrants, free community college tuition and stricter gun control.

"Progressives will be playing defense for many years to come," wrote Jared Bernstein, who served as an economist

Democrats Suffer Steep Losses in States

During President Obama's eight years in office, the Democratic Party lost 968 legislative seats — the biggest reversal during any two-term presidency since World War II. As of September, the Republican Party controlled 31 state legislatures.

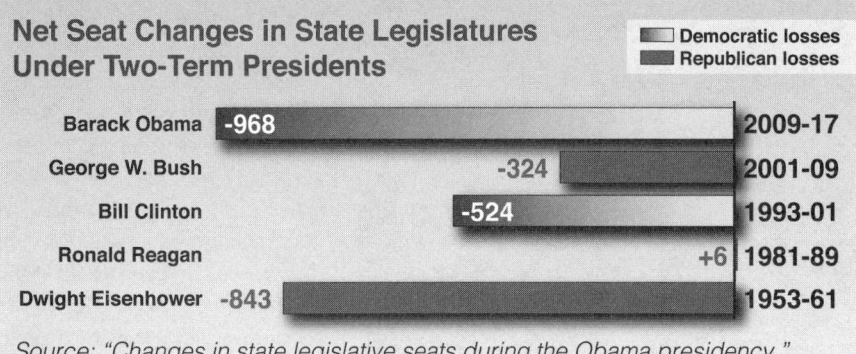

Net Seat Changes in State Legislatures Under Two-Term Presidents

☐ Democratic losses
■ Republican losses

President	Net change	Years
Barack Obama	-968	2009-17
George W. Bush	-324	2001-09
Bill Clinton	-524	1993-01
Ronald Reagan	+6	1981-89
Dwight Eisenhower	-843	1953-61

Source: "Changes in state legislative seats during the Obama presidency," Ballotpedia, Jan. 31, 2017, https://tinyurl.com/y7usbl4a

in the Obama administration. "But let's also make sure we're ready to roll with a true progressive agenda when our time comes." [5]

Elleithee, who is now executive director of the Institute of Politics and Public Service at Georgetown University, says Democratic leaders in Congress are doing what they can to block what they see as the worst GOP excesses, including efforts to roll back parts of the Affordable Care Act. "They've done a good job in coming together in the early days of the Trump administration," he says.

But the party still needs to present a clear sense of how it is going to help the majority of Americans improve their lot in life, he adds. "It's drifted away from having a core theme to becoming a purely coalition party that was speaking to each member of the coalition, African-Americans, Latinos, women and young people and LGBT Americans."

The party's focus on different constituencies, or "identity politics," has become a frequent criticism. Democratic candidates offer a laundry list of proposals aimed at separate groups, such as tuition relief for Millennials or support of Planned Parenthood to appeal to women. This pursuit may have cost Democrats support among the white work-

ing class who had traditionally supported the party, critics of identity politics say.

But even as Democrats try to attract working-class voters, they don't want to alienate members of the demographic groups that have stuck by them, other analysts say. "The fallout among their coalition and the activists they depend on would be huge for Democrats if they were to shift right on things like immigration in a bid to win back some of these Trump voters," says Sam Rosenfeld, a political scientist at Colgate University.

With Trump's victory last fall, Republicans control the White House and both chambers of Congress, while conservatives have a 5-4 majority on the Supreme Court. The GOP dominates state governments as well. Republicans hold 68 of the nation's legislative chambers, having picked up nearly 1,000 seats since the start of Obama's presidency in 2009. (*See graphic, above.*) With the defection of West Virginia Gov. Jim Justice to the GOP on Aug. 3, Democrats are down to just 15 governorships. [6]

"We're at the worst electoral position that the Democratic Party has been in in decades," said Rep. Seth Moulton, D-Mass. "And so when you keep losing like that, you can't keep doing the same old thing." [7]

The party faces a key structural problem: Its voters are concentrated in urban areas, putting the party at a disadvantage in the Electoral College. Indeed, in the 2000 and 2016 elections, the Democratic nominees won the popular vote but lost the presidency because of this geographical imbalance.

In the November election, Clinton carried fewer than 500 counties nationwide out of 3,141. [8] "If more than 50 percent of your '16 voters lived in just nine states," tweeted Dave Wasserman, an election analyst for the *Cook Political Report*, "you're probably not a healthy national party." [9]

Lara Brown, a political scientist at George Washington University, agrees. "If you look at how Democratic progressives are distributed, that's going to keep them in the minority," she says.

"Gerrymandering," the drawing of congressional districts to give one party an advantage over another, adds to Democrats' difficulties. With Republican-dominated legislatures controlling the redistricting process, they have been able to draw district maps that give the GOP big advantages in House contests.

Another key problem is the party's internal divisions that surfaced during the strong run by Sen. Bernie Sanders of Vermont in the 2016 presidential primaries. His supporters and other liberals want to push the party further left and seem uninterested in compromising with more-moderate Democrats. Explaining why some liberals eschew compromise with moderates, Nina Turner, president of Our Revolution, an advocacy group that grew out of Sanders' campaign, said in June, "I don't think it is our job nor our obligation to fit in. It's their job to fit in with us." [10]

Liberals say the party must energize its base by pursuing an aggressive policy agenda. "With its obsessive focus on wooing voters who supported Donald Trump, [the party] is neglecting the cornerstone of its coalition," wrote Steve Phillips, founder of Democracy in Color, a San Francisco-based group that researches race and politics. [11]

But moderates want the party to take centrist positions that will allow it to attract white working-class voters as well as highly educated Republicans in the suburbs who are souring on Trump. "If you just play to your base, that's an electoral dead end," says Evan Bayh, a former Democratic senator from Indiana. "If we make it all or nothing on some of these issues, we're going to end up with nothing. You're only going to win if you find some way to motivate the progressives and at least some of the moderates."

As politicians, pundits and voters ponder the Democrats' future, here are some of the questions they are debating:

Are Democrats moving too far to the left?

On Sept. 13, Sen. Sanders, an independent who was Clinton's chief rival for the Democratic presidential nomination last year, introduced a single-payer health care plan, known as "Medicare for all."

What was once a fringe idea even within Democratic health policy circles appeared to have new momentum, with senators who are considered potential 2020 candidates for president, including Kamala Harris of California and Cory Booker of New Jersey, signing on as co-sponsors. (*See table, right.*) Even more-conservative Democrats such as Sens. Jon Tester of Montana and Joe Manchin of West Virginia said the idea deserved study. "Our view is that within the Democratic Party, this is fast-emerging as a litmus test," said Ben Tulchin, a pollster for Sanders' presidential campaign. [12]

With liberals pushing for true universal health care at a time when Republicans have been attempting to repeal the Affordable Care Act, which relies heavily on government funding to support private insurance plans, some Democrats worried that the Sanders effort threatened to push the party to the left of where most voters are on

Five Democrats to Watch in the Run-Up to 2020

Political observers say the Democratic Party needs dynamic candidates if it is to recapture the White House in 2020. Some see these five politicians as rising stars and potential presidential contenders.

Cory Booker, 48
U.S. senator, New Jersey; former Newark mayor
Strengths: Nearly picked as Hillary Clinton's running mate in 2016, Booker has long been considered an ambitious and talented politician with a strong social media game.
Weaknesses: Some liberals disapprove of his ties to Wall Street or dislike his support for charter schools.

Steve Bullock, 51
Montana governor; former state attorney general
Strengths: Bullock has not only won office in a red state but managed to expand Medicaid and increase higher-education spending. He also is a Washington outsider who could appeal to voters away from the coasts.
Weaknesses: Bullock is little known outside Montana. Also, he opposes liberal priorities such as universal health care and free college tuition.

Kirsten Gillibrand, 50
U.S. senator, New York; former House member
Strengths: Gillibrand champions paid family leave and has taken a leadership role on military and veterans' issues. She has been a fierce Trump critic, particularly regarding his Cabinet appointments.
Weaknesses: She says she is not running. As senator she has fought some Wall Street regulations, and as a House member she took conservative stances on some issues, such as gun owners' rights. But she has voted along liberal lines in the Senate and her "A" rating from the National Rifle Association is now an "F."

Kamala Harris, 52
U.S. senator, California; former state attorney general and San Francisco district attorney
Strengths: Many Democrats admire her outspokenness and say that as an African-American woman she will have great appeal among minorities and women. She holds liberal views on issues such as crime, health care and immigration.
Weaknesses: She was elected to the Senate only last year. Some liberals are unhappy she has accepted campaign contributions from Wall Street donors.

Elizabeth Warren, 68
U.S. senator, Massachusetts; former law professor
Strengths: A powerhouse speaker on liberal causes and an outspoken critic of policies that she says contribute to income inequality, Warren is a hero to many liberals. Her work as an academic led to the creation of the Consumer Financial Protection Bureau.
Weaknesses: Warren will be 71 in 2020, which some critics say is old for a presidential hopeful, and others say she is too controversial to win a general election. She says she is not running.

Getty Images: Win McNamee, William Campbell-Corbis, Mandel Ngan, Michael Kovac, Chip Somodevilla

the issue. Nancy Pelosi, the Democratic leader in the House, declined to endorse the Sanders proposal and said single-payer should not become a litmus test for party politicians. [13]

"If we focus on very, very progressive issues, we risk alienating some voters," says Andrea Dew Steele, president of Emerge America, which recruits and trains female Democratic candidates. "I do worry about our going too far to the left, when we really need to focus on bread-and-butter issues."

Liberal values appear ascendant within the party. According to the Pew Research Center, a nonpartisan think tank in Washington, nearly half of all Democrats — 48 percent — describe themselves as liberal, compared with 36 percent who say they are moderate and 15 percent who consider themselves conservative. By comparison, only 33 percent of Democrats considered themselves liberal in 2008, while 41 percent were self-described moderates and 23 percent conservative. [14]

Energized by Sanders' unexpectedly strong run to Clinton's left last year and angered by the Trump presidency, liberals are demanding that the party follow their lead. "We are not the gate-crashers of today's Democratic Party," Sen. Elizabeth Warren of Massachusetts said at an August gathering of liberals known as Netroots Nation. "We are not a wing of today's Democratic Party. We are the heart and soul of today's Democratic Party."

Liberals maintain that their positions are popular not just among the Democratic Left but the public as a whole. Some recent polls have shown majority support for the single-payer approach. [15] "In general, on economic issues, whether college affordability or minimum wage or universal health care, the American electorate is more progressive than where our politics is now," says Tamara Draut, vice president of policy and research at Demos, a liberal think tank in New York.

Democrats are not moving too far left to win the popular presidential vote,

says Sean Trende, a senior elections analyst with the political website *RealClear-Politics*. But like other observers, Trende warns that the core Democratic vote is poorly distributed in terms of the Electoral College and House districts. And as Steele notes, some issues that play well in liberal coastal cities such as San Francisco may not resonate in the heartland.

Despite the debate between liberals and moderates, Democrats' divide on the issues is not that great, Elleithee says. During last year's campaign, both Clinton and Sanders supported raising the minimum wage, opposed most free-trade deals and backed free college tuition. Sanders wanted a higher minimum wage and more years of free tuition, but their approaches differed in ambition, not direction. "There really aren't ideological differences in the party anymore," Elleithee says. "The policy differences between Clinton and Sanders were a matter of degree."

Similarly, in many of the primary battles already taking place among Democrats, the schism is less about issue positioning than determining whether a candidate is considered too "establishment" and thus is perceived as tainted by long experience, or more of a progressive "outsider." In Minneapolis, the City Council consists of 12 Democrats and one Green Party member and is generally considered a liberal body. Still, left-leaning insurgents are challenging several members of the council and Democratic Mayor Betsy Hodges. "Many of us are facing our own challenges, and they are definitely coming from the left," says council member John Quincy.

But the Democratic Party cannot win by moving further left, warns Third Way's Hatalsky. The good news, from her point of view, is that liberal insurgents tend to lose primary challenges. As Clinton's victory over Sanders showed, there tend to be more moderate voters than far-left liberals.

There is some recent evidence for this argument. This year, the Democratic

nominees in the nation's only two gubernatorial races — Ralph Northam in Virginia and Phil Murphy in New Jersey — are establishment candidates who were able to overcome primary challenges from the left.

Do Democrats need new leaders?

The top Democratic leaders have all been around a long time.

House Minority Leader Pelosi is 77, and the party's other two top House leaders — Minority Whip Steny Hoyer of Maryland and Assistant Minority Leader James Clyburn of South Carolina — are at least that old. Senate Minority Leader Charles Schumer of New York, who took over as that chamber's top Democrat this year, is a comparatively youthful 66, but he has been part of the party's Senate leadership for a dozen years. When *The Washington Post* ranked the party's top 15 presidential contenders for 2020 in September, four of the top five were politicians who will range in age from 71 to 82 by Inauguration Day, 2021. [16]

Rep. Linda Sanchez of California, vice chair of the House Democratic Caucus, said on Oct. 5 that it's time for the party's top three leaders to step down and make way for younger members. "They are all of the same generation, and, again, their contributions to the Congress and the caucus are substantial," she said. "But I think there comes a time when you need to pass that torch. And I think it's time." [17]

A number of Democrats running for House seats next year have said they will not support Pelosi as party leader if they are elected. Some incumbents also have called for her to step down. "President Putin [of Russia] probably has a better approval rating in Georgia than Nancy Pelosi," said Democrat David Kim, a candidate in that state's 7th Congressional District. [18]

Indeed, in Georgia, Pelosi may have contributed to the Democratic loss in a high-profile special House election in June, with Republicans linking Democratic candidate Jon Ossoff to her in ads. "I was kind of skeptical about the idea that Pelosi was hurting Democrats, until that Georgia special election," says *RealClearPolitics* analyst Trende. "I think Pelosi dragged him down. Pelosi has reached the point where if you're a centrist Republican voter who's gettable for the Democrats, she's a big impediment to that happening."

The fights over the leadership of party organs themselves have become proxy battles for different factions that want to see either established leaders or new faces. That played out in the race for chair of the Democratic National Committee last year. Tom Perez, who had served as Labor secretary under President Obama, was cast as the candidate of the party's establishment and eventually won, beating Rep. Keith Ellison of Minnesota, who became deputy chair. Similar battles have played out in state party chair races in states such as California and Maryland.

"That's become the central fight within the Democratic Party," says Lee Drutman, a senior fellow at New America, a left-leaning political think tank in Washington. "The disagreements over policy within the party are small. That means the disagreements are over leadership and style. A lot of the criticism of the Democratic Party, within the party's ranks, is that the people running the party made the wrong strategic investments and didn't invest in party building."

David Carney, a Republican consultant based in New Hampshire, notes that the party out of power never truly has a leader until it picks its next presidential nominee. That person will set the party's tone more clearly and spread its message further than any congressional leader, he says. "The problem they have is the problem we had when we didn't have the White House," he says. "They don't have a single spokesman or agenda."

Numerous Democrats are considered potential presidential contenders, including such relatively youthful figures as Sens. Harris, Booker and Kirsten Gilli-

brand of New York. "Absolutely, we always need new faces, but you're going to see a new Democratic bench over the coming years," Draut of Demos says.

Other analysts defend the current leadership, noting it is battle-tested, adept at raising money and experienced in protecting Democratic interests. They particularly say that Pelosi's strengths should not be undersold. Last year, she easily turned back a leadership challenge from Rep. Tim Ryan of Ohio, who argued

low at the Ethics and Public Policy Center, a conservative think tank in Washington, make a different point: Where the party stands is more important than who its top personalities are.

"Their problem isn't their leadership; their problem is the rigid ideology," Olsen says. "Whoever replaces Pelosi as minority leader won't have her name ID, but unless that person moves to the center, it will basically be a new face in place of a new platform."

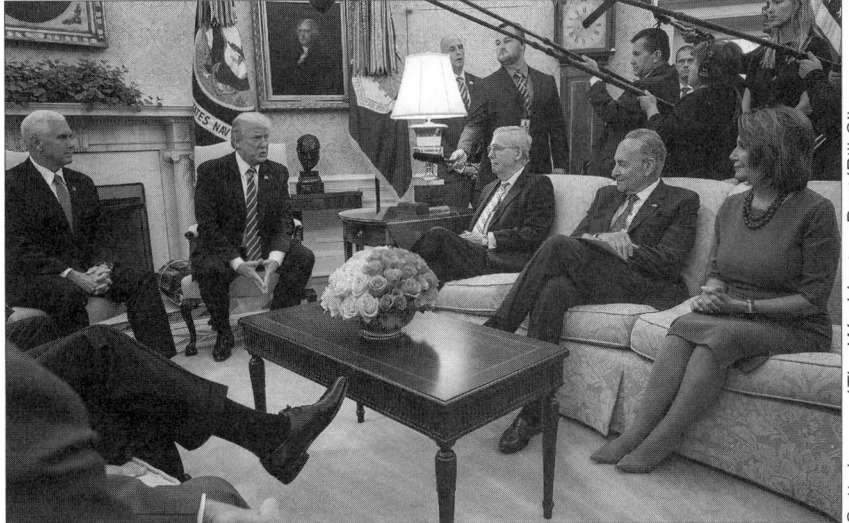

Democrats Sen. Charles Schumer of New York (on couch, center) and Rep. Nancy Pelosi of California (on couch, right) met with President Trump and Republican congressional leaders at the White House on Sept. 6. Supporters of Schumer and Pelosi praise their abilities as deal-makers, but critics say the Democratic Party needs younger leadership.

the party needed a new face. Pelosi is a prodigious fundraiser, and Democrats applaud the way she and Schumer have played their cards thus far as minority leaders in the Trump era.

"This is why we didn't get rid of Pelosi," one House Democratic aide texted a reporter after she, Schumer and Trump agreed on a deal regarding a bill to fund the government and increase the debt ceiling. [19]

"Arguably, Nancy Pelosi has been one of the most successful leaders we've ever had in Congress," Steele of Emerge America says. "I don't think it's time for her to pack her bags right now."

Draut and Henry Olsen, a senior fel-

Can Democrats win back white working-class voters?

Throughout much of the 20th century, white working-class voters were a bedrock of the party. But they have been increasingly voting Republican since the 1980s. In 2016, Donald Trump made further inroads among them, and this success proved to be one of the keys to his election.

Defining the working class is difficult. Many pollsters and pundits use the term to refer to people who have little or no college education, or who work for hourly wages. About one in four white working-class voters who supported Obama in 2008 and 2012 switched to Republicans in 2016. [20]

Democrats Struggled in Electoral College

Many experts say Democratic presidential candidates face an uphill climb in the Electoral College because their supporters are highly concentrated in urban areas and the coasts, which together have fewer electoral votes than states in the interior. In 2016, Democrat Hillary Clinton won the popular vote by 3 million but carried only 20 states and the District of Columbia, worth 232 electoral votes, to Donald Trump's 30 states and 306 electoral votes.

2016 Electoral College Results

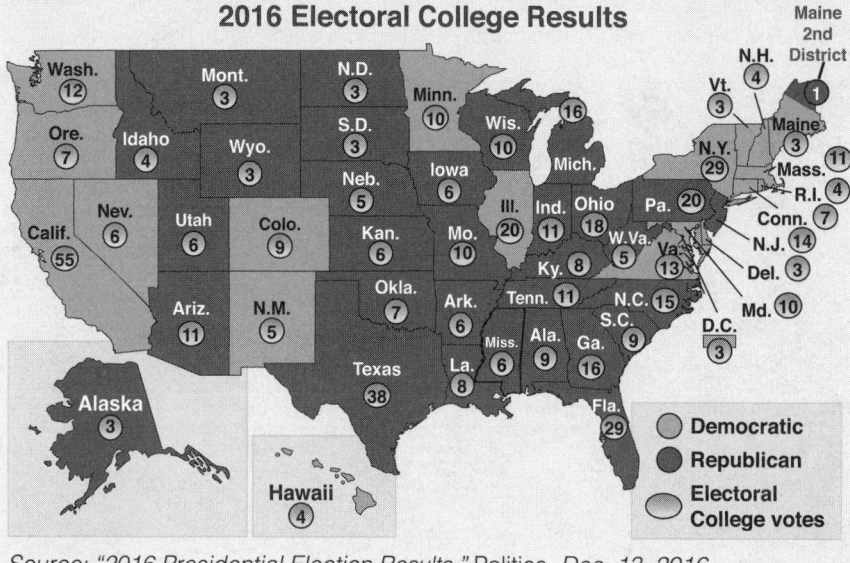

Source: "2016 Presidential Election Results," Politico, Dec. 13, 2016, https://tinyurl.com/y7f4g9p3

"Trump's margin among whites without a college degree is the largest among any candidate in exit polls since 1980," according to the Pew Research Center. Sixty-seven percent of noncollege whites backed Trump, to just 28 percent for Clinton, it said. [21]

Ruy Teixeira, a political demographer at the Center for American Progress, a liberal think tank in Washington, notes that white working-class voters live disproportionately in swing states. More than 200 largely rural or formerly industrial counties that supported Obama voted for Trump. Belmont County, Ohio, backed Obama in 2008 but gave Trump 68 percent of its vote in 2016. Obama carried Trumbull County, Ohio, by 22 percentage points in 2012, but Trump won it by 6 percentage points. [22] Every Iowa county that borders the Mississippi River voted for Obama, but all but

one of them switched to Trump. (The one exception was Scott County, which Trump lost narrowly.) [23]

Because many white working-class voters are not habitual Republicans, Democrats could win them back, a number of political analysts say. "They're a group that has voted for Democrats before," says Justin Gest, author of *The New Minority: White Working Class Politics in an Age of Immigration and Inequality.* "They've voted for Republicans, not voted at all and voted third party. They don't feel their views have been represented in Washington for a long time."

"They didn't vote for Mitt Romney or John McCain," says the Ethics and Public Policy Center's Olsen, referring to the GOP's presidential nominees in 2012 and 2008, respectively. "These are people who are looking for change. If they don't get it, they'll look elsewhere."

Signs of slippage in their support for Trump are emerging. A Quinnipiac University poll in August showed for the first time that Trump had a net negative approval rating among whites without a college degree. [24]

To get the votes of the white working class, Democrats will have to hone a message to show they can help rebuild the economy in struggling parts of the country, says Matt Hennessy, a Democratic consultant in Connecticut. Polling released in May by Priorities USA, a Democratic super PAC, showed that voters who switched support from Obama to Trump were twice as likely to believe that the economic policies put forward by congressional Democrats favor the wealthy than those of Trump (42 percent to 21 percent). [25]

"The big question for the Democratic Party is, how do we reconnect with an economic message that gives hope to people out there who have not benefited from the fundamental shifts in our economy?" Hennessy says.

Democrats are hoping to appeal to blue-collar whites with "A Better Deal," a series of proposals released by congressional leaders in July to create jobs and boost income, such as increasing the minimum wage to $15 an hour and investing in infrastructure. "In the last two elections, Democrats, including in the Senate, failed to articulate a strong, bold economic program for the middle class and those working hard to get there," wrote Schumer, the party's leader in the Senate. "We also failed to communicate our values to show that we were on the side of working people, not the special interests." [26]

But the Democrats' problem with white working class isn't only economic. Many blue-collar voters feel alienated from a party dominated by white professionals in coastal enclaves and college towns, as well as minorities, says Brown, at George Washington University.

Quinnipiac University polling in February found that blue-collar whites were more likely than the nation as a whole to support Trump's ban on immigrants from certain Muslim-majority countries, his plan to build a wall along the Mexican border and his deportation of undocumented immigrants who have not committed serious crimes. [27] White Americans who say their identity as whites is very important and those who believe whites face discrimination are highly likely to back Trump. [28]

Democrats may never win back members of the white working class who share authoritarian leanings or are driven by a sense of racial grievance, says Gest, a political scientist at George Mason University. "Trump was the first American politician to convey what they believe in over a generation, representing precisely the anti-immigrant xenophobia and the law-and-order atmosphere they wanted to create," he says. "The Democrats have no chance at that group of voters, unless they compromise the fundamental aspects of what their party stands for."

Nevertheless, the white working class is huge — at least a third or as much as half of the electorate, depending on how it is measured, Gest says. Many of those voters are concerned primarily with pocketbook issues and could be persuaded to vote Democratic again, if the party crafts the right message, he says. "Democrats must offer a compelling alternative," Gest says. "Otherwise, Donald Trump can ask for more time and can blame his failures on others and institutional obstacles." ∎

BACKGROUND

Jeffersonian Origins

In the 1790s, as a new national government led by President George Washington settled in, arguments grew over the public debt, the powers of the central government, banking and other issues. The fissures resulted in the emergence

Striking McDonald's restaurant employees lock arms before their arrest for blocking an intersection in Los Angeles during nationwide minimum-wage protests on Nov. 29, 2016. The Democrats' "A Better Deal" proposal calls for increasing the minimum wage to $15 an hour.

of a two-party system with one party known as the Federalists, led by Alexander Hamilton, who favored a strong central government and supportive mercantile policies. The other, led by Thomas Jefferson, was first known as the Republican-Democratic Party and later the Democratic Party. Farmers and laborers constituted its core, and an agrarian, anti-commercial outlook defined its vision.

The Democratic Party enjoyed a strong run throughout the first half of the 19th century, thriving during the Jacksonian era. But the divisions of the Civil War split the party into Northern and Southern camps. The Republican Party, formed in 1854 to combat slavery, dominated national politics during and after the war. Of the 17 presidential elections held between 1860 and 1928, Democrats won just four. [29]

The Democratic Party's fortunes changed markedly in the Great Depression. The nation's economic collapse led to the election of Franklin D. Roosevelt as president in 1932 and the creation of the New Deal coalition. Roosevelt wed the party's traditional strength in the "solid South" with low-income workers in the cities, including labor union households and African-Americans. This coalition allowed Democrats to dominate American politics for decades. [30]

Roosevelt put in place new economic programs such as Social Security that appealed to workers, while putting the unemployed to work directly for the government through programs such as the Works Progress Administration. [31] He also pushed for creation of agencies to regulate financial firms, including the Securities and Exchange Commission. "Giant utility holding companies were broken up, farmers gained government support for stable agricultural prices free from speculation, and the chain stores were restrained by laws that blocked them from using predatory pricing to undermine local competition," wrote Matt Stoller, a former analyst with the Senate Budget Committee. [32]

In 1952, Republican Dwight D. Eisenhower broke the Democrats' streak of five straight presidential victories. But the Democrats quickly recovered, regaining control of Congress in 1954. They held the House for the next 40 years and the Senate for another 26 years. [33]

The party's lock on the South held into the 1960s, when President Lyndon B. Johnson successfully pushed for the 1964 Civil Rights Act and Voting Rights Act and implemented his Great Society anti-poverty programs. Johnson feared the push for racial equality would cost the Democrats support in the South, and his fears came to pass, as Republicans began to dominate the region.

GOP's Electoral "Lock"

When Republican Richard M. Nixon ran for president in 1968, he pursued his "Southern strategy," telling reporters that Southerners "didn't want to be treated like national pariahs, they wanted recognition, their right to be heard." [34] Nixon narrowly defeated Hubert Humphrey, Johnson's vice president.

Angered that the Democratic convention had chosen Humphrey over his popular rivals, liberals pushed for changes in the party's selection process. Sen. Eugene McCarthy of Minnesota, who ran as a foe of the Vietnam War, and Sen. Robert F. Kennedy of New York, who was assassinated on the night he won the California primary, had taken 69 percent of the primary vote between them, but almost 25 percent of the nominating convention delegates had been selected up to four years in advance and they went along with party leaders' choice. [35]

McCarthy proposed changing the party rules so that all delegates would be chosen through "procedures open to public participation," in the same year the convention was held. The party merged McCarthy's idea with a proposal from Sen. George McGovern of South Dakota to have delegations reflect the demographic compositions of their states, deciding that the easiest way to satisfy these concerns was to hold more primaries. The party held only 15 primaries in 1958, but by 1980 the number was 35. [36]

These changes helped alter the party's coalition. A strategist named Fred Dutton, who advised the commission overseeing the rule changes, sought to reduce the influence of unions and white working-class voters. Both blocs, Dutton complained, were "a major redoubt of traditional Americanism and of the anti-Negro, anti-youth vote." The future lay in a coalition of African-Americans, feminists and affluent, young, college-educated whites, he argued. [37]

The rule changes paved the way for McGovern's nomination in 1972. "McGovern's party was savagely divided," wrote Nixon biographer John A. Farrell. "The AFL-CIO's George Meany, aghast at the rad-lib poseurs who had usurped the Roosevelt coalition, would sit out the election." Nixon was able to castigate McGovern as the champion of drug use, draft dodgers and abortion supporters. He won a 49-state landslide. [38]

Nixon resigned in August 1974 because of the Watergate scandal. In response to Nixon's troubles, voters sent a huge number of Democrats that fall to Congress. The so-called Watergate babies further pursued social equality and government reform. [39]

In 1980, Republican nominee Ronald Reagan, a former California governor, made inroads among working-class whites in the Midwest and elsewhere, appealing to many Catholics and union households who became known as "Reagan Democrats" as they shifted their allegiance to the GOP. The Republicans regained their first Senate majority in 26 years by capturing 12 Democratic seats. [40]

After Reagan won re-election in 1984 in a landslide, pundits began talking about the GOP enjoying a lock on the Electoral College, thanks to the "Republican L" — the shape made on the map by Republican-leaning states in the Mountain West, the Great Plains and the South. [41] Between 1968 and 1988, Republicans won five of the six presidential elections.

Following the routs of its liberal nominees, more-moderate Democrats argued that the party had to increase its appeal to working-class whites and Southerners by emphasizing traditional values such as work, a meritocratic approach to getting ahead through education and expanding economic opportunity. A group of senators and governors helped form the Democratic Leadership Council (DLC) in 1985 to promote this approach. [42]

Arkansas Gov. Bill Clinton, who chaired the DLC, won the party's nomination in 1992 by emphasizing these ideas. He sought to defuse GOP complaints about Democratic weaknesses on issues such as defense and crime, traveling home during the primaries to oversee the execution of a mentally impaired man. [43] He distanced himself from Jesse Jackson, a veteran civil rights leader and former presidential candidate, in what became known as the "Sister Souljah moment," after a rap artist who had championed the idea of blacks killing whites rather than each other. One of his best-known campaign slogans was a pledge to "end welfare as we know it." [44]

Once in office, Clinton pursued a mix of conservative and liberal priorities — seeking free-trade agreements and balanced budgets, but also proposing a universal health care plan (an effort led by his wife, Hillary). [45] He signed an ambitious crime bill aimed at helping cities hire 100,000 more police and included a ban on certain assault-style weapons. These efforts were unpopular enough to help Republicans regain control of Congress, including their first House majority in 40 years. They also were aided by the party's growing strength in the South, which had seeped down the ballot from the presidential level over the years. [46]

After this rebuke by voters, Clinton followed a more conservative course, signing a GOP bill that overhauled welfare and supporting the Defense of Marriage Act, which denied same-sex couples federal benefits (a decision Clinton later said he regretted). [47] "Clinton moved the Democratic Party past things it had to get beyond, such as welfare," said historian Lewis Gould. "When Democrats essentially eliminated the deficit, a major Republican talking point was eliminated." [48]

Al Gore, Clinton's vice president, became the party's presidential nominee in 2000. He sought to run on Clinton's record of "peace and prosperity," but found himself dragged down by Clinton's scandals, notably his affair with

Continued on p. 856

Chronology

1960s-1970s
Democrats pass liberal legislation in Congress but grow less competitive at the presidential level.

1964
Congress passes the Civil Rights Act under Democratic President Lyndon B. Johnson.

1965
With the help of big Democratic majorities, Johnson pushes an ambitious domestic agenda, including the Voting Rights Act and his Great Society anti-poverty programs.

1966
A backlash against Johnson's agenda leads to Republican gains of 47 House seats, three Senate seats and eight governorships, including in California, where Republican Ronald Reagan won.

1968
Facing a primary challenge from Sen. Eugene McCarthy of Minnesota and setbacks in the Vietnam War, Johnson announces he won't seek a second term. . . . Republican Richard M. Nixon narrowly wins the White House.

1972
Running against anti-war candidate George McGovern, Nixon wins in a landslide.

1974
Watergate scandal forces Nixon to resign.

1980s-1990s
Democrats lose control of Congress but break the GOP "lock" on the White House.

1980
Reagan wins presidency, bringing in the GOP's first Senate majority since 1954.

1985
Pro-business Democratic Leadership Council is founded by officials concerned the party has moved too far left.

1988
With George H.W. Bush's victory, GOP wins its fifth presidential election in six contests

1992
Pulling the Democratic Party to the center on crime and welfare, Bill Clinton reshapes the electoral map in the party's favor.

1994
Running against a failed health plan crafted by Hillary Clinton and a gun control measure, Republicans capture the House for the first time since 1954, winning a majority of Southern seats for the first time. The GOP also retakes the Senate.

2000-Present
Power shifts back and forth between the parties.

2000
Texas Gov. George W. Bush loses the popular vote but wins the Electoral College. With continuing GOP control of Congress, Democrats are shut out of power in Washington for the first time since 1952.

2001
Sen. Jim Jeffords of Vermont breaks ranks with the GOP and caucuses with Democrats, giving them a majority in chamber.

2006
Bush's handling of the Iraq War and Hurricane Katrina helps Democrats retake Congress.

2008
Sen. Barack Obama of Illinois wins the presidency, carrying states that had long voted Republican, such as Indiana and Virginia, and leading the party to a 60-seat majority in the Senate.

2009
Anger over Obama's policies on health and spending leads to a populist movement on the right known as the tea party.

2010
Recession and Obama's policies propel Republicans to a House majority, a six-seat gain in the Senate and their first majority among governors since before the 2006 elections.

2014
Republicans regain the Senate while Democrats win only 188 House seats, matching their lowest total since 1924.

2016
Hillary Clinton is the first woman nominated for president by a major party. . . . She loses to Donald Trump, who becomes the first Republican to carry Michigan, Pennsylvania and Wisconsin since 1984.

2017
Republicans win special election in Georgia that is the most expensive House race in history. . . . Congressional Democrats unveil economic program called "A Better Deal." . . . West Virginia Gov. Jim Justice switches to the GOP, leaving Democrats with only 15 governors, their lowest total in nearly a century.

Democrats Debate a Litmus Test on Abortion

"Every Democrat . . . should support a woman's right to make her own choices."

Heath Mello had a good shot at scoring a rare win for Democrats in Nebraska. Instead, he became the center of a Democratic controversy over abortion rights and lost his bid to become Omaha's mayor.

Mello was backed by, among others, U.S. Sen. Bernie Sanders, a Vermont independent who ran for president as a Democrat last year, and Rep. Keith Ellison of Minnesota, vice chair of the Democratic National Committee (DNC). [1]

The support for Mello, who had cast some votes to limit abortion rights as a state legislator, angered abortion-rights groups. In response, DNC Chair Tom Perez issued a statement saying that all the party's candidates should support abortion rights. "Every Democrat, like every American, should support a woman's right to make her own choices about her body and her health," Perez said. "That is not negotiable and should not change city by city or state by state." [2]

But other party leaders immediately questioned Perez's seemingly absolutist position. They argued that to regain power, Democrats need to appeal to a broad constituency. "This is the Democratic Party," Rep. Nancy Pelosi, D-Calif., the party's leader in the U.S. House, told *The Washington Post*. "This is not a rubber-stamp party." [3]

The Democratic Party's 2016 platform enshrines its support for "safe and legal abortion," pledges to fight GOP efforts to defund Planned Parenthood, which provides abortions and other health services, and calls for an end to the long-standing ban on federal funding for abortions. [4]

The fact that the party favors abortion rights matters more than where an individual candidate might stand on the issue,

argues Andrea Dew Steele, president of Emerge America, a San Francisco-based group that recruits and trains Democratic women candidates. Democratic majorities in the states and in Congress offer the best protection for abortion rights, she says. "We have to focus on power," she says. "What has happened on reproductive rights has been devastating at the state level all over the country."

Rep. Ben Ray Luján of New Mexico, who chairs the Democratic Congressional Campaign Committee (DCCC), said in July the committee's priority will be securing a Democratic majority, and the DCCC will offer financial backing to candidates who oppose abortion rights. "There is not a litmus test for Democratic candidates," Luján said in an interview with *The Hill*. "As we look at candidates across the country, you need to make sure you have candidates that fit the district, that can win in these districts across America." [5]

That position drew criticism from groups allied with the party, such as EMILY's List, a political action committee that seeks to elect Democratic women who support abortion rights, and NARAL Pro Choice America, which promotes abortion rights. Old party hands questioned the congressional campaign committee's decision as well. "There are some issues that you just stand for what you believe in, and the electoral consequences are going to be what they are," says Evan Bayh, a former Democratic senator from Indiana. "A woman's right to choose is one of those issues."

But Democratic leaders would be loath to lose the seats held by the party's relatively few elected officials who oppose abortion, such as U.S. Sen. Bob Casey of Pennsylvania, who faces a challenging re-election battle next year in a state that President Trump carried in 2016. Analysts say the party has to

---

Continued from p. 854

a White House intern. Gore had been a senator representing Tennessee, and there was considerable debate within the party about whether it needed to nominate Southerners to win the White House. (Its three winners between 1964 and 1996 all hailed from the South.) But Gore failed to carry his home state. Republican nominee George W. Bush swept the South on his way to a narrow electoral victory, even though Gore won the popular vote by about 500,000 votes. It was the first time Democrats had lost control of the White House and both congressional chambers since 1952. [49]

Following the terrorist attacks of 2001, the GOP managed to gain seats

in the 2002 midterm elections, a rarity for the president's party. When Bush won re-election two years later, White House adviser Karl Rove and others talked of a "permanent Republican majority." [50] That dream proved to be short-lived. Due to unhappiness with the war in Iraq and the administration's handling of Hurricane Katrina, Democrats recaptured Congress in 2006. [51]

Heading into the 2008 presidential primaries, Hillary Clinton, who had won election to the Senate from New York in 2000, was the heavy favorite. [52] But the field of Democratic contenders included Sen. Barack Obama of Illinois, a rising star in the party since his keynote speech to the 2004 national convention.

Obama was able to tar Clinton for her initial support of the Iraq War. He also was able to restitch parts of the Democratic coalition, winning support from white professionals as well as African-Americans. Obama also excited young voters, who turned out in force for him.

Obama would go on to become the first Democrat to win two consecutive presidential elections with majorities of the vote since Franklin Roosevelt. He put together a winning coalition of young voters, African-Americans, Hispanics, gays and highly educated professionals. In certain ways, it resembled the McGovern coalition of old — but all those groups had gained relative strength since the early 1970s. [53] Like

---

think carefully about what signal it is sending voters when it insists its contenders must support abortion rights. About one in five Democrats believes abortion should be illegal, according to opinion polls. [6]

"For Democrats to win, they have to be able to pull together a broad coalition that includes all sorts of political diversity," says Paul Landow, a political scientist at the University of Nebraska, Omaha.

Most people who support abortion rights already are voting Democratic, while most opponents back the GOP, notes Henry Olsen, a senior fellow at the Ethics and Public Policy Center, a conservative religious and political think tank in Washington. "There are not votes they're going to pick up," Olsen says in regard to those Democrats demanding fealty to abortion rights. "There might be people on the fence who will feel more uncomfortable with them."

Polls have long shown that a majority hold a mixed view — they do not want the procedure banned entirely, but they do not want it legal in all cases, either. [7] From a pragmatic point of view, Democrats would be smart to leave the door open to voters and candidates who have some reservations about abortion, says Lara Brown, a political scientist at George Washington University.

"Most Americans are really in the middle on abortion," she says. "They don't believe that abortion in all cases should be legal, or that allowing abortion in no cases should be the law of the land. Whatever party is going to be more tolerant of a variety of positions will end up winning more voters."

— *Alan Greenblatt*

Democratic mayoral candidate Heath Mello, who as a state legislator had cast some votes to limit abortion rights, concedes to Republican Mayor Jean Stothert in Omaha, Neb., on May 9.

[1] Roseann Moring, "Bernie Sanders stumps for Heath Mello in Omaha, stirs national debate about definition of a progressive," *Omaha World-Herald*, April 21, 2017, http://tinyurl.com/n7g6gfc.

[2] Laura Bassett, "Democratic Party Draws A Line In The Sand On Abortion Rights," *The Huffington Post*, April 21, 2017, http://tinyurl.com/lwaku77.

[3] Karen Tumulty, "Pelosi: Democratic candidates should not be forced to toe party line on abortion," *The Washington Post*, May 2, 2017, http://tinyurl.com/lvg28op.

[4] "2016 Democratic Party Platform," Democratic Platform Committee, July 8-9, 2016, http://tinyurl.com/hsmnjcu.

[5] Ben Kamisar and Reid Wilson, "Dem campaign chief vows no litmus test on abortion," *The Hill*, July 31, 2017, http://tinyurl.com/yawz5fvg.

[6] Hannah Fingerhut, "On abortion, persistent divides between — and within — the two parties," Pew Research Center, July 7, 2017, http://tinyurl.com/ydb4u2u5.

[7] "Public Opinion on Abortion," Pew Research Center, July 7, 2017, http://tinyurl.com/yc2vnavz.

other recent Democrats, Obama failed to win the white vote in either of his elections, but their relative importance was in decline. Non-Hispanic white voters made up 88 percent of the electorate in 1980. By 2012, their share was 72 percent. [54]

Between 1992 and 2012, Democrats won the popular vote in five out of six presidential elections. Given the growth of Hispanics, who tend to give about two-thirds of their vote to Democrats, Republican Party officials worried about winning future elections unless the GOP softened its position on immigration. [55]

Some Democratic pundits began to make a "demographics is destiny" argument, maintaining that the party's future

was bright because of its support among rising shares of the population — notably, Millennials and Hispanics — and the GOP's reliance on older white voters. They also took comfort in the strength of the Democratic "blue wall" — the states, plus the District of Columbia, that had voted for the party every four years from 1992 to 2012 and were worth a combined 242 electoral votes, out of the 270 needed to win the White House. [56]

But it was already clear that the party was in trouble at other levels of government. Republicans won the U.S. House in 2010, in reaction to Obama policies on government spending and health care. They won the Senate in 2014. They also won 11 state legislative chambers, giving

them 68 to the Democrats' 30. They picked up three governorships, for a total of 31. [57] All told, Republicans had "trifectas" — control of the governorship and both legislative chambers in 23 states, to just seven for the Democrats. That was the lowest number of states controlled by Democrats since the Civil War, when the country had 15 fewer states. [58]

Clinton's Second Defeat

Clinton again began the 2016 Democratic nominating cycle as a big favorite. She faced fewer opponents than she had in 2008, none of whom appeared to have the star power of Obama. But

Activists Go to Battle for the Democratic Party

But some worry they could undercut efforts to regain power.

Catherine Vaughan was despondent. A staffer on Hillary Clinton's 2016 presidential campaign in Ohio, coordinating out-of-state volunteers, she watched with shock as the election returns came in and Donald Trump emerged the winner.

But Vaughan didn't sulk for long. Discussing what to do next over drinks with campaign colleagues the night after the election, she helped hatch the idea for what became Flippable, an organization that aims to raise awareness about redistricting and help elect Democrats to state legislatures.

In its first few months of operation, Flippable has raised roughly $500,000, mostly from small donors. "Half a million [dollars] at the state legislative level is significant," says Vaughan, Flippable's CEO. "We're giving people a clear, easy way to participate, by donating or volunteering."

Many new groups have sprung up on the left in response to Trump's presidency, helping to channel the anger of liberals by guiding them toward donating, working on campaigns or lobbying. But some party officials worry these groups will end up stepping on each other's toes, or will fragment the party's message or harm fundraising.

Other Democrats are not worried. "There's a ton of energy on the left," says Joshua Darr, a political scientist at Louisiana State University. "Some of these groups have been effective about getting people to call members of Congress or show up at town halls."

Former campaign staffers run a number of the groups, such as Our Revolution, which sprang out of Vermont insurgent Bernie Sanders' presidential campaign, while others have grown more organically. Indivisible, for instance, grew in response to an online guide posted by a pair of former Capitol Hill staffers that encourages people to engage with the government. Now it claims more than 6,000 chapters around the country.

Some organizations are collaborating with more established ones, such as EMILY's List, which works to elect Democratic women who support abortion rights, and the Democratic Congressional Campaign Committee.

"As long as we're partnering and not trying to duplicate effort, it's exciting we have new people in our field," says Andrea Dew Steele, president of Emerge America, which recruits and trains Democratic women to run for office.

The Democratic National Committee (DNC), meanwhile, is struggling to raise money. In August, the party raised $4.4 million, the latest in a streak of poor months, compared with $7.3 million for the Republican National Committee (RNC). [1] The DNC also is carrying debt, while the RNC is not.

Both major parties have had to compete with super PACs and other groups for funding in recent years. When it comes to raising money, federal campaign finance law puts more restrictions on parties than on outside groups.

But some activists on the left are backing the new groups because they don't like or trust the DNC. Many Sanders supporters believe the party tilted the playing field during the 2016 primaries in favor of Clinton. [2] And parties, as entities, can be hard for

she ran into trouble before the primaries even began, with the revelation that she had used a private server for emails while she was Obama's secretary of State. That seemingly minor issue would continue to dog her throughout the election cycle, keeping her from framing a positive message. Her announcement speech contained applause lines for every Democratic constituency but, her critics said, lacked an overarching theme or rationale for her candidacy. [59]

Her toughest opponent proved to be Bernie Sanders, who had represented Vermont as an independent in the House and Senate since 1991 and was a self-described democratic socialist. Sanders was not expected to present a serious challenge and appeared to be running mainly to push progressive ideas, such as a higher minimum wage and in-

creased taxes on the wealthy. [60]

Those issues resonated with liberals, particularly young voters who were "feeling the Bern." Even though Clinton was running to her husband's left on many issues, the sense that she was not a "true progressive" cost her support. Sanders' frequent attacks against her ties to "Wall Street and other special interests" did not help her. [61]

Sanders and his supporters complained that the primaries were rigged, with DNC Chair Debbie Wasserman Schultz appearing to tilt the rules and procedures, such as the number and timing of debates, in Clinton's favor. Sanders fought Clinton to a draw among white voters in the primaries and caucuses and won 70 percent of voters under 30, but she easily beat him among minorities and self-identified Democrats. [62]

In the general election, Clinton started as the heavy favorite against Donald Trump, a developer and reality television star who had shocked the political world by overcoming a large field of GOP senators and governors to win the Republican nomination. Trump's favorability ratings were the lowest for a major-party candidate in modern polling history. Clinton's, however, were not much better. Although Trump courted controversy throughout the campaign, he stayed on the offense against Clinton, complaining about her emails, which became the subject of a highly publicized FBI investigation, and picking up Sanders' line that she was a captive of Wall Street. [63]

Polls indicated that Clinton would win. In the end, she did carry the popular vote by nearly 3 million. [64] But Trump had busted through the Democrats' blue

outsiders or average citizens to navigate. "The party is the most boring, inane entity on both sides," says David Carney, a GOP consultant based in New Hampshire.

Some of the new groups, such as Swing Left, are willing to support any viable Democrat. Others, such as Our Revolution, want to push the party to make sure it embraces liberal values such as universal health care and free college tuition, causes championed by Sanders. "This isn't about your party; it's about what do you value," says Nina Turner, president of Our Revolution.

In this sense, the new groups on the left seem to parallel the tea party, a decentralized band of conservative activists that sprang up in response to Barack Obama's presidency. Although the tea party helped channel energy on the right, its backing of primary challengers who beat GOP establishment candidates in states such as Delaware, Indiana and Nevada has been widely blamed for costing Republicans winnable Senate seats. [3]

"I don't see how these new groups are going to help Democrats get to the position that they want to be in, which is a party that represents a clear majority of Americans," says Henry Olsen, a senior fellow at the Ethics and Public Policy Center, a conservative think tank in Washington. "The sort of energy they channel doesn't echo the concerns of the people Democrats are trying to get in their camp."

Despite the differences, many Democrats agree on one thing: It is important to win elections. "At this point, these new groups are very helpful," says Lanae Erickson Hatalsky, vice president for the social policy and politics program at Third Way, a centrist

After Hillary Clinton's loss, Catherine Vaughan helped hatch the idea for Flippable, an organization that aims to raise awareness about redistricting and elect Democrats to state legislatures.

Democratic think tank in Washington. "It doesn't seem like an insurgent movement in the party. It seems like a way to channel the energy that's frothing in the party."

— Alan Greenblatt

[1] Aaron Blake, "The DNC's money woes persist," *The Washington Post*, Sept. 21, 2017, http://tinyurl.com/y8shbnuq.

[2] H.A. Goodman, "Debbie Wasserman Schultz And The DNC Favored Hillary Clinton Over Bernie Sanders. Where's The Outrage?" *The Huffington Post*, Aug. 17, 2016, http://tinyurl.com/jdd42lf.

[3] Reid Wilson, "The untold stories of the 2016 battle for the Senate," *The Hill*, Nov. 15, 2016, http://tinyurl.com/gql8j4t.

wall, narrowly winning Michigan, Pennsylvania and Wisconsin — three states that had supported Democrats in every election at least since 1992. While Obama had carried enough of the white working class to keep those Rust Belt states in the Democratic column in 2012, Clinton did not. She won only 78 percent of white Obama voters without a bachelor's degree, according to the Democracy Fund Voter Study Group, a survey by a consortium of political analysts. [65]

It turned out that the Obama coalition was not as supportive of Clinton as forecasters anticipated. Despite Trump's attacks on immigrants and Mexicans, his share of the Hispanic vote (28 percent) was 1-point higher than it had been for GOP nominee Mitt Romney in 2012. Voters under 30 supported Clinton, but not as heavily as they had favored Obama.

The turnout rate dropped substantially among African-Americans, to 59 percent from 66 percent in 2012. [66]

■

CURRENT SITUATION

Improving Prospects

Democrats today are looking for signs of hope. They are finding some. Although fundraising for the Democratic National Committee has been tepid, Democrats are willing to open their wallets to support individual candidates. They showed that with a vengeance

with their backing of Jon Ossoff, the party's candidate in a Georgia special election in June. Thanks to the help of liberal groups, Ossoff raised $23 million for what became the most expensive House race in U.S. history. [67]

He lost, but he took 48 percent of the vote in the June runoff against Republican Karen Handel. That showing was a big improvement over the Democratic performance in the district last November, when the party lost the seat by 24 points. [68] "Ossoff was in a district that Romney carried [in 2012] by 22 points," says Whit Ayres, a consultant to Handel's campaign. "That was a race that never would have been close if we had a more normal Republican in the White House."

Ayres says it is the margin that matters in special elections. If one party is outperforming its normal vote totals, that means it could win more seats than normal in upcoming contests. This prognosis has Democrats excited about their prospects in 2018.

In three dozen special state legislative elections held by Oct. 1, Democrats picked up eight seats, compared with just one pickup for Republicans. [69] What's more, in most of the contests, the Democratic candidates ran well ahead of Clinton's showing in their districts in the presidential contest last year, while Republicans fell behind Trump's totals.

"Democrats are very likely to make gains that could in fact be enough for them to close in on a House majority next year," says John J. Pitney Jr., a government professor at Claremont McKenna College in California.

Some Republicans are bracing for the worst in the 2018 midterms. Nick Ayers, Vice President Mike Pence's chief of staff, reportedly told GOP donors in early October that congressional Republicans will suffer "a gigantic loss" next year if their party is unable to make tangible progress on their legislative agenda. A late-September poll by Quinnipiac found that 78 percent of voters disapprove of the job congressional Republicans are doing. (Democrats did not fare much better: 63 percent disapprove of their performance.) [70]

Democrats are happy with their recruiting efforts thus far. By the end of June, 209 Democratic challengers had registered with the Federal Election Commission and reported raising at least $5,000. That was more than double the number of candidates recruited by the minority party in any election cycle since 2009. By comparison, Republicans had just 78 challengers with at least $5,000 by June 2009, the equivalent point in the party's strong 2010 cycle. "This is unprecedented," said Stephanie Schriock, president of EMILY's List, a political action committee that supports female Democratic candidates who back abortion rights. [71]

The 2018 Map

To win the House, Democrats need a net gain of 24 seats. Their likeliest targets include 23 districts represented by Republicans that voted for Clinton. The Republican incumbents are "strong and good candidates, but a wave can take out a whole lot of good candidates," says Ayres.

But Democrats will still have to catch a lot of breaks to regain control because their vote is heavily concentrated in metropolitan areas. This problem is compounded by gerrymandering, with GOP-controlled state legislatures possessing the ability to draw U.S. House districts that further dilute Democrats' voting power. The Supreme Court is considering a potentially landmark case, *Gill v. Whitford*, that could decide when gerrymandering is unconstitutional. [72]

By one estimate, Democrats could take 54 percent of the votes cast for House candidates nationwide but come away with only 47 percent of the seats. In 2012, Democrats took 51 percent of the House vote but only 46 percent of the seats. [73]

The last time Democrats recaptured the House was 2006, when Rahm Emanuel, then the head of the Democratic Congressional Campaign Committee, went out of his way to recruit centrist Democrats — including opponents of abortion rights — whom he believed could win in more conservative districts. "I purposely recruited candidates who reflected the temperament, tenor and culture of their district," Emanuel, now mayor of Chicago, recalled in May. "I didn't try to elect somebody that fit my image. I tried to help elect somebody that fit the image and the profile of the district." [74]

But the conservative "Blue Dog" Democrats whom Emanuel helped recruit have since been beaten or left office. In 2014, Rep. John Barrow of Georgia, the last white congressional Democrat in the Deep South, was defeated. What was solidly Democratic territory during the 20th century has become solidly Republican. And Democrats are struggling to find winnable districts across the Plains and Midwestern states, outside of cities and college towns.

The picture is not much brighter in the Senate. To regain the majority, Democrats will need a net gain of three seats. Their best targets appear to be Arizona and Nevada, where polls show incumbent Republicans Jeff Flake and Dean Heller, respectively, are vulnerable.

But the reality is that Democrats do not have many targets at all. Republicans will be defending just eight Senate seats in 2018, compared with 25 for Democrats. Democrats will be playing a lot of defense, including in states Trump won easily, such as Indiana, Missouri, Montana, North Dakota and West Virginia. [75] "It's hard to see at this point how Democrats gain many seats, let alone take control of the Senate," Ayres says.

Efforts in the States

Democrats have a lot of ground to make up on the state level. In 2009, 4,082 Democrats were serving in state legislatures, compared with 3,223 Republicans. After last year's elections, those numbers had essentially reversed, with Republicans holding 4,177 state legislative seats and Democrats 3,135. The story is similar in governors' mansions. Democrats started the Obama presidency with 28 governors but now have just 15. Republicans have 34, which ties their all-time high. [76] (Alaska Gov. Bill Walker is independent.)

In contrast to the Senate, Democrats have plenty of pickup opportunities when it comes to governors. They are favorites in Virginia and New Jersey this November. Next year, Republicans will be defending 26 seats, compared with just nine for Democrats. [77]

Many of the Republican seats will be open because of term limits. "Next

Continued on p. 862

At Issue:

Can Democrats win back white working-class voters?

LANAE ERICKSON HATALSKY
VICE PRESIDENT FOR SOCIAL POLICY AND POLITICS, THIRD WAY

WRITTEN FOR *CQ RESEARCHER*, OCTOBER 2017

*W*e all know the stats: In 2016, President Trump dominated among white voters without a college degree. Yet many white working-class voters have long been part of the Democratic coalition, they are open to appeals from Democrats, and the party must bring them back into the fold if it is going to dig out of its electoral hole.

The most compelling reason to believe that at least some of these voters will still support Democrats is that they already have. In 12 heavily white working-class districts that went to Trump, voters simultaneously elected a Democrat to represent them in Congress. If Democrats such as Rep. Cheri Bustos, who won by 20 points in an Illinois district that went to Trump, can have broad appeal with white working-class voters, it's laughable to say those voters aren't "winnable" for Democrats.

What the Democrats who won in Trump districts figured out is the need to focus on what these voters care about most: the economy and jobs. And that's great news, because a jobs message holds serious appeal with the rest of the Democratic coalition, too.

Our recent research with voters who switched support from Barack Obama to Trump, as well as minority and young voters, found near unanimity on this point: Voters of every demographic group want Democrats to be the party of jobs.

This is not a case of needing to appeal to swing voters to the detriment of the rest of the coalition. If Democrats have a message and policies that address economic anxieties caused by the changing economy, it's a win-win.

It's a good thing there is an obvious path for Democrats to appeal to white voters without a college degree, because the party can't win without them. While demographic shifts in the electorate have convinced some analysts that white working-class voters can be cast aside in favor of a new coalition, those rising groups aren't evenly distributed in congressional or state legislative districts. There is simply no mathematical path to taking back the House or reversing historic losses in state legislatures if you take white working class voters off the table.

If Democrats want to take back power, they will have to do it by building a broad coalition with a message and agenda that appeals across race, class and educational lines. If they do that, they can win.

KAY HYMOWITZ
SENIOR FELLOW, MANHATTAN INSTITUTE

WRITTEN FOR *CQ RESEARCHER*, OCTOBER 2017

*b*efore Donald Trump, people on both sides of the aisle presumed that shifting demographics, specifically the large increase in minority voters, would mean Democratic-blue skies as far as the political eye could see. After Trump, farsighted Democrats are scrambling to think of ways to appeal to a white working class they were once confident would be part of their triumphant coalition. The nature of the populism that swept Trump into office suggests they're going to have a tough time of it.

Democrats are comfortable enough speaking to populists' economic complaints. In her new memoir, Hillary Clinton notes how she put forward a number of ideas on this score: job training, health care and tax increases for the rich, presumably to pay for some of the billions she pledged for these programs.

It wasn't just the sensation-seeking media's fault that no one paid attention. For the people she most needed to impress, Clinton and her party personified a ruling class that viewed them as living in a benighted culture. Their accents, their lack of education, their religiosity, their affection for the military, their taste in cars, food and recreation (i.e., hunting) were, well, deplorable.

Future Democrats will also have to transcend white male-hating identity politics. The civil rights movement of the 1960s appealed to American, though patently unrealized, ideals of equality and justice. Today's racial progressivism is predicated on a presumption of total white American iniquity. For populists, the just society imagined by identity-politics Democrats sounds like a zero-sum game. In the past, white men always won. Now, it's payback time.

This polarization, regularly capitalized on by the country's current divider-in-chief, is being played out on professional football fields as I write. Liberals see black football players as protesting the racism they believe is rooted deeply in American identity. Populists see ingrates refusing to show this small respect for a country that has made them millionaire celebrities. Liberals viewed the president's criticism of the players as another example of his racial animus. Populists, who either are themselves, or are close to, someone who had sung the national anthem in uniforms they believed one should be proud to wear, saw hatred for their country.

For Democrats to win over the white working class, they'll have to recover not just vanishing jobs but also a fading language of shared American identity.

Continued from p. 860

year, it's the opposite of the Senate," says Connecticut Gov. Malloy, who chairs the Democratic Governors Association. "Where the map may be harder for our Senate candidates it's easier for us as Democratic governors, with so many Republican governors who are term-limited out and others who aren't running. We feel very good about it."

A number of the states where GOP governors are stepping down, such as Georgia, Idaho, Kansas and South Dakota, lean heavily Republican and are not favorable territory for Democrats. What's

the party at the state level has always been lacking," says Brandon Rottinghaus, a political scientist at the University of Houston. "That has been the Democratic Party's major failing for decades."

Both these Democratic organizations are still being outraised by their Republican counterparts. [81] But Matt Walter, president of the Republican State Leadership Committee (RSLC), notes that outside liberal groups are increasingly interested in state races. Most prominently, the National Democratic Redistricting Committee, which is supported by Obama, raised $10.8 million in the first

ing. Some Democrats viewed his political arm, Organizing for Action, as an end-run around official party organs. [84] "They raised so much money in 2008 and 2012 elections," Drutman says. "They spent it just on ads promoting Obama when they could have been investing it in real party building.

"To me, it's remarkable how much Obama has escaped from blame," he continues. "The way that he let the DNC divert resources away from state parties is total political malpractice." ∎

OUTLOOK

Culture War?

As Democrats and Republicans jockey for power in the coming years, the field of battle will encompass not just ideological fights between left and right but also cultural differences among Americans.

Urban professionals who thrive in the global economy hold far different views than do those Americans in rural communities who feel globalization has left them behind. People who are comfortable with the nation's rapidly changing demographics vote differently than do those who are alarmed by rising immigration.

"Given how diverse the urban centers have become and how much more diverse the Millennial Generation is, it is not surprising that you have this polarization between more diverse, more densely populated areas of the country and more homogenous, less populated areas," says Pitney of Claremont McKenna College. "It's driven not only by economics but by culture."

In the short term, Trump's presidency magnifies these cultural differences. He makes little pretense at being a uniter, his critics say. His language frequently pits "we" against "them." [85] "Trump won

Lt. Gov. Ralph Northam of Virginia, the Democratic nominee for governor, addresses supporters during a primary-night victory party in Arlington, Va., on June 13. Next year Republicans will be defending 26 governorships, compared with just nine for Democrats.

more, Republican governors in typically blue states such as Maryland, Massachusetts, New Hampshire and Vermont all have high approval ratings and may be tough for Democrats to unseat. [78] Still, when *National Journal* ranked governors races in July, the eight states it considered most likely to change hands were all held by the GOP. [79]

The Democratic Governors Association raised $21 million in the first half of the year, a substantial increase over its $13 million haul in the first half of 2013. The Democratic Legislative Campaign Committee also is raising substantially more money than it has in prior cycles. [80] "Investing resources to grow

six months of the year as it works to overcome the Republicans' redistricting advantage. [82] Its fundraising haul got the GOP's attention. "That money is a concern," Walter says. In September, the RSLC announced the creation of the National Republican Redistricting Trust to counter the Democratic effort. [83]

Obama got involved in state legislative races last fall, endorsing about 150 candidates and recording robo-calls for many of them. Drutman, the New America senior fellow, says this was a switch from years of seeming indifference, when Obama aggressively raised money for his presidential campaigns but didn't seem particularly interested in party build-

Getty Images/*The Washington Post*/Ricky Carioti

the presidency by inflaming rather than bridging partisan divisions, and his reflexive response to any opposition or criticism is ad hominem counterattack," says George C. Edwards III, an expert on the presidency at Texas A&M University.

Given Trump's approach to racially polarizing issues, it appears likely that the Democrats will be able to maintain their majorities in the nation's population centers. But their problems with the Electoral College could continue, political analysts say.

"People, including myself, didn't appreciate the disjuncture between demographic change and geographic distribution" in the 2016 election, says Teixeira, a Democratic demographer. While the growth in the minority and immigrant populations helps Democrats, "the way the population is divided up and distributed around the country is not to their advantage."

Millennials have tended to favor Democrats, but as yet their loyalties are not fixed. The share of the vote cast by voters under 30 stayed flat last year, despite their increasing numbers in the population as a whole. [86]

It is possible that Democrats will successfully woo new voters in new places. Ayres, the GOP consultant, notes that in 2016, "for every downscale blue-collar county that Republicans gained, they lost an upscale county that is growing," pointing to traditionally Republican strongholds carried by Clinton such as Cobb County, Ga., Fort Bend County, Texas, and Orange County, Calif., the latter of which last year voted Democratic for president for the first time since 1936. [87]

But New America's Drutman believes that some white working-class voters are unobtainable for the foreseeable future. "My view is that a lot of those Obama-Trump voters aren't coming back as long as issues of American identity are central to our politics," he says. "The party system is organized more and more around questions of American identity." ∎

Notes

[1] Scott Clement and Dan Balz, "Poll finds Trump's standing weakened since springtime," *The Washington Post*, July 16, 2017, http://tinyurl.com/y7rzrasa.

[2] Dan Balz and Scott Clement, "Nearing 100 days, Trump's approval at record lows but his base is holding," *The Washington Post*, April 23, 2017, http://tinyurl.com/n7x47vn.

[3] For background on the Republicans, see Chuck McCutcheon, "Future of the GOP," *CQ Researcher*, Oct. 24, 2014, pp. 889-912.

[4] For background, see Sarah Glazer, "Universal Basic Income," *CQ Researcher*, Sept. 8, 2017, pp. 725-748.

[5] Jared Bernstein, "Is There an Emerging Democratic Agenda," *The New York Times*, June 5, 2017, http://tinyurl.com/y7sy76xe.

[6] Reid Wilson, "Democrats Hit New Low in State Legislatures," *The Hill*, Nov. 18, 2016, http://tinyurl.com/zh3zxzh; Amber Phillips, "West Virginia's governor is switching parties. And Democrats just hit a new low," *The Washington Post*, Aug. 3, 2017, http://tinyurl.com/y9fhnqu7.

[7] "Rep. Seth Moulton Calls For New Leadership Of The Democratic Party," NPR, June 27, 2017, http://tinyurl.com/yc2rjwg3.

[8] Louis Jacobson, "Mike Pence says Donald Trump won most counties by a Republican since Ronald Reagan," *PolitiFact*, Dec. 4, 2016, http://tinyurl.com/jzsg9yc/

[9] Dave Wasserman, Twitter post, Aug. 8, 2017, http://tinyurl.com/ycmks6ym.

[10] Collier Meyerson, "Nina Turner: It Is Not Our Job to Fit Into the Democratic Establishment," *The Nation*, June 30, 2017, http://tinyurl.com/y94ushbs.

[11] Steve Phillips, "The Democratic Party's Billion-Dollar Mistake," *The New York Times*, July 20, 2017, http://tinyurl.com/yagewbok.

[12] Gabriel Debenedetti, "Sanders 'litmus test' alarms Democrats," *Politico*, Aug. 7, 2017, http://tinyurl.com/ycfckotf.

[13] Kelsey Snell and David Weigel, "Pelosi: Single-payer isn't a litmus test for Democrats," *The Washington Post*, Sept. 12, 2017, http://tinyurl.com/y778pah5.

[14] Samantha Smith, "Democratic voters are increasingly likely to call their views liberal," Pew Research Center, Sept. 7, 2017, http://tinyurl.com/ybruz48d.

[15] Jonathan Easley, "Poll: Majority supports single-payer health care," *The Hill*, Sept. 22, 2017, http://tinyurl.com/ybhy9hss.

[16] Aaron Blake, "The top 15 possible 2020 Democratic nominees, ranked," *The Washington Post*, Sept. 8, 2017, http://tinyurl.com/ydczyz89.

[17] Ed O'Keefe, "Top House Democrat: 'I think it's time' for Nancy Pelosi, Steny Hoyer and James Clyburn to go," *The Washington Post*, Oct. 5, 2017, http://tinyurl.com/yc2txa2o.

[18] "'Putin Probably Has Better Approval': Dems Distance Themselves From Pelosi," Fox News, Aug. 16, 2017, http://tinyurl.com/y73ljnzk.

[19] Jeff Stein, Twitter post, Sept. 6, 2017, http://tinyurl.com/y6uj8j3q.

[20] Nate Cohn, "A 2016 Review: Turnout Wasn't the Driver of Clinton's Defeat," *The New York Times*, March 28, 2017, http://tinyurl.com/mgktcby. See also Nate Cohn, "The Obama-Trump Voters Are Real. Here's What They Think," *The New York Times*, Aug. 15, 2017, http://tinyurl.com/yc6dhmtc.

[21] Alec Tyson and Shiva Maniam, "Behind Trump's victory: Divisions by race, gender, education," Pew Research Center, Nov. 9, 2016, http://tinyurl.com/q3wtur8.

[22] Zeke J. Miller and Chris Wilson, "See a Map That Shows Exactly How Donald Trump Won," *Time*, Dec. 1, 2016, http://tinyurl.com/z2rsxry. Ohio results by county in 2016 are available at http://tinyurl.com/odbjhzl; for 2012, at http://tinyurl.com/l27cphb.

[23] Mark Fahey and Nicholas Wells, "The places that flipped and gave the country to Trump," CNBC, http://tinyurl.com/yb9fpvjy; "2016 Iowa Presidential Election Results," *Politico*, Dec. 13, 2016, http://tinyurl.com/p69gx3w.

[24] Danielle Kurtzleben, "Trump Hits New Low With White Non-College Voters," NPR, Aug. 3, 2017, http://tinyurl.com/ycos5cpl.

[25] Greg Sargent, "Why did Trump win? New research by Democrats offers a worrisome answer," *The Washington Post*, May 1, 2017, http://tinyurl.com/ycwjeh7a.

[26] Chuck Schumer, "A Better Deal for American Workers," *The New York Times*, July 24, 2017, http://tinyurl.com/y8s3jsx9.

[27] "American Voters Oppose Trump Immigration Ban, Quinnipiac University National Poll Finds; Big Gender Gap As Voters Disapprove Of Trump," Quinnipiac University, Feb. 7, 2017, http://tinyurl.com/ycub5zap.

[28] Michael Tesler and John Sides, "How political science helps explain the rise of Trump: the role of white identity and grievances," *The Washington Post*, March 3, 2016, http://tinyurl.com/hu8e2fn.

[29] Francie Grace, "What Does 'GOP' Stand For?" CBS News, Dec. 3, 2002, http://tinyurl.com/y9g2ndqm/; "Chronological List of Presidents, First Ladies, and Vice Presidents of the United

States," Library of Congress, March 22, 2017, http://tinyurl.com/znbq84y.

[30] William E. Leuchtenberg, "Franklin D. Roosevelt: The American Franchise," Miller Center, University of Virginia, http://tinyurl.com/yd3vzzk8.

[31] Chip Reid, "FDR's New Deal Blueprint for Obama," CBS News, Dec. 14, 2008, http://tinyurl.com/yavj2u2h.

[32] Matt Stoller, "How Democrats Killed Their Populist Soul," *The Atlantic*, Oct. 24, 2016, http://tinyurl.com/y76q4orh.

[33] For the House, see "Party Divisions of the House of Representatives," U.S. House of Representatives, http://tinyurl.com/ck3x8pb; for the Senate, see "Majority and Minority Leaders," U.S. Senate, http://tinyurl.com/yaxamztm.

[34] John A. Farrell, *Richard Nixon: A Life* (2017), p. 328.

[35] Kevin B. Smith and Alan Greenblatt, *Governing States and Localities*, 6th ed. (2017), p. 169.

[36] John R. Schmidt and Wayne W. Whalen, "Credentials Contests at the 1968 — and 1972 — Democratic National Conventions," *Harvard Law Review*, May 1969, p. 1456; Alan Greenblatt, "History: Winds of War Blew Through Chicago," *CQ Weekly Report*, Aug. 17, 1996, p. 23.

[37] Stoller, *op. cit.*

[38] Farrell, *op. cit.*, p. 473; Max Frankel, "President Won 49 States And 521 Electoral Votes," *The New York Times*, Nov. 9, 1972, http://tinyurl.com/y8cllmrw.

[39] Eric Garcia, "What the Last of the 'Watergate Babies' Can Teach Democrats About Trump," *Roll Call*, July 5, 2017, http://tinyurl.com/y85dujaq; Stoller, *op. cit.*

[40] Stanley B. Greenberg *et al.*, "Reagan Democrats and Barack Obama," Democracy Corps, Aug. 22, 2008, http://tinyurl.com/ybr6rqyd; Lauren Carroll, "Last time GOP defeated two Senate incumbent Democrats? Try 1980," *PolitiFact*, Nov. 2, 2014, http://tinyurl.com/lu6kqjw.

[41] Jason Russell, "Could Trump lose the 'Republican L'?" *Washington Examiner*, Aug. 16, 2016,

http://tinyurl.com/y9d2xj4x.

[42] Al From, *The New Democrats and the Return to Power* (2013), pp. x, 1.

[43] Peter Applebome, "Arkansas Execution Raises Questions on Governor's Politics," *The New York Times*, Jan. 25, 1992, http://tinyurl.com/pxnecq.

[44] Clarence Page, "Bill Clinton's Debt To Sister Souljah," *Chicago Tribune*, Oct. 28, 1992, http://tinyurl.com/y885pl75; Alana Semuels, "The End of Welfare as We Know It," *The Atlantic*, April 21, 2016, http://tinyurl.com/ycfonzc7.

[45] Adam Clymer, Robert Pear and Robin Toner, "What Went Wrong? How the Health Care Campaign Collapsed," *The New York Times*, Aug. 29, 1994, http://tinyurl.com/ydamnj4k.

[46] Inimai M. Chettiar and Lauren-Brooke "L.B." Eisen, "The Complex History of the Controversial 1994 Crime Bill," Brennan Center for Justice, April 14, 2016, http://tinyurl.com/yae5jcwj; Earl Black and Merle Black, *The Rise of Southern Republicans* (2002), p. 329.

[47] Bill Clinton, "Bill Clinton: It's time to overturn DOMA," *The Washington Post*, March 7, 2013, http://tinyurl.com/zxbusqc.

[48] Alan Greenblatt, "Hillary Clinton Is Too Liberal for Bill Clinton," *Politico*, June 2, 2015, http://tinyurl.com/y9vya4db.

[49] "2000 Presidential General Election Results," U.S. Election Atlas, http://tinyurl.com/kx4wf3z; Matt Bai, *The Argument: Billionaires, Bloggers and the Battle to Remake Democratic Politics* (2007), p. 7.

[50] Robin Toner and Carl Hulse, "By Acquiring Full Control of the Congress, Republicans Gained New Responsibility," *The New York Times*, Nov. 10, 2002, http://tinyurl.com/y9ykxuyz; Paul Abrams, "What Karl Rove REALLY Had in Mind for a 'Permanent Republican Majority,' " *The Huffington Post*, Aug. 17, 2007, http://tinyurl.com/39c2m6.

[51] John M. Broder, "Democrats Gain Senate and New Influence," *The New York Times*, Nov. 10, 2006, http://tinyurl.com/y83j4jbf.

[52] Peter Beinart, "The Rise of the New New Left,"

The Daily Beast, Sept. 12, 2013, http://tinyurl.com/y93qhh6y.

[53] Ruy Teixeira and John Halpin, "The Return of the Obama Coalition," Center for American Progress, Nov. 8, 2012, http://tinyurl.com/yaufka9h; Ruy Teixeira and John Halpin, "The Obama Coalition in the 2012 Election and Beyond," Center for American Progress, Dec. 4, 2012, http://tinyurl.com/y94hdaus.

[54] Juana Summers, "The decline of the white voter: How the electorate has changed in 2016," CNN, Nov. 8, 2016, http://tinyurl.com/puryuzo; Chris Cillizza, "How many more white votes did Mitt Romney need to get elected in 2012? A lot," *The Washington Post*, Aug. 4, 2014, http://tinyurl.com/yayqhmx3.

[55] Thomas B. Edsall, "The Republican Autopsy Report," *The New York Times*, March 20, 2013, http://tinyurl.com/ycpkatpm.

[56] Nate Silver, "There Is No 'Blue Wall,' " *Five ThirtyEight*, May 12, 2015, http://tinyurl.com/z8efjdg.

[57] "StateVote 2014: Election Results," National Conference of State Legislatures, Nov. 11, 2014, http://tinyurl.com/k8lw3wz; "Gubernatorial Elections, 2014," Ballotpedia, http://tinyurl.com/ydeg57ny.

[58] "Historical and potential changes in trifectas," Ballotpedia, http://tinyurl.com/yalynhng; Alan Greenblatt, "Republicans Add to Their Dominance of State Legislatures," *Governing*, Nov. 9, 2016, http://tinyurl.com/y7cwgzdd.

[59] Michael S. Schmidt, "Hillary Clinton Used Personal Email Account at State Dept., Possibly Breaking Rules," *The New York Times*, March 2, 2015, http://tinyurl.com/ycexb6t7; Jonathan Allen and Amie Parnes, *Shattered: Inside Hillary Clinton's Doomed Campaign* (2017), p. 17.

[60] "Biographical Directory of the United States Congress 1774-Present," http://tinyurl.com/yav39bjs; Allen and Parnes, *op. cit.*, p. 37.

[61] Colin Wilhelm, "Sanders taunts Clinton again on Wall Street ties," *Politico*, April 17, 2016, http://tinyurl.com/j3vx7kd.

[62] Mark Hensch, "Reid: DNC never gave Sanders a 'fair deal,' " *The Hill*, July 27, 2016, http://tinyurl.com/zjgksyd; Aaron Zitner, Dante Chinni and Brian McGill, "How Hillary Clinton Overcame the Challenge from Sen. Bernie Sanders," *The Wall Street Journal*, June 8, 2016, http://tinyurl.com/j9fnnag.

[63] Harry Enten, "Americans' Distaste For Both Trump And Clinton Is Record-Breaking," *FiveThirtyEight*, May 5, 2016, http://tinyurl.com/zwjzrxb; Angie Drobnic Holan, "In Context: Hillary Clinton and the 'basket of deplorables,' " *PolitiFact*, Sept. 11, 2016, http://tinyurl.com/jmnfaku.

About the Author

Alan Greenblatt is a staff writer at *Governing* magazine. Previously he covered politics and government for NPR and *CQ Weekly*, where he won the National Press Club's Sandy Hume Award for political journalism. He graduated from San Francisco State University in 1986 and received a master's degree in English literature from the University of Virginia in 1988. His *CQ Researcher* reports include "Gentrification," "Future of the GOP," "Immigration Debate," "Media Bias" and "Downtown Revival."

[64] "Official 2016 Presidential Election Results," Federal Election Commission, Jan. 30, 2017, http://tinyurl.com/y7x4l8sb.

[65] Ross Douthat, "The Obama Realignment," *The New York Times*, Nov. 7, 2012, http://tinyurl.com/yalcp8nc; Cohn, "The Obama-Trump Voters Are Real. Here's What They Think," *op. cit.*

[66] Jens Manuel Krogstad and Mark Hugo Lopez, "Hillary Clinton won Latino vote but fell below 2012 support for Obama," Pew Research Center, Nov. 29, 2016, http://tinyurl.com/hro8pnb; Emily Richmond, Mikhail Zinshteyn and Natalie Gross, "Dissecting the Youth Vote," *The Atlantic*, Nov. 11, 2016, http://tinyurl.com/y94q4fc9; and Steven Shepard, "Study: Black turnout slumped in 2016," *Politico*, May 10, 2017, http://tinyurl.com/n8eylsx.

[67] Jonathan Martin and Rachel Shorey, "Ossoff Raises $23 Million in Most Expensive House Race in History," *The New York Times*, June 9, 2017, http://tinyurl.com/y8qvvnfp.

[68] "Georgia's 6th Congressional District election, 2016," Ballotpedia, http://tinyurl.com/ybl2ojek.

[69] Susan Milligan, "Democrats Making Startling Gains in State Legislative Elections," *U.S. News & World Report*, Sept. 14, 2017, http://tinyurl.com/y7t45j87.

[70] Andrew Restuccia and Matthew Nussbaum, "Pence's chief of staff floats 'purge' of anti-Trump Republicans to wealthy donors," *Politico*, Oct. 3, 2017, http://tinyurl.com/yc5au8sz; "Trump Is Not Fit To Be President, American Voters Say," Quinnipiac University poll, Sept. 27, 2017, http://tinyurl.com/y9mypxly.

[71] Michael J. Malbin, "Does the Opening Predict a Wave?" Brookings Institution, July 24, 2017, http://tinyurl.com/y76ax43y; Ed O'Keefe and Mike DeBonis, "Democrats partner with political newcomers aiming to create anti-Trump wave in 2018 midterms," *The Washington Post*, April 21, 2017, http://tinyurl.com/ycg2ytjx.

[72] For background, see Jane Fullerton Lemons, "Redistricting Showdown," *CQ Researcher*, Aug. 25, 2017, pp. 677-700, and Ephrat Livni, "What's at stake in the most important Supreme Court case of the year," *Quartz*, Oct. 3, 2017, http://tinyurl.com/ycxhbhyl.

[73] G. Elliott Morris, "DDHQ 2018 House Midterm Forecast," Decision Desk HQ, Sept. 10, 2017, http://tinyurl.com/yb64agq6; Katie Sanders, "Steny Hoyer: House Democrats won majority of 2012 popular vote," *PolitiFact*, Feb. 19, 2013, http://tinyurl.com/arhfb29.

[74] Edward-Isaac Dovere and Gabriel Debenedetti, "Paging Rahm: House Dems revive 2006 playbook for 2018," *Politico*, May 22, 2017, http://tinyurl.com/y7sh8uyk.

[75] Alan Fram, "Several Democrats facing 2018 re-election are from states Trump carried," The Associated Press, Nov. 11, 2016, http://tinyurl.com/zrsml52.

[76] "2009 State and Legislative Partisan Composition," National Conference of State Legislatures, http://tinyurl.com/y89wzqvj; "State & Legislative Partisan Composition (2016 Election)," National Conference of State Legislatures, http://tinyurl.com/y8z2jkko; "Governors' Party Affiliations, 1900-2017," National Governors Association, http://tinyurl.com/yb8tcsda; and Kurtis Lee, "With party switch in West Virginia, Republicans now have matched record number of governors' seats. Will it last?" *Los Angeles Times*, Aug. 4, 2017, http://tinyurl.com/y8mk7m7p.

[77] Dan Balz, "The future of the Democratic Party could be written in upcoming gubernatorial races," *The Washington Post*, Aug. 5, 2017, http://tinyurl.com/ybjfkf69.

[78] Cameron Easley, "America's Most and Least Popular Governors — July 2017," *Morning Consult*, July 18, 2017, http://tinyurl.com/ydenyo4w.

[79] Jared Leopold, Twitter post, July 26, 2017, http://tinyurl.com/yaqkem3g.

[80] "DGA Announces $21M in Fundraising in First Half of 2017," Democratic Governors Association, July 31, 2017, http://tinyurl.com/ybpwhtq3; Jessica Post, "DLCC Reaffirms Plan to Win Statehouse Majorities at 2017 Annual Meeting," Democratic Legislative Campaign Committee, July 16, 2017, http://tinyurl.com/y8kubtxd.

[81] For governors, see "RGA Sets New Fundraising Record, Brings In $36 Million In First Six Months of 2017," Republican Governors Association, July 11, 2017, http://tinyurl.com/yafxjh6c; for legislators, see Thomas B. Edsall, "Donald Trump Is the Godfather of a Democratic Renaissance," *The New York Times*, Aug. 10, 2017, http://tinyurl.com/y7aybawo.

[82] Edward-Isaac Dovere, "Dem redistricting group clocks $10.8 million in first 6 months," *Politico*, July 31, 2017, http://tinyurl.com/yank9hwg.

[83] David M. Drucker, "Deep-pocketed Republican group ready to battle Obama and Holder over redistricting control," *Washington Examiner*, Sept. 28, 2017, http://tinyurl.com/yb2vftvo.

[84] Edward-Isaac Dovere, "Obama endorses all the way down ballot," *Politico*, Oct. 23, 2016, http://tinyurl.com/h7njstx; Gabriel Debenedetti, "Obama's party-building legacy splits Democrats," *Politico*, Feb. 9, 2017, http://tinyurl.com/jnkfdzb.

[85] Katy Tur, *Unbelievable: My Front-Row Seat to the Craziest Campaign in American History* (2017), p. 80.

[86] Richmond, Zinshteyn and Gross, *op. cit.*

[87] Seema Mehta, "Orange County voted for a Democrat for president for the first time since the Great Depression," *Los Angeles Times*, Nov. 9, 2016, http://tinyurl.com/y7hpborx.

FOR MORE INFORMATION

Center for American Progress, 1333 H St., N.W., 10th Floor, Washington, DC 20005; 202-682-1611; www.americanprogress.org. Liberal think tank that conducts research on income inequality, political demographics and other issues.

Democracy Fund Voter Study Group, 1200 17th St., N.W., Suite 300, Washington, DC 20036; 202-420-7900; www.voterstudygroup.org. Consortium of analysts researching voter ideas and attitudes.

Democratic Legislative Campaign Committee, 1225 I St., N.W., Suite 1250, Washington, DC 20005; 202-449-6740; www.dlcc.org. Democratic Party's primary organization for recruiting and funding candidates for state legislative offices.

Democratic National Committee, 430 S. Capitol St., S.E., Washington, DC 20003; 202-863-8000; www.democrats.org. Democratic Party's "home office," which oversees nomination and support of candidates.

Demos, 80 Broad St., 4th Floor, New York, NY 10004; 212-633-1405; www.demos.org. Liberal think tank that advocates on issues such as campaign finance.

Emerge America, 44 Montgomery St., Suite 2310, San Francisco, CA 94014; 415-344-0323; www.emergeamerica.org. Provides training for Democratic women to run for office at all levels of government in 22 states.

Our Revolution, 603 2nd St., N.E., Washington, DC 20002; ourrevolution.com. Liberal advocacy organization that grew out of Bernie Sanders' presidential campaign.

Third Way, 1025 Connecticut Ave., N.W., Suite 400, Washington, DC 20036; 202-384-1700; www.thirdway.org. Centrist Democratic think tank that conducts research on voter demographics, higher education, health care and other issues.

www.cqresearcher.com Oct. 13, 2017 865

Bibliography

Selected Sources

Books

Allen, Jonathan, and Amie Parnes, *Shattered: Inside Hillary Clinton's Doomed Campaign*, Crown, 2017.

Two journalists granted inside access to the Clinton campaign catalog what they describe as its many mistakes.

Clinton, Hillary Rodham, *What Happened*, Simon & Schuster, 2017.

The 2016 Democratic presidential nominee reflects on her campaign experiences and offers explanations for her loss, ranging from Bernie Sanders' challenge during the primaries to Russian meddling.

Lilla, Mark, *The Once and Future Liberal: After Identity Politics*, Harper, 2017.

A Columbia University humanities professor says liberals have made a mistake by appealing separately to groups based on race or sexual preference, thus encouraging "white, rural, religious Americans to think of themselves as a disadvantaged group whose identity is being threatened or ignored."

Phillips, Steve, *Brown Is the New White: How the Demographic Revolution Has Created a New American Majority*, New Press, 2016.

A social justice organizer and local official examines demographic trends, arguing that the nation's rising number of minorities points the way to creating a progressive majority.

Articles

Dickinson, Tim, "How a New Generation of Progressive Activists Is Leading the Trump Resistance," *Rolling Stone*, Aug. 24, 2017, http://tinyurl.com/y9de97gb.

Donald Trump's election has led to a flowering of new groups that either are trying to get more Democrats elected or want to push the party to the left.

Elliott, Philip, "Divided Democratic Party Debates Its Future as 2020 Looms," *Time*, Sept. 21, 2017, http://tinyurl.com/yb85o4qy.

Democratic strength in the House is limited mostly to coastal districts, with little agreement among elected officials about how best to appeal to voters in the nation's heartland.

Fraga, Bernard L., *et al.*, "Why did Trump win? More whites — and fewer blacks — actually voted," *The Washington Post*, May 8, 2017, http://tinyurl.com/n7ygwhv.

An analysis of voter and census data suggests that black turnout declined drastically in 2016 and rose among whites and other racial and ethnic groups. The shifts were especially pronounced in the key states of Michigan, Wisconsin and Pennsylvania.

Hohmann, James, "The Reagan Democrats are no longer Democrats. Will they ever be again?" *The Washington Post*, Nov. 11, 2016, http://tinyurl.com/zgsswfz.

So-called Reagan Democrats — white working-class voters in the Rust Belt who traditionally supported Democrats but have sometimes supported Republicans — went heavily for Trump in 2016.

Judis, John B., "Redoing the Electoral Math," *The New Republic*, Sept. 21, 2017, http://tinyurl.com/ybk5gto6.

A onetime proponent of the view that the nation's changing demographics are working in the Democrats' favor argues that the party risks losing elections "by relying on narrow racial-ethnic targeting."

Vogel, Kenneth P., "The 'Resistance,' Raising Big Money, Upends Liberal Politics," *The New York Times*, Oct. 8, 2017, http://tinyurl.com/yab8qwae.

More than three dozen political groups on the left have been founded or have reorganized in the wake of the 2016 election, drawing big donors and potentially pulling the party to the left.

Wasserman, David, "The Congressional Map Has A Record-Setting Bias Against Democrats," *FiveThirtyEight*, Aug. 7, 2017, http://tinyurl.com/y7bawxs7.

Democrats have expanded their advantages in large states, while the GOP has consolidated power in small, rural states. That has given the GOP a big edge in the Electoral College, Senate and House.

Reports and Studies

"Insights from the 2016 Voter Survey," Democracy Fund Voter Study Group, June 2017, http://tinyurl.com/ycg42dwx.

A large survey finds that most Democratic voters agree on issues and most voters in general stuck with their preferred party in 2016. White voters who switched from supporting Barack Obama to Trump tended to have concerns about the economy and negative views regarding blacks, Muslims and immigrants.

Hatalsky, Lanae Erickson, and Ryan Pougiales, "Get to Work, Democrats: Become the Jobs Party," Third Way, Sept. 5, 2017, http://tinyurl.com/ycofvxef.

Focus groups of voters show they do not see the Democrats as concentrating on jobs but rather on helping the poor and attacking business. Most of the voters said they believed it would be more productive for Democrats to concentrate on job creation than social issues.

The Next Step:

Additional Articles from Current Periodicals

Abortion Debate

Filipovic, Jill, "Democrats' disastrous mistake on abortion," CNN, Aug. 5, 2017, https://tinyurl.com/ybkmaqcq.

By avoiding a litmus test on abortion rights for candidates, the Democratic Party is insulting women, one of its most important voting blocs, a journalist and author argues.

Foran, Clare, "Should the Democratic Party Reject Pro-Life Candidates?" The Atlantic, Aug. 10, 2017, https://tiny url.com/y7dkrlov.

Winning elections should not take priority over abortion rights, advocates of women's rights say.

Foran, Clare, "What Pro-Life Democrats Want from the DNC," The Atlantic, June 28, 2017, https://tinyurl.com/y89yxsna.

A group known as Democrats for Life of America is urging the party to be inclusive and welcome Democratic candidates who oppose abortion rights.

Economic Issues

Brownstein, Ronald, "Can the Democratic Party Reconcile Two Divergent Economic Visions?" The Atlantic, April 27, 2017, http://tinyurl.com/y7vb2us2.

Democrats are divided into two camps on economic strategy, populists and centrists, impeding their effort to reclaim power, a political analyst says.

Buchanan, Neil H., "The Dems Should Wage All Out War On Our Gatsby Economy," Verdict, Newsweek, Sept. 22, 2017, https://tinyurl.com/yalvjcsm.

Focusing on economic inequality could give the Democratic Party the issue it needs to defeat the GOP, a columnist argues.

Porter, Eduardo, "It's the Economy, Democrats, but Inequality Is Not the Issue," The New York Times, Aug. 15, 2017, https://tinyurl.com/y98dw6hq.

A lack of economic opportunity, not income inequality, is "the great moral cause of our time" and should be what Democrats rally around, says an economics writer.

Potential Leaders

Allen, Jonathan, and Chandelis R. Duster, "Kamala Harris, Booker Are Early 2020 Favs Among Black Leaders," NBC News, Sept. 24, 2017, http://tinyurl.com/ybv3ereb.

Democratic Sens. Kamala Harris of California and Cory Booker of New Jersey are generating the most excitement from African-American leaders ahead of the 2020 presidential campaign.

Caygle, Heather, "The next Kennedy weighs his next move," Politico, Sept. 3, 2017, https://tinyurl.com/yd45wyyn.

Rep. Joe Kennedy, D-Mass., has begun speaking out against President Trump, raising Democrats' hopes that the 36-year-old grandson of Robert F. Kennedy will become a party leader.

Vogel, Kenneth P., and Rachel Shorey, "Long List of Top Democrats Have 2020, and Money, on Their Minds," The New York Times, Sept. 2, 2017, https://tinyurl.com/ych2rzu5.

Deep antipathy to Trump is leading former Vice President Joe Biden and other Democratic leaders to start exploring 2020 presidential runs, say donors and party operatives.

Radical Left

Horton, Alex, "What is the 'alt-left,' which Trump just blamed for some of the violence in Charlottesville?" The Washington Post, Aug. 15, 2017, https://tinyurl.com/y73obkex.

Trump and his supporters have begun using the term "alt-left" to describe anti-Trump protesters and left-wing activists whom conservatives say are responsible for violent incidents in recent months.

Marans, Daniel, "The Radical Left Has Some Advice For Democrats About Confronting Donald Trump," The Huffington Post, Jan. 21, 2017, https://tinyurl.com/y7cqn8cn.

The radical left says the 2016 election loss is proof that the Democratic Party's agenda is too moderate to be successful and should be abandoned for a more liberal approach.

Rothman, Noah, "How the left props up Antifa, and why Nancy Pelosi was right to condemn the violent radicals: Now, who will follow?" New York Daily News, Sept. 1, 2017, https://tinyurl.com/yc9w3zmf.

Democrats should scrutinize the activities of the Antifa, self-styled anti-fascist groups, for committing violence against far-right groups, a columnist argues.

In-depth Reports on Issues in the News

Are you writing a paper?

Need backup for a debate?

Want to become an expert on an issue?

For 90 years, students have turned to *CQ Researcher* for in-depth reporting on issues in the news. Reports on a full range of political and social issues are now available. Following is a selection of recent reports:

Civil Liberties
Privacy and the Internet, 12/15
Intelligence Reform, 5/15
Religion and Law, 11/14

Crime/Law
High-Tech Policing, 4/17
Forensic Science Controversies, 2/17
Jailing Debtors, 9/16
Decriminalizing Prostitution, 4/16
Restorative Justice, 2/16
The Dark Web, 1/16
Immigrant Detention, 10/15

Education
Charter Schools, 3/17
Civic Education, 2/17
Student Debt, 11/16
Apprenticeships, 10/16

Environment/Society
Climate Change and National Security, 9/17
Muslims in America, 7/17
Funding the Arts, 7/17
Hunger in America, 7/17
Future of the Christian Right, 6/17
Trust in Media, 6/17

Health/Safety
Medical Breakthroughs, 9/17
Medical Marijuana, 7/17
Food Labeling, 6/17
Sports and Sexual Assault, 4/17

Politics/Economy
Cyberwarfare Threat, 10/17
Universal Basic Income, 9/17
National Debt, 9/17
North Korea Showdown, 5/17
Rethinking Foreign Aid, 4/17
Immigrants and the Economy, 2/17

Upcoming Reports

Democracies, 10/20/17   Sexual Harrassment, 10/27/17   Military Readiness, 11/3/17

ACCESS

CQ Researcher is available in print and online. For access, visit your library or www.cqresearcher.com.

STAY CURRENT

For notice of upcoming *CQ Researcher* reports or to learn more about *CQ Researcher* products, subscribe to the free email newsletters, *CQ Researcher Alert!* and *CQ Researcher News*: http://cqpress.com/newsletters.

PURCHASE

To purchase a *CQ Researcher* report in print or electronic format (PDF), visit www.cqpress.com or call 866-427-7737. Single reports start at $15. Bulk purchase discounts and electronic-rights licensing are also available.

SUBSCRIBE

Annual full-service *CQ Researcher* subscriptions—including 44 reports a year, monthly index updates, and a bound volume—start at $1,131. Add $25 for domestic postage.

CQ Researcher Online offers a backfile from 1991 and a number of tools to simplify research. For pricing information, call 800-818-7243 or 805-499-9774 or email librarysales@sagepub.com.

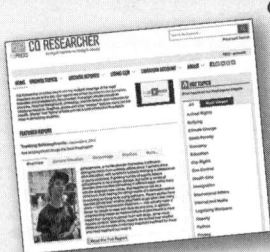

CQ RESEARCHER

CQPRESS

In-depth reports on today's issues

Published by CQ Press, an Imprint of SAGE Publications, Inc.   **www.cqresearcher.com**

Democracy Under Stress

Is representative government in retreat worldwide?

Many democracies in Eastern Europe, the Middle East, Latin America and Southeast Asia are veering toward autocracy, stalling or reversing decades of democratic progress. Leaders have postponed elections, jailed opponents, restricted personal and press freedoms and rewritten constitutions to legalize their actions. Freedoms have eroded in such countries as Russia, Venezuela, Turkey, the Philippines and Poland. In addition, Western democracies are struggling with economic, social and political instability, corruption, immigration and frustrated voters who have turned to populist-nationalist leaders for solutions. Donald Trump, elected president in a wave of populist fervor in the United States, has vowed to stop promoting democracy overseas and to withdraw from some treaties. Meanwhile, Russia seeks to undermine democratic institutions, free elections and liberal Western alliances, and China is wooing developing nations in an effort to show that countries can prosper without the constraints of democracy. Still, some observers are optimistic about democracy's future, saying that new democracies are emerging and others are showing surprising resilience.

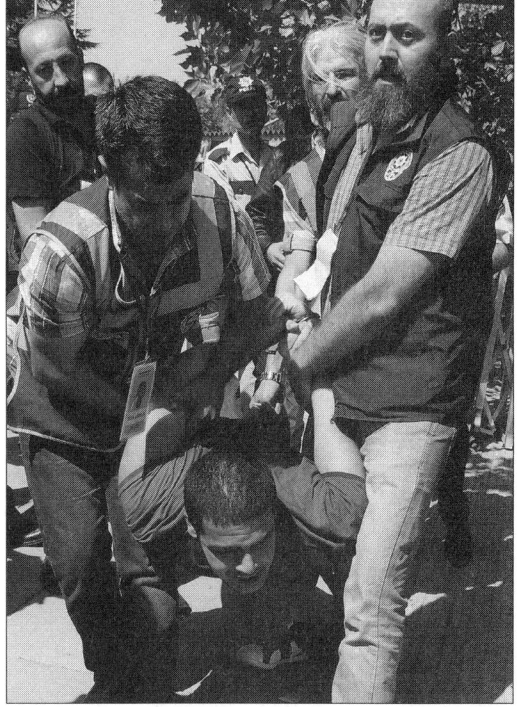

Police detain a protester in Ankara, Turkey, on Sept. 14, 2017, during the trial of two teachers fired during a purge of suspected supporters of a failed coup last year against President Recep Tayyip Erdoğan. Autocratic leaders in a rising number of countries are restricting citizens' rights, reversing years of democratic progress.

CQ Researcher • Oct. 20, 2017 • www.cqresearcher.com
Volume 27, Number 37 • Pages 869-892

I N S I D E THIS REPORT

THE ISSUES 871

BACKGROUND 878

CHRONOLOGY 879

CURRENT SITUATION 883

AT ISSUE......................885

OUTLOOK 886

BIBLIOGRAPHY 890

THE NEXT STEP 891

DEMOCRACIES UNDER STRESS

THE ISSUES

871
- Is China's authoritarian capitalism a viable alternative to democracy?
- Should the United States promote democracy abroad?
- Do the internet and social media strengthen and foster democracy?

BACKGROUND

878 **Greek and Christian Roots**
Athens in the sixth century B.C. became the birthplace of democracy.

878 **Democracy's First Wave**
The English colonies adopted democratic institutions.

882 **Cold War Competition**
After World War II, Western democracies opposed the Soviet Union and other totalitarian states.

882 **Democratic Backsliding**
The United States has struggled to promote democracy abroad, but many fledgling democracies have stumbled.

CURRENT SITUATION

883 **America First**
President Trump seeks foreign aid cuts and an end to most democracy-building efforts.

884 **Embattled Democracies**
Nations worldwide are facing challenges.

OUTLOOK

886 **Dangerous Populist Age**
Rising nationalism threatens democratic principles.

SIDEBARS AND GRAPHICS

872 **Status of Democracy in 2017**
The number of free countries has remained relatively stable since 2000, but democratic norms have eroded significantly in some countries.

876 **Newer Generations Less Supportive of Democracy**
People born after 1970 are less invested in democracy than those born in the 1930s and '40s.

879 **Chronology**
Key events since 1917.

880 **Venezuela Sinks into Dictatorship**
Critics say a power grab by President Nicolás Maduro threatens the once-thriving democracy.

885 **At Issue:**
Is democracy in retreat around the world?

FOR FURTHER RESEARCH

889 **For More Information**
Organizations to contact.

890 **Bibliography**
Selected sources used.

891 **The Next Step**
Additional articles.

891 **Citing *CQ Researcher***
Sample bibliography formats.

Cover: AFP/Getty Images/Adem Altan

CQ RESEARCHER

Oct. 20, 2017
Volume 27, Number 37

EXECUTIVE EDITOR: Thomas J. Billitteri
tjb@sagepub.com

ASSISTANT MANAGING EDITORS: Kenneth Fireman, kenneth.fireman@sagepub.com, Kathy Koch, kathy.koch@sagepub.com, Scott Rohrer, scott.rohrer@sagepub.com

ASSOCIATE MANAGING EDITOR: Val Ellicott

SENIOR CONTRIBUTING EDITOR:
Thomas J. Colin
tom.colin@sagepub.com

CONTRIBUTING WRITERS: Marcia Clemmitt, Sarah Glazer, Alan Greenblatt, Reed Karaim, Barbara Mantel, Patrick Marshall, Tom Price

SENIOR PROJECT EDITOR: Olu B. Davis

EDITORIAL ASSISTANT: Natalia Gurevich

FACT CHECKERS: Eva P. Dasher, Michelle Harris, Betsy Towner Levine, Robin Palmer

SSAGE Publishing | **CQPRESS**

Los Angeles I London I New Delhi
Singapore I Washington DC I Melbourne

An Imprint of SAGE Publications, Inc.

SENIOR VICE PRESIDENT, GLOBAL LEARNING RESOURCES:
Karen Phillips

EXECUTIVE DIRECTOR, ONLINE LIBRARY AND REFERENCE PUBLISHING:
Todd Baldwin

CQ Researcher (ISSN 1056-2036) is printed on acid-free paper. Published weekly, except: (March wk. 4) (May wk. 4) (July wks. 1, 2) (Aug. wks. 2, 3) (Nov. wk. 4) and (Dec. wks. 3, 4). Published by SAGE Publications, Inc., 2455 Teller Rd., Thousand Oaks, CA 91320. Annual full-service subscriptions start at $1,131. For pricing, call 1-800-818-7243. To purchase a *CQ Researcher* report in print or electronic format (PDF), visit www.cqpress.com or call 866-427-7737. Single reports start at $15. Bulk purchase discounts and electronic-rights licensing are also available. Periodicals postage paid at Thousand Oaks, California, and at additional mailing offices. POSTMASTER: Send address changes to *CQ Researcher*, 2600 Virginia Ave., N.W., Suite 600, Washington, DC 20037.

Democracies Under Stress

By Suzanne Sataline

The Issues

One day last May, after a government council in Venezuela announced it would redraft the constitution and delay elections, the bluish mist of tear gas drifted over the streets of Caracas, the capital. A line of young protesters — their T-shirts pulled up over their noses as makeshift gas masks — rushed toward riot police.

Shots rang out. Tear gas canisters exploded over the protesters' heads. Some demonstrators threw Molotov cocktails; others hid behind wooden shields. Engineering student Andres Muñoz said he was in the streets because the police were using force.

"I know that my main duty is to prepare myself for a better future, and that is precisely why I am protesting," said Muñoz, a pseudonym he assumed to protect against reprisals. "This is as much a part of my future as my studies." [1]

Latin America's oldest democracy, with more than 30 million people, has devolved into chaos, with the opposition accusing Venezuelan President Nicolás Maduro of dragging the oil-rich nation into a dictatorship by delaying elections, jailing opposition activists and pressuring lawmakers to overhaul the constitution. Scholars say the country's troubles started decades earlier, when a power-hungry populist leader mismanaged the state-run oil industry and suppressed citizens' rights. (See sidebar, p. 880.)

Like Venezuela, many of the world's representative democracies in recent decades have veered toward autocracy, stalling 30 years of democratic growth. Leaders in some countries in Eastern Europe, the Mediterranean, Latin America and Southeast Asia have postponed

President Nicolás Maduro of Venezuela, Latin America's oldest democracy, has been accused of dragging the oil-rich nation into dictatorship by delaying elections, jailing opposition activists and other actions. Experts blame the decline in democracy in Venezuela and elsewhere in part on resentment over rising immigration and public fury over social changes and economic hardships.

AFP/Getty Images/Rolando Schemidt

elections, jailed opposition activists, restricted human rights and press freedoms and rewritten constitutions to legalize their actions.

"There has been a dramatic shift in global power and behavior, whereby the most important authoritarian countries in the world — first China and Russia, second, Iran and a few others — are more powerful and, in particular, more assertive," says Larry Diamond, a professor of political science and sociology at Stanford University. "Democracy has lost some of its luster, enabling autocrats or elected leaders with authoritarian ambitions to delve into a narrative that says: 'Democracy doesn't work.' " Without forceful checks on authoritarian power, he adds, autocrats will "perceive little or no cost to ruling as nastily as they want."

Experts cite many reasons for the democratic retreat, including a global-ized, increasingly competitive economy that has spurred some politicians to cater to populist fury over social changes and economic hardships. Citizens in democracies also are disheartened when elected officials are guilty of mismanagement and corruption. And, finally, some Western governments have shrunk their long-standing democracy-promotion programs.

Political scientists define a democracy as a political system that lets people or their representatives govern themselves using laws, rather than the authority of a single leader, monarch, party or military dictatorship. Healthy democracies generally have independent judiciaries, protect citizens' civil rights and hold fair elections. [2]

Between 1975 and 2006, the number of democracies grew, as dozens of Latin American and African autocracies and military dictatorships — and then former Soviet satellite states — adopted competitive, multiparty elections, independent judiciaries and civilian rule. By the mid-2000s, many of those fledgling democracies had begun to crumble. [3] (See map, p. 872.)

Then, starting in late 2010, a wave of protests spread across the Middle East, with citizens demanding democratic change, only to see their campaigns for broader rights devolve into civil wars or even more repression. In Egypt, for instance, authoritarian President Hosni Mubarak stepped down in 2011 after months of massive anti-government demonstrations, only to have his popularly elected successor, Mohamed Morsi, ousted by the military in 2013. [4]

Signs of faltering democratic institutions can be seen in a variety of countries or regions, including:

Status of Democracy in 2017

This year, a quarter of the world's 195 countries were listed as not free by Freedom House, a democracy advocacy group. The number of free countries has remained relatively stable since 2000 because as some countries slipped in the rankings — such as when Venezuela fell from partly free to not free this year — others, such as Brazil, Croatia and Tunisia, became more democratic.

A Snapshot of Global Democracy, 2017

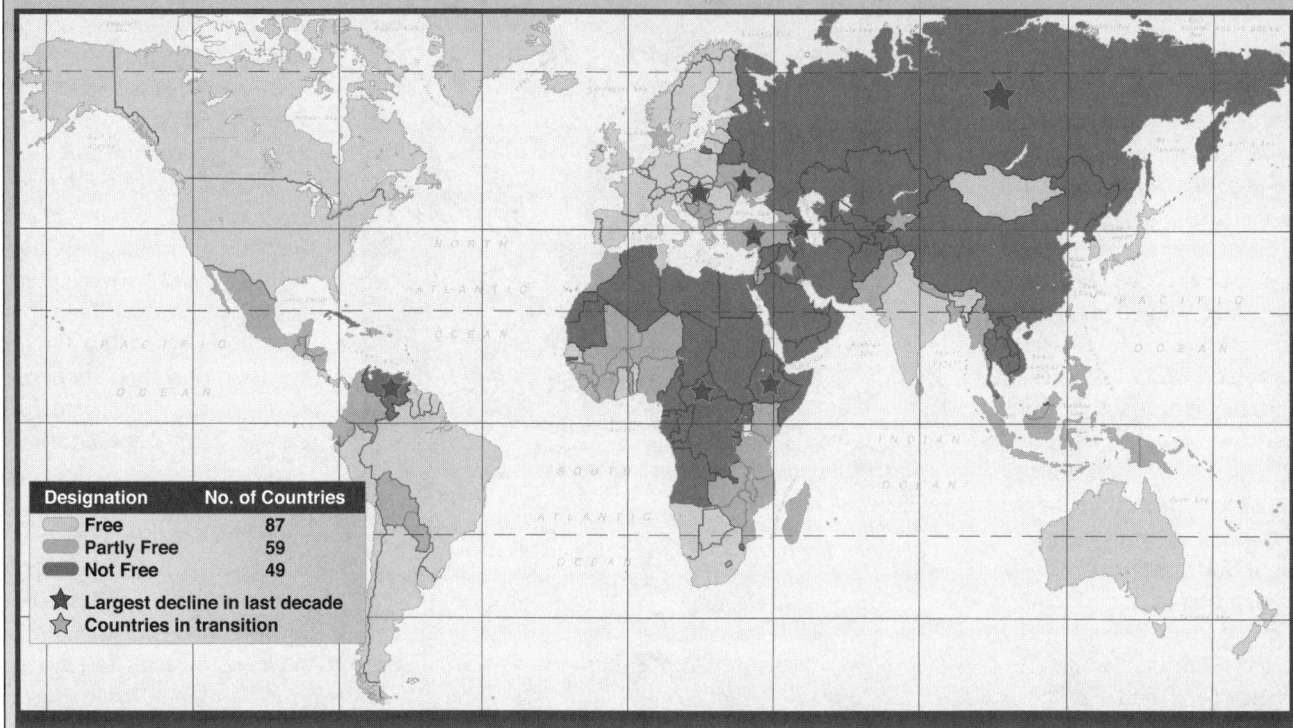

Designation	No. of Countries
Free	87
Partly Free	59
Not Free	49
★ Largest decline in last decade	
☆ Countries in transition	

Countries with Largest Decline in Freedom in the Past Decade

Country	Population (in millions)	Key leader(s)	Key Issues/Prognosis
Azerbaijan	9.9*	President Ilham Aliyev	Constitutional amendments extending the presidential term were passed in allegedly rigged voting.
Central African Republic	5.6	President Faustin-Archange Touadéra	The government is struggling to recover from conflict in 2013 that killed thousands and displaced millions.
Ethiopia	105.3	President Mulatu Teshome	Security forces have responded violently to peaceful protests.
Hungary	9.8*	President János Áder, Prime Minister Viktor Orbán	Orbán has accumulated unprecedented power while praising authoritarian countries such as China and Russia.

• Russia, where President Vladimir Putin has allowed officials to investigate rivals, prevented opponents from running for office and overseen constitutional revisions that will have enabled him to serve, if re-elected in 2018, as either president or prime minister for a total of 24 years. [5]

• Hungary and Poland, where cit- izen fury grew over rapid social and economic changes wrought by global- ization and the European Union's (EU) open-borders policies. That led many citizens to embrace populist leaders' proposals to limit immigrant and refugee rights. Once in power, those leaders have begun to dismantle demo- cratic institutions. [6]

• The Philippines, where citizens and courts until recently have largely lauded President Rodrigo Duterte's vigilante campaign against drug abuse, which triggered thousands of extra- judicial killings of alleged drug sellers and users — a campaign President Trump has praised as an "unbelievable job." [7]

Countries with Largest Decline in Freedom in the Past Decade (Cont.)

Country	Population (in millions)	Key leader(s)	Key Issues/Prognosis
Russia	142*	President Vladimir Putin	Putin has curtailed media freedoms, ended regional elections and harassed political opponents.
Turkey	80.8*	President Recep Tayyip Erdoğan	Government crackdown after failed 2016 coup has led to mass arrests and firings of thousands of perceived enemies.
Ukraine	44*	President Petro Poroshenko	The government has struggled to maintain democratic gains and independence from Russia.
Venezuela	31.3*	President Nicolás Maduro	Maduro has delayed elections and pushed to rewrite the constitution to eliminate the opposition-led legislature.

Top Countries in Democratic Transition in 2017

Country	Population (in millions)	Key leader(s)	Key Issues/Prognosis
Denmark	5.6	Prime Minister Lars Løkke Rasmussen	Parliament is considering restricting immigrant rights.
Ecuador	16.3	President Lenín Moreno	The vice president was recently jailed following a bribery investigation, and Moreno has accused his predecessor, Rafael Correa, of spying on him with hidden cameras.
Iraq	39.2	Prime Minister Haider al-Abadi	The government faces challenges from ISIS and tensions between Sunni and Shiite Muslims.
Kyrgyzstan	5.8	President Almazbek Atambayev	Atambayev's term is expiring, but he may try to become prime minister, a position strengthened in a December 2016 referendum. Sooronbai Jeenbekov, a protégé of Atambayev, was elected on Oct. 15 by a surprisingly large margin.
Philippines	104.2	President Rodrigo Duterte	Extrajudicial killings in Duterte's anti-drug crackdown have taken thousands of lives.
South Africa	54.8	President Jacob Zuma	Rival parties may clash as a new leader is chosen for the African National Congress.
Tanzania	53.9	President John Magufuli	Magufuli faces discontent from semi-autonomous Zanzibar. Threats, attacks and arrests target journalists frequently.
Zimbabwe	13.8	President Robert Mugabe	Politicians are jockeying for position in the struggle to succeed 93-year-old strongman Mugabe.

July 2017 estimate by the CIA World Factbook

Sources: Elen Aghekyan et al., "Populists and Autocrats: The Dual Threat to Global Democracy," Freedom House, 2017, https://tinyurl.com/jkyw8ta; The World Factbook, Central Intelligence Agency, https://tinyurl.com/n27azxz; "Hungary profile — Leaders," BBC News, June 14, 2017, www.bbc.com/news/world-europe-17382823; Roger Southall, "How ANC presidential elections trump South Africa's constitution," University of the Witwatersrand, Johannesburg, June 2, 2017, https://tinyurl.com/y9kogat3; "Tanzania country profile," BBC News, Sept. 21, 2017, https://tinyurl.com/y8u89c39.

• Turkey, where a failed coup in 2016 prompted President Recep Tayyip Erdogan to jail tens of thousands of journalists, teachers and government employees he says opposed him. [8]

• Southeast Asia, where human-rights abuses and crackdowns on freedom are on the rise, notably in Myanmar. The military there has carried out what the United Nations has called ethnic cleansing, which has included rapes, beatings and killings of minority Rohingyans after a militant group attacked police stations. The violence prompted about 500,000 members of the Muslim group to flee Buddhist-dominated Myanmar for neighboring Bangladesh. [9]

• The United States, where voters frustrated with what they call the Washington elite elected populist Republican Trump in 2016. As president he has repeatedly denigrated or attacked democratic institutions such as the press, judiciary, intelligence community and Congress.

• Various countries, such as China, Russia, Egypt and Cambodia, where authoritarian governments have blocked local nongovernmental organizations (NGOs) from providing funds to promote democracy. [10]

"The single biggest factor" causing the decline in democracy, says Diamond, "is that the United States and Europe — the advanced industrial democracies — have pulled away from making the promotion and defense of democracy a high priority."

While some political scientists and pro-democracy groups have criticized Trump for not supporting U.S. democracy-building activities, others point out that the pullback from democracy promotion started under the Obama administration, which rejected the fervid nation-building that the George W. Bush administration began after the Sept. 11, 2001, terrorist attacks on the United States.

Some experts say it may seem paradoxical, but the rise of Islamist terrorism has pushed Western countries to reject

ernment, as Western policymakers and political scientists had assumed they would, according to Joshua Kurlantzick, a Southeast Asia fellow at the Council on Foreign Relations think tank in Washington. [11]

Some political scientists are more optimistic about the state of democracy around the world. "While pluralism is no longer on the rise, democracy has survived in a range of countries with highly unfavorable conditions for fostering democracy," writes Lucan Ahmad Way, a professor of political science at the University of Toronto, pointing to Benin,

strains caused by globalization and the digital revolution.

"Today, China — and to a lesser extent other successful authoritarian capitalists — offer a viable alternative to the leading democracies," wrote Kurlantzick. "In the wake of the global economic crisis and the dissatisfaction with democracy in many developing nations, leaders in Asia, Africa and Latin America are studying the Chinese model far more closely — a model that, eventually, will help undermine democracy in their countries." Such authoritarian capitalists "pose the most serious challenge to democratic capitalism since the rise of communism and fascism in the 1920s and early 1930s," he said. [12]

Democracies have crumbled in places where elected governments have not delivered basic public services and where corrupt judiciaries or police forces have shown bias, according to Diamond. Disillusioned citizens can become receptive to "anti-system" messages by populists promising quick fixes who then try to dismantle democratic structures once in power. When Poland joined the EU in 2004, experts hailed it as a post-communist triumph. Eleven years later, Poland's populist and nationalist right-wing Law and Justice Party won the presidency and a parliamentary majority, and soon sought to control the courts. [13]

Worldwide, several social and economic trends are stressing democracies, says Diamond, and democratic institutions — such as the courts or a free press — have weakened in many developing and post-communist countries where conditions needed to sustain democracy are relatively weak.

In Europe, the EU's open-borders policy for goods and people has allowed many Middle Eastern refugees and African migrants to enter, just as Islamist extremists carried out terror attacks in France, England and elsewhere. Populists fanned the resultant fear of those new arrivals into a seething antagonism toward immigrants and the liberal governments and interest groups that support them. That anger,

President Trump welcomes Egyptian President Abdel Fattah al-Sisi to the White House on April 3, 2017. Some political scientists say that by making al-Sisi and other autocratic leaders among his first invitees to the White House, Trump has sent a strong signal to global leaders that the United States is no longer concerned about protecting democracy or human rights.

Getty Images/Mark Wilson

democracy promotion. The West needs the cooperation of certain autocratic regimes to fight terrorism. "The stomach for democracy promotion has lessened in the last 10 years," says political scientist Brian Klaas, a fellow in comparative politics at the London School of Economics and the author of the 2017 book *The Despot's Accomplice: How the West is Aiding and Abetting the Decline of Democracy.*

As officials in emerging democracies — such as Brazil, Indonesia, South Africa and Turkey — gained power, they often acted as cold realists instead of becoming powerful advocates for representative gov-

the Dominican Republic, El Salvador, Ghana, Mongolia and Romania. In fact, he argues, the last decade could be viewed "as a period of democratic resilience." (*See "At Issue," p. 885.*)

Some democracy experts warn that a number of leaders are attracted to what they call the "authoritarian capitalist" model followed by China, which has achieved rapid economic growth since the 1980s without being hampered by free elections and independent courts. In contrast, many Western democracies have struggled to recover from the 2007-09 recession and are torn by factions and fighting, as their citizens reel from

in turn, made many middle- and lower-income citizens receptive to restrictions on immigrants' rights; in Hungary, the government decided in February to restrict new arrivals to government camps until their legal status is resolved.

Intelligence agencies say Russia has helped some of those anti-immigrant, populist candidates with money, propaganda and so-called disinformation campaigns that aimed to sow confusion during elections in Western democracies such as the United States, France and Germany.

As political scientists, policymakers and government officials evaluate the democratic landscape worldwide, here are some of the questions they are asking:

Is China's authoritarian capitalism a viable alternative to democracy?

Political theorist Daniel A. Bell, a philosophy professor at Tsinghua University in Beijing, touched off a controversy in 2015 when he said, "I disagree with the view that there's only one morally legitimate way of selecting leaders: one person, one vote." [14]

In his book published that year, *The China Model: Political Meritocracy and the Limits of Democracy*, Bell said China's government, far from being an opaque tyranny, offered a "meritocratic" alternative to liberal, multiparty democracy. China chooses leaders based on experience and friendships, without the need for elections, confirmations, public hearings and U.S.-style popular approval. China's model, he said, has worked in a country with a population triple that of the United States. [15]

However, critics say China's so-called meritocracy is riddled with cronyism, and its economy — reliant on government spending and borrowing — could falter as economic growth slows and workers demand higher wages.

China's "authoritarian capitalism" began in the late 1970s when former Premier Deng Xiaoping introduced "socialism with Chinese characteristics." His policies sought to open China to some aspects of capitalism and international trade while retaining the central government's control on individual rights. While economists have credited Deng's policies with making China the world's fastest-growing economy and raising the standard of living for hundreds of millions of citizens, others have criticized the communist government for blocking open elections, imprisoning critics, censoring the press and the internet and barring criticism of the government and its human rights record. [16]

Nevertheless, some political observers have questioned whether the China model proves that prosperity is possible without democracy. China's ability to complete major infrastructure projects, such as a nationwide high-speed rail network, without public hearings or debate showed a country could build wealth and a modern state without bickering legislatures, intrusive judiciaries and a probing, free media. [17]

Moreover, the West has reeled from the recession while China's system appeared to weather it well, although Chinese finances are not transparent. When Western governments were scrambling to save failing banks, China was investing billions worldwide — largely through government-financed construction projects, according to the Council on Foreign Relations' Kurlantzick. Under Beijing's form of capitalism, he wrote, the government controls certain industries, favors certain corporations and influences banks to finance certain firms. When Beijing wants closer ties with, say, Thailand or South Africa, it pressures its state-linked banks to lend money to Chinese companies working abroad, he explained.

However, many economists say China's economy rests on a shaky foundation that relies heavily on construction fueled by state bank loans and has produced gargantuan debt. [18] Other experts say China's political system works well only in theory.

"There is massive factionalism, factional struggle, clientelism, patronage and corruption," wrote Timothy Garton Ash, an Oxford University historian and an expert on authoritarianism. Without free discussion, China allows no consensus or negotiation, perpetuating a system that is, in fact, not meritocratic, he argued. [19] President Xi, who came to power in 2012, has spent much of his first term investigating and even imprisoning party leaders accused of committing theft and amassing fortunes.

"It's actually going to be very difficult for this system to manage the extremely complex challenges it's facing as economic growth slows down, the supply of cheap labor is exhausted, and society becomes increasingly mature and educated, with higher aspirations," Ash wrote. [20]

"They already are in a slowdown," says sociology professor Ho-Fung Hung at Johns Hopkins University, and signs point to growing unemployment. "Unemployment and discontent are the number-one thing they worry about." Political reforms, however, are "the last thing they think of," he says.

Andrew J. Nathan, a Columbia University political scientist, argued that liberal democracy is superior to China's authoritarian model not because of elections but because democracy's independent legislatures and courts hold leaders accountable. "The selection of leaders is very important, but what makes democracy better than authoritarianism is the checking of leaders by the freedom of others," he said. Such limits on power do not exist in China. Rather, "China views democracy promotion, human-rights diplomacy, humanitarian interventions, and the rise of international criminal law . . . as efforts by the Western powers to weaken rivals." [21]

In a notable example, when the U.N. Security Council debated a resolution in 2014 to refer the Syrian civil war and crimes documented there to the International Criminal Court, China joined Russia to veto the move. A nation's internal affairs, Chinese officials argued, are not concerns of other countries. [22]

Should the United States promote democracy abroad?

The State Department says its mission is "to shape and sustain a peaceful,

Newer Generations Less Supportive of Democracy

Older generations — born in the 1930s and '40s — are far more supportive of democracy than generations born after 1970, according to surveys conducted in some of the world's oldest democracies.

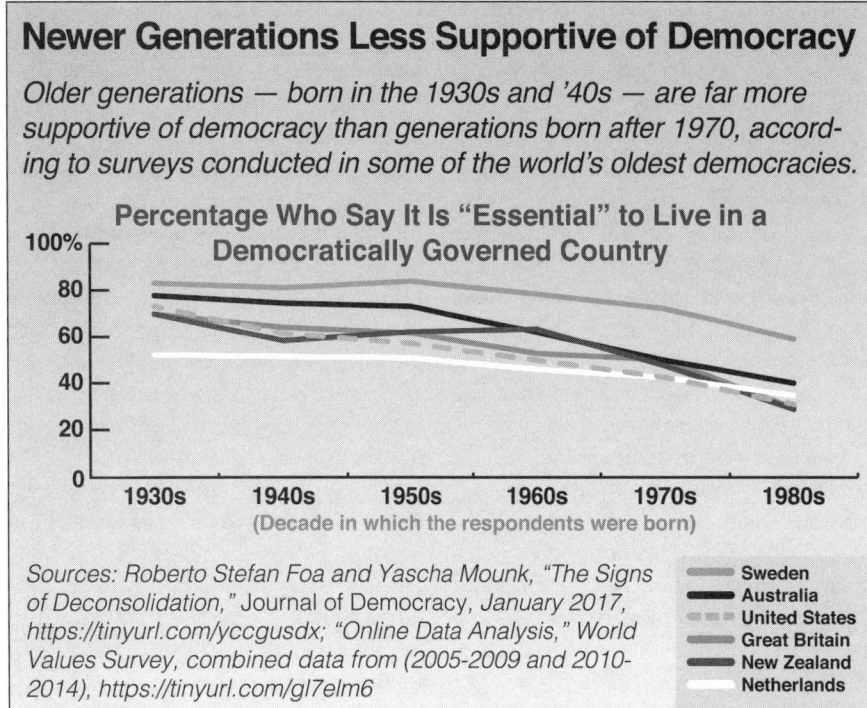

Percentage Who Say It Is "Essential" to Live in a Democratically Governed Country

(Decade in which the respondents were born)

Sources: Roberto Stefan Foa and Yascha Mounk, "The Signs of Deconsolidation," Journal of Democracy, January 2017, https://tinyurl.com/yccgusdx; "Online Data Analysis," World Values Survey, combined data from (2005-2009 and 2010-2014), https://tinyurl.com/gl7elm6

- Sweden
- Australia
- United States
- Great Britain
- New Zealand
- Netherlands

prosperous, just and democratic world and foster conditions for stability and progress." [23] Democracy promotion has been a key U.S. foreign policy goal since the end of World War II, when the United States helped to rebuild former foes Germany and Japan, turning them into powerful democratic allies.

Other U.S. agencies, including the U.S. Agency for International Development, the Millennium Challenge Corp. and the Middle East Partnership Initiative, also strive to promote democracy. [24]

After the Sept. 11, 2001, terrorist attacks, President George W. Bush vowed to create allies in the Middle East by turning autocratic governments into democracies, especially in Iraq and Afghanistan. Those efforts, which continued during Barack Obama's presidency, look to be in peril.

President Trump has proposed an "America first" policy in which the United States focuses on its own goals and does not embroil itself in civil affairs abroad or conduct engage in so-called nation-building. When Trump announced plans to send more troops to Afghanistan, he pointedly rejected the efforts of the

Bush administration, saying, "We are not nation-building again. We are killing terrorists." [25]

To carry out Trump's agenda, Secretary of State Rex Tillerson considered deleting any mention of promoting democracy from the State Department's mission statement. [26] He also proposed slashing spending for programs that promote democratic governance to $1.6 billion in 2018 — down from $2.3 billion in 2016. The proposal "reflects the president's 'America First' agenda that prioritizes the well-being of Americans, bolsters U.S. national security, secures our borders and advances U.S. economic interests," Tillerson said. [27]

Some political scientists say Trump's actions and his decision to welcome several autocratic leaders — Philippine strongman Duterte, Turkey's Erdogan and Egyptian leader Abdel Fattah al-Sisi — as some of his first visitors to the White House sent a strong signal to global leaders that the United States is no longer concerned about protecting democracy or human rights.

Yet, Trump's supporters point out that he has softened his isolationist

tendencies with regard to Venezuela. On Aug. 25, the president imposed sanctions on anyone sending funds that fuel President Maduro's dictatorship. [28] In a Sept. 19 address to the United Nations, Trump urged world leaders to help restore "democracy and political freedoms" in Venezuela, adding, "We are prepared to take further action if the government . . . persists on its path to impose authoritarian rule on the Venezuelan people." [29]

Other political scientists say U.S. skittishness about democracy promotion began in the Obama administration, after what critics called the post-9/11 debacles in Iraq and Afghanistan. Political scientist Klaas said halfhearted attempts to build a democracy in Iraq fed long-standing Muslim rivalries — which had been suppressed by dictator Saddam Hussein — that exploded into a civil war. [30] Such unintended consequences, he said, contributed to a sense in the West that "there are so many fires around the world, maybe we shouldn't make another one."

Reuel Marc Gerecht, a senior fellow at the Foundation for Defense of Democracies, a conservative Washington think tank, said, "Barack Obama came into office mistrusting American hegemony, which had led us into Afghanistan and Iraq." Obama believed in "diplomacy untethered from the use of force," he continued, and tried to persuade Syrian President Bashar al-Assad to leave office and to smooth over relations with Russia's Putin. But U.S. foes saw his outreach as weakness, Gerecht said. [31]

The Obama administration slashed U.S. spending to promote democratic institutions and human rights, from $3.5 billion to $1.9 billion annually between 2010 and 2015, before increasing it to $2.3 billion in 2016, according to Pippa Norris, director of the Electoral Integrity Project, a program at Harvard University and the University of Sydney that assesses elections worldwide. Because the United States has led the spread of democracy and human rights over the years, she said, "any abandonment of this work sends damaging diplomatic signals about America's priorities." [32]

While promoting democracy has enjoyed bipartisan support, some current members of Congress question the effectiveness and appropriateness of past democracy efforts.

"Creating reasonably effective democracies took centuries in the West, and it was often a highly contentious — even violent — process," wrote Stephen M. Walt, a professor of international relations at Harvard University. "To believe the U.S. military could export democracy quickly and cheaply required a degree of hubris that is still breathtaking to recall." [33]

Bruce Fein, a constitutional attorney and conservative activist, wrote that democratically elected leaders "can be every bit as tyrannical and aggressive towards the United States as unelected dictators," citing the election of Islamist extremist leaders of Hamas in the West Bank or the Muslim Brotherhood in Egypt. If a country is "insufficiently mature, literate and homogeneous," democracy degenerates into "majoritarian, sectarian or tribal tyrannies," he continued. [34]

Klaas counters that when America abandons democracy promotion it leaves a vacuum in unstable states that Moscow and Beijing can fill. "It's a global foreign policy battle, and the West's losses are China's and Russia's gains," he said. [35]

Do the internet and social media strengthen and foster democracy?

The internet's power to spread democracy has been undeniable.

Before the wave of popular revolts known as the Arab Spring shook the Middle East in 2010-11, activists, writers and citizens used digital media to help Tunisians, Egyptians, Libyans, Yemenis, Bahrainis, Syrians and others mobilize for political change. Digital media melded journalism, citizen reporting, activism and entertainment, wrote Jeff Ghannam, a journalist and lawyer with the Center for International Media Assistance, a U.S.-government funded nonprofit that pro-

Nanette Castillo grieves beside her son Aldrin, an alleged drug user killed by unidentified assailants, in Manila, Philippines, on Oct. 3, 2017. President Trump has told Philippine President Rodrigo Duterte he is doing an "unbelievable job" with his anti-drug campaign, which has resulted in thousands of extrajudicial killings of alleged drug sellers and users.

AFP/Getty Images/Noel Celis

motes independent media abroad. When Syria barred international news organizations from covering the civil war there, media companies used images and videos sent through social media from citizen journalists. Private, upstart channels offered alternatives to state TV. [36]

"To be sure, these were not Facebook or Twitter revolutions, however much cyberutopians would like them to be," Ghannam wrote. "However, the internet's potential as a tool that can help the process of democratization is undeniable."

In Russia, opposition leader Alexei Navalny's Progress Party has aired investigative reports on YouTube for more than a year documenting the wealth of allies of former President Dmitri Medvedev and Putin. [37] Last spring, after a video accused Medvedev of using friends' charities to hide riches, including mansions and yachts, he apparently accumulated while in office, tens of thousands of citizens demonstrated nationwide. [38]

In China, social media has allowed citizens to air opinions and grievances, despite that nation's heavy censorship. After the July death of Nobel Peace Prize recipient Liu Xioabo — whom the authorities refused to release despite his advanced-stage cancer — citizens flocked online

to pay tribute. Censors quickly scrubbed the comments from social media forums. In 2015, millions of residents downloaded a damning documentary about pollution until censors blocked it. [39]

It is unclear, some academics say, whether such online actions drive long-term commitment to reform. While social media enables organizers to quickly pull off large protests, such actions do not necessarily build permanent opposition movements, according to Zeynep Tufekci, an associate professor of sociology at the University of North Carolina, Chapel Hill, and Christopher Wilson, co-founder of The Engine Room, a Web-based democracy-promotion activist group. Previous large demonstrations, such as the 1963 civil rights March on Washington, required months of preparation that helped to strengthen the movement, they wrote, and helped organizers build future campaigns, such as voter-registration drives in the South. [40]

Several recent social movements have struggled to achieve much beyond large protests. In 2011, Occupy Wall Street activists staged demonstrations in hundreds of cities in more than 80 countries, protesting the role large banks and financial firms played in causing the 2007-08 recession, but few things changed, despite the large crowds. Likewise, protests in Istanbul in 2013 and Hong Kong in 2014 — both of which sought greater political freedoms — did not produce much if any concrete change. [41]

Protests should be only a first, potential step, wrote Tufekci and Wilson, because without follow-up, such as building coalitions, officials will not see such movements as threats.

More ominously, according to Ghannam, the internet can be used by authoritarian governments. The online world operates in the open and is easily viewed by the government and police, he said. China and Russia have detained activists, sometimes in secret, based on what they have written online. [42]

Social media also enables authoritarian governments to undermine democracy, such as efforts by the Russian government to sway the 2016 U.S. election, says Diamond. Governments also can pelt social media with propaganda, fake news and negative publicity that can shape voters' opinions. Some governments are using propaganda, fake news and disinformation "as offensive tools against democracy," says Marc F. Plattner, founding co-editor of the *Journal of Democracy.*

"On the whole, the internet is a plus for freedom, but we're only now starting to grapple with the negative impact," says Arch Puddington, a distinguished fellow for democracy studies at Freedom House, a nonprofit in New York that publishes an annual survey on the status of freedom around the world. "I would expect 10 years from now we are going to see many societies with laws and policies in place that will make the internet less free-wheeling than it is. And some will be enacted by democracies."

Courtney Radsch, advocacy director for the Committee to Protect Journalists, worries that as countries move to ban hate speech, they may end up suppressing free speech. "Governments are calling on private companies to remove content and accounts," she says. "Of course they are going to remove more content than

they should." Governments provide little if any guidance on this, she adds.

In April, the German cabinet passed a bill to combat disinformation and hate speech on social media. It requires media companies to remove hate speech 24 hours after they receive a complaint and to block any other content deemed offensive within seven days. Jewish groups hailed the law. "Jews are exposed to anti-Semitic hatred in social networks on a daily basis," said the Central Council of Jews, a federation of German Jewish organizations. "This law is the logical consequence to effectively limit hate speech." Facebook and free speech activists said the law could smother all kinds of speech. "This law as it stands now will not improve efforts to tackle this important societal problem," Facebook said in a statement. [43]

"Technology moves so fast," says Plattner. "There's a kind of arms race between the people who want to create greater freedom and people who want to create greater oppression." ∎

BACKGROUND

Greek and Christian Roots

Democracy dates to the citizen states and philosophers of ancient Greece. In Athens in the sixth century B.C., as citizens chafed under rule by the elite, philosophers argued that wider citizen participation would best secure the public's loyalty and ensure stability. [44]

The Roman Empire experimented with popular governance, but eventually supplanted it with imperial power. As it did so, a countervailing force emerged that challenged slavery and pagan beliefs — a new religion called Christianity. The influential Christian theologian Augustine argued that community bonds created a moral force for self-governance.

However, after Germanic tribes overran the empire's western flank in the fifth century A.D., the notion of citizen power nearly vanished for several centuries. [45]

In 1215, under pressure from rebel barons, King John in England reluctantly accepted the Magna Carta, which established the notion that a king was subject to laws and that his power could be checked. It also enshrined individual rights, especially the principle of habeas corpus, which allowed a person to challenge his imprisonment in court. [46]

Since its early days, Christianity had promoted the idea that kings were anointed by God. Catholic and Protestant political thinkers began contesting the so-called divine right of kings in the 16th century, and the notion that subjects' could question authority spread during the Protestant Reformation. Opponents of Roman Catholicism challenged religious hierarchy and backed the right of ordinary people to make decisions in their churches and, ultimately, in government. [47]

The concept of democratic rule re-emerged in 17th-century England amid civil wars, as King James — and later his son, Charles I — clashed with Parliament over taxes, religion and other issues. Religious radicals known as Puritans, who wanted to "purify" Anglicanism, fled to North America starting in the early 1600s, where they established the Massachusetts Bay Colony. [48]

Democracy's First Wave

As the English colonies in North America grew in the 17th and 18th centuries, colonial assemblies gained power and stature. These early democratic institutions levied taxes and regulated colonial life. In the 1760s, when British officials attempted to tighten imperial control and tax the colonists, they ignited a rebellion. [49]

On July 4, 1776, the Continental Congress declared the colonies "free

Continued on p. 880

Chronology

1900s-1970s
Dictatorships rise and fall; Western democratic alliances are established.

1917
Russia establishes the world's first government based on communism.

1933
Adolf Hitler seizes power in Germany, setting stage for World War II.

1945
World War II ends; 50 countries form the United Nations.

1947
India wins independence from Britain and later becomes the world's largest democracy.

1948
South Africa establishes apartheid to guarantee white dominance.

1949
Mao Zedong transforms China into a communist state.

1952
European Coal and Steel Community establishes an economic and political alliance that evolves into the European Union in 1993.

1956
Soviet tanks crush pro-democracy uprising in Hungary, killing more than 3,000.

1961
Soviet Union builds the Berlin Wall, separating East Germany from the city's democratic Western half.

1975
Thirty-five nations sign the Helsinki Accords to improve relations between communist countries and the West.

1980s-1990s
Democracy rises in former Soviet-controlled nations.

1989
Chinese soldiers gun down hundreds of pro-democracy protesters in Beijing's Tiananmen Square. . . . The Berlin Wall falls. . . . Pro-democracy demonstrations erupt in Czechoslovakia, Bulgaria, Hungary and Romania.

1990
Lech Walesa becomes Poland's first democratically elected president, marking the end of Soviet control.

1991
Soviet Union is dissolved. The last president, Mikhail Gorbachev, hands power to Russian Federation President Boris Yeltsin. The country struggles to establish democratic institutions.

1994
Anti-aparteid leader Nelson Mandela is released from prison after 29 years and becomes the first democratically elected president of South Africa.

1998
Venezuelans elect populist Hugo Chávez as president; he installs a socialist government.

2000-Present
Democracies falter in Russia, Venezuela and Eastern Europe.

2000
Russia elects former KGB agent Vladimir Putin as president. He consolidates control over the media and courts and ends regional elections.

2009
Venezuelan voters end presidential term limits, letting Chávez rule indefinitely.

2010
Hungarian Prime Minister Viktor Orbán and his Fidesz party take power; constitutional changes give him control over courts.

2011
A Tunisian street vendor commits suicide to protest government oppression, sparking the so-called Arab Spring uprisings in Egypt, Yemen, Libya, Bahrain and Syria that unseat authoritarian leaders, yet new ones replace them.

2014
Thai military suspends the country's constitution and ends democratic rule.

2015
Poland's right-wing Law and Justice Party controls parliament and weakens the constitutional court, politicizes the civil service and restricts the media.

2016
After quelling an attempted coup, Turkish President Recep Tayyip Erdogan blames an old opponent and arrests about 45,000 people, including teachers, journalists and government workers.

2017
Newly elected U.S. President Donald Trump attacks the press, judicial system, Congress and intelligence agencies, disparages NATO and compliments Putin and Philippine President Rodrigo Duterte, who directs a murderous anti-drug campaign that kills thousands of suspected drug dealers and users.

Venezuela Sinks into Dictatorship

Critics say President Nicolás Maduro threatens the once-thriving democracy.

In Venezuela, Latin America's oldest democracy and the country with the world's largest proven oil reserves, grocers' shelves are bare, corruption is rampant and democratic institutions are in tatters. [1]

Venezuela's stunning descent in recent years from a wealthy, stable democracy into a nation gripped by chaos and political intrigue has led to concerns that the country of more than 30 million people could fall permanently into dictatorship.

Elections held Oct. 16 threatened to deepen the country's political crisis by strengthening the ruling Socialist United Party, which won at least 17 of 23 governorships, a result some opposition leaders and the U.S. State Department blamed on fraud. [2]

The shift began under the late Venezuelan president Hugo Chávez, an autocrat elected in a wave of populist enthusiasm in the late 1990s, and continues under his successor, Nicolás Maduro, who has tried to dissolve the country's legislature and rewrite the constitution.

Maduro wants "to eliminate not only our democracy but any institution that still survives in Venezuela," opposition leader Julio Borges said recently. [3]

Ongoing mass demonstrations that began in the spring led to the deaths of about 125 people (as of August), and more than 5,051 people had been arbitrarily detained, according to a United Nations report. [4] Military tribunals have prosecuted hundreds of people protesting Maduro's socialist government on charges that could send them to prison for 30 years.

The protesters say Maduro became more authoritarian as the country's economy deteriorated due to collapsing world oil prices and mismanagement of the state-owned oil industry. Falling oil revenues have triggered massive government borrowing, and production of domestic goods has plummeted. Desperation has grown as food and medicine have run low, creating what Human Rights Watch has called a "humanitarian crisis." [5]

The devolution of Venezuela's democracy is an example of how some longtime democracies have faltered in recent years when authoritarian leaders, buoyed by populist movements, have begun dismantling constitutional protections and destroying checks on their power, usually amid massive economic problems.

But Maduro has not dismantled democracy on his own, according to some of his critics. They say Chávez, who died in 2013, had expanded presidential powers and weakened democracy by, among other things, limiting press freedom and the right to protest. [6] "Democracy was on thin ice by the time [Maduro] came to power," says Michael McCarthy, a research fellow at the Center for Latin American and Latino Studies at American University in Washington.

The conditions that led to Chávez's election in 1998 had begun decades earlier. In the 1970s Venezuela was awash in oil money, making it the richest country in Latin America. But after the oil industry was nationalized in 1976, mismanagement of the industry threw the economy into disarray, with inflation and foreign debt rising sharply in the 1980s and '90s. [7]

When world oil prices fell in the 1980s, Venezuela's government imposed austerity measures. Hundreds of people died in anti-government protests. [8] "From that point on, the system was essentially morally bankrupt," McCarthy says.

Chávez was elected in 1998 after promising to clean up government waste, graft and patronage, redistribute the country's oil wealth and boost social program budgets. [9] He spent oil revenue on education, housing, health and food programs — a component of his wildly popular leftist governing philosophy. The share of households in poverty fell from 55 percent in 1995 to 26 percent in 2009. Unemployment fell from 15 percent when Chávez took office to under 8 percent in June 2009. [10]

Chávez also clashed with the national oil company, Petroleos de Venezuela (PDVSA), which he said was controlled by foreigners and hid profits. Production fell after Chávez cut the company's budget for oil well maintenance. In 2002, Chávez fired at least 20,000 striking PDVSA workers and replaced them with political loyalists. Production fell even lower. [11] He also directed the state to take over food producers, fertilizer plants, farmland, banks, manufacturers, gold production, telecommunications and utilities. [12]

Meanwhile, Chávez capitalized on populist anger by making other sweeping changes. He suspended Supreme Court judges who opposed him and packed the court with allies. [13] A constitutional assembly amended the constitution to eliminate the Senate and authorize Chávez to recall legislators.

Continued from p. 878

and independent states," stating in the Declaration of Independence that governments derive "their just powers from the consent of the governed" and that "whenever any Form of Government becomes destructive of these ends, it is the Right of the People to alter or to abolish it." [50]

After independence was won, the American states in 1787 established a federal government that shared powers among a president, a congress and a judiciary. The American experiment inspired other nations, including France, where citizens launched a revolution of their own in 1789. It ended with a constitution that established the French

Republic and a legislature. Democracy grew in Europe over the next century, especially after the Hapsburg and Hohenzollern empires collapsed. [51]

World War I, and the overthrow of Russia's empire, marked a dire moment for democratic government. The Bolsheviks, the radical wing of a labor party whose members followed the

"The state was gradually eroding the checks and balances," according to Javier Corrales, a political science professor at Amherst College in Massachusetts. "Once you have no way of controlling . . . the executive [by] blocking a spending [bill] or suing him through the courts, the space is completely open for corruption." [14]

When Chavez dies in 2013, Maduro assumed power and was elected as Chavez's successor in a special election. By then, the country was struggling to pay its debts, as world oil prices were tumbling again. His allies have tried to disband the nation's opposition-controlled legislature, first by using the court system. When that failed, Maduro planned to create a new political body, a Constituent Assembly, which would rewrite the country's constitution, grant unlimited power to officials loyal to him and dismantle or reorganize the branches of government viewed as disloyal. [15]

In July, more than 98 percent of Venezuelan voters signaled their disapproval of the Constituent Assembly proposal in a voting exercise, called a popular consultation, organized by opposition parties. [16] Despite the staggering display of public disapproval, the Constituent Assembly was formed after a July 30 vote to elect assembly members. Venezuelans were not given the option to reject the assembly.

Since then the Constituent Assembly has voided the opposition-led legislature and granted itself full authority to write and pass legislation, consolidating control for Maduro's Party. [17]

In July the Trump administration imposed economic sanctions on Venezuela in an effort to block Maduro from altering the nation's constitution, which U.S. officials said could doom Venezuelan democracy. [18] Two months later, Trump attacked Maduro in a speech at the United Nations.

One country leapt to the South American nation's defense — China — an authoritarian communist country. [19]

— Suzanne Sataline

[1] Max Fisher and Amanda Taub, "How Does Populism Turn Authoritarian? Venezuela Is a Case in Point," *The New York Times*, April 1, 2017, https://tinyurl.com/mkufv9w; Juan Carlos Garzón and Robert Muggah, "Venezuela's raging homicide epidemic is going unrecorded," *Los Angeles Times*, March 31, 2017, https://tinyurl.com/y73cl7zb; Jessica Dillinger, "The World's Largest Oil Reserves By Country," *World Atlas*, updated April 25, 2017, https://tinyurl.com/hp7f72a.

[2] Fabiola Sanchez and Christine Armario, "Venezuela opposition looks for answers after election loss," The Associated Press, *The Washington Post*, Oct. 16, 2017, https://tinyurl.com/y7ovwtxk.

[3] Mariana Zuñiga and Nick Miroff, "Maduro wants to rewrite Venezuela's constitution. That's rocket fuel on the fire," *The Washington Post*, June 10, 2017, https://tinyurl.com/y86bz96l.

[4] Brian Ellsworth and Stephanie Nebehay, "U.N. decries excessive force in Venezuela's crackdown on protests," Reuters, Aug. 8, 2017, https://tinyurl.com/yb9m8nqc.

[5] Mercy Benzaquen, "How Food in Venezuela Went From Subsidized to Scarce," *The New York Times*, July 16, 2017, https://tinyurl.com/y8nyd98h; "World Report 2017: Venezuela, Events of 2016," Human Rights Watch, https://tinyurl.com/y7gsyrkc.

[6] "Venezuela: Chávez's Authoritarian Legacy, Dramatic Concentration of Power and Open Disregard for Basic Human Rights," Human Rights Watch, March 5, 2013, https://tinyurl.com/y9sfapow.

[7] Javier Corrales, "Venezuela in the 1980s, the 1990s and beyond, Why Citizen-Detached Parties Imperil Economic Governance," *ReVista: The Harvard Review of Latin America*, Harvard University, 1999, https://tinyurl.com/y8n4gdb4; Alejandro Velasco, "Explaining the Venezuelan Crisis," North American Congress on Latin America, Oct. 28, 2016, https://tinyurl.com/y73bldae; Henkel Garcia U, "Inside Venezuela's economic collapse," *The Conversation*, July 10, 2017, https://tinyurl.com/y7okfj2o.

[8] Simon Romero, "Carlos Andrés Pérez, Former President of Venezuela, Dies at 88," *The New York Times*, Dec. 26, 2010, https://tinyurl.com/y7rz29mq.

[9] Fisher and Taub, *op. cit.*; Brian A. Nelson, "Hugo Chávez, President of Venezuela," *Encyclopædia Britannica*, undated, https://tinyurl.com/ya9kkemg.

[10] Oscar Guardiola-Rivera, "Hugo Chávez kept his promise to the people of Venezuela," *The Guardian*, March 5, 2013, https://tinyurl.com/ybhzlmsq.

[11] Scott Tong, "How oil-rich Venezuela ended up with a miserable economy," Marketplace.org, April 5, 2016, https://tinyurl.com/y7okfj2o.

[12] Steve Mufson, "Conoco, Exxon Exit Venezuela Oil Deals," *The Washington Post*, June 27, 2007, https://tinyurl.com/ybargmbe; Tamsin Carlisle, "Venezuela seizes 60 firms," *The National*, May 9, 2009, https://tinyurl.com/ybwful4u.

[13] Fisher and Taub, *op. cit.*

[14] Javier Corrales, "The Authoritarian Resurgence, Autocratic Legalism in Venezuela," *Journal of Democracy*, April 2015, Volume 26, No. 2, https://tinyurl.com/ya77n9my.

[15] Nicholas Casey, "As Venezuela Prepares to Vote, Some Fear an End to Democracy," *The New York Times*, July 29, 2017, https://tinyurl.com/yan8r6lx.

[16] Ana Vanessa Herrero and Ernestor Londoño, "Venezuelans Rebuke Their President by a Staggering Margin," *The New York Times*, July 16, 2017, https://tinyurl.com/ycljcktu.

[17] Nicholas Casey, "Venezuela's New, Powerful Assembly Takes Over Legislature's Duties," *The New York Times*, Aug. 18, 2017, https://tinyurl.com/y9xvnnpx.

[18] Tracey Wilkinson, "Trump administration hits Venezuela with more sanctions, targeting civilian and military officials," *Los Angeles Times*, July 26, 2017, https://tinyurl.com/ya92njc4.

[19] "China offers support for strife-torn Venezuela at United Nations," Reuters, Sept. 20, 2017, https://tinyurl.com/ya7j6k3e.

writings of German philosopher Karl Marx, overthrew the monarchy. They created the Soviet Union, the world's first communist state. While supporters talked of the wonders of a worker-led government, the system became a brutal dictatorship that eventually killed tens of millions of citizens through starvation, imprisonment and mass executions.

In the 1920s and '30s, with the brutalities almost unknown beyond Soviet borders, people elsewhere — craving stability and economic opportunity, fearful of immigrants and invasions and swayed by powerful propaganda — embraced the idealism of communism, as well as fascism and militarism. Such ideologies soon morphed into autocratic regimes. Fascist

Benito Mussolini overthrew a corrupt democracy in Italy. Meanwhile, authoritarianism spread to Poland and the Baltics, whose fledging post-World War I governments collapsed after military coups. [52]

Adolf Hitler, leader of the National Socialist German Workers' (Nazi) Party, called democracy "a monstrosity of filth and fire" in his book *Mein Kampf*. [53]

After seizing power in Germany and eliminating most citizen protections, Hitler established the Third Reich and launched invasions in late 1939 that led to World War II. Hitler's conquest of most of Europe obliterated the Continent's democracies, including France's, and eventually killed millions, including 6 million Jews in the Holocaust.

Cold War Competition

With the Allies' victory in World War II in 1945, democracy returned to Europe and Japan. The United States helped rebuild ravaged Western economies through the Marshall Plan, which delivered more than $13 billion (about $132 billion today) in aid to European countries. In Japan, U.S. occupying forces imposed military, political, economic and social reforms. Former foes West Germany and Japan eventually flourished as democracies. [54]

The war also ended Europe's colonial regimes, creating many new democracies in Africa and Asia. In Greece, Spain, Argentina, Brazil and Chile, once-autocratic regimes expanded voting rights and civil freedoms. [55]

Soon after the war's end, 50 countries formed the United Nations, which aimed to prevent future wars and promote democratic governments and human rights, a goal laid out in the Universal Declaration of Human Rights in 1948. At about the same time, several European nations formed an economic and political alliance, the European Coal and Steel Community, which eventually became the European Union (EU). [56]

In 1949 Western democracies formed a military alliance, the North Atlantic Treaty Organization (NATO), to match the Soviet Union's united front.

But democracy had formidable foes. A civil war in China ended in 1949 with the victory of Mao Zedong's communist forces, which proceeded to build a one-party state that essentially turned citizens into spies and informers. Tens

of millions died of starvation during the so-called Great Leap Forward, an economic "modernization" effort in 1958-61. Many more died during the Cultural Revolution (1966-76), as the government tried to eliminate "enemies of the revolution." [57]

The Soviet Union, meanwhile, had established impenetrable borders, dubbed the Iron Curtain, between its satellite states in Eastern Europe and democratic Western Europe. Soviet forces tried to block citizens from fleeing the communist-run states in the East to the democratic West; violators were often shot dead. The Berlin Wall that separated East and West Berlin remained in place until citizens tore it down in 1989. [58]

The "Cold War" between nations allied with the United States or the Soviets fanned proxy wars. Civil war erupted in Korea in the early 1950s and Vietnam in the 1960s and '70s. In Africa and Latin America, many former colonial states devolved into military dictatorships, supported by the United States, as they sought to defeat socialist uprisings supported by the Soviet Union or Communist China. [59]

In the late 1980s, the Soviet Union's mounting economic problems — fueled by an inefficient, centrally managed economy — prompted the country to borrow massive amounts of money. Former Soviet leader Mikhail Gorbachev announced new policies of *glasnost* and *perestroika*, or openness and reform. With more freedom to discuss and organize, discontent within the Soviet bloc grew. [60]

On June 12, 1987, in a famous speech in front of West Berlin's Brandenburg Gate, part of the Berlin Wall, U.S. President Ronald Reagan challenged Gorbachev to give his people freedom and "tear down this wall!" [61]

Rather than Reagan's words, the Soviet bloc's faltering economy created the greatest pressure on Gorbachev. As the Soviet Union competed with the United States in expanding its nuclear defenses, it robbed its manufacturing economy of crucial resources. [62] A politically weak-

ened Gorbachev did not interfere when opposition movements arose in satellite states, such as Poland's Solidarity labor movement, which won seats in the Polish legislature in 1989. [63]

After Poland and Hungary gained some freedoms, citizens in East Germany agitated for their government to open the border to the West, sealed since 1961 and manned by armed guards. When the gates opened, suddenly on Nov. 9, 1989, a tide of people crossed to the West, unmolested by the border guards. [64] Two years later, communist hardliners tried to depose Gorbachev in a coup, but military officers and leaders from the autonomous republics refused to cooperate, and on Dec. 31, 1991, the Soviet Union was dissolved. The new leader, President Boris Yeltsin, steered the Russian Federation toward a rudimentary democracy. [65]

Former Soviet republics — Ukraine, Latvia, Lithuania and others — quickly voted for independence. By 2004, after several peaceful protests — the "color revolutions" — voters in former Soviet bloc countries chose new presidents. Many of the emerging states formed democratic governments to qualify for EU membership in what some called the reunification of Europe. [66]

Democratic Backsliding

In the late 1970s, Democratic President Jimmy Carter sought to make human rights central to foreign policy and linked economic and military aid to countries' human-rights records. [67]

The number of world democracies expanded throughout the 1980s and '90s, especially after the Soviet Union ended.

Republican President George W. Bush aggressively promoted democracy after Islamist terrorists attacked the United States on Sept. 11, 2001, arguing that democracy would help alleviate anti-U.S. sentiment in the Middle East and block further attacks on the West.

Yet, the U.S. democracy-promotion campaign of the 2000s had inconsistencies, just as it had during the Cold War, when the United States sometimes supported military dictators who opposed communism. The Bush administration spent billions of dollars, and lost thousands of lives, trying to establish democratic institutions in Iraq, Afghanistan and other nations, while retaining close ties with repressive regimes such as Saudi Arabia, the birthplace of most of the 9/11 terrorists. [68]

However, Bush's efforts to fight Islamist extremists while building new democratic nations in the Middle East largely failed, says author Klaas. Beginning in December 2010, protests and rallies erupted in several Arab states, largely powered by young people's frustration with their autocratic governments and poor job prospects. In Cairo, huge crowds filled the streets for months, demanding that Egyptian President Mubarak resign. [69]

However, the Arab Spring protests did not usher in vast democratic change, except in Tunisia, where democracy remains a work in progress. Egypt elected the religiously conservative Morsi, who was ousted in 2013 by the military, led by Sisi. Since becoming president, Sisi has imposed even more repressive measures than Mubarak's. In Syria, the military remained loyal to Assad and is used as a tool of sectarian power. [70]

During the presidential campaign and after his election in 2008, Democrat Barack Obama vowed to end U.S. involvement in Iraq and Afghanistan, and promoted a policy of restraint in the region as violence grew.

Meanwhile, Putin, first elected president of Russia in 2000, had instituted many changes to ensure his power. His government took over television stations, curtailed media freedoms, ended regional elections, imposed harsh penalties on protesters and harassed political opponents. Many of Putin's critics were killed or died under suspicious circumstances. In 2014, when Ukrainian protests

prodded that country's president to resign, Putin annexed the country's eastern portion, claiming it was historically part of Russia. In response, the West imposed sanctions that, coupled with the collapse of world prices for oil (Russia's major export), severely damaged the Russian economy. [71]

Democracy and human rights faced challenges elsewhere in the West. In Britain, voters backed restrictions on immigrants, as nationalists who opposed the EU's open-border policies blamed new arrivals for taking jobs and dragging down the U.K. economy. In June 2016, British voters stunned the establishment by backing the U.K.'s exit from the European Union. [72]

Five months later the Republican nominee for president, billionaire real estate developer and political neophyte Donald Trump, won an upset victory over Democrat Hillary Clinton. Trump ran a campaign infused with nationalistic slogans that attacked immigrants and refugees, denigrated NATO and vowed to place American interests before those of other nations. In office, he has lambasted Congress and the judiciary, sought to temporarily ban immigrants from certain Muslim-majority nations from entering the United States, and suggested that the press be restricted. His policies prompted many scholars to warn that democracy in America was threatened.

Shortly after his election, the U.S. intelligence community concluded that Russia's intelligence services had meddled in the 2016 presidential election through hacking and planting of "fake news" online that damaged Clinton and favored Trump. In addition, according to the spy agencies, Trump campaign associates communicated with Russians during the election in ways that caused "concern." [73] Senate and House committees opened investigations into the Russian interference.

In May, Trump fired FBI Director James B. Comey, who said later that the president had pressed him to state publicly that Trump was not under in-

vestigation. That month, the Justice Department appointed former FBI Director Robert S. Mueller III to investigate possible ties between the Trump campaign and Russian officials. [74] ■

CURRENT SITUATION

America First

Since taking office, President Trump has insisted that the United States not try to recreate countries "in our own image" or impose democratic policies on others. The administration also proposed cutting aid to developing nations by one-third and diverting the money to national security. [75]

Both the foreign aid and national security communities blasted the plan. Cutting the foreign aid budget would mark "U.S. withdrawal from the world, rather than continued leadership and engagement," says Travis Adkins, senior director for public policy and government relations at InterAction, a Washington alliance of nongovernmental organizations. Sen. Lindsey Graham, a Republican from South Carolina and the chair of the Appropriations Subcommittee on State and Foreign Aid, said cutting aid would damage national security. "Now is not the time for retreat," he said. "Now is the time to double down on diplomacy and development." [76]

The Senate Appropriations Committee approved $51 billion for the State Department, foreign operations and related programs for fiscal 2018 — almost $11 billion above Trump's request. [77]

While disparaging democracy-building, Trump continues to praise authoritarian leaders. Trump said Egyptian strongman al-Sisi was a "fantastic job," and during a May trip to the Middle East he promised to sell weapons to the repressive Saudi Arabian monarchy and urged regional leaders to get tougher on Islamist terrorists — without mentioning that the Saudis had been accused of human-rights abuses. [78]

Human-rights activists say extrajudicial killings and other abuses in Egypt spiked after Trump's trip. "The visit has emboldened Arab rulers that whatever violations they commit against their people are going to be accepted by the Trump administration," said Gamal Eid, executive director of the Arab Network for Human Rights Information. In Egypt, he said, Trump's actions gave Sisi "the green light to increase the repression. He's been empowered." [79]

Obama had frozen part of Egypt's annual military aid package for two years after al-Sisi-led troops overthrew Morsi, and Obama never invited al-Sisi to the White House. In mid-August, the Trump administration said it would cut or delay $290 million in military and economic aid to Egypt after the government passed a law restricting NGOs from engaging in pro-democracy political activity. It was later revealed that the aid was frozen in part because Egyptians were buying contraband weapons from North Korea. [80]

Meanwhile, the congressional and FBI investigations into Russian interference in the 2016 presidential election continue. In September, Facebook CEO Mark Zuckerberg notified Congress that his company had discovered that Russian operatives had paid $100,000 for 3,000 ads posted on 470 phony Facebook pages during the presidential election. The ads aimed to create social chaos, religious and racial division and suppress the vote, said those who had viewed them. Similar ads were discovered on Twitter, Facebook and Google. [81]

The Kremlin's goal is "to encourage discord in American society," said Michael A. McFaul, a former U.S. ambassador to Russia and currently director of the Freeman Spogli Institute for International Studies at Stanford University. Putin believes "our society is imperfect, that our democracy is not better than his, so to

see us in conflict on big social issues is in the Kremlin's interests." [82]

Embattled Democracies

As the European Union prepares for uncertainty after the upcoming departure of Great Britain, member states also must decide how to handle rising populism and nationalism.

In September, when Angela Merkel earned a fourth term as German chancellor, Alternative for Germany won parliamentary representation, the first time a far-right party earned seats in parliament in more than 60 years. [83]

In Poland, where leaders took a cue from nationalist Hungarian Prime Minister Viktor Orbán, Jarosław Kaczyński, leader of the ruling Law and Justice Party, pushed to appoint loyalists to the constitutional court and public broadcasting station. A law passed in July would allow the government to fire Supreme Court judges, the very people responsible for approving election results. After tens of thousands of protesters demanded that Poland's courts remain free, President Andrzej Duda said he would veto the law. [84]

In Turkey, President Erdogan has tried to silence opposition activists after a military coup failed in 2016. A state of emergency remains, and the government has fired or suspended 130,000 workers and arrested about 45,000, including thousands of lawyers, teachers, doctors, journalists and jurists. Recently, hundreds of officials accused of fomenting the plot were sentenced to life in prison. In the spring, voters narrowly approved constitutional amendments that ended the parliamentary system and granted vast powers to the winner of the 2019 presidential election; observers say Erdogan will likely win that. Erdogan's slide toward autocratic rule led the EU Parliament last November to suspend negotiations over Turkey's 1987 application to join. [85]

In Russia, Putin continues to wield enormous control after 17 years as either

president or prime minister. Freedom House rates Russia as "not free" and ranks political rights there among the lowest anywhere. After Russia invaded Ukraine's Crimean region in 2014, Western nations, including the United States, imposed tough economic sanctions that have hampered Russia's economy. [86]

With revenues down, some wages unpaid and poverty rising, opposition leader Navalny's website, which carries investigative pieces detailing what he says are Putin's cronies' corrupt practices, has found a receptive audience. The government has imposed heavy fines on protests deemed illegal and prosecuted Navalny for embezzlement in a case international officials call a sham. [87]

In Southeast Asia, the Philippines' Duterte continues a war on drug users and dealers begun when he took office in June 2016. At least 7,000 Filipinos are dead, most killed without charges or prosecutions. The extrajudicial killings and threats against journalists led Freedom House to reclassify the onetime established democracy as "partly free." Religious and international human-rights groups have condemned the campaign, but Trump has said Duterte is doing an "unbelievable job on the drug problem." [88]

The backsliding on democracy in the former U.S. colony was especially dramatic because the Philippines was known as the "ultimate Third World democracy," with a modern judiciary, free press and speech, a two-party political system with open elections and separation between the church and state, wrote William H. Overholt, a senior fellow at the Asia Center at Harvard University. Moreover, Duterte's predecessor, Benigno Aquino, had set the country on "an upward path of improved growth, democracy and alliance with the United States," he said. [89]

Elsewhere in Southeast Asia, the Rohingya crisis continues to unfold in Myanmar (formerly Burma), once praised as an example of how a former military junta converted to a democratically elected

Continued on p. 886

At Issue:

Is democracy in retreat around the world?

ARCH PUDDINGTON
DISTINGUISHED SCHOLAR FOR DEMOCRACY STUDIES, FREEDOM HOUSE

WRITTEN FOR *CQ RESEARCHER*, OCTOBER 2017

*d*uring the late 20th century, societies everywhere threw off dictatorship and embraced freedom. It was understood that the world's democracies offered peace and prosperity, while authoritarianism brought poverty and oppression.

Today, democracy seems in retreat. Russia and China add layer on layer of repression; new democracies like Poland and Hungary move sharply toward authoritarianism; conditions continue to erode throughout Southeast Asia and the Middle East. Populist parties with nativist streaks are fixtures in Europe, and a populist-nationalist sits in the White House.

Still, things could turn around in the future. Consider these points:

• Both U.S. and European economies are rebounding, with growth rising and unemployment falling. The major democracies remain the world's wealthiest countries.

• The Venezuelan catastrophe has had major ripple effects in the region and beyond, with South American voters rejecting parties associated with the left-wing ideology of former Venezuelan President Hugo Chávez.

• In Europe, centrist forces have maintained government control, even as populist parties have made gains.

• Vladimir Putin's repressive model remains highly unpopular in the Russian neighborhood and beyond. Russian speakers in the Baltics prefer EU democracies to a kleptocratic, propaganda-driven, petro-state. Likewise, the people of Georgia and Ukraine are clearly hostile to the Putin dictatorship. The loss of influence in Ukraine is a major setback for Putin.

• Likewise, the people of Taiwan and Hong Kong have made clear their revulsion at Beijing's police-state regimentation.

• Enthusiasm for democracy remains high throughout Africa. Spurred by unhappy experiences with venal leaders-for-life, opposition parties and civil society have persisted in their drive for honest elections, anticorruption laws and legal reforms.

• U.S. democratic institutions — the media, courts and civil society — have resisted President Trump's agenda and limited the administration's ability to challenge constitutional norms.

Despite some serious setbacks, democracy remains the system of choice for the majority. Freedom's formerly smug advocates, having experienced reversals, are now resisting — focusing on populists at home and autocrats abroad. Meanwhile, as insecure strongmen desperately seek new methods of censorship and political control, the appeal of the China model, Bolivarian socialism and Putinism are fading. Dictatorship is not the wave of the future.

LUCAN AHMAD WAY
PROFESSOR OF POLITICAL SCIENCE, UNIVERSITY OF TORONTO

WRITTEN FOR *CQ RESEARCHER*, OCTOBER 2017

*r*arely have things looked so bad for democracy as they do today. The world's most formidable democracy promoter, the European Union, is in disarray and faces possible disintegration. Far right forces have gained unprecedented support in Europe. Russia and China are resurgent. And most important, the United States itself is now led by a president who openly attacks the foundations of democracy. Democracy is backsliding in three countries where pluralism was once well-established: Venezuela, Hungary and (probably) Poland. The most recent report from Freedom House says the world has witnessed "the 11th straight consecutive year of decline in global freedom."

Overall, however, the case for democratic decline is relatively weak.

According to Freedom House, the number of democracies has remained more or less stable since the start of the millennium — fluctuating between 85 and 90. While several countries that Freedom House ranked as "free" in the late 1990s — including Venezuela — lost that ranking in the 2000s, several other countries became democratic during this same period, including Brazil, Croatia, Serbia and Tunisia.

And although the average Freedom House autocracy score has increased over the last decade — from 3.2 in 2005 to 3.4 in 2016 — the shift has been vanishingly small, and the level of autocracy has decreased very slightly since 2000. In addition, the widely used Polity Data Series index of the level of democracy in countries across the globe indicates that the number of democracies (countries with a score of 7 or above) has increased significantly from 67 in 2000 to 84 in 2016.

Thus, while the last decade has almost universally been seen as a time of democratic deterioration, Freedom House's own data suggests that it may be better understood as a period of democratic resilience. Indeed, while pluralism is no longer on the rise, democracy has survived in a range of countries with highly unfavorable conditions for fostering democracy, such as Benin, the Dominican Republic, El Salvador, Ghana, Mongolia and Romania. The question of why and how so many new democracies have survived in the face of far less favorable international environments merits further study. A better understanding of this democratic survival would help democracy advocates prepare for the all-too-likely day when authoritarian resurgence does, in fact, arrive.

Continued from p. 884

civilian government, led by Nobel Peace Prize-winner Aung San Suu Kyi.* [90]

In late August, after Rohingya rebels attacked a local police station, Myanmar's military torched Rohingya villages and shot residents, forcing some 500,000 Rohingyans to flee to neighboring Bangladesh. Although the Muslim Rohingya have lived in predominantly Buddhist Myanmar for centuries, the current government says they are illegal immigrants and has denied them cit-

took the unprecedented step of annulling the results of the Aug. 8 re-election of President Uhuru Kenyatta. The court said the election was "neither transparent or verifiable" and ordered a new election, scheduled for Oct. 26. [92]

Conservatives also advanced recently. On Oct. 15, right-wing parties in Austria made solid gains in parliamentary elections after promising a hard line on immigration. The conservative People's Party, led by rising political star Sebastian Kurz, 31, won at least 31.7 percent of

Michael Pillsbury, the director of the Center on Chinese Strategy at the Hudson Institute, a conservative think tank in Washington, has argued that if China's economy continues its robust growth — which many economists doubt — and if strict communists maintain control, China could become the dominant world power by mid-century. [95]

But Andrew J. Nathan, a Columbia University political scientist, said many countries would struggle to emulate China. "The Chinese model requires large fiscal resources, technological sophistication, a well-trained and loyal security apparatus, and sufficient political discipline . . . not to take power struggles public," he wrote. [96] ■

Members of Myanmar's Rohingya minority demonstrate in Kuala Lumpur, Malaysia, on Nov. 25, 2016, against persecution of the predominantly Muslim group. In late August, Myanmar's military torched Rohingya villages and shot residents, forcing some 500,000 Rohingyans to flee to neighboring Bangladesh, in what U.N. officials have called a campaign of ethnic cleansing.

izenship, largely because of their Bangladeshi heritage. The situation is a "textbook example of ethnic cleansing," according to the U.N. high commissioner for human rights. Although foreign officials have criticized Suu Kyi for not condemning the army, her advisers say she worries it could antagonize the military and prevent her from building a full democracy. [91]

In a bright spot for democracy, opposition parties and civil society groups in Africa have persistently pushed for elections, legal reforms and anticorruption laws. Kenya's Supreme Court on Sept. 1

the vote, and the far-right Freedom Party won 26 percent. The contest echoed some of the current trends in Europe's 2017 elections, including populist leaders stoking fear of Muslim immigration, disillusion with established politicians and the decline of center-left parties. [93]

Meanwhile, China continues to woo other countries to show that authoritarianism and modernization can coexist. "For now, China is using the U.S. playbook from the 1970s: 'How to be a superpower — use wads of cash and back dictators,' " said Michael Vatikiotis, the Asia regional director at the Geneva-based Centre for Humanitarian Dialogue. "But it's not clear how long that strategy will last." [94]

OUTLOOK

Dangerous Populist Age

The rise of nationalist movements and virulent autocracies presents a growing problem for democratic principles, human rights and independent judiciaries. Facing these pressures, many global leaders and nations will pursue their own narrow interests, unrestrained and unconcerned with global peace, freedom, prosperity and health, according to Freedom House. [97]

The coming years will be "suspended between a continued instability and erosion of democracy globally and the possibility of a full-blown reverse wave of democratic breakdowns," says Stanford professor Diamond. "The prospects for democratic transitions don't look very good," he adds. "The best one could realistically hope for is a kind of stabilization around this rather difficult moment — so not much further deterioration."

"The sheen has been taken off the Washington model," says political scientist Klaas. Some African leaders, for instance, admire China for its strong economy

---

* Aung San Suu Kyi is the state counselor, a position akin to a prime minister.

and governing efficiency, he says, citing several countries where leaders have tried to stay in power by changing their constitutions, such as the Democratic Republic of the Congo, Congo, Rwanda, Burundi, Djibouti, Cameroon, Chad, Uganda, Gabon and Togo. [98]

Yascha Mounk, a lecturer on political theory at Harvard, and Roberto Stefan Foa, a political scientist at the University of Melbourne in Australia, developed a stress test to detect how susceptible democracies are to massive failures. Among other categories, they rate public support for continued democracy, whether citizens support nondemocratic forms of government such as military rule and whether "anti-system parties and movements" are gaining strength by insisting that the government is illegitimate. If support for democracy plummets as the other measures rise, the two professors say, a country is "deconsolidating," a kind of low-grade fever that can lead to a full-blown crisis. [99] (*See graphic, p. 876.*)

Their theory has drawn criticisms, however. Ronald Inglehart, a political scientist at the University of Michigan, has questioned whether Mounk and Foa's methods truly signal democracy's long-term decline. [100]

Along with Stanford University's Diamond, Mounk and Foa say that if nations intend to stop the slide into authoritarianism, politicians and voters must work to counter anti-democratic forces. "In countries where populists have not yet taken power, radical reforms are needed to counteract the social and economic drivers of democratic deconsolidation," Mounk and Foa write. "Establishment politicians with a real commitment to liberal democracy may be more likely to undertake these reforms — and to disregard the protestations of interest groups that oppose them — when they are afraid that anti-system parties are about to take power. In that sense, the dangerous age of populism may harbor an opportunity for righting the ship of state after all." [101]

In his book *The Despot's Accomplice*, Klaas offers 10 principles for promoting democracy and steering foundering democracies and autocracies to freedom. Two involve thinking long-term and not trying to impose democracy through war. [102]

The world's democracies, he suggested, might also establish a "League of Democracies," a sort of U.N. for free trade in which members would be required to support democratic norms. [103]

Diamond says the United States can support ailing democracies by supporting a foreign policy that is not necessarily interventionist but "calls out regressions from democratic norms and standards." ∎

Notes

[1] Virginia Lopez, "On the Frontline of Venezuela's Punishing Protests," *The Guardian*, May 25, 2017, https://tinyurl.com/yaonchdc.

[2] Larry Diamond, *In Search of Democracy* (2015). Also see Larry Diamond and Leonardo Morlino, "The Quality of Democracy: An Overview," *Journal of Democracy*, October 2004, https://tinyurl.com/ycspherk.

[3] "Freedom in the World 2017," Freedom House, 2017, https://tinyurl.com/ybvxftur.

[4] "Middle East and North Africa," Freedom House, undated, https://tinyurl.com/ktav62d "Freedom in the World 2017: Egypt," Freedom House, 2017, https://tinyurl.com/yd4uucmw.

[5] "Freedom in the World 2017: Russia," Freedom House, 2017, https://tinyurl.com/yd7nsu64.

[6] Daniel McLaughlin, "EU rebels Hungary and Poland reaffirm anti-immigrant alliance," *The Irish Times*, Sept. 22, 2017, http://tinyurl.com/y8uvtll3.

[7] "Death toll continues to rise in Duterte's war on drugs," Al-Jazeera, Aug. 17, 2017, https://tinyurl.com/y785wbb5. Also see David Sanger and Maggie Haberman, "Trump Praises Duterte for Philippine Drug Crackdown in Call Transcript," *The New York Times*, May 23, 2017, https://tinyurl.com/ydeqvrjd.

[8] Kareem Shaheen, "Erdogan to continue crackdown as Turkey marks failed coup," *The Guardian*, July 16, 2017, https://tinyurl.com/y9tbaudp.

[9] Vincent Bevins, "It's not just Burma: Human rights are under attack across Southeast Asia, advocates say," *The Washington Post*, Sept. 8, 2017, http://tinyurl.com/y9edl8ht. "Rohingya refugee crisis a 'human rights nightmare,' UN chief tells Security Council," UN News Centre, Sept. 28, 2017, http://tinyurl.com/ybc653fr.

[10] Sarah Bush, "Democracy promotion is failing. Here's why," *The Washington Post*, Nov. 9, 2015, https://tinyurl.com/y99j57o6. Prak Chan Thul, "Cambodia accuses U.S. of political interference, calls US democracy 'bloody and brutal,' " Reuters, Aug. 23, 2017, http://tinyurl.com/ycxy28ow.

[11] Joshua Kurlantzick, "The great democracy meltdown," *The New Republic*, May 19, 2011, https://tinyurl.com/y7vuqwmr. Also see Joshua Kurlantzick, "Why the 'China Model' Isn't Going Away," *The Atlantic*, March 21, 2013, https://tinyurl.com/y8bfkcdx.

[12] *Ibid.*

[13] Diamond, *op. cit.*, pp. 8-9; Amanda Taub, "How Stable are Democracies? 'Warning Signs are Flashing Red,' " *The New York Times*, Nov. 29, 2016, https://tinyurl.com/yardxl9f.

[14] Matt Schiavenza, "Could China's System Replace Democracy?" Asia Society, Jan. 19, 2017, https://tinyurl.com/ycxrwgf9.

[15] Daniel A. Bell et al., "Is the China Model Better Than Democracy?" *Foreign Policy*, Oct 19, 2015, https://tinyurl.com/ybv3bo9m.

[16] Daniel A. Bell, "Chinese Democracy Isn't Inevitable," *The Atlantic*, May 29, 2015, https://tinyurl.com/yc57z49o.

[17] Schiavenza, *op. cit.*

[18] *Ibid.*

[19] Bell et al., *op. cit.*

[20] *Ibid.*

[21] *Ibid.*

[22] *Ibid.*

[23] "U.S. Department of State: Agency Financial Report, Fiscal Year 2016," U.S. Department of State, 2016, https://tinyurl.com/y7wntol7.

[24] "Advancing Freedom and Democracy," U.S. Department of State, undated, https://www.state.gov/j/drl/rls/afdr/.

[25] Krishnadev Calamur, "Trump's Plan for Afghanistan: No Timeline for Exit," *The Atlantic*, Aug. 21, 2017, https://tinyurl.com/y9bju64w.

[26] Joshua Muravchik, "What Trump and Tillerson don't get about democracy promotion," *The Washington Post*, Aug. 4, 2017, https://tinyurl.com/ybrn23zr.

[27] Pippa Norris, "Trump's Global Democracy Retreat," *The New York Times*, Sept. 7, 2017, http://tinyurl.com/yacwfrwf.

[28] Alexandra Ulmer and David Lawder, "Trump slaps sanctions on Venezuela; Maduro sees effort to force default," Reuters, Aug. 25, 2017, https://tinyurl.com/y8upm87b.

[29] Kelly Swanson, "Read: Trump's full speech to the UN General Assembly," *Vox*, Sept.19, 2017, https://tinyurl.com/yc9v6d8x.

[30] Brian Klaas, *The Despot's Accomplice* (2017), p. 63.

[31] Reuel Marc Gerecht, "The World Senses Our Wariness of Power," *The New York Times*, March 11, 2014, https://tinyurl.com/ycz7chve.

[32] Norris, *op. cit.*

[33] Stephen M. Walt, "Why Is America So Bad at Promoting Democracy in Other Countries?" *Foreign Policy*, April 25, 2016, https://tinyurl.com/h6ezfbc.

[34] Bruce Fein, "Stop U.S. Democracy Promotion Abroad," *The Washington Times*, Dec. 24, 2014, https://tinyurl.com/pft962g.

[35] Schiavenza, *op. cit.*

[36] Jeffrey Ghannam, "Digital Media in the Arab World One Year After the Revolutions," Center for International Media Assistance, March 28, 2012, https://tinyurl.com/ydgqy5hy. Also see Zeynep Tufekci and Christopher Wilson, "Social Media and the Decision to Participate in Political Protest: Observations From Tahrir Square," *Journal of Communication*, 2012, pp. 363-379, https://tinyurl.com/ydee7g3c.

[37] "Don't Call him, 'Dimon,' " Anti-Corruption Foundation, March 2, 2017, https://tinyurl.com/yd8opnjv.

[38] Roland Oliphant, "Why are Russians protesting? The investigation accusing the prime minister of corruption that sparked biggest demonstrations in five years," *The Telegraph*, March 27, 2017, https://tinyurl.com/hfbjtsx; Svetlana Reiter and Andrew Osborn, "Anti-Kremlin protesters fill Russian streets, Putin critic Navalny jailed," Reuters, June 11, 2017, https://tinyurl.com/y9dgpzty.

[39] Amy Qin, "Liu Xiaobo's Death Pushes China's Censors Into Overdrive," *The New York Times*, July 17, 2017, https://tinyurl.com/y9mjvzhr. Also see Edward Wong, "China Blocks Web Access to 'Under the Dome' Documentary on Pollution," *The New York Times*, March 6, 2015, https://tinyurl.com/ycwsm4wd.

[40] Tufekci and Wilson, *op. cit.*

[41] Isaac Chotiner, "Has Protesting Become Too Easy?" *Slate*, May 8, 2017, https://tinyurl.com/lkdwz4j.

[42] "Russia enacts 'draconian' law for bloggers and online media," BBC, Aug. 1, 2014, https://tinyurl.com/kakz67p.

[43] Courtney C. Radsch, "Proposed German legislation threatens broad internet censorship," Committee to Protect Journalists, April 20, 2017, https://tinyurl.com/yame2r5v. Also see "Germany approves plans to fine social media firms up to €50m," *The Guardian*, June 30, 2017, https://tinyurl.com/yb5gm4v6.

[44] James T. Kloppenberg, *Toward Democracy: The Struggle for Self-Rule in European and American Thought* (2015), pp. 27-28.

[45] *Ibid.*, pp. 38-43.

[46] Paul Cartledge, *Democracy: A Life* (2016), Kindle location 4835.

[47] Kloppenberg, *op. cit.*

[48] Norman Davies, *The Isles: A History* (1999), pp. 556-561.

[49] "The American Revolution — A Documentary History," The Avalon Project, undated, https://tinyurl.com/y9zk7xfa.

[50] Daniel Thurer and Thomas Burri, "Self-Determination," *Oxford Public International Law*, undated, https://tinyurl.com/japkzpu. See "Declaration of Independence: A Transcription," National Archives, https://tinyurl.com/h2zqchv.

[51] Lyonette Louis-Jacques, "Influence of the U.S. Constitution Abroad," University of Chicago, Sept. 7, 2011, https://tinyurl.com/yce8cka3; Samuel Huntington, *The Third Wave* (1991), p. 17.

[52] Huntington, *ibid.*, p. 18.

[53] Adolf Hitler, *Mein Kampf* (2017; originally published in 1925), p. 74.

[54] "History of the Marshall Plan," George C. Marshall Foundation, undated, https://tinyurl.com/gwfcf9q.

[55] Huntington, *op. cit.*

[56] "History of the European Union," European Union, undated, https://tinyurl.com/gnmkpwy.

[57] Frank Dikotter, "Mao's Great Leap to Famine," *The New York Times*, Dec. 15, 2010, https://tinyurl.com/36bpas8. Also see Austin Ramzy, "China's Cultural Revolution, Explained," *The New York Times*, May 14, 2016, https://tinyurl.com/y7xng7xq.

[58] "Cold War," *Encyclopedia Britannica*, https://tinyurl.com/y8jaecb5.

[59] Odd Arne Westad, *The Cold War: A World History* (2017).

[60] Stephen Kotkin, *Uncivil Society: 1989 and the Implosion of the Communist Establishment* (2010).

[61] Peter Robinson, "Tear Down This Wall," National Archives, Summer 2007, https://tinyurl.com/y783bcrr.

[62] Liam Hoare, "Let's Please Stop Crediting Ronald Reagan for the Fall of the Berlin Wall," *The Atlantic*, Sept. 20, 2012, https://tinyurl.com/yauxsfuu.

[63] Tony Judt, *Postwar: A History of Europe Since 1945* (2005).

[64] Mary Elise Sarotte, *The Collapse: The Accidental Opening of the Berlin Wall* (2014).

[65] Robert Service, *A History of Modern Russia*, 3rd ed. (2009), pp. 497-502.

[66] "European Neighbourhood Policy and Enlargement Negotiations: From 6 to 28 members," European Commission, undated, https://tinyurl.com/y9dkdupy.

[67] "Carter and Human Rights, 1977-1981," Department of State, https://tinyurl.com/l3jzkom.

[68] Shiavenza, *op. cit.*

[69] "Ben Hubbard and Rick Gladstone, "Arab Spring Countries Find Peace Is Harder Than Revolution," *The New York Times*, Aug. 14, 2013, https://tinyurl.com/yct5p6v3.

[70] Amanda Taub, "The unsexy truth about why the Arab Spring failed," *Vox*, Jan. 27, 2016, https://tinyurl.com/ycmvkss2.

[71] "Freedom in the World 2017: Russia," *op. cit.* Also see Steven Lee Myers and Ellen Barry, "Putin Reclaims Crimea for Russia and Bitterly Denounces the West," *The New York Times*, March 18, 2014, https://tinyurl.com/y9coml5z; Rebecca M. Nelson, "U.S. Sanctions and Russia's Economy," Congressional Research Service, Feb. 17, 2017, https://tinyurl.com/yc3npv7a; and Suzanne Sataline, "U.S.-Russia Relations," *CQ Researcher*, Jan. 13, 2017, pp. 25-48.

[72] For background, see Corine Hegland, "European Union's Future," *CQ Researcher*, Dec. 16, 2016, pp. 1037-1060.

[73] "Learn More About the Trump-Russia Imbroglio," NPR, https://tinyurl.com/y9klh6mg.

[74] Matt Apuzzo and Michael S. Schmidt, "Comey Says Trump Pressured Him to 'Lift the Cloud' of Inquiry," *The New York Times*, June 7, 2017, https://tinyurl.com/y7ka9yhf; Rebecca R. Ruiz and Mark Landler, "Robert Mueller, former F.B.I. Director, Is Named Special Counsel for Russia Investigation," *The New York Times*, May 17, 2017, https://tinyurl.com/lq69yck.

About the Author

Suzanne Sataline is a freelance writer and former national correspondent for *The Wall Street Journal*, where she covered religion, politics and health care. She also has worked for *The Boston Globe*, *The New York Daily News* and *The South China Morning Post* in Hong Kong and has written for *The New York Times*, *The New Yorker*, *The Economist*, *The Guardian*, *The Washington Post*, *Popular Science* and *National Geographic*. She was a Nieman fellow at Harvard University.

[75] "Full Transcript and Video: Trump's Speech on Afghanistan," *The New York Times*, Aug. 21, 2017, https://tinyurl.com/ybf9pn4o. Also see Bryant Harris *et al.*, "The End of Foreign Aid as We Know It," *Foreign Policy*, April 24, 2017, https://tinyurl.com/yb5attfc.

[76] For background, see Patrick Marshall, "Rethinking Foreign Aid," *CQ Researcher*, April 14, 2017, pp. 313-336.

[77] Robbie Gramer, "Senate Panel Rejects Trump Plan for Cutting Foreign Assistance," *Foreign Policy*, Sept. 7, 2017, https://tinyurl.com/ybsa35qs.

[78] Phillip Rucker, "Trump keeps praising international strongmen, alarming human rights advocates," *The Washington Post*, May 2, 2017, https://tinyurl.com/yavgtyj5.

[79] Sudarsan Raghavan, "As Trump embraces Egypt's Sissi, abuses rise," *The Washington Post*, Aug. 31, 2017, https://tinyurl.com/y74j6kvo.

[80] *Ibid.*; Joby Warrick, "A North Korean ship was seized off Egypt with a huge cache of weapons destined for a surprising buyer," *The Washington Post*, Oct. 1, 2017, https://tinyurl.com/y6va9v3l.

[81] Adam Entous, Craig Timberg and Elizabeth Dwoskin, "Russians exploited social wedges," *The Washington Post*, Sept. 26, 2017, https://tinyurl.com/y838a7pz; Elizabeth Dwoskin, Adam Entous and Craig Timberg, "Google finds links to Russian disinformation in its services," *The Washington Post*, Oct. 10, 2017, https://tinyurl.com/ybtokgjo.

[82] *Ibid.*

[83] Anoosh Chakelian, "Rise of the Nationalists: A Guide to Europe's Far-Right Parties," *New Statesman*, March 8, 2017, https://tinyurl.com/z6pgcnb.

[84] Anoosh Chakelian, "How Poland's government is weakening democracy," *The Economist*, July 25, 2017, https://tinyurl.com/yd939fpl. Also see Slawomir Sierakowski, "Poland Turns Away from Democracy, Thanks to the U.S.," *The New York Times*, July 24, 2017, https://tinyurl.com/ycr5te35.

[85] Patrick Kingsley, "Over 1,000 People Are Detained in Raids in Turkey," *The New York Times*, April 26, 2017, https://tinyurl.com/mx43kex; Kareem Shaheen, "Turkish court hands down 40 life sentences over plot to kill Erdogan," *The Guardian*, Oct. 4, 2017, https://tinyurl.com/y8ppq56g; and Patrick Kingsley, "Erdogan Claims Vast Powers in Turkey After Narrow Victory in Referendum," *The New York Times*, April 16, 2017, https://tinyurl.com/k9nbhgf.

[86] "Freedom House 2017: Russia," *op. cit.* "America's new economic sanctions may hurt Russia's recovery," *The Economist*, Aug. 5, 2017, https://tinyurl.com/y86so3h9.

[87] Website of Alexei Navalny, https://navalny.com;

FOR MORE INFORMATION

Brookings Institution, 1775 Massachusetts Ave., N.W., Washington, DC 20036; 202-797-6000; www.brookings.edu. A think tank that researches domestic and international issues.

Carnegie Endowment for International Peace, 1779 Massachusetts Ave., N.W., Washington, DC 20036; 202-483-7600; www.ceip.org. An international affairs research organization that reports on the health of democracies and the rule of law.

Center on Democracy, Development, and the Rule of Law, Freeman Spogli Institute for International Studies, Encina Hall, 616 Serra St C100, Stanford University, Stanford, CA 94305-6055; 650-723-4581; https://cddrl.fsi.stanford.edu. A research center that studies how countries can become prosperous and democratic.

Center for Strategic and International Studies, 1800 K St., N.W., Suite 400, Washington, DC 20006; 202-887-0200; www.csis.org. A nonpartisan think tank that evaluates democracy-promotion programs.

Council on Foreign Relations, The Harold Pratt House, 58 East 68th St., New York, NY 10065; 212-434-9400; www.cfr.org. A nonpartisan think tank that studies foreign policy choices facing the U.S. and other countries.

Freedom House, 1850 M St., N.W., 11th floor, Washington, DC 20036; 202-296-5101; https://freedomhouse.org. An independent watchdog group that researches and advocates for democracy, political freedom and human rights.

National Endowment for Democracy, 1101 15th St., N.W., Suite 700, Washington, DC 20005; 202-293-9072; www.ned.org. A foundation financed largely by Congress that funds groups abroad working for democratic goals.

Alexandra Sims, "Vladimir Putin signs law allowing Russia to ignore international human rights rulings," *The Independent*, Dec. 15, 2015, https://tinyurl.com/ose44fc.

[88] "Philippines: Duterte Threatens Human Rights Community," Human Rights Watch, Aug. 17, 2017, https://tinyurl.com/y8vr2f8k; "Freedom in the World 2017: Philippines," Freedom House, 2017, https://tinyurl.com/ydycf84q. Also see Sanger and Haberman, *op. cit.*

[89] William H. Overholdt, "Duterte, democracy and defense," Brookings Institution, Jan. 31, 2017, https://tinyurl.com/jjddgrc.

[90] For background, see Robert Kiener, "Myanmar's New Era," *CQ Global Researcher*, July 17, 2012, pp. 329-352.

[91] Sarah Wildman," Aung San Suu Kyi's disappointing speech about Myanmar's humanitarian catastrophe," *Vox*, Sept. 19, 2017, https://tinyurl.com/ycamrogx; Niharika Mandhana and James Hookway, "Behind the Silence of Myanmar's Aung San Suu Kyi," *The New York Times*, Oct. 6, 2017, https://tinyurl.com/y9x3cpka.

[92] "Kenya's Supreme Court criticises IEBC electoral commission," BBC News, Sept. 20, 2017, https://tinyurl.com/y88cdzh3.

[93] Marcus Walker, "Austria's Right-Wing Parties Enjoy Strong Showing in Parliamentary Elections," *The Wall Street Journal*, Oct. 16, 2017,

https://tinyurl.com/yac4ajea.

[94] Bevins, *op. cit.*

[95] Michael Pillsbury, *The Hundred-Year Marathon: China's Secret Strategy to Replace America as the Global Superpower* (2015), chp. 9. Also see Larry Diamond, Marc F. Plattner and Christopher Walker, eds., *Authoritarianism Goes Global: The Challenge to Democracy* (2016).

[96] Andrew J. Nathan, "China's Challenge," in *Authoritarianism Goes Global, ibid.*, pp. 23-29.

[97] "Freedom in the World 2017: Populists and Autocrats: The Dual Threat to Global Democracy," Freedom House, 2017, https://tinyurl.com/jkyw8ta.

[98] Brian Klaas, "Throw the bums out, African edition," *The Washington Post*, July 28, 2017, https://tinyurl.com/ycg9kwbb.

[99] Amanda Taub, "How Stable Are Democracies? 'Warning Signs Are Flashing Red,' " *op. cit.* Also see Roberto Stefan Foa and Yascha Mounk, "The Signs of Deconsolidation," *Journal of Democracy*, January 2017, https://tinyurl.com/y77roe6q.

[100] Ronald Inglehart, "The Danger of Deconsolidation: How Much Should We Worry?" *Journal of Democracy*, July 2016, https://tinyurl.com/hghco7a.

[101] Foa and Mounk, *op. cit.*

[102] Klaas, *The Despot's Accomplice, op. cit.*

[103] *Ibid.*, pp. 152-154.

Bibliography

Selected Sources

Books

Cartledge, Paul, *Democracy: A Life*, Oxford University Press, 2016.
An authority on ancient Greek culture traces the rudiments of modern democratic society.

Diamond, Larry, *In Search of Democracy*, Routledge, 2016.
One of the world's leading scholars on democracy presents a compendium of articles by him or others evaluating the status and prospects for democracy around the world.

Diamond, Larry, Marc F. Plattner and Christopher Walker, *Authoritarianism Goes Global: The Challenge to Democracy*, Journal of Democracy, 2016.
This collection of journal articles outlines the rise of authoritarianism worldwide.

Klaas, Brian, *The Despot's Accomplice: How the West Is Aiding and Abetting the Decline of Democracy*, Oxford University Press, 2017.
An American political scientist argues that the West has been responsible for the destruction of democracy through careless and narrow-minded foreign policies.

Kloppenberg, James T., *Toward Democracy: The Struggles for Self-Rule in European and American Thought*, Oxford University Press, 2016.
A Harvard historian describes how ideas about self-governing changed over time on both sides of the Atlantic.

Articles

"What's gone wrong with democracy?" *The Economist*, March 1, 2014, https://tinyurl.com/mhsl5pm.
A British business publication reports on democracy's worldwide setbacks.

Filkins, Dexter, "Turkey's Thirty-Year Coup," *The New Yorker*, Oct. 17, 2016, https://tinyurl.com/jq7u9t3.
A veteran reporter explains how a political rivalry between two men helped Turkey tumble from democracy to authoritarianism.

Fisher, Max, and Amanda Taub, "How Venezuela Stumbled to the Brink of Collapse," *The New York Times*, May 14, 2017, https://tinyurl.com/nyuxkrq.
This clear, concise primer describes how Venezuela's oil-rich economy collapsed into bedlam.

Taub, Amanda, "How Stable Are Democracies? 'Warning Signs Are Flashing Red,' " *The New York Times*, Nov. 29, 2016, https://tinyurl.com/y99jqdw3.
A reporter analyzes a government scholar's argument that liberal democracies worldwide may be at risk of decline.

Traub, James, "The Party That Wants to Make Poland Great Again," *The New York Times Magazine*, Nov. 2, 2016, https://tinyurl.com/ya4899rc.
A journalist explores how Poland, which resisted Soviet communism, came to embrace authoritarianism.

Reports and Studies

"The Brookings Democracy Dashboard," The Brookings Institution, June 2, 2016, https://tinyurl.com/y8dg4b5m.
A Washington think tank offers data to evaluate political systems and government performance in the United States.

"Democracy Index 2016," The Economist Intelligence Unit, *The Economist*, accessed on Aug. 29, 2017, https://tinyurl.com/j8tydf2.
A British business publication ranks countries by their civil liberties and the openness of their electoral processes.

"Freedom in the World 2017: Populists and Autocrats: The Dual Threat to Global Democracy," Freedom House, January 2017, https://tinyurl.com/jkyw8ta.
A nonprofit that annually tracks rights and civil liberties worldwide finds that populist and nationalist forces have grown, as has authoritarianism.

Felter, Claire, and Danielle Renwick, "Venezuela in Crisis," Council on Foreign Relations, Aug. 1, 2017, https://tinyurl.com/y7dhj64d.
A New York think tank provides background on the status of governance in South America's oldest democracy.

Foa, Roberto Stefan, and Yascha Mounk, "The Signs of Deconsolidation," *Journal of Democracy*, January 2017, http://tinyurl.com/y7voh95z.
Political scholars argue that young people globally are less invested in democracy than their elders, skeptical of liberal institutions and in search of strong leaders.

Lawson, Marian L., and Susan B. Epstein, "Democracy Promotion: An Objective of U.S. Foreign Assistance," Congressional Research Service, May 31, 2017, https://tinyurl.com/yal89sx3.
Congress' research arm says lawmakers continue to debate the effectiveness and appropriateness of democracy promotion assistance.

Pomerantsev, Peter, and Michael Weiss, "The Menace of Unreality: How the Kremlin Weaponizes Information, Culture and Money," *The Interpreter*, Institute of Modern Russia, November 2014, http://tinyurl.com/khfg2rp.
Journalists assess how state-sponsored hacking and disinformation create scandal and sow doubts about democratic politics.

The Next Step:

Additional Articles from Current Periodicals

China

"Thousands in HK mark China's national day with pro-democracy rally," *The Straits Times*, **Oct. 2, 2017, https://tinyurl.com/ybxfjnbx.**

Following arrests of pro-democracy activists, an "anti-authoritarian" rally was held in Hong Kong to voice growing concern over Beijing's repressive involvement in the city.

"Unlike in Hong Kong, few in Macau demand greater democracy," *The Economist*, **Sept. 14, 2017, https://tinyurl.com/y9myhdnq.**

Although a close neighbor of democratically inclined Hong Kong, the autonomous Chinese region of Macau has welcomed Chinese authority after troops helped with relief efforts in the wake of Typhoon Hato, which struck in August.

Lewis, Margaret K., "Taiwan's Human Rights Revolution and China's Devolution," *The Diplomat*, **Oct. 3, 2017, https://tinyurl.com/yd2rhwnt.**

Taiwan has developed into a full-fledged democracy since its split with China, while China increasingly has devalued citizens' civil liberties.

Nativist Populism

Paauwe, Christiaan, "Don't be relieved by the Dutch election — it's done nothing to stop populism in Europe," *Quartz*, **March 22, 2017, https://tinyurl.com/k8k2lnh.**

Even though the far-right candidate for the Dutch Party for Freedom didn't win the election for prime minister, his rhetoric seeped into the campaigns of other candidates attempting to appeal to his constituents.

Schultheis, Emily, "What Right-Wing Populists Look Like in Norway," *The Atlantic*, **Sept. 12, 2017, https://tinyurl.com/ybeyw7lp.**

The Progress Party in Norway is one of the most successful right-wing populist parties in Europe, but unlike most of its European populist counterparts, its agenda is more moderate, and it plays an active role in Oslo's parliament.

Taub, Amanda, "What the Far Right's Rise May Mean for Germany's Future," *The New York Times*, **Sept. 26, 2017, https://tinyurl.com/y8nynkr9.**

In Germany's recent election, the far-right Alternative for Germany party won 13 percent of the vote, its largest share yet, while mainstream parties lost more than 100 seats in parliament, a record postwar loss.

Russia

Carpenter, Michael, "The 2018 midterms are coming, and Russia is ready," *The Hill*, **Oct. 2, 2017, https://tinyurl.com/ycc5eboy.**

Russia's alleged covert influence in the recent U.S. elections via disinformation campaigns, hacking and murky financing, foreshadows future meddling, a defense expert argues.

Reynolds, Maura, "How to tame Putin," *Politico*, **Oct. 2, 2017, https://tinyurl.com/ybd92yhq.**

Russian President Vladimir Putin's strategy for undermining Western democracy is centered on making Western institutions and societies look dysfunctional compared to the Russian autocracy, according to participants in the recent U.N. General Assembly.

Venezuela

"U.S. not ruling out possible oil embargo on Venezuela: Haley," *Reuters*, **Sept. 21, 2017, https://tinyurl.com/yav7embg.**

The United States is considering imposing an oil embargo on Venezuela if democratic integrity is not restored in Caracas, according to Nikki Haley, U.S. ambassador to the U.N.

Horsey, David, "Venezuela's descent into dictatorship shows democracy can be lost," *Los Angeles Times*, **Aug. 2, 2017, https://tinyurl.com/y73po5wf.**

The ongoing chaos in Venezuela provides a lesson to the United States about how quickly democracy can collapse, a *Los Angeles Times* contributor says.

Tintori, Lillian, "This Isn't the Venezuela I Married," *The New York Times*, **Sept. 13, 2017, https://tinyurl.com/y78cweu8.**

In an op-ed, Venezuelan opposition leader Leopoldo López's wife, who took over the resistance movement after her husband was imprisoned in 2014, describes the current humanitarian crisis under President Nicolás Maduro's regime.

In-depth Reports on Issues in the News

Are you writing a paper?

Need backup for a debate?

Want to become an expert on an issue?

For 90 years, students have turned to *CQ Researcher* for in-depth reporting on issues in the news. Reports on a full range of political and social issues are now available. Following is a selection of recent reports:

Civil Liberties
Privacy and the Internet, 12/15
Intelligence Reform, 5/15
Religion and Law, 11/14

Crime/Law
High-Tech Policing, 4/17
Forensic Science Controversies, 2/17
Jailing Debtors, 9/16
Decriminalizing Prostitution, 4/16
Restorative Justice, 2/16
The Dark Web, 1/16
Immigrant Detention, 10/15

Education
Charter Schools, 3/17
Civic Education, 2/17
Student Debt, 11/16
Apprenticeships, 10/16

Environment/Society
Climate Change and National Security, 9/17
Muslims in America, 7/17
Funding the Arts, 7/17
Hunger in America, 7/17
Future of the Christian Right, 6/17
Trust in Media, 6/17

Health/Safety
Medical Breakthroughs, 9/17
Medical Marijuana, 7/17
Food Labeling, 6/17
Sports and Sexual Assault, 4/17

Politics/Economy
Future of the Democratic Party, 10/17
Cyberwarfare Threat, 10/17
Universal Basic Income, 9/17
National Debt, 9/17
North Korea Showdown, 5/17
Rethinking Foreign Aid, 4/17

Upcoming Reports

Workplace Sexual Harassment, 10/27/17

Military Readiness, 11/3/17

Looted Artifacts, 11/10/17

ACCESS

CQ Researcher is available in print and online. For access, visit your library or www.cqresearcher.com.

STAY CURRENT

For notice of upcoming *CQ Researcher* reports or to learn more about *CQ Researcher* products, subscribe to the free email newsletters, *CQ Researcher Alert!* and *CQ Researcher News*: http://cqpress.com/newsletters.

PURCHASE

To purchase a *CQ Researcher* report in print or electronic format (PDF), visit www.cqpress.com or call 866-427-7737. Single reports start at $15. Bulk purchase discounts and electronic-rights licensing are also available.

SUBSCRIBE

Annual full-service *CQ Researcher* subscriptions—including 44 reports a year, monthly index updates, and a bound volume—start at $1,131. Add $25 for domestic postage.

CQ Researcher Online offers a backfile from 1991 and a number of tools to simplify research. For pricing information, call 800-818-7243 or 805-499-9774 or email librarysales@sagepub.com.

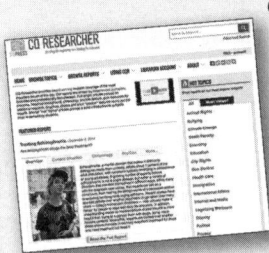

CQ RESEARCHER

CQ PRESS

In-depth reports on today's issues

Published by CQ Press, an Imprint of SAGE Publications, Inc.

www.cqresearcher.com

Workplace Sexual Harassment

Will the latest charges lead to a shift in corporate culture?

C harges of workplace sexual harassment have exploded into the news in recent months as allegations by dozens of women have forced the resignations of such high-profile figures as Uber co-founder Travis Kalanick, Fox TV host Bill O'Reilly and — in perhaps the most spectacular fall from grace — iconic Hollywood producer Harvey Weinstein. Many observers believe the scandals, which involve accusations of harassment, sexual coercion and in some cases rape, mark a turning point in the decades-long battle to change corporate culture so that sexual harassment is no longer tolerated. Human resource managers are beginning to evaluate whether anti-sexual harassment programs might be more effective if they focused on teaching employees to avoid and respond to all types of inappropriate and uncivil behavior rather than simply on teaching them the technicalities of anti-harassment law. At the same time, however, businesses increasingly are requiring employees to sign arbitration agreements that forbid them from taking sexual harassment claims to court, a practice some women's rights advocates say helps perpetuate the behavior.

Movie producer Harvey Weinstein, recently accused of sexual harassment or assault by more than 60 women, joins a long list of media, high tech and other executives who have lost their jobs in the wake of similar allegations. The rash of charges prompted hundreds of thousands of women around the world to report – using the hashtag #MeToo – their own experiences of sexual harassment.

I N S I D E THIS REPORT

THE ISSUES	896
BACKGROUND	901
CHRONOLOGY	903
CURRENT SITUATION	908
AT ISSUE	909
OUTLOOK	910
BIBLIOGRAPHY	914
THE NEXT STEP	915

CQ Researcher • Oct. 27, 2017 • www.cqresearcher.com
Volume 27, Number 38 • Pages 893-916

SAGE Publishing | CQ PRESS
Los Angeles | London | New Delhi
Singapore | Washington DC | Melbourne

RECIPIENT OF SOCIETY OF PROFESSIONAL JOURNALISTS AWARD FOR EXCELLENCE ◆ AMERICAN BAR ASSOCIATION SILVER GAVEL AWARD

WORKPLACE SEXUAL HARASSMENT

CQ RESEARCHER

Oct. 27, 2017
Volume 27, Number 38

EXECUTIVE EDITOR: Thomas J. Billitteri
tjb@sagepub.com

ASSISTANT MANAGING EDITORS: Kenneth Fireman, kenneth.fireman@sagepub.com, Kathy Koch, kathy.koch@sagepub.com, Scott Rohrer, scott.rohrer@sagepub.com

ASSOCIATE MANAGING EDITOR: Val Ellicott

SENIOR CONTRIBUTING EDITOR:
Thomas J. Colin
tom.colin@sagepub.com

CONTRIBUTING WRITERS: Marcia Clemmitt, Sarah Glazer, Alan Greenblatt, Reed Karaim, Barbara Mantel, Patrick Marshall, Tom Price

SENIOR PROJECT EDITOR: Olu B. Davis

EDITORIAL ASSISTANT: Natalia Gurevich

FACT CHECKERS: Eva P. Dasher, Michelle Harris, Betsy Towner Levine, Robin Palmer

Los Angeles I London I New Delhi
Singapore I Washington DC I Melbourne

An Imprint of SAGE Publications, Inc.

SENIOR VICE PRESIDENT, GLOBAL LEARNING RESOURCES:
Karen Phillips

EXECUTIVE DIRECTOR, ONLINE LIBRARY AND REFERENCE PUBLISHING:
Todd Baldwin

CQ Press is a registered trademark of Congressional Quarterly Inc.

CQ Researcher (ISSN 1056-2036) is printed on acid-free paper. Published weekly, except: (March wk. 4) (May wk. 4) (July wks. 1, 2) (Aug. wks. 2, 3) (Nov. wk. 4) and (Dec. wks. 3, 4). Published by SAGE Publications, Inc., 2455 Teller Rd., Thousand Oaks, CA 91320. Annual full-service subscriptions start at $1,131. For pricing, call 1-800-818-7243. To purchase a CQ Researcher report in print or electronic format (PDF), visit www.cqpress. com or call 866-427-7737. Single reports start at $15. Bulk purchase discounts and electronic-rights licensing are also available. Periodicals postage paid at Thousand Oaks, California, and at additional mailing offices. POSTMASTER: Send address changes to CQ Researcher, 2600 Virginia Ave., N.W., Suite 600, Washington, DC 20037.

THE ISSUES

895
• Are workplace training programs on sexual harassment effective?
• Do business policies perpetuate sexual harassment?
• Do policies designed to prevent sexual harassment go too far?

BACKGROUND

901 **Early Problems**
Slaves often were sexually abused.

902 **Early Lawsuits**
The first sexual harassment lawsuits were filed after passage of the 1965 Civil Rights Act.

905 **Landmark Rulings**
The Supreme Court ruled on several significant sexual harassment cases in the 1990s.

907 **Rising Monetary Awards**
Settlement amounts in sexual harassment cases increased after the 1991 Civil Rights Act allowed plaintiffs in employment discrimination cases to seek damages.

CURRENT SITUATION

908 **Social Media Harassment**
Workplace harassers have new outlets to exploit.

908 **California's Problems**
Sexual harassment allegations are roiling Hollywood and Silicon Valley.

OUTLOOK

910 **Changing Mindsets**
Sexual harassment is not just a women's issue.

SIDEBARS AND GRAPHICS

896 **Most Say Sexual Harassment a 'Serious Problem'**
The share of adults who see harassment as a "serious problem" rose from 47 percent in 2011 to nearly 66 percent this month.

897 **EEOC Complaints Highest in Private Sector**
In 2015, 45 percent of charges and complaints filed against private-sector firms involved sexual harassment.

900 **Most Workplace Sexual Harassment Is Verbal**
More than 50 percent of women surveyed complained of leering or ogling.

903 **Chronology**
Key events since 1964.

904 **Women Leaving the Sciences Because of Sexual Harassment**
"This reduces our scientific integrity."

906 **Workers Urged to Report Harassment When They See It**
"We want them to intervene early."

909 **At Issue:**
Is mandatory arbitration harmful to harassment victims?

FOR FURTHER RESEARCH

913 **For More Information**
Organizations to contact.

914 **Bibliography**
Selected sources used.

915 **The Next Step**
Additional articles.

915 **Citing CQ Researcher**
Sample bibliography formats.

Cover: Getty Images/Anadolu Agency/Mustafa Yalcin

Workplace Sexual Harassment

BY SHARON O'MALLEY

THE ISSUES

On her first day as a site reliability engineer at Uber in 2015, Susan J. Fowler got a string of text messages from her new manager saying he was "looking for women to have sex with." [1] She considered the messages "so clearly out of line" that she immediately reported them to the human resources (HR) department at the on-demand car service.

In a detailed blog post about the experience published last February, Fowler said HR acknowledged the manager's behavior was sexual harassment but told her that because the manager was "a high performer," it was "probably just an innocent mistake on his part." An HR representative, she wrote, advised her to change to another team so she would not have to interact with the harasser. The rep also said the manager would probably give her poor marks on her evaluation if she did not switch teams — and HR couldn't stop him, Fowler recalled.

So Fowler joined another team and quit Uber a year later. Her blog post details a year's worth of sexual harassment and retaliation against her and some of her female colleagues. A law firm hired by Uber investigated her allegations and recommended a variety of actions the company should take, including firing 20 employees. [2] In June, CEO Travis Kalanick, who helped found Uber in 2009, stepped down under pressure from investors over the allegations. [3]

Fowler's experience is common in Silicon Valley, where 53 percent of female tech employees said they had experienced sexual harassment and 37 percent said they had witnessed it,

Travis Kalanick stepped down in June as CEO of Uber following reports of widespread sexual harassment and retaliation against women at the car-hailing company. The growing furor over workplace sexual harassment is prompting human-resource managers to evaluate whether companies should focus on teaching employees how to avoid – or respond to – inappropriate and uncivil behavior rather than simply teaching them about anti-harassment law.

according to an August survey by the Washington, D.C., research firm Lincoln Park Strategies. [4] But Kalanick's departure is — or was — unusual in the male-dominated tech culture, where, according to Fowler and others, superstars are shielded from repercussions because they earn so much money for their employers.

Kalanick's departure was followed by a rash of sexual-harassment-related resignations and firings of tech executives, including the founder of 500 Startups, a venture capital company, who called himself "a creep" in a Twitter apology; the co-founder of Binary Capital; and the CEO of Social Finance, or SoFi, which one female former employee described as "a frat house." [5]

Outside of the high-tech world, high-profile resignations over sexual harass-

ment had started earlier: Fox News personality Bill O'Reilly, after costing the network $45 million in settlements with six accusers, lost his job in April, just 10 months after his longtime boss, Roger Ailes, resigned as the media empire's CEO for the same reason. [6] Michael Barnes, the CEO of Signet Jewelers, which owns Kay Jewelers and Jared the Galleria of Jewelry, and world-famous astronomer Geoff Marcy, who taught at the University of California, Berkeley, left their jobs amid multiple allegations of sexual harassment. [7]

Most recently, more than 60 women have accused film producer Harvey Weinstein of sexual harassment or assault. Weinstein has denied the assault charges. [8] On Oct. 14, the board of the Academy of Motion Pictures Arts and Sciences expelled Weinstein, saying it wanted "to send a message that the era of willful ignorance and shameful complicity in sexually predatory behavior and workplace harassment in our industry is over." [9]

Such well-publicized reckonings, some after decades of unpunished misconduct, could signal the start of a culture change in the American workplace, says Melissa Silverstein, founder of Women and Hollywood, which advocates for greater gender diversity in Hollywood. The Weinstein scandal has touched off "a global conversation about sexual harassment" among people who "want to see change," she said. [10]

Since the Weinstein scandal exploded, more than half a million women worldwide — including four U.S. senators — have taken to social media using the hashtag #MeToo to share their own harassment and assault experiences and discuss what needs to change. [11]

Most Say Sexual Harassment a 'Serious Problem'

Nearly two-thirds of American adults polled this month say workplace sexual harassment is a "serious problem," up from 47 percent in 2011. This month's poll also found that more than half of the women surveyed had received unwanted sexual advances they considered inappropriate.

Percentage of Americans Who Say Sexual Harassment Is a "Serious Problem"

Percentage of Women Who Received Unwanted Sexual Advances from a Man

Source: Caitlin Gibson and Emily Guskin, "A majority of Americans now say that sexual harassment is a 'serious problem,'" The Washington Post, Oct. 17, 2017, https://tinyurl.com/ydbmm6u7

"The floodgates have opened," said former Fox News host Gretchen Carlson, who received a $20 million confidential settlement to resolve her sexual harassment suit against Ailes. "Everyone is talking about this now."[12] Media mogul Oprah Winfrey called it a "watershed moment" for women who felt that in order to keep their jobs, "I've got to smile [and] pretend he didn't say that; I've got to pretend he didn't touch me. I think those days are about to be over."[13]

Indeed, a *Washington Post*-ABC News poll after the Weinstein scandal broke found that 64 percent of Americans see workplace sexual harassment as a "serious problem," up from 47 percent in 2011.[14] (*See graph, above.*)

However, skeptics doubt such a cultural shift is occurring or will last. Typically, companies backslide once the corporate mea culpas fade, embarrassed executives settle the lawsuits and the media spotlight focuses elsewhere, says Susan Antilla, a financial writer who authored a book about sexual harassment on Wall Street 15 years ago.[15] "As soon as the spotlight

gets off the case, they go back to where they were," she says.

Still others say public attitudes will be tough to change, given that U.S. voters elected Donald Trump president last year even though 15 women had accused him of sexually harassing or assaulting them and despite revelations that he had settled multiple sexual harassment lawsuits during his business career. He also was caught on tape bragging about sexually assaulting women in 2005. Trump denied the allegations and dismissed the taped conversation as "locker room talk."[16]

"Unfortunately, the lesson that we learned after the election is that sometimes harassers are rewarded," said Fatima Goss Graves, president of the National Women's Law Center, a Washington advocacy group that promotes equality and opportunity for women and families.[17] Author Antilla says, "In this administration, we're not going to see any progress. It's going to go backward."

Workplace sexual harassment is a form of gender discrimination prohibited

under Title VII of the 1964 Civil Rights Act. It can involve unwelcome sexual advances, requests for sexual favors or verbal or physical harassment of a sexual nature toward an employee or job applicant.[18] It also includes offensive comments — even nonsexual ones — about a person's gender. Harassment can occur between men and women or between people of the same gender, and it applies to gay and transgender employees as well. On college campuses, Title IX of the Education Amendments of 1972 protects students who might be harassed by teachers, administrators or other students.[19] Besides the two federal anti-discrimination laws, a variety of state laws prohibit verbal harassment or other sexually threatening behavior such as indecent exposure, groping or stalking someone.[20]

No one really knows how prevalent workplace harassment is because three-quarters of victims never report their experiences or file claims or lawsuits, according to a task force at the Equal Employment Opportunity Commission (EEOC), the federal agency that investigates Title VII violations.[21] About 17 percent of the nearly 7,000 sexual harassment complaints examined by the EEOC in 2016 were filed by males, and 26 percent by LGBT individuals.[22] The *Post*-ABC poll found that 54 percent of female survey respondents said they had received unwanted and inappropriate sexual advances either at work or outside of the workplace.[23]

Others say the proliferation of mandatory confidential arbitration clauses — which require sexual harassment victims to seek redress through an arbitrator and then not discuss the case publicly — hides the true scope of the problem. (*See "At Issue," p. 909.*) "This veil of secrecy protects serial harassers by keeping other potential victims in the dark, and minimizing pressure on companies to fire predators," Carlson wrote in a *New York Times* op-ed in October.[24] Her book, *Be Fierce: Stop Harassment and Take Your Power Back*, was published that month.

EEOC commissioners Chai R. Feld-blum and Victoria A. Lipnic, co-authors of the task force report, wrote that the country has come a long way in the 30 years since the U.S. Supreme Court labeled workplace harassment a form of gender discrimination. But "sadly, [we] still have far to go," they said. [25]

"I'm not quite sure why leaders have not gotten the wake-up call that what they're doing is not working well enough," Feldblum says. "Businesses have not taken the steps they can to change their culture. Leaders will advise them to have an anti-harassment policy and have training, [but] those two elements . . . are not sufficient to change a culture."

However, Cornell University law professor David Sherwyn says most companies have beefed up their anti-harassment policies. [26] "For normal people in normal business, the companies . . . say, 'Get out,' " he says. He ac-knowledges, however, that when the allegations are against people like Bill O'Reilly, who bring in a lot of money, some "companies will look the other way because it's a bottom-line thing."

Harassment "happens less now in cor-porate America," says San Francisco lawyer Harmeet Dhillon, because most companies provide mandatory sensitivity training in order to protect themselves from liability. "To the extent that they think they will have to pay for bad behavior, they will stop the bad behavior," she says.

Companies that offer sensitivity train-ing and create zero-tolerance policies for harassment "are fixing what they can," says Phyllis Hartman, owner of PGHR Consulting, a human resources consulting firm in Pittsburgh, "but the reality is . . . it's more of a company cultural issue." Hartman, a member of a Society for Human Resource Manage-ment committee on ethics and corporate social responsibility, adds: "We need to focus on helping people get along."

Male-dominated industries, such as construction, "still have a good-old-boys mentality," says Karla Y. Epperson, senior HR business partner for the California

EEOC Complaints Highest in Private Sector

Forty-five percent of charges and complaints filed with the U.S. Equal Employment Opportunity Commission (EEOC) in 2015 against private-sector firms involved sexual harassment; in the federal sector, the figure was 7 percent.

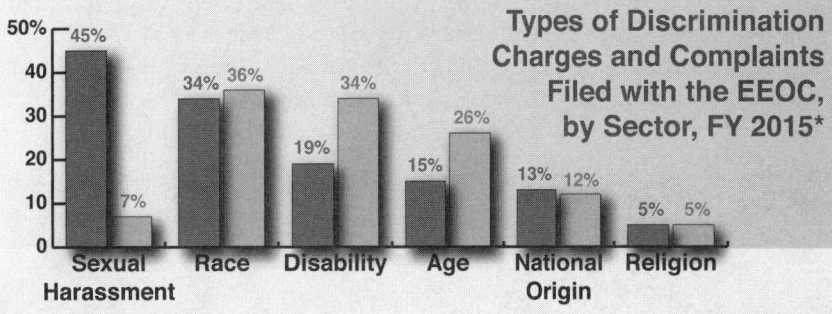

Types of Discrimination Charges and Complaints Filed with the EEOC, by Sector, FY 2015*

Private Sector / Public Sector:
- Sexual Harassment: 45% / 7%
- Race: 34% / 36%
- Disability: 19% / 34%
- Age: 15% / 26%
- National Origin: 13% / 12%
- Religion: 5% / 5%

* Figures total more than 100 percent because a complaint can involve more than one type of discrimination.

Source: Chai R. Feldblum and Victoria A. Lipnic, "Select Task Force on the Study of Harassment in the Workplace," U.S. Equal Employment Opportunity Commission, June 2016, https://tinyurl.com/y8xux2gn

construction company NPL. "And that means, unfortunately, that they cover up certain incidents that should not be covered up."

Feldblum says harassment is often worse in traditionally male fields such as technology, where "women are walk-ing into cultures that often see sexual harassment as a normal way of doing business." Science, engineering and math fields also have high rates of harassment, she says. (*See sidebar, p. 904.*)

Harassment is prevalent in Silicon Valley, says Dhillon, because many of those firms are small startups that are exempt from California's requirement that companies hold biannual sexual harassment training. "There are no checks and balances . . . on their obligations to their workers," she says, "until some-one gets sued." But she continues to see evidence of sexual harassment, she says, in fields where "a powerful man or woman uses a position of power to pressure or demand sexual favors from a subordinate."

Corporate leaders must "do a sig-nificant reset of their culture, and that

starts with an awareness that culture change doesn't happen on its own," says Feldblum. "They need to . . . make it very clear through words and actions that they expect to have no harassment in the workplace."

As sexual harassment and assault cases continue to make headlines, busi-nesses, employees and regulators are asking these questions:

Are workplace training programs on sexual harassment effective?

On an NPL building site in California, a vendor unloading his usual weekly delivery turned casual small talk with a male construction worker toward sex, a conversation the worker later said was unwelcome. But he did not report it to NPL's human resources department until weeks later, after he had attended a mandatory training session on sexual harassment.

NPL's Epperson recounts that the employee had not realized the builder was accountable for the behavior of its vendors. "He thought it was up to the vendor to take action," she says.

But during the training he learned that "if an individual felt harassed by whatever comment or gesture was made by [a vendor's employee], it's still our responsibility to take action."

California, like Connecticut and Maine, requires most businesses to hold regular sexual harassment training for employees. "I think that's a great idea," says Epperson, who has worked at NPL for two years and is the 50-year-old company's first human resources pro-

Former Fox News host Gretchen Carlson received a $20 million settlement to resolve her sexual harassment suit against then-Fox News CEO Roger Ailes, who resigned in June 2016 following numerous reports of sexual harassment. Carlson, who has received hundreds of letters from women saying they, too, had suffered from workplace harassment, said recently: "The floodgates have opened. Everyone is talking about this now."

fessional for the region, which covers California, Texas, Oregon, Washington and Nevada. Members of construction crews often are unaware that they could offend co-workers with graphic stories about sexual exploits, she says. "The training programs that are out there are really beneficial," Epperson says.

It is unclear, however, whether such programs are universally effective. The EEOC task force's review last year of research on sensitivity training unearthed just two studies — both more than 15 years old — addressing whether sexual harassment training prevents the behavior. [27]

One, from 2001, concluded that the training leaves some men feeling threatened and at risk of false accusations. In a stunning finding, that study's co-author, Shereen Bingham, a professor of communication at the University of Nebraska, Omaha, said last year that men who completed a 30-minute training were actually less able to identify coercive behavior toward a subordinate as sexual harassment than men who did not take the training. [28]

The task force complained that most training focuses more on legal definitions and avoiding lawsuits than on stopping bad behavior. "Much of the training done over the past 30 years has not worked as a prevention tool," the EEOC's Feldblum and Lipnic wrote in the report. And "ineffective training can be unhelpful or even counterproductive." [29]

"The training we actually have to do is laughable. It's just terrible," said Leslie Salzinger, a professor of gender and women's studies at the University of California, Berkeley, where a law

school dean, the renowned astronomer Marcy and an assistant basketball coach left the school amid sexual harassment scandals. [30] She criticized the university's training for its lack of discussion about power dynamics and inequality and for focusing on how to supervise harassers, which implies that supervisors would never be the culprits. [31]

The commissioners have advocated a change in the kind of training companies offer, from the typical definitions-based video session to broader, in-person "respectful workplace training," whose premise is that incivility is a gateway to harassment. "It doesn't focus as much on legal definitions as on common sense," says Feldblum, a member of the EEOC since 2010. "It's more about what you should do as opposed to directions on what you shouldn't do."

Fran Sepler, president of the Minneapolis-based human resources consulting firm Sepler & Associates, is working with the EEOC to create respectful workplace training modules. Rather than teaching people what they shouldn't do, the new training is "positive and skill-building." It focuses "on what people should do, and not just with protected classes — but with everybody in the workplace," she says. It discourages "behaviors that are rude and not civil, but which don't rise to the level of unlawful harassment. If you stop those behaviors, you won't get to the level of harassment."

Sepler says sexual harassment training is "too nuanced" for online delivery. She advocates classroom sessions with a live trainer. Epperson, who requires NPL's employees to watch online videos, agrees that face-to-face follow-up with employees is critical to reinforcing their understanding of what the online course teaches.

Still, Epperson says that any sexual harassment training — even a canned version — is better than none. "We can equip people all day long, and if they're going to bury themselves, they're going to bury themselves," she says. "But it cannot be said that the employer didn't do what was in their power to equip that employee with tools and with training."

Cornell law professor Sherwyn says training has become more important as celebrity offenders such as O'Reilly, Kalanick and Weinstein make headlines. "If I were in charge of [human resources] at a large company," Sherwyn says, "I would have stepped up my training, and I would have been prepared for large claims. . . . I would be more serious, because I'd be afraid that more people would say, 'Wow, this stuff that someone accused O'Reilly of, somebody has said that to me.' "

Do business policies perpetuate sexual harassment?

After Uber's Fowler left the team whose manager she said had propositioned her, several of her female colleagues told her the same man had approached them about having sex. HR had told Fowler her report was the first about this manager, she said. But her colleagues said HR told them the same thing when they reported their experiences. [32]

After Fowler's blog went viral, Uber hired former U.S. Attorney General Eric Holder to investigate her claims. One of his recommendations: HR should track complaints and let senior management know if multiple employees have reported the same manager. Then, Holder said, management should intervene. Fowler's abusive supervisor was fired.

Now in private practice in Washington, Holder also recommended that Uber make it clearer to employees how to lodge complaints and give them options for talking to HR, their supervisors, other managers or a helpline. "This encourages employees who may otherwise fear retaliation to come forward," Holder wrote in his report. [33]

It is common for Silicon Valley firms such as Uber not to have such policies in place, says San Francisco lawyer Dhillon, because most started small and without much workplace experience:

"A couple of tech bros get together with one another to start a company; some other bro has money, so they get him in on it. They hire some women. They call them girls."

But even companies with formal procedures and regulations in place are not immune to sexual harassment claims.

Too often, says Washington lawyer Joseph Sellers, business leaders misplace their faith in an announced policy — often a zero-tolerance policy — forbidding sexual harassment. "They believe: 'Resting on the confidence of that policy, we'll have no sexual harassment, and . . . if there is, we won't be held legally responsible,' " says Sellers. "They rely so much on the presence of the policy, so they don't devote resources and attention to protecting against [sexual harassment] in everyday decisions."

Harassment, as a result, is left unchecked, Sellers says.

Management's behavior is more important than policies, Sellers says. "The leadership of the company tends to be viewed as having the most significant influence on whether harassment occurs in the workplace," he says. "It could be that the senior people are engaged in harassment, or they tolerate it, see it, know about it but don't do much about it."

Employees take their cues from "what kind of behavior is permitted, regardless of what the policy says," Sellers adds. "Policies are important, but they are by no means sufficient as a way to protect against workplace harassment."

Dorothy Edwards, president of Alteristic, a Springfield, Va., nonprofit organization that has created programs to prevent sexual violence, says zero-tolerance policies put would-be harassers on notice that they will suffer penalties for misconduct. "That's a good message," she says, "but it doesn't stand alone." Edwards advocates policies that encourage or even require employees to treat each other with respect and to make it safe for victims to report harassment without the fear of retaliation.

Sellers says one policy in particular — the mandatory arbitration contract — can perpetuate sexual harassment. [34]

Some companies require employees to sign a contract upon employment that binds them to work out any grievances with a company-appointed arbitrator. That prevents a woman who claims sexual harassment from suing the company over it; instead, she is required to take her complaint to the arbitrator and abide by that decision.

Those contracts often include confidentiality clauses forbidding an employee who enters into arbitration to talk about the case or any settlement that results from it.

Forcing employees into secret hearings conducted by company-picked decision-makers "silences survivors of sexual harassment," television journalist Carlson said in a Capitol Hill press conference last spring. Lawmakers introduced a bill that would make it easier for sexual harassment victims to avoid forced arbitration. [35]

The EEOC's Feldblum calls confidentiality clauses "problematic in terms of shining sunlight onto problems, especially when you have situations with the superstar harasser — someone who is high value to the company. Things don't get fixed because the incident is swept under the rug." The result, says Sellers, is an experience like Fowler's at Uber: When multiple women complain about the same individual, they don't know about each other. And employees who later encounter the harasser have no warning of that history of misconduct.

Still, says Patricia Wise, a labor and employment lawyer in Toledo, Ohio, who calls herself "no fan of arbitration," the practice gives her management clients an advantage. "If my clients are sued, I would much prefer that they not resolve it through the courts, which is a public forum. Arbitration can be quiet, faster and less expensive [than a lawsuit]. Employees should consider it."

She adds, however: "If I put on my

Most Workplace Sexual Harassment Is Verbal

Most of the sexual harassment women experience at work involves nonphysical behavior such as sexual remarks, teasing or ogling, according to a 2016 online survey of 500 Redbook *readers. Overall, 80 percent of respondents experienced sexual harassment at work, compared with 90 percent in 1976. Some 9,000 women responded to the earlier survey.*

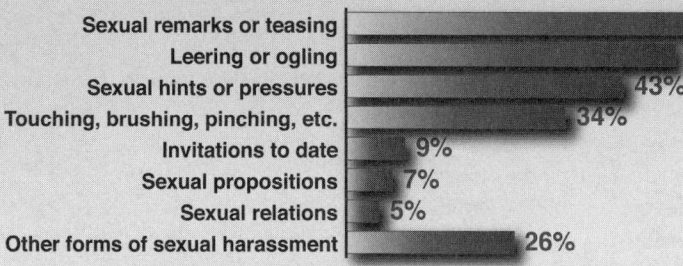

Percentage Who Experienced Various Types of Workplace Sexual Harassment, 2016

Sexual remarks or teasing	64%
Leering or ogling	51%
Sexual hints or pressures	43%
Touching, brushing, pinching, etc.	34%
Invitations to date	9%
Sexual propositions	7%
Sexual relations	5%
Other forms of sexual harassment	26%

Total Who Experienced Sexual Harassment: 80%

Source: Ashley Mateo and Kaitlin Menza, "The Results of a 1976 Survey of Women About Sexual Harassment At Work Remain Virtually Unchanged In 2017," Redbook, *March 27, 2017, https://tinyurl.com/yaczn69y*

other hat, which is that I care about the issue of harassment, I don't think arbitration is the way to go. The arbitrator is going to require an employer . . . to train its managers. It's not the best place for an employee to be. But employees don't have a choice if they sign an arbitration form."

Cornell's Sherwyn disagrees that arbitration harms an employee who has filed a sexual harassment complaint. Going to court, he says, does not guarantee that the case will get publicity. "People get that wrong," he says. "Roger Ailes didn't go to court; Bill O'Reilly didn't go to court. The only reason we know about this is because they're celebrities." He says sexual harassment lawsuits filed by noncelebrities rarely get publicity.

Sherwyn says lawsuits stretch a complaint out over years, while arbitration settles the matter quickly. Anti-arbitration attorneys, he says, "are worried about the 2 percent of cases or fewer that are egregious and deserve to see the light

of day. I'm worried about the 98 percent that are just dealing with people."

Do policies designed to prevent sexual harassment go too far?

Some say sexual harassment training, along with some other workplace practices, is making things worse for women at work.

Psychologist Kim Elsesser, author of the book *Sex and the Office: Women, Men and the Sex Partition That's Dividing the Workplace*, offered this scenario: "Imagine a male executive asks a male employee to join him on a Starbucks run or for a beer after work. No one blinks an eye, a friendship develops, and perhaps a mentor relationship as well. However, if the same male executive invites a woman to join him for coffee or a beer, it's a different story." [36]

Elsesser, a lecturer in women's studies at UCLA, wrote in an op-ed piece for the *Los Angeles Times*: "I'm not suggesting we set the clock back on the progress we've made in trying to de-

crease sexual harassment at work. But I've found that heightened awareness of harassment is also inadvertently leaving many employees overly cautious in interactions with the opposite sex. It's creating a barrier." [37]

Vice President Mike Pence drew barbs in March when a 2002 comment he made to a Capitol Hill newspaper about refusing to dine alone with any woman other than his wife resurfaced in *The Washington Post*. [38] Critics questioned whether his policy meant he would not hire women in leadership positions that might require them to meet with him privately. [39]

Sepler, the Minneapolis HR executive, says policies that are too restrictive can create fear and apprehension among employees, and that can rob women of opportunities. She advocates policies that focus on how to "do things positive" rather than separate men and women. "If I'm a male manager and I'm afraid to be with a female employee," she says, "who's missing the mentoring opportunities?"

In her 2003 book, *Working Together: How Workplace Bonds Strengthen a Diverse Democracy*, New York University law professor Cynthia Estlund argued that zero-tolerance policies banning any sexual references in jokes or conversation among colleagues "threaten both workplace sociability and equality." Even 14 years ago, she said, "the ban on sexual harassment [had] become unmoored from the anti-discrimination norm from which it arose." [40]

But Sepler says policies do not "go too far. I have yet to see a policy that says, don't have a sense of humor; don't enjoy your co-workers; don't go to lunch together. People who think policies have gone too far will look at a perfectly reasonable policy and say it's unfair."

Toledo attorney Wise distinguishes between policies that overcorrect a problem and those that go too far. "We have not overcorrected," she says, "but there is some legitimacy to saying we've gone too far. . . . If I were a man, I probably would stop [complimenting] women; that doesn't rise to the level of sexual harassment." On the other hand, she says, a manager who constantly comments on the appearance of the women who work for him might be guilty of harassment.

Human resources consultant Hartman, however, says compliments about a woman's physical appearance should be verboten in the workplace. "That's not what they're there for," she says. "You can compliment somebody, but why compliment them on their hair or clothes? That's saying that matters more than the work they're doing. What matters is how well the person is doing the job."

Still, she agrees that women lose out when men refuse to travel with them or have private business conversations with them behind a closed office door. "A lot of that kind of travel is what moves a woman's career forward," she says.

A growing cohort of men's activists in Silicon Valley, however, has said tensions over what constitutes sexual harassment have created a "witch hunt" atmosphere in the high-tech world. [41]

The New York Times reported in September that a group of about 200 men in Silicon Valley meets regularly to discuss men's rights and object to what they refer to as "diversity dogma." [42]

But San Francisco attorney Dhillon — who is representing 28-year-old Google engineer James Damore, who lost his job for writing a memo questioning whether women "were biologically less capable of engineering" — says Damore's lawsuit is about discrimination, not sexual harassment. [43]

She claims that some Silicon Valley companies have set high quotas for hiring women. "That's a zero-sum game," she says. "If you're going to have 70 percent [of new positions] set aside for women, and 30 percent set aside for men, that's illegal. I believe what people are entitled to in the workplace is a gender-neutral workplace." ∎

In a video shown on NBC's "Meet the Press" on Oct. 22, Massachusetts Sen. Elizabeth Warren and three other Democratic senators recalled their own experiences with workplace sexual harassment. Warren said when she was a young law professor, a senior faculty member asked her to stop by his office. When she got there, "he slammed the door and lunged for me," she said. "It was like a bad cartoon. He's chasing me around the desk trying to get his hands on me. And I kept saying, 'You don't want to do this. You don't want to do this. . . . Please don't do this.' " The other senators who told their stories were Heidi Heitkamp of North Dakota, Claire McCaskill of Missouri and Mazie Hirono of Hawaii.

BACKGROUND

Early Problems

Sexual harassment has been part of American culture since the early 1600s, when African slaves were brought to Jamestown, Va. [44]

Female slaves were forced into "productive, reproductive and sexual labor crucial to the political economy" at that time, wrote attorney and historian Adrienne D. Davis, the vice provost of Washington University in St. Louis. "Conceiving slavery as sexual harassment sheds light on how slave law was labor law, plantations were workplaces and enslaved women's resistance constituted gender activism." [45]

After the Civil War, women's rights advocates demanded that Philadelphia housekeeper Hester Vaughn, who had come to the United States from England,

be pardoned. Vaughn, who was fired when her employer learned she was pregnant, had been convicted of infanticide and sentenced to death after authorities found her with her dead baby. A backlash from protesters, who argued that Vaughn had been sexually coerced, convinced the governor of Pennsylvania to pardon her. [46]

In the late 19th and early 20th centuries, labor activists and the Woman's Christian Temperance Union attempted to protect women from sexual harassment. Yet through much of the early 20th century, women in clerical and factory jobs silently endured physical and verbal assaults from male colleagues and supervisors. Even labor unions, which negotiated protections for women from work that was too physically demanding, could not shield them from being propositioned by their bosses. Largely left on their own to ward off the advances of lecherous co-workers, women were told by advice handbooks to quit their jobs if they were unable to stop the abuse. [47]

The problem became worse as vast numbers of women began to enter the workforce during World War II. Later, in 1964, Congress passed the Civil Rights Act, including Title VII, which prohibited sex discrimination in the workplace. The next year, the new U.S. Equal Employment Opportunity Commission began to investigate claims of discrimination in employment. Later, Title IX of the Education Amendments of 1972 prohibited sexual harassment at public schools and colleges.

Still, the predatory sexual behavior that women experienced at work continued, even as the feminist movement took hold in cities. In 1975, a group of women's rights activists at Cornell University in Ithaca, N.Y., gave a name to something "they had all experienced but rarely discussed — unwanted sexual demands, comments, looks or sexual touching in the workplace." They called it sexual harassment. [48]

The women organized around a former Cornell colleague, Carmita Wood, who filed a claim for unemployment benefits after she quit her job because of unwelcome touching from her supervisor. She had requested a transfer instead, but Cornell refused and said she did not qualify for benefits because she quit for personal reasons.

Wood and activists at the university's Human Affairs Office formed Working Women United and hosted events at which secretaries, factory workers, mailroom clerks, waitresses and other female wage earners spoke about their experiences. Some reported having to watch their male colleagues masturbate in the workplace. Others said they had been threatened. And nearly all said they had been pressured to have sex or be denied promotions. [49]

The movement gained national attention when in 1975 *The New York Times* reported on the testimony of Lin Farley, director of the Women's Section in Cornell's Human Affairs Office, to the Commission on Human Rights in New York. It was the first time a newspaper used the phrase "sexual harassment," which appeared in the article's headline. [50]

Farley had outlined six behaviors that she considered to be sexual harassment:

- "Constant leering and ogling of a woman's body;
- Continually brushing against a woman's body;
- Forcing a woman to submit to squeezing or pinching;
- Catching a woman alone for forced sexual intimacies;
- Outright sexual propositions, backed by threat of losing a job; and
- Forced sexual relations." [51]

The Times quoted Farley calling the frequency of sexual harassment in the workplace "literally epidemic." [52]

Redbook magazine went further in 1976, calling sexual harassment a "pandemic — an everyday, everywhere occurrence." [53] The magazine conducted a survey of 9,000 female readers; nearly 90 percent of respondents reported they had experienced sexual harassment on the job. In addition, nearly half said they had quit a job because of sexual harassment or knew a woman who had. [54] (*See graphic, p. 900.*)

The new movement sparked a backlash, starting with CNN commentator Rhonda Koenig, who wrote in the February 1976 issue of *Harper's* that "a lot of women would feel deprived without a reasonable quota of sexual harassment per week" and accused feminists of perpetuating the "myth of women as oppressed." [55]

In the same vein, self-described "anti-feminist crusader" Phyllis Schlafly said in 1981 that women who complained had been harassed because they were "asking for it." [56] She told a Senate committee reviewing federal guidelines on harassment that "virtuous women are seldom accosted by unwelcome sexual propositions or familiarities, obscene talk or profane language." [57]

Early Lawsuits

Still, by the early 1970s, the first six sexual harassment lawsuits were filed in federal court under Title VII of the Civil Rights Act, which prohibits employers from discriminating on the basis of race, color, religion, national origin or sex. But defense attorneys successfully argued that the courts "should not be concerned with the social life of company employees" and that because both men and women could suffer from sexual harassment, it did not qualify as discrimination. Plaintiffs lost all but one of those early lawsuits. [58]

The lone breakthrough lawsuit, though, led other courts to recognize harassment based on sex to be within the purview of Title VII. The suit was brought by U.S. Department of Justice employee Diane Williams. Williams, who started working in the agency's Community Relations Service in January 1972, said her boss fired her that September after she rejected his repeated sexual advances. Defense attorneys argued that she was fired not because of her gender — since both men and women are subject to sexual harassment — but because she had snubbed her boss. [59]

The judge disagreed, saying enforcement of Title VII does not depend on "a characteristic peculiar to one of the genders." The victory established *quid pro quo* sexual harassment — when employment or a promotion, for example, depend on providing sexual favors — as a form of sex discrimination in 1976. [60]

Some media organizations mocked the win, calling it an "effort to regulate hanky-panky," Julie Berebitsky wrote in her book *Sex and the Office: A History of Gender, Power, and Desire.* [61]

In 1981, the EEOC added a section on sexual harassment to its guidelines on gender discrimination. The agency acknowledged two kinds of sexual harassment: "*quid pro quo*, as in the

Continued on p. 904

Chronology

1960s-1970s
Sexual harassment becomes illegal.

1964
Title VII of the Civil Rights Act bans employment discrimination based on race, religion, sex or national origin.

1964
New U.S. Equal Employment Opportunity Commission (EEOC) begins investigating discrimination claims.

1976
Sexual harassment plaintiff wins a court case for the first time.

———————•———————

1980s-1990s
EEOC and courts define sexual harassment.

1981
EEOC acknowledges two kinds of sexual harassment: *quid pro quo* and creating a hostile work environment.

1984
U.S. Circuit Court of Appeals says a single, severe workplace incident can constitute sexual harassment.

1986
U.S. Supreme Court rules for victim in its first sexual harassment case.

1991
Law professor Anita Hill accuses Supreme Court nominee Clarence Thomas of persistent sexual harassment when the two worked together years earlier. . . . Former Arkansas state employee Paula Jones drops sexual harassment lawsuit against Gov. Bill Clinton in exchange for $850,000. . . . Federal District Court judge finds that posting pornographic photographs in the workplace constitutes sexual harassment.

1993
Supreme Court rules that a victim does not have to suffer psychological damage for a workplace to be considered hostile.

1995
Sen. Bob Packwood, R-Ore., resigns after dozens of campaign workers accuse him of sexual harassment.

1997
Sexual harassment complaints to EEOC peak at 15,889.

1998
Female employees of Eveleth Taconite Co. iron mine settle the first sexual harassment class-action lawsuit for $3.5 million. . . . Supreme Court rules same-sex sexual harassment is actionable under Title VII. . . . Female employees at a Mitsubishi Motors manufacturing plant win $34 million in sexual harassment suit. . . . Supreme Court says businesses are not liable for a sexual harassment claim if they established procedures for employee redress but the accuser did not follow those procedures.

———————•———————

2000s-Present
Monetary awards in sexual harassment cases skyrocket.

2004
Former Fox News producer Andrea Mackris sues TV personality Bill O'Reilly for $60 million, claiming sexual harassment. She settles for an undisclosed amount of money.

2011
Jury awards Aaron's rental store employee Ashley Alford $95 million — later reduced to $40 million — in a claim against a manager she said sexually harassed her for a year. She eventually settled for $6 million.

2012
A physician's assistant at Sacramento's Mercy Hospital wins largest sexual harassment award ever: $168 million.

2016
Fox News agrees to pay former "Fox & Friends" co-host Gretchen Carlson $20 million to settle sexual harassment lawsuit against Chairman Roger Ailes, who is forced to resign. . . . EEOC task force on harassment says three-quarters of sexual harassment victims never report abuse and calls for overhaul of prevention programs for employees. . . . Fifteen women accuse then-presidential candidate Donald Trump of sexual harassment or assault after the leak of a 2005 "Access Hollywood" video on which he bragged about grabbing women's private parts. . . . Jury awards Houston teenager $8 million in sexual harassment suit against Chipotle, where she worked in 2013.

2017
Fox News fires Bill O'Reilly amid multiple claims of sexual harassment. . . . Uber engineer Susan J. Fowler publishes blog alleging rampant sexual harassment at the on-demand car service, leading to CEO Travis Kalanick's resignation. . . . Fidelity Investments fires well-known stock picker Gavin Baker for allegedly sexually harassing a junior female employee. . . . More than 60 actresses, employees and other women accuse film producer Harvey Weinstein of sexual harassment; some say he raped them; the board fires him. . . . Amazon Studios head Roy Price resigns after a Hollywood producer accuses him of making unwanted sexual advances. . . . Four Democratic senators — Elizabeth Warren, Heidi Heitkamp, Claire McCaskill and Mazie Hirono — make video statements, aired on "Meet the Press" on Oct. 22, about their own experiences with sexual harassment.

Women Leaving the Sciences Because of Sexual Harassment

"This reduces our scientific integrity."

Rebecca Barnes recalls that the first time she presented her doctoral research at a scientific meeting, a male scientist listened politely to her two-minute presentation and then told the blonde Yale University forestry and environmental studies student: " 'You're so much smarter than you look. You should consider dyeing your hair.' "

Not long after, as she prepared for a meeting with a renowned scientist, whom she would accompany to collect water samples from a stream, her professor pulled her into his office to prep her, she says. "You might consider wearing something different," he advised the shorts-clad scientist.

"It's August, and I'm going to be sampling," she says she replied. "What do you expect me to be wearing?"

Barnes is now an assistant professor of environmental science at Colorado College and an investigator on a National Science Foundation-funded team that aims to increase the participation and advancement of women in science and engineering. But many women leave scientific fields before they make it that far, she says, often because they tire of harassment.

Barnes calls the two incidents examples of "a thousand paper cuts" she has endured as a female scientist in a male-dominated field in which young female scientists depend on their male superiors for academic and professional recommendations. And while some people might deem the comments as falling short of harassment, they made her feel "unwelcome" among male scientists, she insists. And she has been sexually harassed "more times than I can count" — in ways she declined to describe for this article — by male scientists, professors and classmates, she says.

Barnes is not alone. In a study of 474 male and female astronomers and planetary scientists published in the *Journal of Geophysical Research* in July, 79 percent of women reported sexist remarks from peers and 44 percent said they heard them from supervisors. Nearly two-thirds of the women said men had questioned their mental abilities, compared with 48 percent of men who reported the same. [1]

Women make up about one-quarter of those in STEM (science, technology, engineering and math) occupations: 24.7 percent of those in computer and math occupations and 15.1 percent of those in architecture and engineering, according to the nonprofit Catalyst, which advocates for diversity in the workplace. [2]

In the astronomy study, women of color reported experiencing the most hostility, including verbal and physical harassment, according to the study by four female scientists. An equal number of white women and women of color said they had been verbally harassed about their gender.

Kathryn Clancy, an associate professor of anthropology at the University of Illinois and lead author of the study, said 28 percent of female scientists of color reported feeling unsafe because of their race or gender. In addition, 18 percent of women of color and 12 percent of white women said they skip professional events because they do not feel safe attending them. [3]

Clancy said the survey covered 2010 through 2015. "This isn't something anyone can point to and say, 'These results are padded by something that happened in 1967,' " she said. "They're feeling unsafe [and] skipping professional events today." [4]

Barnes says the study results ring true. She is a member of the Earth Science Women's Network and says the peer networking group conducted its own study a few years ago and found that 51 percent of its 3,000 members said they had experienced harassment. "These comments that make you feel like you're unwelcome are something that are now far more acknowledged as a problem," she says "We drive [women scientists] away because of the tiny things that happen every day. It's insidious."

In September, the American Geophysical Union (AGU), a professional organization of earth and space scientists, voted to broaden its definition of "scientific misconduct" to include

Continued from p. 902

Williams case, and unwelcome advances and sexual requests that could create a hostile work environment." [62]

Feminist author and attorney Catharine MacKinnon, in her 1979 book *Sexual Harassment of Working Women*, was the first to propose the controversial, two-pronged definition. Ten years after Williams' victory, MacKinnon was co-counsel for the plaintiff in the first sexual harassment case heard by the U.S. Supreme Court.

The high court ruled in 1986 that the sexual harassment of an employee by a supervisor violates the federal law against sex discrimination in the workplace. The case involved a lawsuit filed by Mechelle Vinson, a former teller at a Meritor Savings Bank branch in Washington, D.C., who said her manager pressured her into having sex more than 50 times in the bank. Vinson said she initially rejected the manager's advances but reconsidered because she feared she would lose her job. The court ruled that sexual harassment violates the law if it is "sufficiently severe or pervasive" to create "a hostile or abusive work environment." [63]

It wasn't until 1991, however, that sexual harassment became a national issue when University of Oklahoma law professor Anita Hill accused Supreme Court nominee Clarence Thomas of sexual harassment when she had worked with him years earlier at the EEOC and the U.S. Department of Education. During televised Senate confirmation hearings that gripped the country, Hill said Thomas had invited her on dates and made comments about sex and pornography. Hill never filed charges against Thomas, who denied her claims. The Senate confirmed his appointment to the high court, 52-48, where he remains a justice. [64]

sexual harassment, discrimination and bullying. [5] The organization received four complaints about improper conduct toward women during its own annual meeting in December. [6]

Scientific misconduct — traditionally defined as fabrication, falsification or plagiarism in research — can result in dismissal, the loss of a federal grant, a reprimand or a damaged reputation.

Not every scientist agrees that sexual harassment belongs in the same category as fabricating lab results, however. Mark Frankel, who formerly directed the scientific responsibility program at the American Association for the Advancement of Science in Washington, which calls itself "the world's largest general scientific society," says misconduct applies specifically to scientific research, while harassment is inappropriate in any field. "There is a line between them," Franklel told *Science* magazine. "I would prefer seeing each of them on one side of the line or the other rather than seeing them incorporated." [7]

Alan Price, a former federal scientific misconduct investigator, said investigating research wrongdoing requires different skills from those needed to investigate sexual harassment. Now that the American Geophysical Union has combined them, he said he worries that such investigations "wouldn't be done well." [8]

Barnes says more actions like the AGU's and grants such as the one her team received from the National Science Foundation could help attract more women to scientific fields, and retain them. Women earn about 37 percent of U.S. undergraduate degrees in STEM disciplines and are underrepresented in other scientific fields. For example, women receive just 18 percent of computer science degrees. [9]

Writing in *The Atlantic*, Joan C. Williams and Kate Massinger of the Center for WorkLife Law at the University of California Hastings College of the Law, said within a decade the United States will have a shortage of 1 million college-educated STEM workers, largely because many women drop out of STEM fields

once they become doctoral students. [10]

In a 2014 survey on gender bias against women of color in science, Williams found that one in three female science professors reported sexual harassment. [11] "There's been a lot of talk about how to keep women in the STEM pipeline," Williams and Massinger wrote, "but if fails to make a crucial connection: One reason the pipeline leaks is that women are harassed out of science." [12]

A more diverse scientific community "comes up with better solutions," Barnes says. "[W]e need all hands on deck to figure out climate change and national disasters and energy supply. If we are driving people out of these fields because of bad behavior, that is reducing our scientific integrity."

— *Sharon O'Malley*

[1] Kathryn B. H. Clancy *et al.*, "Double jeopardy in astronomy and planetary science: Women of color face greater risks of gendered and racial harassment," *Journal of Geophysical Research*, July 10, 2017, https://tinyurl.com/y98d96r7.

[2] "Women in Science, Technology, Engineering and Mathematics (STEM)," Catalyst, Dec. 9, 2016, https://tinyurl.com/zberj4q.

[3] Clancy, *op. cit.*

[4] Azeen Ghorayshi, "Many Women of Color Feel Unsafe Working in Science, New Study Finds," *BuzzFeed*, July 10, 2017, https://tinyurl.com/y73zg3t3.

[5] "AGU Scientific Integrity and Professional Ethics," American Geophysical Union, March 2017, https://tinyurl.com/y7zbzffr.

[6] Maggie Kuo, "Geophysics society hopes to define sexual harassment as scientific misconduct," *Science*, April 7, 2017, https://tinyurl.com/ybjoujhn.

[7] *Ibid.*

[8] *Ibid.*

[9] Deborah Bach, "Study examines why some STEM fields have fewer women than others," *Science X*, Oct. 13, 2016, https://tinyurl.com/yb8dyyhs.

[10] Joan C. Williams and Kate Massinger, "How Women Are Harassed Out of Science" *The Atlantic*, July 25, 2106, https://tinyurl.com/luvyuth.

[11] Joan C. Williams, Katherine W. Phillips and Erika V. Hall, "Double Jeopardy? Gender Bias Against Women of Color in Science," WorkLife Law, University of California Hastings College of the Law, 2014, https://tinyurl.com/kkbvykv.

[12] Williams and Massinger, *op. cit.*

That same year, President George H.W. Bush signed the Civil Rights Act of 1991, which gave plaintiffs in employment discrimination suits the right to seek compensatory and punitive damages and to request a jury trial. Previously, plaintiffs could sue only for injunctive relief, including reinstatement to a job they had lost because of the discrimination, or lost pay and benefits. [65]

The publicity surrounding the Senate confirmation hearings, combined with the expanded provisions for victims of workplace discrimination, including sexual harassment, led to a record number

of sexual harassment claims filed with the EEOC that year. One accuser was Arkansas state employee Paula Jones, who filed a sexual harassment lawsuit against President Bill Clinton, claiming he exposed himself to her and requested oral sex when they met in a hotel room in 1991. Clinton denied the allegations. Jones dropped her lawsuit in exchange for $850,000. [66]

By 1997, EEOC had recorded 15,889 charges of sexual harassment, filed both with the agency and its state affiliates, the highest in its history and more than double the 6,127 it logged in 1990. [67]

Landmark Rulings

During the 1990s and early 2000s, federal courts and the Supreme Court ruled on a number of landmark sexual harassment cases, including:

• *Robinson v. Jacksonville Shipyards, 1991* — A federal District Court judge in Jacksonville, Fla., ruled that posting photographs of nude women in the workplace constitutes sexual harassment. Previously, courts had ruled that sexually explicit pictures could "contribute" to an atmosphere of sexual

Workers Urged to Report Harassment When They See It

"We want them to intervene early."

For a variety of reasons, three-quarters of people who experience sexual harassment at work never report it to their supervisors, the company's human resources department, the U.S. Equal Employment Opportunity Commission (EEOC) or a court, according to the EEOC, the federal agency that investigates such allegations. [1]

An EEOC task force on harassment last fall proposed a solution: Companies can teach employees who witness or learn about the harassment to report it on the victim's behalf, says EEOC Commissioner Chai R. Feldblum. Such bystander intervention, she says, is similar to the Department of Homeland Security's anti-terrorism motto: "If you see something, say something."

Bystander intervention is widely taught on college campuses, where students are trained to step in if they suspect sexual violence is about to occur. The theory behind such training is that sexual assaults could be reduced if witnesses other than the victim confronted the offender directly; distracted him before an assault occurred; or reported the incident as the victim's delegate.

Dorothy Edwards, president of Alteristic, a Springfield, Va., firm that creates sexual harassment and assault prevention strategies, says bystander training for sexual harassment covers four areas:

• *Recognizing the warning signs.* "What does harassment look like?" Edwards says. "It's very behavioral. As early as possible, even when it's subtle, we want [every employee] to recognize it. We don't want them to only see it when it's really explicit. We want them to intervene early."

• *Understanding the barriers to getting involved.* Not everyone who witnesses harassment is willing to intervene, Edwards says. Workplaces that train employees to intervene should make it optional. Shy employees, she says, as well as those who do not want to get their peers in trouble or fear retaliation themselves if they report a peer, might never participate in an intervention. She advises managers to make clear that it is OK not to intervene and to offer a confidential way to report misconduct.

• *Implementing the "direct, delegate, distract" strategy.* Direct involves telling the harasser to stop. "Some people can do this, and some people can't," Edwards says. Delegate means reporting the incident to someone else — a human resources manager, a supervisor or even a friend who is willing to tell someone in authority about the incident. Distract involves interrupting

the harassment as it is happening. "Create a distraction to defuse what's going on," Edwards advises. "Say, 'Hey, what's going on?' or 'I need you in my office; can you come here?' or 'Do you have lunch plans? Come with us.'"

• *Focusing on positive behaviors.* If employees intervene only when they catch a harasser in the act, then workplaces will always be reacting rather than preventing, Edwards says. "We need to be shifting norms in a way that makes those behaviors less palatable." The new norm in the workplace, she says, should be that harassment is not OK and that "we look out for each other."

Such training, Edwards says, gives employees tools that they weren't equipped with before to counter the obstacles bystanders often face when deciding whether to intervene: a fear of retaliation; confusion about what constitutes sexual harassment and whether they should report it; and the tendency of bystanders to do nothing if other witnesses are not acting.

At several Oregon construction companies, Edwards' organization is trying out the sexual harassment version of bystander training. She says of the multiyear pilot, which began more than a year ago, employers are starting to embrace the program. "We don't know if it works."

So far, however, Edwards says, employees have called the four-tier approach "more realistic" than a single policy that makes the victim alone responsible for reporting harassment. Real success, she adds, will come when employees, rather than HR, set the tone that sexual harassment in their workplace will not be tolerated.

Companies that conduct bystander training, she says, should start with employees who are the most influential among their peers. "Who are the people who everyone takes their cues from?" Edwards says. "Who is the one in the center of the social life, organizing cocktails after work?

"If you get these socially influential folks to buy in . . . by having them model and endorse these norms, that is more effective than training," Edwards says, and they reinforce the training once the rest of the team has had it.

— Sharon O'Malley

[1] Chai R. Feldblum and Victoria A. Lipnic, "Report of the Co-Chairs of the Select Task Force on the Study of Harassment in the Workplace," U.S. Equal Employment Opportunity Commission, June 2016, http://tinyurl.com/gnrcpnl.

harassment, but the *Robinson* ruling established the pictures themselves amounted to harassment. [68]

• *Harris v. Forklift Systems, 1993* — When a female employee claimed the company's president created a

hostile work environment by making her the target of sexual innuendos and insults, Forklift Systems attorneys argued that no psychological harm occurred. The high court ruled that psychological damage is not

necessary for a workplace to be considered hostile. Justice Sandra Day O'Connor wrote for the court: "Title VII comes into play before the harassing conduct leads to a nervous breakdown." [69]

• *Faragher v. City of Boca Raton and Burlington Industries v. Ellerth, 1998* — These landmark cases led the Supreme Court to clarify that an employer is liable when any of its supervisors sexually harasses a subordinate in a *quid pro quo* situation. However, the high court also said employers are not responsible for sexual harassment by their supervisors if the employer has an established procedure for employees to "seek redress" from sexual harassment; and if the employee took advantage of that procedure. This is why so many companies require employees to take sexual harassment training. [70]

• *Oncale v. Sundowner Offshore Services, 1998* — The Supreme Court unanimously ruled that same-sex sexual harassment is actionable under Title VII. [71]

• *Pennsylvania State Police v. Suders, 2004* — The high court ruled that the employer is automatically liable and may offer no affirmative defense if an employee is forced to quit his or her job because of sexual harassment. [72]

During televised Senate confirmation hearings that gripped the country in 1991, University of Oklahoma law professor Anita Hill accused Supreme Court nominee Clarence Thomas of sexual harassment when she had worked with him years earlier. Hill said Thomas had invited her on dates and made comments about sex and pornography. Hill never filed charges against Thomas, who denied her claims. The Senate narrowly confirmed his appointment to the high court, where he remains a justice.

Getty Images/Bettmann

Rising Monetary Awards

In the years after passage of the Civil Rights Act of 1991, monetary awards in sexual harassment cases pushed well into the millions. Among the highest jury awards and settlements were:

• Female workers at the Mitsubishi Motors plant in Normal, Ill., were awarded $34 million in 1998 after complaining they were subjected to fondling, verbal abuse and obscene jokes and behavior. Some women quit because of it, while others claimed they were denied promotions because they refused managers' sexual advances. [73]

• A jury in 1999 awarded $21 million to the first female millwright at a Chrysler plant in Detroit, who said co-workers showed her sexually explicit photos and called her inappropriate names. However, the Michigan Supreme Court threw out the award in 2004, calling the amount excessive

and "clearly the product of passion and prejudice." [74]

• Six workers won a $30 million award from Ralphs grocery company in Escondido, Calif., in 2002 after complaining that a store manager touched them and threw a 12-pack of soda at them. In 2006, a state appeals court ruled that the award was excessive and reduced it. [75]

• The New York Knicks paid $11.6 million in punitive damages in 2007 to a former team executive who said she was fired after complaining that coach and basketball operations president Isiah Thomas harassed her over a two-year period. [76] The woman eventually settled for an undisclosed additional amount, including back pay, future lost wages and legal fees. [77]

• A jury awarded $10.6 million to an employee of the financial services firm UBS in 2011 after the company fired her for complaining a supervisor

repeatedly commented on the size of her breasts and his penis. [78]

• An employee of an Aaron's rent-to-own franchise won $40 million in 2011 after claiming the store's general manager sexually harassed her for a year. [79] However, the plaintiff eventually settled for a $6 million payout. [80]

• The largest jury award to an individual to date is $168 million in 2012 to Ani Chopourian, a physician's assistant at Mercy General Hospital in Sacramento. She said she asked for help from her supervisor, who laughed when doctors made sexual comments to her, propositioned her, called her "stupid" and stuck her with a needle. [81]

• Fox News agreed to pay former "Fox & Friends" co-host Gretchen Carlson $20 million in 2016 to settle her lawsuit against former Chairman Roger Ailes, whom she accused of sexually harassing her in public, ogling her body and asking her for sex. [82] ∎

CURRENT SITUATION

Social Media Harassment

The EEOC is recommending that businesses include a section on social media use in their sexual harassment policies after the report coauthored by Feldblum and Lipnic, the two co-chairs of the EEOC task force on workplace harassment, called social media "a possible means of workplace harassment." [83]

"Harassment should be in employers' minds as they draft social media policies and, conversely, social media issues should be in employers' minds as they draft anti-harassment policies," wrote Feldblum and Lipnic. [84]

Feldblum says businesses should assign the same penalties for online harassment as for a face-to-face offense. In the report, the authors wrote: "Social media platforms are potential vehicles for workplace-related interactions. And wherever that exists, employers must be aware that harassment may occur." [85]

A 2014 poll by the Pew Research Center, a nonpartisan think tank in Washington, said 6 percent of internet users have been sexually harassed, and 19 percent had witnessed someone else being sexually harassed online. Women ages 18 to 24 are particularly vulnerable, with 25 percent reporting they have been the target of online sexual harassment. Women are more likely than men to be harassed via social media, the poll of 2,849 Web users revealed. [86]

The same state and federal laws that ban sexual harassment in the workplace apply whether the offense occurs in the office, on a business trip, in the field or online. Likewise, anti-harassment laws for students and educators apply outside of the classroom. [87]

However, women have begun using social media to publicize their sexual harassment claims. Uber's Fowler, for example, posted her "strange, fascinating and slightly horrifying story" about systematic sexual harassment on a blog, as did astronomer Joan Schmelz, who wrote that, years ago, a supervisor belittled her, gossiped about her, withheld opportunities and even bad-mouthed her to a prospective employer. [88]

Supporters of the women who accused Fox's O'Reilly of sexual harassment prompted tens of thousands of followers to tweet their objections to O'Reilly's advertisers.

"The scandals around Bill O'Reilly and Uber have shown people there's an easier, quicker way [than going to court] to bring about cultural change," Janine Yancey, founder and CEO of Emtrain, an educational technology company, wrote in her blog. "They can mobilize online to bring a public conscience to the problem and lobby consumers to exert economic pressure on the employer." [89]

And a social media rant can damage a business's reputation. "More and more, stories depicting aggressive corporate cultures are both the source of fascination in a social media-driven world and a potential reputation risk that goes well beyond what a company's current employees and future recruits think of it," Washington Post columnist Jena McGregor agreed. [90]

California's Problems

The Golden State has been particularly beset by sexual harassment problems — in Hollywood, in Silicon Valley and beyond.

After The New York Times and The New Yorker in early October published accusations of sexual misconduct against Oscar-winning film producer Harvey Weinstein, the 65-year-old Hollywood icon flew to Europe for sex-addiction treatment and said, in a statement, "I'm trying to do better." [91]

The Times also reported that Weinstein, who has won six best-picture Oscars, had paid settlements to at least eight actresses and female employees of his companies Miramax and Weinstein Co. — some of them for more than $100,000 — over three decades in connection with the allegations. In his statement, Weinstein admitted: "I appreciate the way I've behaved with colleagues in the past has caused a lot of pain, and I sincerely apologize for it." But he denied several of the allegations "as patently false," his then-lawyer, Lisa Bloom, told The Times. [92] Bloom, a prominent women's rights attorney, dropped Weinstein as a client days after the allegations became public. [93]

Weinstein's accusers include actors Ashley Judd, Gwyneth Paltrow and others who reported unwelcome sexual advances. Some have claimed he forced them to have sex, which Weinstein has denied. [94] After a sixth woman came forward accusing Weinstein of sexual assault, the Los Angeles Police Department opened an investigation into the case. Unlike earlier cases, the latest allegation, by an unnamed Italian actress, occurred in 2013, within the 10-year statute of limitations window. It is the first rape allegation against Weinstein reported in Southern California. New York City police already are looking into two assault allegations, and London's Metropolitan Police are investigating allegations made by three women. [95]

News of the allegations shook the East Coast as well as Hollywood. Weinstein has donated more than $1 million over the years to the campaigns of a number of high-ranking Democrats, including Hillary Clinton and Barack Obama. Plus, he used his influence to persuade others in Hollywood to make sizable donations. [96]

Some politicians — including Sens. Patrick Leahy of Vermont, Richard Blumenthal of Connecticut and Elizabeth Warren of Massachusetts — have vowed to donate the amount of those contributions to charity. [97]

Continued on p. 910

At Issue:

Is mandatory arbitration harmful to harassment victims?

JOSEPH SELLERS
PARTNER, COHEN MILSTEIN SELLERS & TOLL

WRITTEN FOR *CQ RESEARCHER*, OCTOBER 2017

*f*or a number of years, the U.S. Supreme Court has grown increasingly supportive of arbitration agreements entered into by employer and employee. Both sides agree to submit to confidential binding arbitration on any employment-related dispute, including sexual harassment complaints. So you forgo your right to go to court and have a trial by jury. That means you also have given up the opportunity to have a public proceeding.

One of the consequences is that somebody could have just gone through arbitration against Supervisor A, and you could be working under the same supervisor and being harassed, but you would not know that others have made the same claim. You are stuck having to prove your claim from scratch, when having knowledge of a similar claim by a co-worker could help you build your case.

When arbitration is used to resolve a private dispute, nobody knows about it except the employer. You lose the benefit of having rulings that are public and could guide people's conduct in the future.

The more we have decisions entered by arbitrators, the more we are having adjudication that may not reflect the modern workplace. For example, if sexual harassment claims involve gender fluidity, we may never know about them. Arbitrators may be making thoughtful rulings on law in those cases — but they are doing it in private. So we are losing the ability to be guided by the courts in these cases because increasingly, employers are using arbitration as a way to settle workplace disputes.

Another set of issues arises when the arbitration agreements have provisions that prohibit class-action lawsuits. If I and a co-worker both feel we have been harassed and want to adjudicate our claims together, the arbitration agreement says we cannot do that. We have to use separate arbitrators, even though our claims are about the same thing.

Finally, arbitration companies typically are hired by the employers against whom the claims are being made. Judges tend to be a lot more independent. Arbitrators don't have that same liberty. They have less independence than judges, in part, because they might not be selected again if they rule against the employer. This creates at least the perception that some arbitrators have an economic incentive to be beholden to employers.

DAVID SHERWYN
PROFESSOR OF LAW, CORNELL UNIVERSITY

WRITTEN FOR *CQ RESEARCHER*, OCTOBER 2017

*a*long with the spate of sexual harassment cases that have made headlines recently — from Uber, Fox News, the University of California, Berkeley, and others — has come a round of criticism against organizations that require their employees to take their complaints to an arbitrator rather than to a judge.

Personally, I would rather work for a company that has an arbitration policy. Here is why:

• Companies that have pre-dispute mandatory arbitration policies are well versed in the law. They settle cases they cannot win. They cannot use the delays inherent in litigation to draw the process out.

• Arbitration is much quicker than a court case. A victim who can prove sexual harassment to an arbitrator will walk away with an award within the year. That same victim, if she takes her case to court, will wait two or more years for a trial and then has to fear numerous motions, appeals and other delays.

• The privacy of the process is a positive for employees who are harassment victims. Employers, when they become defendants in a lawsuit, tend to tear at an accuser's character and integrity. Unlike private arbitration, litigation leaves a public record that contains those personal details, which colleagues may read if they choose.

• Lawsuits are costly, and pursuing a court case is a huge investment. In fact, the cost of hiring counsel stops many sexual harassment victims from going to court. While most lawyers will take harassment cases on a contingency basis — that is, they will take a part of the settlement rather than charge an hourly fee — they still want substantial "upfront" money. Arbitration is an easier system to be pro se (on one's own behalf) and is less of an investment for lawyers.

• The facts do not support the argument that litigation is superior because the public "needs to know" about the employer's conduct. In fact, more than 85 percent of all harassment claims are dismissed or settled without a judge or jury even being exposed to it. Moreover, fewer than 1 percent of all discrimination charges are resolved at trial, and even fewer court cases involving harassment claims find their way into the headlines. Thus, the contention that litigation brings these cases to the public is simply not true.

The cases of high-profile harassers like Fox News' Bill O'Reilly and Uber's Travis Kalanick became notorious only because the players were already famous.

Arbitration is not perfect, but don't reject it until you compare it to the alternatives.

Continued from p. 908

Some Weinstein accusers, including Lauren Sivan, a reporter for KTTV in Los Angeles, called the revelations a "tipping point" for an industry infamous, in part, for its ubiquitous "casting couch" and discrimination against women directors. [98] "This is the moment we look back on and say, 'That's when it all started to change,' " Jenni Konner the co-showrunner for HBO's "Girls," told *The New York Times*. [99]

But *Times* movie critic Manohla Dargis said she isn't convinced. "I hope she's right," she wrote. "The entertainment in-

in sexual harassment and corporate law. [101]

The same week the Weinstein story broke, Amazon Studios announced that it had suspended president Roy Price after a Hollywood producer accused him of making unwanted sexual advances toward her. [102] He later resigned.

The Weinstein case also reverberated in Northern California, where a bipartisan group of more than 140 state lawmakers, lobbyists and consultants wrote a public letter complaining of pervasive sexual harassment in politics and across all industries.

startup funding for tech companies.

Sen. Hannah-Beth Jackson, a Democrat from Santa Barbara, introduced legislation in August to amend the state's civil rights law to add legal penalties for investors who sexually harass the founders of new tech companies who are seeking financial backing. [104]

"There are too many of these men abusing their power against women who are looking for funding for their ideas, as these women try to break into an industry that is overwhelmingly dominated by men," Jackson told *The Mercury News*.

Jackson introduced the bill after two prominent Silicon Valley venture capitalists — David McClure, founder of the startup accelerator 500 Startups, and Frank Artale, a Seattle-based managing director at Ignition Partners, resigned in response to accusations of sexual harassment. [105]

More recently, Mike Cagney, CEO of online lender Social Finance, announced he would step down after a male employee filed a lawsuit saying he had witnessed the executive harassing female employees and then firing them for reporting it. [106]

Jackson's bill would amend the state's 1959 Unruh Civil Rights Act, which forbids sexual harassment by attorneys, landlords, teachers, physicians and other professionals who do not work at the same company as their victims. Her proposal would add venture capitalists, which means victims could sue them for misconduct with an entrepreneur. [107] ∎

Roy Price, head of Amazon Studios, resigned on Oct. 17 after a Hollywood producer accused him of making unwanted sexual advances toward her. Some observers say the flood of complaints of sexual harassment in the movie industry means such behavior will never again be tolerated. But others, such as New York Times *movie critic Manohla Dargis, are not so sure. "The entertainment industry is extraordinarily forgiving of those who have made it a lot of money," she said.*

Getty Images/Wireimage/Paul Zimmerman

dustry is extraordinarily forgiving of those who have made it a lot of money." [100]

In fact, according to TMZ, Weinstein's 2015 employment contract said if the Weinstein Co. had to pay any new settlements for his sexual or other misconduct, he was required to reimburse the company, plus pay escalating fines, starting at $1 million for the fourth such instance. "That's shocking. It demonstrates the company knew and was willing to sacrifice these targets for the profitability of the company," said Jennifer Drobac, an Indiana University law professor who specializes

"It's a pretty regular thing in Sacramento," said lobbyist Samantha Corbin, who helped coordinate the letter. "A lot of us are fed up with power dynamics that are not on our side." The Weinstein scandal "elevated conversations that already happened under the radar between women colleagues and friends for years." [103]

Elsewhere in California, after the rash of sexual harassment complaints against venture capitalists in Silicon Valley, a state senator has introduced legislation to try to stop financial professionals from making sexual favors a requirement for

OUTLOOK

Changing Mindsets

The problem of sexual harassment, says Ariane Hegewisch, an economist and program director for employment and earnings at the Institute for Women's Policy Research, a think tank in Washington, "will never go away as an issue."

"Good companies," she says, will "deal with it properly" as the number of male and females employees evens out. But a new crop of vulnerable employees has already begun to emerge as more low-skill workers enter the workforce.

A 2016 study from Harvard University predicts that the United States is producing too few college-educated employees to fill all of the jobs that will become available over the next decade. So a growing number of workers without degrees will fill the gaps — if the economy is to continue to grow. [108]

"With lower-skill jobs come a lot of power differences," says Hegewisch. "Unions are having less oversight. Job security is uncertain. It creates a feeling that [the employees] can't change somebody's actions. . . . I don't think that will necessarily get better."

EEOC Commissioner Feldblum is more optimistic, however. She says she believes harassment will be stopped, but adds, "It's not going to happen on its own." The commissioner, whose term at the EEOC expires in 2018, foresees a nationwide campaign that will channel the outrage against the high-profile harassers "into encouraging employers to make systemic culture change."

She says the EEOC will have a role to play, and she plans to be a part of it. The scope of the campaign against sexual harassment, Feldblum says, will have to match that of Mothers Against Drunk Driving and the effort to legalize same-sex marriage. "We should have a concerted public campaign to make harassment not cool in the workplace," she says.

Feldblum notes that changing a national mindset requires the effort of both men and women. "This is not solely a women's issue," she says. "This is a social, cultural issue. I hope that women and men in partnership will lead it."

Toledo attorney Wise ascribes much power to corporate leaders in the shaping of a future without sexual harassment. "They have to decide it is a problem," she says. "It's not something that women can solve on their own. It's got to come from the top of the organization." But, she adds, "I don't see that coming."

Edwards, of Alteristic, however, expects to see "a measurable reduction" in harassment cases within five years. The key, she says, is for companies, one by one, to change their cultures, making sexual harassment so out of norm that nobody would think of engaging in it.

"With any issue like harassment, it is going to be determined by a critical mass setting the norms, by lots of people making small choices," she says. "Very often, when we talk about issues like this, we talk about, 'Hey, it's going to take a long, long time to change the attitudes and make it pervasive.

"But if starting tomorrow, every workplace said, 'We're going to do our own small thing;' if starting tomorrow, every workplace said, 'We're going to create a safe space,' these small choices can have a big impact," she says. ■

Notes

[1] Susan J. Fowler, "Reflecting On One Very, Very Strange Year At Uber," *susanjfowlercom* (blog), Feb. 29, 2017, https://tinyurl.com/j5vvzhu.
[2] Johana Bhuiyan, "The Uber manager who headed Susan Fowler's department has departed," *Recode*, July 11, 2017, https://tinyurl.com/y89amwq4.
[3] Mike Isaac, "Uber Founder Travis Kalanick Resigns as C.E.O.," *The New York Times*, June 21, 2017, https://tinyurl.com/ybw7omfx.
[4] "Tech and Startup Culture Survey," Lincoln Park Strategies, August 2017, https://tinyurl.com/y8jzfyrn.
[5] Alexei Oreskovic and Biz Carson, "The tech investor who apologized for being a 'creep' resigns from 500 Startups after being accused of sexual harassment," *Business Insider*, July 3, 2017, https://tinyurl.com/y8toep47; and Nathaniel Popper and Katie Benner, " 'It Was a Frat House': Inside the Sex Scandal That Toppled SoFi's C.E.O.," *The New York Times*, Sept. 12, 2017, https://tinyurl.com/yaehsjym.

[6] Stephen Bataglio, "Bill O'Reilly reportedly paid $32-million harassment settlement before signing new Fox News contract," *Los Angeles Times*, Oct. 21, 2017, http://tinyurl.com/y7hoxpy5.
[7] Calla Cofield, "Planet Hunter Geoff Marcy Resigns Following Sexual Harassment Investigation," Space.com, Oct. 15, 2015, https://tinyurl.com/y8zvzzyh.
[8] "Harvey Weinstein may be booted from TV Academy," CBS News, Oct. 21, 2017, http://tinyurl.com/y9ah7zsm.
[9] Josh Rottenberg, "Harvey Weinstein expelled from motion picture academy," *Los Angeles Times*, Oct. 14, 2017, https://tinyurl.com/ydgtevog.
[10] "As survivors say #MeToo, what will it take to stop widespread sexual harassment?" PBS News Hour, Oct. 17, 2017, https://tinyurl.com/ycfnvru5.
[11] Lisa Respers France, "#MeToo: Social media flooded with personal stories of assault," CNN, Oct. 16, 2017, https://tinyurl.com/y9z7m7tj. "Women senators say #MeToo, reveal stories of sexual harassment," "Meet the Press," NBC News, Oct. 22, 2017, http://tinyurl.com/y8h3zj59.
[12] David Folkenflik, "Gretchen Carlson On The Spread Of Sexual Harassment In The Workplace," NPR, Oct. 7, 2017, https://tinyurl.com/yckbyg7c.
[13] "Oprah Winfrey says Harvey Weinstein scandal is 'triggering a lot of unreleased pain,' " CBS News, Oct. 18, 2017, https://tinyurl.com/ybq3nfej.
[14] Caitlin Gibson and Emily Guskin, "A majority of Americans now say that sexual harassment is a 'serious problem,' " *The Washington Post*, Oct. 17, 2017, https://tinyurl.com/ycw6oduq.
[15] Antilla's book is *Tales from the Boom-Boom Room: Women vs. Wall Street* (2002).
[16] Danielle Kurtzleben, "1 More Woman Accuses Trump of Inappropriate Sexual Conduct. Here's The Full List," NPR, Oct. 201, 2016, https://tinyurl.com/zn2p62f.
[17] Alex Wagner, "Workplace sexual harassment at a 'tipping point of public attention,' " CBS News, April 20, 2017, https://tinyurl.com/yc2o4e8f.
[18] "Sexual Harassment," U.S. Equal Employment Opportunity Commission, undated, https://tinyurl.com/zowk4k7.
[19] For background see Barbara Mantel, "Campus Sexual Assault," *CQ Researcher*, Oct. 31, 2014, pp. 913-936.
[20] "Street Harassment and the Law: The Best Laws, Advocacy, and Anti-Street Harassment Ordinances," StopStreetHarassment.org, https://tinyurl.com/y7v6af9y.
[21] Chai R. Feldblum and Victoria A. Lipnic, "Report of the Co-Chairs of the Select Task Force on the Study of Harassment in the Workplace," U.S. Equal Employment Opportunity Commission, June 2016, https://tinyurl.com/gnrcpnl.

[22] "Charges Alleging Sex-Based Harassment (Charges filed with EEOC), FY 2010-FY2016," U.S. Equal Employment Opportunity Commission, undated, https://tinyurl.com/jeqyx7k. Also see "LGBT-Based Sex Discrimination Charges (Charges filed with EEOC) FY 2013-FY 2016," EEOC, undated, https://tinyurl.com/y9wsphdj.

[23] Gibson and Guskin, op. cit.

[24] Gretchen Carlson, "Gretchen Carlson: How to Encourage More Women to Report Sexual Harassment," The New York Times, Oct. 10, 2017, https://tinyurl.com/yco7u6ww.

[25] Feldblum and Lipnic, op. cit.

[26] "Women in the Labor Force in 2010," Women's Bureau, U.S. Department of Labor, 2010, https://tinyurl.com/yb4938ft.

[27] Feldblum and Lipnic, op. cit.

[28] Sam Levin, "Sexual harassment training may have reverse effect, research suggests," The Guardian, May 2, 2016, https://tinyurl.com/ydbj7obq.

[29] Feldblum and Lipnic, op. cit.

[30] Sam Levin, "Sexual harassment training 'not as effective' in stopping behavior at work," The Guardian, June 29, 2016, https://tinyurl.com/j54fxua.

[31] Thomas Fuller, "Sexual Harassment Cases Tarnish Berkeley's Image as a Center of Social Activism," The New York Times, March 24, 2016, https://tinyurl.com/ya6l8a8g.

[32] Fowler, op. cit.

[33] "Covington Recommendations for Uber," Covington & Burling LLP, June 2017, https://tinyurl.com/yc2g744z.

[34] For background, see Kenneth Jost, "Arbitrating Disputes," CQ Researcher, March 11, 2016, pp. 241-264.

[35] "Gretchen Carlson says ending mandatory arbitration 'has become my mission,'" Star-Tribune, https://tinyurl.com/y75shq7l.

[36] Kim Elsesser, "How sexual harassment training hurts women," Los Angeles Times, Oct. 9, 2015, https://tinyurl.com/o8zyfvo.

[37] Ibid.

[38] Ashley Parker, "Karen Pence is the vice president's 'prayer warrior,' gut check and shield," The Washington Post, March 28, 2017, https://tinyurl.com/y98redjl.

[39] Emma Gray, "Why It Matters That Pence Won't Have Dinner With a Woman Who Isn't His Wife" The Huffington Post, Aug. 14, 2017, https://tinyurl.com/mafpx25.

[40] Cynthia Estlund, Working Together: How Workplace Bonds Strengthen a Diverse Democracy (2003).

[41] Nellie Bowles, "Push for Gender Equality in Tech? Some Men Say It's Gone Too Far," The New York Times, Sept. 23, 2017, https://tinyurl.com/ybjffmwt.

[42] Ibid.

[43] Ibid.

[44] "Slavery in America," History, undated, https://tinyurl.com/oty4dd8.

[45] Adrienne D. Davis, Slavery and the Roots of Sexual Harassment (2013); Catharine MacKinnon and Reva B. Siegel, eds., Directions in Sexual Harassment (2003).

[46] Amanda Reed, "A Brief History of Sexual Harassment in the United States," National Organization for Women, May 7, 2013, https://tinyurl.com/yac8yz3r.

[47] Ibid.

[48] Carrie N. Baker, The Women's Movement Against Sexual Harassment (2007), pp. 27-28.

[49] Ibid.

[50] Enid Nemy, "Women Begin to Speak Out Against Sexual Harassment," The New York Times, Aug. 19, 1975, https://tinyurl.com/ybuj4ukt.

[51] Ibid.

[52] Ibid.

[53] Julie Berebitsky, Sex and the Office: A History of Gender, Power, and Desire (2012), p. 225.

[54] Kaitlin Menza, "You Have to See Redbook's Shocking 1976 Sexual Harassment Survey," Redbook, Nov. 28, 2016, https://tinyurl.com/y8j69s8y.

[55] Baker, op. cit., p. 36.

[56] "Asking for It?" Time, May 4, 1981,

https://tinyurl.com/y8c23f7w.

[57] Wesley G. Pippert, "Schlafly: Sexual harassment no problem for virtuous women," UPI, April 21, 1981, https://tinyurl.com/ybjjksvf.

[58] Berebitsky, op. cit., p. 239.

[59] Williams v. Saxbe, https://tinyurl.com/y9d4q37h.

[60] Ibid.

[61] Berebitsky, op. cit., p. 241.

[62] Lynn McLain, "The EEOC Sexual Harassment Guidelines: Welcome Advances under Title VII?" University of Baltimore Law Review, winter 1981, https://tinyurl.com/y7ptxtc9.

[63] Stuart Taylor Jr., "Sex Harassment on Job Is Illegal," The New York Times, June 20, 1986, https://tinyurl.com/yakw9ktn. Also see Meritor Savings Bank v. Vinson, http://tinyurl.com/yauxs99p.

[64] Jill Smolowe, "Sex, Lies and Politics: He Said, She Said," Time, Oct. 21, 1991, https://tinyurl.com/y8osay9v.

[65] "The Civil Rights Act of 1991," U.S. Equal Employment Opportunity Commission, undated, https://tinyurl.com/yddzxy9p.

[66] Peter Baker, "Clinton Settles Paula Jones Lawsuit for $850,000," The Washington Post, Nov. 14, 1998, https://tinyurl.com/e26h2.

[67] Carol Kleiman, "Sex Harassment Complaints On Rise," Chicago Tribune, March 7, 1992, https://tinyurl.com/ya88ojfr. "Sexual Harassment Charges EEOC & FEPAs Combined: FY 1997-FY 2011," U.S. Equal Employment Opportunity Commission, undated, http://tinyurl.com/ybajkvmu.

[68] Robinson v. Jacksonville Shipyards, Inc., https://tinyurl.com/y8looc8e.

[69] Harris v. Forklift Systems, https://tinyurl.com/y9spnzhn.

[70] Faragher v. City of Boca Raton, https://tinyurl.com/ycyc8l3m.

[71] Oncale v. Sundowner Offshore Services Inc., https://tinyurl.com/yaa4l2yv.

[72] Pennsylvania State Police v. Suders, https://tinyurl.com/y8h9vq7d.

[73] Stephen Braun, "Mitsubishi to Pay $34 Million in Sex Harassment Case," Los Angeles Times, June 12, 1998, https://tinyurl.com/y7dsffr6.

[74] David Eggert, "Michigan court overturns $21 million sex harassment verdict against automaker," July 22, 2004, The Associated Press, https://tinyurl.com/ycbwd6fm.

[75] Scott Marshall, "Court cuts damages in Ralphs sexual harassment case; justices say amount of punitive damages was excessive," The San Diego Union Tribune, March 2, 2006, https://tinyurl.com/ya4ou87s.

[76] Michael S. Schmidt and Maria Newman, "Jury Awards $11.6 Million to Former Knicks

About the Author

Sharon O'Malley, an assistant professor of journalism at Anne Arundel Community College in Maryland, is a freelance writer, editor, consultant and trainer who has published articles in dozens of newspapers and magazines, including *The Arizona Republic, USA Today, Ladies' Home Journal, Working Woman* and *American Demographics*. For *SAGE Business Researcher* she has written reports on Internships, the Free Economy, Mortgage Finance and Product Recalls.

Executive," *The New York Times*, Oct. 2, 2007, https://tinyurl.com/p26tpl2.

[77] The Associated Press, "Isiah Thomas, Madison Square Garden Settle Sexual Harassment Suit," Fox News, Dec. 10, 2007, https://tinyurl.com/y7o7le8u.

[78] John Vering, "UBS hit with $10.6 million sexual harassment verdict," *Missouri Employment Law Letter*, Nov. 1, 2011.

[79] Nina Mandell, "St. Louis woman awarded $95 million after former boss allegedly masturbated on her," *Daily News*, June 10, 2011, https://tinyurl.com/ycsyxudr.

[80] Catherine Beale, "Was Ashley Alford really awarded $95 million for her lawsuit?" *Quora*, Feb. 23, 2016, https://tinyurl.com/ycucrjrg; *Ashley Alford v. Aaron's Rents Inc.*, No. 3:08-MJR-DGW-683, http://tinyurl.com/y9c69a5s.

[81] Mark Memmott, "California Woman Awarded $168 Million in Workplace Harassment Case," NPR, March 2, 2012, https://tinyurl.com/ya8mx8m9.

[82] Bill Chappell, "Fox Will Pay Gretchen Carlson $20 Million To Settle Sexual Harassment Suit," NPR, Sept. 6, 2016, https://tinyurl.com/howhay6.

[83] Feldblum and Lipnic, *op. cit.*

[84] *Ibid.*

[85] *Ibid.*

[86] Maeve Duggan, "Online Harassment," Pew Research Center, Oct. 22, 2014, https://tinyurl.com/norqoyt.

[87] "Sexual Harassment on the Internet," University of North Carolina School of Law, undated, https://tinyurl.com/ybwjxn5l.

[88] Joan Schmelz, "Coming Out of the Shadows: A Sexual Harassment Story," *Women in Astronomy* (blog), Feb. 17, 2011, https://tinyurl.com/y9xdd822.

[89] Janine Yancey, "The Social Media Fix for Sexual Harassment," *Medium.com* (blog), April 24, 2017, https://tinyurl.com/ycxle6ga.

[90] Jena McGregor, "Why a toxic workplace is now a much bigger liability for companies," *The Washington Post*, Feb. 24, 2017, https://tinyurl.com/ycq8nhg9.

[91] Jodi Kantor and Megan Twohey, "Harvey Weinstein Paid Off Sexual Harassment Accusers for Decades," *The New York Times*, Oct. 5, 2017, https://tinyurl.com/y94p2qjq.

[92] *Ibid.*

[93] Phil McCausland, "Weinstein Loses Adviser Lisa Bloom Amid Harassment Allegations," NBC News, Oct. 8, 2017, https://tinyurl.com/ybv3ndjb.

[94] Ronan Farrow, "From Aggressive Overtures to Sexual Assault: Harvey Weinstein's Accusers Tell Their Stories," *The New Yorker*, Oct. 23, 2017, https://tinyurl.com/ycumybkf. Meredith Mandell, "Could Harvey Weinstein Face Crim-

FOR MORE INFORMATION

Alteristic, 7955 Cameron Brown Court, Springfield, VA 22153; 571-319-0354; alteristic.org. Develops training programs and strategies for sexual assault and harassment prevention, community mobilization and bystander intervention.

California Department of Fair Employment and Housing, 2218 Kausen Drive, Suite 100, Elk Grove, CA 95758; 800-884-1684 in California; 916-227-0551 outside the state; www.dfeh.ca.gov. State agency that enforces California workplace anti-discrimination laws.

Equal Employment Advisory Council, 1501 M St., N.W., Suite 400, Washington, DC 20005; 202-629-5650; www.eeac.org. Advises member companies on compliance with equal employment opportunity and affirmative action regulations.

Equal Employment Opportunity Commission, 131 M St., N.E., Washington, DC 20002; 800-669-4000: www.eeoc.gov. Federal agency that enforces workplace anti-discrimination laws.

Equal Rights Advocates, 1170 Market St., Suite 700, San Francisco, CA 94102; 415-621-0672; www.equalrights.org. Legal organization that works to protect and expand economic and educational access and opportunities for women and girls.

Institute for Women's Policy Research, 200 18th St., N.W., Suite 301, Washington, DC 20036; 202-785-5100; www.iwprorg. Promotes women's issues and policies to strengthen families and communities.

Office for Civil Rights, U.S. Department of Education, 400 Maryland Ave., S.W., Washington, DC 20202; 800-421-3481; ocrcas.ed.gov. Federal agency that enforces Title IX, which bars gender discrimination in education programs that receive federal funding.

---

inal Charges?" NBC News, Oct. 12, 2017, https://tinyurl.com/yczcp4sc.

[95] Richard Winton and Victoria Kim, "Investigation launched after actress tells LAPD she was raped by Harvey Weinstein," *Los Angeles Times*, Oct. 19, 2017, https://tinyurl.com/ybly9fpt.

[96] Peter Overby, "As Democrats Purge Weinstein's Cash, Impact On The Party is Likely To Be Low," NPR, Oct. 12, 2017, https://tinyurl.com/y9ch66xt.

[97] Jonathan Martin, "Democrats, Seeking to Disavow Weinstein, Plan to Give His Donations to Charity," *The New York Times*, Oct. 6, 2017, https://tinyurl.com/yajroulc.

[98] Lindsey Ellefson, "Harvey Weinstein accuser speaks out: 'I hope there's a tipping point,'" CNN, Oct. 11, 2017, https://tinyurl.com/yc229l3u. Also see Luchina Fisher, "How Hollywood's casting couch culture may have contributed to Weinstein's alleged behavior," ABC News, Oct. 12, 2017, https://tinyurl.com/ybooujob.

[99] Megan Twohey, "Harvey Weinstein Is Fired After Sexual Harassment Reports," *The New York Times*, Oct. 8, 2017, https://tinyurl.com/yb4kxz2o.

[100] Manohla Dargis, "Harvey Weinstein Is Gone But Hollywood Still Has a Problem," *The New York Times*, Oct. 11, 2017, https://tinyurl.com/y77rbrjd.

[101] Emily Yoffe, "A bully in the boardroom can be bad for the bottom line," *The Washington Post*, Oct. 22, 2017, p. B1.

[102] John Koblin and Nick Wingfield, "Amazon Studios Chief Suspended After Sexual Harassment Claim," *The New York Times*, Oct. 12, 2017, https://tinyurl.com/ybrnvvz2.

[103] Marisa Lagos and Scott Shafer, " 'Enough': California's Women In Politics Call Out Sexual Harassment," NPR, Oct. 18, 2017, https://tinyurl.com/y8fnka3x.

[104] Marisa Kendall, "New bill would crack down on VC sexual harassment," *The Mercury News*, Aug. 17, 2017, https://tinyurl.com/ybmr5p9c.

[105] Dina Bass, "Seattle Venture Capitalist Artale Leaves After Misconduct Claims," Bloomberg, July 12, 2017, https://tinyurl.com/yap2k8kq.

[106] Clare O'Connor, "SoFi CEO Mike Cagney Resigns Following Sexual Harassment Lawsuit," *Forbes*, Sept. 12, 2017, https://tinyurl.com/y9bbjhdv.

[107] Kendall, *op. cit.*

[108] Gillian B. White, "Are Low-Skill Workers America's Next Great Economic Resource?" *The Atlantic*, Aug. 8, 2016, https://tinyurl.com/y7ooyjme.

Bibliography

Selected Sources

Books

Bennett, Jessica, *Feminist Fight Club: A Survival Manual for a Sexist Workplace*, HarperCollins, 2016.

A journalist blends her personal stories of harassment with an assessment of the gender gap in the American workplace.

Chang, Emily, *Brotopia: Breaking Up the Boys' Club of Silicon Valley*, self-published, available Feb. 13, 2018.

A Bloomberg TV journalist exposes the "bro culture" of Silicon Valley companies, with descriptions of sexual harassment, discrimination and a "toxic culture."

Elsesser, Kim, *Sex and the Office: Women, Men and the Sex Partition That's Dividing the Workplace*, Taylor Trade Publishing, 2013, updated 2015.

A psychologist delves into issues that create barriers between men and women at work, including sexual harassment policies, workplace romances and communication differences.

Articles

Boudreau, John, "Uber Is Finally Realizing HR Isn't Just for Recruiting," *Harvard Business Review*, March 8, 2017, https://tinyurl.com/y8wlp6vk.

The director of the Marshall School of Business and the Center for Effective Organizations at the University of Southern California alleges that Uber's human resources team under company founder Travis Kalanick functioned as a recruiting arm, largely ignoring legal compliance systems and leadership development.

Bowles, Nellie, "Push for Gender Equality in Tech? Some Men Say It's Gone Too Far," *The New York Times*, Sept. 23, 2017, https://tinyurl.com/y9eo98gv.

A growing number of male engineers in Silicon Valley are criticizing tech companies' efforts to diversify their workforces.

Elsesser, Kim, "How sexual harassment training hurts women," *Los Angeles Times*, Oct. 9, 2015, https://tinyurl.com/o8zyfvo.

A researcher who studies business and gender argues that workplace training and policies aimed at stopping sexual harassment are costing women advancement opportunities.

Fowler, Susan J., "Reflecting On One Very, Very Strange Year At Uber," blog, SusanjFowler.com, Feb. 19, 2017, https://tinyurl.com/j5vvzhu.

The engineer whose complaints about sexual harassment led to the dismissal of Uber founder Kalanick alleges that the on-demand car service ignored her claims of sexual harassment and those of other women against a high-performing manager.

Kosoff, Maya, "Silicon Valley's Sexual-Harassment Crisis Keeps Getting Worse," *Vanity Fair*, Sept. 12, 2017, https://tinyurl.com/y7zv3po3.

The sexual harassment claims leveled against the on-demand car service Uber this year are just the tipping point of a widespread sexist culture thriving in Silicon Valley, says a tech writer for *Vanity Fair.*

Levin, Sam, "Sexual harassment training 'not as effective' in stopping behavior at work," *The Guardian*, June 28, 2016, https://tinyurl.com/j54fxua.

The British newspaper looks at studies that question whether sexual harassment training in U.S. workplaces is effective.

Reports and Studies

"Covington Recommendations," Covington & Burling, June 2017, https://tinyurl.com/yc2g744z.

The law firm of former U.S. Attorney General Eric Holder recommends that Uber adopt policies that make it easier for women to report sexual harassment.

"Tech and Startup Culture Survey," Lincoln Park Strategies, August 2017, https://tinyurl.com/yah8wpns.

A survey of 950 tech employees, founders and investors reveals that 53 percent of women and 17 percent of men were sexually harassed on the job.

Clancy, Kathryn B.H., *et al.*, "Double jeopardy in astronomy and planetary science: Women of color face greater risks of gendered and racial harassment," *Journal of Geophysical Research: Planets*, Aug. 4, 2017, https://tinyurl.com/y7facdwm.

An internet-based survey of the workplaces of 474 astronomers and planetary scientists finds that women of color experienced the highest rates of negative workplace experiences, including harassment and assault.

Feldblum, Chai R., and Victoria A. Lipnic, "Select Task Force on the Study of Harassment in the Workplace: Report of Co-Chairs Chai R. Feldblum & Victoria A. Lipnic," U.S. Equal Employment Opportunity Commission, June 2016, https://tinyurl.com/y8xux2gn.

Two Equal Employment Opportunity Commission members summarize the recommendations of a task force on workplace harassment.

Williams, Joan C., Katherine W. Phillips and Erika V. Hall, "Double Jeopardy? Gender Bias against Women of Color in Science," UC Hastings College of the Law, 2014, https://tinyurl.com/kkbvykv.

Three university professors interview 60 women in the fields of science, technology, engineering and math and determine that race shaped their workplace experiences with gender bias.

The Next Step:

Additional Articles from Current Periodicals

Arbitration Clauses

Gillett, Rachel, "Gretchen Carlson says the way we handle sexual harassment 'gags' the women who confront it," *Business Insider*, Oct. 12, 2017, https://tinyurl.com/y96laslg.

A former Fox News host argues that the confidentiality requirements in mandatory arbitration clauses of employment contracts force those who make sexual harassment claims against colleagues to remain silent.

Hafiz, Hiba, "How Legal Agreements Can Silence Victims of Workplace Sexual Assault," *The Atlantic*, Oct. 18, 2017, https://tinyurl.com/y9zodm6j.

Nondisclosure agreements, out-of-court settlements and arbitration provisions can limit an employee's ability to speak about sexual harassment or assault, says a University of Chicago Law School lecturer.

Tiku, Nitasha, "Big Tech Eyes Supreme Court's Employee-Arbitration Case," *Wired*, Oct. 2, 2017, https://tinyurl.com/y6tw3jf7.

Many tech companies place private arbitration clauses in employment contracts, preventing workers from filing class-actions suits, and the Supreme Court will soon decide if that violates federal law.

Hollywood

Desta, Yohana, and Hillary Busis, "These Are the Women Who Have Accused Harvey Weinstein of Sexual Harassment and Assault," *Vanity Fair*, Oct. 12, 2017, https://tinyurl.com/yc2zmldn.

More women in Hollywood are coming forward and accusing mogul Harvey Weinstein of sexual harassment and assault.

Garber, Megan, "In the Valley of the Open Secret," *The Atlantic*, Oct. 11, 2017, https://tinyurl.com/y9vfo9cb.

Although the accusations against Weinstein became public only recently, his conduct was widely known for decades, say Hollywood insiders.

Lynch, John, "James Van Der Beek said he's been sexually harassed by 'older, powerful men' in Hollywood," *Business Insider*, Oct. 12, 2017, https://tinyurl.com/ycey7z9z.

To show his solidarity with the many women speaking out against Weinstein, the former "Dawson's Creek" star describes being groped or sexually harassed by industry executives.

Silicon Valley

Bowles, Nellie, "Push for Gender Equality in Tech? Some Men Say It's Gone Too Far," *The New York Times*, Sept. 23, 2017, https://tinyurl.com/y9eo98gv.

As more tech companies come under fire for sexism and

sexual harassment, some men in Silicon Valley argue that women in tech are exaggerating about the situation.

Dickey, Megan Rose, "Dispatches on diversity: Uber, sexual harassment and venture capital," *TechCrunch*, Sept. 23, 2017, https://tinyurl.com/y74edgqv.

Silicon Valley is constantly changing and innovating, and in order to combat the sexist culture, startups need to foster inclusiveness and diversity, according to participants in September's Tech Crunch Disrupt SF, the annual technology conference hosted by online publisher *TechCrunch*.

Training

Elsesser, Kim, "Meetings In Hotel Rooms: What We Should Be Talking About In Sexual Harassment Training," *Forbes*, Oct. 10, 2017, https://tinyurl.com/yatvfnel.

Meetings in hotel rooms are more common than many think, so sexual harassment training should include instructions on how to handle uncomfortable situations.

Fitts, Alexis Sobel, "When Companies Get Serious About Diversity, They Call Her," *Wired*, July 12, 2017, https://tinyurl.com/y9a3ggg9.

A tech industry diversity expert says the California law requiring that managers get mandatory sexual harassment training for two hours, every two years, is insufficient.

Kessler, Sarah, "Corporate sexual harassment hotlines don't work. They're not designed to," *Quartz*, May 2, 2017, https://tinyurl.com/yck8beb3.

Because employees rarely use corporate hotlines, a more effective tactic for dealing with sexual harassment in the workplace is civility training, says a *Quartz* editor.

CITING CQ RESEARCHER

Sample formats for citing these reports in a bibliography include the ones listed below. Preferred styles and formats vary, so please check with your instructor or professor.

MLA STYLE
    Mantel, Barbara. "Coal Industry's Future." CQ Researcher 17 June 2016: 529-552.

APA STYLE
    Mantel, B. (2016, June 17). Coal Industry's Future. *CQ Researcher, 6*, 529-552.

CHICAGO STYLE
    Mantel, Barbara. "Coal Industry's Future." *CQ Researcher*, June 17, 2016, 529-52.

In-depth Reports on Issues in the News

Are you writing a paper?

Need backup for a debate?

Want to become an expert on an issue?

For 90 years, students have turned to *CQ Researcher* for in-depth reporting on issues in the news. Reports on a full range of political and social issues are now available. Following is a selection of recent reports:

Civil Liberties
Privacy and the Internet, 12/15
Intelligence Reform, 5/15
Religion and Law, 11/14

Crime/Law
High-Tech Policing, 4/17
Forensic Science Controversies, 2/17
Jailing Debtors, 9/16
Decriminalizing Prostitution, 4/16
Restorative Justice, 2/16
The Dark Web, 1/16
Immigrant Detention, 10/15

Education
Charter Schools, 3/17
Civic Education, 2/17
Student Debt, 11/16
Apprenticeships, 10/16

Environment/Society
Climate Change and National Security, 9/17
Muslims in America, 7/17
Funding the Arts, 7/17
Hunger in America, 7/17
Future of the Christian Right, 6/17
Trust in Media, 6/17

Health/Safety
Medical Breakthroughs, 9/17
Medical Marijuana, 7/17
Food Labeling, 6/17
Sports and Sexual Assault, 4/17

Politics/Economy
Democracy Under Stress, 10/17
Cyberwarfare Threat, 10/17
Universal Basic Income, 9/17
National Debt, 9/17
North Korea Showdown, 5/17
Rethinking Foreign Aid, 4/17

Upcoming Reports

Military Readiness, 11/3/17   Looted Artifacts, 11/10/17   Race and College Admissions, 11/17/17

ACCESS

CQ Researcher is available in print and online. For access, visit your library or www.cqresearcher.com.

STAY CURRENT

For notice of upcoming *CQ Researcher* reports or to learn more about *CQ Researcher* products, subscribe to the free email newsletters, *CQ Researcher Alert!* and *CQ Researcher News*: http://cqpress.com/newsletters.

PURCHASE

To purchase a *CQ Researcher* report in print or electronic format (PDF), visit www.cqpress.com or call 866-427-7737. Single reports start at $15. Bulk purchase discounts and electronic-rights licensing are also available.

SUBSCRIBE

Annual full-service *CQ Researcher* subscriptions—including 44 reports a year, monthly index updates, and a bound volume—start at $1,131. Add $25 for domestic postage.

CQ Researcher Online offers a backfile from 1991 and a number of tools to simplify research. For pricing information, call 800-818-7243 or 805-499-9774 or email librarysales@sagepub.com.

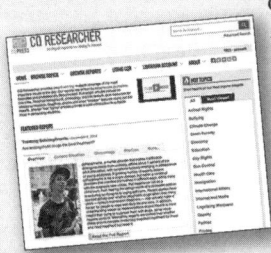

CQ RESEARCHER

CQPRESS

In-depth reports on today's issues

Published by CQ Press, an Imprint of SAGE Publications, Inc.

www.cqresearcher.com

Military Readiness

Is the Pentagon prepared for future threats?

A series of Navy and Air Force accidents this year — reflecting strains on the armed forces from the nearly two-decade fight against terrorism in Afghanistan and elsewhere — is raising pressing questions about whether the Pentagon can handle current conflicts and is ready for the next major confrontation. The United States is by far the world's most formidable military power, but some defense experts say the country needs more troops, planes and ships to confront the growing array of challenges posed by China, Russia, North Korea and Iran. Others say that warnings of a readiness crisis are overblown but that the Pentagon needs to be smarter with the resources it has. Most analysts agree the military must improve training for conventional warfare while modernizing its technology as rivals hone their ability to fight in space and cyberspace. The Trump administration, meanwhile, has ordered the Pentagon to review the nation's nuclear arsenal, which the Obama administration had begun to upgrade in its final years in office. The Pentagon also is reviewing space defenses, as U.S. satellites become more susceptible to attack.

Seven sailors died when the destroyer USS Fitzgerald *collided with a container ship off Japan's coast on June 17. Three other incidents this year involving Navy ships – as well as accidents involving Air Force fighter jets – have raised concerns about whether years of warfare in Afghanistan and Iraq have impaired U.S. military readiness.*

CQ Researcher • Nov. 3, 2017 • www.cqresearcher.com
Volume 27, Number 39 • Pages 917-944

SAGE Publishing

Los Angeles | London | New Delhi
Singapore | Washington DC | Melbourne

RECIPIENT OF SOCIETY OF PROFESSIONAL JOURNALISTS AWARD FOR EXCELLENCE ◆ AMERICAN BAR ASSOCIATION SILVER GAVEL AWARD

I N S I D E THIS REPORT

THE ISSUES **919**

BACKGROUND **925**

CHRONOLOGY **927**

CURRENT SITUATION **933**

AT ISSUE.......................**935**

OUTLOOK **936**

BIBLIOGRAPHY **941**

THE NEXT STEP **942**

CQ RESEARCHER

Nov. 3, 2017
Volume 27, Number 39

EXECUTIVE EDITOR: Thomas J. Billitteri
tjb@sagepub.com

ASSISTANT MANAGING EDITORS: Kenneth
Fireman, kenneth.fireman@sagepub.com,
Kathy Koch, kathy.koch@sagepub.com,
Scott Rohrer, scott.rohrer@sagepub.com

ASSOCIATE MANAGING EDITOR: Val Ellicott

SENIOR CONTRIBUTING EDITOR:
Thomas J. Colin
tom.colin@sagepub.com

CONTRIBUTING WRITERS: Marcia Clemmitt,
Sarah Glazer, Alan Greenblatt, Reed Karaim,
Barbara Mantel, Patrick Marshall, Tom Price

SENIOR PROJECT EDITOR: Olu B. Davis

EDITORIAL ASSISTANT: Natalia Gurevich

FACT CHECKERS: Eva P. Dasher,
Michelle Harris, Betsy Towner Levine,
Robin Palmer

Los Angeles I London I New Delhi
Singapore I Washington DC I Melbourne

An Imprint of SAGE Publications, Inc.

SENIOR VICE PRESIDENT,
GLOBAL LEARNING RESOURCES:
Karen Phillips

EXECUTIVE DIRECTOR, ONLINE LIBRARY AND
REFERENCE PUBLISHING:
Todd Baldwin

CQ Researcher (ISSN 1056-2036) is printed on acid-free paper. Published weekly, except: (March wk. 4) (May wk. 4) (July wks. 1, 2) (Aug. wks. 2, 3) (Nov. wk. 4) and (Dec. wks. 3, 4). Published by SAGE Publications, Inc., 2455 Teller Rd., Thousand Oaks, CA 91320. Annual full-service subscriptions start at $1,131. For pricing, call 1-800-818-7243. To purchase a *CQ Researcher* report in print or electronic format (PDF), visit www.cqpress. com or call 866-427-7737. Single reports start at $15. Bulk purchase discounts and electronic-rights licensing are also available. Periodicals postage paid at Thousand Oaks, California, and at additional mailing offices. POSTMASTER: Send address changes to *CQ Researcher*, 2600 Virginia Ave., N.W., Suite 600, Washington, DC 20037.

THE ISSUES

919 • Is the U.S. military too small?
• Does the procurement process undermine readiness?
• Is the military adequately modernizing its technology?

BACKGROUND

925 **Early Problems**
Americans struggled to field an army during the Revolution.

926 **Wartime Expansion**
President Theodore Roosevelt enlarged the Navy in the early 1900s.

928 **Constant Readiness**
After World War II, the United States and Soviet Union squared off in the Cold War.

931 **Fluctuating Spending**
In the 1990s, a "peace dividend" favored domestic over military spending.

CURRENT SITUATION

933 **Military Strategy**
North Korea threatens to launch an "unimaginable" strike against the United States.

934 **Procurement Fixes**
The Pentagon is focusing on technology and innovation.

OUTLOOK

936 **Evolving Threats**
Cyberspace will be a new battlefield.

SIDEBARS AND GRAPHICS

920 **Middle East Led in Military Spending as Share of GDP**
The United States ranked 18th in 2016, spending 3.3 percent of its GDP on the military. Russia was sixth.

921 **Trump Seeks Increase in Military Spending**
President Trump seeks an increase in military spending in 2018.

924 **Russia and U.S. Hold Largest Nuclear Arsenals**
Eight nations hold the world's estimated 14,905 operational nuclear warheads.

927 **Chronology**
Key events since 1907.

928 **Military Girds for War in Space**
U.S. satellites are "highly vulnerable to attack."

930 **U.S. Is Modernizing Its Nuclear Arsenal**
But experts wonder if President Trump will change Obama-era plan.

935 **At Issue:**
Is the U.S. military in a readiness crisis?

FOR FURTHER RESEARCH

940 **For More Information**
Organizations to contact.

941 **Bibliography**
Selected sources used.

942 **The Next Step**
Additional articles.

943 **Citing *CQ Researcher***
Sample bibliography formats.

Cover: AFP/Getty Images/Kazuhiro Nogi

Military Readiness

BY CHRISTINA L. LYONS

THE ISSUES

This year has not been kind to the U.S. Navy. In January, a guided missile cruiser ran aground in Tokyo Bay. In May, another cruiser collided with a South Korean fishing vessel off the Korean Peninsula, injuring several sailors.

Then, the unthinkable. On June 17, a guided missile destroyer, the *USS Fitzgerald*, collided with a container ship off Japan, killing seven sailors. Two months later, on Aug. 21, an oil tanker struck another destroyer, the *USS John S. McCain*, a little before dawn off the coast of Singapore. The collision flooded machinery, communications equipment and sleeping quarters. Ten sailors died. [1]

"This is a very, very dire circumstance for our Navy," says Lyle Goldstein, an associate professor at the China maritime Studies Institute at the Naval War College in Newport, R.I., referring to the *Fitzgerald* and *McCain* collisions. "It speaks to the possibility that there is some kind of crisis in the force."

Vessels patrolling the Western Pacific are crucial to defending against a possible ballistic missile launch from North Korea, but recent testimony before two House subcommittees cited major gaps in training and maintenance on those ships. [2]

The Navy confirmed that assessment in two reports released on Nov. 1. "The collisions were avoidable," Adm. John Richardson, the chief of naval operations, said in summarizing the reports, which detailed a litany of crew and navigation errors. [3]

Overall, the Navy is struggling to cope with constant deployments, fewer ships and sleep-deprived crews, defense

Army Chief of Staff Gen. Mark Milley testified at a congressional hearing last year that he had "grave concerns" about the Army's ability to fight a major power such as China or Russia. Marine Gen. Joe Dunford, chairman of the Joint Chiefs of Staff, expressed similar concerns, saying that while the military has focused on terrorism, its adversaries "have developed . . . approaches specifically designed to limit our ability to project power."

Getty Images/Alex Wong

analysts say. In the Army, some brigades are exhausted after fighting for 16 years in Afghanistan and 14 years in Iraq. In July, in five separate incidents, Air Force F-16 jet fighters crashed, killing three airmen. [4]

Such problems have raised new concerns about U.S. military readiness amid rising tensions with Russia, China, North Korea and Iran, as well as continuing pressure to contain terrorism in the Middle East, Africa and elsewhere.

Nuclear weapons are also raising alarms. Nuclear war seemed a remote possibility a few years ago, but North Korea's progress developing nuclear weapons has renewed fears that the U.S. nuclear arsenal needs updating. Moreover, U.S. forces also face the prospect of fighting wars in cyberspace and outer space. [5] (*See sidebar, p. 928.*)

The United States remains far and away the world's most formidable military power, spending more on defense than the next eight countries combined. However, the many challenges facing the Army, Navy, Marine Corps and Air Force — including peacekeeping missions and terrorism — have prompted worries about whether the Pentagon has the troops, budget, training and equipment it needs. Defense spending has increased about 70 percent since the Sept. 11, 2001, terrorist attacks on the United States but dropped 16 percent between fiscal 2010 and fiscal 2016. [6]

Army Chief of Staff Gen. Mark Milley told a House Armed Services Committee hearing last year that he had "grave concerns" about whether his forces were prepared to fight a major power such as China or Russia. [7]

Other military leaders say the high priority given to fighting terrorism has hurt the armed forces' readiness for a conventional war. "While we are primarily focused on the threat of violent extremism, our adversaries and our potential adversaries have developed . . . approaches specifically designed to limit our ability to project power," Marine Gen. Joe Dunford, chairman of the Joint Chiefs of Staff, told the committee in June. [8]

Traditionally, U.S. officials and scholars often have defined military readiness as the ability to fight two major wars in different parts of the world at the same time. After the Cold War, some defined it as "two-and-a-half" wars, or two wars sequentially rather than simultaneously. Today, many experts disagree on the definition.

"Readiness is a term that's thrown around a lot lately," says Susanna Blume,

Middle East Led in Military Spending as Share of GDP

Four Middle Eastern nations — Oman, Saudi Arabia, Israel and Jordan — in 2016 were among the global leaders in defense spending as a percentage of gross domestic product (GDP). Oman was first at 13.7 percent. The United States, ranked 18th, spent 3.3 percent of its GDP on its military, behind sixth-ranked Russia at 5.4 percent. In overall spending, however, the United States spends far more on defense than any other nation.

Military Spending as Share of GDP, 2016

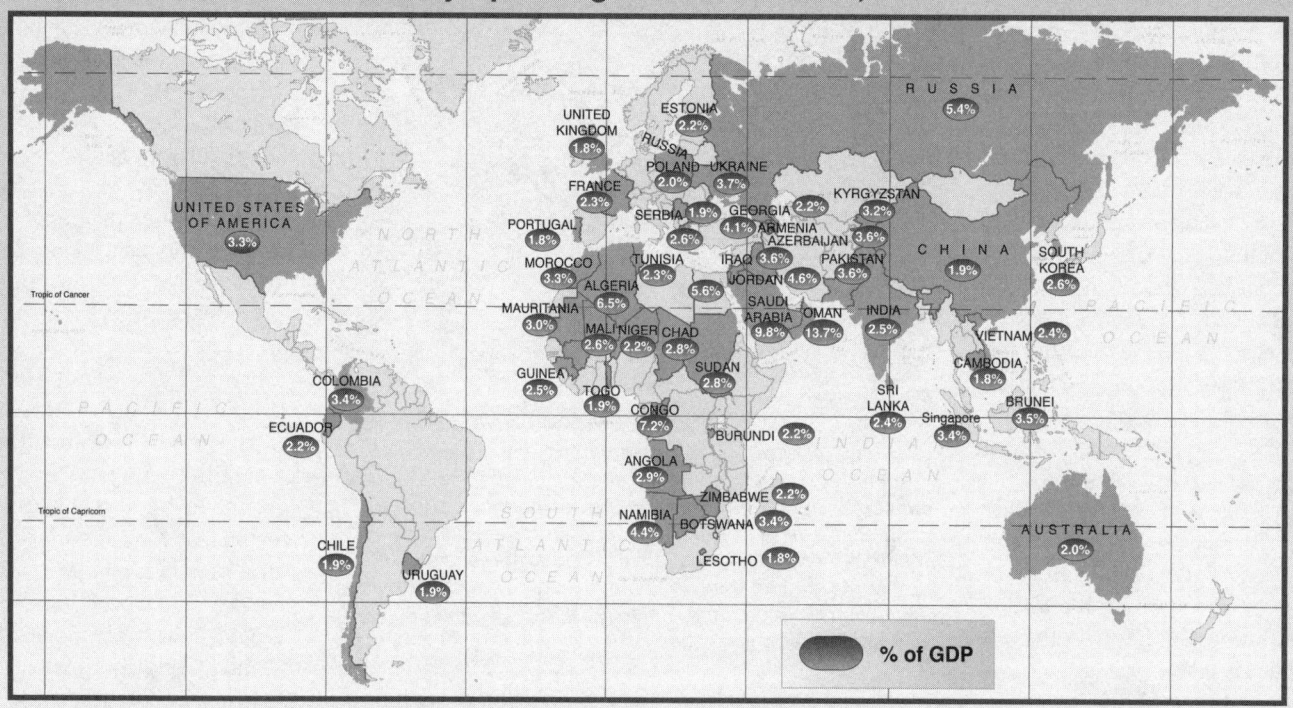

Source: Max Roser and Mohamed Nagdy, "Military Spending," Our World in Data, 2016, https://tinyurl.com/hjm5ewa

a former deputy chief of staff for programs and plans at the Defense Department and now a defense strategy fellow at the Center for a New American Security, a Washington think tank focused on national security issues. "It means a lot of different things to a lot of different people."

In the strictest sense, readiness refers to the ability of each military unit "to execute anticipated tasks for which that unit has been designed," says Michael O'Hanlon, a senior fellow at the Brookings Institution think tank in Washington. He says fears that the U.S. military is facing a readiness "crisis" focus on the most immediate challenges, distracting from the need to modernize and innovate to prepare for future threats.

In Washington, discussions of military preparedness focus heavily on troop strength and budgets. The Pentagon's current budget of about $586 billion pays for more than 1.3 million active-duty troops, including 450,000 deployed overseas. The largest numbers are in Afghanistan (about 11,000) and Kuwait (about 15,000).

U.S. military assets include:

• About 274 Navy ships, submarines and aircraft carriers.

• About 5,400 manned and unmanned aircraft, including 1,303 fighter jets.

• More than 2,800 tanks.

• About 1,650 nuclear warheads deployed on ballistic missiles and bombers, and about 180 tactical nuclear

weapons at bases in Germany, Belgium, the Netherlands, Italy and Turkey. [9]

Some defense analysts say the U.S. military needs to be bigger to deal with growing global demands. Other experts say long-term investments in training and modernizing equipment and technology are more important than increasing troop strength. Some helicopters and other equipment used by the Army are decades out of date.

Getting equipment to troops quickly also aids military readiness, but years-long delays, waste and fraud have hampered the Defense Department's procurement process, according to studies. The Government Accountability Office (GAO) reported in 2009 that only 20 percent of the largest Defense Department programs had been completed on deadline and within budget. [10]

Such delays are not always the Pentagon's fault, some defense analysts say. They note that many defense projects are highly complex and receive lengthy vetting by members of Congress, who compete to place — and preserve — those projects in their districts as a way to boost employment.

President Trump has proposed giving the Pentagon $639.1 billion in fiscal 2018 (which began Oct. 1), but GOP defense hawks on Capitol Hill say that is not enough. That amount includes $64.6 billion for "contingency" war-related operations such as the current missions in Iraq and Afghanistan. [11]

Trump's proposal is about $59 billion — or 10 percent — more than the $580.3 billion the Pentagon received in fiscal 2016. It also is about $52 billion over budget caps that Congress imposed in 2011 to rein in federal spending as part of a process of automatic spending cuts known as sequestration. Many Republicans say the caps have forced Pentagon officials to make damaging cuts to defense programs. [12]

"How the budget was shaped over the years . . . has had an effect on our readiness," says James Jeffrey, a former U.S. ambassador to Turkey and Iraq. He says budget tightening, combined with a continued focus on "region building" in Iraq and Afghanistan, limited military officials' ability to plan and acquire upgraded combat fighting vehicles, jets, helicopters and other equipment.

Pentagon officials are especially irritated by Congress' practice of funding government operations, including defense programs, through stopgap spending bills called continuing resolutions (CR).

David Norquist, the Pentagon's comptroller and chief financial officer, said in September that officials have had to postpone training and hiring and forgo ship maintenance as a result of uncertainty over funding. [13]

Trump Seeks Increase in Military Spending

President Trump has proposed giving the Defense Department about $639 billion in fiscal 2018, a 10 percent increase from fiscal 2016. Among the three major branches, the Air Force would receive the largest amount — $183 billion (left). Operations and maintenance for all branches would get about $272 billion (right).

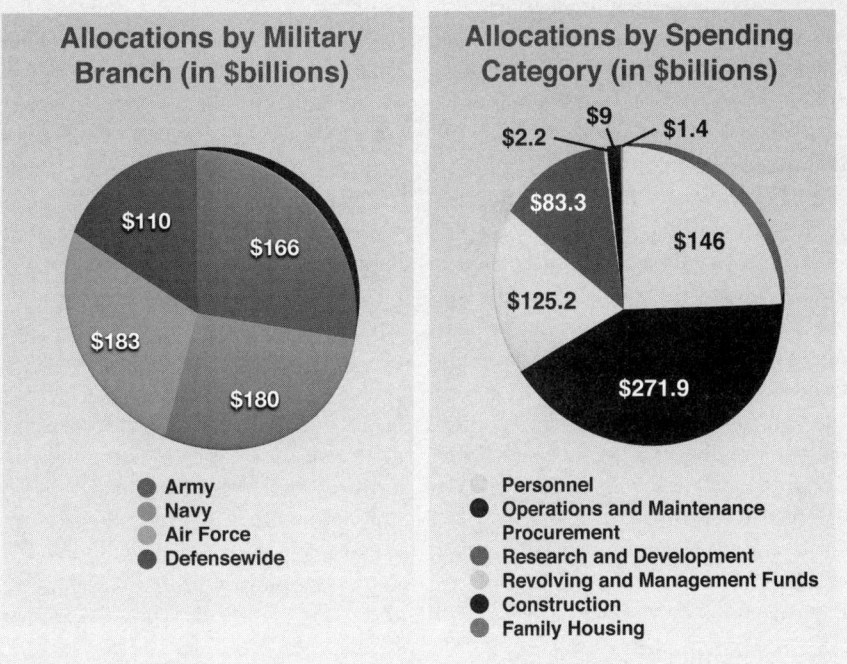

Source: "Defense Budget Overview: United States Department of Defense Fiscal Year 2018 Budget Request," Office of the Under Secretary of Defense (Comptroller), May 2017, p. A-4, https://tinyurl.com/y8p3wzbu

The U.S. military also responds to humanitarian crises, including the recent hurricanes that devastated Puerto Rico. Responding to such emergencies is expected to become more challenging as climate change contributes to more natural disasters, potentially sparking international conflicts over fresh water, food and other resources. [14]

Defense spending in recent years peaked in fiscal 2010 at $691 billion, and Trump's proposal would not bring it up to that level. Some of the country's potential adversaries, meanwhile, have stepped up their military outlays and activities. [15]

China's defense spending increased 26 percent between 2013 and 2016. In addition, since 2014, China has built

3,200 acres of military bases on artificial islands in the South China Sea that U.S. officials say are part of Beijing's plan to dominate Asia. [16]

Russia's military also has become increasingly aggressive, raising alarms among NATO countries in Europe that the United States is pledged to protect under Article 5 of the organization's charter. In September, Russia conducted its largest military exercise in recent history in an area that included the Arctic, the Far East, the Black Sea and Russia's border with Ukraine. The exercise involved tens of thousands of troops, along with warships, submarines, fighter jets, helicopters, tanks, artillery, anti-ship missiles, intercontinental ballistic missiles and swarms of drones. [17]

Another U.S. foe, Iran, says it has increased domestic weapons production 69 percent in the last three years. In January, it conducted its 10th ballistic missile test in two years, raising concerns that it had violated a 2015 agreement with the United States and other world powers to limit its nuclear program in exchange for relief from economic sanctions. According to military reports, 36 U.S. military bases overseas are within range of Iran's missiles. [18]

Joint Chiefs Chairman Dunford last year identified Russia, China, Iran and North Korea, along with Islamic extremism, as the country's top military threats. [19]

But none of those countries matches the United States in military might, analysts say. China, for example, is at low manpower levels, and troops have not faced sustained combat since the Vietnam War and are weak on training, coordination and logistics, according to the Congressional Research Service (CRS), the research arm of Congress. [20]

As the debate about U.S. military readiness continues, here are some of the questions that policymakers and defense experts are asking:

Is the U.S. military too small?

President Trump announced in January that he wanted to oversee "a great rebuilding" of the U.S. military, detailing plans for 540,000 Army troops, 350 Navy ships and a modernized nuclear arsenal. (*See sidebar, p. 930.*)

Pentagon officials and congressional Republicans praised the proposal, although they said it could take years to rebuild the military to something close to Cold War levels, when the Army had more than 750,000 active-duty troops.

That number decreased to about 480,000 during the 1990s, rose after the 2001 terrorist attacks and dropped again beginning in 2011. The Army had 475,000 troops on active duty in fiscal 2016. [21]

As troop numbers have declined, however, their quality has improved, said Steven Kosiak, an adjunct senior fellow at the Center for a New American

Security. Higher spending on military health care and veterans' benefits has attracted more high-quality recruits as measured by "education, aptitude and level of experience," he said. [22]

But demands on U.S. soldiers are increasing, which means troop strength also should increase, some defense experts say.

Since the end of the Cold War, "the range of potential conflicts we have to be ready for has grown exponentially," says Todd Harrison, director of defense budget analysis at the Center for Strategic and International Studies, a Washington think tank that researches national security and other issues.

In addition to conducting counterterrorism operations, today's soldiers must be ready to fight "old-fashioned" conventional wars in places such as North Korea, while also preparing for a potential cyberwar, says James F. Cunningham, a former senior research associate at the American Enterprise Institute, a conservative think tank in Washington.

Yet keeping a full brigade trained and ready is difficult when troops constantly rotate out for home leave or are lost through attrition, Cunningham says. "What we have right now is not sufficient," he says.

Dan Goure, senior vice president of the Lexington Institute, a conservative think tank in Virginia focused on national security and other issues, said today's military "is too small, with too few technological advantages and facing too many threats."

"There is now a very real possibility that in a future conflict . . . U.S. forces could suffer such high casualties that regardless of the outcome, this country will lack the capabilities needed to deal with any other major contingency," Goure said. [23]

The National Commission on the Future of the Army, created by Congress in 2015 to determine how many active-duty and reserve troops the Army needed, concluded that 980,000 — a slightly smaller number than is currently deployed — would be just enough to

meet near-term obligations "with an acceptable level of national risk."

Commission members also noted that budget cuts had forced Army officials to make "many significant trade-offs," including canceling combat training rotations, laying off civilians and deploying regular Army units in lieu of reserve units. By fiscal 2015, budget reductions also had cut the number of active-duty Army air personnel to its lowest level since 1947. [24]

More recently, the Air Force has struggled to compete with commercial airlines for pilots, Lt. Gen. Gina Grosso, deputy chief of staff for manpower, personnel and services for the Air Force, said in March. The branch ended fiscal 2016 short 1,555 pilots, including 1,211 fighter pilots. [25]

Harrison describes the armed forces' current resources as "constrained," and O'Hanlon at the Brookings Institution says the size of the military is "barely sufficient" and should be increased slightly. He also believes the Pentagon needs to set clearer priorities.

Joseph J. Collins, director of the Center for Complex Operations at the National Defense University in Washington, D.C., agrees, saying clearer priorities are even more important than expanding troop strength. "Are we going to face the most intense threats or the most probable?" asks Collins, who served as deputy assistant secretary of Defense for stability operations during the Obama administration.

Goldstein at the Naval War College also cites Pentagon priorities as a problem area, saying Special Forces and military pilots are used so often for expensive counterterrorism operations that they are not getting enough training time for other types of combat.

In the Navy, commanders have "extended deployments; increased operational tempos; and shortened, eliminated, or deferred training and maintenance," according to a 2015 GAO report. [26]

In January, Milley, the Army chief of staff, said spending more money modernizing equipment and technology is more important for military readiness than increasing the size of the armed forces. [27]

Harrison agrees. "A larger military and a larger budget will not necessarily make us strong or safer," he said. "The competition is much more about technology and how well you can deploy the technology." [28]

Does the procurement process undermine readiness?

The F-35 Joint Strike Fighter was designed to do virtually anything the Pentagon desired, serving the Air Force, Marine Corps and Navy and replacing the aging F-18 Hornet and Super Hornet. But the program, which began in 2001, has been plagued with delays and technical problems. [29]

The first four Lockheed Martin-built jets, which cost a combined $400 million, could not launch air-to-air missiles because their wings were too weak. They also lacked a functioning gun and would suddenly roll when flying below the speed of sound. [30]

The F-35 program is now nearly a decade behind schedule and is expected to cost about $406.5 billion for 2,456 planes, more than double its original price tag. It is just one example of the Pentagon's spotty record of accurately estimating the cost of new weapons systems and making sure they are delivered on time and within budget. Other examples include Gerald R. Ford-class supercarriers, Zumwalt-class destroyers and littoral combat ships, which are light frigates designed to transport Special Forces on anti-terrorism missions. [31]

The Defense Department "pays more than anticipated, can buy less than expected, and, in some cases, delivers less capability to the warfighter," the GAO reported in February. And a 2014 report from the Congressional Research Service cited criticisms by defense analysts that Pentagon cost overruns and schedule delays "have a debilitating effect on the nation's military and threat-

en America's technological advantage and military capabilities." The CRS report also noted the Defense Department's efforts to reform its acquisition process "have failed to rein in cost and schedule growth." [32]

Such criticisms, however, overlook the fact that defense projects are highly complex and require thorough vetting by Congress, some defense experts say. "Is it fair to question, how long did

An F-35 Joint Strike Fighter jet is readied for a training mission at Hill Air Force Base in Ogden, Utah, on March 15, 2017. Problems with the F-35 reflect the Pentagon's difficulty in accurately estimating the cost of new weapons systems and making sure they are delivered on time and within budget. The F-35 program is nearly a decade behind schedule and is expected to cost about $406 billion for 2,456 planes, more than double its original price tag.

it take Boeing to build the 787?" asks Alan Estevez, who once handled acquisition duties at the Defense Department and is now an executive at defense contractor Deloitte Consulting.

In addition, the Center for a New American Security's Blume says military projects involve "all kinds of security considerations" that typically are not a factor in non-military projects.

Since 1959, 17 Defense secretaries have pledged to fix the Pentagon's procurement process, but none succeeded, Harvard Business School professor J. Ronald Fox said in 2010. [33]

Part of the problem is that the Defense Department does a poor job monitoring the production line from beginning to end, says Laura Junor, director for research and strategic stud-

ies at the National Defense University in Washington. Managing readiness for war involves ensuring certain equipment is ready and can be sustained throughout the forces, she says. But the department will focus only on preparing equipment for units immediately deploying — not those that aren't scheduled to deploy.

The Marine Corps' F/A-18C Squadron, for example, will look ready when it

deploys on Navy aircraft carriers before the end of the year, Junor says, "but that belies the fact that the Navy depots cannot produce enough working F/A-18s . . . to keep [squadrons] as trained as they should be."

Other examples of supply problems include a satellite communications system designed by Lockheed Martin for the Navy, says Brian Weeden, a former Air Force officer and a technical adviser at the Secure World Foundation in Colorado, which advocates for the peaceful use of outer space. The satellites are in orbit but could be outdated by the time the computers they will link with are installed on ships, submarines and tanks, he says.

"Part of it is timeline," Weeden says. "There is a year or two of debating

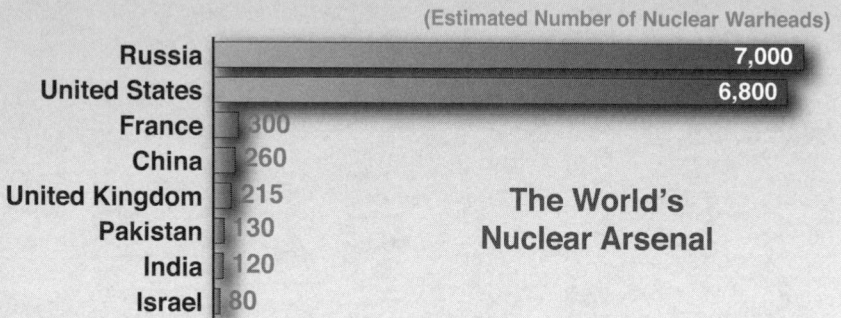

Russia and U.S. Hold Largest Nuclear Arsenals

The estimated 14,905 operational nuclear warheads around the world are held by only eight countries. Russia has the most, with 7,000, followed closely by the United States. The numbers include retired warheads that are still intact. North Korea has produced fissile material for 10 to 20 nuclear warheads but is not thought to have stockpiled any weapons.

(Estimated Number of Nuclear Warheads)

Russia	7,000
United States	6,800
France	300
China	260
United Kingdom	215
Pakistan	130
India	120
Israel	80

The World's Nuclear Arsenal

Source: Martin Armstrong, "The Countries Holding the World's Nuclear Arsenal," Statista, Feb. 28, 2017, https://tinyurl.com/y87xc6rj

warfare requirements, then a couple years to debate a contract, then build it, then to get it out takes another decade. . . . In that decade, technology hasn't stood still, and today's threat hasn't stood still."

Scharre at the Center for a New American Security says 20-to-30-year procurement cycles impede the Defense Department's ability to purchase "fast-developing technology," particularly computer technology.

Congress is another source of delays, partly because lawmakers are reluctant to abandon projects that produce jobs in their districts. Members of Congress from Missouri, for instance, have long pushed for funding Super Hornet fighter jets, largely made at a Boeing facility in St. Louis. [34]

"There seems to be some sort of push to make sure suppliers come from as many states in the union as possible," says Collins at National Defense University. "So once we get big-ticket items on the plate we can't get rid of them."

Blume, the defense strategy fellow, notes that the defense procurement process can move quickly when it has

to. In May 2007, for example, then-Defense Secretary Robert Gates put a high priority on acquiring Mine Resistant, Ambush Protected (MRAP) vehicles to replace Humvees to better protect U.S. troops in Iraq and Afghanistan from roadside bombs. Congress immediately authorized $4 billion, and troops in Iraq were training on the new vehicles by November. Six months later, 3,000 MRAPs were in service in Iraq, and deaths from improvised explosive devices were dropping. [35]

"That's a bit of a success story, in that we were able to move quickly and adapt the process to move materials to the field faster," Blume says.

Is the military adequately modernizing its technology?

Navy officials are investigating whether foreign cyberattacks caused the recent collisions involving the USS John S. McCain and the USS Fitzgerald in the western Pacific. Technology experts consider that unlikely, but North Korea, China, and Russia have been known to jam navigation systems. [36]

All three countries also have demonstrated they are willing to hack into

private-sector computers in the United States and elsewhere to gain a military or political advantage. [37]

In 2015, former Joint Chiefs of Staff Chairman Martin Dempsey said the United States does not have an edge in cyberwarfare, calling it instead a "level playing field." [38]

In March, Air Force Lt. Gen. William J. Bender, chief information officer at the Air Force secretary's office, said the military hopes to make more rapid advances in information technology and data analysis by teaming up with academics and experts in the private sector. [39]

Pentagon officials have been slow to modernize other military technology as well, Rep. Mike Rogers, R-Ala., then-chairman of the House Armed Services Subcommittee on Strategic Forces, said last year. He pointed to the military's continued use of Vietnam-era Huey helicopters to protect intercontinental missile launch facilities around Air Force bases in the northern Great Plains, leaving the nuclear missiles potentially vulnerable to terrorist attack. Congress and the Pentagon delayed a program to replace the helicopters and redirected funds to counterterrorism fights. [40]

Other Army equipment, including some vehicles, was designed in the 1970s and purchased in the 1980s and needs to be replaced, says Jeffrey, the former ambassador to Turkey and Iraq, now a fellow at the Washington Institute for Near East Policy, a foreign policy think tank in Washington.

Meanwhile, Iran, North Korea, China and Russia are developing advanced weapons to challenge U.S. military dominance, including "anti-access area denial" systems that prevent enemy troops from deploying in a particular area and reduce their movement if they make it inside. Such weapons include anti-ship cruise missiles (ASCMs), short- and medium-range ballistic missiles and cruise missiles. [41]

"There's a real concern about the readiness of the Navy, Marine Corps and the Air Force to take on these systems," Jeffrey says.

China and Russia have surpassed the United States in developing anti-ship cruise missiles, according to Goldstein of the Naval War College. "If you put our best ASCM against China's, ours loses hands down," he says. "It's slower, it does not go as far, it doesn't have the kill maneuvers." Russia has an even better ASCM, he says.

"It's like going into a fistfight with someone who has a knife or a gun," Goldstein says.

Artificial intelligence (AI) represents another area where China is investing heavily to deny the United States and other adversaries an advantage. Officials in Beijing said in July they plan to spend billions of dollars to make China a world leader in AI by 2025 through collaboration among military, industry and research groups. [42]

However, in most areas of military technology, including fighter jets, China lags behind the United States, according to Scharre at the Center for a New American Security and other defense experts.

Apart from land-based and submarine-launched missiles, "no Chinese capabilities come close to surpassing those of the U.S.," said Thomas Christensen, director of the China and the World Program at Princeton University. He said that includes cyber capabilities. [43]

Weeden at the Secure World Foundation says China is only just now rolling out technology such as GPS intelligence satellites, which troops use to communicate and to spy on enemy forces. The United States put such satellites into orbit decades ago.

"The perception is they are moving very, very fast," Weeden says of the Chinese. "But that does not mean they're passing us. . . . They've got a long ways to go."

Pentagon officials are working to make sure the United States stays ahead in drone warfare. In October 2016, they dropped more than 100 micro-drones over China Lake, Calif., in the world's largest test of how such devices

The Army's 1st Stryker Brigade Combat Team participates in jungle warfare training at Schofield Barracks in Honolulu on March 1, 2017. The Pentagon's current budget pays for more than 1.3 million active-duty troops, including 450,000 deployed overseas. Some analysts say the U.S. military is too small to deal with growing global demands, but others say long-term investments in training and modern equipment are more important than increasing troop strength.

communicate with each other as part of a swarm, and how they would perform in a military attack. [44]

The Army also used advanced electronic warfare technology to disable "enemy" tanks during a simulation at the Army National Training Center at Fort Irwin, Calif., earlier this year. The exercise used technology to jam the tanks' communications and hack into their computers, forcing the troops inside to stop and get out. [45]

Scharre, author of *Army of None: Autonomous Weapons and the Future of War*, scheduled for release next year, says the Pentagon is working to develop intelligent machines, including unmanned vehicles that will detect enemy threats and make decisions on how to respond. The military also is equipping some aircraft with automatic ground collision avoidance systems that take over control of a plane about to crash. [46]

Scharre says defense officials need to move faster to take advantage of innovation in the private sector, but that has not always gone well. Some companies, including Silicon Valley software startup Palantir, say the Defense Department improperly favors its largest clients when awarding lucrative contracts. In June last year, Palantir sued Pentagon officials, alleging they barred the company from receiving a $206 million contract. In

April, federal officials asked an appeals court to overturn an earlier ruling saying the Army unlawfully refused to consider Palantir's bid. [47]

The Center for a New American Security's Blume acknowledges that military officials have room to improve in making it easier for startups to win government contracts. "There's a lot of red tape, lots of steps, lots of hurdles," she says. ∎

BACKGROUND

Early Problems

English colonists in North America relied on part-time militias, their own martial prowess and occasional help from Britain's army and navy for protection against Indians and French and Spanish forces. When disputes with Parliament and King George III over taxation led to war in April 1775, the colonists lacked the troops, guns, cannons, ships and other military matériel needed for sustained combat operations.

In June 1775, the Continental Congress authorized formation of a full-time army to be commanded by George Washington of Virginia. Congress, however, lacked taxing powers and relied on the newly de- clared 13 states for troops and supplies.

Washington struggled to keep the Continental Army in the field over the next eight years, ultimately fighting a defensive war. [48]

In 1783, the Treaty of Paris ended the war and assured the United States its independence. But wartime memories of ill-clad soldiers freezing at Valley Forge and going into battle short of ammunition contributed to the belief that the fledgling United States needed a stronger central government with taxing powers. In 1787, the Founders crafted the U.S. Constitution, giving Congress the power to "raise and support Armies." At the time, the Army had about 800 men, including officers. [49] In subsequent decades, the United States repeatedly found itself unprepared for war. When war came — with Britain in 1812, the Mexican-American War in 1846 and the Civil War — the government scrambled to build a large professional fighting force. [50]

During the Civil War, the industrialized North had a larger population and greater economic resources than the agricultural South and was able to field a large and well-equipped military. But the South's military leadership proved superior, and Union forces suffered defeat after defeat through 1863 before eventually turning the tide. In late 1864, the Confederacy was running short of troops, guns, am- munition and other supplies, and its armies surrendered in 1865.

After the war, the U.S. decommis- sioned most of its army and navy, keeping small numbers of troops in the West to fight the Indian wars. As the U.S. economy expanded in the late 19th century, the nation moved closer to taking a promi- nent military role globally.

When the Spanish-American War started in April 1898 in Cuba, the U.S. government again mobilized men faster than it could equip them. Less than one-fifth of the nearly 275,000 men mobilized saw combat before the war ended in August. Many who did see action carried obsolete rifles and sweltered in winter uniforms in the

Caribbean heat. And they lacked sufficient "wagons, harnesses, tents, camp equip- ment, and medical supplies," according to military historian James A. Huston. [51]

Nevertheless, by the end of the war, the United States had become a world power.

Wartime Expansion

President Theodore Roosevelt continued to build a navy to challenge those of Great Britain, France and Russia, and particularly to manage increasing tensions with Japan, which dreamed of a Pacific empire after defeating Russia in 1903. [52]

Between 1907 and 1909, Roosevelt sent 16 battleships and accompanying vessels, called the "Great White Fleet," on a 14-month voyage around the world to display U.S. naval power. The fleet, carrying 14,000 sailors and Marines, stopped at 20 ports on six continents. [53]

By then, U.S. shipbuilders could produce 15,000-ton battleships armed with eight-inch guns, and the airplane industry was about to emerge. [54] When the United States declared war on Ger- many in 1917 during World War I, the Army had fewer than 122,000 en- listed men and 6,000 officers, and one- third of those officers had less than a year of service. The National Guard had about 175,000 officers and enlisted men, less than 40 percent of its autho- rized strength.

President Woodrow Wilson signed the Selective Service Act on May 18, 1917, which eventually increased the Army to 500,000 troops. But because of the time needed to train, arm and deploy troops across the Atlantic, only one Army division made it to the war's front lines before 1918. [55]

Equipment and munitions production sputtered initially before picking up and overwhelming railroads. Supplies filled East Coast warehouses because the military did not have enough ships to ferry cargo across the Atlantic. The first squadron of U.S. planes did not fly

over the Western front in France until August 1918, just three months before the war ended. [56]

Similar problems hampered the U.S. military as it entered World War II. Between November 1939 and June 1940, U.S. ac- tive-duty manpower increased by a third and continued to grow rapidly in the months before the country entered the war in December 1941, said Richard K. Betts, a professor of war and peace studies at Columbia University in New York.

Historian Huston said, however, that men "trained with sticks for guns when they might better have remained in shops and factories for another year or two to help produce the weapons and equipment they would need." [57]

On Dec. 7, 1941, after Japanese planes attacked the U.S. naval base at Pearl Harbor, President Franklin D. Roosevelt declared war against Japan, and, days later, against Germany. Within a week of Pearl Harbor, the United States mo- bilized 130,000 troops in the Philippines, including Filipino troops, to defend the islands against a Japanese invasion. [58]

Half of the U.S. fighter pilots dis- patched to protect Clark Field in the Philippines the next day aborted their missions when engine oil shot over their planes' windscreens. Many B-17 bombers did not have tail guns and armor, and crews lacked gunnery train- ing. By Christmas, only a half-dozen U.S. heavy bombers were still in com- mission in the southwest Pacific. [59]

But as the United States shifted to a wartime footing and began to churn out planes, tanks and other supplies, the nation's economic and military might turned the tide against the Axis powers. Meanwhile, U.S. scientists developed an atomic weapon, which they tested in July 1945 after Germany's defeat. Pres- ident Harry S. Truman, hoping to avoid the massive casualties that would result if Allied forces invaded Japan, in August ordered two atomic bombs dropped on Hiroshima and Nagasaki. The bombs destroyed both cities, killing tens of

Continued on p. 928

Chronology

1900s-1940s
U.S. defense spending and troop strength fluctuate.

1907
President Theodore Roosevelt sends "Great White Fleet" of U.S. battleships around the world on a 14-month display of naval power.

1917
U.S. enters World War I. . . . President Woodrow Wilson signs the Selective Service Act requiring eligible men to sign up for military duty.

1941
Japanese planes bomb the U.S. naval base at Pearl Harbor. . . . U.S. enters World War II with a large number of troops but insufficient equipment. . . . Sen. Harry Truman, D-Mo., launches investigation into waste and fraud in defense contracts related to war production.

1945
At war's end, military spending is $85 billion and troop strength estimated at 12 million. . . . U.S. drops atomic bombs on Japan, ending World War II.

1947
Cold War with the Soviet Union begins as U.S. works to contain communism. . . . Annual military spending is $10 billion and the number of troops is estimated at 1.5 million.

1949
U.S. joins North Atlantic Treaty Organization, pledging to defend Allies against Soviet aggression.

1950s-1980s
U.S. military fights communist threat.

1950
Communist North Korea invades South Korea, triggering Korean War.

1953
President Dwight D. Eisenhower emphasizes importance of nuclear firepower over troop size, reduces Army.

1961
President John F. Kennedy boosts defense budget, expands size of armed forces.

1965
U.S. forces in South Vietnam are ill-prepared for guerrilla combat and suffer severe losses against Viet Cong. . . . In January 1973, U.S. and North Vietnam sign peace agreement; U.S. troops pull out in April.

1980
U.S. military helicopters crash in failed mission to rescue hostages in Iran, prompting concerns about military readiness.

1981
President Ronald Reagan pursues largest peacetime buildup of military in U.S. history.

1989
Berlin Wall falls, signaling end of Cold War and making U.S. military readiness less urgent.

1990s-Present
Military spending fluctuates.

1991
U.S. troops liberate Kuwait after Iraqi invasion, boosting confidence in U.S. military readiness.

1993
Clinton administration cuts military personnel; troop strength falls about 19 percent over next eight years.

Sept. 11, 2001
Islamist terrorists crash hijacked planes into World Trade Center and Pentagon. . . . Invasion of Afghanistan begins longest war in U.S. history. . . . Defense spending increases under George W. Bush administration.

2007
Bush submits largest defense budget since Reagan era.

2011
Defense Secretary Robert Gates warns that congressionally mandated caps on defense spending will lead to "hollow force."

2014
U.S. Navy increases patrols in South China Sea after China builds military bases on artificial islands there.

2015
U.S. officials identify cyberattacks and climate change as urgent national security threats.

2016
Defense Department conducts world's largest drone swarm test over China Lake, Calif.

2017
President Trump orders review of nuclear arsenal, proposes 10 percent boost in defense budget. . . . North Korean leader Kim Jong Un and Trump exchange nuclear threats. . . . Navy's readiness questioned after collisions and other accidents. . . . Russia conducts its largest modern military exercise along its western border. . . . Iran conducts ballistic missile tests, potentially violating international agreement aimed at curbing Tehran's nuclear weapons program.

Military Girds for War in Space

U.S. satellites are "highly vulnerable to attack."

With China and Russia rapidly developing the ability to fight in space, the U.S. military's challenges are extending into the cosmos, defense experts say.

The capabilities of the two rivals likely include jamming satellite communications or potentially using a so-called kinetic weapon to destroy satellites, National Intelligence Director Daniel Coats said in May. The Russian military is possibly building an "aircraft-launched missile capable of destroying satellites in low-Earth orbit," he added. [1]

The U.S. military and national security establishment are debating the seriousness of the threats and the steps the Pentagon should take to counter them. The United States is "still a long way ahead" in space defense, although "the Chinese are coming up very fast," says Lyle Goldstein, an associate professor in China maritime studies at the Naval War College in Newport, R.I.

National Security Adviser H.R. McMaster in early October announced he had begun a review that, among other things, aims to deter and defeat adversaries in space and partner with commercial companies to develop space technologies. [2]

The Air Force, meanwhile, plans to appoint a general to act as a "space czar" for that military branch, which has primary oversight of the Pentagon's space activities and is readying other changes designed to protect satellites and spacecraft from cyberattack and enemy missiles. [3]

The Senate blocked a proposal to create a military branch focused on space, which passed the House in July as part of a defense spending bill. Military leaders and the White House opposed a Space Corps as premature and potentially wasteful of resources because it would duplicate much of what the Air Force is already doing. [4]

The U.S. military for decades has used satellites to monitor hostile nations and help direct conventional forces. But Russia and China, defense experts say, are advancing their space capabilities to destroy those satellites, cripple U.S. military operations worldwide and weaken the nation's defenses.

The Center for Strategic and International Studies, a Washington think tank focused on national security issues, on Oct. 3 released a study warning of the potential for a space war that is "more diverse, disruptive, disordered and dangerous" than the space race initiated in 1957 when the Soviet Union launched the first satellite, *Sputnik 1*. [5]

A space war is possible in the near future, and the United States must boost its defense capabilities, says Brian Weeden, a former Air Force officer and a technical adviser for the Secure World Foundation, a Washington nonprofit focused on preventing the militarization of space.

Nearly 1,500 military and civilian satellites orbit the Earth; the United States has 593, while China operates 192 and Russia 135. North Korea in February put its second satellite into orbit. [6]

The U.S. military relies on satellite communications to operate drone aircraft and precision-guided munitions as well as to conduct battlefield reconnaissance. "There is no [sector] of national security that doesn't involve space," Weeden says. "The U.S. is highly dependent on its space systems, and they are highly vulnerable to attack."

Russia tested what national security officials believe was an anti-satellite weapon in December, although it did not hit a target. In May 2014, China launched a rocket which its military said later was to research the magnetic field surrounding the Earth known as the magnetosphere. Weeden found evidence the rocket was designed to launch a "kinetic kill vehicle" that could destroy enemy satellites in high orbits. [7]

Dean Cheng, a senior research fellow at the conservative

Continued from p. 926

thousands of Japanese, and Japan quickly surrendered. [60]

More than 1.2 million officers and nearly 10.8 million enlisted men were on active duty in the U.S. armed forces at the end of the war. Within a year, two-thirds of the officers and three-fourths of the enlisted men had returned to civilian life. [61]

By 1947, military spending had dropped to $10 billion from $83 billion in 1945. In 1949, as tensions with the Soviet Union rose and the Cold War got underway, Truman committed the United States to joining a new Western defense alliance, the North Atlantic Treaty Organization (NATO). [62]

Constant Readiness

After the Japanese surrender, the Soviet Union and the United States temporarily divided responsibility for Korea along the 38th parallel. The United States maintained a small force nearby in Japan and assumed communist forces would remain north of the dividing line. [63]

Instead, North Korea invaded South Korea on June 25, 1950. President Truman provided U.S. air support for South Korea, but it was insufficient. With backing from the United Nations, the United States committed ground troops and regained the initiative under U.S.

Gen. Douglas MacArthur until China intervened in the conflict in late 1950. The war then degenerated into a stalemate that lasted until 1953, when the combatants agreed to an armistice. [64]

After 1950, the United States emphasized a strong defense to contain the communist threat overseas. Over the next three years, the defense budget tripled, and large numbers of troops were deployed to Europe. By then, the Soviets had developed an atomic weapon, and a nuclear arms race began. Readiness had become, in U.S. military and political circles, an "unquestioned virtue," Columbia University's Betts said. In 1953, President Dwight D. Eisenhower substituted nuclear firepower for

Heritage Foundation think tank in Washington, said, "Chinese military writings emphasize the importance of establishing space dominance . . . as the key to winning future wars." [8]

Even while developing their own anti-satellite systems, Russia and China since 2008 have urged the United Nations to adopt a treaty that would ban the use of weapons in space. The United States opposes the treaty, Weeden says, because "it doesn't address any of the problems" about a space war, such as barring lasers or other ground-based anti-satellite weapons.

Meanwhile, the military continues to rely heavily on satellites, with several programs underway to provide more-secure communications for military operations. But some of the programs have been delayed or have exceeded budget estimates, leading to concerns about harm to military readiness.

For instance, the Advanced Extremely High Frequency satellite program, designed to provide more-secure communications for the military, launched its satellite three and a half years late, in 2010, and the program's cost exceeded original estimates by at least 118 percent, according to the Government Accountability Office (GAO). Likewise, the Wideband Global SATCOM, a system to provide communication services for the military and its allies, more than tripled in cost from the original estimate of $1.3 billion to $4.3 billion and became operational nine years late. [9]

Rep. Mike Rogers, R-Ala., chairman of the House Armed Services Subcommittee on Strategic Forces, along with ranking member Jim Cooper, D-Tenn., raised an alarm about the problems. "The current system is wasting billions of dollars and failing to deliver capability to the warfighter. Our adversaries have already reorganized their space programs and are reaping the benefits." [10]

— *Christina L. Lyons*

A ground-based interceptor rocket is launched from Vandenberg Air Force Base in California on May 30, 2017. The rocket successfully intercepted and destroyed a target missile in space.

[1] Daniel Coats, "Worldwide Threat Assessment of the U.S. Intelligence Community," statement before Senate Select Committee on Intelligence, May 11, 2017, p. 9, http://tinyurl.com/y7b9mpar.

[2] Colin Clark, "SecAF Wilson Touts 'Offense' Space Weapons; McMaster Details 'Framework,' " *Breaking Defense*, Oct. 6, 2017, http://tinyurl.com/yc62qubo.

[3] Marcus Weisgerber, "The US Air Force Is Reorganizing to Fight in Space," *Defense One*, April 4, 2017, http://tinyurl.com/ya4n2qth.

[4] Rebecca Khelel, "Top general opposes Space Corps plans," *The Hill*, July 18, 2017, http://tinyurl.com/y7yhw48q.

[5] Todd Harrison, "Escalation and Deterrence in the Second Space Age," Center for Strategic and International Studies, Oct. 3, 2017, http://tinyurl.com/yas9pmxh.

[6] "UCS Satellite Database," Union of Concerned Scientists, http://tinyurl.com/y89xdhu2; Tim Fernholz, "China's secret anti-satellite weapons should be on everyone's radar," *Quartz*, March 19, 2014, http://tinyurl.com/y8epbo6n; and "Controversial Rocket Launch: North Korea successfully places Satellite into Orbit," Spaceflight 101.com, Feb. 7, 2016, http://tinyurl.com/z2jsjvx.

[7] Jim Sciutto, Barbara Starr and Ryan Browne, "Sources: Russia tests anti-satellite weapon," CNN, Dec. 21, 2016, http://tinyurl.com/jn3swxu; Fernholz, *op. cit.*

[8] Patrick Marshall, "New Space Race," *CQ Researcher*, Aug. 4, 2017, p. 664.

[9] Cristina Chaplain, "Space Acquisitions," statement before Subcommittee on Strategic Forces, Armed Services Committee, May 17, 2017, pp. 2-6, http://tinyurl.com/y8r538ee.

[10] "Rogers/Cooper Weigh In On GPS OCX & FAB-T Programs," press release, Committee on Armed Services, July 31, 2017, http://tinyurl.com/y7v97dcx.

force size and reduced Army troop strength over the next eight years. [65]

In 1961, tensions with the Soviets rose over the status of Berlin and the botched Bay of Pigs operation, in which a CIA-backed paramilitary group unsuccessfully invaded Cuba. President John F. Kennedy announced in July he would boost military readiness by requesting an immediate $3.2 billion, increasing the number of Army troops from 875,000 to 1 million, and the Navy and Air Force by 29,000 and 63,000, respectively. Caches of equipment were stockpiled, including new armored personnel carriers, troop-carrying helicopters, M79 grenade launchers and claymore mines. [66] Kennedy got

the Soviet Union to back down in 1962 after Moscow tried to install nuclear missiles in Cuba.

Meanwhile, trouble was brewing in Vietnam, which had been divided along the 17th parallel after the First Indochina War between the French and Viet Minh ended in 1954. Kennedy dispatched military advisers to assist South Vietnam in its fight against the communist-backed North.

By 1965, the United States was sending large numbers of ground troops to Vietnam, but they were ill-prepared for guerrilla combat and found themselves in a protracted war.

They also struggled with equipment problems. The automatic M14 rifle was

heavy, difficult to aim and unreliable and was outperformed by the Soviet-made AK47 used by Viet Cong soldiers. [67] The M16 rifle became the focus of public controversy in 1967 when Rep. James J. Howard, D-N.J., read a letter to colleagues written by a Marine who said almost all Americans killed in the battle for Hill 881 had died because their M16s had jammed. [68]

By November 1967, nearly U.S. 500,000 troops were in Vietnam, and 15,058 had been killed and 109,527 wounded. Public protests in the United States against the war led to violent clashes in cities and on college campuses, and thousands of U.S. military personnel deserted their posts.

U.S. Is Modernizing Its Nuclear Arsenal

But experts wonder how President Trump will change Obama-era plan.

With North Korea conducting nuclear tests and Russia rebuilding its military, U.S. efforts to modernize its nuclear arsenal — begun during Barack Obama's presidency — are taking on renewed urgency.

In January, President Trump signed an executive memorandum ordering the Defense Department to undertake a congressionally mandated review of U.S. nuclear capabilities. It is expected to be completed by the end of the year. [1] After the last review, in 2010, Obama authorized a plan, estimated to cost at least $1 trillion over the next decade, to maintain and modernize the nation's nuclear warheads as well as the planes, missiles and submarines that deliver them. [2]

The U.S. nuclear stockpile totals about 6,800 weapons, down from 31,000 in the 1960s. Some 1,650 are deployed on ground-based intercontinental ballistic missiles (ICBMs), submarine-based missiles and bombers. About 2,800 are retired and awaiting dismantlement, and 2,200 are in reserve and not deployed. Another 150 tactical nuclear weapons, designed to strike targets on the battlefield, are at bases in Belgium, Germany, Italy, the Netherlands and Turkey. [3]

But several experts and officials say the U.S. arsenal is old and its reliability unknown since no nuclear tests have occurred since 1992. "We are fast approaching the point where [failing to modernize aging nuclear weaponry] will put at risk our . . . nuclear deterrent," retired Adm. Cecil Haney, who from 2013 to 2016 was commander of the U.S. Strategic Command that oversees the military's nuclear forces, said in January 2016. [4]

In August, the Air Force awarded contracts to Boeing and Northrop Grumman to continue developing the next generation of land-based Minuteman ICBMs. The companies have three years to develop a model, after which the Air Force will choose one company to build the missiles. [5] The Air Force is spending another $1.8 billion on the initial development of a new nuclear-armed cruise missile that would be fired from existing bombers. [6]

But Trump's intentions on the nuclear arsenal are unclear. At a July meeting of national security leaders, Trump reportedly said the United States should enlarge its arsenal nearly tenfold — a statement he has denied making. [7] When the Pentagon completes its review, Trump could ask the Defense Department to move forward in a number of new directions, says Richard Weitz, director and senior fellow at the Center for Political-Military Analysis at the Hudson Institute, a conservative Washington think tank.

The most controversial step would be to call for developing a new nuclear warhead, which critics fear could lead to a new arms race or increase the chances of the weapon being used. Because current nuclear warheads date to the Cold War, new warheads would be safer and more secure, Weitz says, "and provide better protection from cyber and other threats."

"Another potentially controversial decision [the president] might make is to resume testing of nuclear warheads to make sure they work," a move Congress has rejected before, Weitz says. Testing last occurred on Sept. 23, 1992, in Nevada, according to the Arms Control Association, a pro-disarmament group in Washington. [8]

The association has opposed modernization efforts, warning that it will only accelerate the arms race because Russia and China would feel compelled to respond. Russia has about 7,000 nuclear warheads and China has about 270. [9]

Barry Blechman, co-founder of the Stimson Center, a Washington think tank, said conventional military forces are adequate for most threats and that a modernized, and possibly larger, arsenal is unnecessary to deter a nuclear attack on the United States. [10]

Congressional Republicans in 2015 began pushing for modernization in response to reports that Russia was rebuilding its capabilities. The State Department has accused Russia of violating

---

The White House, under President Lyndon B. Johnson and then President Richard M. Nixon, repeatedly asserted the war was nearly over, while committing an increasing number of troops to the effort. In January 1973, the United States and North Vietnam concluded a peace agreement; American troops were pulled out in April 1973. By July, Congress eliminated the unpopular draft. Fighting between North and South Vietnam continued until April 30, 1975, when North Vietnamese forces captured Saigon. Ultimately, some 59,000 U.S. troops died in the war. [69]

Defense budgets declined steadily for the next seven years. Army Chief of Staff Edward C. Meyer said in 1980 that the cuts had produced a "hollow Army" and that it would cost more than $40 billion beyond planned expenditures over the next five years to rebuild the force to meet a Soviet threat in Europe and cope with dangers in the Persian Gulf, Korea and Latin America. [70]

By September 1981, the Army reported recruitment was up and readiness was improving. In 1982, President Ronald Reagan proposed increased Air Force manpower and more, fighter planes, bombers and new strategic weapons. Congress went along. [71]

Reagan in 1983 undertook the Strategic Defense Initiative, dubbed "Star Wars" by its critics, to develop orbital countermeasures against Soviet intercontinental ballistic missiles. By the end of Reagan's first term, some Americans complained defense spending was nearly 50 percent higher than in 1980 without any evidence readiness had improved. [72]

As the military upgraded its technology, Pentagon officials and military field commanders told Congress in March 1987 that U.S. troops were unprepared for sustained combat. They said funding for new weapons had not left money for ammunition, spare

---

the 1987 Intermediate-Range Nuclear Forces Treaty that bans ground-launched nuclear cruise missiles with a range of 310 to 3,410 miles. [11]

North Korea on July 4 launched its first ICBM possibly capable of reaching the United States. On Sept. 3, the country tested a nuclear weapon seven times the size of the two nuclear bombs dropped on Japan in World War II. [12] "They [North Koreans] are advancing rapidly. . . . We don't have a lot of time," Secretary of State Rex Tillerson said on CBS' "Face the Nation" on Sept. 17 in reference to U.S. modernization efforts. [13]

The U.S. military has about 40 long-range missile interceptors, mostly in Alaska and California, designed to shoot down an incoming missile in space and destroy it using kinetic energy — the force of energy created by the motion of the interceptor, Weitz says. But Weitz says the military lacks the ability to shoot down multiple missiles arriving simultaneously.

In May, the military reported it successfully tested an upgraded interceptor missile, which downed a mock intercontinental ballistic missile over the Pacific Ocean. [14]

However, Weitz says the interceptor's reliability remains in doubt. "We're going to have to get the effectiveness of our existing interceptors higher," he says. "And we need to consider having more interceptors, and we need to develop the next-generation systems."

— Christina L. Lyons

[1] Jeremy Herb, "Trump order sets military buildup in motion," *Politico*, Jan. 27, 2017, http://tinyurl.com/jxplbkn.

[2] Jon B. Wolfsthal, Jeffrey Lewis and Marc Quint, "The Trillion Dollar Nuclear Triad," James Martin Center for Nonproliferation Studies, January 2014, http://tinyurl.com/y8tylsow; John Wagner and Philip Rucker, "Trump warns N. Korea: U.S. nuclear arsenal is 'more powerful than ever before,' " *The Washington Post*, Aug. 9, 2017, http://tinyurl.com/y8g7v4zr. For background, see

William Wanlund, "Modernizing the Nuclear Arsenal," *CQ Researcher*, July 29, 2016, pp. 625-648.

[3] "The dangers of our aging nuclear arsenal," *The Week*, Jan. 17, 2015, http://tinyurl.com/oj8z3dh; Hans M. Kristensen and Robert S. Norris, "Status of World Nuclear Forces," Federation of American Scientists, 2017, https://tinyurl.com/junbna7; Kingston Reif, "U.S. Nuclear Modernization Program," Arms Control Association, August 2017, http://tinyurl.com/7z7yulu; and Robert S. Norris and Hans M. Kristensen, "U.S. tactical nuclear weapons in Europe, 2011," *Bulletin of the Atomic Scientists*, 2011, http://tinyurl.com/ycuvccqk.

[4] "U.S. Nuclear Weapons Capability," 2017 Index of U.S. Military Strength, http://tinyurl.com/yc85a66w; Adm. Cecil Haney, Remarks, Center for Security and International Studies, Jan. 22, 2016, http://tinyurl.com/y9vla2eo.

[5] Aaron Gregg, "Pentagon narrows competition for next big U.S. nuclear missile deterrent," *The Washington Post*, Aug. 22, 2017, http://tinyurl.com/ybkx8xmz.

[6] David E. Sanger and William J. Broad, "Trump Forges Ahead on Costly Nuclear Overhaul," *The New York Times*, Aug. 27, 2017, http://tinyurl.com/ybc6ywqn; Kyle Mizokami, "America Is Building a New, Stealthy Nuclear Cruise Missile," *Popular Mechanics*, Aug. 24, 2017, http://tinyurl.com/y6v8xa8g.

[7] Aaron Blake, "Trump's loose talk on nuclear weapons suddenly becomes very real," *The Washington Post*, Oct. 11, 2017, http://tinyurl.com/y86lqoj7; President Trump, Twitter post, Oct. 11, 2017, http://tinyurl.com/y9w9ohf5.

[8] "23 September 1992 — Last U.S. Nuclear Test," Preparatory Commission for the Comprehensive Nuclear-Test-Ban Treaty Organization, undated, http://tinyurl.com/yclnbajf.

[9] Kristensen and Norris, *op. cit.*

[10] Wanlund, *op. cit.*; Barry Blechman, "A Trillion-Dollar Nuclear Weapon Modernization Is Unnecessary," *The New York Times*, Oct. 26, 2016, http://tinyurl.com/yal6ypxg.

[11] Zachary Keck, "Russia Threatens to Build More Nuclear Weapons," *The National Interest*, May 18, 2015, http://tinyurl.com/yb25asrs; Harvey Day, "Putin says Russia has 'caught up with US missile capabilities' and will respond if America quits Cold War arms treaty," *Daily Mail*, Oct. 19, 2017, http://tinyurl.com/y7zhkpj5.

[12] Choe Sang-Hun, "U.S. Confirms North Korea Fired Intercontinental Ballistic Missile," *The New York Times*, July 4, 2017, http://tinyurl.com/y9jz7s9l; Geoff Brumfiel, "Here Are The Facts About North Korea's Nuclear Test," NPR, Sept. 3, 2017, http://tinyurl.com/yaqgv3k5.

[13] The "Face the Nation" episode can be viewed at http://tinyurl.com/y7qkfgk7.

[14] Barbara Starr and Ryan Browne, "US successfully 'intercepts and destroys' target in missile test," CNN, May 31, 2017, http://tinyurl.com/y7pn6ew4.

parts or adequate medical care for soldiers wounded in battle. [73]

Fears of the Soviet Union subsided after the Berlin Wall dividing communist-controlled East Germany from democratic West Germany fell on Nov. 10, 1989. Two years later the Soviet Union collapsed, breaking into 15 separate countries. The Cold War was over. [74]

Fluctuating Spending

After Iraq invaded neighboring Kuwait in August 1990, the United States sent a half-million troops with advanced weaponry to the region. In January 1991, U.S. forces unleashed their massive firepower in Operation Desert Storm, defeating Iraq in a matter of weeks while suffering negligible casualties. [75]

The operation left the Pentagon and the public satisfied with U.S. military readiness, and the Clinton administration and Congress looked to use the money saved from the postwar "peace dividend" to pay for tax cuts and other domestic needs. [76]

In 1993, President Bill Clinton proposed reducing U.S. troops by 108,000 (from 1.7 million), retiring 28 Navy warships and cutting the number of Air Force fighter wings from 28 to 24. He recommended spending $88 billion less on defense over the next four years than his predecessor had recommended.

Defense Secretary Les Aspen said the military would maintain forces capable of "fighting and winning two major regional conflicts that occur nearly simultaneously." He added, "We are not going to withdraw from our involvement around the world." [77]

But Sen. John McCain, R-Ariz., said in November 1993 that U.S. forces were "going hollow." Russia, Ukraine and Kazakhstan, he warned, possessed nuclear weapons and Iran, North Korea and Iraq were seeking to develop them. [78]

South Korea Flexes Its Military Muscles

South Korea test fires its Hyunmu-2 ballistic missile on Sept. 4, 2017, in response to a nuclear test by North Korea the day before (top). South Korean tanks take part in an exercise on Sept. 6, 2017, near the demilitarized zone (DMZ) separating North and South Korea. The U.S. military has some 23,500 personnel at 83 sites in South Korea, and more than 300 tanks and armored vehicles. Its assets in nearby Japan include dozens of ships and submarines as well as helicopters, tactical fighter jets and surveillance planes. In September, over strong objections from China, the United States finished installing an anti-missile system in South Korea.

During a Senate defense appropriations hearing, Army Chief of Staff Gordon R. Sullivan defended the force reductions, which had allowed the military to focus more on modernization. "The information age is upon us, and [we] must take full advantage of the maturation of information processing technology," he said. [79]

Defense budgets continued to drop through the 1990s, and debates over readiness continued as the military repeatedly deployed overseas — for a military intervention in Haiti in 1994, military operations in Bosnia and Kosovo from 1995 to 1998, maintenance of no-fly zones in Iraq beginning in 1993 and humanitarian operations. [80]

On Sept. 11, 2001, the Islamist terrorist group al Qaeda coordinated attacks involving four hijacked passenger airliners. Two crashed into the World Trade Center in New York City, one hit the Pentagon in Virginia and one crashed into a field near Shanksville, Pa. Most Americans said they supported defense spending increases to invade Afghanistan (where al Qaeda was based) in 2001 and Iraq in 2003.

President George W. Bush in March 2003 announced the launch of Operation Iraqi Freedom against the regime of Saddam Hussein, which allegedly had developed nuclear and biological weapons (reports that were later discredited) and had ties to al Qaeda. Bush warned troops would be facing enemies "with no regard for the conventions of war or rules of morality," suggesting a different type of combat than the U.S. armed forces had faced in previous wars. More than 100,000 U.S. troops had been deployed for the attack. [81]

The 21-day invasion sent Saddam and his leaders into hiding, and coalition forces successfully occupied Baghdad, the site of Iraq government. Estimates on the number of civilian casualties in the initial invasion ranged from 3,200 to 7,500, while about 138 U.S. troops were killed between March 20 and May 1. [82]

The U.S. withdrew many troops, but battles continued during the occupation of Baghdad as sectarian violence spread after U.S. forces captured Saddam in December 2003. In 2004, U.S. troops complained about insufficient and aging equipment. Secretary of Defense Donald Rumsfeld said, "You go to war with the Army you have, not the Army you might want or wish to have at a later time." [83]

In 2007, Bush ordered a "surge" that sent 20,000 more soldiers to Iraq, and Congress authorized another $42.3 billion in war funding. [84]

Between fiscal 2001 and fiscal 2008, defense spending increased by more than 60 percent. In 2007, Bush submitted a defense request of $481.4 billion, the highest amount since the Reagan era. [85]

But funding for overseas military operations declined 70 percent from fiscal 2008 to fiscal 2015 as the wars in Iraq and Afghanistan appeared to wind down. The sharpest decline — from $671 billion to $619 billion — was in 2013, due to President Barack Obama's decision to withdraw troops from those countries and because of automatic funding cuts under sequestration. [86]

In February 2013, Pentagon leaders said the United States might soon have a "hollowed-out" force if it did not increase funding. Defense Secretary Leon Panetta said the "budget uncertainty could prompt the most significant military readiness crisis in more than a decade." [87]

However, Obama told troops that "the time of deploying large ground forces with big military footprints to engage in nation-building overseas" was coming to an end. [88]

In late 2016, news reports revealed the Pentagon had not disclosed a 2015 study by the Defense Business Board, detailing how it could save $125 billion in wasteful spending over five years at the Pentagon. [89] ■

CURRENT SITUATION

Military Strategy

Tensions between the United States and North Korea continue to rise as North Korean leader Kim Jong Un and President Trump exchange nuclear threats. In part, to avoid increasing those tensions, Trump probably will not visit the demilitarized zone (DMZ) between North and South Korea when he travels to Asia in November, a White House official said on Oct. 23. Visiting the DMZ has been standard practice for most U.S. commanders-in-chief since Ronald Reagan's presidency. [90]

North Korea's state-run media said on Oct. 19 the United States will face an "unimaginable" military strike from the communist country at an unexpected time, an apparent response to

joint U.S.-South Korean military exercises just off the Korean Peninsula.

Three days later, Trump said the U.S. military is "prepared for anything" if war breaks out with North Korea. [91]

The United States has nearly 40,000 personnel at 112 bases in Japan and 23,500 at 83 sites in South Korea. U.S.

High-stepping Korean People's Army troops in Pyongyang on April 15, 2017, help mark the 105th anniversary of the birth of the late North Korean leader Kim Il Sung. North Korea has been conducting nuclear tests, and its leader, Kim Jong Un, and President Trump have been exchanging nuclear threats. North Korea's state-run media said on Oct. 19 that the United States will face an "unimaginable" military strike, an apparent response to joint U.S.-South Korean military exercises just off the Korean Peninsula.

military assets in the region include more than 300 tanks and armored vehicles stationed in South Korea; helicopters; tactical fighter jets and surveillance planes; dozens of ships and submarines in Japan, including the USS Ronald Reagan, a nuclear-powered aircraft supercarrier. In Guam, more than 3,800 personnel are stationed at Anderson Air Force Base, headquarters for B-52 bombers and fighter jets. [92]

Adm. Harry Harris, who heads U.S. forces in the Pacific, said in August it would be "foolhardy" for foreign adversaries to take this year's Navy accidents as a sign the United States is unprepared to defend itself in the region.

"The U.S. Navy is large, we have a lot of capacity, and we will bring that capacity forward if we need to," Harris said. [93]

Following the collision involving the McCain, Richardson, the chief of naval

operations, ordered an investigation that he said would "examine the process by which we train and certify our forces . . . to make sure that we're doing everything we can to make them ready for operations and war fighting." Two reports issued by the Navy on Nov. 1 blamed a string of crew, training and

navigation errors for the deadly collisions involving the McCain and the USS Fitzgerald. [94]

In September, over strong objections from China, the United States finished installing an anti-missile system in South Korea known as THAAD (for terminal high altitude area defense). South Korea's new liberal president, Moon Jae-in, initially said he would not allow the final four THAAD launchers to deploy, but he reversed course after North Korea tested an ICBM on July 28. [95]

Also in September, the U.S. and Japanese militaries conducted a joint air exercise over the East China Sea that included two Japanese F-15 fighter jets and two U.S. B1-B bombers. [96]

Recent polling finds mixed opinions on whether the United States should take military action against North Korea in response to Pyongyang's progress toward developing a nuclear missile that could hit this country.

In a CNN poll released in August, 50 percent supported military action. But a CBS News poll found just 29 percent support action, with 60 percent of respondents saying the North Korean threat can be contained in other ways.

Chinese troops fire a howitzer during exercises at a training base in China's Gansu province on Sept. 24, 2017. The country's defense spending increased 26 percent between 2013 and 2016. Since 2014, China has been constructing artificial islands in the South China Sea and installing military bases there that U.S. officials say are part of Beijing's plan to dominate Asia.

Getty Images/Visual China Group

Gallup says its polls show that support for military action has increased between 2003 and this year — from 47 percent to 58 percent. [97]

At the same time, the Pentagon is working to suppress talk of military readiness failures. Defense Secretary James Mattis, for example, has told defense officials to classify all readiness information. This year's National Military Strategy, typically released to the public and scheduled to be updated by 2018, also will be classified. [98]

Trump was similarly tight-lipped when he announced in August that he would send more troops to Afghanistan but did

not specify how many or say what results he expects. [99]

Meanwhile, the Pentagon continues to deal with accidents. In June, the Air Force experienced several accidents in one week that destroyed two F-16 Fighting Falcon fighters and a giant unmanned surveillance drone. [100]

The mishaps have raised questions about pilot training and aircraft maintenance, with top brass blaming tight budgets and an aging fleet.

In August, the Marine Corps ordered all its roughly 1,000 aircraft grounded for 24 hours after two crashes that killed 19 service members. And in September, an explosion at Fort Bragg, N.C., during demolition training killed one soldier and injured seven. [101]

Cunningham, the former American Enterprise Institute research associate, says the Army's 2nd Armored Brigade Combat Team of the 1st Infantry Division

struggled to fill positions and find qualified personnel as it prepared to deploy to Germany in September.

Under a new "sustained readiness model" of training, the brigade's leaders retrained their 4,000 troops to handle conventional, combined-arms battles such as those the United States might experience in a war with North Korea. That marked a break with training that for years focused on counterterrorism.

"It's a product of the concern about being ready to fight for anything," Cunningham says, but added that the brigade had to train with old equipment. "Struggling with a lack of available spare parts and maintenance time, the brigade . . . faces significant equipment readiness shortfalls," the institute concluded in its first report, released in May. [102]

Procurement Fixes

In Washington, the Defense Department is proceeding with congressionally mandated changes to its Office of Acquisition, Technology and Logistics in hopes of streamlining the procurement process.

The plan would divide the undersecretary of acquisitions position into two — an undersecretary for research and engineering and an undersecretary for acquisition and sustainment. The research position would focus on improving innovation and getting new technology to troops on time, the Pentagon's report to Congress said. [103]

Pentagon officials say they are turning more to industry for help in developing new technology and speeding production. The Pentagon is exploring strategies "that promise to accelerate development of military products in line with the accelerated evolution of threats," Adam Jay Harrison, a national security research fellow at New York University, said in August. [104]

Debates about military readiness and defense spending, meanwhile, continue among congressional lawmakers and administration officials.

Continued on p. 936

At Issue:

Is the U.S. military in a readiness crisis?

THOMAS DONNELLY
*CO-DIRECTOR, MARILYN WARE
CENTER FOR SECURITY STUDIES,
AMERICAN ENTERPRISE INSTITUTE*

WRITTEN FOR *CQ RESEARCHER*, NOVEMBER 2017

*t*o describe the problems in manpower, training and equipment faced by the military as a "crisis," as a kind of institutional heart attack, is to misunderstand the maladies plaguing the armed forces. What makes headlines — particularly events like this year's two collisions at sea that claimed the lives of 17 sailors — is more symptom than disease, the result of a larger wasting sickness that has been developing for decades.

The principal cause of this decline is poor nutrition: Since the end of the Cold War, the Pentagon has lost — even when the wartime costs of Iraq and Afghanistan are included — in excess of $7 trillion in investment. Meanwhile, the ever-hectic pace of military operations exacerbates the effects of a calorie-deprived defense diet. Service leaders have made "do more with less" their mantra, but it is not a prescription for long-term health.

What does diminished readiness mean in practice? Consider the Army's 2nd Brigade, 1st Infantry Division. This past month, the "Dagger Brigade" of the "Big Red One" deployed from Fort Riley, Kan., to Germany and Poland as part of the European Reassurance Initiative, the centerpiece of the U.S. effort to bolster deterrence of an increasingly aggressive Russia. The initiative was designed in President Barack Obama's second term and has been carried forward by the Trump administration, and Congress has supported it with billions of dollars.

Despite being an apparently favored child, the Dagger Brigade lacks about one-fifth of its intended personnel. It treats its equipment — particularly its aging M-1 Abrams tanks — with exquisite tenderness, emphasizing stationary gunnery over field maneuver. The result is reduced training opportunity. Not only is the unit's manpower barely adequate but constant turnover — especially of midgrade noncommissioned officers who serve as crew chiefs and in first-line leadership roles — is crippling to unit cohesion.

Indeed, it is difficult to overemphasize how personnel shortages and mismatches contribute to the military's readiness shortfalls. Even more than curtailed modernization or reduced operations and maintenance funding, it is manpower cutbacks that have most sapped the services' strength. When the Navy lacks sufficient numbers of qualified surface warfare officers, accidents at sea are all but inevitable.

Thus, the remedy for the disease isn't a surgical intervention or a miracle medicine — least of all through annual supplements to starvation-level budgets — but rather a long-term program of nourishment, rehabilitation and restoration.

MICHAEL O'HANLON
*SENIOR FELLOW IN FOREIGN POLICY,
BROOKINGS INSTITUTION*

WRITTEN FOR *CQ RESEARCHER*, NOVEMBER 2017

*a*s we begin yet another fiscal year with a stopgap funding measure known as a "continuing resolution" rather than a proper annual budget, Pentagon leaders are understandably frustrated. Such arrangements prevent the Department of Defense from entering multiyear contracts that can save money, interfere with innovation and disrupt training and hiring by leaving planners unsure of what the future holds.

However, these budgetary shenanigans, combined with recent high-profile accidents like last summer's *USS Fitzgerald* and *USS McCain* tragedies, have led numerous officials to wrongly declare a military-readiness crisis. That exaggerates the problem and creates unrealistic expectations of what might be needed, or realistically available, to address it. Pentagon officials need to think of what they can do to mitigate readiness problems by better managing the forces at hand. Numerous options are available:

• The Navy can lighten its busy schedule, allowing sailors more time to train and technicians more time to maintain ships and aircraft, by modifying its operations abroad. Rather than having 100 ships out of a fleet of less than 300 at sea at a time, it can scale back by 10 to 25 percent. It can allow some gaps in forward presence rather than slavishly insisting on maintaining continuous operations in both the Persian Gulf and Pacific fleets. It also can use "crew swaps" more often, keeping surface combatants deployed abroad for one to two years at a time and rotating crews to them by airplane.

• The Air Force can alleviate strain on the Navy's aircraft carriers by stationing more combat aircraft in the Persian Gulf region.

• The Army can permanently base one brigade of combat forces in Korea and another in Poland, rather than maintaining its presence in these countries with unit rotations.

• The Marines can scale back the permanent presence of forces on Okinawa (where they number some 15,000, most on temporary deployment), if Japan would provide more space in ports for prepositioning amphibious U.S. Navy ships. That could allow Marines to fly quickly from California and marry with pre-stationed equipment in a crisis.

Today's military is indeed under strain. But the American armed forces are far from unready, and where they have problems, the defense establishment has many options besides waiting for a big influx of additional dollars.

Statement of Ownership Management, Circulation

Act of Aug. 12, 1970: Section 3685,
Title 39, United States Code

Title of Publication: CQ Researcher. USPS Publication number: 006-785. Date of filing: October 1, 2017. Frequency of issue: Weekly (Except for 3/24, 5/26, 6/30, 8/11, 8/18, 11/24, 12/22, 12/29/17). No. of issues published annually: 44. Annual subscription price for indivduals: $1,246. Annual subscription price for institutions: $1,345. Location of known office of publication: SAGE Publications, Inc., 2455 Teller Road, Thousand Oaks, CA 91320. Names and addresses of publisher and executive editor: Publisher, SAGE Publications, Inc., 2455 Teller Road, Thousand Oaks, CA 91320; Executive Editor, Thomas J. Billitteri, CQ Press, an imprint of SAGE Publications, Inc., 2600 Virginia Avenue, N.W., Suite 600, Washington, D.C. 20037. Owner: SAGE Publications, Inc., McCune Inter-Vivos Trust, David F. McCune, 2455 Teller Road, Thousand Oaks, CA 91320. Known bondholders, mortgagees and other security holders owning or holding 1 percent or more of total amount of bonds, mortgages or other securities: None.

Extent and Nature of Circulation	Average Number of Copies of Each Issue During Preceding 12 months	Actual Number of Copies of Single Issue Published Nearest to Filing Date
A. Total number of copies printed (Net press run)	317	295
B. Paid and/or requested circulation		
(1) Paid/requested outside-county mail subscriptions stated on Form 3541	250	228
(2) Paid in-county subscriptions stated on Form 3541	0	0
(3) Sales through dealers and carriers, street vendors, counter sales, and other non-USPS paid distribution	0	0
(4) Other classes mailed through the USPS	0	0
C. Total paid and/or requested circulation	250	228
D. Free distribution by mail (Samples, complimentary, and other free copies)		
(1) Outside-county as stated on Form 3541	0	0
(2) In-county as stated on Form 3541	0	0
(3) Other classes mailed through the USPS	0	0
E. Free distribution outside the mail (Carriers or other means)	0	0
F. Total free distribution	0	0
G. Total distribution	250	228
H. Copies not distributed	67	67
I. Total	317	295
J. Percent paid and/or requested circulation	100%	100%

Continued from p. 934

In July, the House passed a bill that would authorize about $696 billion for defense spending in fiscal 2018, including $621.5 billion for core operations and $75 billion in war funding. The Senate approved a version in October that would authorize $700 billion, including $640 billion for core operations. Both bills would exceed spending caps set by the 2011 Budget Control Act, which limits Pentagon spending to $549 billion each year. [105]

Republicans and some Democrats continue to blame the automatic spending cuts required under sequestration for damaging military readiness. However, a proposal by Sen. Tom Cotton, R-Ark., to repeal sequestration failed in the Senate in September. [106]

Meanwhile, the House defeated a proposal by Rep. Scott Perry, R-Pa., that would have barred defense officials from addressing climate change. "We would be remiss in our efforts to protect our national security to not fully account for the risk climate change poses to our bases, our readiness and to the fulfillment of our armed forces' mission," said Rep. Elise Stefanik, R-N.Y., who voted against the proposal. [107]

The Pentagon continues to push to close what it says are uneeded military bases. In 2016, it told Congress that if the Defense Department shuttered 22 percent of its bases, the military could use the $2 billion annual savings on "readiness, modernization and other more pressing national security requirements." But the House and Senate rejected base closing proposals this year. Lawmakers with bases in their districts worry that closing them would damage local economies. [108] ∎

OUTLOOK

Evolving Threats

Assessing U.S. military readiness will be as complex in five years as it is now, says Junor at the National Defense University, "but what I hope is that our ability to monitor and manage it will increase." She says data analysis now allows military leaders to see patterns in production lines that could help make Pentagon procurement more efficient.

Scharre at the Center for a New American Security says the United States is the world's only real global military power. "It can go anywhere it wants to . . . and project a significant amount of military capacity," he says.

But U.S. military leaders still face a constantly evolving array of threats.

Cyberwarfare, for example, "affects everything — the control of weapons, the communications between forces, the speed with which things can be done, the way in which one's support systems can be screwed up," says Betts of Columbia University.

Patrolling the seas will remain crucial to military preparedness, according to retired Navy Adm. James Stavridis, dean of the Fletcher School of Law and Diplomacy at Tufts University. "We are not seriously challenged today, but if we neglect fleet size and military spending, the day will come when we cannot take for granted the sea lanes of communication to and from our continent," he said. "This is the basic building block of our [naval] strategy."

Stavridis said the United States will continue to cope with the Chinese military's construction of artificial islands in the South China Sea and will need a long-term maritime plan for dealing with North Korea. [109]

The fight to contain terrorism shows no signs of ending, even though American-backed forces have ousted the Islamic State jihadist group from its base of operations in Raqqa, Syria. [110]

U.S. officials also must reconsider their commitments in Europe, the Middle East and South and East Asia, and develop strategies to tackle climate change, according to Jeremi Suri, a history professor at the University of Texas, Austin, and Benjamin Valentino, an associate professor of government at Dartmouth College. [111]

One key to military readiness is a better system at the Pentagon for setting priorities to make sure troops and other military assets are not stretched too thin, according to Goldstein at the Naval War College.

"A lot of people have been telling us we're the greatest. Maybe this holds for 10 more years," Goldstein says. "If you go in all directions, you can't do everything well . . . you have to choose, you have to make priorities. Yet we refuse. We say we'll do everything."

The Center for a New American Security's Blume warns that if the Pentagon insists on preparing for everything, it will bankrupt the nation. "The appetite for more security is bottomless," she says. ∎

Notes

[1] "US Navy ship and oil tanker collide near Singapore," BBC, Aug. 21, 2017, https://tinyurl.com/ybwfhhqp; Richard C. Paddock, "Re-mains of 10 Sailors Who Died in Navy Collision Are Found," The New York Times, Aug. 27, 2017, https://tinyurl.com/yd27rxdh; Julia Jacobo, Luis Martinez and Emily Shapiro, "USS McCain the 4th Navy warship to crash in Asia this year," ABC News, https://tinyurl.com/ya3ovx74.

[2] Eric P. Schmitt, "Navy Ships Kept at Sea Despite Training and Maintenance Needs, Admiral Says," The New York Times, Sept. 7, 2017, https://tinyurl.com/ychs4sxm; Mike Fabey, "North Korean missiles are testing a stressed U.S. defense net," SpaceNews, Aug. 31, 2017, http://tinyurl.com/y9cna9e2.

[3] Eric P. Schmitt, "Navy Collisions That Killed 17 Sailors Were 'Avoidable,' Official Inquiry Reports," The New York Times, Nov. 1, 2017, http://tinyurl.com/ydb2o8hs.

[4] Dave Philipps and Eric P. Schmitt, "Fatigue and Training Gaps Spell Disaster at Sea, Sailors Warn," The New York Times, Aug.27, 2017, https://tinyurl.com/ybxcw6d5; Kevin Sieff, "In Afghanistan, redeployed U.S. soldiers still coping with demons of post-traumatic stress," The Washington Post, Aug. 18, 2013, https://tinyurl.com/ya9ps3me; and Dave Ruppe, "Five Air Force F-16s Crashed in July," ABC News, Aug. 7, 2017, https://tinyurl.com/y8cx2dpj.

[5] Daniel Goure, "The Measure of a Superpower: A Two Major Regional Contingency Military for the 21st Century," Heritage Foundation, Jan. 25, 2013, https://tinyurl.com/y9d7pzfo; Paul Szoldra, "How the US military is beating hackers at their own game," Business Insider, May 24, 2016, https://tinyurl.com/h8brocx; and Jim Sciutto, "US military prepares for the next frontier: Space war," CNN, Nov. 29, 2016, https://tinyurl.com/jzq3rhp.

[6] Tom O'Connor, "What Russia's Military Looks Like Compared to the U.S.," Newsweek, April 7, 2017, https://tinyurl.com/ybwg32uh; Lauren Carroll, "Obama: US spends more on military than next 8 nations combined," PolitiFact, Jan. 13, 2016, http://tinyurl.com/hnmnyrk; and "Defense Budget Overview," Office of the Under Secretary of Defense (Comptroller), May 2017, https://tinyurl.com/y8p3wzbu.

[7] "U.S. military leaders voice concern about readiness of forces," Reuters, March 16, 2016, https://tinyurl.com/y8szlza8.

[8] Jim Garamone, "Dunford Urges Congress to Protect U.S. Competitive Advantage," U.S. Department of Defense News, June 12, 2017, http://tinyurl.com/y7qfqaha.

[9] Daniel Brown and Skye Gould, "The U.S. has 1.3 million troops stationed around the world — here are the major hotspots," Business Insider, Aug. 31, 2017, https://tinyurl.com/ybnnlxr6; W.J. Hennigan, "U.S. has more troops in Afghanistan than previously disclosed, Pentagon reveals," Los Angeles Times, Aug. 30, 2017, https://tinyurl.com/yaexank2; "U.S. Navy," 2017 Index of Military Strength, Heritage Foundation, https://tinyurl.com/yazxgs43; "U.S. Air Force," 2017 Index of Military Strength, Heritage Foundation, https://tinyurl.com/y7wam7fz; K.K. Rebecca Lai et al., "Is America's Military Big Enough?" The New York Times, March 22, 2017, https://tinyurl.com/ktkc8pt; Kingston Reif, "U.S. Nuclear Modernization Programs," Arms Control Association, August 2017, https://tinyurl.com/7z7yulu; and Julian Borger, "New push to remove tactical nuclear weapons from Europe," The Guardian, Feb. 3, 2012, https://tinyurl.com/ycfzkz2q.

[10] Steven Brill, "Donald Trump, Palantir, And The Crazy Battle To Clean Up A Multibillion-Dollar Military Procurement Swamp," Fortune, https://tinyurl.com/lths7lk.

[11] Ryan Browne and Jeremy Herb, "Congressional Republicans see Trump's defense budget hike as insufficient," CNN, May 23, 2017, https://tinyurl.com/yd3bgah9; Todd Harrison, "The Enduring Dilemma of Overseas Contingency Operations Funding," Defense360, Jan. 11, 2017, https://tinyurl.com/y8votwpq.

[12] "Defense Budget Overview," op. cit.; Annie Lowrey, "Why Sequestration Is Poised to Kill Trump's Budget," The Atlantic, March 16, 2017, https://tinyurl.com/kgzlam4; and Kristina Wong, "Committee chairmen urge Republicans to reverse defense cuts," The Hill, March 10, 2015, https://tinyurl.com/ydz8u8bn.

[13] Vivienne Machi, "Lawmakers, Pentagon Officials Warn of 'Corrosive' Effects of Continuing Resolution (UPDATED)," National Defense Magazine, Sept. 7, 2017, https://tinyurl.com/yc2wsa3o.

[14] "National Security Implications of Climate-Related Risks and a Changing Climate," Department of Defense, July 23, 2015, http://tinyurl.com/p5qlyz9. For background, see William Wanlund, "Climate Change and National Security," CQ Researcher, Sept. 22, 2017, pp. 773-796.

[15] "Defense Budget Overview," op. cit.

[16] James Stavridis, Sea Power: The History and Geopolitics of the World's Oceans (2017), pp. 36-37; Eleanor Ross, "How and Why China is Building Islands in the South China Sea," Newsweek, March 29, 2017, http://tinyurl.com/y9qxh49e.

[17] Eric P. Schmitt, "Vast Exercise Demonstrated Russia's Growing Military Prowess," The New York Times, Oct. 1, 2017, http://tinyurl.com/y9566e7w.

[18] Michael Rubin, "Iran: Domestic Weapons Production up 69 Percent," American Enterprise

Institute, March 13, 2017, https://tinyurl.com/y9bdvt5d; "Iran: US Presence in Bahrain in the Crosshairs?" Foreign Military Studies Office Operational Environment Watch, U.S. Army, March 2017, p. 6, http://tinyurl.com/y85vkyzs; "Iran Tests Ballistic Missile and Rejects 'Threats,'" Reuters, *The New York Times*, Sept. 23, 2017, http://tinyurl.com/y7jtloud.

[19] Colin Clark, "CJCS Dunford Calls For Strategic Shifts; 'At Peace Or At War Is Insufficient,' " *Breaking Defense*, Sept. 21, 2016, https://tinyurl.com/ycob9ku5.

[20] Ian E. Rinehart, "The Chinese Military: Overview and Issues for Congress," summary page, Congressional Research Service, March 24, 2016, http://tinyurl.com/ju29zdc.

[21] Jeremy Herb, "Trump order sets military buildup in motion," *Politico*, Jan. 27, 2017, http://tinyurl.com/jxplbkn; Lawrence Kapp *et al.*, "How Big Should the Army Be? Considerations for Congress," Congressional Research Service, Sept. 2, 2016, p. 2, http://tinyurl.com/yc3me67f.

[22] Steven Kosiak, "Is the U.S. Military Getting Smaller and Older? And How Much Should We Care?" Center for a New American Security, March 14, 2017, p. 6, http://tinyurl.com/hby9fga.

[23] Dan Goure, "Essay: Is the U.S. Military Too Small?" CBS, Nov. 23, 2016, http://tinyurl.com/yczu2wb6.

[24] "Report to the President and the Congress of the United States," National Commission on the Future of the Army, Jan. 28, 2016, pp. 2-3, https://tinyurl.com/ychps9lv.

[25] Statement of Lt. Gen. Gina M. Grosso before the Subcommittee on Personnel, Committee on Armed Services, U.S. House of Representatives, March 29, 2017, http://tinyurl.com/y97639mn.

[26] "Navy Force Structure: Sustainable Plan and Comprehensive Assessment Needed to Mitigate Long-Term Risks to Ships Assigned to Overseas Homeports," Government Accountability Office, May 2015, https://tinyurl.com/yd95vfjj.

[27] Scott Maucione, "Milley joins ranks pleading for readiness over capacity," Federal News Radio, Jan. 12, 2017, http://tinyurl.com/ybhbch38.

[28] Todd Harrison, "Trump's Bigger Military Won't Necessarily Make the US Stronger or Safer," *Defense One*, March 16, 2017, http://tinyurl.com/ydbo3r7q.

[29] Michael Hughes, "What went wrong with the F-35, Lockheed Martin's Joint Strike Fighter?" *The Conversation*, June 13, 2017, http://tinyurl.com/ybzn6uqt.

[30] Carl Prine, "U.S. defense secretary orders review of F-35 Joint Strike Fighter program," *The San Diego Union-Tribune*, Jan. 27, 2017, http://tinyurl.com/y864uwjc.

[31] Hughes, *op. cit.*; Kyle Mizokami, "The Cost of the F-35 Is Going Up Again," *Popular Mechanics*, July 17, 2017, http://tinyurl.com/ydc4kha3/; Doug Cameron and Andrew Tangel, "Donald Trump Presses Fight Over F-35 Jet Costs," *The Wall Street Journal*, Dec. 12, 2017, http://tinyurl.com/y7ss7x72; and Carl Prine, "Pentagon brass seek culture change, innovations in buying weapons," *The San Diego Union-Tribune*, Feb. 22, 2017, http://tinyurl.com/y9kjkvwc.

[32] "High-Risk Series: Progress on Many High-Risk Areas, While Substantial Efforts Needed on Others," Government Accountability Office, February 2017, p. 269, https://tinyurl.com/y83krljd; Moshe Schwartz, "Defense Acquisitions: How DOD Acquires Weapon Systems and Recent Efforts to Reform the Process," Congressional Research Service, May 23, 2014, https://tinyurl.com/ybnzyaa6.

[33] J. Ronald Fox, *Defense Acquisition Reform, 1960-2009: An Elusive Goal* (2010), http://tinyurl.com/ycecz2ky.

[34] Roxana Tiron, "Congress throws Boeing a lifeline for Super Hornet," Bloomberg News, *St. Louis Post-Dispatch*, Jan. 22, 2014, http://tinyurl.com/y8mr7ors.

[35] Adam K. Raymond, "How The Humvee Failed On The Battlefield And Sparked A Culture War Back Home," *Task and Purpose*, March, 18, 2017, http://tinyurl.com/ybenrn85.

[36] Elizabeth Weise, "Could hackers be behind the U.S. Navy collisions" *USA Today*, Aug. 23, 2017, http://tinyurl.com/yakvufmf.

[37] Jeevan Vasagar and Geoff Dyer, "Chinese hackers targeted US aircraft carrier," *Financial Times*, Oct. 21, 2016, https://tinyurl.com/yantc4ej; John Markoff, "Before the Gunfire, Cyberattacks," *The New York Times*, Aug. 12, 2008, https://tinyurl.com/yblvebvo; David E. Sanger and Charlie Savage, "U.S. Says Russia Directed Hacks to Influence Elections," *The New York Times*, Oct. 7, 2016, https://tinyurl.com/y9d297mh; Victor Luckerson, "Everything We Know About the Massive Sony Hack," *Time*, Dec. 4, 2014, https://tinyurl.com/lvy3j5m.

[38] Paul D. Shinkman, "America Is Losing the Cyber War," *U.S. News & World Report*, Sept. 29, 2016, http://tinyurl.com/yda3te7j.

[39] "Lt. Gen. William J. Bender: Breaking Barriers: The Air Force and the Future of Cyberpower," speech at Carnegie Council for Ethics in International Affairs, March 9, 2017, https://tinyurl.com/ycs9zfuv.

[40] John M. Donnelly, "Exclusive: Aging Helicopters Could Make U.S. Nukes Vulnerable to Terrorists," *CQ Roll Call*, Feb. 29, 2016, http://tinyurl.com/yayjzx9m.

[41] Luis Simon, "Demystifying the A2/AD Buzz," *War on the Rocks*, Jan. 4, 2017, https://tinyurl.com/ydg9xs49.

[42] Rahul Chadha, "China is looking to invest billions of dollars into artificial intelligence," *Business Insider*, July 29, 2017, http://tinyurl.com/y8y5enbh.

[43] Thomas J. Christensen, "China's Military Might: First the Good News," Bloomberg View, June 4, 2015, http://tinyurl.com/yctch3x6.

[44] Benjamin Powers, "How Intelligent Drones Are Shaping the Future of Warfare," *Rolling Stone*, March 14, 2017, http://tinyurl.com/grglrkg.

[45] Katherine Owens, "Army electronic warfare technology attacks and causes shift in tank," *Defense Systems*, June 5, 2017, http://tinyurl.com/yc23kzea; Jared Keller, "The Army Can Now Stop Enemy Tanks In Their Tracks Without Firing A Shot," *Task & Purpose*, June 8, 2017, http://tinyurl.com/y9xaw54j.

[46] David Cenciotti, "Watch an F-16's Automatic Ground Collision Avoidance System save an unconscious pilot from certain death," *Business Insider*, Sept. 14, 2016, https://tinyurl.com/ya9wywha.

[47] Patrick Tucker, "The War Over soon-to-be-Outdated Army Intelligence Systems," *Defense*

About the Author

Christina L. Lyons, a freelance journalist in the Washington, D.C., area, writes primarily about U.S. government and politics. She is a contributing author for CQ Press reference books, including *CQ's Guide to Congress*, and was a contributing editor for Bloomberg BNA's *International Trade Daily*. A former editor for Congressional Quarterly, she also was co-author of CQ's *Politics in America 2010*. Lyons began her career as a newspaper reporter in Maryland and then covered environment and health care policy on Capitol Hill. She has a master's degree in political science from American University.

One, July 5, 2016, http://tinyurl.com/y8pfnzou; Daniel Wilson, "Army Says It Didn't Wrongly Reject Palantir For $206M Deal," *Law360*, April 14, 2017, http://tinyurl.com/y7aouz9d; and Jacqueline Klimas and Bryan Bender, "Palantir goes from Pentagon outsider to Mattis' inner circle," *Politico*, June 11, 2017, http://tinyurl.com/y84hm4z6.

[48] E. Wayne Carp, *To Starve the Army at Pleasure: Continental Army Administration and American Political Culture, 1775-1783* (1984), pp. 55-56, http://tinyurl.com/y7yx8lfr.

[49] NCC Staff, "On this day: Congress officially creates the U.S. Army," *Constitution Daily*, National Constitution Center, http://tinyurl.com/ycdfm97y.

[50] Richard K. Betts, *Military Readiness* (1995), pp. 5-6.

[51] James A. Huston, The Sinews of War: Army Logistics 1775-1953, U.S. Army, Office of the Chief of Military History, p. 277, http://tinyurl.com/y9p3b8g7.

[52] Stavridis, *op. cit.*, p. 28; Graham Watson, "The United States Navy: Its Rise to Global Parity, 1900-1922, Naval-History.Net, http://tinyurl.com/yal7dsyv.

[53] "Great White Fleet," Theodore Roosevelt Center at Dickinson State University, undated, http://tinyurl.com/nrvgo7a; McKinley, *op. cit.*

[54] Mackubin Thomas Owens, "How the U.S. Army Came of Age," *National Review*, May 8, 2017, http://tinyurl.com/y9qs9kjw; "Must Exert All Our Power: To Bring a 'Government That Is Running Amuck to Terms," *The New York Times*, April 3, 1917, http://tinyurl.com/ycodxj65; Stavridis, *op. cit.*, p. 75.

[55] "Full text of 'The Queenstown patrol, 1917: the diary of commander Joseph Knefler Taussig, U.S Navy,' " Historical Monograph Series, Naval War College, https://tinyurl.com/ybhb8py6.

[56] Betts, *op. cit.*, pp. 7-8.

[57] *Ibid.*, p. 8; Huston, *op. cit.*, p. 657.

[58] Thomas M. Meagher, *Financing Armed Conflict, Volume 2* (2017), p. 195, https://tinyurl.com/yb9z7brs.

[59] Betts, *op. cit.*, p. 12.

[60] John A. Garrity, *A Short History of the American Nation* (1971), p. 442; This Day in History: Atomic bomb dropped on Hiroshima," The History Channel, undated, http://tinyurl.com/kmftwv7.

[61] U.S. Department of Defense, "Selected Manpower Statistics: Fiscal Year 1988," as quoted in "Downsizing America's Armed Forces," *CQ Researcher*, June 8, 1990.

[62] Robert Higgs, "Policy Analysis: U.S. Military Spending in the Cold War Era: Opportunity Costs, Foreign Crises, and Domestic Constraints," Cato Institute, 1988, p. 2, http://tinyurl.

com/y8oafjs7; "Defense spending and troop levels after major U.S. wars," *PolitiFact*, https://tinyurl.com/yclarn5d.

[63] T.R. Fehrenbach, *This Kind of War: The Classic Korean War History* (1963), p. 27.

[64] Betts, *op. cit.*, pp. 15-16.

[65] *Ibid.*, p. 18; Chester J. Pach Jr., "Dwight D. Eisenhower: Foreign Affairs," Miller Center, University of Virginia, http://tinyurl.com/yaaamecy.

[66] Donald A. Carter, "The U.S. Military Response to the 1960-62 Berlin Crisis," U.S. Army Center of Military History, 2011, p. 2, http://tinyurl.com/yb5grsqu; Charles E. Heller and William A. Stofft, *America's First Battles: 1776-1965* (1986), pp. 300-302.

[67] Heller and Stofft, *op. cit.*, pp. 300-305; Hanson W. Baldwin, "Shortage of Arms and Men Plagues Army and Reserve," *The New York Times*, July 21, 1965, http://tinyurl.com/yavvdju9.

[68] "This Day in History: Congressman claims M-16 is defective," History Channel, undated, http://tinyurl.com/28y29rn.

[69] "Vietnam War," History.com, 2009, http://tinyurl.com/pgmw6nq; Alex Dixon, "July marks 40th anniversary of all-volunteer Army," Army News Service, July 2, 2013, http://tinyurl.com/k9unoz3

[70] Richard Halloran, "$40 Billion is Urged to Modernize Army," *The New York Times*, Nov. 30, 1980, http://tinyurl.com/ycezz3ex.

[71] Betts, *op. cit.*, p. 21; Richard Halloran, "Army Reporting Key Gains in Recruiting and Readiness," *The New York Times*, Sept. 7, 1981, http://tinyurl.com/y88cq8po; Bernard Weinraub, "Congress is in doubt over cost and need in Air Force Buildup," *The New York Times*, April 8, 1982, http://tinyurl.com/yarl97x5.

[72] Philip M. Boffey, " 'Star Wars' and Mankind: Unforeseeable Directions," *The New York Times*, March 8, 1985, http://tinyurl.com/yagylbqq; Betts, *op. cit.*, p. 21.

[73] Richard Halloran, "Despite Arms Buildup, Experts Say U.S. Is Not Ready For War," *The New York Times*, March 24, 1987, http://tinyurl.com/ya9eyyqz.

[74] Laurence Dodds, "Berlin Wall: How the Wall came down, as it happened 25 years ago," *The Telegraph*, Nov. 9, 2014, http://tinyurl.com/pjju9g3.

[75] Betts, *op. cit.*, p. 22.

[76] "Downsizing America's armed forces," *CQ Researcher*, 1990.

[77] Les Aspen, "Report on the Bottom-Up Review," Department of Defense, October 1993, pp. iii, 2, http://tinyurl.com/ycmf5r8m.

[78] "Going Hollow: The Warnings of Our Chiefs of Staff," press release, Office of U.S. Sen. John McCain, Nov. 17, 1993, http://tinyurl.com/yae5aorl.

[79] "Full text of 'Department of Defense appropriations for 1995: hearings before a subcommittee of the Committee on Appropriations, House of Representatives, One Hundred Third Congress, second session,' " Feb. 24, 1994, p. 168, http://tinyurl.com/y7y4yoaw.

[80] "Paying for Military Readiness and Upkeep: Trends in Operations and Maintenance Spending," Congressional Budget Office, September 1997, http://tinyurl.com/yday65sg.

[81] President's Radio Address, "President Discusses Beginning of Operation Iraqi Freedom," The White House, March 22, 2003, http://tinyurl.com/y8dxdng6; "U.S. has 100,000 troops in Kuwait," CNN, Feb. 18, 2003, http://tinyurl.com/y7pnc47y.

[82] Jonathan Steele, "Body counts," *The Guardian*, May 27, 2003, http://tinyurl.com/ycon7h2q; Reuters staff, "Timeline: invasion, surge, withdrawal; U.S. forces in Iraq," Reuters, Dec. 18, 2011, http://tinyurl.com/yacsz95t.

[83] Eric P. Schmitt, "Iraq-Bound Troops Confront Rumsfeld Over Lack of Armor," *The New York Times*, Dec. 8, 2004, http://tinyurl.com/y7ocvwbq.

[84] Thomas Donnelly, "The Readiness Vortex," *Strategika*, May 2016, p. 3, http://tinyurl.com/yclsmfa3; Josh White and Ann Scott Tyson, "Increase in War Funding Sought," *The Washington Post*, Sept. 27, 2007, http://tinyurl.com/yamcal9r.

[85] Anthony H. Cordesman, "The Changing Challenges of US Defense Spending: An Update," Center for Strategic and International Studies, Sept. 24, 2007, http://tinyurl.com/y8wgab7r; Ann Scott Tyson, "Bush's Defense Budget Biggest Since Reagan Era," *The Washington Post*, Feb. 6, 2007, http://tinyurl.com/2q3t63.

[86] Dinah Walker, "Trends in U.S. Military Spending," Maurice R. Greenberg Center for Geo Economic Studies, Council on Foreign Relations, July 15, 2014, p. 1, http://tinyurl.com/y8rvel46; Louis Jacobson and Amy Sherman, "PolitiFact Sheet: Military spending under Obama and Congress," *PolitiFact*, Dec. 14, 2015, http://tinyurl.com/qercoka.

[87] Jared Serbu, "By year's end, troops will be unable to respond to crises, Pentagon says," Federal News Radio, Feb. 4, 2013, http://tinyurl.com/y8yl5m8e; Russell Rumbaugh, "Defining Readiness: Background for Congress," Congressional Research Service, June 14, 2017, p. 1, http://tinyurl.com/y8k4yahj.

[88] President Barack Obama, "Remarks by the President," Joint Base McGuire-Dix-Lakehurst, N.J., Dec. 15, 2014, http://tinyurl.com/y97nwbxt.

[89] Craig Whitlock and Bob Woodward, "Pentagon buries evidence of $125 billion in bureaucratic

waste," *The Washington Post*, Dec. 5, 2016, http://tinyurl.com/y8lfcb39.

[90] David Nakamura, "Trump likely won't visit Korean demilitarized zone during Asia trip, White House says," *The Washington Post*, Oct. 23, 2017, https://tinyurl.com/ybtj7kyo.

[91] Choe Sang-Hun and Austin Ramzy, "South Korea and U.S. Begin Drills as North Warns of Rising Tensions," *The New York Times*, Aug. 21, 2017, http://tinyurl.com/y8wlnfrh; "North Korea warns U.S. of 'unimaginable strike,' " CBS News, Oct. 19, 2017, http://tinyurl.com/ybu9wvm8; and Joshua Nevett, "Donald Trump warns North Korea US is 'totally prepared' for WAR in shock interview," *Daily Star*, Oct. 22, 2017, http://tiny url.com/yan75tt8.

[92] Oliver Holmes, "What is the US military's presence near North Korea?" *The Guardian*, Aug. 9, 2017, https://tinyurl.com/y7pmd9d6.

[93] Tom O'Connor, "U.S. Military Commander Warns Enemies Not To Test Forces After USS John McCain Crash," *Newsweek*, Aug. 22, 2017, https://tinyurl.com/y85zyfck.

[94] John Kirby, "US Navy plans operational pause following warship collisions," CNN, Aug. 21, 2017, https://tinyurl.com/ybhpe6cq; Schmitt, *op. cit.*, Nov. 1, 2017.

[95] Seema Mody, "China lashes out as South Korea puts an American anti-missile system in place," CNBC, March 17, 2017, http://tinyurl.com/y72t9e5d; Bridget Martin, "Moon Jae-In's THAAD Conundrum: South Korea's "candlelight president" faces strong citizen opposition on missile defense," *The Asia Pacific Journal*, Sept. 15, 2017, https://tinyurl.com/yafjl8rb.

[96] The Associated Press, "North Korea calls Trump's threat a 'load of nonsense,' " *Politico*, Aug. 9, 2017, http://tinyurl.com/y8muoa3ej; David E. Sanger and Choe Sang-Hun, "North Korean Nuclear Test Draws U.S. Warning of 'Massive Military Response," *The New York Times*, Sept. 2, 2017, http://tinyurl.com/ybo27 bcc; and Jesse Byrnes, "US, Japan conduct air exercises over East China Sea," *The Hill*, Sept. 9, 2017, http://tinyurl.com/y89qb4lw.

[97] Scott Clement and Emily Guskin, "Polls show mixed support for military action against North Korea, but suggest it could rise," *The Washington Post*, Aug. 10, 2017, http://tinyurl.com/y76r4w3w; Lydia Saad, "More Back U.S. Military Action vs. North Korea Than in 2003," Gallup News, Sept. 15, 2017, http://tinyurl.com/ybvpnneg.

[98] Maggie Ybarra, "How the U.S. Military Is Trying to Mask Its Readiness Crisis," *The National Interest*, May 18, 2017, http://tinyurl.com/yavxvxta; Colin Clark, "CJCS Dunford Calls For Strategic Shifts; 'At Peace Or At War Is Insufficient," *Breaking*

FOR MORE INFORMATION

Center for a New American Security, 1152 15th St., N.W., Suite 950, Washington, DC 20005; 202-456-9400; www.cnas.org. Think tank that researches warfare issues and the status and future of the U.S. military.

Center for Strategic and International Studies, 1616 Rhode Island Ave., N.W., Washington, DC 20036; 202-775-3242; www.csis.org. Think tank that studies the U.S. military and defense issues; affiliated with Georgetown University.

Hudson Institute, 1201 Pennsylvania Ave., N.W., Suite 400, Washington, DC 20004; 202-974-2400; www.hudson.org. Think tank that studies the U.S. military.

National Defense University Institute for National Strategic Studies, Fort Lesley J. McNair, 300 5th Ave., S.W., Washington, DC 20319-5066; 202-685-4700; www.ndu.edu. Researches military readiness and the federal procurement process.

Secure World Foundation, 1779 Massachusetts Ave., N.W., Suite 720, Washington, DC 20036; 202-568-6212. Advocates for the peaceful use of space; researches the status and security of U.S. and foreign orbiting satellites.

Union of Concerned Scientists, 2 Brattle Square, Cambridge, MA 02138-3780; 617-547-5552; www.ucsusa.org. Supports arms control, maintains a database of U.S. and foreign orbiting satellites and tracks development of anti-satellite weapons.

U.S. Naval War College, 686 Cushing Road, Newport, RI 02841-1207; 401-841-1310; usnwc.edu. Studies the U.S. Navy and naval defense programs in China and Russia.

Defense, Sept. 21, 2016, http://tinyurl.com/y8k6m94a.

[99] Julie Hirschfeld Davis and Mark Landler, "Trump Outlines New Afghanistan War Strategy With Few Details," *The New York Times*, Aug. 21, 2017, http://tinyurl.com/y74lorj9.

[100] Kyle Mizokami, "The U.S. Air Force Just Had an Awful Week," *Popular Mechanics*, June 26, 2017, http://tinyurl.com/yaldw9ga.

[101] Ryan Browne, "Military aircraft accidents costing lives, billions of dollars," CNN, June 20, 2016, http://tinyurl.com/y9y9lbgc; "Marine Corps orders all of its aircraft grounded following deadly crashes," Fox News, Aug. 11, 2017, http://tinyurl.com/yb5ozv6x; and Thomas Gibbons-Neff, "One Special Forces soldier killed, seven injured during demolition training," *The Washington Post*, Sept. 14, 2017, http://tinyurl.com/ycpdfm9f.

[102] James M. Cunningham and Thomas Donnelly, "Army Readiness Assessment, Vol. 1," American Enterprise Institute, May 2017, http://tinyurl.com/yawpwwft; Stephanie Casanova, " 'Atlantic Resolve': Dagger Brigade cases colors ahead of deployment," *The Mercury*, Sept. 6, 2017, http://tinyurl.com/yaxmhuez.

[103] "Document: Pentagon Plan to Split Research and Development from Acquisition," *USNI News*, Aug. 2, 2017, http://tinyurl.com/y9bno3ct.

[104] Sydney J. Freedberg Jr., "Army Chief Milley Turns To Industry For Network Overhaul," *Breaking Defense*, July 21, 2017, http://tiny

url.com/y8ysev4p; Adam Jay Harrison, "The Pentagon's Pivot: How Lead Users Are Transforming Defense Product Development," *Defense Horizons*, August 2017, https://tinyurl.com/yahgrp97.

[105] Sheryl Gay Stolberg, "Senate Passes $700 Billion Pentagon Bill, More Money Than Trump Sought," *The New York Times*, Sept. 18, 2017, http://tinyurl.com/y9oqnwp4.

[106] Joe Gould, "GOP senator blasts 'cowardly' Democrats over scuttled sequestration repeal," *Army Times*, Sept. 18, 2017, http://tinyurl.com/y9zw57mz.

[107] Mark Hand, "46 Republicans buck party to help Democrats take down anti-climate action amendment," *Think Progress*, July 14, 2017, http://tinyurl.com/yc8bynvp.

[108] Rebecca Kheel, "Defense experts call on Congress to allow military base closures," *The Hill*, June 19, 2017, https://tinyurl.com/y89ncf39; "Department of Defense Infrastructure Capacity," Department of Defense, March 2016, http://tinyurl.com/y9thwv7z; and Jeff Daniels, "Base closings 'hot potato' issue again as Pentagon insists new round could save tens of billions," CNBC, July 14, 2017, http://tinyurl.com/ycwpcwxu.

[109] Stavridis, *op. cit.*, p. 331.

[110] Anne Barnard and Hwaida Saad, "Raqqa, ISIS 'Capital,' Is Captured, U.S.-Backed Forces Say," *The New York Times*, Oct. 17, 2017, https://tinyurl.com/y7hchp9o.

[111] Suri and Valentino, *op. cit.*

Bibliography

Selected Sources

Books

O'Hanlon, Michael E., *The $650 Billion Bargain: The Case for Modest Growth in America's Defense Budget*, Brookings Institution Press, 2016.

A senior fellow at a centrist Washington think tank argues a slight increase in defense spending could improve the readiness of the U.S. military.

Stavridis, James, *Sea Power: The History and Geopolitics of the World's Oceans*, Penguin Press, 2017.

A retired admiral and former supreme allied commander for global operations at NATO looks at global naval history and the U.S. military's readiness to handle future conflicts at sea.

Suri, Jeremi, and Benjamin Valentino, eds., *Sustainable Security: Rethinking American National Security Strategy*, Oxford University Press, 2016.

Sixteen scholars show how U.S. military institutions and strategies have not changed since the Cold War, and say defense officials need to better prepare for an expanding range of conflicts.

Articles

Brill, Steven, "Donald Trump, Palantir, and the crazy battle to clean up a multibillion-dollar military procurement swamp," *Fortune*, March 27, 2017, http://tinyurl.com/lths7lk.

A Silicon Valley software startup says the Army blocked it from acquiring a lucrative contract for technology that the company says would save soldiers' lives.

Diamond, Christopher, "Report: U.S. military's shrinking size and growing equipment age reflect DOD priorities," *Military Times*, March 15, 2017, http://tinyurl.com/y9lyt6gl.

Despite consistent defense spending increases, the size of the military has been shrinking in recent decades while its equipment has been aging, according to a Center for a New American Security report.

Philipps, Dave, and Eric Schmitt, "Fatigue and Training Gaps Spell Disaster at Sea, Sailors Warn," *The New York Times*, Aug. 27, 2017, http://tinyurl.com/ybxcw6d5.

Current and former Navy ship commanders describe exhausting schedules and maintenance shortfalls that they said could have contributed to two deadly collisions recently between U.S. destroyers and cargo ships.

Powers, Benjamin, "How Intelligent Drones Are Shaping the Future of Warfare," *Rolling Stone*, March 14, 2017, http://tinyurl.com/grglrkg.

Military scholars discuss the expanded use of drones and autonomous weapons systems as part of an effort to modernize the military, and explore related legal questions.

Tirpak, John A., "Combat Forces in Peril," *Air Force Magazine*, July 2017, http://tinyurl.com/y9pnln37.

A former Air Combat Command chief for the Air Force describes the effects of budgetary constraints on readiness and capability, and offers solutions.

Reports and Studies

"U.S. Military Power: What is the status of America's military power?" 2016 Index of U.S. Military Strength, Heritage Foundation, https://tinyurl.com/ojog8sz.

A conservative Washington think tank assesses the size, equipment and capability of the U.S. military and concludes it could not fight two major conflicts at once.

Kosiak, Steven, "Is the U.S. Military Getting Smaller and Older? And How Much Should We Care?" Center for a New American Security, March 14, 2017, https://tinyurl.com/hby9fga.

An adjunct senior fellow at a Washington think tank says the United States still has the world's most formidable military, despite policy decisions that have led to fewer service personnel.

O'Rourke, Ronald, "Navy Force Structure and Shipbuilding Plans: Background and Issues for Congress," Congressional Research Service, Sept. 22, 2017, http://tinyurl.com/y8na4x9p.

The research arm of Congress outlines projected costs and other issues as lawmakers weigh President Trump's proposal to expand the Navy's fleet to 355 ships.

Audio and Video

Bender, William J., "Breaking Barriers: The Air Force and the Future of Cyberpower," Carnegie Council for Ethics in International Affairs, March 9, 2017, http://tinyurl.com/ycs9zfuv.

The chief information officer for the secretary of the Air Force describes efforts to keep up with changes in digital technology and cybersecurity.

Eaglen, MacKenzie, "Space Corps: A new military branch?" American Enterprise Institute, Aug. 4, 2017, http://tinyurl.com/yadazyfc.

A resident fellow at a conservative Washington think tank discusses a House bill that would create a new military service to handle possible conflicts in space.

O'Hanlon, Michael E., "A discussion with Rep. Mac Thornberry on military readiness, modernization, and innovation," Brookings Institution, May 22, 2017, http://tinyurl.com/kkxpflq.

A senior fellow at a centrist Washington think tank talks with the chairman of the House Armed Services Committee about military readiness and other defense-related issues.

The Next Step:

Additional Articles from Current Periodicals

Budget

Elis, Niv, "McCain to vote 'yes' on 2018 budget," *The Hill*, Oct. 17, 2017, https://tinyurl.com/ycrzvagt.

Sen. John McCain, R-Ariz., who had been seeking defense spending increases as a way to improve military readiness, has agreed to support the 2018 budget proposal.

Ham, Carter, "The US Army's Reset Is Underway — and Threatened by Budget Chaos," *Defense One*, Oct. 8, 2017, https://tinyurl.com/y8gvfllv.

The chaotic federal budget approval process is harming military readiness, argues the president of the Association of the U.S. Army, the military branch's advocacy group.

O'Hanlon, Michael E., " 'Military readiness crisis' a risky misdiagnosis," *The Hill*, Oct. 5, 2017, https://tinyurl.com/y8xdkfcb.

Instead of blaming Congress and a dysfunctional budget process for hurting military readiness, the Pentagon should focus on better managing its forces, says a Brookings Institution senior fellow.

China

Buckley, Chris, and Steven Lee Myers, "Xi Jinping Presses Military Overhaul, and Two Generals Disappear," *The New York Times*, Oct. 11, 2017, https://tinyurl.com/y9x618dm.

Chinese President Xi Jinping has moved to shake up the military and strengthen his grip on power.

Rowe, Eric D., "What Is the Likelihood of Cross-Strait Conflict?" *The Diplomat*, Oct. 13, 2017, https://tinyurl.com/ybkp9f6p.

An expert on Taiwan says the island is ill-prepared for an invasion but adds that the odds of China attacking it are "very low."

Venkatachalam, K.S., "Is India's Military Actually Ready for War With China?" *The Diplomat*, Aug. 10, 2017, https://tinyurl.com/ybznvbtk.

The possibility of a war with China over the disputed Doklam plateau in the Himalayas has Indian officials worried.

Disaster Relief

Mitchell, Ellen, "Military stretched thin by hurricane relief efforts," *The Hill*, Sept. 24, 2017, https://tinyurl.com/ybbxoq34.

Hurricanes Maria, Harvey and Irma have strained U.S. military resources after all three storms hit the U.S. mainland and territories in quick succession, officials said.

Pawlyk, Oriana, and Richard Sisk, "Military Response in Puerto Rico Delays Deployments to Afghanistan," *Military.com*, Oct. 5, 2017, https://tinyurl.com/ydeuexjl.

Dispatching military aircraft and ships to Puerto Rico after Hurricane Maria delayed the deployment of troops to Afghanistan, according to a Marine general.

Wang, Christine, "Trump says military should not have to help with food, water distribution in Puerto Rico," *CNBC*, Oct. 16 2017, https://tinyurl.com/y9nc5rr8.

With Puerto Rico struggling to distribute emergency supplies, the military has been pitching in — something it really "shouldn't have to be doing," President Trump said.

North Korea

"Rex Tillerson: US in contact with North Korea," *Al Jazeera*, Sept. 30, 2017, https://tinyurl.com/y9dr96lq.

Secretary of State Rex Tillerson says the United States has open channels of communication with North Korea to see if it is willing to negotiate on its nuclear program.

Scigliano, Eric, "The Book Mattis Reads to Be Prepared for War With North Korea," *Politico*, Oct. 15, 2017, https://tinyurl.com/yb8aumwu.

Defense Secretary Jim Mattis recommended T.R. Fehrenbach's *This Kind of War* as a guide for dealing with North Korea — a 54-year old history of the Korean War that also lamented the decline in U.S. military readiness during the 1950s.

Shinkman, Paul D., "Military Chiefs Back Trump on North Korea," *U.S. News & World Report*, Sept. 27, 2017, https://tinyurl.com/y7e2yejm.

Top defense advisers emphasize that the United States is more than capable of deterring a North Korean attack, but they also stressed the importance of trying to resolve the crisis through diplomacy.

Nuclear Arsenal

Kube, Courtney, *et al.*, "Trump Wanted Tenfold Increase in Nuclear Arsenal, Surprising Military," *NBC News*, Oct. 11, 2017, https://tinyurl.com/y7vjvayc.

President Trump said at a meeting of U.S. security officials over the summer that he wanted to expand the number of U.S. nuclear weapons nearly tenfold to make up for a steady reduction of those weapons since the late 1960s, according to officials at the meeting.

Silva, Cristina, "Did the U.S. Military Just Send One of Its Deadliest Warplanes to North Korea as a Message?" *Newsweek*, Oct. 29, 2017, https://tinyurl.com/yb5f3xmn.

A B-2 stealth bomber, one of the U.S. military's most fearsome planes, flew from Whiteman Air Force Base in Missouri toward the Korean Peninsula in October, presumably as a warning to North Korea amid rising nuclear tensions between Washington and Pyongyang.

Pentagon Waste

Capaccio, Anthony, "F-35s Hobbled by Parts Shortages, Slow Repairs, Audit Finds," Bloomberg, Oct. 23, 2017, https://tinyurl.com/y9pk8lcg.

The F-35 fighter jets made by Lockheed Martin for the Pentagon could not fly 22 percent of the time during the first eight months of 2017 because repair times were twice as long as they should be, according to a draft audit by the Government Accountability Office, the investigative arm of Congress.

Hartung, William, "The scandal of Pentagon spending: Who really gets rich?" Salon, Oct. 15, 2017, https://tinyurl.com/yd37vhtb.

A national security expert at the Center for International Policy, a Washington think tank, says much of the Pentagon's budget pays private corporations to develop unnecessary weapons systems, enriching the companies' executives at taxpayer expense.

Vanden Brook, Tom, "Defense Secretary Mattis rips Pentagon for wasting money on Afghan army uniforms," USA Today, July 24, 2017, https://tinyurl.com/y7neh387.

A special inspector general for the Defense Department says the department has wasted up to $28 million since 2007 buying forest-camouflage uniforms for the Afghan army, even though only 2 percent of Afghanistan is covered by woods.

Space War

"America's fortress: Inside the base that defends U.S. in outer space," CBS News, Oct. 25, 2017, https://tinyurl.com/yd8b66u5.

Colorado's Cheyenne Mountain Air Force Station watches for ballistic missile threats around the clock, a critical national defense role as Russia and China develop weapons that could disable or destroy U.S. military satellites.

Capaccio, Anthony, "U.S. Air Force Space Chief Sees Final Frontier as Battleground," Bloomberg, Oct. 17, 2017, https://tinyurl.com/y92bcqlu.

U.S. military satellites are under increasing threat from adversaries such as China and Russia as well as from the accumulation of space debris, according to Gen. John W. "Jay" Raymond, head of the U.S. Air Force Space Command.

Dillow, Clay, "How the US is gearing up as fear of a space war mounts," CNBC, April 20, 2017, https://tinyurl.com/yce5924y.

U.S. defense officials are teaming up with commercial space start-ups to help protect military satellites and spacecraft from missile attacks and other threats.

Koren, Marina, "America's Space Commanders Rattle Their Lightsabers," The Atlantic, April 5, 2017, https://tinyurl.com/yceeq364.

Recent comments by the vice commander of the Air Force Space Command suggest military officials increasingly believe the country must do more to prepare for possible war in outer space.

Technology

"University of Illinois leads $25 million military technology initiative," Chicago Tribune, Oct. 6, 2017, https://tinyurl.com/yc557qox.

An Illinois university is heading a project that aims to connect soldiers with "smart" armor, communication and weapons technology for use in combat.

Cohen, Zachary, "US launches 'most advanced' stealth sub amid undersea rivalry," CNN, Oct. 26, 2017, https://tinyurl.com/yb3pwubv.

The U.S. Navy has launched a new nuclear-powered, fast-attack submarine to remain competitive with Russia and China in undersea capabilities.

O'Connor, Tom, "U.S. Military Considers New Super-Weapon To Counter Russia's Nuclear Warheads," Newsweek, April 12, 2017, https://tinyurl.com/ybvexgw7.

Russia's advances in nuclear technology have spurred U.S. military officials to consider deploying a futuristic tungsten-based warhead that can travel faster than three times the speed of sounds and can pierce most conventional armor with flaming, metal fragments.

In-depth Reports on Issues in the News

Are you writing a paper?

Need backup for a debate?

Want to become an expert on an issue?

For 90 years, students have turned to *CQ Researcher* for in-depth reporting on issues in the news. Reports on a full range of political and social issues are now available. Following is a selection of recent reports:

Civil Liberties
Privacy and the Internet, 12/15
Intelligence Reform, 5/15
Religion and Law, 11/14

Crime/Law
High-Tech Policing, 4/17
Forensic Science Controversies, 2/17
Jailing Debtors, 9/16
Decriminalizing Prostitution, 4/16
Restorative Justice, 2/16
The Dark Web, 1/16
Immigrant Detention, 10/15

Education
Charter Schools, 3/17
Civic Education, 2/17
Student Debt, 11/16
Apprenticeships, 10/16

Environment/Society
Workplace Sexual Harassment, 10/17
Climate Change and National Security, 9/17
Muslims in America, 7/17
Funding the Arts, 7/17
Hunger in America, 7/17
Trust in Media, 6/17

Health/Safety
Medical Breakthroughs, 9/17
Medical Marijuana, 7/17
Food Labeling, 6/17
Sports and Sexual Assault, 4/17

Politics/Economy
Democracy Under Stress, 10/17
Cyberwarfare Threat, 10/17
Universal Basic Income, 9/17
National Debt, 9/17
North Korea Showdown, 5/17
Rethinking Foreign Aid, 4/17

Upcoming Reports

Stolen Antiquities, 11/10/17   Race and College Admissions, 11/17/17   Future of Marriage, 12/1/17

ACCESS
CQ Researcher is available in print and online. For access, visit your library or www.cqresearcher.com.

STAY CURRENT
For notice of upcoming *CQ Researcher* reports or to learn more about *CQ Researcher* products, subscribe to the free email newsletters, *CQ Researcher Alert!* and *CQ Researcher News*: http://cqpress.com/newsletters.

PURCHASE
To purchase a *CQ Researcher* report in print or electronic format (PDF), visit www.cqpress.com or call 866-427-7737. Single reports start at $15. Bulk purchase discounts and electronic-rights licensing are also available.

SUBSCRIBE
Annual full-service *CQ Researcher* subscriptions—including 44 reports a year, monthly index updates, and a bound volume—start at $1,131. Add $25 for domestic postage.

CQ Researcher Online offers a backfile from 1991 and a number of tools to simplify research. For pricing information, call 800-818-7243 or 805-499-9774 or email librarysales@sagepub.com.

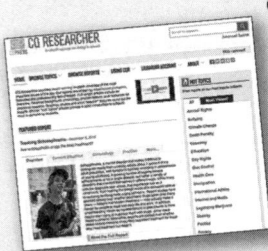

CQ RESEARCHER

CQPRESS

In-depth reports on today's issues

Published by CQ Press, an Imprint of SAGE Publications, Inc. *www.cqresearcher.com*

Stolen Antiquities

Can governments curb trafficking in ancient artifacts?

Reports that the Islamist group ISIS may be funding terrorism by selling looted artifacts from war-torn Iraq and Syria have spurred calls for a new crackdown on the illicit antiquities trade. The United States has banned antiquities imports from Iraq and Syria, and the European Union is considering requiring proof that antiquities entering Europe were legally exported from their home countries, as Germany did last year. Archaeologists favor tougher documentation requirements, but antiquities dealers say such rules are impossible to meet and could destroy the legitimate market. Meanwhile, efforts to have ancient objects returned to their country of origin continue to spark controversy. For years Greece has demanded that Britain relinquish sculptures taken from the Parthenon in the 19th century. In the United States, some archaeologists complain that a 1990 law requiring museums and federal agencies to return skeletal remains of Native Americans to tribes for reburial prevents scientific study of North America's earliest inhabitants.

A police officer in Rome guards an ancient statue recovered with thousands of other artifacts stolen from Italy. Concern about looting of archaeological sites worldwide has intensified in the wake of reports that Islamist groups have looted and trafficked in antiquities, possibly to fund terrorism.

CQ Researcher • Nov. 10, 2017 • www.cqresearcher.com
Volume 27, Number 40 • Pages 945-968

I N S I D E

THIS REPORT

THE ISSUES 947
BACKGROUND 954
CHRONOLOGY 955
AT ISSUE 961
CURRENT SITUATION 962
OUTLOOK 963
BIBLIOGRAPHY 966
THE NEXT STEP 967

THE ISSUES

947
- Should anti-trafficking regulations be strengthened?
- Should archaeological artifacts be returned to their country of origin?
- Has the 1990 law on Native American skeletal remains and other relics fulfilled its goals?

BACKGROUND

954 **Age of Plunder**
Europeans looted artifacts in the 18th and 19th centuries.

956 **Preventing Looting**
A 1970 treaty sought to bar the illicit export of artifacts.

958 **Indian Grave Robbers**
A 1906 law aimed to control the Pueblo artifacts trade.

959 **Antiquities Boom**
A crackdown led to the return of some stolen artifacts.

960 **Conflict Antiquities**
A 2016 act blocked importation of Syrian artifacts.

CURRENT SITUATION

962 **New International Laws**
Europeans seek to stop terrorists from profiting from looting.

962 **Repatriation Issues**
Officials are pressuring museums to return looted artifacts.

962 **Native American Relics**
A bipartisan bill would halt the export of grave relics.

OUTLOOK

963 **Attitude Adjustment**
Archeologists seek a shift in how antiquities are treated.

SIDEBARS AND GRAPHICS

948 **Key Antiquities Legislation**
Lawmakers around the world have tried to control looting for a century.

949 **Archaeologists: Looting Is a Global Problem**
Most say it exists everywhere.

951 **How Looting May Help Terror Groups**
Profits may be used to buy weapons.

955 **Chronology**
Key events since 1799.

956 **Iraqi Jews Want Stolen Documents to Stay in U.S.**
The archive "should not be given back to the thief that stole it."

958 **ISIS "Systematized" Looting, Ex-Official Says**
"The control and sale of looted antiquities is extremely lucrative."

961 **At Issue:**
Should the antiquities trade be legalized in more countries?

FOR FURTHER RESEARCH

965 **For More Information**
Organizations to contact.

966 **Bibliography**
Selected sources used.

967 **The Next Step**
Additional articles.

967 **Citing CQ Researcher**
Sample bibliography formats.

Cover: AFP/Getty Images/Alberto Pizzoli

 **CQ RESEARCHER**

Nov. 10, 2017
Volume 27, Number 40

EXECUTIVE EDITOR: Thomas J. Billitteri
tjb@sagepub.com

ASSISTANT MANAGING EDITORS: Kenneth Fireman, kenneth.fireman@sagepub.com, Kathy Koch, kathy.koch@sagepub.com, Scott Rohrer, scott.rohrer@sagepub.com

ASSOCIATE MANAGING EDITOR: Val Ellicott

SENIOR CONTRIBUTING EDITOR:
Thomas J. Colin
tom.colin@sagepub.com

CONTRIBUTING WRITERS: Marcia Clemmitt, Sarah Glazer, Alan Greenblatt, Reed Karaim, Barbara Mantel, Patrick Marshall, Tom Price

SENIOR PROJECT EDITOR: Olu B. Davis

EDITORIAL ASSISTANT: Natalia Gurevich

FACT CHECKERS: Eva P. Dasher, Michelle Harris, Betsy Towner Levine, Robin Palmer

SAGE Publishing | CQPRESS

Los Angeles | London | New Delhi
Singapore | Washington DC | Melbourne

An Imprint of SAGE Publications, Inc.

SENIOR VICE PRESIDENT, GLOBAL LEARNING RESOURCES:
Karen Phillips

EXECUTIVE DIRECTOR, ONLINE LIBRARY AND REFERENCE PUBLISHING:
Todd Baldwin

CQ Researcher (ISSN 1056-2036) is printed on acid-free paper. Published weekly, except: (March wk. 4) (May wk. 4) (July wks. 1, 2) (Aug. wks. 2, 3) (Nov. wk. 4) and (Dec. wks. 3, 4). Published by SAGE Publications, Inc., 2455 Teller Rd., Thousand Oaks, CA 91320. Annual full-service subscriptions start at $1,131. For pricing, call 1-800-818-7243. To purchase a CQ Researcher report in print or electronic format (PDF), visit www.cqpress. com or call 866-427-7737. Single reports start at $15. Bulk purchase discounts and electronic-rights licensing are also available. Periodicals postage paid at Thousand Oaks, California, and at additional mailing offices. POSTMASTER: Send address changes to CQ Researcher, 2600 Virginia Ave., N.W., Suite 600, Washington, DC 20037.

Stolen Antiquities

THE ISSUES

In packages labeled "ceramic tiles," thousands of ancient Babylonian tablets and cylinder seals from Iraq were smuggled into the United States in 2011, headed for their U.S. buyer — the American arts and crafts chain Hobby Lobby. [1]

In July, the company agreed to forfeit the 5,500 artifacts along with $3 million in a civil settlement with federal prosecutors in Brooklyn, N.Y. [2]

Since 2009, Hobby Lobby's evangelical Christian owners have been collecting ancient objects from the Fertile Crescent — an area of biblical holy lands stretching from the Tigris and Euphrates rivers in the Middle East to the Nile Delta in Egypt — while building a Museum of the Bible in Washington, D.C. [3]

Some experts say the case is illustrative of the worldwide market in ancient artifacts trafficked illegally through smuggling and private transactions outside of the limelight of public auctions. Often, experts say, such items have been looted from archaeological excavations but have phony ownership papers disguising that fact.

Despite a 1970 international treaty ratified by 134 nations aimed at preventing such looting and trafficking, critics say the international antiquities market remains largely self-regulated. [4]

Most countries do not require sellers to reveal details about such sales or provide proof of ownership to buyers. Smugglers exploit weak export-import laws and lax border controls and create false paper trails. And the antiquities market has a long tradition of not asking too many questions about an item's previous owners. [5]

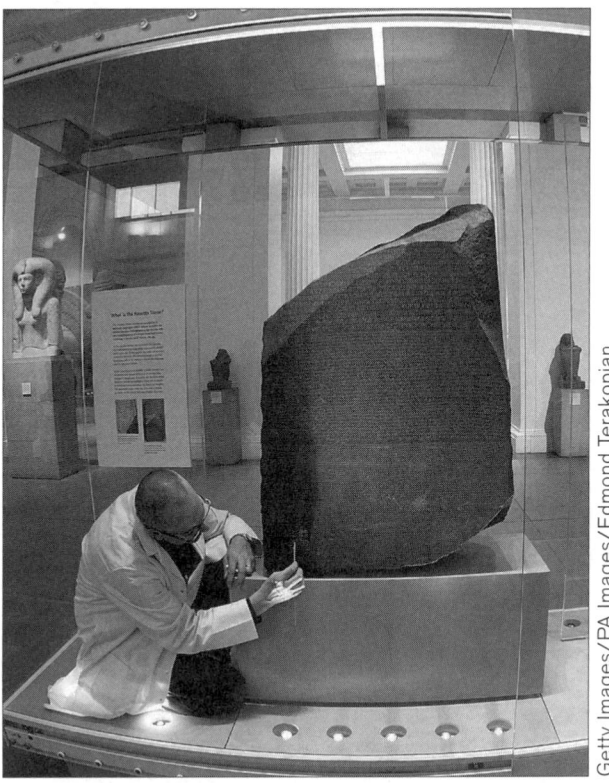

The Rosetta Stone – an ancient Egyptian stone inscribed with text that later provided the key to unlocking hieroglyphics – undergoes conservation at The British Museum in London. The British have owned the stone since 1801, when it was ceded to them by the French. Egypt repeatedly has demanded the relic's return, reflecting the ongoing debate about whether artifacts should be returned to their country of origin.

Getty Images/PA Images/Edmond Terakopian

The laws passed by nations to implement the 1970 treaty vary widely, as does enforcement. Whether an object is "illicit" depends on what country it comes from, whether that nation has prohibited such exports and whether the item left the country before or after the ban was imposed. Finally, criminal prosecutions for violating such laws are rare. For most dealers the more common penalty of forfeiture of trafficked antiquities — the approach used by authorities in the Hobby Lobby case — becomes a cost of doing business, so it is not an effective deterrent, says Patty Gerstenblith, a professor of law at DePaul University in Chicago and an expert on cultural property law.

Although it is unclear how or when the Hobby Lobby purchases left Iraq, prosecutors said the dealers provided conflicting explanations of the items' ownership history. In addition, a cultural property expert advised Hobby Lobby before the sale that certain objects could have been looted from Iraqi sites, which have been pillaged repeatedly since the 1990s. And, under a 1936 Iraqi law, all antiquities — objects at least 200 years old — found in Iraq belong to the state and cannot be exported. [6]

The issue has received renewed attention lately because of United Nations (U.N.) and law enforcement reports that the Islamic State (ISIS) and other terrorist groups have looted and trafficked antiquities, possibly funding terrorism. In response, the international community and the United States have banned the importation of ancient cultural objects from Iraq and Syria, two conflict zones where such looting has been rampant.

The Hobby Lobby case is "a really good example" of how the illicit antiquities market is operating for high-priced artifacts or collections, says Neil Brodie, an archaeologist at the University of Oxford in England, who studies the market. "We don't expect to see them come up for public auction or to be stuck in a gallery's window on Madison Avenue. We expect them to be changing hands in secret transactions in Dubai."

The court filings in the case present a rare snapshot of one route by which illicit archaeological artifacts may be reaching collectors in the United States. According to federal prosecutors, Hobby Lobby agreed to purchase the artifacts for $1.6 million in December 2010 after company president Steve

www.cqresearcher.com   Nov. 10, 2017   947

Key Antiquities Legislation

Law	Country	Year	Description
American Antiquities Act	U.S.	1906	Barred digging on public land without a permit; aimed at controlling Pueblo artifacts trade.
National Stolen Property Act	U.S.	1934	Prohibited movement of stolen or fraudulently acquired goods worth at least $5,000 across state or national borders.
Convention for the Protection of Cultural Property in the Event of Armed Conflict*	129 countries	1954	First international treaty devoted to protecting cultural property during war. Countries agreed to refrain from damaging cultural property within their borders and in other signatory nations.
Convention on the Means of Prohibiting and Preventing the Illicit Import, Export and Transfer of Ownership of Cultural Property*	134 countries	1970	Signatories agreed to require export certificates for artifacts and their return to the source country upon request. Enforcement depended on the strength of each country's implementing law.
Antiquities Law of the State of Israel	Israel	1978	First law in Israel establishing a legal antiquities market through state-licensed dealers. Required dealers to inventory all pre-1700 objects and obtain a license to export an antiquity.
Archaeological Resources Protection Act	U.S.	1979	Imposed fines of up to $20,000 and a year in jail for looting artifacts on Indian or federal land; up to 5 years and $100,000 for second offense.
Convention on Cultural Property Implementation Act	U.S.	1983	Implemented the 1970 treaty in the United States; scope limited by requirement that countries have a bilateral agreement with the U.S. before they can request the U.S. ban imports of imperiled artifacts. Sixteen countries have such agreements.
Egyptian Law on the Protection of Antiquities	Egypt	1983	Declared antiquities discovered after 1983 the property of the Egyptian government and barred export.
Native American Graves Protection and Repatriation Act	U.S.	1990	Required museums and federal agencies to return human remains and funerary objects requested by culturally affiliated Native American tribes for reburial.
Iraq Sanctions Act	U.S.	1990	Banned import of Iraqi antiquities.
Act on the Protection of Cultural Property	Germany	2016	Required documentation that an imported antiquity was legally exported from source country.
Protect and Preserve International Cultural Property Act	U.S.	2016	Restricted importation of Syrian "archeological or ethnological material."
EU Regulation on the Import of Cultural Goods (proposed)	European Union	2016	Would ban the import of goods at least 250 years old without proof of legal export from source country.

* Administered by U.N. Educational, Scientific and Cultural Organization (UNESCO)

Green traveled to the United Arab Emirates to inspect them. However, prosecutors say the company ignored several warnings and "red flags" signaling illegal activity.

A cultural property law expert had warned the company that U.S. Customs officials would likely seize any package from Iraq because of a 1990 U.S. ban on antiquities imports from Iraqi. [7] The packages had falsely listed Turkey or Israel as the country of origin, and one of the dealers involved in the sale instructed Green to wire the money to seven different personal bank accounts. [8]

Green said the company was "new to the world of acquiring these items, and did not fully appreciate the complexities of the acquisitions process." He added that "regrettable mistakes" were made and that he should have "exercised more oversight." [9] He also said the company never purchased "items from dealers in Iraq or from anyone who indicated that they acquired items from that country." He said the company has now "implemented acquisition policies and procedures based on the industry's highest standards." [10]

Experts disagree on the size of the illegal antiquities trade, by its nature an invisible one. That is partly because the definition of antiquities, broadly understood as man-made objects from the ancient past, differs depending on the country, law or organization monitoring or regulating the trade. Estimates of the market value of trafficked artifacts range as high as $7 billion worldwide, according to a widely quoted figure from a U.N. Educational, Scientific and Cultural Organization (UNESCO) official. [11]

But some antiquities dealers and archaeologists, including Oxford's Brodie, consider such figures unrealistically high. The International Association of Dealers in Ancient Art (IADAA) estimates that the legal antiquities market is only $200 million to $250 million a year. [12]

"If the legitimate market is not more than $200 million, how can the illicit market be 40 times as big?" asks Vincent Geerling, chairman of the Zurich-based IADAA, referring to estimates cited in the press. While Brodie thinks Geerling's estimate for the legal market is low, he agrees it would be hard to move billions of dollars' worth of artifacts in the "invisible" or illicit market without being detected.

Some archaeologists say any trade in archeological objects is essentially a "gray" market: While an ancient piece of art may appear legal by the time it shows up in a Madison Avenue gallery, there is usually an illegal link somewhere along the object's journey — whether an illegal export, faked ownership history papers or illegal excavation, according to Donna Yates, an American archaeologist at the University of Glasgow in Scotland, who specializes in antiquities crime.

"There's no way to distinguish" between legal and illicit ancient objects for sale, she says, because "there's no requirement to prove anything sold is legal."

More important than the dollar value of the trade, say many archaeologists, is the damage caused by looters to ancient monuments and archaeological sites — many of which are registered by UNESCO as World

Archaeologists: Looting Is a Global Problem

The vast majority of the 2,358 field archaeologists surveyed in 2013 said antiquities looting exists in nearly every country, and nearly 80 percent said they had personally encountered it.

What Field Archaeologists Say About Antiquities Looting

It exists	97.9%
It exists in all countries	89.6%
Have personally encountered looting	78.5%

Source: Blythe Bowman Proulx, "Archeological Site Looting in 'Glocal' Perspective: Nature, Scope, and Frequency," American Journal of Archaeology, 2013, https://tinyurl.com/yazvt76a

Heritage Sites * — containing important links to understanding the past. Since ISIS' rise, excavation sites in Syria have been bulldozed, "strip-mined and even tunneled" by looters, destroying 2,000 to 3,000 years of buried civilization, according to Michael Danti, academic director of a project to document the damage, the Cultural Heritage Initiatives of the American Schools of Oriental Research.

"That's a cultural loss that's inestimable, says Colgate University archaeologist Danti, whose excavation storerooms in Syria were looted while ISIS controlled the territory.

A survey of archaeologists conducted in 2013 by Blythe Bowman Proulx, an associate professor of criminal justice at Virginia Commonwealth University, found that looting was reported in 103 of the 118 countries with primary archaeological fieldwork locations. "[T]he global looting phenomenon is not an exaggerated problem," Proulx wrote. [13] (*See graph, above.*)

Geerling contends that major artworks from Syria such as Roman mo-

saics are not showing up on the international market, but Brodie says he sees heavy traffic in smaller, portable objects such as coins advertised on eBay and other websites. Such objects are "very difficult for customs and law enforcement to detect," he says.

At least 100,000 antiquities and ancient coins are offered for sale online on any given day, with an estimated value of over $10 million, according to Brodie. [14] He says digging for low-value objects is just as damaging to the historical record contained in archaeological sites as looting for pricier statues or mosaics.

Archaeologists, who often say the existence of an antiquities market incentivizes looters, tend to support tougher legal restrictions, better documentation of provenance (previous ownership) and criminal prosecutions of violators. Dealers and collectors, however, say good ownership documentation has rarely existed.

Radically different views about whether the international trade is inherently criminal comes down to a fundamental difference of opinion over the best home for antiquities. "[T]o participate in the antiquities market is to some extent to participate in, or at least benefit from, criminal enterprise," write Simon Mackenzie and Yates, two

---

* More than 1,000 locations in over 160 countries have been designated for protection as World Heritage Sites for their cultural, historical, scientific, natural or other significance. Of those, 832 have cultural significance.

experts on antiquities trafficking at the University of Glasgow. [15] Archaeologists like Yates often favor keeping ancient objects in their home countries to retain the historical context of an excavation.

But dealers say objects have independent value as works of art and are often safer with collectors and museums than in the chaotic countries or conflict zones where the objects originate.

Moreover, dealers say, strengthening requirements that antiquities are legally imported from their country of origin, as Germany did last year, will drive the trade elsewhere or underground. But supporters of such rules say the days of "don't ask, don't tell" in the antiquities trade are numbered.

The debate has played out in disputes between nations over important pieces of ancient art, such as the long-running struggle between Britain and Greece over the Elgin Marbles, sculptures taken from the Parthenon by British diplomat Lord Thomas Elgin in the 19th century.

Within the United States, the debate about preserving a people's culture has focused on thousands of Native American skeletons and sacred funerary objects in U.S. museums, many plundered from American Indian lands. A 1990 law, the Native American Graves Protection and Repatriation Act (NAGPRA), requires museums and federal agencies to return those remains and objects to culturally affiliated tribes who request them for reburial. However, some archaeologists say ancient bones not clearly linked to a particular tribe should be available for scientific study.

As archeologists, antiquities dealers and regulators try to deal with the widespread looting of cultural objects, here are some of the questions being debated:

Should anti-trafficking regulations be strengthened?

The United States and more than 100 other countries have signed a landmark treaty — the Convention on the Means of Prohibiting and Preventing the Illicit Import, Export and Transfer of Ownership of Cultural Property — that aimed to restrict the importation of illicit cultural objects.

Brokered by UNESCO in 1970, the treaty established the general principle that any antiquity being sold today must have documents showing it was either found before that year or was legally exported from its home country. [16] The treaty said nations rich in archaeological artifacts should require dealers, purchasers or museums to obtain certificates before exporting such items from the country. So-called market countries — those that mainly buy such artifacts — were to ban their import (without proper papers) and penalize violators. In response, many museums changed their policies to ensure that acquisitions have documented provenance going back at least to 1970.

Nevertheless, well into the 1980s "curators didn't demand a bill of sale," says Maxwell Anderson, formerly an assistant curator of Greek and Roman art at the Metropolitan Museum of Art in New York City and now a consulting scholar at the University of Pennsylvania Museum of Archaeology and Anthropology. He says he saw works looted from their country of origin that "ended up in an attractive gallery in a major European city."

In the 1990s, however, some spectacular prosecutions of antiquities traffickers made museums more scrupulous about the need to check an object's history, says Anderson. But other experts say antiquities remains a largely undocumented market, where many objects lack a paper trail of ownership and origin.

Some archaeologists seeking to protect archaeological sites want this to change. To sell a house, one must provide a deed proving ownership, notes Glasgow's Yates. "Some antiquities cost more than a house," she points out, but "when it comes to dealers and auction houses, there's absolutely no requirement to disclose previous own-

ers; and they don't have to share that information with buyers." She adds: "A lot of the market is self-regulated. As we know from banking and finance, self-regulation doesn't work when a lot of money is involved."

When it comes to initial onsite looting and trafficking, the 1970 treaty is only as good as a source country's laws and ability to enforce it, Yates says. Under the U.S. law implementing the treaty — which was not adopted until 1983 — a source country can ask the United States to restrict antiquities imports from that country that are at least 250 years old if the objects are in danger of being pillaged. [17] However, the legislation reduced the treaty's scope by restricting its application to countries that negotiate a bilateral agreement with the United States. Currently, only 16 nations have such agreements because they are cumbersome and expensive to negotiate, Yates says.

Museums and dealers traditionally have relied on self-regulation through trade association codes of ethics. But that has not deterred looting or trafficking. For example, the Association of Art Museum Directors (AAMD), which represents more than 200 directors of leading North American museums, says museums should not acquire an archaeological work unless there is proof the object had been removed from its probable source country before 1970 or was legally exported from the source country after 1970. [18] However, museums can acquire a piece if it is important enough or fills a gap in their collection, according to Gerstenblith, at DePaul University.

Citing concerns that looted artworks are being used to fund terrorism, Germany has gone further than most countries to require expanded documentation to prove an antiquity was exported legally from its source country. A 2016 law shifts the burden of proof to the owner or importer. [19] "It makes the market account for itself," says Yates, who supports the law.

Dealers continue to protest the new German law, saying it is rare that ancient artifacts have the kind of paper trail required. Last year, German antiques and antiquities dealers started moving their businesses abroad in anticipation of the new law, according to the trade press. [20]

In July, European Union (EU) officials announced a similar proposal, calling it a step in fighting terrorism. [21] The proposed rule would ban the import into the EU of goods 250 years old or older without proof of legal export.

"The problem . . . is that antique and ancient objects in circulation for decades have never before required documentation — so none exists," protested a blog posted on the website of the Committee for Cultural Policy, a think tank in Sante Fe, N.M., critical of such restrictions. "Almost no ancient objects have any permit or evidence showing when they were exported from source countries." [22]

In an email response to *CQ Researcher*, an EU spokesperson said, "It is extremely doubtful that items of such high value are never accompanied by evidence documenting their provenance. It's also important for genuine buyers to know that goods [are] not fakes, stolen from museums" or known to the authorities.

Most archaeologically rich nations have patrimony laws, which make antiquities from within their borders the property of the state, prohibit their export and usually make their trade illegal. But such restrictions just ensure "an active, profitable and corrupting black market," the late Stanford law professor John Henry Merryman wrote in a famous 1986 article. [23]

Dealers and the AAMD say if more countries created legal markets it would make the trade more transparent. Israel is the only Middle Eastern country that permits state-licensed dealers to sell antiquities legally for export. Under a 1978 law, dealers must keep an inventory of objects dating from before 1700, and Israel's Antiquities Authority must approve the removal of an antiquity from the country. [24]

How Looting May Help Terror Groups

Terror groups, such as the Islamic State, sometimes called ISIS, ISIL or Daesh, may use profits from selling looted Syrian or Iraqi artifacts on the black market to fund their activities, says the Antiquities Coalition, an international group that fights cultural racketeering. It says terrorist groups can make up to $1 million by selling one "masterpiece," enough to finance sizable arsenals.

What $1 Million Can Buy

11,667 AK47s and

Or

1,250 rocket launchers and

2.5 million bullets

5,000 mortars

Source: "Culture in Conflict: Where Can Daesh Get $1 Million?" Antiquities Coalition, undated, https://tinyurl.com/yabInn3k

But even Israel has run into difficulties. "The dealers that we gave permission to deal antiquities are using our law to deal in looted artifacts," Eitan Klein, deputy director of the Antiquities Authority's Unit for the Prevention of Antiquities Looting, told the *Times of Israel*. [25]

"The legal market in Israel doesn't mean looting stopped in the area," says De Paul University archaeologist Morag Kersel, who has traced pots looted from Jordanian archaeological sites. Looted material still shows up in Israel's market, she says.

Should archaeological artifacts be returned to their country of origin?

Visitors to the Elgin Marbles in London's British Museum have long been greeted with signs and pamphlets defending the museum's continued ownership of this famous frieze from Athens' Parthenon. The fifth-century B.C. sculp-

tures of a religious procession were hacked from the Parthenon in the 19th century by the British ambassador to the Ottoman empire, Lord Elgin, with the permission of the ruling Ottoman government, according to the museum. By staying in the museum, the frieze has been rescued from military destruction and Athenian air pollution and has given millions of people the opportunity to appreciate Hellenic culture, the British Museum argues. [26]

Since the 1980s, however, Greek governments have demanded the sculptures back. "Greece is determined to break the deadlock caused by the continuous refusal of the British government to return the Parthenon sculptures to their country of origin," Lydia Koniordou, the Greek minister of culture, told *The Times* of London in September, saying Greece was not ruling out legal action. [27]

The dispute epitomizes the ongoing debate about where antiquities should reside. Many archaeologists say ancient objects should be exhibited in their proper historical context — in this case at Athens' anthropological museum with views of the sculptures' original home on the Acropolis. Similar debates have swirled around Egypt's effort to repatriate a bust of Queen Nefertiti from a Berlin museum, China's demand for thousands of items in the British museum plundered in war and Nigeria's demand that museums in Boston and London return bronzes looted from southern Nigeria's Benin kingdom 120 years ago. [28]

"It's time to shed our imperialistic cloak," says Marlen Godwin, a spokesperson for the British Committee for the Reunification of the Parthenon Marbles. By letting the broken marble frieze rejoin its other half in the Acropolis museum, she says, "we can put it right."

The Elgin Marbles "are the DNA, in art, of the people of Greece," argued the late Nobel Prize-winning South African writer Nadine Gordimer in a book of essays by prominent intellectuals arguing for their return. "[W]here else should they be but where they were created?" [29]

However, in his landmark 1986 essay, Stanford's Merryman condemned this view as a narrow "nationalist" perspective. He favored a culturally "internationalist" view, which sees historical artifacts as part of the "cultural heritage of all mankind" — not just the heritage of one country. If smog is eating away at the Parthenon, "all of mankind loses something irreplaceable," he wrote. [30]

When a country like Peru has failed to protect its archaeological sites from looting, the artifacts would be better preserved in a rich country like the United States, with museums and collectors "knowledgeable about and respectful of such works," he argued. [31] In a book published last year, *Keeping Their Marbles*, British cultural commentator Tiffany Jenkins sided with Merryman, arguing that a visitor to the British Museum's encyclopedic exhibits

of art from every era and region of the world can better learn how ancient Greek artworks influenced the art, architecture and society of Europe and London itself. The Parthenon marbles' London story "is a major part of that history," she wrote. [32]

The debate continues to divide archaeologists and collectors, with museums taking different sides depending on the artifact in question. However, since the adoption of the 1970 UNESCO convention, law and opinion have been moving closer to the nationalist perspective that antiquities — at least those recently discovered — should go back to their countries of origin. In support of this idea, archaeologically rich countries since the 1900s have enacted patrimony laws, which make all antiquities found within their borders the property of the state and typically outlaw their export. [33]

William Pearlstein, a New York lawyer who has represented antiquities collectors, including the owners of Hobby Lobby, condemns this trend as "rampant nationalism" and says it represents the "collapse of any sense of international exchange" and undermines "the concept of private ownership."

"Our museums would be empty if we were to enforce all these laws," says Kate Fitz Gibbon, executive director of the Committee for Cultural Policy, referring to the national patrimony laws and a U.S. law that makes such objects crossing into the United States stolen property. [34]

Exhibitions of art from other countries "help us to understand our neighbors next door and the cultures they come from," Fitz Gibbon says. "When you see an official policy that encourages blanket nationalization of the entire heritage of a geographic region, that's a dangerous situation."

DePaul's Gerstenblith counters that cultural exchange can occur just as well through long-term loans between countries and their museums — something both the UNESCO convention and the U.S. implementing legislation encouraged.

Peter Der Manuelian, a Harvard University professor of Egyptology and director of the university's Semitic Museum, says the decision about whether to return an artifact to its country of origin should depend on the object's history. While some objects such as the Rosetta Stone were removed as war booty from Egypt, many artifacts left Egypt in the early 1900s under the official "partage" system, which split an expedition's finds between the foreign excavation team and the Cairo museum, he notes. [35]

These objects can be "wonderful cultural ambassadors" educating people around the world about Egypt, Der Manuelian observes. "I think there are great encyclopedic collections around the world that have done a great service," he says. "I would probably not be one to argue that all the Egyptian antiquities at the Louvre should be sent back to Egypt immediately."

Has the 1990 law on Native American skeletal remains and other relics fulfilled its goals?

While international tussles over the Parthenon marbles and Nefertiti's bust grab the world's attention, they are dwarfed in sheer scale by a repatriation debate in the United States involving Native Americans' patrimony. Hundreds of tribes have challenged 1,500 museums in recent years over the fate of some 200,000 Native American skeletons and 1 million funerary items and sacred objects from graves on Indian lands. [36]

Those confrontations — which in some cases have involved legal challenges and in others negotiations — result from long-standing claims of Native Americans, whose rights were codified in the 1990 Native American Graves Protection and Repatriation Act. It requires federal agencies and museums to return human remains and burial objects to lineal descendants and culturally affiliated tribes. NAGPRA was intended to give Native Americans equal rights with other Americans when it comes to reburying ancestors as well as to redress historic wrongs against Indian tribes.

Yet, more than 25 years after NAGPRA's passage, debate continues over the law's original goals and whether they have been met, especially when it comes to early human remains not clearly linked to a particular tribe.

The Society for American Archaeology (SAA) contends the law originally was intended as a compromise between the interests of science in studying the skeletons and that of tribes in reburying their ancestors, says its president, Susan Chandler. Some archaeologists say the law, as implemented, has moved too far in the direction of satisfying tribal claims at the expense of science.

Some groups representing Native Americans, on the other hand, say museums and federal agencies have dragged their feet in returning their ancestors' skeletal remains for proper reburial. [37]

Of the more than 200,000 skeletal remains believed to have been taken from Native American graves, 182,112 ended up in museums or are being held by federal agencies. Only 26 percent of those held in agencies or museums — or about 57,847 — have been returned to tribes or identified as ready to be claimed, according to the National Park Service's National NAGPRA program, which administers the law. [38] About 123,000 are still culturally unidentifiable, according to NAGPRA.

The debate came to a head recently when scientists lost a suit over two skeletons found in 1976 by an archaeology class digging on land in La Jolla, Calif., owned by the University of California, San Diego. The 9,500-year-old skeletons are among the oldest found in the United States.

In 2006, a group of local tribes claimed the skeletons, and the university initiated the process of handing them over. But several archaeologists sued to block the move, arguing that scientists should have a chance to study the skeletons. [39]

Last year, the U.S. Supreme Court declined to hear the case, and the Kumeyaay tribes in San Diego County — the closest geographical tribe — reburied the bones on May 20, 2016. [40]

Archaeologist Robert Bettinger, a plaintiff in the suit and professor emeritus at the University of California, Davis, calls the resolution "a loss for science." If the bones had been made available for DNA analysis, he says, scientists could have learned a great deal about humanity, including how the earliest people arrived on the North American continent.

"This case was about some of the oldest human remains in the New World; the older they are the rarer they get," says Bettinger. "If it's decided you can't study those, that changes the course of science."

But D. Bambi Kraus, president of the National Association of Tribal Historical Preservation Officers, an organization in Washington, D.C., of tribal leaders who implement federal and tribal preservation laws, says Native Americans already have creation stories to explain how they got here. Native Americans are "not looking to Western science to explain their existence. That's just a clash of values, and it's patronizing for a non-Native scientist to think we want to be part of that," she says.

To Elizabeth Weiss, a professor of anthropology at San Jose State University, the law's accommodation to Native American religious beliefs is an "attack on scientific freedom" and violates the Constitution's separation of church and state. The law gives equal weight to Native origin myths and to

A sacred Hopi Indian mask known as the "Hilili" was offered for auction in Paris in 2013 – over the tribe's objections – along with other Hopi relics. In the United States, the ongoing debate over repatriation of relics has focused on the tens of thousands of Native American skeletons and sacred funerary objects in U.S. museums, many plundered from American Indian lands.

scientific evidence in deciding whether a tribe is culturally linked to remains, she has written. [41]

Today, the federally appointed committee that resolves disputes over remains operates in an "environment hostile to science," opening its meetings with a Native American prayer, says Weiss, who is writing a book on the law. Only a handful of studies on Native American bones appear in journals these days, says Weiss, who attributes the small number to NAGPRA's rules. The law's attempt to balance the interests of science and religion is "like mixing oil and water," she says, and was always doomed to fail.

Some archaeologists argue for delaying reburials — particularly remains not yet linked to any tribe — to allow for future technological advances that may enable scientists to discover even more about ancient bones than today's DNA tools, says Keith Kintigh, a pro-

to the tribes comes down to a question of human rights and religious freedom. "At the end of the day it's not about what science can do but about ethical obligations to fellow humans that also have a stake in these cultural items," he says. ■

the Rosetta Stone, which would provide the key to unlocking Egyptian hieroglyphics. When the British defeated the French at Alexandria in 1801, the stone was ceded to the British by treaty. Upon its arrival in Britain, the stone was hailed as a symbol of triumph over the French. Today, it sits in the British Museum, despite repeated demands by Egyptian governments to send it back. [43]

An American service member views looted art treasures at a former Luftwaffe barracks near Königssee, Germany, in May 1945. During World War II, the Nazis seized thousands of paintings and other art objects worth billions of dollars. The widespread theft and destruction of cultural monuments during the war resulted in an international treaty to protect cultural heritage in wartime.

Getty Images/Keystone/Horace Abrahams

fessor of archaeology at Arizona State University, Tempe, and a past president of the SAA.

Choctaw tribe member Joe Watkins, the National Park Service's American Indian liaison officer and an anthropologist at the University of Maryland, College Park, acknowledges that "advances in biological anthropology can be made and derived from information on human remains. But as an American Indian, I recognize [that] the spiritual benefits of being able to rebury" the human remains override the scientific benefits.

Chip Colwell, senior curator at the Denver Museum of Nature and Science, and author of a new book on the debate, *Plundered Skulls and Stolen Spirits*, says the decision about whether to hand over skeletons and sacred objects

BACKGROUND

Age of Plunder

During the 18th and 19th centuries, as England, France and other European countries were expanding their empires, "there was a relatively uncontested free and open dealing in looted cultural objects . . . supported by imperialist values," writes Simon Mackenzie, a professor of criminology, law and society at the University of Glasgow in Scotland. [42]

In one of the most famous finds, following Napoleon's conquest of Egypt, French troops in 1799 stumbled upon

After Napoleon's defeat, Europeans increasingly were interested in acquiring collections from Egypt. And after any British military victory, the British Museum became the "first port of call" for British diplomats with collections to donate, writes British cultural commentator Jenkins. [44]

Throughout the period, adventurers, political leaders and antiquarians raided Italy, Greece and the Middle East, digging deep in the ground or chopping off chunks of monuments in an era when there were few restrictions on carting such materials away. [45]

Other objects were seized under more violent circumstances. In 1897, British troops massacred the inhabitants of the capital of the Benin kingdom in southern Nigeria and hauled off hundreds of bronze sculptures and plaques from the burning palace, selling them off to museums and collectors. In an emotional plea, a Nigerian official in 2012 urged the Boston Museum of Fine Arts, unsuccessfully, to return a collection of Benin bronzes and ivory sculptures that had been donated by New York banker Robert Lehman. [46]

China has appealed to Britain to return 23,000 objects it says were plundered when British troops put down the Boxer Rebellion, a Chinese uprising in 1900 against Western influence. [47]

Many antiquities from the age of plunder ended up in America's first great museums modeled after those in Europe — the Smithsonian Institution, which opened in 1846, and the Metropolitan Museum of Art in New York City, founded in 1870. [48]

Continued on p. 956

Chronology

1700s-1800s
European countries seize artifacts in conquered lands.

1799
The Rosetta Stone, an ancient Egyptian bilingual text used to decipher hieroglyphics, is discovered by the French, who cede it to the victorious British after the Battle of Alexandria in 1801.

1870
Metropolitan Museum of Art, an "encyclopedic" museum covering global art throughout history, is founded in New York.

1901-1954
Countries begin to protect cultural heritage. Nazi Germany loots art owned by Jews.

1906
U.S. Antiquities Act bans digging on federal land without permit.

1932
Greece declares ownership of all cultural property discovered in the country.

1954
International treaty protects cultural property during war.

1970s-1990s
Antiquities trade and looting boom.

1970
UNESCO treaty gives countries the right to recover stolen cultural property from other nations, including the United States.

1979
Archaeological Resources Protection Act toughens penalties for looting Native American sites on federal lands in the United States.

1983
United States adopts law implementing UNESCO treaty, after limiting its scope in response to objections from art dealers and collectors.

1990
Native American Graves Protection and Repatriation Act allows tribes to reclaim looted skeletons and funerary artifacts.

1995
Raid on Italian dealer Giacomo Medici yields thousands of looted antiquities and photos of many already in U.S. museums.

2000-Present
Trafficking trials lead to changes in museum practices.

2002
Raid on Italian dealer Gianfranco Becchina nets thousands of relics.

2003
Appeals court upholds conviction of U.S. dealer Frederick Schultz for conspiracy to receive stolen Egyptian artifacts. . . . More than 13,000 items are stolen from Baghdad Museum after the fall of Iraqi dictator Saddam Hussein following invasion by a U.S.-led coalition.

2005
Italy indicts Marion True, curator of antiquities at the J. Paul Getty Museum in Los Angeles, on charges of conspiring to traffic in illicit antiquities; her trial ends in 2010 with no verdict after statute of limitations expires. . . . Medici is convicted of conspiring to traffic in illegal exports.

2008
Association of Art Museum Directors says museum acquisitions should have documentation back to at least 1970.

2010
Controversial federal regulations enable Indian tribes to claim unidentifiable human remains and funerary objects; archaeologists say the rules impede scientific study.

2015
Islamic State, which controls large swaths of Syria, seizes ancient city of Palmyra, destroys ancient monuments and beheads a longtime antiquities curator.

2016
President Obama blocks imports of archaeological artifacts from Syria; he later agrees to turn over prehistoric Kennewick Man to tribes for reburial. . . . Germany bans importation of artworks that lack export licenses from source countries.

2017
Nine nations sign treaty criminalizing unlawful excavation and trafficking (May). . . . Metropolitan Museum surrenders ancient Greek vase to Italy (July). . . . U.S. collectors surrender bull's head sculpture to Lebanon (October). . . . Proposed STOP Act would prohibit export of Native American artifacts. . . . European Union considers requiring antiquities imports to have valid export licenses (July).

2018
U.S. has until September to return to Iraq a trove of Jewish objects stolen by Saddam Hussein, strongly opposed by U.S. Jewish groups.

Iraqi Jews Want Stolen Documents to Stay in U.S.

The archive "should not be given back to the thief that stole it."

Just days after coalition forces captured Baghdad during the U.S.-led invasion of Iraq in May 2003, several Americans heard about a hidden Jewish archive in President Saddam Hussein's bombed-out intelligence headquarters. [1]

In the facility's flooded basement, U.S. soldiers found 2,700 books and thousands of documents relating to Iraq's Jewish community. The cache included a 16th-century Bible, Torah scrolls, other religious objects, community records and a Jewish calendar from 1971-72 in Hebrew and Arabic, one of the last examples of Hebrew printing in Iraq. [2]

Under an agreement with the Iraqis, U.S. forces sent the waterlogged trove to the United States, where they were dried out, restored and exhibited by the National Archives and Records Administration in Washington. A National Archives exhibit of the recovered documents is on display until Jan. 15 at the Jewish Museum of Maryland in Baltimore. But under the agreement, the archive must be returned to the Iraqi government next September.

Several American Jewish groups oppose the archive's planned return, noting that a succession of Iraqi governments persecuted and expelled their Jewish populations.

"The Jewish community of Iraq was mistreated and forced to flee. Their patrimony — which includes all the religious artifacts, Torahs and personal and communal property — was stolen from them," says Gina Waldman, co-founder and president of the San Francisco-based Jews Indigenous to the Middle East and North Africa. Thus, the archive "should not be given back to the thief that stole it."

Sen. Charles Schumer, D-N.Y., agrees. "This collection . . . belongs to the ancient and proud Iraqi Jewish community," he said. He

wrote to Secretary of State Rex Tillerson on Oct. 3, urging him to work with the Iraqi Jewish community in the United States and abroad to find a permanent home for the collection of Judaica. [3]

The State Department did not respond to *CQ Researcher's* request for comment. However, in October a department spokesman said the archive would be returned next September under the agreement with the Iraqis. "Maintaining the archive outside of Iraq is possible," State Department spokesman Pablo Rodriguez told the Jewish Telegraphic Agency, "but would require a new agreement between the government of Iraq and a temporary host institution or government." [4]

Patty Gerstenblith, a law professor at DePaul University in Chicago and an expert on cultural property law, says if the United States does not return the trove to Iraq it would breach the agreement and violate international law.

The Iraqi Jews, one of the oldest Jewish communities in the world, are believed to have arrived in Babylonia, site of present-day Iraq, in the sixth century B.C. [5] Although 130,000 Jews made up a third of Baghdad's population at the beginning of the 20th century, today only five Jews remain in Iraq, according to Waldman.

Jewish life in Iraq was all but obliterated after the rise of pro-Nazi leaders in the 1930s, the development of the modern Iraqi state and its growing hostility toward Israel. When Nazi sympathizer Rashid Ali became prime minister in 1933, Jews faced discrimination and employment quotas. He invited Nazi propagandists to Baghdad, which became the early base for the Nazis' Middle East intelligence operations during World War II. On April 3, 1941, Ali staged a pro-Nazi coup, but his regime was toppled by the British a month later, and Ali fled to Berlin.

Continued from p. 954

The widespread destruction wreaked by both the Axis and Allied powers during World War II on great cultural monuments and the Nazis' plunder of art in German-occupied areas eventually resulted in an international treaty to protect cultural heritage during wartime. The Nazis seized hundreds of thousands of paintings and art objects worth billions of dollars. After the war, many of the artworks were returned to their country of origin. However, thousands of pieces did not go to their rightful owner or were never relocated. [49] Some are still being discovered in private collections today.

In the wake of the war's massive destruction of cultural heritage, nations signed the Convention for the Protection of Cultural Property in the Event of Armed Conflict in 1954, administered by UNESCO, the first international treaty devoted solely to protecting cultural property in wartime. It has since been ratified by more than 100 countries, including Syria and Iraq. [50]

Preventing Looting

Following growing concerns in the 1960s about archaeological looting, nations adopted the 1970 UNESCO-brokered treaty to prevent the illicit

export of cultural artifacts. It mandated that countries take preventive actions, such as requiring export certificates for culturally significant objects leaving archaeologically rich nations. Most relevant to the United States — one of the world's largest markets for the purchase of antiquities — signatories agreed to limit the import of such objects and to facilitate their return to the country of origin. [51]

"The Age of Piracy is over," declared Thomas Hoving, then director of the Metropolitan Museum of Art, one of many museums that publicly supported the UNESCO treaty. Yet, since then museum officials have "routinely violated the spirit" of the treaty, buying

In June 1941, hundreds of Jews were killed and thousands injured in an anti-Jewish riot known as the Farhood. [6]

The persecution increased in 1948 when Iraq entered the war against the new state of Israel. From 1949 to '51, Jews could leave if they renounced their citizenship and gave up their assets. More than 100,000 Jews left Iraq, most ending up in Israel, the United States or England. [7]

Harold Rhode, an Arabic- and Hebrew-speaking policy analyst on assignment in Baghdad for the secretary of Defense, was part of the group that rescued the documents in 2003. He learned that Iraqi Jews had stored most of their remaining community records and holy books in the women's balcony of the last functioning synagogue, but Hussein's armed henchmen arrived one night in 1984 and carted them away. [8]

Kate Fitz Gibbon, executive director of the Committee for Cultural Policy, a think tank in New Mexico, says the State Department has been too eager to turn over cultural property to its country of origin in the Middle East. [9]

"Despite the egregious abuse of human rights by governments or government-supported militias in Syria, Libya, Egypt and Iraq, the State Department has encouraged making cultural property agreements with these nations," which often means returning historic objects belonging to oppressed communities, she wrote. As recently as 2010, she noted, any person associated with Zionist principles or organizations was subject to punishment by death under Iraq's criminal code. [10]

But Gerstenblith says returning the Jewish artifacts to Baghdad could show Iraqis that "their history is diverse and would be a good thing for Iraqis to learn."

Rhode said he is appalled at the prospect of returning to Iraq the archive he helped to save. "It would be as if Germany demanded material looted from German Jewish communities under the Nazis [be placed] in German government hands," he wrote in 2013. [11]

— *Sarah Glazer*

[1] Harold Rhode, "Outrage: U.S. Returning Artifacts Looted from Iraqi Jews to Iraq, Instead of Lawful Owners," PJ Media, Aug. 26, 2013, https://tinyurl.com/y8y2rltn.

[2] "Discovery and Recovery: Preserving Iraqi Jewish Heritage," Jewish Museum of Maryland, Oct. 15, 2017, https://tinyurl.com/yar4qll2.

[3] "Schumer: State Department Once Again Unwisely Plans to Return Confiscated Judaica Collection to Iraq," press release, Office of Sen. Charles Schumer, U.S. Senate, Oct. 3, 2017, https://tinyurl.com/yc8mev5j.

[4] Josefin Dolstein, "Schumer: Don't Return Trove of Jewish Artifacts to Iraq," Jewish Telegraphic Agency, Oct. 3, 2017, https://tinyurl.com/y8jv7m9f.

[5] "Jewish History," Jews Indigenous to the Middle East and North Africa, 2017, https://tinyurl.com/y78594ex.

[6] "Rashid-Ali-al-Gaylani," *Encyclopedia Britannica*, https://tinyurl.com/ya4mvzce. Also See Bernard Lewis, *The Crisis of Islam: Holy War and Unholy Terror* (2003).

[7] "Jewish History," *op. cit.*

[8] Rhode, *op. cit.* Also see video interview at Iraqi Jewish Archives, https://tinyurl.com/yc4gs3xg.

[9] Under the Convention on Cultural Property Implementation Act of 1983, a country with a bilateral agreement with the United States can seek a U.S. ban on imports of cultural property in danger of being pillaged and demand that any property imported after the date of the agreement be returned to the source country.

[10] Kate Fitz Gibbon, "Iraq, Syria, Libya and Egypt: Beyond Rescuing the Iraqi Jewish Archives," Committee for Culture Policy, Oct. 2, 2017, https://tinyurl.com/y7xuzxtr.

[11] Rhode, *op. cit.*

"ancient art they knew had been illegally excavated," write Jason Felch and Ralph Frammolino, investigative reporters and authors of *Chasing Aphrodite*, which documents some of the more spectacular thefts that ended up at museums. [52]

The treaty covered any cultural property designated by a nation as important for archaeological, historical, artistic, literary or scientific reasons and antiquities more than 100 years old. [53]

American dealers, collectors and some museums feared the treaty would redefine whole categories of traded antiquities as illicit; they sought to limit the government's ability to agree to newly restrictive policies being imposed

by other nations on what the United States could import. That debate is partly why it took more than 10 years for the United States to pass implementing legislation — the Convention on Cultural Property Implementation Act — finally signed in 1983 by President Ronald Reagan. [54]

That act said only nations with a bilateral agreement with the United States — currently only 16 countries — can request an import ban. Under the law, the bans cover only items of "archaeological interest" that are at least 250 years old and of ethnological interest, such as tribal objects. [55] The law also allows the U.S. president to impose emergency import bans on ar-

tifacts in danger of pillage from a country that does not have a bilateral agreement in times of crisis such as civil war. [56] For instance, the United States imposed emergency bans on items coming from Iraq in 1990 and Syria last year. [57]

Many dealers say the treaty changed the rules of the game midstream for a market where artifacts have never been well documented. But Gerstenblith counters that dealers have had notice since 1970.

"It's a choice the market has made not to document over the past 40 to 45 years," she says. Having made that choice, I don't think they should get away with the excuse [that] it's undocumented."

ISIS "Systematized" Looting, Ex-Official Says

"The control and sale of looted antiquities is extremely lucrative."

Looting archaeological sites has long been a common practice among impoverished Syrians. During the ongoing Syrian civil war that began in 2011, rebel forces, regime troops and neighboring Kurdish groups have joined local residents in widespread looting, according to experts.

However, the Islamic State, also known as ISIS, ISIL or Daesh, "industrialized and systematized it," says Amr Al-Azm, a former Syrian antiquities official who is an associate professor of Middle East history and anthropology at Shawnee State University in Portsmouth, Ohio.

After the terrorist group began to occupy large stretches of territory in Syria in 2013 and 2014, it imposed a 20 percent tax on the sale of looted items, Al-Azm says. It also issued digging permits, he says, and joined in the looting, using a network of dealers and routinely using bulldozers and crews of up to 60 people.

"This indicates that the control and sale of looted antiquities is extremely lucrative, well worth the time and financial investment by ISIS," Al-Azm writes in a forthcoming book. [1]

When reports emerged that ISIS was using the antiquities trade to fund its activities, the U.N. Security Council passed resolutions in 2015 and this year urging countries to limit the trade from ISIS-controlled areas and to make involvement in terrorism-related antiquities trading a punishable offense. [2]

Tess Davis, executive director of the Antiquities Coalition, an advocacy group in Washington fighting the illicit antiquities trade, says, "This is an attractive source of terrorist financing." The coalition cites estimates that looters in Syria have removed more than $2 billion worth of antiquities. [3]

But some dealers and experts doubt that ISIS has earned billions from antiquities. Fiona Greenland, a University of Virginia sociologist trained in archaeology, has been studying the likely market value of objects from Dura-Europos, a historic site in Syria dating to 300 B.C. that was heavily looted before and during the Islamic State occupation.

"There's the question of how many objects are worth enough money to generate millions or billions in profit," she says. "The Near Eastern archaeologists with whom I've worked say the majority of objects out of their excavation sites are humble objects — broken pottery, coins, tools, sometimes pieces of mosaic or sculpture. But few are masterpieces" that would fetch hundreds of thousands of dollars, let alone millions, she says.

According to the U.S. government, "ISIL has probably earned several million dollars from antiquities sales since mid-2014, but the precise amount is unknown," said Andrew Keller, the State Department's deputy assistant secretary for counter-threat finance and sanctions. He was speaking at a September 2015 presentation at the Metropolitan Museum of Art in New York City in which he showed photographs from a May 2015 raid on the quarters of Abu Sayyaf, an ISIS leader in charge of uncovering antiquities in Syria. [4]

But Randall Hixenbaugh, a New York City antiquities dealer and appraiser who attended that event, called the ISIS collection displayed in the photos "laughable." The artifacts included fakes, "low-grade" antiquities, tourist items such as a miniature head of Egyptian Queen Nefertiti, and Roman and Islamic coins that are so plentiful they fetch only about $50 each.

Indian Grave Robbers

In the United States, there is a long history of looting Native American graves and pillaging Indian villages.

One of the worst such incidents, called the Sand Creek Massacre, occurred in 1864, when American troops slaughtered an entire Native American village in their sleep. The army took scalps and other objects; some of the remains were sent to the Smithsonian Institution in Washington, D.C. [58]

Under the Theodore Roosevelt administration, Congress passed one of the earliest efforts to halt looting on Native American lands — the American Antiquities Act of 1906 — which made

digging on public lands illegal without a permit. The law aimed to control the enormous trade in artifacts from ancestral Pueblo sites in the Southwest. [59]

However, difficulties in enforcing the law led to the passage in 1979 of the Archaeological Resources Protection Act (ARPA), which imposed fines of up to $20,000 and a year in jail for looting artifacts from archaeological sites on Indian and federal land, and up to five years and $100,000 for a second offense. [60] The largest ARPA case unfolded in 2009, when 24 people were charged with digging up Native American artifacts from federal lands in Utah. [61]

But ARPA did not address an inequity towards Native Americans in

U.S. law. While state laws have long required states to bury paupers and unidentified bodies, such laws did not apply to American Indians. For example, in 1971 a highway construction project in Glenwood, Iowa, uncovered a historic cemetery. The 26 bodies deemed to be white were reburied in the local cemetery, but the remains of a woman and child identified as Native American were sent in a box to the state archaeologist. [62]

To give Indians equal burial rights, Congress in 1990 passed the Native American Graves Protection and Repatriation Act, which said federal agencies and museums must return human remains to Indian descendants or culturally affiliated tribes.

"The market isn't that voracious; it doesn't need more of the same," Hixenbaugh says, putting the total value of the artifacts in the photos at $10,000. [5]

But Al-Azm says some items are more valuable than that. "I have seen looted mosaics ripped out of the ground from Syria and offered to me for sale in Turkey," he says, "and these mosaics fetch tens of thousands of dollars."

Hans-Jakob Schindler, coordinator of the U.N. Security Council's ISIL, Al-Qaeda and Taliban Monitoring Team, says his team has never published a figure for ISIL's looting profits. But "terrorism isn't an expensive business; a couple of thousand will get you very far," he says.

For instance, he says, it cost only about $10,000 for terrorists to carry out the 2015 Paris attack in which several ISIS members with bombs and guns killed 130 people. More importantly, he adds, ISIS is demonstrating to other groups that antiquities are "a viable income source."

Al-Azm says ISIS in Syria probably copied tactics from Tunisian Salafists, or ultraconservative Sunni Muslims, who in 2013 destroyed shrines built by Muslim mystics — the Sufis. The Salafists, who consider Sufis infidels, also looted antiquities and helped turn Tunisia into a trafficking highway.

Tunisian fighters who joined ISIS in Syria will be returning home soon, following recent territorial losses there, Al-Azm says. "If you see a spike in cultural heritage looting [in Tunisia], that means someone is trying to fund themselves," he says, "a potential indicator that ISIS is active again."

— *Sarah Glazer*

In the ancient Syrian city of Palmyra, the Temple of Bel was blown up by the Islamic State in August 2015.

[1] Amr al-Azm, "The Importance of Cultural Heritage in Enhancing a Syrian National Identity and the Role of Local Non-State Actors in Preserving It," in Paul Newsome and Ruth Young, eds., *Post-Conflict Archaeology and Cultural Heritage* (forthcoming, 2018), p. 98.

[2] Resolution 2253, U.N. Security Council, 2015, https://tinyurl.com/yd74yhgl. Resolution 2347, UN Security Council, March 24, 2017, https://tinyurl.com/y7qgpdd3. This resolution urged countries to introduce legislative and other measures to prevent trafficking in cultural property and to make such trafficking that may benefit terrorists a serious crime.

[3] Deborah M. Lehr and Katie A. Paul, "Rocking the Cradle of Civilization," *The Huffington Post*, Sept. 1 2014, https://tinyurl.com/yb3ctr7m.

[4] "Remarks, Andrew Keller," U.S. Department of State, Sept. 29, 2015, https://tinyurl.com/ybrdkznv.

[5] "Rethinking Antiquities," transcript of conference, Cardozo School of Law, New York, March 2016, https://tinyurl.com/y7xkg44s.

However, more than 100,000 Native American human remains now in the hands of museums and federal agencies cannot be clearly linked to a specific tribe. A controversial 2010 regulation directed museums to return such "culturally unidentifiable" skeletons to the tribe that is closest geographically or on whose aboriginal lands the remains were found (if the tribe makes such a claim). [63]

The issue came to the fore in 1996, when two hikers in Kennewick, Wash., found an 8,500-year-old skeleton while wading in the Columbia River. Five tribes, including the local Colvilles, immediately laid claim to the skeleton, which became known as Kennewick Man. But a group of scientists sued to stop the transfer, saying the skeleton was not clearly linked to any tribe and could yield valuable information about early American inhabitants. [64]

After eight years of legal battles, a federal judge, convinced by an analysis of the skull that the skeleton was not Native American, allowed the scientists to study the bones and prevented a reburial. [65] However, a subsequent DNA analysis determined the skeleton was a closer match to the local Colville tribe than to any other modern peoples. [66]

In December 2016, President Obama signed legislation turning the Kennewick Man over to a coalition of tribes that included the Colvilles, who laid the remains to rest in a ritual ceremony last February. [67]

Antiquities Boom

The 1990s and early 2000s saw a boom in the antiquities market coinciding with the rise of extremely wealthy American collectors. In addition, large-scale operations to dig up and sell antiquities illegally were uncovered in several countries. And archaeological source countries, led by Italy, increasingly agitated for the return of their cultural property. [68]

In 1995, Italian and Swiss authorities raided a Geneva warehouse of the antiquities dealer Giacomo Medici, discovering 3,800 looted antiquities and photos of thousands more antiquities, some broken and dirty from recent excavation. From photos found in the warehouse, authorities were able to trace looted artifacts to museums across the United States, Europe and Asia. [69] In another high-profile discovery, Italian and Swiss authorities in May 2002 raided the warehouses of Swiss antiquities dealer Gianfranco Becchina, recovering 5,200 looted antiquities and more than 8,500 photos of artifacts, some pictured with soil still on them that showed they had been dug up recently. [70]

The photos from the raids became known as the Medici and Becchina

stolen from Egypt. The court found that the NSPA, which prohibits dealing in stolen or fraudulently acquired goods valued at $5,000 or more across state or national borders, applied to "property stolen from a foreign government" — in this case Egypt, which asserted ownership under its patrimony law. [72]

U.S. courts have upheld foreign patrimony laws in cases testing whether imported antiquities from countries with such laws were "stolen" under the NSPA. In a landmark 2003 case, *U.S. v. Schultz*,

Schultz served 33 months in federal prison for conspiring to smuggle antiquities out of Egypt by disguising them as cheap souvenirs dipped in plastic and preparing false provenances. [75]

In 2005, Marion True, curator of antiquities at the J. Paul Getty Museum in Los Angeles was indicted by the Italian government on charges of conspiring to traffic in illicit antiquities, many of which had been found in Medici's photos.

Her trial ended in 2010 without a conviction after the statute of limitations expired, but the case had a chilling effect on both potential buyers of antiquities without well-documented provenance and on other museums, according to Anderson, the former Metropolitan Museum of Art assistant curator. U.S. museums returned more than 100 antiquities to Italy during True's five-year trial. [76]

Marion True, former curator of antiquities at the J. Paul Getty Museum in Los Angeles, was indicted by the Italian government in 2005 on charges of conspiring to traffic in illicit antiquities. Her trial ended in 2010 without a conviction after the statute of limitations expired, but the case had a chilling effect on other museums and potential buyers of antiquities that lack proper documentation.

(Getty Images/The Washington Post)

"archives," because they led to hundreds of repatriations around the world and continue to provide evidence that some objects found in museums and private hands had been looted. Medici was convicted in 2005 of receiving stolen goods, illegally exporting artifacts and conspiring to traffic thousands of illegal artifacts. He was sentenced to 10 years in prison and received a 10 million euro fine. [71]

In the 2000s, several spectacular trials led to the return of antiquities from museums to source countries. Frederick Schultz, the former president of the National Association of Dealers in Ancient, Oriental and Primitive Art, was convicted in 2002 under the 1934 National Stolen Property Act (NSPA) of conspiracy to receive antiquities

the Second U.S. Circuit Court of Appeals upheld Schultz's conviction, saying Egypt's patrimony law — designating all antiquities discovered after 1983 as property of the state — had standing in the United States; therefore the property had been stolen.

"If an American conspired to steal the Liberty Bell" and send it to a foreign collector, he would be prosecuted, said U.S. District Judge Jed S. Rakoff. "The same is true" when a U.S. resident conspires to steal Egyptian antiquities, he said. [73]

The judge also criticized the "no questions asked" approach employed for decades by collectors and museums, telling the jury that "to purposefully remain ignorant" of Egypt's patrimony law, as Schultz had claimed, was no excuse. [74]

Conflict Antiquities

The Middle East, an area rich in ancient archaeological sites, has been hard hit by wars, uprisings and terrorism. In 2003, following the fall of Saddam Hussein, more than 13,000 items were stolen from the Iraq Museum. Many were recovered by law enforcement officials, but some are still missing. [77]

Looted items can still be seen for sale on eBay, according to George Washington University archaeologist Eric H. Cline. [78]

Satellite images indicate that looting in Egypt's Nile Valley and delta escalated sharply during the global economic crisis in 2009 and intensified following the so-called Arab Spring political upheavals in 2011, according to research published by University of Alabama researchers last year. [79]

Some of the destruction of cultural icons in that region has been driven by religious intolerance. For instance, in 2001, Muslim extremists in Afghanistan dynamited two colossal sixth-century Buddhist statues in the Bamiyan Valley

Continued on p. 962

At Issue:

Should the antiquities trade be legalized in more countries?

KATE FITZ GIBBON
EXECUTIVE DIRECTOR,
COMMITTEE FOR CULTURAL POLICY

WRITTEN FOR _CQ RESEARCHER_, NOVEMBER 2017

_l_egal markets guided by sensible rules and positive values are often the fastest way to put illegal markets out of business. A regulated trade in ancient art would deincentivize looting. Transparency would earn trust. Collectors would have good title. Source countries could track objects internationally. Worldwide, an inventory of art already in circulation would facilitate legitimate claims for return and allow free trade in other objects, curtail local corruption, eliminate profits from looting and enable global academic access.

Documentation is key. If properly documented, any stolen object can be claimed, and no stolen object can be sold.

In the past, documentation (or provenance) was not considered important. It wasn't required to legally import artworks or for museum acquisition. Most important, it wasn't required because art-source countries never set up systems to enable lawful trade. Many nations simply made everything more than 100 years old illegal to export, from postage stamps to ancient statues, and then ignored or unofficially facilitated the outward flow.

All that has changed. Source nations now argue for universal restitution (even if it means that each country would possess only its own art). U.S. museums cooperate in returns, although they worry about core collections and how best to serve a multicultural population. Digital documentation of collections nowadays sometimes triggers source-country claims.

Museums also are frustrated by acquisition guidelines that require a paper trail back to 1970. Lack of documentation has turned hundreds of thousands of objects into "orphans," unable to be donated to public institutions.

Digital technology can solve the orphan problem and the fate of unprovenanced antiquities. It is feasible to catalog millions of objects, using a descriptive standard such as Object ID and a photograph.

Objects and their provenance could be inventoried on a universally accessible database. After a reasonable period to allow claims, title would be deemed free and clear, unless new information became available. The system could be fee-based, similar to paying for title insurance for one's home. If that fee helps to build museums, secure archaeological sites or foster academic research, so much the better.

The easy part is the technology. The hard part is building trust among foreign governments, museums and collectors. All should see the sense of a global permitting system, fair opportunities to reclaim heritage and secure title. A legal trade in antiquities can serve both our museums and the public.

MORAG KERSEL
ASSOCIATE PROFESSOR OF ANTHROPOLOGY,
DEPAUL UNIVERSITY

WRITTEN FOR _CQ RESEARCHER_, NOVEMBER 2017

_w_hile researching my dissertation on the topic of legalizing the antiquities trade, I collected data from archival documents, archaeological surveys and excavations and interviewed those with a vested interest in the topic — archaeologists, collectors, dealers, government employees, looters, museum professionals and tourists. After three years of research, I arrived at some insights concerning the efficacy of the legal trade to stem looting.

Israel's Antiquities Law of 1978 — which establishes a legal antiquities market in that country — provides a lens to study this issue. Israel's antiquities market, it turns out, encouraged, rather than deterred, looting in Israel and surrounding areas such as Jordan and Palestine. The ready market for material, which looters and middlemen exploited through a loophole in the 1978 law, allowed illegally excavated material to enter the legal market through a laundering process involving an exchange of inventory registry numbers.

Here's how the system worked: Unless buyers (predominantly tourists or pilgrims to the Holy Land) knew to ask for an export license for their purchase, dealers did not need to offer one. As a result, the sale often was not registered with the Israel Antiquities Authority, which oversees antiquities sales. Without an official record of the sale, the inventory number for the artifact could be reused for a similar artifact: One buff-colored Middle Bronze pot looks like the next.

I do not have the temerity to suggest that my early research affected policy or regulations related to the Israeli trade, but it did increase awareness of problems in the antiquities market. In the 10 years since the completion of my dissertation, the Israel Antiquities Authority has enacted a series of measures to tighten loopholes in the system.

The real question is not whether a legal market prevents archaeological looting. The concept of a legal market presents a misleading binary of legal and illegal. In fact, they are often the same thing. There are corrupt actors, illegal elements and loopholes in these markets that make it impossible to consider them "legal."

Given the unequal power balance between First World buyers and Third World suppliers, the focus should be on _demand_ for antiquities without provenance, or what Colgate University associate professor of art and history Elizabeth Marlowe, in her 2013 book _Shaky Ground_, calls "ungrounded" archaeological material. As long as demand for ungrounded antiquities exists, looting will occur.

Continued from p. 960

— a World Heritage Site — after declaring them idolatrous. And in May 2015, in an effort to demonstrate its power and condemn pre-Islamic idol-worshipping, ISIS demolished the 17 A.D. temple dedicated to the Canaanite sky god Baalshamin in Palmyra, Syria. [80]

On March 9, 2016, then-President Obama signed the Protect and Preserve International Cultural Property Act, which blocked the importation of archaeological artifacts from Syria, bringing U.S. policy in line with a U.N. Security Council resolution calling on nations to deny funding to ISIS by preventing antiquities trafficking from Syria and Iraq. [81] ■

CURRENT SITUATION

New International Laws

The European Parliament is expected to consider new rules aimed at blocking terrorists from funding themselves by trafficking antiquities into Europe. European Union regulations, proposed in July, would require antiquities importers to show that an archaeological object was exported legally from the source country if from outside the EU, and to obtain an import license from the EU country where the object is arriving, European Commission spokesperson Vanessa Mock said in an email interview. [82]

EU officials have described the proposed rules as an effort to prevent trade in looted antiquities from the Middle East from being used to finance ISIS' terrorist activities.

However, dealers say the kind of documentation the EU is requiring is not typically available for antiquities and argue that fears about ISIS profiting from trafficking in Syrian antiquities are unfounded. (*See sidebar, p. 958.*)

"Against general expectations, no objects of any importance from Syria have surfaced in Europe or the USA recently," says IADAA Chairman Geerling.

Antiquities dealers blame a new German law passed last year that cracks down on art imports for killing their trade in Germany and forcing them to move their businesses abroad. The German law puts the burden on dealers to prove an antiquity was exported legally from its country of origin and requires a license to export it from Germany. [83]

Court challenges are expected on the grounds that the new German rules violate the German constitution, and a coalition of dealers has filed a complaint with the EU charging its proposed rules violate the EU guarantee of free trade, according to Geerling.

Meanwhile, nine nations, including Greece and Mexico, have signed a new treaty criminalizing unlawful excavation and trafficking in cultural property. The treaty was promulgated in May by the Council of Europe, a human rights organization with 47 member states, including the United States. [84]

Experts say "market" countries such as the United States, with a strong commitment to free enterprise, are unlikely to sign on to the Council of Europe treaty.

Repatriation Issues

In July, the Metropolitan Museum of Art surrendered a 2,300-year-old Greek vase after Manhattan prosecutors served the museum with a warrant for its seizure, citing evidence it had been looted from an ancient Greek site in an area of modern-day Italy that was once part of the ancient Greek empire. [85] Christos Tsirogiannis, a forensic archaeologist who published his suspicions about the vase, said his evidence included photos seized from Medici storehouses in 1995 that showed the vase still encrusted with dirt. [86]

In another case, a 2,300-year-old sculpture of a bull's head that had been on

loan to the Met also came under suspicion and will be repatriated to Lebanon. The Colorado couple that owned it, Lynda and William Beierwaltes, originally said they had bought the sculpture in good faith from a dealer for $1 million in 1996. They filed suit to prevent the Manhattan district attorney from returning it to the Lebanese government.

But in early October, their attorney said they were dropping their suit in the face of "incontrovertible evidence" the sculpture was stolen. According to prosecutors, a state-sponsored excavation in Lebanon uncovered the work in 1967. It was stored and then stolen in 1981 during Lebanon's civil war. [87]

In a new twist, the Manhattan district attorney announced in October he would pursue the return to Lebanon of a second work, an ancient sculpture of a person carrying a calf, seen in a photo accompanying a *House and Garden* magazine profile of the Beierwaltes in June 1998. The sculpture had been sold to another private collector.

Native American Relics

A bipartisan bill introduced in both chambers of Congress aims to stop the export of Native American grave relics and artifacts. The Safeguard Tribal Objects of Patrimony Act of 2017 (STOP Act) was introduced by Sen. Martin Heinrich, D-N.M., in response to a high-profile Paris auction in the summer of 2016, according to a press release from his office. [88]

The Eve auction house in Paris offered for sale a shield from the Acoma Pueblo tribe of New Mexico, over the tribe's protests. Kurt Riley, governor of the tribe, said the shield is a "sacred item which no individual can own." Last year U.S. District Judge Martha Vasquez approved a warrant to repatriate the shield to the Acoma Pueblo. [89]

The French government has said the lack of an explicit U.S. law prohibiting the export of such items prevents the French from enforcing American laws protecting Native American objects in France, according to Heinrich's office. Heinrich's bill would explicitly prohibit the export of items obtained in violation of NAGPRA, which bars trafficking in Native American remains and cultural objects, and other U.S. laws. It also would increase penalties for NAGPRA violations and offer a two-year amnesty for anyone who returns illegally possessed cultural items to Indian tribes. [90]

Native American groups and the Society for American Archaeology support the legislation. Society president Chandler says with federal and state agencies suffering budget cuts, "it's difficult to catch someone looting Indian sites" across the millions of federal acres and called the extent of looting and trafficking "heartbreaking." (Besides the federal law banning digging on federal land, numerous state and local laws prohibit the taking of Native American goods on private land. [91])

However, the bill is opposed by the Antique Tribal Art Dealers Association, an association of collectors and dealers in Rio Rancho, N.M. "Collectors may be pressured to give up objects" that they lawfully own "to tribes that do not want them," the association said. [92] ∎

OUTLOOK

Attitude Adjustment

Continued concern about the looting of archaeological artifacts and the ineffectiveness of existing laws has led some archaeologists to stress the need for a societal change in attitude.

Critics of the trade have taken to referring to looted artifacts as "blood antiquities" — taking a lead from the condemnation of luxury items such as "blood diamonds," fur coats or ivory for their exploitative impact on source communities. [93]

"If you have a big ivory object at the dinner table, your friends are thinking 'dead elephants,' " says Glasgow's Yates. Similarly, she says she would like to "change hearts and minds" of potential buyers through public education about the destructive impact of illegal digging, something she seeks to do with her free online course "Antiquities Trafficking and Art Crime." [94]

The University of Chicago recently held several workshops with experts from academia, the legal profession and the antiquities trade to investigate new approaches to stemming archaeological looting. [95] While no final consensus was achieved among these traditionally warring forces, participants proposed several novel ideas, including taxing antiquities without provenance to help fund more security at archaeological sites. [96]

Other ideas included encouraging museums to take artifacts on long-term loan in lieu of ownership and requiring solid documentation of provenance on donated items before the donor can claim a charitable tax deduction. And more looted items might be seized at the border if international customs rules required more detailed declarations on antiquities, says DePaul's Gerstenblith.

Some archaeologists and collectors also favor the creation of a comprehensive database of artifacts — archaeologists want it for detecting looted items and collectors for assurance that their artifacts are legal. Fitz Gibbon of the Committee for Cultural Policy has proposed such a database.

"After a reasonable period to allow claims, title would be deemed free and clear, unless new information became available," she says.

However, the deep divide between dealers and archaeologists, at least for the present, remains a chasm for some. "If a buyer acquires an object that has been looted, its cultural and scientific value has been destroyed," part of the cultural and historical record of humanity, says Gerstenblith. "If you put that

against the delight a private collector has for something on their mantelpiece, for me, there's no question which one is more important." ∎

Notes

[1] A cylinder seal is a small round tube, typically about one inch in length, engraved with characters and/or figurative scenes, used in ancient times to roll an impression onto a surface, generally wet clay.

[2] "United States Files Civil Action to Forfeit Thousands of Ancient Iraqi Artifacts Imported by Hobby Lobby," press release, U.S. Attorney's Office, Eastern District of New York, U.S. Department of Justice, July 5, 2017, https://tinyurl.com/y73a4h9d.

[3] *Ibid.* Also see David Smith, "Inside the sprawling controversial $500m Museum of the Bible," *The Guardian*, Oct. 16, 2017, https://tinyurl.com/y8uqegwh.

[4] "Illicit Trafficking of Cultural Property," U.N. Educational, Scientific and Cultural Organization, https://tinyurl.com/ydx5pdxf.

[5] Simon Mackenzie and Donna Yates, "What is Grey about the "Grey Market" in Antiquities?" in Jens Beckert and Matías Dewey, eds., *The Architecture of Illegal Markets* (2016), https://tinyurl.com/yc9knvdr.

[6] "U.S. v. Approximately 450 Ancient Cuneiform Tablets and Approximately 3,000 Ancient Clay Bullae," complaint in rem, U.S. District Court, Eastern District of New York, July 5, 2017, p. 10, https://tinyurl.com/ya2q4d2m.

[7] *Ibid.*

[8] *Ibid.*

[9] Alan Fever, "Hobby Lobby Agrees to Forfeit 5,500 Artifacts Smuggled out of Iraq," *The New York Times*, July 5, 2017, https://tinyurl.com/yb427cs7.

[10] "Hobby Lobby to forfeit ancient Iraqi artifacts in settlement with D.O.J.," Reuters, July 5, 2017, https://tinyurl.com/y8amzyko.

[11] "How Terrorists Tap a Black Market Fueled by Stolen Antiquities," NBC News, June 23, 2014, https://tinyurl.com/y99ynj4e. Deborah M. Lehr and Katie A. Paul, "Rocking the Cradle of Civilization," *The Huffington Post*, Sept. 1, 2014, https://tinyurl.com/yb3ctr7m.

[12] The estimate includes Greek, Roman and Near Eastern objects from about 8,000 B.C. to 500 A.D., but not objects from South America, Asia or Africa.

[13] Blythe Bowman Proulx, "Archeological Site Looting in 'Glocal' Perspective: Nature, Scope, and Frequency," *American Journal of Archaeology*, 2013, p. 117, https://tinyurl.com/yazvt76a.

[14] Georgi Kantchev, "Buyer Beware: Looted Antiquities Flood Online Sites like Amazon, Facebook," *The Wall Street Journal*, Nov. 1, 2017, http://tinyurl.com/yddrsyd8.

[15] Mackenzie and Yates, *op. cit.*

[16] Eric Cline, *Three Stones Make a Wall* (2017), p. 330.

[17] See Convention on Cultural Policy Implementation Act, pp. 1-2, https://tinyurl.com/y8ev79se.

[18] "2013 Guidelines on the Acquisition of Archaeological Material and Ancient Art," Association of Art Museum Directors, Jan. 29, 2013, https://tinyurl.com/y7bfhpjh.

[19] "Key Aspects of the New Act on the Protection of Cultural Property," Federal Government Commissioner for Culture and Media, Government of Germany, September 2016, https://tinyurl.com/yc9vrwze.

[20] Roland Arkell, "Sales move out of Germany as controversial culture bill becomes law," *Antiques Trade Gazette*, July 18, 2016, https://tinyurl.com/y98hu6ds.

[21] "Security Union: Cracking down on the illegal import of cultural goods used to finance terrorism," press release, European Commission, July 13, 2017, https://tinyurl.com/y8mu62ay. Also see accompanying Fact Sheet, July 13, 2017, https://tinyurl.com/y7ksmxld.

[22] "New EU Regulations on Art Trade," Committee for Cultural Policy, Aug. 29, 2017, https://tinyurl.com/yaqdp88l.

[23] John Henry Merryman, "Two Ways of Thinking about Cultural Property," *The American Journal of International Law*, October 1986, pp. 831-853, https://tinyurl.com/y9thxdgr.

[24] Michele Chabin, "After the Hobby Lobby Scandal," *Deseret News*, Aug. 17. 2017, https://tinyurl.com/ycs43g97.

[25] *Ibid.*

[26] "The Parthenon Sculptures, Facts and Figures," British Museum, https://tinyurl.com/7uvzs26.

[27] Anthee Carassava," Greece threatens legal action to win back 'stolen' Elgin Marbles," *The Times* (London), Sept. 18, 2017, https://tinyurl.com/yd5jbmu3.

[28] Khanya Mtshali, "British Museum is in talks to return bronze artifacts looted from Benin Kingdom 120 years ago," *Quartz Africa*, Aug. 16, 2017, https://tinyurl.com/yc9addnv.

[29] "Remembering Nadine Gordimer," British Committee for the Reunification of the British Marbles, July 15, 2014, https://tinyurl.com/yam8nktv. Also See Christopher Hitchens, *The Parthenon Marbles: The Case for Reunification* (2008), p. viii.

[30] Merryman, *op. cit.*

[31] *Ibid.*, p. 846.

[32] Tiffany Jenkins, *Keeping their Marbles* (2016), pp. 245-246.

[33] Merryman, *op. cit.*

[34] The National Stolen Property Act (1934) prohibits movement of stolen goods valued at $5,000 or more across state or national borders. U.S. courts have upheld foreign patrimony laws in cases testing whether antiquities imported from those countries were stolen under the U.S. law. *See U.S. v McClain* (1977) 5th Circuit Court of Appeals and *U.S. v. Schultz* (2003) 2nd Circuit Court of Appeals.

[35] "1799 Rosetta Stone Found," This Day in History, https://tinyurl.com/22wwq9r. Napoleon's troops discovered the Rosetta stone in 1799 in Egypt. When the British defeated the French in 1801 they were ceded the stone by treaty.

[36] Chip Colwell, *Plundered Skulls and Stolen Spirits: Inside the Fight to Reclaim Native America's Culture* (2017), pp. 3-4.

[37] Dylan Brown, "The Spoils of Wars and Massacres: NAGPRA 25 Years Later," *Indian Country Today*, June 9, 2015, https://tinyurl.com/y9y7orwb.

[38] According to an Oct. 17, 2017 email from Melanie O'Brien, Program Manager, National NAGPRA Program.

[39] Carl Zimmer, "Tribes' Win in Fight for La Jolla Bones Clouds Hope for DNA Studies," *The New York Times*, Jan. 29, 2016, https://tinyurl.com/ybun3mca.

[40] Dorothy Alther, *White et al. v. California Board of Regents et al.*, Summary from NATHPO program, August 2017, https://tinyurl.com/ycp9r6fh.

[41] Elizabeth Weiss, "The bone battle: The attack on scientific freedom," *Liberty*, December 2009, available at: https://tinyurl.com/yatzodtk. Also See "Determining Cultural Affiliation within NAGPRA," National Park Service, Sept. 1, 2013, https://tinyurl.com/y7u2ff37.

[42] Simon Mackenzie, "While Elgin Marbles debate rages, there is still a market for looted antiquities" *The Conversation*, Feb. 14, 2014, https://tinyurl.com/yda4pjkk.

[43] Jenkins, *op. cit.*, pp. 76-80.

[44] *Ibid.*

[45] *Ibid.*, p. 67.

[46] "Boston's Museum of Fine Arts urged to Return Looted Artifacts to Nigeria," *The Huffington Post*, July 20, 2012, https://tinyurl.com/yb9ccjd3.

[47] "Return the treasures Britain looted, Chinese tell Cameron," Agence France-Press, *Express Tribune*, Dec. 4, 2013, https://tinyurl.com/y9cx96te.

[48] Jenkins, *op. cit.*, pp. 63-65.

[49] "Holocaust Restitution: Recovering Stolen Art," Jewish Virtual Library, updated March 2017, https://tinyurl.com/yaqn4bpc.

[50] "Convention for the Protection of Cultural Property," UNESCO, https://tinyurl.com/y79tm9md.

[51] *Ibid.*

[52] Jason Felch and Ralph Frammolino, *Chasing Aphrodite* (2011), p. 5.

[53] "Convention on the Means of Prohibiting and Preventing the Illicit Import, Export and Transfer of Ownership of Cultural Property," UNESCO, 1970, https://tinyurl.com/ybtely9q.

[54] Merryman, *op. cit.*

[55] "Convention on Cultural Property Implementation Act," https://tinyurl.com/y8ev79se.

[56] "Emergency Implementation of Import Restrictions," https://tinyurl.com/yaeuvvg3.

[57] See PL 114-151, https://tinyurl.com/y9jnub56.

[58] Colwell, *op. cit.*, pp. 84-85.

[59] Cline, *op. cit.*, p. 331.

[60] "The Archaeological Resources Protection Act of 1979," National Park Service, updated March 15, 2016, https://tinyurl.com/y7chazqd.

[61] Cline, *op cit.* Also see, Kirk Johnson, "23 people are arrested or sought in the Looting of Indian Artifacts," *The New York Times*, June 10, 2009, https://tinyurl.com/kjpkug.

[62] Colwell, *op. cit.*, pp. 213, 225-226.

[63] *Ibid.*, p. 253. Native American Graves Protection and Repatriation Act Regulations, Federal Register, March 15, 2010, https://tinyurl.com/ycrh9hlw.

About the Author

Sarah Glazer is a London-based freelancer who contributes regularly to *CQ Researcher*. Her articles on health, education and social-policy issues also have appeared in *The New York Times* and *The Washington Post*. Her recent *CQ Researcher* reports include "Privacy and the Internet" and "Decriminalizing Prostitution." She graduated from the University of Chicago with a B.A. in American history.

64 *Ibid.*, Carl Zimmer, "New DNA Results Show Kennewick Man Was Native American," *The New York Times*, June 18, 2015, https://tinyurl.com/y9brvvh9.

65 Carl Zimmer, "Tribes' Win in Fight for La Jolla Bones Clouds Hope for DNA Studies," *The New York Times*, Jan. 29, 2016, https://tinyurl.com/ybun3mca.

66 Morten Rasmussen *et al.*, "The Ancestry and Affiliations of Kennewick Man," *Nature*, July 23, 2015, https://tinyurl.com/y8y7gtbv.

67 "Tribes Lay Remains of Kennewick Man to Rest," The Associated Press, Feb. 23, 2017, https://tinyurl.com/yd3taa42.

68 Felch and Frammolino, *op. cit.*

69 Application for Turnover Order, filed by Matthew Bogdanos, New York Country District Attorney, Supreme Court of the State of New York, County of New York, p. 33, https://tinyurl.com/y8gu6th5.

70 *Ibid.*, p. 34.

71 *Ibid.*, p. 36.

72 "Egyptian Archaeological Objects," Arthemis Art-Law Centre, University of Geneva, https://tinyurl.com/yc2cfr2y.

73 *Chasing Aphrodite* (2011), *op. cit.*, p. 228. For Appeals Court decision, see: *United States v. Frederick Schultz*, 333 F.3d 393 (2nd Cir. (N.Y.) June 25, 2003) (No. 02-1357), https://tinyurl.com/yakydd2c.

74 *Ibid.*, *Chasing Aphrodite.*

75 Application for Turnover Order, *op. cit.*, p. 43.

76 "Charges Dismissed Against ex-Getty curator Marion True by Italian Judge," *Los Angeles Times*, Oct. 13, 2010, https://tinyurl.com/2ebmwqu.

77 David Randall, "Revealed," *The Independent*, Nov. 13, 2005, https://tinyurl.com/pjk3ugb.

78 Cline, *op. cit.*, p. 328.

79 Tiffany Westry, "UAB Archaeologists Sarah Parcak, Gregory Mumford awarded Antiquity Prize," Alabama News Center, April 27, 2017, https://tinyurl.com/ydyxne2q. For background, see Kenneth Jost, "Financial Crisis," *CQ Researcher*, May 9, 2008, pp. 409-432, and Kenneth Jost, "Unrest in the Arab world," *CQ Researcher*, Feb. 1, 2013, pp. 105-132.

80 Ammar Cheikh Omar, Richard Engel and Aggelos Petropoulos, "Smuggler of stolen artifacts from Palmyra speaks out about ISIS' illicit operation," NBC, April 6, 2016, https://tinyurl.com/ycfusw6c.

81 "President Signs Engel Bill to Stop ISIS from Looting Antiquities," U.S. Committee of the Blue Shield, May 9, 2016, https://tinyurl.com/ydggpdza.

82 Also see "Security Union," press release, European Commission, July 13, 2017, https://tinyurl.com/y8mu62ay.

83 "Key Aspects of the New Act on the Protection of Cultural Property in Germany," *op. cit.*

84 "Combatting illicit trafficking and destruction of cultural property," Council of Europe, May 3, 2017, https://tinyurl.com/ydd6bk6a. Also see Chart of Signatures and Ratifications of Treaty 221, as of Nov. 6, 2017, https://tinyurl.com/ya78st8l.

85 The vase was seized under a New York state law against criminal possession of stolen property.

86 Tom Mashberg, "Ancient Vase Seized from Met Museum on Suspicion It Was Looted," *The New York Times*, July 31, 2017, https://tinyurl.com/ybf75988.

87 Colin Moynihan, "Looted Antiquity, once at Met Museum, to Return to Lebanon," *The New York Times*, Oct. 11, 2017, https://tinyurl.com/yc2ob65j.

88 Sen. Martin Heinrich, "Heinrich introduces bill to prohibit exporting sacred Native American items," U.S. Senate, July 6, 2016, https://tinyurl.com/yb3t7ndp.

89 Lillia McEnaney, "The STOP Act," SAFE, Sept. 9, 2016, https://tinyurl.com/yaqckszt.

90 Heinrich, *op. cit.*

91 Dennis Gaffney, "Indian Artifacts: Understanding the Law," PBS, April 7, 2014, https://tinyurl.com/yd84xf3s.

92 "Update on the Safeguard Tribal Objects of Patrimony Act (STOP Act)," Antique Tribal Art Dealers Association, Nov. 28, 2016, https://tinyurl.com/y9wyp48w. Also see John Molloy, President, "Written Testimony submitted to U.S. Senate Committee on Indian Affairs," Antique Tribal Art Dealers Association, Oct. 24, 2016, https://tinyurl.com/y9j4j88c.

93 Deborah Lehr, "Blood Antiquities," Antiquities Coalition, Feb. 1, 2016, https://tinyurl.com/y9qg9lo6.

94 "Antiquities Trafficking and Art Crime," Future Learn online course, University of Glasgow, https://tinyurl.com/ybd5jv7p.

95 Laura Demanski, "Heritage in Peril," *University of Chicago Magazine*, Summer 2017, https://tinyurl.com/y8whqdon. Also see "The Past for Sale," University of Chicago, https://tinyurl.com/y9luagxp.

96 Lawrence Rothfield, "How Can We Fund the Fight Against Antiquities Looting and Trafficking? A 'Pollution' Tax on the Antiquities Trade," *Antiquities Coalition*, December 2016, https://tinyurl.com/yd8f6a38.

FOR MORE INFORMATION

Anonymous Swiss Collector, www.anonymousswisscollector.com. A weekly compilation of news articles on antiquities thefts and art crime.

Antiquities Coalition, 1875 Connecticut Ave., N.W., Washington, DC 20009; 202-798-5245; https://theantiquitiescoalition.org. Nonprofit advocacy group fighting illicit trade in ancient art.

Committee for Cultural Policy, Box 4881, Santa Fe, NM 87502; 917-546-6724; https://committeeforculturalpolicy.org. Think tank supporting art and antiquities collecting and a legal market in antiquities.

International Association of Dealers in Ancient Art, Seestrasse 92; 8803, Rüschlikon, Zurich, Switzerland; www.iadaa.org. International association of leading dealers in works of ancient art.

Jews Indigenous to the Middle East and North Africa, 415-626-5062; www.jimena.org/. Advocacy group that seeks recognition for Jews displaced from the Middle East and North Africa in the 20th century and seeks to preserve their culture.

National Association of Tribal Historic Preservation Leaders, PO Box 19189, Washington, DC 20036-9189; 202-258-2101; http://nathpo.org. National group of tribal leaders who implement federal and tribal preservation laws.

National NAGPRA Program, National Park Service, 1849 C St., N.W., Mail Stop 7360, Washington, DC 20240; 202-354-2201; https://www.nps.gov/nagpra. Federal program that administers the Native American Graves Protection and Repatriation Act.

Trafficking Culture, SCCJR, University of Glasgow, Ivy Lodge, 63 Gibson St., Glasgow G12 8LR; trafficking culture.org. Research consortium that produces research on the contemporary global trade in looted cultural objects.

Bibliography
Selected Sources

Books

Anderson, Maxwell L., *Antiquities: What Everyone Needs to Know*, Oxford University Press, 2017.

In this primer on antiquities, a consulting scholar at the University of Pennsylvania Museum of Archaeology and Anthropology frames the key debates over the legal and illicit trade.

Cline, Eric H., *Three Stones Make a Wall: The Story of Archaeology*, Princeton University Press, 2017.

A professor of classics and anthropology at George Washington University traces the history of archaeology from an amateur pursuit to today's scientific approaches.

Colwell, Chip, *Plundered Skulls and Stolen Spirits: Inside the Fight to Reclaim Native America's Culture*, University of Chicago Press, 2017.

A senior curator of anthropology at the Denver Museum of Nature & Science describes the debate between scientists and tribes over who gets to keep American Indian bones and sacred objects and how his museum resolved such dilemmas.

Felch, Jason, and Ralph Frammolino, *Chasing Aphrodite: The Hunt for Looted Antiquities at the World's Richest Museum*, Houghton Mifflin Harcourt, 2011.

Two investigative journalists expose the role the J. Paul Getty Museum and other U.S. museums played in the black market for looted antiquities.

Jenkins, Tiffany, *Keeping Their Marbles: How the Treasures of the Past Ended Up in Museums . . . and Why They Should Stay There*, Oxford University Press, 2016.

The Parthenon's Elgin marbles should stay in Britain, says a cultural commentator and sociologist, adding that arguments for repatriating antiquities like the marbles pose a threat to museums and our understanding of past civilizations.

Articles

Demanski, Laura, "Heritage in Peril," *University of Chicago Magazine*, Summer 2017, https://tinyurl.com/y8whqdon.

Experts in archaeology, law and culture convened by the *University of Chicago Magazine* discuss approaches to stopping the illicit trade in archaeological artifacts.

Dolstein, Josefin, "Schumer: Don't return Jewish trove of artifacts to Iraq," *Jewish Telegraphic Agency*, Oct. 3, 2017, https://tinyurl.com/y8jv7m9f.

Sen. Charles Schumer, D-N.Y., joined Jewish groups in protesting the U.S. government's plan to return to the Iraqi government a trove of Jewish books, documents and sacred objects that the Iraqi government stole from Iraqi Jews.

Felch, Jason, "The Sidon Bull's Head: Court Documents

a Journey through the Illicit Antiquities Trade," *Chasing Aphrodite*, Sept. 24, 2017, https://tinyurl.com/ya36ovl8.

An investigative reporter and coauthor of the book *Chasing Aphrodite* traces the journey of an ancient bull's head sculpture from its theft during the Lebanon civil war through the antiquities black market to the Metropolitan Museum of Art.

Kantchev, Georgi, "Buyer Beware: Looted Antiquities Flood Online Sites like Amazon, Facebook," *The Wall Street Journal*, Nov. 1, 2017, https://tinyurl.com/yddrsyd8.

A flood of possibly stolen antiquities is for sale on eBay and WhatsApp at the same time that the Islamic State has been exploiting social media to cut out the middleman in antiquities sales, the business newspaper reports.

Merryman, John Henry, "Two Ways of Thinking about Cultural Property," *The American Journal of International Law*, October 1986, https://tinyurl.com/y8uaqr3v.

In this landmark article, the late Stanford law professor promoted an "internationalist" perspective, treating cultural objects, such as the Elgin marbles in the British Museum, as part of all humans' heritage, rather than the property of Greece.

Moynihan, Colin, "Looted Antiquity, Once at Met Museum, to Return to Lebanon," *The New York Times*, Oct. 11, 2017, https://tinyurl.com/yc2ob65j.

An ancient sculpture of a bull's head, loaned to the Metropolitan Museum of Art in New York City by a Colorado couple, will be returned to Lebanon after the owners accepted proof it was looted during Lebanon's civil war.

Reports and Studies

Brodie, Neal, "How to Control the Internet Market in Antiquities? The Need for Regulation and Monitoring," Antiquities Coalition, July 2017, https://tinyurl.com/ycqewrss.

A University of Oxford archaeologist reports that looted antiquities increasingly are being sold online and says the United States needs stricter oversight of websites such as eBay.

Mackenzie, Simon, and Donna Yates, "What Is Grey about the 'Grey Market' in Antiquities?" in Jens Beckert and Matias Dewey, eds., *The Architecture of Illegal Markets*, 2016, https://tinyurl.com/yc9knvdr.

Two researchers with the Scottish Centre for Crime and Justice Research at the University of Glasgow report that the legitimate antiquities market is "a mix of legality and illegality."

Parcak, Sarah, *et al.*, "Satellite evidence of archaeological site looting in Egypt: 2002-2013," *Antiquity*, February 2016, https://tinyurl.com/ydhwuymk.

This widely cited study based on satellite photos by a University of Alabama, Birmingham, anthropologist found that looting at Egyptian archaeological sites rose in 2009-11, mirrored by increased sales of Egyptian antiquities at Sotheby's auctions.

The Next Step:

Additional Articles from Current Periodicals

Expatriation

"Repatriated Relics on Display at National Museum," *Financial Tribune*, Feb. 9, 2017, https://tinyurl.com/yd3dt9cx.

A February exhibition at the National Museum of Iran displayed hundreds of artifacts, most of which had been looted and returned to Iran from other countries.

Klasfeld, Adam, "Looted 200 A.D. Sarcophagus Returned to Greece," Courthouse News Service, Feb. 10, 2017, https://tinyurl.com/ycnaq92t.

A sarcophagus stolen from Greece in 1989 was discovered for sale in a New York City gallery, and has since been returned.

Mee-yoo, Kwon, "Returned royal seals open to public view," *The Korea Times*, Aug. 21, 2017, https://tinyurl.com/y9ytp528.

Royal seals from the 14th century are on display at the National Palace Museum of Korea, including a few that were looted over 65 years ago and recently returned by the United States.

ISIS

Faucon, Benoit, and Georgi Kantchev, "Prominent Art Family Entangled in ISIS Antiquities-Looting Investigations," *The Wall Street Journal*, May 31, 2017, https://tinyurl.com/y832agpv.

U.S. Immigration and Customs Enforcement authorities are scrutinizing brothers Ali and Hicham Aboutaam, whose family is well known in the international antiquities business, for possibly trading in antiquities looted by ISIS.

McKirdy, Euan, and Radina Gigova, "Russian intel: ISIS planning further destruction of Syria's ancient Palmyra site," CNN, Feb. 13, 2017, https://tinyurl.com/yad9zqq9.

ISIS destroyed many of Palmyra's ancient antiquities and historic monuments after the group occupied the area in 2015.

Wedeman, Ben, "ISIS devastated Mosul Museum, or did it?" CNN, March 13, 2017, https://tinyurl.com/ju25u6j.

Before ISIS got to the Mosul Museum, 1,700 items had been moved to Baghdad in preparation for renovations.

Museum Claims

Barbieri, Claudia, "A Shelter for Art Caught in the Cross-fire," *The New York Times*, March 11, 2017, https://tinyurl.com/y9hwpxfd.

Despite potential controversy, French officials have offered a Louvre building that is under construction as a sanctuary for at-risk artifacts from Middle Eastern conflict zones.

Moynihan, Colin, "Looted Antiquity, Once at Met Museum, to Return to Lebanon," *The New York Times*, Oct. 11 2017,

https://tinyurl.com/yc2ob65j.

An artifact on loan to the Metropolitan Museum of Art from private collectors is being returned to Lebanon after concerns were raised about its origin.

Wamsley, Laurel, "Met Museum Turns Over Ancient Vase Suspected Looted From Italy," NPR, Aug. 1, 2017, https://tinyurl.com/y9ft7tyl.

The Metropolitan Museum of Art turned over an ancient terra cotta vase to the Manhattan district attorney's office, which had issued a warrant for the piece after it was shown to have been looted from Italy in the 1970s.

Native American Relics

"Archaeologists: Looters posting pics of Native American artifacts," CBS 8 San Diego, May 9, 2017, https://tinyurl.com/y7y28cvz.

Tens of thousands of Native American artifact sites in San Diego County are vulnerable to looting, says an archaeologist.

Carpenter, Murray, "Native American Secrets Lie Buried in Huge Shell Mounds," *The New York Times*, Oct. 19, 2017, https://tinyurl.com/yabdpl5q.

Middens, the massive piles of oyster shells left by Native Americans along Maine's coastline, contain important historical information and many have been looted or destroyed.

Eilperin, Juliet, and Darryl Fears, "Trump says he will shrink Bears Ears National Monument, a sacred tribal site in Utah," *The Washington Post*, Oct. 27, 2017, https://tinyurl.com/ybea62y3.

President Trump has approved scaling back the protective boundaries of Bears Ears National Monument.

CITING *CQ RESEARCHER*

Sample formats for citing these reports in a bibliography include the ones listed below. Preferred styles and formats vary, so please check with your instructor or professor.

MLA STYLE
Mantel, Barbara. "Coal Industry's Future." CQ Researcher 17 June 2016: 529-552.

APA STYLE
Mantel, B. (2016, June 17). Coal Industry's Future. *CQ Researcher,* 6, 529-552.

CHICAGO STYLE
Mantel, Barbara. "Coal Industry's Future." *CQ Researcher*, June 17, 2016, 529-52.

In-depth Reports on Issues in the News

Are you writing a paper?

Need backup for a debate?

Want to become an expert on an issue?

For 90 years, students have turned to *CQ Researcher* for in-depth reporting on issues in the news. Reports on a full range of political and social issues are now available. Following is a selection of recent reports:

Civil Liberties
Privacy and the Internet, 12/15
Intelligence Reform, 5/15
Religion and Law, 11/14

Crime/Law
High-Tech Policing, 4/17
Forensic Science Controversies, 2/17
Jailing Debtors, 9/16
Decriminalizing Prostitution, 4/16
Restorative Justice, 2/16
The Dark Web, 1/16
Immigrant Detention, 10/15

Education
Charter Schools, 3/17
Civic Education, 2/17
Student Debt, 11/16

Environment/Society
Military Readiness, 11/17
Climate Change and National Security, 9/17
Muslims in America, 7/17
Funding the Arts, 7/17
Hunger in America, 7/17
Future of the Christian Right, 6/17
Trust in Media, 6/17

Health/Safety
Medical Breakthroughs, 9/17
Medical Marijuana, 7/17
Food Labeling, 6/17
Sports and Sexual Assault, 4/17

Politics/Economy
Democracy Under Stress, 10/17
Cyberwarfare Threat, 10/17
Universal Basic Income, 9/17
National Debt, 9/17
North Korea Showdown, 5/17
Rethinking Foreign Aid, 4/17

Upcoming Reports

Race and College Admissions, 11/17/17   Future of Marriage, 12/1/17   Privatization, 12/8/17

ACCESS

CQ Researcher is available in print and online. For access, visit your library or www.cqresearcher.com.

STAY CURRENT

For notice of upcoming *CQ Researcher* reports or to learn more about *CQ Researcher* products, subscribe to the free email newsletters, *CQ Researcher Alert!* and *CQ Researcher News*: http://cqpress.com/newsletters.

PURCHASE

To purchase a *CQ Researcher* report in print or electronic format (PDF), visit www.cqpress.com or call 866-427-7737. Single reports start at $15. Bulk purchase discounts and electronic-rights licensing are also available.

SUBSCRIBE

Annual full-service *CQ Researcher* subscriptions—including 44 reports a year, monthly index updates, and a bound volume—start at $1,131. Add $25 for domestic postage.

CQ Researcher Online offers a backfile from 1991 and a number of tools to simplify research. For pricing information, call 800-818-7243 or 805-499-9774 or email librarysales@sagepub.com.

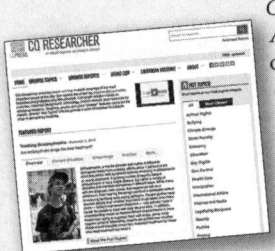

Published by CQ Press, an Imprint of SAGE Publications, Inc.

www.cqresearcher.com

Affirmative Action and College Admissions

Should racial and ethnic preferences continue?

The Supreme Court has upheld the use of race in college admissions, but affirmative action is facing new challenges. Many whites continue to oppose giving preference to minorities to compensate for discrimination and to diversify campuses, and the Trump administration says it may sue universities practicing "intentional" discrimination. Several critics question affirmative action's effectiveness, citing minorities' continued under-representation at elite universities. But affirmative action's defenders say it has helped raise minority representation on campuses, and that most universities rely on a "holistic" admissions approach that looks at applicants' public service, creativity and other attributes, as well as race. Georgetown and other schools are pursuing innovative ways to diversify their student bodies, such as admitting the descendants of slaves owned by their institutions. Meanwhile, activist Edward Blum has filed numerous suits challenging laws and policies that favor minorities over whites.

Demonstrators at the U.S. Supreme Court on Dec. 9, 2015, protest against affirmative action, which they said discriminates against Asian-American applicants to college. The Trump administration is investigating claims that universities are unfairly selecting black and Hispanic applicants over Asian-Americans.

CQ Researcher • Nov. 17, 2017 • www.cqresearcher.com
Volume 27, Number 41 • Pages 969-992

I THIS REPORT

N
S
I
D
E

THE ISSUES	**971**
BACKGROUND	**977**
CHRONOLOGY	**979**
CURRENT SITUATION	**984**
AT ISSUE	**985**
OUTLOOK	**987**
BIBLIOGRAPHY	**990**
THE NEXT STEP	**991**

AFFIRMATIVE ACTION AND COLLEGE ADMISSIONS

THE ISSUES

971 • Should minorities receive preferential treatment in college admissions?
• Should affirmative action be based on income rather than race or ethnicity?
• Does campus diversity improve the quality of education for all students?

BACKGROUND

977 **Search for "Character"** Harvard began using entrance exams in 1905.

978 **Federal Push for Diversity** Affirmative action became federal policy in 1961.

980 **"Mend It, but Don't End It"** President Clinton took a moderate approach to affirmative action in the 1990s.

983 **The Obama Years** The administration emphasized socioeconomic divisions over race.

CURRENT SITUATION

984 **Spending Cutbacks** Federal agencies are reducing enforcement of civil rights laws and regulations.

986 **State-Level Lawsuits** Universities are fending off affirmative-action lawsuits.

OUTLOOK

987 **A Divided Supreme Court** Continued support for affirmative action might depend on President Trump's appointees.

SIDEBARS AND GRAPHICS

972 **Asian-American Students Are No. 1 in Enrollment** All minority enrollment has risen significantly since 1980.

973 **Large Majority Rejects Affirmative Action** Most Americans believe race or ethnicity should not factor into college admissions.

976 **Affirmative Action Barred in Eight States** Most bans apply to college admissions, public employment and contracting.

979 **Chronology** Key events since 1961.

980 **Activist Pushes for a 'Colorblind America'** "Most Americans want to be judged as individuals."

982 **Colleges Seek Novel Ways to Boost Diversity** Increasing community-college transfers is one strategy.

985 **At Issue:** Should affirmative action be based on income instead of race?

FOR FURTHER RESEARCH

989 **For More Information** Organizations to contact.

990 **Bibliography** Selected sources used.

991 **The Next Step** Additional articles.

991 **Citing CQ Researcher** Sample bibliography formats.

CQ RESEARCHER

Nov. 17, 2017
Volume 27, Number 41

EXECUTIVE EDITOR: Thomas J. Billitteri
tjb@sagepub.com

ASSISTANT MANAGING EDITORS: Kenneth Fireman, kenneth.fireman@sagepub.com, Kathy Koch, kathy.koch@sagepub.com, Scott Rohrer, scott.rohrer@sagepub.com

ASSOCIATE MANAGING EDITOR: Val Ellicott

SENIOR CONTRIBUTING EDITOR:
Thomas J. Colin
tom.colin@sagepub.com

CONTRIBUTING WRITERS: Marcia Clemmitt, Sarah Glazer, Alan Greenblatt, Reed Karaim, Barbara Mantel, Patrick Marshall, Tom Price

SENIOR PROJECT EDITOR: Olu B. Davis

EDITORIAL ASSISTANT: Natalia Gurevich

FACT CHECKERS: Eva P. Dasher, Michelle Harris, Betsy Towner Levine, Robin Palmer

Los Angeles I London I New Delhi
Singapore I Washington DC I Melbourne

An Imprint of SAGE Publications, Inc.

SENIOR VICE PRESIDENT, GLOBAL LEARNING RESOURCES:
Karen Phillips

EXECUTIVE DIRECTOR, ONLINE LIBRARY AND REFERENCE PUBLISHING:
Todd Baldwin

CQ Researcher (ISSN 1056-2036) is printed on acid-free paper. Published weekly, except: (March wk. 4) (May wk. 4) (July wks. 1, 2) (Aug. wks. 2, 3) (Nov. wk. 4) and (Dec. wks. 3, 4). Published by SAGE Publications, Inc., 2455 Teller Rd., Thousand Oaks, CA 91320. Annual full-service subscriptions start at $1,131. For pricing, call 1-800-818-7243. To purchase a CQ Researcher report in print or electronic format (PDF), visit www.cqpress. com or call 866-427-7737. Single reports start at $15. Bulk purchase discounts and electronic-rights licensing are also available. Periodicals postage paid at Thousand Oaks, California, and at additional mailing offices. POSTMASTER: Send address changes to CQ Researcher, 2600 Virginia Ave., N.W., Suite 600, Washington, DC 20037.

Cover: Getty Images/*CQ Roll Call*/Bill Clark

Affirmative Action and College Admissions

BY TOM PRICE

THE ISSUES

Abigail Fisher is an unassuming 27-year-old from Sugar Land, Texas, who played the cello and dreamed of attending the University of Texas at Austin, the alma mater of her sister and father.

She also is at the center of a legal storm involving affirmative action. For the past nine years, Fisher has maintained that the university rejected her application in 2008 because she is white, in violation of the U.S. Constitution. Her lawsuit twice landed at the U.S. Supreme Court, most recently producing the landmark 2016 ruling that the school could treat "race as a relevant feature within the broader context of a candidate's application." [1]

Nevertheless, Fisher and an advocacy group backing her, Students for Fair Admissions, filed a new lawsuit in late June in state court, arguing that the university's use of racial preferences in admissions violates state law and the Texas Constitution. [2]

Critics of affirmative action — policies that seek to compensate for racial and ethnic discrimination and to diversify campuses by admitting more African-Americans, Hispanics and other minorities — have long complained that giving preference to minorities in college admissions is a form of reverse discrimination against whites. But the debate is resurfacing, again, in an era of heightened racial tensions in which white supremacists feel emboldened to air their ideology in public, and football players kneel during the National Anthem to protest racial injustice. The United States also is struggling with a contentious transition from America's first black president to a chief executive whose political base includes whites

Abigail Fisher has been challenging University of Texas affirmative-action policies since 2008, when she says the school rejected her application because she is white. Her suit led to the Supreme Court's landmark 2016 ruling that the school could consider race as one of several factors in evaluating a candidate's application.

AP Photo/J. Scott Applewhite

who feel aggrieved because they believe their values are under siege in a nation where minorities will soon constitute a majority of the population.

The Trump administration also worries supporters of affirmative action. The Justice Department's Civil Rights Division is preparing to investigate and possibly sue universities whose admission offices practice "intentional race-based discrimination." And the White House is cutting staff in various agencies' civil rights offices, making it difficult for the government to pursue affirmative-action or discrimination complaints. [3]

Kristen Clarke, president of the liberal Lawyers' Committee for Civil Rights Under Law, called the Justice Department's threat to sue colleges over admissions policies "deeply disturbing. It would be a dog whistle that could invite a lot of chaos and unnecessarily create hysteria among colleges and universities who may fear that the government may come down on them for their efforts to maintain diversity on their campuses." [4]

The Trump administration said it simply is responding to a new challenge to affirmative action that the Obama administration had left unresolved: accusations that Asian-Americans suffer when college admissions offices give preferences to black and Hispanic applicants.

In 2014, 64 Asian-American groups filed a complaint with the Justice Department accusing Harvard University of discriminating against Asian-Americans in its admission policies by holding them to higher standards than other ethnic groups. The same year, Students for Fair Admissions sued Harvard on Asian-Americans' behalf. It filed a separate suit accusing the University of North Carolina of discriminating against both Asian-Americans and whites. [5]

Affirmative action is most controversial at elite private colleges and at flagship public universities where competition for admittance is fiercest. Harvard, for instance, typically rejects 90 percent of applicants, including 1,800 high school valedictorians in one recent year. [6]

Asian-Americans tend to perform better on standardized tests than other ethnic groups, and those who believe they face discrimination cite a 2009 study by Princeton University researchers that found Asian-Americans on average had to score 140 points higher than whites on the Scholastic Aptitude Test (SAT) to win admission to private universities. [7]

Austin Jia, an Asian-American from New Jersey, said he thought he was Ivy League material with his near-perfect SAT score, his 4.42 grade-point

Asian-Americans Are No. 1 in Enrollment

Minority college enrollment has risen significantly since 1980, with Hispanics showing the biggest gains. African-American enrollment recorded the second-biggest increase, rising by 15.5 percentage points between 1980 and 2015. Overall, 62.6 percent of Asian-Americans between ages 18 and 24 were enrolled in college in 2015 — the highest of any demographic group.

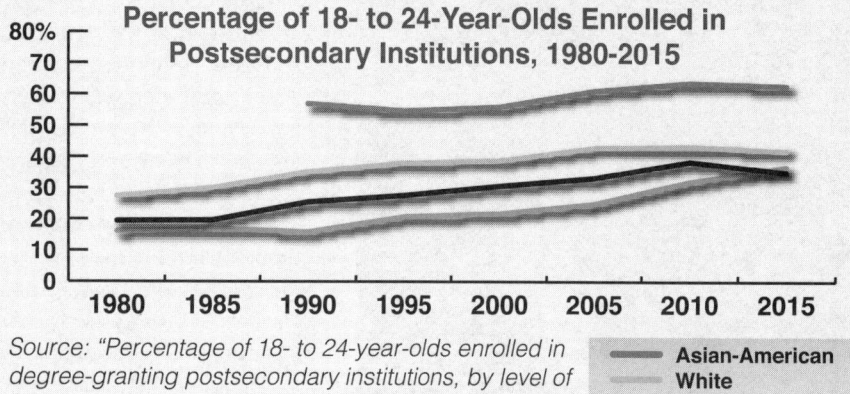

Percentage of 18- to 24-Year-Olds Enrolled in Postsecondary Institutions, 1980-2015

Source: "Percentage of 18- to 24-year-olds enrolled in degree-granting postsecondary institutions, by level of institution and sex and race/ethnicity of student: 1970 through 2015," National Center for Education Statistics, July 2016, https://tinyurl.com/las37rf

Asian-American
White
Black
Hispanic

average and his many Advanced Placement courses and extracurricular activities. But Harvard and several other Ivy League schools rejected his application while admitting classmates with lower SAT scores.

"I felt that the whole concept of meritocracy — which America likes to say it exercises all the time — I felt that principle was defeated a little in my mind," said Jia, now a sophomore at Duke University in Durham, N.C. [8]

Other Asian-Americans support affirmative action. It "benefits everyone," said lawyer Nicole Gon Ochi of Asian Americans Advancing Justice, a civil rights group that supports Harvard's admission policies. "It especially helps traditionally disadvantaged Asian-American students." [9]

Since 1978, the Supreme Court has issued a string of rulings on affirmative action that have established two tenets: Colleges cannot use race as the only criterion for making an admissions decision. But in order to create a diverse student body, they can consider race

as one factor in a "holistic" review of an applicant's qualifications.

Supporters believe affirmative action has largely worked. Overall, minority enrollment for students ages 18 to 24 soared to 41.7 percent in 2014, up from 15.7 percent in 1976, but it fell in a handful of states that have banned race considerations in college admissions. (*See graph above.*) Graduation rates also have improved. Of blacks entering a four-year college in 1996, 39 percent had graduated within six years. For those entering in 2008, 41 percent had graduated by 2014. Hispanics' graduation rates rose even more — from 45.7 percent to 53.5 percent. [10]

Some affirmative-action critics, however, say these statistics do not tell the whole story. Affirmative action can harm minority students by admitting them to programs for which they are not prepared, argue University of California, Los Angeles law professor Richard Sander and former Brookings Institution fellow Stuart Taylor Jr. They say minorities often fail at elite colleges

that give "large preferences" to applicants who have far weaker qualifications than their white peers.

"Large preferences often place students in environments where they can neither learn nor compete effectively — even though these same students would thrive had they gone to less competitive but still quite good schools," wrote Sander and Taylor. [11]

Affirmative-action supporters respond that many minority and low-income applicants are highly qualified and are capable of succeeding at academically competitive schools.

Rod Newhouse, a black graduate of the Massachusetts Institute of Technology, said he was academically unprepared for the elite university but, with tutoring and other help, he was able to travel the "hard, brutal road" to graduation. [12]

Affirmative action's defenders also say these programs are needed to maintain healthy minority enrollment. Despite the Supreme Court rulings allowing consideration of race and ethnicity in admissions, eight states have banned affirmative action at public universities, and minority enrollment has fallen in a number of those places.

For instance, when California banned affirmative action in 1998, blacks made up 8 percent of the freshmen at the University of California's Berkeley and Los Angeles campuses. By 2015 those figures had fallen to 4.3 percent at UCLA and 2.8 percent at Berkeley. [13] And in Michigan, which banned it in 2006, African-American enrollment at the University of Michigan plunged 30 percent in the next seven years. [14]

Meanwhile, the number of colleges considering race in their affirmative-action programs also has fallen, particularly on less selective campuses. Among institutions that accepted 85 percent or more of their applicants, only 35 percent considered race when evaluating applicants in 2014 — down from 60 percent two decades ago. The decline has been less severe at more selective schools that reject at least two-thirds of applicants: 88 percent considered race in 2014, down only 5 percentage points since 1994. [15]

Moreover, African-Americans, who represent about 13 percent of the U.S. population, make up only 9 percent of the freshman class at Ivy League schools and 6 percent of freshmen at 100 elite schools — flagship public universities, top liberal arts colleges and the Ivies. [16]

Elite colleges deny they discriminate against minorities. Harvard officials note that Asian-Americans represent 22 percent of the university's freshman class this year, while making up just 6 percent of the U.S. population. [17] The university said it "considers each applicant as a whole person, and we review many factors, consistent with the legal standards established by the U.S. Supreme Court." [18]

The use of such comprehensive criteria is true of all affirmative-action plans, supporters of the process say. Admissions officers conduct "holistic" reviews that look at "a wide range of qualifications, such as public service, whether students have overcome a variety of difficulties in life, creativity, achievement in art and athletics and leadership qualities," says Michele Moses, associate dean for graduate studies in the University of Colorado School of Education, who studies ethnicity and equal opportunity.

Increasing minority representation improves all students' education by fostering discussions among people with different backgrounds, college officials say. But some analysts challenge that contention and charge that recent college policies seeking to protect students from upsetting speech inhibit open dialogue. [19]

When teaching law classes, "I did not find the discussions to be different based on the race and ethnicity of the students involved," says Roger Clegg, president of the conservative Center for Equal Opportunity, a think tank in Northern Virginia that promotes a "colorblind society." Restriction of campus speech "shows the

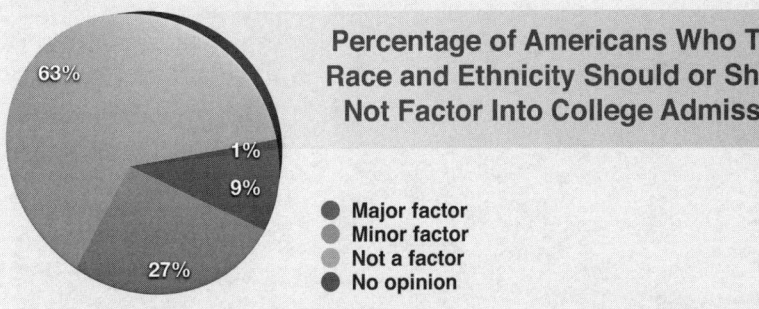

Large Majority Rejects Affirmative Action

Sixty-three percent of Americans believe race or ethnicity should not be a factor in college admissions, according to a 2016 Gallup Poll. Affirmative action's unpopularity stands in stark contrast to Supreme Court rulings that colleges may take race into consideration when deciding which applicants to admit.

Percentage of Americans Who Think Race and Ethnicity Should or Should Not Factor Into College Admissions

63%
1%
9%
27%

- Major factor
- Minor factor
- Not a factor
- No opinion

Source: Frank Newport, "Most in U.S. Oppose Colleges Considering Race in Admissions," Gallup, July 8, 2016, https://tinyurl.com/y8nhaa38

Left is not really interested in diversity when it comes to hearing ideas," he says.

Americans have long felt it is unfair for colleges to consider race or ethnicity in admissions. A 2004 Gallup Poll, for instance, found 69 percent believed admissions should be based "solely on merit." Answering a different question last year, 63 percent said race or ethnicity should not be a factor at all in admissions. [20] (*See graph above.*)

As affirmative action is contested in legislatures and courts of law and public opinion, these are some of the key issues being debated:

Should minorities receive preferential treatment in college admissions?

Although minority enrollment has improved overall since 1976, minorities' continued under-representation on a number of college campuses shows that decades of affirmative action have been targeting the wrong problems, some critics of the practice say. But supporters say centuries of discrimination — from slavery through segregation to lingering inequalities today — leave African-Americans in particular still in need of special assistance to enter and

succeed in higher education.

Minorities' under-representation in college is not the real problem, says Clegg, a former deputy assistant attorney general in the Ronald Reagan and George H.W. Bush administrations. "A disproportional number of African-American men and women . . . are not academically competitive enough to get into our most selective schools," he says.

To change that, he says, the United States must address "social and cultural" issues such as poor-performing public schools in low-income neighborhoods, "black kids being told that doing well in school is acting white" and single parenthood, Clegg says. A one-parent household leads to children having "less support at school, less support doing homework and less supervision," he says, and it often means children do not have a male role model at home. "I don't think the way you correct that is giving them preferences once they apply to colleges and universities."

Some affirmative-action supporters agree that underperforming public schools contribute to minorities' disadvantages in college admissions. "We have disparities by race and income from preschool forward to K-12 education," the University of Colorado's Moses says. "We have to have policies and practices in place well before students apply to college to make a real difference in representation on campus."

But supporters say that is no reason to scrap affirmative action. "There are lots of talented, economically disadvantaged and minority students who can do the work at the most-selective colleges who are not now attending" because

African-American graduates at Harvard University celebrate at commencement on May 25, 2017. Harvard and other elite colleges deny they discriminate in their admission policies. Harvard evaluates each applicant "as a whole person" to make sure students "work with people from different backgrounds, life experiences and perspectives," university spokeswoman Melodie Jackson said.

schools don't do a good-enough job looking for them, says Richard Kahlenberg, a senior fellow at the Century Foundation, a liberal think tank with offices in New York and Washington.

Supporters argue that long-term, systemic discrimination makes affirmative action necessary. This discrimination is "a substantial reason African-Americans achieve [academically] at lower levels and need the compensation that affirmative action provides," says Richard Rothstein, a research associate at the liberal Economic Policy Institute in Washington and author of *The Color of Law: A Forgotten History of How Our Government Segregated America*.

For much of American history, Rothstein says, governments at all levels — including in the North — have imposed segregation, and that requires a government response now.

Not only did government policies force minorities into segregated, inferior schools, Rothstein says, but federal housing policies also supported residential segregation, depressing minorities' ability to build wealth through homeownership. For example, federal housing policy in the 1960s prevented homes in black neighborhoods from qualifying for government-backed mortgages. [21] In addition, minorities historically had little access to high-paying jobs.

The long-term effects of this discrimination continue today, Rothstein says. Median income of non-Hispanic white households last year was $65,041, while it was $47,675 for Hispanics and $39,490 for blacks. [22] The differences in household wealth — accumulated over decades and even generations — is much greater. Fifteen percent of white households are worth more than a million dollars, compared with about 2 percent of black and Hispanic house-

holds. In 2016, median net worth was $171,000 for white families, $20,700 for Hispanics and $17,600 for blacks. Nearly 75 percent of white families own their homes, compared with fewer than half of black and Hispanic families. [23]

Income and wealth have a major impact on higher-education access, affirmative-action advocates say. A study of 38 elite colleges found that more members of the class of 2013 came from the top 1 percent of income-earning families than from the bottom 60 percent. [24] Data from the College Board in 2013 showed that students from families with annual income above $200,000 scored 400 points higher on combined SAT scores than students whose families earned less than $20,000. [25]

Beyond living in high-quality school districts or sending their children to private schools, wealthier families are more likely to invest in tutoring, test preparation and college counseling. [26]

"Especially at selective schools, it's essentially an arms race among students to gather the right SAT score and courses and extracurricular activities and internships," says Jennifer Glynn, research director at the Jack Kent Cooke Foundation in Lansdowne, Va., which supports low-income students from elementary school through postgraduate studies. "Wealthy students can afford to pay for summer experiences and take an unpaid internship. Poor students can't afford to have these additions to their track record."

Clegg, however, argued that past discrimination does not justify affirmative action in admissions because its role in causing white versus minority disparities "is greatly diminished for [college applicants] who were, after all, born late in the Clinton administration — not in slavery or the Jim Crow era." Discrimination "in just about any public transaction, and this includes education, has been illegal for decades," he said. And, he noted, while both Asian-Americans and Latinos have been discriminated against, their educational preparation now is "quite different." [27]

Others counter that discrimination is not in the past — it continues. Douglas Massey, a professor of sociology at Princeton University, said one-third of all African-American city dwellers were living in highly or hypersegregated neighborhoods as of 2010, when the last census took place. [28]

Clegg says that regardless of whether discrimination is responsible for current disparities, discrimination — including against whites and Asian-Americans — is always wrong.

Edward Blum, president of Students for Fair Admissions, which has filed key lawsuits against affirmative-action programs, agrees. "The founding principle of the civil rights movement and the principle that most Americans embrace today is that your race and your ethnicity should not be something that harms your life's endeavors or in the alterative helps you in your life's endeavors," Blum says.

Should affirmative action be based on income rather than race or ethnicity?

For the Century Foundation's Kahlenberg, race-conscious affirmative action has a drawback: It does not give enough consideration to prospective students from economically disadvantaged families, including minorities. "It seems to me that having a multiracial aristocracy is better than an all-white aristocracy, but it's still an aristocracy," he said of the effects of race- and ethnic-conscious admissions at elite colleges and universities. [29]

"When universities have the ability to use race in admissions, they rarely consider economic status," he says. Instead, "universities tend to try to assemble classes that are racially diverse and include upper-middle-class students of all races."

Kahlenberg points to Harvard, which this fall admitted a freshman class with a slight majority of minorities, in part because of a large number of Asian-Americans, who tend to be a highly ed-

ucated and affluent ethnic group. A study published in June found that 15 percent of Harvard's student body came from families in the top 1 percent of income, while only 4.5 percent came from families in the bottom fifth. [30]

Kahlenberg proposes basing affirmative action on economic factors because "it's the fair thing to do," and it still would "produce substantial amounts of racial and ethnic diversity" because minorities tend to have lower incomes and wealth.

"When students have overcome significant economic obstacles and managed to do pretty well academically despite those odds, there's something very special that those students have to offer," he says. "And society ought to recognize these strivers and include them in selective colleges which provide an entrée into the leadership class in society."

Many affirmative-action supporters, however, don't want to drop racial and ethnic preferences.

"I think [economic considerations] should be in addition to race and ethnicity, and not instead of," the University of Colorado's Moses says, because "race and ethnicity continue to be very important factors in American life."

"Race and class, while they overlap, are different things," says Anthony Carnevale, an economist who directs the Georgetown University Center on Education and the Workforce. "They're both disadvantages, but to be poor and black is to be worse than poor. African-Americans as a group have suffered disadvantages at every level of income."

Rothstein of the Economic Policy Institute argues that the Supreme Court has erred in its affirmative-action decisions, which allow, but do not require, race and ethnicity to be considered among other factors. African-Americans — because of government support for slavery and discrimination — have a constitutional right to affirmative action, he says.

"If we're seeking diversity in higher education and seeking to enhance upward mobility, we should certainly give special

consideration to children from lower socioeconomic groups who have made exceptional efforts to attempt to succeed and need the boost of a special lift in the admission process," Rothstein says.

Addressing only economic disadvantage, however, would "mostly overlook a substantial, nonaffluent African-American middle class, sitting between the very poor and the rich," he said. Because of longtime discrimination, "poor whites are less likely to live in high-poverty neighborhoods than poor blacks," he said. "Black middle-class children are more likely to be first in their families to aim for college. While other groups experience hardship and discrimination, few nonblack young people suffer handicaps of similar intensity." [31]

The Cooke Foundation's Glynn says the country is at "a sociological turning point" in understanding the need for affirmative action for the economically disadvantaged.

"We started talking about racial equity gaps 40 years ago, and movement has been made on that front because people have been drawing attention to it," she says. "It is becoming increasingly evident in society that student opportunities for educational advancement strongly correlate with income, and this is something that has not received as much attention to date as other factors."

Currently, Glynn says, "educational attainment gaps based on income are widening, whereas gaps based on race are narrowing." The reading achievement gap between black and white students used to be twice as large as the gap between low-income and higher-income students, for example. Now the reverse is true. [32]

Economically disadvantaged students cannot compete with the résumés of more affluent college applicants, Glynn says.

"Low-income students who may be working to help support the family are not going to engage in the same sort of extracurricular activities that an affluent student who doesn't have to work may engage in," she explains.

Affirmative Action Barred in Eight States

Eight states prohibit preferential treatment for applicants to state-supported universities on the basis of race, sex, ethnicity or national origin. Most of the bans also apply to public employment and public contracting. California was the first state to end affirmative action in its university system.

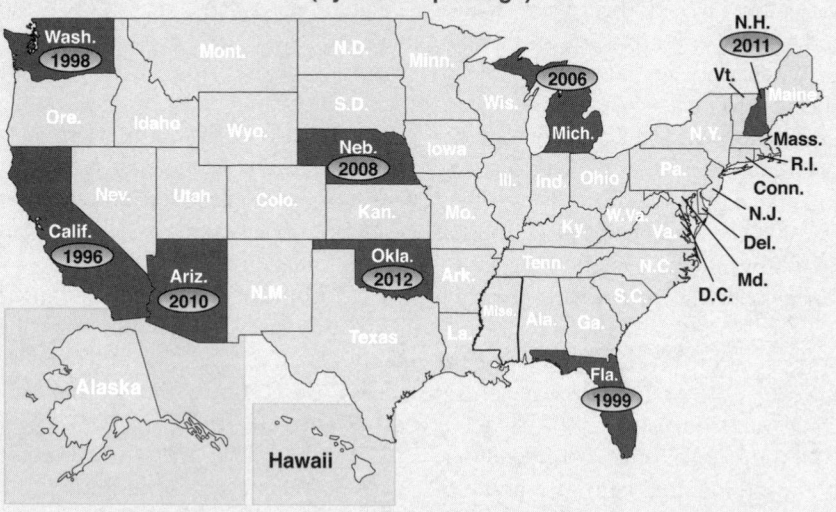

Affirmative-Action Bans in the U.S.*
(by date of passage)

* All bans apply to public employment, public higher education and public contracting except in New Hampshire, whose ban applies to state agencies and public higher education, and Nebraska, whose ban applies only to state colleges and universities.

Source: "Affirmative Action: State Action," National Conference of State Legislatures, April, 2014, https://tinyurl.com/kxhhurj

---

"Yet they still can have the same ability to succeed in college. You're not lowering your standards. You are recognizing that a student who is a high-quality applicant is going to look a little different when they come from a low-income background."

Elite schools should reach out to low-income families because, for them, "enrolling in a top-tier college far from home seems as impossible as taking a trip to Mars," said Cooke Foundation Executive Director Harold Levy. Such students "are unaware of how to apply for scholarships they are eligible to receive. They can't afford SAT or ACT preparation course fees. They can't afford to visit colleges that they are considering attending." [33]

The focus on economic status has won grudging support from affirmative-action opponents such as Blum and Clegg.

"Needs-based affirmative action" is fairer, Blum said. "It cannot be reasonably argued that, in the name of diversity, the daughter of an Asian working-class immigrant should be penalized in her efforts to gain admission to Harvard over the daughter of a successful white, Hispanic or African-American professional." [34]

Clegg says that "if you want to help disadvantaged students, it should be done on the basis of disadvantage, not race and ethnicity." But, he adds, he cannot support the practice when it's "simply a way of achieving surreptitiously a particular racial and ethnic mix."

Does campus diversity improve the quality of education for all students?

Forbidden by the Supreme Court since 1978 from using race or ethnicity as the sole reason to admit applicants, colleges and universities now say they conduct holistic evaluations to build a diverse student body that will enhance the education of all students. Some critics of affirmative action question the educational value of diversity, and some argue that consideration of race is wrong no matter the goal.

Education at the Harvard Business School "at its very core, requires diversity," said the dean, Nitin Nohria. The school's method of teaching, through discussion of case studies, "would collapse without diversity of thought, experiences and backgrounds in our classes," he said. [35]

Emily Choi, an Asian-American junior at Harvard studying history and literature, agrees affirmative action is beneficial. "The diversity at Harvard has been key to my learning," she said, "and I think that if there weren't so many people of different backgrounds, I wouldn't be forced to think about things in new ways." [36]

"Without a truly diverse student body and faculty," said Columbia University President Lee Bollinger, "a university simply will be unable to achieve the highest levels of excellence in teaching, research and intellectual discovery." [37]

Some educators cite personal classroom experiences to demonstrate the value of diversity. Law professors Nancy Leong of the University of Denver and Erwin Chemerinsky of the University of California, Berkeley, wrote that in their constitutional law classes, "we have found no substitute for the firsthand accounts of black and brown men who have been racially profiled, or for the narratives of Japanese-American students whose relatives were sent to internment camps during World War II." [38]

Leong and Chemerinsky also said "extensive research" confirms that "diverse learning environments improve learning, increase interracial understanding and better prepare students for careers in a diverse society."

Psychologists Jonathan Haidt of New York University and Lee Jussim of Rutgers University cited a review of 500 studies that concluded "when people of different races and ethnicities mix together and get to know each other, the effect is generally to reduce prejudice on all sides." [39]

Outside the ivory tower, lack of diversity can cause businesses to make bad decisions, the Century Foundation's Kahlenberg says. For example, he says, "if there are not enough women in the group — or no women — it's easy for a company to think about selling a product in a way that will miss the concerns of women."

The Center for Equal Opportunity's Clegg denounces the quest for diversity as a euphemism that "much of the time cloaks politically correct discrimination on the basis of race, ethnicity and sex."

To the extent that diversity leads to better learning and problem-solving, Clegg says, it is not because of racial or ethnic diversity but because of "cognitive diversity" — differences in how people think. He cites a *Harvard Business Review* article by business-school teachers Alison Reynolds and David Lewis of Great Britain who evaluated a "strategic execution exercise" they run with groups of executives. They found that diversity of age, ethnicity and gender did not improve performance, while cognitive diversity did. Individuals' cognitive diversity develops early in life and is independent of education, culture and "other social conditioning," they said. [40]

Some criticize diversity for obscuring the need to compensate minority groups for the legacy of discrimination. Hanging affirmative action on the value of diversity requires universities to make arguments that are difficult to defend, they say. "If you're in astronomy class, does coming from a certain place with

Rachel Barr, 17, practices for the SATs in Scarborough, Maine, on Feb. 23, 2016. The College Board said in 2013 that students from affluent families scored 400 points higher on combined SAT scores than students whose families earned less than $20,000. One reason, experts say, is that wealthier families are more likely to invest in tutoring, test preparation and college counseling than are those from low-income backgrounds.

a certain background really help out that much?" Harvard Law professor Randall Kennedy asked. [41]

But the University of Colorado's Moses says diversity benefits many sciences. "When it was mostly if not all male doctors doing research on breast cancer, the most favored treatment was radical mastectomy," she says. "When women started to get into the field, you had women's perspectives that maybe not all cases need radical mastectomy. Maybe there could be a lumpectomy.

"The more diversity we have, the more angles to the research that will emerge."

Conservatives also contend that any benefits derived from diversity are negated by actions that curtail free speech, such as protecting students from disturbing classroom content and trying to keep controversial speakers — usually conservatives — off campus.

Moses contends, however, that "to limit some speakers on college campuses is not wrongheaded, and I don't think it hurts diversity of viewpoint." She cites "people wanting to bring in neo-Nazis, white supremacists, people

who claim the Holocaust didn't happen. Not all viewpoints are equal. Some are just wrong and indefensible. It's not going to hurt to not have those aired."

Other affirmative-action supporters disagree.

"I don't want you to be safe, ideologically," Obama White House aide Van Jones, a liberal activist, told students at the University of Chicago. "I don't want you to be safe, emotionally. I want you to be offended every single day on this campus . . . and then to learn how to speak back." [42]

The problem with drawing a line against certain speech, Georgetown's Carnevale says, is "where is the line and who draws it?" ∎

BACKGROUND

Search for "Character"

Harvard began basing admissions on College Entrance Examination

Board tests — precursors to the College Board's SATs — in 1905. [43] The action expanded Harvard's student body from one composed mainly of white Protestants from New England prep schools to one accepting high-achieving high-school graduates from anywhere. Within three years, the entering freshman class became 7 percent Jewish, 9 percent Catholic and 45 percent from public high schools.

By 1922, the freshman class was more than 20 percent Jewish, and Harvard President A. Lawrence Lowell

As a result, Harvard's Jewish population dropped to 15 percent of the student body by 1933. Critics of affirmative action say the subjective criteria enabled the college to put a cap on Jewish enrollment, which they charge the school now is doing with Asian-Americans. [44]

Federal Push for Diversity

Affirmative action became federal policy for the first time in 1961, when President John F. Kennedy's administration

that "you do not take a person who for years has been hobbled by chains and liberate him, bring him up to the starting line of a race, then say, 'You are free to compete with all the others,' and still justly believe that you have been completely fair." Johnson that year expanded on Kennedy's order by requiring contractors and subcontractors to take affirmative action to expand job opportunities for minorities. Women were added the next year. [46]

In 1969, President Richard M. Nixon's administration approved the "Philadelphia Plan" for setting numerical goals for minority hiring on federally funded construction projects. A year later, the plan expanded to include all businesses with 50 or more employees and federal contracts of at least $50,000. The requirements began to make the nebulous concept of affirmative action more concrete by setting goals to match workforce demographics in the area. This period also marked the emergence of complaints about "reverse discrimination" against white males.

Women were added to the Philadelphia Plan in 1971, and the Supreme Court declared such goals and timetables to be constitutional.

Seven years later, the court spoke for the first time on affirmative action in higher education. Allan Bakke, a white former Marine, was rejected twice at the University of California, Davis, medical school. He sued, alleging reverse discrimination. In a landmark case, the court ruled the medical school's decision to reserve 18 percent of entering-class seats for disadvantaged minorities was unconstitutional. However, the justices allowed the university to consider race as one factor when making admissions decisions in order to create a diverse student body that would contribute to a "robust exchange of ideas." [47]

In 1979, President Jimmy Carter instructed all federal agencies to take affirmative action to support female-owned businesses. Conservative Republican Reagan, who was elected president the

Getty Images/Bettmann

Allan Bakke, center, won a landmark "reverse discrimination" suit after twice being rejected by the University of California, Davis, medical school. In 1978 the Supreme Court ruled that the school's decision to reserve 18 percent of entering-class seats for disadvantaged minorities was unconstitutional. However, the justices allowed the university to consider race as one factor when making admissions decisions in order to create a diverse student body.

worried that the growing number of Jews would drive away the Protestants who traditionally dominated the student body.

That year, Harvard expanded the criteria for admission to include a search for "well-rounded" applicants who demonstrated "character" and "leadership." Candidates had to provide letters of reference, write a personal essay, list their extracurricular activities, submit a photograph and offer information about race, color, religious preference, mother's maiden name and father's birthplace. Applicants also had to sit for a personal interview.

ordered federal contractors to take "affirmative action to ensure that applicants are treated equally without regard to race, color, religion, sex, or national origin."

The Congress of Racial Equality (CORE), a civil rights group in New York City, began calling for hiring preferences in 1962. "We are approaching employers with the proposition that they have effectively excluded Negroes from their work force a long time, and they now have a responsibility and obligation to make up for their past sins," the organization announced. [45]

President Lyndon B. Johnson supported that contention, saying in 1965

Continued on p. 980

Chronology

1960s Affirmative action becomes federal policy.

1961
Democratic Kennedy administration orders federal contractors to take "affirmative action" to prevent discrimination against job applicants based on race, color, religion, sex or national origin.

1965
Democratic Johnson administration requires federal contractors to expand job opportunities for minorities and women.

1969
Republican Nixon administration requires numerical goals for minority hiring on federal construction projects.

1978-1995 Courts, presidents revise affirmative-action rules.

1978
Supreme Court bars the University of California, Davis, School of Medicine from reserving spots for disadvantaged minorities but says school can consider race as one factor in making admission decisions.

1981
Republican Reagan administration cuts budgets of Equal Employment Opportunity Commission and Office of Federal Contract Compliance.

1995
Democratic President Bill Clinton, acknowledging problems with affirmative action, says "mend it, but don't end it." . . . University of California votes to phase out race-conscious admissions decisions.

1996-2009 Voters alter affirmative action.

1996
California residents bar public officials from considering race, sex, or ethnicity in employment, contracting and education.

1997
Texas Legislature requires state colleges to open admissions to top 10 percent of graduates from each high school in the state to boost minority enrollment.

2001
Republican President George W. Bush scales back federal legal actions alleging discrimination against minorities and increases actions alleging discrimination against whites.

2003
Supreme Court upholds University of Michigan Law School's practice of considering race as one of many factors in making admissions decisions, but overturns university's policy giving minority undergraduate applicants extra points on school's evaluation scale.

2006
Michigan voters ban preferential treatment of minorities and women in public education, employment and public contracting.

2009
Study finds Asian-Americans must score 140 points higher than whites on SAT to have an equal chance at admission to private universities.

2011-Present Opposition to affirmative action escalates.

2011
Democratic President Barack Obama uses executive orders to advance affirmative action in higher education.

2014
Researchers say 88 percent of the most competitive colleges and universities consider race as a factor in admissions. . . . Sixty-four Asian-American organizations file a federal complaint alleging discrimination by Harvard University.

2015
Students for Fair Admissions files federal suits saying Harvard discriminates against Asian-Americans and the University of North Carolina discriminates against Asians and whites.

2016
Supreme Court rules University of Texas admissions officers can consider race, among many factors, in order to achieve a diverse student body. . . . Gallup Poll finds 66 percent of white Americans, 57 percent of blacks and 47 percent of Latinos believe race and ethnicity should not be a factor in college admissions decisions.

2017
Republican Trump administration begins investigating possible discrimination against Asian-American applicants to Harvard. . . . Candice Jackson, a longtime foe of affirmative action, becomes a top civil rights official at the Department of Education and announces a narrower approach to investigating discrimination complaints. . . . President Trump's fiscal 2018 budget proposes cutting spending on civil rights programs at the departments of Education; Labor and Health and Human Services. . . . Students for Fair Admissions challenges University of Texas affirmative-action plan.

Activist Pushes for a 'Colorblind America'

"Most Americans want to be judged based on who they are as individuals."

Edward Blum, the man behind some of the country's most significant legal attacks on race-based college admissions, went to court for the first time after a failed bid for Congress in 1992.

Campaigning as a Republican in Houston that year, Blum was struck by the bizarre shape of some of the state's congressional districts.

"I discovered how African-Americans were harvested into one district, and straight across the street Hispanics were harvested into a Hispanic congressional district, and catty-cornered to that, whites were put into a different congressional district," he says.

Blum lost that House election to incumbent Craig Washington, a black Democrat. But he had found a cause. He recruited five fellow Republicans to join him in a 1994 lawsuit that said Texas state lawmakers had engaged in racial gerrymandering by redrawing some U.S. House districts to maximize the black or Hispanic vote. In 1996, the Supreme Court agreed, ruling the districts unconstitutional. [1]

"Those who labor and yearn for a colorblind America have won," Blum said after the ruling, "and those who envision an America dominated by race and religious preference have lost." [2]

Since that victory, Blum has filed about 30 lawsuits, most challenging laws or policies favoring minorities over whites. Six of his cases have reached the Supreme Court. Blum has won four of the six, including a landmark case that overturned a key section of the Voting Rights Act in 2013. [3]

"Most Americans — when they apply to a college, when they apply for employment, when they seek a promotion — want to be judged based on who they are as individuals," Blum says. "They don't want to be punished because of their race, nor do they want to be helped because of their race."

Blum, a 65-year-old former stockbroker, is not an attorney. Instead, he recruits plaintiffs, connects them with lawyers, raises money to support the legal proceedings and stands aside.

His ongoing cases include a lawsuit on behalf of a white woman challenging affirmative action at the University of Texas and a suit alleging discrimination against Asian-Americans at Harvard University. He also has sued to stop what he calls discrimination against both Asians-Americans and whites by the University of North Carolina at Chapel Hill.

Harvard and the University of North Carolina deny their admissions policies discriminate. Harvard evaluates each applicant "as a whole person," to make sure students "work with people from different backgrounds, life experiences and perspectives," university spokeswoman Melodie Jackson said. Rick White, UNC's associate vice chancellor for communications and public affairs, said the school admits "undergraduates from every background." [4]

While his 1992 Texas racial gerrymandering case was working its way through the courts, Blum formed the Campaign for a Color-Blind America, which challenged a half-dozen additional congressional and state legislative maps in Virginia, South Carolina, Texas and New York.

In 2005, he created the Project on Fair Representation to oppose race-conscious policies in education, contracting, employment and elections. Three years ago, he founded Students for Fair Admissions, which raises money for suits against affirmative action. The group claims nearly 22,000 students and parents as members.

According to the organization's most-recent IRS filing, it raised $826,664 and spent $545,576 in 2015. [5] Blum says donors include more than 700 individuals and a half-dozen foundations.

Blum's critics call his attacks on affirmative action misguided and say his election-related lawsuits primarily serve GOP political

---

Continued from p. 978

next year, began to roll back some of his predecessors' actions. Between 1981 and '83, Reagan cut the budget of the Equal Employment Opportunity Commission by 12 percent and the Office of Federal Contract Compliance by 34 percent. The compliance office blocked federal contracts for just two companies during Reagan's eight years in office, down dramatically from 13 blocked in Carter's four years. The Justice Department also began opposing some affirmative-action plans.

George H.W. Bush, Reagan's vice president and successor in the White House, compiled a mixed record on

affirmative action. Bush vetoed a bill that would have made it harder for white males to file suits charging reverse discrimination. But he also rejected plans by his White House counsel to outlaw all quotas, set-asides and related affirmative-action measures.

"Mend It, but Don't End It"

Democrat Bill Clinton entered the White House in 1993 expressing ambivalence toward affirmative action. His party relied heavily on minority voters, yet white men were growing

increasingly angry about what they perceived as unfair preferences for minorities and women. "When we hold focus groups, if the issue of affirmative action comes up, you can forget the rest of the session," a Democratic pollster said in 1990. Participants do not want to discuss anything else, he said.

In a 1995 speech, Clinton said he, too, opposed "the unjustified preference of the unqualified over the qualified of any race or gender." But he added that fighting discrimination required the continuation of some affirmative-action policies. He famously proclaimed that his approach was to "mend it, but don't end it."

The day after Clinton's speech, the

ends. Anthony Carnevale, director of the Georgetown University Center on Education and the Workforce, describes Blum and his associates as "fine people" and "idealists."

"They have an aspiration, which is race should not matter," he says. "I just think that isn't a realistic aspiration, because race does matter."

Stephen Spaulding, chief of strategy and external affairs at the good-government group Common Cause, says Blum has taken a "sledgehammer" to election laws "that have brought people into the democratic process so everyone can participate and everyone can be heard."

Blum's most significant case challenged a Voting Rights Act provision that required states and municipalities with a history of discrimination at the ballot box to obtain federal approval before making any changes to their election laws. The challenge, brought by Shelby County, Ala., led to a 2013 Supreme Court ruling that effectively nullified the so-called "pre-clearance" provision. [6]

Some states that had been subject to the provision immediately went to work rewriting their election laws in ways that critics said were designed to suppress the minority vote.

"I worry about it a lot," Blum said of the ruling's impact. "It may be that one or two of the states . . . [have] gone too far." [7]

But he also said the court's decision means "every jurisdiction in the country must be treated equally in our courts when election issues are at stake." [8]

— **Tom Price**

Edward Blum is president of Students for Fair Admissions, which has filed key lawsuits against affirmative-action programs. Blum says college applicants should be judged on an individual basis and not on race or ethnicity.

[1] Krissah Thompson, "Edward Blum defies odds in getting cases to Supreme Court," *The Washington Post*, Feb. 25, 2013, https://tinyurl.com/ybqjwmwp; Alan Bernstein, "GOP suit claims district lines racially gerrymandered, illegal," *Houston Chronicle*, Jan. 27, 1994, p. A-1; and *Bush v. Vera* (94-805), 517 U.S. 952 (1996)," Legal Information Institute, Cornell University Law School, undated, https://tinyurl.com/ycsg8gz5.

[2] Bernstein, *ibid.*; Alan Bernstein and R.G. Ratcliffe, "Justices quash racial districts," *Houston Chronicle*, June 14, 1996, p. A-1.

[3] Ralph K.M. Haurwitz, "Instigator of Fisher v. UT finds solace in wine, noodles," (Austin) *American-Statesman*, June 26, 2016, http://tinyurl.com/ya6kv9wr; Andrew Gumbel, "Man behind gutting of Voting Rights Act: 'I agonize' over decision's impact," *The Guardian*, Jan. 5, 2016, https://tinyurl.com/gpbm3gw.

[4] Anemona Hartocollis and Stephanie Saul, "Affirmative Action Battle Has a New Focus: Asian-Americans," *The New York Times*, Aug. 2, 2017, https://tinyurl.com/y7e7yn2h; Jane Stancill, "Group files suit challenging UNC on use of race in admissions," *The Charlotte Observer*, Nov. 17, 2014, https://tinyurl.com/y9za2qcq.

[5] "Form 990: Return of Organization Exempt from Income Tax," Internal Revenue Service, 2015, https://tinyurl.com/y9529pqr.

[6] Adam Liptak, "Supreme Court Invalidates Key Part of Voting Rights Act," *The New York Times*, June 25, 2013, https://tinyurl.com/o6wuy2y.

[7] Gumbel, *op. cit.*

[8] Michael Wines, "Critics See Efforts by Counties and Towns to Purge Minority Voters From Rolls," *The New York Times*, July 31, 2016, https://tinyurl.com/j3b4q4g.

U.S. Senate defeated legislation that would have banned all affirmative-action preferences. Outside Washington that year, however, the Republican-controlled University of California Board of Regents voted to end affirmative action in admissions at graduate schools, effective in 1997, and for undergraduates the next year. The regents allowed schools to consider socioeconomic factors. In 1996, California voters extended the ban to all public education, employment and contracting. [48]

Meanwhile, Houston voters in 1997 rejected a ballot initiative to end affirmative action in the city. The Texas Legislature that year facilitated minority enrollment in state colleges and universities by requiring them to offer admission to the top 10 percent of graduates from each high school in the state. That percentage was allowed to decrease at the University of Texas at Austin as the number of applications substantially rose. At the Austin campus, enrollment rose for Asian- and Hispanic-Americans between 1997 and 2015 and dipped slightly for blacks. [49]

In 1998, affirmative action won a victory in Congress when the House defeated a bill that would have banned affirmative-action admissions in college programs funded by the federal Higher Education Act. But voters in Washington state prohibited affirmative action in higher education and in public contracting and hiring. And as California's ban for undergraduate admissions took effect in 1998, admissions of African-Americans, Hispanics and Native Americans dropped 61 percent at Berkeley and 36 percent at UCLA.

The Florida Legislature outlawed affirmative action in 2000 but also followed Texas' lead by requiring state universities to open enrollment to the top 20 percent of graduates from each public high school.

California adopted a "dual admissions" plan the next year. The 10-campus University of California system was

Colleges Seek Novel Ways to Boost Diversity

Increasing community-college transfers is one strategy.

Mélisande Short-Colomb had an unusual bit of personal history to share when she filled out an application to Georgetown University earlier this year.

"My story begins simply," she wrote. "My family was sold by the Society of Jesus of Maryland in 1838."

That made Short-Colomb a "legacy," a college applicant who receives preference for admission because of a family connection to an alumnus. In Short-Colomb's case, that connection was her great-great-great grandparents, sold as slaves by Georgetown 180 years ago to help pay off debts at the Jesuit school in Washington. [1]

Legacy admissions tend to be viewed as barriers to campus diversity at elite universities like Georgetown because most recipients come from affluent, white families. However, Georgetown's new policy, created to help atone for the school's past involvement with slavery, is bringing more African-American students to the campus.

Short-Colomb is one of two students (the other is a transfer student) who started classes at Georgetown this fall after being accepted under the new legacy policy. A third is to begin graduate studies in the spring. [2]

Inspired by her ancestry, Short-Colomb has decided to major in African-American studies. At 63, she is far older than her classmates. "There are decades between us," she says, "but I have so much to learn from them, and I think there's a lot they can learn from me."

Other colleges and universities also are reaching beyond traditional admissions procedures to recruit minority and disadvantaged students, even as laws and court decisions restrict their ability to use race or ethnicity as admissions criteria.

A 2014-15 study by the Washington-based American Council on Education, which represents colleges and universities across the country, found that the most popular approach used by four-year, nonprofit institutions was to accept more transfers from community colleges, which tend to enroll higher proportions of minority and lower-income students. Of the 338 four-year schools surveyed, 82 percent said they had entered agreements with community colleges to facilitate such transfers.

More than 70 percent of institutions in the study said they worked to recruit minority and disadvantaged high school graduates. They also said they conducted "holistic" reviews of applications that looked beyond test scores and grades to consider race and ethnicity as well as community service, leadership, special talents and experience overcoming challenging economic circumstances or other hardships.

More than half the schools said they offered summer enrichment programs to attract minority and low-income high school graduates and prepare them for college. A smaller number said they were giving less weight to admissions tests or had made such tests optional. [3]

Eliminating traditional legacy preferences, offering summer enrichment programs, expanding community college transfers and recognizing barriers that low-income students must overcome are especially important for higher minority enrollment, according to the Jack Kent Cooke Foundation in Virginia, which provides financial and other assistance to low-income elementary, high school, college and graduate students.

The foundation's research director, Jennifer Glynn, also said colleges should work with high schools and community organizations to identify outstanding low-income students and pay for such students to visit campus. [4]

Amherst College has been notably successful at creating a diverse student body, according to Richard Rothstein, a research associate at the Economic Policy Institute, a liberal think in Washington that focuses on U.S. workers. [5]

Each spring, the Massachusetts school offers more than 100 applicants a free trip to visit the campus. Each of the applicants

required to open admission to the top 4 percent graduating from each of the state's high schools. The next 8.5 percent of graduates would be admitted at one of the campuses if they completed a two-year program at a community college. [50]

As it had in the Bakke case in 1978, the Supreme Court in 2003 handed down a split decision in a suit involving the University of Michigan. The court upheld the law school's affirmative-action program because the school had a compelling interest in the "educational benefit that flows from student body diversity," and because the school conducted a "highly individualized, holistic review" of each applicant. But the court overturned undergraduate affirmative action at Michigan's College of Literature, Science and the Arts — because blacks, Latinos and American Indians were given 20 extra points on the college's 150-point evaluation scale. The court said this violated its Bakke ruling that race or ethnicity could not be the sole factor in evaluating an application, because the added points guaranteed admission "for virtually every minimally qualified underrepresented minority applicant." [51]

During the first decade of the 21st century, more voters outlawed affirmative action in their states. In 2006, 58 percent of Michigan voters approved banning preferential treatment of minorities and women in public education, employment and public contracting. [52] Four years later, Arizona did the same. In 2008, Nebraska forbade affirmative action by public entities, and voters in Colorado defeated a similar proposal.

Affirmative-action supporters challenged the higher-education provisions of the Michigan ban but lost in the Supreme Court in 2014. The court said in essence that while certain kinds of affirmative action were permissible, they were not required. [53]

is a minority, low-income or first-generation student (the first member of their family to attend college). [6] Those who do enroll receive stipends to pay for career mentoring or to help afford working an unpaid internship.

In other notable efforts:

• George Washington University in Washington made submitting SAT and ACT scores voluntary for applicants in 2015. Freshman enrollment surged from 4.7 percent to 8.8 percent for African-Americans and from 9.2 percent to 10.5 percent for Hispanics. (Half the schools on *U.S. News & World Report*'s list of the top 100 liberal arts colleges have made the tests optional, according to the National Center for Fair and Open Testing in Massachusetts, which advocates reducing use of the tests.) [7]

• The University of Washington in Seattle created a "Geo-Index" in 2015 to measure applicants' experience with adversity. The index is based on where applicants live, the quality of their high schools and other factors, but not on race or ethnicity. The percentage of minority freshmen increased by about two-thirds of 1 percent the next fall. [8]

• In September, Harvard Business School announced a $12.5 million scholarship fund for first-generation college students. It also is attempting to increase its share of minority, low-income and first-generation students by offering summer training programs to rising college seniors. [9]

— *Tom Price*

Mélisande Short-Colomb, 63, in red shirt, was admitted to Georgetown University as a "legacy" applicant because her great-great-great grandparents were slaves sold by Georgetown 180 years ago to help pay the school's debts.

[1] "Enslaved Ancestors Remembered as Retiree Starts as Georgetown Undergrad," Georgetown University, https://tinyurl.com/y8d2cmlp; Terrence McCoy, "Her ancestors were Georgetown's slaves," *The Washington Post*, Aug. 30, 2017, https://tinyurl.com/yabyr5d4.

[2] "Enslaved Ancestors Remembered as Retiree Starts as Georgetown Undergrad," *ibid.*

[3] Lorelle L. Espinosa, Matthew N. Gaertner and Gary Orfield, "Race, Class, and College Access: Achieving Diversity in a Shifting Legal Landscape," American Council on Education, 2015, https://tinyurl.com/ycscnewe.

[4] Jennifer Glynn, "Opening Doors: How Selective Colleges and Universities Are Expanding Access for High-Achieving, Low-Income Students," Jack Kent Cooke Foundation, September 2017, https://tinyurl.com/y7oc6c37.

[5] Valerie Strauss, "Actually, we still need affirmative action for African Americans in college admissions," *The Washington Post*, Aug. 2, 2017, https://tinyurl.com/yb97zvut.

[6] Fred Thys, "Amherst College Makes Sacrifices To Enroll Low-Income Students," WBUR, May 20, 2014, https://tinyurl.com/ybddgp5k.

[7] Scott Jaschik, "Pressure to Build the Class: 2016 Survey of Admissions Directors," *Inside Higher Ed*, Sept. 22, 2016, http://tinyurl.com/y9e5gu2r; Nick Anderson, "George Washington U. gets more diverse after ditching admission test mandate," *The Washington Post*, Nov. 22, 2016, http://tinyurl.com/yd8fnx48.

[8] Eric Hoover, "Defending Diversity," *The Chronicle of Higher Education*, Feb. 26, 2017, http://tinyurl.com/y9g9tzou; "Enrollment Data for Autumn 2016 New Undergraduate Students," Academic and Student Affairs Committee, University of Washington, Nov. 10, 2016, https://tinyurl.com/yccy29v4.

[9] Deirdre Fernandes, "Scholarships will try to lure more first-generation students to Harvard Business School," *The Boston Globe*, Sept. 11, 2017, https://tinyurl.com/ybbddmu3.

Announcing the court's decision, Justice Anthony Kennedy said the case was not about resolving the affirmative-action debate but about "who may resolve it. There is no authority in the Constitution of the United States or in this court's precedents for the judiciary to set aside Michigan laws that submit this policy determination to the voters." [54]

But affirmative-action advocates prevailed in the high court's most recent decision last year, when it upheld the University of Texas' affirmative-action plan. In *Fisher v. University of Texas at Austin*, Abigail Fisher argued the university admitted minority students with weaker academic credentials. [55]

Fisher, however, did not graduate in the top 7 or 8 percent of her class, which would have guaranteed her admission to a state-supported university, although not necessarily the school of her choice. Of the 47 applicants who were admitted with lower grade-point averages and SAT scores than Fisher, only five were minorities. Also denied admission were 168 black and Latino applicants whose grades and scores were as good or better than hers. [56]

In ruling for the university, the court said the school could treat "race as a relevant feature within the broader context of a candidate's application." It added that race could be considered in order to provide "the educational benefits of a diverse student body." [57] In 2015, blacks composed about 4 percent of the school's student body despite making up 12 percent of the state's population. [58]

The Obama Years

The year the University of Texas rejected Fisher's application was the same year that voters made Democrat Barack Obama the first black president in U.S. history.

As president, Obama expressed support for affirmative action but also indicated agreement with the Supreme Court's limited view of what kind of affirmative action passes constitutional muster. Considering race and ethnicity is OK, he said, if a college "decides that there is a value in making sure that folks with different experiences in a classroom will enhance the educational experience of the students, and they do it in a careful way." He added, however, that "most of the time the law's principal job should be as a shield against discrimination, as opposed to a sword to advance a social agenda, because the law is a blunt instrument in these situations." [59]

Moreover, Obama said, "probably the single most important thing I could do for poor black kids is to make sure that they're getting a good K-through-12 education. And, if they're coming out of high school well prepared, then they'll be able to compete for university slots and jobs." [60] He said his well-off daughters should not receive preference over "white kids who have been disadvantaged and have grown up in poverty and shown themselves to have what it takes to succeed." [61]

Obama appointed to his administration some strong affirmative-action proponents, such as Attorney General Eric Holder. The departments of Education and Justice sent a joint letter to higher-education officials in 2013, saying that "racially diverse educational environments help to prepare students to succeed in our increasingly diverse nation" and that "the future workforce of America must be able to transcend the boundaries of race, language and culture as our economy becomes more globally interconnected." [62]

The Office of Federal Contract Compliance Programs in Obama's Labor Department went beyond responding to individual complaints and conducting limited reviews of companies' compliance with the law. It frequently carried out full-scale audits that included visits to a company's multiple locations. [63]

Facing a Republican-dominated Congress beginning in 2011, Obama found that his legislative options were limited. Instead, he used executive orders to make "modest advancements" in affirmative action in higher education and the federal workforce, said Robert C. Smith, a political scientist at San Francisco State University. [64]

To diversify the mix of presidential appointees, Obama's Presidential Personnel Office recruited at historically black colleges and universities and other minority-serving institutions. It also worked with organizations that represent gays, people with disabilities and other groups that traditionally have been under-represented at higher levels of the federal government.

"He wanted to make sure that everybody had an opportunity to serve in this administration and that its diversity reflected the diversity of our country," White House senior adviser Valerie Jarrett said. [65]

The result was the most demographically diverse administration in history, according to Berkeley law school professor Anne Joseph O'Connell, who has studied the top 80 appointees of each president from Jimmy Carter to Obama. As of August 2015, Obama had appointed a majority of women and minorities, the first time that had ever happened, O'Connell said. George W. Bush's top appointees were about a quarter women and minorities, Bill Clinton's were a bit more than one-third. [66] ∎

CURRENT SITUATION

Spending Cutbacks

In addition to promising to investigate — and possibly prosecute — "race-based discrimination" in college admis-

sions, the Trump administration plans to reduce spending by federal agencies that enforce civil rights laws and regulations.

Education Secretary Betsy DeVos has appointed Candice Jackson, a longtime foe of affirmative action, to be deputy assistant secretary in the department's Office for Civil Rights, which does not require Senate confirmation. Jackson also will be acting assistant secretary until that post is filled. President Trump on Oct. 30 nominated Kenneth Marcus, who held the position on an acting basis during the George W. Bush administration and currently is president of the Louis D. Brandeis Center for Human Rights Under Law, which says its mission is "to advance the civil and human rights of the Jewish people and to promote justice for all."

"As with most liberal solutions to a problem," Jackson wrote while she was an undergraduate at Stanford in the mid-1990s, "giving special assistance to minority students is a Band-Aid solution to a deep problem." [67]

As acting assistant secretary, Jackson announced that the department no longer will follow Obama administration guidelines that certain types of civil rights complaints would trigger investigations of whether a pattern of discrimination existed. Some of those inquiries had turned up systemic issues that went beyond the initial complaints.

Department spokeswoman Liz Hall said the change is aimed at reducing a large backlog of complaints from individuals. But Alexandra Brodsky, a fellow at the National Women's Law Center, said the solution to the backlog is "full funding" for the civil rights office so that it has the personnel to investigate complaints in a timely manner. [68]

The president's 2018 budget proposal, which is working its way through Congress, would cut 40 positions at the Education Department's Office for Civil Rights, reduce the Health and Human Services Department's civil

Continued on p. 986

At Issue:

Should affirmative action be based on income instead of race?

RICHARD D. KAHLENBERG
*SENIOR FELLOW, THE CENTURY FOUNDATION,
AND EDITOR,* THE FUTURE OF
AFFIRMATIVE ACTION

WRITTEN FOR *CQ RESEARCHER*, NOVEMBER 2017

*h*arvard University recently boasted that a majority of its incoming class consists of students of color. But a 2017 study by several economists found that more Harvard undergraduates come from the top 10 percent of the income distribution than the bottom 90 percent. Bringing fairly wealthy students of all colors together is not true diversity. Affirmative action needs a 21st-century upgrade to focus on socioeconomic disadvantage.

I'm a liberal who works at a liberal think tank, and most of my friends and colleagues say we should "do both," by which they mean provide preferences in admissions based on race and class. I have been hearing this argument for a quarter century and yet most selective colleges, while providing substantial racial preferences, fail to provide similar preferences to economically disadvantaged students for understandable self-interested reasons.

Colleges compete on the *U.S. News & World Report* rankings, which reward institutions that create small class sizes or to recruit star faculty members, thereby boosting a school's prestige. Enrolling high-achieving, low-income students of all races "diverts" money from efforts to climb the rankings because such students require much more financial aid than wealthy students. In addition, administrators know that a lack of racial diversity on campus is much more visible to the naked eye and culturally embarrassing than a lack of socioeconomic diversity.

Interestingly, the colleges that do tend to have both racial and socioeconomic diversity in their student bodies are those that are barred from using race. These institutions rely exclusively on socioeconomic preferences as a way of indirectly promoting racial diversity. Flagship campuses at the University of Florida, University of Washington and University of Georgia use race-blind economic affirmative action to produce vibrant levels of racial and economic diversity. Because students of color are disproportionately disadvantaged, they disproportionately benefit from economic affirmative action.

Economic affirmative-action programs also remind working-class African-Americans, Latinos, Asians and whites of their common economic interests. These programs benefit the working-class whites that J.D. Vance portrays in *Hillbilly Elegy* as well as the working-class blacks that *The Atlantic*'s Ta-Nehisi Coates writes about. After a presidential election in which a demagogue was able to divide these two constituencies, with disastrous results for the country, finding policies that bring them together should be high on the nation's agenda.

RICHARD ROTHSTEIN
AUTHOR, THE COLOR OF LAW:
A FORGOTTEN HISTORY OF HOW OUR
GOVERNMENT SEGREGATED AMERICA

WRITTEN FOR *CQ RESEARCHER*, NOVEMBER 2017

*p*references for low-income students can replace affirmative action for African-Americans only by stereotyping black families as mostly "low-income." Yet 45 percent of them are in the top 60 percent of all families by income. Preferences for low-income students capture few of these working- and middle-class black applicants who are fully qualified for selective colleges but whose opportunities are limited because of the enduring effects of unconstitutional segregation.

Middle-class wealth, more than income, ensures economic security. It predicts college attendance, childhood expectations that higher education is normal and access to out-of-school programs that enhance college applications. Today, African-American median income is about 60 percent of the white median. But black wealth is only 10 percent of white wealth, a disparity almost entirely attributable to unconstitutional federal policy of the mid-20th century.

Then, the Federal Housing Administration (FHA) financed suburbanization of the nation's white population on the explicit condition that no homes be sold to African-Americans in places like Levittown near New York City, Lakewood near Los Angeles or hundreds of developments in between. The FHA's "Underwriting Manual" warned appraisers against recommending bank guarantees to builders whose subdivisions could include "incompatible racial elements." Federal sponsorship of segregated suburbs continued at least through 1968, when the Fair Housing Act was passed.

White working-class families then bought suburban houses for about $100,000 (in today's currency); they now sell for about $500,000. Across subsequent generations, those families gained hundreds of thousands of dollars in equity, used to send children to college and bequeath assets to heirs. Black families locked into central cities and restricted to urban rentals gained no such wealth.

The racial income gap also partly stems from unconstitutional policy. Social Security and minimum-wage laws were written to exclude predominantly black occupations. The National Labor Relations Act sanctioned government certification of whites-only unions, permitting construction trades to bar black workers from jobs that supported the post-World War II ascendance of many white workers to the middle class.

Other families also have limited wealth, but African-Americans' wealth deficits, as well as other socioeconomic disadvantages, uniquely result from racially targeted civil rights violations and demand remedy through affirmative-action programs.

Continued from p. 984

rights budget by 17 percent and fold the Labor Department's Office of Federal Contract Compliance, which oversees affirmative action and equal employment opportunity regulations for government contractors, into the Equal Employment Opportunity Commission. The administration said these cuts are needed to "reduce operational redundancies" and "promote efficiencies." [69]

But several critics believe the administration's moves, including its promises to investigate college admissions, are an attempt to fire up its conservative, mostly white base. Trump has spoken in support of Confederate memorials, which many African-Americans and others are attempting to remove from public places as symbols of white supremacy. Trump also has become embroiled in a fiery conflict with National Football League players, most of them black, who kneel during the National Anthem to protest what they see as racial prejudice by police and in the judicial system.

"Making whites feel embattled and aggrieved is central to the Trump presidency," wrote *Washington Post* columnist Eugene Robinson in early November. "It is what makes him different from all other recent presidents, perhaps going back as far as Woodrow Wilson, who imposed Jim Crow segregation on the federal workforce." [70]

Attacking affirmative action "touches a lot of issues and talks right to the folks who look at college admissions and believe slots for their kids are being taken, whether it's by illegal immigrants or by other groups," GOP political consultant Brett O'Donnell said. [71]

In a survey last fall, 52 percent of white working-class Americans said discrimination against whites has become as big a problem as discrimination against blacks and other minorities. The survey — by the Public Religion Research Institute and *The Atlantic* magazine — also found that 68 percent of the white working class believe the United States

is in danger of losing its culture and identity. [72]

"I think some whites are disturbed by the progress of African-Americans, which not only includes their admission to institutions of higher education but [also] their occupying positions of influence in the broader society," says the Economic Policy Institute's Rothstein.

State-Level Lawsuits

As Trump revises the government's approach to civil rights issues, colleges and universities are fighting anti-affirmative-action suits in state and federal courts and attempting to implement affirmative-action policies in compliance with court and legislative restrictions.

In the suit it filed in June in Texas state court, Students for Fair Admission is again challenging the University of Texas at Austin's affirmative-action plan — but this time using the state's constitution and laws. [73] It is about the 30th time Blum has filed suit alleging unconstitutional racial preference since he attacked "racial gerrymandering" in Texas congressional districts in 1994. (*See sidebar, p. 980.*)

Blum says he filed the latest suit because "the Texas Constitution is even more strict than the federal Constitution in forbidding the use of racial preferences in college admissions." Abigail Fisher, who graduated from Louisiana State University in 2012, is again the plaintiff.

In response, the university called the suit a "retread" that should be thrown out. Students for Fair Admissions "should not be able to re-litigate this or any other aspect of UT's admissions policy by dressing up the challenge with state law theories they failed to advance the first time around," the university said in a court filing. [74]

Blum's organization also is behind the suit against Harvard that alleges discrimination against Asian-Americans and another that charges the University of North Carolina at Chapel Hill dis-

criminates against both Asian-Americans and whites.

Plaintiffs contend that Harvard and other Ivy League schools set quotas on the number of Asian-Americans they will admit, effectively requiring them to have higher grades and test scores than other minorities and whites. Blum calls it a "triple standard," under which Asians have to meet stiffer requirements than whites who in turn are held to higher standards than other minorities.

In the other suit, Blum's group charges that the University of North Carolina is failing to follow court instructions to create diversity through race-neutral policies if possible. The university could increase financial aid to attract more low-income students, focus recruitment on potential minority applicants or follow other institutions' lead and admit a set percentage of the top students of each high school in the state, the suit suggests. [75]

Rick White, associate vice chancellor for communications and public affairs, said in a statement that "the university stands by its current undergraduate admissions policy and process," adding that the U.S. Department of Education's Office for Civil Rights ruled in 2012 that the school's "use of race in the admissions process is consistent with federal law." [76]

Beyond noting that courts have upheld some forms of affirmative action, including at the University of Texas, affirmative action's defenders point to statistics indicating that minorities still need special help. When Florida banned affirmative action in 1999, the freshman class at the University of Florida in Gainesville the following year was 12 percent black; in 2015, African-Americans were just 6 percent of the freshman class even though blacks represented 17 percent of Florida's population. [77]

The 2016 freshman class at the private California Institute of Technology — a highly rated science and engineering school that a spokeswoman called "as close to a meritocracy as is possible" — was less than 2 percent black. [78] ∎

OUTLOOK

A Divided Supreme Court

Legal scholars say the future of affirmative action could turn on how many Supreme Court justices President Trump gets to appoint.

The court approved the University of Texas' affirmative-action plan last year on a 4-3 vote, with the seat of the late Justice Antonin Scalia, a conservative, vacant and with liberal Justice Elena Kagan recusing herself, presumably because she worked on the case while U.S. solicitor general before she joined the court in 2010.

With newly confirmed conservative Justice Neil Gorsuch expected to be an affirmative-action critic and Kagan expected to support affirmative action in future cases, a Texas-like plan likely would survive on a 5-4 vote. Trump could reverse that outcome if he gets to replace one of the five who appear to support affirmative action. [79]

Although Georgetown's Carnevale foresees minorities becoming more prevalent at U.S. colleges, he doubts their presence on campus will ever equal their share of the national population.

The Economic Policy Institute's Rothstein expects continued progress. "While on the one hand there is the unmasking and enabling and encouraging of white-supremacist groups and attitudes in the society, there is also a much greater willingness than we've had in the past to talk about the history of race in this country and the costs of slavery and Jim Crow," he says. "You have the white-supremacist groups in Charlottesville and on social media. On the other hand, you have white leaders in the South who are presiding over the removal of commemorative statues of the defenders of slavery."

The University of Colorado's Moses says she anticipates continuation of "the incremental program we have seen over the past 40 or 50 years for representation of students of color. It would be amazing to get to a place where there was significant enough educational equity where such modest policies were unnecessary, but we aren't there yet."

But some experts say colleges will have to work harder to win affirmative-action lawsuits in the future by proving the value of diversity on campus and by proving they used race and ethnicity as little as possible.

"The case isn't just about what the student body looks like — it's about knowing whether students are obtaining the benefits of diversity," said Terri Taylor, senior legal and policy adviser at Education Counsel, an education consulting firm. "So that means connecting what's happening in the admissions process . . . to students' experience on campus." [80]

The Center for Equal Opportunity's Clegg predicts affirmative action eventually will fall into disuse. "It's just untenable for our institutions, including our colleges and universities, to divide people according to race and ethnicity and treat them differently in a country that's becoming increasingly multiethnic and multiracial," he says. "The system is going to end because Americans don't like it."

The Century Foundation's Kahlenberg says the use of race in affirmative action is likely to end because it is "very politically unpopular" and "there are potential legal problems there as well." Affirmative action itself will not end, he predicts, but will shift to being based on economics, which he advocates.

The Jack Kent Cooke Foundation's Glynn, another advocate of economics-based affirmative action, agrees. "Attention is increasingly being drawn to the opportunity gaps that exist based on income in this country," she says. "I'm hearing schools talk more about how they are placing increasing attention on the [economic] opportunities students have leading up to admission." ■

Notes

[1] Nikole Hannah-Jones, "What Abigail Fisher's Affirmative Action Case Was Really About," ProPublica, June 23, 2016, https://tinyurl.com/znksurh; Rick Jervis, "Voices: Affirmative action helps, but more is needed," *USA Today*, July 5, 2015, https://tinyurl.com/ycesvwzx; and Anthony Kennedy, *Fisher v. University of Texas at Austin et al.*, U.S. Supreme Court, June 23, 2016, https://tinyurl.com/z4q3uf3.

[2] Ralph K.M. Haurwitz, "UT faces new lawsuit over role of race in admissions policy," *Austin American-Statesman*, June 27, 2017, https://tinyurl.com/ydx82kj9.

[3] Charlie Savage, "Justice Dept. to Take On Affirmative Action in College Admissions," *The New York Times*, Aug. 1, 2017, https://tinyurl.com/yblukuz5; *Students for Fair Admissions, Inc., Plaintiff, v. University of North Carolina, et al.*, U.S. District Court for the Middle District of North Carolina, Nov. 17, 2014, https://tinyurl.com/yctxcfjg.

[4] *Ibid.*

[5] *Students for Fair Admissions, Inc., Plaintiff, v. University of North Carolina, et al., op. cit.*; "U.S. District Court for the Middle District of North Carolina," Nov. 17, 2014, https://tinyurl.com/yctxcfjg; *Students for Fair Admissions, Inc., Plaintiff, v. President and Fellows of Harvard College*, U.S. District Court for the District of Massachusetts Boston Division, Nov. 17, 2014, http://tinyurl.com/yc745jbd.

[6] Jeffrey J. Selingo, "Trump administration is taking aim at affirmative action in college admissions," *The Washington Post*, Aug. 2, 2017, https://tinyurl.com/yccd6x5n.

[7] Jaweed Kaleem, "Asian Americans are divided after the Trump administration's move on affirmative action," *Los Angeles Times*, Aug. 4, 2017, https://tinyurl.com/ybdaqo5e.

[8] Anemona Hartocollis and Stephanie Saul, "Affirmative Action Battle Has a New Focus: Asian-Americans," *The New York Times*, Aug. 2, 2017, https://tinyurl.com/y7e7yn2h.

[9] Kaleem, *op. cit.*

[10] "Graduation rate from first institution attended for first-time, full-time bachelor's degree-seeking students at 4-year postsecondary institutions, by race/ethnicity, time to completion, sex, control of institution, and acceptance rate: Selected cohort entry years, 1996 through 2009," National Center for Education Statistics, U.S. Department of Education, https://tinyurl.com/ybtvx6j7.

[11] Richard Sander and Stuart Taylor Jr., "The Painful Truth About Affirmative Action," *The Atlantic*, Oct. 2, 2012, https://tinyurl.com/y8abjkx3.

[12] Rod Newhouse, "Affirmative action got me into MIT," *The Washington Post*, Aug. 18, 2017, https://tinyurl.com/ya95vyb4.

[13] Lee C. Bollinger, "Affirmative Action as a Tool for a Racially Integrated Society," *The New York Times*, June 22, 2016, https://tinyurl.com/ydbj2wn3.

[14] Valerie Strauss, "Five myths about college admissions," *The Washington Post*, March 24, 2017, https://tinyurl.com/ybdgpmjt.

[15] Jordan Weissmann, "Outside of Elite Colleges, Affirmative Action Is Already Disappearing," *Slate*, Aug. 3, 2017, https://tinyurl.com/y9l44ens.

[16] Collin Binkley, "Ivy League schools brace for scrutiny of race in admissions," The Associated Press, Aug. 6, 2017, https://tinyurl.com/y7lgp3al; Jeremy Ashkenas, Haeyoun Park and Adam Pearce, "Even With Affirmative Action, Blacks and Hispanics Are More Underrepresented at Top Colleges Than 35 Years Ago," *The New York Times*, Aug. 24, 2017, https://tinyurl.com/y8ofb6ta.

[17] Valerie Strauss, "Harvard and the false premise of meritocratic university admissions," *The Washington Post*, Aug. 10, 2017, https://tinyurl.com/yanrovc8.

[18] Stacy Teicher Khadaroo, "A sticky week for college admissions as affirmative, action debate heats up," *The Christian Science Monitor*, Aug. 3, 2017, https://tinyurl.com/yd4fzfsa.

[19] For background, see Sarah Glazer, "Free Speech on Campus," *CQ Researcher*, May 8, 2015, pp. 409-32.

[20] Frank Newport, "Most in U.S. Oppose Colleges Considering Race in Admissions," Gallup, July 8, 2016, https://tinyurl.com/y8nhaa38.

[21] Peter Katel, "Racial Conflict," *CQ Researcher*, Jan. 8, 2016, pp. 25-48.

[22] "Income, Poverty and Health Insurance Coverage in the United States: 2016," U.S. Census Bureau, Sept. 12, 2017, https://tinyurl.com/yau2pfba.

[23] Tracy Jan, "1 in 7 white families are now millionaires," *The Washington Post*, Oct. 3, 2017, https://tinyurl.com/y7p4452o.

[24] Christine Emba, "Black people aren't keeping white Americans out of college," *The Washington Post*, Aug. 4, 2017, https://tinyurl.com/y78ox3n6.

[25] Strauss, *op. cit.*

[26] Valerie Strauss, "Actually, we still need affirmative action for African Americans in college admissions," *The Washington Post*, Aug. 2, 2017, https://tinyurl.com/yb97zvut.

[27] Roger Clegg, "Minority Access to Higher Education," Center for Equal Opportunity, June 2, 2015, https://tinyurl.com/y9lg2bjp.

[28] Douglas S. Massey and Jonathan Tannen, "A Research Note on Trends in Black Hyper-segregation," *Demography*, June 2015, http://tinyurl.com/odta3bf; Kenneth Jost, "Housing Discrimination," *CQ Researcher*, Nov. 6, 2015, pp. 937-60.

[29] Deirdre Fernandes, "Low-income students remain rare at elite universities," *The Boston Globe*, Aug. 12, 2017, https://tinyurl.com/y7as9pl3.

[30] William S. Flanagan and Michael E. Xie, "Median Family Income for Harvard Undergrads Triple National Average, Study Finds," *Harvard Crimson*, Jan. 25, 2017, https://tinyurl.com/ybld5lma.

[31] Strauss, "Actually, we still need affirmative action for African Americans in college admissions," *op. cit.*

[32] Lauren Camera, "Poverty Preference Admissions: The New Affirmative Action?" *U.S. News & World Report*, Jan. 12, 2016, https://tinyurl.com/hbzy4sm.

[33] "Cooke Foundation Report: Top Colleges Should Create Admissions Preference to Help Low-Income Students Overcome Barriers," Jack Kent Cooke Foundation, Jan. 11, 2016, http://tinyurl.com/y7z7yz8c.

[34] Edward Blum, "Harvard's discrimination against Asian Americans must end," *The Washington Post*, Aug. 8, 2017, https://tinyurl.com/yd3ah55z.

[35] Nitin Nohria, "Priorities," Harvard Business School, January 2017, https://tinyurl.com/ybmeljwg.

[36] Hartocollis and Saul, *op. cit.*

[37] Bollinger, *op. cit.*

[38] Nancy Leong and Erwin Chemerinsky, "Don't use Asian Americans to justify anti-affirmative action politics," *The Washington Post*, Aug. 3 2017, https://tinyurl.com/ybfvkxyp.

[39] Jonathan Haidt and Lee Jussim, "Hard Truths About Race on Campus," *The Wall Street Journal*, May 6, 2016, https://tinyurl.com/jn687zc.

[40] Alison Reynolds and David Lewis, "Teams Solve Problems Faster When They're More Cognitively Diverse," *Harvard Business Review*, March 30, 2017, https://tinyurl.com/m9mkqko.

[41] Abby Jackson, "Harvard professor says most people are thinking about diversity on college campuses all wrong," *Business Insider*, Aug. 3, 2017, https://tinyurl.com/yc4tnp73.

[42] Jonathan Haidt, "Van Jones' Excellent Metaphors About the Dangers of Ideological Safety," Heterodox Academy, March 2, 2017, https://tinyurl.com/ycxfrc23.

[43] Peter Katel, "Affirmative Action," *CQ Researcher*, Oct. 17, 2008, pp. 841-64; "More History of Affirmative Action Policies From the 1960s," American Association for Access, Equity And Diversity, https://tinyurl.com/y9yvcquq.

[44] Malcolm Gladwell, "Getting In: The social logic of Ivy League admissions," *The New Yorker*, Oct. 10, 2010, https://tinyurl.com/p77kbf5; Glenn Harlan Reynolds, "Asians get the Ivy League's Jewish treatment," *USA Today*, Nov. 24, 2014, https://tinyurl.com/ycmr7voc.

[45] Katel, "Affirmative Action," *op. cit.*; "More History of Affirmative Action Policies from the 1960s," *op. cit.*

[46] David Leonhardt, "Rethinking Affirmative Action," *The New York Times*, Oct. 14, 2012, https://tinyurl.com/kzk9c4c.

[47] Kurtis Lee and Joy Resmovits, "Justice Department calls for review of race-based college admissions, alarming civil rights groups," *Los Angeles Times*, Aug. 3, 2017, https://tinyurl.com/ycr786xb.

[48] Katel, "Affirmative Action," *op. cit.*

[49] *Ibid.*; Ashkenas, Park and Pearce, *op. cit.*

[50] "Regents Approve 'Dual Admissions' Plan, Expanding UC Access for High-Achieving Students," Office of the President, University of California, Sept. 18, 2001, https://tinyurl.com/yas9l5p5.

[51] *Jennifer Gratz and Patrick Hamacher, Peti-*

About the Author

Tom Price, a contributing writer for *CQ Researcher*, is a Washington-based freelance journalist who previously was a correspondent in the Cox Newspapers Washington Bureau and chief politics writer for *The Dayton Daily News* and *The* (Dayton) *Journal Herald*. He is author or co-author of five books including, with former U.S. Rep. Tony Hall (D-Ohio), *Changing The Face of Hunger: One Man's Story of How Liberals, Conservatives, Democrats, Republicans and People of Faith Are Joining Forces to Help the Hungry, the Poor and the Oppressed.* His previous *CQ Researcher* reports include an examination of college student debt.

tioners v. Lee Bollinger et al., U.S. Supreme Court, June 23, 2003, https://tinyurl.com/yd2jpll2.

[52] Adam Liptak, "Court Backs Michigan on Affirmative Action," The New York Times, April 22, 2014, https://tinyurl.com/kjrgx2e.

[53] Ibid.

[54] Schuette, Attorney General of Michigan, Petitioner v. Coalition to Defend Affirmative Action, Integration and Immigrant Rights and Fight for Equality By Any Means Necessary (BAMN) et al., U.S. Supreme Court, April 22, 2014, https://tinyurl.com/p36rgh7.

[55] Rick Jervis, "Voices: Affirmative action helps, but more is needed," USA Today, July 5, 2015, https://tinyurl.com/ycesvwzx.

[56] Strauss, "Actually, we still need affirmative action for African Americans in college admissions," op. cit.; Fisher v. University of Texas at Austin et al., op. cit.

[57] Fisher v. University of Texas at Austin et al., ibid.

[58] Richard Wolf, "At Texas' flagship university, many fear for diversity," USA Today, Dec. 2, 2015, https://tinyurl.com/yconqafp.

[59] Jeffrey Toobin, "The Obama Brief," The New Yorker, Oct. 27, 2014, https://tinyurl.com/kw6py24.

[60] Scott Jaschik, "Obama on Affirmative Action in Higher Ed," The New Yorker, Oct. 23, 2014, https://tinyurl.com/y8wgna59.

[61] "Obama And Affirmative Action," CBS News, May 14, 2007, https://tinyurl.com/yalyxtbv.

[62] Allie Bidwell, "Obama Administration OK's 'Lawful' College Affirmative Action Programs," U.S. News & World Report, Sept. 27, 2013, https://tinyurl.com/yaasy62e.

[63] Juliet Eilperin, Emma Brown and Darryl Fears, "Trump administration plans to minimize civil rights efforts in agencies," The Washington Post, May 30, 2017, https://tinyurl.com/y77b4gag.

[64] Linda Feldmann, "Was Barack Obama a transformative president?" The Christian Science Monitor, Jan. 18, 2017, https://tinyurl.com/yahxd5dd.

[65] Juliet Eilperin, "Obama has vastly changed the face of the federal bureaucracy," The Washington Post, Sept. 20, 2015, https://tinyurl.com/ybodosx3.

[66] Ibid.

[67] Annie Waldman, "DeVos Pick to Head Civil Rights Office Once Said She Faced Discrimination for Being White," ProPublica, April 14, 2017, https://tinyurl.com/y8v2d935; Valerie Strauss, "Trump taps Jewish community advocate as civil rights chief at Education Department," The Washington Post, Oct. 26, 2017, http://tinyurl.com/ybrnsxg.

FOR MORE INFORMATION

American Civil Liberties Union, 125 Broad St., 18th Floor, New York, NY 10004; 212-549-2500; www.aclu.org. Civil liberties group that supports using affirmative action to achieve equal opportunity.

American Council on Education, 1 Dupont Circle, N.W., Washington, DC 20036; 202-939-9300; www.acenet.edu. Organization representing nearly 1,800 two- and four-year colleges, universities and related organizations across the country.

Center for Equal Opportunity, 7700 Leesburg Pike, Suite 231, Falls Church, VA 22043; 703-442-0066; www.ceousa.org. Conservative think tank that opposes using race or ethnicity as a factor in hiring, contracting, elections and education, including college admissions.

Georgetown University Center on Education and the Workforce, 3300 Whitehaven St., N.W., Suite 3200, Washington, DC 20007; 202-687-7766; https://cew.georgetown.edu. Research institute that studies how race, ethnicity and socioeconomic status affect success in the workplace and at colleges.

Jack Kent Cooke Foundation, 44325 Woodridge Parkway, Lansdowne, VA 20176; 703-723-8000; www.jkcf.org. Provides financial and other assistance to low-income students from elementary school through graduate school.

National Center for Fair & Open Testing, PO Box 300204, Jamaica Plain, MA 02130; 617-477-9792; www.fairtest.org. Research group that advocates limiting or ending the use of SAT and ACT scores in college admissions.

Pew Research Center, 615 L St., N.W., Suite 80, Washington, DC 20036; 202-419-4300; www.pewresearch.org. Researches and reports on education, race, ethnicity and other issues.

Students for Fair Admissions, 2200 Wilson Blvd., Suite 102-13, Arlington, VA 22201; 703-505-1922; https://studentsforfairadmissions.org. Advocacy group that litigates against using race as a factor in college admissions.

[68] Andrew Kreighbaum, "Not Looking for Patterns," Inside Higher Ed, June 16, 2017, https://tinyurl.com/y79vbc2v.

[69] "Editorial: Trump administration systematically dismantling civil rights programs," St. Louis Post-Dispatch, June 18, 2017, https://tinyurl.com/ycguytye; Kreighbaum, op. cit.; and Eilperin, Brown and Fears, op. cit.

[70] Eugene Robinson, "President Trump is the master of abhorrent identity politics," The Washington Post, Nov. 2, 2017, https://tinyurl.com/ycmm565v.

[71] Sari Horwitz and Robert Costa, "Sessions's move to take on affirmative action energizes Trump's base," The Washington Post, Aug. 2, 2017, https://tinyurl.com/y862fyat.

[72] Daniel Cox, Rachel Lienesch and Robert P. Jones, "Beyond Economics: Fears of Cultural Displacement Pushed the White Working Class to Trump," Public Religion Research Institute, May 9, 2017, https://tinyurl.com/y9ckhxpk.

[73] Haurwitz, op. cit.

[74] Ralph K.M. Haurwitz, "UT: Lawsuit challenging use of race in admissions is 'retread' of Fisher," (Austin) American-Statesman, July 31, 2017,

https://tinyurl.com/y9ez8jcn; Eva-Marie Ayala, "Will Trump administration go after affirmative action admissions similar to UT's?" The Dallas Morning News, Aug. 3, 2017, https://tinyurl.com/y8ukewdz.

[75] Jane Stancill, "Group files suit challenging UNC on use of race in admissions," The (Raleigh) News & Observer, Nov. 17, 2014, https://tinyurl.com/yden2b35.

[76] Ibid.

[77] Vivian Yee, "Affirmative Action Policies Evolve, Achieving Their Own Diversity," The New York Times, Aug. 5, 2017, https://tinyurl.com/y7tqk47a.

[78] Ibid.; "Graduation rate from first institution attended for first-time, full-time bachelor's degree-seeking students at 4-year postsecondary institutions, by race/ethnicity, time to completion, sex, control of institution, and acceptance rate: Selected cohort entry years, 1996 through 2009," op. cit.

[79] Eric Hoover, "What Trump's Supreme Court Choice Might Mean for Higher Ed," The Chronicle of Higher Education, Feb. 1, 2017, https://tinyurl.com/hhq4w8f.

[80] Ibid.

Bibliography
Selected Sources

Books

Alon, Sigal, *Race, Class, and Affirmative Action*, Russell Sage Foundation, 2015.

An associate professor in Tel Aviv University's sociology and anthropology department compares race-conscious affirmative-action programs in the United States with class-based policies in Israel and concludes that each method falls short and should be combined.

Kennedy, Randall, *For Discrimination: Race, Affirmative Action, and the Law*, Pantheon, 2013.

A Harvard law professor says affirmative action should be less about diversity and more about compensating victims of discrimination.

Rothstein, Richard, *The Color of Law: A Forgotten History of How Our Government Segregated America*, Liveright, 2017.

A research associate at the liberal Economic Policy Institute says affirmative action is necessary to reverse the effects of government policies that made it harder for black families to build wealth and created racial disparities in education and other areas.

Sander, Richard, and Stuart Taylor Jr., *Mismatch: How Affirmative Action Hurts Students It's Intended to Help and Why Universities Won't Admit It*, Basic Books, 2012.

A UCLA law professor (Sander) and a freelance writer (Taylor) say college students who receive an affirmative-action preference often are less prepared than classmates who did not.

Articles

Blum, Edward, "Harvard's discrimination against Asian Americans must end," *The Washington Post*, Aug. 8, 2017, https://tinyurl.com/yd3ah55z.

A leading opponent of affirmative action says Ivy League schools discriminate against highly qualified Asian-American applicants.

Jaschik, Scott, "The Numbers and the Arguments on Asian Admissions," *Inside Higher Ed*, Aug. 7, 2017, https://tinyurl.com/y7kr6dxu.

A look at the statistics behind the claim that elite colleges reject Asian-American applicants in order to increase enrollment of other minorities.

Leong, Nancy, and Erwin Chemerinsky, "Don't use Asian Americans to justify anti-affirmative action politics," *The Washington Post*, Aug. 3 2017, https://tinyurl.com/ybfvkxyp.

Law professors at the University of Denver (Leong) and the University of California (Chemerinsky) say conservatives use Asian-Americans as "a convenient tool" in arguing against affirmative action.

Newhouse, Rod, "Affirmative action got me into MIT. The cycle that disadvantaged me continues," *The Washington Post*, Aug. 18, 2017, https://tinyurl.com/ya95vyb4.

An African-American graduate from a low-income public high school says he succeeded at an elite university despite being underprepared and that other disadvantaged youths deserve the same opportunity.

Reports and Studies

Espinosa, Lorelle L., Matthew N. Gaertner and Gary Orfield, "Race, Class, and College Access: Achieving Diversity in a Shifting Legal Landscape," American Council on Education, 2015, https://tinyurl.com/ycscnewe.

The top coordinating group for the nation's colleges and universities reviews affirmative-action practices based on a survey of admissions officers at 338 four-year colleges and universities.

Glynn, Jennifer, "Opening Doors: How Selective Colleges and Universities Are Expanding Access for High-Achieving, Low-Income Students," Jack Kent Cooke Foundation, September 2017, https://tinyurl.com/y86dvcfz.

A private foundation that provides financial and other help to low-income students looks at the most effective techniques for expanding college access for such students.

Heriot, Gail, "A 'Dubious Expediency': How Race-Preferential Admissions Policies on Campus Hurt Minority Students," The Heritage Foundation, Aug. 31, 2015, https://tinyurl.com/yboybf9w.

A University of San Diego law professor argues that a lack of highly qualified minority applicants leads top colleges to accept students who often fail.

Jaschik, Scott, and Doug Lederman, eds., "The 2016 Inside Higher Ed Survey of College & University Admissions Directors," *Inside Higher Ed*, undated, https://tinyurl.com/ybhdmb3q.

A publication covering higher education looks at how college admissions officers decide which applicants to accept.

Kennedy, Anthony, "Fisher v. University of Texas at Austin et al.," Supreme Court of the United States, June 23, 2016, https://tinyurl.com/z4q3uf3.

A Supreme Court justice explains why the court ruled that, in order to promote campus diversity, college admissions officers may consider race "as a relevant feature within the broader context of a candidate's application."

The Next Step:

Additional Articles from Current Periodicals

Asian-American Students

Golden, Daniel, "Asian-Americans are indeed treated unfairly in admissions, but the culprit is not affirmative action," *Chicago Tribune*, Aug. 11, 2017, https://tinyurl.com/ybmgw7vg.

"The preferences of privilege," not affirmative action, have hurt Asian-Americans because colleges tend to choose predominately white applicants of higher socioeconomic status over those from other backgrounds, an author argues.

Lee, Stacey, and Kevin K. Kumashiro, "The case for why Asian-Americans need affirmative action in college admissions," *Quartz*, Aug. 13, 2017, https://tinyurl.com/ybznhjd2.

Asian-Americans come from diverse backgrounds, and those from lower-income, less-advantaged families would benefit from affirmative-action programs, say two Asian-American academics.

Wong, Alia, "The Thorny Relationship Between Asians and Affirmative Action," *The Atlantic*, Aug. 3, 2017, https://tinyurl.com/y9vx9jcn.

While research supports the idea that affirmative action harms Asian-American applicants, most statistics do not reflect the complexity of admission policies, says an *Atlantic* contributor.

Economic Disparities

Aisch, Gregor, *et al.*, "Some Colleges Have More Students From the Top 1 Percent Than the Bottom 60. Find Yours," *The New York Times*, Jan. 18, 2017, https://tinyurl.com/jnlrjkm.

Elite universities enroll high-income students at a disproportionately high rate, according to a study by a group seeking to find ways to lift families out of poverty.

Anandalingam, G. Anand, "Rethinking college admissions to serve all segments of society," *The Baltimore Sun*, Sept. 5, 2017, https://tinyurl.com/y82nxnql.

Because college admissions often favor applicants with connections and money, admissions offices need to "end the cronyism," says a professor of management science.

Jost, Ashley, "Washington U. will waive application fees for low-income students," *St. Louis Post-Dispatch*, Oct. 10, 2017, https://tinyurl.com/y9rca7lh.

Washington University has waived its $75 application fee for low-income students as one of a variety of initiatives designed to diversify the student body.

Graduation Rates

Chiles, Nick, "HBCUs Graduate More Poor Black Students Than White Colleges," *NPR*, March 1, 2017, https://tinyurl.com/yazr6rjs.

A study by The Education Trust, a Washington group working to improve academic achievement, found that historically black colleges and universities are more successful at graduating low-income black students than white institutions.

Hess, Abigail, "Bill Gates: US college dropout rates are 'tragic,'" *CNBC*, Oct. 10, 2017, https://tinyurl.com/yasx4qrg.

Microsoft founder Bill Gates lauded Georgia State University for its high graduation rates for minorities and low-income students, accomplished by accepting more at-risk applicants than other universities and dedicating resources to support the students.

State Bans

"Diversity rising at UC Santa Cruz decades after affirmative action ban," *Santa Cruz Sentinel*, Aug. 9, 2017, https://tinyurl.com/y7mse36n.

Despite the state's ban on affirmative action in public school admissions, the University of California, Santa Cruz, has increased campus diversity by encouraging minority students to apply.

O'Connor, Madison, "How MSU deals with decade-old affirmative action ban," *The State News*, Jan. 12, 2017, https://tinyurl.com/yao7ft7b.

In the years since Michigan voters banned affirmative action in admissions decisions, Michigan State University has pursued an aggressive minority-recruitment strategy.

Slagter, Martin, "UM alumni look to boost minority enrollment with $30M scholarship expansion," *Michigan Live*, May 3, 2017, https://tinyurl.com/y9vm66n6.

With black student enrollment declining since the state banned affirmative action in college admissions in 2006, the University of Michigan's Alumni Association is investing $30 million in a merit scholarship program.

CITING CQ RESEARCHER

Sample formats for citing these reports in a bibliography include the ones listed below. Preferred styles and formats vary, so please check with your instructor or professor.

MLA STYLE
Mantel, Barbara. "Coal Industry's Future." CQ Researcher 17 June 2016: 529-552.

APA STYLE
Mantel, B. (2016, June 17). Coal Industry's Future. *CQ Researcher, 6*, 529-552.

CHICAGO STYLE
Mantel, Barbara. "Coal Industry's Future." *CQ Researcher*, June 17, 2016, 529-52.

In-depth Reports on Issues in the News

Are you writing a paper?

Need backup for a debate?

Want to become an expert on an issue?

For 90 years, students have turned to *CQ Researcher* for in-depth reporting on issues in the news. Reports on a full range of political and social issues are now available. Following is a selection of recent reports:

Civil Liberties
Privacy and the Internet, 12/15
Intelligence Reform, 5/15
Religion and Law, 11/14

Crime/Law
High-Tech Policing, 4/17
Forensic Science Controversies, 2/17
Jailing Debtors, 9/16
Decriminalizing Prostitution, 4/16
Restorative Justice, 2/16
The Dark Web, 1/16
Immigrant Detention, 10/15

Education
Charter Schools, 3/17
Civic Education, 2/17
Student Debt, 11/16
Apprenticeships, 10/16

Environment/Society
Stolen Antiquities, 11/17
Climate Change and National Security, 9/17
Muslims in America, 7/17
Funding the Arts, 7/17
Hunger in America, 7/17
Future of the Christian Right, 6/17

Health/Safety
Medical Breakthroughs, 9/17
Medical Marijuana, 7/17
Food Labeling, 6/17
Sports and Sexual Assault, 4/17

Politics/Economy
Democracy Under Stress, 10/17
Cyberwarfare Threat, 10/17
Universal Basic Income, 9/17
National Debt, 9/17
North Korea Showdown, 5/17
Rethinking Foreign Aid, 4/17

—— Upcoming Reports ——

Future of Marriage, 12/1/17   Privatization, 12/8/17   Species Extinction, 12/15/17

ACCESS
CQ Researcher is available in print and online. For access, visit your library or www.cqresearcher.com.

STAY CURRENT
For notice of upcoming *CQ Researcher* reports or to learn more about *CQ Researcher* products, subscribe to the free email newsletters, *CQ Researcher Alert!* and *CQ Researcher News*: http://cqpress.com/newsletters.

PURCHASE
To purchase a *CQ Researcher* report in print or electronic format (PDF), visit www.cqpress.com or call 866-427-7737. Single reports start at $15. Bulk purchase discounts and electronic-rights licensing are also available.

SUBSCRIBE
Annual full-service *CQ Researcher* subscriptions—including 44 reports a year, monthly index updates, and a bound volume—start at $1,131. Add $25 for domestic postage.

CQ Researcher Online offers a backfile from 1991 and a number of tools to simplify research. For pricing information, call 800-818-7243 or 805-499-9774 or email librarysales@sagepub.com.

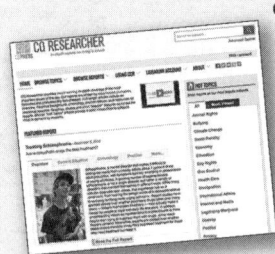

CQ RESEARCHER

CQ PRESS

In-depth reports on today's issues

Published by CQ Press, an Imprint of SAGE Publications, Inc.

www.cqresearcher.com

Future of Marriage

Are traditional unions becoming obsolete?

A mericans, especially young adults, are less likely than ever to see marriage as essential for a happy, fulfilled life. Women's increasing economic and social independence and the country's growing tolerance for nontraditional lifestyles have led many young people to rank matrimony behind such goals as an advanced degree or better job. Most Millennials say they see a wedding in their future, but a significant share of that generation views marriage as an outdated institution out of step with the demands and opportunities of contemporary culture. At the same time, many couples are remaining single or cohabitating because of high debt, job instability and other financial challenges. That has made marriage increasingly the province of the wealthy and well-educated, leading some experts to argue that the government should do more to help boost marriage rates. Meanwhile, online dating sites and mobile apps are growing in popularity, inspiring new research on the permanence of marriages made in cyberspace.

Andrew Schwaab, a pitcher for the Tampa Yankees minor league baseball team, proposes to his stunned girlfriend, Lauren Stoeckle, before a game in Lakeland, Fla., on June 17, 2017. Marriage rates in the United States have fallen nearly 30 percent since 1990, especially among people in their 20s to mid-30s, known as Millennials.

I N S I D E THIS REPORT

THE ISSUES **995**

BACKGROUND **1001**

CHRONOLOGY **1003**

CURRENT SITUATION **1007**

AT ISSUE.....................**1009**

OUTLOOK **1010**

BIBLIOGRAPHY **1014**

THE NEXT STEP **1015**

CQ Researcher • Dec. 1, 2017 • www.cqresearcher.com
Volume 27, Number 42 • Pages 993-1016

RECIPIENT OF SOCIETY OF PROFESSIONAL JOURNALISTS AWARD FOR
EXCELLENCE ◆ AMERICAN BAR ASSOCIATION SILVER GAVEL AWARD

SAGE Publishing
Los Angeles | London | New Delhi
Singapore | Washington DC | Melbourne

CQ RESEARCHER

Dec. 1, 2017
Volume 27, Number 42

EXECUTIVE EDITOR: Thomas J. Billitteri
tjb@sagepub.com

ASSISTANT MANAGING EDITORS: Kenneth Fireman, kenneth.fireman@sagepub.com, Kathy Koch, kathy.koch@sagepub.com, Scott Rohrer, scott.rohrer@sagepub.com

ASSOCIATE MANAGING EDITOR: Val Ellicott

SENIOR CONTRIBUTING EDITOR:
Thomas J. Colin
tom.colin@sagepub.com

CONTRIBUTING WRITERS: Marcia Clemmitt, Sarah Glazer, Alan Greenblatt, Reed Karaim, Barbara Mantel, Patrick Marshall, Tom Price

SENIOR PROJECT EDITOR: Olu B. Davis

EDITORIAL ASSISTANT: Natalia Gurevich

FACT CHECKERS: Eva P. Dasher, Michelle Harris, Betsy Towner Levine, Robin Palmer

Los Angeles | London | New Delhi
Singapore | Washington DC | Melbourne

An Imprint of SAGE Publications, Inc.

SENIOR VICE PRESIDENT,
GLOBAL LEARNING RESOURCES:
Karen Phillips

EXECUTIVE DIRECTOR, ONLINE LIBRARY AND
REFERENCE PUBLISHING:
Todd Baldwin

CQ Researcher (ISSN 1056-2036) is printed on acid-free paper. Published weekly, except: (March wk. 4) (May wk. 4) (July wks. 1, 2) (Aug. wks. 2, 3) (Nov. wk. 4) and (Dec. wks. 3, 4). Published by SAGE Publications, Inc., 2455 Teller Rd., Thousand Oaks, CA 91320. Annual full-service subscriptions start at $1,131. For pricing, call 1-800-818-7243. To purchase a *CQ Researcher* report in print or electronic format (PDF), visit www.cqpress. com or call 866-427-7737. Single reports start at $15. Bulk purchase discounts and electronic-rights licensing are also available. Periodicals postage paid at Thousand Oaks, California, and at additional mailing offices. POSTMASTER: Send address changes to *CQ Researcher*, 2600 Virginia Ave., N.W., Suite 600, Washington, DC 20037.

THE ISSUES

995 • Does growing income inequality discourage marriage?
• Should government policies do more to encourage marriage?
• Does online dating lead to stronger marriages?

BACKGROUND

1001 **Evolution of Marriage**
Marriage was typically an economic decision.

1002 **Pursuing Happiness**
Marriage became the norm after the Enlightenment.

1005 **Cultural Storm**
Social changes in the 1960's and '70's roiled the 1950's model of marriage.

1006 **Modern Polygamy**
Some Muslim and Mormon communities in the U.S. permit multiple wives.

CURRENT SITUATION

1007 **Same-Sex Marriages**
They have increased since a 2015 Supreme Court decision.

1008 **Similar Trends Worldwide**
Lack of financial security concerns couples globally.

1008 **Intermarriage Rising**
An increasing number of Americans have a spouse of a different race or ethnicity.

1010 **Births Outside Marriage**
The number has been increasing.

OUTLOOK

1010 **More Changes Coming**
Experts say marriage will continue evolving.

SIDEBARS AND GRAPHICS

996 **Marriage Declines Among Young Adults**
Many attribute delays to financial concerns.

997 **U.S. Marriage Rate Declines**
They have fallen almost 30 percent since 1990.

999 **Marriage Gap Widens Based on Education Level**
In the past 25 years, the marriage rate dropped much less for college-educated adults than those who didn't attend college.

1000 **Majority of Never-Married Adults Want to Marry**
Forty-one percent say they don't want to, or are not sure.

1003 **Chronology**
Key events since 1519.

1004 **Divorce Rising Among Older Americans**
"Why be miserable?"

1006 **Facebook Era Is Not Always a Friend of Marriage**
Experts say social media contribute to divorce rates.

1009 **At Issue:**
Is marriage becoming obsolete?

FOR FURTHER RESEARCH

1013 **For More Information**
Organizations to contact.

1014 **Bibliography**
Selected sources used.

1015 **The Next Step**
Additional articles.

1015 **Citing *CQ Researcher***
Sample bibliography formats.

Cover: AP Photo/Four Seam Images/Mike Janes

Future of Marriage

BY JANE FULLERTON LEMONS

THE ISSUES

In her mother's generation, Justine Cook would have been considered something of an oddity. At 33, Cook is single and has been with her boyfriend off and on for 13 years. Now living in Washington, D.C., they want to marry eventually, she says, but lack of money has put those plans on hold.

"We don't really have the disposable income," the fourth-grade teacher says. "We have rent and [graduate school] loans. Even just a ring and a small party is outside of what we're capable of."

Today, a smaller proportion of Americans, particularly Millennials (those in their 20s through mid-30s), are marrying, and increasingly they are delaying marriage until later in life. Many say they want to achieve other goals first, such as an advanced degree, a more fulfilling career or, like Cook, financial security.

In 2016, the average age for first-time marriage in the United States was at an all-time high — 27.4 for women and 29.5 for men. In 2015, the share of married Americans was at its lowest point (50 percent) since 1920. In 2014, for the first time, the number of unmarried American adults outnumbered those who were married. [1]

Major cultural shifts over the past several decades have altered Americans' perspectives on marriage. Compared to just a few decades ago, the country is far more tolerant of cohabitation, same-sex marriage, sex outside of marriage, single parenthood, unions between people of different races and ethnicities and an individual's decision to simply choose not to marry.

Pop culture today reflects these changes: Rather than the 1950s ideal

Courtesy Justine Cook

Justine Cook, 33, a fourth-grade teacher in Washington, D.C., wants to marry her longtime boyfriend but says financial concerns are holding them back. Americans increasingly are delaying marriage until later in life to achieve other goals first, such as an advanced degree, a more fulfilling career or, like Cook, financial security.

of husbands as breadwinners and wives as homemakers, Hollywood now routinely portrays working women in powerful jobs, men staying home with the children and gay men and women in successful unions. [2]

And young adults are far more likely than their parents to view marriage as outdated and to believe that children do not have to grow up in a two-parent home to be happy. Forty-four percent of Millennials surveyed by the Pew Research Center, a think tank in Washington, D.C., said marriage is becoming obsolete. [3]

"Young adults look different from prior generations in almost every regard: how much education they have, their work experiences, when they start a family and even who they live with growing up," the Census Bureau reported earlier this year. [4]

But while Millennials do not view marriage as a required rite of passage, most see it as a goal in their own lives, eventually. [5] "They seem to recognize that marriage has more potential to be mutually rewarding for those who truly want it, precisely because it's no longer a mandatory institution with rigid rules," says Stephanie Coontz, who teaches history and family studies at The Evergreen State College in Olympia, Wash.

Experts also link declining marriage rates to women's growing economic independence. As wages for men have fallen, more women are working and their lifestyle choices have expanded. Women are less likely than ever before to view marriage as crucial for financial security, and are less willing to marry someone who makes less money than they do.

"Women have raised the bar," says Isabel V. Sawhill, a senior fellow at the Brookings Institution, a think tank in Washington. "Marriage is now an option, not a necessity, from an economic standpoint."

Brad Wilcox, director of the National Marriage Project at the University of Virginia, attributes the country's retreat from marriage to "economic, policy and cultural shifts that all combined in the '60s and '70s to undercut the economic and legal and cultural foundation of a strong and stable marriage-centered family system."

Technology has played several roles in these cultural trends. Contraception and internet dating have made sex more accessible — or, in the case of pornography sites, less necessary, said Mark Regnerus, a sociologist at the University of Texas at Austin and author of *Cheap Sex: The Transformation of Men, Marriage, and Monogamy.* Such factors, he said, "have created a massive

Marriage Declines Among Young Adults

The percentage of people marrying young has declined by almost 40 percentage points over the past few generations. Millennials cite financial concerns as a main reason for delaying marriage.

Percentage of Each Generation Who Married, Ages 18-32
(by year of survey)

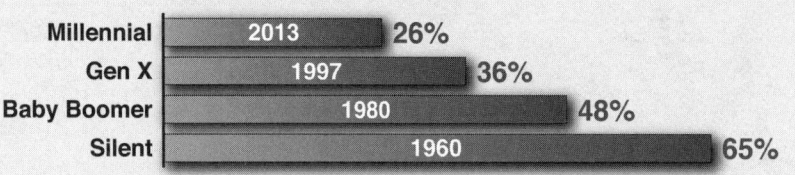

Millennial	2013	26%
Gen X	1997	36%
Baby Boomer	1980	48%
Silent	1960	65%

Source: "Millennials in Adulthood," Pew Research Center, March 7, 2014, https://tinyurl.com/y7ayuhu8

slowdown in the development of committed relationships, especially marriage," among young adults. [6]

Defenders of dating sites say they help people meet others with similar interests and that couples who wed after meeting online have lower rates of marital breakup. A recent study by Josue Ortega, a lecturer in economics at the University of Essex in Britain, and Philipp Hergovich, a doctoral candidate in economics at the University of Vienna in Austria, predicts that "marriages created in a society with online dating tend to be stronger." [7]

Developments in fertility technology have made parenthood feasible later in life. More than half of Millennial women say they would consider freezing their eggs, and 37 percent are open to using in vitro fertilization to get pregnant. [8]

"A combination of things is pushing Millennials to wait longer to start families," said Valerie Landis, who founded the egg freezing website Eggsperience. "Millennial women are focusing on their career success, online dating has made relationships more casual, and the tough economy has shifted Millennials' timelines for having their first child back." [9]

In addition, Jean Twenge, a professor of psychology at San Diego State University, said many young adults today are not in any rush to grow up: "The

entire developmental path from infancy to full adulthood has slowed." [10]

The marriage rate for young U.S. adults has dropped steadily since 1970, a trend that eventually could produce the largest proportion of unmarried young adults in modern history, the Pew Research Center said in 2014. [11]

Economics is a big factor. "Most unmarried Millennials (69 percent) say they would like to marry, but many, especially those with lower levels of income and education, lack what they deem to be a necessary prerequisite — a solid economic foundation," Pew reported. [12]

Student-loan debts are a major hurdle for many Millennials. They create economic insecurity, "which makes commitment to long-term life choices of any kind more challenging," according to American Student Assistance, a nonprofit in Boston that provides students with advice and other services to help them advance their educations. The group reported that 21 percent of student loan borrowers it surveyed said the loan obligations influenced their decision to delay marriage. [13]

However, Americans without college degrees lead the decline in marriage rates. Marriage has "evolved from a marker of conformity to a marker of prestige . . . a status one builds up to," said Andrew Cherlin, who teaches sociology and public

policy at Johns Hopkins University in Baltimore. [14]

Pew researchers report that never-married adults with family incomes under $75,000 are more likely than those with higher incomes to say that not being financially secure is a major reason they are not married. [15]

Marriage is falling most steeply among whites. In 1980, 81 percent of newlyweds were white. In 2015, that had dropped to 66 percent. The percentage of Hispanic and Asian newlyweds surged over that period, largely due to significant growth in the overall population of both groups. The percentage of black newlyweds remained unchanged, at 9 percent. [16]

Meanwhile, more unmarried U.S. adults are choosing to live together. Overall, the number of cohabiting couples has risen about 29 percent since 2007, and among people 50 and older, the increase is about 75 percent. [17]

Marriage allows couples to share household chores and save on taxes, and many researchers say children are happier and healthier when raised in a two-parent household. But experts disagree on whether the federal government should do more to promote marriage, with some arguing that government programs should instead focus on providing prospective parents, married or not, with long-term support systems, such as job training. [18]

Supreme Court decisions also have changed the marital landscape in the United States. Same-sex marriages surged after the court ruled in June 2015 that gays have a constitutional right to marry. [19]

In other marriage-related trends:

• About 26 percent of Millennials are married, much lower than previous generations in that age group: Generation X (36 percent) and Baby Boomers (48 percent). [20] (*See graph above.*)

• Marriage rates are declining much more slowly (4 percentage points since 1990) for those with a college degree than for those with only a high school diploma (13 percentage points). [21]

Experts are split on how marriage will fare as an institution in the United States.

"Marriage is in trouble," says Sawhill at the Brookings Institution. It's changing in a major way, and I don't think it's going to be as important in the future as it was in the past."

But Wilcox, at the National Marriage Project, says marriage remains "the gold standard when it comes to commitment, stability and social recognition in the U.S."

As researchers study changing trends in marriage, here are some of the questions they are asking:

Does growing income inequality discourage marriage?

Increasingly, marriage rates are linked closely to socio-economic status. In 2008, for instance, marriage rates among college-educated 30-year-olds for the first time surpassed those without a college degree. Seven years later, 65 percent of Americans with a four-year college degree were married, compared with 50 percent of those with only a high school diploma. [22]

"More and more, people now see the institution of marriage as a capstone to young adult life," says Alan Hawkins, associate director of the School of Family Life at Brigham Young University in Salt Lake City, Utah. "It's the mark of achievement — when you get a certain level of economic stability, psychological stability, that then the field is ripe and, 'I'm ready for marriage.'"

But if a college-and-career track "seems like a pipe dream" due to tough financial circumstances, marriage "seems a long way off and maybe unachievable," Hawkins says. "The stairs to that door are long and steep and costly. It makes marriage seem like a fantasy."

People in such situations delay marriage — or forgo it altogether — while searching for other ways to form relationships and families, Hawkins says.

Cherlin, at Johns Hopkins University, has tracked similar patterns. "College-educated Americans constitute the win-

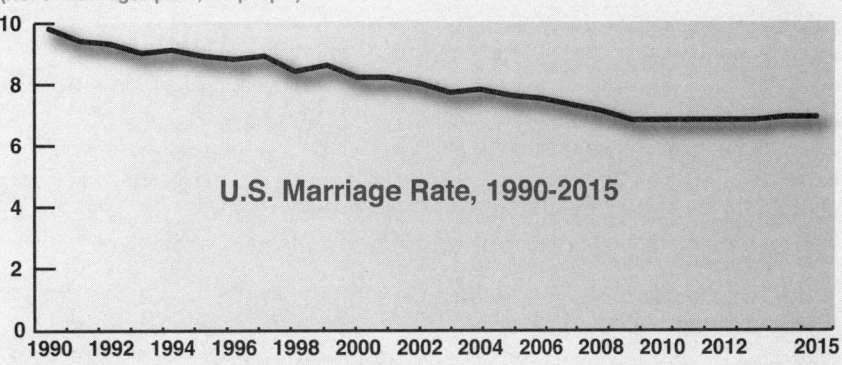

U.S. Marriage Rate Declines

The marriage rate in the United States has fallen from 9.8 marriages per 1,000 people in 1990 to 6.9 in 2015, about a 30 percent drop.

(No. of marriages per 1,000 people)

U.S. Marriage Rate, 1990-2015

Source: "Marriage rate in the United States from 1990 to 2015 (per 1,000 of population)," National Center for Health Statistics, Centers for Disease Control and Prevention, Statista, January 2017, https://tinyurl.com/yabc8g86

ners in our new economy, and they are sticking with long-term marriage as a context for rearing children," he said. [23]

The American Enterprise Institute, a conservative think tank in Washington, and the Institute for Family Studies, a research group that promotes marriage, said in a report that: "The retreat from marriage — a retreat that has been concentrated among lower-income Americans — plays a key role in the changing economic fortunes of American family life." [24]

American University economics professor Robert I. Lerman, who co-authored the report, said there has been a massive amount of "economic and political commentary on inequality and opportunity and stagnant middle-class incomes, but only rarely do we see a mention of this key factor of the changing structure of American families." [25]

Falling marriage rates parallel a decline in wages for male workers. In 2014, the typical male full-time worker earned $50,383. In 1973, that same worker earned $53,294, measured in 2014 dollars. In inflation-adjusted terms, the average wage for men peaked more than 40 years ago. [26] "It's hard to get ahead," says Ron Haskins, a senior fellow

at the Brookings Institution think tank and co-director of the group's Center on Children and Families.

Women's participation in the workforce has nearly doubled since 1950 — from under 34 percent to 57 percent. [27] And women workers — particularly younger ones — have narrowed the salary gap with men. [28]

In the 1950s, high school graduates were the most likely to marry, but as economic prospects declined for young men and increased for young women, that has reversed.

"One thing that really stands in the way of marriage among lower-income people is the woman's sense that she's not willing to take that step with a guy who might be a drag on her," says Coontz at Evergreen State College, who also directs research and public education at the Council on Contemporary Families, based at the University of Texas, Austin, which disseminates research on American families. "Of course, men, too, are looking for someone who can be an economic help and not a burden on them."

Other experts focus more on the flip side of the link between marriage rates and income and education levels.

They cite evidence that, as marriage rates continue their sharp declines among lower-income Americans, the gap between rich and poor is growing wider.

Marriage rates among women have declined most sharply for those with the least education and, consequently, the fewest job opportunities, says Haskins. "The reason this is important is that single women and their children are five times as likely to be poor as women who are married," he says. "So married couples are way better off financially."

Gregg Pitts, left, and Brooks Brunson of Washington, D.C., read to their adopted son on May 19, 2016. Their marriage in 2013 reflected one of the major cultural shifts in Americans' perspectives on marriage in recent decades. Polls show that the country has become increasingly tolerant of cohabitation, same-sex marriage, single parenthood and unions between people of different races or ethnicities.

AP Photo/Jacquelyn Martin

Pew researchers say college graduates, who have outpaced noncollege-educated Americans in earnings gains since 1970, "have fortified their financial advantage . . . because of their greater tendency to be married." [29]

Other studies have tracked Americans' preference for marrying others with similar educations and income prospects, a tendency researchers call "assortative mating." [30]

"Better educated people are increasingly more likely to marry other better-educated people while those with less formal schooling are more likely to

choose a less well-educated partner," according to a Pew analysis of findings by the National Bureau of Economic Research, a nonprofit organization in Cambridge, Mass., that studies economic trends. "As a consequence, income inequality has increased because education is strongly correlated with income — the more schooling you have, the more money you typically earn." [31]

When noncollege-educated men and women do marry each other, however, their finances typically do not improve, studies show, while the opposite is true for marriages involving two college-educated partners. Since 1960, the earnings of husbands and wives with only a high-school diploma have fallen 20 percentage points relative to average income levels, according to the National Bureau of Economic Research. Earnings for highly educated husbands and wives, meanwhile, increased by 43 points. [32]

At least two economic policy analysts, however, reject the notion that today's marriage trends contribute to income disparity. Sean McElwee, a policy analyst at Demos, a liberal think tank in New

York City, and Marshall I. Steinbaum, an economist at the Washington Center for Equitable Growth, a liberal group in Washington that researches the causes of income inequality, say economic and employment factors alone are responsible for making wealthy Americans richer and lower-income Americans poorer.

"The causes of rising inequality are the same reasons why household structure has changed: stagnant wages, labor market detachment and job lock," the two wrote in *The New Republic*, a liberal magazine.* [33]

McElwee and Steinbaum cite studies showing that marriage rates are high among armed forces members, because the military provides stable employment and a safety net to help families raise children.

"The evidence shows that family structure has changed because economic opportunities for most people have worsened," McElwee and Steinbaum wrote. [34]

Researchers have tried to find out how the 2007-09 recession affected marriage rates, but the results are unclear, according to Philip Cohen, a professor of sociology at the University of Maryland, College Park. [35]

There is evidence, however, that the end of the 2007-09 recession brought an increase in divorces, as couples who had postponed splitting up saw their finances improve.

"This is exactly what happened in the 1930s," Cherlin said. "The divorce rate dropped during the Great Depression not because people were happier with their marriages, but because they couldn't afford to get divorced." [36]

Should government policies do more to encourage marriage?

Federal, state and local governments play an active role in the lives of married

---

* Labor market detachment refers to people who stop looking for work. Job lock occurs when workers feel they cannot freely give up a job because doing so would mean losing health and other benefits.

couples in myriad ways — issuing marriage licenses, crafting divorce laws, providing special tax status and enforcing laws against polygamy.

When Congress enacted welfare reform in 1996, it built in family-related provisions that funded teen pregnancy prevention efforts, strengthened procedures for establishing paternity, toughened enforcement of child support laws and expanded benefits for two-parent families. [37]

More recently, the federal Office of Family Assistance awarded grants to 91 groups in 27 states and one territory designed to "promote healthy marriage," among other goals. Supporters of such measures say they help reduce poverty and protect children by making families more stable. [38]

"By most measures, marriage helps keep children out of poverty," according to a 2002 report from the Urban Institute, a think tank in Washington that researches income disparity. "If government-funded initiatives could promote healthy marriages, child poverty would almost certainly decline." [39]

Hawkins, of Brigham Young University, said "there is a role for the states and the federal government to make sure that we're not penalizing marriage" in areas such as tax law and assistance to low-income Americans. Marriage "is a bedrock of our society, and it contributes in many ways that we often take for granted," he says. "The federal government and the state governments need to support this kind of social infrastructure as much as they support the economic infrastructure of roads and bridges and sewer lines."

Wilcox, of the National Marriage Project, also favors government social welfare programs that encourage marriage — or at least remove disincentives to marry. "People are not indifferent to their bank accounts and their budgets," he says.

Wilcox co-authored a 2016 study that found 82 percent of unmarried couples earning between $24,000 and $79,000 would be penalized, if they married,

Marriage Gap Widens Based on Education Level

Between 1990 and 2015, the marriage rate dropped 13 percentage points among U.S. adults who never attended college. For college-educated men and women, the drop was only 4 percentage points.

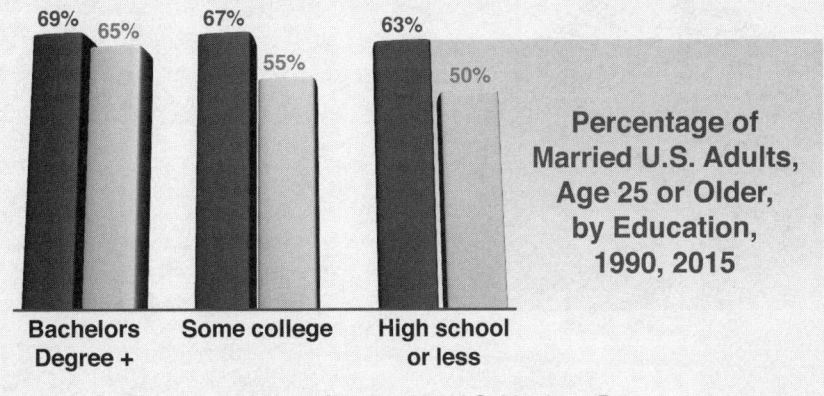

Percentage of Married U.S. Adults, Age 25 or Older, by Education, 1990, 2015

Bachelors Degree +   Some college   High school or less

69% 65%   67% 55%   63% 50%

Source: Kim Parker and Renee Stepler, "As U.S. Marriage Rate Hovers at 50%, Education Gap in Marital Status Widens," Pew Research Center, Sept. 14, 2017, https://tinyurl.com/yargyuc7

■ 1990
■ 2015

through lower levels of Medicaid, food stamps or other benefits.

"No one wants to see government efforts to support the lower-middle class undermine the stability of the very families they are intended to help," the report said. [40]

Haskins, at the Brookings Institution, is even more emphatic about the need for government action on issues affecting marriage. "We should do everything we can to remove disincentives to marriage, through the tax code especially, but also through welfare programs," he says.

Critics of such steps, however, warn against implementing policies that discriminate against unmarried Americans. [41]

Yale Law School professor Anne Alstott, an expert in taxation and social policy, argues that "the model of two married and co-resident parents is no longer standard," and that tax provisions specifically aimed at married couples should be eliminated. [42]

Some researchers say the Healthy Marriage Initiative — a George W. Bush administration program designed to encourage low-income people to marry as a way to improve their finances —

has been largely ineffective. "When faced with a myriad of social issues, building intimate relationships is just not high on their priority lists," Matthew D. Johnson, a professor of psychology at Binghamton University in New York, said of couples who participated in the program. [43]

And in a paper written for the Federal Reserve Bank of Atlanta, researchers said that welfare reform legislation enacted in 1996, despite containing pro-marriage provisions, "may have actually decreased the incentives to be married by giving women greater financial independence via the program's new emphasis on work." [44]

Critics of marriage promotion policies say they may encourage women to remain in abusive relationships and overlook the sacrifices made by single parents working hard to raise children despite limited resources. [45]

"Such programs intrude on personal privacy, may ignore the risk of domestic violence and may coerce women to marry," said Timothy J. Casey, a lawyer for the advocacy group Legal Momentum (formerly the NOW Legal Defense and Education Fund), which provides legal advice aimed at protecting women's economic security. [46]

Majority of Never-Married Adults Want to Marry

Fifty-eight percent of never-married U.S. adults say they want to get married eventually, while 41 percent say they do not or are not sure.

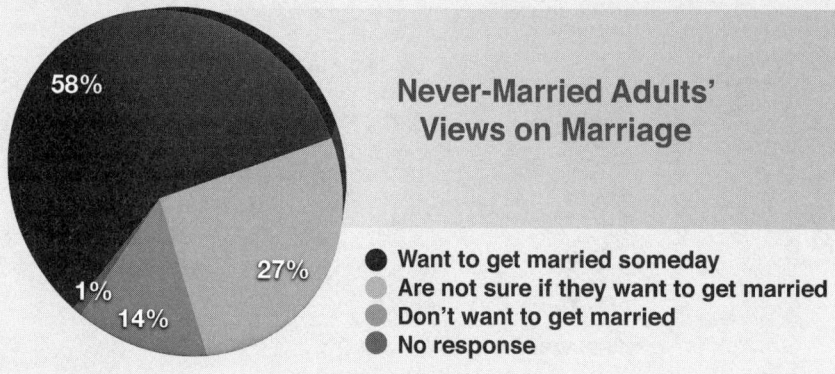

Never-Married Adults' Views on Marriage

- 58%
- 27%
- 14%
- 1%

● Want to get married someday
● Are not sure if they want to get married
● Don't want to get married
● No response

Source: Kim Parker and Renee Stepler, "As U.S. Marriage Rate Hovers at 50%, Education Gap in Marital Status Widens," Pew Research Center, Sept. 14, 2017, https://tinyurl.com/yargyuc7

Libertarians such as Sen. Rand Paul, R-Ky., argue that marriage is a private realm and government should stay out of it.

"Since government has been involved in marriage, they have done what they always do — taxed it, regulated it, and now redefined it," Paul wrote after the Supreme Court legalized same-sex marriage in 2015. "It is hard to argue that government's involvement in marriage has made it better, a fact also not surprising to those who believe government does little right." [47]

Paul questioned whether government officials should grant special benefits to married couples or even issue marriage licenses. "Perhaps the time has come to examine whether or not governmental recognition of marriage is a good idea," he wrote.

Does online dating lead to stronger marriages?

More people continue to turn to the internet to meet their partners. Nearly one of four heterosexual couples meets online. For gay couples, the rate is about two of every three. [48]

Fifteen percent of U.S. adults say they have used online dating sites or mobile dating apps. The two age groups that

are behind much of the increase in the apps' popularity are 18- to 24-year-olds and 55- to 64-year-olds, according to the Pew Research Center. [49]

Pew also found that 41 percent of Americans know someone who uses an online dating service, and 29 percent know someone who married or entered into a long-term partnership with a person after initially meeting that person via online dating. [50]

Other research shows that one-third of marriages now begin online — and that such matches may be more successful than marriages that do not. Marriages that began online were slightly less likely to result in separation or divorce "and were associated with slightly higher marital satisfaction among those respondents who remained married," according to a 2012 study by researchers from the University of Chicago and Harvard University. [51]

Coontz, at Evergreen State College, agrees that online dating may result in stronger marriages. "Those who do find a match seem to do very well with it," she says.

Dating apps have been particularly helpful for older Americans, who might otherwise have limited opportunities

to meet people. "It means there is a lot more choice out there," Coontz says. Some people may feel overwhelmed by all the choices available online, she says, "[but] for others it means, 'I really do have a shot at meeting somebody that I wouldn't have had 30 years ago.' "

Stanford University sociologist Michael Rosenfeld said his research shows that dating websites such as Match.com and eHarmony, offer significant benefits "for people who have a hard time finding partners in their day-to-day, face-to-face life." That's particularly relevant for single, older people because so many of their peers are already in relationships. [52]

He also said couples who meet online move more quickly to wedding plans, largely because online daters focus only on potential partners with similar interests and typically communicate with each other more before meeting for the first time.

"When you're using online dating, and there's the possibility of selecting on characteristics that you know you're going to like, you're going to know a lot more about people before a first date," he said. [53]

Of couples who meet through online dating and stay together, about half get married within four years, Rosenfeld said. That compares to 10 years for half the couples who stay together after meeting offline. His research also suggests that online dating is popular because it meshes with the increasingly prevalent view among young people that there is no reason to hurry to get married.

"People used to marry in their early 20s, which meant that most dating that was done, or most courting that was done, was done with the intention of settling down right away," he said. "And that's not the life that young people lead anymore." [54]

However, online dating also plays to tendencies that are not conducive to marriage, critics say. All that swiping and scrolling, they say, can encourage people to treat potential dates as commodities, and the vast array of choices invites indecision. Behavioral experts also note that online profiles often contain exaggerations or outright lies, and can lead to unrealistic expectations. [55]

"In this social environment, studies show a decline in the ability to form secure attachments — the kind where you trust and share your life," Sherry Turkle, a psychologist at the Massachusetts Institute of Technology, wrote in *Reclaiming Conversation: The Power of Talk in a Digital Age*. "Ironically, our new efficient quests for romance are tied up in behavior that discourages empathy and intimacy." [56]

Mobile dating apps, such as Tinder or Grindr, have been criticized for fueling a culture of hook-ups rather than long-term relationships. "There is no dating. There's no relationships," a woman identified only as Amanda told *Vanity Fair* in referring to dating apps. "They're rare. You can have a fling that could last like seven, eight months and you could never actually call someone your 'boyfriend.' " [57]

But Rosenfeld said online dating can go well beyond the superficial. "People looking for longer-term relationships exclusively tend to choose the dating websites where profiles are more lengthy and text-driven" than the mobile apps, he said. "If you're looking for a life partner, online dating is pretty good for that." [58] ∎

BACKGROUND

Evolution of Marriage

Modern Americans tend to think of marriage in terms of a loving, lifelong commitment. But for most of human history, love and religion had little to do with marriage.

Although pairing up to produce offspring is as old as human history, the

Working to keep their marriages strong, the seven Quincy, Ill., couples above – all married for more than 40 years – have been meeting monthly ever since they attended a Marriage Encounter get-together 35 years ago. "I think this group has kept us grounded in our relationship," said Cathy Tate, first row, third from left. "We've supported each other with raising kids."

first recorded evidence of formal marriage ceremonies uniting one woman and one man dates back more than 4,000 years ago to Mesopotamia. The institution has been in a continuous state of evolution ever since. [59]

Marriage has different meanings around the world. Individual cultures, religions and social classes have distinct marital standards and expectations, both currently and historically.

"Whenever people talk about traditional marriage or traditional families, historians throw up their hands," said Steven Mintz, a historian at the University of Texas, Austin. "We say, 'When and where?' " [60]

Coontz, at Evergreen State College, said marriage has taken so many different forms over time "that trying to define it by its most frequently encountered functions does not really help us understand what any particular society's marriage system is or how and why such a system changes over time."

"We also can't claim some groups did not have 'real' marriage just because

their marriage practices were not 'typical,' " Coontz wrote in her book, *Marriage, A History: How Love Conquered Marriage.* [61]

Throughout most of recorded time, marriage was an economic and social arrangement — a contract between families, with property, inheritances and other nonromantic realities taking precedence over love. The man and woman involved typically had little or no say when it came to their future spouse. This was particularly true among the upper classes.

For thousands of years, beginning with the earliest civilizations, Coontz wrote, "the economic functions of marriage were far more important to the middle and lower classes than were its personal satisfactions, while among the upper classes, the political functions of marriage took first place," such as expanding political power or forging military alliances [62]

While marriage in the lower classes had less political intrigue, it was still ruled by practical calculations rather than personal desires. As societies transitioned from hunting and gathering to agriculture, families needed labor and the ability to maintain control of their land. Marriage was a less formal affair, and the state often did not get involved.

Arranged marriages remain common today, especially in countries such as India. More than half the marriages worldwide today are arranged. And while some couples have more input into the process than their historical predecessors, some countries have high

The Koran advises Muslim men they may take up to four wives, but only if they can "deal justly" with each of them. [65]

In a handful of cultures, women take multiple husbands, a practice known as polyandry. Several factors, such as men outnumbering women or a lack of usable farmland, can encourage this custom. For instance, in Tibet, where large tracts of arable land are scarce, a family might marry all of its men to one woman so they can all work one plot of land and avoid scrounging for

sake of pleasure, concubines for the daily health of our bodies, and wives to bear us lawful offspring and be the faithful guardians of our homes." [68]

Monogamy developed as the cultural norm later in the history of marital evolution, according to anthropologists. [69]

For several centuries after the fall of the Roman Empire, the Catholic Church battled against rulers who wanted to take additional wives, according to Coontz. The church eventually prevailed, and by the 9th century monogamy was central to the notion of marriage in Christian cultures.

Along with these various forms of heterosexual marriage, same-sex marriage recurred throughout history. Mesopotamian prayers have been found for such couples, and in the Native American tradition, "two-spirit people" had relationships with both sexes. Evidence has been discovered, dating from between 1050 and 1150, of ceremonies that some believe amounted to the Christian church's blessing of same-sex unions. [70]

Historians have widely documented that relationships existed between same-sex couples in ancient Greek and Roman civilizations. They were first dubbed marriages in ancient Rome, where emperors Nero and Elagabalus publicly married men. [71]

Runners kiss during a mass wedding and vow renewal ceremony before the Rock 'n' Roll Las Vegas Marathon on Nov. 12, 2017. In 2016, the average age for first-time marriage in the United States was at an all-time high — 27.4 for women and 29.5 for men. In 2015, the share of married Americans was 50 percent, the lowest since 1920.

AP Photo/John Locher

Pursuing Happiness

rates of forced marriage and marriages involving child brides. [63]

In many cultures, marriage has involved more than the two-person model familiar to modern Americans. Polygamy, the practice of marrying multiple spouses, has been widely accepted under various laws, religions and customs throughout history. The ancient Hebrews practiced the most common form of polygamy, in which a man has multiple wives. The Bible cites several examples, including King Solomon, who had 700 wives and 300 concubines. [64]

individual plots to farm. Polyandry is still widely practiced in Tibet, though it is technically illegal. [66]

Spartan women had far more authority and rights inside and outside marriage than other women in ancient Greece. In ancient Egypt, wives had the same power as husbands except in employment. They could choose their own husbands and divorce a husband who no longer pleased them. [67]

The ancient Greek statesman Demosthenes summed up the 4th century B.C. view on marriage and sexual partners for men: "We have courtesans for the

By the 17th and 18th centuries, several changes were taking place that affected the view of marriage and its role in society. Enlightenment thinkers introduced the idea that life was about the pursuit of happiness, giving rise to the more modern concept that people could marry for love rather than for economic or political needs. At the same time, the Industrial Revolution was creating a larger middle class and increasing economic stability, meaning more people could afford to choose whom they wanted to marry. [72]

Continued on p. 1004

Chronology

1500s-1700s
Marriages are commonly arranged as business transactions.

1519
Martin Luther delivers sermons praising marriage at a time when celibacy is linked to a higher state of spirituality.

1691
Virginia becomes first colony in North America to ban interracial marriage.

1753
Marriage Act is first legislation in England and Wales requiring a formal religious ceremony of marriage.

1800s-1940s
Polygamy, interracial marriage outlawed.

1856
Republican Party platform refers to Mormons' practice of polygamy as one of the "twin relics of barbarism," alongside slavery.

1879
Supreme Court upholds federal law banning polygamy (*Reynolds v. United States*).

1883
Supreme Court upholds Alabama's ban on interracial marriage (*Pace v. Alabama*).

1890
Mormon church ends its support for polygamy.

1900
Married women can own property in their own name in every state.

1907
Congress revokes U.S. citizenship for women who marry non-citizens.

1940
Congress changes 1907 law to sever link between women's marital status and citizenship.

1960s-1970s
The sexual revolution and the civil rights and women's rights movements affect marriage.

1960
The share of married adults peaks at 72 percent. . . . Food and Drug Administration approves birth control pill.

1964
Civil Rights Act prohibits discrimination based on gender.

1965
Landmark Supreme Court decision (*Griswold v. Connecticut*) overturns a Connecticut law banning married couples from using contraceptives, establishing the right to marital privacy.

1967
Supreme Court rejects state miscegenation laws in landmark ruling (*Loving v. Virginia*).

1970
Jack Baker and Michael McConnell apply for a marriage license in Minnesota the year after the Stonewall riots in New York City launched the gay rights movement.

1972
Supreme Court says unmarried people have the same right to possess contraceptives as married people (*Eisenstadt v. Baird*).

1974
Equal Credit Opportunity Act allows women to have credit cards in their own names.

1978
Pregnancy Discrimination Act bars discrimination against pregnant women in the workplace.

1980-Present
Support for gay marriage increases.

1980
U.S. divorce rate peaks at about 50 percent.

1993
Marital rape is a crime in all states.

1996
Defense of Marriage Act (DOMA) defines marriage as the union of one man and one woman, and denies same-sex couples the federal benefits available to other married couples.

2013
Supreme Court strikes down DOMA but leaves in place laws banning same-sex marriage (*United States v. Windsor*).

2015
Supreme Court rules that the constitutionally protected right to marry applies to same-sex couples just as it applies to opposite-sex couples (*Obergefell v. Hodges*).

2017
Number of Americans getting married continues to decline. . . . Supreme Court declines to hear a challenge to a Utah law banning polygamy, meaning the practice remains illegal.

Divorce Is Rising Among Older Americans

"It's such a gift to be here. Why be miserable?"

Susan Fischer (not her real name) divorced her husband just five months shy of their 25th wedding anniversary. Reflecting on the split, the suburban Washington, D.C., resident says they had been living "very inauthentically," with each partner wanting something different from the marriage.

"I really wanted this perfect marriage and to grow old with him," says Fischer, who asked to remain anonymous to protect her amicable relationship with her ex-husband. "Now, a few years later, I've recreated a whole new life for myself, and I'm so glad I'm not doing this another 25 years, just staying in a miserable situation."

Fischer is part of a new trend in the United States. Although the nation's overall divorce rate is stabilizing, the rate among Americans 50 and over has doubled in the past 25 years and is still rising.

The divorce rate has doubled since 1990 for those 50 and over, jumping from five out of every 1,000 married individuals in 1990 to 10 of every 1,000 in 2015, according to the Pew Research Center in Washington. The increase was even steeper for those 65 and older, with the divorce rate tripling since 1990 to six of every 1,000 married people. [1]

Stephanie Coontz, a historian of marriage and families at The Evergreen State College in Olympia, Wash., calls these "gray divorces" a mixed bag.

She recalls how an unhappily married couple who used to live in her neighborhood would sit in lawn chairs on opposite sides of their yard. "The good news is that people no longer have to do that," she says, meaning such couples can split up. "The bad news is there are risks to divorce at a later age."

In addition to the potential financial concerns of ending a marriage, Coontz says, both men and women face the possibility of losing social networks built as a couple. As they age, they also could be dealing with health issues without the support of a spouse.

Isabel V. Sawhill, a senior fellow in economic studies at the Brookings Institution, a Washington think tank, views the trend through a similar lens. "It's all about the fact that we're living longer," she says.

Older couples' lives no longer center on work and raising children, Sawhill says. When they reach their 50s and 60s, "[they] say, 'Now what?,'" she says. "They didn't used to say 'now what?' They retired and died. But now they want to make the most of

that third phase of life." Sociologists Susan L. Brown and I-Fen Lin of Bowling Green State University in Ohio said many older couples getting divorced are in second or third marriages.

"Older individuals are more often in remarriages, not first marriages, and remarriages have long been more likely than first marriages to end through divorce," they said. "People who have been divorced in the past are more willing to divorce again in the event a marriage becomes unsatisfying." [2]

But that's only part of the story. Brown and Lin also documented an increase in the breakup rate of older people in their first marriages. "More than half of gray divorces are to couples in first marriages," they said. "Long-term marriages are not immune to divorce — more than 55 percent of gray divorces involved a split for couples who had been married more than 20 years."

Higher education levels typically mean lower divorce rates, but that does not hold true in this demographic, said Brown and Lin. They said these marriages were not marked by discord or violence. Instead, the couples were unwilling to stay in an "empty shell" arrangement.

"This reflects the shifting meaning of marriage in contemporary America," Brown and Lin said. "Today, most people hold marriage to a higher standard than in the past. . . . If spouses no longer derive satisfaction from their marriage, divorce is seen as a viable solution and carries far less social stigma than the past." [3]

Fischer, who remains on good terms with her former husband and in-laws, says she realized she had choices that women in previous generations did not. "It's not like you give up; you just want to be happy," she says. "Nowadays, you can be who you want to be in life."

Fischer says she is glad she struck out on her own. "We're being who we were meant to be, and we couldn't do that together," she says. "It's such a gift to be here. Why be miserable?"

— Jane Fullerton Lemons

[1] Renee Stepler, "Led by Baby Boomers, divorce rates climb for America's 50+ population," Pew Research Center, March 9, 2017, https://tinyurl.com/zvogsl5; Brigid Schulte, "Till Death Do Us Part? No way. Gray Divorce on the Rise," *The Washington Post*, Oct. 8, 2014, https://tinyurl.com/y8yqruvc.
[2] Susan L. Brown and I-Fen Lin, "Gray Divorce: A Growing Risk Regardless of Class or Education," Council on Contemporary Families, Oct. 8, 2014, https://tinyurl.com/y8bt9unp.
[3] *Ibid.*

Continued from p. 1002

Coontz's writes that it was only about 200 years ago "that men and women began to wrest control over the right to marry from the hands of parents, church and state. And only in the last hundred years have women had the independence to make their marital

choices without having to bow to economic need and social pressure." [73]

Despite these changes, however, hurdles still existed when it came to marriage. In the United States, for example, a 1907 law said that women who married noncitizens would lose their U.S. citizenship. That changed in

1940, when Congress enacted a new law saying a woman's citizenship was no longer tied to her marital status and those who had lost their citizenship could regain it. [74]

Miscegenation laws prohibiting interracial marriage, dating from the days of slavery, remained in place until 1967, when the U.S. Supreme Court, in the landmark *Loving v. Virginia* case, ruled that such laws were unconstitutional. [75]

For years, laws treated married women differently from their husbands. Beginning in 1839, states began passing laws allowing married women to own property in their own name. In the 1970s, laws were changed to outlaw marital rape, allow women to open credit cards in their own name and curtail job discrimination on the basis of being pregnant or having preschool children. [76]

Cultural Storm

Many Americans still view marriage through the lens of the 1950s, the era of the breadwinner husband and homemaker wife that is commonly seen as the pinnacle of marital success. Coontz called this postwar period "a lull before the long-predicted storm" of the sexual revolution and the widespread cultural changes of the 1960s and '70s. "[T]his stability was the result of a unique moment of equilibrium in the expansion of economic, political and personal options," she wrote. [77]

It took 150 years to establish the 1950s model of marriage, but only 25 years to dismantle it, Coontz wrote. Contributing factors included the invention of reliable birth control, an economy that required two incomes and modern conveniences that reduced the homemaker's workload. The civil rights movement, antiwar protests and the feminist movement raised questions about societal norms, including women's role in marriage. [78]

Those developments laid the groundwork for even more change, such as the overturning, decades later, of laws banning interracial and gay marriage. By 1980, half of all Americans who got married would end up divorced.

As these cultural shifts played out, economic factors began affecting family structure and marriage rates. Beginning in 1964, with President Lyndon B. Johnson's War on Poverty, the government

Emily Helfgot, a school curriculum specialist, and Robert Weinstein, a librarian, discovered that they lived in the same Brooklyn, N.Y., neighborhood after meeting online. They married three years later. Nearly one of four heterosexual couples meets online. For gay couples, the rate is about two of every three. "For all the pitfalls, annoyances and tumult of online dating, I'm so glad I did it!" Helfgot said.

AFP/Getty Images/Jewel Samad

began implementing programs aimed at helping low-income families and individuals. More than 50 years later, scholars continue to debate whether they helped lift people out of poverty or created a culture of dependency. [79]

In particular, critics contend welfare programs discouraged parents from getting married and may have contributed to rising rates of nonmarital births. [80]

In the 1990s, President Bill Clinton championed welfare reform that, among other things, was designed to encourage two-parent families and reduce nonmarital births. Researchers remain divided on how effective the law has been in that regard. After increasing for decades, unwed births began to level off in the mid-1990s, while teen births have declined significantly since the early 1990s. But experts say it is difficult to link those trends directly to changes in welfare policy because of other factors, such as increases in both abstinence rates and birth control use. [81]

Meanwhile, the movement to legalize same-sex marriage continued to strengthen. It began in 1970, when Jack Baker and Michael McConnell applied for a marriage license in Minnesota the year after the

Stonewall riots in New York City launched the gay rights movement. [82]

In 1993, the Hawaii Supreme Court ruled that same-sex marriages could not be denied unless there was a "compelling reason" to do so. Lawmakers in Hawaii and other states responded with legislation to ban gay marriage. [83]

In 1996, Congress passed — and Clinton signed — the Defense of Marriage Act (DOMA), which defined marriage as the union of one man and one woman and denied same-sex couples the federal benefits available to other married couples. [84]

The following year, Hawaii became the first state to offer domestic partnership benefits to same-sex couples, and other states began passing laws to outlaw gay marriage. In 2000, Vermont became the first state to grant the full benefits of marriage to same-sex couples.

A pair of key Supreme Court decisions followed. In 2013, the court declared DOMA unconstitutional, saying it denied same-sex couples the "equal liberty" guaranteed by the Fifth Amendment. That ruling left in place state laws banning same-sex marriage, but not for long. In 2015, the court legalized

Facebook Era Is Not Always a Friend of Marriage

Social media are contributing to higher divorce rates, experts say.

Social media and the internet have opened up new ways to find love. They also have opened up new ways for a marriage to fail.

One in three divorces can be traced to an "online affair" — an affair that begins with electronic communications, according to McKinley Irvin, a national family-law firm based in Seattle that specializes in divorce. Attorneys regularly use information gleaned from texts, emails and other electronic communications as evidence in divorce proceedings. Social media postings in particular can provide clues about finances and infidelity, sometimes with accompanying photos, or about a spouse's unhappiness with the marriage. [1]

In other findings:

• Researchers who conducted a 2014 study published in the journal *Computers in Human Behavior* reported that heavy use of Facebook is "a positive, significant predictor of divorce rate and spousal troubles."

• 15 percent of couples believe the internet poses the greatest threat to marriage, according to a January poll taken by 60 Minutes and *Vanity Fair.*

• A 2015 survey by a British law firm found that nearly 25 percent of married couples in Britain argued at least once a week over social media use, and one in seven of those surveyed said they had considered getting divorced because of their partner's activities on Facebook, Skype, Snapchat, Twitter or WhatsApp. [2]

Experts say excessive use of social media can lead to jealousy, arguments and doubts about the relationship. [3]

"Facebook-induced jealousy may lead to arguments concerning past partners," said Russell Clayton, former director of the Cognition and Emotion Lab in the School of Communication at the University of Missouri and now at Florida State University. "Excessive Facebook users are more likely to connect or reconnect with other Facebook users, including previous partners, which may lead to emotional and physical cheating." [4]

The study reported in *Computers in Human Behavior* reached the same conclusions, finding that excessive use of Facebook is contributing to higher divorce rates and reduced marital happiness: "Although it may seem surprising that a Facebook profile, a relatively small factor compared to other drivers of human behavior, could have a significant statistical relationship with divorce rates and marital satisfaction, it nonetheless seems to be the case," the study said. And Facebook's impact on marriage raises "profound questions about the role of social media in daily lives." [5]

When couples head to divorce court, social media and digital devices provide "a treasure trove of incriminating information" for bickering spouses and their attorneys to exploit, according to the American Academy of Matrimonial Lawyers. [6]

In a Connecticut divorce case, for instance, a judge ordered the couple to exchange passwords for Facebook and other social networking sites after the husband suspected his wife had posted incriminating information. [7]

In August 2015, hackers released the names and personal information of 37 million users of Ashley Madison, a dating website aimed at married people seeking to have an affair. [8]

The American Academy of Matrimonial Lawyers said 97 percent of its members have seen an increase in evidence taken from smartphones and other wireless devices, including texts, emails, internet search histories, call histories and GPS locations. In addition, 67 percent of divorce lawyers, it said, are gathering evidence

---

same-sex marriage throughout the country in its landmark 5-4 decision in *Obergefell v. Hodges.* [85]

In some ways, the changes to marriage over the past century have brought the institution closer to the egalitarian model of some ancient societies — in which both spouses have equal say in taking care of the house — than to the the era of economically driven, arranged marriages. That is largely due to changing views on what is acceptable regarding premarital sex, divorce, remarriage, cohabitation and out-of-wedlock births — the very trends at play in modern marriage.

"Some people note this resemblance between modern family relations and the informal sexual and marital norms of many [ancient] societies and worry that we are throwing away the advantages of civilization," Coontz wrote in her book. "They hope to reinstitutionalize marriage as the main mechanism that regulates sexuality, legitimizes children, organizes the division of labor between men and women, and redistributes resources to dependents. But the last century of social change makes this highly unlikely." [86]

Modern Polygamy

In recent times, there has been a growing trend against polygamy, recognized in about 850 societies — primarily in Asia, Africa and the Middle East. As immigrants from those countries have moved to other countries, they have brought their marriage practices with them, raising legal and cultural issues for countries where the practice is illegal. [87]

In the United States, polygamy is illegal in all 50 states and the District of Columbia, but researchers estimate that up to 150,000 people continue to take multiple wives, mostly in Muslim immigrant communities and among fundamentalist Mormons in Utah and nearby states. [88]

Polygamy was a significant tenet of the early Church of Jesus Christ of Latter-day Saints (the Mormons) in the mid-1800s. Mormonism's founders, Joseph Smith and Brigham Young, each had multiple wives. The church ended the practice in 1890, paving the way for Utah to gain statehood, and formally prohibited the practice in 1904. [89]

from apps, and the top three apps are those for social media sites: Facebook (41 percent), Twitter (17 percent) and Instagram (16 percent). [9]

"In the past, a suspicious spouse might have turned to a private investigator for this kind of detailed information, but nowadays most people willingly carry around some kind of wireless tracking device everywhere they go," in the form of a cellphone, said James McLaren, the academy's president. "As with almost every aspect of our lives, smartphones and other wireless devices are having a big impact on the ways in which couples divorce." [10]

New York attorney Alison Keil said she advises her clients "to be smart about what they write, send and post online. As a rule of thumb, you should never post something that you would not want your worst enemy to see, which, in a contested divorce, just may end up being your spouse." [11]

— *Jane Fullerton Lemons*

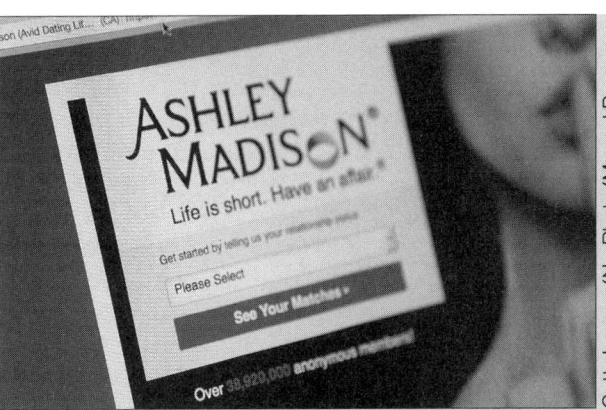

In 2015, hackers released the names of 37 million users of Ashley Madison, a dating website aimed at married people seeking to have an affair.

[1] "Digital Divorce: A Guide for Social Media & Digital Communications in Divorce," McKinley Irvin, https://tinyurl.com/yamhvmzf; Samantha Yule, "Facebook now crops up in a third of divorce cases over cheating and old flames," *The Mirror*, Jan. 20, 2015, https://tinyurl.com/mv2jkrd.

[2] Amy Laskowski, "Could Facebook Use End a Marriage," *BU Today*, June 2, 2014, https://tinyurl.com/knasa9e; Sebastian Valenzuela *et al.*, "Social network sites, marriage well-being and divorce: Survey and state-level evidence from the United States," *Computers in Human Behavior*, 2014, https://tinyurl.com/ya46qkzj; "60 Minutes/Vanity Fair Poll: Marriage," cbsnews.com, Jan. 5, 2017, https://tinyurl.com/y9jmap3f; "Social Media Is The New Marriage Minefield," Slater and Gordon Law Firm, April 30, 2015, https://tinyurl.com/y78wd3hn.

[3] Amanda Chatel, "Why Social Media Causes Divorces, And 7 Ways It's Ruining Your Relationship," *Bustle*, July 29, 2015, https://tinyurl.com/y7vzscgn; Danielle Page, "5 Ways Marriage Is Harder in 2017 (and What You Can Do

About It)," NBC News, June 6, 2017, https://tinyurl.com/y7df4ur7.

[4] Nathan Hurst, "Excessive Facebook Use Can Damage Relationships, MU Study Finds," University of Missouri, June 3, 2013, https://tinyurl.com/n9xszrn.

[5] Sebastián Valenzuela, Daniel Halpern and James E. Katz, "Social network sites, marriage well-being and divorce: Survey and state-level evidence from the United States," *Computers in Human Behavior*, July 2014, https://tinyurl.com/ycgoxaub.

[6] "Huge Increase of Texts and App Evidence in Divorces Say Nation's Top Lawyers: Smart Phones and Other Wireless Devices Yielding Treasure Trove of Incriminating Information," American Academy of Matrimonial Lawyers, June 8, 2015, https://tinyurl.com/ybddyoy8.

[7] Kashmir Hill, "Judge Orders Divorcing Couple To Swap Facebook And Dating Site Passwords," *Forbes*, Nov. 7, 2011, https://tinyurl.com/y93y3ust.

[8] Daniel Victor, "The Ashley Madison Data Dump, Explained," *The New York Times*, Aug. 19, 2015, https://tinyurl.com/y737zbaf.

[9] "Huge Increase of Texts and App Evidence in Divorces Say Nation's Top Lawyers: Smart Phones and Other Wireless Devices Yielding Treasure Trove of Incriminating Information," *op. cit.*

[10] *Ibid.*

[11] Alison Keil, "Is Social Media Related to Higher Divorce Rates?" Divorceify, March 9, 2017, https://tinyurl.com/y8ddszda.

Although many American polygamists live in the legal shadows, some have spoken out publicly on the issue, and polygamous families have been featured in TV programs, such as HBO's fictional "Big Love" and the TLC network's reality show "Sister Wives." [90]

The Brown family from "Sister Wives" sued to overturn Utah law that made polygamy a crime. Although a federal judge initially sided with the family, a federal appeals court overturned that ruling. In January, the U.S. Supreme Court declined to hear the family's appeal in *Brown v. Buhman*, meaning polygamy remains illegal. [91]

George Washington University law professor Jonathan Turley, who represented the Browns in their litigation,

said many of those on his staff who worked on the case "believed strongly that every family has a fundamental right to follow their own faiths so long as they did not harm others." [92] ■

CURRENT SITUATION

Same-Sex Marriages

Same-sex marriages in the United States are surging in the wake of the Supreme Court's 2015 landmark

ruling in *Obergefell v. Hodges*. Nearly 1.1 million U.S. adults are married to someone of the same sex. Of those approximately 547,000 same-sex couples, an estimated 157,000 married since the court's decision. [93]

Surveys conducted by Gallup earlier this year indicate that 10.2 percent of lesbian, gay, bisexual or transgender (LGBT) adults are married to a same-sex spouse — up from 7.9 percent in the months leading up to the ruling. As a result, about 61 percent of same-sex, cohabiting couples are now married — up from 38 percent before the ruling. [94]

The U.S. public's views on same-sex marriages have changed markedly in the past 10 years. In 2007, 54 percent of Americans opposed such unions.

In 2017, opposition has dropped to 32 percent, with a solid majority of people — 62 percent — saying they support the right of same-sex couples to marry. [95]

Americans who identify as LGBT cite the same reasons for getting married as heterosexuals. Love topped the list for both groups, followed by companionship. However, LGBT Americans were twice as likely to cite legal rights and benefits as an important reason for getting married.

"As Americans attend the weddings of their friends, family and work colleagues, research shows that support for marriage equality will continue to grow," said demographer Gary J. Gates of the Williams Institute at UCLA School of Law. [96]

Coontz, at Evergreen State College, views gay unions as a natural next

the way for gay marriage, Coontz says, adding that she is curious to watch those marriages develop.

Similar Trends Worldwide

Marriage rates are declining in other countries for at least one of the same reasons they are declining in the United States — lack of financial security.

"The lack of stable jobs and absence of credit have become disincentives to forming a family," said Teresa Castro-Martin, a professor of population studies research at the Spanish National Research Council, a government research institute in Madrid, Spain. [97]

10 years later than in the 1980s. And the number of children born out of wedlock in Poland is at record highs.

"Marriage has traditionally been a rite of passage to adulthood, but it has lost its centrality," said Castro-Martin.

In 2014, Antonio Golini, then-chairman of Italy's National Institute of Statistics, said falling marriage rates are the result of cultural and economic factors. "The cultural causes are that marriage has become less important from a religious and civil point of view, because many young people live together without marrying," he said. [99]

As marriage rates decline worldwide, so has the number of weddings. There were fewer weddings in Poland in 2013 than in any year since 1945. The same was true in Italy. Weddings in France are at historic lows.

In the United States, the number of weddings fell an estimated 0.5 percent last year, to about 2.2 million. About 310,000 U.S. business provide wedding-related services. In 2016, the average cost of a wedding in the United States reached an all-time high of $35,329. [100]

Intermarriage Rising

Fifty years after the Supreme Court struck down laws banning interracial marriage in *Loving v. Virginia*, the number of Americans married to someone of a different race or ethnicity continues to rise.

In 2015, 17 percent of newlyweds — one in six — were married to someone of a different race or ethnicity. That was more than five times the number in 1967, the year the court issued its landmark ruling. [101]

A Pew analysis of Census Bureau data also found that one in 10 married Americans in 2015 — not just newlyweds — had a spouse of a different race or ethnicity.

"The growth in intermarriage has coincided with shifting societal norms as

Getty Images/*The Washington Post*/Michael S. Williamson

Interracial couples like Ron Campbell, a City Council member in Leesburg, Va., and his wife, Barbara Lawrence, were able to marry legally in Virginia thanks to the Supreme Court's 1967 Loving v. Virginia *ruling, which outlawed state anti-miscegenation laws. In the 50 years since the landmark decision, the percentage of newlyweds married to someone of a different race or ethnicity has risen more than fivefold, to 17 percent.*

step after the breakdown of gender and racial barriers to marriage. "Same-sex marriage was an outcome of the changes that heterosexuals made in the institution of marriage," she says.

The advent of more egalitarian marriages based on love and desire rather than financial concerns helped pave

According to the most recent data, countries in the European Union reported an average marriage rate of 4.6 first-time marriages per 1,000 people, below the U.S. rate of 6.9 per 1,000 people. [98]

In Spain, couples married at an average age of 37.2 in 2014 — almost

Continued on p. 1010

At Issue:

Is marriage becoming obsolete?

ISABEL V. SAWHILL
SENIOR FELLOW, BROOKINGS INSTITUTION AND AUTHOR, GENERATION UNBOUND: DRIFTING INTO SEX AND PARENTHOOD WITHOUT MARRIAGE

WRITTEN FOR *CQ RESEARCHER*, DECEMBER 2017

*i*s marriage obsolete? I hope not, but I don't think it's coming back. Marriage in the United States has been declining steadily for almost five decades. Granted it is still alive and well among the most educated, but they are only about 30 percent of the population. Among the youngest generation, regardless of education, the majority of children are now born outside of marriage.

Marriage has had positive effects on the well-being of families and the life trajectories of children, according to the experts. For these reasons, many people, myself included, hope it can be restored to a more prominent place in our society.

That said, there are many reasons to be pessimistic.

First, major demographic trends are hard to reverse. Whether it is declining fertility, new opportunities for women, the greater acceptance of gays or many other trends, once they achieve a certain momentum, they are hard to reverse.

Second, groups with the lowest marital rates — minorities and the young — are becoming a larger share of the population. (More education could partially or completely offset this effect.)

Third, the trend is evident in all advanced countries, suggesting that it has little to do with policies or cultural factors that are specific to the United States.

Finally, the major factor driving the trend is the fact that women are no longer dependent on men for economic or social support. Marriage is now an option, not a necessity. And as more people opt to forgo marriage, being unmarried, including having a child on one's own, can become the new normal.

While I am not optimistic about future trends, I don't think marriage is going to disappear. It still confers many benefits, including the greater income that comes from pooling resources; higher success rates for the children of marital unions; and the kind of adult intimacy, security and companionship that aren't as easily available to those who are single.

However, if the decline continues, as I expect it to, then we need to worry more about children who increasingly are being deprived of a stable family environment. If the old social norm was "don't have a child outside of marriage," the new social norm needs to be "don't have a child until you and your partner want one" and are ready to make the commitment that parenthood should entail.

ALAN J. HAWKINS
ASSOCIATE DIRECTOR, SCHOOL OF FAMILY LIFE, BRIGHAM YOUNG UNIVERSITY

WRITTEN FOR *CQ RESEARCHER*, DECEMBER 2017

i've been carefully observing changes to the institution of marriage for 30 years. And changing it is. But I think it's hard to make a case stick that marriage is becoming obsolete, if by obsolete you mean "no longer useful."

A large majority of adults still marry (and remarry). Most never-married adults still say they hope to do so at some point. At least for the well-educated — those who are often at the vanguard of cultural change — divorce rates are significantly lower than they were for their parents' generation. And research continues to find that getting and staying married is associated with a wide range of psychological, financial and health benefits for adults. Perhaps most important, research is continually affirming the value of stable, healthy marriages to children's well-being.

Yes, there are popular voices arguing that marriage is "past its prime." And granted, nearly half of Millennials report that they think marriage is becoming obsolete. Perhaps Millennials' responses to pollsters, however, reflects more their desires to be approving of all different kinds of family forms than their doubts about the value of marriage as an institution. (In the same poll, nearly the same proportion of Millennials say the growing variety of family arrangements is a good thing.) Moreover, for those disadvantaged Millennials who have grown up with few models of healthy marriages in their lives, their views on the obsolescence of marriage may say more about their discouraged dreams than their objective assessment of marriage. And in fact, a large majority of Millennials, advantaged and disadvantaged, still say they want to join this institution.

There are voices arguing that marriage is a "vestige," a remnant of an earlier time before the sexual revolution reshaped both public and private life. But research that documents changes to marriage also provides compelling evidence that marriage continues to play a crucial role in society.

No doubt marriage's mettle will be tested over the coming years. For instance, many social scientists and legal scholars are questioning the merits of marital monogamy and whether marriage should be remodeled to make room for more colorful conceptions of the meaning of fidelity. I struggle to see exactly how this gathering storm and other future forces will batter the boundaries of marriage.

Right now, I'm betting on the fundamental resiliency of this venerable institution.

Continued from p. 1008

Americans have become more accepting of marriages involving spouses of different races and ethnicities, even within their own families," the report found.

Intermarriage rates for black newlyweds account for much of the overall increase. The share of recently married blacks with a spouse of a different race or ethnicity more than tripled between 1980 and 2015 — from 5 percent to 18 percent. Among recently married whites, intermarriage rates increased from 4 percent to 11 percent over that period. [102]

The overall numbers are similar among those who live together but are not married. About 18 percent of cohabiting adults have a partner of a different race or ethnicity, according to Pew. Among those under age 50, the number is roughly one of every five. [103]

At the same time, Pew found that one in seven U.S. infants under a year of age were multiracial or multiethnic in 2015, nearly triple the share in 1980. [104]

In addition, about 24 percent of adopted children in the United States were placed with a parent of a race different from their own, according to data from the 2010 census. That is up from 17 percent in 2000. [105]

"Today the race mixing that supremacists feared is growing apace, and interracial dating, marriage, adoption and friendship are occurring at rates that were unfathomable 50 years ago," Georgetown University law professor Sheryll Cashin wrote in a *New York Times* essay, "How Interracial Love Is Saving America." [106]

The evolving state of marriage and families has caught the attention of advertisers, whose campaigns have begun to reflect these changes. Interracial families are featured in TV ads for Cheerios and Swiffer housecleaning products, and gay couples are featured in ads for Chevrolet and Banana Republic.

"People seem to have decided diversity can be used as a statement," said Jaime Prieto, president of global brand management at the advertising firm Ogilvy. "It's an interesting shift." [107]

Births Outside Marriage

The cultural shifts affecting views on marriage also have led to an increase in the number of children born to single women. Forty percent of the babies delivered in the United States in 2014 were born to unmarried women, according to a Pew analysis of government data. That is almost twice the percentage of 30 years earlier. [108]

Sawhill at the Brookings Institution, author of *Generation Unbound: Drifting into Sex and Parenthood without Marriage*, finds these numbers alarming. [109] She says 73 percent of pregnancies among single women under 30 are unplanned — a trend directly related to the falling marriage rate, rising cohabitation and society's growing acceptance of unwed pregnancy.

"The old social norm was, don't have a child outside of marriage," Sawhill says. "The new norm should be, in my view, that you shouldn't have a child until you and your partner really want to be parents."

In 2014, fewer than half — 46 percent — of children younger than 18 in the United States lived with two married, heterosexual parents in their first marriage, according to a Pew census analysis. In 1960, 73 percent of children fit that description. The Pew study also found that about one-third of children live with an unmarried parent, up from 9 percent in 1960 and 19 percent in 1980. [110] ∎

OUTLOOK

More Changes

Marriage will continue to evolve beyond its transformation over the past few decades, researchers say. Brigham Young's Hawkins believes Americans will spend another couple of decades "slogging through" the recent cultural and economic shifts that have altered views on marriage.

"This is a long-term adjustment process that's going on as a society," he says. "We've had this dramatic sexual revolution and dramatic economic changes, and those things coming together have just battered this ship. I don't think it's going to sink, but I think we are a decade or two, or maybe a generation away, from a more stable social world."

Hawkins is optimistic that congressional lawmakers will come up with policies to support marriage so more people can attain it.

Evergreen State College's Coontz says "the future depends on decisions we make right now" to close the growing gaps in income and education levels reflected in marriage rates. "If we continue to acquiesce to this incredible surge in inequality," she says, "that's going to have very different consequences for the future than if we make a societal decision that everybody should have the right to a job that pays a living wage and to be able to get off that job in time to spend with whomever they want to count as family."

Policymakers need to craft laws — in parental leave, child care and other areas — that support families, she says. "We're taking a big risk with the quality of married life and the future of married life if we fail to address those problems," she says.

However, Haskins at the Brookings Institution has found that reversing decades of declining marriage rates "is turning out to be exceptionally difficult," citing the ineffectiveness of some past government efforts to promote marriage.

Given current trends in marriage rates and nonmarital births, "millions of American children over the next several decades will live in families headed by single mothers," Haskins said. [111]

Regnerus, the University of Texas sociologist, predicts that "pornography . . . will have become conventional by 2030," further hampering the sort of relationships that can lead to marriage. "Cheap sex slows down the road to marriage, makes its would-be participants think twice about it, and draws their attention toward consumption rather than production," he wrote. [112]

Other researchers say even as marriage rates fall, Americans are more likely than ever to marry someone from a different racial, ethnic or religious background. "This churning, this turnover in our intimate partnerships is creating complex families on a scale we've not seen before," said Cherlin at Johns Hopkins University. "It's a mistake to think this is the endpoint of enormous change. We are still very much in the midst of it." [113]

Hawkins remains optimistic that marriage will survive.

"The data are overwhelming about how valuable the institution is to our society," he says. "I just think it's going to take us a long time to really see that marriage is something that isn't conservative or progressive. It's just good stuff." ■

Notes

[1] Gretchen Livingston and Andrea Caumont, "5 facts on love and marriage in America," Pew Research Center, Feb. 13, 2017, https://tinyurl.com/z3t5kgs; Stephanie Hanes, "Singles nation: Why so many Americans are unmarried," *The Christian Science Monitor*, June 14, 2015, https://tinyurl.com/y78nvaqu.

[2] Gretchen Livingston and Andrea Caumont, "5 facts on love and marriage in America," Pew Research Center, Feb. 13, 2017, https://tinyurl.com/z3t5kgs.

[3] Wendy Wang and Paul Taylor, "For Millennials, Parenthood Trumps Marriage," Pew Research Center, March 9, 2011, https://tinyurl.com/lfl2nhy.

[4] Jennifer Calfas, "Millennials Want Jobs and Education, Not Marriage and Kids," *Time*, April 20, 2017, https://tinyurl.com/n2tpmtt.

[5] Wang and Taylor, *op. cit.*

[6] Julie Beck, "Love in the Time of Individualism," *The Atlantic*, Sept. 22, 2017, https://tinyurl.com/y9rplo4y.

[7] Josue Ortega and Philipp Hergovich, "The Strength of Absent Ties: Social Integration via Online Dating," arvix.org, Oct. 2, 2017, https://tinyurl.com/y7edkphf.

[8] "The State of Fertility Report 2017," *Healthline*, undated, https://tinyurl.com/ya3xvnco.

[9] *Ibid.*

[10] Jean Twenge, "Why today's teens aren't in any hurry to grow up," *The Conversation*, Sept. 19, 2017, https://tinyurl.com/yczz4yoq.

[11] Wendy Wang and Kim Parker, "Record Share of Americans Have Never Married," Pew Research Center, Sept. 24, 2014, https://tinyurl.com/m9w37a7.

[12] Bruce Drake, "6 new findings about Millennials," Pew Research Center, March 7, 2014, https://tinyurl.com/nutkq9x.

[13] "Life Delayed: The Impact of Student Debt on the Daily Lives of Young Americans," American Student Assistance, 2015, https://tinyurl.com/y8rdar4m.

[14] Claire Cain Miller, "How Did Marriage Become a Mark of Privilege?" *The New York Times*, Sept. 25, 2017, https://tinyurl.com/y9wzbg8h; Andrew J. Cherlin, "The Deinstitutionalization of American Marriage," *Journal of Marriage and Family*, November 2004, https://tinyurl.com/yaf9gfnf.

[15] Kim Parker and Renee Stepler, "As U.S. marriage rate hovers at 50%, education gap in marital status widens," Pew Research Center, Sept. 14, 2017, https://tinyurl.com/yargyuc7.

[16] Gretchen Livingston and Anna Brown, "Trends and patterns in intermarriage," Pew Research Center, May 18, 2017, https://tinyurl.com/y8k9alq9.

[17] Meg Murphy, "NowUKnow: Why Millennials Refuse to Get Married," Bentley University, undated, https://tinyurl.com/lffxe8t; Renee Stepler, "Number of U.S. adults cohabiting with a partner continues to rise, especially among those 50 and older," Pew Research Center, April 6, 2017, https://tinyurl.com/ydhlggdv.

[18] Geraldine Sealey, "Should the Government Push Marriage?" ABC News, undated, https://tinyurl.com/y9bmoogt.

[19] Richard Wolf, "Gay marriages up 33% in year since Supreme Court ruling," *USA Today*, June 22, 2016, https://tinyurl.com/ydauhjsz.

[20] "Millennials in Adulthood," Pew Research Center, March 7, 2014, https://tinyurl.com/pbpw3tv; Drake, *op. cit.*

[21] Parker and Stepler, *op. cit.*

[22] Richard V. Reeves, Isabel V. Sawhill and Eleanor Krause, "The most educated women are the most likely to be married," Brookings Institution, Aug. 19, 2016, https://tinyurl.com/zrm9xyu; Parker and Stepler, *op. cit.*

[23] Andrew J. Cherlin, "In the Season of Marriage, a Question. Why Bother?" *The New York Times*, April 27, 2013, https://tinyurl.com/mgva8vx.

[24] Robert I. Lerman and W. Bradford Wilcox, "For richer, for poorer: How family structures

economic success in America," American Enterprise Institute and Institute for Family Studies, Oct. 28, 2014, https://tinyurl.com/y8br8vyh.

[25] Katherine Peralta, "Want More Money? Get Married," *U.S. News & World Report*, Oct. 28, 2014, https://tinyurl.com/y6tvte5l.

[26] David Wessel, "The typical male U.S. worker earned less in 2014 than in 1973," Brookings Institution, Sept. 18, 2015, https://tinyurl.com/ya42o55l; Drew DeSilver, "For most workers, real wages have barely budged for decades," Pew Research Center, Oct. 9, 2014, https://tinyurl.com/qxuhn2o.

[27] "Average wages for all workers, men and women, have increased as a result of women joining the workforce," *Science Daily*, Oct. 11, 2017, https://tinyurl.com/y83r6uar.

[28] Anna Brown and Eileen Patten, "The narrowing, but persistent, gender gap in pay," Pew Research Center, April 3, 2017, https://tinyurl.com/l8gfgfk.

[29] Richard Fry and D'Vera Cohn, "Women, Men and the New Economics of Marriage," Pew Research Center, Jan. 9, 2010, https://tinyurl.com/b4v6896.

[30] Jeremy Greenwood *et al.*, "Marry Your Like: Assortative Mating and Income Inequality," National Bureau of Economic Research, May 2014, https://tinyurl.com/yb9wmg94.

[31] *Ibid.*; Rich Morin, "New academic study links rising income inequality to 'assortative mating,' " Pew Research Center, Jan. 29, 2014, https://tinyurl.com/nz4755e.

[32] Morin, *ibid.*

[33] McElwee, Sean, and Marshall I. Steinbaum, "No, The Decline in Marriage Did Not Increase Inequality," *The New Republic*, Jan. 16, 2015, https://tinyurl.com/y9gcxzgw.

[34] *Ibid.*

[35] Philip N. Cohen, "How The American Family Was Affected By The Great Recession," *Pacific Standard*, Feb. 5, 2015, https://tinyurl.com/yaw7u7po.

[36] Emily Alpert Reyes, "Divorces rise as economy recovers, study finds," *Los Angeles Times*, Jan. 27, 2014, https://tinyurl.com/ya47ysky.

[37] Robert I. Lerman, "Should Government Promote Healthy Marriages?" Urban Institute, May 31, 2002, https://tinyurl.com/yb3cvs4e.

[38] "Healthy Marriage & Responsible Fatherhood," Office of Family Assistance, U.S. Department of Health and Human Services, undated, https://tinyurl.com/y7nzc57v.

[39] Lerman, *op. cit.*

[40] W. Bradford Wilcox, Angela Rachidi and Joseph Price, "Marriage, Penalized: Does Social-Welfare Policy Affect Family Formation?" American

Enterprise Institute and Institute for Family Studies, July 26, 2016, https://tinyurl.com/y9aj5p5u.

[41] Dylan Matthews, "The case for cutting the link between taxes and marriage," *The Washington Post*, June 27, 2013, https://tinyurl.com/yc8tcdo5.

[42] Anne Alstott, "Updating the Welfare State: Marriage, the Income Tax, and Social Security in the Age of Individualism," *Tax Law Review*, 2013, https://tinyurl.com/ydhcft89.

[43] Noah Rubinstein, "Why the Healthy Marriage Initiative Doesn't Work," GoodTherapy.org, May 31, 2012, https://tinyurl.com/y8wl6phq.

[44] Marianne P. Bitler *et al.*, "The Impact of Welfare Reform on Marriage and Divorce," Working Paper Series, Federal Reserve Bank of Atlanta, June 2002, https://tinyurl.com/y7owu4rb.

[45] *Ibid*.

[46] Robert Pear and David D. Kirkpatrick, "Bush Plans $1.5 Billion Drive For Promotion of Marriage," *The New York Times*, Jan. 14, 2004, https://tinyurl.com/y95bwabp.

[47] Rand Paul, "Rand Paul: Government Should Get Out of the Marriage Business Altogether," *Time*, June 29, 2015, https://tinyurl.com/o5qx4s7.

[48] Roberto A. Ferdman, "How well online dating works, according to someone who has been studying it for years," *The Washington Post*, March 23, 2016, https://tinyurl.com/ybqjes7u.

[49] Aaron Smith, "15% of American Adults Have Used Online Dating Sites or Mobile Dating Apps," Pew Research Center, Feb. 11, 2016, https://tinyurl.com/hxbmg5k; Aaron Smith and Maeve Duggan, "Online Dating and Relationships," Pew Research Center, Oct. 21, 2013, https://tinyurl.com/qcm929c.

[50] Smith, *op. cit.*

[51] Drake Baer, "How Online Dating is Creating Stronger Marriages," *Thrive Global*, Oct. 17, 2017, https://tinyurl.com/y9dlrpbt; John T. Cacioppo *et al.*, "Marital satisfaction and break-ups differ across on-line and off-line meeting venues," Proceedings of the National Academy of Sciences, June 18, 2013, https://tinyurl.com/y7mnv4wg.

[52] Ferdman, *op. cit.*

[53] *Ibid*.

[54] *Ibid*.

[55] Rebecca Adams, "7 Drawbacks Of Online Dating, According To Science," *The Huffington Post*, July 7, 2015, https://tinyurl.com/ybu66sxm.

[56] Sherry Turkle, *Reclaiming Conversation: The Power of Talk in a Digital Age* (2016), https://tinyurl.com/yaw9odno.

[57] Nancy Jo Sales, "Tinder and the Dawn of the 'Dating Apocalypse,'" *Vanity Fair*, September 2015, https://tinyurl.com/y74vj7nk.

[58] Ferdman, *op. cit.*

[59] "The origins of marriage," *The Week*, Jan. 1, 2007, https://tinyurl.com/yadu667v.

[60] "How marriage has changed over centuries," *The Week*, June 1, 2012, https://tinyurl.com/kf5pale.

[61] Stephanie Coontz, *Marriage, a History: How Love Conquered Marriage* (2006), p. 28, https://tinyurl.com/y92lrqyh.

[62] *Ibid*.

[63] Léa Rose Emery, "What Modern Arranged Marriages Really Look Like," *Brides*, Sept. 9, 2017, https://tinyurl.com/yb4bqoah; Laura Ling, "Where Do Arranged Marriages Still Exist?" *Now This World*, April 18, 2015, https://tinyurl.com/yd3gt5mn.

[64] "1 Kings 11:3," BibleHub.com, https://tinyurl.com/y7tc89lh.

[65] Nicholas Bala *et al.*, "An International Review of Polygamy: Legal and Policy Implications for Canada," November 2005, https://tinyurl.com/y786ohmj.

[66] Stephanie Weber, "Yes, There Is a Marriage Practice Where Women Have Multiple Husbands," *Modern Notion*, Dec. 16, 2015, https://tinyurl.com/y9sjbvs9.

[67] "Spartan Women," *Legends & Chronicles*, undated, https://tinyurl.com/y9nex26h; Joshua J. Mark, "Women in Ancient Egypt," Ancient History Encyclopedia, Nov. 4, 2016, https://tinyurl.com/y9obzhox.

[68] William Harlan Hale, *Horizon History of Ancient Greece* (2017).

[69] Carl Zimmer, "Monogamy and Human Evolution," *The New York Times*, Aug. 2, 2013,

https://tinyurl.com/qyl8g9y.

[70] Alex Gendler, "The history of marriage," TEDEd, undated, https://tinyurl.com/yd5sdgcg; Dalton Walker, "Going Far From Home to Feel at Home," *The New York Times*, July17, 2007, https://tinyurl.com/ya2jfdhr; David W. Dunlap, "John E. Boswell, 47, Historian Of Medieval Gay Culture, Dies," *The New York Times*, Dec. 25, 1994, https://tinyurl.com/y9dkea5w.

[71] Laura Geggel, "Same-Sex Marriage in History: What the Supreme Court Missed," *Live Science*, May 5, 2015, https://tinyurl.com/ybhspfpe.

[72] "How marriage has changed over centuries," *op. cit.*

[73] Coontz, *Marriage, a History: How Love Conquered Marriage, op. cit.*

[74] Meg Hacker, "When Saying 'I Do' Meant Giving Up Your U.S. Citizenship," *Prologue Magazine*, National Archives, undated, https://tinyurl.com/zw5cbqf.

[75] Sheryl Gay Stolberg, "50 Years After Loving v. Virginia," *The New York Times*, June 11, 2017, https://tinyurl.com/ybjfcj3o; "Loving v. Virginia," Oyez, June 12, 1967, https://tinyurl.com/zvfhu7d.

[76] "Timeline of Legal History of Women in the United States," National Women's History Project, undated, https://tinyurl.com/hlmnfqy; Samantha Allen, "Marital Rape Is Semi-Legal in 8 States," *Daily Beast*, June 9, 2015, https://tinyurl.com/ycv7yakm.

[77] Coontz, *Marriage, a History: How Love Conquered Marriage, op. cit.*

[78] For background, see David Masci, "Legacy of the Vietnam War," *CQ Researcher*, Feb. 18, 2000, pp. 113-136, and Sarah Glazer, "Women's Rights," *CQ Researcher*, April 3, 2012, pp. 153-180.

[79] Dylan Matthews, "Everything you need to know about the war on poverty," *The Washington Post*, Jan. 8, 2014, https://tinyurl.com/y9oqlcsf; Drew DeSilver, "Who's poor in America? 50 years into the 'War on Poverty,' a data portrait," Pew Research Center, Jan. 13, 2014, https://tinyurl.com/lw5gs33.

[80] Robert Rector, "How Welfare Undermines Marriage and What to Do About It," The Heritage Foundation, Nov. 17, 2014, https://tinyurl.com/y86ryapq.

[81] Isabel V. Sawhill, R. Kent Weaver and Ron Haskins, "Welfare Reform: An Overview of Effects to Date," Brookings Institution, Jan. 1, 2001, https://tinyurl.com/y9u3gcan; Julien O. Teitler *et al.*, "Effects of Welfare Participation on Marriage," *Journal of Marriage and Family*, Oct. 23, 2009, https://tinyurl.com/yabvb2mg; Jordan Weissmann, "The Failure of Welfare Reform," *Slate*, June 1, 2016, https://tinyurl.com/zz8cqd4.

About the Author

Jane Fullerton Lemons is a freelance writer in Northern Virginia with more than 25 years of journalism experience. A former Washington bureau chief for the *Arkansas Democrat-Gazette* and *Farm Journal* magazine, she has covered the White House, Congress, food policy and health care. She recently completed a master's degree in creative nonfiction from Goucher College in Towson, Md.

[82] "A Timeline of the Legalization of Same-Sex Marriage in the U.S.," Georgetown Law Library, undated, https://tinyurl.com/ycqtfb9y.

[83] "Same-Sex Marriage Laws," National Conference of State Legislatures, June 26, 2015, https://tinyurl.com/pcadok6.

[84] Robert Barnes, "Supreme Court strikes down key part of Defense of Marriage Act," *The Washington Post*, June 26, 2013, https://tinyurl.com/y98obppy.

[85] Eyder Peralta, "Court Overturns DOMA, Sidesteps Broad Gay Marriage Ruling," NPR, June 26, 2013, https://tinyurl.com/y9dg7ngj; Adam Liptak, "Supreme Court Ruling Makes Same-Sex Marriage a Right Nationwide," *The New York Times*, June 26, 2015, https://tinyurl.com/gq2suhg; *Obergefell et al., v. Hodges, Director, Ohio Department of Health, et al.*, U.S. Supreme Court, October Term 2014, https://tinyurl.com/gquwvbl.

[86] Coontz, *Marriage, a History: How Love Conquered Marriage, op. cit.*

[87] Bala *et al., op. cit.*

[88] Casey E. Faucon, "Marriage Outlaws: Regulating Polygamy in America," *Duke Journal of Gender Law & Policy*, Fall 2014, https://tinyurl.com/y9bbvyzm; Barbara Bradley Hagerty, "Some Muslims in U.S. Quietly Engage in Polygamy," NPR, May 27, 2008, https://tinyurl.com/2vbrcpe.

[89] Holly Munson, "Utah's very interesting path to statehood," *Constitution Daily*, Jan. 4, 2013, https://tinyurl.com/y8bkfazl.

[90] "Sister Wives," TLC, undated, https://tinyurl.com/y9waccgc.

[91] Nate Carlisle, "Polygamy remains a crime as U.S. Supreme Court won't hear case from 'Sister Wives,'" *The Salt Lake Tribune*, Jan. 23, 2017, https://tinyurl.com/y6vgpmjg; "Brown v. Buhman," SCOTUSblog, Supreme Court of the United States Blog, https://tinyurl.com/y7unlyd8.

[92] Jonathan Turley, "Supreme Court Turns Down Sister Wives Petition," blog, Jan. 23, 2017, https://tinyurl.com/yc5h8zay.

[93] Adam P. Romero, "Estimates of Marriages of Same-Sex Couples at the Two-Year Anniversary of Obergefell v. Hodges," The Williams Institute at UCLA School of Law, June 23, 2017.

[94] Jeffrey M. Jones, "In U.S., 10.2% of LGBT Adults Now Married to Same-Sex Spouse," Gallup, June 22, 2017, https://tinyurl.com/y99gcdpj.

[95] David Masci, Anna Brown and Jocelyn Kiley, "5 facts about same-sex marriage," Pew Research Center, June 26, 2017, https://tinyurl.com/ycyyul6x.

[96] "96,000 Same-sex Couples Married Since Supreme Court Decision, Accounting for More Than 1 in 10 Summer Weddings," The Williams Institute at UCLA School of Law, Nov. 5, 2015, https://tinyurl.com/y7s7m3w4.

[97] Lizzy Davies *et al.*, "Marriage falls out of favour for young Europeans as austerity and apathy bite," *The Guardian*, July 25, 2014, https://tinyurl.com/ya74sb29.

[98] Ben Steverman, "Why You're Being Invited to Fewer Weddings," Bloomberg, July 28, 2017, https://tinyurl.com/ycbwyd6s.

[99] Davies, *op. cit.*

[100] Steverman, *op. cit.*; Maggie Seaver, "The National Average Cost of a Wedding Hits $35,329," *The Knot*, undated, https://tinyurl.com/zabfk58.

[101] Gretchen Livingston and Anna Brown, "Intermarriage in the U.S. 50 Years After Loving v. Virginia," Pew Research Center, May 18, 2017, https://tinyurl.com/y9lytt68.

[102] *Ibid.*

[103] Gretchen Livingston, "Among U.S. cohabiters, 18% have a partner of a different race or ethnicity," Pew Research Center, June 8, 2017, https://tinyurl.com/yckxg9dy.

[104] Gretchen Livingston, "The rise of multiracial and multiethnic babies in the U.S." Pew Research Center, June 6, 2017, https://tinyurl.com/ya65kaso.

[105] Rose M. Kreider and Daphne A. Lofquist, "Adopted Children and Stepchildren: 2010," U.S. Census Bureau, April 2014, https://tinyurl.com/yc2w4vtp.

[106] Sheryll Cashin, "How Interracial Love Is Saving America," *The New York Times*, June 3, 2017, https://tinyurl.com/yade8d7u.

[107] Natalie Zmuda, "Ad Campaigns Are Finally reflecting Diversity of U.S.," *AdAge*, March 10, 2014, https://tinyurl.com/mfruuvy.

[108] Gretchen Livingston, "Births Outside of Marriage Decline for Immigrant Women," Pew Research Center, Oct. 26, 2016, https://tinyurl.com/yasvx5sy; "Unmarried Childbearing," National Center for Health Statistics, Centers for Disease Control and Prevention, https://tinyurl.com/n5sunjv.

[109] Isabel V. Sawhill, "Beyond Marriage," *The New York Times*, Sept. 13, 2014, https://tinyurl.com/y9jgkz5g.

[110] Gretchen Livingston, "Fewer than half of U.S. kids today live in a 'traditional' family," Pew Research Center, Dec. 22, 2014, https://tinyurl.com/l5ww4eq.

[111] Ron Haskins, "Marriage, Parenthood and Public Policy," Brookings Institution, June 19, 2014, https://tinyurl.com/ybxss2oa.

[112] Mark Regnerus, *Cheap Sex: The Transformation of Men, Marriage, and Monogamy* (2017), p. 417.

[113] Natalie Angier, "The Changing American Family," *The New York Times*, Nov. 25, 2013, https://tinyurl.com/qauc6pk.

FOR MORE INFORMATION

American Enterprise Institute, 1150 17th St., N.W., Washington, DC 20036; 202-862-5800; https://www.aei.org. Conservative think tank that focuses on government, politics, economics and social welfare.

Brookings Institution, 1775 Massachusetts Ave., N.W., Washington, DC 20036; 202-797-6000; www.brookings.edu. Centrist think tank that conducts research on a wide variety of issues, including the economy and the family.

Council on Contemporary Families, 305 E. 23rd St., G1800, Austin, TX 78712; 512-471-8339; https://contemporaryfamilies.org. Nonpartisan organization based at the University of Texas that studies American families.

National Center for Family and Marriage Research, 005 Williams Hall, Bowling Green State University, Bowling Green, OH 43403; 419-372-3119; www.bgsu.edu/ncfmr.html. Studies the well-being of children, adults, families and communities.

National Marriage Project, PO Box 400766, Charlottesville, VA 22904; 434-321-8601; http://nationalmarriageproject.org. Nonpartisan initiative at the University of Virginia that analyzes issues related to marriage and family.

Pew Research Center, 1615 L St., N.W., Suite 700, Washington, DC 20036; 202-419-4300; www.pewresearch.org. Nonpartisan think tank that conducts polling and demographic research to explore the issues and trends shaping the nation.

Williams Institute, UCLA School of Law, Box 951476, Los Angeles, CA 90095-1476; 310-267-4382; https://williamsinstitute.law.ucla.edu/. Think tank at the University of California that conducts research on sexual orientation and gender identity.

Bibliography
Selected Sources

Books

Cherlin, Andrew J., *The Marriage-Go-Round: The State of Marriage and the Family in America Today*, Vintage, 2010.

A sociologist looks at how Americans' belief in two contradictory ideals — marriage and individualism — shape the state of marriage.

Coontz, Stephanie, *Marriage, a History: How Love Conquered Marriage*, Penguin Books, 2006.

An historian traces the evolution of marriage, from ancient civilizations to modern times, to show how the institution shifted from an economic and political arrangement to one centered on love.

Sawhill, Isabel V., *Generation Unbound: Drifting into Sex and Parenthood without Marriage*, Brookings Institution Press, 2014.

A social researcher surveys the impact of family structure on children, offering policy solutions for lowering the rate of out-of-wedlock births.

Articles

Angier, Natalie, "The Changing American Family," *The New York Times*, Nov. 25, 2013, https://tinyurl.com/qauc6pk.

A special issue of *Science Times* examines the changing definition of family, and profiles those affected by it.

Dominus, Susan, "Is an Open Marriage a Happier Marriage?" *The New York Times Magazine*, May 11, 2017, https://tinyurl.com/lrddku3.

A writer profiles couples in non-monogamous marriages.

Haskins, Ron, and Isabel V. Sawhill, "The Decline of the American Family: Can Anything Be Done to Stop the Damage?" *Annals of the American Academy of Political and Social Science*, Aug. 17, 2016, https://tinyurl.com/y7pebczg.

Two Brookings Institution researchers examine changes affecting American families, including the decline of marriage and the rise of births among unmarried couples.

Khazan, Olga, "We Expect Too Much From Our Romantic Partners," *The Atlantic*, Sept. 29, 2017, https://tinyurl.com/y93m4hvh.

A psychologist describes how marriage has changed in recent history and how individual expectations have contributed to its evolution.

Zagorsky, Jay L., "Why are fewer people getting married?" *The Conversation*, June 1, 2016, https://tinyurl.com/y8ay8ehd.

Marriage rates are dropping because the costs of merging two lives outweigh the benefits, an economist says.

Reports and Studies

"The Decline of Marriage And Rise of New Families," Pew Research Center, Nov. 18, 2010, https://tinyurl.com/y7xk7ppj.

An analysis of Census Bureau data over the past 50 years details the decline of marriage and the rise of new family structures.

Daugherty, Jill, and Casey Copen, "Trends in Attitudes About Marriage, Childbearing, and Sexual Behavior: United States, 2002, 2006-2010, and 2011-2013," Centers for Disease Control and Prevention, March 17, 2016, https://tinyurl.com/y76dobgq.

A National Center for Health Statistics report shows a wide variety of attitudes about marriage, cohabitation and sexual behavior.

Eickmeyer, Kasey J., *et al.*, "Crossover In The Median Age At First Marriage And First Birth: Thirty-Five Years Of Change," National Center for Family and Marriage Research, Bowling Green State University, October 2017, https://tinyurl.com/yafwfa2j.

The median age when women first marry has surpassed the median age when they first give birth, researchers at Bowling Green conclude.

Gates, Gary J., and Taylor N.T. Brown, "Marriage and Same-Sex Couples after Obergefell," The Williams Institute at UCLA School of Law, November 2015, https://tinyurl.com/y9yxpcdb.

Same-sex unions have increased since the Supreme Court decision legalized gay marriage in 2015.

Kennedy, Sheela, and Steven Ruggles, "Breaking Up Is Hard to Count: The Rise of Divorce in the United States, 1980-2010," *Demography*, January 2014, https://tinyurl.com/ycnjpb2b.

Two demographers make the case that the divorce rate is increasing.

Lewis, Jamie M., and Rose M. Kreider, "Remarriage in the United States," American Community Survey Reports, March 2015, https://tinyurl.com/y73nsv38.

Half of men and 54 percent of women have married only once, according to an analysis of Census Bureau data.

Wilcox, W. Bradford, Angela Rachidi and Joseph Price, "Marriage, Penalized: Does Social-Welfare Policy Affect Family Formation?" American Enterprise Institute and Institute for Family Studies, July 26, 2016, https://tinyurl.com/y9aj5p5u.

Marriage advocates look at the ramifications of government policies involving marriage.

The Next Step:

Additional Articles from Current Periodicals

Marital Industry

"Spending skyrockets for gay weddings," *Washington Blade*, **March 31, 2017, https://tinyurl.com/y97govb5.**

Spending on same-sex weddings, especially those involving lesbian couples, has surged since the Supreme Court legalized gay marriages in 2015, according to research by a wedding planning company and a cable TV channel aimed at LGBT viewers.

Foster, Brooke Lea, "Want a Fabulous Wedding? Consider Eloping," *The New York Times*, **July 12, 2017, https://tinyurl.com/y8kas4zf.**

Some engaged couples are opting to spend their money on destination weddings or expensive honeymoons rather than on ceremonies that involve a large guest list.

Vasel, Kathryn, "Couples are spending a record amount to get married," **CNN, Feb. 2, 2017, https://tinyurl.com/hsmhdca.**

The average number of guests at weddings in the United States has dropped, but the average cost of weddings hit a record $35,329 last year, according to The Knot, a wedding planning company.

Marriage Alternatives

Dominus, Susan, "Is an Open Marriage a Happier Marriage?" *The New York Times*, **May 11, 2017, https://tinyurl.com/lwbjnlx.**

A couple explores the possibilities of an open marriage, a growing trend in the changing culture of marriage.

Manning, Kay, "Why more couples over 50 are cohabiting, not marrying," *Chicago Tribune*, **Oct. 19, 2017, https://tinyurl.com/ya4t24ou.**

A desire to maintain individual freedoms has contributed to a 75 percent increase in cohabitating U.S. adults over the past decade.

McGowan, Emma, "7 Alternatives To Traditional Marriage," *Bustle*, **April 4, 2017, https://tinyurl.com/yb7ewl3f.**

Two women — one a licensed therapist — have written a book that says alternatives to traditional marriage are emerging to suit modern lifestyles and needs.

Millennials

Calfas, Jennifer, "Millennials Want Jobs and Education, Not Marriage and Kids," *Time*, **April 20, 2017, https://tinyurl.com/n2tpmtt.**

Millennials prioritize personal achievements in education and their careers ahead of marriage and family.

Cao, Rachel, "Dogs trump marriage, kids for young buyers of first homes," **CNBC, July 30, 2017, https://tinyurl.com/ya9hlm97.**

About 33 percent of Millennials make dog-friendly features a top priority when buying a house, while only 25 percent think first of marriage and family, according to a survey.

Larsen, Vicki, "Millennials are open to an age-old idea about marriage: that it should be temporary," *Quartz*, **April 10, 2017, https://tinyurl.com/ybx4gbja.**

Millennials are open to "beta marriage," a short-term commitment in which a couple test their relationship.

Social Media

"Facebook Divorce," *FindLaw*, **undated, https://tinyurl.com/y9knm3ce.**

Divorce lawyers are increasingly using Facebook and other social networking sites to gather evidence for their clients in divorce and child custody cases.

Gollayan, Christian, "Dating apps could be leading to more interracial marriages," *The New York Post*, **Oct. 30, 2017, https://tinyurl.com/y8wm9bh4.**

The spike in interracial marriages coincides with the startup dates for various dating apps and online matchmaking sites, according to the National Academy of Sciences.

Morgan, Richard, "Ashley Madison is back — and claims surprising user numbers," *The New York Post*, **May 21, 2017, https://tinyurl.com/ydyzh5zv.**

A website that caters to married men and women looking to have an affair reports gaining about 400,000 new customers each month this year, despite a data breach in 2015.

CITING CQ RESEARCHER

Sample formats for citing these reports in a bibliography include the ones listed below. Preferred styles and formats vary, so please check with your instructor or professor.

MLA STYLE

Mantel, Barbara. "Coal Industry's Future." CQ Researcher 17 June 2016: 529-552.

APA STYLE

Mantel, B. (2016, June 17). Coal Industry's Future. CQ Researcher, 6, 529-552.

CHICAGO STYLE

Mantel, Barbara. "Coal Industry's Future." CQ Researcher, June 17, 2016, 529-52.

In-depth Reports on Issues in the News

Are you writing a paper?

Need backup for a debate?

Want to become an expert on an issue?

For 90 years, students have turned to *CQ Researcher* for in-depth reporting on issues in the news. Reports on a full range of political and social issues are now available. Following is a selection of recent reports:

Civil Liberties
Privacy and the Internet, 12/15
Intelligence Reform, 5/15
Religion and Law, 11/14

Crime/Law
High-Tech Policing, 4/17
Forensic Science Controversies, 2/17
Jailing Debtors, 9/16
Decriminalizing Prostitution, 4/16
Restorative Justice, 2/16
The Dark Web, 1/16
Immigrant Detention, 10/15

Education
Affirmative Action and College Admissions, 11/17
Charter Schools, 3/17
Civic Education, 2/17
Student Debt, 11/16

Environment/Society
Stolen Antiquities, 11/17
Climate Change and National Security, 9/17
Muslims in America, 7/17
Funding the Arts, 7/17
Hunger in America, 7/17

Health/Safety
Medical Breakthroughs, 9/17
Medical Marijuana, 7/17
Food Labeling, 6/17
Sports and Sexual Assault, 4/17

Politics/Economy
Democracy Under Stress, 10/17
Cyberwarfare Threat, 10/17
Universal Basic Income, 9/17
National Debt, 9/17
North Korea Showdown, 5/17
Rethinking Foreign Aid, 4/17

Upcoming Reports

Privatizing Government Services, 12/8/17   Species Extinction, 12/15/17   Future of Puerto Rico, 1/5/18

ACCESS

CQ Researcher is available in print and online. For access, visit your library or www.cqresearcher.com.

STAY CURRENT

For notice of upcoming *CQ Researcher* reports or to learn more about *CQ Researcher* products, subscribe to the free email newsletters, *CQ Researcher Alert!* and *CQ Researcher News*: http://cqpress.com/newsletters.

PURCHASE

To purchase a *CQ Researcher* report in print or electronic format (PDF), visit www.cqpress.com or call 866-427-7737. Single reports start at $15. Bulk purchase discounts and electronic-rights licensing are also available.

SUBSCRIBE

Annual full-service *CQ Researcher* subscriptions—including 44 reports a year, monthly index updates, and a bound volume—start at $1,131. Add $25 for domestic postage.

CQ Researcher Online offers a backfile from 1991 and a number of tools to simplify research. For pricing information, call 800-818-7243 or 805-499-9774 or email librarysales@sagepub.com.

![CQ PRESS logo] **CQ RESEARCHER**

In-depth reports on today's issues

Published by CQ Press, an Imprint of SAGE Publications, Inc.   **www.cqresearcher.com**

Privatizing Government Services

Do business-run public services save taxpayers money?

President Trump has said he wants to turn over certain public functions, including air traffic control, to profit-making private contractors. While his specific intentions remain unclear, supporters of privatization contend it would save money and inject competition into what they claim is a bureaucratic system that lacks efficiency and innovation, discourages cost cutting and falls prey to political whim. Opponents argue, however, that privatization often fails to reduce costs and undermines democracy by putting private business in charge of vital public services. Republican President Ronald Reagan advocated privatization in the 1980s, and it has grown under both Republican and Democratic administrations to include charter schools, municipal water systems and military operations. Still, some of the fervor for privatization has cooled in recent years, especially after studies found higher rates of civil rights abuses, medical neglect and assaults on guards in privately run prisons than in government facilities.

Demonstrators in Boston on March 13, 2017, protest plans to let private firms handle driver and maintenance jobs for the city's public transit system. Supporters say privatization saves money and spurs innovation, while opponents say it does not always save money and that private businesses should not control vital public services.

I N S I D E THIS REPORT

THE ISSUES **1019**

BACKGROUND **1025**

CHRONOLOGY **1027**

CURRENT SITUATION **1030**

AT ISSUE.....................**1033**

OUTLOOK **1034**

BIBLIOGRAPHY **1038**

THE NEXT STEP **1039**

CQ Researcher • Dec. 8, 2017 • www.cqresearcher.com
Volume 27, Number 43 • Pages 1017-1040

RECIPIENT OF SOCIETY OF PROFESSIONAL JOURNALISTS AWARD FOR EXCELLENCE ◆ AMERICAN BAR ASSOCIATION SILVER GAVEL AWARD

CQ RESEARCHER

Dec. 8, 2017
Volume 27, Number 43

EXECUTIVE EDITOR: Thomas J. Billitteri
tjb@sagepub.com

ASSISTANT MANAGING EDITORS: Kenneth
Fireman, kenneth.fireman@sagepub.com,
Kathy Koch, kathy.koch@sagepub.com,
Scott Rohrer, scott.rohrer@sagepub.com

ASSOCIATE MANAGING EDITOR: Val Ellicott

SENIOR CONTRIBUTING EDITOR:
Thomas J. Colin
tom.colin@sagepub.com

CONTRIBUTING WRITERS: Marcia Clemmitt,
Sarah Glazer, Alan Greenblatt, Reed Karaim,
Barbara Mantel, Patrick Marshall, Tom Price

SENIOR PROJECT EDITOR: Olu B. Davis

EDITORIAL ASSISTANT: Natalia Gurevich

FACT CHECKERS: Eva P. Dasher,
Michelle Harris, Betsy Towner Levine,
Robin Palmer

Los Angeles | London | New Delhi
Singapore | Washington DC | Melbourne

An Imprint of SAGE Publications, Inc.

SENIOR VICE PRESIDENT,
GLOBAL LEARNING RESOURCES:
Karen Phillips

EXECUTIVE DIRECTOR, ONLINE LIBRARY AND
REFERENCE PUBLISHING:
Todd Baldwin

CQ Press is a registered trademark of Congressional
Quarterly Inc.

CQ Researcher (ISSN 1056-2036) is printed on acid-free
paper. Published weekly, except: (March wk. 4) (May
wk. 4) (July wks. 1, 2) (Aug. wks. 2, 3) (Nov. wk. 4)
and (Dec. wks. 3, 4). Published by SAGE Publications,
Inc., 2455 Teller Rd., Thousand Oaks, CA 91320. Annual
full-service subscriptions start at $1,131. For pricing,
call 1-800-818-7243. To purchase a CQ Researcher report
in print or electronic format (PDF), visit www.cqpress.
com or call 866-427-7737. Single reports start at $15.
Bulk purchase discounts and electronic-rights licensing
are also available. Periodicals postage paid at Thousand
Oaks, California, and at additional mailing offices.
POSTMASTER: Send address changes to CQ Researcher, 2600 Virginia Ave., N.W., Suite 600, Washington,
DC 20037.

THE ISSUES

1019
• Does privatizing government services save taxpayers
money?
• Does privatization make
government less accountable
to voters?
• Do privatized toll roads and
other user-fee-based projects
hurt low-income citizens?

BACKGROUND

1025 **Starting Small**
Public education spread in
the 19th century.

1025 **Era of Big Government**
FDR's New Deal programs
included public-works projects.

1025 **Privatization Movement**
A 1962 book garnered support
for the approach.

1028 **Privatization Backlash**
President Barack Obama
sought to end private prisons.

CURRENT SITUATION

1030 **Infrastructure Needs**
President Trump's rebuilding
plan remains unclear.

1031 **Charter Schools**
They continue to grow in
the United States.

1032 **Privatizing Prisons**
Trump's support has revived
the private-prison industry.

1034 **Air Traffic Control**
Opponents say privatization
benefits airlines at consumers'
expense.

OUTLOOK

1034 **Continuing Pressure**
Privatization is expected to
grow, but slowly.

SIDEBARS AND GRAPHICS

1020 **Private-Prison Population**
Declining
Prisoner counts at for-profit
facilities have fallen in recent
years.

1021 **Public-Private Projects**
Span 11 States, Puerto
Rico
Texas, Florida and Virginia
spend the most.

1024 **Contractors Outnumber**
Troops in Afghanistan
The Department of Defense
had 25,000 private U.S.
contractors in Afghanistan
in 2016.

1027 **Chronology**
Key events since 1944.

1028 **Blackwater Founder Urges**
Trump to Privatize Afghan
War
Critics warn contractors' be-
havior "has really poisoned
the well."

1030 **Should Airport Security**
Be Privatized — Again?
Backers see benefits, but foes
fear a lack of accountability.

1033 **At Issue:**
Should the U.S. use private
capital to rebuild infrastructure?

FOR FURTHER RESEARCH

1037 **For More Information**
Organizations to contact.

1038 **Bibliography**
Selected sources used.

1039 **The Next Step**
Additional articles.

1039 **Citing CQ Researcher**
Sample bibliography formats.

Cover: Getty Images/*The Boston Globe*/David L. Ryan

Privatizing Government Services

BY REED KARAIM

THE ISSUES

President Trump arrived in office as a champion of privatization — letting private industry finance and manage many government services and projects.

Trump's $1 trillion privatization plan includes giving incentives to state and local governments to sell airports, bridges or highway rest stops to private companies, which would then recoup their costs through tolls and other fees. [1]

Yet, in a meeting with Democratic lawmakers in September, Trump indicated he had changed his mind, specifically about public-private partnerships, in which investors pay for infrastructure in return for future profits. "He dismissed it categorically and said it doesn't work," said Rep. Brian Higgins, D-N.Y., who attended the session. [2]

The president's apparent ambivalence about at least some types of privatization reflects a larger debate in U.S. policy circles about the effectiveness of the approach. Proponents say turning over government responsibilities to private enterprise lowers costs and improves efficiency by bringing competitive forces to bear. Opponents say it often allows corporations to profit at taxpayers' expense by giving them monopolistic control over assets that should be publicly held, weakens government oversight over those assets and undermines democracy.

"People are harmed by badly run government programs," wrote E. S. Savas, a father of the U.S. privatization movement, in his landmark 2000 book, *Privatization and Public-Private Partnerships*. "The purpose of privatization is

Garbage collection in Seattle is handled by Waste Management Inc., which serves 21 million customers in the United States and Canada. Privatization first gained popularity in the United States in the 1980s, when city officials found that garbage collection by private firms was more economical than by city workers.

Getty Images/Bloomberg/David Ryder

to improve government performance and thereby improve the lives of those most dependent on government, while saving money and improving services for all taxpayers." [3]

But critics say studies have raised doubts about the savings and quality of the services rendered by private companies. More fundamentally, they say, privatizing government services can remove them from the control of elected officials and the voters.

"The government exercises sovereign powers," wrote Paul Verkuil, a legal scholar and author of *Outsourcing Sovereignty: Why Privatization of Government Threatens Democracy and What We Can Do About It.* "When those powers are delegated to outsiders, the capacity to govern is undermined." [4]

Privatization has become a significant force at all levels of government since the 1980s. Private companies now operate prisons, public charter schools, municipal water systems, highways, public parking, trash pickup — and even traffic enforcement through private traffic cameras. [5] Private security forces served in Iraq during U.S. military involvement there, and the Internal Revenue Service (IRS) began using private agencies to collect unpaid taxes this year. [6]

"It's become accepted. You really see it everywhere now," Savas says.

Both advocates and critics of privatization cite examples to support their views. For instance, critics cite the case of Chicago, which has leased its parking meters to a private company for 75 years to obtain a much-needed $1.16 billion infusion of cash. The city's inspector general later found that Chicago had leased the meters for nearly $1 billion less than what they would generate in revenue over that 75 years. [7]

Privatization proponents cite a public-private partnership between Virginia and a financial and construction consortium to build express toll lanes and other improvements on a crowded section of Interstate 66 outside of Washington, D.C. The project is expected to save the state $2.5 billion in construction and maintenance costs. [8]

The state "knew what they wanted to get done," says Robert Puentes, president and CEO of the Eno Center for Transportation, a think tank in Washington. "They figured out what it would cost them and they said, 'Let's put it out for bid and see if somebody else can provide a better deal.' "

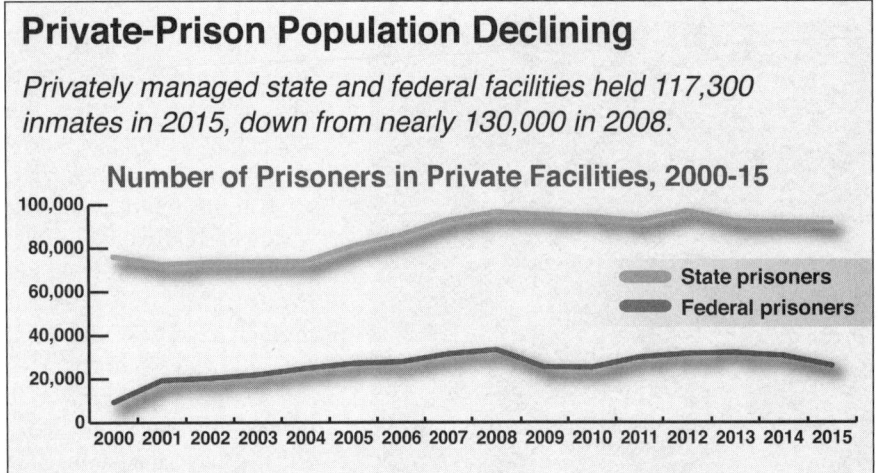

Private-Prison Population Declining

Privately managed state and federal facilities held 117,300 inmates in 2015, down from nearly 130,000 in 2008.

Number of Prisoners in Private Facilities, 2000-15

Legend: State prisoners, Federal prisoners

Source: "Publications & Products: National Prisoner Statistics (NPS) Program," Bureau of Justice Statistics, undated, https://tinyurl.com/ycfmked7

Government privatizes in three ways:

• Selling off public property to private enterprises, often to free government officials from the burden of managing the property while providing a one-time shot of cash for government agencies.

• Establishing private-public partnerships, in which investors pay for building or maintaining a highway, bridge or other public asset in return for long-term profits, often collected through tolls or other fees.

• Outsourcing public services, such as trash pickup or data management, by hiring a private contractor to provide the services.

Outsourcing has been one of the most popular vehicles for privatizing governmental responsibilities. According to one estimate, about $1 trillion of the $6 trillion in annual federal, state and local government spending goes to private contractors, according to Donald Cohen, executive director of In the Public Interest, a policy and research institute in Oakland, Calif., that is a foremost critic of privatization. [9]

Local governments have been particularly attracted to the privatization model, with private contractors providing nearly 40 percent of municipal services in 2012, according to research by Mildred Warner, a professor of city and regional planning at Cornell University in Ithaca, N.Y. [10]

But the federal government also has increasingly turned to private companies. The administration of President Ronald Reagan, who ran for office promising to shrink the role of government, gave life to the modern privatization movement at the federal level in the 1980s. [11] Still, the trend to use private contractors has grown during both Republican and Democratic administrations.

The growth was particularly strong in the first decade of the 21st century, as the U.S. government expanded the use of private contractors during the war and reconstruction in Iraq. In 2000, federal contracting stood at about $200 billion. It grew to about $550 billion in 2011, before falling back to less than $450 billion in 2013, the latest year for which figures are available. Sixty percent of that money went for services. [12]

The growth of privatization has been accompanied by a corresponding reduction in the federal workforce. In 1984, at the end of Reagan's first term, there were roughly 2.2 million federal workers. When President Barack Obama took office 25 years later, there were 200,000 fewer, although the nation's population, economy and federal budget had all grown significantly. The decline has led some analysts to suggest

the government faces a shortage of necessary employees. [13]

While many privatization advocates support the idea of shrinking the number of full-time government employees, critics say that even when services are outsourced, federal workers are still needed to manage and monitor contractors to ensure they are meeting expectations and serving the public good.

"The question is always in the standards, the oversight, the accountability," says Cohen.

The debate is likely to intensify in 2018. While Trump may have doubts about the effectiveness of private-public partnerships, his administration still supports privatizing the nation's air traffic control system, parts of the Department of Veterans Affairs' health care services and federal prisons.

As analysts, lawmakers and the public consider the pros and cons of privatization, here are some of the questions being asked:

Does privatizing government services save taxpayers money?

The single biggest argument made by advocates of privatizing government services is that it saves taxpayers money while providing for superior service through better-run operations.

Privatization's proponents say introducing competition through a bidding process leads to more efficient operations compared to government offices and departments, which they say operate as de facto monopolies.

The Reason Foundation, a libertarian, pro-privatization think tank in Los Angeles, says a review of more than 100 studies of outsourced government services found savings ranging from 5 percent to 50 percent. [14] "The evidence from competitive contracting of municipal services [and] state services is that in extreme cases [savings] can be 50 to 60 percent, but more likely, . . . 20 to 30 percent," says Robert Poole, director of transportation policy at the foundation.

However, other studies cast doubt on the savings from outsourcing. At the federal level, a 2012 study by the Project on Government Oversight, a watchdog group in Washington that monitors waste in federal spending, concluded that contracting out services was, on average, nearly twice as expensive as it would have been to pay federal employees to do the work. [15]

Conversely, at the municipal level, a report by In the Public Interest, the think tank that is skeptical of privatization, found that outsourcing often achieved savings by paying privates employees less and providing fewer benefits. "A growing body of evidence and industry wage data suggest an alarming trend: Outsourcing public services sets off a downward spiral in which reduced worker wages and benefits can hurt the local economy and overall stability of middle and working class communities," the report concluded. [16]

Views also are split over having private companies invest in public infrastructure. Poole says studies have found that letting a private contractor build and manage highways through a public-private partnership can save from 10 percent to 30 percent, and, he says, such partnerships provide other benefits that do not necessarily show up in the initial financial equation.

"Maintenance is built in and guaranteed [in the contracts], and one of the biggest problems we have with highways is deferred maintenance," he says. Private financiers recognize the need for a maintenance reserve, Poole continues, "because they know if the toll road is competing with free roads and it's not in tip-top shape, they're not going to get the business."

But Elizabeth McNichols, a budget analyst with the Center on Budget and Policy Priorities, a liberal Washington think tank, says because private investors need to make a profit on their infrastructure projects, it is unlikely that significant savings will materialize. "I don't think, generally, the taxpayer comes out well

because the private sector is going to invest in something where they feel like they can make profit," she says.

Public-Private Projects Span 11 States, Puerto Rico

Public-private infrastructure projects are widespread across the continental United States and Puerto Rico, with billions of dollars in roads, bridges and tunnels completed or in progress. Texas, Florida and Virginia have the highest total dollar value in projects.

Public-Private Projects Completed or in Progress
(by total cost)

Texas $7.5 billion	North Tarrant Express 35W (segments 3A and 3B), $1.6 billion
	SH 130 (segments 5-6), $1.3 billion
	North Tarrant Express I-820 and SH 121/183 (segments 1 and 2A), $2 billion
	LBJ Express, $2.6 billion
Florida $5.2 billion	I-4 Ultimate, $2.3 billion
	I-595 Corridor roadway improvements, $1.8 billion
	Port of Miami Tunnel, $1.1 billion
Virginia $5.5 billion	Dulles Greenway, $350 million
	Capital Beltway High Occupancy Toll (HOT) lanes (I-495), $2.1 billion
	Elizabeth River tunnels (Downtown/Midtown Tunnel), $2.1 billion
	I-95 HOV/HOT lanes, $923 million
California $1.6 billion	Presidio Parkway (Phase II), $852 million
	SR-91 express lanes,* $135 million
	South Bay Expressway,* $658 million
New Jersey/New York $1.4 billion	Goethals Bridge replacement, $1.4 billion
Indiana $1.3 billion	Ohio River bridges East End Crossing, $981 million
	I-69 Section 5, $325 million
Pennsylvania $899 million	Pennsylvania Rapid Bridge Replacement Project, $899 million
North Carolina $655 million	I-77 express lanes, $655 million
Colorado $521 million	U.S. 36 express lanes (Phase II), $521 million
Ohio $429 million	Southern Ohio Veterans Memorial Highway, $429 million
Puerto Rico $127 million	Teodoro Moscoso Bridge, $127 million

* Now under public management and operation.

Source: "Interactive Map: New Build Facilities," Center for Innovative Finance Support, U.S. Department of Transportation, Federal Highway Administration, Aug. 2, 2017, https://tinyurl.com/yat44o3t

Although Trump has not spoken publicly about his changing views on public-private partnerships since the meeting with Democrats in September, an unnamed White House official said after the meeting that there are "legitimate questions" about a public-private approach, which is "certainly not the silver bullet for all of our nation's infrastructure problems." The administration would continue to consider all viable options, the official said. [17]

Kevin DeGood, director of infrastructure policy at the Center for American Progress, a liberal Washington research and policy group, questions the logic of private financing "at this time." He says that since governments currently can borrow money at extremely lost cost — by issuing bonds at about 3 percent — it makes more fiscal sense for states and cities to pursue projects on their own.

"Private equity investors in infrastructure projects are . . . looking [for return] rates of 12 to 15 percent," he says, or about four times the cost of government borrowing the money and doing it themselves.

A 2012 study by the nonpartisan Congressional Budget Office (CBO) found that public-private partnerships "have built highways slightly less expensively and slightly more quickly, compared with the traditional public sector approach." [18] However, when factoring in other considerations, such as the risk that taxpayers will ultimately have to pick up losses from failing projects, the CBO concluded, "the cost of financing a highway project privately is roughly equal to the cost of financing it publicly." [19]

McNichols believes that contracting with private construction companies, whether through outsourcing or private-public partnerships, builds in another layer of expenses that do not show up in the contract price. "With privatization, if you're doing it right, you have to put out bids; you have to monitor the project; you're creating a whole set of costs on top of government doing the job itself."

But Puentes, of the Eno Center for Transportation, says public officials can take the cost of management into account when considering bids, and with a well-written contract can still find solutions that benefit both taxpayers and investors.

"You can figure out ways you can take advantage of private sector expertise and resources and public expertise to meet both public and private goals," he says.

Does privatization make government less accountable to voters?

A fundamental area of disagreement between privatization skeptics and supporters is whether the public will be able to adequately monitor and control what is happening with their tax dollars

"When power is shunted into private hands, there is less opportunity for public engagement, public participation," says Jon Michaels, a professor of law at the University of California Los Angeles (UCLA) and author of *Constitutional Coup: Privatization's Threat to the American Republic*. "We're just seeing a greater sense in which government is not a shared enterprise."

While government bureaucrats are often maligned, Michaels says, "Civil servants are servants of the state" and, in a democratic government, they must respond to the competing forces in the political process — internal pressures from lawmakers and other government officials as well as external pressures from public interest groups and engaged citizens. Private contractors, he says, answer first to their owners or shareholders and secondly to their government administrators.

Separating government operations from the civil service and democratic process represents a fundamental challenge to the American way of government, Michaels argues.

But privatization's supporters believe private contractors are more responsive to the public's needs and wishes than public officials and administrators. Privatization "makes government more accountable. This is true for all kinds of government services, including municipal services," the Reason Foundation's Poole says. "Most city governments, when they're the monopoly provider, tend not to have quantitative performance measures, and they certainly don't hold managers of those services accountable. When you do a contract for street sweeping or garbage collection, you put in performance indicators [that must be met.] Studies have found this makes possible huge improvements in performance, and it means the companies are being held accountable."

Poole believes the same is true for public-private partnerships used to build and operate toll roads and other infrastructure. "You build in all kinds of performance requirements and penalties," he says. For instance, the lease for the 156-mile Indiana Toll Road has "standards for the maximum number of hours a dead animal can be on the road before it has to be cleared, and for pavement quality, pavement roughness, etc. This creates much more accountability."

Privatization opponents, however, point out that Indiana originally leased the toll road to an international consortium in 2006 for 75 years, but the consortium went bankrupt in 2014. Vice President Mike Pence championed the controversial project when he was governor of Indiana. While Pence boasts that Indiana got corporations to invest in infrastructure that would otherwise have been funded by taxpayers, opponents say Indiana sold off valuable public assets that were then badly mismanaged. [20]

Aman Banerji, a program manager at the Roosevelt Institute, a liberal think tank in New York, says the kind of standards Poole referred to do not always exist: "Often, . . . private contractors are not held to the same standards that public institutions are." This is particularly true, he says, for privately operated charter schools, which receive public money but often do not have to meet the same standards as other public schools. [21]

Other analysts say contracting makes government both less responsive and less transparent. "You're increasing the distance between the person who wants the work and [who] does the work," says In the Public Interest's Cohen. "You're adding layers of bureaucracy and putting up walls — contractors have claimed they don't have to let the public know what they're doing because it involves trade secrets."

For example, he says, the private consortium that built State Highway 130, a toll road in Texas, went bankrupt last year, leaving the state to assume responsibility for the crumbling road. The investors refused to release the traffic projections they made when taking on the project, which they said had made the road feasible. [22] "There are times when we [taxpayers] want something that's important information, and they say you can't have it," Cohen says.

But Chris Edwards, director of tax policy studies at the Cato Institute, a libertarian think tank in Washington, counters that if governments fail to require transparency from private partners it is not the fault of privatization. "State governments can write bad public-private-partnership contracts just like they can write bad contracts under their regular procurement practices," he says. "It's unfair to say private-public partnerships are worse, or this is a new problem."

Rather, he says, "Government bureaucracies are secretive and often less transparent than nonprofit entities or publicly traded corporations."

Savas, who is a public policy professor at Baruch College in the City University of New York system and worked in New York City government in the 1970s, agrees. He says protections afforded to unionized public employees can make them indifferent to consumers. Privatization, he says, removes "a layer of power that prevents effective response to public complaints."

But DeGood, of the Center for American Progress, says privatization can make government less responsive to the public by distorting the decision-making process toward projects likely to provide a good return for investors. Government, he says, should be focusing on citizens' needs. For example, he says, less prosperous areas might most need improved infrastructure, but private investors might see such areas as risky for investment because they may provide a lower rate of return.

A driver pays a toll in Ocala, Fla. Privatization has grown in recent years under both Republican and Democratic administrations to include charter schools, privately operated municipal water systems, military operations, corporate-owned toll roads and prisons.

"If you construct a problem as simply a narrow business one, you're going to get one answer," DeGood says, but politics and governing are hard because business factors "aren't the only considerations."

Do toll roads and other pay-to-use projects hurt low-income citizens more than others?

Privatizing infrastructure often involves imposing tolls or user fees to cover the cost of building, managing and maintaining the facility and provide profits to investors. And if the private companies take over existing services,

such as water and sewage treatment facilities, a higher rate structure can result.

"What you see in privatization is increased fees and increased costs," says Cohen, because money that could be directed to a service gets diverted to profits, CEO salaries and debt service if the company borrowed money to buy the property.

For example, he says, after Coatesville, Pa., privatized its water services, "the rates went way up, and [some customers] were forced into bankruptcy." A *New York Times* investigation in 2016 documented several cases in which private companies raised rates significantly after taking over municipal water systems. [23]

An earlier study by In the Public Interest examined rate hikes that followed the privatization of 10 large municipal water systems in the late 1990s and early 2000s. After 11 years of private control, water bills in the communities had nearly tripled, and those increases fell most heavily on the poorest parts of the population, according to Cohen. [24]

Spokespeople for the private companies say many of the systems they acquired were sold by cash-strapped

Contractors Outnumber Troops in Afghanistan

The Department of Defense employed more than 25,000 private contractors in Afghanistan at the end of 2016, more than twice the number of U.S. troops.

U.S. Armed Forces and Contractors in Afghanistan, 2007-17

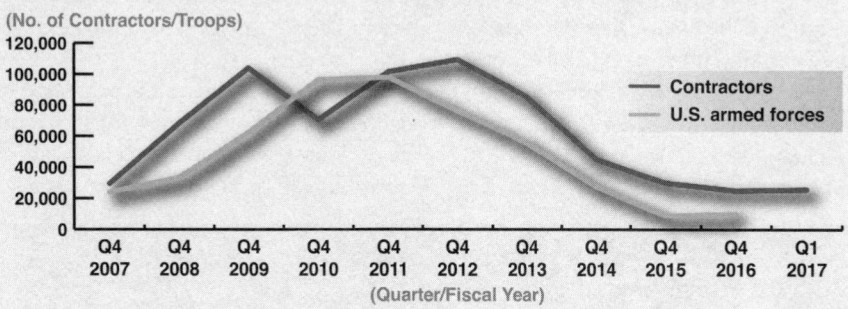

Note: U.S. armed forces figures include all active and reserve personnel.

Source: Heidi M. Peters et al., "Department of Defense Contractor and Troop Levels in Iraq and Afghanistan: 2007-2017," Congressional Research Service, April 28, 2017, https://tinyurl.com/lch975o

municipalities that had not been maintaining the facilities properly, requiring significant investments to meet or maintain public health standards.

"Keeping rates down may sound like the ultimate righteous good for ratepayers, but the truth is, not if you're failing to provide basic care and maintenance," said Megan Matson, a partner at Table Rock Capital, a private equity firm that invested in the water and sewage system in Rialto, Calif. [25]

Privatization's critics say economic inequity can also become most pronounced on toll roads, especially those where drivers can pay extra for access to special lanes that allow them to avoid congestion. Popularly dubbed "Lexus Lanes," they have proven controversial. "This is a plan for the 'highway of the 1 percent,' " said Stewart Fefer, a Floridian who participated in a protest against a planned toll lane on an interstate highway in Tampa. [26]

But the Reason Foundation's Poole says the data from the transponders used by drivers to pay tolls indicate that most people who set up accounts to access the lanes use them sparingly.

"Most people use the pay lanes for a specific purpose," he says, such as "when the value of being on time is greater than the cost of paying the toll: if you're running late to pick up your kids from daycare, for example. So ordinary people, not just the affluent, see opportunities where it makes sense for them."

Privatization supporters say if drivers want to avoid toll lanes or highways, they can use regular lanes or other, free roads. But critics note that some private infrastructure projects include non-compete clauses that bar the state government from building a free road that would compete with the private highway.

The Cato Institute's Edwards says tolls do not make sense on some roads and that other accommodations, such as increased mass transit, should be incorporated into a private-public partnership plan to ensure that the system serves all taxpayers. But he disputes the idea that tolls are inherently unfair to the poor, citing the recent private investment in Interstate 66 in Northern Virginia as an example.

However, on Dec. 3, when the new I-66 express lanes opened on a 10-mile stretch between I-495 and the District of Columbia, tolls during peak travel times spiked. They reached $40 on the second day of operation, prompting commuters to complain that only wealthy drivers could afford the new lanes. Transportation officials said drivers could avoid a toll by carrying a passenger or using alternative roads, which critics said are congested. [27]

"If Virginia didn't get the private money for the Beltway expansions, perhaps they would have had to raise their gas tax, which is a regressive tax," he says. (A regressive tax is one applied uniformly, regardless of the payer's income, so it takes a larger percentage of a low-wage earner's income than from high-income earners.)

However, UCLA's Michaels notes the working class or poorer citizens often have the longest commutes because rents and housing costs are cheaper farther from urban centers. Thus, toll roads force poorer citizens to either pay more or spend more time on the road than drivers who can afford a speedier commute.

Still, Jacob Leibenluft, a senior adviser at the Center on Budget and Policy Priorities, says sometimes toll roads can effectively channel people toward mass transit, reducing traffic congestion and automobile emissions, and thus benefiting the entire community.

"It really depends on the project," says Leibenluft. "There are places where there might be value in tolls, where we want fewer people to drive." But if toll roads or express lanes are built to serve a wealthy community, diverting infrastructure priorities toward areas where private investors see the greatest chance for profits, he says, the equation clearly favors the wealthy.

"Anything that discourages investment in communities that have the greatest infrastructure needs and the least ability to pay is going to contribute to inequities," he says. ■

BACKGROUND

Starting Small

In the early days of the United States, federal and state governments had fewer resources than they do today, and much of what are now regarded as government responsibilities were handled privately.

Education remained largely a private matter until the middle of the 19th century. Although the Massachusetts Colony passed a law in 1647 requiring towns to provide public education, it wasn't until the mid-1800s that the idea of public education began to take hold across most of the nation. Before that, education was often provided at home or through churches, private schools that catered to the wealthy or apprenticeship programs that focused on trades. Public education did not become compulsory in all 50 states until 1918. [28]

Many of the early nation's roads and bridges also were built by private companies. In some cases, streets and local roads were constructed and maintained by communities, with local citizens required to spend a certain amount of time each month working on them. But from the 1780s through the middle of the 19th century, a nation impatient for a better long-distance transportation system turned to private projects. [29]

The building spree began with bridges. Fifty-nine private toll bridge companies were chartered in the Northeast from 1786 to 1798. Private turnpikes, or toll roads, soon followed. The first such road, running 62 miles from Philadelphia to Lancaster, Pa., was completed in 1794. By 1810, 398 private turnpikes had been incorporated, mostly in the East. A smaller boom in private tolls would also occur later in the West. [30]

But at the end of the 19th century and in the first decades of the 20th century, public sentiment began to favor public ownership of roads and bridges. The rise of the Progressive movement, which sought to rein in big business and create greater social equality, expanded the role of government. Most toll roads closed or became part of state highway systems. [31]

By the 1920s, the transition to public ownership of highways and bridges was complete. "Throughout most of twentieth-century America, roads were widened and new bridges built almost exclusively when politicians appropriated the funds to have the work done," wrote Henry Petroski, a professor of civil engineering and history at Duke University in North Carolina, in his history of America's transportation infrastructure, *The Road Not Taken*. [32]

Era of Big Government

The Progressive era sparked expansion of the public sector. But the expansion was dwarfed by the explosive growth of the federal government in the 1930s under President Franklin D. Roosevelt's New Deal programs that aimed to help the economy recover from the Great Depression (1929-1939). Dams, public power systems, roads, bridges and public buildings were built with public funds, contributing to dramatic growth of federal responsibility and spending. [33]

One of the nation's largest public infrastructure projects, the Interstate Highway System, was initiated in the 1950s by President Dwight D. Eisenhower. As a young Army officer in 1919, Eisenhower had crossed the United States to promote the Army's Motor Transport Corps. The 3,200-mile trip from Washington to San Francisco took 62 days. Later, while serving as supreme commander of allied forces in Europe during World War II, Eisenhower was impressed by Germany's controlled-access, high-speed highway system, known as the autobahn. When elected president, he supported an effort to build a similar highway system in the United States, both as a matter of national defense and to improve cross-country transportation. [34]

In 1956, Eisenhower signed the Federal-Aid Highway Act, which authorized $25 billion for construction of a national Interstate Highway System. To pay for the massive project, the law increased the federal gasoline tax and put the money in a highway trust fund, which financed the federal government's 90 percent share of the highway system, with states paying the remaining costs. [35]

By the 1980s, when the system was completed, the United States had what was considered the world's best public highway system.

At the time, few people thought about turning over municipally owned utilities, such as water or power systems, to private companies. There were no private prisons or publicly funded, privately run charter schools. But as discontent with government grew in the late 1970s and early '80s, attitudes began to change.

Privatization Movement

Austrian economist Frederick von Hayek is considered the intellectual founder of the privatization movement. In his 1944 book *The Road to Serfdom*, he argued that government control of economic planning leads to tyranny. While Hayek's work continues to be popular with today's economic conservatives, it had little impact on public policy at the time. [36]

In the United States, Hayek's ideas were furthered by economist Milton Friedman, whose 1962 book *Capitalism and Freedom* characterized government as an inefficient and unresponsive public monopoly. Friedman believed privatizing government services would increase competition and improve performance. [37] His ideas gained currency in conservative circles as discontent with the quality of public services in some cities led officials to begin experimenting with more privatization.

In 1973 Baruch College's Savas was working as a New York deputy city administrator when Mayor John Lindsay asked him to look into problems with clearing the streets after a major snowstorm. Savas' examination led him to conclude that the city's sanitation department, which was responsible for

Immigrants and their supporters demonstrate in New York City on Aug. 2, 2017, holding up photos of families separated when relatives were detained in privately run immigrant detention centers. U.S. Immigration and Customs Enforcement hires private firms to detain immigrants awaiting hearings on their status.

street cleaning, would benefit from private competition.

Although Savas' proposal failed in the face of opposition from public employees and members of the Lindsay administration, he became a foremost advocate of privatization, publishing more than a dozen books promoting the approach.

Savas says privatization first gained popularity at the municipal level. "One way it spread was starting with solid-waste management, garbage collection," he says, an area where private contractors were often able to offer less-expensive bids. "In many cities, city councilmen were not full time, they were often businessmen," he says, "so [they] were very prone to try to use competition in these sectors."

Privatization, he adds, evolved from there. "The idea started spreading all over the country. It started with outsourcing [and] gradually expanded to the notion of selling off various government assets not being used, which made sense," Savas says.

Reagan's election in 1980 gave privatization an advocate in the White House. Many in the privatization movement say Reagan was inspired by British Prime Minister Margaret Thatcher. "Thatcher had already started privatizing public enterprises," explains the Reason Foundation's Poole, also an early U.S. advocate of privatization.

After being elected in 1979, Thatcher had moved to privatize many state-owned ventures, such as energy and steel companies, British Airways and automaker Jaguar — the kind of enterprises that had never been state-owned in the United States. [38] The Reagan administration studied the feasibility of privatizing a range of government agencies, including the Postal Service, the air traffic control system, passenger railway Amtrak and other agencies. [39]

However, facing opposition in a Democratic-controlled Congress, the administration advanced only limited proposals. Reagan did privatize Conrail,

the government-owned freight railroad, in 1987. [40] But it would take a Democratic president, Bill Clinton, to advance the movement further.

Clinton was elected in 1992 promising to reinvent government and trim 100,000 workers from the federal workforce. He directed Vice President Al Gore to head a special commission to study making government more efficient. The results led to a wave of outsourcing of a wide range of government services to private contractors. [41]

"Clinton is the first president after World War II to decrease the number of federal employees," says UCLA's Michaels. He also accelerated the sale of government assets.

"Ironically, there was more real privatization under the Clinton administration than the Reagan administration," a Reason Foundation report concluded. [42] Under Clinton, the federal government sold off the Elk Hills Naval Petroleum Reserve; the U.S. Enrichment Corp., which processed uranium for nuclear power plants; and part of the electromagnetic spectrum that could be used for broadcasting. [43]

Privatization accelerated further under Republican President George W. Bush, elected in 2000, particularly the outsourcing of military services during the wars in Afghanistan and Iraq. By 2011, the Defense Department had more private contract personnel in the two countries — at 155,000 — than military personnel, who numbered 145,000. [44] (See sidebar, p. 1028.)

From 2000 to 2006, U.S. spending on private contractors — both military and civilian — more than doubled, to a record $412 billion in 2006, according to a report prepared in 2007 by the Democratic majority staff of the House Committee on Oversight and Government Reform. "Since 2000, spending on federal contracts has grown more than twice as fast as other discretionary federal spending," said the report. "For the first time, the federal government now spends over 40 cents

Continued on p. 1028

Chronology

1944-1976
Modern privatization movement begins.

1944
Conservative economist Friedrich von Hayek argues in *The Road to Serfdom* that big government is tyrannical.

1962
Conservative economist Milton Friedman says privatizing government services introduces beneficial competition.

1971
A study of New York's sanitation department convinces deputy city administrator E. S. Savas that privatizing the service would improve it. He goes on to become a leading privatization advocate.

1976
The Reason Foundation, a libertarian think tank, begins advocating for privatization.

1980s-1992
President Ronald Reagan vows to shrink the federal government; privatization grows at the state and local levels.

1980
Frustration with inefficient and costly government services helps lead to Reagan's election.

1983
Corrections Corporation of America, the country's first private prison company, is founded.

1987
Reagan's budget includes more privatization proposals than recommended by any previous president. Congress blocks most of the plans.

1992
City Academy in St. Paul, Minn., becomes the nation's first charter school; charter schools, which can be privately owned, receive public funds.

1990s-2008
Privatization is embraced by both political parties with the election of Democratic President Bill Clinton.

1993
Newly elected President Clinton promises to eliminate 100,000 federal jobs. . . . Government privatizes the U.S. Enrichment Corp., which contracts with the Department of Energy to produce enriched uranium for power plants.

1995
A task force chaired by Vice President Al Gore recommends more privatization of federal services.

1998
Clinton administration completes $3.6 billion sale of the Elk Hills Naval Petroleum Reserve to a private company.

2000
The number of charter schools reaches nearly 2,000.

2001
Following the 9/11 attacks, U.S. government creates Transportation Security Administration (TSA) to do airport screenings once done by private contractors.

2008
A Congressional Research Service study finds that private contractors make up 67 percent of U.S. military forces in Afghanistan.

2010-Present
President Barack Obama reduces private contracting at the federal level; President Trump seeks to reverse that policy.

2010
More than 128,000 men and women are held in private prisons at the state and federal level.

2011
Republican congressional leaders unveil a plan to privatize part of Amtrak. The plan fails to get through Congress.

2012
Obama administration promotes "insourcing," which returns some privately contracted services to federal employees.

2016
Obama administration announces plan to phase out private prisons after an audit finds they have more safety and security problems than government-run facilities (August). . . . President-elect Donald Trump promises a massive infrastructure-building project that administration officials say will largely depend on private investors (November).

2017
Trump administration rescinds Obama administration decision on private prisons, saying the U.S. Bureau of Prisons needs greater flexibility (February). . . . Trump says he does not believe partnerships where private companies invest in and manage transportation infrastructure work, casting doubt on his administration's plans (September).

Blackwater Founder Urges Trump to Privatize Afghan War

Critics warn contractors' behavior "has really poisoned the well."

Early this year as President Trump weighed his options for the Afghan conflict, two of his top advisers, Steve Bannon and Trump's son-in-law Jared Kushner, met with two businessmen who had a proposal for what to do next: privatize the war. [1]

The businessmen — Erik Prince, founder of Blackwater Worldwide, a security contracting firm that had been heavily involved in Iraq, and Stephen Feinberg, who owns DynCorp International, a major military contractor — proposed contracting the war out to a 5,500-person private force. This force, made up mostly of former Special Operations troops, would work closely with the Afghan military but report to an appointed American "viceroy" who would answer only to the U.S. president. Their proposal included setting up a 90-plane private air force to assist in the fight against the Taliban, the extremist movement trying to topple the Afghan government. [2]

The idea seems to have little support in government, but it is not out of line with recent practice. During the United States' 16-year involvement in Afghanistan and 14 years in Iraq, the U.S. military has increasingly relied on private contractors to help fulfill its mission.

At the end of last year, the U.S. military employed 25,197 contract personnel in Afghanistan, compared with 9,800 uniformed U.S. military personnel there. While the contractors included people working in a wide variety of support positions, more than 3,000 were security personnel. [3]

In March 2011, when the U.S. military had a large presence in Iraq and Afghanistan battling Islamist insurgents, the Defense Department had 155,000 contract personnel in the two countries, compared with 145,000 uniformed service members. [4]

Prince's proposal, nevertheless, attracted considerable criticism from U.S. military analysts and was reportedly unpopular with Trump's military advisers, including Defense Secretary James Mattis and National Security Adviser H.R. McMaster. They are said to fear that a private force would be more expensive than

Prince predicted and would be resisted by regional allies. [5]

Molly Dunigan, associate director of the defense and political sciences department at the RAND Corp., a research institute in Santa Monica, Calif., says the United States has relied on private contractors to support its military since the American Revolution. But the use of armed security contractors who can end up in firefights and other deadly situations is new, she says.

Military officials say they must rely more heavily on contractors because Congress and the executive branch have capped the number of uniformed personnel, leaving the military shorthanded in Iraq and Afghanistan. [6] Dunigan and others, however, say the expanded use of private security personnel can cause problems because of training and command-and-control issues.

"There are issues in terms of contractors operating in a counterinsurgency environment and how they interact with locals," Dunigan says. "They're typically perceived as part of the American force, but they don't necessarily abide by the same doctrines or the same norms of behavior."

Private contractors' behavior was at the center of a highly controversial incident during the Iraq War when Blackwater personnel opened fire on civilians in Nisour Square in Baghdad, killing 17 people. Iraqis were enraged, and the government demanded that Blackwater leave the country. [7] The four guards involved in the shooting later were found guilty of murder, manslaughter and weapons charges in U.S. courts, although part of the sentences were later overturned. [8] (Private security contractors have been connected to several other incidents that outraged the populace in Iraq and Afghanistan, including the shooting of civilians under questionable circumstances and cases of torture and sexual abuse.) [9]

Prince sold Blackwater in 2010 and is not directly involved in security contracting. But in a *Wall Street Journal* opinion piece and several interviews, he has said a private force would be more effective than a traditional military force in Afghanistan. [10] He compared the idea to the East India Company, a private trading

---

Continued from p. 1026

of every discretionary dollar on contracts with private companies." [45]

The report raised concern about the growing number of government contracts being signed without competitive bidding. It also identified 187 federal contracts with private contractors over six years valued at $1.1 trillion that involved "significant waste, fraud, abuse or mismanagement." [46]

In one area — airport security — the government took a decidedly dif-

ferent tack on privatization after the Sept. 11, 2001, terrorist attacks during Bush's first year in office. Within weeks, Congress crafted legislation creating the Transportation Security Administration, which replaced private airport security companies with federal agents at all U.S. airports. President Bush signed the bill into law on Nov. 19, 2001, creating a new federal agency that today has 60,000 employees, including 44,000 screening agents. [47] (*See sidebar, p. 1030.*)

Privatization Backlash

Obama's election in 2008 brought a Democratic administration into office that, analysts say, was less enthusiastic about many aspects of privatization than previous administrations. [48] While the new administration supported the continued expansion of charter schools, it began to promote "insourcing," or using government personnel to perform work previously done by contractors.

firm that at times maintained its own army and helped Britain manage its empire during the 17th, 18th and 19th centuries.

"We've fought for the last 15 years with the First Infantry Division model, now we should fight with an East India Company model and do it much cheaper," Prince told Fox News. [11]

Although Trump has expressed doubts about the U.S. approach to the war, he decided to follow the recommendation of his military advisers and announced in August he would send more U.S. troops to Afghanistan. According to administration officials, about 4,000 additional troops were to join the 8,500 U.S. military personnel already in the country. [12]

Prince, however, says he thinks Trump eventually will turn to a private force. "Whether it's six months or a year, I don't think the president wants to go into the [2018 congressional elections] with thousands of American soldiers at risk," he said. [13]

But David Sedney, a former deputy U.S. ambassador to Afghanistan, said Afghans would "never accept" privatization of the U.S. military forces there because past experience with private security personnel created "political toxicity." Afghans have said private security personnel in Afghanistan have acted as if they were above the law. [14]

"Bad behavior on the part of private security companies has really poisoned the well," he said. [15]

— Reed Karaim

A U.S. security contractor working with the Army's 10th Mountain Division patrols in Ghazni, Afghanistan, on May 19, 2013.

[1] Mark Landler, Eric Schmitt and Michael Gordon, "Trump Aides Recruited Businessmen to Devise Options for Afghanistan," *The New York Times*, July 10, 2017, https://tinyurl.com/y8ft5rc7.

[2] Jim Michaels, "Trump White House weighs unprecedented plan to privatize much of the war in Afghanistan," *USA Today*, Aug. 8, 2017, https://tinyurl.com/y8olr96x.

[3] Heidi Peters, Moshe Schwartz and Lawrence Kapp, "Department of Defense Contractor and Troop Levels in Iraq and Afghanistan: 2007-2017," Congressional Research Service, April 28, 2017, https://tinyurl.com/lch975o.

[4] Moshe Schwartz and Joyprada Swain, "Department of Defense Contractors in Afghanistan and Iraq: Background and Analysis," Congressional Research Service, May 13, 2011, https://tinyurl.com/yab8sxpl.

[5] Rosie Gray, "Erik Prince's Plan to Privatize the War in Afghanistan," *The Atlantic*, Aug. 18, 2017, https://tinyurl.com/y83vdlzh.

[6] Peters, Schwartz and Kapp, *op. cit.*

[7] Amit R. Paley, "Iraq Demands Expulsion of Contractor Blackwater, Compensation for Killings," *The Washington Post*, Oct. 15, 2007, https://tinyurl.com/yb7ku9us.

[8] Matt Apuzo, "In Blackwater Case, Court Rejects a Murder Conviction and Voids 3 Sentences," *The New York Times*, Aug. 4, 2017, https://tinyurl.com/y7pgz9e6.

[9] Moshe Schwartz, "The Department of Defense's Use of Private Security Contractors in Iraq and Afghanistan: Background, Analysis, and Options for Congress," Congressional Research Service, Sept. 29, 2009, https://tinyurl.com/ybez6mu2; James Glanz and Andrew Lehren, "Use of Contractors Added to War's Chaos in Iraq," *The New York Times*, Oct. 23, 2010, https://tinyurl.com/ybr7szeu.

[10] Erik D. Prince, "The MacArthur Model for Afghanistan," *The Wall Street Journal*, May 31, 2017, https://tinyurl.com/yav8j77d.

[11] "Blackwater Founder: Ironically 'The Left Loved The USSR' 30 Years Ago," Fox News Insider, May 17, 2017, https://tinyurl.com/mu2qjza.

[12] David Nakamura and Abby Phillip, "Trump announces new strategy for Afghanistan that calls for a troop increase," *The Washington Post*, Aug. 21, 2017, https://tinyurl.com/y9bdrj8g.

[13] Steven Nelson, "Erik Prince believes Trump will eventually privatize Afghanistan War," *Washington Examiner*, Nov. 6, 2017, https://tinyurl.com/y77ldkgj.

[14] Paul Tait, "Afghanistan orders ban on private security firms," Reuters, Aug. 17, 2017, https://tinyurl.com/y778jhol.

[15] Nelson, *op. cit.*

It also opposed having private companies run federal prisons.

Private prisons had become big business. In 2015, the most recent year for which statistics are available, roughly 8 percent of the 1.53 million people held in state and federal prisons were held in private facilities in 29 states and the federal prison system, an 83 percent jump from 1999, according to the Pew Research Center, a think tank in Washington. [49] U.S. Immigration and Customs Enforcement also contracts with private companies to detain immigrants awaiting hearings on their status.

However, a decade of studies by the Justice Department, the American Civil Liberties Union and others had documented problems at private prisons that included more frequent assaults on guards and prisoners than in public prisons, civil rights abuses and medical neglect. [50] Some state studies have also shown that private prisons do not save taxpayers money. [51]

Yet, a peer-reviewed 2014 study by economists at Temple University — commissioned by the corrections industry and published independently — found that, when all costs were taken into account, private state-run prisons did provide savings of between 14 and 58 percent over government-run state prisons. [52]

Nevertheless, after a government audit found that private prisons had more safety and security problems than government-run prisons, the Obama administration announced in August of 2016 that it would phase out the federal

Should Airport Security Be Privatized — Again?

Backers see cost savings and better security, but foes fear a lack of accountability.

Airport security screening has a unique history that illustrates the constant back-and-forth pull between public and private operations of government services.

Before the Sept. 11, 2001, terrorist attacks, private contractors conducted passenger screening at airports. Then, 19 hijackers boarded four commercial airliners carrying box cutters, which they used to take control of the planes and crash them into the World Trade Center in New York City and the Pentagon near Washington, D.C. A fourth plane crashed in rural Pennsylvania. In all, nearly 3,000 people were killed.

Within weeks, Congress voted to create the Transportation Security Administration (TSA), which today has more than 44,000 federal security officers who continue to provide airport screening. [1]

But discontent with the federalized service, particularly the long lines at some airports that critics blame on the TSA, has led to repeated calls to return the responsibility to private contractors. The push to reprivatize airport security comes from conservative think tanks, such as the Heritage Foundation, along with some senior Republican lawmakers, including Rep. Michael McCaul, R-Texas, head of the House Committee on Homeland Security, and Rep. Darrell Issa, R-Calif. [2]

Privatization foes, however, say private airport security did not work well before 2001 and would not work well again because, the opponents contend, these contractors focus on the bottom line over security.

Although no one has introduced legislation, Issa reflected the view of privatization supporters earlier this year when he

described the airport security system as "broken." If the United States wants to speed up and improve screening, Issa said, "the solution couldn't be any simpler: Let's get the TSA out of the airport screening business altogether." Citing various studies, he said private screeners at 22 airports outperformed their public counterparts in terms of efficiency and safety because of better morale and higher employee retention rates. [3]

"Ultimately, allowing private companies to take over administration of our airports' security, under the TSA's guidelines, would unleash the markets' power of innovation to improve customer service and undo years of bureaucracy that has squandered billions of dollars dedicated to airport security and done much to make traveling more miserable," Issa said.

But other analysts say the history of airport security illustrates the dangers of privatizing a service essential to public safety. In a 2007 book, legal scholar Paul R. Verkuil argued the pre-9/11 approach had a fundamental flaw: Security was the responsibility of the airlines, which contracted the work out to private companies.

"Not surprisingly, these contracts went to the lowest bidders," wrote Verkuil. "As a result, these private security firm employees were poorly trained, lacking language skills and otherwise unqualified (they were sometimes convicted felons)." [4]

Through the contracting process, Verkuil said, "airlines treated the security functions as a cost control item and forced the quality of services downward. In these circumstances, it should have been no surprise that the airport security system failed in its essential purpose." [5]

use of private prisons, an order that Trump would later rescind. [53]

During the Obama administration, the Defense Department also had begun to hire thousands of employees to replace contractors, part of what Defense Secretary Robert Gates termed an effort to shrink a bloated Pentagon bureaucracy that included too many private contractors. [54]

A backlash against privatization was also emerging in some city governments, fed by cases such as Chicago's parking meter privatization, which is expected to cost the city nearly $1 billion in lost revenue over the life of the contract but also included non-compete clauses that restricted the city's ability to build new parking garages or close streets for festivals. [55]

The bankruptcies of the companies

that built the Indiana Toll Road, once held up as a model of a public-private partnership, and Texas State Highway 130, increased skepticism among some state officials. In 2014, 18 states considered legislation to limit state contracting, and three — Oregon, Nebraska and Maryland — passed laws imposing such restrictions, according to In the Public Interest. [56]

"The ideological fervor for privatization has ebbed," John D. Donahue, an expert on privatization at Harvard's Kennedy School of Government, said that year. [57]

Analysts note, however, that many states and cities continued to turn to privatization. The election of Trump, a former real estate developer, in 2016 also brought a drastic shift in favor of private business at the top level of government. ∎

CURRENT SITUATION

Infrastructure Needs

President Trump's 2018 budget in May proposed spending $200 billion for infrastructure over 10 years. Critics noted that it also included $255 billion in cuts of existing infrastructure programs, amounting to an overall reduction in federal infrastructure spending. But administration officials said some of the money being trimmed was for

The TSA's creation was an acknowledgment that for certain government responsibilities, cost and profit calculations cannot be the primary concerns, he said. "The reasons that Congress took this action reflect concerns with public values and inherent government functions, essential considerations that are often left out of the debate over privatization."

The United States took additional steps to improve security aboard airliners, such as deploying federal marshals on planes, and no U.S. airliner has been hijacked since 9/11. But privatization's advocates say the current system is bloated, expensive and not customer friendly. In Europe, they say, privatized systems do a better job with fewer resources. [6]

In addition, said Issa, studies show that airport screeners still miss a high percentage of dangerous objects. He added there is no evidence that federalizing airport security has improved security. [7] Contracting out screening would "would go a long way to helping improve the experience fliers face at our nation's airports," he said. [8]

But Aman Banerji, a program manager who works on privatization issues at the Roosevelt Institute, a liberal think tank in New York, says that while the TSA is badly run, "We're papering over the cracks by pretending that the problems will be fixed by private contractors. I think it's a good example of the way we use bad management as an argument for privatization. In reality, when you look at the way privatization plays out, you just shift from a public monopoly to a private monopoly [for a service]. There's no way that makes government more accountable."

— *Reed Karaim*

New automated security-screening lanes funded by American Airlines and installed by the Transportation Security Administration check travelers at Miami International Airport on Oct. 24, 2017.

Getty Images/Joe Raedle

[1] "House, Senate pass aviation security bill," CNN, Nov. 16, 2001, https://tinyurl.com/y8mywd4n; "TSA at a Glance," Transportation Security Administration, https://tinyurl.com/yclwnnqu.

[2] David Inserra, "Time to Privatize the TSA," Heritage Foundation, July 19, 2017, https://tinyurl.com/y7of7uh3. Keith Laing, "TSA Failures Spark Calls for Privatization," *The Hill*, June 9, 2015, https://tinyurl.com/y8pas4fd.

[3] Darrell Issa, "A simple solution to the TSA breakdown," CNN, May 26, 2016, https://tinyurl.com/hl38s4z.

[4] Paul Verkuil, *Outsourcing Sovereignty: Why Privatization of Government Threatens Democracy and What We Can Do About it* (2007), p. 58.

[5] *Ibid.*

[6] Inserra, *op. cit.*

[7] Thomas Frank, "Most fake bombs missed by screeners," *USA Today*, Oct. 22, 2007, https://tinyurl.com/yctzyvtf.

[8] Issa, *op. cit.*

administration and oversight and not for infrastructure. [58]

The budget did not spell out how federal money would be leveraged with private investment to reach $1 trillion in spending. However, several of Trump's principal advisers, including Pence and Transportation Secretary Elaine Chao, favor relying on private investment. [59]

Other analysts say any final plan must include privatization. "If they want to get to a trillion dollars, it's going to be really hard for them to do without private finance," says Cohen, of In the Public Interest, because "the other choice is public finance or, even better, public funding, . . . and this Congress isn't going to do it."

Savas believes private capital could provide a much needed boost. "America has great infrastructure needs . . . and here's an opportunity to tap the private sector," he says. "As long as it's managed well, the basic idea is good."

While the administration's infrastructure plan remains on hold, state and local governments continue to privatize highway, bridge and water and sewer projects. In Arizona, Republican Gov. Doug Ducey is asking the U.S. Department of Transportation to allow the state to privatize rest stops along interstate highways, bringing in private businesses such as restaurants or gas stations that would pay to upgrade the facilities. The idea is opposed by the National Association

of Truck Stop Owners, which says it would hurt existing businesses operating at rest stops. [60]

Los Angeles International Airport is seeking a private partner to build, operate and maintain an "automated people-moving system" to transport travelers to car rental facilities as part of a $14 billion upgrade in airport facilities. [61]

Charter Schools

The charter school movement continues to grow, despite a backlash in some areas. Earlier in the year, Kentucky became the 44th state to allow charters, which are tuition-free, taxpayer-supported independently run public schools. Other states also took steps to increase public funding for charters or to give them access to new revenue streams. [62]

For-profit companies managed more than 900 charter schools around the United States in the 2014-2015 school year, according to one study. [63] Many others are operated by nonprofit entities, some of which contract out their management to private, for-profit companies. [64]

Since the first charters opened in the 1990s, the movement has grown rapidly, and today 3.1 million students attend more than 6,900 charter schools. [65] Education Secretary Betsy DeVos was a leading advocate for charter schools before joining the Trump administration, and the administration has pledged $20 billion to promote charter schools and vouchers that provide aid for students to attend private schools. [66]

In September, the Department of Education announced it would provide $253 million in grants to expand charter schools. "These grants will help supplement state-based efforts to give students access to more options for their education," said DeVos. [67] The two largest grants went to the Indiana and Minnesota, and $16 million was earmarked to spur the creation of up to 25 charter schools in Oklahoma, nearly doubling that state's count. [68]

But elsewhere resistance has grown. In New Jersey, the state education department denied two applications for new charters in Paterson, where local activists have opposed them, which they say are siphoning revenue from traditional public schools. [69]

In November, New York state officials for the first time rejected charter applications for two schools. The state Board of Regents, which is expected to approve several other new charters, said the proposed curriculums in the rejected applications were not innovative and the board feared the charters would drain resources from existing schools, a concern expressed by local opponents to the schools. [70]

The most heated recent struggle over charter schools has been in Los Angeles, where a coalition led by the teachers union opposed a plan, led by a private foundation, to drastically expand the number of charters in the city. [71] In a bitter election last May, charter supporters won a majority on the city's school board after outspending their opponents in the most expensive campaign in the school board's history. [72] The new board this fall exempted charter schools from some district rules. [73]

Charter school supporters say they improve education by creating competition, opening up the education market to alternatives beyond a one-size-fits-all public school system. "They were intended to create a new path, new opportunities and new patterns of accountability. They have done better in all these areas," said Jeanne Allen, founder and CEO of the Center for Education Reform, a charter advocacy organization in Washington. [74]

But some education experts say the idea that privatization does a better job is simplistic when applied to education. Privatization can work well for public services when the effectiveness of the contract can be easily measured, said Samuel E. Abrams, director of the National Center for the Study of Privatization in Education at Teachers College, Columbia University, in New York. But privatization does not work well for complex services where effectiveness is hard to measure, he said. [75]

"In the case of schooling, which is a classic complex service, the direct consumer is a child, who [cannot] judge whether classes are being properly taught," Abrams said. "The parent, taxpayer and legislator are at a necessary distance. And standardized testing as a check on quality is rife with problems." [76]

Privatizing Prisons

The Trump administration's support for private prisons has breathed new life into the industry, analysts say. CoreCivic, the nation's largest private prison firm, recently announced it will be expanding into operating halfway houses. [77]

After Obama's Justice Department announced it would phase out the use of private facilities for federal prisoners, the stock prices of the two largest private corrections companies, GEO Group and Corrections Corporation of America (now CoreCivic), fell significantly. [78] But both stocks rebounded after Trump's election and an announcement by Attorney General Jeff Sessions last February that the administration was rescinding Obama's order. [79]

Critics say profits depend on keeping facilities full, and many private prison contracts have lock-up quotas that require state or local governments to keep prisons filled to a certain occupancy level — some as high as 100 percent — or pay for the unused beds. [80] In addition, a study by In the Public Interest found that prisoners in private facilities had higher recidivism rates. [81]

"We don't believe privatized prisons should exist, period, or detention centers," says In the Public Interest's Cohen. Private companies' interests "are completely contrary to the public's interests," he added. "They make more money if there's a head in a bed. We don't want heads in beds. We want people to ultimately get out and live productive lives."

But Amanda Gilchrist, a spokesperson for CoreCivic, says it has begun an effort to reduce recidivism and has lobbied for state and federal policies to bring down the level of repeat offenders. "CoreCivic has made significant commitments to address the recidivism crisis in America that we believe are unmatched by any corrections system — public or private," says Gilchrist.

The company's goal, Gilchrist says, is to help rehabilitate prisoners. To that end, she say, CoreCivic is committing increased resources to education, voca-

Continued on p. 1034

At Issue:

Should the U.S. use private capital to rebuild infrastructure?

ROBERT POOLE
TRANSPORTATION POLICY DIRECTOR,
REASON FOUNDATION

WRITTEN FOR *CQ RESEARCHER*, DECEMBER 2017

*a*merica's 20th-century infrastructure model is broken
and needs replacing. This model calls for separate contracts for design and construction — and leaves maintenance to the vagaries of politics. Far better stewardship results
from the newer model, which uses private companies that design,
build, finance, operate and maintain (DBFOM) an infrastructure
project. Under this approach, the winning company signs a contract to do all those things for terms of 40 to 50 years.

This long-term approach yields much better projects,
whether new construction or rebuilding aging facilities. First,
design and construction are integrated, which minimizes costly
change orders. Second, the same entity that creates the project
is responsible for long-term operations and maintenance. That
means the design seeks to minimize life-cycle costs, not just
initial costs — producing far better value for the money spent.
Also, maintenance is guaranteed for the life of the agreement.

Moreover, if customers finance the project through fees, the
developer/operator has incentives to design it to attract as many
customers as possible, and to serve them well. And this type of
financing shifts a major risk from taxpayers to investors.

These differences are especially important for mega-projects,
which have a well-documented history of cost overruns, late completion and overly optimistic traffic and revenue forecasts. (Recall
Boston's "Big Dig" and any number of urban rail projects.)

If the United States shifted to DBFOM for most or all major
infrastructure rebuilding, the benefits would include:

• Higher infrastructure investment, particularly if the long-
term agreements are based on user fees (e.g., Interstate tolls).

• Getting many needed reconstruction and modernization projects done years or decades sooner, thanks to the availability of
private equity capital (more than $300 billion of which has been
raised by infrastructure investment funds in the past decade).

• Better project selection, thanks to more rigorous
benefit/cost analysis and the need for the projects to show a
positive return on investment (no more "bridges to nowhere").

• New federal and state corporate tax revenue, to the extent that the resulting concession companies are profitable.

Moreover, DBFOM infrastructure projects are highly attractive to public employee pension funds that need to diversify
their portfolios to earn higher real returns.

If this model sounds familiar, it should: It's how investor-
owned electric, gas and water utilities operate. A much larger
portion of U.S. infrastructure should adopt this proven model.

DONALD COHEN
EXECUTIVE DIRECTOR,
IN THE PUBLIC INTEREST

WRITTEN FOR *CQ RESEARCHER*, DECEMBER 2017

*t*he infrastructure debate is often convoluted and detached
from people's everyday lives, but it's important. At its
core, the debate is a battle over crucial public assets and
the role of government itself.

That's why privatization must be avoided, whether it's outsourcing the operations or maintenance of public assets, relying on private financing — known as "public-private partnerships" — or selling off what the public owns to private
investors and multinational corporations. Not only is privatization
often less transparent and more expensive than public ownership, but it also cedes key aspects of public control to the
private sector. If we're going to meet the challenges of the
21st century — declining global competitiveness, skyrocketing
economic inequality and rapid climate change — we need
more democratic decision-making, not less.

Some local and state governments have already turned to
privatization with alarming results. Chicago's contract with a
Wall Street-led group to run the city's downtown parking
meters requires the public to make up for lost revenue from
policy changes such as new bike or bus lanes — for the next
66 years. If that wasn't enough, parking meter rates more than
doubled in the contract's first five years.

A private group operating a parkway in Denver once stopped
the city from making improvements to a nearby public road,
citing contract language that prevented improvements that
"might hurt the parkway financially" by providing an alternative
route for travelers.

In Virginia, a long-term contract with an Australian corporation
penalizes the public for increased carpooling on the Capital
Beltway's high-occupancy express toll lanes.

Recently, public-private partnerships increasingly have been
structured with large contractually obligated payments that last
for decades. Such "availability payments" can squeeze other
areas of public budgets, such as education or emergency services, without the traditional flexibility of public debt.

Ultimately, the larger and more difficult question is not how
we borrow the money to rebuild our infrastructure but how we
pay back what we borrow. There's no free lunch. Whether
we use direct federal spending, cheap municipal bonds or expensive private financing, the burden falls on all of us. Privatization is not only the most expensive way forward, but it also
distorts the role of government by giving private investors
control over our shared public assets.

Continued from p. 1032

tional training and addiction treatment. "Additionally, CoreCivic has invested $250 million to build an expanding network of residential re-entry centers around the country," or halfway houses, she says. "These facilities help inmates transition back into their communities."

Air traffic controllers staff the control tower at Portland International Jetport in Maine on Oct. 26, 2017. President Trump supports transferring air traffic control from the Federal Aviation Administration to a nonprofit corporation. Major U.S. airlines and the air traffic controllers' union support the idea.

Getty Images/The Portland Press Herald/Derek Davis

Air Traffic Control

Trump supports privatizing air traffic control, transferring it from the Federal Aviation Administration (FAA), which oversees aircraft traffic across the country, into a separate nonprofit corporation. [82]

The administration's plan is modeled closely on legislation introduced by Rep. Bill Shuster, R-Pa., chairman of the House Transportation and Infrastructure Committee. Shuster's plan aims to modernize the aging air traffic control system, with the costs borne by carriers through user fees established by a 13-member governing board. The idea is supported both by the major U.S. airlines and the air traffic controllers' union. [83]

Puentes, of the Eno Transportation Center, says the proposal would allow airlines and airports to make needed long-term investments to upgrade the system, something Congress, because of its annual spending and budget battles, hasn't done. "Congress can't authorize money in the way it needs to for long-term investment," Puentes says.

By creating a private, nonprofit corporation to manage the system, something several European nations have already done, "you can spin it off from the FAA and set up an entity that can start to deliver this modern system we've been talking about for a long time," Puentes says.

However, opponents of the proposal, especially those involved in providing air service to small, rural communities, see it as a power grab by the major airlines. "This is an attempt to really get more control over the system and be able to direct the infrastructure investment and resources toward the hubs that they [the major airlines] care about," says Selena Shilad, executive director of the Alliance for Aviation Across America, a

coalition representing small airports, businesses and other groups.

Modernizing the system can be done without privatization if the government adequately funded the FAA, Shilad says. Maintain an equitable system that treats all parts of America fairly is essential, she says.

"The FAA makes sure we maintain public transportation both big and small," Shilad says. "If you transition that to a governance board that's overseen by private interests, a 13-person board dominated and heavily influenced by the airlines and larger private interests, then we're concerned about how smaller airports would fare."

Others, such as retired U.S. Airways pilot Sully Sullenberger, famous for landing a disabled passenger jet in the Hudson River in 2009, argued in an op-ed that privatizing air traffic control operations would threaten passenger safety and access to aviation. [84]

Air traffic privatization also faces powerful resistance from lawmakers wary of giving up federal control of the system, fearing it could leave the major airlines with too much power over commercial aviation. Prospects for the legislation passing are considered uncertain. [85]

In July, for instance, a Senate Appropriations subcommittee rejected President Trump's proposal, citing concerns that the nonprofit corporation would not have congressional oversight. [86] ∎

OUTLOOK

Continuing Pressure

Outsourcing, forming public-private partnerships and selling public assets to private companies are a significant part of how the U.S. government operates. No privatization expert sees that halting over the next five to 10 years, but some believe the trend may slow or face more pushback.

"I can imagine a state of equilibrium developing," says Baruch College's Savas. "The last time I looked, about 30 percent of American cities had outsourced one or more of their major municipal services. Is that going to grow? I suspect it's going to grow slowly."

That could change, he adds, depending on the resolution of a case to be heard by the U.S. Supreme Court next year. The court will decide whether unions can require everyone in a unionized workplace to pay union fees. Previous courts have held that mandatory fees were justified because benefits negotiated by a union affect everyone in the workplace. [87] The current court is widely expected to overturn that ruling, allowing employees to opt out of paying union fees, which could seriously weaken public employee unions.

"If the Supreme Court ruling makes every state essentially a right-to-work state . . . it would become easier for cities and states to exercise good managerial judgment and make good policy decisions about when it makes sense to introduce competition into public services," Savas says. While such a decision would not directly result in more privatization, it could eventually weaken public unions, making more outsourcing possible.

Even though Trump's comments have cast doubt on his commitment to public-private partnerships for rebuilding infrastructure, the Reason Foundation's Poole hopes the administration moves ahead with its original plan to seek significant private investment in new infrastructure.

"The money is sitting there. It's waiting," he says. "I see this big shortfall particularly of transportation infrastructure. It's a problem waiting to be solved by private investment if we can just get a clear path to let it happen."

The Cato Institute's Edwards says budget pressures will force the federal government to embrace more privatization. "There's always going to be resistance to tax increases. There's going to be less and less federal money as

entitlement programs continue to expand," he says. "I think there's going to be continuing pressure on the United States to look to privatization."

In the near term, he believes, successful privatization in one area could lead the government to embrace more of it elsewhere. "To me, air traffic control, if they do that, it will spur lots more similar efforts," Edwards says.

But UCLA's Michaels says several of Trump's cabinet appointments of people openly hostile to the government agencies they now head, such as Environmental Protection Agency administrator Scott Pruitt, have created a backlash against anti-government rhetoric and privatization.

"Last year, I would have said . . . there's going to just be this slow trickle away, until one day we wake up and say, 'Wow we don't have a government,' " Michaels says. "Now, I think people are starting to rally behind the bureaucrats, as silly as it sounds. . . . We're seeing a rediscovery of an appreciation of a strong, independent civil service."

The Roosevelt Foundation's Banerji agrees that the Trump cabinet, which includes several members who worked in the industries they are now regulating, is energizing opponents of privatization. More of the public, he says, is aware that "there is this collection of people profiting off government."

Still, he believes opponents are unlikely to change the federal approach, especially with regard to privatizing air traffic control and other government functions. "I think what we're likely to see in the next five years or so, at the state and local level, is people pushing back very strongly against the privatization of public services," Banerji says. "But at the national level, we're likely to see the opposite."

However, Cohen, of In the Public Interest, says it will be difficult to slow down corporate efforts to promote privatization at the local level. "All these companies are bigger and more capable," he says.

"Twenty-five years ago they didn't know how to work city halls and state governments," he continues. "Now they know how to do it. There's a whole industry of lobbyists and deal-doers, . . . and if you're a mayor and they say, 'I can take your trash off your hands and it will save you money and it will save you headaches,' you say, 'Sure.' " ∎

Notes

[1] Michael Laris, "Trump advisers call for privatizing some public assets to build new infrastructure," *The Washington Post*, May 23, 2017, https://tinyurl.com/yawackc7.

[2] Tony Newmyer and Damian Paletta, "Trump backs off vow that private sector should help pay for infrastructure package," *The Washington Post*, Sept. 26, 2017, https://tinyurl.com/y9tjp3nr.

[3] E. S. Savas, *Privatization and Public-Private Partnerships* (2000), p. XIV.

[4] Paul Verkuil, *Outsourcing Sovereignty: Why Privatization of Government Threatens Democracy and What We Can Do About it* (2007), p. 1.

[5] Erika Eichelberger, "Who Really Runs Your City?" *Talking Points Memo*, 2016, https://tinyurl.com/z87cgyt.

[6] Sean McFate, "America's Addiction to Mercenaries," *The Atlantic*, Aug. 12, 2016, https://tinyurl.com/y9zzfn9b. "Private Debt Collection," The Internal Revenue Service, Aug. 7, 2017, https://tinyurl.com/j6t3td8.

[7] David Hoffman, "Report of Inspector General's Finding and Recommendations: An Analysis of the Lease of the City's Parking Meters," Office of the Inspector General, City of Chicago, June 2, 2009, https://tinyurl.com/y9npx8v7.

[8] Michael Martz and Robert Zullo, "Virginia awards contract for I-66 under new approach that saves state $2.5 billion," *The Richmond Times Dispatch*, Nov. 3, 2016, https://tinyurl.com/yaqzv6cw.

[9] Molly Ball, "The Privatization Backlash," *The Atlantic*, April 23, 2014, https://tinyurl.com/ybnvjzdk. Also see "Pay to Prey, Governors Facilitate the Predatory Outsourcing of America's Public Services," Center for Media and Democracy, 2014, https://tinyurl.com/ydbn9lm4.

[10] Eichelberger, *op. cit.*

[11] For background, see Richard L. Worsnop, "Privatization," *CQ Researcher*, Nov. 13, 1992, pp. 977-1000.

[12] Steven Pearlstein, "The federal outsourcing boom and why it's failing Americans," *The Washington Post*, Jan. 31, 2014, https://tinyurl.com/y8oy6e3f.

[13] John DiIulio Jr. and Paul Verkuil, "Want a leaner government? Hire more federal workers," *The Washington Post*, April 21, 2016, https://tinyurl.com/y82quacf.

[14] Leonard Gilroy, "Local Government Privatization 101," The Reason Foundation, March 16, 2010, https://tinyurl.com/36modc8.

[15] "Bad Business: Billions of Taxpayer Dollars Wasted on Hiring Contractors," Project on Government Oversight, 2012, https://tinyurl.com/6lrp8ja.

[16] "Race to the Bottom: How Outsourcing Public Services Rewards Corporations and Punishes the Middle Class," In the Public Interest, June 2014, https://tinyurl.com/hq9mpcw.

[17] Newmyer and Paletta, *op. cit.*

[18] "Using Public-Private Partnerships to Carry Out Highway Projects," Congressional Budget Office, January 2012, https://tinyurl.com/y7z3fhte.

[19] *Ibid.*

[20] Lydia O'Neal and David Sirota, "Trump's Infrastructure Plan is Actually Pence's — And It's All About Privatization," *Newsweek*, Sept. 4, 2017, https://tinyurl.com/y8wns48x.

[21] For background, see Reed Karaim, "Charter Schools," *CQ Researcher*, March 10, 2017, pp. 217-240.

[22] Donald Cohen, "The Fastest Road in America Is Falling Apart. Here's Why," *HuffPost*, Sept. 23, 2017, https://tinyurl.com/yawxebw4.

[23] Danielle Ivory, Ben Protess and Griff Palmer, "In American Towns, Private Profits from Public Works," *The New York Times*, Dec. 24, 2016, https://tinyurl.com/ybaynpdk.

[24] "Selling Out Consumers: How Water Prices Increased After 10 of the Largest Water System Sales," In the Public Interest, June 2011, https://tinyurl.com/yba8q6es.

[25] Ivory, Protess and Palmer, *op. cit.*

[26] Yvette Hammett, "Tampa's toll-lanes plan intrusive, elitist, obsolete, protestors say," *Tampa Bay Times*, Feb. 6, 2016, https://tinyurl.com/ycval58g.

[27] David Hedgpeth, "$34.50 for 10 Miles? New Tolls on I-66 Kick Off With Some High Rates," *The Washington Post*, Dec. 4, 2017, https://tinyurl.com/yd4lmqxh; Dana Hedgpeth and Luz Lazo, "I-66 toll hits $40 on day 2. Virginia transportation chief: 'No one has to pay a toll,' " *The Washington Post*, Dec. 5, 2017, https://tinyurl.com/y9c6jrbj.

[28] "History of education in the United States," K12ademics.com, 2017, https://tinyurl.com/y7fkmzh4.

[29] Daniel Klein and John Majewski, "Turnpikes and Toll Roads in Nineteenth-Century America," EH.net, https://tinyurl.com/yafw87fg.

[30] *Ibid.*

[31] *Ibid.*

[32] Henry Petroski, *The Road Taken: The History and Future of America's Infrastructure* (2016), p. 117.

[33] For background, see C. Hankin, "The Supreme Court and the New Deal," *Editorial Research Reports*, 1935 (Vol. I), and B. W. Patch, "New Deal Aims and the Constitution," *Editorial Research Reports*, 1936 (Vol. 2); both available at https://tinyurl.com/7hve5.

[34] Petroski, *op. cit.*, pp. 41-49.

[35] *Ibid.*, p. 48.

[36] Donald Cohen, "The History of Privatization," *Talking Points Memo*, 2016, https://tinyurl.com/j9gv8lr.

[37] *Ibid.*

[38] Richard Seymour, "A short history of privatisation in the UK: 1979-2012," *The Guardian*, March 29, 2012, https://tinyurl.com/jmn9j2t.

[39] Robert Poole, "Ronald Reagan and the Privatization Revolution," Reason Foundation, June 8, 2004, https://tinyurl.com/y9whbrat.

[40] James Sterngold, "85% U.S. Stake in Conrail Sold for $1.6 Billion," *The New York Times*, March 27, 1987, https://tinyurl.com/y89eou3f.

[41] Cohen, "The History of Privatization," *op. cit.*

[42] Poole, *op. cit.*

[43] *Ibid.*

[44] Moshe Schwartz and Joyprada Swain, "Department of Defense Contractors in Afghanistan and Iraq: Background and Analysis," Congressional Research Service, May 13, 2011, https://tinyurl.com/yab8sxpl.

[45] "More Dollars Less Sense: Worsening Contracting Trends Under the Bush Administration," U.S. House of Representatives, Committee on Oversight and Government Reform, Majority Staff, June 2007, p. i.

[46] *Ibid.*

[47] For background, see Martin Kady II, "Homeland Security," *CQ Researcher*, Sept. 12, 2003, pp. 749-772; "TSA at a Glance," Transportation Security Administration, https://tinyurl.com/yclwnnqu.

[48] Cohen, "The History of Privatization," *op. cit.*

[49] Abigail Geiger, "U.S. private prison population has declined in recent years," Pew Research Center, April 11, 2017, https://tinyurl.com/y8myljlb.

[50] "Banking on Bondage: Private Prisons and Mass Incarceration," American Civil Liberties Union, November 2011, https://tinyurl.com/pj8qdo6; "Emerging Issues on Privatized Prisons," Department of Justice, February 2001, https://tinyurl.com/bqlg9gt; Brendan Fischer, "Violence, Abuse and Death at For-Profit Prisons: A GEO Group Rap Sheet," PRWatch, Center for Media and Democracy, Sept. 26, 2013, https://tinyurl.com/y7uxr6xy.

[51] Megan Mumford, Diane Whitmore Schanzenbach and Ryan Nunn, "The economics of private prisons," Brookings Institution, Oct. 20, 2016, https://tinyurl.com/yahrjf87.

[52] Simon Hakim and Erwin Blackstone, "Prison Break: A New Approach to Public Cost and Safety," The Independent Institute, June 2014, https://tinyurl.com/yaojdbus.

[53] Eileen Sullivan, "Obama administration to end use of private prisons," PBS News Hour, Aug. 18, 2016, https://tinyurl.com/y8h4rwlq.

[54] Matthew Weigelt, "Obama official hits campaign trail to sell insourcing," *Washington Technology*, Jan. 12, 2010, https://tinyurl.com/y85pvelv; Greg Jaffe, "Gates: Cuts in Pentagon bureaucracy needed to help maintain military force," *The Washington Post*, May 2010, https://tinyurl.com/35x5vco.

[55] Ball, *op. cit.*

[56] *Ibid.*

[57] *Ibid.*

[58] Patrick Gillespie, "Trump's $1 trillion infrastructure promise has an obstacle: His own budget cut," CNN, June 9, 2017, https://tinyurl.com/y8fn3c55.

About the Author

Reed Karaim, a freelance writer in Tucson, Ariz., has written for *The Washington Post, U.S. News & World Report, Smithsonian, American Scholar, USA Weekend* and other publications. He is the author of the novel *If Men Were Angels*, which was selected for the Barnes & Noble Discover Great New Writers series. He is also the winner of the Robin Goldstein Award for Outstanding Regional Reporting and other journalism honors. Karaim is a graduate of North Dakota State University in Fargo.

[59] Laris, *op. cit.*; O'Neal and Sirota, *op. cit.*

[60] Howard Fischer, "Arizona makes pitch for permission to privatize public rest stops," Tucson.com, Nov. 3, 2017, https://tinyurl.com/ydyga44n.

[61] Jodi Richards, "Los Angeles International uses private-public partnerships to build automated people mover and consolidated rental car facility," *Airport Improvement*, May-June 2017, https://tinyurl.com/ycods4ca.

[62] Todd Ziebarth, "State Legislative Session Highlights for Public Charter Schools," National Alliance for Public Charter Schools, October 2017, https://tinyurl.com/ydze3o3s.

[63] Bruce Baker and Gary Miron, "The Business of Charter Schooling: Understanding the Policies that Charter Operators Use for Financial Benefit," National Education Policy Center, Colorado University, December 2015, https://tinyurl.com/jnludyq.

[64] Karaim, *op. cit.*

[65] "2016 Annual Report," National Alliance for Public Charter Schools, May 2017, https://tinyurl.com/y9epu7jv.

[66] Karaim, *op. cit.*, p. 221.

[67] "U.S. Department of Education Awards $253 Million in Grants to Expand Charter Schools," U.S. Department of Education, Sept. 28, 2017, https://tinyurl.com/yaevhqmf.

[68] "Awards," Office of Innovation and Improvement, U.S. Department of Education, Sept. 28, 2917, https://tinyurl.com/y8dlf7sb. Ben Felder, "Feds send $16.5M to Oklahoma for charter schools," *NewsOK*, Sept. 29, 2017, https://tinyurl.com/yd7pldea.

[69] Joe Malinconico, "Charter school applications in Paterson rejected by New Jersey," NorthJersey.com, Nov. 9, 2017, https://tinyurl.com/ycgwg68d.

[70] James Mulder, "NY rejects state's first 'agribased' rural charter school in Cortland," Syracuse.com, Nov. 14, 2017, https://tinyurl.com/ycalr4l8.

[71] Karaim, *op. cit.*, p. 231.

[72] Howard Blume and Shelby Grad, "Major changes could come to L.A. schools after charter school movement's big win," *Los Angeles Times*, May 17, 2017, https://tinyurl.com/mja8ljs.

[73] Howard Blume, "Agreement paves way for L.A. Unified to approve most old and new charter schools," *Los Angeles Times*, Nov. 7, 2017, https://tinyurl.com/y7mbgkvs.

[74] Karaim, *op. cit.*, p. 220.

[75] Valerie Strauss, "Why the movement to privatize public education is a very bad idea," *The Washington Post*, July 14, 2016, https://tinyurl.com/ybtf6nd6.

FOR MORE INFORMATION

American Federation of Government Employees, 80 F St., N.W., Washington, DC 20001; 202-737-8700; www.afge.org. Largest federal employee union, with more than 700,000 members; opposes outsourcing and the privatization of federal agencies.

American Society of Civil Engineers, 1801 Alexander Bell Drive, Reston, VA 20191; 800-548-2723; www.asce.org. Publishes the annual "Report Card for America's Infrastructure," assessing the state of the nation's roads, bridges, water systems, power grid and other key infrastructure; also estimates the cost of unmet maintenance and needed upgrades.

Center for American Progress, 1333 H St., N.W., Washington, DC 20005; 202-682-1611; https://www.americanprogress.org. An independent liberal-leaning policy institute engaged in national economic and policy debates.

Center on Budget and Policy Priorities, 820 First St., N.E., Suite 510, Washington, DC 20002; 202-408-1080; www.cbpp.org. Think tank that promotes federal and state policies designed to reduce poverty and economic inequality and studies privatization efforts.

Eno Center for Transportation, 1710 Rhode Island Ave., N.W., Suite 500, Washington, DC 20036; 202-879-4700; www.enotrans.org. Think tank that monitors public policy affecting the nation's transportation system and tracks transportation-related public-private partnerships.

Heritage Foundation, 214 Massachusetts Ave., N.E., Washington, DC 20002-4999; 202-546-4400; www.heritage.org. A prominent public policy think tank that promotes conservative ideas.

In the Public Interest, 1939 Harrison St., Suite 150, Oakland, CA 94612; 202-429-5091; www.inthepublicinterest.org. Think tank focused on privatization and government contracting; publishes "Weekly Privatization Report" on activities at all levels of government.

Reason Foundation, 1747 Connecticut Ave., N.W., Washington, DC 20009; 202-986-0916; http://reason.org. Libertarian think tank that promotes privatization. Publishes annual report tracking privatization trends in local, state and federal government.

Roosevelt Institute, 570 Lexington Ave., 18th Floor New York, NY 10022; 212-444-9130; http://rooseveltinstitute.org. A liberal think tank dedicated to carrying on the legacy and ideals of Franklin and Eleanor Roosevelt.

[76] *Ibid.*

[77] Geert de Lombaerde, "CoreCivic buys halfway houses in three states," *Nashville Post*, Nov. 9, 2017, https://tinyurl.com/yalrpjp8.

[78] Christopher Ingram, "Private prison stocks collapse after Justice Department promises to phase them out," *The Washington Post*, Aug. 18, 2016.

[79] Heather Long, "Private prison stocks up 100% since Trump win," CNN Money, Feb. 24, 2017, https://tinyurl.com/y9eg7nrf.

[80] Joe Watson, "Report Finds Two-Thirds of Private Prison Contracts Include 'Lockup Quotas,'" *Prison Legal News*, July 31, 2015, https://tinyurl.com/z7szbbm.

[81] "How Private Prison Companies Increase Recidivism," In the Public Interest, June 2016, https://tinyurl.com/za7og9j.

[82] Julie Hirschfield Davis, "Trump Backs Air Traffic Control Privatization," *The New York Times*, June 5, 2017, https://tinyurl.com/ya9xglng.

[83] *Ibid.*

[84] Sully Sullenberger, "Miracle on Hudson pilot: Don't privatize air traffic control," *USA Today*, Oct. 18, 2017, https://tinyurl.com/yckvrlcc.

[85] Jacob Fischler, "Holding Pattern, A chairman's plan for air traffic control is still circling the House, unable to land," *CQ Weekly*, Nov. 13, 2017.

[86] Bart Jansen, "Senate panel rejects air-traffic control privatization," *USA Today*, July 25, 2017, https://tinyurl.com/y85nhl7e.

[87] David Savage, "Supreme Court poised to deal a sharp blow to unions for teachers and public employees," *Los Angeles Times*, Sept. 28, 2017, https://tinyurl.com/ydapgumr.

Bibliography

Selected Sources

Books

Gonzalez, Joaquin III, and Roger Kemp, *Privatization in Practice: Reports on Trends, Cases and Debates in Public Service by Business and Nonprofits*, 2nd ed., McFarland, 2016.

A collection of essays, edited by two public administration professors from Golden State University in San Francisco, explores the pluses and minuses of privatizing government services.

Michaels, Jon, *Constitutional Coup: Privatization's Threat to the American Republic*, Harvard University Press, 2017.

A law professor at the University of California, Los Angeles, argues that privatization threatens America's system of government by usurping power from civil servants and other participants in the democratic process.

Savas, E. S., *Privatization and Public-Private Partnerships*, 2nd ed., Chatham House, 1990.

A public affairs professor at the City University of New York who is considered a founder of the modern privatization movement outlines his ideas about the practical applications of the theory in this landmark book on the topic.

Verkuil, Paul, *Outsourcing Sovereignty: Why Privatization of Government Functions Threatens Democracy and What We Can Do About It*, Cambridge University Press, 2007.

A legal scholar concludes that privatizing essential functions undermines government officials and democratic practices.

Articles

Alexander, Brian, "Privatization Is Changing America's Relationship With Its Physical Stuff," *The Atlantic*, July 12, 2017, https://tinyurl.com/y7s8w8pr.

Privatization is turning citizens into customers, the author argues.

Bauer, Shane, "My four months as a private prison guard," *Mother Jones*, July/August 2016, https://tinyurl.com/yd7sc6fm.

An award-winning undercover investigation at a private prison in Louisiana finds violent conditions and an overworked staff.

Ivory, Danielle, Ben Protess and Griff Palmer, "In American Towns, Private Profits from Public Works," *The New York Times*, Dec. 24, 2016, https://tinyurl.com/ycmmx753.

An analysis of public works projects financed by Wall Street firms found that taxpayers often end up paying a much higher cost for utility bills because of contracts that guarantee certain returns for financial firms.

Manson, Katrina, "Erik Prince offers private military force in Afghanistan," *Financial Times*, Aug. 7, 2017, https://tinyurl.com/y9bqpv6j.

The founder of Blackwater, which provided private security forces for the U.S. government in Iraq before being shut down for abusive use of force, proposes creating a new private military force for Afghanistan.

O'Neal, Lydia, and David Sirota, "Trump's Infrastructure Plan is Actually Pence's — And It's All About Privatization," *Newsweek*, Sept. 4, 2017, https://tinyurl.com/y8wns48x.

President Trump's plan to use private financing for infrastructure spending are traced to Indiana's approach to building a private toll road, which eventually went bankrupt.

Porter, Eduardo, "When Public Outperforms Private in Services," *The New York Times*, Jan. 15, 2013, https://tinyurl.com/ybfozocv.

A review of privatized government enterprises here and abroad finds that such projects are successful when the privatized enterprises are given clear-cut goals and are rewarded for reaching those goals.

Reports and Studies

"Building America While Building the Middle Class: Best Practices for P3 Infrastructure Projects," In the Public Interest and Partnership for Working Families, March 9, 2016, https://tinyurl.com/y8ehnc9k.

A liberal think tank and a public interest advocacy group outline safeguards to ensure that taxpayers and workers benefit from public-private infrastructure projects.

Chassy, Paul, and Scott Amey, "Bad Business: Billions of Taxpayer Dollars Wasted on Hiring Contractors," Project on Government Oversight, Sept. 12, 2011, https://tinyurl.com/6lrp8ja.

Outsourcing government jobs to private contractors can end up costing more than having the government perform the same job in-house, according to a study by an organization dedicated to eliminating government waste.

Edwards, Chris, "Options for Federal Privatization and Reform Lessons from Abroad," Cato Institute, June 28, 2016, https://tinyurl.com/ya7g89nu.

A libertarian think tank outlines reasons for privatizing much of the federal government's operations and assets, including air traffic control, Amtrak and the U.S. Postal Service.

Stuart, Austill, and Leonard Gilroy, eds., "Annual Privatization Report 2017," Reason Foundation, https://tinyurl.com/y98ep6jm.

A libertarian think tank releases a yearly report tracking privatization trends in local, state and federal government in a variety of areas, including prisons and air and surface transportation.

The Next Step:

Additional Articles from Current Periodicals

Air Traffic Control

Davis, Julie Hirschfeld, "Trump Backs Air Traffic Control Privatization," *The New York Times*, June 5, 2017, https://tinyurl.com/ya9xglng.

President Trump endorsed a proposal to privatize air traffic control, but the move had no binding effect.

Jansen, Bart, "Senate panel rejects air-traffic control privatization," *USA Today*, July 25, 2017, https://tinyurl.com/y85nhl7e.

A Senate Appropriations subcommittee rejected President Trump's proposal to move air traffic controllers from the Federal Aviation Administration to a nonprofit corporation.

Sullenberger, Sully, "Miracle on Hudson pilot: Don't privatize air traffic control," *USA Today*, Oct. 18, 2017, https://tinyurl.com/yckvrlcc.

The retired airline pilot, famous for safely landing a disabled passenger jet in the Hudson River in 2009, argues in an op-ed that privatizing air-traffic control would threaten passenger safety.

Infrastructure Projects

Goldstein, Matthew, and Patricia Cohen, "Public-Private Projects Where the Public Pays and Pays," *The New York Times*, June 6, 2017, https://tinyurl.com/ycktaevb.

Supporters of public-private partnerships say infrastructure projects are completed faster and less expensively when the private sector is involved, but experts say there is little evidence such partnerships benefit taxpayers in the long term.

McWhirter, Cameron, "Indiana Highway Gives 'Black Eye' to Private Investment in Infrastructure," *The Wall Street Journal*, Aug. 9, 2017, https://tinyurl.com/y9urc84d.

A public-private Indiana highway project that is two years behind schedule and only 60 percent finished reflects the pitfalls of privatizing infrastructure projects.

Siegel, Josh, "Puerto Rico's oversight board considering privatization of 'failing' power utility," *Washington Examiner*, Nov. 7, 2017, https://tinyurl.com/y8mo84zj.

Puerto Rico's oversight board and Gov. Ricardo Rossello are divided on whether privatizing the bankrupt, state-run Puerto Rico Electric Power Authority is the best way to restore full power to the island.

Military Contractors

Carter, Philip, "No More Private Wars," *Slate*, Aug. 8, 2017, https://tinyurl.com/yaaqgjom.

A senior fellow at the Center for a New American Security, a national security think tank, says there is little evidence private contractors perform better than U.S. troops in combat.

Prince, Erik, "Erik Prince: Contractors, Not Troops, Will Save Afghanistan," *The New York Times*, Aug. 30, 2017, https://tinyurl.com/ybaswwty.

The founder of the security company formerly known as Blackwater USA says the best strategy for ending the war in Afghanistan is to withdraw most U.S. troops and use private contractors and U.S. Special Operations personnel to support the Afghan Army.

Zaleski, Andrew, "Lockheed Martin invests millions in defense start-ups to fast-track R&D," *CNBC*, Nov. 2, 2017, https://tinyurl.com/y7a6bnjr.

Defense contractors, including Lockheed Martin Ventures, have invested millions of dollars in startups working on innovations — in artificial intelligence, cybersecurity, space and other areas — that could be used for military purposes.

Protests

Yen, Hope, "After vets protests, new deal struck to end VA budget crisis," The Associated Press, PBS, July 28, 2017, https://tinyurl.com/ydcl4x7e.

Congressional lawmakers reached agreement in July on emergency money for the Veterans Affairs Department after veterans' groups protested that the House's original proposal tilted too far toward private-sector care.

Young, Anna, "Opponents Protest Potential County Airport Privatization Plan," *The Examiner*, July 19, 2017, https://tinyurl.com/y995b7bj.

More than 100 opponents of a plan to privatize the public airport in Westchester County, N.Y., said at a protest in July that the proposal would threaten air and water quality.

CITING CQ RESEARCHER

Sample formats for citing these reports in a bibliography include the ones listed below. Preferred styles and formats vary, so please check with your instructor or professor.

MLA STYLE

Mantel, Barbara. "Coal Industry's Future." CQ Researcher 17 June 2016: 529-552.

APA STYLE

Mantel, B. (2016, June 17). Coal Industry's Future. *CQ Researcher*, 6, 529-552.

CHICAGO STYLE

Mantel, Barbara. "Coal Industry's Future." *CQ Researcher*, June 17, 2016, 529-52.

In-depth Reports on Issues in the News

Are you writing a paper?

Need backup for a debate?

Want to become an expert on an issue?

For 90 years, students have turned to *CQ Researcher* for in-depth reporting on issues in the news. Reports on a full range of political and social issues are now available. Following is a selection of recent reports:

Civil Liberties
Privacy and the Internet, 12/15
Intelligence Reform, 5/15
Religion and Law, 11/14

Crime/Law
High-Tech Policing, 4/17
Forensic Science Controversies, 2/17
Jailing Debtors, 9/16
Decriminalizing Prostitution, 4/16
Restorative Justice, 2/16
The Dark Web, 1/16
Immigrant Detention, 10/15

Education
Affirmative Action and College Admissions, 11/17
Charter Schools, 3/17
Civic Education, 2/17
Student Debt, 11/16

Environment/Society
Future of Marriage, 12/17
Stolen Antiquities, 11/17
Climate Change and National Security, 9/17
Muslims in America, 7/17
Funding the Arts, 7/17

Health/Safety
Medical Breakthroughs, 9/17
Medical Marijuana, 7/17
Food Labeling, 6/17
Sports and Sexual Assault, 4/17

Politics/Economy
Democracy Under Stress, 10/17
Cyberwarfare Threat, 10/17
Universal Basic Income, 9/17
National Debt, 9/17
North Korea Showdown, 5/17
Rethinking Foreign Aid, 4/17

Upcoming Reports

Species Extinction, 12/15/17   Citizen Protests, 1/5/18   Future of Puerto Rico, 1/12/18

ACCESS

CQ Researcher is available in print and online. For access, visit your library or www.cqresearcher.com.

STAY CURRENT

For notice of upcoming *CQ Researcher* reports or to learn more about *CQ Researcher* products, subscribe to the free email newsletters, *CQ Researcher Alert!* and *CQ Researcher News*: http://cqpress.com/newsletters.

PURCHASE

To purchase a *CQ Researcher* report in print or electronic format (PDF), visit www.cqpress.com or call 866-427-7737. Single reports start at $15. Bulk purchase discounts and electronic-rights licensing are also available.

SUBSCRIBE

Annual full-service *CQ Researcher* subscriptions—including 44 reports a year, monthly index updates, and a bound volume—start at $1,131. Add $25 for domestic postage.

CQ Researcher Online offers a backfile from 1991 and a number of tools to simplify research. For pricing information, call 800-818-7243 or 805-499-9774 or email librarysales@sagepub.com.

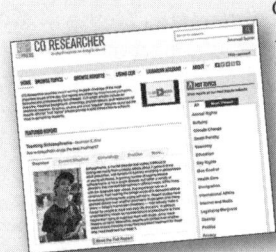

CQ RESEARCHER

CQPRESS

In-depth reports on today's issues

Published by CQ Press, an Imprint of SAGE Publications, Inc.   **www.cqresearcher.com**

Species Extinction

Is a mass die-off underway?

Fossil-fuel burning, deforestation, overhunting and other human activities are driving more and more animals, birds and plants to extinction, scientists say. Since 1970, the number of vertebrates — mammals, reptiles, amphibians, birds and fish — has dropped by more than half, and almost 200 species have become extinct. The loss of so many species in such a short time signals that a mass extinction, in which at least 75 percent of all species disappear, is occurring, many researchers say. A mass extinction would take place over thousands of years, endangering the global food supply and perhaps even human survival. But other scientists deny such a catastrophe has begun. The losses are part of the planet's evolutionary history, they say, noting that as species die new ones take their place. Still, both sides agree that humans must do better at protecting Earth's biodiversity — the web of dependency that ties together plants, animals and humans. Many scientists say that adopting biodiversity-friendly alternatives, such as using renewable fuels and better managing suburban sprawl, could significantly slow the disappearance of plants and wild animals.

An estimated 900 mountain gorillas remain on Earth, including this silverback in Virunga National Park in the Democratic Republic of the Congo. Many scientists say the current extinction rate of plant and animal species is at least 100 times higher than the historical average. Some argue this indicates Earth is undergoing a mass extinction, or the loss of more than 75 percent of all species.

CQ Researcher • Dec. 15, 2017 • www.cqresearcher.com
Volume 27, Number 44 • Pages 1041-1064

THIS REPORT

I N S I D E	
THE ISSUES	.................**1043**
BACKGROUND	.............**1049**
CHRONOLOGY	.............**1051**
CURRENT SITUATION	......**1056**
AT ISSUE	....................**1057**
OUTLOOK	..................**1059**
BIBLIOGRAPHY	.............**1062**
THE NEXT STEP	............**1063**

Species Extinction

The Issues

1043
- Is a mass extinction underway?
- Could humans survive a mass extinction?
- Can species extinctions be slowed, stopped or reversed?

Background

1049   **Life History**
Fossils uncovered in North America led a French scientist in the 1790s to suspect that species can become extinct.

1050   **Climate and Ecology**
An 1820s French physicist first described the "greenhouse effect."

1052   **Mass Extinctions Revisited**
A paleontologist in the 1950s revived studies of prehistoric die-offs.

1054   **Species on the Brink**
The Baiji dolphin and other species became extinct in the early 2000s despite increased conservation efforts.

Current Situation

1056   **Trump Administration**
President Trump is scaling back environmental regulations that protect wildlife.

1058   **Global Developments**
Governments worldwide are doubling down on conservation efforts.

Outlook

1059   **Action Urged**
Experts say aggressive steps are needed to prevent a mass extinction.

Sidebars and Graphics

1044   **Thousands of Species on Path to Extinction**
In addition to species at risk of extinction, thousands more are in decline at unknown rates.

1045   **Asteroids, Volcanoes Caused Mass Extinctions**
Earth has experienced five major die-offs in its 4.5 billion-year history.

1048   **Scientists Count Rising Number of Species**
Researchers say 25,821 species are under threat in 2017.

1051   **Chronology**
Key events since 1796.

1052   **Scientists Link Biodiversity Threats to Human Survival**
"We remain organisms absolutely dependent on other organisms."

1054   **Entrepreneur Brings Business Skills to Conservation Movement**
The goal "is to see populations of threatened animals stabilize."

1057   **At Issue:**
Should cost factor into whether a species is listed as endangered?

For Further Research

1061   **For More Information**
Organizations to contact.

1062   **Bibliography**
Selected sources used.

1063   **The Next Step**
Additional articles.

1063   **Citing CQ Researcher**
Sample bibliography formats.

Cover: Getty Images/LightRocket/Thierry Falise

 **CQ RESEARCHER**

Dec. 15, 2017
Volume 27, Number 44

EXECUTIVE EDITOR: Thomas J. Billitteri
tjb@sagepub.com

ASSISTANT MANAGING EDITORS: Kenneth Fireman, kenneth.fireman@sagepub.com, Kathy Koch, kathy.koch@sagepub.com, Scott Rohrer, scott.rohrer@sagepub.com

ASSOCIATE MANAGING EDITOR: Val Ellicott

SENIOR CONTRIBUTING EDITOR:
Thomas J. Colin
tom.colin@sagepub.com

CONTRIBUTING WRITERS: Marcia Clemmitt, Sarah Glazer, Alan Greenblatt, Reed Karaim, Barbara Mantel, Patrick Marshall, Tom Price

SENIOR PROJECT EDITOR: Olu B. Davis

EDITORIAL ASSISTANT: Natalia Gurevich

FACT CHECKERS: Eva P. Dasher, Michelle Harris, Betsy Towner Levine, Robin Palmer

SAGE Publishing | **CQPRESS**

Los Angeles I London I New Delhi
Singapore I Washington DC I Melbourne

An Imprint of SAGE Publications, Inc.

SENIOR VICE PRESIDENT, GLOBAL LEARNING RESOURCES:
Karen Phillips

EXECUTIVE DIRECTOR, ONLINE LIBRARY AND REFERENCE PUBLISHING:
Todd Baldwin

CQ Researcher (ISSN 1056-2036) is printed on acid-free paper. Published weekly, except: (March wk. 4) (May wk. 4) (July wks. 1, 2) (Aug. wks. 2, 3) (Nov. wk. 4) and (Dec. wks. 3, 4). Published by SAGE Publications, Inc., 2455 Teller Rd., Thousand Oaks, CA 91320. Annual full-service subscriptions start at $1,131. For pricing, call 1-800-818-7243. To purchase a CQ Researcher report in print or electronic format (PDF), visit www.cqpress.com or call 866-427-7737. Single reports start at $15. Bulk purchase discounts and electronic-rights licensing are also available. Periodicals postage paid at Thousand Oaks, California, and at additional mailing offices. POSTMASTER: Send address changes to CQ Researcher, 2600 Virginia Ave., N.W., Suite 600, Washington, DC 20037.

Species Extinction

BY MARCIA CLEMMITT

THE ISSUES

Toughie was no ordinary frog. To his many fans, his death last year at the Atlanta Botanical Garden was as sad as the passing of a family pet. But for scientists, Toughie's death represented something more ominous. He was the last-known member of a species — Rabbs' fringe-limbed tree frog — that scientists had discovered only a dozen years ago in the tree canopies of central Panama.

Now they fear the bug-eyed amphibians are extinct. Toughie died of natural causes, but the rest of the species probably died from a fungus, likely dispersed through the exportation of frogs for medical and scientific use, which has destroyed hundreds of amphibian populations worldwide in the past 30 years. [1]

The amphibians' disappearance is part of a global trend that has scientists warning that Earth could be experiencing a mass extinction of wildlife — the loss of 75 percent or more of the planet's 8.7 million plant and animal species — as has happened five times in Earth's 4.5 billion-year history.

A mass extinction would take place over thousands of years, eventually endangering the global food supply and perhaps even human survival. So rapidly and widely have populations of many animals decreased over the past several decades that the situation is best described as a "case of biological annihilation," said Rodolfo Dirzo, a professor of biology at Stanford University in Palo Alto, Calif., and co-author of a study on animal-population declines. [2]

Climate change, deforestation, poaching and suburban sprawl are among the causes behind the disappearance of

The last known Rabbs' fringe-limbed tree frog on Earth died last year at the Atlanta Botanical Garden, leading scientists to believe the species is now extinct. Extinction threatens 41 percent of amphibian species and 25 percent of mammal species. Many plant and animal populations have declined rapidly over the past several decades, due largely to climate change, deforestation, poaching and suburban sprawl.

Courtesy Atlanta Botanical Garden

wild-animal and -plant populations, many scientists say. These researchers warn that losses to the planet's biodiversity — the profusion of plants and animals that work together to support life — threaten human societies by endangering food supplies and perhaps even the future of homo sapiens. [3]

In mid-November, more than 15,300 scientists from 184 countries sent a "warning to humanity" that humans "have unleashed a mass extinction event, the sixth in roughly 540 million years, wherein many current life forms could be annihilated or at least committed to extinction by the end of this century." [4]

Others, however, say fears of a mass extinction are overblown.

"Many now assume that we are in the midst of a human-caused 'Sixth Mass Extinction' . . . but we're not," said Stewart Brand, an entrepreneur and writer who specializes in environmental and social sustainability. "The five historic mass ex-

tinctions eliminated 70 percent or more of all species in a relatively short time. That is not going on now." [5]

Regardless of which side is right, scientists' understanding of both past mass extinctions and present-day threats to wild animals and plants has greatly improved in recent decades. Among their findings:

- More than 99 percent of species that have ever existed are now extinct. [6]
- The number of vertebrates dropped by up to 58 percent between 1970 and 2012. For example, habitat loss and unsustainable hunting have drastically driven down the numbers of elephants and pangolins, scale-covered mammals found in Africa. [7]
- Wildlife now makes up only 3 percent of Earth's land animals, by weight (biomass), with the other 97 percent consisting of humans, livestock and pets. Marine species are harder to count, but a similar transformation has occurred in the oceans, where the number of large predators, including cod and tuna, has dropped by up to 90 percent since 1950, mostly from overfishing. [8]
- Extinction threatens 41 percent of amphibian species and 25 percent of mammal species. [9]

The loss of habitats from human-related activities is a major factor driving the decline of wildlife populations. Since 1900, as the human population has soared from 1.6 billion to 7.6 billion, land mammals have steadily lost territory. In a study of 177 wild mammal species, researchers said all lost at least 30 percent of their ranges, and more than 40 percent lost 80 percent or more. [10]

Also hard hit are coral reefs, large undersea ridges made of calcium carbonate secreted by tiny marine animals,

Thousands of Species on Path to Extinction

The threats facing living things extend beyond endangered species — those at risk of extinction — to those in decline at unknown rates.

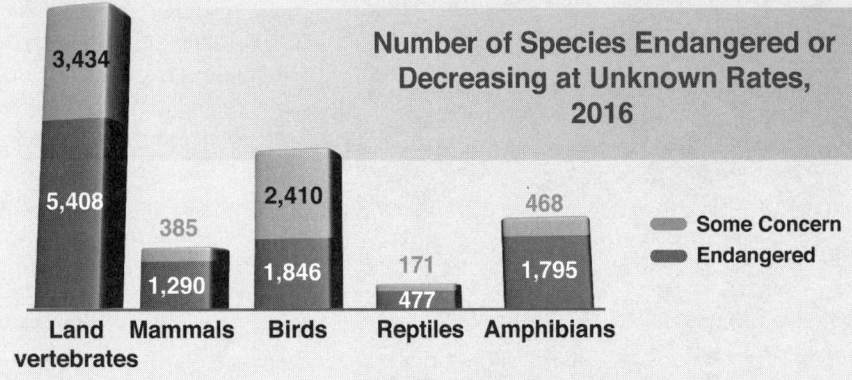

Source: Gerardo Ceballos et al., "Biological annihilation via the ongoing sixth mass extinction signaled by vertebrate population losses and declines," Proceedings of the National Academy of Sciences Online, March 28, 2017, p. 5, https://tinyurl.com/yb3m7nod

which have fallen victim to climate warming and ocean acidification. These valuable undersea ecosystems provide nitrogen and other nutrients as well as shelter to many marine species, protect shorelines from storms and serve as nurseries for fish. However, 19 percent of the world's coral reefs are already dead, while 38 percent of coral species are vulnerable to extinction. [11]

Despite such clear evidence of humans' power to drive extinctions, the popular notion persists that it takes an asteroid strike or other catastrophic event to cause widespread extinctions, scientists say. "People say, 'We're just humans. We're not destroying these things,' " says Simon Darroch, an assistant professor of earth and environmental sciences at Vanderbilt University in Nashville, Tenn. But not only is it possible for one animal species to drive other species to extinction, it's almost certainly happened before, says Darroch.

Recent research suggests that about 540 million years ago the Earth's first large extinction — called the End-Ediacaran, and not quite one of the big five mass extinctions — occurred after some animals evolved new abilities to change the environment, such as by burrowing tunnels on the seafloor, he says. Previously dominant species were unable to adapt to changes made by these "ecosystem engineers," and widespread extinction followed, Darroch says.

Today, humans are the ecosystem engineers, he says. From paving over wetlands to poaching elephants, "humans aren't good at promoting species richness," he says. "And the idea should really be in the public consciousness. We shouldn't be surprised about it."

Louise Glew, the global lead scientist at the conservation group World Wildlife Fund, says there has been "a very rapid loss of species, of biodiversity. And from a scientific standpoint, there's very little doubt humans are responsible."

One 2017 estimate found that 200 species of vertebrates have gone extinct in the last 100 years. By contrast, "if subjected to the estimated 'background' or 'normal' extinction rate prevailing in the last 2 million years, the 200 ver-

tebrate species . . . would have taken . . . up to 10,000 [years] to disappear," three researchers wrote in the Proceedings of the National Academy of Sciences. [12]

Brand agrees that the decline in wild-animal populations is a serious problem, one that can sometimes damage entire ecosystems. But talk of a mass extinction being underway "introduces an emotional charge that makes the problem seem cosmic and overwhelming rather than local and solvable," he wrote. [13]

Several scientists also note that throughout Earth's history, as some species go extinct, others that are better adapted to current conditions evolve and replace them.

"Extinction is the engine of evolution, the mechanism by which natural selection prunes the poorly adapted and allows the hardiest to flourish," wrote R. Alexander Pyron, an associate professor of biology at George Washington University. "Species constantly go extinct," and all species are endangered. [14]

Unquestionably, however, humans could do much more to preserve species, many scientists say. For example, exploiting technology to halt overfishing could save fish populations, such as the bluefin tuna, said Chris D. Thomas, a professor of conservation biology at the United Kingdom's University of York. By 2100, technology should be developed to replace as much as possible of the wild-caught and farmed fish in today's diets with edible fish tissues cultured in factories, he said. [15]

Reluctance to change habits or fear that protecting biodiversity could harm the economy often block such proposals, scientists say. In October, the House Committee on Natural Resources approved and sent five bills to the full House designed to limit the scope of the 1973 Endangered Species Act, which grants federal protection to species under threat. Committee Chairman Bob Bishop, R-Utah, has said he would "love to invalidate the act," which he calls a federal power grab that prevents residents from controlling their own land. The legislation's prospects are uncertain, but most observers agree that its chances have improved with Republicans controlling Congress and the White House. [16]

In reducing the size of the Bears Ears National Monument, home to numerous endangered species, President Trump said in early December, "Some people think that the natural resources of Utah should be controlled by a small handful of very distant bureaucrats located in Washington. And guess what? They're wrong." [17]

Ultimately, what to do about such questions rests with the public, many scientists say.

"Public awareness waxes and wanes," says ecologist Bradley Cardinale, a professor at the University of Michigan's School for Environment and Sustainability in Ann Arbor. "We've had 20 years now where biodiversity hasn't been on the radar screen," he says. "Nevertheless, many people have the strong feeling that they are impacted by nature. I think we're at the beginning of another wave of awareness."

As scientists, lawmakers and the public debate the effect of species loss on their lives, here are some of the questions being asked:

Is a mass extinction underway?

A surprisingly large number of animal species have gone extinct over the past few centuries, biologists say. "There's nothing magical about this planet that protects biodiversity. It's been lost before," says Jonathan Payne, a professor of geological sciences at Stanford University in Palo Alto, Calif.

Less clear, however, is whether these losses constitute a "mass extinction," similar to the five major mass extinctions in Earth's history, each of which wiped out at least three-quarters of all species. (*See chart, above.*) The first occurred about 440 million years ago, probably due to extreme cooling and falling sea levels. Subsequent extinctions

---

Asteroids, Volcanoes Caused Mass Extinctions

Planet Earth has experienced five major mass extinctions in its 4.5 billion-year history. The largest, the Permian, wiped out 96 percent of species as well as Earth's forests and coral reefs. The most well-known extinction, the Cretaceous-Tertiary, claimed about 80 percent of animal species, including the dinosaurs.

The Five Biggest Mass Extinctions in Earth's History

Extinction	Period	Description
Ordovician-Silurian	440 million years ago	When most plants and animals, including jawless fish, lived in tropical waters, extreme cooling and falling sea levels killed about 85 percent of species.
Late Devonian	365 million years ago	When most species still lived in the sea, oceanic "dead zones" likely caused by de-oxygenation killed three-quarters of species.
Permian	250 million years ago	The so-called Great Dying destroyed about 96 percent of species, likely due to climate warming caused by volcanic eruptions. Scientists believe Earth's ecosystems needed 10 million to 15 million years to recover.
Triassic-Jurassic	200 million years ago	About three-fourths of species died from uncertain causes, possibly climate warming caused by volcanic eruptions, clearing the way for dinosaurs to dominate Earth.
Cretaceous-Tertiary	65 million years ago	Climate change caused by volcanic eruptions and/or an asteroid strike killed off the dinosaurs. Most mammals, which were then small, survived and eventually came to dominate the planet as they grew in size, number and complexity.

Sources: "Big Five mass extinction events," BBC Nature, 2017, https://tinyurl.com/cw2x786; Michael J. Benton, "Mass Extinctions," New Scientist, March 5, 2011, https://tinyurl.com/mgl9bfh

---

occurred about 365 million years ago, possibly due to deoxygenation of the oceans; about 250 million years ago, likely due to climate warming because of volcanic eruptions; about 200 million years ago, for uncertain reasons; and about 65 million years ago, possibly due to an asteroid strike and volcanic eruptions. [18]

Douglas Erwin, curator of Paleozoic invertebrates at the Smithsonian Na-

tional Museum of Natural History in Washington, said humans are doing plenty of damage to many species, but it is inaccurate to say that a sixth mass extinction is underway.

Erwin compares a mass extinction to a large electrical blackout. Both power grids and ecosystems are complex interacting webs, or networks, and they collapse in similar ways, he said. In 2003, for example, a software bug in a power plant's control room in Ohio caused a blackout that spread quickly from Ohio and Michigan, east to New York City and north to Toronto. The small localized failure thus triggered a cascade of secondary failures across the network, Erwin said. [19]

Tusks of elephants killed by poachers for their ivory are shown in Bayanga, Central African Republic, on March 16, 2015. In Mali in West Africa, civil conflict left elephants unprotected, and poachers killed 163 animals, more than a third of the nation's northern herd, between 2012 and 2017. This year, Mali's government has successfully protected the herd.

Likewise, in mass extinctions, "there's a very rapid collapse of the ecosystems" as food webs and other interactions among organisms fail in unexpected ways, Erwin said. As with a massive power blackout, evidence of an ecosystem collapse is unmistakable. Such evidence is currently lacking, he said. [20]

Paul Olsen, a professor of biology and paleo environment at Columbia University in New York City, argues that a human-driven mass extinction has been ongoing for 50,000 years.

According to Olsen, it began when "humans spread out of Africa and wiped out all the megafauna," or large animals, including the woolly mammoths in Europe and North America.

Then humans began destroying wildlife habitats, polluting the air and water and changing the climate, all still ongoing today, he said. [21]

Other scientists who believe a sixth mass extinction is underway point to amphibians as evidence.

Amphibians — cold-blooded vertebrates such as frogs, most of which spend part of their lives in water and part on land — evolved about 360 million years ago and persisted in similar form through the last three mass extinctions, says David Wake, a professor emeritus of integrative biology at the University of California, Berkeley. "They have evolved many ways to cope" with environmental changes, such as hibernating under mud for years without food or water. "They are very fit organisms," he says.

Now, however, hundreds of amphibian species have disappeared in the past 20 to 30 years, says Vance Vredenburg, an associate professor of biology at San Francisco State University.

Habitat loss, climate change and pollution are all stressing amphibian populations. But the prime culprit, he says, is a fungal disease that likely spread worldwide when frogs were farmed as food and exported for medical and scientific use.

"The amphibians are a harbinger, showing us where things may be going," says Vredenburg. "In the big picture, the deep perspective, we really do believe we've entered a sixth mass extinction."

Humans have always had an underappreciated ability to change ecosystems and put stress on other species, says Roy Plotnick, a professor of earth and environmental sciences at the University of Illinois, Chicago. To grasp this, he says, compare human hunting and fishing to the behavior of other predators. "Humans go after the big and the healthy animals," he says, threatening the survival of prey communities by picking off the very animals likely to raise healthy offspring to adulthood. "Other predators simply don't do that," he says. Instead, they mainly kill weaker prey.

Those scientists who doubt that a mass extinction is already underway nevertheless argue that a tipping point may be nearing, at which a mass extinction becomes possible or even inevitable.

Growing evidence suggests that after an ecosystem has experienced a long series of changes, at some point a single, small external event could trigger a massive loss, wrote Anthony Barnosky, a professor of integrative biology at the University of California, Berkeley, in a 2011 paper. For instance, a small increase in the number of fish harvested from a marine fishery may suddenly and unexpectedly cause an entire species to collapse. [22]

Some extinction skeptics argue that talk of a sixth extinction paints a misleading picture of nature — namely, how resilient species and ecosystems can be. This resilience is evident in the number of new species that are evolving as others go extinct, said the University of York's Thomas.

As humans move around the globe, they carry organisms with them, ranging from bacteria to rodents and livestock. When these animals and plants reach their new homes, some evolve into new species, better suited to those environments, he said. "In the human era we are seeing great losses [of species]," Thomas said. "But we are also seeing all these biological gains of new animals and plants spreading around the world, new hybrids coming into existence." [23]

Examples include the house sparrow, originally a native of Asian prairies but now common worldwide. The bird also is evolving new variations. The sparrows in cold regions are larger than those in warmer climes. In Italy, the house sparrow "met up with the Spanish sparrow and they hybridized, and there's now a new species called the Italian sparrow," Thomas said. [24]

Could humans survive a mass extinction?

Evidence that the loss of a species affects humans is easy to find, says Stuart Pimm, a professor of conservation ecology at Duke University in Durham, N.C. For example, marine biologists "feel that a huge threat is the overfishing that's wiped out large species — predators such as sharks," threatening the survival of ocean fishing grounds and the lower-income communities that depend on them, he says. Loss of a major species, especially a predator, often leads to other species' extinction, sometimes causing an entire ecosystem to collapse.

The famous *Joy of Cooking* cookbook, first published in 1931 and most recently in 2006, inadvertently tells the tale of dwindling fish species, says Pimm. Produced under the supervision of three generations of one family, *Joy of Cooking* began with cod and herring recipes, shifted to sea bass and orange roughie in the late 20th century and now features recipes for tilapia, which is mostly raised on fish farms. Those are not a sign of changed tastes but a sign of the decline of many fish, he says.

But while many scientists agree that humans eventually could face extreme difficulties if large numbers of species die off, others say humans' ability to manipulate the environment suggests that homo sapiens can likely survive a mass extinction.

Today, wild forests have almost disappeared, human-generated trash and industrial pollution are everywhere and human-created carbon-dioxide emissions may be altering the climate more quickly than at any time in Earth's history, said Erle Ellis, a professor of geography and environmental systems at the University of Maryland, Baltimore County. Nevertheless, "over the last two centuries . . . most humans have enjoyed longer, healthier and freer lives" than ever. There seems to be no reason that can't continue, he said. [25]

"[The] sixth mass extinction on Earth is going to happen," said Annalee Newitz, a science and technology journalist who wrote the 2013 book *Scatter, Adapt, and Remember: How Humans Will Survive a Mass Extinction*. But humans have a long history of altering the environment to meet their needs, so optimism is warranted, she wrote. [26]

Building underground cities and colonizing space to escape problems on Earth will be in the mix, wrote Newitz. Geoengineers also are devising ways to "cool the planet down and remove carbon dioxide from the atmosphere" to make Earth more hospitable for humans and the organisms and ecosystems that supply food and other needs, she said. Dumping the mineral lime into the oceans could cool the planet by doubling the oceans' ability to absorb carbon dioxide, for example. Most geoengineering ideas remain theoretical and would likely be extremely expensive to implement, but futurists predict that effective and affordable methods will be found, Newitz said. [27]

Other observers are less optimistic, predicting that, while some humans may survive a mass extinction, the human population will shrink substantially.

Climate change could reach a tipping point as soon as a century from now, after which any further increase in temperature would be "deadly," says Gerta Keller, a professor of geosciences at Princeton University in New Jersey. For humans, "the best-case scenario will be moving to cooler latitudes. But a lot less food will be grown. Populations will decrease. There will be war, famine and fighting for space in those cooler latitudes. In the worst-case scenario, those things could wipe us out."

The story of life on Earth is the story of species becoming dominant and then disappearing, said Kenneth Lacovara, founding dean of Rowan University's School of the Earth and Environment in Glassboro, N.J. "The lesson from all of paleontology is things don't last forever. Worlds don't have to have humans, just as they don't have to have dinosaurs." [28]

Humans have always depended for survival on other species and on multiple ecosystems, many scientists note. Moreover, researchers continue to discover unexpected ways in which a species' loss may put humans' well-being and even their lives at risk.

For example, research in Kenya shows that the loss of large species such as zebras, giraffes and elephants from an area often triggers a population explosion among rodents. In turn, the disease-carrying ectoparasites that live on rodents increase, raising the risks of disease transmission to humans and other animals, said Stanford's Dirzo. [29]

Three-quarters of the world's food supply comes from just 12 crops and five animal species, according to a report from the agricultural-development research group Bioversity International in Rome. Meanwhile, tens of thousands of edible wild or rarely cultivated species are being pushed toward extinction, a potentially life-threatening

Scientists Count Rising Number of Species

The International Union for Conservation of Nature (IUCN) gathers data on an ever-growing number of species in order to monitor their status. In the last 17 years, the number of species the IUCN assessed for extinction threats grew nearly sixfold, from 16,510 to 91,523. Over that period the number of species found under threat of extinction — the "Red List" — also rose, but at a slower rate.

(No. of Species)

Number of Species Inventoried by IUCN, 2000-17

Species assessed
Threatened species

"Red List"

2000 2001 2002 2003 2004 2005 2006 2007 2008 2009 2010 2011 2012 2013 2014 2015 2016 2017

Source: "An expanding Red List: knowledge gaps and fully assessed groups," International Union for Conservation of Nature, 2017, https://tinyurl.com/y9bg3k75

outcome for humans, says the group. These vanishing species — and their genetic diversity — would be the only backstops against famine if currently farmed species encounter a disease to which they have no resistance or prove unable to adapt to climate changes. [30]

The World Wildlife Fund's Glew says, "The number of people who depend on marine-caught fish is very large," and the stocks are dwindling. Less fish consumed means a less healthy diet; in children, for instance, a protein-deficient diet can have severe consequences, Glew says.

Numerous organisms are on the brink of extinction whose loss would greatly affect humans, says Plotnick of the University of Illinois. For example, many bat populations face numerous stresses, including a deadly fungal disease, and if a bat population is lost "then insect populations could explode," increasing the spread of often-deadly insect-borne disease. As such changes driven by species loss accumulate, they "may well make it impossible to sustain ourselves."

Natural ecosystems, not human engineering, provide necessities such as

clean water, flood control and home-building materials for much of the world's population, says Berkeley's Wake. Loss of species and ecosystems has already drastically diminished those resources in some poor countries. "When you see a civilization that's depleted its natural resources, there's no chance that it can be a stable society," he says.

Can species extinctions be slowed, stopped or reversed?

Humans have already claimed more than 50 percent of Earth's land mass for monoculture agriculture and human habitation, says Michigan's Cardinale, "and this habitat loss is driving extinctions." Nevertheless, portions of that land — both rural and urban — can be made hospitable for wild species again, he says.

Restoring habitat to whatever extent possible is crucial. "Absolutely, cities can be transformed" to permit more wild species to share the space with humans, Cardinale says. One way is to use native plants — which can provide food and habitat for native birds and insects — as ground cover to prevent soil erosion.

With about 17 percent of North American bird species in decline, sprawling urban and suburban areas can be redesigned to provide habitat, many environmentalists say.

Breaking up lawns with the right kind of shrubs, mowing a bit less often to make grassy areas hospitable to native pollinators such as bees, and keeping pet cats indoors are proven ways to bring more native wildlife, especially birds, back to town, said Susanna Lerman, a U.S. Department of Agriculture research ecologist and an adjunct faculty member at the University of Massachusetts, Amherst. [31]

Some urban and suburban areas around the world are already creating more wild-species habitat.

Baltimore County, Md., requires 80 percent of trees planted on county land to be tall canopy trees — half of them oak — rather than flowering trees or other smaller trees. Native trees, especially oaks, harbor many more caterpillars, a favorite bird food. [32]

In an effort to restore native pollinators and other dwindling species, the United Kingdom's Prince Charles in 2013 created a program to re-establish native-wildflower meadows around the country, including in cities such as London. Since the 1930s, U.K. meadow habitat has declined by 97 percent. So far, the program has created 90 meadows, covering about 1,000 acres. [33]

Meanwhile, "creating multifunctional [farm] landscapes capable of producing high [crop] yields for humans while enabling [wild] species to live and move are increasingly common management strategies in Europe, Japan and some other developed nations," said the University of Maryland's Ellis. [34]

In Iowa, where monoculture farming dominates, bringing native habitats back into the land-use mix can benefit farms while increasing wildlife numbers, say Matthew Liebman, a professor of agronomy, and Lisa Schulte-Moore, a professor of natural resource ecology and management at Iowa State University, in Ames. Sixty-three percent of Iowa's land area and 82 percent of its crop area have been given over to corn and soybean farming in recent decades. This monoculture land-use pattern has increased soil erosion, degraded water quality (due to fertilizer, herbicide and pesticide runoff) and caused herbicide-resistant weeds to proliferate, Liebman and Schulte-Moore said. [35]

Now research demonstrates that interspersing Iowa's single-crop fields with strips of native prairie plants provides habitat that attracts native insects — increasing biodiversity while decreasing soil erosion, fertilizer runoff and the need for herbicides, the Iowa State scientists said. [36]

One of the most ambitious proposals for preserving biodiversity comes from E.O. Wilson, a professor emeritus of entomology at Harvard University. He proposes setting aside half the planet's land and half its seas as refuges for wild species. Currently, only 15 percent of the land and 3 percent of the oceans are protected for wildlife. [37]

The 50 percent goal can be reached by allowing "large and small fragments around the world to remain relatively natural, without removing people living there or changing property rights," wrote Wilson. This set-aside could conceivably save more than 90 percent of species and most kinds of ecosystems, he calculates.

But while science has shown that at least some species loss can be stemmed and native wild plants and animals brought back to the land, a substantial barrier to doing it remains, many scientists say. Humans may not think the effort is worthwhile.

"The public looks at these things and says, 'Yeah, [species are] changing but it's all still the same,' " says Princeton's Keller. "That's a big problem. They don't see what scientists see," so many are reluctant to change habitual ways, she says.

Winning agreement among humans with competing interests about which

actions to take is likely the most daunting challenge that species conservation faces, said the University of Maryland's Ellis. Conservatives, businesses and many landowners have long complained that protecting species is costly and harms the economy. Rep. Pete Olson, R-Texas, recently called the Endangered Species Act "a political weapon for extreme environmentalists." [38]

Ellis said setting aside 10 percent of farmland for wild-species prairie plots may require some landowners to give up some cropland, potentially leading to resentments and conflict. That makes conservation "a demanding social project" that "requires intensive and ongoing negotiations and investments shared among landowners, governments, the public, businesses and other stakeholders." [39]

Meanwhile, de-extinction technologies that could revive some extinct species — or plausible substitutes for them — are on the horizon, although not yet operational. These technologies use methods such as combining an extinct animal's DNA with that of a closely related living species to create a hybrid animal.

Such technologies hold promise, but they are expensive and might siphon resources from conservation efforts, many scientists say, so their use should be scrutinized in each case. For example, bringing back a recently extinct species might make sense if the species' habitat is still intact and its return would restore an ecosystem to wholeness, said Stanford's Dirzo. [40]

But if reviving an animal would not help restore a valuable ecosystem, de-extinction should probably not be used, many scientists say.

"If this is always going to be a zoo animal, then stop," said Ben Novak, lead scientist at Revive & Restore, a San Francisco group that studies and implements biotech conservation methods. "The goals have to be about ecological restoration and function." [41] ■

BACKGROUND

Life History

The theory that human activities, such as fossil-fuel use, single-crop agriculture, urban sprawl and overfishing, may be leading to a "mass extinction" of most plant and animal species has emerged over the past few decades. The scientific ideas that led many researchers to that conclusion, however, have been accumulating for two centuries. Before that, the idea that any animals had become extinct was all but unthinkable. [42]

About 200 years ago, paleontologists began announcing extraordinary findings: Studies of fossils showed that animal species quite different from modern-day ones had apparently lived in the far distant past, then vanished from the planet. Until then, most Westerners believed the biblical account of creation: the Earth was about 6,000 years old, and God created all living creatures in six days.

Adventurers have always come upon unusual sights, but 18th-century European explorers in North America's forests, in particular, seemed to turn up even more remains of strange animals than others. These included the skeletons of what seemed to be elephants — but five or six times as large as living elephants and with carnivores' teeth. At the time, people assumed the creatures still existed somewhere on the largely unexplored planet. The giant elephant never turned up, however, but more unusual bones and fossils did. Even bones of a huge winged, lizard-like animal — the pterodactyl — were found and assembled.

In the 1790s the French naturalist Georges Cuvier, then the world's greatest expert on animal anatomy, began careful study of the bones, concluding that the strange animals had become extinct. Moreover, Cuvier argued, a series of catastrophic changes on the planet had likely wiped the animals out. [43]

While Cuvier's pronouncements initially shocked the scientific world, his idea that different animals roamed the planet in different eras, before vanishing, took hold over the next few decades. By the early 19th century, the idea that both the Earth itself and the living things on it had histories became an important theme across the sciences.

Some hypothesized that Earth's history was more one of gradual transitions than of the sudden extinction-triggering changes Cuvier envisioned.

The most famous of these "gradualists" was the British biologist Charles Darwin.

Early study of the work of Scottish geologist Charles Lyell convinced Darwin that most of Earth's landforms likely formed gradually over long periods rather than in single cataclysmic events. After an earthquake struck in Chile, Darwin observed that a beach had risen eight feet. Clearly, a series of earthquakes occurring over hundreds of years, he concluded, could eventually raise a mountain range thousands of feet. [44]

Darwin extended the gradualism idea to two key questions about biology: how and why species go extinct, and where new species come from.

In his landmark 1859 book, *On the Origin of Species*, Darwin laid out his theory of evolution by natural selection. He proposed that inherited traits that better allow an organism to successfully reproduce accumulate over many generations, slowly changing an old species into a new one. Accordingly, each new

A humpback whale breaches off Australia's Gold Coast on June 9, 2016. Humpbacks were hunted nearly to extinction by the 1960s, when only an estimated 1,600 existed worldwide. The U.S. Endangered Species Act is credited with saving the whales, now numbering about 20,000 worldwide, as well as the bald eagle, grizzly bear, California condor and Florida manatee.

species is "produced and maintained by having some advantage over those with which it comes into competition; and the consequent extinction of less favoured forms almost inevitably follows," he wrote. [45]

Climate and Ecology

Earth's history also involves its so-called carbon cycle — the complicated process by which that vital chemical element circulates among plants and animals, through rocks and into the sea and the atmosphere, altering them as it goes. The carbon cycle is central to today's debates about climate change, and it, too was

first carefully analyzed by 19th-century scientists.

In the 1820s, French physicist Joseph Fourier described what was later named "the greenhouse effect" — that particular gases in Earth's atmosphere hold onto the sun's heat. [46]

In 1859, Irish physicist John Tyndall discovered that carbon dioxide was one of what today are called greenhouse gases. And in 1896, Swedish scientist Svante Arrhenius predicted that if the amount of atmospheric carbon dioxide doubled, the Earth's average atmospheric temperature would rise by about 9 degrees Fahrenheit. That is well off today's best estimate of just over 5 degrees, but not bad given the limited measuring and computational capacities of his time. [47]

Natural philosophers as far back as ancient Greece had speculated about how organisms interact with each other and the environment to create ecosystems. But the study of such interactive systems, called ecology, achieved status as a science only in the 20th century.

Widely considered the founder of ecological science, G. Evelyn Hutchinson, a professor of biology at Yale University in New Haven, Conn., brought mathematics to the field, studying how and why animal populations change in size and makeup over time and how the changes related to their environments. [48]

Out of such studies came a new focus on the meaning of life's immense diversity. Biological diversity — a term later shortened to biodiversity — comes in three forms:

- **Genetic diversity** — the different inheritable traits that members of a species pass on to offspring. A population with greater genetic diversity is more likely to produce some offspring that can survive environmental changes. [49]

- **Species diversity** — the number of species in existence (about 8.7 million).

Continued on p. 1052

Chronology

50,000 B.C.-A.D. 1800s

As humans spread across the planet, overhunting on several continents threatens large animals with extinction.

1796

French anatomist Georges Cuvier argues that catastrophic prehistoric events pushed animals such as mastodons and pterodactyls to extinction.

1859

Irish physicist John Tyndall finds that carbon dioxide helps the atmosphere hold heat.

1890s

Decades of habitat loss and overhunting by white hunters nearly drive the Great Plains bison to extinction.

1900s-1970s

Researchers explore the decline of wild species.

1901

Upset about the loss of bison and other animals, President Theodore Roosevelt establishes 150 national forests as well as 18 national monuments and numerous parks and game reserves, to protect U.S. wilderness.

1914

The last passenger pigeon in North America dies; the species, once numbering in the billions, was killed off by humans.

1934

An international treaty protects whales by setting catch limits.

1936

Tasmanian tigers, the world's largest carnivorous marsupial, become extinct.

1965

Columbia University paleontologist Norman Newell revives interest in catastrophic losses of species.

1970

World Wildlife Fund begins tracking biodiversity through its Living Planet Index.

1973

The Endangered Species Act provides federal protection for species threatened by extinction.

1978

In a ruling that added to the controversy over the Endangered Species Act, the Supreme Court halts construction of a Tennessee dam because its completion would threaten the endangered snail darter.

1980s-Present

Concerns grow that human activities are leading to a sixth major mass extinction.

1980

Geologist Walter Alvarez of the University of California, Berkeley, presents evidence that an asteroid strike may have killed off the dinosaurs.

1991

As the Soviet Union collapses, soaring poverty in Central Asia leads to overhunting and a massive die-off of the saiga antelope.

1992

The first international treaty committing nations to sustainable use of natural resources — the U.N. Convention on Biological Diversity — is signed at the Earth Summit.

1993

President Bill Clinton signs the Convention on Biological Diversity, but Senate Republicans block ratification, citing concerns about financing and the treaty's effect on land-use policies. The convention takes effect in December after 30 nations ratify it.

2002

Biodiversity Convention sets targets for reducing "unprecedented" biodiversity losses by 2010. The European Union and 195 countries have ratified or legally approved the treaty.

2012

Civil conflict in Mali in West Africa leaves elephants unprotected from ivory traffickers, who kill more than a third of that nation's northern herd between 2012 and 2017.

2016

Norway becomes the first government to announce it will not buy products, such as palm oil, that lead to deforestation.

2017

The Trump administration says it will shrink two sites in Utah that President Barack Obama in 2016 designated as protected national monuments and might weaken land-use restrictions on several more. . . . House Committee on Natural Resources approves and sends for House approval five bills to limit the scope of the Endangered Species Act. . . . Interior Department rejects 25 petitions for species to be added to the endangered species list. . . . An international scientific team completes an "atlas of life" to improve conservation efforts, adding location and population data for 10,064 reptile species to those already listed for 10,000 bird, 5,000 mammal and 6,000 amphibian species.

Scientists Link Biodiversity Threats to Human Survival

"We remain organisms absolutely dependent on other organisms."

Humans may appear to be masters of the planet, but some scientists say appearances are deceiving. "Soon we'll have the ability to reach other star systems, and the planets that circle them," wrote E.O. Wilson, a well-known champion of biodiversity and a professor emeritus of entomology at Harvard University. "Yet we ourselves, our physical bodies, have stayed as vulnerable as when we evolved millions of years ago. We remain organisms absolutely dependent on other organisms" for such basics as food, shelter and even oxygen to breathe. [1]

This vulnerability is due to biodiversity — the complex web of interrelationships that ties together the fates of Earth's plants, animals and humans.

While much is unknown about how biodiversity works, scientists increasingly worry that environmental damage and the loss of species put human survival at serious risk. Pulling one string of the biodiversity web, they say, leads to unforeseen, and often bad, consequences.

"If fungal diseases wipe out bats, for example, then what's going to happen with insect populations that bats eat? And how will that affect humans?" asks Roy Plotnick, a professor of earth and environmental sciences at the University of Illinois, Chicago.

In addition, three-quarters of the world's food supply comes from just 12 crops and five animal species, only a few varieties of which are widely cultivated, according to a report from the agricultural-development research group Bioversity International in Rome. Limited biodiversity led to the Irish potato famine of the mid-1800s, in which a million people starved to death because the genetically similar potatoes grown in Ireland were susceptible to a disease that turned them into inedible slime. [2]

Today, many of the tens of thousands of edible plant and animal species — including both those that grow wild and those that are cultivated in only a few places — are being pushed toward extinction, said Ann Tutwiler, Bioversity International's director general. [3]

At least 1,000 cultivated species — many of high value to humans — are endangered, she said. Malnutrition is widespread because in some poverty-stricken regions, human diets are "based on a narrow set of commodities" that supply only a limited number of nutrients, said Tutwiler. Many currently untapped species could help prevent famine, because some are more disease-resistant and adaptable to climate change than many cultivated varieties. [4]

Although not every extinction is a tragedy, assuring a livable future for humanity still means trying to save as many species as possible, said Chris D. Thomas, a professor of biology at England's University of York and the author of the 2017 book *Inheritors of the Earth*.

According to some estimates a mass extinction — when three-quarters of all species are lost — could occur in the next 10,000 years if current extinction rates do not slow, Thomas noted. "This is risky, given that species represent our planet's biological parachute. All future ecosystems will be formed from the descendants of existing species, and we do not know which of today's currently rare species will be important components of future ecosystems (especially if humans alter the planet in yet another, unexpected way)," he told an interviewer. [5]

Nevertheless, species extinctions are inevitable in a fast-changing world, and as many as 30 to 40 percent of all animal species might go extinct in the "near future," said R. Alexander Pyron,

Continued from p. 1050

Also can refer to the often large number that make up a single ecosystem, such as a forest. [50] Many species within an ecosystem are interdependent, such as when a species of bat drinks a plant's nectar and, in turn, disperses its pollen.

• **Ecosystem diversity** — the variety of Earth's interactive biological communities, from those living on Alpine slopes to the microbes in a human gut. These communities, too, perform different functions, such as when forests absorb carbon dioxide in the air and emit oxygen that animals breathe.

Ecologists' study of biodiversity has led to conclusions about how human activity affects it. One of ecology's

most concrete and widely applicable findings, for example, is the "species-area relationship." Simply put, it holds that the larger an ecosystem area is, the more species that area contains, and that the relationship between ecosystem size and species number can be expressed as a mathematical formula.

Thus, if a grassland was home to 100 species of birds, and half of it was converted into farmland or shopping malls, the species-area relationship can calculate "the proportion of bird species . . . that would be lost," wrote science journalist Elizabeth Kolbert. "Very roughly speaking, the answer is 10 percent" over time. [51]

Mass Extinctions Revisited

French animal anatomist Cuvier's notion that occasional catastrophic mass extinctions killed off most existing life forms made a comeback in the mid-20th century.

Invertebrate paleontologist Norman Newell, a professor of geology at Columbia University, began mulling the possibility of mass extinctions in the 1950s, as he studied the disappearance of some mollusks from the fossil record in several places from about 250 million years ago. Newell concluded that a climate change resulting from the carbon cycle caused a drastic sea-level drop

an associate professor of biology at George Washington University in Washington, D.C. "But both the planet and humanity can probably survive and even thrive in a world with fewer species." Conservation must focus on species and habitats that appear vital for humans to survive, such as crop-pollinating bees, he said. [6]

The challenge is deciding which species and ecosystems to target first for rescue, some scientists say. Sustained research over the past quarter century has begun to provide answers, says Bradley Cardinale, a professor at the University of Michigan's School for Environment and Sustainability in Ann Arbor.

In 2008, for example, Cardinale was on a research team that analyzed 40 studies of grassland ecosystems and the genetics of 177 flowering plants that lived in them. The aim: to figure out which flower species are most important to keeping grasslands healthy and thriving. [7] Among other "services" they supply, grasslands act as carbon sinks to help control atmospheric warming, slow rainwater runoff to prevent soil erosion and provide food and range for many species, such as pollinators.

The researchers found that the most genetically unique species in any ecosystem is the most crucial in sustaining the ecosystem's health. Buttercups, for instance, are a genetically unique grassland species, and if they disappear no other plants can easily replace them. Daisies and sunflowers, by contrast, are close genetic relatives and if one species vanished, the other could fill its role.

So, the study concluded, if confronted with a choice, save the buttercups.

— *Marcia Clemmitt*

A horse grazes in a meadow of buttercups. Unlike daisies and sunflowers, buttercups are a genetically unique species and difficult to replace if they become extinct, researchers say.

[2] "Monoculture and the Irish Potato Famine: cases of missing genetic variation," Understanding Evolution, UC Berkeley, https://tinyurl.com/yconakex; Damian Carrington, "Sixth mass extinction of wildlife also threatens global food supplies," *The Guardian*, Sept. 26, 2017, https://tinyurl.com/ycfqpfbv; and "Mainstreaming Agrobiodiversity in Sustainable Food Systems," Bioversity International, September 2017, https://tinyurl.com/y8gq36jp.

[3] Quoted in Carrington, *ibid.*

[4] *Ibid.*

[5] "Inheritors of the Earth: An interview with Chris D. Thomas," The Hoopoe blog, July 6, 2017, https://tinyurl.com/yb66u5kp.

[6] R. Alexander Pyron, "We don't need to save endangered species. Extinction is part of evolution," *The Washington Post*, Nov. 22, 2017, https://tinyurl.com/ybdjaav9.

[7] Gail Gallessich, "Current Mass Extinction Spurs Major Study of Which Plants to Save," *The Current*, University of California, Santa Barbara, Oct. 20, 2008, https://tinyurl.com/y9jn2dv6.

[1] Edward O. Wilson, *Half-Earth: Our Planet's Fight for Life* (2016), p. 13.

that led to the mass extinction, and he later hypothesized that another might be in the offing, driven by human activities such as fossil-fuel burning and population growth. [52]

Then, in 1980, a scientific team led by Walter Alvarez, a professor of geology at the University of California, Berkeley, shifted public fascination with the most recent mass extinction — 65 million years ago — into overdrive.

Alvarez's team, which included his father, Luis, a Nobel Prize-winning physicist, announced they had found evidence of a large asteroid or comet strike that likely killed off the dinosaurs. Around the world, layers of sedimentary rock laid down about the time dinosaurs

disappeared contain high levels of the element iridium — extremely rare in the Earth's crust — and shattered quartz grains that are evidence of a cosmic-level impact, Alvarez said. [53]

While the sci-fi drama of a massive rock from the sky killing off dinosaurs entranced the public, scientists increasingly pursued mass-extinction research on several fronts. The asteroid story is "dramatic and sexy, but it's a fairy tale," says Princeton's Keller.

Her study of the dinosaur die-off zeroed in on massive volcanic eruptions that occurred in the so-called Deccan Traps of west-central India, an area as large as Texas, New Mexico, Arizona and California combined. The dinosaur

extinction occurred in the middle of the biggest eruption and took place very rapidly, making the volcanoes an obvious culprit, Keller says.

The devastating killing power behind both an asteroid strike and a volcanic eruption is rapid climate warming, Keller explains. An asteroid releases greenhouse gases as it breaks apart carbon-containing rocks, while volcanoes violently emit hot greenhouse gases and melted rock into the atmosphere. But an asteroid's impact is equivalent to just one Deccan eruption, and the Deccan Traps erupted many times, making their effect much greater than an asteroid and a more likely mass-extinction cause, she argues.

Entrepreneur Brings Business Skills to Conservation Movement

The goal "is to see populations of threatened animals stabilize."

In 1994, Silicon Valley entrepreneur Charles Knowles sold the software company he founded five years earlier and devoted himself to a quite different enterprise: helping "charismatic megafauna" — large, popular animals such as snow leopards and elephants — survive warfare, climate change, overhunting and other threats to their wilderness habitats.

To do it, Knowles used his entrepreneurial skills to help small nonprofit conservation groups around the world improve their operations. In 2002, he founded the Wildlife Conservation Network (WCN) in San Francisco to expand on that work.

"WCN focuses on key species that have a big impact on their environment and tend to need a lot of space," Knowles said. "The theory is that by preserving this physically and ecologically significant animal, you're also preserving its habitat and the animals and plants that share it." The ultimate goal, he added, "is to see populations of threatened animals stabilize or increase in the wild." [1]

The network seeks out conservationists who have turned creative ideas into strong practical programs to help local areas protect threatened species, then helps those leaders get funding and strengthen their operations for the long haul, Knowles said. [2]

That is where his group, staffed mainly by people with business and administrative experience, can provide expertise and guidance, Knowles said. WCN helps local conservation groups improve marketing and strategic planning. It also helps groups network with each other and with potential funders. [3]

Today's extinction threats come mostly from human activities. What's more, these threats grow as human problems such as war and climate change become more intense, conservation experts say.

That was the case with the approximately 470-elephant herd that forages for food and water across a 12,400-square-mile stretch of desert in Mali, West Africa. While high temperatures and drought worsened by climate change make life hard for the elephants, the most recent threat to their safety comes from warfare. [4]

In northern Mali, a brutal, ongoing civil conflict that began in 2012 has left that section of the country essentially ungoverned, and ivory traffickers took advantage of the chaos to plunder the herds. Poachers killed 163 elephants for their tusks between 2012 and 2017, a rate that could wipe out the approximately 300 remaining elephants over the next three years. This year, though, a brigade of rangers and army forces deployed by the Mali government has successfully protected the herd.

"The poaching didn't start until there was conflict," said Susan Canney, a research associate in zoology at England's Oxford University and director of the Mali Elephant Project, a conservation group. [5]

Social problems also threaten animal species around the globe.

In the vast semi-arid lands of Russia and Central Asia, the saiga antelope faced a massive die-off beginning in 1991. Experts blamed the collapse of the Soviet Union, which wrecked the region's economies. As poverty and hunger drove local populations to overhunt the migratory saiga, its numbers dropped by 95 percent in 15 years. [6]

In northern Kenya, poor management of livestock-grazing land by formerly nomadic communities threatens a local zebra species — Grevy's zebra — of which fewer than 2,500 survive. The zebras are well suited for the dry lands they inhabit and can survive five days without water. However, overgrazing left the land bare and dangerously diminished the zebras' habitat, according to the Wildlife Conservation Network. [7]

The WCN and other funders seek out local conservation groups whose programs address human social problems in tandem with the rescue of species.

Research and debate on the asteroid and volcanic eruption theories continue. In any case, scientific interest in mass extinctions increased beginning in the 1980s. And as researchers zeroed in on climate change as a major contributing cause of past extinctions, speculation grew about the possibility of another mass extinction occurring.

Over the past quarter century, geologists have increasingly turned up evidence that "the five worst episodes in earth history" — the mass extinctions — "have all been associated with violent changes in the planet's carbon cycle," wrote science journalist Peter Brannen. [54]

The 1992 United Nations Earth Summit in Rio de Janeiro marked the coming-of-age of scientific concern about human-driven species loss and its potential consequences, says Michigan's Cardinale. After the meeting, scientists began large-scale data collection and stepped-up research into the causes of and potential fixes for biodiversity losses.

In addition, the U.N. Convention on Biological Diversity, through which nations commit themselves to supporting research on biodiversity and managing their natural resources, was introduced at the meeting and went into force the next year. President Bill Clinton signed the convention, but the Senate has not ratified it because Republican senators worry that it might lead to land-use restrictions. [55]

Species on the Brink

In the 25 years since the convention put the issue of biodiversity and present-day extinctions on the world stage, societies have struggled to reconcile human priorities with conservation.

Among the species lost is the Baiji dolphin, a native of China's Yangtze River. Last spotted in 2002 (except for an unconfirmed 2016 sighting), it was declared extinct in 2006 from overfishing,

In Kenya, the Grevy's Zebra Trust helps nomadic herders-turned-settled farmers learn to manage grazing lands scientifically to ensure good crops of native grasses that feed both cattle and zebra. "The survival of Grevy's zebra and people's livelihoods are inextricably linked," said Belinda Macky, founder and executive director of the trust. "They rely on the same habitat." [8]

A northern region of Kenya, El Barta, still has ample grazing land for Grevy's zebra, but two local tribes, the Samburu and Turkana, have had many disputes over resources. Another Trust project, the Zebra Ambassador program, is designed to create a working relationship between the two tribes and to find ways to resolve conflicts by bringing them together to collect data on the zebras.

Wild species face a particularly difficult struggle when nearby human societies grapple with poverty and other problems, conservationists say. In Zimbabwe in southern Africa, economic stress is the biggest threat to the endangered wild-dog population, said Peter Blinston, managing director of the WCN-sponsored group Painted Dog Conservation. Chronic widespread poverty has reduced "the value of a human life, let alone that of wildlife," he said. [9]

— *Marcia Clemmitt*

A Grevy's zebra stands in the shade in Samburu National Reserve in Kenya. Overgrazing has dangerously diminished the zebras' habitat, and they number about 2,500.

Getty Images/LightRocket/Wolfgang Kaehler

[1] Sara Gaiser, "Wildlife Conservation Network co-founder Charles Knowles on bringing awareness about vanishing species," *San Francisco Examiner*, Oct. 14, 2011, https://tinyurl.com/yaaqrpmf.

[2] Eliza Ridgeway, "Saving species: Los Altos Hills resident brings entrepreneurial edge to conservation," *Los Altos Town Crier*, July 1, 2009, https://tinyurl.com/y7fst3e7.

[3] *Ibid.*

[4] Mark Rivett-Carnac, "Mali's Desert Elephants, on Edge of Annihilation, Get a Fighting Chance," *The New York Times*, Oct. 29, 2017, https://tinyurl.com/y8kqtd34.

[5] *Ibid.*

[6] "Saiga Antelope," Wildlife Conservation Network, https://tinyurl.com/ycptcum5.

[7] "Grevy's Zebra," Wildlife Conservation Network, https://tinyurl.com/y6ubxqm8.

[8] *Ibid.*

[9] Rhett A. Butler, "Painted dog population falls 99%, but community efforts could save species," *Mongabay*, Sept. 28, 2008, https://tinyurl.com/ycwkalfp.

pollution and other problems. [56] West Africa's western black rhino was declared extinct in 2011, and several other rhinoceros species are endangered. Many are illegally killed for their horns, prized as medicine and as a status symbol in some East Asian countries. [57]

Other species on the brink of extinction have been rescued, however.

Among animals listed for protection under the U.S. Endangered Species Act, the humpback whale had been hunted nearly to extinction by the 1960s, when only an estimated 1,600 existed worldwide. Today, the population has rebounded to about 20,000. Scientists also credit the act with saving the bald eagle, grizzly bear, California condor and Florida manatee. [58]

The population of mountain gorillas, in central Africa's forests, had dwindled to fewer than 300 by the 1970s but stands at around 900 today, thanks to efforts in several countries. In the east-central African nation of Rwanda — which is still recovering from civil war and genocidal violence that erupted in the early 1990s [59] — a population of about 250 gorillas rose to 480 by 2015. The Rwandan gorillas are the centerpiece of an eco-tourism industry the government hopes can rebuild the nation's struggling economy. [60]

Many conservation efforts remain highly controversial, even leading to violence in some cases, as in long-running disputes over deforestation in Brazil's Amazon rainforest.

In October 2016, Luiz Araujo, environmental secretary for the town of Altamira in northern Brazil, was shot to death, apparently by paid assassins. The area is the site of bitter battles among business people who want to clear the forests for soy plantations and cattle-grazing, government officials who try to enforce rules limiting deforestation and indigenous groups who live in the Amazon. The rainforest, which covers about 2.1 million square miles — nearly 10 times the size of Texas — is home to a huge variety of plant and animal species and helps to cool Earth's atmosphere by removing carbon dioxide. [61]

Demonstrators at Utah's Capitol on Feb. 2, 2017, protest President Trump's plan to shrink protected monument lands. Trump announced in early December that he would downsize Utah's Grand Staircase and Bears Ears National Monuments by a combined 2 million acres to allow drilling and mining.

Getty Images/LightRocket/Pacific Press/Michael Nigro

"We do not know what happened to [Araujo], but it's a common occurrence in this country that people attempting to defend the environment are murdered by *pistoleiros* [gunmen]," said Olavo Perin Galvao, an agent with Institute of Environment and Renewable Natural Resources, a Brazilian government agency. [62] ■

CURRENT SITUATION

Trump Administration

As part of its efforts to boost the economy and reduce regulatory burdens for businesses, landowners, developers and hunters, the Trump administration is scaling back many policies that help preserve wildlife.

In April, President Trump ordered a review of 27 federally owned sites — primarily large wilderness areas home to numerous species — that the last three presidents have designated as protected national monuments under the 1906 Antiquities Act. [63]

Trump announced in early December that he would shrink Utah's Grand Staircase and Bears Ears national monuments by a combined 2 million acres to allow drilling and mining. Then, on Dec. 5, Interior Secretary Ryan Zinke proposed reducing two more sites and recommended revamping usage rules for several other sites to ensure that livestock grazing and commercial fishing would be allowed. [64]

Conservationists reacted with alarm to the moves. Michael Brune, executive director of the environmental group Sierra Club, warned that the president is trying "to undercut the principle of permanent protection that underpins the security of all America's wildlife refuges, national monuments and national parks." Others stressed that Bears Ears and other monuments support a variety of wildlife, including mule deer, elk, prairie dog, Botta's pocket gopher and white-tailed antelope squirrel, and say that development would threaten their habitats. [65]

But Western state lawmakers argue the monument designations amount to federal overreach that harms local economies. "When you turn the management over to the tree-huggers, the bird and bunny lovers and the rock lickers, you turn your heritage over," said Utah state Rep. Mike Noel, a Republican. [66]

In Congress, some House and Senate Republicans have long complained that the Endangered Species Act and other environmental laws place the interests of wildlife above the interests of humans. In 2017, committees in both the House and the Senate have introduced bills aimed at limiting the laws' scope.

The House Committee on Natural Resources in October approved five bills to curtail the act. Analysts say they doubt the Senate will go along with such a drastic move. However, a government spending bill amended with one or more specific provisions aimed at weakening the law remains a possibility. Rep. Bishop of Utah and others say the economic impact of designating a species as endangered must be considered. (*See "At Issue," p. 1057.*) [67]

Environmental Protection Agency (EPA) Administrator Scott Pruitt said in June the administration will withdraw an Obama administration rule intended to clarify which waterways fall under the anti-pollution standards of the 1972 Clean Water Act. [68] Under the rule, the Clean Water Act would apply to all "relatively permanent" small streams that feed into larger waterways; wetlands near waterways or the coast; and some isolated wetlands fed by groundwater and rain, even if the sites are wet only at certain times of the year.

Continued on p. 1058

At Issue:

Should cost factor into whether a species is listed as endangered?

ROBERT GORDON
SENIOR RESEARCH FELLOW, HERITAGE FOUNDATION

WRITTEN FOR *CQ RESEARCHER*, DECEMBER 2017

i n 1978, a tiny fish shut down a nearly completed dam. The Supreme Court ruled that the snail darter had to be saved, "whatever the cost."

Turned out, the U.S. Fish and Wildlife Service had significantly undercounted the fish, and Congress intervened so the dam could be completed. It was a clear sign the Endangered Species Act (ESA) would be a mess.

Today, the Fish and Wildlife Service lists more than 1,650 species as "threatened" or "endangered." The agency claims the listing process is purely science-based, but that's not quite the case. The ESA requires the agency to use "the best available data" to place a species on the protected list. But often, the best available evidence is neither accurate nor reliable.

The agency compounds this problem by refusing to honestly consider the economic impact of its rules. Once a species is not-so-scientifically listed as "threatened" or "endangered," it is illegal to harm it. Additionally, the agency is supposed to designate each listed species' critical habitat. Adversely modifying that habitat is prohibited.

Importantly, the law allows the agency to exclude areas from critical habitat when the economic costs outweigh the benefits. But although that provision is on the books, it is not in the Fish and Wildlife Service's playbook.

The agency has a history of failing to designate critical habitat when species are listed. Instead it has misinterpreted the prohibition against harm as a way to regulate any habitat it chooses. When it does designate critical habitat, it often uses "low-ball" economic-impact estimates to avoid limits to its regulation.

The costs are large. The agency and countless other federal and state bureaucracies spend over $1.4 billion annually to comply with the Endangered Species Act. And that doesn't include cost estimates for recovering most of the listed species.

Where estimates are available, they often are massive. The agency estimates the cost of recovering just four aquatic invertebrates, a beetle and about a dozen wetland plants at over $1 billion. And these figures don't reflect the economic impact on affected property owners and businesses.

"Whatever the cost" spending and economic burden from limitless regulation doesn't work well. In the law's 44-year history, fewer than 40 domestic species have been "recovered," and some of them never really were endangered.

High cost, poor performance: It's the very definition of unsustainable.

NORA APTER
LEGISLATIVE ADVOCATE, NATURAL RESOURCES DEFENSE COUNCIL

WRITTEN FOR *CQ RESEARCHER*, DECEMBER 2017

w hen you go to the doctor's office, you are looking for a diagnosis of whether you are sick. The answer to that question does not depend on the cost of treatment.

In the same way, the Endangered Species Act asks wildlife scientists to determine whether a population is healthy. It does not ask not how much it will cost to save it from extinction.

Indeed, current law prescribes that listing decisions under the Endangered Species Act be based solely on the best available science. Convoluting that process by adding cost as a determining factor in whether a species deserves to be protected or wiped off the planet completely is not only nonsensical, it is uneconomical.

Including cost as a factor in listing decisions would block much-needed protections for imperiled plants and wildlife in decline. Furthermore, while costs are already considered when it comes to identifying and implementing species recovery plans, it is beyond the ability of economists to determine the true cost or benefit of species conservation.

That doesn't mean the species lacks value. It just means our economy alone cannot tell us what it is worth.

Plants and animals provide us with demonstrable benefits, some of which we can quantify. Wildlife-related recreation and tourism, for example, generates nearly $900 billion each year and supports 7.6 million jobs. A third of our food is pollinated by birds, bats and insects, saving us billions of dollars each year in agricultural services and helping ensure global food security. Many critical medicines have come from flora and fauna — from Houston toads to Florida alligators. Endangered Species Act protections allow us to continue discovering such cures.

Other benefits are simply incalculable: Ecological biodiversity supports healthy natural systems that we humans need to survive. Remove one species from the intricate web of life and there may be hell to pay, even if we cannot put a price tag on such unintended consequences.

Recent scientific studies have concluded that the world is facing a sixth mass extinction; it is estimated that one in six species will be extinct by the end of the century.

As a species that depends on these dying breeds for our own survival, we must ask ourselves not "how much would it cost" to save a species, but "how much more can we afford to lose?"

Continued from p. 1056

A number of scientists argue these waters need protection because many animal and plant species depend on their being pollution free.

Builders, farmers and the oil and gas industry said the rule could leave them liable for pollution in waterways that are no more than ditches, and in February Trump signed an order to pave "the way for elimination of this very destructive and horrible rule." [69]

In October, the U.S. Fish and Wildlife Service rejected 25 petitions asking that the Department of Interior list a number of species, such as the Florida Keys mole skink and the Pacific walrus, as endangered or threatened. In defending the rejections, the agency said in a statement, "We considered and thoroughly evaluated the best scientific and commercial information available regarding the past, present and future stressors and threats." Conservation groups, however, saw the rejection as further evidence of the administration's hostility to helping endangered species. [70]

A month later, the Fish and Wildlife Service said it was reversing an Obama-era ban against the importation of African elephant tusks and hides aimed at discouraging poaching. [71] "Legal, well-regulated sport hunting as part of a sound management program can benefit certain species by providing incentives to local communities to conserve those species," the Wildlife Service said. Animal rights groups protested, saying the administration's policy calls for killing an endangered species to save it. After the outcry, Trump said in mid-November he would consider reinstating the ban. [72]

Trump's proposal to expand the wall on the Mexican border to curb illegal immigration from Mexico and Central America would shrink and fragment the habitats of many threatened species, according to conservationists. Along the U.S.-Mexico border, about 654 miles of intermittent walls and fences — about a third of the

border's length — are already in place. Under consideration as the site for new walls are two Texas wildlife refuges. [73]

To survive, most species need the freedom to move over a fairly large area so they can gain access to mates and food and water in the dry region, wildlife biologists say. But many species, including jaguars and even low-flying birds and butterflies, won't go over tall, solid barriers. [74]

In addition, Trump's June decision to pull the United States out of the international Paris agreement on climate change will have consequences for multiple species by making it harder to meet climate goals, environmentalists warn. In fact, a recent study concluded that even if the original Paris agreement accomplished its goal of limiting the global average temperature increase to 2 degrees Celsius by century's end, 5 percent of the world's species would still go extinct because of climate issues. If temperature increases exceed that amount, species losses will be even higher, environmentalists say. [75]

Global Developments

Worldwide, governments and intergovernmental organizations are initiating programs on habitat destruction and biodiversity loss.

Norway in 2016 announced that its government agencies would no longer purchase products with ingredients, such as palm oil and tropical lumber, known to contribute to deforestation where they are grown and harvested. Deforestation worsens climate change and destroys habitat. While many private companies have pledged to cut these goods from their supply chains, Norway was the first national government to do so. [76]

Deciding which species to target for conservation and how to rescue them requires a massive knowledge

base, much of which is still lacking. Scientists increasingly are working together to build that knowledge. In October, a team added the final section — reptiles — to an "atlas of life." The atlas now shows the location of 10,064 reptile species, about 99 percent of those known. The reptiles join the geographical listing of the world's known vertebrate species, including some 10,000 birds, 5,000 mammals and 6,000 amphibians. [77]

"Now conservation has the data and tools required to bring planning up to the same level as the businesses and governments who might have an eye on land for other uses," said Richard Greyner, lead researcher and an associate professor of geography at England's Oxford University. [78]

Efforts to slow species loss include getting people to change their habits to allowing wildlife and humans to live side by side more easily. (See sidebar, p. 1054.)

Throughout southern Africa, the environmental group Cheetah Conservation Fund (CCF), based in Namibia, is working with livestock farmers to help stabilize the declining cheetah population. Farmers must graze their flocks across southern Africa's often dry landscapes and have understandable reservations about the speedy carnivorous cats.

CCF is giving farmers guard dogs to protect livestock and a free "Carnivore Tracker" cellphone app so residents can report big-cat sightings in real time. Farmers with guard dogs report a 70 percent reduction in livestock loss "and have become very tolerant toward having predators as their neighbors," said CCF Executive Director Laurie Marker. [79]

In northern Colombia, deforestation and the illegal trade in exotic pets have imperiled the tiny cotton-top tamarin monkey. By publicizing the monkeys' plight, the group has enlisted local farm families in the fight to preserve the habitat of the tamarins, which never leave the treetops, according to the conservation group Proyecto Titi. [80]

The group also works with farmers and ranchers to retain or replace forest trees in selected areas of their land to create "corridors" that connect the region's now isolated forested plots and allow tamarins and other wildlife to access additional habitat. [81] ■

OUTLOOK

Action Urged

Some scientists envision a day when humans may peaceably share the planet with other species. As the world grows more interconnected and human population growth levels off, "it is an increasingly imaginable, if daunting, prospect that our societies might yet pool our resources to construct, connect, and sustain a global ecological niche that includes the rest of life on Earth," the University of Maryland's Ellis said. [82]

Others are not so sanguine. "Avoiding a true sixth mass extinction will require rapid, greatly intensified efforts to conserve already threatened species and to alleviate pressures on their populations — notably habitat loss, overexploitation for economic gain, and climate change," a recent study by six biologists concluded. [83]

The most effective way to slow the loss of wild species is to alleviate human poverty, said renowned chimpanzee expert Jane Goodall. "[If] you're living in desperate poverty, you're going to continue destroying the environment in order to live," she said, such as cutting down the last trees "in a desperate effort to grow food." [84]

In addition, said Goodall, the "wealthy need to start thinking about their environmental footprint — what do I buy, what do I eat . . . where did it come from?"

But persuading the public to change their ways — for the sake of wild nature — is a difficult argument to make, Goodall and others say. One place to start, though, is by showing politicians and others that fostering biodiversity does not mean wrecking the economy, says Duke's Pimm.

"There's a tendency to portray environmental causes as being somehow antithetical to business, but that's a really serious mistake," he says. "People debate the value of national parks, but 3 million people visit them a year, and they drop hundreds of dollars a day. Somebody might want a uranium mine in one of them. But the parks, just as they are, have a dramatic national impact, including economically."

Ultimately, though, the decision to make species and habitat preservation a top priority may come down to the uncertain answer to this question: Can humans adapt if the vast majority of ecosystem types and species vanish, or would a large-scale extinction seriously harm humans as well?

Some scientists argue that, with those answers unknown, caution requires slowing species loss as much as possible.

"Biodiversity as a whole forms a shield protecting each of the species that together compose it, ourselves included," said Harvard entomologist Wilson. [85]

Scientists already know that, in at least some situations, "as more and more species vanish or drop to near extinction" in an ecosystem, "the rate of extinction of the survivors accelerates," and "biodiversity reaches a tipping point at which the ecosystem collapses," Wilson wrote. Based on that knowledge, caution dictates slowing species loss, he argued. [86]

Other scientists, however, note that both humans and some ecosystems have already shown they can adapt to change without catastrophe. For example, in the heavily populated eastern United States, humans cut down most of the virgin forest hundreds of years ago, yet the area is again heavily forest-

ed — albeit with a different plant mix — and both the woods and the humans are healthy, said George Washington University's Pyron. [87]

There's no reason to think that will not persist, he said. "Thirty to 40 percent of species may be threatened with extinction in the near future, and their loss may be inevitable. But both the planet and humanity can probably survive or even thrive in a world with fewer species. We don't depend on polar bears for our survival, and even if their eradication has a domino effect that eventually affects us, we will find a way to adapt." ■

Notes

[1] John R. Platt, "The Rabbs' Tree Frog Just Went Extinct," *Scientific American*, Sept. 28, 2016, https://tinyurl.com/y7qw6ce6.

[2] Rob Jordan, "Prelude to global extinction: Stanford biologists say disappearance of species tells only part of the only part of the story of human impact on Earth's animals," Stanford News Service, July 10, 2017, https://tinyurl.com/y79k7ucz; Gerardo Ceballos, Paul R. Ehrlich and Rodolfo Dirzo, "Biological annihilation via the ongoing sixth mass extinction signaled by vertebrate population losses and declines," Proceedings of the National Academy of Sciences, July 25, 2017, https://tinyurl.com/y8byq25a.

[3] For background, see Reed Karaim, "Vanishing Biodiversity," *CQ Researcher*, Nov. 6, 2012, pp. 497-520.

[4] William J. Ripple *et al.*, "World Scientists' Warning to Humanity: A Second Notice," *BioScience*, Nov. 13, 2017, https://tinyurl.com/y7ndulkl.

[5] Stewart Brand, "Rethinking Extinction," *Aeon*, April 21, 2015, https://tinyurl.com/zgcprz7.

[6] Michael J. Benton, "Mass Extinctions," *New Scientist*, March 5, 2011.

[7] "Living Planet Report 2016," World Wildlife Fund, https://tinyurl.com/y9qgu66a; Damian Carrington, "World on tract to lose two-thirds of wild animals by 2020, major report warns," *The Guardian*, Oct. 26, 2016, https://tinyurl.com/zpwlctu; and William J. Ripple *et al.*, "Bushmeat hunting and extinction risk to the world's mammals," Royal Society Open Science, Oct. 19,

2016, https://tinyurl.com/ybgsbt7y.

[8] Peter Brannen, *The Ends of the World* (2017), p. 238.

[9] "Action on the ground," International Union for Conservation of Nature, https://tinyurl.com/yd47lqjd.

[10] Ceballos, Ehrlich and Dirzo, *op. cit.*

[11] "Human Impact on the Reef," Biodiscovery and the Great Barrier Reef, https://tinyurl.com/l6cr4fy; Edward O. Wilson, *Half-Earth: Our Planet's Fight for Life* (2016), pp. 68-69.

[12] Ceballos *et al.*, *op. cit.*

[13] Brand, *op. cit.*

[14] R. Alexander Pyron, "We don't need to save endangered species. Extinction is part of evolution," *The Washington Post*, Nov. 22, 2017, https://tinyurl.com/y7l38shj.

[15] Leon, "Inheritors of the Earth: An Interview with Chris D. Thomas," The Hoopoe blog, July 6, 2017, https://tinyurl.com/ydggkdg9; Paige Browning, "Those farmed salmon have reached the Pacific Ocean. (That's not good.)," *Kuow*, Aug. 25, 2017, https://tinyurl.com/yc9k5foq.

[16] Darryl Fears, "Powerful lawmaker wants to 'invalidate' the Endangered Species Act. He's getting close," *The Washington Post*, Nov. 5, 2017, https://tinyurl.com/y9f3mssu.

[17] Josh Dawsey and Juliet Eilperin, "Trump shrinks two huge national monuments in Utah, drawing praise and protests," *The Washington Post*, Dec. 4, 2017, https://tinyurl.com/y8bf44ef.

[18] Benton, *op. cit.*

[19] Brannen, *op. cit.*, pp. 244ff.

[20] Peter Brannen, "Earth Is Not in the Midst of a Sixth Mass Extinction," *The Atlantic*, June 13, 2017, https://tinyurl.com/ydxugmlp.

[21] Quoted in Brannen, *Ends of the Earth*, *op. cit.*, p. 11.

[22] "Has Earth's sixth mass extinction already arrived?" *op. cit.*

[23] Ferris Jabr, "The case that humans are creating new species despite killing off so many," *Vox*, Oct. 23, 2017, https://tinyurl.com/ybsflkzm.

[24] *Ibid.*

[25] Erle Ellis, "The Planet of No Return," *The Breakthrough*, Winter 2012, https://tinyurl.com/y8pp6o4b.

[26] Annalee Newitz, "The Sixth Mass Extinction Is Upon Us. Can Humans Survive?" *Newsweek*, May 6, 2013, https://tinyurl.com/y9xfydmb.

[27] *Ibid.*

[28] "Why Dinosaurs Matter debuts at #1 in Paleontology on Amazon," *Rowan Today*, Sept. 26, 2017, https://tinyurl.com/ycxn2c3j.

[29] Bjorn Carey, "Stanford biologist warns of early stages of Earth's 6th mass extinction event," *Stanford News*, July 24, 2014, https://tinyurl.com/n2jrokn; Rodolfo Dirzo *et al.*, "Defaunation in the Anthropocene," *Science*, July 25, 2014, https://tinyurl.com/yd56xe6r.

[30] "Mainstreaming Agrobiodiversity in Sustainable Food Systems," *Bioversity International*, September 2017, https://tinyurl.com/ybvk3fg7.

[31] Richard Conniff, "Urban Nature: How to Foster Biodiversity in the World's Cities," *Yale Environment 360*, Jan. 6, 2014, https://tinyurl.com/y8gtkaxk.

[32] *Ibid.*

[33] *Ibid.*; Coronation Meadows, https://tinyurl.com/m9sunac.

[34] Erle Ellis, "Nature for the People," *The Breakthrough*, Summer 2017, https://tinyurl.com/ya793lf6.

[35] Matthew Liebman and Lisa Schulte-Moore, "Enhancing agroecosystem performance and Resilience through Increased Diversification of Landscapes and Cropping Systems," *Elementa*, 2015, https://tinyurl.com/ycxhupc7.

[36] *Ibid.*

[37] E.O. Wilson, "The Global Solution to Extinction," *The New York Times*, March 12, 2016, https://tinyurl.com/y8m52mwc; Wilson, Half-Earth, *op. cit.*, pp. 3ff.

[38] Ellis, "Nature for the People," *op. cit.*; Fears, *op. cit.*

[39] Ellis, *ibid.*

[40] "Back from the Dead: Why De-extinction May Save Humanity," NBC News, July 24,

2014, https://tinyurl.com/hazqoug.

[41] Quoted in David Schultz, "Should we bring extinct species back from the dead?" *Science*, Sept. 26, 2016, https://tinyurl.com/zgzx4h2.

[42] For background, see Brannen, *op. cit.*, and Elizabeth Kolbert, *The Sixth Extinction* (2014).

[43] Kolbert, *op. cit.*, p. 92ff; "Extinctions: Georges Cuvier," Understanding Evolution, University of California, Berkeley, https://tinyurl.com/ybdoh38r.

[44] Kolbert, *ibid.*, p. 52.

[45] Charles Darwin, *On the Origin of Species* (2003), p. 294.

[46] Brannen, *op. cit.*, p. 48.

[47] Justin Gillis, "A Change in Temperature," *The New York Times*, May 13, 2013, https://tinyurl.com/cjwul58.

[48] Patrick Lynch, "Ecology, evolution, & climate change: G. Evelyn Hutchinson and the founding of modern ecology," *Yale News*, Nov. 21, 2015, https://tinyurl.com/ybzpojlh.

[49] "Monoculture and the Irish Potato Famine: cases of missing genetic variation," Understanding Evolution, https://tinyurl.com/yconakex.

[50] "How many species on Earth? About 8.7 million, new estimate says," *Science Daily*, Aug. 24, 2011, https://tinyurl.com/7ovp4v2.

[51] Kolbert, *op. cit.*, p. 166.

[52] Jeremy Pearce, "Norman Newell, 96, Scientist Who Studied Dying Species, Has Died," *The New York Times*, April 23, 2005, https://tinyurl.com/yccdkn2l.

[53] Kolbert, *op. cit.*, pp. 70ff.

[54] Brannen, *op. cit.*, p. 6.

[55] Convention on Biological Diversity, United Nations 1992, https://tinyurl.com/6h3g26u.

[56] Laura Moss, "10 animals presumed extinct in the last decade," Mother Nature Network, Oct. 10, 2016, https://tinyurl.com/y8kbd5jr.

[57] Daniel Boettcher, "Western black rhino declared extinct," BBC News, Nov. 10, 2011, https://tinyurl.com/yb6w8k4m.

[58] Darryl Fears, "These creatures faced extinction. The Endangered Species Act saved them," *The Washington Post*, March 11, 2017, https://tinyurl.com/y9ky3hrq.

[59] For background, see Josh Kron, "Conflict in Congo," *CQ Global Researcher*, April 5, 2011, pp. 157-82.

[60] Dominique Mosbergen, "Humans Almost Drove These 6 Animals to Extinction. But We Saved Them Instead," *The Huffington Post*, Jan. 26, 2017, https://tinyurl.com/yaszjncp; Kevin Sack, "Trekking With the Gorillas of Rwanda," *The New York Times*, Oct. 23, 2015, https://tinyurl.com/ycqp3k5c.

[61] For background, see Brian Beary, "Brazil on the Rise," *CQ Global Researcher*, June 7,

About the Author

Marcia Clemmitt is a veteran social-policy reporter who previously served as editor in chief of *Medicine & Health* and staff writer for *The Scientist*. She has also been a high school math and physics teacher. She holds a liberal arts and sciences degree from St. John's College, Annapolis, and a master's degree in English from Georgetown University. Her recent *CQ Researcher* reports include "The Dark Web" and "Emerging Infectious Diseases."

2011, pp. 263-290. Also see Doug Struck, "Disappearing Forests," *CQ Global Researcher*, Jan. 18, 2011, pp. 27-52.

[62] Vincent Bevins, "The debate over saving rain forests has gotten ugly. Now a Brazilian environmental official is dead," *Los Angeles Times*, Oct. 14, 2016, https://tinyurl.com/j3eouan.

[63] Julie Turkewitz and Lisa Friedman, "Interior Secretary Proposes Shrinking Four National Monuments," *The New York Times*, Aug. 24, 2017, https://tinyurl.com/y8jgwlat; Lisa Friedman, Nadja Popvich and Matt McCann, "27 National Monuments Are Under Review. Here Are Five to Watch," *The New York Times*, Aug. 16 2017, https://tinyurl.com/y9c48was; Annie Sneed, "Conservative Hunters & Fishers May Help Determine the Fate of National Monuments," *Scientific American*, Oct. 30, 2017, https://tinyurl.com/yct8b5w6.

[64] Ryan K. Zinke, "Memorandum for the President," Dec. 5, 2017, https://tinyurl.com/y92e6fst; Juliet Eilperin, "Zinke backs shrinking more national monuments and shifting management of 10," *The Washington Post*, Dec. 5, 2017, https://tinyurl.com/ydhc2j62.

[65] Michael Brune, "No Shame, No Future," *The Huffington Post*, Dec. 6, 2017, https://tinyurl.com/y7rre8d7; "Presidential Proclamation — Establishment of the Bears Ears National Monument," The White House, Dec. 28, 2016, https://tinyurl.com/kz7ezxz.

[66] Quoted in Turkewitz and Friedman, *op. cit.*

[67] Monica Trauzzi, "E&E News' Hiar discusses efforts to reform landmark law," E&E TV, April 21, 2017, https://tinyurl.com/y7eognlu; House Committee Advances Five Bills to Cripple Endangered Species Act, July 18, 2017, Center for Biological Diversity, https://tinyurl.com/y96dk2sp.

[68] Susan Phillips, "Trump plans to ditch Obama's protection for small wetlands and waterways," State Impact/NPR, Feb. 27, 2017, https://tinyurl.com/yapgffxm; Steven Mufson and Juliet Eilperin, "EPA to scrap wetland, stream protection rule issued under Obama," *Press Herald*, June 28, 2017, https://tinyurl.com/yd5ytsah.

[69] Quoted in Mufson and Eilperin, *ibid.*

[70] Chris Mooney and Dino Grandoni, "Interior Department rejects 25 endangered species petitions, including several linked to climate change," *The Washington Post*, Oct. 5, 2017, https://tinyurl.com/y8dadzy8.

[71] For background, see Robert Kiener, "Wildlife Smuggling," *CQ Global Researcher*, Oct. 1, 2010, pp. 235-262.

[72] Anne Gearan, "Trump calls elephant hunting a 'horror show' and suggests he'll enforce a

FOR MORE INFORMATION

Amphibia Web, https://amphibiaweb.org. Searchable website run by university-based researchers that provides information on the world's amphibian species and the threats they face.

BiodiversityMapping.org, http://biodiversitymapping.org/wordpress/index.php/home. Website run by an international team of environmental researchers that posts maps of species biodiversity.

International Union for Conservation of Nature, Rue Mauverney 28, 1196 Gland, Switzerland; +41 22 9990000; www.iucn.org. Membership group for governments and citizens' organizations that publishes authoritative data and provides expert advice on biodiversity issues.

Natural Resources Defense Council, 40 W. 20th St., 11th Floor, New York, NY 10011; 212-727-2700; www.nrdc.org. Membership group that supports research, legal analysis and legislative advocacy for environmental causes, including species protection.

United Nations Convention on Biological Diversity, www.cbd.int. Website that posts facts, history, news and progress updates on the international treaty to protect biodiversity.

U.S. Fish and Wildlife Service, 1849 C St., N.W., Washington, DC 20240; 202-208-6541; www.fws.gov. Federal agency charged with helping to preserve wildlife and wildlife habits, and protecting threatened and endangered species.

Wildlife Conservation Network, 209 Mississippi St., San Francisco, CA 94107; 415-202-6380; https://wildnet.org. Nonprofit that provides funding, advice and other help to local animal-conservation groups in 37 countries.

World Wildlife Fund, 1250 24th St., N.W., Washington, DC 20037; 202-293-4800; www.worldwildlife.org. Membership organization that conducts environmental research and conservation projects in 100 countries.

ban on trophy imports," *The Washington Post*, Nov. 19, 2017, https://tinyurl.com/ycu5vfmk.

[73] Eliza Barclay and Sarah Frostenson, "The ecological disaster that is Trump's border wall: a visual guide," *Vox*, Oct. 29, 2017, https://tinyurl.com/krsslzy; Cally Carswell, "Trump's Wall May Threaten Thousands of Animal Species on the U.S.-Mexico Border," *Scientific American*, May 10, 2017, https://tinyurl.com/ya4v9q9e.

[74] Barclay and Frostenson, *ibid.*

[75] Jeremy Hance, "What does the Paris agreement mean for the world's other 8 million species?" *The Guardian*, June 2, 2017, https://tinyurl.com/ydd7j6kp.

[76] Aidan Quigley, "Norway adopts world's first zero deforestation policy: What does that mean?" *The Christian Science Monitor*, June 8, 2016, https://tinyurl.com/yavmnk7m.

[77] David Moscato, "The reptiles of the world have been added to the 'atlas of life,' " Earth Touch News, Oct. 11, 2017, https://tinyurl.com/yalljcpr; "Scientists complete conservation 'atlas

of life,' " University of Oxford, Oct. 9, 2017, https://tinyurl.com/yclzmmsc.

[78] Moscato, *ibid.*

[79] Laurie Marker, "Conservation Efforts Helped by Farmers Using Cell Phones," *The Huffington Post*, Sept. 27, 2017, https://tinyurl.com/y8nxukuo.

[80] "Cotton-top Tamarin," Wildlife Conservation Network, https://tinyurl.com/y7kky2vm.

[81] "Titi Tidbits: June Edition," *Proyecto Titi*, June 2017, https://tinyurl.com/yao5n4fm.

[82] Ellis, *op. cit.*

[83] Gerardo Ceballos *et al.*, "Accelerated modern human-induced species losses: Entering the sixth mass extinction," *Science Advances*, June 19, 2015, https://tinyurl.com/pksl8ow.

[84] Jane Goodall, "Giving Up Hope Won't Save the Planet, Ending Poverty Might," NBC News, Oct. 24, 2017, https://tinyurl.com/y75bunde.

[85] Wilson, *op. cit.*, p. 14.

[86] *Ibid.*, p. 16.

[87] Pyron, *op. cit.*

Bibliography

Selected Sources

Books

Brannen, Peter, *The Ends of the World: Volcanic Apocalypses, Lethal Oceans, and Our Quest to Understand Earth's Past Mass Extinctions*, Ecco, 2017.

A science journalist examines the research showing that climate changes played a major role in Earth's five mass extinctions. Scientists weigh in on what this finding may mean for the planet today.

Kolbert, Elizabeth, *The Sixth Extinction — An Unnatural History*, Henry Holt & Co., 2014.

In this Pulitzer Prize-winning book, a science journalist explains how 200 years of study by paleontologists and ecologists taught scientists that Earth's history included a series of mass extinctions.

Newitz, Annalee, *Scatter, Adapt, and Remember: How Humans Will Survive a Mass Extinction*, Doubleday, 2013.

A technology journalist who believes that a catastrophic extinction event is in the offing describes proposals that futurists say could allow humanity to survive. These range from removing excess carbon dioxide from the atmosphere to creating "space elevators" that could transport humans to other planets.

Thomas, Chris D., *Inheritors of the Earth: How Nature Is Thriving in an Age of Extinction*, PublicAffairs, 2017.

A professor of conservation biology at England's University of York argues that nature is more resilient than many believe.

Wilson, Edward O., *Half-Earth: Our Planet's Fight for Life*, Liveright Publishing, 2017.

A professor emeritus in entomology at Harvard University proposes setting aside half of the land and half the surface of the oceans as areas in which wildlife would receive protection. Doing so could save about 90 percent of species, he says.

Articles

Brand, Stewart, "Rethinking Extinction," *Aeon*, April 21, 2015, https://tinyurl.com/zgcprz7.

An author and entrepreneur concerned with social and environmental sustainability argues that although many wildlife species are under stress, a sixth mass extinction is not underway. He says claims about a mass extinction create hopelessness among the public, which could doom promising efforts to put Earth's wildlife on a firmer footing.

Carrington, Damian, "Oceans under greatest threat in history, warns Sir David Attenborough," *The Guardian*, Dec. 5, 2017, https://tinyurl.com/yd3bdcg3.

Plastic waste and noise from shipping, cruise tourism and fossil-fuel extraction threaten marine animals and habitat, says a new documentary.

Carswell, Cally, "Trump's Wall May Threaten Thousands of Animal Species on the U.S.-Mexico Border," *Scientific American*, May 10, 2017, https://tinyurl.com/y9w8rmcp.

Walls placed at the U.S.-Mexican border to prevent illegal immigration threaten wildlife populations' access to water and food in one of the largest wilderness areas on the continent, conservation advocates say.

Ellis, Erle, "Nature for the People," *The Breakthrough*, Summer 2017, https://tinyurl.com/y8wktlts.

A professor of geography and environmental systems at the University of Maryland, Baltimore County, says that with better management, humans can shrink the amount of land they use to allow more room for the preservation of wildlife.

Pyron, R. Alexander, "We don't need to save endangered species. Extinction is part of evolution," *The Washington Post*, Nov. 22, 2017, https://tinyurl.com/ybdjaav9.

An associate professor of biology at George Washington University argues that because extinction is a natural result of environmental changes, efforts to save endangered species are a waste of time.

Reports and Studies

"Living Planet Report 2016," World Wildlife Fund, 2016, https://tinyurl.com/y7kqosxu.

This biannual report by an international environmental group details the state of the world's wildlife and of human activities that affect it.

"Mainstreaming Agrobiodiversity in Sustainable Food Systems: Scientific Foundations for an Agrobiodiversity Index," Bioversity International, 2017, https://tinyurl.com/y86jffrd.

With climate change threatening many plant species that humans depend on for survival, an agriculture-sustainability research group in Rome says using more diverse plant and animal food sources could prevent severe food shortages.

"Supplement: Recreating the Wild: De-extinction, Technology, and the Ethics of Conservation," The Hastings Center Report, July/August 2017, https://tinyurl.com/yc6rqvyw.

A group of scholars assembled by a bioethics-research center in upstate New York discusses the current status of "de-extinction" technology to bring back species that have died off and the questions its use would raise.

"Top 10 Species Priorities for a New Administration: Removing the Walls to Recovery," Endangered Species Coalition, December 2016, https://tinyurl.com/yd43gmmn.

U.S. conservation groups list which issues they believe the Trump administration must address to preserve species, including the native bees that pollinate most of Hawaii's plants, and why.

The Next Step:

Additional Articles from Current Periodicals

Biodiversity

"Western Ghats' biodiversity 'faces threat,' says report," *Economic Times*, Nov. 20, 2017, https://tinyurl.com/y89u3no6.

Population growth and climate change threaten India's Western Ghats, a mountainous region that is a World Heritage Site, says the International Union for Conservation of Nature.

Hone, Dave, "Past extinctions point to a current and future biodiversity crisis," *The Guardian*, July 19, 2017, https://tinyurl.com/yaqcffa7.

Climate change will harm Earth's biodiversity — the complex interrelationships among plants, animals and humans — and hasten species extinction, says a University of London lecturer.

Macauley, Conor, "Hard Brexit 'risks' biodiversity in Ireland," BBC News, Nov. 28, 2017, https://tinyurl.com/ybywq8ur.

Environmentalists say that when the United Kingdom leaves the European Union, Ireland's species will be further endangered because most of Ireland's biodiversity laws are EU protections..

Declining Habitats

Fraňková, Ruth, "Alarm Called Over Endangered Moravian Amazon," Radio Prague, Oct. 11, 2017, https://tinyurl.com/y7mu6tds.

Woodlands along the Morava and Dyje rivers in Czech Republic, home to a rich variety of trees and species, are facing losses on a similar level to many endangered tropical habitats.

Mooney, Chris, "72 percent of the world's most majestic coral reefs have been hit by major heat stress since 2014," *The Washington Post*, June 23, 2017, https://tinyurl.com/y9okx23d.

Twenty-one of 29 coral reefs on UNESCO'S list of World Heritage sites, including Australia's Great Barrier Reef, have suffered severe heat stress over the past few years and could disappear by century's end, according to the organization.

Worland, Justin, "More than 700 North American Bee Species Are Headed Toward Extinction," *Time*, March 2, 2017, https://tinyurl.com/hhokxlk.

Habitat loss and pesticide use are the two main factors driving the decline of bee species in North America.

Environmental Policy

Falk, Pamela, "U.N. environment chief warns 'we're facing an ocean Armageddon,' " CBS News, Dec. 5, 2017, https://tinyurl.com/ydyu8e5w.

The U.N. Environment Assembly will push for a nonbinding treaty banning plastic waste from the seas.

Sudarshan, Anant, "Environmental Policies Demand Innovation. India Is Taking The Next Step," *Forbes*, June 22,

2017, https://tinyurl.com/y7f6pj6p.

The Indian state of Maharashtra has introduced an environmental regulation that rates industrial plants on the amount of air pollution they produce and posts the results online.

Super, David A., "GOP could cut environmental review policy like loggers clear forests," *The Hill*, Dec. 4, 2017, https://tinyurl.com/y9s6y24l.

The National Environmental Policy Act, a bipartisan measure passed in 1969 to protect the environment, is under threat in Congress, says a Georgetown law professor.

Recovery Efforts

"Peregrine Falcon achieves landmark recovery but salmon struggle," Committee on the Status of Endangered Wildlife in Canada, Canada NewsWire, Dec. 4, 2017, https://tinyurl.com/yde2uwdv.

A ban on the insecticide DDT and a breeding program have elevated the peregrine falcon to a "not at risk" species.

Hackwell, Kevin, "Stars of the Red List: two kiwi species are no longer Endangered," Bird Life International, Dec. 5, 2017, https://tinyurl.com/y9ts3pho.

Two species of New Zealand kiwi have been downgraded from "endangered" to "vulnerable," thanks to concentrated efforts by government bodies, conservation groups and Maori communities.

McGuigan, Connor, "Trump Administration Finalizes Flawed Mexican Wolf Recovery Plan," *Sierra Magazine*, Dec. 1, 2017, https://tinyurl.com/y9twac74.

Environmentalists have sharply criticized the Trump administration's recovery plan for the Mexican gray wolf, alleging that the plan will actually lead to their extinction.

CITING CQ RESEARCHER

Sample formats for citing these reports in a bibliography include the ones listed below. Preferred styles and formats vary, so please check with your instructor or professor.

MLA STYLE

Mantel, Barbara. "Coal Industry's Future." CQ Researcher 17 June 2016: 529-552.

APA STYLE

Mantel, B. (2016, June 17). Coal Industry's Future. CQ Researcher, 6, 529-552.

CHICAGO STYLE

Mantel, Barbara. "Coal Industry's Future." CQ Researcher, June 17, 2016, 529-52.

In-depth Reports on Issues in the News

Are you writing a paper?

Need backup for a debate?

Want to become an expert on an issue?

For 90 years, students have turned to *CQ Researcher* for in-depth reporting on issues in the news. Reports on a full range of political and social issues are now available. Following is a selection of recent reports:

Civil Liberties
Privacy and the Internet, 12/15
Intelligence Reform, 5/15
Religion and Law, 11/14

Crime/Law
High-Tech Policing, 4/17
Forensic Science Controversies, 2/17
Jailing Debtors, 9/16
Decriminalizing Prostitution, 4/16
Restorative Justice, 2/16
The Dark Web, 1/16
Immigrant Detention, 10/15

Education
Affirmative Action and College Admissions, 11/17
Charter Schools, 3/17
Civic Education, 2/17
Student Debt, 11/16

Environment/Society
Future of Marriage, 12/17
Stolen Antiquities, 11/17
Climate Change and National Security, 9/17
Muslims in America, 7/17
Funding the Arts, 7/17

Health/Safety
Medical Breakthroughs, 9/17
Medical Marijuana, 7/17
Food Labeling, 6/17
Sports and Sexual Assault, 4/17

Politics/Economy
Privatizing Government Services, 12/17
Democracy Under Stress, 10/17
Cyberwarfare Threat, 10/17
Universal Basic Income, 9/17
National Debt, 9/17
North Korea Showdown, 5/17

Upcoming Reports

Citizen Protests, 1/5/18   Future of Puerto Rico, 1/12/18   Disaster Relief, 1/19/18

ACCESS

CQ Researcher is available in print and online. For access, visit your library or www.cqresearcher.com.

STAY CURRENT

For notice of upcoming *CQ Researcher* reports or to learn more about *CQ Researcher* products, subscribe to the free email newsletters, *CQ Researcher Alert!* and *CQ Researcher News*: http://cqpress.com/newsletters.

PURCHASE

To purchase a *CQ Researcher* report in print or electronic format (PDF), visit www.cqpress.com or call 866-427-7737. Single reports start at $15. Bulk purchase discounts and electronic-rights licensing are also available.

SUBSCRIBE

Annual full-service *CQ Researcher* subscriptions—including 44 reports a year, monthly index updates, and a bound volume—start at $1,131. Add $25 for domestic postage.

CQ Researcher Online offers a backfile from 1991 and a number of tools to simplify research. For pricing information, call 800-818-7243 or 805-499-9774 or email librarysales@sagepub.com.

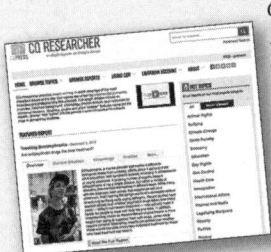

Published by CQ Press, an Imprint of SAGE Publications, Inc.

www.cqresearcher.com

Index

January 1991– December 2017

❖ *CQ Researcher* reports are indexed by title under boldface topic headings.

- Titles are followed by the date the report appeared and the first page number of its print version.

- Page numbers followed by an asterisk refer to a sidebar or the "At Issue" (Pro/Con) feature.

- Page numbers preceded by a double asterisk refer to an issue that has been updated.

❖ This index is updated monthly and available at: http://library.cqpress.com/static.php?page=admin

❖ *CQ Researcher* can be accessed online at: www.cqresearcher.com

Los Angeles I London I New Delhi
Singapore I Washington DC I Melbourne

Published by CQ Press, an Imprint of SAGE Publications, Inc.

	Date	Page
Abortion. *See also Birth control*		
Abortion Clinic Protests	04/07/95	297
Abortion Debates	03/21/03	249
Abortion Debates	09/10/10	725
Abortion Debates	03/21/14	265
Abortion Showdowns	09/22/06	769
Catholic Church in the U.S.	09/08/95	784*
Embryo Research	12/17/99	1065
Feminism's Future	02/28/97	181*
Fetal Tissue Research	08/16/91	561
Global Population Growth	01/16/15	49
Population and the Environment	07/17/98	607*
Population Growth	07/16/93	601
Religion and Law	11/07/14	937
Religion and Politics	07/30/04	637
Reproductive Ethics	04/08/94	289
Roe v. Wade at 25	11/28/97	1033
Supreme Court's Future	01/28/05	77
Supreme Court Preview	09/17/93	817
Teenagers and Abortion	07/05/91	441
Teen Pregnancy	03/26/10	265*
Women and Human Rights	04/30/99	367*
Abu Musab al-Zarqawi		
Global Jihad	10/14/05	857
Accidents. *See Occupational health and safety; Safety;*		
Traffic accidents		
Acquired immune deficiency syndrome. *See AIDS disease*		
Addiction. *See Drug abuse*		
Adolescents and youth. *See also Colleges and universities;*		
Elementary and secondary education; Children's health		
and safety		
Advertising Overload	01/23/04	49
Arts Education	03/16/12	253
Boys' Emotional Needs	06/18/99	521
Broadcast Indecency	04/16/04	321
Changing U.S. Electorate	05/30/08	**457
Charter Schools	03/10/17	217
Childhood Depression	07/16/99	593
Child Poverty	04/07/00	281
Child Welfare Reform	04/22/05	345
Chronic Fatigue Syndrome	04/05/02	289
College Rankings	01/02/15	1
Combating Plagiarism	09/19/03	773
Community Prosecution	12/15/00	1016*
Consumer Debt	11/15/96	1009
Cosmetic Surgery	04/15/05	317
Covering the Uninsured	06/14/02	521
Cyberbullying	05/02/08	385
Cyber-Predators	03/01/02	169
Cyber Socializing	07/28/06	625
Declining Crime Rates	04/04/97	289
Digital Education	12/02/11	1001
Draft Debates	08/19/05	661

	Date	Page
Dropout Rate	06/13/14	505
Drug Safety	03/11/05	221
Eating Disorders	02/10/06	**121
Extreme Sports	04/03/09	297
Financial Literacy	09/04/09	717
Free Speech on Campus	05/08/15	409
The Future of Baseball	09/25/98	839*
Future of Books	05/29/09	**473
Future of the GOP	03/20/09	249
Future of Marriage	05/07/04	397
Future of the Music Industry	11/21/03	989
Gang Crisis	05/14/04	421
Gender and Learning	05/20/05	445
Girls' Rights	04/17/15	337
Hazing	01/09/04	1
Highway Safety	07/14/95	609
Homeless Students	04/05/13	305
Home Schooling	03/07/14	217
Home Schooling Debate	01/17/03	25
Homework Debate	12/06/02	993
HPV Vaccine	05/11/07	409
Human Trafficking and Slavery	03/26/04	273
Illegal Immigration	05/06/05	393
Immigrants and the Economy	02/24/17	169
Impact of the Internet on Thinking	09/24/10	773
Increase in Autism	06/13/03	**545
Juvenile Justice	02/25/94	169
Juvenile Justice	11/07/08	913
Kids in Prison	04/27/01	345
Manipulating the Human Genome	06/19/15	529
Media Violence	02/14/14	145
Mental Illness Medication Debate	02/06/04	101
Millennial Generation	06/26/15	553
Mothers' Movement	04/04/03	297
Movie Ratings	03/28/03	273
National Service	06/30/06	577
Native Americans	05/08/92	400
Native American Youths	04/24/15	361
No Child Left Behind	05/27/05	469
Parental Rights	10/25/96	950*
Paying College Athletes	07/11/14	577
Pornography	10/21/16	865
Preventing Bullying	12/10/10	**1013
Preventing Juvenile Crime	03/15/96	217
Preventing Obesity	10/01/10	797
Prisoners and Mental Illness	03/13/15	241
Prostitution Debate	05/23/08	433
Race and Education	09/05/14	721
Racial Conflict	01/08/16	25
Reality TV	08/27/10	677
Reforming Big-Time College Sports	03/19/04	249
Restorative Justice	02/05/16	121
Rethinking Foreign Aid	04/14/17	313
Rising College Costs	12/05/03	1013

	Date	Page
School Desegregation	04/23/04	345
School Discipline	05/09/14	409
School Violence	10/09/98	881
School Vouchers Showdown	02/15/02	121
Sentencing Debates	11/05/04	925
Sex Offenders	09/08/06	721
Sex on Campus	11/04/94	961
Sexual Abuse and the Clergy	05/03/02	393
Sexually Transmitted Diseases	12/03/04	997
Soccer in America	04/22/94	337
Social Networking	09/17/10	749
Student Journalism	06/05/98	481
Students Under Stress	07/13/07	577
Teaching Critical Thinking	04/10/15	313
Teenage Suicide	06/14/91	369
Teen Driving	01/07/05	1
Teen Drug Use	06/03/11	481
Teen Pregnancy	03/26/10	265*
Teen Sex	09/16/05	761
Teen Spending	05/26/06	457
Teen Suicide	09/12/14	745
Tobacco Industry	12/10/04	**1025
Transgender Rights	12/11/15	1033
Treating Schizophrenia	12/05/14	1009
The Value of a College Education	11/20/09	981
Understanding Autism	08/01/14	649
Vaccine Controversies	02/19/16	169
Video Games	11/10/06	**937
Video Games and Learning	02/12/16	145
Violence in Schools	09/11/92	785
Virtual Reality	02/26/16	193
Young Voters	10/02/15	817
Youth Gangs	10/11/91	753
Youth Suicide	02/13/04	125
Youth Unemployment	03/14/14	241

Adolescents and youth — Alcohol and drug use

AB and IP Programs	03/03/06	193
Alcohol Advertising	03/14/97	217
Athletes and Drugs	07/26/91	513
Bullying	02/04/05	101
Celebrity Culture	03/18/05	245
Drinking on Campus	03/20/98	241
Drinking on Campus	08/18/06	649
Drug-Policy Debate	07/28/00	610*
Drug Testing	11/20/98	1006*
Greek Life on Campus	11/20/15	985
High School Sports	09/22/95	825
Juvenile Justice	11/07/08	913
Marijuana Laws	02/11/05	125
Medical Marijuana	08/20/99	711*
Medication Abuse	10/09/09	837
Methamphetamine	07/15/05	589
Native American Youths	04/24/15	361

	Date	Page
Preventing Hazing	02/08/13	133
Preventing Teen Drug Use	07/28/95	657
Preventing Teen Drug Use	03/15/02	217
Reforming Big-Time College Sports	03/19/04	249
Rethinking Ritalin	10/22/99	922*
Social Media Explosion	01/25/13	81
Sports and Drugs	07/23/04	618*
Teen Driving	01/07/05	1
Treating Addiction	05/02/14	385
Underage Drinking	03/13/92	217
War on Drugs	03/19/93	254*
War on Drugs	06/02/06	481
Youth Violence	03/05/10	193*

Adolescents and youth — Employment

Closing In on Tobacco	11/12/99	977
Fast-Food Shake-Up	11/08/91	825
Future Job Market	01/11/02	1
High-Tech Labor Shortage	04/24/98	370*
Job Stress	08/04/95	695*
National Service	06/25/93	553
The Value of a College Education	11/20/09	981
Youth Apprenticeships	10/23/92	905
Youth Unemployment	03/14/14	241

Adolescents and youth — Pregnancy

Abortion Debates	03/21/03	249
Abortion Showdowns	09/22/06	769
Birth-Control Debate	06/24/05	565
Child Welfare Reform	04/22/05	345
Encouraging Teen Abstinence	07/10/98	577
Girls' Rights	04/17/15	337
Infant Mortality	07/31/92	652
Preventing Teen Pregnancy	05/14/93	409
Sexually Transmitted Diseases	12/03/04	997
Teenagers and Abortion	07/05/91	441
Teen Pregnancy	03/26/10	265*
Tobacco Industry	12/10/04	**1025
Welfare, Work and the States	12/06/96	1069*

Adoption

Abortion Debates	03/21/03	249
Adoption	11/26/93	1033
Adoption Controversies	09/10/99	777
Child Welfare Reform	04/22/05	345
Foster Care Reform	01/09/98	1
Gay Marriage	09/05/03	721
Gay Rights	03/05/93	210*
Gay Rights Update	04/14/00	305
Native Americans' Future	07/12/96	617*

Advanced Placement (AP)

AB and IP Programs	03/03/06	193
Racial Diversity in Public Schools	09/14/07	**745
Students Under Stress	07/13/07	577
Teaching Critical Thinking	04/10/15	313

	Date	Page		Date	Page
Advertising. *See also Political advertising*			Civil Liberties in Wartime	12/14/01	1017
Advertising Overload	01/23/04	49	Closing Guantánamo	02/27/09	**177
Advertising Under Attack	09/13/91	657	Combat Journalism	04/12/13	329
Alcohol Advertising	03/14/97	217	Cost of the Iraq War	04/25/08	361*
Celebrity Culture	03/18/05	245	Drone Warfare	08/06/10	653
Centennial Olympic Games	04/05/96	289	Exporting Democracy	04/01/05	269
Children's Television	08/15/97	734*	Foreign Aid and National Security	06/17/11	529
The Consumer Culture	11/19/99	1007*	Government Secrecy	02/11/11	121
Dietary Supplements	09/03/04	709	Intelligence Reforms	01/25/02	49
Digital Commerce	02/05/99	98*	International Law	12/17/04	1049
Digital Journalism	05/30/14	457	Interrogating the CIA	09/25/09	789
Drinking on Campus	03/20/98	253*	Islamic Fundamentalism	03/24/00	241
Drug Company Ethics	06/06/03	521*	Military Suicides	09/23/11	781*
E-Cigarettes	09/19/14	769	New Defense Priorities	09/13/02	721
Future of Newspapers	01/20/06	49	The Obama Presidency	01/30/09	73
The Growing Influence of Boycotts	01/04/91	1	Policing the Borders	02/22/02	145
Media Violence	02/14/14	145	Privatizing the Military	07/13/12	597
The New Corporate Philanthropy	02/27/98	186*	Prosecuting Terrorists	03/12/10	**217*
Online Dating	03/20/15	265	Reforming Veterans' Health Care	11/21/14	985
Online Privacy	11/06/09	**933	Remembering 9/11	09/02/11	701*
Preventing Teen Drug Use	07/28/95	663*	Treatment of Detainees	08/25/06	673
Reforming Big-Time College Sports	03/19/04	249	U.S.-British Relations	11/05/10	917*
Regulating the Internet	06/30/95	568*	U.S.-Pakistan Relations	08/05/11	653*
Regulating Pharmaceuticals	10/11/13	861	War on Terrorism	10/12/01	817
Regulating Tobacco	09/30/94	852*	Weapons of Mass Destruction	03/08/02	193
Sex, Violence and the Media	11/17/95	1025*	Women and Human Rights	04/30/99	353
Soccer in America	04/22/94	342*	Women in Combat	05/13/16	433
Teen Driving	01/07/05	1	Women in the Military	11/13/09	957
Teen Drug Use	06/03/11	481	Wounded Veterans	08/31/07	697
Teens and Tobacco	12/01/95	1065	**Africa**		
Television's Future	02/16/07	145	Aiding Africa	08/29/03	697
Tobacco Industry	12/10/04	**1025	AIDS Update	12/04/98	1062*
Trust in Media	06/09/17	481	Assessing the Threat From al Qaeda	06/27/14	553
Underage Drinking	03/13/92	217	Assisting Refugees	02/07/97	104*
Affirmative action			Battling HIV/AIDS	10/26/07	889
Affirmative Action	09/21/01	737	Children in Crisis	08/31/01	657
Affirmative Action	10/17/08	**841	Democracy in Africa	03/24/95	241
Affirmative Action and			Ecotourism	10/20/06	865
College Admissions	11/17/17	969	Emerging Infectious Diseases	02/13/15	145
The Black Middle Class	01/23/98	49	Ending Poverty	09/09/05	733
Diversity in Hollywood	08/05/16	649	European Migration Crisis	07/31/15	649
Diversity in the Workplace	10/10/97	889	Famine in Africa	11/08/02	921
Getting into College	02/23/96	169	Foreign Aid and National Security	06/17/11	529
Race in America	07/11/03	603*	Foreign Aid After Sept. 11	04/26/02	361
Racial Diversity in Public Schools	09/14/07	**745	Girls' Rights	04/17/15	337
Racial Quotas	05/17/91	277	Global AIDS Crisis	10/13/00	809
Racial Tensions in Schools	01/07/94	1	Global Food Crisis	06/27/08	553
Rethinking Affirmative Action	04/28/95	369	Global Hunger	08/08/14	673
Supreme Court Controversies	09/28/12	813	Global Jihad	10/14/05	857
Afghanistan			Global Refugee Crisis	07/09/99	569
Afghanistan Dilemma	08/07/09	**669*	Global Water Shortages	12/15/95	1113
America at War	07/23/10	**605	Homegrown Jihadists	09/03/10	701
Assessing the Threat From al Qaeda	06/27/14	553	Human Rights in China	07/25/08	601
Caring for Veterans	04/23/10	361	Human Rights Issues	10/30/09	909

	Date	Page
Human Trafficking and Slavery	03/26/04	273
Oil Diplomacy	01/24/03	49
Pandemic Threat	06/02/17	457
Philanthropy in America	12/08/06	1009
Reforming the U.N.	06/24/16	553
Religious Persecution	11/21/97	1009
Rethinking Foreign Aid	04/14/17	313
Sexually Transmitted Diseases	12/03/04	997
South Africa's Future	01/14/94	25
Stopping Genocide	08/27/04	685
Terrorism in Africa	07/10/15	577
Transnational Crime	08/29/14	697
Water Shortages	08/01/03	649
Women and Human Rights	04/30/99	353
World Hunger	10/25/91	814

African-Americans

Adoption	11/26/93	1033
Adoption Controversies	09/10/99	777
Affirmative Action	10/17/08	**841
Affirmative Action and College Admissions	11/17/17	969
Asian Americans	12/13/91	960
Asthma Epidemic	12/24/99	1093*
Black Colleges	12/12/03	1045
The Black Middle Class	01/23/98	49
Breast Cancer	04/02/10	289
Census Controversey	05/14/10	433
Changing Demographics	11/16/12	989
Changing U.S. Electorate	05/30/08	**457
Charter Schools	12/20/02	1033
College Football	11/18/11	977
College Sports	08/26/94	745
Consumer Debt	03/02/07	193
Debate Over Immigration	07/14/00	580*
Democracy in Africa	03/24/95	246*
Discipline in Schools	02/15/08	145
Diversity in Hollywood	08/05/16	649
Diversity in the Workplace	10/10/97	889
Domestic Poverty	09/07/07	**721
Dropout Rate	06/13/14	505
Drug-Policy Debate	07/28/00	612*
Electing Minorities	08/12/94	697
Encouraging Teen Abstinence	07/10/98	594*
Evaluating Head Start	08/26/05	685
Far-Right Extremism	09/18/15	769
Fighting Crime	02/08/08	121
Fighting Urban Poverty	07/17/15	601
Financial Literacy	09/04/09	717
The Future of Baseball	09/25/98	839*
Future of the GOP	03/20/09	249
Future of Marriage	12/01/17	993
Future of the Middle Class	04/08/16	313
Gentrification	02/20/15	169
Gun Control Debate	11/12/04	949

	Date	Page
Hate Crimes	01/08/93	1
Hate Groups	05/08/09	421
Hispanic Americans	10/30/92	935
Historic Preservation	10/07/94	876*
Housing Discrimination	02/24/95	169
Intelligence Testing	07/30/93	649
Jailing Debtors	09/16/16	745
The Jury System	11/10/95	993
Juvenile Justice	11/07/08	913
Mortgage Crisis	11/02/07	**913
Muslims in America	04/30/93	361
New Military Culture	04/26/96	361
The Obama Legacy	11/04/16	913
The Obama Presidency	01/30/09	73
Obesity Epidemic	01/31/03	78*
Peace Corps' Challenges in the 1990s	01/25/91	49
Police Corruption	11/24/95	1041
Police Misconduct	04/06/12	301
Policing the Police	03/17/00	209
Preventing Hazing	02/08/13	133
Preventing Teen Pregnancy	05/14/93	409
Protestants Today	12/07/07	1009
Public Defenders	04/18/08	337*
Public Housing	09/10/93	793
Race and Education	09/05/14	721
Race and Politics	07/18/08	577
Race in America	07/11/03	593
Racial Conflict	01/08/16	25
Racial Diversity in Public Schools	09/14/07	**745
Racial Quotas	05/17/91	277
Racial Tensions in Schools	01/07/94	1
Reassessing the Nation's Gun Laws	03/22/91	157
Rebuilding New Orleans	02/03/06	97
Redistricting Disputes	03/12/04	221
Redistricting: Drawing Power with a Map	02/15/91	97
Redistricting Showdown	08/25/17	677
Reforming Big-Time College Sports	03/19/04	249
Reparations Movement	06/22/01	529
Rethinking Affirmative Action	04/28/95	382*
Rethinking School Integration	10/18/96	913
Revising No Child Left Behind	04/16/10	337
School Desegregation	04/23/04	345
School Vouchers	04/09/99	281
School Vouchers Showdown	02/15/02	121
Sentencing Debates	11/05/04	925
Sentencing Reform	01/10/14	25
Sexually Transmitted Diseases	12/03/04	997
Should the U.S. Reinstate the Draft?	01/11/91	17
Student Aid	01/25/08	73
Teaching History	09/29/95	849
Teens and Tobacco	12/01/95	1082*
Unions at a Crossroads	08/07/15	673
Upward Mobility	04/29/05	369

	Date	Page
Worker Retraining	01/21/94	62*
Wrongful Convictions	04/17/09	**345
Youth Unemployment	03/14/14	241
Youth Violence	03/05/10	193*
Zero Tolerance	03/10/00	185

Agency for International Development

	Date	Page
Aiding Africa	08/29/03	697
Famine in Africa	11/08/02	921
Foreign Aid After Sept. 11	04/26/02	361
Global Hunger	08/08/14	673
Reassessing Foreign Aid	09/27/96	841
Rethinking Foreign Aid	04/14/17	313
Trouble in South America	03/14/03	225

Aging. *See Elderly*

Agriculture. *See also Forests and forestry*

	Date	Page
Animal Rights	05/24/91	316*
Animal Rights	01/08/10	1
Biofuels Boom	09/29/06	793
Biotech Foods	03/30/01	249
Bush and the Environment	10/25/02	865
California: Enough Water for the Future?	04/19/91	221
Child Labor and Sweatshops	08/16/96	732*
Coastal Development	08/21/98	739*
Consumer Safety	10/12/07	841
Crisis on the Plains	05/09/03	417
Domestic Drones	10/18/13	885
Factory Farms	01/12/07	25
Farm Policy	12/02/94	1057
Farm Policy	08/10/12	693
Farm Subsidies	05/17/02	433
Fighting over Animal Rights	08/02/96	673
Food Labeling	06/16/17	509
Food Policy Debates	10/03/14	817
Food Safety	11/01/02	897
Food Safety	12/17/10	1037
Food Safety Battle: Organic v. Biotech	09/04/98	761
Genetically Modified Food	08/31/12	717
Global Food Crisis	06/27/08	553
Global Hunger	08/08/14	673
Global Water Shortages	12/15/95	1113
Hunger in America	07/07/17	557
Illegal Immigration	05/06/05	393
The New Environmentalism	12/01/06	985
Pesticide Controversies	06/05/15	481
Reforming the Corps	05/30/03	497
Regulating Pesticides	01/28/94	73
Regulating Pesticides	08/06/99	665
Reviving Rural Economies	03/31/17	265
Slow Food Movement	01/26/07	73
Tobacco Industry	12/10/04	**1025
U.S. Trade Policy	01/29/93	84*
U.S. Trade Policy	09/13/13	765
Water Crisis in the West	12/09/11	1025

	Date	Page
Water Shortages	08/01/03	649
Water Shortages	06/18/10	529
World Hunger	10/25/91	818

AIDS disease

	Date	Page
Aiding Africa	08/29/03	697
AIDS Update	12/04/98	1049
Alternative Medicine	01/31/92	79*
Battling HIV/AIDS	10/26/07	889
Birth Control Choices	07/29/94	649
Birth-Control Debate	06/24/05	565
Blood Supply Safety	11/11/94	985
Children in Crisis	08/31/01	657
Combating AIDS	04/21/95	345
Emerging Infectious Diseases	02/13/15	145
Famine in Africa	11/08/02	935*
Fighting over Animal Rights	08/02/96	677*
Gay Rights	03/05/93	204*
Girls' Rights	04/17/15	337
Global AIDS Crisis	10/13/00	809
Infant Mortality	07/31/92	651
New Military Culture	04/26/96	377*
Philanthropy in America	12/08/06	1009
Pornography	10/21/16	865
Privacy in the Workplace	11/19/93	1023*
Prostitution	06/11/93	505
Prostitution Debate	05/23/08	433
Sexually Transmitted Diseases	12/03/04	997
Women and AIDS	12/25/92	1121

Air pollution. *See also Global warming*

	Date	Page
Acid Rain: New Approach to Old Problem	03/08/91	129
Air Pollution and Climate Control	11/13/15	961
Air Pollution Conflict	11/14/03	965
Alternative Energy	02/25/05	173
Asbestos Litigation	05/02/03	398*
Bush and the Environment	10/25/02	865
China Today	04/04/14	289
Climate Change	01/27/06	73
Climate Change	06/14/13	521
Coal's Comeback	10/05/07	817
Coal Industry's Future	06/17/16	529
Crackdown on Smoking	12/04/92	1066*
Electric Cars	07/09/93	577
Environmental Movement at 25	03/31/95	280*
Flexible Work Arrangements	08/14/98	715*
Future of the Arctic	09/20/13	789
The Greening of Eastern Europe	11/15/91	849
Indoor Air Pollution	10/27/95	945
Human Rights in China	07/25/08	601
Jobs vs. Environment	05/15/92	422
Lead Poisoning	06/19/92	537
Managing Wildfires	11/02/12	941
National Parks	01/17/14	49
New Air Quality Standards	03/07/97	193

	Date	Page
The New Environmentalism	12/01/06	985
Oil Imports	08/23/91	585
Regulating Toxic Chemicals	07/18/14	601
SUV Debate	05/16/03	460*
Traffic Congestion	05/06/94	385

Air transportation

Airline Industry Problems	09/24/99	825
Airline Safety	10/08/93	865
Airline Safety	05/15/15	433
Domestic Drones	10/18/13	885
Future of the Airline Industry	06/21/02	545
Future of the Airlines	03/07/08	217
Homeland Security	09/12/03	749
Homeland Security	02/13/09	129
Privatizing Government Services	12/08/17	1017
Re-examining 9/11	06/04/04	493

Alcohol

Advertising Overload	01/23/04	49
Alcohol Advertising	03/14/97	217
Athletes and Drugs	07/26/91	519*
Combating Addiction	02/09/07	121
Crime on Campus	02/04/11	97
Diet and Health	02/23/01	129
Drinking on Campus	03/20/98	241
Drinking on Campus	08/18/06	649
Drug-Policy Debate	07/28/00	599*
Drug Testing	11/20/98	1001
Drunken Driving	10/06/00	793
Ending Homelessness	06/18/04	541
Future of Cars	07/25/14	625
Hazing	01/09/04	1
Highway Safety	07/14/95	609
Native Americans	05/08/92	394*
Native Americans' Future	07/12/96	608*
Preventing Hazing	02/08/13	133
Preventing Teen Drug Use	03/15/02	217
Reducing Traffic Deaths	02/17/17	145
Socially Responsible Investing	08/29/08	673
Teen Driving	01/07/05	1
Treating Addiction	01/06/95	14*
Treating Addiction	05/02/14	385
Underage Drinking	03/13/92	217
Youth Suicide	02/13/04	125

Alternative fuels

Alternative Energy	07/10/92	573
Alternative Energy	02/25/05	173
Confronting Warming	01/09/09	1
Biofuels Boom	09/29/06	793
Bush and the Environment	10/25/02	865
Electric Cars	07/09/93	577
Energy and Climate	07/24/09	621
Energy Efficiency	05/19/06	433
Energy Security	02/01/02	84*

	Date	Page
Future of the Airlines	03/07/08	217
Modernizing the Grid	02/19/10	145
Oil Diplomacy	01/24/03	49
Oil Imports	08/23/91	599
Oil Production in the 21st Century	08/07/98	682*
Renewable Energy	11/07/97	961
SUV Debate	05/16/03	449

Alternative medicine

Alternative Medicine	01/31/92	73
Alternative Medicine	09/06/13	741
Alternative Medicine's Next Phase	02/14/97	121
Chronic Fatigue Syndrome	04/05/02	289
Dietary Supplements	07/08/94	590*
Dietary Supplements	09/03/04	709
Drug-Resistant Bacteria	06/04/99	489*
Fighting Cancer	01/22/16	73
Homeopathy Debate	12/19/03	1069
Lyme Disease	11/08/13	957
Marijuana Industry	10/16/15	865
Marijuana Laws	02/11/05	125
Medical Marijuana	07/21/17	605
Prayer and Healing	01/14/05	25
Rethinking Ritalin	10/22/99	905
Treating Alzheimer's Disease	07/24/15	625

Alternative sentences

Civic Renewal	03/21/97	252*
Community Prosecution	12/15/00	1009
Jailing Debtors	09/16/16	745
Juvenile Justice	02/25/94	180*
Native American Youths	04/24/15	361
Prison-Building Boom	09/17/99	801
Prison Overcrowding	02/04/94	105*
Punishing Sex Offenders	01/12/96	25
Reforming Juvenile Justice	09/11/15	745
Restorative Justice	02/05/16	121
School Discipline	05/09/14	409
Sentencing Debates	11/05/04	925
Sentencing Reform	01/10/14	25
Women in Prison	03/03/17	193

American Indians. *See Native Americans*

American Library Association

The Future of Libraries	05/23/97	457
Hard Times for Libraries	06/26/92	553

Americans with Disabilities Act, 1990

The Disabilities Act	12/27/91	993
Implementing the Disabilities Act	12/20/96	1105
Mental Health Policy	09/12/97	793

Amtrak. *See Railroads*

Animals. *See also Endangered species; Wildlife*

America's Pampered Pets	12/27/96	1129
Animal Intelligence	10/22/10	869
Animal Rights	05/24/91	301
Animal Rights	01/08/10	1

	Date	Page
Biology and Behavior	04/03/98	295*
The Cloning Controversy	05/09/97	409
'Designer' Humans	05/18/01	433*
Disappearing Species	11/30/07	985
Factory Farms	01/12/07	25
Fighting over Animal Rights	08/02/96	673
Hunting Controversy	01/24/92	49
Invasive Species	10/05/01	785
Invasive Species	02/17/12	153
Marine Mammals vs. Fish	08/28/92	737*
Organ Transplants	08/11/95	705
Pesticide Controversies	06/05/15	481
Protecting the Oceans	10/17/14	865
Protecting Wetlands	10/03/08	793*
Prozac Controversy	08/19/94	734*
Species Extinction	12/15/17	1041
Zoos in the 21st Century	04/28/00	353

Anorexia nervosa. *See Eating disorders*

Anti-Ballistic Missile Treaty, 1972. *See Treaties and international agreements; International relations — U.S. foreign policy*

Antitrust law. *See also Business and industry*

Airline Industry Problems	09/24/99	825
Antitrust Policy	06/12/98	505
The Business of Sports	02/10/95	121
Digital Commerce	02/05/99	89
Google's Dominance	11/11/11	953
Paying for College	11/20/92	1017*
Reforming Big-Time College Sports	03/19/04	249
Wealth and Inequality	04/18/14	337

Aquaculture

Fish Farming	07/27/07	625
Protecting the Oceans	10/17/14	865
Saving the Oceans	11/04/05	933

Arab-Americans

Middle East Tensions	10/27/06	**889
Muslims in America	04/30/93	361
Muslims in America	07/28/17	629
Race in America	07/11/03	612*
Understanding Islam	11/03/06	913
War on Terrorism	10/12/01	817

Arafat, Yasser. *See Middle East*

Archaeology

Archaeology Today	05/24/02	457
Historic Preservation	10/07/94	870*
Is America Allowing Its Past to Be Stolen? 33	01/18/91	
Stolen Antiquities	11/10/17	945

Arctic National Wildlife Refuge

Arctic Development	12/02/16	989
Bush and the Environment	10/25/02	865
Domestic Energy Development	09/30/05	809
Energy Efficiency	05/19/06	433

	Date	Page
Energy Policy	05/25/01	441
Energy Security	02/01/02	73
Future of the Arctic	09/20/13	789
Oil Imports	08/23/91	601*

Armed forces. *See Military service*

Arms control

Arms Sales	12/09/94	1081
Banning Land Mines	08/08/97	697
Bush's Defense Strategy	09/07/01	703*
Chemical and Biological Weapons	01/31/97	73
Confronting Iraq	10/04/02	793
Defeating the Islamic State	04/01/16	289
Defense Priorities	07/30/99	658*
Ethics of War	12/13/02	1013
European Unrest	01/09/15	25
Future of NATO	02/28/03	177
Gun Rights Debates	10/31/08	**889
Haiti's Dilemma	02/18/05	149
Missile Defense	09/08/00	689
Modernizing the Nuclear Arsenal	07/29/16	625
Non-Proliferation Treaty at 25	01/27/95	73
North Korean Crisis	04/11/03	321
Nuclear Arms Cleanup	06/24/94	553
Nuclear Proliferation	06/05/92	481
Nuclear Proliferation and Terrorism	04/02/04	297
Police Tactics	12/12/14	1033
Robotic Warfare	01/23/15	73
U.S.-Iran Relations	03/04/16	217
U.S. Policy in Asia	11/27/92	1025
U.S.-Russia Relations	01/18/02	32*
U.S.-Russian Relations	05/22/98	457
The United Nations and Global Security	02/27/04	173
United Nations at 50	08/18/95	745*
Weapons of Mass Destruction	03/08/02	193

Army Corps of Engineers

Coastal Development	08/21/98	721
Reforming the Corps	05/30/03	497

Army, U.S. *See Military service*

U.S. Global Engagement	05/16/14	433

Artificial intelligence

Artificial Intelligence	11/14/97	985
Artificial Intelligence	04/22/11	361
Future of Computers	05/26/00	449
Government Surveillance	08/30/13	717
Insurance Fraud	10/11/96	906*
Robotic Warfare	01/23/15	73
Robotics and the Economy	09/25/15	793

Arts

Arts Education	03/16/12	253
Arts Funding	10/21/94	913
Funding the Arts	07/14/17	581
Humanities Education	12/06/13	1029
Stolen Antiquities	04/13/07	313

	Date	Page
Asbestos		
Asbestos Litigation	05/02/03	393
Indoor Air Pollution	10/27/95	957*
Science in the Courtroom	10/22/93	922*
Worker Safety	05/21/04	445
Asia		
Battling HIV/AIDS	10/26/07	889
China After Deng	06/13/97	505
China and the South China Sea	01/20/17	49
China Today	08/04/00	625
China Today	04/04/14	289
Deflation Fears	02/13/98	121
Democracy in Asia	07/24/98	625
Ecotourism	10/20/06	865
Emerging India	04/19/02	329
Fighting SARS	06/20/03	569
Future of the Arctic	09/20/13	789
Future of Korea	05/19/00	425
Global AIDS Crisis	10/13/00	814*
Global Hunger	08/08/14	673
Human Trafficking and Slavery	03/26/04	273
Immigrants and the Economy	02/24/17	169
International Monetary Fund	01/29/99	65
New Era in Asia	02/14/92	121
Pandemic Threat	06/02/17	457
Religious Persecution	11/21/97	1009
Taiwan, China, and the U.S.	05/24/96	457
U.S.-Europe Relations	03/23/12	277
U.S. Policy in Asia	11/27/92	1025
U.S.-Vietnam Relations	12/03/93	1057
Asian-Americans		
Affirmative Action and College Admissions	11/17/17	969
Asian Americans	12/13/91	945
Debate Over Immigration	07/14/00	580*
Electing Minorities	08/12/94	711*
Gang Crisis	05/14/04	421
Hate Crimes	01/08/93	1
The New Immigrants	01/24/97	49
Race in America	07/11/03	593
Racial Quotas	05/17/91	285*
School Desegregation	04/23/04	356*
Assisted suicide		
Assisted Suicide	02/21/92	145
Assisted Suicide	05/17/13	449
Assisted Suicide Controversy	05/05/95	393
Caring for the Dying	09/05/97	769
Right to Die	05/13/05	421
Asylum. *See Political asylum*		
Athletes. *See Sports*		
Attention deficit disorder		
Rethinking Ritalin	10/22/99	905

	Date	Page
Australia		
Caring for the Dying	09/05/97	782*
Gun Control Standoff	12/19/97	1116*
Protecting the Oceans	10/17/14	865
Reparations Movement	06/22/01	529
Automobiles and automobile industry. *See also* ***Highways and roads; Traffic accidents***		
Aggressive Driving	07/25/97	649*
Air Pollution Conflict	11/14/03	965
Alternative Energy	07/10/92	584*
Alternative Energy	02/25/05	173
Arbitrating Disputes	03/11/16	241
Auto Industry's Future	01/21/00	17
Auto Industry's Future	02/06/09	**105
Auto Safety	10/26/01	873
Biofuels Boom	09/29/06	793
Business Bankruptcy	04/10/09	321
Buying Green	02/29/08	193
Cell Phone Safety	03/16/01	201
Confronting Warming	01/09/09	1
Distracted Driving	05/04/12	401
Electric Cars	07/09/93	577
Energy and the Environment	03/03/00	174*
Energy Efficiency	05/19/06	433
Energy Security	02/01/02	73
Future of Amtrak	10/18/02	841
Future of Cars	07/25/14	625
Global Warming Update	11/01/96	966*
High-Speed Trains	05/01/09	**397
Labor Movement's Future	06/28/96	571*
Mass Transit Boom	01/18/08	49
The New Environmentalism	12/01/06	985
Oil Imports	08/23/91	585
Oil Jitters	01/04/08	**1
Recession's Regional Impact	02/01/91	74*
Reducing Your Carbon Footprint	12/05/08	985
Reducing Traffic Deaths	02/17/17	145
Renewable Energy	11/07/97	972*
SUV Debate	05/16/03	449
Teen Driving	01/07/05	1
Traffic Congestion	05/06/94	385
Traffic Congestion	08/27/99	729
Transportation Policy	07/04/97	577
The U.S. and Japan	05/31/91	342*
U.S. Auto Industry	10/16/92	881
U.S. Trade Policy	01/29/93	73
Avian Flu		
Avian Flu Threat	01/13/06	25
Pandemic Threat	06/02/17	457
Aviation. *See Air transportation*		
Baby Boomers		
Aging Baby Boomers	10/19/07	865
Aging Population	07/15/11	577

	Date	Page
Baby Boomers at Midlife	07/31/98	649
Budget Deficit	12/09/05	1029
Caring for the Dying	09/05/97	787*
Caring for the Elderly	02/20/98	160*
College Rankings	01/02/15	1
Medicare Reform	08/22/03	673
Millennial Generation	06/26/15	553
The New Corporate Philanthropy	02/27/98	184*
Overhauling Social Security	05/12/95	417
Pension Crisis	02/17/06	145
Preventing Memory Loss	04/04/08	289*
Religion in America	11/25/94	1033
Retirement Security	05/31/02	481
Saving Social Security	10/02/98	857
Smart Growth	05/28/04	469
Social Security Reform	09/24/04	781
Treating Alzheimer's Disease	07/24/15	625

Balkans

Democracy in Eastern Europe	10/08/99	865
Economic Sanctions	10/28/94	954*
Ethics of War	12/13/02	1013
Europe's New Right	02/12/93	121
Foreign Policy Burden	08/20/93	721
Future of NATO	02/28/03	177
Privatizing the Military	06/25/04	565
Torture	04/18/03	345
The United Nations and Global Security	02/27/04	173
War Crimes	07/07/95	585

Bankruptcy

Accountants Under Fire	03/22/02	241
Auto Industry's Future	02/06/09	**105
Business Bankruptcy	04/10/09	321
Consumer Debt	11/15/96	1009
Consumer Debt	03/02/07	193
Financial Literacy	09/04/09	717
Future of the Airline Industry	06/21/02	545
Pension Crisis	02/17/06	145
Regulating Credit Cards	10/10/08	817*
Student Debt	11/18/16	965
Teen Spending	05/26/06	457

Banks and banking

Business Bankruptcy	04/10/09	321
Cyber-Crime	04/12/02	305
The Dark Web	01/15/16	49
Digital Currency	09/26/14	793
The Federal Reserve	09/01/00	673
The Federal Reserve	01/03/14	1
Holocaust Reparations	03/26/99	257
Housing Discrimination	02/24/95	169
Housing Discrimination	11/06/15	937
Jobs in the '90s	02/28/92	179
Mortgage Crisis	11/02/07	**913
Mutual Funds	05/20/94	449*

	Date	Page
Preparing for Disaster	08/02/13	669
Recession's Regional Impact	02/01/91	75*
Regulating Credit Cards	10/10/08	817*
Transnational Crime	08/29/14	697
Y2K Dilemma	02/19/99	137

Battered women. *See Domestic violence*

Bilingual education

Bilingual Education	08/13/93	697
Debate over Bilingualism	01/19/96	49
Hispanic Americans	10/30/92	946*
Hispanic-Americans' New Clout	09/18/98	809

Bin Laden, Osama

Civil Liberties in Wartime	12/14/01	1017
Democracy in the Arab World	01/30/04	73
Future of NATO	02/28/03	177
The Future of U.S.-Russia Relations	01/18/02	25
Hating America	11/23/01	869
Intelligence Reforms	01/25/02	49
Islamic Fundamentalism	03/24/00	241
New Defense Priorities	09/13/02	721
The Obama Legacy	11/04/16	913
Policing the Borders	02/22/02	145
Rebuilding Afghanistan	12/21/01	1041
Re-examining 9/11	06/04/04	493
Smallpox Threat	02/07/03	105
Treatment of Detainees	08/25/06	673
War on Terrorism	10/12/01	817
Weapons of Mass Destruction	03/08/02	193

Bioethics. *See Medical ethics*

Biological diversity. *See Environmental protection*

Biological weapons

Chemical and Biological Weapons	01/31/97	73
Chemical and Biological Weapons	12/13/13	1053
Confronting Iraq	10/04/02	793
Ethics of War	12/13/02	1013
Future of NATO	02/28/03	177
Homeland Security	09/12/03	749
Homeland Security	02/13/09	129
Pandemic Threat	06/02/17	457
Smallpox Threat	02/07/03	105
Weapons of Mass Destruction	03/08/02	193

Biology — Study and teaching

Animal Intelligence	10/22/10	869
Animal Rights	05/24/91	308*
Evolution vs. Creationism	08/22/97	745
Fighting over Animal Rights	08/02/96	689*
Fighting SARS	06/20/03	569
Gender and Learning	05/20/05	445

Biotechnology

Biofuels Boom	09/29/06	793
Biology and Behavior	04/03/98	306*
Blood Supply Safety	11/11/94	985

	Date	Page
'Designer' Humans	05/18/01	425
Famine in Africa	11/08/02	921
Fighting Cancer	01/22/16	73
Food Policy Debates	10/03/14	817
Food Safety	06/04/93	497*
Food Safety	11/01/02	897
Food Safety Battle: Organic v. Biotech	09/04/98	761
Gene Therapy	10/18/91	777
Gene Therapy's Future	12/08/95	1089
Human Genome Research	05/12/00	401
Manipulating the Human Genome	06/19/15	529
Organ Shortage	02/21/03	153
Stem Cell Research	09/01/06	**697
Vaccine Controversies	02/19/16	169

Birth control. *See also Abortion*

	Date	Page
Abortion Debates	03/21/03	249
Abortion Debates	03/21/14	265
Birth Control Choices	07/29/94	649
Birth-Control Debate	06/24/05	565
Catholic Church in the U.S.	09/08/95	777
Encouraging Teen Abstinence	07/10/98	577
Parental Rights	10/25/96	937
Population and the Environment	07/17/98	601
Population Growth	07/16/93	601
Preventing Teen Pregnancy	05/14/93	409
Religion and Law	11/07/14	937
Sexually Transmitted Diseases	12/03/04	997
Teen Pregnancy	03/26/10	265*
The United Nations and Global Security	02/27/04	173
Welfare Reform	08/03/01	606*
Women's Health	11/07/03	941

Birth defects

	Date	Page
Human Genome Research	05/12/00	401
Infant Mortality	07/31/92	652
Mosquito-Borne Disease	07/22/16	601
Pandemic Threat	06/02/17	457
Right to Die	05/13/05	421

Blacks. *See African-Americans*

Blogs

	Date	Page
Blog Explosion	06/09/06	**505
Press Freedom	02/05/10	97

Bonds. *See Stocks and bonds*

Books. *See also Libraries*

	Date	Page
Combating Plagiarism	09/19/03	773
The Future of Books	06/23/00	545
Reading Crisis?	02/22/08	169

Bosnia

	Date	Page
Ethics of War	12/13/02	1013
Foreign Policy and Public Opinion	07/15/94	601
Foreign Policy Burden	08/20/93	726*
Privatizing the Military	06/25/04	565
Stopping Genocide	08/27/04	685
The United Nations and Global Security	02/27/04	173

	Date	Page
United Nations at 50	08/18/95	729
War Crimes	07/07/95	585

Boycotts

	Date	Page
Advertising Under Attack	09/13/91	657
The Growing Influence of Boycotts	01/04/91	1
Israeli-Palestinian Conflict	06/21/13	545
Threatened Fisheries	08/02/02	624*

Brady bill

	Date	Page
Gang Crisis	05/14/04	421
Gun Control	06/10/94	505
Gun Control Debate	11/12/04	949
Gun Control Standoff	12/19/97	1119*
Reassessing the Nation's Gun Laws	03/22/91	157
States and Federalism	09/13/96	793
Suburban Crime	09/03/93	780*

Brain. *See also Mental health and illness*

	Date	Page
Alzheimer's Disease	07/24/92	617
Alzheimer's Disease	05/15/98	433
Animal Intelligence	10/22/10	869
Artificial Intelligence	11/14/97	985
Biology and Behavior	04/03/98	289
Chronic Fatigue Syndrome	04/05/02	289
Embryo Research	12/3/99	1078*
Gender and Learning	05/20/05	445
Impact of the Internet on Thinking	09/24/10	773
Increase in Autism	06/13/03	**545
Intelligence Testing	07/30/93	649
Learning Disabilities	12/10/93	1081
Mental Health Insurance	03/29/02	265
Professional Football	01/29/10	**73
Prozac Controversy	08/19/94	721
Rethinking Ritalin	10/22/99	905
Right to Die	05/13/05	421
Sleep Deprivation	06/26/98	553
Sleep Deprivation	02/12/10	121
Treating Alzheimer's Disease	07/24/15	625
Treating Schizophrenia	12/05/14	1009
Understanding Autism	08/01/14	649
Youth Suicide	02/13/04	125

Branch Davidians. *See Cults*

Brazil

	Date	Page
Biofuels Boom	09/29/06	793
Mosquito-Borne Disease	07/22/16	601
Troubled Brazil	04/07/17	289

Broadcasting. *See Television and radio*

Budget deficit

	Date	Page
Assessing the New Health Care Law	09/21/12	789
Budget Deficit	12/09/05	1029
Government Spending	07/12/13	597
Health-Care Reform	06/11/10	**505
Humanities Education	12/06/13	1029
The National Debt	11/14/08	937
National Debt	03/18/11	241

	Date	Page
National Debt	09/01/17	701
New Space Race	08/04/17	653
Budget surplus		
Budget Surplus	04/13/01	297
Bush's Defense Strategy	09/07/01	689
The National Debt	11/14/08	937
National Debt	03/18/11	241
National Debt	09/01/17	701
Buildings and construction industry		
Aging Infrastructure	09/28/07	**793
Asbestos Litigation	05/02/03	393
Confronting Warming	01/09/09	1
Earthquake Research	12/16/94	1105
Implementing the Disabilities Act	12/20/96	1105
Property Rights	03/04/05	197
Recession's Regional Impact	02/01/91	74*
Smart Growth	05/28/04	469
Worker Safety	05/21/04	445
Bulimia. *See Eating disorders*		
Bush, George		
Business' Role in Education	11/22/91	873
Confronting Iraq	10/04/02	793
Disaster Response	10/15/93	906*
Ethics of War	12/13/02	1013
Presidential Libraries	03/16/07	241
Presidential Power	11/15/02	945
Privatizing Government Services	08/09/96	712*
Racial Quotas	05/17/91	277
Redistricting Disputes	03/12/04	221
School Choice	05/10/91	253
U.S.-Vietnam Relations	12/03/93	1070*
Bush, George W.		
Abortion Debates	03/21/03	249
Abortion Showdowns	09/22/06	769
Affordable Housing	02/09/01	104*
Aiding Africa	08/29/03	697
Air Pollution Conflict	11/14/03	965
Alternative Energy	02/25/05	173
Biofuels Boom	09/29/06	793
Birth-Control Debate	06/24/05	565
Budget Deficit	12/09/05	1029
Budget Surplus	04/13/01	297
Bush Presidency	02/02/01	65
Bush's Defense Strategy	09/07/01	689
Campaign Finance Showdown	11/22/02	969
Change in Latin America	07/21/06	601
Civil Liberties Debates	10/24/03	893*
Climate Change	01/27/06	73
Coal Mining Safety	03/17/06	241
Confronting Iraq	10/04/02	793
Corporate Crime	10/11/02	817
Cost of the Iraq War	04/25/08	361*
Cyberpolitics	09/17/04	757

	Date	Page
Dealing With the "New" Russia	06/06/08	481
Democracy in the Arab World	01/30/04	73
Democrats in Congress	06/08/07	505
Disaster Preparedness	11/18/05	**981
Draft Debates	08/19/05	661
Drug Company Ethics	06/06/03	521
Electing the President	04/20/07	337
Electoral College	12/08/00	977
Ending Homelessness	06/18/04	541
Ending Poverty	09/09/05	733
Energy Efficiency	05/19/06	433
Energy Policy	05/25/01	447*
Energy Security	02/01/02	73
Ethics of War	12/13/02	1013
Evaluating Head Start	08/26/05	685
Exporting Democracy	04/01/05	269
Faith-Based Initiatives	05/04/01	377*
Farm Subsidies	05/17/02	433
Free-Press Disputes	04/08/05	293
Future of the GOP	03/20/09	249
Future of Marriage	05/07/04	397
Future of NATO	02/28/03	177
Gay Marriage	09/05/03	721
Government Secrecy	12/02/05	1005
Homeland Security	09/12/03	749
Human Trafficking and Slavery	03/26/04	273
Identity Theft	06/10/05	517
Illegal Immigration	05/06/05	393
Interrogating the CIA	09/25/09	789
The Iraq War: 10 Years Later	03/01/13	205
Judges and Politics	07/27/01	577
Latino Voters	04/03/15	289
Medical Malpractice	02/14/03	129
Medicare Reform	08/22/03	673
Mental Illness Medication Debate	02/06/04	101
Middle East Peace	01/21/05	53
Middle East Tensions	10/27/06	**889
New Defense Priorities	09/13/02	721
New Strategy in Iraq	02/23/07	169
No Child Left Behind	05/27/05	469
North Korean Crisis	04/11/03	321
Nuclear Energy	03/10/06	217
Nuclear Proliferation and Terrorism	04/02/04	297
The Obama Presidency	01/30/09	73
Oil Diplomacy	01/24/03	49
The Partisan Divide	04/30/04	373
Political Conventions	08/08/08	649
Port Security	04/21/06	337
Presidential Libraries	03/16/07	241
Presidential Power	11/15/02	945
Presidential Power	02/24/06	169
Presidential Power	03/06/15	217
Preventing Teen Drug Use	03/15/02	217
Privacy in Peril	11/17/06	961

	Date	Page
Race in America	07/11/03	593
Rebuilding Afghanistan	12/21/01	1041
Rebuilding Iraq	07/11/03	625*
Redistricting Disputes	03/12/04	221
Re-examining 9/11	06/04/04	493
Reforming the Corps	05/30/03	497
Religion and Politics	07/30/04	637
Religion in Schools	01/12/01	1
Remembering 9/11	09/02/11	701*
Retirement Security	05/31/02	481
Revising No Child Left Behind	04/16/10	337
Right to Die	05/13/05	421
Rising Health Costs	04/07/06	289
School Desegregation	04/23/04	345
Science and Politics	08/20/04	661
Sexually Transmitted Diseases	12/03/04	997
Smallpox Threat	02/07/03	105
Social Security	06/03/16	481
Social Security Reform	09/24/04	781
Stem Cell Research	09/01/06	**697
Stimulating the Economy	01/10/03	1
Supreme Court's Future	01/28/05	77
Teacher Shortages	08/24/01	633
Teen Sex	09/16/05	761
Testing in Schools	04/20/01	321
Transatlantic Tensions	07/13/01	533
Treatment of Detainees	08/25/06	673
Treatment of Veterans	11/19/04	973
Trouble in South America	03/14/03	225
Unemployment Benefits	04/25/03	369*
The United Nations and Global Security	02/27/04	173
Upward Mobility	04/29/05	369
U.S.-British Relations	11/05/10	917*
U.S.-Mexico Relations	11/09/01	921
U.S. Policy on Iran	11/16/07	961
Voting Controversies	09/15/06	745
War in Iraq	10/21/05	881
War on Drugs	06/02/06	481
Weapons of Mass Destruction	03/08/02	193
Wounded Veterans	08/31/07	697

Business and industry. *See also Antitrust law; Corporate mergers; Employment and unemployment; International trade; Privatization; Wages and salaries*

	Date	Page
3D Printing	12/07/12	1037
Accountants Under Fire	03/22/02	241
Airline Industry Problems	09/24/99	825
Air Pollution Conflict	11/14/03	965
Airline Safety	10/08/93	865
Airline Safety	05/15/15	433
Alternative Energy	07/10/92	573
Alternative Energy	02/25/05	173
Antitrust Policy	06/12/98	505
Apprenticeships	10/14/16	841
Arbitrating Disputes	03/11/16	241

	Date	Page
Arctic Development	12/02/16	989
Arms Sales	12/09/94	1081
Artificial Intelligence	04/22/11	361
Asbestos Litigation	05/02/03	393
Attracting Jobs	03/02/12	205
Auto Industry's Future	02/06/09	**105
Betting on Sports	10/28/16	889
Big-Box Stores	09/10/04	733
Big Data and Privacy	10/25/13	909
Broadcast Indecency	04/16/04	321
Business Bankruptcy	04/10/09	321
Business Ethics	05/06/11	409
The Business of Sports	02/10/95	121
Buying Green	02/29/08	193
Campaign Finance	05/06/16	409
Campaign Finance Debates	05/28/10	457
Celebrity Culture	03/18/05	245
Centennial Olympic Games	04/05/96	289
Charitable Giving	11/12/93	993*
Charter Schools	03/10/17	217
Child-Care Options	05/08/98	409
Child Labor and Sweatshops	08/16/96	721
Civic Renewal	03/21/97	241
Class Action Lawsuits	05/13/11	433
Coal Mining Safety	03/17/06	241
College Football	11/18/11	977
College Rankings	01/02/15	1
Computer Hacking	09/16/11	757*
Consumer Safety	10/12/07	841
Corporate Crime	10/11/02	817
Corporate Social Responsibility	08/03/07	649
Cosmetic Surgery	04/15/05	317
Crisis on the Plains	05/09/03	417
Curbing CEO Pay	03/09/07	217
Cyber-Crime	04/12/02	305
Cybersecurity	09/26/03	811*
Cybersecurity	02/26/10	169
Cyberwarfare Threat	10/06/17	821
The Dark Web	01/15/16	49
Debating Hip-Hop	06/15/07	529
Decriminalizing Prostitution	04/15/16	337
Defeating the Islamic State	04/01/16	289
Democrats' Future	10/29/10	893
Dietary Supplements	09/03/04	709
Dietary Supplements	10/30/15	913
Digital Commerce	02/05/99	89
Digital Currency	09/26/14	793
Digital Journalism	05/30/14	457
Distance Learning	12/07/01	993
Diversity in Hollywood	08/05/16	649
Doctor Shortage	08/28/15	697
Domestic Drones	10/18/13	885
Downward Mobility	07/23/93	625
Drinking Water Safety	07/15/16	577

	Date	Page		Date	Page
Drug Company Ethics	06/06/03	521	Internet Regulation	04/13/12	325
Drug Safety	03/11/05	221	Internet Shopping	06/28/13	573
Emerging China	11/11/05	957	Jobs in the '90s	02/28/92	169
Energy and Climate	07/24/09	621	Journalism Standards in the		
Energy Policy	05/20/11	457	Internet Age	10/08/10	821
Energy Security	02/01/02	73	Journalism Under Fire	12/25/98	1121
Euro Crisis	10/05/12	841	Judicial Elections	04/24/09	373
Executive Pay	07/11/97	601	Labor Unions' Future	09/02/05	**709
Exporting Jobs	02/20/04	149	Latino Voters	04/03/15	289
Fairness in Salaries	05/29/92	457	Limiting Lawsuits	12/19/08	1033
Far-Right Extremism	09/18/15	769	Managing Public Lands	11/04/11	929
Fast-Food Shake-Up	11/08/91	825	Managing Western Lands	04/22/16	361
The Federal Reserve	01/03/14	1	Marijuana Industry	10/16/15	865
Fighting Gangs	10/09/15	841	Media Ownership	10/10/03	**845
Fighting Urban Poverty	07/17/15	601	Media Violence	02/14/14	145
Financial Bailout	10/24/08	**865	Medical Marijuana	07/21/17	605
Financial Crisis	05/09/08	409	Mental Illness Medication Debate	02/06/04	101
Financial Industry Overhaul	07/30/10	629	Military Readiness	11/03/17	917
Financial Misconduct	01/20/12	53	Millennial Generation	06/26/15	553
Food Labeling	06/16/17	509	Minimum Wage	12/16/05	1053
Food Policy Debates	10/03/14	817	Minimum Wage	01/24/14	72
Fracking Controversy	12/16/11	1049	Muslims in America	07/28/17	629
Funding the Arts	07/14/17	581	Nanotechnology	06/11/04	517
Future Job Market	01/11/02	1	Nanotechnology	06/10/16	505
Future of the Airline Industry	06/21/02	545	NASA's Future	05/23/03	489*
Future of the Airlines	03/07/08	217	National Debt	09/01/17	701
The Future of Baseball	09/25/98	833	Native American Sovereignty	05/05/17	385
Future of Books	05/29/09	**473	New Challenges in Space	07/23/99	617
Future of the Democratic Party	10/13/17	845	New Space Race	08/04/17	653
Future of the GOP	10/24/14	889	NFL Controversies	09/04/15	721
Future of Journalism	03/27/09	**273	The New Corporate Philanthropy	02/27/98	169
Future of Libraries	07/29/11	625	The New Volunteerism	12/13/96	1081
Future of Marriage	12/01/17	993	Nonprofit Groups and Partisan Politics	11/14/14	961
Future of the Middle Class	04/08/16	313	The Obama Legacy	11/04/16	913
Future of Newspapers	01/20/06	49	The Obama Presidency	01/30/09	73
Future of Telecommunications	04/23/99	329	'Occupy' Movement	01/13/12	25
The Future of Television	12/23/94	1129	Offshore Drilling	06/25/10	553
Genetically Modified Food	08/31/12	717	Online Dating	03/20/15	265
Gentrification	02/20/15	169	Online Privacy	11/06/09	**933
The Gig Economy	03/18/16	265	Patent Controversies	02/27/15	193
The Glass Ceiling	10/29/93	937	Pension Crisis	02/17/06	145
Google's Dominance	11/11/11	953	Political Polling	02/06/15	121
The Growing Influence of Boycotts	01/04/91	1	Pornography	10/21/16	865
Gulf Coast Restoration	08/26/11	677*	Port Security	04/21/06	337
Health-Care Reform	08/28/09	693*	Prescription Drug Costs	05/20/16	457
Housing Discrimination	11/06/15	937	Prescription Drug Prices	07/17/92	610*
Human Spaceflight	10/16/09	861	Presidential Power	03/06/15	217
Identity Theft	06/10/05	517	Preventing Disease	01/06/12	1
Illegal Immigration	05/06/05	393	Privacy and the Internet	12/04/15	1009
Immigrants and the Economy	02/24/17	169	Privatizing Government Services	12/08/17	1017
Impact of the Internet on Thinking	09/24/10	773	Privatizing the Military	06/25/04	565
Implementing the Disabilities Act	12/20/96	1105	Privatizing the Military	07/13/12	597
Immigrant Detention	10/23/15	889	Professional Football	01/29/10	**73
Income Inequality	04/17/98	337	Property Rights	06/16/95	513

	Date	Page
Property Rights	03/04/05	197
Protecting the Power Grid	11/11/16	941
Protecting Whistleblowers	03/31/06	265
Public-Works Projects	02/20/09	153
Puerto Rico: The Struggle over Status	02/08/91	81
Race in America	07/11/03	593
Reading Crisis?	02/22/08	169
Rebuilding Iraq	07/11/03	637*
Redistricting Showdown	08/25/17	677
Reducing Your Carbon Footprint	12/05/08	985
Reducing Traffic Deaths	02/17/17	145
Reforming School Funding	12/10/99	1052*
Reforming the FDA	06/06/97	481
Reforming the U.N.	06/24/16	553
Regulating Lobbying	06/06/14	481
Regulating Nonprofits	12/26/97	1129*
Regulating the Internet	06/30/95	561
Regulating Toxic Chemicals	01/23/09	49
Religion and Law	11/07/14	937
Religious Freedom	01/01/16	1
Restructuring the Electric Industry	01/17/97	25
Revitalizing the Cities	10/13/95	910*
Reviving Manufacturing	07/22/11	601
Reviving Rural Economies	03/31/17	265
Robotic Warfare	01/23/15	73
Robotics and the Economy	09/25/15	793
Science and Politics	08/20/04	661
School Reform	04/29/11	385
Smart Cities	07/27/12	645
Social Media Explosion	01/25/13	81
Social Networking	09/17/10	749
Social Security	06/03/16	481
Social Security Reform	09/24/04	781
Socially Responsible Investing	08/29/08	673
Software Piracy	05/21/93	433
Solar Energy Controversies	04/29/16	385
Space Program	02/24/12	177
Space Program's Future	12/24/93	1143*
Stimulating the Economy	01/10/03	1
The Stock Market	05/02/97	385
Stock Market Troubles	01/16/04	25
Stolen Antiquities	11/10/17	945
Student Debt	10/21/11	877
Supreme Court Controversies	09/28/12	813
SUV Debate	05/16/03	449
Tax Reform	03/22/96	241
Teaching Critical Thinking	04/10/15	313
Telecommuting	07/19/13	621
Think Tanks in Transition	09/29/17	797
Threatened Fisheries	08/02/02	617
Tobacco Industry	12/10/04	**1025
Too Many Lawsuits?	05/22/92	433
Transatlantic Tensions	07/13/01	566*
Troubled Brazil	04/07/17	289

	Date	Page
Trump Presidency	01/06/17	1
Trust in Media	06/09/17	481
Underground Economy	03/04/94	193
Unemployment Benefits	04/25/03	369
Unions at a Crossroads	08/07/15	673
Universal Basic Income	09/08/17	725
Upward Mobility	04/29/05	369
U.S. Auto Industry	10/16/92	881
U.S.-China Relations	05/07/10	**409
U.S.-Iran Relations	03/04/16	217
U.S.-Mexico Relations	09/02/16	697
U.S. Trade Policy	09/13/13	765
Vaccine Controversies	02/19/16	169
Video Games and Learning	02/12/16	145
Virtual Reality	02/26/16	193
Whistleblowers	12/05/97	1057
Whistleblowers	01/31/14	97
Women and Sports	03/25/11	265
Women in Combat	05/13/16	433
Women in Leadership	09/23/16	769
Women in Prison	03/03/17	193
Work, Family and Stress	08/14/92	689
Workplace Sexual Harassment	10/27/17	893
Worker Safety	05/21/04	445
Worker Safety	10/04/13	837
Y2K Dilemma	02/19/99	137
Young Voters	10/02/15	817
Youth Apprenticeships	10/23/92	905
Youth Unemployment	03/14/14	241

Business and industry — Environmental issues

	Date	Page
Acid Rain: New Approach to Old Problem	03/08/91	129
Air Pollution and Climate Control	11/13/15	961
Air Pollution Conflict	11/14/03	965
Alternative Energy	02/25/05	173
Asbestos Litigation	05/02/03	393
Auto Industry's Future	02/06/09	**105
Biofuels Boom	09/29/06	793
Bush and the Environment	10/25/02	865
Buying Green	02/29/08	193
Cleaning Up Hazardous Wastes	08/23/96	745
Coal Industry's Future	06/17/16	529
Crisis on the Plains	05/09/03	434*
The Economics of Recycling	03/27/98	265
Energy and the Environment	03/03/00	161
Energy Security	02/01/02	73
Environmental Justice	06/19/98	529
Food Safety Battle: Organic v. Biotech	09/04/98	761
Future of the Airlines	03/07/08	217
Garbage Crisis	03/20/92	241
Global Warming Treaty	01/26/01	53*
Global Warming Update	11/01/96	961
The Growing Influence of Boycotts	01/04/91	1
Historic Preservation	10/07/94	865

	Date	Page		Date	Page
Jobs vs. Environment	05/15/92	409	Identity Theft	06/10/05	517
Modernizing the Grid	02/19/10	145	Illegal Immigration	05/06/05	393
Nanotechnology	06/11/04	517	Immigration Reform	09/24/93	841
New Air Quality Standards	03/07/97	193	Jobs vs. Environment	05/15/92	409
The New Environmentalism	12/01/06	985	Latinos' Future	10/17/03	869
Nuclear Energy	03/10/06	217	Learning to Read	05/19/95	441
Oil Spills	01/17/92	25	Mandatory Sentencing	05/26/95	480*
Ozone Depletion	04/03/92	289	Marijuana Laws	02/11/05	125
Pesticide Controversies	06/05/15	481	Medical Marijuana	08/20/99	716*
Protecting the Oceans	10/17/14	865	Networking the Classroom	10/20/95	926*
Reforming the Corps	05/30/03	497	Oil Imports	08/23/91	599*
Regulating Toxic Chemicals	07/18/14	601	Pornography	10/21/16	865
Renewable Energy	11/07/97	961	Prisoner Reentry	12/04/09	1005
Saving the Rain Forests	06/11/99	512*	Redistricting Disputes	03/12/04	221
SUV Debate	05/16/03	460*	Redistricting: Drawing Power		
Threatened Fisheries	08/02/02	617	with a Map	02/15/91	108
Traffic Congestion	05/06/94	401*	Rethinking Affirmative Action	04/28/95	386*
Water Shortages	08/01/03	649	Rethinking the Death Penalty	11/16/01	960*
Cable television			State Budget Crises	10/03/03	827*
Alcohol Advertising	03/14/97	217	State Budget Crisis	09/11/09	741
Broadcast Indecency	04/16/04	321	Testing Term Limits	11/18/94	1016*
Future of Journalism	03/27/09	**273	Three-Strikes Laws	05/10/02	427*
The Future of Telecommunications	04/23/99	329	Traffic Congestion	05/06/94	385
The Future of Television	12/23/94	1129	Water Shortages	08/01/03	649
Future of TV	04/11/14	313	Year-Round Schools	05/17/96	447*
Indecency on Television	11/09/12	965	**Campaign finance**		
Media Ownership	10/10/03	**845	Campaign Finance	05/06/16	409
Media Violence	02/14/14	145	Campaign Finance Debates	05/28/10	457
Pay-Per-View TV	10/04/91	729	Campaign Finance Reform	02/09/96	121
Paying College Athletes	07/11/14	577	Campaign Finance Reform	03/31/00	257
Polarization in America	02/28/14	193	Campaign Finance Reform	06/13/08	505
Public Broadcasting	09/18/92	809	Campaign Finance Showdown	11/22/02	969
California			China After Deng	06/13/97	516*
Assisted Suicide	02/21/92	145	Corporate Crime	10/11/02	817
Assisted Suicide Controversy	05/05/95	406*	Cyberpolitics	09/17/04	757
Big-Box Stores	09/10/04	733	Electing the President	04/20/07	337
Bilingual Education	08/13/93	712*	Future of the GOP	10/24/14	889
California: Enough Water for the Future?	04/19/91	221	Income Inequality	12/03/10	989
Celebrity Culture	03/18/05	245	Judicial Elections	04/24/09	373
Crackdown on Smoking	12/04/92	1062	Low Voter Turnout	10/20/00	833
Cracking Down on Immigration	02/03/95	97	The New Immigrants	01/24/97	56*
Downsizing Prisons	03/11/11	217	The Partisan Divide	04/30/04	384*
Drug-Policy Debate	07/28/00	593	Political Polling	02/06/15	121
Earthquake Research	12/16/94	1105	Populism and Party Politics	09/09/16	721
Earthquake Threat	04/09/10	313	Presidential Election	02/03/12	101
Gay Marriage	03/15/13	257	Presidential Libraries	03/16/07	241
Gay Marriage Showdowns	09/26/08	**769	Regulating Nonprofits	12/26/97	1129
Getting into College	02/23/96	169	Social Media and Politics	10/12/12	865
Global Water Shortages	12/15/95	1128*	Supreme Court Controversies	09/28/12	813
Gridlock in Washington	04/30/10	385	Voting Controversies	02/21/14	169
Gun Control Standoff	12/19/97	1120*	**Canada**		
High-Speed Rail	04/16/93	328*	Acid Rain: New Approach to		
High-Speed Trains	05/01/09	**397	Old Problem	03/08/91	129
Hispanic-Americans' New Clout	09/18/98	809	Blood Supply Safety	11/11/94	998*

	Date	Page
Border Security	09/27/13	813
Courts and the Media	09/23/94	830*
Deepening Canadian Crisis over Quebec	04/12/91	205
Fighting SARS	06/20/03	569
Future of the Arctic	09/20/13	789
Gay Marriage	09/05/03	721
Marijuana Laws	02/11/05	125
Movie Ratings	03/28/03	279*
Native Americans	05/08/92	396*
Oil Diplomacy	01/24/03	63*
Quebec Sovereignty	10/06/95	873
Rethinking NAFTA	06/07/96	481
Retiree Health Benefits	12/06/91	937*
U.S. Trade Policy	01/29/93	83*

Cancer

Advances in Cancer Research	08/25/95	753
Alternative Medicine	01/31/92	73
Asbestos Litigation	05/02/03	393
Biology and Behavior	04/03/98	294*
Birth Control Choices	07/29/94	649
Breast Cancer	06/27/97	553
Breast Cancer	04/02/10	289
Cancer Treatments	09/11/98	785
Cell Phone Safety	03/16/01	201
Diet and Health	02/23/01	129*
Electromagnetic Fields	04/26/91	237
Fighting Cancer	01/22/16	73
Gene Therapy's Future	12/08/95	1095*
Indoor Air Pollution	10/27/95	945
Marijuana Laws	02/11/05	125
Medical Breakthroughs	09/15/17	749
Patenting Human Genes	05/31/13	473
Prescription Drug Costs	05/20/16	457
Preventing Cancer	01/16/09	25
Regulating Pesticides	01/28/94	73
Tobacco Industry	12/10/04	**1025
Women's Health	11/07/03	941
Women's Health Issues	05/13/94	409
Worker Safety	05/21/04	445

Capital punishment. *See Death penalty*

Carbon dioxide emissions. *See Global warming*

Careers. *See Job training; Wages and salaries*

Carpal tunnel syndrome

Repetitive Stress Injuries	06/23/95	537

Cars. *See Automobiles and automobile industry*

Catholic Church

Abortion Debates	03/21/03	249
Abortion Debates	03/21/14	265
Birth-Control Debate	06/24/05	565
Castro's Next Move	12/12/97	1081
Catholic Church in the U.S.	09/08/95	777

	Date	Page
Child Sexual Abuse	01/15/93	32*
Future of the Catholic Church	01/19/07	49
Future of the Catholic Church	06/07/13	497
Future of the Christian Right	06/23/17	533
Future of the Papacy	02/26/99	161
Latinos' Future	10/17/03	869
Religion and Law	11/07/14	937
Religion and Politics	07/30/04	637
Sex Offenders	09/08/06	721
Sexual Abuse and the Clergy	05/03/02	393
Troubled Brazil	04/07/17	289

Catholic schools

Boys' Emotional Needs	06/18/99	534*
School Vouchers	04/09/99	281
School Vouchers Showdown	02/15/02	121

Cattle. *See Livestock and ranching*

Celebrities

Celebrity Advocacy	05/11/12	425
Celebrity Culture	03/18/05	245
Diversity in Hollywood	08/05/16	649
Medication Abuse	10/09/09	837
Offshore Drilling	06/25/10	553
Philanthropy in America	12/08/06	1009
Sex Scandals	01/22/10	49
Transgender Rights	12/11/15	1033
Vaccine Controversies	02/19/16	169
Workplace Sexual Harassment	10/27/17	893

Cellular telephones

Cell Phone Safety	03/16/01	201
Distracted Driving	05/04/12	401
Future of Recycling	12/14/07	1033
Rising College Costs	12/05/03	1026*
Social Media Explosion	01/25/13	81

Censorship

Combat Journalism	04/12/13	329
Controlling the Internet	05/12/06	409
The Dark Web	01/15/16	49
Debating Hip-Hop	06/15/07	529
Free-Press Disputes	04/08/05	293
Free Speech at Risk	04/26/13	377
Free Speech on Campus	05/08/15	409
Google's Dominance	11/11/11	953
Improving Cybersecurity	02/15/13	157
Movie Ratings	03/28/03	273
The Obscenity Debate	12/20/91	969
Press Freedom	02/05/10	97
Religious Repression	11/01/13	933
Restoring Ties With Cuba	06/12/15	505
Resurgent Russia	02/07/14	121
School Censorship	02/19/93	145
Sex, Violence and the Media	11/17/95	1017
Shock Jocks	06/01/07	**481
Student Journalism	06/05/98	481

	Date	Page
Unrest in Turkey	01/29/16	97
U.S.-China Relations	05/07/10	**409

Census. *See also Population, Redistricting*

	Date	Page
Census 2000	05/01/98	385
Census Controversey	05/14/10	433
Crisis on the Plains	05/09/03	417
Helping the Homeless	01/26/96	78*
The Homeless	08/07/92	665
Illegal Immigration	04/24/92	366*
Latinos' Future	10/17/03	869
Latino Voters	04/03/15	289
Millennial Generation	06/26/15	553
Muslims in America	07/28/17	629
Native Americans	05/08/92	389*
Redistricting Debates	02/25/11	169
Redistricting Disputes	03/12/04	221
Redistricting Showdown	08/25/17	677
Religion in America	11/25/94	1040*

Central America

	Date	Page
Central American Gangs	01/30/15	97
Debate Over Immigration	07/14/00	582*
Foreign Aid After Sept. 11	04/26/02	361
Gang Crisis	05/14/04	421
Illegal Immigration	04/24/92	372
Immigrant Detention	10/23/15	889

Central Intelligence Agency

	Date	Page
Civil Liberties Debates	10/24/03	893
Cybersecurity	09/26/03	797
Government Secrecy	12/02/05	1005
Homeland Security	09/12/03	749*
Intelligence Reform	05/29/15	457
Intelligence Reforms	01/25/02	49
Interrogating the CIA	09/25/09	789
The New CIA	12/11/92	1073
Policing the Borders	02/22/02	145
Privacy in Peril	11/17/06	961
Re-examining 9/11	06/04/04	493
Reforming the CIA	02/02/96	97
Restoring Ties With Cuba	06/12/15	505
Reviving Rural Economies	03/31/17	265
Torture	04/18/03	345
Treatment of Detainees	08/25/06	673

Charities and nonprofit organizations. *See also Voluntarism*

	Date	Page
Arts Funding	10/21/94	913
Assisting Refugees	02/07/97	97
Blighted Cities	11/12/10	941*
Celebrity Advocacy	05/11/12	425
Charitable Giving	11/12/93	985
Corporate Social Responsibility	08/03/07	649
Fairness in Salaries	05/29/92	470*
Faith-Based Initiatives	05/04/01	377
Foreign Aid After Sept. 11	04/26/02	361
Future of Journalism	03/27/09	**273
Haiti's Dilemma	02/18/05	149

	Date	Page
Helping the Homeless	01/26/96	73
The Homeless	08/07/92	665
Housing the Homeless	10/10/14	841
Humanities Education	12/06/13	1029
Hunger in America	07/07/17	557
National Service	06/30/06	577
The New Corporate Philanthropy	02/27/98	169
The New Volunteerism	12/13/96	1081
Nonprofit Groups and Partisan Politics	11/14/14	961
Philanthropy in America	12/08/06	1009
Reassessing Foreign Aid	09/27/96	841
Regulating Nonprofits	12/26/97	1129
Role of Foundations	01/22/99	49
School Choice Debate	07/18/97	632*
Sexual Abuse and the Clergy	05/03/02	393
Socially Responsible Investing	08/29/08	673
Stolen Antiquities	11/10/17	945
Straining the Safety Net	07/31/09	645
Tax Reform	03/22/96	241
Think Tanks in Transition	09/29/17	797
Youth Volunteerism	01/27/12	77

Charter schools

	Date	Page
Attack on Public Schools	07/26/96	656*
Charter Schools	12/20/02	1033
Charter Schools	03/10/17	217
Fixing Urban Schools	04/27/07	**361
Home Schooling Debate	01/17/03	25
Private Management of Public Schools	03/25/94	282*
Privatizing Government Services	12/08/17	1017
Race and Education	09/05/14	721
Revising No Child Left Behind	04/16/10	337
School Reform	04/29/11	385
School Vouchers	04/09/99	281
School Vouchers Showdown	02/15/02	121
Special Education	11/10/00	905

Chechnya

	Date	Page
The Future of U.S.-Russia Relations	01/18/02	37*
Resurgent Russia	02/07/14	121
Russia and the Former Soviet Republics	06/17/05	541
Russia's Political Future	05/03/96	399*
U.S. Global Engagement	05/16/14	433

Chemical weapons

	Date	Page
Chemical and Biological Weapons	01/31/97	73
Confronting Iraq	10/04/02	793
Ethics of War	12/13/02	1013
Weapons of Mass Destruction	03/08/02	193

Chemicals and chemical industry

	Date	Page
Air Pollution and Climate Control	11/13/15	961
Breast Cancer	04/02/10	289
Chemical and Biological Weapons	12/13/13	1053
Ozone Depletion	04/03/92	289
Pesticide Controversies	06/05/15	481
Regulating Pesticides	01/28/94	73

	Date	Page
Regulating Pesticides	08/06/99	665
Regulating Toxic Chemicals	01/23/09	49

Chesapeake Bay

	Date	Page
Water Quality	11/24/00	953

Child abuse

	Date	Page
Catholic Church in the U.S.	09/08/95	792*
Children in Crisis	08/31/01	657
Child Sexual Abuse	01/15/93	25
Child Welfare	08/26/16	673
Child Welfare Reform	04/22/05	345
Cyber-Predators	03/01/02	169
Eating Disorders	12/18/92	1108
Foster Care Crisis	09/27/91	705
Foster Care Reform	01/09/98	1
Girls' Rights	04/17/15	337
Human Trafficking and Slavery	03/26/04	273
Infant Mortality	07/31/92	652
Parental Rights	10/25/96	937
Prayer and Healing	01/14/05	25
Punishing Sex Offenders	01/12/96	25
Recovered-Memory Debate	07/05/96	577
Sex Offenders	09/08/06	721
Sexual Abuse and the Clergy	05/03/02	393
Treating Anxiety	02/08/02	97
Violence in Schools	09/11/92	785
Women and Human Rights	04/30/99	353

Child care

	Date	Page
Child Care	12/17/93	1105
Child-Care Options	05/08/98	409
Child Welfare Reform	04/22/05	345
Future of Feminism	04/14/06	313
Mothers' Movement	04/04/03	297
State Budget Crises	10/03/03	832*
Women and Work	07/26/13	645

Child custody and support

	Date	Page
Child Custody and Support	01/13/95	25
Children and Divorce	06/07/91	358*
Children and Divorce	01/19/01	25*
Child Poverty	10/28/11	901
Child Welfare	08/26/16	673
Child Welfare Reform	04/22/05	345
Gay Rights	03/05/93	210*
Mothers' Movement	04/04/03	297

Child welfare

	Date	Page
Adoption	11/26/93	1033
Child Poverty	04/07/00	281
Child Poverty	10/28/11	901
Children in Crisis	08/31/01	657
Child Welfare	08/26/16	673
Child Welfare Reform	04/22/05	345
Foster Care Crisis	09/27/91	705
Foster Care Reform	01/09/98	1
Girls' Rights	04/17/15	337

	Date	Page
The Homeless	08/07/92	675*
Housing the Homeless	10/10/14	841
Kids in Prison	04/27/01	345
Native American Youths	04/24/15	361
Privacy and the Internet	12/04/15	1009
Rethinking Foreign Aid	04/14/17	313
Treating Addiction	01/06/95	6*
Welfare, Work and the States	12/06/96	1057

Children. *See also Adolescents and youth; Adoption; Elementary and secondary education; Family*

Children — Health and safety

	Date	Page
Aggressive Driving	07/25/97	649
Asthma Epidemic	12/24/99	1092*
Boys' Emotional Needs	06/18/99	521
Bullying	02/04/05	101
Childhood Depression	07/16/99	593
Childhood Immunizations	06/18/93	529
Child Labor and Sweatshops	08/16/96	721
Child Poverty	04/07/00	281
Child Welfare	08/26/16	673
Children in Crisis	08/31/01	657
Children's Legal Rights	04/23/93	337
Children's Television	08/15/97	721
Child Welfare Reform	04/22/05	345
Chronic Fatigue Syndrome	04/05/02	289
Closing in on Tobacco	11/12/99	977
Combating Infectious Diseases	06/09/95	505*
Consumer Safety	10/12/07	841
Covering the Uninsured	06/14/02	521
Cyberbullying	05/02/08	385
Cyber-Predators	03/01/02	169
Dieting and Health	04/14/95	321
DNA Databases	05/28/99	466*
Drinking Water Safety	07/15/16	577
Drug-Resistant Bacteria	06/04/99	479*
Drug Safety	03/11/05	221
Eating Disorders	12/18/92	1109
Emerging Infectious Diseases	02/13/15	145
Fatherhood Movement	06/02/00	473
Fighting Superbugs	08/24/07	673
Food Safety	11/01/02	897
Future of Marriage	05/07/04	397
Girls' Rights	04/17/15	337
Gun Control	03/08/13	233
Gun Rights Debates	10/31/08	**889
Gun Violence	05/25/07	457
Head Start	04/09/93	297*
Highway Safety	07/14/95	623*
Homeless Students	04/05/13	305
Homework Debate	12/06/02	993
Housing the Homeless	10/10/14	841
HPV Vaccine	05/11/07	409
Hunger in America	12/22/00	1050*
Immigrants and the Economy	02/24/17	169

	Date	Page		Date	Page
Increase in Autism	06/13/03	**545	**China**		
Indecency on Television	11/09/12	965	China After Deng	06/13/97	505
Infant Mortality	07/31/92	641	China and the South China Sea	01/20/17	49
Internet Privacy	11/06/98	967*	China Today	08/04/00	625
Job Stress	08/04/95	695*	China Today	04/04/14	289
Kids in Prison	04/27/01	345	Climate Change	06/14/13	521
Lead Poisoning	06/19/92	525	Coal's Comeback	10/05/07	817
Marriage and Divorce	05/10/96	409	Consumer Safety	10/12/07	841
Medicaid Reform	07/16/04	589	Controlling the Internet	05/12/06	409
Mental Illness Medication Debate	02/06/04	106*	Cybersecurity	02/26/10	169
Mosquito-Borne Disease	07/22/16	601	The Dark Web	01/15/16	49
Mothers' Movement	04/04/03	297	Democracy in Asia	07/24/98	625
Movie Ratings	03/28/03	273	Emerging China	11/11/05	957
Obesity and Health	01/15/99	40*	Exporting Jobs	02/20/04	149
Obesity Epidemic	01/31/03	73	Fighting SARS	06/20/03	569
Physical Fitness	11/06/92	953	Foreign Aid and National Security	06/17/11	529
Prayer and Healing	01/14/05	25	Foreign Aid After Sept. 11	04/26/02	361
Preventing Bullying	12/10/10	**1013	Free Speech at Risk	04/26/13	377
Preventing Teen Drug Use	07/28/95	670*	Future of Recycling	12/14/07	1033
Reality TV	08/27/10	677	Google's Dominance	11/11/11	953
Reforming the FDA	06/06/97	496*	Human Rights in China	07/25/08	601
Regulating Pesticides	01/28/94	73	Human Rights Issues	10/30/09	909
Regulating Tobacco	09/30/94	841	Illegal Immigration	04/24/92	376
Rethinking Ritalin	10/22/99	905	Immigrants and the Economy	02/24/17	169
Right to Die	05/13/05	421	Improving Cybersecurity	02/15/13	157
School Discipline	05/09/14	409	Internet Shopping	06/28/13	573
School Violence	10/09/98	881	New Challenges in Space	07/23/99	634*
Sex Offenders	09/08/06	721	New Era in Asia	02/14/92	121
Sexual Abuse and the Clergy	05/03/02	393	New Space Race	08/04/17	653
Sexually Transmitted Diseases	12/03/04	997	Oil Jitters	01/04/08	**1
Sleep Deprivation	06/26/98	553	Panama Canal	11/26/99	1017
Sleep Deprivation	02/12/10	121	Pandemic Threat	06/02/17	457
Social Networking	09/17/10	749	Religious Persecution	11/21/97	1009
Sugar Controversies	11/30/12	1013	Reviving Manufacturing	07/22/11	601
Teen Driving	01/07/05	1	Smart Cities	07/27/12	645
Teen Suicide	09/12/14	745	Space Program	02/24/12	177
Teens and Tobacco	12/01/95	1065	Taiwan, China, and the U.S.	05/24/96	457
Tobacco Industry	12/10/04	**1025	Torture	04/18/03	345
Treating Anxiety	02/08/02	97	The United Nations and		
TV Violence	03/26/93	265	Global Security	02/27/04	173
Understanding Autism	08/01/14	649	U.S.-China Relations	05/07/10	**409
Vaccine Controversies	08/25/00	641	U.S.-China Trade	04/15/94	313
Vaccine Controversies	02/19/16	169	U.S.-Europe Relations	03/23/12	277
Violence in Schools	09/11/92	785	U.S. Policy in Asia	11/27/92	1025
Women and AIDS	12/25/92	1121	Weapons of Mass Destruction	03/08/02	193
Work, Family and Stress	08/14/92	689			
Youth Fitness	09/26/97	841	**Christian Coalition**		
Youth Violence	03/05/10	193*	Bullying	02/04/05	101
Chile			Future of the Christian Right	06/23/17	533
			Parental Rights	10/25/96	937
Foreign Aid After Sept. 11	04/26/02	361	Protestants Today	12/07/07	1009
Rethinking NAFTA	06/07/96	497*	Religion and Politics	10/14/94	889
Saving Social Security	10/02/98	865*	Rise of Megachurches	09/21/07	769
Trouble in South America	03/14/03	225	Teaching Values	06/21/96	529

	Date	Page
Christians. *See also Catholic Church*		
Abortion Debates	03/21/14	265
Abortion Showdowns	09/22/06	769
Birth-Control Debate	06/24/05	565
Cloning Debate	10/22/04	877
Embryo Research	12/17/99	1065
Evangelical Christians	09/14/01	713
Faith-Based Initiatives	05/04/01	377
Future of the Christian Right	06/23/17	533
Gay Marriage	09/05/03	721
Global AIDS Crisis	10/13/00	809
Government and Religion	01/15/10	25
Home Schooling	03/07/14	217
Home Schooling Debate	01/17/03	25
The New Millennium	10/15/99	889
Parental Rights	10/25/96	937
Prayer and Healing	01/14/05	25
Protestants Today	12/07/07	1009
Religion and Law	11/07/14	937
Religion and Politics	10/14/94	889
Religion and Politics	07/30/04	637
Religion in America	11/25/94	1033
Religion in Schools	01/12/01	1
Religion in the Workplace	08/23/02	649
Religious Freedom	01/01/16	1
Religious Persecution	11/21/97	1009
Religious Repression	11/01/13	933
Right to Die	05/13/05	421
Rise of Megachurches	09/21/07	769
School Censorship	02/19/93	145
Science and Politics	08/20/04	661
Science and Religion	03/22/13	281
Searching for Jesus	12/11/98	1073
Sexual Abuse and the Clergy	05/03/02	393
Sexually Transmitted Diseases	12/13/04	997
Teaching Values	06/21/96	529
Terrorism in Africa	07/10/15	577
Understanding Mormonism	10/19/12	889
Church-state separation. *See First Amendment*		
Churches. *See Religion*		
Cigarettes. *See Tobacco*		
Cities and towns		
Big-Box Stores	09/10/04	733
Blighted Cities	11/12/10	941*
Census Controversey	05/14/10	433
Coal Industry's Future	06/17/16	529
Downtown Renaissance	06/23/06	**553
Drinking Water Safety	07/15/16	577
Ending Homelessness	06/18/04	541
Fighting Crime	02/08/08	121
Fighting Urban Poverty	07/17/15	601
Fixing Urban Schools	04/27/07	**361
Gentrification	02/20/15	169

	Date	Page
Housing Discrimination	11/06/15	937
Housing the Homeless	12/18/09	1053
Housing the Homeless	10/10/14	841
Immigrants and the Economy	02/24/17	169
Mass Transit	12/09/16	1013
Mass Transit Boom	01/18/08	49
Millennial Generation	06/26/15	553
Property Rights	03/04/05	197
Reviving Rural Economies	03/31/17	265
Smart Cities	07/27/12	645
Smart Growth	05/28/04	469
Civil rights and liberties. *See Democracy; First Amendment*		
Academic Freedom	10/07/05	833
Affirmative Action	10/17/08	**841
Affirmative Action and College Admissions	11/17/17	969
Anti-Semitism	05/12/17	409
Big Data and Privacy	10/25/13	909
Birth-Control Debate	06/24/05	565
Border Security	09/27/13	813
Campaign Finance Showdown	11/22/02	969
Charter Schools	12/20/02	1033
Children's Legal Rights	04/23/93	337
Civic Education	02/03/17	97
Civic Renewal	03/21/97	241
Civil Liberties Debates	10/24/03	893
Civil Liberties in Wartime	12/14/01	1017
Closing Guantánamo	02/27/09	**177
Combating Terrorism	07/21/95	633
Courts and the Media	09/23/94	817
Crackdown on Smoking	12/04/92	1049
Crime Victims' Rights	07/22/94	625
Cyberbullying	05/02/08	385
Cyber-Crime	04/12/02	305
Cyber-Predators	03/01/02	169
Death Penalty Debate	03/10/95	193
Death Penalty Debates	11/19/10	965
Death Penalty Update	01/08/99	1
Declining Crime Rates	04/04/97	306*
DNA Databases	05/28/99	449
Domestic Drones	10/18/13	885
Domestic Partners	09/04/92	761
Drug-Policy Debate	07/28/00	612*
Drug Testing	11/20/98	1001
Electing Minorities	08/12/94	697
Environmental Justice	06/19/98	529
Exporting Democracy	04/01/05	269
The FBI Under Fire	04/11/97	313
Fighting SARS	06/20/03	569
Free Speech on Campus	05/08/15	409
Future of the Airline Industry	06/21/02	545
Gay Marriage	03/15/13	257

	Date	Page		Date	Page
Gay Marriage Showdowns	09/26/08	**769	School Desegregation	04/23/04	345
Gay Rights	03/05/93	193	School Vouchers Showdown	02/15/02	121
Government Surveillance	08/30/13	717	Sentencing Debates	11/05/04	925
The Growing Influence of Boycotts	01/04/91	1	Serial Killers	10/31/03	917
Gun Control	06/10/94	505	Sexual Harassment	08/09/91	537
Gun Control Debate	11/12/04	949	Sports and Sexual Assault	04/28/17	361
Haiti's Dilemma	02/18/05	149	Student Rights	06/05/09	501
Hate Crimes	01/08/93	1	Supreme Court Preview	09/17/93	817
Hate Groups	05/08/09	421	Torture	04/18/03	345
Helping the Homeless	01/26/96	89*	Transgender Rights	12/11/15	1033
Homeland Security	09/12/03	749	Treatment of Detainees	08/25/06	673
Housing Discrimination	11/06/15	937	Voting Controversies	02/21/14	169
Illegal Immigration	04/24/92	361	War on Terrorism	10/12/01	817
Illegal Immigration	05/06/05	393	Women in Leadership	09/23/16	769
Immigrant Detention	10/23/15	889	Young Voters	10/02/15	817
Immigration Conflict	03/09/12	229			

Clean Air Act Amendments, 1990. *See Air pollution; Global warming*

Climate change. *See Global warming*

Clinton, Bill

	Date	Page
Jailing Debtors	09/16/16	745
Kids in Prison	04/27/01	345
Latinos' Future	10/17/03	869
Legal-Aid Crisis	10/07/11	829
Libraries and the Internet	06/01/01	465
Native American Sovereignty	05/05/17	385
Native American Youths	04/24/15	361
The Obama Legacy	11/04/16	913
The Obscenity Debate	12/20/91	969
Parental Rights	10/25/96	937
Plea Bargaining	02/12/99	127*
Police Brutality	09/06/91	633
Police Misconduct	04/06/12	301
Police Tactics	12/12/14	1033
Policing the Borders	02/22/02	145
Presidential Power	11/15/02	945
Preventing Bullying	12/10/10	**1013
Prison Overcrowding	02/04/94	102*
Privacy in Peril	11/17/06	961
Prostitution	06/11/93	505
Public Defenders	04/18/08	337*
Punishing Sex Offenders	01/12/96	25
Race and Education	09/05/14	721
Race in America	07/11/03	593
Racial Conflict	01/08/16	25
Racial Diversity in Public Schools	09/14/07	**745
Racial Profiling	11/22/13	1005
Racial Quotas	05/17/91	277
Reassessing the Nation's Gun Laws	03/22/91	157
Redistricting Disputes	03/12/04	221
Redistricting: Drawing Power with a Map	02/15/91	97
Re-examining 9/11	06/04/04	493
Religion and Law	11/07/14	937
Religion in Schools	02/18/94	145
Religion in Schools	01/12/01	1
Remembering 9/11	09/02/11	701*
Restorative Justice	02/05/16	121

	Date	Page
Air Pollution Conflict	11/14/03	965
Bush Presidency	02/02/01	82*
Campaign Finance Showdown	11/22/02	969
Closing In on Tobacco	11/12/99	991*
Cyberpolitics	09/17/04	757
Drug Company Ethics	06/06/03	521
Electing the President	04/20/07	337
The Federal Judiciary	03/13/98	217
Foreign Policy and Public Opinion	07/15/94	601
Foreign Policy Burden	08/20/93	721
Gays in the Military	09/18/09	**765
Gun Control Debate	11/12/04	949
Independent Counsels	02/21/97	145
Independent Counsels Re-examined	05/07/99	377
Line-Item Veto	06/20/97	529
Missile Defense	09/08/00	689
National Education Standards	05/14/99	401
National Service	06/25/93	553
National Service	06/30/06	577
Non-Proliferation Treaty at 25	01/27/95	86*
North Korean Crisis	04/11/03	321
Northern Ireland Cease-Fire	09/15/95	801
Partisan Divide	04/30/04	373
Partisan Politics	03/19/99	233
Philanthropy in America	12/08/06	1009
Political Conventions	08/08/08	649
Political Scandals	05/27/94	457
Politicians and Privacy	04/17/92	337
Presidential Libraries	03/16/07	241
Re-examining 9/11	06/04/04	493
Reforming the CIA	02/02/96	97
Reforming Veterans' Health Care	11/21/14	985
Reinventing Government	02/17/95	145
Religion and Politics	10/14/94	889
Saving Open Spaces	11/05/99	953

	Date	Page
Social Security Reform	09/24/04	781
Talk Show Democracy	04/29/94	361
Tax Reform	03/22/96	241
U.S.-British Relations	01/30/98	73
U.S.-British Relations	11/05/10	917*
U.S.-China Trade	04/15/94	313
U.S.-Russian Relations	05/22/98	457
U.S. Trade Policy	01/29/93	88*
Welfare Experiments	09/16/94	793
Welfare, Work and the States	12/06/96	1057

Clinton, Hillary Rodham

Campaign Finance Debates	05/28/10	457
Changing U.S. Electorate	05/30/08	**457
Children's Legal Rights	04/23/93	348*
Electing the President	04/20/07	337
First Ladies	06/14/96	505
Future of the Democratic Party	10/13/17	845
Independent Counsels Re-examined	05/07/99	377
Mental Illness	08/06/93	673
The Obama Legacy	11/04/16	913
Political Conventions	08/08/08	649
Political Scandals	05/27/94	457
Populism and Party Politics	09/09/16	721
Talk Show Democracy	04/29/94	374*
Teaching Values	06/21/96	534*
U.S.-China Relations	05/07/10	**409
Women and Human Rights	04/30/99	353
Women in Leadership	09/23/16	769
Women in Politics	03/21/08	265

Cloning

The Cloning Controversy	05/09/97	409
Embryo Research	12/17/99	1065
Food Safety	11/01/02	897
Mass Extinction	09/15/00	728*
Organ Shortage	02/21/03	153

Clothing and dress

Animal Rights	05/24/91	311*
Child Labor and Sweatshops	08/16/96	721
Preventing Juvenile Crime	03/15/96	224*

Coaching. *See Sports*

Coal

Acid Rain: New Approach to Old Problem	03/08/91	129
Air Pollution and Climate Control	11/13/15	961
Air Pollution Conflict	11/14/03	965
Alternative Energy	07/10/92	573
Alternative Energy	02/25/05	173
Coal's Comeback	10/05/07	817
Coal Industry's Future	06/17/16	529
Coal Mining Safety	03/17/06	241
Confronting Warming	01/09/09	1
Energy and Climate	07/24/09	621
Energy Policy	05/25/01	455*

	Date	Page
Energy Policy	05/20/11	457
Energy Security	02/01/02	73
Mine Safety	06/24/11	553
The Politics of Energy	03/05/99	185
Renewable Energy	11/07/97	961
Reviving Rural Economies	03/31/17	265

Coastal areas

Climate Change	01/27/06	73
Climate Change and National Security	09/22/17	773
Coastal Development	08/21/98	721
Coastal Development	02/22/13	181
Disaster Preparedness	11/18/05	**981
Protecting the Oceans	10/17/14	865
Rebuilding New Orleans	02/03/06	97
Reforming the Corps	05/30/03	497
Threatened Coastlines	02/07/92	97
Water Shortages	08/01/03	649

Cocaine. *See Drug abuse*

Cold fusion. *See Nuclear fusion*

Cold War

Dealing With the "New" Russia	06/06/08	481
Democracies Under Stress	10/20/17	869
European Unrest	01/09/15	25
Intelligence Reform	05/29/15	457
Military Readiness	11/03/17	917
Restoring Ties With Cuba	06/12/15	505
U.S. Global Engagement	05/16/14	433
U.S.-Russia Relations	01/13/17	25

Colleges and universities

AB and IP Programs	03/03/06	193
Academic Freedom	10/07/05	833
Academic Politics	02/16/96	145
Affirmative Action	09/21/01	737
Affirmative Action	10/17/08	**841
Affirmative Action and College Admissions	11/17/17	969
Anti-Semitism	05/12/17	409
Apprenticeships	10/14/16	841
Archaeology Today	05/24/02	457
Big Data and Privacy	10/25/13	909
Black Colleges	12/12/03	1045
Campus Sexual Assault	10/31/14	913
Career Colleges	01/07/11	1
Cheating in Schools	09/22/00	745
College Rankings	01/02/15	1
Combating Plagiarism	09/19/03	773
Combating Scientific Misconduct	01/10/97	1
Community Colleges	04/21/00	329
Community Colleges	05/01/15	385
Contingent Work Force	10/24/97	948*
Crime on Campus	02/04/11	97
Cults in America	05/07/93	402*
Cyber-Crime	04/12/02	305

	Date	Page
Cyber Socializing	07/28/06	625
Discipline in Schools	02/15/08	145
Distance Learning	12/07/01	993
Drinking on Campus	03/20/98	241
Drinking on Campus	08/18/06	649
Education and Gender	06/03/94	481
Free Speech on Campus	05/08/15	409
Future of Books	05/29/09	**473
Future of the Middle Class	04/08/16	313
Future of the Music Industry	11/21/03	989
Future of Public Universities	01/18/13	53
Gender and Learning	05/20/05	445
Getting into College	02/23/96	169
Grade Inflation	06/07/02	505
Greek Life on Campus	11/20/15	985
Gun Rights Debates	10/31/08	**889
Gun Violence	05/25/07	457
Hate Crimes	01/08/93	1
Hazing	01/09/04	1
Homeless Students	04/05/13	305
Home Schooling	03/07/14	217
Home Schooling Debate	01/17/03	39*
Hospitals' Financial Woes	08/13/99	697*
Humanities Education	12/06/13	1029
Illegal Immigration	05/06/05	393
Immigration Debate	02/01/08	**97
Income Inequality	12/03/10	989
Internet Accuracy	08/01/08	625
Jobs Outlook	06/04/10	481
Law Schools	04/19/13	353
Liberal Arts Education	04/10/98	313
Living-Wage Movement	09/27/02	782*
National Service	06/25/93	553
Paying for College	11/20/92	1001
Plagiarism and Cheating	01/04/13	1
Prayer and Healing	01/14/05	25
Preventing Hazing	02/08/13	133
Preventing Teen Drug Use	03/15/02	217
Race and Education	09/05/14	721
Race in America	07/11/03	603*
Racial Quotas	05/17/91	277
Racial Tensions in Schools	01/07/94	1
Rethinking Affirmative Action	04/28/95	375*
Rising College Costs	12/05/03	1013
Science in America	01/11/08	25
Science and Politics	08/20/04	661
Sex on Campus	11/04/94	961
Sexual Harassment	04/27/12	377
Single-Sex Education	07/12/02	569
Social Networking	09/17/10	749
Special Education	11/10/00	919*
State Budget Crisis	09/11/09	741
Student Activism	08/28/98	745

	Date	Page
Student Aid	01/25/08	73
Student Debt	10/21/11	877
Student Journalism	06/05/98	481
Teacher Education	10/17/97	913
Teaching Critical Thinking	04/10/15	313
Treating Anxiety	02/08/02	97
Treatment of Veterans	11/19/04	984*
Underage Drinking	03/13/92	217
Upward Mobility	04/29/05	369
Women and Sports	03/25/11	265
Women and Work	07/26/13	645
Worker Retraining	01/21/94	55*
Year-Round Schools	05/17/96	446*
Youth Volunteerism	01/27/12	77

Colleges and universities — Sports

	Date	Page
'Alt-Right' Movement	03/17/17	241
Athletes and Drugs	07/26/91	513
College Football	11/18/11	977
College Sports	08/26/94	745
Eating Disorders	12/18/92	1103
Gender and Learning	05/20/05	445
Gender Equity in Sports	04/18/97	337
Getting into College	02/23/96	186*
Guns on Campus	01/27/17	73
Paying College Athletes	07/11/14	577
Press Freedom	02/05/10	97
Reforming Big-Time College Sports	03/19/04	249
Repetitive Stress Injuries	06/23/95	548*
Shock Jocks	06/01/07	**481
Soccer in America	04/22/94	350*
Sports and Drugs	07/23/04	**613
Sports and Sexual Assault	04/28/17	361
Sportsmanship	03/23/01	225
Student Aid	01/25/08	73
Student Debt	11/18/16	965
The Value of a College Education	11/20/09	981
Women and Sports	03/06/92	193

Colombia

	Date	Page
Children in Crisis	08/31/01	657
Democracy in Latin America	11/03/00	896*
Privatizing the Military	06/25/04	565
Reforming Big-Time College Sports	03/19/04	249
Trouble in South America	03/14/03	241*

Colorado

	Date	Page
Cleaning Up Hazardous Wastes	08/23/96	745
Parental Rights	10/25/96	937
Redistricting Disputes	03/12/04	221
Reforming Big-Time College Sports	03/19/04	249
Saving Open Spaces	11/05/99	965*
Urban Sprawl in the West	10/03/97	865
Water Shortages	08/01/03	661*

Columbine High School. *See Littleton, Colo.*

	Date	Page
Communication. *See Telecommunications*		
Communism and communist countries		
Aid to Russia	03/12/93	217
Castro's Next Move	12/12/97	1081
China After Deng	06/13/97	505
China Today	04/04/14	289
Cuba in Crisis	11/29/91	897
Cuba's Future	07/20/07	601
Cyberwarfare Threat	10/06/17	821
Dealing With the "New" Russia	06/06/08	481
Democracy in Eastern Europe	10/08/99	876*
Emerging China	11/11/05	957
Emerging India	04/19/02	329
European Unrest	01/09/15	25
The Greening of Eastern Europe	11/15/91	849
Intelligence Reform	05/29/15	457
Military Readiness	11/03/17	917
New Era in Asia	02/14/92	121
Policing the Borders	02/22/02	145
Religious Persecution	11/21/97	1009
Restoring Ties With Cuba	06/12/15	505
Russia and the Former Soviet Republics	06/17/05	541
Russia's Political Future	05/03/96	385
U.S.-China Relations	05/07/10	**409
U.S. Global Engagement	05/16/14	433
Community colleges		
College Rankings	01/02/15	1
Community Colleges	04/21/00	329
Community Colleges	05/01/15	385
Distance Learning	12/07/01	993
Nursing Shortage	09/20/02	757*
Paying for College	11/20/92	1018*
Worker Retraining	01/21/94	55*
Community service. *See Voluntarism*		
Commuting. *See also Telecommuting*		
Affordable Housing	02/09/01	94*
Mass Transit	12/09/16	1013
Millennial Generation	06/26/15	553
Smart Growth	05/28/04	469
Traffic Congestion	05/06/94	385
Traffic Congestion	08/27/99	729
Computers. *See also Internet*		
3D Printing	12/07/12	1037
Artificial Intelligence	11/14/97	985
Artificial Intelligence	04/22/11	361
Big Data and Privacy	10/25/13	909
Computer Hacking	09/16/11	757*
Controlling the Internet	05/12/06	409
Cyberbullying	05/02/08	385
Cyber-Crime	04/12/02	305
Cyber-Predators	03/01/02	169
Cybersecurity	09/26/03	797

	Date	Page
Cyber Socializing	07/28/06	625
Cyberwarfare Threat	10/06/17	821
The Dark Web	01/15/16	49
Digital Currency	09/26/14	793
Digital Education	12/02/11	1001
Digital Journalism	05/30/14	457
Distance Learning	12/07/01	993
Employee Benefits	02/04/00	65
Examining Forensics	07/17/09	597
Future of Computers	05/26/00	449
Future of the Music Industry	11/21/03	989
Future of Recycling	12/14/07	1033
The Future of Television	12/23/94	1136*
Government Surveillance	08/30/13	717
Hard Times for Libraries	06/26/92	565*
High-Tech Labor Shortage	04/24/98	361
Identity Theft	06/10/05	517
Impact of the Internet on Thinking	09/24/10	773
Improving Cybersecurity	02/15/13	157
Internet Accuracy	08/01/08	625
Internet Regulation	04/13/12	325
Nanotechnology	06/11/04	517
Networking the Classroom	10/20/95	921
Online Privacy	11/06/09	**933
Preventing Bullying	12/10/10	**1013
Privacy and the Internet	12/04/15	1009
Protecting the Power Grid	11/11/16	941
Reading Crisis?	02/22/08	169
Recession's Regional Impact	02/01/91	75*
Redistricting Disputes	03/12/04	221
Redistricting: Drawing Power with a Map	02/15/91	101*
Regulating the New Economy	10/19/01	849
Repetitive Stress Injuries	06/23/95	537
Rising College Costs	12/05/03	1026*
Robotics and the Economy	09/25/15	793
Smart Cities	07/27/12	645
Social Media Explosion	01/25/13	81
Social Media and Politics	10/12/12	865
Social Networking	09/17/10	749
Software Piracy	05/21/93	433
Teacher Education	10/17/97	926*
Television's Future	02/16/07	145
Video Games	11/10/06	**937
Video Games and Learning	02/12/16	145
Virtual Reality	02/26/16	193
Work, Family and Stress	08/14/92	703*
Worker Safety	05/21/04	451*
Y2K Dilemma	02/19/99	137
Congress, U.S.		
Campaign Finance Reform	02/09/96	121
Campaign Finance Showdown	11/22/02	969
Census 2000	05/01/98	403*

	Date	Page
Census Controversey	05/14/10	433
Civic Renewal	03/21/97	246*
Democrats in Congress	06/08/07	505
Democrats' Future	10/29/10	893
Domestic Energy Development	09/30/05	809
Domestic Violence	01/06/06	1
Draft Debates	08/19/05	661
Drug Testing	11/20/98	1015*
Electing Minorities	08/12/94	697
Evaluating Head Start	08/26/05	685
Foreign Aid After Sept. 11	04/26/02	361
Future of the GOP	03/20/09	249
Future of the GOP	10/24/14	889
Governing Washington, D.C.	11/22/96	1033
Gridlock in Washington	04/30/10	385
Homeland Security	09/12/03	749
Humanities Education	12/06/13	1029
Independent Counsels	02/21/97	145
Interrogating the CIA	09/25/09	789
Lies and Politics	02/18/11	145
Line-Item Veto	06/20/97	529
Lobbying Boom	07/22/05	613
Medicaid Reform	07/16/04	589
Mental Illness Medication Debate	02/06/04	101
Middle East Tensions	10/27/06	**889
Minimum Wage	12/16/05	1053
NASA's Future	05/23/03	473
New Strategy in Iraq	02/23/07	169
The Partisan Divide	04/30/04	384
Partisan Politics	03/19/99	233
Political Scandals	05/27/94	457
Pork Barrel Politics	06/16/06	529
Presidential Power	11/15/02	945
Rebuilding Iraq	07/11/03	625
Rebuilding New Orleans	02/03/06	97
Redistricting Debates	02/25/11	169
Redistricting Disputes	03/12/04	221
Re-examining the Constitution	09/07/12	741
Re-examining 9/11	06/04/04	493
Reforming the Corps	05/30/03	497
Regulating Lobbying	06/06/14	481
Right to Die	05/13/05	421
Science and Politics	08/20/04	661
Sex Scandals	01/22/10	49
Sexual Harassment	08/09/91	551*
States and Federalism	10/15/10	845
Supreme Court's Future	01/28/05	77
Tea Party Movement	03/19/10	**241*
Telecommuting	07/19/13	621
Term Limits	01/10/92	1
Testing Term Limits	11/18/94	1009
Treating Schizophrenia	12/05/14	1009
Treatment of Veterans	11/19/04	973
U.S.-British Relations	11/05/10	917*

	Date	Page
War in Iraq	10/21/05	881
Women in Politics	03/21/08	265
Congress, U.S. — Legislative outlooks		
Abortion Debates	03/21/03	265*
Abortion Debates	09/10/10	725
Abortion Debates	03/21/14	265
Abortion Showdowns	09/22/06	769
Afghanistan Dilemma	08/07/09	**669*
Age Discrimination	08/01/97	687*
Aging Infrastructure	09/28/07	**793
Aiding Africa	08/29/03	697
Air Pollution Conflict	11/14/03	965
Alzheimer's Disease	05/15/98	433
America at War	07/23/10	**605
American Indians	04/28/06	**361
Animal Rights	01/08/10	1
Apprenticeships	10/14/16	841
Arbitrating Disputes	03/11/16	241
Asbestos Litigation	05/02/03	393
Assessing the New Health Care Law	09/21/12	789
Auto Industry's Future	02/06/09	**105
Betting on Sports	10/28/16	889
Biofuels Boom	09/29/06	793
Birth-Control Debate	06/24/05	565
Blighted Cities	11/12/10	941*
Breast Cancer	04/02/10	289
Broadcast Indecency	04/16/04	321
Business Bankruptcy	04/10/09	321
Business Ethics	05/06/11	409
Buying Green	02/29/08	193
Campaign Finance	05/06/16	409
Campaign Finance Debates	05/28/10	457
Caring for the Dying	09/05/97	784*
Caring for Veterans	04/23/10	361
Celebrity Advocacy	05/11/12	425
Central American Gangs	01/30/15	97
Child-Care Options	05/08/98	423*
Child Custody and Support	01/13/95	39*
Children and Divorce	06/07/91	362
Child Poverty	10/28/11	901
Child Welfare	08/26/16	673
Child Welfare Reform	04/22/05	345
Civil Liberties Debates	10/24/03	893
Cleaning Up Hazardous Wastes	08/23/96	745
Climate Change	06/14/13	521
Climate Change and National Security	09/22/17	773
Closing Guantanamo	09/30/16	793
Coal Mining Safety	03/17/06	241
Coal's Comeback	10/05/07	817
Coastal Development	08/21/98	736*
Coastal Development	02/22/13	181
Combating Addiction	02/09/07	121
Combating Terrorism	07/21/95	633
Computer Hacking	09/16/11	757*

	Date	Page		Date	Page
Confronting Iraq	10/04/02	793	Gays in the Military	09/18/09	**765
Consumer Safety	10/12/07	841	Gentrification	02/20/15	169
Cost of the Iraq War	04/25/08	361*	The Gig Economy	03/18/16	265
Crime on Campus	02/04/11	97	Global Population Growth	01/16/15	49
Crisis on the Plains	05/09/03	438*	Google's Dominance	11/11/11	953
Cuba's Future	07/20/07	601	Government Spending	07/12/13	597
Curbing CEO Pay	03/09/07	217	Gulf Coast Restoration	08/26/11	677*
Cyberwarfare Threat	10/06/17	821	Gun Control	03/08/13	233
D.C. Voting Rights	04/11/08	313*	Gun Control Debate	11/12/04	949
Death Penalty Debate	03/10/95	206*	Gun Control Standoff	12/19/97	1105
Debate over Bilingualism	01/19/96	49	Gun Rights Debates	10/31/08	**889
Debt Collectors	07/20/12	621	Gun Violence	05/25/07	457
Democrats in Congress	06/08/07	505	Guns on Campus	01/27/17	73
Dietary Supplements	07/08/94	577	Health-Care Reform	08/28/09	693*
Dietary Supplements	09/03/04	709	Health-Care Reform	06/11/10	**505
Dietary Supplements	10/30/15	913	Helping the Homeless	01/26/96	90*
Distracted Driving	05/04/12	401	High-Speed Trains	05/01/09	**397
Domestic Poverty	09/07/07	**721	High-Tech Labor Shortage	04/24/98	378*
Downsizing Prisons	03/11/11	217	Highway Safety	07/14/95	622*
Dropout Rate	06/13/14	505	Homeland Security	09/12/03	749
Drug Company Ethics	06/06/03	521	The Homeless	08/07/92	676
Drugmakers Under Siege	09/03/99	753	Homeless Students	04/05/13	305
Drug Safety	03/11/05	221	Housing Discrimination	11/06/15	937
Earthquake Threat	04/09/10	313	Housing the Homeless	12/18/09	1053
E-Cigarettes	09/19/14	769	Human Rights Issues	10/30/09	909
Electing the President	04/20/07	337	Human Spaceflight	10/16/09	861
Embryo Research	12/17/99	1065	Human Trafficking and Slavery	03/26/04	273
Ending Homelessness	06/18/04	541	Identity Theft	06/10/05	517
Energy and Climate	07/24/09	621	Illegal Immigration	05/06/05	393
Energy Efficiency	05/19/06	433	Immigrants and the Economy	02/24/17	169
Energy Policy	05/20/11	457	Immigration Conflict	03/09/12	229
Environmental Movement at 25	03/31/95	273	Immigration Debate	02/01/08	**97
Executive Pay	07/11/97	615*	Improving Cybersecurity	02/15/13	157
Exporting Jobs	02/20/04	149	Income Inequality	12/03/10	989
Extreme Weather	09/09/11	733*	Increase in Autism	06/13/03	**553*
Farm Policy	12/02/94	1057	Independent Counsels	02/21/97	145
Farm Policy	08/10/12	693	Independent Counsels Re-examined	05/07/99	377
Farm Subsidies	05/17/02	433	Indoor Air Pollution	10/27/95	960*
Financial Bailout	10/24/08	**865	Infant Mortality	07/31/92	658
Financial Crisis	05/09/08	409	Insurance Fraud	10/11/96	904*
Financial Industry Overhaul	07/30/10	629	Intelligence Reforms	01/25/02	49
Fish Farming	07/27/07	625	Internet Regulation	04/13/12	325
Fixing Urban Schools	04/27/07	**361	Internet Shopping	06/28/13	573
Foreign Aid and National Security	06/17/11	529	IRS Reform	01/16/98	25
Fracking Controversy	12/16/11	1049	Jobs vs. Environment	05/15/92	409
Free-Press Disputes	04/08/05	293	Jobs Outlook	06/04/10	481
Funding the Arts	07/14/17	581	Latino Voters	04/03/15	289
Future of the Airlines	03/07/08	217	Lead Poisoning	06/19/92	542
Future of the Democratic Party	10/13/17	845	Legalizing Marijuana	06/12/09	**525
Future of Homeownership	12/14/12	1061	Limiting Lawsuits	12/19/08	1033
Future of the Middle Class	04/08/16	313	Managed Care	04/12/96	329*
The Future of Television	12/23/94	1129	Managing Nuclear Waste	01/28/11	73
Future of TV	04/11/14	313	Managing Public Lands	11/04/11	929
Gang Crisis	05/14/04	421	Managing Western Lands	04/22/16	361

	Date	Page		Date	Page
Managing Wildfires	11/02/12	941	Prisoners and Mental Illness	03/13/15	241
Marijuana Industry	10/16/15	865	Privacy and the Internet	12/04/15	1009
Mass Transit	12/09/16	1013	Privacy in Peril	11/17/06	961
Media Ownership	10/10/03	**845	Privatizing Government Services	12/08/17	1017
Medical Breakthroughs	09/15/17	749	Privatizing the Military	06/25/04	565
Medical Malpractice	02/14/03	129	Privatizing the Military	07/13/12	597
Medicare Reform	08/22/03	673	Property Rights	06/16/95	513
Mental Health Policy	05/10/13	425	Protecting Endangered Species	04/19/96	337
Mexico's Drug War	12/12/08	1009	Protecting the Oceans	10/17/14	865
Middle-Class Squeeze	03/06/09	201	Protecting the Power Grid	11/11/16	941
Military Readiness	11/03/17	917	Protecting Wetlands	10/03/08	793*
Military Suicides	09/23/11	781*	Protecting Whistleblowers	03/31/06	265
Mine Safety	06/24/11	553	Real ID	05/04/07	385
Mortgage Crisis	11/02/07	**913	Reassessing Foreign Aid	09/27/96	841
Mosquito-Borne Disease	07/22/16	601	Reducing Your Carbon Footprint	12/05/08	985
Nanotechnology	06/10/16	505	Reforming the U.N.	06/24/16	553
The National Debt	11/14/08	937	Reforming Veterans' Health Care	11/21/14	985
National Debt	03/18/11	241	Regulating Credit Cards	10/10/08	817*
National Debt	09/01/17	701	Regulating Nonprofits	12/26/97	1129
National Education Standards	05/14/99	401	Regulating Pesticides	01/28/94	73
Native Americans	05/08/92	398	Regulating Pesticides	08/06/99	682*
New Space Race	08/04/17	653	Regulating Pharmaceuticals	10/11/13	861
Nonprofit Groups and Partisan Politics	11/14/14	961	Regulating Toxic Chemicals	01/23/09	49
Nuclear Disarmament	10/02/09	**813	Regulating Toxic Chemicals	07/18/14	601
Nuclear Energy	03/10/06	217	Religion and Law	11/07/14	937
Nuclear Power	06/10/11	505	Religious Persecution	11/21/97	1009
Nuclear Proliferation and Terrorism	04/02/04	297	Renewable Energy	11/07/97	978*
The Obama Presidency	01/30/09	73	Repetitive Stress Injuries	06/23/95	537
Offshore Drilling	06/25/10	553	Rethinking Affirmative Action	04/28/95	369
Oil Jitters	01/04/08	**1	Rethinking Foreign Aid	04/14/17	313
Online Privacy	11/06/09	**933	Rethinking Retirement	06/19/09	549
Opioid Crisis	10/07/16	817	Revising No Child Left Behind	04/16/10	337
Overhauling Social Security	05/12/95	417	Revitalizing the Cities	10/13/95	909*
Patent Controversies	02/27/15	193	Reviving Rural Economies	03/31/17	265
Patent Disputes	12/15/06	1033	Rising Health Costs	04/07/06	289
Patients' Rights	02/06/98	112*	Robotic Warfare	01/23/15	73
Patient Safety	02/10/12	125	Roe v. Wade at 25	11/28/97	1033
Peace Corps Challenges	01/11/13	29	Saving Open Spaces	11/05/99	966*
Pension Crisis	02/17/06	145	School Reform	04/29/11	385
Polarization in America	02/28/14	193	School Vouchers Showdown	02/15/02	121
Police Tactics	12/12/14	1033	Sentencing Debates	11/05/04	925
Policing the Borders	02/22/02	145	Sex Offenders	09/08/06	721
Populism and Party Politics	09/09/16	721	Sexual Assault in the Military	08/09/13	693
Pornography	10/21/16	865	Shock Jocks	06/01/07	**481
Port Security	04/21/06	337	Social Networking	09/17/10	749
Prescription Drug Costs	05/20/16	457	Solar Energy Controversies	04/29/16	385
Presidential Libraries	03/16/07	241	Space Program	02/24/12	177
Presidential Power	11/15/02	952*	Stem Cell Research	09/01/06	**697
Presidential Power	03/06/15	217	Stimulating the Economy	01/10/03	17*
Press Freedom	02/05/10	97	The Stock Market	05/02/97	401*
Preventing Cancer	01/16/09	25	Straining the Safety Net	07/31/09	645
Preventing Obesity	10/01/10	797	Student Aid	01/25/08	73
Primary Care	03/17/95	234*	Student Debt	10/21/11	877
Prison Reform	04/06/07	289	Supreme Court's Future	01/28/05	77

	Date	Page
Teacher Education	10/17/97	930*
Teaching Critical Thinking	04/10/15	313
Testing Term Limits	11/18/94	1009
Think Tanks in Transition	09/29/17	797
Treating Alzheimer's Disease	07/24/15	625
Treating Depression	06/26/09	573
Three-Strikes Laws	05/10/02	417
Transportation Policy	07/04/97	577
Treatment of Detainees	08/25/06	673
Underage Drinking	03/13/92	217
Unemployment Benefits	04/25/03	369
United Nations at 50	08/18/95	729
Universal Basic Income	09/08/17	725
Universal Coverage	03/30/07	265
Upward Mobility	04/29/05	369
U.S.-Pakistan Relations	08/05/11	653*
U.S. Policy on Iran	11/16/07	961
U.S.-Russia Relations	01/13/17	25
Vanishing Jobs	03/13/09	225
Voter Rights	05/18/12	449
Voting Controversies	09/15/06	745
Voting Controversies	02/21/14	169
Water Shortages	06/18/10	529
Weapons of Mass Destruction	03/08/02	193
Whistleblowers	12/05/97	1072*
Whistleblowers	01/31/14	97
Wind Power	04/01/11	289
Women in Combat	05/13/16	433
Women in the Military	11/13/09	957
Worker Safety	05/21/04	445
Worker Safety	10/04/13	837
The Working Poor	11/03/95	984*
Wounded Veterans	08/31/07	697
Youth Violence	03/05/10	193*

Conservation. *See also Endangered species; Environmental Protection*

Alternative Energy	02/25/05	173
Archaeology Today	05/24/02	457
Arctic Development	12/02/16	989
Bush and the Environment	10/25/02	865
Buying Green	02/29/08	193
California: Enough Water for the Future?	04/19/91	221
Crisis on the Plains	05/09/03	439*
Disappearing Species	11/30/07	985
Ecotourism	10/20/06	865
Endangered Species Act	06/03/05	**493
Energy and the Environment	03/03/00	161
Energy Efficiency	05/19/06	433
Energy Security	02/01/02	73
Farm Policy	08/10/12	693
Global Hunger	08/08/14	673
Global Water Shortages	12/15/95	1113
Hunting Controversy	01/24/92	49

	Date	Page
Mass Transit Boom	01/18/08	49
National Forests	10/16/98	905
National Parks	05/28/93	457
National Parks	01/17/14	49
National Parks Under Pressure	10/06/06	817
The Obama Legacy	11/04/16	913
Oil Jitters	01/04/08	**1
Pesticide Controversies	06/05/15	481
Protecting the National Parks	06/16/00	521
Protecting the Oceans	10/17/14	865
Public Land Policy	06/17/94	529
Reducing Your Carbon Footprint	12/05/08	985
Reforming the Corps	05/30/03	497
Regulating Toxic Chemicals	07/18/14	601
Saving Open Spaces	11/05/99	953
Saving the Forests	09/20/91	681
Saving the Rain Forests	06/11/99	497
Smart Growth	05/28/04	469
SUV Debate	05/16/03	449
Threatened Fisheries	08/02/02	617
Troubled Brazil	04/07/17	289
Water Shortages	08/01/03	649

Constitution, U.S. *See also Civil rights and liberties; First Amendment*

Affirmative Action	10/17/08	**841
Campaign Finance Showdown	11/22/02	985*
Civic Education	02/03/17	97
Civil Liberties Debates	10/24/03	893
Closing Guantánamo	02/27/09	**177
Cyberbullying	05/02/08	385
Death Penalty Debates	11/19/10	965
Free-Press Disputes	04/08/05	293
Future of Marriage	05/07/04	397
Gay Marriage	03/15/13	257
Gay Marriage Showdowns	09/26/08	**769
Gender Pay Gap	03/14/08	241
Gun Control Debate	11/12/04	949
International Law	12/17/04	1049
Latino Voters	04/03/15	289
Line-Item Veto	06/20/97	529
Presidential Power	11/15/02	945
Presidential Power	02/24/06	169
Presidential Power	03/06/15	217
Preventing Bullying	12/10/10	**1013
Property Rights	06/16/95	513
Public Defenders	04/18/08	337*
Racial Diversity in Public Schools	09/14/07	**745
Racial Profiling	11/22/13	1005
Reassessing the Nation's Gun Laws	03/22/91	157
Redistricting Disputes	03/12/04	221
Re-examining the Constitution	09/07/12	741
School Vouchers Showdown	02/15/02	121
Sentencing Debates	11/05/04	925
Supreme Court Controversies	09/28/12	813

	Date	Page
Term Limits	01/10/92	1
Testing Term Limits	11/18/94	1009
Three-Strikes Laws	05/10/02	417

Consumerism

	Date	Page
Advertising Overload	01/23/04	49
Alternative Energy	02/25/05	173
Buying Green	02/29/08	193
Celebrity Culture	03/18/05	245
Consumer Debt	03/02/07	193
The Consumer Culture	11/19/99	1001
Financial Literacy	09/04/09	717
Food Policy Debates	10/03/14	817
Limiting Lawsuits	12/19/08	1033
Media Violence	02/14/14	145
Millennial Generation	06/26/15	553
Professional Football	01/29/10	**73
Protecting the Oceans	10/17/14	865
Reducing Your Carbon Footprint	12/05/08	985
Rise of Megachurches	09/21/07	769
Teen Spending	05/26/06	457
Video Games and Learning	02/12/16	145

Consumer prices

	Date	Page
America's Pampered Pets	12/27/96	1129
Big-Box Stores	09/10/04	733
Child Labor and Sweatshops	08/16/96	721
Civic Renewal	03/21/97	241
College Rankings	01/02/15	1
Doctor Shortage	08/28/15	697
Drugmakers Under Siege	09/03/99	753
The Economics of Recycling	03/27/98	265
Energy Security	02/01/02	73
Fast-Food Shake-Up	11/08/91	825
Gentrification	02/20/15	169
Jobs in the '90s	02/28/92	182*
Liberal Arts Education	04/10/98	313
Managed Care	04/12/96	313
Mental Illness Medication Debate	02/06/04	101
Oil Production in the 21st Century	08/07/98	673
Paying for College	11/20/92	1001
Prescription Drug Prices	07/17/92	597
Restructuring the Electric Industry	01/17/97	25
Rethinking NAFTA	06/07/96	481
Rising College Costs	12/05/03	1013
Space Program's Future	04/25/97	372*
Stimulating the Economy	01/10/03	1
U.S. Auto Industry	10/16/92	881
Wealth and Inequality	04/18/14	337

Consumer protection

	Date	Page
Advertising Overload	01/23/04	49
Advertising Under Attack	09/13/91	657
Airline Industry Problems	09/24/99	825
Animal Rights	05/24/91	301
Antitrust Policy	06/12/98	510*
Arbitrating Disputes	03/11/16	241

	Date	Page
Betting on Sports	10/28/16	889
Caring for the Elderly	02/20/98	145
Charter Schools	03/10/17	217
Class Action Lawsuits	05/13/11	433
Coal Industry's Future	06/17/16	529
Consumer Debt	03/02/07	193
Consumer Safety	10/12/07	841
Corporate Crime	10/11/02	817
Cosmetic Surgery	04/15/05	317
Cyber-Crime	04/12/02	305
Cyber-Predators	03/01/02	169
Cyberwarfare Threat	10/06/17	821
Debt Collectors	07/20/12	621
Decriminalizing Prostitution	04/15/16	337
Dietary Supplements	07/08/94	577
Dietary Supplements	09/03/04	709
Dietary Supplements	10/30/15	913
Digital Currency	09/26/14	793
Drinking Water Safety	07/15/16	577
Drugmakers Under Siege	09/03/99	753
Drug Safety	03/11/05	221
E-Cigarettes	09/19/14	769
Electromagnetic Fields	04/26/91	237
Fighting over Animal Rights	08/02/96	673
Financial Misconduct	01/20/12	53
Food Irradiation	06/12/92	505
Food Labeling	06/16/17	509
Food Safety	06/04/93	481
Genetically Engineered Foods	08/05/94	673
The Growing Influence of Boycotts	01/04/91	1
High-Impact Litigation	02/11/00	93*
Homeopathy Debate	12/19/03	1069
Housing Discrimination	11/06/15	937
Identity Theft	06/10/05	517
Insurance Fraud	10/11/96	889
Internet Shopping	06/28/13	573
Managing Managed Care	04/16/99	305
Marijuana Industry	10/16/15	865
Media Violence	02/14/14	145
Medical Marijuana	07/21/17	605
Mortgage Crisis	11/02/07	**913
Mosquito-Borne Disease	07/22/16	601
Mutual Funds	05/20/94	433
Nanotechnology	06/11/04	517
Obesity and Health	01/15/99	25
Online Dating	03/20/15	265
Pornography	10/21/16	865
Privacy and the Internet	12/04/15	1009
Privatizing Government Services	12/08/17	1017
Reducing Traffic Deaths	02/17/17	145
Regulating Credit Cards	10/10/08	817*
Regulating Pesticides	01/28/94	73
Regulating Pesticides	08/06/99	665
Regulating Pharmaceuticals	10/11/13	861

	Date	Page
Stock Market Troubles	01/16/04	25
Student Debt	10/21/11	877
Vaccine Controversies	02/19/16	169
Whistleblowers	12/05/97	1057

Contraceptives. *See Birth control*

Copyright

Clashing over Copyright	11/08/96	985
Combating Plagiarism	09/19/03	773
Copyright and the Internet	09/29/00	769
Cyber-Crime	04/12/02	305
Future of Libraries	07/29/11	625
Future of the Music Industry	11/21/03	989
Internet Regulation	04/13/12	325
Patent Controversies	02/27/15	193
Plagiarism and Cheating	01/04/13	1
Regulating the Internet	06/30/95	566*
Software Piracy	05/21/93	433

Corporate mergers. *See also Business and industry*

Antitrust Policy	06/12/98	505
Baby Boomers at Midlife	07/31/98	649
Business Bankruptcy	04/10/09	321
Corporate Crime	10/11/02	817
Cosmetic Surgery	04/15/05	317
Financial Bailout	10/24/08	**865
Financial Crisis	05/09/08	409
Financial Industry Overhaul	07/30/10	629
Future of Journalism	03/27/09	**273
The Future of Telecommunications	04/23/99	329
Journalism Under Fire	12/25/98	1135*
The Politics of Energy	03/05/99	200*
Wealth and Inequality	04/18/14	337

Corruption

Rethinking Foreign Aid	04/14/17	313
Troubled Brazil	04/07/17	289

Cosmetics — Testing. *See Animals*

Cosmetic Surgery

Celebrity Culture	03/18/05	245
Cosmetic Surgery	04/15/05	317

Courts. *See also Supreme Court*

Abortion Debates	03/21/03	249
Abortion Debates	09/10/10	725
Abortion Debates	03/21/14	265
Abortion Showdowns	09/22/06	769
Advertising Overload	01/23/04	49
Affirmative Action and		
College Admissions	11/17/17	969
Air Pollution and Climate Control	11/13/15	961
Air Pollution Conflict	11/14/03	965
Arbitrating Disputes	03/11/16	241
Asbestos Litigation	05/02/03	393
Assisted Suicide	02/21/92	145
Assisted Suicide Controversy	05/05/95	393
Betting on Sports	10/28/16	889

	Date	Page
Birth-Control Debate	06/24/05	565
Boys' Emotional Needs	06/18/99	538*
Breast Cancer	04/02/10	289
Cameras in the Courtroom	01/14/11	25
Campaign Finance Debates	05/28/10	457
Campaign Finance Showdown	11/22/02	980*
Caring for the Dying	09/05/97	769
Central American Gangs	01/30/15	97
Children's Legal Rights	04/23/93	337
Child Welfare	08/26/16	673
Child Welfare Reform	04/22/05	345
Civil Liberties Debates	10/24/03	893
Class Action Lawsuits	05/13/11	433
Closing Guantánamo	02/27/09	**177
Closing Guantanamo	09/30/16	793
Closing In on Tobacco	11/12/99	977
Cosmetic Surgery	04/15/05	317
Courts and the Media	09/23/94	817
Crackdown on Sexual Harassment	07/19/96	625
Crime Victims' Rights	07/22/94	625
Cyber-Crime	04/12/02	305
The Dark Web	01/15/16	49
Death Penalty Controversies	09/23/05	785
Death Penalty Update	01/08/99	1
Debt Collectors	07/20/12	621
DNA Databases	05/28/99	449
Domestic Partners	09/04/92	761
Downsizing Prisons	03/11/11	217
Drug-Policy Debate	07/28/00	593
Drug-Policy Debate	07/28/00	599*
Environmental Justice	06/19/98	529
Examining Forensics	07/17/09	597
Eyewitness Testimony	10/14/11	853
Far-Right Extremism	09/18/15	769
The Federal Judiciary	03/13/98	217
Fighting Gangs	10/09/15	841
Forensic Science Controversies	02/10/17	121
Foster Care Reform	01/09/98	6*
Free-Press Disputes	04/08/05	293
Future of the Music Industry	11/21/03	989
Gay Marriage	09/05/03	721
Gay Marriage	03/15/13	257
Gay Marriage Showdowns	09/26/08	**769
Gentrification	02/20/15	169
Google's Dominance	11/11/11	953
Greek Life on Campus	11/20/15	985
Helping the Homeless	01/26/96	73
High-Impact Litigation	02/11/00	89
Homegrown Jihadists	09/03/10	701
Housing Discrimination	11/06/15	937
Immigrant Detention	10/23/15	889
International Law	12/17/04	1049
Jailing Debtors	09/16/16	745
Judges and Politics	07/27/01	1003*

	Date	Page
Judicial Elections	04/24/09	373
The Jury System	11/10/95	993
Juvenile Justice	02/25/94	169
Juvenile Justice	11/07/08	913
Latino Voters	04/03/15	289
Law Schools	04/19/13	353
Legal-Aid Crisis	10/07/11	829
Limiting Lawsuits	12/19/08	1033
Marijuana Industry	10/16/15	865
Marijuana Laws	02/11/05	125
Medical Malpractice	02/14/03	129
Mental Health Policy	09/12/97	793
Mine Safety	06/24/11	553
NFL Controversies	09/04/15	721
No Child Left Behind	05/27/05	469
Opioid Crisis	10/07/16	817
Patent Controversies	02/27/15	193
Patent Disputes	12/15/06	1033
Plea Bargaining	02/12/99	113
Police Tactics	12/12/14	1033
Presidential Power	11/15/02	945
Presidential Power	03/06/15	217
Prison Reform	04/06/07	289
Prisoners and Mental Illness	03/13/15	241
Privacy and the Internet	12/04/15	1009
Property Rights	06/16/95	513
Property Rights	03/04/05	197
Prosecuting Terrorists	03/12/10	**217*
Prosecutors and the Law	11/09/07	937
Prosecutors and Politics	06/22/07	553
Public Defenders	04/18/08	337*
Punishing Sex Offenders	01/12/96	25
Race in America	07/11/03	593
Redistricting	02/16/01	113
Redistricting Debates	02/25/11	169
Redistricting Disputes	03/12/04	221
Redistricting: Drawing Power with a Map	02/15/91	97
Redistricting Showdown	08/25/17	677
Reforming Juvenile Justice	09/11/15	745
Reforming School Funding	12/10/99	1041
Religious Freedom	01/01/16	1
Restorative Justice	02/05/16	121
Rethinking School Integration	10/18/96	913
Right to Die	05/13/05	421
Robotic Warfare	01/23/15	73
Robotics and the Economy	09/25/15	793
School Censorship	02/19/93	145
School Choice Debate	07/18/97	630*
School Desegregation	04/23/04	345
School Funding	08/27/93	745
School Vouchers Showdown	02/15/02	121
Science and Politics	08/20/04	661
Science in the Courtroom	10/22/93	913

	Date	Page
Sentencing Debates	11/05/04	925
Serial Killers	10/31/03	917
Sex Offenders	09/08/06	721
Sexual Abuse and the Clergy	05/03/02	393
Sexual Assault in the Military	08/09/13	693
Sexual Harassment	04/27/12	377
Sleep Deprivation	06/26/98	570*
Solitary Confinement	09/14/12	765
States and Federalism	09/13/96	798*
Stock Market Troubles	01/16/04	25
Stolen Antiquities	11/10/17	945
Supreme Court Controversies	09/28/12	813
Supreme Court's Future	01/28/05	77
Three-Strikes Laws	05/10/02	417
Tobacco Industry	12/10/04	**1025
Too Many Lawsuits?	05/22/92	433
Transgender Issues	05/05/06	385
Unions at a Crossroads	08/07/15	673
Vaccine Controversies	08/25/00	650*
Voting Controversies	09/15/06	745
War Crimes	07/07/95	585
Women and Sports	03/25/11	265
Women in Prison	03/03/17	193
Workplace Sexual Harassment	10/27/17	893
Wrongful Convictions	04/17/09	**345
Young Voters	10/02/15	817

Creationism

	Date	Page
Evolution vs. Creationism	08/22/97	745
Intelligent Design	07/29/05	637
Religion in Schools	01/12/01	11*
Science and Religion	03/22/13	281

Credit cards

	Date	Page
The Consumer Culture	11/19/99	1001
Consumer Debt	11/15/96	1009
Consumer Debt	03/02/07	193
Cyber-Crime	04/12/02	305
Debt Collectors	07/20/12	621
Identity Theft	06/10/05	517
Student Aid	01/25/08	73
Teen Spending	05/26/06	457

Crime and criminals

	Date	Page
Accountants Under Fire	03/22/02	241
Betting on Sports	10/28/16	889
Biology and Behavior	04/03/98	289
Business Ethics	05/06/11	409
Border Security	09/27/13	813
Cameras in the Courtroom	01/14/11	25
Campus Sexual Assault	10/31/14	913
Central American Gangs	01/30/15	97
Child Sexual Abuse	01/15/93	25
Child Welfare	08/26/16	673
Child Welfare Reform	04/22/05	345
Civic Renewal	03/21/97	252*
Closing Guantanamo	09/30/16	793

	Date	Page		Date	Page
Combating Terrorism	07/21/95	633	Internet Regulation	04/13/12	325
Community Policing	02/05/93	97	Is America Allowing Its Past to Be		
Community Prosecution	12/15/00	1009	Stolen?	01/18/91	33
Computer Hacking	09/16/11	757*	Jailing Debtors	09/16/16	745
Corporate Crime	10/11/02	817	Job Stress	08/04/95	688*
Courts and the Media	09/23/94	817	The Jury System	11/10/95	993
Crime on Campus	02/04/11	97	Juvenile Justice	02/25/94	169
Crime Victims' Rights	07/22/94	625	Juvenile Justice	11/07/08	913
Criminal Records and Employment	04/20/12	349	Kids in Prison	04/27/01	345
Cyber-Crime	04/12/02	305	Labor Unions' Future	09/02/05	**709
Cyber-Predators	03/01/02	169	Legalizing Marijuana	06/12/09	**525
Cybersecurity	02/26/10	169	Mafia Crackdown	03/27/92	265
Cyberwarfare Threat	10/06/17	821	Mandatory Sentencing	05/26/95	465
Death Penalty Debate	03/10/95	193	Marijuana Laws	02/11/05	125
Death Penalty Debates	11/19/10	965	Medical Marijuana	08/20/99	721*
Death Penalty Update	01/08/99	1	Mental Illness	08/06/93	673
Declining Crime Rates	04/04/97	289	Mexico's Future	10/26/12	913
Democracy in Latin America	11/03/00	881	Native American Sovereignty	05/05/17	385
Digital Currency	09/26/14	793	NFL Controversies	09/04/15	721
DNA Databases	05/28/99	449	The Obscenity Debate	12/20/91	969
Domestic Violence	11/15/13	981	Online Dating	03/20/15	265
Downsizing Prisons	03/11/11	217	Opioid Crisis	10/07/16	817
Drug-Policy Debate	07/28/00	593	Plea Bargaining	02/12/99	113
Examining Forensics	07/17/09	597	Police Misconduct	04/06/12	301
Eyewitness Testimony	10/14/11	853	Police Tactics	12/12/14	1033
Fighting Crime	02/08/08	121	Policing the Borders	02/22/02	145
Fighting Gangs	10/09/15	841	Policing the Police	03/17/00	209
Financial Misconduct	01/20/12	53	Pork Barrel Politics	06/16/06	529
Forensic Science Controversies	02/10/17	121	Preventing Hazing	02/08/13	133
Free-Press Disputes	04/08/05	293	Preventing Juvenile Crime	03/15/96	217
Future of the Music Industry	11/21/03	989	Prison-Building Boom	09/17/99	801
Gambling in America	03/07/03	201	Prison Overcrowding	02/04/94	97
Gambling Under Attack	09/06/96	785*	Prison Reform	04/06/07	289
Gang Crisis	05/14/04	421	Prisoner Reentry	12/04/09	1005
Government Secrecy	02/11/11	121	Prisoners and Mental Illness	03/13/15	241
Government Surveillance	08/30/13	717	Privacy and the Internet	12/04/15	1009
Greek Life on Campus	11/20/15	985	Privatizing the Military	06/25/04	565
Gun Control	06/10/94	505	Prosecutors and the Law	11/09/07	937
Gun Control	03/08/13	233	Prostitution	06/11/93	505
Gun Control Debate	11/12/04	949	Protecting Whistleblowers	03/31/06	265
Gun Control Standoff	12/19/97	1105	Public Defenders	04/18/08	337*
Gun Rights Debates	10/31/08	**889	Public Housing	09/10/93	793
Gun Violence	05/25/07	457	Punishing Sex Offenders	01/12/96	25
Guns on Campus	01/27/17	73	Racial Profiling	11/22/13	1005
Hate Crimes	01/08/93	1	Recovered-Memory Debate	07/05/96	577
Hazing	01/09/04	1	Reforming Big-Time College Sports	03/19/04	249
High-Tech Policing	04/21/17	337	Reforming Juvenile Justice	09/11/15	745
Human Trafficking and Slavery	03/26/04	273	Regulating the Internet	06/30/95	561
Identity Theft	06/10/05	517	Restorative Justice	02/05/16	121
Illegal Immigration	04/24/92	361	Science in the Courtroom	10/22/93	920*
Illegal Immigration	05/06/05	393	School Violence	10/09/98	881
Improving Cybersecurity	02/15/13	157	Sentencing Debates	11/05/04	925
Insurance Fraud	10/11/96	889	Sentencing Reform	01/10/14	25
Intelligence Reform	05/29/15	457	Serial Killers	10/31/03	917

	Date	Page
Sex Offenders	09/08/06	721
Sex on Campus	11/04/94	961
Sexual Abuse and the Clergy	05/03/02	393
Software Piracy	05/21/93	433
Solitary Confinement	09/14/12	765
Sports and Drugs	07/23/04	**613
Sports and Sexual Assault	04/28/17	361
Stock Market Troubles	01/16/04	25
Stolen Antiquities	04/13/07	313
Stolen Antiquities	11/10/17	945
Suburban Crime	09/03/93	769
Supreme Court Preview	09/17/93	817
Teen Driving	01/07/05	1
Teen Drug Use	06/03/11	481
Terrorism in Africa	07/10/15	577
Three-Strikes Laws	05/10/02	417
Transnational Crime	08/29/14	697
Treating Addiction	01/06/95	17*
Treating Addiction	05/02/14	385
Troubled Brazil	04/07/17	289
TV Violence	03/26/93	279*
U.S.-Mexico Relations	09/02/16	697
Violence Against Women	02/26/93	169
Violence in Schools	09/11/92	785
War Crimes	07/07/95	585
War on Drugs	03/19/93	241
War on Drugs	06/02/06	481
Women in Prison	03/03/17	193
Workplace Sexual Harassment	10/27/17	893
Wrongful Convictions	04/17/09	**345
Youth Gangs	10/11/91	753
Youth Violence	03/05/10	193*

Cuba

Castro's Next Move	12/12/97	1081
Closing Guantánamo	02/27/09	**177
Closing Guantanamo	09/30/16	793
Cuba in Crisis	11/29/91	897
Cuba's Future	07/20/07	601
Economic Sanctions	10/28/94	937
Intelligence Reform	05/29/15	457
Latino Voters	04/03/15	289
Oil Production in the 21st Century	08/07/98	689*
Presidential Power	03/06/15	217
Restoring Ties With Cuba	06/12/15	505

Cults

Cults in America	05/07/93	385
The FBI Under Fire	04/11/97	313
Preparing for Disaster	08/02/13	669

Cyber Politics

| Campaign Finance Reform | 06/13/08 | 505 |

Czech Republic and Czechoslovakia

Democracy in Eastern Europe	10/08/99	865
Expanding NATO	05/16/97	433
The Greening of Eastern Europe	11/15/91	849

Dance

	Date	Page
Arts Education	03/16/12	253
Arts Funding	10/21/94	913
Centennial Olympic Games	04/05/96	297*
Funding the Arts	07/14/17	581

Date rape

Domestic Violence	11/15/13	981
Preventing Teen Drug Use	03/15/02	217
Sex on Campus	11/04/94	961
Violence Against Women	02/26/93	169

Day care. ***See Child care***

"Deadbeat Dads." ***See Child custody and support***

Dean, Howard

| Cyberpolitics | 09/17/04 | 757 |

Death penalty

Crime Victims' Rights	07/22/94	625
Death Penalty Controversies	09/23/05	785
Death Penalty Debate	03/10/95	193
Death Penalty Debates	11/19/10	965
Death Penalty Update	01/08/99	1
Human Rights	11/13/98	982*
Juvenile Justice	11/07/08	913
Kids in Prison	04/27/01	361*
Public Defenders	04/18/08	337*
Race in America	07/11/03	593
Rethinking the Death Penalty	11/16/01	945
Sentencing Debates	11/05/04	925
Sentencing Reform	01/10/14	25
Transatlantic Tensions	07/13/01	564*
Wrongful Convictions	04/17/09	**345

Defense. ***See Military policy***

Democracy

Aid to Russia	03/12/93	217
Aiding Africa	08/29/03	697
The British Monarchy	03/08/96	193
China After Deng	06/13/97	513*
Civic Education	02/03/17	97
Civic Journalism	09/20/96	817
Confronting Iraq	10/04/02	806*
Conspiracy Theories	10/23/09	885
Cuba's Future	07/20/07	601
Democracies Under Stress	10/20/17	869
Democracy in Africa	03/24/95	241
Democracy in Asia	07/24/98	625
Democracy in Eastern Europe	10/08/99	865
Democracy in Latin America	11/03/00	881
Democracy in the Arab World	01/30/04	73
Emerging India	04/19/02	329
Exporting Democracy	04/01/05	269
Free Speech at Risk	04/26/13	377
Future of Journalism	03/27/09	**273
Human Rights in China	07/25/08	601
Human Rights Issues	10/30/09	909

	Date	Page
Islamic Fundamentalism	03/24/00	241
Judicial Elections	04/24/09	373
Media Bias	05/03/13	401
Mexico's Emergence	07/19/91	489
'Occupy' Movement	01/13/12	25
Populism and Party Politics	09/09/16	721
Race in America	07/11/03	593
Reform in Iran	12/18/98	1097
Religious Freedom	01/01/16	1
Restoring Ties With Cuba	06/12/15	505
Resurgent Russia	02/07/14	121
Rethinking Foreign Policy	02/02/07	97
Russia and the Former Soviet Republics	06/17/05	541
Russia's Political Future	05/03/96	385
South Africa's Future	01/14/94	25
Taiwan, China, and the U.S.	05/24/96	457
Trouble in South America	03/14/03	225
Unrest in the Arab World	02/01/13	105
U.S. Global Engagement	05/16/14	433
Voting Controversies	09/15/06	745

Democratic Party

Air Pollution Conflict	11/14/03	965
Black Middle Class	01/23/98	66*
Campaign Finance	05/06/16	409
Campaign Finance Debates	05/28/10	457
Campaign Finance Reform	02/09/96	134*
Changing Demographics	11/16/12	989
Changing U.S. Electorate	05/30/08	**457
Cyberpolitics	09/17/04	757
D.C. Voting Rights	04/11/08	313*
Democrats in Congress	06/08/07	505
Democrats' Future	10/29/10	893
Feminism's Future	02/28/97	183*
Future of the Democratic Party	10/13/17	845
Future of the GOP	03/20/09	249
Future of the GOP	10/24/14	889
Gridlock in Washington	04/30/10	385
Health-Care Reform	08/28/09	693*
Hispanic-Americans' New Clout	09/18/98	809
Labor Movement's Future	06/28/96	553
Latino Voters	04/03/15	289
Lies and Politics	02/18/11	145
Media Bias	05/03/13	401
Millennial Generation	06/26/15	553
National Debt	03/18/11	241
The New Immigrants	01/24/97	56*
Nonprofit Groups and Partisan Politics	11/14/14	961
The Obama Legacy	11/04/16	913
The Obama Presidency	01/30/09	73
'Occupy' Movement	01/13/12	25
The Partisan Divide	04/30/04	373
Partisan Politics	03/19/99	233
Polarization in America	02/28/14	193

	Date	Page
Political Conventions	08/08/08	649
Political Polling	02/06/15	121
Populism and Party Politics	09/09/16	721
Presidential Election	02/03/12	101
Presidential Power	03/06/15	217
Prosecutors and Politics	06/22/07	553
Race and Politics	07/18/08	577
Redistricting Debates	02/25/11	169
Redistricting Disputes	03/12/04	221
Redistricting: Drawing Power with a Map	02/15/91	97
Redistricting Showdown	08/25/17	677
Regulating Lobbying	06/06/14	481
Religion and Politics	07/30/04	637
Rethinking Affirmative Action	04/28/95	369
Rising College Costs	12/05/03	1013
Social Media and Politics	10/12/12	865
Tax Reform	03/22/96	241
Term Limits	01/10/92	1
Third-Party Prospects	12/22/95	1137
Voting Controversies	09/15/06	745
Women in Politics	03/21/08	265
Wounded Veterans	08/31/07	697
Young Voters	10/02/15	817

Depression, Mental. *See Mental health and illness*

Deregulation. *See Regulation and deregulation*

Developing countries

Aiding Africa	08/29/03	697
Arms Sales	12/09/94	1088*
Change in Latin America	07/21/06	601
Cheating in Schools	09/22/00	758*
Childhood Immunizations	06/18/93	546*
Child Labor and Sweatshops	08/16/96	721
Children in Crisis	08/31/01	657
Climate Change	06/14/13	521
Democracies Under Stress	10/20/17	869
Democracy in Africa	03/24/95	241
Democracy in the Arab World	01/30/04	73
Drug Company Ethics	06/06/03	534*
Emerging Infectious Diseases	02/13/15	145
Ending Poverty	09/09/05	733
Exporting Democracy	04/01/05	269
Exporting Jobs	02/20/04	149
Fair Trade Labeling	05/18/07	433
Famine in Africa	11/08/02	921
Foreign Aid and National Security	06/17/11	529
Foreign Aid After Sept. 11	04/26/02	361
Future of the Catholic Church	06/07/13	497
Global AIDS Crisis	10/13/00	809
Global Hunger	08/08/14	673
Global Population Growth	01/16/15	49
Global Refugee Crisis	07/09/99	569
The Greening of Eastern Europe	11/15/91	865*
Human Trafficking and Slavery	03/26/04	273

	Date	Page
International Monetary Fund	01/29/99	65
Mexico's Emergence	07/19/91	489
Nuclear Proliferation	06/05/92	481
Ozone Depletion	04/03/92	289
Peace Corps' Challenges in the 1990s	01/25/91	49
Philanthropy in America	12/08/06	1009
Population Growth	07/16/93	601
Puerto Rico: The Struggle over Status	02/08/91	81
Reassessing Foreign Aid	09/27/96	841
Rebuilding Iraq	07/11/03	625
Rethinking Foreign Aid	04/14/17	313
Saving the Forests	09/20/91	681
Saving the Rain Forests	06/11/99	497
Sexual Abuse and the Clergy	05/03/02	393
Terrorism in Africa	07/10/15	577
Three-Strikes Laws	05/10/02	417
Trouble in South America	03/14/03	225
Water Shortages	08/01/03	649
World Hunger	10/25/91	801

Diet. *See Food and nutrition*

Disabled

Arts Education	03/16/12	253
Asbestos Litigation	05/02/03	393
Centennial Olympic Games	04/05/96	306*
Charter Schools	12/20/02	1033
Child-Care Options	05/08/98	422*
Covering the Uninsured	06/14/02	521
Cracking Down on Immigration	02/03/95	109*
The Disabilities Act	12/27/91	993
Election Reform	11/02/01	908*
Implementing the Disabilities Act	12/20/96	1105
Learning Disabilities	12/10/93	1081
Medical Breakthroughs	09/15/17	749
Medical Malpractice	02/14/03	129
Mental Health Policy	09/12/97	793
Mental Illness	08/06/93	679*
No Child Left Behind	05/27/05	469
Reforming Veterans' Health Care	11/21/14	985
Rethinking Ritalin	10/22/99	905
Retirement Security	05/31/02	481
Right to Die	05/13/05	421
Special Education	11/10/00	905
Treatment of Veterans	11/19/04	973

Disadvantaged. *See Poverty*

Discrimination

Affirmative Action and College Admissions	11/17/17	969
Age Discrimination	08/01/97	673
Asian Americans	12/13/91	945
Biology and Behavior	04/03/98	289
Black Colleges	12/12/03	1045
The Black Middle Class	01/23/98	49
Charter Schools	12/20/02	1033

	Date	Page
Civil Liberties Debates	10/24/03	893
Crackdown on Sexual Harassment	07/19/96	625
Crackdown on Smoking	12/04/92	1063*
Criminal Records and Employment	04/20/12	349
Diabetes Epidemic	03/09/01	192*
The Disabilities Act	12/27/91	993
Diversity in Hollywood	08/05/16	649
Diversity in the Workplace	10/10/97	889
Domestic Partners	09/04/92	761
Educating Gifted Students	03/28/97	265
Education and Gender	06/03/94	481
Education Standards	03/11/94	217
European Unrest	01/09/15	25
Future of the Airline Industry	06/21/02	557*
Gay Rights	03/05/93	202*
Gender and Learning	05/20/05	445
Gender Pay Gap	03/14/08	241
Getting into College	02/23/96	169
The Glass Ceiling	10/29/93	937
Housing Discrimination	02/24/95	169
Housing Discrimination	11/06/15	937
Illegal Immigration	04/24/92	361
Implementing the Disabilities Act	12/20/96	1105
Jailing Debtors	09/16/16	745
Latinos' Future	10/17/03	869
Medicare Reform	08/22/03	681*
Mental Health Policy	09/12/97	793
Muslims in America	07/28/17	629
Native American Youths	04/24/15	361
Northern Ireland Cease-Fire	09/15/95	812*
The Obama Legacy	11/04/16	913
Policing the Borders	02/22/02	145
Privacy Under Attack	06/15/01	505
Race and Education	09/05/14	721
Race in America	07/11/03	593
Racial Conflict	01/08/16	25
Racial Diversity in Public Schools	09/14/07	**745
Racial Quotas	05/17/91	277
Racial Tensions in Schools	01/07/94	1
Redistricting Showdown	08/25/17	677
Reforming the CIA	02/02/96	110*
Religion in the Workplace	08/23/02	649
Rethinking Affirmative Action	04/28/95	369
School Choice	05/10/91	253
School Desegregation	04/23/04	345
Sexual Harassment	08/09/91	537
Sexual Harassment	04/27/12	377
Transgender Rights	12/11/15	1033
Women and AIDS	12/25/92	1138
Women and Sports	03/06/92	193
Women and Sports	03/25/11	265
Women in Combat	05/13/16	433
Women in Leadership	09/23/16	769
Women in the Military	09/25/92	833

	Date	Page
Diseases and health problems. *See also AIDS disease;* *Cancer; Drug abuse; Medical care; Mental health and* *illness; Tobacco*		
Air Pollution and Climate Control	11/13/15	961
Alternative Medicine	09/06/13	741
Alzheimer's Disease	07/24/92	617
Alzheimer's Disease	05/15/98	433
American Indians	04/28/06	**361
Asbestos Litigation	05/02/03	393
Assisted Suicide	02/21/92	145
Assisted Suicide	05/17/13	449
Asthma Epidemic	12/26/99	1089
Avian Flu Threat	01/13/06	25
Battling HIV/AIDS	10/26/07	889
Biotech Foods	03/30/01	249
Birth-Control Debate	06/24/05	565
Blood Supply Safety	11/11/94	985
Breast Cancer	04/02/10	289
Caring for the Elderly	10/13/06	841
Cell Phone Safety	03/16/01	201
Childhood Immunizations	06/18/93	529
Child Welfare Reform	04/22/05	345
Chronic Fatigue Syndrome	04/05/02	289
Combating Infectious Diseases	06/09/95	489
Cosmetic Surgery	04/15/05	317
Covering the Uninsured	06/14/02	521
Diabetes Epidemic	03/09/01	185
Diet and Health	02/23/01	129
Dietary Supplements	09/03/04	709
Dietary Supplements	10/30/15	913
Dieting and Health	04/14/95	321
The Disabilities Act	12/27/91	997*
Doctor Shortage	08/28/15	697
Drinking Water Safety	07/15/16	577
Drug-Resistant Bacteria	06/04/99	473
Drug Safety	03/11/05	221
Eating Disorders	12/18/92	1097
Eating Disorders	02/10/06	**121
E-Cigarettes	09/19/14	769
Embryo Research	12/17/99	1065
Emerging Infectious Diseases	02/13/15	145
Ending Poverty	09/09/05	733
Fighting Cancer	01/22/16	73
Fighting SARS	06/20/03	569
Fighting Superbugs	08/24/07	673
Food Labeling	06/16/17	509
Food Safety	06/04/93	481
Food Safety	11/01/02	897
Food Safety	12/17/10	1037
Genes and Health	01/21/11	49
Gene Therapy	10/18/91	777
Gene Therapy's Future	12/08/95	1089
Global Hunger	08/08/14	673
Heart Health	09/12/08	721

	Date	Page
Human Genome Research	05/12/00	401
Impact of the Internet on Thinking	09/24/10	773
Increase in Autism	06/13/03	**545
Indoor Air Pollution	10/27/95	945
Infant Mortality	07/31/92	641
Invasive Species	10/05/01	785
Lead Poisoning	06/19/92	525
Limiting Lawsuits	12/19/08	1033
Lyme Disease	11/08/13	957
Mad Cow Disease	03/02/01	161
Manipulating the Human Genome	06/19/15	529
Marijuana Laws	02/11/05	125
Medicaid Reform	07/16/04	589
Medical Breakthroughs	09/15/17	749
Medical Malpractice	02/14/03	129
Medical Mistakes	02/25/00	137
Mental Health Insurance	03/29/02	265
Mental Health Policy	05/10/13	425
Mental Illness Medication Debate	02/06/04	101
Military Suicides	09/23/11	781*
Mosquito-Borne Disease	07/22/16	601
Native Americans	05/08/92	399
NFL Controversies	09/04/15	721
Obesity and Health	01/15/99	25
Obesity Epidemic	01/31/03	73
Opioid Crisis	10/07/16	817
Organ Donations	04/15/11	337
Organ Shortage	02/21/03	153
Organ Transplants	08/11/95	705
Pandemic Threat	06/02/17	457
Patenting Human Genes	05/31/13	473
Patient Safety	02/10/12	125
Pesticide Controversies	06/05/15	481
Prayer and Healing	01/14/05	25
Prescription Drug Costs	05/20/16	457
Preventing Cancer	01/16/09	25
Preventing Disease	01/06/12	1
Preventing Memory Loss	04/04/08	289*
Preventing Obesity	10/01/10	797
Prison Health Care	01/05/07	1
Prisoners and Mental Illness	03/13/15	241
Privacy in the Workplace	11/19/93	1023*
Professional Football	01/29/10	**73
Prolonging Life	09/30/11	805*
Prostitution	06/11/93	505
Prostitution Debate	05/23/08	433
Protecting the Oceans	10/17/14	865
Reforming Veterans' Health Care	11/21/14	985
Regulating Pesticides	01/28/94	73
Regulating Pesticides	08/06/99	665
Regulating Toxic Chemicals	01/23/09	49
Regulating Toxic Chemicals	07/18/14	601
Repetitive Stress Injuries	06/23/95	537
Rethinking Foreign Aid	04/14/17	313

	Date	Page
Rethinking Ritalin	10/22/99	905
Right to Die	05/13/05	421
Sexually Transmitted Diseases	12/03/04	997
Sleep Deprivation	06/26/98	553
Sleep Deprivation	02/12/10	121
Smallpox Threat	02/07/03	105
Social Security	06/03/16	481
Stem Cell Research	09/01/06	**697
Students Under Stress	07/13/07	577
Sugar Controversies	11/30/12	1013
Threatened Fisheries	08/02/02	634*
Tobacco Industry	12/10/04	**1025
Treating Addiction	05/02/14	385
Treating ADHD	08/03/12	669
Treating Alzheimer's	03/04/11	193
Treating Alzheimer's Disease	07/24/15	625
Treating Anxiety	02/08/02	97
Treating Depression	06/26/09	573
Treatment of Veterans	11/19/04	973
Troubled Brazil	04/07/17	289
Understanding Autism	08/01/14	649
Universal Coverage	03/30/07	265
Vaccine Controversies	08/25/00	641
Vaccine Controversies	02/19/16	169
Water Quality	02/11/94	121
Weapons of Mass Destruction	03/08/02	193
Women's Health	11/07/03	941

District of Columbia

	Date	Page
D.C. Voting Rights	04/11/08	313*
Downtown Renaissance	06/23/06	**553
Foster Care Crisis	09/27/91	719*
Governing Washington, D.C.	11/22/96	1033
Gun Control Debate	11/12/04	949
Infant Mortality	07/31/92	647*
Public Housing	09/10/93	793
Student Journalism	06/05/98	498*

Diversity awareness training

	Date	Page
Diversity in Hollywood	08/05/16	649
Diversity in the Workplace	10/10/97	894*
Police Corruption	11/24/95	1058*
Policing the Police	03/17/00	209
Race in America	07/11/03	593
Racial Profiling	11/22/13	1005
Religion in the Workplace	08/23/02	649

Divorce. *See Family*

DNA analysis

	Date	Page
Biology and Behavior	04/03/98	289
DNA Databases	05/28/99	449
Eyewitness Testimony	10/14/11	853
Forensic Science Controversies	02/10/17	121
Genes and Health	01/21/11	49
Human Genome Research	05/12/00	401
Manipulating the Human Genome	06/19/15	529

	Date	Page
Mass Extinction	09/15/00	728*
Medical Breakthroughs	09/15/17	749
Patenting Human Genes	05/31/13	473
Privacy in the Workplace	11/19/93	1023*
Public Defenders	04/18/08	337*
Science in the Courtroom	10/22/93	924*
Serial Killers	10/31/03	917
Wrongful Convictions	04/17/09	**345

Doctors. *See Physicians*

Domestic partners. *See Family*

Domestic violence

	Date	Page
Domestic Violence	01/06/06	1
Domestic Violence	11/15/13	981
Future of Marriage	05/07/04	397
Gay Marriage	09/05/03	736*
Girls' Rights	04/17/15	337
Native American Youths	04/24/15	361
NFL Controversies	09/04/15	721
Transgender Rights	12/11/15	1033
Treating Anxiety	02/08/02	97
Violence Against Women	02/26/93	169
Women and Human Rights	04/30/99	366*
Women in Prison	03/03/17	193

"Downsizing." *See Corporate mergers*

Draft. *See Military service*

Drinking. *See Alcohol; Drunken driving*

Drinking water

	Date	Page
Bush and the Environment	10/25/02	865
Fracking Controversy	12/16/11	1049
Global Hunger	08/08/14	673
Global Water Shortages	12/15/95	1113
Regulating Toxic Chemicals	07/18/14	601
Water Quality	02/11/94	121
Water Shortages	08/01/03	649

Drought

	Date	Page
Climate Change and National Security	09/22/17	773
Global Food Crisis	06/27/08	553

Drug abuse. *See also Alcohol*

	Date	Page
AIDS Update	12/04/98	1055*
American Indians	04/28/06	**361
Athletes and Drugs	07/26/91	513
Centennial Olympic Games	04/05/96	289
Childhood Depression	07/16/99	593
Child Poverty	10/28/11	901
Combating Addiction	02/09/07	121
Combating AIDS	04/21/95	350*
Community Prosecution	12/15/00	1014*
Dietary Supplements	10/30/15	913
Downsizing Prisons	03/11/11	217
Drug-Policy Debate	07/28/00	593
Ending Homelessness	06/18/04	541
Faith-Based Initiatives	05/04/01	382*

	Date	Page
High School Sports	09/22/95	825
Infant Mortality	07/31/92	650
Legalizing Marijuana	06/12/09	**525
Marijuana Industry	10/16/15	865
Marijuana Laws	02/11/05	125
Medical Marijuana	08/20/99	705
Medical Marijuana	07/21/17	605
Methamphetamine	07/15/05	589
Mexico's Drug War	12/12/08	1009
Opioid Crisis	10/07/16	817
Preventing Teen Drug Use	03/15/02	217
Prison Health Care	01/05/07	1
Prostitution	06/11/93	505
Prostitution Debate	05/23/08	433
Regulating Tobacco	09/30/94	841
Rethinking Ritalin	10/22/99	905
Sports and Drugs	07/23/04	**613
Student Rights	06/05/09	501
Teen Driving	01/07/05	1
Teen Drug Use	06/03/11	481
Three-Strikes Laws	05/10/02	417
Treating Addiction	01/06/95	1
Treating Addiction	05/02/14	385
Treating ADHD	08/03/12	669
War on Drugs	03/19/93	241
War on Drugs	06/02/06	481
Women and AIDS	12/25/92	1121
The Working Poor	11/03/95	982*

Drug abuse — Testing

	Date	Page
Drug Testing	11/20/98	1001
Medication Abuse	10/09/09	837
Privacy in the Workplace	11/19/93	1021*
Sentencing Debates	11/05/04	925

Drug traffic

	Date	Page
Afghanistan Dilemma	08/07/09	**669*
Central American Gangs	01/30/15	97
Change in Latin America	07/21/06	601
Declining Crime Rates	04/04/97	289
Democracy in Latin America	11/03/00	896*
Drug-Policy Debate	07/28/00	593
Foreign Aid After Sept. 11	04/26/02	383*
Gangs in the U.S.	07/16/10	581
Haiti's Dilemma	02/18/05	149
Legalizing Marijuana	06/12/09	**525
Mandatory Sentencing	05/26/95	465
Mexico's Drug War	12/12/08	1009
Mexico's Future	09/19/97	817
Mexico's Future	10/26/12	913
Prison-Building Boom	09/17/99	801
Prisoner Reentry	12/04/09	1005
Reassessing the Nation's Gun Laws	03/22/91	157
Rethinking Ritalin	10/22/99	922*
Sentencing Debates	11/05/04	925

	Date	Page
Three-Strikes Laws	05/10/02	417
Transnational Crime	08/29/14	697
Treating Addiction	01/06/95	10*
Underground Economy	03/04/94	193
U.S.-Mexico Relations	11/09/01	921
U.S.-Mexico Relations	09/02/16	697
War on Drugs	03/19/93	241
War on Drugs	06/02/06	481
Youth Gangs	10/11/91	753

Drugs and pharmaceutical industry

	Date	Page
Advances in Cancer Research	08/25/95	753
Advertising Overload	01/23/04	56*
AIDS Update	12/04/98	1049
Alternative Medicine's Next Phase	02/14/97	121
Alzheimer's Disease	05/15/98	433
Assisted Suicide Controversy	05/05/95	406*
Asthma Epidemic	12/24/99	1096*
Avian Flu Threat	01/13/06	25
Baby Boomers at Midlife	07/31/98	649
Biology and Behavior	04/03/98	307*
Birth Control Choices	07/29/94	649
Birth-Control Debate	06/24/05	565
Cancer Treatments	09/11/98	785
Childhood Depression	07/16/99	593
Childhood Immunizations	06/18/93	529
Chronic Fatigue Syndrome	04/05/02	289
Combating AIDS	04/21/95	345
Cosmetic Surgery	04/15/05	317
Covering the Uninsured	06/14/02	521
Depression	10/09/92	857
Dietary Supplements	09/03/04	709
Dietary Supplements	10/30/15	913
Dieting and Health	04/14/95	339*
Drug Company Ethics	06/06/03	521
Drugmakers Under Siege	09/03/99	753
Drug-Resistant Bacteria	06/04/99	473
Drug Safety	03/11/05	221
Emerging Infectious Diseases	02/13/15	145
Fighting Cancer	01/22/16	73
Gene Therapy's Future	12/08/95	1089
Legalizing Marijuana	06/12/09	**525
Limiting Lawsuits	12/19/08	1033
Marijuana Laws	02/11/05	125
Medical Marijuana	08/20/99	705
Medicare Reform	08/22/03	673
Medication Abuse	10/09/09	837
Mental Illness Medication Debate	02/06/04	101
Nanotechnology	06/11/04	517
The New Corporate Philanthropy	02/27/98	174*
Obesity and Health	01/15/99	25
Opioid Crisis	10/07/16	817
Organ Shortage	02/21/03	153
Organ Transplants	08/11/95	713*

	Date	Page
Patent Disputes	12/15/06	1033
Prescription Drug Costs	05/20/16	457
Prescription Drug Prices	07/17/92	597
Preventing Cancer	01/16/09	25
Prisoners and Mental Illness	03/13/15	241
Prozac Controversy	08/19/94	721
Punishing Sex Offenders	01/12/96	32*
Reforming the FDA	06/06/97	481
Regulating Pharmaceuticals	10/11/13	861
Rethinking Ritalin	10/22/99	905
Rising Health Costs	04/07/06	289
Saving the Rain Forests	06/11/99	497
Science in the Courtroom	10/22/93	913
Sexually Transmitted Diseases	12/03/04	997
Sleep Deprivation	06/26/98	553
Treating Addiction	01/06/95	16*
Treating Addiction	05/02/14	385
Treating Alzheimer's	03/04/11	193
Treating Alzheimer's Disease	07/24/15	625
Treating Anxiety	02/08/02	104*
Treating Schizophrenia	12/05/14	1009
Vaccine Controversies	08/25/00	641
Vaccine Controversies	02/19/16	169
Women's Health	11/07/03	941
Youth Suicide	02/13/04	125

Drunken driving
Drinking on Campus	03/20/98	241
Drinking on Campus	08/18/06	649
Drunken Driving	10/06/00	793
Highway Safety	07/14/95	609
Reducing Traffic Deaths	02/17/17	145
Teen Driving	01/07/05	1
Underage Drinking	03/13/92	217

E-mail
Advertising Overload	01/23/04	49
Cyber-Predators	03/01/02	169
Cybersecurity	09/26/03	797
Privacy in the Workplace	11/19/93	1013*
Regulating the Internet	06/30/95	561

Earmarks
Pork Barrel Politics	06/16/06	529

Earth Day
Bush and the Environment	10/25/02	865
Environmental Movement at 25	03/31/95	273

Earthquakes
Disaster Response	10/15/93	889
Earthquake Research	12/16/94	1105
Earthquake Threat	04/09/10	313

Eastern Europe
Blighted Cities	11/12/10	941*
Democracies Under Stress	10/20/17	869
Democracy in Eastern Europe	10/08/99	865
Europe 1992	06/28/91	417

	Date	Page
European Migration Crisis	07/31/15	649
European Unrest	01/09/15	25
Expanding NATO	05/16/97	433
Future of NATO	02/28/03	177
The Greening of Eastern Europe	11/15/91	849
Human Trafficking and Slavery	03/26/04	273
Peace Corps' Challenges in the 1990s	01/25/91	49
Privatizing Government Services	08/09/96	708*
Russia's Political Future	05/03/96	385

Eating disorders
Depression	10/09/92	869
Eating Disorders	12/18/92	1097
Eating Disorders	02/10/06	**121
Obesity Epidemic	01/31/03	73
Prozac Controversy	08/19/94	721
Women's Health	11/07/03	941

Economic conditions
3D Printing	12/07/12	1037
Affordable Housing	02/09/01	89
Aging Baby Boomers	10/19/07	865
Aging Population	07/15/11	577
America's Border Fence	09/19/08	745
Antitrust Policy	06/12/98	505
Arctic Development	12/02/16	989
Arms Sales	12/09/94	1097*
Assessing the New Health Care Law	09/21/12	789
Attracting Jobs	03/02/12	205
Auto Industry's Future	02/06/09	**105
Big-Box Stores	09/10/04	733
Budget Surplus	04/13/01	307*
Business Bankruptcy	04/10/09	321
Changing Demographics	11/16/12	989
Child Poverty	10/28/11	901
Child Welfare	08/26/16	673
Coal Industry's Future	06/17/16	529
College Rankings	01/02/15	1
Community Colleges	05/01/15	385
Confronting Warming	01/09/09	1
The Consumer Culture	11/19/99	1001
Consumer Debt	11/15/96	1009
Cost of the Iraq War	04/25/08	361*
Covering the Uninsured	06/14/02	521
Criminal Records and Employment	04/20/12	349
Crisis on the Plains	05/09/03	417
Curbing CEO Pay	03/09/07	217
Cyber-Crime	04/12/02	321*
Debate Over Immigration	07/14/00	569
Debt Collectors	07/20/12	621
Democracy in Latin America	11/03/00	881
Democrats' Future	10/29/10	893
Deflation Fears	02/13/98	121
Domestic Poverty	09/07/07	**721
Downtown Renaissance	06/23/06	**553
Downward Mobility	07/23/93	625

	Date	Page
Dropout Rate	06/13/14	505
Ending Homelessness	06/18/04	541
Euro Crisis	10/05/12	841
Exporting Jobs	02/20/04	149
Famine in Africa	11/08/02	921
The Federal Reserve	09/01/00	673
The Federal Reserve	01/03/14	1
Fighting Urban Poverty	07/17/15	601
Financial Bailout	10/24/08	**865
Financial Crisis	05/09/08	409
Financial Industry Overhaul	07/30/10	629
Financial Literacy	09/04/09	717
Financial Misconduct	01/20/12	53
Fracking Controversy	12/16/11	1049
Future of the Airline Industry	06/21/02	545
Future of Homeownership	12/14/12	1061
Future Job Market	01/11/02	1
Future of the Middle Class	04/08/16	313
Government Spending	07/12/13	597
Hate Groups	05/08/09	421
Health-Care Reform	06/11/10	**505
High-Speed Trains	05/01/09	**397
Homeless Students	04/05/13	305
Housing the Homeless	12/18/09	1053
Identity Theft	06/10/05	517
Illegal Immigration	04/24/92	361
Illegal Immigration	05/06/05	393
Immigrants and the Economy	02/24/17	169
Immigration Conflict	03/09/12	229
Income Inequality	04/17/98	337
Income Inequality	12/03/10	989
Internet Regulation	04/13/12	325
The Iraq War: 10 Years Later	03/01/13	205
Jailing Debtors	09/16/16	745
Jobs in the '90s	02/28/92	169
Jobs Outlook	06/04/10	481
Latinos' Future	10/17/03	869
Law Schools	04/19/13	353
Legal-Aid Crisis	10/07/11	829
Middle-Class Squeeze	03/06/09	201
Millennial Generation	06/26/15	553
Minimum Wage	01/24/14	72
Mortgage Crisis	11/02/07	**913
Mutual Funds	05/20/94	433
The National Debt	11/14/08	937
National Debt	03/18/11	241
National Debt	09/01/17	701
The Obama Presidency	01/30/09	73
'Occupy' Movement	01/13/12	25
Oil Jitters	01/04/08	**1
Preparing for Disaster	08/02/13	669
Presidential Election	02/03/12	101
Public-Works Projects	02/20/09	153
Puerto Rico: The Struggle over Status	02/08/91	81

	Date	Page
Racial Conflict	01/08/16	25
Racial Diversity in Public Schools	09/14/07	**745
Recession's Regional Impact	02/01/91	65
Regulating Credit Cards	10/10/08	817*
Rethinking Retirement	06/19/09	549
Retirement Security	05/31/02	481
Reviving Manufacturing	07/22/11	601
Reviving Rural Economies	03/31/17	265
Rise of Megachurches	09/21/07	769
Saving Social Security	10/02/98	857
Science and Religion	03/22/13	281
Science in America	01/11/08	25
State Budget Crises	10/03/03	821
State Budget Crisis	09/11/09	741
Stimulating the Economy	01/10/03	1
The Stock Market	05/02/97	385
Stock Market Troubles	01/16/04	25
Straining the Safety Net	07/31/09	645
Student Aid	01/25/08	73
Student Debt	10/21/11	877
Student Debt	11/18/16	965
Tax Reform	03/22/96	241
Teen Pregnancy	03/26/10	265*
Truck Safety	03/12/99	209
Underground Economy	03/04/94	193
Unemployment Benefits	04/25/03	369
Universal Basic Income	09/08/17	725
Upward Mobility	04/29/05	369
U.S. Auto Industry	10/16/92	884*
The Value of a College Education	11/20/09	981
Vanishing Jobs	03/13/09	225
Water Crisis in the West	12/09/11	1025
Wealth and Inequality	04/18/14	337
Welfare Reform	04/10/92	327
Women and Work	07/26/13	645
Women in Leadership	09/23/16	769
Worker Safety	10/04/13	837
The Working Poor	11/03/95	969
Youth Unemployment	03/14/14	241

Economic conditions — International

	Date	Page
Aid to Russia	03/12/93	217
Aiding Africa	08/29/03	697
Castro's Next Move	12/12/97	1081
China After Deng	06/13/97	505
Declining Birthrates	11/21/08	961
Deflation Fears	02/13/98	121
Democracy in the Arab World	01/30/04	73
Earthquake Threat	04/09/10	313
Emerging China	11/11/05	957
Euro Crisis	10/05/12	841
European Monetary Union	11/27/98	1025
European Union's Future	12/16/16	1037
Exporting Jobs	02/20/04	149
Fair Trade Labeling	05/18/07	433

	Date	Page		Date	Page
Famine in Africa	11/08/02	921	The Gig Economy	03/18/16	265
Fighting SARS	06/20/03	581*	Global Population Growth	01/16/15	49
Future of the Catholic Church	06/07/13	497	Global Water Shortages	12/15/95	1113
The Future of U.S.-Russia Relations	01/18/02	25	Historic Preservation	10/07/94	865
Global Food Crisis	06/27/08	553	Jobs vs. Environment	05/15/92	409
Global Hunger	08/08/14	673	Managing Western Lands	04/22/16	361
The Greening of Eastern Europe	11/15/91	849	National Parks	05/28/93	457
Haiti's Dilemma	02/18/05	149	Native Americans	05/08/92	400
Holocaust Reparations	03/26/99	257	Native Americans' Future	07/12/96	601
Immigrant Detention	10/23/15	889	Peace Corps Challenges	01/11/13	29
International Monetary Fund	01/29/99	65	Population and the Environment	07/17/98	601
Japan in Crisis	07/26/02	593	Prescription Drug Costs	05/20/16	457
Mexico's Future	09/19/97	817	Property Rights	03/04/05	197
The New CIA	12/11/92	1073	Protecting Endangered Species	04/19/96	337
Oil Jitters	01/04/08	**1	Puerto Rico: The Struggle over Status	02/08/91	81
Peace Corps Challenges	01/11/13	29	Reassessing Foreign Aid	09/27/96	841
Privatization	11/13/92	991*	Reforming the U.N.	06/24/16	553
Reform in Iran	12/18/98	1097	Regulating the New Economy	10/19/01	849
Reforming the CIA	02/02/96	97	Revitalizing the Cities	10/13/95	897
Resurgent Russia	02/07/14	121	Saving Open Spaces	11/05/99	953
Rethinking Foreign Aid	04/14/17	313	Solar Energy Controversies	04/29/16	385
Reviving Manufacturing	07/22/11	601	Stimulating the Economy	01/10/03	1
Saving Social Security	10/02/98	871*	Threatened Coastlines	02/07/92	97
Smart Cities	07/27/12	645	Trouble in South America	03/14/03	225
South Africa's Future	01/14/94	25	Troubled Brazil	04/07/17	289
Stolen Antiquities	11/10/17	945	Upward Mobility	04/29/05	369
Student Aid	01/25/08	73	Water Crisis in the West	12/09/11	1025
Russia's Political Future	05/03/96	385	Worker Safety	10/04/13	837
Trouble in South America	03/14/03	225	Youth Unemployment	03/14/14	241
Troubled Brazil	04/07/17	289	**Economic espionage**		
Underground Economy	03/04/94	206*	The New CIA	12/11/92	1089
Universal Basic Income	09/08/17	725	Reforming the CIA	02/02/96	97
Unrest in Turkey	01/29/16	97	**Economic sanctions**		
U.S.-Europe Relations	03/23/12	277	Economic Sanctions	10/28/94	937
U.S. Global Engagement	05/16/14	433	Reform in Iran	12/18/98	1097
U.S.-Russia Relations	01/13/17	25	South Africa's Future	01/14/94	39*
U.S.-Russian Relations	05/22/98	457	U.S.-Russia Relations	01/13/17	25
U.S. Trade Policy	09/13/13	765	U.S.-Vietnam Relations	12/03/93	1068*
Y2K Dilemma	02/19/99	137	**Ecotourism**		
Economic development			Ecotourism	10/20/06	865
Aiding Africa	08/29/03	697	Panama Canal	11/26/99	1031*
Change in Latin America	07/21/06	601	Saving the Rain Forests	06/11/99	506*
Coastal Development	08/21/98	721	**Education.** *See Colleges and universities; Education standards; Elementary and secondary education; Libraries; Preschool education; Special education; Student aid*		
Declining Birthrates	11/21/08	961			
Democracy in the Arab World	01/30/04	73			
Downtown Renaissance	06/23/06	**553			
Earthquake Threat	04/09/10	313	**Education Amendments Act, 1972 (Title IX)**		
Emerging India	04/19/02	329	Affirmative Action and		
Energy Security	02/01/02	73	College Admissions	11/17/17	969
Exporting Jobs	02/20/04	149	Campus Sexual Assault	10/31/14	913
Famine in Africa	11/08/02	921	College Rankings	01/02/15	1
Farm Subsidies	05/17/02	438*	College Sports	08/26/94	745
Gambling Under Attack	09/06/96	769	Dropout Rate	06/13/14	505
Gentrification	02/20/15	169			

	Date	Page
Funding the Arts	07/14/17	581
Future of Books	05/29/09	**473
Gender Equity in Sports	04/18/97	337
High School Sports	09/22/95	825
Humanities Education	12/06/13	1029
Race and Education	09/05/14	721
Reforming Big-Time College Sports	03/19/04	249
Revising No Child Left Behind	04/16/10	337
School Discipline	05/09/14	409
Single-Sex Education	07/12/02	580*
Soccer in America	04/22/94	351*
State Budget Crisis	09/11/09	741
Student Debt	11/18/16	965
Women and Sports	03/06/92	193
Women in Sports	05/11/01	401
Women and Sports	03/25/11	265
Youth Fitness	09/26/97	846*

Education standards

	Date	Page
AB and IP Programs	03/03/06	193
Affirmative Action	10/17/08	**841
American Indians	04/28/06	**361
Apprenticeships	10/14/16	841
Bilingual Education vs. English Immersion	12/11/09	1029
Career Colleges	01/07/11	1
Charter Schools	12/20/02	1033
Charter Schools	03/10/17	217
Cheating in Schools	09/22/00	745
Civic Education	02/03/17	97
College Football	11/18/11	977
College Rankings	01/02/15	1
Combating Plagiarism	09/19/03	773
Community Colleges	05/01/15	385
Digital Education	12/02/11	1001
Educating Gifted Students	03/28/97	265
Education Standards	03/11/94	217
Fixing Urban Schools	04/27/07	**361
Future of Libraries	07/29/11	625
Future of Public Universities	01/18/13	53
Gender and Learning	05/20/05	445
Government and Religion	01/15/10	25
Grade Inflation	06/07/02	505
Home Schooling	03/07/14	217
Home Schooling Debate	01/17/03	25
Homework Debate	12/06/02	993
Impact of the Internet on Thinking	09/24/10	773
Internet Accuracy	08/01/08	625
Low Voter Turnout	10/20/00	833
National Education Standards	05/14/99	401
Native American Youths	04/24/15	361
No Child Left Behind	05/27/05	469
Paying College Athletes	07/11/14	577
Plagiarism and Cheating	01/04/13	1
Racial Conflict	01/08/16	25

	Date	Page
Racial Diversity in Public Schools	09/14/07	**745
Reading Crisis?	02/22/08	169
Reforming Big-Time College Sports	03/19/04	249
Reforming School Funding	12/10/99	1047*
Revising No Child Left Behind	04/16/10	337
School Funding	08/27/93	760*
School Reform	04/29/11	385
School Vouchers	04/09/99	281
School Vouchers Showdown	02/15/02	121
Science in America	01/11/08	25
Student Aid	01/25/08	73
Student Debt	10/21/11	877
Students Under Stress	07/13/07	577
Teacher Education	10/17/97	913
Teaching Critical Thinking	04/10/15	313
Teaching History	09/29/95	849
Teaching Math and Science	09/06/02	697
Upward Mobility	04/29/05	369
The Value of a College Education	11/20/09	981
Video Games and Learning	02/12/16	145
Youth Volunteerism	01/27/12	77

Egypt

	Date	Page
Archaeology Today	05/24/02	457
Democracy in the Arab World	01/30/04	73
European Migration Crisis	07/31/15	649
Exporting Democracy	04/01/05	269
Foreign Aid After Sept. 11	04/26/02	361
Reassessing Foreign Aid	09/27/96	848*
Understanding Islam	11/03/06	913
Unrest in the Arab World	02/01/13	105

Elderly. *See also Social Security*

	Date	Page
Age Discrimination	08/01/97	673
Alzheimer's Disease	07/24/92	617
Alzheimer's Disease	05/15/98	433
Assisted Suicide	02/21/92	145
Baby Boomers at Midlife	07/31/98	649
Cancer Treatments	09/11/98	803*
Caring for the Elderly	02/20/98	145
Caring for the Elderly	10/13/06	841
Changing Demographics	11/16/12	989
Covering the Uninsured	06/14/02	521
Cracking Down on Immigration	02/03/95	109*
Drug Company Ethics	06/06/03	521
Flexible Work Arrangements	08/14/98	715*
Medicare Reform	08/22/03	673
Medicaid Reform	07/16/04	589
National Service	06/30/06	577
Patients' Rights	02/06/98	108*
Preventing Memory Loss	04/04/08	289*
Prolonging Life	09/30/11	805*
Retiree Health Benefits	12/06/91	921
Retirement Security	05/31/02	481
Right to Die	05/13/05	421
Rising Health Costs	04/07/06	289

	Date	Page
Treating Alzheimer's	03/04/11	193
Treating Alzheimer's Disease	07/24/15	625
Youth Fitness	09/26/97	858*

Elections. *See also Campaign finance; Presidential elections; Term limits; Voting and voting rights*

	Date	Page
Campaign Finance	05/06/16	409
Civic Education	02/03/17	97
Cyberwarfare Threat	10/06/17	821
Defeating the Islamic State	04/01/16	289
Democracies Under Stress	10/20/17	869
Future of the Christian Right	06/23/17	533
Future of the Democratic Party	10/13/17	845
Judicial Elections	04/24/09	373
Latino Voters	04/03/15	289
The Obama Legacy	11/04/16	913
Political Polling	02/06/15	121
Populism and Party Politics	09/09/16	721
Presidential Power	03/06/15	217
Redistricting Showdown	08/25/17	677
Regulating Lobbying	06/06/14	481
Social Security	06/03/16	481
Think Tanks in Transition	09/29/17	797
Trump Presidency	01/06/17	1
U.S.-Iran Relations	03/04/16	217
U.S.-Mexico Relations	09/02/16	697
U.S.-Russia Relations	01/13/17	25
Voting Controversies	02/21/14	169

Electric cars. *See Automobiles and automobile industry*

Electric power

	Date	Page
Acid Rain: New Approach to Old Problem	03/08/91	129
Aging Infrastructure	09/28/07	**793
Air Pollution and Climate Control	11/13/15	961
Air Pollution Conflict	11/14/03	965
Alternative Energy	07/10/92	573
Alternative Energy	02/25/05	173
Buying Green	02/29/08	193
Coal's Comeback	10/05/07	817
Confronting Warming	01/09/09	1
Electromagnetic Fields	04/26/91	237
Energy and the Environment	03/03/00	161
Energy Policy	05/20/11	457
Future of Cars	07/25/14	625
Modernizing the Grid	02/19/10	145
Nanotechnology	06/11/04	517
Nuclear Power	06/10/11	505
The Politics of Energy	03/05/99	185
Preparing for Disaster	08/02/13	669
Protecting the Power Grid	11/11/16	941
Reducing Your Carbon Footprint	12/05/08	985
Renewable Energy	11/07/97	961
Restructuring the Electric Industry	01/17/97	25
Setting Environmental Priorities	05/21/99	438*
Solar Energy Controversies	04/29/16	385

	Date	Page
Will Nuclear Power Get Another Chance?	02/22/91	113
Wind Power	04/01/11	289

Electromagnetic waves

	Date	Page
Airline Safety	10/08/93	882*
Archaeology Today	05/24/02	457
Electromagnetic Fields	04/26/91	237
Preparing for Disaster	08/02/13	669
Science in the Courtroom	10/22/93	913

Electronic surveillance

	Date	Page
Big Data and Privacy	10/25/13	909
Border Security	09/27/13	813
Cyber-Crime	04/12/02	305
Domestic Drones	10/18/13	885
Government Surveillance	08/30/13	717
Nanotechnology	06/11/04	517
Privacy in the Workplace	11/19/93	1009
Privacy Under Attack	06/15/01	505

Elementary and secondary education

	Date	Page
AB and IP Programs	03/03/06	193
Advertising Overload	01/23/04	49
Arts Education	03/16/12	253
Arts Funding	10/21/94	921*
Attack on Public Schools	07/26/96	649
Bilingual Education	08/13/93	697
Bilingual Education vs. English Immersion	12/11/09	1029
Boys' Emotional Needs	06/18/99	521
Bullying	02/04/05	101
Business' Role in Education	11/22/91	873
Catholic Church in the U.S.	09/08/95	791*
Charter Schools	12/20/02	1033
Charter Schools	03/10/17	217
Cheating in Schools	09/22/00	745
Childhood Depression	07/16/99	593
Children's Television	08/15/97	721
Child Welfare Reform	04/22/05	345
Combating Plagiarism	09/19/03	779*
Consumer Debt	11/15/96	1020*
Debate over Bilingualism	01/19/96	49
Diabetes Epidemic	03/09/01	192*
The Digital Divide	01/28/00	58*
Discipline in Schools	02/15/08	145
Distance Learning	12/07/01	993
Educating Gifted Students	03/28/97	265
Education and Gender	06/03/94	481
Education Standards	03/11/94	217
Encouraging Teen Abstinence	07/10/98	577
Evolution vs. Creationism	08/22/97	745
Faith-Based Initiatives	05/04/01	391*
Financial Literacy	09/04/09	717
Fixing Urban Schools	04/27/07	**361
Free-Press Disputes	04/08/05	293
Gangs in the U.S.	07/16/10	581

	Date	Page
Gay Rights	03/05/93	207*
Gender and Learning	05/20/05	445
Gender Equity in Sports	04/18/97	337
Getting into College	02/23/96	169
Girls' Rights	04/17/15	337
Head Start	04/09/93	289
High School Sports	09/22/95	825
Hispanic Americans	10/30/92	929
Hispanic-Americans' New Clout	09/18/98	823*
Homeless Students	04/05/13	305
Home Schooling	09/09/94	769
Home Schooling	03/07/14	217
Home Schooling Debate	01/17/03	25
Homework Debate	12/06/02	993
Implementing the Disabilities Act	12/20/96	1105
Intelligence Testing	07/30/93	649
Intelligent Design	07/29/05	637
Jobs in the '90s	02/28/92	169
Kids in Prison	04/27/01	350*
Learning Disabilities	12/10/93	1081
Learning to Read	05/19/95	441
Libraries and the Internet	06/01/01	477*
National Debt	03/18/11	241
National Education Standards	05/14/99	401
National Service	06/25/93	564*
Networking the Classroom	10/20/95	921
The New Volunteerism	12/13/96	1086*
No Child Left Behind	05/27/05	469
Parental Rights	10/25/96	937
Parents and Schools	01/20/95	49
Patriotism in America	06/25/99	545
Peace Corps Challenges	01/11/13	29
Physical Fitness	11/06/92	958*
Plagiarism and Cheating	01/04/13	1
Preventing Hazing	02/08/13	133
Preventing Juvenile Crime	03/15/96	217
Preventing Teen Drug Use	07/28/95	657
Private Management of Public Schools	03/25/94	265
Privatization	11/13/92	988*
Professional Football	01/29/10	**73
Public Broadcasting	09/18/92	827*
Public-Employee Unions	04/08/11	313
Race and Education	09/05/14	721
Racial Diversity in Public Schools	09/14/07	**745
Racial Tensions in Schools	01/07/94	1
Reforming School Funding	12/10/99	1041
Religion in Schools	01/12/01	1
Rethinking School Integration	10/18/96	913
Revising No Child Left Behind	04/16/10	337
School Censorship	02/19/93	145
School Choice Debate	07/18/97	625
School Desegregation	04/23/04	345
School Funding	08/27/93	745

	Date	Page
School Reform	04/29/11	385
School Violence	10/09/98	881
School Vouchers	04/09/99	281
School Vouchers Showdown	02/15/02	121
Science and Religion	03/22/13	281
Science in America	01/11/08	25
Single-Sex Education	07/12/02	569
Sexually Transmitted Diseases	12/03/04	997
Sleep Deprivation	06/26/98	553
Special Education	11/10/00	905
Student Journalism	06/05/98	481
Student Rights	06/05/09	501
Teacher Education	10/17/97	913
Teacher Shortages	08/24/01	633
Teaching Critical Thinking	04/10/15	313
Teaching History	09/29/95	849
Teaching Math and Science	09/06/02	697
Teaching Values	06/21/96	529
Teenage Suicide	06/14/91	385*
Teen Driving	01/07/05	1
Teen Sex	09/16/05	761
Testing in Schools	04/20/01	321
Treating ADHD	08/03/12	669
Upward Mobility	04/29/05	369
Violence in Schools	09/11/92	785
Year-Round Schools	05/17/96	433
Youth Apprenticeships	10/23/92	905
Youth Fitness	09/26/97	841
Youth Violence	03/05/10	193*
Zero Tolerance	03/10/00	185

Embryos. *See Fetal tissue research*

Employee-assistance programs

	Date	Page
Job Stress	08/04/95	681
Retirement Security	05/31/02	481
Treating Addiction	01/06/95	15*
Unemployment Benefits	04/25/03	369

Employment and unemployment. *See also Discrimination; Job stress; Job training; Occupational health and safety; Pensions; Social Security; Wages and salaries*

	Date	Page
Accountants Under Fire	03/22/02	252*
Affirmative Action	10/17/08	**841
America's Border Fence	09/19/08	745
Apprenticeships	10/14/16	841
Arms Sales	12/09/94	1089*
Artificial Intelligence	04/22/11	361
Attracting Jobs	03/02/12	205
Auto Industry's Future	02/06/09	**105
Bilingual Education	08/13/93	734*
Business Bankruptcy	04/10/09	321
Business Ethics	05/06/11	409
Career Colleges	01/07/11	1
Child-Care Options	05/08/98	409
Child Labor and Sweatshops	08/16/96	721
Class Action Lawsuits	05/13/11	433

	Date	Page
Coal Industry's Future	06/17/16	529
Community Colleges	05/01/15	385
Contingent Work Force	10/24/97	937
Crackdown on Smoking	12/04/92	1049
Criminal Records and Employment	04/20/12	349
Curbing CEO Pay	03/09/07	217
Debate Over Immigration	07/14/00	569
Decriminalizing Prostitution	04/15/16	337
Diversity in the Workplace	10/10/97	889
Domestic Partners	09/04/92	761
Domestic Poverty	09/07/07	**721
Downward Mobility	07/23/93	625
Dropout Rate	06/13/14	505
Drug Testing	11/20/98	1001
Employee Benefits	02/04/00	65
European Union's Future	12/16/16	1037
European Unrest	01/09/15	25
Exporting Jobs	02/20/04	149
Fairness in Salaries	05/29/92	457
Fast-Food Shake-Up	11/08/91	825
The Federal Reserve	01/03/14	1
Fighting Urban Poverty	07/17/15	601
Flexible Work Arrangements	08/14/98	697
Future Job Market	01/11/02	1
Future of Feminism	04/14/06	313
Future of the European Union	10/28/05	909
Gentrification	02/20/15	169
Future of the Middle Class	04/08/16	313
The Gig Economy	03/18/16	265
Global Population Growth	01/16/15	49
High-Tech Labor Shortage	04/24/98	361
Housing the Homeless	10/10/14	841
Housing Discrimination	11/06/15	937
Illegal Immigration	04/24/92	361
Illegal Immigration	05/06/05	393
Immigrants and the Economy	02/24/17	169
Immigration Debate	02/01/08	**97
Immigration Reform	09/24/93	841
Implementing the Disabilities Act	12/20/96	1105
Income Inequality	12/03/10	989
Intelligence Testing	07/30/93	649
Job Stress	08/04/95	681
Jobs in the '90s	02/28/92	169
Jobs vs. Environment	05/15/92	409
Jobs Outlook	06/04/10	481
Labor Movement's Future	06/28/96	553
Latinos' Future	10/17/03	869
Law Schools	04/19/13	353
Liberal Arts Education	04/10/98	313
Living-Wage Movement	09/27/02	769
Managing Managed Care	04/16/99	317*
Middle-Class Squeeze	03/06/09	201
Millennial Generation	06/26/15	553
Minimum Wage	12/16/05	1053

	Date	Page
Minimum Wage	01/24/14	72
Mothers' Movement	04/04/03	297
National Service	06/25/93	553
Native American Sovereignty	05/05/17	385
Native American Youths	04/24/15	361
NFL Controversies	09/04/15	721
The Obama Legacy	11/04/16	913
'Occupy' Movement	01/13/12	25
Paying for College	11/20/92	1001
Prison-Building Boom	09/17/99	813*
Prisoner Reentry	12/04/09	1005
Privacy in the Workplace	11/19/93	1009
Public-Employee Unions	04/08/11	313
Public-Works Projects	02/20/09	153
Recession's Regional Impact	02/01/91	65
Rethinking NAFTA	06/07/96	481
Rethinking Retirement	06/19/09	549
Retirement Security	05/31/02	481
Reviving Manufacturing	07/22/11	601
Reviving Rural Economies	03/31/17	265
Rising College Costs	12/05/03	1013
Robotics and the Economy	09/25/15	793
Science in America	01/11/08	25
Sexual Harassment	04/27/12	377
Should the U.S. Reinstate the Draft?	01/11/91	17
Sleep Deprivation	06/26/98	561*
Solar Energy Controversies	04/29/16	385
Stimulating the Economy	01/10/03	1
Straining the Safety Net	07/31/09	645
Teaching Critical Thinking	04/10/15	313
Telecommuting	07/19/13	621
Too Many Lawsuits?	05/22/92	440
Transatlantic Tensions	07/13/01	566*
Underground Economy	03/04/94	193
Unemployment Benefits	04/25/03	369
Unions at a Crossroads	08/07/15	673
Universal Basic Income	09/08/17	725
Upward Mobility	04/29/05	369
U.S. Auto Industry	10/16/92	895
The Value of a College Education	11/20/09	981
Vanishing Jobs	03/13/09	225
Welfare Reform	04/10/92	313
Welfare, Work and the States	12/06/96	1057
Whistleblowers	12/05/97	1057
Work, Family and Stress	08/14/92	689
Worker Retraining	01/21/94	49
Worker Safety	10/04/13	837
The Working Poor	11/03/95	969
Youth Apprenticeships	10/23/92	905
Youth Unemployment	03/14/14	241

Endangered species

	Date	Page
Animal Rights	01/08/10	1
Bush and the Environment	10/25/02	865
Disappearing Species	11/30/07	985

	Date	Page		Date	Page
Ecotourism	10/20/06	865	Managing Nuclear Waste	01/28/11	73
Endangered Species	06/21/91	393	Managing Public Lands	11/04/11	929
Endangered Species Act	10/01/99	849	Managing Western Lands	04/22/16	361
Endangered Species Act	06/03/05	**493	Modernizing the Grid	02/19/10	145
Environmental Movement at 25	03/31/95	283*	Native American Sovereignty	05/05/17	385
Hunting Controversy	01/24/92	49	Nuclear Energy	03/10/06	217
Jobs vs. Environment	05/15/92	409	Nuclear Power	06/10/11	505
Marine Mammals vs. Fish	08/28/92	737	The Obama Presidency	01/30/09	73
Mass Extinction	09/15/00	713	Offshore Drilling	06/25/10	553
National Parks	01/17/14	49	Oil Diplomacy	01/24/03	49
National Parks Under Pressure	10/06/06	817	Oil Imports	08/23/91	585
Property Rights	06/16/95	513	Oil Jitters	01/04/08	**1
Protecting Endangered Species	04/19/96	337	The Politics of Energy	03/05/99	185
Protecting Wetlands	10/03/08	793*	Presidential Power	03/06/15	217
Public Land Policy	06/17/94	542*	Protecting the Power Grid	11/11/16	941
Saving the Forests	09/20/91	697*	Reducing Your Carbon Footprint	12/05/08	985
Saving the Rain Forests	06/11/99	497	Renewable Energy	11/07/97	961
Science and Politics	08/20/04	661	Socially Responsible Investing	08/29/08	673
Setting Environmental Priorities	05/21/99	425	Solar Energy Controversies	04/29/16	385
Slow Food Movement	01/26/07	73	SUV Debate	05/16/03	449
Species Extinction	12/15/17	1041	Troubled Brazil	04/07/17	289
Threatened Fisheries	08/02/02	617	U.S.-Iran Relations	03/04/16	217
Transnational Crime	08/29/14	697	Utility Deregulation	01/14/00	1
			Wind Power	04/01/11	289

Energy policy. *See also Coal; Electric power; Nuclear power plants; Petroleum*

English language. *See Official English*

Enron Corp. Scandal

Air Pollution and Climate Control	11/13/15	961
Air Pollution Conflict	11/14/03	965
Alternative Energy	07/10/92	573
Alternative Energy	02/25/05	173
Arctic Development	12/02/16	989
Biofuels Boom	09/29/06	793
Bush and the Environment	10/25/02	865
Buying Green	02/29/08	193
Climate Change	01/27/06	73
Climate Change	06/14/13	521
Coal's Comeback	10/05/07	817
Confronting Iraq	10/04/02	793
Confronting Warming	01/09/09	1
Dealing With the "New" Russia	06/06/08	481
Domestic Energy Development	09/30/05	809
Energy and Climate	07/24/09	621
Energy and the Environment	03/03/00	161
Energy Efficiency	05/19/06	433
Energy Policy	05/25/01	441
Energy Policy	05/20/11	457
Energy Security	02/01/02	73
Fracking Controversy	12/16/11	1049
Future of the Arctic	09/20/13	789
Future of Recycling	12/14/07	1033
The Future of U.S.-Russia Relations	01/18/02	40*
Global Warming Treaty	01/26/01	41
Gulf Coast Restoration	08/26/11	677*
Homeland Security	09/12/03	761*
Jobs Outlook	06/04/10	481

Enron Corp. Scandal

Accountants Under Fire	03/22/02	241
Corporate Crime	10/11/02	817
Financial Misconduct	01/20/12	53
Stock Market Troubles	01/16/04	25

Environmental protection

Acid Rain: New Approach to Old Problem	03/08/91	129
Advertising Under Attack	09/13/91	671*
Affordable Housing	02/09/01	103*
Aging Infrastructure	09/28/07	**793
Air Pollution and Climate Control	11/13/15	961
Air Pollution Conflict	11/14/03	965
Alternative Energy	07/10/92	573
Alternative Energy	02/25/05	173
Animal Intelligence	10/22/10	869
Arctic Development	12/02/16	989
Asbestos Litigation	05/02/03	393
Biofuels Boom	09/29/06	793
Biotech Foods	03/30/01	249
Bush and the Environment	10/25/02	865
Buying Green	02/29/08	193
Cleaning Up Hazardous Wastes	08/23/96	745
Climate Change	01/27/06	73
Climate Change	06/14/13	521
Coal's Comeback	10/05/07	817
Coal Industry's Future	06/17/16	529
Coastal Development	08/21/98	721
Coastal Development	02/22/13	181

	Date	Page		Date	Page
The Consumer Culture	11/19/99	1005*	National Parks Under Pressure	10/06/06	817
Disappearing Species	11/30/07	985	New Air Quality Standards	03/07/97	193
Domestic Energy Development	09/30/05	809	The New CIA	12/11/92	1085*
Downtown Renaissance	06/23/06	**553	The New Environmentalism	12/01/06	985
Drinking Water Safety	07/15/16	577	Nuclear Arms Cleanup	06/24/94	553
The Economics of Recycling	03/27/98	265	Nuclear Fusion	01/22/93	59*
Ecotourism	10/20/06	865	Offshore Drilling	06/25/10	553
Electric Cars	07/09/93	577	Oil Imports	08/23/91	585
Endangered Species	06/21/91	393	Oil Spills	01/17/92	25
Endangered Species Act	10/01/99	849	Ozone Depletion	04/03/92	289
Endangered Species Act	06/03/05	**493	Pandemic Threat	06/02/17	457
Energy and Climate	07/24/09	621	Pesticide Controversies	06/05/15	481
Energy and the Environment	03/03/00	161	Population and the Environment	07/17/98	601
Energy Policy	05/25/01	441	Population Growth	07/16/93	601
Energy Policy	05/20/11	457	Preventing Cancer	01/16/09	25
Energy Security	02/01/02	73	Property Rights	06/16/95	513
Environmental Justice	06/19/98	529	Protecting Endangered Species	04/19/96	337
Environmental Movement at 25	03/31/95	273	Protecting the National Parks	06/16/00	521
Extreme Sports	04/03/09	297	Protecting the Oceans	10/17/14	865
Famine in Africa	11/08/02	921	Protecting Wetlands	10/03/08	793*
Farm Policy	12/02/94	1057	Public Land Policy	06/17/94	529
Farm Policy	08/10/12	693	Reducing Your Carbon Footprint	12/05/08	985
Farm Subsidies	05/17/02	433	Reforming the Corps	05/30/03	497
Food Policy Debates	10/03/14	817	Regulating Pesticides	01/28/94	73
Food Safety Battle: Organic v. Biotech	09/04/98	761	Regulating Pesticides	08/06/99	665
Future of Amtrak	10/18/02	841	Regulating Toxic Chemicals	07/18/14	601
Future of Recycling	12/14/07	1033	Renewable Energy	11/07/97	961
Garbage Crisis	03/20/92	241	Restructuring the Electric Industry	01/17/97	31*
Genetically Engineered Foods	08/05/94	686*	Saving Open Spaces	11/05/99	953
Genetically Modified Food	08/31/12	717	Saving the Forests	09/20/91	681
Global Warming Treaty	01/26/01	41	Saving the Oceans	11/04/05	933
Global Warming Update	11/01/96	961	Saving the Rainforests	06/11/99	511*
Global Water Shortages	12/15/95	1113	Science and Politics	08/20/04	661
The Greening of Eastern Europe	11/15/91	849	Setting Environmental Priorities	05/21/99	425
The Growing Influence of Boycotts	01/04/91	1	Smart Cities	07/27/12	645
Gulf Coast Restoration	08/26/11	677*	Smart Growth	05/28/04	469
Human Rights in China	07/25/08	601	Socially Responsible Investing	08/29/08	673
Indoor Air Pollution	10/27/95	945	Species Extinction	12/15/17	1041
Invasive Species	10/05/01	785	SUV Debate	05/16/03	449
Invasive Species	02/17/12	153	Synthetic Biology	04/25/14	361
Jobs vs. Environment	05/15/92	409	Threatened Coastlines	02/07/92	97
Managing Public Lands	11/04/11	929	Threatened Fisheries	08/02/02	617
Managing Western Lands	04/22/16	361	Traffic Congestion	08/27/99	739*
Managing Wildfires	11/02/12	941	Troubled Brazil	04/07/17	289
Marine Mammals vs. Fish	08/28/92	737	Urban Sprawl in the West	10/03/97	865
Mass Extinction	09/15/00	713	Utility Deregulation	01/14/00	8*
Mass Transit Boom	01/18/08	49	Water Quality	02/11/94	121
Mexico's Emergence	07/19/91	503*	Water Quality	11/24/00	953
Mine Safety	06/24/11	553	Water Shortages	08/01/03	649
Modernizing the Grid	02/19/10	145	Water Shortages	06/18/10	529
National Forests	10/16/98	905	Will Nuclear Power Get Another		
National Parks	05/28/93	457	Chance?	02/22/91	113
National Parks	01/17/14	49	Wind Power	04/01/11	289

	Date	Page
Equal Employment Opportunity Commission		
Age Discrimination	08/01/97	673
Crackdown on Sexual Harassment	07/19/96	625
Latinos' Future	10/17/03	869
Mental Health Policy	09/12/97	793
Sexual Harassment	08/09/91	537
Women and Work	07/26/13	645
Workplace Sexual Harassment	10/27/17	893
Ergonomics		
Worker Safety	05/21/04	456*
Espionage. *See Intelligence service*		
Ethanol		
Global Food Crisis	06/27/08	553
Ethical and moral issues. *See also Ethics in government;*		
Medical ethics; Religion		
Accountants Under Fire	03/22/02	241
Air Pollution and Climate Control	11/13/15	961
Animal Rights	05/24/91	301
Assisted Suicide	05/17/13	449
Broadcast Indecency	04/16/04	321
Bullying	02/04/05	101
Business Ethics	05/06/11	409
Campus Sexual Assault	10/31/14	913
Catholic Church in the U.S.	09/08/95	777
Cell Phone Safety	03/16/01	208*
Cheating in Schools	09/22/00	745
Civic Renewal	03/21/97	241
The Cloning Controversy	05/09/97	409
Combating Plagiarism	09/19/03	773
Combating Scientific Misconduct	01/10/97	1
Computer Hacking	09/16/11	757*
The Consumer Culture	11/19/99	1001
Digital Journalism	05/30/14	457
Disappearing Species	11/30/07	985
Doctor Shortage	08/28/15	697
Drug Company Ethics	06/06/03	521
Drug Safety	03/11/05	221
Encouraging Teen Abstinence	07/10/98	577
Ethics of War	12/13/02	1013
Financial Misconduct	01/20/12	53
Forensic Science Controversies	02/10/17	121
Free-Press Disputes	04/08/05	293
Future of the Catholic Church	01/19/07	49
Future of the Catholic Church	06/07/13	497
Future of the Christian Right	06/23/17	533
Future of the Music Industry	11/21/03	989
Gays in the Military	09/18/09	**765
Genetically Modified Food	08/31/12	717
Girls' Rights	04/17/15	337
Greek Life on Campus	11/20/15	985
Guns on Campus	01/27/17	73
High School Sports	09/22/95	825
Housing Discrimination	11/06/15	937

	Date	Page
Human Trafficking and Slavery	03/26/04	273
Hunger in America	07/07/17	557
Hunting Controversy	01/24/92	49
Immigrant Detention	10/23/15	889
Interrogating the CIA	09/25/09	789
Jailing Debtors	09/16/16	745
Journalism Standards in the		
Internet Age	10/08/10	821
Journalism Under Fire	12/25/98	1129*
Lead Poisoning	06/19/92	529*
Manipulating the Human Genome	06/19/15	529
Marriage and Divorce	05/10/96	409
Medical Marijuana	07/21/17	605
Mothers' Movement	04/04/03	297
Nanotechnology	06/10/16	505
Parental Rights	10/25/96	937
Patenting Human Genes	05/31/13	473
Patriotism in America	06/25/99	545
Plagiarism and Cheating	01/04/13	1
Police Tactics	12/12/14	1033
Prayer and Healing	01/14/05	25
Prisoners and Mental Illness	03/13/15	241
Privacy and the Internet	12/04/15	1009
Protestants Today	12/07/07	1009
Punishing Sex Offenders	01/12/96	25
Race in America	07/11/03	593
Reforming Big-Time College Sports	03/19/04	249
Reforming Juvenile Justice	09/11/15	745
Regulating Lobbying	06/06/14	481
Religious Freedom	01/01/16	1
Reproductive Ethics	05/15/09	449
Restorative Justice	02/05/16	121
Right to Die	05/13/05	421
Robotics and the Economy	09/25/15	793
Sentencing Debates	11/05/04	925
Sex on Campus	11/04/94	961
Sexually Transmitted Diseases	12/03/04	997
Sports and Drugs	07/23/04	**613
Sportsmanship	03/23/01	225
Stock Market Troubles	01/16/04	25
Stolen Antiquities	11/10/17	945
Stopping Genocide	08/27/04	685
Teaching Values	06/21/96	529
Three-Strikes Laws	05/10/02	417
Tobacco Industry	12/10/04	**1025
Torture	04/18/03	345
Transgender Rights	12/11/15	1033
Understanding Mormonism	10/19/12	889
Vaccine Controversies	02/19/16	169
Workplace Sexual Harassment	10/27/17	893
Ethnic groups. *See Minorities*		
Ethics in government		
Campaign Finance	05/06/16	409
Drug Safety	03/11/05	221

	Date	Page
Fighting SARS	06/20/03	569
Future of the GOP	10/24/14	889
Independent Counsels	02/21/97	145
Political Scandals	05/27/94	457
Politicians and Privacy	04/17/92	337
Pork Barrel Politics	06/16/06	529
Privatizing the Military	06/25/04	565
Property Rights	03/04/05	197
Protecting Whistleblowers	03/31/06	265
Think Tanks in Transition	09/29/17	797
Whistleblowers	01/31/14	97

Europe and European Union

	Date	Page
'Alt-Right' Movement	03/17/17	241
Avian Flu Threat	01/13/06	25
Declining Birthrates	11/21/08	961
Democracy in Eastern Europe	10/08/99	865
Drinking on Campus	08/18/06	649
Euro Crisis	10/05/12	841
Europe 1992	06/28/91	417
European Union's Future	12/16/16	1037
European Monetary Union	11/27/98	1025
European Unrest	01/09/15	25
Europe's New Right	02/12/93	121
Expanding NATO	05/16/97	433
Exporting Democracy	04/01/05	269
Food Safety Battle: Organic v. Biotech	09/04/98	
768	*	
Future of NATO	02/28/03	177
Future of the European Union	10/28/05	909
Future of Marriage	05/07/04	405*
Global Jihad	10/14/05	857
The Greening of Eastern Europe	11/15/91	866
Internet Privacy	11/06/98	962*
Mad Cow Disease	03/02/01	161
Middle East Tensions	10/27/06	**889
Missile Defense	09/08/00	700*
NATO's Changing Role	08/21/92	713
Oil Spills	01/17/92	36*
Population and the Environment	07/17/98	612*
Populism and Party Politics	09/09/16	721
Religious Persecution	11/21/97	1009
Resurgent Russia	02/07/14	121
Revitalizing the Cities	10/13/95	902*
Russia and the Former Soviet Republics	06/17/05	541
Transatlantic Tensions	07/13/01	553
Universal Basic Income	09/08/17	725
U.S. Auto Industry	10/16/92	894
U.S.-British Relations	01/30/98	73
U.S.-British Relations	11/05/10	917*
U.S.-Europe Relations	03/23/12	277
U.S. Global Engagement	05/16/14	433
U.S.-Russia Relations	01/13/17	25
U.S. Trade Policy	09/13/13	765

	Date	Page
Euthanasia		
Assisted Suicide	02/21/92	145
Assisted Suicide Controversy	05/05/95	393
Caring for the Dying	09/05/97	780*
Right to Die	05/13/05	421
Everglades		
Invasive Species	02/17/12	153
Jobs vs. Environment	05/15/92	423*
National Parks	05/28/93	462*
Reforming the Corps	05/30/03	497
Evolution		
Evolution vs. Creationism	08/22/97	745
Intelligent Design	07/29/05	637
Religion in Schools	01/12/01	11*
Science and Religion	03/22/13	281
Synthetic Biology	04/25/14	361
Teaching Math and Science	09/06/02	697

Executions. See Death penalty

Exercise. See Physical fitness

Export controls

	Date	Page
Internet Privacy	11/06/98	961*
Non-Proliferation Treaty at 25	01/27/95	89*
Nuclear Proliferation	06/05/92	481

Exports. See International trade

Extraterrestrial life

	Date	Page
Pursuing the Paranormal	03/29/96	265
The Search for Extraterrestrials	03/05/04	197
Search for Life on New Planets	06/20/14	529

Family. See also Adoption; Parents

	Date	Page
Alzheimer's Disease	07/24/92	630*
Alzheimer's Disease	05/15/98	433
Birth-Control Debate	06/24/05	565
Child Care	12/17/93	1122*
Children and Divorce	06/07/91	349
Children and Divorce	01/19/01	25
Children's Legal Rights	04/23/93	337
Child Sexual Abuse	01/15/93	25
Child Welfare	08/26/16	673
Child Welfare Reform	04/22/05	345
Declining Birthrates	11/21/08	961
Domestic Partners	09/04/92	761
Domestic Violence	01/06/06	1
Domestic Violence	11/15/13	981
Foster Care Crisis	09/27/91	705
Foster Care Reform	01/09/98	1
Future of Feminism	04/14/06	313
Future of Marriage	05/07/04	397
Future of Marriage	12/01/17	993
Gay Marriage	09/05/03	721
Gay Marriage	03/15/13	257
Gay Marriage Showdowns	09/26/08	**769
Gentrification	02/20/15	169
Girls' Rights	04/17/15	337

	Date	Page
Homeless Students	04/05/13	305
Housing the Homeless	10/10/14	841
Immigrant Detention	10/23/15	889
Marriage and Divorce	05/10/96	409
Millennial Generation	06/26/15	553
Mothers' Movement	04/04/03	297
New Military Culture	04/26/96	378*
Opioid Crisis	10/07/16	817
Preventing Teen Pregnancy	05/14/93	409
Primary Care	03/17/95	217
Prostitution Debate	05/23/08	433
Recovered-Memory Debate	07/05/96	577
Religion in America	11/25/94	1033
Reproductive Ethics	05/15/09	449
Right to Die	05/13/05	421
Teen Pregnancy	03/26/10	265*
Treating Alzheimer's Disease	07/24/15	625
Understanding Autism	08/01/14	649

Family — Economic aspects

Black Middle Class	01/23/98	63*
Caring for Veterans	04/23/10	361
Charitable Giving	11/12/93	991*
Child-Care Options	05/08/98	409
Child Poverty	04/07/00	281
Child Poverty	10/28/11	901
Children and Divorce	06/07/91	358*
Child Welfare Reform	04/22/05	345
Consumer Debt	11/15/96	1009
Covering the Uninsured	06/14/02	521
Declining Birthrates	11/21/08	961
Ending Homelessness	06/18/04	541
Future of Homeownership	12/14/12	1061
Gender Pay Gap	03/14/08	241
Getting into College	02/23/96	169
Income Inequality	04/17/98	337
Middle-Class Squeeze	03/06/09	201
Mothers' Movement	04/04/03	297
Paying for College	11/20/92	1001
Paying for Retirement	11/05/93	961
Reviving Rural Economies	03/31/17	265
School Vouchers	04/09/99	281
School Vouchers Showdown	02/15/02	121
Straining the Safety Net	07/31/09	645
Tax Reform	03/22/96	241
Underground Economy	03/04/94	197*
Vanishing Jobs	03/13/09	225
Welfare Experiments	09/16/94	793
Welfare Reform	04/10/92	313
Welfare, Work and the States	12/06/96	1066*
Women and Work	07/26/13	645
Work, Family and Stress	08/14/92	689
The Working Poor	11/03/95	969
Wounded Veterans	08/31/07	697

	Date	Page
Famine		
Climate Change and National Security	09/22/17	773
Global Food Crisis	06/27/08	553
Global Hunger	08/08/14	673
Farming. *See Agriculture*		
Fast-food restaurants		
Fast-Food Shake-Up	11/08/91	825
Food Policy Debates	10/03/14	817
Minimum Wage	01/24/14	72
Obesity and Health	01/15/99	25
Obesity Epidemic	01/31/03	73
Fathers		
Adoption	11/26/93	1033
Child Care	12/17/93	1119*
Domestic Violence	01/06/06	1
Fatherhood Movement	06/02/00	473
Gay Marriage	09/05/03	732*
Federal Bureau of Investigation		
Civil Liberties Debates	10/24/03	893
Combating Terrorism	07/21/95	633
Cyber-Crime	04/12/02	305
Cyber-Predators	03/01/02	169
Cybersecurity	09/26/03	797
The FBI Under Fire	04/11/97	313
Forensic Science Controversies	02/10/17	121
Future of the Airline Industry	06/21/02	545
Gang Crisis	05/14/04	421
Homegrown Jihadists	09/03/10	701
Homeland Security	09/12/03	749
Identity Theft	06/10/05	517
Insurance Fraud	10/11/96	901*
Intelligence Reform	05/29/15	457
Intelligence Reforms	01/24/02	49
Marijuana Industry	10/16/15	865
Policing the Borders	02/22/02	145
Presidential Power	11/15/02	945
Re-examining 9/11	06/04/04	493
Serial Killers	10/31/03	917
War on Terrorism	10/12/01	817
Weapons of Mass Destruction	03/08/02	193
Federal Communications Commission		
Broadcast Indecency	04/16/04	321
Children's Television	08/15/97	721
The Future of Telecommunications	04/23/99	329
The Future of Television	12/23/94	1129
Future of TV	04/11/14	313
Indecency on Television	11/09/12	965
Media Ownership	10/10/03	**845
Media Violence	02/14/14	145
Paying College Athletes	07/11/14	577
Pay-Per-View TV	10/04/91	729
Reality TV	08/27/10	677
Shock Jocks	06/01/07	**481

	Date	Page
Talk Show Democracy	04/29/94	377*
Transition to Digital TV	06/20/08	529

Federal Election Commission

	Date	Page
Campaign Finance Reform	02/09/96	126*
Campaign Finance Showdown	11/22/02	969
Redistricting Showdown	08/25/17	677
Voting Controversies	09/15/06	745
Voting Controversies	02/21/14	169

Federal Emergency Management Agency

	Date	Page
Coastal Development	02/22/13	181
Disaster Preparedness	11/18/05	**981
Rebuilding New Orleans	02/03/06	97

Federal government. *See also Congress, U.S.; Regulation and deregulation; specific agencies and programs*

	Date	Page
Aging Infrastructure	09/28/07	**793
Air Pollution Conflict	11/14/03	965
American Indians	04/28/06	**361
Census Controversey	05/14/10	433
Charter Schools	03/10/17	217
Conspiracy Theories	10/23/09	885
Cosmetic Surgery	04/15/05	317
Democrats' Future	10/29/10	893
Disaster Preparedness	11/18/05	**981
Drone Warfare	08/06/10	653
Drug Safety	03/11/05	221
Ending Homelessness	06/18/04	541
Exporting Democracy	04/01/05	269
Financial Bailout	10/24/08	**865
Financial Industry Overhaul	07/30/10	629
Free-Press Disputes	04/08/05	293
Future of the Airline Industry	06/21/02	545
Future of the GOP	10/24/14	889
Future of Homeownership	12/14/12	1061
Gangs in the U.S.	07/16/10	581
Government Spending	07/12/13	597
Gridlock in Washington	04/30/10	385
Homeland Security	09/12/03	749
Homeland Security	02/13/09	129
Homeless Students	04/05/13	305
Human Spaceflight	10/16/09	861
Humanities Education	12/06/13	1029
Legal-Aid Crisis	10/07/11	829
Managing Nuclear Waste	01/28/11	73
Marijuana Industry	10/16/15	865
Medicaid Reform	07/16/04	589
Medical Breakthroughs	09/15/17	749
Medical Marijuana	07/21/17	605
Nanotechnology	06/11/04	517
Nanotechnology	06/10/16	505
The National Debt	11/14/08	937
National Debt	03/18/11	241
National Service	06/25/93	553
The Obama Presidency	01/30/09	73

	Date	Page
Patent Controversies	02/27/15	193
Patent Disputes	12/15/06	1033
Patenting Human Genes	05/31/13	473
Policing the Borders	02/22/02	145
Privatizing Government Services	08/09/96	697
Privatizing Government Services	12/08/17	1017
Prosecutors and Politics	06/22/07	553
Prostitution Debate	05/23/08	433
Protecting Whistleblowers	03/31/06	265
Public-Employee Unions	04/08/11	313
Public-Works Projects	02/20/09	153
Pursuing the Paranormal	03/29/96	265
Re-examining the Constitution	09/07/12	741
Reinventing Government	02/17/95	145
Renewable Energy	11/07/97	961
Reviving Manufacturing	07/22/11	601
Smart Growth	05/28/04	469
Space Program	02/24/12	177
State Budget Crises	10/03/03	837*
States and Federalism	09/13/96	793
States and Federalism	10/15/10	845
Tea Party Movement	03/19/10	**241*
Three-Strikes Laws	05/10/02	417
Trump Presidency	01/06/17	1
Water Shortages	08/01/03	665*
Y2K Dilemma	02/19/99	137
Water Crisis in the West	12/09/11	1025
Whistleblowers	01/31/14	97
Wind Power	04/01/11	289

Federal lands

	Date	Page
Arctic Development	12/02/16	989
Bush and the Environment	10/25/02	865
Domestic Energy Development	09/30/05	809
Energy Security	02/01/02	73
Environmental Movement at 25	03/31/95	286*
Managing Public Lands	11/04/11	929
Managing Western Lands	04/22/16	361
National Forests	10/16/98	905
National Parks	05/28/93	457
National Parks	01/17/14	49
National Parks Under Pressure	10/06/06	817
Protecting the Oceans	10/17/14	865
Public Land Policy	06/17/94	529
Reforming the Corps	05/30/03	497
Saving Open Spaces	11/05/99	953
Setting Environmental Priorities	05/21/99	440*

Federal Reserve

	Date	Page
Deflation Fears	02/13/98	121
The Federal Reserve	09/01/00	673
The Federal Reserve	01/03/14	1
Financial Bailout	10/24/08	**865
Financial Crisis	05/09/08	409
Financial Industry Overhaul	07/30/10	629

	Date	Page
The National Debt	11/14/08	937
National Debt	03/18/11	241
Stimulating the Economy	01/10/03	1
The Stock Market	05/02/97	385

Federalism

Deepening Canadian Crisis over		
Quebec	04/12/91	205
Marijuana Laws	02/11/05	125
National Education Standards	05/14/99	401
No Child Left Behind	05/27/05	469
Setting Environmental Priorities	05/21/99	431*
States and Federalism	09/13/96	793

Fetal tissue research

Embryo Research	12/17/99	1065
Fetal Tissue Research	08/16/91	561
Manipulating the Human Genome	06/19/15	529
Organ Shortage	02/21/03	153
Organ Transplants	08/11/95	718*
Treating Alzheimer's Disease	07/24/15	625

Film. *See Movies*

Financial Aid

Future of Public Universities	01/18/13	53
Student Debt	11/18/16	965

Firearms. *See also Arms control; Weapons*

3D Printing	12/07/12	1037
Arms Sales	12/09/94	1092*
Declining Crime Rates	04/04/97	289
Discipline in Schools	02/15/08	145
Fighting Crime	02/08/08	121
Fighting Gangs	10/09/15	841
Future of the Airline Industry	06/21/02	561*
Gang Crisis	05/14/04	421
Gangs in the U.S.	07/16/10	581
Gun Control	06/10/94	505
Gun Control	03/08/13	233
Gun Control Debate	11/12/04	949
Gun Control Standoff	12/19/97	1105
Gun Rights Debates	10/31/08	**889
Gun Violence	05/25/07	457
Guns on Campus	01/27/17	73
Haiti's Dilemma	02/18/05	149
High-Impact Litigation	02/11/00	89
Hunting Controversy	01/24/92	49
Juvenile Justice	02/25/94	169
Mexico's Drug War	12/12/08	1009
Mexico's Future	10/26/12	913
Police Tactics	12/12/14	1033
Reassessing the Nation's Gun Laws	03/22/91	167*
School Violence	10/09/98	881
Suburban Crime	09/03/93	782*
Violence in Schools	09/11/92	785
Youth Gangs	10/11/91	753
Youth Suicide	02/13/04	131*

	Date	Page
First Amendment		
Abortion Debates	03/21/03	255*
Advertising Overload	01/23/04	49
Advertising Under Attack	09/13/91	657
'Alt-Right' Movement	03/17/17	241
Broadcast Indecency	04/16/04	321
Campaign Finance Debates	05/28/10	457
Campaign Finance Reform	02/09/96	121
Civic Education	02/03/17	97
Computer Hacking	09/16/11	757*
Courts and the Media	09/23/94	817
Crackdown on Sexual Harassment	07/19/96	642*
Cults in America	05/07/93	385
Cyberbullying	05/02/08	385
Cyber-Predators	03/01/02	169
The Dark Web	01/15/16	49
Digital Commerce	02/05/99	89
Evolution vs. Creationism	08/22/97	749*
Faith-Based Initiatives	05/04/01	377
Free-Press Disputes	04/08/05	293
Free Speech at Risk	04/26/13	377
Free Speech on Campus	05/08/15	409
Future of Journalism	03/27/09	**273
Government and Religion	01/15/10	25
Government Secrecy	02/11/11	121
Hate Crimes	01/08/93	1
Libraries and the Internet	06/01/01	465
Movie Ratings	03/28/03	273
The Obscenity Debate	12/20/91	969
'Occupy' Movement	01/13/12	25
Press Freedom	02/05/10	97
Preventing Bullying	12/10/10	**1013
Protestants Today	12/07/07	1009
Regulating the Internet	06/30/95	561
Religion and Politics	10/14/94	889
Religion in Schools	02/18/94	145
Religion in Schools	01/12/01	1
Religious Freedom	01/01/16	1
Religious Repression	11/01/13	933
Rise of Megachurches	09/21/07	769
School Censorship	02/19/93	145
School Choice Debate	07/18/97	630*
School Vouchers	04/09/99	281
Sex, Violence and the Media	11/17/95	1017
Sexual Harassment	08/09/91	537
Student Journalism	06/05/98	481
Student Rights	06/05/09	501
Trust in Media	06/09/17	481

First Ladies

First Ladies	06/14/96	505

Fish and fishing

Acid Rain: New Approach to Old		
Problem	03/08/91	129
Coastal Development	08/21/98	739*

	Date	Page
Disappearing Species	11/30/07	985
Endangered Species	06/21/91	406*
Endangered Species Act	10/01/99	854*
Endangered Species Act	06/03/05	**493
Fish Farming	07/27/07	625
Food Safety	06/04/93	481
Gulf Coast Restoration	08/26/11	677*
Invasive Species	02/17/12	153
Marine Mammals vs. Fish	08/28/92	737
Offshore Drilling	06/25/10	553
Pesticide Controversies	06/05/15	481
Protecting Endangered Species	04/19/96	337
Protecting the Oceans	10/17/14	865
Protecting Wetlands	10/03/08	793*
Saving the Oceans	11/04/05	933
Threatened Fisheries	08/02/02	617
Water Shortages	06/18/10	529

Fitness. *See Physical fitness*

Flag desecration

Patriotism in America	06/25/99	545

Floods

Climate Change and National Security	09/22/17	773
Coastal Development	08/21/98	721
Coastal Development	02/22/13	181
Disaster Response	10/15/93	889
Extreme Weather	09/09/11	733*
Farm Policy	12/02/94	1072*
Global Food Crisis	06/27/08	553
Reforming the Corps	05/30/03	497
Threatened Coastlines	02/07/92	97
Water Shortages	08/01/03	649

Florida

Bilingual Education	08/13/93	708*
Cuba in Crisis	11/29/91	908*
Cuba's Future	07/20/07	601
Disaster Response	10/15/93	889
Electoral College	12/08/00	977
High-Speed Rail	04/16/93	327*
Kids in Prison	04/27/01	364*
Reforming the Corps	05/30/03	497
Rethinking the Death Penalty	11/16/01	960*
Water Quality	11/24/00	967*

Food and Drug Administration, U.S.

Birth-Control Debate	06/24/05	565
Cancer Treatments	09/11/98	785
Closing In on Tobacco	11/12/99	977
Consumer Safety	10/12/07	841
Cosmetic Surgery	04/15/05	317
Dietary Supplements	07/08/94	577
Dietary Supplements	09/03/04	709
Dietary Supplements	10/30/15	913
Drug Company Ethics	06/06/03	521
Drugmakers Under Siege	09/03/99	753

	Date	Page
Drug Safety	03/11/05	221
Fish Farming	07/27/07	625
Food Irradiation	06/12/92	505
Food Labeling	06/16/17	509
Food Safety	06/04/93	481
Food Safety	11/01/02	897
Food Safety	12/17/10	1037
Genetically Engineered Foods	08/05/94	673
Marijuana Laws	02/11/05	125
Medical Breakthroughs	09/15/17	749
Obesity Epidemic	01/31/03	73
Prescription Drug Prices	07/17/92	606*
Preventing Obesity	10/01/10	797
Prozac Controversy	08/19/94	721
Reforming the FDA	06/06/97	481
Regulating Pharmaceuticals	10/11/13	861
Regulating Tobacco	09/30/94	841
Regulating Toxic Chemicals	01/23/09	49
Tobacco Industry	12/10/04	**1025
Women's Health	11/07/03	941

Food and nutrition

Advances in Cancer Research	08/25/95	760*
Advertising Overload	01/23/04	49
Biotech Foods	03/30/01	249
Children in Crisis	08/31/01	671*
Child Poverty	10/28/11	901
Consumer Safety	10/12/07	841
Diet and Health	02/23/01	129
Dietary Supplements	07/08/94	577
Dietary Supplements	09/03/04	709
Dietary Supplements	10/30/15	913
Dieting and Health	04/14/95	321
Drugmakers Under Siege	09/03/99	767*
Drug-Resistant Bacteria	06/04/99	482*
Eating Disorders	12/18/92	1097
Factory Farms	01/12/07	25
Fair Trade Labeling	05/18/07	433
Farm Policy	08/10/12	693
Fast-Food Shake-Up	11/08/91	825
Fish Farming	07/27/07	625
Food Irradiation	06/12/92	505
Food Labeling	06/16/17	509
Food Policy Debates	10/03/14	817
Food Safety	06/04/93	481
Food Safety	11/01/02	897
Food Safety	12/17/10	1037
Food Safety Battle: Organic v. Biotech	09/04/98	761
Genetically Engineered Foods	08/05/94	673
Genetically Modified Food	08/31/12	717
Heart Health	09/12/08	721
Hunger in America	07/07/17	557
Lead Poisoning	06/19/92	539
Mad Cow Disease	03/02/01	161
Obesity and Health	01/15/99	25

	Date	Page
Obesity Epidemic	01/31/03	73
Preventing Disease	01/06/12	1
Preventing Obesity	10/01/10	797
Prolonging Life	09/30/11	805*
Regulating Pesticides	01/28/94	73
Regulating Pesticides	08/06/99	665
Rethinking Ritalin	10/22/99	916*
Slow Food Movement	01/26/07	73
Sugar Controversies	11/30/12	1013
Threatened Fisheries	08/02/02	634*
Treating ADHD	08/03/12	669
Treating Alzheimer's	03/04/11	193

Food stamps

Child Poverty	10/28/11	901
Farm Policy	08/10/12	693
Hunger in America	12/22/00	1033
Hunger in America	07/07/17	557
Welfare, Work and the States	12/06/96	1062*

Food supply

Animal Rights	05/24/91	301
Factory Farms	01/12/07	25
Farm Policy	12/02/94	1057
Farm Subsidies	05/17/02	433
Food Labeling	06/16/17	509
Food Policy Debates	10/03/14	817
Food Safety	11/01/02	897
Food Safety	12/17/10	1037
Fighting over Animal Rights	08/02/96	673
Future of Recycling	12/14/07	1033
Global Hunger	08/08/14	673
Hunger in America	12/22/00	1033
Hunger in America	07/07/17	557
Marine Mammals vs. Fish	08/28/92	737
Population and the Environment	07/17/98	601
Preparing for Disaster	08/02/13	669
Protecting the Oceans	10/17/14	865
Slow Food Movement	01/26/07	73
World Hunger	10/25/91	801

Football. *See Sports*

Foreign aid

Aid to Russia	03/12/93	217
Aiding Africa	08/29/03	697
Assisting Refugees	02/07/97	97
Calculating the Costs of the Gulf War	03/15/91	145
China Today	04/04/14	289
Defeating the Islamic State	04/01/16	289
Democracies Under Stress	10/20/17	869
Democracy in Africa	03/24/95	241
Emerging India	04/19/02	329
Ending Poverty	09/09/05	733
Euro Crisis	10/05/12	841
European Union's Future	12/16/16	1037
Famine in Africa	11/08/02	921
Foreign Aid and National Security	06/17/11	529

	Date	Page
Foreign Aid After Sept. 11	04/26/02	361
Global Hunger	08/08/14	673
The Greening of Eastern Europe	11/15/91	849
Haiti's Dilemma	02/18/05	149
Hating America	11/23/01	969
Israel at 50	03/06/98	193
North Korean Crisis	04/11/03	321
Population Growth	07/16/93	601
Reassessing Foreign Aid	09/27/96	841
Rebuilding Afghanistan	12/21/01	1041
Rebuilding Iraq	07/11/03	625
Reforming the U.N.	06/24/16	553
Resurgent Russia	02/07/14	121
Rethinking Foreign Aid	04/14/17	313
Russia's Political Future	05/03/96	396*
Terrorism in Africa	07/10/15	577
Trouble in South America	03/14/03	225
Unrest in Turkey	01/29/16	97
U.S. Global Engagement	05/16/14	433
U.S.-Pakistan Relations	08/05/11	653*
World Hunger	10/25/91	801

Foreign languages

Bilingual Education	08/13/93	697
Bilingual Education vs. English Immersion	12/11/09	1029
Debate over Bilingualism	01/19/96	49
Electing Minorities	08/12/94	704*
Future of Language	11/17/00	929

Foreign policy. *See International relations*

Foreign relations. *See International relations*

Forests and forestry

Acid Rain: New Approach to Old Problem	03/08/91	129
Bush and the Environment	10/25/02	865
Disappearing Species	11/30/07	985
Endangered Species	06/21/91	393
Endangered Species Act	06/03/05	**493
Jobs vs. Environment	05/15/92	409
Managing Public Lands	11/04/11	929
Managing Wildfires	11/02/12	941
National Forests	10/16/98	905
National Parks	01/17/14	49
Protecting Endangered Species	04/19/96	337
Protecting the National Parks	06/16/00	521
Public Land Policy	06/17/94	529
Saving the Forests	09/20/91	681
Species Extinction	12/15/17	1041

Former Soviet Union. *See Soviet Union (Former)*

Fossil fuels. *See Coal; Petroleum*

Foster care

Adoption	11/26/93	1033
Child Welfare	08/26/16	673
Foster Care Crisis	09/27/91	705

	Date	Page
Foster Care Reform	01/09/98	1
France		
Blood Supply Safety	11/11/94	997*
Future of NATO	02/28/03	177
Future of the European Union	10/28/05	909
High-Speed Rail	04/16/93	313
NATO's Changing Role	08/21/92	729*
The United Nations and Global Security	02/27/04	173
Fraternities		
Drinking on Campus	08/18/06	649
Greek Life on Campus	11/20/15	985
Hazing	01/09/04	1
Preventing Hazing	02/08/13	133
Fraud		
Aiding Africa	08/29/03	708*
Alternative Medicine's Next Phase	02/14/97	138*
Business Ethics	05/06/11	409
Caring for the Elderly	02/20/98	145
Cheating in Schools	09/22/00	745
Combating Scientific Misconduct	01/10/97	1
Consumer Debt	11/15/96	1018*
Cyber-Crime	04/12/02	305
Digital Commerce	02/05/99	106*
Digital Currency	09/26/14	793
The Disabilities Act	12/27/91	1005*
Identity Theft	06/10/05	517
Insurance Fraud	10/11/96	889
Real ID	05/04/07	385
Reforming Big-Time College Sports	03/19/04	249
Reforming Veterans' Health Care	11/21/14	985
Regulating Nonprofits	12/26/97	1129
Stock Market Troubles	01/16/04	25
Voter Rights	05/18/12	449
Voting Controversies	02/21/14	169
Whistleblowers	12/05/97	1057
Whistleblowers	01/31/14	97
Free Speech		
'Alt-Right' Movement	03/17/17	241
Campaign Finance Reform	06/13/08	505
Civic Education	02/03/17	97
The Dark Web	01/15/16	49
Democracies Under Stress	10/20/17	869
Free Speech on Campus	05/08/15	409
Privacy and the Internet	12/04/15	1009
Religious Freedom	01/01/16	1
Religious Repression	11/01/13	933
Trust in Media	06/09/17	481
Unrest in Turkey	01/29/16	97
Free trade and protection		
Aiding Africa	08/29/03	697
Deepening Canadian Crisis over Quebec	04/12/91	214*

	Date	Page
Europe 1992	06/28/91	429
Fair Trade Labeling	05/18/07	433
Foreign Aid After Sept. 11	04/26/02	361
Mexico's Emergence	07/19/91	489
New Era in Asia	02/14/92	137*
NFL Controversies	09/04/15	721
Rethinking NAFTA	06/07/96	481
Unions at a Crossroads	08/07/15	673
U.S. Trade Policy	09/13/13	765
World Trade	06/09/00	497
Freedom of Information Act		
The FBI Under Fire	04/11/97	328*
Government Secrecy	12/02/05	1005
Press Freedom	02/05/10	97
Privacy in Peril	11/17/06	961
Freedom of speech. ***See First Amendment***		
Freedom of the press. ***See First Amendment***		
Fuel. ***See Gasoline; Petroleum***		
Gambling		
American Indians	04/28/06	**361
Betting on Sports	10/28/16	889
Combating Addiction	02/09/07	121
Gambling Boom	03/18/94	241
Gambling in America	03/07/03	201
Gambling Under Attack	09/06/96	769
Native American Sovereignty	05/05/17	385
Native Americans	05/08/92	391*
Native Americans' Future	07/12/96	601
Gangs		
Community Prosecution	12/15/00	1016*
Declining Crime Rates	04/04/97	289
Discipline in Schools	02/15/08	145
Central American Gangs	01/30/15	97
Fighting Crime	02/08/08	121
Fighting Gangs	10/09/15	841
Gang Crisis	05/14/04	421
Gangs in the U.S.	07/16/10	581
Mexico's Drug War	12/12/08	1009
Preventing Juvenile Crime	03/15/96	217
School Violence	10/09/98	892*
Violence in Schools	09/11/92	797
Youth Gangs	10/11/91	753
Garbage. ***See Waste products; Landfills***		
Gasoline		
Alternative Energy	02/25/05	173
Auto Industry's Future	02/06/09	**105
Biofuels Boom	09/29/06	793
Lead Poisoning	06/19/92	536
Oil Diplomacy	01/24/03	49
The Politics of Energy	03/05/99	192*
SUV Debate	05/16/03	449
Transportation Policy	07/04/97	593*
Gays. ***See Homosexuals***		

	Date	Page
Gender equity		
Boys' Emotional Needs	06/18/99	521
Class Action Lawsuits	05/13/11	433
College Sports	08/26/94	759*
Debating Hip-Hop	06/15/07	529
Diversity in Hollywood	08/05/16	649
Education and Gender	06/03/94	481
Gender and Learning	05/20/05	445
Gender Equity in Sports	04/18/97	337
Gender Pay Gap	03/14/08	241
Girls' Rights	04/17/15	337
Future of the Catholic Church	06/07/13	497
Future of Feminism	04/14/06	313
Income Inequality	04/17/98	346*
Mothers' Movement	04/04/03	297
Saving Social Security	10/02/98	863*
Sexual Assault in the Military	08/09/13	693
Single-Sex Education	07/12/02	569
Treating Anxiety	02/08/02	100*
Understanding Mormonism	10/19/12	889
Video Games and Learning	02/12/16	145
Women and Work	07/26/13	645
Women in Leadership	09/23/16	769
Women in Politics	03/21/08	265
Women in the Military	11/13/09	957
Women's Health Issues	05/13/94	409
General Agreement on Tariffs and Trade (GATT)		
Farm Policy	12/02/94	1071*
U.S. Trade Policy	01/29/93	73
Generation X		
Feminism's Future	02/28/97	169
Low Voter Turnout	10/20/00	833
Mothers' Movement	04/04/03	302*
Online Dating	03/20/15	265
Overhauling Social Security	05/12/95	417
Religion in America	11/25/94	1033
Retirement Security	05/31/02	481
Genetics. *See also DNA analysis*		
Advances in Cancer Research	08/25/95	753
Alzheimer's Disease	05/15/98	441*
Biology and Behavior	04/03/98	289
Biotech Foods	03/30/01	249
Birth-Control Debate	06/24/05	565
Cancer Treatments	09/11/98	785
Cell Phone Safety	03/16/01	201
The Cloning Controversy	05/09/97	409
'Designer' Humans	05/18/01	425
Diabetes Epidemic	03/09/01	185
Drugmakers Under Siege	09/03/99	770*
Drug-Resistant Bacteria	06/04/99	473
Embryo Research	12/17/99	1065
Emerging Infectious Diseases	02/13/15	145
Famine in Africa	11/08/02	921
Fish Farming	07/27/07	625

	Date	Page
Food Safety Battle: Organic v. Biotech	09/04/98	761
Gay Rights	03/05/93	193
Gender and Learning	05/20/05	445
Genes and Health	01/21/11	49
Gene Therapy	10/18/91	777
Gene Therapy's Future	12/08/95	1089
Genetically Engineered Foods	08/05/94	673
Genetically Modified Food	08/31/12	717
Human Genome Research	05/12/00	401
Increase in Autism	06/13/03	**545
Intelligence Testing	07/30/93	649
Manipulating the Human Genome	06/19/15	529
Medical Breakthroughs	09/15/17	749
Obesity and Health	01/15/99	25
Organ Shortage	02/21/03	153
Patenting Human Genes	05/31/13	473
Privacy Under Attack	06/15/01	505
Prolonging Life	09/30/11	805*
Reproductive Ethics	04/08/94	289
Sports and Drugs	07/23/04	624*
Treating Alzheimer's	03/04/11	193
Treating Alzheimer's Disease	07/24/15	625
Treating Schizophrenia	12/05/14	1009
Vaccine Controversies	08/25/00	641
Vaccine Controversies	02/19/16	169
Genocide		
Stopping Genocide	08/27/04	685
The United Nations and Global Security	02/27/04	173
Geology		
Earthquake Research	12/16/94	1105
Geothermal energy		
Alternative Energy	07/10/92	587
Renewable Energy	11/07/97	961
Germany		
Apprenticeships	10/14/16	841
The Economics of Recycling	03/27/98	276*
Ethics of War	12/13/02	1013
European Unrest	01/09/15	25
Europe's New Right	02/12/93	121
Future of NATO	02/28/03	177
Future of the European Union	10/28/05	909
Holocaust Reparations	03/26/99	257
Sports and Drugs	07/23/04	**613
War Crimes	07/07/95	585
Year-Round Schools	05/17/96	440*
Youth Apprenticeships	10/23/92	917*
Gifted and talented children		
AB and IP Programs	03/03/06	193
Bilingual Education	08/13/93	702*
Educating Gifted Students	03/28/97	265
Grade Inflation	06/07/02	505
Intelligence Testing	07/30/93	654*

	Date	Page
Gingrich, Newt		
Campaign Finance Reform	02/09/96	135*
Glass ceiling. *See Discrimination; Sex discrimination*		
Globalization		
Aiding Africa	08/29/03	697
Apprenticeships	10/14/16	841
Auto Industry's Future	02/06/09	**105
Child Labor and Sweatshops	08/16/96	732*
Contingent Work Force	10/24/97	937
Corporate Social Responsibility	08/03/07	649
Cracking Down on Immigration	02/03/95	104*
Emerging India	04/19/02	329
European Monetary Union	11/27/98	1025
European Union's Future	12/16/16	1037
Expanding NATO	05/16/97	433
Exporting Jobs	02/20/04	149
Foreign Aid After Sept. 11	04/26/02	361
Future of Language	11/17/00	929
Future of the European Union	10/28/05	909
Globalization Backlash	09/28/01	761
Global Refugee Crisis	07/09/99	569
Human Rights	11/13/98	933*
Human Rights in China	07/25/08	601
International Monetary Fund	01/29/99	65
NFL Controversies	09/04/15	721
Oil Production in the 21st Century	08/07/98	678
Population and the Environment	07/17/98	601
Populism and Party Politics	09/09/16	721
Reassessing Foreign Aid	09/27/96	841
Rethinking NAFTA	06/07/96	481
Reviving Rural Economies	03/31/17	265
Rethinking Foreign Aid	04/14/17	313
Saving the Rain Forests	06/11/99	512*
Setting Environmental Priorities	05/21/99	432*
Transatlantic Tensions	07/13/01	533
Transnational Crime	08/29/14	697
Unions at a Crossroads	08/07/15	673
Universal Basic Income	09/08/17	725
Upward Mobility	04/29/05	369
U.S. Trade Policy	01/29/93	73
U.S. Trade Policy	09/13/13	765
Worker Safety	10/04/13	837
World Trade	06/09/00	497
Global warming. *See also Air pollution*		
Air Pollution and Climate Control	11/13/15	961
Air Pollution Conflict	11/14/03	965
Alternative Energy	07/10/92	573
Alternative Energy	02/25/05	173
Arctic Development	12/02/16	989
Bush and the Environment	10/25/02	865
Buying Green	02/29/08	193
Celebrity Advocacy	05/11/12	425
Climate Change	01/27/06	73
Climate Change	06/14/13	521

	Date	Page
Climate Change and National Security	09/22/17	773
Coal's Comeback	10/05/07	817
Coastal Development	02/22/13	181
Confronting Warming	01/09/09	1
Corporate Social Responsibility	08/03/07	649
Disappearing Species	11/30/07	985
Ecotourism	10/20/06	865
Endangered Species Act	06/03/05	**493
Energy and Climate	07/24/09	621
Energy and the Environment	03/03/00	161
Extreme Weather	09/09/11	733*
Future of the Arctic	09/20/13	789
Future of Recycling	12/14/07	1033
Global Warming Treaty	01/26/01	41
Global Warming Update	11/01/96	961
Global Water Shortages	12/15/95	1127*
Invasive Species	02/17/12	153
National Parks Under Pressure	10/06/06	817
Native American Sovereignty	05/05/17	385
The New Environmentalism	12/01/06	985
Nuclear Energy	03/10/06	217
Oil Diplomacy	01/24/03	63*
Ozone Depletion	04/03/92	294
The Politics of Energy	03/05/99	202*
Preparing for Disaster	08/02/13	669
Protecting the Oceans	10/17/14	865
Public-Works Projects	02/20/09	153
Reducing Your Carbon Footprint	12/05/08	985
Reforming the U.N.	06/24/16	553
Renewable Energy	11/07/97	974*
Rethinking Foreign Aid	04/14/17	313
Saving the Forests	09/20/91	681
Science and Politics	08/20/04	661
Setting Environmental Priorities	05/21/99	425
Socially Responsible Investing	08/29/08	673
Species Extinction	12/15/17	1041
Threatened Coastlines	02/07/92	97
Water Shortages	08/01/03	657*
Water Shortages	06/18/10	529
Will Nuclear Power Get Another Chance?	02/22/91	113
Gore, Al		
Electoral College	12/08/00	977
Reinventing Government	02/17/95	145
Setting Environmental Priorities	05/21/99	425
Voting Controversies	09/15/06	745
Great Britain		
Apprenticeships	10/14/16	841
Betting on Sports	10/28/16	889
The British Monarchy	03/08/96	193
DNA Databases	05/28/99	461*
European Union's Future	12/16/16	1037
Future of the European Union	10/28/05	909
Gun Control Standoff	12/19/97	1116*

	Date	Page
Middle East Tensions	10/27/06	**889
Northern Ireland Cease-Fire	09/15/95	801
Populism and Party Politics	09/09/16	721
Taiwan, China, and the U.S.	05/24/96	468*
U.S.-British Relations	01/30/98	73

Greenhouse effect. *See Global warming*

Greenspan, Alan
| The Federal Reserve | 09/01/00 | 673 |
| Social Security Reform | 09/24/04 | 781 |

Gulf War. *See Persian Gulf War*

Gun control. *See also Firearms*
| Gun Violence | 05/25/07 | 457 |
| Guns on Campus | 01/27/17 | 73 |

Gypsies. *See Roma*

Habeas corpus reform
Death Penalty Controversies	09/23/05	785
Death Penalty Debate	03/10/95	193
Death Penalty Update	01/08/99	1

Habitat for Humanity
| Affordable Housing | 02/09/01 | 103* |

Haiti
Economic Sanctions	10/28/94	937
Foreign Aid After Sept. 11	04/26/02	361
Foreign Policy and Public Opinion	07/15/94	601
Haiti's Dilemma	02/18/05	149
Illegal Immigration	04/24/92	361

Handguns. *See Firearms*

Handicapped. *See Disabled*

Hate crimes
'Alt-Right' Movement	03/17/17	241
Asian Americans	12/13/91	960
Bullying	02/04/05	101
Europe's New Right	02/12/93	121
Hate Crimes	01/08/93	1
New Military Culture	04/26/96	361
Race in America	07/11/03	593
Racial Conflict	01/08/16	25
Transgender Rights	12/11/15	1033

Hazing
Greek Life on Campus	11/20/15	985
Hazing	01/09/04	1
Preventing Hazing	02/08/13	133

Hawaii
| Marriage and Divorce | 05/10/96 | 420* |
| Native Americans' Future | 07/12/96 | 612* |

Hazardous substances. *See also Nuclear waste; Pesticides; Tobacco; Waste products*
Acid Rain: New Approach to Old Problem	03/08/91	129
Arctic Development	12/02/16	989
Asbestos Litigation	05/02/03	393
Blood Supply Safety	11/11/94	985

	Date	Page
Breast Cancer	06/27/97	560*
Cleaning Up Hazardous Wastes	08/23/96	745
Drug Safety	03/11/05	221
Electromagnetic Fields	04/26/91	237
Environmental Justice	06/19/98	529
Environmental Movement at 25	03/31/95	288*
Food Irradiation	06/12/92	505
Food Safety	06/04/93	481
Food Safety Battle: Organic v. Biotech	09/04/98	761
Garbage Crisis	03/20/92	241
Genetically Engineered Foods	08/05/94	673
The Greening of Eastern Europe	11/15/91	849
Indoor Air Pollution	10/27/95	945
Lead Poisoning	06/19/92	525
Nanotechnology	06/11/04	517
Ozone Depletion	04/03/92	289
Panama Canal	11/26/99	1031*
Pesticide Controversies	06/05/15	481
Policing the Borders	02/22/02	145
Protecting the Oceans	10/17/14	865
Regulating Toxic Chemicals	01/23/09	49
Regulating Toxic Chemicals	07/18/14	601
Science in the Courtroom	10/22/93	923*
Setting Environmental Priorities	05/21/99	425
Synthetic Biology	04/25/14	361
Tobacco Industry	12/10/04	**1025
Water Quality	02/11/94	121
Weapons of Mass Destruction	03/08/02	193

Head Start. *See Preschool education*

Health. *See Diseases and health problems; Food and nutrition; Medical care; Physical fitness*

Health-care reform. *See also Medical Care — costs control*
Abortion Debates	09/10/10	725
Abortion Debates	03/21/14	265
Alternative Medicine	09/06/13	741
Covering the Uninsured	06/14/02	521
Democrats' Future	10/29/10	893
Doctor Shortage	08/28/15	697
Drug Company Ethics	06/06/03	521
Fighting Cancer	01/22/16	73
First Ladies	06/14/96	505
Gridlock in Washington	04/30/10	385
Health-Care Reform	08/28/09	693*
Lies and Politics	02/18/11	145
Medicaid Reform	07/16/04	589
Medical Malpractice	02/14/03	129
Medicare Reform	08/22/03	673
The Obama Legacy	11/04/16	913
The Obama Presidency	01/30/09	73
Primary Care	03/17/95	217
Prison Health Care	01/05/07	1
Prisoners and Mental Illness	03/13/15	241
Prozac Controversy	08/19/94	736*
Regulating Pharmaceuticals	10/11/13	861

	Date	Page
Retirement Security	05/31/02	481
Rising Health Costs	04/07/06	289
Robotics and the Economy	09/25/15	793
States and Federalism	10/15/10	845
Tea Party Movement	03/19/10	**241*
Universal Coverage	03/30/07	265
Vaccine Controversies	02/19/16	169

Health insurance

	Date	Page
Abortion Debates	09/10/10	725
Abortion Debates	03/21/14	265
Advances in Cancer Research	08/25/95	770*
Aging Baby Boomers	10/19/07	865
Aging Population	07/15/11	577
Alternative Medicine	01/31/92	88
Alternative Medicine	09/06/13	741
Alzheimer's Disease	07/24/92	617
Baby Boomers at Midlife	07/31/98	657*
Birth-Control Debate	06/24/05	565
Breast Cancer	04/02/10	289
Cancer Treatments	09/11/98	794*
Caring for the Elderly	02/20/98	162*
Caring for Veterans	04/23/10	361
Covering the Uninsured	06/14/02	521
Domestic Partners	09/04/92	761
Drug Company Ethics	06/06/03	521
Eating Disorders	02/10/06	**121
Emergency Medicine	01/05/96	1
Employee Benefits	02/04/00	65
Fighting Superbugs	08/24/07	673
Health-Care Reform	08/28/09	693*
Insurance Fraud	10/11/96	889
Managed Care	04/12/96	313
Managing Managed Care	04/16/99	305
Medicaid Reform	07/16/04	589
Medical Malpractice	02/14/03	129
Medicare Reform	08/22/03	673
Mental Health Insurance	03/29/02	265
Mental Health Policy	09/12/97	793
Mental Illness	08/06/93	673
Mental Illness Medication Debate	02/06/04	101
Middle-Class Squeeze	03/06/09	201
The Obama Legacy	11/04/16	913
The Obama Presidency	01/30/09	73
Organ Shortage	02/21/03	153
Patients' Rights	02/06/98	97
Prescription Drug Costs	05/20/16	457
Prescription Drug Prices	07/17/92	597
Prison Health Care	01/05/07	1
Reproductive Ethics	04/08/94	289
Reproductive Ethics	05/15/09	449
Rethinking Retirement	06/19/09	549
Retiree Health Benefits	12/06/91	921
Retirement Security	05/31/02	481
Reviving Rural Economies	03/31/17	265

	Date	Page
Rising Health Costs	04/07/06	289
Treating Anxiety	02/08/02	97
Treating Alzheimer's Disease	07/24/15	625
Treating Depression	06/26/09	573
Universal Coverage	03/30/07	265
Women and AIDS	12/25/92	1138
Wounded Veterans	08/31/07	697
Youth Suicide	02/13/04	125

Health maintenance organizations

	Date	Page
Covering the Uninsured	06/14/02	521
Doctor Shortage	08/28/15	697
Drugmakers Under Siege	09/03/99	753
Emergency Medicine	01/05/96	1
Health-Care Reform	08/28/09	693*
Managed Care	04/12/96	313
Managing Managed Care	04/16/99	305
Patients' Rights	02/06/98	97
Primary Care	03/17/95	217
Universal Coverage	03/30/07	265

Heart disease

	Date	Page
Breast Cancer	06/27/97	558*
Obesity Epidemic	01/31/03	73
Organ Shortage	02/21/03	153
Organ Transplants	08/11/95	705
Physical Fitness	11/06/92	967*
Tobacco Industry	12/10/04	**1025
Women's Health Issues	05/13/94	409

High-speed rail. *See Railroads*

Highways and roads

	Date	Page
Aggressive Driving	07/25/97	649
Aging Infrastructure	09/28/07	**793
Auto Safety	10/26/01	873
Distracted Driving	05/04/12	401
Future of Amtrak	10/18/02	841
Future of Cars	07/25/14	625
Highway Safety	07/14/95	609
Mass Transit Boom	01/18/08	49
National Forests	10/16/98	921*
Privatization	11/13/92	992
Privatizing Government Services	08/09/96	713*
Privatizing Government Services	12/08/17	1017
Public-Works Projects	02/20/09	153
Reducing Traffic Deaths	02/17/17	145
Smart Growth	05/28/04	469
SUV Debate	05/16/03	449
Teen Driving	01/07/05	1
Traffic Congestion	05/06/94	385
Traffic Congestion	08/27/99	729
Transportation Policy	07/04/97	577
Truck Safety	03/12/99	209

Hispanics

	Date	Page
Affirmative Action	09/21/01	737
Affirmative Action	10/17/08	**841

	Date	Page
Alcohol Advertising	03/14/97	221*
America's Border Fence	09/19/08	745
Bilingual Education vs. English Immersion	12/11/09	1029
Central American Gangs	01/30/15	97
Census Controversey	05/14/10	433
Changing U.S. Electorate	05/30/08	**457
Cuba in Crisis	11/29/91	908*
Debate over Bilingualism	01/19/96	49
Debate Over Immigration	07/14/00	580*
Democrats' Future	10/29/10	893
Diversity in the Workplace	10/10/97	889
Domestic Poverty	09/07/07	**721
Dropout Rate	06/13/14	505
Electing Minorities	08/12/94	697
Evaluating Head Start	08/26/05	685
Fighting Crime	02/08/08	121
Hate Groups	05/08/09	421
Hispanic Americans	10/30/92	929
Hispanic-Americans' New Clout	09/18/98	809
Illegal Immigration	05/06/05	393
Immigrant Detention	10/23/15	889
Immigration Debate	02/01/08	**97
Latinos' Future	10/17/03	869
Latino Voters	04/03/15	289
Mortgage Crisis	11/02/07	**913
No Child Left Behind	05/27/05	469
Police Misconduct	04/06/12	301
Protestants Today	12/07/07	1009
Race and Politics	07/18/08	577
Race in America	07/11/03	593
Racial Diversity in Public Schools	09/14/07	**745
Racial Tensions in Schools	01/07/94	1
Redistricting Disputes	03/12/04	221
Redistricting: Drawing Power with a Map	02/15/91	97
Restoring Ties With Cuba	06/12/15	505
Rethinking School Integration	10/18/96	918*
Reviving Rural Economies	03/31/17	265
School Desegregation	04/23/04	345
School Vouchers Showdown	02/15/02	121
Sexually Transmitted Diseases	12/03/04	997
Student Aid	01/25/08	73
Trump Presidency	01/06/17	1
U.S.-Mexico Relations	09/02/16	697
Worker Retraining	01/21/94	62*
Youth Unemployment	03/14/14	241

History — Study and teaching

	Date	Page
Archaeology Today	05/24/02	457
Black Colleges	12/12/03	1056*
Conspiracy Theories	10/23/09	885
Historic Preservation	10/07/94	865
School Censorship	02/19/93	159*

	Date	Page
Searching for Jesus	12/11/98	1073
Teaching History	09/29/95	849

HIV infection. *See AIDS disease*

HMOs. *See Health maintenance organizations*

Holistic medicine

	Date	Page
Alternative Medicine	09/06/13	741
Alternative Medicine's Next Phase	02/14/97	133*
Drug-Resistant Bacteria	06/04/99	489*
Prayer and Healing	01/14/05	25

Hollywood. *See Movies*

Holocaust

	Date	Page
Anti-Semitism	05/12/17	409
Ethics of War	12/13/02	1013
Holocaust Reparations	03/26/99	257
Reparations Movement	06/22/01	529
Stopping Genocide	08/27/04	685

Home Schooling

	Date	Page
Home Schooling	09/09/94	769
Home Schooling	03/07/14	217
Home Schooling Debate	01/17/03	25
Parental Rights	10/25/96	942

Homeland Security

	Date	Page
Assessing the Threat From al Qaeda	06/27/14	553
Chemical and Biological Weapons	12/13/13	1053
Civil Liberties Debates	10/24/03	893
Climate Change and National Security	09/22/17	773
Confronting Iraq	10/04/02	793
Cyber-Crime	04/12/02	305
Cybersecurity	09/26/03	797
Cybersecurity	02/26/10	169
Cyberwarfare Threat	10/06/17	821
Energy Security	02/01/02	73
Exporting Democracy	04/01/05	269
Far-Right Extremism	09/18/15	769
Future of the Airline Industry	06/21/02	545
Government Surveillance	08/30/13	717
Homeland Security	09/12/03	749
Homeland Security	02/13/09	129
Illegal Immigration	05/06/05	393
Intelligence Reform	05/29/15	457
Modernizing the Nuclear Arsenal	07/29/16	625
New Defense Priorities	09/13/02	721
Policing the Borders	02/22/02	145
Port Security	04/21/06	337
Preparing for Disaster	08/02/13	669
Presidential Power	11/15/02	945
Presidential Power	02/24/06	169
Privacy in Peril	11/17/06	961
Protecting the Power Grid	11/11/16	941
Remembering 9/11	09/02/11	701*
Smallpox Threat	02/07/03	105
Torture	04/18/03	345

	Date	Page
War on Terrorism	10/12/01	817
Weapons of Mass Destruction	03/08/02	193

Homeless persons
Charitable Giving	11/12/93	996*
Declining Crime Rates	04/04/97	289
Ending Homelessness	06/18/04	541
Hard Times for Libraries	06/26/92	562
Helping the Homeless	01/26/96	73
The Homeless	08/07/92	665
Homeless Students	04/05/13	305
Housing the Homeless	12/18/09	1053
Housing the Homeless	10/10/14	841
Treatment of Veterans	11/19/04	973

Homeopathic medicine. *See Alternative medicine*

Homosexuals
Adoption Controversies	09/10/99	782*
Biology and Behavior	04/03/98	298*
Bullying	02/04/05	101
Catholic Church in the U.S.	09/08/95	788*
Diversity in the Workplace	10/10/97	900*
Domestic Partners	09/04/92	761
Employee Benefits	02/04/00	72*
Future of the Catholic Church	01/19/07	49
Future of the Catholic Church	06/07/13	497
Gay Marriage	09/05/03	721
Gay Marriage	03/15/13	257
Gay Marriage Showdowns	09/26/08	**769
Gay Rights	03/05/93	193
Gay Rights Update	04/14/00	305
Gays in the Military	09/18/09	**765
Hate Crimes	01/08/93	1
Homeless Students	04/05/13	305
Human Rights Issues	10/30/09	909
Marriage and Divorce	05/10/96	420*
New Military Culture	04/26/96	361
Politicians and Privacy	04/17/92	351*
Religion and Law	11/07/14	937
Religious Freedom	01/01/16	1
Revitalizing the Cities	10/13/95	908*
School Censorship	02/19/93	145
Sexual Abuse and the Clergy	05/03/02	393
Sexually Transmitted Diseases	12/03/04	997
Teaching Values	06/21/96	529
Transgender Issues	05/05/06	385
Transgender Rights	12/11/15	1033
Women and AIDS	12/25/92	1121
Women and Sports	03/06/92	199
Women in the Military	09/25/92	850*

Hong Kong
China After Deng	06/13/97	510*
Taiwan, China, and the U.S.	05/24/96	468*
U.S.-China Trade	04/15/94	327*

	Date	Page

Hormone-replacement therapy
Baby Boomers at Midlife	07/31/98	660*
Breast Cancer	06/27/97	553
Women's Health	11/07/03	941
Women's Health Issues	05/13/94	423*

Hospices
Assisted Suicide Controversy	05/05/95	400*
Caring for the Dying	09/05/97	769

Hospitals
Caring for Veterans	04/23/10	361
Covering the Uninsured	06/14/02	521
Doctor Shortage	08/28/15	697
Drug-Resistant Bacteria	06/04/99	473
Emergency Medicine	01/05/96	1
Emerging Infectious Diseases	02/13/15	145
Fighting SARS	06/20/03	569
Fighting Superbugs	08/24/07	673
Hospitals' Financial Woes	08/13/99	689
Managing Managed Care	04/16/99	305
Medical Malpractice	02/14/03	129
Medicare Reform	08/22/03	673
Organ Shortage	02/21/03	153
Pandemic Threat	06/02/17	457
Patient Safety	02/10/12	125
Prayer and Healing	01/14/05	25
Right to Die	05/13/05	421
Treatment of Veterans	11/19/04	973
Wounded Veterans	08/31/07	697

Housing. *See also Public housing*
Affordable Housing	02/09/01	89
Blighted Cities	11/12/10	941*
Buying Green	02/29/08	193
Consumer Debt	03/02/07	193
Downward Mobility	07/23/93	643*
Ending Homelessness	06/18/04	541
Financial Bailout	10/24/08	**865
Financial Crisis	05/09/08	409
Financial Industry Overhaul	07/30/10	629
Future of Homeownership	12/14/12	1061
Gentrification	02/20/15	169
Helping the Homeless	01/26/96	73
The Homeless	08/07/92	665
Homeless Students	04/05/13	305
Housing Discrimination	02/24/95	169
Housing Discrimination	11/06/15	937
Housing the Homeless	12/18/09	1053
Housing the Homeless	10/10/14	841
Implementing the Disabilities Act	12/20/96	1117*
Indoor Air Pollution	10/27/95	945
Lead Poisoning	06/19/92	525
Middle-Class Squeeze	03/06/09	201
Mortgage Crisis	11/02/07	**913
The Obama Presidency	01/30/09	73

	Date	Page
Racial Tensions in Schools	01/07/94	1
Reducing Your Carbon Footprint	12/05/08	985
Regulating Credit Cards	10/10/08	817*
Smart Growth	05/28/04	469
Urban Sprawl in the West	10/03/97	865

Human Genome Project. *See Genetics*

Human rights

Castro's Next Move	12/12/97	1081
Celebrity Advocacy	05/11/12	425
China After Deng	06/13/97	505
China and the South China Sea	01/20/17	49
Closing Guantanamo	09/30/16	793
Decriminalizing Prostitution	04/15/16	337
Democracy in Asia	07/24/98	625
Democracy in Eastern Europe	10/08/99	876*
Emerging China	11/11/05	957
Ethics of War	12/13/02	1013
European Migration Crisis	07/31/15	649
Free Speech on Campus	05/08/15	409
Girls' Rights	04/17/15	337
Global Population Growth	01/16/15	49
Human Rights	11/13/98	977
Human Rights in China	07/25/08	601
Human Rights Issues	10/30/09	909
Human Trafficking and Slavery	03/26/04	273
Immigrant Detention	10/23/15	889
International Law	12/17/04	1049
North Korea Showdown	05/19/17	433
Racial Conflict	01/08/16	25
Religious Persecution	11/21/97	1009
Religious Repression	11/01/13	933
Restoring Ties With Cuba	06/12/15	505
Resurgent Russia	02/07/14	121
Rethinking Foreign Aid	04/14/17	313
Stopping Genocide	08/27/04	685
Terrorism in Africa	07/10/15	577
Torture	04/18/03	345
Transgender Rights	12/11/15	1033
Transnational Crime	08/29/14	697
Treatment of Detainees	08/25/06	673
Unrest in Turkey	01/29/16	97
U.S.-China Relations	05/07/10	**409
U.S.-China Trade	04/15/94	313
U.S. Global Engagement	05/16/14	433
U.S.-Russia Relations	01/13/17	25
War Crimes	07/07/95	585
Women and Human Rights	04/30/99	353

Hungary

Expanding NATO	05/16/97	433
The Greening of Eastern Europe	11/15/91	849
Peace Corps' Challenges in the 1990s	01/25/91	49

Hunger

Celebrity Advocacy	05/11/12	425
Famine in Africa	11/08/02	921

	Date	Page
Food Policy Debates	10/03/14	817
Foreign Aid and National Security	06/17/11	529
Housing the Homeless	10/10/14	841
Hunger in America	12/22/00	1033
Hunger in America	07/07/17	557
World Hunger	10/25/91	801

Hunting

Endangered Species Act	06/03/05	**493
Hunting Controversy	01/24/92	49

Hurricanes and storms

Aging Infrastructure	09/28/07	**793
Coastal Development	08/21/98	721
Coastal Development	02/22/13	181
Disaster Response	10/15/93	889
Extreme Weather	09/09/11	733*
Preparing for Disaster	08/02/13	669
Rebuilding New Orleans	02/03/06	97
Threatened Coastlines	02/07/92	97
Youth Volunteerism	01/27/12	77

Hydroelectric power

Renewable Energy	11/07/97	961
Setting Environmental Priorities	05/21/99	438*

Hypnosis

Recovered-Memory Debate	07/05/96	577
Treating Anxiety	02/08/02	97

Illegal aliens. *See Immigration and emigration*

Immigration and emigration

Adoption Controversies	09/10/99	787*
America's Border Fence	09/19/08	745
Asian Americans	12/13/91	945
Assisting Refugees	02/07/97	110*
Bilingual Education	08/13/93	697
Border Security	09/27/13	813
Castro's Next Move	12/12/97	1093*
Catholic Church in the U.S.	09/08/95	785*
Census Controversey	05/14/10	433
Central American Gangs	01/30/15	97
Changing Demographics	11/16/12	989
Civil Liberties in Wartime	12/14/01	1029*
Cracking Down on Immigration	02/03/95	97
Cuba in Crisis	11/29/91	908*
Cuba's Future	07/20/07	601
Debate Over Bilingualism	01/19/96	49
Debate Over Immigration	07/14/00	569
Declining Birthrates	11/21/08	961
Drone Warfare	08/06/10	653
European Migration Crisis	07/31/15	649
Europe's New Right	02/12/93	121
European Union's Future	12/16/16	1037
Exporting Jobs	02/20/04	149
Fighting Gangs	10/09/15	841
Gangs in the U.S.	07/16/10	581
Gay Marriage	03/15/13	257

	Date	Page
Global Population Growth	01/16/15	49
Global Refugee Crisis	07/09/99	569
Haiti's Dilemma	02/18/05	149
High-Tech Labor Shortage	04/24/98	361
Hispanic Americans	10/30/92	929
Hispanic-Americans' New Clout	09/18/98	809
Homeland Security	09/12/03	749
Homeland Security	02/13/09	129
Human Trafficking and Slavery	03/26/04	273
Illegal Immigration	04/24/92	361
Illegal Immigration	05/06/05	393
Immigrant Detention	10/23/15	889
Immigrants and the Economy	02/24/17	169
Immigration Conflict	03/09/12	229
Immigration Debate	02/01/08	**97
Immigration Reform	09/24/93	841
Insurance Fraud	10/11/96	893*
Latinos' Future	10/17/03	869
Latino Voters	04/03/15	289
Mexico's Emergence	07/19/91	499*
Mexico's Future	09/19/97	832*
The New Immigrants	01/24/97	49
The Obama Legacy	11/04/16	913
Policing the Borders	02/22/02	154*
Population and the Environment	07/17/98	609*
Population Growth	07/16/93	601
Presidential Power	03/06/15	217
Race in America	07/11/03	593
Real ID	05/04/07	385
Re-examining 9/11	06/04/04	493
Reviving Rural Economies	03/31/17	265
Science in America	01/11/08	25
States and Federalism	10/15/10	845
Terrorism in Africa	07/10/15	577
Trump Presidency	01/06/17	1
Underground Economy	03/04/94	207*
U.S.-Mexico Relations	11/09/01	921
U.S.-Mexico Relations	09/02/16	697
War on Terrorism	10/12/01	817
Welfare, Work and the States	12/06/96	1062*
The Working Poor	11/03/95	975*

Impeachment

The Federal Judiciary	03/13/98	234*
Partisan Politics	03/19/99	250*
Presidential Power	03/06/15	217

Imports. *See International trade*

Incest. *See Sex crimes*

Income. *See Wages and salaries*

Income tax

Age Discrimination	08/01/97	684*
Calculating the Costs of the Gulf War	03/15/91	153*
Governing Washington, D.C.	11/22/96	1049*
Income Inequality	04/17/98	345*

	Date	Page
Income Inequality	12/03/10	989
IRS Reform	01/16/98	25
Marriage and Divorce	05/10/96	414*
National Debt	09/01/17	701
Social Security: The Search for Fairness	04/05/91	189
Stimulating the Economy	01/10/03	1
Tax Reform	03/22/96	241
Underground Economy	03/04/94	193
Wealth and Inequality	04/18/14	337
The Working Poor	11/03/95	969

Independent counsels

Independent Counsels	02/21/97	145
Independent Counsels Re-examined	05/07/99	377
Partisan Politics	03/19/99	233
Political Scandals	05/27/94	474*
Presidential Power	03/06/15	217

Independent political candidates

The Partisan Divide	04/30/04	389*
Partisan Politics	03/19/99	242*
Third-Party Prospects	12/22/95	1137

India

Coal's Comeback	10/05/07	817
Democracy in Asia	07/24/98	625
Emerging India	04/19/02	329
Exporting Jobs	02/20/04	149
Human Trafficking and Slavery	03/26/04	273
Nuclear Proliferation	06/05/92	481
Nuclear Proliferation and Terrorism	04/02/04	297
Oil Jitters	01/04/08	**1
Weapons of Mass Destruction	03/08/02	193

Individual retirement accounts (IRAs)

IRS Reform	01/16/98	38*
Overhauling Social Security	05/12/95	417
Paying for Retirement	11/05/93	961
Saving Social Security	10/02/98	857
Social Security: The Search for Fairness	04/05/91	201*

Indonesia

Democracy in Asia	07/24/98	625

Industry. *See Business and industry*

Infant mortality

Infant Mortality	07/31/92	641
Native Americans	05/08/92	399

Infertility

The Cloning Controversy	05/09/97	409
Embryo Research	12/17/99	1065
Reproductive Ethics	04/08/94	302*

Inflation

Affordable Housing	02/09/01	89
Deflation Fears	02/13/98	121
The Federal Reserve	09/01/00	673

Insomnia. *See Sleep disorders*

	Date	Page
Insurance. *See also Health insurance*		
Caring for the Elderly	10/13/06	841
Coastal Development	08/21/98	721
Coastal Development	02/22/13	181
Disaster Response	10/15/93	889
Farm Policy	08/10/12	693
Holocaust Reparations	03/26/99	257
Insurance Fraud	10/11/96	889
Medical Malpractice	02/14/03	129
Medicare Reform	08/22/03	673
Reproductive Ethics	05/15/09	449
Too Many Lawsuits?	05/22/92	440
Universal Coverage	03/30/07	265
Intellectual property rights		
Clashing over Copyright	11/08/96	985
Cyber-Crime	04/12/02	305
Future of the Music Industry	11/21/03	989
Software Piracy	05/21/93	433
U.S. Trade Policy	01/29/93	84*
Intelligence service		
Border Security	09/27/13	813
Cybersecurity	09/26/03	797
Gay Rights	03/05/93	202*
Government Surveillance	08/30/13	717
Homeland Security	09/12/03	749
Intelligence Reform	05/29/15	457
Intelligence Reforms	01/25/02	49
The New CIA	12/11/92	1073
Policing the Borders	02/22/02	145
Presidential Power	02/24/06	169
Re-examining 9/11	06/04/04	493
Reforming the CIA	02/02/96	97
Torture	04/18/03	345
Weapons of Mass Destruction	03/08/02	193
Whistleblowers	01/31/14	97
Intelligence tests		
Artificial Intelligence	04/22/11	361
Intelligence Testing	07/30/93	649
Intelligent design		
Intelligent Design	07/29/05	637
Science and Religion	03/22/13	281
Internal Revenue Service, U.S.		
IRS Reform	01/16/98	25
Nonprofit Groups and Partisan Politics	11/14/14	961
Regulating Nonprofits	12/26/97	1129
Underground Economy	03/04/94	193
International Atomic Energy Agency (IAEA)		
The United Nations and		
Global Security	02/27/04	173
U.S.-Iran Relations	03/04/16	217
International Baccalaureate (IB)		
AB and IP Programs	03/03/06	193
Racial Diversity in Public Schools	09/14/07	**745

	Date	Page
International courts		
Ethics of War	12/13/02	1025*
Government Secrecy	02/11/11	121
Human Rights	11/13/98	933*
International Law	12/17/04	1049
Stopping Genocide	08/27/04	685
Terrorism in Africa	07/10/15	577
Torture	04/18/03	345
U.S. Global Engagement	05/16/14	433
War Crimes	07/07/95	585
International Monetary Fund		
Deflation Fears	02/13/98	127*
Famine in Africa	11/08/02	937*
Globalization Backlash	09/28/01	761
International Monetary Fund	01/29/99	65
Trouble in South America	03/14/03	225
International relations. *See also Military policy; Treaties and international agreements*		
Adoption Controversies	09/10/99	787*
America's Border Fence	09/19/08	745
Apprenticeships	10/14/16	841
Arctic Development	12/02/16	989
Assessing the Threat From al Qaeda	06/27/14	553
Assisting Refugees	02/07/97	97
Border Security	09/27/13	813
Central American Gangs	01/30/15	97
China and the South China Sea	01/20/17	49
China Today	04/04/14	289
Closing Guantanamo	09/30/16	793
Confronting Iraq	10/04/02	793
Death Penalty Update	01/08/99	14*
Defeating the Islamic State	04/01/16	289
Democracy in Eastern Europe	10/08/99	865
Democrats in Congress	06/08/07	505
Emerging Infectious Diseases	02/13/15	145
Ethics of War	12/13/02	1013
Euro Crisis	10/05/12	841
Europe 1992	06/28/91	417
European Migration Crisis	07/31/15	649
European Monetary Union	11/27/98	1025
European Union's Future	12/16/16	1037
European Unrest	01/09/15	25
Expanding NATO	05/16/97	433
Exporting Democracy	04/01/05	269
Famine in Africa	11/08/02	921
Future of the Arctic	09/20/13	789
Future of NATO	02/28/03	177
Girls' Rights	04/17/15	337
Global AIDS Crisis	10/13/00	809
Global Population Growth	01/16/15	49
Global Refugee Crisis	07/09/99	569
Global Warming Update	11/01/96	961
Global Water Shortages	12/15/95	1113
Government Secrecy	02/11/11	121

	Date	Page
Government Surveillance	08/30/13	717
Haiti's Dilemma	02/18/05	149
Hating America	11/23/01	969
Human Rights	11/13/98	977
Intelligence Reform	05/29/15	457
International Law	12/17/04	1049
International Monetary Fund	01/29/99	65
Israel at 50	03/06/98	193
Mexico's Drug War	12/12/08	1009
Mexico's Future	10/26/12	913
Middle East Conflict	04/06/01	273
Middle East Peace	01/21/05	53
Modernizing the Nuclear Arsenal	07/29/16	625
NATO's Changing Role	08/21/92	713
New Space Race	08/04/17	653
North Korean Crisis	04/11/03	321
The Obama Presidency	01/30/09	73
Oil Jitters	01/04/08	**1
Peace Corps Challenges	01/11/13	29
Populism and Party Politics	09/09/16	721
Privacy and the Internet	12/04/15	1009
Privatizing the Military	07/13/12	597
Prospects for Mideast Peace	08/30/02	673
Race in America	07/11/03	593
Reforming the U.N.	06/24/16	553
Resurgent Russia	02/07/14	121
Rise in Counterinsurgency	09/05/08	697
Terrorism in Africa	07/10/15	577
Transnational Crime	08/29/14	697
Trump Presidency	01/06/17	1
United Nations at 50	08/18/95	729
Universal Basic Income	09/08/17	725
Unrest in the Arab World	02/01/13	105
Unrest in Turkey	01/29/16	97
U.S.-China Relations	05/07/10	**409
U.S.-Europe Relations	03/23/12	277
U.S.-Iran Relations	03/04/16	217
U.S.-Mexico Relations	09/02/16	697
U.S.-Pakistan Relations	08/05/11	653*
U.S.-Russia Relations	01/13/17	25
U.S. Trade Policy	09/13/13	765
War Crimes	07/07/95	585
Weapons of Mass Destruction	03/08/02	193
Whistleblowers	01/31/14	97

International relations — Issues and problems

	Date	Page
Cyberwarfare Threat	10/06/17	821
The Iraq War: 10 Years Later	03/01/13	205
North Korea Showdown	05/19/17	433
Stolen Antiquities	11/10/17	945
U.S.-Iran Relations	03/04/16	217
U.S.-Mexico Relations	09/02/16	697

International relations — U.S. foreign policy

	Date	Page
Aid to Russia	03/12/93	217
Aiding Africa	08/29/03	697

	Date	Page
Air Pollution Conflict	11/14/03	965
America at War	07/23/10	**605
Calculating the Costs of the Gulf War	03/15/91	145
Castro's Next Move	12/12/97	1081
Change in Latin America	07/21/06	601
China After Deng	06/13/97	505
China Today	08/04/00	625
Combating Terrorism	07/21/95	633
Confronting Iraq	10/04/02	793
Cuba in Crisis	11/29/91	897
Cuba's Future	07/20/07	601
Defense Priorities	07/30/99	641
Democracies Under Stress	10/20/17	869
Democracy in Africa	03/24/95	258*
Democracy in Asia	07/24/98	625
Democracy in Eastern Europe	10/08/99	872*
Democracy in the Arab World	01/30/04	73
Democrats in Congress	06/08/07	505
Drone Warfare	08/06/10	653
Economic Sanctions	10/28/94	937
Expanding NATO	05/16/97	433
Exporting Democracy	04/01/05	269
First Ladies	06/14/96	508*
Foreign Aid and National Security	06/17/11	529
Foreign Aid After Sept. 11	04/26/02	361
Foreign Policy and Public Opinion	07/15/94	601
Foreign Policy Burden	08/20/93	721
Free Speech at Risk	04/26/13	377
Future of Korea	05/19/00	425
Future of NATO	02/28/03	177
The Future of U.S.-Russia Relations	01/18/02	25
Government Secrecy	02/11/11	121
Haiti's Dilemma	02/18/05	149
Immigrant Detention	10/23/15	889
International Law	12/17/04	1049
The Iraq War: 10 Years Later	03/01/13	205
Israel at 50	03/06/98	193
Israeli-Palestinian Conflict	06/21/13	545
Japan in Crisis	07/26/02	593
Mexico's Emergence	07/19/91	489
Mexico's Future	09/19/97	817
Middle East Peace	01/21/05	53
Middle East Tensions	10/27/06	**889
Military Readiness	11/03/17	917
The New CIA	12/11/92	1073
New Era in Asia	02/14/92	121
New Strategy in Iraq	02/23/07	169
North Korean Crisis	04/11/03	337*
Northern Ireland Cease-Fire	09/15/95	801
Nuclear Proliferation and Terrorism	04/02/04	297
The Obama Legacy	11/04/16	913
Oil Diplomacy	01/24/03	49
Oil Production in the 21st Century	08/07/98	678*
The Palestinians	08/30/91	623

	Date	Page
Panama Canal	11/26/99	1017
Peace Corps' Challenges in the 1990s	01/25/91	49
Policing the Borders	02/22/02	145
The Politics of Energy	03/05/99	199*
Presidential Power	11/15/02	945
Prospects for Mideast Peace	08/30/02	673
Quebec Sovereignty	10/06/95	873
Reassessing Foreign Aid	09/27/96	841
Rebuilding Iraq	07/11/03	625
Reform in Iran	12/18/98	1097
Reforming the CIA	02/02/96	97
Religious Persecution	11/21/97	1009
Resurgent Russia	02/07/14	121
Rethinking Foreign Aid	04/14/17	313
Rethinking Foreign Policy	02/02/07	97
Rise in Counterinsurgency	09/05/08	697
Russia and the Former Soviet		
Republics	06/17/05	541
Russia's Political Future	05/03/96	385
South Africa's Future	01/14/94	39*
Soviet Republics Rebel	07/12/91	465
Stopping Genocide	08/27/04	685
Taiwan, China, and the U.S.	05/24/96	457
Torture	04/18/03	345
Treatment of Detainees	08/25/06	673
Trouble in South America	03/14/03	225
Understanding Islam	11/03/06	913
United Nations at 50	08/18/95	729
Unrest in the Arab World	02/01/13	105
U.S.-British Relations	01/30/98	73
U.S.-British Relations	11/05/10	917*
U.S.-China Relations	05/07/10	**409
U.S.-China Trade	04/15/94	313
U.S. Global Engagement	05/16/14	433
U.S.-Iran Relations	03/04/16	217
U.S.-Pakistan Relations	08/05/11	653*
U.S. Policy in Asia	11/27/92	1025
U.S. Policy on Iran	11/16/07	961
U.S.-Russian Relations	05/22/98	457
U.S.-Vietnam Relations	12/03/93	1057
War in Iraq	10/21/05	881
Weapons of Mass Destruction	03/08/02	193
Women and Human Rights	04/30/99	353

International trade — Issues and problems

	Date	Page
Aiding Africa	08/29/03	697
Asbestos Litigation	05/02/03	409*
Child Labor and Sweatshops	08/16/96	721
China After Deng	06/13/97	521*
China Today	04/04/14	289
Cuba's Future	07/20/07	601
The Consumer Culture	11/19/99	1006*
Deflation Fears	02/13/98	121
Economic Sanctions	10/28/94	937

	Date	Page
Emerging China	11/11/05	957
Endangered Species Act	10/01/99	856*
Fair Trade Labeling	05/18/07	433
Food Safety	11/01/02	897
Foreign Aid After Sept. 11	04/26/02	361
Foreign Policy Burden	08/20/93	721
Global Food Crisis	06/27/08	553
Human Rights in China	07/25/08	601
Identity Theft	06/10/05	517
International Law	12/17/04	1049
Mexico's Future	10/26/12	913
The New Corporate Philanthropy	02/27/98	182*
New Era in Asia	02/14/92	138*
The Obama Legacy	11/04/16	913
Port Security	04/21/06	337
Recession's Regional Impact	02/01/91	65
Reforming the CIA	02/02/96	97
Religious Persecution	11/21/97	1025*
Rethinking NAFTA	06/07/96	481
Stolen Antiquities	11/10/17	945
Trouble in South America	03/14/03	225
Troubled Brazil	04/07/17	289
Truck Safety	03/12/99	222*
U.S.-Iran Relations	03/04/16	217
U.S. Trade Policy	01/29/93	73
Worker Safety	10/04/13	837
World Trade	06/09/00	497

International trade — Products and services

	Date	Page
Airline Industry Problems	09/24/99	836*
Airline Safety	10/08/93	865
Arms Sales	12/09/94	1081
Cuba's Future	07/20/07	601
Emerging India	04/19/02	329
Exporting Jobs	02/20/04	149
Fair Trade Labeling	05/18/07	433
Farm Policy	12/02/94	1057
Fast-Food Shake-Up	11/08/91	839
Food Safety	11/01/02	897
Food Safety	12/17/10	1037
Nuclear Proliferation	06/05/92	481
Oil Imports	08/23/91	585
Oil Production in the 21st Century	08/07/98	673
Oil Spills	01/17/92	25
The Politics of Energy	03/05/99	185
Prostitution	06/11/93	516*
Protecting Endangered Species	04/19/96	348*
Regulating Pesticides	01/28/94	73
Regulating Tobacco	09/30/94	847*
Reviving Manufacturing	07/22/11	601
Software Piracy	05/21/93	433
U.S. Auto Industry	10/16/92	881
U.S.-British Relations	11/05/10	917*
U.S. Trade Policy	09/13/13	765

	Date	Page
Internet. *See also Computers*		
Adoption Controversies	09/10/99	790*
Alcohol Advertising	03/14/97	234*
'Alt-Right' Movement	03/17/17	241
Big Data and Privacy	10/25/13	909
Blog Explosion	06/09/06	**505
Broadcast Indecency	04/16/04	326*
Cameras in the Courtroom	01/14/11	25
Campaign Finance Reform	03/31/00	269*
Cheating in Schools	09/22/00	754*
Civil Liberties in Wartime	12/14/01	1017
Clashing over Copyright	11/08/96	985
Combat Journalism	04/12/13	329
Combating Plagiarism	09/19/03	773
Computer Hacking	09/16/11	757*
Computers and Medicine	10/27/00	857
Controlling the Internet	05/12/06	409
Copyright and the Internet	09/29/00	769
Criminal Records and Employment	04/20/12	349
Cyberbullying	05/02/08	385
Cyber-Crime	04/12/02	305
Cyberpolitics	09/17/04	757
Cybersecurity	09/26/03	797
Cybersecurity	02/26/10	169
Cyber-Predators	03/01/02	169
Cyber Socializing	07/28/06	625
Cyberwarfare Threat	10/06/17	821
The Dark Web	01/15/16	49
Digital Commerce	02/05/99	89
Digital Currency	09/26/14	793
Digital Education	12/02/11	1001
Distance Learning	12/07/01	993
The Digital Divide	01/28/00	41
Digital Journalism	05/30/14	457
Drugmakers Under Siege	09/03/99	762*
Energy and the Environment	03/03/00	173*
Examining Forensics	07/17/09	597
Free-Press Disputes	04/08/05	304*
Free Speech at Risk	04/26/13	377
Future of Books	05/29/09	**473
Future of Journalism	03/27/09	**273
Future of Language	11/17/00	929
The Future of Libraries	05/23/97	457
Future of Libraries	07/29/11	625
Future of Marriage	05/07/04	409*
Future of Marriage	12/01/17	993
Future of Public Universities	01/18/13	53
The Future of Telecommunications	04/23/99	329
Future of the Music Industry	11/21/03	989
Future of Newspapers	01/20/06	49
Gambling in America	03/07/03	201
Google's Dominance	11/11/11	953
Government Secrecy	02/11/11	121
Government Surveillance	08/30/13	717

	Date	Page
High-Tech Policing	04/21/17	337
Homeland Security	09/12/03	749
Human Rights in China	07/25/08	601
Identity Theft	6/10/05	517
Impact of the Internet on Thinking	09/24/10	773
Improving Cybersecurity	02/15/13	157
Internet Accuracy	08/01/08	625
Internet Privacy	11/06/98	953
Internet Regulation	04/13/12	325
Internet Shopping	06/28/13	573
IRS Reform	01/16/98	36*
Israeli-Palestinian Conflict	06/21/13	545
Journalism Standards in the Internet Age	10/08/10	821
Journalism Under Fire	12/25/98	1121
Libraries and the Internet	06/01/01	465
Lies and Politics	02/18/11	145
Low Voter Turnout	10/20/00	844*
Media Bias	05/03/13	401
Medication Abuse	10/09/09	837
Online Dating	03/20/15	265
Online Privacy	11/06/09	**933
Plagiarism and Cheating	01/04/13	1
Press Freedom	02/05/10	97
Preventing Bullying	12/10/10	**1013
Privacy and the Internet	12/04/15	1009
Privacy Under Attack	06/15/01	505
Prostitution Debate	05/23/08	433
Reading Crisis?	02/22/08	169
Regulating the Internet	06/30/95	561
Regulating the New Economy	10/19/01	849
Rising College Costs	12/05/03	1026*
Smart Cities	07/27/12	645
Social Media Explosion	01/25/13	81
Social Media and Politics	10/12/12	865
Social Networking	09/17/10	749
Student Journalism	06/05/98	499*
Student Rights	06/05/09	501
Telecommuting	07/19/13	621
Television's Future	02/16/07	145
U.S.-China Relations	05/07/10	**409
U.S.-Russia Relations	01/13/17	25
Video Games	11/10/06	**937
Video Games and Learning	02/12/16	145
Virtual Reality	02/26/16	193
Iran		
Chemical and Biological Weapons	12/13/13	1053
Computer Hacking	09/16/11	757*
Economic Sanctions	10/28/94	944*
Exporting Democracy	04/01/05	269
Hating America	11/23/01	969
The Iraq War: 10 Years Later	03/01/13	205
Islamic Fundamentalism	03/24/00	241
Middle East Tensions	10/27/06	**889

	Date	Page
New Strategy in Iraq	02/23/07	169
Nuclear Disarmament	10/02/09	**813
Nuclear Energy	03/10/06	217
Nuclear Proliferation and Terrorism	04/02/04	297
Oil Jitters	01/04/08	**1
Oil Production in the 21st Century	08/07/98	673
Reform in Iran	12/18/98	1097
Rethinking Foreign Policy	02/02/07	97
Understanding Islam	11/03/06	913
The United Nations and Global Security	02/27/04	173
U.S.-Europe Relations	03/23/12	277
U.S.-Iran Relations	03/04/16	217
U.S. Policy on Iran	11/16/07	961
War on Terrorism	10/12/01	817
Women and Human Rights	04/30/99	353

Iran-contra affair

	Date	Page
Independent Counsels	02/21/97	158*
Political Scandals	05/27/94	470*
Reforming the CIA	02/02/96	111*
U.S. Policy on Iran	11/16/07	961

Iraq

	Date	Page
Alternative Energy	02/25/05	173
America at War	07/23/10	**605
Assessing the Threat From al Qaeda	06/27/14	553
Assisting Refugees	02/07/97	109*
Calculating the Costs of the Gulf War	03/15/91	145
Caring for Veterans	04/23/10	361
Celebrity Culture	03/18/05	245
Chemical and Biological Weapons	01/31/97	84*
Chemical and Biological Weapons	12/13/13	1053
Combat Journalism	04/12/13	329
Confronting Iraq	10/04/02	793
Cost of the Iraq War	04/25/08	361*
Defeating the Islamic State	04/01/16	289
Democracy in the Arab World	01/30/04	73
Democrats in Congress	06/08/07	505
Draft Debates	08/19/05	661
Drone Warfare	08/06/10	653
Economic Sanctions	10/28/94	937
Examining Forensics	07/17/09	597
Exporting Democracy	04/01/05	269
Foreign Aid and National Security	06/17/11	529
Future of NATO	02/28/03	177
Global Jihad	10/14/05	857
Government Secrecy	12/02/05	1005
Government Secrecy	02/11/11	121
Hating America	11/23/01	969
International Law	12/17/04	1049
Interrogating the CIA	09/25/09	789
The Iraq War: 10 Years Later	03/01/13	205
Middle East Tensions	10/27/06	**889
Military Suicides	09/23/11	781*
New Defense Priorities	09/13/02	735*
New Strategy in Iraq	02/23/07	169

	Date	Page
Nuclear Proliferation	06/05/92	481
Nuclear Proliferation and Terrorism	04/02/04	297
The Obama Presidency	01/30/09	73
Oil Diplomacy	01/24/03	49
Oil Jitters	01/04/08	**1
Oil Production in the 21st Century	08/07/98	673
Privatizing the Military	06/25/04	565
Privatizing the Military	07/13/12	597
Prosecuting Terrorists	03/12/10	**217*
Rebuilding Iraq	07/11/03	625
Reforming Veterans' Health Care	11/21/14	985
Remembering 9/11	09/02/11	701*
Rethinking Foreign Policy	02/02/07	97
Rise in Counterinsurgency	09/05/08	697
Smallpox Threat	02/07/03	118*
Stolen Antiquities	04/13/07	313
Stolen Antiquities	11/10/17	945
Stopping Genocide	08/27/04	685
Torture	04/18/03	345
Treatment of Detainees	08/25/06	673
Treatment of Veterans	11/19/04	973
Understanding Islam	11/03/06	913
The United Nations and Global Security	02/27/04	173
U.S. Policy on Iran	11/16/07	961
War in Iraq	10/21/05	881
War on Terrorism	10/12/01	817
Women in Combat	05/13/16	433
Women in the Military	11/13/09	957
Wounded Veterans	08/31/07	697

IRAs. *See Individual retirement accounts*

Ireland

	Date	Page
Northern Ireland Cease-Fire	09/15/95	801

Irradiation. *See Radiation*

Islam

	Date	Page
Assessing the Threat From al Qaeda	06/27/14	553
Closing Guantanamo	09/30/16	793
Defeating the Islamic State	04/01/16	289
Democracy in the Arab World	01/30/04	73
Emerging India	04/19/02	329
Free Speech at Risk	04/26/13	377
Future of the European Union	10/28/05	909
Global Jihad	10/14/05	857
Hating America	11/23/01	969
Homegrown Jihadists	09/03/10	701
The Iraq War: 10 Years Later	03/01/13	205
Islamic Fundamentalism	03/24/00	241
Middle East Tensions	10/27/06	**889
Muslims in America	04/30/93	361
Muslims in America	07/28/17	629
Oil Diplomacy	01/24/03	49
Policing the Borders	02/22/02	145
Rebuilding Iraq	07/11/03	625
Reform in Iran	12/18/98	1097
Religion and Law	11/07/14	937

	Date	Page		Date	Page
Religious Freedom	01/01/16	1	**Jews**		
Religious Persecution	11/21/97	1009	Anti-Semitism	05/12/17	409
Religious Repression	11/01/13	933	Hate Crimes	01/08/93	1
Remembering 9/11	09/02/11	701*	Holocaust Reparations	03/26/99	257
Russia and the Former Soviet			Israel at 50	03/06/98	202*
Republics	06/17/05	541	Middle East Peace	01/21/05	53
Terrorism in Africa	07/10/15	577	Middle East Tensions	10/27/06	**889
Understanding Islam	11/03/06	913	Prospects for Mideast Peace	08/30/02	673
Unrest in the Arab World	02/01/13	105	Religion and Politics	07/30/04	642*
Unrest in Turkey	01/29/16	97	Religion in Schools	02/18/94	159*
U.S.-Iran Relations	03/04/16	217	Religious Repression	11/01/13	933
U.S. Policy on Iran	11/16/07	961	Reparations Movement	06/22/01	529
War on Terrorism	10/12/01	817	Searching for Jesus	12/11/98	1084*
Women and Human Rights	04/30/99	353	Stolen Antiquities	11/10/17	945
Israel			**Job discrimination.** *See Discrimination*		
Anti-Semitism	05/12/17	409	**Job stress**		
Confronting Iraq	10/04/02	793	Flexible Work Arrangements	08/14/98	705*
Democracy in the Arab World	01/30/04	73	Job Stress	08/04/95	681
Foreign Aid and National Security	06/17/11	529	Jobs in the '90s	02/28/92	169
Foreign Aid After Sept. 11	04/26/02	361	Work, Family and Stress	08/14/92	689
Global Water Shortages	12/15/95	1113	**Job training**		
Human Rights Issues	10/30/09	909	Apprenticeships	10/14/16	841
Israel at 50	03/06/98	193	Business Ethics	05/06/11	409
Israeli-Palestinian Conflict	06/21/13	545	Career Colleges	01/07/11	1
Middle East Conflict	04/06/01	273	Community Colleges	05/01/15	385
Middle East Peace	01/21/05	53	Domestic Poverty	09/07/07	**721
Middle East Tensions	10/27/06	**889	Dropout Rate	06/13/14	505
Oil Diplomacy	01/24/03	49	Fighting Urban Poverty	07/17/15	601
The Palestinians	08/30/91	609	Future Job Market	01/11/02	1
Prospects for Mideast Peace	08/30/02	673	Future of the Middle Class	04/08/16	313
Reassessing Foreign Aid	09/27/96	848*	The Gig Economy	03/18/16	265
Torture	04/18/03	345	Income Inequality	04/17/98	353*
Understanding Islam	11/03/06	913	Jobs Outlook	06/04/10	481
Japan			Liberal Arts Education	04/10/98	313
Asian Americans	12/13/91	945	Nursing Shortage	09/20/02	745
Auto Industry's Future	01/21/00	26*	Solar Energy Controversies	04/29/16	385
Chemical and Biological Weapons	01/31/97	86*	Straining the Safety Net	07/31/09	645
Declining Birthrates	11/21/08	961	Student Journalism	06/05/98	481
Deflation Fears	02/13/98	133*	Teacher Education	10/17/97	913
Earthquake Research	12/16/94	1122*	Teaching Critical Thinking	04/10/15	313
Ethics of War	12/13/02	1013	Universal Basic Income	09/08/17	725
Europe 1992	06/28/91	432	Upward Mobility	04/29/05	369
Japan in Crisis	07/26/02	593	The Value of a College Education	11/20/09	981
Modernizing the Nuclear Arsenal	07/29/16	625	Vanishing Jobs	03/13/09	225
New Era in Asia	02/14/92	121	Welfare Experiments	09/16/94	793
Nuclear Fusion	01/22/93	66*	Women in Combat	05/13/16	433
The Obama Presidency	01/30/09	73	Worker Retraining	01/21/94	49
The U.S. and Japan	05/31/91	325	Youth Apprenticeships	10/23/92	905
U.S. Auto Industry	10/16/92	881	Youth Unemployment	03/14/14	241
U.S. Policy in Asia	11/27/92	1025	**Jobs.** *See Employment and unemployment*		
U.S. Trade Policy	01/29/93	73	**Journalism**		
U.S. Trade Policy	09/13/13	765	Blog Explosion	06/09/06	**505
War Crimes	07/07/95	585	Business Bankruptcy	04/10/09	321
Year-Round Schools	05/17/96	440*			

	Date	Page
Celebrity Culture	03/18/05	245
Child Sexual Abuse	01/15/93	36*
Civic Journalism	09/20/96	817
Civil Liberties Debates	10/24/03	893
Civil Liberties in Wartime	12/14/01	1017
Combat Journalism	04/12/13	329
Combating Plagiarism	09/19/03	773
Copyright and the Internet	09/29/00	783*
Courts and the Media	09/23/94	817
Crime Victims' Rights	07/22/94	638*
Digital Journalism	05/30/14	457
Evangelical Christians	09/14/01	718*
Fairness in Salaries	05/29/92	466*
Feminism's Future	02/28/97	176*
Free-Press Disputes	04/08/05	293
Free Speech at Risk	04/26/13	377
Foreign Policy and Public Opinion	07/15/94	601
Future of Journalism	03/27/09	**273
Future of Newspapers	01/20/06	49
Globalization Backlash	09/28/01	775*
Human Rights in China	07/25/08	601
Internet Accuracy	08/01/08	625
Journalism Standards in the Internet Age	10/08/10	821
Journalism Under Fire	12/25/98	1121
Lies and Politics	02/18/11	145
Media Bias	05/03/13	401
Media Ownership	10/10/03	**845
The Partisan Divide	04/30/04	373
Partisan Politics	03/19/99	233
Patriotism in America	06/25/99	551
Political Conventions	08/08/08	649
Political Scandals	05/27/94	457
Politicians and Privacy	04/17/92	337
Press Freedom	02/05/10	97
Pursuing the Paranormal	03/29/96	272*
Religion in America	11/25/94	1050*
School Censorship	02/19/93	153*
Serial Killers	10/31/03	920*
Sex Scandals	01/22/10	49
Social Media and Politics	10/12/12	865
Student Journalism	06/05/98	481
Talk Show Democracy	04/29/94	361
Trump Presidency	01/06/17	1
Trust in Media	06/09/17	481
TV Violence	03/26/93	282*
Women in Politics	03/21/08	265
Women and Sports	03/06/92	200*

Judicial system. *See Courts*

Justice Department, U.S.

Antitrust Policy	06/12/98	505
Civil Liberties in Wartime	12/14/01	1017
Closing In on Tobacco	11/12/99	977
Corporate Crime	10/11/02	817

	Date	Page
Cyber-Predators	03/01/02	169
Eyewitness Testimony	10/14/11	853
Forensic Science Controversies	02/10/17	121
Gang Crisis	05/14/04	421
Government Secrecy	02/11/11	121
Homegrown Jihadists	09/03/10	701
Independent Counsels Re-examined	05/07/99	377
Interrogating the CIA	09/25/09	789
Legal-Aid Crisis	10/07/11	829
Mafia Crackdown	03/27/92	265
Police Tactics	12/12/14	1033
Policing the Borders	02/22/02	145
Presidential Power	11/15/02	945
Prosecuting Terrorists	03/12/10	**217*
Prosecutors and Politics	06/22/07	553
Race in America	07/11/03	593
Redistricting Disputes	03/12/04	221
Wealth and Inequality	04/18/14	337
Women in Prison	03/03/17	193

Juvenile delinquency

Bullying	02/04/05	101
Childhood Depression	07/16/99	611*
Death Penalty Update	01/08/99	7*
Declining Crime Rates	04/04/97	289
Dropout Rate	06/13/14	505
Gang Crisis	05/14/04	421
Juvenile Justice	02/25/94	169
Juvenile Justice	11/07/08	913
Kids in Prison	04/27/01	345
Preventing Juvenile Crime	03/15/96	217
Preventing Teen Drug Use	03/15/02	217
Reforming Juvenile Justice	09/11/15	745
School Violence	10/09/98	881
Teen Driving	01/07/05	1
Underage Drinking	03/13/92	217
Violence in Schools	09/11/92	785
Women in Prison	03/03/17	193
Youth Gangs	10/11/91	753

Kerry, John

Cyberpolitics	09/17/04	757
Social Security Reform	09/24/04	781

Kevorkian, Jack

Assisted Suicide	02/21/92	145
Assisted Suicide Controversy	05/05/95	393

Klu Klux Klan

'Alt-Right' Movement	03/17/17	241
Far-Right Extremism	09/18/15	769
Hate Groups	05/08/09	421

Korea (North)

Economic Sanctions	10/28/94	945*
Foreign Aid After Sept. 11	04/26/02	361
Future of Korea	05/19/00	425
Military Readiness	11/03/17	917

	Date	Page
New Era in Asia	02/14/92	121
Non-Proliferation Treaty at 25	01/27/95	87*
North Korean Crisis	04/11/03	321
North Korea Showdown	05/19/17	433
Nuclear Proliferation	06/05/92	481
Nuclear Proliferation and Terrorism	04/02/04	297
Rethinking Foreign Policy	02/02/07	97
U.S. Policy in Asia	11/27/92	1025
Weapons of Mass Destruction	03/08/02	193

Korea (South)

	Date	Page
Democracy in Asia	07/24/98	625
Foreign Aid After Sept. 11	04/26/02	361
Future of Korea	05/19/00	425
New Era in Asia	02/14/92	121
North Korean Crisis	04/11/03	321
U.S. Policy in Asia	11/27/92	1025
U.S. Trade Policy	09/13/13	765

Kosovo

	Date	Page
Defense Priorities	07/30/99	641
Ethics of War	12/13/02	1013
Global Refugee Crisis	07/09/99	569
Reforming the U.N.	06/24/16	553
Resurgent Russia	02/07/14	121
Stopping Genocide	08/27/04	685
The United Nations and Global Security	02/27/04	173

Kyoto Protocol on global warming

	Date	Page
Air Pollution Conflict	11/14/03	965
Alternative Energy	02/25/05	173
Bush and the Environment	10/25/02	865
Global Warming Treaty	01/26/01	41
Reforming the U.N.	06/24/16	553
Setting Environmental Priorities	05/21/99	425
The United Nations and Global Security	02/27/04	173

Labeling in packaging

	Date	Page
Consumer Safety	10/12/07	841
Dietary Supplements	09/03/04	709
Dietary Supplements	10/30/15	913
Fair Trade Labeling	05/18/07	433
Fast-Food Shake-Up	11/08/91	840
Food Labeling	06/16/17	509
Food Safety	06/04/93	498*
Food Safety	11/01/02	897
Food Safety Battle: Organic v. Biotech	09/04/98	761
Genetically Engineered Foods	08/05/94	687*
Genetically Modified Food	08/31/12	717
Nanotechnology	06/10/16	505
The Obscenity Debate	12/20/91	982*

Labor. *See Employment and unemployment*

Labor unions

	Date	Page
Attracting Jobs	03/02/12	205
Auto Industry's Future	02/06/09	**105
Big-Box Stores	09/10/04	733
The Business of Sports	02/10/95	121

	Date	Page
Child Labor and Sweatshops	08/16/96	721
Coal Industry's Future	06/17/16	529
Contingent Work Force	10/24/97	937
Curbing CEO Pay	03/09/07	217
Exporting Jobs	02/20/04	149
Fairness in Salaries	05/29/92	468*
Future of the Airline Industry	06/21/02	545
Future of the Middle Class	04/08/16	313
The Growing Influence of Boycotts	01/04/91	1
Labor Movement's Future	06/28/96	553
Labor Unions' Future	09/02/05	**709
Living-Wage Movement	09/27/02	769
Minimum Wage	01/24/14	72
'Occupy' Movement	01/13/12	25
Paying College Athletes	07/11/14	577
Privatizing Government Services	08/09/96	697
Public-Employee Unions	04/08/11	313
Regulating Nonprofits	12/26/97	1142*
Rethinking NAFTA	06/07/96	481
Retiree Health Benefits	12/06/91	921
School Reform	04/29/11	385
Teacher Education	10/17/97	929*
Unions at a Crossroads	08/07/15	673
Upward Mobility	04/29/05	369
Worker Safety	05/21/04	445
Youth Apprenticeships	10/23/92	909*

Land mines

	Date	Page
Banning Land Mines	08/08/97	697

Land use policy

	Date	Page
Arctic Development	12/02/16	989
Big-Box Stores	09/10/04	733
China and the South China Sea	01/20/17	49
Coal Industry's Future	06/17/16	529
Crisis on the Plains	05/09/03	417
Energy Security	02/01/02	73
Gentrification	02/20/15	169
Managing Western Lands	04/22/16	361
Privatizing Government Services	12/08/17	1017
Public Land Policy	06/17/94	529
Reforming the Corps	05/30/03	497
Saving Open Spaces	11/05/99	953
Smart Growth	05/28/04	469
Traffic Congestion	05/06/94	393*
Urban Sprawl in the West	10/03/97	865

Landfills

	Date	Page
The Economics of Recycling	03/27/98	265
Future of Recycling	12/14/07	1033
Garbage Crisis	03/20/92	241

Languages. *See Foreign languages; Official English*

Latin America

	Date	Page
Central American Gangs	01/30/15	97
Change in Latin America	07/21/06	601
Cuba's Future	07/20/07	601

	Date	Page
Democracy in Latin America	11/03/00	881
Ecotourism	10/20/06	865
Foreign Aid After Sept. 11	04/26/02	361
Globalization Backlash	09/28/01	761
Mexico's Drug War	12/12/08	1009
Oil Diplomacy	01/24/03	49
Oil Jitters	01/04/08	**1
Policing the Borders	02/22/02	145
Privatizing Government Services	08/09/96	708*
Restoring Ties With Cuba	06/12/15	505
Rethinking NAFTA	06/07/96	481
Saving the Forests	09/20/91	681
Saving the Rain Forests	06/11/99	497
Torture	04/18/03	356*
Trouble in South America	03/14/03	225
Troubled Brazil	04/07/17	289
U.S.-Mexico Relations	09/02/16	697

Latinos. *See Hispanics*

Law enforcement. *See Police and law enforcement*

Lawyers. *See also Independent counsels*

Asbestos Litigation	05/02/03	393
Combating Scientific Misconduct	01/10/97	1
Death Penalty Debates	11/19/10	965
Eyewitness Testimony	10/14/11	853
Fairness in Salaries	05/29/92	464*
Fighting over Animal Rights	08/02/96	680*
High-Impact Litigation	02/11/00	89
Judicial Elections	04/24/09	373
The Jury System	11/10/95	993
Law Schools	04/19/13	353
Legal-Aid Crisis	10/07/11	829
Limiting Lawsuits	12/19/08	1033
Medical Malpractice	02/14/03	129
Prosecuting Terrorists	03/12/10	**217*
Prosecutors and the Law	11/09/07	937
Prosecutors and Politics	06/22/07	553
Public Defenders	04/18/08	337*
Too Many Lawsuits?	05/22/92	433
Wrongful Convictions	04/17/09	**345

Lead poisoning

Drinking Water Safety	07/15/16	577
Indoor Air Pollution	10/27/95	957*
Lead Poisoning	06/19/92	525
New Air Quality Standards	03/07/97	193

Learning disabilities

Boys' Emotional Needs	06/18/99	521
Homework Debate	12/06/02	993
Implementing the Disabilities Act	12/20/96	1105
Learning Disabilities	12/10/93	1081

Lebanon

Middle East Tensions	10/27/06	**889

	Date	Page
Leisure		
Ecotourism	10/20/06	865
Gambling Under Attack	09/06/96	769
National Forests	10/16/98	905
National Parks	05/28/93	457
National Parks Under Pressure	10/06/06	817
Online Dating	03/20/15	265
Protecting the National Parks	06/16/00	521
Work, Family and Stress	08/14/92	689
Year-Round Schools	05/17/96	433

Lesbians. *See Homosexuals*

Libertarian Party

Testing Term Limits	11/18/94	1020*
Third-Party Prospects	12/22/95	1144*

Libraries

Civil Liberties Debates	10/24/03	893
Clashing over Copyright	11/08/96	985
Distance Learning	12/07/01	993
Future of Books	06/23/00	545
Future of Books	05/29/09	**473
The Future of Libraries	05/23/97	457
Future of Libraries	07/29/11	625
Hard Times for Libraries	06/26/92	549
Libraries and the Internet	06/01/01	465
Presidential Libraries	03/16/07	241
Reading Crisis?	02/22/08	169
Regulating the Internet	06/30/95	561
School Censorship	02/19/93	145

Library of Congress

The Future of Libraries	05/23/97	457
Hard Times for Libraries	06/26/92	554*

Libya

Economic Sanctions	10/28/94	945*
European Migration Crisis	07/31/15	649
Nuclear Proliferation and Terrorism	04/02/04	297
Terrorism in Africa	07/10/15	577

Liquor. *See Alcohol*

Literacy and illiteracy

Impact of the Internet on Thinking	09/24/10	773
Internet Accuracy	08/01/08	625
Learning to Read	05/19/95	441
The New Volunteerism	12/13/96	1088*
No Child Left Behind	05/27/05	469
Reading Crisis?	02/22/08	169
Teaching Critical Thinking	04/10/15	313
Video Games	11/10/06	**937

Littleton, Colo., school shootings, 1999

Boys' Emotional Needs	06/18/99	521
Bullying	02/04/05	101
Childhood Depression	07/16/99	593
Discipline in Schools	02/15/08	145

	Date	Page
Gang Crisis	05/14/04	421
Gun Control	03/08/13	233
Gun Rights Debates	10/31/08	**889
Gun Violence	05/25/07	457
School Discipline	05/09/14	409
School Violence	10/09/98	881
Smart Growth	05/28/04	469
Livestock and ranching		
Biotech Foods	03/30/02	262*
The Cloning Controversy	05/09/97	409
Crisis on the Plains	05/09/03	417
Drug-Resistant Bacteria	06/04/99	473
Farm Subsidies	05/17/02	433
Food Labeling	06/16/17	509
Food Safety	11/01/02	897
Genetically Engineered Foods	08/05/94	673
Mad Cow Disease	03/02/01	161
Managing Western Lands	04/22/16	361
Pandemic Threat	06/02/17	457
Public Land Policy	06/17/94	529
Regulating Pharmaceuticals	10/11/13	861
Water Shortages	08/01/03	649
Lobbying and lobbyists		
Covering the Uninsured	06/14/02	521
Dietary Supplements	09/03/04	709
Fairness in Salaries	05/29/92	466*
Nonprofit Groups and Partisan Politics	11/14/14	961
Pork Barrel Politics	06/16/06	529
Regulating Lobbying	06/06/14	481
Regulating Nonprofits	12/26/97	1129
Regulating Tobacco	09/30/94	841
Stock Market Troubles	01/16/04	25
Think Tanks in Transition	09/29/17	797
The U.S. and Japan	05/31/91	341*
Local government. *See Cities and towns*		
Logging. *See Forests and forestry*		
Long-term health care		
Alzheimer's Disease	05/15/98	433
Caring for the Elderly	02/20/98	145
Caring for the Elderly	10/13/06	841
Drug Company Ethics	06/06/03	521
Medicaid Reform	07/16/04	589
Los Angeles, Calif.		
Community Policing	02/05/93	97
Drug Company Ethics	06/06/03	521
Gang Crisis	05/14/04	421
Police Brutality	09/06/91	633
Prison Reform	04/06/07	289
Water Shortages	08/01/03	649
Lotteries. *See Gambling*		
Louisiana		
Charter Schools	03/10/17	217
Electing Minorities	08/12/94	714*

	Date	Page
Rebuilding New Orleans	02/03/06	97
Threatened Coastlines	02/07/92	109*
Low income. *See Poverty*		
Magnet schools		
Rethinking School Integration	10/18/96	924*
School Choice	05/10/91	259*
School Desegregation	04/23/04	345
School Vouchers Showdown	02/15/02	121
Malcolm X		
Muslims in America	04/30/93	361
Mammography		
Advances in Cancer Research	08/25/95	764*
Breast Cancer	06/27/97	553
Women's Health Issues	05/13/94	423*
Managed medical care		
Caring for the Dying	09/05/97	777*
Caring for the Elderly	02/20/98	145
Caring for the Elderly	10/13/06	841
Covering the Uninsured	06/14/02	521
Doctor Shortage	08/28/15	697
Emergency Medicine	01/05/96	1
Hospitals' Financial Woes	08/13/99	689
Managed Care	04/12/96	313
Managing Managed Care	04/16/99	305
Medicare Reform	08/22/03	673
Mental Health Insurance	03/29/02	281*
Mental Health Policy	09/12/97	804*
Patients' Rights	02/06/98	97
Right to Die	05/13/05	421
Mandatory sentencing		
Drug-Policy Debate	07/28/00	593
Forensic Science Controversies	02/10/17	121
Jailing Debtors	09/16/16	745
Mandatory Sentencing	05/26/95	465
Prison-Building Boom	09/17/99	801
Prison Overcrowding	02/04/94	97
Sentencing Debates	11/05/04	925
Sentencing Reform	01/10/14	25
Three-Strikes Laws	05/10/02	417
War on Drugs	03/19/93	252*
Women in Prison	03/03/17	193
Mandela, Nelson		
South Africa's Future	01/14/94	31*
Marijuana		
Alternative Medicine's Next Phase	02/14/97	121
Drug-Policy Debate	07/28/00	593
Drug Testing	11/20/98	1001
Legalizing Marijuana	06/12/09	**525
Marijuana Industry	10/16/15	865
Marijuana Laws	02/11/05	125
Medical Marijuana	08/20/99	705
Medical Marijuana	07/21/17	605
Medication Abuse	10/09/09	837

	Date	Page
Mexico's Future	10/26/12	913
Presidential Power	03/06/15	217
Preventing Teen Drug Use	07/28/95	657
Preventing Teen Drug Use	03/15/02	233*
Teen Drug Use	06/03/11	481
Treating Addiction	01/06/95	8*
Treating Addiction	05/02/14	385
War on Drugs	06/02/06	481

Marriage. *See Family*

Mars

	Date	Page
Human Spaceflight	10/16/09	861
NASA's Future	05/23/03	473
Space Program	02/24/12	177
Space Program's Future	04/25/97	361
Uncertain Future for Man in Space	03/29/91	173

Mass transit

	Date	Page
Future of Amtrak	10/18/02	841
Mass Transit	12/09/16	1013
Mass Transit Boom	01/18/08	49
Smart Growth	05/28/04	469
Traffic Congestion	08/27/99	729

Mbeki, Thabo

	Date	Page
Global AIDS Crisis	10/13/00	821*

McCain, John

	Date	Page
Campaign Finance Reform	06/13/08	505

McCain-Feingold Act

	Date	Page
Campaign Finance Reform	06/13/08	505

McDonald's

	Date	Page
Fast-Food Shake-Up	11/08/91	825
Historic Preservation	10/07/94	882*

Meat. *See Food and nutrition*

Media. *See Journalism; Television and radio*

Medicaid

	Date	Page
Aging Baby Boomers	10/19/07	865
Aging Population	07/15/11	577
AIDS Update	12/04/98	1063*
Alzheimer's Disease	05/15/98	433
Assessing the New Health Care Law	09/21/12	789
Birth-Control Debate	06/24/05	565
Caring for the Elderly	02/20/98	145
Caring for the Elderly	10/13/06	841
Covering the Uninsured	06/14/02	521
Emergency Medicine	01/05/96	1
Government Spending	07/12/13	597
Health-Care Reform	08/28/09	693*
Health-Care Reform	06/11/10	**505
Infant Mortality	07/31/92	641
Medicaid Reform	07/16/04	589
Mental Illness Medication Debate	02/06/04	101
Organ Donations	04/15/11	337
Prescription Drug Costs	05/20/16	457
Right to Die	05/13/05	421
State Budget Crises	10/03/03	821

	Date	Page
States and Federalism	10/15/10	845
Trump Presidency	01/06/17	1

Medical care. *See also Diseases and health problems;*
Health insurance

	Date	Page
Aging Baby Boomers	10/19/07	865
Aging Population	07/15/11	577
AIDS Update	12/04/98	1049
Alternative Medicine	01/31/92	73
Alternative Medicine's Next Phase	02/14/97	121
Alzheimer's Disease	07/24/92	617
Asbestos Litigation	05/02/03	393
Assessing the New Health Care Law	09/21/12	789
Assisted Suicide	05/17/13	449
Assisted Suicide Controversy	05/05/95	393
Banning Land Mines	08/08/97	710*
Battling HIV/AIDS	10/26/07	889
Cancer Treatments	09/11/98	803*
Caring for the Dying	09/05/97	769
Caring for the Elderly	02/20/98	145
Caring for the Elderly	10/13/06	841
Caring for Veterans	04/23/10	361
Childhood Immunizations	06/18/93	529
Combating AIDS	04/21/95	345
Computers and Medicine	10/27/00	857
Cosmetic Surgery	04/15/05	317
Covering the Uninsured	06/14/02	521
Debt Collectors	07/20/12	621
Doctor Shortage	08/28/15	697
Drug Company Ethics	06/06/03	521
Drug Safety	03/11/05	221
Emergency Medicine	01/05/96	1
Emerging Infectious Diseases	02/13/15	145
Fighting Cancer	01/22/16	73
Fighting SARS	06/20/03	569
Fighting Superbugs	08/24/07	673
Genes and Health	01/21/11	49
Head Start	04/09/93	297*
Health-Care Reform	08/28/09	693*
Health-Care Reform	06/11/10	**505
Homeopathy Debate	12/19/03	1069
Increase in Autism	06/13/03	**545
Infant Mortality	07/31/92	641
Latino Voters	04/03/15	289
Legalizing Marijuana	06/12/09	**525
Lyme Disease	11/08/13	957
Managing Managed Care	04/16/99	305
Medicaid Reform	07/16/04	589
Medical Malpractice	02/14/03	129
Medical Marijuana	07/21/17	605
Medical Mistakes	02/25/00	137
Medicare Reform	08/22/03	673
Mental Health Policy	05/10/13	425
Mental Illness Medication Debate	02/06/04	101
Middle-Class Squeeze	03/06/09	201

	Date	Page		Date	Page
Mosquito-Borne Disease	07/22/16	601	Health-Care Reform	06/11/10	**505
Native Americans' Future	07/12/96	608*	Heart Health	09/12/08	721
Nursing Shortage	09/20/02	745	Hospitals' Financial Woes	08/13/99	689
Opioid Crisis	10/07/16	817	Managed Care	04/12/96	313
Organ Donations	04/15/11	337	Managing Managed Care	04/16/99	305
Organ Shortage	02/21/03	153	Medicaid Reform	07/16/04	589
Pandemic Threat	06/02/17	457	Medical Malpractice	02/14/03	129
Patients' Rights	02/06/98	97	Medicare Reform	08/22/03	673
Patient Safety	02/10/12	125	Mental Health Insurance	03/29/02	265
Paying College Athletes	07/11/14	577	Mental Illness Medication Debate	02/06/04	101
Peace Corps Challenges	01/11/13	29	Middle-Class Squeeze	03/06/09	201
Prayer and Healing	01/14/05	25	National Debt	09/01/17	701
Prescription Drug Costs	05/20/16	457	Nursing Shortage	09/20/02	745
Preventing Cancer	01/16/09	25	Organ Shortage	02/21/03	153
Preventing Disease	01/06/12	1	Patients' Rights	02/06/98	97
Preventing Memory Loss	04/04/08	289*	Prescription Drug Costs	05/20/16	457
Primary Care	03/17/95	217	Prescription Drug Prices	07/17/92	597
Prison Health Care	01/05/07	1	Preventing Cancer	01/16/09	25
Rating Doctors	05/05/00	377	Preventing Disease	01/06/12	1
Re-examining the Constitution	09/07/12	741	Preventing Teen Pregnancy	05/14/93	409
Reforming the FDA	06/06/97	481	Primary Care	03/17/95	217
Reforming Veterans' Health Care	11/21/14	985	Retiree Health Benefits	12/06/91	930*
Right to Die	05/13/05	421	Rising Health Costs	04/07/06	289
Sexually Transmitted Diseases	12/03/04	997	Social Security	06/03/16	481
Supreme Court Controversies	09/28/12	813	Talk Show Democracy	04/29/94	374*
Torture	04/18/03	352*	Too Many Lawsuits?	05/22/92	443
Treating Addiction	05/02/14	385	Treating Alzheimer's Disease	07/24/15	625
Treating ADHD	08/03/12	669	Treatment of Veterans	11/19/04	973
Treating Anxiety	02/08/02	97	**Medical ethics**		
Treating Depression	06/26/09	573	Abortion Debates	03/21/03	249
Treatment of Veterans	11/19/04	973	Abortion Debates	03/21/14	265
Understanding Autism	08/01/14	649	Advances in Cancer Research	08/25/95	769*
Universal Coverage	03/30/07	265	Assisted Suicide	02/21/92	145
Vaccine Controversies	08/25/00	641	Assisted Suicide Controversy	05/05/95	393
Women in the Military	11/13/09	957	Biology and Behavior	04/03/98	289
Women's Health	11/07/03	941	Caring for the Dying	09/05/97	769
Women's Health Issues	05/13/94	409	The Cloning Controversy	05/09/97	409
Wounded Veterans	08/31/07	697	Cosmetic Surgery	04/15/05	317
Youth Suicide	02/13/04	125	Covering the Uninsured	06/14/02	521
Medical care — Cost control			'Designer' Humans	05/18/01	425
Alzheimer's Disease	05/15/98	433	Drug Company Ethics	06/06/03	521
Assessing the New Health Care Law	09/21/12	789	Drug Safety	03/11/05	221
Assisted Suicide	02/21/92	145	Embryo Research	12/17/99	1065
Assisted Suicide Controversy	05/05/95	399*	Fetal Tissue Research	08/16/91	561
Asbestos Litigation	05/02/03	393	Fighting SARS	06/20/03	576*
Childhood Immunizations	06/18/93	529	Gene Therapy	10/18/91	777
Closing In on Tobacco	11/12/99	977	Gene Therapy's Future	12/08/95	1089
Cost of the Iraq War	04/25/08	361*	Health-Care Reform	08/28/09	693*
Covering the Uninsured	06/14/02	521	Homeopathy Debate	12/19/03	1069
Doctor Shortage	08/28/15	697	Human Genome Research	05/12/00	401
Drug Company Ethics	06/06/03	521	Internet Privacy	11/06/98	966*
Emergency Medicine	01/05/96	1	Managed Care	04/12/96	313
Fighting Cancer	01/22/16	73	Marijuana Industry	10/16/15	865
Health-Care Reform	08/28/09	693*	Marijuana Laws	02/11/05	125

	Date	Page		Date	Page
Medical Breakthroughs	09/15/17	749	Examining Forensics	07/17/09	597
Medical Malpractice	02/14/03	129	Fetal Tissue Research	08/16/91	561
Medical Marijuana	07/21/17	605	Fighting over Animal Rights	08/02/96	673
Medical Mistakes	02/25/00	137	Fighting Cancer	01/22/16	73
Medication Abuse	10/09/09	837	Fighting SARS	06/20/03	569
Organ Donations	04/15/11	337	Fighting Superbugs	08/24/07	673
Organ Shortage	02/21/03	158*	Food Labeling	06/16/17	509
Organ Transplants	08/11/95	705	Genes and Health	01/21/11	49
Patients' Rights	02/06/98	103*	Gene Therapy	10/18/91	777
Prayer and Healing	01/14/05	25	Gene Therapy's Future	12/08/95	1089
Prescription Drug Costs	05/20/16	457	Human Genome Research	05/12/00	401
Preventing Memory Loss	04/04/08	289*	Increase in Autism	06/13/03	**545
Privacy Under Attack	06/15/01	505	Lead Poisoning	06/19/92	529*
Professional Football	01/29/10	**73	Lyme Disease	11/08/13	957
Reforming Veterans' Health Care	11/21/14	985	Mad Cow Disease	03/02/01	161
Reproductive Ethics	04/08/94	289	Medical Breakthroughs	09/15/17	749
Right to Die	05/13/05	421	Medical Marijuana	08/20/99	705
Stem Cell Research	09/01/06	**697	Mental Health Insurance	03/29/02	265
Teen Drug Use	06/03/11	481	Mental Health Policy	05/10/13	425
Too Many Lawsuits?	05/22/92	443	Mental Illness Medication Debate	02/06/04	101
Treating Schizophrenia	12/05/14	1009	Mosquito-Borne Disease	07/22/16	601
Vaccine Controversies	02/19/16	169	Nanotechnology	06/11/04	517
Medical research			New Air Quality Standards	03/07/97	193
3D Printing	12/07/12	1037	Organ Donations	04/15/11	337
Abortion Debates	09/10/10	725	Organ Shortage	02/21/03	153
Advances in Cancer Research	08/25/95	753	Organ Transplants	08/11/95	705
Alternative Medicine	01/31/92	73	Pandemic Threat	06/02/17	457
Alternative Medicine	09/06/13	741	Patient Safety	02/10/12	125
Alzheimer's Disease	07/24/92	622*	Prayer and Healing	01/14/05	25
Alzheimer's Disease	05/15/98	433	Prescription Drug Costs	05/20/16	457
Animal Rights	05/24/91	301	Preventing Cancer	01/16/09	25
Animal Rights	01/08/10	1	Preventing Memory Loss	04/04/08	289*
Baby Boomers at Midlife	07/31/98	649	Reforming the FDA	06/06/97	481
Battling HIV/AIDS	10/26/07	889	Regulating Pharmaceuticals	10/11/13	861
Biology and Behavior	04/03/98	289	Reproductive Ethics	04/08/94	289
Birth-Control Debate	06/24/05	565	Saving the Forests	09/20/91	697*
Blood Supply Safety	11/11/94	985	Science in America	01/11/08	25
Breast Cancer	06/27/97	553	Science and Politics	08/20/04	661
Breast Cancer	04/02/10	289	Sexually Transmitted Diseases	12/03/04	997
Cancer Treatments	09/11/98	785	Sleep Deprivation	06/26/98	553
Childhood Depression	07/16/99	593	Sleep Deprivation	02/12/10	121
Chronic Fatigue Syndrome	04/05/02	289	Space Program's Future	12/24/93	1133*
The Cloning Controversy	05/09/97	409	Stem Cell Research	09/01/06	**697
Combating AIDS	04/21/95	345	Treating ADHD	08/03/12	669
Combating Infectious Diseases	06/09/95	489	Treating Alzheimer's	03/04/11	193
Combating Scientific Misconduct	01/10/97	1	Treating Alzheimer's Disease	07/24/15	625
Depression	10/09/92	857	Treating Anxiety	02/08/02	97
Diabetes Epidemic	03/09/01	185	Treating Depression	06/26/09	573
Drug Company Ethics	06/06/03	521	Treating Schizophrenia	12/05/14	1009
Drugmakers Under Siege	09/03/99	753	Treatment of Veterans	11/19/04	973
Drug Safety	03/11/05	221	Understanding Autism	08/01/14	649
Electromagnetic Fields	04/26/91	237	Vaccine Controversies	02/19/16	169
Embryo Research	12/17/99	1065	Women and AIDS	12/25/92	1121
			Women's Health	11/07/03	941

	Date	Page
Medicare		
Aging Baby Boomers	10/19/07	865
Alternative Medicine	09/06/13	741
Alzheimer's Disease	05/15/98	433
Assessing the New Health Care Law	09/21/12	789
Caring for the Elderly	02/20/98	145
Caring for the Elderly	10/13/06	841
Covering the Uninsured	06/14/02	521
Drug Company Ethics	06/06/03	521
Drugmakers Under Siege	09/03/99	753
Health-Care Reform	08/28/09	693*
Health-Care Reform	06/11/10	**505
Hospitals' Financial Woes	08/13/99	689
Managing Managed Care	04/16/99	323*
Medicaid Reform	07/16/04	589
Medicare Reform	08/22/03	673
National Debt	03/18/11	241
Patients' Rights	02/06/98	109*
Prescription Drug Prices	07/17/92	607
Retiree Health Benefits	12/06/91	930*
Retirement Security	05/31/02	481
Right to Die	05/13/05	421
Social Security	06/03/16	481
Social Security Reform	09/24/04	781
Medvedev, Dmitry		
Dealing With the "New" Russia	06/06/08	481
Melatonin		
Alternative Medicine's Next Phase	02/14/97	132*
Baby Boomers at Midlife	07/31/98	660*
Sleep Deprivation	06/26/98	564*
Mental health and illness		
Adoption	11/26/93	1044*
Advances in Cancer Research	08/25/95	766*
Aggressive Driving	07/25/97	649
Alternative Medicine	01/31/92	73
Alzheimer's Disease	07/24/92	617
American Indians	04/28/06	**361
America's Pampered Pets	12/27/96	1129
Boys' Emotional Needs	06/18/99	521
Child Sexual Abuse	01/15/93	25
Childhood Depression	07/16/99	593
Children and Divorce	06/07/91	349
Children and Divorce	01/19/01	25
Chronic Fatigue Syndrome	04/05/02	289
Combating Addiction	02/09/07	121
Death Penalty Debate	03/10/95	199*
Death Penalty Debates	11/19/10	965
Depression	10/09/92	857
Disaster Response	10/15/93	902*
Downward Mobility	07/23/93	625
Drug Safety	03/11/05	221
Eating Disorders	12/18/92	1097
Eating Disorders	02/10/06	**121
Educating Gifted Students	03/28/97	273*

	Date	Page
Ending Homelessness	06/18/04	541
Gambling Boom	03/18/94	241
Gambling Under Attack	09/06/96	776*
Gun Control	03/08/13	233
Gun Rights Debates	10/31/08	**889
Gun Violence	05/25/07	457
Helping the Homeless	01/26/96	73
The Homeless	08/07/92	681*
Housing the Homeless	10/10/14	841
Increase in Autism	06/13/03	**545
Job Stress	08/04/95	681
Marriage and Divorce	05/10/96	409
Mental Health Insurance	03/29/02	265
Mental Health Policy	09/12/97	793
Mental Health Policy	05/10/13	425
Mental Illness	08/06/93	673
Mental Illness Medication Debate	02/06/04	101
Military Suicides	09/23/11	781*
Native American Youths	04/24/15	361
NFL Controversies	09/04/15	721
Prayer and Healing	01/14/05	25
Politicians and Privacy	04/17/92	346*
Preventing Memory Loss	04/04/08	289*
Prisoners and Mental Illness	03/13/15	241
Professional Football	01/29/10	**73
Prozac Controversy	08/19/94	721
Punishing Sex Offenders	01/12/96	25
Recovered-Memory Debate	07/05/96	577
Reforming Veterans' Health Care	11/21/14	985
Rethinking the Death Penalty	11/16/01	953*
Serial Killers	10/31/03	917
Sexual Abuse and the Clergy	05/03/02	407*
Sleep Deprivation	02/12/10	121
Solitary Confinement	09/14/12	765
Students Under Stress	07/13/07	577
Teenage Suicide	06/14/91	369
Teen Suicide	09/12/14	745
Torture	04/18/03	352*
Transgender Issues	05/05/06	385
Treating ADHD	08/03/12	669
Treating Alzheimer's	03/04/11	193
Treating Alzheimer's Disease	07/24/15	625
Treating Anxiety	02/08/02	97
Treating Depression	06/26/09	573
Treating Schizophrenia	12/05/14	1009
Treatment of Veterans	11/19/04	973
Understanding Autism	08/01/14	649
Whistleblowers	12/05/97	1064*
Youth Suicide	02/13/04	125
Mercenaries. *See Private Military Contractors (PMCs)*		
Mergers. *See Corporate mergers*		
Methamphetamine		
Methamphetamine	07/15/05	589
War on Drugs	06/02/06	481

	Date	Page
Methanol. *See Alternative fuels*		
Mexican Americans		
America's Border Fence	09/19/08	745
Border Security	09/27/13	813
Hispanic Americans	10/30/92	929
Hispanic-Americans' New Clout	09/18/98	809
Immigration Debate	02/01/08	**97
Latino Voters	04/03/15	289
Trump Presidency	01/06/17	1
U.S.-Mexico Relations	09/02/16	697
Mexico		
America's Border Fence	09/19/08	745
Border Security	09/27/13	813
Central American Gangs	01/30/15	97
Change in Latin America	07/21/06	601
Debate Over Immigration	07/14/00	582*
Democracy in Latin America	11/03/00	881
Exporting Jobs	02/20/04	149
Illegal Immigration	04/24/92	361
Illegal Immigration	05/06/05	393
Immigrants and the Economy	02/24/17	169
Immigration Debate	02/01/08	**97
International Law	12/17/04	1049
Mexico's Drug War	12/12/08	1009
Mexico's Emergence	07/19/91	489
Mexico's Future	09/19/97	817
Mexico's Future	10/26/12	913
Policing the Borders	02/22/02	145
Rethinking NAFTA	06/07/96	481
Truck Safety	03/12/99	222*
Trump Presidency	01/06/17	1
U.S.-Mexico Relations	11/09/01	921
U.S.-Mexico Relations	09/02/16	697
Worker Retraining	01/21/94	66*
Microsoft Corp.		
Antitrust Policy	06/12/98	505
Cybersecurity	09/26/03	797
Exporting Jobs	02/20/04	149
Online Privacy	11/06/09	**933
Middle class		
Affordable Housing	02/09/01	89
The Black Middle Class	01/23/98	49
Future of the Middle Class	04/08/16	313
Middle-Class Squeeze	03/06/09	201
Student Aid	01/25/08	73
Vanishing Jobs	03/13/09	225
Middle East		
Archaeology Today	05/24/02	457
Assessing the Threat From al Qaeda	06/27/14	553
Blighted Cities	11/12/10	941*
Calculating the Costs of the Gulf War	03/15/91	145
Civil Liberties in Wartime	12/14/01	1017
Confronting Iraq	10/04/02	793

	Date	Page
Defeating the Islamic State	04/01/16	289
Democracy in the Arab World	01/30/04	73
Democrats' Future	10/29/10	893
Energy Security	02/01/02	73
European Migration Crisis	07/31/15	649
Exporting Democracy	04/01/05	269
Foreign Aid After Sept. 11	04/26/02	361
Free Speech at Risk	04/26/13	377
Global Jihad	10/14/05	857
Global Refugee Crisis	07/09/99	572*
Global Water Shortages	12/15/95	1113
Hating America	11/23/01	969
Israel at 50	03/06/98	193
Middle East Conflict	04/06/01	273
Middle East Peace	01/21/05	53
Middle East Tensions	10/27/06	**889
Military Readiness	11/03/17	917
New Strategy in Iraq	02/23/07	169
Nuclear Proliferation	06/05/92	493
Nuclear Proliferation and Terrorism	04/02/04	297
The Obama Legacy	11/04/16	913
Oil Diplomacy	01/24/03	49
Oil Jitters	01/04/08	**1
The Palestinians	08/30/91	609
Policing the Borders	02/22/02	145
The Politics of Energy	03/05/99	199*
Prospects for Mideast Peace	08/30/02	673
Rebuilding Iraq	07/11/03	625
Reform in Iran	12/18/98	1097
Religious Persecution	11/21/97	1009
Rethinking Foreign Policy	02/02/07	97
Rise in Counterinsurgency	09/05/08	697
Understanding Islam	11/03/06	913
The United Nations and Global Security	02/27/04	173
Unrest in the Arab World	02/01/13	105
Unrest in Turkey	01/29/16	97
War in Iraq	10/21/05	881
War on Terrorism	10/12/01	820*
Water Quality	02/11/94	138*
Weapons of Mass Destruction	03/08/02	193
Military police		
Haiti's Dilemma	02/18/05	149
Military policy		
Afghanistan Dilemma	08/07/09	**669*
America at War	07/23/10	**605
Artificial Intelligence	04/22/11	361
Assisting Refugees	02/07/97	103*
Banning Land Mines	08/08/97	697
Bush's Defense Strategy	09/07/01	689
Chemical and Biological Weapons	01/31/97	73
China and the South China Sea	01/20/17	49
Civil Liberties in Wartime	12/14/01	1017
Climate Change and National Security	09/22/17	773

	Date	Page		Date	Page
Closing Guantánamo	02/27/09	**177	Unrest in the Arab World	02/01/13	105
Closing Guantanamo	09/30/16	793	U.S. Policy in Asia	11/27/92	1025
Costs of the Gulf War	03/15/91	145	U.S.-British Relations	01/30/98	81*
Confronting Iraq	10/04/02	793	U.S.-China Relations	05/07/10	**409
Cybersecurity	09/26/03	808*	U.S.-Europe Relations	03/23/12	277
Cybersecurity	02/26/10	169	The U.S. and Japan	05/31/91	325
Defeating the Islamic State	04/01/16	289	U.S.-Pakistan Relations	08/05/11	653*
Defense Priorities	07/30/99	641	War in Iraq	10/21/05	881
Democrats in Congress	06/08/07	505	Weapons of Mass Destruction	03/08/02	193
Disaster Preparedness	11/18/05	**981	Whistleblowers	01/31/14	97
Drone Warfare	08/06/10	653	Women in Combat	05/13/16	433
Ethics of War	12/13/02	1013	Women in the Military	11/13/09	957
Expanding NATO	05/16/97	433	**Military service**		
Exporting Democracy	04/01/05	269	America at War	07/23/10	**605
Foreign Policy and Public Opinion	07/15/94	611*	Calculating the Costs of the Gulf War	03/15/91	145
Foreign Policy Burden	08/20/93	721	Draft Debates	08/19/05	661
Future of NATO	02/28/03	177	Drone Warfare	08/06/10	653
Gay Marriage	03/15/13	257	Gay Rights	03/05/93	193
Gays in the Military	09/18/09	**765	Gay Rights Update	04/14/00	305
Global Refugee Crisis	07/09/99	569	Gays in the Military	09/18/09	**765
Government Secrecy	02/11/11	121	Legacy of the Vietnam War	02/18/00	113
Government Spending	07/12/13	597	Military Suicides	09/23/11	781*
International Law	12/17/04	1049	New Military Culture	04/26/96	361
Interrogating the CIA	09/25/09	789	Privatizing the Military	06/25/04	565
The Iraq War: 10 Years Later	03/01/13	205	Reforming Veterans' Health Care	11/21/14	985
Israel at 50	03/06/98	209*	Sexual Assault in the Military	08/09/13	693
Military Readiness	11/03/17	917	Treating Depression	06/26/09	573
Military Suicides	09/23/11	781*	Treatment of Veterans	11/19/04	973
Missile Defense	09/08/00	689	Upward Mobility	04/29/05	369
NATO's Changing Role	08/21/92	713	Women in Combat	05/13/16	433
New Challenges in Space	07/23/99	631*	Women in the Military	09/25/92	850*
The New CIA	12/11/92	1073	**Millennium**		
New Defense Priorities	09/13/02	721	Millennial Generation	06/26/15	553
New Era in Asia	02/14/92	121	The New Millennium	10/15/99	889
New Strategy in Iraq	02/23/07	169	**Mineral resources and mining**		
North Korean Crisis	04/11/03	321	Asbestos Litigation	05/02/03	393
Nuclear Disarmament	10/02/09	**813	Cleaning Up Hazardous Wastes	08/23/96	745
Nuclear Proliferation and Terrorism	04/02/04	297	Coal Mining Safety	03/17/06	241
Panama Canal	11/26/99	1017	Energy Security	02/01/02	73
Police Tactics	12/12/14	1033	Future of the Arctic	09/20/13	789
Presidential Power	11/15/02	945	Public Land Policy	06/17/94	529
Preventing Hazing	02/08/13	133	Regulating Toxic Chemicals	07/18/14	601
Privatizing the Military	06/25/04	565	Worker Safety	05/21/04	445
Privatizing the Military	07/13/12	597	**Minimum wage**		
Prosecuting Terrorists	03/12/10	**217*	Domestic Poverty	09/07/07	**721
Pursuing the Paranormal	03/29/96	265	Dropout Rate	06/13/14	505
Reassessing Foreign Aid	09/27/96	847*	Ending Homelessness	06/18/04	541
Rebuilding Afghanistan	12/21/01	1057*	Fighting Urban Poverty	07/17/15	601
Reforming the CIA	02/02/96	97	Income Inequality	04/17/98	337
Rise in Counterinsurgency	09/05/08	697	Living-Wage Movement	09/27/02	769
Robotic Warfare	01/23/15	73	Minimum Wage	12/16/05	1053
Sexual Assault in the Military	08/09/13	693	Minimum Wage	01/24/14	72
Sexual Harassment	04/27/12	377	The Working Poor	11/03/95	977*
Treatment of Detainees	08/25/06	673	Youth Unemployment	03/14/14	241

	Date	Page
Minorities		
Affirmative Action	09/21/01	737
Affirmative Action	10/17/08	**841
Affirmative Action and		
College Admissions	11/17/17	969
Aging Population	07/15/11	577
AIDS Update	12/04/98	1049
Alcohol Advertising	03/14/97	221*
Arts Education	03/16/12	253
Asian Americans	12/13/91	945
Bilingual Education	08/13/93	697
Bilingual Education vs. English		
Immersion	12/11/09	1029
Birth-Control Debate	06/24/05	565
Black Colleges	12/12/03	1045
The Black Middle Class	01/23/98	49
Census 2000	05/01/98	385
Census Controversey	05/14/10	433
Changing Demographics	11/16/12	989
Changing U.S. Electorate	05/30/08	**457
Charter Schools	12/20/02	1033
Chronic Fatigue Syndrome	04/05/02	289
Cleaning Up Hazardous Wastes	08/23/96	752*
Consumer Debt	03/02/07	193
Criminal Records and Employment	04/20/12	349
Debate over Bilingualism	01/19/96	49
Debating Hip-Hop	06/15/07	529
Discipline in Schools	02/15/08	145
Diversity in Hollywood	08/05/16	649
Diversity in the Workplace	10/10/97	889
Doctor Shortage	08/28/15	697
Domestic Poverty	09/07/07	**721
Dropout Rate	06/13/14	505
Educating Gifted Students	03/28/97	265
Education Standards	03/11/94	217
Electing Minorities	08/12/94	697
Environmental Justice	06/19/98	529
Europe's New Right	02/12/93	121
Eyewitness Testimony	10/14/11	853
Fighting Gangs	10/09/15	841
Fixing Urban Schools	04/27/07	**361
Forensic Science Controversies	02/10/17	121
Foster Care Reform	01/09/98	14*
The Future of Baseball	09/25/98	839*
Future of the Airline Industry	06/21/02	545
Future of the GOP	03/20/09	249
Future of Homeownership	12/14/12	1061
Gangs in the U.S.	07/16/10	581
Getting into College	02/23/96	169
The Glass Ceiling	10/29/93	937
Grade Inflation	06/07/02	505
Hate Crimes	01/08/93	1
Hispanic Americans	10/30/92	929
Hispanic-Americans' New Clout	09/18/98	809

	Date	Page
Housing Discrimination	02/24/95	169
Housing Discrimination	11/06/15	937
Housing the Homeless	10/10/14	841
Immigration Conflict	03/09/12	229
Infant Mortality	07/31/92	641
Intelligence Testing	07/30/93	654*
Jailing Debtors	09/16/16	745
Living-Wage Movement	09/27/02	769
Mafia Crackdown	03/27/92	270*
Muslims in America	04/30/93	361
Muslims in America	07/28/17	629
National Education Standards	05/14/99	401
Native Americans	05/08/92	385
Native Americans' Future	07/12/96	601
Native American Youths	04/24/15	361
The New Immigrants	01/24/97	49
New Military Culture	04/26/96	361
No Child Left Behind	05/27/05	469
Obesity Epidemic	01/31/03	78*
Organ Donations	04/15/11	337
Police Misconduct	04/06/12	301
Policing the Borders	02/22/02	145
Prisoner Reentry	12/04/09	1005
Property Rights	03/04/05	197
Puerto Rico: The Struggle over Status	02/08/91	81
Race and Education	09/05/14	721
Race in America	07/11/03	593
Racial Conflict	01/08/16	25
Racial Diversity in Public Schools	09/14/07	**745
Racial Quotas	05/17/91	277
Racial Tensions in Schools	01/07/94	1
Redistricting	02/16/01	113
Redistricting Debates	02/25/11	169
Redistricting Disputes	03/12/04	221
Redistricting Showdown	08/25/17	677
Reproductive Ethics	05/15/09	449
Rethinking Affirmative Action	04/28/95	369
Rethinking School Integration	10/18/96	913
Revitalizing the Cities	10/13/95	904*
School Choice	05/10/91	253
School Desegregation	04/23/04	345
School Discipline	05/09/14	409
School Vouchers Showdown	02/15/02	121
Sentencing Reform	01/10/14	25
Shock Jocks	06/01/07	**481
Soviet Republics Rebel	07/12/91	465
Straining the Safety Net	07/31/09	645
Student Aid	01/25/08	73
Talk Show Democracy	04/29/94	379*
Teacher Shortages	08/24/01	633
Three-Strikes Laws	05/10/02	417
Upward Mobility	04/29/05	369
Voter Rights	05/18/12	449
Women and Human Rights	04/30/99	353

	Date	Page
Women and Sports	03/06/92	206*
Women in Prison	03/03/17	193
Young Voters	10/02/15	817
Youth Gangs	10/11/91	753
Youth Unemployment	03/14/14	241
Youth Violence	03/05/10	193*

Missile-defense systems
	Date	Page
Bush's Defense Strategy	09/07/01	689
Defense Priorities	07/30/99	641
Military Readiness	11/03/17	917
Missile Defense	09/08/00	689
Modernizing the Nuclear Arsenal	07/29/16	625
New Challenges in Space	07/23/99	631*
New Defense Priorities	09/13/02	721
North Korea Showdown	05/19/17	433
Nuclear Proliferation and Terrorism	04/02/04	297
Transatlantic Tensions	07/13/01	533
Weapons of Mass Destruction	03/08/02	193

Mobile phones. *See Cellular telephones; Telecommunications*

Monetary policy
	Date	Page
Deflation Fears	02/13/98	121
Digital Currency	09/26/14	793
Euro Crisis	10/05/12	841
European Monetary Union	11/27/98	1025
European Union's Future	12/16/16	1037
The Federal Reserve	01/03/14	1
Financial Bailout	10/24/08	**865
Financial Crisis	05/09/08	409
Financial Industry Overhaul	07/30/10	629
The National Debt	11/14/08	937
National Debt	03/18/11	241
National Debt	09/01/17	701
Stimulating the Economy	01/10/03	1

Monopoly. *See Antitrust law; Economic conditions*

Montreal Protocol
	Date	Page
Global Warming Update	11/01/96	969*
Ozone Depletion	04/03/92	299*
Setting Environmental Priorities	05/21/99	439*

Morals. *See Ethical and moral issues*

Mothers Against Drunk Driving
	Date	Page
Alcohol Advertising	03/14/97	230*
Drunken Driving	10/06/00	793
Teen Driving	01/07/05	1

Movie industry
	Date	Page
Attracting Jobs	03/02/12	205
Clashing over Copyright	11/08/96	985
Copyright and the Internet	09/29/00	769
Diversity in Hollywood	08/05/16	649
Fairness in Salaries	05/29/92	463*
Movie Ratings	03/28/03	273
Pay-Per-View TV	10/04/91	729

	Date	Page
Workplace Sexual Harassment	10/27/17	893

Movies
	Date	Page
Artificial Intelligence	11/14/97	990*
Asian Americans	12/13/91	959*
The Cloning Controversy	05/09/97	420*
Encouraging Teen Abstinence	07/10/98	588*
The FBI Under Fire	04/11/97	318*
Helping the Homeless	01/26/96	86*
Internet Regulation	04/13/12	325
Mafia Crackdown	03/27/92	276*
Media Violence	02/14/14	145
Mental Illness	08/06/93	684*
Movie Ratings	03/28/03	273
Muslims in America	04/30/93	361*
The Obscenity Debate	12/20/91	980*
Searching for Jesus	12/11/98	1087*
Sex, Violence and the Media	11/17/95	1017
Teaching History	09/29/95	862*
Youth Gangs	10/11/91	765*

Multicultural education
	Date	Page
Academic Politics	02/16/96	145
Liberal Arts Education	04/10/98	313
Racial Tensions in Schools	01/07/94	17*
Teaching History	09/29/95	849

Museums
	Date	Page
Archaeology Today	05/24/02	473*
Is America Allowing Its Past to Be Stolen?	01/18/91	33
Native Americans	05/08/92	399
Stolen Antiquities	04/13/07	313
Stolen Antiquities	11/10/17	945
Teaching History	09/29/95	858*

Music
	Date	Page
Clashing over Copyright	11/08/96	985
Copyright and the Internet	09/29/00	769
Debating Hip-Hop	06/15/07	529
Fairness in Salaries	05/29/92	463*
Future of the Music Industry	11/21/03	989
Internet Regulation	04/13/12	325
The Obscenity Debate	12/20/91	969
Pay-Per-View TV	10/04/91	733*
Plagiarism and Cheating	01/04/13	1
Sex, Violence and the Media	11/17/95	1028*
Teenage Suicide	06/14/91	381*
TV Violence	03/26/93	276*

Mutual funds
	Date	Page
Mutual Funds	05/20/94	433
Socially Responsible Investing	08/29/08	673
Stock Market Troubles	01/16/04	25

NAACP. *See National Association for the Advancement of Colored People*

NAFTA. *See North American Free Trade Agreement*

	Date	Page
Nanotechnology		
Nanotechnology	06/11/04	517
U.S. Trade Policy	09/13/13	765
Narcotics. *See Drug abuse; Drug traffic*		
National Aeronautics and Space Administration (NASA)		
NASA's Future	05/23/03	473
Networking the Classroom	10/20/95	926*
New Challenges in Space	07/23/99	617
New Space Race	08/04/17	653
Ozone Depletion	04/03/92	289
The Search for Extraterrestrials	03/05/04	197
Search for Life on New Planets	06/20/14	529
Space Program	02/24/12	177
Space Program's Future	12/24/93	1129
Space Program's Future	04/25/97	361
Uncertain Future for Man on Space	03/29/91	173
National Association for the Advancement of Colored People (NAACP)		
The Black Middle Class	01/23/98	61*
Diversity in Hollywood	08/05/16	649
Redistricting Disputes	03/12/04	221
School Desegregation	04/23/04	345
Voting Controversies	02/21/14	169
National Collegiate Athletic Association (NCAA)		
Paying College Athletes	07/11/14	577
Reforming Big-Time College Sports	03/19/04	249
Sports and Sexual Assault	04/28/17	361
National Education Association		
Charter Schools	12/20/02	1033
Grade Inflation	06/07/02	505
Teacher Education	10/17/97	924*
National Endowment for the Arts		
Arts Funding	10/21/94	913
Funding the Arts	07/14/17	581
Humanities Education	12/06/13	1029
National Highway Traffic Safety Administration		
Future of Cars	07/25/14	625
SUV Debate	05/16/03	454*
Teen Driving	01/07/05	1
Truck Safety	03/12/99	209
National Institutes of Health, U.S.		
Alternative Medicine	01/31/92	73
Alternative Medicine	09/06/13	741
Alternative Medicine's Next Phase	02/14/97	121
Avian Flu Threat	01/13/06	25
Chronic Fatigue Syndrome	04/05/02	289
Combating Scientific Misconduct	01/10/97	1
Embryo Research	12/17/99	1065
Fetal Tissue Research	08/16/91	561
Fighting SARS	06/20/03	569
Food Labeling	06/16/17	509
Gene Therapy	10/18/91	777

	Date	Page
Gene Therapy's Future	12/08/95	1089
Increase in Autism	06/13/03	**545
Manipulating the Human Genome	06/19/15	529
Medical Breakthroughs	09/15/17	749
Pandemic Threat	06/02/17	457
Reforming Veterans' Health Care	11/21/14	985
Science and Politics	08/20/04	672*
Stem Cell Research	09/01/06	**697
Treating Alzheimer's Disease	07/24/15	625
Women's Health Issues	05/13/94	416*
Nationalism		
'Alt-Right' Movement	03/17/17	241
Centennial Olympic Games	04/05/96	289
Deepening Canadian Crisis over Quebec	04/12/91	205
Democracy in the Arab World	01/30/04	73
Europe's New Right	02/12/93	121
European Union's Future	12/16/16	1037
Quebec Sovereignty	10/06/95	873
Soviet Republics Rebel	07/12/91	465
U.S.-Russian Relations	05/22/98	474*
National Labor Relations Board		
Future of the Airline Industry	06/21/02	545
Labor Movement's Future	06/28/96	564*
National Parks		
Bush and the Environment	10/25/02	865
Is America Allowing Its Past to Be Stolen?	01/18/91	33
Managing Public Lands	11/04/11	929
Managing Western Lands	04/22/16	361
National Parks	05/28/93	457
National Parks	01/17/14	49
National Parks Under Pressure	10/06/06	817
Protecting the National Parks	06/16/00	521
National Performance Review		
Reinventing Government	02/17/95	145
National Public Radio		
Public Broadcasting	09/18/92	821*
National Rifle Association		
Gun Control	03/08/13	233
Gun Control Debate	11/12/04	949
Mexico's Drug War	12/12/08	1009
National Science Foundation		
Combating Scientific Misconduct	01/10/97	1
National service. *See Voluntarism*		
Native Americans		
Adoption	11/26/93	1047*
Alcohol Advertising	03/14/97	221*
American Indians	04/28/06	**361
Archaeology Today	05/24/02	457
Bilingual Education vs. English Immersion	12/11/09	1029

	Date	Page
Child Welfare	08/26/16	673
Crisis on the Plains	05/09/03	417
Environmental Justice	06/19/98	534*
Gambling Boom	03/18/94	241
Gambling in America	03/07/03	201
Gambling Under Attack	09/06/96	769
Is America Allowing Its Past to Be Stolen?	01/18/91	33
Managing Western Lands	04/22/16	361
Native Americans	05/08/92	385
Native Americans' Future	07/12/96	601
Native American Sovereignty	05/05/17	385
Native American Youths	04/24/15	361
Parental Rights	10/25/96	942*
Quebec Sovereignty	10/06/95	887*
Religion in the Workplace	08/23/02	649
Reparations Movement	06/22/01	536*
Stolen Antiquities	11/10/17	945
Women in Prison	03/03/17	193

NATO. *See North Atlantic Treaty Organization*

Natural gas

	Date	Page
Air Pollution Conflict	11/14/03	976*
Alternative Energy	07/10/92	584
Alternative Energy	02/25/05	173
Electric Cars	07/09/93	582*
Energy Policy	05/25/01	454*
Energy Policy	05/20/11	457
Fracking Controversy	12/16/11	1049
Future of the Arctic	09/20/13	789
Renewable Energy	11/07/97	961

Natural resources. *See Agriculture; Conservation; Energy policy; Forests and forestry; Water resources; Wildlife*

Navy, U.S. *See Military service*

Nazis

	Date	Page
Ethics of War	12/13/02	1013
Holocaust Reparations	03/26/99	257
Reparations Movement	06/22/01	529
Stopping Genocide	08/27/04	685
War Crimes	07/07/95	598*

Neo-Nazis

	Date	Page
'Alt-Right' Movement	03/17/17	241
Anti-Semitism	05/12/17	409
Europe's New Right	02/12/93	121
European Unrest	01/09/15	25
Far-Right Extremism	09/18/15	769

Netherlands

	Date	Page
Aggressive Driving	07/25/97	662*
Assisted Suicide	02/21/92	158*
Assisted Suicide Controversy	05/05/95	404*
Caring for the Dying	09/05/97	780*

Nevada

	Date	Page
Nuclear Waste	06/08/01	489
Prostitution	06/11/93	505

New England. *See Northeastern states*

New York

	Date	Page
Coastal Development	02/22/13	181
Community Policing	02/05/93	110*
Death Penalty Debate	03/10/95	193
Declining Crime Rates	04/04/97	289
The Homeless	08/07/92	676
Mafia Crackdown	03/27/92	265
Policing the Police	03/17/00	209
Re-examining 9/11	06/04/04	493

News media, Newspapers. *See Journalism*

Noise pollution

	Date	Page
Indoor Air Pollution	10/27/95	958*

Nonprofit organizations. *See Charities and nonprofit organizations*

North American Free Trade Agreement (NAFTA)

	Date	Page
Deepening Canadian Crisis over Quebec	04/12/91	214*
Exporting Jobs	02/20/04	149
Illegal Immigration	04/24/92	379
Immigration Reform	09/24/93	854*
Income Inequality	04/17/98	352*
International Law	12/17/04	1049
Mexico's Emergence	07/19/91	501*
Mexico's Future	09/19/97	817
Mexico's Future	10/26/12	913
Quebec Sovereignty	10/06/95	880*
Rethinking NAFTA	06/07/96	481
Truck Safety	03/12/99	222*
Trump Presidency	01/06/17	1
Unions at a Crossroads	08/07/15	673
U.S. Auto Industry	10/16/92	897*
U.S.-Mexico Relations	11/09/01	921
U.S.-Mexico Relations	09/02/16	697
U.S. Trade Policy	01/29/93	73
Worker Retraining	01/21/94	66*
Worker Safety	05/21/04	445

North Atlantic Treaty Organization (NATO)

	Date	Page
Afghanistan Dilemma	08/07/09	**669*
Cyberwarfare Threat	10/06/17	821
Dealing With the "New" Russia	06/06/08	481
Defense Priorities	07/30/99	641
Expanding NATO	05/16/97	433
Foreign Policy Burden	08/20/93	721
Future Job Market	01/11/02	1
Future of NATO	02/28/03	177
Global Refugee Crisis	07/09/99	569
NATO's Changing Role	08/21/92	713
Resurgent Russia	02/07/14	121
Russia's Political Future	05/03/96	401*
Stopping Genocide	08/27/04	685
U.S.-Europe Relations	03/23/12	277
U.S.-Russia Relations	01/13/17	25

	Date	Page
U.S.-Russian Relations	05/22/98	457
North Korea. *See Korea (North)*		
Northeastern states		
Marine Mammals vs. Fish	08/28/92	747
Recession's Regional Impact	02/01/91	65
Northern Ireland		
Northern Ireland Cease-Fire	09/15/95	801
U.S.-British Relations	01/30/98	84*
Northern spotted owl		
Endangered Species	06/21/91	409*
Jobs vs. Environment	05/15/92	409
Protecting Endangered Species	04/19/96	337
Public Land Policy	06/17/94	542*
Nuclear fusion		
Energy and the Environment	03/03/00	165*
Nuclear Fusion	01/22/93	49
Will Nuclear Power Get Another Chance?	02/22/91	119*
Nuclear power plants		
Air Pollution Conflict	11/14/03	976*
Alternative Energy	07/10/92	582*
Energy Policy	05/25/01	455*
Energy Security	02/01/02	73
Managing Nuclear Waste	01/28/11	73
Nuclear Energy	03/10/06	217
Nuclear Fusion	01/22/93	49
Nuclear Waste	06/08/01	489
The Politics of Energy	03/05/99	193*
U.S.-Iran Relations	03/04/16	217
U.S. Policy on Iran	11/16/07	961
Will Nuclear Power Get Another Chance?	02/22/91	113
Nuclear test ban treaties		
Emerging India	04/19/02	329
Military Readiness	11/03/17	917
Modernizing the Nuclear Arsenal	07/29/16	625
Non-Proliferation Treaty at 25	01/27/95	73
North Korea Showdown	05/19/17	433
Nuclear Arms Cleanup	06/24/94	553
Nuclear Proliferation	06/05/92	497*
Nuclear Proliferation and Terrorism	04/02/04	297
Weapons of Mass Destruction	03/08/02	193
Nuclear waste		
Food Irradiation	06/12/92	511
Managing Nuclear Waste	01/28/11	73
Nuclear Arms Cleanup	06/24/94	553
Nuclear Energy	03/10/06	217
Nuclear Power	06/10/11	505
Nuclear Waste	06/08/01	489
The Politics of Energy	03/05/99	193*
Will Nuclear Power Get Another Chance?	02/22/91	123*
Worker Safety	05/21/04	445

	Date	Page
Nuclear weapons		
Confronting Iraq	10/04/02	793
Emerging India	04/19/02	329
Ethics of War	12/13/02	1013
The Future of U.S.-Russia Relations	01/18/02	32*
Homeland Security	02/13/09	129
Managing Nuclear Waste	01/28/11	73
Middle East Tensions	10/27/06	**889
Military Readiness	11/03/17	917
Missile Defense	09/08/00	689
Modernizing the Nuclear Arsenal	07/29/16	625
New Defense Priorities	09/13/02	726*
Non-Proliferation Treaty at 25	01/27/95	73
North Korea Showdown	05/19/17	433
North Korean Crisis	04/11/03	329*
Nuclear Arms Cleanup	06/24/94	553
Nuclear Disarmament	10/02/09	**813
Nuclear Proliferation	06/05/92	481
Nuclear Proliferation and Terrorism	04/02/04	297
Policing the Borders	02/22/02	145
Rethinking Foreign Policy	02/02/07	97
Russia and the Former Soviet Republics	06/17/05	541
The United Nations and Global Security	02/27/04	173
U.S.-Iran Relations	03/04/16	217
U.S. Policy on Iran	11/16/07	961
U.S.-Russian Relations	05/22/98	457
Weapons of Mass Destruction	03/08/02	193
Nursing		
Doctor Shortage	08/28/15	697
Nursing Shortage	09/20/02	745
Primary Care	03/17/95	230*
Nursing homes		
Caring for the Elderly	02/20/98	145
Caring for the Elderly	10/13/06	841
Medicaid Reform	07/16/04	589
Retirement Security	05/31/02	481
Worker Safety	05/21/04	445
Nutrition. *See Food and nutrition*		
Obama, Barack		
Afghanistan Dilemma	08/07/09	**669*
America at War	07/23/10	**605
Campaign Finance Reform	06/13/08	505
China and the South China Sea	01/20/17	49
Civic Education	02/03/17	97
Closing Guantánamo	02/27/09	**177
Closing Guantanamo	09/30/16	793
Conspiracy Theories	10/23/09	885
Democrats' Future	10/29/10	893
Financial Industry Overhaul	07/30/10	629
Future of the Democratic Party	10/13/17	845
Gays in the Military	09/18/09	**765
Gridlock in Washington	04/30/10	385
Hate Groups	05/08/09	421

	Date	Page
Health-Care Reform	08/28/09	693*
High-Speed Trains	05/01/09	**397
Human Rights Issues	10/30/09	909
Human Spaceflight	10/16/09	861
Interrogating the CIA	09/25/09	789
Israeli-Palestinian Conflict	06/21/13	545
Lies and Politics	02/18/11	145
Media Bias	05/03/13	401
Nuclear Disarmament	10/02/09	**813
The Obama Legacy	11/04/16	913
The Obama Presidency	01/30/09	73
Presidential Election	02/03/12	101
Privatizing Government Services	12/08/17	1017
Redistricting Showdown	08/25/17	677
Revising No Child Left Behind	04/16/10	337
Social Media and Politics	10/12/12	865
Space Program	02/24/12	177
States and Federalism	10/15/10	845
Supreme Court Controversies	09/28/12	813
Trump Presidency	01/06/17	1
U.S.-British Relations	11/05/10	917*
U.S.-China Relations	05/07/10	**409
U.S.-Europe Relations	03/23/12	277
The Value of a College Education	11/20/09	981
Vanishing Jobs	03/13/09	225

Obesity

Diabetes Epidemic	03/09/01	185
Dieting and Health	04/14/95	321
Eating Disorders	12/18/92	1097
Hunger in America	12/22/00	1046*
Obesity and Health	01/15/99	25
Obesity Epidemic	01/31/03	73
Physical Fitness	11/06/92	964*
Preventing Disease	01/06/12	1
Smart Growth	05/28/04	474*
Sugar Controversies	11/30/12	1013
Women's Health	11/07/03	941

Obscenity. *See Pornography*

Obsessive-compulsive disorders

Prozac Controversy	08/19/94	721

Occupational health and safety

Child Labor and Sweatshops	08/16/96	721
Coal Industry's Future	06/17/16	529
Coal Mining Safety	03/17/06	241
Crackdown on Smoking	12/04/92	1049
Decriminalizing Prostitution	04/15/16	337
Drug Testing	11/20/98	1001
Electromagnetic Fields	04/26/91	237
Indoor Air Pollution	10/27/95	953*
Job Stress	08/04/95	681
Labor Unions' Future	09/02/05	**709
Lead Poisoning	06/19/92	534*
Mine Safety	06/24/11	553

	Date	Page
Nuclear Power	06/10/11	505
Peace Corps Challenges	01/11/13	29
Prison Reform	04/06/07	289
Privacy in the Workplace	11/19/93	1013*
Regulating Pesticides	08/06/99	678*
Repetitive Stress Injuries	06/23/95	537
Worker Safety	05/21/04	445
Worker Safety	10/04/13	837

Occupations. *See Employment and unemployment; Wages and salaries*

Oceans

Arctic Development	12/02/16	989
Climate Change	01/27/06	73
Fish Farming	07/27/07	625
Marine Mammals vs. Fish	08/28/92	737
Oil Spills	01/17/92	25
Renewable Energy	11/07/97	975*
Saving the Oceans	11/04/05	933
Species Extinction	12/15/17	1041
Threatened Coastlines	02/07/92	97
Threatened Fisheries	08/02/02	617
Water Shortages	08/01/03	649

Official English

Bilingual Education	08/13/93	713*
Bilingual Education vs. English Immersion	12/11/09	1029
Debate over Bilingualism	01/19/96	49
Future of Language	11/17/00	929
Latinos' Future	10/17/03	869
Puerto Rico's Status	10/23/98	936*

Oil industry. *See Petroleum*

Oklahoma City, Okla., bombing, 1995

Combating Terrorism	07/21/95	633
Treating Anxiety	02/08/02	97

Old age. *See Elderly*

Olympic games

Athletes and Drugs	07/26/91	513
Centennial Olympic Games	04/05/96	289
Extreme Sports	04/03/09	297
Gender Equity in Sports	04/18/97	337
Human Rights in China	07/25/08	601
Mosquito-Borne Disease	07/22/16	601
Pay-Per-View TV	10/04/91	729
Resurgent Russia	02/07/14	121
Sports and Drugs	07/23/04	**613
Sports and Sexual Assault	04/28/17	361
Women and Sports	03/06/92	193

OPEC. *See Organization of Petroleum Exporting Countries*

Operation rescue

Abortion Clinic Protests	04/07/95	297
Abortion Debates	03/21/03	249

	Date	Page
Oregon		
Assisted Suicide Controversy	05/05/95	393
Caring for the Dying	09/05/97	769
Jobs vs. Environment	05/15/92	409
Medicaid Reform	07/16/04	589
Prison Overcrowding	02/04/94	111*
Right to Die	05/13/05	421
Smart Growth	05/28/04	469
Organ transplants		
Fetal Tissue Research	08/16/91	561
Fighting over Animal Rights	08/02/96	673
Organ Donations	04/15/11	337
Organ Shortage	02/21/03	153
Organ Transplants	08/11/95	705
Organic farming and food		
Buying Green	02/29/08	193
Crisis on the Plains	05/09/03	417
Factory Farms	01/12/07	25
Farm Subsidies	05/17/02	433
Fish Farming	07/27/07	625
Food Labeling	06/16/17	509
Food Safety	11/01/02	897
Food Safety Battle: Organic v. Biotech	09/04/98	761
Hunger in America	07/07/17	557
Medical Marijuana	07/21/17	605
Reducing Your Carbon Footprint	12/05/08	985
Regulating Pesticides	01/28/94	73
Regulating Pesticides	08/06/99	665
Slow Food Movement	01/26/07	73
Organization of American States		
Democracy in Latin America	11/03/00	893*
Organization of Petroleum Exporting Countries (OPEC)		
Air Pollution Conflict	11/14/03	976*
Energy Security	02/01/02	73
Oil Diplomacy	01/24/03	49
Oil Imports	08/23/91	585
Oil Jitters	01/04/08	**1
Oil Production in the 21st Century	08/07/98	673
Ozone		
Air Pollution and Climate Control	11/13/15	961
Arctic Development	12/02/16	989
Bush and the Environment	10/25/02	865
New Air Quality Standards	03/07/97	193
Ozone Depletion	04/03/92	289
Pacific Northwest		
Jobs vs. Environment	05/15/92	409
Marine Mammals vs. Fish	08/28/92	750
Packaging		
Fast-Food Shake-Up	11/08/91	825
Garbage Crisis	03/20/92	241
The Obscenity Debate	12/20/91	982*

	Date	Page
Pain management		
Assisted Suicide Controversy	05/05/95	406*
Caring for the Dying	09/05/97	769
Marijuana Laws	02/11/05	125
Medical Marijuana	07/21/17	605
Regulating Pharmaceuticals	10/11/13	861
Pakistan		
Afghanistan Dilemma	08/07/09	**669*
Emerging India	04/19/02	329
Exporting Democracy	04/01/05	269
Homegrown Jihadists	09/03/10	701
Middle East Tensions	10/27/06	**889
Nuclear Proliferation	06/05/92	481
Nuclear Proliferation and Terrorism	04/02/04	297
U.S.-Pakistan Relations	08/05/11	653*
Weapons of Mass Destruction	03/08/02	193
Palestinians		
Democracy in the Arab World	01/30/04	73
Global Water Shortages	12/15/95	1113
Human Rights Issues	10/30/09	909
Israel at 50	03/06/98	193
Israeli-Palestinian Conflict	06/21/13	545
Middle East Conflict	04/06/01	273
Middle East Peace	01/21/05	53
Middle East Tensions	10/27/06	**889
The Obama Presidency	01/30/09	73
The Palestinians	08/30/91	609
Prospects for Mideast Peace	08/30/02	673
Understanding Islam	11/03/06	913
Panama Canal		
Panama Canal	11/26/99	1017
Panhandling. *See Homeless persons*		
Paralympic Games		
Centennial Olympic Games	04/05/96	306*
Implementing the Disabilities Act	12/20/96	1118*
Paranormal phenomena		
Pursuing the Paranormal	03/29/96	265
Parents — Rights. *See also Family*		
Abortion Showdowns	09/22/06	769
Adoption	11/26/93	1033
Bullying	02/04/05	101
Charter Schools	12/20/02	1033
Child Care	12/17/93	1105
Child Custody and Support	01/13/95	25
Children's Television	08/15/97	721
Child Welfare	08/26/16	673
Child Welfare Reform	04/22/05	345
Cyberbullying	05/02/08	385
Cyber Socializing	07/28/06	625
Drinking on Campus	03/20/98	241
Encouraging Teen Abstinence	07/10/98	592*
Fatherhood Movement	06/02/00	473

	Date	Page
Future of Feminism	04/14/06	313
Gay Marriage	09/05/03	732*
Gay Rights	03/05/93	210*
Gay Rights Update	04/14/00	305
Head Start	04/09/93	289
Home Schooling	09/09/94	769
Home Schooling Debate	01/17/03	25
Immigrant Detention	10/23/15	889
Increase in Autism	06/13/03	**545
Infant Mortality	07/31/92	657*
Mothers' Movement	04/04/03	297
Movie Ratings	03/28/03	273
Parental Rights	10/25/96	937
Parents and Schools	01/20/95	49
Preventing Bullying	12/10/10	**1013
Preventing Juvenile Crime	03/15/96	217
Right to Die	05/13/05	421
School Censorship	02/19/93	145
School Choice Debate	07/18/97	625
School Vouchers Showdown	02/15/02	121
Sex, Violence and the Media	11/17/95	1017
Sportsmanship	03/23/01	225
Students Under Stress	07/13/07	577
Teaching Values	06/21/96	529
Teenagers and Abortion	07/05/91	441
Teen Driving	01/07/05	1
Treating Addiction	01/06/95	6*
Treating Anxiety	02/08/02	108*
Unemployment Benefits	04/25/03	385*
Underage Drinking	03/13/92	217
Vaccine Controversies	02/19/16	169
Video Games	11/10/06	**937
Youth Fitness	09/26/97	854*

Patents

3D Printing	12/07/12	1037
Drugmakers Under Siege	09/03/99	753
Future of Books	05/29/09	**473
Genes and Health	01/21/11	49
Gene Therapy's Future	12/08/95	1089
Patent Controversies	02/27/15	193
Patent Disputes	12/15/06	1033
Patenting Human Genes	05/31/13	473
Prescription Drug Costs	05/20/16	457
Software Piracy	05/21/93	433
U.S. Trade Policy	01/29/93	73

PATRIOT Act

Civil Liberties Debates	10/24/03	893
Civil Liberties in Wartime	12/14/01	1017
Homeland Security	09/12/03	749
Intelligence Reforms	01/24/02	49
Policing the Borders	02/22/02	145
Presidential Power	11/15/02	945
Presidential Power	02/24/06	169
Presidential Power	03/06/15	217

Patriotism

	Date	Page
Patriotism in America	06/25/99	545

Pay. *See Wages and salaries*

Payroll taxes. *See Social Security*

Peace Corps

National Service	06/25/93	553
National Service	06/30/06	577
Peace Corps Challenges	01/11/13	29
Peace Corps' Challenges in the 1990s	01/25/91	49

Peacekeeping

China and the South China Sea	01/20/17	49
North Korea Showdown	05/19/17	433
Privatizing the Military	06/25/04	565
The United Nations and Global Security	02/27/04	173

Pedestrian safety

Aggressive Driving	07/25/97	649
High-Tech Policing	04/21/17	337
Transportation Policy	07/04/97	577

Pensions. *See Social Security; Retirement*

Rethinking Retirement	06/19/09	549

People for the Ethical Treatment of Animals

Animal Rights	05/24/91	301
Fighting over Animal Rights	08/02/96	673

People's Republic of China. *See China*

Perot, Ross

Third-Party Prospects	12/22/95	1137

Persian Gulf War, 1991

Calculating the Costs of the Gulf War	03/15/91	145
Chemical and Biological Weapons	01/31/97	73
Chemical and Biological Weapons	12/13/13	1053
China Today	08/04/00	633*
Confronting Iraq	10/04/02	793
Defense Priorities	07/30/99	641
Democracy in the Arab World	01/30/04	73
Oil Diplomacy	01/24/03	49
Oil Imports	08/23/91	585
Oil Spills	01/17/92	25
The Palestinians	08/30/91	609
Recession's Regional Impact	02/01/91	65
Reforming Veterans' Health Care	11/21/14	985
Should the U.S. Reinstate the Draft?	01/11/91	17
Weapons of Mass Destruction	03/08/02	193
Women in the Military	09/25/92	833

Peru

Democracy in Latin America	11/03/00	881
Privatizing the Military	06/25/04	565
Trouble in South America	03/14/03	225

Pesticides

Breast Cancer	06/27/97	560*
Food Labeling	06/16/17	509
Food Safety	06/04/93	481
Food Safety Battle: Organic v. Biotech	09/04/98	761

	Date	Page
Pesticide Controversies	06/05/15	481
Regulating Pesticides	01/28/94	73
Regulating Pesticides	08/06/99	665
Species Extinction	12/15/17	1041

Petroleum

	Date	Page
Air Pollution Conflict	11/14/03	976*
Alternative Energy	07/10/92	573
Arctic Development	12/02/16	989
Calculating the Costs of the		
Gulf War	03/15/91	145
China and the South China Sea	01/20/17	49
Cost of the Iraq War	04/25/08	361*
Democracy in the Arab World	01/30/04	73
Domestic Energy Development	09/30/05	809
Energy and Climate	07/24/09	621
Energy Policy	05/25/01	454*
Energy Policy	05/20/11	457
Energy Security	02/01/02	73
Future of the Arctic	09/20/13	789
The Future of U.S.-Russia Relations	01/18/02	40*
Gulf Coast Restoration	08/26/11	677*
Hating America	11/23/01	982*
Lead Poisoning	06/19/92	536
Mass Transit Boom	01/18/08	49
Mexico's Emergence	07/19/91	497
Offshore Drilling	06/25/10	553
Oil Diplomacy	01/24/03	49
Oil Imports	08/23/91	585
Oil Jitters	01/04/08	**1
Oil Production in the 21st Century	08/07/98	673
Oil Spills	01/17/92	25
The Politics of Energy	03/05/99	185
Rebuilding Iraq	07/11/03	632*
Reform in Iran	12/18/98	1110*
Renewable Energy	11/07/97	961
Socially Responsible Investing	08/29/08	673
SUV Debate	05/16/03	449
Universal Basic Income	09/08/17	725

Pets

	Date	Page
America's Pampered Pets	12/27/96	1129
Animal Intelligence	10/22/10	869
Caring for the Elderly	02/20/98	150*
Fighting over Animal Rights	08/02/96	691*
Invasive Species	02/17/12	153

Philanthropy. *See Charities and nonprofit organizations; Voluntarism*

Philippines

	Date	Page
China and the South China Sea	01/20/17	49
U.S. Policy in Asia	11/27/92	1025

Phonics. *See Reading*

Physical fitness

	Date	Page
Aging Baby Boomers	10/19/07	865
Aging Population	07/15/11	577
Baby Boomers at Midlife	07/31/98	649
Diabetes Epidemic	03/09/01	185
Dieting and Health	04/14/95	321
Eating Disorders	12/18/92	1097
Heart Health	09/12/08	721
Obesity Epidemic	01/31/03	86*
Physical Fitness	11/06/92	953
Preventing Disease	01/06/12	1
Preventing Obesity	10/01/10	797
Professional Football	01/29/10	**73
Prolonging Life	09/30/11	805*
Sports and Drugs	07/23/04	**613
Treating Alzheimer's	03/04/11	193
Youth Fitness	09/26/97	841

Physicians. *See also Medical malpractice*

	Date	Page
Alternative Medicine	01/31/92	73
Assisted Suicide	02/21/92	145
Assisted Suicide	05/17/13	449
Assisted Suicide Controversy	05/05/95	393
Caring for the Dying	09/05/97	769
Computers and Medicine	10/27/00	863*
Cosmetic Surgery	04/15/05	317
Doctor Shortage	08/28/15	697
Fairness in Salaries	05/29/92	464*
Fighting Superbugs	08/24/07	673
Health-Care Reform	08/28/09	693*
Homeopathy Debate	12/19/03	1069
Managed Care	04/12/96	313
Managing Managed Care	04/16/99	305
Marijuana Laws	02/11/05	125
Medicaid Reform	07/16/04	589
Medical Malpractice	02/14/03	129
Medical Mistakes	02/25/00	137
Medication Abuse	10/09/09	837
Mental Illness	08/06/93	690*
Mental Illness Medication Debate	02/06/04	101
Patients' Rights	02/06/98	97
Primary Care	03/17/95	217
Rating Doctors	05/05/00	377
Right to Die	05/13/05	421
Smallpox Threat	02/07/03	105

Plastics

	Date	Page
The Economics of Recycling	03/27/98	265
Future of Recycling	12/14/07	1033
Garbage Crisis	03/20/92	253*

Plutonium

	Date	Page
Nuclear Arms Cleanup	06/24/94	553
Nuclear Proliferation	06/05/92	496*

Poland

	Date	Page
Democracy in Eastern Europe	10/08/99	865
Expanding NATO	05/16/97	433
The Greening of Eastern Europe	11/15/91	849
Peace Corps' Challenges in the 1990s	01/25/91	49

	Date	Page			Date	Page
Police and law enforcement				Prostitution	06/11/93	505
Age Discrimination	08/01/97	673		Prostitution Debate	05/23/08	433
Aggressive Driving	07/25/97	649		Punishing Sex Offenders	01/12/96	25
Anti-Semitism	05/12/17	409		Pursuing the Paranormal	03/29/96	280*
Campus Sexual Assault	10/31/14	913		Race in America	07/11/03	593
Central American Gangs	01/30/15	97		Racial Profiling	11/22/13	1005
Combating Terrorism	07/21/95	633		Reducing Traffic Deaths	02/17/17	145
Community Policing	02/05/93	97		Reforming the CIA	02/02/96	97
Crime on Campus	02/04/11	97		Robotic Warfare	01/23/15	73
Crime Victims' Rights	07/22/94	636*		School Discipline	05/09/14	409
Cyber-Predators	03/01/02	169		Serial Killers	10/31/03	917
Cyber Socializing	07/28/06	625		Sexual Abuse and the Clergy	05/03/02	393
The Dark Web	01/15/16	49		Sleep Deprivation	02/12/10	121
Declining Crime Rates	04/04/97	289		Sports and Sexual Assault	04/28/17	361
Decriminalizing Prostitution	04/15/16	337		State Budget Crises	10/03/03	821
DNA Databases	05/28/99	449		Stock Market Troubles	01/16/04	25
Domestic Drones	10/18/13	885		Stolen Antiquities	11/10/17	945
Drug-Policy Debate	07/28/00	593		Suburban Crime	09/03/93	769
Examining Forensics	07/17/09	597		Three-Strikes Laws	05/10/02	417
Eyewitness Testimony	10/14/11	853		Torture	04/18/03	345
Far-Right Extremism	09/18/15	769		Trump Presidency	01/06/17	1
The FBI Under Fire	04/11/97	313		Underage Drinking	03/13/92	217
Fighting Crime	02/08/08	121		U.S.-Mexico Relations	09/02/16	697
Fighting Gangs	10/09/15	841		War on Drugs	03/19/93	241
Forensic Science Controversies	02/10/17	121		Women in Prison	03/03/17	193
Future of the Airline Industry	06/21/02	545		Youth Gangs	10/11/91	753
Gang Crisis	05/14/04	421		**Political action committees**		
Gangs in the U.S.	07/16/10	581		Campaign Finance	05/06/16	409
Globalization Backlash	09/28/01	761		Campaign Finance Reform	02/09/96	121
Gun Control Debate	11/12/04	949		Campaign Finance Reform	03/31/00	257
Guns on Campus	01/27/17	73		Campaign Finance Showdown	11/22/02	969
Haiti's Dilemma	02/18/05	149		Electing the President	04/20/07	337
High-Tech Policing	04/21/17	337		Political Polling	02/06/15	121
Homeland Security	09/12/03	749		Populism and Party Politics	09/09/16	721
Human Trafficking and Slavery	03/26/04	273		Tea Party Movement	03/19/10	**241*
Identity Theft	06/10/05	517		**Political advertising**		
Illegal Immigration	04/24/92	361		Advertising Under Attack	09/13/91	668*
Illegal Immigration	05/06/05	393		Campaign Finance	05/06/16	409
Immigration Conflict	03/09/12	229		Campaign Finance Showdown	11/22/02	969
Jailing Debtors	09/16/16	745		Cyberpolitics	09/17/04	757
Mafia Crackdown	03/27/92	265		Electing the President	04/20/07	337
Mental Health Policy	05/10/13	425		Labor Movement's Future	06/28/96	568*
Methamphetamine	07/15/05	589		Political Consultants	10/04/96	865
Native American Sovereignty	05/05/17	385		Political Polling	02/06/15	121
Opioid Crisis	10/07/16	817		Populism and Party Politics	09/09/16	721
Police Brutality	09/06/91	633		Regulating Nonprofits	12/26/97	1135*
Police Corruption	11/24/95	1041		Think Tanks in Transition	09/29/17	797
Police Misconduct	04/06/12	301		Trust in Media	06/09/17	481
Police Tactics	12/12/14	1033		Young Voters	10/02/15	817
Policing the Borders	02/22/02	145		**Political asylum**		
Policing the Police	03/17/00	209		Assisting Refugees	02/07/97	111*
Presidential Power	11/15/02	945		Central American Gangs	01/30/15	97
Preventing Teen Drug Use	03/15/02	217		European Migration Crisis	07/31/15	649
Property Rights	06/16/95	524*		European Union's Future	12/16/16	1037

	Date	Page
European Unrest	01/09/15	25
Europe's New Right	02/12/93	121
Global Refugee Crisis	07/09/99	576*
Illegal Immigration	04/24/92	361
Illegal Immigration	05/06/05	393
Immigrant Detention	10/23/15	889
The Iraq War: 10 Years Later	03/01/13	205
North Korea Showdown	05/19/17	433
Terrorism in Africa	07/10/15	577

"Political correctness"

Academic Politics	02/16/96	145
Racial Quotas	05/17/91	292*
Racial Tensions in Schools	01/07/94	13*

Political ethics. *See Ethics in government*

Politics. *See also Special interest groups*

'Alt-Right' Movement	03/17/17	241
Arctic Development	12/02/16	989
Birth-Control Debate	06/24/05	565
Blog Explosion	06/09/06	**505
Campaign Finance	05/06/16	409
Campaign Finance Reform	02/09/96	121
Campaign Finance Reform	03/31/00	257
Campaign Finance Showdown	11/22/02	969
Celebrity Culture	03/18/05	256*
Change in Latin America	07/21/06	601
Changing Demographics	11/16/12	989
Changing U.S. Electorate	05/30/08	**457
Charter Schools	03/10/17	217
China and the South China Sea	01/20/17	49
Civic Education	02/03/17	97
Computer Hacking	09/16/11	757*
Conspiracy Theories	10/23/09	885
Cost of the Iraq War	04/25/08	361*
Cyberpolitics	09/17/04	757
Cyberwarfare Threat	10/06/17	821
D.C. Voting Rights	04/11/08	313*
Debating Hip-Hop	06/15/07	529
Democrats in Congress	06/08/07	505
Downsizing Prisons	03/11/11	217
Drug Testing	11/20/98	1015*
Electing the President	04/20/07	337
Evangelical Christians	09/14/01	713
First Ladies	06/14/96	505
Future of the Christian Right	06/23/17	533
Future of the Democratic Party	10/13/17	845
Future of the GOP	10/24/14	889
Gay Marriage	09/05/03	742*
Gay Rights	03/05/93	203*
Gridlock in Washington	04/30/10	385
Hunger in America	07/07/17	557
Independent Counsels	02/21/97	145
Independent Counsels Re-examined	05/07/99	377
Internet Accuracy	08/01/08	625

	Date	Page
Judges and Politics	07/27/01	577
Judicial Elections	04/24/09	373
Latinos' Future	10/17/03	869
Lies and Politics	02/18/11	145
Lobbying Boom	07/22/05	613
Media Bias	05/03/13	401
Muslims in America	07/28/17	629
National Debt	09/01/17	701
The Obama Legacy	11/04/16	913
'Occupy' Movement	01/13/12	25
The Partisan Divide	04/30/04	373
Partisan Politics	03/19/99	233
Polarization in America	02/28/14	193
Political Consultants	10/04/96	865
Political Conventions	08/08/08	649
Political Scandals	05/27/94	457
Politicians and Privacy	04/17/92	337
Populism and Party Politics	09/09/16	721
Pork Barrel Politics	06/16/06	529
Presidential Election	02/03/12	101
Prosecutors and Politics	06/22/07	553
Protestants Today	12/07/07	1009
Public-Employee Unions	04/08/11	313
Race and Politics	07/18/08	577
Race in America	07/11/03	598*
Redistricting Debates	02/25/11	169
Redistricting Disputes	03/12/04	221
Redistricting: Drawing Power with a Map	02/15/91	97
Redistricting Showdown	08/25/17	677
Regulating Lobbying	06/06/14	481
Religion and Politics	07/30/04	637
Rethinking Foreign Aid	04/14/17	313
Science and Politics	08/20/04	661
Sex Scandals	01/22/10	49
Social Media Explosion	01/25/13	81
Social Media and Politics	10/12/12	865
State Budget Crises	10/03/03	821
Supreme Court Controversies	09/28/12	813
Tea Party Movement	03/19/10	**241*
Term Limits	01/10/92	1
Think Tanks in Transition	09/29/17	797
Third-Party Prospects	12/22/95	1137
Trump Presidency	01/06/17	1
Trust in Media	06/09/17	481
Understanding Mormonism	10/19/12	889
U.S.-Mexico Relations	09/02/16	697
U.S.-Russia Relations	01/13/17	25
Voter Rights	05/18/12	449
Voting Controversies	02/21/14	169
Women in Leadership	09/23/16	769
Women in Politics	03/21/08	265

Pollution. *See Air pollution; Hazardous substances; Water pollution*

	Date	Page
Popular culture		
Celebrity Culture	03/18/05	245
Cosmetic Surgery	04/15/05	317
Reality TV	08/27/10	677
U.S.-British Relations	11/05/10	917*
Population. *See also Census*		
Blighted Cities	11/12/10	941*
Census Controversey	05/14/10	433
Climate Change and National Security	09/22/17	773
Crisis on the Plains	05/09/03	417
Debate Over Immigration	07/14/00	580*
Declining Birthrates	11/21/08	961
Emerging India	04/19/02	342*
Foreign Aid After Sept. 11	04/26/02	361
Future of the Democratic Party	10/13/17	845
Gentrification	02/20/15	169
Global Hunger	08/08/14	673
Global Population Growth	01/16/15	49
Latinos' Future	10/17/03	869
Muslims in America	07/28/17	629
Population and the Environment	07/17/98	601
Population Growth	07/16/93	601
Reassessing Foreign Aid	09/27/96	841
Redistricting Debates	02/25/11	169
Redistricting Showdown	08/25/17	677
Rethinking Foreign Aid	04/14/17	313
Smart Growth	05/28/04	469
Universal Basic Income	09/08/17	725
Water Shortages	08/01/03	649
Women and Human Rights	04/30/99	365*
World Hunger	10/25/91	801
Pornography		
Broadcast Indecency	04/16/04	326*
Crackdown on Sexual Harassment	07/19/96	642*
Cyber-Predators	03/01/02	169
Digital Commerce	02/05/99	89
The Future of Libraries	05/23/97	472*
Libraries and the Internet	06/01/01	465
The Obscenity Debate	12/20/91	969
Pornography	10/21/16	865
Privacy and the Internet	12/04/15	1009
Regulating the Internet	06/30/95	561
Sex, Violence and the Media	11/17/95	1017
Violence Against Women	02/26/93	177*
Postal Service, U.S.		
Job Stress	08/04/95	688*
Privatizing Government Services	08/09/96	697
Poverty		
AB and IP Programs	03/03/06	193
Abortion Debates	03/21/03	249
Affordable Housing	02/09/01	89
American Indians	04/28/06	**361
Asthma Epidemic	12/24/99	1089
Birth-Control Debate	06/24/05	565

	Date	Page
Change in Latin America	07/21/06	601
Charitable Giving	11/12/93	985
Childhood Immunizations	06/18/93	529
Children in Crisis	08/31/01	657
Child Poverty	04/07/00	281
Child Poverty	10/28/11	901
Child Welfare	08/26/16	673
Child Welfare Reform	04/22/05	345
Community Prosecution	12/15/00	1009
Consumer Debt	03/02/07	193
Covering the Uninsured	06/14/02	521
Cyberpolitics	09/17/04	757
Debating Hip-Hop	06/15/07	529
Declining Crime Rates	04/04/97	289
Democracy in Latin America	11/03/00	881
The Digital Divide	01/28/00	41
Distance Learning	12/07/01	993
Domestic Poverty	09/07/07	**721
Educating Gifted Students	03/28/97	265
Emergency Medicine	01/05/96	1
Ending Poverty	09/09/05	733
Environmental Justice	06/19/98	529
Evaluating Head Start	08/26/05	685
Fighting Crime	02/08/08	121
Fighting Urban Poverty	07/17/15	601
Fixing Urban Schools	04/27/07	**361
Future of the Catholic Church	06/07/13	497
Gentrification	02/20/15	169
Girls' Rights	04/17/15	337
Haiti's Dilemma	02/18/05	149
Head Start	04/09/93	289
Helping the Homeless	01/26/96	73
The Homeless	08/07/92	665
Housing the Homeless	10/10/14	841
Human Trafficking and Slavery	03/26/04	273
Hunger in America	12/22/00	1033
Hunger in America	07/07/17	557
Income Inequality	04/17/98	337
Infant Mortality	07/31/92	641
Jailing Debtors	09/16/16	745
Lead Poisoning	06/19/92	531
Legal-Aid Crisis	10/07/11	829
Living-Wage Movement	09/27/02	785*
Medicaid Reform	07/16/04	589
Middle-Class Squeeze	03/06/09	201
Native American Sovereignty	05/05/17	385
Native American Youths	04/24/15	361
Networking the Classroom	10/20/95	931*
The New Volunteerism	12/13/96	1081
No Child Left Behind	05/27/05	469
Philanthropy in America	12/08/06	1009
Preventing Obesity	10/01/10	797
Preventing Teen Pregnancy	05/14/93	409
Public Defenders	04/18/08	337*

	Date	Page
Public Housing	09/10/93	793
Puerto Rico: The Struggle over Status	02/08/91	81
Reforming School Funding	12/10/99	1041
Revising No Child Left Behind	04/16/10	337
Reviving Rural Economies	03/31/17	265
School Vouchers	04/09/99	281
School Vouchers Showdown	02/15/02	121
Sexually Transmitted Diseases	12/03/04	997
Should the U.S. Reinstate the Draft?	01/11/91	17
State Budget Crises	10/03/03	832*
Straining the Safety Net	07/31/09	645
Student Aid	01/25/08	73
Teacher Education	10/17/97	918*
Trouble in South America	03/14/03	225
Unemployment Benefits	04/25/03	369
Universal Basic Income	09/08/17	725
Upward Mobility	04/29/05	369
Welfare Experiments	09/16/94	793
Welfare Reform	08/03/01	601
Welfare, Work and the States	12/06/96	1057
The Working Poor	11/03/95	969
Youth Unemployment	03/14/14	241
Youth Volunteerism	01/27/12	77

POWs/MIAs. *See Prisoners of war*

Prayer

Prayer and Healing	01/14/05	25

Pregnancy. *See also Abortion; Adolescents and youth —*
Pregnancy

Abortion Debates	03/21/03	249
Abortion Debates	03/21/14	265
Abortion Showdowns	09/22/06	769
AIDS Update	12/04/98	1064*
Birth Control Choices	07/29/94	649
Electromagnetic Fields	04/26/91	244*
Gene Therapy	10/18/91	790*
Girls' Rights	04/17/15	337
Infant Mortality	07/31/92	641
Lead Poisoning	06/19/92	534*
Mosquito-Borne Disease	07/22/16	601
Mothers' Movement	04/04/03	297
Reproductive Ethics	04/08/94	289
Reproductive Ethics	05/15/09	449
Teen Pregnancy	03/26/10	265*
Women's Health	11/07/03	941

Preschool education

Child Care	12/17/93	1105
Evaluating Head Start	08/26/05	685
Head Start	04/09/93	289
School Vouchers Showdown	02/15/02	121

Presidency, U.S.

Affirmative Action and College Admissions	11/17/17	969

	Date	Page
Bush Presidency	02/02/01	65
Campaign Finance Reform	02/09/96	132*
Campaign Finance Reform	03/31/00	257
Democrats in Congress	06/08/07	505
Electing the President	04/20/07	337
First Ladies	06/14/96	505
Line-Item Veto	06/20/97	529
The Obama Legacy	11/04/16	913
The Obama Presidency	01/30/09	73
The Partisan Divide	04/30/04	373
Partisan Politics	03/19/99	250*
Political Conventions	08/08/08	649
Political Polling	02/06/15	121
Politicians and Privacy	04/17/92	344
Presidential Election	02/03/12	101
Presidential Libraries	03/16/07	241
Presidential Power	11/15/02	945
Presidential Power	02/24/06	169
Presidential Power	03/06/15	217
Prosecutors and Politics	06/22/07	553
Re-examining the Constitution	09/07/12	741
Religion in America	11/25/94	1044*
Social Media and Politics	10/12/12	865
State Budget Crises	10/03/03	821
Tea Party Movement	03/19/10	**241*
Term Limits	01/10/92	12

Presidential elections

Campaign Finance	05/06/16	409
Future of the Democratic Party	10/13/17	845
Future of the GOP	10/24/14	889
Political Conventions	08/08/08	649
Political Polling	02/06/15	121
Populism and Party Politics	09/09/16	721
Unions at a Crossroads	08/07/15	673
Voting Controversies	02/21/14	169
Young Voters	10/02/15	817

Presidential election, 1996

China After Deng	06/13/97	516*
Labor Movement's Future	06/28/96	553
The New Immigrants	01/24/97	56*
Political Consultants	10/04/96	865
Rethinking NAFTA	06/07/96	481
Tax Reform	03/22/96	241

Presidential election, 2000

Cyberpolitics	09/17/04	757
Electoral College	12/08/00	977
Election Reform	11/02/01	897
Latino Voters	04/03/15	289
Legacy of the Vietnam War	02/18/00	128*
The Partisan Divide	04/30/04	373
Voting Controversies	09/15/06	745
Voting Controversies	02/21/14	169

	Date	Page
Presidential election, 2004		
Blog Explosion	06/09/06	**505
Cyberpolitics	09/17/04	757
Electing the President	04/20/07	337
Exporting Jobs	02/20/04	149
The Partisan Divide	04/30/04	373
Presidential Power	03/06/15	217
Religion and Politics	07/30/04	637
Social Security Reform	09/24/04	781
Worker Safety	05/21/04	445
Voting Controversies	09/15/06	745
Presidential election, 2008		
Changing U.S. Electorate	05/30/08	**457
Political Conventions	08/08/08	649
Presidential Power	03/06/15	217
Race and Politics	07/18/08	577
Women in Politics	03/21/08	265
Presidential election, 2012		
Latino Voters	04/03/15	289
Presidential Election	02/03/12	101
Presidential election, 2016		
'Alt-Right' Movement	03/17/17	241
Anti-Semitism	05/12/17	409
Arctic Development	12/02/16	989
Campaign Finance	05/06/16	409
Charter Schools	03/10/17	217
China and the South China Sea	01/20/17	49
Civic Education	02/03/17	97
Cyberwarfare Threat	10/06/17	821
Future of the Christian Right	06/23/17	533
Future of the Democratic Party	10/13/17	845
Immigrants and the Economy	02/24/17	169
Muslims in America	07/28/17	629
The Obama Legacy	11/04/16	913
Populism and Party Politics	09/09/16	721
Redistricting Showdown	08/25/17	677
Rethinking Foreign Aid	04/14/17	313
Reviving Rural Economies	03/31/17	265
Social Security	06/03/16	481
Trump Presidency	01/06/17	1
Trust in Media	06/09/17	481
U.S.-Mexico Relations	09/02/16	697
U.S.-Russia Relations	01/13/17	25
Women in Leadership	09/23/16	769
Press. *See Journalism*		
Preventive medicine		
AIDS Update	12/04/98	1049
Asthma Epidemic	12/24/99	1089
Doctor Shortage	08/28/15	697
Prisoners of war (POWs/MIAs)		
Ethics of War	12/13/02	1013
Intelligence Reform	05/29/15	457

	Date	Page
Presidential Power	11/15/02	945
Torture	04/18/03	345
Treatment of Detainees	08/25/06	673
U.S.-Vietnam Relations	12/03/93	1057
War Crimes	07/07/95	585
Prisons and prisoners		
Census Controversey	05/14/10	433
Closing Guantánamo	02/27/09	**177
Closing Guantanamo	09/30/16	793
Death Penalty Update	01/08/99	1
Downsizing Prisons	03/11/11	217
Gangs in the U.S.	07/16/10	581
Interrogating the CIA	09/25/09	789
Juvenile Justice	11/07/08	913
Kids in Prison	04/27/01	345
Mandatory Sentencing	05/26/95	465
Mental Illness Medication Debate	02/06/04	112*
Organ Shortage	02/21/03	167*
Policing the Borders	02/22/02	145
Prison-Building Boom	09/17/99	801
Prison Health Care	01/05/07	1
Prison Overcrowding	02/04/94	97
Prison Reform	04/06/07	289
Prisoner Reentry	12/04/09	1005
Prisoners and Mental Illness	03/13/15	241
Privatization	11/13/92	985*
Privatizing Government Services	08/09/96	710*
Privatizing Government Services	12/08/17	1017
Public Defenders	04/18/08	337*
Reforming Juvenile Justice	09/11/15	745
Restorative Justice	02/05/16	121
Sentencing Debates	11/05/04	925
Solitary Confinement	09/14/12	765
State Budget Crisis	09/11/09	741
Torture	04/18/03	345
War on Drugs	03/19/93	241
Women and Human Rights	04/30/99	368*
Women in Prison	03/03/17	193
Wrongful Convictions	04/17/09	**345
Privacy		
Adoption Controversies	09/10/99	777
AIDS Update	12/04/98	1049
Artificial Intelligence	04/22/11	361
Big Data and Privacy	10/25/13	909
Civic Renewal	03/21/97	257*
Computers and Medicine	10/27/00	857
Cyber-Predators	03/01/02	169
Cybersecurity	02/26/10	169
Cyberwarfare Threat	10/06/17	821
The Dark Web	01/15/16	49
DNA Databases	05/28/99	449
Domestic Drones	10/18/13	885
Drug Testing	11/20/98	1001

	Date	Page
Future of Marriage	12/01/17	993
Gay Rights	03/05/93	205*
Google's Dominance	11/11/11	953
Government Surveillance	08/30/13	717
High-Tech Policing	04/21/17	337
Identity Theft	06/10/05	517
Intelligence Reform	05/29/15	457
Internet Privacy	11/06/98	953
Internet Shopping	06/28/13	573
Online Privacy	11/06/09	**933
Patients' Rights	02/06/98	104*
Policing the Borders	02/22/02	159*
Politicians and Privacy	04/17/92	337
Privacy and the Internet	12/04/15	1009
Privacy in Peril	11/17/06	961
Privacy in the Workplace	11/19/93	1009
Privacy Under Attack	06/15/01	505
Regulating the Internet	06/30/95	561
Sex Scandals	01/22/10	49
Social Media Explosion	01/25/13	81
Social Media and Politics	10/12/12	865
Social Networking	09/17/10	749
Sports and Sexual Assault	04/28/17	361
Whistleblowers	01/31/14	97

Private Military Contractors (PMCs)

	Date	Page
Privatizing Government Services	12/08/17	1017
Privatizing the Military	06/25/04	565

Privatization

	Date	Page
Business' Role in Education	11/22/91	887
Foster Care Reform	01/09/98	1
Hard Times for Libraries	06/26/92	555
Health-Care Reform	08/28/09	693*
Prison-Building Boom	09/17/99	801
Private Management of Public Schools	03/25/94	265
Privatization	11/13/92	977
Privatizing Government Services	08/09/96	697
Privatizing Government Services	12/08/17	1017
Privatizing the Military	06/25/04	565
Public Broadcasting	09/18/92	825*
Public Land Policy	06/17/94	539*
Reassessing Foreign Aid	09/27/96	849*
Reforming the FDA	06/06/97	497*
Reinventing Government	02/17/95	145
Saving Social Security	10/02/98	857
Social Security	06/03/16	481
Social Security Reform	09/24/04	781
Social Security: The Search for Fairness	04/05/91	189
Space Program's Future	04/25/97	375*
Welfare, Work and the States	12/06/96	1070*

Product liability

	Date	Page
Consumer Safety	10/12/07	841
E-Cigarettes	09/19/14	769

	Date	Page
Regulating Tobacco	09/30/94	854*
Regulating Toxic Chemicals	07/18/14	601
Teens and Tobacco	12/01/95	1078*
Tobacco Industry	12/10/04	**1025
Too Many Lawsuits?	05/22/92	433

Professional sports. *See Sports*

Property rights

	Date	Page
California: Enough Water for the Future?	04/19/91	231*
Endangered Species Act	10/01/99	849
Gentrification	02/20/15	169
Global Water Shortages	12/15/95	1129*
Government and Religion	01/15/10	25
Managing Western Lands	04/22/16	361
Native Americans' Future	07/12/96	601
Native American Sovereignty	05/05/17	385
Property Rights	06/16/95	513
Property Rights	03/04/05	197
Saving Open Spaces	11/05/99	953
School Funding	08/27/93	761*
Smart Growth	05/28/04	469
Stolen Antiquities	04/13/07	313
Stolen Antiquities	11/10/17	945
Threatened Coastlines	02/07/92	97
Urban Sprawl in the West	10/03/97	865

Prostitution

	Date	Page
Prostitution	06/11/93	505
Prostitution Debate	05/23/08	433
Women and Human Rights	04/30/99	353

Prozac. *See Mental health and illness*

Psychiatry. *See Mental health and illness*

Public broadcasting

	Date	Page
Public Broadcasting	09/18/92	809
Public Broadcasting	10/29/99	929

Public health

	Date	Page
AIDS Update	12/04/98	1049
Asbestos Litigation	05/02/03	393
Asthma Epidemic	12/24/99	1089
Birth-Control Debate	06/24/05	565
Breast Cancer	06/27/97	553
Combating Infectious Diseases	06/09/95	489
Covering the Uninsured	06/14/02	521
Dietary Supplements	09/03/04	709
Dietary Supplements	10/30/15	913
Disaster Preparedness	11/18/05	**981
Doctor Shortage	08/28/15	697
Drinking Water Safety	07/15/16	577
Drug Company Ethics	06/06/03	521
Drugmakers Under Siege	09/03/99	760*
Drug-Resistant Bacteria	06/04/99	473
Fighting SARS	06/20/03	569

	Date	Page
Food Labeling	06/16/17	509
Food Safety	11/01/02	897
Homeopathy Debate	12/19/03	1069
Hunger in America	07/07/17	557
Increase in Autism	06/13/03	**545
Mosquito-Borne Disease	07/22/16	601
Obesity Epidemic	01/31/03	73
Opioid Crisis	10/07/16	817
Pandemic Threat	06/02/17	457
Pesticide Controversies	06/05/15	481
Pornography	10/21/16	865
Smallpox Threat	02/07/03	105
Sexually Transmitted Diseases	12/03/04	997
Tobacco Industry	12/10/04	**1025
Understanding Autism	08/01/14	649

Public housing

	Date	Page
Housing Discrimination	11/06/15	937
Housing the Homeless	12/18/09	1053
Public Housing	09/10/93	793

Public lands. *See Federal lands*

Public opinion

	Date	Page
Foreign Policy and Public Opinion	07/15/94	601
Legacy of the Vietnam War	02/18/00	116*

Public schools. *See Elementary and secondary education*

Public utilities

	Date	Page
Alternative Energy	07/10/92	590
Drinking Water Safety	07/15/16	577
Homeland Security	09/12/03	761*
Modernizing the Grid	02/19/10	145
Public-Works Projects	02/20/09	153
Restructuring the Electric Industry	01/17/97	25
Solar Energy Controversies	04/29/16	385
Utility Deregulation	01/14/00	1

Publishing Industry

	Date	Page
Digital Journalism	05/30/14	457
Future of Books	05/29/09	**473

Puerto Rico

	Date	Page
Hispanic Americans	10/30/92	944*
Prescription Drug Prices	07/17/92	610*
Puerto Rico: The Struggle over Status	02/08/91	81
Puerto Rico's Status	10/23/98	929

Putin, Vladimir

	Date	Page
Dealing With the "New" Russia	06/06/08	481
Democracies Under Stress	10/20/17	869
U.S.-Russia Relations	01/13/17	25

Quebec

	Date	Page
Deepening Canadian Crisis over Quebec	04/12/91	205
Quebec Sovereignty	10/06/95	873

Racial profiling

	Date	Page
Civil Liberties in Wartime	12/14/01	1033*
Extreme Sports	04/03/09	297

	Date	Page
High-Tech Policing	04/21/17	337
Muslims in America	07/28/17	629
Police Misconduct	04/06/12	301
Race in America	07/11/03	593
Racial Conflict	01/08/16	25
Racial Profiling	11/22/13	1005
Redistricting Showdown	08/25/17	677
Understanding Islam	11/03/06	913

Racism

	Date	Page
Affirmative Action	09/21/01	737
Affirmative Action and College Admissions	11/17/17	969
'Alt-Right' Movement	03/17/17	241
Anti-Semitism	05/12/17	409
Asian Americans	12/13/91	945
Black Colleges	12/12/03	1045
Black Middle Class	01/23/98	49
Death Penalty Update	01/08/99	1
Debating Hip-Hop	06/15/07	529
Discipline in Schools	02/15/08	145
Diversity in Hollywood	08/05/16	649
Drug-Policy Debate	07/28/00	612*
Environmental Justice	06/19/98	529
Far-Right Extremism	09/18/15	769
Free Speech at Risk	04/26/13	377
Free Speech on Campus	05/08/15	409
Greek Life on Campus	11/20/15	985
Hate Crimes	01/08/93	1
Hate Groups	05/08/09	421
Housing Discrimination	11/06/15	937
Income Inequality	04/17/98	344*
The Jury System	11/10/95	993
Native Americans' Future	07/12/96	601
Native American Youths	04/24/15	361
New Military Culture	04/26/96	361
Police Brutality	09/06/91	633
Police Corruption	11/24/95	1041
Police Tactics	12/12/14	1033
Policing the Borders	02/22/02	145
Policing the Police	03/17/00	209
Property Rights	03/04/05	197
Prosecutors and the Law	11/09/07	937
Race and Education	09/05/14	721
Race and Politics	07/18/08	577
Race in America	07/11/03	593
Racial Conflict	01/08/16	25
Racial Diversity in Public Schools	09/14/07	**745
Racial Profiling	11/22/13	1005
Racial Tensions in Schools	01/07/94	1
Reality TV	08/27/10	677
School Desegregation	04/23/04	345
Shock Jocks	06/01/07	**481
Suburban Crime	09/03/93	769
Understanding Mormonism	10/19/12	889

	Date	Page
Radiation		
Electromagnetic Fields	04/26/91	237
Food Irradiation	06/12/92	505
Nuclear Power	06/10/11	505
Nuclear Waste	06/08/01	497*
Ozone Depletion	04/03/92	289
Will Nuclear Power Get Another		
Chance?	02/22/91	113
Radio. *See Television and radio*		
Railroads		
Future of Amtrak	10/18/02	841
High-Speed Rail	04/16/93	313
Traffic Congestion	08/27/99	742*
Transportation Policy	07/04/97	593*
Rain forests		
Ecotourism	10/20/06	865
Saving the Forests	09/20/91	681
Ranching. *See Livestock and ranching*		
Rap music. *See Music*		
Rape. *See Sex crimes*		
Reading. *See Literacy and illiteracy*		
Real estate		
Blighted Cities	11/12/10	941*
Downtown Renaissance	06/23/06	**553
Financial Bailout	10/24/08	**865
Financial Crisis	05/09/08	409
Financial Industry Overhaul	07/30/10	629
Gentrification	02/20/15	169
Housing Discrimination	02/24/95	169
Indoor Air Pollution	10/27/95	951*
Recession's Regional Impact	02/01/91	65
Smart Growth	05/28/04	469
Wealth and Inequality	04/18/14	337
Recession. *See Economic conditions*		
Recreation. *See Leisure; Sports*		
Recycling		
The Economics of Recycling	03/27/98	265
Environmental Movement at 25	03/31/95	288*
Future of Recycling	12/14/07	1033
Garbage Crisis	03/20/92	241
Lead Poisoning	06/19/92	537
Managing Nuclear Waste	01/28/11	73
Red Cross		
Blood Supply Safety	11/11/94	985
Ethics of War	12/13/02	1013
First Ladies	06/14/96	505
National Service	06/30/06	577
Philanthropy in America	12/08/06	1009
Redistricting. *See also Census*		
Census Controversey	05/14/10	433
Future of the Democratic Party	10/13/17	845

	Date	Page
The Partisan Divide	04/30/04	373
Race in America	07/11/03	598*
Redistricting	02/16/01	113
Redistricting Debates	02/25/11	169
Redistricting Disputes	03/12/04	221
Redistricting: Drawing Power		
with a Map	02/15/91	97
Redistricting Showdown	08/25/17	677
Refugees		
Assisting Refugees	02/07/97	97
Defeating the Islamic State	04/01/16	289
Ethics of War	12/13/02	1013
European Migration Crisis	07/31/15	649
Europe's New Right	02/12/93	121
Global Hunger	08/08/14	673
Global Refugee Crisis	07/09/99	569
Human Trafficking and Slavery	03/26/04	273
The Iraq War: 10 Years Later	03/01/13	205
Middle East Peace	01/21/05	53
Reforming the U.N.	06/24/16	553
Restoring Ties With Cuba	06/12/15	505
Terrorism in Africa	07/10/15	577
Unrest in the Arab World	02/01/13	105
Regulation and deregulation		
Accountants Under Fire	03/22/02	257*
Advertising Overload	01/23/04	49
Airline Industry Problems	09/24/99	825
Airline Safety	10/08/93	865
Airline Safety	05/15/15	433
Air Pollution and Climate Control	11/13/15	961
Air Pollution Conflict	11/14/03	965
Alternative Energy	02/25/05	173
Antitrust Policy	06/12/98	505
Arbitrating Disputes	03/11/16	241
Arctic Development	12/02/16	989
Auto Safety	10/26/01	873
Betting on Sports	10/28/16	889
Biology and Behavior	04/03/98	299*
Broadcast Indecency	04/16/04	321
Bush and the Environment	10/25/02	880*
Bush Presidency	02/02/01	82*
Campaign Finance	05/06/16	409
Career Colleges	01/07/11	1
Caring for the Elderly	02/20/98	152*
Child-Care Options	05/08/98	409
The Cloning Controversy	05/09/97	409
Coal Industry's Future	06/17/16	529
Combating Scientific Misconduct	01/10/97	1
Corporate Crime	10/11/02	817
Cosmetic Surgery	04/15/05	317
Decriminalizing Prostitution	04/15/16	337
Debt Collectors	07/20/12	621
Dietary Supplements	07/08/94	577

	Date	Page		Date	Page
Dietary Supplements	09/03/04	709	Renewable Energy	11/07/97	961
Dietary Supplements	10/30/15	913	Restructuring the Electric Industry	01/17/97	25
Digital Commerce	02/05/99	89	Right to Die	05/13/05	421
Digital Currency	09/26/14	793	Role of Foundations	01/22/99	49
The Digital Divide	01/28/00	57*	School Vouchers	04/09/99	281
Digital Journalism	05/30/14	457	School Vouchers Showdown	02/15/02	121
Domestic Drones	10/18/13	885	Sleep Deprivation	06/26/98	553
Drugmakers Under Siege	09/03/99	767*	Smart Growth	05/28/04	469
Drug Safety	03/11/05	221	Solar Energy Controversies	04/29/16	385
Drunken Driving	10/06/00	793	Stimulating the Economy	01/10/03	1
Embryo Research	12/17/99	1065	The Stock Market	05/02/97	393*
Endangered Species Act	10/01/99	849	Stock Market Troubles	01/16/04	25
Environmental Movement at 25	03/31/95	273	Sugar Controversies	11/30/12	1013
Financial Bailout	10/24/08	**865	Synthetic Biology	04/25/14	361
Financial Crisis	05/09/08	409	Tea Party Movement	03/19/10	**241*
Financial Industry Overhaul	07/30/10	629	Teen Driving	01/07/05	1
Financial Misconduct	01/20/12	53	Teens and Tobacco	12/01/95	1065
Food Labeling	06/16/17	509	Tobacco Industry	12/10/04	**1025
Fracking Controversy	12/16/11	1049	Truck Safety	03/12/99	209
Future of the Airlines	03/07/08	217	Underground Economy	03/04/94	193
Future of the GOP	10/24/14	889	Unions at a Crossroads	08/07/15	673
The Future of Telecommunications	04/23/99	329	U.S.-Iran Relations	03/04/16	217
The Future of Television	12/23/94	1129	Utility Deregulation	01/14/00	1
Future of the Music Industry	11/21/03	989	Water Crisis in the West	12/09/11	1025
Gene Therapy's Future	12/08/95	1102*	Wind Power	04/01/11	289
Genetically Engineered Foods	08/05/94	684*	Women's Health	11/07/03	957*
Guns on Campus	01/27/17	73	Worker Safety	05/21/04	445
Homeopathy Debate	12/19/03	1069	**Rehnquist, William H.**		
Home Schooling	09/09/94	769	Supreme Court Preview	09/17/93	817
Improving Cybersecurity	02/15/13	157	Supreme Court's Future	01/28/05	77
Indecency on Television	11/09/12	965	**Religion. *See also Ethical and moral issues***		
Internet Privacy	11/06/98	953	Abortion Debates	03/21/14	265
Managing Managed Care	04/16/99	305	Alternative Medicine	01/31/92	87*
Marijuana Industry	10/16/15	865	Birth-Control Debate	06/24/05	565
Marijuana Laws	02/11/05	125	Castro's Next Move	12/12/97	1085*
Media Ownership	10/10/03	**845	Catholic Church in the U.S.	09/08/95	777
Medical Marijuana	07/21/17	605	Changing Demographics	11/16/12	989
Mental Illness Medication Debate	02/06/04	101	Charitable Giving	11/12/93	1002*
Mine Safety	06/24/11	553	Cults in America	05/07/93	385
Modernizing the Grid	02/19/10	145	Defeating the Islamic State	04/01/16	289
Nonprofit Groups and Partisan Politics	11/14/14	961	Democracy in the Arab World	01/30/04	73
Nuclear Power	06/10/11	505	Disappearing Species	11/30/07	985
Political Polling	02/06/15	121	Domestic Partners	09/04/92	761
The Politics of Energy	03/05/99	185	Embryo Research	12/17/99	1077*
Privatizing Government Services	12/08/17	1017	Emerging India	04/19/02	351*
Privatizing the Military	07/13/12	597	Evangelical Christians	09/14/01	713
Property Rights	06/16/95	513	Evolution vs. Creationism	08/22/97	745
Reforming the FDA	06/06/97	481	Faith-Based Initiatives	05/04/01	377
Regulating Nonprofits	12/26/97	1129	Free Speech at Risk	04/26/13	377
Regulating Pesticides	08/06/99	665	Future of the Catholic Church	01/19/07	49
Regulating Tobacco	09/30/94	841	Future of the Catholic Church	06/07/13	497
Regulating Toxic Chemicals	01/23/09	49	Future of the Christian Right	06/23/17	533
Regulating the Internet	06/30/95	561	Future of the Papacy	02/26/99	161
Regulating the New Economy	10/19/01	849	Gay Marriage	09/05/03	726*

	Date	Page
Global Jihad	10/14/05	857
Government and Religion	01/15/10	25
Helping the Homeless	01/26/96	73
Home Schooling Debate	01/17/03	25
Islamic Fundamentalism	03/24/00	241
Israel at 50	03/06/98	206*
Marriage and Divorce	05/10/96	409
Muslims in America	04/30/93	361
Muslims in America	07/28/17	629
The New Millennium	10/15/99	889
Nonprofit Groups and Partisan Politics	11/14/14	961
Northern Ireland Cease-Fire	09/15/95	812*
Parental Rights	10/25/96	937
Population Growth	07/16/93	610*
Prayer and Healing	01/14/05	25
Preparing for Disaster	08/02/13	669
Prison-Building Boom	09/17/99	815*
Protestants Today	12/07/07	1009
Religion and Law	11/07/14	937
Religion and Politics	10/14/94	889
Religion and Politics	07/30/04	637
Religion in America	11/25/94	1033
Religion in Schools	02/18/94	145
Religion in Schools	01/12/01	1
Religion in the Workplace	08/23/02	649
Religious Freedom	01/01/16	1
Religious Persecution	11/21/97	1009
Religious Repression	11/01/13	933
Rise of Megachurches	09/21/07	769
School Censorship	02/19/93	157*
School Choice	05/10/91	256
School Choice Debate	07/18/97	625
School Vouchers	04/09/99	281
School Vouchers Showdown	02/15/02	121
Science and Religion	03/22/13	281
The Search for Extraterrestrials	03/05/04	197
Searching for Jesus	12/11/98	1073
Sexual Abuse and the Clergy	05/03/02	393
Student Rights	06/05/09	501
Supreme Court Preview	09/17/93	817
Teaching Values	06/21/96	529
Understanding Islam	11/03/06	913
Understanding Mormonism	10/19/12	889
U.S.-Iran Relations	03/04/16	217
Women and Human Rights	04/30/99	353

Renewable energy resources

	Date	Page
Air Pollution and Climate Control	11/13/15	961
Air Pollution Conflict	11/14/03	976*
Alternative Energy	07/10/92	573
Alternative Energy	02/25/05	173
Biofuels Boom	09/29/06	793
Bush and the Environment	10/25/02	865
Coal Industry's Future	06/17/16	529
Energy Efficiency	05/19/06	433

	Date	Page
Energy Policy	05/25/01	455*
Energy Policy	05/20/11	457
Energy Security	02/01/02	73
Jobs Outlook	06/04/10	481
Managing Public Lands	11/04/11	929
Modernizing the Grid	02/19/10	145
Nanotechnology	06/11/04	517
The Politics of Energy	03/05/99	185
Protecting the Power Grid	11/11/16	941
Renewable Energy	11/07/97	961
Solar Energy Controversies	04/29/16	385
Vanishing Jobs	03/13/09	225
Water Crisis in the West	12/09/11	1025
Wind Power	04/01/11	289

Reparations

	Date	Page
Holocaust Reparations	03/26/99	257
Reparations Movement	06/22/01	529*

Repetitive stress injuries

	Date	Page
Repetitive Stress Injuries	06/23/95	537

Reproduction. *See Pregnancy*

Republic of China. *See Taiwan*

Republican Party

	Date	Page
Abortion Debates	09/10/10	725
Abortion Debates	03/21/14	265
Academic Freedom	10/07/05	833
Air Pollution Conflict	11/14/03	965
Assessing the New Health Care Law	09/21/12	789
Birth-Control Debate	06/24/05	565
The Black Middle Class	01/23/98	66*
Budget Deficit	12/09/05	1029
Campaign Finance	05/06/16	409
Campaign Finance Debates	05/28/10	457
Campaign Finance Reform	02/09/96	134*
Changing Demographics	11/16/12	989
Changing U.S. Electorate	05/30/08	**457
Cracking Down on Immigration	02/03/95	112*
Cyberpolitics	09/17/04	757
D.C. Voting Rights	04/11/08	313*
Democrats in Congress	06/08/07	505
Democrats' Future	10/29/10	893
Environmental Movement at 25	03/31/95	290*
Exporting Democracy	04/01/05	269
The Federal Judiciary	03/13/98	217
Feminism's Future	02/28/97	184*
Future of the Christian Right	06/23/17	533
Future of the Democratic Party	10/13/17	845
Future of the GOP	03/20/09	249
Future of the GOP	10/24/14	889
Gridlock in Washington	04/30/10	385
Health-Care Reform	06/11/10	**505
Hispanic-Americans' New Clout	09/18/98	809
Housing Discrimination	02/24/95	184*
Labor Movement's Future	06/28/96	553

	Date	Page
Latino Voters	04/03/15	289
Lies and Politics	02/18/11	145
Lobbying Boom	07/22/05	613
Media Bias	05/03/13	401
Millennial Generation	06/26/15	553
Minimum Wage	12/16/05	1053
Muslims in America	07/28/17	629
National Debt	03/18/11	241
National Debt	09/01/17	701
Nonprofit Groups and Partisan Politics	11/14/14	961
Non-Proliferation Treaty at 25	01/27/95	90*
The Obama Legacy	11/04/16	913
The Obama Presidency	01/30/09	73
The Partisan Divide	04/30/04	373
Partisan Politics	03/19/99	233
Polarization in America	02/28/14	193
Political Conventions	08/08/08	649
Political Polling	02/06/15	121
Populism and Party Politics	09/09/16	721
Presidential Election	02/03/12	101
Presidential Power	03/06/15	217
Prosecutors and Politics	06/22/07	553
Protestants Today	12/07/07	1009
Race and Politics	07/18/08	577
Redistricting Debates	02/25/11	169
Redistricting: Drawing Power with a Map	02/15/91	97
Redistricting Showdown	08/25/17	677
Regulating Lobbying	06/06/14	481
Regulating Nonprofits	12/26/97	1129
Reinventing Government	02/17/95	145
Religion and Politics	10/14/94	889
Religion and Politics	07/30/04	637
Rethinking Affirmative Action	04/28/95	369
Revitalizing the Cities	10/13/95	909*
Rising College Costs	12/05/03	1013
Science and Politics	08/20/04	661
Social Media and Politics	10/12/12	865
State Budget Crises	10/03/03	821
States and Federalism	09/13/96	793
Tax Reform	03/22/96	241
Tea Party Movement	03/19/10	**241*
Term Limits	01/10/92	1
Think Tanks in Transition	09/29/17	797
Third-Party Prospects	12/22/95	1137
Voting Controversies	09/15/06	745
Women in Politics	03/21/08	265
Wounded Veterans	08/31/07	697
Young Voters	10/02/15	817

Respiratory diseases

	Date	Page
Air Pollution Conflict	11/14/03	965
Fighting SARS	06/20/03	569
New Air Quality Standards	03/07/97	193
Pandemic Threat	06/02/17	457

Restaurants

	Date	Page
Crackdown on Smoking	12/04/92	1049
Fast-Food Shake-Up	11/08/91	825
Food Safety	06/04/93	481
Food Safety Battle: Organic v. Biotech	09/04/98	766*
Historic Preservation	10/07/94	870*
Hunger in America	07/07/17	557
Obesity Epidemic	01/31/03	94*
Threatened Fisheries	08/02/02	617

Retail trade

	Date	Page
Big-Box Stores	09/10/04	733
Child Labor and Sweatshops	08/16/96	721
The Consumer Culture	11/19/99	1001
Digital Commerce	02/05/99	89
Drugmakers Under Siege	09/03/99	762*
Future of the Music Industry	11/21/03	989
Jobs in the '90s	02/28/92	182
Minimum Wage	01/24/14	72
Religion in the Workplace	08/23/02	665*

Retirement

	Date	Page
Accountants Under Fire	03/22/02	252*
Age Discrimination	08/01/97	673
Aging Baby Boomers	10/19/07	865
Aging Population	07/15/11	577
Budget Deficit	12/09/05	1029
Corporate Crime	10/11/02	817
Declining Birthrates	11/21/08	961
Employee Benefits	02/04/00	65
Future of the Middle Class	04/08/16	313
Middle-Class Squeeze	03/06/09	201
Overhauling Social Security	05/12/95	417
Paying for Retirement	11/05/93	961
Pension Crisis	02/17/06	145
Rethinking Retirement	06/19/09	549
Retiree Health Benefits	12/06/91	921
Retirement Security	05/31/02	481
Rising Health Costs	04/07/06	289
Saving Social Security	10/02/98	857
Smart Growth	05/28/04	469
Social Security Reform	09/24/04	781
Socially Responsible Investing	08/29/08	673
State Budget Crisis	09/11/09	741

Rights. *See Civil rights and liberties; Property rights*

Ritalin. *See Attention Deficit Disorder*

Roads. *See Highways and roads*

Robotics

	Date	Page
Artificial Intelligence	11/14/97	985
Future Job Market	01/11/02	13*
Medical Breakthroughs	09/15/17	749
Nanotechnology	06/11/04	517
Robotic Warfare	01/23/15	73
Robotics and the Economy	09/25/15	793
Space Program's Future	04/25/97	361

	Date	Page
Roma (Gypsies)		
Democracy in Eastern Europe	10/08/99	882*
Roman Catholics. *See Catholic Church*		
Romania		
The Greening of Eastern Europe	11/15/91	849
Ruby Ridge, Idaho, shootout		
The FBI Under Fire	04/11/97	315*
Russia. *See also Soviet Union (Former)*		
Aid to Russia	03/12/93	217
Arctic Development	12/02/16	989
Bush's Defense Strategy	09/07/01	689
Chemical and Biological Weapons	12/13/13	1053
Cyberwarfare Threat	10/06/17	821
Defense Priorities	07/30/99	641
Democracies Under Stress	10/20/17	869
Democracy in Eastern Europe	10/08/99	873*
European Unrest	01/09/15	25
Expanding NATO	05/16/97	433
Exporting Democracy	04/01/05	269
Free Speech at Risk	04/26/13	377
Future of NATO	02/28/03	177
The Future of U.S.-Russia Relations	01/18/02	25
Human Spaceflight	10/16/09	861
International Monetary Fund	01/29/99	65
Military Readiness	11/03/17	917
Missile Defense	09/08/00	689
NASA's Future	05/23/03	473
New Challenges in Space	07/23/99	617
New Space Race	08/04/17	653
Nuclear Disarmament	10/02/09	813
Nuclear Proliferation and Terrorism	04/02/04	297
Oil Diplomacy	01/24/03	49
Religious Persecution	11/21/97	1009
Restoring Ties With Cuba	06/12/15	505
Resurgent Russia	02/07/14	121
Russia and the Former Soviet Republics	06/17/05	541
Russia's Political Future	05/03/96	385
Soviet Republics Rebel	07/12/91	465
Space Program	02/24/12	177
Space Program's Future	12/24/93	1129
Space Program's Future	04/25/97	361
Transnational Crime	08/29/14	697
Unrest in Turkey	01/29/16	97
U.S. Global Engagement	05/16/14	433
U.S.-Russia Relations	01/13/17	25
U.S.-Russian Relations	05/22/98	457
Weapons of Mass Destruction	03/08/02	193
Whistleblowers	01/31/14	97
Rwanda		
Assisting Refugees	02/07/97	97
Ethics of War	12/13/02	1013
Famine in Africa	11/08/02	921
Foreign Policy and Public Opinion	07/15/94	601
Stopping Genocide	08/27/04	685
The United Nations and Global Security	02/27/04	173
War Crimes	07/07/95	585
Saddam Hussein		
Chemical and Biological Weapons	12/13/13	1053
Confronting Iraq	10/04/02	793
Democracy in the Arab World	01/30/04	73
Economic Sanctions	10/28/94	937
Ethics of War	12/13/02	1013
Future of NATO	02/28/03	177
Hating America	11/23/01	969
The Iraq War: 10 Years Later	03/01/13	205
New Defense Priorities	09/13/02	721
Nuclear Proliferation	06/05/92	481
Oil Diplomacy	01/24/03	49
Oil Production in the 21st Century	08/07/98	673
Presidential Power	11/15/02	945
Rebuilding Iraq	07/11/03	625
Reform in Iran	12/18/98	1097
Stopping Genocide	08/27/04	685
War Crimes	07/07/95	585
War on Terrorism	10/12/01	817
Weapons of Mass Destruction	03/08/02	193
Safety. *See also Occupational health and safety; Traffic accidents*		
3D Printing	12/07/12	1037
Aging Infrastructure	09/28/07	**793
Airline Safety	10/08/93	865
Airline Safety	05/15/15	433
Auto Safety	10/26/01	873
Cell Phone Safety	03/16/01	201
Coal Industry's Future	06/17/16	529
Combat Journalism	04/12/13	329
Consumer Safety	10/12/07	841
Cybersecurity	02/26/10	169
Dietary Supplements	10/30/15	913
Domestic Drones	10/18/13	885
Earthquake Threat	04/09/10	313
Extreme Sports	04/03/09	297
Gun Control	03/08/13	233
Managing Wildfires	11/02/12	941
Marijuana Industry	10/16/15	865
Nanotechnology	06/11/04	517
Nuclear Power	06/10/11	505
Patient Safety	02/10/12	125
Pesticide Controversies	06/05/15	481
Prison Reform	04/06/07	289
Regulating Toxic Chemicals	07/18/14	601
Robotics and the Economy	09/25/15	793
Sleep Deprivation	02/12/10	121
Synthetic Biology	04/25/14	361
Teen Driving	01/07/05	1
Worker Safety	10/04/13	837

	Date	Page
Salaries. *See Wages and salaries*		
Sales tax		
Digital Commerce	02/05/99	89
IRS Reform	01/16/98	38*
Tax Reform	03/22/96	241
Salmonella		
Food Irradiation	06/12/92	505
Food Safety	06/04/93	481
Food Safety	11/01/02	897
SAT tests		
Affirmative Action and College Admissions	11/17/17	969
Attack on Public Schools	07/26/96	649
Education and Gender	06/03/94	488*
Getting into College	02/23/96	169
Grade Inflation	06/07/02	505
Implementing the Disabilities Act	12/20/96	1116*
Learning to Read	05/19/95	446*
Students Under Stress	07/13/07	577
Teaching Critical Thinking	04/10/15	313
Testing in Schools	04/20/01	328*
Scholarships. *See Student aid*		
School choice		
Attack on Public Schools	07/26/96	662*
Business' Role in Education	11/22/91	885*
Charter Schools	12/20/02	1033
Home Schooling	03/07/14	217
Home Schooling Debate	01/17/03	25
No Child Left Behind	05/27/05	469
Private Management of Public Schools	03/25/94	265
Privatization	11/13/92	988*
Racial Diversity in Public Schools	09/14/07	**745
Religion in Schools	01/12/01	1
School Choice	05/10/91	253
School Choice Debate	07/18/97	625
School Desegregation	04/23/04	345
School Vouchers	04/09/99	281
School Vouchers Showdown	02/15/02	121
School funding		
Advertising Overload	01/23/04	49
Arts Education	03/16/12	253
Charter Schools	12/20/02	1033
College Rankings	01/02/15	1
Community Colleges	05/01/15	385
Fixing Urban Schools	04/27/07	**361
No Child Left Behind	05/27/05	469
Reforming School Funding	12/10/99	1041
Schools. *See Elementary and secondary education*		
Science and technology. *See also Medical research*		
3D Printing	12/07/12	1037
Acid Rain: New Approach to Old Problem	03/08/91	132*
Airline Safety	05/15/15	433

	Date	Page
Alternative Energy	07/10/92	573
Alternative Energy	02/25/05	173
Animal Intelligence	10/22/10	869
Artificial Intelligence	04/22/11	361
Animal Rights	01/08/10	1
Artificial Intelligence	11/14/97	985
Big Data and Privacy	10/25/13	909
Biofuels Boom	09/29/06	793
Biotech Foods	03/30/01	249
Breast Cancer	04/02/10	289
California: Enough Water for the Future?	04/19/91	224*
Cell Phone Safety	03/16/01	213*
Cheating in Schools	09/22/00	754*
Climate Change	06/14/13	521
College Rankings	01/02/15	1
Combat Journalism	04/12/13	329
Combating Scientific Misconduct	01/10/97	1
Crisis on the Plains	05/09/03	430*
Cyber-Crime	04/12/02	305
Cyberpolitics	09/17/04	757
Cybersecurity	09/26/03	797
Cybersecurity	02/26/10	169
Debt Collectors	07/20/12	621
Digital Education	12/02/11	1001
Distracted Driving	05/04/12	401
Doctor Shortage	08/28/15	697
Domestic Drones	10/18/13	885
Drug Company Ethics	06/06/03	521
Earthquake Research	12/16/94	1105
Earthquake Threat	04/09/10	313
Emerging India	04/19/02	329
Energy and Climate	07/24/09	621
Examining Forensics	07/17/09	597
Extreme Weather	09/09/11	733*
Fighting Cancer	01/22/16	73
Forensic Science Controversies	02/10/17	121
Free Speech at Risk	04/26/13	377
Future of Books	05/29/09	**473
Future of Homeownership	12/14/12	1061
Future of Libraries	07/29/11	625
The Future of Television	12/23/94	1129
Future of the Music Industry	11/21/03	989
Gender and Learning	05/20/05	445
Genes and Health	01/21/11	49
Genetically Modified Food	08/31/12	717
Global Water Shortages	12/15/95	1113
High-Tech Labor Shortage	04/24/98	361
High-Tech Policing	04/21/17	337
Homeopathy Debate	12/19/03	1069
Human Genome Research	05/12/00	401
Human Spaceflight	10/16/09	861
Immigrants and the Economy	02/24/17	169
Internet Regulation	04/13/12	325

	Date	Page
Journalism Standards in the Internet Age	10/08/10	821
Manipulating the Human Genome	06/19/15	529
Medical Breakthroughs	09/15/17	749
Mine Safety	06/24/11	553
Modernizing the Grid	02/19/10	145
Nanotechnology	06/11/04	517
Nanotechnology	06/10/16	505
NASA's Future	05/23/03	473
The New CIA	12/11/92	1073
New Space Race	08/04/17	653
Nuclear Arms Cleanup	06/24/94	564*
Nuclear Disarmament	10/02/09	**813
Nuclear Fusion	01/22/93	49
Nuclear Proliferation and Terrorism	04/02/04	297
Oil Production in the 21st Century	08/07/98	685*
Online Privacy	11/06/09	**933
Organ Donations	04/15/11	337
Patient Safety	02/10/12	125
Preventing Memory Loss	04/04/08	289*
Prolonging Life	09/30/11	805*
Pursuing the Paranormal	03/29/96	265
Reading Crisis?	02/22/08	169
Reality TV	08/27/10	677
Reducing Traffic Deaths	02/17/17	145
Regulating Toxic Chemicals	01/23/09	49
Reproductive Ethics	05/15/09	449
Science in America	01/11/08	25
Science in the Courtroom	10/22/93	913
Science and Politics	08/20/04	661
Science and Religion	03/22/13	281
The Search for Extraterrestrials	03/05/04	197
Search for Life on New Planets	06/20/14	529
Smart Cities	07/27/12	645
Social Media Explosion	01/25/13	81
Solar Energy Controversies	04/29/16	385
Space Program	02/24/12	177
Space Program's Future	12/24/93	1129
Space Program's Future	04/25/97	361
Stem Cell Research	09/01/06	**697
Synthetic Biology	04/25/14	361
Teaching Math and Science	09/06/02	697
Television's Future	02/16/07	145
Transition to Digital TV	06/20/08	529
Treating Alzheimer's	03/04/11	193
Treating Alzheimer's Disease	07/24/15	625
Treating Schizophrenia	12/05/14	1009
Uncertain Future for Man in Space	03/29/91	173
Virtual Reality	02/26/16	193
Weapons of Mass Destruction	03/08/02	193
Wrongful Convictions	04/17/09	**345

Scientists

	Date	Page
Animal Rights	01/08/10	1
Combating Scientific Misconduct	01/10/97	1

	Date	Page
Gender and Learning	05/20/05	445
NASA's Future	05/23/03	473
Nuclear Proliferation	06/05/92	486*
The Search for Extraterrestrials	03/05/04	197
Science in America	01/11/08	25
Science and Politics	08/20/04	661
Science and Religion	03/22/13	281
Species Extinction	12/15/17	1041
Synthetic Biology	04/25/14	361

Second Amendment. *See Firearms*

Secondhand smoke. *See Tobacco*

Segregation. *See Civil rights and liberties; Discrimination*

Self-employment

Aging Baby Boomers	10/19/07	865
Contingent Work Force	10/24/97	937
Future of the Middle Class	04/08/16	313
The Glass Ceiling	10/29/93	947*

Sentencing guidelines. *See also Alternative sentences*

Forensic Science Controversies	02/10/17	121
Jailing Debtors	09/16/16	745
Mandatory Sentencing	05/26/95	465
Plea Bargaining	02/12/99	125*
Prisoners and Mental Illness	03/13/15	241
Prosecutors and the Law	11/09/07	937
Punishing Sex Offenders	01/12/96	25
Reforming Juvenile Justice	09/11/15	745
Sentencing Debates	11/05/04	925
Sentencing Reform	01/10/14	25
Women in Prison	03/03/17	193

Sept. 11, 2001

Academic Freedom	10/07/05	833
Afghanistan Dilemma	08/07/09	**669*
Civil Liberties Debates	10/24/03	893
Civil Liberties in Wartime	12/14/01	1017
Conspiracy Theories	10/23/09	885
Foreign Aid After Sept. 11	04/26/02	361
Future of the Airline Industry	06/21/02	545
Government Secrecy	12/02/05	1005
Hating America	11/23/01	969
Homegrown Jihadists	09/03/10	701
Homeland Security	09/12/03	749
Homeland Security	02/13/09	129
Intelligence Reforms	01/25/02	49
International Law	12/17/04	1049
Interrogating the CIA	09/25/09	789
New Defense Priorities	09/13/02	721
Port Security	04/21/06	337
Presidential Power	11/15/02	945
Presidential Power	02/24/06	169
Presidential Power	03/06/15	217
Prosecuting Terrorists	03/12/10	**217*
Real ID	05/04/07	385

	Date	Page		Date	Page
Re-examining 9/11	06/04/04	493	Gender Equity in Sports	04/18/97	337
Reforming the U.N.	06/24/16	553	The Glass Ceiling	10/29/93	937
Remembering 9/11	09/02/11	701*	Lead Poisoning	06/19/92	534*
Torture	04/18/03	345	Mothers' Movement	04/04/03	297
Treatment of Detainees	08/25/06	673	Prostitution Debate	05/23/08	433
Understanding Islam	11/03/06	913	Racial Quotas	05/17/91	277
War in Iraq	10/21/05	881	Reforming the CIA	02/02/96	110*
War on Terrorism	10/12/01	817	Transgender Issues	05/05/06	385
Weapons of Mass Destruction	03/08/02	193	Transgender Rights	12/11/15	1033

Serbia

	Date	Page		Date	Page
			Women and Sports	03/06/92	193
Ethics of War	12/13/02	1013	Women and Work	07/26/13	645
Stopping Genocide	08/27/04	685	Women in the Military	09/25/92	833
War Crimes	07/07/95	585	Women in the Military	11/13/09	957

SETI Institute

Sex education

	Date	Page		Date	Page
The Search for Extraterrestrials	03/05/04	197	Abortion Showdowns	09/22/06	769
Search for Life on New Planets	06/20/14	529	Battling HIV/AIDS	10/26/07	889
			Encouraging Teen Abstinence	07/10/98	577

Sex crimes. *See also Child abuse*

	Date	Page		Date	Page
			Gay Rights	03/05/93	207*
Campus Sexual Assault	10/31/14	913	Girls' Rights	04/17/15	337
College Football	11/18/11	977	HPV Vaccine	05/11/07	409
Cyber-Predators	03/01/02	169	Parental Rights	10/25/96	946*
Cyber Socializing	07/28/06	625	Preventing Teen Pregnancy	05/14/93	409
Decriminalizing Prostitution	04/15/16	337	Sexually Transmitted Diseases	12/03/04	997
DNA Databases	05/28/99	449	Teaching Values	06/21/96	534*
Feminism's Future	02/28/97	182*	Teen Pregnancy	03/26/10	265*
Girls' Rights	04/17/15	337	Teen Sex	09/16/05	761
Greek Life on Campus	11/20/15	985			

Sexual behavior. *See also Homosexuals; Pornography; Pregnancy*

	Date	Page		Date	Page
Human Trafficking and Slavery	03/26/04	273			
The Obscenity Debate	12/20/91	985	AIDS Update	12/04/98	1049
Pornography	10/21/16	865	Battling HIV/AIDS	10/26/07	889
Privacy and the Internet	12/04/15	1009	Broadcast Indecency	04/16/04	321
Prosecutors and the Law	11/09/07	937	Campus Sexual Assault	10/31/14	913
Prostitution	06/11/93	505	Catholic Church in the U.S.	09/08/95	777
Prostitution Debate	05/23/08	433	Children's Television	08/15/97	721
Punishing Sex Offenders	01/12/96	25	Cyber-Predators	03/01/02	169
Reforming Big-Time College Sports	03/19/04	249	Decriminalizing Prostitution	04/15/16	337
Reforming the U.N.	06/24/16	553	Domestic Violence	11/15/13	981
Serial Killers	10/31/03	917	Encouraging Teen Abstinence	07/10/98	577
Sex Offenders	09/08/06	721	Feminism's Future	02/28/97	183*
Sex on Campus	11/04/94	961	Future of Marriage	05/07/04	397
Sexual Abuse and the Clergy	05/03/02	393	Future of the Catholic Church	01/19/07	49
Sexual Assault in the Military	08/09/13	693	Global AIDS Crisis	10/13/00	809
Sports and Sexual Assault	04/28/17	361	HPV Vaccine	05/11/07	409
Treating Anxiety	02/08/02	97	Indecency on Television	11/09/12	965
Violence Against Women	02/26/93	169	Marriage and Divorce	05/10/96	409
War Crimes	07/07/95	590*	Political Scandals	05/27/94	457
Women and Human Rights	04/30/99	353	Politicians and Privacy	04/17/92	337
Workplace Sexual Harassment	10/27/17	893	Pornography	10/21/16	865
			Preventing Teen Pregnancy	05/14/93	409

Sex discrimination. *See also Sexual harassment*

	Date	Page		Date	Page
			Privacy and the Internet	12/04/15	1009
Crackdown on Sexual Harassment	07/19/96	625	Prostitution	06/11/93	505
Democracy in the Arab World	01/30/04	73	Prostitution Debate	05/23/08	433
Education and Gender	06/03/94	481	Sex on Campus	11/04/94	961
Feminism's Future	02/28/97	169	Sex Scandals	01/22/10	49
Gender and Learning	05/20/05	445			

	Date	Page
Sex, Violence and the Media	11/17/95	1017
Sexually Transmitted Diseases	12/03/04	997
Teen Pregnancy	03/26/10	265*
Teen Sex	09/16/05	761
Transgender Rights	12/11/15	1033
TV Violence	03/26/93	176*
Women and AIDS	12/25/92	1121
Workplace Sexual Harassment	10/27/17	893

Sexual harassment

Academic Politics	02/16/96	162*
Bullying	02/04/05	101
Crackdown on Sexual Harassment	07/19/96	625
Crime on Campus	02/04/11	97
Cyber-Predators	03/01/02	169
Education and Gender	06/03/94	494*
New Military Culture	04/26/96	370*
Political Scandals	05/27/94	462*
Sexual Assault in the Military	08/09/13	693
Sexual Harassment	08/09/91	537
Sexual Harassment	04/27/12	377
Sports and Sexual Assault	04/28/17	361
Women and Sports	03/06/92	200*
Women in the Military	09/25/92	833
Women in the Military	11/13/09	957
Workplace Sexual Harassment	10/27/17	893

Sexually transmitted diseases. *See also AIDS disease*

Battling HIV/AIDS	10/26/07	889
Encouraging Teen Abstinence	07/10/98	577
HPV Vaccine	05/11/07	409
Mosquito-Borne Disease	07/22/16	601
Pornography	10/21/16	865
Prostitution Debate	05/23/08	433
Sexually Transmitted Diseases	12/03/04	997

Sharon, Ariel. *See Middle East*

Simpson, O.J.

Courts and the Media	09/23/94	817
The Jury System	11/10/95	993

Single-parent families. *See Family*

Single-sex education

Boys' Emotional Needs	06/18/99	521
Education and Gender	06/03/94	481
Racial Tensions in Schools	01/07/94	18*
Single-Sex Education	07/12/02	569

Sinn Fein. *See Ireland*

Sleep disorders

Chronic Fatigue Syndrome	04/05/02	289
Homework Debate	12/06/02	1002*
Sleep Deprivation	06/26/98	553
Sleep Deprivation	02/12/10	121
Truck Safety	03/12/99	209

Small business

Aging Baby Boomers	10/19/07	865
Asian Americans	12/13/91	945

	Date	Page
The Glass Ceiling	10/29/93	947*
Implementing the Disabilities Act	12/20/96	1105
Minimum Wage	01/24/14	72

Smoking. *See Tobacco*

Social Media

Cyberwarfare Threat	10/06/17	821
Future of Marriage	12/01/17	993
Trust in Media	06/09/17	481

Social Security

Age Discrimination	08/01/97	682*
Aging Baby Boomers	10/19/07	865
Aging Population	07/15/11	577
Budget Deficit	12/09/05	1029
Government Spending	07/12/13	597
Middle-Class Squeeze	03/06/09	201
National Debt	03/18/11	241
Overhauling Social Security	05/12/95	417
Privatizing Government Services	08/09/96	704*
Rethinking Retirement	06/19/09	549
Retirement Security	05/31/02	481
Saving Social Security	10/02/98	857
Social Security Reform	09/24/04	781
Social Security: The Search for Fairness	04/05/91	189

Social services. *See Welfare and social services*

Soft Money

Campaign Finance Reform	06/13/08	505

Solar energy

Air Pollution and Climate Control	11/13/15	961
Alternative Energy	07/10/92	586
Coal Industry's Future	06/17/16	529
Confronting Warming	01/09/09	1
Nanotechnology	06/11/04	517
Renewable Energy	11/07/97	961
Solar Energy Controversies	04/29/16	385

Solid waste. *See Waste products*

Somalia

European Migration Crisis	07/31/15	649
Famine in Africa	11/08/02	921
Foreign Policy Burden	08/20/93	721
Privatizing the Military	06/25/04	565

South Africa

Democracy in Africa	03/24/95	252*
Economic Sanctions	10/28/94	942*
South Africa's Future	01/14/94	25

South America

Democracies Under Stress	10/20/17	869
Foreign Aid After Sept. 11	04/26/02	361
Saving the Rain Forests	06/11/99	497
Troubled Brazil	04/07/17	289
War on Drugs	06/02/06	481

South Dakota

Abortion Showdowns	09/22/06	769

	Date	Page
South Korea. *See Korea (South)*		
Soviet Union (Former). *See also Russia*		
Aid to Russia	03/12/93	217
Conspiracy Theories	10/23/09	885
Cuba in Crisis	11/29/91	897
Defense Priorities	07/30/99	641
Democracy in Eastern Europe	10/08/99	873*
European Unrest	01/09/15	25
Expanding NATO	05/16/97	433
Global Refugee Crisis	07/09/99	574*
Missile Defense	09/08/00	689
Modernizing the Nuclear Arsenal	07/29/16	625
NATO's Changing Role	08/21/92	713
The New CIA	12/11/92	1073
New Challenges in Space	07/23/99	617
New Space Race	08/04/17	653
Non-Proliferation Treaty at 25	01/27/95	73
Nuclear Arms Cleanup	06/24/94	553
Nuclear Disarmament	10/02/09	**813
Nuclear Proliferation	06/05/92	481
Nuclear Proliferation and Terrorism	04/02/04	297
Oil Production in the 21st Century	08/07/98	673
Religious Persecution	11/21/97	1009
Resurgent Russia	02/07/14	121
Russia and the Former Soviet Republics	06/17/05	541
Russia's Political Future	05/03/96	385
Soviet Republics Rebel	07/12/91	465
Space Program's Future	12/24/93	1129
Space Program's Future	04/25/97	361
Uncertain Future for Man in Space	03/29/91	173
U.S. Global Engagement	05/16/14	433
U.S.-Russia Relations	01/13/17	25
U.S.-Russian Relations	05/22/98	457
Will Nuclear Power Get Another Chance?	02/22/91	113
Weapons of Mass Destruction	03/08/02	193
Space programs		
Conspiracy Theories	10/23/09	885
Human Spaceflight	10/16/09	861
NASA's Future	05/23/03	473
Military Readiness	11/03/17	917
New Challenges in Space	07/23/99	617
New Space Race	08/04/17	653
The Search for Extraterrestrials	03/05/04	197
Search for Life on New Planets	06/20/14	529
Space Program	02/24/12	177
Space Program's Future	12/24/93	1129
Space Program's Future	04/25/97	361
Uncertain Future for Man in Space	03/29/91	173
U.S.-Russian Relations	05/22/98	468*
Spanish		
Bilingual Education	08/13/93	697
Hispanic-Americans' New Clout	09/18/98	809

	Date	Page
Latino Voters	04/03/15	289
Puerto Rico's Status	10/23/98	936*
Special education		
Air Pollution Conflict	11/14/03	965
Charter Schools	12/20/02	1044*
Child-Care Options	05/08/98	422*
Educating Gifted Students	03/28/97	265
Home Schooling Debate	01/17/03	25
Increase in Autism	06/13/03	**558*
Learning Disabilities	12/10/93	1081
No Child Left Behind	05/27/05	469
Special Education	11/10/00	905
Special-interest groups		
Affirmative Action and College Admissions	11/17/17	969
'Alt-Right' Movement	03/17/17	241
Animal Rights	01/08/10	1
Campaign Finance Reform	02/09/96	121
Campaign Finance Reform	03/31/00	257
Campaign Finance Showdown	11/22/02	969
Charter Schools	03/10/17	217
Crackdown on Smoking	12/04/92	1049
Cyberpolitics	09/17/04	757
D.C. Voting Rights	04/11/08	313*
Environmental Movement at 25	03/31/95	284*
Feminism's Future	02/28/97	183*
Future of the Democratic Party	10/13/17	845
Future of the GOP	10/24/14	889
Guns on Campus	01/27/17	73
The Growing Influence of Boycotts	01/04/91	1
Gridlock in Washington	04/30/10	385
Hunting Controversy	01/24/92	49
Judicial Elections	04/24/09	373
Lobbying Boom	07/22/05	613
Media Ownership	10/10/03	**850*
Patriotism in America	06/25/99	558*
Polarization in America	02/28/14	193
Political Polling	02/06/15	121
Populism and Party Politics	09/09/16	721
Presidential Power	03/06/15	217
Privatizing Government Services	12/08/17	1017
Redistricting Showdown	08/25/17	677
Regulating Nonprofits	12/26/97	1129
Religion and Politics	10/14/94	889
Religion in Schools	02/18/94	145
Rethinking Foreign Aid	04/14/17	313
School Censorship	02/19/93	145
Stolen Antiquities	11/10/17	945
Student Activism	08/28/98	745
Talk Show Democracy	04/29/94	361
Tea Party Movement	03/19/10	**241*
Testing Term Limits	11/18/94	1020*
Think Tanks in Transition	09/29/17	797
U.S.-Russia Relations	01/13/17	25

	Date	Page
Special olympics		
Centennial Olympic Games	04/05/96	306*
Special prosecutors. *See Independent counsels*		
Sport-utility vehicles		
Alternative Energy	02/25/05	173
Auto Industry's Future	01/21/00	17
Auto Safety	10/26/01	873
Oil Diplomacy	01/24/03	49
SUV Debate	05/16/03	449
Traffic Congestion	08/27/99	739*
Sports		
Athletes and Drugs	07/26/91	513
Arbitrating Disputes	03/11/16	241
Attracting Jobs	03/02/12	205
Betting on Sports	10/28/16	889
The Business of Sports	02/10/95	121
Centennial Olympic Games	04/05/96	289
College Football	11/18/11	977
College Sports	08/26/94	745
Drug Testing	11/20/98	1012*
Eating Disorders	12/18/92	1097
Executive Pay	07/11/97	608*
Extreme Sports	04/03/09	297
Fairness in Salaries	05/29/92	462*
The Future of Baseball	09/25/98	833
Future of Public Universities	01/18/13	53
Future of TV	04/11/14	313
Gambling Boom	03/18/94	241
Gender Equity in Sports	04/18/97	337
Getting into College	02/23/96	186*
Hazing	01/09/04	1
High School Sports	09/22/95	825
Hunting Controversy	01/24/92	49
Implementing the Disabilities Act	12/20/96	1118*
Marine Mammals vs. Fish	08/28/92	751*
Native Americans	05/08/92	388
Native American Youths	04/24/15	361
NFL Controversies	09/04/15	721
Organ Transplants	08/11/95	708*
Pay-Per-View TV	10/04/91	729
Paying College Athletes	07/11/14	577
Physical Fitness	11/06/92	953
Preventing Hazing	02/08/13	133
Professional Football	01/29/10	**73
Reforming Big-Time College Sports	03/19/04	249
Soccer in America	04/22/94	337
Sports and Drugs	07/23/04	**613
Sports and Sexual Assault	04/28/17	361
Sportsmanship	03/23/01	225
Women and Sports	03/06/92	193
Women and Sports	03/25/11	265
Women in Sports	05/11/01	401
Youth Fitness	09/26/97	841

	Date	Page
Starr, Kenneth W.		
Independent Counsels	02/21/97	145
Independent Counsels Re-examined	05/07/99	377
State government		
Abortion Debates	09/10/10	725
Abortion Showdowns	09/22/06	769
Adoption Controversies	09/10/99	780*
Affirmative Action	10/17/08	**841
Air Pollution Conflict	11/14/03	965
Animal Rights	01/08/10	1
Assessing the New Health Care Law	09/21/12	789
Assisted Suicide	05/17/13	449
Assisted Suicide Controversy	05/05/95	396*
Attack on Public Schools	07/26/96	666*
Attracting Jobs	03/02/12	205
Bilingual Education	08/13/93	711*
Biofuels Boom	09/29/06	793
Birth-Control Debate	06/24/05	565
Blighted Cities	11/12/10	941*
Budget Surplus	04/13/01	312*
Cameras in the Courtroom	01/14/11	25
Campaign Finance Reform	03/31/00	270*
Census Controversey	05/14/10	433
Child Poverty	10/28/11	901
Child Welfare Reform	04/22/05	345
Cleaning Up Hazardous Wastes	08/23/96	748*
Closing In on Tobacco	11/12/99	977
Coal Mining Safety	03/17/06	241
Coastal Development	02/22/13	181
Confronting Warming	01/09/09	1
Cracking Down on Immigration	02/03/95	97
Crime Victims' Rights	07/22/94	637*
Criminal Records and Employment	04/20/12	349
Cyberbullying	05/02/08	385
D.C. Voting Rights	04/11/08	313*
Death Penalty Controversies	09/23/05	785
Death Penalty Debates	11/19/10	965
Death Penalty Update	01/08/99	5*
Debate over Bilingualism	01/19/96	52*
Democrats' Future	10/29/10	893
Discipline in Schools	02/15/08	145
Distracted Driving	05/04/12	401
Domestic Partners	09/04/92	761
Downsizing Prisons	03/11/11	217
The Economics of Recycling	03/27/98	268*
Educating Gifted Students	03/28/97	268*
Education Standards	03/11/94	217
Electing Minorities	08/12/94	710*
Energy and Climate	07/24/09	621
Extreme Sports	04/03/09	297
Evolution vs. Creationism	08/22/97	745
Fighting Crime	02/08/08	121
Free-Press Disputes	04/08/05	293
Future of the Airlines	03/07/08	217

	Date	Page		Date	Page
Future of the Democratic Party	10/13/17	845	Mental Health Policy	05/10/13	425
Future of Libraries	07/29/11	625	Mental Illness Medication Debate	02/06/04	101
Future of Public Universities	01/18/13	53	Mexico's Drug War	12/12/08	1009
Future of Recycling	12/14/07	1033	Middle-Class Squeeze	03/06/09	201
Gambling Boom	03/18/94	241	Mine Safety	06/24/11	553
Gambling in America	03/07/03	201	National Education Standards	05/14/99	401
Gangs in the U.S.	07/16/10	581	New Air Quality Standards	03/07/97	193
Garbage Crisis	03/20/92	241	The New Environmentalism	12/01/06	985
Gay Marriage	03/15/13	257	No Child Left Behind	05/27/05	469
Gay Marriage Showdowns	09/26/08	**769	Parental Rights	10/25/96	940*
Gay Rights	03/05/93	208*	Port Security	04/21/06	337
Genetically Modified Food	08/31/12	717	Preventing Bullying	12/10/10	**1013
Government and Religion	01/15/10	25	Preventing Juvenile Crime	03/15/96	230*
Government Spending	07/12/13	597	Prison-Building Boom	09/17/99	801
Gridlock in Washington	04/30/10	385	Prison Overcrowding	02/04/94	97
Gulf Coast Restoration	08/26/11	677*	Prisoner Reentry	12/04/09	1005
Gun Control	03/08/13	233	Private Management of Public Schools	03/25/94	265
Gun Control Standoff	12/19/97	1105	Privatizing Government Services	08/09/96	697
Gun Rights Debates	10/31/08	**889	Privatizing Government Services	12/08/17	1017
Gun Violence	05/25/07	457	Property Rights	06/16/95	517*
Hard Times for Libraries	06/26/92	549	Prosecuting Terrorists	03/12/10	**217*
Hate Crimes	01/08/93	13*	Prosecutors and the Law	11/09/07	937
Health-Care Reform	06/11/10	**505	Prostitution Debate	05/23/08	433
High-Speed Trains	05/01/09	**397	Protecting Wetlands	10/03/08	793*
Home Schooling	09/09/94	776*	Public Defenders	04/18/08	337*
Homeland Security	09/12/03	749	Public-Employee Unions	04/08/11	313
The Homeless	08/07/92	665	Punishing Sex Offenders	01/12/96	28*
Housing the Homeless	12/18/09	1053	Race and Politics	07/18/08	577
HPV Vaccine	05/11/07	409	Real ID	05/04/07	385
Immigration Conflict	03/09/12	229	Rebuilding New Orleans	02/03/06	97
Immigration Debate	02/01/08	**97	Redistricting Debates	02/25/11	169
Immigration Reform	09/24/93	841	Redistricting: Drawing Power		
Infant Mortality	07/31/92	641	with a Map	02/15/91	97
Insurance Fraud	10/11/96	894*	Re-examining the Constitution	09/07/12	741
Internet Shopping	06/28/13	573	Reforming School Funding	12/10/99	1041
Judges and Politics	07/27/01	577	Reinventing Government	02/17/95	145
Judicial Elections	04/24/09	373	Renewable Energy	11/07/97	976*
Juvenile Justice	11/07/08	913	Restructuring the Electric Industry	01/17/97	25
Legal-Aid Crisis	10/07/11	829	Revising No Child Left Behind	04/16/10	337
Legalizing Marijuana	06/12/09	**525	Roe v. Wade at 25	11/28/97	1040*
Limiting Lawsuits	12/19/08	1033	Right to Die	05/13/05	421
Line-Item Veto	06/20/97	529	Saving Open Spaces	11/05/99	953
Living-Wage Movement	09/27/02	769	School Choice Debate	07/18/97	628*
Managing Managed Care	04/16/99	318*	School Funding	08/27/93	745
Mandatory Sentencing	05/26/95	469*	School Reform	04/29/11	385
Marijuana Industry	10/16/15	865	School Vouchers Showdown	02/15/02	121
Marijuana Laws	02/11/05	125	Sex Offenders	09/08/06	721
Marriage and Divorce	05/10/96	409	Sex Scandals	01/22/10	49
Mass Transit	12/09/16	1013	Sleep Deprivation	02/12/10	121
Mass Transit Boom	01/18/08	49	Smart Growth	05/28/04	469
Medicaid Reform	07/16/04	589	Solitary Confinement	09/14/12	765
Medical Marijuana	08/20/99	708*	State Budget Crises	10/03/03	821
Medical Marijuana	07/21/17	605	State Budget Crisis	09/11/09	741
Mental Health Policy	09/12/97	800*	States and Federalism	09/13/96	793

	Date	Page
States and Federalism	10/15/10	845
Stem Cell Research	09/01/06	**697
Stimulating the Economy	01/10/03	12*
Teacher Education	10/17/97	921*
Teen Drug Use	06/03/11	481
Testing Term Limits	11/18/94	1009
Threatened Coastlines	02/07/92	97
Too Many Lawsuits?	05/22/92	433
Transportation Policy	07/04/97	577
Universal Basic Income	09/08/17	725
Urban Sprawl in the West	10/03/97	881*
Vanishing Jobs	03/13/09	225
Voter Rights	05/18/12	449
Voting Controversies	09/15/06	745
Water Crisis in the West	12/09/11	1025
Water Shortages	06/18/10	529
Welfare Experiments	09/16/94	793
Welfare Reform	04/10/92	313
Welfare, Work and the States	12/06/96	1057
Women in Politics	03/21/08	265
The Working Poor	11/03/95	969
Wrongful Convictions	04/17/09	**345
Year-Round Schools	05/17/96	436*

Steel industry

The Economics of Recycling	03/27/98	265
Recession's Regional Impact	02/01/91	67*

Stem cells

Embryo Research	12/17/99	1065
Fighting Cancer	01/22/16	73
Medical Breakthroughs	09/15/17	749
Organ Shortage	02/21/03	153*
Stem Cell Research	09/01/06	**697

Steroids

Athletes and Drugs	07/26/91	513
Centennial Olympic Games	04/05/96	289
Dietary Supplements	10/30/15	913
Sports and Drugs	07/23/04	**613

Stocks and bonds

Accountants Under Fire	03/22/02	241
Aging Baby Boomers	10/19/07	865
Business Ethics	05/06/11	409
Corporate Crime	10/11/02	817
Curbing CEO Pay	03/09/07	217
Executive Pay	07/11/97	601
Fairness in Salaries	05/29/92	462
The Federal Reserve	01/03/14	1
Financial Bailout	10/24/08	**865
Financial Crisis	05/09/08	409
Financial Literacy	09/04/09	717
Financial Industry Overhaul	07/30/10	629
Financial Misconduct	01/20/12	53
Mutual Funds	05/20/94	433
Nanotechnology	06/11/04	517

	Date	Page
Overhauling Social Security	05/12/95	422*
Rethinking Retirement	06/19/09	549
Retirement Security	05/31/02	481
Saving Social Security	10/02/98	857
Stimulating the Economy	01/10/03	1
The Stock Market	05/02/97	385
Socially Responsible Investing	08/29/08	673
Stock Market Troubles	01/16/04	25
Tax Reform	03/22/96	241

Storms. *See Hurricanes and storms*

Strikes

The Future of Baseball	09/25/98	848*
Labor Movement's Future	06/28/96	570*

Student aid

Affirmative Action and College Admissions	11/17/17	969
Apprenticeships	10/14/16	841
Caring for Veterans	04/23/10	361
College Rankings	01/02/15	1
Community Colleges	05/01/15	385
Consumer Debt	03/02/07	193
Doctor Shortage	08/28/15	697
Financial Literacy	09/04/09	717
Getting into College	02/23/96	169
Humanities Education	12/06/13	1029
Law Schools	04/19/13	353
National Service	06/25/93	553
Paying for College	11/20/92	1001
Regulating Credit Cards	10/10/08	817*
Rising College Costs	12/05/03	1013
School Vouchers	04/09/99	281
School Vouchers Showdown	02/15/02	121
Student Aid	01/25/08	73
Student Debt	10/21/11	877
Student Debt	11/18/16	965
Upward Mobility	04/29/05	369
The Value of a College Education	11/20/09	981
Women and Sports	03/06/92	193
Wounded Veterans	08/31/07	697

Suburban areas

The Black Middle Class	01/23/98	55*
Census Controversey	05/14/10	433
Changing U.S. Electorate	05/30/08	**457
Downtown Renaissance	06/23/06	**553
Revitalizing the Cities	10/13/95	897
Rise of Megachurches	09/21/07	769
Saving Open Spaces	11/05/99	953
School Funding	08/27/93	745
Setting Environmental Priorities	05/21/99	442*
Smart Growth	05/28/04	469
Suburban Crime	09/03/93	769
Traffic Congestion	08/27/99	729
Urban Sprawl in the West	10/03/97	865

	Date	Page
Sudan		
Human Rights Issues	10/30/09	909
Human Trafficking and Slavery	03/26/04	273
Stopping Genocide	08/27/04	685
Sudden Infant Death Syndrome		
Infant Mortality	07/31/92	651*
Suicide. *See also Assisted suicide*		
Assisted Suicide	05/17/13	449
Childhood Depression	07/16/99	593
Drug Safety	03/11/05	221
Homework Debate	12/06/02	993
Gun Control	06/10/94	514*
Middle East Peace	01/21/05	53
Military Suicides	09/23/11	781*
Native Americans	05/08/92	400
Native American Youths	04/24/15	361
Prospects for Mideast Peace	08/30/02	686*
Teenage Suicide	06/14/91	369
Teen Suicide	09/12/14	745
Youth Suicide	02/13/04	125
Superfund		
Asbestos Litigation	05/02/03	393
Cleaning Up Hazardous Wastes	08/23/96	745
Supreme Court		
Abortion Debates	03/21/14	265
Abortion Showdowns	09/22/06	769
Advertising Overload	01/23/04	49
Affirmative Action	09/21/01	737
Affirmative Action	10/17/08	**841
Affirmative Action and		
College Admissions	11/17/17	969
Age Discrimination	08/01/97	673
Alcohol Advertising	03/14/97	229*
Antitrust Policy	06/12/98	505
Arbitrating Disputes	03/11/16	241
Broadcast Indecency	04/16/04	326*
Cameras in the Courtroom	01/14/11	25
Campaign Finance Debates	05/28/10	457
Campaign Finance Showdown	11/22/02	969
Caring for the Dying	09/05/97	769
Civil Liberties Debates	10/24/03	893
Class Action Lawsuits	05/13/11	433
Death Penalty Debate	03/10/95	193
Death Penalty Debates	11/19/10	965
Downsizing Prisons	03/11/11	217
Electing Minorities	08/12/94	697
Eyewitness Testimony	10/14/11	853
Free-Press Disputes	04/08/05	293
Future of the Christian Right	06/23/17	533
Future of Marriage	12/01/17	993
Gay Marriage	09/05/03	721
Gay Marriage	03/15/13	257
Gays in the Military	09/18/09	**765

	Date	Page
Gender Pay Gap	03/14/08	241
Government and Religion	01/15/10	25
The Growing Influence of Boycotts	01/04/91	9*
Gun Control Standoff	12/19/97	1119*
Hate Crimes	01/08/93	1
High School Sports	09/22/95	825
Immigration Conflict	03/09/12	229
Indecency on Television	11/09/12	965
International Law	12/17/04	1049
Learning Disabilities	12/10/93	1081
Limiting Lawsuits	12/19/08	1033
Line-Item Veto	06/20/97	544*
Marijuana Laws	02/11/05	125
Muslims in America	07/28/17	629
Native American Sovereignty	05/05/17	385
Nonprofit Groups and Partisan Politics	11/14/14	961
Patent Controversies	02/27/15	193
Parental Rights	10/25/96	950*
Patenting Human Genes	05/31/13	473
Plea Bargaining	02/12/99	122*
Police Brutality	09/06/91	643*
Police Misconduct	04/06/12	301
Policing the Borders	02/22/02	145
Policing the Police	03/17/00	209
Presidential Power	11/15/02	945
Presidential Power	02/24/06	169
Presidential Power	03/06/15	217
Press Freedom	02/05/10	97
Privacy and the Internet	12/04/15	1009
Property Rights	06/16/95	513
Property Rights	03/04/05	197
Prosecuting Terrorists	03/12/10	**217*
Prosecutors and Politics	06/22/07	553
Public Defenders	04/18/08	337*
Racial Diversity in Public Schools	09/14/07	**745
Racial Quotas	05/17/91	288*
Redistricting Showdown	08/25/17	677
Re-examining the Constitution	09/07/12	741
Re-examining 9/11	06/04/04	493
Reforming Big-Time College Sports	03/19/04	249
Reforming Juvenile Justice	09/11/15	745
Religion and Law	11/07/14	937
Religion in Schools	02/18/94	145
Religion in Schools	01/12/01	1
Religion in the Workplace	08/23/02	649
Religious Freedom	01/01/16	1
Rethinking Affirmative Action	04/28/95	381*
Rethinking School Integration	10/18/96	913
Rethinking the Death Penalty	11/16/01	945
Right to Die	05/13/05	421
Roe v. Wade at 25	11/28/97	1033
School Choice	05/10/91	260*
School Desegregation	04/23/04	345
School Vouchers	04/09/99	281

	Date	Page
School Vouchers Showdown	02/15/02	121
Science in the Courtroom	10/22/93	913
Sentencing Debates	11/05/04	925
Sexual Harassment	04/27/12	377
Solitary Confinement	09/14/12	765
States and Federalism	10/15/10	845
Stem Cell Research	09/01/06	**697
Student Journalism	06/05/98	481
Student Rights	06/05/09	501
Supreme Court Controversies	09/28/12	813
Supreme Court Preview	09/17/93	817*
Supreme Court's Future	01/28/05	77
Testing Term Limits	11/18/94	1009
Threatened Coastlines	02/07/92	111*
Three-Strikes Laws	05/10/02	417
Treatment of Detainees	08/25/06	673
Trump Presidency	01/06/17	1
Voting Controversies	09/15/06	745
Women in Prison	03/03/17	193
Workplace Sexual Harassment	10/27/17	893

Surveillance. *See Electronic surveillance*

Sweatshops

	Date	Page
Child Labor and Sweatshops	08/16/96	721
Corporate Social Responsibility	08/03/07	649

Syria

	Date	Page
Chemical and Biological Weapons	12/13/13	1053
Defeating the Islamic State	04/01/16	289
European Migration Crisis	07/31/15	649
Stolen Antiquities	11/10/17	945

Taiwan

	Date	Page
China Today	08/04/00	625
China Today	04/04/14	289
New Era in Asia	02/14/92	121
Taiwan, China, and the U.S.	05/24/96	457
U.S.-China Trade	04/15/94	320*
U.S. Policy in Asia	11/27/92	1025

Tariffs

	Date	Page
China Today	04/04/14	289
Mexico's Emergence	07/19/91	489
U.S.-China Trade	04/15/94	313
U.S.-Iran Relations	03/04/16	217
U.S. Policy in Asia	11/27/92	1041*
U.S. Trade Policy	01/29/93	73

Tax evasion

	Date	Page
IRS Reform	01/16/98	34*
Tax Reform	03/22/96	241
Underground Economy	03/04/94	193

Taxation. *See also Business and industry; Taxation; Income tax; User fees*

	Date	Page
Alternative Energy	07/10/92	589*
Attracting Jobs	03/02/12	205
Betting on Sports	10/28/16	889
Budget Deficit	12/09/05	1029

	Date	Page
Budget Surplus	04/13/01	297
Business Bankruptcy	04/10/09	321
Child-Care Options	05/08/98	409
Climate Change	06/14/13	521
Energy Policy	05/20/11	457
Gambling Boom	03/18/94	241
Government Spending	07/12/13	597
Historic Preservation	10/07/94	865
Income Inequality	12/03/10	989
Internet Shopping	06/28/13	573
Legalizing Marijuana	06/12/09	**525
Line-Item Veto	06/20/97	543*
Marijuana Industry	10/16/15	865
National Debt	03/18/11	241
National Debt	09/01/17	701
Nonprofit Groups and Partisan Politics	11/14/14	961
Public-Works Projects	02/20/09	153
Reforming School Funding	12/10/99	1041
Regulating Nonprofits	12/26/97	1129
Saving Open Spaces	11/05/99	953
School Vouchers	04/09/99	281
School Vouchers Showdown	02/15/02	121
State Budget Crises	10/03/03	821
State Budget Crisis	09/11/09	741
Stimulating the Economy	01/10/03	1
Tax Reform	03/22/96	241
Tea Party Movement	03/19/10	**241*
Tobacco Industry	12/10/04	**1025
Wealth and Inequality	04/18/14	337

Teachers. *See Elementary and secondary education*

Technology. *See Science and technology*

Teenagers. *See Adolescents and youth*

Telecommunications. *See also Cellular telephones*

	Date	Page
Advertising Overload	01/23/04	49
Cyber-Crime	04/12/02	305
The Future of Telecommunications	04/23/99	329
Future of TV	04/11/14	313
New Challenges in Space	07/23/99	617
Regulating the New Economy	10/19/01	849

Telecommuting

	Date	Page
Flexible Work Arrangements	08/14/98	697
Telecommuting	07/19/13	621
Traffic Congestion	05/06/94	390*
Work, Family and Stress	08/14/92	706*

Television and radio

	Date	Page
Advertising Overload	01/23/04	49
Advertising Under Attack	09/13/91	657
Alcohol Advertising	03/14/97	217
Assisting Refugees	02/07/97	105*
Broadcast Indecency	04/16/04	321
The Business of Sports	02/10/95	132*
Cameras in the Courtroom	01/14/11	25
Celebrity Culture	03/18/05	245

	Date	Page
Centennial Olympic Games	04/05/96	289
Children's Television	08/15/97	721
College Sports	08/26/94	754*
The Consumer Culture	11/19/99	1007*
Cosmetic Surgery	04/15/05	317
Courts and the Media	09/23/94	817
Cyberbullying	05/02/08	385
Death Penalty Debate	03/10/95	210*
Emergency Medicine	01/05/96	8*
Extreme Sports	04/03/09	297
Food Safety Battle: Organic v. Biotech	09/04/98	772*
Foreign Policy and Public Opinion	07/15/94	601
Free-Press Disputes	04/08/05	293
Funding the Arts	07/14/17	581
Future of Journalism	03/27/09	**273
The Future of Television	12/23/94	1129
Future of TV	04/11/14	313
The Growing Influence of Boycotts	01/04/91	1
Hispanic-Americans' New Clout	09/18/98	818*
Indecency on Television	11/09/12	965
Journalism Standards in the Internet Age	10/08/10	821
Journalism Under Fire	12/25/98	1121
Latino Voters	04/03/15	289
Lies and Politics	02/18/11	145
Media Bias	05/03/13	401
Media Ownership	10/10/03	**845
Obesity Epidemic	01/31/03	86*
The Obscenity Debate	12/20/91	983
The Partisan Divide	04/30/04	373
Patriotism in America	06/25/99	545
Pay-Per-View TV	10/04/91	729
Paying College Athletes	07/11/14	577
Political Conventions	08/08/08	649
Political Scandals	05/27/94	457
Preventing Bullying	12/10/10	**1013
Public Broadcasting	09/18/92	809
Public Broadcasting	10/29/99	929
Pursuing the Paranormal	03/29/96	265
Reading Crisis?	02/22/08	169
Reality TV	08/27/10	677
Reassessing the Nation's Gun Laws	03/22/91	157
Reforming Big-Time College Sports	03/19/04	249
School Violence	10/09/98	888*
Sex Scandals	01/22/10	49
Sex, Violence and the Media	11/17/95	1017
Shock Jocks	06/01/07	**481
Soccer in America	04/22/94	354*
Talk Show Democracy	04/29/94	361
Television's Future	02/16/07	145
Transition to Digital TV	06/20/08	529
Trust in Media	06/09/17	481
TV Violence	03/26/93	265

	Date	Page
Violence in Schools	09/11/92	802*
Women and Sports	03/06/92	200*
Women and Sports	03/25/11	265
Young Voters	10/02/15	817
Term limits		
Term Limits	01/10/92	1
Testing Term Limits	11/18/94	1009
Terrorism		
Academic Freedom	10/07/05	833
Afghanistan Dilemma	08/07/09	**669*
Airline Safety	10/08/93	874*
Airline Safety	05/15/15	433
America at War	07/23/10	**605
Anti-Semitism	05/12/17	409
Assessing the Threat From al Qaeda	06/27/14	553
Border Security	09/27/13	813
Chemical and Biological Weapons	01/31/97	73
Chemical and Biological Weapons	12/13/13	1053
Civil Liberties Debates	10/24/03	893
Civil Liberties in Wartime	12/14/01	1017
Closing Guantánamo	02/27/09	**177
Closing Guantanamo	09/30/16	793
Combating Terrorism	07/21/95	633
Cost of the Iraq War	04/25/08	361*
Cyber-Crime	04/12/02	322*
Cybersecurity	09/26/03	797
Cybersecurity	02/26/10	169
Death Penalty Update	01/08/99	1
Defeating the Islamic State	04/01/16	289
Democracy in the Arab World	01/30/04	73
Drone Warfare	08/06/10	653
Energy Security	02/01/02	73
European Migration Crisis	07/31/15	649
Exporting Democracy	04/01/05	269
Far-Right Extremism	09/18/15	769
Fighting Crime	02/08/08	121
Food Safety	11/01/02	897
Future of Amtrak	10/18/02	853*
Future of NATO	02/28/03	177
Future of the Airline Industry	06/21/02	545
Global Jihad	10/14/05	857
Government Secrecy	12/02/05	1005
Government Surveillance	08/30/13	717
Hating America	11/23/01	969
Homegrown Jihadists	09/03/10	701
Homeland Security	09/12/03	749
Homeland Security	02/13/09	129
Illegal Immigration	05/06/05	393
Improving Cybersecurity	02/15/13	157
Intelligence Reforms	01/25/02	49
International Law	12/17/04	1049
Interrogating the CIA	09/25/09	789
The Iraq War: 10 Years Later	03/01/13	205

	Date	Page
Middle East Peace	01/21/05	53
Middle East Tensions	10/27/06	**889
Military Readiness	11/03/17	917
Modernizing the Nuclear Arsenal	07/29/16	625
Muslims in America	04/30/93	361
Nuclear Proliferation and Terrorism	04/02/04	297
The Obama Presidency	01/30/09	73
Policing the Borders	02/22/02	145
Port Security	04/21/06	337
Preparing for Disaster	08/02/13	669
Presidential Power	11/15/02	945
Presidential Power	03/06/15	217
Prosecuting Terrorists	03/12/10	**217*
Protecting the Power Grid	11/11/16	941
Protecting Whistleblowers	03/31/06	265
Puerto Rico: The Struggle over Status	02/08/91	91*
Real ID	05/04/07	385
Re-examining 9/11	06/04/04	493
Reforming the U.N.	06/24/16	553
Remembering 9/11	09/02/11	701*
Resurgent Russia	02/07/14	121
Smallpox Threat	02/07/03	118*
Stolen Antiquities	11/10/17	945
Terrorism in Africa	07/10/15	577
Torture	04/18/03	361*
Treating Anxiety	02/08/02	97
Treatment of Detainees	08/25/06	673
Understanding Islam	11/03/06	913
Unrest in the Arab World	02/01/13	105
Unrest in Turkey	01/29/16	97
U.S. Global Engagement	05/16/14	433
U.S.-Pakistan Relations	08/05/11	653*
U.S. Policy on Iran	11/16/07	961
War on Terrorism	10/12/01	817
Weapons of Mass Destruction	03/08/02	193
Worker Safety	05/21/04	445

Texas
Death Penalty Debates	11/19/10	965
Debate over Bilingualism	01/19/96	60*
High School Sports	09/22/95	837*
High-Speed Rail	04/16/93	327*
Illegal Immigration	05/06/05	393
Protecting Endangered Species	04/19/96	337
Redistricting Disputes	03/12/04	221
Rethinking the Death Penalty	11/16/01	960*
Testing in Schools	04/20/01	332*

Textbooks
Education and Gender	06/03/94	496*
Evolution vs. Creationism	08/22/97	745
Government and Religion	01/15/10	25
Home Schooling Debate	01/17/03	30*
Teaching History	09/29/95	849
School Censorship	02/19/93	145
School Funding	08/27/93	756*

Thailand
	Date	Page
Human Trafficking and Slavery	03/26/04	273
Prostitution	06/11/93	516*

Thalidomide
Cancer Treatments	09/11/98	798*
Reforming the FDA	06/06/97	493*

Third World. *See Developing countries*

Timber industry. *See Forests and forestry*

Title IX. *See Education Amendments Act*

Tobacco
Advertising Overload	01/23/04	49
Advertising Under Attack	09/13/91	657
Closing In on Tobacco	11/12/99	977
Crackdown on Smoking	12/04/92	1049
Drug-Policy Debate	07/28/00	599*
High-Impact Litigation	02/11/00	102*
Indoor Air Pollution	10/27/95	945
Limiting Lawsuits	12/19/08	1033
Preventing Cancer	01/16/09	25
Preventing Disease	01/06/12	1
Preventing Teen Drug Use	07/28/95	657
Prolonging Life	09/30/11	805*
Reforming the FDA	06/06/97	481
Regulating Tobacco	09/30/94	841
Science and Politics	08/20/04	661
Socially Responsible Investing	08/29/08	673
Teens and Tobacco	12/01/95	1065
Tobacco Industry	12/10/04	**1025
Women's Health	11/07/03	952*

Torture. *See Violence; War crimes*

Toxic substances. *See Hazardous substances*

Trade. *See International trade*

Traffic accidents
Aggressive Driving	07/25/97	649
Aging Infrastructure	09/28/07	**793
Auto Safety	10/26/01	873
Distracted Driving	05/04/12	401
Drinking on Campus	03/20/98	241
Drunken Driving	10/06/00	793
Highway Safety	07/14/95	609
Reducing Traffic Deaths	02/17/17	145
Sleep Deprivation	06/26/98	553
Sleep Deprivation	02/12/10	121
SUV Debate	05/16/03	454*
Teen Driving	01/07/05	1
Too Many Lawsuits?	05/22/92	440
Truck Safety	03/12/99	209
Underage Drinking	03/13/92	217
U.S. Auto Industry	10/16/92	896*
U.S.-Mexico Relations	11/09/01	921

Traffic congestion
Flexible Work Arrangements	08/14/98	697
Future of Cars	07/25/14	625

	Date	Page		Date	Page
Mass Transit	12/09/16	1013	Ethics of War	12/13/02	1013
Mass Transit Boom	01/18/08	49	European Monetary Union	11/27/98	1025
Smart Growth	05/28/04	469	European Union's Future	12/16/16	1037
Telecommuting	07/19/13	621	Future of NATO	02/28/03	177
Traffic Congestion	05/06/94	385	Human Rights	11/13/98	977
Traffic Congestion	08/27/99	729	Human Trafficking and Slavery	03/26/04	273
Transportation Policy	07/04/97	577	International Law	12/17/04	1049

Transit Systems

			Invasive Species	10/05/01	785
High-Speed Trains	05/01/09	**397	Kids in Prison	04/27/01	361*
Mass Transit	12/09/16	1013	Military Readiness	11/03/17	917

Transportation. *See also Air transportation; Automobiles and auto industry; Railroads; Highways and roads*

			Missile Defense	09/08/00	689
Affordable Housing	02/09/01	94*	Native Americans' Future	07/12/96	610*
Future of Amtrak	10/18/02	841	Nuclear Arms Cleanup	06/24/94	553
Future of the Airline Industry	06/21/02	545	Nuclear Proliferation	06/05/92	481
Future of the Airlines	03/07/08	217	Nuclear Proliferation and Terrorism	04/02/04	297
Future of Cars	07/25/14	625	Panama Canal	11/26/99	1017
High-Speed Rail	04/16/93	313	Reforming the U.N.	06/24/16	553
High-Speed Trains	05/01/09	**397	Setting Environmental Priorities	05/21/99	425
Mass Transit	12/09/16	1013	Sports and Drugs	07/23/04	**613
Mass Transit Boom	01/18/08	49	Stolen Antiquities	11/10/17	945
Public-Works Projects	02/20/09	153	Stopping Genocide	08/27/04	685
Reducing Traffic Deaths	02/17/17	145	U.S.-Iran Relations	03/04/16	217
Transportation Policy	07/04/97	577	U.S. Trade Policy	09/13/13	765
Truck Safety	03/12/99	209	Women and Human Rights	04/30/99	353
U.S.-Mexico Relations	11/09/01	921			

Transsexuals

Trucks and trucking

			Auto Safety	10/26/01	873
Transgender Issues	05/05/06	385	Highway Safety	07/14/95	620*
Transgender Rights	12/11/15	1033	Sleep Deprivation	06/26/98	553

Travel and tourist trade. *See also Ecotourism*

			SUV Debate	05/16/03	449
Airline Industry Problems	09/24/99	842*	Truck Safety	03/12/99	209
Castro's Next Move	12/12/97	1081	U.S.-Mexico Relations	11/09/01	921

Tuberculosis

Coastal Development	08/21/98	721			
Ecotourism	10/20/06	865	Battling HIV/AIDS	10/26/07	889
Future of the Airline Industry	06/21/02	545	Combating Infectious Diseases	06/09/95	496*
Gambling Boom	03/18/94	245*	Women and AIDS	12/25/92	1134

Tuition vouchers

Historic Preservation	10/07/94	865			
National Forests	10/16/98	905	Attack on Public Schools	07/26/96	662*
National Parks	05/28/93	457	Private Management of Public Schools	03/25/94	276*
Prostitution	06/11/93	516*	Privatization	11/13/92	988*
Restoring Ties With Cuba	06/12/15	505	School Choice	05/10/91	253

Treaties and international agreements. *See also North American Free Trade Agreement; International relations*

			School Choice Debate	07/18/97	625
			School Desegregation	04/23/04	345
Air Pollution Conflict	11/14/03	965	School Vouchers	04/09/99	281
Arctic Development	12/02/16	989	School Vouchers Showdown	02/15/02	121

Trump, Donald J.

Banning Land Mines	08/08/97	697			
Chemical and Biological Weapons	01/31/97	73	'Alt-Right' Movement	03/17/17	241
Children's Legal Rights	04/23/93	345*	Anti-Semitism	05/12/17	409
China and the South China Sea	01/20/17	49	China and the South China Sea	01/20/17	49
Closing Guantanamo	09/30/16	793	Civic Education	02/03/17	97
Decriminalizing Prostitution	04/15/16	337	Cyberwarfare Threat	10/06/17	821
Defeating the Islamic State	04/01/16	289	Democracies Under Stress	10/20/17	869
Endangered Species Act	06/03/05	**493	Future of the Christian Right	06/23/17	533
			Future of the Democratic Party	10/13/17	845
			High-Tech Policing	04/21/17	337

	Date	Page
Hunger in America	07/07/17	557
Immigrants and the Economy	02/24/17	169
Military Readiness	11/03/17	917
Muslims in America	07/28/17	629
National Debt	09/01/17	701
North Korea Showdown	05/19/17	433
The Obama Legacy	11/04/16	913
Populism and Party Politics	09/09/16	721
Privatizing Government Services	12/08/17	1017
Redistricting Showdown	08/25/17	677
Rethinking Foreign Aid	04/14/17	313
Reviving Rural Economies	03/31/17	265
Trump Presidency	01/06/17	1
Trust in Media	06/09/17	481
U.S.-Mexico Relations	09/02/16	697
U.S.-Russia Relations	01/13/17	25

Turkey
Democracies Under Stress	10/20/17	869
Future of the European Union	10/28/05	909
Unrest in Turkey	01/29/16	97

UFOs
| Pursuing the Paranormal | 03/29/96 | 265 |
| The Search for Extraterrestrials | 03/05/04 | 197 |

Unemployment. *See Employment and unemployment*

Unification Church
| Cults in America | 05/07/93 | 385 |

Unions. *See Labor unions*

United Nations
Aiding Africa	08/29/03	697
Childhood Immunizations	06/18/93	546*
Children in Crisis	08/31/01	657
Confronting Iraq	10/04/02	793
Economic Sanctions	10/28/94	937
Emerging India	04/19/02	329
Ending Poverty	09/09/05	733
Ethics of War	12/13/02	1013
European Unrest	01/09/15	25
Foreign Aid After Sept. 11	04/26/02	361
Foreign Policy Burden	08/20/93	721
Global Food Crisis	06/27/08	553
Haiti's Dilemma	02/18/05	149
Human Rights	11/13/98	977
Human Rights Issues	10/30/09	909
Improving Cybersecurity	02/15/13	157
International Law	12/17/04	1049
Israeli-Palestinian Conflict	06/21/13	545
Middle East Tensions	10/27/06	**889
Non-Proliferation Treaty at 25	01/27/95	73
Nuclear Disarmament	10/02/09	**813
Population Growth	07/16/93	601
Privatizing the Military	06/25/04	565
Rebuilding Afghanistan	12/21/01	1057*
Rebuilding Iraq	07/11/03	625

	Date	Page
Reforming the U.N.	06/24/16	553
Rethinking Foreign Aid	04/14/17	313
Stopping Genocide	08/27/04	685
Torture	04/18/03	345
Treatment of Detainees	08/25/06	673
The United Nations and Global Security	02/27/04	173
United Nations at 50	08/18/95	729
U.S. Global Engagement	05/16/14	433
War Crimes	07/07/95	585
Weapons of Mass Destruction	03/08/02	193
Women and Human Rights	04/30/99	353

United States
| Dealing With the "New" Russia | 06/06/08 | 481 |

Universities. *See Colleges and universities*

Urban areas. *See Cities and towns*

User fees
Hard Times for Libraries	06/26/92	553
National Parks	05/28/93	457
Reforming the FDA	06/06/97	481
Transportation Policy	07/04/97	580*

Utilities. *See Public utilities*

Vaccines
AIDS Update	12/04/98	1049
Avian Flu Threat	01/13/06	25
Childhood Immunizations	06/18/93	529
Combating AIDS	04/21/95	345
Combating Infectious Diseases	06/09/95	489
Emerging Infectious Diseases	02/13/15	145
Fighting Superbugs	08/24/07	673
HPV Vaccine	05/11/07	409
Increase in Autism	06/13/03	**561*
Pandemic Threat	06/02/17	457
Prescription Drug Costs	05/20/16	457
Sexually Transmitted Diseases	12/03/04	997
Smallpox Threat	02/07/03	105
Understanding Autism	08/01/14	649
Vaccine Controversies	08/25/00	641
Vaccine Controversies	02/19/16	169

Values. *See Ethical and moral issues*

Vegetarianism
| Animal Rights | 05/24/91 | 318* |

Venezuela
| Democracies Under Stress | 10/20/17 | 869 |

Veterans
Caring for Veterans	04/23/10	361
Reforming Veterans' Health Care	11/21/14	985
Wounded Veterans	08/31/07	697

Veterinary medicine
America's Pampered Pets	12/27/96	1129
Drug-Resistant Bacteria	06/04/99	473
Prozac Controversy	08/19/94	734*

	Date	Page
Victims' rights. *See Crime and criminals*		
Video games		
Betting on Sports	10/28/16	889
Digital Education	12/02/11	1001
Media Violence	02/14/14	145
Reading Crisis?	02/22/08	169
Video Games	11/10/06	**937
Video Games and Learning	02/12/16	145
Virtual Reality	02/26/16	193
Vietnam		
Combat Journalism	04/12/13	329
Global Refugee Crisis	07/09/99	574*
Legacy of the Vietnam War	02/18/00	113
New Era in Asia	02/14/92	121
Privatizing the Military	06/25/04	565
Should the U.S. Reinstate the Draft?	01/11/91	17
Treatment of Veterans	11/19/04	973
U.S.-Vietnam Relations	12/03/93	1057
Weapons of Mass Destruction	03/08/02	193
Wounded Veterans	08/31/07	697
Violence		
Aggressive Driving	07/25/97	649
'Alt-Right' Movement	03/17/17	241
Anti-Semitism	05/12/17	409
Biology and Behavior	04/03/98	289
Boys' Emotional Needs	06/18/99	521
Bullying	02/04/05	101
Campus Sexual Assault	10/31/14	913
Central American Gangs	01/30/15	97
Childhood Depression	07/16/99	593
Children in Crisis	08/31/01	657
Children's Television	08/15/97	721
Child Welfare	08/26/16	673
Child Welfare Reform	04/22/05	345
Combat Journalism	04/12/13	329
Combating Terrorism	07/21/95	633
Cyberbullying	05/02/08	385
Defeating the Islamic State	04/01/16	289
Democracy in Latin America	11/03/00	881
Discipline in Schools	02/15/08	145
Domestic Violence	11/15/13	981
Europe's New Right	02/12/93	121
Extreme Sports	04/03/09	297
Far-Right Extremism	09/18/15	769
Fighting Crime	02/08/08	121
Fighting Gangs	10/09/15	841
Forensic Science Controversies	02/10/17	121
Future of TV	04/11/14	313
Gang Crisis	05/14/04	421
Gangs in the U.S.	07/16/10	581
Greek Life on Campus	11/20/15	985
Gun Control	06/10/94	505
Gun Control	03/08/13	233
Gun Control Debate	11/12/04	949

	Date	Page
Gun Rights Debates	10/31/08	**889
Gun Violence	05/25/07	457
Guns on Campus	01/27/17	73
Haiti's Dilemma	02/18/05	149
Hate Crimes	01/08/93	1
Hate Groups	05/08/09	421
Hazing	01/09/04	1
High-Tech Policing	04/21/17	337
Housing Discrimination	11/06/15	937
Indecency on Television	11/09/12	965
The Iraq War: 10 Years Later	03/01/13	205
Job Stress	08/04/95	688*
Juvenile Justice	02/25/94	186*
Media Violence	02/14/14	145
Mental Illness	08/06/93	678*
Mexico's Future	10/26/12	913
Middle East Peace	01/21/05	53
Movie Ratings	03/28/03	273
NFL Controversies	09/04/15	721
Northern Ireland Cease-Fire	09/15/95	801
Patriotism in America	06/25/99	558*
Police Misconduct	04/06/12	301
Police Tactics	12/12/14	1033
Preventing Bullying	12/10/10	**1013
Preventing Juvenile Crime	03/15/96	217
Prison Overcrowding	02/04/94	97
Prisoners and Mental Illness	03/13/15	241
Privacy and the Internet	12/04/15	1009
Privatizing the Military	07/13/12	597
Prozac Controversy	08/19/94	737*
Racial Conflict	01/08/16	25
Reassessing the Nation's Gun Laws	03/22/91	157
Reforming Juvenile Justice	09/11/15	745
Religious Freedom	01/01/16	1
Restorative Justice	02/05/16	121
School Discipline	05/09/14	409
School Violence	10/09/98	881
Sentencing Reform	01/10/14	25
Serial Killers	10/31/03	917
Sex, Violence and the Media	11/17/95	1017
Sexual Assault in the Military	08/09/13	693
Soccer in America	04/22/94	349*
Socially Responsible Investing	08/29/08	673
South Africa's Future	01/14/94	25
Suburban Crime	09/03/93	769
Terrorism in Africa	07/10/15	577
Transgender Rights	12/11/15	1033
Treating Depression	06/26/09	573
Troubled Brazil	04/07/17	289
TV Violence	03/26/93	265
Unions at a Crossroads	08/07/15	673
Unrest in Turkey	01/29/16	97
U.S.-Mexico Relations	09/02/16	697
Video Games and Learning	02/12/16	145

	Date	Page
Violence Against Women	02/26/93	169
Violence in Schools	09/11/92	785
Women and Human Rights	04/30/99	353
Youth Violence	03/05/10	193*
Zero Tolerance	03/10/00	185

Violence Against Women Act (VAWA)
	Date	Page
Domestic Violence	01/06/06	1
Domestic Violence	11/15/13	981

Vitamins and minerals. *See Food and nutrition*

Voluntarism. *See also Charities and nonprofit organizations*
	Date	Page
Celebrity Advocacy	05/11/12	425
Civic Renewal	03/21/97	244*
Corporate Social Responsibility	08/03/07	649
Ending Homelessness	06/18/04	556*
Future Job Market	01/11/02	8*
Hunger in America	07/07/17	557
Invasive Species	10/05/01	796*
National Service	06/25/93	553
National Service	06/30/06	577
The New Corporate Philanthropy	02/27/98	169
The New Volunteerism	12/13/96	1081
Parents and Schools	01/20/95	49
Peace Corps Challenges	01/11/13	29
Peace Corps' Challenges in the 1990s	01/25/91	49
Youth Volunteerism	01/27/12	77

Voting and voting rights
	Date	Page
Asian Americans	12/13/91	962
Campaign Finance	05/06/16	409
Campaign Finance Showdown	11/22/02	969
Changing Demographics	11/16/12	989
Changing U.S. Electorate	05/30/08	**457
Civic Education	02/03/17	97
D.C. Voting Rights	04/11/08	313*
Electing Minorities	08/12/94	697
Electing the President	04/20/07	337
Election Reform	11/02/01	897
Future of the Democratic Party	10/13/17	845
Future of the GOP	03/20/09	249
Haiti's Dilemma	02/18/05	149
Hispanic-Americans' New Clout	09/18/98	809
Latino Voters	04/03/15	289
Lies and Politics	02/18/11	145
Low Voter Turnout	10/20/00	833
Partisan Politics	03/19/99	233
Political Conventions	08/08/08	649
Political Polling	02/06/15	121
Populism and Party Politics	09/09/16	721
Presidential Election	02/03/12	101
Prison-Building Boom	09/17/99	817*
Race and Politics	07/18/08	577
Race in America	07/11/03	593
Real ID	05/04/07	385
Redistricting Debates	02/25/11	169

	Date	Page
Redistricting Disputes	03/12/04	221
Redistricting: Drawing Power with a Map	02/15/91	97
Redistricting Showdown	08/25/17	677
Re-examining the Constitution	09/07/12	741
Term Limits	01/10/92	1
Third-Party Prospects	12/22/95	1137
Voter Rights	05/18/12	449
Voting Controversies	09/15/06	745
Voting Controversies	02/21/14	169
Young Voters	10/02/15	817

Wages and salaries
	Date	Page
Apprenticeships	10/14/16	841
Auto Industry's Future	02/06/09	**105
Big-Box Stores	09/10/04	733
The Business of Sports	02/10/95	121
Child Care	12/17/93	1105
Child Labor and Sweatshops	08/16/96	721
College Football	11/18/11	977
Community Colleges	05/01/15	385
Contingent Work Force	10/24/97	937
Corporate Crime	10/11/02	817
Corporate Social Responsibility	08/03/07	649
Curbing CEO Pay	03/09/07	217
Doctor Shortage	08/28/15	697
Domestic Poverty	09/07/07	**721
Downward Mobility	07/23/93	629*
Dropout Rate	06/13/14	505
Employee Benefits	02/04/00	65
Executive Pay	07/11/97	601
Fairness in Salaries	05/29/92	457
Fighting Urban Poverty	07/17/15	601
The Future of Baseball	09/25/98	833
Future of Feminism	04/14/06	313
Future of the Middle Class	04/08/16	313
Future of Public Universities	01/18/13	53
Gender Pay Gap	03/14/08	241
Gentrification	02/20/15	169
The Gig Economy	03/18/16	265
The Glass Ceiling	10/29/93	937
Health-Care Reform	08/28/09	693*
High-Tech Labor Shortage	04/24/98	361
Housing the Homeless	10/10/14	841
Illegal Immigration	05/06/05	393
Immigration Debate	02/01/08	**97
Income Inequality	04/17/98	337
Income Inequality	12/03/10	989
Jobs in the '90s	02/28/92	169
Labor Unions' Future	09/02/05	**709
Living-Wage Movement	09/27/02	769
Middle-Class Squeeze	03/06/09	201
Minimum Wage	12/16/05	1053
Minimum Wage	01/24/14	72
'Occupy' Movement	01/13/12	25

	Date	Page
Paying for College	11/20/92	1006*
Paying for Retirement	11/05/93	961
Public-Employee Unions	04/08/11	313
Overhauling Social Security	05/12/95	417
Rethinking Retirement	06/19/09	549
Reviving Manufacturing	07/22/11	601
Rising College Costs	12/05/03	1013
Social Security Reform	09/24/04	781
Stimulating the Economy	01/10/03	1
Stock Market Troubles	01/16/04	25
Teacher Shortages	08/24/01	640*
Telecommuting	07/19/13	621
Unions at a Crossroads	08/07/15	673
Universal Basic Income	09/08/17	725
Universal Coverage	03/30/07	265
Upward Mobility	04/29/05	369
Vanishing Jobs	03/13/09	225
Women and Work	07/26/13	645
Women in Leadership	09/23/16	769
Worker Retraining	01/21/94	56*
The Working Poor	11/03/95	969
Youth Apprenticeships	10/23/92	918*
Youth Unemployment	03/14/14	241

Wall Street. *See Stocks and bonds*

War crimes
Closing Guantánamo	02/27/09	**177
Closing Guantanamo	09/30/16	793
Ethics of War	12/13/02	1013
Famine in Africa	11/08/02	921
International Law	12/17/04	1049
Interrogating the CIA	09/25/09	789
Rebuilding Iraq	07/11/03	625
Reforming the U.N.	06/24/16	553
Stopping Genocide	08/27/04	685
War Crimes	07/07/95	585
Women and Human Rights	04/30/99	353

Washington, D.C. *See District of Columbia*

Washington (State)
Assisted Suicide	02/21/92	145
Assisted Suicide Controversy	05/05/95	406*
Gun Control Standoff	12/19/97	1120*
Jobs vs. Environment	05/15/92	409
Punishing Sex Offenders	01/12/96	25
School Choice Debate	07/18/97	629*

Waste products. *See also Nuclear waste*
The Economics of Recycling	03/27/98	265
Environmental Movement at 25	03/31/95	288*
Fast-Food Shake-Up	11/08/91	825
Future of Recycling	12/14/07	1033
Garbage Crisis	03/20/92	241
Panama Canal	11/26/99	1031*
Renewable Energy	11/07/97	970*
Setting Environmental Priorities	05/21/99	438*

Water pollution. *See also Water resources*
	Date	Page
Acid Rain: New Approach to Old Problem	03/08/91	129
Arctic Development	12/02/16	989
Bush and the Environment	10/25/02	865
Coastal Development	08/21/98	739*
Drinking Water Safety	07/15/16	577
Environmental Movement at 25	03/31/95	283*
Farm Subsidies	05/17/02	433
Fish Farming	07/27/07	625
Fracking Controversy	12/16/11	1049
The Greening of Eastern Europe	11/15/91	849
Gulf Coast Restoration	08/26/11	677*
Jobs vs. Environment	05/15/92	423
Lead Poisoning	06/19/92	538
Managing Wildfires	11/02/12	941
Marine Mammals vs. Fish	08/28/92	754
Offshore Drilling	06/25/10	553
Oil Spills	01/17/92	25
Protecting the Oceans	10/17/14	865
Protecting Wetlands	10/03/08	793*
Reforming the Corps	05/30/03	497
Regulating Toxic Chemicals	07/18/14	601
Saving the Oceans	11/04/05	933
Setting Environmental Priorities	05/21/99	425
Threatened Coastlines	02/07/92	107
Threatened Fisheries	08/02/02	617
Water Quality	02/11/94	121
Water Quality	11/24/00	953
Water Shortages	08/01/03	649
Water Shortages	06/18/10	529

Water resources. *See also Water pollution*
Aging Infrastructure	09/28/07	**793
California: Enough Water for the Future?	04/19/91	221
Crisis on the Plains	05/09/03	434*
Drinking Water Safety	07/15/16	577
Farm Policy	08/10/12	693
Farm Subsidies	05/17/02	433
Fish Farming	07/27/07	625
Global Water Shortages	12/15/95	1113
Protecting the Oceans	10/17/14	865
Protecting Wetlands	10/03/08	793*
Public-Works Projects	02/20/09	153
Reforming the Corps	05/30/03	497
Urban Sprawl in the West	10/03/97	880*
Water Crisis in the West	12/09/11	1025
Water Shortages	08/01/03	649
Water Shortages	06/18/10	529

Watergate scandal. *See Independent counsels*

Weapons. *See also Arms control; Firearms*
Arms Sales	12/09/94	1081
Banning Land Mines	08/08/97	697
Calculating the Costs of the Gulf War	03/15/91	145

	Date	Page
Chemical and Biological Weapons	01/31/97	73
Confronting Iraq	10/04/02	793
Defense Priorities	07/30/99	641
Future of NATO	02/28/03	177
Gun Control	03/08/13	233
Gun Control Debate	11/12/04	949
Gun Rights Debates	10/31/08	**889
Gun Violence	05/25/07	457
Guns on Campus	01/27/17	73
Homeland Security	09/12/03	764*
Military Readiness	11/03/17	917
Missile Defense	09/08/00	689
New Challenges in Space	07/23/99	631*
North Korean Crisis	04/11/03	321
Nuclear Proliferation and Terrorism	04/02/04	297
Panama Canal	11/26/99	1031*
Police Tactics	12/12/14	1033
Policing the Borders	02/22/02	145
Rise in Counterinsurgency	09/05/08	697
Robotic Warfare	01/23/15	73
Smallpox Threat	02/07/03	105
U.S.-Iran Relations	03/04/16	217
War on Terrorism	10/12/01	833*
Weapons of Mass Destruction	03/08/02	193

Welfare and social services

Assisting Refugees	02/07/97	97
Caring for Veterans	04/23/10	361
Child-Care Options	05/08/98	409
Child Poverty	04/07/00	281
Child Poverty	10/28/11	901
Child Welfare	08/26/16	673
Child Welfare Reform	04/22/05	345
Cost of the Iraq War	04/25/08	361*
Covering the Uninsured	06/14/02	521
Domestic Poverty	09/07/07	**721
Encouraging Teen Abstinence	07/10/98	577
Ending Homelessness	06/18/04	541
Faith-Based Initiatives	05/04/01	377
Fighting Urban Poverty	07/17/15	601
Future of Marriage	05/07/04	397
Head Start	04/09/93	289
Helping the Homeless	01/26/96	73
The Homeless	08/07/92	665
Housing Discrimination	11/06/15	937
Housing the Homeless	10/10/14	841
Hunger in America	12/22/00	1033
Hunger in America	07/07/17	557
Illegal Immigration	04/24/92	361
Immigration Reform	09/24/93	841
Minimum Wage	01/24/14	72
National Debt	03/18/11	241
National Service	06/25/93	553
Native Americans' Future	07/12/96	601
The New Immigrants	01/24/97	49

	Date	Page
The New Volunteerism	12/13/96	1081
Nonprofit Groups and Partisan Politics	11/14/14	961
Preventing Teen Pregnancy	05/14/93	409
Privatization	11/13/92	983*
Race in America	07/11/03	593
Social Security	06/03/16	481
State Budget Crisis	09/11/09	741
States and Federalism	09/13/96	793
Straining the Safety Net	07/31/09	645
Teen Pregnancy	03/26/10	265*
Universal Basic Income	09/08/17	725
Upward Mobility	04/29/05	369
Welfare Experiments	09/16/94	793
Welfare Reform	08/03/01	601
Welfare, Work and the States	12/06/96	1057
The Working Poor	11/03/95	969
Wounded Veterans	08/31/07	697

West Bank

Global Water Shortages	12/15/95	1113
Israel at 50	03/06/98	193
Middle East Conflict	04/06/01	273
Middle East Peace	01/21/05	53
The Palestinians	08/30/91	609
Prospects for Mideast Peace	08/30/02	673

Wetlands

Endangered Species	06/21/91	393
Reforming the Corps	05/30/03	513*
Saving the Oceans	11/04/05	933
Threatened Coastlines	02/07/92	97

Whistleblowers

Accountants Under Fire	03/22/02	241
Combating Scientific Misconduct	01/10/97	6*
Corporate Crime	10/11/02	817
Government Secrecy	12/02/05	1005
Protecting Whistleblowers	03/31/06	265
Stock Market Troubles	01/16/04	25
Whistleblowers	12/05/97	1057
Whistleblowers	01/31/14	97

Whitewater scandal. *See Independent counsels*

Wildlife

America's Pampered Pets	12/27/96	1140*
Animal Intelligence	10/22/10	869
Animal Rights	01/08/10	1
Crisis on the Plains	05/09/03	439*
Disappearing Species	11/30/07	985
Endangered Species	06/21/91	393
Endangered Species Act	10/01/99	849
Environmental Movement at 25	03/31/95	286*
Hunting Controversy	01/24/92	49
Invasive Species	02/17/12	153
Managing Public Lands	11/04/11	929
Managing Wildfires	11/02/12	941
Marine Mammals vs. Fish	08/28/92	737

	Date	Page
National Parks	01/17/14	49
Protecting Endangered Species	04/19/96	337
Protecting Wetlands	10/03/08	793*
Threatened Fisheries	08/02/02	617
Transnational Crime	08/29/14	697
Zoos in the 21st Century	04/28/00	353

Women

	Date	Page
Academic Politics	02/16/96	145
Aiding Africa	08/29/03	712*
Boys' Emotional Needs	06/18/99	521
Changing U.S. Electorate	05/30/08	**457
Children and Divorce	06/07/91	357
Cosmetic Surgery	04/15/05	317
Crime on Campus	02/04/11	97
Democracy in the Arab World	01/30/04	73
Domestic Violence	01/06/06	1
Education and Gender	06/03/94	481
Emerging India	04/19/02	338*
Exporting Democracy	04/01/05	269
Feminism's Future	02/28/97	169
Fighting Gangs	10/09/15	841
First Ladies	06/14/96	505
Foreign Aid and National Security	06/17/11	529
Future of the Catholic Church	06/07/13	497
Future of Feminism	04/14/06	313
Future of Marriage	05/07/04	397
Future of Marriage	12/01/17	993
Gender and Learning	05/20/05	445
Gender Pay Gap	03/14/08	241
Global Refugee Crisis	07/09/99	586*
Human Trafficking and Slavery	03/26/04	273
Japan in Crisis	07/26/02	604*
Jobs Outlook	06/04/10	481
Marriage and Divorce	05/10/96	409
Mothers' Movement	04/04/03	297
The Obscenity Debate	12/20/91	969
Prostitution	06/11/93	505
Racial Quotas	05/17/91	277
Rebuilding Afghanistan	12/21/01	1048*
Reform in Iran	12/18/98	1103*
Retirement Security	05/31/02	496*
Saving Social Security	10/02/98	863*
Sexual Assault in the Military	08/09/13	693
Single-Sex Education	07/12/02	569
Teaching History	09/29/95	860*
Telecommuting	07/19/13	621
Understanding Mormonism	10/19/12	889
Video Games and Learning	02/12/16	145
Violence Against Women	02/26/93	169
War Crimes	07/07/95	590*
Welfare Reform	04/10/92	313
Women and Human Rights	04/30/99	353
Women in Leadership	09/23/16	769
Women in Politics	03/21/08	265

	Date	Page
Women and Sports	03/25/11	265
Women and Work	07/26/13	645
Women in Prison	03/03/17	193
Women in Sports	05/11/01	401
Women in the Military	11/13/09	957
Workplace Sexual Harassment	10/27/17	893

Women athletes

	Date	Page
College Sports	08/26/94	745
Eating Disorders	12/18/92	1102
Eating Disorders	02/10/06	**121
Gender Equity in Sports	04/18/97	337
High School Sports	09/22/95	825
Soccer in America	04/22/94	351*
Women and Sports	03/06/92	193
Women and Sports	03/25/11	265
Youth Fitness	09/26/97	846*

Women — Employment

	Date	Page
Big-Box Stores	09/10/04	733
Child Care	12/17/93	1105
Class Action Lawsuits	05/13/11	433
Contingent Work Force	10/24/97	937
Crackdown on Sexual Harassment	07/19/96	625
Diversity in the Workplace	10/10/97	889
Fairness in Salaries	05/29/92	457
Feminism's Future	02/28/97	169
Foreign Aid After Sept. 11	04/26/02	370*
Future of Feminism	04/14/06	313
Future of Marriage	05/07/04	397
Gender and Learning	05/20/05	445
Gender Pay Gap	03/14/08	241
The Glass Ceiling	10/29/93	937
Income Inequality	04/17/98	346*
Mothers' Movement	04/04/03	297
Paying for Retirement	11/05/93	978*
Rethinking Affirmative Action	04/28/95	369
Sexual Harassment	08/09/91	537
Sexual Harassment	04/27/12	377
Women and Sports	03/06/92	204*
Women and Work	07/26/13	645
Work, Family and Stress	08/14/92	689

Women — Health. *See also Abortion; Pregnancy*

	Date	Page
Abortion Debates	03/21/03	249
Advances in Cancer Research	08/25/95	753
Battling HIV/AIDS	10/26/07	889
Birth Control Choices	07/29/94	649
Birth-Control Debate	06/24/05	565
Breast Cancer	06/27/97	553
Chronic Fatigue Syndrome	04/05/02	289
Cosmetic Surgery	04/15/05	317
Dieting and Health	04/14/95	331*
Domestic Violence	11/15/13	981
Eating Disorders	12/18/92	1097
Girls' Rights	04/17/15	337
Mosquito-Borne Disease	07/22/16	601

	Date	Page
Sexually Transmitted Diseases	12/03/04	997
Treating Anxiety	02/08/02	97
Women and AIDS	12/25/92	1121
Women's Health	11/07/03	941
Women's Health Issues	05/13/94	409

Women — Military service

New Military Culture	04/26/96	361
Sexual Assault in the Military	08/09/13	693
Should the U.S. Reinstate the Draft?	01/11/91	17
Women in Combat	05/13/16	433
Women in the Military	09/25/92	833
Women in the Military	11/13/09	957

World Bank

Emerging India	04/19/02	329
Famine in Africa	11/08/02	937*
Foreign Aid After Sept. 11	04/26/02	361
Globalization Backlash	09/28/01	761
Global Water Shortages	12/15/95	1113
Rethinking Foreign Aid	04/14/17	313
Trouble in South America	03/14/03	225

	Date	Page

World Trade Organization

China After Deng	06/13/97	518*
China Today	08/04/00	625
Foreign Aid After Sept. 11	04/26/02	361
Globalization Backlash	09/28/01	761
International Law	12/17/04	1049
U.S. Trade Policy	09/13/13	765
World Trade	06/09/00	497

World Wide Web. *See Internet*

Youth. *See Adolescents and youth*

Yugoslavia

Defense Priorities	07/30/99	641
Democracy in Eastern Europe	10/08/99	865
Economic Sanctions	10/28/94	945*
Europe's New Right	02/12/93	121
Global Refugee Crisis	07/09/99	569
NATO's Changing Role	08/21/92	713
Stopping Genocide	08/27/04	685
United Nations at 50	08/18/95	729
War Crimes	07/07/95	585